The Pocket Interlinear New Testament

The Pocket Interlinear New Testament

Numerically Coded to Strong's Exhaustive Concordance

Jay P. Green, Sr., *Editor*

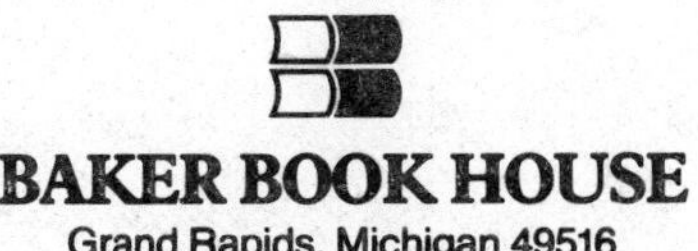

BAKER BOOK HOUSE
Grand Rapids, Michigan 49516

Reprinted 1988 by
Baker Book House Company
with permission of copyright owner

ISBN: 0-8010-3825-1

Printed in the United States of America

PREFACE

"Every Scripture (is) God-breathed, and (is) profitable for teaching, for reproof, for correction, for instruction in righteousness, so that the man of God may be fitted out, having been fully furnished for every good work"

— 2 Timothy 3:16.

This Pocket Interlinear New Testament is presented to you and to all the Christian community with much exultation, tempered by fear and trembling and awe toward our almighty God and Savior, Jesus Christ.

It is hoped that you will discern that we have fully believed all the words of this holy Book, handling it with reverence, knowing that *"man shall not live by bread alone, but by every word that proceeds out of the mouth of God"* — Matthew 4:4, and that these words did not come *"by the will of man, but men spoke from God, being borne along by (the) Holy Spirit"* — 2 Peter 1:21. It also has been written that each of the sons of men shall be judged by the words of this Book: *"And if anyone hears My words, and does not believe, I do not judge him, . . . the word which I spoke is that which will judge him in the last day"* — John 12:47,48. And the words of this Book being the ones that will judge every person who has lived in all the ages, then how important it must be that very words of God, and no other, shall be contained in a portable book, to be distributed far and wide, in a form and in a commonly understood language which can be easily and immediately taken into the heart and into the consciousness of all who have the privilege to read them. With these considerations in mind, and in holy fear inculcated by our God, we have sought to provide in *The Interlinear Hebrew-Greek-English Bible* all the original God-breathed Hebrew, Aramaic and Greek words. And after much prayer and laborious study, it was concluded that this could best be done by providing you with the two attested texts that alone have been uniquely preserved whole, and accepted in all generations, in all lands, by the vast majority of God's people, as their 'received texts.' Other texts have been put forth from time to time, but none have been found true and powerful enough to displace these two texts: The Masoretic Text of the Old Testament, and the Received Text of the New Testament.

THE GREEK TEXT IN THIS VOLUME

The Greek text herein is purportedly that which underlies the *King James Version*, as reconstructed by F. H. A. Scrivener in 1894. It thus differs to a degree from all previously printed editions of the Received Text (there are over 250 differences, most of them quite minor, between this text and the Stephens 1550 'standard' *Textus Receptus*). The present text was typeset in England for the Trinitarian Bible Society, and corresponds to *The New Testament in the Original Greek according to the Text Followed in the Authorized Version*, edited by F. H. A. Scrivener, and originally published by Cambridge University Press in 1894 and 1902. The present Trinitarian Bible Society edition of the Greek New Testament was published in 1976.

Careful study, however, will show that this present text does not agree 100% with the text used by the KJV translators, though virtually always it does so. In places it has a different reading than that found in the KJV (*e.g.* Matthew 12:24,27, Gk. *Beelzeboul*; KJV has *"Beelzebub"* — John 8:21, Gk. *sin*; KJV, *"sins"* — John 10:16, Gk. *one flock*; KJV, *one fold"* — 1 Corinthians 14:10, KJV has *of these,"* but it is omitted in the Greek — 1 Corinthians 16:1, the KJV has *"churches," without any MSS support at all;* the Greek has *church*. In other places the present text gives Greek words where the KJV translators indicated by italics that they had none (the following KJV italicised words are actually given in the Greek of this TBS edition: Mark 8:14, *the disciples*; Mark 9:42, *these*; John 8:6, *as though he heard them not*; Acts 1:4, *them*; 1 John 3:16; *of God*. Some of these readings do have minority MSS support — see *Majority Text Notes* in the appendix of this volume — it seems clear that these readings were not in the text chosen by the KJV translators. Nevertheless, to all intents and purposes, the TBS edition faithfully reproduces the KJV Greek text, as nearly as could be done at this date.

THE ENGLISH TRANSLATIONS

There are two translations in this volume, one appearing as the literal translation of the Greek words, with English equivalents placed directly under each of the Greek words, and the other, *A Literal Translation of the Bible* on the side of the page, serving to provide a straight-forward translation for the purpose of making it easy for the reader to see the proper word order in English, and thus to easily assimilate the message given in God's word on that page. Both translations are accomplished in a word-for-word translation. The 'conceptual idea' form of 'translating' the word of God has been rejected, studiously avoided because no person has the right, nor the inspiration, to rewrite God's word to conform it to his or her own concepts. Those passing off their conceptual ideas are, in our opinion, despising the words originally given, and carefully preserved, by God the Spirit through the prophets and apostles. It is only a dodge to give the paraphraser an opportunity to *"be as God,"* as Satan promised in his lie to Eve.

INTERPRETATIONS

In the matter of interpretation, or as some would call it, bias, there is no hesitation on our part to admit to the fact that there are many interpretive decisions that must be made in any translation of the Bible. It has been our determination to let the text say what it says. And so no particular set of beliefs has been inserted into the text by these translations. Nevertheless, by the very fact that a true translation must take into consideration the entire context of a word, or phrase, or sentence, or verse, interpretation must be present in making that translation. This is especially so in those places where a Greek word, apart from the context, may be correctly translated by several different English words. For instance, it does make a difference whether a person is "saved," or "cured." And conceivably there could be differences of opinion in the choice of an English word to express a Greek word in such cases.

If a list of interpretive renditions were to be compiled, these at least should be noted as present in this volume: *(s)* Punctuation has been added, and the original manuscripts have none; *(b)* capitals and small letters have been added, and the original manuscripts had only capital letters. Especially we have attempted to aid the reader by capitalizing pronouns connected to a Person of the Godhead. Without a doubt, there is room for differences of opinion here. In those places quoted from the Old Testament, the New Testament writers nearly always have fixed the deity of the Persons quoted, so these are not so interpretative. But in another class of places, where we have endeavored to capitalize, or not to capitalize pronouns — according to whether the persons addressing Jesus acknowledged Him as God — there is room for much difference of opinion. *(c)* Words have sometimes been added to aid the English reader to follow the sense, in which case those supplied words are in parentheses under the Greek, or in italics in the marginal English translation.

PRESUPPOSITIONS

Being a willing slave of our God and Savior, Jesus Christ, and joyfully submitting to His higher thoughts, we gladly admit to a number of presuppositions: *(a)* We have acted on the premise that *"the Scriptures cannot be broken"* (John 10:35), meaning that not an iota or a point of them has been lost; and having the firm conviction that each word was God-breathed, and that having had such an origin God Himself has taken it upon Himself to also carefully preserve His words for us even to this day, we have not dared to change a word, or to supply a word without designating it as uninspired by parentheses or by italics. If God has appeared at places to use an ambiguous word, we have tried to leave it that way, etc. *(b)* We have presupposed that Jesus Christ is not only our personal Savior and Lord, but that the Scriptures clearly reveal Him as equal with God the Father and with God the Holy Spirit, that He is in fact one of the three Persons in the Godhead; that He came to earth to give Himself as a fully-paid ransom for many; that He both lived and died as a substitute for the sins of all those who shall come to a saving knowledge and belief in Him; that He has risen to sit at the right of God the Father, ruling the world from there, interceding for and providentially guiding His own, until that day when He will destroy the earth by fire, and shall then come to receive all of them to a place at His right hand; and finally that He will sit as supreme Judge of all men of all ages, and that He will use the words of the Bible to judge the deeds of each and every person who will have inhabited the earth, casting all unbelievers into everlasting fiery punishment, and sitting all true believers at His feet to learn from Him *"the depths of the riches and of (the) wisdom and knowledge of God"* throughout all eternity.

DISTINCTIVE TRANSLATIONS

For easy apprehension, and continuity with the Old Testament, we have translated the Greek representing the names of the Old Testament characters and places by the same English names that were used there.

Due to the principle of translating each Greek word literally, a number of translations have emerged that are quite different from other versions:

The Greek word designating the mother of Jesus has always been translated "Mary," but most often the Greek word is actually **Μαριάμ**, properly meaning Mariam, or Miriam, rather than Mary. So we have given it. It is not that we think we can at this late date change her name in the mind of others from Mary to Mariam, but that we simply translated its literal meaning. It does answer to the question that some have raised, as to why there would be two Marys in one family.

In translating the Greek words for *"I am"* in certain places we have capitalized these words: *viz. I AM* (see John 8:59 and other places). It is our firm conviction that in those cases Jesus is identifying Himelf as

Jehovah (*Jehovah* properly translated, *I AM THAT I AM*). *Jesus* is of course the English name assigned to a word that means *Jehovah is salvation*.

Under the Greek we have translated literally, *"to the ages,"* though we surely believe that the words are a clear idiomatic expression for *"forever."* In the translation in the margin we have reversed this. Likewise we have translated under the Greek *"clean"* heart, but firmly believe that *"pure* could be idiomatically used.

We have tried to translate various places in a way that would not be misleading as to sex. Many times other translators have put *"any man"* where *"anyone"* was literally correct. Male pronouns and male references abound in the Scriptures. There is no good reason for supplying additional male references.

This is now the only interlinear New Testament in current, proper English. All others continue to use Elizabethan-age English. The Bible was written in simple, common Hebrew and Greek words, with no special language used when addressing God. Why now encase the Bible in a stilted language of another age, whether it be Latin or Elizabethan English. Tyndale wrote that every plowboy should be able to understand the Scriptures in his own language. Otherwise, why not leave it in the original languages?

Our constant aim in translation has been to represent the meaning of the Greek words in English as precisely and accurately as the English language will allow. This has included an attempt to display the meaning of compound Greek words so that the parts of them are expressed in the translation. For example, in John 8:7, Jesus did not merely rise, or stand up — He had bent down, and now he was bending back up — by which words we can visualize exactly what He was doing. This principle may have been imperfectly applied, but in succeeding editions an attempt will be made to achieve more of this type of accuracy.

There has been a conscious recognition of the value of consistency in translation. And although we believe we have achieved more consistency than in other versions, there is recognition on our part that there is yet more to be done in this area.

TRANSLATION PROBLEMS, CHALLENGES

Just as there are difficult places to understand, so there are difficult places to translate. And sometimes the difficulty is not so much in assigning meanings to the Greek words as it is in punctuating them so as to catch the apostle's meaning. One example of this is 1 Corinthians 12:2.

Among the many decisions made, some may want to challenge the translation chosen. In many places a Greek word has been left untranslated, usually a particle or an article, where it would be redundant or otherwise unsuitable to English transmission. Where the Greek order or words is difficult to English readers, superior numbers have not been used, because it is believed that the reader may more easily see the English order by referring to the translation in the margin. In most cases the literal translation of each word is given, rather than an idiomatic phrase, where it was considered more explanatory of the meaning than the idiom would supply. In some places where the present tense in Greek takes an English past for proper English, the past tense has been used in translation. But in a great many cases this has not been done, depending on the reader to realize the differences in the two languages. This is also true of the aorist. In fact we doubt that the New Testament writers themselves used the aorist in the strict (or, restricted) way that Greek grammarians interpret it today.

Due to space problems, a true translation of the participle has not always been given under the Greek.

For example, where the English words "having been" would be proper, "being" has often been given. In other places where the Greek word is short, but the English equivalent is long, a substitution may have been given (*e.g.* "by" instead of "through"). In the case of the double-negative construction in the Greek, it is often left as literally translated, rather than to change one negative to a positive in order to make good English out of it. In some cases the added strength of the double-negative, as intended in the Greek, has been transmitted by the use of punctuation.

Many other problems are encountered in rendering Greek into English. The reader is referred to other introductions to the Greek New Testament, especially to those in other interlinear New Testaments.

RESPONSIBILITY FOR THE TRANSLATIONS

The English translations in this volume, both the literal translation under the Greek words, and the translation named *A Literal Translation of the Bible*, are the work of Jay P. Green, Sr., improved and corrected by the suggestions of others who have reviewed these pages (both in the original manuscript, and in the many printings of this volume since). The responsibility for the assignment of English equivalents belongs to Jay P. Green, Sr., since he was the sole judge of what would, or would not, be allowed in either of the English translations.

In each printed volume an invitation will be given to all lovers of God's word to submit suggestions for improvement of these translations. May God be pleased to use us collectively to achieve the most accurate translation possible in the English language!

JAY P. GREEN, SR.
General Editor

PREFACE

TO THE SECOND EDITION

This much-improved Second Edition of *The Interlinear Greek-English New Testament* has been made more useful in many ways:

First, much credit must go to the host of serious students of the Bible who have purchased the tens of thousands of copies of the First Edition. Many of these have sent in suggestions for improvement, and most of those suggestions have been incorporated into this Second Edition.

Secondly, being convinced that they would save much more time and energy to those studying the New Testament, we have added to this volume the numbers assigned to each Greek word by James Strong in his *Strong's Exhaustive Concordance*. This has added one hundred pages to the volume, but it should prove to be well worth the extra cost.

Thirdly, the First Edition of *A Literal Translation of the Bible* has been printed in the margin. This also has benefited from a host of suggestions by others who are vitally interested in achieving the most accurate Bible translation possible in the English language. Proofreading by Philip Rosenbaum, and others, has been invaluable in eliminating errors and in improving the English translation in a goodly number of places.

Fourthly, the introduction of *A Literal Translation of the Bible* in the margins, and the re-typesetting of thousands of the lines of the interlineary portion of this volume, has now given it a far better appearance, and a much more readable character.

As General Editor and Translator, my heartfelt thanks must be expressed to all of you who have followed the leading of God the Spirit to participate in this effort to aid the readers and users of this volume.

SOME NOTES ON THE USE OF THE NUMBERING SYSTEM

In order to save both time and energy, and also to enhance general knowledge of the meaning of the individual Greek words, James Strong devised a number system for the Greek words of the New Testament, and he incorporated those numbers into his Greek Lexicon, which appeared in his *Exhaustive Concordance* in the last century. In recent years these numbers have been added to many of the Hebrew and Greek study volumes, such as *The Englishman's Greek Concordance, Thayer's Greek-English Lexicon, Englishman's Hebrew Concordance, Gesenius Hebrew-Chaldee Lexicon;* also the new *Concise Lexicon to the Biblical Languages* has the Strong's numbers in both the Hebrew and Greek sections. To complete the perfect circle of usefulness for serious Bible students, it was important that the Bible itself be numbered with these numbers. This has now been done in both this volume, and in the other three volumes of *The Interlinear Hebrew-Greek-English Bible*.

Please note the following suggestions for understanding the numbering system:

1. Because some Greek words are shorter than the numbers, where they appear close together, they are sometimes separated by a /. Also, in cases where many of these shorter words follow one another, there is not enough room to allow for all the numbers to be placed above the Greek words. In such a case the use of an asterisk above one or more of the words will indicate to the reader that the number for that word or

words will appear in the verse margin to the left of the line.

2. In order to avoid confusion and congestion which would be caused by the numbering some of the very common, short Greek words, these numbers have not been given above the words. The reader should not have any difficulty in finding the numbers of these words, usually articles and/or conjunctions, which nearly always are the following:

NOTE: Frequent words not numbered; **δέ** (1161); **καί** (2532—and, but); **ὁ, ἡ, τό** (3588—the).

3. Since some combinations of Greek words, usually two or three words following one another, have a combined meaning, or an idiomatic meaning, Strong assigned different numbers to the combination. In such cases you will find equal signs preceding and following the number, so that it will be seen that the one number covers all the words between the equal signs.

JAY P. GREEN, SR.
General Editor

CONTENTS

THE GREEK ALPHABET

The Greek alphabet has twenty-four letters: —

Form.		Equivalent.	Name.	
Α	α	a	ἄλφα	*Alpha*
Β	β	b	βῆτα	*Beta*
Γ	γ	g	γάμμα	*Gamma*
Δ	δ	d	δέλτα	*Delta*
Ε	ε	e (*short*)	εἶ, ἒ ψῑλόν	*Epsīlon*
Ζ	ζ	z	ζῆτα	*Zeta*
Η	η	e (*long*)	ἦτα	*Eta*
Θ	θ ϑ	th	θῆτα	*Theta*
Ι	ι	i	ἰῶτα	*Iota*
Κ	κ	k *or hard* c	κάππα	*Kappa*
Λ	λ	l	λά(μ)βδα	*Lambda*
Μ	μ	m	μῦ	*Mu*
Ν	ν	n	νῦ	*Nu*
Ξ	ξ	x	ξεῖ, ξῖ	*Xi*
Ο	ο	o (*short*)	οὖ, ὂ μῑκρόν	*Omīcron*
Π	π	p	πεῖ, πῖ	*Pi*
Ρ	ρ	r	ῥῶ	*Rho*
Σ	σ ς	s	σίγμα	*Sigma*
Τ	τ	t	ταῦ	*Tau*
Υ	υ	(u) y	ὖ, ὖ ψῑλόν	*Upsīlon*
Φ	φ	ph	φεῖ, φῖ	*Phi*
Χ	χ	kh	χεῖ, χῖ	*Chi*
Ψ	ψ	ps	ψεῖ, ψῖ	*Psi*
Ω	ω	o (*long*)	ὦ, ὦ μέγα	*Omĕga*

N. At the end of a word the form ς is used, elsewhere the form σ; thus, σύστασις.

ΕΥΑΓΓΕΛΙΟΝ

GOSPEL

ΤΟ ΚΑΤΑ ΜΑΤΘΑΙΟΝ

THE ACCORDING TO MATTHEW

THE GOSPEL
ACCORDING TO
MATTHEW

A LITERAL TRANSLATION OF THE BIBLE

CHAPTER 1

[1]The Book of the generation of Jesus Christ *the* son of David, *the* son of Abraham: [2]Abraham fathered Isaac, and Isaac fathered Jacob, and Jacob fathered Judah and his brothers. [3]And Judah fathered Pharez and Zarah out of Tamar; and Pharez fathered Hezron; and Hezron fathered Aram; [4]and Aram fathered Amminadab; and Amminadab fathered Nahshon; and Nahshon fathered Salmon; [5]and Salmon fathered Boaz out of Rahab; and Boaz fathered Obed out of Ruth; and Obed fathered Jesse; [6]and Jesse fathered David the king.

And David the king fathered Solomon out of *her who had been the wife* of Uriah; [7]and Solomon fathered Rehoboam; and Rehoboam fathered Abijah; and Abijah fathered Asa; [8]and Asa fathered Jehoshaphat; and Jehoshaphat fathered Jehoram; and Jehoram fathered Uzziah; [9]and Uzziah fathered Jotham; and Jotham fathered Ahaz; and Ahaz fathered Hezekiah; [10]and Hezekiah fathered Manasseh; and Manasseh fathered Amon; and Amon fathered Josiah; [11]and Josiah fathered Jehoiachin and his brothers,

CHAPTER 1

976 1078 2424 5547 5207 1138 5207
1 Βίβλος γενέσεως Ἰησοῦ Χριστοῦ, υἱοῦ Δαβίδ, υἱοῦ
(The) Book of generation of Jesus Christ, son of David, son
11
Ἀβραάμ.
of Abraham.
11 1080 2464 2464 1080
2 Ἀβραὰμ ἐγέννησε τὸν Ἰσαάκ· Ἰσαὰκ δὲ ἐγέννησε τὸν
Abraham fathered Isaac, Isaac and fathered
2384 2384 1080 2455 80
Ἰακώβ· Ἰακὼβ δὲ ἐγέννησε τὸν Ἰούδαν καὶ τοὺς ἀδελφοὺς
Jacob, Jacob and fathered Judah and the brothers
846 2455 1080 5329 2196 1537
3 αὐτοῦ· Ἰούδας δὲ ἐγέννησε τὸν Φαρὲς καὶ τὸν Ζαρὰ ἐκ τῆς
of him, Judah And fathered Pharez and Zarah out of
2283 5329 1080 5329 5329 1080
Θάμαρ· Φαρὲς δὲ ἐγέννησε τὸν Ἑσρώμ· Ἑσρὼμ δὲ ἐγέννησε
Tamar; Pharez and fathered Hezron; Hezron and fathered
689 689 1080 284 284
4 τὸν Ἀράμ· Ἀρὰμ δὲ ἐγέννησε τὸν Ἀμιναδάβ· Ἀμιναδὰβ
Aram; Aram and fathered Amminadab; Amminadab
1080 3476 3476 1080
δὲ ἐγέννησε τὸν Ναασσών· Ναασσὼν δὲ ἐγέννησε τὸν
and fathered Nahshon; Nahshon and fathered
4533 4533 1080 1003 1537 4477
5 Σαλμών· Σαλμὼν δὲ ἐγέννησε τὸν Βοὸζ ἐκ τῆς Ῥαχάβ·
Salmon; Salmon and fathered Boaz out of Rahab'
1003 1080 5601 1537 4503 5601
Βοὸζ δὲ ἐγέννησε τὸν Ὠβὴδ ἐκ τῆς Ῥούθ· Ὠβὴδ δὲ
Boaz and fathered Obed out of Ruth; Obed and
1080 2421 2421 1080 1138
6 ἐγέννησε τὸν Ἰεσσαί· Ἰεσσαὶ δὲ ἐγέννησε τὸν Δαβὶδ τὸν
fathered Jesse; Jesse and fathered David the
935
βασιλέα.
king.
1138 932 1080 4672 1537
Δαβὶδ δὲ ὁ βασιλεὺς ἐγέννησε τὸν Σολομῶντα ἐκ τῆς
David And the king fathered Solomon out of the
3774 4672 1080 4497 4497
7 τοῦ Οὐρίου· Σολομὼν δὲ ἐγέννησε τὸν Ῥοβοάμ· Ῥοβοὰμ
(wife) of Uriah; Solomon and fathered Rehoboam; Rehoboam
1080 7 7 1080 760 760
8 δὲ ἐγέννησε τὸν Ἀβιά· Ἀβιὰ δὲ ἐγέννησε τὸν Ἀσά· Ἀσὰ
and fathered Abijah; Abijah and fathered Asa; Asa
1080 2498 2498 1080
δὲ ἐγέννησε τὸν Ἰωσαφάτ· Ἰωσαφὰτ δὲ ἐγέννησε τὸν
and fathered Jehoshaphat; Jehoshaphat and fathered
2496 2496 1080 5604 5604 1080
9 Ἰωράμ· Ἰωρὰμ δὲ ἐγέννησε τὸν Ὀζίαν· Ὀζίας δὲ ἐγέννησε
Jehoram; Jehoram and fathered Uzziah; Uzziah and fathered
2488 2488 1080 881 881
τὸν Ἰωάθαμ· Ἰωάθαμ δὲ ἐγέννησε τὸν Ἄχαζ· Ἄχαζ δὲ
Jotham; Jotham and fathered Ahaz; Ahaz and
1080 1478 1478 1080 3128
10 ἐγέννησε τὸν Ἐζεκίαν· Ἐζεκίας δὲ ἐγέννησε τὸν Μανασσῆ·
fathered Hezekiah; Hezekiah and fathered Manasseh;
3128 1080 300 300 1080
Μανασσῆς δὲ ἐγέννησε τὸν Ἀμών· Ἀμὼν δὲ ἐγέννησε τὸν
Manasseh and fathered Amon; Amon and fathered
2502 2502 1080 2428
11 Ἰωσίαν· Ἰωσίας δὲ ἐγέννησε τὸν Ἰεχονίαν καὶ τοὺς
Josiah; Josiah and fathered Jehoiachin and the

at the carrying away of Babylon.

[12]And after the carrying away of Babylon, Jehoiachin fathered Shealtiel; and Shealtiel fathered Zerubbabel; [13]and Zerubbabel fathered Abiud; and Abiud fathered Eliakim; and Eliakim fathered Azor; [14]and Azor fathered Sadoc; and Sadoc fathered Achim; and Achim fathered Eliud; [15]and Eliud fathered Eleazar; and Eleazar fathered Matthan; and Matthan fathered Jacob; [16]and Jacob fathered Joseph, the *betrothed* husband of Mary, of whom Jesus was born, who is called Christ.

[17]So all the generations from Abraham to David *were* fourteen generations; and from David to the carrying away to Babylon, fourteen generations; and from the carrying away to Babylon until Christ, fourteen generations.

[18]Now the birth of Jesus Christ was this way —for His mother Mary had been betrothed to Joseph—before they came together, she was discovered *to be* pregnant in womb by *the* Holy Spirit. [19]But her husband Joseph being just, and not willing to make her a public example, *he* purposed to put her away secretly. [20]And *as* he *was* thinking about these things, behold, an angel of *the* Lord was seen by him in a dream, saying, Joseph, son of David, do not be afraid to take Mary *as* your wife. For that in her is fathered by *the* Holy Spirit. [21]And she will bear a son; and you shall call His name Jesus; for He shall save His

80 846 1909 3350 897
ἀδελφοὺς αὐτοῦ, ἐπὶ τῆς μετοικεσίας Βαβυλῶνος.
brothers of him, at the deportation of Babylon.

3326 3350 897 2423 1080
12 Μετὰ δὲ τὴν μετοικεσίαν Βαβυλῶνος, Ἰεχονίας ἐγέννησε
after And the deportation of Babylon, Jehoichin fathered

4528 4528 1080 2216
τὸν Σαλαθιήλ· Σαλαθιὴλ δὲ ἐγέννησε τὸν Ζοροβάβελ·
Shealtiel; Shealtiel and fathered Zerubbabel;

2216 1080 10 10 1080
13 Ζοροβάβελ δὲ ἐγέννησε τὸν Ἀβιούδ· Ἀβιοὺδ δὲ ἐγέννησε
Zerubbabel and fathered Abiud; Abiud and fathered

1662 1662 1080 107 107
14 τὸν Ἐλιακείμ· Ἐλιακεὶμ δὲ ἐγέννησε τὸν Ἀζώρ· Ἀζὼρ δὲ
Eliakim; Eliakim and fathered Azor; Azor and

1080 4524 4524 1080 885 885
ἐγέννησε τὸν Σαδώκ· Σαδὼκ δὲ ἐγέννησε τὸν Ἀχείμ· Ἀχεὶμ
fathered Sadoc; Sadoc and fathered Achim; Achim

1080 1664 1664 1080 1648
15 δὲ ἐγέννησε τὸν Ἐλιούδ· Ἐλιοὺδ δὲ ἐγέννησε τὸν Ἐλεάζαρ·
and fathered Eliud; Eliud and fathered Eleazar;

1648 1080 3157 3157 1080
Ἐλεάζαρ δὲ ἐγέννησε τὸν Ματθάν· Ματθὰν δὲ ἐγέννησε τὸν
Eleazer and fathered Matthan; Matthan and fathered

2384 2384 1080 2501 435 3137
16 Ἰακώβ· Ἰακὼβ δὲ ἐγέννησε τὸν Ἰωσὴφ τὸν ἄνδρα Μαρίας,
Jacob; Jacob and fathered Joseph the husband of Mariam,

1537 1080 2424 3004 5547
ἐξ ἧς ἐγεννήθη Ἰησοῦς ὁ λεγόμενος Χριστός.
out of who was born Jesus, (the) One) called Christ.

3956 3767 1074 575 11 2193 1138 1074
17 Πᾶσαι οὖν αἱ γενεαὶ ἀπὸ Ἀβραὰμ ἕως Δαβὶδ γενεαὶ
all Then the generations from Abraham until David, generations

1180 575 1138 2193 3350 897
δεκατέσσαρες· καὶ ἀπὸ Δαβὶδ ἕως τῆς μετοικεσίας Βαβυλῶνος
fourteen; and from David until the deporation to Babylon,

1074 1180 575 3350 897
γενεαὶ δεκατέσσαρες· καὶ ἀπὸ τῆς μετοικεσίας Βαβυλῶνος
generations fourteen; and from the deporation to Babylon

2193 5547 1074 1180
ἕως τοῦ Χριστοῦ γενεαὶ δεκατέσσαρες.
until the Christ, generations fourteen.

2424 5547 1083 3779 2258 3423
18 Τοῦ δὲ Ἰησοῦ Χριστοῦ ἡ γέννησις οὕτως ἦν. μνηστευθεί-
Now of Jesus Christ the birth thus was: being betrothed

1063 3384 848 3137 2501 4280
σης γὰρ τῆς μητρὸς αὐτοῦ Μαρίας τῷ Ἰωσήφ, πρὶν ἢ
for the mother of Him, Mariam, to Joseph, before

4905 846 2147 1722 1064 2192 1537 4151
συνελθεῖν αὐτούς, εὑρέθη ἐν γαστρὶ ἔχουσα ἐκ Πνεύματος
joining of them, she was found in womb, pregnant by Spirit

40 2501 435 846 1342 5607 3361 2309
19 Ἁγίου. Ἰωσὴφ δὲ ὁ ἀνὴρ αὐτῆς, δίκαιος ὤν, καὶ μὴ θέλων
Holy. Joseph And the husband of her, just being, and not willing

846 3856 1014 2977 630 846
αὐτὴν παραδειγματίσαι, ἐβουλήθη λάθρα ἀπολῦσαι αὐτήν.
her to expose publicly, purposed secretly to put away her.

5023 848 1760 2400 32 2962 2596
20 ταῦτα δὲ αὐτοῦ ἐνθυμηθέντος, ἰδού, ἄγγελος Κυρίου κατ'
these things And he meditating on, behold, an angel of (the) Lord by

3677 5316 846 3004 2501 5207 1138 3361 5399
ὄναρ ἐφάνη αὐτῷ, λέγων, Ἰωσήφ, υἱὸς Δαβίδ, μὴ φοβηθῇς
a dream as seen by him, saying, Joseph, son of David, not do fear

3880 3137 1135 4675 1063 1722 846
παραλαβεῖν Μαριὰμ τὴν γυναῖκά σου· τὸ γὰρ ἐν αὐτῇ
to take Mariam (as) the wife of you. that For in her

1080 1537 4151 2076 40 5088 5207
21 γεννηθὲν ἐκ Πνεύματός ἐστιν Ἁγίου. τέξεται δὲ υἱόν, καὶ
begotten by (the) Spirit is Holy. she will bear And a son, and

2564 3686 848 2424 846 1063 4982 3992
καλέσεις τὸ ὄνομα αὐτοῦ Ἰησοῦν· αὐτὸς γὰρ σώσει τὸν λαὸν
you shall call the name of Him Jesus. He For will save the people

848 575 266 848 5124 3650 1096
22 αὐτοῦ ἀπὸ τῶν ἁμαρτιῶν αὐτῶν. τοῦτο δὲ ὅλον γέγονεν,
of Him from the sins of them. this Now all happened
2443 4151 4483 5259 2962 1223 4396
ἵνα πληρωθῇ τὸ ῥηθὲν ὑπὸ τοῦ Κυρίου διὰ τοῦ προφήτου,
that be fulfilled that spoken by the Lord through the prophet,
3004 2400 3933 1722 1064 2192 5088 5207
23 λέγοντος, Ἰδού, ἡ παρθένος ἐν γαστρὶ ἕξει καὶ τέξεται υἱόν,
saying, Behold, the virgin in womb will conceive and will bear a son
2564 3686 848 1694 3739/2076 3177
καὶ καλέσουσι τὸ ὄνομα αὐτοῦ Ἐμμανουήλ, ὅ ἐστι μεθερμη-
and they will call the name of Him Emmanuel, which is, translated,
3326 2257 2316 1326 2881 575
24 νευόμενον, Μεθ' ἡμῶν ὁ Θεός. διεγερθεὶς δὲ ὁ Ἰωσὴφ ἀπὸ
with us God. being aroused And Joseph from
5258 4160 5613 4367 848 32 2962
τοῦ ὕπνου ἐποίησεν ὡς προσέταξεν αὐτῷ ὁ ἄγγελος Κυρίου·
the sleep, he did as commanded him the angel of (the) Lord,
3880 1135 848 3756 1097 846
καὶ παρέλαβε τὴν γυναῖκα αὐτοῦ, καὶ οὐκ ἐγίνωσκεν αὐτὴν
and took (as) the wife of him, and not did know her
2193 3739 5088 5207 848 4416 2564
25 ἕως οὗ ἔτεκε τὸν υἱὸν αὐτῆς τὸν πρωτότοκον· καὶ ἐκάλεσε
until she bore the son of her, the firstborn. And he called
3686 848 2424
τὸ ὄνομα αὐτοῦ ἸΗΣΟΥΝ.
the name of Him, JESUS.

CHAPTER 2

2424 1080 1722 965 2449 1722
1 Τοῦ δὲ Ἰησοῦ γεννηθέντος ἐν Βηθλεὲμ τῆς Ἰουδαίας, ἐν
And Jesus having been born in Bethlehem of Judea, in
2250 2264 935 2400 3087 575 395
ἡμέραις Ἡρῴδου τοῦ βασιλέως, ἰδού, μάγοι ἀπὸ ἀνατολῶν
(the) days of Herod the king, Behold, Magi from (the) east
3854 1519 2414 3004 4226 2076 5088
2 παρεγένοντο εἰς Ἱεροσόλυμα, λέγοντες, Ποῦ ἐστὶν ὁ τεχθεὶς
arrived into Jerusalem, saying, where is he born
935 2453 1492 1063 848 792 1722
βασιλεὺς τῶν Ἰουδαίων; εἴδομεν γὰρ αὐτοῦ τὸν ἀστέρα ἐν
king of the Jews? we saw For of him the star in
395 2064 4352 846 191
3 τῇ ἀνατολῇ, καὶ ἤλθομεν προσκυνῆσαι αὐτῷ. ἀκούσας δὲ
the east, and came to worship him. hearing And
2264 935 5015 3956 2414 3326
Ἡρῴδης ὁ βασιλεὺς ἐταράχθη, καὶ πᾶσα Ἱεροσόλυμα μετ'
Herod the king was troubled, and all Jerusalem with
848 4863 3956 749 1122
4 αὐτοῦ. καὶ συναγαγὼν πάντας τοὺς ἀρχιερεῖς καὶ γραμ-
him. And gathering all the chief priests and scribes
2992 4441 3844 846 4226 5547
ματεῖς τοῦ λαοῦ, ἐπυνθάνετο παρ' αὐτῶν ποῦ ὁ Χριστὸς
of the people, he inquired from them where the Christ
1080 2036 846 1722 965 2449
5 γεννᾶται. οἱ δὲ εἶπον αὐτῷ, Ἐν Βηθλεὲμ τῆς Ἰουδαίας·
was to be born. they And said to him, In Bethlehem of Judea.
3779 1063 1125 1223 4396 4771 965
6 οὕτω γὰρ γέγραπται διὰ τοῦ προφήτου, Καὶ σὺ Βηθλεέμ,
thus For it has been written by the prophet, And you, Bethlehem,
1095 2455 3760 1646 1488 1722 2232 2448 1537
γῆ Ἰούδα, οὐδαμῶς ἐλαχίστη εἶ ἐν τοῖς ἡγεμόσιν Ἰούδα· ἐκ
land of Judah, not at all least are you among the governors of Judah out of
4675 1063 1831 2233 3748 4166 2992
σοῦ γὰρ ἐξελεύσεται ἡγούμενος, ὅστις ποιμανεῖ τὸν λαόν
of you for will come out a Governor who will shepherd the people
3450 2474 5119 2264 2977 2564
7 μου τὸν Ἰσραήλ. τότε Ἡρῴδης, λάθρα καλέσας τοὺς
of Me, (even) Israel. Then Herod, secretly calling the
3097 198 3844 846 5550 5316
μάγους, ἠκρίβωσε παρ' αὐτῶν τὸν χρόνον τοῦ φαινο-
Magi, asked exactly from them the time of the appearing

people from their sins.

[22]Now all this happened so that might be fulfilled that spoken by the Lord through the prophet, saying, [23]"Behold! The virgin will conceive in *her* womb, and will bear a son; and they will call His name Emmanuel", which translated is, God with us.

[24]And being aroused from sleep, Joseph did as the angel of *the* Lord commanded him, and took his wife; [25]and did not know her until she bore her son, the Firstborn. And he called His name Jesus.

CHAPTER 2

[1]Now when Jesus had been born in Bethlehem of Judea in *the* days of Herod the king, behold, wise men arrived from *the* east to Jerusalem, [2]saying, Where is He born king of the Jews? For we saw His star in the east and have come to worship Him. [3]But Herod the king having heard *this*, *he* was troubled, and all Jerusalem with him. [4]And having gathered all the chief priests and scribes of the people, he asked of them where the Christ was to be born. [5]And they said to him, In Bethlehem of Judea, for so it has been written by the prophet,

[6]"And you, Bethlehem in the land of Judah, in no way are you least among the governors of Judah, for out of you shall come a Governor who shall shepherd My people Israel."

[7]Then secretly calling the wise men, Herod asked of them exactly the time of the

792 3992 846 1519 965 2036 4198
8 μένου ἀστέρος. καὶ πέμψας αὐτοὺς εἰς Βηθλεὲμ εἶπε, Πορευ-
star. And sending them to Bethlehem, he said, Having
199 1833 4012 3813 1875 2147
θέντες ἀκριβῶς ἐξετάσατε περὶ τοῦ παιδίου· ἐπὰν δὲ εὕρητε,
gone, exactly inquire about the child. when And you find,
518 3427 3704 2504 2064 4352 846
ἀπαγγείλατέ μοι, ὅπως κἀγὼ ἐλθὼν προσκυνήσω αὐτῷ.
report to me, so that I also coming may worship him.
191 935 4198 2400
9 οἱ δὲ ἀκούσαντες τοῦ βασιλέως ἐπορεύθησαν· καὶ ἰδού, ὁ
they And having heard the king departed. And, behold, the
792 3739 1492 1722 395 4254 846 2193 1492
ἀστήρ, ὃν εἶδον ἐν τῇ ἀνατολῇ, προῆγεν αὐτούς, ἕως ἐλθὼν
star which they saw in the east went before them until coming
2476 1883 3756 2258 3813 1492 792
10 ἔστη ἐπάνω οὗ ἦν τὸ παιδίον. ἰδόντες δὲ τὸν ἀστέρα,
it stood over where was the child. seeing And the star,
5463 5479 3173 4970 2064 1519
11 ἐχάρησαν χαρὰν μεγάλην σφόδρα. καὶ ἐλθόντες εἰς τὴν
they rejoiced a joy great, exceedingly. And coming into the
3614 2147 3813 3326 3137 3384 848
οἰκίαν, εἶδον τὸ παιδίον μετὰ Μαρίας τῆς μητρὸς αὐτοῦ,
house, they saw the child with Mariam the mother of Him.
4098 4352 846 455
καὶ πεσόντες προσεκύνησαν αὐτῷ, καὶ ἀνοίξαντες τοὺς
And falling down, they worshiped Him. And opening the
2344 846 4374 846 1435 5557
θησαυροὺς αὐτῶν προσήνεγκαν αὐτῷ δῶρα, χρυσὸν καὶ
treasures of them, they offered to Him gifts: gold and
3030 4686 5537 2596 3677 3361
12 λίβανον καὶ σμύρναν. καὶ χρηματισθέντες κατ' ὄναρ μὴ
frankincense and myrrh. And having been warned by a dream not
344 4314 2264 1223 243 3598 402 1519
ἀνακάμψαι πρὸς Ἡρῴδην, δι' ἄλλης ὁδοῦ ἀνεχώρησαν εἰς
to return to Herod, by another way they departed into
5861 848
τὴν χώραν αὐτῶν.
the country of them.

402 846 2400 32 2962
13 Ἀναχωρησάντων δὲ αὐτῶν, ἰδού, ἄγγελος Κυρίου
having departing Now they, behold, an angel of (the) Lord
5316 2596 3677 2501 3004 1453 3880
φαίνεται κατ' ὄναρ τῷ Ἰωσήφ, λέγων, Ἐγερθεὶς παράλαβε
appears by a dream to Joseph, saying, Rise up; take with (you)
3813 3384 848 5343 1519 125
τὸ παιδίον καὶ τὴν μητέρα αὐτοῦ, καὶ φεῦγε εἰς Αἴγυπτον,
the child and the mother of Him, and flee into Egypt
2468 1563 2193 302 2036 4671 3195 1063 2264 2212
καὶ ἴσθι ἐκεῖ ἕως ἂν εἴπω σοι· μέλλει γὰρ Ἡρῴδης ζητεῖν τὸ
and be there until I shall say to you. is about For Herod to seek the
3813 3384 848 5243 3880
14 παιδίον, τοῦ ἀπολέσαι αὐτό. ὁ δὲ ἐγερθεὶς παρέλαβε τὸ
child, to destroy Him. he And rising up took along the
3813 3384 848 3571 402 1519
παιδίον καὶ τὴν μητέρα αὐτοῦ νυκτός, καὶ ἀνεχώρησεν εἰς
child and the mother of Him by night, and departed into
125 2258 1563 2193 5054 2264 2443
15 Αἴγυπτον, καὶ ἦν ἐκεῖ ἕως τῆς τελευτῆς Ἡρῴδου· ἵνα
Egypt. And he was there until the end of Herod; that
4137 4483 5259 2962 1223 4396
πληρωθῇ τὸ ῥηθὲν ὑπὸ τοῦ Κυρίου διὰ τοῦ προφήτου,
be fulfilled that spoken by the Lord through the prophet,
3004 1537 125 2561 5207 3450 5119
16 λέγοντος, Ἐξ Αἰγύπτου ἐκάλεσα τὸν υἱόν μου. τότε
saying, Out of Egypt I have called the Son of Me. Then
2264 1492 3754 1702 5259 3097 2373
Ἡρῴδης, ἰδὼν ὅτι ἐνεπαίχθη ὑπὸ τῶν μάγων, ἐθυμώθη
Herod, seeing that he was mocked by the Magi, was enraged
3029 649 337 3956 3816 1722
λίαν, καὶ ἀποστείλας ἀνεῖλε πάντας τοὺς παῖδας τοὺς ἐν
greatly, and sending, he killed all the male-children in

star appearing. [8]And sending them to Bethlehem, he said, Having gone, search carefully for the child. And when you find *him*, bring me word again so that coming I may also worship him.

[9]And having heard the king, they departed. And, behold! The star which they saw in the east went before them until it had come and stood over where the child was. [10]And seeing the star, they rejoiced exceedingly *with* a great joy. [11]And having come into the house, they saw the child with His mother Mary. And falling down, they worshiped Him. And opening their treasures, they presented gifts to Him: gold and frankincense and myrrh. [12]And having been warned by a dream not to return to Herod, they went away into their own country by another way.

[13]And they having departed, an angel of *the* Lord appeared to Joseph by a dream, saying, Rise up! Take the child and His mother with *you*, and flee into Egypt. And be there until I shall tell you. For Herod is about to look for the child in order to destroy Him. [14]And having risen up, he took along the child and His mother by night, and withdrew into Egypt. [15]And he was there until the end of Herod, that might be fulfilled that spoken by the Lord through the prophet, saying, "Out of Egypt I have called My Son."

[16]Then having seen that he was fooled by the wise men, Herod was greatly enraged; and having sent, he killed all the boys in Bethle-

hem and in all its districts, from two years old and under—according to the time which he exactly asked from the wise men. [17]Then was fulfilled that spoken by Jeremiah the prophet, saying: [18]"A voice was heard in Ramah, wailing and bitter weeping, and great mourning, Rachel weeping for her children, and would not be comforted, because they were *not*."

[19]But Herod having expired, behold, an angel of *the* Lord appears to Joseph by a dream in Egypt, [20]saying, Rising up, take along the child and His mother, and pass over into *the* land of Israel; for those seeking the soul of the child have expired. [21]And rising up, he took along the child and His mother and came into *the* land of Israel. [22]But hearing that Archelaus reigned over Judea in place of his father Herod, he feared to go there. And having been warned by a dream, he departed into the parts of Galilee. [23]And coming he lived in a city called Nazareth; so as to fulfill that spoken by the prophets, "He shall be called a Nazarene.

CHAPTER 3

[1]Now in those days John the Baptist came preaching in the wilderness of Judea, [2]and saying, Repent! For the kingdom of Heaven has drawn near. [3]For this is he spoken of by Isaiah the prophet, saying: "The voice of *one* crying in the wilderness! Prepare the way of *the* Lord! Make His paths straight!"

[4]And John himself had

965 1722 3956 3725 846 575 1332
Βηθλεὲμ καὶ ἐν πᾶσι τοῖς ὁρίοις αὐτῆς, ἀπὸ διετοῦς καὶ
Bethlehem and in all the districts of it, from two years and
2736 2596 5350 3739 198 3844 3097
κατωτέρω, κατὰ τὸν χρόνον ὃν ἠκρίβωσε παρὰ τῶν μάγων.
under, according to the time which he exactly asked from the Magi.
5119 4137 4483 5259 2408 4396
17 τότε ἐπληρώθη τὸ ῥηθὲν ὑπὸ Ἱερεμίου τοῦ προφήτου,
Then was fulfilled that spoken by Jeremiah the prophet,
3004 5456 4671 191 2355 2805
18 λέγοντος, Φωνὴ ἐν Ῥαμᾷ ἠκούσθη, θρῆνος καὶ κλαυθμὸς
saying, A voice in Rama was heard, lamenting and weeping
3602 4183 4478 2799 5043 848
καὶ ὀδυρμὸς πολύς, Ῥαχὴλ κλαίουσα τὰ τέκνα αὐτῆς, καὶ
and mourning much; Rachel weeping for the children of her, and
3756 2309 3870 3754 3756 1526 5053
19 οὐκ ἤθελε παρακληθῆναι, ὅτι οὐκ εἰσί. τελευτήσαντος δὲ
not willing to be comforted, because not they were. having expired But
2264 2400 32 2962 2596 3677 5316
τοῦ Ἡρῴδου, ἰδού, ἄγγελος Κυρίου κατ' ὄναρ φαίνεται τῷ
Herod, behold, an angel of (the) Lord by a dream appears
2501 1722 125 3004 1453 3880 3813
20 Ἰωσὴφ ἐν Αἰγύπτῳ, λέγων, Ἐγερθεὶς παράλαβε τὸ παιδίον
to Joseph in Egypt, saying, Rising up, take along the child
3384 848 4198 1519 1093 2474 2348
καὶ τὴν μητέρα αὐτοῦ, καὶ πορεύου εἰς γῆν Ἰσραήλ· τεθνή-
and the mother of Him, and pass over into (the) land of Israel; have
1063 2212 5590 3813 1453
21 κασι γὰρ οἱ ζητοῦντες τὴν ψυχὴν τοῦ παιδίου. ὁ δὲ ἐγερθεὶς
expired for those seeking the soul of the child. he And rising up
3880 3813 3384 848 2064 1519
παρέλαβε τὸ παιδίον καὶ τὴν μητέρα αὐτοῦ, καὶ ἦλθεν εἰς
took along the child and the mother of Him, and came into
1093 2474 191 3754 345 936 1909
22 γῆν Ἰσραήλ. ἀκούσας δὲ ὅτι Ἀρχέλαος βασιλεύει ἐπὶ τῆς
(the) land of Israel. Hearing But that Archelaus reigns over
2449 473 2264 3962 848 5399 1563
Ἰουδαίας ἀντὶ Ἡρῴδου τοῦ πατρὸς αὐτοῦ, ἐφοβήθη ἐκεῖ
Judea in place of Herod the father of him, he feared there
565 5537 2596 3677 402 1519 3313
ἀπελθεῖν· χρηματισθεὶς δὲ κατ' ὄναρ, ἀνεχώρησεν εἰς τὰ μέρη
to go. being warned And by a dream, he departed into the parts
1056 2064 1730 1519 4172 3004
23 τῆς Γαλιλαίας, καὶ ἐλθὼν κατῴκησεν εἰς πόλιν λεγομένην
of Galilee. And having come, he dwelt in a city called
3480 3704 4137 4483 1223 4396 3754
Ναζαρέθ· ὅπως πληρωθῇ τὸ ῥηθὲν διὰ τῶν προφητῶν ὅτι
Nazareth; thus to fulfill that spoken through the prophet:
3480 2564
Ναζωραῖος κληθήσεται.
A Nazarene He shall be called.

CHAPTER 3

1722 2250 1565 3854 2491
1 Ἐν δὲ ταῖς ἡμέραις ἐκείναις παραγίνεται Ἰωάννης ὁ
in Now days those comes John the
910 2474 1722 2048 2449 3004
βαπτιστής, κηρύσσων ἐν τῇ ἐρήμῳ τῆς Ἰουδαίας, καὶ λέγων,
Baptist proclaiming in the wilderness of Judea, and saying,
3340 1488 1063 932 3772 3778
2 Μετανοεῖτε· ἤγγικε γὰρ ἡ βασιλεία τῶν οὐρανῶν. οὗτος
Repent! has come near For the kingdom of the heavens. this
1063 2076 4483 5259 2268 4396 3004
3 γάρ ἐστιν ὁ ῥηθεὶς ὑπὸ Ἡσαΐου τοῦ προφήτου, λέγοντος,
For is he spoken of by Isaiah the prophet, saying,
5456 994 1722 2048 2090 3598 2962
Φωνὴ βοῶντος ἐν τῇ ἐρήμῳ, Ἑτοιμάσατε τὴν ὁδὸν Κυρίου·
A voice of (one) crying in the wilderness: Prepare the way of (the) Lord;
2117 4160 5147 848 848 2491 2192
4 εὐθείας ποιεῖτε τὰς τρίβους αὐτοῦ. αὐτὸς δὲ ὁ Ἰωάννης εἶχε
straight make the paths of Him, he Now, John, had

his clothing from hairs of a camel, and a belt of leather about his loin. And his food was locusts and wild honey.

5 Then Jerusalem and all Judea went out to him, and all the neighborhood of the Jordan; 6 and were baptized by him in the Jordan, confessing their sins. 7 But seeing many of the Pharisees and Sadducees coming to his baptism, he said to them, Offspring of vipers! Who warned you to flee from the wrath to come? 8 Therefore, bring forth fruits worthy of repentance. 9 And do not think to say within yourselves, We have a father, Abraham. For I say to you that God is able to raise up children to Abraham from these stones. 10 But already the axe is even laid at the root of the trees; therefore, any tree not producing good fruit is cut down, and is thrown into fire. 11 I indeed baptize you in water to repentance; but He who *is* coming after me is stronger than I, whose sandals I am not fit to carry. He will baptize you in *the* Holy Spirit and fire; 12 whose fan *is* in His hand, and He will cleanse His floor, and will gather His wheat into the barn. But He will burn up the chaff with fire that cannot be put out.

13 Then Jesus arrived from Galilee to the Jordan, to John, to be baptized by him. 14 But John restrained Him, saying, I have need to be baptized by You, and do You come to me? 15 But

1742 848 575 2359 2574 2223 1193
τὸ ἔνδυμα αὐτοῦ ἀπὸ τριχῶν καμήλου, καὶ ζώνην δερ-
the clothing of him from hairs of a camel, and a belt of
4012 3751 848 5160 848 2258
ματίνην περὶ τὴν ὀσφὺν αὐτοῦ· ἡ δὲ τροφὴ αὐτοῦ ἦν
leather around the loin of him. the And food of him was
200 3192 66 5119 1607 4314 846
5 ἀκρίδες καὶ μέλι ἄγριον. τότε ἐξεπορεύετο πρὸς αὐτὸν
locusts and honey wild. Then went out to him
2414 3956 2449 3956 4066
Ἱεροσόλυμα καὶ πᾶσα ἡ Ἰουδαία καὶ πᾶσα ἡ περίχωρος τοῦ
Jerusalem and all Judea, and all the neighborhood of the
2446 907 1722 2446 5259 846
6 Ἰορδάνου· καὶ ἐβαπτίζοντο ἐν τῷ Ἰορδάνῃ ὑπ' αὐτοῦ,
Jordan; and were baptized in the Jordan by him,
1843 266 848 1492 4183
7 ἐξομολογούμενοι τὰς ἁμαρτίας αὐτῶν. Ἰδὼν δὲ πολλοὺς τῶν
having confessed the sins of them. seeing And many of the
5330 4523 2064 1909 908
Φαρισαίων καὶ Σαδδουκαίων ἐρχομένους ἐπὶ τὸ βάπτισμα
Pharisees and Sadducees coming on the baptism
848 2036 846 1081 2191 5102 5263 5213
αὐτοῦ, εἶπεν αὐτοῖς, Γεννήματα ἐχιδνῶν, τίς ὑπέδειξεν ὑμῖν
of him, he said to them, Offspring of vipers! Who warned you
5343 575 3195 3709 4160 3767 2590
8 φυγεῖν ἀπὸ τῆς μελλούσης ὀργῆς; ποιήσατε οὖν καρποὺς
to flee from the coming wrath? Produce, then, fruits
514 3341 3361 1380 3004 1722 1438
9 ἀξίους τῆς μετανοίας· καὶ μὴ δόξητε λέγειν ἐν ἑαυτοῖς,
worthy of repentance; and not do think to say in yourselves
3962 2192 11 3004 1063 5213 3754 1410
Πατέρα ἔχομεν τὸν Ἀβραάμ· λέγω γὰρ ὑμῖν ὅτι δύναται ὁ
A father we have Abraham. I say For to you that is able
2316 1537 3037 5130 1453 5043 11 2235
10 Θεὸς ἐκ τῶν λίθων τούτων ἐγεῖραι τέκνα τῷ Ἀβραάμ. ἤδη
God out of stones these to raise up children to Abraham. already
513 4314 4491 1186 2749 3956 3767
δὲ καὶ ἡ ἀξίνη πρὸς τὴν ῥίζαν τῶν δένδρων κεῖται· πᾶν οὖν
And even the axe at the root of the trees is laid. any Then
1186 3361 4160 2590 2570 1581 1519 4442
δένδρον μὴ ποιοῦν καρπὸν καλὸν ἐκκόπτεται καὶ εἰς πῦρ
tree not producing fruit good is cut off, and into fire
906 1473 3303 907 5209 1722 5204 1519 3341
11 βάλλεται. ἐγὼ μὲν βαπτίζω ὑμᾶς ἐν ὕδατι εἰς μετάνοιαν· ὁ
is thrown. I indeed baptize you in water to repentance. He
3694 3450 2064 2478 3450 2076 3739 3756 1510
δὲ ὀπίσω μου ἐρχόμενος ἰσχυρότερός μου ἐστιν, οὗ οὐκ εἰμὶ
But after me coming stronger than me is, of whom not I am
2425 5266 941 846 5209 907 1722
ἱκανὸς τὰ ὑποδήματα βαστάσαι· αὐτὸς ὑμᾶς βαπτίσει ἐν
worthy the sandals to bear. He you will baptize in
4151 40 4442 3739 4425 1722 5495 848
12 Πνεύματι Ἁγίῳ καὶ πυρί. οὗ τὸ πτύον ἐν τῇ χειρὶ αὐτοῦ,
(the) Spirit Holy and fire; of whom the fan (is) the hand of Him.
1245 257 848 4863 4621
καὶ διακαθαριεῖ τὴν ἅλωνα αὐτοῦ, καὶ συνάξει τὸν σῖτον
And He will cleanse the floor of Him, and will gather the wheat
848 1519 596 892 2618 4442
αὐτοῦ εἰς τὴν ἀποθήκην, τὸ δὲ ἄχυρον κατακαύσει πυρὶ
of Him into the barn, the But chaff He will burn with fire
762 5119 3854 2424 575 1056
13 ἀσβέστῳ. Τότε παραγίνεται ὁ Ἰησοῦς ἀπὸ τῆς Γαλιλαίας
unquenchable. Then arrives Jesus from Galilee
1909 2446 4314 2491 907 5259
ἐπὶ τὸν Ἰορδάνην πρὸς τὸν Ἰωάννην, τοῦ βαπτισθῆναι ὑπ'
at the Jordan to John, to be baptized by
846 2491 1254 846 3004 1473 5532
14 αὐτοῦ. ὁ δὲ Ἰωάννης διεκώλυεν αὐτόν, λέγων, Ἐγὼ χρε-
him, But John restrained Him, saying, I need
2192 5259 4675 907 4771 2064 4314 3165 611
ἴαν ἔχω ὑπὸ σοῦ βαπτισθῆναι, καὶ σὺ ἔρχῃ πρός με; ἀποκ-
have by You to be baptized; and You come to me? an-

answering, Jesus said to him, Allow it now, for it is becoming to us this way to fulfill all righteousness. Then he allowed Him. [16]And having been baptized, Jesus went up immediately from the water. And, behold! The heavens were opened to Him, and He saw the Spirit of God coming down as a dove, and coming upon Him. [17]And behold! A voice out of Heaven, saying, This is My Son, the Beloved, in whom I have found delight.

CHAPTER 4

[1]Then Jesus was led up, into the wilderness by the Spirit, to be tempted by the Devil. [2]And having fasted forty days and forty nights, afterwards He hungered. [3]And coming near to Him, the Tempter said, If You are *the* Son of God, speak that these stones may become loaves. [4]But answering, He said, It has been written: "Man shall not live by bread alone, but by every word going out of *the* mouth of God."

[5]Then the Devil takes Him to the holy city and *he* set Him on the wing of the temple. [6]And *he* said to Him, If You are *the* Son of God, throw Yourself down; for it has been written: "He shall give His angels charge concerning You, and they shall bear You on *their* hands, lest You strike Your foot against a stone." [7]Jesus said to him, Again it has been written: "You shall not tempt *the* Lord your God." [8]Again the Devil takes Him to a very high mountain, and *he* showed to Him all the kingdoms of the world, and

2424 2036 4314 846 863 737 3779 1063
15 ριθεὶς δὲ ὁ Ἰησοῦς εἶπε πρὸς αὐτόν, Ἄφες ἄρτι· οὕτω γὰρ
swering But Jesus said to him, Allow (it) now; thus for
4241 2076 2254 4137 3956 1343 5119
πρέπον ἐστὶν ἡμῖν πληρῶσαι πᾶσαν δικαιοσύνην. τότε
fitting it is to us to fulfill all righteousness. Then
863 846 907 2424 305 2117 5259
16 ἀφίησιν αὐτόν. καὶ βαπτισθεὶς ὁ Ἰησοῦς ἀνέβη εὐθὺς ἀπὸ τοῦ
he allows Him. And being baptized, Jesus went up at once from the
5204 2400 455 846 3772 1492
ὕδατος· καὶ ἰδού, ἀνεῴχθησαν αὐτῷ οἱ οὐρανοί, καὶ εἶδε τὸ
water. And, behold, were opened to Him the heavens; and He saw the
4151 2316 2597 5816 4058 2064
Πνεῦμα τοῦ Θεοῦ καταβαῖνον ὡσεὶ περιστερὰν καὶ ἐρχόμε
Spirit of God descending as a dove, and coming
1909 846 2400 5456 1537 3772 3004
17 νον ἐπ' αὐτόν. καὶ ἰδού, φωνὴ ἐκ τῶν οὐρανῶν, λέγουσα,
upon Him. And, behold, a voice out of the heavens, saying,
3778 2076 5207 3450 27 1722 3739 2106
Οὗτός ἐστιν ὁ υἱός μου ὁ ἀγαπητός, ἐν ᾧ εὐδόκησα.
This is the Son of Me, the Beloved, in whom I have found delight.

CHAPTER 4

5119 2424 321 1519 2048 5259 4151
1 Τότε ὁ Ἰησοῦς ἀνήχθη εἰς τὴν ἔρημον ὑπὸ τοῦ Πνεύ-
Then Jesus was led up into the wilderness by the Spirit,
3985 5259 1228 3522
2 ματος, πειρασθῆναι ὑπὸ τοῦ διαβόλου. καὶ νηστεύσας
to be tested by the Devil. And having fasted
2250 5062 3571 5062 5305
ἡμέρας τεσσαράκοντα καὶ νύκτας τεσσαράκοντα, ὕστερον
days forty and nights forty, afterward
3983 4334 846 3985 2036 1487 5207
3 ἐπείνασε. καὶ προσελθὼν αὐτῷ ὁ πειράζων εἶπεν, Εἰ υἱὸς
He hungered. And coming near Him, the Tempter said, If Son
1487 2316 2036 2443 3037 3778 740 1096
4 εἶ τοῦ Θεοῦ, εἰπὲ ἵνα οἱ λίθοι οὗτοι ἄρτοι γένωνται. ὁ δὲ
You are of God, say that stones these loaves may become. He But
611 2036 1125 3756 1909 740 3441 2198
ἀποκριθεὶς εἶπε, Γέγραπται, Οὐκ ἐπ' ἄρτῳ μόνῳ ζήσεται
answering said, It has been written: Not on bread alone shall live
444 235 1909 3956 4487 1607 1223 4750
ἄνθρωπος, ἀλλ' ἐπὶ παντὶ ῥήματι ἐκπορευομένῳ διὰ στό-
man, but on every word proceeding through (the)
2316 5119 3880 846 1228 1519
5 ματος Θεοῦ. τότε παραλαμβάνει αὐτὸν ὁ διάβολος εἰς τὴν
mouth of God. Then takes Him the Devil into the
40 4172 2476 846 1909 4418 2411
ἁγίαν πόλιν, καὶ ἵστησιν αὐτὸν ἐπὶ τὸ πτερύγιον τοῦ ἱεροῦ,
holy city, and sets Him on the wing of the Temple,
3004 846 1487 5207 1488 2316 906 4572 2736
6 καὶ λέγει αὐτῷ, Εἰ υἱὸς εἶ τοῦ Θεοῦ, βάλε σεαυτὸν κάτω·
and says to Him, If Son You are of God throw Yourself down;
1125 1063 3754 32 848 1781 4012
γέγραπται γὰρ ὅτι Τοῖς ἀγγέλοις αὐτοῦ ἐντελεῖται περὶ
it has been written for: To the angels of Him He will give charge about
4675 1909 5495 142 4571 3379 4350 4314
σοῦ, καὶ ἐπὶ χειρῶν ἀροῦσί σε, μήποτε προσκόψῃς πρὸς
You; and on hands they will bear You, lest You strike against
3037 4228 4675 5346 846 2424 3825 1125
7 λίθον τὸν πόδα σοῦ. ἔφη αὐτῷ ὁ Ἰησοῦς, Πάλιν γέγραπται,
a stone the foot of You. said to him Jesus, Again, it has been written,
3756 1598 2962 2316/4675 3825 3880
8 Οὐκ ἐκπειράσεις Κύριον τὸν Θεόν σου. πάλιν παραλαμβάνει
Not you shall tempt (the) Lord God of you. Again takes
846 1228 1519 3735 5308 3029 1166 846
αὐτὸν ὁ διάβολος εἰς ὄρος ὑψηλὸν λίαν, καὶ δείκνυσιν αὐτῷ
Him the Devil to a mount high exceeding, and shows Him
3956 932 2889 1391 848
9 πάσας τὰς βασιλείας τοῦ κόσμου καὶ τὴν δόξαν αὐτῶν, καὶ
all the kingdoms of the world, and the glory of them; and

their glory. [9]And *he* said to
Him, I will give all these
things to You if falling down
You will worship me.

[10]Then Jesus said to him,
Go, Satan! For it has been
written: "You shall worship
the Lord your God, and you
shall serve Him only."
[11]Then the Devil left Him.
And behold! Angels came
near and served Him.
[12]But Jesus hearing that
John was delivered up, He
withdrew into Galilee.
[13]And leaving Nazareth,
coming He lived at Caper-
naum, in *the* districts of
Zebulun and Naphtali;
[14]so that might be fulfilled
that spoken by Isaiah the
prophet, saying: [15]"Land of
Zebulun and land of Naph-
tali, way of *the* sea, beyond
the Jordan, Galilee of the
nations: [16]the people sitting in the darkness saw a
great Light; and to those
sitting in *the* region and
shadow of death, Light
sprang up to them."

[17]From that time Jesus
began to preach and to say,
Repent! For the kingdom of
Heaven has drawn near.
[18]And walking beside the
sea of Galilee, Jesus saw
two brothers, Simon called
Peter, and his brother
Andrew, casting a net into
the sea—for they were
fishers. [19]And He says to
them, Come after Me, and I
will make you fishers of
men. [20]And leaving the
nets, they immediately followed Him. [21]And going on
from there, He saw two
other brothers, James the
son of Zebedee, and his
brother John, in the boat
with their father Zebedee,
mending their nets. And He

3004 846 5023 3956 4671 1325 1437 4698 4352
λέγει αὐτῷ, Ταῦτα πάντα σοι δώσω, ἐὰν πεσὼν προσ-
says to Him, These things all to You I will give, if falling down You
3427 5119 3004 846 2424 5217 4567
10 κυνήσῃς μοι. τότε λέγει αὐτῷ ὁ Ἰησοῦς, Ὕπαγε, Σατανᾶ
will worship me. Then says to him Jesus, Go, Satan
1125 1063 2962 2316 4675 4352
γέγραπται γάρ, Κύριον τὸν Θεόν σου προσκυνήσεις, καὶ
It has been written for: (The) Lord God of you you shall worship, and
846 3441 3000 5119 863 846 1228
11 αὐτῷ μόνῳ λατρεύσεις. τότε ἀφίησιν αὐτὸν ὁ διάβολος· καὶ
Him only you shall serve. Then leaves Him the Devil, and
2400 22 4334 1247 846 191
12 ἰδού, ἄγγελοι προσῆλθον καὶ διηκόνουν αὐτῷ. Ἀκούσας δὲ
behold, angels came near and ministered to Him. having heard But
2424 3754 2391 3860 402 1519
ὁ Ἰησοῦς ὅτι Ἰωάννης παρεδόθη, ἀνεχώρησεν εἰς τὴν
Jesus that John was delivered up, He withdrew into
1056 2641 3478 2064 2730
13 Γαλιλαίαν· καὶ καταλιπὼν τὴν Ναζαρὲθ ἐλθὼν κατῴκησεν
Galilee. And having left Nazareth, having come, He lived
1519 2584 3864 1722 3725 2194
εἰς Καπερναοὺμ τὴν παραθαλασσίαν, ἐν ὁρίοις Ζαβουλὼν
in Capernaum beside the sea, in districts of Zebulun
3508 2443 4137 4483 1223 2268 4396
14 καὶ Νεφθαλείμ· ἵνα πληρωθῇ τὸ ῥηθὲν διὰ Ἡσαΐου τοῦ προ-
and Naphtali that may be fulfilled that spoken by Isaiah the
3004 1093 2194 1093 3508 3598
15 φήτου, λέγοντος, Γῆ Ζαβουλὼν καὶ γῆ Νεφθαλείμ, ὁδὸν
prophet saying, Land of Zebulun and land of Naphtali, way
2281 4008 2446 1056 1484 2992
16 θαλάσσης, πέραν τοῦ Ἰορδάνου, Γαλιλαία τῶν ἐθνῶν, ὁ λαὸς
of (the) sea beyond the Jordan, Galilee of the nations; the people
2521 1722 4655 1492 5457 3173 2521 1722
ὁ καθήμενος ἐν σκότει εἶδε φῶς μέγα, καὶ τοῖς καθημένοις ἐν
having sat in darkness saw a light great, and to those having sat in
5561 4639 2288 5457 393 846
χώρᾳ καὶ σκιᾷ θανάτου, φῶς ἀνέτειλεν αὐτοῖς.
a region and shadow of death, light sprang up to them.
575 5119 756 2424 2784 3004
17 Ἀπὸ τότε ἤρξατο ὁ Ἰησοῦς κηρύσσειν καὶ λέγειν,
From then began Jesus to proclaim and to say,
3340 1448 1063 932 3772
Μετανοεῖτε· ἤγγικε γὰρ ἡ βασιλεία τῶν οὐρανῶν.
Repent! has come near For the kingdom of the heavens.
4043 2424 3844 2281
18 Περιπατῶν δὲ ὁ Ἰησοῦς παρὰ τὴν θάλασσαν τῆς
walking And Jesus beside the sea
1056 1492 1417 80 4613 3004 4074
Γαλιλαίας εἶδε δύο ἀδελφούς, Σίμωνα τὸν λεγόμενον Πέτρον,
of Galilee saw two brothers, Simon being called Peter
406 80 848 906 293
καὶ Ἀνδρέαν τὸν ἀδελφὸν αὐτοῦ, βάλλοντας ἀμφίβληστρον
and Andrew the brother of him, casting a net
1519 2281 2258 1063 231 3004 846 1205
19 εἰς τὴν θάλασσαν· ἦσαν γὰρ ἁλιεῖς. καὶ λέγει αὐτοῖς, Δεῦτε
into the sea. they were For fishers. And He says to them, Come
3694 3450 4160 5209 231 444 2112
20 ὀπίσω μου, καὶ ποιήσω ὑμᾶς ἁλιεῖς ἀνθρώπων. οἱ δὲ εὐθέως
after Me, and I will make you fishers of men. they And at once
863 1350 190 846 4260 1564
21 ἀφέντες τὰ δίκτυα ἠκολούθησαν αὐτῷ. καὶ προβὰς ἐκεῖθεν,
forsaking the nets followed Him. And going on from there
1492 243 1417 80 2385 2199
εἶδεν ἄλλους δύο ἀδελφούς, Ἰάκωβον τὸν τοῦ Ζεβεδαίου καὶ
He saw other two brothers, James the (son) of Zebedee, and
2491 80 848 1722 4143 3326 2199
Ἰωάννην τὸν ἀδελφὸν αὐτοῦ, ἐν τῷ πλοίῳ μετὰ Ζεβεδαίου
John the brother of him, in the boat with Zebedee
3962 848 2675 1350 848
τοῦ πατρὸς αὐτῶν, καταρτίζοντας τὰ δίκτυα αὐτῶν·
the father of them, mending the nets of them,

called them. 22And at once
leaving the boat and their
father, they followed Him.

23And Jesus went around
all Galilee teaching in their
synagogues, and preaching
the gospel of the kingdom;
and healing every disease
and every *one of the* ill-
nesses among the people.

24And the report of Him
went out into all Syria. And
they brought to Him all the
ones having illness, suffering various diseases and
torments; also *those* having
been demon-possessed;
and lunatics, and paralytics;
and He healed them. 25And
many crowds followed Him
from Galilee and Decapolis,
and Jerusalem, and Judea,
and beyond the Jordan.

CHAPTER 5
1But seeing the crowds,
He went up into the moun-
tain, and seating Himself,
His disciples came near to
Him. 2And opening His
mouth, He taught them,
saying:

3Blessed *are* the poor in
spirit! For theirs is the
kingdom of the Heavens.

4Blessed *are* they who
mourn! For they shall be
comforted.

5Blessed *are* the meek!
For they shall inherit the
earth.

6Blessed *are* they who
hunger and thirst after
righteousness! For they
shall be filled.

7Blessed *are* the merci-
ful! For they shall obtain
mercy.

8Blessed *are* the pure in
heart! For they shall see
God.

2563 846 2112 863 4143
22 καὶ ἐκάλεσεν αὐτούς. οἱ δὲ εὐθέως ἀφέντες τὸ πλοῖον καὶ τὸν
And He called them. they And at once forsaking the boat and the
3962 848 190 846
πατέρα αὐτῶν ἠκολούθησαν αὐτῷ.
father of them followed Him.
4013 3650 1056 2424 1321
23 Καὶ περιῆγεν ὅλην τὴν Γαλιλαίαν ὁ Ἰησοῦς, διδάσκων
And went about all Galilee Jesus, teaching
1722 4864 848 2784 2098
ἐν ταῖς συναγωγαῖς αὐτῶν, καὶ κηρύσσων τὸ εὐαγγέλιον
in the synagogues of them, and proclaiming the gospel
932 2323 3956 3554 3956
τῆς βασιλείας, καὶ θεραπεύων πᾶσαν νόσον καὶ πᾶσαν
of the kingdom, and healing every disease and every
3119 2992 565 189 848 1519 3650
24 μαλακίαν ἐν τῷ λαῷ. καὶ ἀπῆλθεν ἡ ἀκοὴ αὐτοῦ εἰς ὅλην
sicknesses among the people. And went the report of Him into all
4947 4374 846 3956 2560
τὴν Συρίαν· καὶ προσήνεγκαν αὐτῷ πάντας τοὺς κακῶς
Syria. And they brought to Him all those illness
2192 4164 3554 931 4912
ἔχοντας, ποικίλαις νόσοις καὶ βασάνοις συνεχομένους, καὶ
having, various diseases and torments suffering, and
1139 4583 3885
δαιμονιζομένους, καὶ σεληνιαζομένους, καὶ παραλυτικούς·
demon-possessed, and lunatics, and paralytics.
2323 846 190 846 3793
25 καὶ ἐθεράπευσεν αὐτούς. καὶ ἠκολούθησαν αὐτῷ ὄχλοι
And He healed them. And followed Him crowds
4183 575 1056 1179 2414
πολλοὶ ἀπὸ τῆς Γαλιλαίας καὶ Δεκαπόλεως καὶ Ἱεροσολύμων
many from Galilee and Decapolis and Jerusalem
2449 4008 2446
καὶ Ἰουδαίας καὶ πέραν τοῦ Ἰορδάνου.
and Judea, and beyond the Jordan.

CHAPTER 5

1492 3793 305 1519 3735 2523
1 Ἰδὼν δὲ τοὺς ὄχλους ἀνέβη εἰς τὸ ὄρος καὶ καθίσαντος
seeing And the crowds, He went into the mount and sitting down
846 4334 846 3101 848 455
2 αὐτοῦ, προσῆλθον αὐτῷ οἱ μαθηταὶ αὐτοῦ· καὶ ἀνοίξας
Himself, came near to Him the disciples of Him. And opening
4750 848 1321 846 3004
τὸ στομα αὐτοῦ, ἐδίδασκεν αὐτούς, λέγων,
the mouth of Him, He taught them, saying,
3107 4434 4151 3754 848 2076
3 Μακάριοι οἱ πτωχοὶ τῷ πνεύματι· ὅτι αὐτῶν ἐστιν ἡ
Blessed (are) the poor in spirit, because of them is the
932 3772
βασιλεία τῶν οὐρανῶν.
kingdom of the heavens.
3107 3996 3754 846 3870
4 Μακάριοι οἱ πενθοῦντες· ὅτι αὐτοὶ παρακληθήσονται.
Blessed (are) the (ones) mourning, because they shall be comforted.
3107 4239 3754 846 2816 1093
5 Μακάριοι οἱ πρᾳεῖς· ὅτι αὐτοὶ κληρονομήσουσι τὴν γῆν.
Blessed (are) the meek, because they shall inherit the earth.
3107 3983 1372 1343
6 Μακάριοι οἱ πεινῶντες καὶ διψῶντες τὴν δικαιοσύνην·
Blessed (are) the (ones) hungering and thirsting (after) righteousness,
3754 846 5526
ὅτι αὐτοὶ χορτασθήσονται.
because they shall be filled.
3107 1655 3754 846 1653
7 Μακάριοι οἱ ἐλεήμονες· ὅτι αὐτοὶ ἐλεηθήσονται.
Blessed (are) the merciful, because they shall receive mercy.
3107 2513 2588 3754 846 2316
8 Μακάριοι οἱ καθαροὶ τῇ καρδίᾳ· ὅτι αὐτοὶ τὸν Θεὸν
Blessed (are) the pure in heart, because they God

[9]Blessed *are* the peacemakers! For they shall be called sons of God.

[10]Blessed *are* they who have been persecuted for righteousness' sake! For theirs is the kingdom of Heaven.

[11]Blessed are you when they shall reproach you, and persecute *you*, and shall say every evil word against you, lying, on account of Me. [12]Rejoice and leap for joy, for your reward *is* great in Heaven; for in this way they persecuted the prophets who *were* before you.

[13]You are the salt of the earth; but if the salt becomes tasteless, with what shall it be salted? For it has strength for nothing any more, but to be thrown out, and to be trampled under by men.

[14]You are the light of the world, a city situated on a mountain cannot be hidden. [15]Nor do they light a lamp and put it under the grain measure, but on the lampstand; and it shines for all who *are* in the house. [16]So let your light shine before men, so that they may see your good works, and may glorify your Father in Heaven.

[17]Do not think that I came to annul the Law or the Prophets; I did not come to annul, but to fulfill. [18]Truly I say to you, Until the heavens and the earth pass away, in no way shall one iota or one tittle pass away from the law until all comes to pass. [19]Whoever then shall break one of these commandments, the least, and shall teach men so, he shall be called least in the kingdom of Heaven. But

3700
ὄψονται.
shall see.
3107 1518 3754 846 5207 2316 2564
9 Μακάριοι οἱ εἰρηνοποιοί· ὅτι αὐτοὶ υἱοὶ Θεοῦ κληθήσονται.
Blessed (are) the peacemakers, because they sons of God shall be called.
3107 1377 1752 1343 3754 848
10 Μακάριοι οἱ δεδιωγμένοι ἕνεκεν δικαιοσύνης· ὅτι αὐτῶν
Blessed (are) those being persecuted because of righteousness, for of them
2076 932 3772 3107 2075 3752 3679
11 ἐστιν ἡ βασιλεία τῶν οὐρανῶν. Μακάριοί ἐστε, ὅταν ὀνειδί-
is the kingdom of the heavens. Blessed are you when they will
5209 1377 2036 3956 4190 4487
σωσιν ὑμᾶς καὶ διώξωσι, καὶ εἴπωσι πᾶν πονηρὸν ῥῆμα
reproach you and persecute, and shall say every evil word
2596 5216 5574 1752 1700 5463 21
12 καθ' ὑμῶν ψευδόμενοι, ἕνεκεν ἐμοῦ. χαίρετε καὶ ἀγαλλιᾶσθε,
against you, lying, for the sake of Me; rejoice and be glad,
3754 3408 5216 4183 1722 3772 3779 1063 1377
ὅτι ὁ μισθὸς ὑμῶν πολὺς ἐν τοῖς οὐρανοῖς· οὕτω γὰρ ἐδίω-
because the reward of you (is) great in the heavens. thus For they per-
4396 4253 5216
ξαν τοὺς προφήτας τοὺς πρὸ ὑμῶν.
secuted the prophets before you.
5210 2075 217 1093 1437 217 3471 1722
13 Ὑμεῖς ἐστε τὸ ἅλας τῆς γῆς· ἐὰν δὲ τὸ ἅλας μωρανθῇ, ἐν
You are the salt of the earth. if But the salt be tasteless, by
5101 233 1519 3762 2480 2089 1508 906 1854
τίνι ἁλισθήσεται ; εἰς οὐδὲν ἰσχύει ἔτι, εἰ μὴ βληθῆναι ἔξω
what shall it be salted? for nothing it is strong still, except to be thrown out,
2662 5259 444 5210 2075 5457
14 καὶ καταπατεῖσθαι ὑπὸ τῶν ἀνθρώπων. ὑμεῖς ἐστε τὸ φῶς
and to be trampled under by men. You are the light
2889 3756 1410 4172 2928 1863 3735
τοῦ κόσμου· οὐ δύναται πόλις κρυβῆναι ἐπάνω ὄρους
of the world; not is able a city to be hidden on a mount
2749 3761 2545 3088 5087 846 5259
15 κειμένη· οὐδὲ καίουσι λύχνον καὶ τιθέασιν αὐτὸν ὑπὸ τὸν
situated. Nor do they light a lamp and place it under the
3426 235 1909 3087 2989 3956 1722
μόδιον, ἀλλ' ἐπὶ τὴν λυχνίαν, καὶ λάμπει πᾶσι τοῖς ἐν τῇ
grain-measure, but on the lampstand, and it lightens all those in the
3614 3779 2989 5457 5216 1715 444
16 οἰκίᾳ. οὕτω λαμψάτω τὸ φῶς ὑμῶν ἔμπροσθεν τῶν ἀνθρώ-
house. Thus let shine the light of you before men.
3704 1492 5216 2570 2041 1392
πων, ὅπως ἴδωσιν ὑμῶν τὰ καλὰ ἔργα, καὶ δοξάσωσι τὸν
so that they may see of you the good works, and may glorify the
3962 5216 1722 3772
πατέρα ὑμῶν τὸν ἐν τοῖς οὐρανοῖς.
Father of you in the heavens.
3361 3543 3754 2064 2647 3551
17 Μὴ νομίσητε ὅτι ἦλθον καταλῦσαι τὸν νόμον ἢ τοὺς
Not do think that I came to annul the law or the
4396 3756 2064 2647 235 4137 281
18 προφήτας· οὐκ ἦλθον καταλῦσαι ἀλλὰ πληρῶσαι. ἀμὴν
prophets. Not I came to annul, but to fulfill. truly
1063 3004 5213 2193 302 3928 3772 2228 1093 2503
γὰρ λέγω ὑμῖν, ἕως ἂν παρέλθῃ ὁ οὐρανὸς καὶ ἡ γῆ, ἰῶτα
For I say to you, Until pass away the heavens and the earth, iota
1520 2228 3391 2762 3364 3928 575 3551 2193 302
ἓν ἢ μία κεραία οὐ μὴ παρέλθῃ ἀπὸ τοῦ νόμου, ἕως ἂν
one or one point in no way shall pass away from the law, until
3956 1096 3739 1437 3767 3089 3391 1785 5130
19 πάντα γένηται. ὃς ἐὰν οὖν λύσῃ μίαν τῶν ἐντολῶν τούτων
all things occur. Whoever, then, relaxes one of commandments these
1646 1321 3779 444 1646
τῶν ἐλαχίστων, καὶ διδάξῃ οὕτω τοὺς ἀνθρώπους, ἐλά-
the least, and teaches so men, least
2564 1722 932 3772 3739 302
χιστος κληθήσεται ἐν τῇ βασιλείᾳ τῶν οὐρανῶν· ὃς δ' ἂν
he shall be called in the kingdom of the heavens. who But ever

whoever does and teaches *them*, this one shall be called great in the kingdom of the Heavens. [20]For I say to you, If your righteousness shall not exceed *that of* the scribes and Pharisees, in no way shall you go into the kingdom of Heaven.

[21]You have heard that it was said to the ancients: "Do not commit murder!" And, "Whoever commits murder shall be liable to the Judgment." [22]But I say to you, Everyone who is angry with his brother without a cause shall be liable to the Judgment. And whoever says to his brother, Raca, shall be liable to the sanhedrin; but whoever says, Fool! shall be liable *to be thrown* into the fire of Hell.

[23]Therefore, if you offer your gift on the altar, and remember there that your brother has something against you, [24]leave your gift there before the altar, and go. First, be reconciled to your brother, and then coming, offer your gift.

[25]Be well-intentioned toward your opponent quickly, while you are in the way with him, that the opponent not deliver you to the judge, and the judge deliver you to the officer, and you be thrown into prison. [26]Truly, I say to you, In no way shall you come out from there until you pay the last kodrantes.

[27]You have heard that it was said to the ancients: "Do not commit adultery." [28]But I say to you, Everyone looking at a woman to lust after her has already committed adultery with her in his heart. [29]But if your right eye offends you, take it out and throw *it* from you—for it is profitable to you that one of your members should perish, and all your body not be thrown into Hell. [30]And if your right

4160 1321 3778 3173 2564 1722 932
ποιήσῃ καὶ διδάξῃ, οὗτος μέγας κληθήσεται ἐν τῇ βασιλείᾳ
does (them) and teaches, this one great shall be called in the kingdom
3772 3004 1063 5213 3754 3362 4052
20 τῶν οὐρανῶν. λέγω γὰρ ὑμῖν ὅτι ἐὰν μὴ περισσεύσῃ ἡ
of the heavens. I say For to you that if not shall exceed the
1343 5216 4119 1122 5330
δικαιοσύνη ὑμῶν πλεῖον τῶν γραμματέων καὶ Φαρισαίων,
righteousness of you more than the scribes and Pharisees,
3364 1525 1519 932 3772
οὐ μὴ εἰσέλθητε εἰς τὴν βασιλείαν τῶν οὐρανῶν.
in no way shall you go into the kingdom of the heavens.
191 3754 4483 744 3756 5407 3739
21 Ἠκούσατε ὅτι ἐρρέθη τοῖς ἀρχαίοις, Οὐ φονεύσεις· ὃς
You heard that it was said to the ancients: Not do murder; who
1161 302 5407 1777 2071 2920 1473 3004 5213
22 δ' ἂν φονεύσῃ, ἔνοχος ἔσται τῇ κρίσει· ἐγὼ δὲ λέγω ὑμῖν
and ever murders, liable shall be to the Judgment. I But say to you
3754 3956 3710 80 848 1500 1777 2071
ὅτι πᾶς ὁ ὀργιζόμενος τῷ ἀδελφῷ αὐτοῦ εἰκῇ ἔνοχος ἔσται
that each who is angry with the brother of him without cause liable shall be
2920 3739 302 2036 80 846 4469 1777
τῇ κρίσει· ὃς δ' ἂν εἴπῃ τῷ ἀδελφῷ αὐτοῦ, Ρακά, ἔνοχος
to the Judgment. who and ever says to the brother of him, Raca, liable
2071 4892 3739 2036 3474 1777 2071 1722
•302 ἔσται τῷ συνεδρίῳ· ὃς δ' ἂν εἴπῃ, Μωρέ, ἔνοχος ἔσται εἰς
shall be to the sanhedrin; who and ever says, Fool, liable shall be into
1067 4442 1437 3767 4374 1435 4675
23 τὴν γέενναν τοῦ πυρός. ἐὰν οὖν προσφέρῃς τὸ δῶρόν σου
the Gehenna of fire. If, then, you offer the gift of you
1909 2379 2546 3415 3754 80 4675 2192
ἐπὶ τὸ θυσιαστήριον, κἀκεῖ μνησθῇς ὅτι ὁ ἀδελφός σου ἔχει
on the altar, and there remember that the brother of you has
5100 2596 4675 863 1563 1435 4675 1715 2379
24 τι κατὰ σοῦ, ἄφες ἐκεῖ τὸ δῶρόν σου ἔμπροσθεν τοῦ θυσια-
some-thing against you, leave there the gift of you before the altar,
5217 4412 1259 80 4675
στηρίου, καὶ ὕπαγε, πρῶτον διαλλάγηθι τῷ ἀδελφῷ σου,
and go; first be reconciled to the brother of you,
5119 2064 4374 1435 4675 2468 2132
25 καὶ τότε ἐλθὼν πρόσφερε τὸ δῶρόν σου. ἴσθι εὐνοῶν τῷ
and then coming offer the gift of you. Be well-minded with the
476 4675 5035 2193 3755 1488 1722 3598 3326 846
ἀντιδίκῳ σου ταχύ, ἕως ὅτου εἶ ἐν τῇ ὁδῷ μετ' αὐτοῦ,
opponent of you quickly, until that you are in the way with him,
3379 4571 3860 476 2923 2923 4571
μήποτέ σε παραδῷ ὁ ἀντίδικος τῷ κριτῇ, καὶ ὁ κριτής σε
lest you deliver the opponent to the judge, and the judge you
3860 5257 1519 5438 906 281 3004
26 παραδῷ τῷ ὑπηρέτῃ, καὶ εἰς φυλακὴν βληθήσῃ. ἀμὴν λέγω
deliver to the officer, and into prison you be thrown. Truly, I say
4671 3364 1831 1564 2193 302 591 2078
σοι, οὐ μὴ ἐξέλθῃς ἐκεῖθεν, ἕως ἂν ἀποδῷς τὸν ἔσχατον
to you, in no way shall you exit from there until you pay the last
2835 191 3754 4483 744 3756 3431
27 κοδράντην. Ἠκούσατε ὅτι ἐρρέθη τοῖς ἀρχαίοις, Οὐ μοιχεύ-
28 kodrantes. You heard that it was said to the ancients, Not commit
1473 3004 5213 3754 3956 991 1135 4314
σεις· ἐγὼ δὲ λέγω ὑμῖν, ὅτι πᾶς ὁ βλέπων γυναῖκα πρὸς τὸ
adul-tery. I But I say to you that each one looking at a woman to
1937 846 2235 3431 846 1722 2588 848
ἐπιθυμῆσαι αὐτῆς ἤδη ἐμοίχευσεν αὐτὴν ἐν τῇ καρδίᾳ αὐτοῦ.
lust after her already has committed adultery with her in the heart of him.
•1188 1487 3788 4675 4624 4571 1807 846
29 εἰ δὲ ὁ ὀφθαλμός σου ὁ δεξιὸς σκανδαλίζει σε, ἔξελε αὐτὸν
if But the eye of you right offends you, take out it
906 575 4675 4851 1063 4671 2443 622 1722
καὶ βάλε ἀπὸ σοῦ· συμφέρει γάρ σοι ἵνα ἀπόληται ἓν τῶν
and throw (it) from you. profitable For to you that should perish one of the
3196 4675 3361 3650 4983 4675 906 1519 1067
30 μελῶν σου, καὶ μὴ ὅλον τὸ σῶμά σου βληθῇ εἰς γέενναν. καὶ
parts of you, and not all the body of you be cast into Gehenna. And

hand causes you to offend, cut it off and throw *it* from you—for it is profitable to you that one of your members should perish, and all your body not be thrown into Hell.

[31]It was also said, Whoever puts away his wife, let him give her a bill of divorce. [32]But I say to you, Whoever puts away his wife, apart from a matter of fornication, makes her commit adultery. And whoever shall marry the one put away commits adultery.

[33]Again, you have heard that it was said to the ancients: "You shall not swear falsely, but shall give your oaths to the Lord." [34]But I say to you, Do not swear *at* all, neither by Heaven, because it is God's throne; [35]nor by the earth, because it is the footstool of His feet; nor by Jerusalem, because it is *the* city of the great King. [36]Nor shall you swear by your head, because you are not able to make one hair white or black. [37]But let your word be Yes, yes; No, no. For whatever is more than these is from evil.

[38]You have heard that it was said: "An eye for an eye, and a tooth for a tooth;" [39]but I say to you, Do not resist the evil; but whoever strikes you on the right cheek, turn the other to him also. [40]And to him desiring to sue you, and to take your tunic, allow him also *to have* the coat. [41]And whoever shall compel you to go one mile, go two with him. [42]He asking you to give, and he wishing to borrow from you, do not turn away.

[43]You have heard that it was said, "You shall love your neighbor and hate your

1487 1188 4675 5495 4624 4571 1581 846 906
εἰ ἡ δεξιά σου χεὶρ σκανδαλίζει σε, ἔκκοψον αὐτὴν καὶ βάλε
if the right of you hand causes to offend you, cut off it and throw
575 4675 4851 1063 4671 2443 622 1520 3196 4675
ἀπὸ σοῦ συμφέρει γάρ σοι ἵνα ἀπόληται ἓν τῶν μελῶν σου,
from you. profitable For you that should perish one of the parts of you
3361 3650 4983 4675 906 1519 1067 4483 3754
31 καὶ μὴ ὅλον τὸ σῶμά σου βληθῇ εἰς γέενναν. ἐρρέθη δὲ ὅτι
and not all the body of you be cast into Gehenna. it was said And
3739 302 630 1135 848 1325 848 647
Ὃς ἂν ἀπολύσῃ τὴν γυναῖκα αὐτοῦ, δότω αὐτῇ ἀποσ-
Whoever puts away the wife of him, let him give her a bill
•3739 1473 3004 5213 3754 •302 630 1135
32 τάσιον· ἐγὼ δὲ λέγω ὑμῖν, ὅτι ὃς ἂν ἀπολύσῃ τὴν γυναῖκα
of divorce. I But say to you that whoever puts away the wife
848 3924 3056 4202 4160 846 3429
αὐτοῦ, παρεκτὸς λόγου πορνείας, ποιεῖ αὐτὴν μοιχᾶσθαι·
of him, apart from a matter of fornication, makes her commit adultery;
37391437 630 1060 3429
καὶ ὃς ἐὰν ἀπολελυμένην γαμήσῃ μοιχᾶται.
and whoever the put away one shall marry commits adultery.
3825 191 3754 4483 744 3756 1964
33 Πάλιν ἠκούσατε ὅτι ἐρρέθη τοῖς ἀρχαίοις, Οὐκ ἐπιορκή-
Again, you heard that it was said to the ancients, Not you shall per-
591 2962 3727 4675 1473 3004
34 σεις, ἀποδώσεις δὲ τῷ Κυρίῳ τοὺς ὅρκους σου· ἐγὼ δὲ λέγω
jure, shall deliver but to the Lord the oaths of you. I But say
5213 3361 3660 3654 3383 1722 3772 3754 2362 2076
ὑμῖν μὴ ὀμόσαι ὅλως· μήτε ἐν τῷ οὐρανῷ, ὅτι θρόνος ἐστὶ
to you, Not do swear (at) all, neither by Heaven, because throne it is
2316 3383 1722 1093 3754 5286 2076 4228
35 τοῦ Θεοῦ· μήτε ἐν τῇ γῇ, ὅτι ὑποπόδιόν ἐστι τῶν ποδῶν
of God; neither by the earth, because footstool it is of the feet
848 3383 1519 2414 3754 4172 2076 3173
αὐτοῦ· μήτε εἰς Ἱεροσόλυμα, ὅτι πόλις ἐστὶ τοῦ μεγάλου
of Him; neither to Jerusalem, because city it is of the great
935 3383 1722 2776 4675 3660 3754 3756 1410
36 βασιλέως· μήτε ἐν τῇ κεφαλῇ σου ὀμόσῃς, ὅτι οὐ δύνασαι
King; neither by the head of you swear, because not you are able
3391 2359 3022 2228 3189 4160 2077 3056
37 μίαν τρίχα λευκὴν ἢ μέλαιναν ποιῆσαι. ἔστω δὲ ὁ λόγος
one hair white or black to make. let be But the word
5216 3483 3483 3756 3756 4053 5130 1537 4190
ὑμῶν, ναὶ ναί, οὒ οὔ· τὸ δὲ περισσὸν τούτων ἐκ τοῦ πονηροῦ
of you, Yes, yes, no, no. the And excess of these out of the evil one
2076 191 3754 4483 3788 473 3788
38 ἐστιν. Ἠκούσατε ὅτι ἐρρέθη, Ὀφθαλμὸν ἀντὶ ὀφθαλμοῦ, καὶ
is. You heard that it was said, An eye instead of an eye, and
3599 473 3599 1473 3004 5213 3361 436
39 ὀδόντα ἀντὶ ὀδόντος· ἐγὼ δὲ λέγω ὑμῖν μὴ ἀντιστῆναι τῷ
a tooth instead of a tooth. I But say to you, Not do resist the
4190 235 3748 4571 4474 1909 1188 4675 4600
πονηρῷ· ἀλλ' ὅστις σε ῥαπίσει ἐπὶ τὴν δεξιάν σου σιαγόνα,
evil, but who you strikes on the right of you cheek
4762 846 243 2309 4671 2919
40 στρέψον αὐτῷ καὶ τὴν ἄλλην· καὶ τῷ θέλοντί σοι κριθῆναι
turn to him also the other; and he wishing you to sue,
5509 4675 2983 863 846 2440
41 καὶ τὸν χιτῶνά σου λαβεῖν, ἄφες αὐτῷ καὶ τὸ ἱμάτιον· καὶ
and the tunic of you to take, allow him also the coat. And
3748 4571 29 3400 1722 5217 3326 846 1417
42 ὅστις σε ἀγγαρεύσει μίλιον ἕν, ὕπαγε μετ' αὐτοῦ δύο. τῷ
who you shall compel to go mile one, go with him two. He
154 4571 1325 2309 575 4675 1155 3361
αἰτοῦντί σε δίδου· καὶ τὸν θέλοντα ἀπὸ σοῦ δανείσασθαι μὴ
asking you to give, and he wishing from you to borrow, not
654
ἀποστραφῇς.
do turn away.
191 3754 4483 25 4139 4675
43 Ἠκούσατε ὅτι ἐρρέθη, Ἀγαπήσεις τὸν πλησίον σου, καὶ
You heard that it was said, You shall love the neighbor of you and

enemy;" [44]but I say to you, Love your enemies, bless those cursing you; do well to those hating you, and pray for those abusing and persecuting you; [45]so that you may be sons of your Father in Heaven. Because He causes the sun to rise on *the* evil and *the* good, and sends rain on *the* just and unjust. [46]For if you love those loving you, what reward do you have? Do not the tax-collectors do the same? [47]And if you only greet your brothers, what exceptional *thing* do you do? Do not the tax-collectors do so? [48]Therefore, you be perfect, even as your Father in Heaven is perfect.

3404 2190 4675 1473 3004 5213 25
44 μισήσεις τὸν ἐχθρόν σου· ἐγὼ δὲ λέγω ὑμῖν, ἀγαπᾶτε τοὺς
you shall hate the enemy of you. I But I say to you, Love the
2190 5216 2127 2672 5209 2573
ἐχθροὺς ὑμῶν, εὐλογεῖτε τοὺς καταρωμένους ὑμᾶς, καλῶς
enemies of you, bless those cursing you, well
4160 3404 5209 4336 5228
ποιεῖτε τοὺς μισοῦντας ὑμᾶς, καὶ προσεύχεσθε ὑπὲρ τῶν
do to those hating you, and pray on behalf of those
1908 5209 1377 5209 3704 1096
45 ἐπηρεαζόντων ὑμᾶς, καὶ διωκόντων ὑμᾶς· ὅπως γένησθε
abusing you and persecuting you; so that you may be
5207 3962 5216 1722 3772 3754 2246 848
υἱοὶ τοῦ πατρὸς ὑμῶν τοῦ ἐν οὐρανοῖς, ὅτι τὸν ἥλιον αὐτοῦ
sons of the Father of you in (the) heavens. Because the sun of Him
393 1909 4190 18 1026 1909
ἀνατέλλει ἐπὶ πονηροὺς καὶ ἀγαθούς, καὶ βρέχει ἐπὶ
He makes rise on (the) evil and (the) good, and sends rain on
1342 94 1437 1063 25 25
46 δικαίους καὶ ἀδίκους. ἐὰν γὰρ ἀγαπήσητε τοὺς ἀγαπῶντας
(the) just and (the) unjust. if For you love those loving
5209 5101 3408 2192 3780 5057 846
ὑμᾶς, τίνα μισθὸν ἔχετε; οὐχὶ καὶ οἱ τελῶναι τὸ αὐτὸ
you, what reward have you? Not even do the tax-collectors the same
4160 1437 782 80 5216 3440
47 ποιοῦσι; καὶ ἐὰν ἀσπάσησθε τοὺς ἀδελφοὺς ὑμῶν μόνον,
practice? And if you greet the brothers of you only,
5101 4053 4160 3780 5057 3779 4160
τί περισσὸν ποιεῖτε; οὐχὶ καὶ οἱ τελῶναι οὕτω ποιοῦσιν;
what exceptional do you? Not do even the tax-collectors so do?
2071 3767 5210 5046 5618 3962 5216 1722
48 ἔσεσθε οὖν ὑμεῖς τέλειοι, ὥσπερ ὁ πατὴρ ὑμῶν ὁ ἐν τοῖς
be then You perfect, even as the Father of you in the
3772 5046 2076
οὐρανοῖς τέλειός ἐστι.
heavens perfect is.

CHAPTER 6

[1]Be careful not to do your merciful deeds before men in order to be seen by them. Otherwise, you have no reward from your Father in Heaven. [2]Therefore, when you do merciful deeds, do not trumpet before you, as the hypocrites do in the synagogues and in the streets, so that they may be glorified by men. Truly I say to you, they have their reward. [3]But you doing merciful deeds, do not let your left know what your right *hand* does, [4]so that your merciful deeds may be in secret. And your Father seeing in secret Himself will repay you in the open.

4337 1654 5216 3361 4160 1715
1 Προσέχετε τὴν ἐλεημοσύνην ὑμῶν μὴ ποιεῖν ἔμπροσθεν
Take care the merciful deeds of you not to do before
444 4314 2300 846 =1490 ==
τῶν ἀνθρώπων, πρὸς τὸ θεαθῆναι αὐτοῖς· εἰ δὲ μήγε,
men, in order to be seen of them. if But not,
3408 3756 2192 3844 3962 5216 1722 3772
μισθὸν οὐκ ἔχετε παρὰ τῷ πατρὶ ὑμῶν τῷ ἐν τοῖς οὐρανοῖς.
reward not you have from the Father of you in the heavens
3752 3767 4160 1654 3361 4537 1715
2 Ὅταν οὖν ποιῇς ἐλεημοσύνην, μὴ σαλπίσῃς ἔμπροσθέν
when Then you do merciful deeds, not do trumpet before
4675 5618 5273 4160 1722 4864
σου, ὥσπερ οἱ ὑποκριταὶ ποιοῦσιν ἐν ταῖς συναγωγαῖς καὶ
you, as the hypocrites do in the synagogues and
1722 4505 3704 1392 5259 444
ἐν ταῖς ῥύμαις, ὅπως δοξασθῶσιν ὑπὸ τῶν ἀνθρώπων·
in the streets, so that they may be glorified by men.
281 3004 5213 568 3408 848 4675 4160
3 ἀμὴν λέγω ὑμῖν, ἀπέχουσι τὸν μισθὸν αὐτῶν. σοῦ δὲ ποιοῦν-
Truly, I say to you, they have the reward of them. you But doing
1654 3361 1097 710 4675 5101 4160
τος ἐλεημοσύνην, μὴ γνώτω ἡ ἀριστερά σου τί ποιεῖ ἡ
merciful deeds, not do let know the left of you what does the
1188 4675 3704 5600 4675 1654 1722 2927
4 δεξιά σου, ὅπως ᾖ σου ἡ ἐλεημοσύνη ἐν τῷ κρυπτῷ· καὶ ὁ
right of you, so that of you the merciful deeds in secret, and the
3962 4675 991 1722 2927 848 591 4671 1722
πατήρ σου ὁ βλέπων ἐν τῷ κρυπτῷ αὐτὸς ἀποδώσει σοι ἐν
Father of you seeing in secret Him(self) will repay you in
5318
τῷ φανερῷ.
the open.

[5]And when you pray, you shall not be as the hypocrites, for they love to pray standing in the synagogues, and in the corners of the open streets, so that they may be seen of men. Truly I say to you, they have their reward. [6]But you, when you pray, enter into your room, and shutting your door, pray to your Father in secret. And your Father seeing in secret will repay you in the open. [7]But when you pray, do not babble vain words, as the nations, for they think that they shall be heard in their much speaking. [8]Then do not be like them, for your Father knows what things you have need of before you ask Him. [9]Therefore, you *should* pray this way:

Our Father *who is* in Heaven, let be sanctified Your name. [10]Let Your kingdom come; let Your will be done, as *it is* in Heaven, also on earth. [11]Give us today our daily bread, [12]and forgive us our debts as we also forgive our debtors. [13]And do not lead us into temptation, but deliver us from evil; for Yours is the kingdom, and the power, and the glory to forever. Amen.

[14]For if you forgive men their offenses, your heavenly Father will also forgive you. [15]But if you will not forgive men their offenses, neither will your Father forgive your offenses.

[16]And when you fast, do not be as the hypocrites,

3752 4336 3756 2071 5618 5273 3754
5 Καὶ ὅταν προσεύχῃ, οὐκ ἔσῃ ὥσπερ οἱ ὑποκριταί, ὅτι
And when you pray, not you shall be as the hypocrites, because
5368 1722 4864 1722 1137
φιλοῦσιν ἐν ταῖς συναγωγαῖς καὶ ἐν ταῖς γωνίαις τῶν
they love in the synagogues and in the corners of the
4113 2476 4336 3704 302 5316
πλατειῶν ἑστῶτες προσεύχεσθαι, ὅπως ἂν φανῶσι τοῖς
open streets standing to pray, so that may they appear
444 281 3004 5213 3754 568 3408
ἀνθρώποις· ἀμὴν λέγω ὑμῖν ὅτι ἀπέχουσι τὸν μισθὸν
to men. Truly, I say to you that they have the reward
848 4771 3752 4336 1525 1519 5009 4675
6 αὐτῶν. σὺ δέ, ὅταν προσεύχῃ, εἴσελθε εἰς τὸ ταμιεῖόν σου,
of them. you But, when you pray, enter into the room of you
2808 2374 4675 4336 3962 4675
καὶ κλείσας τὴν θύραν σου, πρόσευξαι τῷ πατρί σου τῷ
and shutting the door of you, pray to the Father of you
1722 2927 3962 4675 991 1722 2927
ἐν τῷ κρυπτῷ· καὶ ὁ πατήρ σου ὁ βλέπων ἐν τῷ κρυπτῷ
in secret; and the Father of you seeing in secret
591 4671 1722 5318 4336 3361 945
7 ἀποδώσει σοι ἐν τῷ φανερῷ. προσευχόμενοι δὲ μὴ βαττο-
will repay you in the open. when praying But, not do use
5618 1482 1380 1063 3754 1733 4180
λογήσητε, ὥσπερ οἱ ἐθνικοί· δοκοῦσι γὰρ ὅτι ἐν τῇ πολυ-
vain repetition, as the nations; they think for that in much
848 1522 3361 3754 3666 846
8 λογίᾳ αὐτῶν εἰσακουσθήσονται. μὴ οὖν ὁμοιωθῆτε αὐτοῖς·
speaking of them they will be heard. not Then do be like them,
1492 1063 3962 5216 3739 5532 2192 4253 5209
οἶδε γὰρ ὁ πατὴρ ὑμῶν ὧν χρείαν ἔχετε, πρὸ τοῦ ὑμᾶς
knows for the Father of you what things need you have before you
154 846 3779 3767 4336 5210 3962 2257
9 αἰτῆσαι αὐτόν. οὕτως οὖν προσεύχεσθε ὑμεῖς· Πάτερ ἡμῶν
ask Him. So then pray you, Father of us
1722 3772 37 3686 4675 2064
10 ὁ ἐν τοῖς οὐρανοῖς, ἁγιασθήτω τὸ ὄνομά σου· ἐλθέτω ἡ
in the heavens, let be sanctified the name of You. Let come the
932 4675 1096 2307 4675 5613 • 3772
•1722 βασιλεία σου· γενηθήτω τὸ θέλημά σου, ὡς ἐν οὐρανῷ, καὶ
kingdom of You; let be done the will of You, as in Heaven, also
1909 1093 740 2257 1967 1325 2254
11 ἐπὶ τῆς γῆς· τὸν ἄρτον ἡμῶν τὸν ἐπιούσιον δὸς ἡμῖν
on the earth. The bread of us daily, give to us
4594 863 2254 3783 2257 5613 2249
12 σήμερον· καὶ ἄφες ἡμῖν τὰ ὀφειλήματα ἡμῶν, ὡς καὶ ἡμεῖς
today, and forgive us the debts of us, as also we
863 3781 2257 3361 1533 2248 1519
13 ἀφίεμεν τοῖς ὀφειλέταις ἡμῶν· καὶ μὴ εἰσενέγκῃς ἡμᾶς εἰς
forgive the debtors of us. And not lead us into
3986 235 4508 2248 575 4190 3754 4675
πειρασμόν, ἀλλὰ ῥῦσαι ἡμᾶς ἀπὸ τοῦ πονηροῦ. ὅτι σοῦ
temptation, but deliver us from evil; because of You
2076 932 1411 1391 1519 165
ἐστιν ἡ βασιλεία καὶ ἡ δύναμις καὶ ἡ δόξα εἰς τοὺς αἰῶνας.
is the kingdom, and the power, and the glory to the ages.
281 1437 1063 863 444 3900
14 ἀμήν. ἐὰν γὰρ ἀφῆτε τοῖς ἀνθρώποις τὰ παραπτώματα
Amen. if For you forgive men the trespasses
848 863 5213 3962 5216 3770 1437
15 αὐτῶν, ἀφήσει καὶ ὑμῖν ὁ πατὴρ ὑμῶν ὁ οὐράνιος· ἐὰν δὲ
of them, will forgive also you the Father of you heavenly. if But
3361 863 444 3900 848 3761
μὴ ἀφῆτε τοῖς ἀνθρώποις τὰ παραπτώματα αὐτῶν, οὐδὲ ὁ
not you forgive men the trespasses of them, neither the
3962 5216 863 3900 5216
πατὴρ ὑμῶν ἀφήσει τὰ παραπτώματα ὑμῶν.
Father of you will forgive the trespasses of you.
3752 3522 3361 1906 5618 5273
16 Ὅταν δὲ νηστεύητε, μὴ γίνεσθε ὥσπερ οἱ ὑποκριταί
when And you fast, not do be as the hypocrites,

darkening the face, for they disfigure their faces so that they may appear to men to be fasting. Truly I say to you that they have their reward. [17]But you *in* fasting, anoint your head and wash your face, [18]so as not to appear to men to be fasting, but to your Father in secret. And your Father seeing in secret will repay you in the open.

[19]Do not treasure up for you treasures on the earth, where moth and rust cause to vanish, and where thieves dig through and steal. [20]But treasure up for you treasures in Heaven, where neither moth nor rust cause to vanish, and where thieves do not dig through and steal. [21]For where your treasure is, there your heart will be also.

[22]The lamp of the body is the eye. If, then, your eye is sound, all your body is light. [23]But if your eye is evil, all your body is dark. If, then, the light in you is darkness, how great *is* the darkness! [24]No one is able to serve two lords; for either he will hate the one, and he will love the other; or he will cleave to the one, and he will despise the other. You are not able to serve God and wealth. [25]Because of this, I say to you, Do not be anxious for your soul, what you eat and what you drink; nor for your body, what you put on. Is not the soul more than the food, and the body than the clothing? [26]Observe the birds of the heaven, that they do not sow, nor do they reap, nor

4659 853 1063 4383 848 3704
σκυθρωποί· ἀφανίζουσι γὰρ τὰ πρόσωπα αὑτῶν, ὅπως
darkening the face; they disfigure for the faces of them so as

5316 444 3522 281 3004 5213 3754
φανῶσι τοῖς ἀνθρώποις νηστεύοντες· ἀμὴν λέγω ὑμῖν ὅτι
they appear to men fasting. Truly, I say to you that

568 3408 848 4771 3522 218 4675
17 ἀπέχουσι τὸν μισθὸν αὑτῶν. σὺ δὲ νηστεύων ἄλειψαί σου
they have the reward of them. you But (in) fasting, anoint of you

2776 4383 4675 3538 3704 3361 5316
18 τὴν κεφαλήν, καὶ τὸ πρόσωπόν σου νίψαι, ὅπως μὴ φανῇς
the head, and the face of you wash, so as not to appear

444 3522 235 3962 4675 1722
τοῖς ἀνθρώποις νηστεύων, ἀλλὰ τῷ πατρί σου τῷ ἐν τῷ
to men fasting, but to the Father of you in

2927 3962 4675 991 1722 2927 591
κρυπτῷ· καὶ ὁ πατήρ σου ὁ βλέπων ἐν τῷ κρυπτῷ ἀποδώ-
secret; and the Father of you seeing in secret will repay

4671 1722 5318
σει σοι ἐν τῷ φανερῷ.
you in the open.

3361 2343 5213 2344 1909 1093 3699 4597
19 Μὴ θησαυρίζετε ὑμῖν θησαυροὺς ἐπὶ τῆς γῆς, ὅπου σὴς
Not do treasure up for you treasures on the earth, where moth

1035 853 3699 2812 1358
καὶ βρῶσις ἀφανίζει, καὶ ὅπου κλέπται διορύσσουσι καὶ
and rust cause to vanish, and where thieves dig through and

2813 2343 5213 2344 1722 3772
20 κλέπτουσι· θησαυρίζετε δὲ ὑμῖν θησαυροὺς ἐν οὐρανῷ,
steal. treasure up But for you treasures in Heaven,

3699 3777 4597 3777 1035 853 3699 2812 3756
ὅπου οὔτε σὴς οὔτε βρῶσις ἀφανίζει, καὶ ὅπου κλέπται οὐ
where neither moth nor rust cause to vanish, and where thieves not

1358 3761 2813 3699 1063 2076 2344
21 διορύσσουσιν οὐδὲ κλέπτουσιν. ὅπου γάρ ἐστιν ὁ θησαυρὸς
dig through nor steal. where For is the treasure

5216 1563 2071 2588 5216 3088 4983
22 ὑμῶν, ἐκεῖ ἔσται καὶ ἡ καρδία ὑμῶν. ὁ λύχνος τοῦ σώματός
of you, there will be also the heart of you. The lamp of the body

2076 3788 1437 3767 3788 4675 573 5600 3650
ἐστιν ὁ ὀφθαλμός· ἐὰν οὖν ὁ ὀφθαλμός σου ἁπλοῦς ᾖ, ὅλον
is the eye. If, then, the eye of you sound be, all

4983 4675 5460 2071 1437 3788 4675 4190
23 τὸ σῶμά σου φωτεινὸν ἔσται· ἐὰν δὲ ὁ ὀφθαλμός σου πονη-
the body of you light is. if But the eye of you evil

5600 3650 4983 4675 4652 2071 1487 3767 5457
ρὸς ᾖ, ὅλον τὸ σῶμά σου σκοτεινὸν ἔσται. εἰ οὖν τὸ φῶς τὸ
be, all the body of you dark is. If, then, the light

1722 4671 4655 2076 4655 4214 3762 1410 1417
24 ἐν σοὶ σκότος ἐστί, τὸ σκότος πόσον; οὐδεὶς δύναται δυσὶ
in you darkness is, the darkness how great! No one is able two

2962 1398 2228 1063 1520 3404 2087
κυρίοις δουλεύειν· ἢ γὰρ τὸν ἕνα μισήσει, καὶ τὸν ἕτερον
lords to serve, either For the one he will hate, and the other

25 2228 1520 472 2087 2706
ἀγαπήσει· ἢ ἑνὸς ἀνθέξεται, καὶ τοῦ ἑτέρου καταφρονήσει.
he will love, or one he will cleave to, and the other he will despise.

3756 1410 2316 1398 3126 1223 5124 3004
25 οὐ δύνασθε Θεῷ δουλεύειν καὶ μαμμωνᾷ. διὰ τοῦτο λέγω
not you are able God to serve and wealth. Because of this, I say,

5213 336 3309 5590 5216 5101 5315 5101 4095
ὑμῖν, μὴ μεριμνᾶτε τῇ ψυχῇ ὑμῶν, τί φάγητε καὶ τί πίητε·
to you, not do be anxious for the soul of you, what you eat, and what drink;

3366 4983 5216 5101 1746 3780 5590 4119
μηδὲ τῷ σώματι ὑμῶν, τί ἐνδύσησθε. οὐχὶ ἡ ψυχὴ πλεῖόν
nor for the body of you, what you put on. not the soul more

2076 5160 4983 1742 1689
26 ἐστι τῆς τροφῆς, καὶ τὸ σῶμα τοῦ ἐνδύματος; ἐμβλέψατε
is than the food, and the body than the clothing? Look

1519 4071 3772 3754 3756 4687 3761 2325
εἰς τὰ πετεινὰ τοῦ οὐρανοῦ, ὅτι οὐ σπείρουσιν, οὐδὲ θερί-
at the birds of the heaven, that not they sow, nor do they

NOTE: Frequent words not numbered: δέ(1161); καί(2531)—and, but; ὁ, ἡ, τό (3588, the)— * above word, look in verse margin for No.

do *they* gather into barns; yet your heavenly Father feeds them. Do you not rather excel them?

[27]But who of you *by* being anxious is able to add one cubit onto his stature?

[28]And why are you anxious about clothing? Consider the lilies of the field, how they grow. They do not labor nor do they spin; [29]but I say to you that not even Solomon in all his glory was clothed as one of these. [30]If God so enrobes the grass of the field—*which* is today, and is thrown into a furnace tomorrow—*will He* not much rather you, littlefaiths? [31]Then do not be anxious, saying, What may we eat? Or, what may we drink? Or, what may clothe us? [32]For after all these things the nations seek. For your heavenly Father knows that you have need of all these things. [33]But seek first the kingdom of God and His righteousness, and all these things will be added to you. [34]Then do not be anxious for tomorrow. For the morrow will be anxious of itself. Sufficient to *each* day *is* its *own* badness.

CHAPTER 7

[1]Do not judge, that you may not be judged; [2]for with whatever judgment you judge, you will be judged; and with whatever measure you measure, it will be measured again to you. [3]But why do you look on the twig that *is* in the eye of your brother, but do not see the log in your eye? [4]Or how will you say to your brother, Allow me to cast out the twig from your eye; and behold, the log *is* in your eye! [5]Hypocrite, first

3761 4863 1519 596 3962 5216
ζουσιν, οὐδὲ συνάγουσιν εἰς ἀποθήκας, καὶ ὁ πατὴρ ὑμῶν ὁ
reap, not do gather into barns; yet the Father of you
3770 5142 846 4756 5210 3123 1308 846
οὐράνιος τρέφει αὐτά· οὐχ ὑμεῖς μᾶλλον διαφέρετε αὐτῶν;
heavenly feeds them. Not do you rather excel them?
5101 1537 5216 3309 1410 4369 1909
27 τίς δὲ ἐξ ὑμῶν μεριμνῶν δύναται προσθεῖναι ἐπὶ τὴν
who But of you being anxious is able to add onto the
2244 848 4083 1520 4012 1742 5101 3309
28 ἡλικίαν αὐτοῦ πῆχυν ἕνα; καὶ περὶ ἐνδύματος τί μεριμνᾶτε;
stature of him cubit one? And concerning clothing, why are you anxious?
2648 2918 68 4459 837 3756 2872
καταμάθετε τὰ κρίνα τοῦ ἀγροῦ, πῶς αὐξάνει· οὐ κοπιᾷ,
Consider the lilies of the field, how they grow; not they labor
3761 3514 3004 5213 3754 3761 4672 1722 3956
29 οὐδὲ νήθει· λέγω δὲ ὑμῖν ὅτι οὐδὲ Σολομὼν ἐν πάσῃ τῇ
nor spin. I say But to you that not even Solomon In all the
1391 848 4016 5613 1520 5130 1487 5528
30 δόξῃ αὐτοῦ περιεβάλετο ὡς ἓν τούτων. εἰ δὲ τὸν χόρτον τοῦ
glory of him was clothed as one of these. if But the grass of the
68 4594 5607 839 1519 2823 906
ἀγροῦ, σήμερον ὄντα, καὶ αὔριον εἰς κλίβανον βαλλόμενον,
field, today being, and tomorrow into a furnace being thrown,
2316 3779 294 3756 4183 3123 5209 3640
ὁ Θεὸς οὕτως ἀμφιέννυσιν, οὐ πολλῷ μᾶλλον ὑμᾶς, ὀλιγό-
God thus enrobes; not much more (are) you, little-
3361 3767 3309 3004 5101 5315 2228 5101
31 πιστοι; μὴ οὖν μεριμνήσητε, λέγοντες, Τί φάγωμεν, ἢ τί
faiths? not Then be anxious, saying, What may we eat? Or, what
4095 2228 5101 4016 3956 1063 5023 1484
32 πίωμεν, ἢ τί περιβαλώμεθα; πάντα γὰρ ταῦτα τὰ ἔθνη
may we drink? Or, what may clothe us? all For these things the nations
1934 1492 1063 3962 5216 3770 3754 5535
ἐπιζητεῖ· οἶδε γὰρ ὁ πατὴρ ὑμῶν ὁ οὐράνιος ὅτι χρῄζετε
seek. knows For the Father of you heavenly that you need
5130 537 2212 4412 932
33 τούτων ἁπάντων. ζητεῖτε δὲ πρῶτον τὴν βασιλείαν τοῦ
these of all. seek But first the kingdom
2315 1343 848 5023 3956 4369
Θεοῦ καὶ τὴν δικαιοσύνην αὐτοῦ, καὶ ταῦτα πάντα προσ-
of God and the righteousness of Him, and these things all will be
5213 3361 3767 3309 1519 839 1063
34 τεθήσεται ὑμῖν. μὴ οὖν μεριμνήσητε εἰς τὴν αὔριον· ἡ γὰρ
added to you. not Then do be anxious for the morrow; the for
839 3309 1438 713 2250 2549
αὔριον μεριμνήσει τὰ ἑαυτῆς. ἀρκετὸν τῇ ἡμέρᾳ ἡ κακία
morrow will be anxious of itself. Sufficient to the day (is) the badness
848
αὐτῆς.
of it.

CHAPTER 7

3361 2919 2443 3361 2919 1722 3739 1063 2917 2919
1 Μὴ κρίνετε, ἵνα μὴ κριθῆτε· ἐν ᾧ γὰρ κρίματι κρίνετε,
2 Not do judge, that not you be judged. in what For judgment you
2919 1722/3739/3358 3354 488 judge,
κριθήσεσθε· καὶ ἐν ᾧ μέτρῳ μετρεῖτε, ἀντιμετρηθήσεται
you will be judged. and in what measure you measure, it will be measured
5213/5101 991 2595 1722 3788 80
3 ὑμῖν. τί δὲ βλέπεις τὸ κάρφος τὸ ἐν τῷ ὀφθαλμῷ τοῦ ἀδελφοῦ
to you. why But do you see the twig in the eye of the brother
4675 1722 4674 3788 1385 3756 2657 2228 4459
4 σου, τὴν δὲ ἐν τῷ σῷ ὀφθαλμῷ δοκὸν οὐ κατανοεῖς; ἢ πῶς
of you, the but in the of you eye log not you perceive? Or how
2046 80 4675 863 1544 2595 575
ἐρεῖς τῷ ἀδελφῷ σου, Ἄφες ἐκβάλω τὸ κάρφος ἀπὸ τοῦ
will you say to the brother of you. Permit (me) to take out the twig from the,
*1385 3788 4675 2400 1722 3788 4675
ὀφθαλμοῦ σου· καὶ ἰδού, ἡ δοκὸς ἐν τῷ ὀφθαλμῷ σου;
the eye of you, and behold, the log (is) in the eye of you?

cast the log out of your eye, and then you will see clearly to cast the twig out of the eye of your brother.

[6]Do not give that which *is* holy to the dogs, nor throw your pearls before the pigs, that they should not trample them with their feet, and turning they may tear you.

[7]Ask, and it will be given to you; seek, and you will find; knock, and it will be opened to you. [8]For each one that asks receives and the *one* that seeks finds; and to the *one* knocking, it will be opened. [9]Or what man of you is there, if his son should ask a loaf of him, will he give him a stone? [10]And if he should ask a fish, will he give him a snake? [11]If, then, you, being evil, know to give good gifts to your children, how much more will your Father who *is* in Heaven give good things to those that ask Him?

[12]Therefore, all things, whatever you desire that men should do to you, so also you should do to them; for this is the Law and the Prophets.

[13]Go in through the narrow gate; for wide is the gate, and broad *is* the way that leads to death. And many are the ones who go through it. [14]For narrow is the gate, and constricted *is* the way that leads into life, and few are the ones who find it.

[15]But beware of the false prophets who come to you in sheep's clothing, but inside they are plundering

5273 1544 4412 1385 1537 3788 4675
5 ὑποκριτά, ἔκβαλε πρῶτον τὴν δοκὸν ἐκ τοῦ ὀφθαλμοῦ σου,
Hypocrite! take out First the log out of the eye of you.
5119 1227 1544 2595 1537 3788
καὶ τότε διαβλέψεις ἐκβαλεῖν τὸ κάρφος ἐκ τοῦ ὀφθαλμοῦ
and then you will see clearly to take out the twig out of the eye
80 4675
τοῦ ἀδελφοῦ σου.
of the brother of you.

3361 1325 40 2965 3366 906 3135
6 Μὴ δῶτε τὸ ἅγιον τοῖς κυσί· μηδὲ βάλητε τοὺς μαργαρί-
Not do give the holy to the dogs, nor throw the pearls
5216 1715 5519 3379 2662
τας ὑμῶν ἔμπροσθεν τῶν χοίρων, μήποτε καταπατήσωσιν
of you before the pigs, lest they trample
846 1722 4228 848 4762 4486 5209
αὐτοὺς ἐν τοῖς ποσὶν αὐτῶν, καὶ στραφέντες ῥήξωσιν ὑμᾶς.
them with the feet of them, and turning they tear you

154 1325 5213 2212 2147
7 Αἰτεῖτε, καὶ δοθήσεται ὑμῖν· ζητεῖτε, καὶ εὑρήσετε·
Ask, and it will be given to you; seek, and you will find;
2925 455 5213 3956 1063 154 2983
8 κρούετε, καὶ ἀνοιγήσεται ὑμῖν. πᾶς γὰρ ὁ αἰτῶν λαμβάνει,
knock, and it will be opened to you. each For asking, receives;
2212 2147 2925 455 5100
9 καὶ ὁ ζητῶν εὑρίσκει, καὶ τῷ κρούοντι ἀνοιγήσεται. ἢ τίς
and he seeking, finds; and to the (one) knocking, it will be opened. Or who
2076 1537 5216 444 3739 1437 154 5207 848 740
ἐστιν ἐξ ὑμῶν ἄνθρωπος, ὃν ἐὰν αἰτήσῃ ὁ υἱὸς αὐτοῦ ἄρτον,
is of you a man, who if should ask the son of him a loaf,
3361 3037 1929 846 1437 2486 154 3361 3789
10 μὴ λίθον ἐπιδώσει αὐτῷ; καὶ ἐὰν ἰχθὺν αἰτήσῃ, μὴ ὄφιν
not a stone he will give him? And if a fish he should ask, a snake
1929 846 1487 3767 5210 4190 5607 1492 1390
11 ἐπιδώσει αὐτῷ; εἰ οὖν ὑμεῖς, πονηροὶ ὄντες, οἴδατε δόματα
he will give him? If, then, you, evil being, know gifts
18 1325 5043 5216 4214 3123 3962
ἀγαθὰ διδόναι τοῖς τέκνοις ὑμῶν, πόσῳ μᾶλλον ὁ πατὴρ
good to give to the children of you, how much more the Father
5216 1722 3772 1325 18 154 846
ὑμῶν ὁ ἐν τοῖς οὐρανοῖς δώσει ἀγαθὰ τοῖς αἰτοῦσιν αὐτόν;
of you in the heavens will give good things to those asking Him!

3956 3767 3745/302 2309 2443 4160 5213 444
12 πάντα οὖν ὅσα ἂν θέλητε ἵνα ποιῶσιν ὑμῖν οἱ ἄνθρωποι,
all things Then, what ever you desire that may do to you men,
3779 5210 4160 846 3778 1063 2076 3551
οὕτω καὶ ὑμεῖς ποιεῖτε αὐτοῖς· οὗτος γάρ ἐστιν ὁ νόμος καὶ
so also you do to them. this For is the Law and
4396
οἱ προφῆται.
the Prophets.

1525 1223 4728 4439 3754 4116 4439
13 Εἰσέλθετε διὰ τῆς στενῆς πύλης· ὅτι πλατεῖα ἡ πύλη, καὶ
Enter in through the narrow gate, because wide (is) the gate and
2149 3598 520 1519 684 4183
εὐρύχωρος ἡ ὁδὸς ἡ ἀπάγουσα εἰς τὴν ἀπώλειαν, καὶ πολλοί
broad (is) the way leading away into destruction; and many
1526 1525 1223 846 3754 4728 4439
14 εἰσιν οἱ εἰσερχόμενοι δι' αὐτῆς· ὅτι στενὴ ἡ πύλη, καὶ
are those entering in through it; because narrow the gate, and
2346 3598 520 1519 2222 3641
τεθλιμμένη ἡ ὁδὸς ἡ ἀπάγουσα εἰς τὴν ζωήν, καὶ ὀλίγοι
constricted (is) the way leading away into Life; and few
1526 2147 846
εἰσιν οἱ εὑρίσκοντες αὐτήν.
are those finding it.

4337 575 5578 3748 2064
15 Προσέχετε δὲ ἀπὸ τῶν ψευδοπροφητῶν, οἵτινες ἔρχονται
take care But from the false prophets, who come
4314 5209 1722 1742 4263 2081 1526 3074
πρὸς ὑμᾶς ἐν ἐνδύμασι προβάτων, ἔσωθεν δέ εἰσι λύκοι
to you in clothing of sheep; within but they are wolves

wolves. [16]From their fruits you shall know them. Do they gather grapes from thorns, or figs from thistles? [17]So every good tree produces good fruits; but the corrupt tree produces evil fruits. [18]A good tree cannot produce evil fruits, nor a corrupt tree produce good fruits. [19]Every tree not producing good fruit is cut out and is thrown into fire. [20]Then surely from their fruits you shall know them.

[21]Not everyone who says to Me, Lord, Lord, will enter into the kingdom of Heaven, but the ones who do the will of My Father in Heaven. [22]Many will say to Me in that day, Lord, Lord, did we not prophesy in Your name, and in Your name cast out demons, and in Your name do many works of power? [23]And then I will declare to them, I never knew you; depart from Me, those working lawlessness!

[24]Therefore, everyone who hears these words from Me, and does them, I will compare him to a wise man who built his house on the rock; [25]and the rains came down, and the waters came up, and the winds blew, and fell against that house; but it did not fall, for it had been founded on the rock. [26]And everyone who hears these words of Mine, and who does not do them, *he* shall be compared to a foolish man who built his house on the sand; [27]and the rain came down, and the rivers came up, and the winds blew, and beat

727 575 2590 848 1921 846
16 ἅρπαγες. ἀπὸ τῶν καρπῶν αὐτῶν ἐπιγνώσεσθε αὐτούς
plundering. From the fruits of them, you shall know them.
3385 4816 575 173 4718 575 5146
μήτι συλλέγουσιν ἀπὸ ἀκανθῶν σταφυλήν, ἢ ἀπὸ τριβόλων
Neither do they gather from thorns grapes, or from thistles
4810 3779 3956 1186 18 2590 2570 4160
17 σῦκα; οὕτω πᾶν δένδρον ἀγαθὸν καρποὺς καλοὺς ποιεῖ
figs? So every tree good fruits good produces
4550 1186 2590 4190 4160 3756 1410
18 τὸ δὲ σαπρὸν δένδρον καρποὺς πονηροὺς ποιεῖ. οὐ δύναται
the But corrupt tree fruits evil produces. Not is able
1186 18 2590 4190 4160 3761 1186
δένδρον ἀγαθὸν καρποὺς πονηροὺς ποιεῖν, οὐδὲ δένδρον
a tree good fruits evil to produce; nor a tree
4550 2590 2570 4160 3956 1186 3361 4160
19 σαπρὸν καρποὺς καλοὺς ποιεῖν. πᾶν δένδρον μὴ ποιοῦν
corrupt fruits good to produce. Every tree not producing
2590 2570 1581 1519 4442 906 686 575
20 καρπὸν καλὸν ἐκκόπτεται καὶ εἰς πῦρ βάλλεται. ἄραγε ἀπὸ
fruits good is cut out, and into fire is thrown. Surely, from
2590 848 1921 846 3756 3956 3004
21 τῶν καρπῶν αὐτῶν ἐπιγνώσεσθε αὐτούς. οὐ πᾶς ὁ λέγων
the fruits of them you will know them. Not everyone saying
3427 2962 2962 1525 1519 932
μοι, Κύριε, Κύριε, εἰσελεύσεται εἰς τὴν βασιλείαν τῶν
to Me, Lord, Lord, will enter into the kingdom of the
3772 235 4160 2307 3962 3450 1722
οὐρανῶν· ἀλλ' ὁ ποιῶν τὸ θέλημα τοῦ πατρός μου τοῦ ἐν
heavens, but those doing the will of the Father of Me in
3772 4183 2046 3427 1722 1565 2250 2962 2962
22 οὐρανοῖς. πολλοὶ ἐροῦσί μοι ἐν ἐκείνῃ τῇ ἡμέρᾳ, Κύριε, Κύριε,
(the) heavens. Many will say to Me in that day, Lord, Lord,
3756 4674 3686 4395 4674 3686
οὐ τῷ σῷ ὀνόματι προεφητεύσαμεν, καὶ τῷ σῷ ὀνόματι
not in Your name did we prophesy, and in Your name
1140 1544 4674 3686 1411 4183
δαιμόνια ἐξεβάλομεν, καὶ τῷ σῷ ὀνόματι δυνάμεις πολλὰς
demons cast out, and in Your name works of power many
4160 5119 3670 846 3754 3763
23 ἐποιήσαμεν; καὶ τότε ὁμολογήσω αὐτοῖς, ὅτι οὐδέποτε
we performed? And then I will declare to them, Never
1097 5209 672 575 1700 2038
ἔγνων ὑμᾶς· ἀποχωρεῖτε ἀπ' ἐμοῦ οἱ ἐργαζόμενοι τὴν
I knew you; depart from Me, those working
458 3956 3767 3748 191 3450 3056 5128
24 ἀνομίαν. πᾶς οὖν ὅστις ἀκούει μου τοὺς λόγους τούτους καὶ
lawlessness. Everyone then who hears from Me words these, and
4160 846 3666 846 435 5429 3748 3618
ποιεῖ αὐτούς, ὁμοιώσω αὐτὸν ἀνδρὶ φρονίμῳ, ὅστις ᾠκοδό-
does them, I will compare him to a man prudent, who built
3614 848 1909 4073 2597 1028
25 μησε τὴν οἰκίαν αὐτοῦ ἐπὶ τὴν πέτραν· καὶ κατέβη ἡ βροχὴ
the house of him on the rock. And came down the rain,
2064 4215 4154 417 4363
καὶ ἦλθον οἱ ποταμοὶ καὶ ἔπνευσαν οἱ ἄνεμοι, καὶ προσ-
and came up the rivers, and blew the winds, and fell
3614 1565 3756 4098 2311 1063 1909
έπεσον τῇ οἰκίᾳ ἐκείνῃ, καὶ οὐκ ἔπεσε· τεθεμελίωτο γὰρ ἐπὶ
against house that; yet not it fell; it had been founded for on
4073 3956 191 3450 3056 5128
26 τὴν πέτραν. καὶ πᾶς ὁ ἀκούων μου τοὺς λόγους τούτους
the rock. And everyone hearing of Me words these,
3361 4160 846 3666 435 3474 3748
καὶ μὴ ποιῶν αὐτούς, ὁμοιωθήσεται ἀνδρὶ μωρῷ, ὅστις
and not doing them, will be compared to a man foolish, who
3618 3614 848 1909 285 2597
27 ᾠκοδόμησε τὴν οἰκίαν αὐτοῦ ἐπὶ τὴν ἄμμον· καὶ κατέβη ἡ
built the house of him on the sand; and came down the
1028 2064 4215 4154 417
βροχὴ καὶ ἦλθον οἱ ποταμοὶ καὶ ἔπνευσαν οἱ ἄνεμοι, καὶ
rain. and came up the rivers, and blew the winds, and

against that house; and it fell, and great was the fall of it.

28 And it happened, when Jesus had finished these sayings, the crowds were astonished at His teaching. 29 For He was teaching them as having authority, and not as the scribes.

4350 3614 1565 4098 2258 4431
προσέκοψαν τῇ οἰκίᾳ ἐκείνῃ, καὶ ἔπεσε· καὶ ἦν ἡ πτῶσις
beat against house that; and it fell, and was the collapse
848 3173
αὐτῆς μεγάλη.
of it great.
1096 3753 4931 2424 3056 5128
28 Καὶ ἐγένετο ὅτε συνετέλεσεν ὁ Ἰησοῦς τοὺς λόγους τού-
And happened, when had finished Jesus sayings these,
1605 3793 1909 1322 848 2258 1063
29 τους, ἐξεπλήσσοντο οἱ ὄχλοι ἐπὶ τῇ διδαχῇ αὐτοῦ· ἦν γὰρ
were astonished the crowds at the teaching of him. He was For
1321 846 5613 1849 2192 3756 5613 1122
διδάσκων αὐτοὺς ὡς ἐξουσίαν ἔχων, καὶ οὐχ ὡς οἱ γραμ-
teaching them as authority having, and not as the
ματεῖς.
scribes.

CHAPTER 8

1 And He having come down from the mount, great crowds followed Him. 2 And behold, coming up, a leper worshiped Him, saying, Lord, If You will, You are able to cleanse me. 3 And stretching out His hand, Jesus touched him, saying, I will! Be cleansed! And instantly his leprosy was cleansed. 4 And Jesus said to him, See *that* you tell no one, but go, show yourself to the priest, and offer the gift which Moses commanded, for a testimony to them.

5 And Jesus entering into Capernaum, a centurion came near to Him, begging Him, 6 and saying, Lord, my boy has been laid in the house, a paralytic, being grievously tormented. 7 And Jesus said to him, I will come and heal him. 8 And answering, the centurion said, Lord, I am not worthy that You should enter under my roof; but only speak a word, and my boy will be healed. 9 For I am also a man under authority, having soldiers under myself. And I say to this one, Go; and he goes; and to another,

CHAPTER 8

1 2597 846 575 3735 190 846
Καταβάντι δὲ αὐτῷ ἀπὸ τοῦ ὄρους, ἠκολούθησαν αὐτῷ
having come down And He from the mount followed Him
2 3793 4183 2400 3015 2064 4352 846
ὄχλοι πολλοί καὶ ἰδού, λεπρὸς ἐλθὼν προσεκύνει αὐτῷ,
crowds great. And behold, a leper having come worshiped Him,
3004 2962 1437 2309 1410 3165 2511 1614
3 λέγων, Κύριε, ἐὰν θέλῃς, δύνασαί με καθαρίσαι. καὶ ἐκτείνας
saying, Lord, if You will, You are able me to cleanse. And stretching
5495 680 846 2424 3004 2309 2511
τὴν χεῖρα, ἥψατο αὐτοῦ ὁ Ἰησοῦς, λέγων, Θέλω, καθαρί-
the hand, touched him Jesus, saying, I will, be
2112 2511 848 3014 3004
4 σθητι. καὶ εὐθέως ἐκαθαρίσθη αὐτοῦ ἡ λέπρα. καὶ λέγει
cleansed! And instantly was cleansed of Him the leprosy. And says
846 2424 3708 3367 2036 235 5217 4572
αὐτῷ ὁ Ἰησοῦς, Ὅρα μηδενὶ εἴπῃς· ἀλλ' ὕπαγε, σεαυτὸν
to him Jesus, See (that) no one you tell, but go, yourself
1166 2409 4374 1435 4367
δεῖξον τῷ ἱερεῖ, καὶ προσένεγκε τὸ δῶρον ὃ προσέταξε
show to the priest, and offer the gift which ordered
3475 1519 3142 846
Μωσῆς, εἰς μαρτύριον αὐτοῖς.
Moses, for a testimony to them.
1525 2424 1519 2584 4334
5 Εἰσελθόντι δὲ τῷ Ἰησοῦ εἰς Καπερναούμ, προσῆλθεν
having entered And Jesus into Capernaum, came near
846 1543 3870 846 3004 2962
αὐτῷ ἑκατόνταρχος παρακαλῶν αὐτόν, καὶ λέγων, Κύριε,
to Him a centurion beseeching Him, and saying, Lord,
3816 3450 906 1722 3614 3885 1171 928
6 ὁ παῖς μου βέβληται ἐν τῇ οἰκίᾳ παραλυτικός, δεινῶς βασανι-
the child of me has been laid in the house a paralytic, grievously being
3004 846 2424 1473 2064 2323
7 ζόμενος. καὶ λέγει αὐτῷ ὁ Ἰησοῦς, Ἐγὼ ἐλθὼν θεραπεύσω
tormented. And says to him Jesus, I coming will heal
846 611 1543 5346 2962 3756 1510
8 αὐτόν. καὶ ἀποκριθεὶς ὁ ἑκατόνταρχος ἔφη, Κύριε, οὐκ εἰμὶ
him. And answering, the centurion said, Lord, not I am
2425 2443 3450 5259 4721 1525 235 3440 2036
ἱκανὸς ἵνα μου ὑπὸ τὴν στέγην εἰσέλθῃς· ἀλλὰ μόνον εἰπὲ
worthy that of me under the roof You may enter, but only say
3056 2390 3816 3450 1063 1473 444
9 λόγον, καὶ ἰαθήσεται ὁ παῖς μου. καὶ γὰρ ἐγὼ ἄνθρωπός
a word, and will be healed the child of me, also For I a man
1510 5259 1849 2192 5259 1683 4757 3004
εἰμι ὑπὸ ἐξουσίαν, ἔχων ὑπ' ἐμαυτὸν στρατιώτας· καὶ λέγω
am under authority, having under myself soldiers; and I say
5129 4198 4198 243 2063
τούτῳ, Πορεύθητι, καὶ πορεύεται· καὶ ἄλλῳ, Ἔρχου, καὶ
to this (one), Go! And he goes. And to another, Come! And

Come; and he comes; and to my slave, Do this; and he does *it*.

[10]And hearing, Jesus marveled, and said to those following. Truly I say to you, Not even in Israel did I find such faith. [11]But I say to you that many will come from east and west, and will recline with Abraham and Isaac and Jacob in the kingdom of Heaven; [12]but the sons of the kingdom shall be cast out into the outer darkness; there shall be weeping and gnashing of the teeth. [13]And Jesus said to the centurion, Go, and as you have believed, so let it be to you. And his boy was healed in that hour.

[14]And coming to the house of Peter, Jesus saw his mother-in-law laid out and in a fever. [15]And He touched her hand, and her fever left her. And she rose up and served them.

[16]And evening having come on, they brought to Him many possessed by demons. And He cast out the spirits by a word, and He healed all those having illness; [17]so that it might be fulfilled that spoken by Isaiah the prophet, saying, "He took *upon Himself* our weaknesses, and bore *our* sicknesses."

[18]And seeing great crowds around Him, Jesus gave orders to go away to the other side. [19]And one, a scribe, coming near, said to Him, Teacher, I will follow You wherever you may go. [20]And Jesus said to him, The foxes have holes, and the birds of the heaven have nests, but the Son of man has nowhere He may lay *His* head. [21]And another of His disciples

2064 1401 3450 4160 5124 4160
ἔρχεται· καὶ τῷ δούλῳ μου, Ποίησον τοῦτο, καὶ ποιεῖ.
he comes. And to the slave of me, Do this! And he does.
191 2424 2296 2036 190
10 ἀκούσας δὲ ὁ Ἰησοῦς ἐθαύμασε, καὶ εἶπε τοῖς ἀκολουθοῦσιν,
hearing And, Jesus marveled, and said to those following,
281 3004 5213 3761 1722 2474 5118 4102
Ἀμὴν λέγω ὑμῖν, οὐδὲ ἐν τῷ Ἰσραὴλ τοσαύτην πίστιν
Truly, I say to you, Not even in Israel such faith
2147 3004 5213 3754 4183 575 395 1424
11 εὗρον. λέγω δὲ ὑμῖν, ὅτι πολλοὶ ἀπὸ ἀνατολῶν καὶ δυσμῶν
I found. I say And to you that many from east and west
2240 347 3326 11 2464
ἥξουσι, καὶ ἀνακλιθήσονται μετὰ Ἀβραὰμ καὶ Ἰσαὰκ καὶ
will come, and will recline with Abraham and Isaac and
2384 1722 932 3772 5207 932
12 Ἰακὼβ ἐν τῇ βασιλείᾳ τῶν οὐρανῶν· οἱ δὲ υἱοὶ τῆς βασιλείας
Jacob in the kingdom of the heavens. the But sons of the kingdom
1544 1519 4655 1857 1563 2071
ἐκβληθήσονται εἰς τὸ σκότος τὸ ἐξώτερον· ἐκεῖ ἔσται ὁ
shall be cast out into the darkness outer; there shall be
2805 1030 3599 2036 2424
13 κλαυθμὸς καὶ ὁ βρυγμὸς τῶν ὀδόντων. καὶ εἶπεν ὁ Ἰησοῦς
weeping and gnashing of the teeth. And said Jesus
1543 5217 5613 4100 1096 4671
τῷ ἑκατοντάρχῳ, Ὕπαγε, καὶ ὡς ἐπίστευσας γενηθήτω σοι.
to the centurion, Go! And as you believed, let it be to you.
2390 3816 848 1722 5610 1565
καὶ ἰάθη ὁ παῖς αὐτοῦ ἐν τῇ ὥρᾳ ἐκείνῃ.
And was healed the child of him in hour that.
2064 2424 1519 3614 4074 1492
14 Καὶ ἐλθὼν ὁ Ἰησοῦς εἰς τὴν οἰκίαν Πέτρου, εἶδε τὴν
And having come Jesus into the house of Peter, He saw the
3994 848 906 4445 680
15 πενθερὰν αὐτοῦ βεβλημένην καὶ πυρέσσουσαν, καὶ ἥψατο
mother-in-law of him having been laid and fever-stricken. And He touched
5495 848 863 846 4446 1453
τῆς χειρὸς αὐτῆς, καὶ ἀφῆκεν αὐτὴν ὁ πυρετός· καὶ ἠγέρθη,
the hand of her, and left her the fever. And she arose
1247 846 3798 1096 4374 846
16 καὶ διηκόνει αὐτοῖς. ὀψίας δὲ γενομένης προσήνεγκαν αὐτῷ
and ministered to them. evening And having come, they brought to Him
1139 4183 1544 4151 3056
δαιμονιζομένους πολλούς· καὶ ἐξέβαλε τὰ πνεύματα λόγῳ,
demon-possessed many. And He cast out the spirits by a word;
3956 2560 2192 2323 3704 4137
17 καὶ πάντας τοὺς κακῶς ἔχοντας ἐθεράπευσεν· ὅπως πληρωθῇ
and all those illness having, He healed; so as may be fulfilled
4483 1223 2268 4396 3004 848
τὸ ῥηθὲν διὰ Ἡσαΐου τοῦ προφήτου, λέγοντος, Αὐτὸς τὰς
that spoken through Isaiah the prophet, saying, He the
769 2257 2983 3554 941
ἀσθενείας ἡμῶν ἔλαβε, καὶ τὰς νόσους ἐβάστασεν.
weaknesses of us took, and the sicknesses He bore.
1492 2424 4183 3793 4012 848 2753
Ἰδὼν δὲ ὁ Ἰησοῦς πολλοὺς ὄχλους περὶ αὐτόν, ἐκέλευσεν
seeing And Jesus great crowds around Him, He ordered
565 1519 4008 4334 1519 1122 2036
18 ἀπελθεῖν εἰς τὸ πέραν. καὶ προσελθὼν εἷς γραμματεὺς εἶπεν
to go away to the other side. And coming near one scribe said
846 1320 190 4671 3699 1437 565
19 αὐτῷ, Διδάσκαλε, ἀκολουθήσω σοι ὅπου ἐὰν ἀπέρχῃ. καὶ
to Him, Teacher, I will follow you whereever you go. And
3004 846 2424 258 5454 2192
20 λέγει αὐτῷ ὁ Ἰησοῦς, Αἱ ἀλώπεκες φωλεοὺς ἔχουσι, καὶ τὰ
says to him Jesus, The foxes holes have and the
4071 3772 2682 5207 444
πετεινὰ τοῦ οὐρανοῦ κατασκηνώσεις· ὁ δὲ υἱὸς τοῦ ἀνθρώ-
birds of the heaven nests, the but Son of
3756 2192 4226 2776 2827 2084 3101
21 που οὐκ ἔχει ποῦ τὴν κεφαλὴν κλίνῃ. ἕτερος δὲ τῶν μαθητῶν
man not has where the head He may lay. another And of the disciples

said to Him, Lord, allow me
first to go away and bury my
father. [22]But Jesus said to
him, Follow Me, and allow
the dead to bury their own
dead.

[23]And He entering into
the boat, His disciples
followed Him. [24]And, behold, a great storm rose up
in the sea, so that the boat
was covered by the waves;
but He was sleeping. [25]And
coming near, His disciples
awakened Him, saying,
Lord, save us! We are perishing. [26]And He said to
them, Why are you afraid,
littlefaiths? Then rising up,
He rebuked the winds and
the sea. And there was a
great calm. [27]And the men
marveled, saying, What
kind *of man* is this, that
even the winds and the sea
obey Him?

[28]And when He had
come to the other side, into
the country of the
Gergesenes, two demon-
possessed ones met Him,
coming out of the tombs,
very violent, so that no one
was able to pass through
that way. [29]And, behold!
They cried out, saying,
What *is* to us and to You,
Jesus, Son of God? Have
You come here before time
to torment us?

[30]And far off from them
there was a herd of many
pigs feeding. [31]And the
demons begged Him, say-
ing, If You cast us out, allow
us to go away into the herd
of pigs. [32]And He said to
them, Go! And coming out,
these went away into the
herd of pigs. And, behold,
all the herd of pigs rushed

848 2036 846 2962 2010 3427 4412 565
αὐτοῦ εἶπεν αὐτῷ, Κύριε, ἐπίτρεψόν μοι πρῶτον ἀπελθεῖν
of Him said to Him, Lord, allow me first to go away
2290 3962 3450 2424 2036 846 190
22 καὶ θάψαι τὸν πατέρα μου. ὁ δὲ Ἰησοῦς εἶπεν αὐτῷ, Ἀκολού-
and to bury the father of me. And Jesus said to him, Follow
3427 863 3498 2290 1438 3498
θει μοι, καὶ ἄφες τοὺς νεκροὺς θάψαι τοὺς ἑαυτῶν νεκρούς.
Me, and allow the dead to bury the of themselves dead.
1684 846 1519 4143 190 846
23 Καὶ ἐμβάντι αὐτῷ εἰς τὸ πλοῖον, ἠκολούθησαν αὐτῷ οἱ
And having entered He into the boat, followed Him the
3101 848 2400 4578 3173 1096 1722 2281
24 μαθηταὶ αὐτοῦ. καὶ ἰδού, σεισμὸς μέγας ἐγένετο ἐν τῇ θα-
disciples of Him. And behold, a shaking great occurred in the
5620 4143 2572 5259 2949
λάσσῃ, ὥστε τὸ πλοῖον καλύπτεσθαι ὑπὸ τῶν κυμάτων·
sea, so that the boat was covered by the waves.
846 2518 4334 3101 848
25 αὐτὸς δὲ ἐκάθευδε. καὶ προσελθόντες οἱ μαθηταὶ αὐτοῦ
He But was sleeping. And coming near, the disciples of Him
1453 846 3004 2962 4982 2248 622
ἤγειραν αὐτόν, λέγοντες, Κύριε, σῶσον ἡμᾶς, ἀπολλύμεθα.
aroused Him, saying, Lord, save us; we are perishing.
3004 846 5102 1169 2075 3640 5119 1453
26 καὶ λέγει αὐτοῖς, Τί δειλοί ἐστε, ὀλιγόπιστοι ; τότε ἐγερθεὶς
And He says to them, Why afraid are you, little-faiths? Then arising.
2008 417 2281 1096 1055
ἐπετίμησε τοῖς ἀνέμοις καὶ τῇ θαλάσσῃ, καὶ ἐγένετο γαλήνη
He rebuked the wind and the sea, and there was a calm
3173 444 2296 3004 4217
27 μεγάλη. οἱ δὲ ἄνθρωποι ἐθαύμασαν, λέγοντες, Ποταπός
great. the And men marveled, saying, Of what kind
2076 3778 3754 417 2281 5219
ἐστιν οὗτος, ὅτι καὶ οἱ ἄνεμοι καὶ ἡ θάλασσα ὑπακούουσιν
is this, that even the winds and the sea obey
846
αὐτῷ ;
Him?
2064 846 1519 4008 1519 5561
28 Καὶ ἐλθόντι αὐτῷ εἰς τὸ πέραν εἰς τὴν χώραν τῶν
And having come He to the other side, into the country of the
1086 5221 846 1417 1139 1537
Γεργεσηνῶν, ὑπήντησαν αὐτῷ δύο δαιμονιζόμενοι ἐκ τῶν
Gergesenes, met Him two demon-possessed out of the
3419 1831 5467 3029 5620 3361 2480 5100
μνημείων ἐξερχόμενοι, χαλεποὶ λίαν, ὥστε μὴ ἰσχύειν τινὰ
tombs coming out, violent exceedingly, so as not was able any
3928 1223 3598 1565 2400 2896 3004
29 παρελθεῖν διὰ τῆς ὁδοῦ ἐκείνης· καὶ ἰδού, ἔκραξαν λέγοντες,
to pass through way that. And behold, they cried out, saying,
5101 2254 4671 2424 5207 2316 2064 5602 4253 2540
Τί ἡμῖν καὶ σοί, Ἰησοῦ, υἱὲ τοῦ Θεοῦ ; ἦλθες ὧδε πρὸ καιροῦ
What to us and to You, Jesus, Son of God? Come You here before time
928 2248 2258 3112 575 846 34 5519
30 βασανίσαι ἡμᾶς ; ἦν δὲ μακρὰν ἀπ' αὐτῶν ἀγέλη χοίρων
to torment us? was And at a distance from them a herd of pigs
4183 1006 1142 3870 846
31 πολλῶν βοσκομένη. οἱ δὲ δαίμονες παρεκάλουν αὐτόν,
many feeding. the And demons begged Him,
3004 1487 1544 2248 2010 2254 565 1519
λέγοντες, Εἰ ἐκβάλλεις ἡμᾶς, ἐπίτρεψον ἡμῖν ἀπελθεῖν εἰς τὴν
saying, If You expel us, allow us to go away into the
34 5519 2036 846 5217
32 ἀγέλην τῶν χοίρων. καὶ εἶπεν αὐτοῖς, Ὑπάγετε. οἱ δὲ
herd. of the pigs. And He said to them, Go! those And
1831 565 1519 34 5519 2400
ἐξελθόντες ἀπῆλθον εἰς τὴν ἀγέλην τῶν χοίρων· καὶ ἰδού,
coming out went away into the herd of the pigs. And behold,
3729 3956 34 5519 2596 2911 1519
ὥρμησε πᾶσα ἡ ἀγέλη τῶν χοίρων κατὰ τοῦ κρημνοῦ εἰς
rushed all the herd of the pigs down the cliff into

down the cliff into the sea, and died in the waters.

33But those who fed *them* fled, and going into the city, *they* told all the things of the demon-possessed ones. 34And, behold, all the city went out to meet with Jesus. And seeing Him, they begged that He move away from their borders.

CHAPTER 9

1And entering into the boat, He passed over and came to *His* own city. 2And, behold, they brought a paralytic lying on a cot to Him. And seeing their faith, Jesus said to the paralytic, Be comforted, child. Your sins have been forgiven you. 3And, behold, some of the scribes said within themselves, This one blasphemes. 4And seeing their thoughts, Jesus said, Why do you think evil in your hearts? 5For what is easier, to say, *Your* sins have been forgiven you; or to say, Rise up and walk? 6But that you may know that the Son of man has authority on earth to forgive sins, then He said to the paralytic, Rising up, lift up your cot and go to your house. 7And rising up, he went away to his house.

8And seeing, the crowds marveled, and *they* glorified God who gave such authority to men.

9And passing from there, Jesus saw a man named Matthew sitting at the tax office. And *He* said to him, Follow Me. And rising up, he followed Him.

2281 599 1722 5204 1006
33 τὴν θάλασσαν, καὶ ἀπέθανον ἐν τοῖς ὕδασιν. οἱ δὲ βόσκοντες
the sea, and died in the waters. those But feeding
5343 565 1519 4172 518 3956
ἔφυγον, καὶ ἀπελθόντες εἰς τὴν πόλιν ἀπήγγειλαν πάντα,
fled, and having gone into the city told all things,
1139 2400 3956 4172 1831
34 καὶ τὰ τῶν δαιμονιζομένων. καὶ ἰδού, πᾶσα ἡ πόλις ἐξῆλ-
and the (things) of the demon-possessed. And behold, all the city went
•1519 4877 2424 1492 846 3870
θεν εἰς συνάντησιν τῷ Ἰησοῦ· καὶ ἰδόντες αὐτόν, παρεκά-
out to meet with Jesus; and seeing Him, they
3704 3327 575 3725 848
λεσαν ὅπως μεταβῇ ἀπὸ τῶν ὁρίων αὐτῶν.
begged that He move from the borders of them.

CHAPTER 9

1684 1519 4143 1276 2064 1519 2398
1 Καὶ ἐμβὰς εἰς τὸ πλοῖον διεπέρασε καὶ ἦλθεν εἰς τὴν ἰδίαν
And entering into the boat, He passed over and came into the own
4172 2400 4374 846 3885 1909 2825
2 πόλιν. καὶ ἰδού, προσέφερον αὐτῷ παραλυτικὸν ἐπὶ κλίνης
city. And behold, they brought to Him a paralytic on a cot
906 1492 2424 4102 848 2036
βεβλημένον· καὶ ἰδὼν ὁ Ἰησοῦς τὴν πίστιν αὐτῶν εἶπε τῷ
laid out. And seeing Jesus the faith of them, He said to the
3885 2293 5043 863 4671 266
παραλυτικῷ, Θάρσει, τέκνον· ἀφέωνταί σοι αἱ ἁμαρτίαι
paralytic, Be comforted, child; have been forgiven you the sins
4675 2400 5100 1122 2036 1722 1438
3 σου. καὶ ἰδού, τινὲς τῶν γραμματέων εἶπον ἐν ἑαυτοῖς,
of you. And behold, some of the scribes said within themselves,
3778 987 1492 2424 1761 848
4 Οὗτος βλασφημεῖ. καὶ ἰδὼν ὁ Ἰησοῦς τὰς ἐνθυμήσεις αὐτῶν
This (one) blasphemes. And seeing Jesus the thoughts of them
2036 2444 5210 1760 4190 1722 2588 5216
εἶπεν, Ἱνατί ὑμεῖς ἐνθυμεῖσθε πονηρὰ ἐν ταῖς καρδίαις ὑμῶν;
He said, Why do you think evil in the hearts of you?
5101 1063 2076 2123 2036 863 4671
5 τί γάρ ἐστιν εὐκοπώτερον, εἰπεῖν, Ἀφέωνταί σοι αἱ
what For is easier, to say, Have been forgiven you the
266 2228 2036 1453 4043 2443 1492
6 ἁμαρτίαι· ἢ εἰπεῖν, Ἔγειραι καὶ περιπάτει; ἵνα δὲ εἰδῆτε,
sins; or to say, Rise up and walk? that But you may know
3754 1849 2192 5207 444 1909 1093 863
ὅτι ἐξουσίαν ἔχει ὁ υἱὸς τοῦ ἀνθρώπου ἐπὶ τῆς γῆς ἀφιέναι
that authority has the Son of man on the earth to forgive
266 5119 3004 3885 1453 142 4675
ἁμαρτίας (τότε λέγει τῷ παραλυτικῷ), Ἐγερθεὶς ἆρόν σου
sins — then He says to the paralytic, Having risen, lift your
2825 5217 1519 3624 4675 1453 565
7 τὴν κλίνην, καὶ ὕπαγε εἰς τὸν οἶκόν σου. καὶ ἐγερθεὶς ἀπῆλ-
cot, and go to the house of you. And rising up, he went
1519 3624 848 1492 3793 2296
8 θεν εἰς τὸν οἶκον αὐτοῦ. ἰδόντες δὲ οἱ ὄχλοι ἐθαύμασαν, καὶ
away to the house of him. having seen And the crowds marveled, and
1392 2316 1325 1849 5108
ἐδόξασαν τὸν Θεόν, τὸν δόντα ἐξουσίαν τοιαύτην τοῖς
glorified God, the (One) giving authority such
444
ἀνθρώποις.
to men.
3855 2424 1564 1492 444 2521
9 Καὶ παράγων ὁ Ἰησοῦς ἐκεῖθεν εἶδεν ἄνθρωπον καθήμενον
And passing by Jesus from there saw a man sitting
1909 5058 3156 3004 3004 846
ἐπὶ τὸ τελώνιον, Ματθαῖον λεγόμενον, καὶ λέγει αὐτῷ,
at the tax-office, Matthew called; and says to him,
190 3427 450 190 846
Ἀκολούθει μοι. καὶ ἀναστὰς ἠκολούθησεν αὐτῷ.
Follow me. And rising up, he followed Him.

10 And it happened as He reclined in the house, behold, coming many tax-collectors and sinners were reclining with Jesus and His disciples. 11 And seeing, the Pharisees said to His disciples, Why does your teacher eat with tax-collectors and sinners? 12 But Jesus hearing, He said to them, The ones who are strong have no need of a physician, but the ones who are sick. 13 But going, learn what *this* is, "I desire mercy, and not sacrifice." For I did not come to call righteous *ones*, but sinners to repentance.

14 Then the disciples of John came to Him, saying, Why do we and the Pharisees fast much, and Your disciples do not fast? 15 And Jesus said to them, Can the sons of the bridechamber mourn as long as the bridegroom is with them? But the days will come when the bridegroom will have been taken from them; and then they will fast. 16 But no one puts a piece of new cloth onto an old garment. For its filling up takes away from the garment, and a worse tear takes *its* place. 17 Nor do they put new wine into old skins; otherwise, the skins are burst, and the wine pours out, and the skins will be ruined. But they put new wine into new skins, and both are preserved together.

18 As He spoke these things to them, behold, coming up a ruler bowed before Him, saying, My daughter has just now died; but coming lay Your hand on her, and she will live.

1096 846 345 1722 3614 2400
10 Καὶ ἐγένετο αὐτοῦ ἀνακειμένου ἐν τῇ οἰκίᾳ, καὶ ἰδού,
And it happened He reclining in the house, and behold,
4183 5057 268 2064 4873
πολλοὶ τελῶναι καὶ ἁμαρτωλοὶ ἐλθόντες συνανέκειντο τῷ
many tax-collectors and sinners having come were reclining
2424 3101 846 1492 5330
11 Ἰησοῦ καὶ τοῖς μαθηταῖς αὐτοῦ. καὶ ἰδόντες οἱ Φαρισαῖοι
with Jesus and the disciples of Him. And having seen, the Pharisees
2036 3101 846 1302 3326 5057
εἶπον τοῖς μαθηταῖς αὐτοῦ, Διατί μετὰ τῶν τελωνῶν καὶ
said to the disciples of Him, Why with the tax-collectors and
268 2068 1320 5216 2424 191
12 ἁμαρτωλῶν ἐσθίει ὁ διδάσκαλος ὑμῶν; ὁ δὲ Ἰησοῦς ἀκούσας
sinners eats the teacher of you? But Jesus having heard,
2036 846 3756 5532 2192 2480 2395 235
εἶπεν αὐτοῖς, Οὐ χρείαν ἔχουσιν οἱ ἰσχύοντες ἰατροῦ, ἀλλ'
He said to them, Not need have those being strong of a healer, but
2560 2192 4198 3129 5101 2076 1656
13 οἱ κακῶς ἔχοντες. πορευθέντες δὲ μάθετε τί ἐστιν, Ἔλεον
those illness having. having gone But, learn what it is: mercy
2309 3756 2378 3756 1063 2064 2564 1342 235
θέλω, καὶ οὐ θυσίαν· οὐ γὰρ ἦλθον καλέσαι δικαίους, ἀλλ'
I desire, and not sacrifice; not for I came to call righteous (ones) but
268 1519 3341
ἁμαρτωλοὺς εἰς μετάνοιαν.
sinners to repentance.
5119 4334 846 3101 2491 3004
14 Τότε προσέρχονται αὐτῷ οἱ μαθηταὶ Ἰωάννου, λέγοντες,
Then came near to Him the disciples of John, saying,
1302 2249 5330 3522 4183
Διατί ἡμεῖς καὶ οἱ Φαρισαῖοι νηστεύομεν πολλά, οἱ δὲ
Why we and the Pharisees do fast much, the but
3101 4675 3756 3522 2036 846 2424 3361
15 μαθηταί σου οὐ νηστεύουσι; καὶ εἶπεν αὐτοῖς ὁ Ἰησοῦς, Μὴ
disciples of You not do fast? And said to them Jesus, not
1410 5207 3567 3996 1909 3745 3326 846
δύνανται οἱ υἱοὶ τοῦ νυμφῶνος πενθεῖν, ἐφ' ὅσον μετ' αὐτῶν
Are able the sons of the bridechamber to mourn as long as with them
2076 3566 2064 2250 3752 522 575
16 ἐστιν ὁ νυμφίος; ἐλεύσονται δὲ ἡμέραι ὅταν ἀπαρθῇ ἀπ'
is the bridegroom? will come But days when will have been taken from
846 3566 5119 3522 3762 1911
αὐτῶν ὁ νυμφίος, καὶ τότε νηστεύσουσιν. οὐδεὶς δὲ ἐπιβάλ-
them the bridegroom, and then they will fast. no one But puts
1915 4470 46 1909 2440 3820 142
λει ἐπίβλημα ῥάκους ἀγνάφου ἐπὶ ἱματίῳ παλαιῷ· αἴρει
a piece of cloth unfulled on a garment old; takes away
1063 4138 846 575 2440 5501
γὰρ τὸ πλήρωμα αὐτοῦ ἀπὸ τοῦ ἱματίου, καὶ χεῖρον
for the fullness of it from the garment, and a worse
4978 1096 3761 906 3631 3501 1519 779
17 σχίσμα γίνεται. οὐδὲ βάλλουσιν οἶνον νέον εἰς ἀσκοὺς
tear occurs. Neither do they put wine new into wineskins
3820 1490 4486 779 3631
παλαιούς· εἰ δὲ μήγε, ῥήγνυνται οἱ ἀσκοί, καὶ ὁ οἶνος
old; otherwise are burst the wineskins, and the wine
1632 779 622 235 906 3631
ἐκχεῖται, καὶ οἱ ἀσκοὶ ἀπολοῦνται· ἀλλὰ βάλλουσιν οἶνον
pours out, and the wineskins will be ruined; but they put wine
3501 1519 779 2537 297 4933
νέον εἰς ἀσκοὺς καινούς, καὶ ἀμφότερα συντηροῦνται.
new into wineskins fresh, and both are preserved together.
5023 846 2980 846 2400 758 1520 2064
18 Ταῦτα αὐτοῦ λαλοῦντος αὐτοῖς, ἰδού, ἄρχων εἷς ἐλθὼν
(As) these things He is speaking to them, behold, a ruler one coming
4352 846 3004 3754 2364 3450 737 5053
προσεκύνει αὐτῷ, λέγων ὅτι Ἡ θυγάτηρ μου ἄρτι ἐτελεύ-
worshiped Him, saying, — The daughter of me just now has
235 2064 2007 5495 4675 1909 846
τησεν· ἀλλὰ ἐλθὼν ἐπίθες τὴν χεῖρά σου ἐπ' αὐτήν, καὶ
died, but coming lay the hand of You on her, and

[19]And rising up, Jesus and His disciples followed him. [20]And, behold, a woman who had a flow of blood for twelve years came near, behind *Him, and* touched the fringe of His robe. [21]For she said within herself, If only I shall touch His robe, I will be cured. [22]But turning and seeing her, Jesus said, Be comforted, daughter; your faith has healed you. And the woman was healed from that hour. [23]And coming into the house of the ruler, and seeing the flute-players and the crowd causing a tumult, [24]Jesus said to them, Go back, for the little girl has not died, but she sleeps. And they laughed at Him. [25]But when the crowd had been put out, entering He took hold of her hand, and the little girl rose up. [26]And this report went out into all that land.

[27]And Jesus passing on from there, two blind ones followed Him, crying and saying, Have pity on us, Son of David. [28]And coming into the house, the blind ones came near to Him. And Jesus said to them, Do you believe that I am able to do this? And they said to Him, Yes, Lord. [29]Then He touched their eyes, saying, According to your faith let it be to you. [30]And their eyes were opened. And Jesus strictly ordered them, saying, See, let no one know.

[31]But going out, they made Him known in all that land.

[32]And as they were going out, behold, they brought to Him a dumb man possessed by a demon. [33]And the demon being cast out,

2198 1453 2424 190 846
19 ζήσεται. καὶ ἐγερθεὶς ὁ Ἰησοῦς ἠκολούθησεν αὐτῷ καὶ οἱ
she will live. And rising up, — Jesus followed him, and the
3101 848 2400 1135 131 1427 2094
20 μαθηταὶ αὐτοῦ. καὶ ἰδού, γυνὴ αἱμορροοῦσα δώδεκα ἔτη,
disciples of Him. And, behold, a woman having a flow of blood twelve years
4334 3693 680 2899 2440
προσελθοῦσα ὄπισθεν, ἥψατο τοῦ κρασπέδου τοῦ ἱματίου
coming near behind, touched the fringe of the garment
848 3004 1063 1722 1438 1437 3440 680 2440
21 αὐτοῦ. ἔλεγε γὰρ ἐν ἑαυτῇ, Ἐὰν μόνον ἅψωμαι τοῦ ἱματίου
of Him. she said For within herself, If only I shall touch the garment
848 4982 2424 1994 1492 846
22 αὐτοῦ, σωθήσομαι. ὁ δὲ Ἰησοῦς ἐπιστραφεὶς καὶ ἰδὼν αὐτὴν
of Him, I shall be cured.— But Jesus having turned and seeing her
2036 2293 2364 4102 4675 4982 4571 4982
εἶπε, Θάρσει, θύγατερ· ἡ πίστις σου σέσωκέ σε. καὶ ἐσώθη
said, Be comforted, daughter; the faith of you has saved you.. And was saved
1135 575 5610 1565 2064 2424 1519
23 ἡ γυνὴ ἀπὸ τῆς ὥρας ἐκείνης. καὶ ἐλθὼν ὁ Ἰησοῦς εἰς την
the woman from — hour that. And coming Jesus into the
3614 758 1492 834 3793
οἰκίαν τοῦ ἄρχοντος, καὶ ἰδὼν τοὺς αὐλητὰς καὶ τὸν ὄχλον
house of the ruler, and seeing the flute-players and the crowd
2350 3004 846 402 3756 1063 599
24 θορυβούμενον, λέγει αὐτοῖς, Ἀναχωρεῖτε· οὐ γὰρ ἀπέθανε
causing a tumult, said to them. Go back not for has died
2877 235 2518 2606 846 3753
25 τὸ κοράσιον, ἀλλὰ καθεύδει. καὶ κατεγέλων αὐτοῦ. ὅτε δὲ
the girl, but she sleeps. And they laughed at Him. when But
1544 3793 1525 2902 5495 848
ἐξεβλήθη ὁ ὄχλος, εἰσελθὼν ἐκράτησε τῆς χειρὸς αὐτῆς, καὶ
had been put the crowd, entering He took hold of the hand of her, and
1453 2877 1831 5345 3778 1519 3650
26 ἠγέρθη τὸ κοράσιον. καὶ ἐξῆλθεν ἡ φήμη αὕτη εἰς ὅλην τὴν
arose the girl. And went out the report this into all —
1093 1565
γῆν ἐκείνην.
land that.

3855 1564 2424 190 846 1417
27 Καὶ παράγοντι ἐκεῖθεν τῷ Ἰησοῦ, ἠκολούθησαν αὐτῷ δύο
And passing on from there — Jesus, followed Him two
5185 2896 3004 1653 2248 5207 1138
τυφλοί, κράζοντες καὶ λέγοντες, Ἐλέησον ἡμᾶς, υἱὲ Δαβίδ.
blind ones, crying and saying, Have pity on us, Son of David.
2064 1519 3614 4334 846 5185
28 ἐλθόντι δὲ εἰς τὴν οἰκίαν, προσῆλθον αὐτῷ οἱ τυφλοί, καὶ
coming And into the house, came near to Him the blind ones and
3004 846 2424 4100 3754 1410 5124 4160
λέγει αὐτοῖς ὁ Ἰησοῦς, Πιστεύετε ὅτι δύναμαι τοῦτο ποιῆ-
said to them Jesus, Do you believe that I am able this to do?
3004 846 3483 2962 5119 680 3788
29 σαι; λέγουσιν αὐτῷ, Ναί, Κύριε. τότε ἥψατο τῶν ὀφθαλμῶν
They say to Him, Yes, Lord. Then He touched the eyes
848 3004 2596 4102 5216 1096 5213
30 αὐτῶν, λέγων, Κατὰ τὴν πίστιν ὑμῶν γενηθήτω ὑμῖν. καὶ
of them, saying, According to the faith of you let it be to you. And
455 848 3788 1690 846
ἀνεῴχθησαν αὐτῶν οἱ ὀφθαλμοί· καὶ ἐνεβριμήσατο αὐτοῖς ὁ
were opened their eyes; and strictly ordered them
2424 3004 3708 3367 1097 1831
31 Ἰησοῦς, λέγων, Ὁρᾶτε μηδεὶς γινωσκέτω. οἱ δὲ ἐξελθόντες
Jesus, saying, See, no one let know. they But going out
1310 846 1722 3650 1093 1565
διεφήμισαν αὐτὸν ἐν ὅλῃ τῇ γῇ ἐκείνῃ.
declared Him in all land that.
846 1831 2400 4374 846 444
32 Αὐτῶν δὲ ἐξερχομένων, ἰδού, προσήνεγκαν αὐτῷ ἄνθρω-
(as) they And were going out, behold, they brought to Him a man
2974 1139 1544 1140
33 πον κωφὸν δαιμονιζόμενον. καὶ ἐκβληθέντος τοῦ δαιμονίου,
dumb demon-possessed. And having been cast out the demon,

2980 2974 2296 3793 3004
ἐλάλησεν ὁ κωφός· καὶ ἐθαύμασαν οἱ ὄχλοι, λέγοντες,
spoke the dumb. And marveled the crowds, saying,
3762 5316 3779 1722 2474 5330
34 Οὐδέποτε ἐφάνη οὕτως ἐν τῷ Ἰσραήλ. οἱ δὲ Φαρισαῖοι
Never was it seen thus in Israel. the But Pharisees
3004 1722 758 1140 1544
ἔλεγον, Ἐν τῷ ἄρχοντι τῶν δαιμονίων ἐκβάλλει τὰ
said, By the prince of the demons He casts out the
1140
δαιμόνια.
demons.

4013 2424 4172 3956 2968
35 Καὶ περιῆγεν ὁ Ἰησοῦς τὰς πόλεις πάσας καὶ τὰς κώμας,
And went about Jesus the cities all and the villages,
1321 1722 4864 848 2784
διδάσκων ἐν ταῖς συναγωγαῖς αὐτῶν, καὶ κηρύσσων τὸ
teaching in the synagogues of them, and proclaiming the
2098 932 2323 3956 3554
εὐαγγέλιον τῆς βασιλείας, καὶ θεραπεύων πᾶσαν νόσον καὶ
gospel of the kingdom, and healing every sickness and
3956 3119 1722 2992 1492 3793 4697
36 πᾶσαν μαλακίαν ἐν τῷ λαῷ. Ἰδὼν δὲ τοὺς ὄχλους, ἐσπλαγ-
every weakness in the people. seeing And the crowds, He was moved
4012 848 3754 2258 1590 4496
χνίσθη περὶ αὐτῶν, ὅτι ἦσαν ἐκλελυμένοι καὶ ἐρριμμένοι
with pity for them, because they were tired and scattered
5616 4263 3361 2192 4166 5119 3004 3101
37 ὡσεὶ πρόβατα μὴ ἔχοντα ποιμένα. τότε λέγει τοῖς μαθηταῖς
as sheep not having a shepherd Then He says to the disciples
848 3303 2326 4183 2040 3641
αὐτοῦ, Ὁ μὲν θερισμὸς πολύς, οἱ δὲ ἐργάται ὀλίγοι·
of Him, the Indeed harvest (is) great the but workmen few;
1189 3767 2962 2326 3704 1544 2040
38 δεήθητε οὖν τοῦ Κυρίου τοῦ θερισμοῦ, ὅπως ἐκβάλῃ ἐργάτας
pray then the Lord of the harvest, that He may send workmen
1519 2326 848
εἰς τὸν θερισμὸν αὐτοῦ.
into the harvest of Him.

the dumb one spoke. And the crowds marveled, saying, Never was it seen this way in Israel. [34]But the Pharisees said, He casts out the demons by the ruler of the demons.

[35]And Jesus went about all the cities and the villages teaching in their synagogues, and proclaiming the gospel of the kingdom, and healing every sickness and every weakness of body among the people. [36]And seeing the crowds, He was moved with pity for them, because they were tired and scattered, like sheep having no shepherd. [37]Then He said to His disciples, The harvest truly *is* great, but the workers few. [38]Pray then that the Lord of the harvest may send out workers into His harvest.

CHAPTER 10

4341 1427 3101 848 1325
1 καὶ προσκαλεσάμενος τοὺς δώδεκα μαθητὰς αὐτοῦ, ἔδωκεν
And having called near the twelve disciples of Him, He gave
846 1849 4151 169 5620 1544
αὐτοῖς ἐξουσίαν πνευμάτων ἀκαθάρτων. ὥστε ἐκβάλλειν
to them authority over spirits unclean so as to cast out
846 2323 3956 3554 3956 3119
αὐτά, καὶ θεραπεύειν πᾶσαν νόσον καὶ πᾶσαν μαλακίαν.
them, and to heal every disease and every weakness.
1429 652 3686 2076 5023
2 Τῶν δὲ δώδεκα ἀποστόλων τὰ ὀνόματά ἐστι ταῦτα·
the And twelve apostles the names are these:
4413 4613 3004 4074 406 80
πρῶτος Σίμων ὁ λεγόμενος Πέτρος, καὶ Ἀνδρέας ὁ ἀδελφὸς
first Simon who is called Peter, and Andrew the brother
848 2385 2199 2491 80
αὐτοῦ· Ἰάκωβος ὁ τοῦ Ζεβεδαίου, καὶ Ἰωάννης ὁ ἀδελφὸς
of him; James the (son of) Zebedee, and John the brother
848 5376 918 2381 3156
3 αὐτοῦ· Φίλιππος, καὶ Βαρθολομαῖος· Θωμᾶς, καὶ Ματθαῖος
of him; Philip, and Bartholomew, Thomas, and Matthew
5057 2385 256 3002
ὁ τελώνης· Ἰάκωβος ὁ τοῦ Ἀλφαίου, καὶ Λεββαῖος ὁ
the tax-collector; James the (son) of Alpheus, and Lebbeus who
1941 2280 4613 2581 2455
4 ἐπικληθεὶς Θαδδαῖος· Σίμων ὁ Κανανίτης, καὶ Ἰούδας
was surnamed Thaddeus; Simon the Canaanite, and Judas
2469 3860 846 5128 1427
5 Ἰσκαριώτης ὁ καὶ παραδοὺς αὐτόν. τούτους τοὺς δώδεκα
Iscariot who also betrayed Him. These twelve

CHAPTER 10

[1]And having called His twelve disciples, He gave them authority over unclean spirits, so as to throw them out, and to heal every disease and every weakness of body.

[2]And the names of the twelve apostles are these: First, Simon who is called Peter, and his brother Andrew; James the *son* of Zebedee, and his brother John; [3]Philip, and Bartholomew; Thomas, and Matthew the tax-collector; James the *son* of Alpheus, and Lebbeus, whose last name *was* Thaddeus; [4]Simon the Canaanite, and Judas Iscariot, who also betrayed Him.

5 Jesus sent these twelve out, charging them, saying: Do not go into the way of *the* nations, and do not go into a city of *the* Samaritans; 6 but rather go to the lost sheep of *the* house of Israel. 7 And going on, proclaim, saying, The kingdom of Heaven has drawn near.

8 Heal sick ones, cleanse lepers, raise dead ones, cast out demons. You have freely received, freely give. 9 Do not provide gold, nor silver, nor copper in your belt; 10 nor provision-bag for *the* road, nor two tunics, nor sandals, nor staves. For the worker is worthy of his food.

11 And into whatever city or village you enter, ask who in it is worthy; and remain there until you go out. 12 But entering into the house, greet it; 13 and if the house truly is worthy, let your peace come upon it. But if it is not worthy, let your peace return to you. 14 And whoever will not receive you, nor will hear your words, having gone out of that house or city, shake off the dust from your feet. 15 Truly I say to you, It will be more bearable to the land of Sodom and Gomorrah in Judgment Day than for that city.

16 Behold, I send you out as sheep in *the* midst of wolves. Therefore, be wise as serpents, and harmless as doves. 17 But beware of men. For they will betray you to sanhedrins, and they will will be brought before governors and kings for My sake, for a testimony to them and to the nations.

649 2424 3853 846 3004
ἀπέστειλεν ὁ Ἰησοῦς, παραγγείλας αὐτοῖς, λέγων,
sent out — Jesus, having charged them, saying,
1519 3598 1484 3361 565 1519 4172 4541
Εἰς ὁδὸν ἐθνῶν μὴ ἀπέλθητε, καὶ εἰς πόλιν Σαμαρειτῶν
Into the way of nations not do go, and into a city of (the) Samaritans
3361 1525 4198 3123 4314 4263
6 μὴ εἰσέλθητε· πορεύεσθε δὲ μᾶλλον πρὸς τὰ πρόβατα τὰ
not do enter, go but rather to the sheep, the
622 3624 2474 4198 2784 3004
7 ἀπολωλότα οἴκου Ἰσραήλ. πορευόμενοι δὲ κηρύσσετε, λέγον-
lost of (the) house of Israel. going on. And proclaim, saying,
3754 1448 932 3772 770
8 τες ὅτι Ἤγγικεν ἡ βασιλεία τῶν οὐρανῶν. ἀσθενοῦντας
— Has drawn near the kingdom of the heavens. Sick ones
2323 3015 2511 3498 1483 1140
θεραπεύετε, λεπροὺς καθαρίζετε, νεκροὺς ἐγείρετε, δαιμόνια
heal, lepers cleanse, dead ones raise, demons
1544 1482 2983 1432 1325 3361 2932
9 ἐκβάλλετε. δωρεὰν ἐλάβετε, δωρεὰν δότε. μὴ κτήσησθε
cast out. Freely you received, freely give. Not provide
5557 3366 696 3366 5478 1519 2223 5216
χρυσόν, μηδὲ ἄργυρον, μηδὲ χαλκὸν εἰς τὰς ζώνας ὑμῶν,
gold, nor silver, nor copper in the belts of you,
3361 4082 1519 3598 3366 1417 5509 3366 5266
10 μὴ πήραν εἰς ὁδόν, μηδὲ δύο χιτῶνας, μηδὲ ὑποδήματα,
nor a bag for (the) way, nor two tunics, nor sandals,
3366 4464 574 1063 2040 5160 848 2076
μηδὲ ῥάβδους· ἄξιος γὰρ ὁ ἐργάτης τῆς τροφῆς αὐτοῦ ἐστιν.
nor staves, worthy for the worker of the food of him is.
1519 * 302 4172 2968 1525 1833 5101 1722 846
*3739 εἰς ἣν δ' ἂν πόλιν ἢ κώμην εἰσέλθητε, ἐξετάσατε τίς ἐν αὐτῇ
11 **into what And ever city village you enter, ask who in it**
514 2076 2546 3306 2193 302 1831 1525
12 ἄξιός ἐστι· κἀκεῖ μείνατε, ἕως ἂν ἐξέλθητε. εἰσερχόμενοι δὲ
worthy is, and there remain until you go out. entering But
1519 3614 782 846 1437 3303 * 3614 574
*2228 εἰς τὴν οἰκίαν, ἀσπάσασθε αὐτήν. καὶ ἐὰν μὲν ᾖ ἡ οἰκία ἀξία,
13 **into the house, greet it; and if indeed be the house worthy,**
2164 1575 5216 1909 846 1437 3361 574 1515
ἐλθέτω ἡ εἰρήνη ὑμῶν ἐπ' αὐτήν· ἐὰν δὲ μη ῃ ἀξία, ἡ εἰρήνη
let come the peace of you on it; if But not it is worthy, the peace
5216 4314 5209 1994 3739 1437 3361 1209 5209
14 ὑμῶν πρὸς ὑμᾶς ἐπιστραφήτω. καὶ ὃς ἐὰν μὴ δέξηται ὑμᾶς
of you to you let return. And whoever not will receive you
3366 191 3056 5216 1831 3614 2228
μηδὲ ἀκούσῃ τοὺς λόγους ὑμῶν, ἐξερχόμενοι τῆς οἰκίας ἢ τῆς
nor will hear the words of you, going out (of) the house or —
4172 1565 1621 2868 4228 5216
πόλεως ἐκείνης, ἐκτινάξατε τὸν κονιορτὸν τῶν ποδῶν ὑμῶν.
city that shake off the dust of the feet of you.
281 3004 5213 414 2071 1093 4670 1111
15 ἀμὴν λέγω ὑμῖν, ἀνεκτότερον ἔσται γῇ Σοδόμων καὶ Γομόρ-
Truly I say to you, More bearable it will be to the land of Sodom and Gomor-
1722 2250 2920 2228 4172 1565
ρων ἐν ἡμέρᾳ κρίσεως, ἢ τῇ πόλει ἐκείνῃ.
rah in (the) day of judgment than city that.
2400 1473 649 5209 5613 4263 1722 3319 3074
16 Ἰδού, ἐγὼ ἀποστέλλω ὑμᾶς ὡς πρόβατα ἐν μέσῳ λύκων·
Behold, I send out you as sheep in (the) midst of wolves;
1096 3767 5429 5613 3789 185 5613 4058
γίνεσθε οὖν φρόνιμοι ὡς οἱ ὄφεις, καὶ ἀκέραιοι ὡς αἱ περιστε-
you be then wise as — serpents and harmless as — doves.
4337 575 444 3860 1063
17 ραί. προσέχετε δὲ ἀπὸ τῶν ἀνθρώπων· παραδώσουσι γὰρ
beware And from — men; they will betray For
5209 1519 4892 1722 4864 848 3146
ὑμᾶς εἰς συνέδρια, καὶ ἐν ταῖς συναγωγαῖς αὐτῶν μαστιγώ-
you to sanhedrins and in the synagogues of them they will
5209 1909 2232 935 71
18 σουσιν ὑμᾶς· καὶ ἐπὶ ἡγεμόνας δὲ καὶ βασιλεῖς ἀχθήσεσθε
scourge you; and before governors also and kings you will be brought

[19]But when they deliver you up, do not be anxious how or what you should say, for it is given to you in that hour what you should say. [20]For you are not the *ones* speaking, but the Spirit of your Father who speaks in you. [21]But brother will betray brother to death, and *the* father *his* child. And children will rise up against parents and will put them to death. [22]And you will be hated by all on account of My name; but the *one* enduring to *the* end shall be saved. [23]But when they persecute you in this city, flee to another. For truly I say to you, In no way will you have finished the cities of Israel until the Son of man comes.

[24]A disciple is not above the teacher, nor a slave above his lord. [25]*It is* enough for the disciple *to* become as his teacher, and the slave as his lord. If they call the Master of the house Beelzebub, how much more those of His household?

[26]Therefore, you should not fear them, for nothing is covered which will not be uncovered; and hidden, which will not be made known. [27]What I say to you in the darkness, speak in the light. And what you hear in the ear, proclaim on the housetops. [28]And you should not fear the *ones* killing the body, but not being able to kill the soul. But rather fear Him being able to destroy both soul and body in Hell.

[29]Are not two sparrows sold for an assarion? Yet not one of them shall fall to the ground without your Father. [30]But even the hairs of your

1752 1700 1519 3142 846 1484 3752
19 ἕνεκεν ἐμοῦ, εἰς μαρτύριον αὐτοῖς καὶ τοῖς ἔθνεσιν. ὅταν δὲ
for My sake, for a testimony to them and to the nations. when But
3860 5209 3361 3309 4459 5101 2980
παραδιδῶσιν ὑμᾶς, μὴ μεριμνήσητε πῶς ἢ τί λαλήσητε·
they deliver up you, not be anxious how or what you may say;
1325 1063 52131722 1565 5610 5101 2980 3756 1063
20 δοθήσεται γὰρ ὑμῖν ἐν ἐκείνῃ τῇ ὥρᾳ τί λαλήσετε· οὐ γὰρ
it is given for to you in that hour what you may say; not for
5210 2075 2980 235 4151 3962 5216
ὑμεῖς ἐστε οἱ λαλοῦντες, ἀλλὰ τὸ Πνεῦμα τοῦ πατρος υμων
you are the (ones) speaking, but the Spirit of the Father of you
2980 1722 5213 3860 80 80 1519
21 τὸ λαλοῦν ἐν ὑμῖν. παραδώσει δὲ ἀδελφὸς ἀδελφὸν εἰς
which speaks in you. will deliver up But brother brother to
2288 3962 5043 1881 5043 1909
θάνατον, καὶ πατὴρ τέκνον· καὶ ἐπαναστήσονται τέκνα ἐπὶ
death, and Father (the) child; and will rise up children against
1118 2289 846 2071 3404 5259
22 γονεῖς, καὶ θανατώσουσιν αὐτούς. καὶ ἔσεσθε μισούμενοι ὑπὸ
parents, and put to death them. And you will be (being) hated by
3956 1223 3686 3450 5278 1519 5056 3778
πάντων διὰ τὸ ὄνομά μου· ὁ δὲ ὑπομείνας εἰς τέλος, οὗτος
all because of the name of Me. he But enduring to (the) end, this (one)
4982 3752 1377 5209 1722 4172 5026
23 σωθήσεται. ὅταν δὲ διώκωσιν ὑμᾶς ἐν τῇ πόλει ταύτῃ,
shall be saved. when But they persecute you in city this,
5343 1519 243 281 1063 3004 5213 3364-- 5055
φεύγετε εἰς τὴν ἄλλην· ἀμὴν γὰρ λέγω ὑμῖν, οὐ μὴ τελέσητε
flee to another; truly for I say to you, In no way will you finish
4172 2474 2193 302 2064 5207 444
τὰς πόλεις τοῦ Ἰσραήλ, ἕως ἂν ἔλθῃ ὁ υἱὸς τοῦ ἀνθρώπου.
the cities of Israel, until may come the Son of man
3756 2076 3101 3228 1320 3761 1401
24 Οὐκ ἔστι μαθητὴς ὑπὲρ τὸν διδάσκαλον, οὐδὲ δοῦλος
Not is a disciple above the teacher, nor a slave
5228 2962 848 713 3101 2443 1096 5613
25 ὑπὲρ τὸν κύριον αὐτοῦ. ἀρκετὸν τῷ μαθητῇ ἵνα γένηται ὡς
above the Lord of him. (It is) enough for the disciple (to) become as
1320 848 1401 5613 2962 848 1487
ὁ διδάσκαλος αὐτοῦ, καὶ ὁ δοῦλος ὡς ὁ κύριος αὐτοῦ. εἰ τὸν
the teacher of him, and the slave as the the lord of him. If the
3617 954 2564 4214 3123
οἰκοδεσπότην Βεελζεβοὺβ ἐκάλεσαν, πόσῳ μᾶλλον τοὺς
master of the house Beelzebub they called, how much more those
3615 848 3361 3767 5399 846 3762 1063 2076
26 οἰκιακοὺς αὐτοῦ; μὴ οὖν φοβηθῆτε αὐτούς· οὐδὲν γάρ ἐστι
of his household? Not, then, you should fear them, nothing for is
2572 3756 601 2927 3756
κεκαλυμμένον ὃ οὐκ ἀποκαλυφθήσεται· καὶ κρυπτὸν ὃ οὐ
covered which will not be uncovered, and hidden which not
1097 3739 3004 5213 1722 4653 2036 1722 5457
27 γνωσθήσεται. ὃ λέγω ὑμῖν ἐν τῇ σκοτίᾳ, εἴπατε ἐν τῷ φωτί·
will be made known. What I say to you in the dark, you say in the light;
3739 1519 3775 191 2784 1909 1430 3361
28 καὶ ὃ εἰς τὸ οὖς ἀκούετε, κηρύξατε ἐπὶ τῶν δωμάτων. καὶ μὴ
and what in the ear you hear, proclaim on the housetops. And not
5399 575 615 4983 5590
φοβηθῆτε ἀπὸ τῶν ἀποκτεινόντων τὸ σῶμα, τὴν δὲ ψυχὴν
you should fear – the (ones) killing the body, the but soul
3361 1410 615 5399 3123 1410
μὴ δυναμένων ἀποκτεῖναι· φοβήθητε δὲ μᾶλλον τὸν δυνά-
not being able to kill; fear but rather the (one)
5590 4893 622 1722 1067 3780 1417
29 μενον καὶ ψυχὴν καὶ σῶμα ἀπολέσαι ἐν γεέννῃ. οὐχὶ δύο
being able both the soul and the body to destroy in Gehenna. Are not two
4765 787 4453 1722 1587 846 3756 4098
στρουθία ἀσσαρίου πωλεῖται; καὶ ἓν ἐξ αὐτῶν οὐ πεσεῖται
sparrows for an assarion sold? And one of them not shall fall
1909 1093 427 3962 5216 2359
30 ἐπὶ τὴν γῆν ἄνευ τοῦ πατρὸς ὑμῶν· ὑμῶν δὲ καὶ αἱ τρίχες τῆς
on the earth without the Father of you. of you But even the hairs of the

head are all numbered. [31]Then do not fear; you are better than many sparrows. [32]Then everyone who shall confess Me before men, I will also confess him before My Father in Heaven. [33]But whoever may deny Me before men, I also will deny him before My Father in Heaven.

[34]Do not think that I came to bring peace on earth. I did not come to bring peace, but a sword. [35]I came to dissever a man from his father, and a daughter from her mother; and a daughter-in-law from her mother-in-law. [36]And a man's enemies *shall be* those of his *own* house. [37]He that loves father or mother above Me is not worthy of Me. And he that loves son or daughter above Me is not worthy of Me. [38]And whoever does not take up his cross and follow after Me is not worthy of Me. [39]The *one* finding his soul shall lose it. And the *one* losing his soul on account of Me shall find it. [40]The *one* receiving you receives Me; and the *one* receiving Me receives Him who sent Me. [41]The *one* receiving a prophet in *the* name of a prophet will receive a prophet's reward; and the *one* receiving a just *one* in the name of a just *one* will receive a just *one's* reward. [42]And whoever gives drink to one of these little ones, only a cup of cold *water,* in the name of a disciple, truly I say to you, In no way will he lose his reward.

2776 3956 705 1526|3361|3767 5399 4183
31 κεφαλῆς πᾶσαι ἠριθμημέναι εἰσί. μὴ οὖν φοβηθῆτε· πολλῶν
head all numbered are. not Then fear; many
4765 1308 5210 3956 3767 3748 3670 1722
32 στρουθίων διαφέρετε ὑμεῖς. πᾶς οὖν ὅστις ὁμολογήσει ἐν
sparrows excell you. Everyone then who shall confess
1698 1715 444 3670 2504 1722 846
ἐμοὶ ἔμπροσθεν τῶν ἀνθρώπων, ὁμολογήσω κἀγὼ ἐν αὐτῷ
Me before men, will confess I also him
1715 3962 3450 1722 3772 3748 302
33 ἔμπροσθεν τοῦ πατρός μου τοῦ ἐν οὐρανοῖς. ὅστις δ' ἂν
before the Father of Me in Heaven whoever and shall
720 3165 1715 444 720 846
ἀρνήσηταί με ἔμπροσθεν τῶν ἀνθρώπων, ἀρνήσομαι αὐτὸν
deny Me before men, will deny him
2504 1715 3962 3450 1722 3772
κἀγὼ ἔμπροσθεν τοῦ πατρός μου τοῦ ἐν οὐρανοῖς.
I also before the Father of Me who (is) in Heaven.
3361 3543 3754 2064 906 1575 1909 1093 3756
34 Μὴ νομίσητε ὅτι ἦλθον βαλεῖν εἰρήνην ἐπὶ τὴν γῆν· οὐκ
Not think that I came to cast peace on the earth; not
2064 906 1515 235 3162 2064 1093 1369
35 ἦλθον βαλεῖν εἰρήνην, ἀλλὰ μάχαιραν. ἦλθον γὰρ διχάσαι
came to cast peace but a sword. I came For to dissever
444 2596 3962 848 2364 2596
ἄνθρωπον κατὰ τοῦ πατρὸς αὐτοῦ, καὶ θυγατέρα κατὰ τῆς
a man with the father of him, and a daughter with the
3384 848 3565 2596 3994 848
36 μητρὸς αὐτῆς, καὶ νύμφην κατὰ τῆς πενθερᾶς αὐτῆς· καὶ
mother of her, and a bride with the mother-in-law of her, and
2190 444 3615 848 5368 3962
37 ἐχθροὶ τοῦ ἀνθρώπου οἱ οἰκιακοὶ αὐτοῦ. ὁ φιλῶν πατέρα ἢ
enemies of the man those of the house of him He loving father or
3384 5228 1691 3756 2076 3450 514 5368 5207
μητέρα ὑπὲρ ἐμέ, οὐκ ἔστι μου ἄξιος· καὶ ὁ φιλῶν υἱὸν ἢ
mother above Me not is of Me worthy; and he loving son or
2364 5228 1691 3756 2076 3450 514 3739 3756 2983
38 θυγατέρα ὑπὲρ ἐμέ, οὐκ ἔστι μου ἄξιος· καὶ ὃς οὐ λαμβάνει
daughter instead of Me, not is of Me worthy. And who not takes up
4716 848 190 3694 3450 3756 2076 3450
τὸν σταυρὸν αὐτοῦ καὶ ἀκολουθεῖ ὀπίσω μου, οὐκ ἔστι μου
the cross of him and follow after Me not is of Me
514 2147 5590 898 622 846
39 ἄξιος. ὁ εὑρὼν τὴν ψυχὴν αὐτοῦ ἀπολέσει αὐτήν· καὶ ὁ
worthy. He finding the soul of him will lose it, and he
622 5590 848 1752 1700 2147 846
ἀπολέσας τὴν ψυχὴν αὐτοῦ ἕνεκεν ἐμοῦ εὑρήσει αὐτήν.
losing the soul of him for sake My will find it.
1209 5209 1696 1209 1691 1209 1209
40 Ὁ δεχόμενος ὑμᾶς ἐμὲ δέχεται· καὶ ὁ ἐμὲ δεχόμενος δέχεται
He receiving you Me. receives, and he Me receiving receives
649 3165 1209 4396 1519 3685
41 τὸν ἀποστείλαντά με. ὁ δεχόμενος προφήτην εἰς ὄνομα
the (One) sending Me. He receiving a prophet in (the) name
4396 3408 4396 2983 1209
προφήτου μισθὸν προφήτου λήψεται· καὶ ὁ δεχόμενος
of a prophet (the) reward of a prophet will receive; and he receiving
1342 1519 3686 1342 3408 1342 2983 3739 302
42 δίκαιον εἰς ὄνομα δικαίου μισθὸν δικαίου λήψεται. καὶ ὃς ἐὰν
(one) just in the name of a just (one), reward a just will receive. And whoever
4222 1520 3398 5130 4221 5593 3440
ποτίσῃ ἕνα τῶν μικρῶν τούτων ποτήριον ψυχροῦ μόνον
gives drink to one little ones of these a cup of cold (water) only
1519 3686 3101 281 3004 5213 --3364-- 622
εἰς ὄνομα μαθητοῦ, ἀμὴν λέγω ὑμῖν, οὐ μὴ ἀπολέσῃ τὸν
in (the) name of a disciple, truly I say to you, in no way will he lose the
3408 848
μισθὸν αὐτοῦ.
reward of him.

CHAPTER 11

1 And it happened, when Jesus finished commanding His twelve disciples, He left there to teach and to proclaim in their cities.
2 But hearing in the prison of the works of Christ, sending two of his disciples, 3 John said to Him, Are You the One coming, or are we to look for another? 4 And answering, Jesus said to them, Going, relate to John what you hear and see: 5 The blind receive sight, and the lame walk; lepers are cleansed, and the deaf hear; the dead are raised, and the poor are given the gospel.

6 And blessed is he, whoever shall not be offended in Me.
7 But as these were going, Jesus began to say to the crowds about John, What did you go out into the wilderness to see? A reed being shaken with the wind? 8 But what did you go out to see? A man clothed in soft clothing? Behold, those wearing soft things are in the houses of kings. 9 But what did you go out to see? A prophet? Yes, I say to you, and *one* more excellent than a prophet. 10 For this is *the one* about whom it has been written: "Behold, I send My messenger before Your face, who shall prepare Your way before You." 11 Truly I say to you, Not has arisen among *those* born of a woman *any* greater than John the Baptist. But the least in the kingdom of Heaven is greater than he is. 12 But from the days of John the Baptist until now,

CHAPTER 11

1096 3753 5055 2424 1299
1 Καὶ ἐγένετο ὅτε ἐτέλεσεν ὁ Ἰησοῦς διατάσσων τοῖς
And it was, when finished Jesus giving command to the
1427 3101 848 3327 1564 1321
δώδεκα μαθηταῖς αὐτοῦ, μετέβη ἐκεῖθεν τοῦ διδάσκειν καὶ
twelve disciples of Him, He moved from there to teach and
2784 1722 4142 848
κηρύσσειν ἐν ταῖς πόλεσιν αὐτῶν.
to proclaim in the cities of them.
2491 191 1722 1201 2041
2 Ὁ δὲ Ἰωάννης ἀκούσας ἐν τῷ δεσμωτηρίῳ τὰ ἔργα τοῦ
But John having heard in the prison the works
5547 3992 1417 3101 848 2036 846 4771
3 Χριστοῦ, πέμψας δύο τῶν μαθητῶν αὐτοῦ, εἶπεν αὐτῷ, Σὺ
of Christ, sending two of the disciples of him, said to Him, You
1487 2064 2228 2087 4328 611
4 εἶ ὁ ἐρχόμενος, ἢ ἕτερον προσδοκῶμεν; καὶ ἀποκριθεὶς ὁ
are the coming (one), or another may we expect? And answering -
2424 2036 846 4198 518 2491 3739
Ἰησοῦς εἶπεν αὐτοῖς, Πορευθέντες ἀπαγγείλατε Ἰωάννῃ ἃ
Jesus said to them, Going relate to John what
191 991 5185 308 5560 4043
5 ἀκούετε καὶ βλέπετε· τυφλοὶ ἀναβλέπουσι, καὶ χωλοὶ περι-
you hear and see: blind ones receive sight, and lame ones walk
3015 2511 2974 191 3498
πατοῦσι, λεπροὶ καθαρίζονται, καὶ κωφοὶ ἀκούουσι, νεκροὶ
about; lepers are cleansed, and deaf ones hear; dead ones
1453 4434 2097 3107 2076
6 ἐγείρονται, καὶ πτωχοὶ εὐαγγελίζονται· καὶ μακάριός ἐστιν,
are raised and poor ones are evanelized; and blessed he is
3739 1437 3361 4624 1722 1698 5130 4198
7 ὃς ἐὰν μὴ σκανδαλισθῇ ἐν ἐμοί. τούτων δὲ πορευομένων,
whoever not shall be offended in Me. (as) these But were going,
756 2424 3004 3793 4012 2491 5101
ἤρξατο ὁ Ἰησοῦς λέγειν τοῖς ὄχλοις περὶ Ἰωάννου, Τί
began - Jesus to say to the crowds concerning John, What
1831 1519 2048 2300 2563 5259 417
ἐξήλθετε εἰς τὴν ἔρημον θεάσασθαι; κάλαμον ὑπὸ ἀνέμου
went you out to the wilderness to view? A reed by wind
4531 235 5101 1831 1492 444 1722 3120
8 σαλευόμενον; ἀλλὰ τί ἐξήλθετε ἰδεῖν; ἄνθρωπον ἐν μαλακοῖς
being shaken? But what did you go out to see? A man in soft
2440 294 2400 3120 5409 1722
ἱματίοις ἠμφιεσμένον; ἰδού, οἱ τὰ μαλακὰ φοροῦντες ἐν τοῖς
garments clothed? Behold, those the soft wearing in the
3624 935 1526 235 5101 1831 1492 4396
9 οἴκοις τῶν βασιλέων εἰσίν. ἀλλὰ τί ἐξήλθετε ἰδεῖν; προφήτην;
houses of kings are. But what went you out to see? A prophet?
3483 3004 5213 4055 4396 3778 1063
10 ναί, λέγω ὑμῖν, καὶ περισσότερον προφήτου· οὗτος γάρ
Yea, I say to you, and (one) more excellent than a prophet. this For
2076 4012 3739 1125 2400 1473 649
ἐστι περὶ οὗ γέγραπται, Ἰδού, ἐγὼ ἀποστέλλω τὸν
is (he) about whom it has been written, Behold, I send forth the
32 3450 4253 4383 4675 3739 2680
ἄγγελόν μου πρὸ προσώπου σου, ὃς κατασκευάσει τὴν
messenger of Me before the face of you, who shall prepare the
3598 4675 1715 4675 281 3004 5213 3756 1453 1722
11 ὁδόν σου ἔμπροσθέν σου. ἀμὴν λέγω ὑμῖν, οὐκ ἐγήγερται ἐν
way of you before you. Truly I say to you, not has arisen in
1084 1135 3187 2491 910
γεννητοῖς γυναικῶν μείζων Ἰωάννου τοῦ Βαπτιστοῦ· ὁ δὲ
(those) born of a woman a greater (than) John the Baptist; the but
3398 1722 932 3772 3187 846 2076
μικρότερος ἐν τῇ βασιλείᾳ τῶν οὐρανῶν μείζων αὐτοῦ ἐστιν.
lesser in the kingdom of the heavens greater (than) he is.
575 2250 2491 910 2193 737
12 ἀπὸ δὲ τῶν ἡμερῶν Ἰωάννου τοῦ βαπτιστοῦ ἕως ἄρτι ἡ
from And the days of John the Baptist until now the

the kingdom of Heaven suffers violence, and the violent seize it. [13]For all the Prophets and the Law prophesied until John. [14]And if you are willing to receive, he is Elijah, the *one* about to come. [15]The *one* having ears to hear, let him hear.

[16]But to what shall I compare this generation? It is like little children sitting in *the* markets, and calling to their mates, [17]and saying, We piped to you, and you did not dance; we mourned to you, and you did not wail. [18]For John came neither eating nor drinking, and they say, He has a demon. [19]The Son of man came eating and drinking, and they say, Behold, a gluttonous man and a winedrinker, and a friend of taxcollectors, and of sinners. And wisdom was justified by her children.

[20]Then He began to reproach the cities in which most of His powerful *acts* had occurred, for they did not repent. [21]Woe to you, Chorazin! Woe to you, Bethsaida! For if the powerful *acts* which have taken place in you had happened in Tyre and Sidon, they would have repented long ago in sackcloth and ashes. [22]But I say to you, It shall be more bearable for Tyre and Sidon in Judgment Day than for you. [23]And you, Capernaum, who have been exalted to the heaven, *you* will be thrown down to Hades. For if the powerful *acts* happening in you had taken place in Sodom, it have remained until today. [24]But I say to you, It will be more bearable for the land of Sodom in Judgment day than for you.

[25]Answering at that time, Jesus said, I praise You, Father, Lord of Heaven and

932 3772 971 97? 726
βασιλεία τῶν οὐρανῶν βιάζεται, καὶ βιασταὶ ἁρπάζουσιν
kingdom of the heavens suffers violence, and the violent seize
846 3956 1063 4396 3551 2193 2491
13 αὐτήν. πάντες γὰρ οἱ προφῆται καὶ ὁ νόμος ἕως Ἰωάννου
it. all For the prophets and the law until John
4395 1487 2309 1209 846 2076 2243
14 προεφήτευσαν· καὶ εἰ θέλετε δέξασθαι, αὐτός ἐστιν Ἠλίας ὁ
prophesied; and if you are willing to receive, he is Elijah, he
3195 2064 2192 3775 191 191 5101
15 μέλλων ἔρχεσθαι. ὁ ἔχων ὦτα ἀκούειν ἀκουέτω. τίνι δὲ
16 about to come. He having ears to hear, let him hear. to what But
3666 1074 5026 3664 2076 3808 1722
ὁμοιώσω τὴν γενεὰν ταύτην; ὁμοία ἐστὶ παιδαρίοις ἐν
shall I compare generation this? like It is to little children in
58 2521 4377 2083 848
ἀγοραῖς καθημένοις, καὶ προσφωνοῦσι τοῖς ἑταίροις αὐτῶν,
markets sitting, and calling to the mates of them,
3004 832 5213 3756 3738 2354
17 καὶ λέγουσιν, Ηὐλήσαμεν ὑμῖν, καὶ οὐκ ὠρχήσασθε· ἐθρηνή-
and saying, We piped to you and not you did dance; we
5213 3756 2875 2064 1063 2491 3383 2068
18 σαμεν ὑμῖν, καὶ οὐκ ἐκόψασθε. ἦλθε γὰρ Ἰωάννης μήτε ἐσθίων
mourned to you and not you did wail. came For John neither eating
3383 4095 3004 1140 2192 2064 5207
19 μήτε πίνων, καὶ λέγουσι, Δαιμόνιον ἔχει. ἦλθεν ὁ υἱὸς τοῦ
nor drinking, and they say, A demon he has. Came the Son
444 2068 4095 3004 2400 444
ἀνθρώπου ἐσθίων καὶ πίνων, καὶ λέγουσιν, Ἰδού, ἄνθρωπος
of man eating and drinking, and they say, Behold, a man
5314 3630 5057 5384 268
φάγος καὶ οἰνοπότης, τελωνῶν φίλος καὶ ἁμαρτωλῶν. καὶ
gluttonous, and a winedrinker, of tax-collectors a friend and of sinners. And
1344 4678 575 5043 848
ἐδικαιώθη ἡ σοφία ἀπὸ τῶν τέκνων αὐτῆς.
was justified wisdom by the children of her.
5119 756 3679 4172 1722 3739 1096
20 Τότε ἤρξατο ὀνειδίζειν τὰς πόλεις ἐν αἷς ἐγένοντο αἱ
Then He began to reproach the cities in which had occurred the
4118 1411 848 3754 3756 3340 3759 4671
21 πλεῖσται δυνάμεις αὐτοῦ, ὅτι οὐ μετενόησαν. Οὐαί σοι,
most powerful (acts) of His; because not they repented. Woe to you,
5523 3759 4671 966 3754 1486 1722 5184 4605
Χοραζίν, οὐαί σοι, Βηθσαϊδά, ὅτι εἰ ἐν Τύρῳ καὶ Σιδῶνι
Chorazin; woe to you, Bethsaida! Because if in Tyre and Sidon
1096 1411 1096 1722 5213 3819 302 1722 4526
ἐγένοντο αἱ δυνάμεις αἱ γενόμεναι ἐν ὑμῖν, πάλαι ἂν ἐν σάκκῳ
occurred the powerful (acts) happening in you, long ago in sackcloth
4700 3340 4133 3004 5213 5184 4605
22 καὶ σποδῷ μετενόησαν. πλὴν λέγω ὑμῖν, Τύρῳ καὶ Σιδῶνι
and ashes they had repented. However, I say to you, For Tyre and for Sidon
414 2071 1722 2250 2920 2228 5213 4771 2584
23 ἀνεκτότερον ἔσται ἐν ἡμέρᾳ κρίσεως, ἢ ὑμῖν. καὶ σύ, Καπερ-
more tolerable it will be in (the) day of judgment than for you; and you, Ca-
2193 3772 5312 2193 86 2601
ναούμ, ἡ ἕως τοῦ οὐρανοῦ ὑψωθεῖσα, ἕως ᾅδου καταβιβα-
pernaum, who to the heaven have been exalted, to Hades will be cast
3754 1487 1722 4670 1096 1411 1096
σθήσῃ· ὅτι εἰ ἐν Σοδόμοις ἐγένοντο αἱ δυνάμεις αἱ γενόμεναι ἐν
down, because if in Sodom occurred the powerful (acts) happening in
4671 3306 302 3360 4594 4133 3004 5213 3754 1093
24 σοί, ἔμειναν ἂν μέχρι τῆς σήμερον. πλὴν λέγω ὑμῖν, ὅτι γῇ
you, it would last until today. However, I tell you that for land
4670 414 2071 1722 2250 2920 2228 4671
Σοδόμων ἀνεκτότερον ἔσται ἐν ἡμέρᾳ κρίσεως, ἢ σοί.
of Sodom more tolerable it will be in (the) day of judgment than for you.
1722 1565 2540 611 2424 2036 1843
25 Ἐν ἐκείνῳ τῷ καιρῷ ἀποκριθεὶς ὁ Ἰησοῦς εἶπεν Ἐξομολο-
At that – time answering Jesus said, I give praise
4671 3962 2962 3772 1093 3754
γοῦμαί σοι, πάτερ, Κύριε τοῦ οὐρανοῦ καὶ τῆς γῆς, ὅτι
to You, Father, Lord of the heaven and of the earth, for

613 5023 575 4680 4908 601
ἀπέκρυψας ταῦτα ἀπὸ σοφῶν καὶ συνετῶν. καὶ ἀπεκάλυψας
You hid these things from sophisti- and cunning, and revealed
846 3516 3483 cated 3962 3754 3779 1096 2107
26 αὐτὰ νηπίοις. ναί ὁ πατήρ, ὅτι οὕτως ἐγένετο εὐδοκία
them to babes. Yea, Father, because thus it was well-pleasing
1715 4675 3956 3427 3860 5259 3962 3450
27 ἔμπροσθέν σου. πάντα μοι παρεδόθη ὑπὸ τοῦ πατρός μου·
before You. All things to Me were yielded by the Father of Me;
3762 1921 5207 --1508-- 3962 3761
καὶ οὐδεὶς ἐπιγινώσκει τὸν υἱόν, εἰ μὴ ὁ πατήρ· οὐδὲ τὸν
and no one knows the Son except the Father, nor the
3962 5100 1921 --1508-- 5207 3739 1437 1014
πατέρα τις ἐπιγινώσκει. εἰ μὴ ὁ υἱός. καὶ ᾧ ἐὰν βούληται ὁ
Father anyone does know, except the Son, and to whomever wills the
5207 601 1205 4314 3165 3956 2872
28 υἱὸς ἀποκαλύψαι. δεῦτε πρός με πάντες οἱ κοπιῶντες καὶ
Son to reveal. Come to Me, all the (ones) laboring and
5412 2504 373 5209 142 2218
29 πεφορτισμένοι, κἀγὼ ἀναπαύσω ὑμᾶς. ἄρατε τὸν ζυγόν
being burdened, and I will give rest you. Take the yoke
3450 1909 5209 3129 575 1700 3754 4235 1510 5011
μου ἐφ' ὑμᾶς καὶ μάθετε ἀπ' ἐμοῦ, ὅτι πρᾶός εἰμι καὶ ταπεινὸς
of Me on you and learn from Me, because meek I am and lowly
2588 2147 372 5590 5216
30 τῇ καρδίᾳ· καὶ εὑρήσετε ἀνάπαυσιν ταῖς ψυχαῖς ὑμῶν. ὁ
– in heart, and you will find rest to the souls of you; the
1063 2218 3450 5543 5413 3450 1645 2076
γὰρ ζυγός μου χρηστός, καὶ τὸ φορτίον μου ἐλαφρόν ἐστιν.
for yoke of Me pleasant and the burden of Me light is.

CHAPTER 12

1722 1565 2540 4198 2424 4521 1223
1 Ἐν ἐκείνῳ τῷ καιρῷ ἐπορεύθη ὁ Ἰησοῦς τοῖς σάββασι διὰ
At that time went Jesus on the Sabbath through
4702 3101 848 3983 756
τῶν σπορίμων· οἱ δὲ μαθηταὶ αὐτοῦ ἐπείνασαν, καὶ ἤρξαντο
the grainfields; the and disciples of Him hungered, and began
5089 4719 2068 5330 1492 2036
2 τίλλειν στάχυας καὶ ἐσθίειν. οἱ δὲ Φαρισαῖοι ἰδόντες εἶπον
to pluck ears and to eat. the But Pharisees seeing, said
846 2400 3101 4675 4160 3739 3756 1832 4160
αὐτῷ, Ἰδού, οἱ μαθηταί σου ποιοῦσιν ὃ οὐκ ἔξεστι ποιεῖν
to Him, behold, the disciples of You are doing what not it is lawful to do
1722 4521 2036 846 3756 314 5101 4160
3 ἐν σαββάτῳ. ὁ δὲ εἶπεν αὐτοῖς, Οὐκ ἀνέγνωτε τί ἐποίησε
on a sabbath. He And said to them, Not did you read what did
1138 3753 3983 848 3326 846 4459 1525
4 Δαβίδ, ὅτε ἐπείνασεν αὐτὸς καὶ οἱ μετ' αὐτοῦ· πῶς εἰσῆλθεν
David, when he hungered Himself and those with him? How he went in
1519 3624 2316 740 4286
εἰς τὸν οἶκον τοῦ Θεοῦ, καὶ τοὺς ἄρτους τῆς προθέσεως
into the house of God, and the loaves of the presentation
5315 3739 3756 1832 2258 846 5315 3761 3326 846
ἔφαγεν, οὓς οὐκ ἐξὸν ἦν αὐτῷ φαγεῖν, οὐδὲ τοῖς μετ' αὐτοῦ,
he ate, which not lawful it was for him to eat, nor for those with him,
--1508-- 2409 3441 2228 3756 314 1722 3551 3754
5 εἰ μὴ τοῖς ἱερεῦσι μόνοις; ἢ οὐκ ἀνέγνωτε ἐν τῷ νόμῳ, ὅτι
except for the priests only? Or not did you read in the law that
4521 2409 1722 2411 4521 953
τοῖς σάββασιν οἱ ἱερεῖς ἐν τῷ ἱερῷ τὸ σάββατον βεβηλοῦσι,
on the sabbaths the priests in the Temple the sabbath profane,
338 1526 3004 5213 3754 2411 3187 2076
6 καὶ ἀναίτιοί εἰσι; λέγω δὲ ὑμῖν ὅτι τοῦ ἱεροῦ μείζων ἐστὶν
and guiltless are? I say But to you that the Temple a greater than is
5602 1487 1097 5101 2076 1656 2309 3756 2378
7 ὧδε. εἰ δὲ ἐγνώκειτε τί ἐστιν, Ἔλεον θέλω καὶ οὐ θυσίαν,
here. if But you had known what it is, Mercy I desire, and not sacrifice,
3756 302 2613 338 2962 1063 2076
8 οὐκ ἂν κατεδικάσατε τοὺς ἀναιτίους. κύριος γάρ ἐστι καὶ τοῦ
not would you have judged the guiltless. Lord For is also of the

of earth, because You hid these things from *the* sophisticated and cunning, and revealed them to babes. [26]Yes, Father, for so it was pleasing before You. [27]All things were yielded up to Me by My Father; and no one knows the Son except the Father; nor does anyone know the Father, except the Son, and *he* to whom the Son wills to reveal *Him*.

[28]Come to Me, all those laboring and being burdened, and I will give you rest. [29]Take My yoke upon you, and learn from Me, because I am meek and lowly in heart; and you will find rest to your souls. [30]For My yoke is easy, and My burden is light.

CHAPTER 12

[1]At that time on the sabbath, Jesus went through the grain fields. And His disciples were hungry, and began to pluck ears and to eat. [2]But seeing, the Pharisees said to Him, Behold, your disciples are doing what it is not lawful to do on the sabbath. [3]But He said to them, Have you not read what David did when he and those with him hungered? [4]How he entered into the house of God and he ate the Loaves of Presentation, which it was not lawful for him to eat, nor for those with him, but for the priests only? [5]Or have you not read in the Law that on the sabbaths the priests in the temple profane the sabbath, and are guiltless? [6]But I say to you, One greater than the temple is here. [7]But if you had known what *this* is, "I desire mercy, and not sacrifice," you would not have condemned the guiltless.

NOTE: Frequent words not numbered: δέ(1161); καί(2531)—and, but; ὁ, ἡ, τό (3588, the)— * above word, look in verse margin for No.

man is also Lord of the sabbath.

[9]And moving from there, He came into their synagogue. [10]And, behold, a man having *a* withered hand was there. And they asked Him, saying, Is it lawful to heal on the sabbaths?—that they might accuse Him. [11]But He said to them, What man of you will be, who will have one sheep, and if this one fall into a pit on the sabbaths, will he not lay hold of it and raise *it* up? [12]How much more, then, does a man excel a sheep! So that it is lawful to do well on the sabbaths. [13]Then He said to the man, Stretch out your hand! And he stretched out. And it was restored sound as the other.

[14]But *as* they *were* leaving, the Pharisees took up a council against Him, how they might destroy Him. [15]But knowing, Jesus withdrew from there. And many crowds followed Him; and He healed them all, [16]and warned them that they should not make Him manifest. [17]So that might be fulfilled that spoken through Isaiah the prophet, saying, [18]"Behold My child whom I chose, My Beloved, in whom My soul has delighted! I will put My Spirit on Him, and He will declare judgment to the nations. [19]He will not strive nor cry out, nor will anyone hear His voice in the streets. [20]A bruised reed He will not break, and smoking flax He will not quench, until He bring forth judgment to victory. [21]And the nations will hope in His name."

[22]Then one having been demon-possessed was led to Him, blind and dumb.

4521 5207 444
σαββάτου ὁ υἱὸς τοῦ ἀνθρώπου.
Sabbath the Son – of man.
3327 1564 2064 1519 4864 848
9 Καὶ μεταβὰς ἐκεῖθεν ἦλθεν εἰς τὴν συναγωγὴν αὐτῶν. καὶ
10 And moving from there He came into the synagogue of them. And
2400 444 2258 5495 2192 3584 1905
ἰδού, ἄνθρωπος ἦν τὴν χεῖρα ἔχων ξηράν· καὶ ἐπηρώτησαν
behold, a man was, the hand having withered, and they questioned
846 3004 1487 1832 4521 2323 2443
αὐτόν, λέγοντες, Εἰ ἔξεστι τοῖς σάββασι θεραπεύειν; ἵνα
Him, saying, If it is lawful on the Sabbaths to heal? That
2723 846 2036 846 5101 2071 1537
11 κατηγορήσωσιν αὐτοῦ. ὁ δὲ εἶπεν αὐτοῖς, Τίς ἔσται ἐξ
they might accuse Him. He But said to them, What will be of
5216 444 3739 2192 4263 1520 1437 1706 5124
ὑμῶν ἄνθρωπος, ὃς ἕξει πρόβατον ἕν, καὶ ἐὰν ἐμπέσῃ τοῦτο
you a man who will have sheep one, and if fall (in) this
4521 1519 999 3780 2902 846 1453
τοῖς σάββασιν εἰς βόθυνον, οὐχὶ κρατήσει αὐτὸ καὶ ἐγερεῖ;
on the Sabbaths into a pit, not will he lay hold of it and raise (it)?
4214 3767 1308 444 4263 5620 1832
12 πόσῳ οὖν διαφέρει ἄνθρωπος προβάτου. ὥστε ἔξεστι τοῖς
How much then surpasses a man a sheep! So that it is lawful on the
4521 2573 4160 5119 3004 444 1614
13 σάββασι καλῶς ποιεῖν. τότε λέγει τῷ ἀνθρώπῳ, Ἔκτεινον
Sabbaths well to do. Then He says to the man, Stretch out
5495 4675 1614 600 5199 5613
τὴν χεῖρά σου. καὶ ἐξέτεινε, καὶ ἀποκατεστάθη ὑγιὴς ὡς ἡ
the hand of you, and he stretched and it was restored sound as the
243 5330 4824 2983 2596 846
14 ἄλλη. οἱ δὲ Φαρισαῖοι συμβούλιον ἔλαβον κατ' αὐτοῦ
other. the But Pharisees a council took against Him,
1831 3704 846 622 2424 1097
15 ἐξελθόντες, ὅπως αὐτὸν ἀπολέσωσιν. ὁ δὲ Ἰησοῦς γνοὺς
they having left, how Him they might destroy. But Jesus knowing
402 1564 190 848 3793 4183
ἀνεχώρησεν ἐκεῖθεν· καὶ ἠκολούθησαν αὐτῷ ὄχλοι πολλοί,
withdrew from there. And followed Him crowds many,
2323 846 3956 2008 846
16 καὶ ἐθεράπευσεν αὐτοὺς πάντας, καὶ ἐπετίμησεν αὐτοῖς,
and He healed them all, and warned them
2443 3361 5318 846 4160 3704 4137
17 ἵνα μὴ φανερὸν αὐτὸν ποιήσωσιν· ὅπως πληρωθῇ τὸ
that not manifest Him they should make; so that may be fulfilled that
4483 1223 2268 4396 3004 2400 3816
18 ῥηθὲν διὰ Ἠσαΐου τοῦ προφήτου, λέγοντος, Ἰδού, ὁ παῖς
spoken through Isaiah the prophet, saying, Behold, the child
3450 3739 140 27 3450 1519 3739 2106 5590
μου ὃν ᾑρέτισα· ὁ ἀγαπητός μου εἰς ὃν εὐδόκησεν ἡ ψυχή
of Me whom I chose, the beloved of Me in whom has delighted the soul
3450 5087 4151 3450 1909 846 2920 1484
μου θήσω τὸ πνεῦμά μου ἐπ' αὐτόν καὶ κρίσιν τοῖς ἔθνεσιν
of Me. I will put the Spirit of Me on Him, and judgment to the nations
518 3756 2051 3761 2905 3761 191 5100 1722
19 ἀπαγγελεῖ. οὐκ ἐρίσει, οὐδὲ κραυγάσει· οὐδὲ ἀκούσει τις ἐν
He will declare. Not He will strive, nor cry out, nor will hear any in
4113 5456 848 2563 4937
20 ταῖς πλατείαις τὴν φωνὴν αὐτοῦ. κάλαμον συντετριμμένον
the streets the voice of Him. A reed bruised
3756 2608 3043 5188 3756 4570 2193 302 1544
οὐ κατεάξει, καὶ λίνον τυφόμενον οὐ σβέσει· ἕως ἂν ἐκβάλῃ
not He will break, and flax smoking not He will quench, until He expel
1519 3534 2920 1722 3686 848 1484 1679
21 εἰς νῖκος τὴν κρίσιν. καὶ ἐν τῷ ὀνόματι αὐτοῦ ἔθνη ἐλπιοῦσι.
to victory the judgment. And in the name of Him nations will hope.
5119 4374 846 1139 5185
22 Τότε προσηνέχθη αὐτῷ δαιμονιζόμενος, τυφλὸς καὶ
Then was brought to Him a demon-possessed one blind and
2974 2323 846 5620 5185 2974
κωφός· καὶ ἐθεράπευσεν αὐτόν, ὥστε τὸν τυφλὸν καὶ κωφὸν
dumb; and He healed him, so that the blind and dumb

And He healed him, so that the blind and dumb one could both both speak and see. [23]And all the crowds were amazed, and said, Is this not the son of David? [24]But hearing, the Pharisees said, This *one* does not cast out demons except by Beelzebub, ruler of the demons. [25]But Jesus knowing their thoughts, He said to them, Every kingdom divided against itself is brought to ruin. And every city or house divided against itself will not stand. [26]And if Satan throws out Satan, he was divided against himself. How then will his kingdom stand? [27]And if I throw out the demons by Beelzebub, by whom do your sons throw them out? Because of this, they shall be your judges. [28]But if I cast out the demons by the Spirit of God, then the kingdom of God has come on you. [29]Or how is anyone able to enter the house of the strong one and plunder his goods, if he does not first tie up the strong one; and then he will plunder his house?

[30]The *one* who is not with Me is against Me; and the *one* who does not gather with Me scatters. [31]Because of this, I say to you, Every sin and blasphemy shall be forgiven to men, but the blasphemy concerning the Spirit shall not be forgiven to men. [32]And whoever speaks a word against the Son of man, it shall be forgiven him. But whoever speaks against the Holy Spirit, it shall not be forgiven him, not in this age, nor in the coming *one*.

[33]Either make the tree good, and its fruit good; or make the tree corrupt, and its fruit corrupt; for the tree

2980 991 1839 3956 3793
23 καὶ λαλεῖν καὶ βλέπειν. καὶ ἐξίσταντο πάντες οἱ ὄχλοι καὶ
both could speak and see. And were amazed all the crowds, and
3004 3385 3778 2076 5207 1138 5330
24 ἔλεγον, Μήτι οὗτός ἐστιν ὁ υἱὸς Δαβίδ ; οἱ δὲ Φαρισαῖοι
said, Not this is the son of David? the But Pharisees
191 2036 3778 3756 1544 1140 1508
ἀκούσαντες εἶπον, Οὗτος οὐκ ἐκβάλλει τὰ δαιμόνια, εἰ μὴ
hearing said, This (one) not casts out the demons except
1722 954 758 1140 1492
25 ἐν τῷ Βεελζεβοὺλ ἄρχοντι τῶν δαιμονίων. εἰδὼς δὲ ὁ
by Beelzebub, ruler of the demons. knowing But
2424 1761 848 2036 856 3956 932
Ἰησοῦς τὰς ἐνθυμήσεις αὐτῶν εἶπεν αὐτοῖς, Πᾶσα βασιλεία
Jesus the thoughts of them, He said to them, Every kingdom
3307 2596 1438 2049 3956 4172 2228 3614
μερισθεῖσα καθ' ἑαυτῆς ἐρημοῦται· καὶ πᾶσα πόλις ἢ οἰκία
divided against itself is brought to ruin, and every city or house
3307 2596 1438 3756 2476 1487 4567
26 μερισθεῖσα καθ' ἑαυτῆς οὐ σταθήσεται. καὶ εἰ ὁ Σατανᾶς τὸν
divided against itself not will stand, and if — Satan —
4567 1544 1909 1438 3307 4459 3767 2476
Σατανᾶν ἐκβάλλει, ἐφ' ἑαυτὸν ἐμερίσθη· πῶς οὖν σταθήσεται
Satan casts out, against himself he was divided. How then will stand
932 848 1487 1473 1722 954 1544
27 ἡ βασιλεία αὐτοῦ ; καὶ εἰ ἐγὼ ἐν Βεελζεβοὺλ ἐκβάλλω τὰ
the kingdom of him? And if I by Beelzebub cast out the
1140 5207 5216 1722 5101 1544 1223 5124 846
δαιμόνια, οἱ υἱοὶ ὑμῶν ἐν τίνι ἐκβάλλουσι ; διὰ τοῦτο αὐτοὶ
demons, the sons of you by whom do they cast out? By this they
5216 2071 2923 1487 1473 1722 4151 2316 1544
28 ὑμῶν ἔσονται κριταί. εἰ δὲ ἐγὼ ἐν Πνεύματι Θεοῦ ἐκβάλλω
of you shall be judges. if But I by (the) Spirit of God cast out
1140 686 5348 1909 5209 932 2316/2228
29 τὰ δαιμόνια, ἄρα ἔφθασεν ἐφ' ὑμᾶς ἡ βασιλεία τοῦ Θεοῦ. ἢ
the demons, then has come upon you the kingdom of God. Or
4459 1410 5100 1525 1519 3614 2478
πῶς δύναταί τις εἰσελθεῖν εἰς τὴν οἰκίαν τοῦ ἰσχυροῦ καὶ τὰ
how can anyone enter into the house of the strong one and the
4632 848 1283 3362 4412 1210 2478
σκεύη αὐτοῦ διαρπάσαι, ἐὰν μὴ πρῶτον δήσῃ τὸν ἰσχυρόν ;
vessels of him to plunder, if not first he binds the strong one?
5119 3614 848 1283 3361 1560 3326 1700
30 καὶ τότε τὴν οἰκίαν αὐτοῦ διαρπάσει. ὁ μὴ ὢν μετ' ἐμοῦ,
And then the house of him he will plunder. He not being with Me
2596 1700 2076 3361 4863 3326 1700 4650 1223
31 κατ' ἐμοῦ ἐστι, καὶ ὁ μὴ συνάγων μετ' ἐμοῦ, σκορπίζει. διὰ
against Me is; and he not gathering with Me scatters. Because
5124 3004 5213 3956 266 988 863
τοῦτο λέγω ὑμῖν, Πᾶσα ἁμαρτία καὶ βλασφημία ἀφεθήσεται
of this I say to you, Every sin and blasphemy shall be forgiven
444 4151 988 3756 863
τοῖς ἀνθρώποις· ἡ δὲ τοῦ Πνεύματος βλασφημία οὐκ ἀφεθή-
to men; the but of the Spirit blasphemy not will be
444 3739 302 2036 3056 2596 5207
32 σεται τοῖς ἀνθρώποις. καὶ ὃς ἂν εἴπῃ λόγον κατὰ τοῦ υἱοῦ
forgiven to men. And whoever speaks a word against the Son
444 863 846 3739 302 2036 2596
τοῦ ἀνθρώπου, ἀφεθήσεται αὐτῷ· ὃς δ' ἂν εἴπῃ κατὰ τοῦ
of man, It will be forgiven him; but whoever speaks against the
4151 40 3756 863 846 3777 1722 5129
Πνεύματος τοῦ Ἁγίου, οὐκ ἀφεθήσεται αὐτῷ, οὔτε ἐν τούτῳ
Spirit the Holy, not it shall be forgiven him, neither in this
165 3777 1722 3195 2228 4160 1186
33 τῷ αἰῶνι οὔτε ἐν τῷ μέλλοντι. ἢ ποιήσατε τὸ δένδρον
age nor in the coming (one). Either make the tree
2570 2590 848 2570 2228 4160 2686
καλόν, καὶ τὸν καρπὸν αὐτοῦ καλόν, ἢ ποιήσατε τὸ δένδρον
good and the fruit of it good, or make the tree
4550 2590 848 4550 1531 1063 2590
σαπρόν, καὶ τὸν καρπὸν αὐτοῦ σαπρόν· ἐκ γὰρ τοῦ καρποῦ
corrupt and the fruit of it corrupt; of for the fruit

NOTE: Frequent words not numbered: δέ(1161); καί(2531)—and, but; ὁ, ἡ, τό (3588, the)— • above word, look in verse margin for No.

34 Offspring of vipers! How can you being evil speak good things? For out of the abundance of the heart the mouth speaks. 35 TEhe good man out of the good treasure of the heart brings forth good things. And the evil man out of the evil treasure puts forth evil things. 36 But I say to you that every idle word, whatever men may speak, they shall give an account of it in Judgment Day. 37 For by your words you will be justified, and by your words you will be condemned.

38 Then some of the scribes and Pharisees answered, saying, Teacher, we desire to see a sign from you. 39 But answering He said to them, An evil and adulterous generation seeks a sign, and a sign shall not be given to it, except the sign of Jonah the prophet. 40 For even as Jonah was in the belly of the huge fish three days and three nights, so shall the Son of man be in the heart of the earth three days and three nights.

41 Men, Ninevites, will stand up in the Judgment with this generation, and will condemn it. For they repented at the preaching of Jonah; and, behold, a Greater-than-Jonah *is* here. 42 *The* queen of *the* south will be raised in the Judgment with this generation, and will condemn it. For she came from the ends of the earth to hear the wisdom of Solomon; and, behold, a Greater-than-Solomon *is* here.

43 But when the unclean spirit goes from a man, he goes through dry places seeking rest, and does not

1186 1097 1081 2191 4459 1410
34 τὸ δένδρον γινώσκεται. γεννήματα ἐχιδνῶν, πῶς δύνασθε
the tree is known. Offspring of vipers! How can you
18 2980 4190 5601 1537 1063 4051
ἀγαθὰ λαλεῖν, πονηροὶ ὄντες; ἐκ γὰρ τοῦ περισσεύματος
good things speak, evil being? out of For the abundance
2588 4750 2980 18 444 1537
35 τῆς καρδίας τὸ στόμα λαλεῖ. ὁ ἀγαθὸς ἄνθρωπος ἐκ τοῦ
of the heart the mouth speaks. The good man out of the
18 2344 2588 1544 18
ἀγαθοῦ θησαυροῦ τῆς καρδίας ἐκβάλλει τὰ ἀγαθά· καὶ ὁ
good treasure of the heart puts forth the good things, and the
4190 444 1537 4190 2344 1544
πονηρὸς ἄνθρωπος ἐκ τοῦ πονηροῦ θησαυροῦ ἐκβάλλει
evil man out of the evil treasure puts forth
4190 3004 5213 3754 3956 4487 692 1437 2980
36 πονηρά. λέγω δὲ ὑμῖν, ὅτι πᾶν ῥῆμα ἀργόν, ὃ ἐὰν λαλή-
evil things. I say But to you, that every word idle whatever may speak
444 591 4012 848 3056 1722
σωσιν οἱ ἄνθρωποι, ἀποδώσουσι περὶ αὐτοῦ λόγον ἐν
— men, they will give concerning it account in
2250 2920 1537 1063 3056 4675 1344 1537
37 ἡμέρᾳ κρίσεως. ἐκ γὰρ τῶν λόγων σου δικαιωθήσῃ, καὶ ἐκ
(the) day of judgment, by For the words of you you will be justified, and by
3056 4675 2613
τῶν λόγων σου καταδικασθήσῃ.
the words of you you will be condemned.
5119 611 5100 1122 5330
38 Τότε ἀπεκρίθησάν τινες τῶν γραμματέων καὶ Φαρισαίων,
Then answered some of the scribes and Pharisees,
3004 1320 2309 575 4675 4592 1492
39 λέγοντες, Διδάσκαλε, θέλομεν ἀπὸ σοῦ σημεῖον ἰδεῖν. ὁ δὲ
saying, Teacher, we wish from You a sign to see. He But
611 2036 846 1074 4190 3428 4592
ἀποκριθεὶς εἶπεν αὐτοῖς, Γενεὰ πονηρὰ καὶ μοιχαλὶς σημεῖον
answering said to them, generation An evil and adulterous a sign
1934 4592 3756 1325 846 1508 4592
ἐπιζητεῖ· καὶ σημεῖον οὐ δοθήσεται αὐτῇ, εἰ μὴ τὸ σημεῖον
seeks, and a sign not shall be given to it except the sign
2495 4396 5618 1063 2258 2495 1722 2836
40 Ἰωνᾶ τοῦ προφήτου. ὥσπερ γὰρ ἦν Ἰωνᾶς ἐν τῇ κοιλίᾳ
of Jonah the prophet. even as For was Jonah in the belly
2785 5140 2250 5140 3571 3779 2071 5207
τοῦ κήτους τρεῖς ἡμέρας καὶ τρεῖς νύκτας, οὕτως ἔσται ὁ υἱὸς
of the huge fish three days and three nights, so will be the Son
444 1722 2588 1093 5140 2250 5140
τοῦ ἀνθρώπου ἐν τῇ καρδίᾳ τῆς γῆς τρεῖς ἡμέρας καὶ τρεῖς
— of man in the heart of the earth three days and three
3571 435 3536 450 1722 2920 3326
41 νύκτας. ἄνδρες Νινευῖται ἀναστήσονται ἐν τῇ κρίσει μετὰ
nights. Men, Ninevites will stand up in the judgment with
1074 5026 2632 846 3754 3340
τῆς γενεᾶς ταύτης καὶ κατακρινοῦσιν αὐτήν· ὅτι μετενόησαν
— generation this and will condemn it; because they repented
1519 2782 2495 2400 4119 2495 5602 938
42 εἰς τὸ κήρυγμα Ἰωνᾶ· καὶ ἰδού, πλεῖον Ἰωνᾶ ὧδε. βασίλισσα
at the preaching of Jonah, and behold, a greater than Jonah (is) here. (The) queen
3558 1453 1722 2920 3326 1074 5026
νότου ἐγερθήσεται ἐν τῇ κρίσει μετὰ τῆς γενεᾶς ταύτης καὶ
of (the) south will be raised in the judgment with — generation this and
2632 846 3754 2064 1537 4009 1093
κατακρινεῖ αὐτήν· ὅτι ἦλθεν ἐκ τῶν περάτων τῆς γῆς
will condemn it; because she came out of the limits of the earth
191 4678 4672 2400 4119 4672
ἀκοῦσαι τὴν σοφίαν Σολομῶντος· καὶ ἰδού, πλεῖον Σολο-
to hear the wisdom of Solomon, and, behold, a greater- than Solo-
5602 3752 169 4151 1831 575
43 μῶντος ὧδε. ὅταν δὲ τὸ ἀκάθαρτον πνεῦμα ἐξέλθῃ ἀπὸ τοῦ
(is) here. when Now the unclean spirit goes out from —
444 1330 1223 504 5117 2212 372
ἀνθρώπου, διέρχεται δι' ἀνύδρων τόπων, ζητοῦν ἀνάπαυσιν,
a man, he goes through dry places seeking rest,

NOTE: Frequent words not numbered: δέ(1161); καί(2531)—and, but; ὁ, ἡ, τό (3588, the)— * above word, look in verse margin for No

find *it.* 44Then he says, I will return to my house from which I came out. And coming, he finds *it* standing empty, swept and decorated. 45Then he goes and takes with him seven other spirits more evil than him*self*, and entering dwells there. And the last things of that man become worse than the first. So it will be also to this evil generation.

46But while He was yet speaking to the crowds, behold, His mother and brothers were standing outside, seeking to speak to Him. 47Then one said to Him, Behold, Your mother and Your brothers are standing outside, seeking to speak to You. 48But answering, He said to the *one* speaking to Him, Who is My mother? And who are My brothers? 49And stretching out His hand to His disciples, He said, Behold, My mother and My brothers. 50For whoever shall do the will of My Father in Heaven, that one is My brother and sister and mother.

3756 2147 5119 3004 1994 1519 3624 3450
44 καὶ οὐχ εὑρίσκει. τότε λέγει, Ἐπιστρέψω εἰς τὸν οἶκόν μου
and not does find. Then he says, I will return to the house of me,
3606 1831 2064 2147 4980 4563
ὅθεν ἐξῆλθον· καὶ ἐλθὸν εὑρίσκει σχολάζοντα, σεσαρωμένον,
from where I came, and coming he finds (it) standing empty, being swept
2885 5119 4198 3880 3326
45 καὶ κεκοσμημένον. τότε πορεύεται καὶ παραλαμβάνει μεθ'
and being decorated. Then he goes and takes along with
1438 2033 2087 4151 4191 1438
ἑαυτοῦ ἑπτὰ ἕτερα πνεύματα πονηρότερα ἑαυτοῦ, καὶ
him seven other spirits more evil (than) him, and
1525 2730 1563 1096 2078 444
εἰσελθόντα κατοικεῖ ἐκεῖ· καὶ γίνεται τὰ ἔσχατα τοῦ ἀνθρώ-
entering dwells there; and becomes the last things of man
1525 5501 4413 2779 2071 1074
που ἐκείνου χείρονα τῶν πρώτων. οὕτως ἔσται καὶ τῇ γενεᾷ
that worse than the first. Thus it will be also to gene-
5026 4190
ταύτῃ τῇ πονηρᾷ.
ration this evil.

2089 846 2980 3793 2400 3384
46 Ἔτι δὲ αὐτοῦ λαλοῦντος τοῖς ὄχλοις, ἰδού, ἡ μήτηρ καὶ
while But He is speaking to the crowds, behold the mother and
80 848 2476 1854 2212 846 2980
οἱ ἀδελφοὶ αὐτοῦ εἱστήκεισαν ἔξω, ζητοῦντες αὐτῷ λαλῆσαι.
the brothers of Him stood outside, seeking to Him to speak.
2036 5100 846 2400 3384 4675 80 5675 1854
47 εἶπε δέ τις αὐτῷ, Ἰδού, ἡ μήτηρ σου καὶ οἱ ἀδελφοί σου ἔξω
said And one to Him, Behold, the mother of You and the brothers of You out
2476 2212 4671 2980 611 2036
48 ἑστήκασι, ζητοῦντές σοι λαλῆσαι. ὁ δὲ ἀποκριθεὶς εἶπε τῷ
are standing, seeking to You to speak. He And answering said to the
2036 846 5101 2076 3384 3450 5101 1526
εἰπόντι αὐτῷ, Τίς ἐστιν ἡ μήτηρ μου; καὶ τίνες εἰσὶν οἱ
(one) saying to Him, Who is the mother of Me, and who are the
80 3450 1614 5495 848 1909
49 ἀδελφοί μου; καὶ ἐκτείνας τὴν χεῖρα αὐτοῦ ἐπὶ τοὺς
brothers of Me? And stretching out the hand of Him on the
3101 848 2036 2400 3384 3450 80 3450
μαθητὰς αὐτοῦ εἶπεν, Ἰδού, ἡ μήτηρ μου καὶ οἱ ἀδελφοί μου.
disciples of Him He said, Behold, the mother of Me and the brothers of Me.
3748 1063 302 4160 2307 3962 3450 1722
50 ὅστις γὰρ ἂν ποιήσῃ τὸ θέλημα τοῦ πατρός μου τοῦ ἐν
who For ever does the will of the Father of Me the in
3772 846 3450 80 79 3384 2076
οὐρανοῖς, αὐτός μου ἀδελφὸς καὶ ἀδελφὴ καὶ μήτηρ ἐστίν.
heavens, he of Me brother and sister and mother is.

CHAPTER 13

1And going out from the house in that day, Jesus sat down by the sea. 2And great crowds were gathered to Him, so that boarding the boat, He sat down. And all the crowd stood on the shore. 3And He spoke to them many things in parables, saying:

Behold, the sower went out to sow. 4And in his sowing, some fell by the roadside, and the birds came and ate them. 5And

CHAPTER 13

1722 2250 1565 1831 2424 575 3614
1 Ἐν δὲ τῇ ἡμέρᾳ ἐκείνῃ ἐξελθὼν ὁ Ἰησοῦς ἀπὸ τῆς οἰκίας
in And day that going forth Jesus from the house
2521 3844 2281 4863 4314 846
2 ἐκάθητο παρὰ τὴν θάλασσαν. καὶ συνήχθησαν πρὸς αὐτὸν
He sat down by the sea. And were assembled to Him
3793 4183 5620 846 1519 4143 1684 2521
ὄχλοι πολλοί, ὥστε αὐτὸν εἰς τὸ πλοῖον ἐμβάντα καθῆσθαι·
crowds great, so that He into the boat entering sat down
3956 3793 1909 123 2476 2980
3 καὶ πᾶς ὁ ὄχλος ἐπὶ τὸν αἰγιαλὸν εἱστήκει. καὶ ἐλάλησεν
and all the crowd on the shore stood. And He spoke
846 4183 1722 3850 3004 2400 1831
αὐτοῖς πολλὰ ἐν παραβολαῖς, λέγων, Ἰδού, ἐξῆλθεν ὁ
to them many things in parables, saying, Behold, went out the
4687 4687 1722 4687 846 3739 3303 4098
4 σπείρων τοῦ σπείρειν. καὶ ἐν τῷ σπείρειν αὐτόν, ἃ μὲν ἔπεσε
(one) sowing to sow, and in the sowing of him, some truly fell
3814 3598 2064 4071 2719 846
παρὰ τὴν ὁδόν· καὶ ἦλθε τὰ πετεινὰ καὶ κατέφαγεν αὐτά.
by the wayside, and came the birds and ate them.

other fell on the stony places where they did not have much earth; and it immediately sprang up, because *it* had no deepness of earth. [6]And *the* sun rising, it was scorched; and because of having no root, it was dried up. [7]And other fell on the thorns, and the thorns grew up and choked them. [8]And other fell on the good ground, and yielded fruit; indeed one a hundred*fold*, and one sixty, and one thirty. [9]The *one* having ears to hear, let him hear.

[10]And coming near, the disciples said to Him, Why do You speak to them in parables? [11]And answering He said to them, Because it has been given to you to know the mysteries of the kingdom of Heaven, but it has not been given to those. [12]For whoever has, to him will be given, and he will have over-abundance. But whoever does not have, even what he has will be taken from him. [13]Because of this, I speak to them in parables, because seeing they do not see, and hearing they do not hear, nor do they understand. [14]And the prophecy of Isaiah is fulfilled on them, which says, "In hearing you will hear, and in no way understand; and seeing you will see, yet in no way perceive. [15]For the heart of this people has grown fat, and they heard sluggishly with the ears; and they have closed their eyes, that they not see with the eyes, or hear with the ears, and understand with the heart, and be converted, and I heal them." [16]But your eyes are blessed, because they see; and your ears, because they hear. [17]For truly I tell you that many prophets and righteous ones desired to see what you see, and did not see; and to hear what

243 4098 1909 4075 3699 3756 2192 1093 4183
5 ἄλλα δὲ ἔπεσεν ἐπὶ τὰ πετρώδη. ὅπου οὐκ εἶχε γῆν πολλήν·
other and fell upon the rocky places, where not they had earth much
2112 1816 1223 3361 2192 899 1093 2246
6 καὶ εὐθέως ἐξανέτειλε, διὰ τὸ μὴ ἔχειν βάθος γῆς· ἡλίου δὲ
and at once it sprang up because not having depth of earth; sun and
393 2739 1223 3361 2192 4491
ἀνατείλαντος ἐκαυματίσθη, καὶ διὰ τὸ μὴ ἔχειν ῥίζαν,
rising, it was scorched, and.because of— not having root,
3583 243 4098 1909 173 305
7 ἐξηράνθη. ἄλλα δὲ ἔπεσεν ἐπὶ τὰς ἀκάνθας, καὶ ἀνέβησαν αἱ
it was dried. other And fell upon the thorns, and grew up the
173 638 846 243 4098 1909 1093
8 ἄκανθαι καὶ ἀπέπνιξαν αὐτά. ἄλλα δὲ ἔπεσεν ἐπὶ τὴν γῆν
thorns and choked them. other And fell upon the earth
2570 1325 2590 3303 1540 1835
τὴν καλήν, καὶ ἐδίδου καρπόν, ὃ μὲν ἑκατόν, ὃ δὲ ἑξήκοντα,
— good, and yielded fruit, one indeed a hundred, one and sixty
5144 2192 3775 191 191
9 ὃ δὲ τριάκοντα. ὁ ἔχων ὦτα ἀκούειν ἀκουέτω.
one and thirty. The (one) having ears to hear, let him hear.
4334 3101 2036 846 1302
10 Καὶ προσελθόντες οἱ μαθηταὶ εἶπον αὐτῷ, Διατί ἐν
And having come, the disciples said to Him, Why in
3850 2980 846 611 2036 846 3754
11 παραβολαῖς λαλεῖς αὐτοῖς; ὁ δὲ ἀποκριθεὶς εἶπεν αὐτοῖς ὅτι
parables do You speak to them? He And answering said to them, Because
5213 1325 1097 3466 932
Ὑμῖν δέδοται γνῶναι τὰ μυστήρια τῆς βασιλείας τῶν
to you it has been given to know the mysteries of the kingdom of the
3772 1565 3756 1325 3748 1063 2192 1325
12 οὐρανῶν, ἐκείνοις δὲ οὐ δέδοται. ὅστις γὰρ ἔχει, δοθήσεται
heavens, to those but not it has been given, whoever for has, will be given
846 4052 3748 3756 2192 2192
αὐτῷ καὶ περισσευθήσεται· ὅστις δὲ οὐκ ἔχει, καὶ ὃ ἔχει,
to him, and he will have abundance; who but not has, even what he has
142 575 846 1223 5124 1722 3850 846 2980
13 ἀρθήσεται ἀπ᾽ αὐτοῦ. διὰ τοῦτο ἐν παραβολαῖς αὐτοῖς λαλῶ,
will be taken from him. Because of this, in parables to them I speak,
3754 991 3756 991 191 3756 191
ὅτι βλέποντες οὐ βλέπουσι, καὶ ἀκούοντες οὐκ ἀκούουσιν,
because seeing not they see, and hearing not they hear,
3761 4920 378 1909 846 4394
14 οὐδὲ συνιοῦσι. καὶ ἀναπληροῦται ἐπ᾽ αὐτοῖς ἡ προφητεία
neither understand. And is fulfilled upon them the prophecy
2268 3004 189 191 3764 3361 4920
Ἡσαΐου, ἡ λέγουσα, Ἀκοῇ ἀκούσετε καὶ οὐ μὴ συνῆτε· καὶ
of Isaiah, which says, In hearing you will hear and in no way know, and
991 991 3756 3361 1492 3975 1063 2588
15 βλέποντες βλέψετε, καὶ οὐ μὴ ἴδητε. ἐπαχύνθη γὰρ ἡ καρδία
seeing you will see and in no way perceive; has grown fat for the heart
2992 5127 3775 917 191
τοῦ λαοῦ τούτου, καὶ τοῖς ὠσὶ βαρέως ἤκουσαν, καὶ τοὺς
of people this and with the ears heavily they heard, and the
3788 848 2576 3379 1492 3788
ὀφθαλμοὺς αὐτῶν ἐκάμμυσαν· μήποτε ἴδωσι τοῖς ὀφθαλμοῖς,
eyes of them they closed, lest they see with the eyes
3775 191 2588 4920 1994
καὶ τοῖς ὠσὶν ἀκούσωσι, καὶ τῇ καρδίᾳ συνῶσι, καὶ ἐπι-
and with the ears they hear, and with the heart understand, and be
2390 846 5216 3107 3788
16 στρέψωσι, καὶ ἰάσωμαι αὐτούς. ὑμῶν δὲ μακάριοι οἱ ὀφθαλ-
converted, and I heal them. of you But blessed (are) the eyes,
3754 991 3775 5216 3754 191 281 1063
17 μοί, ὅτι βλέπουσι· καὶ τὰ ὦτα ὑμῶν, ὅτι ἀκούει. ἀμὴν γὰρ
because they see, and the ears of you, because they hear. truly For
3004 5213 3754 4183 4396 1342 1937
λέγω ὑμῖν ὅτι πολλοὶ προφῆται καὶ δίκαιοι ἐπεθύμησαν
I say to you, that many prophets and righteous (ones) desired
1492 991 3756 1492 191 3739 191
ἰδεῖν ἃ βλέπετε, καὶ οὐκ εἶδον· καὶ ἀκοῦσαι ἃ ἀκούετε, καὶ
to see what you see, and not did see; and to hear what you hear, and

NOTE: Frequent words not numbered: **δέ**(1161); **καί**(2531)—and, but; **ὁ, ἡ, τό** (3588, the)— * above word, look in verse margin for No.

you hear, and did not hear. [18]Then hear the parable of the sower: [19]Everyone hearing the word of the kingdom, and not understanding, *then* the evil one comes and catches away that which was sown in his heart. This is that sown by the roadside. [20]And that sown on the stony places is this: the *one* hearing the word, and immediately receiving it with joy, [21]but has no root in himself, but is temporary—and tribulation, or persecution occurring because of the word, he is at once offended.

[22]And that sown into the thorns is this: the *one* hearing the word, and the anxiety of this age, and the deceit of riches, choke the word, and it becomes unfruitful.

[23]But that sown on the good ground is this: the*one* hearing the word, and understanding *it;* who indeed brings forth and produces fruit: one truly a hundred*fold;* and one sixty, and one thirty.

[24]He put before them another parable, saying: The kingdom of Heaven is compared to a man sowing good seed in his fields. [25]But while the men *were* sleeping, his enemy came and sowed darnel in the midst of the wheat, and went away. [26]And when the blade sprouted and produced fruit, then the darnel also appeared. [27]And coming near the slaves of the housemaster said to him, Sir, did you not sow good seed in your field? Then from where does it have the darnel? [28]And he said to them, A man, an enemy did this. And the slaves said to him,

3756 191 5210 3767 191 3850
18 οὐκ ἤκουσαν. ὑμεῖς οὖν ἀκούσατε τὴν παραβολὴν τοῦ
not did hear. You therefore hear the parable of the
4687 3956 191 3056 932
19 σπείροντος. παντὸς ἀκούοντος τὸν λόγον τῆς βασιλείας καὶ
sower: Everyone hearing the word of the kingdom and
3361 4920 2064 4190 726 4687
μὴ συνιέντος, ἔρχεται ὁ πονηρος, καὶ ἁρπάζει τὸ ἐσπαρ-
not understands, comes the evil one and catches away that which was
1722 2588 848 3778 2076 3844 3598
μένον ἐν τῇ καρδίᾳ αὐτοῦ· οὗτός ἐστιν ὁ παρὰ τὴν ὁδὸν
sown in the heart of him. This is the (word) by the wayside
4687 1909 4075 4687 3778 2076
20 σπαρείς. ὁ δὲ ἐπὶ τὰ πετρώδη σπαρείς, οὗτός ἐστιν ὁ τὸν
sown. the (word) and on the rocky places was sown, this is the (one) the
3056 191 2117 3326 5479 2983 846 3756
21 λόγον ἀκούων, καὶ εὐθὺς μετὰ χαρᾶς λαμβάνων αὐτόν· οὐκ
word hearing, and at once with joy receiving it; no
2192 4491 1722 1438 235 4340 2076 1096
ἔχει δὲ ῥίζαν ἐν ἑαυτῷ, ἀλλὰ πρόσκαιρός ἐστι· γενομένης δὲ
has but root in himself, but temporary is; occurring but
2347/2228 1375 1223 3056 2117 4624
22 θλίψεως ἢ διωγμοῦ διὰ τὸν λόγον, εὐθὺς σκανδαλίζεται. ὁ
tribulation or persecution through the word, at once he is offended.. he who
1519 173 4687 3778 2076 3056 191
δὲ εἰς τὰς ἀκάνθας σπαρείς, οὗτός ἐστιν ὁ τὸν λόγον ἀκούων,
And in the thorns sown, this is the (one) the word hearing,
3308 165 5127 539 4149
καὶ ἡ μέριμνα τοῦ αἰῶνος τούτου καὶ ἡ ἀπάτη τοῦ πλούτου
and the anxiety of the age this and the deceit of riches
4846 3056 175 1096 1909 1093
23 συμπνίγει τὸν λόγον, καὶ ἄκαρπος γίνεται. ὁ δὲ ἐπὶ τὴν γῆν
choke the word, and unfruitful it becomes. he But on the earth
2570 4687 3778 2076 3056 191
τὴν καλὴν σπαρείς, οὗτός ἐστιν ὁ τὸν λόγον ἀκούων καὶ
good was sown, this is the (one) the word hearing and
4920 3739 1211 2592 4160 3303 1540
συνιών· ὃς δὴ καρποφορεῖ, καὶ ποιεῖ ὁ μὲν ἑκατόν, ὁ δὲ
understands; who indeed bears fruit and produces one truly a hundred, one and
1835 5144
ἑξήκοντα, ὁ δὲ τριάκοντα.
sixty, one and thirty.
243 3850 3908 846 3004 3666
24 Ἄλλην παραβολὴν παρέθηκεν αὐτοῖς, λέγων, Ὡμοιώθη
Another parable He put before them, saying, is likened
932 3772 444 4687 2570
ἡ βασιλεία τῶν οὐρανῶν ἀνθρώπῳ σπείραντι καλὸν
the kingdom of the heavens to a man sowing good
4690 68 848 2518 444
25 σπέρμα ἐν τῷ ἀγρῷ αὐτοῦ· ἐν δὲ τῷ καθεύδειν τοὺς ἀνθρώ-
seed in the fields of him: in but the sleeping of the men
2064 848 2190 4687 2215 303 3319
πους, ἦλθεν αὐτοῦ ὁ ἐχθρὸς καὶ ἔσπειρε ζιζάνια ἀνὰ μέσον
came his enemy and sowed darnel amidst
4621 565 3753 985 5528
26 τοῦ σίτου, καὶ ἀπῆλθεν. ὅτε δὲ ἐβλάστησεν ὁ χόρτος καὶ
the wheat, and went away. when And sprouted the blade, and
2590 4160 5119 5316 2215 4334
27 καρπὸν ἐποίησε, τότε ἐφάνη καὶ τὰ ζιζάνια. προσελθόντες
fruit produced, then appeared also the darnel. coming near
1401 3617 2036 846 2962 3780
δὲ οἱ δοῦλοι τοῦ οἰκοδεσπότου εἶπον αὐτῷ, Κύριε, οὐχὶ
And the slaves of the master of the house said to him, Lord not
2570 4690 4687 1722 4674 68 4159 3767 2192
καλὸν σπέρμα ἔσπειρας ἐν τῷ σῷ ἀγρῷ ; πόθεν οὖν ἔχει τὰ
good seed did you sow in the of you field? Whence then has it the
2215 5346 846 2190 444 5124 4160
28 ζιζάνια ; ὁ δὲ ἔφη αὐτοῖς, Ἐχθρὸς ἄνθρωπος τοῦτο ἐποίησεν.
darnel? he And said to them, An enemy, a man, this did.
1401 2036 846 2209 3767 565 4816
οἱ δὲ δοῦλοι εἶπον αὐτῷ, Θέλεις οὖν ἀπελθόντες συλλέξωμεν
the And slaves said to him, Will you then having gone out we may collect

Do you desire, then, that going out we should gather them? [29]But he said, No, lest gathering the darnel you should uproot the wheat with them. [30]Allow both to grow together until the harvest. And in the time of the harvest I will say to the reapers, First gather the darnel, and bind them into bundles to burn them; but gather the wheat into my granary.

[31]He put another parable before them, saying: The kingdom of Heaven is compared to a grain of mustard, which taking a man sowed in his field; [32]which indeed is less than all the seeds, but when it is grown it is greater than the plants, and becomes a tree, so that the birds of the heaven come and roost in its branches.

[33]He spoke another parable to them: The kingdom of Heaven is compared to leaven, which taking, a woman hid in three measures of meal, until the whole was leavened.

[34]Jesus spoke all these things in parables to the crowds; and He did not speak to them without a parable; [35]so that was fulfilled that spoken through the prophet, saying: "I will open My mouth in parables; I will say things hidden from *the* foundation of *the* world."

[36]Then sending away the crowds, Jesus came into the house. And His disciples came to Him, saying, Explain to us the parable of the darnel of the field. [37]And answering He said to them, The *one* sowing the good seed is the Son of

846 5346 3756 3379 4816 2215
29 αὐτά; ὁ δὲ ἔφη, Οὔ· μήποτε, συλλέγοντες τὰ ζιζάνια,
them? he But said, No, lest collecting the darnel
1610 260 846 4621 853 4885
30 ἐκριζώσητε ἅμα αὐτοῖς τὸν σῖτον. ἄφετε συναυξάνεσθαι
you may uproot with them the wheat. Allow to grow together
297 3360 2326 1722 2540 2326
ἀμφότερα μέχρι τοῦ θερισμοῦ· καὶ ἐν τῷ καιρῷ τοῦ θερισμοῦ
both until the harvest; and in the time of the harvest
2046 2327 4816 4412 2215
ἐρῶ τοῖς θερισταῖς, Συλλέξατε πρῶτον τὰ ζιζάνια, καὶ
I will say to the reapers, Collect first the darnel, and
1210 846 1519 1197 4314 2618 846
δήσατε αὐτὰ εἰς δέσμας πρὸς τὸ κατακαῦσαι αὐτά· τὸν δὲ
bind them into bundles in order to burn them; the but
4621 4863 1519 596 3450
σῖτον συναγάγετε εἰς τὴν ἀποθήκην μου.
wheat bring together into the granary of me.

243 3850 3908 846 3004 3664
31 Ἄλλην παραβολὴν παρέθηκεν αὐτοῖς, λέγων, Ὁμοία
Another parable He presented to them, saying, Like
2076 932 3772 2848 4615 3739 2983
ἐστὶν ἡ βασιλεία τῶν οὐρανῶν κόκκῳ σινάπεως, ὃν λαβὼν
is the kingdom of the heavens to a grain of mustard, which taking
444 4687 1722 68 848 3739 3398 3303
32 ἄνθρωπος ἔσπειρεν ἐν τῷ ἀγρῷ αὐτοῦ· ὃ μικρότερον μέν
a man sowed in the field of him, which lesser truly
2076 3956 4690 3752 837 3187
ἐστι πάντων τῶν σπερμάτων· ὅταν δὲ αὐξηθῇ, μεῖζον τῶν
is than all the seeds, when but it is grown, greater than the
3001 2076 1096 1186 5620 2064 4071
λαχάνων ἐστί, καὶ γίνεται δένδρον, ὥστε ἐλθεῖν τὰ πετεινὰ
plants is, and becomes a tree, so that come the birds
3772 2681 1722 2798 848
τοῦ οὐρανοῦ καὶ κατασκηνοῦν ἐν τοῖς κλάδοις αὐτοῦ.
of the heaven and roost in the branches of it.

243 3850 2980 846 3664 2076
33 Ἄλλην παραβολὴν ἐλάλησεν αὐτοῖς, Ὁμοία ἐστὶν ἡ
Another parable He spoke to them: Like is the
932 3772 2219 3739 2983 1135 1470
βασιλεία τῶν οὐρανῶν ζύμῃ, ἣν λαβοῦσα γυνὴ ἐνέκρυψεν
kingdom of the heavens to leaven, which taking a woman hid
1519 224 4568 5140/2193/3739 2220 3650
εἰς ἀλεύρου σάτα τρία, ἕως οὗ ἐζυμώθη ὅλον.
in meal measures three, until was leavened the whole.

5023 3956 2980 2424 1722 3850
34 Ταῦτα πάντα ἐλάλησεν ὁ Ἰησοῦς ἐν παραβολαῖς τοῖς
These things all spoke — Jesus in parables to the
3793 5565 3850 3756 2980 846 3704
35 ὄχλοις, καὶ χωρὶς παραβολῆς οὐκ ἐλάλει αὐτοῖς· ὅπως
crowds, and without a parable not He spoke to them; so that
4137 4483 1223 4396 3004 455
πληρωθῇ τὸ ῥηθὲν διὰ τοῦ προφήτου, λέγοντος, Ἀνοίξω
was fulfilled that spoken through the prophet, saying, I will open
1722 3850 4750 3450 2044 2928 576
ἐν παραβολαῖς τὸ στόμα μου, ἐρεύξομαι κεκρυμμένα ἀπὸ
in parables the mouth of Me; I will utter things hidden from
2602 2889
καταβολῆς κόσμου.
(the) foundation of (the) world.

5119 863 3793 2064 1519 3614 2424
36 Τότε ἀφεὶς τοὺς ὄχλους ἦλθεν εἰς τὴν οἰκίαν ὁ Ἰησοῦς· καὶ
Then sending away the crowds, came into the house — Jesus; and
4334 846 3101 848 3004 5419 2254
προσῆλθον αὐτῷ οἱ μαθηταὶ αὐτοῦ, λέγοντες, Φράσον ἡμῖν
came to Him the disciples of Him, saying, Explain to us
3850 2215 68 611
37 τὴν παραβολὴν τῶν ζιζανίων τοῦ ἀγροῦ. ὁ δὲ ἀποκριθεὶς
the parable of the darnel of the field. He And answering
2036 846 4687 2570 4690 2076 5207
εἶπεν αὐτοῖς, Ὁ σπείρων τὸ καλὸν σπέρμα ἐστὶν ὁ υἱὸς τοῦ
said to them, The (one) sowing the good seed is the Son —

man. [38]And the field is the
world; and the good seed,
these are the sons of the
kingdom; but the darnel are
the sons of the evil one.
[39]And the enemy who
sowed them is the Devil;
and the harvest is the end of
the age; and the angels are
the reapers. [40]Then as the
darnel is gathered and is
consumed in the fire, so it
will be in the end of this
age. [41]The Son of man will
send forth His angels, and
they will gather out of His
kingdom all the offenses,
and those who practice
lawlessness. [42]And they
will throw them into the
furnace of fire; there will be
weeping and gnashing of
the teeth. [43]Then the
righteous will shine out like
the sun in the kingdom of
their Father. The *one* having
ears to hear, let him hear.

[44]Again, the kingdom of
Heaven is compared to
treasure hidden in the field,
which finding, a man hid;
and for the joy of it he goes
and sells all things, as many
as he has, and buys that
field.

[45]Again, the kingdom of
Heaven is compared to a
man, a merchant seeking
excellent pearls; [46]who
finding one very precious
pearl, going away has sold
all things, as many as he
had, and bought it.

[47]Again, the kingdom of
Heaven is compared to a
drag net thrown into the
sea, and gathering together
of every kind; [48]which,
when it was filled, drawing
it up on the shore, and

444 68 2076 2889 2570 4690
38 ἀνθρώπου· ὁ δὲ ἀγρός ἐστιν ὁ κόσμος· τὸ δὲ καλὸν σπέρμα,
of man; the and field is the world; the and good seed
3778 1526 5207 932 2215 1526 5207
οὗτοί εἰσιν οἱ υἱοὶ τῆς βασιλείας· τὰ δὲ ζιζάνιά εἰσιν οἱ υἱοὶ
these are the sons of the kingdom; the but darnel are the sons
4190 2190 4687 846 2076 1228
39 τοῦ πονηροῦ· ὁ δὲ ἐχθρὸς ὁ σπείρας αὐτά ἐστιν ὁ διάβολος·
of the evil one; the and enemy who sowed them is the Devil;
2326 4930 165 2076 2327
ὁ δὲ θερισμὸς συντέλεια τοῦ αἰῶνός ἐστιν· οἱ δὲ θερισταὶ
the and harvest (the) completion of the age is, the and reapers
32 1526 5618 3767 4816 2215 4442
40 ἄγγελοί εἰσιν. ὥσπερ οὖν συλλέγεται τὰ ζιζάνια καὶ πυρὶ
angels are. As therefore is collected the darnel, and in fire
2618 3779 2071 1722 4930 165
κατακαίεται, οὕτως ἔσται ἐν τῇ συντελείᾳ τοῦ αἰῶνος
is consumed, thus it shall be in the completion of the age
5127 649 5207 444 32
41 τούτου. ἀποστελεῖ ὁ υἱὸς τοῦ ἀνθρώπου τοὺς ἀγγέλους
this. Shall send out the Son of man the angels
848 4816 1537 932 848 3956
αὐτοῦ, καὶ συλλέξουσιν ἐκ τῆς βασιλείας αὐτοῦ πάντα τὰ
of Him, and they will collect out of the kingdom of Him all the
4625 4160 458 906
42 σκάνδαλα καὶ τοὺς ποιοῦντας τὴν ἀνομίαν, καὶ βαλοῦσιν
offenses and those who practice lawlessness, and they will cast
846 2575 4442 1563 2071 2805
αὐτοὺς εἰς τὴν κάμινον τοῦ πυρός· ἐκεῖ ἔσται ὁ κλαυθμὸς καὶ
them into the furnace of the fire: there shall be the weeping and
1030 3599 5119 1342 1584 5613
43 ὁ βρυγμὸς τῶν ὀδόντων. τότε οἱ δίκαιοι ἐκλάμψουσιν ὡς ὁ
the gnashing of the teeth. Then the righteous will shine forth as the
2246 932 3962 848 2192 3775 191
ἥλιος ἐν τῇ βασιλείᾳ τοῦ πατρὸς αὐτῶν. ὁ ἔχων ὦτα ἀκούειν
sun in the kingdom of the Father of them. He having ears to hear,
191
ἀκουέτω.
let him hear.
3825 3664 2076 932 3772 2344
44 Πάλιν ὁμοία ἐστὶν ἡ βασιλεία τῶν οὐρανῶν θησαυρῷ
Again like is the kingdom of the heavens to treasure
2928 1722 68 3739 2147 444 2928 575
κεκρυμμένῳ ἐν τῷ ἀγρῷ, ὃν εὑρὼν ἄνθρωπος ἔκρυψε· καὶ ἀπὸ
hid in the field, which having found a man hid, and from
5479 848 5217 3956 3745 2192 4453
τῆς χαρᾶς αὐτοῦ ὑπάγει, καὶ πάντα ὅσα ἔχει πωλεῖ, καὶ
the joy of it he goes, and all things what- he has, he sells, and
59 68 1565 ever
ἀγοράζει τὸν ἀγρὸν ἐκεῖνον.
buys field that.
3525 3664 2076 932 3772 444
45 Πάλιν ὁμοία ἐστὶν ἡ βασιλεία τῶν οὐρανῶν ἀνθρώπῳ
Again like is the kingdom of the heavens to a man
1713 2212 2570 3135 3739 2147 1520 4186
46 ἐμπόρῳ ζητοῦντι καλοὺς μαργαρίτας· ὃς εὑρὼν ἕνα πολύ-
a merchant seeking excellent pearls; who finding one very
3135 565 4097 3956 3745 2192
τιμον μαργαρίτην, ἀπελθὼν πέπρακε πάντα ὅσα εἶχε, καὶ
precious pearl, going away has sold all things that he has, and
59 846
ἠγόρασεν αὐτόν.
bought it.
3825 3664 2076 932 3772 4522
47 Πάλιν ὁμοία ἐστὶν ἡ βασιλεία τῶν οὐρανῶν σαγήνῃ
Again like is the kingdom of the heavens to a net
906 1519 2281 1537 3956 1085 4863
βληθείσῃ εἰς τὴν θάλασσαν, καὶ ἐκ παντὸς γένους συναγα-
thrown into the sea, and of every kind gathering
3739 3753 4137 307 1909 123
48 γούσῃ· ἥν, ὅτε ἐπληρώθη, ἀναβιβάσαντες ἐπὶ τὸν αἰγιαλόν,
together; which when it was filled, drawing up onto the shore,

sitting down, *they* gathered the good into containers, and they threw out the rotten. 49So it will be in the end of the age: the angels will go out and will separate the wicked from *the* midst of the righteous; 50and will throw them into the furnace of fire; there will be weeping and gnashing of the teeth.

51Jesus said to them, Have you understood all these things? They said to Him, Yes, Lord. 52And He said to them, Because of this every scribe schooled to the kingdom of Heaven is like a man, a master of a house, who puts forth out of his treasure new and old.

53And it happened, when Jesus had finished these parables, He moved from there. 54And coming into His own country, He taught them in their synagogue, so that they were astonished, and said, Where did this one *get* this wisdom, and the powerful works? 55Is this not the carpenter's son? *Is* not his mother called Mary, and his brothers, James, and Joses, and Simon, and Judas? 56And are not his sisters all with us? From where then did this one *get* all these things? 57And they were offended in Him. But Jesus said to them, A prophet is not without honor, except in his own homeland, and in his own house. 58And He did not do many works of power there because of their unbelief.

2523 4816 2570 1519 30 4550
καὶ καθίσαντες, συνέλεξαν τὰ καλὰ εἰς ἀγγεῖα, τὰ δὲ σαπρὰ
and sitting down, (men) collected the good into vessels, the and corrupt
1854 906 3779 2071 1722 4930 165 1831
49 ἔξω ἔβαλον. οὕτως ἔσται ἐν τῇ συντελείᾳ τοῦ αἰῶνος· ἐξελεύ-
out they threw. So it will be in the completion of the age: will go
32 873 4190 1537 3319
σονται οἱ ἄγγελοι, καὶ ἀφοριοῦσι τοὺς πονηροὺς ἐκ μέσου
out the angels, and will separate the evil from (the) midst
1342 906 846 1519 2575 4442
50 τῶν δικαίων, καὶ βαλοῦσιν αὐτοὺς εἰς τὴν κάμινον τοῦ πυρός·
of the righteous, and will throw them into the furnace of the fire;
1563 2071 2805 1030 3599
ἐκεῖ ἔσται ὁ κλαυθμὸς καὶ ὁ βρυγμὸς τῶν ὀδόντων.
there will be the weeping and the gnashing of the teeth.
3004 846 2424 4920 5023 3956 3004
51 Λέγει αὐτοῖς ὁ Ἰησοῦς, Συνήκατε ταῦτα πάντα; λέγουσιν
says to them Jesus, Did you discern these things all? They say
846 3483 2962 2036 846 1223 5124 3956 1122
52 αὐτῷ, Ναί, Κύριε. ὁ δὲ εἶπεν αὐτοῖς, Διὰ τοῦτο πᾶς γραμ-
to Him, Yes, Lord. He And said to them, Because of this every scribe
3101 1519 932 3772 3664
ματεὺς μαθητευθεὶς εἰς τὴν βασιλείαν τῶν οὐρανῶν ὅμοιός
discipled into the kingdom of the heavens like
2076 444 3617 3748 1544 1537 2344
ἐστιν ἀνθρώπῳ οἰκοδεσπότῃ, ὅστις ἐκβάλλει ἐκ τοῦ θησαυ-
is to a man, a master of a house, who puts forth out of the treasure
848 2537 3820
ροῦ αὐτοῦ καινὰ καὶ παλαιά.
of him new and old.
1093 3753 5055 2424 3850 5025
53 Καὶ ἐγένετο ὅτε ἐτέλεσεν ὁ Ἰησοῦς τὰς παραβολὰς ταύτας,
And it was, when had ended Jesus parables these,
3332 1564 2064 3968 848 1321
54 μετῆρεν ἐκεῖθεν· καὶ ἐλθὼν εἰς τὴν πατρίδα αὐτοῦ ἐδίδασκεν
He moved from there; and coming into the country of Him, He taught
846 1722 4864 848 5620 1605 846
αὐτοὺς ἐν τῇ συναγωγῇ αὐτῶν, ὥστε ἐκπλήττεσθαι αὐτοὺς
them in the synagogue of them, so that were astounded they,
3004 4159 5129 4678 3778 1411 3756
55 καὶ λέγειν, Πόθεν τούτῳ ἡ σοφία αὕτη καὶ αἱ δυνάμεις; οὐχ
even to say, Whence to this one wisdom this, and the works of power? Not
3778 2076 5045 5207 3780 3384 846
οὗτός ἐστιν ὁ τοῦ τέκτονος υἱός; οὐχὶ ἡ μήτηρ αὐτοῦ
this is the of the carpenter son? (Is) not the mother of him
3004 3137 80 848 2385 2500
λέγεται Μαριάμ, καὶ οἱ ἀδελφοὶ αὐτοῦ Ἰάκωβος καὶ Ἰωσῆς
called Mary, and the brothers of him James and Joses
4613 2455 79 848 3780 3956
56 καὶ Σίμων καὶ Ἰούδας; καὶ αἱ ἀδελφαὶ αὐτοῦ οὐχὶ πᾶσαι
and Simon and Judas? And the sisters of him not all
4314 2248 1526 4159 3767 5129 5023 3956
57 πρὸς ἡμᾶς εἰσι; πόθεν οὖν τούτῳ ταῦτα πάντα; καὶ
with us are? Whence then to this (one) these things all? And
4624 1722 846 2424 2036 846 3756
ἐσκανδαλίζοντο ἐν αὐτῷ ὁ δὲ Ἰησοῦς εἶπεν αὐτοῖς, Οὐκ
they were offended in Him. But Jesus said to them, Not
2036 4396 820 -1508- 1722 3968 848 1722
ἔστι προφήτης ἄτιμος, εἰ μὴ ἐν τῇ πατρίδι αὐτοῦ καὶ ἐν τῇ
is a prophet honorless, except in the homeland of him, and in the
3614 848 3756 4160 1563 1411 4183 1223
58 οἰκίᾳ αὐτοῦ. καὶ οὐκ ἐποίησεν ἐκεῖ δυνάμεις πολλάς, διὰ
house of him. And not He did there power-works many, because
570 848
τὴν ἀπιστίαν αὐτῶν.
of the unbelief of them.

CHAPTER 14

1At that time Herod the tetrarch heard the fame of

1722 1565 2540 191 2264 5076
1 Ἐν ἐκείνῳ τῷ καιρῷ ἤκουσεν Ἡρώδης ὁ τετράρχης τὴν
At that time heard Herod the tetrarch the

Jesus. [2]And *he* said to his servants, This is John the Baptist. He has risen from the dead, and because of this powerful works are working in him. [3]For seizing John, Herod bound him and put *him* into prison, because of Herodias, the wife of his brother Philip. [4]For John said to him, It is not lawful for you to have her. [5]And desiring to kill him, he feared the multitude, because they held him as a prophet.

[6]But a birthday *feast for* Herod being held, the daughter of Herodias danced in the midst, and pleased Herod. [7]So then he promised with an oath to give her whatever she should ask. [8]But she being urged on by her mother, she says, Give me here on a platter the head of John the Baptist. [9]And the king was grieved, but because of the oaths, and those who had reclined with *him,* he ordered *it* to be given. [10]And sending, he beheaded John in the prison. [11]And his head was brought on a platter, and was given to the girl; and she brought *it* to her mother. [12]And coming, his disciples took the body and buried it; and coming, *they* reported to Jesus.

[13]And hearing, Jesus withdrew from there in a boat, into a desert place apart.

[14]And hearing, the crowds followed Him on foot from the cities. And going out, Jesus saw a great crowd, and was filled with pity toward them. And He healed their infirm ones. [15]And evening coming, His

189 2424 2036 3816 848 3778 2076
2 ἀκοὴν Ἰησοῦ, καὶ εἶπε τοῖς παισὶν αὐτοῦ, Οὗτός ἐστιν
fame of Jesus, and said to the servants of him, This is
2491 910 846 1453 575 3498
Ἰωάννης ὁ Βαπτιστής· αὐτὸς ἠγέρθη ἀπὸ τῶν νεκρῶν, καὶ
John the Baptist; he is risen from the dead, and
1223 5124 1411 1754 1722 846 1063 2264
3 διὰ τοῦτο αἱ δυνάμεις ἐνεργοῦσιν ἐν αὐτῷ. ὁ γὰρ Ἡρώδης
because of this the powerful operate in him. For Herod
1722 2902 works 1210 846 5087 5438
κρατήσας τὸν Ἰωάννην ἔδησεν αὐτὸν καὶ ἔθετο ἐν φυλακῇ,
having seized — John bound him and put in prison,
1223 2266 1135 5376 80 848
διὰ Ἡρωδιάδα τὴν γυναῖκα Φιλίππου τοῦ ἀδελφοῦ αὐτοῦ.
because of Herodias the wife of Philip, the brother of him.
3004 1063 846 2491 3756 1832 4671 2192 846
4 ἔλεγε γὰρ αὐτῷ ὁ Ἰωάννης, Οὐκ ἔξεστί σοι ἔχειν αὐτήν.
said For to him John, Not it is lawful for you to have her.
2309 846 615 5399 3793 3754 5613
5 καὶ θέλων αὐτὸν ἀποκτεῖναι, ἐφοβήθη τὸν ὄχλον, ὅτι ὡς
And wishing him to kill, he feared the crowd, because as
4396 846 2192 1077 71 2264
6 προφήτην αὐτὸν εἶχον. γενεσίων δὲ ἀγομένων τοῦ Ἡρώδου,
a prophet him they held. a birthday But being held of Herod,
3738 2364 2266 1722 3319
ὠρχήσατο ἡ θυγάτηρ τῆς Ἡρωδιάδος ἐν τῷ μέσῳ, καὶ
danced the daughter — of Herodias in the midst, and
700 2264 3526 3326 3727 3670 846 1325
7 ἤρεσε τῷ Ἡρώδῃ. ὅθεν μεθ' ὅρκου ὡμολόγησεν αὐτῇ δοῦναι
pleased Herod. Whence with an oath he acknowledged to her to give
1437 154 4264 5259 3384
8 ὃ ἐὰν αἰτήσηται. ἡ δέ, προβιβασθεῖσα ὑπὸ τῆς μητρὸς
whatever she might ask. she So being urged on by the mother
848 1325/3427/5346 5602/1909/4094 2776 2491
αὐτῆς, Δός μοι, φησίν, ὧδε ἐπὶ πίνακι τὴν κεφαλὴν Ἰωάννου
of her, Give me, she says, here on a platter the head of John
910 3076 935 1223 3727
9 τοῦ Βαπτιστοῦ. καὶ ἐλυπήθη ὁ βασιλεύς, διὰ δὲ τοὺς ὅρκους
the Baptist. And was grieved the king, because of but the oaths
4873 2753 1325 3992
10 καὶ τοὺς συνανακειμένους ἐκέλευσε δοθῆναι· καὶ πέμψας
and those who reclined with (him), he ordered (it) be given. And sending
607 2491 1722 5438 5342
11 ἀπεκεφάλισε τὸν Ἰωάννην ἐν τῇ φυλακῇ. καὶ ἠνέχθη ἡ
he beheaded — John in the prison. And was brought the
2776 848 1909 4094 1325 2877 5342
κεφαλὴ αὐτοῦ ἐπὶ πίνακι, καὶ ἐδόθη τῷ κορασίῳ· καὶ ἤνεγκε
head of him on a platter, and was given to the girl, and she brought
3384 848 4334 3101 848 142
12 τῇ μητρὶ αὐτῆς. καὶ προσελθόντες οἱ μαθηταὶ αὐτοῦ ἦραν
to the mother of her. And having come the disciples of him took
4983 2290 846 2064 518
τὸ σῶμα, καὶ ἔθαψαν αὐτό καὶ ἐλθόντες ἀπήγγειλαν τῷ
the body, and buried it; and coming told —
2424
Ἰησοῦ.
to Jesus. 191 2424 402 1564 1722 4143 1519
13 Καὶ ἀκούσας ὁ Ἰησοῦς ἀνεχώρησεν ἐκεῖθεν ἐν πλοίῳ εἰς
And hearing Jesus withdrew from there in a boat into
2048 5117 2596 2398 191 3793 190
ἔρημον τόπον κατ' ἰδίαν· καὶ ἀκούσαντες οἱ ὄχλοι ἠκολού-
a desert place privately. And having heard the crowds followed
846 3979 575 4172 1831 2424
14 θησαν αὐτῷ πεζῇ ἀπὸ τῶν πόλεων. καὶ ἐξελθὼν ὁ Ἰησοῦς
Him on foot from the cities. And going out — Jesus
1492 4183 3793 4697 1909 846
εἶδε πολὺν ὄχλον, καὶ ἐσπλαγχνίσθη ἐπ' αὐτούς, καὶ
saw great a crowd, and was filled with pity toward them, and
2323 732 848 3798 1096
15 ἐθεράπευσε τοὺς ἀρρώστους αὐτῶν. ὀψίας δὲ γενομένης,
He healed the infirm of them. evening And coming,

disciples came near to Him, saying, The place is desert, and the hour is already gone. Dismiss the crowds, that going away into the villages they may buy provisions for themselves. [16]But Jesus said to them, They have no need to go away. You give them *food* to eat. [17]But they said to Him, We have nothing here except five loaves and two fish. [18]And He said, Bring them here to Me. [19]And commanding the crowds to recline on the grass, and taking the five loaves and two fish, looking up to Heaven, He blessed. And breaking, He gave the loaves to the disciples, and the disciples *gave* to the crowds. [20]And all ate, and were satisfied. And they took up the left over pieces, twelve handbaskets full. [21]And the ones eating were about five thousand men, besides women and children.

[22]And immediately Jesus made His disciples get into a boat, and to go before Him to the other side, until He should dismiss the crowds. [23]And having dismissed the crowds, He went up into the mountain alone to pray. And evening coming on, He was there alone. [24]But the boat was now in *the* middle of the sea, tossed by the waves, for the wind was contrary. [25]But in the fourth watch of the night, Jesus went out to them, walking on the sea. [26]And seeing Him walking on the sea, the disciples were troubled, saying, It is a ghost! And they cried out from the fear. [27]But immediately Jesus spoke to

4334 846 3101 848 3004 2048
προσῆλθον αὐτῷ οἱ μαθηταὶ αὐτοῦ, λέγοντες, Ἔρημός
came near to Him the disciples of Him, saying, Desert
2076 5117 5610 2235 3928 630
ἐστιν ὁ τόπος, καὶ ἡ ὥρα ἤδη παρῆλθεν· ἀπόλυσον τοὺς
is the place, and the hour already is gone by. Dismiss the
3793 2443 565 1519 2968 59 1438
ὄχλους, ἵνα ἀπελθόντες εἰς τὰς κώμας ἀγοράσωσιν ἑαυτοῖς
crowds, that going away into the villages they may buy for themselves
1033 2424 2036 846 3756 5532 2192
16 βρώματα. ὁ δὲ Ἰησοῦς εἶπεν αὐτοῖς, Οὐ χρείαν ἔχουσιν
foods. But Jesus said to them, Not need they have
565 1325 846 5210 5315 3004 846
17 ἀπελθεῖν· δότε αὐτοῖς ὑμεῖς φαγεῖν. οἱ δὲ λέγουσιν αὐτῷ,
to go away; give to them you to eat. they But say to Him,
3756 2192 5602 1508 4002 740 1417 2486 2036
18 Οὐκ ἔχομεν ὧδε εἰ μὴ πέντε ἄρτους καὶ δύο ἰχθύας. ὁ δὲ εἶπε,
Not we have here except five loaves and two fish. He And said,
5342 3427 846 5602 2753 3793 347
19 Φέρετέ μοι αὐτοὺς ὧδε. καὶ κελεύσας τοὺς ὄχλους ἀνακλιθῆ-
Bear to Me them here. And commanding the crowds to recline
1909 5528 2963 4002 740
ναι ἐπὶ τοὺς χόρτους, καὶ λαβὼν τοὺς πέντε ἄρτους καὶ τοὺς
on the grass, and taking the five loaves and the
1417 2486 308 1519 3772 2127
δύο ἰχθύας, ἀναβλέψας εἰς τὸν οὐρανόν, εὐλόγησε, καὶ
two fish, looking up to the Heaven, He blessed, and
2806 1325 3101 740 3101
κλάσας ἔδωκε τοῖς μαθηταῖς τοὺς ἄρτους, οἱ δὲ μαθηταὶ τοῖς
breaking He gave to the disciples the loaves, the and disciples to the
3793 5315 3956 5526 142
20 ὄχλοις. καὶ ἔφαγον πάντες, καὶ ἐχορτάσθησαν· καὶ ἦραν τὸ
crowds. And ate all and were satisfied; and they took the
4052 2801 1427 2894 4134
21 περισσεῦον τῶν κλασμάτων, δώδεκα κοφίνους πλήρεις. οἱ
excess of the fragments, twelve handbaskets full. the (ones)
2068 2258 435 5616 4000 5565 1135
δὲ ἐσθίοντες ἦσαν ἄνδρες ὡσεὶ πεντακισχίλιοι, χωρὶς γυναι-
and eating were men about five thousand, apart from women
3813
κῶν καὶ παιδίων.
and children.
2112 315 2424 3101 848
22 Καὶ εὐθέως ἠνάγκασεν ὁ Ἰησοῦς τοὺς μαθητὰς αὐτοῦ
And instantly constrained Jesus the disciples of Him
1684 1519 4143 4254 848 1519 4008
ἐμβῆναι εἰς τὸ πλοῖον, καὶ προάγειν αὐτὸν εἰς τὸ πέραν,
to enter into the boat and to go before Him to the other side,
2193 3739 630 3793 530 3793
23 ἕως οὗ ἀπολύσῃ τοὺς ὄχλους. καὶ ἀπολύσας τοὺς ὄχλους,
until He should dismiss the crowds. And having dismissed the crowds,
305 1519 3735 2596 2398 4336 3798 1096
ἀνέβη εἰς τὸ ὄρος κατ' ἰδίαν προσεύξασθαι· ὀψίας δὲ γενο-
He went into the mountain apart in order to pray. evening And oc-
3441 2258 1563 4143 2235 3319 2281
24 μένης, μόνος ἦν ἐκεῖ. τὸ δὲ πλοῖον ἤδη μέσον τῆς θαλάσσης
curring alone He was there. the And Boat now amidst the sea
2258 928 5259 2949 2258 1063 1727
ἦν, βασανιζόμενον ὑπὸ τῶν κυμάτων· ἦν γὰρ ἐναντίος ὁ
was, being tossed by the waves; was for contrary the
417 5067 5438 3571 565 4314 846
25 ἄνεμος. τετάρτῃ δὲ φυλακῇ τῆς νυκτὸς ἀπῆλθε πρὸς αὐτοὺς
wind. in fourth But watch of the night went toward them
2424 4043 1909 2281 1492 846
26 ὁ Ἰησοῦς, περιπατῶν ἐπὶ τῆς θαλάσσης. καὶ ἰδόντες αὐτὸν
Jesus, walking on the sea. And seeing Him
3101 1909 2281 4043 5015
οἱ μαθηταὶ ἐπὶ τὴν θάλασσαν περιπατοῦντα ἐταράχθησαν,
the disciples on the sea walking they were troubled,
3004 3754 5326 2076 575 5401 2896
λέγοντες ὅτι Φάντασμά ἐστι· καὶ ἀπὸ τοῦ φόβου ἔκραξαν.
saying, A phantom it is, and out of fear they cried out.

them, saying, Be comforted! I AM! Do not fear. [28]And answering Him, Peter said, Lord, if it is You, command me to come to You on the waters. [29]And He said, Come! And going down from the boat, Peter walked on the waters to go to Jesus. [30]But seeing the strong wind, he was afraid, and beginning to sink, he cried out, saying, Lord, save me! [31]And immediately stretching out the hand, Jesus took hold of him, and said to him, Little-faith, why did you doubt? [32]And coming into the boat, the wind ceased. [33]And those in the boat came and worshiped Him, saying, Truly, You are the Son of God.

[34]And having passed over, they came to the land of Gennesaret. [35]And recognizing Him, the men of that place sent to all that neighborhood, and brought to Him all those who had illness. [36]And *they* begged Him that they might touch the fringe of His robe. And as many as touched were made perfectly well.

2112 2980 846 2424 3004 2293 1473
27 εὐθέως δὲ ἐλάλησεν αὐτοῖς ὁ Ἰησοῦς, λέγων, Θαρσεῖτε· ἐγώ
at once But spoke to them Jesus, saying, Be comforted, I
1510 3361 5399 611 846 4074 2036 2962
28 εἰμι· μὴ φοβεῖσθε. ἀποκριθεὶς δὲ αὐτῷ ὁ Πέτρος εἶπε, Κύριε,
AM! not Do fear. answering And Him Peter said, Lord,
1487/4771/1488/ 2753/3165/4314/4571/2064/1909 5204 2036
29 εἰ σὺ εἶ, κέλευσόν με πρός σε ἐλθεῖν ἐπὶ τὰ ὕδατα. ὁ δὲ εἶπεν,
if You are, command me to You to come on the waters. He And said,
2064 2597 575 4143 4074 4043
Ἐλθέ. καὶ καταβὰς ἀπὸ τοῦ πλοίου ὁ Πέτρος περιεπάτησεν
Come! And descending from the boat, — Peter walked
1909 5204 2064 4314 2424 991
30 ἐπὶ τὰ ὕδατα, ἐλθεῖν πρὸς τὸν Ἰησοῦν. βλέπων δὲ τὸν
on the waters, to come toward — Jesus. seeing But the
417 2478 5399 756 2670
ἄνεμον ἰσχυρὸν ἐφοβήθη· καὶ ἀρξάμενος καταποντίζεσθαι
wind strong, he was frightened, and beginning to sink
2896 3004 2962 4982 3165 2112 2424 1614
31 ἔκραξε, λέγων, Κύριε, σῶσόν με. εὐθέως δὲ ὁ Ἰησοῦς ἐκτείνας
he cried out, saying, Lord, save me! instantly And — Jesus extending
5495 1949 848 3004 846 3640
τὴν χεῖρα ἐπελάβετο αὐτοῦ, καὶ λέγει αὐτῷ, Ὀλιγόπιστε,
the hand took hold of him, and says to him, Little-faith,
1519/5101 1365 1684 846 1519 4143
32 εἰς τί ἐδίστασας; καὶ ἐμβάντων αὐτῶν εἰς τὸ πλοῖον,
why did you doubt? And going up they into the boat,
2869 417 1722 4143 2064 4352
33 ἐκόπασεν ὁ ἄνεμος· οἱ δὲ ἐν τῷ πλοίῳ ἐλθόντες προσεκύνησαν
ceased the wind. the (ones) And in the boat coming worshiped
846 3004 230 2316 5207 1488
αὐτῷ, λέγοντες, Ἀληθῶς Θεοῦ υἱὸς εἶ.
Him, saying Truly of God Son You are!
1276 2064 1519 1093 1082
34 Καὶ διαπεράσαντες ἦλθον εἰς τὴν γῆν Γεννησαρέτ. καὶ
35 And passing over they came into the land of Gennesaret. And
1921 846 435 5117 1567 649
ἐπιγνόντες αὐτὸν οἱ ἄνδρες τοῦ τόπου ἐκείνου ἀπέστειλαν
recognizing Him the men of place that sent
1519 3650 4066 1565 4374 846
εἰς ὅλην τὴν περίχωρον ἐκείνην, καὶ προσήνεγκαν αὐτῷ
into all — neighborhood that, and brought to Him
3956 2560 2192 3870 846 2443
36 πάντας τοὺς κακῶς ἔχοντας· καὶ παρεκάλουν αὐτόν, ἵνα
all those illness having, and begged Him that
3440 680 2899 2440 848
μόνον ἅψωνται τοῦ κρασπέδου τοῦ ἱματίου αὐτοῦ· καὶ
only they might touch the fringe of the garment of Him. And
3745 680 1295
ὅσοι ἥψαντο διεσώθησαν.
as many as touched were made perfectly well.

CHAPTER 15

[1]Then the scribes and Pharisees came to Jesus from Jerusalem, saying, [2]Why do your disciples transgress the tradition of the elders? For they do not wash their hands when they eat bread. [3]But answering He said to them, Why do you also transgress the command of God on account of your tradition?

5119 4334 2424 575 2414
1 Τότε προσέρχονται τῷ Ἰησοῦ οἱ ἀπὸ Ἱεροσολύμων
Then approach — to Jesus the (ones) from Jerusalem,
1122 5330 3004 1302 3101 4675
2 γραμματεῖς καὶ Φαρισαῖοι, λέγοντες, Διατί οἱ μαθηταί σου
scribes and Pharisees, saying, Why the disciples of you
3845 3862 4245 3756 1063
παραβαίνουσι τὴν παράδοσιν τῶν πρεσβυτέρων; οὐ γὰρ
transgress the tradition of the elders? not For
3538 5495 848 3752 740 2068
3 νίπτονται τὰς χεῖρας αὐτῶν, ὅταν ἄρτον ἐσθίωσιν. ὁ δὲ
they wash the hands of them, when bread they eat. He But
611 2036 846 1302 5210 3845
ἀποκριθεὶς εἶπεν αὐτοῖς, Διατί καὶ ὑμεῖς παραβαίνετε τὴν
answering said to them, Why also do you transgress the
1785 2316 1223 3862 5216 1063 2316
4 ἐντολὴν τοῦ Θεοῦ διὰ τὴν παράδοσιν ὑμῶν; ὁ γὰρ Θεὸς
command of God on account of the tradition of you? For God

[4]For God commanded, saying, "Honor your father and mother," and, "The *one* speaking evil of father or mother, by death let him die." [5]But you say, Whoever says to the father or the mother, A gift, whatever you would gain from me; [6]and in no way he honors his father or his mother; and you annulled the command of God on account of your tradition. [7]Hypocrites! Well did Isaiah prophesy concerning you, saying: [8]"This people draws near to Me with their mouth, and with their lips honor Me; but their heart is far from Me.

[9]But in vain they worship Me, teaching *as* doctrines *the* ordinances of men." [10]And calling near the crowd, He said to them, Hear and understand: [11]It is not that which has entered into the mouth that defiles the man, but that which has come out of the mouth, this defiles the man.

[12]Then coming the disciples said to Him, You know that hearing the saying, the Pharisees were offended? [13]But answering He said, Every plant which My heavenly Father has not planted shall be rooted up. [14]Leave them alone. They are blind leaders of the blind; and if the blind lead the blind, both will fall into a pit.

[15]And answering Peter said to Him, Explain this parable to us. [16]But Jesus said, Are you also still without understanding? [17]Do you not yet perceive that everything entering into the mouth goes into the belly, and is thrown out into *the* wastebowl? [18]But the things which have come out of the mouth come forth from the heart, and these defile the man.

1781 3004 5091 3962 4675 3384
ἐνετείλατο, λέγων, Τίμα τὸν πατέρα σοῦ, καὶ τὴν μητέρα·
commanded, saying, Honor the father of you, and the mother;
2551 3962 2228 3384 2288 5053
καί, Ὁ κακολογῶν πατέρα ἢ μητέρα θανάτῳ τελευτάτω·
and, The (one) speaking evil of father or mother by death let him end.
5210 3004 3739 302 2036 3962 2228 3384 1435
5 ὑμεῖς δὲ λέγετε, Ὃς ἂν εἴπῃ τῷ πατρὶ ἢ τῇ μητρί, Δῶρον,
you But say, Whoever says to the father or the mother, A gift,
3739 1437 1537 1700 5623 =3364= 5091 3962
ὃ ἐὰν ἐξ ἐμοῦ ὠφεληθῇς, καὶ οὐ μὴ τιμήσῃ τὸν πατέρα
whatever by me you would gain, and in no way he honors the father
848 2228 3384 848 208 1785
6 αὐτοῦ ἢ τὴν μητέρα αὐτοῦ· καὶ ἠκυρώσατε τὴν ἐντολὴν τοῦ
of him or the mother of him; and you annulled the command —
2316 1223 3862 5216 5273 2573 4395
7 Θεοῦ διὰ τὴν παράδοσιν ὑμῶν. ὑποκριταί, καλῶς προεφή-
of God on account of tradition your. Hypocrites! Well proph-
4012 5216 2268 3004 1448 3427 2992 3778
8 τευσε περὶ ὑμῶν Ἡσαΐας, λέγων, Ἐγγίζει μοι ὁ λαὸς οὗτος
esied concerning you Isaiah, saying, Draws near to Me people this
4750 848 5491 3165 5091 2228 2588
τῷ στόματι αὐτῶν, καὶ τοῖς χείλεσί με τιμᾷ· ἡ δὲ καρδία
with the mouth of them, and with the lips Me it honors; the but heart
848 4206 568 575 1700 3155 4576 3165
9 αὐτῶν πόρρω ἀπέχει ἀπ' ἐμοῦ. μάτην δὲ σέβονταί με.
of them far is away from Me. in vain But they adore Me
1321 1319 1778 444 4341
10 διδάσκοντες διδασκαλίας ἐντάλματα ἀνθρώπων. καὶ προσκα-
teaching (as) teachings ordinances of men. And calling
3793 2036 846 191 4920 3756
11 λεσάμενος τὸν ὄχλον, εἶπεν αὐτοῖς, Ἀκούετε καὶ συνίετε. οὐ
near the crowd, He said to them, Hear and understand, not
1525 1519 4750 2840 444 235
τὸ εἰσερχόμενον εἰς τὸ στόμα κοινοῖ τὸν ἄνθρωπον· ἀλλὰ τὸ
the (thing) entering into the mouth defiles the man, but the (thing)
1607 1537 4750 5124 2840 444
ἐκπορευόμενον ἐκ τοῦ στόματος, τοῦτο κοινοῖ τὸν ἄνθρωπον.
coming forth from the mouth, this defiles the man,
5119 4334 3101 848 2036 846 1492 3754
12 τότε προσελθόντες οἱ μαθηταὶ αὐτοῦ εἶπον αὐτῷ, Οἶδας ὅτι
Then coming the disciples to Him, they said to Him, Know You that
5330 191 3056 4624
13 οἱ Φαρισαῖοι ἀκούσαντες τὸν λόγον ἐσκανδαλίσθησαν; ὁ
the Pharisees hearing the saying were offended? He
611 2036 3956 5451 3739 3756 5452 3962
δὲ ἀποκριθεὶς εἶπε, Πᾶσα φυτεία, ἣν οὐκ ἐφύτευσεν ὁ πατήρ
But answering said, Every plant which not has planted the Father
3450 3770 1610 863 846 3595 1526
14 μου ὁ οὐράνιος, ἐκριζωθήσεται. ἄφετε αὐτούς· ὁδηγοί εἰσι
of Me the heavenly shall be rooted up. Leave them; leaders they are
5185 5185 5185 5185 1437 3594 297 1519
τυφλοὶ τυφλῶν· τυφλὸς δὲ τυφλὸν ἐὰν ὁδηγῇ, ἀμφότεροι εἰς
blind of blind; blind and blind if lead, both into
999 4098 611 4074 2036 846
15 βόθυνον πεσοῦνται. ἀποκριθεὶς δὲ ὁ Πέτρος εἶπεν αὐτῷ,
a pit will fall. answering And Peter said to Him,
5419 2254 3850 5026 2424 2036
16 Φράσον ἡμῖν τὴν παραβολὴν ταύτην. ὁ δὲ Ἰησοῦς εἶπεν,
Explain to us parable this. But Jesus said,
188 5210 801 2075 3768 3539 3754 3956
17 Ἀκμὴν καὶ ὑμεῖς ἀσύνετοί ἐστε; οὔπω νοεῖτε, ὅτι πᾶν τὸ
Yet also you unintelligent are? Not yet you perceive that everything
1531 1519 4750 1519 2836 5562 1519
εἰσπορευόμενον εἰς τὸ στόμα εἰς τὴν κοιλίαν χωρεῖ, καὶ εἰς
entering into the mouth into the stomach goes, and into
856 1544 1607 1537 4750
18 ἀφεδρῶνα ἐκβάλλεται; τὰ δὲ ἐκπορευόμενα ἐκ τοῦ στόματος
(the) wastebowl is thrown out; the but (things) coming forth from the mouth
1537 2588 1831 2518 2840 444 1537
19 ἐκ τῆς καρδίας ἐξέρχεται, κἀκεῖνα κοινοῖ τὸν ἄνθρωπον. ἐκ
from the heart come forth, and those defile the man. from

[19]For out of the heart come forth evil thoughts, murders, adulteries, fornications, thefts, lies, blasphemies. [20]These things are the things defiling the man. But eating with unwashed hands does not defile the man.

[21]And going out from there, Jesus withdrew to the parts of Tyre and Sidon. [22]And, behold, a woman of Canaan coming forth from those borders cried out to Him, saying, Have pity on me, Lord, Son of David! My daughter is vilely demon-possessed. [23]But He did not answer her a word. And coming near, His disciples asked Him, saying, Send her away, for she cries out after us. [24]But answering He said, I was not sent except to the lost sheep of *the* house of Israel. [25]But coming she worshiped Him, saying, Lord, help me! [26]But answering He said, It is not good to take the bread of the children and to throw *it* to the little dogs. [27]But she said, Yes, Lord; for even the little dogs eat of the crumbs falling from the table of their lords. [28]Then answering Jesus said to her, O woman, your faith *is* great; let it be to you as you desire. And her daughter was healed from that hour.

[29]And moving from there, Jesus came beside the Sea of Galilee. And going up into the mountain, He sat there. [30]And great crowds came to Him, having with them *those* lame, blind, dumb, maimed, and many others. And they flung them

1063 2588 1831 1261 4190 5408
γὰρ τῆς καρδίας ἐξέρχονται διαλογισμοὶ πονηροί, φόνοι,
For the heart come forth thoughts evil, murders,

3430 4202 2829 5577 988
μοιχεῖαι, πορνεῖαι, κλοπαί, ψευδομαρτυρίαι, βλασφημίαι·
adulteries, fornications, thefts, false witnessing, blasphemies;

5023 2076 2840 444 449
20 ταῦτά ἐστι τὰ κοινοῦντα τὸν ἄνθρωπον· τὸ δὲ ἀνίπτοις
these things are the (ones) defiling the man; but with unwashed

5495 5315 3756 2840 444
χερσὶ φαγεῖν οὐ κοινοῖ τὸν ἄνθρωπον.
hands to eat not defiles the man.

1831 1564 2424 402 1519 3313
21 Καὶ ἐξελθὼν ἐκεῖθεν ὁ Ἰησοῦς ἀνεχώρησεν εἰς τὰ μέρη
And going out from there Jesus withdrew into the parts

5184 4605 2400 1135 5478 575 3725
22 Τύρου καὶ Σιδῶνος. καὶ ἰδού, γυνὴ Χαναναία ἀπὸ τῶν ὁρίων
of Tyre and Sidon. And behold, a woman Canaanite from borders

1565 1831 2905 846 3004 1653
ἐκείνων ἐξελθοῦσα ἐκραύγασεν αὐτῷ, λέγουσα, Ἐλέησόν
those coming forth cried out to Him, saying, Have pity on

3165 2962 5207 1138 2364 3450 2560 1139
23 με, Κύριε, υἱὲ Δαβίδ· ἡ θυγάτηρ μου κακῶς δαιμονίζεται. ὁ
me, Lord, Son of David; the daughter of me badly is demon-possessed. He

3756 611 846 3056 4334 3101
δὲ οὐκ ἀπεκρίθη αὐτῇ λόγον. καὶ προσελθόντες οἱ μαθηταὶ
But not answered her a word. And coming near, His disciples

848 2065 846 3004 630 846 3754
αὐτοῦ ἠρώτων αὐτόν, λέγοντες, Ἀπόλυσον αὐτήν, ὅτι
of Him asked Him, saying, Send away her because

2896 3693 2257 611 2036 3756 649
24 κράζει ὄπισθεν ἡμῶν. ὁ δὲ ἀποκριθεὶς εἶπεν, Οὐκ ἀπεστάλην
she cries out after us. He But answering said, not I was sent

1508 1519 4263 622 3624 2474
25 εἰ μὴ εἰς τὰ πρόβατα τὰ ἀπολωλότα οἴκου Ἰσραήλ. ἡ δὲ
except to the sheep lost of (the) house of Israel. she but

2064 4352 846 3004 2962 997 3450
26 ἐλθοῦσα προσεκύνει αὐτῷ λέγουσα, Κύριε, βοήθει μοι. ὁ δὲ
coming worshiped Him, saying, Lord, help me! He But

611 2036 3756 2076 2570 2983 740
ἀποκριθεὶς εἶπεν, Οὐκ ἔστι καλὸν λαβεῖν τὸν ἄρτον τῶν
answering said, not it is good to take the bread of the

5043 906 2952 2036 3483 2962
27 τέκνων, καὶ βαλεῖν τοῖς κυναρίοις. ἡ δὲ εἶπε, Ναί, Κύριε· καὶ
children and to throw to the dogs. she And said, Yes, Lord, even

1063 2952 2068 575 5589 4098
γὰρ τὰ κυνάρια ἐσθίει ἀπὸ τῶν ψιχίων τῶν πιπτόντων
For the dogs eat from the crumbs falling

575 5132 2962 848 5119 611
28 ἀπὸ τῆς τραπέζης τῶν κυρίων αὐτῶν. τότε ἀποκριθεὶς ὁ
from the table of the lords of them. Then answering

2424 2036 846 5599 1135 3173 4675 4102
Ἰησοῦς εἶπεν αὐτῇ, Ὦ γύναι, μεγάλη σου ἡ πίστις·
Jesus said to her, O woman, great (is) of you the faith;

1096 4671 5613 2309 2390 2364 848 575
γενηθήτω σοι ὡς θέλεις. καὶ ἰάθη ἡ θυγάτηρ αὐτῆς ἀπὸ τῆς
let it be to you as you will. And was healed the daughter of her from

5610 1565
ὥρας ἐκείνης.
hour that.

3327 1564 2424 2064 3844 2281
29 Καὶ μεταβὰς ἐκεῖθεν ὁ Ἰησοῦς ἦλθε παρὰ τὴν θάλασσαν
And moving from there Jesus came beside the Sea

1056 305 1519 3735 2521 1563
30 τῆς Γαλιλαίας· καὶ ἀναβὰς εἰς τὸ ὄρος ἐκάθητο ἐκεῖ. καὶ
of Galilee; and going up into the mountain He sat there. And

4334 846 3793 4183 2192 3326 1438 5560
προσῆλθον αὐτῷ ὄχλοι πολλοί, ἔχοντες μεθ' ἑαυτῶν χωλούς,
came to Him crowds great, having with themselves (the) lame,

5185 2974 2948 2087 4183 4496
τυφλούς, κωφούς, κυλλούς, καὶ ἑτέρους πολλούς, καὶ ἔρριψαν
blind, dumb, maimed, and others many: and they flung

down at the feet of Jesus. And He healed them; [31]so that the crowds marveled, seeing the dumb speaking, the maimed sound, the lame walking, and the blind seeing. And they glorified the God of Israel.

[32]But having called near His disciples, Jesus said, I am filled with pity on the crowd, because they already have remained with Me three days, and have nothing they may eat. And I do not desire to send them away fasting, that they may not faint in the way. [33]And His disciples said to Him, From where in a desert *will come* to us so many loaves as to satisfy so great a crowd? [34]And Jesus said to them, How many loaves do you have? And they said, Seven, and a few small fish. [35]And He ordered the crowds to recline on the ground. [36]And taking the seven loaves and the fish, giving thanks, He broke and gave to His disciples, and the disciples to the crowd. [37]And all ate, and were satisfied. And they took up the left over pieces, seven lunch-baskets full. [38]And the ones eating were four thousand men, besides women and children.

[39]And sending away the crowds, He went into the boat, and came to the borders of Magdala.

CHAPTER 16

[1]And coming, the Pharisees and Sadducees asked Him to show them a sign out of Heaven, tempting Him [2]But answering He said to them, Evening coming on, you say, Clear sky; for the heaven is red. [3]And at morning, Today a

846 3844 4228 2424 2323 846
αὐτοὺς παρὰ τοὺς πόδας τοῦ Ἰησοῦ καὶ ἐθεράπευσεν αὐτούς·
them at the feet of Jesus; and He healed them;
5620 3793 2296 991 2974 2980
31 ὥστε τοὺς ὄχλους θαυμάσαι, βλέποντας κωφοὺς λαλοῦντας,
so that the crowds (had)l to marvel, seeing dumb ones speaking,
2948 5199 5560 4043 5185
κυλλοὺς ὑγιεῖς, χωλοὺς περιπατοῦντας, καὶ τυφλοὺς
maimed ones sound lame ones walking, and blind ones
991 1392 2316 2474
βλέποντας· καὶ ἐδόξασαν τὸν Θεὸν Ἰσραήλ.
seeing; and they glorified the God of Israel.
2424 4341 3101 848 2036
32 Ὁ δὲ Ἰησοῦς προσκαλεσάμενος τοὺς μαθητὰς αὐτοῦ εἶπε,
And Jesus having called near the disciples of Him said,
4697 1909 3793 3754 2235 2250 5140 4357
Σπλαγχνίζομαι ἐπὶ τὸν ὄχλον, ὅτι ἤδη ἡμέρας τρεῖς προσ-
I am filled with pity on the crowd, because now days three they
3427 3756 2192 5101 5715 630
μένουσί μοι, καὶ οὐκ ἔχουσι τί φάγωσι· καὶ ἀπολῦσαι
remain with Me, and not have anything they may eat; and to send away
846 3523 3756 2192 3379 1590 1722 3598
33 αὐτοὺς νήστεις οὐ θέλω, μήποτε ἐκλυθῶσιν ἐν τῇ ὁδῷ. καὶ
them fasting not I desire, lest they be weary in the way. And
3004 846 3101 848 4159 2254 1722 2047
λέγουσιν αὐτῷ οἱ μαθηταὶ αὐτοῦ, Πόθεν ἡμῖν ἐν ἐρημίᾳ
say to Him the disciples of Him, From where to us in a desert
740 5118 5620 5526 3793 5118
34 ἄρτοι τοσοῦτοι, ὥστε χορτάσαι ὄχλον τοσοῦτον; καὶ
loaves so many as to satisfy a crowd so great? And
3004 846 2424 4214 740 2192 2036
λέγει αὐτοῖς ὁ Ἰησοῦς, Πόσους ἄρτους ἔχετε; οἱ δὲ εἶπον,
said to them Jesus, How many loaves have you? they And said,
2033 3641 2485 2753 3793 377
35 Ἑπτά, καὶ ὀλίγα ἰχθύδια. καὶ ἐκέλευσε τοῖς ὄχλοις ἀναπε-
Seven, and a few small fish. And He ordered the crowd to recline
1909 1093 2983 2033 740
36 σεῖν ἐπὶ τὴν γῆν· καὶ λαβὼν τοὺς ἑπτὰ ἄρτους καὶ τοὺς
on the ground; and taking the seven loaves and the
2486 2168 2806 1325 3101 848
ἰχθύας, εὐχαριστήσας ἔκλασε, καὶ ἔδωκε τοῖς μαθηταῖς αὐτοῦ,
fish, giving thanks He broke, and gave to the disciples of Him,
3101 3793 5315 3956 5526
37 οἱ δὲ μαθηταὶ τῷ ὄχλῳ. καὶ ἔφαγον πάντες καὶ ἐχορτά-
the and disciples to the crowd. And ate all, and were
142 4052 2801 2033
σθησαν· καὶ ἦραν τὸ περισσεῦον τῶν κλασμάτων, ἑπτὰ
filled and they took up the excess of the fragments, seven
4711 4134 2068 2258 5070
38 σπυρίδας πλήρεις. οἱ δὲ ἐσθίοντες ἦσαν τετρακισχίλιοι
lunch-baskets full. the And (ones) eating were four thousand
435 5565 1135 3813 630
39 ἄνδρες, χωρὶς γυναικῶν καὶ παιδίων. καὶ ἀπολύσας τοὺς
men apart from women and children. And sending away the
3793 1684 1519 4143 2064 1519 3125 3093
ὄχλους ἐνέβη εἰς τὸ πλοῖον, καὶ ἦλθεν εἰς τὰ ὅρια Μαγδαλά.
crowds, He went into the boat, and came into the borders of Magdala.

CHAPTER 16

4334 5330 4523 3985
1 Καὶ προσελθόντες οἱ Φαρισαῖοι καὶ Σαδδουκαῖοι πειρά-
And coming the Pharisees and Sadducees tempting
1905 846 4592 1537 3772 1925
ζοντες ἐπηρώτησαν αὐτὸν σημεῖον ἐκ τοῦ οὐρανοῦ ἐπιδεῖξαι
asked Him a sign from Heaven to show
846 611 2036 846 3798 1096
2 αὐτοῖς. ὁ δὲ ἀποκριθεὶς εἶπεν αὐτοῖς, Ὀψίας γενομένης
them. He But answering said to them, Evening coming on
3004 2105 4449 1063 3772 4404 4594
3 λέγετε, Εὐδία· πυρράζει γὰρ ὁ οὐρανός. καὶ πρωΐ, Σήμερον
you say, Clear sky; is red for the heaven. And at morning, Today

storm; for the sky is red, being overcast. Hypocrites! You indeed know how to discern face of the heaven, but you cannot the signs the times. [4]An evil and adulterous generation seeks a sign, and a sign will not be given to it, except the sign of Jonah the prophet. And leaving them, He went away.

[5]And His disciples coming to the other side, they forgot to take loaves. [6]And Jesus said to them, Watch! And beware of the leaven of the Pharisees and Sadducees. [7]And they easoned among themselves, saying, Because we did not take loaves. [8]And knowing Jesus said to them, Why do you reason among yourselves because you took no loaves, little-faiths? [9]Do you not perceive nor recall the five loaves of the five thousand, and how many baskets you took up? [10]Nor the seven loaves of the four thousand, and how many lunch-baskets you took up? [11]How do you not perceive that *it was* not about loaves that I said to you to take heed from the leaven of the Pharisees and Sadducees? [12]Then they knew that He did not say to take heed from the leaven of bread, but from the teaching of the Pharisees and Sadducees.

[13]And coming into the parts of Caesarea of Philip, Jesus questioned His disciples, saying, Whom do men say Me to be, the Son of man? [14]And they said, Some *say* John the Baptist; and others Elijah; and others Jeremiah, or one of the prophets. [15]He said to them, But you, whom do

5494 4449 1063 4768 3772 5273
χειμών· πυρράζει γὰρ στυγνάζων ὁ οὐρανός. ὑποκριταί,
a storm; is red for being overcast the heaven. Hypocrites!
3303 4383 3772 1097 1252
τὸ μὲν πρόσωπον τοῦ οὐρανοῦ γινώσκετε διακρίνειν, τὰ
the Indeed face of the heaven you know to discern, the
4592 2540 3756 1410 1074 4190
4 δὲ σημεῖα τῶν καιρῶν οὐ δύνασθε; γενεὰ πονηρὰ καὶ
but signs of the times not you are able. A generation evil and
3428 4592 1934 4592 3756 1325 846
μοιχαλὶς σημεῖον ἐπιζητεῖ· καὶ σημεῖον οὐ δοθήσεται αὐτῇ,
adulterous a sign seeks; and a sign not shall be given to it,
1508 4592 2495 4396 2641
εἰ μὴ τὸ σημεῖον Ἰωνᾶ τοῦ προφήτου. καὶ καταλιπὼν
except the sign of Jonah the prophet. And forsaking
846 565
αὐτούς, ἀπῆλθε.
them He went away.
2064 3101 848 1519 4008 1950
5 Καὶ ἐλθόντες οἱ μαθηταὶ αὐτοῦ εἰς τὸ πέραν ἐπελάθοντο
And coming the disciples of Him to the other side they forgot
740 2983 2424 2036 846 3708 4337
6 ἄρτους λαβεῖν. ὁ δὲ Ἰησοῦς εἶπεν αὐτοῖς, Ὁρᾶτε καὶ προσ-
loaves to take. And Jesus said to them, Beware and take
575 2219 5330 4523
7 έχετε ἀπὸ τῆς ζύμης τῶν Φαρισαίων καὶ Σαδδουκαίων. οἱ
heed from the leaven of the Pharisees and the Sadducees. they
1260 1722 1438 3004 3754 740 3756
δὲ διελογίζοντο ἐν ἑαυτοῖς, λέγοντες ὅτι Ἄρτους οὐκ
But reasoned among themselves, saying, Because loaves not
2983 1097 2424 2036 846 5101 1260
8 ἐλάβομεν. γνοὺς δὲ ὁ Ἰησοῦς εἶπεν αὐτοῖς, Τί διαλογίζεσθε
we took. knowing And Jesus said to them, Why do you reason
1722 1438 3640 3754 740 3756 2983 3768
9 ἐν ἑαυτοῖς, ὀλιγόπιστοι, ὅτι ἄρτους οὐκ ἐλάβετε; οὔπω
among yourselves, little-faiths, because loaves not you took? not
3539 3761 3421 4002 740 4000
νοεῖτε, οὐδὲ μνημονεύετε τοὺς πέντε ἄρτους τῶν πεντακι-
you perceive not remember the five loaes of the five
4214 2894 2983 3711 2033
10 σχιλίων, καὶ πόσους κοφίνους ἐλάβετε; οὐδὲ τοὺς ἑπτὰ
thousand, and how many baskets you took? Neither the seven
740 5010 4214 4711 2983
ἄρτους τῶν τετρακισχιλίων, καὶ πόσας σπυρίδας ἐλάβετε;
loaves of the four thousand, and how many lunch-baskets you took?
4459 3756 3539 3754 3756 4012 740 2036 5213 4337 575
11 πῶς οὐ νοεῖτε, ὅτι οὐ περὶ ἄρτου εἶπον ὑμῖν προσέχειν ἀπὸ
How not perceive that not about loaves I said to you to take heed from
2219 5330 4523 5119 4920
12 τῆς ζύμης τῶν Φαρισαίων καὶ Σαδδουκαίων; τότε συνῆκαν
the leaven of the Pharisees and Sadducees. Then they knew
3754 3756 2036 4337 575 2219 740 235 575
ὅτι οὐκ εἶπε προσέχειν ἀπὸ τῆς ζύμης τοῦ ἄρτου, ἀλλ' ἀπὸ
that not He said to take heed from the leaven of bread, but from
1322 5330 4523
τῆς διδαχῆς τῶν Φαρισαίων καὶ Σαδδουκαίων.
the teaching of the Pharisees and Sadducees.
2064 2424 1519 3313 2542 5376
13 Ἐλθὼν δὲ ὁ Ἰησοῦς εἰς τὰ μέρη Καισαρείας τῆς Φιλίππου
coming And Jesus into the parts of Caesarea of Philip
2065 3101 848 3004 5101 3165 3004
ἠρώτα τοὺς μαθητὰς αὐτοῦ, λέγων, Τίνα με λέγουσιν οἱ
He queried the disciples of Him, saying, Whom Me do say
444 1511 5207 444 2036 3303
14 ἄνθρωποι εἶναι, τὸν υἱὸν τοῦ ἀνθρώπου; οἱ δὲ εἶπον, Οἱ μὲν
men to be, the Son of man? they And said, Some
2491 910 243 2243 2087
Ἰωάννην τὸν Βαπτιστήν· ἄλλοι δὲ Ἠλίαν· ἕτεροι δὲ
(say) John the Baptist; others and Elijah; others and
2408 2228 1520 4396 3004 846 5210 5101
15 Ἱερεμίαν, ἢ ἕνα τῶν προφητῶν. λέγει αὐτοῖς, Ὑμεῖς δὲ τίνα
Jeremiah, or one of the prophets. He says to them, you But, whom

you say Me to be? [16]And answering, Simon Peter said, You are the Christ, the Son of the living God. [17]And answering Jesus said to him, Blessed are you, Simon, son of Jonah, for flesh and blood did not reveal *it* to you, but My Father in Heaven. [18]And I also say to you that you are Peter, and on this rock I will build My church, and *the* gates of Hades will not prevail against her. [19]And I will give to you the keys of the kingdom of Heaven. And whatever you bind on earth shall occur, having already been bound in Heaven. And whatever you may loose on the earth shall be, having been already loosed in Heaven. [20]Then He warned His disciples that they should tell no one that He is Jesus the Christ.

3165 3004 1511 611 4613 4074 2036 4771 1488
16 με λέγετε εἶναι ; ἀποκριθεὶς δὲ Σίμων Πέτρος εἶπε, Σὺ εἶ ὁ
Me do you say to be? answering And Simon Peter said, You are the
5547 5207 2316 2198 611
17 Χριστός, ὁ υἱὸς τοῦ Θεοῦ τοῦ ζῶντος. καὶ ἀποκριθεὶς ὁ
Christ, the Son of God the living. And answering
2424 2036 846 3107 1488 4613 =920= 3754 4561
Ἰησοῦς εἶπεν αὐτῷ, Μακάριος εἶ, Σίμων Βὰρ Ἰωνᾶ, ὅτι σὰρξ
Jesus said to him, Blessed are you, Simon Bar-jonah because flesh
129 3756 601 4671 235 3962 3450 1722
καὶ αἷμα οὐκ ἀπεκάλυψέ σοι, ἀλλ' ὁ πατήρ μου ὁ ἐν τοῖς
and blood not did reveal to you, but the Father of Me in the
3772 2504 4671 3004 3754/4771/1487/4074 1909 5026
18 οὐρανοῖς. κἀγὼ δέ σοι λέγω, ὅτι σὺ εἶ Πέτρος, καὶ ἐπὶ ταύτῃ
heavens. I also And to you say, You are Peter, and on this
4073 3618 3450 1577 4439 86
τῇ πέτρᾳ οἰκοδομήσω μου τὴν ἐκκλησίαν, καὶ πύλαι ᾅδου
rock I will build of Me the church, and (the) gates of Hades
3756 2729 846 1325 4671 2807
19 οὐ κατισχύσουσιν αὐτῆς. καὶ δώσω σοὶ τὰς κλεῖς τῆς
not will prevail against her. And I will give to you the keys of the
932 3772 1437 1210 1909 1093 2071
βασιλείας τῶν οὐρανῶν· καὶ ὃ ἐὰν δήσῃς ἐπὶ τῆς γῆς, ἔσται
kingdom of the heavens, and whatever you bind on the earth shall be,
1210 1722 3772 1437 3089 1909 1093
δεδεμένον ἐν τοῖς οὐρανοῖς· καὶ ὃ ἐὰν λύσῃς ἐπὶ τῆς γῆς,
having been bound in the heavens, and whatever you loose on the earth
2071 3089 1722 3772 5119 1291
20 ἔσται λελυμένον ἐν τοῖς οὐρανοῖς. τότε διεστείλατο τοῖς
shall be, having been loosed in the heavens. Then He warned the
3101 848 2443 3367 2036 3754 846 2076 2424
μαθηταῖς αὐτοῦ ἵνα μηδενὶ εἴπωσιν ὅτι αὐτός ἐστιν Ἰησοῦς
disciples of Him that to no one they may tell that He is Jesus
5547
ὁ Χριστός.
the Christ.

[21]From that time Jesus began to show to His disciples that it was necessary for Him to go away to Jerusalem, and to suffer many things from the elders and chief priests and scribes, and to be killed, and to be raised on the third day. [22]And having taken Him near, Peter began to rebuke Him, saying, *God be* gracious to You, Lord; this shall never be to You. [23]But turning He said to Peter, Go behind Me, Satan! You are an offense to Me, for you do not think of the things of God, but the things of men.

575 5119 756 2424 1166 3101
21 Ἀπὸ τότε ἤρξατο ὁ Ἰησοῦς δεικνύειν τοῖς μαθηταῖς
From then began Jesus to show to the disciples
848\3754\1163 846 565 1519 2414 4183
αὐτοῦ ὅτι δεῖ αὐτὸν ἀπελθεῖν εἰς Ἱεροσόλυμα, καὶ πολλὰ
of Him that it behoves Him to go away to Jerusalem, and many things
3958 575 4245 749 1122
παθεῖν ἀπὸ τῶν πρεσβυτέρων καὶ ἀρχιερέων καὶ γραμ-
to suffer from the elders and chief priests and scribes
615 5154 2250 1453
ματέων, καὶ ἀποκτανθῆναι, καὶ τῇ τρίτῃ ἡμέρᾳ ἐγερθῆναι.
and to be killed, and on the third day to be raised.
4355 846 4074 756 2008 846
22 καὶ προσλαβόμενος αὐτὸν ὁ Πέτρος ἤρξατο ἐπιτιμᾶν αὐτῷ
And taking near Him, Peter began to rebuke Him,
3004 2436 4671 2962 =3364- 2071 4671 5124 4762
23 λέγων, Ἵλεώς σοι, Κύριε· οὐ μὴ ἔσται σοι τοῦτο. ὁ δὲ στραφεὶς
saying, Gracious to You, Lord, never shall be to You this. He But turning
2036 4074 5217 3694 3450 4567 4625 3450
εἶπε τῷ Πέτρῳ, Ὕπαγε ὀπίσω μου, Σατανᾶ, σκάνδαλόν μου
said to Peter, Go behind Me, Satan, an offense to Me
1488/3754/3756/5426 2316 235 444
εἶ· ὅτι οὐ φρονεῖς τὰ τοῦ Θεοῦ, ἀλλὰ τὰ τῶν ἀνθρώπων.
you are, for not you think the things of God, but the things of men.

[24]Then Jesus said to His disciples, If anyone desires to come after Me, let him deny himself, and let him bear his cross, and let him follow Me. [25]For whoever may desire to save his soul will lose it. But whoever may lose his soul for My

5119 2424 2036 3101 848 =1536= 2309 3694
24 τότε ὁ Ἰησοῦς εἶπε τοῖς μαθηταῖς αὐτοῦ, Εἴ τις θέλει ὀπίσω
Then Jesus said to the disciples of Him, If anyone desires after
3450 2064 533 1438 142 4716
μου ἐλθεῖν, ἀπαρνησάσθω ἑαυτόν, καὶ ἀράτω τὸν σταυρὸν
Me to come, let him deny himself, and let him bear the cross
848 190 3427 3739 1063 302 2309 5590
25 αὐτοῦ, καὶ ἀκολουθείτω μοι. ὃς γὰρ ἂν θέλῃ τὴν ψυχὴν
of him, and let him follow Me. whoever For may desire the soul
848 4982 622 846 3739 302 622 5590
αὐτοῦ σῶσαι ἀπολέσει αὐτήν· ὃς δ' ἂν ἀπολέσῃ τὴν ψυχὴν
of him to save he will lose it; and whoever may lose the soul

NOTE: Frequent words not numbered: δέ(1161); καί(2531)—and, but; ὁ, ἡ, τό (3588, the)— * above word, look in verse margin for No.

sake will find it. [26]For what
will a man be benefited if he
should gain the whole
world, but forfeits his soul?
Or what will a man give *as*
an exchange *for* his soul?
[27]For the Son of man is
about to come in the glory
of His Father, with His
angels. And then He will
give reward to each
according to his works.
[28]Truly I say to you, There
are some standing here
who in no way will taste of
death until they see the
Son of man coming in His
kingdom.

848 1752 1700 2147 846 5101 1063 5623 444
26 αὐτοῦ ἕνεκεν ἐμοῦ εὑρήσει αὐτήν· τί γὰρ ὠφελεῖται ἄνθρω-
of him for the sake of Me, he will find it. what For will be benefited a man
1437 2889 3650 2770 5590 848
πος ἐὰν τὸν κόσμον ὅλον κερδήσῃ, τὴν δὲ ψυχὴς αὐτοῦ
if the world whole he should gain, the but soul of him?
2210 5102 1325 444 465 5590
27 ζημιωθῇ ; ἢ τί δώσει ἄνθρωπος ἀντάλλαγμα τῆς ψυχῆς
forfeits? Or what will give a man (as) an exchange (for) the soul
848 3195 1063 5207 444 2064 1722
αὐτοῦ ; μέλλει γὰρ ὁ υἱὸς τοῦ ἀνθρώπου ἔρχεσθαι ἐν τῇ
of him? is about For the Son – of man to come in the
1391 3962 848 3326 32 848
δόξῃ τοῦ πατρὸς αὐτοῦ μετὰ τῶν ἀγγέλων αὐτοῦ, καὶ
glory of the Father of Him with the angels of Him, and
5119 591 1538 2596 4234 848 281 3004
28 τότε ἀποδώσει ἑκάστῳ κατὰ τὴν πρᾶξιν αὐτοῦ. ἀμὴν λέγω
then He will reward to each according to the works of him. Truly I say
5213 1526 5100 5602 2476 3748 =3364= 1089
ὑμῖν, εἰσί τινες τῶν ὧδε ἑστηκότων, οἵτινες οὐ μὴ γεύ-
to you, there are some – here standing who not at all will
2288 2193 302 1492 5207 444
σωνται θανάτου, ἕως ἂν ἴδωσι τὸν υἱὸν τοῦ ἀνθρώπου
taste of death until they see the Son – of man
2064 1722 932 848
ἐρχόμενον ἐν τῇ βασιλείᾳ αὐτοῦ.
coming in the kingdom of Him.

CHAPTER 17

CHAPTER 17

[1]And after six days,
Jesus took Peter and
James, and his brother
John, and brought them up
into a high mountain apart.
[2]And He was transfigured
before them, and His face
shone like the sun, and His
clothing became white as
the light. [3]And, behold!
Moses and Elijah appeared
to them, talking with Him.
[4]And answering Peter said
to Jesus, Lord, it is good for
us to be here. If You will, let
us make three tents here,
one for You, one for Moses,
and one for Elijah. [5]While
he *was* yet speaking,
behold, a radiant cloud
overshadowed them. And,
behold, a voice out of the
cloud saying, This is My
Son, the Beloved, in whom
I delight; hear Him. [6]And
hearing, the disciples fell
on their face and and were
greatly terrified. [7]And
coming near, Jesus
touched them and said,

3326 2250 1803 3880 2424 4074
1 Καὶ μεθ' ἡμέρας ἓξ παραλαμβάνει ὁ Ἰησοῦς τὸν Πέτρον καὶ
And after days six takes – Jesus – Peter and
2385 2491 80 848 399
Ἰάκωβον καὶ Ἰωάννην τὸν ἀδελφὸν αὐτοῦ, καὶ ἀναφέρει
James and John the brother of him, and leads up
846 1519 3735 5308 2596 2398 3339
2 αὐτοὺς εἰς ὄρος ὑψηλὸν κατ' ἰδίαν. καὶ μετεμορφώθη
them into mountain a high privately. And He was transfigured
1715 846 2989 4383 848 5613
ἔμπροσθεν αὐτῶν, καὶ ἔλαμψε τὸ πρόσωπον αὐτοῦ ὡς ὁ
before them, and shone the face of Him like the
2246 2440 848 1096 3022 5613 5457 2400
3 ἥλιος, τὰ δὲ ἱμάτια αὐτοῦ ἐγένετο λευκὰ ὡς τὸ φῶς. καὶ ἰδού,
sun, the and garments of Him became white as the light, and behold,
3700 846 3475 2243 3326 848 4814
ὤφθησαν αὐτοῖς Μωσῆς καὶ Ἠλίας, μετ' αὐτοῦ συλλαλοῦν-
appeared to them Moses and Elijah with Him talking to-
611 4074 2036 2424 2962 2570
4 τες. ἀποκριθεὶς δὲ ὁ Πέτρος εἶπε τῷ Ἰησοῦ, Κύριε, καλόν
gether answering And – Peter said – to Jesus, Lord, good
2036 2248 5602 1511 1487 2309 4160 5602 5140 4633
ἐστιν ἡμᾶς ὧδε εἶναι· εἰ θέλεις, ποιήσωμεν ὧδε τρεῖς σκηνάς,
it is for us here to be. If You desire, let us make here three tents,
4671 3391 3475 3391 3391 2243 2089 846 2980
5 σοὶ μίαν, καὶ Μωσῇ μίαν, καὶ μίαν Ἠλίᾳ. ἔτι αὐτοῦ λαλοῦν-
for You one, and for Moses one, and one for Elijah. While he (was) speaking,
2400 3507 5460 1982 846 2400
τος, ἰδού, νεφέλη φωτεινὴ ἐπεσκίασεν αὐτούς· καὶ ἰδού,
behold, a cloud radiant overshadowed them, and behold,
5456 1537 3507 3004 3778 2076 5207 3450
φωνὴ ἐκ τῆς νεφέλης, λέγουσα, Οὗτός ἐστιν ὁ υἱός μου
a voice out of the cloud, saying, This is the Son of Me,
27 1722 3739 2106 846 191 191
6 ὁ ἀγαπητός, ἐν ᾧ εὐδόκησα· αὐτοῦ ἀκούετε. καὶ ἀκούσαντες
the beloved, in whom I delight; of Him hear. And hearing,
3101 4098 1909 4383 848 5399
οἱ μαθηταὶ ἔπεσον ἐπὶ πρόσωπον αὐτῶν, καὶ ἐφοβήθησαν
the disciples fell on the face of them, and were terrified
4970 4334 2424 680 846 2036
7 σφόδρα. καὶ προσελθὼν ὁ Ἰησοῦς ἥψατο αὐτῶν καὶ εἶπεν,
greatly. And coming near, Jesus touched them, and said,

NOTE: Frequent words not numbered: δέ(1161); καί(2531)—and, but; ὁ, ἡ, τό (3588, the)— * above word, look in verse margin for No.

Rise up, and do not be terrified. [8]And lifting up their eyes, they did not see anyone except Jesus alone.

[9]And as they were coming down from the mountain, Jesus charged them, saying, Tell the vision to no one until the Son of man is raised from the dead. [10]And His disciples asked Him, saying, Why then do the scribes say that Elijah must come first? [11]And answering Jesus said to them, Elijah indeed comes first, and shall restore all things. [12]But I say to you, Elijah has already come, and they did not know him, but did to him whatever they desired. So also the Son of man is about to suffer by them. [13]Then the disciples understood that He spoke to them about John the Baptist

[14]And they coming to the crowd, a man came near to Him, kneeling down to Him, and saying, [15]Lord, pity my son. For he is moonstruck and suffers miserably. For he often falls into the fire, and often into the water. [16]And I brought him to Your disciples, and they were not able to heal him. [17]And answering Jesus said, O faithless and perverted generation! How long will I be with you? How long shall I bear with you? Bring him here to Me. [18]And Jesus rebuked him, and the demon came out from him; and the boy was healed from that hour.

[19]Then coming up to Jesus privately, the disciples said, Why were we not able to cast him out?

1453 3361 5399 1869 3788
8 Ἐγέρθητε καὶ μὴ φοβεῖσθε. ἐπάραντες δὲ τοὺς ὀφθαλμοὺς
Arise, and not fear. lifting up And the eyes
848 3762 1492 --1508-- 2424 3441
αὐτῶν, οὐδένα εἶδον, εἰ μὴ τὸν Ἰησοῦν μόνον.
of them, no one they saw except Jesus alone.
2597 846 575 3735 1781
9 Καὶ καταβαινόντων αὐτῶν ἀπὸ τοῦ ὄρους, ἐνετείλατο
And coming down they from the mountain, enjoined
846 2424 3004 3367 2036 3705 2193 3739
αὐτοῖς ὁ Ἰησοῦς, λέγων, Μηδενὶ εἴπητε τὸ ὅραμα, ἕως οὗ ὁ
them — Jesus, saying, To no one tell the vision, until the
5207 4415 1537 3498 450 1905
10 υἱὸς τοῦ ἀνθρώπου ἐκ νεκρῶν ἀναστῇ. καὶ ἐπηρώτησαν
Son — of man from the dead is raised. And questioned
846 3101 848 3004 5101 3767 1122
αὐτὸν οἱ μαθηταὶ αὐτοῦ λέγοντες, Τί οὖν οἱ γραμματεῖς
Him the disciples of Him saying, Why then the scribes
3004 3754 2243 1163 2064 4412 2424 611
11 λέγουσιν ὅτι Ἠλίαν δεῖ ἐλθεῖν πρῶτον ; ὁ δὲ Ἰησοῦς ἀποκρι-
say that Elijah it behoves to come first? And Jesus, answering
2036 846 2243 3303 2064 4412 600
θεὶς εἶπεν αὐτοῖς, Ἠλίας μὲν ἔρχεται πρῶτον, καὶ ἀποκατα-
said to them, Elijah indeed comes first and shall restore
3956 3004 5213 3754 2243 2235 2064 3756
12 στήσει πάντα· λέγω δὲ ὑμῖν ὅτι Ἠλίας ἤδη ἦλθε, καὶ οὐκ
all things; I tell but you that Elijah already is come, and not
1921 846 235 4160 1722 846 3745 2309
ἐπέγνωσαν αὐτόν, ἀλλ' ἐποίησαν ἐν αὐτῷ ὅσα ἠθέλησαν·
they knew him, but did to him whatever they wished
3779 5207 444 3195 3958 5259 846
οὕτω καὶ ὁ υἱὸς τοῦ ἀνθρώπου μέλλει πάσχειν ὑπ' αὐτῶν.
thus also the Son of man is about to suffer by them
5119 4920 3101 3754 4012 2491 910
13 τότε συνῆκαν οἱ μαθηταὶ ὅτι περὶ Ἰωάννου τοῦ Βαπτιστοῦ
Then understood the disciples that concerning John the Baptist
2036 846
εἶπεν αὐτοῖς.
He spoke to them.
2064 846 4314 3793 4334 846
14 Καὶ ἐλθόντων αὐτῶν πρὸς τὸν ὄχλον, προσῆλθεν αὐτῷ
And having come they toward the crowd, came near to Him
444 1120 846 3004 2962 1653 3450
15 ἄνθρωπος γονυπετῶν αὐτῷ καὶ λέγων, Κύριε, ἐλέησόν μου
a man kneeling down to Him and saying, Lord, pity of me
5207 3754 4583 2560 3968 4178 1063
τὸν υἱόν, ὅτι σεληνιάζεται καὶ κακῶς πάσχει· πολλάκις γὰρ
the son, because he is moonstruck and illness suffers; often for
4098 1519 4442 4178 1519 5204 4374
16 πίπτει εἰς τὸ πῦρ, καὶ πολλάκις εἰς τὸ ὕδωρ. καὶ προσήνεγκα
he falls into the fire, and often into the water. And I brought
846 3101 4675 3756 1410 846
αὐτὸν τοῖς μαθηταῖς σου, καὶ οὐκ ἠδυνήθησαν αὐτὸν
him to the disciples of You, and not they were able him
2323 611 2424 2036 5599 1074 571
17 θεραπεῦσαι. ἀποκριθεὶς δὲ ὁ Ἰησοῦς εἶπεν, Ὦ γενεὰ ἄπιστος
to heal. answering And Jesus said, O generation faithless
1294 2193 4219 2071 3326 5216 2193 4219
καὶ διεστραμμένη, ἕως πότε ἔσομαι μεθ' ὑμῶν ; ἕως πότε
and perverted, until when shall I be with you? Until when
430 5216 5342 3427 846 5602 2008 846
18 ἀνέξομαι ὑμῶν ; φέρετέ μοι αὐτὸν ὧδε. καὶ ἐπετίμησεν αὐτῷ
shall I endure you? Bring to Me him here. And rebuked it
2424 1831 575 846 1140 2323
ὁ Ἰησοῦς, καὶ ἐξῆλθεν ἀπ' αὐτοῦ τὸ δαιμόνιον, καὶ ἐθεραπεύ-
— Jesus, and came out from him the demon, and was healed
3816 575 5610 1565 5119 4334
19 θη ὁ παῖς ἀπὸ τῆς ὥρας ἐκείνης. τότε προσελθόντες οἱ
the boy from — hour that. Then coming up the
3101 2424 2596 2398 2036 1302 2249 3756 1410
μαθηταὶ τῷ Ἰησοῦ κατ' ἰδίαν εἶπον, Διατί ἡμεῖς οὐκ ἠδυνή-
disciples — to Jesus privately said, Why we not were

[20]And Jesus said to them, Because of your unbelief. For truly I say to you, If you have faith as a grain of mustard, you will say to this mountain, Move from here to there! And it will move. And nothing shall be impossible to you. [21]But this kind does not go out except by prayer and fasting.

[22]And while they were staying in Galilee, Jesus said to them, The Son of man is about to be delivered into *the* hands of men. [23]And they will kill Him; and on the third day He will be raised. And they grieved exceedingly.

[24]And they coming into Capernaum, those receiving the didrachmas came to Peter and said, Does your teacher not pay the didrachmas? [25]He said, Yes. And when he entered into the house, Jesus anticipated him, saying, What do you think, Simon? From whom do the kings of the earth receive custom or tribute? From their sons or from strangers? [26]Peter said to Him, From strangers. Jesus said to him, Then truly the sons are free. [27]But that we may not offend them, going to the sea, throw in a hook, and take the first fish coming up. And opening its mouth, you will find a stater. Taking that, give to them for you and Me.

1544 846 2424 2036 846 1223
20 θημεν ἐκβαλεῖν αὐτό ; ὁ δὲ Ἰησοῦς εἶπεν αὐτοῖς, Διὰ τὴν
able to cast out him? And Jesus said to them, Through the
570 5216 281 1063 3004 5213 1437 2192 4102 5613
ἀπιστίαν ὑμῶν. ἀμὴν γὰρ λέγω ὑμῖν, ἐὰν ἔχητε πίστιν ὡς
unbelief of you. truly For I say to you, if you have faith as
2848 4615 2046 3735 5129 3327 1782
κόκκον σινάπεως, ἐρεῖτε τῷ ὄρει τούτῳ, Μετάβηθι ἐντεῦθεν
a grain of mustard, you will say to mountain this, Move from here
1563 3327 3762 101 5213 5124
21 ἐκεῖ, καὶ μεταβήσεται· καὶ οὐδὲν ἀδυνατήσει ὑμῖν. τοῦτο δὲ
to there and it will move, and nothing shall be impossible to you. this But
1085 3756 1607 1508 1722 4335 3521
τὸ γένος οὐκ ἐκπορεύεται εἰ μὴ ἐν προσευχῇ καὶ νηστείᾳ.
kind not does go out except by prayer and fasting.
390 846 1722 1056 2036 846
22 Ἀναστρεφομένων δὲ αὐτῶν ἐν τῇ Γαλιλαίᾳ, εἶπεν αὐτοῖς
while were remaining And they in Galilee, said to them
2424 3195 5207 444 3860 1519
ὁ Ἰησοῦς, Μέλλει ὁ υἱὸς τοῦ ἀνθρώπου παραδίδοσθαι εἰς
Jesus, is about the Son -- of man to be delivered into
5495 444 615 846 5154
23 χεῖρας ἀνθρώπων, καὶ ἀποκτενοῦσιν αὐτόν, καὶ τῇ τρίτῃ
(the) hands of men, and they will kill Him, and on the third
2250 1453 3076 4970
ἡμέρᾳ ἐγερθήσεται. καὶ ἐλυπήθησαν σφόδρα.
day He will be raised. And they grieved exceedingly.
2064 846 1519 2584 4334
24 Ἐλθόντων δὲ αὐτῶν εἰς Καπερναούμ, προσῆλθον οἱ τὰ
coming And they into Capernaum came up those the
1323 2983 4074 2036 1320
δίδραχμα λαμβάνοντες τῷ Πέτρῳ καὶ εἶπον, Ὁ διδάσκαλος
didrachmas receiving to Peter, and said, The teacher
5216 3756 5055 1323 3004 3483 3753 1525 1519
25 ὑμῶν οὐ τελεῖ τὰ δίδραχμα ; λέγει, Ναί. καὶ ὅτε εἰσῆλθεν εἰς
of you not pays the didrachma? He says, Yes. And when he entered into
3614 4399 846 2424 3004 5101 4671
τὴν οἰκίαν, προέφθασεν αὐτὸν ὁ Ἰησοῦς, λέγων, Τί σοι
the house, anticipated him — Jesus, saying, What you
1380 4613 935 1093 575 5101 2983
δοκεῖ, Σίμων ; οἱ βασιλεῖς τῆς γῆς ἀπὸ τίνων λαμβάνουσι
think, Simon? The kings of the earth, from whom do they receive
5056 2228 2778 575 5207 848 2228 575
τέλη ἢ κῆνσον ; ἀπὸ τῶν υἱῶν αὐτῶν, ἢ ἀπὸ τῶν
custom or poll-tax? From the sons of them, or from the
245 3004 846 4074 575 245
26 ἀλλοτρίων ; λέγει αὐτῷ ὁ Πέτρος, Ἀπὸ τῶν ἀλλοτρίων.
strangers? says to Him Peter, From the strangers.
5346 846 2424 686 1658 1526 5207 2443 3361
27 ἔφη αὐτῷ ὁ Ἰησοῦς, Ἄραγε ἐλεύθεροί εἰσιν οἱ υἱοί. ἵνα δὲ μὴ
said to him Jesus, Then indeed free are the sons. that But not
4624 846 4198 1519 2281 906
σκανδαλίσωμεν αὐτούς, πορευθεὶς εἰς τὴν θάλασσαν βάλε
we may offend them, having gone to the sea, throw
44 305 4413 2486 142
ἄγκιστρον, καὶ τὸν ἀναβάντα πρῶτον ἰχθὺν ἆρον· καὶ
a hook, and the coming up first fish take, and
455 4750 848 2147 4715 1565 2983
ἀνοίξας τὸ στόμα αὐτοῦ, εὑρήσεις στατῆρα· ἐκεῖνον λαβὼν
opening the mouth of it, you will find a stater; that taking
1325 846 473 1700 4675
δὸς αὐτοῖς ἀντὶ ἐμοῦ καὶ σοῦ.
give them for Me and you.

CHAPTER 18

[1]In that hour the disciples came to Jesus, saying, Who then is greater in the kingdom of Heaven?

1722 1565 5610 4334 3101 2424
1 Ἐν ἐκείνῃ τῇ ὥρᾳ προσῆλθον οἱ μαθηταὶ τῷ Ἰησοῦ,
In that — hour came up the disciples — to Jesus.
3004 5101 686 3187 2076 1722 932 3772
λέγοντες Τίς ἄρα μείζων ἐστὶν ἐν τῇ βασιλείᾳ τῶν οὐρα-
saying, Who then greater is in the kingdom of the heavens?

[2]And having called forward
a little child, Jesus set him
in their midst. [3]And *He*
said, Truly I say to you,
Unless you convert, and
become as the little children, not at all can you enter
into the kingdom of
Heaven.
[4]Therefore, whoever will
humble himself as this little
child, this one is the greater
in the kingdom of Heaven.
[5]And whoever will receive
one such little child in My
name receives Me. [6]But
whoever causes one of
these little *ones* believing in
Me to offend, it is better for
him that a millstone turned
by an ass be hung on his
neck, and he be sunk in the
depth of the sea. [7]Woe to
the world from *its* offenses!
It is *a* necessity for the
offenses to come, yet woe
to that man through whom
the offense comes! [8]And if
your hand or your foot
offends you, cut it off and
throw *it* from you—it is
good for you to enter into
life lame or maimed, than
having two hands or two
feet to be thrown into the
everlasting fire. [9]And if
your eye offends you, pluck
it out and throw *it* from
you—for it is good for you
to enter into life one-eyed
than having two eyes to be
thrown into the Hell of fire.

[10]See *that* you do not
despise one of these little
ones, for I tell you that their
angels in Heaven contin-
ually look on the face of My
Father in Heaven. [11]For the
Son of man has come to
save that which was lost.
[12]What do you think? If
there be to any man a
hundred sheep, and one of
them strays away, will he

4341 2424 3813 2476
2 νῶν; καὶ προσκαλεσάμενος ὁ Ἰησοῦς παιδίον ἔστησεν
And calling forward — Jesus a child, He set
846 1722 3319 848 2036 281 3004 5213 1437 336
3 αὐτὸ ἐν μέσῳ αὐτῶν, καὶ εἶπεν, Ἀμὴν λέγω ὑμῖν, ἐὰν μὴ
him in the midst of them, and said, Truly I say to you, except
4762 1096 5613 3813 =3364= 1525 1519
στραφῆτε καὶ γένησθε ὡς τὰ παιδία, οὐ μὴ εἰσέλθητε εἰς τὴν
you convert and become as the children, cannot you enter into the
932 3772 3748 3767 5013 1438 5613
4 βασιλείαν τῶν οὐρανῶν. ὅστις οὖν ταπεινώσῃ ἑαυτὸν ὡς τὸ
kingdom of the heavens. Whoever then will humble himself as —
3813 5124 3778 2076 3187 1722 932
παιδίον τοῦτο, οὗτός ἐστιν ὁ μείζων ἐν τῇ βασιλείᾳ τῶν
child this, this (one) is the greater in the kingdom of the
3772 3739 1437 1209 3813 5108 1722 1909
5 οὐρανῶν. καὶ ὃς ἐὰν δέξηται παιδίον τοιοῦτον ἓν ἐπὶ τῷ
heavens. And whoever receives child such one on the
3686 3450 1691 1209 3739 302 4624 1520
6 ὀνόματί μου, ἐμὲ δέχεται· ὃς δ' ἂν σκανδαλίσῃ ἕνα τῶν
name of Me, Me receives. who But ever causes to offend one of
3398 5130 4100 1519 1691 4851 846 2443
μικρῶν τούτων τῶν πιστευόντων εἰς ἐμέ, συμφέρει αὐτῷ ἵνα
little (ones) these — believing in Me, it is gain for him that
2910 3458 3684 1909 5137 848 2670
κρεμασθῇ μύλος ὀνικὸς ἐπὶ τὸν τράχηλον αὐτοῦ, καὶ κατα-
be hung a millstone an ass's on the neck of him, and he be
1722 3989 2281 3759 2889
7 ποντισθῇ ἐν τῷ πελάγει τῆς θαλάσσης. οὐαὶ τῷ κόσμῳ
sunk in the depth of the sea. Woe to the world
575 4625 318 1063 2076 2064 4625
ἀπὸ τῶν σκανδάλων· ἀνάγκη γάρ ἐστιν ἐλθεῖν τὰ σκάνδαλα·
from offenses; necessity for it to come the offenses,
4133 3759 444 1565 1223 3739 4625
πλὴν οὐαὶ τῷ ἀνθρώπῳ ἐκείνῳ, δι' οὗ τὸ σκάνδαλον
yet woe to man that through whom the offense
2064 1487 5495 4675 4228 4675 4624
8 ἔρχεται. εἰ δὲ ἡ χείρ σου ἢ ὁ πούς σου σκανδαλίζει σε,
comes! if And the hand of you or the foot of you offends you,
1581 846 906 575 4675 2570 4671 2076 1525
ἔκκοψον αὐτὰ καὶ βάλε ἀπὸ σοῦ· καλόν σοι ἐστὶν εἰσελθεῖν
cut off it and throw from you; good for you it is to enter
1519 2222 5560 2228 2948 2228 1417 5495 2228 1417 4228
εἰς τὴν ζωὴν χωλὸν ἢ κυλλόν, ἢ δύο χεῖρας ἢ δύο πόδας
into — life lame or maimed than two hands or two feet
2192 906 1519 4442 166 1487 3788
9 ἔχοντα βληθῆναι εἰς τὸ πῦρ τὸ αἰώνιον. καὶ εἰ ὁ ὀφθαλμός
having to be thrown into the fire everlasting. And if the eye
4675 4625 4571 1807 846 906 575 4675 2570
σου σκανδαλίζει σε, ἔξελε αὐτὸν καὶ βάλε ἀπὸ σοῦ· καλόν
of you offends you, pluck out it and throw from you; good
4671 2076 3442 1519 2222 1525 2228 1417 3788
σοι ἐστὶ μονόφθαλμον εἰς τὴν ζωὴν εἰσελθεῖν, ἢ δύο ὀφθαλ-
for you it is one-eyed into life to enter, than two eyes
2192 906 1519 1067 4442 3708 3361
10 μοὺς ἔχοντα βληθῆναι εἰς τὴν γέενναν τοῦ πυρός. ὁρᾶτε μὴ
having to be thrown into Gehenna of fire. See (that) not
2706 1520 3398 5130 3004 1063 5213
καταφρονήσητε ἑνὸς τῶν μικρῶν τούτων, λέγω γὰρ ὑμῖν
you despise one of little ones these; I for you
3754 32 848 1722 3772 1223 3956 991
ὅτι οἱ ἄγγελοι αὐτῶν ἐν οὐρανοῖς διὰ παντὸς βλέπουσι τὸ
that the angels of them in heavens always behold the
4383 3962 3450 3772 2064 1063
11 πρόσωπον τοῦ πατρός μου τοῦ ἐν οὐρανοῖς. ἦλθε γὰρ ὁ
face of the Father of Me in heavens. is come For the
5207 444 4982 622 5102 5213 1380 1437
12 υἱὸς τοῦ ἀνθρώπου σῶσαι τὸ ἀπολωλός. τί ὑμῖν δοκεῖ; ἐὰν
Son of man to save that which was lost. What to you seems; if
1096 5100 444 1540 4263 4105 1520 1537
γένηταί τινι ἀνθρώπῳ ἑκατὸν πρόβατα, καὶ πλανηθῇ ἓν ἐξ
there be to any man a hundred sheep, and strays one of

not leave the ninety-nine on the mountains; *and* going seek the straying *one*? [13]And if he happens to find it, truly I say to you that he rejoices over it more than over the ninety-nine not going astray. [14]So it is not *the* will before your Father in Heaven that one of these little *ones* should perish.

[15]But if your brother sins against you, go and reprove him between you and him alone. If he hears you, you have gained your brother. [16]But if he does not hear, take one or two more with you, so that on *the* mouth of two or three witnesses every word may stand. [17]But if he fails to hear them, tell *it* to the church. And if he also fails to hear the church, let him be to you as the nations and the tax-collector. [18]Truly I say to you, Whatever you bind on the earth shall occur, having been already bound in Heaven. And whatever you loose on the earth shall be, having been already loosed in Heaven. [19]Again I say to you, If two of you agree on earth as to anything, whatever they shall ask, it shall be to them from My Father in Heaven. [20]For where two or three are gathered together in My name, there I am in their midst.

[21]Then coming up to Him, Peter said, Lord, how often shall my brother sin against me, and I forgive him? Until seven times? [22]Jesus said to him, I do not say to you, Until seven times, but, Until seventy times seven. [23]For this reason the kingdom of

846 3780 863 1768 1909 3735 4198
αὐτῶν· οὐχὶ ἀφεὶς τὰ ἐννενηκονταεννέα, ἐπὶ τὰ ὄρη πορευθεὶς
them, not will he leave the ninety-nine on the mounts, going
2212 4105 1437 1096 2147 846 281
13 ζητεῖ τὸ πλανώμενον; καὶ ἐὰν γένηται εὑρεῖν αὐτό, ἀμὴν
he seeks the straying (one)? And if he happens to find it, truly
3004 5213 3754 5463 1909 846 3123 2228 1909 1768
λέγω ὑμῖν ὅτι χαίρει ἐπ' αὐτῷ μᾶλλον, ἢ ἐπὶ τοῖς ἐννενη-
I say to you that he rejoices over it more than over the ninety-
3361 4105 3779 3756 2076 2307
14 κονταεννέα τοῖς μὴ πεπλανημένοις. οὕτως οὐκ ἔστι θέλημα
nine — not going astray. So not it is the will
1715 3962 5216 1722 3772 2443 622
ἔμπροσθεν τοῦ πατρὸς ὑμῶν τοῦ ἐν οὐρανοῖς, ἵνα ἀπόληται
before the Father of you in Heaven that should perish
1520 3398 5130
εἷς τῶν μικρῶν τούτων.
one of little (ones) these.
1437 264 1519 4571 80 4675 5217
15 Ἐὰν δὲ ἁμαρτήσῃ εἰς σὲ ὁ ἀδελφός σου, ὕπαγε καὶ
if But sins against you the brother of you, go and
1651 846 3342 4675 846 3441 1437 4675
ἔλεγξον αὐτὸν μεταξὺ σοῦ καὶ αὐτοῦ μόνου. ἐάν σου
reprove him between you and him alone. If you
191 2770 80 4675 1437 3361 191
16 ἀκούσῃ, ἐκέρδησας τὸν ἀδελφόν σου· ἐὰν δὲ μὴ ἀκούσῃ,
he hear, you have gained the brother of you; if but not he hear,
3880 3326 4675 2089 1520 1417 2443 1909 4750 1417
παράλαβε μετὰ σοῦ ἔτι ἕνα ἢ δύο, ἵνα ἐπὶ στόματος δύο
take along with you besides one or two, that upon (the) mouth of two
3144 2228 5140 2476 3956 4487 1437 3878
17 μαρτύρων ἢ τριῶν σταθῇ πᾶν ῥῆμα. ἐὰν δὲ παρακούσῃ
witnesses or three may stand every word. if But he fails to hear
846 2036 1577 1437 1577
αὐτῶν, εἰπὲ τῇ ἐκκλησίᾳ· ἐὰν δὲ καὶ τῆς ἐκκλησίας
them, tell to the church; if and even the church
3878 2077 4671 5618 1482 5057 281
18 παρακούσῃ, ἔστω σοι ὥσπερ ὁ ἐθνικὸς καὶ ὁ τελώνης. ἀμὴν
he fails to hear, let him be to you as the nations and the tax-collector. Truly
3004 5213 3745 1437 1210 1909 1093 2071 1210 1722
λέγω ὑμῖν, ὅσα ἐὰν δήσητε ἐπὶ τῆς γῆς, ἔσται δεδεμένα ἐν
I say to you, whatever you bind on the earth shall occur, being bound in
3772 3745 1437 3089 1909 1093 2071 3089
τῷ οὐρανῷ· καὶ ὅσα ἐὰν λύσητε ἐπὶ τῆς γῆς, ἔσται λελυμένα
Heaven; and whatever you loose on the earth shall occur, being
1722 3772 3825 3004 5213 3754 1437 1417 5216 4856 loosed
19 ἐν τῷ οὐρανῷ. πάλιν λέγω ὑμῖν, ὅτι ἐὰν δύο ὑμῶν συμφωνή-
in Heaven. Again, I say to you that if two of you may agree
1909 1093 4012 3956 4229 3739 1437 154
σωσιν ἐπὶ τῆς γῆς περὶ παντὸς πράγματος οὗ ἐὰν αἰτή-
on the earth concerning every matter, whatever they
1096 846 3844 3962 3450 1722
σωνται, γενήσεται αὐτοῖς παρὰ τοῦ πατρός μου τοῦ ἐν
may ask it shall occur to them from the Father of Me in
3772 3757 1063 1526 1417 2228 5140 4863 1519 1699
20 οὐρανοῖς. οὗ γάρ εἰσι δύο ἢ τρεῖς συνηγμένοι εἰς τὸ ἐμὸν
heavens. where For are two or three gathered together in My
3686 1563 1519 1722 3319 846
ὄνομα, ἐκεῖ εἰμι ἐν μέσῳ αὐτῶν.
name. there I am in midst of them.
5119 4334 846 4074 2036 2962 4212
21 Τότε προσελθὼν αὐτῷ ὁ Πέτρος εἶπε, Κύριε, ποσάκις
Then coming up to Him Peter said, Lord, how often
264 1519 1691 80 3450 863 846 2193
ἁμαρτήσει εἰς ἐμὲ ὁ ἀδελφός μου, καὶ ἀφήσω αὐτῷ; ἕως
shall sin against me the brother of me, and I forgive him? Until
2034 3004 846 2424 3956 3004 4671 2193 2034
22 ἑπτάκις; λέγει αὐτῷ ὁ Ἰησοῦς, Οὐ λέγω σοι ἕως ἑπτάκις,
seven times? Says to him Jesus, not I say to you until seven times,
235 2193 1441 2033 1223 5121 3666
23 ἀλλ' ἕως ἑβδομηκοντάκις ἑπτά. διὰ τοῦτο ὡμοιώθη ἡ
but until seventy times seven. For this reason was likened the

Heaven has been compared to a man, a king who decided to take account with his slaves. 24 And when he began to reckon, one debtor of ten thousand talents was brought near to him. 25 But he not having *any* to pay, the lord commanded him to be sold, also his wife and children, and all things, as much as he had, even to pay back. 26 Then falling down, the slave bowed the knee to him, saying, Lord, have patience with me, and I will pay all to you. 27 And being filled with pity, the lord of that slave released him, and forgave him the loan. 28 But going out, that slave found one of his fellow-slaves who owed him a hundred denarii. And seizing him, he choked *him,* saying, Pay me whatever you owe. 29 Then falling down at his feet, his fellow-slave begged him, saying, Have patience with me, and I will pay all to you. 30 But he would not, but going away he threw him into prison, until he pay back the *amount* owing.

31 But his fellow-slaves seeing the things happening, they were greatly grieved. And coming *they* reported to their lord all the things happening. 32 Then calling him near, his lord said to him, Wicked slave! I forgave you all that debt, since you begged me. 33 Ought you not also to favor your fellow-slave, as I also favored you? 34 And being angry, his lord delivered him up to the tormentors until he pay back all that debt to him. 35 So also My heavenly Father will do to

932 3772 444 935 3739 2309
βασιλεία τῶν οὐρανῶν ἀνθρώπῳ βασιλεῖ, ὃς ἠθέλησε
kingdom of the heavens to a man, a king, who decided
4868 3056 3326 1401 848 756
24 συνᾶραι λόγον μετὰ τῶν δούλων αὐτοῦ. ἀρξαμένου δὲ
to take account with the slaves of him. beginning And
846 4868 4374 846 1520 3781 3463
αὐτοῦ συναίρειν, προσηνέχθη αὐτῷ εἷς ὀφειλέτης μυρίων
him to reckon, was brought near to him one debtor of ten thousand
5007 3361 2192 846 591 2753 846
25 ταλάντων. μὴ ἔχοντος δὲ αὐτοῦ ἀποδοῦναι, ἐκέλευσεν αὐτὸν
talents. not having And he to repay, commanded him
2962 848 4097 1135 848
ὁ κύριος αὐτοῦ πραθῆναι, καὶ τὴν γυναῖκα αὐτοῦ καὶ τὰ
the lord of him to be sold, and the wife of him and the
5043 3956 3745 2192 591 4098 3767
26 τέκνα, καὶ πάντα ὅσα εἶχε, καὶ ἀποδοθῆναι. πεσὼν οὖν ὁ
children, and all as much as he had, and to pay back. Falling then the
1401 4352 846 3004 2962 3114 1909
δοῦλος προσεκύνει αὐτῷ, λέγων, Κύριε, μακροθύμησον ἐπ'
slave bowed the knee to him, saying, Lord, have patience over
1698 3956 4671 591 4697 2962
27 ἐμοί, καὶ πάντα σοι ἀποδώσω. σπλαγχνισθεὶς δὲ ὁ κύριος
me, and all to you I will repay. filled with pity And, the lord
1401 1565 630 846 1156 863
τοῦ δούλου ἐκείνου ἀπέλυσεν αὐτόν, καὶ τὸ δάνειον ἀφῆκεν
slave of that released him, and the loan forgave
846 1831 1401 1565 2147 1520 4889
28 αὐτῷ. ἐξελθὼν δὲ ὁ δοῦλος ἐκεῖνος εὗρεν ἕνα τῶν συνδούλων
him. going out But slave that found one of the fellow-slaves
848 3739 3784 846 1540 1220 2902
αὐτοῦ, ὃς ὤφειλεν αὐτῷ ἑκατὸν δηνάρια, καὶ κρατήσας
of him, who owed him a hundred denarii, and seizing
846 4155 3004 591 3427 -3748- 3784 4098 3767
29 αὐτὸν ἔπνιγε, λέγων, Ἀπόδος μοι ὅ τι ὀφείλεις. πεσὼν οὖν
him he throttled, saying, Pay back to me what ever you owe Falling then
4889 848 1519 4228 848 3870 846
ὁ σύνδουλος αὐτοῦ εἰς τοὺς πόδας αὐτοῦ παρεκάλει αὐτόν,
the fellow-slave of him to the feet of him begged him,
3004 3114 1909 1698 3956 591 4671
λέγων, Μακροθύμησον ἐπ' ἐμοί, καὶ πάντα ἀποδώσω σοι.
saying, Have patience over me and all I will repay to you.
3756 2309 235 565 906 846 1519 5438
30 ὁ δὲ οὐκ ἤθελεν, ἀλλ' ἀπελθὼν ἔβαλεν αὐτὸν εἰς φυλακήν,
he but not willed (it), but going away threw him into prison
2193 3757 591 3784 1492 4889 848
31 ἕως οὗ ἀποδῷ τὸ ὀφειλόμενον. ἰδόντες δὲ οἱ σύνδουλοι αὐτοῦ
until he pay back that owing. seeing And the fellow-slaves of him
1096 3076 4970 2064 1285
τὰ γενόμενα ἐλυπήθησαν σφόδρα· καὶ ἐλθόντες διεσάφησαν
that occurring, they were greived greatly, and coming reported
2962 848 3956 1096 5119 4341
32 τῷ κυρίῳ αὐτῶν πάντα τὰ γενόμενα. τότε προσκαλεσά-
to the lord of them all the (things) occurring. Then calling near
846 2962 848 3004 846 1401 4190
μενος αὐτὸν ὁ κύριος αὐτοῦ λέγει αὐτῷ, Δοῦλε πονηρέ,
him, the lord of him says to him, slave Wicked,
3956 3782 1565 863 4671 1893 3870 3165
πᾶσαν τὴν ὀφειλὴν ἐκείνην ἀφῆκά σοι, ἐπεὶ παρεκάλεσάς με·
all debt that I forgave you, since you begged me.
3767 1163 4571 1653 4889 4675 5613 1473 4571
33 οὐκ ἔδει καὶ σὲ ἐλεῆσαι τὸν σύνδουλόν σου, ὡς καὶ ἐγώ σε
not Must be even you to favor the fellow-slave of you, as also I you
1653 3710 2962 898 3860 846
34 ἠλέησα; καὶ ὀργισθεὶς ὁ κύριος αὐτοῦ παρέδωκεν αὐτὸν
had favored. And being angry, the lord of him delivered him
930 2193 3739 591 3956 3784 846
τοῖς βασανισταῖς, ἕως οὗ ἀποδῷ πᾶν τὸ ὀφειλόμενον αὐτῷ.
to the tormentors, until that he repay all that debt to him.
3779 3962 3450 2032 4160 5213 -3362=
35 οὕτω καὶ ὁ πατήρ μου ὁ ἐπουράνιος ποιήσει ὑμῖν, ἐὰν μὴ
So also the Father of Me heavenly will do to you, unless

NOTE: Frequent words not numbered: δέ(1161); καί(2531)—and, but; ὁ, ἡ, τό (3588, the)— * above word, look in verse margin for No.

you unless each of you from your hearts forgive his brother their offenses.

CHAPTER 19

1 And it happened when Jesus had finished these words, He moved from Galilee and came into the borders of Judea beyond the Jordan. 2 And great crowds followed Him; and He healed them there.

3 And the Pharisees came near to Him, tempting Him, and saying to Him, Is it lawful for a man to put away his wife for every reason? 4 But answering He said to them, Have you not read that He who created them from the beginning created them male and female? 5 And He said, "For this reason a man shall leave father and mother, and shall be joined to his wife, and the two shall become one flesh." 6 So that they are no longer two, but one flesh. Therefore, what God has joined together, let not man separate.

7 They said to Him, Why then did Moses command to give a bill of divorce, and to put her away? 8 He said to them, In view of your hardheartedness Moses allowed you to put away your wives. But from the beginning it was not so. 9 And I say to you, Whoever shall put away his wife, if not for fornication, and shall marry another, *that one* commits adultery. And the *one* who marries her *who was* put away commits adultery.

10 His disciples said to Him, If the case of the man be so with his wife, it is not good to marry. 11 But He said to them, Not all receive this word, but *those* to

863 1538 80 848 575 2588 5216
ἀφῆτε ἕκαστος τῷ ἀδελφῷ αὐτοῦ ἀπὸ τῶν καρδιῶν ὑμῶν τὰ
you forgive each one the brother of him from the hearts of you the
3900 848
παραπτώματα αὐτῶν.
offenses of them.

CHAPTER 19

1096 3753 5055 2424 3056 5128
1 Καὶ ἐγένετο ὅτε ἐτέλεσεν ὁ Ἰησοῦς τοὺς λόγους τούτους,
And it was, when ended – Jesus – words these,
3332 575 1056 2064 1519 3725
μετῆρεν ἀπὸ τῆς Γαλιλαίας, καὶ ἦλθεν εἰς τὰ ὅρια τῆς
He moved from – Galilee and came into the borders –
2449 4008 2446 190 846
2 Ἰουδαίας πέραν τοῦ Ἰορδάνου. καὶ ἠκολούθησαν αὐτῷ
of Judea, across the Jordan. And followed Him
3793 4183 2323 846 1563
ὄχλοι πολλοί, καὶ ἐθεράπευσεν αὐτοὺς ἐκεῖ.
crowds much, and He healed them there.
4334 846 5330 3985 846
3 Καὶ προσῆλθον αὐτῷ οἱ Φαρισαῖοι πειράζοντες αὐτόν,
And approached him the Pharisees, tempting Him
3004 846/1487 1832 444 630
καὶ λέγοντες αὐτῷ, Εἰ ἔξεστιν ἀνθρώπῳ ἀπολῦσαι τὴν
and saying to Him, If it is lawful for a man to put away the
1135 848 2596 3956 156 611 2036
4 γυναῖκα αὐτοῦ κατὰ πᾶσαν αἰτίαν ; ὁ δὲ ἀποκριθεὶς εἶπεν
wife of him for every reason? He And answering said
848 3756 314 3754 4160 575 746 730
αὐτοῖς, Οὐκ ἀνέγνωτε ὅτι ὁ ποιήσας ἀπ' ἀρχῆς ἄρσεν καὶ
to them, not Did you read that He making from beginning male and
2338 4160 846 2036 1752 5127 2641
5 θῆλυ ἐποίησεν αὐτούς, καὶ εἶπεν, Ἕνεκεν τούτου καταλείψει
female made them? And He said, For the sake of this shall leave
444 3962 3384 4347
ἄνθρωπος τὸν πατέρα καὶ τὴν μητέρα, καὶ προσκολληθή-
a man – father and – mother, and shall be joined to
1135 848 2071 1417 1519 4561 3391
σεται τῇ γυναικὶ αὐτοῦ, καὶ ἔσονται οἱ δύο εἰς σάρκα μίαν ;
the wife of him; and shall be the two for flesh one;
5620 3765 1526 1417 235 4561 3391 3767 2316 4801
6 ὥστε οὐκέτι εἰσὶ δύο, ἀλλὰ σὰρξ μία· ὃ οὖν ὁ Θεὸς συνέζευξεν,
so that no longer are they two, but flesh one. What then God yoked together
444 3361 5563 3004 846 5101 3767 3475
7 ἄνθρωπος μὴ χωριζέτω. λέγουσιν αὐτῷ, Τί οὖν Μωσῆς
man do not let separate. They say to Him, Why then Moses
1781 1325 975 647 630
ἐνετείλατο δοῦναι βιβλίον ἀποστασίου, καὶ ἀπολῦσαι
did command to give a bill of divorce, and to put away
846 3004 846 3754 3475 4314 4641
8 αὐτήν ; λέγει αὐτοῖς ὅτι Μωσῆς πρὸς τὴν σκληροκαρδίαν
her? He says to them, – Moses in view of the hardheartedness
5216 2010 5213 630 1135 5216 575
ὑμῶν ἐπέτρεψεν ὑμῖν ἀπολῦσαι τὰς γυναῖκας ὑμῶν· ἀπ'
of you allowed you to put away the wives of you. from
•3739 746 3756 1096 3779 3004 5213 3754 • 302 630
9 ἀρχῆς δὲ οὐ γέγονεν οὕτω. λέγω δὲ ὑμῖν ὅτι ὃς ἂν ἀπολύσῃ
the beginning but not it was so. I say And to you that whoever puts away
1135 848 =1508= 1909 4202 1060 243
τὴν γυναῖκα αὐτοῦ, εἰ μὴ ἐπὶ πορνείᾳ, καὶ γαμήσῃ ἄλλην,
the wife of him, if not for fornication, and shall marry another,
3429 630 1060 3429 3004
10 μοιχᾶται· καὶ ὁ ἀπολελυμένην γαμήσας μοιχᾶται. λέγουσιν
commits adultery and he her put away marrying commits adultery. Say
846 3101 848 1487 3779 2076 156
αὐτῷ οἱ μαθηταὶ αὐτοῦ, Εἰ οὕτως ἐστὶν ἡ αἰτία τοῦ
to Him the disciples of Him, If thus is the case of the
444 3326 1135 3756 4851 1060 2036
11 ἀνθρώπου μετὰ τῆς γυναικός, οὐ συμφέρει γαμῆσαι. ὁ δὲ εἶπεν
man with the wife, not it is gain to marry. He But said

NOTE: Frequent words not numbered: δέ(1161); καί(2531)—and, but; ὁ, ἡ, τό (3588, the)— * above word, look in verse margin for No.

whom it is given. 12 For there are eunuchs who were born thus from *their* mother's womb, and there are eunuchs who were made eunuchs by men; and there are eunuchs who made eunuchs *of* themselves for the sake of the kingdom of Heaven. He who is able to receive, let him receive *it.*

13 Then little children were brought to Him, that He might lay hands on them and might pray. But the disciples rebuked them. 14 But Jesus said, Allow the little children and do not prevent them to come to Me; for of such is the kingdom of Heaven. 15 And laying hands on them, He went away from there.

16 And, behold, coming near one said to Him, Good Teacher, what good thing shall I do that I may have eternal life? 17 And He said to him, Why do you call Me good? No one *is* good except One, God! But if you desire to enter into life, keep the commandments. 18 He said to Him, Which? And Jesus said, "You shall not commit murder; do not commit adultery; do not steal; do not bear false witness; 19 honor your father and your mother;" and, "You shall love your neighbor as yourself." 20 The young man said to Him, All these things I have kept from my youth. What do I still lack? 21 Jesus said to him, If you desire to be perfect, go sell your property and give to *the* poor, and you will have treasure in Heaven; and come, follow Me. 22 But hearing the word, being grieved, the young man went away—for he had many possessions.

NOTE: F---

846 3756 3956 5562 3056 5126 235 3739
αὐτοῖς, Οὐ πάντες χωροῦσι τὸν λόγον τοῦτον, ἀλλ' οἷς
to them, Not all make room for word this. Only to whom
1325 1526 1063 2135 3748 1537 2836 3384
12 δέδοται. εἰσὶ γὰρ εὐνοῦχοι, οἵτινες ἐκ κοιλίας μητρὸς
it is given, there are For eunuchs who from (the) womb of a mother
1080 3779 1526 2135 3748 2134
ἐγεννήθησαν οὕτω· καί εἰσιν εὐνοῦχοι, οἵτινες εὐνουχίσθησαν
were born so; and there are eunuchs who were made eunuchs
5259 444 1526 2135 3748 2134
ὑπὸ τῶν ἀνθρώπων· καί εἰσιν εὐνοῦχοι, οἵτινες εὐνούχισαν
by men; and there are eunuchs who made eunuchs
1438 1223 932 3772 1410
ἑαυτοὺς διὰ τὴν βασιλείαν τῶν οὐρανῶν. ὁ δυνάμενος
(of) themselves due to the kingdom of the heavens. The (one) able
5562 5562
χωρεῖν χωρείτω.
to receive, let him receive (it).

5119 4374 846 3813 2443 5495 2007
13 Τότε προσηνέχθη αὐτῷ παιδία, ἵνα τὰς χεῖρας ἐπιθῇ
Then were brought to Him children, that — hands He might lay
846 4336 3101 2008 846
αὐτοῖς, καὶ προσεύξηται· οἱ δὲ μαθηταὶ ἐπετίμησαν αὐτοῖς.
on them and to pray; the but disciples rebuked them.
2424 2036 863 3813 3361 2967 846
14 ὁ δὲ Ἰησοῦς εἶπεν, Ἄφετε τὰ παιδία, καὶ μὴ κωλύετε αὐτὰ
— But Jesus said, Permit the children, and not do prevent them
2064 4314 3165 1063 5108 2076 932
ἐλθεῖν πρός με· τῶν γὰρ τοιούτων ἐστὶν ἡ βασιλεία τῶν
to come to Me; — for of such is the kingdom of the
3772 2007 846 5495 4198 1564
15 οὐρανῶν. καὶ ἐπιθεὶς αὐτοῖς τὰς χεῖρας, ἐπορεύθη ἐκεῖθεν.
heavens. And laying on them — hands, He went away from there.
2400 1520 4334 2036 846 1320 18
16 Καὶ ἰδού, εἷς προσελθὼν εἶπεν αὐτῷ, Διδάσκαλε ἀγαθέ,
And behold! One coming near said to Him, teacher Good
5101 18 4160 2443 2192 2222 166 2036 846
17 τί ἀγαθὸν ποιήσω, ἵνα ἔχω ζωὴν αἰώνιον ; ὁ δὲ εἶπεν αὐτῷ,
what good shall I do that I may have life eternal? He And said to him,
5101 3165 3004 18 3762 18 1508 1520 2316 1487
Τί με λέγεις ἀγαθόν ; οὐδεὶς ἀγαθός, εἰ μὴ εἷς, ὁ Θεός. εἰ δὲ
Why Me you call good? No one (is) good except One, — God. if But
2309 1525 1519 2222 5083 1755 3004
18 θέλεις εἰσελθεῖν εἰς τὴν ζωήν, τήρησον τὰς ἐντολάς. λέγει
you desire to enter into — life, keep the commands. He says
846 4169 2424 2036 3756 5407 3756 3431
αὐτῷ, Ποίας ; ὁ δὲ Ἰησοῦς εἶπε, Τὸ οὐ φονεύσεις· οὐ μοιχεύ-
to Him, Which? — And Jesus said, not You shall murder; not commit
3756 2813 3756 5576 5091 3962
19 σεις· οὐ κλέψεις· οὐ ψευδομαρτυρήσεις· τίμα τὸν πατέρα
adultery; not steal; not bear false witness; honor — father
4675 3384 25 4139 4675 5613
σου καὶ τὴν μητέρα· καί, ἀγαπήσεις τὸν πλησίον σου ὡς
your and — mother; and, you shall love the neighbor of you as
4572 3004 846 3495 3956 5023 5442
20 σεαυτόν. λέγει αὐτῷ ὁ νεανίσκος, Πάντα ταῦτα ἐφυλαξάμην
yourself. says to Him The young man, All these things I have kept
1537 3503 3450 5101 2089 5302 5346 846 2424 1487 2309
21 ἐκ νεότητός μου· τί ἔτι ὑστερῶ ; ἔφη αὐτῷ ὁ Ἰησοῦς, Εἰ θέλεις
from my youth; What yet do I lack? said to him — Jesus, If you wish
5046 1511 1217 4453 4675 5224 1325
τέλειος εἶναι, ὕπαγε, πώλησόν σου τὰ ὑπάρχοντα καὶ δὸς
perfect to be, go sell your — property and give
4434 2192 2344 1722 3772 1204 190
πτωχοῖς, καὶ ἕξεις θησαυρὸν ἐν οὐρανῷ· καὶ δεῦρο, ἀκολούθει
to (the) poor, and you will have treasure in Heaven; and come, follow
3427 191 3495 3056 565 3076
22 μοι. ἀκούσας δὲ ὁ νεανίσκος τὸν λόγον ἀπῆλθε λυπούμενος·
Me. hearing But the young man the word went away grieving,
2258 1063 2192 2933 4183
ἦν γὰρ ἔχων κτήματα πολλά.
he was for having possessions many.

23 And Jesus said to His disciples, Truly I say to you that a rich man will with great difficulty enter into the kingdom of Heaven. 24 And again I say to you, It is easier for a camel to pass through a needle's eye than for a rich man to enter the kingdom of God. 25 And His disciples were exceedingly astonished when they heard this, saying, Who then can be saved? 26 But looking on *them,* Jesus said to them, With men this is impossible, but with God all things are possible.

27 Then answering, Peter said to Him, Behold, we left all things and followed You. What then shall be to us? 28 And Jesus said to them, Truly I say to you, You who have followed Me; in the regeneration, when the Son of man sits on the throne of His glory, you also will sit on twelve thrones, judging the twelve tribes of Israel. 29 And everyone who left houses, or brothers, or sisters, or father, or mother, or wife, or children, or lands, for My name's sake shall receive a hundredfold, and shall inherit everlasting life. 30 But many first *ones* shall be last, and last *ones* first.

2424 2036 3101 848 281 3004 5213
23 Ὁ δὲ Ἰησοῦς εἶπε τοῖς μαθηταῖς αὐτοῦ, Ἀμὴν λέγω ὑμῖν
And Jesus said to the disciples of Him, Truly, I say to you
3754 1423 4145 1525 1519 932
ὅτι δυσκόλως πλούσιος εἰσελεύσεται εἰς τὴν βασιλείαν τῶν
that with difficulty a rich man will enter into the kingdom of the
3772 3825 3004 5213 2123 2076 2574
24 οὐρανῶν. πάλιν δὲ λέγω ὑμῖν, εὐκοπώτερόν ἐστι κάμηλον
heavens. again And I tell you easier It is a camel
1223 5169 4476 1330 4145 1519 932
διὰ τρυπήματος ῥαφίδος διελθεῖν, ἢ πλούσιον εἰς τὴν βασι-
through (the) eye of a needle to pass, than a rich man into the king-
2316 1525 191 3101 848
25 λείαν τοῦ Θεοῦ εἰσελθεῖν. ἀκούσαντες δὲ οἱ μαθηταὶ αὐτοῦ
dom of God to enter. having heard And the disciples of Him
1605 4970 3004 5101 1686 1410 4982
ἐξεπλήσσοντο σφόδρα, λέγοντες, Τίς ἄρα δύναται σωθῆναι;
were astonished exceedingly, saying, Who then is able to be saved?
1689 2424 2036 846 3844 444 5124
26 ἐμβλέψας δὲ ὁ Ἰησοῦς εἶπεν αὐτοῖς, Παρὰ ἀνθρώποις τοῦτο
looking But – Jesus said to them, With men this
102 2076 3844 2316 3956 1415 2076 5119
27 ἀδύνατόν ἐστι, παρὰ δὲ Θεῷ πάντα δυνατά ἐστι. Τότε
impossible is, with But God all things possible are Then
611 4074 2036 846 2400 2249 863
ἀποκριθεὶς ὁ Πέτρος εἶπεν αὐτῷ, Ἰδού, ἡμεῖς ἀφήκαμεν
answering – Peter said to Him. Behold, we left
3956 190 4671 5101 686 2071 2254 2424
28 πάντα καὶ ἠκολουθήσαμέν σοι· τί ἄρα ἔσται ἡμῖν; ὁ δὲ Ἰη-
all things and followed You. What then shall be to us? – And
2036 846 281 3004 5213 3754 5210 190
σοῦς εἶπεν αὐτοῖς, Ἀμὴν λέγω ὑμῖν ὅτι ὑμεῖς οἱ ἀκολουθή-
Jesus said to them, Truly I tell you that you the (ones) having
3427 1722 3824 3752 2523 5207
σαντές μοι, ἐν τῇ παλιγγενεσίᾳ ὅταν καθίσῃ ὁ υἱὸς τοῦ
followed Me, in the regeneration, when sits the Son –
444 1909 2362 1391 848 2523 5210 1909
ἀνθρώπου ἐπὶ θρόνου δόξης αὐτοῦ, καθίσεσθε καὶ ὑμεῖς ἐπὶ
of man on (the) throne of glory of Him, You will sit even you on
1427 2362 2919 1427 5443 2474
δώδεκα θρόνους, κρίνοντες τὰς δώδεκα φυλὰς τοῦ Ἰσραήλ.
twelve thrones judging the twelve tribes of Israel.
3956 3739 863 3614 2228 80 2228 79 2228 3962
29 καὶ πᾶς ὃς ἀφῆκεν οἰκίας, ἢ ἀδελφούς, ἢ ἀδελφάς, ἢ πατέρα,
And everyone who left houses, or brothers, or sisters, or father,
2228 3384 2228 1135 2228 5043 2228 68 1752 3686
ἢ μητέρα, ἢ γυναῖκα, ἢ τέκνα, ἢ ἀγρούς, ἕνεκεν τοῦ ὀνόματός
or mother, or wife, or children, or lands, for the sake of the name
3450 1542 2983 2222 166 2816
μου, ἑκατονταπλασίονα λήψεται, καὶ ζωὴν αἰώνιον κλη-
of Me, a hundredfold shall receive, and life eternal shall
4183 2071 4413 2078 2078
30 ρονομήσει. πολλοὶ δὲ ἔσονται πρῶτοι ἔσχατοι, καὶ ἔσχατοι
inherit. many But shall be first last, and last
4413
πρῶτοι.
first.

CHAPTER 20

1 For the kingdom of Heaven is like a man, a housemaster, who went out when *it was* early to hire workers into his vineyard. 2 And agreeing with the workers for a denarius *for* the day, he sent them into

3664 1063 2076 932 3772 444
1 ὁμοία γάρ ἐστιν ἡ βασιλεία τῶν οὐρανῶν ἀνθρώπῳ
like For is the kingdom of the heavens to a man,
3617 3748 1831 260 4404 3409 2040
οἰκοδεσπότῃ, ὅστις ἐξῆλθεν ἅμα πρωῒ μισθώσασθαι ἐργάτας
a housemaster, who went out when early to hire workmen
1519 290 848 4856 3313 2040
2 εἰς τὸν ἀμπελῶνα αὐτοῦ. συμφωνήσας δὲ μετὰ τῶν ἐργατῶν
into the vineyard of him. agreeing And with the workmen
1537 1220 2250 649 846 1519 290
ἐκ δηναρίου τὴν ἡμέραν, ἀπέστειλεν αὐτοὺς εἰς τὸν ἀμπελῶνα
for a denarius the day, he sent them into the vineyard

his vineyard. [3]And going out about the third hour, he saw others standing idle in the market. [4]And he said to them, You also go into the vineyard, and I will give you whatever is just. And they went. [5]Again, going out about *the* sixth and ninth hour, he did the same.

[6]And going out about the eleventh hour, he found others standing idle, and said to them, Why do you stand here idle all day? [7]They said to him, Because no one has hired us. He said to them, You also go into the vineyard, and you will receive whatever is just. [8]But evening coming, the lord of the vineyard said to his manager, Call the workers and pay them the wage, beginning from the last to the first. [9]And the ones coming the eleventh hour each received a denarius.

[10]And coming the first supposed that they would receive more. And they also each received a denarius. [11]And receiving *it,* they murmured against the housemaster, [12]saying, These last have performed one hour, and you have made them equal to us who have borne the burden and the heat of the day. [13]But answering he said to one of them, Friend, I am not unjust to you. Did you not agree to a denarius with me? [14]Take yours and go. But I desire to give to this last as also to you. [15]Or is it not lawful for me to do what I desire with my things? Or is your eye evil because I am good? [16]So the last shall be first, and the first last; for many are called, but few chosen.

848 1831 4012 5154 5610 1492 243
3 αὐτοῦ. καὶ ἐξελθὼν περὶ τὴν τρίτην ὥραν, εἶδεν ἄλλους
of him. And going out about the third hour, he saw others
2476 1722 58 692 2538 2036 5217
4 ἑστῶτας ἐν τῇ ἀγορᾷ ἀργούς· κἀκείνοις εἶπεν, Ὑπάγετε καὶ
standing in the market idle, and to them said, Go also
5210 1519 290 1437 1342 1325 5213
5 ὑμεῖς εἰς τὸν ἀμπελῶνα, καὶ ὃ ἐὰν ᾖ δίκαιον δώσω ὑμῖν. οἱ
you into the vineyard, and whatever is just I will give you. they
565 3825 1831 4012 1622 1766 5610
δὲ ἀπῆλθον. πάλιν ἐξελθὼν περὶ ἕκτην καὶ ἐννάτην ὥραν,
And went. Again going out about (the) sixth and ninth hour,
4160 5615 4012 1734 5610 1831
6 ἐποίησεν ὡσαύτως. περὶ δὲ τὴν ἑνδεκάτην ὥραν ἐξελθών,
he did likewise. about And the eleventh hour, going out,
2147 243 2476 692 3004 846 5101 5602
εὗρεν ἄλλους ἑστῶτας ἀργούς, καὶ λέγει αὐτοῖς, Τί ὧδε
he found others standing idle, and says to them, Why here
2476 3650 2250 692 3004 846 3754
7 ἑστήκατε ὅλην τὴν ἡμέραν ἀργοί; λέγουσιν αὐτῷ, Ὅτι
do you stand all the day idle? They say to him, Because
3762 2248 3409 3004 846 5217 5210 1519
οὐδεὶς ἡμᾶς ἐμισθώσατο. λέγει αὐτοῖς, Ὑπάγετε καὶ ὑμεῖς εἰς
no one us has hired. He says to them, Go also you into
290 1437 /2228/1342 2983 3798 1096
8 τὸν ἀμπελῶνα, καὶ ὃ ἐὰν ᾖ δίκαιον λήψεσθε. ὀψίας δὲ γενο-
the vineyard, and whatever is just you will receive. eve But com-
3004 2962 290 2012 848
μένης λέγει ὁ κύριος τοῦ ἀμπελῶνος τῷ ἐπιτρόπῳ αὐτοῦ,
ing, says the lord of the vineyard to the manager of him,
2564 2040 591 846 3408
Κάλεσον τοὺς ἐργάτας, καὶ ἀπόδος αὐτοῖς τὸν μισθόν,
Call the workmen, and pay them the wage,
756 575 2078 2193 4413 2064
9 ἀρξάμενος ἀπὸ τῶν ἐσχάτων ἕως τῶν πρώτων. καὶ ἐλθόντες
beginning from the last ones until the first. And coming,
4012 1734 5610 2983 303 1220 2064
10 οἱ περὶ τὴν ἑνδεκάτην ὥραν ἔλαβον ἀνὰ δηνάριον. ἐλθόντες
those about the eleventh hour received each a denarius. coming
4413 3543 3754 4119 2983 2983
δὲ οἱ πρῶτοι ἐνόμισαν ὅτι πλείονα λήψονται· καὶ ἔλαβον καὶ
And the first supposed that more they will get; and they got also
846 303 1220 2983 1111 2596
11 αὐτοὶ ἀνὰ δηνάριον. λαβόντες δὲ ἐγόγγυζον κατὰ τοῦ
themselves each a denarius. receiving And they murmured against the
3617 3004 3754 3778 2078 3391 5610
12 οἰκοδεσπότου, λέγοντες ὅτι Οὗτοι οἱ ἔσχατοι μίαν ὥραν
housemaster, saying, These last one hour
4160 2470 2254 846 4160 941
ἐποίησαν, καὶ ἴσους ἡμῖν αὐτοὺς ἐποίησας, τοῖς βαστάσασι
performed and equal to us them you have made, who have borne
922 2250 2942 611
13 τὸ βάρος τῆς ἡμέρας καὶ τὸν καύσωνα. ὁ δὲ ἀποκριθεὶς
the burden of the day and the heat. he But answering
2036 1520 846 2083 3756 91 4571 3780 1220
εἶπεν ἑνὶ αὐτῶν, Ἑταῖρε, οὐκ ἀδικῶ σε· οὐχὶ δηναρίου
said to one of them, Friend, not I am unjust to you; not of a denarius
4856 3427 142 4674 5217 2309 5129
14 συνεφώνησάς μοι; ἆρον τὸ σὸν καὶ ὕπαγε· θέλω δὲ τούτῳ
you agreed with me? Take — yours and go; I desire But to this
2078 1325 5613 4671 2228 3756 1832 3427 4160 3739
15 τῷ ἐσχάτῳ δοῦναι ὡς καὶ σοί. ἢ οὐκ ἔξεστί μοι ποιῆσαι ὃ
— last to give as also to you. Or not is it lawful for me to do what
2309 1722 1689 1487 3788 4675 4190 2076 3754
θέλω ἐν τοῖς ἐμοῖς; εἰ ὁ ὀφθαλμός σου πονηρός ἐστιν, ὅτι
I desire in the things of me; or the eye of you evil is, because
1473 18 1510 3779 2071 2078 4413
16 ἐγὼ ἀγαθός εἰμι; οὕτως ἔσονται οἱ ἔσχατοι πρῶτοι, καὶ οἱ
I good am? So shall be the last first, and the
4413 2078 4183 1063 1526 2822 3641 1588
πρῶτοι ἔσχατοι· πολλοὶ γάρ εἰσι κλητοί, ὀλίγοι δὲ ἐκλεκτοί.
first last; many for are called, few but chosen.

[17]And going up to Jeru-
salem, Jesus took the
twelve disciples aside in
the way, and said to them,
[18]Behold, we are going up
to Jerusalem, and the Son
of man will be betrayed to
the chief priests and
scribes. And they will
condemn Him to death.
[19]And they will deliver Him
up to the heathen to mock,
and to scourge, and to
crucify. And the third day
He will rise again.

[20]Then the mother of the
sons of Zebedee came near
to Him, along with her sons,
bowing the knee and
asking something from
Him. [21]And He said to her,
What do you desire? She
said to Him, Say that these
two sons of mine may sit
one on Your right, and one
on *Your* left in Your
kingdom. [22]But answering
Jesus said, You do not
know what you ask. Are you
able to drink the cup which I
am about to drink, and to be
baptized with the baptism
with which I am to be
baptized? They said to Him,
We are able. [23]And He said
to them, Indeed you shall
drink My cup, and you shall
be baptized with the bap-
tism with which I am bap-
tized; but to sit off My right
and off My left *hand* is not
Mine to give, but *to those*
for whom it was prepared
by My Father.
[24]And hearing, the ten
were indignant about the
two brothers. [25]But having
called them, Jesus said,
You know that the rulers of
the nations exercise lordship over them, and the
great ones exercise authority over them. [26]But it will
not be so among you. But
whoever desires to become
great among you, let him be
your servant. [27]And whoever desires to be first
among you, let him be your

305 2424 1519 2414 3880
17 Καὶ ἀναβαίνων ὁ Ἰησοῦς εἰς Ἱεροσόλυμα παρέλαβε τοὺς
And going up Jesus to Jerusalem He took the
1427 3101 2596 2398 1722 3598 2036 846 2400
18 δώδεκα μαθητὰς κατ' ἰδίαν ἐν τῇ ὁδῷ, καὶ εἶπεν αὐτοῖς, Ἰδού,
twelve disciples privately, in the way and said to them, Behold,
305 1519 2414 5207 444
ἀναβαίνομεν εἰς Ἱεροσόλυμα, καὶ ὁ υἱὸς τοῦ ἀνθρώπου
we are going up to Jerusalem and the Son of man
3860 749 1122 2632
παραδοθήσεται τοῖς ἀρχιερεῦσι καὶ γραμματεῦσι· καὶ κατα-
will be delivered up to the chief priests and scribes. And they
846 2288 3860 846
19 κρινοῦσιν αὐτὸν θανάτῳ, καὶ παραδώσουσιν αὐτὸν τοῖς
will condemn Him to death. And they will deliver up Him to the
1484 1519 1702 3146 4717
ἔθνεσιν εἰς τὸ ἐμπαῖξαι καὶ μαστιγῶσαι καὶ σταυρῶσαι·
nations to mock and to scourge and to crucify
5154 2250 450
καὶ τῇ τρίτῃ ἡμέρᾳ ἀναστήσεται.
And the third day He will rise again.
5119 4334 846 3384 5207 2199 3326
20 Τότε προσῆλθεν αὐτῷ ἡ μήτηρ τῶν υἱῶν Ζεβεδαίου μετὰ
Then came near to Him the mother of the sons of Zebedee with
5207 848 4352 154 5100 3844 848
τῶν υἱῶν αὐτῆς, προσκυνοῦσα καὶ αἰτοῦσά τι παρ' αὐτοῦ.
the sons of her, bowing the knee and asking something from Him.
2036 846 5101 2309 3004 846 2036 2443 2523
21 ὁ δὲ εἶπεν αὐτῇ, Τί θέλεις; λέγει αὐτῷ, Εἰπὲ ἵνα καθίσωσιν
He And said to her, What desire you? She says to Him, Say that may sit
1519 3778 1417 5207 2450 *1537 1188 4675 1520 1537 2176
οὗτοι οἱ δύο υἱοί μου, εἷς ἐκ δεξιῶν σου, καὶ εἷς ἐξ εὐωνύμων,
these the two sons of me, one on the right of You and one on the left
1722 932 4675 611 2424 2036 3756
22 ἐν τῇ βασιλείᾳ σου. ἀποκριθεὶς δὲ ὁ Ἰησοῦς εἶπεν, Οὐκ
in the kingdom of You. answering But Jesus said, not
1492 5101 154 1410 4095 4221 1473 3195
οἴδατε τί αἰτεῖσθε. δύνασθε πιεῖν τὸ ποτήριον ὃ ἐγὼ μέλλω
You know what you ask. Can you drink the cup which I am about
4095 908 3739 1473 907 907
πίνειν, καὶ τὸ βάπτισμα ὃ ἐγὼ βαπτίζομαι βαπτισθῆναι;
to drink, and the baptism which I am baptized to be baptized?
3004 846 1410 3004 846 3303
23 λέγουσιν αὐτῷ, Δυνάμεθα. καὶ λέγει αὐτοῖς, Τὸ μὲν
They say to Him, We can. And He says to them, the indeed
4221 3450 4095 908 3739 1473 907
ποτήριόν μου πίεσθε, καὶ τὸ βάπτισμα ὃ ἐγὼ βαπτίζομαι
cup of Me you will drink, and the baptism which I am baptised
907 2523 1537 1188 3450 1537 2176
βαπτισθήσεσθε· τὸ δὲ καθίσαι ἐκ δεξιῶν μου καὶ ἐξ εὐωνύμων
you will be baptized (with), but to sit off the right of Me and off the left
3450 3756 2076 1699 1325 235 3739 2090 5259
μου, οὐκ ἔστιν ἐμὸν δοῦναι, ἀλλ' οἷς ἡτοίμασται ὑπὸ τοῦ
of Me, not is Mine to give, but for whom it was prepared by the
3962 3450 191 1176 23 4012
24 πατρός μου. καὶ ἀκούσαντες οἱ δέκα ἠγανάκτησαν περὶ τῶν
Father of Me. And having heard the ten were indignant about the
1417 80 2424 4341 846 2036
25 δύο ἀδελφῶν. ὁ δὲ Ἰησοῦς προσκαλεσάμενος αὐτοὺς εἶπεν,
two brothers. – But Jesus having called near them said,
1492 3754 758 1484 2634 846
Οἴδατε ὅτι οἱ ἄρχοντες τῶν ἐθνῶν κατακυριεύουσιν αὐτῶν,
You know that the rulers of the nations exercise lordship over them;
3173 2715 846 3756 3779 2071
26 καὶ οἱ μεγάλοι κατεξουσιάζουσιν αὐτῶν. οὐχ οὕτως δὲ ἔσται
and the great ones exercise authority over them. not so But it will be
1722 5213 235 1437 2309 1722 5213 3173 1096 2077 5216
ἐν ὑμῖν· ἀλλ' ὃς ἐὰν θέλῃ ἐν ὑμῖν μέγας γενέσθαι ἔστω ὑμῶν
among you; but whoever would among you great become, let him be of you
1249 3739 1437 2309 1722 5213 1511 4413 2077 5216
27 διάκονος· καὶ ὃς ἐὰν θέλῃ ἐν ὑμῖν εἶναι πρῶτος ἔστω ὑμῶν
a servant. And whoever desires among you to be first, he shall be of you

NOTE: Frequent words not numbered: δέ(1161); καί(2531)—and, but; ὁ, ἡ, τό (3588, the)— * above word, look in verse margin for No.

slave; 28 even as the Son of man did not come to be served, but to serve; and to give His life a ransom for many.

29 And as they were going out from Jericho, a great crowd followed Him. 30 And, behold, two blind ones sitting beside the way, hearing that Jesus is passing by, *they* cried out, saying, Have mercy on us, Lord, Son of David! 31 But the crowd rebuked them, that they be quiet. But they cried out more, saying, Have mercy on us, Lord, Son of David! 32 And stopping, Jesus called them, and said, What do you desire that I do to you? 33 They said to Him, Lord, that our eyes may be opened. 34 And moved with pity, Jesus touched their eyes. And instantly their eyes received sight, and they followed Him.

1401 5618 5207 444 3756 2064 1247
28 δοῦλος· ὥσπερ ὁ υἱὸς τοῦ ἀνθρώπου οὐκ ἦλθε διακονηθῆναι,
a slave even as the Son of man not did come to be served
235 1247 1325 5590 848 3083 473
ἀλλὰ διακονῆσαι, καὶ δοῦναι τὴν ψυχὴν αὐτοῦ λύτρον ἀντὶ
but to serve, and to give the life of Him a ransom for
4183
πολλῶν.
many.
1607 846 575 2410 190
29 Καὶ ἐκπορευομένων αὐτῶν ἀπὸ Ἱεριχώ, ἠκολούθησεν
And going out they from Jericho, followed
846 3793 4183 2400 1417 5185 2521 3844
30 αὐτῷ ὄχλος πολύς. καὶ ἰδού, δύο τυφλοὶ καθήμενοι παρὰ
Him a crowd great. And behold, two blind (ones) sitting beside
3598 191 3754 2424 3855 2896
τὴν ὁδόν, ἀκούσαντες ὅτι Ἰησοῦς παράγει, ἔκραξαν,
the way, hearing that Jesus is passing by, cried out,
3004 1653 2248 2962 5207 1138 3793
31 λέγοντες, Ἐλέησον ἡμᾶς, Κύριε, υἱὸς Δαβίδ. ὁ δὲ ὄχλος
saying, Have pity on us, Lord, Son of David. the But crowd
2008 846 2443 4623 3185 2896
ἐπετίμησεν αὐτοῖς ἵνα σιωπήσωσιν. οἱ δὲ μεῖζον ἔκραζον,
rebuked them, that they be silent they But more cried out
3004 1653 2248 2962 5207 1138 2476
32 λέγοντες, Ἐλέησον ἡμᾶς, Κύριε, υἱὸς Δαβίδ. καὶ στὰς ὁ
saying, Have mercy on us, Lord, Son of David. And stopping
2424 5455 846 2036 5101 2309 4160 5213
Ἰησοῦς ἐφώνησεν αὐτούς, καὶ εἶπε, Τί θέλετε ποιήσω ὑμῖν;
Jesus called them, and said, What do you desire I do to you?
3004 846 2962 2443 455 2257 3788
33 λέγουσιν αὐτῷ, Κύριε, ἵνα ἀνοιχθῶσιν ἡμῶν οἱ ὀφθαλμοί.
They say to Him, Lord, that may be opened of us the eyes.
4697 2424 680 3788 848
34 σπλαγχνισθεὶς δὲ ὁ Ἰησοῦς ἥψατο τῶν ὀφθαλμῶν αὐτῶν·
moved with pity And Jesus touched the eyes of them,
2112 308 848 3788 190
καὶ εὐθέως ἀνέβλεψαν αὐτῶν οἱ ὀφθαλμοί, καὶ ἠκολούθησαν
and instantly received sight of them the eyes, and they followed
846
αὐτῷ.
Him.

CHAPTER 21

1 And when they drew near to Jerusalem and came to Bethphage, toward the Mount of Olives, then Jesus sent two disciples, 2 saying to them, Go into the village opposite you, and immediately you will find an ass tied, and a colt with her. Loosen *them and* lead *them* to Me. 3 And if anyone says anything to you, you shall say, The Lord has need of them. And he will send them at once.

4 But all this happened that might be fulfilled that which was spoken by the prophet, saying, 5 Tell the daughter of Zion, Behold, your King comes to you, meek and mounted on a

3753 1448 1519 2414 2064 1519 967
1 Καὶ ὅτε ἤγγισαν εἰς Ἱεροσόλυμα, καὶ ἦλθον εἰς Βηθφαγῆ
And when they drew near to Jerusalem, and came into Bethphage,
4314 3735 1636 5119 2424 649 1417
πρὸς τὸ ὄρος τῶν ἐλαιῶν, τότε ὁ Ἰησοῦς ἀπέστειλε δύο
toward the mount of the olives, then Jesus sent two
3101 3004 846 4198 1519 2968 561
2 μαθητάς, λέγων αὐτοῖς, Πορεύθητε εἰς τὴν κώμην τὴν ἀπέ-
disciples, telling them, You go into the village, that
5216 2112 2147 3688 1210 4454
ναντι ὑμῶν, καὶ εὐθέως εὑρήσετε ὄνον δεδεμένην, καὶ πῶλον
opposite you, and at once you will find an ass tied, and a colt
3326 846 3089 71 3427 1437 5100 5213 2936 5100
3 μετ' αὐτῆς· λύσαντες ἀγάγετέ μοι. καὶ ἐάν τις ὑμῖν εἴπῃ τι,
with her. Loosen (and) lead to Me. And if any to you says anything,
2046 3754 2962 846 5532 2192 2112 649
ἐρεῖτε ὅτι Ὁ Κύριος αὐτῶν χρείαν ἔχει· εὐθέως δὲ ἀποστελεῖ
you shall say, The Lord of them need has; at once and he will send
846 5124 3650 1096 2443 4137 4483 1223
4 αὐτούς. τοῦτο δὲ ὅλον γέγονεν, ἵνα πληρωθῇ τὸ ῥηθὲν διὰ
them. this But all happened that may be fulfilled that spoken by
4396 3004 2036 2364 4622 2400
5 τοῦ προφήτου, λέγοντος, Εἴπατε τῇ θυγατρὶ Σιών, Ἰδού,
the prophet, saying, Tell the daughter of Zion, Behold,
935 4675 2064 4671 4239 1910 1909 3688
ὁ βασιλεύς σου ἔρχεταί σοι, πραῢς καὶ ἐπιβεβηκὼς ἐπὶ ὄνον
the king of you comes to you, meek and mounted on an ass,

colt, *the* son of an ass."
[6]And the disciples going and doing as Jesus ordered them, [7]they led the ass and the colt. And *they* put on them their garments; and He sat on them.

[8]And most of *the* crowd spread their garments on the road. And others were cutting branches from the trees and were spreading them in the road. [9]And the crowd, the ones going before and the ones following, were crying out, saying, Hosanna to the Son of David! Blessed *is* He coming in *the* name of *the* Lord! Hosanna in the highest! [10]And as He entered into Jerusalem, all the city was shaken, saying, Who is this? [11]And the crowds said, This is Jesus, the Prophet, the *one* from Nazareth of Galilee.

[12]And Jesus entered into the temple of God and threw out all those selling and buying in the temple. And He overthrew the tables of the moneychangers, and the seats of those selling the doves. [13]And He said to them, It has been written, "My house shall be called a house of prayer," but you have made it a den of robbers.
[14]And blind and lame ones came to Him in the temple, and He healed them. [15]But the chief priests and the scribes, seeing the wonders which He did, and the children crying out in the temple, and saying, Hosanna to the Son of David, they were incensed. [16]And *they* said to Him, Do you hear what these say? And Jesus said to them,

4454 5207 5268 4198 3101
6 καὶ πῶλον υἱὸν ὑποζυγίου. πορευθέντες δὲ οἱ μαθηταί, καὶ
even a colt (the) son of an ass. having gone And the disciples, and
4160 2531 4367 846 2424 71
7 ποιήσαντες καθὼς προσέταξεν αὐτοῖς ὁ Ἰησοῦς, ἤγαγον
having done as ordered them — Jesus, they led
3688 4454 2007 1883 846
τὴν ὄνον καὶ τὸν πῶλον, καὶ ἐπέθηκαν ἐπάνω αὐτῶν τὰ
the ass and the colt, and put upon them the
2440 848 1940 1883 846 4118
8 ἱμάτια αὐτῶν, καὶ ἐπεκάθισαν ἐπάνω αὐτῶν. ὁ δὲ πλεῖστος
garments of them; and He sat on them. the And most of
3793 4766 1438 2440 1722 3598 243
ὄχλος ἔστρωσαν ἑαυτῶν τὰ ἱμάτια ἐν τῇ ὁδῷ· ἄλλοι δὲ
(the) crowd strewed of themselves the garments on the way. others And
2875 2798 575 1186 4766 1722
ἔκοπτον κλάδους ἀπὸ τῶν δένδρων, καὶ ἐστρώννυον ἐν τῇ
were cutting branches from the trees and were spreading in the
3598 3793 4254 190
9 ὁδῷ. οἱ δὲ ὄχλοι οἱ προάγοντες καὶ οἱ ἀκολουθοῦντες
way. the And crowds, those going before and the (ones) following,
2896 3004 5614 5207 1138 2127
ἔκραζον, λέγοντες, Ὡσαννὰ τῷ υἱῷ Δαβίδ· εὐλογημένος ὁ
were crying out, saying, Hosanna to the Son of David! Blessed (is) He
2064 1722 3686 2962 5614 1722 5310
ἐρχόμενος ἐν ὀνόματι Κυρίου· Ὡσαννὰ ἐν τοῖς ὑψίστοις.
coming in (the) name of the Lord; Hosanna in the highest!
1525 846 1519 2424 4579 3956
10 καὶ εἰσελθόντος αὐτοῦ εἰς Ἱεροσόλυμα, ἐσείσθη πᾶσα ἡ
And entering He into Jerusalem, was shaken all the
4172 3004 5101 2076 3778 3793 3004
11 πόλις, λέγουσα, Τίς ἐστιν οὗτος; οἱ δὲ ὄχλοι ἔλεγον,
city, saying, Who is this? the And crowds said,
3778 2076 2424 4396 575 3478
Οὗτός ἐστιν Ἰησοῦς ὁ προφήτης, ὁ ἀπὸ Ναζαρὲθ τῆς
This is Jesus the prophet, the (one) from Nazareth —
1056
Γαλιλαίας.
of Galilee.

1525 2424 1519 2411 2316 1544
12 Καὶ εἰσῆλθεν ὁ Ἰησοῦς εἰς τὸ ἱερὸν τοῦ Θεοῦ, καὶ ἐξέβαλε
And went in Jesus into the Temple of God, and threw out
3956 4453 59 1722 2411
πάντας τοὺς πωλοῦντας καὶ ἀγοράζοντας ἐν τῷ ἱερῷ, καὶ
all those selling and buying in the Temple. And
5132 2855 2690
τὰς τραπέζας τῶν κολλυβιστῶν κατέστρεψε, καὶ τὰς
the tables of the moneychangers He overthrew, and the
2515 4453 4058 3004 846
13 καθέδρας τῶν πωλούντων τὰς περιστεράς. καὶ λέγει αὐτοῖς,
seats of the (ones) selling the doves. And He says to them,
1125 3624 3450 3624 4335 2564
Γέγραπται, Ὁ οἶκός μου οἶκος προσευχῆς κληθήσεται·
it has been written, The house of Me a house of prayer shall be called;
5210 846 4160 4693 3027 4334
14 ὑμεῖς δὲ αὐτὸν ἐποιήσατε σπήλαιον λῃστῶν. καὶ προσῆλθον
you but it have made (it) a den of robbers. And came near
846 5185 5560 1722 2411 2323 846
αὐτῷ τυφλοὶ καὶ χωλοὶ ἐν τῷ ἱερῷ· καὶ ἐθεράπευσεν αὐτούς.
to Him blind and lame in the Temple. and He healed them.
1492 749 1122 2297 3739
15 ἰδόντες δὲ οἱ ἀρχιερεῖς καὶ οἱ γραμματεῖς τὰ θαυμάσια ἃ
seeing But the chief priests and the scribes the wonders which
4160 3816 2896 1722 2411 3004
ἐποίησε, καὶ τοὺς παῖδας κράζοντας ἐν τῷ ἱερῷ, καὶ λέγον-
He did and the children crying out in the Temple, and saying,
5614 5207 1138 23 2036 846
16 τας, Ὡσαννὰ τῷ υἱῷ Δαβίδ, ἠγανάκτησαν, καὶ εἶπον αὐτῷ,
Hosanna to the Son of David, they were incensed, and said to Him,
191 5101 3778 3004 2424 3004 846 3483
Ἀκούεις τί οὗτοι λέγουσιν; ὁ δὲ Ἰησοῦς λέγει αὐτοῖς, Ναί·
Do you hear what these say? And Jesus says to them, Yes,

NOTE: Frequent words not numbered: δέ (1161); καί (2531)—and, but; ὁ, ἡ, τό (3588, the)— * above word, look in verse margin for No.

Yes. Did you never read, "Out of *the* mouth of babes and sucklings You have perfected praise"? [17]And leaving them, He went out of the city to Bethany, and spent the night there.

[18]And returning early to the city, He hungered. [19]And seeing one fig-tree by the road, He went up *to* it, and found nothing on it except leaves only. And He said to it, Let there be no more fruit from you forever. And the fig-tree immediately dried up. [20]And seeing, the disciples marveled, saying, How quickly the fig-tree is dried up! [21]And answering Jesus said to them, Truly I say to you, If you have faith and do not doubt, not only will you do the *miracle* of the fig-tree, but even if you should say to this mountain, Be taken up and thrown into the sea—it will be *so*. [22]And all things, whatever you may ask in prayer, believing, you shall receive.

[23]And He coming into the temple, the chief priests and elders of the people came near to Him *as He was* teaching, saying, By what authority do you do you do these things? And who gave to you this authority? [24]And answering Jesus said to them, I also will ask you one thing, which if you tell Me, I also will tell you by what authority I do these things. [25]The baptism of John, from where was it? From Heaven, or from men? [26]And they reasoned among themselves, saying, If we should say, From Heaven, he will say to us, Then why did you not believe him? But if we should say, From men, we fear the people. For all hold

3762 314 3754 1537 4750 3516 2337
οὐδέποτε ἀνέγνωτε ὅτι Ἐκ στόματος νηπίων καὶ θηλα-
n never Did you read, Out of (the) mouth of babes and sucking
2675 136 2641 846 1831
17 ζόντων κατηρτίσω αἶνον ; καὶ καταλιπὼν αὐτοὺς ἐξῆλθεν
(ones) You have perfected praise? And leaving them He went
1854 4172 1519 963 835 2563
ἔξω τῆς πόλεως εἰς Βηθανίαν, καὶ ηὐλίσθη ἐκεῖ.
out of the city to Bethany, and lodged there.
4405 1877 1519 4172 3983 1492
18 Πρωΐας δὲ ἐπανάγων εἰς τὴν πόλιν, ἐπείνασε· καὶ ἰδὼν
19 early. And returning to the city, He hungered. And seeing
4808 3391 1909 3598 2064 1909 846 3762 2147
συκῆν μίαν ἐπὶ τῆς ὁδοῦ, ἦλθεν ἐπ' αὐτήν, καὶ οὐδὲν εὗρεν
fig-tree one on the way, He went up (to) it, and nothing found
1722 846 =1508= 5444 3440 3004 846 3371 1537 4675
ἐν αὐτῇ εἰ μὴ φύλλα μόνον· καὶ λέγει αὐτῇ, Μηκέτι ἐκ σοῦ
in it, except leaves only, and He says to it, No longer of you
2590 1096 1519 165 3583 3916
καρπὸς γένηται εἰς τὸν αἰῶνα. καὶ ἐξηράνθη παραχρῆμα ἡ
fruit may be to the age. And was dried up instantly the
4808 1492 3101 2296 3004 4459
20 συκῆ. καὶ ἰδόντες οἱ μαθηταὶ ἐθαύμασαν, λέγοντες, Πῶς
fig-tree. And seeing the disciples marveled, saying, How
3916 3583 4808 611 2424
21 παραχρῆμα ἐξηράνθη ἡ συκῆ ; ἀποκριθεὶς δὲ ὁ Ἰησοῦς
instantly was withered the fig-tree! answering And Jesus
2036 846 281 3004 5213 1437 2192 4102 3361
εἶπεν αὐτοῖς, Ἀμὴν λέγω ὑμῖν, ἐὰν ἔχητε πίστιν, καὶ μὴ
said to them, Truly I say to you, If you have faith and not
1252 3756 3440 4808 4160 235 2579
διακριθῆτε, οὐ μόνον τὸ τῆς συκῆς ποιήσετε, ἀλλὰ κἂν τῷ
do doubt, not only that of the fig-tree you will do, but also if to
3735 5129 2036 142 906 1519 2281
ὄρει τούτῳ εἴπητε, Ἄρθητι καὶ βλήθητι εἰς τὴν θάλασσαν,
mountain this you say, Be taken and thrown into the sea,
1096 3956 3745 302 154 1722 4335
22 γενήσεται. καὶ πάντα ὅσα ἂν αἰτήσητε ἐν τῇ προσευχῇ,
it will be. And all things, whatever you ask in prayer,
4100 2983
πιστεύοντες, λήψεσθε.
believing, you will receive.
2064 846 1519 2411 4334 846 1321
23 Καὶ ἐλθόντι αὐτῷ εἰς τὸ ἱερόν, προσῆλθον αὐτῷ διδά-
And coming He into the Temple, approached to Him teach-
749 4245 2992 3004
σκοντι οἱ ἀρχιερεῖς καὶ οἱ πρεσβύτεροι τοῦ λαοῦ, λέγοντες,
ing the chief priests and the elders of the people, saying
1722 4169 1849 5023 4160 5101 4671 1325
Ἐν ποίᾳ ἐξουσίᾳ ταῦτα ποιεῖς ; καὶ τίς σοι ἔδωκε τὴν
By what authority these things do you? And who to you gave —
1849 5026 611 2424 2036 846
24 ἐξουσίαν ταύτην ; ἀποκριθεὶς δὲ ὁ Ἰησοῦς εἶπεν αὐτοῖς,
authority this? answering And — Jesus said to them,
2065 5209 2504 3056 1520 3739 1437 2036 3427 2505
Ἐρωτήσω ὑμᾶς κἀγὼ λόγον ἕνα, ὃν ἐὰν εἴπητέ μοι, κἀγὼ
will question you I also word one, which if you tell Me, I also
5213 2046 4169 1849 5023 4160 908 2491
25 ὑμῖν ἐρῶ ἐν ποίᾳ ἐξουσίᾳ ταῦτα ποιῶ. τὸ βάπτισμα Ἰωάννου
you I will tell by what authority these I do: The baptism of John,
4159 2258 1537 3772 2228 1537 444 1260
πόθεν ἦν ; ἐξ οὐρανοῦ ἢ ἐξ ἀνθρώπων ; οἱ δὲ διελογίζοντο
whence was it? From Heaven or from men? they And reasoned
3844 1438 3004 1437 2036 1537 3772 2046 2254
παρ' ἑαυτοῖς, λέγοντες, Ἐὰν εἴπωμεν, ἐξ οὐρανοῦ, ἐρεῖ ἡμῖν,
by themselves, saying, If we say from Heaven, He will say to us
1302 3767 3756 4100 846 1437 2036 1537 444
26 Διατί οὖν οὐκ ἐπιστεύσατε αὐτῷ ; ἐὰν δὲ εἴπωμεν, ἐξ ἀνθρώ-
Why then not you did believe him? if But we say from men,
5399 3793 3956 1063 2192 2491
πων, φοβούμεθα τὸν ὄχλον· πάντες γὰρ ἔχουσι τὸν Ἰωάννην
we fear the crowd. all For hold John

John to be a prophet. [27]And answering Jesus they said, We do not know. And He said to them, Neither do I tell you by what authority I do these things.

[28]But what do you think? A man had two children, and coming to the first he said, Child, go today; work in my vineyard. [29]And answering he said, I will not. But afterward, feeling sorry, he went. [30]And coming to the second, he said the same. And answering he said, I *go,* sir, but did not leave. [31]Which of the two did the will of the father? They said to Him, The first. Jesus said to them, Truly I say to you, The tax-collectors and the harlots go before you into the kingdom of God. [32]For John came to you in *the* way of righteousness, and you did not believe him. But the tax-collectors and the harlots believed him. And seeing, you did not repent afterwards to believe him.

[33]Hear another parable: There was a certain man, a housemaster who planted a vineyard and placed a hedge around it, and dug a winepress in it, and built a tower. And *he* rented it to vinedressers, and left the country. [34]And when the season of the fruits came, he sent his slaves to the vinedressers to receive his fruits. [35]And the vinedressers taking his slaves, they beat this one, and they killed one; and they stoned another. [36]Again he sent other slaves, more than the first. And they did the same

5613 4396 611 2424 2036 3756
27 ὡς προφήτην. καὶ ἀποκριθέντες τῷ Ἰησοῦ εἶπον, Οὐκ
as a prophet. And answering Jesus they said, not
1492 5346 846 846 3761 1473 3004 5213 4169
οἴδαμεν. ἔφη αὐτοῖς καὶ αὐτός, Οὐδὲ ἐγὼ λέγω ὑμῖν ἐν ποίᾳ
we do know. said to them And He, Neither I tell you by what
1849 5023 4160 5101 5213 1380 444 2192
28 ἐξουσίᾳ ταῦτα ποιῶ. τί δὲ ὑμῖν δοκεῖ; ἄνθρωπος εἶχε
authority these things I do. what But to you seems it? A man had
5043 1417 4334 4413 2036 5043 5217
τέκνα δύο, καὶ προσελθὼν τῷ πρώτῳ εἶπε, Τέκνον, ὕπαγε,
children two, and having come to the first he said, Child, go,
4594 2038 1722 290 3450 611 2036
29 σήμερον ἐργάζου ἐν τῷ ἀμπελῶνί μου. ὁ δὲ ἀποκριθεὶς εἶπεν,
today work in the vineyard of me. he And answering said
3756 2309 5305 3338 565 4334
30 Οὐ θέλω· ὕστερον δὲ μεταμεληθείς, ἀπῆλθε. καὶ προσελθὼν
not I will. afterwards But feeling sorry he went. And having come
1208 2036 5615 611 2036 1473
τῷ δευτέρῳ εἶπεν ὡσαύτως. ὁ δὲ ἀποκριθεὶς εἶπεν, Ἐγώ,
to the second, he said likewise. he And answering said, I (go),
2962 3756 565 5101 1537 1417 4160 2307
31 κύριε· καὶ οὐκ ἀπῆλθε. τίς ἐκ τῶν δύο ἐποίησε τὸ θέλημα
lord, and not did leave. Who of the two did the will
3962 3004 846 4413 3004 846
τοῦ πατρός; λέγουσιν αὐτῷ, Ὁ πρῶτος. λέγει αὐτοῖς ὁ
of the father? They say to Him, The first. says to them
2424 281 3004 5213 3754 5057 4204
Ἰησοῦς, Ἀμὴν λέγω ὑμῖν, ὅτι οἱ τελῶναι καὶ αἱ πόρναι
Jesus, Truly I say to you, that the tax-collectors and the harlots
4254 5209 1519 932 2316 2064 1063
32 προάγουσιν ὑμᾶς εἰς τὴν βασιλείαν τοῦ Θεοῦ. ἦλθε γὰρ
go before you into the kingdom of God. came For
4314 5209 2491 1722 3588 1343 3756 4100
πρὸς ὑμᾶς Ἰωάννης ἐν ὁδῷ δικαιοσύνης, καὶ οὐκ ἐπιστεύ-
to you John in (the) way of righteousness, and not you did
846 5457 4204 4100 846
σατε αὐτῷ· οἱ δὲ τελῶναι καὶ αἱ πόρναι ἐπίστευσαν αὐτῷ·
believe him; the but tax-collectors and the harlots believed him.
5210 1492 3756 3338 5305 4100
ὑμεῖς δὲ ἰδόντες οὐ μετεμελήθητε ὕστερον τοῦ πιστεῦσαι
you And seeing, not felt sorry afterwards to believe
846
αὐτῷ.
him.
243 3850 191 444 5100 2258 3617
33 Ἄλλην παραβολὴν ἀκούσατε. ἄνθρωπός τις ἦν οἰκοδε-
Another parable hear: A man certain was a house-
3748 5452 290 5418 846
σπότης, ὅστις ἐφύτευσεν ἀμπελῶνα, καὶ φραγμὸν αὐτῷ
master, who planted a vineyard, and a hedge it
4060 3736 1722 846 3025 3618 4444
περιέθηκε, καὶ ὤρυξεν ἐν αὐτῷ ληνόν, καὶ ᾠκοδόμησε πύργον,
put around, and dug in it a winepress, and built a tower,
1554 846 1092 589 3753
34 καὶ ἐξέδοτο αὐτὸν γεωργοῖς, καὶ ἀπεδήμησεν. ὅτε δὲ
and rented it to vinedressers, and departed. when And
1448 2540 2590 649 1401
ἤγγισεν ὁ καιρὸς τῶν καρπῶν, ἀπέστειλε τοὺς δούλους
drew near the time of the fruits, he sent the slaves
848 4314 1092 2983 2590 848
αὐτοῦ πρὸς τοὺς γεωργούς, λαβεῖν τοὺς καρποὺς αὐτοῦ·
of him to the vinedressers, to receive the fruits of it.
3739 2983 1092 1401 848 3739/ /3303/1194
35 καὶ λαβόντες οἱ γεωργοὶ τοὺς δούλους αὐτοῦ, ὃν μὲν ἔδειραν,
And taking the vinedressers, slaves of him, this one they beat,
3739 615 3036 3825 649
36 ὃν δὲ ἀπέκτειναν, ὃν δὲ ἐλιθοβόλησαν. πάλιν ἀπέστειλεν
one and they killed; one and they stoned. Again he sent
243 1401 4119 4413 4160 846
ἄλλους δούλους πλείονας τῶν πρώτων· καὶ ἐποίησαν αὐτοῖς
other slaves, more (than) the first, and they did to them

NOTE: Frequent words not numbered: δέ(1161); καί(2531)—and, but; ὁ, ἡ, τό (3588, the)— * above word look in verse margin for No.

to them. [37]And at last he sent his son to them, saying, They will have respect for my son. [38]But seeing the son, the vinedressers said among themselves, This is the heir. Come, let us kill him, and get hold of his inheritance. [39]And taking him, they threw *him* out of the vineyard, and killed *him*.

[40]Therefore, when the lord of the vineyard comes, what will he do to these vinedressers? [41]They said to Him, Bad men! He will miserably destroy them, and he will rent out the vineyard to other vinedressers who will give to him the fruits in their seasons. [42]Jesus said to them, Did you never read in the Scriptures, "*The* Stone which the builders rejected is the One that has become the head of *the* corner. This was from the Lord, and it is a wonder in our eyes"?

[43]Because of this I say to you, The kingdom of God will be taken from you, and it will be given to a nation bringing forth the fruits of it. [44]And he who falls on this Stone will be broken; but on whomever it falls, it will grind him to powder. [45]And hearing His parables, the chief priests and the Pharisees knew that He was speaking about them. [46]And seeking to lay hold of Him, they feared the crowds, because they held Him as a prophet.

5615 5305 649 4314 846 5207
37 ὡσαύτως. ὕστερον δὲ ἀπέστειλε πρὸς αὐτοὺς τὸν υἱὸν
likewise. later But he sent to them the son
848 3004 1788 5207 3450 1092
38 αὐτοῦ, λέγων, Ἐντραπήσονται τὸν υἱόν μου. οἱ δὲ γεωργοὶ
of him, saying, They will respect the son of me. the But vinedressers
1492 5207 2036/1722/1437 3778 2076 2818
ἰδόντες τὸν υἱὸν εἶπον ἐν ἑαυτοῖς, Οὗτός ἐστιν ὁ κληρονόμος· –
seeing the son said among themselves, This is the heir;
1205 615 846 2722 2817
δεῦτε, ἀποκτείνωμεν αὐτόν, καὶ κατάσχωμεν τὴν κληρονο-
come, let us kill him, and let us possess the inheritance
848 2983 846 1544 1854 290
39 μίαν αὐτοῦ. καὶ λαβόντες αὐτὸν ἐξέβαλον ἔξω τοῦ ἀμπε-
of him. And taking him, they threw out the vine-
615 3752 3767 2064 2962
40 λῶνος καὶ ἀπέκτειναν ὅταν οὖν ἔλθῃ ὁ κύριος τοῦ
yard and killed When therefore comes the lord of the
290 5101 4160 1092 1565 3004
41 ἀμπελῶνος, τί ποιήσει τοῖς γεωργοῖς ἐκείνοις; λέγουσιν
vineyard, what will he do to vinedressers those? They say
846 2556 2560 622 846 290
αὐτῷ, Κακοὺς κακῶς ἀπολέσει αὐτούς, καὶ τὸν ἀμπελῶνα
to Him, Bad men, badly he will destroy them, and the vineyard
1554 243 1092 3748 591 846
ἐκδόσεται ἄλλοις γεωργοῖς, οἵτινες ἀποδώσουσιν αὐτῷ
he will give out to other vinedressers, who will render to him
2590 1722 2540 848 3004 846 2424
42 τοὺς καρποὺς ἐν τοῖς καιροῖς αὐτῶν. λέγει αὐτοῖς ὁ Ἰησοῦς,
the fruits in the seasons of them. says to them Jesus,
3762 314 1722 1124 3037 3739 593
Οὐδέποτε ἀνέγνωτε ἐν ταῖς γραφαῖς, Λίθον ὃν ἀπεδοκί-
never Did you read in the Scriptures: A stone which rejected
3618 3778 1096 1519 2776
μασαν οἱ οἰκοδομοῦντες, οὗτος ἐγενήθη εἰς κεφαλὴν
the builders, this (one) became — head
1137 3844 2962 1096 3778 2076 2298 1722
γωνίας· παρὰ Κυρίου ἐγένετο αὕτη, καὶ ἔστι θαυμαστὴ ἐν
of corner; from (the) Lord happened this, and it is a wonder in
3788 2257 1223 5124 3004 5213 3754 142 575
43 ὀφθαλμοῖς ἡμῶν; διὰ τοῦτο λέγω ὑμῖν ὅτι ἀρθήσεται ἀφ'
(the) eyes of us? Because of this I tell you, that will be taken from
5216 932 2316 1325 1484 4160
ὑμῶν ἡ βασιλεία τοῦ Θεοῦ, καὶ δοθήσεται ἔθνει ποιοῦντι
you the kingdom — of God, and will be given to a nation producing
2590 846 4098 1909 3037 5126
44 τοὺς καρποὺς αὐτῆς καὶ ὁ πεσὼν ἐπὶ τὸν λίθον τοῦτον,
the fruits of it. And the (one) falling on — stone this
4917 1909 3739 302 4098 3039 846
45 συνθλασθήσεται· ἐφ' ὃν δ' ἂν πέσῃ, λικμήσει αὐτόν. καὶ
will be broken up; upon whom but ever it fall, it will pulverize him. And
191 749 5330 3850
ἀκούσαντες οἱ ἀρχιερεῖς καὶ οἱ Φαρισαῖοι τὰς παραβολὰς
hearing the chief priests and the Pharisees the parables
848 1097 3754 4012 846 3004 2212 846
46 αὐτοῦ ἔγνωσαν ὅτι περὶ αὐτῶν λέγει. καὶ ζητοῦντες αὐτὸν
of Him, they knew that about them He says; and seeking Him
2902 5399 3793 1894 5613 4396
κρατῆσαι, ἐφοβήθησαν τοὺς ὄχλους, ἐπειδὴ ὡς προφήτην
to seize, they feared the crowds, because as a prophet
846 2192
αὐτὸν εἶχον.
Him they held.

CHAPTER 22

[1]And answering Jesus again spoke to them in parables, saying: [2]The kingdom of Heaven is compared to a man, a king,

CHAPTER 22

611 2424 3825 2036 846 1722 3850
1 Καὶ ἀποκριθεὶς ὁ Ἰησοῦς πάλιν εἶπεν αὐτοῖς ἐν παρα-
And answering Jesus again spoke to them in parables,
3004 3666 932 3772 444
2 βολαῖς, λέγων, Ὡμοιώθη ἡ βασιλεία τῶν οὐρανῶν ἀνθρώπῳ
saying, is likened the kingdom of the heavens to a man,

who made a wedding feast for his son. [3]And *he* sent his slaves to call those who had been invited to the wedding feast; but they did not desire to come. [4]Again, he sent other slaves, saying, Tell the *ones* invited, Behold, I have prepared my supper; my oxen, and the fatlings are killed, and all things ready; come to the wedding feast. [5]But not caring they went away, one to *his* own field, and one to *his* trading. [6]And the rest, seizing his slaves, insulted and killed *them*. [7]And hearing, the king became angry. And sending his armies, *he* destroyed those murderers, and burned their city. [8]Then he said to his slaves, Indeed, the wedding feast is ready, but those who had been invited were not worthy. [9]Therefore, go onto the exits of the highways and call to the wedding feast as many as you may find.

[10]And going out into the highways, those slaves gathered all, as many as they found, both evil and good. And the wedding feast was filled with reclining guests. [11]And the king coming in to look over those reclining, he saw a man there not being dressed *in* a wedding garment. [12]And he said to him, Friend, how did you come in here, not having a wedding garment? But he was silent. [13]Then the king said to the servants, Binding his feet and hands, take him away, and throw *him* out into the outer darkness. There shall be weeping and gnashing of the teeth. [14]For many are called, but few chosen.

935 3748 4160 1062 5207 848 649
3 βασιλεῖ, ὅστις ἐποίησε γάμους τῷ υἱῷ αὐτοῦ· καὶ ἀπέστειλε
a king, who made a wedding feast to the son of him. And he sent
1401 848 2564 2564 1519
τοὺς δούλους αὐτοῦ καλέσαι τοὺς κεκλημένους εἰς τοὺς
the slaves of him to call the (ones) being called to the
1062 3756 2309 2064 3825 649 243
4 γάμους, καὶ οὐκ ἤθελον ἐλθεῖν. πάλιν ἀπέστειλεν ἄλλους
wedding. And not they desired to come. Again he sent other
1401 3004 2036 2563 2400 712
δούλους, λέγων, Εἴπατε τοῖς κεκλημένοις, Ἰδού, τὸ ἄριστόν
slaves, saying, Tell the (ones) called, Behold, the supper
3450 2090 5022 3450 4619 2380
μου ἡτοίμασα, οἱ ταῦροί μου καὶ τὰ σιτιστὰ τεθυμένα, καὶ
of me I have readied; the oxen of me and the fatted beasts are killed, and
3956 2092 1205 1519 1062 272
5 πάντα ἕτοιμα· δεῦτε εἰς τοὺς γάμους. οἱ δὲ ἀμελήσαντες
all things ready. Come to the wedding feast. they But not caring
565 3303 1519 2398 68 1519 1711
ἀπῆλθον, ὁ μὲν εἰς τὸν ἴδιον ἀγρόν, ὁ δὲ εἰς τὴν ἐμπορίαν
went off, one, to the own field, one and to the trading
848 3062 2902 1401 848
6 αὐτοῦ· οἱ δὲ λοιποὶ κρατήσαντες τοὺς δούλους αὐτοῦ
of him; the and rest seizing the slaves of him
5195 615 191 935 3710
7 ὕβρισαν καὶ ἀπέκτειναν. ἀκούσας δὲ ὁ βασιλεὺς ὠργίσθη,
insulted and killed. hearing And the king became angry,
3992 4753 848 622 5406
καὶ πέμψας τὰ στρατεύματα αὐτοῦ ἀπώλεσε τοὺς φονεῖς
and sending the armies of him destroyed murderers
1565 4172 848 1714 5119 3004
8 ἐκείνους, καὶ τὴν πόλιν αὐτῶν ἐνέπρησε. τότε λέγει τοῖς
those, also the city of them burned. Then he says to the
1401 848 3303 1062 2092 2076 2563
δούλοις αὐτοῦ, Ὁ μὲν γάμος ἕτοιμός ἐστιν, οἱ δὲ κεκλημένοι
slaves of him, the Indeed wedding ready is, those but called
3756 2258 514 4198 3767 1909 1327 3598
9 οὐκ ἦσαν ἄξιοι. πορεύεσθε οὖν ἐπὶ τὰς διεξόδους τῶν ὁδῶν,
not were worthy. You go therefore onto the exits of the ways,
3745 302 2147 2564 1519 1062 1831
10 καὶ ὅσους ἂν εὕρητε, καλέσατε εἰς τοὺς γάμους. καὶ ἐξελ-
and as many as you find call to the feast. And going
1401 1565 1519 3598 4863 3956
θόντες οἱ δοῦλοι ἐκεῖνοι εἰς τὰς ὁδοὺς συνήγαγον πάντας
forth slaves those into the ways gathered all
3745 2147 4190 5037 18 4130
ὅσους εὗρον, πονηρούς τε καὶ ἀγαθούς· καὶ ἐπλήσθη ὁ
as many as they found; evil both and good; and was filled the
1062 345 1525 935 2300
11 γάμος ἀνακειμένων. εἰσελθὼν δὲ ὁ βασιλεὺς θεάσασθαι τοὺς
wedding with recliners. coming in And the king to view those
345 1492 1563 444 3756 1745 1742
ἀνακειμένους εἶδεν ἐκεῖ ἄνθρωπον οὐκ ἐνδεδυμένον ενουμα
reclining he saw there a man not being dressed (in) a dress
1062 3004 846 2083 4459 1525 5602 3361 2192
12 γάμου· καὶ λέγει αὐτῷ, Ἑταῖρε, πῶς εἰσῆλθες ὧδε μὴ ἔχων
of wedding. And he said to him, Friend, how did you enter here not having
1742 1062 5392 5119 2036 932
13 ἔνδυμα γάμου; ὁ δὲ ἐφιμώθη. τότε εἶπεν ὁ βασιλεὺς τοῖς
a dress of wedding? he But was silent. Then said the king to the
1249 1210 848 4228 5495 142 848
διακόνοις, Δήσαντες αὐτοῦ πόδας καὶ χεῖρας, ἄρατε αὐτὸν
servants, Binding of him (the) feet and hands, take away him
1544 1519 4655 1857 1563 2071 2805
14 καὶ ἐκβάλετε εἰς τὸ σκότος τὸ ἐξώτερον· ἐκεῖ ἔσται ὁ κλαυθμὸς
and throw out into the darkness outer, there shall be the weeping
1030 3599 4183 1063 1526 2822 3641
καὶ ὁ βρυγμὸς τῶν ὀδόντων. πολλοὶ γάρ εἰσι κλητοί, ὀλίγοι
and the gnashing of the teeth. many For are called, few
1588
δὲ ἐκλεκτοί.
but chosen.

NOTE: Frequent words not numbered: δέ(1161); καί(2531)—and, but; ὁ, ἡ, τό (3588, the)— * above word, look in verse margin for No.

[15]Then going, the Pharisees took counsel so as they might trap Him in words. [16]And they sent to Him their disciples with the Herodians, saying, Teacher, we know that you are true, and teach the way of God in truth; and it does not concern you about anyone, for you do not look to *the* face of men. [17]Then tell us, what do you think? Is it lawful to give tribute to Caesar, or not?

[18]But knowing their wickedness, Jesus said, Why do you test Me, hypocrites? [19]Show Me the tribute coin. And they brought a denarius to Him. [20]And He said to them, Whose image and superscription is this? [21]They said to Him, Caesar's. Then He said to them, Then give to Caesar the things of Caesar, and to God the things of God.

[22]And hearing, they marveled. And leaving Him, they went away.

[23]On that day Sadducees came to Him, who say there is no resurrection. And they questioned Him, [24]saying, Teacher, Moses said, If any should die not having children, his brother shall marry his wife, and shall raise up seed to his brother. [25]And seven brothers were with us. And having married, the first expired, and not having seed left his wife to his brother. [26]In the same way also the second, and the third, until the seven. [27]And last of all the woman also died. [28]Then in the resurrection, of which of the seven will she be wife? For all had her. [29]And

5119 4198 5330 4824 2983 3704
15 Τότε πορευθέντες οἱ Φαρισαῖοι συμβούλιον ἔλαβον ὅπως
Then going the Pharisees counsel took so as
846 3802 1722 3056 649 846
16 αὐτὸν παγιδεύσωσιν ἐν λόγῳ. καὶ ἀποστέλλουσιν αὐτῷ
Him they might trap in discourse. And they send forth to Him
3101 848 3326 2265 3004
τοὺς μαθητὰς αὐτῶν μετὰ τῶν Ἡρωδιανῶν, λέγοντες,
the disciples of them with the Herodians, saying,
1320 1492 3754 227 1488 3598 2316
Διδάσκαλε, οἴδαμεν ὅτι ἀληθὴς εἶ, καὶ τὴν ὁδὸν τοῦ Θεοῦ
Teacher, we know that truthful you are, and the way – of God
1722 225 1321 3756 3199 4671 4012 3762 3756 1063
ἐν ἀληθείᾳ διδάσκεις, καὶ οὐ μέλει σοι περὶ οὐδενός, οὐ γὰρ
in truth you teach. and not it concerns you about no one; not for
991 1519 4383 444 2036 3767 2254 5101 4671
17 βλέπεις εἰς πρόσωπον ἀνθρώπων. εἰπὲ οὖν ἡμῖν, τί σοι
you look to face of men. Tell therefore us, what you
1380 1832 1325 2778 2541 2228 3756 1097
18 δοκεῖ; ἔξεστι δοῦναι κῆνσον Καίσαρι, ἢ οὔ; γνοὺς δὲ ὁ
think: Is it lawful to give tribute to Caesar, or not? knowing But –
2424 4189 848 2036 5101 3165 2985 5273
Ἰησοῦς τὴν πονηρίαν αὐτῶν εἶπε, Τί με πειράζετε, ὑπο-
Jesus the wickedness of them, said, Why Me you tempt, hypo-
1925 3427 3546 2778 4374
19 κριταί; ἐπιδείξατέ μοι τὸ νόμισμα τοῦ κήνσου. οἱ δὲ προσ-
crites? Show Me the coin of the tribute. they And brought
846 1220 3004 846 5101 1504
20 ἤνεγκαν αὐτῷ δηνάριον. καὶ λέγει αὐτοῖς, Τίνος ἡ εἰκὼν
to Him a denarius. And He says to them, Of whom – image
3778 1923 3004 846 2541 5119 3004
21 αὕτη καὶ ἡ ἐπιγραφή; λέγουσιν αὐτῷ, Καίσαρος. τότε λέγει
this and – superscription? They say to Him, Of Caesar. Then He says
846 591 3767 2541 2541
αὐτοῖς, Ἀπόδοτε οὖν τὰ Καίσαρος Καίσαρι· καὶ τὰ τοῦ
to them, Render then the things of Caesar to Caesar, and the things
2316 2316 191 2296 863 846
22 Θεοῦ τῷ Θεῷ. καὶ ἀκούσαντες ἐθαύμασαν· καὶ ἀφέντες αὐτὸν
of God – to God. And hearing they marveled, and leaving Him
565
ἀπῆλθον.
they went away.
1722 1565 2250 4334 846 4523
23 Ἐν ἐκείνῃ τῇ ἡμέρᾳ προσῆλθον αὐτῷ Σαδδουκαῖοι, οἱ
On that – day approaching to Him Sadducees, who
3004 3361 1511 386 1905 846
λέγοντες μὴ εἶναι ἀνάστασιν, καὶ ἐπηρώτησαν αὐτόν,
are saying not to be a resurrection. And they questioned Him.
3004 1320 3475 2036 1437 5100 599 3361
24 λέγοντες, Διδάσκαλε, Μωσῆς εἶπεν, Ἐάν τις ἀποθάνῃ μὴ
saying, Teacher, Moses said, If any (man) die not
2192 5043 1918 80 848 1135
ἔχων τέκνα, ἐπιγαμβρεύσει ὁ ἀδελφὸς αὐτοῦ τὴν γυναῖκα
having children, shall take to wife the brother of him the wife
848 450 4690 80 848 2258
25 αὐτοῦ, καὶ ἀναστήσει σπέρμα τῷ ἀδελφῷ αὐτοῦ. ἦσαν δὲ
of him and shall raise up seed to the brother of him. were And
3844 2254 2033 80 4413 1060 5053
παρ' ἡμῖν ἑπτὰ ἀδελφοί· καὶ ὁ πρῶτος γαμήσας ἐτελεύτησε·
with us seven brothers; and the first having married ended (his life),
3361 2192 4690 863 1135 848 80
καὶ μὴ ἔχων σπέρμα, ἀφῆκε τὴν γυναῖκα αὐτοῦ τῷ ἀδελφῷ
and not having seed left the wife of him to the brother
848 3668 1208 5154 2193 2033
26 αὐτοῦ. ὁμοίως καὶ ὁ δεύτερος, καὶ ὁ τρίτος, ἕως τῶν ἑπτά.
of him; likewise also the second, and the third, until the seven.
5305 3956 599 1135 1722 3767 386
27 ὕστερον δὲ πάντων ἀπέθανε καὶ ἡ γυνή. ἐν τῇ οὖν ἀναστάσει,
28
last And of all died also the woman. in the Then resurrection,
5101 2033 2071 1135 3956 1063 2192 846
τίνος τῶν ἑπτὰ ἔσται γυνή; πάντες γὰρ ἔσχον αὐτήν.
of which of the seven will she be wife? all For had her.

- • above word, look in verse margin for No

answering Jesus said to them, You err, not knowing the Scriptures, nor the power of God. [30]For in the resurrection they neither marry nor are given in marriage, but they are as the angels of God in Heaven. [31]But concerning the resurrection of the dead, have you not read that spoken to you by God, saying: [32]"I am the God of Abraham, and the God of Isaac, and the God of Jacob"? God is not God of the dead, but of the living. [33]And hearing, the crowds were astonished at His teaching.

[34]But hearing that He had silenced the Sadducees, the Pharisees were gathered together. [35]And one of them, a lawyer, questioned *Him*, testing Him, and saying, [36]Teacher, which *is the* great commandment in the Law? [37]And Jesus said to him, "You shall love *the* Lord your God with all your heart, and with all your soul, and with all your mind." [38]This is *the* first and great commandment. [39]And *the* second *is* like it: "You shall love your neighbor as yourself." [40]On these two commandments all the Law and the Prophets hang.

[41]But the Pharisees having been gathered, Jesus questioned them, [42]saying, What do you think about the Christ? Whose son is He? They say to Him, David's. [43]He said to them, Then how does David in Spirit call Him Lord, saying, [44]"The Lord said to my Lord, Sit on My right until I place Your enemies as a footstool for Your feet"? [45]Then if David calls Him Lord, how is He his son? [46]And no one was able to

611 2424 2036 846 4105 3361 1492
29 ἀποκριθεὶς δὲ ὁ Ἰησοῦς εἶπεν αὐτοῖς, Πλανᾶσθε, μὴ εἰδότες
answering And – Jesus said to them, You err, not knowing
1124 3366 1411 2316 1722 1063 386
30 τὰς γραφάς, μηδὲ τὴν δύναμιν τοῦ Θεοῦ. ἐν γὰρ τῇ ἀναστά-
the Scriptures, nor the power – of God. in For the resurrection
3777 1060 3777 1547 235 5613 32
σει οὔτε γαμοῦσιν, οὔτε ἐκγαμίζονται, ἀλλ' ὡς ἄγγελοι τοῦ
neither they marry, nor are given in marriage; but as angels –
2316 1722 3772 1526 4012 386 3498
31 Θεοῦ ἐν οὐρανῷ εἰσι. περὶ δὲ τῆς ἀναστάσεως τῶν νεκρῶν,
of God. in Heaven they are. about But the resurrection of the dead,
3756 314 4483 5213 5259 2316 3004 1473
32 οὐκ ἀνέγνωτε τὸ ῥηθὲν ὑμῖν ὑπὸ τοῦ Θεοῦ, λέγοντος, Ἐγώ
not have you read that spoken to you by God, saying, I
1510 2316 11 2316 2464 2316 2384
εἰμι ὁ Θεὸς Ἀβραάμ, καὶ ὁ Θεὸς Ἰσαάκ, καὶ ὁ Θεὸς Ἰακώβ;
am the God of Abraham, and the God of Isaac, and the God of Jacob?
3756 2076 2316 2316 3498 235 2198 191
33 οὐκ ἔστιν ὁ Θεὸς Θεὸς νεκρῶν, ἀλλὰ ζώντων. καὶ ἀκού-
not is God God of the dead, but of (the) living. And having
3793 1605 1909 1322 848
σαντες οἱ ὄχλοι ἐξεπλήσσοντο ἐπὶ τῇ διδαχῇ αὐτοῦ.
heard, the crowds were astounded at the teaching of Him.
5330 191 3754 5392 4523
34 Οἱ δὲ Φαρισαῖοι, ἀκούσαντες ὅτι ἐφίμωσε τοὺς Σαδδου-
the But Pharisees hearing that He silenced the Sadducees,
4863 1909 846 1905 1520 1537
35 καίους, συνήχθησαν ἐπὶ τὸ αὐτό. καὶ ἐπηρώτησεν εἷς ἐξ
were assembled together, and questioned one of
846 3544 3985 846 3004 1320
36 αὐτῶν νομικός, πειράζων αὐτόν, καὶ λέγων, Διδάσκαλε,
them, a lawyer, tempting Him; and saying, Teacher,
4169 1785 3173 1722 3551 2424 2036 846
37 ποία ἐντολὴ μεγάλη ἐν τῷ νόμῳ; ὁ δὲ Ἰησοῦς εἶπεν αὐτῷ,
which command (is) great in the Law? And Jesus said to him,
25 2962 2316 4675 1722 3650 2588 4675
Ἀγαπήσεις Κύριον τὸν Θεόν σου, ἐν ὅλῃ τῇ καρδίᾳ σου,
You shall love the Lord the God of you, with all the heart of you,
1722 3650 5590 4675 1722 3650 1271 4675 3778
38 καὶ ἐν ὅλῃ τῇ ψυχῇ σου, καὶ ἐν ὅλῃ τῇ διανοίᾳ σου. αὕτη
and with all the soul of you, and with all the mind of you. This
2076 4413 3173 1785 1208 3664 846
39 ἐστὶ πρώτη καὶ μεγάλη ἐντολή. δευτέρα δὲ ὁμοία αὐτῇ,
is the first and great commandment; second and like to it,
25 4139 4675 5613 4572 1722 5025
40 Ἀγαπήσεις τὸν πλησίον σου ὡς σεαυτόν. ἐν ταύταις ταῖς
You shall love the neighbor of you as yourself. In these
1417 1785 3650 3551 4396 2910
δυσὶν ἐντολαῖς ὅλος ὁ νόμος καὶ οἱ προφῆται κρέμανται.
two commandments all the Law and the prophets hang.
4863 5330 1905 846
41 Συνηγμένων δὲ τῶν Φαρισαίων, ἐπηρώτησεν αὐτοὺς ὁ
having been assembled But the Pharisees, questioned them
2424 3004 5101 5213 1380 4012 5547 5101 5207
42 Ἰησοῦς, λέγων, Τί ὑμῖν δοκεῖ περὶ τοῦ Χριστοῦ; τίνος υἱός
Jesus, saying, What to you seems about the Christ? Of whom son
2076 3004 846 1138 3004 846 4459 3767
43 ἐστι; λέγουσιν αὐτῷ, Τοῦ Δαβίδ. λέγει αὐτοῖς, Πῶς οὖν
is He? They say to Him, Of David. He says to them, How then
1138 1722 4151 2962 846 2564 3004 2036
44 Δαβὶδ ἐν πνεύματι Κύριον αὐτὸν καλεῖ, λέγων, Εἶπεν ὁ
David by (the) Spirit Lord Him does call, saying, Said the
2962 2962 3450 2521 1537 1188 3450 2193 302 5087
Κύριος τῷ Κυρίῳ μου, Κάθου ἐκ δεξιῶν μου, ἕως ἂν θῶ τοὺς
Lord to the Lord of Me, Sit on the right of Me until I put the
2190 4675 5286 4228 4675 1487 3767 1138
45 ἐχθρούς σου ὑποπόδιον τῶν ποδῶν σου; εἰ οὖν Δαβὶδ
enemies of You (as) a footstool of the feet of You? If, then, David
2564 846 2962 4459 5207 848 2076 3762 1410
46 καλεῖ αὐτὸν Κύριον, πῶς υἱὸς αὐτοῦ ἐστι; καὶ οὐδεὶς ἐδύνατο
calls Him Lord, how a son of him is He? And no one was able

NOTE: Frequent words not numbered: δέ(1161); καί(2531)—and, but; ὁ, ἡ, τό (3588, the)— * above word, look in verse margin for No.

answer Him a word, nor did anyone dare from that day to question Him any more.

CHAPTER 23

[1]Then Jesus spoke to the crowd and to His disciples, [2]saying, The scribes and the Pharisees sat down on Moses' seat. [3]Then all things, whatever they tell you to keep, keep and do. But do not do according to their works; for they say, and do not do. [4]For they bind heavy and hard to bear burdens, and lay *them* on the shoulders of men; but they do not desire to move them with their finger. [5]And they do all their works to be seen by men. And they make their phylacteries broad, and enlarge the borders of their robes.

[6]And *they* love the first couch in the suppers, and the first seats in the synagogues, [7]and the greetings in the markets, and to be called by men, Rabbi, Rabbi. [8]But do not you be called Rabbi; for One is your leader, the Christ, and you are all brothers. [9]And call no one father on earth, for one is your Father, the *One* in Heaven. [10]Nor be called leaders, for One is your Leader, the Christ. [11]But the greater of you shall be your servant. [12]And whoever will exalt himself shall be humbled. And whoever will humble himself shall be exalted.

[13]But woe to you, scribes and Pharisees, hypocrites! For you shut up the

846 611 3056 3761 5111 5100 575 1565
αὐτῷ ἀποκριθῆναι λόγον· οὐδὲ ἐτόλμησέ τις ἀπ' ἐκείνης τῆς
Him to answer a word, nor dared anyone from that
2250 1905 846 3765
ἡμέρας ἐπερωτῆσαι αὐτὸν οὐκέτι.
day to question Him no longer.

CHAPTER 23

5119 2424 2980 3793 3101
1 Τότε ὁ Ἰησοῦς ἐλάλησε τοῖς ὄχλοις καὶ τοῖς μαθηταῖς
Then – Jesus spoke to the crowd and to the disciples
848 3004 1909 3475 2515 2523
2 αὐτοῦ, λέγων, Ἐπὶ τῆς Μωσέως καθέδρας ἐκάθισαν οἱ
of Him, saying, On the of Moses seat sat the
1122 5330 3956 3767 3745 302 2036
3 γραμματεῖς καὶ οἱ Φαρισαῖοι· πάντα οὖν ὅσα ἂν εἴπωσιν
scribes and the Pharisees. All things, then, whatever they tell
5213 5083 5083 4160 2596 2041 848 3361
ὑμῖν τηρεῖν, τηρεῖτε καὶ ποιεῖτε· κατὰ δὲ τὰ ἔργα αὐτῶν μὴ
you to keep, keep and do. after But the works of them not
4160 3004 1063 3756 4160 1195 1063 5413
4 ποιεῖτε, λέγουσι γὰρ καὶ οὐ ποιοῦσι. δεσμεύουσι γὰρ φορτία
do you. they say For and not do. they bind For burdens
926 1419 2007 1909 5606
βαρέα καὶ δυσβάστακτα, καὶ ἐπιτιθέασιν ἐπὶ τοὺς ὤμους
heavy, and hard to bear, and lay (them) on the shoulders
444 1147 848 3756 2309 2795
τῶν ἀνθρώπων, τῷ δὲ δακτύλῳ αὐτῶν οὐ θέλουσι κινῆσαι
of men; (with) the but finger of them not they wish to move
846 3956 2041 848 4160 4314 2300
5 αὐτά. πάντα δὲ τὰ ἔργα αὐτῶν ποιοῦσι πρὸς τὸ θεαθῆναι
them. all. But the works of them they do in order to be seen
444 4115 5440 848
τοῖς ἀνθρώποις· πλατύνουσι δὲ τὰ φυλακτήρια αὐτῶν, καὶ
by men; they broaden And the phylacteries of them, and
3170 2899 2440 848 5368 5037
6 μεγαλύνουσι τὰ κράσπεδα τῶν ἱματίων αὐτῶν· φιλοῦσί τε
enlarge the fringes of the garments of them; they love and
4411 1722 1173 4410
τὴν πρωτοκλισίαν ἐν τοῖς δείπνοις, καὶ τὰς πρωτοκαθεδρίας
the first couch in the suppers, and the first seats
1722 4864 783 1722 58
7 ἐν ταῖς συναγωγαῖς, καὶ τοὺς ἀσπασμοὺς ἐν ταῖς ἀγοραῖς,
in the synagogues, and the greetings in the markets
2564 5259 444 4461 4461 5210 3361
8 καὶ καλεῖσθαι ὑπὸ τῶν ἀνθρώπων, ῥαββί, ῥαββί· ὑμεῖς δὲ μὴ
and to be called by men, Rabbi, Rabbi! you But not
2564 4561 1520 1063 2076 5216 2519 5547
κληθῆτε ῥαββί· εἷς γάρ ἐστιν ὑμῶν ὁ καθηγητής, ὁ Χριστός·
be called Rabbi; one for is of you the leader, the Christ,
3956 5210 80 2075 3962 3361 2564 5216
9 πάντες δὲ ὑμεῖς ἀδελφοί ἐστε. καὶ πατέρα μὴ καλέσητε ὑμῶν
all and you brothers are. And Father not call of you
1909 1093 1519 1063 2076 3962 5216 1722 3772
ἐπὶ τῆς γῆς· εἷς γάρ ἐστιν ὁ πατὴρ ὑμῶν, ὁ ἐν τοῖς οὐρανοῖς.
on the earth; one for is the Father of you, the (One) in the heavens
3366 2564 2519 1520 1063 5216 2076 2519
10 μηδὲ κληθῆτε καθηγηταί· εἷς γὰρ ὑμῶν ἐστιν ὁ καθηγητής,
Neither be called leaders; One for of you is the Leader
5547 3187 5216 2071 5216 1249 3748
11 ὁ Χριστός. ὁ δὲ μείζων ὑμῶν ἔσται ὑμῶν διάκονος. ὅστις δὲ
12 the Christ. the And greater of you shall be of you a servant, whoever And
5312 1438 5013 3748 5013
ὑψώσει ἑαυτόν, ταπεινωθήσεται· καὶ ὅστις ταπεινώσει
will exalt himself shall be humbled, and whoever will humble
1438 5312
ἑαυτόν, ὑψωθήσεται.
himself shall be exalted.
3759 5213 1122 5330 5273 3754
13 Οὐαὶ δὲ ὑμῖν, γραμματεῖς καὶ Φαρισαῖοι, ὑποκριταί, ὅτι
woe But to you, scribes and Pharisees, hypocrites! Because

NOTE: Frequent words not numbered: δέ(1161); καί(2531)—and, but; ὁ, ἡ, τό (3588, the)— * above word, look in verse margin for No.

kingdom of Heaven before men; for you do not enter, nor do you allow those entering to go in.

[14]Woe to you, scribes and Pharisees, hypocrites! For you devour the houses of widows, and pray at length as a pretext. Because of this you will receive more abundant judgment.

[15]Woe to you, scribes and Pharisees, hypocrites! For you go about the sea and the dry *land* to make one proselyte; and when he has become *so*, you make him twofold more a son of Hell than yourselves.

[16]Woe to you, blind guides, who say, Whoever swears by the temple, it is nothing; but whoever swears by the gold of the temple is a debtor. [17]Fools and blind! For which is greater, the gold, or the temple that sanctifies the gold? [18]And *you say*, Whoever swears by the altar, it is nothing; but whoever swears by the gift on it, *he is* a debtor. [19]Fools and blind! For which is greater, the gift, or the altar that sanctifies the gift? [20]Then the *one* swearing by the altar swears by it, and by all things on it. [21]And the *one* swearing by the temple swears by it, and by the *One* dwelling in it. [22]And the *one* swearing by Heaven swears by the throne of God, and by the *One* sitting on it.

[23]Woe to you, scribes and Pharisees, hypocrites! For you pay tithes of mint and dill and cummin, and you have left aside the weightier *matters* of the Law: judgment, and mercy,

2808 932 3772 1715 444
κλείετε τὴν βασιλείαν τῶν οὐρανῶν ἔμπροσθεν τῶν ἀνθρώ-
you shut the kingdom of the heavens before men;
5210 1063 3756 1525 3761 1525
πων· ὑμεῖς γὰρ οὐκ εἰσέρχεσθε, οὐδὲ τοὺς εἰσερχομένους
you for not do enter, nor the (ones) entering
868 1525
ἀφίετε εἰσελθεῖν.
do you allow to enter.
3759 5213 1122 5330 5273 3754
14 Οὐαὶ ὑμῖν, γραμματεῖς καὶ Φαρισαῖοι, ὑποκριταί, ὅτι
Woe to you, scribes and Pharisees, hypocrites! Because
2719 3614 5503 4392 3117
κατεσθίετε τὰς οἰκίας τῶν χηρῶν, καὶ προφάσει μακρὰ
you devour the houses of the widows, and as a pretext (are) long
4336 1223 5124 2983 4055 2917
προσευχόμενοι· διὰ τοῦτο λήψεσθε περισσότερον κρίμα.
praying. Because of this you will receive more abundant judgment.
3759 5213 1122 5330 5273 3754
15 Οὐαὶ ὑμῖν, γραμματεῖς καὶ Φαρισαῖοι, ὑποκριταί, ὅτι
Woe to you, scribes and Pharisees, hypocrites! Because
4013 2281 3584 4160 1520 4339
περιάγετε τὴν θάλασσαν καὶ τὴν ξηρὰν ποιῆσαι ἕνα προσή-
you go about the sea and the dry (land) to make one prose-
3752 1096 4160 846 5207 1067 1362
λυτον, καὶ ὅταν γένηται, ποιεῖτε αὐτὸν υἱὸν γεέννης διπλό-
lyte, and when he becomes, you make him a son of Gehenna twofold
5216
τερον ὑμῶν.
more than you.
3759 5213 3595 5185 3004 3739 302 3660 1722
16 Οὐαὶ ὑμῖν, ὁδηγοὶ τυφλοί, οἱ λέγοντες, Ὃς ἂν ὀμόσῃ ἐν
Woe to you, leaders blind, the (ones) saying, Whoever swears by
3485 3762 2075 3739 302 3660 1722 5557 3485
τῷ ναῷ, οὐδέν ἐστιν· ὃς δ' ἂν ὀμόσῃ ἐν τῷ χρυσῷ τοῦ ναοῦ,
the Temple, nothing it is; who but ever swears by the gold of the Temple,
3784 3474 5185 5101 1063 3187 2076 5557 2228
17 ὀφείλει. μωροὶ καὶ τυφλοί· τίς γὰρ μείζων ἐστίν, ὁ χρυσός, ἢ
is a debtor. Fools and blind! what For greater is, the gold or
3485 37 5558 3739 1437 3660 1722
18 ὁ ναὸς ὁ ἁγιάζων τὸν χρυσόν; καί, Ὃς ἐὰν ὀμόσῃ ἐν τῷ
The Temple sanctifying the gold? And, whoever swears by the
2379 3762 2076 3739 302 3660 1722 1435
θυσιαστηρίῳ, οὐδέν ἐστιν· ὃς δ' ἂν ὀμόσῃ ἐν τῷ δώρῳ τῷ
altar, nothing it is; who but ever swears by the gift
1883 846 3784 3474 5185 5101 1063 3187
19 ἐπάνω αὐτοῦ, ὀφείλει. μωροὶ καὶ τυφλοί· τί γὰρ μεῖζον,
upon it, (is) a debtor. Fools and blind! what For is greater
1435 2228 2379 37 1435 3767
20 τὸ δῶρον, ἢ τὸ θυσιαστήριον τὸ ἁγιάζον τὸ δῶρον; ὁ οὖν
the gift or the altar sanctifying the gift? he Then
3660 1722 2379 3660 1722 846 1722 3956
ὀμόσας ἐν τῷ θυσιαστηρίῳ ὀμνύει ἐν αὐτῷ καὶ ἐν πᾶσι τοῖς
swearing by the altar swears by it and by all the things
1883 846 3660 1722 3485 3660 1722 846 1722
21 ἐπάνω αὐτοῦ· καὶ ὁ ὀμόσας ἐν τῷ ναῷ ὀμνύει ἐν αὐτῷ καὶ ἐν
upon it; and he swearing by the Temple swears by it and by
2730 846 3660 1722 3772 3660
22 τῷ κατοικοῦντι αὐτόν· καὶ ὁ ὀμόσας ἐν τῷ οὐρανῷ ὀμνύει
the (One) inhabiting it. And the (one) swearing by Heaven swears
1722 2362 2316 1722 2521 1883 846
ἐν τῷ θρόνῳ τοῦ Θεοῦ καὶ ἐν τῷ καθημένῳ ἐπάνω αὐτοῦ.
by the throne of God and by the (one) sitting upon it.
3759 5213 1122 5330 5273 3754
23 Οὐαὶ ὑμῖν, γραμματεῖς καὶ Φαρισαῖοι, ὑποκριταί, ὅτι
Woe to you, scribes and Pharisees, hypocrites! Because
586 2238 432 2951
ἀποδεκατοῦτε τὸ ἡδύοσμον καὶ τὸ ἄνηθον καὶ τὸ κύμινον,
you tithe the mint and the dill and the cummin,
863 926 3551 2920
καὶ ἀφήκατε τὰ βαρύτερα τοῦ νόμου, τὴν κρίσιν καὶ τὸν
and you have left the weightier matters of the law, judgment and

and faith. It was right to do these, and not to have left those aside. 24 Blind guides, straining out the gnat, but swallowing the camel!

25 Woe to you, scribes and Pharisees, hypocrites! For you cleanse the outside of the cup and of the dish, but within they are full of robbery and excess. 26 Blind Pharisee! First cleanse the inside of the cup and of the dish, that the outside of them may become clean also.

27 Woe to you, scribes and Pharisees, hypocrites! For you are like whitened graves which outwardly indeed appear beautiful, but within are full of bones of *the* dead, and of all uncleanness. 28 So you also indeed outwardly appear righteous to men, but within are full of hypocrisy and lawlessness.

29 Woe to you, scribes and Pharisees, hypocrites! For you build the tombs of the prophets, and adorn the tombs of the righteous. 30 And you say, If we had been in the days of our fathers, we would not have been partakers with them in the blood of the prophets. 31 So you witness to yourselves, that you are the sons of those who murdered the prophets. 32 And you fill up the measure of your fathers. 33 Serpents, offspring of vipers! How shall you escape the judgment of Hell? 34 Because of this, behold, I send to you prophets and wise ones and scribes. And *some* of them you will kill and crucify; and *some* of them

1656 4102 5023 1163 4160 2548 3361 863
ἔλεον καὶ τὴν πίστιν· ταῦτα ἔδει ποιῆσαι, κἀκεῖνα μὴ ἀφιέναι.
mercy and faith; these things one needs to do, and those not to leave
3595 5185 1368 2971 2574
24 ὁδηγοὶ τυφλοί, οἱ διϋλίζοντες τὸν κώνωπα, τὴν δὲ κάμηλον
leaders Blind, the (ones) straining out the gnat, the but camel
2666
καταπίνοντες.
swallowing.

3759 5213 1122 5330 5273 3754
25 Οὐαὶ ὑμῖν, γραμματεῖς καὶ Φαρισαῖοι, ὑποκριταί, ὅτι
Woe to you, scribes and Pharisees, hypocrites! Because
2511 1855 4221 3953
καθαρίζετε τὸ ἔξωθεν τοῦ ποτηρίου καὶ τῆς παροψίδος,
you cleanse the outside of the cup and the dish,
2081 1073 1537 724 192 5330 5185
26 ἔσωθεν δὲ γέμουσιν ἐξ ἁρπαγῆς καὶ ἀκρασίας. Φαρισαῖε τυφλέ,
within but they are full of robbery and excess. Pharisee Blind,
2511 4412 1787 4221 3953
καθάρισον πρῶτον τὸ ἐντὸς τοῦ ποτηρίου καὶ τῆς παροψί-
cleanse first the inside of the cup and of the dish,
2443 1096 1623 846 2513
δος, ἵνα γένηται καὶ τὸ ἐκτὸς αὐτῶν καθαρόν.
that may become also the outside of them clean.

3759 5213 1122 5330 5273 3754
27 Οὐαὶ ὑμῖν, γραμματεῖς καὶ Φαρισαῖοι, ὑποκριταί, ὅτι
Woe to you, scribes and Pharisees, hypocrites! Because
3945 5028 2867 3748 1855 3303
παρομοιάζετε τάφοις κεκονιαμένοις, οἵτινες ἔξωθεν μὲν
you are like graves whitewashed, who outwardly indeed
5316 5611 2081 1073 3747 3498
φαίνονται ὡραῖοι, ἔσωθεν δὲ γέμουσιν ὀστέων νεκρῶν καὶ
appear beautiful, within but are full of bones of the dead and
3956 167 3779 5210 1855 3303 5316
28 πάσης ἀκαθαρσίας. οὕτω καὶ ὑμεῖς ἔξωθεν μὲν φαίνεσθε τοῖς
of all uncleanness. So also you outwardly indeed appear —
444 1342 2081 3324 2075 5212
ἀνθρώποις δίκαιοι, ἔσωθεν δέ μεστοί ἐστε ὑποκρίσεως καὶ
to men righteous, within but full are of hypocrisy and
458
ἀνομίας.
lawlessness.

3759 5213 1122 5330 5273 3754
29 Οὐαὶ ὑμῖν, γραμματεῖς καὶ Φαρισαῖοι, ὑποκριταί, ὅτι
Woe to you, scribes and Pharisees, hypocrites! Because
3618 5028 4396 2885
οἰκοδομεῖτε τοὺς τάφους τῶν προφητῶν, καὶ κοσμεῖτε τὰ
you build the graves of the prophets, and decorate the
3419 1342 3004 1487 2258 1722 2250
30 μνημεῖα τῶν δικαίων, καὶ λέγετε, Εἰ ἦμεν ἐν ταῖς ἡμέραις
monuments of the righteous, and say, If we had been in the days
3962 2257 3756 302 2258 2844 846 1722
τῶν πατέρων ἡμῶν, οὐκ ἂν ἦμεν κοινωνοὶ αὐτῶν ἐν τῷ
of the fathers of us, not would we have been sharers of them in the
129 4396 5620 3140 1438 3754 5207
31 αἵματι τῶν προφητῶν. ὥστε μαρτυρεῖτε ἑαυτοῖς ὅτι υἱοί
blood of the prophets. So you witness to yourselves that sons
2075 5407 4396 5210 4137
32 ἐστε τῶν φονευσάντων τοὺς προφήτας· καὶ ὑμεῖς πληρώσατε
you are of those murdering the prophets and you fill up
3358 3962 5216 3789 1081 2191
33 τὸ μέτρον τῶν πατέρων ὑμῶν. ὄφεις, γεννήματα ἐχιδνῶν,
the measure of the fathers of you. Serpents! Offspring of vipers!
4459 5343 575 2920 1067 1223 5124 2400
34 πῶς φύγητε ἀπὸ τῆς κρίσεως τῆς γεέννης; διὰ τοῦτο, ἰδού,
How do you escape from the judgment — of Gehenna? Therefore, behold,
1473 649 4314 5209 4396 4680 1122
ἐγὼ ἀποστέλλω πρὸς ὑμᾶς προφήτας καὶ σοφοὺς καὶ γραμ-
I send to you prophets and wise ones and scribes;
1537 846 615 4717 1537
ματεῖς· καὶ ἐξ αὐτῶν ἀποκτενεῖτε καὶ σταυρώσετε, καὶ ἐξ
and of them you will kill and crucify; and of

NOTE: Frequent words not numbered: δέ(1161); καί(2531)—and, but; ὁ, ἡ, τό (3588, the)— * above word, look in verse margin for No.

you will flog in your synagogues, and will persecute from city to city; [35]so that should come on you all *the* righteous blood poured out on the earth, from the blood of righteous Abel to the blood of Zechariah the son of Berechiah, whom you murdered between the temple and the altar. [36]Truly I say to you, All these things will come on this generation.

[37]Jerusalem, Jerusalem, the *one* killing the prophets and stoning those sent to her. How often I desired to gather your children in the way a bird gathers her chicks from under *her* wings! And you did not desire it. [38]Behold, your house is left to you desolate. [39]For I say to you, In no way shall you see Me from now on until you say, "Blessed is He who comes in *the* name of *the* Lord."

CHAPTER 24

[1]And going out, Jesus left the temple. And His disciples came to show Him the buildings of the temple. [2]But Jesus said to them, Do you not see all these things? Truly I say to you, There will not at all be left *one* stone on *a* stone which in no way will not be thrown down.

[3]And as He was sitting on the Mount of Olives, the disciples came to Him privately, saying, Tell us, when will these things be? And, What is the sign of Your coming and of the end of the age? [4]And answering Jesus said to them, See that not any leads you astray. [5]For many will come in My name, saying, I

846 3146 1722 4864 5216 1377
αὐτῶν μαστιγώσετε ἐν ταῖς συναγωγαῖς ὑμῶν καὶ διώξετε
them you will scourge in the synagogues of you, and persecute
575 4172 1519 4172 3704 2064 1909 5209 3956 129 1342
35 ἀπὸ πόλεως εἰς πόλιν· ὅπως ἔλθῃ ἐφ' ὑμᾶς πᾶν αἷμα δίκαιον
from city to city; so comes upon you all blood righteous
1632 1909 1093 575 129 6
ἐκχυνόμενον ἐπὶ τῆς γῆς, ἀπὸ τοῦ αἵματος Ἄβελ τοῦ
being poured out on the earth, from the blood of Abel the
1342 2193 129 2197 5207 914 3739
δικαίου, ἕως τοῦ αἵματος Ζαχαρίου υἱοῦ Βαραχίου, ὃν
righteous, to the blood of Zachariah (the) son of Barachiah, whom
5407 3342 3485 2379 281
36 ἐφονεύσατε μεταξὺ τοῦ ναοῦ καὶ τοῦ θυσιαστηρίου. ἀμὴν
you murdered between the Temple and the altar. Truly
3004 5213 2240 5023 3956 1909 1074 5026
λέγω ὑμῖν, ἥξει ταῦτα πάντα ἐπὶ τὴν γενεὰν ταύτην.
I say to you, will come all these things on — generation this.
2419 2419 615 4396
37 Ἱερουσαλήμ, Ἱερουσαλήμ, ἡ ἀποκτείνουσα τοὺς προφή-
Jerusalem, Jerusalem, the (one) killing the prophets
3036 649 4314 848
τας καὶ λιθοβολοῦσα τοὺς ἀπεσταλμένους πρὸς αὐτήν,
and stoning the (ones) sent to her,
4212 2309 1996 5043 4675 3739 5158
ποσάκις ἠθέλησα ἐπισυναγαγεῖν τὰ τέκνα σου, ὃν τρόπον
how often I desired to gather together the children of you, in the way
1996 3733 3556 1438 5259 4420
ἐπισυνάγει ὄρνις τὰ νοσσία ἑαυτῆς ὑπὸ τὰς πτέρυγας, καὶ
gathers together a bird the young of her under the wings, and
3767 2309 2400 863 5213 3624 5216 2048
38 οὐκ ἠθελήσατε. ἰδού, ἀφίεται ὑμῖν ὁ οἶκος ὑμῶν ἔρημος.
not you desired. Behold, is left to you the house of you desolate;
3004 1063 5213 =3364= 3165 1492 575 737 2193 302 2036
39 λέγω γὰρ ὑμῖν, Οὐ μή με ἴδητε ἀπ' ἄρτι, ἕως ἂν εἴπητε,
I say For to you, Not at all Me shall you see from now until you say,
2127 2064 1722 3686 2962
Εὐλογημένος ὁ ἐρχόμενος ἐν ὀνόματι Κυρίου.
Blessed the (one) coming in (the) name of (the) Lord.

CHAPTER 24

1831 2424 4198 575 2411
1 Καὶ ἐξελθὼν ὁ Ἰησοῦς ἐπορεύετο ἀπὸ τοῦ ἱεροῦ· καὶ
And going forth — Jesus went away from the Temple, and
4334 3101 848 1925 846 3619
προσῆλθον οἱ μαθηταὶ αὐτοῦ ἐπιδεῖξαι αὐτῷ τὰς οἰκοδομὰς
came up the disciples of Him to show Him the buildings
2411 2424 2036 846 3756 991 3956
2 τοῦ ἱεροῦ. ὁ δὲ Ἰησοῦς εἶπεν αὐτοῖς, Οὐ βλέπετε πάντα
of the Temple — And Jesus said to them, Not you see all
5023 281 3004 5213 3756 3361 863 5602 3037 1909 3037 3739
ταῦτα; ἀμὴν λέγω ὑμῖν, οὐ μὴ ἀφεθῇ ὧδε λίθος ἐπὶ λίθον, ὃς
these? Truly I say to you, Not at all will be left here stone on stone which
=3364= 2647
οὐ μὴ καταλυθήσεται.
not at all shall be thrown down.
2521 846 1909 3735 1636 4334
3 Καθημένου δὲ αὐτοῦ ἐπὶ τοῦ ὄρους τῶν ἐλαιῶν, προσῆλ-
sitting And He on the mount of the olives, came
846 3101 2596 2398 3004 2036 2254 4129
θον αὐτῷ οἱ μαθηταὶ κατ' ἰδίαν, λέγοντες, Εἰπὲ ἡμῖν, πότε
up to Him the disciples privately, saying, Tell us, when
5023 2071 5102 4592 4674 3952
ταῦτα ἔσται; καὶ τί τὸ σημεῖον τῆς σῆς παρουσίας, καὶ τῆς
these things will be; and what the sign of Your presence, and of the
4930 165 611 2424 2036 846
4 συντελείας τοῦ αἰῶνος; καὶ ἀποκριθεὶς ὁ Ἰησοῦς εἶπεν αὐτοῖς,
termination of the age? And answering — Jesus said to them,
991 3361 5100 5209 4105 4183 1063 2064 1909
5 Βλέπετε, μή τις ὑμᾶς πλανήσῃ. πολλοὶ γὰρ ἐλεύσονται ἐπὶ
See, not any you misleads. many For will come on

NOTE: Frequent words not numbered: δέ(1161); καί(2531)—and, but; ὁ, ἡ, τό (3588, the)— * above word look in verse margin for No.

am the Christ. And *they* will cause many to err. [6]But you are going to hear of wars and rumors of wars. See, do not be disturbed. For all things must take place, but the end is not yet. [7]For nation will be raised against nation, and kingdom against kingdom; and there will be famines and plagues and earthquakes against *many* places. [8]But all these *are* a beginning of throes. [9]Then they will deliver you up to affliction, and will kill you; and you will be hated by all nations for My name's sake. [10]And then many will be offended, and they will deliver up one another, and will hate one another. [11]And many false prophets will be raised, and will cause many to err. [12]And because lawlessness shall have been multiplied, the love of many will grow cold. [13]But the *one* who endures to *the* end, that one will be saved.

[14]And this gospel of the kingdom shall be preached in all the earth, for a testimony to all the nations; and then will come the end.

[15]Then when you see the abomination of desolation which was spoken of by Daniel the prophet, standing in *the* holy place—the *one* reading, let him understand—[16]then let those in Judea flee on the mountains; [17]the *one* on the housetop, let him not come down to take anything out of his house; [18]and the *one* in the field, let him not turn back to take his garment. [19]But woe to the *woman* being with child and to those suckling in those days! [20]And pray that your flight will not be in winter, nor on a sabbath. [21]For

3686 3450 3004 1473 1510 5547 4187
τῷ ὀνόματί μου, λέγοντες, Ἐγώ εἰμι ὁ Χριστός· καὶ πολλοὺς
the name of Me, saying, I am the Christ, and many
4105 3195 191 4171 189
6 πλανήσουσι. μελλήσετε δὲ ἀκούειν πολέμους καὶ ἀκοὰς
will cause to err. you will be about But to hear of wars and rumors
4171 3708 3361 2360 1163 1063 3956 1096 235
πολέμων· ὁρᾶτε, μὴ θροεῖσθε· δεῖ γὰρ πάντα γενέσθαι· ἀλλ'
of wars. See, do not be upset; it is right for all things to happen, but
3768 2076 5056 1453 1063 1484 1909 1484
7 οὔπω ἐστὶ τὸ τέλος. ἐγερθήσεται γὰρ ἔθνος ἐπὶ ἔθνος, καὶ
not yet is the end. will be raised For nation against nation, and
932 1909 932 2071 3042 3061
βασιλεία ἐπὶ βασιλείαν· καὶ ἔσονται λιμοὶ καὶ λοιμοὶ καὶ
kingdom against kingdom, and there will be famines and plagues and
4578 2596 5117 3956 5023 746 5604 5119
8 σεισμοὶ κατὰ τόπους. πάντα δὲ ταῦτα ἀρχὴ ὠδίνων. τότε
9 earthquakes against places. all these things But beginning of throes. Then
3860 5209 1519 2347 615 5209
παραδώσουσιν ὑμᾶς εἰς θλῖψιν, καὶ ἀποκτενοῦσιν ὑμᾶς· καὶ
they will deliver up you to affliction, and will kill you, and
2071 3404 5259 3956 1484 1223 3686 3450
ἔσεσθε μισούμενοι ὑπὸ πάντων τῶν ἐθνῶν διὰ τὸ ὄνομά μου.
you will be hated by all the nations for the name of Me.
5119 4624 4183 240 3860
10 καὶ τότε σκανδαλισθήσονται πολλοί, καὶ ἀλλήλους παραδώ-
And then will be offended many, and one another will
3404 240 4183 5578
11 σουσι, καὶ μισήσουσιν ἀλλήλους. καὶ πολλοὶ ψευδοπρο-
deliver, and they will hate one another. And many false
1453 4105 4183 1223
12 φῆται ἐγερθήσονται, καὶ πλανήσουσι πολλούς. καὶ διὰ τὸ
prophets will be raised up, and will cause to err many; and because of
4129 458 5594 26
πληθυνθῆναι τὴν ἀνομίαν, ψυγήσεται ἡ ἀγάπη τῶν
shall have been multiplied lawlessness, will grow cold the love of the
4183 5278 1519 5056 3778 4982
13 πολλῶν· ὁ δὲ ὑπομείνας εἰς τέλος, οὗτος σωθήσεται. καὶ
14 many. the (one) But enduring to (the) end, this one will be saved. And
2784 5124 2098 932 1722 3650
κηρυχθήσεται τοῦτο τὸ εὐαγγέλιον τῆς βασιλείας ἐν ὅλῃ
will be proclaimed this gospel of the kingdom in all
3625 1519 3142 3956 1484 5119 2240
τῇ οἰκουμένῃ εἰς μαρτύριον πᾶσι τοῖς ἔθνεσι· καὶ τότε ἥξει
the inhabited earth for a testimony to all the nations, and then will come
5056
τὸ τέλος.
the end.

3752 3767 1492 946 2050 4483 1223
15 Ὅταν οὖν ἴδητε τὸ βδέλυγμα τῆς ἐρημώσεως, τὸ ῥηθὲν διὰ
When then you see the abomination of desolation spoken via
1158 4396 2476 1722 5117 40 314
Δανιὴλ τοῦ προφήτου, ἑστὼς ἐν τόπῳ ἁγίῳ (ὁ ἀναγινώ-
Daniel the prophet, standing in place holy (the one reading
3539 5119 1722 2449 5343 1909
16 σκων νοείτω), τότε οἱ ἐν τῇ Ἰουδαίᾳ φευγέτωσαν ἐπὶ τὰ
let him understand) then the(se) in Judea, let them flee upon the
3735 1909 1430 3361 2597 142 5100 1537
17 ὄρη· ὁ ἐπὶ τοῦ δώματος μὴ καταβαινέτω ἆραί τι ἐκ τῆς
mounts, he on the housetop not let him descend to take a thing from the
3614 848 1722 68 3361 1994 3684
18 οἰκίας αὐτοῦ· καὶ ὁ ἐν τῷ ἀγρῷ μὴ ἐπιστρεψάτω ὀπίσω
house of him; and the (one) in the field, not let him return behind
142 2440 848 3759 1722 1064 2192
19 ἆραι τὰ ἱμάτια αὐτοῦ. οὐαὶ δὲ ταῖς ἐν γαστρὶ ἐχούσαις καὶ
to take the garment of him. Woe And to the(se) in womb having and
2337 1722 1565 2250 4336
20 ταῖς θηλαζούσαις ἐν ἐκείναις ταῖς ἡμέραις. προσεύχεσθε δὲ
to those suckling in those – days. pray And
2443 3361 1096 5437 5216 5494 3366 1722 4521
ἵνα μὴ γένηται ἡ φυγὴ ὑμῶν χειμῶνος, μηδὲ ἐν σαββάτῳ·
that not will occur the flight of you of winter, nor on a sabbath;

NOTE: Frequent words not numbered: δέ(1161); καί(2531)—and, but; ὁ, ἡ, τό (3588, the)— a above word, look in verse margin for No.

there will be great affliction, such as has not happened from *the* beginning of *the* world until now; no, nor ever will be. [22]And except those days were shortened, not any flesh would be saved—but on account of the elect, those days will be shortened. [23]Then if anyone says to you, Behold, here *is* the Christ; or, Here! Do not believe. [24]For false christs and false prophets will rise up. And *they* will give great signs and wonders, so as to lead astray, if possible, even the elect. [25]Behold, I tell you beforehand. [26]Then if they say to you, Behold, He is in the wilderness; do not go out. Behold, *He is* in the inner rooms; do not believe. [27]For as the lightning comes forth from *the* east and shines as far as *the* west, so also will be the coming of the Son of man. [28]For wherever the dead body may be, there the eagles will be gathered.

[29]And immediately after the affliction of those days, the sun will be darkened, and the moon will not give her light, and the stars will fall from the heaven, and the powers of the heavens will be shaken. [30]And then the sign of the Son of man will appear in the heavens. And then all the tribes of the land will wail. And they will see the Son of man coming on the clouds of heaven with power and much glory. [31]And He will send His angels with a great sound of a trumpet, and they will gather His elect from the four winds; from *the* ends of *the* heavens to their ends.

2071 1063 5119 2347 3173 3634 3756 1096 575 746
21 ἔσται γὰρ τότε θλίψις μεγάλη, οἵα οὐ γέγονεν ἀπ' ἀρχῆς
will be for then affliction great, such as not has occurred from origin
2889 2193 3568 3761 =3364= 1096 =1508= 2856
22 κόσμου ἕως τοῦ νῦν, οὐδ' οὐ μὴ γένηται. καὶ εἰ μὴ ἐκολοβώ-
of world until now; neither by no means occur. And except were cut
2250 1565 3756 302 4982 3956 4561 1223
θησαν αἱ ἡμέραι ἐκεῖναι, οὐκ ἂν ἐσώθη πᾶσα σάρξ· διὰ δὲ
short days those, not would be saved any flesh; because of the
1588 2856 2250 1565 5119 1437
23 τοὺς ἐκλεκτοὺς κολοβωθήσονται αἱ ἡμέραι ἐκεῖναι. τότε ἐάν
the elect will be cut short days those. Then if
5100/5213/2036 2400 5602 5547 2228 5602 3361 4100
τις ὑμῖν εἴπῃ, Ἰδού, ὧδε ὁ Χριστός, ἢ ὧδε, μὴ πιστεύσητε.
anyone to you says, Behold, here the Christ; or, Here; not believe
1453 1063 5580 5578
24 ἐγερθήσονται γὰρ ψευδόχριστοι καὶ ψευδοπροφῆται, καὶ
will arise for false Christ and false prophets, and
1325 4592 3173 5059 5620 4105
δώσουσι σημεῖα μεγάλα καὶ τέρατα, ὥστε πλανῆσαι, εἰ
they will give signs great and wonders, so as to cause to err, if
1415 1588 2400 4280 5213 1437 3767
25 δυνατόν, καὶ τοὺς ἐκλεκτούς. ἰδού, προείρηκα ὑμῖν. ἐὰν οὖν
26 possible, even the elect. Behold, I tell before to you. If then
2036 5213 2400 1722 2048 2076 3361 1831 2400
εἴπωσιν ὑμῖν, Ἰδού, ἐν τῇ ἐρήμῳ ἐστί, μὴ ἐξέλθητε· ἰδού,
they say to you, Behold, in the desert He is, not go forth: Behold,
1722 5009 3361 4100 5618 1063 796
27 ἐν τοῖς ταμείοις, μὴ πιστεύσητε. ὥσπερ γὰρ ἡ ἀστραπὴ
in the private rooms. not believe. as For the lightning
1831 575 395 5316 2193 1424 3779
ἐξέρχεται ἀπὸ ἀνατολῶν καὶ φαίνεται ἕως δυσμῶν, οὕτως
comes forth from (the) east and shines as far as (the) west, so
2071 3952 5207 444 3699 1063
28 ἔσται καὶ ἡ παρουσία τοῦ υἱοῦ τοῦ ἀνθρώπου. ὅπου γὰρ
will be also the coming of the Son of man. wherever For
1437 5600 4430 1563 4863 105
ἐὰν ᾖ τὸ πτῶμα, ἐκεῖ συναχθήσονται οἱ ἀετοί.
if may be the carcase, there will be gathered the eagles.

2112 3326 2347 2250 1565 2246
29 Εὐθέως δὲ μετὰ τὴν θλῖψιν τῶν ἡμερῶν ἐκείνων, ὁ ἥλιος
immediately And after the affliction – of days those, the sun
4654 4582 3756 1325 5338 848
σκοτισθήσεται, καὶ ἡ σελήνη οὐ δώσει τὸ φέγγος αὐτῆς,
will be darkened, and the moon not will give the light of her,
792 4098 575 3772 1411
καὶ οἱ ἀστέρες πεσοῦνται ἀπὸ τοῦ οὐρανοῦ, καὶ αἱ δυνάμεις
and the stars will fall from – heaven, and the powers
3772 4531 5119 5316
30 τῶν οὐρανῶν σαλευθήσονται. καὶ τότε φανήσεται τὸ
of the heavens will be shaken. And then will appear the
4592 5207 444 1722 3772 5119
σημεῖον τοῦ υἱοῦ τοῦ ἀνθρώπου ἐν τῷ οὐρανῷ· καὶ τότε
sign of the Son – of man in the heavens; and then
2875 3956 5443 1093 3700 5207
κόψονται πᾶσαι αἱ φυλαὶ τῆς γῆς, καὶ ὄψονται τὸν υἱὸν τοῦ
will wail all the tribes of the land, and they will see the Son –
444 2064 1909 3507 3772 3326
ἀνθρώπου ἐρχόμενον ἐπὶ τῶν νεφελῶν τοῦ οὐρανοῦ μετὰ
of man coming on the clouds of heaven with
1411 1391 4183 649 32
31 δυνάμεως καὶ δόξης πολλῆς. καὶ ἀποστελεῖ τοὺς ἀγγέλους
power and glory much; and He will send the angels
848 3326 4536 5456 3173 1996
αὐτοῦ μετὰ σάλπιγγος φωνῆς μεγάλης, καὶ ἐπισυνάξουσι
of Him with a trumpet sound great, and they will gather
1588 848 1537 5064 417 575 206
τοὺς ἐκλεκτοὺς αὐτοῦ ἐκ τῶν τεσσάρων ἀνέμων, ἀπ' ἄκρων
the elect of Him out of the four winds from (the) ends
3772 2193 206 848
οὐρανῶν ἕως ἄκρων αὐτῶν.
of the heavens to (the) ends of them.

[32]But learn the parable of the fig-tree: When its branch becomes tender, and it puts out leaves, you know that the summer *is* near; [33]so also you when you see all these things, know that it is near, at *the* doors. [34]Truly I say to you, In no way will this generation pass away until all these things have occurred. [35]The heavens and the earth will pass away, but My words will not at all pass away.. [36]But about that day and the hour, no one knows, neither the angels of Heaven, except My Father only. [37]But as the days of Noah, so also will be the coming of the Son of man. [38]For as they were in the days before the flood: eating, and drinking, marrying, and giving in marriage, until *the* day *when* Noah went into the ark—[39]and they did not know until the flood came and took all away—so also will be the coming of the Son of man. [40]At that time two will be out in the field; the one is taken away, and the one is left; [41]two grinding at the mill; one is taken, and one is left.

[42]Watch, then, for you do not know in what hour your Lord comes. [43]But know this, that if the housemaster had known in what watch the thief comes, he would have watched, and not have allowed his house to be dug through. [44]Because of this, you also be ready, for in that hour you think not, the Son of man comes. [45]Who then is the faithful and wise servant, whom his lord has set over his household, to give to

575 4818 3129 3850 3752 2235
32 Ἀπὸ δὲ τῆς συκῆς μάθετε τὴν παραβολήν· ὅταν ἤδη ὁ
from And the fig-tree learn the parable: When now the
2798 846 1096 527 5444 1631 1097
κλάδος αὐτῆς γένηται ἁπαλός, καὶ τὰ φύλλα ἐκφύῃ, γινώ-
branch of it becomes tender, and the leaves it puts out, you
3754 1451 2330 3779 5210 3752 1492 3956
33 σκετε ὅτι ἐγγὺς τὸ θέρος· οὕτω καὶ ὑμεῖς, ὅταν ἴδητε πάντα
know that near (is) the summer: so also you when you see all
5023 1097 3754 1451 2076 1909 2374 281 3004
34 ταῦτα, γινώσκετε ὅτι ἐγγύς ἐστιν ἐπὶ θύραις. ἀμὴν λέγω
these things know that near it is on (the) doors. Truly I say
5213 3756 3361 3928 1074 3778 2193 302 3956 5023
ὑμῖν, οὐ μὴ παρέλθῃ ἡ γενεὰ αὕτη, ἕως ἂν πάντα ταῦτα
to you, In no way passes away generation this until all these things
1096 3772 1093 3928 3056
35 γένηται. ὁ οὐρανὸς καὶ ἡ γῆ παρελεύσονται, οἱ δὲ λόγοι
have occurred. The heavens and the earth will pass away, the but words
3450 =3364= 3928 4012 2250 1565
36 μου οὐ μὴ παρέλθωσι. περὶ δὲ τῆς ἡμέρας ἐκείνης καὶ τῆς
of Me in no way may pass away. about But day that and the
5610 3762 1492 3761 32 3772 =1508=
ὥρας οὐδεὶς οἶδεν, οὐδὲ οἱ ἄγγελοι τῶν οὐρανῶν, εἰ μὴ ὁ
hour no one knows, neither the angels of the Heaven, except the
3962 3450 3441 5618 2250 3575 3779
37 πατήρ μου μόνος. ὥσπερ δὲ αἱ ἡμέραι τοῦ Νῶε, οὕτως
Father of Me only. as But the days of Noah, so
2071 3952 5207 444 5618 1063
38 ἔσται καὶ ἡ παρουσία τοῦ υἱοῦ τοῦ ἀνθρώπου. ὥσπερ γὰρ
will be also the coming of the Son of man. as For
2258 1722 2250 4253 2627 5176
ἦσαν ἐν ταῖς ἡμέραις ταῖς πρὸ τοῦ κατακλυσμοῦ τρώγοντες
they were in the days before the flood, eating
4095 1060 1547 891 3739 2250
καὶ πίνοντες, γαμοῦντες καὶ ἐκγαμίζοντες, ἄχρι ἧς ἡμέρας
and drinking marrying and giving in marriage, until which day
1525 3575 1519 2787 3756 1097 2193 2064
39 εἰσῆλθε Νῶε εἰς τὴν κιβωτόν, καὶ οὐκ ἔγνωσαν, ἕως ἦλθεν
entered Noah into the ark, and not did know until came
2627 142 537 3779 2071 3952
ὁ κατακλυσμὸς καὶ ἦρεν ἅπαντας, οὕτως ἔσται καὶ ἡ παρου-
the flood and took all, so will be the coming
5207 444 5119 1417 2071 1722 68
40 σία τοῦ υἱοῦ τοῦ ἀνθρώπου. τότε δύο ἔσονται ἐν τῷ ἀγρῷ·
of the Son of man. Then two will be in the field.
1520 3880 1520 863 1417 229
41 ὁ εἷς παραλαμβάνεται, καὶ ὁ εἷς ἀφίεται. δύο ἀλήθουσαι ἐν
the one is taken away and the one is left. Two grinding in
3459 3391 3880 3391 863 1127
42 τῷ μύλωνι· μία παραλαμβάνεται, καὶ μία ἀφίεται. γρηγο-
the mill, one is taken away and one is left. Watch
3761 3754 3756 1492 4169 5510 2962 5216 2064
ρεῖτε οὖν, ὅτι οὐκ οἴδατε ποίᾳ ὥρᾳ ὁ Κύριος ὑμῶν ἔρχεται.
therefore that not you know on what hour the Lord of you is coming.
1565 1097 3754 1487 1492 3617 4169 5438
43 ἐκεῖνο δὲ γινώσκετε, ὅτι εἰ ᾔδει ὁ οἰκοδεσπότης ποίᾳ φυλακῇ
this And know, that if knew the housemaster in what watch
2812 2064 1127 302 3756 302 1439 1358
ὁ κλέπτης ἔρχεται, ἐγρηγόρησεν ἄν, καὶ οὐκ ἂν εἴασε διο-
the thief is coming, he would have watched and not might allow to be
3614 848 1223 5124 5210 1096
44 ρυγῆναι τὴν οἰκίαν αὐτοῦ. διὰ τοῦτο καὶ ὑμεῖς γίνεσθε
dug through the house of him. Therefore also you be
3739 2092 3754 5610 3756 1380 5207 444 2064
ἕτοιμοι· ὅτι ᾗ ὥρᾳ οὐ δοκεῖτε, ὁ υἱὸς τοῦ ἀνθρώπου ἔρχεται.
ready, because that hour not you think the Son — of man comes.
5101 686 2076 4103 1401 5429 3739 2525
45 τίς ἄρα ἐστὶν ὁ πιστὸς δοῦλος καὶ φρόνιμος, ὃν κατέστησεν ὁ
Who then is the faithful slave and prudent whom appointed the
2962 848 1909 2322 848 1325 846
κύριος αὐτοῦ ἐπὶ τῆς θεραπείας αὐτοῦ, τοῦ διδόναι αὐτοῖς
lord of him over the service of him — to give to them

them the food in season?
46 Blessed *is* that servant
whom his lord shall find so
doing when he comes.
47 Truly I say to you, He will
set him over all his sub-
stance. 48 But if that wicked
servant says in his heart, My
lord delays to come, 49 and
begins to beat *his* fellow-
servants, and to eat and to
drink with the drunkards,
50 the lord of that slave will
come in a day in which he
does not expect, and in an
hour which he does not
know, 51 and will cut him in
two, and will appoint his
portion with the hypocrtes.
There will be weeping and
gnashing of the teeth.

5160 1722 2540 3107 1401 1565 3739 2064
46 τὴν τροφὴν ἐν καιρῷ; μακάριος ὁ δοῦλος ἐκεῖνος, ὃν ἐλθὼν
the food in season? Blessed (is) – slave that whom coming
2962 848 2147 4160 3779 281 3004 5213
47 ὁ κύριος αὐτοῦ εὑρήσει ποιοῦντα οὕτως. ἀμὴν λέγω ὑμῖν,
the lord of him will find doing so. Truly I say to you,
3754 1909 3956 5224 848 2525 846
ὅτι ἐπὶ πᾶσι τοῖς ὑπάρχουσιν αὐτου καταστήσει αὐτόν.
that over all the goods of him he will appoint him.
1437 2036 2556 1401 1565 1722 2588 848
48 ἐὰν δὲ εἴπῃ ὁ κακὸς δοῦλος ἐκεῖνος ἐν τῇ καρδίᾳ αὐτοῦ,
if But says – wicked slave that in the heart of him,
5549 2962 3450 2064 756 5180 4889
49 Χρονίζει ὁ κύριός μου ἐλθεῖν, καὶ ἄρξηται τύπτειν τοὺς συν-
delays the lord of me to come, and should begin to beat the fellow-
2068 4095 3326 3184 2040
50 δούλους, ἐσθίειν δὲ καὶ πίνειν μετὰ τῶν μεθυόντων, ἥξει ὁ
slaves, to eat and, and to drink with the (ones) drunk, comes the
2962 1401 1565 1722 2250 3739 3756 4328 1722
κύριος τοῦ δούλου ἐκείνου ἐν ἡμέρᾳ ᾗ οὐ προσδοκᾷ, καὶ ἐν
lord of slave that on a day which not he expects, and in
5610 3739 3756 1097 1371 846 3313
51 ὥρᾳ ᾗ οὐ γινώσκει, καὶ διχοτομήσει αὐτόν, καὶ τὸ μέρος
an hour which not he knows, and will cut in two him, and the portion
848 3326 5273 5087 1563 2071 2805
αὐτοῦ μετὰ τῶν ὑποκριτῶν θήσει· ἐκεῖ ἔσται ὁ κλαυθμὸς καὶ
of him with the hypocrites will put; there will be the weeping and
1030 3599
ὁ βρυγμὸς τῶν ὀδόντων.
the gnashing of the teeth.

CHAPTER 25

CHAPTER 25

1 Then the kingdom of
Heaven shall be compared
to ten virgins who took their
lamps and went out to a
meeting of the bridegroom.
2 And five of them were
wise, and five foolish.
3 Those *being* foolish,
taking their lamps did not
take oil with them. 4 But the
wise took oil in their vessels
with their lamps. 5 But the
bridegroom delaying, all
nodded and slept. 6 And *at*
midnight a cry occurred:
Behold the bridegroom
comes! Go out to meet him.
7 Then all those virgins
rose up and prepared their
lamps. 8 And the foolish
said to the wise, Give us
some of your oil, for our
lamps are going out. 9 But
the wise answered, saying,
No, lest there not be

5119 3666 932 3772 1176 3933
1 Τότε ὁμοιωθήσεται ἡ βασιλεία τῶν οὐρανῶν δέκα παρθέ-
Then shall be compared the kingdom of the heavens to ten virgins,
3748 2983 2985 848 1831 1519
νοις, αἵτινες λαβοῦσαι τὰς λαμπάδας αὐτῶν ἐξῆλθον εἰς
who taking the lamps of them went out to
529 3566 4002 2258 1537 846 5429
2 ἀπάντησιν τοῦ νυμφίου. πέντε δὲ ἦσαν ἐξ αὐτῶν φρόνιμοι,
a meeting of the bridegroom. five And were of them prudent
4002 3474 3748 3474 2983 2985
3 καὶ αἱ πέντε μωραί. αἵτινες μωραι, λαβοῦσαι τὰς λαμπάδας
and – five fools those (being) fools, having taken the lamps
1438 3756 2983 3326 1438 1637 5429
4 ἑαυτῶν, οὐκ ἔλαβον μεθ' ἑαυτῶν ἔλαιον· αἱ δὲ φρόνιμοι
of them, not did take with themselves oil; the but prudent
2983 1637 1722 30 848 3326 2985
ἔλαβον ἔλαιον ἐν τοῖς ἀγγείοις αὐτῶν μετὰ τῶν λαμπάδων
took oil in the the vessels of them with the lamps
848 5549 3566 3573 3956
5 αὐτῶν. χρονίζοντος δὲ τοῦ νυμφίου, ἐνύσταξαν πᾶσαι καὶ
of them. delaying But the bridegroom, nodded all and
2518 3319 3571 2906 1096 2400
6 ἐκάθευδον. μέσης δὲ νυκτὸς κραυγὴ γέγονεν, Ἰδού, ὁ
slept (at) mid- And night, a cry occurred: Behold, the
3566 2064 1831 1519 529 846 5119
7 νυμφίος ἔρχεται, ἐξέρχεσθε εἰς ἀπάντησιν αὐτοῦ. τότε
bridegroom comes! Go forth to a meeting of him. Then
1453 3956 3993 1565 2885
ἠγέρθησαν πᾶσαι αἱ παρθένοι ἐκεῖναι, καὶ ἐκόσμησαν τὰς
arose all virgins those, and prepared the
2985 848 3474 5429 2036 1325
8 λαμπάδας αὐτῶν. αἱ δὲ μωραὶ ταῖς φρονίμοις εἶπον, Δότε
lamps of them, the And fools to the prudent said, Give
5213 1537 1637 5216 3754 2985 2257 4570
ἡμῖν ἐκ τοῦ ἐλαίου ὑμῶν, ὅτι αἱ λαμπάδες ἡμῶν σβέννυνται.
us the oil of you, for the lamps of us are going out.
611 5429 3004 3379 3756
9 ἀπεκρίθησαν δὲ αἱ φρόνιμοι, λέγουσαι, Μήποτε οὐκ
answered But the prudent, saying, (No,) lest not

enough for us and you. But rather go to those who sell, and buy for yourselves. [10]But they going away to buy, the bridegroom came. And those ready went in with him to the wedding feast; and the door was shut. [11]And afterwards the rest of the virgins also came, saying, Lord, Lord, open to us. [12]But answering he said, Truly I say to you, I do not know you. [13]Therefore, watch, for you do not know the day nor the hour in which the Son of man comes.

[14]For *it is* as if a man going abroad called *his* own slaves and delivered his goods to them. [15]And to one indeed he gave five talents, and to another two, and to another, one—to each according to his ability. And *he* went abroad at once. [16]And going, the *one* who received the five talents worked with them, and made another five talents. [17]In the same way, the *one* with the two also *did*; he also gained another two. [18]But going away, the *one* who received the one dug in the earth and hid his lord's silver. [19]And after much time, the lord of those slaves came and took account with them. [20]And coming up, the *one* who received five talents brought another five talents near, saying, Lord, you delivered five talents to me. Behold, I gained another five talents above them. [21]And his lord said to him, Well *done*, good and faithful slave. You were faithful over a few things, I will set you over many. Enter into the joy of your lord. [22]And the *one* who received two talents, coming up also said, Lord,

714 2254 5213 4198 3123 4314
ἀρκέσῃ ἡμῖν καὶ ὑμῖν· πορεύεσθε δὲ μᾶλλον πρὸς τοὺς
it suffices to us and to you. go But rather to the (Ones)
4453 59 1438 565 846
10 πωλοῦντας καὶ ἀγοράσατε ἑαυταῖς. ἀπερχομένων δὲ αὐτῶν
selling and buy for yourselves. going away And they
59 2064 3566 2092 1525 3326
ἀγοράσαι, ἦλθεν ὁ νυμφίος· καὶ αἱ ἕτοιμοι εἰσῆλθον μετ᾽
to buy, came the bridegroom and the ready (ones) went in with
846 1062 2808 2374 5305
11 αὐτοῦ εἰς τοὺς γάμους, καὶ ἐκλείσθη ἡ θύρα. ὕστερον δὲ
him to the wedding feast, and was shut the door. later And
2064 3062 3933 3004 2962 2962
ἔρχονται καὶ αἱ λοιπαὶ παρθένοι, λέγουσαι, Κύριε, κύριε,
come also the remaining virgins, saying, Lord, Lord,
455 2254 611 2036 281 3004 5213 3756
12 ἄνοιξον ἡμῖν. ὁ δὲ ἀποκριθεὶς εἶπεν, Ἀμὴν λέγω ὑμῖν, οὐκ
open to us. he But answering said, Truly I say to you, not
1491 5209 1127 3767 3754 3756 1492 2250 3761
13 οἶδα ὑμᾶς. γρηγορεῖτε οὖν, ὅτι οὐκ οἴδατε τὴν ἡμέραν οὐδὲ
I know you. Watch, therefore, for not you know the day nor
5610 1722 * 5207 444 2064
*3739 τὴν ὥραν, ἐν ᾗ ὁ υἱὸς τοῦ ἀνθρώπου ἔρχεται.
the hour in which the Son of man comes.

5618 1063 444 589 2564 2398
14 Ὥσπερ γὰρ ἄνθρωπος ἀποδημῶν ἐκάλεσε τοὺς ἰδίους
(it is) as if For a man going abroad called the own
1401 3860 846 5224 848
15 δούλους, καὶ παρέδωκεν αὐτοῖς τὰ ὑπάρχοντα αὐτοῦ· καὶ
slaves, and delivered to them the goods of him, and
3303 1325 4002 5007 3739 1417 3739 1722 1538 2596
ᾧ μὲν ἔδωκε πέντε τάλαντα, ᾧ δὲ δύο, ᾧ δὲ ἕν, ἑκάστῳ κατὰ
to one he gave five talents; to one and two; to and one; to each by
indeed 2398 1411 589 one 2112 4198
16 τὴν ἰδίαν δύναμιν· καὶ ἀπεδήμησεν εὐθέως. πορευθεὶς δὲ ὁ
the own ability, and went abroad Immediately. going And he
4002 5007 2983 2038 1722 846 4160
τὰ πέντε τάλαντα λαβὼν εἰργάσατο ἐν αὐτοῖς, καὶ ἐποίησεν
the five talents. Likewise, also the (one) the two; gained also
243 4002 5007 5615 1417 2770
17 ἄλλα πέντε τάλαντα. ὡσαύτως καὶ ὁ τὰ δύο ἐκέρδησε καὶ
other five talents. Likewise, also the (one) the two; gained also
846 243 1417 1520 2983 565 3736 1722
18 αὐτὸς ἄλλα δύο. ὁ δὲ τὸ ἓν λαβὼν ἀπελθὼν ὤρυξεν ἐν τῇ
he other two. he But the one receiving, going away dug in the
1093 613 694 2962 848 3326
19 γῇ, καὶ ἀπέκρυψε τὸ ἀργύριον τοῦ κυρίου αὐτοῦ. μετὰ δὲ
earth, and hid the silver of the lord of him. after And
5550 4183 2064 2962 1401 1565
χρόνον πολὺν ἔρχεται ὁ κύριος τῶν δούλων ἐκείνων, καὶ
time much comes the lord — of slaves those, and
4868 3326 846 3056 4334 4002
20 συναίρει μετ᾽ αὐτῶν λόγον. καὶ προσελθὼν ὁ τὰ πέντε
takes with them account. And coming up, the (one) the five
5007 2983 4374 243 4002 5007 3004
τάλαντα λαβὼν προσήνεγκεν ἄλλα πέντε τάλαντα, λέγων,
talents receiving brought near other five talents, saying,
2962 4002 5007 3427 3860 2396 243 4002
Κύριε, πέντε τάλαντά μοι παρέδωκας· ἴδε, ἄλλα πέντε
Lord, five talents to me you delivered. Behold, other five
5007 2770 1909 846 5346 846 2962 848
21 τάλαντα ἐκέρδησα ἐπ᾽ αὐτοῖς. ἔφη δὲ αὐτῷ ὁ κύριος αὐτοῦ,
talents I gained over them. said And to him the lord of him,
2095 1401 18 4103 1909 3641 2258 4103 1909 4183
Εὖ, δοῦλε ἀγαθὲ καὶ πιστέ, ἐπὶ ὀλίγα ἦς πιστός, ἐπὶ πολλῶν
Well, slave good and faithful, over a few you were faithful, over many
4571 2525 1525 1519 5479 2962 4675
σε καταστήσω· εἴσελθε εἰς τὴν χαρὰν τοῦ κυρίου σου.
you I will set. Enter into the joy of the lord of you.
4334 1417 5007 2983 2036 2962
22 προσελθὼν δὲ καὶ ὁ τὰ δύο τάλαντα λαβὼν εἶπε, Κύριε,
coming up And also the (one) the two talents receiving said, Lord,

you delivered two talents to me. Behold, I have gained two other talents above them. [23]His lord said to him, Well *done,* good and faithful slave. You were faithful over a few things; I will set you over many. Enter into the joy of your lord. [24]And the *one* who received the one talent also coming up, *he* said, Lord, I knew you, that you are a hard man, reaping where you did not sow, and gathering where you did not scatter. [25]And being afraid, going away, I hid your talent in the earth. Behold, you have yours. [26]And answering his lord said to him, Evil and slothful slave! You knew that I reap where I did not sow, and gather where I did not scatter. [27]Then you ought to have put my silver to the bankers; and coming I would have received my own with interest. [28]Therefore, take the talent from him, and give *it* to him who has the ten talents. [29]For to each who has, *more* will be given, and he will abound. But from him who does not have, even that which he has will be taken from him. [30]And throw the worthless slave out into the outer darkness. There will be weeping and gnashing of the teeth.

[31]But when the Son of man comes in His glory, and all the holy angels with Him, then He will sit on the throne of His glory. [32]And before Him shall be gathered all the nations, and He will separate them from one another, as the shepherd separates the sheep from the goats. [33]And indeed *He* will set the sheep off His right, but the goats off *the* left *hand.*

1417 5007 3427 3860 2396 243 1417 5007
δύο τάλαντά μοι παρέδωκας· ἴδε, ἄλλα δύο τάλαντα
two talents to me you delivered. Behold, other two talents
2770 1909 846 5346 846 2962 848 2095 1401
23 ἐκέρδησα ἐπ' αὐτοῖς. ἔφη αὐτῷ ὁ κύριος αὐτοῦ, Εὖ, δοῦλε
I gained over them. said to him The lord of him, Well, slave
18 4103 1909 3641 2258 4103 1909 4183 4571
ἀγαθὲ καὶ πιστέ, ἐπὶ ὀλίγα ἦς πιστός, ἐπὶ πολλῶν σε
good and faithful over a few you were faithful; over many you
2525 1525 1519 5479 2962 4675 4334
24 καταστήσω· εἴσελθε εἰς τὴν χαρὰν τοῦ κυρίου σου. προσ-
I will set. Enter into the joy of the lord of you. coming
1520 5007 2983 2036 2962 1097
ελθὼν δὲ καὶ ὁ τὸ ἓν τάλαντον εἰληφὼς εἶπε, Κύριε, ἔγνων
up And also the (one) the one talent having received said, Lord, I knew
4571 3754 4642 1488 444 2325 3699 3756 4687
σε ὅτι σκληρὸς εἶ ἄνθρωπος, θερίζων ὅπου οὐκ ἔσπειρας, καὶ
you, that hard you are a man, reaping where not you sowed, and
4863 3606 3756 1287 5399 565
25 συνάγων ὅθεν οὐ διεσκόρπισας· καὶ φοβηθείς, ἀπελθὼν
gathering from where not you scattered; and fearing, going away,
2928 5007 4675 1722 1093 2396 2192 4674
ἔκρυψα τὸ τάλαντόν σου ἐν τῇ γῇ· ἴδε, ἔχεις τὸ σόν.
I hid the talent of you in the earth. Behold, you have yours.
611 2962 848 2036 846 4190 1401
26 ἀποκριθεὶς δὲ ὁ κύριος αὐτοῦ εἶπεν αὐτῷ, Πονηρὲ δοῦλε καὶ
answering And, the lord of him said to him, Evil slave and
3636 1492 3754 2325 3699 3756 4687 4863 3606
ὀκνηρέ, ᾔδεις ὅτι θερίζω ὅπου οὐκ ἔσπειρα, καὶ συνάγω ὅθεν
slothful, you knew that I reap where not I sowed, and I gather where
3756 1287 1163 3767 4571 906 694 3450
27 οὐ διεσκόρπισα· ἔδει οὖν σε βαλεῖν τὸ ἀργύριόν μου τοῖς
not I scattered. It behoved then you to put the silver of me to the
5133 2064 1473 2864 302 1699 4862
τραπεζίταις, καὶ ἐλθὼν ἐγὼ ἐκομισάμην ἂν τὸ ἐμὸν σὺν
bankers, and coming I would have received again mine with
5110 142 3767 575 846 5007 1325
28 τόκῳ. ἄρατε οὖν ἀπ' αὐτοῦ τὸ τάλαντον, καὶ δότε τῷ
interest. Take, therefore, from him the talent, and give to him
2192 1176 5007 1063 2192 3956 1325
29 ἔχοντι τὰ δέκα τάλαντα. τῷ γὰρ ἔχοντι παντὶ δοθήσεται,
having the ten talents. to him For having, each will be given
4052 575 3361 2192 3739 2192
καὶ περισσευθήσεται· ἀπὸ δὲ τοῦ μὴ ἔχοντος, καὶ ὃ ἔχει,
and he will abound; from but the (one) not having, even what he has
142 575 846 888 1401 1544
30 ἀρθήσεται ἀπ' αὐτοῦ. καὶ τὸν ἀχρεῖον δοῦλον ἐκβάλλετε
will be taken from him. And the worthless slave throw out
1519 4655 1857 1563 2071 2805
εἰς τὸ σκότος τὸ ἐξώτερον. ἐκεῖ ἔσται ὁ κλαυθμὸς καὶ ὁ
into the darkness outer; there will be the weeping and the
1030 3599
βρυγμὸς τῶν ὀδόντων.
gnashing of the teeth.

3752 2064 5207 444 1722 1391 848
31 Ὅταν δὲ ἔλθῃ ὁ υἱὸς τοῦ ἀνθρώπου ἐν τῇ δόξῃ αὐτοῦ,
when And comes the Son of man in the glory of Him,
3956 40 32 3326 846 5119 2523 1909
καὶ πάντες οἱ ἅγιοι ἄγγελοι μετ' αὐτοῦ, τότε καθίσει ἐπὶ
and all the holy angels with Him, then He will sit on
2362 1391 848 4863 1715 846
32 θρόνου δόξης αὐτοῦ, καὶ συναχθήσεται ἔμπροσθεν αὐτοῦ
a throne of glory of Him, and will be assembled before Him
3956 1484 873 846 575 240 5618
πάντα τὰ ἔθνη, καὶ ἀφοριεῖ αὐτοὺς ἀπ' ἀλλήλων, ὥσπερ ὁ
all the nations, and He will part them from one another, as the
4166 863 4263 575 2056 2476
33 ποιμὴν ἀφορίζει τὰ πρόβατα ἀπὸ τῶν ἐρίφων· καὶ στήσει
shepherd parts the sheep from the goats, and will set
3303 4263 1537 1188 848 2055 1537 2176
τὰ μὲν πρόβατα ἐκ δεξιῶν αὐτοῦ, τὰ δὲ ἐρίφια ἐξ εὐωνύμων.
the even sheep off right his, the but goats off (the) left.

[34]Then the King will say to those on His right, Come, the blessed of My Father. Inherit the kingdom prepared for you from *the* foundation of *the* world. [35]For I hungered, and you gave Me *food* to eat; I thirsted, and you gave Me drink; I was a stranger, and you took Me in; [36]naked, and you clothed Me; I was sick, and you visited Me; I was in prison, and you came to Me. [37]Then the righteous will answer, saying, Lord, when did we see You hungry, and fed *You;* or thirsting, and gave *You* drink? [38]And when did we see You a stranger, and took *You* in; or naked, and clothed *You?* [39]And when did we see You sick, or in prison, and came to You? [40]And answering, the King will say to them, Truly I say to you, Inasmuch as you did *it* to one of these, the least of My brothers, you did *it* to Me.

[41]Then He will also say to those on *His* left, Go away from Me, cursed ones, into the everlasting fire having been prepared for the Devil and his angels. [42]For I hungered, and you gave Me nothing to eat; I thirsted, and you gave me nothing to drink; [43]I was a stranger, and you did not take Me in; naked, and you did not clothe Me; sick, and in prison, and you did not visit Me. [44]Then they also will answer Him, saying, Lord, when did we see You hungering, or thirsting or a stranger, or naked, or sick, or in prison, and did not minister to You? [45]Then He will answer them, saying, Truly I say to you, Inasmuch as you did not do *it* to one of these, the least, neither did you do *it* to Me. [46]And these shall go away into

5119 2046 932 1537 1188 848 1205 2127
34 τότε ἐρεῖ ὁ βασιλεὺς τοῖς ἐκ δεξιῶν αὐτοῦ, Δεῦτε, οἱ εὐλογη-
Then will say the King to those off the right of Him, Come, the blessed
3962 3450 2816 2090
μένοι τοῦ πατρός μου, κληρονομήσατε τὴν ἡτοιμασμένην
of the Father of Me; inherit the prepared
5213 935 575 2602 2889 3983 1063
35 ὑμῖν βασιλείαν ἀπὸ καταβολῆς κόσμου. ἐπείνασα γάρ, καὶ
for you kingdom from foundation of (the) world. I hungered For, and
1325 3427 5315 1372 4222 3165 3581 2252
ἐδώκατέ μοι φαγεῖν· ἐδίψησα, καὶ ἐποτίσατέ με· ξένος ἤμην,
you gave Me to eat; I thirsted, and you gave drink Me; an alien I was
4863 3165 1131 4016 3165 770
36 καὶ συνηγάγετέ με· γυμνός, καὶ περιεβάλετέ με· ἠσθένησα,
and you took in Me; naked, and you clothed Me: I was sick,
1980 3165 1722 5438 2252 2064 4314 3165
καὶ ἐπεσκέψασθέ με· ἐν φυλακῇ ἤμην, καὶ ἤλθετε πρός με.
and you visited Me in prison I was, and you came to Me.
5119 611 846 1342 3004 2962
37 τότε ἀποκριθήσονται αὐτῷ οἱ δίκαιοι, λέγοντες, Κύριε,
Then will answer Him the righteous, saying, Lord,
5119 4571 1492 3983 5142 2228 1372
πότε σὲ εἴδομεν πεινῶντα, καὶ ἐθρέψαμεν; ἢ διψῶντα, καὶ
when You did we see hungering, and fed, or thirsting, and
4222 4219 4571 149: 581 486
38 ἐποτίσαμεν; πότε δέ σε εἴδομεν ξένον, καὶ συνηγάγομεν;
gave drink; when and You did we see an alien, and gathered (You) in;
2228 1131 4016 4219 4571 1492 611 2228 1722
39 ἢ γυμνόν, καὶ περιεβάλομεν; πότε δέ σε εἴδομεν ἀσθενῆ, ἢ ἐν
or naked, and clothed? when And You did we see sick, or in
5438 2064 4314 4571 611 935 2046
40 φυλακῇ, καὶ ἤλθομεν πρός σε; καὶ ἀποκριθεὶς ὁ βασιλεὺς ἐρεῖ
prison, and came to You? And answering the King will say
846 281 3004 5213 1909 3745 4160 1520 5130
αὐτοῖς, Ἀμὴν λέγω ὑμῖν, ἐφ' ὅσον ἐποιήσατε ἑνὶ τούτων τῶν
to them, Truly I say to you, inasmuch as you did to one of these the
80 3450 1646 1698 4160 5119 2046
41 ἀδελφῶν μου τῶν ἐλαχίστων, ἐμοὶ ἐποιήσατε. τότε ἐρεῖ καὶ
brothers of Me the least, to Me you did. Then He says also
1537 2176 4198 575 1700 2672 1519
τοῖς ἐξ εὐωνύμων, Πορεύεσθε ἀπ' ἐμοῦ, οἱ κατηραμένοι, εἰς
to those off (the) left, Go from Me, those cursed into
4442 166 2090 1228
τὸ πῦρ τὸ αἰώνιον, τὸ ἡτοιμασμένον τῷ διαβόλῳ καὶ τοῖς
the fire — everlasting — having been prepared for the Devil and the
32 848 3983 1063 3756 1325 3427 5315
42 ἀγγέλοις αὐτοῦ. ἐπείνασα γάρ, καὶ οὐκ ἐδώκατέ μοι φαγεῖν·
angels of him. I hungered For, and not you gave Me to eat;
1372 3756 4222 3165 3581 2252 3756 4863
43 ἐδίψησα, καὶ οὐκ ἐποτίσατέ με· ξένος ἤμην, καὶ οὐ συνηγά-
I thirsted, and not you gave drink to Me; an alien I was, and not you gathered
3165 1131 3756 4016 3165 772 1722
γετέ με· γυμνός, καὶ οὐ περιεβάλετέ με· ἀσθενής, καὶ ἐν
in Me; naked, and not you clothed Me; sick, and in
5438 3756 1980 3165 5119 611
44 φυλακῇ, καὶ οὐκ ἐπεσκέψασθέ με. τότε ἀποκριθήσονται
prison, and not you visited Me. Then will answer
846 846 3004 2962 4219 4571 1492 3983
αὐτῷ καὶ αὐτοί, λέγοντες, Κύριε, πότε σὲ εἴδομεν πεινῶντα,
Him also they, saying, Lord, when You did we see hungering,
2228 1372 3581 2228 1131 2228 772 2228 1722 5438
ἢ διψῶντα, ἢ ξένον, ἢ γυμνόν, ἢ ἀσθενῆ, ἢ ἐν φυλακῇ, καὶ
or thirsting, or an alien, or naked, or sick, or in prison, and
3756 1247 4671 5119 611 846 3004
45 οὐ διηκονήσαμέν σοι; τότε ἀποκριθήσεται αὐτοῖς, λέγων,
not did minister to You? Then He will answer them, saying,
281 3004 5213 1909 3785 3756 4160 1520 5130
Ἀμὴν λέγω ὑμῖν, ἐφ' ὅσον οὐκ ἐποιήσατε ἑνὶ τούτων τῶν
Truly I say to you, Insasmuch as not you did to one of these the
1646 3761 1698 4160 565 3778
46 ἐλαχίστων, οὐδὲ ἐμοὶ ἐποιήσατε. καὶ ἀπελεύσονται οὗτοι
least (ones), neither to Me you did. And will go away these

NOTE: Frequent words not numbered: δέ(1161); καί(2531)—and, but; ὁ, ἡ, τό (3588, the)— * above word, look in verse margin for No.

everlasting punishment,
but the righteous into
everlasting life.

CHAPTER 26

1 And it happened when
Jesus finished all these
sayings, He said to His disciples, 2 You know that the
Passover is coming after
two days, and the Son of
man is betrayed to be crucified. 3 Then the chief
priests and the scribes and
the elders of the people
were assembled to the
court of the high priest, the
one named Caiaphas. 4 And
they plotted together in
order that they might seize
Jesus by guile, and kill *Him*.
5 But they said, Not during
the feast, that there be no
uproar among the people.

6 And Jesus being in
Bethany in Simon the
leper's house, 7 a woman
came to Him having an
alabaster vial of ointment,
very precious. And *she*
poured *it* on His head as He
reclined. 8 But seeing, His
disciples were indignant,
saying, For what *is* this
waste? 9 For this ointment
could have been sold for
much, and be given to *the*
poor. 10 But knowing, Jesus
said to them, Why do you
cause trouble to the
woman? For she worked a
good work toward Me.
11 For you always have the
poor with you, but you do
not always have Me. 12 For
in putting this ointment on
My body, she did *it* in order
to bury Me. 13 Truly I say to
you, Wherever this gospel
is proclaimed in all the
world, what she did also
will be spoken of as a
memorial of her.

1519 2851 166 1342 1519 2222 166
εἰς κόλασιν αἰώνιον· οἱ δὲ δίκαιοι εἰς ζωὴν αἰώνιον.
into punishment eternal, the but righteous into life eternal.

CHAPTER 26

1096 3753 5055 2424 3956 3956
1 Καὶ ἐγένετο ὅτε ἐτέλεσεν ὁ Ἰησοῦς πάντας τοὺς λόγους
And it was, when ended Jesus all sayings
5128 2036 3101 848 1492 3754 3326 1417
2 τούτους, εἶπε τοῖς μαθηταῖς αὐτοῦ, Οἴδατε ὅτι μετὰ δύο
these, He said to the disciples of Him, You know that after two
2250 3857 1096 5207 444 3860
ἡμέρας τὸ πάσχα γίνεται, καὶ ὁ υἱὸς τοῦ ἀνθρώπου παραδί-
days the Passover comes, and the Son of man is be-
1519 4717 5119 4863 749
3 δοται εἰς τὸ σταυρωθῆναι. τότε συνήχθησαν οἱ ἀρχιερεῖς
trayed to be crucified. Then were assembled the chief priests
1122 4245 2992 1519
καὶ οἱ γραμματεῖς καὶ οἱ πρεσβύτεροι τοῦ λαοῦ εἰς τὴν
and the scribes and the elders of the people to the
833 749 3004 2533 4823
4 αὐλὴν τοῦ ἀρχιερέως τοῦ λεγομένου Καϊάφα, καὶ συνεβου-
court of the high priest being named Caiaphas, and consulted
2443 2424 2902 1388 615
λεύσαντο ἵνα τὸν Ἰησοῦν κρατήσωσι δόλῳ καὶ ἀπο-
together that Jesus they might seize by guile, and
3004 3361 1722 1859 2443 3361 2351
5 κτείνωσιν. ἔλεγον δέ, Μὴ ἐν τῇ ἑορτῇ, ἵνα μὴ θόρυβος
kill (Him). they said But, Not at the feast, that not a turmoil
1096 1722 2992
γένηται ἐν τῷ λαῷ.
occur among the people.
2424 1096 1722 963 1722 3614 4613
6 Τοῦ δὲ Ἰησοῦ γενομένου ἐν Βηθανίᾳ ἐν οἰκίᾳ Σίμωνος τοῦ
And Jesus being in Bethany in (the) house of Simon the
3015 4334 846 1135 211 3414 2192
7 λεπροῦ, προσῆλθεν αὐτῷ γυνὴ ἀλάβαστρον μύρου ἔχουσα
leper, came up to Him a woman an alabaster vial of ointment having
927 2708 1909 2776 848 345
βαρυτίμου, καὶ κατέχεεν ἐπὶ τὴν κεφαλὴν αὐτοῦ ἀνακει-
very precious, and poured (it) on the head of Him reclining.
1492 3101 848 23 3004
8 μένου. ἰδόντες δὲ οἱ μαθηταὶ αὐτοῦ ἠγανάκτησαν, λέγοντες,
seeing And the disciples of Him were indignant, saying,
1519 5101 684 3778 1410 1063 5124 3414
9 Εἰς τί ἡ ἀπώλεια αὕτη; ἠδύνατο γὰρ τοῦτο τὸ μύρον
To what — waste this? could For this ointment
4097 4183 1325 4434 1097 2424
10 πραθῆναι πολλοῦ, καὶ δοθῆναι πτωχοῖς. γνοὺς δὲ ὁ Ἰησοῦς
have been sold of much, and to be given to (the) poor? knowing And Jesus
2036 846 5101 2873 3930 1135 2041 1063
εἶπεν αὐτοῖς, Τί κόπους παρέχετε τῇ γυναικί; ἔργον γὰρ
said to them, Why trouble do you cause to the woman? work For
2570 2038 1519 1691 3842 1063 4434 2192
11 καλὸν εἰργάσατο εἰς ἐμέ. πάντοτε γὰρ τοὺς πτωχοὺς ἔχετε
a good she worked toward Me, always for the poor you have
3326 1438 1691 3756 3842 2192 906 1063 3778
12 μεθ' ἑαυτῶν, ἐμὲ δὲ οὐ πάντοτε ἔχετε. βαλοῦσα γὰρ αὕτη
with yourselves, Me but not always you have. putting For she
3864 5124 1909 4983 3450 4314 1779
τὸ μύρον τοῦτο ἐπὶ τοῦ σώματός μου, πρὸς τὸ ἐνταφιάσαι
ointment this on the body of Me, in order to bury
3165 4160 281 3004 5213 3699 1737 2784 2098
13 με ἐποίησεν. ἀμὴν λέγω ὑμῖν, ὅπου ἐὰν κηρυχθῇ τὸ εὐαγ-
Me she did (it). Truly I say to you, wherever is proclaimed gospel
5124 1722 3650 2889 2980 4160
γέλιον τοῦτο ἐν ὅλῳ τῷ κόσμῳ, λαληθήσεται καὶ ὃ ἐποίησεν
this in all the world, will be spoken also what did
3778 1519 3422 848
αὕτη, εἰς μνημόσυνον αὐτῆς.
she for a memorial of her.

14 Then one of the twelve, the *one* named Judas Iscariot, going to the chief priests 15 said, What will you give to me, and I will deliver Him up to you? And they weighed to him thirty silver pieces. 16 And from then he sought opportunity that he might betray Him.

17 And on the first *day* of unleavened *bread* the disciples came to Jesus, saying to Him, Where do you desire we should prepare for You to eat the Passover? 18 And He said, Go into the city to a certain one and say to him, The Teacher says, My time is near; to you I will prepare the Passover with My disciples. 19 And the disciples did as Jesus ordered them, and prepared the Passover.

20 And evening coming, He reclined with the Twelve. 21 And as they were eating, He said, Truly I say to you that one of you will betray Me. 22 And grieving exceedingly, they began to say to Him, each of them, Lord, Not I am *the one*? 23 But answering He said, The *one* dipping the hand with Me in the dish will betray Me. 24 Indeed, *the* Son of man goes, as it has been written about Him. But woe to that man by whom the Son of man is betrayed. It were good for him if that man was never born. 25 And answering the *one* betraying Him, Judas, said, Not I am *the one*, Rabbi? He said to him, You said *it*.

26 And *as* they ate, taking the bread and blessing *it*, Jesus broke and gave to the disciples; and said, Take, eat; this is My body. 27 And taking the cup, and giving

5119 4198 1519 1427 3004 2455
14 Τότε πορευθεὶς εἷς τῶν δώδεκα, ὁ λεγόμενος Ἰούδας
Then going one of the twelve, he said (to be) Judas
2469 4314 749 2036 5101 2309 3427 1325
15 Ἰσκαριώτης, πρὸς τοὺς ἀρχιερεῖς, εἶπε, Τί θέλετέ μοι δοῦναι,
Iscariot, to the chief priests, said, What will You Me to give,
2504 5213 3860 846 2476 846 5144
κἀγὼ ὑμῖν παραδώσω αὐτόν; οἱ δὲ ἔστησαν αὐτῷ τριά-
and I to you will deliver up Him? they And weighed him thirty
694 575 5119 2212 2120 2443 846
16 κοντα ἀργύρια. καὶ ἀπὸ τότε ἐζήτει εὐκαιρίαν ἵνα αὐτὸν
silver pieces. And from then he sought opportunity that Him
3860
παραδῷ.
he might deliver.

4413 106 4334 3101
17 Τῇ δὲ πρώτῃ τῶν ἀζύμων προσῆλθον οἱ μαθηταὶ τῷ
on the And first unleavened came the disciples to
2424 3004 846 4226 2309 2090 4671 5315
Ἰησοῦ, λέγοντες αὐτῷ, Ποῦ θέλεις ἑτοιμάσωμέν σοι φαγεῖν
Jesus, saying to Him, Where will You we may prepare for You to eat
3957 2036 5217 1519 4172 4314
18 τὸ πάσχα; ὁ δὲ εἶπεν, Ὑπάγετε εἰς τὴν πόλιν πρὸς τὸν
the Passover? He And said, Go into the city to such
1170 2036 846 1320 3004 2540 3450
δεῖνα, καὶ εἴπατε αὐτῷ, Ὁ διδάσκαλος λέγει, Ὁ καιρός μου
a one, and say to him, The Teacher says, The time of Me
1451 2076 4314 4571 4160 3957 3326 3101 3450
ἐγγύς ἐστι· πρὸς σὲ ποιῶ τὸ πάσχα μετὰ τῶν μαθητῶν μου.
near is; toward you I make the Passover, with the disciples of Me.
4160 3101 5613 4929 846 2424
19 καὶ ἐποίησαν οἱ μαθηταὶ ὡς συνέταξεν αὐτοῖς ὁ Ἰησοῦς, καὶ
And did the disciples as ordered them – Jesus, and
2090 3957 3798 1096 345 3326
20 ἡτοίμασαν τὸ πάσχα. ὀψίας δὲ γενομένης ἀνέκειτο μετὰ τῶν
prepared the Passover. evening And coming, He reclined with the
1427 2068 846 2036 281 3004 5213
21 δώδεκα. καὶ ἐσθιόντων αὐτῶν εἶπεν, Ἀμὴν λέγω ὑμῖν ὅτι
twelve. And eating they, He said, Truly I say to you that
1519 1537 5216 3860 3165 3076 4970 756
22 εἷς ἐξ ὑμῶν παραδώσει με. καὶ λυπούμενοι σφόδρα ἤρξαντο
one of you will betray Me. And grieving exceedingly they bega
3004 846 1538 846 3385 1473 1570 2962
23 λέγειν αὐτῷ ἕκαστος αὐτῶν, Μήτι ἐγώ εἰμι, Κύριε; ὁ δὲ
to say to Him, each of them, Not I am (he), Lord? He But
611 2036 1686 3326 1700 1722 5165
ἀποκριθεὶς εἶπεν, Ὁ ἐμβάψας μετ' ἐμοῦ ἐν τῷ τρυβλίῳ τὴν
answering said, The (one) dipping with Me in the dish the
5495 3778 3165 3860 3303 5207 444 5217
24 χεῖρα, οὗτός με παραδώσει. ὁ μὲν υἱὸς τοῦ ἀνθρώπου ὑπάγει,
hand, Me will betray. the Indeed Son of man goes
2531 1125 4012 846 3759 444 1565
καθὼς γέγραπται περὶ αὐτοῦ· οὐαὶ δὲ τῷ ἀνθρώπῳ ἐκείνῳ,
as it has been written about Him woe but to man that
1223 3639 5207 444 3860 2570 2258 846 1487
δι' οὗ ὁ υἱὸς τοῦ ἀνθρώπου παραδίδοται· καλὸν ἦν αὐτῷ εἰ
by whom the Son of man is betrayed; good were it for him if
3756 1080 444 1565 611 2455
25 οὐκ ἐγεννήθη ὁ ἄνθρωπος ἐκεῖνος. ἀποκριθεὶς δὲ Ἰούδας ὁ
not was born man that. answering And Judas who
3860 846 2036 3385 1473 1510 4461 3004 846
παραδιδοὺς αὐτὸν εἶπε, Μήτι ἐγώ εἰμι, ῥαββί; λέγει αὐτῷ,
was betraying Him said, Not I am, Rabbi? He says to him
4771 2036 2068 846 2983 2424 740
26 Σὺ εἶπας. ἐσθιόντων δὲ αὐτῶν. λαβὼν ὁ Ἰησοῦς τὸν ἄρτον,
You said (it). eating And they, taking Jesus the bread
2127 2806 1325 3101 2036
καὶ εὐλογήσας, ἔκλασε καὶ ἐδίδου τοῖς μαθηταῖς, καὶ εἶπε,
and blessing, He broke and gave to the disciples, and said,
2983 5315 5124 2076 4983 3450 2983
27 Λάβετε, φάγετε· τοῦτό ἐστι τὸ σῶμά μου. καὶ λαβὼν τὸ
Take, eat, this is the body of Me. And taking the

thanks, He gave to them, saying, Drink all of it. [28]For this is My blood of the New Covenant which concerning many is being poured out for forgiveness of sins. [29]But I say to you, I will not at all drink of this fruit of the vine after this, until that day when I drink it new with you in the kingdom of My Father.

[30]And singing a hymn, they went into the Mount of Olives. [31]Then Jesus said to them, You all will be offended in Me during this night. For it has been written, "I will smite the Shepherd, and the sheep of the flock will be scattered. [32]But after My resurrection I will go before you into Galilee. [33]And answering Peter said to Him, Even if all will be offended in You, I will never be offended. [34]Jesus said to him, Truly I say to you, During this night, before *the* cock crows, you will deny Me three times. [35]Peter said to Him, Even if it were necessary for me to die with You, I will in no way deny You. And all the disciples said the same.

[36]Then Jesus came with them to a place called Gethsemane. And He said to the disciples, Sit here until going away I shall pray there. [37]And taking along Peter and the two sons of Zebedee, He began to grieve and to be deeply troubled. [38]Then He said to them, My soul is deeply grieved, even unto death. Stay here and watch with Me.

[39]And going forward a little, He fell on His face, praying and saying, My

4221 2168 1325 846 3004 4095
ποτήριον, καὶ εὐχαριστήσας, ἔδωκεν αὐτοῖς, λέγων, Πίετε
cup, and giving thanks, He gave to them, saying, Drink
1537 846 3956 5124 1063 2076 129 3450 2537
28 ἐξ αὐτοῦ πάντες· τοῦτο γάρ ἐστι τὸ αἷμά μου, τὸ τῆς καινῆς
of it all; this for is the blood of Me – of the New
1242 4012 4183 1632 1519 859 266
διαθήκης, τὸ περὶ πολλῶν ἐκχυνόμενον εἰς ἄφεσιν ἁμαρτιῶν.
Covenant, which concern many is being poured out for forgiveness of sins.
3004 5213/3754 =3364= 4095/575/737/1537/5127 1081
29 λέγω δὲ ὑμῖν ὅτι οὐ μὴ πίω ἀπ' ἄρτι ἐκ τούτου τοῦ γεννή-
I say And to you that never will I drink from now of this fruit
288 2193 2250 1565 3752 846 4095
ματος τῆς ἀμπέλου, ἕως τῆς ἡμέρας ἐκείνης ὅταν αὐτὸ πίνω
of the vine until – day that when it I drink
3326 5216 2537 1722 932 3962 3450
μεθ' ὑμῶν καινὸν ἐν τῇ βασιλείᾳ τοῦ πατρός μου.
with you new in the kingdom of the Father of Me.
5214 1831 1519 3735 1636
30 Καὶ ὑμνήσαντες ἐξῆλθον εἰς τὸ ὄρος τῶν ἐλαιῶν.
And having sung a hymn they went into the mount of the olives.
5119 3004 846 2424 3956 5210 4624
31 Τότε λέγει αὐτοῖς ὁ Ἰησοῦς, Πάντες ὑμεῖς σκανδαλισθή-
Then says to them Jesus, All you will be offended
1722 1698 1722 3571 5026 1125 1063 3960
σεσθε ἐν ἐμοὶ ἐν τῇ νυκτὶ ταύτῃ· γέγραπται γάρ, Πατάξω
in Me during night this; it has been written for, I will strike
4166 1287 4263
τὸν ποιμένα, καὶ διασκορπισθήσεται τὰ πρόβατα τῆς
the shepherd, and will be scattered the sheep of the
4167 3326 1453 3165 4254 5209 1519
32 ποίμνης. μετὰ δὲ τὸ ἐγερθῆναί με, προάξω ὑμᾶς εἰς τὴν
flock; after but the rising (of) Me, I will go before you to –
1056 611 4074 2036 846 1499 3956
33 Γαλιλαίαν. ἀποκριθεὶς δὲ ὁ Πέτρος εἶπεν αὐτῷ, Εἰ καὶ πάντες
Galilee. answering And Peter said to Him, If even all
4624 1722 4671 1473 3762 4624
σκανδαλισθήσονται ἐν σοί, ἐγὼ οὐδέποτε σκανδαλισθή-
be offended in You, I never will be offended.
5346 846 2424 281 3004 4671 3754 1722 5026
34 σομαι. ἔφη αὐτῷ ὁ Ἰησοῦς, Ἀμὴν λέγω σοι ὅτι ἐν ταύτῃ τῇ
said to him Jesus, Truly I say to you that in this
3571 4250 220 5455 5151 533 3165 3004
35 νυκτί, πρὶν ἀλέκτορα φωνῆσαι, τρὶς ἀπαρνήσῃ με. λέγει
night, before (the) cock crows, thrice you will deny Me. Says
846 4074 1163 3165 4862 4671 599 =3364= 4571
αὐτῷ ὁ Πέτρος, Κἂν δέῃ με σὺν σοὶ ἀποθανεῖν, οὐ μή σε
to Him – Peter, Even if need I with You to die, in no way You
533 3668 3956 3101 2036
ἀπαρνήσομαι. ὁμοίως καὶ πάντες οἱ μαθηταὶ εἶπον.
I will deny. Likewise also all the disciples said.
5119 2064 3326 846 2424 1519 5564 3004
36 Τότε ἔρχεται μετ' αὐτῶν ὁ Ἰησοῦς εἰς χωρίον λεγόμενον
Then comes with them – Jesus to a place called
1068 3004 3101 2523 847 2193 3739
Γεθσημανῆ, καὶ λέγει τοῖς μαθηταῖς, Καθίσατε αὐτοῦ, ἕως οὗ
Gethsemane, and says to the disciples, Sit on this until
565 4336 1563 3880 4074
37 ἀπελθὼν προσεύξωμαι ἐκεῖ. καὶ παραλαβὼν τὸν Πέτρον καὶ
going away I shall pray there. And taking along – Peter and
1417 5207 2199 756 3076 85
τοὺς δύο υἱοὺς Ζεβεδαίου, ἤρξατο λυπεῖσθαι καὶ ἀδημονεῖν.
the two sons of Zebedee, He began to grieve and be distressed.
5119 3004 846 4036 2076 5590 3450 2193 2288
38 τότε λέγει αὐτοῖς, Περίλυπός ἐστιν ἡ ψυχή μου ἕως θανάτου·
Then He says to them, Deeply grieved is the soul of Me unto death;
3306 5602 1127 3326 1700 4281 3397
39 μείνατε ὧδε καὶ γρηγορεῖτε μετ' ἐμοῦ. καὶ προελθὼν μικρόν,
remain here and watch with Me. And going forward a little
4098 1909 4383 848 4336 3004
ἔπεσεν ἐπὶ πρόσωπον αὐτοῦ προσευχόμενος καὶ λέγων,
He fell on (the) face of Him, praying and saying,

Father, if it is possible, let this cup pass from Me; yet, not as I will, but as You *will*. [40]And He came to the disciples and found them sleeping. And *He* said to Peter, So! Were you not able to watch one hour with Me? [41]Watch and pray that you do not enter into temptation. The Spirit indeed *is* willing, but the flesh is weak. [42]Again, going away a second time, He prayed, saying, My Father, if this cup cannot pass away from Me without my drinking it, let Your will be done. [43]And coming He again found them sleeping, for their eyes were heavy.

[44]And leaving them, going away again, He prayed a third *time*, saying the same thing. [45]Then He came to His disciples and said to them, Sleep on, and rest *for* what *time* remains. Behold, the hour draws near, and the Son of man is betrayed into *the* hands of sinners. [46]Rise up, let us go. Behold, the *one* betraying Me draws near.

[47]And as He was yet speaking, behold, Judas came, one of the Twelve. And with him was a numerous crowd with swords and clubs, from the chief priests and elders of the people. [48]And the *one* betraying Him gave them a sign, saying, Whomever I may kiss, it is He; seize Him. [49]And coming up at once to Jesus, he said, Greetings, Rabbi. And *he* ardently kissed

3962 3450 1487 1415 2076 3928 575 1700 4221
Πάτερ μου, εἰ δυνατόν ἐστι, παρελθέτω ἀπ' ἐμοῦ τὸ ποτή-
Father of Me, if possible it is, let pass from Me cup
5124 4133 3756 5613 1473 2309 235 5613 4771 2064
40 ριον τοῦτο· πλὴν οὐχ ὡς ἐγὼ θέλω, ἀλλ' ὡς σύ. καὶ ἔρχεται
this; yet not as I will, but as You. And He comes
4314 3101 2147 846 2518
πρὸς τοὺς μαθητάς, καὶ εὑρίσκει αὐτοὺς καθεύδοντας, καὶ
toward the disciples and finds them sleeping, and
3004 4074 3779 3756 2480 3391 5610 1127
λέγει τῷ Πέτρῳ, Οὕτως οὐκ ἰσχύσατε μίαν ὥραν γρηγορῆ-
says to Peter, So, not were you able one hour to watch
3326 1700 1127 4336 2443 3361
41 σαι μετ' ἐμοῦ; γρηγορεῖτε καὶ προσεύχεσθε, ἵνα μὴ
with Me? Watch and pray lest
1525 1519 3986 3303 4151 4289
εἰσέλθητε εἰς πειρασμόν· τὸ μὲν πνεῦμα πρόθυμον, ἡ δὲ
you enter into temptation; the indeed spirit (is) eager, the but
4561 772 3825 1537 1208 565 4336
42 σὰρξ ἀσθενής. πάλιν ἐκ δευτέρου ἀπελθὼν προσηύξατο,
flesh (is) weak. Again, for a second (time) going away He prayed,
3004 3962 3450 1487 3756 1410 5124 4221
λέγων, Πάτερ μου, εἰ οὐ δύναται τοῦτο τὸ ποτήριον
saying, Father of Me, if not can this cup
3928 575 1700 =3362= 846 4095 1096 2307
παρελθεῖν ἀπ' ἐμοῦ, ἐὰν μὴ αὐτὸ πίω, γενηθήτω τὸ θέλημά
pass away from Me unless it I drink, let be done the will
4675 2064 2147 846 3825 2518 2258
43 σου. καὶ ἐλθὼν εὑρίσκει αὐτοὺς πάλιν καθεύδοντας, ἦσαν
of You. And coming He finds them again sleeping, were
1063 848 3788 916 863 846
44 γὰρ αὐτῶν οἱ ὀφθαλμοὶ βεβαρημένοι. καὶ ἀφεὶς αὐτοὺς
for of them the eyes heavy. And leaving them
565 3825 4336 1537 5154 846 3056
ἀπελθὼν πάλιν προσηύξατο ἐκ τρίτου, τὸν αὐτὸν λόγον
going away again, He prayed a third (time), the same word
2036 5119 2064 4314 3101 848 3004
45 εἰπών. τότε ἔρχεται πρὸς τοὺς μαθητὰς αὐτοῦ, καὶ λέγει
saying. Then He comes to the disciples of Him, and says
846 2518 3063 373 2400 1448
αὐτοῖς, Καθεύδετε τὸ λοιπὸν καὶ ἀναπαύεσθε· ἰδού, ἤγγικεν
to them, Sleep (for) what remains and rest; behold, draws near
5610 5207 444 3860 1519 5495
ἡ ὥρα, καὶ ὁ υἱὸς τοῦ ἀνθρώπου παραδίδοται εἰς χεῖρας
the hour and the Son of man is betrayed into hands
268 1453 71 2400 1448 3860
46 ἁμαρτωλῶν. ἐγείρεσθε, ἄγωμεν. ἰδού, ἤγγικεν ὁ παραδι-
of sinners. Rise, let us go. Behold, draws near the (one)
3165
δούς με.
betraying Me.

2089 846 2980 2400 2455 1519 1427
47 Καὶ ἔτι αὐτοῦ λαλοῦντος, ἰδού, Ἰούδας εἷς τῶν δώδεκα
And while He was speaking, behold Judas, one of the twelve,
2064 3326 846 3793 4193 3326 3162
ἦλθε, καὶ μετ' αὐτοῦ ὄχλος πολὺς μετὰ μαχαιρῶν καὶ
came, and with him a crowd numerous with swords and
3586 575 749 4245 2992
48 ξύλων, ἀπὸ τῶν ἀρχιερέων καὶ πρεσβυτέρων τοῦ λαοῦ. ὁ
clubs, from the chief priests and elders of the people, he
3860 846 1325 846 4592 3004 3739
δὲ παραδιδοὺς αὐτὸν ἔδωκεν αὐτοῖς σημεῖον, λέγων, Ὃν
And betraying Him gave to them a sign, saying, Whom-
302 5368 846 2076 2902 846 2112
49 ἂν φιλήσω, αὐτός ἐστι· κρατήσατε αὐτόν. καὶ εὐθέως
ever I may kiss, He it is; seize Him. And at once
4334 2424 2036 5463 4461 2705
προσελθὼν τῷ Ἰησοῦ εἶπε, Χαῖρε, ῥαββί· καὶ κατεφίλησεν
coming up, they laid on the hands, on Jesus, and
846 2424 2036 846 2083 1909 3739 3918 5119
50 αὐτόν. ὁ δὲ Ἰησοῦς εἶπεν αὐτῷ, Ἑταῖρε, ἐφ' ᾧ πάρει; τότε
Him. – But Jesus said to him, Friend, why are you here? Then

Him. 50 But Jesus said to him, Friend, why are you here? Then coming up, they laid hands on Jesus and seized Him. 51 And, behold, one of those with Jesus, stretching out the hand, drew his sword and struck the slave of the high priest, *and* took off his ear. 52 Then Jesus said to him, Put your sword back into its place. For all who take *the* sword shall perish by a sword. 53 Or do you think that I am not able now to call on My Father, and He will place beside Me more than twelve legions of angels? 54 How then should the Scriptures be fulfilled, that it must happen this way?

55 In that hour Jesus said to the crowds, Have you come out to take Me with swords and clubs, as against a robber? I sat with you daily, teaching in the temple, and you did not lay hands on Me. 56 But all this is happening that the Scriptures of the prophets may be fulfilled.
Then all the disciples ran away, forsaking Him.

57 And those who had seized Jesus led *Him* away to Caiaphas the high priest, where the scribes and the elders were assembled. 58 And Peter followed Him from a distance, even to the court of the high priest. And going inside, *he* sat with the under-officers to see the end. 59 And the chief priests and the elders and the whole sanhedrin looked for false testimony against Jesus, so that they might put Him to death. 60 And not *any were* found, even though *there were* many false witnesses coming forward, they did not find *any*. But at last two false witnesses came up,

4334 1911 5495 1909 2424
προσελθόντες ἐπέβαλον τὰς χεῖρας ἐπὶ τὸν Ἰησοῦν, καὶ
coming up, they laid on the hands, on Jesus, and
2902 846 2400 1519 3326 2424 1614
51 ἐκράτησαν αὐτόν. καὶ ἰδού, εἷς τῶν μετὰ Ἰησοῦ, ἐκτείνας
seized Him. And behold, one of those with Jesus, stretching
5495 645 3162 848 3960
τὴν χεῖρα, ἀπέσπασε τὴν μάχαιραν αὐτοῦ, καὶ πατάξας τὸν
the hand, drew the sword of him, and striking the
1401 749 851 848 5621 5119 3004
52 δοῦλον τοῦ ἀρχιερέως ἀφεῖλεν αὐτοῦ τὸ ὠτίον. τότε λέγει
slave of the high priest took off of him the ear. Then says
846 2424 654 4675 3162 1519
αὐτῷ ὁ Ἰησοῦς, Ἀπόστρεψόν σου τὴν μάχαιραν εἰς τὸν
to him -- Jesus, Put back of you the sword to the
5117 848 3956 1063 2983 3162 1722 3162
τόπον αὐτῆς· πάντες γὰρ οἱ λαβόντες μάχαιραν ἐν μαχαίρᾳ
place of it; all for those taking (the) sword by a sword
622 2228 1380 3754 3756 1140 737 3870
53 ἀπολοῦνται. ἢ δοκεῖς ὅτι οὐ δύναμαι ἄρτι παρακαλέσαι τὸν
shall perish. Or think you that not I can now call upon the
3962 3450 3936 3427 4119 2228 1427 3003
πατέρα μου, καὶ παραστήσει μοι πλείους ἢ δώδεκα λεγεῶνας
Father of Me, and He will place near Me more than twelve legions
32 4459 3767 4137 1124 3754 3779 1163
54 ἀγγέλων; πῶς οὖν πληρωθῶσιν αἱ γραφαί, ὅτι οὕτω δεῖ
of angels? How, then, should be fulfilled the Scriptures that so it must
1096 1722 1565 5610 2036 2424 3793 5613
55 γενέσθαι; ἐν ἐκείνῃ τῇ ὥρᾳ εἶπεν ὁ Ἰησοῦς τοῖς ὄχλοις, Ὡς
be? In that hour said Jesus to the crowds, As
1909 3027 1831 3326 3162 3586 4815
ἐπὶ λῃστὴν ἐξήλθετε μετὰ μαχαιρῶν καὶ ξύλων συλλαβεῖν
on a robber came you with swords and clubs together to take
3165 2596 2250 4314 5209 2516 1321 1722 2411
με; καθ' ἡμέραν πρὸς ὑμᾶς ἐκαθεζόμην διδάσκων ἐν τῷ ἱερῷ,
Me? Daily with you I sat teaching in the Temple,
56 3756 2902 3165 5124 3650 1096 2443 4137
καὶ οὐκ ἐκρατήσατέ με. τοῦτο δὲ ὅλον γέγονεν, ἵνα πληρωθῶ-
and not you seized Me. this But all has happened that may be ful-
1124 4396 5119 3101 3956
σιν αἱ γραφαὶ τῶν προφητῶν. τότε οἱ μαθηταὶ πάντες
filled the Scriptures of the prophets. Then the disciples all
863 846 5343
ἀφέντες αὐτὸν ἔφυγον.
leaving Him fled.
2902 2424 520 4314 2533
57 Οἱ δὲ κρατήσαντες τὸν Ἰησοῦν ἀπήγαγον πρὸς Καϊάφαν
those But seizing – Jesus led away to Caiaphas
749 3699 1122 4245
τὸν ἀρχιερέα, ὅπου οἱ γραμματεῖς καὶ οἱ πρεσβύτεροι
the high priest, where the scribes and the elders
4863 4074 190 846 575 3113
58 συνήχθησαν. ὁ δὲ Πέτρος ἠκολούθει αὐτῷ ἀπὸ μακρόθεν,
were assembled. And Peter followed Him from afar
2193 833 749 1525 2090 2521
ἕως τῆς αὐλῆς τοῦ ἀρχιερέως, καὶ εἰσελθὼν ἔσω ἐκάθητο
up to the court of the high priest, and entering within sat
3326 5257 1492 5056 749
59 μετὰ τῶν ὑπηρετῶν, ἰδεῖν τὸ τέλος. οἱ δὲ ἀρχιερεῖς καὶ οἱ
with the under-officers to see the end. the And chief priests and the
4245 4892 3650 2212 5577
πρεσβύτεροι καὶ τὸ συνέδριον ὅλον ἐζήτουν ψευδομαρτυ-
elders and the sanhedrin whole sought false testimony
2596 2424 3704 846 2289 3756
60 ρίαν κατὰ τοῦ Ἰησοῦ, ὅπως αὐτὸν θανατώσωσι. καὶ οὐχ
against Jesus so as Him they might execute, but not
2147 4183 5575 4334 3756
εὗρον· καὶ πολλῶν ψευδομαρτύρων προσελθόντων, οὐχ
did find even many false witnesses coming forward not
2147 5305 4334 1417 5575 2036
εὗρον. ὕστερον δὲ προσελθόντες δύο ψευδομάρτυρές εἶπον,
did find. at last But coming up two false witnesses said,

[61] saying, This one said, I am able to destroy the temple of God, and in three days to build it. [62]And standing up, the high priest said to Him, Do you answer nothing? What do these witness against you? [63]But Jesus kept silent. And answering the high priest said to Him, I adjure you by the living God that you tell us if you are the Christ, the Son of God. [64]Jesus said to him, You said *it*. I tell you more. From this time you shall see the Son of man sitting off *the* right *hand* of power, and coming on the clouds of the heavens.

[65]Then the high priest tore his garments, saying, He blasphemed! Why do we have any more need of witnesses? Behold, now you have heard his blasphemy. [66]What does it seem to you? And answering they said, He is liable to death. [67]Then they spat in His face, and beat Him with the fist; and *some* slapped *Him*, [68]saying, Prophesy to us, Christ. Who is the *one* that struck you?

[69]And Peter sat outside in the court. And one girl came near to him, saying, And you were with Jesus the Galilean. [70]But he denied before all, saying, I do not know what you say. [71]And he going out into the porch, another saw him, and said to those there, And this one was with Jesus the Nazarene. [72]And again he denied with an oath, I do not know the man. [73]And after a little, coming near, those standing by said to Peter, Truly you also are of them, for even your speech makes you known. [74]Then he began to curse and to

3778 5346 1410 2647 3485 2316 1223
61 Οὗτος ἔφη, Δύναμαι καταλῦσαι τὸν ναὸν τοῦ Θεοῦ, καὶ διὰ
This one said, I am able to destroy the Temple of God, and via
5140 2250 3618 846 450 749
62 τριῶν ἡμερῶν οἰκοδομῆσαι αὐτόν. καὶ ἀναστὰς ὁ ἀρχιερεὺς
three days to build it. And standing up the high priest
2036 846 3762 611 5101 3778 4675 2649
εἶπεν αὐτῷ, Οὐδὲν ἀποκρίνῃ; τί οὗτοί σου καταμαρτυροῦ-
said to Him, Nothing do you reply of what these of you do witness
2424 4623 611 749 2036
63 σιν; ὁ δὲ Ἰησοῦς ἐσιώπα. καὶ ἀποκριθεὶς ὁ ἀρχιερεὺς εἶπεν
against? But Jesus kept silent. And answering, the high priest said
846 1844 4571 2596 2316 2198 2443 2254
αὐτῷ, Ἐξορκίζω σε κατὰ τοῦ Θεοῦ τοῦ ζῶντος, ἵνα ἡμῖν
to Him, I adjure you by God the living that us
2036 1487 4771 1488 5547 5207 2316 3004 846
εἴπῃς εἰ σὺ εἶ ὁ Χριστός, ὁ υἱὸς τοῦ Θεοῦ. λέγει αὐτῷ ὁ
you tell if you are the Christ, the Son of God! Says to him –
2424 4771 2036 4133 3004 5213 575 737 3700
64 Ἰησοῦς, Σὺ εἶπας. πλὴν λέγω ὑμῖν, ἀπ' ἄρτι ὄψεσθε τὸν
Jesus, You said (it). Yet I tell you, from now you will see the
5207 444 2521 1537 1188 1411
υἱὸν τοῦ ἀνθρώπου καθήμενον ἐκ δεξιῶν τῆς δυνάμεως καὶ
Son of man sitting off (the) right (hand) of power and
2064 1909 3507 3772 5119 749
65 ἐρχόμενον ἐπὶ τῶν νεφελῶν τοῦ οὐρανοῦ. τότε ὁ ἀρχιερεὺς
coming on the clouds – of Heaven. Then the high priest
1284 2440 848 3004 3754 987 5102 2089
διέρρηξε τὰ ἱμάτια αὐτοῦ, λέγων ὅτι Ἐβλασφήμησε· τί ἔτι
tore the garments of him, saying, – He blasphemed; Why yet
5532 2192 3144 2396 3568 191 988
χρείαν ἔχομεν μαρτύρων; ἴδε, νῦν ἠκούσατε τὴν βλασφημίαν
need have we of witnesses? Behold, now, you heard the blasphemy.
848 5101 5213 1380 611 2036 1777
66 αὐτοῦ. τί ὑμῖν δοκεῖ; οἱ δὲ ἀποκριθέντες εἶπον, Ἔνοχος
of him. What to you seems it? they And answering said, Liable
2288 2076 5119 1716 1519 4383 848
67 θανάτου ἐστί. τότε ἐνέπτυσαν εἰς τὸ πρόσωπον αὐτοῦ καὶ
of death he is. Then they spat in the face of Him, and
2852 846 4474 3004 4395
68 ἐκολάφισαν αὐτόν· οἱ δὲ ἐρράπισαν, λέγοντες, Προφή-
beat with the fist Him, the and slapped (Him), saying, Prophesy
2254 5547 5101 2076 3817 4571
τευσον ἡμῖν, Χριστέ, τίς ἐστιν ὁ παίσας σε;
to us, Christ, who is it, the (one) having struck you?
4074 1854 2521 1722 833 4334
69 Ὁ δὲ Πέτρος ἔξω ἐκάθητο ἐν τῇ αὐλῇ· καὶ προσῆλθεν
And Peter outside sat in the court; and came near
846 3391 3814 3004 4771 2588 3326 2424
αὐτῷ μία παιδίσκη, λέγουσα, Καὶ σὺ ἦσθα μετὰ Ἰησοῦ τοῦ
to him one maid, saying, And you were with Jesus the
1057 720 1715 3956 3004 3756
70 Γαλιλαίου. ὁ δὲ ἠρνήσατο ἔμπροσθεν πάντων, λέγων, Οὐκ
Galilean. he But denied before all, saying, not
1492 5101 3004 1831 846 1519 4440 1491
71 οἶδα τί λέγεις. ἐξελθόντα δὲ αὐτὸν εἰς τὸν πυλῶνα, εἶδεν
I know what you say. going out And he into the porch, saw
846 243 3004 1563 3778 2258 3326 2424
αὐτὸν ἄλλη, καὶ λέγει τοῖς ἐκεῖ, Καὶ οὗτος ἦν μετὰ Ἰησοῦ
him another, and says to those there. And this one was with Jesus
3480 3825 720 3326 3727 3754 3756
72 τοῦ Ναζωραίου. καὶ πάλιν ἠρνήσατο μεθ' ὅρκου ὅτι Οὐκ
the Nazarene. And again he denied, with an oath, not
1492 444 3326 3397 4334 2476
73 οἶδα τὸν ἄνθρωπον. μετὰ μικρὸν δὲ προσελθόντες οἱ ἑστῶτες
I know the man. after a little And coming near those standing
2036 4074 230 3771 1537 846 1488 1063
εἶπον τῷ Πέτρῳ, Ἀληθῶς καὶ σὺ ἐξ αὐτῶν εἶ· καὶ γὰρ ἡ
said to Peter, Truly also you of them are, even for the
2981 4675 1212 4571 4160 5119 756 2653
74 λαλιά σου δῆλόν σε ποιεῖ. τότε ἤρξατο καταναθεματίζειν καὶ
speech of you manifest you makes. Then he began to curse and

swear, I do not know the man. And immediately a cock crowed. [75]And Peter recalled the word of Jesus, saying to him, Before a cock crows, you will deny Me three times. And going out, he wept bitterly.

CHAPTER 27

[1]And *it* becoming early morning, all the chief priests and the elders of the people took counsel together against Jesus, so as to put Him to death. [2]And binding Him, they led *Him* away and delivered Him to Pontius Pilate the governor.

[3]Then the *one* betraying Him, seeing that He was condemned, sorrowing Judas returned the thirty pieces of silver to the chief priests and the elders, [4]saying, I sinned, betraying innocent blood. But they said, What *is it* to us? You see *to it*. [5]And tossing the silver pieces into the temple, he left. And going away *he* hanged himself. [6]And taking the pieces of silver, the chief priests said, It is not lawful to put them into the treasury, since it is *the* price of blood. [7]And taking counsel, they bought of them the potter's field, for burial for the strangers. [8]So that field was called Field of Blood until today. [9]Then was fulfilled that spoken through Jeremiah the prophet, saying, "And I took the thirty pieces of silver, the price of Him who was priced, on whom they of the sons of Israel set a price, [10]and gave them for the potter's field, as the Lord directed me."

[11]And Jesus stood before the governor. And the governor questioned Him,

3660 3754 3756 1492 444 2112 220
ὀμνύειν ὅτι Οὐκ οἶδα τὸν ἄνθρωπον. καὶ εὐθέως ἀλέκτωρ
to swear, - not I know the man. And immediately a cock
5455 3415 4074 4487 2424
75 ἐφώνησε. καὶ ἐμνήσθη ὁ Πέτρος τοῦ ῥήματος τοῦ Ἰησοῦ
crowed. And remembered Peter the word of Jesus,
2046 846 3754 4250 220 5455 5151 533
εἰρηκότος αὐτῷ ὅτι Πρὶν ἀλέκτορα φωνῆσαι, τρὶς ἀπαρνήσῃ
saying to him, Before a cock crows thrice you will deny
3165 1831 1854 2799 4090
με. καὶ ἐξελθὼν ἔξω ἔκλαυσε πικρῶς.
Me. And going forth outside he wept bitterly.

CHAPTER 27

4405 1096 4824 2983 3956
1 Πρωΐας δὲ γενομένης, συμβούλιον ἔλαβον πάντες οἱ
early morning And occurring, counsel together took all the
749 4245 2992 2596 2424
ἀρχιερεῖς καὶ οἱ πρεσβύτεροι τοῦ λαοῦ κατὰ τοῦ Ἰησοῦ,
chief priests and the elders of the people against Jesus,
5620 2289 846 1210 846 520
2 ὥστε θανατῶσαι αὐτόν· καὶ δήσαντες αὐτὸν ἀπήγαγον καὶ
so as to execute Him And binding Him, they led away and
3860 846 4194 4091 2232
παρέδωκαν αὐτὸν Ποντίῳ Πιλάτῳ τῷ ἡγεμόνι.
delivered Him to Pontius Pilate the governor.
5119 1492 2455 3860 846 3754 2632
3 Τότε ἰδὼν Ἰούδας ὁ παραδιδοὺς αὐτὸν ὅτι κατεκρίθη,
Then seeing Judas, the (one) betraying Him, that He was condemned,
3338 654 5144 694 749
μεταμεληθεὶς ἀπέστρεψε τὰ τριάκοντα ἀργύρια τοῖς ἀρχιε-
sorrowing returned the thirty pieces of silver to the chief
4245 3004 264 3860
4 ρεῦσι καὶ τοῖς πρεσβυτέροις, λέγων, Ἥμαρτον παραδοὺς
priests and the elders, saying, I sinned, betraying
129 121 2036 5101 4314 2248 4771 3700 4496
5 αἷμα ἀθῷον. οἱ δὲ εἶπον, Τί πρὸς ἡμᾶς; σὺ ὄψει. καὶ ῥίψας
blood innocent. they But said, What to us? You see (to it) And tossing
694 1722 3485 402 565 519
τὰ ἀργύρια ἐν τῷ ναῷ, ἀνεχώρησε· καὶ ἀπελθὼν ἀπήγξατο.
the silver pieces into the temple, he left, and going away hanged himself
749 2983 694 2036 3756 1832
6 οἱ δὲ ἀρχιερεῖς λαβόντες τὰ ἀργύρια εἶπον, Οὐκ ἔξεστι
the But chief priests taking the silver pieces said, not It is lawful
906 846 1519 2878 1893 5092 129 2076 4824
βαλεῖν αὐτὰ εἰς τὸν κορβανᾶν, ἐπεὶ τιμὴ αἵματός ἐστι. συμ-
to put them into the treasury, since price of blood it is.
2983 59 1537 846 68
7 βούλιον δὲ λαβόντες ἠγόρασαν ἐξ αὐτῶν τὸν ἀγρὸν τοῦ
counsel And taking, they bought of them the field of the
2763 1519 5027 3581 1352 2564 68 1565
8 κεραμέως, εἰς ταφὴν τοῖς ξένοις. διὸ ἐκλήθη ὁ ἀγρὸς ἐκεῖνος
potter for burial for the strangers. Thus was called field that,
68 129 2193 4594 5119 4137 4483
9 ἀγρὸς αἵματος, ἕως τῆς σήμερον. τότε ἐπληρώθη τὸ ῥηθὲν
Field of Blood, until — today. Then was fulfilled that spoken
1223 2408 4396 3004 2983
διὰ Ἱερεμίου τοῦ προφήτου, λέγοντος, Καὶ ἔλαβον τὰ
through Jeremiah the prophet, saying, And I took the
5144 694 5092 5091 3739 5091
τριάκοντα ἀργύρια, τὴν τιμὴν τοῦ τετιμημένου, ὃν ἐτιμή-
thirty silver pieces, the price of the (one) priced, whom they
575 5207 2474 1325 846 1519 68
10 σαντο ἀπὸ υἱῶν Ἰσραήλ· καὶ ἔδωκαν αὐτὰ εἰς τὸν ἀγρὸν
priced from sons of Israel, and gave them for the field
2763 2505 4929 3427 2962
τοῦ κεραμέως, καθὰ συνέταξέ μοι Κύριος.
of the potter, as directed me the Lord.
2424 2476 1715 2232 1905
11 Ὁ δὲ Ἰησοῦς ἔστη ἔμπροσθεν τοῦ ἡγεμόνος· καὶ ἐπηρώ-
And Jesus stood before the governor, and questioned

saying, Are you the king of the Jews? And Jesus said to him, You say *it*. [12]And when He was accused by the chief priests and the elders, He answered nothing. [13]Then Pilate said to Him, Do you not hear how many things they testify against you? [14]And He did not answer him, not even to one word, so that the governor greatly marveled.

[15]And at a feast the governor customarily released one prisoner to the crowd, whom they wished. [16]And they had then a notable prisoner named Barabbas. [17]Then they having been assembled, Pilate said to them, Whom do you wish I may release to you, Barabbas, or Jesus called Christ? [18]For he knew they delivered Him up through envy.

[19]But as he was sitting on the judgment seat, his wife sent to him, saying, Let nothing *be* to you and that just one. For I have suffered many things today by a dream because of him. [20]But the chief priests and the elders persuaded the crowds, that they should ask *for* Barabbas, and to destroy Jesus. [21]And answering the governor said to them, From the two, which do you wish that I release to you? And they said, Barabbas. [22]Pilate said to them, What then should I do *to* Jesus called Christ? [23]They all said to him, Let him be crucified. But the governor said, For what wrong did he do? But they the more cried out, saying, Let him be crucified. [24]And seeing that nothing *is* gained, but rather an uproar occurs, taking water Pilate washed *his* hands before the crowd, saying, I am

846 2232 3004 4771 1488 935
τησεν αὐτὸν ὁ ἡγεμών, λέγων, Σὺ εἶ ὁ βασιλεὺς τῶν
Him the governor, saying, You are the king of the

2453 5346 846 4771 3004 1722
12 Ἰουδαίων; ὁ δὲ Ἰησοῦς ἔφη αὐτῷ, Σὺ λέγεις. καὶ ἐν τῷ
Jews? And Jesus said to him, You say (it). And in the

2723 846 5259 749 4245
κατηγορεῖσθαι αὐτὸν ὑπὸ τῶν ἀρχιερέων καὶ τῶν πρε-
accusing (of) Him by the chief priests and the

3762 611 5119 3004 846 4091
13 σβυτέρων, οὐδὲν ἀπεκρίνατο. τότε λέγει αὐτῷ ὁ Πιλάτος,
elders, nothing He answered. Then says to Him Pilate,

3756 191 4214 5675 2649 3756 611
14 Οὐκ ἀκούεις πόσα σοῦ καταμαρτυροῦσι; καὶ οὐκ ἀπεκρίθη
do not you hear what you they witness against? And not He answered

846 4314 3761 1722 4487 5620 2296 2232 3029
αὐτῷ πρὸς οὐδὲ ἓν ῥῆμα, ὥστε θαυμάζειν τὸν ἡγεμόνα λίαν.
him, to not even one word, so as to marvel the governor much

2596 1859 1486 2232 630 1520 3793
15 κατὰ δὲ ἑορτὴν εἰώθει ὁ ἡγεμὼν ἀπολύειν ἕνα τῷ ὄχλῳ
at And a feast used the governor to release one to the crowd

1198 3739 2309 2192 5119 1198 1978 3004
16 δέσμιον, ὃν ἤθελον. εἶχον δὲ τότε δέσμιον ἐπίσημον, λεγό-
prisoner, whom they wished. they had And then a prisoner notable called

912 4863 3767 846 2036 846
17 μενον Βαραββᾶν. συνηγμένων οὖν αὐτῶν, εἶπεν αὐτοῖς ὁ
Barabbas. having assembled then they said to them

4091 5101 2309 630 5213 912 2424
Πιλάτος, Τίνα θέλετε ἀπολύσω ὑμῖν; Βαραββᾶν, ἢ Ἰησοῦν
Pilate, Whom wish you I may release to you, Barabbas, or Jesus

3004 5547 1492 1063 3754 1223 5355 3862
18 τὸν λεγόμενον Χριστόν; ᾔδει γὰρ ὅτι διὰ φθόνον παρέδωκαν
called Christ? he knew For that through envy they delivered

846 2521 846 1909 968 649
19 αὐτόν. καθημένου δὲ αὐτοῦ ἐπὶ τοῦ βήματος, ἀπέστειλε
Him. sitting And he on the tribunal sent

4314 846 1135 848 3004 3367 4671
πρὸς αὐτὸν ἡ γυνὴ αὐτοῦ, λέγουσα, Μηδέν σοι καὶ τῷ
to him the wife of him, saying, Nothing to you and to

1342 1565 4183 1063 3958 4594 2596 3677 1223
δικαίῳ ἐκείνῳ· πολλὰ γὰρ ἔπαθον σήμερον κατ᾽ ὄναρ δι᾽
just one that; many things for I suffered today by a dream through

846 749 4245 3982
20 αὐτόν. οἱ δὲ ἀρχιερεῖς καὶ οἱ πρεσβύτεροι ἔπεισαν τοὺς
him. the But chief priests and the elders persuaded the

3793 2443 154 912 2424
ὄχλους ἵνα αἰτήσωνται τὸν Βαραββᾶν, τὸν δὲ Ἰησοῦν
crowds that they should ask Barabbas, and Jesus

622 611 2232 2036 846 5101
21 ἀπολέσωσιν. ἀποκριθεὶς δὲ ὁ ἡγεμὼν εἶπεν αὐτοῖς, Τίνα
to destroy. answering And the governor said to them, Which

2309 575 1417 630 5213 2036 912
θέλετε ἀπὸ τῶν δύο ἀπολύσω ὑμῖν; οἱ δὲ εἶπον, Βαραββᾶν.
wish you from the two I may release to you? they And said, Barabbas.

3004 846 4091 5101 3767 4160 2424 3004
22 λέγει αὐτοῖς ὁ Πιλάτος, Τί οὖν ποιήσω Ἰησοῦν τὸν λεγό-
Says to them, Pilate, What then may I do (to) Jesus called

5597 3004 846 3956 4717
23 μενον Χριστόν; λέγουσιν αὐτῷ πάντες, Σταυρωθήτω. ὁ
Christ? They say to him all, Let him be crucified. the

2232 5346 5101 1063 2556 4160 4057
δὲ ἡγεμὼν ἔφη, Τί γὰρ κακὸν ἐποίησεν; οἱ δὲ περισσῶς
But governor said, what For badness did he? they But more

2896 3004 4717 1492 4091 3754
24 ἔκραζον, λέγοντες, Σταυρωθήτω. Ἰδὼν δὲ ὁ Πιλάτος ὅτι
cried out, saying, Let him be crucified! seeing And Pilate that

3762 5623 235 3123 2351 1096 2983 5204
οὐδὲν ὠφελεῖ, ἀλλὰ μᾶλλον θόρυβος γίνεται, λαβὼν ὕδωρ,
nothing is gained, but rather an uproar occurs, taking water

633 5495 561 3793 3004 121
ἀπενίψατο τὰς χεῖρας ἀπέναντι τοῦ ὄχλου, λέγων, Ἀθῷός
he washed the hands before the crowd, saying, Innocent

innocent of the blood of this just one; you will see. [25]And answering all the people said, His blood *be* on us and on our children. [26]Then he released Barabbas to them. But having flogged Jesus, he delivered *Him* up that He might be crucified.

[27]Then taking Jesus into the praetorium, the soldiers of the governor gathered all the cohort against Him. [28]And stripping Him, they put a scarlet cloak around Him. [29]And plaiting a crown of thorns, they placed *it* on His head, and a reed in His right *hand*. And bowing the knee before Him, they mocked at Him, saying, Hail, king of the Jews. [30]And spitting at Him, *they* took the reed and struck at His head. [31]And when they had mocked Him, they stripped off His cloak, and they put His garments on Him and led Him away to crucify *Him*.

[32]And going out they found a man, a Cyrenean named Simon. They forced this one to bear His cross. [33]And coming to a place called Golgotha, which is called, Place of a Skull, [34]they gave Him vinegar mingled with gall to drink. And having tasted, He would not drink. [35]And having crucified Him, they divided His garments, casting a lot—that might be fulfilled that spoken by the prophet, "They divided My garments *to* themselves, and they cast a lot over My clothing." [36]And sitting down, they guarded Him there. [37]And they put up

1510 575 129 1342 5127 5210 3700
25 εἰμι ἀπὸ τοῦ αἵματος τοῦ δικαίου τούτου· ὑμεῖς ὄψεσθε. καὶ
I am from the blood of righteous one this, you will see. And
611 3956 2992 2036 129 848 1909 2248 1909
ἀποκριθεὶς πᾶς ὁ λαὸς εἶπε, Τὸ αἷμα αὐτοῦ ἐφ' ἡμᾶς καὶ ἐπὶ
answering, all the people said, The blood of him on us and on
5043 2267 5119 630 846 912
26 τὰ τέκνα ἡμῶν. τότε ἀπέλυσεν αὐτοῖς τὸν Βαραββᾶν· τὸν
the children of us. Then he released to them Barabbas
2424 5417 3860 2443 4717
δὲ Ἰησοῦν φραγελλώσας παρέδωκεν ἵνα σταυρωθῇ.
But Jesus having whipped, he delivered that he might be crucified.
5119 4757 2232 3880
27 Τότε οἱ στρατιῶται τοῦ ἡγεμόνος, παραλαβόντες τὸν
Then the soldiers of the governor, taking
2424 1519 4232 4863 1909 846 3650
Ἰησοῦν εἰς τὸ πραιτώριον, συνήγαγον ἐπ' αὐτὸν ὅλην τὴν
Jesus into the praetorium, gathered against Him all the
4686 1562 846 4060 846 5511
28 σπεῖραν· καὶ ἐκδύσαντες αὐτόν, περιέθηκαν αὐτῷ χλαμύδα
cohort. And stripping Him, they put around Him a cloak
2847 4120 4735 1537 173 2007
29 κοκκίνην. καὶ πλέξαντες στέφανον ἐξ ἀκανθῶν, ἐπέθηκαν
scarlet, and plaiting a crown of thorns, they placed
1909 2776 848 2563 1909 1188 848
ἐπὶ τὴν κεφαλὴν αὐτοῦ, καὶ κάλαμον ἐπὶ τὴν δεξιὰν αὐτοῦ·
on the head of Him, and a reed upon the right of Him.
1120 1715 846 1702 846
καὶ γονυπετήσαντες ἔμπροσθεν αὐτοῦ ἐνέπαιζον αὐτῷ,
And bowing the kneed in front of Him they mocked at Him,
3004 5463 935 2453 1715
30 λέγοντες, Χαῖρε, ὁ βασιλεὺς τῶν Ἰουδαίων· καὶ ἐμπτύσαντες
saying, Hail, king of the Jews; and spitting
1519 846 2983 2563 5180 1519 2776
εἰς αὐτόν, ἔλαβον τὸν κάλαμον, καὶ ἔτυπτον εἰς τὴν κεφαλὴν
at Him took the reed and struck at the head
848 3753 1702 846 1562 846
31 αὐτοῦ. καὶ ὅτε ἐνέπαιξαν αὐτῷ, ἐξέδυσαν αὐτὸν τὴν
of Him. And when they mocked at Him, they stripped off Him the
5511 1745 846 2440 848 520
χλαμύδα, καὶ ἐνέδυσαν αὐτὸν τὰ ἱμάτια αὐτοῦ, καὶ ἀπή-
cloak and put on Him the garments of Him, and led
846 1519 4717
γαγον αὐτὸν εἰς τὸ σταυρῶσαι.
away Him to – crucify.
1831 2147 444 2956 3686
32 Ἐξερχόμενοι δὲ εὗρον ἄνθρωπον Κυρηναῖον, ὀνόματι
going forth And they found a man, a Cyrenian, by name
2613 5126 29 2443 142 4716 848
Σίμωνα· τοῦτον ἠγγάρευσαν ἵνα ἄρῃ τὸν σταυρὸν αὐτοῦ.
Simon. This one they compelled, that he bear the cross of Him.
2064 1519 5117 3004 1115 3739 2076 3004
33 καὶ ἐλθόντες εἰς τόπον λεγόμενον Γολγοθᾶ, ὅς ἐστι λεγόμενος
And coming to a place called Golgotha, which is saying,
2898 5117 1325 846 4095 3690 3326 5521 3396
34 κρανίου τόπος, ἔδωκαν αὐτῷ πιεῖν ὄξος μετὰ χολῆς μεμιγ-
Of a skull place, they gave Him to drink vinegar with gall being
1089 3756 2309 4095 4717
35 μένον· καὶ γευσάμενος οὐκ ἤθελε πιεῖν. σταυρώσαντες δὲ
mixed; and having tasted (it), not He would drink. crucifying And
846 1266 2440 848 906 2819
αὐτόν, διεμερίσαντο τὰ ἱμάτια αὐτοῦ, βάλλοντες κλῆρον·
Him, they divided the garments of Him, casting a lot
2443 4137 4483 5259 4396 1266
ἵνα πληρωθῇ τὸ ῥηθὲν ὑπὸ τοῦ προφήτου, Διεμερίσαντο τὰ
that may be fulfilled the spoken by the prophet, They divided the
2440 3450 1438 1909 2441 3450 906 2819
ἱμάτιά μου ἑαυτοῖς, καὶ ἐπὶ τὸν ἱματισμόν μου ἔβαλον κλῆρον.
garments of Me themselves and on the clothing of Me they cast a lot.
2521 5083 846 1563 2007 1883
36 καὶ καθήμενοι ἐτήρουν αὐτὸν ἐκεῖ. καὶ ἐπέθηκαν ἐπάνω τῆς
37 And sitting down they guarded Him there. And they placed above the

over His head His charge, *it* having been written: THIS IS JESUS THE KING OF THE JEWS. [38]Then two robbers were crucified with Him, one off *the* right, and one off *the* left *of Him.*

[39]But those passing by blasphemed Him, shaking their heads, [40]and saying, *You* destroying the temple, and building it in three days, if you are the Son of God, come down from the cross. [41]And in the same way the chief priests with the scribes and elders, mocking said, [42]He saved others; he is not able to save himself. If he is the king of Israel, let him come down now from the cross, and we will believe him. [43]He trusted on God. Let Him rescue him now, if He desires him. For he said, I am Son of God. [44]And also the robbers crucified with Him reviled Him, *saying* the same.

[45]And from *the* sixth hour there was darkness over all the land until *the* ninth hour. [46]And about the ninth hour Jesus cried out with a loud voice, saying, Eli, Eli, lama sabachthani—that is, My God, My God, why did You forsake Me? [47]And hearing, some of those standing there said, This one calls Elijah. [48]And at once one of them running and taking a sponge, and filling *it* with vinegar, put *it* on a reed and gave drink to Him. [49]But the rest said, Let be; let us see if Elijah comes to save him.

[50]And crying again with a loud voice, Jesus released *His* spirit. [51]And, behold, the veil of the temple was torn into two from top to

2776 848 156 848 1125 3778 2076
κεφαλῆς αὐτοῦ τὴν αἰτίαν αὐτοῦ γεγραμμένην, Οὗτός ἐστιν
the head of Him the charge of Him, having been written, THIS IS
2424 935 2453 5119 4717 4862
38 Ἰησοῦς ὁ βασιλεὺς τῶν Ἰουδαίων. τότε σταυροῦνται σὺν
JESUS THE KING OF THE JEWS. Then are crucified with
846 1417 3027 1520 1537 1188 1519 1537 2176
39 αὐτῷ δύο λῃσταί, εἷς ἐκ δεξιῶν καὶ εἷς ἐξ εὐωνύμων. οἱ δὲ
Him two robbers, one of (the) right and one off (the) left. those And
3899 987 846 2795 2776
παραπορευόμενοι ἐβλασφήμουν αὐτόν, κινοῦντες τὰς κεφα-
passing by blasphemed Him, shaking the heads
848 3004 2647 3485
40 λὰς αὐτῶν, καὶ λέγοντες, Ὁ καταλύων τὸν ναὸν καὶ ἐν
of them, and saying, The (one) destroying the temple and in
5140 2250 3618 4982 4572 1487 5207 1488
τρισὶν ἡμέραις οἰκοδομῶν, σῶσον σεαυτόν· εἰ υἱὸς εἶ τοῦ
three days building (it), save yourself, if Son You are
2316 2597 575 4716 3618
41 Θεοῦ, κατάβηθι ἀπὸ τοῦ σταυροῦ. ὁμοίως δὲ καὶ οἱ
of God, come down from the cross. likewise And also the
749 1702 3326 1122 4245
ἀρχιερεῖς ἐμπαίζοντες μετὰ τῶν γραμματέων καὶ πρεσ-
chief priests mocking with the scribes and elders
3004 243 4982 1438 3756 1410 4982
42 βυτέρων ἔλεγον, Ἄλλους ἔσωσεν, ἑαυτὸν οὐ δύναται σῶσαι.
said, Others He saved, Himself not He is able to save.
1487 935 2474 2076 2597 3568 575 4716
εἰ βασιλεὺς Ἰσραήλ ἐστι, καταβάτω νῦν ἀπὸ τοῦ σταυροῦ,
If king of Israel He is, let Him descend now from the cross,
4100 846 3983 1909 2316 4506
43 καὶ πιστεύσομεν αὐτῷ. πέποιθεν ἐπὶ τὸν Θεόν· ῥυσάσθω
and we will believe Him. He trusted on God, let Him rescue
3568 846 1487 2309 846 2036 1063 3754 2316 1519 5207
νῦν αὐτόν, εἰ θέλει αὐτόν. εἶπε γὰρ ὅτι Θεοῦ εἰμι υἱός. τὸ
now Him, if He desires Him. He said For, of God I am Son. the
846 3027 4957 846 3679
44 δ' αὐτὸ καὶ οἱ λῃσταὶ οἱ συσταυρωθέντες αὐτῷ ὠνείδιζον
And same also the robbers crucified together with Him reproached
846
αὐτῷ.
Him.

575 1622 5610 4655 1096 1909 3956 1093
45 Ἀπὸ δὲ ἕκτης ὥρας σκότος ἐγένετο ἐπὶ πᾶσαν τὴν γῆν
from And sixth hour darkness occurred over all the land
2193 5610 1766 4012 1766 560 310
46 ἕως ὥρας ἐννάτης· περὶ δὲ τὴν ἐννάτην ὥραν ἀνεβόησεν ὁ
until hour (the) ninth. about And the ninth hour cried out
2424 5456 3173 3004 2241 2241 2982 4518
Ἰησοῦς φωνῇ μεγάλῃ, λέγων, Ἠλί, Ἠλί, λαμὰ σαβαχθανί;
Jesus a voice great, saying, Eli, Eli, lama sabachthani?
=5123 = 2076 2316 3450 2316 3450 2444 3165 1459 5100
τοῦτ' ἔστι, Θεέ μου, Θεέ μου, ἱνατί με ἐγκατέλιπες; τινὲς
this is, God of Me, God of Me, why Me did You forsake? some
1563 2476 191 3004 3754 2243 5455
47 δὲ τῶν ἐκεῖ ἑστώτων ἀκούσαντες ἔλεγον ὅτι Ἠλίαν φωνεῖ
And of those there standing hearing said, Elijah calls
3778 2112 5143 1520 1537 846 2983 4699
48 οὗτος. καὶ εὐθέως δραμὼν εἷς ἐξ αὐτῶν, καὶ λαβὼν σπόγγον,
this one. And at once running one of them and taking a sponge
4130 5037 3690 4060 2563 4222 846
49 πλήσας τε ὄξους, καὶ περιθεὶς καλάμῳ, ἐπότιζεν αὐτόν. οἱ δὲ
filling and with vinegar, and put on a reed, gave to drink Him. the But
3062 3004 863 1492 1487 2064 2243 4982 846
λοιποὶ ἔλεγον, Ἄφες, ἴδωμεν εἰ ἔρχεται Ἠλίας σώσων αὐτόν.
rest said, Leave! Let us see if comes Elijah to save Him.
2424 3825 2896 5456 3173 863 4151
50 ὁ δὲ Ἰησοῦς πάλιν κράξας φωνῇ μεγάλῃ ἀφῆκε τὸ πνεῦμα.
And Jesus again crying with a voice great released the spirit
2400 2665 3485 4977 1519 1417 575
51 καὶ ἰδού, τὸ καταπέτασμα τοῦ ναοῦ ἐσχίσθη εἰς δύο ἀπὸ
And behold, the veil of the Temple was torn into two, from

bottom. And the earth quaked, and the rocks were sheared! [52]And the tombs were opened, and many bodies of the saints who had fallen asleep were raised. [53]And coming forth out of the tombs after His resurrection, *they* entered into the holy city and were revealed to many.

[54]But the centurion and those guarding Jesus with him, seeing the earthquake and the things taking place, *they* feared exceedingly, saying, Truly this One was Son of God.

[55]And many women were there, watching from afar off, *those* who followed Jesus from Galilee, ministering to Him; [56]among whom was Mary Magdalene, and Mary the mother of James and Joses, and the mother of the sons of Zebedee.

[57]And evening having come, a rich man from Arimathea, Joseph by name, who also himself was discipled to Jesus; [58]coming up to Pilate, this one asked the body of Jesus. Then Pilate commanded the body to be given. [59]And taking the body, Joseph wrapped it in clean linen [60]and laid it in his new tomb, which he had cut out in the rock. And rolling a great stone to the door of the tomb, *he* departed. [61]And there was Mary Magdalene and the other Mary sitting across from the grave.

[62]And on the morrow, which is after the Preparation, the chief priests and the Pharisees were assembled to Pilate, [63]saying, Lord, we have recalled that that deceiver said while

509 2193 2736 1093 4579 4073 4977
ἄνωθεν ἕως κάτω· καὶ ἡ γῆ ἐσείσθη καὶ αἱ πέτραι ἐσχίσθη-
above until below and the earth was shaken, and the rocks were
3419 455 4183 4983
52 σαν· καὶ τὰ μνημεῖα ἀνεῴχθησαν· καὶ πολλὰ σώματα τῶν
torn, and the tombs were opened, and many bodies of the
2837 40 1453 1831 1537 3419
53 κεκοιμημένων ἁγίων ἠγέρθη· καὶ ἐξελθόντες ἐκ τῶν μνημείων
having fallen asleep saints were raised; and coming forth out of the tombs
3326 1454 848 1525 1519 40 4172
μετὰ τὴν ἔγερσιν αὐτοῦ εἰσῆλθον εἰς τὴν ἁγίαν πόλιν, καὶ
after the rising of Him entered into the holy city and
1718 4183 1543 3326 846
54 ἐνεφανίσθησαν πολλοῖς. ὁ δὲ ἑκατόνταρχος καὶ οἱ μετ᾽ αὐτοῦ
were manifested to many. the And centurion and those with him
5083 2424 1492 4578 1096
τηροῦντες τὸν Ἰησοῦν, ἰδόντες τὸν σεισμὸν καὶ τὰ γενόμενα,
guarding Jesus, seeing the earthquake and the happenings,
5399 4970 3004 230 2316 5207 2258
ἐφοβήθησαν σφόδρα, λέγοντες, Ἀληθῶς Θεοῦ υἱὸς ἦν
feared exceedingly, saying, Truly of God Son was
3778 2258 1563 1135 4183 575 3113 2334
55 οὗτος. ἦσαν δὲ ἐκεῖ γυναῖκες πολλαὶ ἀπὸ μακρόθεν θεωροῦ-
this One. were And there women many from afar beholding
3748 190 2424 575 1056
σαι, αἵτινες ἠκολούθησαν τῷ Ἰησοῦ ἀπὸ τῆς Γαλιλαίας,
who followed — Jesus from — Galilee,
1247 846 1722 3739 2258 3137 3094
56 διακονοῦσαι αὐτῷ· ἐν αἷς ἦν Μαρία ἡ Μαγδαληνή, καὶ
ministering to Him; among whom was Mary the Magdalene, and
3137 2385 2500 3384 3384
Μαρία ἡ τοῦ Ἰακώβου καὶ Ἰωσῆ μήτηρ, καὶ ἡ μήτηρ τῶν
Mary the of James and Joses mother, and the mother of the
5207 2199
υἱῶν Ζεβεδαίου.
sons of Zebedee.
3798 1096 2064 444 4145 575
57 Ὀψίας δὲ γενομένης, ἦλθεν ἄνθρωπος πλούσιος ἀπὸ
evening And having come, came a man rich from
707 5122 2501 3739 846 3100
Ἀριμαθαίας, τοὔνομα Ἰωσήφ, ὃς καὶ αὐτὸς ἐμαθήτευσε τῷ
Arimathea, by name Joseph, who also himself was discipled
2424 3778 4334 4091 154 4983
58 Ἰησοῦ· οὗτος προσελθὼν τῷ Πιλάτῳ, ᾐτήσατο τὸ σῶμα
to Jesus; this one coming up to Pilate asked the body
2424 5119 4091 2753 591 4983
τοῦ Ἰησοῦ. τότε ὁ Πιλάτος ἐκέλευσεν ἀποδοθῆναι τὸ σῶμα.
of Jesus. Then Pilate commanded to be given the body.
2983 4983 2501 1794 846 4616
59 καὶ λαβὼν τὸ σῶμα ὁ Ἰωσὴφ ἐνετύλιξεν αὐτὸ σινδόνι
And taking the body, Joseph wrapped it in linen
2513 5087 846 1722 2537 848 3419 3739
60 καθαρᾷ, καὶ ἔθηκεν αὐτὸ ἐν τῷ καινῷ αὐτοῦ μνημείῳ, ὃ
clean, and placed it in the new of him tomb, which
2998 1722 4073 4351 3037 3173
ἐλατόμησεν ἐν τῇ πέτρᾳ· καὶ προσκυλίσας λίθον μέγαν τῇ
he had hewed in the rock, and having rolled a stone great to the
2374 3419 565 2258 1563 3137 3094
61 θύρα τοῦ μνημείου, ἀπῆλθεν. ἦν δὲ ἐκεῖ Μαρία ἡ Μαγδαληνή,
door of the tomb, he went away. was And there Mary the Magdalene,
243 3137 2521 561 5028
καὶ ἡ ἄλλη Μαρία, καθήμεναι ἀπέναντι τοῦ τάφου.
and the other Mary, sitting opposite the grave.
1887 3748 2076 3326 3904 4863
62 Τῇ δὲ ἐπαύριον, ἥτις ἐστὶ μετὰ τὴν Παρασκευήν, συνή-
on the And morrow, which is after the Preparation, were
749 5330 4314 4091 3004
63 χθησαν οἱ ἀρχιερεῖς καὶ οἱ Φαρισαῖοι πρὸς Πιλάτον, λέγοντες,
assembled the chief priests and the Pharisees to Pilate, saying,
2962 3415 3754 1565 4108 2036 2089/2198/3326
Κύριε, ἐμνήσθημεν ὅτι ἐκεῖνος ὁ πλάνος εἶπεν ἔτι ζῶν, Μετὰ
Sir, we have recalled that that — deceiver said yet living, After

living. After three days I will rise. 64 Therefore, command that the grave be secured until the third day, that his disciples may not come by night and steal him away, and may say to the people, He is raised from the dead. And the last deception will be worse than the first. 65 And Pilate said to them, You have a guard; go away; make *it as* secure as you know *how*. 66 And going, they made the grave secure, sealing the stone, along with the guard.

5140 2250 1453 2753 3767 805
64 τρεῖς ἡμέρας ἐγείρομαι. κέλευσον οὖν ἀσφαλισθῆναι τὸν
three days I arise. Command then to be made secure the
5028/2193 5154 2250 3379 2064 3101
τάφον ἕως τῆς τρίτης ἡμέρας· μήποτε ἐλθόντες οἱ μαθηταὶ
grave until the third day, lest coming the disciples
848 3571 2813 846 2036 2092 1453
αὐτοῦ νυκτὸς κλέψωσιν αὐτόν, καὶ εἴπωσι τῷ λαῷ, Ἠγέρ-
of him by night may steal him and may say to the people, He is
575 3498 2071 2078 4106 5501
θη ἀπὸ τῶν νεκρῶν· καὶ ἔσται ἡ ἐσχάτη πλάνη χείρων τῆς
raised from the dead, and will be the last deceit worse than the
4413 5346 846 4091 2192 2892
65 πρώτης. ἔφη δὲ αὐτοῖς ὁ Πιλάτος, Ἔχετε κουστωδίαν·
first. Said and to them — Pilate, You have a guard;
5217 805 5613 1492 4198 805
66 ὑπάγετε, ἀσφαλίσασθε ὡς οἴδατε. οἱ δὲ πορευθέντες ἠσφαλί-
go, make secure as you know. they And going made
5028 4972 3037 3326
σαντο τὸν τάφον, σφραγίσαντες τὸν λίθον, μετὰ τῆς
secure the grave, sealing the stone, with the
κουστωδίας.
guard.

CHAPTER 28

1 After the sabbaths, at the dawning into the first of *the* sabbaths, Mary Magdalene and the other Mary came to see the grave. 2 And, behold! A great earthquake occurred! For coming down from Heaven, and coming up, an angel of *the* Lord rolled away the stone from the door, and was sitting on it. 3 And his face was as lightning, and his clothing white as snow. 4 And those keeping guard were shaken from the fear of him, and they became as dead. 5 But answering the angel said to the women, You must not fear, for I know that you seek Jesus, He having been crucified.

6 He is not here, for He was raised, as He said. Come, see the place where the Lord was lying. 7 And going quickly say to His disciples that He was raised from the dead. And, behold, He goes before you into Galilee. You will see Him there. See, I told you. 8 And going away from the tomb quickly, with fear and great joy, they ran

CHAPTER 28

3796 4521 2020 1519 3391 4521
1 Ὀψὲ δὲ σαββάτων, τῇ ἐπιφωσκούσῃ εἰς μίαν σαββάτων,
after But the sabbaths, at the dawning into the first of (the) sabbaths
2064 3137 3094 243 3137 2334
ἦλθε Μαρία ἡ Μαγδαληνή, καὶ ἡ ἄλλη Μαρία, θεωρησαι
came Mary the Magdalene and the other Mary to view
5028 2400 4578 1096 3173 32 1080
2 τὸν τάφον. καὶ ἰδού, σεισμὸς ἐγένετο μέγας· ἄγγελος γὰρ
the grave. And, behold, an earthquake occurred great; an angel for
2962 2597 1537 3772 4334 617
Κυρίου καταβὰς ἐξ οὐρανοῦ, προσελθὼν ἀπεκύλισε τὸν
of (the) Lord descending from Heaven, and coming up rolled away the
3037 575 2374 2521 1883 846 2258
3 λίθον ἀπὸ τῆς θύρας, καὶ ἐκάθητο ἐπάνω αὐτοῦ. ἦν δὲ ἡ
stone from the door, and sitting on it. was And the
2397 848 5613 796 1742 848 3022 5616
ἰδέα αὐτοῦ ὡς ἀστραπή, καὶ τὸ ἔνδυμα αὐτοῦ λευκὸν ὡσεὶ
look of him as lightning, and the dress of him white as
5510 575 5401 846 4579 5083
4 χιών. ἀπὸ δὲ τοῦ φόβου αὐτοῦ ἐσείσθησαν οἱ τηροῦντες
snow. from and the fear of him were shaken those guarding
1096 5616 3498 611 32 2036
5 καὶ ἐγένοντο ὡσεὶ νεκροί. ἀποκριθεὶς δὲ ὁ ἄγγελος εἶπε ταῖς
and they became as dead. answering And the angel said to the
1135 3361 5399 5210 1492 1063 3754 2424
γυναιξί, Μὴ φοβεῖσθε ὑμεῖς· οἶδα γὰρ ὅτι Ἰησοῦν τὸν
women, Do not fear you; I know for that Jesus the (One)
4717 2212 3756 2076 5602 1453 1063 2531
6 ἐσταυρωμένον ζητεῖτε. οὐκ ἔστιν ὧδε· ἠγέρθη γάρ, καθὼς
having been crucified you seek. not He is here; He was raised for, as
2036 1205 1492 5117 3699 2749 2962 5035
7 εἶπε. δεῦτε, ἴδετε τὸν τόπον ὅπου ἔκειτο ὁ Κύριος. καὶ ταχὺ
He said; come, see the place where lay the Lord. And quickly
4198 2036 3101 848 3754 1453 575
πορευθεῖσαι εἴπατε τοῖς μαθηταῖς αὐτοῦ ὅτι Ἠγέρθη ἀπὸ
going tell to the disciples of Him that He was raised from
3498 2400 4254 5209 1519 1056 1563
τῶν νεκρῶν· καὶ ἰδού, προάγει ὑμᾶς εἰς τὴν Γαλιλαίαν· ἐκεῖ
the dead, and, behold, He goes before you into — Galilee. There
846 3700 2400 2036 5213 1831 5035 575
8 αὐτὸν ὄψεσθε· ἰδού, εἶπον ὑμῖν. καὶ ἐξελθοῦσαι ταχὺ ἀπὸ
Him you will see. Behold, I told you. And going away quickly from
3419 3326 5401 5479 3173 5143
τοῦ μνημείου μετὰ φόβου καὶ χαρᾶς μεγάλης, ἔδραμον
the tomb, with fear and joy great, they ran

to tell *it* to His disciples. [9]But as they were going to tell *it* to His disciples, behold, Jesus also met them, saying, Hail! And coming near, they seized His feet, and worshiped Him. [10]Then Jesus said to them, Do not fear. Go tell your brothers that they may go into Galilee, and there they will see Me.

[11]And they having left, behold, some of the guard coming into the city reported to the chief priests all things that occurred. [12]And being assembled with the elders, and taking counsel, *they* gave enough silver to the soldiers, [13]saying, Say that his disciples came *and* stole him by night, we being asleep. [14]And if this is heard by the governor, we will persuade him, and will make you free from anxiety. [15]And taking the silver, they did as they were taught. And this reort was spread by the Jews until today.

[16]But the eleven disciples went into Galilee, to the mount where Jesus appointed them. [17]And seeing Him, they worshiped Him. But they doubted. [18]And coming up Jesus talked with them, saying, All authority in Heaven and on earth was given to Me. [19]Going, then, disciple all nations, baptizing them into the name of the Father and of the Son and of the Holy Spirit; [20]teaching

518 3101 846 5613 4198 518
9 ἀπαγγεῖλαι τοῖς μαθηταῖς αὐτοῦ. ὡς δὲ ἐπορεύοντο ἀπαγ-
to announce to the disciples of Him. as But they were going to
3101 846 2400 2424 528
γεῖλαι τοῖς μαθηταις αὐτοῦ, καὶ ἰδού, ὁ Ἰησοῦς ἀπήντησεν
tell (it) to the disciples of Him, also behold, – Jesus met
848 3004 5463 4334 2902
αὐταῖς, λέγων, Χαίρετε. αἱ δὲ προσελθοῦσαι ἐκράτησαν
them, saying, Hail! they And coming near seized
846 4228 4352 846 5119 3004
10 αὐτοῦ τοὺς πόδας, καὶ προσεκύνησαν αὐτῷ. τότε λέγει
of Him the feet, and worshiped Him. Then says
846 2424 3361 5399 5217 518
αὐταῖς ὁ Ἰησοῦς· Μὴ φοβεῖσθε· ὑπάγετε, ἀπαγγείλατε τοῖς
to them – Jesus, Do not fear. Go, announce to the
80 3450 2443 565 1519 1056 2546 3165
ἀδελφοῖς μου ἵνα ἀπέλθωσιν εἰς τὴν Γαλιλαίαν, κἀκεῖ με
brothers of Me that they may go into Galilee, and there Me
3700
ὄψονται.
they will see.

4198 848 2400 5100 2892
11 Πορευομένων δὲ αὐτῶν, ἰδού, τινὲς τῆς κουστωδίας
going And they, behold, some of the guard
2064 1519 4172 518 749 537
ἐλθόντες εἰς τὴν πόλιν ἀπήγγειλαν τοῖς ἀρχιερεῦσιν ἅπαντα
coming into the city announced to the chief priests all things
1096 4863 3326 4245 4824
12 τὰ γενόμενα. καὶ συναχθέντες μετὰ τῶν πρεσβυτέρων, συμ-
that occurred. And being assembled with the elders,
5037 2983 694 2425 1325 4757
βούλιόν τε λαβόντες, ἀργύρια ἱκανὰ ἔδωκαν τοῖς στρατιώ-
counsel and taking, silver enough gave to the soldiers,
3004 2036 3754 3101 848 3571
13 ταις, λέγοντες, Εἴπατε ὅτι Οἱ μαθηταὶ αὐτοῦ νυκτὸς
saying, Say, The disciples of Him by night
2064 2813 846 2257 2837 1437 191
14 ἐλθόντες ἔκλεψαν αὐτὸν ἡμῶν κοιμωμένων. καὶ ἐὰν ἀκουσθῇ
coming stole Him, we being asleep. And if is heard
5124 1909 2232 2249 3982 846 5209
τοῦτο ἐπὶ τοῦ ἡγεμόνος, ἡμεῖς πείσομεν αὐτόν, καὶ ὑμᾶς
this before the governor, we will persuade him, and you
275 4160 2983 694 4160
15 ἀμερίμνους ποιήσομεν. οἱ δὲ λαβόντες τὰ ἀργύρια ἐποίη-
free from anxiety we will make. they And taking the silver did
5613 1321 1310 3056 3778 3844
σαν ὡς ἐδιδάχθησαν. καὶ διεφημίσθη ὁ λόγος οὗτος παρὰ
as they were taught. And was spread – saying this by
2453 3360 4594
Ἰουδαίοις μέχρι τῆς σήμερον.
Jews until – today.

1733 3101 4198 1519 1056 1519
16 Οἱ δὲ ἕνδεκα μαθηταὶ ἐπορεύθησαν εἰς τὴν Γαλιλαίαν, εἰς
the And eleven disciples went to – Galilee, to
3735 3757 5021 846 2424 1492 846
17 τὸ ὄρος οὗ ἐτάξατο αὐτοῖς ὁ Ἰησοῦς. καὶ ἰδόντες αὐτὸν
the mount where appointed them – Jesus. And seeing Him,
4352 846 1365 4334
18 προσεκύνησαν αὐτῷ· οἱ δὲ ἐδίστασαν. καὶ προσελθὼν ὁ
they worshiped Him, they but doubted. And coming up –
2424 2980 846 3004 1325 3427 3956 1849
Ἰησοῦς ἐλάλησεν αὐτοῖς, λέγων, Ἐδόθη μοι πᾶσα ἐξουσία
Jesus talked with them, saying, was given Me All authority
1722 3772 1909 1093 4198 3767 3100 3956
19 ἐν οὐρανῷ καὶ ἐπὶ γῆς. πορευθέντες οὖν μαθητεύσατε πάντα
in Heaven and upon earth. Having gone, then, disciple all
1484 907 846 1519 3686 3962
τὰ ἔθνη, βαπτίζοντες αὐτοὺς εἰς τὸ ὄνομα τοῦ Πατρὸς καὶ
the nations, baptizing them into the name of the Father and
5207 40 4151 1321 846
20 τοῦ Υἱοῦ καὶ τοῦ Ἁγίου Πνεύματος· διδάσκοντες αὐτοὺς
of the Son and of the Holy Spirit, teaching them

them to observe all things, whatever I commanded you. And, behold, I am with you all the days until the completion of the age. Amen.

5083 3956 3745 1781 5213 2400 1473 3326
τηρεῖν πάντα ὅσα ἐνετειλάμην ὑμῖν· καὶ ἰδού, ἐγὼ μεθ᾽
to observe all things whatever I commanded you; and,behold, I with
5216 1510 3956 2250 2193 4930 165
ὑμῶν εἰμι πάσας τὰς ἡμέρας ἕως τῆς συντελείας τοῦ αἰῶνος.
you am all the days until the completion of the age.
281
᾽Αμήν.
Amen.

ΕΥΑΓΓΕΛΙΟΝ
GOSPEL
ΤΟ ΚΑΤΑ ΜΑΡΚΟΝ
THE ACCORDING TO MARK

THE GOSPEL
ACCORDING TO
MARK
A LITERAL TRANSLATION
OF THE BIBLE

CHAPTER 1

[1]The beginning of the gospel of Jesus Christ, *the* Son of God, [2]as it has been written in the Prophets, "Behold, I send My messenger before Your face, who will prepare Your way before You; [3]*the* voice of one crying in the wilderness. Prepare the way of *the* Lord, make His paths straight."

[4]John came baptizing in the wilderness, and proclaiming a baptism of repentance for forgiveness of sins. [5]And all the Judean country, and those of Jerusalem went out to him, and were all baptized by him in the Jordan River, confessing their sins. [6]And John was clothed in camel's hair, and a leather girdle about his loin; and eating locusts and wild honey. [7]And he proclaimed, saying, He who comes after me is mightier than I, of whom I am not fit to stoop down to loosen the thong of His sandals. [8]I indeed baptized you in water, but He will baptize you in *the* Holy Spirit.

[9]And it happened in those days, Jesus came from Nazareth of Galilee, and was baptized by John in the Jordan. [10]And going up from the water immediately, He saw the heavens being torn, and the Spirit coming down as a dove upon Him.

CHAPTER 1

746 2098 2424 5547 5207 2316
1 Ἀρχὴ τοῦ εὐαγγελίου Ἰησοῦ Χριστοῦ, υἱοῦ τοῦ Θεοῦ·
(The) beginning of the gospel of Jesus Christ, Son of God.
5613 1125 1722 4396 2400 1473 649
2 Ὡς γέγραπται ἐν τοῖς προφήταις, Ἰδού, ἐγὼ ἀποστέλλω
As it has been written in the prophets, Behold, I send
32 3450 4253 4383 4675 3739 2680
τὸν ἄγγελόν μου πρὸ προσώπου σου, ὃς κατασκευάσει τὴν
the messenger of Me before (the) face of you who will prepare the
3598 4675 1715 4675 5456 994 1722 2048
3 ὁδόν σου ἔμπροσθέν σου. φωνὴ βοῶντος ἐν τῇ ἐρήμῳ,
way of You before You. (The) voice of one crying in the wilderness.
2090 3598 2912 2117 4160 5147
Ἑτοιμάσατε τὴν ὁδὸν Κυρίου· εὐθείας ποιεῖτε τὰς τρίβους
Prepare the way of (the) Lord; straight make the paths
848 1096 2491 907 1722 2048 2784
4 αὐτοῦ. ἐγένετο Ἰωάννης βαπτίζων ἐν τῇ ἐρήμῳ, καὶ κηρύσ-
of Him. came John baptizing in the desert, and proclaim-
908 3341 1519 859 266 1607
5 σων βάπτισμα μετανοίας εἰς ἄφεσιν ἁμαρτιῶν. καὶ ἐξεπορεύ-
ing a baptism of repentance for forgiveness of sins. And went out
4314 846 3956 2449 5561 2415
ετο πρὸς αὐτὸν πᾶσα ἡ Ἰουδαία χώρα, καὶ οἱ Ἱεροσολυμῖται,
to him all the Judean country, and the Jerusalemites,
907 3956 1722 2446 4215 5259 846
καὶ ἐβαπτίζοντο πάντες ἐν τῷ Ἰορδάνῃ ποταμῷ ὑπ' αὐτοῦ,
and were baptised all in the Jordan River by him,
1843 266 848 2258 2491
6 ἐξομολογούμενοι τὰς ἁμαρτίας αὐτῶν. ἦν δὲ Ἰωάννης
having confessed the sins of them. was And John
1746 2359 2574 2223 1193 4012
ἐνδεδυμένος τρίχας καμήλου, καὶ ζώνην δερματίνην περὶ
being clothed in hair of a camel, and a girdle leather about
3751 848 2068 200 3192 66
τὴν ὀσφὺν αὐτοῦ, καὶ ἐσθίων ἀκρίδας καὶ μέλι ἄγριον.
the loin of him, and eating locusts and honey wild.
2784 3004 2064 2478 3450 3694
7 καὶ ἐκήρυσσε, λέγων, Ἔρχεται ὁ ἰσχυρότερός μου ὀπίσω
And he proclaimed, saying, Comes He stronger than me after
3450 3739 3756 1510 2425 2955 3089 2438
μου, οὗ οὐκ εἰμὶ ἱκανὸς κύψας λῦσαι τὸν ἱμάντα τῶν
me, of whom not I am fit stooping down to loosen the thong of the
5266 348 1473 3303 907 5209 1722 5204 846
8 ὑποδημάτων αὐτοῦ. ἐγὼ μὲν ἐβάπτισα ὑμᾶς ἐν ὕδατι· αὐτὸς
sandals of Him. I indeed baptised you in water, He
907 5209 4151 40
δὲ βαπτίσει ὑμᾶς ἐν Πνεύματι Ἁγίῳ.
but will baptize you in (the) Spirit Holy.
1096 1722 1565 2250 2064 2424 575
9 Καὶ ἐγένετο ἐν ἐκείναις ταῖς ἡμέραις, ἦλθεν Ἰησοῦς ἀπὸ
And it was in those days, came Jesus from
3478 1056 907 5259 2491 1519
Ναζαρὲθ τῆς Γαλιλαίας, καὶ ἐβαπτίσθη ὑπὸ Ἰωάννου εἰς τὸν
Nazareth of Galilee and was baptized by John in the
2446 2112 305 575 5204 1492
10 Ἰορδάνην. καὶ εὐθέως ἀναβαίνων ἀπὸ τοῦ ὕδατος, εἶδε
Jordan. And immediately going up from the water, he saw
4977 3772 4151 5616 4058
σχιζομένους τοὺς οὐρανούς, καὶ τὸ Πνεῦμα ὡσεὶ περιστερὰν
being torn the heavens, and the Spirit as a dove

NOTE: Frequent words not numbered: δέ(1161); καί(2531)—and, but; ὁ, ἡ, τό (3588, the)— * above word, look in verse margin for No.

11 And there was a voice out of the heavens, You are My Son, the Beloved, in whom I take delight.

12 And the Spirit at once drove Him out into the wilderness. 13 And He was there in the wilderness forty days, being tempted by Satan, and was with the wild beasts. And the angels ministered to Him.

14 And after John was delivered up, Jesus came into Galilee, proclaiming the gospel of the kingdom of God, 15 and saying, The time has been fulfilled, and the kingdom of God draws near. Repent and believe in the gospel.

16 And walking along beside the Sea of Galilee, He saw Simon and his brother Andrew casting a small net in the sea; for they were fishers. 17 And Jesus said to them, Come after Me, and I will make you to become fishers of men.

18 And leaving their nets, they immediately followed Him. 19 And going forward from there a little, He saw James the *son* of Zebedee, and his brother John. And they *were* in the boat mending the nets. 20 And at once He called them. And leaving their father Zebedee in the boat with the hired servants, they went after Him.

21 And they passed along into Capernaum. And entering into the synagogue, at once He taught on the sabbaths. 22 And

2597 1909 846 5456 1096 1537 3772
11 καταβαῖνον ἐπ' αὐτόν· καὶ φωνὴ ἐγένετο ἐκ τῶν οὐρανῶν,
coming down upon Him. And a voice there was out of the heavens:
4571 1487 5207 3450 27 1722 3739 2106
Σὺ εἶ ὁ υἱός μου ὁ ἀγαπητός, ἐν ᾧ εὐδόκησα.
You are the Son of Me, the Beloved, in whom I take delight.
2117 4151 846 1544 1519 2048
12 Καὶ εὐθὺς τὸ Πνεῦμα αὐτὸν ἐκβάλλει εἰς τὴν ἔρημον. καὶ
13 And instantly the Spirit Him thrusts into the desert. And
2258/1563/1722 2048 2250 5062 3985 5259
ἦν ἐκεῖ ἐν τῇ ἐρήμῳ ἡμέρας τεσσαράκοντα πειραζόμενος ὑπὸ
He was there in the desert days forty being tempted by
4567 2258 3326 2342 32 1247
τοῦ Σατανᾶ, καὶ ἦν μετὰ τῶν θηρίων, καὶ οἱ ἄγγελοι διη-
Satan, and was with the wild beasts, and the angels
846
κόνουν αὐτῷ.
ministered to Him.
3326 3860 2491 2064 2424
14 Μετὰ δὲ τὸ παραδοθῆναι τὸν Ἰωάννην, ἦλθεν ὁ Ἰησοῦς
after And was delivered up John, came Jesus
1519 1056 2784 2098 932
εἰς τὴν Γαλιλαίαν, κηρύσσων τὸ εὐαγγέλιον τῆς βασιλείας
into Galilee, proclaiming the gospel of the kingdom
2316 3004 3754 4137 2540 1448
15 τοῦ Θεοῦ, καὶ λέγων ὅτι Πεπλήρωται ὁ καιρός, καὶ ἤγγικεν
of God, and saying, Has been fulfilled the time, and draws near
932 2316 3340 4100 1722
ἡ βασιλεία τοῦ Θεοῦ· μετανοεῖτε, καὶ πιστεύετε ἐν τῷ
the kingdom of God; repent and believe in the
2098
εὐαγγελίῳ.
gospel.
4043 3844 2281 1056 1492
16 Περιπατῶν δὲ παρὰ τὴν θάλασσαν τῆς Γαλιλαίας εἶδε
walking along And beside the Sea of Galilee, He saw
4613 406 80 848 906
Σίμωνα καὶ Ἀνδρέαν τὸν ἀδελφὸν αὐτοῦ, βάλλοντας
Simon and Andrew the brother of him casting
293 1722 2281 2258 1063 231 2036
17 ἀμφίβληστρον ἐν τῇ θαλάσσῃ· ἦσαν γὰρ ἁλιεῖς. καὶ εἶπεν
a small net in the sea; they were for fishers. And said
846 2424 1205 3694 3450 4160 5209
αὐτοῖς ὁ Ἰησοῦς, Δεῦτε ὀπίσω μου, καὶ ποιήσω ὑμᾶς
to them Jesus, Come after Me, and I will make you
1096 231 444 2112 863 1350
18 γενέσθαι ἁλιεῖς ἀνθρώπων. καὶ εὐθέως ἀφέντες τὰ δίκτυα
to become fishers of men. And at once leaving the nets
848 190 846 4260 1564 3644
19 αὐτῶν, ἠκολούθησαν αὐτῷ. καὶ προβὰς ἐκεῖθεν ὀλίγον,
of them, they followed Him. And going forward from there a bit,
1492 2385 2199 1491
εἶδεν Ἰάκωβον τὸν τοῦ Ζεβεδαίου, καὶ Ἰωάννην τὸν
He saw James the (son) of Zebedee and John the
80 848 846 1722 4143 2675
ἀδελφὸν αὐτοῦ, καὶ αὐτοὺς ἐν τῷ πλοίῳ καταρτίζοντας τὰ
brother of him, and they in the boat mending the
1350 2112 2564 846 863 3962
20 δίκτυα. καὶ εὐθέως ἐκάλεσεν αὐτούς· καὶ ἀφέντες τὸν πατέρα
nets. And at once He called them. And leaving the father
848 2199 1722 4143 3326 3411 565
αὐτῶν Ζεβεδαῖον ἐν τῷ πλοίῳ μετὰ τῶν μισθωτῶν ἀπῆλθον
of them, Zebedee, in the boat with the hired servants, they went
3694 846
ὀπίσω αὐτοῦ.
after Him.
1531 1519 2584 2112
21 Καὶ εἰσπορεύονται εἰς Καπερναούμ· καὶ εὐθέως τοῖς
And they passed along into Capernaum, and at once on the
4521 1525 1519 4864 1321
22 σάββασιν εἰσελθὼν εἰς τὴν συναγωγήν ἐδίδασκε. καὶ
sabbaths entering into the synagogue He taught. And

they were astonished at His teaching, for He was teaching them as having authority, and not as the scribes. [23]And a man with an unclean spirit was in their synagogue. And he cried out, [24]saying, What *is* to us and to You, Jesus, Nazarene? Have You come to destroy us? I know You, who You are, the Holy One of God. [25]And Jesus rebuked him, saying, Be quiet, and come out of him. [26]And the unclean spirit convulsing him, and crying out with a loud voice, he came out of him. [27]And all were astonished, so as to discuss to themselves, saying, What is this? What new teaching *is* this, that He commands even the unclean spirits with authority, and they obey Him? [28]And His fame went out at once into all the Galilean neighborhood.

[29]And at once going out of the synagogue, they came into the house of Simon and Andrew, with James and John. [30]And the mother-in-law of Simon was laid out, stricken by fever. And at once they spoke to Him about her. [31]And coming near, He raised her up, holding her hand. And the fever left her instantly; and she served them.

[32]And evening coming, when the sun set, they brought to Him all those having illness, and those having been demon-possessed. [33]And the whole city was gathered at the door. [34]And He healed many who had illness of various diseases. And he cast out many demons, and did not allow the demons to speak, because they knew Him.

1605 1909 1322 848 2258 1063 1321
ἐξεπλήσσοντο ἐπὶ τῇ διδαχῇ αὐτοῦ· ἦν γὰρ διδάσκων
they were astounded at the teaching of Him, He was for teaching
846 5613 1849 2192 3756 5613 1122
23 αὐτοὺς ὡς ἐξουσίαν ἔχων, καὶ οὐχ ὡς οἱ **γραμματεῖς**. καὶ
them as authority having, and not as the scribes. And
2258 1722 4864 848 444 1722 4151 169
ἦν ἐν τῇ συναγωγῇ αὐτῶν ἄνθρωπος ἐν πνεύματι ἀκαθάρτῳ,
was in the synagogue of them a man with a spirit unclean;
349 3004 1436 5101 2254 4671 2424 3479
24 καὶ ἀνέκραξε, λέγων, Ἔα, τί ἡμῖν καὶ σοί, Ἰησοῦ Ναζαρηνέ;
and he cried out, saying, Ah! What to us and to You, Jesus, Nazarene?
488 2064 622 2248 1492 4571 5101 * 40 2316
25 ἦλθες ἀπολέσαι ἡμᾶς; οἶδά σε τίς εἶ, ὁ ἅγιος τοῦ Θεοῦ. καὶ
Came You to destroy us? I know You who You the Holy of God. And
2008 846 2424 3004 are, 5392 1831
ἐπετίμησεν αὐτῷ ὁ Ἰησοῦς, λέγων, Φιμώθητι, καὶ ἔξελθε
rebuked him Jesus, saying, Be quiet, and come
1537 846 4682 846 4151 169
ἐξ αὐτοῦ. καὶ σπαράξαν αὐτὸν τὸ πνεῦμα τὸ ἀκάθαρτον καὶ
out of him. And convulsing him the spirit unclean, and
2896 5456 3173 183 1537 846 2284
27 κράξαν φωνῇ μεγάλῃ, ἐξῆλθεν ἐξ αὐτοῦ. καὶ ἐθαμβήθησαν
crying out with a voice great he came out of him. And were astounded
3956 5620 4802 4314 846 3004 5101 2076
πάντες, ὥστε συζητεῖν πρὸς αὐτούς, λέγοντας, Τί ἐστι
all, so as to discuss to themselves, saying, What is
5124 5101 1322 2537 3778 3754 2596 1849
τοῦτο; τίς ἡ διδαχὴ ἡ καινὴ αὕτη, ὅτι κατ' ἐξουσίαν καὶ
this? What teaching new (is) this, that with authority even
4151 169 2004 5219
τοῖς πνεύμασι τοῖς ἀκαθάρτοις ἐπιτάσσει, καὶ ὑπακούουσιν
the spirits – unclean he commands, and they obey
846 1831 189 846 2117 1519 3650 4066
28 αὐτῷ; ἐξῆλθε δὲ ἡ ἀκοὴ αὐτοῦ εὐθὺς εἰς ὅλην τὴν περίχωρον
Him? went out And the fame of Him at once in all the neighborhood
1056
τῆς Γαλιλαίας.
of Galilee.

2112 1537 4864 1831 2064 1519
29 Καὶ εὐθέως ἐκ τῆς συναγωγῆς ἐξελθόντες, ἦλθον εἰς τὴν
And at once out of the synagogue going forth, they came into the
3614 4613 406 3326 2385 1491
οἰκίαν Σίμωνος καὶ Ἀνδρέου, μετὰ Ἰακώβου καὶ Ἰωάννου.
house of Simon and Andrew, with James and John.
3994 4163 2621 4445 2112
30 ἡ δὲ πενθερὰ Σίμωνος κατέκειτο πυρέσσουσα, καὶ εὐθέως
the And mother-in-law of Simon was laid fever-stricken. And at once
3004 846 4012 846 4334 1453 846
31 λέγουσιν αὐτῷ περὶ αὐτῆς· καὶ προσελθὼν ἤγειρεν αὐτήν,
they say to Him about her. And coming near He raised her,
2902 5495 848 863 846 4446
κρατήσας τῆς χειρὸς αὐτῆς· καὶ ἀφῆκεν αὐτὴν ὁ πυρετὸς
holding the hand of her, and left her the fever
2112 1247 846
εὐθέως, καὶ διηκόνει αὐτοῖς.
at once. And she served them.
3798 1096 3753 1416 2246 5342 4314 846
32 Ὀψίας δὲ γενομένης, ὅτε ἔδυ ὁ ἥλιος, ἔφερον πρὸς αὐτὸν
evening and coming, when set the sun, they brought to Him
3956 2560 2192 1139
33 πάντας τοὺς κακῶς ἔχοντας καὶ τοὺς δαιμονιζομένους· καὶ
all the (ones) illness having, and the (ones) demon-possessed. And
4172 3650 1996 2258 4314 2374 2323
34 ἡ πόλις ὅλη ἐπισυνηγμένη ἦν πρὸς τὴν θύραν. καὶ ἐθεράπευσε
the city whole having gathered was at the door. And He healed
4183 1544 2192 4164 3554 1140
πολλοὺς κακῶς ἔχοντας ποικίλαις νόσοις, καὶ δαιμόνια
many illness having of various diseases, and demons
4183 2560 3756 863 2980 1140 3754 1492
πολλὰ ἐξέβαλε, καὶ οὐκ ἤφιε λαλεῖν τὰ δαιμόνια, ὅτι ᾔδεισαν
many He cast out, and not allowed to speak the demons, because they knew

[35]And rising up quite early in *the* night, He went out and went away into a desert place. And *He* was praying there [36]And Simon and those with him searched for Him. [37]And finding Him, they said to Him, All are seeking You. [38]And He said to them, Let us go into the neighboring towns, that I may proclaim there also. For *it was* for this I came forth. [39]And He was proclaiming in their synagogues in all Galilee, and casting out the demons.

[40]And a leper came to Him, begging Him, and falling on *his* knees to Him, and saying to Him, If You will, You are able to make me clean. [41]And being moved with pity, reaching out the hand, Jesus touched him, and said to him, I am willing. Be made clean! [42]And He having spoken, instantly the leprosy departed from him, and he was made clean. [43]And strictly warning him, He at once put him out, [44]and said to him, See, tell no one a thing, but go show yourself to the priest, and offer what Moses directed concerning your cleansing, for a testimony to them. [45]But going out he began to proclaim much, and to spread about the matter, so that He no longer could openly enter into a city. But He was outside in desert places. And they came to Him from every quarter.

CHAPTER 2

[1]And again He entered into Capernaum after *some* days. And it was heard that He was in *a* house. [2]And at once many were gathered,

846
αὐτόν.
Him.
4404 1773 3029 450 1831 565
35 Καὶ πρωῒ ἔννυχον λίαν ἀναστὰς ἐξῆλθε, καὶ ἀπῆλθεν εἰς
And early in night quite rising up He went out, and went away to
2048 5117 2546 4336 2614 846
36 ἔρημον τόπον, κἀκεῖ προσηύχετο. καὶ κατεδίωξαν αὐτὸν ὁ
a desert place, and there was praying. And searched for Him
4613 3326 846 2147 846 3004 846
37 Σίμων καὶ οἱ μετ' αὐτοῦ· καὶ εὑρόντες αὐτὸν λέγουσιν αὐτῷ
Simon and those with him, and finding Him they say to Him,
3754 3956 2122 4571 3004 846 71 1519
38 ὅτι Πάντες ζητοῦσί σε. καὶ λέγει αὐτοῖς, Ἄγωμεν εἰς τὰς
— All are seeking You. And He says to them, Let us go into the
2192 2969 2443 2546 2784 1519 5124 1063
ἐχομένας κωμοπόλεις, ἵνα κἀκεῖ κηρύξω· εἰς τοῦτο γὰρ
neighboring towns, that there also I may proclaim. for this For
1831 2258 2784 4864 848 1519
39 ἐξελήλυθα. καὶ ἦν κηρύσσων ἐν ταῖς συναγωγαῖς αὐτῶν εἰς
came forth. And He was proclaiming in the synagogues of them in
3650 1056 1140 1544
ὅλην τὴν Γαλιλαίαν, καὶ τὰ δαιμόνια ἐκβάλλων.
all Galilee, and the demons casting out.
2064 4314 848 3015 3870 848
40 Καὶ ἔρχεται πρὸς αὐτὸν λεπρός, παρακαλῶν αὐτὸν καὶ
And comes to Him a leper, begging Him and
1120 - 846 3004 846 3754 1437 2309 1410
γονυπετῶν αὐτόν, καὶ λέγων αὐτῷ ὅτι Ἐὰν θέλῃς, δύνασαί
falling on knees to Him, and saying to Him, If You will, You are able
3165 2511 2424 4687 1614
41 με καθαρίσαι. ὁ δὲ Ἰησοῦς σπλαγχνισθείς, ἐκτείνας τὴν
me to make clean. And Jesus being filled with pity, reaching out the
5495 680 846 3004 846 2309 2511
χεῖρα, ἥψατο αὐτοῦ, καὶ λέγει αὐτῷ. Θέλω, καθαρίσθητι.
hand, He touched him, and says to him, I am willing, be made clean.
2036 846 2112 565 575 846 3014
42 καὶ εἰπόντος αὐτοῦ εὐθέως ἀπῆλθεν ἀπ' αὐτοῦ ἡ λέπρα,
And having spoken He, instantly departed from him the leprosy,
2511 1690 846 2112 1544
43 καὶ ἐκαθαρίσθη. καὶ ἐμβριμησάμενος αὐτῷ, εὐθέως ἐξέβαλεν
and he was cleansed. And strictly warning him, immediately He put out
846 3004 846 3708 3367 3367 2036 235
44 αὐτόν, καὶ λέγει αὐτῷ, Ὅρα, μηδενὶ μηδὲν εἴπῃς· ἀλλ'
him, and says to him, See, no one nothing tell, but
5217 4572 1166 2409 4374 4012
ὕπαγε, σεαυτὸν δεῖξον τῷ ἱερεῖ, καὶ προσένεγκε περὶ τοῦ
go yourself show to the priest and offer concerning the
2512 4675 4367 3475 1519 3142 846
καθαρισμοῦ σου ἃ προσέταξε Μωσῆς, εἰς μαρτύριον αὐτοῖς.
cleansing of you, what ordered Moses, for a testimony to them.
1831 756 2784 4183 1310
45 ὁ δὲ ἐξελθὼν ἤρξατο κηρύσσειν πολλὰ καὶ διαφημίζειν τὸν
he But going out began to proclaim much, and to spread about the
3056 5620 3371 846 1410 5320 1519 4172
λόγον, ὥστε μηκέτι αὐτὸν δύνασθαι φανερῶς εἰς πόλιν
matter, so as no longer He to be able openly into a city
1525 235 1854 1722 2048 5117 2258 2064 4314
εἰσελθεῖν, ἀλλ' ἔξω ἐν ἐρήμοις τόποις ἦν· καὶ ἤρχοντο πρὸς
to enter, but outside on desert places He was, and they came to
846 3836
αὐτὸν πανταχόθεν.
Him from every quarter.

CHAPTER 2

3825 1525 1519 2584 1223 2250
1 Καὶ πάλιν εἰσῆλθεν εἰς Καπερναοὺμ δι' ἡμερῶν· καὶ
And again He entered into Capernaum through days. d
191 3754/1919/3624/2076 2112 4863 4183
2 ἠκούσθη ὅτι εἰς οἶκόν ἐστι. καὶ εὐθέως συνήχθησαν πολλοί,
it was heard that in (a) house He is. And at once were assembled many.

so as none any longer had room, not even to the door. And He spoke the word to them. 3 And they came to Him carrying a paralytic, being borne by four. 4 And not being able to draw near to Him, due to the crowd, they unroofed the roof where He was. And digging through, they lowered the cot on which the paralytic was lying. 5 And seeing their faith, Jesus said to the paralytic, Child, your sins are forgiven to you. 6 But some of the scribes were sitting there, and reasoning in their hearts, 7 Why does this one speak blasphemies this way? Who is able to forgive sins, except One, God? 8 And instantly knowing in His spirit that they reasoned this way within themselves, Jesus said to them, Why do you reason these things in your hearts? 9 Which is easier? To say to the paralytic, *Your* sins are forgiven to you; or to say, Rise up and take your cot and walk? 10 But that you may know that the Son of man has authority to forgive sins on the earth, He said to the paralytic, 11 I say to you, Rise up and take up your cot, and go to your house. 12 And at once he rose up. And taking his cot, he went out before all; so that all were amazed and glorified God, saying, Never did we see *it* this way.

13 And he went out by the sea again. And all the crowd came to Him. And He taught them. 14 And passing on, He saw Levi the *son* of Alpheus sitting at the

5620 3371 5562 3366 4314 2374 2980
ὥστε μηκέτι χωρεῖν μηδὲ τὰ πρὸς τὴν θύραν· καὶ ἐλάλει
so as no longer to have room not even to the door, and He spoke
846 3056 2064 4314 846 3885
3 αὐτοῖς τὸν λόγον. καὶ ἔρχονται πρὸς αὐτόν, παραλυτικὸν
to them the word. And they come to Him a paralytic
5342 142 5259 5064 3361 1410
4 φέροντες, αἰρόμενον ὑπὸ τεσσάρων. καὶ μὴ δυνάμενοι
carrying, being borne by four. And not being able
4331 846 1223 3793 648 4721
προσεγγίσαι αὐτῷ διὰ τὸν ὄχλον, ἀπεστέγασαν τὴν στέγην
to draw near to Him through the crowd, they unroofed the roof
3699 2258 1846 5465 2895 1909/3759
ὅπου ἦν, καὶ ἐξορύξαντες χαλῶσι τὸν κράββατον ἐφ' ᾧ ὁ
where He was, and digging through they lower the cot on which the
3885 2621 1492 2424 4102 848
5 παραλυτικὸς κατέκειτο. ἰδὼν δὲ ὁ Ἰησοῦς τὴν πίστιν αὐτῶν
paralytic was lying. seeing And Jesus the faith of them,
3004 3885 5043 863 4671 266
λέγει τῷ παραλυτικῷ, Τέκνον, ἀφέωνταί σοι αἱ ἁμαρτίαι
He says to the paralytic, Child, are forgiven to you the sins
4675 2258 5100 1122 1563 2521
6 σου. ἦσαν δέ τινες τῶν γραμματέων ἐκεῖ καθήμενοι, καὶ
of you. were But some of the scribes there sitting, and
1260 1722 2588 848 5101 3778 3779
7 διαλογιζόμενοι ἐν ταῖς καρδίαις αὐτῶν, Τί οὗτος οὕτω
reasoning in the hearts of them, Why this one thus
2980 988 5101 1410 863 266 1508 1519
λαλεῖ βλασφημίας; τίς δύναται ἀφιέναι ἁμαρτίας εἰ μὴ εἷς,
speaks blasphemies? Who is able to forgive sins except one?
2316 2112 1921 2424 4151 848
8 ὁ Θεός; καὶ εὐθέως ἐπιγνοὺς ὁ Ἰησοῦς τῷ πνεύματι αὐτοῦ
God? And instantly knowing Jesus in the spirit of Him
3754 3779 1261 1722 1438 2036 846 5101 5023
ὅτι οὕτως διαλογίζονται ἐν ἑαυτοῖς, εἶπεν αὐτοῖς, Τί ταῦτα
that so the reasoning among themselves, He says to them, Why these things
1260 1722 2588 5216 5101/2076/ 2123
9 διαλογίζεσθε ἐν ταῖς καρδίαις ὑμῶν; τί ἐστιν εὐκοπώτερον,
do you reason in the hearts of you? What is easier,
2036 3885 863 4671 266 2228 2036
εἰπεῖν τῷ παραλυτικῷ, Ἀφέωνταί σοι αἱ ἁμαρτίαι, ἢ εἰπεῖν,
to say to the paralytic, are forgiven to you the sins, or to say,
1453 142 4675 2895 4043 2443
10 Ἔγειραι, καὶ ἆρόν σου τὸν κράββατον, καὶ περιπάτει; ἵνα
Rise and take up of you the cot and walk? that
1492 3754 1849 2192 5207 444 863 1909
δὲ εἰδῆτε ὅτι ἐξουσίαν ἔχει ὁ υἱὸς τοῦ ἀνθρώπου ἀφιέναι ἐπὶ
But you know that authority has the Son of man to forgive on
1093 266 3004 3885 4671 3004
11 τῆς γῆς ἁμαρτίας (λέγει τῷ παραλυτικῷ), Σοὶ λέγω,
the earth sins, He says to the paralytic, To you I say,
1453 142 2895 4675 5217 1519
ἔγειραι, καὶ ἆρον τὸν κράββατόν σου, καὶ ὕπαγε εἰς τὸν
Rise up and take up the cot of you, and walk? that
3624 4675 1453 2112 142 2895
12 οἶκόν σου. καὶ ἠγέρθη εὐθέως, καὶ ἄρας τὸν κράββατον,
house of you. And he arose at once, and taking up the cot
1831 1726 3956 5620 1839 3956
ἐξῆλθεν ἐναντίον πάντων· ὥστε ἐξίστασθαι πάντας, καὶ
he went out before all, so as to be astounded all, and
1392 2316 3004 3754 3763 3779 1492
δοξάζειν τὸν Θεόν, λέγοντας ὅτι Οὐδέποτε οὕτως εἴδομεν.
to glorify – God, saying, Never thus we saw.
1831 3825 3844 2281 3956 3793
13 Καὶ ἐξῆλθε πάλιν παρὰ τὴν θάλασσαν· καὶ πᾶς ὁ ὄχλος
And He went out again by the sea. And all the crowd
2064 4314 846 1321 846 3855
14 ἤρχετο πρὸς αὐτόν, καὶ ἐδίδασκεν αὐτούς. καὶ παράγων
came to Him, and He taught them. And passing along
1492 3018 256 2521 1909 5058
εἶδε Λευὶν τὸν τοῦ Ἀλφαίου καθήμενον ἐπὶ τὸ τελώνιον, καὶ
He saw Levi the (son) of Alpheus sitting at the tax-office, and

tax-office. And *He* said to
him, Follow Me. And rising
up, he followed Him.
15 And it happened as He
reclined in his house, even
many tax-collectors and
sinners reclined with Jesus
and His disciples, for they
were many. And they
followed Him. 16 And the
scribes and Pharisees seeing Him eating with tax-
collectors and sinners, *they*
said to His disciples, Why
is it that He eats and drinks
with the tax-collectors and
sinners? 17 And hearing,
Jesus said to them, Those
who are strong have no
need of a physician, but
those who have illness. I
did not come to call the
righteous to repentance,
but sinners.

18 And John's disciples,
and those of the Pharisees,
were fasting. And they
came and said to Him, Why
do John's disciples and
those of the Pharisees fast,
but your disciples do not
fast? 19 And Jesus said to
them, Can the sons of the
bridechamber fast while the
groom is with them? What
time they have the groom
with them, they cannot fast.
20 But the days will come
when the groom will be
taken away from them, and
then they will fast in those
days. 21 And no one sews a
patch of unmilled cloth on
an old garment, else *it* takes
away its fullness, the new
from the old, and a worse
tear occurs. 22 And no one
puts new wine into old
skins, else the new wine
will burst the skins and the
wine pours out, and the

3004 846 190 3427 450 190
λέγει αὐτῷ, Ἀκολούθει μοι. καὶ ἀναστὰς ἠκολούθησεν
says to him, Follow Me. And rising up he followed
846 1096 1722 2621 846 1722 3614
15 αὐτῷ. καὶ ἐγένετο ἐν τῷ κατακεῖσθαι αὐτὸν ἐν τῇ οἰκίᾳ
Him. And it was, while reclined He in the house
846 4183 5057 268 4873
αὐτοῦ. καὶ πολλοὶ τελῶναι καὶ ἁμαρτωλοὶ συνανέκειντο τῷ
of him, and many tax-collectors and sinners reclined with
2424 3101 848 2258 1063 4183
Ἰησοῦ καὶ τοῖς μαθηταῖς αὐτοῦ· ἦσαν γὰρ πολλοί, καὶ
Jesus and the disciples of Him. they were For many, and
190 846 1122 5330
16 ἠκολούθησαν αὐτῷ. καὶ οἱ γραμματεῖς καὶ οἱ Φαρισαῖοι,
they followed Him. And the scribes and the Pharisees
1492 846 2068 3326 5057 268
ἰδόντες αὐτὸν ἐσθίοντα μετὰ τῶν τελωνῶν καὶ ἁμαρτωλῶν,
seeing Him eating with tax-collectors and sinners,
3004 3101 848 5101/3754/3326 5057
ἔλεγον τοῖς μαθηταῖς αὐτοῦ, Τί ὅτι μετὰ τῶν τελωνῶν καὶ
said to the disciples of Him, Why that with the tax-collectors and
268 2068 4095 191 2424 3004
17 ἁμαρτωλῶν ἐσθίει καὶ πίνει ; καὶ ἀκούσας ὁ Ἰησοῦς λέγει
sinners does He eat and drink? And hearing Jesus says
846 3756 5532 2192 2480 2395 235
αὐτοῖς, Οὐ χρείαν ἔχουσιν οἱ ἰσχύοντες ἰατροῦ, ἀλλ' οἱ
to them, Not need have those being strong of a physician, but those
2560 2192 3756 2064 2564 1342 235 268
κακῶς ἔχοντες. οὐκ ἦλθον καλέσαι δικαίους, ἀλλὰ ἁμαρ-
illness having. not I came to call righteous ones, but sin-
1519 3341
τωλοὺς εἰς μετάνοιαν.
ners to repentance.
2258 3101 2491 5330
18 Καὶ ἦσαν οἱ μαθηταὶ Ἰωάννου καὶ οἱ τῶν Φαρισαίων
And were the disciples of John and those of the Pharisees

3522 2064 3004 846 1302
νηστεύοντες· καὶ ἔρχονται καὶ λέγουσιν αὐτῷ, Διατί οἱ
fasting. And they come and say to Him, Why do the
3101 2491 5330 3522
μαθηταὶ Ἰωάννου καὶ οἱ τῶν Φαρισαίων νηστεύουσιν, οἱ
disciples of John and those of the Pharisees fast,
4671 3101 3756/3522 2036 846 2424
19 δὲ σοὶ μαθηταὶ οὐ νηστεύουσι ; καὶ εἶπεν αὐτοῖς ὁ Ἰησοῦς,
but Your disciples not do fast? And said to them Jesus,
3361 1410 5207 3567 1722/3739 3566 3326
Μὴ δύνανται οἱ υἱοὶ τοῦ νυμφῶνος, ἐν ᾧ ὁ νυμφίος μετ'
Not are able the sons of the bridechamber, while the groom with
846 2076 3522 3745 5550 3326 1438 2592
αὐτῶν ἐστι, νηστεύειν ; ὅσον χρόνον μεθ' ἑαυτῶν ἔχουσι τὸν
them is, to fast? What time with them they have the
3566 3756 1410 3522 2064 2250 3752
20 νυμφίον, οὐ δύνανται νηστεύειν· ἐλεύσονται δὲ ἡμέραι ὅταν
bridegroom, not they are able to fast. will come But days when
522 575 846 3566 5119 3522 1722
ἀπαρθῇ ἀπ' αὐτῶν ὁ νυμφίος, καὶ τότε νηστεύσουσιν ἐν
will be taken away from them the bridegroom, and then they will fast in
1565 2250 3762 1915 4470 46
21 ἐκείναις ταῖς ἡμέραις. καὶ οὐδεὶς ἐπίβλημα ῥάκους ἀγνάφου
those days. And no one a patch of cloth unfulled
1976 1909 2440 3820 =1490=== 142 4138
ἐπιρράπτει ἐπὶ ἱματίῳ παλαιῷ· εἰ δὲ μή, αἴρει τὸ πλήρωμα
sews on a garment old; else takes away the fullness
848 2537 3820 5501 4978 1096
αὐτοῦ τὸ καινὸν τοῦ παλαιοῦ, καὶ χεῖρον σχίσμα γίνεται.
of it the new (from) the old, and a worse tear occurs.
3762 906 3631 3501 1519 779 3820 =1490=
22 καὶ οὐδεὶς βάλλει οἶνον νέον εἰς ἀσκοὺς παλαιούς· εἰ δὲ μή,
And no one puts wine new into wineskins old; if but not,
4486 3631 3501 779 3635 1632
ῥήσσει ὁ οἶνος ὁ νέος τοὺς ἀσκούς, καὶ ὁ οἶνος ἐκχεῖται καὶ οἱ
will burst the wine new the wineskins, and the wine pours out, and the

skins will be destroyed. But new wine is put into fresh skins.

[23]And it happened He went along through the grainfields in the sabbaths. And His disciples began to make way, plucking the heads *of grain.* [24]And the Pharisees said to Him, Behold, why do they do that which is not lawful on the sabbaths? [25]And He said to them, Did you never read what David did when he had need and hungered, he and those with him, [26]how he entered the house of God in *the days of* Abiathar the high priest, and ate the Showbread, which it is not lawful to eat, except for the priests, and *he* even gave to those being with him? [27]And He said to them, The sabbath came into being for man's sake, not man for the sabbath's sake. [28]So then the Son of man is Lord of the sabbath also.

CHAPTER 3

[1]And again He entered into the synagogue. And there was a man who had a withering *of* the hand. [2]And they watched Him, whether He will heal him on the sabbaths, that they might accuse Him. [3]And He said to the man who had a withering *of* the hand, Rise up into the middle. [4]And He said to them, *Is it* lawful to do good on the sabbaths, or to do evil? To save a soul, or to kill? But they were silent. [5]And having looked around *on* them with anger, being greatly grieved over the hardness of their heart, He said to the man, Stretch out your hand! And he stretched out, and his hand

779 622 235 3631 3501 1519 779 2537
ἀσκοὶ ἀπολοῦνται· ἀλλὰ οἶνον νέον εἰς ἀσκοὺς καινοὺς
skins will be destroyed; but wine new into wineskins fresh
992
βλητέον.
is to be put.

1096 3899 846 1722 4521 1223
23 Καὶ ἐγένετο παραπορεύεσθαι αὐτὸν ἐν τοῖς σάββασι διὰ
And it happened, went along He in the sabbaths through
4702 756 3101 848 3598 4160
τῶν σπορίμων, καὶ ἤρξαντο οἱ μαθηταὶ αὐτοῦ ὁδὸν ποιεῖν
the grainfields, and began the disciples of Him (a) way to make
5089 4719 5330 3004 846
24 τίλλοντες τοὺς στάχυας. καὶ οἱ Φαρισαῖοι ἔλεγον αὐτῷ,
plucking the ears (of grain). And the Pharisees said to Him,
2396/5101/ 4160 1722 4421 3756 1832 846
25 Ἴδε, τί ποιοῦσιν ἐν τοῖς σάββασιν ὃ οὐκ ἔξεστι; καὶ αὐτὸς
Behold, why do they in the sabbaths what not is lawful? And He
3004 846 3763 314 5101 4160 1138 3753
ἔλεγεν αὐτοῖς, Οὐδέποτε ἀνέγνωτε τί ἐποίησε Δαβίδ, ὅτε
said to them, never Did you read what did David when
5532 2192 3983 846 3326 846 4459
26 χρείαν ἔσχε καὶ ἐπείνασεν αὐτὸς καὶ οἱ μετ' αὐτοῦ; πῶς
need he had, and hungered, he and the (ones) with him; how
1525 1519 3624 2316/1909 8 749
εἰσῆλθεν εἰς τὸν οἶκον τοῦ Θεοῦ ἐπὶ Ἀβιάθαρ τοῦ ἀρχιερέως,
he entered into the house of God on Abiathar the high priest,
740 4286 5315 3739/3756 1832
καὶ τοὺς ἄρτους τῆς προθέσεως ἔφαγεν, οὓς οὐκ ἔξεστι
and the loaves of the presentation ate, which not is lawful
5315 =1508= 2409 1325 4862 846 5607
φαγεῖν εἰ μὴ τοῖς ἱερεῦσι, καὶ ἔδωκε καὶ τοῖς σὺν αὐτῷ οὖσι;
to eat except the priests, and gave also to those with him being?
3004 846 4521 1223 444 1096
27 καὶ ἔλεγεν αὐτοῖς, Τὸ σάββατον διὰ τὸν ἄνθρωπον ἐγένετο,
And He said to them, The sabbath for the sake of man came into being,
3756 444 1223 4521 5620 2962 2076 5207
28 οὐχ ὁ ἄνθρωπος διὰ τὸ σάββατον· ὥστε Κύριός ἐστιν ὁ υἱὸς
not man for the sake of the sabbath; so then Lord is the Son
444 4521
τοῦ ἀνθρώπου καὶ τοῦ σαββάτου.
of man also of the sabbath.

CHAPTER 3

1525 3825 1519 4864 2258/1563/ 444
1 Καὶ εἰσῆλθε πάλιν εἰς τὴν συναγωγήν, καὶ ἦν ἐκεῖ ἄνθρω-
And He entered again into the synagogue, and was there a
3583 2192 5495 3906 846 1487
2 πος ἐξηραμμένην ἔχων τὴν χεῖρα. καὶ παρετήρουν αὐτὸν εἰ
man a withering having (of) the hand. And they watched Him, if
4521 2323 846 2443 2723 846
τοῖς σαββασι θεραπεύσει αὐτόν, ἵνα κατηγορήσωσιν αὐτοῦ.
on the sabbaths He will heal him, that they might accuse Him.
3004 444 3583 2192 5495
3 καὶ λέγει τῷ ἀνθρώπῳ τῷ ἐξηραμμένην ἔχοντι τὴν χεῖρα,
And He says to the man a withering having (of) the hand,
1453 1519 3319 3004 846 1832 4521
4 Ἔγειραι εἰς τὸ μέσον. καὶ λέγει αὐτοῖς, Ἔξεστι τοῖς σάββασιν
Rise up into the midst. And He says to them, Lawful on the sabbaths
15 2228 2554 5590 4982 2228/ 615
ἀγαθοποιῆσαι, ἢ κακοποιῆσαι; ψυχὴν σῶσαι, ἢ ἀπο-
to do good, or to do evil; a soul to save, or to
4623 4017 846 3326
5 κτεῖναι; οἱ δὲ ἐσιώπων. καὶ περιβλεψάμενος αὐτοὺς μετ'
kill? they But were silent. And looking around (on) them with
3709 4818 1909 4457 2588 848
ὀργῆς, συλλυπούμενος ἐπὶ τῇ πωρώσει τῆς καρδίας αὐτῶν
anger, being greatly grieved on the hardness of the heart of them,
3004 444 1614 5495 4675 1614
λέγει τῷ ἀνθρώπῳ, Ἔκτεινον τὴν χεῖρά σου. καὶ ἐξέτεινε.
He says to the man, Stretch out the hand of you. And he stretched,

was restored sound as the other. [6]And going out the Pharisees at once took counsel with the Herodians against Him, how they might destroy Him.

[7]And Jesus withdrew to the sea with His disciples; and a great multitude from Galilee and from Judea followed Him; [8]also *some* from Jerusalem, and from Idumea, and beyond the Jordan; also those around Tyre and Sidon, a great multitude came to Him, hearing how much He was doing. [9]And He spoke to His disciples that a small boat should stay near to Him because of the crowd, that they might not press upon Him. [10]For He healed many, so that they fell on Him, that they might touch Him, as many as had plagues. [11]And when the unclean spirits saw Him, *they* fell down before Him, and cried out, saying, You are the Son of God! [12]And He warned them very much, that they should not reveal Him.

[13]And He went up into the mountain, and He called near whom He desired. And they went to Him. [14]And He made *disciples of* twelve, that they might be with Him, and that He might send them to proclaim, [15]and to have authority to heal diseases and to cast out the demons. [16]And He put on Simon *the* name Peter. [17]And on James *the* son of Zebedee, and John the brother of James, He put on them *the* names Boanerges, which is, Sons of Thunder. [18]Also *He appointed* Andrew, and Philip, and Bartholomew, and Matthew, and Thomas, and James the *son* of

600 5495 848 5199 5613 243
6 καὶ ἀποκατεστάθη ἡ χεὶρ αὐτοῦ ὑγιὴς ὡς ἡ ἄλλη. καὶ
and was restored the hand of him sound as the other. And
1831 5330 2112 3326 2265
ἐξελθόντες οἱ Φαρισαῖοι εὐθέως μετὰ τῶν Ἡρωδιανῶν
going out the Pharisees immediately with the Herodians
4824 4160 2596 846 3704 846 622
συμβούλιον ἐποίουν κατ' αὐτοῦ, ὅπως αὐτὸν ἀπολέσωσι.
counsel made against Him, how that Him they might destroy.
2424 402 3326 3101 848 4314
7 Καὶ ὁ Ἰησοῦς ἀνεχώρησε μετὰ τῶν μαθητῶν αὐτοῦ πρὸς
And Jesus withdrew with the disciples of Him to
2281 4183 4128 575 1056 190
τὴν θάλασσαν· καὶ πολὺ πλῆθος ἀπὸ τῆς Γαλιλαίας ἠκολού-
the sea; and a great multitude from Galilee followed
846 575 2449 575 2414
8 θησαν αὐτῷ, καὶ ἀπὸ τῆς Ἰουδαίας, καὶ ἀπὸ Ἱεροσολύμων,
Him; and from Judea, and from Jerusalem.
575 2401 4008 2446
καὶ ἀπὸ τῆς Ἰδουμαίας, καὶ πέραν τοῦ Ἰορδάνου, καὶ οἱ
and from Idumea, and beyond the Jordan, and those
4012 5184 4605 4128 4183 191 3745
περὶ Τύρον καὶ Σιδῶνα, πλῆθος πολύ, ἀκούσαντες ὅσα
around Tyre and Sidon; a multitude great, hearing what
4160 2064 4314 846 2036 3101 848
9 ἐποίει, ἦλθον πρὸς αὐτόν. καὶ εἶπε τοῖς μαθηταῖς αὐτοῦ
He was doing came to Him. And He told the disciples of Him
2443 4142 4342 846 1223 3793 2443 3361
ἵνα πλοιάριον προσκαρτερῇ αὐτῷ διὰ τὸν ὄχλον, ἵνα μὴ
that a small boat should stay near Him because of the crowd, that not
2346 846 4183 1063 2323 5620 1968
10 θλίβωσιν αὐτόν. πολλοὺς γὰρ ἐθεράπευσεν, ὥστε ἐπιπί-
they press on Him. many For He healed, so that (they) fell
846 2443/846 680 3745 2192 3148
11 πτειν αὐτῷ, ἵνα αὐτοῦ ἅψωνται, ὅσοι εἶχον μάστιγας. καὶ τὰ
upon Him, that Him they might touch, as many as had plagues; and the
4151 169 3752 846 2334 4363
πνεύματα τὰ ἀκάθαρτα, ὅταν αὐτὸν ἐθεώρει, προσέπιπτεν
spirits unclean when Him they saw fell before
846 2896 3004 3754/4771/1488/5207 2316
12 αὐτῷ, καὶ ἔκραζε, λέγοντα ὅτι Σὺ εἶ ὁ υἱὸς τοῦ Θεοῦ. καὶ
Him and cried out, saying, You are the Son of God. And
4183 2008 846 2443/3361/846 5318 4160
πολλὰ ἐπετίμα αὐτοῖς ἵνα μὴ αὐτὸν φανερὸν ποιήσωσι.
much He warned them that not Him manifest they should make.
305 1519 3735 4341 3739 2309
13 Καὶ ἀναβαίνει εἰς τὸ ὄρος, καὶ προσκαλεῖται οὓς ἤθελεν
And He goes up into the mountain, and called near whom wished
846 565 4314 846 4160 1427 2443
14 αὐτός· καὶ ἀπῆλθον πρὸς αὐτόν. καὶ ἐποίησε δώδεκα, ἵνα
He, and they went to Him. And He made twelve that
5600 3326 846 2443 649 846 2784
15 ὦσι μετ' αὐτοῦ, καὶ ἵνα ἀποστέλλῃ αὐτοὺς κηρύσσειν καὶ
they may be with Him, and that He might send them to proclaim, and
2192 1849 2323 3554 1544
ἔχειν ἐξουσίαν θεραπεύειν τὰς νόσους, καὶ ἐκβάλλειν τὰ
to have authority to heal the diseases, and to cast out the
1140 2007 4613 3696 4074 2385
16 δαιμόνια· καὶ ἐπέθηκε τῷ Σίμωνι ὄνομα Πέτρον· καὶ Ἰάκωβον
17 demons. And He put upon Simon a name, Peter; and James,
2199 2491 80 2385
τὸν τοῦ Ζεβεδαίου, καὶ Ἰωάννην τὸν ἀδελφὸν τοῦ Ἰακώβου·
the (son) of Zebedee, and John the brother of James.
2007 486 3686 993 3603 2076 5207
καὶ ἐπέθηκεν αὐτοῖς ὀνόματα Βοανεργές, ὅ ἐστιν, Υἱοὶ
and He put upon them (the) names Boanerges, which is, Sons
1027 408 5376 918
18 βροντῆς· καὶ Ἀνδρέαν, καὶ Φίλιππον, καὶ Βαρθολομαῖον,
of Thunder; and Andrew and Philip; and Bartholomew
3156 2381 2385 256
καὶ Ματθαῖον, καὶ Θωμᾶν, καὶ Ἰάκωβον τὸν τοῦ Ἀλφαίου,
and Matthew; and Thomas; and James the (son) of Alpheus,

Alpheus, and Thaddeus, and Simon the Canaanite, [19]and Judas Iscariot, who also betrayed Him.

[20]And He came into a house. And again a crowd came together, so as they were not able even to eat bread. [21]And hearing, those with Him went out to take hold *of* Him; for they said, He is out of wits. [22]And coming down from Jerusalem, the scribes said, He has Beelzebub, and he cast out demons by the ruler of the demons. [23]And calling them near, He spoke to them in parables, *saying,* How can Satan cast out Satan? [24]And if a kingdom is divided against itself, that kingdom cannot stand. [25]And if a house is divided against itself, that house is not able to stand. [26]And if Satan rises upon himself, and has been divided, he is not able to stand, but he has an end. [27]No one is able in any way to plunder the goods of the strong one, entering into his house, unless he first tie up the strong one; and then he will plunder his house.

[28]Truly I say to you, All the sins will be forgiven to the sons of men, and whatever blasphemies they have blasphemed. [29]But whoever commits blasphemy against the Holy Spirit has no forgiveness to eternity, but is liable to eternal judgment—[30]because they said, He has an unclean spirit.

[31]Then His mother and brothers came. And standing outside, *they* sent to Him, calling Him. [32]And a crowd sat around Him. And they said to Him, Behold, Your mother and Your brothers seek You outside.

2280 4613 2581 2455
19 καὶ Θαδδαῖον, καὶ Σίμωνα τὸν Κανανίτην, καὶ Ἰούδαν
and Thaddeus, and Simon the Canaanite, and Judas
2469 3739 3860 846
Ἰσκαριώτην, ὃς καὶ παρέδωκεν αὐτόν.
Iscariot, who also betrayed Him.
2064 1519 3624 4905 3825 3793 5620
20 Καὶ ἔρχονται εἰς οἶκον· καὶ συνέρχεται πάλιν ὄχλος, ὥστε
And He comes into a house; and comes together again a crowd, so as
3361 1410 846 3383 740 5315 191
21 μὴ δύνασθαι αὐτοὺς μήτε ἄρτον φαγεῖν. καὶ ἀκούσαντες οἱ
not are able they not even bread to eat. And having heard those
3844 846 1831 2902 846 3004 1063 3754
παρ' αὐτοῦ ἐξῆλθον κρατῆσαι αὐτόν· ἔλεγον γὰρ ὅτι
with Him went forth to take hold (of) Him, they said for,
1839 1122 575 2414 2597
22 Ἐξέστη. καὶ οἱ γραμματεῖς οἱ ἀπὸ Ἱεροσολύμων καταβάντες
He is insane. And the scribes from Jersualem coming down
3004 3754 954 2192 3754 1722 758
ἔλεγον ὅτι Βεελζεβοὺλ ἔχει, καὶ ὅτι Ἐν τῷ ἄρχοντι τῶν
said, Beelzebub He has, and, By the ruler of the
1140 1544 1140 4341
23 δαιμονίων ἐκβάλλει τὰ δαιμόνια. καὶ προσκαλεσάμενος
demons he casts out the demons. And calling near
846 1722 3850 3004 846 4450 1410 4567
αὐτούς, ἐν παραβολαῖς ἔλεγεν αὐτοῖς, Πῶς δύναται Σατανᾶς
them, in parables He spoke to them, How is able Satan
4567 1544 1437 932 1909 1438 3307 3756
24 Σατανᾶν ἐκβάλλειν; καὶ ἐὰν βασιλεία ἐφ' ἑαυτὴν μερισθῇ, οὐ
Satan to cast out? And if a kingdom against itself is divided, not
1410 2476 932 1565 1437 3614 1909
25 δύναται σταθῆναι ἡ βασιλεία ἐκείνη. καὶ ἐὰν οἰκία ἐφ'
is able to stand kingdom that. And if a house against
1438 3307 3756 1410 2476 3614 1565 1487
26 ἑαυτὴν μερισθῇ, οὐ δύναται σταθῆναι ἡ οἰκία ἐκείνη. καὶ εἰ
itself is divided, not is able to stand house that. And if
4567 450 1909 1438 3307 3756 1410
ὁ Σατανᾶς ἀνέστη ἐφ' ἑαυτὸν καὶ μεμέρισται, οὐ δύναται
Satan rises upon himself and has been divided, not he is able
2476 235 5056 2192 /3756/ 1410 3762 4632
27 σταθῆναι, ἀλλὰ τέλος ἔχει. οὐ δύναται οὐδεὶς τὰ σκεύη τοῦ
to stand, but and end he has. not is able No one the goods of the
2478 1525 1519 3614 848 1283 =3362=
ἰσχυροῦ, εἰσελθὼν εἰς τὴν οἰκίαν αὐτοῦ, διαρπάσαι, ἐὰν μὴ
strong one having entered into the house of him, to plunder, unless
4412 2478 1210 5119 3614 848 1283
πρῶτον τὸν ἰσχυρὸν δήσῃ, καὶ τότε τὴν οἰκίαν αὐτοῦ διαρ-
first the strong one he bind, and then the house of him he will
281 3004 5213 3754 3956 863 265
28 πάσει. ἀμὴν λέγω ὑμῖν, ὅτι πάντα ἀφεθήσεται τὰ ἁμαρτή-
plunder. Truly I say to you, that all will be forgiven the sins
5207 444 988 3745 302
ματα τοῖς υἱοῖς τῶν ἀνθρώπων, καὶ βλασφημίαι ὅσας ἂν
of the sons of men, and blasphemies whatever
987 2739 302 987 1519 4151
29 βλασφημήσωσιν· ὃς δ' ἂν βλασφημήσῃ εἰς τὸ Πνεῦμα τὸ
they have blasphemed, who but ever blasphemes against the Spirit
40 3756 2192 859 1519 165 235 1777 2076
Ἅγιον, οὐκ ἔχει ἄφεσιν εἰς τὸν αἰῶνα, ἀλλ' ἔνοχός ἐστιν
Holy, not has forgiveness unto the age, but liable is
2496 2920 3754 3004 4151 169 2192
30 αἰωνίου κρίσεως. ὅτι ἔλεγον, Πνεῦμα ἀκάθαρτον ἔχει.
of an eternal judgment; for they said, A spirit unclean He has.
2064 3767 80 3384 848 1854
31 Ἔρχονται οὖν οἱ ἀδελφοὶ καὶ ἡ μήτηρ αὐτοῦ, καὶ ἔξω
come Then the brothers and the mother of Him, and outside
2476 649 4314 846 5455 846
32 ἑστῶτες ἀπέστειλαν πρὸς αὐτόν, φωνοῦντες αὐτόν. καὶ
standing sent to Him, calling Him. And
2521 3793 4012 846 2036 846 2400 3384
ἐκάθητο ὄχλος περὶ αὐτόν· εἶπον δὲ αὐτῷ, Ἰδού, ἡ μήτηρ
sat a crowd around Him. they said And to Him, Behold the mother

33And He answered them, saying, Who is My mother or My brothers? 34And having looked around *on* those sitting around Him in a circle, He said, Behold, My mother and My brothers!

35For whoever does the will of God, this one is My brother, and My sister, and My mother.

4675 80 4675 1854 2272 4571 611 846
33 σου καὶ οἱ ἀδελφοί σου ἔξω ζητοῦσί σε. καὶ ἀπεκρίθη αὐτοῖς
of you and the brothers of you outside seek You. And He answered them,
3004 5101 2076 3384 3450 2228 80 3450
34 λέγων, Τίς ἐστιν ἡ μήτηρ μου ἢ οἱ ἀδελφοί μου; καὶ
saying, Who is the mother of Me or the brothers of Me? And
4017 2945 4012 846 2521 3004
περιβλεψάμενος κύκλῳ τοὺς περὶ αὐτὸν καθημένους, λέγει,
having looked around in a circle (at) those around Him sitting, He says
2896 3384 3450 80 3450 3739/1063/302/ 4160
35 Ἴδε, ἡ μήτηρ μου καὶ οἱ ἀδελφοί μου. ὃς γὰρ ἂν ποιήσῃ τὸ
Behold, the mother of Me and the brothers of Me! who For ever does the
2307 2316 3778 80 3450 79 3450
θέλημα τοῦ Θεοῦ, οὗτος ἀδελφός μου καὶ ἀδελφή μου καὶ
will of God, this one brother of Me and sister of Me and
3384 2076
μήτηρ ἐστί.
mother is.

CHAPTER 4

1And again He began to teach by the sea. And a large crowd was gathered to Him, so that He entered into the boat in order to sit in the sea. And all the crowd were on the land toward the sea. 2And He taught them many things in parables, and said to them in His teaching: 3Listen! Behold, the sower went out to sow. 4And as he sowed, it happened that one indeed fell by the wayside; and the birds of the heaven came and ate it up. 5And another fell on the stony place where it did not have much earth. And it sprang up at once, due to not having deepness of earth. 6And *the* sun rising, it was scorched. And through not having root, it was dried out.

7And another fell into the thorns, and the thorns grew up and choked it, and it did not yield fruit. 8And another fell into the good ground, and yielded fruit, going up and increasing; and one bore thirty, and one sixty, and one a hundred*fold*. 9And He said to them, The *one* having ears to hear, let him hear.

10And when He was alone, those around Him,

3825 756 1221 3844 2281
1 Καὶ πάλιν ἤρξατο διδάσκειν παρὰ τὴν θάλασσαν. καὶ
And again He began to teach by the sea. And
4863 4314 846 3793 4183 5620 846 1684 1519
συνήχθη πρὸς αὐτὸν ὄχλος πολύς, ὥστε αὐτὸν ἐμβάντα εἰς
is assemble to Him a crowd large, so that He entering into
4143 2521 1722 2281 3956 3793 4314
τὸ πλοῖον καθῆσθαι ἐν τῇ θαλάσσῃ· καὶ πᾶς ὁ ὄχλος πρὸς
the boat (had) to sit in the sea, and all the crowd toward
2281 1909 1093 2258 1321 846 1722
2 τὴν θάλασσαν ἐπὶ τῆς γῆς ἦν. καὶ ἐδίδασκεν αὐτοὺς ἐν
the sea on the land were. And He taught them in
3850 4183 3004 846 1722 1322 846
παραβολαῖς πολλά, καὶ ἔλεγεν αὐτοῖς ἐν τῇ διδαχῇ αὐτοῦ,
parables many things, and said to them in the teaching of Him,
191 2400 1831 4687 4687 1096
3 Ἀκούετε· ἰδού, ἐξῆλθεν ὁ σπείρων τοῦ σπεῖραι· καὶ ἐγένετο
4 Hear! Behold, went out the (one) sowing to sow. And it was,
1722 4687 3739/3303/4098 3844 3598 2064
ἐν τῷ σπείρειν, ὃ μὲν ἔπεσε παρὰ τὴν ὁδόν, καὶ ἦλθε τὰ
while sowing one indeed fell by the way, and came the
4071 3772 2719 846 243 4098
5 πετεινὰ τοῦ οὐρανοῦ καὶ κατέφαγεν αὐτό. ἄλλο δὲ ἔπεσεν
birds of the heaven and devoured it. other And fell
1909 4075 3699 3756 2192 1093 4183 2112
ἐπὶ τὸ πετρῶδες, ὅπου οὐκ εἶχε γῆν πολλήν· καὶ εὐθέως
on the rocky place where not it had earth much, and at once
1816 1223 3361 2192 899 1093 2246 393
6 ἐξανέτειλε, διὰ τὸ μὴ ἔχειν βάθος γῆς· ἡλίου δὲ ἀνατείλαντος
it sprang up, due to not having depth of earth. sun And arising,
2739 1223 3361 2192 4491 3583 243
7 ἐκαυματίσθη, καὶ διὰ τὸ μὴ ἔχειν ῥίζαν ἐξηράνθη. καὶ ἄλλο
it was scorched, and through not to have root it was dried up. And other
4098 1519 173 305 173 4846
ἔπεσεν εἰς τὰς ἀκάνθας, καὶ ἀνέβησαν αἱ ἄκανθαι, καὶ συνέ-
fell into the thorns, and grew the thorns and choked
846 2590 3756 1325 243 4098 1519
8 πνιξαν αὐτό, καὶ καρπὸν οὐκ ἔδωκε. καὶ ἄλλο ἔπεσεν εἰς τὴν
it. and fruit not it did give. And other fell into the
1093 2570 1325 2590 305
γῆν τὴν καλήν· καὶ ἐδίδου καρπὸν ἀναβαίνοντα καὶ
earth good, and gave fruit going up and
837 5342 1520 5144 1520 1835
αὐξάνοντα, καὶ ἔφερεν ἓν τριάκοντα, καὶ ἓν ἑξήκοντα, καὶ
increasing, and bore one thirty, and one sixty, and
1520 1540 3004 846 2192 3775 191 191
9 ἓν ἑκατόν. καὶ ἔλεγεν αὐτοῖς, Ὁ ἔχων ὦτα ἀκούειν ἀκουέτω.
one a hundred. And He said to them, He having ears to hear, let him hear.
3753 1096 2651 2065 846 4012
10 Ὅτε δὲ ἐγένετο καταμόνας, ἠρώτησαν αὐτὸν οἱ περὶ
when And He became alone, asked Him those around

with the Twelve, asked Him *as to* the parable. [11]And He said to them, To you has been given to know the mystery of the kingdom of God. But to these, those outside, all things *are* being *given* in parables, [12]that seeing they may see and not perceive; and hearing they may hear, and not understand, lest they should convert, and sins be forgiven to them. [13]And He said to them, Do you not know this parable? And how will you know all parables?

[14]The sower sows the word. [15]And these are those by the wayside, where the word is sown. And when they hear, Satan comes at once and takes the word having been sown in their hearts. [16]And likewise, these are the ones being sown on the stony places, who, when they hear the word, immediately receive it with joy, [17]yet they have no root in themselves, but are temporary. Then trouble or persecution having occurred through the word, immediately they are offended.

[18]These are those being sown into the thorns, those hearing the word, [19]and the cares of this age, and the deceitfulness of riches, and the lusts about other things entering in, *they* choke the word, and it becomes unfruitful. [20]And these are those being sown on the good ground, who hear and welcome the word, and bring forth fruit —one thirty, and one sixty, and one a hundred*fold*.

[21]And He said to them, Does the lamp come that it may be put under the grain measure, or under the bed? *Is it* not that it may be put on the lampstand? [22]For not

846 4862 1427 3850 3004 846
11 αὐτὸν σὺν τοῖς δώδεκα τὴν παραβολήν. καὶ ἔλεγεν αὐτοῖς,
Him with the twelve the parable. and He said to them,
5213 1325 1097 3466 932
Ὑμῖν δέδοται γνῶναι τὸ μυστήριον τῆς βασιλείας τοῦ
To you has been given to know the mystery of the kingdom
2316 1565 1854/1722 3850 3956 1096
Θεοῦ· ἐκείνοις δὲ τοῖς ἔξω, ἐν παραβολαῖς τὰ πάντα γίνεται·
of God; to these but those outside in parables all things became
2443 991 991 3361 1492 191
12 ἵνα βλέποντες βλέπωσι, καὶ μὴ ἴδωσι· καὶ ἀκούοντες
that seeing they may see, and not perceive; and hearing
191 3361 4920 3379 1994
ἀκούωσι, καὶ μὴ συνιῶσι· μήποτε ἐπιστρέψωσι, καὶ
they may hear, and not understand, lest they should convert, and
863 846 265 3004 846 3756 1492
13 ἀφεθῇ αὐτοῖς τὰ ἁμαρτήματα. καὶ λέγει αὐτοῖς, Οὐκ οἴδατε
be forgiven them the sins. And He says to them, not Know you
3850 5026 4459 3956 3850
τὴν παραβολὴν ταύτην; καὶ πῶς πάσας τὰς παραβολὰς
parable this? And how all the parables
1097 4687 3056 4687 3778 1526
14 γνώσεσθε; ὁ σπείρων τὸν λόγον σπείρει. οὗτοι δέ εἰσιν οἱ
15 will you know? He sowing the word sows. these And are those
3844 3598 4567 4687 3056 3752 191
παρὰ τὴν ὁδόν, ὅπου σπείρεται ὁ λόγος, καὶ ὅταν ἀκούσω-
by the way, where is sown the word; and when they hear,
2112 2064 4567 142 3056
σιν, εὐθέως ἔρχεται ὁ Σατανᾶς καὶ αἴρει τὸν λόγον τὸν
immediately comes — Satan and takes the word —
4687 1722 2588 848 3778 1526 3668
16 ἐσπαρμένον ἐν ταῖς καρδίαις αὐτῶν. καὶ οὗτοί εἰσιν ὁμοίως
having been sown in the hearts of them. And these are likewise
1909 4075 4587 3739 3752 191
οἱ ἐπὶ τὰ πετρώδη σπειρόμενοι, οἵ, ὅταν ἀκούσωσι τὸν
these on the rocky places being sown, who when they hear the
3056 2112 3326 5479 2983 846 3756
17 λόγον, εὐθέως μετὰ χαρᾶς λαμβάνουσιν αὐτόν, καὶ οὐκ
word, immediately with joy they receive it, and not
2192 4491 1722 1438 235 4340 1526 1534 1096
ἔχουσι ῥίζαν ἐν ἑαυτοῖς, ἀλλὰ πρόσκαιροί εἰσιν· εἶτα γενο-
they have root in themselves, but temporary they are; then having
2347 2228 1375 1223 3056 2112 4624
μένης θλίψεως ἢ διωγμοῦ διὰ τὸν λόγον, εὐθέως σκανδαλί-
become trouble or persecution through the word, immediately they are
3778 1526 1519 173 4687 3778
18 ζονται. καὶ οὗτοί εἰσιν οἱ εἰς τὰς ἀκάνθας σπειρόμενοι, οἱ τὸν
offended. And these are those into the thorns being sown; those the
3056 191 3308 165 5127
19 λόγον ἀκούοντες, καὶ αἱ μέριμναι τοῦ αἰῶνος τούτου, καὶ ἡ
word hearing, and the cares of age this, and the
539 4149 4012 3062 1939
ἀπάτη τοῦ πλούτου, καὶ αἱ περὶ τὰ λοιπὰ ἐπιθυμίαι
deceitfulness — of riches, and the about the other things desires
1531 4846 3056 175
εἰσπορευόμεναι συμπνίγουσι τὸν λόγον, καὶ ἄκαρπος
entering in choke the word, and unfruitful
1096 3778 1526 1909 1093 2570 4687
20 γίνεται. καὶ οὗτοί εἰσιν οἱ ἐπὶ τὴν γῆν τὴν καλὴν σπαρέντες,
it becomes. And these are the (ones) on the earth — good being sown,
3748 191 3056 3858 2592
οἵτινες ἀκούουσι τὸν λόγον, καὶ παραδέχονται, καὶ καρ-
who hear the word, and welcome (it), and bring
1520 5144 1520 1835 1520 1540
ποφοροῦσιν, ἓν τριάκοντα, καὶ ἓν ἑξήκοντα, καὶ ἓν ἑκατόν.
forth fruit, one thirty, and one sixty, and one a hundred.
3004 846 3385 3088 2064 2443 5259
21 Καὶ ἔλεγεν αὐτοῖς, Μήτι ὁ λύχνος ἔρχεται ἵνα ὑπὸ τὸν
And He said to them, Not (is) the lamp come that under the
3426 5087/2228/5259 2825 3756/2443/1909 3087
μόδιον τεθῇ ἢ ὑπὸ τὴν κλίνην; οὐχ ἵνα ἐπὶ τὴν λυχνίαν
bushel it be placed, or under the couch? (is it) not that on the lampstand

anything is hidden but that it will be revealed; nor *anything* become covered but that it will come to light. [23]If anyone has ears to hear, let him hear.

[24]And He said to them, Be careful what you hear. With what measure you measure, it will be measured to you, and more will be given to you, the *ones* hearing. [25]For whoever may have, *more* will be given to him; and *the one* who does not have, even what he has will be taken from him.

[26]And He said, So is the kingdom of God, as if a man should cast seed on the earth, [27]and should sleep, and rise night and day, and the seed should sprout and lengthen of itself, as he does not know—[28]for of itself the earth bears fruit: first greenery, then an ear, then full grain in the ear. [29]And when the fruit yields, immediately he sends forth the sickle, for the harvest has come.

[30]And He said, To what shall we compare the kingdom of God? Or with what parable shall we compare it? [31]*It is* like a grain of mustard, which, when it is sown on the earth, it is less than all the seeds of those on the earth. [32]And when it is sown, *it* comes up, and becomes greater than all the plants, and produces great branches, so as to enable the birds of the heaven to roost under its shade.

[33]And with many such parables He spoke the word to them, even as they were able to hear. [34]But He did not speak to them without a parable. And He explained all things to His disciples privately.

2007 3756 1063/2076/5101/2927 3739/+3362= 5319 3761
22 ἐπιτεθῇ ; οὐ γάρ ἐστί τι κρυπτόν, ὃ ἐὰν μὴ φανερωθῇ· οὐδὲ
it be placed? not For is a thing hidden which if not it may be re- nor
1096 614 235 2443/1519 5318 2064 vealed 2192
23 ἐγένετο ἀπόκρυφον, ἀλλ' ἵνα εἰς φανερὸν ἔλθῃ. εἴ τις ἔχει
1536 became covered, but that to light it may come. If any have
3775 191 191 3004 846 991 5101 191
24 ὦτα ἀκούειν ἀκουέτω. καὶ ἔλεγεν αὐτοῖς, Βλέπετε τί ἀκούετε.
ears to hear, let him hear. And He them, Be careful what you hear
1722/3739/3354 3354 3354 explained 5213 4369
ἐν ᾧ μέτρῳ μετρεῖτε μετρηθήσεται ὑμῖν, καὶ προστεθήσεται
in what measure you measure it will be measured to you. And it will be added
5213 191 3739 1063/302 2192 1325 846
25 ὑμῖν τοῖς ἀκούουσιν. ὃς γὰρ ἂν ἔχῃ, δοθήσεται αὐτῷ· καὶ
to you, the (ones) hearing. who For ever may have, it will be to him; and
3739/3756/2192 3739/2192 142 575 846 given
ὃς οὐκ ἔχει, καὶ ὃ ἔχει ἀρθήσεται ἀπ' αὐτοῦ.
who not has, even what he has will be taken from him.

3004 3779 2076 932 2316 5613/1437
26 Καὶ ἔλεγεν, Οὕτως ἐστὶν ἡ βασιλεία τοῦ Θεοῦ, ὡς ἐὰν
And He said, Thus is the kingdom God, as if
444 906 4703 1909 1093 2518
27 ἄνθρωπος βάλῃ τὸν σπόρον ἐπὶ τῆς γῆς, καὶ καθεύδῃ καὶ
a man should cast the seed on the earth, and should sleep and
1453 3571 2250 4703 985
ἐγείρηται νύκτα καὶ ἡμέραν, καὶ ὁ σπόρος βλαστάνῃ καὶ
rise night and day, and the seed should sprout and
3373 5613/3756/1492 846 844 1063 1093 2592
28 μηκύνηται ὡς οὐκ οἶδεν αὐτός. αὐτομάτη γὰρ ἡ γῆ καρπο-
lengthen as not knows he of itself, for the earth bears
4412 5528 1534 4719 1534 4134 4621 1722
φορεῖ, πρῶτον χόρτον, εἶτα στάχυν, εἶτα πλήρη σῖτον ἐν
fruit, first greenery, then an ear, then full grain in
4719 3752 3860 2590 2112 649
29 τῷ στάχυϊ. ὅταν δὲ παραδῷ ὁ καρπός, εὐθέως ἀποστέλλει
the ear. when But yields the fruit, immediately he sends forth
1407 3754 3936 2326
τὸ δρέπανον, ὅτι παρέστηκεν ὁ θερισμός.
the sickle, because stands ready the harvest.

3004 5101 3666 932 2316
30 Καὶ ἔλεγε, Τίνι ὁμοιώσωμεν τὴν βασιλείαν τοῦ Θεοῦ;
And He said, How may we compare the kingdom of God,
1722 4169 3850 3846 846 5613 2848
31 ἢ ἐν ποίᾳ παραβολῇ παραβάλωμεν αὐτήν; ὡς κόκκῳ
or by what parable may we compare it? As to a grain
4615 3739 3752 4687 1909 1093 3398 3956
σινάπεως, ὅς, ὅταν σπαρῇ ἐπὶ τῆς γῆς, μικρότερος πάντων
of mustard, which when it is sown on the earth, lesser than all
4690 2076 1909 1093 3752 4687
32 τῶν σπερμάτων ἐστὶ τῶν ἐπὶ τῆς γῆς· καὶ ὅταν σπαρῇ,
the seeds it is of those on the earth. And when it is sown,
305 1096 3956 3001 3187
ἀναβαίνει, καὶ γίνεται πάντων τῶν λαχάνων μείζων, καὶ
comes up, and becomes than all the plants greater, and
4160 2798 3173 5620 1410 5259 4639
ποιεῖ κλάδους μεγάλους, ὥστε δύνασθαι ὑπὸ τὴν σκιὰν
makes branches great, so as to be able under the shade
848 4071 3772 2681
αὐτοῦ τὰ πετεινὰ τοῦ οὐρανοῦ κατασκηνοῦν.
of it the birds of the heaven to roost.

5108 3850 4183 2980 846
33 Καὶ τοιαύταις παραβολαῖς πολλαῖς ἐλάλει αὐτοῖς τὸν
And such parables many He spoke to them the
3056 2531 1410 191 5565 3850 3756
34 λόγον, καθὼς ἠδύναντο ἀκούειν· χωρὶς δὲ παραβολῆς οὐκ
word, even as they were able to hear; without and a parable not
2980 846 2596 2398 3101 848 1956
ἐλάλει αὐτοῖς· κατ' ἰδίαν δὲ τοῖς μαθηταῖς αὐτοῦ ἐπέλυε
He spoke to them, privately but to the disciples of Him, He explained
3956
πάντα.
all things.

35 And evening having come, He said to them on that day, Let us pass over to the other side. 36 And dismissing the crowd, they took Him along, as He was in the boat. And other small boats also were with Him. 37 And a great windstorm occurred, and the waves beat into the boat, so that it was filled already. 38 And He was on the stern, sleeping on the headrest. And they awakened Him, and said to Him, Teacher, does it not matter to You that we are perishing? 39 And being awakened, He rebuked the wind, and said to the sea, Silence! Be still! And the wind ceased, and there was a great calm. 40 And He said to them, Why are you so fearful? How do you not have faith? 41 And they feared a great fear, and said to one another, Who then is this, that even the wind and the sea obey Him?

CHAPTER 5

1 And they came to the other side of the sea, to the country of the Gadarenes. 2 And He coming out from the boat, immediately out of the tombs a man with an unclean spirit met Him, 3 who had *his* abode among the tombs, and no one was able to bind him, not even with chains; 4 because he had often been bound with fetters and chains, and the chains had been torn by him, and the fetters had been shattered. And no one was able to subdue him. 5 And continually night and day in the hills, and in the tombs, he was crying and cutting himself with stones. 6 And seeing Jesus from afar, he ran and bowed the

3004 846 1722 1565 2250 3798 1096
35 Καὶ λέγει αὐτοῖς ἐν ἐκείνῃ τῇ ἡμέρᾳ, ὀψίας γενομένης,
And He says to them on that day, evening having come,
1330 1519 4008 863 3793 3880
36 Διέλθωμεν εἰς τὸ πέραν. καὶ ἀφέντες τὸν ὄχλον, παραλαμ-
Let us pass over to the other side. And dismissing the crowd, they take
846 5613/2258/1722 4143 243 4142
βάνουσιν αὐτὸν ὡς ἦν ἐν τῷ πλοίῳ. καὶ ἄλλα δὲ πλοιάρια
along Him as He was in the boat. also other And small boats
2258 3326/846 1096 2978 417 3173
37 ἦν μετ' αὐτοῦ. καὶ γίνεται λαῖλαψ ἀνέμου μεγάλη τὰ δὲ
were with Him. And occurs a storm of wind great the and
2949 1911 1519 4143 5620 846 2235 1072
κύματα ἐπέβαλλεν εἰς τὸ πλοῖον, ὥστε αὐτὸ ἤδη γεμίζεσθαι.
waves beat into the boat, so as it already was filled.
2258 846 1909 4403 1909 4344 2518
38 καὶ ἦν αὐτὸς ἐπὶ τῇ πρύμνῃ ἐπὶ τὸ προσκεφάλαιον καθεύδων·
And was He on the stern, on the headrest sleeping.
1326 846 3004 846 1320 3756
καὶ διεγείρουσιν αὐτόν, καὶ λέγουσιν αὐτῷ, Διδάσκαλε, οὐ
And they awaken Him and say to Him, Teacher, not
3199 4671 3754 622 1326 2008
39 μέλει σοι ὅτι ἀπολλύμεθα; καὶ διεγερθεὶς ἐπετίμησε τῷ
it matters to You that we are perishing? And being awakened He rebuked the
417 2036 2281 4623 5392 2869
ἀνέμῳ, καὶ εἶπε τῇ θαλάσσῃ, Σιώπα, πεφίμωσο. καὶ ἐκόπα-
wind, and said to the sea, Silence! Be still! And cut off
417 1096 1055 3173 2036 846
40 σεν ὁ ἄνεμος, καὶ ἐγένετο γαλήνη μεγάλη. καὶ εἶπεν αὐτοῖς,
the wind, and there was a calm great. And He said to them,
5101 1169/2075/3779 4459/3756 2192 4102 5399
41 Τί δειλοί ἐστε οὕτω; πῶς οὐκ ἔχετε πίστιν; καὶ ἐφοβήθησαν
Why fearful are you so? How not have you faith? And they feared
5401 3173 3004 4314 240 5101 686 3778
φόβον μέγαν, καὶ ἔλεγον πρὸς ἀλλήλους, Τίς ἄρα οὗτός
a fear great, and said to one another, Who then this One
2078 3754 417 2281 5219 846
ἐστιν, ὅτι καὶ ὁ ἄνεμος καὶ ἡ θάλασσα ὑπακούουσιν αὐτῷ;
is, that even the wind and the sea obey Him?

CHAPTER 5

2064 1519 4008 2281 1519 5561
1 Καὶ ἦλθον εἰς τὸ πέραν τῆς θαλάσσης, εἰς τὴν χώραν τῶν
And they came to the other side of the sea, into the country of the
1046 1831 846 1537 4143 2112
2 Γαδαρηνῶν. καὶ ἐξελθόντι αὐτῷ ἐκ τοῦ πλοίου, εὐθέως
Gadarenes. And coming out He from the boat, immediately
528 846 1537 3419 444 1722 4151
ἀπήντησεν αὐτῷ ἐκ τῶν μνημείων ἄνθρωπος ἐν πνεύματι
met Him out of the tombs a man in a spirit
169 3739 2731 2192 1722 3419
3 ἀκαθάρτῳ, ὃς τὴν κατοίκησιν εἶχεν ἐν τοῖς μνημείοις· καὶ
unclean, who the dwelling had among the tombs, and
3777 254 3762 1410 846 1210 1223 846
4 οὔτε ἁλύσεσιν οὐδεὶς ἠδύνατο αὐτὸν δῆσαι, διὰ τὸ αὐτὸν
not with chains no one was able him to bind, because that he
4178 3976 254 1210 1288 5259
πολλάκις πέδαις καὶ ἁλύσεσι δεδέσθαι, καὶ διεσπᾶσθαι ὑπ'
often with fetters and chains had been bound, and had been torn by
846 254 3976 4937 3762
αὐτοῦ τὰς ἁλύσεις, καὶ τὰς πέδας συντετρῖφθαι· καὶ οὐδεὶς
him the chains, and the fetters had been broken, and no one
846 2480 1150 1223 3956 3571 2250
5 αὐτὸν ἴσχυε δαμάσαι· καὶ διὰ παντός, νυκτὸς καὶ ἡμέρας,
him was able to subdue; and through all, night and day.
1722 3735 1722 3418 2258 2896 2629
ἐν τοῖς ὄρεσι καὶ ἐν τοῖς μνήμασιν ἦν κράζων καὶ κατακόπτων
among the hills and in the tombs he was crying and cutting
1438 3037 1492 2424 575 3113 5143
6 ἑαυτὸν λίθοις. Ἰδὼν δὲ τὸν Ἰησοῦν ἀπὸ μακρόθεν, ἔδραμε
himself with stones. seeing And Jesus from afar, he ran

knee to Him. [7]And crying with a loud voice, he said, What *is* to me and to You, Jesus, Son of the most high God? I adjure You *by* God not to torment me. [8]For He said to him, Unclean spirit, come out of the man! [9]And He asked him, What *is* your name? And he replied, saying, My name is Legion, because we are many. [10]And he begged Him very much that He would not send them outside the country. [11]And a great herd of pigs were feeding there near the mountain. [12]And all the demons begged Him, saying, Send us into the pigs, that we may enter into them. [13]And Jesus immediately allowed them. And coming out, the unclean spirits entered into the pigs, and the herd rushed down the cliff into the sea—and they were about two thousand—and *they* were choked in the sea. [14]And those who fed the pigs fled, and *they* told *it* to the city, and to the fields. And they came out to see what was happening.

[15]And they came to Jesus, and stared at the one *who had been* demon-possessed, sitting and being clothed, and being in his senses, the one who had the legion. And they feared. [16]And those who had seen related how it happened to the demon-possessed one, and about the pigs.

[17]And they began to beg Him to depart from their borders. [18]And He having entered into the boat, the *former* demoniac begged Him, that he be with Him. [19]But Jesus did not allow him, but said to him, Go to your house, to your own, and announce to them

4352 846 2896 5456 3173 2036 5101
7 καὶ προσεκύνησεν αὐτῷ, καὶ κράξας φωνῇ μεγάλῃ εἶπε, Τί
and bowed the knee to Him, and crying with a voice great said, What
1698 4671 2424 5207 2316 5310 3726 4571
ἐμοὶ καὶ σοί, Ἰησοῦ, υἱὲ τοῦ Θεοῦ τοῦ ὑψίστου ; ὁρκίζω σε
to me and to You, Jesus,, Son of God the Most High? I adjure You
2316 3361 3165 928 3004 1063 846 1831
8 τὸν Θεόν, μή με βασανίσῃς. ἔλεγε γὰρ αὐτῷ, Ἔξελθε, τὸ
(by) God not me torment. He said For to him, Come out, the
4151 169 1537 444 1905
9 πνεῦμα τὸ ἀκάθαρτον, ἐκ τοῦ ἀνθρώπου. καὶ ἐπηρώτα
spirit unclean, out of the man! And He questioned
846 5101 4671 3686 611 3004 3003 3686
αὐτόν, Τί σοι ὄνομα ; καὶ ἀπεκρίθη, λέγων, Λεγεὼν ὄνομά
him, What (is) to you name? And he answered, saying, Legion (the) name
3427/3754/ 4183 2070 3870 846 4183 2443 3361
10 μοι, ὅτι πολλοί ἐσμεν. καὶ παρεκάλει αὐτὸν πολλά, ἵνα μὴ
of me, for many we are. And he begged Him much, that not
846 649 1854 5561 2258 1563 4314 3735
11 αὐτοὺς ἀποστείλῃ ἔξω τῆς χώρας. ἦν δὲ ἐκεῖ πρὸς τὰ ὄρη
them He would send outside the country. was And there near the mount
34 5519 3173 1006 3870 846
12 ἀγέλη χοίρων μεγάλη βοσκομένη· καὶ παρεκάλεσαν αὐτὸν
herd of pigs a great feeding; and begged Him
3956 1142 3004 3992 2248/1519 5519
πάντες οἱ δαίμονες, λέγοντες, Πέμψον ἡμᾶς εἰς τοὺς χοίρους,
all the demons, saying, Send us into the pigs.
2443 1519 846 1525 2010 846 2112
13 ἵνα εἰς αὐτοὺς εἰσέλθωμεν. καὶ ἐπέτρεψεν αὐτοῖς εὐθέως ὁ
that into them we may enter. And allowed them immediately
2424 1831 4151 169 1525
Ἰησοῦς. καὶ ἐξελθόντα τὰ πνεύματα τὰ ἀκάθαρτα εἰσῆλθον
Jesus. And coming out, the spirits unclean entered
1519 5519 3729 34 2592 2911
εἰς τοὺς χοίρους· καὶ ὥρμησεν ἡ ἀγέλη κατὰ τοῦ κρημνοῦ
into the pigs, and rushed the herd down the precipice
1519 2281 2258 1367 4155 1722
εἰς τὴν θάλασσαν· ἦσαν δὲ ὡς δισχίλιοι· καὶ ἐπνίγοντο ἐν τῇ
into the sea, they were And about two thousand and were in the
2281 1006 5519 5343 ᶜchoked 312
14 θαλάσσῃ. οἱ δὲ βόσκοντες τοὺς χοίρους ἔφυγον, καὶ ἀνήγ-
sea. those And feeding the pigs fled, and told
1519 4172 1519 68 1831 1492
γειλαν εἰς τὴν πόλιν καὶ εἰς τοὺς ἀγρούς. καὶ ἐξῆλθον ἰδεῖν
(it) to the city, and to the fields. And they came out to see
5101/2076 1096 2064 4314 2424
15 τί ἐστι τὸ γεγονός· καὶ ἔρχονται πρὸς τὸν Ἰησοῦν, καὶ
what is that having occurred, and they come to Jesus, and
2334 1139 2521 2439
θεωροῦσι τὸν δαιμονιζόμενον καθήμενον καὶ ἱματισμένον
gaze upon the demon-possessed one sitting and having been robed
4993 2192 3003 5399
καὶ σωφρονοῦντα, τὸν ἐσχηκότα τὸν λεγεῶνα· καὶ ἐφοβήθη-
and being in his senses, the (one) having had the legion, and they feared.
1334 846 1492 4459 1096
16 σαν. καὶ διηγήσαντο αὐτοῖς οἱ ἰδόντες πῶς ἐγένετο τῷ
And related to them the (ones) seeing how it occurred to
1139 4012 5519 756 3870 the
17 δαιμονιζομένῳ, καὶ περὶ τῶν χοίρων. καὶ ἤρξαντο παρα-
demon-possessed one and about the pigs. And they began to beg
846 565 575 3725 848 1684
18 καλεῖν αὐτὸν ἀπελθεῖν ἀπὸ τῶν ὁρίων αὐτῶν. καὶ ἐμβάντος
Him to depart from the territory of them. And entering
848 1519 4143 3870 846 1139 2443
5600 αὐτοῦ εἰς τὸ πλοῖον, παρεκάλει αὐτὸν ὁ δαιμονισθείς, ἵνα ᾖ
He into the boat, begged Him the demoniac, that he b
3326 846 2424 3756 863 846 235 3004 846
19 μετ' αὐτοῦ. ὁ δὲ Ἰησοῦς οὐκ ἀφῆκεν αὐτόν, ἀλλὰ λέγει αὐτῷ,
with Him. – But Jesus not did allow him, but says to him
5217 1519 3624 4675 4314 4674 312
Ὕπαγε εἰς τὸν οἶκόν σου πρὸς τοὺς σούς, καὶ ἀνάγγειλον
Go to the house of you to those of you, and announce

what the Lord has done to you, and favored you. [20]And he left and began to proclaim in Decapolis what Jesus did to him. And all marveled.

[21]And Jesus having crossed over in the boat again to the other side, a large crowd gathered upon Him; and He was by the sea. [22]And, behold one of the synagogue rulers named Jairus came. And seeing Him, *he* fell at His feet. [23]And he begged Him very much, saying, My daughter is at the last end. *I pray* that You will come *and* lay hands on her, that *she* may be cured, and live. [24]And He went with him. And a large crowd followed Him, and pressed on Him.

[25]And a certain woman being with a flow of blood twelve years, [26]and who had suffered many things by many physicians, and had spent all things that she had, and gaining nothing, but rather coming to worse, [27]hearing about Jesus, coming in the crowd behind *Him*, she touched His garment. [28]For she said, If I may but touch His garments, I will be cured. [29]And instantly the fountain of her blood was dried up, and she knew in *her* body that she was healed of the plague. [30]And knowing instantly within Himself that power had gone forth out of Him, turning in the crowd, Jesus said, Who touched My garments? [31]And His disciples said to Him, You see the crowd pressing on You, and do You say, Who touched Me? [32]And He looked around to see the *one* who had done this. [33]And the woman

846 3745/4671 2962 4160 1653 4571 565
20 αὐτοῖς ὅσα σοι ὁ Κύριος ἐποίησε, καὶ ἠλέησέ σε. καὶ ἀπῆλθε
to them how to you the Lord has done, and favored you. And he left
756 2784 1722 1179 3745 4160 846
καὶ ἤρξατο κηρύσσειν ἐν τῇ Δεκαπόλει ὅσα ἐποίησεν αὐτῷ ὁ
and began to proclaim in Decapolis how much did to him
2424 3956 2296
Ἰησοῦς· καὶ πάντες ἐθαύμαζον.
Jesus. And all marvelled.
1276 2424 1722 4143 3825 1519
21 Καὶ διαπεράσαντος τοῦ Ἰησοῦ ἐν τῷ πλοίῳ πάλιν εἰς τὸ
And crossing over — Jesus in the boat again to the
4008 4863 3793 4183 1909 846 2258 3844
πέραν, συνήχθη ὄχλος πολὺς ἐπ' αὐτόν, καὶ ἦν παρὰ τὴν
other side, was collected a crowd big upon Him, and He was by the
2281 2400 2064 1520 752
22 θάλασσαν. καὶ ἰδού, ἔρχεται εἷς τῶν ἀρχισυναγώγων,
sea. And behold, comes one of the synagogue chiefs,
3686 2383 1492 846 4098 4314 4228
ὀνόματι Ἰάειρος, καὶ ἰδὼν αὐτόν, πίπτει πρὸς τοὺς πόδας
by name Jairus, and seeing Him he falls at the feet
848 3870 846 4183 3004 3754 2365
23 αὐτοῦ, καὶ παρεκάλει αὐτὸν πολλά, λέγων ὅτι Τὸ θυγάτριόν
of Him, and begs Him much, saying, — The daughter
3450 2079 2192/2443/2064 2007 846 5495 3704
μου ἐσχάτως ἔχει· ἵνα ἐλθὼν ἐπιθῇς αὐτῇ τὰς χεῖρας, ὅπως
of me (is) at the last end, that coming You may lay on her the hands, that (she)
4982 2198 565 3326 846 190
24 σωθῇ καὶ ζήσεται. καὶ ἀπῆλθε μετ' αὐτοῦ· καὶ ἠκολούθει
be cured and may live. And He went with him. And followed
846 3793 4183 4918 846
αὐτῷ ὄχλος πολύς, καὶ συνέθλιβον αὐτόν.
Him a crowd great, and pressed upon Him.
1135 5100 5607 1722 4511 129 2094 1427
25 Καὶ γυνή τις οὖσα ἐν ῥύσει αἵματος ἔτη δώδεκα, καὶ
26 And a woman certain being in a flow of blood years twelve, and
4183 3958 5259 4183 2395 1159
πολλὰ παθοῦσα ὑπὸ πολλῶν ἰατρῶν, καὶ δαπανήσασα τὰ
many things suffering by many physicians, and having spent that
3844 1438 3956 3367 5623 235 3123
παρ' ἑαυτῆς πάντα, καὶ μηδὲν ὠφεληθεῖσα, ἀλλὰ μᾶλλον
by her all things, and nothing having been gained, but rather
1519 5501 2064 191 4012 2424 2064
27 εἰς τὸ χεῖρον ἐλθοῦσα, ἀκούσασα περὶ τοῦ Ἰησοῦ, ἐλθοῦσα
to the worse having come, hearing about — Jesus, coming
1722 3793 3693 680 2440 848 3004 1063
28 ἐν τῷ ὄχλῳ ὄπισθεν, ἥψατο τοῦ ἱματίου αὐτοῦ· ἔλεγε γὰρ
in the crowd behind she touched the garment of Him. she said For
3754 2579 2440 848 680 4982
29 ὅτι Κἂν τῶν ἱματίων αὐτοῦ ἅψωμαι, σωθήσομαι. καὶ
— if but the garments of Him I may touch, I will be cured. And
2112 3583 4077 129 848 1097
εὐθέως ἐξηράνθη ἡ πηγὴ τοῦ αἵματος αὐτῆς, καὶ ἔγνω τῷ
instantly was dried up the fountain of the blood of her, and she knew in
4983 3754 2390 575 3148 2112 2424
30 σώματι ὅτι ἴαται ἀπὸ τῆς μάστιγος. καὶ εὐθέως ὁ Ἰησοῦς
(her) body that she is healed of the plague. And instantly Jesus
1994 1722 1438 1537 846 1411 1831
ἐπιγνοὺς ἐν ἑαυτῷ τὴν ἐξ αὐτοῦ δύναμιν ἐξελθοῦσαν,
knowing within Himself that out of Him power had gone forth,
1994 1722 3793 3004 5101 3450 680 2440
ἐπιστραφεὶς ἐν τῷ ὄχλῳ, ἔλεγε, Τίς μου ἥψατο τῶν ἱματίων;
turning in the crowd said, Who of Me touched the garments?
3004 846 3101 848 991 3793
31 καὶ ἔλεγον αὐτῷ οἱ μαθηταὶ αὐτοῦ, Βλέπεις τὸν ὄχλον
And said to Him the disciples of Him, You see the crowd
4918 4571 3004 5101 3450 680 4017
32 συνθλίβοντά σε, καὶ λέγεις, Τίς μου ἥψατο; καὶ περιεβλέ-
pressing upon You, and You say, Who of Me touched? And He looked
1492 5124 4160 1135 5399
33 πετο ἰδεῖν τὴν τοῦτο ποιήσασαν. ἡ δὲ γυνὴ φοβηθεῖσα καὶ
around to see the (one) this having done. the And woman fearing and

being afraid and trembling, knowing what had happened on her, she came and fell down before Him, and told Him all the truth. [34]And He said to her, Daughter, your faith has healed you. Go in peace, and be whole from your plague.

[35]As He was speaking, they came from the synagogue ruler, saying, Your daughter has died. Why do you still trouble the Teacher? [36]But hearing the word spoken, Jesus said to the synagogue the synagogue ruler at once, Do not fear; only believe. [37]And He did not allow anyone to go with Him except Peter and James and John, the brother of James. [38]And they came into the synagogue ruler's house. And He saw a tumult, and weeping and much wailing.

[39]And going in, He said to them, Why do you make a tumult and weep? The child has not died, but is sleeping. [40]And they laughed at Him. But putting all out, He took along the father and the mother of the child, and those with Him, and passed on into where the child was lying. [41]And taking hold of the child's hand, He said to her, Talitha koumi; which is, being translated, Little girl, I say to you, Rise up! [42]And immediately the little girl rose up and walked. For she was twelve years *old*. And they were amazed with great amazement. [43]And very much He directed them that no one should know this. And *He* said to give her *something* to eat.

5141 1492 1096 1909 846 2064 4363
τρέμουσα, εἰδυῖα ὃ γέγονεν ἐπ' αὐτῇ, ἦλθε καὶ προσέπεσεν
trembling, knowing what happened on her, came and fell before
846 2036 846 3956 225 2036 846
34 αὐτῷ, καὶ εἶπεν αὐτῷ πᾶσαν τὴν ἀλήθειαν. ὁ δὲ εἶπεν αὐτῇ,
Him, and told Him all the truth. He And said to her
2364 4102 4675 4982 4571 5217 1519 1515
Θύγατερ, ἡ πίστις σου σέσωκέ σε· ὕπαγε εἰς εἰρήνην, καὶ
Daughter, the faith of you has healed you; go in peace, and
2468 5199 575 3148 4675
ἴσθι ὑγιὴς ἀπὸ τῆς μάστιγός σου.
be whole from the plague of you.
2089 846 2980 2064 575 752
35 Ἔτι αὐτοῦ λαλοῦντος, ἔρχονται ἀπὸ τοῦ ἀρχισυναγώ-
While He was speaking, they come from the synagogue
3004 3754 2364 4675 599 5101/2089 4660
γου, λέγοντες ὅτι Ἡ θυγάτηρ σου ἀπέθανε· τί ἔτι σκύλλεις
chief, saying, The daughter of you has died; why still trouble
1320 2424 2112 191 3056
36 τὸν διδάσκαλον; ὁ δὲ Ἰησοῦς εὐθέως ἀκούσας τὸν λόγον
the Teacher? But Jesus immediately, hearing the word
2980 3004 752 3361 5399 3440
λαλούμενον λέγει τῷ ἀρχισυναγώγῳ, Μὴ φοβοῦ, μόνον
spoken, says to the synagogue chief, Do not fear; only
4100 3756 863 3762 846 4870 1488
37 πίστευε. καὶ οὐκ ἀφῆκεν οὐδένα αὐτῷ συνακολουθῆσαι, εἰ
believe. And not He did allow no one Him to accompany, ex-
3361 4074 2385 2491 80 2385
μὴ Πέτρον καὶ Ἰάκωβον καὶ Ἰωάννην τὸν ἀδελφὸν Ἰακώβου.
cept Peter and James, and John the brother of James.
2064 1519 3624 752 2334
38 καὶ ἔρχεται εἰς τὸν οἶκον τοῦ ἀρχισυναγώγου, καὶ θεωρεῖ
And they come into the house of the synagogue-chief, and He sees
2351 2799 214 4183
39 θόρυβον, καὶ κλαίοντας καὶ ἀλαλάζοντας πολλά. καὶ
a tumult, and weeping and wailing much. And
1525 3004 846 5101 2350 2799
εἰσελθὼν λέγει αὐτοῖς, Τί θορυβεῖσθε καὶ κλαίετε; τὸ
entering He says to them, Why do you make a tumult and weep? The
3813 3756 599 235 2518 2606 846
40 παιδίον οὐκ ἀπέθανεν, ἀλλὰ καθεύδει. καὶ κατεγέλων αὐτοῦ.
child not has died, but sleeps. And they laughed at Him.
1544 537 3880 3962
ὁ δέ, ἐκβαλὼν ἅπαντας, παραλαμβάνει τὸν πατέρα τοῦ
He But putting out all takes along the father of the
3813 3384 3326 846 1531
παιδίου καὶ τὴν μητέρα καὶ τοὺς μετ' αὐτοῦ, καὶ εἰσπορεύε-
child and the mother and those with Him, and passes into
3699 2258 3813 345 2902
41 ται ὅπου ἦν τὸ παιδίον ἀνακείμενον. καὶ κρατήσας τῆς
where was the child lying. And taking hold of the
5495 3813 3004 846 5008 2891 3739 2076
χειρὸς τοῦ παιδίου, λέγει αὐτῇ, Ταλιθά, κοῦμι· ὅ ἐστι
hand of the child, He says to her, Talitha, koumi; which is,
3177 2877 4671 3004 1453
42 μεθερμηνευόμενον, Τὸ κοράσιον, σοὶ λέγω, ἔγειραι. καὶ
being translated, Little girl, to you I say, Arise! And
2112 450 2877 4043 2258/ 1063 2094
εὐθέως ἀνέστη τὸ κοράσιον καὶ περιεπάτει, ἦν γὰρ ἐτῶν
instantly rose up the little girl and walked. she was For of years
1427 1839 1611 3173 1291
43 δώδεκα· καὶ ἐξέστησαν ἐκστάσει μεγάλῃ. καὶ διεστείλατο
twelve. And they were amazed with amazement great. And He ordered
846 4183 2443 3367 1097 5124 2036 1325
αὐτοῖς πολλὰ ἵνα μηδεὶς γνῷ τοῦτο· καὶ εἶπε δοθῆναι
them much that no one should know this, and said to give
846 5315
αὐτῇ φαγεῖν.
to her to eat.

CHAPTER 6

[1]And He went out from there, and came to His native-place. And His disciples followed Him. [2]And a sabbath occurring, He began to teach in the synagogue. And hearing many were amazed, saying, From where *came* these things to this one? And what *is* the wisdom given to him, that even such works of power come about through his hands? [3]Is this one not the carpenter, the son of Mary, and brother of James and Joseph and Judas and Simon? And are not his sisters here with us? And they were offended in Him. [4]And Jesus said to them, A prophet is not without honor, except in his native-place, and among the relatives, and in his *own* house. [5]And he could do no work of power there, except He performed healing on a few infirm ones, laying on *His* hands. [6]And He marveled because of their unbelief.

And He went around the villages in a circuit, teaching.

[7]And He called the Twelve near, and began to send them out two by two. And *He* gave them authority *over* the unclean spirits, [8]and charged them that they take nothing in *the* way, except only a staff—no bag, no bread, no copper in the belt; [9]but having tied on sandals, and not putting on two tunics. [10]And He said to them, Wherever you enter into a house, remain there until you go out from there. [11]And as many as will not receive you, nor hear from

CHAPTER 6

1831 1564 2064 1519 3968 848
1 Καὶ ἐξῆλθεν ἐκεῖθεν, καὶ ἦλθεν εἰς τὴν πατρίδα αὐτοῦ·
And He went out from there and comes to the native-place of Him.
190 846 3101 848 1096
2 καὶ ἀκολουθοῦσιν αὐτῷ οἱ μαθηταὶ αὐτοῦ. καὶ γενομένου
and follow Him the disciples of Him. And occurring
4521 756 1722 4864 1322 4183
σαββάτου, ἤρξατο ἐν τῇ συναγωγῇ διδάσκειν· καὶ πολλοὶ
a sabbath, He began in the synagogue to teach, and many
191 1605 3004 4159 5129 5023
ἀκούοντες ἐξεπλήσσοντο, λέγοντες, Πόθεν τούτῳ ταῦτα;
hearing were astonished, saying, From where to this one these things?
5101 4678 1325 846 3754 1411 5108
καὶ τίς ἡ σοφία ἡ δοθεῖσα αὐτῷ, ὅτι καὶ δυνάμεις τοιαῦται
and what the wisdom given to Him that even works of power such
1223 5495 848 1096 3756 3778 2076 5045
3 διὰ τῶν χειρῶν αὐτοῦ γίνονται; οὐχ οὗτός ἐστιν ὁ τέκτων,
through the hands of Him coming about? Not this one is the carpenter,
5207 3137 80 2385 2500 2455
ὁ υἱὸς Μαρίας, ἀδελφὸς δὲ Ἰακώβου καὶ Ἰωσῆ καὶ Ἰούδα
the son of Mary, brother and of James and Joseph and Judas
4613 3756 1526 79 848 5612 4314 2248
καὶ Σίμωνος; καὶ οὐκ εἰσὶν αἱ ἀδελφαὶ αὐτοῦ ὧδε πρὸς ἡμᾶς;
and Simon? And not are the sisters of Him here with us?
4624 1722 846 3004 846 2424 3754
4 καὶ ἐσκανδαλίζοντο ἐν αὐτῷ. ἔλεγε δὲ αὐτοῖς ὁ Ἰησοῦς ὅτι
And they were offended in Him. said And to them — Jesus, —
3756 2076 4396 820 =1508=1722 3968 848
Οὐκ ἔστι προφήτης ἄτιμος, εἰ μὴ ἐν τῇ πατρίδι αὐτοῦ, καὶ
Not is a prophet unhonored, except in the native place of him, and
1722 4773 1722 3614 848 3756 1410
5 ἐν τοῖς συγγενέσι καὶ ἐν τῇ οἰκίᾳ αὐτοῦ. καὶ οὐκ ἠδύνατο
among the relatives, and in the house of him. And not He could
1563 3762 1411 4160 =1508= 3641 732
ἐκεῖ οὐδεμίαν δύναμιν ποιῆσαι, εἰ μὴ ὀλίγοις ἀρρώστοις
there no work of power do, except on a few infirm ones
2007 5495 2323 2296 1223 570
6 ἐπιθεὶς τὰς χεῖρας, ἐθεράπευσε. καὶ ἐθαύμαζε διὰ τὴν ἀπι-
laying on the hands He healed. And He marveled through the un-
848
στίαν αὐτῶν.
belief of them.
4013 2968 2945 1321
Καὶ περιῆγε τὰς κώμας κύκλῳ διδάσκων.
And He went around the villages in circuit teaching.
4341 1427 756 846
7 Καὶ προσκαλεῖται τοὺς δώδεκα, καὶ ἤρξατο αὐτοὺς
And He calls near the twelve, and began them
649 1417 1417 1325 846 1849
ἀποστέλλειν δύο δύο, καὶ ἐδίδου αὐτοῖς ἐξουσίαν τῶν
to send out two by two, and gave to them authority (over) the
4151 169 3853 846 2443
8 πνευμάτων τῶν ἀκαθάρτων. καὶ παρήγγειλεν αὐτοῖς ἵνα
spirits — unclean, and charged them that
3367 142 1519 3598 =1508= 4464 3440 3361 4082 3361
μηδὲν αἴρωσιν εἰς ὁδόν, εἰ μὴ ῥάβδον μόνον· μὴ πήραν, μὴ
nothing they take in (the) way, except a staff only not a bag, nor
740 3361 1519 2223 5475 535 5265
9 ἄρτον, μὴ εἰς τὴν ζώνην χαλκόν· ἀλλ' ὑποδεδεμένους
bread, nor in the belt copper; but having tied under
4547 3361 1746 1417 5509 3004
10 σανδάλια· καὶ μὴ ἐνδύσασθαι δύο χιτῶνας. καὶ ἔλεγεν
sandals, and not put on two tunics. And He said
846 3699 1437 1525 1519 3614 1563 3306 2193 303
αὐτοῖς, Ὅπου ἐὰν εἰσέλθητε εἰς οἰκίαν, ἐκεῖ μένετε ἕως ἂν
to them, Wherever you enter into a house, there remain until
1831 1564 3745 302 3361 1209 5209 3366
11 ἐξέλθητε ἐκεῖθεν. καὶ ὅσοι ἂν μὴ δέξωνται ὑμᾶς, μηδὲ
you go out from there. And as many as not will receive you, nor

you, having gone out from there, shake off the dust under your feet for a testimony to them. Truly I say to you, it will be more bearable for Sodom or Gomorrah in Judgment Day than for that city. [12]And going out they proclaimed that *men* should repent. [13]And they cast out many demons, and anointed with oil and healed many sick ones.

[14]And Herod the king heard; for His name became publicly known. And he said, John the Baptist has been raised from the dead, and because of this the works of power operate in him.

[15]Others said, He is Elijah; and others said, He is a prophet, or as one of the prophets. [16]But hearing, Herod said, This one is John, whom I beheaded. He has risen from the dead.

[17]For having sent, Herod himself had seized John, and bound him in the prison, because of Herodias the wife of his brother Philip; because he had married her. [18]For John had said to Herod, It is not lawful for you to have the wife of your brother. [19]And Herodias held it against him, and desired to kill him, but was not able. [20]For Herod feared John, knowing him *to be* a holy and just man, and kept him safe. And hearing him, he did many things, and gladly heard from him.

[21]And a suitable day having come, when Herod made a supper for his great ones on his birthday, also the chiliarchs, and the first ones of Galilee. [22]And the daughter of Herodias herself entering, and dancing,

191 5216 1607 1564 1621
ἀκούσωσιν ὑμῶν, ἐκπορευόμενοι ἐκεῖθεν, ἐκτινάξατε τὸν
hear from you, going out from there shake off the
5522 5270 4228 5216 1519 3142 846
χοῦν τὸν ὑποκάτω τῶν ποδῶν ὑμῶν εἰς μαρτύριον αὐτοῖς.
dust under the feet of you for a testimony to them.
281 3004 5213 414 2071 4670 2228 1116 1722
ἀμὴν λέγω ὑμῖν, ἀνεκτότερον ἔσται Σοδόμοις ἢ Γομόρροις ἐν
Truly I say to you, more tolerable it will be for Sodom or Gomorrah in
2250 2920 2228 4172 1565 1831 2784
12 ἡμέρᾳ κρίσεως, ἢ τῇ πόλει ἐκείνῃ. καὶ ἐξελθόντες ἐκήρυσσον
day of judgment, than for city that. And going out they preached
2443 3340 1140 4183 1544
13 ἵνα μετανοήσωσι· καὶ δαιμόνια πολλὰ ἐξέβαλλον, καὶ
that (men) should repent. And demons many they cast out; and
218 1637 4183 732 2323
ἤλειφον ἐλαίῳ πολλοὺς ἀρρώστους καὶ ἐθεράπευον.
anointed with oil many sick ones, and healed.
191 935 2264 5318 1063 1096
14 Καὶ ἤκουσεν ὁ βασιλεὺς Ἡρώδης, φανερὸν γὰρ ἐγένετο τὸ
And heard the king, Herod. manifest For became the
3686 848 3004 3754 2491 907 1537 3498
ὄνομα αὐτοῦ, καὶ ἔλεγεν ὅτι Ἰωάννης ὁ βαπτίζων ἐκ νεκρῶν
name of Him. And he said, John the Baptist from the dead
1453 1223 5124 1754 1411 1722 846
ἠγέρθη, καὶ διὰ τοῦτο ἐνεργοῦσιν αἱ δυνάμεις ἐν αὐτῷ.
has been raised; because of this operate the works of power in him.
243 3004 3754 2243 2076 243 3004 3754 4396
15 ἄλλοι ἔλεγον ὅτι Ἠλίας ἐστίν· ἄλλοι δὲ ἔλεγον ὅτι Προφήτης
Others said, Elijah he is; others and said, a prophet
2228 2076 *5613/1519 4396 191 2264 2036
16 ἐστίν, ἢ ὡς εἷς τῶν προφητῶν. ἀκούσας δὲ ὁ Ἡρώδης εἶπεν
he is, or as one of the prophets. hearing But, Herod said,
3754 3739 1473 607 2491 3778 2076 846
ὅτι Ὃν ἐγὼ ἀπεκεφάλισα Ἰωάννην, οὗτός ἐστιν· αὐτὸς
— whom I beheaded, John, this one he is. He
1453 1537 3498 846 1063 2264 649
17 ἠγέρθη ἐκ νεκρῶν. αὐτὸς γὰρ ὁ Ἡρώδης ἀποστείλας
is risen from the dead. himself For — Herod sending
2902 2491 1210 846 1722 5438
ἐκράτησε τὸν Ἰωάννην, καὶ ἔδησεν αὐτὸν ἐν τῇ φυλακῇ,
had seized — John, and bound him in the prison,
1223 2266 1135 5376 80 848
διὰ Ἡρωδιάδα τὴν γυναῖκα Φιλίππου τοῦ ἀδελφοῦ αὐτοῦ,
because of Herodias the wife of Philip, the brother of him;
3754 846 1060 3004 1063 2491 2264
18 ὅτι αὐτὴν ἐγάμησεν. ἔλεγε γὰρ ὁ Ἰωάννης τῷ Ἡρώδῃ
because her he had married. had said For John to Herod.
3754 3756 1832 4671 2192 1135 80 4675
ὅτι Οὐκ ἔξεστί σοι ἔχειν τὴν γυναῖκα τοῦ ἀδελφοῦ σου.
— not it is lawful for you to have the wife of the brother of you.
2266 1758 846 2309 846 615
19 ἡ δὲ Ἡρωδιὰς ἐνεῖχεν αὐτῷ, καὶ ἤθελεν αὐτὸν ἀποκτεῖναι·
And Herodias held it against him, and wished him to kill,
3756 1410 1063 2264 5399 2491
20 καὶ οὐκ ἠδύνατο· ὁ γὰρ Ἡρώδης ἐφοβεῖτο τὸν Ἰωάννην,
and not was able; for Herod feared John,
1492 846 435 1342 40 4933 846
εἰδὼς αὐτὸν ἄνδρα δίκαιον καὶ ἅγιον, καὶ συνετήρει αὐτόν·
knowing him a man just and holy, and kept safe him,
191 846 4183 4160 2234 846 191
καὶ ἀκούσας αὐτοῦ, πολλὰ ἐποίει, καὶ ἡδέως αὐτοῦ ἤκουε.
and hearing him, many things he did, and gladly from him heard.
1096 2250 2121 3753 2264 1077
21 καὶ γενομένης ἡμέρας εὐκαίρου, ὅτε Ἡρώδης τοῖς γενεσίοις
And coming a day suitable when Herod on the birth-feast
848 1173 4160 3175 848
αὐτοῦ δεῖπνον ἐποίει τοῖς μεγιστᾶσιν αὐτοῦ καὶ τοῖς
of Him a supper made for the great ones of him, and the
5506 4413 1056 1525
22 χιλιάρχοις καὶ τοῖς πρώτοις τῆς Γαλιλαίας, καὶ εἰσελθούσης
chiliarchs, and the first ones — of Galilee. And entering

she also pleased Herod and those reclining with *him.* The king said to the girl, Ask me whatever you wish, and I will give it to you. [23]And he swore to her, Whatever you ask me, I will give to you, up to half of my kingdom. [24]And going out, she said to her mother, What shall I ask? And she said, The head of John the Baptist. [25]And immediately, going in with haste to the king, she asked, saying, I desire that at once you give to me the head of John the Baptist on a platter. [26]And becoming deeply grieved, because of

2364 846 2266 3738
τῆς θυγατρὸς αὐτῆς τῆς Ἡρωδιάδος καὶ ὀρχησαμένης, καὶ
the daughter of her, – of Herodias, and dancing, and

700 2264 4873 2036
ἀρεσάσης τῷ Ἡρώδῃ καὶ τοῖς συνανακειμένοις, εἶπεν ὁ
she pleased – Herod and those reclining with (him). said the

935 2877 154 3165 1437 2309 1325
βασιλεὺς τῷ κορασίῳ, Αἴτησόν με ὃ ἐὰν θέλῃς, καὶ δώσω
king to the girl, Ask me whatever you wish, and I will give

4671 3660 846 3754/3739/1437/3165/ 154 1325 4671
23 σοί· καὶ ὤμοσεν αὐτῇ ὅτι Ὃ ἐάν με αἰτήσῃς, δώσω σοί,
to you. And he swore to her, – Whatever me you ask, I will give to you,

2193 2255 932 3450 1831 2036
24 ἕως ἡμίσους τῆς βασιλείας μου. ἡ δὲ ἐξελθοῦσα εἶπε τῇ
up to half of the kingdom of me. she and going out said to the

3384 848 5101 154 2036 2776
μητρὶ αὐτῆς, Τί αἰτήσομαι; ἡ δὲ εἶπε, Τὴν κεφαλὴν
mother of her, What shall I ask? she And said, The head

2491 910 1525 2112 3326
25 Ἰωάννου τοῦ Βαπτιστοῦ. καὶ εἰσελθοῦσα εὐθέως μετὰ
of John the Baptist. And entering immediately with

4710 4314 935 154 3004 2309 2443
σπουδῆς πρὸς τὸν βασιλέα, ᾐτήσατο, λέγουσα, Θέλω ἵνα
haste to the king, she asked, saying, I desire that

3427 1325 1824 1909 4094 2776 2491
μοι δῷς ἐξαυτῆς ἐπὶ πίνακι τὴν κεφαλὴν Ἰωάννου τοῦ
to me you give at once on a dish the head of John the

910 4036 1096 935 1223
26 Βαπτιστοῦ. καὶ περίλυπος γενόμενος ὁ βασιλεύς, διὰ τοὺς
Baptist. And deeply grieved becoming the king, because of the

the oaths and those reclining together, the king did not wish to reject her. [27]And the king sending a guardsman at once, he ordered his head to be brought. [28]And going he beheaded him in the prison, and brought his head on a platter, and gave it to the girl. And the girl gave it to her mother. [29]And hearing, his disciples went and took his corpse and placed it in a tomb.

3727 4873 3756 2309 846 114
ὅρκους καὶ τοὺς συνανακειμένους οὐκ ἠθέλησεν αὐτὴν ἀθε-
oaths, and those reclining together not did wish her to

2112 649 935 4688
27 τῆσαι. καὶ εὐθέως ἀποστείλας ὁ βασιλεὺς σπεκουλάτωρα
reject. And at once sending the king a guardsman

2004 5342 2776 848 565
28 ἐπέταξεν ἐνεχθῆναι τὴν κεφαλὴν αὐτοῦ. ὁ δὲ ἀπελθὼν
he ordered to be brought the head of him, he And going

607 846 1722 5438 5342 2776
ἀπεκεφάλισεν αὐτὸν ἐν τῇ φυλακῇ, καὶ ἤνεγκε τὴν κεφαλὴν
beheaded him in the prison, and brought the head

848 1909 4094 1325 846 2877
αὐτοῦ ἐπὶ πίνακι, καὶ ἔδωκεν αὐτὴν τῷ κορασίῳ· καὶ τὸ
of him on a dish, and gave it to the girl; and the

2877 1325 846 3384 848 191
29 κοράσιον ἔδωκεν αὐτὴν τῇ μητρὶ αὐτῆς. καὶ ἀκούσαντες
girl gave it to the mother of her. And hearing

3101 848 2064 142 4430 848
οἱ μαθηταὶ αὐτοῦ ἦλθον, καὶ ἦραν τὸ πτῶμα αὐτοῦ, καὶ
the disciples of him went and took the cor[illegible] of him, and

5087 846 1722 3419
ἔθηκαν αὐτὸ ἐν μνημείῳ.
placed it in a tomb.

[30]And the apostles gathered to Jesus. And *they* told Him all things, even what they did, and what they taught. [31]And He said to them, *You* yourselves come apart into a desert place, and rest a little. For those coming, and those going were many; and they did not even have opportunity to eat. [32]And they departed by boat into a desert place apart.

4863 652 4314 2424
30 Καὶ συνάγονται οἱ ἀπόστολοι πρὸς τὸν Ἰησοῦν, καὶ
And are assembled the apostles to Jesus, and

518 846 3956 3745 4160 3745 1321
ἀπήγγειλαν αὐτῷ πάντα, καὶ ὅσα ἐποίησαν καὶ ὅσα ἐδί-
told Him all things, even what they did and what they

2036 846 1205 5210 846 2596 2398 1519
31 δαξαν. καὶ εἶπεν αὐτοῖς, Δεῦτε ὑμεῖς αὐτοὶ κατ' ἰδίαν εἰς
taught. And He said to them, Come yourselves privately to

2048 5117 373 3641 2258 1063
ἔρημον τόπον, καὶ ἀναπαύεσθε ὀλίγον. ἦσαν γὰρ οἱ
a desert place, and rest a little. were For those

2064 5217 4183 3761 5315 2119
ἐρχόμενοι καὶ οἱ ὑπάγοντες πολλοί, καὶ οὐδὲ φαγεῖν ηὐκαί-
coming and the (ones) going many, and not even to eat they had

565 1519 2048 5117 4143 2596 2398
32 ρουν. καὶ ἀπῆλθον εἰς ἔρημον τόπον τῷ πλοίῳ κατ' ἰδίαν.
opportunity. And they left into a desert place, by the boat, privately.

[33]And the crowds saw them going, and many recognized Him. And *they* ran together on foot there, from all the cities, and came before them, and came together to Him. [34]And going out Jesus saw a large crowd, and had pity on them, because they were as sheep having no shepherd. And He began to teach them many things. [35]And *it* now becoming a late hour, drawing near to Him, the disciples said, The place is desert, and *it is* now a late hour. [36]Send them away, that going away to the surrounding fields and villages they may buy bread for themselves. For they do not have what they may eat. [37]And answering He said to them, You give them *food* to eat. And they said to Him, Going should we buy two hundred denarii of bread, and give them to eat? [38]And He said to them, How many loaves do you have? Go and see. And knowing, they said, Five, and two fish.

[39]And He ordered them all to recline, group *by* group on the green grass. [40]And they sat, group *by* group, by hundred and by fifty.

[41]And taking the five loaves and the two fish, looking up to Heaven, He blessed, and broke the loaves, and gave to His disciples, that they might set before them. And He divided the two fish to all. [42]And all ate, and were satisfied. [43]And they took up twelve handbaskets full *of* fragments; also from the fish. [44]And those eating were about five thousand men.

1492 846 5217 3793 1921 846
33 καὶ εἶδον αὐτοὺς ὑπάγοντας οἱ ὄχλοι, καὶ ἐπέγνωσαν αὐτὸν
And saw them going the crowds, and recognized Him
4183 3979 575 3956 4172 4936 1563
πολλοί, καὶ πεζῇ ἀπὸ πασῶν τῶν πόλεων συνέδραμον ἐκεῖ,
many, and on foot from all the cities ran together there,
4281 846 4905 4314 846
34 καὶ προῆλθον αὐτούς, καὶ συνῆλθον πρὸς αὐτόν. καὶ
and came before them, and came together to Him. And
1831 1492 2424 4183 3793 4697
ἐξελθὼν εἶδεν ὁ Ἰησοῦς πολὺν ὄχλον, καὶ ἐσπλαγχνίσθη
going out saw Jesus a much crowd, and had compassion
1909 846 3754 2258 5613 4263 3361 2192 4166
ἐπ' αὐτοῖς, ὅτι ἦσαν ὡς πρόβατα μὴ ἔχοντα ποιμένα· καὶ
on them, because they were as sheep not having a shepherd. And
756 1321 846 4183 2235 5610 4183
35 ἤρξατο διδάσκειν αὐτοὺς πολλά. καὶ ἤδη ὥρας πολλῆς
He began to teach them many things. And now an hour a much
1096 4334 846 3101 848 3004
γενομένης, προσελθόντες αὐτῷ οἱ μαθηταὶ αὐτοῦ λέγουσιν
occurring drawing near to Him the disciples of Him said,
3754 2048 2076 5119 2235 5610 4183 630
36 ὅτι Ἔρημός ἐστιν ὁ τόπος, καὶ ἤδη ὥρα πολλή· ἀπόλυσον
desert is The place, and now a hour much. Send away
846 2443 565 1519 2945 68 2968
αὐτούς, ἵνα ἀπελθόντες εἰς τοὺς κύκλῳ ἀγροὺς καὶ κώμας
them, that going away to the surrounding fields and village
59 1438 740 5101/1063 5315 3756 2192
ἀγοράσωσιν ἑαυτοῖς ἄρτους. τί γὰρ φάγωσιν οὐκ ἔχουσιν.
they may buy for themselves bread. what For they may eat not they have.
611 2036 846 1325 846 5210 5315
37 ὁ δὲ ἀποκριθεὶς εἶπεν αὐτοῖς, Δότε αὐτοῖς ὑμεῖς φαγεῖν. καὶ
He But answering said to them, Give them you to eat. And
3004 846 565 59 1250 1220
λέγουσιν αὐτῷ, Ἀπελθόντες ἀγοράσωμεν διακοσίων δηνα-
they say to Him, Going, should we buy two hundred de-
740 1325 846 5315 3004 846
38 ρίων ἄρτους, καὶ δῶμεν αὐτοῖς φαγεῖν; ὁ δὲ λέγει αὐτοῖς,
narii of bread, and give them to eat? He And says to them
4214 740 2192 5217 1492 1097
Πόσους ἄρτους ἔχετε; ὑπάγετε καὶ ἴδετε. καὶ γνόντες
How many loaves do you have? Go and see. And knowing
3004 4002 1417 2486 2004 846 347
39 λέγουσι, Πέντε, καὶ δύο ἰχθύας. καὶ ἐπέταξεν αὐτοῖς ἀνα-
they say, Five, and two fish. And He ordered them to
3956 4849 4849 1909 5515 5528
κλῖναι πάντας συμπόσια συμπόσια ἐπὶ τῷ χλωρῷ χόρτῳ.
recline all, companies (by) companies on the green grass.
377 4237 4237 303 1540 303 4004
40 καὶ ἀνέπεσον πρασιαὶ πρασιαί, ἀνὰ ἑκατὸν καὶ ἀνὰ πεντή-
And they sat group (by) group by hundred and by fifty
2983 4002 740 1417 2486
41 κοντα. καὶ λαβὼν τοὺς πέντε ἄρτους καὶ τοὺς δύο ἰχθύας,
And taking the five loaves and the two fish,
308 1519 3772 2127 2622
ἀναβλέψας εἰς τὸν οὐρανόν, εὐλόγησε, καὶ κατέκλασε τοὺς
looking up to Heaven, He blessed, and broke the
740 1325 3101 848 2443 3908
ἄρτους, καὶ ἐδίδου τοῖς μαθηταῖς αὐτοῦ ἵνα παραθῶσιν
loaves, and gave to the disciples of Him, that they may set before
846 1417 2486 3307 3956 5315 3956
42 αὐτοῖς· καὶ τοὺς δύο ἰχθύας ἐμέρισε πᾶσι. καὶ ἔφαγον πάντες,
them. And the two fish He divided to all. And ate all,
5526 142 2801 1427 2894
43 καὶ ἐχορτάσθησαν· καὶ ἦραν κλασμάτων δώδεκα κοφίνους
and were satisfied. And they took fragments, twelve handbaskets
4134 575 2486 2258 5315
44 πλήρεις, καὶ ἀπὸ τῶν ἰχθύων. καὶ ἦσαν οἱ φαγόντες τοὺς
full, and from the fish. And were the (ones) eating the
740 5616 4000 435
ἄρτους ὡσεὶ πεντακισχίλιοι ἄνδρες.
loaves about five thousand men.

45 And at once He constrained His disciples to enter into the boat, and to go before to the other side, to Bethsaida, until He should dismiss the crowd. 46 And taking leave *of* them, He went away to the mountain to pray. 47 And *it* becoming evening, the boat was in *the* middle of the sea, and He alone on the land. 48 And He saw them being distressed in the rowing, for the wind was contrary to them. And *it was* about the fourth watch of the night *when* He came toward them, walking on the sea. And *He* willed to go by them. 49 But seeing Him walking on the sea, they thought *it* to be a ghost. And *they* cried out. 50 For all saw Him, and were troubled. And immediately He spoke to them and said to them, Have courage. I AM! Do not fear. 51 And He went up to them into the boat, and the wind was cut off. And they were amazed, exceedingly beyond measure within themselves, and marveled. 52 For they did not understand *the miracle* of the loaves; for their hearts were hardened.

53 And crossing over, they came into the land of Gennesaret, and drew to shore. 54 And they coming out of the boat, at once knowing Him, 55 they ran around all that neighborhood. *And* they began to carry about those having illness on cots *to* where they heard that He was. 56 And wherever He went into villages or cities or fields, they laid the ailing *ones* in the markets, and begged Him if only they may touch the fringe of His garment. And as many as touched Him were healed.

2112 315 3101 848 1684 1519
45 Καὶ εὐθέως ἠνάγκασε τοὺς μαθητὰς αὐτοῦ ἐμβῆναι εἰς τὸ
And at once He constrained the disciples of Him to enter into the
4143 4254 1519 4008 4314 966 2193
πλοῖον, καὶ προάγειν εἰς τὸ πέραν πρὸς Βηθσαϊδά, ἕως
boat, and to go before to the other side, to Bethsaida, until
846 630 3793 657 846
46 αὐτὸς ἀπολύσῃ τὸν ὄχλον. καὶ ἀποταξάμενος αὐτοῖς,
He should dismiss the crowd. And taking leave (of) them,
565 1519 3735 4336 3798 1096
47 ἀπῆλθεν εἰς τὸ ὄρος προσεύξασθαι. καὶ ὀψίας γενομένης,
He went away to the mountain to pray. And evening occurring,
2258 4143 1722 3319 2281 846 3441 909
ἦν τὸ πλοῖον ἐν μέσῳ τῆς θαλάσσης, καὶ αὐτὸς μόνος ἐπὶ τῆς
was the boat in (the) midst of the sea, and He alone on the
1093 1492 846 928 1722 1643 2258
48 γῆς. καὶ εἶδεν αὐτοὺς βασανιζομένους ἐν τῷ ἐλαύνειν, ἦν
land. And He saw them being distressed in the row(ing), was
1063 417 1727 846 4012 5067 5438 417
γὰρ ὁ ἄνεμος ἐναντίος αὐτοῖς, καὶ περὶ τετάρτην φυλακὴν
for the wind contrary to them, and about (the) fourth watch
3571 2064 4314 846 4043 1909
τῆς νυκτὸς ἔρχεται πρὸς αὐτούς, περιπατῶν ἐπὶ τῆς
of the night He comes toward them, walking on the
2281 2309 3928 846 1492 846
49 θαλάσσης· καὶ ἤθελε παρελθεῖν αὐτούς. οἱ δέ, ἰδόντες αὐτὸν
sea; and willed to go by them. they But, seeing Him
4043 1909 2281 1380 5326 1511
περιπατοῦντα ἐπὶ τῆς θαλάσσης, ἔδοξαν φάντασμα εἶναι,
walking on the sea, thought a ghost (it) to be,
349 3956 1063 846 1492 5015
50 καὶ ἀνέκραξαν· πάντες γὰρ αὐτὸν εἶδον, καὶ ἐταράχθησαν.
and cried out. all For Him saw, and were troubled.
2112 2980 3326 846 3004 846 2293
καὶ εὐθέως ἐλάλησε μετ' αὐτῶν, καὶ λέγει αὐτοῖς, Θαρσεῖτε·
And immediately He spoke with them, and says to them, Have courage,
1473 1510/3361 5399 305 4314 846 1519 4143
51 ἐγώ εἰμι, μὴ φοβεῖσθε. καὶ ἀνέβη πρὸς αὐτοὺς εἰς τὸ πλοῖον,
I AM! Do not fear. And He went up to them into the boat,
2869 417 3029 1537 4053 1722 1438
καὶ ἐκόπασεν ὁ ἄνεμος· καὶ λίαν ἐκ περισσοῦ ἐν ἑαυτοῖς
and was cut the wind. And exceedingly beyond measure in themselves
1839 2296 3756 1063 4920 1909 740
52 ἐξίσταντο, καὶ ἐθαύμαζον. οὐ γὰρ συνῆκαν ἐπὶ τοῖς ἄρτοις·
they were amazed, and marveled. not For they understood by the loaves,
2258 1063 2588 848 4456
ἦν γὰρ ἡ καρδία αὐτῶν πεπωρωμένη.
were for the hearts of them hardened.
1276 2064 1909 1093 1082
53 Καὶ διαπεράσαντες ἦλθον ἐπὶ τὴν γῆν Γεννησαρέτ, καὶ
And crossing over they came onto the land of Gennesaret, and
4358 1831 848 1537 4143
54 προσωρμίσθησαν. καὶ ἐξελθόντων αὐτῶν ἐκ τοῦ πλοίου,
drew to shore. And coming out they out of the boat,
2112 1921 846 4063 3650 4066
55 εὐθέως ἐπιγνόντες αὐτόν, περιδραμόντες ὅλην τὴν περίχω-
at once knowing Him they ran around all neighborhood
1565 756 1909 2895 2560
ρον ἐκείνην, ἤρξαντο ἐπὶ τοῖς κραββάτοις τοὺς κακῶς
that, they began on the cots those illness
2192 4064 3699 191 3754/1563/2076 3699 302
56 ἔχοντας περιφέρειν, ὅπου ἤκουον ὅτι ἐκεῖ ἐστι. καὶ ὅπου ἂν
having to carry about, where they heard that there He is. And wherever
1531 1519 2968 2228/4172/2228 68 1722 58
εἰσεπορεύετο εἰς κώμας ἢ πόλεις ἢ ἀγρούς, ἐν ταῖς ἀγοραῖς
He entered into villages or cities or fields, in the markets
5087 770 3870 846 2443
ἐτίθουν τοὺς ἀσθενοῦντας, καὶ παρεκάλουν αὐτὸν ἵνα κἂν
they laid the ailing (ones), and begged Him that if even
2899 2440 848 680 3745 302
τοῦ κρασπέδου τοῦ ἱματίου αὐτοῦ ἅψωνται· καὶ ὅσοι ἂν
the fringe of the garment of Him they may touch; and as many as

680 846 4982
ἥπτοντο αὐτοῦ ἐσῴζοντο.
touched Him were cured.

CHAPTER 7

[1]And the Pharisees were assembled to Him, also some of the scribes, coming from Jerusalem. [2]And seeing some of His disciples eating bread with unclean hands, that is unwashed *hands,* they found fault. [3]For the Pharisees and all the Jews do not eat unless they wash the hands with *the* fist, holding the tradition of the elders. [4]And *coming* from the market, they do not eat unless they wash themselves. And there are many other things which they received to hold: washings of cups, and of utensils, and of bronze vessels, and couches. [5]Then the Pharisees and scribes questioned Him, Why do your disciples not walk according to the tradition of the elders, but eat bread with unwashed hands? [6]And answering He said to them, Well did Isaiah prophesy concerning you, hypocrites; as it has been written: "This people honors Me with the lips, but their heart is far away from Me; [7]and in vain they worship Me, teaching *as* doctrines *the* commandments of men." [8]For forsaking the commandment bf God, you hold the tradition of men: washings of utensils and cups, and many other such like things you do. [9]And He said to them, Do you *do* well to set aside the commandment of God so that you may keep your tradition? [10]For Moses said, "Honor your father and your mother;" and, "The *one* speaking evil of father

CHAPTER 7

4863 4314 846 5330 5100
1 Καὶ συνάγονται πρὸς αὐτὸν οἱ Φαρισαῖοι, καί τινες τῶν
And were assembled to Him the Pharisees, and some of the
1122 2065 575 2414 1492 5100
2 γραμματέων, ἐλθόντες ἀπὸ Ἱεροσολύμων· καὶ ἰδόντες τινὰς
scribes, coming from Jerusalem. And seeing some
3101 848 2839 5495 = 5123 = 449
τῶν μαθητῶν αὐτοῦ κοιναῖς χερσί, τοῦτ᾿ ἔστιν ἀνίπτοις,
of the disciples of Him with unclean hands, that is unwashed,
2068 740 3201 1063 5330 3956
3 ἐσθίοντας ἄρτους ἐμέμψαντο. οἱ γὰρ Φαρισαῖοι καὶ πάντες
eating bread, they found fault. the For Pharisees and all
2453 =3362 = 4435 3538 5495 3756
οἱ Ἰουδαῖοι, ἐὰν μὴ πυγμῇ νίψωνται τὰς χεῖρας, οὐκ
the Jews unless with (the) fist they wash the hands, not
2068 2902 3862 4245
ἐσθίουσι, κρατοῦντες τὴν παράδοσιν τῶν πρεσβυτέρων·
do they eat, holding the tradition of the elders.
575 58 = 3362= 907 3756 2068
4 καὶ ἀπὸ ἀγορᾶς, ἐὰν μὴ βαπτίσωνται, οὐκ ἐσθίουσι· καὶ
And from market unless they wash themselves, not they eat, and
243 4183 2076 3739 3880 2902 909
ἄλλα πολλά ἐστιν ἃ παρέλαβον κρατεῖν, βαπτισμοὺς
other things many there are which they received to hold, washings
4221 3582 5473 2825 1899
5 ποτηρίων καὶ ξεστῶν καὶ χαλκίων καὶ κλινῶν. ἔπειτα
of cups and of utensils and of bronze vessels and couches. Then
1905 846 5330 1122 1302
ἐπερωτῶσιν αὐτὸν οἱ Φαρισαῖοι καὶ οἱ γραμματεῖς, Διατί οἱ
question Him the Pharisees and the scribes, Why the
3101 4675 3756 4043 2596 3862
μαθηταί σου οὐ περιπατοῦσι κατὰ τὴν παράδοσιν τῶν
disciples of you not walk according to the tradition of the
4245 235 449 5495 2098 740
πρεσβυτέρων, ἀλλὰ ἀνίπτοις χερσὶν ἐσθίουσι τὸν ἄρτον;
elders, but with unwashed hands eat the bread?
611 2036 846 3754 2573 4395
6 ὁ δὲ ἀποκριθεὶς εἶπεν αὐτοῖς ὅτι Καλῶς προεφήτευσεν
He And answering said to them, Well prophesied
2268 4012 5216 5273 5613 1125 3778
Ἠσαΐας περὶ ὑμῶν τῶν ὑποκριτῶν, ὡς γέγραπται, Οὗτος ὁ
Isaiah concerning you, hypocrites, as it has been written, This
2992 5491 3165/5091 2588 848 4206 568
λαὸς τοῖς χείλεσί με τιμᾷ, ἡ δὲ καρδία αὐτῶν πόρρω ἀπέχει
people with the lips Me honors, the but heart of them far is away
575 1700 3155 4576 3165 1321 1319
7 ἀπ᾿ ἐμοῦ. μάτην δὲ σέβονταί με, διδάσκοντες διδασκαλίας
from Me; in vain and they worship Me, teaching (as) teachings
1778 444 863 1063 1785 2316
8 ἐντάλματα ἀνθρώπων. ἀφέντες γὰρ τὴν ἐντολὴν τοῦ Θεοῦ,
commandments of men. forsaking For the commandment – of God,
2902 3862 444 909
κρατεῖτε τὴν παράδοσιν τῶν ἀνθρώπων, βαπτισμοὺς
you hold the tradition – of men washings
3582 4221 243 3946 5108 4183
ξεστῶν καὶ ποτηρίων· καὶ ἄλλα παρόμοια τοιαῦτα πολλὰ
of utensils and cups and other like things such many
4160 3004 846 2573 114 1785
9 ποιεῖτε. καὶ ἔλεγεν αὐτοῖς, Καλῶς ἀθετεῖτε τὴν ἐντολὴν τοῦ
you do. And He said to them, Well do you set aside the commandment
2316 2443 3862 4216 5083 3475 1063 2036
10 Θεοῦ, ἵνα τὴν παράδοσιν ὑμῶν τηρήσητε. Μωσῆς γὰρ εἶπε,
of God, that the tradition of you you may keep. Moses For said,
5091 3962 4675 3384 4675 2551
Τίμα τὸν πατέρα σου καὶ τὴν μητέρα σου· καί, Ὁ κακολογῶν
Honor the father of you and the mother of you, and, He speaking evil

or mother, let him expire by death." [11]But you say, If a man says to *his* father or mother, Corban, which is; A gift!—whatever you may profit by me. [12]And you no longer allow him to do anything for his father or his mother, [13]making the word of God of no effect by your tradition which you delivered. And many such like things you do.

[14]And calling all the crowd near, He said to them, All hear Me, and understand. [15]There is nothing from outside the man which entering into him which is able to defile *him*. But the things going out from him, those are the things defiling the man.

[16]If anyone has ears to hear, let him hear.

[17]And when He entered into a house from the crowd, His disciples questioned Him about the parable. [18]And He said to them, Are you also so undiscerning? Do you not perceive that all that enters from the outside into the man is not able to defile him? [19]*This is* because it does not enter into his heart, but into the belly, and goes out into the wastebowl, purging all the foods. [20]And He said, That passing out of the man, *it is* that defiles the man. [21]For from within, out of the heart of men, pass out the evil thoughts, adulteries, fornications, murders, [22]thefts, greedy desires, iniquities, deceit, lustful desires, a wicked eye, blasphemy, pride, foolishness—[23]all these evil things pass out from within and defile the man.

3962 2228 3384 2288 5053 5210 3004 1437
11 πατέρα ἢ μητέρα θανάτῳ τελευτάτω· ὑμεῖς δὲ λέγετε, Ἐὰν
of father or mother by death let him end. you But say, If
2036 444 3962 2228 3384 2878 3603 2076
εἴπῃ ἄνθρωπος τῷ πατρὶ ἢ τῇ μητρί, Κορβᾶν, ὅ ἐστι,
says a man to the father or to the mother, Corban– which is,
1435 1437/1537/1700 5623 3765 863 846
12 δῶρον, ὃ ἐὰν ἐξ ἐμοῦ ὠφεληθῇς· καὶ οὐκέτι ἀφίετε αὐτὸν
A gift – whatever by me you might profit;and no longer you allow him
3762 4160 3962 848 2228 3384 848 208
13 οὐδὲν ποιῆσαι τῷ πατρὶ αὐτοῦ ἢ τῇ μητρὶ αὐτοῦ, ἀκυ-
nothing to do for the father of him or the mother of him, making
3056 2316 3862 5216 3739 3860
ροῦντες τὸν λόγον τοῦ Θεοῦ τῇ παραδόσει ὑμῶν ᾗ παρεδώ-
void the word – of God by the tradition of you which you
3946 5108 4183 4160 4341
14 κατε· καὶ παρόμοια τοιαῦτα πολλὰ ποιεῖτε. καὶ προσκαλε-
delivered. And like things such many you do. And calling near
3956 3793 3004 846 191 3450
σάμενος πάντα τὸν ὄχλον, ἔλεγεν αὐτοῖς, Ἀκούετέ μου
(Him) all the crowd, He said to them, Hear Me
3956 4920 3762 2076 1855 444
15 πάντες, καὶ συνίετε. οὐδέν ἐστιν ἔξωθεν τοῦ ἀνθρώπου
all, and understand. nothing There is from outside the man
1531 1519 846 3739 1410 846 2840 235
εἰσπορευόμενον εἰς αὐτόν, ὃ δύναται αὐτὸν κοινῶσαι· ἀλλὰ
having entered into him which is able him to profane; but
1607 575 846 1565 2076 2840
τὰ ἐκπορευόμενα ἀπ' αὐτοῦ, ἐκεῖνά ἐστι τὰ κοινοῦντα τὸν
the things going out from him, those are the things profaning the
444 =1536=/2192/3715/ 191 191 3753 1525
16 ἄνθρωπον. εἴ τις ἔχει ὦτα ἀκούειν ἀκουέτω. καὶ ὅτε εἰσῆλθεν
17 man. If anyone has ears to hear, let him hear. And when He entered
1519 3624 575 3793 1905 846 3101
εἰς οἶκον ἀπὸ τοῦ ὄχλου, ἐπηρώτων αὐτὸν οἱ μαθηταὶ
into a house from the crowd, questioned Him the disciples
848 4012 3850 3004 846 3779
18 αὐτοῦ περὶ τῆς παραβολῆς. καὶ λέγει αὐτοῖς, Οὕτω καὶ
of Him about the parable. And He says to them, Thus also
5210 801 2075/3756/3539/3754/3956 1855 1531
ὑμεῖς ἀσύνετοί ἐστε ; οὐ νοεῖτε ὅτι πᾶν τὸ ἔξωθεν εἰσπορευό-
you undiscerning are? Not perceive you that all that from outside enter-
1519 444 3756 1410 846 2840 3754
19 μενον εἰς τὸν ἄνθρωπον οὐ δύναται αὐτὸν κοινῶσαι, ὅτι
ing into man not is able him to profane because
3756 1531 846 1519 2588 235 1519
οὐκ εἰσπορεύεται αὐτοῦ εἰς τὴν καρδίαν, ἀλλ' εἰς τὴν
not it does enter of him into the heart, but into the
2836 1519 856 1607 2511
κοιλίαν· καὶ εἰς τὸν ἀφεδρῶνα ἐκπορεύεται, καθαρίζον
belly, and into the waste-bowl goes out, purging
3956 1033 3004 3754 1537 444
20 πάντα τὰ βρώματα. ἔλεγε δὲ ὅτι Τὸ ἐκ τοῦ ἀνθρώπου
all the foods? He said And, That out of the man
1607 1565 2840 444 2081 1063
21 ἐκπορευόμενον, ἐκεῖνο κοινοῖ τὸν ἄνθρωπον. ἔσωθεν γάρ,
having passed out, that profanes the man. from within For,
1537 2588 444 1261 2556
ἐκ τῆς καρδίας τῶν ἀνθρώπων, οἱ διαλογισμοὶ οἱ κακοὶ
out of the heart of men the thoughts evil
1607 3430 4202 5408 2829 4124
22 ἐκπορεύονται, μοιχεῖαι, πορνεῖαι, φόνοι, κλοπαί, πλεονεξίαι,
pass out, adulteries, fornications, murders, thefts, greedy desires,
4189 1388 766 3788 4190 988
πονηρίαι, δόλος, ἀσέλγεια, ὀφθαλμὸς πονηρός, βλασφημία,
iniquities, deceit, lustful desires, an eye wicked, blasphemy,
5243 877 3956 5023 4190 2081
23 ὑπερηφανία, ἀφροσύνη· πάντα ταῦτα τὰ πονηρὰ ἔσωθεν
pride, foolishness — all these evil things from within
1607 2840 444
ἐκπορεύεται, καὶ κοινοῖ τὸν ἄνθρωπον.
pass out and profane the man.

[24]And rising up from there, He went away into the borders of Tyre and Sidon. And entering into the house, He desired no one to know. But He could not be hidden. [25]But hearing about Him, a woman came up, *(one* whose daughter had an unclean spirit. *And she* fell down at His feet. [26]And the woman was a Greek, a Syrophoenician by race. And she asked Him, that He would cast out the demon from her daughter. [27]And Jesus said to her, First, allow the children to be satisfied; for it is not good to take the children's bread and to throw *it* to the dogs. [28]But she answered and said to Him, Yes, Lord; for even the dogs under the table eat from the crumbs of the children. [29]And He said to her, Because of this word, go. The demon has gone out from your daughter. [30]And going away to her house, she found the demon had gone out, and *her* daughter was laid on the couch.

[31]And again going out from the borders of Tyre and Sidon, He came to the Sea of Galilee, in the midst of the borders of *the* Decapolis. [32]And they brought a deaf one to Him, hardly speaking. And they begged Him, that He put *His* hand on him. [33]And taking him away, apart from the crowd, He put His fingers into his ears; and spitting, He touched his tongue; [34]and looking up into Heaven, He groaned, and said to him, Ephphatha! which is, Be opened! [35]And instantly his ears were opened, and the bond of his tongue was loosened, and

1564 450 565 1519 3181 5184
24 Καὶ ἐκεῖθεν ἀναστὰς ἀπῆλθεν εἰς τὰ μεθόρια Τύρου καὶ
And from there rising up He went away into the borders of Tyre and
4605 1525 1519 3614 3762 2309 1097
Σιδῶνος. καὶ εἰσελθὼν εἰς τὴν οἰκίαν, οὐδένα ἤθελε γνῶναι,
Sidon. And entering into the house, no one He desired to know.
3756 1410 2990 191 1063 1135 4012 846
25 καὶ οὐκ ἠδυνήθη λαθεῖν. ἀκούσασα γὰρ γυνὴ περὶ αὐτοῦ,
But not He could be hidden. hearing For a woman about Him,
3739/2192 2365 848 4151 169 2064
ἧς εἶχε τὸ θυγάτριον αὐτῆς πνεῦμα ἀκάθαρτον, ἐλθοῦσα
of whom had the daughter of her a spirit unclean, coming
4363 4314 4228 848 2258 1135 1674
26 προσέπεσε πρὸς τοὺς πόδας αὐτοῦ· ἦν δὲ ἡ γυνὴ Ἑλληνίς,
fell down to the feet of Him; was and the woman a Greek,
4949 1085 2065 848 2443 1140
Συροφοίνισσα τῷ γένει· καὶ ἠρώτα αὐτὸν ἵνα τὸ δαιμόνιον
a Syrophoenician by race. And she asked Him that the demon
1544 1537 2364 848 2424 2036 846
27 ἐκβάλλῃ ἐκ τῆς θυγατρὸς αὐτῆς. ὁ δὲ Ἰησοῦς εἶπεν αὐτῇ,
He would expel from the daughter of her. And Jesus said to her,
863 4412 5526 5043 3756 1063 2570 2076
Ἄφες πρῶτον χορτασθῆναι τὰ τέκνα· οὐ γάρ καλόν ἐστι
Allow first to be satisifed the children; not for good is
2983 740 5043 906 2952
28 λαβεῖν τὸν ἄρτον τῶν τέκνων καὶ βαλεῖν τοις κυναρίοις. ἡ
to take the bread of the children and to throw to the dogs. she
611 3004 846 3483 2962 1063 2952
δὲ ἀπεκρίθη καὶ λέγει αὐτῷ, Ναί, Κύριε· καὶ γὰρ τὰ κυνάρια
And answered and says to Him, Yes, Lord; even for the dogs
5270 5132 2068 575 5589 3813
ὑποκάτω τῆς τραπέζης ἐσθίει ἀπὸ τῶν ψιχίων τῶν παιδίων.
under the table eat from the crumbs of the children.
2036 846 1223 5126 3056 5217 1831
29 καὶ εἶπεν αὐτῇ, Διὰ τοῦτον τὸν λόγον ὕπαγε· ἐξελήλυθε τὸ
And He said to her, Because of this word, go; has gone out the
1140 1537 2364 4675 565 1519 3624
30 δαιμόνιον ἐκ τῆς θυγατρός σου. καὶ ἀπελθοῦσα εἰς τὸν οἶκον
demon from the daughter of you. And going away to the house
848 2147 1140 1831 2364
αὐτῆς, εὗρε τὸ δαιμόνιον ἐξεληλυθός, καὶ τὴν θυγατέρα
of her, she found the demon had gone out, and the daughter
906 1909 2825
βεβλημένην ἐπὶ τῆς κλίνης.
was laid on the couch.
3825 1831 1537 3725 5184 4605 2064
31 Καὶ πάλιν ἐξελθὼν ἐκ τῶν ὁρίων Τύρου καὶ Σιδῶνος, ἦλθε
And again going out from the borders of Tyre and Sidon, He came
4314 2281 1056 303 3319 3725
πρὸς τὴν θάλασσαν τῆς Γαλιλαίας, ἀνὰ μέσον τῶν ὁρίων
to the sea — of Galilee in the midst of the borders
1179 5342 846 2974 3424
32 Δεκαπόλεως. καὶ φέρουσιν αὐτῷ κωφὸν μογιλάλον, καὶ
of (the) Decapolis. And they bring to Him a deaf one, hardly speaking, and
3870 846 2443 2007 846 5495 618
33 παρακαλοῦσιν αὐτὸν ἵνα ἐπιθῇ αὐτῷ τὴν χεῖρα. καὶ ἀπολα-
they begged Him that He put on him the hand. And taking
846 575 3793 2398 906 1147
βόμενος αὐτὸν ἀπὸ τοῦ ὄχλου κατ' ἰδίαν, ἔβαλε τοὺς δα-
away him from the crowd, privately He put the
848/1519 3775 848 4429 680
κτύλους αὐτοῦ εἰς τὰ ὦτα αὐτοῦ, καὶ πτύσας ἥψατο τῆς
fingers of Him into the ears of him, and spitting He touched the
1100 848 308 1519 3772 4727
34 γλώσσης αὐτοῦ, καὶ ἀναβλέψας εἰς τὸν οὐρανόν, ἐστέναξε,
tongue of him, and looking up into — Heaven, He groaned,
3004 846 2188 2076 1272 2112
35 καὶ λέγει αὐτῷ, Ἐφφαθά, ὅ ἐστι, Διανοίχθητι. καὶ εὐθέως
and says **to him, Ephphatha, which is, Be opened! And instantly**
1272 848 189 3089 1199 1100
διηνοίχθησαν αὐτοῦ αἱ ἀκοαί· καὶ ἐλύθη ὁ δεσμὸς τῆς γλώσ-
were opened of him the ears, and was loosened the bond of the tongue

he spoke correctly. 36 And He ordered them, that they should tell no one. But as much as He ordered them, much more abundantly they proclaimed. 37 And they were most exceedingly amazed, saying, He has done all things well. He makes even the deaf to hear, and the dumb to speak.

CHAPTER 8

1 The crowd being very great in those days, and not having anything they may eat, Jesus calling His disciples near, He said to them, 2 I have pity on the crowd, because now three days they remain with Me, and they do not have what they may eat. 3 And if I send them away fasting to their house, they will faint in the way, for some of them come from afar. 4 And His disciples answered Him, From where will anyone here be able to satisfy these *with* bread on a desert?

5 And He asked them, How many loaves do you have? And they said, Seven. 6 And He ordered the crowd to recline on the ground. And taking the seven loaves, giving thanks, He broke and gave to His disciples, that they might serve. And they served the crowd. 7 And they had a few fish. And blessing, He said *for* these also to be served. 8 And they ate, and were satisfied. And *they* took up over and above seven lunch-baskets *of* fragments. 9 And those eating were about four thousand. And He sent them away. 10 And at once entering into the boat with His disciples, He came into the region of Dalmanutha.

848 2980 3723 1291 846 2443
36 σης αὐτοῦ, καὶ ἐλάλει ὀρθῶς. καὶ διεστείλατο αὐτοῖς ἵνα
of him, and He spoke correctly. And He ordered them that
3367 2036 3745 846 846 1291 3123
μηδενὶ εἴπωσιν· ὅσον δὲ αὐτὸς αὐτοῖς διεστέλλετο, μᾶλλον
no one they should tell; as much as but He them ordered, much
4054 2784 5249 1605
37 περισσότερον ἐκήρυσσον. καὶ ὑπερπερισσῶς ἐξεπλήσσοντο,
more abundantly they proclaimed. And most exceedingly they were amazed.
3004 2573 3956 4160 2974 4160
λέγοντες, Καλῶς πάντα πεποίηκε· καὶ τοὺς κωφοὺς ποιεῖ
saying, Well all things He has done, even the deaf He makes
191 216 2980
ἀκούειν, καὶ τοὺς ἀλάλους λαλεῖν.
to hear, and the dumb to speak.

CHAPTER 8

1722 1565 2250 3827 3793 5607
1 Ἐν ἐκείναις ταῖς ἡμέραις, παμπόλλου ὄχλου ὄντος, καὶ
In those days very great the crowd being, and
3361 2192 5101 5315 4341 2424
μὴ ἐχόντων τί φάγωσι, προσκαλεσάμενος ὁ Ἰησοῦς τοὺς
not having anything they may eat, having called near Jesus the
3101 848 3004 846 4697 1909 3793
2 μαθητὰς αὐτοῦ λέγει αὐτοῖς, Σπλαγχνίζομαι ἐπὶ τὸν ὄχλον·
disciples of Him, He says to them, I have pity on the crowd
3754/2235/ 2250 5140 4357 3427 3756 2192 5100
ὅτι ἤδη ἡμέρας τρεῖς προσμένουσί μοι, καὶ οὐκ ἔχουσι τί
because now days three they continue with Me, and not have what
5315 1437 630 846 3523 1519 3624 848
3 φάγωσι· καὶ ἐὰν ἀπολύσω αὐτοὺς νήστεις εἰς οἶκον αὐτῶν,
they may eat; and if I send away them fasting to (the) house of them,
1590 1722 3598 5100 1063 846 3113 2240
ἐκλυθήσονται ἐν τῇ ὁδῷ· τινὲς γὰρ αὐτῶν μακρόθεν ἥκασι.
they will faint in the way; some for of them from afar are come.
611 846 3101 848 4159 5128
4 καὶ ἀπεκρίθησαν αὐτῷ οἱ μαθηταὶ αὐτοῦ, Πόθεν τούτους
And answered Him the disciples of Him, From where these
1410 5100 5602 5526 740 1909 2047
δυνήσεταί τις ὧδε χορτάσαι ἄρτων ἐπ' ἐρημίας; καὶ
will be able anyone here to satisfy (with) bread on a desert? And
1908 846 4214 2192 740 2036 2033
5 ἐπηρώτα αὐτούς, Πόσους ἔχετε ἄρτους; οἱ δὲ εἶπον, Ἑπτά.
He asked them, How many have you loaves? they And said, Seven.
3853 3793 377 1909 1093 2983
6 καὶ παρήγγειλε τῷ ὄχλῳ ἀναπεσεῖν ἐπὶ τῆς γῆς· καὶ λαβὼν
And he ordered the crowd to recline on the ground. And taking
2033 740 2168 2806 1325
τοὺς ἑπτὰ ἄρτους, εὐχαριστήσας ἔκλασε καὶ ἐδίδου τοῖς
the seven loaves, giving thanks, He broke and gave to the
3101 848 2443 3908 3908 3793
μαθηταῖς αὐτοῦ, ἵνα παραθῶσι· καὶ παρέθηκαν τῷ ὄχλῳ.
disciples of Him, that they may serve. And they served the crowd
2192 2485 3641 2127 2036 3908
7 καὶ εἶχον ἰχθύδια ὀλίγα· καὶ εὐλογήσας εἶπε παραθεῖναι καὶ
And they had fish a few. And blessing He said to be served also
846 5315 5526 142 4051
8 αὐτά. ἔφαγον δέ, καὶ ἐχορτάσθησαν· καὶ ἦραν περισσεύματα
these. they ate And, and were satisfied, and took up over and above
2801 2033 4711 2258 5315 5613
9 κλασμάτων ἑπτὰ σπυρίδας. ἦσαν δὲ οἱ φαγόντες ὡς
fragments, seven baskets, were And those eating about
5070 630 846 2112 1684 1519
10 τετρακισχίλιοι· καὶ ἀπέλυσεν αὐτούς. καὶ εὐθέως ἐμβὰς εἰς
four thousand. And He sent away them. And at once entering into
4143 3326 3101 848 2064 1519 3313
τὸ πλοῖον μετὰ τῶν μαθητῶν αὐτοῦ, ἦλθεν εἰς τὰ μέρη
the boat with the disciples of Him, He came into the region
1148
Δαλμανουθά.
of Dalmanutha.

[11]And the Pharisees went out and began to argue with Him, seeking from Him a sign from Heaven, tempting Him. [12]And groaning in His spirit, He said, Why does this generation seek a sign? Truly I say to you, *As* if this generation will be given a sign! [13]And leaving them, again entering into the boat, He went away to the other side.

[14]And the disciples forgot to take loaves. And they did not have *any* with them, except one loaf in the boat. [15]And He charged them, saying, See! Beware of the leaven of the Pharisees, and of the leaven of Herod. [16]And they reasoned with one another, saying, Because we have no loaves. [17]And knowing, Jesus said to them, Why do you reason because you have no loaves? Do you not yet perceive nor realize? Have you still hardened your heart? [18]Having eyes, do you not see? And having ears, do you not hear? And do you not remember?

[19]When I broke the five loaves to the five thousand, how many handbaskets full of fragments did you take up? They said to Him, Twelve. [20]And when the seven to the four thousand, how many lunchbaskets did you take up *with the* fillings of fragments? And they said, Seven. [21]And He said to them, How do you not understand?

[22]And He came to Bethsaida. And they carried a blind one to Him, and begged Him that He would touch him. [23]And laying hold of the blind one's hand, He led him forth outside the village. And spitting into his eyes, laying *His* hands on him, He asked

1831 5330 756 4802 846
11 Καὶ ἐξῆλθον οἱ Φαρισαῖοι, καὶ ἤρξαντο συζητεῖν αὐτῷ,
And went out the Pharisees and began to argue with Him,
2212 3844 846 4592 575 3772 3985
ζητοῦντες παρ' αὐτοῦ σημεῖον ἀπὸ τοῦ οὐρανοῦ, πειρά-
seeking from Him a sign from Heaven, tempting
846 389 4151 848 3004
12 ζοντες αὐτόν. καὶ ἀναστενάξας τῷ πνεύματι αὐτοῦ λέγει,
Him And groaning in the spirit of Him, He says,
5101 1074 3778 4592 1934 281 3004 5213 1487
Τί ἡ γενεὰ αὕτη σημεῖον ἐπιζητεῖ; ἀμὴν λέγω ὑμῖν, εἰ
Why generation this a sign! seeks? Truly I say to you, (As) if
1325 1074 5026 4592 863 846 1684
13 δοθήσεται τῇ γενεᾷ ταυτῃ σημεῖον. καὶ ἀφεὶς αὐτούς, ἐμβὰς
will be given generation this a sign! And leaving them, entering
4172/1519 4143 565 1519 4008
πάλιν εἰς τὸ πλοῖον, ἀπῆλθεν εἰς τὸ πέραν.
again into the boat, He went away to the other side.
1950 3101 2983 740 =1508=1520
14 Καὶ ἐπελάθοντο οἱ μαθηταὶ λαβεῖν ἄρτους, καὶ εἰ μὴ ἕνα
And forgot the disciples to take loaves, and except one
740 3756 2192 3326 1438 1722 4143 1291
15 ἄρτον οὐκ εἶχον μεθ' ἑαυτῶν ἐν τῷ πλοίῳ. καὶ διεστέλλετο
loaf not they had with them in the boat. And He charged
846 3004 3708 991 575 2219
αὐτοῖς, λέγων, Ὁρᾶτε, βλέπετε ἀπὸ τῆς ζύμης τῶν
them, saying, See, Look out! From the leaven of the
5330 2219 2264 1260 4314
16 Φαρισαίων καὶ τῆς ζύμης Ἡρώδου. καὶ διελογίζοντο πρὸς
Pharisees, and of the leaven of Herod. And they reasoned with
240 3004 3754 740 3756 2192 1097
17 ἀλλήλους, λέγοντες ὅτι Ἄρτους οὐκ ἔχομεν. καὶ γνοὺς ὁ
one another, saying, Because Loaves not we have. And knowing
2424 3004 846 5101 1260 3754 740 3756 2192
Ἰησοῦς λέγει αὐτοῖς, Τί διαλογίζεσθε ὅτι ἄρτους οὐκ ἔχετε;
Jesus says to them, Why do you reason because loaves not you have?
3768 3539 3761 4920 2089 4456 2192
οὔπω νοεῖτε, οὐδὲ συνίετε; ἔτι πεπωρωμένην ἔχετε τὴν
not yet Do you perceive nor realize? yet hardened have you the
2588 5216 3788 2192 3756 991 3775
18 καρδίαν ὑμῶν; ὀφθαλμοὺς ἔχοντες οὐ βλέπετε: καὶ ὦτα
heart of you? eyes having, not do you see? And ears
2192 3756 191 3756 3421 3753 4002
19 ἔχοντες οὐκ ἀκούετε; καὶ οὐ μνημονεύετε; ὅτε τοὺς πέντε
having, not do you hear? And not do you remember when the five
740 2806 1519 4000 4214 2894
ἄρτους ἔκλασα εἰς τοὺς πεντακισχιλίους, πόσους κοφίνους
loaves I broke to the five thousand, how many handbaskets
4134 2801 142 3004 846 1427 3753
20 πλήρεις κλασμάτων ἤρατε; λέγουσιν αὐτῷ, Δώδεκα. Ὅτε
full of fragments you took? They say to Him, Twelve. when
2033 1519 5070 4214 479
δὲ τοὺς ἑπτὰ εἰς τοὺς τετρακισχιλίους, πόσων σπυρίδων
And the seven to the four thousand, of how many baskets
4138 2801 142 2036 2033
21 πληρώματα κλασμάτων ἤρατε; οἱ δὲ εἶπον, Ἑπτά. καὶ
(the) fillings of fragments you took? they And said, Seven. And
3004 846 4459 3756 4920
ἔλεγεν αὐτοῖς, Πῶς οὐ συνίετε;
He said to them, How not do you understand?
2064 1519 966 5342 846 5185
22 Καὶ ἔρχεται εἰς Βηθσαϊδά. καὶ φέρουσιν αὐτῷ τυφλόν,
And He comes to Bethsaida. And they bear to Him a blind one,
2870 846 2443 846 680 1949
23 καὶ παρακαλοῦσιν αὐτὸν ἵνα αὐτοῦ ἅψηται. καὶ ἐπιλαβό-
and beg Him that him He would touch. And laying
5495 5185 1806 846 1854
μενος τῆς χειρὸς τοῦ τυφλοῦ, ἐξήγαγεν αὐτὸν ἔξω τῆς
hold of the hand of the blind one, He led forth him outside the
2768 4429 1519 3659 848 2007 5495
κώμης· καὶ πτύσας εἰς τὰ ὄμματα αὐτοῦ, ἐπιθεὶς τὰς χεῖρας
village. And having spit into the eyes of him, having laid the hands

him if he saw anything. [24]And looking, he said, I see men as trees walking. [25]Then He placed *His* hands on his eyes again, and made him look up. And he was restored, and saw all clearly. [26]And He sent him to his house, saying, You may not go into the village, nor may tell anyone in the village.

[27]And Jesus and His disciples went out to the villages of Caesarea of Philip. And in the way He questioned His disciples, saying to them, Whom do men say Me to be? [28]And they answered, John the Baptist; and others *say* Elijah; but others, one of the prophets. [29]And He said to them, And you, whom do you say Me to be? And answering Peter said to Him, You are the Christ. [30]And He warned them that they may tell no one about Him. [31]And He began to teach them that it is necessary for the Son of man to suffer many things, and to be rejected of the elders and chief priests and scribes, and to be killed, and after three days to rise again. [32]And He spoke the word openly. And taking Him aside, Peter began to rebuke Him. [33]But turning around and seeing His disciples, He rebuked Peter, saying, Go behind Me, Satan, because you do not mind the things of God, but the things of men.

[34]And calling near the crowd with His disciples, he said to them, Whoever desires to come after Me,

846 1905 846 =1536= 991 308 3004
24 αὐτῷ, ἐπηρώτα αὐτὸν εἴ τι βλέπει. καὶ ἀναβλέψας ἔλεγε,
on him, He asked him if anything he sees. And looking, he said,
991 444 3754 1186 4043 1534
25 Βλέπω τοὺς ἀνθρώπους ὡς δένδρα περιπατοῦντας. εἶτα
I see men, as trees walking. Then
3825 2007 5495 1909 3788 848
πάλιν ἐπέθηκε τὰς χεῖρας ἐπὶ τοὺς ὀφθαλμοὺς αὐτοῦ, καὶ
again He placed the hands upon the eyes of him, and
4160 846 308 600 1689
ἐποίησεν αὐτὸν ἀναβλέψαι. καὶ ἀποκατεστάθη, καὶ ἐνέβλεψε
made him look up. And he was restored, and saw
5081 537 649 846 1519 3624
26 τηλαυγῶς ἅπαντας. καὶ ἀπέστειλεν αὐτὸν εἰς τὸν οἶκον
clearly all And He sent him to the house
848 3004 3366 1519 2968 1525 3366 2036
αὐτοῦ, λέγων, Μηδὲ εἰς τὴν κώμην εἰσέλθῃς, μηδὲ εἴπῃς
of him, saying, Not into the village you may go in, nor may tell
5100/1722 2968
τινὶ ἐν τῇ κώμῃ.
anyone in the village.

1831 2424 3101 848 1519
27 Καὶ ἐξῆλθεν ὁ Ἰησοῦς καὶ οἱ μαθηταὶ αὐτοῦ εἰς τὰς
And went out Jesus and the disciples of Him to the
2968 2542 5376 1722 3598 1905
κώμας Καισαρείας τῆς Φιλίππου· καὶ ἐν τῇ ὁδῷ ἐπηρώτα
villages of Caesarea of Philip. And in the way He questioned
3101 848 3004 846 5101 3165 3004
τοὺς μαθητὰς αὐτοῦ, λέγων αὐτοῖς, Τίνα με λέγουσιν οἱ
the disciples of Him, saying to them, Whom me say the
444 1511 611 2491 910
28 ἄνθρωποι εἶναι; οἱ δὲ ἀπεκρίθησαν, Ἰωάννην τὸν Βαπτι-
men to be? they And answered, John the Baptist;
243 2243 243 1520 4396
29 στήν· καὶ ἄλλοι Ἠλίαν, ἄλλοι δὲ ἕνα τῶν προφητῶν. καὶ
and others Elijah; others but, one of the prophets. And
846 3004 846 5210 5101/3165/3004 1511 611
αὐτὸς λέγει αὐτοῖς, Ὑμεῖς δὲ τίνα με λέγετε εἶναι; ἀποκριθεὶς
He says to them, you And, whom Me say you to be? answering
4074 3004 846 4771/1488 5547 2008
30 δὲ ὁ Πέτρος λέγει αὐτῷ, Σὺ εἶ ὁ Χριστός. καὶ ἐπετίμησεν
And Peter says to Him, You are the Christ! And He warned
846 2443 3367 3004 4012 846 356 1321
31 αὐτοῖς, ἵνα μηδενὶ λέγωσι περὶ αὐτοῦ. καὶ ἤρξατο διδάσκειν
them, that no one they may tell about Him. And He began to teach
846 3754 1163 5207 444 4183 3958
αὐτούς, ὅτι δεῖ τὸν υἱὸν τοῦ ἀνθρώπου πολλὰ παθεῖν, καὶ
them that it behoves the Son of man many things to suffer, and
593 575 4245 749
ἀποδοκιμασθῆναι ἀπὸ τῶν πρεσβυτέρων καὶ ἀρχιερέων καὶ
to be rejected of the elders and chief priests and
1122 615 3326 5140 2250
γραμματέων, καὶ ἀποκτανθῆναι, καὶ μετὰ τρεῖς ἡμέρας
scribes, and to be killed, and after three days
450 3954 3056 2980 4355
32 ἀναστῆναι· καὶ παρρησίᾳ τὸν λόγον ἐλάλει. καὶ προσλαβό-
to rise again. And openly the word He spoke. And taking aside
846 4074 756 2008 846 1994
33 μενος αὐτὸν ὁ Πέτρος ἤρξατο ἐπιτιμᾷν αὐτῷ. ὁ δὲ ἐπιστρα-
Him, — Peter began to rebuke Him. He But turning
1492 3101 848 2008 4074
φεὶς, καὶ ἰδὼν τοὺς μαθητὰς αὐτοῦ, ἐπετίμησε τῷ Πέτρῳ,
around and seeing the disciples of Him rebuked Peter,
3004 5217 3694 3450 4567 3754/3756 5426
λέγων, Ὕπαγε ὀπίσω μου, Σατανᾶ· ὅτι οὐ φρονεῖς τὰ τοῦ
saying, Get behind Me, Satan, because not you mind the things
2316 235 444 4341
34 Θεοῦ, ἀλλὰ τὰ τῶν ἀνθρώπων. καὶ προσκαλεσάμενος τὸν
of God, but the things of men. And calling near the
3793 4862 3101 848 2036 846 3748 2309
ὄχλον σὺν τοῖς μαθηταῖς αὐτοῦ, εἶπεν αὐτοῖς, Ὅστις θέλει
crowd with the disciples of Him, He said to them, Whoever desires

let him deny himself and take his cross, and let him follow Me. [35]For whoever desires to save his soul, *he* shall lose it. But whoever shall lose his soul for My sake and the gospel, that one shall save it. [36]For what shall it profit a man if he gain the whole world, yet damage his soul? [37]Or what shall a man give *as* an exchange *for* his soul?

[38]For whoever may be ashamed of Me and My words in this adulterous and sinful generation, the Son of man will also be ashamed of him when He comes in the glory of His Father, along with the holy angels.

CHAPTER 9

[1]And He said to them, Truly I say to you, There are some of those standing here who in no way shall taste of death until they see the kingdom of God coming in power.

[2]And after six days Jesus takes along Peter and James and John, and carries them into a high mount apart, alone. And He was transfigured before them. [3]And His garments became shining, very white like snow, such as a fuller on earth is not able to whiten. [4]And Elijah with Moses was seen by them, and they were speaking with Jesus. [5]And answering Peter said to Jesus, Rabbi, it is good *for* us to be here; and, Let us make three tabernacles, one for You, and one for Moses, and one for Elijah. [6]For he did not know what to say,

3694 3450 2064 533 1438 142
ὀπίσω μου ἐλθεῖν, ἀπαρνησάσθω ἑαυτόν, καὶ ἀράτω τὸν
after Me to come, let him deny himself and take the
4716 848 190 3427/3739/1063/302/2309
35 σταυρὸν αὐτοῦ, καὶ ἀκολουθείτω μοι. ὃς γὰρ ἂν θέλῃ τὴν
cross of him, and let him follow Me. who For ever desires the
5590 848 4982 622 846 3739/ 302/ 622
ψυχὴν αὐτοῦ σῶσαι, ἀπολέσει αὐτήν· ὃς δ' ἂν ἀπολέσῃ τὴν
soul of him to save, shall lose it; who but ever may lose the
5590 848 1752 1700 2098 3778 4982
ψυχὴν αὐτοῦ ἕνεκεν ἐμοῦ καὶ τοῦ εὐαγγελίου, οὗτος σώσει
soul of him for the sake of Me and the gospel, this one will save
846 5101 1063 5623 444 1437 2770
36 αὐτήν. τί γὰρ ὠφελήσει ἄνθρωπον, ἐὰν κερδήσῃ τὸν
it. what For shall it profit a man if he gain the
2889 3650 2210 559 848 2228/5101/1325
37 κόσμον ὅλον, καὶ ζημιωθῇ τὴν ψυχὴν αὐτοῦ; ἢ τί δώσει
world whole, yet damage the soul of him. Or what shall give
444 465 5590 848 3739/1063/302
38 ἄνθρωπος ἀντάλλαγμα τῆς ψυχῆς αὐτοῦ; ὃς γὰρ ἂν ἐπαι-
a man (as) an exchange (for) the soul of him? who For ever may be
1870 3165 1699 3056 1722 1074 5026
σχυνθῇ με καὶ τοὺς ἐμοὺς λόγους ἐν τῇ γενεᾷ ταύτῃ τῇ
ashamed of Me and My words in generation this
3428 268 5207 444 1870
μοιχαλίδι καὶ ἁμαρτωλῷ, καὶ ὁ υἱὸς τοῦ ἀνθρώπου ἐπαι-
adulterous and sinful, *also the Son of man will be
846 3752 2064 1722 1391 3962
σχυνθήσεται αὐτόν, ὅταν ἔλθῃ ἐν τῇ δόξῃ τοῦ πατρὸς
ashamed of him, when He comes in the glory of the Father
848 3326 32 40
αὐτοῦ μετὰ τῶν ἀγγέλων τῶν ἁγίων.
of him, with the angels — holy.

CHAPTER 9

3004 846 281 3004 5213 3754/1526/5100
1 καὶ ἔλεγεν αὐτοῖς, Ἀμὴν λέγω ὑμῖν, ὅτι εἰσί τινες τῶν
And He said to them, Truly I say to you, that are some of those
5602 2476 3748 =3364= 1089 2288 2193 302
ὧδε ἑστηκότων, οἵτινες οὐ μὴ γεύσωνται θανάτου, ἕως ἂν
here standing who in no way shall taste of death until
1492 932 2316 2064 1722 1411
ἴδωσι τὴν βασιλείαν τοῦ Θεοῦ ἐληλυθυῖαν ἐν δυνάμει.
they see the kingdom of God having come in power.
3326 2250 1803 3880 2424 4074
2 Καὶ μεθ' ἡμέρας ἓξ παραλαμβάνει ὁ Ἰησοῦς τὸν Πέτρον
And after days six takes along — Jesus — Peter
2385 2491 399 846
καὶ τὸν Ἰάκωβον καὶ τὸν Ἰωάννην, καὶ ἀναφέρει αὐτοὺς
and — James and — John, and carries them
1519 3735 5308 2596 2398 3441 3339 1715
εἰς ὄρος ὑψηλὸν κατ' ἰδίαν μόνους· καὶ μετεμορφώθη ἔμπρο-
into a mount high, privately, alone. And He was transfigured before
846 2440 848 1096 4744 3022
3 σθεν αὐτῶν· καὶ τὰ ἱμάτια αὐτοῦ ἐγένετο στίλβοντα, λευκὰ
them. And the garments of Him became shining, white
3029/5613/5510/3634 1102 1909 1093/3756 1410 3021
λίαν ὡς χιών, οἷα γναφεὺς ἐπὶ τῆς γῆς οὐ δύναται λευκᾶναι
very, as snow, such as a fuller on the earth not is able to whiten.
3700 846 2243 4862 3475 2258 4814
4 καὶ ὤφθη αὐτοῖς Ἡλίας σὺν Μωσεῖ, καὶ ἦσαν συλλαλοῦντε
And was seen by them Elijah with Moses, and they were speaking with
2424 611 4074 3004 2424 4461
5 τῷ Ἰησοῦ. καὶ ἀποκριθεὶς ὁ Πέτρος λέγει τῷ Ἰησοῦ, Ῥαββί,
Jesus. And answering Peter says to Jesus, Rabbi,
2570 2076 2248 5602 1511 4160 4633 5140
καλόν ἐστιν ἡμᾶς ὧδε εἶναι· καὶ ποιήσωμεν σκηνὰς τρεῖς,
good it is us here to be, and, Let us make tents three
4671 3391 3475 3391 2243 3391 3756 1063 1492 5101
6 σοὶ μίαν, καὶ Μωσεῖ μίαν, καὶ Ἠλίᾳ μίαν. οὐ γὰρ ᾔδει τί
for You one, and for Moses one, and for Elijah one. not For he knew what

NOTE: Frequent words not numbered. δέ(1161); καί(2531)–and, but; ὁ, ἡ, τό (3588, the)— * above word, look in verse margin for No.

for they were very fearful. [7]And a cloud was overshadowing them, and a voice came out of the cloud, saying, This is My Son, the Beloved; hear Him. [8]And suddenly looking around, they saw no one any longer, but Jesus alone with them.

[9]And as they were coming down from the mount, He commanded them that they should tell no one what they saw, except when the Son of man should rise from *the* dead. [10]And they held the word to themselves, debating what *it* is to rise from *the* dead.

[11]And they asked Him, saying, Do *not* the scribes say that Elijah must come first? [12]And answering He said to them, Indeed Elijah coming first restores all things. And how it has been written of the Son of man that He suffer many things, and be despised! [13]But I say to you, Elijah also has come, and they did to him whatever they desired, even as it has been written of him.

[14]And coming to the disciples, He saw a great crowd around them, and scribes arguing with them. [15]And at once all the crowd seeing Him were greatly amazed. And running up, *they* greeted Him. [16]And He questioned the scribes, What are you arguing with them? [17]And one answered out of the crowd, saying, Teacher, I brought my son to You, having a dumb spirit. [18]And wherever it seizes him, it dashes him; and he foams and gnashes his teeth. And

2980 2258 1063 1630 1096 3507 1982
7 λαλήσῃ· ἦσαν γὰρ ἔκφοβοι. καὶ ἐγένετο νεφέλη ἐπισκιάζουσα
to say, they were for very fearful. And was a cloud overshadowing
846 2064 5456 1537 3507 3004 3778 2076
αὐτοῖς· καὶ ἦλθε φωνὴ ἐκ τῆς νεφέλης, λέγουσα, Οὗτός ἐστιν
them, and came a voice out of the cloud, saying, This is
5207 3450 27 846 191 1819
8 ὁ υἱός μου ὁ ἀγαπητός· αὐτοῦ ἀκούετε. καὶ ἐξάπινα
the Son of Me, the Beloved· Him hear. And suddenly,
4017 3765 3762 1492 235 2424
περιβλεψάμενοι, οὐκέτι οὐδένα εἶδον, ἀλλὰ τὸν Ἰησοῦν
looking around, no longer no one they saw, but — Jesus
3440 3326 1438
μόνον μεθ' ἑαυτῶν.
alone with themselves.

2597 846 575 3735 1291
9 Καταβαινόντων δὲ αὐτῶν ἀπὸ τοῦ ὄρους, διεστείλατο
as were descending And they from the mountain, He commanded
846 2443 3367 1334 3739 1492 =1508= 3752 5207
αὐτοῖς ἵνα μηδενὶ διηγήσωνται ἃ εἶδον, εἰ μὴ ὅταν ὁ υἱὸς
them that to no one they should tell what they saw, except when the Son
444 1537 3498 450 3056 2902
10 τοῦ ἀνθρώπου ἐκ νεκρῶν ἀναστῇ. καὶ τὸν λόγον ἐκράτησαν
— of man from (the) dead may rise. And the word they held
4314 1438 4802 5101/2076 1537 3498 450
πρὸς ἑαυτούς, συζητοῦντες τί ἐστι τὸ ἐκ νεκρῶν ἀναστῆναι.
to themselves, debating what is (it) from (the) dead to rise.
1905 846 3004 3754 3004 1122
11 καὶ ἐπηρώτων αὐτόν, λέγοντες ὅτι Λέγουσιν οἱ γραμματεῖς
And they asked Him, saying, Do (not) say the scribes
3754 2243 1163 2064 4412 611 2036 846
12 ὅτι Ἠλίαν δεῖ ἐλθεῖν πρῶτον; ὁ δὲ ἀποκριθείς, εἶπεν αὐτοῖς,
that Elijah it behoves to come first? He And answering said to them,
2243 3303 2064 4412 600 3956 4459
Ἠλίας μὲν ἐλθὼν πρῶτον, ἀποκαθιστᾷ πάντα· καὶ πῶς
Elijah indeed having come first restores all things. And how
1125 1909 5207 444 2443 4183 3958
γέγραπται ἐπὶ τὸν υἱὸν τοῦ ἀνθρώπου, ἵνα πολλὰ πάθῃ
has it been written on the Son — of man, that many things He suffer
1847 235 3004 5213 3754 2243 2064
13 καὶ ἐξουδενωθῇ. ἀλλὰ λέγω ὑμῖν ὅτι καὶ Ἠλίας ἐλήλυθε,
and be despised. But I say to you, that also Elijah has come,
4160 846 3745 2309 2531 1125 1909
καὶ ἐποίησαν αὐτῷ ὅσα ἠθέλησαν, καθὼς γέγραπται ἐπ'
and they did to him whatever they desired, even as it has been written of
846
αὐτόν.
him.

2064 4314 3101 1492 3793 4183 4012
14 Καὶ ἐλθὼν πρὸς τοὺς μαθητάς, εἶδεν ὄχλον πολὺν περὶ
And coming to the disciples, He saw a crowd great around
846 1122 4802 846 2112
15 αὐτούς, καὶ γραμματεῖς συζητοῦντας αὐτοῖς. καὶ εὐθέως
them, and scribes arguing with them. And at once
3956 3793 1492 846 1568 4370
πᾶς ὁ ὄχλος ἰδὼν αὐτὸν ἐξεθαμβήθη, καὶ προστρέχοντες
all the crowd seeing Him were greatly amazed, and running up
782 846 1905 1122 5101
16 ἠσπάζοντο αὐτόν. καὶ ἐπηρώτησε τοὺς γραμματεῖς, Τί
greeted Him. And He questioned the scribes, What
4802 4314 846 611 1520/1537 3793
17 συζητεῖτε πρὸς αὐτούς; καὶ ἀποκριθεὶς εἷς ἐκ τοῦ ὄχλου
are you arguing with them? And answered one out of the crowd,
2036 1320 5342 5207 3450 4314 4571 2192
εἶπε, Διδάσκαλε, ἤνεγκα τὸν υἱόν μου πρός σε, ἔχοντα
said, Teacher, I brought the son of me to You, having
4151 216 3699 302 846 2638 4486
18 πνεῦμα ἄλαλον. καὶ ὅπου ἂν αὐτὸν καταλάβῃ, ῥήσσει
a spirit dumb; and wherever him it seizes, it dashes
846 875 5149 3599 848
αὐτόν· καὶ ἀφρίζει, καὶ τρίζει τοὺς ὀδόντας αὐτοῦ, καὶ
him, and he foams, and gnashes the teeth of him and

he wastes away. And I told Your disciples, that they might expel it. And they were not able. [19]And answering them He said, O unbelieving generation! How long will I be with you? How long shall I endure you? Bring him to Me. [20]And they brought him to Him. And seeing Him, the spirit immediately convulsed him. And falling on the ground, he wallowed, foaming. [21]And He questioned his father, How long a time is it while this has happened to him? And he said, From childhood. [22]And often it threw him both into fire and into water, that it might destroy him. But if You are able to do anything, help us, having pity on us. [23]And Jesus said to him, If you are able to believe, all things are possible to those believing. [24]And immediately crying out, the father of the child said with tears, Lord, I believe! Help my unbelief! [25]And seeing that a crowd is running together, Jesus rebuked the unclean spirit, saying to it, Dumb and deaf spirit, I command you, Come out from him, and you may no more go into him! [26]And crying out, and convulsing him very much, it came out. And he became as if dead, so as *for* many to say that he died. [27]But taking hold of his hand, Jesus raised him up, and he stood up. [28]And He entering into a house, His disciples questioned Him privately, *Why* were we not able to cast it out? [29]And He said to them, This kind can go out by nothing except by prayer and fasting.

3583 2036 3101 5675 2443 846 1544
ξηραίνεται· καὶ εἶπον τοῖς μαθηταῖς σου ἵνα αὐτὸ ἐκβάλωσι,
he wastes away. And I told the disciples of You that it they might expel,
3756 2480 611 846 3004 5599 1074
19 καὶ οὐκ ἴσχυσαν. ὁ δὲ ἀποκριθεὶς αὐτῷ λέγει, Ὦ γενεὰ
and not they were able. He And answering them says, O generation
571 2192 3421 4314 5209 2071 2193 4219 430
ἄπιστος, ἕως πότε πρὸς ὑμᾶς ἔσομαι; ἕως πότε ἀνέξομαι
unbelieving, until when with you will I be? Until when shall I endure
5216 5342 846 4314/3165 5342 846 4314 846
20 ὑμῶν; φέρετε αὐτὸν πρός με. καὶ ἤνεγκαν αὐτὸν πρὸς αὐτόν·
you? Bring him to Me. And they brought him to Him.
1492 846 2112 4151 4682 846
καὶ ἰδὼν αὐτόν, εὐθέως τὸ πνεῦμα ἐσπάραξεν αὐτόν· καὶ
And seeing Him, instantly the spirit convulsed him; and
4098 1909 1093 2947 875 1905
21 πεσὼν ἐπὶ τῆς γῆς, ἐκυλίετο ἀφρίζων. καὶ ἐπηρώτησε τὸν
falling on the ground, he wallowed, foaming. And He questioned the
3962 848 4214 5550 2076 5613 5124 1096 846
πατέρα αὐτοῦ, Πόσος χρόνος ἐστὶν ὡς τοῦτο γέγονεν αὐτῷ;
father of him, How long a time is it while this has happened to him?
2036 3812 4178 846 1519 4442 906
22 ὁ δὲ εἶπε, Παιδιόθεν. καὶ πολλάκις αὐτὸν καὶ εἰς πῦρ ἔβαλε
he And said, From childhood. And often him both into fire it threw
1519 5204 2443 622 846 235 =1536= 1410
καὶ εἰς ὕδατα, ἵνα ἀπολέσῃ αὐτόν· ἀλλ᾽ εἴ τι δύνασαι,
and into water, that it might destroy him. But if anything You can do,
997 2254 4697 1909 2248 2424 2036
23 βοήθησον ἡμῖν, σπλαγχνισθεὶς ἐφ᾽ ἡμᾶς. ὁ δὲ Ἰησοῦς εἶπεν
help us, having pity on us. And Jesus said
846 1487 1410 4100 3956 1415
αὐτῷ τό, Εἰ δύνασαι πιστεῦσαι, πάντα δυνατὰ τῷ
to him, If you are able to believe, all things (are) possible to the
4100 2112 2896 3962 3813 3326
24 πιστεύοντι. καὶ εὐθέως κράξας ὁ πατὴρ τοῦ παιδίου, μετὰ
believing. And immediately crying out the father of the child, with
1144 3004 4100 2962 997 3450 570
δακρύων ἔλεγε, Πιστεύω, Κύριε, βοήθει μου τῇ ἀπιστίᾳ.
tears, said, I believe! Lord, help of me the unbelief!
1492 2424 3754 1998 3793 2008
25 Ἰδὼν δὲ ὁ Ἰησοῦς ὅτι ἐπισυντρέχει ὄχλος, ἐπετίμησε τῷ
seeing And Jesus that is running together a crowd, rebuked the
4151 169 3004 846 4151 216
πνεύματι τῷ ἀκαθάρτῳ, λέγων αὐτῷ, Τὸ πνεῦμα τὸ ἄλαλον
spirit unclean, saying to it, spirit Dumb
2974 1473 4671 2004 1831 1537 846 3371
καὶ κωφόν, ἐγώ σοι ἐπιτάσσω, ἔξελθε ἐξ αὐτοῦ, καὶ μηκέτι
and deaf, I you command, Come forth from him, and no more
1525 1519 846 2896 4183 4682 846
26 εἰσέλθῃς εἰς αὐτόν. καὶ κράξαν, καὶ πολλὰ σπαράξαν αὐτόν,
may you go into him. And crying out, and much convulsing him,
1831 1096 5616 3498 5620 4183 3004 3754
ἐξῆλθε· καὶ ἐγένετο ὡσεὶ νεκρός, ὥστε πολλοὺς λέγειν ὅτι
it came out. And he became as if dead, so as many to say that
599 2424 2902 846 5495 1453
27 ἀπέθανεν. ὁ δὲ Ἰησοῦς κρατήσας αὐτὸν τῆς χειρός, ἤγειρεν
he died. — But Jesus having taken hold of him the hand raised
846 450 1525 846 1519 3624
28 αὐτόν· καὶ ἀνέστη. καὶ εἰσελθόντα αὐτὸν εἰς οἶκον, οἱ
him, and he stood up. And entering He into a house, the
3101 848 1905 846 2596 2398 3754 2249 3756
μαθηταὶ αὐτοῦ ἐπηρώτων αὐτὸν κατ᾽ ἰδίαν ὅτι Ἡμεῖς οὐκ
disciples of Him questioned Him privately, (Why) we not
1410 1544 846 2036 846 5124
29 ἠδυνήθημεν ἐκβαλεῖν αὐτό; καὶ εἶπεν αὐτοῖς, Τοῦτο τὸ
were able to cast out it? And He said to them, This
1085 1722 3762 1410 1831 =1508= 1722 4335
γένος ἐν οὐδενὶ δύναται ἐξελθεῖν, εἰ μὴ ἐν προσευχῇ καὶ
kind by nothing can go out, except by prayer and
3521
νηστείᾳ.
fasting.

[30]And going forth from there, they passed by through Galilee. And He desired that no one know. [31]For He taught His disciples, and said to them, The Son of man is betrayed into *the* hands of men, and they will kill Him. And being killed, He will rise up the third day. [32]But they did not know the word, and feared to question Him.

[33]And they came to Capernaum. And having come into the house, He questioned them, What were you disputing to yourselves in the way? [34]And they were silent, for they argued with one another in the way *as to* who was greater. [35]And sitting, He called the Twelve and said to them, If anyone desires to be first, he shall be last of all, and servant of all. [36]And taking a child, He set it in their midst, and having embraced it, He said to them, [37]Whoever receives one of such children on My name receives Me. And whoever receives Me, *he* not *only* receives Me, but the *One* having My name receives Me. And whoever receives Me, *he* not *only* receives Me, but He sending Me.

[38]And John answered Him, saying, Teacher, we saw someone casting out demons in Your name, who does not follow us. And we forbade him, because he does not follow us. [39]But Jesus said, Do not forbid him. For there is no one who shall do a work of power in My name, yet be able to speak evil of Me quickly. [40]For who is not against us is for us. [41]For whoever gives you a cup of cold water to drink in My name, because you are of Christ, truly I say to you, In

1564 1831 3899 1223 1056
30 Καὶ ἐκεῖθεν ἐξελθόντες παρεπορεύοντο διὰ τῆς Γαλιλαίας·
And from there going forth, they passed by through Galilee.
3756 2309 2443 5100 1097 1321 1063 3101
31 καὶ οὐκ ἤθελεν ἵνα τις γνῷ. ἐδίδασκε γὰρ τοὺς μαθητὰς
And not He desired that anyone know; He taught for the disciples
848 3004 846 3754 5207 444 3860
αὐτοῦ, καὶ ἔλεγεν αὐτοῖς ὅτι Ὁ υἱὸς τοῦ ἀνθρώπου παραδί-
of Him, and said to them, The Son of man is
1519 5495 444 615 846
δοται εἰς χεῖρας ἀνθρώπων, καὶ ἀποκτενοῦσιν αὐτόν· καὶ
betrayed into hands of men, and they will kill Him; and
615 5154 2250 450 50
32 ἀποκτανθείς, τῇ τρίτῃ ἡμέρᾳ ἀναστήσεται. οἱ δὲ ἠγνόουν
having been killed, the third day He will rise up. they But knew not
4487 5399 846 1905
τὸ ῥῆμα, καὶ ἐφοβοῦντο αὐτὸν ἐπερωτῆσαι.
the word, and feared Him to question.
2064 1519 2584 1722 3614 1096
33 Καὶ ἦλθεν εἰς Καπερναούμ· καὶ ἐν τῇ οἰκίᾳ γενόμενος
And they came to Capernaum. And in the house having come;
1905 846 5101 1722 3590 4314 1438 1260
ἐπηρώτα αὐτούς, Τί ἐν τῇ ὁδῷ πρὸς ἑαυτοὺς διελογίζεσθε;
He questioned them, What in the way toward yourselves were you arguing?
4623 4314 240 1063 1256 1722 3598
34 οἱ δὲ ἐσιώπων· πρὸς ἀλλήλους γὰρ διελέχθησαν ἐν τῇ ὁδῷ,
they And were quiet with one another, for they argued in the way
5102 3187 2523 5455 1427 3004
35 τίς μείζων. καὶ καθίσας ἐφώνησε τοὺς δώδεκα, καὶ λέγει
who (was) greater. And sitting He called the twelve and says
846 =1536= 2309 4413 1511 2071 3956 2078
αὐτοῖς, Εἴ τις θέλει πρῶτος εἶναι, ἔσται πάντων ἔσχατος,
to them, If anyone desires first to be, he shall be of all last,
3956 1249 2983 3813 2476 846
36 καὶ πάντων διάκονος. καὶ λαβὼν παιδίον, ἔστησεν αὐτὸ
and of all servant. And taking a child, He set it
1722 3319 846 1723 846 2036 846
ἐν μέσῳ αὐτῶν· καὶ ἐναγκαλισάμενος αὐτό, εἶπεν αὐτοῖς·
in (the) midst of them, and having embraced it, He said to them,
3739/1437/1520 5108 3813 1209 1909 3686
37 Ὃς ἐὰν ἓν τῶν τοιούτων παιδίων δέξηται ἐπὶ τῷ ὀνόματί
Whoever one — of such children receives on the name
3450 1691 1209 3739/1437/1691 1209 3756 1691 1209
μου, ἐμὲ δέχεται· καὶ ὃς ἐὰν ἐμὲ δέξηται, οὐκ ἐμὲ δέχεται,
of Me, Me receives; and whoever Me receives, not Me receives,
235 649 3165
ἀλλὰ τὸν ἀποστείλαντά με.
but the (One) having sent Me.
611 846 2491 3004 1320
38 Ἀπεκρίθη δὲ αὐτῷ ὁ Ἰωάννης, λέγων, Διδάσκαλε,
answered And Him — John, saying, Teacher,
1492 1722 3686 4675 1544 1140 3739
εἴδομέν τινα ἐν τῷ ὀνόματί σου ἐκβάλλοντα δαιμόνια, ὃς
we saw someone in the name of You casting out demons, who
3756 190 2254 2967 846 3754 3756
οὐκ ἀκολουθεῖ ἡμῖν· καὶ ἐκωλύσαμεν αὐτόν, ὅτι οὐκ
not does follow us; and we forbade him, because not
190 2254 2424 2036 3361 2967 846
39 ἀκολουθεῖ ἡμῖν. ὁ δὲ Ἰησοῦς εἶπε, Μὴ κωλύετε αὐτόν·
he follows us. — But Jesus said, not Do forbid him;
3762 1063 2076 3739 4160 1411 1909 3686 3450
οὐδεὶς γάρ ἐστιν ὃς ποιήσει δύναμιν ἐπὶ τῷ ὀνόματί μου,
no one for is who shall do a work of power on the name of Me,
1410 5035 2551 3165 1063 3756 2076 2596
40 καὶ δυνήσεται ταχὺ κακολογῆσαί με. ὃς γὰρ οὐκ ἔστι καθ'
yet be able quickly to speak evil of Me. who For not is against
2254 5228 2254 2076 3739/1063/302 4222 5209 4221
41 ἡμῶν, ὑπὲρ ἡμῶν ἐστιν. ὃς γὰρ ἂν ποτίσῃ ὑμᾶς ποτήριον
us, for us is. who For ever gives drink you a cup
5204 1722 3686 3450 3754 5547 2075 281 3004
ὕδατος ἐν τῷ ὀνόματί μου, ὅτι Χριστοῦ ἐστέ, ἀμὴν λέγω
of water in the name of Me, because of Christ you are, truly I say

no way he will lose his reward. [42]And whoever causes one of these little ones that believe in Me to offend, it is good for him if rather a millstone be laid about his neck, and he be thrown into the sea.

[43]And if your hand offend you, cut it off. For it is profitable for you to enter into life maimed, than having two hands to go away into Hell, into the fire that cannot be put out, [44]where their worm does not die, and the fire is not put out. [45]And if your foot causes you to offend, cut it off, for it is profitable for you to enter into life lame, than having two feet to be thrown into Hell, into the fire that cannot be put out, [46]where their worm does not die, and the fire is not put out. [47]And if your eye offends you, cast it out. For it is profitable for you to enter into the kingdom of God one-eyed, than having two eyes to be thrown into the Hell of fire, [48]where their worm does not die, and the fire is not put out.

[49]For everyone will be salted with fire, and every sacrifice will be salted with salt. [50]Salt *is* good, but if the salt becomes saltless, by what will you season? Have salt in yourselves, and be at peace with one another.

5213 3364 622 3408 848 3739/302 4624
42 ὑμῖν, οὐ μὴ ἀπολέσῃ τὸν μισθὸν αὐτοῦ. καὶ ὃς ἂν σκαν-
to you, in no way he will lose the reward of him. And whoever causes to
1520 3398 5130 4100 1519 1691
δαλίσῃ ἕνα τῶν μικρῶν τούτων τῶν πιστευόντων εἰς ἐμέ,
offend one – little (ones) of these – believing in Me,
2570 2076 846 3123 1487 4029 3037 3457 4012
καλόν ἐστιν αὐτῷ μᾶλλον εἰ περίκειται λίθος μυλικὸς περὶ
good is it for him rather if be laid about of a stone of a mill around
5137 848 906 1519 2281
43 τὸν τράχηλον αὐτοῦ, καὶ βέβληται εἰς τὴν θάλασσαν. καὶ
the neck of him, and he be thrown into the sea. And
1437 4624 4571 5495 4675 609 846 2570 4671
ἐὰν σκανδαλίζῃ σε ἡ χείρ σου, ἀπόκοψον αὐτήν· καλόν σοι
if offend you the hand of you, cut off it; well for you
2076 2948 1519 2222 1525 2228 1417 5495 2192
ἐστι κυλλὸν εἰς τὴν ζωὴν εἰσελθεῖν, ἢ τὰς δύο χεῖρας ἔχοντα
is it maimed into life to enter, than the two hands having
565 1519 1067 1519 4442 762 3699
44 ἀπελθεῖν εἰς τὴν γέενναν, εἰς τὸ πῦρ τὸ ἄσβεστον. ὅπου ὁ
to go away into Gehenna, into the fire unquenchable, where the
4663 848 3756 5053 4442 3756 4570
45 σκώληξ αὐτῶν οὐ τελευτᾷ, καὶ τὸ πῦρ οὐ σβέννυται. καὶ
worm of them not has an end, and the fire not is quenched. And
1437 4228 4675 4624 4571 609 846 2570 2076
ἐὰν ὁ πούς σου σκανδαλίζῃ σε, ἀπόκοψον αὐτόν· καλόν ἐστί
if the foot of you causes to offend you, cut off it; well is it
4571 1525 1519 2222 5560 2228 1417 4228 2192
σοι εἰσελθεῖν εἰς τὴν ζωὴν χωλόν, ἢ τοὺς δύο πόδας ἔχοντα
you to enter into life lame, that the two feet having
906 1519 1067 1519 4442 762 3699
46 βληθῆναι εἰς τὴν γέενναν, εἰς τὸ πῦρ τὸ ἄσβεστον, ὅπου
to be thrown into Gehenna, into the fire unquenchable, where
4663 848 3756 5053 4442 3756 4570
47 ὁ σκώληξ αὐτῶν οὐ τελευτᾷ, καὶ τὸ πῦρ οὐ σβέννυται. καὶ
the worm of them not has an end, and the fire not is quenched. And
1437 3788 4675 4624 4571 1544 846 2570
ἐὰν ὁ ὀφθαλμός σου σκανδαλίζῃ σε, ἔκβαλε αὐτόν· καλόν
if the eye of you offends you, cast out it; well
4671 2076 3442 1525 1519 932 2316
σοι ἐστὶ μονόφθαλμον εἰσελθεῖν εἰς τὴν βασιλείαν τοῦ Θεοῦ,
for you it is one-eyed to enter into the kingdom of God,
2228 1417 3788 2192 906 1519 1067
ἢ δύο ὀφθαλμοὺς ἔχοντα βληθῆναι εἰς τὴν γέενναν τοῦ
than two eyes having to be thrown into the Gehenna
4442 3699 4663 848 3756 5053 4442 3756
48 πυρός, ὅπου ὁ σκώληξ αὐτῶν οὐ τελευτᾷ, καὶ τὸ πῦρ οὐ
of fire, where the worm of them not has an end, and the fire not
4570 3956 1063 4442 233 3956 2378 251
49 σβέννυται. πᾶς γὰρ πυρὶ ἁλισθήσεται, καὶ πᾶσα θυσία ἁλὶ
is quenched. everyone For with fire will be salted, and every sacrifice with
233 2570 217 1437 217 358 1048 salt
50 ἁλισθήσεται. καλὸν τὸ ἅλας· ἐὰν δὲ τὸ ἅλας ἄναλον γένηται,
will be salted. Good (is) the salt, if but the salt saltless becomes,
1722/5101/846 741 2192 1722 1438 217 1574
ἐν τίνι αὐτὸ ἀρτύσετε; ἔχετε ἐν ἑαυτοῖς ἅλας, καὶ εἰρηνεύετε
by what it will you season? Have in yourselves salt, and be at peace
1722 240
ἐν ἀλλήλοις.
among one another.

CHAPTER 10

[1]And rising up from there, He came into the borders of Judea by the other side of the Jordan. And again crowds came together to Him, and as He usually did, He again taught them.

2547 450 2064 1519 3725 2449 1223
1 Κἀκεῖθεν ἀναστὰς ἔρχεται εἰς τὰ ὅρια τῆς Ἰουδαίας διὰ
And from there arising, He comes into the borders – of Judea by
4008 2446 4848 3825 3793
τοῦ πέραν τοῦ Ἰορδάνου· καὶ συμπορεύονται πάλιν ὄχλοι
the other side of the Jordan. And came together again crowds
4314 846 5613 1486 3825 1321 846
2 πρὸς αὐτόν· καί, ὡς εἰώθει, πάλιν ἐδίδασκεν αὐτούς. καὶ
with Him, and as He did usually, again He taught them. And

[2]And coming near the Pharisees asked Him if it is lawful for a man to put away a wife, testing Him. [3]But answering He said to them, What did Moses command you? [4]And they said, Moses allowed to write a bill of divorce, and to put away. [5]And answering Jesus said to them, With respect to your hardheartedness he wrote this command to you. [6]But from the beginning of creation God made them male and female. [7]Because of this a man shall leave his father

4334 5330 1905 846 1487 1832
προσελθόντες οἱ Φαρισαῖοι ἐπηρώτησαν αὐτόν, Εἰ ἔξεστιν
coming up the Pharisees questioned Him, if (it is) lawful
435 1135 630 3985 846 611
3 ἀνδρὶ γυναῖκα ἀπολῦσαι, πειράζοντες αὐτόν. ὁ δὲ ἀποκρι-
for a man a wife to dismiss, testing Him. He And answering
2036 846 5101 5213 1781 3474 2036
4 θεὶς εἶπεν αὐτοῖς, Τί ὑμῖν ἐνετείλατο Μωσῆς; οἱ δὲ εἶπον,
said to them, What you did command Moses? they And said,
3475 2010 975 647 1125 630
Μωσῆς ἐπέτρεψε βιβλίον ἀποστασίου γράψαι, καὶ ἀπολῦ-
Moses allowed a roll of divorce to write, and to dismiss.
611 2424 2036 846 4314
5 σαι. καὶ ἀποκριθεὶς ὁ Ἰησοῦς εἶπεν αὐτοῖς, Πρὸς τὴν
And answering, Jesus said to them, For the
4641 5216 1125 5213 1785 5026
σκληροκαρδίαν ὑμῶν ἔγραψεν ὑμῖν τὴν ἐντολὴν ταύτην·
hardheartedness of you he wrote to you commandment this.
575 746 2937 730 2338 4160 846
6 ἀπὸ δὲ ἀρχῆς κτίσεως, ἄρσεν καὶ θῆλυ ἐποίησεν αὐτοὺς ὁ
from But beginning of creation male and female made them, –
2316 1752 5152 2641 444 3962 848
7 Θεός. ἕνεκεν τούτου καταλείψει ἄνθρωπος τὸν πατέρα αὐτοῦ
God. On account of this shall leave a man the father of him

and mother, and shall be joined to his wife, [8]and the two shall be one flesh; so that they no longer are two, but one flesh. [9]Therefore, what God yoked together, let not man put apart [10]And again in the house His disciples asked Him about the same. [11]And He said to them, Whoever puts away his wife, and shall marry another commits adultery against her. [12]And if a woman puts away her husband and marries another, she commits adultery.

3384 4347 4314 1135
καὶ τὴν μητέρα· καὶ προσκολληθήσεται πρὸς τὴν γυναῖκα
and the mother, and shall be joined to the wife
848 2071 1417 1519 4561 3391 5620 3765 1526
8 αὐτοῦ, καὶ ἔσονται οἱ δύο εἰς σάρκα μίαν. ὥστε οὐκέτι εἰσὶ
of him, and shall become the two into flesh one; so as no longer are they
1417 235 3391 4561 3767 2316 4801 444 3361
9 δύο, ἀλλὰ μία σάρξ. ὃ οὖν ὁ Θεὸς συνέζευξεν, ἄνθρωπος μὴ
two, but one flesh. What then God yoked together, man not
5563 1722 3614 3825 3101 848 4012
10 χωριζέτω. καὶ ἐν τῇ οἰκίᾳ πάλιν οἱ μαθηταὶ αὐτοῦ περὶ τοῦ
let put apart. And in the house again the disciples of Him about the
846 1905 846 3004 846 3739/1437 630
11 αὐτοῦ ἐπηρώτησαν αὐτόν. καὶ λέγει αὐτοῖς, Ὃς ἐὰν ἀπο-
same questioned Him. And He says to them, Whoever may
1135 848 1060 243 3429 1909
λύσῃ τὴν γυναῖκα αὐτοῦ καὶ γαμήσῃ ἄλλην, μοιχᾶται ἐπ'
dismiss the wife of him and marry another is in adultery with
846 1437 1135 630 435 848 1060
12 αὐτήν· καὶ ἐὰν γυνὴ ἀπολύσῃ τὸν ἄνδρα αὐτῆς καὶ γαμηθῇ
her; and if a woman may dismiss husband her and marries
243 3429
ἄλλῳ, μοιχᾶται.
another she commits adultery.

[13]And they brought children to Him, that He might touch them. But the disciples rebuked those carrying *them.* [14]But seeing, Jesus was indignant. And He said to them, Allow the children to come to Me, and do not hinder them. For of such is the kingdom of God. [15]Truly I say to you, Whoever does not receive the kingdom of God as a child may in no way enter into it. [16]And having taken them in *His* arms, laying hands on them, He blessed them.

4374 846 3813 2443 680 846
13 Καὶ προσέφερον αὐτῷ παιδία ἵνα ἅψηται αὐτῶν· οἱ δὲ
And they carried to Him children, that He might touch them. the But
3101 2008 4374 1492 2424
14 μαθηταὶ ἐπετίμων τοῖς προσφέρουσιν. ἰδὼν δὲ ὁ Ἰησοῦς
disciples rebuked the (ones) carrying (them). seeing But Jesus
23 2036 846 863 3813 2064
ἠγανάκτησε, καὶ εἶπεν αὐτοῖς, Ἄφετε τὰ παιδία ἔρχεσθαι
was indignant, and He said to them, Allow the children to come
4314 3165 3361 2967 846 1063 5108 2076
πρός με, καὶ μὴ κωλύετε αὐτά· τῶν γὰρ τοιούτων ἐστὶν ἡ
to Me; and not forbid them; of these for such is the
932 2316 281 3004 5213 3739/1437/3361 1209
15 βασιλεία τοῦ Θεοῦ. ἀμὴν λέγω ὑμῖν, ὃς ἐὰν μὴ δέξηται τὴν
kingdom of God. Truly I say to you, Whoever not receives the
932 2316 5613 3813 =3364= 1525 1519 846
βασιλείαν τοῦ Θεοῦ ὡς παιδίον, οὐ μὴ εἰσέλθῃ εἰς αὐτήν.
kingdom of God as a child, in no way may enter into it.
1723 846 5087 5495 1909 846
16 καὶ ἐναγκαλισάμενος αὐτά, τιθεὶς τὰς χεῖρας ἐπ' αὐτά,
And having taken in arms them, having laid the hands on them.
2127 846
ηὐλόγει αὐτά.
He blessed them.

17 And He having gone out into *the* highway, running up and kneeling down to Him, one questioned Him, Good Teacher, what shall I do that I may inherit eternal life? 18 But Jesus said to him, Why do you call Me good? No one *is* good except One, God. 19 You know the commandments:

Do not commit adultery; do not commit murder; do not steal; do not bear false witness; do not defraud; honor your father and mother. 20 And answering he said to Him, Teacher, I observed all these from my youth. 21 And looking at him, Jesus loved him, and said to him, One *thing* is lacking to you. Go, sell what things you have, and give to the poor. And you will have treasure in Heaven. And come, follow Me, taking up the cross. 22 But being sad at the word, he went away grieving; for he had many possessions.

23 And looking around Jesus said to His disciples, How hardly those having riches will enter into the kingdom of God! 24 And the disciples were astonished at His words. And answering again Jesus said to them, Children, how hard it is for those trusting on riches to enter into the kingdom of God! 25 It is easier *for* a camel to pass through the eye of the

needle, than *for* a rich one to enter into the kingdom of God. 26 And they were exceedingly astonished, saying to themselves, And who is able to be saved? 27 But looking at them, Jesus said, From men *it is* impossible, but not from God—for all

1607 846 1519 3598 4370 1520
17 Καὶ ἐκπορευομένου αὐτοῦ εἰς ὁδόν, προσδραμὼν εἷς καὶ
And going forth Him into (the) way, running up one and
1120 846 1905 846 1320 18 5101
γονυπετήσας αὐτὸν ἐπηρώτα αὐτόν, Διδάσκαλε ἀγαθέ, τί
kneeling down to Him questioned Him, teacher Good, What
4160 2443 2222 166 2816 2424
18 ποιήσω ἵνα ζωὴν αἰώνιον κληρονομήσω; ὁ δὲ Ἰησοῦς
shall I do that life eternal I may inherit? – And Jesus
2036 846 5101/3165/3004 18 3752 18 =1508= 1520
εἶπεν αὐτῷ, Τί με λέγεις ἀγαθόν; οὐδεὶς ἀγαθός, εἰ μὴ εἷς, ὁ
said to him, Why Me call you good? No one (is) good, except one, –
2316 1785 1492 3361 3431 3361 5407 3361
19 Θεός. τὰς ἐντολὰς οἶδας, Μὴ μοιχεύσῃς, μὴ φονεύσῃς, μὴ
God. The commandments you know: Do not adultery; do not murder, do not
2813 3361 5576 3361 650 5091
κλέψῃς, μὴ ψευδομαρτυρήσῃς, μὴ ἀποστερήσῃς, τίμα τὸν
steal, do not bear false witness' do not defraud; honor the
3962 4675 3384 611 2036 846
20 πατέρα σου καὶ τὴν μητέρα. ὁ δὲ ἀποκριθεὶς εἶπεν αὐτῷ,
father of you and the mother. he And answering said to Him,
1320 5023 3956 5442 1537 3503 3450
21 Διδάσκαλε, ταῦτα πάντα ἐφυλαξάμην ἐκ νεότητός μου. ὁ δὲ
Teacher, these All I observed from youth of me. But
2424 1689 846 25 846 2036 846
Ἰησοῦς ἐμβλέψας αὐτῷ ἠγάπησεν αὐτόν, καὶ εἶπεν αὐτῷ,
Jesus, looking at him, loved him, and said to him,
1520/4671/ 5302 5217 3745 2192 4453 1325
Ἕν σοι ὑστερεῖ· ὕπαγε, ὅσα ἔχεις πώλησον, καὶ δὸς τοῖς
One to you is lacking; go, what things you have sell, and give to the
4434 2192 2344 1722 3772 1204 190
πτωχοῖς, καὶ ἕξεις θησαυρὸν ἐν οὐρανῷ· καὶ δεῦρο, ἀκολούθει
poor: and you will have treasure in Heaven; and come, follow
3427 142 4716 4768 1909 3056 565
22 μοι, ἄρας τὸν σταυρόν. ὁ δὲ στυγνάσας ἐπὶ τῷ λόγῳ ἀπῆλθε
Me, taking up the cross. he But being sad at the word went away
3076 2258 1063 2192 2933 4183
λυπούμενος· ἦν γὰρ ἔχων κτήματα πολλά.
grieving; he was for having possessions many.
4017 2424 3004 3101 848
23 Καὶ περιβλεψάμενος ὁ Ἰησοῦς λέγει τοῖς μαθηταῖς αὐτοῦ,
And looking around, – Jesus says to the disciples of Him,
4459 1423 5536 2192 1519 932
Πῶς δυσκόλως οἱ τὰ χρήματα ἔχοντες εἰς τὴν βασιλείαν τοῦ
How hardly the (ones) the riches having into the kingdom
2316 1525 3101 2284 1909
24 Θεοῦ εἰσελεύσονται. οἱ δὲ μαθηταὶ ἐθαμβοῦντο ἐπὶ τοῖς
of God will enter. the And disciples were amazed at the
3056 848 2424 3825 611 3004 846
λόγοις αὐτοῦ. ὁ δὲ Ἰησοῦς πάλιν ἀποκριθεὶς λέγει αὐτοῖς,
words of Him. And Jesus again anwering says to them,
5043 4459 1422 2076 3982 1909
Τέκνα, πῶς δύσκολόν ἐστι τοὺς πεποιθότας ἐπὶ τοῖς
Children, how hard it is for those trusting on the
5536 1519 932 2316 1525 2123
25 χρήμασιν εἰς τὴν βασιλείαν τοῦ Θεοῦ εἰσελθεῖν. εὐκοπώ-
riches into the kingdom of God to enter! Easier
2076 2574 1223 5168 4476
τερόν ἐστι κάμηλον διὰ τῆς τρυμαλιᾶς τῆς ῥαφίδος
it is (for) a camel through the eye of the needle
1525 2228 4145 1519 932 2316 1525
διελθεῖν, ἢ πλούσιον εἰς τὴν βασιλείαν τοῦ Θεοῦ εἰσελθεῖν.
to pass, than (for) a rich one into the kingdom of God to enter.
4057 1605 3004 4314 1438
26 οἱ δὲ περισσῶς ἐξεπλήσσοντο, λέγοντες πρὸς ἑαυτούς, Καὶ
they But exceedingly were astonished, saying, to themselves, And
5101 1410 4982 1689 846 2424 3004
27 τίς δύναται σωθῆναι; ἐμβλέψας δὲ αὐτοῖς ὁ Ἰησοῦς λέγει,
who is able to be saved? looking at And them, Jesus says,
3844 444 102 235 3756 3844 2316 3956
Παρὰ ἀνθρώποις ἀδύνατον, ἀλλ' οὐ παρὰ τῷ Θεῷ· πάντα
From men (it is) impossible; but not from – God; all things

things are possible from God. [28]And Peter began to say to Him, Behold, we left all and followed You. [29]But answering Jesus said, Truly I say to you, There is no one who forsook house, or brothers, or sisters, or father, or mother, or wife, or children, or lands, for My sake and the gospel, [30]that will not receive a hundredfold now in this time; houses and brothers and sisters and mothers and children and lands, with persecutions; and in the coming age, eternal life. [31]But many first shall be last, and the last *shall be* first.

[32]And they were in the highway, going up to Jerusalem. And Jesus was going before them, and they were astonished, and following *Him* were afraid. And taking the Twelve again, He began to tell them the things about to happen to Him: [33]Behold, we are going up to Jerusalem. And the Son of man will be betrayed to the chief priests and to the scribes. And they will condemn Him to death, and will deliver Him up to the nations. [34]And they will mock Him, and will flog Him, and will spit at Him, and will kill Him. And on the third day He will rise again.

[35]And coming up to Him, James and John, the sons of Zebedee, said, Teacher, we desire that whatever we may ask You would do for us. [36]And He said to them, What do you desire for Me to do for you? [37]And they said to Him, Give us that we may sit one off *the* right of

1063 1415 2076 3844 2316 756 4074
28 γὰρ δυνατά ἐστι παρὰ τῷ Θεῷ. καὶ ἤρξατο ὁ Πέτρος
for possible are from God. And began Peter
3004 846 2400 2249 863 3956 190
λέγειν αὐτῷ, Ἰδού, ἡμεῖς ἀφήκαμεν πάντα, καὶ ἠκολουθή-
to say to Him, Behold, we forsook all, and have followed
4671 611 2424 2036 281 3004 5213
29 σαμέν σοι. ἀποκριθεὶς δὲ ὁ Ἰησοῦς εἶπεν, Ἀμὴν λέγω ὑμῖν,
You. answering But — Jesus said, Truly I say to you,
3762 2076 3739 863 3614 2228 80 2228 79 2228
οὐδείς ἐστιν ὃς ἀφῆκεν οἰκίαν, ἢ ἀδελφούς, ἢ ἀδελφάς, ἢ
no one there is who forsook house, or brothers, or sisters, or
3962 2228 3384 2228 1135 2228 5043 2228 68 1752
πατέρα, ἢ μητέρα, ἢ γυναῖκα, ἢ τέκνα, ἢ ἀγρούς, ἕνεκεν
father, or mother, or wife, or children, or fields, for the sake
1700 2098 1437 3361 2983 1542
30 ἐμοῦ καὶ τοῦ εὐαγγελίου, ἐὰν μὴ λάβῃ ἑκατονταπλασίονα
of Me and the gospel, except he receives a hundredfold
3568/1722 2540 5129 3614 80 79
νῦν ἐν τῷ καιρῷ τούτῳ, οἰκίας καὶ ἀδελφοὺς καὶ ἀδελφὰς
now in — time this, houses, and brothers, and sisters,
3384 5043 68 3326 1375 1722
καὶ μητέρας καὶ τέκνα καὶ ἀγρούς, μετὰ διωγμῶν, καὶ ἐν τῷ
and mothers, and children, and fields, with persecutions: and in the
165 2064 2222 166 4183 2071
31 αἰῶνι τῷ ἐρχομένῳ ζωὴν αἰώνιον. πολλοὶ δὲ ἔσονται
age — coming, life eternal. many And will be
4413 2078 2078 4413
πρῶτοι ἔσχατοι, καὶ οἱ ἔσχατοι πρῶτοι.
first last; and the last, first.
2258 1722 3598 305 1519 2414
32 Ἦσαν δὲ ἐν τῇ ὁδῷ ἀναβαίνοντες εἰς Ἱεροσόλυμα· καὶ
they were ,And in the way, going up to Jerusalem. And
2258 4254 846 2424 2284
ἦν προάγων αὐτοὺς ὁ Ἰησοῦς, καὶ ἐθαμβοῦντο, καὶ
was going before them — Jesus, and they were astonished and
190 5399 3880 3825
ἀκολουθοῦντες ἐφοβοῦντο. καὶ παραλαβὼν πάλιν τοὺς
following were afraid And having taken again the
1427 756 846 3004 3195 846 4819
δώδεκα, ἤρξατο αὐτοῖς λέγειν τὰ μέλλοντα αὐτῷ συμβαίνειν
twelve, He began them to tell the things about to Him to happen,
3754 2400 305 1519 2414 5207
33 ὅτι Ἰδού, ἀναβαίνομεν εἰς Ἱεροσόλυμα, καὶ ὁ υἱὸς τοῦ
— Behold, we are going up to Jerusalem, and the Son —
444 3860 749 1122
ἀνθρώπου παραδοθήσεται τοῖς ἀρχιερεῦσι καὶ τοῖς γραμ-
of man will be betrayed to the chief priests and to the
2632 846 2288 3860
ματεῦσι, καὶ κατακρινοῦσιν αὐτὸν θανάτῳ, καὶ παραδώ-
scribes, and they will condemn Him to death, and will deliver
846 1484 1702 846
34 σουσιν αὐτὸν τοῖς ἔθνεσι, καὶ ἐμπαίξουσιν αὐτῷ, καὶ
up Him to the nations. And they will mock Him, and
3146 846 1716 846 615
μαστιγώσουσιν αὐτόν, καὶ ἐμπτύσουσιν αὐτῷ, καὶ ἀπο-
will scourge Him, and will spit at Him, and will
846 5154 2250 450
κτενοῦσιν αὐτόν· καὶ τῇ τρίτῃ ἡμέρᾳ ἀναστήσεται.
kill Him; and on the third day He will rise again.
4365 846 2385 1491
35 Καὶ προσπορεύονται αὐτῷ Ἰάκωβος καὶ Ἰωάννης οἱ
And come up to Him James and John, the
5207 2199 3004 1320 2309 2443 1437
υἱοὶ Ζεβεδαίου, λέγοντες, Διδάσκαλε, θέλομεν ἵνα ὃ ἐὰν
sons of Zebedee, saying, Teacher, we desire that whatever
154 4160 2254 2036 846 5101 2309
36 αἰτήσωμεν, ποιήσῃς ἡμῖν. ὁ δὲ εἶπεν αὐτοῖς, Τί θέλετε
we may ask You would do for us. He And said to them, What desire
4160 3165 5213 2036 846 1325 2254 2443 1520/1537
37 ποιῆσαί με ὑμῖν; οἱ δὲ εἶπον αὐτῷ, Δὸς ἡμῖν, ἵνα εἷς ἐκ
to do Me for you? they And said to Him, Give us that one off

You, and one off *the* left of You, in Your glory. [38]But Jesus said to them, You do not know what you ask. Are you able to drink the cup which I drink, and to be baptized *with* the baptism I am baptized *with*? [39]And they said to Him, We are able. But Jesus said to them, Indeed you will drink the cup which I drink, and you will be baptized *with* the baptism *with* which I am baptized. [40]But to sit off My right and off My left is not Mine to give, but for whom it has been prepared.

[41]And hearing, the ten began to be indignant about James and John. [42]But having called them near, Jesus said to them, You know that those seeming to rule the nations lord it over them, and their great ones exercise authority over them. [43]But it shall not be so among you, but whoever desires to become great among you shall be your servant. [44]And whoever of you desires to become first, *he* shall be slave of all. [45]For even the Son of man did not come to be served, but to serve, and to give His soul *as* a ransom for many.

[46]And they came to Jericho. And He and His disciples and a large crowd going out from Jericho, a son of Timeus, Bartimeus the blind, sat beside the highway, begging. [47]And hearing that it was Jesus the Nazarene, he began to cry out and to say, Son of David, Jesus, have mercy on me! [48]And many warned him that he be quiet. But he much more cried out, Son of David, have mercy on me! [49]And standing still, Jesus said for

1188 4675 1520/1537 2176 4675 2523 1722 1391
δεξιῶν σου καὶ εἰς ἐξ εὐωνύμων σου καθίσωμεν ἐν τῇ δόξῃ
(the) right of You and one off (the) left of You we may sit in the glory
4675 2424 2036 846 3756 1492 5101 154
38 σου. ὁ δὲ Ἰησοῦς εἶπεν αὐτοῖς, Οὐκ οἴδατε τί αἰτεῖσθε.
of You. And Jesus said to them, not You know what you ask.
1410 4095 4221 3739/1473/4095 908 3739
δύνασθε πιεῖν τὸ ποτήριον ὃ ἐγὼ πίνω, καὶ τὸ βάπτισμα ὃ
Can you drink the cup which I drink, and the baptism which
1473 907 907 2036 846 1410
39 ἐγὼ βαπτίζομαι βαπτισθῆναι; οἱ δὲ εἶπον αὐτῷ, Δυνάμεθα.
I am baptized to be baptized (with)? they And said to Him, We can.
2424 2036 846 3303 4221 3739/1473 4095
ὁ δὲ Ἰησοῦς εἶπεν αὐτοῖς, Τὸ μὲν ποτήριον ὃ ἐγὼ πίνω
-- And Jesus said to them, the Indeed cup which I drink
4095 908 3739 1473 907 907
πίεσθε· καὶ τὸ βάπτισμα ὃ ἐγὼ βαπτίζομαι βαπτισθήσεσθε·
you will drink, and the baptism which I am baptized (with) you will be baptized;
2523 1537 1188 3450 1537 2176 3450 3756 2076
40 τὸ δὲ καθίσαι ἐκ δεξιῶν μου καὶ ἐξ εὐωνύμων μου οὐκ ἔστιν
but to sit off (the) right of Me and off (the) left of Me not is
1699 1325 235 3739 2090 191 1176
41 ἐμὸν δοῦναι, ἀλλ' οἷς ἡτοίμασται. καὶ ἀκούσαντες οἱ δέκα
Mine to give, but for whom it has been prepared. And hearing the ten
756 23 4012 2385 2491 2424
42 ἤρξαντο ἀγανακτεῖν περὶ Ἰακώβου καὶ Ἰωάννου. ὁ δὲ Ἰησοῦς
began to be indignant about James and John. -- But Jesus
4341 846 3004 846 1492 3754 1380
προσκαλεσάμενος αὐτοὺς λέγει αὐτοῖς, Οἴδατε ὅτι οἱ δοκοῦν-
having called near them says to them, You know that those seem-
757 1484 1634 846 3173
τες ἄρχειν τῶν ἐθνῶν κατακυριεύουσιν αὐτῶν· καὶ οἱ μεγάλοι
ing to rule the nations lord it over them, and the great (ones)
848 2715 848 3756 3779 2071 1722 5213
43 αὐτῶν κατεξουσιάζουσιν αὐτῶν. οὐχ οὕτω δὲ ἔσται ἐν ὑμῖν·
of them exercise authority over them. not so But to be among you;
235/3739/1437/2309 1096 3173 1722/5213 2071 1249 5216
ἀλλ' ὃς ἐὰν θέλῃ γενέσθαι μέγας ἐν ὑμῖν, ἔσται διάκονος ὑμῶν·
but whoever desires to become great among you, shall be servant of you;
3739/302/2309/5216 1096 4413 2071 3956 1401
44 καὶ ὃς ἂν θέλῃ ὑμῶν γενέσθαι πρῶτος, ἔσται πάντων δοῦλος.
and whoever desires of you to become first, shall be of all slave.
1063 5207 444 3756 2064 1247
45 καὶ γὰρ ὁ υἱὸς τοῦ ἀνθρώπου οὐκ ἦλθε διακονηθῆναι,
even For the Son -- of man not did come to be served,
235 1247 1325 5590 848 3083 473
ἀλλὰ διακονῆσαι, καὶ δοῦναι τὴν ψυχὴν αὐτοῦ λύτρον ἀντὶ
but to serve and to give the soul of Him a ransom for
4183
πολλῶν.
many.

2064 1519 2410 1607 848 575
46 Καὶ ἔρχονται εἰς Ἱεριχώ· καὶ ἐκπορευομένου αὐτοῦ ἀπὸ
And they come to Jericho. And going out He from
2410 3101 848 3793 2425 5207
Ἱεριχώ, καὶ τῶν μαθητῶν αὐτοῦ, καὶ ὄχλου ἱκανοῦ, υἱὸς
Jericho, and the disciples of Him, and a crowd large, son
5090 924 5185 2521 3844 3598
Τιμαίου Βαρτίμαιος ὁ τυφλὸς ἐκάθητο παρὰ τὴν ὁδὸν
of Timaeus Bartimaeus the blind sat by the way,
4319 191 3754 2424 3480 2076
47 προσαιτῶν. καὶ ἀκούσας ὅτι Ἰησοῦς ὁ Ναζωραῖός ἐστιν,
begging. And having heard that Jesus the Nazarene it is,
756 2896 3004 5207 1138 2424 1653
ἤρξατο κράζειν καὶ λέγειν, Ὁ υἱὸς Δαβίδ, Ἰησοῦ, ἐλέησόν
he began to cry out and to say, -- Son of David, Jesus. have mercy on
3165 2008 846 4183 2443 4623 4183
48 με. καὶ ἐπετίμων αὐτῷ πολλοί, ἵνα σιωπήσῃ· ὁ δὲ πολλῷ
me! And warned him many, that he be quiet. he But much
3123 2896 5207 1138 1653 3165 2476 2424
49 μᾶλλον ἔκραζεν, Υἱὲ Δαβίδ, ἐλέησόν με. καὶ στὰς ὁ Ἰησοῦς
more cried out, Son of David, have mercy on me! And standing Jesus

him to be called. And they called the blind *one*, saying to him, Be comforted, rise up. He calls you. [50]And throwing away his garment, rising up, he came to Jesus. [51]And answering Jesus said to him, What do you desire I should do to you? And the blind *one* said to Him, My Lord, that I may see again. [52]And Jesus said to him, Go, your faith has healed you. And instantly he saw again, and followed Jesus in the highway.

CHAPTER 11

[1]And when they drew near to Jerusalem, to Bethphage and Bethany, toward the Mount of Olives, He sent two of His disciples, [2]and said to them, Go into the village opposite you. And going into it at once, you will find a colt tied, on which no one of men has sat. Untying it, bring *it*. [3]And if anyone says to you, Why do you do this? say, The Lord has need of it. And he will at once send it here.

[4]And they departed and found the colt tied at the door outside, by the crossway; and they untied it. [5]And some of those standing there said to them, What are you doing, untying the colt? [6]And they said to them as Jesus commanded. And they let them go. [7]And they led the colt to Jesus. And they threw their garments on it, and He sat on it. [8]And many spread their garments on the highway, and others were cutting branches from the trees, and were spreading *them* on the highway. [9]And those going before, and those following after, were crying out, saying,

2036 846 5455 5455 5185 3004
εἶπεν αὐτὸν φωνηθῆναι· καὶ φωνοῦσι τὸν τυφλόν, λέγοντες
said for him to be called. And they call the blind (one), saying.
846 2293 1453 5455 4571 577 2440
50 αὐτῷ, Θάρσει· ἔγειραι, φωνεῖ σε. ὁ δὲ ἀποβαλὼν τὸ ἱμάτιον
to him, Be comforted, arise, He calls you. he And casting away the garment
848 450 2064 4314 2424 611 3004
51 αὐτοῦ ἀναστὰς ἦλθε πρὸς τον Ἰησοῦν. καὶ ἀποκριθεὶς λέγει
of him, rising up, came to — Jesus. And answering says
846 2424 5101 2309 4160 4671 5185 2036
αὐτῷ ὁ Ἰησοῦς, Τί θέλεις ποιήσω σοί; ὁ δὲ τυφλὸς εἶπεν
to him — Jesus, What desire you I do for you? the And blind one said
846 4462 2443 308 2424 2036 846
52 αὐτῷ, Ῥαββονί, ἵνα ἀναβλέψω. ὁ δὲ Ἰησοῦς εἶπεν αὐτῷ,
to Him, My Lord, that I may see again. And Jesus said to him,
5217 4102 4675 4982 4571 2112 308
Ὕπαγε· ἡ πίστις σου σέσωκέ σε. καὶ εὐθέως ἀνέβλεψε, καὶ
Go. the faith of you has cured you. And instantly he saw again, and
190 2424 1722 3598
ἠκολούθει τῷ Ἰησοῦ ἐν τῇ ὁδῷ.
followed — Jesus in the way.

CHAPTER 11

3753 1448 1519 2419 1519 967
1 Καὶ ὅτε ἐγγίζουσιν εἰς Ἱερουσαλήμ, εἰς Βηθφαγὴ καὶ
And when they draw near to Jerusalem, to Bethphage and
963 4314 3735 1636 649 1417
Βηθανίαν, πρὸς τὸ ὄρος τῶν ἐλαιῶν, ἀποστέλλει δύο τῶν
Bethany, towards the mount — of olives, He sends two of the
3101 848 3004 846 5217 1519 2968
2 μαθητῶν αὐτοῦ, καὶ λέγει αὐτοῖς, Ὑπάγετε εἰς τὴν κώμην
disciples of Him and says to them, Go into the village
2713 5216 2112 1531 1519 846
τὴν κατέναντι ὑμῶν· καὶ εὐθέως εἰσπορευόμενοι εἰς αὐτὴν
— opposite you, and at once entering into it
2147 4454 1210 1909/3739/3762 444 2523
εὑρήσετε πῶλον δεδεμένον, ἐφ᾽ ὃν οὐδεὶς ἀνθρώπων κεκάθικε·
you will find a colt having been tied, on which no one of men has sat.
3089 846 71 1437 5100/5213/2036/5101/ 4160
3 λύσαντες αὐτὸν ἀγάγετε. καὶ ἐάν τις ὑμῖν εἴπῃ, Τί ποιεῖτε
Loosing it, lead. And if anyone to you says, Why do you do
5124 2036 3754 2962 848 5532 2192 2112
τοῦτο; εἴπατε ὅτι Ὁ Κύριος αὐτοῦ χρείαν ἔχει· καὶ εὐθέως
this? Say, The Lord of it need has, and at once
846 659 5602 565 2147 4454
4 αὐτὸν ἀποστελεῖ ὧδε. ἀπῆλθον δὲ καὶ εὗρον τὸν πῶλον
it he will send here. they departed And and found the colt
1210 4314 2374 1854 1909 296
δεδεμένον πρὸς τὴν θύραν ἔξω ἐπὶ τοῦ ἀμφόδου, καὶ
having been tied to the door outside on the crossway, and
3089 846 5100 1563 2476 3004 846
5 λύουσιν αὐτόν. καί τινες τῶν ἐκεῖ ἑστηκότων ἔλεγον αὐτοῖς,
they loosen it. And some of those there standing said to them,
5101 4160 3089 4454 2036 846 2531
6 Τί ποιεῖτε λύοντες τὸν πῶλον; οἱ δὲ εἶπον αὐτοῖς καθὼς
What do you do loosening the colt? they And said to them as
1781 2424 863 846 71
7 ἐνετείλατο ὁ Ἰησοῦς· καὶ ἀφῆκαν αὐτούς. καὶ ἤγαγον τὸν
commanded — Jesus, and they let go them. And they led the
4454 4314 2424 1911 846 2440
πῶλον πρὸς τὸν Ἰησοῦν, καὶ ἐπέβαλον αὐτῷ τὰ ἱμάτια
colt to — Jesus; and they throw on it the garments
848 2523 1909 846 4183 2440 848
8 αὐτῶν, καὶ ἐκάθισεν ἐπ᾽ αὐτῷ. πολλοὶ δὲ τὰ ἱμάτια αὐτῶν
of them and He sat on it. many And the garments of them
4766 1519 3598 243 4746 2875 1537
ἔστρωσαν εἰς τὴν ὁδόν· ἄλλοι δὲ στοιβάδας ἔκοπτον ἐκ
scattered into the way, others and branches were cutting from
1186 4766 1519 3598 4254
9 τῶν δένδρων, καὶ ἐστρώννυον εἰς τὴν ὁδόν. καὶ οἱ προάγον-
the trees, and were scattering into the way. And those going be-

Hosanna! Blessed *is* the *One* coming in *the* name of *the* Lord! 10 Blessed *is* the coming kingdom of our father David in *the* name of *the* Lord! Hosanna in the highest!

11 And Jesus entered into Jerusalem, and into the temple. And having looked around at all things, the hour already being late, He went out to Bethany with the Twelve.

12 And on the morrow, they going out from Bethany, He hungered. 13 And seeing afar off a fig-tree having leaves, He went *toward it*, if perhaps He would find anything on it. And coming on it, He found nothing except leaves, for it was not *the* time of figs. 14 And answering Jesus said to it, Let no one eat fruit of you any more forever. And His disciples heard.

15 And they came to Jerusalem. And entering into the temple, Jesus began to throw out those selling and buying in the temple; also He overturned the tables of the moneychangers, and the seats of those selling the doves. 16 And *He* did not allow any to carry a vessel through the temple. 17 And *He* taught, saying to them, Has it not been written, "My house shall be called a house of prayer for all the nations"? But you have made it a den of robbers. 18 And the scribes and the chief priests heard. And they sought how they might destroy Him; for they feared Him; because all the crowd was astonished at His teaching.

190 2896 3004 5614
τες καὶ οἱ ἀκολουθοῦντες ἔκραζον, λέγοντες, Ὡσαννά·
fore and those following, cried out, saying, Hosanna!
2127 2064 1722 3686 2962 2127
10 εὐλογημένος ὁ ἐρχόμενος ἐν ὀνόματι Κυρίου· εὐλογημένη
Blessed (be) the (One) coming in (the) name of (the) Lord! Blessed
2064 932 1722 3686 2962 3962 2257
ἡ ἐρχομένη βασιλεία ἐν ὀνόματι Κυρίου τοῦ πατρὸς ἡμῶν
the coming kingdom in (the) name of (the) Lord, of the father of us
1138 5614 1722 5310
Δαβίδ· Ὡσαννὰ ἐν τοῖς ὑψίστοις.
David! Hosanna in the highest!
1525 1519 2414 2424 1519 2411
11 Καὶ εἰσῆλθεν εἰς Ἱεροσόλυμα ὁ Ἰησοῦς, καὶ εἰς τὸ ἱερόν·
And entered into Jerusalem Jesus, and into the Temple
4017 3956 3798 2235 5607 5610
καὶ περιβλεψάμενος πάντα, ὀψίας ἤδη οὔσης τῆς ὥρας,
and looking around at all things, late already being the hour,
1831 1519 963 3326 1427
ἐξῆλθεν εἰς Βηθανίαν μετὰ τῶν δώδεκα.
He went out to Bethany with the twelve.
1887 1831 848 575 963
12 Καὶ τῇ ἐπαύριον ἐξελθόντων αὐτῶν ἀπὸ Βηθανίας,
And on the morrow having gone out they from Bethany,
3983 1492 4808 3113 2192 5444 2064
13 ἐπείνασε. καὶ ἰδὼν συκῆν μακρόθεν, ἔχουσαν φύλλα, ἦλθεν
He hungered. And seeing a fig-tree afar off having leaves, He came
1487/686 2147 5100/1722/846 2064 1909 846 3762
εἰ ἄρα εὑρήσει τι ἐν αὐτῇ· καὶ ἐλθὼν ἐπ' αὐτήν, οὐδὲν
if perhaps He will find any in it. And coming upon it, nothing
2147 =1508= 5444 3756/1063/2258/ 2540 4810 611
14 εὗρεν εἰ μὴ φύλλα· οὐ γὰρ ἦν καιρὸς σύκων. καὶ ἀποκριθεὶς
He found except leaves; not for it was time of figs. And answering
2424 2036 846 3371 1537/4675/1519 165 3367
ὁ Ἰησοῦς εἶπεν αὐτῇ, Μηκέτι ἐκ σοῦ εἰς τὸν αἰῶνα μηδεὶς
– Jesus said to it, No more from you to the age no one
2590 5315 191 3101 848
καρπὸν φάγοι. καὶ ἤκουον οἱ μαθηταὶ αὐτοῦ.
fruit may eat. And heard the disciples of Him.
2064 1519 2414 1525 2424 1519
15 Καὶ ἔρχονται εἰς Ἱεροσόλυμα· καὶ εἰσελθὼν ὁ Ἰησοῦς εἰς
And they come to Jerusalem. And entering Jesus into
2411 756 1544 4453 59
τὸ ἱερὸν ἤρξατο ἐκβάλλειν τοὺς πωλοῦντας καὶ ἀγοράζοντας
the Temple, He began to cast out those selling, and buying
1722 2411 5132 2855
ἐν τῷ ἱερῷ· καὶ τὰς τραπέζας τῶν κολλυβιστῶν, καὶ τὰς
in the Temple, and the tables of the moneychangers, and the
2515 4453 4058 2690
16 καθέδρας τῶν πωλούντων τὰς περιστερὰς κατέστρεψε· καὶ
seats of those selling the doves He overturned, and
3756 863 2443/5100/ 1308 4632 1223 2411 1321
17 οὐκ ἤφιεν ἵνα τις διενέγκῃ σκεῦος διὰ τοῦ ἱεροῦ. καὶ ἐδίδασκε,
not did allow that any may carry a vessel through the Temple, and taught,
3004 846 3756 1125 3754 3624 3450 3624
λέγων αὐτοῖς, Οὐ γέγραπται ὅτι Ὁ οἶκός μου οἶκος
saying to them, not Has it been written that the house of Me a house
4335 2564 3956 1484 5210 4160
προσευχῆς κληθήσεται πᾶσι τοῖς ἔθνεσιν; ὑμεῖς δὲ ἐποιή-
of prayer shall be called for all the nations? you But have
846 4693 3027 191 1122
18 σατε αὐτὸν σπήλαιον λῃστῶν. καὶ ἤκουσαν οἱ γραμματεῖς
made it a den of robbers. And heard the scribes
749 2212 4459 846 622
καὶ οἱ ἀρχιερεῖς, καὶ ἐζήτουν πῶς αὐτὸν ἀπολέσουσιν·
and the chief priests, and they sought how Him they might destroy;
5399 1063 846 3754 3956 3793 1605 1909
ἐφοβοῦντο γὰρ αὐτόν, ὅτι πᾶς ὁ ὄχλος ἐξεπλήσσετο ἐπὶ
they feared for Him; because all the crowd was astounded at
1322 848
τῇ διδαχῇ αὐτοῦ.
the teaching of Him.

19And when evening
came, He went outside the
city. 20And passing along
early, they saw the fig-tree
withered from *the* roots.
21And remembering, Peter
said to Him, Rabbi, behold,
the fig-tree which You
cursed has withered. 22And
answering Jesus said to
them, Have faith *in* God.
23For truly I say to you,
Whoever says to this
mountain, Be taken up and
be thrown into the sea; and
does not doubt in his heart,
but believes that what he
says will happen, it will be
to him, whatever he says.
24Therefore I say to you, All
things, whatever you ask,
praying, believe that you
will receive, and it will be to
you. 25And when you stand
praying, if you have any-
thing against anyone, forgive *it*, so that your Father in
Heaven may also forgive
your sins. 26But if you do
not forgive, neither will your
Father in Heaven forgive
your sins.

27And they came again to
Jerusalem. And as He was
walking in the temple,
the chief priests and the
scribes and the elders came
to Him. 28And they said to
Him, By what authority do
you do these things? And
who gave you this authority
that you do these things?
29And answering Jesus said
to them, I will also ask you
one thing, and answer Me,
and I will tell you by what
authority I do these things.
30The baptism of John, was
it from Heaven, or from
men? Answer Me. 31And
they argued to themselves,
saying, If we say, From
Heaven, he will say, Why
then did you not believe
him? 32But if we say, From

3753 3796 1096 1607 1854 4172
19 Καὶ ὅτε ὀψὲ ἐγένετο, ἐξεπορεύετο ἔξω τῆς πόλεως.
And when evening came, He went forth out of the city.
4404 3899 1492 4808 3583
20 Καὶ πρωῒ παραπορευόμενοι, εἶδον τὴν συκῆν ἐξηραμ-
And in the morning passing along they saw the fig-tree withered
1537 4491 363 4074 3004 846
21 μένην ἐκ ῥιζῶν. καὶ ἀναμνησθεὶς ὁ Πέτρος λέγει αὐτῷ,
from (the) roots. And remembering – Peter says to Him,
4461 2396 4808/3739 2672 3583 611
22 Ῥαββί, ἴδε, ἡ συκῆ ἣν κατηράσω ἐξήρανται. καὶ ἀποκριθεὶς
Rabbi, behold, the fig-tree which You cursed has withered. And answering
2424 3004 846 2192 4102 2316 281 2063 3004
23 Ἰησοῦς λέγει αὐτοῖς, Ἔχετε πίστιν Θεοῦ. ἀμὴν γὰρ λέγω
Jesus says to them, Have faith (in) God. truly For I say
3739 5213/3754//302/2036 3735 5129 142 906 1519
ὑμῖν ὅτι ὃς ἂν εἴπῃ τῷ ὄρει τούτῳ, Ἄρθητι, καὶ βλήθητι εἰς
to you that whoever says – mountain to this, Be taken, and be thrown into
2281 3361 1252 1722 2588 848 235
τὴν θάλασσαν, καὶ μὴ διακριθῇ ἐν τῇ καρδίᾳ αὐτοῦ, ἀλλὰ
the sea, and not does doubt in the heart of him, but
4100 3754/3739/3004 1096 2071 846/3739/1437/2036/1223
24 πιστεύσῃ ὅτι ἃ λέγει γίνεται· ἔσται αὐτῷ ὃ ἐὰν εἴπῃ. διὰ
believes that what he says occurs, it will be to him, whatever he says. There-
5124 3004 5213 3956 3745 302 4336 154
τοῦτο λέγω ὑμῖν, Πάντα ὅσα ἂν προσευχόμενοι αἰτεῖσθε,
fore, I say to you, All things whatever praying you ask,
4100 3754 2983 2071 5213 3752 4739
25 πιστεύετε ὅτι λαμβάνετε, καὶ ἔσται ὑμῖν. καὶ ὅταν στήκητε
believe that you receive, and it will be to you. And when you stand
4336 863 1487/5100/2192 2596 5100 2443
προσευχόμενοι, ἀφίετε εἴ τι ἔχετε κατά τινος· ἵνα καὶ ὁ
praying, forgive if anything you have against any, that also the
3962 5216 1722 3772 863 5213 3900
πατὴρ ὑμῶν ὁ ἐν τοῖς οὐρανοῖς ἀφῇ ὑμῖν τὰ παραπτώματα
Father of you – in the heavens may forgive you the transgressions
5216/1487 5210 3756 863 3761 3962 5216 1722
26 ὑμῶν. εἰ δὲ ὑμεῖς οὐκ ἀφίετε, οὐδὲ ὁ πατὴρ ὑμῶν ὁ ἐν τοῖς
of you. if But you not do forgive, neither the Father of you – in the
3772 863 3900 5216
οὐρανοῖς ἀφήσει τὰ παραπτώματα ὑμῶν.
heavens will forgive the transgressions of you.

2064 3825 1519 2414 1722 2411
27 Καὶ ἔρχονται πάλιν εἰς Ἱεροσόλυμα· καὶ ἐν τῷ ἱερῷ
And they come again to Jerusalem. And in the Temple
4043 846 2064 4314 846 749
περιπατοῦντος αὐτοῦ, ἔρχονται πρὸς αὐτὸν οἱ ἀρχιερεῖς
walking Him, come to Him the chief priests
1122 4245 3004 846
28 καὶ οἱ γραμματεῖς καὶ οἱ πρεσβύτεροι, καὶ λέγουσιν αὐτῷ,
and the scribes and the elders, and they say to Him,
1722 4169 1849 5023 4160 5101 4671 1849
Ἐν ποίᾳ ἐξουσίᾳ ταῦτα ποιεῖς; καὶ τίς σοι τὴν ἐξουσίαν
By what authority these things do You? And who You authority
5026 1325 2443 5023 4160 2424 611
29 ταύτην ἔδωκεν ἵνα ταῦτα ποιῇς; ὁ δὲ Ἰησοῦς ἀποκριθεὶς
this gave that these things You do? But Jesus answering
2036 846 1905 5209 2504 1520 3056
εἶπεν αὐτοῖς, Ἐπερωτήσω ὑμᾶς κἀγὼ ἕνα λόγον, καὶ
said to them, I will ask you, I also, one thing, and
611 3427 2046/5213/1722/4169 1849 5023 4160
ἀποκρίθητέ μοι, καὶ ἐρῶ ὑμῖν ἐν ποίᾳ ἐξουσίᾳ ταῦτα ποιῶ.
answer to Me, and I will tell you by what authority these things I do.
908 2491 1537 3772 2258/2228/1537 444
30 τὸ βάπτισμα Ἰωάννου ἐξ οὐρανοῦ ἦν, ἢ ἐξ ἀνθρώπων;
The baptism of John, out of Heaven was it, or out of men?
611 3427 3049 4314 1438 3004
31 ἀποκρίθητέ μοι. καὶ ἐλογίζοντο πρὸς ἑαυτούς, λέγοντες,
Answer Me. And they argued with themselves, saying,
1437 2036 1537 3772 2046 1302 3767/3756 4100
Ἐὰν εἴπωμεν, Ἐξ οὐρανοῦ, ἐρεῖ, Διατί οὖν οὐκ ἐπιστεύσατε
If we say, Out of Heaven, He will say, Why then not did you believe

NOTE: Frequent words not numbered: δέ(1161); καί(2531)—and, but; ὁ, ἡ, τό (3588, the)— * above word, look in verse margin for No.

men—they feared the people. For all held that John really was a prophet. [33]And answering they said to Jesus, We do not know. And answering Jesus said to them, Neither do I tell you by what authority I do these things.

CHAPTER 12

[1]And He began to speak to them in parables:

A man planted a vineyard, and set a fence around *it*, and dug a winevat, and built a tower. And *he* let it out to vinedressers, and went away. [2]And at the season he sent a slave to the vinedressers, that he might receive from the vinedressers the fruit of the vineyard. [3]But taking him, they beat *him*, and sent *him* away empty. [4]And again he sent to them another slave. And stoning that one, they struck *him* in the head, and sent *him* away, insulting him. [5]And again he sent another, and they killed that one; also many others, indeed beating these, and killing these.

[6]Yet having one son, his own beloved, then he sent him to them also, last *of all*, saying, They will have respect for my son. [7]But these vinedressers said to themselves, This is the heir; come, let us kill him and the inheritance will be ours. [8]And taking *him*, they killed him, and threw *him* outside the vineyard. [9]What, then, will the lord of the vineyard do? He will come and will destroy the vinedressers, and will give the vineyard to others. [10]Have you not

846 235 1437 2036 1537 444 5399
32 αὐτῷ; ἀλλ' ἐὰν εἴπωμεν, Ἐξ ἀνθρώπων, ἐφοβοῦντο τὸν
him? But if we say, Out of men — they feared the
2992 537 1063 2192 2491 3754 3689 4396
λαόν· ἅπαντες γὰρ εἶχον τὸν Ἰωάννην, ὅτι ὄντως προφήτης
people, all for held John, that really a prophet
2258 611 3004 2424 3756 1492
33 ἦν. καὶ ἀποκριθέντες λέγουσι τῷ Ἰησοῦ, Οὐκ οἴδαμεν. καὶ ὁ
he was. And answering they say to Jesus, not We do know. And
2424 611 3004 846 3761 1473 3004 5213/1722/4169
Ἰησοῦς ἀποκριθεὶς λέγει αὐτοῖς, Οὐδὲ ἐγὼ λέγω ὑμῖν ἐν ποίᾳ
Jesus answering says to them, Neither I tell you by what
1849 5023 4160
ἐξουσίᾳ ταῦτα ποιῶ.
authority these things I do.

CHAPTER 12

756 846 1722 3850 3004 290
1 Καὶ ἤρξατο αὐτοῖς ἐν παραβολαῖς λέγειν, Ἀμπελῶνα
And He began to them in parables to speak. a vineyard
5452 444 4060 5418 3736
ἐφύτευσεν ἄνθρωπος, καὶ περιέθηκε φραγμόν, καὶ ὤρυξεν
planted A man, and put around (it) a fence, and dug
5276 3618 4444 1554 846
ὑπολήνιον, καὶ ᾠκοδόμησε πύργον, καὶ ἐξέδοτο αὐτὸν
a winevat, and built a tower, and gave out it
1092 589 649 4314 1092
2 γεωργοῖς, καὶ ἀπεδήμησε. καὶ ἀπέστειλε πρὸς τοὺς γεωργοὺς
to vinedressers, and went away. And he sent to the vinedressers
2540 1401 2443 3844 1092 2983 575
τῷ καιρῷ δοῦλον, ἵνα παρὰ τῶν γεωργῶν λάβῃ ἀπὸ τοῦ
at the time a slave, that from the vinedressers he receive from the
2590 290 2983 846 1194
3 καρποῦ τοῦ ἀμπελῶνος. οἱ δὲ λαβόντες αὐτὸν ἔδειραν, καὶ
fruit of the vineyard. they But having taken, him beat, and
849 2756 3825 649 4314 846 243
4 ἀπέστειλαν κενόν. καὶ πάλιν ἀπέστειλε πρὸς αὐτοὺς ἄλλον
sent (him) away empty. And again he sent to them another
1401 2548 3036 2775 649
δοῦλον· κἀκεῖνον λιθοβολήσαντες ἐκεφαλαίωσαν, καὶ ἀπέ-
slave; that one having stoned they struck in the head and sent
821 3825 243 649 2548
5 στειλαν ἠτιμωμένον. καὶ πάλιν ἄλλον ἀπέστειλε· κἀκεῖνον
(him) away, insulting him. And again another he sent; that one
615 4183 243 3303 1194
ἀπέκτειναν· καὶ πολλοὺς ἄλλους, τοὺς μὲν δέροντες, τοὺς
they killed; and many others, these indeed beating, these
615 2089/3767/1520/5207/2192 27 848
6 δὲ ἀποκτείνοντες. ἔτι οὖν ἕνα υἱὸν ἔχων ἀγαπητὸν αὐτοῦ,
and killing. Still, then, one son having beloved his own,
649 846 4314 846 2078 3004 3754
ἀπέστειλε καὶ αὐτὸν πρὸς αὐτοὺς ἔσχατον, λέγων ὅτι
he sent also him to them last, saying,
1788 5207 3450 1565 1092 2036
7 Ἐντραπήσονται τὸν υἱόν μου. ἐκεῖνοι δὲ οἱ γεωργοὶ εἶπον
They will respect the son of me. those But vinedressers said
4314 1438 3754 3778 2076 2818 1205 615
πρὸς ἑαυτοὺς ὅτι Οὗτός ἐστιν ὁ κληρονόμος· δεῦτε, ἀπο-
to themselves, This is the heir, come, let us
846 2257 2071 2817 2983
8 κτείνωμεν αὐτόν, καὶ ἡμῶν ἔσται ἡ κληρονομία. καὶ λαβόντες
kill him, and of us will be the inheritance. And taking
846 615 1544 1854 290 5101
9 αὐτὸν ἀπέκτειναν, καὶ ἐξέβαλον ἔξω τοῦ ἀμπελῶνος. τί οὖν
him they killed, and cast (him) outside the vineyard. What then
4160 2962 290 2064 622
ποιήσει ὁ κύριος τοῦ ἀμπελῶνος; ἐλεύσεται καὶ ἀπολέσει
will do the lord of the vineyard? He will come and will destroy
1092 1325 290 243 3761
10 τοὺς γεωργούς, καὶ δώσει τὸν ἀμπελῶνα ἄλλοις. οὐδὲ τὴν
the vinedressers, and will give the vineyard to others. not even

even read this Scripture, "*The* Stone which the builders rejected, this one became head of *the* corner; [11]this came about from *the* Lord, and it is marvelous in our eyes"? [12]And they sought to seize Him, yet feared the crowd. For they knew that He spoke the parable against them. And leaving Him, they went away.

[13]And they sent some of the Pharisees and of the Herodians to Him, that they might catch Him in a word. [14]And coming they said to Him, Teacher, we know that you are true, and there is not a care to you about anyone, for you do not look to *the* face of men, but teach on the way of God *in* truth: Is it lawful to give tribute to Caesar, or not? [15]Should we give, or should we not give? But knowing their hypocrisy, He said to them, Why do you tempt Me? Bring Me a denarius, that I may see. [16]And they brought *one*. And He said to them, Whose image and superscription *is* this? And they said to Him, Caesar's. [17]And answering Jesus said to them, Render the things of Caesar to Caesar, and the things of God to God. And they marveled at Him.

[18]And Sadducees came to Him, who say there is no resurrection. And they questioned Him, saying, [19]Teacher, Moses wrote for us that if a brother of anyone should die and leave behind a wife, and leave no children, that his brother should take his wife and raise up seed to his brother. [20]Then there were seven brothers.

1124 5026 314 3037 3739 593
γραφὴν ταύτην ἀνέγνωτε, Λίθον ὃν ἀπεδοκίμασαν οἱ
scripture this Did you read? (The) Stone which rejected those
3618 3778 1096 1519 2776 1137 3844
11 οἰκοδομοῦντες, οὗτος ἐγενήθη εἰς κεφαλὴν γωνίας· παρὰ
building, this one became for head of (the) corner; from
2962 1096 3778 2076 2298 1722 3788
Κυρίου ἐγένετο αὕτη, καὶ ἔστι θαυμαστὴ ἐν ὀφθαλμοῖς
(the) Lord occurred this, and it is marvelous in eyes
2254 2212 846 2902 5399
12 ἡμῶν; καὶ ἐζήτουν αὐτὸν κρατῆσαι, καὶ ἐφοβήθησαν τὸν
of us? And they sought Him to seize, and feared the
3793 1097 1063 3754 4314 846 3850
ὄχλον· ἔγνωσαν γὰρ ὅτι πρὸς αὐτοὺς τὴν παραβολὴν
crowd; they knew for that to them the parable
2036 863 846 565
εἶπε· καὶ ἀφέντες αὐτὸν ἀπῆλθον.
He told. And leaving Him, they went away.
649 4314 846 5100 5330
13 Καὶ ἀποστέλλουσι πρός αὐτόν τινας τῶν Φαρισαίων καὶ
And they send to Him some of the Pharisees and
2265 2443 846 64 3056
14 τῶν Ἡρωδιανῶν, ἵνα αὐτὸν ἀγρεύσωσι λόγῳ. οἱ δὲ
the Herodians, that Him they might catch in a word. they And
2064 3004 846 1320 1492 3754 227
ἐλθόντες λέγουσιν αὐτῷ, Διδάσκαλε, οἴδαμεν ὅτι ἀληθὴς
having come say to Him, Teacher, we know that true
1488 3756 3199 4671 4012 3762 3756 1063 991 1519 4383
εἶ, καὶ οὐ μέλει σοι περὶ οὐδενός· οὐ γὰρ βλέπεις εἰς πρό-
you are, and not a care to you about no one; not for you look to (the)
444 235 1909 225 3598 2316
σωπον ἀνθρώπων, ἀλλ' ἐπ' ἀληθείας τὴν ὁδὸν τοῦ Θεοῦ
face of men, but on truth the way — of God
1321 1832 2778 2541 1325 2228/3756 1325
15 διδάσκεις· ἔξεστι κῆνσον Καίσαρι δοῦναι ἢ οὔ; δῶμεν, ἢ
teach: Is it lawful tribute to Caesar to give, or not? Should we give or
3361 1325 1492 848 5272 2036 846
μὴ δῶμεν; ὁ δὲ εἰδὼς αὐτῶν τὴν ὑπόκρισιν εἶπεν αὐτοῖς,
not should we give? He But knowing their hypocrisy said to them,
5101/3165 3985 5342 3427 1220 2443/1492 5342
16 Τί με πειράζετε; φέρετέ μοι δηνάριον, ἵνα ἴδω. οἱ δὲ ἤνεγκαν.
Why Me tempt you? Bring Me a denarius, that I may see. they And brought.
3004 846 5101 1504 3778 1923
καὶ λέγει αὐτοῖς, Τίνος ἡ εἰκὼν αὕτη καὶ ἡ ἐπιγραφή; οἱ
And He says to them, Whose (is) image this and superscription? they
2036 846 2541 611 2424 2036
17 δὲ εἶπον αὐτῷ, Καίσαρος. καὶ ἀποκριθεὶς ὁ Ἰησοῦς εἶπεν
And said to Him, Caesar's. And answering, Jesus said
846 591 2541 2541 2316
αὐτοῖς, Ἀπόδοτε τὰ Καίσαρος Καίσαρι, καὶ τὰ τοῦ Θεοῦ
to them, Render the things of Caesar to Caesar, and the things of God
2316 2296 1909 846
τῷ Θεῷ. καὶ ἐθαύμασαν ἐπ' αὐτῷ.
to God. And they marveled at Him.
2064 4523 4314 846 3748 3004
18 Καὶ ἔρχονται Σαδδουκαῖοι πρὸς αὐτόν, οἵτινες λέγουσιν
And come Sadducees to Him, who say
386 3361 1511 1905 846 3004
ἀνάστασιν μὴ εἶναι· καὶ ἐπηρώτησαν αὐτόν, λέγοντες,
a resurrection not to be, and questioned Him, saying,
1320 3475 1125 2254 3754/1437 5100 80
19 Διδάσκαλε, Μωσῆς ἔγραψεν ἡμῖν, ὅτι ἐάν τινος ἀδελφὸς
Teacher, Moses wrote to us that if of anyone a brother
599 2641 1135 5043/3361/863/2443
ἀποθάνῃ, καὶ καταλίπῃ γυναῖκα, καὶ τέκνα μὴ ἀφῇ, ἵνα
should die and leave behind a wife, and children not leave, that
2983 80 848 1135 848 1817
λάβῃ ὁ ἀδελφὸς αὐτοῦ τὴν γυναῖκα αὐτοῦ, καὶ ἐξαναστήσῃ
should take the brother of him the wife of him and should raise up
4690 80 848 2033 3767 80 2258
20 σπέρμα τῷ ἀδελφῷ αὐτοῦ· ἑπτὰ οὖν ἀδελφοὶ ἦσαν· καὶ ὁ
seed to the brother of him. Seven then brothers were; and the

And the first took a wife, and dying, *he* left no seed. [21]And the second took her, and died, and neither did he leave seed; and the third likewise. [22]And the seven took her, and left no seed. Last of all, the woman also died. [23]Therefore, in the resurrection, when they rise again, of which of them will she be the wife? For the seven had her *as* wife. [24]And answering Jesus said to them, Do you not err because of this, not knowing the Scriptures, nor the power of God? [25]For when they rise again from the dead, they neither marry nor are given in marriage, but are as angels in Heaven. [26]But concerning the dead, that they are raised, have you not read in the book of Moses, as God spoke to him at the Bush, saying, "I *am* the God of Abraham, and the God of Isaac, and the God of Jacob"? [27]He is not the God of *the* dead, but God of *the* living. Therefore, you greatly err.

[28]And coming up one of the scribes, hearing them arguing, knowing that He answered them well, *he* questioned Him, What is *the* first commandment of all? [29]And Jesus answered him, *The* first of all the commandments *is*: "Hear, Israel. *The* Lord our God is one Lord, [30]and you shall love *the* Lord your God with all your heart, and with all your soul and with all your mind, and with all your strength." This is the first commandment. [31]And *the* second *is* like this, "You shall love your neighbor as yourself." There is not

4413 2983 1135 599 3756 863 4690
πρῶτος ἔλαβε γυναῖκα, καὶ ἀποθνήσκων οὐκ ἀφῆκε σπέρμα·
first took a wife, and dying not did leave seed.
1208 2983 846 599 3751 846
21 καὶ ὁ δεύτερος ἔλαβεν αὐτήν, καὶ ἀπέθανε, καὶ οὐδὲ αὐτὸς
And the second took her, and died, and neither he
863 4690 5154 5615 2983 846
22 ἀφῆκε σπέρμα· καὶ ὁ τρίτος ὡσαύτως. καὶ ἔλαβον αὐτὴν
left behind seed. And the third likewise. And took her
2033 3756 863 4690 2078 3956 599
οἱ ἑπτά, καὶ οὐκ ἀφῆκαν σπέρμα. ἐσχάτη πάντων ἀπέθανε
the seven, and not did leave seed. Last of all died
1135 1722 3767 386 3752 450 5101
23 καὶ ἡ γυνή. ἐν τῇ οὖν ἀναστάσει, ὅταν ἀναστῶσι, τίνος
also the wife. In the then resurrection, when they rise again, of which
846 2071 1135 1063 2033 2192 846 1135
αὐτῶν ἔσται γυνή; οἱ γὰρ ἑπτὰ ἔσχον αὐτὴν γυναῖκα.
of them will she be wife? the For seven had her (as) wife.
611 2424 2036 846 3756 1223 5124
24 καὶ ἀποκριθεὶς ὁ Ἰησοῦς εἶπεν αὐτοῖς, Οὐ διὰ τοῦτο
And answering, – Jesus said to them, Not therefore
4105 3361 1492 1124 3366 1411
πλανᾶσθε, μὴ εἰδότες τὰς γραφάς, μηδὲ τὴν δύναμιν τοῦ
do you err, not knowing the Scriptures, nor the power –
2316 3752 1063 1537 3498 450 3777 1060
25 Θεοῦ; ὅταν γὰρ ἐκ νεκρῶν ἀναστῶσιν, οὔτε γαμοῦσιν,
of God? when For from (the) dead they rise again, neither they marry,
3777 1061 235 1526/5613 32 1722 3772
οὔτε γαμίσκονται, ἀλλ' εἰσὶν ὡς ἄγγελοι οἱ ἐν τοῖς οὐρανοῖς.
nor are given in marriage, but are as angels – in the heavens.
4012 3498 2754 1453 3756 314 1722
26 περὶ δὲ τῶν νεκρῶν, ὅτι ἐγείρονται, οὐκ ἀνέγνωτε ἐν τῇ
about But the dead, that they are raised, not did you read in the
976 3475 1909 942 5613/2036/ 846 2316 3004
βίβλῳ Μωσέως, ἐπὶ τῆς βάτου, ὡς εἶπεν αὐτῷ ὁ Θεός, λέγων,
roll of Moses at the Bush, as spoke to him God, saying,
1473 2316 11 2316 2464 2316 2384
Ἐγὼ ὁ Θεὸς Ἀβραάμ, καὶ ὁ Θεὸς Ἰσαάκ, καὶ ὁ Θεὸς Ἰακώβ;
I (am) the God of Abraham, and the God of Isaac, and the God of Jacob?
3756 2076 2316 3498 235 2316 2198 5210 3767 4183
27 οὐκ ἔστιν ὁ Θεὸς νεκρῶν, ἀλλὰ Θεὸς ζώντων· ὑμεῖς οὖν πολὺ
not He is the God of (the) dead, but God of (the) living You then much
4105
πλανᾶσθε.
err.

4334 1520 1122 191 846
28 Καὶ προσελθὼν εἷς τῶν γραμματέων, ἀκούσας αὐτῶν
And coming up one of the scribes, hearing them
4802 1492 3754 2573 846 611 1905
συζητούντων, εἰδὼς ὅτι καλῶς αὐτοῖς ἀπεκρίθη, ἐπηρώ-
arguing, knowing that well to them He answered, asked
846 4169 2076 4413 3956 1785
29 τησεν αὐτόν, Ποία ἐστὶ πρώτη πασῶν ἐντολή; ὁ δὲ
Him, What is (the) first of all commandments? – And
2424 611 846 3754 4413 3954 1785
Ἰησοῦς ἀπεκρίθη αὐτῷ ὅτι Πρώτη πασῶν τῶν ἐντολῶν.
Jesus answered him, The first of all commandments? (is)
191 2414 2962 2316 2257 2962 1520 2076
30 Ἄκουε, Ἰσραήλ· Κύριος ὁ Θεὸς ἡμῶν, Κύριος εἷς ἐστί· καὶ
Hear, Israel, Lord the God of us Lord one is, and
25 2962 2316 4675 1537/3650 2588 4675
ἀγαπήσεις Κύριον τὸν Θεόν σου ἐξ ὅλης τῆς καρδίας σου,
you shall love the Lord the God of you from all the heart of you,
1537/3650 5590 4675 1537/3650 1271 4675
καὶ ἐξ ὅλης τῆς ψυχῆς σου, καὶ ἐξ ὅλης τῆς διανοίας σου,
and from all the soul of you, and from all the mind of you,
1537/3650 2479 4675 3778 4413 1781 1208
31 καὶ ἐξ ὅλης τῆς ἰσχύος σου. αὕτη πρώτη ἐντολή. καὶ δευτέρα
and from all the strength of you. This the first commandment; and second
3664 3778 25 4139 4675/5613 4572 3173
ὁμοία αὕτη, Ἀγαπήσεις τὸν πλησίον σου ὡς σεαυτόν. μείζων
like this, You shall love the neighbor of you as yourself. Greater

another commandment greater than these. [32]And the scribe said to Him, *You say* well, Teacher. You have spoken according to truth, that God is one, and there is no other besides Him; [33]and to love Him from all the heart, and from all the understanding, and from all the soul, and from all the strength; and to love *one's* neighbor as oneself, is more than all the burnt offerings and the sacrifices. [34]And seeing that he answered intelligently, Jesus said to him, You are not far from the kingdom of God. And no one dared to question Him any more.

[35]And teaching in the temple, answering Jesus said, How do the scribes say that Christ is the son of David? [36]For David himself said by the Holy Spirit, "The Lord said to my Lord, Sit off My right until I place Your enemies *as* a footstool for Your feet." [37]Then David himself calls Him Lord. And from where is He his son? And the large crowd heard Him gladly.

[38]And He said to them in His teaching, Be careful of the scribes, those desiring to walk about in robes, and greetings in the markets, [39]and chief seats in the synagogues, and chief couches in the dinners, [40]those devouring the houses of widows, and for a pretense praying at length. These shall receive more abundant judgment.

[41]And sitting down opposite the treasury, Jesus watched how the crowd threw copper coins into the treasury. And many rich

5130 243 1785 3756/2076 2036 846 1122
32 τούτων ἄλλη ἐντολὴ οὐκ ἔστι. καὶ εἶπεν αὐτῷ ὁ γραμματεύς,
(than) these other command not is. And said to Him the scribe,
2573 1320 1909 225 2036 3754/1519/2076/2316
Καλῶς, διδάσκαλε, ἐπ' ἀληθείας εἶπας ὅτι εἷς ἐστι Θεός, καὶ
Well, Teacher, by truth you say that one is God, and
3756 2076 243 4133 846 25 846 1537
33 οὐκ ἔστιν ἄλλος πλὴν αὐτοῦ. καὶ τὸ ἀγαπᾷν αὐτὸν ἐξ
not there is another besides Him; and – to love Him out of
3650 2588 1537/3650 4907 1537/3650
ὅλης τῆς καρδίας, καὶ ἐξ ὅλης τῆς συνέσεως, καὶ ἐξ ὅλης τῆς
all the heart, and out of all the understanding, and out of all the
5590 1537/3650 2479 25 4139
ψυχῆς, καὶ ἐξ ὅλης τῆς ἰσχύος, καὶ τὸ ἀγαπᾷν τὸν πλησίον
soul, and from all the strength; and – to love the neighbor
5613 1438 4119 2076 3956 3646
ὡς ἑαυτόν, πλεῖόν ἐστι πάντων τῶν ὁλοκαυτωμάτων καὶ
as oneself, more is than all the burnt offerings and
2378 2424 1492 846 3754 3562
34 τῶν θυσιῶν. καὶ ὁ Ἰησοῦς ἰδὼν αὐτὸν ὅτι νουνεχῶς
the sacrifices. And – Jesus seeing him, that intelligently
611 2036 846 3756/ 3112 1488/575 932
ἀπεκρίθη, εἶπεν αὐτῷ, Οὐ μακρὰν εἶ ἀπὸ τῆς βασιλείας τοῦ
he answered, said to him, Not far are you from the kingdom
2316 3762 3765 5111 846 1905
Θεοῦ. καὶ οὐδεὶς οὐκέτι ἐτόλμα αὐτὸν ἐπερωτῆσαι.
of God. And no one no more dared Him to question.
611 2424 3004 1321 1722 2411 4459
35 Καὶ ἀποκριθεὶς ὁ Ἰησοῦς ἔλεγε, διδάσκων ἐν τῷ ἱερῷ, Πῶς
And answering, – Jesus said, teaching in the Temple, How
3004 1122 3754 5547 5207 2076 1138
λέγουσιν οἱ γραμματεῖς ὅτι ὁ Χριστὸς υἱός ἐστι Δαβίδ;
say the scribes that the Christ son is of David?
848 1063 1138 2036 1722 4151 40 2036
36 αὐτὸς γὰρ Δαβὶδ εἶπεν ἐν τῷ Πνεύματι τῷ Ἁγίῳ, Εἶπεν ὁ
himself For David said in the Spirit – Holy, Said the
2962 2962 3450 2521 1537 1188 3450 2193 302/5087
Κύριος τῷ Κυρίῳ μου, Κάθου ἐκ δεξιῶν μου, ἕως ἂν θῶ τοὺς
Lord to the Lord of me, Sit off (the) right of Me until I put the
2190 4675 5286 4228 4675 846 3767 1138
37 ἐχθρούς σου ὑποπόδιον τῶν ποδῶν σου. Αὐτὸς οὖν Δαβὶδ
enemies of You (as) a footstool for the feet of You. Himself, Then, David
3004 846 2962 4159 5207 848 2076 4183
λέγει αὐτὸν Κύριον· καὶ πόθεν υἱὸς αὐτοῦ ἐστι; καὶ ὁ πολὺς
says Him (to be) Lord, and from where son of him is He? And the large
3793 191 846 2234
ὄχλος ἤκουεν αὐτοῦ ἡδέως.
crowd heard Him gladly.
3004 846 1722 1322 848 991 575
38 Καὶ ἔλεγεν αὐτοῖς ἐν τῇ διδαχῇ αὐτοῦ, Βλέπετε ἀπὸ τῶν
And He said to them in the teaching of Him, Be careful from the
1122 2309 1722 4749 4043
γραμματέων, τῶν θελόντων ἐν στολαῖς περιπατεῖν, καὶ
scribes, the (ones) desiring in robes to walk about, and
783 1722 58 4410 1722
39 ἀσπασμοὺς ἐν ταῖς ἀγοραῖς, καὶ πρωτοκαθεδρίας ἐν ταῖς
greetings in the markets, and chief seats in the
4864 4411 1722 1173 2719
40 συναγωγαῖς, καὶ πρωτοκλισίας ἐν τοῖς δείπνοις· οἱ κατε-
synagogues, and chief couches in the dinners; the (ones)
3614 5503 4392 3117
σθίοντες τὰς οἰκίας τῶν χηρῶν, καὶ προφάσει μακρὰ
devouring the houses of the widows, and for a pretence lengthily
4336 3778 2963 4055 2917
προσευχόμενοι· οὗτοι λήψονται περισσότερον κρίμα.
praying; these will receive more abundant judgment.
2523 2424 2713 1049
41 Καὶ καθίσας ὁ Ἰησοῦς κατέναντι τοῦ γαζοφυλακίου
And sitting Jesus opposite the treasury,
2334 4459 3793 906 5475 1519 1049
ἐθεώρει πῶς ὁ ὄχλος βάλλει χαλκὸν εἰς τὸ γαζοφυλάκιον·
He watched how the crowd cast copper coins into the treasury.

ones threw in much. [42]And coming one poor widow threw in two lepta, which is a kodrantes. [43]And having called His disciples near, He said to them, Truly I say to you that this poor widow has thrown *in* more than all of those casting into the treasury. [44]For all threw *in* out of that abounding to them, but she out of her poverty threw *in* all, as much as she had, her whole livelihood.

4183 4145 906 4183 2064 3391
42 καὶ πολλοὶ πλούσιοι ἔβαλλον πολλά. καὶ ἐλθοῦσα μία
And many rich ones cast in much; and coming one
5503 4434 906 3016 1417 3739 2076 2835
43 χήρα πτωχὴ ἔβαλε λεπτὰ δύο, ὅ ἐστι κοδράντης. καὶ
widow poor cast lepta two, which is a quadrans. And
4341 3101 848 3004 846 281
προσκαλεσάμενος τοὺς μαθητὰς αὐτοῦ, λέγει αὐτοῖς, Ἀμὴν
having called near the disciples of Him, He says to them, Truly
3004 5213 3754 5503 3778 4434 4119 3956
λέγω ὑμῖν ὅτι ἡ χήρα αὕτη ἡ πτωχὴ πλεῖον πάντων
I say to you that – widow, this – poor more than all
906 906 1519 1049 3956 1063
44 βέβληκε τῶν βαλόντων εἰς τὸ γαζοφυλάκιον· πάντες γὰρ
has cast the (ones) casting into the treasury; all for
1537 4052 846 906 3778 1537
ἐκ τοῦ περισσεύοντος αὐτοῖς ἔβαλον· αὕτη δὲ ἐκ τῆς
out of that abounding to them cast, she but out of the
5304 848 3956 3745 2192 906 3650 979
ὑστερήσεως αὐτῆς πάντα ὅσα εἶχεν ἔβαλεν, ὅλον τὸν βίον
poverty of her all, as much as she had cast all the living
848
αὐτῆς.
of her.

CHAPTER 13

[1]And as He was going out of the temple, one of His disciples said to Him, Teacher, see what kind of stones and what kind of buildings! [2]And answering Jesus said to him, Do you see these great buildings? Not one stone shall be left upon *a* stone which shall not be thrown down.

[3]And *as* He *was* sitting in the Mount of Olives opposite the temple, Peter and James and John and Andrew questioned Him privately: [4]Tell us when these things shall be? And what *is* the sign when all these things are about to be done? [5]And answering Jesus began to say to them, Be careful that no one lead you astray. [6]For many will come in My name, saying I AM! And they will lead many astray. [7]But when you hear *of* wars and rumors of wars, do not be disturbed; for it must occur—but the end is not yet. [8]For nation will be raised against nation, and kingdom against kingdom. And there shall be earthquakes in many places; and

1607 846 1537 2411 3004 846 1520
1 Καὶ ἐκπορευομένου αὐτοῦ ἐκ τοῦ ἱεροῦ, λέγει αὐτῷ εἷς
And going forth He out of the Temple, says to Him one
3101 848 1320 2396 4217 3037
τῶν μαθητῶν αὐτοῦ, Διδάσκαλε, ἴδε, ποταποὶ λίθοι καὶ
of the disciples of Him, Teacher, Behold, what kind of stones and
4217 3619 2424 611 2036 846
2 ποταπαὶ οἰκοδομαί. καὶ ὁ Ἰησοῦς ἀποκριθεὶς εἶπεν αὐτῷ,
what kind of buildings! And – Jesus answering said to him,
991 5025 3173 3619 =3364= 863 3037
Βλέπεις ταύτας τὰς μεγάλας οἰκοδομάς; οὐ μὴ ἀφεθῇ λίθος
Do you see these – great buildings? In no way will be left stone
3361/1909 3037/3739/3756 * 2647
ἐπὶ λίθῳ, ὃς οὐ μὴ καταλυθῇ.
upon stone that not at all (will) be thrown down.
2521 846 1519 3735 1636 2713
3 Καὶ καθημένου αὐτοῦ εἰς τὸ ὄρος τῶν ἐλαιῶν κατέναντι
And sitting He in the mount of the olives opposite
2411 1905 846 2596 2398 4074 2385
τοῦ ἱεροῦ, ἐπηρώτων αὐτὸν κατ' ἰδίαν Πέτρος καὶ Ἰάκωβος
the Temple, questioned Him privately Peter and James
2491 406 2036/5213 4219 5023 2071
4 καὶ Ἰωάννης καὶ Ἀνδρέας, Εἰπὲ ἡμῖν, πότε ταῦτα ἔσται;
and John and Andrew, Tell us, when these things will be?
5101 4592 3752 3195 3956 5023 4931
καὶ τί τὸ σημεῖον ὅταν μέλλῃ πάντα ταῦτα συντελεῖσθαι;
And what the sign when are about all these things to be accomplished
2424 611 846 756 3004 991 3361/5100
5 ὁ δὲ Ἰησοῦς ἀποκριθεὶς αὐτοῖς ἤρξατο λέγειν, Βλέπετε μή τις
And Jesus answering to them began to say, Watch (that) not any
5209 4105 4183 1063 2064 1909 3686 3450
6 ὑμᾶς πλανήσῃ. πολλοὶ γὰρ ἐλεύσονται ἐπὶ τῷ ὀνόματί μου,
you lead astray many For will come on the name of Me,
3004 3754/ 1473/ 1510 4183 4105 3752
7 λέγοντες ὅτι Ἐγώ εἰμι· καὶ πολλοὺς πλανήσουσιν. ὅταν δὲ
saying, – I AM! And many they will lead astray. when But
191 4171 189 4171 3361 2360 1163
ἀκούσητε πολέμους καὶ ἀκοὰς πολέμων, μὴ θροεῖσθε· δεῖ
you hear (of) wars and rumors of wars, do not be alarmed. it must
1063 1096 235 3768 5056 1453 1063 1484
8 γὰρ γενέσθαι· ἀλλ' οὔπω τὸ τέλος. ἐγερθήσεται γὰρ ἔθνος
For happen, but not yet the end. will be raised For nation
1909 1484 932 1909 932 2071 4578
ἐπὶ ἔθνος, καὶ βασιλεία ἐπὶ βασιλείαν· καὶ ἔσονται σεισμοὶ
against nation, and kingdom against kingdom; and shall be earthquakes

there shall be famines and
troubles. These things *are*
the beginnings of an-
guishes.

9 But you yourselves be
careful, for they will deliver
you up to sanhedrins and to
synagogues. You will be
beaten, and you will be led
before governors and kings
for My sake, for a testimony
to them. 10 And the gospel
must first be proclaimed to
all the nations. 11 But
whenever they lead you
away, delivering *you,* do not
be anxious beforehand,
what you should say, nor
meditate. But whatever
may be given to you in that
hour, speak that. For you
are not those speaking, but
the Holy Spirit.
12 And a brother will
deliver up a brother to
death, and a father the
child. And children will rise
up on parents, and will put
them to death. 13 And you
will be hated by all on
account of My name. But
the *one* enduring to the
end, that *one* will be saved.
14 But when you see the
abomination of desolation,
the *one* spoken of by Daniel
the prophet, standing
where it ought not—he
reading, let him understand
—then let those in Judea
flee into the mountains.
15 And he on the housetop,
let him not go down into
the house, nor go in to take
anything out of his house.
16 And the *one* in the field,
let him not return to the
things behind, to take his
garment. 17 But woe to the
ones holding *a child* in
womb, and to those giving
suck in those days! 18 And
pray that your flight will not
be in winter; 19 for there will
be affliction *in* those days,
such as has not been the
like from *the* beginning of
creation which God created

2596 5117 2071 3042 5016 746 5604
κατὰ τόπους, καὶ ἔσονται λιμοὶ καὶ ταραχαί· ἀρχαὶ ὠδίνων
In many places; and shall be famines and troubles. Beginnings of travails
5023
ταῦτα.
these things (are).
991 5210 1438 3860 1063 5209/1519
9 Βλέπετε δὲ ὑμεῖς ἑαυτούς· παραδώσουσι γὰρ ὑμᾶς εἰς
watch But you yourselves; they will deliver for you to
4892 1519 4864 1194 1909 2232
συνέδρια, καὶ εἰς συναγωγὰς δαρήσεσθε, καὶ ἐπὶ ἡγεμόνων
sanhedrins, and to synagogues—you will be beaten; and before rulers
935 2476 1752 1700/1519 3142 846
καὶ βασιλέων ἀχθήσεσθε ἕνεκεν ἐμοῦ, εἰς μαρτύριον αὐτοῖς.
and kings you will be led for the sake of Me, for a testimony to them.
1519/3956 1484 4412 2784 2098
10 καὶ εἰς πάντα τὰ ἔθνη δεῖ πρῶτον κηρυχθῆναι τὸ εὐαγγέλιον
And to all the nations must first be proclaimed the gospel.
3752 71 5209 3860 3361 4305 5101
11 ὅταν δὲ ἀγάγωσιν ὑμᾶς παραδιδόντες, μὴ προμεριμνᾶτε τί
when And they lead away you, delivering (you), not be anxious before what t
2980 3366 3191 235/3739/1437/1325/5213/1722/ 1565
λαλήσητε, μηδὲ μελετᾶτε· ἀλλ' ὃ ἐὰν δοθῇ ὑμῖν ἐν ἐκείνῃ τῇ
you may say, not meditate, but whatever is given you in that
5610 5124 2980 3756/1063/ 2075 5210 2980 235
ὥρᾳ, τοῦτο λαλεῖτε· οὐ γάρ ἐστε ὑμεῖς οἱ λαλοῦντες, ἀλλὰ
hour, this speak; not for are you the (ones) speaking, but
4151 40 3860 80 80 1519
12 τὸ Πνεῦμα τὸ Ἅγιον. παραδώσει δὲ ἀδελφὸς ἀδελφὸν εἰς
the Spirit — Holy. will deliver And a brother a brother to
2288 3962 5043 1881 5043 1909
θάνατον, καὶ πατὴρ τέκνον· καὶ ἐπαναστήσονται τέκνα ἐπὶ
to death, and a father a child; and will rise up children upon
1118 2289 846 2071 3404
13 γονεῖς, καὶ θανατώσουσιν αὐτούς· καὶ ἔσεσθε μισούμενοι
parents, and will put to death them; and you will be hated
5259 3956 1223 3686 3450 5278 1519 5056
ὑπὸ πάντων διὰ τὸ ὄνομά μου· ὁ δὲ ὑπομείνας εἰς τέλος,
by all on account of the name of Me. he But enduring to the end,
3778 4982
οὗτος σωθήσεται.
this (one) will be saved.
3752 1492 946 2050 4483
14 Ὅταν δὲ ἴδητε τὸ βδέλυγμα τῆς ἐρημώσεως, τὸ ῥηθὲν
when But you see the abomination — of desolation the (one) spoken
5259 1158 4396 2476 3699/3756/1163 314
ὑπὸ Δανιὴλ τοῦ προφήτου, ἑστὼς ὅπου οὐ δεῖ (ὁ ἀναγινώ-
by Daniel the prophet, standing where not it ought, he reading
3539 5119 1722 2449 5343 1519
σκων νοείτω), τοτε οἱ ἐν τῇ Ἰουδαίᾳ φευγέτωσαν εἰς τὰ
let him understand, then those in Judea, let them flee into the
3735 1909 1430 3361 2597 1519 3614
15 ὄρη· ὁ δὲ ἐπὶ τοῦ δώματος μὴ καταβάτω εἰς τὴν οἰκίαν,
mounts. he And on the housetop, not let him descend into the house,
3366 1525 142 5100 1537 3614 848 1519
16 μηδὲ εἰσελθέτω ἆραί τι ἐκ τῆς οἰκίας αὐτοῦ· καὶ ὁ εἰς τὸν
nor enter to take anything out of the house of him; and he in the
68 5607/3361 1994 1519 3694 142 2440
ἀγρὸν ὢν μὴ ἐπιστρεψάτω εἰς τὰ ὀπίσω, ἆραι τὸ ἱμάτιον
field, being, not let him return to the things behind to take the garment
848 3759 1722 1064 2192 2337
17 αὐτοῦ. οὐαὶ δὲ ταῖς ἐν γαστρὶ ἐχούσαις καὶ ταῖς θηλαζού-
of him. woe But to those in womb holding, and to those giving
1722 1565 2250 4336 2443/3361 1096
18 σαις ἐν ἐκείναις ταῖς ἡμέραις. προσεύχεσθε δὲ ἵνα μὴ γένηται
suck in those days. pray But that not may occur
5437 5216 5494 2071 1063 2250 1565 2347
19 ἡ φυγὴ ὑμῶν χειμῶνος. ἔσονται γὰρ αἱ ἡμέραι ἐκεῖναι θλίψις,
the flight of you in winter, will be for days those affliction
3634/3756 1096 5108 575 746 2937 3739 2936
οἵα οὐ γέγονε τοιαύτη ἀπ' ἀρχῆς κτίσεως ἧς ἔκτισεν ὁ
such as not has been the like from beginning of creation which created

until now, and never *will* be. [20]And if *the* Lord had not shortened the days, not any flesh would be saved; but because of the elect whom He chose, He has shortened the days. [21]And then if anyone says to you, Behold, here *is* the Christ! Or, Behold, there! You shall not believe. [22]For false christs and false prophets will be raised, and they will give signs and wonders in order to lead astray, if possible, even the elect. [23]But you be careful. Behold, I have foretold you all things.

[24]But in those days, after that affliction, the sun will be darkened, and the moon will not give her light; [25]and the stars of the heaven will be falling, and the powers in the heavens will be shaken. [26]And then they will see the Son of man coming in clouds with much power and glory. [27]And then He will send His angels and will gather His elect from the four winds, from *the* end of earth to *the* end of Heaven.

[28]And from the fig-tree learn the parable: When its branch becomes tender and puts out leaves, you know the summer is near. [29]So you also, when you see these things happening, know that it is near, at *the* doors. [30]Truly I say to you, Not at all will this generation pass away until all these things occur. [31]The heaven and the earth will pass away, but My words will not at all pass away. [32]But concerning that day and the hour, no one knows, not the angels, those in Heaven, nor the

2316 2193 3568 3756/3361 1096 =1508= 2962
20 Θεὸς ἕως τοῦ νῦν, καὶ ου μὴ γένηται. καὶ εἰ μὴ Κύριος
God until — now, and in no way may be. And unless (the) Lord
2856 2250 3956/302 4982 3956 4561 235 1223
ἐκολόβωσε τὰς ἡμέρας, οὐκ ἂν ἐσώθη πᾶσα σάρξ· ἀλλὰ διὰ
had shortened the days, not would be saved any flesh; but because of
1588 3739 1586 2856 2250
21 τοὺς ἐκλεκτοὺς, οὓς ἐξελέξατο, ἐκολόβωσε τὰς ἡμέρας. καὶ
the elect whom He elected, He shortened the days. And
5119/1437/5101/5213/2036/2400/602 5547 2228/2400/1563 3361
τότε ἐάν τις ὑμῖν εἴπῃ, Ἰδού, ὧδε ὁ Χριστός, ἤ Ἰδού, ἐκεῖ, μὴ
then if anyone to you says, Behold, here the Christ, or behold, there, not
4100 1453 1063 5580 5578
22 πιστεύσητε. ἐγερθήσονται γαρ ψευδόχριστοι καὶ ψευδο-
believe. will be raised For false Christs and false
1325 4592 5059 4314 635
προφῆται, καὶ δώσουσι σημεῖα καὶ τέρατα, πρὸς τὸ ἀπο-
prophets, and they will give signs and wonders in order to lead
1487 1415 1588 5210 991
23 πλανᾷν, εἰ δυνατόν, καὶ τοὺς ἐκλεκτούς. ὑμεῖς δὲ βλέπετε·
astray, if possible, even the elect. you But watch.
2400 4280 5213 3956
Ἰδού, προείρηκα ὑμῖν πάντα.
Behold, I have told before you all things.

235/1722 1565 2250 3326 2347 1565
24 Ἀλλ' ἐν ἐκείναις ταῖς ἡμέραις, μετὰ τὴν θλῖψιν ἐκείνην, ὁ
But in those — days, after — affliction that, the
2247 4654 4582 3756 1325 5338
ἥλιος σκοτισθήσεται, καὶ ἡ σελήνη οὐ δώσει τὸ φέγγος
sun will be darkened, and the moon not will give the light
848 792 3772 2071 1601
25 αὐτῆς, καὶ οἱ ἀστέρες τοῦ οὐρανοῦ ἔσονται ἐκπίπτοντες,
of her. And the stars of the heaven will be falling,
1411 1722 3772 4531 5119
26 καὶ αἱ δυνάμεις αἱ ἐν τοῖς οὐρανοῖς σαλευθήσονται. καὶ τότε
and the powers in the heavens will be shaken. And then
3700 5207 444 2064 1772 3507
ὄψονται τὸν υἱὸν τοῦ ἀνθρώπου ἐρχόμενον ἐν νεφέλαις
they will see the Son — of man coming in clouds
3326 1411 4183 1391 5119 649
27 μετὰ δυνάμεως πολλῆς καὶ δόξης. καὶ τότε ἀποστελεῖ τοὺς
with power much and glory. And then He will send the
32 848 1996 1588 848 1537
ἀγγέλους αὐτοῦ, καὶ ἐπισυνάξει τοὺς ἐκλεκτοὺς αὐτοῦ ἐκ
angels of Him, and they will gather the elect of Him out of
5064 417 575 206 1093 2193 206 3772
τῶν τεσσάρων ἀνέμων, ἀπ' ἄκρου γῆς ἕως ἄκρου οὐρανοῦ.
the four winds, from (the) end of earth to (the) end of heaven.
575 4808 3129 3850 3752 846
28 Ἀπὸ δὲ τῆς συκῆς μάθετε τὴν παραβολήν· ὅταν αὐτῆς
from And the fig-tree learn the parable: when of it
2235 2798 527 1096 1631 5444 1097
ἤδη ὁ κλάδος ἁπαλὸς γένηται καὶ ἐκφύῃ τὰ φύλλα, γινώ-
now the branch tender becomes and puts out the leaves, you
3754 1451 2330 2076 3779 5210 3752 5023
29 σκετε ὅτι ἐγγὺς τὸ θέρος ἐστίν· οὕτω καὶ ὑμεῖς, ὅταν ταῦτα
know that near the summer is. So also you, when these things
1492 1096 1097 3754 1451 2076 1909 2374 281
30 ἴδητε γινόμενα, γινώσκετε ὅτι ἐγγύς ἐστιν ἐπὶ θύραις. ἀμὴν
you see happening, know that near is it, at (the) doors. Truly
3004/5213/3754/3756/3361 3928 1074 3778 3360/3739
λέγω ὑμῖν ὅτι οὐ μὴ παρέλθῃ ἡ γενεὰ αὕτη, μέχρις οὗ
I say to you that in no way will pass away generation this until
3956 5023 1096 3772 1093 3928
31 πάντα ταῦτα γένηται. ὁ οὐρανὸς καὶ ἡ γῆ παρελεύσονται·
all these things happen. The heaven and the earth will pass away
3056 3450/3756/3361 3928 4012 2250
32 οἱ δὲ λόγοι μου οὐ μὴ παρέλθωσι. περὶ δὲ τῆς ἡμέρας
the but words of Me in no way will pass away. concerning But day
1565 5610 3762 1492 3761 32 1722
ἐκείνης καὶ τῆς ὥρας οὐδεὶς οἶδεν, οὐδὲ οἱ ἄγγελοι οἱ ἐν
that and the hour no one knows, not the angels in

Son, except the Father.
33Be careful; be wakeful,
and pray. For you do not
know when the time is.
34As a man going away,
leaving his house, and
giving his slaves authority,
and to each his work—and
he commanded the door-
keeper, that he watch—
35then you watch, for you do
not know when the lord of
the house is coming, *at*
evening, or at midnight, or
at cock-crowing, or early;
36so that he may not come
suddenly *and* find you
sleeping. 37And what I say
to you, I say to all. Watch!

3772 3761 5207=1508= 3962 991 . 69
33 οὐρανῷ, οὐδὲ ὁ υἱός, εἰ μὴ ὁ πατήρ. βλέπετε, ἀγρυπνεῖτε καὶ
Heaven, not the Son, except the Father. watch, be wakeful, and
4336 3756 1492 1063 4219 2540 2076 5613
34 προσεύχεσθε· οὐκ οἴδατε γὰρ πότε ὁ καιρός ἐστιν. ὡς
pray not you know For when the time is. As
444 590 863 3614 848 1325
ἄνθρωπος ἀπόδημος ἀφεὶς τὴν οἰκίαν αὐτοῦ, καὶ δοὺς τοῖς
a man going abroad, leaving the house of him, and giving to the
1401 848 1849 1538 2041 848
δούλοις αὐτοῦ τὴν ἐξουσίαν, καὶ ἑκάστῳ τὸ ἔργον αὐτοῦ,
slaves of him the authority, and to each the work of him,
2377 1781 2443 1127 1127 3767
35 καὶ τῷ θυρωρῷ ἐνετείλατο ἵνα γρηγορῇ. γρηγορεῖτε οὖν
and the doorkeeper he ordered that he should watch You watch, then,
3756 1492 1063 4219 2962 3614 2064 3797 2228
οὐκ οἴδατε γὰρ πότε ὁ κύριος τῆς οἰκίας ἔρχεται, ὀψέ, ἢ
not you know for when the lord of the house comes, evening, or
3317 219 2228 4404 3361 2064 1810
36 μεσονυκτίου, ἢ ἀλεκτοροφωνίας, ἢ πρωΐ· μὴ ἐλθὼν ἐξαίφνης
at midnight, or at cock-crowing, or early; lest coming suddenly
2147 5209 2518 3739 5213 3004 3956 3004
37 εὕρῃ ὑμᾶς καθεύδοντας. ἃ δὲ ὑμῖν λέγω πᾶσι λέγω,
he find you sleeping. what And to you I say, to all I say,
1127
Γρηγορεῖτε.
Watch!

CHAPTER 14

2258 3956 106 3326 1417 2250
1 Ἦν δὲ τὸ πάσχα καὶ τὰ ἄζυμα μετὰ δύο ἡμέρας· καὶ
it was And the Passover and the unleavened (bread) after two days. And
2212 749 1122 4459 8436/1722 1388
ἐζήτουν οἱ ἀρχιερεῖς καὶ οἱ γραμματεῖς πῶς αὐτὸν ἐν δόλῳ
sought the chief priests and the scribes how Him by guile
2902 615 3004 3361 1722 1859
2 κρατήσαντες ἀποκτείνωσιν· ἔλεγον δέ, Μὴ ἐν τῇ ἑορτῇ,
seizing they might kill. they said And, Not at the feast,
3379 2351 2071 2992
μήποτε θόρυβος ἔσται τοῦ λαοῦ.
lest a tumult will be of the people.
5607 846 1722 963 1722 3614 4613
3 Καὶ ὄντος αὐτοῦ ἐν Βηθανίᾳ, ἐν τῇ οἰκίᾳ Σίμωνος τοῦ
And being He in Bethany in the house of Simon the
3015 2621 846 2064 1135 2192 211
λεπροῦ, κατακειμένου αὐτοῦ, ἦλθε γυνὴ ἔχουσα ἀλάβαστρον
leper, having reclined He, came a woman having an alabaster vial
3464 3487 4101 4185 4937
μύρου νάρδου πιστικῆς πολυτελοῦς· καὶ συντρίψασα τὸ
of ointment of nard pure costly. And breaking the
211 2708 848 2596 2776 2258
4 ἀλάβαστρον, κατέχεεν αὐτοῦ κατὰ τῆς κεφαλῆς. ἦσαν δέ
alabaster vial she poured (it) of Him down the head. were And
5100 23 4314 1438 3004 1519/5100
τινες ἀγανακτοῦντες πρὸς ἑαυτούς, καὶ λέγοντες, Εἰς τί ἡ
some being indignant to themselves, and saying, To what
684 3778 3464 1096 1410 1063 5124
5 ἀπώλεια αὕτη τοῦ μύρου γέγονεν; ἠδύνατο γὰρ τοῦτο
waste this of the ointment has occurred? could For this
4097 1883 5145 1220 1325
πραθῆναι ἐπάνω τριακοσίων δηναρίων, καὶ δοθῆναι τοῖς
be sold (for) over three hundred denarii, and to be given to the
4434 1690 846 2424 2036 863
6 πτωχοῖς. καὶ ἐνεβριμῶντο αὐτῇ. ὁ δὲ Ἰησοῦς εἶπεν, Ἄφετε
poor. And they were incensed with her. But Jesus said, Let alone
•2873 846 5101 846 • 3930 2570 2041 2038
αὐτήν· τί αὐτῇ κόπους παρέχετε; καλὸν ἔργον εἰργάσατο
her Why to her troubles do you cause? a good work she worked
1519/1691/ 3842 1063 4434 2192 3326 1438
7 εἰς ἐμέ. πάντοτε γὰρ τοὺς πτωχοὺς ἔχετε μεθ' ἑαυτῶν, καὶ
to Me. always For the poor you have with yourselves, and

CHAPTER 14

1And it was the Passover,
and the *Feast of* Un-
leavened *Bread* after two
days. And the chief priests
and the scribes were seeking how they might get
hold of Him by guile, *and*
might kill *Him*. 2But they
said, Not during the feast,
lest there will be a tumult of
the people.
3And He being in Beth-
any in the house of Simon
the leper, as He reclined, a
woman came, having an
alabaster vial of pure, costly
ointment of nard. And
breaking the alabaster vial,
she poured *it* down His
head. 4And some were be-
ing indignant to them-
selves, and saying, To what
has this waste of the
ointment occurred? 5For
this could be sold *for* over
three hundred denarii, and
to be given to the poor. And
they were incensed with
her.
6But Jesus said, Let her
alone. Why do you cause
her troubles? She worked a
good work toward Me. 7For
you have the poor with you

always, and when you wish, you can do well toward them. But you do not have Me always. 8What this one held, she did. She took beforehand to anoint My body for the burial. 9Truly I say to you, Wherever this gospel is proclaimed in all the world, what this *one* did will also be spoken of for a memorial of her.

10And Judas Iscariot, one of the Twelve, went away to the chief priests, that he might betray Him to them. 11And hearing, they rejoiced and promised to give him silver. And he sought how he might opportunely betray Him.

12And on the first day of the unleavened *bread,* when they killed the passover, His disciples said to Him, Where do you desire *that* going we may prepare that You may eat the passover? 13And He sent two of His disciples, and said to them, Go into the city. And you will meet a man carrying a pitcher of water. Follow him. 14And wherever he goes in, say to the housemaster, The Teacher says, Where is the guest room where I may eat the passover with My disciples? 15And he will show you a large upper room, having been spread *and* made ready. Prepare for us there. 16And His disciples went out and came into the city, and found *it* as He told them. And they prepared the passover.

17And evening having come, He came with the Twelve. 18And as they were reclining and eating, Jesus said, Truly I say to you, One of you will betray Me, the *one* eating with Me. 19And they began to be grieved,

3752 2309 1410 846 2095 4160 1691 3756 3842
ὅταν θέλητε δύνασθε αὐτοὺς εὖ ποιῆσαι· ἐμὲ δὲ οὐ πάντοτε
when you wish you are able (to) them well to do, Me but not always
2192 2192 3778 4160 4301 3462 3450
8 ἔχετε. ὃ εἶχεν αὕτη ἐποίησε· προέλαβε μυρίσαι μου τὸ
you have. What held this one, she did; she took beforehand to anoint of Me the
4983 1519 1780 281 3004 5213 3699 302
9 σῶμα εἰς τὸν ἐνταφιασμόν. ἀμὴν λέγω ὑμῖν, ὅπου ἂν
body for the burial. Truly I say to you, where ever
2784 2098 5124 1519 3650 2889 3739
κηρυχθῇ τὸ εὐαγγέλιον τοῦτο εἰς ὅλον τὸν κόσμον, καὶ ὃ
is proclaimed gospel this into all the world, also what
4160 3778 2980 1519 3422 846
ἐποίησεν αὕτη λαληθήσεται εἰς μνημόσυνον αὐτῆς.
did this (one) will be spoken for a memorial of her.
2455 2469 1520 1427 565
10 Καὶ ὁ Ἰούδας ὁ Ἰσκαριώτης, εἷς τῶν δώδεκα, ἀπῆλθε
And Judas Iscariot, one of the twelve, went away
4314 749 2443 3860 846 846 191
11 πρὸς τοὺς ἀρχιερεῖς, ἵνα παραδῷ αὐτὸν αὐτοῖς. οἱ δὲ ἀκού-
to the chief priests, that he might betray Him to them. they And
5463 1861 846 694 1325
σαντες ἐχάρησαν, καὶ ἐπηγγείλαντο αὐτῷ ἀργύριον δοῦναι·
hearing rejoiced and promised him silver to give.
2212 4459 2122 846 3860
καὶ ἐζήτει πῶς εὐκαίρως αὐτὸν παραδῷ.
And he sought how opportunely Him he might betray.
4413 2250 106 3753 3957 2380
12 Καὶ τῇ πρώτῃ ἡμέρᾳ τῶν ἀζύμων, ὅτε τὸ πάσχα ἔθυον,
And on the first day of the unleavened, when the Passover they killed
3004 846 3101 848 4226 2309 565
λέγουσιν αὐτῷ οἱ μαθηταὶ αὐτοῦ, Ποῦ θέλεις ἀπελθόντες
say to Him the disciples of Him, Where do You wish going
209 2443 5315 3957 649 1417
13 ἑτοιμάσωμεν ἵνα φάγῃς τὸ πάσχα; καὶ ἀποστέλλει δύο τῶν
we may prepare that You eat the Passover? And He sends two of the
3101 848 3004 846 5217 1519 4172
μαθητῶν αὐτοῦ, καὶ λέγει αὐτοῖς, Ὑπάγετε εἰς τὴν πόλιν,
disciples of Him, and says to them, Go into the city,
528 5213 444 2765 5204 941
καὶ ἀπαντήσει ὑμῖν ἄνθρωπος κεράμιον ὕδατος βαστάζων·
and will meet you a man a pitcher of water carrying;
190 846 3699 1437 1525 2036
14 ἀκολουθήσατε αὐτῷ, καὶ ὅπου ἐὰν εἰσέλθῃ, εἴπατε τῷ
follow him. And where ever he enters, tell the
3617 3754 1320 3004 4226 2076 2646
οἰκοδεσπότῃ ὅτι Ὁ διδάσκαλος λέγει, Ποῦ ἐστι τὸ κατά-
housemaster, The Teacher says, Where is the guest-
3699 3957 3326 3101 3450 5315
15 λυμα, ὅπου τὸ πάσχα μετὰ τῶν μαθητῶν μου φάγω; καὶ
room where the Passover with the disciples of Me I may eat? And
846 5213 1166 508 3173 4766 2092 1563
αὐτὸς ὑμῖν δείξει ἀνώγεον μέγα ἐστρωμένον ἕτοιμον· ἐκεῖ
he you will show an upper room large being spread, ready. There
2090 2254 1831 3101 848 2064
16 ἑτοιμάσατε ἡμῖν. καὶ ἐξῆλθον οἱ μαθηταὶ αὐτοῦ, καὶ ἦλθον
you prepare for us. And went forth the disciples of Him, and came
1519 4172 2147 2531 2036 846 2090
εἰς τὴν πόλιν, καὶ εὗρον καθὼς εἶπεν αὐτοῖς, καὶ ἡτοίμασαν
into the city, and found as He told them, and they prepared
3957
τὸ πάσχα.
the Passover.
3798 1096 2064 3326 1427 345
17 Καὶ ὀψίας γενομένης ἔρχεται μετὰ τῶν δώδεκα. καὶ ἀνακει-
18 And evening occurring, He comes with the twelve. And reclining
846 2068 2036 2424 281 3004
μένων αὐτῶν καὶ ἐσθιόντων, εἶπεν ὁ Ἰησοῦς, Ἀμὴν λέγω
they, and eating, said Jesus, Truly I say
5213 3754/1519/1537/5216 3860 3165 2068 3326 1700
19 ὑμῖν, ὅτι εἷς ἐξ ὑμῶν παραδώσει με, ὁ ἐσθίων μετ' ἐμοῦ. οἱ
to you that one from you will betray Me, the (one) eating with Me, they

and to say to Him one by one, Not at all I, *is it*? And another, Not at all I, *is it*? [20]But answering He said to them, *It is* one from the Twelve, the *one* dipping in the dish with Me. [21]Truly the Son of man goes as it has been written concerning Him, but woe to that man by whom the Son of man is betrayed! It were good for him if that man had never been born.

[22]And *as* they *were* eating, Jesus taking a loaf, blessing, He broke and gave to them. And *He* said, Take, eat, this is My body. [23]And taking the cup, giving thanks, He gave to them. And they all drank out of it. [24]And He said to them, This is My blood, that of the New Covenant, which is poured out concerning many. [25]Truly I say to you, I will not at all drink of the fruit of the vine any more until that day when I drink it new in the kingdom of God.

[26]And singing a hymn, they went into the Mount of Olives.

[27]And Jesus said to them, All of you will be offended in Me in this night, because it has been written: "I will strike the Shepherd, and the sheep will be scattered." [28]But after My resurrection, I will go before you into Galilee. [29]But Peter said to Him, Even if all shall be offended, yet not I. [30]And Jesus said to him, Truly I say to you that today, in this night, before *the* cock crows twice, you will deny Me three times. [31]But he said more fervently, If it were needful for me to die with You, in no way will I deny

756 3076 3004 846 =1527= 1520 3361
δὲ ἤρξαντο λυπεῖσθαι, καὶ λέγειν αὐτῷ εἷς καθ' εἷς, Μή τι
And began to be grieved, and to say to Him one by one, Not at all
1473 243 =3385= 1473 611 2036 846
20 ἐγώ; καὶ ἄλλος, Μή τι ἐγώ; ὁ δὲ ἀποκριθεὶς εἶπεν αὐτοῖς,
I? And another, Not at all I? He And answering said to them,
1519/1537 1427 1686 3326 1700/1519 5165
Εἷς ἐκ τῶν δώδεκα, ὁ ἐμβαπτόμενος μετ' ἐμοῦ εἰς τὸ τρυβλίον.
One from the twelve, the (one) dipping in with Me in the dish.
3303/5207 444 5217 2531 1125 4012
21 ὁ μὲν υἱὸς τοῦ ἀνθρώπου ὑπάγει, καθὼς γέγραπται περὶ
the Indeed Son of man is going as it has been written about
846 3759 444 1565 1223/3739 5207
αὐτοῦ· οὐαὶ δὲ τῷ ἀνθρώπῳ ἐκείνῳ δι' οὗ ὁ υἱὸς τοῦ
Him. woe But to man that through whom the Son
444 3860 2570/2258/846 1487/3756 1080
ἀνθρώπου παραδίδοται· καλὸν ἦν αὐτῷ εἰ οὐκ ἐγεννήθη ὁ
of man is betrayed; good were it for him if not was born
444 1565
ἄνθρωπος ἐκεῖνος.
man that.
2068 846 2983 2424 740 2127
22 Καὶ ἐσθιόντων αὐτῶν, λαβὼν ὁ Ἰησοῦς ἄρτον εὐλογήσας
And eating they, taking Jesus a loaf, blessing,
2806 1325 846 2036 2983 5315 5124
ἔκλασε, καὶ ἔδωκεν αὐτοῖς, καὶ εἶπε, Λάβετε, φάγετε· τοῦτό
He broke and gave to them, and said, Take, eat, this
2076 4983 3450 2983 4221 2168
23 ἐστι τὸ σῶμά μου. καὶ λαβὼν τὸ ποτήριον εὐχαριστήσας
is the body of Me. And taking the cup, giving thanks,
1325 846 4095 1537 846 3956 2036 846
24 ἔδωκεν αὐτοῖς· καὶ ἔπιον ἐξ αὐτοῦ πάντες. καὶ εἶπεν αὐτοῖς,
He gave to them, and drank from it all. And He said to them,
5124 2076 129 3450 2537 1242 4012
Τοῦτό ἐστι τὸ αἷμά μου, τὸ τῆς καινῆς διαθήκης, τὸ περὶ
This is the blood of Me, that of the New Covenant concerning
4183 1632 281 3004 5213 3754 3765 =3364= 4095
25 πολλῶν ἐκχυνόμενον. ἀμὴν λέγω ὑμῖν ὅτι οὐκέτι οὐ μὴ πίω
many being poured out. Truly I say to you — no more, not at all, I may drink
1537 1081 288 2193 2250 1565 3752
ἐκ τοῦ γεννήματος τῆς ἀμπέλου, ἕως τῆς ἡμέρας ἐκείνης ὅταν
of the offspring of the vine until day that when
846 4095 2537 1722 932 2316
αὐτὸ πίνω καινὸν ἐν τῇ βασιλείᾳ τοῦ Θεοῦ.
it I drink new in the kingdom of God.
5214 1831 1519 3735 1636
26 Καὶ ὑμνήσαντες ἐξῆλθον εἰς τὸ ὄρος τῶν ἐλαιῶν.
And having sung a hymn they went into the mount of the olives.
3004 846 2424 3754 3956 4624
27 Καὶ λέγει αὐτοῖς ὁ Ἰησοῦς ὅτι Πάντες σκανδαλισθήσεσθε
And says to them Jesus, All you will be offended
1722/1698/1722 3571 5026 3754 1125 3960
ἐν ἐμοὶ ἐν τῇ νυκτὶ ταύτῃ· ὅτι γέγραπται, Πατάξω τὸν
in Me in night this, because it has been written: I will strike the
4160 1287 4263 235 3326
28 ποιμένα, καὶ διασκορπισθήσεται τὰ πρόβατα. ἀλλὰ μετὰ
Shepherd, and will be scattered the sheep. But after
1453 3165 4254 5209 1519 1056
29 τὸ ἐγερθῆναί με, προάξω ὑμᾶς εἰς τὴν Γαλιλαίαν. ὁ δὲ
the arising of Me, I will go before you into Galilee. And
4074 5346 846 1487 3956 4624 235
Πέτρος ἔφη αὐτῷ, Καὶ εἰ πάντες σκανδαλισθήσονται, ἀλλ'
Peter said to Him, Even if all shall be offended, yet
3767 1473 3004 846 2424 281 3004 4671 3754
30 οὐκ ἐγώ. καὶ λέγει αὐτῷ ὁ Ἰησοῦς, Ἀμὴν λέγω σοι, ὅτι
not I. And says to him Jesus, Truly I say to you,
4594 1722 3571 5026 4250/2228/1364 220 5455
σήμερον ἐν τῇ νυκτὶ ταύτῃ, πρὶν ἢ δὶς ἀλέκτορα φωνῆσαι,
Today, in night this, before twice (the) cock sounds,
5151 533 3165 1537 4053 3004 3123 1437 3165
31 τρίς ἀπαρνήσῃ με. ὁ δὲ ἐκ περισσοῦ ἔλεγε μᾶλλον, Ἐὰν με
thrice you will deny Me. He But exceedingly said more, If me

You. And also all said the same.

[32]And they came to a place which *was* named Gethsemane. And He said to His disciples, Sit here while I pray. [33]And He took along Peter and James and John with Him. And He began to be much amazed, and to be deeply troubled. [34]And *He* said to them, My soul is deeply grieved, unto death. Remain here and watch. [35]And going forward a little, He fell on the ground, and prayed that if it were possible, the hour might pass from Him. [36]And He said, Abba, Father, all things *are* possible to You; take this cup from Me. Yet not what I will, but what You *will*. [37]And He came and found them sleeping. And *He* said to Peter, Simon, do you sleep? Were you not strong enough to watch one hour? [38]Watch and pray, that you may not enter into temptation. The spirit truly *is* willing, but the flesh *is* weak. [39]And going away again, He prayed, saying the same thing. [40]And returning He found them sleeping again, for their eyes were heavy. And they did not know what to answer Him. [41]And He came a third time, and said to them, Sleep on now, and rest. It is enough. The hour has come. Behold, the Son of man is betrayed into the hands of sinners. [42]Rise up, let us go. Behold, the *one* betraying Me has drawn near.

[43]And immediately, as He was yet speaking, Judas

1163 4880 4671 3364 4571 533 5615
δέῃ συναποθανεῖν σοι, οὐ μή σε ἀπαρνήσομαι. ὡσαύτως
must die with You, in no way You will I deny. likewise
3956 3004
δὲ καὶ πάντες ἔλεγον.
And also all said.

2064 1519 5564 3739 3686 1068
32 Καὶ ἔρχονται εἰς χωρίον οὗ τὸ ὄνομα Γεθσημανῆ· καὶ
And they come to a place of which the name (was) Gethsemane. And
3004 3101 848 2523 5602 2193 4336
λέγει τοῖς μαθηταῖς αὐτοῦ, Καθίσατε ὧδε, ἕως προσεύξω-
He says to the disciples of Him, Sit here while I pray
3880 4074 2385
33 μαι. καὶ παραλαμβάνει τὸν Πέτρον καὶ τὸν Ἰάκωβον καὶ
And He takes along Peter and James and
2491 3326 1438 756 1568 85
Ἰωάννην μεθ' ἑαυτοῦ, καὶ ἤρξατο ἐκθαμβεῖσθαι καὶ ἀδη-
John with Him. And He began to be much amazed, and to be
3004 846 4036 2076 5590 3450 2193
34 μονεῖν. καὶ λέγει αὐτοῖς, Περίλυπός ἐστιν ἡ ψυχή μου ἕως
distressed, and says to them, Deeply grieved is the soul of Me unto
2288 3306 5602 1127 4281 3397
35 θανάτου· μείνατε ὧδε καὶ γρηγορεῖτε. καὶ προελθὼν μικρόν,
death. Remain here and watch. And going forward a little,
4098 1909 1093 4336 2443/1487/1415 2076
ἔπεσεν ἐπὶ τῆς γῆς, καὶ προσηύχετο ἵνα, εἰ δυνατόν ἐστι,
He fell on the ground, and prayed that if possible it is
3928 575 846 5610 3004 5 3962
36 παρέλθῃ ἀπ' αὐτοῦ ἡ ὥρα. καὶ ἔλεγεν, Ἀββᾶ, ὁ πατήρ,
might pass from Him the hour. And He said, Abba, Father,
3956 1415 4671 3911 4221 575 1700 5124
πάντα δυνατά σοι. παρένεγκε τὸ ποτήριον ἀπ' ἐμοῦ τοῦτο·
all things possible to You. Remove cup from Me this;
235 3756/5101/1473/2309 235/5101/4771 2064 2147
37 ἀλλ' οὐ τί ἐγὼ θέλω, ἀλλὰ τί σύ. καὶ ἔρχεται καὶ εὑρίσκει
but not what I desire, but what You. And He comes and finds
846 2518 3004 4074 4613 2518
αὐτοὺς καθεύδοντας, καὶ λέγει τῷ Πέτρῳ, Σίμων, καθεύδεις;
them sleeping, and says to Peter, Simon, do you sleep?
3756 2480 3391 5610 1127 1127
38 οὐκ ἴσχυσας μίαν ὥραν γρηγορῆσαι; γρηγορεῖτε καὶ
not were you strong one hour to watch? Watch and
4336 2443/3361 1525 1519 3986 3303 4151
προσεύχεσθε, ἵνα μὴ εἰσέλθητε εἰς πειρασμόν. τὸ μὲν πνεῦμα
pray, that not you enter into temptation; the indeed spirit
4289 4561 772 3825 565 4336
39 πρόθυμον, ἡ δὲ σὰρξ ἀσθενής. καὶ πάλιν ἀπελθὼν προσηύ-
(is) eager, the but flesh (is) weak. And again going away He prayed
846 3056 2036 5290 2147 846
40 ξατο, τὸν αὐτὸν λόγον εἰπών. καὶ ὑποστρέψας εὗρεν αὐτοὺς
the same word saying. And having returned He found them
3825 2518 2258 1063 3788 848 916
πάλιν καθεύδοντας· ἦσαν γὰρ οἱ ὀφθαλμοὶ αὐτῶν βεβαρη-
again sleeping, were for the eyes of them heavy.
3756 1492 5101 846 611 2064
41 μένοι, καὶ οὐκ ᾔδεισαν τί αὐτῷ ἀποκριθῶσι. καὶ ἔρχεται τὸ
And not they knew what Him to answer. And He comes the
5154 3004 846 2518 3063 373
τρίτον, καὶ λέγει αὐτοῖς, Καθεύδετε τὸ λοιπὸν καὶ ἀναπαύε-
third, and says to them, Sleep now and rest;
566 2064 5610 2400 3860 5207
σθε. ἀπέχει· ἦλθεν ἡ ὥρα· ἰδού, παραδίδοται ὁ υἱὸς τοῦ
it is enough; has come the hour; behold, is betrayed the Son —
444 1519 5495 268 1453 71
42 ἀνθρώπου εἰς τὰς χεῖρας τῶν ἁμαρτωλῶν. ἐγείρεσθε, ἄγωμεν·
of man into the hands of the sinners. Rise up, let us go;
2400 3860 3165 1448
ἰδού, ὁ παραδιδούς με ἤγγικε.
behold, the (one) betraying Me has drawn near.

2112 2089 846 2980 3854 2455
43 Καὶ εὐθέως, ἔτι αὐτοῦ λαλοῦντος, παραγίνεται Ἰούδας,
And at once, yet He speaking, comes up Judas.

:ame up, being one of the
Twelve. And with him *was*
a great crowd with swords
and clubs, from the chief
priests and the scribes and
the elders. [44]And the *one*
betraying Him had given
them a sign, saying,
Whomever I kiss, *it* is He;
seize Him, and lead *Him*
away safely. [45]And coming,
at once coming near to
Him, he said, Rabbi, Rabbi!
And *he* ardently kissed
Him. [46]And they laid their
hands on Him and seized
Him. [47]But a certain one of
those standing by, drawing
a sword, struck the slave of
the high priest, and took off
his ear. [48]And answering
Jesus said to them, Have
you come out with swords
and clubs to take Me, as
against a robber? [49]I was
with you daily teaching in
the temple, and you did not
seize Me. But *it is* that the
Scriptures may be fulfilled.

And leaving Him, all fled.
And one, a certain young
man, was following Him,
having thrown a linen cloth
around *his* naked *body*. And
the young men caught him.
But he, leaving behind the
linen cloth, fled from them
naked.

[53]And they led Jesus
away to the high priest. And
all the chief priests and the
elders and the scribes came
together to him. [54]And
Peter followed Him from a
distance, to the inside of
the court of the high priest.
And he was sitting with the
under-officers, also warming himself near the light.
And the chief priests
and the whole sanhedrin
sought testimony against
Jesus, to put Him to death.
And *they* did not find

1520/5607 1427 3326 846 3793 4183 3326 3162
εἷς ὢν τῶν δώδεκα, καὶ μετ' αὐτοῦ ὄχλος πολὺς μετὰ μαχαι-
one being of the twelve, and with him a crowd large with swords
3586 3844 749 1122
ρῶν καὶ ξύλων, παρὰ τῶν ἀρχιερέων καὶ τῶν γραμματέων
and clubs from the chief priests and the scribes
4245 1325 3860 846
44 καὶ τῶν πρεσβυτέρων. δεδώκει δὲ ὁ παραδιδοὺς αὐτὸν
and the elders. had given And the (one) betraying Him
4953 846 3004 3739/302/ 5368 846 2076 2902
σύσσημον αὐτοῖς, λέγων, Ὃν ἂν φιλήσω, αὐτός ἐστι κρατή-
a signal them, saying, Whomever I kiss, He it is; seize
846 520 806 2064 2112
45 σατε αὐτόν, καὶ ἀπαγάγετε ἀσφαλῶς. καὶ ἐλθών, εὐθέως
Him, and lead away securely. And coming, at once
4334 846 3004 4461 4461 2705
προσελθὼν αὐτῷ λέγει, Ῥαββί, ῥαββί· καὶ κατεφίλησεν
coming near to Him, he says, Rabbi, Rabbi; and fervently kissed
846 1911 1909 846 5495 848
46 αὐτόν. οἱ δὲ ἐπέβαλον ἐπ' αὐτὸν τὰς χεῖρας αὐτῶν, καὶ
Him. they And laid on Him the hands of them and
2902 846 1510 5100 3936 4685
47 ἐκράτησαν αὐτόν. εἷς δέ τις τῶν παρεστηκότων σπασά-
seized Him. one But certain of the (ones) standing by, drawing
3162 3817 1401 749
μενος τὴν μάχαιραν ἔπαισε τὸν δοῦλον τοῦ ἀρχιερέως, καὶ
the sword struck the slave of the high priest, and
851 848 5621 611 2424 2036
48 ἀφεῖλεν αὐτοῦ τὸ ὠτίον. καὶ ἀποκριθεὶς ὁ Ἰησοῦς εἶπεν
took off of him the ear. And answering — Jesus said
846 5613/1909 3027 1831 3326 3162 3586
αὐτοῖς, Ὡς ἐπὶ λῃστὴν ἐξήλθετε μετὰ μαχαιρῶν καὶ ξύλων
to them, As against a robber come you out with swords and clubs
4865 3165 2596 2250 2252 4314 5209 1722 2411
49 συλλαβεῖν με; καθ' ἡμέραν ἤμην πρὸς ὑμᾶς ἐν τῷ ἱερῷ
to take Me? Daily I was with you in the Temple
1321 3756 2902 3165 235 2443 4137
διδάσκων, καὶ οὐκ ἐκρατήσατέ με· ἀλλ' ἵνα πληρωθῶσιν αἱ
teaching, and not you did seize Me; but that may be fulfilled the
1124 863 846 3956 5343
50 γραφαί. καὶ ἀφέντες αὐτὸν πάντες ἔφυγον.
Scriptures. And forsaking Him, all fled.
1519/5100 3495 190 846 4016
51 Καὶ εἷς τις νεανίσκος ἠκολούθει αὐτῷ, περιβεβλημένος
And one certain young man was following Him, having thrown about
4616 1909 1131 2902 846 3495
52 σινδόνα ἐπὶ γυμνοῦ. καὶ κρατοῦσιν αὐτὸν οἱ νεανίσκοι· ὁ
a linen cloth on (his) naked (body) And seized him the young men. he
2641 4616 1131 5343 575 846
δὲ καταλιπὼν τὴν σινδόνα γυμνὸς ἔφυγεν ἀπ' αὐτῶν.
But forsaking the linen cloth naked fled from them.
520 2424 4314 749 4905
53 Καὶ ἀπήγαγον τὸν Ἰησοῦν πρὸς τὸν ἀρχιερέα· καὶ συνέρ-
And they led away Jesus to the high priest, and come
846 3956 749 4245
χονται αὐτῷ πάντες οἱ ἀρχιερεῖς καὶ οἱ πρεσβύτεροι καὶ οἱ
together to him all the chief priests and the elders and the
1122 4074 575 3113 190 846
54 γραμματεῖς. καὶ ὁ Πέτρος ἀπὸ μακρόθεν ἠκολούθησεν αὐτῷ
scribes. And Peter from afar followed Him,
2193/2080/1519 833 749 2258 4775
ἕως ἔσω εἰς τὴν αὐλὴν τοῦ ἀρχιερέως· καὶ ἦν συγκαθήμενος
until within, in the court of the high priest; and was sitting together
3326 5257 2328 4314 5457
55 μετὰ τῶν ὑπηρετῶν, καὶ θερμαινόμενος πρὸς τὸ φῶς. οἱ δὲ
with the attendants, and warming himself toward the light. the And
749 3650 4892 2212 2596 2424
ἀρχιερεῖς καὶ ὅλον τὸ συνέδριον ἐζήτουν κατὰ τοῦ Ἰησοῦ
chief priests and all the sanhedrin sought against — Jesus
3141 1519 2289 846 3756 2147
μαρτυρίαν, εἰς τὸ θανατῶσαι αὐτόν· καὶ οὐχ εὕρισκον.
witness, for the putting to death Him, and not did find.

any. 56For many bore false witness against Him, but their testimonies were not alike. 57And standing up, some falsely testified against Him, saying, 58We heard Him saying, I will throw down this temple made with hands, and through three days I will build another not made with hands. 59And neither in this was their testimony alike. 60And standing up in the middle, the high priest questioned Jesus, saying, Do you not answer? Nothing? What do these testify against you? 61But He was silent, and answered nothing. Again the high priest questioned Him, and said to Him, Are you the Christ, the son of the Blessed? 62And Jesus said, I AM! And you will see the Son of man sitting off *the* right *hand* of power, and coming with the clouds of the heaven. 63And tearing his garments, the high priest said, Why do we still have need of witnesses?

64You heard the blasphemy. What does it seem to you? And they all condemned Him to be liable, *even* of death. 65And some began to spit at Him, and to cover His face, and to beat Him with a fist, and to say to Him, Prophesy! And the under-officers struck Him with slaps.

66And Peter being in the court below, one of the maids of the high priest came. 67And seeing Peter warming himself, looking at him, *she* said, And you were with Jesus the Nazarene. 68But he denied, saying, I do not know nor understand what you say. And he went out into the forecourt. And a cock crowed. 69And seeing

4183 1063 5576 2596 846 2470
56 πολλοὶ γὰρ ἐψευδομαρτύρουν κατ' αὐτοῦ, καὶ ἴσαι αἱ
many For falsely testified against Him, and identical the
3141 3756 2258 5100 450 5576
57 μαρτυρίαι οὐκ ἦσαν. καί τινες ἀναστάντες ἐψευδομαρτύρουν
testimonies not were. And some standing up falsely testified
2596 846 3004 3754 2249 191 846 3004
58 κατ' αὐτοῦ, λέγοντες ὅτι Ἡμεῖς ἠκούσαμεν αὐτοῦ λέγοντος
against Him, saying, — We heard Him saying
3754/1473 2647 3485 5126 5499
ὅτι Ἐγὼ καταλύσω τὸν ναὸν τοῦτον τὸν χειροποίητον, καὶ
— I will throw down Temple this — made with hands, and
1223 5140 2250 243 886 3618
59 διὰ τριῶν ἡμερῶν ἄλλον ἀχειροποίητον οἰκοδομήσω. καὶ
through three days another not made with hands I will build. And
3761 3779 2470/2258 3141 848 450 749
60 οὐδὲ οὕτως ἴση ἦν ἡ μαρτυρία αὐτῶν. καὶ ἀναστὰς ὁ ἀρχιε-
neither thus identical was the witness of them. And standing up the high
1519 3319 1905 2424 3004 3756 611
ρεὺς εἰς τὸ μέσον ἐπηρώτησε τὸν Ἰησοῦν, λέγων, Οὐκ ἀπο-
priest in the midst, he questioned Jesus, saying, Do not you
1519 3319 5101 3778 4675 2649 4623
61 κρίνῃ οὐδὲν; τί οὗτοί σου καταμαρτυροῦσιν; ὁ δὲ ἐσιώπα,
answer—nothing, what these you testify against? He But was silent,
3762 611 3825 749 1905 846
καὶ οὐδὲν ἀπεκρίνατο. πάλιν ὁ ἀρχιερεὺς ἐπηρώτα αὐτόν, καὶ
and nothing answered. Again the high priest questioned Him, and
3004 846 4771/1488 5547 5207 2128
62 λέγει αὐτῷ, Σὺ εἶ ὁ Χριστός, ὁ υἱὸς τοῦ εὐλογητοῦ; ὁ δὲ
says to Him, You are the Christ the Son of the Blessed (One)? And
2424 2036 1473 1510 3700 5207 444
Ἰησοῦς εἶπεν, Ἐγώ εἰμι. καὶ ὄψεσθε τὸν υἱὸν τοῦ ἀνθρώπου
Jesus said, I AM! And you will see the Son of man
2521 1537 1188 1411 2064 3326
καθήμενον ἐκ δεξιῶν τῆς δυνάμεως, καὶ ἐρχόμενον μετὰ τῶν
sitting off (the) right of the Power, and coming with the
3507 3772 749 1284
63 νεφελῶν τοῦ οὐρανοῦ. ὁ δὲ ἀρχιερεὺς διαρρήξας τοὺς
clouds of Heaven. the And high priest, tearing the
5509 848 3004 5101 2089 5532 2192 3144
χιτῶνας αὐτοῦ λέγει, Τί ἔτι χρείαν ἔχομεν μαρτύρων;
garments of him, says, Why still need do we have of witnesses
191 988 5101 5213 5316 3956
64 ἠκούσατε τῆς βλασφημίας· τί ὑμῖν φαίνεται; οἱ δὲ πάντες
You heard the blasphemy. What to you appears it? they And all
2632 846 1511 1777 2288 756 5100
65 κατέκριναν αὐτὸν εἶναι ἔνοχον θανάτου. καὶ ἤρξαντό τινες
condemned Him to be liable of death. And began some
1716 846 4028 4383 848
ἐμπτύειν αὐτῷ, καὶ περικαλύπτειν τὸ πρόσωπον αὐτοῦ,
to spit at Him, and to cover the face of Him,
2852 846 3004 846 4395
καὶ κολαφίζειν αὐτόν, καὶ λέγειν αὐτῷ, Προφήτευσον· καὶ
and to beat with a fist Him, and to say to Him, Prophesy! And
5257 4475 846 906
οἱ ὑπηρέται ῥαπίσμασιν αὐτὸν ἔβαλλον.
the attendants with slaps Him struck.
5607 4074/1722 833 2736 2064 3391
66 Καὶ ὄντος τοῦ Πέτρου ἐν τῇ αὐλῇ κάτω, ἔρχεται μία τῶν
And being Peter in the court below, comes one of the
3814 749 1492 4074 2328
67 παιδισκῶν τοῦ ἀρχιερέως, καὶ ἰδοῦσα τὸν Πέτρον θερμαινό-
maids of the high priest, and seeing Peter warming
1689 846 3004 4771/3326 3479
μενον, ἐμβλέψασα αὐτῷ λέγει, Καὶ σὺ μετὰ τοῦ Ναζαρηνοῦ
himself, looking at him, says, And you with the Nazarene
2424 2258 720 3004 3756 1492 3761
68 Ἰησοῦ ἦσθα. ὁ δὲ ἠρνήσατο, λέγων, Οὐκ οἶδα, οὐδὲ
Jesus were. he But denied, saying, not I know, nor
1987 5101/4771/3004 1831 1854 1519 4259
ἐπίσταμαι τί σὺ λέγεις. καὶ ἐξῆλθεν ἔξω εἰς τὸ προαύλιον·
understand what you say. And he went outside into the forecourt;

im again, the maid began
› say to those standing by,
his one is of them. [70]And
gain he denied. And after a
ttle, those standing by
gain said to Peter, Truly
ou are from them, for you
re both a Galilean and your
peech agrees. [71]But he
egan to curse and to
wear, I do not know this
nan whom you speak of.
[72]And a second time a cock
rowed. And Peter remem-
ered the word Jesus said
o him, Before a cock crows
wice, you will deny Me
hree times. And thinking
›n *it,* he wept.

CHAPTER 15

[1]And immediately in the
norning, the chief priests
vith the elders and scribes
nd all the sanhedrin form-
ng a council, binding
Jesus, *they* led *Him* away
nd delivered *Him* to Pilate.
[2]And Pilate questioned
Him, Are you the king of the
Jews? And answering He
said to him, You say *it.*
[3]And the chief priests
urgently accused Him *of*
many things. But He
answered nothing. [4]But
Pilate again questioned
Him, saying, Do you answer
nothing? Behold, how
many things they testify
against you. [5]But Jesus
answered nothing any
more; so as *for* Pilate to
marvel.
[6]And at a feast he re-
leased to them one
prisoner, whomever they
asked. [7]And there was
one called Barabbas, hav-
ing been bound with the
insurgents, who in the
insurrection had committed
murder. [8]And crying aloud,
the crowd began to beg
him to do as he always did
to them. [9]But Pilate

220 5455 3814 1492 846 3825
69 καὶ ἀλέκτωρ ἐφώνησε. καὶ ἡ παιδίσκη ἰδοῦσα αὐτὸν πάλιν
and a cock crowed. And the maid seeing him again
756 3004 3936 3754 3778 1537 846 2076
ἤρξατο λέγειν τοῖς παρεστηκόσιν ὅτι Οὗτος ἐξ αὐτῶν ἐστίν.
began to say to those standing by, This one of them is.
3825 720 3326 3397 3825 3936
70 ὁ δὲ πάλιν ἠρνεῖτο. καὶ μετὰ μικρὸν πάλιν οἱ παρεστῶτες
he But again denied. And after a little again the (ones) standing by
3004 4074 230 1537 846 1488 1063 1057
ἔλεγον τῷ Πέτρῳ, Ἀληθῶς ἐξ αὐτῶν εἶ· καὶ γὰρ Γαλιλαῖος
said to Peter, Truly of them you are; even for a Galilean
1488 2981 4675 3662 756 332
71 εἶ, καὶ ἡ λαλιά σου ὁμοιάζει. ὁ δὲ ἤρξατο ἀναθεματίζειν καὶ
you and the speech of you agrees. he And began to curse and
are, 3660/3754/3756/1492 444 5126 3739 3004
72 ὀμνύειν ὅτι Οὐκ οἶδα τὸν ἄνθρωπον τοῦτον ὃν λέγετε. καὶ
to swear, not I know man this whom you say. And
1537 1208 220 5455 363 4074
ἐκ δευτέρου ἀλέκτωρ ἐφώνησε. καὶ ἀνεμνήσθη ὁ Πέτρος τοῦ
for a second time a cock crowed. And remembered Peter the
4487 3739 2036 846 2424 3754 4250 220
ῥήματος οὗ εἶπεν αὐτῷ ὁ Ἰησοῦς ὅτι Πρὶν ἀλέκτορα
word that said to him Jesus, Before a cock
5455 1364 533 3165 5151 1911 2799
φωνῆσαι δίς, ἀπαρνήσῃ με τρίς. καὶ ἐπιβαλὼν ἔκλαιε.
crows twice, you will deny Me thrice. And thinking on (it), he wept.

CHAPTER 15

2112 1909 4404 4824 4160
1 Καὶ εὐθέως ἐπὶ τὸ πρωῒ συμβούλιον ποιήσαντες οἱ
And immediately on (morn) early, a council having made the
749 3326 4245 1122 3650
ἀρχιερεῖς μετὰ τῶν πρεσβυτέρων καὶ γραμματέων, καὶ ὅλον
chief priests with the elders and scribes, and all
4892 1210 2424 667 3860
τὸ συνέδριον, δήσαντες τὸν Ἰησοῦν ἀπήνεγκαν καὶ παρέδω-
the sanhedrin, having bound Jesus led (Him) away and delivered
4091 1905 846 4091 4771/1488
2 καν τῷ Πιλάτῳ. καὶ ἐπηρώτησεν αὐτὸν ὁ Πιλάτος, Σὺ εἶ ὁ
(Him) – to Pilate. And questioned Him – Pilate, You are the
935 2453 611 2036 846 4771
βασιλεὺς τῶν Ἰουδαίων; ὁ δὲ ἀποκριθεὶς εἶπεν αὐτῷ, Σὺ
king of the Jews? He And answering said to him, You
3004 2723 846 749 4183
3 λέγεις. καὶ κατηγόρουν αὐτοῦ οἱ ἀρχιερεῖς πολλά· αὐτὸς δὲ
say (it). And accused Him the chief priests many things, He but
3762 611 4091 3825 1905 846
4 οὐδὲν ἀπεκρίνατο. ὁ δὲ Πιλάτος πάλιν ἐπηρώτησεν αὐτόν,
nothing answered. – But Pilate again questioned Him,
3004 3756 611 3762 2396 4214 4675 2649
λέγων, Οὐκ ἀποκρίνῃ οὐδέν; ἴδε, πόσα σου καταμαρτυ-
saying, not Do you answer nothing? Behold, how many things you they testify
2424 3765 3762 611 5620 2296
5 ροῦσιν. ὁ δὲ Ἰησοῦς οὐκέτι οὐδὲν ἀπεκρίθη, ὥστε θαυμάζειν
against. – But Jesus no more nothing answered, so as to marvel
4091
τὸν Πιλάτον.
Pilate.
2596 1859 630 846 1520 1198 4007
6 Κατὰ δὲ ἑορτὴν ἀπέλυεν αὐτοῖς ἕνα δέσμιον, ὅνπερ
at And a feast he released to them one prisoner, whomever
154 2258 3004 912 3326 4955
7 ᾐτοῦντο. ἦν δὲ ὁ λεγόμενος Βαραββᾶς μετὰ τῶν συστασια-
they asked. was And one called Barabbas with the insurgents
1210 3748 1722 4714 5408 4160
8 στῶν δεδεμένος, οἵτινες ἐν τῇ στάσει φόνον πεποιήκεισαν. καὶ
having been bound, who in the insurrection murder had committed. And
310 3793 756 154 2531 104 4160 846
ἀναβοήσας ὁ ὄχλος ἤρξατο αἰτεῖσθαι καθὼς ἀεὶ ἐποίει αὐτοῖς.
crying aloud the crowd began to beg as always he did for them.

answered them, saying, Do you desire I should release to you the king of the Jews? [10]For he knew that the chief priests had delivered Him up through envy. [11]But the chief priests stirred up the crowd, that rather he should release Barabbas to them. [12]But answering again Pilate said to them, What then do you desire I do to *him* whom you call king of the Jews? [13]And again they cried out, Crucify him! [14]But Pilate said to them, For what evil did he do? But they much more cried out, Crucify him! [15]And deciding to do the easiest to the crowd, Pilate released Barabbas to them. And having flogged *Him, he* delivered up Jesus, that He might be crucified.

[16]And the soldiers led Him away inside the court, which is *the* praetorium. And they called together all the cohort. [17]And they put purple on Him, and they plaited and placed a crown of thorns on Him. [18]And they began to salute Him,

Hail, King of the Jews! [19]And they struck His head with a reed, and spat at Him. And placing the knees, *they* bowed down to Him. [20]And when they had mocked Him, they took the purple off Him, and put His own garments on Him. and they led Him out, that they might crucify Him. [21]And they forced one passing by, Simon, a Cyrenian, coming from a field, the father of Alexander and Rufus, that he might carry His cross.

[22]And they brought Him to Golgotha Place, which translated is, Place of a Skull. [23]And they gave Him

4091 611 846 3004 2309 630 521
9 ὁ δὲ Πιλάτος ἀπεκρίθη αὐτοῖς, λέγων, Θέλετε ἀπολύσω ὑμ
– But Pilate answered them, saying, Desire you I may release to
935 2453 1097 1063 3754/1223 535 yo
10 τὸν βασιλέα τῶν Ἰουδαίων; ἐγίνωσκε γὰρ ὅτι διὰ φθόνο
the king of the Jews? he knew For that for envy
3860 846 749 383
11 παραδεδώκεισαν αὐτὸν οἱ ἀρχιερεῖς. οἱ δὲ ἀρχιερεῖς ἀνέσε
had delivered over Him the chief priests. the But chief priests stirred
3793 2443 3123 912 630 846
σαν τὸν ὄχλον, ἵνα μᾶλλον τὸν Βαραββᾶν ἀπολύσῃ αὐτοῖ
up the crowd, that rather – Barabbas he should release to the
4091 611 3825 2036 846 5101/3767 230
12 ὁ δὲ Πιλάτος ἀποκριθεὶς πάλιν εἶπεν αὐτοῖς, Τί οὖν θέλε
– But Pilate answering again said to them, What then wish y
2896 3004 935 2453 3825
13 ποιήσω ὃν λέγετε βασιλέα τῶν Ἰουδαίων; οἱ δὲ πάλι
I do (with) whom you call king of the Jews? they And agai
4160 4717 846 4091 3004 846 51
14 ἔκραξαν, Σταύρωσον αὐτόν. ὁ δὲ Πιλάτος ἔλεγεν αὐτοῖς, Τ
cried out, Crucify Him! – But Pilate said to them, wh
1063 2556 4160 4056 2896 4717
γὰρ κακὸν ἐποίησεν; οἱ δὲ περισσοτέρως ἔκραξαν, Σταυ
For evil did he do? they And much more cried out, Crucify
846 4091 1014 3793 2425
15 ρωσον αὐτόν. ὁ δὲ Πιλάτος βουλόμενος τῷ ὄχλῳ τὸ ἱκανὸ
Him! – But Pilate deciding the crowd the easiest
4160 630 846 912 3860
ποιῆσαι, ἀπέλυσεν αὐτοῖς τὸν Βαραββᾶν· καὶ παρέδωκε τὸ
to do released to them Barabbas, and delivered up –
2424 5417 2443 4717
Ἰησοῦν, φραγελλώσας, ἵνα σταυρωθῇ.
Jesus, having flogged (Him), that He might be crucified
4757 520 846 2080 833/3603/2076
16 Οἱ δὲ στρατιῶται ἀπήγαγον αὐτὸν ἔσω τῆς αὐλῆς, ὅ ἐστι
the And soldiers led away Him inside the court, which is
4232 4779 3650 4686
17 πραιτώριον, καὶ συγκαλοῦσιν ὅλην τὴν σπεῖραν. κ
praetorium, and they call together all the cohort. An
1746 846 4209 4060 846 41
ἐνδύουσιν αὐτὸν πορφύραν, καὶ περιτιθέασιν αὐτῷ π
they put on Him purple, and placed around Him ha
174 4735 756 782 846
18 ξαντες ἀκάνθινον στέφανον, καὶ ἤρξαντο ἀσπάζεσθαι αὐτ
plaited a thorny crown. And they began to salute H
5463 935 2453 5180 846
19 Χαῖρε, βασιλεῦ τῶν Ἰουδαίων· καὶ ἔτυπτον αὐτοῦ τ
Hail, King of the Jews! And they struck of Him the
2776 2563 1716 846 5087 1119
κεφαλὴν καλάμῳ, καὶ ἐνέπτυον αὐτῷ, καὶ τιθέντες τὰ γόνα
head with a reed, and spit at Him; and placing the kn
4352 846 3753 1702 846 1562
20 προσεκύνουν αὐτῷ. καὶ ὅτε ἐνέπαιξαν αὐτῷ, ἐξέδυσ
did homage to Him. And when they had mocked Him, they took
846 4209 1746 846 2440 23
αὐτὸν τὴν πορφύραν, καὶ ἐνέδυσαν αὐτὸν τὰ ἱμάτια τὰ ἴδ
Him the purple, and put on Him the garments, his ow
1806 846 2443 4717 846
21 Καὶ ἐξάγουσιν αὐτὸν ἵνα σταυρώσωσιν αὐτόν. κ
And they lead forth Him, that they might crucify Him. A
29 3855 5100 4613 2956 2064
ἀγγαρεύουσι παράγοντά τινα Σίμωνα Κυρηναῖον, ἐρχόμε
they compel passing by a certain Simon, a Cyrenian coming
575 68 3962 223 4504 2443 1
ἀπ' ἀγροῦ, τὸν πατέρα Ἀλεξάνδρου καὶ Ῥούφου, ἵνα ἄ
from a field, the father of Alexander and of Rufus, that he b
4716 846 5342 846 1909 1115 51
22 τὸν σταυρὸν αὐτοῦ. καὶ φέρουσιν αὐτὸν ἐπὶ Γολγοθᾶ τοπ
the cross of Him. And they bring Him to Golgotha pla
3739/2076 3177 2898 5117 1325 8
23 ὅ ἐστι μεθερμηνευόμενον, κρανίου τόπος. καὶ ἐδίδουν αὐ
which is, being translated, of a Skull Place. And they gave H

wine having been spiced
with myrrh to drink. But He
did not take *it.* 24And
having crucified Him, they
divided His garments, casting a lot on them, who *and*
what *each* should take.
25And it was *the* third hour,
and they crucified Him.
26And the superscription of
His charge was written over
Him, THE KING OF THE
JEWS. 27And they cruci-
fied two robbers with Him,
one off *the* right, and one off
the left of Him.

28And the Scripture was
fulfilled which says, "And
He was numbered with *the*
lawless." 29And those
passing by blasphemed
Him, shaking their heads,
and saying, Aha! *You* razing
the temple, and in three
days building *it,* 30save
yourself, and come down
from the cross. 31And also
the chief priests and the
scribes mocking to one
another said the same, He
saved others; he is not able
to save himself. 32The
Christ, the King of Israel?
Let him now come down
from the cross, that we may
see and believe. And the
ones crucified with Him
insulted Him.

33And *it* being *the* sixth
hour, darkness came over
all the land until *the* ninth
hour. 34And at the ninth
hour Jesus cried with a loud
voice, saying, Eloi, Eloi,
lama sabachthani? which
being translated is, My
God, My God, why did You
forsake Me? 35And hearing,
some of those standing by
said, Behold, he calls Elijah.
36And one running up, and
filling a sponge with
vinegar, and putting it on a
reed, gave Him to drink. *But
they* said, Leave *alone,* let
us see if Elijah comes to
take Him down.

37And letting out a great

4095 4669 3631 3756 2983 4717
24 πιεῖν ἐσμυρνισμένον οἶνον· ὁ δὲ οὐκ ἔλαβε. καὶ σταυρώσαντες
to drink spiced with myrrh wine. He but not did take. And having crucified
846 1266 2440 848 906 2819 1909
αὐτόν, διεμέριζον τὰ ἱμάτια αὐτοῦ, βάλλοντες κλῆρον ἐπ'
Him, they divided the garments of Him, casting a lot on
846 5101/5101/142/2258 5610 5154 4717 846
25 αὐτά, τίς τί ἄρῃ. ἦν δὲ ὥρα τρίτη, καὶ ἐσταύρωσαν αὐτόν.
them, who what may take. was And hour third, and they crucified Him.
2258 1923 156 848 1924
26 καὶ ἦν ἡ ἐπιγραφὴ τῆς αἰτίας αὐτοῦ ἐπιγεγραμμένη, Ὁ
And was the superscription of the accusa- tion of Him written over (Him), THE
935 2453 4862 846 4717 1417
27 βασιλεὺς τῶν Ἰουδαίων. καὶ σὺν αὐτῷ σταυροῦσι δύο
KING OF THE JEWS. And with Him they crucify two
3027 1520 1537 1188 1520/1537 2176 848
28 λῃστάς, ἕνα ἐκ δεξιῶν καὶ ἕνα ἐξ εὐωνύμων αὐτοῦ. καὶ
robbers, one off (the) right, and one off (the) left of Him. And
4137 1124 3004 3326 459 3049
ἐπληρώθη ἡ γραφὴ ἡ λέγουσα, Καὶ μετὰ ἀνόμων ἐλογίσθη.
was fulfilled the scripture which says, And with (the) lawless He was counted.
3899 987 846 2795
29 καὶ οἱ παραπορευόμενοι ἐβλασφήμουν αὐτόν, κινοῦντες τὰς
And those passing by blasphemed Him, shaking the
2776 848 3004 3758 2647 3485
κεφαλὰς αὐτῶν, καὶ λέγοντες, Οὐά, ὁ καταλύων τὸν ναόν,
heads of them, and saying, Aha, the (one) razing the temple
1722 5140 2250 3618 4982 4572 2597
30 καὶ ἐν τρισὶν ἡμέραις οἰκοδομῶν, σῶσον σεαυτόν. καὶ κατάβα
and in three days building, save yourself, and come down
575 4716 4982 749 1702
31 ἀπὸ τοῦ σταυροῦ. ὁμοίως δὲ καὶ οἱ ἀρχιερεῖς ἐμπαίζοντες
from the cross. likewise And also the chief priests mocking
4314 240 3326 1122 3004 243
πρὸς ἀλλήλους μετὰ τῶν γραμματέων ἔλεγον, Ἄλλους
to one another, with the scribes, said, Others
4982 1438 3756 1410 4482 5547 935
32 ἔσωσεν, ἑαυτὸν οὐ δύναται σῶσαι. ὁ Χριστὸς ὁ βασιλεὺς
he saved, himself not he is able to save; the Christ, the king
2474 2597 3568 575 4716 2443 1492
τοῦ Ἰσραὴλ καταβάτω νῦν ἀπὸ τοῦ σταυροῦ, ἵνα ἴδωμεν
— of Israel, let Him descend now from the cross, that we may see
4100 4957 846 3679
καὶ πιστεύσωμεν. καὶ οἱ συνεσταυρωμένοι αὐτῷ ὠνείδιζον
and believe. And the (ones) being crucified with Him insulted
846
αὐτόν.
Him.
1096 5610 1623 4655 1096 1909/3650 1093
33 Γενομένης δὲ ὥρας ἕκτης, σκότος ἐγένετο ἐφ' ὅλην τὴν γῆν
occurring And hour sixth, darkness came over all the land
2193 5610 1766 5610 1766 994 2424
34 ἕως ὥρας ἐννάτης. καὶ τῇ ὥρᾳ τῇ ἐννάτῃ ἐβόησεν ὁ Ἰησοῦς
until hour ninth. And at the hour ninth cried Jesus
5456 3173 3004 1682 1682 2982 4518
φωνῇ μεγάλῃ, λέγων, Ἐλωΐ, Ἐλωΐ, λαμμᾶ σαβαχθανί;
with a voice great, saying, Eloi, Eloi, Lama sabachthani?
3739/2076 3177 2316 3450 2316 3450/1519/5101/•
•3165 ὅ ἐστι μεθερμηνευόμενον, Ὁ Θεός μου, ὁ Θεός μου, εἰς τί με
which is, being translated, The God of Me, the God of Me, why Me
1459 5100 3936 191
35 ἐγκατέλιπες; καί τινες τῶν παρεστηκότων ἀκούσαντες
did You forsake? And some of the (ones) standing by hearing
3004 2400 2243 5455 5143 1520 1072
36 ἔλεγον, Ἰδού, Ἠλίαν φωνεῖ. δραμὼν δὲ εἷς, καὶ γεμίσας
said, Behold, Elijah he calls. running And one, and filling
4699 3690 4060 5037 2563 4222 846 3004
σπόγγον ὄξους, περιθείς τε καλάμῳ, ἐπότιζεν αὐτόν, λέγων,
a sponge of vinegar, putting it and on a reed, gave to drink Him, saying,
863 1492 1487 2064 2243 2507 846
37 Ἄφετε, ἴδωμεν εἰ ἔρχεται Ἠλίας καθελεῖν αὐτόν. ὁ δὲ
Leave, let us see if comes Elijah to take down Him. But

cry, Jesus expired. [38]And the veil of the temple was torn into two, from top to bottom. [39]And standing off across from Him, seeing that *He* had cried out so, *and* He expired, the centurion said, Truly, this Man was Son of God.

[40]And also women were watching from a distance, among whom also was Mary Magdalene; also Mary the mother of James the less, and of Joses, and Salome, [41]who also followed Him and ministered to Him when He was in Galilee; and many other *women* who came up to Jerusalem with Him.

[42]And *it* becoming evening already, since it was *the* preparation, that is, *the* day before sabbath, [43]Joseph of Arimathea came, an honorable councillor, who himself was also waiting for the kingdom of God. *And* taking courage, he went in to Pilate and begged the body of Jesus. [44]And Pilate wondered if He had already dead. And calling the centurion near, he asked him if He died long ago. [45]And knowing from the centurion, he granted the body to Joseph. [46]And having bought a linen cloth, and having taken Him down, he wrapped *Him* in the linen, and laid Him in a tomb which was cut out of rock. And *he* rolled a stone against the mouth of the tomb. [47]And Mary Magdalene, and Mary of Joses, saw where He was laid.

2424 863 5456 3173 1606 2665
38 Ἰησοῦς ἀφεὶς φωνὴν μεγάλην ἐξέπνευσε. καὶ τὸ καταπέτασμα
Jesus letting out a voice great expired. And the veil
3485 4977 1519/1417/575 509 2193 2736 1492
39 τοῦ ναοῦ ἐσχίσθη εἰς δύο ἀπὸ ἄνωθεν ἕως κάτω. Ἰδὼν δὲ ὁ
of the temple was torn into two, from top to bottom. seeing And the
2760 3936 1537 1727 846 3754 3779
κεντυρίων ὁ παρεστηκὼς ἐξ ἐναντίας αὐτοῦ ὅτι οὕτω
centurion standing near off the opposite of Him, that thus
2896 1606 2036 230 444 3778 5207
κράξας ἐξέπνευσεν, εἶπεν, Ἀληθῶς ὁ ἄνθρωπος οὗτος υἱὸς
having cried out, He expired, said, Truly, man this Son
2258/2316 2258 1135 575 3113 2334
40 ἦν Θεοῦ. ἦσαν δὲ καὶ γυναῖκες ἀπὸ μακρόθεν θεωροῦσαι,
was of God. were And also women from afar watching,
1722/3739/2258 3137 3094 3137
ἐν αἷς ἦν καὶ Μαρία ἡ Μαγδαληνή, καὶ Μαρία ἡ τοῦ
among whom was also Mary the Magdalene, and Mary the
2385 3398 2500 3384 4539 3739
41 Ἰακώβου τοῦ μικροῦ καὶ Ἰωσῆ μήτηρ καὶ Σαλώμη, αἳ καί,
of James the less, and of Joses mother and Salome, who also
3753/2258/1722 1056 190 846 1247
ὅτε ἦν ἐν τῇ Γαλιλαίᾳ, ἠκολούθουν αὐτῷ, καὶ διηκόνουν
when He in Galilee had followed Him, and ministered
846 243 4183 2872 846 1519
αὐτῷ, καὶ ἄλλαι πολλαὶ αἱ συναναβᾶσαι αὐτῷ εἰς
to Him, and other (women) many who came up with Him to
2414
Ἱεροσόλυμα.
Jerusalem.
2235/3798 1096 1893/2258 3904 3603 2076
42 Καὶ ἤδη ὀψίας γενομένης, ἐπεὶ ἦν Παρασκευή, ὅ ἐστι
And now evening occurring, since it was (the) preparation which is
4315 2064 2501 575 707 2158
43 προσάββατον, ἦλθεν Ἰωσὴφ ὁ ἀπὸ Ἀριμαθαίας, εὐσχήμων
(the) day before sabbath, coming Joseph from Arimathea, an honorable
1010 3739 846 2258 4327 932
βουλευτής, ὃς καὶ αὐτὸς ἦν προσδεχόμενος τὴν βασιλείαν
councillor, who also (him)self was expecting the kingdom
2316 5111 1525 4314 4091 154
τοῦ Θεοῦ· τολμήσας εἰσῆλθε πρὸς Πιλάτον, καὶ ᾐτήσατο
— of God, taking courage went in to Pilate, and asked
4983 2424 4091 2296 1487/2235
44 τὸ σῶμα τοῦ Ἰησοῦ. ὁ δὲ Πιλάτος ἐθαύμασεν εἰ ἤδη
the body — of Jesus. — And Pilate marveled if already
2348 4341 2760 1905
τέθνηκε· καὶ προσκαλεσάμενος τὸν κεντυρίωνα, ἐπηρώτησεν
He had died, and having called near the centurion, he questioned
846/1487/3819 599 1087 575 2760
45 αὐτὸν εἰ πάλαι ἀπέθανε. καὶ γνοὺς ἀπὸ τοῦ κεντυρίωνος,
him if long ago He died. And knowing from the centurion
1433 4983 2501 59 4616
46 ἐδωρήσατο τὸ σῶμα τῷ Ἰωσήφ. καὶ ἀγοράσας σινδόνα,
he granted the body to Joseph. And buying a linen cloth
2507 846 1750 4616 2698 846
καὶ καθελὼν αὐτόν, ἐνείλησε τῇ σινδόνι, καὶ κατέθηκεν αὐτὸν
and taking Him, he wrapped in the linen, and laid Him
1722 3419/3739/2258/ 2998 1537 4073 4351
ἐν μνημείῳ, ὃ ἦν λελατομημένον ἐκ πέτρας· καὶ προσεκύλισε
in a tomb, which was cut out of rock, and rolled
3037 1909 2374 3419 3137 3094
47 λίθον ἐπὶ τὴν θύραν τοῦ μνημείου. ἡ δὲ Μαρία ἡ Μαγδαληνὴ
a stone against the door of the tomb. And Mary the Magdalene
3137 2500 233 4226 5087
καὶ Μαρία Ἰωσῆ ἐθεώρουν ποῦ τίθεται.
and Mary of Joses beheld where He had been laid.

CHAPTER 16

[1]And the sabbath passing, Mary Magdalene and

1230 4521 3137 3094
1 Καὶ διαγενομένου τοῦ σαββάτου, Μαρία ἡ Μαγδαληνὴ
And passing the sabbath, Mary the Magdalene,

Mary the *mother* of James
and Salome, bought spices
so that coming they might
anoint Him. [2]And very early
on the first of the sabbaths,
the sun rising, they came
upon the tomb. [3]And they
said to themselves, Who
will roll away the stone from
the door of the tomb for
us? [4]And looking up, they
saw that the stone had
been rolled back; for it was
very large. [5]And entering
into the tomb, they saw a
young man sitting on the
right, having been clothed
in a white robe. And they
were much amazed. [6]But
He said to them, Do not be
amazed. You seek Jesus
the Nazarene, who has
been crucified. He was
raised. He is not here. See
the place where they put
Him? [7]But go, say to the
disciples and to Peter, He
goes before you into Galilee. You will see Him there,
even as He told you. [8]And
going out quickly, they fled
from the tomb. And trem-
bling and ecstasy took hold
of them. And they told no
one, not a thing, for they
were afraid.
[9]And rising early on the
first of the week, He first
appeared to Mary Magda-
lene, from whom He had
cast out seven demons.
[10]That *one* had gone *and*
reported to those who had
been with Him, *who were*
mourning and weeping.
[11]And those hearing that He
lives, and was seen by her,
they did not believe.

[12]And after these things,
He was revealed in a
different form to two of
them walking *and* going
into the country. [13]And
going those reported to the
rest. Neither did they
believe those.

3137 2385 4539 59 759
καὶ Μαρία ἡ τοῦ Ἰακώβου καὶ Σαλώμη ἠγόρασαν ἀρώματα,
and Mary the (mother) of James and Salome bought spices
2443 2064 218 846 3029 4404 3391
2 ἵνα ἐλθοῦσαι ἀλείψωσιν αὐτόν. καὶ λίαν πρωῒ τῆς μιᾶς
that coming they might anoint Him. And very early on the first
4521 2064 1909 3419 393
σαββάτων ἔρχονται ἐπὶ τὸ μνημεῖον, ἀνατείλαντος τοῦ
of the sabbaths they come upon the tomb, rising the
2246 3004 4314 1438 5101 617 2254
3 ἡλίου. καὶ ἔλεγον πρὸς ἑαυτάς, Τίς ἀποκυλίσει ἡμῖν τὸν
sun. And they said to themselves, Who will roll away for us the
3037 1537 2374 3419 308
4 λίθον ἐκ τῆς θύρας τοῦ μνημείου; καὶ ἀναβλέψασαι
stone from the door of the tomb? And looking up
2334 3754 617 3037 2258 1063 3173
θεωροῦσιν ὅτι ἀποκεκύλισται ὁ λίθος· ἦν γὰρ μέγας
they see that has been rolled back the stone. it was For great
4970 1525 1519 3419 1492 3495
5 σφόδρα. καὶ εἰσελθοῦσαι εἰς τὸ μνημεῖον, εἶδον νεανίσκον
exceedingly. And having entered into the tomb, they saw a young man
2521 1722 1188 4016 4749 3022
καθήμενον ἐν τοῖς δεξιοῖς, περιβεβλημένον στολὴν λευκήν·
sitting on the right, having been clothed (in) a robe white.
1568 3004 846 3361 1568
6 καὶ ἐξεθαμβήθησαν. ὁ δὲ λέγει αὐταῖς, Μὴ ἐκθαμβεῖσθε·
And they were much amazed. he But says to them, not Be much amazed;
2424 2212 3479 4717 1453
Ἰησοῦν ζητεῖτε τὸν Ναζαρηνὸν τὸν ἐσταυρωμένον· ἠγέρθη,
Jesus you seek, the Nazarene; having been crucified, He was raised
3756 2076 5602 2396 5117 3699 5087 846 235
7 οὐκ ἔστιν ὧδε· ἴδε, ὁ τόπος ὅπου ἔθηκαν αὐτόν. ἀλλ'
not He is here; behold, the place where they put Him. But
5217 2036 3101 848 4074 3754
ὑπάγετε, εἴπατε τοῖς μαθηταῖς αὐτοῦ καὶ τῷ Πέτρῳ ὅτι
go tell the disciples of Him, and — Peter, —
4254 5209 1519 1056 1563 846 3700 2531
Προάγει ὑμᾶς εἰς τὴν Γαλιλαίαν· ἐκεῖ αὐτὸν ὄψεσθε, καθὼς
He goes before you into — Galilee; there Him you will see, even as
2036 5213 1831 5035 5343 575 3419
8 εἶπεν ὑμῖν. καὶ ἐξελθοῦσαι ταχὺ ἔφυγον ἀπὸ τοῦ μνημείου·
He told you. And going out quickly, they fled from the tomb.
2192 846 5156 1611 3762 3762 2036
εἶχε δὲ αὐτὰς τρόμος καὶ ἔκστασις· καὶ οὐδενὶ οὐδὲν εἶπον,
held And them trembling and ecstasy; and no one nothing they told;
5399 1063
ἐφοβοῦντο γάρ.
they were afraid for.
450 4404 4413 4521 5316 4412
9 Ἀναστὰς δὲ πρωῒ πρώτῃ σαββάτου ἐφάνη πρῶτον
having risen And early on the first of the week, He appeared first
3137 3094 575 3739 1544 2033 1140
Μαρίᾳ τῇ Μαγδαληνῇ, ἀφ' ἧς ἐκβεβλήκει ἑπτὰ δαιμόνια.
to Mary the Magdalene, from whom He had cast seven demons.
1565 4198 518 3326 846 1096
10 ἐκείνη πορευθεῖσα ἀπήγγειλε τοῖς μετ' αὐτοῦ γενομένοις,
That (one) having gone reported to the (ones) with Him having been,
3996 2799 2548 191 3754 2198
11 πενθοῦσι καὶ κλαίουσι. κἀκεῖνοι ἀκούσαντες ὅτι ζῇ καὶ
mourning and weeping. And those hearing that He lives and
2300 5259 846 569
ἐθεάθη ὑπ' αὐτῆς ἠπίστησαν.
was seen by her they disbelieved.
3326 5023 1417/1537 846 4043 5319
12 Μετὰ δὲ ταῦτα δυσὶν ἐξ αὐτῶν περιπατοῦσιν ἐφανερώθη
after And these things to two of them walking He was revealed
1722/2087/3444 4198 1519 68 2548 565
13 ἐν ἑτέρᾳ μορφῇ, πορευομένοις εἰς ἀγρόν. κἀκεῖνοι ἀπελθόντες
in a different form, going into the country. And those going
518 3062 3761 1565 4100
ἀπήγγειλαν τοῖς λοιποῖς· οὐδὲ ἐκείνοις ἐπίστευσαν.
reported to the rest; neither those they believed.

NOTE: Frequent words not numbered: δέ(1161); καί(2531)—and, but; ὁ, ἡ, τό (3588, the)— * above word, look in verse margin for No.

14 Afterward, as they reclined, He was revealed to the Eleven. And *He* reproached their unbelief and hardness of heart, because they did not believe those who had seen Him, having been raised. 15 And He said to them, Going into all the world, preach the gospel to all the creation. 16 The one believing and being baptized will be saved. And the *one* not believing will be condemned. 17 And signs will follow to those believing these things: they will cast out demons in My name; they will speak new languages; 18 they will take up snakes; and if they drink anything deadly, it will in no way hurt them; they will lay hands on *the* sick, and they will be well.

19 Then indeed, after speaking to them, the Lord was taken up into Heaven, and sat off *the* right of God.

20 And going out they preached everywhere, the Lord working with *them,* and confirming the word by the signs following. Amen.

5305 345 846 1733 5319
14 Ὕστερον ἀνακειμένοις αὐτοῖς τοῖς ἕνδεκα ἐφανερώθη, καὶ
Later as reclined they to the eleven He was revealed, and
3679 570 848 4641 3754
ὠνείδισε τὴν ἀπιστίαν αὐτῶν καὶ σκληροκαρδίαν, ὅτι τοῖς
reproached the unbelief of them and hardness of heart, because those
2300 846 1453 3756 4100 2036
15 θεασαμένοις αὐτὸν ἐγηγερμένον οὐκ ἐπίστευσαν. καὶ εἶπεν
having seen Him having been raised not they believed. And He said
846 4198 1519 2889 537 2784
αὐτοῖς, Πορευθέντες εἰς τὸν κόσμον ἅπαντα, κηρύξατε τὸ
to them, Going into the world all, preach the
2098 3956 2937 4100 907
16 εὐαγγέλιον πάσῃ τῇ κτίσει. ὁ πιστεύσας καὶ βαπτισθεὶς
gospel to all the creation. The (one) believing and being baptized
4982 569 2632 4592
17 σωθήσεται· ὁ δὲ ἀπιστήσας κατακριθήσεται. σημεῖα δὲ τοῖς
will be saved; he but not believing will be condemned. signs And to those
4100 5023 3877 1722 3686 3450
πιστεύσασι ταῦτα παρακολουθήσει· ἐν τῷ ὀνόματί μου
believing these will follow, in the name of Me
1140 1544 1100 2980 2537 3789
18 δαιμόνια ἐκβαλοῦσι· γλώσσαις λαλήσουσι καιναῖς· ὄφεις
demons they will cast out; languages they shall speak new; snakes
142 2579 2286 5100 4095 =3364= 846 984 1909
ἀροῦσι· κἂν θανάσιμόν τι πίωσιν, οὐ μὴ αὐτοὺς βλάψει· ἐπὶ
they will take; and if deadly anything they drink, in no way them it will hurt; on
732 5495 2007 2573 2192
ἀρρώστους χεῖρας ἐπιθήσουσι, καὶ καλῶς ἕξουσιν.
infirm ones hands they will place, and wellness they will have.
3303/3767/ 2962 3326 2980 846 353 1519
19 Ὁ μὲν οὖν Κύριος, μετὰ τὸ λαλῆσαι αὐτοῖς, ἀνελήφθη εἰς
The indeed then Lord, after the speaking to them, was taken up into
3772 2523 1537 1188 2316 1565
20 τὸν οὐρανόν, καὶ ἐκάθισεν ἐκ δεξιῶν τοῦ Θεοῦ. ἐκεῖνοι δὲ
— Heaven, and sat off (the) right of God, they But
1831 2784 3837 2962 4903
ἐξελθόντες ἐκήρυξαν πανταχοῦ, τοῦ Κυρίου συνεργοῦντος,
having gone out preached everywhere, the Lord working with (them)
3056 950 1223 1872
καὶ τὸν λόγον βεβαιοῦντος διὰ τῶν ἐπακολουθούντων
and the word confirming through the accompanying
4592 281
σημείων. Ἀμήν.
signs Amen.

THE GOSPEL
ACCORDING TO
LUKE
A LITERAL TRANSLATION
OF THE BIBLE

[1]Since many took in hand
to draw up an account concerning the matters having
been borne out among us,
[2]as those from *the* beginning delivered to us, be-
coming eyewitnesses and
ministers of the word, [3]it
seemed good also to me,
having traced out all things
accurately from the first, to
write in order to you, most
excellent Theophilus, [4]that
you may know the certainty
concerning the words
which you were taught.
[5]In the days of Herod the
king of Judea, there was a
certain priest named Zacharias, of *the* daily course of
Abijah. And his wife *was* of
the daughters of Aaron, and
her name *was* Elizabeth.
[6]And they were both
righteous before God, walking blameless in all the
commandments and ordi-
nances of the Lord. [7]And no
child was *born* to them,
because Elizabeth was barren. And both were ad-
vanced in their days.

[8]And it happened in his
serving as priest in the
order of his course before
God, [9]according to the
custom of the priests,
entering into the temple of
the Lord, *it was Zacharias'*
lot to burn incense. [10]And
all the multitude of the
people was praying outside
at the hour of incense.
[11]And an angel of *the* Lord

ΕΥΑΓΓΕΛΙΟΝ
GOSPEL
ΤΟ ΚΑΤΑ ΛΟΥΚΑΝ
THE ACCORDING TO LUKE

CHAPTER 1

1895 4183 2021 392 1335
1 Ἐπειδήπερ πολλοὶ ἐπεχείρησαν ἀνατάξασθαι διήγησιν
Since many took in hand to draw up an account
4012 4135 1722 2254 4229 2531
2 περὶ τῶν πεπληροφορημένων ἐν ἡμῖν πραγμάτων, καθὼς
concerning the having been fully borne out among us matters, as
3860 2254 575 746 845 5257
παρέδοσαν ἡμῖν οἱ ἀπ' ἀρχῆς αὐτόπται καὶ ὑπηρέται
delivered to us the (ones) from beginning, eyewitnesses and ministers
1097 3056 1380 2504 3877 509
3 γενόμενοι τοῦ λόγου, ἔδοξε κἀμοί, παρηκολουθηκότι ἄνωθεν
becoming of the word, it seemed good also to me, following from the first
3956 199 2517 4671 1125 2903 2321 2443
4 πᾶσιν ἀκριβῶς, καθεξῆς σοι γράψαι, κράτιστε Θεόφιλε, ἵνα
all things accurately, in order to you to write, most excellent Theophilus, that
1921 4012 3739 2727 3056 803
ἐπιγνῷς περὶ ὧν κατηχήθης λόγων τὴν ἀσφάλειαν.
you may know about which you were (in) words the certainty.
1096/1722 taught 2250 2264 735
5 Ἐγένετο ἐν ταῖς ἡμέραις Ἡρώδου τοῦ βασιλέως τῆς
There was in the days of Herod the king –
2449 2409 5100 3686 2197 1537 2183 7
Ἰουδαίας ἱερεύς τις ὀνόματι Ζαχαρίας, ἐξ ἐφημερίας Ἀβιά·
of Judea, a priest certain by name Zacharias, of (the) daily course of Abia,
1135 848 1527 2364 2 3686
καὶ ἡ γυνὴ αὐτοῦ ἐκ τῶν θυγατέρων Ἀαρών, καὶ τὸ ὄνομα
and the wife of him of the daughters of Aaron, and the name
848 1665 2258 1342 297 1799
6 αὐτῆς Ἐλισάβετ. ἦσαν δὲ δίκαιοι ἀμφότεροι ἐνώπιον τοῦ
of her Elizabeth. they were And righteous both in (the) sight of
2316 4198 1722/3956 1785 1345
Θεοῦ, πορευόμενοι ἐν πάσαις ταῖς ἐντολαῖς καὶ δικαιώμασι
God, walking in all the commandments and ordinances
2962 273 3756 2258 846 5043 2530
7 τοῦ Κυρίου ἄμεμπτοι. καὶ οὐκ ἦν αὐτοῖς τέκνον, καθότι
of the Lord blameless. And not was to them a child, because
1665 2258 4723 297 4260 1722
ἡ Ἐλισάβετ ἦν στεῖρα, καὶ ἀμφότεροι προβεβηκότες ἐν ταῖς
– Elizabeth was barren, and both advanced in the
2250 848 2258
ἡμέραις αὐτῶν ἦσαν.
days of them were.
1096 1722 2407 846 1722 5010 2183
8 Ἐγένετο δὲ ἐν τῷ ἱερατεύειν αὐτὸν ἐν τῇ τάξει τῆς ἐφη-
it was And, in the serving as priest of him in the order of the
848 1725 2316 2596 1485 2405
9 μερίας αὐτοῦ ἔναντι τοῦ Θεοῦ, κατὰ τὸ ἔθος τῆς ἱερατείας,
course of him before God, according to the custom of the priests,
2975 2370 1575 1519 3485 2962
10 ἔλαχε τοῦ θυμιάσαι εἰσελθὼν εἰς τὸν ναὸν τοῦ Κυρίου. καὶ
(his) lot to burn incense entering into the temple of the Lord. And
3956 4128 2992 2258 4336 1854 4610
πᾶν τὸ πλῆθος τοῦ λαοῦ ἦν προσευχόμενον ἔξω τῇ ὥρᾳ
all the multitude of the people was praying outside at the hour
2368 3700 846 32 2962 2456 1537
11 τοῦ θυμιάματος. ὤφθη δὲ αὐτῷ ἄγγελος Κυρίου, ἑστὼς ἐκ
of incense appeared And to him an angel of (the) standing on

appeared to him, standing on *the* right of the altar of incense. [12]And seeing *this*, Zacharias was troubled, and fear fell on him. [13]But the angel said to him, Do not fear, Zacharias, because your prayer was heard, and your wife Elizabeth will bear a son to you; and you shall call his name John. [14]And he will be joy and exultation to you, and many will rejoice over his birth. [15]For he shall be great in the eyes of the Lord; and he shall not drink wine or strong drink. And he will be filled of *the* Holy Spirit, even from his mother's womb. [16]And he will turn many of the sons of Israel to *the* Lord their God.

[17]And he will go out before Him in *the* spirit and power of Elijah, to turn *the* hearts of fathers to *their* children, and disobedient ones to *the* wisdom of *the* just, to make ready a people having been prepared for *the* Lord.

[18]And Zacharias said to the angel, By what shall I know this? For I am old, and my wife is advanced in her days.

[19]And answering, the angel said to him, I am Gabriel, who stands before God, and I was sent to speak to you and to announce to you *the* good news of these things. [20]And behold, you shall be silent and not able to speak until the day in which these things take place, because you did not believe my words, which shall be fulfilled in their season.

[21]And the people were expecting Zacharias, and they wondered at his delay in the temple. [22]But coming out, he was not able to speak to them, and they recognized that he had seen a vision in the

1188 2379 2368 5015
δεξιῶν τοῦ θυσιαστηρίου τοῦ θυμιάματος. καὶ ἐταράχθη
(the) right of the altar of incense. And was troubled
2197 1492 5401 1968 1909 846 2036 4314
13 Ζαχαρίας ἰδών, καὶ φόβος ἐπέπεσεν ἐπ' αὐτόν. εἶπε δὲ πρὸς
Zacharias seeing, and fear fell upon him. said But to
846 32 3361 5399 2197 1360 1522
αὐτὸν ὁ ἄγγελος, Μὴ φοβοῦ, Ζαχαρία· διότι εἰσηκούσθη ἡ
him the angel. Do not fear, Zacharias because was heard the
1162 4675 1135 4675 1665 1080 5207 4671
δέησίς σου, καὶ ἡ γυνή σου Ἐλισάβετ γεννήσει υἱόν σοι, καὶ
request of you, and the wife of you, Elizabeth, will bear a son to you, and
2563 3685 848 2491 2071 5479 4671
14 καλέσεις τὸ ὄνομα αὐτοῦ Ἰωάννην. καὶ ἔσται χαρά σοι καὶ
you shall call the name of him John. And he shall be joy to you and
20 4183 1909 1083 848 5463
ἀγαλλίασις, καὶ πολλοὶ ἐπὶ τῇ γεννήσει αὐτοῦ χαρήσονται.
exultation, and many over the birth of him will rejoice.
2071 1063 3173 1799 2962 3631 4608
15 ἔσται γὰρ μέγας ἐνώπιον τοῦ Κυρίου, καὶ οἶνον καὶ σίκερα
he will be For great in the eyes of the Lord, and wine and strong drink
3364 4095 4151 40 4130 2089 2836
•1537 οὐ μὴ πίῃ, καὶ Πνεύματος Ἁγίου πλησθήσεται ἔτι ἐκ κοιλίας
not at all he may drink, and of (the) Spirit Holy he will be filled even from womb
3384 848 4183 5207 2474 1994
16 μητρὸς αὐτοῦ. καὶ πολλοὺς τῶν υἱῶν Ἰσραὴλ ἐπιστρέψει
of mother of him. And many of the sons of Israel he will turn
1909 2962 2316 848 846 4281
17 ἐπὶ Κύριον τὸν Θεὸν αὐτῶν· καὶ αὐτὸς προελεύσεται
onto (the) Lord, the God of them; and he will go ahead
1799 846 1722 4151 1411 2243 1994
ἐνώπιον αὐτοῦ ἐν πνεύματι καὶ δυνάμει Ἠλίου, ἐπιστρέψαι
before Him in (the) spirit and power of Elijah, to turn
2588 3962 1909 5043 545 1722 5428
καρδίας πατέρων ἐπὶ τέκνα, καὶ ἀπειθεῖς ἐν φρονήσει
(the) hearts of fathers onto children, and disobedient to (the) wisdom
1342 2090 2962 2992 2680 2036
18 δικαίων, ἑτοιμάσαι Κυρίῳ λαὸν κατεσκευασμένον. καὶ εἶπε
of (the) just, to prepare for (the) Lord a people having been prepared. And said
2197 4314 32 2596 5101 1097 5124
Ζαχαρίας πρὸς τὸν ἄγγελον, Κατὰ τί γνώσομαι τοῦτο;
Zacharias to the angel, By what shall I know this?
1473 1063 1510 4246 1135 3450 4260 1722
ἐγὼ γάρ εἰμι πρεσβύτης, καὶ ἡ γυνή μου προβεβηκυῖα ἐν
I For am old, and the wife of me is advanced in
2250 848 611 32 2036 846
19 ταῖς ἡμέραις αὐτῆς. καὶ ἀποκριθεὶς ὁ ἄγγελος εἶπεν αὐτῷ,
the days of her. And answering the angel said to him,
1473 1510 1043 3936 1799 2316
Ἐγώ εἰμι Γαβριὴλ ὁ παρεστηκὼς ἐνώπιον τοῦ Θεοῦ· καὶ
I am Gabriel, the (one) standing by before God, and
649 2980 4314 4571 2097 4671
ἀπεστάλην λαλῆσαι πρός σε, καὶ εὐαγγελίσασθαί σοι
I was sent to speak to you, and to give good news to you
5023 2400 2071 4623 3361 1410 2980
20 ταῦτα. καὶ ἰδού, ἔσῃ σιωπῶν καὶ μὴ δυνάμενος λαλῆσαι,
of these. And, behold, you will be silent and not able to speak
891 2258 2250 1096 5023 473 3739 3756 4100
ἄχρι ἧς ἡμέρας γένηται ταῦτα, ἀνθ' ὧν οὐκ ἐπίστευσας
until which day occurs these things, because not you believed
3056 3450 3748 4137 1519 2540
τοῖς λόγοις μου, οἵτινες πληρωθήσονται εἰς τὸν καιρὸν
the words of me, which will be fulfilled in the time
848 2258 2992 4328 2197
21 αὐτῶν. καὶ ἦν ὁ λαὸς προσδοκῶν τὸν Ζαχαρίαν· καὶ
of them. And were the people expecting Zacharias, and
2296 1722 5549 846 1722 3485 1831 3756
22 ἐθαύμαζον ἐν τῷ χρονίζειν αὐτὸν ἐν τῷ ναῷ. ἐξελθὼν δὲ οὐκ
they marveled in the delay of him in the temple coming out. And not
1410 2980 846 1921 3754 3701
ἠδύνατο λαλῆσαι αὐτοῖς· καὶ ἐπέγνωσαν ὅτι ὀπτασίαν
he was able to speak to them, and they knew that a vision

temple. And he was making signs to them, and continued dumb.

[23]And it happened when the days of his service were fulfilled, he went away to his house. [24]And after these days his wife Elizabeth conceived. And she hid herself five months, saying, [25]So has the Lord done to me in *the* days in which He looked on *me* to take away my reproach among men.

[26]And in the sixth month, the angel Gabriel was sent by God to a city of Galilee named Nazareth, [27]to a virgin who had been betrothed to a man whose name *was* Joseph, of *the* house of David; and the virgin's name *was* Mary. [28]And entering, the angel said to her, Hail, *one* having received grace! The Lord *is* with you. You *are* blessed among women! [29]And seeing *this*, she was disturbed at his word, and considered what kind of greeting this might be. [30]And the angel said to her, Do not fear, Mary, for you have found favor from God. [31]And behold! You will conceive in *your* womb and bear a Son; and you will call His name Jesus. [32]This One will be great and will be called Son of *the* Most High. And the Lord God will give Him the throne of His father David. [33]And He will reign over the house of Jacob forever, and of His kingdom there will be no end.

[34]But Mary said to the angel, How will this be since I do not know a man? [35]And answering, the angel said to her, *The* Holy Spirit will come upon you, and *the* power of *the* Most High will overshadow you—and for this reason that holy *One* being born of you will

3708 1722 3485 846 2258 1269 846
ἑώρακεν ἐν τῷ ναῷ· καὶ αὐτὸς ἦν διανεύων αὐτοῖς, καὶ
he had seen in the Temple. And he was signaling to them, and
1265 2974 1096 5613 4130 2250
23 διέμενε κωφός. καὶ ἐγένετο, ὡς ἐπλήσθησαν αἱ ἡμέραι τῆς
remained dumb. And it was, as were fulfilled the days of the
3009 848 565 1519 3624 848
λειτουργίας αὐτοῦ, ἀπῆλθεν εἰς τὸν οἶκον αὐτοῦ.
service of him, he went away to the house of him.
3326 5025 2250 4815 1665 1135
24 Μετὰ δὲ ταύτας τὰς ἡμέρας συνέλαβεν Ἐλισάβετ ἡ γυνὴ
after And these days, conceived Elizabeth the wife
848 4032 1438 3376 4002 3004 3754
αὐτοῦ, καὶ περιέκρυβεν ἑαυτὴν μῆνας πέντε, λέγουσα ὅτι
of him, and hid herself months five, saying,
3779 3427 4160 2962 1722 2250 3739 1896 851
25 Οὕτω μοι πεποίηκεν ὁ Κύριος ἐν ἡμέραις αἷς ἐπεῖδεν ἀφελεῖν
Thus to me has done the Lord in days in which He saw to remove
3681 3450 1722 444
τὸ ὄνειδός μου ἐν ἀνθρώποις.
the reproach of me among men.
1722 3376 1623 649 32 1063
26 Ἐν δὲ τῷ μηνὶ τῷ ἕκτῳ ἀπεστάλη ὁ ἄγγελος Γαβριὴλ
in And the month sixth was sent the angel Gabriel
5259 2316 1519 4172 1056 3739 3686 3478
ὑπὸ τοῦ Θεοῦ εἰς πόλιν τῆς Γαλιλαίας, ᾗ ὄνομα Ναζαρέθ,
by God to a city of Galilee, to which (the) name was Nazareth,
3739/4314 3933 3423 435 3686 2501
27 πρὸς παρθένον μεμνηστευμένην ἀνδρί, ᾧ ὄνομα Ἰωσήφ,
to a virgin having been betrothed to a man whose name (was) Joseph
1537 3624 1138 3686 3933 3137
28 ἐξ οἴκου Δαβίδ· καὶ τὸ ὄνομα τῆς παρθένου Μαριάμ. καὶ
of (the) house of David, and the name of the virgin (was) Mariam. And
1525 32 4314 846 2036 5463 5487
εἰσελθὼν ὁ ἄγγελος πρὸς αὐτὴν εἶπε, Χαῖρε, κεχαριτωμένη·
entering, the angel to her said, Hail, (one) receiving grace,
2962 3326 4675 2127 4771 1722 1135 1492
29 ὁ Κύριος μετὰ σου, εὐλογημένη σὺ ἐν γυναιξίν. ἡ δὲ ἰδοῦσα
the Lord (is) with you. Blessed (are) you among women. she And seeing,
1298 1909 3056 848 1260 4217
διεταράχθη ἐπὶ τῷ λόγῳ αὐτοῦ, καὶ διελογίζετο ποταπὸς
was disturbed at the word of him, and considered of what kind
1498 783 3778 2036 32 846 3361 5399
30 εἴη ὁ ἀσπασμὸς οὗτος. καὶ εἶπεν ὁ ἄγγελος αὐτῇ, Μὴ φοβοῦ,
may be greeting this. And said the angel to her, Do not fear
3137 2147 1063 5485 3844 2316 2400 4815
31 Μαριάμ· εὗρες γὰρ χάριν παρὰ τῷ Θεῷ. καὶ ἰδού, συλλήψῃ
Mariam, you found for favor with God. And, lo, you will conceive
1722 1064 5088 5207 2564 3686 848
ἐν γαστρί, καὶ τέξῃ υἱόν, καὶ καλέσεις τὸ ὄνομα αὐτοῦ
in womb and bear a son, and you will call the name of Him
2424 3778 2071 3173 5207 5310 2564
32 Ἰησοῦν. οὗτος ἔσται μέγας, καὶ υἱὸς ὑψίστου κληθήσεται·
Jesus. This One will be great, and Son of Most High will be called,
1325 846 2962 2316 2362 1138 3962
καὶ δώσει αὐτῷ Κύριος ὁ Θεὸς τὸν θρόνον Δαβὶδ τοῦ πατρὸς
and will give Him (the) Lord God the throne of David the father
848 936 1909 3624 2384 1519 165
33 αὐτοῦ, καὶ βασιλεύσει ἐπὶ τὸν οἶκον Ἰακὼβ εἰς τοὺς αἰῶνας,
of Him; and He will reign over the house of Jacob to the ages,
932 848 3756 2071 5056 2036 3137 4314
34 καὶ τῆς βασιλείας αὐτοῦ οὐκ ἔσται τέλος. εἶπε δὲ Μαριὰμ πρὸς
and of the kingdom of Him not will be an end. said And Mariam to
32 4459 2071 5124 1893 435 3756 1097
35 τὸν ἄγγελον, Πῶς ἔσται τοῦτο, ἐπεὶ ἄνδρα οὐ γινώσκω ; καὶ
the angel, How will be this, since a man not I know? And
611 32 2036 846 4151 40 1904
ἀποκριθεὶς ὁ ἄγγελος εἶπεν αὐτῇ, Πνεῦμα Ἅγιον ἐπελεύσεται
answering, the angel said to her, (The) Spirit Holy will come up
1909 4571 1411 5310 1982 4671 1312 1080
ἐπὶ σέ, καὶ δύναμις ὑψίστου ἐπισκιάσει σοι· διὸ καὶ τὸ γεννώ-
upon you, and power of (the) Most High will overshadow you, so also that being

NOTE: Frequent words not numbered: δέ(1161); καί(2531)—and, but; ὁ, ἡ, τό (3588, the)— • above word, look in verse margin for No.

be called Son of God.
36And behold, your kins-
woman Elizabeth! She also
conceived a son in her old
age, and this is *the* sixth
month to her who *was*
called barren; 37for nothing
shall be impossible with
God. 38And Mary said, Be-
hold, the slave of *the* Lord!
May it be to me according
to your word. And the angel
departed from her.

39And rising up in these
days, Mary went into the
hill-country with haste to a
city of Judah. 40And *she*
entered into the house of
Zacharias, and greeted
Elizabeth. 41And it hap-
pened, as Elizabeth heard
Mariam's greeting, the
babe in her womb leaped,
and Elizabeth was filled of
the Holy Spirit. 42And *she*
cried out with a loud voice
and said, Blessed *are* you
among women, and bles-
sed *is* the fruit of your
womb. 43And from where
is this to me, that the
mother of my Lord comes to
me? 44For behold, as the
sound of your greeting
came to my ears, the babe
in my womb leaped in
exultation. 45And blessed
is she believing, because
there will be a completion
to the things spoken to her
from *the* Lord.

46And Mariam said, My
soul magnifies the Lord,
47and my spirit exulted in
God My Savior. 48For He
looked upon the humili-
ation of His bondslave. For,
behold, from now on all
generations will count me
blessed. 49For the Mighty
One did great things to me,
and holy *is* His name.
50And His mercy *is* to
generations of generations
to those fearing Him. 51He

1537 4675 40 2563 5207 2316 2400 1665
36 μενον ἐκ σοῦ ἅγιον κληθήσεται υἱὸς Θεοῦ. καὶ ἰδού, Ἐλισάβετ
born of you holy will be called Son of God. And, behold, Elizabeth
4773 4675 846 4815 5207 1722 1094 848
ἡ συγγενής σου, καὶ αὐτὴ συνειληφυῖα υἱὸν ἐν γήρᾳ αὐτῆς·
the relative of you, also she conceived a son in old age of her,
3778 3376 1623 2076 846 2564 4723 3754
37 καὶ οὗτος μὴν ἕκτος ἐστὶν αὐτῇ τῇ καλουμένῃ στείρᾳ. ὅτι
and this month sixth is with her, the (one) called barren; because
3756 101 3844 2316 3956 4487 2036 3137
38 οὐκ ἀδυνατήσει παρὰ τῷ Θεῷ πᾶν ῥῆμα. εἶπε δὲ Μαριάμ,
not will be impossible with God every word. said And Mariam,
2400 1399 2962 1096 3427 2596 4487 4675
Ἰδού, ἡ δούλη Κυρίου· γένοιτό μοι κατὰ τὸ ῥῆμά σου. καὶ
Behold, the slave of (the) Lord; may it be to me as the word of you. And
565 575 846 32
ἀπῆλθεν ἀπ αὐτῆς ὁ ἄγγελος.
went away from her the angel.
450 3137 1722 2250 5025 4198
39 Ἀναστᾶσα δὲ Μαριὰμ ἐν ταῖς ἡμέραις ταύταις ἐπορεύθη
rising up And Mariam in days these, she went
1519 3714 3326 4710 1519/4172 2448 1525
εἰς τὴν ὀρεινὴν μετὰ σπουδῆς, εἰς πόλιν Ἰούδα, καὶ εἰσῆλθεν
to the hill-country with haste, to a city of Judah and entered
1519 3624 2197 782 1665
40 εἰς τὸν οἶκον Ζαχαρίου, καὶ ἠσπάσατο τὴν Ἐλισάβετ καὶ
into the house of Zacharias, and greeted Elizabeth. And
1096 5613 191 1665 783 3137
41 ἐγένετο ὡς ἤκουσεν ἡ Ἐλισάβετ τὸν ἀσπασμὸν τῆς Μαρίας,
it was, as heard Elizabeth the greeting of Mariam,
4640 1025 1722 2836 848 4130 4151
ἐσκίρτησε τὸ βρέφος ἐν τῇ κοιλίᾳ αὐτῆς· καὶ ἐπλήσθη Πνεύ-
leaped the babe in the womb of her, and was filled of (the)
40 1665 400 5456 3173
42 ματος Ἁγίου ἡ Ἐλισάβετ, καὶ ἀνεφώνησε φωνῇ μεγάλῃ
Spirit Holy Elizabeth, and she called out with a voice great,
2036 2127 4771 1722 1135 2127
καὶ εἶπεν, Εὐλογημένη σὺ ἐν γυναιξί, καὶ εὐλογημένος ὁ
and said, Blessed (are) you among women, and blessed (is) the
2590 2836 4675 4159 3427 5124 2443 2064
43 καρπὸς τῆς κοιλίας σου. καὶ πόθεν μοι τοῦτο, ἵνα ἔλθῃ ἡ
fruit of the womb of you. And whence to me this, that comes the
3384 2962 3450 4314 3165 2400 1063 5613 1096 5456
44 μήτηρ τοῦ Κυρίου μου πρός με; ἰδοὺ γάρ, ὡς ἐγένετο ἡ φωνὴ
mother of the Lord of me to me? behold For, as came the sound
783 4675 1519 3775 3450 4640 1722 20
τοῦ ἀσπασμοῦ σου εἰς τὰ ὦτά μου, ἐσκίρτησεν ἐν ἀγαλλιάσει
of the greeting of you to the ears of me, leaped in exultation
1025 1722 2836/3450 3107 4100 3754
45 τὸ βρέφος ἐν τῇ κοιλίᾳ μου. καὶ μακαρία ἡ πιστεύσασα, ὅτι
the babe in the womb of me. And blessed the (one) believing, because
2071 5050 2980 846 3844 2962
ἔσται τελείωσις τοῖς λελαλημένοις αὐτῇ παρὰ Κυρίου. καὶ
will be a completion to the things spoken to her from (the) Lord. And
2036 3137 3170 5590 3450 2962
46 εἶπε Μαριάμ, Μεγαλύνει ἡ ψυχή μου τὸν Κύριον, καὶ
said Mariam, magnifies The soul of me the Lord, and
21 4151 3450 1909 2316 4990 3450 3754
47 ἠγαλλίασε τὸ πνεῦμά μου ἐπὶ τῷ Θεῷ τῷ σωτῆρί μου. ὅτι
exulted the spirit of me on God the Savior of me; because
1914 1909 5014 1399 848 2400 1063
48 ἐπέβλεψεν ἐπὶ τὴν ταπείνωσιν τῆς δούλης αὐτοῦ. ἰδοὺ γάρ,
He looked upon the humiliation of the bondslave of Him. behold For,
575 3568 3106 3165 3956 1074 3754 4160 3427
ἀπὸ τοῦ νῦν μακαριοῦσί με πᾶσαι αἱ γενεαί. ὅτι ἐποίησέ μοι
from — now will count blessed me all the generations: for did to me
3167 1415 40 3686 848
49 μεγαλεῖα ὁ δυνατός, καὶ ἅγιον τὸ ὄνομα αὐτοῦ. καὶ τὸ
great things the Mighty One. And holy the name of Him, and the
1656 848 1519 1074 1074 5399 846
50 ἔλεος αὐτοῦ εἰς γενεὰς γενεῶν τοῖς φοβουμένοις αὐτόν.
mercy of Him to generations of generations to those fearing Him.

NOTE: Frequent words not numbered: δέ(1161); καί(2531)—and, but; ὁ, ἡ, τό (3588, the)— * above word, look in verse margin for No.

performed mighti*ly* with His arm; He scattered proud ones in *the* thought of their heart. [52]He put down powerful ones from thrones, and exalted lowly ones. [53]He filled *the* hungry with good things, and He sent *the* rich away empty. [54]He helped His servant Israel in order to remember mercy, [55]even as He spoke to our fathers, to Abraham, and to his seed forever.

4160 2904 1722 1023 848 1287 5244
51 ἐποίησε κράτος ἐν βραχίονι αὐτοῦ· διεσκόρπισεν ὑπερη-
He did might(ily) with (the) arm of Him; He scattered proud
1271 2588 848 2507 1413 575
52 φάνους διανοίᾳ καρδίας αὐτῶν. καθεῖλε δυνάστας ἀπὸ
ones in (the) thought of the heart of them; He pulled down potentates from
2362 5312 5011 3983 1705
53 θρόνων, καὶ ὕψωσε ταπεινούς. πεινῶντας ἐνέπλησεν
thrones, and exalted humble ones. hungering ones He filled
18 4147 1821 2756 482
54 ἀγαθῶν, καὶ πλουτοῦντας ἐξαπέστειλε κενούς. ἀντελάβετο
of good things, and rich ones He sent away empty. He succored
2474 3816 848 3415 1656 2531 2980
55 Ἰσραὴλ παιδὸς αὐτου, μνησθῆναι ἐλέους (καθὼς ἐλάλησε
Israel (the) servant of Him, to remember mercy, even as He spoke
4314 3962 2257 11 4690
πρὸς τοὺς πατέρας ἡμῶν) τῷ Ἀβραὰμ καὶ τῷ σπέρματι
to the fathers of us, — to Abraham and to the seed
848 1519 165
αὐτοῦ εἰς τὸν αἰῶνα.
of him to the age.

[56]And Mariam remained with her about three months, and returned to her house.

3306 3137 4862 846 5616 3376 5140 5290
56 Ἔμεινε δὲ Μαριὰμ σὺν αὐτῇ ὡσεὶ μῆνας τρεῖς, καὶ ὑπέ-
remained And Mariam with her about months three, and
1519 3624 848
στρεψεν εἰς τὸν οἶκον αὐτῆς.
returned to the house of her.

[57]And the time was fulfilled to Elizabeth *for* her to bear; and she bore a son. [58]And the neighbors and her relatives heard that *the* Lord magnified His mercy with her, and they rejoiced with her. [59]And it happened on the eighth day, they came to circumcise the child, and were calling it by his father's name, Zacharias. [60]And his mother answered, saying, Not so, but he shall be called John. [61]And they said to her, No one is among your kindred who is called by this name. [62]And they signaled to his father, what he might desire him to be called. [63]And asking for a writing tablet, he wrote, saying, John is his name. And all marveled. [64]And instantly his mouth was opened, and his tongue *loosed,* and he spoke, blessing God. [65]And fear came on all those living around them, and in all the hill-country of Judea all these things were talked

1665 4130 5550 5088 846
57 Τῇ δὲ Ἐλισάβετ ἐπλήσθη ὁ χρόνος τοῦ τεκεῖν αὐτήν,
- And to Elizabeth was fulfilled the time to bear her,
1080 5207 191 4040 4773
58 καὶ ἐγέννησεν υἱόν. καὶ ἤκουσαν οἱ περίοικοι καὶ οἱ συγ-
and she bore a son. And heard the neighbors and the
848 3754 3170 2962 1656 848 3326
γενεῖς αὐτῆς ὅτι ἐμεγάλυνε Κύριος τὸ ἔλεος αὐτοῦ μετ'
relatives of her that magnified (the) Lord the mercy of Him with
846 4796 846 1096 1722 3590 2250
59 αὐτῆς, καὶ συνέχαιρον αὐτῇ. καὶ ἐγένετο ἐν τῇ ὀγδόῃ ἡμέρᾳ,
her, and they rejoiced with her. And it was, on the eighth day,
2064 4059 3813 2564 846 1909
ἦλθον περιτεμεῖν τὸ παιδίον· καὶ ἐκάλουν αὐτὸ ἐπὶ τῷ
they came to circumcise the child, and were calling it by the
3686 3962 848 2197 611
60 ὀνόματι τοῦ πατρὸς αὐτοῦ Ζαχαρίαν. καὶ ἀποκριθεῖσα ἡ
name of the father of him, Zacharias. And answering the
3384 848 2036 3780 235 2563 2491
61 μήτηρ αὐτοῦ εἶπεν, Οὐχί, ἀλλὰ κληθήσεται Ἰωάννης. καὶ
mother of him said, Not so, but he shall be called John. And
2036 4314 846 2754 3762 2076 1722 4772 4675
εἶπον πρὸς αὐτὴν ὅτι Οὐδείς ἐστιν ἐν τῇ συγγενείᾳ σου
they said to her, No one there is in the kindred of you
3739 2563 3686 5129 1770 3962 848
62 ὃς καλεῖται τῷ ὀνόματι τούτῳ. ἐνένευον δὲ τῷ πατρὶ αὐτοῦ,
who is called by name this. they signaled And to the father of him
5101/302/2309 2564 846 156 4093
63 τὸ τί ἂν θέλοι καλεῖσθαι αὐτόν. καὶ αἰτήσας πινακίδιον
what may he desire to be called him. And asking for a tablet,
1125 3004 2491 2076 3686 848 2296
64 ἔγραψε, λέγων, Ἰωάννης ἐστὶ τὸ ὄνομα αὐτοῦ· καὶ ἐθαύ-
he wrote, saying, John is the name of him. And
3956 455 4750 848 3916
μασαν πάντες. ἀνεῴχθη δὲ τὸ στόμα αὐτοῦ παραχρῆμα
marveled all. was opened And the mouth of him instantly,
1100 848 2980 2127 2316
65 καὶ ἡ γλῶσσα αὐτοῦ, καὶ ἐλάλει εὐλογῶν τὸν Θεόν. καὶ
and the tongue of him, and he spoke blessing — God. And
1096 1909 3956 5401 4039 846
ἐγένετο ἐπὶ πάντας φόβος τοὺς περιοικοῦντας αὐτούς· καὶ
came upon all fear the (ones) living around them, and
1722 3650 3714 2449 1255 3956 4487
ἐν ὅλῃ τῇ ὀρεινῇ τῆς Ἰουδαίας διελαλεῖτο πάντα τὰ ῥήματα
in all the hill-country — of Judea were talked over all — facts

NOTE: Frequent words not numbered: δέ (1161); καί (2531)—and, but; ὁ, ἡ, τό (3588, the)— * above word, look in verse margin for No.

about. [66]And all who heard
laid *them* up in their hearts,
saying, What then will this
child be? And the hand of
the Lord was with him.

[67]And his father Zach-
arias was filled of *the* Holy
Spirit, and prophesied, saying, [68]Blessed be *the* Lord,
the God of Israel, because
He visited and worked
redemption for His people.
[69]And *He* raised up a Horn
of salvation for us in the
house of His servant David;
[70]even as He spoke through
the mouth of His holy
prophets from the age *before:* [71]Salvation from our
enemies, and from *the*
hand of all those hating
us; [72]to execute mercy
with our fathers, and to
remember His holy cove-
nant, [73]*the* oath which He
swore to our father Abra-
ham, [74]to give to us *that we*
being delivered out of our
enemies' hand, in order to
serve Him without fear,
[75]in consecration and righteousness before Him all
the days of our life. [76]And
you, child, will be called
Prophet of *the* Most High;
for you will go before *the*
face of *the* Lord to prepare
His ways, [77]to give a
knowledge of salvation to
His people by forgiveness
of their sins, [78]through *the*
tender bowels of mercy of
our God, in which *the*
Dayspring from on high *will*
visit us, [79]to appear to
those sitting in darkness
and in shadow of death, to
direct our feet into *the* way
of peace.

[80]And the child grew,
and became strong in
spirit. And *he* was in the
deserts until *the* day of his
showing to Israel.

5023 5087 3956 191 1722 2588 848
66 ταῦτα. καὶ ἔθεντο πάντες οἱ ἀκούσαντες ἐν τῇ καρδίᾳ αὐτῶν,
these. And laid up all the (ones) hearing in the heart of them.
3004 5101 686 3813 5124 2071 5495 2962
λέγοντες, Τί ἄρα τὸ παιδίον τοῦτο ἔσται ; καὶ χεὶρ Κυρίου
saying, What then child this will be? And (the) hand Lord's
2258 3326 846
ἦν μετ' αὐτοῦ.
was with him.
2197 3962 848 4130 4151
67 Καὶ Ζαχαρίας ὁ πατὴρ αὐτοῦ ἐπλήσθη Πνεύματος
And Zacharias the father of him was filled of (the) Spirit
40 4395 3004 2128 2962
68 Ἁγίου, καὶ προεφήτευσε, λέγων, Εὐλογητὸς Κύριος ὁ
Holy, and prophesied saying, Blessed (be the) Lord the
2316 2474 3754 1980 4160 3085
Θεὸς τοῦ Ἰσραήλ, ὅτι ἐπεσκέψατο καὶ ἐποίησε λύτρωσιν
God of Israel, because He visited and worked redemption
2992 848 1453 2768 4991 2254/1722 3624
69 τῷ λαῷ αὐτοῦ, καὶ ἤγειρε κέρας σωτηρίας ἡμῖν ἐν τῷ οἴκῳ
for the people of Him, and raised a horn of salvation for us in the house
1138 3816 848 2531 2980 1223 4750
70 Δαβὶδ τοῦ παιδὸς αὐτοῦ (καθὼς ἐλάλησε διὰ στόματος τῶν
of David the servant of Him; even as He spoke through (the) mouth of the
40 575 165 4396 848 4991 1537
71 ἁγίων τῶν ἀπ' αἰῶνος προφητῶν αὐτοῦ), σωτηρίαν ἐξ
holy – from (the) age prophets of Him, salvation out of
2190 2257 1537 5495 3956 3404 2248
ἐχθρῶν ἡμῶν, καὶ ἐκ χειρὸς πάντων τῶν μισούντων ἡμᾶς·
(the) enemies of us, and out of hand of all the (ones) hating us,
4160 1656 3326 3962 2257 3415
72 ποιῆσαι ἔλεος μετὰ τῶν πατέρων ἡμῶν, καὶ μνησθῆναι
to execute mercy with the fathers of us, and to remember
1242 40 848 3727/3739/3660 4314 11
73 διαθήκης ἁγίας αὐτοῦ, ὅρκον ὃν ὤμοσε πρὸς Ἀβραὰμ τὸν
(the) covenant holy of Him, (the) oath which He swore to Abraham the
3962 2257 1325 2254 870 1537 5495
74 πατέρα ἡμῶν, τοῦ δοῦναι ἡμῖν, ἀφόβως, ἐκ χειρὸς τῶν
father of us, to give to us without fear out of (the) hand of the
2190 2257 4506 3000 846 1722 3742
75 ἐχθρῶν ἡμῶν ῥυσθέντας, λατρεύειν αὐτῷ ἐν ὁσιότητι καὶ
enemies of us being delivered to serve Him in consecration and
1343 1799 846 3956 2250 2222
δικαιοσύνῃ ἐνώπιον αὐτοῦ πάσας τὰς ἡμέρας τῆς ζωῆς
righteousness before Him all the days of the life
2257 4771 3813 4396 5310 2564
76 ἡμῶν. καὶ σύ, παιδίον, προφήτης ὑψίστου κληθήσῃ·
of us. And you, child, a prophet of (the) Most High will be called
4313 1063 4253 4383 2962 2090 3598
προπορεύσῃ γὰρ πρὸ προσώπου Κυρίου ἑτοιμάσαι ὁδοὺς
you will go for before (the) face of (the) Lord to prepare (the) ways
848 1325 1108 4991 2992 848 1722
77 αὐτοῦ· τοῦ δοῦναι γνῶσιν σωτηρίας τῷ λαῷ αὐτοῦ ἐν
of Him, – to give a knowledge of salvation to the people of Him by
859 266 848 1223 4698 1656 2316 2257
78 ἀφέσει ἁμαρτιῶν αὐτῶν, διὰ σπλάγχνα ἐλέους Θεοῦ ἡμῶν,
forgiveness of sins of them, through (the) bowels of mercy of God of us,
1722 3737 1980 2248 395 1537 5311 2014 1722
79 ἐν οἷς ἐπεσκέψατο ἡμᾶς ἀνατολὴ ἐξ ὕψους, ἐπιφᾶναι τοῖς ἐν
in which (will visit) us the) Dayspring from on high, to appear to those in
4655 4639 2288 2521 2720
σκότει καὶ σκιᾷ θανάτου καθημένοις, τοῦ κατευθῦναι τοὺς
darkness and in shadow of death sitting, to direct the
4228 2257 1519 3598 1515
πόδας ἡμῶν εἰς ὁδὸν εἰρήνης.
feet of us into a way of peace.
3813 837 2901 4151 2258 1722
80 Τὸ δὲ παιδίον ηὔξανε καὶ ἐκραταιοῦτο πνεύματι, καὶ ἦν ἐν
the And child grew and became strong in spirit, and was in
2048 2193 2250 323 848 4314 2474
ταῖς ἐρήμοις ἕως ἡμέρας ἀναδείξεως αὐτοῦ πρὸς τὸν Ἰσραήλ.
the deserts until (the) day of showing of him to Israel.

CHAPTER 2

[1]And it happened in those days, a decree went out from Caesar Augustus *for* all the habitable world to be registered. [2]This registration first occurred *under* the governing of Syria *by* Cyrenius. [3]And all went to be registered, each to *his* own city. [4]And Joseph also went from Galilee, out of *the* city of Nazareth to Judea, to *the* city of David which is called Bethlehem, because of his being of *the* house and family of David, [5]to be registered with Mary, she having been betrothed to him *as* wife, *she* being pregnant. [6]And it happened *as* they were there, the days were fulfilled *for* her to bear. [7]And she bore her son, the Firstborn. And she wrapped Him, and laid Him in the manger—because there was no place for them in the inn.

[8]And shepherds were in the same country, living in the fields, and keeping guard over their flock *by* night. [9]And, behold, an angel of *the* Lord came on them. And *the* glory of *the* Lord shone around them. And they feared with a great fear. [10]And the angel said to them, do not fear. For, behold, I announce good news to you, a great joy, which will be to all people, [11]because today a Savior, who is Christ *the* Lord, was born to you in *the* city of David. [12]And this *is* a sign to you: You will find a babe having been wrapped, lying in the manger. [13]And suddenly there was with the angel a multitude of *the* heavenly host, praising God

CHAPTER 2

1096 1722 2250 1565 1831 1378 3844
1 Ἐγένετο δὲ ἐν ταῖς ἡμέραις ἐκείναις, ἐξῆλθε δόγμα παρὰ
it was And, in — days those, went out a decree from
2541 828 583 3956 3625
Καίσαρος Αὐγούστου, ἀπογράφεσθαι πᾶσαν τὴν οἰκου-
Caesar Augustus to be registered all the inhabited
3778 582 4413 1096 2230
2 μένην. αὕτη ἡ ἀπογραφὴ πρώτη ἐγένετο ἡγεμονεύοντος τῆς
earth. This registration first was (during the) governing of
4947 2958 4198 3956 583
3 Συρίας Κυρηνίου. καὶ ἐπορεύοντο πάντες ἀπογράφεσθαι,
Syria (by) Cyrenius. And went all to be registered,
1538 1519 2398 4172 305 2501 575
4 ἕκαστος εἰς τὴν ἰδίαν πόλιν. ἀνέβη δὲ καὶ Ἰωσὴφ ἀπὸ τῆς
each one into (his) own city. went up And also Joseph from —
1056 1537 4172 3478 1519 2449 1519 4172
Γαλιλαίας, ἐκ πόλεως Ναζαρέθ, εἰς τὴν Ἰουδαίαν, εἰς πόλιν
Galilee out of (the) city Nazareth to Judea, into (the) city
1138 3748 2563 965 1223 1511 846 1537 3624
Δαβίδ, ἥτις καλεῖται Βηθλεέμ, διὰ τὸ εἶναι αὐτὸν ἐξ οἴκου καὶ
of David which is called Bethlehem, because of being him of (the) house and
3965 1138 583 4862 3137 3423
5 πατριᾶς Δαβίδ, ἀπογράψασθαι σὺν Μαριὰμ τῇ μεμνηστευ-
family of David; to be registered with Mariam the (one) being be-
846 1135 5607 1471 1096 1722 1511
6 μένῃ αὐτῷ γυναικί, οὔσῃ ἐγκύῳ. ἐγένετο δὲ ἐν τῷ εἶναι
trothed to him (as) wife, being pregnant. it was And, in being
846 1563 4130 2250 5088 846
7 αὐτοὺς ἐκεῖ, ἐπλήσθησαν αἱ ἡμέραι τοῦ τεκεῖν αὐτήν. καὶ
they there, were fulfilled the days (for) the bearing (of) her; and
5088 5207 848 4416 4683
ἔτεκε τὸν υἱὸν αὐτῆς τὸν πρωτότοκον, καὶ ἐσπαργάνωσεν
she bore the son of her, the first-born, and she wrapped
846 347 846 1722 5336 1360 3756 2258 846
αὐτόν, καὶ ἀνέκλινεν αὐτὸν ἐν τῇ φάτνῃ, διότι οὐκ ἦν αὐτοῖς
Him and laid Him in the manger, because not was for them
5117 1722 2646
τόπος ἐν τῷ καταλύματι.
a place in the inn.

4166 2258 1722 5561 846 63
8 Καὶ ποιμένες ἦσαν ἐν τῇ χώρᾳ τῇ αὐτῇ ἀγραυλοῦντες καὶ
And shepherds were in the country same living in the fields and
5442 5438 3571 1909 4167 848
φυλάσσοντες φυλακὰς τῆς νυκτὸς ἐπὶ τὴν ποίμνην αὐτῶν.
keeping guard of the night over the flock of them.
2400 32 2962 2186 846 1391 2962
9 καὶ ἰδού, ἄγγελος Κυρίου ἐπέστη αὐτοῖς, καὶ δόξα Κυρίου
And behold, an angel of (the) Lord came on them, and (the) glory of Lord
4034 846 5399 5401 3173 2036
10 περιέλαμψεν αὐτούς· καὶ ἐφοβήθησαν φόβον μέγαν. καὶ εἶπεν
shone around them, and they feared (with) a fear great. And said
846 32 3361 5399 2400 1063 2097
αὐτοῖς ὁ ἄγγελος, Μὴ φοβεῖσθε· ἰδοὺ γάρ, εὐαγγελίζομαι
to them the angel, Do not fear, behold for, I give good news
5213 5479 3173 3788 2071 3956 2992 3754 5088
11 ὑμῖν χαρὰν μεγάλην, ἥτις ἔσται παντὶ τῷ λαῷ· ὅτι ἐτέχθη
to you, a joy great, which will be to all the people, because was born
5213 4594 4990 3739 2076 5547 2962 1722 4172 1138
ὑμῖν σήμερον Σωτήρ, ὅς ἐστι Χριστὸς Κύριος, ἐν πόλει Δαβίδ.
to you today a Savior, who is Christ (the) Lord, into the city of David.
5124 5213 4592 2147 1025 4683
12 καὶ τοῦτο ὑμῖν τὸ σημεῖον· εὑρήσετε βρέφος ἐσπαργανω-
And this to you· a sign, you will find a babe having been
2749 1722 5336 1810 1096 4862
13 μένον, κείμενον ἐν τῇ φάτνῃ. καὶ ἐξαίφνης ἐγένετο σὺν τῷ
wrapped, lying in manger. And suddenly there was with the
32 4128 4756 3770 134 2316
ἀγγέλῳ πλῆθος στρατιᾶς οὐρανίου, αἰνούντων τὸν Θεόν,
angel a multitude of (the) host heavenly, praising God

and saying, [14]Glory to God in the highest, and peace on earth, good will among men.

[15]And it happened as the angels departed from them into Heaven, even the men, the shepherds, said to one another, Indeed, let us go over to Bethlehem, and let us see this thing which has occurred, which the Lord made known to us. [16]And hurrying they came and sought out both Mary and Joseph, and the babe lying in the manger. [17]And seeing, they publicly told about the word spoken to them about this Child. [18]And all those hearing marveled about the things spoken to them by the shepherds. [19]And Mary kept all these words, meditating in her heart. [20]And the shepherds returned, glorifying and praising God for all things which they heard and saw, even as was spoken to them.

[21]And when eight days were fulfilled to circumcise the child, His name was called Jesus, *the name* called by the angel before He was conceived in the womb.

[22]And when the days of her cleansing according to the Law of Moses were fulfilled, they took Him up to Jerusalem to present *Him* to the Lord, [23]as it has been written in *the* Law of the Lord: "Every male opening a womb shall be called holy to the Lord;" [24]and to offer a sacrifice according to that said in the Law of *the* Lord, a pair of turtledoves, or two nestlings of doves.

3004 1391 1722 5310 2316 1909 1093 1515
14 καὶ λεγόντων, Δόξα ἐν ὑψίστοις Θεῷ, καὶ ἐπὶ γῆς εἰρήνη·
and saying, Glory in the highest to God, and on earth peace,
1722 444 2107
ἐν ἀνθρώποις εὐδοκία.
in men, good will.
1096 5613 565 575 846 1519 3772
15 Καὶ ἐγένετο, ὡς ἀπῆλθον ἀπ' αὐτῶν εἰς τὸν οὐρανὸν οἱ
And it was, as departed from them into – Heaven the
32 444 4166 2036 4314 240
ἄγγελοι, καὶ οἱ ἄνθρωποι οἱ ποιμένες εἶπον πρὸς ἀλλήλους,
angels, even the men, the shepherds, said to one another,
1330 1211 2193 965 1492 4487 5124
Διέλθωμεν δὴ ἕως Βηθλεέμ, καὶ ἴδωμεν τὸ ῥῆμα τοῦτο τὸ
Let us go indeed unto Bethlehem, and let us see – thing this –
1096 3739 2962 1107 2254 2064 4692
16 γεγονός, ὃ ὁ Κύριος ἐγνώρισεν ἡμῖν. καὶ ἦλθον σπεύσαντες,
having occurred, which the Lord made known to us. And they came, hurrying,
429 5037 3137 2501 1025
καὶ ἀνεῦρον τήν τε Μαριὰμ καὶ τὸν Ἰωσήφ, καὶ τὸ βρέφος
and sought out – both Mariam and – Joseph, and the babe
2749 1722 5336 1492 1232 4012
17 κείμενον ἐν τῇ φάτνῃ. ἰδόντες δὲ διεγνώρισαν περὶ τοῦ
lying in the manger. seeing And, they publicly told about the
4487 2980 846 4012 3813 5127
ῥήματος τοῦ λαληθέντος αὐτοῖς περὶ τοῦ παιδίου τούτου.
saying spoken to them about child this.
3956 191 2296 4012 2980
18 καὶ πάντες οἱ ἀκούσαντες ἐθαύμασαν περὶ τῶν λαληθέντων
And all those hearing marveled concerning the things spoken
5259 4166 4314 846 3137 3956
19 ὑπὸ τῶν ποιμένων πρὸς αὐτούς. ἡ δὲ Μαριὰμ πάντα
by the shepherds to them. And Mariam all
4933 4487 5023 4820 1722 2588
συνετήρει τὰ ῥήματα ταῦτα, συμβάλλουσα ἐν τῇ καρδίᾳ
kept sayings these, meditating in the heart
848 1994 4166 1392 134
20 αὐτῆς. καὶ ἐπέστρεψαν οἱ ποιμένες, δοξάζοντες καὶ αἰνοῦντες
of her. And returned the shepherds, glorifying and praising
2316 1909 3956 373 191 1492 2531 2980
τὸν Θεὸν ἐπὶ πᾶσιν οἷς ἤκουσαν καὶ εἶδον, καθὼς ἐλαλήθη
– God at all things which they heard and saw, even as was spoken
4314 846
πρὸς αὐτούς.
to them.
3753 4130 2250 3638 4059
21 Καὶ ὅτε ἐπλήσθησαν ἡμέραι ὀκτὼ τοῦ περιτεμεῖν τὸ
And when were fulfilled days eight to circumcise the
3813 2563 3686 848 2424 2563 5259
παιδίον, καὶ ἐκλήθη τὸ ὄνομα αὐτοῦ Ἰησοῦς, τὸ κληθὲν ὑπὸ
child, and was called the name of Him Jesus, that called by
32 4253 4865 846 1722 2836
τοῦ ἀγγέλου πρὸ τοῦ συλληφθῆναι αὐτὸν ἐν τῇ κοιλίᾳ.
the angel before – was conceived Him in the womb.
3753 4130 2250 2572 848
22 Καὶ ὅτε ἐπλήσθησαν αἱ ἡμέραι τοῦ καθαρισμοῦ αὐτῆς
And when were fulfilled the days of the cleansing of her,
2596 3551 3475 321 846 1519 2414
κατὰ τὸν νόμον Μωσέως, ἀνήγαγον αὐτὸν εἰς Ἱεροσόλυμα,
according to the law of Moses, they took up Him to Jerusalem
3936 2962 2531 1125 1722/3551 2962
23 παραστῆσαι τῷ Κυρίῳ (καθὼς γέγραπται ἐν νόμῳ Κυρίου
to present to the Lord, as it has been written in (the) law of the Lord.
3754 3956 730 1272 3388 40 2962 2564
ὅτι Πᾶν ἄρσεν διανοῖγον μήτραν ἅγιον τῷ Κυρίῳ κληθήσε-
– Every male opening a womb holy to the Lord shall be
1325 2378 2596 2046 1722 3551
24 ται·), καὶ τοῦ δοῦναι θυσίαν κατὰ τὸ εἰρημένον ἐν νόμῳ
called; and to give a sacrifice according to that said in the law
2962 2201 5167 2228 1417 3502 4058
Κυρίου, Ζεῦγος τρυγόνων ἢ δύο νεοσσοὺς περιστερῶν. καὶ
of (the) Lord: a pair of turtledoves, or two nestlings of doves. And

[25]And, behold, there was a man in Jerusalem whose name *was* Simeon. And this man *was* righteous and devout, eagerly expecting *the* Consolation of Israel. And *the* Holy Spirit was upon him. [26]And it happened to him, having been divinely-instructed by the Holy Spirit, *he was* not to see death before he would see the Christ of *the* Lord. [27]And by the Spirit he came into the temple. And *as* the parents *were* bringing in the child Jesus *for* them to do according to the custom of the the Law concerning Him, [28]even *Simeon* received Him into his arms. And *he* blessed God and said, [29]Now You will let Your slave go in peace, Master, according to Your word; [30]because my eyes saw Your Salvation, [31]which You prepared before *the* face of all the peoples; [32]a Light for revelation *to the* nations, and *the* Glory of Your people Israel.

[33]And Joseph was marveling, also His mother, at the things being said concerning Him. [34]And Simeon blessed them, and said to His mother Mary, Behold, this One is set for *the* fall and rising up of many in Israel, and for a sign spoken against; [35]yea, a sword also will pierce your own soul, so that *the* thoughts of many hearts may be revealed.

[36]And there was Anna, a prophetess, a daughter of Phanuel, of *the* tribe of Asher—she *was* advanced in many days, having lived seven years with a husband from her virginity; [37]and she *was* a widow eighty-four years—who did not depart from the temple,

2400 2258 444 1722 2419 3739 3686 4826
25 Ἰδού, ἦν ἄνθρωπος ἐν Ἱερουσαλήμ, ᾧ ὄνομα Συμεών, καὶ ὁ
behold, was a man in Jerusalem, to whom name Simeon. And
444 3778 1342 2126 4327
ἄνθρωπος οὗτος δίκαιος καὶ εὐλαβής, προσδεχόμενος
man this (was) righteous and devout, eagerly expecting
3874 2474 4151 40 2258 1909 846
παράκλησιν τοῦ Ἰσραήλ, καὶ Πνεῦμα Ἅγιον ἦν ἐπ' αὐτόν.
(the) consolation of Israel; and (the) Spirit Holy was upon him.
2258 846 5537 5259 4151
26 καὶ ἦν αὐτῷ κεχρηματισμένον ὑπὸ τοῦ Πνεύματος τοῦ
And was to him, having been instructed by the Spirit
40 3361 1492 2288 4250 2228 1492 5547 2962
Ἁγίου, μὴ ἰδεῖν θάνατον πρὶν ἢ ἴδῃ τὸν Χριστὸν Κυρίου.
Holy, not to see death before that he sees the Christ of (the) Lord.
2064/1722 4151 1519 2411 1722 1521
27 καὶ ἦλθεν ἐν τῷ Πνεύματι εἰς τὸ ἱερόν· καὶ ἐν τῷ εἰσαγαγεῖν
And he came by the Spirit into the Temple; and in the bringing in
1118 3813 2424 4160 846 2596
τοὺς γονεῖς τὸ παιδίον Ἰησοῦν, τοῦ ποιῆσαι αὐτοὺς κατὰ
the parents the child Jesus to do them according
1480 3551 4012 846 846 1209 846
28 τὸ εἰθισμένον τοῦ νόμου περὶ αὐτοῦ, καὶ αὐτὸς ἐδέξατο αὐτὸ
to the custom of the law concerning Him; and he received Him
1519 43 848 2127 2316 2036
εἰς τὰς ἀγκάλας αὐτοῦ, καὶ εὐλόγησε τὸν Θεόν, καὶ εἶπε,
in the arms of him, and blessed — God and said,
3568 630 1401 4675 1203 2596 4487 4675
29 Νῦν ἀπολύεις τὸν δοῦλόν σου, δέσποτα, κατὰ τὸ ῥῆμά σου,
Now let go the slave of You, Master, according to the word of You
1722 1515 3754 1492 3788 3450 4992 4675 3739
30 ἐν εἰρήνῃ· ὅτι εἶδον οἱ ὀφθαλμοί μου τὸ σωτήριόν σου, ὃ
in peace; because saw the eyes of me the salvation of You which
2090 2596 4383 3956 2992 5457 1519
31 ἡτοίμασας κατὰ πρόσωπον πάντων τῶν λαῶν· φῶς εἰς
You prepared before (the) face of all the peoples; a light for
602 1484 1391 2992 4675 2474 2258
32 ἀποκάλυψιν ἐθνῶν, καὶ δόξαν λαοῦ σου Ἰσραήλ. καὶ ἦν
revelation (to the) nations, and a glory of people of You Israel. And was
2501 3384 848 2296 1909 2980
33 Ἰωσὴφ καὶ ἡ μήτηρ αὐτοῦ θαυμάζοντες ἐπὶ τοῖς λαλου-
Joseph and the mother of Him marveling at the things being
4012 846 2127 846 4826 2036
34 μένοις περὶ αὐτοῦ. καὶ εὐλόγησεν αὐτοὺς Συμεών, καὶ εἶπε
said about Him. And blessed them Simeon, and said
4314 3137 3384 848 2400 3778 2749 1519
πρὸς Μαριὰμ τὴν μητέρα αὐτοῦ, Ἰδού, οὗτος κεῖται εἰς
to Mariam the mother of Him, Behold, this (One) is set for
4431 386 4183 1722 2474 1519 4592
πτῶσιν καὶ ἀνάστασιν πολλῶν ἐν τῷ Ἰσραήλ, καὶ εἰς σημεῖον
fall and rising of many in Israel, and for a sign
483 4675 846 5590 1330
35 ἀντιλεγόμενον· καὶ σοῦ δὲ αὐτῆς τὴν ψυχὴν διελεύσεται
being spoken against, and of you also of her soul will pierce
4501 3700 302 601 1537 4183 2588
ῥομφαία· ὅπως ἂν ἀποκαλυφθῶσιν ἐκ πολλῶν καρδιῶν
a sword, so as may be revealed of many hearts
1261 2258 451 4398 2364 5323
36 διαλογισμοί. καὶ ἦν Ἄννα προφῆτις, θυγάτηρ Φανουήλ,
(the) thoughts. And was Anna a prophetess, a daughter of Phanuel,
1537 5443 768 3778 4260 1722 2250 4183
ἐκ φυλῆς Ἀσήρ (αὕτη προβεβηκυῖα ἐν ἡμέραις πολλαῖς,
of (the) tribe of Asher; she advanced in days many,
2198 2094 3326 435 2033 575 3932 848
ζήσασα ἔτη μετὰ ἀνδρὸς ἑπτὰ ἀπὸ τῆς παρθενίας αὐτῆς,
having lived years with a husband seven from the virginity of her,
3778 5503 5613 2094 3589 5064 3739 3756 868
37 καὶ αὕτη χήρα ὡς ἐτῶν ὀγδοηκοντατεσσάρων), ἣ οὐκ ἀφί-
and she a widow years eighty-four, who not
575 2411 3521 1162 3000
στατο ἀπὸ τοῦ ἱεροῦ, νηστείαις καὶ δεήσεσι λατρεύουσα
departed from the Temple, with fasting and petitionings serving

serving night and day with
fastings and prayers.
38 And coming on at the very
hour, she gave thanks to
the Lord, and spoke con-
cerning Him to all those in
Jerusalem eagerly expect-
ing redemption. 39 And as
they finished all things
according to the Law of *the*
Lord, they returned to Galilee, to Nazareth their city.

40 And the Child grew,
and became strong in
spirit, being filled with
wisdom. And the grace of
God was upon Him.

41 And His parents went
into Jerusalem year by year
at the Feast of the Pass-
over. 42 And when He was
twelve years *old*, they
going up to Jerusalem
according to the custom of
the Feast, 43 and fulfilling
the days, in their returning,
the boy Jesus stayed in
Jerusalem. And Joseph and
His mother did not know.
44 But supposing Him to be
in the company, they went a
day on the way. And they
looked for Him among the
relatives and friends. 45 And
not finding Him, they re-
turned to Jerusalem, looking for Him.
46 And it happened after
three days they found Him
in the temple, sitting in *the*
midst of the teachers, even
hearing them and questioning them. 47 And all those
hearing Him were amazed
at His intelligence and
His answers. 48 And see-
ing Him, they were
astounded. And His mother
said to Him, Child, why did
You do so to us? Behold,
Your father and I were
looking for You, greatly
distressed. 49 And He said
to them, Why did you look
for me? Did you not know
that I must be *busy* in the
affairs of My Father? 50 And
they did not understand the

3571 2250 3778 846 5610 2186 437
38 νύκτα καὶ ἡμέραν. καὶ αὕτη αὐτῇ τῇ ὥρᾳ ἐπιστᾶσα ἀνθω-
night and day. And she at the very hour coming on, she
2962 2980 4012 846 3956
μολογεῖτο τῷ Κυρίῳ, καὶ ἐλάλει περὶ αὐτοῦ πᾶσι τοῖς
gave thanks to the Lord, and spoke concerning Him to all those
4327 3085 1722 2419 5613 5055
39 προσδεχομένοις λύτρωσιν ἐν Ἱερουσαλήμ. καὶ ὡς ἐτέλεσαν
expecting eagerly redemption in Jerusalem. And as they finished
537 2596 3551 2962 5290 1519
ἅπαντα τὰ κατὰ τὸν νόμον Κυρίου, ὑπέστρεψαν εἰς τὴν
all things according to the law of (the) Lord, they returned to
1056 1519 4172 848 3478
Γαλιλαίαν, εἰς τὴν πόλιν αὐτῶν Ναζαρέθ.
Galilee, to the city of them, Nazareth.
3813 837 2901 4151 4137
40 Τὸ δὲ παιδίον ηὔξανε, καὶ ἐκραταιοῦτο πνεύματι, πληρού-
the And child grew, and became strong in spirit being
4678 5485 2316 2258 1909 846
μενον σοφίας· καὶ χάρις Θεοῦ ἦν ἐπ' αὐτό.
filled with wisdom, and the grace of God was upon Him.
4198 1118 848 2596 2094 1519 2419
41 Καὶ ἐπορεύοντο οἱ γονεῖς αὐτοῦ κατ' ἔτος εἰς Ἱερουσαλὴμ
And went the parents of Him year by year into Jerusalem
1859 3957 3753 1096 2094 1427 305
42 τῇ ἑορτῇ τοῦ πάσχα. καὶ ὅτε ἐγένετο ἐτῶν δώδεκα, ἀναβάν-
at the feast of the Passover. And when He was years twelve, going up
846 1519 2414 2596 1485 1859
43 των αὐτῶν εἰς Ἱεροσόλυμα κατὰ τὸ ἔθος τῆς ἑορτῆς, καὶ
them to Jerusalem according to the custom of the feast, and
5048 2250 1722 5290 846 5278
τελειωσάντων τὰς ἡμέρας, ἐν τῷ ὑποστρέφειν αὐτούς, ὑπέ-
fulfilling the days, in the returning of them,
2424 3816 1722 2419 3756 1097 2501
μεινεν Ἰησοῦς ὁ παῖς ἐν Ἱερουσαλὴμ καὶ οὐκ ἔγνω Ἰωσὴφ
stayed Jesus the boy in Jerusalem; and not did know Joseph
3384 848 3543 846 1722 4923 1511
44 καὶ ἡ μήτηρ αὐτοῦ· νομίσαντες δὲ αὐτὸν ἐν τῇ συνοδίᾳ εἶναι,
and the mother of Him. supposing But Him in the company to be,
2064 2250 3598 327 846 1722 4773
ἦλθον ἡμέρας ὁδόν καὶ ἀνεζήτουν αὐτὸν ἐν τοῖς συγγενέσι
they went a day on the way, and looked for Him among the relatives
•1722 1110 3361 2147 846 5290 1519
45 καὶ ἐν τοῖς γνωστοῖς· καὶ μὴ εὑρόντες αὐτόν, ὑπέστρεψαν εἰς
and among the friends, and not finding Him, they returned into
2419 2212 846 1096 3326 2250
46 Ἱερουσαλήμ, ζητοῦντες αὐτόν. καὶ ἐγένετο, μεθ' ἡμέρας
Jerusalem seeking Him. And it was, after days
5140 2147 846 1722 2411 2516 1722 3319
τρεῖς εὗρον αὐτὸν ἐν τῷ ἱερῷ, καθεζόμενον ἐν μέσῳ τῶν
three they found Him in the Temple, sitting in (the) midst of the
1320 191 846 1905 846
47 διδασκάλων, καὶ ἀκούοντα αὐτῶν, καὶ ἐπερωτῶντα αὐτούς.
teachers, even hearing them and questioning them
1839 3956 191 846 1909 4907
ἐξίσταντο δὲ πάντες οἱ ἀκούοντες αὐτοῦ ἐπὶ τῇ συνέσει καὶ
were amazed And all those hearing Him at the intelligence and
612 848 1492 846 1605
48 ταῖς ἀποκρίσεσιν αὐτοῦ. καὶ ἰδόντες αὐτὸν ἐξεπλάγησαν·
the answers of Him. And seeing Him, they were astounded.
4314 846 3384 848 2036 5043 5101 4160
καὶ πρὸς αὐτὸν ἡ μήτηρ αὐτοῦ εἶπε, Τέκνον, τί ἐποίησας
and to Him the mother of Him said, Child, why did You do
2254 3779 2400 3962 4675 2504 3600 2212
ἡμῖν οὕτως; ἰδού, ὁ πατήρ σου κἀγὼ ὀδυνώμενοι ἐζητοῦμέν
to us thus? Behold, the father of You and I greatly distressed are seeking
4571 2036 4314 846 5101 3754 2212 3165 3756 1492 3754
49 σε. καὶ εἶπε πρὸς αὐτούς, Τί ὅτι ἐζητεῖτέ με; οὐκ ᾔδειτε ὅτι ἐν
You. And He said to them, Why that you sought Me? not know that in
3962 3450 1163 1511 3165 846 3756 4920
50 τοῖς τοῦ πατρός μου δεῖ εἶναί με; καὶ αὐτοὶ οὐ συνῆκαν τὸ
the (affairs) of Father My must be Me? And they not understood the

word which He spoke to them. [51]And He went with them, and came to Nazareth, and was being subject to them. And His mother carefully kept all these words in her heart.

[52]And Jesus progressed *in* wisdom and stature and favor before God and men.

CHAPTER 3

[1]And in *the* fifteenth year of the government of Tiberius Caesar, Pontius Pilate governing Judea, and Herod ruling as tetrarch of Galilee; and his brother Philip ruling as tetrarch of Iturea and *the* Trachonitis country; and Lysanias ruling as tetrarch of Abilene, [2]upon *the* high priesthood of Anna and Caiaphas, *the* word of God came on John the son of Zacharias in the desert. [3]And he came into the neighborhood of the Jordan, proclaiming a baptism of repentance for forgiveness of sins, [4]as it has been written in *the* roll of *the* words of Isaiah the prophet, saying: "*The* voice of *one* crying in the wilderness, Prepare the way of *the* Lord, make His paths straight—[5]every valley shall be filled up, and every mountain and hill shall be made low; and the crooked *places* shall be *made* into straight; and the rough into smooth ways; [6]and all flesh shall see the salvation of God."

[7]Then he said to the crowds going out to be baptized by him, Offspring of vipers! Who warned you to flee from the coming

4487 3739 2980 846 2597 3326 846 2064
51 ῥῆμα ὃ ἐλάλησεν αὐτοῖς. καὶ κατέβη μετ' αὐτῶν, καὶ ἦλθεν
word which He spoke to them. And He went with them, and came
1519 3478 2258 5293 846 3384
εἰς Ναζαρέθ· καὶ ἦν ὑποτασσόμενος αὐτοῖς· καὶ ἡ μήτηρ
to Nazareth, and was being subject to them. And the mother
848 1301 3956 4487 5023 1722 2588
αὐτοῦ διετήρει πάντα τὰ ῥήματα ταῦτα ἐν τῇ καρδίᾳ
of Him carefully kept all sayings these in the heart
848
αὐτῆς.
of her.

2424 4298 4678 2244 5485 3844
52 Καὶ Ἰησοῦς προέκοπτε σοφίᾳ καὶ ἡλικίᾳ, καὶ χάριτι παρὰ
And Jesus progressed (in) wisdom and stature and favor before
2316 444
Θεῷ καὶ ἀνθρώποις.
God and men.

CHAPTER 3

1722 2094 4003 2231 5086
1 Ἐν ἔτει δὲ πεντεκαιδεκάτῳ τῆς ἡγεμονίας Τιβερίου
in (the) year And fifteenth of the government of Tiberius
2831 2230 4194 4091 2449
Καίσαρος, ἡγεμονεύοντος Ποντίου Πιλάτου τῆς Ἰουδαίας,
Caesar, (in the) governing of Pontius Pilate of Judea
5075 1056 2264 5376
καὶ τετραρχοῦντος τῆς Γαλιλαίας Ἡρώδου, Φιλίππου δὲ
and ruling as tetrarch of Galilee Herod, Philip and
80 848 5075 2484
τοῦ ἀδελφοῦ αὐτοῦ τετραρχοῦντος τῆς Ἰτουραίας καὶ
the brother of him ruling as tetrarch of Iturea and
5139 5561 3078 9 5075
2 Τραχωνίτιδος χώρας, καὶ Λυσανίου τῆς Ἀβιληνῆς τετραρ-
of Trachonitis country, and Lysanias of Abilene ruling as
1909 749 452 2533 1096 4487
χοῦντος, ἐπ' ἀρχιερέων Ἄννα καὶ Καϊάφα, ἐγένετο ῥῆμα
tetrarch, at high priesthood of Anna and Caiphas, came a word
2316 1909 2491 2197 5207 1722 2048
Θεοῦ ἐπὶ Ἰωάννην τὸν τοῦ Ζαχαρίου υἱὸν ἐν τῇ ἐρήμῳ. καὶ
of God upon John the of Zachariah son in the desert. And
2064 1519 3956 4066 2446 2784
3 ἦλθεν εἰς πᾶσαν τὴν περίχωρον τοῦ Ἰορδάνου, κηρύσσων
he came into all the neighborhood of the Jordan, proclaiming
908 3341 1519 859 266 5613 1125 1722
4 βάπτισμα μετανοίας εἰς ἄφεσιν ἁμαρτιῶν· ὡς γέγραπται ἐν
a baptism of repentance for foregiveness of sins, as it has been written in
976 3056 2268 4396 3004 5456
βίβλῳ λόγων Ἡσαΐου τοῦ προφήτου, λέγοντος, Φωνὴ
(the) roll of (the) words of Isaiah the prophet, saying, (The) voice
994 1722 2048 2090 3598 2962 2117
βοῶντος ἐν τῇ ἐρήμῳ, Ἑτοιμάσατε τὴν ὁδὸν Κυρίου· εὐθείας
of (one) crying in the wilderness; prepare the way of (the) Lord, straight
4160 5747 848 3956 5327 4137
5 ποιεῖτε τὰς τρίβους αὐτοῦ. πᾶσα φάραγξ πληρωθήσεται,
make the paths of Him; every valley shall be filled up,
3956 3735 1015 5013 2511
καὶ πᾶν ὄρος καὶ βουνὸς ταπεινωθήσεται· καὶ ἔσται τὰ
and every mountain and hill shall be laid low; and shall be the
4646 1519 2117 5138 1519 3598 3006
6 σκολιὰ εἰς εὐθεῖαν, καὶ αἱ τραχεῖαι εἰς ὁδοὺς λείας· καὶ
crooked into straight, and the rough (places) into ways a smooth; and
3700 3956 4561 4992 2316
ὄψεται πᾶσα σὰρξ τὸ σωτήριον τοῦ Θεοῦ.
shall see all flesh the salvation of God.

3004 3767 1607 3793 907 5259
7 Ἔλεγεν οὖν τοῖς ἐκπορευομένοις ὄχλοις βαπτισθῆναι ὑπ'
He said therefore to the having gone out crowds to be baptized by
846 1081 2191 5101 5263 5213 5343 575
αὐτοῦ, Γεννήματα ἐχιδνῶν, τίς ὑπέδειξεν ὑμῖν φυγεῖν ἀπὸ
him, Offspring of vipers! Who warned you to flee from

wrath? [8]Therefore, bring forth fruits worthy of repentance, and do not begin to say within yourselves, We have Abraham *as* father. For I say to you that God is able to raise up children to Abraham out of these stones. [9]And also the axe is already laid to the root of the trees; therefore, every tree not producing good fruit is being cut down and being thrown into *the* fire. [10]And the crowd asked him, saying, What then shall we do? [11]And answering he said to them, The *one* that has two tunics, let him give to him that has not. And the *one* that has foods, let him do the same.

[12]And tax-collectors also came to be baptized. And they said to him, Teacher, what shall we do? [13]And he said to them, Continue to do no more than that commanded to you. [14]And also ones serving as soldiers asked him, saying, And we, what shall we do? And he said to them, Do not oppress anyone, nor accuse falsely; and be satisfied with your pay.

[15]But the people *were* expecting, and all reasoning in their hearts about John, lest perhaps he is the Christ. [16]John answered all, saying, I indeed baptize you with water; but He stronger than I comes, of whom I am not fit to loosen the latchet of His sandals. He will baptize you in *the* Holy Spirit and fire; [17]whose sifting fan *is* in His hand; and He will fully purge His threshing-floor, and will gather the wheat into His barn—but He will burn the chaff with fire that cannot be put out.

3195 3709 4160 3767 2590 514
8 τῆς μελλούσης ὀργῆς; ποιήσατε οὖν καρποὺς ἀξίους τῆς
the coming wrath? Produce therefore fruits worthy —
3341 3361 756 3004 1722 1438 3962 2192
μετανοίας· καὶ μὴ ἄρξησθε λέγειν ἐν ἑαυτοῖς, Πατέρα ἔχομεν
of repentance; and not do begin to say among yourselves, Father we have
11 3004 1063 5213 3754 1410 2316 1537
τὸν Ἀβραάμ· λέγω γὰρ ὑμῖν ὅτι δύναται ὁ Θεὸς ἐκ τῶν
Abraham. I say For to you that is able God out of
3037 5130 1453 5043 11 2235 513
9 λίθων τούτων ἐγεῖραι τέκνα τῷ Ἀβραάμ. ἤδη δὲ καὶ ἡ ἀξίνη
stones these to raise up children (to) Abraham. already And even the axe
4314 4491 1186 2749 3956 3767 1186
πρὸς τὴν ῥίζαν τῶν δένδρων κεῖται· πᾶν οὖν δένδρον μὴ
to the root of the trees is laid; every therefore tree not
4160 2590 2570 1581 1519 4442 906
ποιοῦν καρπὸν καλὸν ἐκκόπτεται καὶ εἰς πῦρ βάλλεται. καὶ
producing fruit good is being cut down and into fire being cast. And
1905 846 3793 3004 5101 3767 4160
10 ἐπηρώτων αὐτὸν οἱ ὄχλοι λέγοντες, Τί οὖν ποιήσομεν;
asked him the crowd, saying, What, then, may we do?
611 3004 846 2192 1417 5509 3330
11 ἀποκριθεὶς δὲ λέγει αὐτοῖς, Ὁ ἔχων δύο χιτῶνας μεταδότω
answering And he says to them, He having two tunics, let him impart
3361 2192 2192 1033 3668 4160 2064
τῷ μὴ ἔχοντι· καὶ ὁ ἔχων βρώματα ὁμοίως ποιείτω. ἦλθον
to the (one) not having; and the (one) having foods likewise let him do. came
5057 907 2036 4314 846
12 δὲ καὶ τελῶναι βαπτισθῆναι, καὶ εἶπον πρὸς αὐτόν,
And also tax-collectors to be baptized, and said to him,
1320 5101 4160 2036 4314 846 3367
13 Διδάσκαλε, τί ποιήσομεν; ὁ δὲ εἶπε πρὸς αὐτούς, Μηδὲν
Teacher, what may we do? he And said to them, Nothing
4119 3844 1299 5213 4238 1905
πλέον παρὰ τὸ διατεταγμένον ὑμῖν πράσσετε. ἐπηρώ-
more besides that commanded to you keep doing. asked
846 4754 3004 2248 5101
14 των δὲ αὐτὸν καὶ στρατευόμενοι, λέγοντες, Καὶ ἡμεῖς τί
— And him also ones serving as soldiers, saying, And we, what
4160 2036 4314 846 3367 1286
ποιήσομεν; καὶ εἶπε πρὸς αὐτούς, Μηδένα διασείσητε,
may we do? And he said to them, No one oppress,
3366 4811 714 3800 5216
μηδὲ συκοφαντήσητε· καὶ ἀρκεῖσθε τοῖς ὀψωνίοις ὑμῶν.
nor accuse falsely; and be satisfied with the pay of you.
4328 2992 1260 3956
15 Προσδοκῶντος δὲ τοῦ λαοῦ, καὶ διαλογιζομένων πάντων
expecting And the people, and reasoning all
1722 2588 848 4012 2491 3379 846
ἐν ταῖς καρδίαις αὐτῶν περὶ τοῦ Ἰωάννου, μήποτε αὐτὸς
in the hearts of them about John, lest perhaps he
1498 5547 611 2491 537 3004 1473
16 εἴη ὁ Χριστός, ἀπεκρίνατο ὁ Ἰωάννης, ἅπασι λέγων, Ἐγὼ
is the Christ, answered John to all, saying, I
3303 5204 907 5209 2064 2478 3450 3739
μὲν ὕδατι βαπτίζω ὑμᾶς· ἔρχεται δὲ ὁ ἰσχυρότερός μου, οὗ
indeed with water baptize you; comes but (He) stronger than me, of whom
3756 1510 2425 3089 2438 5256
οὐκ εἰμὶ ἱκανὸς λῦσαι τὸν ἱμάντα τῶν ὑποδημάτων αὐτοῦ·
not I am fit to loose the latchet of the sandals of Him;
846 5209 907 1722 4151 40 4442 3739
17 αὐτὸς ὑμᾶς βαπτίσει ἐν Πνεύματι Ἁγίῳ καὶ πυρί· οὗ τὸ
He you will baptize in (the) Spirit Holy and fire; of whom the
4425 1722 5495 848 1245 257 848
πτύον ἐν τῇ χειρὶ αὐτοῦ, καὶ διακαθαριεῖ τὴν ἅλωνα αὐτοῦ,
fan (is) in the hand of Him, and He will fully purge the threshing-floor of Him,
•596 4863 4621 1519 848 892
καὶ συνάξει τὸν σῖτον εἰς τὴν ἀποθήκην αὐτοῦ, τὸ δὲ ἄχυρον
and will gather the wheat into the barn of Him; the but chaff
2618 4442 762
κατακαύσει πυρὶ ἀσβέστῳ.
He will burn up with fire unquenchable.

18And then indeed ex-
horting many different
things, he announced the
gospel to the people. 19But
Herod the tetrarch, having
been reproved by him
concerning his brother
Philip's wife, Herodias,
and concerning all *the* evil
things Herod did, 20he
also added this above all,
he even shut up John in
the prison.
21And it happened in the
baptizing *of* all the people,
Jesus also being baptized,
and praying., the heaven
was opened, 22and the
Holy Spirit came down in a
bodily form as a dove upon
Him. And there was a voice
out of Heaven, saying, You
are My Son, the Beloved;
I am delighted in You.
**23And Jesus Himself was
beginning to be about thirty
years *old*, being, as was
supposed, the son of Jo-
seph, the *son* of Heli, 24the
son of Matthat, the *son* of
Levi, the *son* of Melchi, the
son of Janna, the *son* of
Joseph, 25the *son* of Mattathias, the *son* of Amos, the
son of Nahum, the *son* of
Esli, the *son* of Naggai, 26the
son of Maath, the *son* of
Mattathias, the *son* of
Semei, the *son* of Joseph,
the *son* of Judah, 27the *son*
of Joannes, the *son* of
Rhesa, the *son* of Zerubbabel, the *son* of Shealtiel,
the *son* of Neri, 28the *son* of
Melchi, the *son* of Addi, the
son of Cosam, the *son* of
Elmodam, the *son* of Er,
29the *son* of Joses, the *son*
of Eliezer, the *son* of Jorim,
the *son* of Matthat, the *son*
of Levi, 30the *son* of
Simeon, the *son* of Judah,
the *son* of Joseph, the *son*
of Jonan, the *son* of Eliakim, 31the *son* of Melea,
the *son* of Menam, the *son*
of Mattatha, the *son* of
Nathan, the *son* of David,
32the *son* of Jesse, the *son*
of Obed, the *son* of Boaz,
the *son* of Salmon, the *son*
of Nahshon, 33the *son* of
Amminadab, the *son* of**

4183 3303 3767 2087 3870 2097
18 Πολλὰ μὲν οὖν καὶ ἕτερα παρακαλῶν εὐηγγελίζετο τὸν
Many things indeed then and different exhorting, he preached the gospel to the
2992 2264 5076 1651 5258 846
19 λαόν· ὁ δὲ Ἡρώδης ὁ τετράρχης, ἐλεγχόμενος ὑπ' αὐτοῦ
people. – But Herod the tetrarch, being reproved by him
4012 2266 1135 5376 80 848
περὶ Ἡρωδιάδος τῆς γυναικὸς Φιλίππου τοῦ ἀδελφοῦ αὐτοῦ,
concerning Herodias the wife of Philip the brother of him,
4012 3956 3739 4160 4190 2264 4369
καὶ περὶ πάντων ὧν ἐποίησε πονηρῶν ὁ Ἡρώδης, προσέ-
and concerning all things which did evil – Herod, he
5124 1909 3956 2623 2491 1722
20 θηκε καὶ τοῦτο ἐπὶ πᾶσι, καὶ κατέκλεισε τὸν Ἰωάννην ἐν τῇ
added also this above all, even he shut up – John in the
5438
φυλακῇ.
prison.
1096 1722 907 537 2992
21 Ἐγένετο δὲ ἐν τῷ βαπτισθῆναι ἅπαντα τὸν λαόν, καὶ
it was And in the baptizing (of) all the people, also
2424 907 4336 455
Ἰησοῦ βαπτισθέντος καὶ προσευχομένου, ἀνεῳχθῆναι τὸν
Jesus being baptized and praying, was opened the
3772 2597 4151 40 4984
22 οὐρανόν, καὶ καταβῆναι τὸ Πνεῦμα τὸ Ἅγιον σωματικῷ
heaven and came down the Spirit – Holy in a bodily
1491 5616 4058 1909 846 5456 1537 3772
εἴδει ὡσεὶ περιστερὰν ἐπ' αὐτόν, καὶ φωνὴν ἐξ οὐρανοῦ
form as a dove upon Him, and a voice out of Heaven
1096 3004 4771 1488 5207 3450 27 1722 4671
γενέσθαι, λέγουσαν, Σὺ εἶ ὁ υἱός μου ὁ ἀγαπητός, ἐν σοὶ
occurred, saying, You are the Son of Me, the Beloved: in You
2106
ηὐδόκησα.
I am delighted.
846 2258 2424 5616 2094 5144 756
23 Καὶ αὐτὸς ἦν ὁ Ἰησοῦς ὡσεὶ ἐτῶν τριάκοντα ἀρχόμενος,
And Himself was Jesus about years (old) thirty beginning
5607 5613 3543 5207 2511 2242 3158
24 ὤν (ὡς ἐνομίζετο) υἱὸς Ἰωσήφ, τοῦ Ἠλί, τοῦ Ματθάτ, τοῦ
being, as was supposed, son of Joseph, of Heli of Matthat,
3018 3197 2388 2501 3161
25 Λευΐ, τοῦ Μελχί, τοῦ Ἰαννά, τοῦ Ἰωσήφ, τοῦ Ματταθίου
of Levi, of Melchi, of Janna, of Joseph, of Mattathias,
301 3486 2069 3477 3092
26 τοῦ Ἀμώς, τοῦ Ναούμ, τοῦ Ἐσλί, τοῦ Ναγγαί, τοῦ Μαάθ,
– of Amos, of Nahum, of Esli, of Naggai, of Maath,
3161 4584 2501 2455
τοῦ Ματταθίου, τοῦ Σεμεΐ, τοῦ Ἰωσήφ, τοῦ Ἰούδα, τοῦ
– of Mattathias, of Semei, of Joseph, of Judah,
2490 4488 2216 4528
27 Ἰωαννᾶ, τοῦ Ῥησά, τοῦ Ζοροβάβελ, τοῦ Σαλαθιήλ, τοῦ
of Joannes, of Rhesa, of Zerubbabel, of Salathiel,
3518 3197 78 2973 1678
28 Νηρί, τοῦ Μελχί, τοῦ Ἀδδί, τοῦ Κωσάμ, τοῦ Ἐλμωδάμ,
of Neri, – of Melchi, – of Addi, – of Cosam, – of Elmodam,
2262 2499 1663 2497 3158
29 τοῦ Ἤρ, τοῦ Ἰωσή, τοῦ Ἐλιέζερ, τοῦ Ἰωρείμ, τοῦ Ματθάτ,
of Er, of Joseph, of Eliezer, of Joreim, of Matthat,
3018 4826 2455 2501 2494
30 τοῦ Λευΐ, τοῦ Σιμεών, τοῦ Ἰούδα, τοῦ Ἰωσήφ, τοῦ Ἰωνάν,
– of Levi, – of Simeon, – of Judah, – of Joseph, – of Jonan,
1662 3190 3104 3160
31 τοῦ Ἐλιακείμ, τοῦ Μελεᾶ, τοῦ Μενάμ, τοῦ Ματταθά, τοῦ
– of Eliakim, – of Melea, – of Menam, – of Mattatha, –
3481 1138 2421 5601 1003
32 Ναθάν, τοῦ Δαβίδ, τοῦ Ἰεσσαί, τοῦ Ὠβήδ, τοῦ Βοόζ, τοῦ
of Nathan, – of David, – of Jesse, – of Obed, – of Boaz, –
4533 3476 284 689
33 Σαλμών, τοῦ Ναασσών, τοῦ Ἀμιναδάβ, τοῦ Ἀράμ, τοῦ
of Salmon, – of Nahshon, – of Amminadab, – of Ram, –

NOTE: Frequent words not numbered: δέ(1161); καί(2531)—and, but; ὁ, ἡ, τό (3588, the)— * above word, look in verse margin for No.

Aram, the *son* of Hezron, the *son* of Pharez, the *son* of Judah, [34]the *son* of Jacob, the *son* of Isaac, the *son* of Abraham, the *son* of Terah, the *son* of Nahor, [35]the *son* of Serug, the *son* of Reu, the *son* of Peleg, the *son* of Eber, the *son* of Salah, [36]the *son* of Cainan, the *son* of Arphaxad, the *son* of Shem, the *son* of Noah, the *son* of Lamech, [37]the *son* of Methuselah, the *son* of Enoch, the *son* of Jared, the *son* of Mahalaleel, the *son* of Cainan, [38]the *son* of Enos, the *son* of Seth, the *son* of Adam, the *son* of God.

CHAPTER 4

[1]And full of *the* Holy Spirit, Jesus returned from the Jordan, and was led by the Spirit into the wilderness [2]forty days, being tested by the Devil. And He ate nothing in those days, and they being ended, He afterwards hungered. [3]And the Devil said to Him, If You are Son of God, speak to this stone that it become a loaf. [4]And Jesus answered to him, saying, It has been written: "Man shall not live on bread alone, but on every word of God." [5]And leading Him up into a high mountain, the Devil showed Him all the kingdoms of the world in a moment of time. [6]And the Devil said to Him, I will give all this authority and their glory to You, because it has been delivered to me, and I give it to whomever I wish; [7]then if You worship before me, all will be Yours. [8]And answering to him, Jesus said, Get behind Me, Satan! For it has been written: "You shall worship *the* Lord your God, and Him only you shall serve."

[9]And he led Him to Jerusalem, and stood Him on

2074 5329 2455 2384 2464
34 Ἑσρώμ, τοῦ Φαρές, τοῦ Ἰούδα, τοῦ Ἰακώβ, τοῦ Ἰσαάκ·
of Hezron, of Pharez, of Judah, of Jacob, of Isaac,
11 2291 3493 4562
35 τοῦ Ἀβραάμ, τοῦ Θάρα, τοῦ Ναχώρ, τοῦ Σαρούχ, τοῦ
– of Abraham, of Terah, – of Nahor, – of Serug, –
4466 5317 1443 4527 2536
Ῥαγαῦ, τοῦ Φαλέκ, τοῦ Ἔβερ, τοῦ Σαλά, τοῦ Καϊνάν, τοῦ
of Reu, of Peleg, – of Eber, – of Salah, – of Cainan, –
742 4590 3575 2984 3103
36 Ἀρφαξάδ, τοῦ Σήμ, τοῦ Νῶε, τοῦ Λάμεχ, τοῦ Μαθουσάλα,
of Arphaxad, – of Shem, – of Noah, – of Lamech, – of Methuselah,
1802 1 2391 3121 2536
37 τοῦ Ἐνώχ, τοῦ Ἰαρέδ, τοῦ Μαλελεήλ, τοῦ Καϊνάν, τοῦ
– of Enoch, – of Jared, – of Mahalaleel, – of Cainan, –
1800 4589 76 2316
38 Ἐνώς, τοῦ Σήθ, τοῦ Ἀδάμ, τοῦ Θεοῦ.
of Enos, – of Seth, – of Adam, – of God.

CHAPTER 4

2424 4151 40 4134 5290 575
1 Ἰησοῦς δὲ Πνεύματος Ἁγίου πλήρης ὑπέστρεψεν ἀπὸ τοῦ
Jesus And of (the) Spirit Holy full returned from the
2446 71 1722 4151 1519 2048 2250
2 Ἰορδάνου, καὶ ἤγετο ἐν τῷ Πνεύματι εἰς τὴν ἔρημον, ἡμέρας
Jordan, and was led by the Spirit into the wilderness, days
5062 3985 5259 1228 3756
τεσσαράκοντα πειραζόμενος ὑπὸ τοῦ διαβόλου. καὶ οὐκ
forty being tempted by the Devil. And not
5315 3762 1722 2250 1565 4931
ἔφαγεν οὐδὲν ἐν ταῖς ἡμέραις ἐκείναις· καὶ συντελεσθεισῶν
He ate, nothing in days those; and being ended
848 5304 3983 2036 846 1228 1223 1487
3 αὐτῶν, ὕστερον ἐπείνασε. καὶ εἶπεν αὐτῷ ὁ διάβολος, Εἰ
them, afterwards He hungered. And said to Him the Devil, If
5207 1488 2316 2036 3037 5129 2443 1096 740
υἱὸς εἶ τοῦ Θεοῦ, εἰπὲ τῷ λίθῳ τούτῳ ἵνα γένηται ἄρτος.
Son you are of God say to stone this that it become a loaf.
611 2424 4314 846 3004 1125 3754
4 καὶ ἀπεκρίθη Ἰησοῦς πρὸς αὐτόν, λέγων, Γέγραπται ὅτι
And made answer Jesus to him, saying, It has been written,
3756/1909/740 3441 2198 444 235/1909/3956
Οὐκ ἐπ' ἄρτῳ μόνῳ ζήσεται ὁ ἄνθρωπος, ἀλλ' ἐπὶ παντὶ
Not on bread only shall live man, but on every
4487 2316 321 846 1228 1519 3735
5 ῥήματι Θεοῦ. καὶ ἀναγαγὼν αὐτὸν ὁ διάβολος εἰς ὄρος
word of God. And leading up Him the Devil into a mount
5308 1166 846 3956 932 3625
ὑψηλὸν ἔδειξεν αὐτῷ πάσας τὰς βασιλείας τῆς οἰκουμένης
high, he showed Him all the kingdoms of the habitable world
1722 4743 5550 2036 846 1228 4671 1325
6 ἐν στιγμῇ χρόνου. καὶ εἶπεν αὐτῷ ὁ διάβολος, Σοὶ δώσω τὴν
in a moment of time. And said to Him the Devil, To you I will give
1849 5026 537 1391 848 3754 1698
ἐξουσίαν ταύτην ἅπασαν καὶ τὴν δόξαν αὐτῶν· ὅτι ἐμοὶ
authority this all and the glory of them, because to me
3860 3739 1437 2309 1325 846 4771 3767 1437
7 παραδέδοται, καὶ ᾧ ἐὰν θέλω δίδωμι αὐτήν. σὺ οὖν ἐὰν
it has been delivered, and to whomever I wish I give it; you, then, if
4352 1799 3450 2071 4675 3956 611
8 προσκυνήσῃς ἐνώπιόν μου, ἔσται σου πάντα. καὶ ἀποκρι-
you worship before me, will be of you all. And answering
846 2036 2424 5217 3694 3450 4567
θεὶς αὐτῷ εἶπεν ὁ Ἰησοῦς, Ὕπαγε ὀπίσω μου, Σατανᾶ·
to him said Jesus, Get behind Me, Satan!
1125 1063 4352 2962 2316 4675
γέγραπται γάρ, Προσκυνήσεις Κύριον τὸν Θεόν σου, καὶ
it has been written For, You shall worship (the) Lord the God of you, and
846 3441 3000 71 846 1519 2419
9 αὐτῷ μόνῳ λατρεύσεις. καὶ ἤγαγεν αὐτὸν εἰς Ἱερουσαλήμ,
Him only you shall serve. And he led Him to Jerusalem,

the pinnacle of the temple, and said to Him, If You are the Son of God, throw Yourself down from here; 10 for it has been written: "He will command His angels about You, and to preserve You; 11 that on *their* hands they shall bear You, lest you strike Your foot against a stone." 12 And answering Jesus said to him, It has been said: "You shall not tempt *the* Lord your God." 13 And having finished every temptation, the Devil departed from Him until a time.

14 And Jesus returned in the power of the Spirit to Galilee. And a rumor went out through all the neighborhood about Him. 15 And He taught in their synagogues, being glorified by all.

16 And He came to Nazareth, where He was brought up. And He went in, as *was* His custom, on the day of the sabbaths, into the synagogue, and stood up to read. 17 And *the* roll of Isaiah the prophet was handed to Him. And unrolling the book, He found the place where it was written: 18 "*The* Spirit of *the* Lord is upon Me; therefore He anointed Me to preach the gospel to *the* poor; He has sent Me to heal the brokenhearted, to preach deliverance to captives, and new sight to *the* blind; to send away crushed ones in deliverance; 19 to preach an acceptable year of *the* Lord." 20 And rolling up the roll, returning *it* to the attendant, He sat down. And the eyes of all in the synagogue were fixed on Him. 21 And He began to

2476 846 1909 4419 2411 2036
καὶ ἔστησεν αὐτὸν ἐπὶ τὸ πτερύγιον τοῦ ἱεροῦ, καὶ εἶπεν
and stood Him on the pinnacle of the Temple, and said
846 1487 5207 1488 2316 906 4572 1782 2736
αὐτῷ, Εἰ ὁ υἱὸς εἶ τοῦ Θεοῦ, βάλε σεαυτὸν ἐντεῦθεν κάτω·
to Him, If the Son you are of God, throw yourself from here down;
1125 1063 3754 32 848 1781 4012
10 γέγραπται γὰρ ὅτι Τοῖς ἀγγέλοις αὐτοῦ ἐντελεῖται περὶ
it has been written For, To the angels of Him He will command about
4675 1314 4571 3756 1909 5495 142 4571
11 σοῦ, τοῦ διαφυλάξαι σε· καὶ ὅτι Ἐπὶ χειρῶν ἀροῦσί σε,
You to preserve You and, In (their) hands they will bear You,
3379 4350 4314 3037 4228 4675 611
12 μήποτε προσκόψῃς πρὸς λίθον τὸν πόδα σου. καὶ ἀπο-
lest You strike against a stone the foot of You. And answering
2036 846 2424 3754 2046 3756 1598
κριθεὶς εἶπεν αὐτῷ ὁ Ἰησοῦς ὅτι Εἴρηται, Οὐκ ἐκπειράσεις
said to him Jesus, It has been said, not You shall tempt
2962 2316 4675 4391 3956 3986
13 Κύριον τὸν Θεόν σου. καὶ συντελέσας πάντα πειρασμὸν ὁ
(the) Lord the God of you. And having finished every temptation, the
1228 868 575 846 891 2540
διάβολος ἀπέστη ἀπ' αὐτοῦ ἄχρι καιροῦ.
Devil departed from Him until a season.
5290 2424 1722 1411 4151
14 Καὶ ὑπέστρεψεν ὁ Ἰησοῦς ἐν τῇ δυνάμει τοῦ Πνεύματος
And returned – Jesus in the power of the Spirit
1519 1056 5345 1831 2596 3650 4066
εἰς τὴν Γαλιλαίαν· καὶ φήμη ἐξῆλθε καθ' ὅλης τῆς περιχώρου
to – Galilee; and a rumor went out through all the neighborhood
4012 846 846 1321 1722 4864
15 περὶ αὐτοῦ. καὶ αὐτὸς ἐδίδασκεν ἐν ταῖς συναγωγαῖς
concerning Him. And He taught in the synagogues
848 1392 5259 3956
αὐτῶν, δοξαζόμενος ὑπὸ πάντων.
of them, being glorified by all.
2064 1519 3478 3757 2258 5112
16 Καὶ ἦλθεν εἰς τὴν Ναζαρέθ, οὗ ἦν τεθραμμένος· καὶ
And He came to – Nazareth, where He was brought up and
1525 2596 1486 846 1722 2250 4521
εἰσῆλθε, κατὰ τὸ εἰωθὸς αὐτῷ, ἐν τῇ ἡμέρᾳ τῶν σαββάτων
He went in as (was) the custom to Him, on the day of the sabbaths,
1519 4864 450 314 1929
17 εἰς τὴν συναγωγήν, καὶ ἀνέστη ἀναγνῶναι. καὶ ἐπεδόθη
into the synagogue and stood up to read. And was handed
846 975 2268 4396 380
αὐτῷ βιβλίον Ἠσαΐου τοῦ προφήτου. καὶ ἀναπτύξας τὸ
to Him a roll of Isaiah the prophet. And having unrolled the
975 2147 5117 3757 2258 1125 4151 2962
18 βιβλίον, εὗρε τὸν τόπον οὗ ἦν γεγραμμένον, Πνεῦμα Κυρίου
roll, He found the place where it was written, (the) Spirit of (the) Lord
1909 1691 3757 1752 5548 3165 2097 4434 649
ἐπ' ἐμέ, οὗ εἵνεκεν ἔχρισέ με εὐαγγελίζεσθαι πτωχοῖς· ἀπέ-
(is) on Me; therefore He anointed Me to preach the gospel to (the) poor; He
3165 2390 4937 2588
σταλκέ με ἰάσασθαι τοὺς συντετριμμένους τὴν καρδίαν·
has sent Me to heal the broken (in) heart,
2784 164 859 5185 309
κηρύξαι αἰχμαλώτοις ἄφεσιν, καὶ τυφλοῖς ἀνάβλεψιν,
to preach to captives deliverance, and to (the) blind new sight,
649 2532 1722 859 2784 1763
19 ἀποστεῖλαι τεθραυσμένους ἐν ἀφέσει, κηρύξαι ἐνιαυτὸν
to send away crushed ones in deliverance, to preach a year
2962 1184 4428 975 591 5257
20 Κυρίου δεκτόν. καὶ πτύξας τὸ βιβλίον, ἀποδοὺς τῷ ὑπηρέτῃ,
(the) acceptable. And closing the roll, returning (it) to the attendant
Lord 2523 3956 1722 4864 3788 2258
ἐκάθισε· καὶ πάντων ἐν τῇ συναγωγῇ οἱ ὀφθαλμοὶ ἦσαν
He sat. And of all in the synagogue the eyes were
816 846 756 3104 4314 846 3754
21 ἀτενίζοντες αὐτῷ. ἤρξατο δὲ λέγειν πρὸς αὐτοὺς ὅτι
fixed on Him. He began And to say to them,

NOTE: Frequent words not numbered: δέ(1161); καί(2531)—and, but; ὁ, ἡ, τό (3588, the)— * above word, look in verse margin for No.

say to them, Today this Scripture has been fulfilled in your ears. 22 And all bore witness to Him, and marveled at the gracious words coming out of His mouth. And they said, Is this not the son of Joseph? 23 And He said to them, Surely you will speak this parable to Me, Physician, heal yourself. What things we heard *were* happening in Capernaum, do also here in your native-place. 24 But He said, Truly I say to you that no prophet is acceptable in his native-place. 25 But truthfully I say to you, There were many widows in Israel in the days of Elijah, when the heaven was shut up over three years and six months, when a great famine came on all the land; 26 and *yet* Elijah was sent to none of them except to Zarephath of Sidon, to a widow woman. 27 And many lepers were in Israel during the *time* of Elisha the prophet, and none of them was made clean except Naaman the Syrian.

28 And all were filled *with* anger, hearing these things in the synagogue. 29 And rising up, they threw Him outside the city, and led Him up to the brow of the hill on which their city was built, in order to throw Him down. 30 But He went away, passing through their midst.

31 And He went down to Capernaum, a city of Galilee. And He was teaching them *on* the sabbaths. 32 And they were astonished at His teaching, because His word was with authority. 33 And in the synagogue was a man who had a spirit of an unclean

4594 4137 1124 3778 1722 3775 5216
Σήμερον πεπλήρωται ἡ γραφὴ αὕτη ἐν τοῖς ὠσὶν ὑμῶν
Today has been fulfilled scripture this in the ears of you.
3956 3140 846 2296 1909 3056
22 καὶ πάντες ἐμαρτύρουν αὐτῷ, καὶ ἐθαύμαζον ἐπὶ τοῖς λόγοις
And all bore witness to Him and marveled at the words
5485 1807 1537 4750 848
τῆς χάριτος τοῖς ἐκπορευομένοις ἐκ τοῦ στόματος αὐτοῦ, καὶ
- of grace proceeding from the mouth of Him. And
3004 3756 3778 2076 5207 2501 2036 4314 846
23 ἔλεγον, Οὐχ οὗτός ἐστιν ὁ υἱὸς Ἰωσήφ; καὶ εἶπε πρὸς αὐτούς.
they said, Not this is the son of Joseph? And He said to them,
3843 2046 3427 3850 5026 2395 2323
Πάντως ἐρεῖτέ μοι τὴν παραβολὴν ταύτην, Ἰατρέ, θερά-
Surely you will say to Me parable this, Physician, heal
4572 3745 191 1096 1722 2584
πευσον σεαυτόν· ὅσα ἠκούσαμεν γενόμενα ἐν τῇ Καπερναούμ,
yourself! What things we heard happening in Capernaum,
4160 5602 1722 3968 4675 2036 281 281
24 ποίησον καὶ ὧδε ἐν τῇ πατρίδι σου. εἶπε δέ, Ἀμὴν λέγω
do also here in the native-place of you. He said And, Truly, I say
5213 3754 3762 4396 1184 2076 1722 3968 848
ὑμῖν ὅτι οὐδεὶς προφήτης δεκτός ἐστιν ἐν τῇ πατρίδι αὐτοῦ.
to you that no prophet acceptable is in the native-place of him.
1909 225 3004 5213 4183 5593 2258/1722
25 ἐπ' ἀληθείας δὲ λέγω ὑμῖν, πολλαὶ χῆραι ἦσαν ἐν ταῖς
on a truth But I say to you, Many widows were in the
2250 2243 1722 2474 3753 2808 3772 1909
ἡμέραις Ἠλίου ἐν τῷ Ἰσραήλ, ὅτε ἐκλείσθη ὁ οὐρανὸς ἐπὶ
days of Elijah in Israel, when was shut up the heaven over
2094 5140 3376 1803 5613 1096 3042 3173 1909 3956
ἔτη τρία καὶ μῆνας ἕξ, ὡς ἐγένετο λιμὸς μέγας ἐπὶ πᾶσαν τὴν
years three and months six, when came a famine great upon all the
1093 4314 3762 846 3992 2243 -1508- 1519
26 γῆν· καὶ πρὸς οὐδεμίαν αὐτῶν ἐπέμφθη Ἠλίας, εἰ μὴ εἰς
land; and to no one of them was sent Elijah except to
4558 4605 4314 1135 5503 4183
27 Σάρεπτα τῆς Σιδῶνος πρὸς γυναῖκα χήραν. καὶ πολλοὶ
Zarephath of Sidon, to a woman, a widow. And many
3015 2258 1909 1666 4396 1722 2474
λεπροὶ ἦσαν ἐπὶ Ἐλισσαίου τοῦ προφήτου ἐν τῷ Ἰσραήλ·
lepers were during Elisha the prophet in – Israel,
3762 846 2511 -1508- 3497 4948
28 καὶ οὐδεὶς αὐτῶν ἐκαθαρίσθη, εἰ μὴ Νεεμὰν ὁ Σύρος. καὶ
and none of them was cleansed except Naaman the Syrian. And
4130 3956 2372 1722 4864 191
ἐπλήσθησαν πάντες θυμοῦ ἐν τῇ συναγωγῇ, ἀκούοντες
were filled all (with) anger in the synagogue hearing
5023 450 1544 846 1854 4172
29 ταῦτα, καὶ ἀναστάντες ἐξέβαλον αὐτὸν ἔξω τῆς πόλεως, καὶ
these things, and rising up they threw Him outside the city, and
71 846 2193 3790 3735 1909/3739 4172
ἤγαγον αὐτὸν ἕως τῆς ὀφρύος τοῦ ὄρους ἐφ' οὗ ἡ πόλις
led Him up to the brow of the hill on which the city
848 3618 1519 2630 846 846
30 αὐτῶν ᾠκοδόμητο, εἰς τὸ κατακρημνίσαι αὐτόν. αὐτὸς δὲ
of them was built, in order to throw down Him. He But
1330 1223 3319 846 4198
διελθὼν διὰ μέσου αὐτῶν ἐπορεύετο.
passing through (the) midst of them went away.

2718 1519 2584 4172 1056
31 Καὶ κατῆλθεν εἰς Καπερναοὺμ πόλιν τῆς Γαλιλαίας· καὶ
And He went down to Capernaum, a city – of Galilee. And
2258 1321 848 1722 4521 1605
32 ἦν διδάσκων αὐτοὺς ἐν τοῖς σάββασι. καὶ ἐξεπλήσσοντο
He was teaching them in the sabbaths. And they were astounded
1909 1322 848 3754 1722 1849 2258 3056 848
33 ἐπὶ τῇ διδαχῇ αὐτοῦ, ὅτι ἐν ἐξουσίᾳ ἦν ὁ λόγος αὐτοῦ. καὶ
at the teaching of Him, for with authority was the word of Him. And
1722 4864 2258 444 2192 4151 1140
ἐν τῇ συναγωγῇ ἦν ἄνθρωπος ἔχων πνεῦμα δαιμονίου
in the synagogue there was a man having a spirit of a demon

demon. And he cried out with a loud voice, 34 saying, Aha! What *is* to us and to You, Jesus, Nazarene? Did You come to destroy us? I know You, who You are, the Holy One of God. 35 And Jesus rebuked him, saying, Be silent, and come out from him! And throwing him into the midst, the demon came out from him, not harming him. 36 And astonishment came on all. And they spoke with one another saying, What word *is* this, that He commands the unclean spirits with authority and power, and they come out? 37 And a report about Him went out into every place of the neighborhood.

169 349 5456 3173 3004 1436 5102 2254
34 ἀκαθάρτου, καὶ ἀνέκραξε φωνῇ μεγάλῃ, λέγων, Ἔα, τί ἡμῖν
unclean, and cried out with a voice great, saying, Aha! What to us
4671 2424 3479 2064 622 2248 1492
καὶ σοί, Ἰησοῦ Ναζαρηνέ; ἦλθες ἀπολέσαι ἡμᾶς; οἶδά
and to You, Jesus, Nazarene? Did You come to destroy us? I know
*1486 4571 5101 * 40 2316 2008 846 2424
35 σε τίς εἶ, ὁ ἅγιος τοῦ Θεοῦ. καὶ ἐπετίμησεν αὐτῷ ὁ Ἰησοῦς,
You, who You are, the holy One of God. And rebuked him Jesus,
3004 5392 1831 1537 846 4496 846
λέγων, Φιμώθητι, καὶ ἔξελθε ἐξ αὐτοῦ. καὶ ῥίψαν αὐτὸν τὸ
saying, Be silent, and come out from him. And throwing him the
1140 1519 3319 1831 575 846 3367 984
36 δαιμόνιον εἰς τὸ μέσον ἐξῆλθεν ἀπ' αὐτοῦ, μηδὲν βλάψαν
demon in the midst came out from him, nothing injuring
846 1096 2285 1909 3956 4814
αὐτόν. καὶ ἐγένετο θάμβος ἐπὶ πάντας, καὶ συνελάλουν πρὸς
him. And came astonishment on all, and they spoke with
240 3004 5101 3056 3778 3754 1722 1849
ἀλλήλους, λέγοντες, Τίς ὁ λόγος οὗτος, ὅτι ἐν ἐξουσίᾳ καὶ
one another, saying, What (is) word this, that with authority and
1411 2004 169 4151 1831
δυνάμει ἐπιτάσσει τοῖς ἀκαθάρτοις πνεύμασι, καὶ ἐξέρχον-
power He commands the unclean spirits, and they come
1607 2279 4012 846 1519 3956 5117
37 ται; καὶ ἐξεπορεύετο ἦχος περὶ αὐτοῦ εἰς πάντα τόπον τῆς
out? And went forth a rumor concerning Him into every place of the
4066
περιχώρου.
neighborhood.

38 And rising up from the synagogue, He went into the house of Simon. And the mother-in-law of Simon was being seized with a great fever. And they asked Him concerning her. 39 And standing over her, He rebuked the fever; and it left her. And rising up instantly, she served them. 40 And the sun sinking, all, as many as had sick ones with various diseases, brought them to Him. And laying hands on each one of them, He healed them. 41 And also demons came out from many, crying out and saying, You are the Christ, the Son of God! And rebuking *them,* He did not

450 1537 4864 1525 1519 3614
38 Ἀναστὰς δὲ ἐκ τῆς συναγωγῆς, εἰσῆλθεν εἰς τὴν οἰκίαν
rising up And from the synagogue, He went into the house
4613 3994 4613 2258 4912 4446
Σίμωνος· ἡ πενθερὰ δὲ τοῦ Σίμωνος ἦν συνεχομένη πυρετῷ
of Simon. The mother-in-law And of Simon was being seized with a fever
3173 2065 846 4012 846 2186
39 μεγάλῳ· καὶ ἠρώτησαν αὐτὸν περὶ αὐτῆς. καὶ ἐπιστὰς
great, and they ask Him concerning her. And standing
1883 846 2008 4446 863 846
ἐπάνω αὐτῆς, ἐπετίμησε τῷ πυρετῷ, καὶ ἀφῆκεν αὐτήν·
over her, He rebuked the fever; and it left her.
3916 450 1247 846
παραχρῆμα δὲ ἀναστᾶσα διηκόνει αὐτοῖς.
at once And rising up she served them.
1416 2246 3956 3745 2192 770
40 Δύνοντος δὲ τοῦ ἡλίου, πάντες ὅσοι εἶχον ἀσθενοῦντας
sinking And the sun, all, as many as had sick ones
3554 4164 71 846 4314 846 1520
νόσοις ποικίλαις ἤγαγον αὐτοὺς πρὸς αὐτόν· ὁ δὲ ἑνὶ
with various diseases, brought them to Him. He And one
1538 846 5495 2007 2323 846
ἑκάστῳ αὐτῶν τὰς χεῖρας ἐπιθεὶς ἐθεράπευσεν αὐτούς.
each of them the hands laying on healed them.
1831 1140 575 4183 2896
41 ἐξήρχετο δὲ καὶ δαιμόνια ἀπὸ πολλῶν, κράζοντα καὶ
came out And also demons from many, crying out and
3004 3754 4771 * 5547 5207 2316 2008
*1488 λέγοντα ὅτι Σὺ εἶ ὁ Χριστὸς ὁ υἱὸς τοῦ Θεοῦ. καὶ ἐπιτιμῶν
saying, You are the Christ, the Son of God. And rebuking
3756 1439 846 2980 3754 1492 5547 846 1511
οὐκ εἴα αὐτὰ λαλεῖν, ὅτι ᾔδεισαν τὸν Χριστὸν αὐτὸν εἶναι.
not He allowed them to speak, for they knew the Christ Him to be.

allow them to speak; for they knew Him to be the Christ. 42 And day coming, going out He went into a desert place. And the crowds looked for Him, and came up to Him, and held Him fast, not to pass away from them. 43 But He said to

1096 2250 1831 4198 1519 2048 5117
42 Γενομένης δὲ ἡμέρας, ἐξελθὼν ἐπορεύθη εἰς ἔρημον τόπον,
coming and day, going out He went to a desert place.
3793 2212 846 2064 2193 846
καὶ οἱ ὄχλοι ἐζήτουν αὐτόν, καὶ ἦλθον ἕως αὐτοῦ, καὶ
And the crowds looked for Him, and came up to Him, and
2722 846 3361 4198 575 846 2036
43 κατεῖχον αὐτὸν τοῦ μὴ πορεύεσθαι ἀπ' αὐτῶν. ὁ δὲ εἶπε
held fast Him, not to pass from them. He But said

them. It is right for Me to preach the gospel, the kingdom of God, to the other cities, because I was sent on this *mission*.

[44]And He was proclaiming in the synagogues of Galilee.

CHAPTER 5

[1]And it happened that the crowd was pressing on Him to hear the word of God. And He was standing by Lake Gennesaret. [2]And He saw two boats standing by the lake, but the fishermen had left them and were washing the nets. [3]And entering into one of the boats, which was Simon's, He asked him to put out a little from the land. And sitting down, He taught the crowd from the boat. [4]And as He quit speaking, He said to Simon, Put out into the deep, and let down your nets for a haul. [5]And answering Simon said to Him, Master, laboring all through the night we took nothing. But at Your word I will let down the net. [6]And doing this, they netted a great multitude of fish; and their net was being torn.

[7]And they signaled the partners, those in the other boat, to come *and* help them. And they came and filled both the boats, so that they were sinking. [8]And seeing, Simon Peter fell at the knees of Jesus, saying, Depart from me, for I am a sinful man, Lord. [9]For astonishment took hold of him, and all those with him, at the haul of fish which they took; [10]and in the same way also, James and John, *the* sons of Zebedee,

4314 846 3754 2087 4172 2097
πρὸς αὐτοὺς ὅτι Καὶ ταῖς ἑτέραις πόλεσιν εὐαγγελίσασθαί
to them. Also to the other cities to preach the gospel
3165 1163 932 2316 3754 1519 5124 649
με δεῖ τὴν βασιλείαν τοῦ Θεοῦ· ὅτι εἰς τοῦτο ἀπέσταλμαι.
Me it behoves the kingdom of God, for on this I was sent.
2258 2784 1722 4864 1056
44 Καὶ ἦν κηρύσσων ἐν ταῖς συναγωγαῖς τῆς Γαλιλαίας.
And He was proclaiming in the synagogues of Galilee.

CHAPTER 5

1096 1722 3793 1945 846 191
1 Ἐγένετο δὲ ἐν τῷ τὸν ὄχλον ἐπικεῖσθαι αὐτῷ τοῦ ἀκούειν
it was And in the crowd pressing on Him to hear
3056 2316 846 2258 2476 3844 3041
τὸν λόγον τοῦ Θεοῦ, καὶ αὐτὸς ἦν ἑστὼς παρὰ τὴν λίμνην
the word of God, even He was standing by the lake
1082 1492 1417 4143 2476 3844 3041
2 Γεννησαρέτ· καὶ εἶδε δύο πλοῖα ἑστῶτα παρὰ τὴν λίμνην·
Gennesaret. And He saw two boats standing by the lake;
231 576 575 846 637 1350
οἱ δὲ ἁλιεῖς ἀποβάντες ἀπ' αὐτῶν ἀπέπλυναν τὰ δίκτυα.
the but fishermen having gone from them were washing the nets.
1684 1519 1722 4143 3739 2258 4613 2065
3 ἐμβὰς δὲ εἰς ἓν τῶν πλοίων, ὃ ἦν τοῦ Σίμωνος, ἠρώτησεν
entering And into one of the boats, which was Simon's. He asked
846 575 1093 1877 3641 2523
αὐτὸν ἀπὸ τῆς γῆς ἐπαναγαγεῖν ὀλίγον. καὶ καθίσας
him from the land to put out a little. And sitting
1321 1537 4143 3793 5613 3973
4 ἐδίδασκεν ἐκ τοῦ πλοίου τοὺς ὄχλους. ὡς δὲ ἐπαύσατο
He taught from the boat the crowd. as And He quit
2980 2036 4314 4613 1877 1519 899
λαλῶν, εἶπε πρὸς τὸν Σίμωνα, Ἐπανάγαγε εἰς τὸ βάθος,
Speaking, He said to Simon, Put out into the deep,
5465 1350 5216 1519 61 611
5 καὶ χαλάσατε τὰ δίκτυα ὑμῶν εἰς ἄγραν. καὶ ἀποκριθεὶς ὁ
and let down the nets of you for a haul. And answering
4613 2036 846 1988 1223 3650 3571 2872
Σίμων εἶπεν αὐτῷ, Ἐπιστάτα, δι' ὅλης τῆς νυκτὸς κοπιά-
Simon said to Him, Master, through all the night laboring
3762 2983 1909 4487 4675 5465
σαντες οὐδὲν ἐλάβομεν· ἐπὶ δὲ τῷ ῥήματί σου χαλάσω τὸ
nothing we took, at but the word of You I will let down the
1350 5124 4160 4788 2486 4128
6 δίκτυον. καὶ τοῦτο ποιήσαντες, συνέκλεισαν ἰχθύων πλῆθος
net. And this doing, they enclosed of fish a multitude
4183 1284 1350 848 2956
7 πολύ· διερρήγνυτο δὲ τὸ δίκτυον αὐτῶν· καὶ κατένευσαν
much was being torn and the net of them. And they signaled
3353 1722 2087 4143 2064 4815
τοῖς μετόχοις τοῖς ἐν τῷ ἑτέρῳ πλοίῳ, τοῦ ἐλθόντας συλ-
the partners, those in the other boat, coming to
846 2064 4130 297
λαβέσθαι αὐτοῖς· καὶ ἦλθον καὶ ἔπλησαν ἀμφότερα τὰ
help them; and they came and filled both the
4143 5620 1036 846 1492 4613 4074
8 πλοῖα, ὥστε βυθίζεσθαι αὐτά. Ἰδὼν δὲ Σίμων Πέτρος
boats, so as were sinking they. having seen And Simon Peter
4363 1119 2424 3005 1831 575 1700
προσέπεσε τοῖς γόνασι τοῦ Ἰησοῦ, λέγων, Ἔξελθε ἀπ' ἐμοῦ,
fell at the knees of Jesus, saying, Depart from me,
3754 435 268 1510 2962 2285 1063 4023
9 ὅτι ἀνὴρ ἁμαρτωλός εἰμι, Κύριε. θάμβος γὰρ περιέσχεν
because a man sinful I am. Lord. astonishment For seized
846 3956 4862 846 1909 61 2486
αὐτὸν καὶ πάντας τοὺς σὺν αὐτῷ, ἐπὶ τῇ ἄγρᾳ τῶν ἰχθύων
him and all the (ones) with him at the haul – of fish
3739 4815 3668 2385 2491 5207
10 ᾗ συνέλαβον· ὁμοίως δὲ καὶ Ἰάκωβον καὶ Ἰωάννην, υἱοὺς
which they took; likewise and both James and John, sons

who were partners with Simon. And Jesus said to Simon, Do not fear. From now on you will be taking men alive. [11]And bringing the boats down onto the land, forsaking all things, they followed Him.

[12]And it happened, in His being in one of the cities, even behold, a man full of leprosy. And seeing Jesus, falling on *his* face, he begged Him, saying, Lord, if You choose, You are able to cleanse me. [13]And stretching out the hand, He touched him, saying, I will; be cleansed! And instantly the leprosy departed from him. [14]And He charged him to tell no one, but going away, show yourself to the priest, and offer concerning your cleansing, as Moses commanded, for a testimony to them.

[15]But the word about Him spread even more. And large crowds were coming to hear, and to be healed from their infirmities by Him. [16]But He was drawing back in the desert, and praying.

[17]And it happened on one of the days, even He was teaching. And Pharisees and teachers of *the* Law were sitting by, who were coming out of every village of Galilee and Judea, and Jerusalem. And *the* power of *the* Lord was there, for the curing of them. [18]And, behold, men carrying on a cot a man who was paralyzed. And they sought to bring him in, and to lay *him* before Him. [19]And not finding a way through *which* they might bring him in through the crowd, going up on the housetop, they let him down through the tiles with

2199 3739 2258 2844 4613 2036 4314
Ζεβεδαίου, οἳ ἦσαν κοινωνοὶ τῷ Σίμωνι. καὶ εἶπε πρὸς τὸν
of Zebedee, who were sharers with Simon. And said to
4613 2424 3361 5399 575 3568 444 2071
Σίμωνα ὁ Ἰησοῦς, Μὴ φοβοῦ· ἀπὸ τοῦ νῦν ἀνθρώπους ἔσῃ
Simon – Jesus, Not do fear; from – now men you will be
2221 2609 4143 1909 1093 863
11 ζωγρῶν. καὶ καταγαγόντες τὰ πλοῖα ἐπὶ τὴν γῆν, ἀφέντες
taking alive. And bringing down the boats onto the land, forsaking
537 190 846
ἅπαντα, ἠκολούθησαν αὐτῷ.
all things, they followed Him.
1096 1722 1511 846 1722 3391 4172
12 Καὶ ἐγένετο, ἐν τῷ εἶναι αὐτὸν ἐν μιᾷ τῶν πόλεων, καὶ
And it was, in the being of Him in one of the cities, and
2400 435 4134 3014 1492 2424 4098
ἰδού, ἀνὴρ πλήρης λέπρας· καὶ ἰδὼν τὸν Ἰησοῦν, πεσὼν
behold, a man full of leprosy; and seeing – Jesus, having fallen
1909 4383 1189 846 3004 2962 1437 2309
ἐπὶ πρόσωπον, ἐδεήθη αὐτοῦ, λέγων, Κύριε, ἐὰν θέλῃς,
on (his) face, he begged Him, saying, Lord, if You choose,
1410 3165 2511 1614 5495 680 846
13 δύνασαί με καθαρίσαι. καὶ ἐκτείνας τὴν χεῖρα ἥψατο αὐτοῦ,
You are able Me to cleanse. And stretching the hand He touched him,
2036 2309 2511 2112 3014 565 575
εἰπών, Θέλω, καθαρίσθητι. καὶ εὐθέως ἡ λέπρα ἀπῆλθεν ἀπ'
saying, I will, be cleansed! And instantly the leprosy departed from
846 846 3853 846 3367 2036 235
14 αὐτοῦ. καὶ αὐτὸς παρήγγειλεν αὐτῷ μηδενὶ εἰπεῖν· ἀλλὰ
him. And He charged him no one to tell, but
565 1166 4572 2409 4374 4012
ἀπελθὼν δεῖξον σεαυτὸν τῷ ἱερεῖ, καὶ προσένεγκε περὶ τοῦ
going away show yourself to the priest, and offer concerning the
2512 4675 2531 4367 3475 1519 3142
καθαρισμοῦ σου, καθὼς προσέταξε Μωσῆς, εἰς μαρτύριον
cleansing of you, as commanded Moses, for a testimony
846 1330 3123 3056 4012 846 4905
15 αὐτοῖς. διήρχετο δὲ μᾶλλον ὁ λόγος περὶ αὐτοῦ· καὶ συν-
to them. spread But even more the word concerning Him, and were
3793 4183 191 2323 5259 846
ήρχοντο ὄχλοι πολλοὶ ἀκούειν, καὶ θεραπεύεσθαι ὑπ' αὐτοῦ
coming crowds great to hear, and to be healed by Him
575 769 848 846 2258 5298 1722
16 ἀπὸ τῶν ἀσθενειῶν αὐτῶν. αὐτὸς δὲ ἦν ὑποχωρῶν ἐν ταῖς
from the infirmities of them. He But was withdrawing in the
2048 4336
ἐρήμοις καὶ προσευχόμενος.
desert and praying.
1096 1722 3391 2250 846 2258 1321
17 Καὶ ἐγένετο ἐν μιᾷ τῶν ἡμερῶν, καὶ αὐτὸς ἦν διδάσκων·
And it was, on one of the days, and He was teaching,
2258 2521 5330 3547 3739 2258
καὶ ἦσαν καθήμενοι Φαρισαῖοι καὶ νομοδιδάσκαλοι, οἳ ἦσαν
and were sitting Pharisees and teachers of law, who were
2064 1537 3956 2968 1056 2449
ἐληλυθότες ἐκ πάσης κώμης τῆς Γαλιλαίας καὶ Ἰουδαίας καὶ
coming out of every village of Galilee and Judea and
2419 1411 2962 2258 1519 2390 846
Ἱερουσαλήμ· καὶ δύναμις Κυρίου ἦν εἰς τὸ ἰᾶσθαι αὐτούς.
Jerusalem. And power of (the) Lord was, to the curing (of) them.
2400 435 5342 1909 2825 444 3739 2258 3886
18 καὶ ἰδού, ἄνδρες φέροντες ἐπὶ κλίνης ἄνθρωπον ὃς ἦν παρα-
And, behold, men carrying on a cot a man who was
2312 846 1533 5087 1799
λελυμένος, καὶ ἐζήτουν αὐτὸν εἰσενεγκεῖν καὶ θεῖναι ἐνώπιον
paralyzed; and they sought him to bring in and to lay before
846 3361 2147 1223 4119 1533 846 1223
19 αὐτοῦ· καὶ μὴ εὑρόντες διὰ ποίας εἰσενέγκωσιν αὐτὸν διὰ
Him. And not finding by what way they may bring in him through
3793 305 1909 1430 1223 2766
τὸν ὄχλον, ἀναβάντες ἐπὶ τὸ δῶμα, διὰ τῶν κεράμων
the crowd, going up on the housetop, through the tiles

2524 846 4862 2826 1519 3319 1715
καθῆκαν αὐτὸν σὺν τῷ κλινιδίῳ εἰς τὸ μέσον ἔμπροσθεν τοῦ
they let down him with the cot into the midst in front of —
2424 1492 4102 848 2036 846 444
20 Ἰησοῦ καὶ ἰδὼν τὴν πίστιν αὐτῶν, εἶπεν αὐτῷ, Ἄνθρωπε,
Jesus. And seeing the faith of them, He said to him, Man,
863 4671 266 4675 756 1260
21 ἀφέωνταί σοι αἱ ἁμαρτίαι σου. καὶ ἤρξαντο διαλογίζεσθαι
have been forgiven you the sins of you. And began to reason
1122 5330 3004 5101 2076 3778
οἱ γραμματεῖς καὶ οἱ Φαρισαῖοι, λέγοντες, Τίς ἐστιν οὗτος
the scribes and the Pharisees, saying, Who is this one
3739 2980 988 5101 1410 863 266 –1508–
ὃς λαλεῖ βλασφημίας; τίς δύναται ἀφιέναι ἁμαρτίας, εἰ μὴ
who speaks blasphemies? Who is able to forgive sins, except
3441 2316 1921 2424 1261
22 μόνος ὁ Θεός; ἐπιγνοὺς δὲ ὁ Ἰησοῦς τοὺς διαλογισμοὺς
only God? knowing But Jesus the reasonings
848 611 2036 4314 846 5101 1260 1722
αὐτῶν ἀποκριθεὶς εἶπε πρὸς αὐτούς, Τί διαλογίζεσθε ἐν ταῖς
of them, answering said to them, Why do you reason in the
2588 5216 5101 2076 2123 2036 863
23 καρδίαις ὑμῶν; τί ἐστιν εὐκοπώτερον, εἰπεῖν, Ἀφέωνταί
hearts of you? What is easier, to say, Have been forgiven
4671 266 4675 2228 2036 1453 4043 2443
σοι αἱ ἁμαρτίαι σου, ἢ εἰπεῖν, Ἔγειραι καὶ περιπάτει; ἵνα
you the sins of you, or to say, Rise up and walk? that
1492 3754 1849 2192 5207 444 1909 1093
24 δὲ εἰδῆτε ὅτι ἐξουσίαν ἔχει ὁ υἱὸς τοῦ ἀνθρώπου ἐπὶ τῆς γῆς
But you may know authority has the Son of man on the earth
863 266 2036 3886 4671 3004
ἀφιέναι ἁμαρτίας (εἶπε τῷ παραλελυμένῳ), Σοὶ λέγω,
to forgive sins, He said to the paralytic, To you I say,
1453 142 2826 4675 4198 1519 3624
ἔγειραι, καὶ ἄρας τὸ κλινίδιόν σου, πορεύου εἰς τὸν οἶκόν
Rise up, and taking the cot of you, go to the house
4675 3916 450 1799 846 142 1909 3739
25 σου. καὶ παραχρῆμα ἀναστὰς ἐνώπιον αὐτῶν, ἄρας ἐφ᾽ ᾧ
of you. And at once rising up before them, taking on which
2621 565 1519 3624 848 1392 2316
κατέκειτο, ἀπῆλθεν εἰς τὸν οἶκον αὐτοῦ, δοξάζων τὸν Θεόν.
he was lying, he went to the house of him, glorifying God.
1611 2983 537 1392 2316
26 καὶ ἔκστασις ἔλαβεν ἅπαντας, καὶ ἐδόξαζον τὸν Θεόν, καὶ
And amazement seized all, and they glorified God, and
4130 5401 3004 3754 1492 3861
ἐπλήσθησαν φόβου, λέγοντες ὅτι Εἴδομεν παράδοξα
were filled (with) fear, saying, We saw wonderful things
4594
σήμερον.
today.
3326 5023 1831 2300 5057 3686
27 Καὶ μετὰ ταῦτα ἐξῆλθε, καὶ ἐθεάσατο τελώνην, ὀνόματι
And after these things He went, and saw a tax-collector, by name
3018 2521 1909 5058 2036 846 190
Λευΐν, καθήμενον ἐπὶ τὸ τελώνιον, καὶ εἶπεν αὐτῷ, Ἀκολού-
Levi, sitting at the custom-house, and said to him, Follow
3427 2641 537 450 190 846
28 θει μοι. καὶ καταλιπὼν ἅπαντα, ἀναστὰς ἠκολούθησεν αὐτῷ.
Me! And having left all things, rising up he followed Him.
4160 1403 3173 3018 846 1722 3614 848
29 καὶ ἐποίησε δοχὴν μεγάλην ὁ Λευῒς αὐτῷ ἐν τῇ οἰκίᾳ αὐτοῦ·
And made a feast great Levi for Him in the house of him;
2258 3793 5057 4183 243 3739 2252 3326
καὶ ἦν ὄχλος τελωνῶν πολύς, καὶ ἄλλων οἳ ἦσαν μετ᾽
and was a crowd of tax-collectors, much, and of others who were with
846 2621 1111 1122 848
30 αὐτῶν κατακείμενοι. καὶ ἐγόγγυζον οἱ γραμματεῖς αὐτῶν
them having reclined. And murmured the scribes of them
5330 4314 3101 848 3004 1302
καὶ οἱ Φαρισαῖοι πρὸς τοὺς μαθητὰς αὐτοῦ, λέγοντες, Διατί
and the Pharisees at the disciples of Him, saying, Why

the cot, into the midst, in front of Jesus. [20]And seeing their faith, He said to him, Man, your sins have been forgiven you. [21]And the scribes and the Pharisees began to reason, saying, Who is this who speaks blasphemies? Who is able to forgive sins, except God alone? [22]But knowing their thoughts, answering Jesus said to them, Why do you reason in your hearts?

[23]Which is easier, to say, Your sins have been forgiven you; or to say, Rise up and walk? [24]But that you may know that the Son of man has authority on the earth to forgive sins, He said to the paralytic, I say to you, Rise up, and take your cot *and* go to your house.

[25]And rising up at once before them, taking up *that* on which he was lying, he went to his house, glorifying God. [26]And amazement seized all, and they glorified God, and were filled *with* fear, saying, We saw wonderful things today.

[27]And after these things, He went out and saw a tax-collector named Levi, sitting at the tax office. And *He* said to him, Follow Me! [28]And leaving all, rising up he followed Him. [29]And Levi made a great feast for Him in his house. And there was a crowd of many tax-collectors reclining, and of others who were with them. [30]And their scribes and the Pharisees murmured at His disciples, saying, Why do

you eat and drink with tax-collectors and sinners? [31]And answering Jesus said to them, Those who are sound have no need of a physician, but those who have illness. [32]I did not come to call the righteous, but sinners to repentance.

[33]But they said to Him, Why do John's disciples fast often, and make prayers, and likewise those of the Pharisees, but those *close* to You eat and drink? [34]But He said to them, You are not able to make the sons of the bridechamber fast while the bridegroom is with them. [35]But days will come, even when the bridegroom is taken away from them, then in those days they will fast.

[36]And He also told a parable to them: No one puts a piece of a new garment on an old garment; otherwise, both the new will tear, and *it* does not match *the* piece from the new. [37]And no one puts new wine into old skins; otherwise, the new wine will burst the skins, and it will be poured out, and the skins will perish. [38]But new wine is to be put into new skins, and both are preserved together. [39]And no one drinking old *wine* immediately desires new; for he says, The old is better.

CHAPTER 6

[1]And it happened on the second chief sabbath, He passed along through the sown fields. And His disciples plucked the heads, and were eating, rubbing with the hands. [2]But some of the Pharisees said to them, Why do you do that which is not lawful to do on

3326 5057 268 2068 4095
μετὰ τελωνῶν καὶ ἁμαρτωλῶν ἐσθίετε καὶ πίνετε ; καὶ
with tax-collectors and sinners do you eat and drink? And
611 2424 2036 4314 4846 3756 5532 2192
31 ἀποκριθεὶς ὁ Ἰησοῦς εἶπε πρὸς αὐτούς, Οὐ χρείαν ἔχουσιν
answering Jesus said to them, Not need have
5198 2395 235 2560 2192 3756 2064
32 οἱ ὑγιαίνοντες ἰατροῦ, ἀλλ' οἱ κακῶς ἔχοντες. οὐκ ἐλήλυθα
those being sound of a physician, but those illness having. not I have come
2564 1342 235 268 1519 3341
καλέσαι δικαίους, ἀλλὰ ἁμαρτωλοὺς εἰς μετάνοιαν. οἱ δὲ
to call righteous ones, but sinners to repentance. they But
2036 4314 846 1302 3101 2491 3522
33 εἶπον πρὸς αὐτόν, Διατί οἱ μαθηταὶ Ἰωάννου νηστεύουσι
said to Him, Why the disciples of John fast
4437 1162 4160 3668 5330
πυκνά, καὶ δεήσεις ποιοῦνται, ὁμοίως καὶ οἱ τῶν Φαρισαίων·
often, and prayers make, likewise also those of the Pharisees,
4671 2068 4095 2036 4314 846 3361
34 οἱ δὲ σοὶ ἐσθίουσι καὶ πίνουσιν ; ὁ δὲ εἶπε πρὸς αὐτούς, Μὴ
those but to you eat and drink? He But said to them, Not
3739 1410 5207 3567 1722* 3566 3326 846
δύνασθε τοὺς υἱοὺς τοῦ νυμφῶνος, ἐν ᾧ ὁ νυμφίος μετ' αὐτῶν
are able the sons of the bride-chamber, while the groom with them
2076 4160 3522 2064 2250 3752
35 ἐστι, ποιῆσαι νηστεύειν ; ἐλεύσονται δὲ ἡμέραι, καὶ ὅταν
is to make to fast, will come but days, and when
522 575 846 3566 5119 3522 1722
ἀπαρθῇ ἀπ' αὐτῶν ὁ νυμφίος, τότε νηστεύσουσιν ἐν
is taken away from them the bridegroom then they will fast in
1565 2250 3004 3850 4314 846
36 ἐκείναις ταῖς ἡμέραις. ἔλεγε δὲ καὶ παραβολὴν πρὸς αὐτοὺς
those days. He told And also a parable to them,
3754/3762 1915 2440 2537 1911 1909 2440
ὅτι Οὐδεὶς ἐπίβλημα ἱματίου καινοῦ ἐπιβάλλει ἐπὶ ἱμάτιον
– No one a piece of a garment new puts on a garment
3820 -- 1490 -- 2537 4977 3820
παλαιόν· εἰ δὲ μήγε, καὶ τὸ καινὸν σχίζει, καὶ τῷ παλαιῷ
old, otherwise, both the new will tear, and with the old
3756 4856 1915 575 2537 3762 906
37 οὐ συμφωνεῖ ἐπίβλημα τὸ ἀπὸ τοῦ καινοῦ. καὶ οὐδεὶς βάλλει
not does agree (the) piece from the new. And no one puts
3631 3501 1519 779 3820 -- 1490 -- 4486 3501 3631
οἶνον νέον εἰς ἀσκοὺς παλαιούς· εἰ δὲ μήγε, ῥήξει ὁ νέος οἶνος
wine fresh into wineskins old; otherwise, will burst the fresh wine
779 846 1632 779 622
τοὺς ἀσκούς, καὶ αὐτὸς ἐκχυθήσεται, καὶ οἱ ἀσκοὶ ἀπολοῦν-
the wineskins, and it will be poured out, and the wineskins will
235 3331 3501/1519/779 2537 992 297
38 ται. ἀλλὰ οἶνον νέον εἰς ἀσκοὺς καινοὺς βλητέον. καὶ ἀμφό-
perish. But wine fresh into wineskins new is to be put, and both
4933 3762 4095 3820 2112 2309
τεροι συντηροῦνται. καὶ οὐδεὶς πιὼν παλαιὸν εὐθέως θέλει
are preserved together. And no one drinking old at once desires
3501 3004 1063 3820 5543 2076
νέον· λέγει γάρ, Ὁ παλαιὸς χρηστότερός ἐστιν.
new; he says, for, The old better is.

CHAPTER 6

1096 1722 4521 1207 1279
1 Ἐγένετο δὲ ἐν σαββάτῳ δευτεροπρώτῳ διαπορεύεσθαι
it was And on a sabbath the second chief, passed along
846 1223 4702 5089 3101 848
αὐτὸν διὰ τῶν σπορίμων· καὶ ἔτιλλον οἱ μαθηταὶ αὐτοῦ
He through the sown fields, and plucked the disciples of Him
4719 2068 5597 5495 5100
2 τοὺς στάχυας, καὶ ἤσθιον, ψώχοντες ταῖς χερσί. τινὲς δὲ τῶν
the heads, and were eating, rubbing with the hands. some And of the
5330 2036 846 5101 4160 3739 3756 1832 4160 1722
Φαρισαίων εἶπον αὐτοῖς, Τί ποιεῖτε ὃ οὐκ ἔξεστι ποιεῖν ἐν
Pharisees said to them, Why do you what not is lawful to do on

NOTE: Frequent words not numbered: δέ(1161); καί(2531)—and, but; ὁ, ἡ, τό (3588, the)— * above word, look in verse margin for No.

the sabbaths? [3]And
answering Jesus said to
them, Have you never read
this, what David did when
he hungered, and those being with him? [4]How he
went into the house of God,
and he took the Show-
bread, and ate, and even
gave to those with him—
which it is not lawful to eat,
except only the priests?
[5]And He said to them, The
Son of man is Lord of the
sabbath also.

[6]And it also happened on
another sabbath, He going
into the synagogue and
teaching. And a man was
there, and his right hand
was withered. [7]And the
scribes and the Pharisees
kept close by Him, *to see* if
He would heal on the
sabbath, so that they might
find a charge against Him.
[8]But He knew their reasonings. And *He* said to the
man having the withered
hand, Rise up, and stand in
the middle! And rising up,
he stood. [9]Then Jesus
said to them, I will ask you
one *thing,* Is it lawful to do
good on the sabbaths, or to
do ill; to save a soul, or to
destroy *it?* [10]And having
looked around at them all,
He said to the man, Stretch
out your hand! And he did
so. And his hand was
restored sound as the
other. [11]But they were
filled *with* madness, and
talked to one another *as to*
what they might do to
Jesus.

[12]And it happened in
these days, He went out
into the mountain to pray.
And He was spending the
night in prayer to God.

[13]And when it became day,
He called His disciples,

4521 611 4314 846 2036 2424
3 τοις σάββασι ; καὶ ἀποκριθεὶς πρὸς αὐτοὺς εἶπεν ὁ Ἰησοῦς,
the sabbaths? And answering to them said Jesus,
3761 5124 314 3739 4160 1138 3698 3983
Οὐδὲ τοῦτο ἀνέγνωτε, ὃ ἐποίησε Δαβίδ, ὁπότε ἐπείνασεν
Not this you read, what did David when he hungered
846 3326 846 5607 5613 1525 1519 3624
4 αὐτὸς καὶ οἱ μετ᾽ αὐτοῦ ὄντες ; ὡς εἰσῆλθεν εἰς τὸν οἶκον τοῦ
he and those with him being? As he entered into the house
2316 740 4286 2983 5315
Θεοῦ, καὶ τοὺς ἄρτους τῆς προθέσεως ἔλαβε, καὶ ἔφαγε, καὶ
of God, and the loaves of the presentation he took and ate, and
1325 3326 846 3739 3756 1832 5315 -1508- 3441
ἔδωκε καὶ τοῖς μετ᾽ αὐτοῦ, οὓς οὐκ ἔξεστι φαγεῖν εἰ μὴ μόνους
gave even to those with him, which not it is lawful to eat except only
2409 3004 846 3754 2962 2076 5207
5 τοὺς ἱερεῖς ; καὶ ἔλεγεν αὐτοῖς ὅτι Κύριός ἐστιν ὁ υἱὸς τοῦ
the priests? And he said to them, Lord is The Son
444 4521
ἀνθρώπου καὶ τοῦ σαββάτου.
of man even of the sabbath.
1096 1722 2089 4521 1525 846 1519
6 Ἐγένετο δὲ καὶ ἐν ἑτέρῳ σαββάτῳ εἰσελθεῖν αὐτὸν εἰς τὴν
it was And also on another sabbath, entering He into the
4864 1321 2258 1563 444 5495
συναγωγὴν καὶ διδάσκειν· καὶ ἦν ἐκεῖ ἄνθρωπος, καὶ ἡ χεὶρ
synagogue and teaching; and was there a man, and the hand
848 1188 2258 3584 3906 846 1122
7 αὐτοῦ ἡ δεξιὰ ἦν ξηρα. παρετήρουν δὲ αὐτὸν οἱ γραμματεῖς
of him, the right, was withered. kept close by And Him the scribes
5330 1487 1722 4521 2323 2443 2147
καὶ οἱ Φαρισαῖοι, εἰ ἐν τῷ σαββάτῳ θεραπεύσει· ἵνα εὕρωσι
and the Pharisees, if on the sabbath He will heal, that they may find
2724 846 846 1492 1261 848
8 κατηγορίαν αὐτοῦ. αὐτὸς δὲ ᾔδει τοὺς διαλογισμοὺς αὐτῶν,
an accusation of Him. He But knew the reasonings of them,
2036 444 3584 2192 5495 1453
καὶ εἶπε τῷ ἀνθρώπῳ τῷ ξηρὰν ἔχοντι τὴν χεῖρα, Ἔγειραι,
and said to the man withered having the hand, Rise up
2476 1519 3319 450 2476 2036 3767 2424
9 καὶ στῆθι εἰς τὸ μέσον. ὁ δὲ ἀναστὰς ἔστη. εἶπεν οὖν ὁ Ἰησοῦς
and stand, in the middle! he And rising up stood. said Then Jesus
4314 846 1905 5209 5101 1832 4521
πρὸς αὐτούς, Ἐπερωτήσω ὑμᾶς τί, Ἔξεστι τοῖς σάββασιν,
to them, I will ask you one: Is it lawful on the sabbaths
15 2228 2554 5590 4982 2228 622
ἀγαθοποιῆσαι ἢ κακοποιῆσαι ; ψυχὴν σῶσαι ἢ ἀπολέσαι ;
to do good, or to do ill? A soul to save, or to destroy?
4017 3956 846 2036 444
10 καὶ περιβλεψάμενος πάντας αὐτούς, εἶπε τῷ ἀνθρώπῳ,
And looking around at all (of) them, He said to the man,
1614 5495 4675 4160 3779 600
Ἔκτεινον τὴν χεῖρά σου. ὁ δὲ ἐποίησεν οὕτω. καὶ ἀποκατε-
Stretch out the hand of you. he And did so. And was
5495 848 5199 5613 243 846 4130
11 στάθη ἡ χεὶρ αὐτοῦ ὑγιὴς ὡς ἡ ἄλλη. αὐτοὶ δὲ ἐπλήσθησαν
restored the hand of him sound as the other. they But were filled
454 1255 4314 240 5101 302 4160
ἀνοίας· καὶ διελάλουν πρὸς ἀλλήλους, τί ἂν ποιήσειαν τῷ
(with) madness and talked to one another, what they might do
2424
Ἰησοῦ.
to Jesus.
1096 1722 2250 5025 1821 1519 3735
12 Ἐγένετο δὲ ἐν ταῖς ἡμέραις ταύταις ἐξῆλθεν εἰς τὸ ὄρος
it was And in days these, He went out into the mount
4336 2258 1273 1722 4335
προσεύξασθαι· καὶ ἦν διανυκτερεύων ἐν τῇ προσευχῇ τοῦ
to pray, and He was spending the night in prayer
2316 3753 1096 2250 4377 3101
13 Θεοῦ. καὶ ὅτε ἐγένετο ἡμέρα, προσεφώνησε τοὺς μαθητὰς
of God. And when it became day, He called to the disciples

also choosing out twelve from them, whom He also named apostles: [14]Simon, whom He also named Peter; and his brother Andrew; James and John; Philip and Bartholomew; [15]Matthew and Thomas; James the *son* of Alpheus, and Simon, the *one* being called Zealot; [16]Judas *brother* of James, and Judas Iscariot, who also became *the* betrayer.

[17]And coming down with them, he stood on a level place. And a crowd of His disciples, and a great multitude of the people from all Judea and Jerusalem, and *from* the coast country of Tyre and Sidon, *were there*. *These* came to hear Him, and to be healed from their diseases—[18]also those who had been tormented by unclean spirits. And they were healed. [19]And all the crowd sought to touch Him, because power went out from Him and healed all.

[20]And lifting up His eyes to His disciples, He said:

Blessed *are* the poor, for the kingdom of God is yours.

[21]Blessed *are* those hungering now, for you will be filled.

Blessed *are* those weeping now, for you will laugh.

[22]Blessed *are* you when men hate you, and when they cut you off, and will reproach *you*, and will cast out your name as evil, on account of the Son of man —[23]rejoice in that day, and leap for joy; for, behold, your reward *is* much in Heaven! For their fathers did according to these things to the prophets.

[24]But woe to you, rich ones, for you have your

848 1586 575 846 1427 3739 652
αὐτοῦ· καὶ ἐκλεξάμενος ἀπ' αὐτῶν δώδεκα, οὓς καὶ ἀποστό-
of Him, and elected from them twelve, whom also apostles
3687 4613 3739 3607 4074 406
14 λους ὠνόμασε, Σίμωνα ὃν καὶ ὠνόμασε Πέτρον, καὶ Ἀνδρέαν
He named: Simon, whom also He named Peter; and Andrew
80 848 2385 2491 5376
τὸν ἀδελφὸν αὐτοῦ, Ἰάκωβον καὶ Ἰωάννην, Φίλιππον καὶ
the brother of him; James and John; Philip and
918 3156 2381 2385
15 Βαρθολομαῖον, Ματθαῖον καὶ Θωμᾶν, Ἰάκωβον τὸν τοῦ
Bartholomew; Matthew and Thomas; James the (son) —
256 4613 2583 2208 2455
16 Ἀλφαίου, καὶ Σίμωνα τὸν καλούμενον Ζηλωτήν, Ἰούδαν
of Alpheus; and Simon the (one) being called Zealot; Judas
2385 2455 2469 3739 1096 4273
Ἰακώβου, καὶ Ἰούδαν Ἰσκαριώτην, ὃς καὶ ἐγένετο προδό-
of James; and Judas Iscariot, who also became betrayer.
2591 3326 848 2476 1909 5117 3977
17 της, καὶ καταβὰς μετ' αὐτῶν, ἔστη ἐπὶ τόπου πεδινοῦ, καὶ
And coming down with them, He stood on a place level, and
3793 3101 848 4128 4183 2992 575
ὄχλος μαθητῶν αὐτοῦ, καὶ πλῆθος πολὺ τοῦ λαοῦ ἀπὸ
crowd of disciples of Him, and a multitude much of the people from
3956 2449 2419 3882
πάσης τῆς Ἰουδαίας καὶ Ἱερουσαλήμ, καὶ τῆς παραλίου
all — Judea and Jerusalem, and the coast country
5184 4605 3739 2064 191 846 2390
Τύρου καὶ Σιδῶνος, οἳ ἦλθον ἀκοῦσαι αὐτοῦ, καὶ ἰαθῆναι
of Tyre and Sidon, who came to hear Him, and to be cured
575 3554 848 3791 5259 4151
18 ἀπὸ τῶν νόσων αὐτῶν· καὶ οἱ ὀχλούμενοι ὑπὸ πνευμάτων
from the diseases of them, and those having been by spirits
169 2323 tormented 3793 2212
19 ἀκαθάρτων, καὶ ἐθεραπεύοντο. καὶ πᾶς ὁ ὄχλος ἐζήτει
unclean, and they were healed. And all the crowd sought
680 846 3754 1411 3844 846 1831 2390
ἅπτεσθαι αὐτοῦ· ὅτι δύναμις παρ' αὐτοῦ ἐξήρχετο καὶ ἰᾶτο
to touch Him, because power from Him went out and cured
3956
πάντας.
all.
846 1869 3788 848 1519 3101
20 Καὶ αὐτὸς ἐπάρας τοὺς ὀφθαλμοὺς αὐτοῦ εἰς τοὺς μαθητὰς
And He lifting up the eyes of Him to the disciples
848 3004 3107 4434 3754 5212 2076
αὐτοῦ ἔλεγε, Μακάριοι οἱ πτωχοί, ὅτι ὑμετέρα ἐστὶν ἡ
of Him said, Blessed (are) the poor, because yours is the
932 2316 3107 3983 3568 3754 5526
21 βασιλεία τοῦ Θεοῦ. μακάριοι οἱ πεινῶντες νῦν, ὅτι χορτασθή-
kingdom of God. Blessed (are) those hungering now, for you will be
3107 2799 3568 3754 1070 3107
σεσθε. μακάριοι οἱ κλαίοντες νῦν, ὅτι γελάσετε. μακάριοί
filled. Blessed (are) those weeping now, because you will laugh. Blessed
2075 3752 3404 5209 444 3752 873
22 ἐστε, ὅταν μισήσωσιν ὑμᾶς οἱ ἄνθρωποι, καὶ ὅταν ἀφο-
are you when hate you — men, and when they
5209 3679 1544 3686 5216
ρίσωσιν ὑμᾶς, καὶ ὀνειδίσωσι, καὶ ἐκβάλωσι τὸ ὄνομα ὑμῶν
separate you, and will reproach, and will cast out the name of you
5613 4190 1752 5207 444 5463 1722
23 ὡς πονηρόν, ἕνεκα τοῦ υἱοῦ τοῦ ἀνθρώπου. χαίρετε ἐν
as evil, for the sake of the Son — of man. Rejoice in
1565 2250 4640 2400 1063 3408 5216
ἐκείνῃ τῇ ἡμέρᾳ καὶ σκιρτήσατε· ἰδοὺ γάρ, ὁ μισθὸς ὑμῶν
that — day and leap for joy, behold For, the reward of you
4183 1722 3772 2596 5024 1063 4160 4396
πολὺς ἐν τῷ οὐρανῷ· κατὰ ταῦτα γὰρ ἐποίουν τοῖς προφή-
much in — Heaven! according to these For did to the prophets
3962 848 4133 3759 5213 4145
24 ταις οἱ πατέρες αὐτῶν. πλὴν οὐαὶ ὑμῖν τοῖς πλουσίοις,
the fathers of them. But woe to you the rich ones,

NOTE: Frequent words not numbered: δέ(1161); καί(2531)—and, but; ὁ, ἡ, τό (3588, the)— * above word, look in verse margin for No.

comfort! [25]Woe to you, those having been filled, for you will hunger! Woe to you, those laughing now, for you will mourn and lament! [26]Woe to you when all men speak well *of* you, for their fathers did according to these things to the false prophets.

[27]But I say to you, those hearing: Love your enemies; do good to those hating you; [28]bless those cursing you; and pray for those insulting you. [29]To those striking you on the cheek, turn the other also. And from those taking your garment, do not keep back the tunic also. [30]And to everyone asking you, give. And do not ask back from those taking your things. [31]And according as you desire that men should do to you, you also do the same to them. [32]And if you love those who love you, what thanks is there to you? For even sinners love those who love them. [33]And if you do good to those who do good to you, what thanks is there to you? For even the sinners do the same. [34]And if you lend *to those* from whom you hope to receive, what thanks is there to you? For even the sinners lend to sinners, so that they may receive the same.

[35]But love your enemies, and do good, and lend, hoping for nothing *in return;* and your reward will be much; and you will be sons of the Most High, for He is kind to the unthankful and evil ones. [36]Therefore, be merciful, even as your Father also is merciful.

3754 568 3874 5216 3759 5213 1705
25 ὅτι ἀπέχετε τὴν παράκλησιν ὑμῶν. οὐαὶ ὑμῖν, οἱ ἐμπεπλη-
because you have the comfort of you! Woe to you, those having
3754 3983 3759 5213 1070 3568 3754
σμένοι, ὅτι πεινάσετε. οὐαὶ ὑμῖν, οἱ γελῶντες νῦν, ὅτι
been filled, for you will hunger! Woe to you, those laughing now, for
3996 2799 3759/5213/3752 2573 5209 2036
26 πενθήσετε καὶ κλαύσετε. οὐαὶ ὑμῖν, ὅταν καλῶς ὑμᾶς εἴπωσι
you will mourn and lament! Woe to you, when well (of) you speak
3956 444 2596 5024 1063 4160 5578
πάντες οἱ ἄνθρωποι· κατὰ ταῦτα γὰρ ἐποίουν τοῖς ψευδο-
all men; according to these For did to the false
3962 848
προφήταις οἱ πατέρες αὐτῶν.
prophets the fathers of them.
235 5213 3004 191 25 2190
27 Ἀλλ' ὑμῖν λέγω τοῖς ἀκούουσιν, Ἀγαπᾶτε τοὺς ἐχθροὺς
But to you I say, those hearing, Love the enemies
5216 2573 4160 3404 5209 2127
28 ὑμῶν, καλῶς ποιεῖτε τοῖς μισοῦσιν ὑμᾶς, εὐλογεῖτε τοὺς
of you; well do to those hating you; bless those
2672 5213 4336 5228 1908
καταρωμένους ὑμῖν, καὶ προσεύχεσθε ὑπὲρ τῶν ἐπηρεαζόν-
cursing you; and pray for those insulting
5209 5180 4571 1909 4600 3930
29 των ὑμᾶς. τῷ τύπτοντί σε ἐπὶ τὴν σιαγόνα, πάρεχε καὶ τὴν
you. To those striking you on the cheek, turn also the
243 575 142 4675 2440
ἄλλην· καὶ ἀπὸ τοῦ αἴροντός σου τὸ ἱμάτιον, καὶ τὸν
other; and from those taking of you the garment, also the
5509 3361 2967 3956 154 4571 1325
30 χιτῶνα μὴ κωλύσῃς. παντὶ δὲ τῷ αἰτοῦντί σε δίδου· καὶ
tunic not do keep back. To everyone And asking you, give; and
575 142 4674/3361/523 2531 2309/2443
31 ἀπὸ τοῦ αἴροντος τὰ σὰ μὴ ἀπαίτει. καὶ καθὼς θέλετε ἵνα
from those taking your things, not do ask back. And as you desire that
4160 5213 444 5210 4160 846 3668
ποιῶσιν ὑμῖν οἱ ἄνθρωποι, καὶ ὑμεῖς ποιεῖτε αὐτοῖς ὁμοίως.
may do to you men, also you do to them likewise.
1487 25 25 5209 4169 5213 5485
32 καὶ εἰ ἀγαπᾶτε τοὺς ἀγαπῶντας ὑμᾶς, ποία ὑμῖν χάρις
And if you love those loving you, what to you thanks
2076 1063 268 25 846 25
ἐστί; καὶ γὰρ οἱ ἁμαρτωλοὶ τοὺς ἀγαπῶντας αὐτοὺς ἀγα-
is there? even For the sinners those loving them love.
1437 15 15 5209
33 πῶσι. καὶ ἐὰν ἀγαθοποιῆτε τοὺς ἀγαθοποιοῦντας ὑμᾶς,
And if you do good to those doing good to you,
4169 5213 5485 2076 1063 268 846
ποία ὑμῖν χάρις ἐστί; καὶ γὰρ οἱ ἁμαρτωλοὶ τὸ αὐτὸ
what to you thanks is there? even For the sinners the same
4160 1437 1155 3844 3739 1679 618
34 ποιοῦσι. καὶ ἐὰν δανείζητε παρ' ὧν ἐλπίζητε ἀπολαβεῖν,
do. And if you lend from whom you hope to receive,
4169 5213 5485 2076 1063 268 268
ποία ὑμῖν χάρις ἐστί; καὶ γὰρ οἱ ἁμαρτωλοὶ ἁμαρτωλοῖς
what to you thanks is there? even For the sinners to sinners
1155 2443 615 2470 4133 25
35 δανείζουσιν, ἵνα ἀπολάβωσι τὰ ἴσα. πλὴν ἀγαπᾶτε τοὺς
lend, that they may receive the same. But love the
2190 5216 15 1155 3367 560
ἐχθροὺς ὑμῶν, καὶ ἀγαθοποιεῖτε, καὶ δανείζετε, μηδὲν ἀπελ-
enemies of you, and do good and lend, nothing
2071 3408 5216 4183 2511 5207
πίζοντες· καὶ ἔσται ὁ μισθὸς ὑμῶν πολύς, καὶ ἔσεσθε υἱοὶ τοῦ
despairing, and will be the reward of you much; and you will be sons of the
5310 3754 846 5543 2076 1909 884
ὑψίστου· ὅτι αὐτὸς χρηστός ἐστιν ἐπὶ τοὺς ἀχαρίστους καὶ
most High because He kind is to the unthankful and
4190 1096 3767 3629 2531 3962
36 πονηρούς. γίνεσθε οὖν οἰκτίρμονες, καθὼς καὶ ὁ πατὴρ
evil ones. Be then merciful, even as also the Father

37 Judge not, and in no way be judged. Do not condemn, and in no way you will be condemned. Forgive, and you will be forgiven. 38 Give, and good measure will be given to you, pressed down and shaken together, and running over, they will give into your bosom. For the same measure which you measure, it will be measured back to you.

39 And He spoke a parable to them: A blind one is not able to guide a blind one. Will they not both fall into the ditch? 40 A disciple is not above his teacher, but everyone who has been perfected will be like his teacher. 41 But why do you look on the twig in your brother's eye, but do not consider the log in *your* own eye? 42 Or how can you say to your brother, Brother, let me pull out the twig in your eye, not yourself seeing the log in your eye? Hypocrite! First take the log out of your eye, and then you will see clearly to take out the twig in your brother's eye. 43 For there is not a good tree that produces bad fruit, nor a bad tree that produces good fruit. 44 For each tree is known from *its* own fruit. For they do not gather figs from thorns, nor do they gather grapes from a bramble bush. 45 The good man brings forth good out of the good treasure of his heart. And the evil man brings forth evil out of the evil treasure of his heart, for his mouth speaks out of the abundance of his heart.

5216 3629 2076 3361 2919 --3364-- 2919 3361 2613
37 ὑμῶν οἰκτίρμων ἐστί. μὴ κρίνετε, καὶ οὐ μὴ κριθῆτε. μὴ κατα-
of you merciful is. not Judge, and in no way be judged; do not
--3364-- 2613 630 630
δικάζετε, καὶ οὐ μὴ καταδικασθῆτε· ἀπολύετε, καὶ ἀπολυθή-
condemn, and in no way you will be condemned; forgive, and you will be
1325 1325 5213 3358 2570 4085
38 σεσθε· δίδοτε, καὶ δοθήσεται ὑμῖν· μέτρον καλόν, πεπιε-
forgiven; give, and will be given to you measure good, pressed
4531 5240 1325 1519
σμένον καὶ σεσαλευμένον καὶ ὑπερεκχυνόμενον δώσουσιν εἰς
down and shaken together and running over shall they give into
2859 5216 1063 846 3358 3739 3354 488
τὸν κόλπον ὑμῶν. τῷ γὰρ αὐτῷ μέτρῳ ᾧ μετρεῖτε ἀντι-
the bosom of you. the For same measure which you mete, it will
5213
μετρηθήσεται ὑμῖν.
be measured back to you.
2036 3850 846 3385 1410 5185 5185
39 Εἶπε δὲ παραβολὴν αὐτοῖς, Μήτι δύναται τυφλὸς τυφλὸν
He spoke And a parable to them, Not is able a blind one a blind one
3594 3780 297 1519 999 4098 3756/2076
ὁδηγεῖν; οὐχὶ ἀμφότεροι εἰς βόθυνον πεσοῦνται; οὐκ ἔστι
guide. not Will they into the ditch fall in? Not is
3101 5228 1320 848 2675
40 μαθητὴς ὑπὲρ τὸν διδάσκαλον αὐτοῦ· κατηρτισμένος δὲ
a disciple above the teacher of him, having been perfected but
3956 2071 5613 1320 848 5101 991 2595
41 πᾶς ἔσται ὡς ὁ διδάσκαλος αὐτοῦ. τί δὲ βλέπεις τὸ κάρφος
everyone will be as the teacher of him. why And do you see the twig
1722 3788 80 4675 1385 1722
τὸ ἐν τῷ ὀφθαλμῷ τοῦ ἀδελφοῦ σου, τὴν δὲ δοκὸν τὴν ἐν
in the eye of the brother of you, the but log in
2398 3788 3756 2657 2228 4459 1410 3004
42 τῷ ἰδίῳ ὀφθαλμῷ οὐ κατανοεῖς; ἢ πῶς δύνασαι λέγειν τῷ
(your) own eye not you consider? Or how are you able to say to the
80 4675 80 863 1544 2595 1722
ἀδελφῷ σου, Ἀδελφέ, ἄφες ἐκβάλω τὸ κάρφος τὸ ἐν τῷ
brother of you, Brother, allow I may take out the twig — in the
3788 4675 846 1722 3788 4675 1385 3756
ὀφθαλμῷ σου, αὐτὸς τὴν ἐν τῷ ὀφθαλμῷ σου δοκὸν οὐ
eye of you, yourself the in the eye of you log not
991 5273 1544 4412 1385 1537
βλέπων; ὑποκριτά, ἔκβαλε πρῶτον τὴν δοκὸν ἐκ τοῦ
seeing? Hypocrite, take out first the log out of the
3788 4675 5119 1227 1544 2595
ὀφθαλμοῦ σου, καὶ τότε διαβλέψεις ἐκβαλεῖν τὸ κάρφος τὸ
eye of you, and then you will se clearly to take out the twig
1722 3788 80 4675 3756 1063 2076 1186
43 ἐν τῷ ὀφθαλμῷ τοῦ ἀδελφοῦ σου. οὐ γάρ ἐστι δένδρον
in the eye of the brother of you. not For is a tree
2570 4160 2590 4550 3761 1086 4550 4160
καλὸν ποιοῦν καρπὸν σαπρόν· οὐδὲ δένδρον σαπρὸν ποιοῦν
good producing fruit bad, nor tree a bad producing
2590 2570 1538 1063 1186 1537 2398 2590
44 καρπὸν καλόν. ἕκαστον γὰρ δένδρον ἐκ τοῦ ἰδίου καρποῦ
fruit good. each For tree out of the own fruit
1087 1163 1537 173 4816 4810 3761 1537
γινώσκεται. ου γὰρ ἐξ ἀκανθῶν συλλέγουσι σῦκα, οὐδὲ ἐκ
is known. not For out of thorns do they gather figs, nor out of
942 5166 4718 18 444 1537
45 βάτου τρυγῶσι σταφυλήν. ὁ ἀγαθὸς ἄνθρωπος ἐκ τοῦ
a bramble gather grapes. The good man out of the
18 2344 2588 848 4393 18
ἀγαθοῦ θησαυροῦ τῆς καρδίας αὐτοῦ προφέρει τὸ ἀγαθόν
good treasure of the heart of him brings forth the good;
4190 444 1537 4190 2344
καὶ ὁ πονηρὸς ἄνθρωπος ἐκ τοῦ πονηροῦ θησαυροῦ τῆς
and the evil man out of the evil treasure of the
2588 848 4393 4190 1537 1063 4051
καρδίας αὐτοῦ προφέρει τὸ πονηρόν· ἐκ γὰρ τοῦ περισσεύ-
heart of him brings forth the evil; out of for the abundance

[46]And why do you call Me Lord, Lord, and do not do what I say? [47]Everyone coming to Me and hearing My words, and doing them, I will show you to whom he is like: [48]He is like a man building a house, who dug and deepened, and laid a foundation on the rock. And a flood having occurred, the stream burst against that house, and could not shake it, for it had been founded on the rock. [49]But he who heard and did not perform, *he* is like a man having built *his* house on the earth without a foundation, on which the stream burst, and it immediately fell; and the ruin of that house was great.

CHAPTER 7

[1]And when He had completed all His words in the ears of the people, He went into Capernaum.

[2]And a certain slave of a centurion, *one* dear to him, having illness was about to expire. [3]And hearing about Jesus, he sent elders of the Jews to Him, asking Him that He might come *to* restore his slave. [4]And coming to Jesus, they earnestly begged Him, saying, He to whom You give this is worthy. [5]For he loves our nation, and he built the synagogue for us. [6]And Jesus went with them. But He being yet not far away from the house, the centurion sent friends

2588 2980 4750 848
ματος τῆς καρδίας λαλεῖ τὸ στόμα αὐτοῦ.
of the heart speaks the mouth of him.
5101 3165 2564 2962 2962 3756 4160 3739 3004
46 Τί δέ με καλεῖτε, Κύριε, Κύριε, καὶ οὐ ποιεῖτε ἃ λέγω
why And Me do you call, Lord, Lord, and not do what I say?
3956 2064 4314 3165 191 3450 3056
47 πᾶς ὁ ἐρχόμενος πρός με καὶ ἀκούων μου τῶν λόγων καὶ
Everyone coming to Me and hearing of Me the words, and
4160 846 5263 5213 5101 2076 3664 3664 2076
48 ποιῶν αὐτούς, ὑποδείξω ὑμῖν τίνι ἐστὶν ὅμοιος· ὅμοιός ἐστιν
doing them, I will show you to whom he is like. like He is
444 3618 3614 3739 4626 900
ἀνθρώπῳ οἰκοδομοῦντι οἰκίαν, ὃς ἔσκαψε καὶ ἐβάθυνε, καὶ
a man building a house, who dug and deepened, and
5087 2310 1909 4073 4132 1096
ἔθηκε θεμέλιον ἐπὶ τὴν πέτραν· πλημμύρας δὲ γενομένης,
laid a foundation on the rock; a flood and happening,
4366 4215 3614 1565 3756 2480
προσέρρηξεν ὁ ποταμὸς τῇ οἰκίᾳ ἐκείνῃ καὶ οὐκ ἴσχυσε
burst against the stream house that, and not could
4531 846 2311 1063 1909 4073
49 σαλεῦσαι αὐτήν· τεθεμελίωτο γὰρ ἐπὶ τὴν πέτραν. ὁ δὲ
shake it, it had been founded for on the rock. he But
191 3361 4160 3664 2576 444 3615
ἀκούσας καὶ μὴ ποιήσας ὅμοιός ἐστιν ἀνθρώπῳ οἰκοδομή-
heard and not performed like is to a man having
3614 1909 1093 5565 2310 3739 4366
σαντι οἰκίαν ἐπὶ τὴν γῆν χωρὶς θεμελίου· ᾗ προσέρρηξεν ὁ
built a house on the earth without a foundation, on which burst the
4215 2112 4098 1096 4485
ποταμός, καὶ εὐθέως ἔπεσε, καὶ ἐγένετο τὸ ῥῆγμα τῆς
stream, and immediately it fell, and was the ruin
3614 1565 3173
οἰκίας ἐκείνης μέγα.
house of that great.

CHAPTER 7

1893 4137 3956 4487 848 1519 189
1 Ἐπεὶ δὲ ἐπλήρωσε πάντα τὰ ῥήματα αὐτοῦ εἰς τὰς ἀκοὰς
when And He completed all the words of Him in the ears
2992 1525 1519 2584
τοῦ λαοῦ, εἰσῆλθεν εἰς Καπερναούμ.
of the people, He went into Capernaum.
1543 5100 1401 2560 2192 3195
2 Ἑκατοντάρχου δέ τινος δοῦλος κακῶς ἔχων ἤμελλε
of a centurion And a certain slave illness having was about
5053 3739 2258 846 1784 191 4012 2424
3 τελευτᾶν, ὃς ἦν αὐτῷ ἔντιμος. ἀκούσας δὲ περὶ τοῦ Ἰησοῦ
to expire, who was to him dear. hearing And about Jesus
649 4314 846 4245 2453
ἀπέστειλε πρὸς αὐτὸν πρεσβυτέρους τῶν Ἰουδαίων,
he sent to Him elders of the Jews
2065 846 3700 2064 1295 1401 848
ἐρωτῶν αὐτόν, ὅπως ἐλθὼν διασώσῃ τὸν δοῦλον αὐτοῦ. οἱ
asking Him that coming He might restore the slave of him. the
3854 4314 2424 3870 846
4 δέ, παραγενόμενοι πρὸς τὸν Ἰησοῦν, παρεκάλουν αὐτὸν
And coming to — Jesus begged Him
4709 3004 3754 514 2076 3739 3930 5124
σπουδαίως, λέγοντες ὅτι ἄξιός ἐστιν ᾧ παρέξει τοῦτο
earnestly, saying, worthy He is for whom You give this
25 1063 1484 2257 4864 846
5 ἀγαπᾷ γὰρ τὸ ἔθνος ἡμῶν, καὶ τὴν συναγωγὴν αὐτὸ
he loves For the nation of us, and the synagogue he
3618 2254 2424 4198 3767 846 223
6 ᾠκοδόμησεν ἡμῖν. ὁ δὲ Ἰησοῦς ἐπορεύετο σὺν αὐτοῖς. ἤδη
built for us. And Jesus went with them. yet
846 3754 3112 568 575 3614 3992 4314
δὲ αὐτοῦ οὐ μακρὰν ἀπέχοντος ἀπὸ τῆς οἰκίας, ἔπεμψε πρὸ
And Him not far being away from the house, sent to

o Him, saying to Him, ord, do not trouble, for I m not worthy that You ome under my roof. [7]For his reason I did not count nyself worthy to come to ou. But say in a word, and et my servant be cured. For I also am a man having een set under authority, aving soldiers under myelf. And I say to this one, ol And he goes. And *to* nother, Come! And he omes. And *to* my slave, o this! And he does *it*.

[9]And hearing these things, Jesus marveled at him. And turning to the crowd following Him, He said, I say to you, I did not find such faith in Israel. [10]And those sent, returning to the house, found the sick slave well.

[11]And it happened on the next *day*, He went into a city being called Nain. And many of His disciples went with Him, also a great crowd. [12]And as He drew near to the gate of the city, even behold, *one* having died was being borne, an only son born to his mother; and she was a widow. And a considerable crowd of the city was with her. [13]And seeing her, the Lord felt pity over her; and said to her, Stop weeping. [14]And coming up, He touched the coffin; and those carrying *it* stood still. And He said, Young man, I say to you, arise! [15]And the dead one sat up and began to speak. And He gave him to his mother. [16]And fear took hold of all; and they glorified God, saying, A great prophet has risen up among us; and, God has visited His

846 1543 5384 3004 846 2962 3361
αὐτὸν ὁ ἑκατόνταρχος φίλους, λέγων αὐτῷ, Κύριε, μὴ
Him the centurion friends, saying to Him, Lord, not

4660 3756 1063 1510 2425 2443 5259 4721 3450
σκύλλου· οὐ γάρ εἰμι ἱκανὸς ἵνα ὑπὸ τὴν στέγην μου
do trouble. not For I am worthy that under the roof of me

1525 1352 3761 1683 515 4314 4571 2064 235
7 εἰσέλθῃς· διὸ οὐδὲ ἐμαυτὸν ἠξίωσα πρός σε ἐλθεῖν· ἀλλὰ
You enter. Therefore not myself I counted worthy to You to come, but

2036 3056 2390 3816 3450 1063 1473 444
8 εἰπὲ λόγῳ, καὶ ἰαθήσεται ὁ παῖς μου. καὶ γὰρ ἐγὼ ἄνθρωπός
say in a word, and let be cured the servant of me. even For I a man

1510 5259 1849 5021 2192 5259 1683 4757
εἰμι ὑπὸ ἐξουσίαν τασσόμενος, ἔχων ὑπ᾽ ἐμαυτὸν στρατιώ-
am under authority being set, having under myself soldiers,

3004 5129 4198 4198 235
τας, καὶ λέγω τούτῳ, Πορεύθητι, καὶ πορεύεται· καὶ ἄλλῳ,
and I tell this one, Go, and he goes; and another,

2064 2064 1401 3450 4160 5124
Ἔρχου, καὶ ἔρχεται· καὶ τῷ δούλῳ μου, Ποίησον τοῦτο, καὶ
Come, and he comes; and the slave of me, Do this, and

4160 191 5023 2424 2296 846
9 ποιεῖ. ἀκούσας δὲ ταῦτα ὁ Ἰησοῦς ἐθαύμασεν αὐτόν, καὶ
he does. hearing And these things, Jesus marveled at him, and

4762 190 846 3793 2036 3004 5213 3761
στραφεὶς τῷ ἀκολουθοῦντι αὐτῷ ὄχλῳ εἶπε, Λέγω ὑμῖν, οὐδὲ
turning to the ones following Him crowd said, I say to you, not

1722 2474 5118 4102 2147 5290
10 ἐν τῷ Ἰσραὴλ τοσαύτην πίστιν εὗρον. καὶ ὑποστρέψαντες οἱ
in Israel such faith I found. And returning those

3992 1519 3624 2147 770 1401
πεμφθέντες εἰς τὸν οἶκον εὗρον τὸν ἀσθενοῦντα δοῦλον
sent to the house found the sick slave

5198
ὑγιαίνοντα.
well.

1096 1722 1836 4198 1519 4172 2563
11 Καὶ ἐγένετο ἐν τῇ ἑξῆς, ἐπορεύετο εἰς πόλιν καλουμένην
And it was, on the next (day) He went into a city being called

3484 4848 846 3101 848 2425
Ναΐν· καὶ συνεπορεύοντο αὐτῷ οἱ μαθηταὶ αὐτοῦ ἱκανοί,
Nain, and went with Him the disciples of Him many,

3793 4183 5613 1448 4439 4172 2400
12 καὶ ὄχλος πολύς. ὡς δὲ ἤγγισε τῇ πύλῃ τῆς πόλεως, καὶ ἰδού,
and a crowd much. as And He drew near to the gate of the city, even behold

1580 2348 5207 3439 3384 848
ἐξεκομίζετο τεθνηκώς, υἱὸς μονογενὴς τῇ μητρὶ αὐτοῦ, καὶ
was being borne, having died, son an only born to the mother of him; and

846 2258 5503 3793 4172 2425 2258 4862 846
αὕτη ἦν χήρα· καὶ ὄχλος τῆς πόλεως ἱκανὸς ἦν σὺν αὐτῇ.
this was a widow. And a crowd of the city considerable was with her.

1492 846 2962 4697 1909 846 2036
13 καὶ ἰδὼν αὐτὴν ὁ Κύριος ἐσπλαγχνίσθη ἐπ᾽ αὐτῇ, καὶ εἶπεν
And seeing her, the Lord felt pity over her, and said

846 3361 2799 4334 680 4673
14 αὐτῇ, Μὴ κλαῖε. καὶ προσελθὼν ἥψατο τῆς σοροῦ· οἱ δὲ
to her, Stop weeping. And coming up, He touched the coffin, those and

941 2476 2036 3495 4671 3004
βαστάζοντες ἔστησαν. καὶ εἶπε, Νεανίσκε, σοὶ λέγω,
bearing stood still. And He said, Young man, to you I say,

1453 339 3498 756 2980
15 ἐγέρθητι. καὶ ἀνεκάθισεν ὁ νεκρός, καὶ ἤρξατο λαλεῖν. καὶ
Arise! And sat up the dead one, and began to speak; and

1325 846 3384 848 2983 5401 537
16 ἔδωκεν αὐτὸν τῇ μητρὶ αὐτοῦ. ἔλαβε δὲ φόβος ἅπαντας, καὶ
He gave him to the mother of him. took And fear all, and

1391 2316 3004 3754 4396 3173 1453
ἐδόξαζον τὸν Θεόν, λέγοντες ὅτι Προφήτης μέγας ἐγήγερται
they glorified God, saying, A prophet great has risen up

1722 2254 3754 1980 2316 2992 848
17 ἐν ἡμῖν, καὶ ὅτι Ἐπεσκέψατο ὁ Θεὸς τὸν λαὸν αὐτοῦ. καὶ
among us, and, has visited God the people of Him. And

people. 17And this word about Him went out in all Judea, and in all the neighborhood.

18And His disciples reported to John about all these things. 19And having called near a certain two of his disciples, John sent to Jesus, saying, Are You the One coming? Or should we expect another? 20And having come to Him, the men said, John the Baptist sent us to You, saying, Are You the One coming, or should we expect another? 21And in the same hour He healed many from diseases and plagues and evil spirits. And He gave to many blind ones *ability* to see. 22And answering Jesus said to them, Going, report to John what you saw and heard: Blind ones see again; lame ones walk about; lepers are being cleansed; deaf ones hear; dead ones are raised; poor ones are given the gospel. 23And blessed is *he* who is not offended in Me.

24And John's messengers going away, He began to speak to the crowds about John: What did you go out to the wilderness to see? A reed being shaken by the wind? 25But what did you go out to see? A man who had been dressed in soft clothing? Behold, those in splendid clothing and being in luxury are in king's palaces. 26But what did you go out to see? A prophet? Yes, I say to you, even more than a prophet. 27This is he about whom it has been written: "Behold, I send My messenger before

1831 3056 3778 1722 3650 2449 4012 846
ἐξῆλθεν ὁ λόγος οὗτος ἐν ὅλῃ τῇ Ἰουδαίᾳ περὶ αὐτοῦ, κα
went out word this in all Judea concerning Him, an
1722 3956 4066
ἐν πάσῃ τῇ περιχώρῳ.
in all the neighborhood.
518 2491 3101 848 4012 3956
18 Καὶ ἀπήγγειλαν Ἰωάννῃ οἱ μαθηταὶ αὐτοῦ περὶ πάντων
And reported to John the disciples of him about all
5130 4341 1417 5100 3101
19 τούτων. καὶ προσκαλεσάμενος δύο τινὰς τῶν μαθητῶ
these things. And having called near two a certain of the disciple
848 2491 3992 4314 2424 3004 4771 1488
αὐτοῦ ὁ Ἰωάννης ἔπεμψε πρὸς τὸν Ἰησοῦν, λέγων, Σὺ εἶ
of him, — John sent to — Jesus, saying, you Are
2064 2228 243 4328 3854 4314
20 ἐρχόμενος, ἢ ἄλλον προσδοκῶμεν; παραγενόμενοι δὲ πρὸ
coming One? Or another should we expect? coming And to
846 435 2036 2491 910 649
αὐτὸν οἱ ἄνδρες εἶπον, Ἰωάννης ὁ Βαπτιστὴς ἀπέσταλκε
Him the men said, John the Baptist sent
2248 4314 4571 3004 4771 1488 2064 2228 243 4328
ἡμᾶς πρός σε, λέγων, Σὺ εἶ ὁ ἐρχόμενος, ἢ ἄλλον προσδοκῶ
us to You, saying, you Are the coming One, or another should we
1722 846 5610 2323 4183 575 3554
21 μεν; ἐν αὐτῇ δὲ τῇ ὥρᾳ ἐθεράπευσε πολλοὺς ἀπὸ νόσων κα
expect? In the same And hour He healed many from diseases and
3148 4151 4190 5185 4183
μαστίγων καὶ πνευμάτων πονηρῶν, καὶ τυφλοῖς πολλοῖ
plagues and spirits evil; and blind ones to many
5483 991 611 2424 2036 846
22 ἐχαρίσατο τὸ βλέπειν. καὶ ἀποκριθεὶς ὁ Ἰησοῦς εἶπεν αὐτοῖς
He gave to see. And answering — Jesus said to them,
4198 518 2491 3739 1492 191
Πορευθέντες ἀπαγγείλατε Ἰωάννῃ ἃ εἴδετε καὶ ἠκούσατε
Going report to John what you saw and heard:
3754 5185 308 5560 4043 3015
ὅτι τυφλοὶ ἀναβλέπουσι, χωλοὶ περιπατοῦσι, λεπρο
— Blind ones see again; lame ones walk about; lepers
2511 2974 191 3498 1453 4434
καθαρίζονται, κωφοὶ ἀκούουσι, νεκροὶ ἐγείρονται, πτωχο
are being cleansed; deaf ones hear; dead ones are raised; poor ones
2097 3107 2076 3739 1437 3361 4624
23 εὐαγγελίζονται· καὶ μακάριός ἐστιν, ὃς ἐὰν μὴ σκανδαλισθῇ
are given the gospel; and blessed is whoever not is offended
1722 1698
ἐν ἐμοί.
in Me.
565 32 2491 756 3004
24 Ἀπελθόντων δὲ τῶν ἀγγέλων Ἰωάννου, ἤρξατο λέγειν
going away And the messengers of John, He began to s
4314 3793 4012 2491 5101 1831 1519
πρὸς τοὺς ὄχλους περὶ Ἰωάννου, Τί ἐξεληλύθατε εἰς τὴ
to the crowds about John, What did you go out to
2048 2300 2563 5259 417 4531 235
ἔρημον θεάσασθαι; κάλαμον ὑπὸ ἀνέμου σαλευόμενον; ἀλλ
wilderness to see? A reed by wind being shaken? Bu
5101 1831 1492 444 1722 3120 2440
25 τί ἐξεληλύθατε ἰδεῖν; ἄνθρωπον ἐν μαλακοῖς ἱματίοις
what did you go out to see? A man in soft clothing
294 2400 1722 2441 1741 5172
ἠμφιεσμένον; Ἰδού, οἱ ἐν ἱματισμῷ ἐνδόξῳ καὶ τρυφῇ
having been dressed? Behold, those in clothing splendid and in luxury
5225 1722 933 1526 235 5101 1831
26 ὑπάρχοντες ἐν τοῖς βασιλείοις εἰσίν. ἀλλὰ τί ἐξεληλύθα
being in king's palaces are. But what did you go
1492 4396 3483 3004 5213 4054 4396
ἰδεῖν; προφήτην; ναί, λέγω ὑμῖν, καὶ περισσότερον προ
to see? A prophet? Yes, I say to you, Even more than a
3778 2076 4012 3739 1125 2400 1473 649
27 φήτου. οὗτός ἐστι περὶ οὗ γέγραπται, Ἰδού, ἐγὼ ἀπο-
prophet! This is (he) about whom it has been written, Behold, I

Your face, who will prepare Your way before You." [28]For I say to you, Among *those* born of a woman, no prophet is greater than John the Baptist. But the least *one* in the kingdom of God is greater than he is.

[29]And all the people and the tax-collectors hearing, *they* justified God, being baptized *with* the the baptism of John. [30]But the Pharisees and the lawyers set aside God's counsel as to themselves, not being baptized by him. [31]And the Lord said, Then to what shall I compare the men of this generation? And to what are they like? [32]They are like children sitting in a market and calling to one another, and saying, We piped to you, and you did not dance; we mourned to you, and you did not weep. [33]For John the Baptist has come neither eating bread nor drinking wine, and you say, He has a demon. [34]The Son of man has come eating and drinking, and you say, Behold, a man, a glutton and a drunkard; a friend of tax-collectors and sinners. [35]But wisdom was justified from all her children.

[36]And a certain one of the Pharisees asked Him that He eat with him. And going into the Pharisee's house, He reclined. [37]And, behold, a woman who was a sinner in the city, knowing that He reclined in the Pharisee's house, taking an alabaster vial of ointment, [38]and standing at His feet, weeping behind *Him, she* began to wash His feet with tears. And she

32 3450 4253 4383 4675 3739 2680
στέλλω τὸν ἄγγελόν μου πρὸ προσώπου σου, ὃς κατα-
send the messenger of Me before (the) face of You, who will
3598 4675 1715 4675 3004 1063 5213 3187
28 σκευάσει τὴν ὁδόν σου ἔμπροσθέν σου. λέγω γὰρ ὑμῖν, μείζων
prepare the way of You before You. I say For to you, greater
1722 1084 1135 4396 2491 910
ἐν γεννητοῖς γυναικῶν προφήτης Ἰωάννου τοῦ Βαπτιστοῦ
among (those) born of women prophet than John the Baptist
3762 2076 3398 1722 932 2316
οὐδείς ἐστιν· ὁ δὲ μικρότερος ἐν τῇ βασιλείᾳ τοῦ Θεοῦ
no one is. the But least (one) in the kingdom – of God
3187 846 2076 3956 2992 191 5057
29 μείζων αὐτοῦ ἐστι. καὶ πᾶς ὁ λαὸς ἀκούσας καὶ οἱ τελῶναι
greater tha he is. And all the people hearing, and the tax-collectors,
1344 2316 907 908 2491
ἐδικαίωσαν τὸν Θεόν, βαπτισθέντες τὸ βάπτισμα Ἰωάννου·
justified God, being baptized (with) the baptism of John.
5330 3544 1012 2316
30 οἱ δὲ Φαρισαῖοι καὶ οἱ νομικοὶ τὴν βουλὴν τοῦ Θεοῦ
the But Pharisees and the lawyers the counsel – of God
114 1519 1438 3361 907 5259 846 2036
ἠθέτησαν εἰς ἑαυτούς, μὴ βαπτισθέντες ὑπ᾽ αὐτοῦ. εἶπε δὲ
set aside, for themselves not had been baptized by him. said And
2962 5101 3767 3666 444 1074
31 ὁ Κύριος, Τίνι οὖν ὁμοιώσω τοὺς ἀνθρώπους τῆς γενεᾶς
the Lord, To what then shall I liken the men generation
5026 5101 1526 3664 3664 1526 3813 1722
32 ταύτης, καὶ τίνι εἰσὶν ὅμοιοι ; ὅμοιοί εἰσι παιδίοις τοῖς ἐν
of this, and to what are they like? like They are (to) children in
58 2521 4377 240
ἀγορᾷ καθημένοις, καὶ προσφωνοῦσιν ἀλλήλοις, καὶ
a market sitting and calling to one another, and
3004 832 5213 3756 3738 2354
λέγουσιν, Ηὐλήσαμεν ὑμῖν, καὶ οὐκ ὠρχήσασθε· ἐθρηνή-
saying, We piped to you, and not you danced; we
5213 3756 2799 2064 1063 2491
33 σαμεν ὑμῖν, καὶ οὐκ ἐκλαύσατε. ἐλήλυθε γὰρ Ἰωάννης ὁ
mourned to you, and not you wept. has come For John the
910 3383 740 2068 3383 3621 4095 3004
Βαπτιστὴς μήτε ἄρτον ἐσθίων μήτε οἶνον πίνων, καὶ λέγετε,
Baptist not bread eating, nor wine drinking, and you say,
1140 2192 2064 5207 444 2068
34 Δαιμόνιον ἔχει. ἐλήλυθεν ὁ υἱὸς τοῦ ἀνθρώπου ἐσθίων καὶ
A demon he has. has come The Son of man eating and
4095 3004 2400 444 5314 3630
πίνων, καὶ λέγετε, Ἰδού, ἄνθρωπος φάγος καὶ οἰνοπότης,
drinking, and you say, Behold, a man, a glutton and a winebibber,
5057 5384 268 1314 4678 575
35 τελωνῶν φίλος καὶ ἁμαρτωλῶν. καὶ ἐδικαιώθη ἡ σοφία ἀπὸ
of tax-collectors friend and sinners. And was justified wisdom from
5043 848 3956
τῶν τέκνων αὐτῆς πάντων.
the children of her all.

2064 5100 846 5330 2443 5315 3326
36 Ἠρώτα δέ τις αὐτὸν τῶν Φαρισαίων ἵνα φάγῃ μετ᾽
asked And a certain Him of the Pharisees, that He eat with
846 1525 1519 3614 5330 347
αὐτοῦ· καὶ εἰσελθὼν εἰς τὴν οἰκίαν τοῦ Φαρισαίου ἀνεκλίθη.
him. And going into the house of the Pharisee He reclined
2400 1135 1722 4172 3798 2258 268 1921
37 καὶ ἰδού, γυνὴ ἐν τῇ πόλει, ἥτις ἦν ἁμαρτωλός, ἐπιγνοῦσα
And behold, a woman in the city who was a sinner, knowing
3754 345 1722 3614 5330 2965 211
ὅτι ἀνάκειται ἐν τῇ οἰκίᾳ τοῦ Φαρισαίου, κομίσασα ἀλά-
that He had reclined in the house of the Pharisee, taking an
3464 2476 3814 4228 848 3694
38 βαστρον μύρου, καὶ στᾶσα παρὰ τοὺς πόδας αὐτοῦ ὀπίσω
alabaster of ointment, and standing at the feet of Him behind
vial 2799 756 1026 4228 848 1144
κλαίουσα, ἤρξατο βρέχειν τοὺς πόδας αὐτοῦ τοῖς δάκρυσι,
weeping, began to wet the feet of Him with the tears

was wiping with the hairs of her head. And *she* ardently kissed His feet, and *was* anointing *them* with the ointment. [39]But seeing, the Pharisee who invited Him spoke within himself, saying, This one, if he were a prophet, would

him *is*; for she is a sinner. [40]And answering Jesus said to the man, Simon, I have a thing to say to you. And he said, Teacher, say *it*. [41]There were two debtors to a certain creditor: the one owed five hundred denarii, and *the* other fifty. [42]But they not having *a thing* to pay, he freely forgave both. Then which of them do *you* say will love him most? [43]And answering Simon said, I suppose *the one* to whom he freely forgave the most. And He said to him, You have judged rightly. [44]And turning to the woman, He said to Simon, Do you see this woman? I came into your house. You did not give water for My feet, but she washed My feet with tears, and wiped off with the hairs of her head. [45]You gave Me no kiss, but she from *when* I entered did not stop fervently kissing My feet. [46]You did not anoint My head with oil, but she anointed My feet with ointment. [47]For this reason I say to you, her many sins are forgiven, for she loved much. But to whom little is forgiven, he loves little.

[48]And He said to her, Your sins are forgiven. [49]And those reclining with *Him* began to say within themselves, Who is this who even forgives sins? [50]But He said to the woman, Your faith has saved you. Go in peace.

2359 2776 848 1591 2705
καὶ ταῖς θριξὶ τῆς κεφαλῆς αὐτῆς ἐξέμασσε, καὶ κατεφίλε
and with the hairs of the head of her she was wiping, and kissing
4228 848 218 3464 1492 5330
39 τοὺς πόδας αὐτοῦ. καὶ ἤλειφε τῷ μύρῳ. Ἰδὼν δὲ ὁ Φαρισαῖος
the feet of Him, and anointing with the ointment. seeing And the Phari
•2258 2564 846 2036 1722 1438 3004 3778 1487 see
ὁ καλέσας αὐτὸν εἶπεν ἐν ἑαυτῷ λέγων, Οὗτος, εἰ ἦν
having invited Him, he spoke in himself, saying, This one, if he wa
4396 1097 302 5101 4217 1135 3748
προφήτης, ἐγίνωσκεν ἂν τίς καὶ ποταπὴ ἡ γυνὴ ἥτις
a prophet have known would who and what the woman (is) w
680 846 3754 268 2076 611
40 ἅπτεται αὐτοῦ. ὅτι ἁμαρτωλός ἐστι. καὶ ἀποκριθεὶς ὁ
touches him, because a sinner she is. And answering
2424 2036 4314 846 4613 2192 4671 5101 2036 5346
Ἰησοῦς εἶπε πρὸς αὐτόν, Σίμων, ἔχω σοί τι εἰπεῖν. ὁ δέ φησι,
Jesus said to him, Simon, I have to you a thing to he And says,
1320 2036 1417 5533 2258 say. 1157 5100
41 Διδάσκαλε, εἰπέ. Δύο χρεωφειλέται ἦσαν δανειστῇ τινί·
Teacher, say. Two debtors were to a creditor certain
1520 3784 1220 4001 2087 4004 3361
42 ὁ εἷς ὤφειλε δηνάρια πεντακόσια, ὁ δὲ ἕτερος πεντήκοντα. μὴ
The one owed denarii five hundred, the and (the) other fifty. not
2192 846 591 297 5483 5101
ἐχόντων δὲ αὐτῶν ἀποδοῦναι, ἀμφοτέροις ἐχαρίσατο. τίς
having And them (a thing) to repay, both he freely forgave. Who
3767 846 2036 4119 846 25 611
43 οὖν αὐτῶν, εἰπέ, πλεῖον αὐτὸν ἀγαπήσει; ἀποκριθεὶς δὲ ὁ
then of them say (you) more him will love? answering And
4613 2036 5274 3754 3739 4119 5483
Σίμων εἶπεν, Ὑπολαμβάνω ὅτι ᾧ τὸ πλεῖον ἐχαρίσατο. ὁ
Simon said, I suppose to whom the more he freely forgave. He
2036 846 3723 2919 4762 4314
44 δὲ εἶπεν αὐτῷ, Ὀρθῶς ἔκρινας. καὶ στραφεὶς πρὸς τὴν
And said to him, Rightly you judged. And turning to the
1135 4613 5346 991 5026 1135
γυναῖκα, τῷ Σίμωνι ἔφη, Βλέπεις ταύτην τὴν γυναῖκα;
woman, to Simon He said, Do you see this woman?
1525 4675 1519 3614 5204 1909 4228 3450 3756
εἰσῆλθόν σου εἰς τὴν οἰκίαν, ὕδωρ ἐπὶ τοὺς πόδας μου οὐκ
I went of you into the house, water on the feet of Me not
1325 3778 1144 1626 3450 4228
ἔδωκας· αὕτη δὲ τοῖς δάκρυσιν ἔβρεξέ μου τοὺς πόδας, καὶ
you gave. she But with the tears wet of Me the feet, and
2359 2776 848 1591 5370 3427 3756 1325
45 ταῖς θριξὶ τῆς κεφαλῆς αὐτῆς ἐξέμαξε. φίλημά μοι οὐκ ἔδωκας·
with the hairs – head of her wiped off. A kiss to Me not you gave,
3778 575 3739 1525 3756 1257 2705 3650
αὕτη δέ, ἀφ' ἧς εἰσῆλθον, οὐ διέλιπε καταφιλοῦσά μου τοὺς
she but from (when) I entered not did stop fervently kissing of Me the
4228 1637 2776 3450 3756 218 3778 3464
46 πόδας. ἐλαίῳ τὴν κεφαλήν μου οὐκ ἤλειψας· αὕτη δὲ μύρῳ
feet. With oil the head of Me not you anointed, she but with
218 3450 4228 3739 5464 3004 4671 863 ointmen
47 ἤλειψέ μου τοὺς πόδας. οὗ χάριν, λέγω σοι, ἀφέωνται αἱ
anointed of Me the feet. For this reason I say to you, are forgiven the
266 848 4187 3754 25 4183 3739 3641
ἁμαρτίαι αὐτῆς αἱ πολλαί, ὅτι ἠγάπησε πολύ· ᾧ δὲ ὀλίγον
sins of her many, because she loved much, to whom but little
863 3641 25 2036 846 863 4675
48 ἀφίεται, ὀλίγον ἀγαπᾷ. εἶπε δὲ αὐτῇ, Ἀφέωνταί σου αἱ
is forgiven, little he loves. He said And to her, are forgiven of you The
266 756 4873 3004 1722 1438
49 ἁμαρτίαι. καὶ ἤρξαντο οἱ συνανακείμενοι λέγειν ἐν ἑαυτοῖς,
sins. And began those reclining with (Him) to say in themselves
5101 3778 2076 3739 266 863 2036 4314
Τίς οὗτός ἐστιν ὃς καὶ ἁμαρτίας ἀφίησιν; εἶπε δὲ πρὸς τὴν
Who this is, who even sins forgives? He said But to the
1135 4102 4675 4982 4571 4198 1519 1515
50 γυναῖκα, Ἡ πίστις σου σέσωκέ σε· πορεύου εἰς εἰρήνην.
woman, The faith of you has saved you; Go in peace.

CHAPTER 8

[1]And it happened afterwards, even He traveled in every city and village, preaching and announcing the gospel of the kingdom of God. And the Twelve *were* with Him; [2]also certain women who were healed from evil spirits and infirmities: Mary having been called Magdalene, from whom seven demons had gone out; [3]and Joanna, (the) wife of Chuza, Herod's steward; and Susanna; and many others, who were ministering to Him of their possessions.

[4]And a great crowd coming together, and those in each city coming to Him, He spoke through a parable:

[5]The sower went out to sow his seed. And as he sowed, some fell by the wayside, and was trampled; and the birds of the heaven ate it. [6]And other fell on the rock, and sprouting, it dried up, because of not having moisture. [7]And other fell in *the* midst of the thorns, and springing up with the thorns, *they* choked it. [8]And other fell on the good ground, and springing up, it produced fruit a hundredfold. Saying these things, He cried out, The one having ears to hear, let him hear.

[9]And His disciples questioned Him, saying, What might this parable be? [10]And He said, To you it has been given to know the mysteries of the kingdom of God, but to the rest in parables, that seeing they might not see, and hearing they might not understand. [11]And this is the parable: The seed is the word of

CHAPTER 8

1096 1722 2517 846 1353 2596 4172
1 Καὶ ἐγένετο ἐν τῷ καθεξῆς, καὶ αὐτὸς διώδευε κατὰ πόλιν
And it was afterwards, and He traveled through every city
2968 2784 2097 932
κάὶ κώμην, κηρύσσων, καὶ εὐαγγελιζόμενος τὴν βασιλείαν
and village, preaching and announcing the gospel of the kingdom
2316 1427 4862 846 1135 5100 3739
2 τοῦ Θεοῦ· καὶ οἱ δώδεκα σὺν αὐτῷ, καὶ γυναῖκές τινες αἳ
— of God, and the twelve with Him, also women certain who
2258 2323 575 4151 4190
ἦσαν τεθεραπευμέναι ἀπὸ πνευμάτων πονηρῶν καὶ
were healed from spirits evil and
169 3137 2563 3094 575 3739 1140
ἀσθενειῶν, Μαρία ἡ καλουμένη Μαγδαληνή, ἀφ' ἧς δαιμόνια
infirmities; Mary being called Magdalene, from whom demons
2033 1831 2489 1135 5529 2012 2264
3 ἑπτὰ ἐξεληλύθει, καὶ Ἰωάννα γυνὴ Χουζᾶ ἐπιτρόπου Ἡρώ-
seven had gone out; and Joanna, wife of Chuza, steward of
4677 2087 4183 3748 1247
δου, καὶ Σουσάννα, καὶ ἕτεραι πολλαί, αἵτινες διηκόνουν
Herod; and Susanna; and others many; who ministered
846 575 5224 848
αὐτῷ ἀπὸ τῶν ὑπαρχόντων αὐταῖς.
to Him from the possessions of them.

4896 3793 4183 2596 4172 1975
4 Συνιόντος δὲ ὄχλου πολλοῦ, καὶ τῶν κατὰ πόλιν ἐπιπο-
coming together And crowd a much, and those in each city coming
4314 846 2036 1223 3850 1831
ρευομένων πρὸς αὐτόν, εἶπε διὰ παραβολῆς, Ἐξῆλθεν ὁ
to Him, He said through a parable: Went out the
4687 4687 4703 848 1722 4687
5 σπείρων τοῦ σπεῖραι τὸν σπόρον αὐτοῦ καὶ ἐν τῷ σπείρειν
(one) sowing to sow the seed of him. And in the sowing
846 3739 3303 4098 3844 3598 2662
αὐτόν, ὃ μὲν ἔπεσε παρὰ τὴν ὁδόν, καὶ κατεπατήθη, καὶ τὰ
of him, the one fell by the way, and was trampled; and the
4071 3772 2719 846 2087 4098
6 πετεινὰ τοῦ οὐρανοῦ κατέφαγεν αὐτό. καὶ ἕτερον ἔπεσεν
birds of the heaven ate it. And other fell
1909 4073 5453 3583 1223 3361 2192 2429
ἐπὶ τὴν πέτραν, καὶ φυὲν ἐξηράνθη, διὰ τὸ μὴ ἔχειν ἰκμάδα.
on the rock, and growing it dried up, because of not having moisture.
2087 4098 1722 3319 173 4855
7 καὶ ἕτερον ἔπεσεν ἐν μέσῳ τῶν ἀκανθῶν, καὶ συμφυεῖσαι αἱ
And other fell amidst the thorns, and growing up with the
173 1970 846 2087 4098 1909 1093
8 ἄκανθαι ἀπέπνιξαν αὐτό. καὶ ἕτερον ἔπεσεν ἐπὶ τὴν γῆν τὴν
thorns choked it. And other fell on the earth the
18 5453 4160 2590 1542
ἀγαθήν, καὶ φυὲν ἐποίησε καρπὸν εκατονταεκατοντα-
good, and growing it produced fruit a hundredfold.
5023 3004 5455 2192 3775 191 191
ταῦτα λέγων ἐφώνει, Ὁ ἔχων ὦτα ἀκούειν ἀκουέτω.
these things saying He called, Those having ears to hear, let him hear.
1905 846 3101 848 3004 5101
9 Ἐπηρώτων δὲ αὐτὸν οἱ μαθηταὶ αὐτοῦ, λέγοντες, Τίς
questioned And Him the disciples of Him, saying, What
1498 3850 3778 2036 5213 1325 1097
10 εἴη ἡ παραβολὴ αὕτη; ὁ δὲ εἶπεν, Ὑμῖν δέδοται γνῶναι τὰ
might be parable this? He And said, To you it was given to know the
3466 932 2316 3062 1722
μυστήρια τῆς βασιλείας τοῦ Θεοῦ· τοῖς δὲ λοιποῖς ἐν
mysteries of the kingdom of God, to the but rest in
3850 2443 991 3361 991 191 3361
παραβολαῖς, ἵνα βλέποντες μὴ βλέπωσι, καὶ ἀκούοντες μὴ
parables, that seeing not they might see, and hearing not
4920 2076 3778 3850 4703 2076
11 συνιῶσιν. ἔστι δὲ αὕτη ἡ παραβολή· ὁ σπόρος ἐστὶν ὁ
they might know, is And this the parable: The seed is the

God. [12]And those by the wayside are those who hear, then the Devil comes and takes away the word from their heart, lest believing they may be saved. [13]And those on the rock *are* those who, when they hear, receive the word with joy; and these have no root, those believing for a time, and in time of trial draw back. [14]And those falling in the thorns, these are those hearing, but under cares and riches and pleasures of life, having moved along, they are choked, and do not bear to maturity. [15]And those in the good ground, these are *the ones* who in a right and good heart, hearing the word, they hold *it* and bear fruit in patience.

[16]But no one lighting a lamp covers it with a vessel, or puts *it* underneath a couch, but puts *it* on a lampstand, that those coming in may see the light. [17]For nothing is hidden which will not be revealed; nor secret which will not be known and come to be revealed. [18]Then observe how you hear; for whoever may have, it will be given to him; and whoever may not have, even what he seems to have will be taken from him.

[19]And His mother and His brothers came to Him, and were not able to come up with Him through the crowd. [20]And it was told to Him, saying, Your mother and Your brothers are standing outside, wishing to see You. [21]And answering He said to them, My mother and My brothers are these, the ones hearing the word of God, and doing it.

3056 2316 3844 3598 1526 191
12 λόγος τοῦ Θεοῦ. οἱ δὲ παρὰ τὴν ὁδὸν εἰσὶν οἱ ἀκούοντες,
word — of God. the And (ones) by the way are those hearing;
1534 2064 1228 142 3056 575 2588
εἶτα ἔρχεται ὁ διάβολος καὶ αἴρει τὸν λόγον ἀπὸ τῆς καρδίας
then comes the Devil and takes the word from the heart
848 2443 3361 4100 4982 1909
13 αὐτῶν, ἵνα μὴ πιστεύσαντες σωθῶσιν. οἱ δὲ ἐπὶ τῆς
of them, that not believing they may be saved. those And on the
4073 3739 3752 191 3326 5479 1209 3056
πέτρας οἳ, ὅταν ἀκούσωσι, μετὰ χαρᾶς δέχονται τὸν λόγον,
rock who when they hear with joy receive the word;
3778 4491 3756 2192 3739 4314 2540 4100
καὶ οὗτοι ῥίζαν οὐκ ἔχουσιν, οἳ πρὸς καιρὸν πιστεύουσι,
and these root not do have, who for a time believe,
1722 2510 3986 868 1519 173
14 καὶ ἐν καιρῷ πειρασμοῦ ἀφίστανται. τὸ δὲ εἰς τὰς ἀκάνθας
and in time of trial draw back. those And in the thorns
4098 3778 1526 191 5259 3308
πεσόν, οὗτοί εἰσιν οἱ ἀκούσαντες, καὶ ὑπὸ μεριμνῶν καὶ
falling, these are those hearing, and under cares and
4129 2237 979 4198 4846
πλούτου καὶ ἡδονῶν τοῦ βίου πορευόμενοι συμπνίγονται,
riches and pleasures of life moving along, they are choked
3756 5052 1722 2570 1093 3778 1526
15 καὶ οὐ τελεσφοροῦσι. τὸ δὲ ἐν τῇ καλῇ γῇ, οὗτοί εἰσιν
and not do bear to maturity. those And in the good earth, these are
3748 1722 2588 2570 18 191 3056
οἵτινες ἐν καρδίᾳ καλῇ καὶ ἀγαθῇ, ἀκούσαντες τὸν λόγον
(those) who in a heart right and good hearing the word,
2722 2592 1722 5281
κατέχουσι, καὶ καρποφοροῦσιν ἐν ὑπομονῇ.
they hold (it), and bear fruit in patience.
3762 3088 681 2572 846 4632 2228 5270
16 Οὐδεὶς δὲ λύχνον ἅψας καλύπτει αὐτὸν σκεύει, ἢ ὑποκάτω
no one But a lamp having lit covers it with a vessel, or underneath
2825 5087 235 1909 3087 2007 2443 1531
κλίνης τίθησιν, ἀλλ᾽ ἐπὶ λυχνίας ἐπιτίθησιν, ἵνα οἱ εἰσπορευό-
a couch puts (it), but on a lampstand puts (it), that those coming in
991 5457 3756 1063 2076 2927 3739 3756 5318
17 μενοι βλέπωσι τὸ φῶς. οὐ γάρ ἐστι κρυπτόν, ὃ οὐ φανερὸν
may see the light. not For is hidden which not revealed
1096 3761 614 3739 3756 1097 1519
γενήσεται· οὐδὲ ἀπόκρυφον, ὃ οὐ γνωσθήσεται καὶ εἰς
will be, nor secret which not will be known and to (be)
5318 2064 991 3767 4459 191 3739 1063 302 2192
18 φανερὸν ἔλθῃ. βλέπετε οὖν πῶς ἀκούετε· ὃς γὰρ ἂν ἔχῃ,
revealed come. see Therefore how you hear; who for ever has,
1325 846 3739/302/3361/2192 1380 2192 142
δοθήσεται αὐτῷ· καὶ ὃς ἂν μὴ ἔχῃ, καὶ ὃ δοκεῖ ἔχειν ἀρθή-
it will be given to him; and who ever not has, even what he seems to have will
575 846
σεται ἀπ᾽ αὐτοῦ.
be taken from him.
3854 4314 846 3384 80
19 Παρεγένοντο δὲ πρὸς αὐτὸν ἡ μήτηρ καὶ οἱ ἀδελφοὶ
came And to Him the mother and the brothers
848 3756 1410 4940 846 1223 3793
αὐτοῦ, καὶ οὐκ ἠδύναντο συντυχεῖν αὐτῷ διὰ τὸν ὄχλον.
of Him, and not were able to come up with Him through the crowd.
518 846 3004 3384 4675
20 καὶ ἀπηγγέλη αὐτῷ, λεγόντων, Ἡ μήτηρ σου καὶ οἱ
And it was told to Him, saying, The mother of You and the
80 4675 2476 1854 1492 4571 2309 611
ἀδελφοί σου ἑστήκασιν ἔξω, ἰδεῖν σε θέλοντες. ὁ δὲ ἀποκριθεὶς
brothers of You are standing outside to see You desiring. He And answering
2036/4314 846 3384 3450 80 3450/3778 1526
21 εἶπε πρὸς αὐτούς, Μήτηρ μου καὶ ἀδελφοί μου οὗτοί εἰσιν
said to them, Mother of Me and brothers of Me these are,
3056 2316 191 4160 846
οἱ τὸν λόγον τοῦ Θεοῦ ἀκούοντες καὶ ποιοῦντες αὐτόν.
those the word of God hearing and doing it.

[22]And it happened on one of the days that He and His disciples entered into a boat. And He said to them, Let us go over to the other side of the lake; and they put out to sea. [23]And as they sailed He fell asleep. And a storm of wind came onto the lake, and they were being filled and were in danger. [24]And coming up they awakened Him, saying, Master! Master! We are perishing! And being aroused, He rebuked the wind and the roughness of the water; and they ceased; and there was a calm. [25]And He said to them, Where is your faith? And being afraid, they marveled, saying to one another, Who then is this One, that He commands even the wind and the water, and they obey Him?

[26] And they sailed down to the country of the Gadarenes, which is across from Galilee. [27]And He going out onto the land, a certain man out of the city met Him, who had demons from a long time—and he put no garment on. And he did not stay in a house, but among the tombs. [28]And seeing Jesus, and crying out, he fell down before Him, and with a loud voice said, What to me and to You, Jesus, Son of God the Most High? I beg You, do not torment me. [29]For He charged the unclean spirit to come out of the man. For many times it had seized him, and he was bound with with chains and fetters, being guarded. And tearing apart the bonds, he was driven by the demons into the deserts. [30]And Jesus asked him, saying, What is your name? And he said, Legion, because many demons entered into

1096 1722 3391 2250 846 1634 1519 4143
22 Καὶ ἐγένετο ἐν μιᾷ τῶν ἡμερῶν, καὶ αὐτὸς ἐνέβη εἰς πλοῖον
And it was on one of the days, and He entered into a boat,
3101 848 2036 4314 846 1330 1519
καὶ οἱ μαθηταὶ αὐτοῦ, καὶ εἶπε πρὸς αὐτούς, Διέλθωμεν εἰς
also the disciples of Him; and He said to them, Let us go over to
4008 3041 321 4126 846
23 τὸ πέραν τῆς λίμνης· καὶ ἀνήχθησαν. πλεόντων δὲ αὐτῶν
the other side of the lake; and they put out to sea. sailing And them,
879 2597 2978 417/1519 3041
ἀφύπνωσε· καὶ κατέβη λαῖλαψ ἀνέμου εἰς τὴν λίμνην, καὶ
He fell asleep. And came down a storm of wind onto the lake, and
4845 2793 4334 1326
24 συνεπληροῦντο, καὶ ἐκινδύνευον. προσελθόντες δὲ διήγειραν
they were being filled, and were in danger. coming up And they awoke
846 3004 1988 1988 622
αὐτόν, λέγοντες, Ἐπιστάτα, ἐπιστάτα, ἀπολλύμεθα. ὁ δὲ
Him, saying, Master! Master! We are perishing. He And
1453 2008 417 2830 5204
ἐγερθεὶς ἐπετίμησε τῷ ἀνέμῳ καὶ τῷ κλύδωνι τοῦ ὕδατος·
being aroused rebuked the wind and the roughness of the water,
3973 1096 1055 2036 846 4226
25 καὶ ἐπαύσαντο, καὶ ἐγένετο γαλήνη. εἶπε δὲ αὐτοῖς, Ποῦ
and they ceased; and there was a calm. He said And to them, Where
2076 4102 5216 5399 2296 3004
ἐστιν ἡ πίστις ὑμῶν; φοβηθέντες δὲ ἐθαύμασαν, λέγοντες
is the faith of you? fearing And, they marveled, saying,
4314 240 5101 686 3778 2076 3754 417
πρὸς ἀλλήλους, Τίς ἄρα οὗτός ἐστιν, ὅτι καὶ τοῖς ἀνέμοις
to one another, Who then this One is, that even the wind
2004 5204 5219 846
ἐπιτάσσει καὶ τῷ ὕδατι, καὶ ὑπακούουσιν αὐτῷ;
He commands and the water, and they obey Him?
2668 1519 5561 1046 3140
26 Καὶ κατέπλευσαν εἰς τὴν χώραν τῶν Γαδαρηνῶν, ἥτις
And they sailed down to the country of the Gadarenes, which
2076 495 1056 1831 846 1909
27 ἐστὶν ἀντιπέραν τῆς Γαλιλαίας. ἐξελθόντι δὲ αὐτῷ ἐπὶ τὴν
is opposite Galilee. going out And Him onto the
1093 5221 846 435 5101 1537 4172 3739 2192 1140
γῆν, ὑπήντησεν αὐτῷ ἀνήρ τις ἐκ τῆς πόλεως, ὃς εἶχε δαι-
land, met Him a man certain out of the city, who had
1537 5550 2425 2440 3756 1737
μόνια ἐκ χρόνων ἱκανῶν, καὶ ἱμάτιον οὐκ ἐνεδιδύσκετο, καὶ
demons from a time long. and a garment not he put on, and
1722 3614 3756 3306 235 1722 3418 1492
28 ἐν οἰκίᾳ οὐκ ἔμενεν, ἀλλ' ἐν τοῖς μνήμασιν. ἰδὼν δὲ τὸν
in a house not he stayed, but among the tombs. seeing And
2424 349 4363 846 5456 3173
Ἰησοῦν, καὶ ἀνακράξας, προσέπεσεν αὐτῷ, καὶ φωνῇ μεγάλῃ
Jesus, and crying out, he fell down before Him, and with a voice great
2036 5101 1698 4671 2424 5207 2316 5310
εἶπε, Τί ἐμοὶ καὶ σοί, Ἰησοῦ, υἱὲ τοῦ Θεοῦ τοῦ ὑψίστου;
said, What to me and to You, Jesus, Son of God the Most High?
1189 4675/3361/3165/ 928 3853 1063 4151
29 δέομαί σου, μή με βασανίσῃς. παρήγγειλε γὰρ τῷ πνεύματι
I beg You, not me do torment. He charged For the spirit
169 1831 575 444 4183 1063
τῷ ἀκαθάρτῳ ἐξελθεῖν ἀπὸ τοῦ ἀνθρώπου· πολλοῖς γὰρ
unclean to come out from the man. many For
5550 4884 846 1196 254 3976
χρόνοις συνηρπάκει αὐτόν, καὶ ἐδεσμεῖτο ἁλύσεσι καὶ πέδαις
times it had seized him, and he was bound with chains and fetters,
5442 1284 1199 1643 5259
φυλασσόμενος, καὶ διαρρήσσων τὰ δεσμὰ ἠλαύνετο ὑπὸ τοῦ
being guarded, and tearing apart the bonds, he was driven by the
1142 1519 2048 1905 846 2424
30 δαίμονος εἰς τὰς ἐρήμους. ἐπηρώτησε δὲ αὐτὸν ὁ Ἰησοῦς,
demons into the deserts. questioned And Him Jesus,
3004 5101 4671 2076 3686 2036 3003 3754 1140
λέγων, Τί σοι ἐστὶν ὄνομα; ὁ δὲ εἶπε, Λεγεών· ὅτι δαιμόνια
saying. What to you is (the) name? he And said, Legion, because demons

him. [31]And they begged Him that He not order them to go away into the abyss. [32]And there was a herd of many pigs feeding there in the mount. And they begged Him that He would allow them to enter into those. And He allowed them. [33]And coming out from the man, the demons entered into the pigs, and the herd rushed down the cliff into the lake, and was choked. [34]And seeing the thing, those feeding *the pigs* fled. And leaving, *they* reported to the city and to the farms. [35]And they went out to see the thing happening, and came to Jesus. And *they* found the man from whom the demons had gone out, sitting at the feet of Jesus, clothed and of sound mind. And they were afraid. [36]And those seeing also related to them how the demon-possessed one was healed. [37]And all the multitude of the neighborhood of the Gadarenes were seized with a great fear. And *they* asked Him to depart from them. And entering into the boat, He returned.

[38]And the man from whom the demons had gone out begged Him, *desiring* to be with Him. But Jesus sent him away, saying, [39]Go back to your house and tell what God did to you. And he went away proclaiming through all the city what things Jesus did to him.

[40]And it happened *as* Jesus returned, the crowd gladly received Him, for they were all waiting for Him. [41]And, behold, a man whose name (was) Jairus came, and this one was a

4183 1525 1519 846 3870 846 2443 3363
31 πολλὰ εἰσῆλθεν εἰς αὐτόν. καὶ παρεκάλουν αὐτὸν ἵνα μὴ
many entered into him. And they begged Him that not

2004 846 1519 12 565 2258 1563 34
32 ἐπιτάξῃ αὐτοῖς εἰς τὴν ἄβυσσον ἀπελθεῖν. ἦν δὲ ἐκεῖ ἀγέλη
He order them into the abyss to go away. was And there a herd

5519 2425 1006 1722 3735 3870
χοίρων ἱκανῶν βοσκομένων ἐν τῷ ὄρει· καὶ παρεκάλουν
pigs of many feeding in the mountain; and they begged

846 2443 2010 846 1519 1565 1525 2010
αὐτὸν ἵνα ἐπιτρέψῃ αὐτοῖς εἰς ἐκείνους εἰσελθεῖν. καὶ ἐπέτρε-
Him that He would let them into those to enter. And He let

846 1831 1140 575 444
33 ψεν αὐτοῖς. ἐξελθόντα δὲ τὰ δαιμόνια ἀπὸ τοῦ ἀνθρώπου
them. coming out And the demons from the man

1525 1519 5519 3729 34 2596
εἰσῆλθεν εἰς τοὺς χοίρους· καὶ ὥρμησεν ἡ ἀγέλη κατὰ τοῦ
entered into the pigs, and rushed the herd down the

2911 1519 3041 638 1492
34 κρημνοῦ εἰς τὴν λίμνην, καὶ ἀπεπνίγη. ἰδόντες δὲ οἱ
precipice into the lake, and was choked. seeing And those

1006 1096 5343 565 518
βόσκοντες τὸ γεγενημένον ἔφυγον, καὶ ἀπελθόντες ἀπήγ-
feeding the thing happening, they fled; and leaving (they)

1519 4172 1519 68 1831 1492
35 γειλαν εἰς τὴν πόλιν καὶ εἰς τοὺς ἀγρούς. ἐξῆλθον δὲ ἰδεῖν
reported to the city and to the farms. they went And to see

1096 2064 4314 2424 2147 2521
τὸ γεγονός· καὶ ἦλθον πρὸς τὸν Ἰησοῦν, καὶ εὗρον καθή-
the thing happening and came to — Jesus, and found sitting

444 575/3739 1140 1831 2439
μενον τὸν ἄνθρωπον ἀφ' οὗ τὰ δαιμόνια ἐξεληλύθει, ἱματι-
the man from whom the demons had gone out, clothed

4993 3844 4228 2424
σμένον καὶ σωφρονοῦντα, παρὰ τοὺς πόδας τοῦ Ἰησοῦ· καὶ
and of sound mind, at the feet of Jesus. And

5399 518 846 1492 4459 4982
36 ἐφοβήθησαν. ἀπήγγειλαν δὲ αὐτοῖς καὶ οἱ ἰδόντες πῶς ἐσώθη
they were afraid. related And to them also those seeing how was healed

1139 2065 846 537 4128
37 ὁ δαιμονισθείς. καὶ ἠρώτησαν αὐτὸν ἅπαν τὸ πλῆθος τῆς
the demon-possessed. And asked Him all the multitude of the

4066 1046 565 575 846 3754 5401
περιχώρου τῶν Γαδαρηνῶν ἀπελθεῖν ἀπ' αὐτῶν, ὅτι φόβῳ
neighborhood of the Gadarenes to depart from them, for with a fear

3173 4912 846 1684 1519 4143 5290
μεγάλῳ συνείχοντο· αὐτὸς δὲ ἐμβὰς εἰς τὸ πλοῖον ὑπέ-
great they were seized; He and entering into the boat

1189 846 435 575 3739 1831
38 στρεψεν. ἐδέετο δὲ αὐτοῦ ὁ ἀνὴρ ἀφ' οὗ ἐξεληλύθει τὰ
returned. begged And Him the man from whom had gone out the

1140 1511 4862 846 630 846 2424 3004
δαιμόνια εἶναι σὺν αὐτῷ. ἀπέλυσε δὲ αὐτὸν ὁ Ἰησοῦς λέγων,
demons to be with Him; dismissed But him Jesus, saying,

5290 1519 3614 4675 1334 3746 4160 4671
39 Ὑπόστρεφε εἰς τὸν οἶκόν σου. καὶ διηγοῦ ὅσα ἐποίησέ σοι
Return to the house of you, and relate what did to you

2316 565 2596 3650 4172 2784 3745
ὁ Θεός. καὶ ἀπῆλθε, καθ' ὅλην τὴν πόλιν κηρύσσων ὅσα
— God. And he went away through all the city proclaiming what things

4160 846 2424
ἐποίησεν αὐτῷ ὁ Ἰησοῦς.
did to him — Jesus.

1096 1722 5290 2424 588
40 Ἐγένετο δὲ ἐν τῷ ὑποστρέψαι τὸν Ἰησοῦν, ἀπεδέξατο
it was And, in the returning Jesus, gladly received

846 3793 2258 1063 3956 4328 846
41 αὐτὸν ὁ ὄχλος· ἦσαν γὰρ πάντες προσδοκῶντες αὐτόν. καὶ
Him the crowd; they were for all expecting Him. And

2400 2064 435 3739 3686 2383 846 758
ἰδού, ἦλθεν ἀνὴρ ᾧ ὄνομα Ἰάειρος, καὶ αὐτὸς ἄρχων τῆς
behold, came a man to whom name Jairus, and this one a ruler of the

synagogue ruler. And falling at the feet of Jesus, he begged Him to come into his house, [42]because an only daughter was born to him, about twelve years *old*, and she was dying. And in His going, the crowd pressed on Him.

[43]And a woman being in a flow of blood from twelve years, who had spent *her* whole living on physicians, *and* could not be cured by anyone, [44]coming up behind, she touched the border of His garment. And instantly the flow of her blood stopped. [45]And Jesus said, Who *was* touching Me? And all having denied, Peter and those with Him said, Master, the crowds press on You and jostle. And do You say, Who *was* touching Me? [46]But Jesus said, Someone touched Me; for I knew power had gone out from Me. [47]And seeing that she was not hidden, the woman came trembling, and kneeled down before Him, *and* told Him before all the people for what reason she touched Him, and how *she* was instantly cured. [48]And He said to her, Daughter, be comforted. Your faith has healed you. Go in peace.

[49]*As* He was yet speaking, someone came from the synagogue ruler, saying to him, Your daughter has expired. Do not trouble the Teacher. [50]But hearing, Jesus answered him, saying, Do not fear; only believe, and she will be healed. [51]And coming into the house, He did not allow anyone to enter except Peter and James and John, and the father and mother of the child. [52]And all were

4864 5225 4098 3844 4228 2424
συναγωγῆς ὑπῆρχε, καὶ πεσὼν παρὰ τοὺς πόδας τοῦ Ἰησοῦ
synagogue was. And falling at the feet of Jesus,
3870 846 1525 1519 3624 848 3754 2364
42 παρεκάλει αὐτὸν εἰσελθεῖν εἰς τὸν οἶκον αὐτοῦ· ὅτι θυγάτηρ
he begged Him to come into the house of him, because daughter
3439 2258 846 5613 2091 1427 3778 599
μονογενὴς ἦν αὐτῷ ὡς ἐτῶν δώδεκα, καὶ αὕτη ἀπέθνη-
an only born was to him, about years twelve, and she was dying.
1722 5217 846 3793 4846 846
σκεν. ἐν δὲ τῷ ὑπάγειν αὐτὸν οἱ ὄχλοι συνέπνιγον αὐτόν.
in And the going (of) Him, the crowd pressed upon Him.
1135 5607 1722 4511 129 575 2094 1427 3748
43 Καὶ γυνὴ οὖσα ἐν ῥύσει αἵματος ἀπὸ ἐτῶν δώδεκα, ἥτις
And a woman being in a flow of blood from years twelve, who
1519 2395 4321 3650 979 3756 2480
εἰς ἰατροὺς προσαναλώσασα ὅλον τὸν βίον οὐκ ἴσχυσεν
to physicians had spent whole (her) living, not could
5259 3762 2323 4334 3693 680
44 ὑπ' οὐδενὸς θεραπευθῆναι, προσελθοῦσα ὄπισθεν, ἥψατο
by no one be cured, having come up behind, she touched
2899 2440 848 3916 2476
τοῦ κρασπέδου τοῦ ἱματίου αὐτοῦ· καὶ παραχρῆμα ἔστη
the border of the garment of Him, and immediately stopped
4511 129 848 2036 2424 5101
45 ἡ ῥύσις τοῦ αἵματος αὐτῆς. καὶ εἶπεν ὁ Ἰησοῦς, Τίς ὁ
the flow of the blood of her. And said Jesus, Who
680 3450 720 3956 2036 4074
ἁψάμενός μου; ἀρνουμένων δὲ πάντων, εἶπεν ὁ Πέτρος καὶ
(was) touching Me? denying And all, said Peter and
3326 846 1988 3793 4912 4571
οἱ μετ' αὐτοῦ, Ἐπιστάτα, οἱ ὄχλοι συνέχουσί σε, καὶ
those with Him, Master, the crowds press upon You and
598 3004 5101 680 3450 2424
46 ἀποθλίβουσι, καὶ λέγεις, Τίς ὁ ἁψάμενός μου; ὁ δὲ Ἰησοῦς
jostle. And do You say, Who was touching Me? But Jesus
2036 680 3450 5100 1473 1063 1097 1411 1831
47 εἶπεν, Ἥψατό μού τις· ἐγὼ γὰρ ἔγνων δύναμιν ἐξελθοῦσαν
said, touched Me Someone; I for knew power (was) going
575 1700 1492 1135 3754 3756 2990 5141 2064
ἀπ' ἐμοῦ. ἰδοῦσα δὲ ἡ γυνὴ ὅτι οὐκ ἔλαθε, τρέμουσα ἦλθε,
from Me. seeing And the woman that not she was hid, trembling came
4363 846 1223 3739 156 680 846
καὶ προσπεσοῦσα αὐτῷ, δι' ἣν αἰτίαν ἥψατο αὐτοῦ
and kneeled down before Him, for what cause she touched Him
518 846 1799 3956 2992 5613 2390
48 ἀπήγγειλεν αὐτῷ ἐνώπιον παντὸς τοῦ λαοῦ, καὶ ὡς ἰάθη
she declared to Him before all the people, and how was cured
3916 2036 846 2293 2364 4102
49 παραχρῆμα. ὁ δὲ εἶπεν αὐτῇ, Θάρσει, θύγατερ, ἡ πίστις
immediately. He And said to her, Be comforted, daughter, the faith
4675 4992 4571 4198 1519 1575
σου σέσωκέ σε· πορεύου εἰς εἰρήνην.
of you has healed you; go in peace.
2089 846 2980 2064/5100/3844 752
Ἔτι αὐτοῦ λαλοῦντος, ἔρχεταί τις παρὰ τοῦ ἀρχισυναγώ-
Yet Him speaking, comes someone from the synagogue ruler
3004 846 3754 2348 2364 4675 3361 4660
γου, λέγων αὐτῷ ὅτι Τέθνηκεν ἡ θυγάτηρ σου· μὴ σκύλλε
saying to him. has expired The daughter of you, not trouble
1320 2424 191 611 846
50 τὸν διδάσκαλον. ὁ δὲ Ἰησοῦς ἀκούσας ἀπεκρίθη αὐτῷ,
the Teacher. But Jesus hearing answered him,
3004 3361 5399 3440 4100 4982 1525
λέγων, Μὴ φοβοῦ· μόνον πίστευε, καὶ σωθήσεται. εἰσελθὼν
saying, Do not fear; only believe, and she will be healed. coming
1519 3614 3756 863 1525 3762 --1508- 4074
51 δὲ εἰς τὴν οἰκίαν, οὐκ ἀφῆκεν εἰσελθεῖν οὐδένα, εἰ μὴ Πέτρον
And to the house, not He allowed to enter anyone except Peter
2385 2491 3962 3816
καὶ Ἰάκωβον καὶ Ἰωάννην, καὶ τὸν πατέρα τῆς παιδὸς καὶ
and James and John, and the father of the child, and

weeping and bewailing
her. But He said, Stop
weeping. She has not died,
but is sleeping. [53]And they
scoffed at Him, knowing
that she died. [54]But putting all outside, and taking
hold of her hand, He called
out, saying, Child, rise up!
[55]And her spirit returned,
and she rose up immediately. And He ordered *some-
thing* to eat be given to
her. [56]And her parents
were amazed. But He
charged them to tell no one
of that *which* occurred.

3384 2799 3956 2875 846
52 τὴν μητέρα. ἔκλαιον δὲ πάντες, καὶ ἐκόπτοντο αὐτήν. ὁ δὲ
the mother. were weeping And all and bewailing her. He But
2036 3361 2799 3756 599 235 2518 2606
53 εἶπε, Μὴ κλαίετε· οὐκ ἀπέθανεν, ἀλλὰ καθεύδει. καὶ κατε-
said, Stop weeping! not she died, but sleeps. And they
846 1492 3754 599 846 1544 1854
γέλων αὐτοῦ, εἰδότες ὅτι ἀπέθανεν. αὐτὸς δὲ ἐκβαλὼν ἔξω
ridiculed Him, knowing that she died. He But putting outside
3956 2902 5495 848 5455 3004
54 πάντας, καὶ κρατήσας τῆς χειρὸς αὐτῆς, ἐφώνησε λέγων,
all, and taking hold of the hand of her, He called out, saying,
3816 1453 1994 4151 848 450
55 Ἡ παῖς ἐγείρου. καὶ ἐπέστρεψε τὸ πνεῦμα αὐτῆς. καὶ ἀνέστη
Child, arise! And returned the spirit of her, and she arose
3916 1299 846 1325 5315 1839
56 παραχρῆμα· καὶ διέταξεν αὐτῇ δοθῆναι φαγεῖν. καὶ ἐξέστη-
immediately. And He ordered her to be given to eat. And were
1118 848 3853 846 3367 2036
σαν οἱ γονεῖς αὐτῆς· ὁ δὲ παρήγγειλεν αὐτοῖς μηδενὶ εἰπεῖν
amazed the parents of her. He But charged them to no one to tell
1096
τὸ γεγονός.
the thing (which) happened.

CHAPTER 9

[1]And having called to-
gether His twelve disciples,
He gave them power and
authority over all the
demons, and to heal
diseases. [2]And *He* sent
them to proclaim the kingdom of God, and to heal the
ones being sick. [3]And He
said to them, Take nothing
for the way, neither staffs,
nor moneybags, nor bread,
nor silver, nor each to
have two tunics. [4]And into
whatever house you enter,
remain there, and go out
from there. [5]And as many
as may not receive you,
going out from that city
even shake off the dust
from your feet, for a testimony against them. [6]And
going out they passed
through the villages preaching the gospel, and healing
everywhere.

[7]And Herod the tetrarch
heard all the things hap-
pening by Him, and was
puzzled, because of the
saying by some that John
had been raised from *the*
dead; [8]and by some that
Elijah had appeared. And

4779 1427 3101 848 1325
1 Συγκαλεσάμενος δὲ τοὺς δώδεκα μαθητὰς αὐτοῦ, ἔδωκεν
having called together And the twelve disciples of Him, He gave
846 1411 1849 1909 3956 1140
αὐτοῖς δύναμιν καὶ ἐξουσίαν ἐπὶ πάντα τὰ δαιμόνια, καὶ
them power and authority over all the demons, and
3554 2323 649 846 2784
2 νόσους θεραπεύειν. καὶ ἀπέστειλεν αὐτοὺς κηρύσσειν τὴν
diseases to heal. And He sent them to proclaim the
932 2316 2390 770 2036
3 βασιλείαν τοῦ Θεοῦ, καὶ ἰᾶσθαι τοὺς ἀσθενοῦντας. καὶ εἶπε
kingdom -- of God, and to cure those being sick. And He said
4314 846 3367 142 1519 3598 3383 4464
πρὸς αὐτούς, Μηδὲν αἴρετε εἰς τὴν ὁδόν· μήτε ῥάβδους,
to them, Nothing take for the way, neither staffs,
3383 4082 3383 740 3383 694 3383 303 1417
μήτε πήραν, μήτε ἄρτον, μήτε ἀργύριον, μήτε ἀνὰ δύο
nor moneybags, nor bread, nor silver, nor each two
5509 2192 1519 3739 302 3614 1525 1563 3306
4 χιτῶνας ἔχειν. καὶ εἰς ἣν ἂν οἰκίαν εἰσέλθητε, ἐκεῖ μένετε, καὶ
tunics to have. And into whatever house you go in, there remain, and
1564 1837 3745 302 3361 1209 5209 1831
5 ἐκεῖθεν ἐξέρχεσθε. καὶ ὅσοι ἂν μὴ δέξωνται ὑμᾶς, ἐξερχό-
from there go out. And as many as not may receive you, going
575 4172 1565 2868 575
μενοι ἀπὸ τῆς πόλεως ἐκείνης καὶ τὸν κονιορτὸν ἀπὸ τῶν
out from — city that even the dust from the
4228 5216 660 1519 3142 1909 846 1831
6 ποδῶν ὑμῶν ἀποτινάξατε εἰς μαρτύριον ἐπ' αὐτούς. ἐξερχό-
feet of you shake off, for a testimony against them. going
1330 2596 2968 2097
μενοι δὲ διήρχοντο κατὰ τὰς κώμας, εὐαγγελιζόμενοι καὶ
out And they passed through the villages preaching the gospel and
2323 3837
θεραπεύοντες πανταχοῦ.
healing everywhere.
191 2264 5076 1096 5259 846
7 Ἤκουσε δὲ Ἡρώδης ὁ τετράρχης τὰ γινόμενα ὑπ' αὐτοῦ
heard And Herod the tetrarch the things happening by Him
3956 1280 1223 3004 5259 5100 3754
πάντα· καὶ διηπόρει, διὰ τὸ λέγεσθαι ὑπό τινων ὅτι
all, and was puzzled, because of the saying by some that
2491 1453 1537 3498 5259 5100 3754 2243
8 Ἰωάννης ἐγήγερται ἐκ νεκρῶν· ὑπό τινων δὲ ὅτι Ἠλίας
John has been raised from the dead, by some and that Elijah

others *said,* A prophet of the ancients rose again. [9]And Herod said, I beheaded John, but who is this about whom I hear such things? And he sought to see Him.

[10]And returning the apostles told Him what things they did. And taking them He went out privately to a desert place of a city called Bethsaida. [11]But knowing *this,* the crowds followed Him. And having received them, He spoke to them about the kingdom of God. And He cured those having need of healing. [12]But the day began to wane, and coming up the Twelve said to Him, Let the crowd go, that going to the surrounding villages and farms they may lodge, and find food supplies, because here we are in a desert place. [13]But He said to them, You give them to eat. But they said, There are not to us more than five loaves and two fish, unless going we buy foods for all this people. [14]For there were about five thousand men. But He said to His disciples, Make them recline in groups, by fifties. [15]And they did so, and made all recline. [16]And taking the five loaves and the two fish, looking up to Heaven, He blessed them, and broke, and gave to the disciples to set before the crowd. [17]And they ate and were all satisfied. And twelve handbaskets of fragments of that left over to them were taken up.

5316 243 3754 4396 1520 744 450
ἐφάνη ἄλλων δὲ ὅτι Προφήτης εἷς τῶν ἀρχαίων ἀνέστη
had appeared; others and that a prophet of the ancients rose again.
2036 2264 2491 1473 607 5101
9 καὶ εἶπεν ὁ Ἡρῴδης, Ἰωάννην ἐγὼ ἀπεκεφάλισα· τίς δέ
And said Herod, John I beheaded, who but
2076 3778 4012 3756 1473 191 5118 2212 1492
ἐστιν οὗτος, περὶ οὗ ἐγὼ ἀκούω τοιαῦτα; καὶ ἐζήτει ἰδεῖν
is this about whom I hear such things? And he tried to see
846
αὐτόν.
Him.
5290 652 1334 846 3745
10 Καὶ ὑποστρέψαντες οἱ ἀπόστολοι διηγήσαντο αὐτῷ ὅσα
And having returned the apostles told Him what
4160 3880 846 5298 2596 2398
ἐποίησαν. καὶ παραλαβὼν αὐτούς, ὑπεχώρησε κατ' ἰδίαν
they did. And taking them, He departed privately
1519 5117 2048 4172 2563 966 3793
11 εἰς τόπον ἔρημον πόλεως καλουμένης Βηθσαϊδά. οἱ δὲ ὄχλοι
to a place desert of a city called Bethsaida. the But crowds
1097 190 846 1209 846 2980
γνόντες ἠκολούθησαν αὐτῷ· καὶ δεξάμενος αὐτούς, ἐλάλει
having known followed Him. And having received them, He spoke
846 4012 932 2316 5532
αὐτοῖς περὶ τῆς βασιλείας τοῦ Θεοῦ, καὶ τοὺς χρείαν
to them about the kingdom — of God, and those need
2192 2322 2390 2250 756 2827 4334
12 ἔχοντας θεραπείας ἰᾶτο. ἡ δὲ ἡμέρα ἤρξατο κλίνειν· προσ-
having of healing He cured. the But day began to decline; coming
1427 2036 846 630 3793
ελθόντες δὲ οἱ δώδεκα εἶπον αὐτῷ, Ἀπόλυσον τὸν ὄχλον,
up and the twelve said to Him, Let go the crowd,
2443 565 1519 2945 2968 68 2647
ἵνα ἀπελθόντες εἰς τὰς κύκλῳ κώμας καὶ τοὺς ἀγροὺς κατα-
that going to the around villages and the farms they
2147 1979 3754 5602 1722 2048 5117
λύσωσι, καὶ εὕρωσιν ἐπισιτισμόν· ὅτι ὧδε ἐν ἐρήμῳ τόπῳ
may lodge, and may find food supplies, because here in a desert place
2070 2036 4314 846 1325 846 5210 5315
13 ἐσμέν. εἶπε δὲ πρὸς αὐτούς, Δότε αὐτοῖς ὑμεῖς φαγεῖν. οἱ δὲ
we are. He said And to them, give them You to eat. they But
2036 3756 1526 2254 4192 2228 4002 740 1417 2486
εἶπον, Οὐκ εἰσὶν ἡμῖν πλεῖον ἢ πέντε ἄρτοι καὶ δύο ἰχθύες,
said, Not is to us more than five loaves and two fish,
1509 4198 2249 59 1519 3956 2992
εἰ μήτι πορευθέντες ἡμεῖς ἀγοράσωμεν εἰς πάντα τὸν λαὸν
unless going we may buy for all people
5126 1033 2258 1063 5316 435 4000
14 τοῦτον βρώματα. ἦσαν γὰρ ὡσεὶ ἄνδρες πεντακισχίλιοι.
this foods. there were For about men five thousand.
2036 4314 3101 848 2625 846
εἶπε δὲ πρὸς τοὺς μαθητὰς αὐτοῦ, Κατακλίνατε αὐτοὺς
He said And to the disciples of Him, Cause to recline them
2828 303 4004 4160 3779 347
15 κλισίας ἀνὰ πεντήκοντα. καὶ ἐποίησαν οὕτω, καὶ ἀνέκλιναν
in groups by fifties. And they did so, and caused to recline
537 2983 4002 740 1417 2486
16 ἅπαντας. λαβὼν δὲ τοὺς πέντε ἄρτους καὶ τοὺς δύο ἰχθύας,
all. taking And the five loaves and the two fish,
308 1519 3772 2127 846 2622
ἀναβλέψας εἰς τὸν οὐρανόν, εὐλόγησεν αὐτούς, καὶ κατέ-
looking up to Heaven, He blessed them, and broke
1325 3101 3908 3793
17 κλασε, καὶ ἐδίδου τοῖς μαθηταῖς παρατιθέναι τῷ ὄχλῳ. καὶ
and gave to the disciples to set before the crowd. And
5315 5526 3956 142 4052
ἔφαγον καὶ ἐχορτάσθησαν πάντες· καὶ ἤρθη τὸ περισσεῦσαν
they ate and were filled all; and were taken the excess
846 2801 2894 1427
αὐτοῖς κλασμάτων, κόφινοι δώδεκα.
to them of fragments, baskets twelve.

18 And it happened *as* He was praying alone, the disciples were with Him. And He questioned them, saying, Whom do the crowds say Me to be? 19 And answering they said, John the Baptist; and others, Elijah; and others that some prophet of the ancients has risen again. 20 And He said to them, But whom do you say Me to be? And answering Peter said, The Christ of God. 21 And strictly warning them, He ordered to tell no one this, 22 saying, The Son of man must suffer many things, and be rejected by the elders and chief priests and scribes, and be killed, and be raised the third day. 23 And He said to all, If anyone desires to come after Me, let him deny himself and take up his cross daily. And let him follow Me. 24 For whoever desires to save his soul, he will lose it. But whoever loses his soul for My sake, this one will save it. 25 For what is a man profited gaining the whole world, but destroying himself or suffering loss? 26 For whoever is ashamed of Me and My words, the Son of man will be ashamed of that one when He comes in His glory, and *that* of the Father, and of the holy angels.

27 But truly I say to you, There are some of those standing here who in no way shall taste of death until they see the kingdom of God.

28 And about eight days after these sayings, it happened: also taking Peter and John and James, He

1096 1722 1511 846 4336 2651
18 Καὶ ἐγένετο ἐν τῷ εἶναι αὐτὸν προσευχόμενον καταμόνας,
And it was, (as) was Him praying alone,
4895 846 3101 1905 846 3004
συνῆσαν αὐτῷ οἱ μαθηταί· καὶ ἐπηρώτησεν αὐτούς, λέγων,
were with Him the disciples, and He questioned them, saying,
5101 3165 3004 3793 1511 611 2036
19 Τίνα με λέγουσιν οἱ ὄχλοι εἶναι ; οἱ δὲ ἀποκριθέντες εἶπον,
Whom Me say the crowds to be? they And answering said,
2491 910 2431 2213 243 3754
Ἰωάννην τὸν Βαπτιστήν· ἄλλοι δὲ Ἠλίαν· ἄλλοι δέ, ὅτι
John the Baptist; others but Elijah; others and that
4396 5100 744 450 2036 846 5210
20 προφήτης τις τῶν ἀρχαίων ἀνέστη. εἶπε δὲ αὐτοῖς, Ὑμεῖς
prophet a certain of the ancients rose again. He said And to them, you
5101 3165 3004 1511 611 4074 2036
δὲ τίνα με λέγετε εἶναι ; ἀποκριθεὶς δὲ ὁ Πέτρος εἶπε, Τὸν
And, whom Me say to be? answering And Peter said, The
5547 2316 2008 846 3853
21 Χριστὸν τοῦ Θεοῦ. ὁ δὲ ἐπιτιμήσας αὐτοῖς παρήγγειλε
Christ of God. He But warning them ordered
3367 2036 5124 2036 3754 1163 5207 444
22 μηδενὶ εἰπεῖν τοῦτο, εἰπὼν ὅτι Δεῖ τὸν υἱὸν τοῦ ἀνθρώπου
no one to tell this, saying that it behoves the Son of man
4183 3958 593 575 4245
πολλὰ παθεῖν, καὶ ἀποδοκιμασθῆναι ἀπὸ τῶν πρεσβυτέ-
many things to suffer, and to be rejected from the elders
749 1122 615
ρων καὶ ἀρχιερέων καὶ γραμματέων, καὶ ἀποκτανθῆναι,
and chief priests and scribes, and to be killed,
5154 2250 1453 3004 4314 3956 1487 5100
23 καὶ τῇ τρίτῃ ἡμέρᾳ ἐγερθῆναι. ἔλεγε δὲ πρὸς πάντας, Εἴ τις
and the third day to be raised. He said And to all, If anyone
2309 3694 3450 2064 533 1438 142
θέλει ὀπίσω μου ἐλθεῖν, ἀπαρνησάσθω ἑαυτόν, καὶ ἀράτω
desires after Me to come, let him deny himself and take up
4716 848 2250 190 3427 3739
24 τὸν σταυρὸν αὐτοῦ καθ' ἡμέραν, καὶ ἀκολουθείτω μοι. ὃς
the cross of Him daily. And let him follow Me. whoever
1063 302 2309 5590 848 4982 622 848 3739
γὰρ ἂν θέλῃ τὴν ψυχὴν αὐτοῦ σῶσαι, ἀπολέσει αὐτήν· ὃς
For shall desire the soul of him to save, he will lose it; whoever
302 622 5590 848 1752 1700 3778 4982
δ' ἂν ἀπολέσῃ τὴν ψυχὴν αὐτοῦ ἕνεκεν ἐμοῦ, οὗτος σώσει
But shall lose the soul of him for My sake, this one will save
846 5101 1063 5623 444 2770 2889
25 αὐτήν. τί γὰρ ὠφελεῖται ἄνθρωπος, κερδήσας τὸν κόσμον
it. what For is profited a man gaining the world
3650 1438 622 2228/2210 3739/1063/302 1870
26 ὅλον, ἑαυτὸν δὲ ἀπολέσας ἢ ζημιωθείς ; ὃς γὰρ ἂν ἐπαισχυνθῇ
whole, himself but destroying or suffering loss? whoever For is ashamed of
3165 1699 3056 5126 5207 444
με καὶ τοὺς ἐμοὺς λόγους, τοῦτον ὁ υἱὸς τοῦ ἀνθρώπου
Me and — My words, this one the Son — of man
1870 3752 2064 1722 1391 848
ἐπαισχυνθήσεται, ὅταν ἔλθῃ ἐν τῇ δόξῃ αὐτοῦ καὶ τοῦ
will be ashamed of when He comes in the glory of Him, and of the
3962 40 32 3004 5213 230
27 πατρὸς καὶ τῶν ἁγίων ἀγγέλων. λέγω δὲ ὑμῖν ἀληθῶς,
Father, and of the holy angels. I say But to you truly,
1526 5100 5602 2476 3739 3364 1089 2288
εἰσί τινες τῶν ὧδε ἑστηκότων, οἳ οὐ μὴ γεύσονται θανάτου,
are some of those here standing who in no way shall taste of death
2193 302 1492 932 2316
ἕως ἂν ἴδωσι τὴν βασιλείαν τοῦ Θεοῦ.
until they see the kingdom — of God.
1096 3329 3056 5128 5616 2250 3638
28 Ἐγένετο δὲ μετὰ τοὺς λόγους τούτους ὡσεὶ ἡμέραι ὀκτώ,
it was And, after sayings these, about days eight,
3880 4074 2491 2385
καὶ παραλαβὼν τὸν Πέτρον καὶ Ἰωάννην καὶ Ἰάκωβον,
and taking — Peter and John and James,

305 1519 3735 4336 1096 1722
29 ἀνέβη εἰς τὸ ὄρος προσεύξασθαι. καὶ ἐγένετο, ἐν τῷ
He went into the mountain to pray. And became in the
4336 846 1491 4383 848 2087
προσεύχεσθαι αὐτόν, τὸ εἶδος τοῦ προσώπου αὐτοῦ ἕτερον,
praying (of) Him the appearance of the face of Him different
2441 848 3022 1823 2400
30 καὶ ὁ ἱματισμὸς αὐτοῦ λευκὸς ἐξαστράπτων. καὶ ἰδού,
and the clothing of Him white dazzling. And, behold,
435 1417 4814 846 3748 2258 3475
ἄνδρες δύο συνελάλουν αὐτῷ, οἵτινες ἦσαν Μωσῆς καὶ
men two talked with Him, who were Moses and
2243 3739 3700 1722 1391 3004 1841 848 3739
31 Ἠλίας, οἳ ὀφθέντες ἐν δόξῃ ἔλεγον τὴν ἔξοδον αὐτοῦ ἣν
Elijah, who appearing in glory spoke of the exodus of Him, which
3195 4137 1722 2419 4074 4862 846
32 ἔμελλε πληροῦν ἐν Ἱερουσαλήμ. ὁ δὲ Πέτρος καὶ οἱ σὺν αὐτῷ
He was about to finish in Jerusalem. And Peter and those with him
2258 916 5258 1235 1492
ἦσαν βεβαρημένοι ὕπνῳ· διαγρηγορήσαντες δὲ εἶδον τὴν
were being pressed down with sleep. awakening fully But they saw the
1391 848 1417 435 4921 846
δόξαν αὐτοῦ, καὶ τοὺς δύο ἄνδρας τοὺς συνεστῶτας αὐτῷ.
glory of Him, and the two men standing with Him.
1096 1722 1316 846 575 846 2036
33 καὶ ἐγένετο, ἐν τῷ διαχωρίζεσθαι αὐτοὺς ἀπ' αὐτοῦ, εἶπεν
And it was, in the parting (of) them from Him, said
4074 4314 2424 1988 2570 2076 2248
ὁ Πέτρος πρὸς τὸν Ἰησοῦν, Ἐπιστάτα, καλόν ἐστιν ἡμᾶς
Peter to Jesus, Master, good it is (for) us
5602 1511 4160 4633 5140 3391 4671
ὧδε εἶναι· καὶ ποιήσωμεν σκηνὰς τρεῖς, μίαν σοί, καὶ
here to be, and let us make tents three, one for You, and
3474 3391 3393 2243 3361 1492 3739 3004 5023
34 Μωσεῖ μίαν, καὶ μίαν Ἠλίᾳ· μὴ εἰδὼς ὃ λέγει. ταῦτα δὲ
Moses one, and one for Elijah, not knowing what he says. these And
846 3004 1096 3507 1982 846
αὐτοῦ λέγοντος, ἐγένετο νεφέλη καὶ ἐπεσκίασεν αὐτούς·
him saying, came a cloud and overshadowed them;
5399 1722 1565 1525 1519 3507
35 ἐφοβήθησαν δὲ ἐν τῷ ἐκείνους εἰσελθεῖν εἰς τὴν νεφέλην. καὶ
they feared and in the of those entering into the cloud. And
5456 1096 1537 3507 3004 3778 2076 5207
φωνὴ ἐγένετο ἐκ τῆς νεφέλης, λέγουσα, Οὗτός ἐστιν ὁ υἱός
a voice came out of the cloud, saying, This is the Son
3450 27 846 191 1722 1096
36 μου ὁ ἀγαπητός· αὐτοῦ ἀκούετε. καὶ ἐν τῷ γενέσθαι τὴν
of Me, the Beloved; Him hear. And in the occurring of the
5456 2147 2424 3440 846 4601
φωνήν, εὑρέθη ὁ Ἰησοῦς μόνος. καὶ αὐτοὶ ἐσίγησαν, καὶ
voice, was found Jesus alone. And they were quiet; and
3762 518 1722 1565 2250 3762 3739
οὐδενὶ ἀπήγγειλαν ἐν ἐκείναις ταῖς ἡμέραις οὐδὲν ὧν
to no one reported in those days, nothing which
3708
ἑωράκασιν.
they had seen.
1096 1722 1836 2250 2718 846 575
37 Ἐγένετο δὲ ἐν τῇ ἑξῆς ἡμέρᾳ, κατελθόντων αὐτῶν ἀπὸ
it was And, on the next day, coming down them from
3735 4876 846 3793 4183 2400 435
38 τοῦ ὄρους, συνήντησεν αὐτῷ ὄχλος πολύς. καὶ ἰδού, ἀνὴρ
the mountain, met Him a crowd much. And, behold, a man
575 3793 310 3004 1320 1189 4675
ἀπὸ τοῦ ὄχλου ἀνεβόησε, λέγων, Διδάσκαλε, δέομαί σου,
from the crowd called aloud, saying, Teacher, I beg You,
1914 1909 5207 3450 3754 3439 2076 3427
39 ἐπίβλεψον ἐπὶ τὸν υἱόν μου, ὅτι μονογενής ἐστί μοι· καὶ
to look at the son of me, because only born he is to me, and
2400 4151 2983 846 1810 2896
ἰδού, πνεῦμα λαμβάνει αὐτόν, καὶ ἐξαίφνης κράζει, καὶ
behold, a spirit takes him, and suddenly cries out, and

went into the mountain to pray. [29]And in His praying the appearance of His face became different, and His clothing *was* dazzling white. [30]And, behold, two men talked with Him, who were Moses and Elijah. [31]Appearing in glory, *they* spoke of His exodus, which He was about to accomplish in Jerusalem. [32]But Peter and those with him were pressed down with sleep. But fully awakening they saw His glory, and the two men standing with Him. [33]And it happened in their parting from Him, Peter said to Jesus, Master, it is good for *us* to be here. And, Let us make three tabernacles, one for You, and one for Moses, and one for Elijah —not knowing what he said. [34]And he saying these things, a cloud came and overshadowed them. And they feared *as* those entered into the cloud. [35]And a voice came out of the cloud, saying, This is My Son, the Beloved; hear Him! [36]And *as* the voice occurred, Jesus was found alone. And they were quiet. And *they* reported to no one in those days, nothing which they had seen.

[37]And it happened on the next day, they coming down from the mountain, a huge crowd met Him. [38]And, behold, a man called aloud from the crowd, saying, Teacher, I beg You to look at my son, because he is my only-born. [39]And, behold, a spirit takes him, and *he* suddenly cries out; and *it*

throws him into convulsions, with foaming. And *it* departs from him with pain, bruising him. [40]And I begged Your disciples, that they cast it out. And they were not able. [41]And answering Jesus said, O unbelieving and generation which has been perverted, how long shall I be with you and bear with you? Bring your son here. [42]But as *he* was yet coming up, the demon tore him and violently convulsed *him*. But Jesus rebuked the unclean spirit and healed the child, and gave him back to his father. [43]And all were astonished at the majesty of God.

And as all were marveling at all things which He did, Jesus said to His disciples, [44]You lay into your ears these sayings; for the Son of man is about to be betrayed into *the* hands of men. [45]But they did not understand this saying, and it was veiled from them so that they might not perceive it. And they feared to ask Him about this word.

[46]But an argument came in among them, who might be *the* greater of them. [47]And seeing the argument of their heart, taking a child, Jesus stood it beside Himself, [48]and said to them, Whoever receives this child on My name receives Me. And whoever receives Me receives Him who sent Me. For the one being least among you all, this one shall be great.

4682 846 3326 876 3425 672 575
σπαράσσει αὐτὸν μετὰ ἀφροῦ, καὶ μόγις ἀποχωρεῖ ἀπ'
convulses him with foam, and with pain departs from
846 4937 846 1189 3101 4675
40 αὐτοῦ, συντρῖβον αὐτόν. καὶ ἐδεήθην τῶν μαθητῶν σου
him, bruising him. And I begged the disciples of You
2443 1544 846 3756 1410 611
41 ἵνα ἐκβάλλωσιν αὐτό, καὶ οὐκ ἠδυνήθησαν. ἀποκριθεὶς δὲ
that they cast out it, and not they were able. answering And
2424 2036 5599 1074 571 1294 2193
ὁ Ἰησοῦς εἶπεν, Ὦ γενεὰ ἄπιστος καὶ διεστραμμένη, ἕως
– Jesus said, O generation unbelieving and having been perverted, until
4219 2071 4314 5209 430 5216 4317
πότε ἔσομαι πρὸς ὑμᾶς, καὶ ἀνέξομαι ὑμῶν; προσάγαγε
when shall I be with you, and endure you? Bring
5602 5207 4675 2089 4334 846 4486
42 ὧδε τὸν υἱόν σου. ἔτι δὲ προσερχομένου αὐτοῦ, ἔρρηξεν
here the son of you. yet But (as was) coming up him, tore
846 1140 4952 2008
αὐτὸν τὸ δαιμόνιον καὶ συνεσπάραξεν· ἐπετίμησε δὲ ὁ
him the demon and violently convulsed. rebuked But
2424 4151 169 2390 3816
Ἰησοῦς τῷ πνεύματι τῷ ἀκαθάρτῳ, καὶ ἰάσατο τὸν παῖδα,
Jesus the spirit unclean, and healed the child,
591 846 3962 848 1605
43 καὶ ἀπέδωκεν αὐτὸν τῷ πατρὶ αὐτοῦ. ἐξεπλήσσοντο δὲ
and restored him to the father of him. were astounded And
3856 1909 3168 2316
πάντες ἐπὶ τῇ μεγαλειότητι τοῦ Θεοῦ.
all at the majesty of God.
3956 2296 1909 3956 3739 4160
Πάντων δὲ θαυμαζόντων ἐπὶ πᾶσιν οἷς ἐποίησεν ὁ
all And marveling at all things which He did
2424 2036 4314 3101 848 5087 5210 1519
44 Ἰησοῦς, εἶπε πρὸς τοὺς μαθητὰς αὐτοῦ, Θέσθε ὑμεῖς εἰς τὰ
Jesus said to the disciples of Him, Lay you into the
3775 5216 3056 5128 1063 5207 444
ὦτα ὑμῶν τοὺς λόγους τούτους· ὁ γὰρ υἱὸς τοῦ ἀνθρώπου
ears of you sayings these; the for Son of man
3195 3860 1519 5495 444 50
45 μέλλει παραδίδοσθαι εἰς χεῖρας ἀνθρώπων. οἱ δὲ ἠγνόουν
is about to be betrayed into (the) hands of men. they But knew not
4487 5124 2258 3871 575 846 2443
τὸ ῥῆμα τοῦτο, καὶ ἦν παρακεκαλυμμένον ἀπ' αὐτῶν, ἵνα
word this, and it was having been veiled from them that
3361 143 846 5399 2065 846 4012
μὴ αἴσθωνται αὐτό· καὶ ἐφοβοῦντο ἐρωτῆσαι αὐτὸν περὶ
not they perceive it. And they feared to ask Him about
4487 5127
τοῦ ῥήματος τούτου.
word this.
1525 1261 1722 846 5101 302 1498 3187
46 Εἰσῆλθε δὲ διαλογισμὸς ἐν αὐτοῖς, τὸ τίς ἂν εἴη μείζων
came in But an argument among them, – who might be greater
846 2424 1492 1261 2588
47 αὐτῶν. ὁ δὲ Ἰησοῦς ἰδὼν τὸν διαλογισμὸν τῆς καρδίας
of them. – And Jesus having seen the argument of the heart
848 1949 3813 2476 846 3844 1438
αὐτῶν, ἐπιλαβόμενος παιδίου, ἔστησεν αὐτὸ παρ' ἑαυτῷ,
of them, taking a child, stood it beside Himself,
2036 846 3739 1437 1209 5124 3813 1909
48 καὶ εἶπεν αὐτοῖς, Ὃς ἐὰν δέξηται τοῦτο τὸ παιδίον ἐπὶ τῷ
and said to them, Whoever receives this child upon the
3686 3450 1691 1209 3739 1437 1691 1209 1209
ὀνόματί μου ἐμὲ δέχεται· καὶ ὃς ἐὰν ἐμὲ δέξηται δέχεται τὸν
name of Me, Me receives. And whoever Me receives receives the (One)
649 3165 1063 3398 1722 3956 5213 5225
ἀποστείλαντά με· ὁ γὰρ μικρότερος ἐν πᾶσιν ὑμῖν ὑπάρχων
having sent Me. the For lesser among all you being,
3778 2071 3173
οὗτος ἔσται μέγας.
this one shall be great.

NOTE: Frequent words not numbered. δέ(1161); καί(2531)—and, but; ὁ, ἡ, τό (3588, the)— * above word, look in verse margin for No.

49 And answering John said, Master, we saw someone casting out demons on Your name, and we forbade him because he does not follow with us. 50 And Jesus said to them, Do not forbid; for whoever is not against us is for us.

51 And it happened in the fulfilling *of* the days of His taking up, even He set His face to go to Jerusalem.

52 And *He* sent messengers before His face. And going they went into a village of Samaritans, so as to make ready for Him. 53 And they did not receive Him, because His face was going toward Jerusalem. 54 And seeing, His disciples James and John said, Lord, do You desire *that* we tell fire to come down from Heaven, and to destroy them, even as Elijah did? 55 But turning He rebuked them, and *then He* said, You do not know of what spirit you are. 56 For the Son of man did not come to destroy men's lives, but to save. And they went to another village.

57 And it happened as they were going in the way, one said to Him, I will follow You everywhere You may go, Lord. 58 And Jesus said to him, The foxes have holes, and the birds of the heaven nests, but the Son of man has nowhere He may lay *His* head. 59 And He said to another, Follow Me. But he said, Lord, allow me to go first to bury my father. 60 But Jesus said to

611 2491 2036 1988 1492 5100
49 Ἀποκριθεὶς δὲ ὁ Ἰωάννης εἶπεν, Ἐπιστάτα, εἴδομέν τινα
answering And John said, Master, we saw someone
1909 3686 4675 1544 1140 2967
ἐπὶ τῷ ὀνόματί σου ἐκβάλλοντα τὰ δαιμόνια· καὶ ἐκωλύ-
on the name of You casting out — demons, and we pre-
846 3754 3756 190 3326 2257 2036 4314
50 σαμεν αὐτόν, ὅτι οὐκ ἀκολουθεῖ μεθ' ἡμῶν. καὶ εἶπε πρὸς
vented him, because not he follows with us. And said to
846 2424 3361 2967 3739 1063 3756 2076 2596 2257
αὐτὸν ὁ Ἰησοῦς, Μὴ κωλύετε· ὃς γὰρ οὐκ ἔστι καθ' ἡμῶν
them — Jesus, Do not prevent; whoever for not is against us,
5228 2257 2076
ὑπὲρ ἡμῶν ἐστιν
for us is.

1096 1722 4845 2250
51 Ἐγένετο δὲ ἐν τῷ συμπληροῦσθαι τὰς ἡμέρας τῆς
it was And in the fulfilling (of) the days of the
354 848 846 4383 848 4741
ἀναλήψεως αὐτοῦ, καὶ αὐτὸς τὸ πρόσωπον αὐτοῦ ἐστήριξε
taking up of Him, even He the face of Him set
4198 1519 2419 649 32
52 τοῦ πορεύεσθαι εἰς Ἱερουσαλήμ, καὶ ἀπέστειλεν ἀγγέλους
to go to Jerusalem, and sent messengers
4253 4198 848 4198 1525 1519 2968
πρὸ προσώπου αὐτοῦ· καὶ πορευθέντες εἰσῆλθον εἰς κώμην
before the face of Him. And going they went into a village
4541 5620 2090 846 3756 1209 846
53 Σαμαρειτῶν, ὥστε ἑτοιμάσαι αὐτῷ. καὶ οὐκ ἐδέξαντο αὐτόν,
of Samaritans, so as to prepare for Him. And not they received Him,
3754 4383 848 2258 4198 1519 2419
ὅτι τὸ πρόσωπον αὐτοῦ ἦν πορευόμενον εἰς Ἱερουσαλήμ.
because the face of Him was going to Jerusalem.
1492 3101 848 2385 2491 2036
54 Ἰδόντες δὲ οἱ μαθηταὶ αὐτοῦ Ἰάκωβος καὶ Ἰωάννης εἶπον,
seeing And the disciples of Him, James and John said,
2962 2309 2036 4442 2597 575 3772
Κύριε, θέλεις εἴπωμεν πῦρ καταβῆναι ἀπὸ τοῦ οὐρανοῦ, καὶ
Lord, desire You (that) we tell fire to come down from Heaven and
355 846 5613 2243 4160 4762
55 ἀναλῶσαι αὐτούς, ὡς καὶ Ἠλίας ἐποίησε; στραφεὶς δὲ
to destroy them, as also Elijah did? turning But
2008 846 2036 3756 1492 3634 4151
ἐπετίμησεν αὐτοῖς, καὶ εἶπεν, Οὐκ οἴδατε οἵου πνεύματός
He rebuked them, and said, Not you know of what spirit
2075 5210 1063 5207 444 3756 2064 5590
56 ἐστε ὑμεῖς· ὁ γὰρ υἱὸς τοῦ ἀνθρώπου οὐκ ἦλθε ψυχὰς
are you. the For Son of man not did come the souls
444 622 235 4982 4198 1519
ἀνθρώπων ἀπολέσαι, ἀλλὰ σῶσαι. καὶ ἐπορεύθησαν εἰς
of men to destroy, but to save. And they went to
2087 2968
ἑτέραν κώμην.
another village.

1096 4198 848 1722 3598 2036 5100 4314
57 Ἐγένετο δὲ πορευομένων αὐτῶν ἐν τῇ ὁδῷ, εἶπέ τις πρὸς
it was And, going them in the way, said one to
846 190 4671 3699 302 565 2962 2036
αὐτόν, Ἀκολουθήσω σοι ὅπου ἂν ἀπέρχῃ, Κύριε. καὶ εἶπεν
Him, I will follow You wherever may You go, Lord. And said
846 2424 258 5454 2192
58 αὐτῷ ὁ Ἰησοῦς, Αἱ ἀλώπεκες φωλεοὺς ἔχουσι, καὶ τὰ
to him Jesus, The foxes holes have, and the
4071 3772 2682 5207 444
πετεινὰ τοῦ οὐρανοῦ κατασκηνώσεις· ὁ δὲ υἱὸς τοῦ ἀνθρώ-
birds of the heaven nests; the but Son of man
3756 2192 4226 2776 2827 2036 4314 2087
59 που οὐκ ἔχει ποῦ τὴν κεφαλὴν κλίνῃ. εἶπε δὲ πρὸς ἕτερον,
not has where the head He may lay. He said And to another,
190 3427 2036 2962 2010 3427 565
Ἀκολούθει μοι. ὁ δὲ εἶπε, Κύριε, ἐπίτρεψόν μοι ἀπελθόντι
Follow Me. he But said, Lord, allow me going

him, Leave the dead to bury their dead, but going out, you announce the kingdom of God. [61]And also another said, I will follow You, Lord, but first allow me to take leave of those in my house. [62]But Jesus said to him, No one putting his hand on the plow, and looking at the things behind, is fit for the kingdom of God.

4412 2290 3962 3450 2036 846 2424
60 πρῶτον θάψαι τὸν πατέρα μου. εἶπε δὲ αὐτῷ ὁ Ἰησοῦς,
first to bury the father of me. said But to him – Jesus,
863 3498 2290 1438 3498 4771
Ἄφες τοὺς νεκροὺς θάψαι τοὺς ἑαυτῶν νεκρούς· σὺ δὲ
Leave the dead to bury the of themselves dead, you but
565 1229 932 2316 2036
61 ἀπελθὼν διάγγελλε τὴν βασιλείαν τοῦ Θεοῦ. εἶπε δὲ καὶ
going out announce the kingdom – of God. said And also
2087 190 4671 2963 4412 2010 3427
ἕτερος, Ἀκολουθήσω σοι, Κύριε· πρῶτον δὲ ἐπίτρεψόν μοι
another, I will follow You, Lord; first but allow me
657 1519 3624 3450 2036 4314 846
62 ἀποτάξασθαι τοῖς εἰς τὸν οἶκόν μου. εἶπε δὲ πρὸς αὐτὸν ὁ
to take leave of those in the house of me. said But to him
2424 3762 1911 5495 848 1909 723
Ἰησοῦς, Οὐδείς, ἐπιβαλὼν τὴν χεῖρα αὐτοῦ ἐπ' ἄροτρον,
Jesus, No one putting the hand of him on the plow
991 1519 3694 2111 2076 1519 932
καὶ βλέπων εἰς τὰ ὀπίσω, εὔθετός ἐστιν εἰς τὴν βασιλείαν
and looking at the things behind fit is for the kingdom
2316
τοῦ Θεοῦ.
– of God.

CHAPTER 10

[1]And after these things the Lord also appointed seventy others, and sent them two by two before His face into every city and place, even *to* where He was about to come. [2]Therefore He said to them, Indeed the harvest *is* much, but the laborers *are* few. Therefore, pray *to* the Lord of the harvest, that He send out workers into His harvest. [3]Go! Behold, I send you out as lambs in *the* midst of wolves. [4]Do not carry a purse, nor a moneybag, nor sandals; and greet no one by the way. [5]And into whatever house you may enter, first say, Peace to this house. [6]And if a son of peace is truly there, your peace shall rest on it; but if not so, it shall return to you. [7]And remain in the same house, eating and drinking the things *shared* by them; for the laborer is worthy of his hire. Do not move from house to house. [8]And into whatever city you enter, and they receive you, eat

CHAPTER 10

3326 5023 322 2962 2087 1440
1 Μετὰ δὲ ταῦτα ἀνέδειξεν ὁ Κύριος καὶ ἑτέρους ἑβδομή-
after And these things appointed the Lord and others seventy
649 846 303 1417 4253 4383
κοντα, καὶ ἀπέστειλεν αὐτοὺς ἀνὰ δύο πρὸ προσώπου
and sent them two by two before (the) face
848 1519 3956 4172 5117 3759 3195 846 2064
αὐτοῦ εἰς πᾶσαν πόλιν καὶ τόπον οὗ ἔμελλεν αὐτὸς ἔρχεσθαι.
of Him into every city and place where was about He to come.
3004 3767 4314 846 3303 2326 4183 2040
2 ἔλεγεν οὖν πρὸς αὐτούς, Ὁ μὲν θερισμὸς πολύς, οἱ δὲ ἐργάται
He said Then to them, the Indeed harvest (is) much, the but workers
3641 1189 3767 2962 2326 3704 1544
ὀλίγοι· δεήθητε οὖν τοῦ Κυρίου τοῦ θερισμοῦ, ὅπως ἐκβάλλῃ
few; pray therefore of the Lord of the harvest, that He send out
2040 1519 2326 848 5217 2400 1473 649
3 ἐργάτας εἰς τὸν θερισμὸν αὐτοῦ. ὑπάγετε· ἰδού, ἐγὼ ἀπο-
workers into the harvest of Him. Go! Behold! I send
5209 5613 704 1722 3319 3074 3361 941 905
4 στέλλω ὑμᾶς ὡς ἄρνας ἐν μέσῳ λύκων. μὴ βαστάζετε βαλάν-
out you as lambs in (the) midst of wolves. Not do carry a
3361 4082 3366 5266 3367 2596
τιον, μὴ πήραν, μηδὲ ὑποδήματα· καὶ μηδένα κατὰ τὴν
purse, nor a moneybag, nor sandals; and no one by the
3598 782 1519 3739 302 3614 1525 4412
5 ὁδὸν ἀσπάσησθε. εἰς ἣν δ' ἂν οἰκίαν εἰσέρχησθε, πρῶτον
way greet. into whatever And may house you enter, first
*5600 3004 1515 3624 5129 1437 3303 * 1563 5207
6 λέγετε, Εἰρήνη τῷ οἴκῳ τούτῳ. καὶ ἐὰν μὲν ᾖ ἐκεῖ ὁ υἱὸς
say, Peace house to this. And if indeed is there a son
1515 1879 1909 846 1515 5216 =1490=
εἰρήνης, ἐπαναπαύσεται ἐπ' αὐτὸν ἡ εἰρήνη ὑμῶν· εἰ δὲ
of peace, shall rest upon it the peace of you; if but
1490 1909 5209 344 1722 846 3614 3306 2068
7 μήγε, ἐφ' ὑμᾶς ἀνακάμψει. ἐν αὐτῇ δὲ τῇ οἰκίᾳ μένετε, ἐσθίον-
not so, on you it shall return. In same And the house remain, eating
4095 3844 846 514 1063 2040
τες καὶ πίνοντες τὰ παρ' αὐτῶν· ἄξιος γὰρ ὁ ἐργάτης τοῦ
and drinking the things with them; worthy for the worker of the
3408 848 2076 3361 3327 1537 3614 1519 3614
8 μισθοῦ αὐτοῦ ἐστι. μὴ μεταβαίνετε ἐξ οἰκίας εἰς οἰκίαν. καὶ
pay of him is. Do not move from house to house. And
*3739 1519 * 302 4172 1525 1209 5209 2068
εἰς ἣν δ' ἂν πόλιν εἰσέρχησθε, καὶ δέχωνται ὑμᾶς, ἐσθίετε τὰ
into what- may city you enter, and they receive you, eat the things
ever

the things set before you. [9]And heal the sick in it, and say to them, The kingdom of God has drawn near to you. [10]But into whatever city you enter, and they do not receive you, going out into its streets, say, [11]Even the dust clinging to us out of your city, we shake off against you! Yet know this, that the kingdom of God has drawn near to you!

[12]And I say to you that it shall be more bearable for Sodom in that day than for that city! [13]Woe to you, Chorazin! Woe to you, Bethsaida! For if the works of power which have been occurring in you had occurred in Tyre and Sidon, they would have repented long ago, sitting in sackcloth and ashes! [14]But it will be more bearable for Tyre and Sidon in the Judgment than for you. [15]And you, Capernaum, were you not exalted to Heaven? You will be thrust down to Hades!

[16]The one hearing you *also* hears Me, and the one rejecting you *also* rejects Me, and the one rejecting Me *also* rejects the *One* having sent Me.

[17]And the seventy returned with joy, saying, Lord, even the demons are subject to us through Your Name. [18]And He said to them, I saw Satan falling out of Heaven as lightning! [19]Behold, I have given you the authority to tread on snakes and scorpions, and on all the power of the Enemy, and nothing shall hurt you, not at all. [20]But stop rejoicing in this, that the *evil* spirits submit to you. But rather rejoice that your names are written in Heaven.

3908 5213 2323 1722 846 772
9 παρατιθέμενα ὑμῖν, καὶ θεραπεύετε τοὺς ἐν αὐτῇ ἀσθενεῖς,
being set before you, and heal the in it sick,
3004 846 1448 1908 5209 932 2316
καὶ λέγετε αὐτοῖς, Ἤγγικεν ἐφ' ὑμᾶς ἡ βασιλεία τοῦ Θεοῦ.
and say to them, has drawn near on you the kingdom of God.
3739 1519* 302 4172 1525 3361 1209 5209 1831
10 εἰς ἣν δ' ἂν πόλιν εἰσέρχησθε, καὶ μὴ δέχωνται ὑμᾶς, ἐξελ-
And into whatever city you enter, and not they receive you, going
1519 4113 848 2036 2868
11 θόντες εἰς τὰς πλατείας αὐτῆς εἴπατε, Καὶ τὸν κονιορτὸν τὸν
out into the streets of it say, Even the dust
2853 2254 1537 4172 5216 631 5213
κολληθέντα ἡμῖν ἐκ τῆς πόλεως ὑμῶν ἀπομασσόμεθα ὑμῖν·
clinging to us out of the city of you we shake off to you
4133 5124 1097 3754 1448 1908 5209 932
πλὴν τοῦτο γινώσκετε, ὅτι ἤγγικεν ἐφ' ὑμᾶς ἡ βασιλεία τοῦ
yet this know, that has drawn near on you the kingdom
2316 3004 5213 3754 4670 1722 2250 1565 414
12 Θεοῦ. λέγω δὲ ὑμῖν, ὅτι Σοδόμοις ἐν τῇ ἡμέρᾳ ἐκείνῃ ἀνε-
of God. I say And to you that for Sodom in — day that more
2071 2228 4172 1565 3759 4671 5523 3759
13 κτότερον ἔσται, ἢ τῇ πόλει ἐκείνῃ. οὐαί σοι, Χωραζίν, οὐαί
tolerable it will be than city for that. Woe to you, Chorazin! Woe
1487 4671 966 3754 * 1722 5184 4605 1096 1411
σοι, Βηθσαϊδά· ὅτι εἰ ἐν Τύρῳ καὶ Σιδῶνι ἐγένοντο αἱ δυνά-
to you, Bethsaida! For if in Tyre and Sidon happened the works
1096 1722 5213 3819 302 1722 4526 4700
μεις αἱ γενόμεναι ἐν ὑμῖν, πάλαι ἂν ἐν σάκκῳ καὶ σποδῷ
of power happening in you, long ago in sackcloth and ashes
2521 3340 4133 5184 4605 414
14 καθήμεναι μετενόησαν. πλὴν Τύρῳ καὶ Σιδῶνι ἀνεκτότερον
sitting they would have repented. But for Tyre and Sidon more tolerable
2071/1722 2920/2228/5213 4771 2584 2193
15 ἔσται ἐν τῇ κρίσει, ἢ ὑμῖν. καὶ σύ, Καπερναούμ, ἡ ἕως τοῦ
it will be in the Judgment than for you. And you, Capernaum, unto
3772 5312 2193 86 2601 191
16 οὐρανοῦ ὑψωθεῖσα, ἕως ᾅδου καταβιβασθήσῃ. ὁ ἀκούων
Heaven were you lifted? To Hades you will come down. Those hearing
5216 1700 191 114 5209 1691 114 1691
ὑμῶν ἐμοῦ ἀκούει· καὶ ὁ ἀθετῶν ὑμᾶς ἐμὲ ἀθετεῖ· ὁ δὲ ἐμὲ
you Me hears, and he rejecting you Me rejects; he and Me
114 114 649 3165
ἀθετῶν ἀθετεῖ τὸν ἀποστείλαντά με.
rejecting rejects the (One) having sent Me.
5290 1440 3326 5479 3004
17 Ὑπέστρεψαν δὲ οἱ ἑβδομήκοντα μετὰ χαρᾶς, λέγοντες,
returned And the seventy with joy, saying,
2962 1140 5293 2254 1722 3686
Κύριε, καὶ τὰ δαιμόνια ὑποτάσσεται ἡμῖν ἐν τῷ ὀνόματί
Lord, even the demons submit to us in the name
4675 2036 846 2334 4567 5613 796
18 σου. εἶπε δὲ αὐτοῖς, Ἐθεώρουν τὸν Σατανᾶν ὡς ἀστραπὴν
of You. He said But to them, I saw Satan as lightning
1537 3772 4098 2400 1325 5213 1849
19 ἐκ τοῦ οὐρανοῦ πεσόντα. ἰδού, δίδωμι ὑμῖν τὴν ἐξουσίαν
out of Heaven fall. Behold! I have given you the authority
3961 1883 3789 4651 1909 3956
τοῦ πατεῖν ἐπάνω ὄφεων καὶ σκορπίων, καὶ ἐπὶ πᾶσαν τὴν
to tread on snakes and scorpions, and on all the
1411 2190 3762 5209 =3364= 91 4133
20 δύναμιν τοῦ ἐχθροῦ· καὶ οὐδὲν ὑμᾶς οὐ μὴ ἀδικήσει. πλὴν
power of the enemy, and nothing you in no way shall hurt. But
1722 5129 3361 5463 3754 4151 5213 5293
ἐν τούτῳ μὴ χαίρετε ὅτι τὰ πνεύματα ὑμῖν ὑποτάσσεται·
in this stop rejoicing that the spirits to you submit
5463 3123 3754 3686 5216 1125 1722
χαίρετε δὲ μᾶλλον ὅτι τὰ ὀνόματα ὑμῶν ἐγράφη ἐν τοῖς
rejoice but rather that the names of you are written in the
3772
οὐρανοῖς.
heavens.

21 In the same hour Jesus
rejoiced in the Spirit, and
said, I praise You, Father,
Lord of Heaven and of earth,
that You hid these things
from *the* sophisticated and
cunning, and revealed them
to babes; yes, Father, because so it was pleasing
before You. 22 All things
were delivered to Me by My
Father, and no one knows
who the Son is except the
Father; and who is the
Father, except the Son, and
he to whom the Son may
desire to reveal *Him*. 23 And
having turned to the dis-
ciples alone, He said,
Blessed *are* the eyes seeing
what you see. 24 For I say to
you that many prophets and
kings desired to see what
you see, and did not see;
and to hear what you hear,
and did not hear.

25 And behold, a certain
doctor of the Law stood up,
testing Him and saying,
Teacher, What shall I do
that I may inherit eternal
life? 26 And He said to him,
What has been written in
the Law? How do you read
it? 27 And answering he said,
You shall love *the* Lord your
God with all your heart, and
with all your soul, and with
all your strength, and with
all your mind; and your
neighbor as yourself. 28 And
He said to him, You have
answered rightly; do this,
and you shall live. 29 But
desiring to justify himself,
he said to Jesus, And who
is my neighbor? 30 And
taking *it* up, Jesus said, A
certain man was going
down from Jerusalem to
Jericho, and fell in with
robbers, who both stripping
him and laying on wounds,

1722 846 5610 21 4151 2424
21 Ἐν αὐτῇ τῇ ὥρᾳ ἠγαλλιάσατο τῷ πνεύματι ὁ Ἰησοῦς
In same the hour exulted in the Spirit Jesus
2036 1843 4671 3962 2962 3772
καὶ εἶπεν, Ἐξομολογοῦμαί σοι, πάτερ, Κύριε τοῦ οὐρανοῦ
and said, I praise You, Father, Lord of Heaven
1093 3754 613 5023 575 4680 4908
καὶ τῆς γῆς, ὅτι ἀπέκρυψας ταῦτα ἀπὸ σοφῶν καὶ συνετῶν,
and of earth, for You hid these things from sophisticated and cunning,
601 846 3516 3483 3962 3754 3779
καὶ ἀπεκάλυψας αὐτὰ νηπίοις· ναί, ὁ πατήρ, ὅτι οὕτως
and revealed them to babes; yes, Father, because thus
1096 2107 1715 4675 3956 3860 3427 5259
22 ἐγένετο εὐδοκία ἔμπροσθέν σου. πάντα παρεδόθη μοι ὑπὸ
it was well-pleasing before You. All things were delivered to Me by
3962 3450 3762 1097 5101 2076 5207 =1508=
τοῦ πατρός μου· καὶ οὐδεὶς γινώσκει τίς ἐστιν ὁ υἱός, εἰ μὴ
the Father of Me, and no one knows who is the Son, except
3962 5101 2076 3962 =1508= 5207 3739 1437
ὁ πατήρ, καὶ τίς ἐστιν ὁ πατήρ, εἰ μὴ ὁ υἱός, καὶ ᾧ ἐὰν
the Father, and who is the Father, except the Son, and whoever
935 5207 601 4762 4314
23 βούληται ὁ υἱὸς ἀποκαλύψαι. καὶ στραφεὶς πρὸς τοὺς
may desire the Son to reveal (Him). And turning to the
3101 2398 2036 3107 3788 991
μαθητὰς κατ' ἰδίαν εἶπε, Μακάριοι οἱ ὀφθαλμοὶ οἱ βλέποντες
disciples, privately He said, Blessed the eyes seeing
3739 991 3004 1063 5213 3754 4183 4396
24 ἃ βλέπετε. λέγω γὰρ ὑμῖν, ὅτι πολλοὶ προφῆται καὶ
what you see. I say For to you that many prophets and
935 2309 1492 3739 5210 991 3756 1492
βασιλεῖς ἠθέλησαν ἰδεῖν ἃ ὑμεῖς βλέπετε, καὶ οὐκ εἶδον· καὶ
kings desired to see what you see, and not did see; and
191 3739 191 3756 191
ἀκοῦσαι ἃ ἀκούετε, καὶ οὐκ ἤκουσαν.
to hear what you hear, and not did hear.
2400 3544 5100 450 1598 846
25 Καὶ ἰδού, νομικός τις ἀνέστη, ἐκπειράζων αὐτόν, καὶ
And, behold, lawyer a certain stood up, tempting Him, and
3004 1320 5101 4160 2222 166 2816
λέγων, Διδάσκαλε, τί ποιήσας ζωὴν αἰώνιον κληρονομήσω ;
said, Teacher, what doing life eternal I may inherit?
2036 4314 846 1722 3551 5101 1125 4459
26 ὁ δὲ εἶπε πρὸς αὐτόν, Ἐν τῷ νόμῳ τί γέγραπται ; πῶς
He And said to him, In the law what is written? How
314 611 2036 25 2962
27 ἀναγινώσκεις ; ὁ δὲ ἀποκριθεὶς εἶπεν, Ἀγαπήσεις Κύριον
do you read? he And answering said, You shall love (the) Lord
2316 4675 1537 3650 2588 4675 1537 3650
τὸν Θεόν σου, ἐξ ὅλης τῆς καρδίας σου, καὶ ἐξ ὅλης τῆς
the God of you from all the heart of you, and from all the
5590 4675 1537 3650 2479 4675 1537 3650
ψυχῆς σου, καὶ ἐξ ὅλης τῆς ἰσχύος σου, καὶ ἐξ ὅλης τῆς
soul of you; and the neighbor of you as yourself. He said And
1271 4675 4139 4675 5613 4572 2036
28 διανοίας σου· καὶ τὸν πλησίον σου ὡς σεαυτόν. εἶπε δὲ
mind of you; and the neighbor of you as yourself. He said And
846 3723 611 5124 4160 2198 2309
29 αὐτῷ, Ὀρθῶς ἀπεκρίθης· τοῦτο ποίει, καὶ ζήσῃ. ὁ δὲ θέλων
to him, Rightly you answered; this do, and you will live • he But willing
1344 1438 2036 4314 2424 2076 3450
•5101 δικαιοῦν ἑαυτὸν εἶπε πρὸς τὸν Ἰησοῦν, Καὶ τίς ἐστί μου
to justify himself said to Jesus, And who is of me
4139 5274 2424 2036 444 5100
30 πλησίον ; ὑπολαβὼν δὲ ὁ Ἰησοῦς εἶπεν, Ἄνθρωπός τις
neighbor? Taking (it) up And, Jesus said, man A certain
1597 575 2419 1519 2410 3027
κατέβαινεν ἀπὸ Ἰερουσαλὴμ εἰς Ἰεριχώ, καὶ λῃσταῖς
was going down from Jerusalem to Jericho, and robbers
4045 3739 1562 846 4127 2007
περιέπεσεν, οἳ καὶ ἐκδύσαντες αὐτὸν καὶ πληγὰς ἐπιθέντες
fell in with, who both stripping him and blows laying on,

going away, leaving *him* being half-dead. [31]But by a coincidence, a certain priest was going on that road; and seeing him, he passed on the opposite *side*. [32]And in the same way a Levite, also being at the place, coming and seeing him, he passed on the opposite *side*. [33]But a certain traveling Samaritan came upon him, and seeing him, *he* was filled with pity. [34]And coming near, *he* bound up his wounds, pouring on oil and wine. And putting him on his own animal, *he* brought him to an inn, and cared for him. [35]And going forth on the morrow, taking out two denarii, he gave *them* to the innkeeper, and said to him, Care for him, and whatever more you spend, I on my return will repay to you.

[36]Who, then, of these three seems to you to have become a neighbor to the one having fallen among the robbers? [37]And he said, The *one* doing the *deed of* mercy with him. Then Jesus said to him, Go, and you do likewise.

[38]And as they went on, it happened *that* He also entered into a certain village. And a certain woman, Martha by name, received Him into her house. [39]And she had a sister being called Mary, who also *was* sitting alongside, at the feet of Jesus, *and* heard His word. [40]But Martha was distracted about much serving. And coming on she said, Lord, *Is it* not a care to You that my sister left me alone to serve? Then tell her that she should help me. [41]But answering Jesus said to her, Martha, Martha, you are anxious and troubled about many things, [42]but

565 863 2253 5177 2596 4795
31 ἀπῆλθον, ἀφέντες ἡμιθανῆ τυγχάνοντα. κατὰ συγκυρίαν
went away, leaving (him) half-dead being. by a coincidence
2407 5100 2597 1722 3598 1565 1492 846
δὲ ἱερεύς τις κατέβαινεν ἐν τῇ ὁδῷ ἐκείνῃ· καὶ ἰδὼν αὐτὸν
And priest a certain was going in way that, and seeing him
492 3668 3019 1096 2596
32 ἀντιπαρῆλθεν. ὁμοίως δὲ καὶ Λευίτης γενόμενος κατὰ τὸν
passed opposite. likewise And also a Levite being at the
5117 2064 1492 492 4541 5100
33 τόπον ἐλθὼν καὶ ἰδὼν ἀντιπαρῆλθε. Σαμαρείτης δέ τις
place, coming and seeing, passed opposite. Samaritan But one
3593 2064 2596 846 1492 846 4697
ὁδεύων ἦλθε κατ' αὐτόν, καὶ ἰδὼν αὐτὸν ἐσπλαγχνίσθη,
traveling came upon him, and seeing him was filled with pity.
4334 2611 5134 846 2022
34 καὶ προσελθὼν κατέδησε τὰ τραύματα αὐτοῦ, ἐπιχέων
And coming up he bound up the wounds of him, pouring
1637 3631 1931 846 1909 2398 2934
ἔλαιον καὶ οἶνον· ἐπιβιβάσας δὲ αὐτὸν ἐπὶ τὸ ἴδιον κτῆνος,
oil and wine, placing and him on the own beast
71 846 1519 3829 1959 846 1909
35 ἤγαγεν αὐτὸν εἰς πανδοχεῖον, καὶ ἐπεμελήθη αὐτοῦ. καὶ ἐπὶ
brought him to an inn, and cared for him. And on
839 1831 1544 1417 1220 1325 3830
τὴν αὔριον ἐξελθών, ἐκβαλὼν δύο δηνάρια ἔδωκε τῷ παν-
the morrow going out, taking out two denarii he gave to the inn-
2036 846 1959 846 =3748= 302
δοχεῖ, καὶ εἶπεν αὐτῷ, Ἐπιμελήθητι αὐτοῦ· καὶ ὅ τι ἂν
keeper, and said to him, Care for him, and whatever
4325 1473 1722 1880 3165 591 4671
προσδαπανήσῃς, ἐγὼ ἐν τῷ ἐπανέρχεσθαί με ἀποδώσω σοι.
you spend more, I in the returning (of) me will repay you.
5101 3767 5130 5140 1380 4671 4139 1096
36 τίς οὖν τούτων τῶν τριῶν δοκεῖ σοι πλησίον γεγονέναι
Who, then, of these three seems it to you neighbor to have become
1706 1519 3027 2036 4160
37 τοῦ ἐμπεσόντος εἰς τοὺς λῃστάς; ὁ δὲ εἶπεν, Ὁ ποιήσας τὸ
of those falling among the robbers? he And said, The (one) doing the
1656 3326 846 2036 3767 846 2424 4698
ἔλεος μετ' αὐτοῦ. εἶπεν οὖν αὐτῷ ὁ Ἰησοῦς, Πορεύου, καὶ
mercy with him. said Then to him Jesus, Go, and
4771 4160 3668
σὺ ποίει ὁμοίως.
you do likewise.
1096 1722 4198 846 846 1525
38 Ἐγένετο δὲ ἐν τῷ πορεύεσθαι αὐτούς, καὶ αὐτὸς εἰσῆλθεν
it occurred And in the going (of) them, also He entered
1519 2968 5100 1135 5100 3686 3136 5264
εἰς κώμην τινά· γυνὴ δέ τις ὀνόματι Μάρθα ὑπεδέξατο
into village a certain. Woman And a certain by name Martha received
846 1519 3624 848 3592 2258 79 2564
39 αὐτὸν εἰς τὸν οἶκον αὐτῆς. καὶ τῇδε ἦν ἀδελφὴ καλουμένη
Him into the house of her. And to this was a sister being called
3137 3739 3869 3844 4228 2424
Μαρία, ἣ καὶ παρακαθίσασα παρὰ τοὺς πόδας τοῦ Ἰησοῦ
Mary, who also sitting beside at the feet of Jesus
191 3056 848 3136 4049 4012
40 ἤκουε τὸν λόγον αὐτοῦ. ἡ δὲ Μάρθα περιεσπᾶτο περὶ
heard the word of Him. But Martha was distracted about
4183 1248 2186 2036 2962 3756 3199 4671 3754
πολλὴν διακονίαν· ἐπιστᾶσα δὲ εἶπε, Κύριε, οὐ μέλει σοι ὅτι
much serving; coming on And she said, Lord, not a care to You that
79 3450 3440 3165 2641 1247 2036 3767 846
ἡ ἀδελφή μου μόνην με κατέλιπε διακονεῖν; εἰπὲ οὖν αὐτῇ
the sister of me alone me left to serve? tell Then her
2443 3427 4878 611 2036 846 2424
41 ἵνα μοι συναντιλάβηται. ἀποκριθεὶς δὲ εἶπεν αὐτῇ ὁ Ἰησοῦς,
that me she should help. answering And said to her Jesus
3136 3136 3309 5182 4012 4183 1520
Μάρθα, Μάρθα, μεριμνᾷς καὶ τυρβάζῃ περὶ πολλά· ἑνὸς
Martha, Martha, you are anxious and troubled about many things of one

there is need of *only* one; and Mary chose the good part, which shall not be taken from her.

CHAPTER 11

[1]And it happened *as* He *was* praying in a certain place, when He ceased, one of His disciples said to Him, Lord teach us to pray, as John also taught his disciples. [2]And He said to them: When you pray, say,

Our Father who *is* in Heaven, hallowed be Your name; let Your kingdom come; let Your will be done on earth as *it* also *is* in Heaven. [3]Give us our needed bread day by day; [4]and forgive us our sins, for we ourselves also forgive everyone indebted to us. And lead us not into temptation, but deliver us from evil.

[5]And He said to them, Who of you shall have a friend, and will come to him at midnight and say to him, Friend, lend me three loaves. [6]*For* a friend of mine arrived to me from a journey, and I do not have what I may set before him. [7]And that one answering from within may say, Do not cause me troubles. The door has already been shut, and my children are in bed with me. I cannot rise up to give to you. [8]I say to you, Even if rising up he will not give to him because he is *a* friend, yet because of his shameless insisting, rising up he will give him as many as he needs. [9]And I say to you, Ask, and it will be given to you. Seek, and you will

2076 5532 3137 18 3310 1586 3748
42 δέ ἐστι χρεία· Μαρία δὲ τὴν ἀγαθὴν μερίδα ἐξελέξατο, ἥτις
but is need; Mary and the good part chose, which
3756 851 575 846
οὐκ ἀφαιρεθήσεται ἀπ᾽ αὐτῆς.
not shall be taken from her.

CHAPTER 11

1096 1722 1511 846 1722 5117 5100 4336
1 Καὶ ἐγένετο ἐν τῷ εἶναι αὐτὸν ἐν τόπῳ τινὶ προσευχό-
And it was in the being (of) Him in place a certain praying,
5613 3973 2036 3101 848 4314
μενον, ὡς ἐπαύσατο, εἶπέ τις τῶν μαθητῶν αὐτοῦ πρὸς
as He ceased, said a certain one of the disciples of Him, to
846 2962 1321 2248 4336 2531
αὐτόν, Κύριε, δίδαξον ἡμᾶς προσεύχεσθαι, καθὼς καὶ
Him, Lord, teach us to pray, even as also
2491 1321 3101 848 2036 846
2 Ἰωάννης ἐδίδαξε τοὺς μαθητὰς αὐτοῦ. εἶπε δὲ αὐτοῖς,
John taught the disciples of him. He said And to them,
3752 4336 3004 3962 2257 1722 3772
Ὅταν προσεύχησθε, λέγετε, Πάτερ ἡμῶν ὁ ἐν τοῖς οὐρανοῖς
When you pray, say, Father Our, who in the heavens,
37 3686 4675 2064 932 4675 1096
ἁγιασθήτω τὸ ὄνομά σου. ἐλθέτω ἡ βασιλεία σου. γενηθήτω
holy be the name of You; let come the kingdom of You. Let be done
2307 4675 5613 1722 3772 1909 1093 740
3 τὸ θέλημά σου, ὡς ἐν οὐρανῷ, καὶ ἐπὶ τῆς γῆς. τὸν ἄρτον
the will of You, as in Heaven, also on the earth. The bread
2257 1967 1325 2254 2596 2250 863
4 ἡμῶν τὸν ἐπιούσιον δίδου ἡμῖν τὸ καθ᾽ ἡμέραν. καὶ ἄφες
of us the needed give us day by day. And forgive
5213 266 2257 1093 846 863 3956
ἡμῖν τὰς ἁμαρτίας ἡμῶν, καὶ γὰρ αὐτοὶ ἀφίεμεν παντὶ
us the sins of us, also for ourselves we forgive everyone
3784 2254 3361 1533 2248 1519 3986 235
ὀφείλοντι ἡμῖν. καὶ μὴ εἰσενέγκῃς ἡμᾶς εἰς πειρασμόν, ἀλλὰ
indebted to us. And do not lead us into temptation, but
4506 2248 575 4190
ῥῦσαι ἡμᾶς ἀπὸ τοῦ πονηροῦ.
deliver us from evil.
2036 4314 846 5101 1537 5216 2192 5384 4198
5 Καὶ εἶπε πρὸς αὐτούς, Τίς ἐξ ὑμῶν ἕξει φίλον, καὶ πορεύ-
And He said to them, Who of you shall have a friend, and will
4314 846 3317 2036 846 5384
σεται πρὸς αὐτὸν μεσονυκτίου, καὶ εἴπῃ αὐτῷ, Φίλε,
come to him at midnight, and say to him, Friend,
5531 3427 5140 740 1896 5384 3450 3850 1537
6 χρῆσόν μοι τρεῖς ἄρτους, ἐπειδὴ φίλος μου παρεγένετο ἐξ
lend me three loaves, since a friend of me arrived off
3598 4314 3165 3756 2192 3739 3908 846 2548
7 ὁδοῦ πρός με, καὶ οὐκ ἔχω ὃ παραθήσω αὐτῷ· κἀκεῖνος
a journey to me, and not I have what I may set before him; and that one
2081 611 2036 3361 3427 2873 3930 2235
ἔσωθεν ἀποκριθεὶς εἴπῃ, Μή μοι κόπους πάρεχε· ἤδη ἡ
within answering may say, Not me troubles cause; now the
2374 2808 3813 3450 3326 1700 1519 2845
θύρα κέκλεισται, καὶ τὰ παιδία μου μετ᾽ ἐμοῦ εἰς τὴν κοίτην
door has been shut, and the children of me with me in the bed
1526 3756 1410 450 1325 4671 3004 5213 1499=
8 εἰσίν· οὐ δύναμαι ἀναστὰς δοῦναί σοι. λέγω ὑμῖν, εἰ καὶ
are; not I am able rising up to give you. I say to you, if even
3756 1325 848 450 1223 1511 848 5384 1223 1065
οὐ δώσει αὐτῷ ἀναστάς, διὰ τὸ εἶναι αὐτοῦ φίλον, διά γε
not he will give him, rising up on account of being of him friend, yet because of
335 848 1453 1325 846 3745 5535
τὴν ἀναίδειαν αὐτοῦ ἐγερθεὶς δώσει αὐτῷ ὅσων χρῄζει.
the importunity of him rising he will give him as many as he needs.
2504 5213 3004 154 1325 5213 2212
9 κἀγὼ ὑμῖν λέγω, Αἰτεῖτε, καὶ δοθήσεται ὑμῖν· ζητεῖτε, καὶ
And I to you say, Ask, and it will be given to you; seek, and

find; knock, and it will be opened to you. [10]For everyone asking receives, and the *one* seeking finds; and to the *one* knocking, it will be opened. [11]And what father of you, *if* the son asks *for* bread, will he give him a stone? And if a fish, will he give him a snake instead of a fish? [12]And if he should ask an egg, will he give him a scorpion? [13]Then if you being evil know to give good gifts to your children, how much more the Father out of Heaven will give *the* Holy Spirit to those asking Him.

[14]And he was casting out a demon, and it was dumb. And it happened *as* the demon *was* going out, the dumb one spoke. And the crowds marveled. [15]But some of them said, He casts out the demons by Beelzebub the chief of the demons. [16]And tempting *Him*, others were seeking a sign from Heaven from Him. [17]But knowing their thoughts, He said to them, Every kingdom divided against itself is brought to ruin, and a house against a house falls. [18]And also if Satan is divided against himself, how shall his kingdom stand?—because you say I cast out the demons by Beelzebub. [19]And if I cast out the demons by Beelzebub, by whom do your sons cast out? Because of this they shall be your judges. [20]But if I cast out the demons by *the* finger of God, then the kingdom of God has come upon you.

[21]When the strong one who has been armed guards his dwelling, his goods are in peace. [22]But as soon as one stronger than he comes, *he* overcomes him; he takes away his armor on which he

2147 2925 455 5213 3956 1063 154
10 εὑρήσετε· κρούετε, καὶ ἀνοιγήσεται ὑμῖν. πᾶς γὰρ ὁ αἰτῶν
you will find; knock, and it will be opened to you. everyone For asking
2983 2212 2167 2925 455
λαμβάνει· καὶ ὁ ζητῶν εὑρίσκει· καὶ τῷ κρούοντι ἀνοιγή-
receives, and the (one) seeking finds, and to the (one) knocking, it will be
5101 5216 3962 154 5207 740 3361
11 σεται. τίνα δὲ ὑμῶν τὸν πατέρα αἰτήσει ὁ υἱὸς ἄρτον, μὴ
opened. what And of you father (of whom) asks the son bread,
3037 1929 846 1487 2486 3361 473 2486 3799
λίθον ἐπιδώσει αὐτῷ; εἰ καὶ ἰχθύν, μὴ ἀντὶ ἰχθύος ὄφιν
a stone will he give him? if And a fish, instead of a fish, a snake
1929 846 2228 1437 154 5609 3361 1929 846
12 ἐπιδώσει αὐτῷ; ἢ καὶ ἐὰν αἰτήσῃ ὠόν, μὴ ἐπιδώσει αὐτῷ
will he give him? Or also if he should ask an egg, will he give to him
4651 1487 3767 5210 4190 5225 1492 18
13 σκορπίον; εἰ οὖν ὑμεῖς πονηροὶ ὑπάρχοντες οἴδατε ἀγαθὰ
a scorpion? If, then, you evil being know good
1390 1325 5043 5216 4214 3123 3962
δόματα διδόναι τοῖς τέκνοις ὑμῶν, πόσῳ μᾶλλον ὁ πατὴρ
gifts to give to the children of you, how much more the Father
1537 3772 1325 4151 40 154 846
ὁ ἐξ οὐρανοῦ δώσει Πνεῦμα Ἅγιον τοῖς αἰτοῦσιν αὐτόν;
of Heaven will give (the) Spirit Holy to those asking Him.
2259 1544 1140 846 2258 2974 1096
14 Καὶ ἦν ἐκβάλλων δαιμόνιον, καὶ αὐτὸ ἦν κωφόν. ἐγένετο
And He was casting out a demon, and it was dumb. it was
1140 1831 2980 2974
δέ, τοῦ δαιμονίου ἐξελθόντος, ἐλάλησεν ὁ κωφός· καὶ
And, the demon going out, spoke the dumb one. And
2296 3793 5100 1537 846 2036 1722 954
15 ἐθαύμασαν οἱ ὄχλοι. τινὲς δὲ ἐξ αὐτῶν εἶπον, Ἐν Βεελζεβοὺλ
marveled the crowds. some But of them said, By Beelzebub
758 1140 1544 1140 2087
16 ἄρχοντι τῶν δαιμονίων ἐκβάλλει τὰ δαιμόνια. ἕτεροι δὲ
the chief of the demons He casts out the demons. others And
3985 4592 3844 846 2212 1537 3772 846
17 πειράζοντες σημεῖον παρ' αὐτοῦ ἐζήτουν ἐξ οὐρανοῦ. αὐτὸς
tempting, a sign from Him were seeking from Heaven He
1492 848 1270 2036 846 3956 932
δὲ εἰδὼς αὐτῶν τὰ διανοήματα εἶπεν αὐτοῖς, Πᾶσα βασιλεία
But knowing of them the thoughts said to them, Every kingdom
1909 1438 1266 2049 3624 1909 3624
ἐφ' ἑαυτὴν διαμερισθεῖσα ἐρημοῦται· καὶ οἶκος ἐπὶ οἶκον,
against itself divided is brought to ruin, and a house against a house
4098 1487 4567 1909 1438 1266 4459
18 πίπτει. εἰ δὲ καὶ ὁ Σατανᾶς ἐφ' ἑαυτὸν διεμερίσθη, πῶς
falls. if And also Satan against himself is divided, how
2476 932 848 3754 3004 1722 954
σταθήσεται ἡ βασιλεία αὐτοῦ; ὅτι λέγετε, ἐν Βεελζεβοὺλ
shall stand the kingdom of him? Because you say by Beelzebub
1544 3165 1140 1487 1473 1722 954 1544
19 ἐκβάλλειν με τὰ δαιμόνια. εἰ δὲ ἐγὼ ἐν Βεελζεβοὺλ ἐκβάλλω
casting out I (am) the demons. if But I by Beelzebub cast out
1140 5207 5216 1722 5101 1544 1223 5124
τὰ δαιμόνια, οἱ υἱοὶ ὑμῶν ἐν τίνι ἐκβάλλουσι; διὰ τοῦτο
the demons, the sons of you, by what do they cast out? Therefore
2923 5216 846 2071 1487 1722 1147 2316 1544
20 κριταὶ ὑμῶν αὐτοὶ ἔσονται εἰ δὲ ἐν δακτύλῳ Θεοῦ ἐκβάλλω
judges of you they shall be. if But by (the) finger of God I cast out
1140 686 5348 1909 5209 932 2316
τὰ δαιμόνια, ἄρα ἔφθασεν ἐφ' ὑμᾶς ἡ βασιλεία τοῦ Θεοῦ.
the demons, then came upon you the kingdom — of God.
3752 2478 2528 5442 1438 833
21 ὅταν ὁ ἰσχυρὸς καθωπλισμένος φυλάσσῃ τὴν ἑαυτοῦ αὐλήν,
When the strong one being armed guards the dwelling of him,
1722 1515 2076 5274 848 1875 2478
22 ἐν εἰρήνῃ ἐστὶ τὰ ὑπάρχοντα αὐτοῦ· ἐπὰν δὲ ὁ ἰσχυρότερος
in peace are the goods of him. when But one stronger
846 1904 3528 846 3833 846 142
αὐτοῦ ἐπελθὼν νικήσῃ αὐτόν, τὴν πανοπλίαν αὐτοῦ αἴρει
(than) him coming overcomes him; the armor of him he takes

relied, and deals out his arms. [23]The *one* not being with Me is against Me. And the *one* not gathering with me scatters.

[24]When the unclean spirit goes out from the man, he goes through dry places seeking rest. And not finding, *he* says, I will return to my house from where I came out. [25]And coming he finds *it* swept and decorated. [26]Then he goes and takes seven other spirits more wicked than himself; and entering he dwells there. And the last things of that man become worse than the first.

[27]And *as* He spoke these things, it happened that a certain woman lifted up *her* voice out of the crowd *and* said to Him, Blessed *is* the womb having borne You, and *the* breasts which You sucked. [28]But He said, No; rather, blessed *are* those hearing the word of God, and keeping it.

[29]But the crowds pressing on *Him,* He began to say, This is an evil generation. It seeks a sign, and a sign will not be given to it, except the sign of Jonah the prophet. [30]For Jonah became a sign to the Ninevites; so also the Son of man will be to this generation. [31]*The* queen of *the* south will be raised in the Judgment with the men of this generation, and will condemn them, because she came from the ends of the earth to hear the wisdom of Solomon. And, behold, a Greater-than-Solomon *is* here. [32]Men, Ninevites will rise up in the Judgment with this generation, and will condemn it, because they repented at the

1909 3739 3982 4661 848 1239 3361 5607
23 ἐφ' ᾗ ἐπεποίθει, καὶ τὰ σκῦλα αὐτοῦ διαδίδωσιν. ὁ μὴ ὢν
on which he relied, and the arms of him distributes. The (one) not being
3326 1700 2596 1700 2076 3361 4863 3326 1700 4650
μετ' ἐμοῦ κατ' ἐμοῦ ἐστι· καὶ ὁ μὴ συνάγων μετ' ἐμοῦ σκορπί-
with Me, against Me is! And he not gathering with Me, scatters!
3752 169 4151 1831 575 444
24 ζει. ὅταν τὸ ἀκάθαρτον πνεῦμα ἐξέλθῃ ἀπὸ τοῦ ἀνθρώπου,
When the unclean spirit goes out from the man,
1330 1223 504 5117 2212 372 3361
διέρχεται δι' ἀνύδρων τόπων, ζητοῦν ἀνάπαυσιν· καὶ μὴ
he goes through dry places seeking rest, and not
2147 3004 5290 1519 3624 3450 3606 1831
εὑρίσκον λέγει, Ὑποστρέψω εἰς τὸν οἶκόν μου ὅθεν ἐξῆλθον.
finding says, I will return to the house of me from where I came.
2064 2147 4563 2885 5119
25 καὶ ἐλθὸν εὑρίσκει σεσαρωμένον καὶ κεκοσμημένον. τότε
And coming he finds (it) having been swept and decorated. Then
4198 3880 2033 2087 4151 4191
26 πορεύεται καὶ παραλαμβάνει ἑπτὰ ἕτερα πνεύματα πονηρό-
he goes and takes seven other spirits more wicked
1438 1525 2730 1563 1096
τερα ἑαυτοῦ, καὶ εἰσελθόντα κατοικεῖ ἐκεῖ· καὶ γίνεται τὰ
(than) himself, and entering he lives there; and becomes the
2078 444 1565 5501 4413
ἔσχατα τοῦ ἀνθρώπου ἐκείνου χείρονα τῶν πρώτων.
last things man of that worse (than) the first.
1096 1722 3004 848 5023 1869 5100 1135
27 Ἐγένετο δὲ ἐν τῷ λέγειν αὐτὸν ταῦτα, ἐπάρασά τις γυνὴ
it And in the saying (of) Him these things, lifting a certain woman
5456 1537 3793 2036 846 3107 2836 941
φωνὴν ἐκ τοῦ ὄχλου εἶπεν αὐτῷ, Μακαρία ἡ κοιλία ἡ βαστά-
(her) voice out of the crowd said to Him, Blessed the womb having
4571 3149 3739 2337 846 2036 3304
28 σασά σε, καὶ μαστοὶ οὓς ἐθήλασας. αὐτὸς δὲ εἶπε, Μενοῦνγε
borne You, and breasts which You sucked. He But said, No, rather
3107 191 3056 2316 5442
μακάριοι οἱ ἀκούοντες τὸν λόγον τοῦ Θεοῦ καὶ φυλάσσοντες
blessed those hearing the word of God and keeping
846
αὐτόν.
it.
3793 1865 756 3004 1074
29 Τῶν δὲ ὄχλων ἐπαθροιζομένων ἤρξατο λέγειν, Ἡ γενεὰ
the And crowds pressing upon (Him), He began to say, generation
3778 4191 2076 4592 1934 4592 3756 1325
αὕτη πονηρά ἐστι· σημεῖον ἐπιζητεῖ, καὶ σημεῖον οὐ δοθή-
This an evil is. a sign It seeks, and a sign not will
846 =1508= 4592 2495 4396 2531
30 σεται αὐτῇ, εἰ μὴ τὸ σημεῖον Ἰωνᾶ τοῦ προφήτου. καθὼς
be given to it, except the sign of Jonah the prophet. even as
1063 1096 2495 4592 3536 3779 2071
γὰρ ἐγένετο Ἰωνᾶς σημεῖον τοῖς Νινευΐταις οὕτως ἔσται
For became Jonah a sign to the Ninevites; so will be
5207 444 1074 5026 938 3558
31 καὶ ὁ υἱὸς τοῦ ἀνθρώπου τῇ γενεᾷ ταύτῃ. βασίλισσα νότου
also the Son of man generation to this. (The) queen of south
1453 2920 3326 435 1074 5026
ἐγερθήσεται ἐν τῇ κρίσει μετὰ τῶν ἀνδρῶν τῆς γενεᾶς ταύτης,
will be raised in the Judgment with the men generation of this
2632 846 3754 2064 1537 4009 1093
καὶ κατακρινεῖ αὐτούς· ὅτι ἦλθεν ἐκ τῶν περάτων τῆς γῆς
and will condemn them; because she came from the ends of the earth
191 4678 4672 2400 4119 4672
ἀκοῦσαι τὴν σοφίαν Σολομῶντος, καὶ ἰδού, πλεῖον Σολομῶν-
to hear the wisdom of Solomon, and behold, a greater-than-Solomon
5602 435 3535 450 2722 2920 3326
32 τος ὧδε. ἄνδρες Νινευὶ ἀναστήσονται ἐν τῇ κρίσει μετὰ τῆς
(is) here. Men, Ninevites, will rise up in the Judgment with
1074 5026 2632 846 3754 3340
γενεᾶς ταύτης, καὶ κατακρινοῦσιν αὐτήν· ὅτι μετενόησαν
generation this, and will condemn it, because they repented

preaching of Jonah. And, behold, a Greater-than-Jonah *is* here.

33But no one having lit a lamp places *it* in secret, nor under the grain-measure, but on the lamp-stand, that the ones entering may see the light. 34The lamp of the body is the eye. Then when your eye is sound, also all your body is light. But when it is evil, also your body *is* dark.

35Watch, then, that the light in you is not darkness. 36If, then, your whole body *is* light, not having any part dark, all will be light, as when the lamp enlightens you with *its* shining.

37And *as He was* speaking, a certain Pharisee asked Him that He would dine with him. And going in, He reclined. 38But watching, the Pharisee marveled that He did not first wash before the dinner. 39But the Lord said to him, Now you Pharisees cleanse the outside of the cup and of the dish, but your inside is full of robbery and evil. 40Fools! Did not He who made the outside also make the inside? 41But give alms *of* the things which are within, and behold, all things *are* clean to you.

42But woe to you, Pharisees, for you pay tithes of the mint, and the rue, and every plant, and pass by the judgment and the love of God. It was right to do these things, but not to leave aside those. 43Woe to you, Pharisees! For you love the chief seat in the synagogues, and the greetings

1519 2782 2495 2400 4119 2495 5602
εἰς τὸ κήρυγμα Ἰωνᾶ, καὶ ἰδού, πλεῖον Ἰωνᾶ ὧδε.
at the preaching of Jonah; and behold, a greater than Jonah (is) here.
3762 3088 681 1519 2927 5087 3761 5259
33 Οὐδεὶς δὲ λύχνον ἅψας εἰς κρυπτὸν τίθησιν, οὐδὲ ὑπὸ τὸν
No one But a lamp having lit in secret places (it), nor under the
3426 235 1909 3087 2443 1531
μόδιον, ἀλλ' ἐπὶ τὴν λυχνίαν, ἵνα οἱ εἰσπορευόμενοι τὸ
grain-measure, but on the lampstand, that the (ones) entering the
5338 991 3088 4983 2076 3788
34 φέγγος βλέπωσιν. ὁ λύχνος τοῦ σώματός ἐστιν ὁ ὀφθαλμός·
light may see. The lamp of the body is the eye.
3752 3767 3788 4675 573 5600 3650 4983 4675
ὅταν οὖν ὁ ὀφθαλμός σου ἁπλοῦς ᾖ, καὶ ὅλον τὸ σῶμά σου
when Then the eye of you single is, also all the body of you
5460 2076 1875 4190 5600 4983 4675 4652
φωτεινόν ἐστιν· ἐπὰν δὲ πονηρὸς ᾖ, καὶ τὸ σῶμά σου σκο-
bright is; when but evil it is, also the body of you (is)
4648 3767 3361 5457 1722 4671 4655 2076 1487 3767
35 τεινόν. σκόπει οὖν μὴ τὸ φῶς τὸ ἐν σοὶ σκότος ἐστίν. εἰ οὖν
dark. Watch, then, lest the light — in you darkness is. If, then,
4983 4675 3650 5460 3361 2192 5100 3313 4652
36 τὸ σῶμά σου ὅλον φωτεινόν μὴ ἔχον τι μέρος σκοτεινόν
the body of you whole (is) bright, not having any part dark,
2071 5460 3650 5613 3752 3088 796
ἔσται φωτεινὸν ὅλον, ὡς ὅταν ὁ λύχνος τῇ ἀστραπῇ
will be bright all, as when the lamp with the shining
5461 4571
φωτίζῃ σε.
enlightens you.
1722 2980 2065 846 5330 5100 3700
37 Ἐν δὲ τῷ λαλῆσαι, ἠρώτα αὐτὸν Φαρισαῖός τις ὅπως
in And the speaking, asked Him Pharisee certain that
709 3844 846 1525 377 5330
38 ἀριστήσῃ παρ' αὐτῷ· εἰσελθὼν δὲ ἀνέπεσεν. ὁ δὲ Φαρισαῖος
He would dine with him; entering and He reclined. the But Pharisee
1492 2296 3754 3756 4412 907 4253 712
ἰδὼν ἐθαύμασεν ὅτι οὐ πρῶτον ἐβαπτίσθη πρὸ τοῦ ἀρίστου.
seeing marveled, that not first He washed before the dinner.
2036 2962 4314 846 3568 5210 5330
39 εἶπε δὲ ὁ Κύριος πρὸς αὐτόν, Νῦν ὑμεῖς οἱ Φαρισαῖοι τὸ
said But the Lord to him, Now you Pharisees the
1855 4221 4094 2511
ἔξωθεν τοῦ ποτηρίου καὶ τοῦ πίνακος καθαρίζετε, τὸ δὲ
outside of the cup and of the dish cleanse, the but
2081 5216 1073 724 4189 878 3756
40 ἔσωθεν ὑμῶν γέμει ἁρπαγῆς καὶ πονηρίας. ἄφρονες, οὐχ
inside of you is full of robbery and evil. Fools! Did not
4160 1855 2081 4160 4133
ὁ ποιήσας τὸ ἔξωθεν καὶ τὸ ἔσωθεν ἐποίησε; πλὴν τὰ
the (One) making the outside also the inside make? But (of) the
5213 1751 1325 1654 2400 3956 2513 things
41 ἐνόντα δότε ἐλεημοσύνην· καὶ ἰδού, πάντα καθαρὰ ὑμῖν
being within give alms, and behold! all things clean to you
2076
ἐστιν.
is.
235 3759 5213 5330 3754 586
42 Ἀλλ' οὐαὶ ὑμῖν τοῖς Φαρισαίοις, ὅτι ἀποδεκατοῦτε τὸ
But woe to you Pharisees, because you tithe the
2238 4076 3956 3001 3928
ἡδύοσμον καὶ τὸ πήγανον καὶ πᾶν λάχανον, καὶ παρέρ-
mint and the rue, and every plant, and pass
2920 26 2316 5023 1163
χεσθε τὴν κρίσιν καὶ τὴν ἀγάπην τοῦ Θεοῦ· ταῦτα ἔδει
by the judgment and the love of God; these things must
4160 2548 3361 863 3759 5213 5330
43 ποιῆσαι, κἀκεῖνα μὴ ἀφιέναι. οὐαὶ ὑμῖν τοῖς Φαρισαίοις,
(you) do, and those not to leave aside. Woe to you, Pharisees,
3754 25 4410 1722 4864
ὅτι ἀγαπᾶτε τὴν πρωτοκαθεδρίαν ἐν ταῖς συναγωγαῖς,
because you love the chief seat in the synagogues,

in the marketplaces. [44]Woe to you, scribes and Pharisees! Hypocrites! For you are as the unseen tombs, and the men walking above do not know.

[45]And answering one of the lawyers said to Him, Teacher, saying these things you also insult us. [46]And He said, Woe to you also, lawyers! Because you burden men *with* burdens hard to bear, and *you* yourselves do not touch the burdens with one of your fingers. [47]Woe to you! Because you build the tombs of the prophets, and your fathers killed them. [48]So you bear witness and consent to the works of your fathers; for they indeed killed them, and you build their tombs. [49]And because of this the wisdom of God said, I will send prophets and apostles to them, and they will kill and drive out *some* of them, [50]that the blood of all the prophets which has been shed from *the* foundation of the world may be required from this generation, [51]from the blood of Abel until the blood of Zechariah *who* perished between the altar and the House. Yea, I say to you, it will be required from this generation. [52]Woe to you, lawyers! because you took the key of knowledge; you yourselves did not enter, and you kept out the ones entering.

[53]And as He was saying these things to them, the scribes and the Pharisees began to be terribly angry, and to draw Him out concerning many things, [54]lying in ambush for Him, and

783 1722 58 3759 5213 1122
44 καὶ τοὺς ἀσπασμοὺς ἐν ταῖς ἀγοραῖς. οὐαὶ ὑμῖν, γραμματεῖς
and the greetings in the markets! Woe to you, scribes
5330 5273 3754 2075 5613 3419 82
καὶ Φαρισαῖοι, ὑποκριταί, ὅτι ἐστὲ ὡς τὰ μνημεῖα τὰ ἄδηλα,
and Pharisees, hypocrites! For you are as the tombs unseen
444 4043 1883 3756 1492
καὶ οἱ ἄνθρωποι οἱ περιπατοῦντες ἐπάνω οὐκ οἴδασιν.
and the men walking over not do know.
611 5101 3544 3004 846 1320
45 Ἀποκριθεὶς δέ τις τῶν νομικῶν λέγει αὐτῷ, Διδάσκαλε,
answering And one of the lawyers says to Him, Teacher,
5023 3004 2248 5195 2036 5213
46 ταῦτα λέγων καὶ ἡμᾶς ὑβρίζεις. ὁ δὲ εἶπε, Καὶ ὑμῖν τοῖς
these things saying also us You insult. He And said, Also to you
3544 3759 3754 5412 444 5413
νομικοῖς οὐαί, ὅτι φορτίζετε τοὺς ἀνθρώπους φορτία
lawyers, woe! Because you burden — men (with) burdens
1419 846 1520 1147 5216 3756
δυσβάστακτα, καὶ αὐτοὶ ἑνὶ τῶν δακτύλων ὑμῶν οὐ
difficult to carry, and yourselves with one of the fingers of you not
4379 5413 3759 5213 3754 3618
47 προσψαύετε τοῖς φορτίοις. οὐαὶ ὑμῖν, ὅτι οἰκοδομεῖτε τὰ
you touch the burdens. Woe to you, because you build the
3419 4396 3962 5216 615
μνημεῖα τῶν προφητῶν, οἱ δὲ πατέρες ὑμῶν ἀπέκτειναν
tombs of the prophets, the and fathers of you killed
846 686 3140 4909 2041
48 αὐτούς. ἄρα μαρτυρεῖτε καὶ συνευδοκεῖτε τοῖς ἔργοις τῶν
them! Then witnesses and consent to the works of the
3962 5216 3754 846 3303 615 846 5210
πατέρων ὑμῶν· ὅτι αὐτοὶ μὲν ἀπέκτειναν αὐτούς, ὑμεῖς δὲ
fathers of you; for they indeed killed them, you but
3618 848 3419 1223 5124 4678
49 οἰκοδομεῖτε αὐτῶν τὰ μνημεῖα. διὰ τοῦτο καὶ ἡ σοφία τοῦ
build of them the tombs. Because of this also the wisdom
2316 2036 649 1519 846 4396 652
Θεοῦ εἶπεν, Ἀποστελῶ εἰς αὐτοὺς προφήτας καὶ ἀποστό-
of God said, I will send to them prophets and apostles,
1537 848 615 1559 2443
50 λους, καὶ ἐξ αὐτῶν ἀποκτενοῦσι καὶ ἐκδιώξουσιν· ἵνα
and of them they will kill and drive out, that
1567 129 3956 4396 1632
ἐκζητηθῇ τὸ αἷμα πάντων τῶν προφητῶν τὸ ἐκχυνόμενον
may be required the blood of all the prophets having been shed
575 2602 2889 575 1074 5026 575
51 ἀπὸ καταβολῆς κόσμου ἀπὸ τῆς γενεᾶς ταύτης, ἀπὸ τοῦ
from (the) foundation of world from generation this, from the
129 6 2193 129 2197 622
αἵματος Ἄβελ ἕως τοῦ αἵματος Ζαχαρίου τοῦ ἀπολομένου
blood of Abel until the blood of Zechariah (who) perished
3342 2379 3624 3483 3004 5213
μεταξὺ τοῦ θυσιαστηρίου καὶ τοῦ οἴκου· ναί, λέγω ὑμῖν,
between the altar and the house; yes, I say to you,
1567 575 1074 5026 3759 5213
52 ἐκζητηθήσεται ἀπὸ τῆς γενεᾶς ταύτης. οὐαὶ ὑμῖν τοῖς
it will be required from generation this. Woe to you,
3544 3754 142 2807 1108 846 3756
νομικοῖς, ὅτι ἤρατε τὴν κλεῖδα τῆς γνώσεως· αὐτοὶ οὐκ
lawyers! Because you took the key of knowledge; yourselves not
1525 1525 2967
εἰσήλθετε, καὶ τοὺς εἰσερχομένους ἐκωλύσατε.
you entered, and those having entered you kept out.
3004 846 5023 4314 846 756
53 Λέγοντος δὲ αὐτοῦ ταῦτα πρὸς αὐτούς, ἤρξαντο οἱ
as was saying And He these things to them, began the
1122 5330 1171 1758 653
γραμματεῖς καὶ οἱ Φαρισαῖοι δεινῶς ἐνέχειν, καὶ ἀποστο-
scribes and the Pharisees terribly to be angry, and to draw
846 4012 4119 1748 846
54 ματίζειν αὐτὸν περὶ πλειόνων, ἐνεδρεύοντες αὐτόν, καὶ
out Him concerning many things, lying in wait for Him, and

seeking to catch something out of His mouth, that they might accuse Him.

CHAPTER 12

[1]At which time the myriads of the crowd being gathered together, so as to trample on one another, He began to say to His disciples first, Take heed to yourselves of the leaven of the Pharisees, which is hypocrisy. [2]But there is nothing which has been completely concealed which will not be uncovered, nor hidden which will not be known. [3]For this reason, whatever you said in the darkness will be heard in the light; and whatever you spoke in the ear in the secret rooms will be proclaimed on the housetops. [4]But I say to you, My friends, Stop being afraid of the ones killing the body, and after these things not having anything more *they can* do. [5]But I will warn you whom you should fear; fear the ones who after the killing have authority to cast into Hell; yea, I say to you, fear that One!

[6]Are not five sparrows sold for two assaria? And not one of them has been forgotten before God. [7]But even the hairs of your head have all been numbered. Then stop being afraid; you differ from many sparrows. [8]But I say to you, Everyone who may confess Me before men, the Son of man will also confess him before the angels of God, [9]but the *one* denying Me before men will be denied before the angels of God.

[10]And everyone who shall say a word against the Son

2212 2340 5100 1537 4750 848 2443 2723
ζητοῦντες θηρεῦσαί τι ἐκ τοῦ στόματος αὐτοῦ, ἵνα κατηγορή-
seeking to catch some- from the mouth of Him, that they might
846 thing
σωσιν αὐτοῦ.
accuse Him.

CHAPTER 12

1722 3739 1996 3461 3793 5620
1 Ἐν οἷς ἐπισυναχθεισῶν τῶν μυριάδων τοῦ ὄχλου, ὥστε
In which things being assembled the thousands of the crowd, so as
2662 240 756 3004 4314 3101
καταπατεῖν ἀλλήλους, ἤρξατο λέγειν πρὸς τοὺς μαθητὰς
to trample on one another, He began to say to the disciples
848 4412 4337 1438 575 2219
αὐτοῦ πρῶτον, Προσέχετε ἑαυτοῖς ἀπὸ τῆς ζύμης τῶν
of Him first, Beware to yourselves from the leaven of the
5330 3748 2076 5272 3762 4780
2 Φαρισαίων, ἥτις ἐστὶν ὑπόκρισις. οὐδὲν δὲ συγκεκαλυμ-
Pharisees, which is hypocrisy. nothing And being completely
2076 3739 3756 601 2927 3739 3756
μένον ἐστὶν, ὃ οὐκ ἀποκαλυφθήσεται, καὶ κρυπτόν, ὃ οὐ
concealed is, which not will be uncovered; and hidden, which not
1097 473/3739/3745/1722 4653 2036/1722 5457
3 γνωσθήσεται. ἀνθ' ὧν ὅσα ἐν τῇ σκοτίᾳ εἴπατε, ἐν τῷ φωτὶ
will be known. Therefore, what in the darkness you said, in the light
191 3739 4314 3775 2980 5009
ἀκουσθήσεται· καὶ ὃ πρὸς τὸ οὖς ἐλαλήσατε ἐν τοῖς ταμείοις,
it will be heard; and what to the ear you spoke in the secret rooms,
2784 1909 1430 3004 5213 5384
4 κηρυχθήσεται ἐπὶ τῶν δωμάτων. λέγω δὲ ὑμῖν τοῖς φίλοις
will be proclaimed on the housetops. I say But to you, the friends
3450 3361 5399 575 615 4983
μου, Μὴ φοβηθῆτε ἀπὸ τῶν ἀποκτεινόντων τὸ σῶμα, καὶ
of Me, Stop being afraid from those killing the body, and
3326 5023 3361 2192 4054 5100 4160 5263
5 μετὰ ταῦτα μὴ ἐχόντων περισσότερόν τι ποιῆσαι. ὑποδείξω
after these things not having anything more to do. I will warn
5213 5101 5399 5399 3326 615
δὲ ὑμῖν τίνα φοβηθῆτε· φοβήθητε τὸν μετὰ τὸ ἀποκτεῖναι
But you whom you should fear, fear the (One) after the killing
1849 2192 1685 1519 1067 3483 3004 5213
ἐξουσίαν ἔχοντα ἐμβαλεῖν εἰς τὴν γέενναν· ναί, λέγω ὑμῖν,
authority having to throw into Gehenna. Yes, I say to you,
5126 5399 3780 4002 4765 4453 787
6 τοῦτον φοβήθητε. οὐχὶ πέντε στρουθία πωλεῖται ἀσσαρίων
this one fear! not five sparrows Are sold (for) assaria
1417 1520 1537 846 3756 2076 1950 1799
δύο ; καὶ ἓν ἐξ αὐτῶν οὐκ ἔστιν ἐπιλελησμένον ἐνώπιον τοῦ
two? And one of them not is having been forgotten before —
2316 235 2359 2776 5216 3956 705
7 Θεοῦ. ἀλλὰ καὶ αἱ τρίχες τῆς κεφαλῆς ὑμῶν πᾶσαι ἠρίθ-
God. But even the hairs of the head of you all have been
3361 3767 5399 4183 4765 1308
μηνται. μὴ οὖν φοβεῖσθε· πολλῶν στρουθίων διαφέρετε.
numbered. stop, Then, being afraid; from many sparrows you differ.
3004 5213 3956 3739 302 3670 1722 1698 1715
8 λέγω δὲ ὑμῖν, Πᾶς ὃς ἂν ὁμολογήσῃ ἐν ἐμοὶ ἔμπροσθεν τῶν
I say And to you, everyone who confesses — Me before —
444 5207 444 3670 1722 846
ἀνθρώπων, καὶ ὁ υἱὸς τοῦ ἀνθρώπου ὁμολογήσει ἐν αὐτῷ
men, also the Son of man will confess him
1715 32 2316 720 3165
9 ἔμπροσθεν τῶν ἀγγέλων τοῦ Θεοῦ· ὁ δὲ ἀρνησάμενός με
before the angels of God, the But denying Me
1799 444 533 (one) 1799
ἐνώπιον τῶν ἀνθρώπων ἀπαρνηθήσεται ἐνώπιον τῶν
before men will be denied before the
32 2316 3956 3739 2046 3056 1519 1519 5207
10 ἀγγέλων τοῦ Θεοῦ. καὶ πᾶς ὃς ἐρεῖ λόγον εἰς τὸν υἱὸν τοῦ
angels — of God. And everyone who says a word against the Son —

of man, it shall be forgiven Him; but the ones blaspheming against the Holy Spirit, *it* will not be forgiven. [11]But when they bring you in before synagogues and rulers, and the authorities, do not be anxious how or what you shall reply, or what you should say; [12]for the Holy Spirit will teach you in the same hour what you ought to say.

[13]And one from the crowd said to Him, Teacher, tell my brother to divide the inheritance with me. [14]But He said to him, Man, who appointed Me a judge or a divider over you?

[15]And He said to them, Beware, and keep back from covetousness; for one's life is not in the abundance of the things which are to him. [16]And He spoke a parable to them, saying, A certain rich man produced well *from* the land. [17]And he reasoned within himself, saying, What may I do, for I have nowhere I may gather my fruits? [18]And he said, I will do this; I will tear down my barns, and I will build larger; and I will gather there all my produce and my goods. [19]And I will say to my soul, Soul, you have many goods laid *up* for many years; take rest; eat, drink, be glad. [20]But God said to him, Fool! This night they demand your soul from you; and that which you prepared, to whom will it be? [21]So *is* he treasuring up for himself, and not being rich toward God.

[22]And He said to His disciples, Because of this I say to you, do not be anxious as to your life, what you should eat; nor as to the body, what you should put on. [23]The life is more than the food, and the body than the

444 863 846 1519 40 4151
ἀνθρώπου, ἀφεθήσεται αὐτῷ· τῷ δὲ εἰς τὸ ˚Ἅγιον Πνεῦμα
of man, it will be forgiven him, those but against the Holy Spirit
987 3756 863 3752 4374 5209
11 βλασφημήσαντι οὐκ ἀφεθήσεται. ὅταν δὲ προσφέρωσιν ὑμᾶς
blaspheming not will be forgiven. when And they bring in you
1909 4864 746 1849 3361
ἐπὶ τὰς συναγωγὰς καὶ τὰς ἀρχὰς καὶ τὰς ἐξουσίας, μὴ
before synagogues and rulers and authorities, do not
3309 4459/2228/5101/ 626 2228/5101 2036 1063
12 μεριμνᾶτε πῶς ἢ τί ἀπολογήσησθε, ἢ τί εἴπητε· τὸ γὰρ
be anxious how or what you may answer, or what you may say; the for
40 4151 1321 5209 1722 846 5610 3739 1163 2036
˚Ἅγιον Πνεῦμα διδάξει ὑμᾶς ἐν αὐτῇ τῇ ὥρᾳ, ἃ δεῖ εἰπεῖν.
Holy Spirit will teach you in same the hour what must you say.
2036 5100 846 1537 3793 1320 2036 80
13 Εἶπε δέ τις αὐτῷ ἐκ τοῦ ὄχλου, Διδάσκαλε, εἰπὲ τῷ ἀδελφῷ
said And one to Him from the crowd, Teacher, tell the brother
3450 3307 3326 1700 2817 2036 84
14 μου μερίσασθαι μετ' ἐμοῦ τὴν κληρονομίαν. ὁ δὲ εἶπεν αὐτῷ,
of me to divide with me the inheritance. He But said to him,
444 5101 3165 2525 1348 2228 3312 1909 5209
˚Ἄνθρωπε, τίς με κατέστησε δικαστὴν ἢ μεριστὴν ἐφ' ὑμᾶς;
Man, who Me appointed a judge or a divider over you?
2036 4314 846 3708 5442 575 4124
15 εἶπε δὲ πρὸς αὐτούς, Ὁρᾶτε καὶ φυλάσσεσθε ἀπὸ τῆς πλεονε-
He said And to them, Beware, and keep back from covetous-
3754 3756 1722 4052 5100 2222 848 2076 1537
ξίας· ὅτι οὐκ ἐν τῷ περισσεύειν τινὶ ἡ ζωὴ αὐτοῦ ἐστὶν ἐκ
ness; for not in the abundance to anyone the life of him is out of
5224 846 2036 3850 4314 846
16 τῶν ὑπαρχόντων αὐτοῦ. εἶπε δὲ παραβολὴν πρὸς αὐτούς,
the things existing of him. He spoke And a parable to them,
3004 444 5100 4145 2164 5561
17 λέγων, Ἀνθρώπου τινὸς πλουσίου εὐφόρησεν ἡ χώρα· καὶ
saying, of a man certain rich produced well The land. And
1260 1438 3004 5101 4160 3754 3756 2192 4226
διελογίζετο ἐν ἑαυτῷ λέγων, Τί ποιήσω, ὅτι οὐκ ἔχω ποῦ
he reasoned within himself, saying, What may I do? For not I have where
4863 2590 3450 2036 5124 4160 2507
18 συνάξω τοὺς καρπούς μου; καὶ εἶπε, Τοῦτο ποιήσω· καθελῶ
I may gather the fruits of me? And he said, This I will do; I will raze
3450 596 3187 3618 4863
μου τὰς ἀποθήκας, καὶ μείζονας οἰκοδομήσω, καὶ συνάξω
of me the barns, and larger I will build; and I will gather
1563 3956 1081 3450 18 3450 2046
19 ἐκεῖ πάντα τὰ γενήματά μου καὶ τὰ ἀγαθά μου. καὶ ἐρῶ
there all the produce of me and the goods of me; and I will say
5590 3450 5590 2192 4183 18 2749 1519 2094
τῇ ψυχῇ μου, Ψυχή, ἔχεις πολλὰ ἀγαθὰ κείμενα εἰς ἔτη
to the soul of me, Soul, you have many goods laid (up) for years
4183 373 5315 4095 2165 2036 846
20 πολλά· ἀναπαύου, φάγε, πίε, εὐφραίνου. εἶπε δὲ αὐτῷ ὁ
many; take rest, eat, drink, be glad. said But to him
2316 878 5026 3571 5590 4675 523
Θεός, ˚Ἄφρον, ταύτῃ τῇ νυκτὶ τὴν ψυχήν σου ἀπαιτοῦσιν
God, Fool! This night the soul of you they demand
575 4675 3739 2090 5101 2071 3779 2343
21 ἀπὸ σοῦ· ἃ δὲ ἡτοίμασας, τίνι ἔσται; οὕτως ὁ θησαυρίζων
from you; that and you prepared, to whom will it be? So the (one) treasuring
1438 3361 1519 2316 4147
ἑαυτῷ, καὶ μὴ εἰς Θεὸν πλουτῶν.
for himself, and not to God being rich.
2036 4314 3101 848 1223 5124 5213 3004
22 Εἶπε δὲ πρὸς τοὺς μαθητὰς αὐτοῦ, Διὰ τοῦτο ὑμῖν λέγω,
He said And to the disciples of Him, For this reason to you I say,
3361 3309 5590 5216 5101 5315 3366 4983
μὴ μεριμνᾶτε τῇ ψυχῇ ὑμῶν, τί φάγητε· μηδὲ τῷ σώματι,
Stop being anxious for the soul of you, what you eat, nor for the body,
5101 1746 5590 4119 2076 5160 4983
23 τί ἐνδύσησθε. ἡ ψυχὴ πλεῖόν ἐστι τῆς τροφῆς, καὶ τὸ σῶμα
what you put on. The soul more is (than) the food, and the body

clothing. [24]Consider the ravens, for they do not sow, nor do they reap; to which there is no storehouse or barn, and God feeds them. How much rather you differ from the birds! [25]And who of you *by* being anxious is able to add one cubit to his stature? [26]Therefore, if you are not able to do even *the* least, why are you anxious about the rest?

[27]Consider the lilies, how they grow; they do not labor, nor do they spin; but I say to you, Not even Solomon in all his glory was clothed as one of these. [28]But if God so dresses the grass, which today *is* in the field, and tomorrow is thrown into the oven, how much rather you, *O* little-faiths? [29]And you stop seeking what you may eat, or what you may drink; and stop being in anxiety. [30]For all the nations of the world seek after these things; and your Father knows that you need these things. [31]But seek the kingdom of God, and all these things will be added to you. [32]Stop being afraid, little flock, because your Father was pleased to give you the kingdom.

[33]Sell your possessions, and give alms. Make for yourselves purses that do not grow old, an unfailing treasure in Heaven, where a thief cannot come near, nor moth can corrupt. [34]For where your treasure is, there your heart will be also.

[35]Let your loins be girded about, and the lamps burning; [36]and you *be* like men awaiting their lord when he returns from the feasts, so that *he* coming and knocking, they will at once

1742 2657 2876 3754 3756 4687
24 τοῦ ἐνδύματος. κατανοήσατε τοὺς κόρακας, ὅτι οὐ σπεί-
(than) the clothing. Consider the ravens, for not they
3761 2325 3739 3756 2076 5009 3761 596
ρουσιν, οὐδὲ θερίζουσιν, οἷς οὐκ ἔστι ταμεῖον οὐδὲ ἀποθήκη,
sow, nor do they reap, to which not is storehouse nor barn,
2316 5142 846 4214 3123 5210 1308
καὶ ὁ Θεὸς τρέφει αὐτούς· πόσῳ μᾶλλον ὑμεῖς διαφέρετε τῶν
and God feeds them; by how much rather you differ from the
4071 5101 1537 5216 3309 1410 4369 1909
25 πετεινῶν ; τίς δὲ ἐξ ὑμῶν μεριμνῶν δύναται προσθεῖναι ἐπὶ
birds. who And of you being anxious is able to add on
2244 848 4083 1520 1487 3767 3777 1646
26 τὴν ἡλικίαν αὐτοῦ πῆχυν ἕνα ; εἰ οὖν οὔτε ἐλάχιστον
the stature of him cubit one. If, then, not (the) least
1410 5101 4012 3062 3309 2657
δύνασθε, τί περὶ τῶν λοιπῶν μεριμνᾶτε ; κατανοήσατε τὰ
you are able, why about the other things are you anxious? Consider the
2918 4459 837 3756 2872 3761 3514 3004 5213 3761
27 κρίνα πῶς αὐξάνει· οὐ κοπιᾷ, οὐδὲ νήθει· λέγω δὲ ὑμῖν, οὐδὲ
lilies, how they grow, not they labor, nor spin. I say But to you, Not
2672 1722 3956 1391 848 4016 5613 1722 5130
Σολομὼν ἐν πάσῃ τῇ δόξῃ αὐτοῦ περιεβάλετο ὡς ἓν τούτων.
Solomon in all the glory of him was clothed as one of these.
1487 5528 1722 68 4594 5607 839 1519
28 εἰ δὲ τὸν χόρτον ἐν τῷ ἀγρῷ σήμερον ὄντα, καὶ αὔριον εἰς
if And the grass in the field, today (is) which, and tomorrow into
2823 906 2316 3779 294 4214 3123
κλίβανον βαλλόμενον, ὁ Θεὸς οὕτως ἀμφιέννυσι. πόσῳ μᾶλλον
an oven is thrown, God so clothes, by how much rather
5209 3640 5210 3361 2212 5101 5315 2228 5101
29 ὑμᾶς, ὀλιγόπιστοι ; καὶ ὑμεῖς μὴ ζητεῖτε τί φάγητε, ἢ τί
you, little-faiths? And you not shall seek what you eat, or what
4095 3361 3349 5123 1063 3956 1484
30 πίητε· καὶ μὴ μετεωρίζεσθε. ταῦτα γὰρ πάντα τὰ ἔθνη τοῦ
you drink, and stop being in anxiety. these things For all the nations of the
2889 1934 5216 3962 1492 3754 5536 5130
κόσμου ἐπιζητεῖ· ὑμῶν δὲ ὁ πατὴρ οἶδεν ὅτι χρῄζετε τούτων.
world seek after; of you But the Father knows that you need these.
4133 2212 932 2316 5023 3956
31 πλὴν ζητεῖτε τὴν βασιλείαν τοῦ Θεοῦ, καὶ ταῦτα πάντα
But you seek the kingdom of God, and these things all
4369 5213 3361 5399 3398 4168 3754
32 προστεθήσεται ὑμῖν. μὴ φοβοῦ, τὸ μικρὸν ποίμνιον· ὅτι
will be added to you. Stop fearing, – little flock; because
2106 3962 5216 1325 5213 932
εὐδόκησεν ὁ πατὴρ ὑμῶν δοῦναι ὑμῖν τὴν βασιλείαν.
was pleased the Father of you to give you the kingdom.
4453 5224 5216 1325 1654
33 πωλήσατε τὰ ὑπάρχοντα ὑμῶν καὶ δότε ἐλεημοσύνην.
Sell the possessions of you and give alms;
4160 1438 905 3361 3822 2344
ποιήσατε ἑαυτοῖς βαλάντια μὴ παλαιούμενα, θησαυρὸν
make for yourselves purses not growing old, a treasure
413 1722 3772 3699 2812 3756 1448 3761
ἀνέκλειπτον ἐν τοῖς οὐρανοῖς, ὅπου κλέπτης οὐκ ἐγγίζει οὐδὲ
unfailing in the heavens, where a thief not can approach, nor
4597 1311 3699 1063 2076 2344 5216 1563
34 σὴς διαφθείρει· ὅπου γάρ ἐστιν ὁ θησαυρὸς ὑμῶν, ἐκεῖ καὶ
moth can corrupt; where for is the treasure of you, there also
2588 5216 2071
ἡ καρδία ὑμῶν ἔσται.
the heart of you will be.
2077 5216 3751 4024 3085
35 Ἔστωσαν ὑμῶν αἱ ὀσφύες περιεζωσμέναι, καὶ οἱ λύχνοι
Let be of you the loins having been girded, and the lamps
2545 5210 3664 444 4327
36 καιόμενοι· καὶ ὑμεῖς ὅμοιοι ἀνθρώποις προσδεχομένοις τὸν
burning; and you like men awaiting the
2962 1438 4219 360 1537 1062 2443 2064
κύριον ἑαυτῶν, πότε ἀναλύσει ἐκ τῶν γάμων, ἵνα, ἐλθόντος
lord of themselves, when he returns from the feasts, that, coming

open to him. [37]Blessed *are* those slaves whom the lord will find watching when *he* comes. Truly I say to you that he will gird himself and will make them recline. And coming up *he* will serve them. [38]And if he comes in the second watch, even in the third watch he comes and finds *it* so, blessed are those slaves. [39]But know this, that if the house-master had known the hour the thief is coming, he would have watched and would not have allowed his house to be dug through. [40]And you, then, be ready; for in the hour you think not, the Son of man comes.

[41]And Peter said to Him, Lord, do You speak this parable to us, or also to all? [42]And the Lord said, Who then is the faithful and wise steward whom the lord will set over his house servants, to give the portion of their food in season? [43]Blessed *is* that slave *when* his lord comes *and* will find *him* so doing. [44]Truly I say to you, he will set him over all his possessions. [45]But if that slave says in his heart, My lord delays to come, and begins to beat the men servants and the female servants, and to eat and to drink, and be a drunk, [46]the lord of that slave will come in the day in which he does not expect, and in an hour which he does not know. And *he* will cut him apart and will put his portion with the unbelievers. [47]But that slave knowing the will of his Lord, and did not prepare, nor did according to

2925 2112 455 846 3107 1401
37 καὶ κρούσαντος, εὐθέως ἀνοίξωσιν αὐτῷ. μακάριοι οἱ δοῦλοι
and knocking, at once they will open to him. Blessed slaves
1565 3739 2064 2962 2147 1127 281
ἐκεῖνοι, οὓς ἐλθὼν ὁ κύριος εὑρήσει γρηγοροῦντας· ἀμὴν
those, whom coming the lord will find watching; truly
3004 5213 3754 4024 347 846 3928
λέγω ὑμῖν ὅτι περιζώσεται καὶ ἀνακλινεῖ αὐτούς, καὶ παρ-
I say to you that he will gird himself and cause to recline them, and coming
1247 846 1437 2064 1208 5438
38 ελθὼν διακονήσει αὐτοῖς. καὶ ἐὰν ἔλθῃ ἐν τῇ δευτέρᾳ φυλακῇ,
up to will serve them. And if he come in the second watch,
1722 5154 5438 2064 2147 3779 3107 1525
καὶ ἐν τῇ τρίτῃ φυλακῇ ἔλθῃ, καὶ εὕρῃ οὕτω μακάριοί εἰσιν
even in the third watch he come, and find (it) so, blessed are
1401 1565 5124 1097 3754 1487 1492 3617
39 οἱ δοῦλοι ἐκεῖνοι. τοῦτο δὲ γινώσκετε, ὅτι εἰ ᾔδει ὁ οἰκοδε-
— slaves those. this But know, that if had known the house-
4169 5610 2812 2064 1127 302
σπότης ποίᾳ ὥρᾳ ὁ κλέπτης ἔρχεται, ἐγρηγόρησεν ἄν, καὶ
master in what hour the thief is coming, he would have watched, and
3756 302 863 1358 3624 848 5210 3767
40 οὐκ ἂν ἀφῆκε διορυγῆναι τὸν οἶκον αὐτοῦ. καὶ ὑμεῖς οὖν
not have allowed to be dug through the house of him. And you, then,
•5610 2064 2092 3754 3739 • 3756 1380 5207 444
γίνεσθε ἕτοιμοι· ὅτι ᾗ ὥρᾳ οὐ δοκεῖτε ὁ υἱὸς τοῦ ἀνθρώπου
be prepared, for the hour not you think the Son of man
2064
ἔρχεται.
comes.
2036 846 4074 2962 4314 2248 3850
41 Εἶπε δὲ αὐτῷ ὁ Πέτρος, Κύριε, πρὸς ἡμᾶς τὴν παραβολὴν
said And to Him Peter, Lord, to us parable
5026 3004 2228 4314 3956 2036 2962 5101 686
42 ταύτην λέγεις, ἢ καὶ πρὸς πάντας; εἶπε δὲ ὁ Κύριος, Τίς ἄρα
this do You say, or also to all? said And the Lord, Who then
2076 4103 3623 5429 3739 2525
ἐστὶν ὁ πιστὸς οἰκονόμος καὶ φρόνιμος, ὃν καταστήσει ὁ
is the faithful steward and prudent, whom will appoint the
2962 1909 2322 848 1325 1722 2540
κύριος ἐπὶ τῆς θεραπείας αὐτοῦ, τοῦ διδόναι ἐν καιρῷ τὸ
lord over the houseservants of him, to give in season the
4620 3117 1401 1565 3739 2064 2962
43 σιτομέτριον; μακάριος ὁ δοῦλος ἐκεῖνος, ὃν ἐλθὼν ὁ κύριος
portion of food? Blessed — slave that, whom coming the lord
848 2147 4160 3779 230 3004 5213 3754 1909
44 αὐτοῦ εὑρήσει ποιοῦντα οὕτως. ἀληθῶς λέγω ὑμῖν ὅτι ἐπὶ
of him will find doing so. Truly I say to you that over
3956 5224 848 2525 846 1437 2036
45 πᾶσι τοῖς ὑπάρχουσιν αὐτοῦ καταστήσει αὐτόν. ἐὰν δὲ εἴπῃ
all the possessions of him he will appoint him. if But says
1401 1565 2588 848 5549 2962 3450
ὁ δοῦλος ἐκεῖνος ἐν τῇ καρδίᾳ αὐτοῦ, Χρονίζει ὁ κυριός μου
— slave that in the heart of him, Delays the lord of me
2064 756 5180 3816 3814
ἔρχεσθαι, καὶ ἄρξηται τύπτειν τοὺς παῖδας καὶ τὰς παιδί-
to come, and begins to beat the menservants and the maid-
2068 5037 4095 3182 2240 2962
46 σκας, ἐσθίειν τε καὶ πίνειν καὶ μεθύσκεσθαι ἥξει ὁ κυριος τοῦ
servants, to eat both and to drink and to become drunk, will come the lord of
3739 1401 1565 1722 2250 3739 3756 4328 1722 5610 • 3756
δούλου ἐκείνου ἐν ἡμέρᾳ ᾗ οὐ προσδοκᾷ, καὶ ἐν ὥρᾳ ᾗ οὐ
slave that in a day in which not he expects, and in an hour which
3326 1097 1371 846 3313 848 • not
γινώσκει· καὶ διχοτομήσει αὐτόν, καὶ τὸ μέρος αὐτοῦ μετὰ
he knows, and will cut apart him, and the portions of him with
571 5087 1565 1401 1097 2307
47 τῶν ἀπίστων θήσει. ἐκεῖνος δὲ ὁ δοῦλος ὁ γνοὺς τὸ θέλημα
the unbelievers will place. that But slave knowing the will
2962 1438 3361 2090 3366 4160 4314
τοῦ κυρίου ἑαυτοῦ, καὶ μὴ ἑτοιμάσας μηδὲ ποιήσας πρὸς τὸ
of the Lord of him, and not did prepare nor did according to the

His will, will be beaten with many *stripes*. [48]But he not knowing, and doing *things* worthy of stripes, will be beaten with few. And everyone given much, much will be demanded from him. And to whom much was deposited, more exceedingly they will ask him.

[49]I came to hurl fire into the earth; and what will I if it already was lit? [50]But I have a baptism to be immersed in, and how am I pressed until it is done! [51]Do you think that I came to give peace in the earth? No, I say to you, but rather division. [52]For from now on five in one house will have been divided, three against two, and two against three. [53]Father will be divided against son, and son against father; mother against daughter, and daughter against mother; mother-in-law against her daughter-in-law, and *the* daughter-in-law against her mother-in-law.

[54]And He also said to the crowds, When you see the cloud rising up from *the* west, you immediately say, A storm is coming; and it happens so. [55]And when a south wind *is* blowing, you say, There will be heat; and it occurs. [56]Hypocrites! You know to discern the face of the earth and of the heaven, but how *is it* you do not discern this time? [57]And why do you not judge what *is* right even of yourselves? [58]For as you go with your adversary to a magistrate, give pains in the way to be set free from him, that he not drag you to the judge, and the judge deliver you to the officer, and the officer throw you into prison. [59]I say to you, In no way may you leave there until you pay even the last lepton.

2307 848 1194 4183 3361 1097 4160
48 θέλημα αὐτοῦ, δαρήσεται πολλάς· ὁ δὲ μὴ γνούς, ποιήσας
will of Him, will be beaten with many. he But not knowing, doing
514 4127 1194 3641 3956 3739 1325 4183
δὲ ἄξια πληγῶν, δαρήσεται ὀλίγας. παντὶ δὲ ᾧ ἐδόθη πολύ,
and worthy of stripes will be beaten with few. everyone And given much,
4183 2212 3844 846 3739 3908 4183
πολὺ ζητηθήσεται παρ' αὐτοῦ· καὶ ᾧ παρέθεντο πολύ,
much will be demanded from him; and to whom was deposited much,
4054 154 846
περισσότερον αἰτήσουσιν αὐτόν.
more exceedingly they will ask him.
*1487 4442 2064 906 1519 1093 5101 2309 *2235 381
49 Πῦρ ἦλθον βαλεῖν εἰς τὴν γῆν, καὶ τί θέλω εἰ ἤδη ἀνήφθη ;
Fire I came to cast into the earth, and what will I if already it was lit?
908 2192 907 4459 4912 2193 3756
50 βάπτισμα δὲ ἔχω βαπτισθῆναι, καὶ πῶς συνέχομαι ἕως οὗ
a baptism And I have to be baptized, and how I am compressed until
5055 1380 3754 1515 3854 1325 1093
51 τελεσθῇ. δοκεῖτε ὅτι εἰρήνην παρεγενόμην δοῦναι ἐν τῇ γῇ ;
it is finished! Think that peace I came to give in the earth?
3780 3004 5213 235 2228 1267 2071 1063 575
52 οὐχί, λέγω ὑμῖν, ἀλλ' ἢ διαμερισμόν. ἔσονται γὰρ ἀπὸ τοῦ
No, I say to you, but rather division. will be For from
3568 4002 1722 3624 1520 1266 5140 1909 1417
νῦν πέντε ἐν οἴκῳ ἑνὶ διαμεμερισμένοι, τρεῖς ἐπὶ δυσί, καὶ
now five in house one having been divided; three against two, and
1417 1909 5140 1266 3962 1909 5207 5207 1909
53 δύο ἐπὶ τρισί. διαμερισθήσεται πατὴρ ἐφ' υἱῷ, καὶ υἱὸς ἐπὶ
two against three will be divided; father against son, and son against
3962 3384 1909 2364 2364 3384 3994
πατρί· μήτηρ ἐπὶ θυγατρί, καὶ θυγάτηρ ἐπὶ μητρί πενθερὰ
father; mother against daughter, and daughter against mother; mother-in-law
1909 3565 848 3565 3994 848
ἐπὶ τὴν νύμφην αὐτῆς, καὶ νύμφη ἐπὶ τὴν πενθερὰν αὐτῆς.
against the daughter-in-law of her, and daughter-in-law against the mother-in-law of her
3004 3793 3752 1492 3507
54 Ἔλεγε δὲ καὶ τοῖς ὄχλοις, Ὅταν ἴδητε τὴν νεφέλην
He said And also to the crowds, When you see the cloud
393 575 1424 2112 3004 3655 2064
ἀνατέλλουσαν ἀπὸ δυσμῶν, εὐθέως λέγετε Ὄμβρος ἔρχεται·
rising up from (the) west, at once you say, A storm is coming
1096 3779 3752 3558 4154 3004 3754
55 καὶ γίνεται οὕτω. καὶ ὅταν νότον πνέοντα, λέγετε ὅτι
and it happens so. And when a south wind (is) blowing you say that
2742 2071 1096 5273 4383
56 Καύσων ἔσται· καὶ γίνεται. ὑποκριταί, τὸ πρόσωπον τοῦ
heat will be, and it happens. Hypocrites! The face of the
3772 1093 1492 1381 2540
οὐρανοῦ καὶ τῆς γῆς οἴδατε δοκιμάζειν· τὸν δὲ καιρὸν
heaven and the earth you know to discern, but time
5126 4459 3756 1381 5101 575 1438 3756 2919
57 τοῦτον πῶς οὐ δοκιμάζετε ; τί δὲ καὶ ἀφ' ἑαυτῶν οὐ κρίνετε
this how not do you discern? why And even from yourselves not do judge
1342 5613 1063 5217 3326 476 4675 1909
58 τὸ δίκαιον ; ὡς γὰρ ὑπάγεις μετὰ τοῦ ἀντιδίκου σου ἐπ'
the righteous? as For you go with the adversary of you to
758 3598 1325 2039 525 575 846
ἄρχοντα, ἐν τῇ ὁδῷ δὸς ἐργασίαν ἀπηλλάχθαι ἀπ' αὐτοῦ·
a magistrate, in the way give pains to be freed from him,
3379 2694 4571 4314 2923 2923 4571
μήποτε κατασύρῃ σε πρὸς τὸν κριτήν, καὶ ὁ κριτής σε
that not he drag you to the judge, and the judge you
3860 4233 4233 4571 906 1519 5438
παραδῷ τῷ πράκτορι, καὶ ὁ πράκτωρ σε βάλλῃ εἰς φυλακήν.
will deliver to the officer, and the officer you throw into prison.
3004 4671 =3364= 1831 1564 2193 3739 2078
59 λέγω σοι, οὐ μὴ ἐξέλθῃς ἐκεῖθεν, ἕως οὗ καὶ τὸ ἔσχατον
I say to you, in no way may you leave there until even the last
3016 591
λεπτὸν ἀποδῷς.
lepton you pay.

red: δέ(1161); καί(2531)—and, but; ὁ, ἡ, τό (3588, the)— * above word, look in verse margin for No.

CHAPTER 13

[1]And some were present at the same time reporting to Him about the Galileans, whose blood Pilate mixed with their sacrifices. [2]And answering Jesus said to them, Do you think that these Galileans were sinners beyond all the Galileans, because they suffered such things? [3]No, I say to you; but if you do not repent, you will all perish in the same way. [4]Or those eighteen on whom the tower in Siloam fell, and killed them, do you think that they were sinners beyond all men who lived in Jerusalem? [5]No, I say to you; but if you do not repent, you will all perish in the same way.

[6]And He spoke this parable:

A certain one had planted a fig-tree in his vineyard. And He came looking for fruit on it, and did not find *any*. [7]And he said to the vinedresser, Behold, three years I come looking for fruit on this fig-tree, and found none. Cut it down, and why does it waste the ground? [8]And the vinedresser said to him, Sir, leave it also this year, until I shall dig around it and throw manure; [9]and *see* if it indeed makes fruit. But if not, in the future you may cut it down.

[10]And He was teaching in one of the synagogues on *one of* the sabbaths. [11]And, behold, there was a woman having a spirit of infirmity eighteen years, and was bent together, and was not able to be completely erect. [12]And seeing her, Jesus called *her* near,

CHAPTER 13

3918 5100 846 2540 518
1 Παρῆσαν δέ τινες ἐν αὐτῷ τῷ καιρῷ ἀπαγγέλλοντες
were present And some at same the time reporting
846 4012 1057 3739 129 4091 3396 3326
αὐτῷ περὶ τῶν Γαλιλαίων, ὧν τὸ αἷμα Πιλάτος ἔμιξε μετὰ
to Him about the Galileans, of whom the blood Pilate mixed with
2378 848 611 2424 2036 846
2 τῶν θυσιῶν αὐτῶν. καὶ ἀποκριθεὶς ὁ Ἰησοῦς εἶπεν αὐτοῖς,
the sacrifices of them. And answering — Jesus said to them,
1380 3754 1057 3778 268 3844 3956
Δοκεῖτε ὅτι οἱ Γαλιλαῖοι οὗτοι ἁμαρτωλοὶ παρὰ πάντας
Do you think that Galileans those sinners above all
1057 1097 3754 5108 3958 3780
3 τοὺς Γαλιλαίους ἐγένοντο, ὅτι τοιαῦτα πεπόνθασιν; οὐχί,
the Galileans were, because these things they have suffered? No.
3004 5213 235 1437 3361 3340 3956 5615
λέγω ὑμῖν· ἀλλ' ἐὰν μὴ μετανοῆτε, πάντες ὡσαύτως
I say to you, but except you repent, all likewise
622 2228 1565 1176 3638 1909 3739 4098
4 ἀπολεῖσθε. ἢ ἐκεῖνοι οἱ δέκα καὶ ὀκτώ, ἐφ' οὓς ἔπεσεν ὁ
you will perish. Or those ten and eight on whom fell the
4444 4611 615 846 1380 3754
πύργος ἐν τῷ Σιλωὰμ καὶ ἀπέκτεινεν αὐτούς, δοκεῖτε ὅτι
tower in — Siloam, and killed them, do you think that
3778 3781 1096 3844 3956 444
οὗτοι ὀφειλέται ἐγένοντο παρὰ πάντας ἀνθρώπους τοὺς
they debtors were above all men, those
2730 2419 3780 3004 5213 235 1437
5 κατοικοῦντας ἐν Ἱερουσαλήμ; οὐχί, λέγω ὑμῖν· ἀλλ' ἐὰν
dwelling in Jerusalem? No, I say to you, but ex-
3361 3340 3956 3668 622 3004 5026
6 μὴ μετανοῆτε, πάντες ὁμοίως ἀπολεῖσθε. ἔλεγε δὲ ταύτην
cept you repent, all likewise you will perish. He told And this
3850 4808 2192 5100 1722 290 848
τὴν παραβολήν· Συκῆν εἶχέ τις ἐν τῷ ἀμπελῶνι αὐτοῦ
— parable: A fig-tree had a certain in the vineyard of him
5452 2064 2590 2212 1722 846 3756
πεφυτευμένην· καὶ ἦλθε καρπὸν ζητῶν ἐν αὐτῇ, καὶ οὐχ
planted, and came fruit seeking in it, and not
2147 2036 4314 289 2400 5140 2094
7 εὗρεν. εἶπε δὲ πρὸς τὸν ἀμπελουργόν, Ἰδού, τρία ἔτη
he found. he said And to the vinedresser, Behold, three years
2064 2212 2590 4808 5026 3756 2147
ἔρχομαι ζητῶν καρπὸν ἐν τῇ συκῇ ταύτῃ, καὶ οὐχ εὑρίσκω·
I come seeking fruit on — fig-tree this, and not do find;
1581 846 2444 1093 2673 611
8 ἔκκοψον αὐτήν· ἱνατί καὶ τὴν γῆν καταργεῖ; ὁ δὲ ἀποκριθεὶς
cut down it; why even the ground it spoils? he And answering
3004 846 2962 863 846 5124 2094 2193 3755
λέγει αὐτῷ, Κύριε, ἄφες αὐτὴν καὶ τοῦτο τὸ ἔτος, ἕως ὅτου
said to him, Lord, leave it also this year, until
4626 4012 846 906 2874 2579 3303 4160
9 σκάψω περὶ αὐτήν, καὶ βάλω κοπρίαν· κἂν μὲν ποιήσῃ
I may dig around it, and throw manure; and if indeed it makes
2590 =1490= 1519 3195 1581 846
καρπόν· εἰ δὲ μήγε, εἰς τὸ μέλλον ἐκκόψεις αὐτήν.
fruit; if but not, in the future you may cut down it.
2258 1320 1722 3391 4864 4521
10 Ἦν δὲ διδάσκων ἐν μιᾷ τῶν συναγωγῶν ἐν τοῖς σάββασι·
He was And teaching in one of the synagogues on the sabbaths.
2400 1135 2258 4151 2192 769 2094 1176
11 καὶ ἰδού, γυνὴ ἦν πνεῦμα ἔχουσα ἀσθενείας ἔτη δέκα καὶ
And behold! A woman was a spirit having of infirmity years eighteen
3638 2258 4794 3361 1410 352 1519
ὀκτώ, καὶ ἦν συγκύπτουσα, καὶ μὴ δυναμένη ἀνακύψαι εἰς
and was bent together, and not was able to be erect to
3338 1492 846 2424 4377
12 τὸ παντελές. ἰδὼν δὲ αὐτὴν ὁ Ἰησοῦς προσεφώνησε, καὶ
the fullest. seeing And her, Jesus called near and

nd said to her, Woman,
ou have been freed from
our infirmity. [13]And He
id hands on her. And in-
tantly she was made erect,
nd glorified God. [14]But
nswering, the synagogue
ıler, being angry that
esus healed on the sab-
ath, said to the crowd,
here are six days in which
is right to work. Therefore,
oming in these, be healed,
nd not on the sabbath day.
Then the Lord answered
im and said, Hypocrites!
ach one of you on the
abbath, does he not untie
is ox or ass from the
anger, and leading *it*
way give *it* drink? [16]And
is one being a daughter of
braham, whom Satan has
ound, lo, eighteen years,
as it not right to free *her*
om this bond on the sab-
ath day? [17]And on His say-
g these things, all who
pposed Him were put to
hame. And all the crowd
joiced over all the
orious things taking place
y Him.

[18]And He said, What is
e kingdom of God like?
nd to what shall I compare
[19]It is like a grain of
ustard, which a man
king threw into his
arden. And it grew and
ecame a great tree; and
e birds of the heaven
erched in its branches.
And again He said, To
hat shall I compare the
ngdom of God? [21]It is like
aven, which taking a
oman hid in three
easures of meal, until all
as leavened.

[22]And He went through
y cities and villages,
aching, and making pro-
ress toward Jerusalem.
And one said to Him, Lord,
re the ones being saved
w? But He said to them,
Labor to enter in through

2036 846 1135 630 769 4675
13 εἶπεν αὐτῇ, Γύναι, ἀπολέλυσαι της ἀσθενείας σοῦ. καὶ
said to her, Woman, you have been freed from the infirmity of you. And
2007 846 5495 611 461
ἐπεθηκεν αὐτῇ τὰς χεῖρας· καὶ παραχρῆμα ἀνωρθώθη,
He laid on her the hands, and immediately she was made erect
1392 2316 611 752
14 καὶ ἐδόξαζε τὸν Θεόν. ἀποκριθεὶς δὲ ὁ ἀρχισυνάγωγος,
and glorified — God. answering But the synagogue ruler,
23 3754 4521 2323 2424 3004
ἀγανακτῶν ὅτι τῷ σαββάτῳ ἐθεράπευσεν ὁ Ἰησοῦς, ἔλεγε
being angry that on the sabbath healed Jesus, said
3793 1803 2250 1526 1722 3739 1163 2038 1722 5025
τῷ ὄχλῳ, Ἓξ ἡμέραι εἰσὶν ἐν αἷς δεῖ ἐργάζεσθαι· ἐν ταύταις
to the crowd, Six days there are in which it is right to work; on these
3767 2064 2323 3361 2250 4521
οὖν ἐρχόμενοι θεραπεύεσθε, καὶ μὴ τῇ ἡμέρᾳ τοῦ σαββάτου.
then coming be healed, and not on the day of the sabbath.
611 3767 846 2962 2036 5273 1538
15 ἀπεκρίθη οὖν αὐτῷ ὁ Κύριος, καὶ εἶπεν, Ὑποκριτά, ἕκαστος
answered Then him the Lord, and said, Hypocrites! Each one
5216 4521 3756 3089 1016 848 2228 3688 575
ὑμῶν τῷ σαββάτῳ οὐ λύει τὸν βοῦν αὐτοῦ ἢ τὸν ὄνον ἀπὸ
of you on the sabbath, not loosen the ox of him or the ass from
5336 520 4222 5026 2364
16 τῆς φάτνης, καὶ ἀπαγαγὼν ποτίζει; ταύτην δέ, θυγατέρα
the manger, and leading away give drink? this one And, a daughter
11 5607 3739 1210 4567 2400 1176 3638
Ἀβραὰμ οὖσαν, ἣν ἔδησεν ὁ Σατανᾶς, ἰδού, δέκα καὶ ὀκτὼ
of Abraham being, whom bound Satan, behold, ten and eight
2094 3756 1163 3089 575 1199 5127 2250
ἔτη, οὐκ ἔδει λυθῆναι ἀπὸ τοῦ δεσμοῦ τούτου τῇ ἡμέρᾳ τοῦ
years, not was it right to free from bond this on the day of the
4521 5023 3004 846 2617
17 σαββάτου; καὶ ταῦτα λέγοντος αὐτοῦ, κατῃσχύνοντο
sabbath? And these things saying Him, were put to shame
3956 480 846 3956 3793 5463 1909
πάντες οἱ ἀντικείμενοι αὐτῷ· καὶ πᾶς ὁ ὄχλος ἔχαιρεν ἐπὶ
all those opposing Him, and all the crowd rejoiced over
3956 1741 1096 5259 846
πᾶσι τοῖς ἐνδόξοις τοῖς γινομένοις ὑπ' αὐτοῦ.
all the glorious things — happening by Him.
3004 5101 3664 2076 932 2316 5101
18 Ἔλεγε δέ, Τίνι ὁμοία ἐστὶν ἡ βασιλεία τοῦ Θεοῦ; καὶ τίνι
He said And, To what like is the kingdom — of God, and to what
3666 846 3664 2076 2848 4615 3739 2983
19 ὁμοιώσω αὐτήν; ὁμοία ἐστὶ κόκκῳ σινάπεως, ὃν λαβὼν
may I compare it? like It is a grain of mustard, which taking
444 906 1519 2779 1438 837 1096
ἄνθρωπος ἔβαλεν εἰς κῆπον ἑαυτοῦ· καὶ ηὔξησε, καὶ ἐγένετο
a man threw into a garden of himself; and it grew, and became
1519/1186 3173 4071 3772 2681
εἰς δένδρον μέγα, καὶ τὰ πετεινὰ τοῦ οὐρανοῦ κατεσκήνωσεν
into a tree great, and the birds of the heaven perched
2798 848 3825 2036 5101 3666
20 ἐν τοῖς κλάδοις αὐτοῦ. καὶ πάλιν εἶπε, Τίνι ὁμοιώσω τὴν
in the branches of it. And again He said, To what may I compare the
932 2316 3664 2076 2219 3739 2983 1135
21 βασιλείαν τοῦ Θεοῦ; ὁμοία ἐστὶ ζύμῃ, ἣν λαβοῦσα γυνὴ
kingdom — of God? like It is to leaven, which taking a woman
1470 1519 224 4568 5140 2193 3739 2220 3650
ἐνέκρυψεν εἰς ἀλεύρου σάτα τρία, ἕως οὗ ἐζυμώθη ὅλον.
hid in of meal measures three, until were leavened all.
1279 2596 4172 2968 1321
22 Καὶ διεπορεύετο κατὰ πόλεις καὶ κώμας διδάσκων, καὶ
And he traveled throughout cities and villages teaching, and
4197 4160 1519 2419 2036 5100 846 2962
23 πορείαν ποιούμενος εἰς Ἱερουσαλήμ. εἶπε δέ τις αὐτῷ, Κύριε,
progress making toward Jerusalem. said And one to Him, Lord,
1487 3641 4982 2036 4314 846 75
24 εἰ ὀλίγοι οἱ σωζόμενοι; ὁ δὲ εἶπε πρὸς αὐτούς, Ἀγωνίζεσθε
If few those being saved? He And said to them. Strive

the narrow gate; for I say to you that many will seek to enter in, and will not have strength. [25]From the time the Master of the house rises up, and He shuts the door, and you begin to stand outside and to knock at the door, saying, Lord, Lord, open to us. And answering He will say to you, I do not know you. From where are you? [26]Then you will begin to say, We ate and drank before You, and You taught in our streets. [27]And He will say, I tell you, I do not know you, from where you are. Stand back from Me, all workers of unrighteousness. [28]There will be weeping and gnashing of the teeth when you see Abraham and Isaac and Jacob, and all the prophets, in the kingdom of God, but you being thrust outside.

[29]And they will come from east and west, and from north and south, and will recline in the kingdom of God. [30]And, behold, there are last ones who will be first, and there are first ones who will be last.

[31]In the same day certain Pharisees came saying to *Him*, Go out and go on from here, for Herod desires to kill you. [32]And He said to them, Going, say to that fox, Behold, today and tomorrow I cast out demons, and I complete cures, and the third *day* I am perfected. [33]But today and tomorrow, and on the following *day*, I must travel on. For it is not possible for a prophet to perish outside Jerusalem. [34]Jerusalem! Jerusalem! The *one* killing the prophets, and stoning the ones that have been sent to her; how often I desired to gather your children in the

1525 1220 4728 4439 3754 4183 3004 5213
εἰσελθεῖν διὰ τῆς στενῆς πύλης· ὅτι πολλοί, λέγω ὑμῖν,
to enter through the narrow gate. that many I say to you,
2212 1525 3756 2480 575 3739 302 1453
25 ζητήσουσιν εἰσελθεῖν, καὶ οὐκ ἰσχύσουσιν. ἀφ' οὗ ἂν ἐγερθῇ ὁ
will seek to enter in, and not will have strength. From when is risen t
3617 608 2274 756 1854
οἰκοδεσπότης καὶ ἀποκλείσῃ τὴν θύραν, καὶ ἄρξησθε ἔξω
housemaster, and he shuts the door, and you begin outside
2476 2925 2374 3004 2962 2962
ἑστάναι καὶ κρούειν τὴν θύραν, λέγοντες, Κύριε, Κύριε,
to stand and to knock the door, saying, Lord, Lord,
455 2254 611 2046 5213 3756 1492 5209 4159
ἄνοιξον ἡμῖν· καὶ ἀποκριθεὶς ἐρεῖ ὑμῖν, Οὐκ οἶδα ὑμᾶς, πόθεν
open to us, and answering He say to you, not I know you, from wher
2075 5119 756 3004 5315 1799 4675
26 ἐστέ· τότε ἄρξεσθε λέγειν, Ἐφάγομεν ἐνώπιόν σου καὶ
you are. Then you will begin to say, We ate before You and
4095 1722 4113 2257 1321 2046
27 ἐπίομεν, καὶ ἐν ταῖς πλατείαις ἡμῶν ἐδίδαξας. καὶ ἐρεῖ,
drank, and in the streets of us You taught. And He will say
1700 3004 5213 3756 1492 5209 4159 2075 868 575
Λέγω ὑμῖν, οὐκ οἶδα ὑμᾶς πόθεν ἐστέ· ἀπόστητε ἀπ' ἐμοῦ
I tell you, not I know you, from where you are. Stand back from M
3956 2040 93 1563 2071 2805
28 πάντες οἱ ἐργάται τῆς ἀδικίας. ἐκεῖ ἔσται ὁ κλαυθμὸς καὶ ὁ
all the workers of unrighteousness. There will be the weeping and the
1030 3599 3752 3700 11 2464
βρυγμὸς τῶν ὀδόντων, ὅταν ὄψησθε Ἀβραὰμ καὶ Ἰσαὰκ
gnashing of the teeth, when you see Abraham and Isaac
2384 3956 4396 1722 932
καὶ Ἰακὼβ καὶ πάντας τοὺς προφήτας ἐν τῇ βασιλείᾳ τοῦ
and Jacob and all the prophets in the kingdom
2316 5209 1544 1854 2240 575 395
29 Θεοῦ, ὑμᾶς δὲ ἐκβαλλομένους ἔξω. καὶ ἥξουσιν ἀπὸ ἀνατο-
of God, you and being thrust outside. And they will come from east
1424 575 1005 3558 341
λῶν καὶ δυσμῶν, καὶ ἀπὸ βορρᾶ καὶ νότου, καὶ ἀνακλιθή-
and west, and from north and south, and will recline
932 2316 2400 1526 2078 3739
30 σονται ἐν τῇ βασιλείᾳ τοῦ Θεοῦ. καὶ ἰδού, εἰσὶν ἔσχατοι οἳ
in the kingdom of God. And behold, are last ones wh
2071 4413 1526 4412 3739 2071 2078
ἔσονται πρῶτοι, καὶ εἰσὶ πρῶτοι οἳ ἔσονται ἔσχατοι.
will be first, and are first ones who will be last.
1722 846 2250 4334 5100 5330 3004
31 Ἐν αὐτῇ τῇ ἡμέρᾳ προσῆλθόν τινες Φαρισαῖοι, λέγοντες
In same the day came to (Him certain Pharisees, saying,
846 1831 4198 1782 3754 2264 2307 457
αὐτῷ, Ἔξελθε καὶ πορεύου ἐντεῦθεν, ὅτι Ἡρῴδης θέλει σε
to Him, Go out and go on from here, because Herod desires you
615 2036 846 4198 2036 258
32 ἀποκτεῖναι. καὶ εἶπεν αὐτοῖς, Πορευθέντες εἴπατε τῇ ἀλώπεκι
to kill. And He said to them, Going, say fox
5026 2400 1544 1140 2392 2005 4594
ταύτῃ, Ἰδού, ἐκβάλλω δαιμόνια καὶ ἰάσεις ἐπιτελῶ σήμερον
to that, Behold, I cast out demons and cures I finish today,
839 5154 4198 4133 1163 3165 4594
33 καὶ αὔριον, καὶ τῇ τρίτῃ τελειοῦμαι. πλὴν δεῖ με σήμερον
and tomorrow, and the third (day) I am perfected. But must I today
839 2192 4198 3754 3756 1735
καὶ αὔριον καὶ τῇ ἐχομένῃ πορεύεσθαι· ὅτι οὐκ ἐνδέχεται
and tomorrow and on the following travel on, because not it is possible
4396 622 1854 2419 2419 2419
34 προφήτην ἀπολέσθαι ἔξω Ἱερουσαλήμ. Ἱερουσαλήμ, Ἱερου-
a prophet to perish outside Jerusalem. Jerusalem! Jeru-
615 4396 3036
σαλήμ, ἡ ἀποκτείνουσα τοὺς προφήτας, καὶ λιθοβολοῦσα
salem! The (one) killing the prophets, and stoning
649 4314 846 4212 2309 1996
τοὺς ἀπεσταλμένους πρὸς αὐτήν, ποσάκις ἠθέλησα ἐπισυνά-
those having been sent to her. How often I desired to gather

way a hen *gathers* her
brood under the wings;
and you did not desire *it*..
35Behold! Your house is
left to you desolate. And
truly I say to you, You shall
not at all see Me until it
come when you say,
Blessed *is* the *One* coming
in *the* name of *the* Lord.

1And it occurred on His
going into a house of one
of the Pharisee leaders on
a sabbath to eat bread,
even they were closely
observing Him. 2And be-
hold, a certain man was
dropsical before Him. 3And
answering Jesus said to
the lawyers and Pharisees,
asking whether it is lawful
to heal on the sabbath.
4And they were silent. And
taking the *man*, He cured
him, and let *him* go. 5And
answering to them He said,
Whose ass or ox of yours
shall fall into a pit, and he
will not at once pull it up on
the sabbath day? 6 And
they were not able to reply
to Him against these
things.

7And He spoke a
parable to those who had
been invited, noting how
they were choosing the
chief seats, saying to them,
8When you are invited by
anyone to wedding feasts,
do not recline at the chief
seat, lest *one* more honorable *than* you be invited by
him; 9and he coming to
you, and he inviting, will
say to you, Give this one
place. And then you begin
with shame to take the last
place. 10But when you are
invited, going in recline at
the last place, so that when
he inviting you may come,
he *may* say to you, Friend,
go up higher. Then glory
will be to you before those
reclining with you. 11For

5043 4675 3739 5158 3733 1438 3555 5259
ξαι τὰ τέκνα σου, ὃν τρόπον ὄρνις τὴν ἑαυτῆς νοσσιὰν ὑπὸ
the children of you in the way a hen (gathers) her brood under
4420 3756 2309 2400 863 5213 3614
35 τὰς πτέρυγας, καὶ οὐκ ἠθελήσατε. ἰδού, ἀφίεται ὑμῖν ὁ οἶκος
wings, and not you desired (it). Behold, is left to you the house
5216 2048 281 3004 5213 3754 3756 3361 • 1492 2192 302
3165 ὑμῶν ἔρημος· ἀμὴν δὲ λέγω ὑμῖν ὅτι Οὐ μή με ἴδητε ἕως ἂν
of you desolate. truly And I say to you that in no way Me shall you see until
2240 3753 2036 2127 2064 1722 3686 2962
ἥξῃ, ὅτε εἴπητε, Εὐλογημένος ὁ ἐρχόμενος ἐν ὀνόματι Κυρίου.
it come when you say, Blessed the (One) coming in (the) name of (the) Lord.

CHAPTER 14

1096 1722 2064 846 1519 3624 5100
1 Καὶ ἐγένετο ἐν τῷ ἐλθεῖν αὐτὸν εἰς οἶκόν τινος τῶν
And it was in the going (of) Him into a house of one of the
758 5330 4521 5315 740
ἀρχόντων τῶν Φαρισαίων σαββάτῳ φαγεῖν ἄρτον, καὶ
leaders of the Pharisees on a sabbath to eat bread, and
846 2258 3906 846 2400 444 5100
2 αὐτοὶ ἦσαν παρατηρούμενοι αὐτόν. καὶ ἰδού, ἄνθρωπός τις
they were carefully watching Him. And, behold, man a certain
2258 5203 1715 846 611 2424
3 ἦν ὑδρωπικὸς ἔμπροσθεν αὐτοῦ. καὶ ἀποκριθεὶς ὁ Ἰησοῦς
was dropsical before Him. And answering Jesus
2036 4314 3544 5330 3004 1487 1832
εἶπε πρὸς τοὺς νομικοὺς καὶ Φαρισαίους, λέγων, Εἰ ἔξεστι
said to the lawyers and Pharisees, saying, If it is lawful
4521 2323 2270 1949
4 τῷ σαββάτῳ θεραπεύειν; οἱ δὲ ἡσύχασαν. καὶ ἐπιλαβόμενος
on the sabbath to heal; they and were silent. And taking (him),
2390 846 630 611 4314 846
5 ἰάσατο αὐτόν, καὶ ἀπέλυσε. καὶ ἀποκριθεὶς πρὸς αὐτοὺς
He cured him, and dismissed (him). And answering to them
2036 5101 5216 3681 2228 1016 1519 5421 1706 3756
εἶπε, Τίνος ὑμῶν ὄνος ἢ βοῦς εἰς φρέαρ ἐμπεσεῖται, καὶ οὐκ
He said, Of whom of you an ass or ox into a pit should fall, and not
2112 385 846 2250 4521
6 εὐθέως ἀνασπάσει αὐτὸν ἐν τῇ ἡμέρᾳ τοῦ σαββάτου; καὶ
at once he will pull up it on the day of the sabbath? And
3756 2484 470 846 4314 5023
οὐκ ἴσχυσαν ἀνταποκριθῆναι αὐτῷ πρὸς ταῦτα.
not they were able to reply to Him against these things.
3004 4314 2564 3850 1907 4459
7 Ἔλεγε δὲ πρὸς τοὺς κεκλημένους παραβολήν, ἐπέχων πῶς
He told And to those having been invited a parable noting how
4411 1586 3104 4314 846 3752
8 τὰς πρωτοκλισίας ἐξελέγοντο, λέγων πρὸς αὐτούς, Ὅταν
the chief seats they were choosing, saying to them, When
2564 5259 5102 1519 1062 3361 2625 1519 4411
κληθῇς ὑπό τινος εἰς γάμους, μὴ κατακλιθῇς εἰς τὴν πρωτοκλι-
you are invited by one to feasts, do not recline at the chief seat,
3379 1784 4675 5600 2564 5259 846
9 σίαν· μήποτε ἐντιμότερός σου ᾖ κεκλημένος ὑπ' αὐτοῦ, καὶ
lest (one) more honorable (than) be invited by him, and
1325 2064 4571 848 2564 you 2046 4671 • 5129 5117
ἐλθὼν ὁ σὲ καὶ αὐτὸν καλέσας ἐρεῖ σοι, Δὸς τούτῳ τόπον· καὶ
coming he to you and him inviting will say to you, Give this one place. And
5119 756 3326 152 2078 5117 2722 235
10 τότε ἄρξῃ μετ' αἰσχύνης τὸν ἔσχατον τόπον κατέχειν. ἀλλ'
then you begin with shame the last place to take. But
3752 2564 4198 377 1519 2078 5117
ὅταν κληθῇς, πορευθεὶς ἀνάπεσον εἰς τὸν ἔσχατον τόπον·
when you are invited, going recline in the last place,
2443 3752 2064 2564 4571 2036 4671 5384 4320
ἵνα, ὅταν ἔλθῃ ὁ κεκληκώς σε, εἴπῃ σοι, Φίλε, προσανάβηθι
that when comes he inviting you, he say to you, Friend, go up
511 5119 2071 4671 1391 1799 4873
ἀνώτερον· τότε ἔσται σοι δόξα ἐνώπιον τῶν συνανακειμένων
higher. Then will be to you glory before those reclining with

everyone exalting himself will be humbled; and the *one* humbling himself will be exalted.

[12]And He also said to him who had invited Him, When you make a dinner or supper, do not call your friends, nor your brothers, nor your relatives, nor rich neighbors, lest they also should invite you in return, and it become a repayment to you. [13]But when you make a party, call the poor, the crippled, the lame, the blind; [14]and then you will be blessed, for they have nothing to repay you. For it will be repaid to you in the resurrection of the just.

[15]And one of those reclining with *Him*, hearing these things, *he* said to Him, Blessed *are* those eating bread in the kingdom of God. [16]But He said to him, A certain man made a great supper, and invited many. [17]And he sent his slave at the supper hour to say to those who had been invited, Come, for now all is ready. [18]And all with one *mind* began to beg off. The first said to him, I have bought a field, and I have need to go out and see it; I ask you, have me excused. [19]And another said, I bought five yoke of oxen, and I am going to try them out; I ask you, have me excused. [20]And another said, I married a wife, and for this reason I am not able to come. [21]And having come up that slave reported these things to his lord, then being angry the housemaster said to his slave, Go out quickly into the streets and lanes of the

4671 3754 3956 5312 1438 5013 5013
11 σοι. ὅτι πᾶς ὁ ὑψῶν ἑαυτὸν ταπεινωθήσεται, καὶ ὁ ταπεινῶν
you. For everyone exalting himself will be humbled; and he humblin
1438 5312
ἑαυτὸν ὑψωθήσεται.
himself will be exalted.
3004 2564 846 3752 4160 712 222
12 Ἔλεγε δὲ καὶ τῷ κεκληκότι αὐτόν, Ὅταν ποιῇς ἄριστον ἢ
He said And also to those inviting Him, When you make a dinner o
1173 3361 5455 5384 4675 3366 80 4675
δεῖπνον, μὴ φώνει τοὺς φίλους σου, μηδὲ τοὺς ἀδελφούς σου
a supper, do not call the friends of you, nor the brothers of yo
3366 4773 4675 3366 1069 4145 3379
μηδὲ τοὺς συγγενεῖς σου, μηδὲ γείτονας πλουσίους· μήποτ
nor the relatives of you, nor neighbors rich, lest
846 1571 479 1096 4671 468
καὶ αὐτοί σε ἀντικαλέσωσι, καὶ γένηταί σοι ἀνταπόδομα
also they you invite in return, and it becomes to you a repaymen
235 3752 4160 1403 2564 4434 376 5560
13 ἀλλ' ὅταν ποιῇς δοχήν, κάλει πτωχούς, ἀναπήρους, χωλούς,
But when a party you make, invite poor ones, maimed ones, lame ones
5185 3107 2071 3754 3756 2192 467
14 τυφλούς· καὶ μακάριος ἔσῃ, ὅτι οὐκ ἔχουσιν ἀνταποδοῦναί
blind ones, and blessed you will be, for not they have (with which) to repa
4671 467 1063 4671/1722 467
σοι· ἀνταποδοθήσεται γάρ σοι ἐν τῇ ἀναστάσει τῶν
you. it will be repaid For to you in the resurrection of th
1342
δικαίων.
just.
191 5100 4873 5023 2036 846
15 Ἀκούσας δέ τις τῶν συνανακειμένων ταῦτα εἶπεν αὐτῷ
hearing And one of those reclining with these things said to H
3107 3739 5315 740 1722 932 2316
16 Μακάριος, ὃς φάγεται ἄρτον ἐν τῇ βασιλείᾳ τοῦ Θεοῦ. ὁ δὲ
Blessed those eating bread in the kingdom of God. He B
2036 846 444 5100 4160 1173 3173
εἶπεν αὐτῷ, Ἄνθρωπός τις ἐποίησε δεῖπνον μέγα, καὶ
said to him, man A certain made a supper great, an
2564 4183 649 1401 848 5610
17 ἐκάλεσε πολλούς· καὶ ἀπέστειλε τὸν δοῦλον αὐτοῦ τῇ ὥρᾳ
invited many, and sent the slave of him at the hour
1173 2036 2564 2064 3754 223
τοῦ δείπνου εἰπεῖν τοῖς κεκλημένοις, Ἔρχεσθε, ὅτι ἤδη
of the supper to say to those having been invited, Come, because nov
2092 2076 3956 756 575 3391 3868
18 ἕτοιμά ἐστι πάντα. καὶ ἤρξαντο ἀπὸ μιᾶς παραιτεῖσθαι
ready it is all. And they began with one (mind) to beg off
3956 4413 2036 846 68 59 2192
πάντες. ὁ πρῶτος εἶπεν αὐτῷ, Ἀγρὸν ἠγόρασα, καὶ ἔχω
all. The first said to him, A field I have bought, and I hav
318 1831 1492 846 2065 4571 2192 3165 3868
ἀνάγκην ἐξελθεῖν καὶ ἰδεῖν αὐτόν· ἐρωτῶ σε, ἔχε με παρῃτη-
need to go out and to see it; I ask you, have me excuse
2087 2036 2201 1016 59 4002
19 μένον. καὶ ἕτερος εἶπε, Ζεύγη βοῶν ἠγόρασα πέντε, καὶ
And another said, yoke of oxen I bought five, and
4198 1381 846 2065 4571 2192/3165 3868
πορεύομαι δοκιμάσαι αὐτά· ἐρωτῶ σε, ἔχε με παρῃτημένον.
I am going to try out them; I ask you, have me excused.
2087 2036 1135 1060 1223 5124 3756 1410
20 καὶ ἕτερος εἶπε, Γυναῖκα ἔγημα, καὶ διὰ τοῦτο οὐ δύναμαι
And another said, a wife I married, and for this reason not I am ab
2064 3854 1401 1565 518
21 ἐλθεῖν. καὶ παραγενόμενος ὁ δοῦλος ἐκεῖνος ἀπήγγειλε τῷ
to come. And coming up slave that reported to the
2962 848 5023 5119 3710 3617 2036
κυρίῳ αὐτοῦ ταῦτα. τότε ὀργισθεὶς ὁ οἰκοδεσπότης εἶπε τῷ
lord of him these things. Then being angry the housemaster said to t
1401 848 1831 5030 1519 4113 4505
δούλῳ αὐτοῦ, Ἔξελθε ταχέως εἰς τὰς πλατείας καὶ ῥύμας τῆς
slave of him, Go out quickly into the streets and lanes of th

city, and bring in here the poor and maimed and lame and blind ones. [22]And the slave said, Sir, *it* has been done as you ordered, and still there is room. [23]And the lord said to the slave, Go out into the highways and hedges and compel *them* to come in, so that my house may be filled. [24]For I say to you that not one of those men who had been invited shall taste of my supper.

[25]And great crowds came together to Him. And turning He said to them, [26]If anyone comes to Me and does not hate his father, and mother, and wife, and children, and brothers and sisters, and also his own soul, too, he cannot be My disciple. [27]And whoever does not bear his cross and *does not* come after Me, he is not able to be My disciple. [28]For which of you, desiring to build a tower does not first sit down and count the cost, whether he has the things to finish; [29]that having laid a foundation, and not having strength to finish all, those seeing begin to mock him, [30]saying, This man began to build, and did not have strength to finish. [31]Or what king going to attack another king in war does not first sit down *and* take counsel whether he is able with ten thousands to meet those coming upon him with twenty thousands?

[32]But if not, he being still far off, sending a delegation he asks the things for peace. [33]So then everyone of you who does not abandon all

4172 4434 376 5660
πόλεως, καὶ τοὺς πτωχοὺς καὶ ἀναπήρους καὶ χωλοὺς καὶ
city and the poor and maimed and lame and
5185 1521 5602 2036 1401 2962 1096 5613
22 τυφλοὺς εἰσάγαγε ὧδε. καὶ εἶπεν ὁ δοῦλος, Κύριε, γέγονεν ὡς
blind bring in here. And said the slave, Lord, has occurred as
2004 2089 5117 2076 2036 2962 4314
23 ἐπέταξας, καὶ ἔτι τόπος ἐστί. καὶ εἶπεν ὁ κύριος πρὸς τὸν
you ordered, and yet room there is. And said the lord to the
1401 1831 1519 3598 5418 315
δοῦλον, Ἔξελθε εἰς τὰς ὁδοὺς καὶ φραγμούς, καὶ ἀνάγκασον
slave, Go out into the ways and hedges, and compel (them)
1525 2443 1072 3624 3450 3004 1063 5213 3754 3762
24 εἰσελθεῖν, ἵνα γεμισθῇ ὁ οἶκός μου. λέγω γὰρ ὑμῖν ὅτι οὐδεὶς
to come in, that may be filled the house of me. I say For to you that not one
435 1565 2564 1089 3450
τῶν ἀνδρῶν ἐκείνων τῶν κεκλημένων γεύσεταί μου τοῦ
— men of those — having been invited shall taste of me the
1173
δείπνου.
supper.

4848 846 3793 4183 4762 2036
25 Συνεπορεύοντο δὲ αὐτῷ ὄχλοι πολλοί· καὶ στραφεὶς εἶπε
came together And to Him crowds many; and turning He said
4314 846 =1536= 2064 4314 3165 3756 3404 3962
26 πρὸς αὐτούς, Εἴ τις ἔρχεται πρός με, καὶ οὐ μισεῖ τὸν πατέρα
to them, If anyone comes to Me, and not hates the father
1438 3384 1135 5043
ἑαυτοῦ, καὶ τὴν μητέρα, καὶ τὴν γυναῖκα, καὶ τὰ τέκνα, καὶ
of him and the mother, and the wife, and the children, and
80 79 2089 1438 5590
τοὺς ἀδελφούς, καὶ τὰς ἀδελφάς, ἔτι δὲ καὶ τὴν ἑαυτοῦ ψυχήν,
the brothers, and the sisters, besides and even the of himself soul,
3756 1410 3450 3101 1511 3783 3756 941
27 οὐ δύναταί μου μαθητὴς εἶναι. καὶ ὅστις οὐ βαστάζει τὸν
not he is able of Me a disciple to be. And who not does bear the
4716 848 2064 3694 3450 3756 1410 3450
σταυρὸν αὐτοῦ καὶ ἔρχεται ὀπίσω μου, οὐ δύναταί μου
cross of him and comes after Me, not he is able of Me
•1537 1511 3101 5101 1063* 5216 2309 4444 3618
28 εἶναι μαθητής. τίς γὰρ ἐξ ὑμῶν, θέλων πύργον οἰκοδομῆσαι,
to be a disciple. who For of you desiring a tower to build,
3780 4412 2523 5585 1160 1487 2192 4314
οὐχὶ πρῶτον καθίσας ψηφίζει τὴν δαπάνην, εἰ ἔχει τὰ πρὸς
does not first sitting count the cost, if he has that to
535 2443 3379 5087 846 2310 3361
29 ἀπαρτισμόν; ἵνα μήποτε, θέντος αὐτοῦ θεμέλιον καὶ μὴ
bring to completion; lest laying him a foundation, and not
2480 1615 3956 2334 756 1702
ἰσχύοντος ἐκτελέσαι, πάντες οἱ θεωροῦντες ἄρξωνται ἐμπαί-
having strength to finish all, those seeing begin to mock
846 3004 3754 3778 444 756 3618
30 ζειν αὐτῷ, λέγοντες ὅτι Οὗτος ὁ ἄνθρωπος ἤρξατο οἰκοδο-
him, saying, — This man began to build,
3756 2480 1615 2228 5101 935 4198
31 μεῖν, καὶ οὐκ ἴσχυσεν ἐκτελέσαι. ἢ τίς βασιλεὺς πορευόμενος
and not had strength to finish. Or what king going
4820 2087 935 1519 4171 3780 2523 4412
συμβαλεῖν ἑτέρῳ βασιλεῖ εἰς πόλεμον οὐχὶ καθίσας πρῶτον
to attack another king at war does not sitting first
1011 1487 1415 2076 1176 5505 528
βουλεύεται εἰ δυνατός ἐστιν ἐν δέκα χιλιάσιν ἀπαντῆσαι
take counsel whether able he is with ten thousands to meet
3326 1501 5505 2064 1909 846 = 1490 =
32 τῷ μετὰ εἴκοσι χιλιάδων ἐρχομένῳ ἐπ᾽ αὐτόν; εἰ δὲ μήγε,
those with twenty thousands coming upon him? Otherwise,
2089 846 4206 5607 4242 649 2065
ἔτι αὐτοῦ πόρρω ὄντος, πρεσβείαν ἀποστείλας ἐρωτᾷ τὰ
yet him afar being, a delegation sending he asks the
4214 1515 3779 3767 3956 1537 5216 3739 3756 657 things
33 πρὸς εἰρήνην. οὕτως οὖν πᾶς ἐξ ὑμῶν ὃς οὐκ ἀποτάσσεται
for peace. So, then everyone of you who not does abandon

NOTE: Frequent words not numbered: δέ(1161); καί(2531)—and, but; ὁ, ἡ, τό (3588, the)— * above word, look in verse margin for No.

his possessions is not able to be My disciple. [34]The salt *is* good, but if the salt becomes tasteless, with what will it be seasoned? [35]It is not fit for soil nor for fertilizer; they throw it out. The *one* having ears to hear, let him hear.

CHAPTER 15

[1]And all the tax-collectors and sinners were coming near to Him, to hear Him. [2]And the Pharisees and the scribes murmured, saying, This one receives sinners and eats with them.

[3]And He spoke to them this parable, saying, [4]What man of you having a hundred sheep, and losing one of them, does not leave the ninety-nine in the desert, and goes after the lost *one* until he finds it? [5]And finding *it*, he puts *it* on his shoulders, rejoicing. [6]And coming to the house, he calls together the friends and neighbors, saying to them, Rejoice with me, for I have found my sheep that had been lost. [7]I say to you that so is joy in Heaven over one sinner repenting, than over ninety-nine righteous ones who have no need of repentance.

[8]Or what woman having ten drachmas, if she loses one drachma does not light a lamp and sweep the house, and look carefully until she finds *it*? [9]And finding *it* she calls together the friends and neighbors, saying, Rejoice with me, for I have found the drachma which I lost. [10]So I say to you, there is joy

3956 1439 5224 3756 1410 3450 151
πᾶσι τοῖς ἑαυτοῦ ὑπάρχουσιν, οὐ δύναταί μου εἶνα
to all the of himself possessions not is able of Me to be
3101 2570 217 1437 217 3471 1722 510
34 μαθητής. καλὸν τὸ ἅλας· ἐὰν δὲ τὸ ἅλας μωρανθῇ, ἐν τίν
a disciple. Good (is) the salt; if but the salt becomes useless, with w
741 3777 1519 1093 3771 1519 2874 2111 2076
35 ἀρτυθήσεται ; οὔτε εἰς γῆν οὔτε εἰς κοπρίαν εὔθετόν ἐστι
will it be seasoned? Not for soil nor for manure fit it is.
1854 906 846 2192 3775 191 191
ἔξω βάλλουσιν αὐτό. ὁ ἔχων ὦτα ἀκούειν ἀκουέτω.
out They throw it. The (one) having ears to hear, let him hear.

CHAPTER 15

2258 1448 846 3956 5057
1 Ἦσαν δὲ ἐγγίζοντες αὐτῷ πάντες οἱ τελῶναι καὶ οἱ
were And drawing near to Him all the tax-collectors and the
268 191 846 1234 5330
2 ἁμαρτωλοί, ἀκούειν αὐτοῦ. καὶ διεγόγγυζον οἱ Φαρισαῖοι
sinners to hear Him. And murmured the Pharisees
1122 3004 3754 3778 268 4327
καὶ οἱ γραμματεῖς λέγοντες ὅτι Οὗτος ἁμαρτωλοὺς προσδέ-
and the scribes, saying – This one sinners receives,
4906 846
χεται, καὶ συνεσθίει αὐτοῖς.
and eats with them.
2036 4314 846 3850 5026 3004 510
3 Εἶπε δὲ πρὸς αὐτοὺς τὴν παραβολὴν ταύτην, λέγων, Τίς
He spoke and to them – parable this, saying, What
444 1537 5216 2192 1540 4263 622 1520
4 ἄνθρωπος ἐξ ὑμῶν ἔχων ἑκατὸν πρόβατα, καὶ ἀπολέσας ἓν
man of you having a hundred sheep, and losing one
1537 846 3756 2641 1768 2018
ἐξ αὐτῶν, οὐ καταλείπει τὰ ἐννενηκονταεννέα ἐν τῇ ἐρήμῳ,
of them, not does leave the ninety-nine in the desert
4198 1909 622 2193 2147 846 2147
5 καὶ πορεύεται ἐπὶ τὸ ἀπολωλός, ἕως εὕρῃ αὐτό ; καὶ εὑρὼν
and goes after the lost (one) until he finds it? And findin
2007 1909 5606 1438 5463 2064 1519
6 ἐπιτίθησιν ἐπὶ τοὺς ὤμους ἑαυτοῦ χαίρων. καὶ ἐλθὼν εἰς τὸν
puts (it) on the shoulders of himself, rejoicing. And coming to th
3624 4779 5384 1069 3004 846
οἶκον, συγκαλεῖ τοὺς φίλους καὶ τοὺς γείτονας, λέγων αὐτοῖς,
house, he calls together the friends and the neighbors, saying to them,
4796 3427 3754 2147 4263 3450 622
Συγχάρητέ μοι, ὅτι εὗρον τὸ πρόβατόν μου τὸ ἀπολωλός.
Rejoice with me, for I have found the sheep of me having been lost
3004 5213 3754 3779 5479 2071 1722 3772 1909 1520 268
7 λέγω ὑμῖν ὅτι οὕτω χαρὰ ἔσται ἐν τῷ οὐρανῷ ἐπὶ ἑνὶ ἁμαρ-
I say to you that thus joy is in Heaven over one
3340 2228 1909 1769 1342 3748
τωλῷ μετανοοῦντι, ἢ ἐπὶ ἐννενηκονταεννέα δικαίοις, οἵτινες
sinner repenting, than over ninety-nine righteous ones wh
3756 5532 2192 3341
οὐ χρείαν ἔχουσι μετανοίας.
no need have of repentance.
2228 5101 1135 1406 2192 1176 1437 622 1406
8 Ἢ τίς γυνὴ δραχμὰς ἔχουσα δέκα, ἐὰν ἀπολέσῃ δραχμὴν
Or what woman drachmas having ten, if she loses drachma
3391 3780 681 3088 4563 3614 2218
μίαν, οὐχὶ ἅπτει λύχνον, καὶ σαροῖ τὴν οἰκίαν, καὶ ζητεῖ
one, does not light a lamp and sweep the house, and seek
1960 2193 3755 2147 2147 4779
9 ἐπιμελῶς ἕως ὅτου εὕρῃ ; καὶ εὑροῦσα συγκαλεῖται τὰς
carefully until she finds? And finding she calls together the
5384 1069 3004 4796 3427 3754 2147
φίλας καὶ τὰς γείτονας, λέγουσα, Συγχάρητέ μοι, ὅτι εὗρον
friends and the neighbors, saying, Rejoice with me, for I have
1096 1406 3739 622 3779 3004 5213 5479
10 τὴν δραχμὴν ἣν ἀπώλεσα. οὕτω, λέγω ὑμῖν, χαρὰ γίνεται
the drachma which I lost. So, I say to you, joy there is found

before the angels of God
over one sinner repenting.

[11]And He said, A certain
man had two sons; [12]and
the younger of them said to
the father, Father give me
that part of the property
falling *to me*. And he
divided the living to them.
[13]And not many days after,
gathering up all things, the
younger son went away to
a distant country. And there
he wasted his property,
living dissolutely. [14]But
having spent all his things,
a severe famine came
throughout that country;
and he began to be in need.
[15]And going he was joined
to one of the citizens of that
country. And he sent him
into his fields to feed pigs.

[16]And he longed to fill his
stomach from the husks
which the pigs ate; but no
one gave to him. [17]But
coming to himself, he said,
How many servants of my
father have plenty of
loaves, and I am perishing
with famine. [18]Rising up I
will go to my father, and I
will say to him, Father, I
sinned against Heaven and
before you; [19]and I am no
longer worthy to be called
your son. Make me as one
of your servants. [20]And
rising up he came to his
father. But he yet being far
away, his father saw him
and was moved with pity.
And running *he* fell on his
neck and fervently kissed
him. [21]And the son said to
him, Father, I have sinned
against Heaven and before
you, and I no longer am
worthy to be called your
son. [22]But the father said
to his slaves, Bring out the

1799 32 2316 1909 1520 268
ἐνώπιον τῶν ἀγγέλων τοῦ Θεοῦ ἐπὶ ἑνὶ ἁμαρτωλῷ
before the angels of God over one sinner
3340
μετανοοῦντι.
repenting.
2036 444 5100 2192 1417 5207 2036 3501
11 Εἶπε δέ, Ἄνθρωπός τις εἶχε δύο υἱούς· καὶ εἶπεν ὁ νεώτερος
12 He said And, man a certain had two sons. And said the younger
846 3962 3962 1325 3427 1911 3313
αὐτῶν τῷ πατρί, Πάτερ, δός μοι τὸ ἐπιβάλλον μέρος τῆς
of them to the father, Father, give me the falling (to me) share of the
3776 1244 846 979 3326 3756 4183
13 οὐσίας. καὶ διεῖλεν αὐτοῖς τὸν βίον. καὶ μετ' οὐ πολλὰς
property. And he divided to them the living. And after not many
2250 4863 537 3501 5207 589 1519
ἡμέρας συναγαγὼν ἅπαντα ὁ νεώτερος υἱὸς ἀπεδήμησεν εἰς
days, gathering all things, the younger son went away to
5561 3117 1563 1287 3776 848 2198
χώραν μακράν, καὶ ἐκεῖ διεσκόρπισε τὴν οὐσίαν αὐτοῦ, ζῶν
a country distant, and there scattered the property of him, living
811 1159 846 3956 1096 3042
14 ἀσώτως. δαπανήσαντος δὲ αὐτοῦ πάντα, ἐγένετο λιμὸς
dissolutely. having spent But him all things, came famine
2478 2596 5561 1565 846 756 5302
ἰσχυρὸς κατὰ τὴν χώραν ἐκείνην, καὶ αὐτὸς ἤρξατο ὑστερεῖ-
a severe throughout country that; and he began to be in
4198 2853 1520 4177 5561
15 σθαι. καὶ πορευθεὶς ἐκολλήθη ἑνὶ τῶν πολιτῶν τῆς χώρας
need. And going he was joined to one of the citizens country
1565 3992 846 1519 68 848 1006
ἐκείνης· καὶ ἔπεμψεν αὐτὸν εἰς τοὺς ἀγροὺς αὐτοῦ βόσκειν
of that, and he sent him into the fields of him to feed
5519 1937 1072 2836 848 575
16 χοίρους. καὶ ἐπεθύμει γεμίσαι τὴν κοιλίαν αὐτοῦ ἀπὸ τῶν
pigs. And he longed to fill the stomach of him from the
2769 3739 2068 5519 3762 1325 846 1519
κερατίων ὧν ἤσθιον οἱ χοῖροι· καὶ οὐδεὶς ἐδίδου αὐτῷ. εἰς
husks which ate the pigs; and no one gave to him. to
1438 2064 2036 4214 3407 3962 3450 4052
17 ἑαυτὸν δὲ ἐλθὼν εἶπε, Πόσοι μίσθιοι τοῦ πατρός μου περισ-
himself But coming, he said, How many servants of the father of me
740 1473 3042 622 450 4198
18 σεύουσιν ἄρτων, ἐγὼ δὲ λιμῷ ἀπόλλυμαι· ἀναστὰς πορεύ-
abound in loaves, I but with famine am perishing. Rising up I will
4314 3962 3450 2046 846 3962 264
σομαι πρὸς τὸν πατέρα μου, καὶ ἐρῶ αὐτῷ, Πάτερ, ἥμαρτον
go to the father of me, and I will say to him, Father, I sinned
1519 3772 1799 4675 3765 1510 514 2564
19 εἰς τὸν οὐρανὸν καὶ ἐνώπιόν σου· καὶ οὐκέτι εἰμὶ ἄξιος κληθῆ-
against Heaven, and before you; and no longer am I worthy to be
5207 4675 4160 3165 5613 1520 3407 4675
ναι υἱός σου· ποίησόν με ὡς ἕνα τῶν μισθίων σου. καὶ
called son of you. Make me as one of the servants of you. And
450 2064 4314 3962 1438 2089 846 3112
20 ἀναστὰς ἦλθε πρὸς τὸν πατέρα ἑαυτοῦ. ἔτι δὲ αὐτοῦ μακρὰν
rising up he came to the father of himself. yet But him afar
568 1492 846 3962 848 4697
ἀπέχοντος, εἶδεν αὐτὸν ὁ πατὴρ αὐτοῦ, καὶ ἐσπλαγχνίσθη,
being away, saw him the father of him, and was moved with pity;
5143 1968 1909 5137 848 2705
καὶ δραμὼν ἐπέπεσεν ἐπὶ τὸν τράχηλον αὐτοῦ, καὶ κατε-
and running fell upon the neck of him, and fervently
846 2036 846 5207 3962 264 1519
21 φίλησεν αὐτόν. εἶπε δὲ αὐτῷ ὁ υἱός, Πάτερ, ἥμαρτον εἰς τὸν
kissed him. said And to him the son, Father, I sinned against
3772 1799 4675 3765 1510 514 2564
οὐρανὸν καὶ ἐνώπιόν σου, καὶ οὐκέτι εἰμὶ ἄξιος κληθῆναι
Heaven and before you; and no longer am I worthy to be called
5207 4675 2036 3962 4314 1401 848 1627
22 υἱός σου. εἶπε δὲ ὁ πατὴρ πρὸς τοὺς δούλους αὐτοῦ, Ἐξε-
son of you. said But the father to the slaves of him, Bring

best robe and clothe him, and give a ring for his hand, and sandals for *his* feet. 23And bring the fattened calf; slaughter *it*, and let us eat and be merry; 24for this son of mine was dead, and lived again; and was lost, and was found. And they began to be merry.

25And his older son was in a field. And as he drew near, coming to the house, he heard music and dances. 26And calling one of the children to *him*, he asked what these things might be. 27And he said to him, Your brother came, and your father slaughtered the fattened calf, because he received him back in *good* health. 28But he was angry, and did not desire to go in. Then coming out his father begged him. 29But answering he said to *his* father, Behold, so many years I serve you, and never have I transgressed a command of yours. And you never gave a goat *to me* so that I might be merry with my friends. 30But when this son of yours came, the *one* devouring your living with harlots, you killed the fattened calf for him. 31But he said to him, Child, you always are with me, and all *of* my things are yours. 32But to be merry and to rejoice *was* right, for this brother of yours was dead, and lived again; and being lost, also *he* was found.

4749 4413 1746 846
νέγκατε τὴν στολὴν τὴν πρώτην καὶ ἐνδύσατε αὐτόν, καὶ
out robe the first, and clothe him, and
1325 1146 1519 5495 848 5266 1519
δότε δακτύλιον εἰς τὴν χεῖρα αὐτοῦ, καὶ ὑποδήματα εἰς τοὺς
give a ring to the hand of him, and sandals to the
4228 5342 3448 4618 2380
23 πόδας· καὶ ἐνέγκαντες τὸν μόσχον τὸν σιτευτὸν θύσατε, καὶ
feet; and bring the calf fattened, kill, and
5315 2165 3754 3778 5207 3450 3498 2258
24 φαγόντες εὐφρανθῶμεν· ὅτι οὗτος ὁ υἱός μου νεκρὸς ἦν, καὶ
eating let us be merry; because this son of me dead was, and
326 622 2258 2147 756
ἀνέζησε· καὶ ἀπολωλὼς ἦν, καὶ εὑρέθη. καὶ ἤρξαντο
lived again; and lost was, and was found. And they began
2165 2258 5207 848 4245 1722 68
25 εὐφραίνεσθαι. ἦν δὲ ὁ υἱὸς αὐτοῦ ὁ πρεσβύτερος ἐν ἀγρῷ·
to be merry. was but the son of him older in a field;
5613 2064 1448 3614 191 4858
καὶ ὡς ἐρχόμενος ἤγγισε τῇ οἰκίᾳ, ἤκουσε συμφωνίας καὶ
and as coming he drew near to the house, he heard music and
5525 4341 1520 3816 4441
26 χορῶν. καὶ προσκαλεσάμενος ἕνα τῶν παίδων, ἐπυνθάνετο
dances. And having called near one of the children, he inquired
5101 1498 5023 2036 846 3754 80 4675 2240
27 τί εἴη ταῦτα. ὁ δὲ εἶπεν αὐτῷ ὅτι Ὁ ἀδελφός σου ἥκει· καὶ
what may be this. he And said to him, The brother of you came, and
2380 3962 4675 3448 4618 3754
ἔθυσεν ὁ πατήρ σου τὸν μόσχον τὸν σιτευτόν, ὅτι
killed the father of you the calf fattened, because
5198 846 618 3710 3756 2309
28 ὑγιαίνοντα αὐτὸν ἀπέλαβεν. ὠργίσθη δέ, καὶ οὐκ ἤθελεν
being in health him he received back. he was angry But, and not desired
1525 3767 3962 848 1831 3870 846
29 εἰσελθεῖν· ὁ οὖν πατὴρ αὐτοῦ ἐξελθὼν παρεκάλει αὐτόν. ὁ δὲ
to go in. the Then father of him coming out begged him. he But
611 2036 3962 2400 5118 2094 1398 4671
ἀποκριθεὶς εἶπε τῷ πατρί, Ἰδού, τοσαῦτα ἔτη δουλεύω σοι,
answering said to the father, Behold, so many years I serve you,
3762 1785 4675 3928 1698 3762
καὶ οὐδέποτε ἐντολήν σου παρῆλθον, καὶ ἐμοὶ οὐδέποτε
and never a command of you I transgressed; and to me never
1325 2056 2443 3326 5384 3450 2165 3753
30 ἔδωκας ἔριφον, ἵνα μετὰ τῶν φίλων μου εὐφρανθῶ. ὅτε δὲ ὁ
you gave a goat that with the friends of me I might be merry. when But
5207 4675 3778 2719 4675 979 3326 4204
υἱός σου οὗτος ὁ καταφαγών σου τὸν βίον μετὰ πορνῶν
son of you this, having devoured of you the living with harlots,
2064 2380 846 3448 4618 2036
ἦλθεν, ἔθυσας αὐτῷ τὸν μόσχον τὸν σιτευτόν. ὁ δὲ εἶπεν
came, you killed for him the calf fattened. he And said
846 5043 4771 3842 3326 1700 3956 1699 4674
31 αὐτῷ, Τέκνον, σὺ πάντοτε μετ᾽ ἐμοῦ εἶ, καὶ πάντα τὰ ἐμὰ σά
to him, Child, you always with me are, and all things (of) mine yours
2076 2165 5463 1163 3754 80 4675
32 ἐστιν. εὐφρανθῆναι δὲ καὶ χαρῆναι ἔδει· ὅτι ὁ ἀδελφός σου
are. to be merry And, and to rejoice, must be, for the brother of you
3778 3498 326 622 2258 2147
οὗτος νεκρὸς ἦν, καὶ ἀνέζησε· καὶ ἀπολωλὼς ἦν, καὶ εὑρέθη.
this dead was, and lived again, and having been lost also was found

CHAPTER 16

CHAPTER 16

1And He also said to His disciples, A certain man was rich, *and he* had a steward, and this one was accused to him as wasting his goods. 2And calling

3004 4314 3101 848 444 5100 2258
1 Ἔλεγε δὲ καὶ πρὸς τοὺς μαθητὰς αὐτοῦ, Ἄνθρωπός τις ἦν
He said And also to the disciples of Him, man A certain was
4145 3739 2192 3623 3778 1225 846 5613
πλούσιος, ὃς εἶχεν οἰκονόμον· καὶ οὗτος διεβλήθη αὐτῷ ὡς
rich, who had a steward, and this one was accused to him as
1287 5224 848 5455 846
2 διασκορπίζων τὰ ὑπάρχοντα αὐτοῦ. καὶ φωνήσας αὐτὸν
wasting the possessions of him. And calling him,

him, he said to him, What *is* this I hear about you? Give the account of your stewardship, for you can no longer be steward. [3]And the steward said within himself, What shall I do, for my lord is taking away the stewardship from me? I am not able to dig, and I am ashamed to beg. [4]I know what I will do, that when I am removed *from* the stewardship, they will receive me into their houses. [5]And calling to him each one of the debtors of his lord, he said to the first, How much do you owe my lord? [6]And he said, A hundred baths of oil. And he said to him, Take your statements, and sitting, quickly write fifty. [7]Then he said to another, And you, how much do you owe? And he said a hundred cors of wheat. And he said to him, Take your statement and write eighty. [8]And the lord praised the unrighteous steward, because he acted prudently. For the sons of this age are more prudent than the sons of light themselves are in their generation. [9]And I say to you, Make to yourselves friends by the unrighteous mammon, that when it fails they may take you into the eternal dwellings. [10]He faithful in *the* least is also faithful in much. And he unrighteous in *the* least is also unrighteous in much.

[11]Then if you were not faithful in the unrighteous mammon, who will entrust the true to you? [12]And if you were not faithful in that of another, who will give to you that *which is* yours? [13]No servant is able to serve two lords; for either he will hate the one, and he will love the other; or he will cling to one, and he

2036 846 5101 5124 191 4012 4675 591 3056
εἶπεν αὐτῷ, Τί τοῦτο ἀκούω περὶ σοῦ ; ἀπόδος τὸν λόγον
he said to him, What (is) this I hear about you? Render the account
3622 4675 3756 1063 1410 2089 3621 2036
3 τῆς οἰκονομίας σου· οὐ γὰρ δυνήσῃ ἔτι οἰκονομεῖν. εἶπε δὲ
of the stewardship of you; not for you can longer be steward. said And
1722 1438 3623 5101 4160 3754 2962 3450 851
ἐν ἑαυτῷ ὁ οἰκονόμος, Τί ποιήσω, ὅτι ὁ κύριός μου ἀφαι-
within himself the steward, What may I do, because the lord of me takes
3622 575 1700 4626 3756 2480 1871
ρεῖται τὴν οἰκονομίαν ἀπ' ἐμοῦ ; σκάπτειν οὐκ ἰσχύω, ἐπαι-
away the stewardship from me? to dig not I am able; to
153 1097 5101 4160 2443 3752 3179
4 τεῖν αἰσχύνομαι. ἔγνων τί ποιήσω, ἵνα, ὅταν μετασταθῶ
beg I am ashamed I know what I may so, that when I am removed
3622 1209 3165 1519 3624 848
5 τῆς οἰκονομίας, δέξωνταί με εἰς τοὺς οἴκους αὐτῶν. καὶ
(from) the stewardship, they receive me into the houses of them. And
4341 1520 1538 5533 2962
προσκαλεσάμενος ἕνα ἕκαστον τῶν χρεωφειλετῶν τοῦ κυρίου
having called near one each of the debtors of the lord
1438 3004 4413 4214 3784 2962 3450
ἑαυτοῦ, ἔλεγε τῷ πρώτῳ, Πόσον ὀφείλεις τῷ κυρίῳ μου ;
of himself, he said to the first, How much do you owe to the lord of me?
2036 1540 943 1637 2036 846 1209 4675
6 ὁ δὲ εἶπεν, Ἑκατὸν βάτους ἐλαίου. καὶ εἶπεν αὐτῷ, Δέξαι σου
he And said, a hundred baths of oil. And he said to him, Take of you
1121 2593 5030 1125 4004 1899
τὸ γράμμα, καὶ καθίσας ταχέως γράψον πεντήκοντα. ἔπειτα
the statements, and sitting quickly write fifty. Then
2087 2036 4771 4214 3784 2036 1540 2884
7 ἑτέρῳ εἶπε, Σὺ δὲ πόσον ὀφείλεις ; ὁ δὲ εἶπεν, Ἑκατὸν κόρους
to another he said, you And how much owe you? he And said, A hundred cors
4621 3004 846 1209 4675 1121 1125
σίτου. καὶ λέγει αὐτῷ, Δέξαι σου τὸ γράμμα, καὶ γράψον
of wheat. And he said to him, Take of you the statement, and write
3589 1867 2962 3623 93
8 ὀγδοήκοντα. καὶ ἐπῄνεσεν ὁ κύριος τὸν οἰκονόμον τῆς ἀδικίας
eighty. And praised the lord the steward of unrighteousness
3754 5430 4160 3754 5207 165
•5127 ὅτι φρονίμως ἐποίησεν· ὅτι οἱ υἱοὶ τοῦ αἰῶνος •τούτου
because prudently he acted. For the sons — age of this
5429 5228 5207 5457 1519 1074
φρονιμώτεροι ὑπὲρ τοὺς υἱοὺς τοῦ φωτὸς εἰς τὴν γενεὰν
more prudent than the sons of the light in the generation
1438 1526 2504 5213 3004 4160 1438 5384 1537
9 ἑαυτῶν εἰσί. κἀγὼ ὑμῖν λέγω, Ποιήσατε ἑαυτοῖς φίλους ἐκ
of themselves are. And I to you say, Make to yourselves friends by
3126 93 2443 3752 1587 1209
τοῦ μαμωνᾶ τῆς ἀδικίας, ἵνα, ὅταν ἐκλίπητε, δέξωνται
the mammon of unrighteousness, that when it fails, they may receive
5209 1519 166 4633 4103 1646
10 ὑμᾶς εἰς τὰς αἰωνίους σκηνάς. ὁ πιστὸς ἐν ἐλαχίστῳ καὶ ἐν
you into the eternal dwellings. He faithful in least also in
4183 4103 2076 1722 1646 94 1722 4183
πολλῷ πιστός ἐστι. καὶ ὁ ἐν ἐλαχίστῳ ἄδικος καὶ ἐν πολλῷ
much faithful is; and he in least (is) unrighteous also in much
•1722 94 2076 1487 3767• 94 3126 4103 3756 1096
11 ἄδικός ἐστιν. εἰ οὖν ἐν τῷ ἀδίκῳ μαμωνᾷ πιστοὶ οὐκ ἐγένεσθε,
unrighteous is. If, then, in the unrighteous mammon faithful not you were,
228 5101 5213 4100 1487 1722 245
12 τὸ ἀληθινὸν τίς ὑμῖν πιστεύσει ; καὶ εἰ ἐν τῷ ἀλλοτρίῳ
the true who to you will entrust? And if in that of another
4103 3756 1096 5212 5101 5213 1325 3762
13 πιστοὶ οὐκ ἐγένεσθε, τὸ ὑμέτερον τίς ὑμῖν δώσει ; οὐδεὶς
faithful not you were, that being yours (is) who to you will give? No
3610 1410 1417 2962 1398 2228 1063 1520
οἰκέτης δύναται δυσὶ κυρίοις δουλεύειν· ἢ γὰρ τὸν ἕνα
houseslave is able two lords to serve; either for the one
3404 2087 25 2228 1520 472
μισήσει, καὶ τὸν ἕτερον ἀγαπήσει· ἢ ἑνὸς ἀνθέξεται, καὶ τοῦ
he will hate, and the other he will love, or one he will cling to, and the

will despise the other. You are unable to serve God and mammon.

[14]And being lovers of money, the Pharisees also heard all these things; and they derided Him. [15]And He said to them, You are those justifying yourselves before men, but God knows your hearts; for the thing highly prized among men is a hateful thing before God. [16]The Law and the Prophets *were* until John; from then the kingdom of God is being preached, and everyone is pressing into it. [17]But it is easier *for* the heaven and the earth to pass away than one tittle of the law to fail. [18]Everyone putting away his wife, and marrying another, commits adultery. And everyone marrying her who has been put away from a husband commits adultery.

[19]And there was a certain rich man, and *he was* accustomed to don a purple robe and fine linen, making merry in luxury day by day. [20]And there was a certain poor one named Lazarus, who had been laid at his porch, being plagued by sores, [21]and longing to be filled from the crumbs that were falling from the table of the rich one. But even the dogs coming licked his sores. [22]And it happened, the poor one died, and was carried away by the angels into the bosom of Abraham. And the rich one also died, and was buried. [23]And being in torments in Hell, lifting up his eyes, he sees Abraham afar off, and Lazarus in his bosoms. [24]And send Lazarus that he may

2087 2706 3756 1410 2316 1398 3126
ἑτέρου καταφρονήσει. οὐ δύνασθε Θεῷ δουλεύειν καὶ μαμωνᾷ.
other he will despise. not You are able God to serve and mammon.
191 5023 3956 5330 5366
Ἤκουον δὲ ταῦτα πάντα καὶ οἱ Φαρισαῖοι φιλάργυροι
heard And these things all also the Pharisees, money-lovers
5225 1592 846 2036 846
14 ὑπάρχοντες, καὶ ἐξεμυκτήριζον αὐτόν. καὶ εἶπεν αὐτοῖς,
being; and they derided Him. And He said to them,
5210 2075 1344 1438 1799 444
15 Ὑμεῖς ἐστε οἱ δικαιοῦντες ἑαυτοὺς ἐνώπιον τῶν ἀνθρώπων
You are those justifying yourselves before men,
2316 1097 2588 5216 3754 444
ὁ δὲ Θεὸς γινώσκει τὰς καρδίας ὑμῶν· ὅτι τὸ ἐν ἀνθρώποις
But God knows the hearts of you; for the thing among men
5308 946 1799 2316 2076 3551
16 ὑψηλὸν βδέλυγμα ἐνώπιον τοῦ Θεοῦ ἐστιν. ὁ νόμος καὶ οἱ
highly prized an abomination before God is. The Law and the
4396 2193 2491 575 5119 932 2316
προφῆται ἕως Ἰωάννου· ἀπὸ τότε ἡ βασιλεία τοῦ Θεοῦ
Prophets (were) until John; from then the kingdom of God
2097 3956 1519 846 971 2123
17 εὐαγγελίζεται, καὶ πᾶς εἰς αὐτὴν βιάζεται. εὐκοπώτερον δέ
is being preached; and everyone into it is pressing. easier But
2076 3772 1093 3928 2228 3551 3391
ἐστι τὸν οὐρανὸν καὶ τὴν γῆν παρελθεῖν, ἢ τοῦ νόμου μίαν
it is the heaven and the earth to pass away, than of the law one
2762 4098 3956 630 1135 848
18 κεραίαν πεσεῖν. πᾶς ὁ ἀπολύων τὴν γυναῖκα αὐτοῦ καὶ
tittle to fall. Everyone putting away the wife of him and
1060 2087 3431 3956 630 575 435
γαμῶν ἑτέραν μοιχεύει· καὶ πᾶς ὁ ἀπολελυμένην ἀπὸ ἀνδρὸς
marrying another commits adultery and everyone having been put away her from a husband
1060 3431
γαμῶν μοιχεύει.
marrying, commits adultery.
*2258 444 5101 * 4145 1737 4209
19 Ἄνθρωπος δέ τις ἦν πλούσιος, καὶ ἐνεδιδύσκετο πορφύραν
man And a certain was rich, and customarily donned a purple robe
1040 2165 2596 2250 2988 4434
20 καὶ βύσσον, εὐφραινόμενος καθ' ἡμέραν λαμπρῶς. πτωχὸς
and fine linen, having been merry day by day in luxury. poor one
5100 2258 3686 2976 3756 906 4314 4440
δέ τις ἦν ὀνόματι Λάζαρος, ὃς ἐβέβλητο πρὸς τὸν πυλῶνα
And a was by name Lazarus who had been laid at the porch
848 1669 1937 5526 575
21 αὐτοῦ ἡλκωμένος καὶ ἐπιθυμῶν χορτασθῆναι ἀπὸ τῶν
of him, being sore-plagued and desiring to be filled from the
5589 4098 575 5132 4145
ψιχίων τῶν πιπτόντων ἀπὸ τῆς τραπέζης τοῦ πλουσίου·
crumbs that were falling from the table of the rich one.
235 2965 2064 625 1668 848
ἀλλὰ καὶ οἱ κύνες ἐρχόμενοι ἀπέλειχον τὰ ἕλκη αὐτοῦ.
But even the dogs coming licked the sores of him.
1096 599 4434 667 846
22 ἐγένετο δὲ ἀποθανεῖν τὸν πτωχόν, καὶ ἀπενεχθῆναι αὐτὸν
it was And, died the poor one, and was carried away him
5259 32 1519 2859 11 599
ὑπὸ τῶν ἀγγέλων εἰς τὸν κόλπον τοῦ Ἀβραάμ· ἀπέθανε δὲ
by the angels into the bosom of Abraham. died And
4145 2290 86 1869
23 καὶ ὁ πλούσιος, καὶ ἐτάφη. καὶ ἐν τῷ ᾅδῃ ἐπάρας τοὺς
also the rich one, and was buried. And in Hades lifting up the
3788 848 5225 1722 931 3704 11
ὀφθαλμοὺς αὐτοῦ, ὑπάρχων ἐν βασάνοις, ὁρᾷ τὸν Ἀβραὰμ
eyes of him, being in torments, he sees Abraham
575 3113 2976 2859 848 846
24 ἀπὸ μακρόθεν, καὶ Λάζαρον ἐν τοῖς κόλποις αὐτοῦ. καὶ αὐτὸς
from afar, and Lazarus in the bosoms of him. and he
5455 2036 3962 11 1653 3165 3992
φωνήσας εἶπε, Πάτερ Ἀβραάμ, ἐλέησόν με, καὶ πέμψον
calling said, Father Abraham, pity me, and send

dip the tip of his finger in water and cool my tongue; for I am suffering in this flame. 25 But Abraham said, Child, remember that you fully received your good things in your lifetime, and Lazarus likewise the bad things. But now he is comforted, and you are suffering. 26 And besides all these things, a great chasm has been fixed between us, and you, so that those desiring to pass from here to you are not able, nor can they pass from there to us. 27 And he said, Then I beg you, father, that you send him to my father's house; 28 for I have five brothers, so that he may witness to them, that they not also come to this place of torment. 29 Abraham said to him, They have Moses and the Prophets; let them hear them. 30 But he said, No, father Abraham, but if one should go from *the* dead to them, they will repent. 31 And he said to him, If they will not hear Moses and the Prophets, they will not be persuaded even if one from *the* dead should rise.

2976 2443 911 206 1147 858 5204
Λάζαρον, ἵνα βάψῃ τὸ ἄκρον τοῦ δακτύλου αὐτοῦ ὕδατος,
Lazarus, that he may dip the tip of the finger of him of water,
2711 1100 3450 3754 3600
καὶ καταψύξῃ τὴν γλῶσσάν μου· ὅτι ὀδυνῶμαι ἐν τῇ
and may cool the tongue of me because I am suffering in
5395 5026 2036 11 5043 3415 3754 618
25 φλογὶ ταύτῃ. εἶπε δὲ Ἀβραάμ, Τέκνον, μνήσθητι ὅτι ἀπέ-
flame this. said But Abraham, Child, remember that fully re-
4771 18 4675 1722 2222 4675 2976 3668
λαβες σὺ τὰ ἀγαθά σου ἐν τῇ ζωῇ σου, καὶ Λάζαρος ὁμοίως
ceived you things good of you in the life of you, and Lazarus likewise
2556 2568 3592 3870 4771 3600 1909
26 τὰ κακά· νῦν δὲ ὅδε παρακαλεῖται, σὺ δὲ ὀδυνᾶσαι. καὶ ἐπὶ
the bad. now But here he is comforted, you but are suffering. And besides
3956 5125 3342 2257 5216 5490 3173 4741
πᾶσι τούτοις, μεταξὺ ἡμῶν καὶ ὑμῶν χάσμα μέγα ἐστή-
all these things, between us and you a chasm great has
3704 2309 1224 1782 4314 5209 3361
ρικται, ὅπως οἱ θέλοντες διαβῆναι ἐντεῦθεν πρὸς ὑμᾶς μὴ
been fixed so that those desiring to pass from here to you not
1410 3366 1564 4314 2248 1276 2036
27 δύνωνται, μηδὲ οἱ ἐκεῖθεν πρὸς ἡμᾶς διαπερῶσιν. εἶπε δέ,
are able, not those from there to us may cross over. he said And,
2065 3767 4571 3962 2443 3992 846 1519 3614
Ἐρωτῶ οὖν σε, πάτερ, ἵνα πέμψῃς αὐτὸν εἰς τὸν οἶκον τοῦ
I ask Then you, father, that you send him to the house of the
3962 3450 2192 1063 4002 80 3704 1263
28 πατρός μου, ἔχω γὰρ πέντε ἀδελφούς, ὅπως διαμαρτύρηται
father of me; I have for five brothers; so that he may witness
846 2443 3363 846 2064 1519 5117 5126
αὐτοῖς, ἵνα μὴ καὶ αὐτοὶ ἔλθωσιν εἰς τὸν τόπον τοῦτον τῆς
to them, that not also they come to place this
931 3004 846 11 2192 3475
29 βασάνου. λέγει αὐτῷ Ἀβραάμ, Ἔχουσι Μωσέα καὶ τοὺς
of torment. says to him Abraham, They have Moses and the
4396 191 846 2036 3780 3962
30 προφήτας· ἀκουσάτωσαν αὐτῶν. ὁ δὲ εἶπεν, Οὐχί, πάτερ
prophets, let them hear them. he But said, No, father
11 235 1437 5100 575 3498 4198 4314 846
Ἀβραάμ· ἀλλ' ἐάν τις ἀπὸ νεκρῶν πορευθῇ πρὸς αὐτούς,
Abraham, but if one from (the) dead should go to them,
3340 2036 846 1487 3475 4396
31 μετανοήσουσιν. εἶπε δὲ αὐτῷ, Εἰ Μωσέως καὶ τῶν προφη-
they will repent. he said And to him, If Moses and the prophets
3756 191 3761 1437 5100 1537 3498 450
τῶν οὐκ ἀκούουσιν, οὐδέ, ἐάν τις ἐκ νεκρῶν ἀναστῇ,
not they will hear, not even if one from (the) dead should rise
3982
πεισθήσονται.
will they be persuaded.

CHAPTER 17

1 And He said to the disciples, It is impossible that the offenses should not come, but woe *to him* by whom they come. 2 It is profitable for him if a millstone turned by an ass is put around his neck, and he be thrown into the sea, than that he should offend one of these little ones. 3 Take heed to yourselves. And if your brother sins against you, rebuke him; and if he repents, forgive him. 4 And if seven times of

CHAPTER 17

2036 4314 3101 418 2076 3361
1 Εἶπε δὲ πρὸς τοὺς μαθητάς, Ἀνένδεκτόν ἐστι τοῦ μὴ
He said And to the disciples, Impossible it is — not
2064 4625 3759 1223 3739 2064 3081 846
2 ἐλθεῖν τὰ σκάνδαλα· οὐαὶ δὲ δι' οὗ ἔρχεται. λυσιτελεῖ αὐτῷ
should come offenses, woe but through whom they come It profits him
1487 3458 3684 4029 4012 5137 848
εἰ μύλος ὀνικὸς περίκειται περὶ τὸν τράχηλον αὐτοῦ, καὶ
If a millstone of an ass is put around the neck of him, and
4496 1519 2281 2228 2443 4624 1520
ἔρριπται εἰς τὴν θάλασσαν, ἢ ἵνα σκανδαλίσῃ ἕνα τῶν
he be cast into the sea, than that he should offend one
3398 5130 4337 1438 1437 264 1519 4571
3 μικρῶν τούτων. προσέχετε ἑαυτοῖς. ἐὰν δὲ ἁμάρτῃ εἰς σὲ ὁ
little one of these. Take heed to yourselves. If And sins against you the
80 4675 2068 846 1437 3340 863
ἀδελφός σου, ἐπιτίμησον αὐτῷ· καὶ ἐὰν μετανοήσῃ, ἄφες
brother of you, rebuke him; and if he repents, forgive

the day he sins against you, and seven times of the day turns to you saying, I repent; you shall forgive him.

[5]And the apostles said to the Lord, Give us more faith. [6]But the Lord said, If you had faith as a grain of mustard, you may say to this sycamine tree, Be rooted up, and be planted in the sea! And it would obey you. [7]But which of you having a slave plowing or feeding will say at once *to him* coming out of the field, Come, recline? [8]But will he not say to him, Prepare something what I may eat, and having girded yourself serve me until I eat and drink; and after these things you shall eat and drink? [9]*Does* he have thanks to that slave because he did the things commanded of him? I think not. [10]So also when you have done all things commanded you, you say, We are unprofitable slaves, for we have done what we ought to do.

[11]And it happened in His going to Jerusalem, even He passed through *the* midst of Samaria and Galilee. [12]And He entering into a certain village, ten leprous men met Him, who stood afar off. [13]And they lifted *their* voice, saying, Jesus, Master, pity us. [14]And seeing *them*, He said to them, Going, show yourselves to the priests. And it happened in their going they were cleansed. [15]And one of them, seeing that he was cured, returned glorifying God with a loud voice. [16]And *he* fell on *his* face at His feet,

846 1437 2034 2250 264 1519 4571
4 αὐτῷ. καὶ ἐὰν ἑπτάκις τῆς ἡμέρας ἁμάρτῃ εἰς σέ, καὶ
him. And if seven times of the day he sins against you, and
2034 2250 1994 1909 4571 3004 3340
ἑπτάκις τῆς ἡμέρας ἐπιστρέψῃ ἐπί σε, λέγων, Μετανοῶ,
seven times of the day turns to you, saying, I repent,
863 846
ἀφήσεις αὐτῷ.
you shall forgive him.
2036 652 2962 4369 2254 4102
5 Καὶ εἶπον οἱ ἀπόστολοι τῷ Κυρίῳ, Πρόσθες ἡμῖν πίστιν.
And said the apostles to the Lord, Add to us faith.
2036 2962 1487 2192 4102 5613 2848 4615
6 εἶπε δὲ ὁ Κύριος, Εἰ εἴχετε πίστιν ὡς κόκκον σινάπεως,
said And the Lord, If you have faith as a grain of mustard,
3004 302 4807 5026 1610 5452
ἐλέγετε ἂν τῇ συκαμίνῳ ταύτῃ, Ἐκριζώθητι, καὶ φυτεύθητι
you may say — sycamine to this, Be rooted up, and be planted
2281 5219 302 5213 5101 1537 5216 1401
7 ἐν τῇ θαλάσσῃ· καὶ ὑπήκουσεν ἂν ὑμῖν. τίς δὲ ἐξ ὑμῶν δοῦλον
in the sea; even it would obey you. who But of you a slave
2192 722 2228 4165 3739 1525 1537
ἔχων ἀροτριῶντα ἢ ποιμαίνοντα, ὃς εἰσελθόντι ἐκ τοῦ
having plowing or shepherding, who (to him) come out of the
68 2046 2112 3928 377 235 3780 2046
8 ἀγροῦ ἐρεῖ εὐθέως, Παρελθὼν ἀνάπεσαι· ἀλλ' οὐχὶ ἐρεῖ
field will say immediately, Having come, recline? But not will say
846 2090 5101 1172 4024 1247
αὐτῷ, Ἑτοίμασον τί δειπνήσω, καὶ περιζωσάμενος διακόνει
to him, Prepare something I may eat; and having girded yourself serve
3427 2193 5315 4095 3326 5023 5315 4095
μοι, ἕως φάγω καὶ πίω· καὶ μετὰ ταῦτα φάγεσαι καὶ πίεσαι
me until I eat and drink; and after these things eat and drink
4771 3361 5485 2192 1401 1565 3754 4160 1299
9 σύ; μὴ χάριν ἔχει τῷ δούλῳ ἐκείνῳ ὅτι ἐποίησε τὰ δια-
you. — thanks Does he have slave to that because he did the things
846 3756 1380 3779 5210 3752 4160
10 ταχθέντα αὐτῷ; οὐ δοκῶ. οὕτω καὶ ὑμεῖς, ὅταν ποιήσητε
commanded of him? not I think. So also you, when you have done
3956 1299 5213 3004 3754 1401 888 2070
πάντα τὰ διαταχθέντα ὑμῖν, λέγετε ὅτι Δοῦλοι ἀχρεῖοί ἐσμεν·
all things commanded you, say, Slaves unprofitable we are;
3754 3739 3784 4160 4160
ὅτι ὃ ὠφείλομεν ποιῆσαι πεποιήκαμεν.
what we ought to do, we have done.
1096 4198 846 1519 2419
11 Καὶ ἐγένετο ἐν τῷ πορεύεσθαι αὐτὸν εἰς Ἱερουσαλήμ, καὶ
And it was, in the going of Him to Jerusalem, even
846 1330 1223 3318 4540 1056
12 αὐτὸς διήρχετο διὰ μέσου Σαμαρείας καὶ Γαλιλαίας. καὶ
He passed through (the)midst of Samaria and Galilee. And
1525 846 1519 5100 2968 528 846 1176
εἰσερχομένου αὐτοῦ εἴς τινα κώμην, ἀπήντησαν αὐτῷ δέκα
having entered Him into certain a village, met Him ten
3015 435 3739 2476 4207 846 142 5456
13 λεπροὶ ἄνδρες, οἳ ἔστησαν πόρρωθεν· καὶ αὐτοὶ ἦραν φωνήν,
leprous men, who stood afar off, and they lifted voice,
3004 2424 1988 1653 2248 1492 2036
14 λέγοντες, Ἰησοῦ, ἐπιστάτα, ἐλέησον ἡμᾶς. καὶ ἰδὼν εἶπεν
saying, Jesus, Master, pity us. And seeing He said
846 4198 1925 1438 2409
αὐτοῖς, Πορευθέντες ἐπιδείξατε ἑαυτοὺς τοῖς ἱερεῦσι. καὶ
to them, Going, show yourselves to the priests. And
1096 1722 5217 846 2511 1520 1537
15 ἐγένετο ἐν τῷ ὑπάγειν αὐτούς, ἐκαθαρίσθησαν. εἷς δὲ ἐξ
it was, in the going (of) them, they were cleansed. one But of
846 1492 3754 2390 5290 3326 5456 3173
αὐτῶν, ἰδὼν ὅτι ἰάθη, ὑπέστρεψε, μετὰ φωνῆς μεγάλης
them, seeing that he was cured, returned with a voice great
1392 2316 4098 1909 4383 3844
16 δοξάζων τὸν Θεόν· καὶ ἔπεσεν ἐπὶ πρόσωπον παρὰ τοὺς
glorifying — God, and fell upon (his) face at the

thanking Him. And he was a Samaritan. [17]And answering Jesus said, Were not the ten cleansed? But where *are* the nine? [18]Were not *any* found returning to give glory to God except this stranger? [19]And He said to him, Rising up, go! Your faith has cured you.

[20]And being questioned by the Pharisees *as to* when the kingdom of God comes, He answered them and said, The kingdom of God does not come with observation; [21]nor will they say, Lo, here! Or, Lo, there! For behold the kingdom of God is in your midst.

[22]And He said to the disciples, Days will come when you will long to see one of the days of the Son of man, and will not see. [23]And they will say to you, Lo, here! Or, Lo, there! Do not go away, nor follow. [24]For as the lightning which lights up, flashing from the *one part* under heaven and shines to the *other part* under heaven, so also will the Son of man be in His day. [25]And He must suffer many things, and be rejected from this generation. [26]And as it was in the days of Noah, so also it will be in the days of the Son of man. [27]They were eating, drinking, marrying, giving in marriage, until *the* day Noah went into the ark. And the flood came and destroyed all. [28]And likewise, as it was in the days of Lot, they were eating, drinking, buying, selling, planting, building; [29]but on *the* day Lot went out from Sodom, it rained fire and brimstone from

4228 848 2168 846 846 2258 4541
πόδας αὐτοῦ, εὐχαριστῶν αὐτῷ· καὶ αὐτὸς ἦν Σαμαρείτης.
feet of Him, thanking Him; and he was a Samaritan.
611 2424 2036 3780 1176 2511
17 ἀποκριθεὶς δὲ ὁ Ἰησοῦς εἶπεν, Οὐχὶ οἱ δέκα ἐκαθαρίσθησαν;
answering And — Jesus said, Not the ten were cleansed?
1767 4226 3756 2147 5290 1325 1391
18 οἱ δὲ ἐννέα ποῦ; οὐχ εὑρέθησαν ὑποστρέψαντες δοῦναι δόξαν
the But nine, where? not Were found returning to give glory
2316 1508 241 3778 2036 846 450
19 τῷ Θεῷ, εἰ μὴ ὁ ἀλλογενὴς οὗτος, καὶ εἶπεν αὐτῷ, Ἀναστὰς
to God, except stranger this? And He said to him, Rising up
4198 4102 4675 4982 4571
πορεύου· ἡ πίστις σου σέσωκέ σε.
go! The faith of you has healed you.
1905 5259 5330 4219 2064
20 Ἐπερωτηθεὶς δὲ ὑπὸ τῶν Φαρισαίων, πότε ἔρχεται ἡ
being questioned And by the Pharisees, when comes the
932 2316 611 846 2036 3756 2064
βασιλεία τοῦ Θεοῦ, ἀπεκρίθη αὐτοῖς καὶ εἶπεν, Οὐκ ἔρχεται
kingdom — of God, He answered them and said, does not come
932 2316 3326 3907 3761 2046
21 ἡ βασιλεία τοῦ Θεοῦ μετὰ παρατηρήσεως· οὐδὲ ἐροῦσιν,
The kingdom of God with observation, nor will they say,
2400 5602 2228 2400 1563 2400 1063 932 2316 1787
Ἰδοὺ ὧδε, ἤ, Ἰδοὺ ἐκεῖ. Ἰδοὺ γάρ, ἡ βασιλεία τοῦ Θεοῦ ἐντὸς
Behold, here; or behold, there. behold For, the kingdom — of God within
5216 2076
ὑμῶν ἐστίν.
you is.
2036 4314 3101 2064 2250 3753
22 Εἶπε δὲ πρὸς τοὺς μαθητάς, Ἐλεύσονται ἡμέραι ὅτε
He said And to the disciples, will come Days when
1937 3391 2250 5207 444 1492
ἐπιθυμήσετε μίαν τῶν ἡμερῶν τοῦ υἱοῦ τοῦ ἀνθρώπου ἰδεῖν,
you will long one of the days of the Son — of man to see,
3756 3700 2046 5213 2400 5602 2228 2400 1563 3361
23 καὶ οὐκ ὄψεσθε. καὶ ἐροῦσιν ὑμῖν, Ἰδοὺ ὧδε, ἤ, Ἰδοὺ ἐκεῖ· μὴ
and not will see. And they will say to you, Behold here, or, behold, there; not
565 3366 1377 5618 1063 796 797
24 ἀπέλθητε, μηδὲ διώξητε. ὥσπερ γὰρ ἡ ἀστραπὴ ἡ ἀστρά-
do go away, nor follow. as For the lightning which lights up
1537 5229 3772 1519 5229 3772 2989 2071
πτουσα ἐκ τῆς ὑπ' οὐρανὸν εἰς τὴν ὑπ' οὐρανὸν λάμπει, οὕτως
flashing out of that under heaven to that under heaven shines, so
2071 5207 444 1722 2250 848 4412
ἔσται καὶ ὁ υἱὸς τοῦ ἀνθρώπου ἐν τῇ ἡμέρᾳ αὐτοῦ. πρῶτον
will be also the Son — of man in the day of Him. first
1163 846 4183 3958 593 575
25 δὲ δεῖ αὐτὸν πολλὰ παθεῖν καὶ ἀποδοκιμασθῆναι ἀπὸ τῆς
But must Him many things suffer, and to be rejected from —
1074 5026 2531 1096 2250 3575
26 γενεᾶς ταύτης. καὶ καθὼς ἐγένετο ἐν ταῖς ἡμέραις τοῦ Νῶε,
generation this. And as it was in the days — of Noah,
3779 2071 2250 5207 444
οὕτως ἔσται καὶ ἐν ταῖς ἡμέραις τοῦ υἱοῦ τοῦ ἀνθρώπου.
so it will be also in the days of the Son — of man.
2068 4095 1061 1547 891 3739 2250
27 ἤσθιον, ἔπινον, ἐγάμουν, ἐξεγαμίζοντο, ἄχρι ἧς ἡμέρας
They were eating, drinking, marrying, giving in marriage, until which day
1525 3575 1519 2787 2064 2627
εἰσῆλθε Νῶε εἰς τὴν κιβωτόν, καὶ ἦλθεν ὁ κατακλυσμός, καὶ
went in Noah into the ark. And came the Flood and
622 537 3668 5613 1096 2250
28 ἀπώλεσεν ἅπαντας. ὁμοίως καὶ ὡς ἐγένετο ἐν ταῖς ἡμέραις
destroyed all. Likewise also, as it was in the days
3091 2068 4095 59 4453 5452
Λώτ· ἤσθιον, ἔπινον, ἠγόραζον, ἐπώλουν, ἐφύτευον,
of Lot, they were eating, drinking, buying, selling, planting,
3618 2228 2250 1831 3091 575 4670 1026
29 ᾠκοδόμουν· ᾗ δὲ ἡμέρᾳ ἐξῆλθε Λὼτ ἀπὸ Σοδόμων, ἔβρεξε
building; on which but day went out Lot from Sodom, it rained

Heaven and destroyed all. 30 Even so it will be in the day the Son of man is revealed.

31 In that day *he* who will be on the housetop, let him not come down to take his goods *from* the house. And likewise, he in the field, let him not return to the things behind. 32 Remember Lot's wife. 33 Whoever seeks to save his life, he will lose it. And whoever will lose it, *he* will preserve it. 34 I say to you, In that night two will be on one bed; the one will be taken, and the other will be left. 35 Two will be grinding together, one will be taken, and the other will be left. 36 Two will be in the field; one will be taken, and the other will be left. 37 And answering they said to Him, Where, Lord? And He said to them, Where the body *is,* there the eagles will be gathered together.

4442 2303 575 3772 622 537 2596
30 πῦρ καὶ θεῖον ἀπ' οὐρανοῦ, καὶ ἀπώλεσεν ἅπαντας· κατὰ
fire and brimstone from heaven and destroyed all. Accord-
5024 2071 3739 2250 5207 444 601
ταὐτὰ ἔσται ᾗ ἡμέρᾳ ὁ υἱὸς τοῦ ἀνθρώπου ἀποκαλύπτεται
ing to this it will be in the day the Son of man is revealed.
1722 1565 2250 3739 2071 1909 1430
31 ἐν ἐκείνῃ τῇ ἡμέρᾳ, ὃς ἔσται ἐπὶ τοῦ δώματος, καὶ τὰ
In that — day, who will be on the housetop, and the
4632 848 1722 3614 3361 2597 142 846
σκεύη αὐτοῦ ἐν τῇ οἰκίᾳ, μὴ καταβάτω ἆραι αὐτά· καὶ ὁ
goods of him in the house, not let him descend to take them; and he
1722 68 3668 3361 1994 1519 3694
32 ἐν τῷ ἀγρῷ ὁμοίως μὴ ἐπιστρεψάτω εἰς τὰ ὀπίσω. μνη-
in the field likewise, not let him turn back to the things behind. Re-
3421 135 3091 3739 1437 2212 5590
33 μονεύετε τῆς γυναικὸς Λώτ. ὃς ἐὰν ζητήσῃ τὴν ψυχὴν
member the wife of Lot. Whoever seeks the soul
848 4982 622 846 3739 1437 622 846
αὐτοῦ σῶσαι ἀπολέσει αὐτήν· καὶ ὃς ἐὰν ἀπολέσῃ αὐτήν
of him to save, he will lose it; and whoever will lose it.
2225 846 3004 5213 5026 3571 2071 1417
34 ζωογονήσει αὐτήν. λέγω ὑμῖν, ταύτῃ τῇ νυκτὶ ἔσονται δύο
will preserve it. I say to you, in this — night will be two
1909 2825 3391 1520 3880 2087 863
ἐπὶ κλίνης μιᾶς· ὁ εἷς παραληφθήσεται, καὶ ὁ ἕτερος ἀφεθή-
on bed one; the one will be taken, and the other will
1417 2071 229 1909 846 3391 3880
35 σεται. δύο ἔσονται ἀλήθουσαι ἐπὶ τὸ αὐτό ἡ μία παρα-
be left. Two will be grinding together; the one will
2087 863 1417 2071
36 ληφθήσεται, καὶ ἡ ἑτέρα ἀφεθήσεται. δύο ἔσονται ἐν τῷ
be taken, and the other will be left. Two will be in the
1520 3880 2087 863
37 ἀγρῷ ὁ εἷς παραληφθήσεται, καὶ ὁ ἕτερος ἀφεθήσεται. καὶ
field; the one will be taken, and the other will be left. And
611 3004 846 4226 2962 2036 846
ἀποκριθέντες λέγουσιν αὐτῷ, Ποῦ, Κύριε; ὁ δὲ εἶπεν αὐτοῖς,
answering they say to Him, Where, Lord? He And said to them,
3699 4483 1563 4863 105
Ὅπου τὸ σῶμα, ἐκεῖ συναχθήσονται οἱ ἀετοί.
Where the body (is), there will be gathered the eagles.

CHAPTER 18

1 And He also spoke a parable to them to *teach* it is always right to pray, and not to faint, 2 saying, A certain judge was in a certain city, not fearing God and not respecting man. 3 And a widow was in that city, and she came to him, saying, Avenge me from my adversary. 4 And for a time he would not. But after these things he said to himself, Even if I do not fear God, and do not respect man, 5 yet because this widow causes me trouble, I will avenge her, that coming in *the* end she may not subdue me. 6 And

CHAPTER 18

3004 3850 846 4314 1163 3842
1 Ἔλεγε δὲ καὶ παραβολὴν αὐτοῖς πρὸς τὸ δεῖν πάντοτε
He told And also a parable to them to (teach) it is right always
4336 3361 1573 3004 2923 5101 2258 • 5100
2 προσεύχεσθαι, καὶ μὴ ἐκκακεῖν, λέγων, Κριτής τις ἦν ἔν τινι
1722 to pray, and not to faint, saying, A judge certain was in a
4172 2316 3361 5399 444 3361 1788
πόλει, τὸν Θεὸν μὴ φοβούμενος, καὶ ἄνθρωπον μὴ ἐντρεπό-
city, God not fearing and man not respecting.
5503 2258 1722 4172 1565 2064 4314 846
3 μενος· χήρα δὲ ἦν ἐν τῇ πόλει ἐκείνῃ, καὶ ἤρχετο πρὸς αὐτόν
a widow And was in city that, and she came to him,
3004 1556 3165 575 476 3450 3756
4 λέγουσα, Ἐκδίκησόν με ἀπὸ τοῦ ἀντιδίκου μου. καὶ οὐκ
saying, Avenge me from the adversary of me. And not
2309 1909 5550 3326 5023 2036 1722 1438
ἠθέλησεν ἐπὶ χρόνον· μετὰ δὲ ταῦτα εἶπεν ἐν ἑαυτῷ, Εἰ
he would for a time; after but these things he said in himself, If
2316 3756 5399 444 3756 1788
καὶ τὸν Θεὸν οὐ φοβοῦμαι, καὶ ἄνθρωπον οὐκ ἐντρέπομαι·
even God not I fear, and man not respect,
1223 1065 3930 3427 2873 5503 5026 1556
5 διά γε τὸ παρέχειν μοι κόπον τὴν χήραν ταύτην, ἐκδικήσω
because yet causes me trouble widow this, I will avenge
846 2443 3363 1519 5056 2064 5299 3165 2036
6 αὐτήν, ἵνα μὴ εἰς τέλος ἐρχομένη ὑπωπιάζῃ με. εἶπε δὲ ὁ
her, that not in(the) end coming she subdue me. said And the

the Lord said, Hear what the unrighteous judge says; [7]and will God not at all execute the avenging of His elect, those crying to Him day and night, also being patient over them? [8]I say to you that He will carry out the avenging of them speedily. But the Son of man coming then, will He find faith on the earth?

[9]And He also spoke this parable to some *of* those relying on themselves, that they are righteous, and despising the rest:

[10]Two men went up into the temple to pray, the one a Pharisee, and the other a tax-collector. [11]The Pharisee *was* standing, praying these things to himself: God, I thank You that I am not as the rest of men, rapacious, unrighteous, adulterers, or even as this tax-collector. [12]I fast twice *in* the week, I tithe all things, as many as I get. [13]And standing at a distance, the tax-collector would not even lift up *his* eyes to Heaven, but smote on his breast, saying, God, be merciful to me, the sinner! [14]I say to you, This one went down to his house having been justified, rather than that one. For everyone exalting himself will be humbled. And the *one* humbling himself will be exalted.

[15]And they brought infants to Him also, that He might touch them. But seeing, the disciples rebuked them. [16]But Jesus called them near, saying, Allow the children to come to Me, and do not prevent them. For of such is the

2962 191 5101 2923 93 3004 2316
7 Κύριος, Ἀκούσατε τί ὁ κριτὴς τῆς ἀδικίας λέγει. ὁ δὲ Θεὸς
Lord, Hear what the judge of unrighteousness says; — and God
3364= 4160 1557 1588 848
οὐ μὴ ποιήσει τὴν ἐκδίκησιν τῶν ἐκλεκτῶν αὐτοῦ τῶν
in no way will execute the avenging of the elect of Him, those
994 4314 846 2250 3571 3114
βοώντων πρὸς αὐτὸν ἡμέρας καὶ νυκτός, καὶ μακροθυμῶν
crying to Him day and night, and being patient
1909 846 3004 5213 3754 4160 1557 846
8 ἐπ' αὐτοῖς; λέγω ὑμῖν ὅτι ποιήσει τὴν ἐκδίκησιν αὐτῶν ἐν
over them? I say to you that He will execute the avenging of them
5034 4133 5207 444 2064 687 2147
τάχει. πλὴν ὁ υἱὸς τοῦ ἀνθρώπου ἐλθὼν ἄρα εὑρήσει τὴν
speedily But the Son of man coming then, will He find
4102 1909 1093
πίστιν ἐπὶ τῆς γῆς;
faith on the earth?
2036 4314 5100 3982 1909 1438 3754
9 Εἶπε δὲ καὶ πρός τινας τοὺς πεποιθότας ἐφ' ἑαυτοῖς ὅτι
He spoke And also to some (of) those relying on themselves that
1524 1342 1848 3062 3850
εἰσὶ δίκαιοι, καὶ ἐξουθενοῦντας τοὺς λοιπούς, τὴν παρα-
they are righteous, also despising the rest parable
5026 444 1417 305 1519 2411
10 βολὴν ταύτην· Ἄνθρωποι δύο ἀνέβησαν εἰς τὸ ἱερὸν
this, men Two went up to the Temple
4336 1520 5330 2087 5057
11 προσεύξασθαι· ὁ εἷς Φαρισαῖος, καὶ ὁ ἕτερος τελώνης. ὁ
to pray, the one a Pharisee, and the other a tax-collector. The
5330 2476 4314 1438 5023 4336
Φαρισαῖος σταθεὶς πρὸς ἑαυτὸν ταῦτα προσηύχετο, Ὁ
Pharisee standing, to himself these things praying,
2316 2168 4671 3754 3756 1510 5618 3062
Θεός, εὐχαριστῶ σοι ὅτι οὐκ εἰμὶ ὥσπερ οἱ λοιποὶ τῶν
God, I thank You that not I am as the rest
444 727 94 3432 2228 5613 3778
ἀνθρώπων, ἅρπαγες, ἄδικοι, μοιχοί, ἢ καὶ ὡς οὗτος ὁ
of men, rapacious, unrighteous, adulterers, or even as this
5057 3522 1364 4521 586 3956
12 τελώνης. νηστεύω δὶς τοῦ σαββάτου, ἀποδεκατῶ πάντα
tax-collector. I fast twice (in) the week; I tithe all things,
3745 2932 5057 3113 2476 3756 2309 3761
13 ὅσα κτῶμαι. καὶ ὁ τελώνης μακρόθεν ἑστὼς οὐκ ἤθελεν οὐδὲ
as many as I get. And the tax-collector afar off standing not would not even,
3788 1519 3772 1869 235 5180 1519
τοὺς ὀφθαλμοὺς εἰς τὸν οὐρανὸν ἐπᾶραι, ἀλλ' ἔτυπτεν εἰς τὸ
the eyes to Heaven lift up, but smote on the
4738 848 3004 2316 2433 3427 268
στῆθος αὐτοῦ, λέγων, Ὁ Θεός, ἱλάσθητί μοι τῷ ἁμαρτωλῷ.
breast of him, saying, God, be merciful to me the sinner.
3004 5213 2597 3778 1344 1519 3624 848
14 λέγω ὑμῖν, κατέβη οὗτος δεδικαιωμένος εἰς τὸν οἶκον αὐτοῦ
I say to you, went down this one having been justified to the house of him,
2229 1565 3754 3956 5312 1438 5013 5013
ἢ ἐκεῖνος· ὅτι πᾶς ὁ ὑψῶν ἑαυτὸν ταπεινωθήσεται, ὁ δὲ τα-
than that one, for everyone exalting himself will be humbled. he And
1438 5312
πεινῶν ἑαυτὸν ὑψωθήσεται.
humbling himself will be exalted.
4374 846 1025 2443 846 680
15 Προσέφερον δὲ αὐτῷ καὶ τὰ βρέφη, ἵνα αὐτῶν ἅπτηται·
they brought And to Him also the babes, that them He might touch;
1492 3101 2008 846 2424
ἰδόντες δὲ οἱ μαθηταὶ ἐπετίμησαν αὐτοῖς. ὁ δὲ Ἰησοῦς
seeing but, the disciples rebuked them, But Jesus
4341 846 2036 863 3813 2064
16 προσκαλεσάμενος αὐτὰ εἶπεν, Ἄφετε τὰ παιδία ἔρχεσθαι
having called near them, saying, Allow the children to come
4314 3165 2967 846 1063 5108 2076
πρός με, καὶ μὴ κωλύετε αὐτά· τῶν γὰρ τοιούτων ἐστὶν ἡ
to Me, and not do prevent them, for of such is the

kingdom of God. [17]Truly I say to you, Whoever does not receive the kingdom of God like a child, not at all will enter into it.

[18]And a certain ruler asked Him, saying, Good Teacher, what may I do to inherit eternal life? [19]But Jesus said to him, Why do you say Me *to be* good? No one *is* good, except One: God. [20]You know the commandments: Do not commit adultery, do not murder, do not steal; do not bear false witness; honor your father and your mother. [21]And he said, I have kept all these from my youth. [22]And hearing these things, Jesus said to him, Yet one thing is lacking to you: sell all, as much as you have, and give to *the* poor, and you will have treasure in Heaven. And come, follow Me. [23]But hearing these things, he became very much grieved, for he was exceedingly rich.

[24]And seeing him having become very much grieved, Jesus said, How hardly those having riches shall enter into the kingdom of God! [25]For it is easier *for* a camel to go in through a needle's eye than *for* a rich one to enter into the kingdom of God. [26]And those hearing said, And who is able to be saved? [27]But He said, The things impossible with men are possible with God.

[28]And Peter said, Behold, we left all and followed You. [29]And He said to them, Truly I say to you, There is no one who has left house, or parents, or brothers, or wife, or children, for the sake of the kingdom of God, [30]who shall not receive many times more in this time,

932 2316 281 3004 5213 3739 1437 3361 1209
17 βασιλεία τοῦ Θεοῦ. ἀμὴν λέγω ὑμῖν, ὃς ἐὰν μὴ δέξηται τὴν
kingdom – of God. Truly I say to you, whoever not receives the
932 2316 5613 3813 =3764= 1525 1519 846
βασιλείαν τοῦ Θεοῦ ὡς παιδίον, οὐ μὴ εἰσέλθῃ εἰς αὐτήν.
kingdom – of God as a child, in no way enters into it.
1905 5100 846 758 3004 1320
18 Καὶ ἐπηρώτησέ τις αὐτὸν ἄρχων, λέγων, Διδάσκαλε
And questioned a certain Him ruler, saying, teacher
68 5101 4160 2222 166 2816 2036
19 ἀγαθέ, τί ποιήσας ζωὴν αἰώνιον κληρονομήσω; εἶπε δὲ
Good, what doing life eternal I may inherit? said And
846 2424 5101 3165 3004 18 3762 18 =1508=
αὐτῷ ὁ Ἰησοῦς, Τί με λέγεις ἀγαθόν; οὐδεὶς ἀγαθός, εἰ μὴ
to him – Jesus, Why Me you say (is) good? No one (is) good, except
1519 2316 1785 1492 3361 3431 3361 5407
20 εἷς, ὁ Θεός. τὰς ἐντολὰς οἶδας, Μὴ μοιχεύσῃς, μὴ φονεύσῃς,
One, God. The commands you know, Not do adultery, not kill.
3361 2813 3361 5576 5091 3962 4675
μὴ κλέψῃς, μὴ ψευδομαρτυρήσῃς, τίμα τὸν πατέρα σου καὶ
not steal, not bear false witness, honor the father of you and
3384 4675 2036 5023 3956 1442 1537
21 τὴν μητέρα σου. ὁ δὲ εἶπε, Ταῦτα πάντα ἐφυλαξάμην ἐκ
the mother of you. he And said, these things All I have kept from
3503 3450 191 5023 2424 2036 846 2089
22 νεότητός μου. ἀκούσας δὲ ταῦτα ὁ Ἰησοῦς εἶπεν αὐτῷ, Ἔτι
youth my. hearing But these things, Jesus said to him, Yet
1722 4671 3007 3956 3745 2192 4453 1239 4434
ἕν σοι λείπει· πάντα ὅσα ἔχεις πώλησον, καὶ διάδος πτωχοῖς,
one to you is lacking: all, as much as you have, sell, and distribute to (the)
2192 2344 1722 3772 1204 190 3427 **poor,**
καὶ ἕξεις θησαυρὸν ἐν οὐρανῷ· καὶ δεῦρο, ἀκολούθει μοι. ὁ δὲ
and you will have treasure in Heaven; and come, follow Me. he But
191 5023 4036 1096 2258 1063 4145 4970
23 ἀκούσας ταῦτα περίλυπος ἐγένετο· ἦν γὰρ πλούσιος σφόδρα.
hearing these things very grieved became, he was for rich exceedingly.
2400 846 2424 4036 1096 2036 4459
24 Ἰδὼν δὲ αὐτὸν ὁ Ἰησοῦς περίλυπον γενόμενον εἶπε, Πῶς
seeing And him, Jesus very grieved having become said, How
1423 5536 2192 1525 1519
δυσκόλως οἱ τὰ χρήματα ἔχοντες εἰσελεύσονται εἰς τὴν
hardly those riches having shall enter into the
932 2316 2123 1063 2076 2574 1223
25 βασιλείαν τοῦ Θεοῦ. εὐκοπώτερον γάρ ἐστι κάμηλον διὰ
kingdom of God. easier For it is (for) a camel through
5168 4476 1525 2228 4145 1519 932
τρυμαλιᾶς ῥαφίδος εἰσελθεῖν, ἢ πλούσιον εἰς τὴν βασιλείαν
(the) eye of a needle to go in, than a rich one into the kingdom
2316 1525 2036 191 1410
26 τοῦ Θεοῦ εἰσελθεῖν. εἶπον δὲ οἱ ἀκούσαντες, Καὶ τίς δύναται
– of God to enter. said And those hearing, And who is able
4982 2036 102 3844 444 1415
27 σωθῆναι; ὁ δὲ εἶπε, Τὰ ἀδύνατα παρὰ ἀνθρώποις δυνατά
to be saved? He And said, The things impossible with men possible
2076 3844 2316 2036 4074 2400 2249 863
28 ἐστι παρὰ τῷ Θεῷ. εἶπε δὲ ὁ Πέτρος, Ἰδού, ἡμεῖς ἀφή-
is with God. said And Peter, Behold, we
3956 190 4571 2036 846
29 καμεν πάντα, καὶ ἠκολουθήσαμέν σοι. ὁ δὲ εἶπεν αὐτοῖς,
left all and followed You. He And said to them,
281 3004 5213 3754 3762 2076 3739 863 3614 2228
Ἀμὴν λέγω ὑμῖν ὅτι οὐδείς ἐστιν ὃς ἀφῆκεν οἰκίαν, ἢ
Truly I say to you that no one there is who has left house, or
1118 2228 80 2228 1135 2228 5043 1752 932
γονεῖς, ἢ ἀδελφούς, ἢ γυναῖκα, ἢ τέκνα, ἕνεκεν τῆς βασιλείας
parents, or brothers, or wife, or children for the sake of the kingdom
2316 3739 =3364= 618 4179 2540
30 τοῦ Θεοῦ, ὃς οὐ μὴ ἀπολάβῃ πολλαπλασίονα ἐν τῷ καιρῷ
of God, who not shall receive many times more in time
5129 1722 165 2064 2222 166
31 τούτῳ, καὶ ἐν τῷ αἰῶνι τῷ ἐρχομένῳ ζωὴν αἰώνιον.
this and in the age coming life everlasting.

NOTE: Frequent words not numbered: δέ (1161); καί (2531)—and, but; ὁ, ἡ, τό (3588, the)— * above word, look in verse margin for No.

[31]And taking the Twelve, He said to them, Behold, we are going up to Jerusalem, and all things will be fulfilled which have been written through the prophets to the Son of man. [32]For He will be delivered up to the nations, and will be mocked, and will be insulted, and will be spat upon. [33]And flogging *Him*, they will kill Him. And on the third day He will rise again. [34]And they did not understand these things—nothing! And this saying had been hidden from them, and they did not know the things being said.

[35]And it happened *as* He drew near to Jericho, a certain blind one sat by the highway, begging. [36]And a crowd passing through, he asked what this might be. [37]And they reported to him that Jesus the Nazarene is passing by. [38]And he cried out, saying, Jesus, son of David, pity me! [39]And those going before rebuked him, that he be quiet. But he much more cried out, Son of David, pity me! [40]And standing still, Jesus commanded him to be brought to Him. [41]And drawing near him, He asked him, saying, What do you desire I do to you? And he said, Lord, that I may see again. [42]And Jesus said to him, See again! Your faith has healed you. [43]And instantly he saw again. And *he* followed Him, glorifying God. And seeing, all the people gave praise to God.

3880 1427 2036 4314 846 2400
Παραλαβὼν δὲ τοὺς δώδεκα, εἶπε πρὸς αὐτούς, Ἰδού,
taking And the twelve, He said to them, Behold,
305 1519 2414 5055 3956
ἀναβαίνομεν εἰς Ἱεροσόλυμα, καὶ τελεσθήσεται πάντα τὰ
we are going up to Jerusalem, and will be completed all things
1125 1223 4396 5207 444
γεγραμμένα διὰ τῶν προφητῶν τῷ υἱῷ τοῦ ἀνθρώπου.
having been written via the prophets to the Son of man
3860 1063 1484 1702
32 παραδοθήσεται γὰρ τοῖς ἔθνεσι, καὶ ἐμπαιχθήσεται, καὶ
He will be delivered for to the nations, and will be mocked, and
5195 1716 3146
33 ὑβρισθήσεται, καὶ ἐμπτυσθήσεται, καὶ μαστιγώσαντες
will be insulted, and will be spat upon. And having scourged
615 846 2250 5054 450
ἀποκτενοῦσιν αὐτόν· καὶ τῇ ἡμέρᾳ τῇ τρίτῃ ἀναστήσεται.
they will kill Him; and on the day third He will rise again.
846 3762 5130 4920 2258 4487 5124
34 καὶ αὐτοὶ οὐδὲν τούτων συνῆκαν, καὶ ἦν τὸ ῥῆμα τοῦτο
And they none of these things understood, and was saying this
2928 575 846 3756 1097 3004
κεκρυμμένον ἀπ' αὐτῶν, καὶ οὐκ ἐγίνωσκον τὰ λεγόμενα.
having been hidden from them; and not they knew the things being said.
1096 1722 1448 846 1519 2410 5185 5100
35 Ἐγένετο δὲ ἐν τῷ ἐγγίζειν αὐτὸν εἰς Ἱεριχώ, τυφλός τις
it was And in the drawing near (of) Him to Jericho, blind one a certain
2521 3844 3598 4319 191 3793
36 ἐκάθητο παρὰ τὴν ὁδὸν προσαιτῶν· ἀκούσας δὲ ὄχλου
sat by the way begging. hearing And a crowd
1279 4441 5101 1498 5124 518
37 διαπορευομένου, ἐπυνθάνετο τί εἴη τοῦτο. ἀπήγγειλαν δὲ
passing through, he asked what might be this. they reported And
846 3754 2424 3480 3928 994
38 αὐτῷ ὅτι Ἰησοῦς ὁ Ναζωραῖος παρέρχεται. καὶ ἐβόησε,
to him that Jesus the Nazarene is passing by. And he cried,
3004 2424 5207 1138 1653 3165 4254
39 λέγων, Ἰησοῦ, υἱὲ Δαβίδ, ἐλέησόν με. καὶ οἱ προάγοντες
saying, Jesus, son of David, pity me. And those going before
2008 846 2443 4623 846 4183 3123
ἐπετίμων αὐτῷ ἵνα σιωπήσῃ· αὐτὸς δὲ πολλῷ μᾶλλον
rebuked him, that he be quiet. he But by much more
2896 5207 1138 1653 3165 2476 2424 2753
40 ἔκραζεν, Υἱὲ Δαβίδ, ἐλέησόν με. σταθεὶς δὲ ὁ Ἰησοῦς ἐκέλευσεν
cried out, Son of David, pity me. standing And Jesus commanded
846 71 4314 846 1448 846 1905
41 αὐτὸν ἀχθῆναι πρὸς αὐτόν· ἐγγίσαντος δὲ αὐτοῦ ἐπηρώ-
him to be brought to Him. drawing near And him, He asked
846 3004 5101 4671 2309 4160 2036 2962
τησεν αὐτόν, λέγων, Τί σοι θέλεις ποιήσω; ὁ δὲ εἶπε, Κύριε,
him, saying, What to you wish I do? he And said, Lord,
2443 308 2424 2036 846 308
42 ἵνα ἀναβλέψω. καὶ ὁ Ἰησοῦς εἶπεν αὐτῷ, Ἀνάβλεψον· ἡ
that I may see again. And Jesus said to him, See again! The
4102 4675 4982 4571 3916 308
43 πίστις σου σέσωκέ σε. καὶ παραχρῆμα ἀνέβλεψε, καὶ
faith of you has healed you. And at once he saw again, and
190 846 1392 2316 3956 2992 1492
ἠκολούθει αὐτῷ, δοξάζων τὸν Θεόν· καὶ πᾶς ὁ λαὸς ἰδὼν
followed Him, glorifying God. And all the people seeing
1325 136 2316
ἔδωκεν αἶνον τῷ Θεῷ.
gave praise to God.

CHAPTER 19

[1]And going in, He passed through Jericho. [2]And, behold, a man called by name Zaccheus. And he was a chief tax-collector,

CHAPTER 19

1525 1330 2410 2400 435
1 Καὶ εἰσελθὼν διήρχετο τὴν Ἱεριχώ. καὶ ἰδού, ἀνὴρ
2 And entering He traversed Jericho. And behold, a man
3686 2564 2195 846 2258 759
ὀνόματι καλούμενος Ζακχαῖος, καὶ αὐτὸς ἦν ἀρχιτελώνης,
by name being called Zaccheus; and he was a chief tax-collector

and he was rich. 3And he was seeking to see Jesus, who He is. And He was not able, because of the crowd, and he was little in stature. 4And running ahead, he went up onto a sycamore-tree, so that he might see Him; for He was going to pass through that way. 5And as He came to the place, looking up, Jesus saw him, and said to him, Zaccheus, hurry, come down, for today I must stay in your house. 6And hastening he came down and welcomed Him, rejoicing.

7And seeing, all murmured, saying, He has gone in to stay with a sinful man. 8But standing, Zaccheus said to the Lord, Behold, Lord, half of my possessions I give to the poor. And if I accused anyone falsely, I restore *it* fourfold. 9And Jesus said to him, Today salvation has come to this house; for he also is a son of Abraham. 10For the Son of man came to seek and to save the lost.

11But as they were hearing these things, He spoke, adding a parable, because He was near to Jerusalem, and they thought that the kingdom of God was immediately to be revealed:

12Then He said: A certain wellborn man went to a distant country to receive a kingdom for himself, and to return. 13And calling ten of his slaves, He gave to them ten minas, and said to them, Trade until I come. 14But his citizens hated him, and sent a delegation after him, saying, We do not desire this one to reign over us. 15And it happened *as*

3778 2258 4145 2212 1492 2424 5101 2076
3 καὶ οὗτος ἦν πλούσιος. καὶ ἐζήτει ἰδεῖν τὸν Ἰησοῦν τίς ἐστι,
and he was rich. And he sought to see Jesus, who He is.
3756 1410 575 3793 3754 2244 3398 2258
καὶ οὐκ ἠδύνατο ἀπὸ τοῦ ὄχλου, ὅτι τῇ ἡλικίᾳ μικρὸς ἦν.
And not he was able from the crowd, because in stature little he was.
4390 1715 305 1909 4809 2443 1492
4 καὶ προδραμὼν ἔμπροσθεν ἀνέβη ἐπὶ συκομωραίαν ἵνα ἴδῃ
And running ahead before, he went up onto a sycamore-tree, that he see
846 3754 1223 1565 3195 1330 5613 2064 1909
5 αὐτόν· ὅτι δι' ἐκείνης ἤμελλε διέρχεσθαι. καὶ ὡς ἦλθεν ἐπὶ
Him, because via that (way) He was going to pass. And as He came upon
5117 308 2424 1492 846 2036 4314
τὸν τόπον, ἀναβλέψας ὁ Ἰησοῦς εἶδεν αὐτόν, καὶ εἶπε πρὸς
the place. looking up Jesus saw him, and said to
846 2195 4692 2597 4594 1063 1722
αὐτόν, Ζακχαῖε, σπεύσας κατάβηθι· σήμερον γὰρ ἐν τῷ
him, Zaccheus, making haste, come down; today for in the
3624 4675 1163 3165 3306 4692 2597 5264
6 οἴκῳ σου δεῖ με μεῖναι. καὶ σπεύσας κατέβη, καὶ ὑπεδέξατο
house of you must Me to stay. And hastening he came down, and welcomed
846 5463 1492 537 1234 3004
7 αὐτὸν χαίρων. καὶ ἰδόντες ἅπαντες διεγόγγυζον, λέγοντες
Him, rejoicing. And seeing all murmured, saying,
3754 3844 268 435 1525 2647 2476
8 ὅτι Παρὰ ἁμαρτωλῷ ἀνδρὶ εἰσῆλθε καταλῦσαι. σταθεὶς δὲ
— With a sinful man He went in to lodge. standing And
2195 2036 4314 2962 2400 2255
Ζακχαῖος εἶπε πρὸς τὸν Κύριον, Ἰδού, τὰ ἡμίση τῶν
Zaccheus said to the Lord, Behold, the half of the
5224 3450 2962 1325 4434 1536 5100
ὑπαρχόντων μου, Κύριε, δίδωμι τοῖς πτωχοῖς· καὶ εἴ τινός
possessions of me, Lord, I give to the poor; and if anyone
5100 4811 591 5073 2036 4314
9 τι ἐσυκοφάντησα, ἀποδίδωμι τετραπλοῦν. εἶπε δὲ πρὸς
anything I accused falsely, I restore fourfold said And to
846 2424 3754 4594 4991 3614 5129 1096
αὐτὸν ὁ Ἰησοῦς ὅτι Σήμερον σωτηρία τῷ οἴκῳ τούτῳ ἐγέ-
him — Jesus, — Today salvation — house to this is
2530 846 5207 11 2076 2064 1063 5207
10 νετο, καθότι καὶ αὐτὸς υἱὸς Ἀβραάμ ἐστιν. ἦλθε γὰρ ὁ υἱὸς
come, because even he a son of Abraham is. came for the Son
444 2212 4982 622
τοῦ ἀνθρώπου ζητῆσαι καὶ σῶσαι τὸ ἀπολωλός.
of man to seek and to save the thing being lost.
191 846 5023 4369 2036 3850
11 Ἀκουόντων δὲ αὐτῶν ταῦτα, προσθεὶς εἶπε παραβολήν,
hearing And them these things, adding He told a parable,
1223 1451 846 1511 2419 1380 846 3754
διὰ τὸ ἐγγὺς αὐτὸν εἶναι Ἱερουσαλήμ, καὶ δοκεῖν αὐτοὺς ὅτι
because near He was to Jerusalem, and thought they that
3916 3195 932 2316 398
12 παραχρῆμα μέλλει ἡ βασιλεία τοῦ Θεοῦ ἀναφαίνεσθαι.
immediately was about the kingdom — of God to be revealed.
2036 3767 444 5100 2104 4198 1519 5561 3117
13 εἶπεν οὖν, Ἄνθρωπός τις εὐγενὴς ἐπορεύθη εἰς χώραν μακράν,
He said, then, man a certain well-born went to a country distant
2983 1438 932 5290 2563 1176
λαβεῖν ἑαυτῷ βασιλείαν, καὶ ὑποστρέψαι. καλέσας δὲ δέκα
to receive for himself a kingdom, and to return. having called And ten
1401 1438 1325 846 1176 3414 2036 4314
14 δούλους ἑαυτοῦ, ἔδωκεν αὐτοῖς δέκα μνᾶς, καὶ εἶπε πρὸς
slaves of himself, He gave to them ten minas, and said to
846 4231 2193 2064 4177
αὐτούς, Πραγματεύσασθε ἕως ἔρχομαι. οἱ δὲ πολῖται
them, Trade until I come. the But citizens
848 3404 846 649 4242 3694
αὐτοῦ ἐμίσουν αὐτόν, καὶ ἀπέστειλαν πρεσβείαν ὀπίσω
of him hated him, and sent a delegation after
846 3004 3756 2309 5126 936 1909 2248
αὐτοῦ, λέγοντες, Οὐ θέλομεν τοῦτον βασιλεῦσαι ἐφ' ἡμᾶς.
him, saying, not We desire this one to reign over us.

he returned, having received the kingdom, he even said *for* those slaves to be called to him, *those* to whom he gave the silver; that he might know what each had gained by trading. [16]And the first came, saying, Lord, your mina has gained ten minas. [17]And he said to him, Well done, good slave! Because you were faithful in a least thing, have authority over ten cities. [18]And the second came, saying, Lord, your mina has made five minas. [19]And he said to this one also, And you be over five cities. [20]And another came, saying, Lord, behold your mina which I had kept in a handkerchief. [21]For I feared you, because you are an exacting man, taking what you did not lay down, and reaping what you did not sow. [22]But he said to him, I will judge you out of your own mouth, wicked slave. You knew that I am an exacting man, taking what I did not lay down, and reaping what I did not sow. [23]And why did you not give my silver on the *bank* table? And coming I might have exacted it with interest. [24]And to those standing by, he said, Take the mina from him, and give it to him who has ten minas.

[25]And they said to him, Lord, he has ten minas. [26]For I say to you, To everyone who has, it will be given. And from the *one* who does not have, even what he has will be taken from him. [27]But these enemies of mine, those not desiring me to reign over them, bring here and execute *them* before me.

[28]And saying these things, He went in front, going up to Jerusalem.

1096 1880 846 2983 932
15 καὶ ἐγένετο ἐν τῷ ἐπανελθεῖν αὐτὸν λαβόντα τὴν βασιλείαν,
And it was, in the returning (of) him, having received the kingdom,
2036 5455 846 1401 5128 3739 1325
καὶ εἶπε φωνηθῆναι αὐτῷ τοὺς δούλους τούτους, οἷς ἔδωκε
even he said to be called to him — slaves those to whom he gave
694 2443 1097 5101 5101 1281 3854
16 τὸ ἀργύριον, ἵνα γνῷ τίς τί διεπραγματεύσατο. παρε-
the silver, that he know what each had gained by trading. came
4413 3004 2962 3414 4675 4333
γένετο δὲ ὁ πρῶτος, λέγων, Κύριε, ἡ μνᾶ σου προσειργάσατο
And the first, saying, Lord, the mina of you has gained
•1722 1176 3414 2036 846 2095 18 1401 3754 • 1646
17 δέκα μνᾶς. καὶ εἶπεν αὐτῷ, Εὖ, ἀγαθὲ δοῦλε· ὅτι ἐν ἐλαχίστῳ
ten minas. And he said to him, Well, good slave, for in a least thing
4103 1096 2468 1849 2192 1883 1176 4172
18 πιστὸς ἐγένου, ἴσθι ἐξουσίαν ἔχων ἐπάνω δέκα πόλεων. καὶ
faithful you were; be authority having over ten cities. And
2064 1208 3004 2962 3414 4675 4160 4002
ἦλθεν ὁ δεύτερος, λέγων, Κύριε, ἡ μνᾶ σου ἐποίησε πέντε
came the second, saying, Lord, Behold, the mina of you which I had
3414 2036 5129 4771 1096 1883 4002 4172
19 μνᾶς. εἶπε δὲ καὶ τούτῳ, Καὶ σὺ γίνου ἐπάνω πέντε πόλεων.
minas. he said And also to this, And you be over five cities.
2087 2064 3004 2962 2400 3414 4675 3739 2192
20 καὶ ἕτερος ἦλθε, λέγων, Κύριε, ἰδού, ἡ μνᾶ σου, ἣν εἶχον
And another came, saying, Lord, Behold, the mina of you which I had
606 4676 5399 1063 4571 3754 444
21 ἀποκειμένην ἐν σουδαρίῳ· ἐφοβούμην γάρ σε, ὅτι ἄνθρωπος
reserved in a napkin; I feared for you, for a man
840 1488 142 3739 3756 5087 2325 3739 3756 4687
αὐστηρὸς εἶ· αἴρεις ὃ οὐκ ἔθηκας, καὶ θερίζεις ὃ οὐκ ἔσπειρας.
exacting you are, taking what not you lay, and reaping what not you sowed.
3004 846 1537 4750 4675 2919 4571 4190 1401
22 λέγει δὲ αὐτῷ, Ἐκ τοῦ στόματός σου κρινῶ σε, πονηρὲ δοῦλε.
he says And to him, From the mouth of you I will judge you, wicked slave.
1492 3754 1473 444 840 1510 142 3739 3756 5087
ᾔδεις ὅτι ἐγὼ ἄνθρωπος αὐστηρός εἰμι, αἴρων ὃ οὐκ ἔθηκα,
You knew that I an exacting man am, taking what not I laid,
2325 3739 3756 4687 1302 3756 1325 694
23 καὶ θερίζων ὃ οὐκ ἔσπειρα· καὶ διατί οὐκ ἔδωκας τὸ ἀργύριόν
and reaping what not I sowed. And why not did you give the silver
3450 1909 5132 1473 2064 4862 5110 302 4238
μου ἐπὶ τὴν τράπεζαν, καὶ ἐγὼ ἐλθὼν σὺν τόκῳ ἂν ἔπραξα
of me on the (bank) table? And I coming, with interest may have exacted
846 3936 2036 142 575 846
24 αὐτό; καὶ τοῖς παρεστῶσιν εἶπεν, Ἄρατε ἀπ' αὐτοῦ τὴν
it. And to those standing by he said, Take from him the
3414 1325 1176 3414 2192 2036 846
25 μνᾶν, καὶ δότε τῷ τὰς δέκα μνᾶς ἔχοντι. καὶ εἶπον αὐτῷ,
mina, and give to the (one) ten minas having. And they said to him,
2962 2192 1176 3414 3004 1063 5213 3754 3956 2192
26 Κύριε, ἔχει δέκα μνᾶς. λέγω γὰρ ὑμῖν, ὅτι παντὶ τῷ ἔχοντι
Lord, he has ten minas. I say For to you, that to everyone having,
1325 575 3361 2192 3739 2192 142
δοθήσεται· ἀπὸ δὲ τοῦ μὴ ἔχοντος, καὶ ὃ ἔχει ἀρθήσεται
it will be given, from and the (one) not having, even what he has will be taken
575 846 4133 2190 3450 1565 3361 2309
27 ἀπ' αὐτοῦ. πλὴν τοὺς ἐχθρούς μου ἐκείνους, τοὺς μὴ θελή-
from him. But — enemies of me these, those not
3165 936 1909 846 71 5602
σαντάς με βασιλεῦσαι ἐπ' αὐτούς, ἀγάγετε ὧδε, καὶ
desiring me to reign over them, bring here, and
2695 1715 3450
κατασφάξατε ἔμπροσθέν μου.
execute before me.
2036 5023 4198 1715 305
28 Καὶ εἰπὼν ταῦτα, ἐπορεύετο ἔμπροσθεν, ἀναβαίνων εἰς
And saying these things, He went in front, going up to
Ἱεροσόλυμα.
Jerusalem.

29 And it happened as He drew near to Bethphage and Bethany toward the Mount called Of Olives, He sent two of His disciples, 30 saying, Go into the village opposite *you,* in which having entered you will find a colt which has been tied up; on which no one of men ever yet sat. Untying it, bring *it.* 31 And if anyone asks, Why do you untie *it?* You shall say to them, The Lord has need of it. 32 And going, those having been sent found as He told them. 33 And *as* they were untying the colt, its owners said to them, Why do you untie the colt? 34 And they said, The Lord has need of it. 35 And they led it to Jesus. And throwing their garments on the colt, they put Jesus on *it.* 36 And as He went, they were spreading their garments in the highway.

37 And as He was already drawing near to the descent of the Mount of Olives,, all the multitude of the disciples began rejoicing, to praise God with a loud voice concerning all *the* works of power which they saw, 38 saying,

Blessed *is* the One coming in the name of the Lord, the King. Peace in Heaven, and glory in *the* highest!

39 And some of the Pharisees from the crowd said to Him, Teacher, rebuke your disciples. 40 And answering He said to them, I say to you, If these should be silent, the stones will cry out.

41 And as He drew near, seeing the city, He wept

1096 5613 1448 1519 967 963 4314
29 Καὶ ἐγένετο ὡς ἤγγισεν εἰς Βηθφαγὴ καὶ Βηθανίαν πρὸς
And it was, as He drew near to Bethphage and Bethany toward
3735 2564 1636 649 1417 3101
τὸ ὄρος τὸ καλούμενον ἐλαιῶν, ἀπέστειλε δύο τῶν μαθητῶν
the mount — being called of olives, He sent two of the disciples
848 2036 5217 1519 2713 2968 1722 3739
30 αὐτοῦ, εἰπών, Ὑπάγετε εἰς τὴν κατέναντι κώμην· ἐν ᾗ
of Him, saying, Go into the opposite village, in which
1531 2147 4454 1210 1909 3739 3762
εἰσπορευόμενοι εὑρήσετε πῶλον δεδεμένον, ἐφ' ὃν οὐδεὶς
having entered you will find a colt having been tied, on which no one
4455 444 2523 3089 846 71
πώποτε ἀνθρώπων ἐκάθισε· λύσαντες αὐτὸν ἀγάγετε. καὶ
ever yet of men sat. Having untied it, bring (it). And
1437 5100 5209 2065 1302 3089 3779 2046 846 3754
31 ἐάν τις ὑμᾶς ἐρωτᾷ, Διατί λύετε; οὕτως ἐρεῖτε αὐτῷ ὅτι
if anyone you asks, Why do you untie, thus you shall say to them,—
2962 848 5532 2192 565 649
32 Ὁ Κύριος αὐτοῦ χρείαν ἔχει. ἀπελθόντες δὲ οἱ ἀπεσταλ-
The Lord of it need has. having gone And, those having been
2147 2531 2036 846 3089 846
33 μένοι εὗρον καθὼς εἶπεν αὐτοῖς. λυόντων δὲ αὐτῶν τὸν
sent found as He told them. untying And them the
4454 2036 2962 848 4314 846 5101 3089
πῶλον, εἶπον οἱ κύριοι αὐτοῦ πρὸς αὐτούς, Τί λύετε τὸν
colt, said the owners of it to them, Why do you untie the
4454 2036 2962 848 5532 2192
34 πῶλον; οἱ δὲ εἶπον, Ὁ Κύριος αὐτοῦ χρείαν ἔχει. καὶ
colt? they And said, The Lord of it need has. And
71 846 4314 2524 1977 1438
35 ἤγαγον αὐτὸν πρὸς τὸν Ἰησοῦν· καὶ ἐπιρρίψαντες ἑαυτῶν
they led it to Jesus, and throwing of themselves
2440 1909 4454 1913 2424 4198
τὰ ἱμάτια ἐπὶ τὸν πῶλον ἐπεβίβασαν τὸν Ἰησοῦν. πορευο-
the garments on the colt, they put on (it) Jesus. going
848 5291 2440 848 1722 3598
36 μένου δὲ αὐτοῦ, ὑπεστρώννυον τὰ ἱμάτια αὐτῶν ἐν τῇ ὁδῷ.
And Him, they spread out the garments of them in the way.
1488 848 2235 4314 2600 3735
37 ἐγγίζοντος δὲ αὐτοῦ ἤδη πρὸς τῇ καταβάσει τοῦ ὄρους τῶν
drawing near And Him now to the descent of the mount of the
1636 756 537 4128 3101 5463
ἐλαιῶν, ἤρξαντο ἅπαν τὸ πλῆθος τῶν μαθητῶν χαίροντες·
olives, began all the multitude of the disciples rejoicing
134 2316 5456 3173 4012 3956 3739 1492 1411
αἰνεῖν τὸν Θεὸν φωνῇ μεγάλῃ περὶ πασῶν ὧν εἶδον δυνά-
to praise God with a voice great about all which they saw, works
3004
38 μεων, λέγοντες,
of power, saying,
2127 2064 935 1722 3686 2962
Εὐλογημένος ὁ ἐρχόμενος βασιλεὺς ἐν ὀνόματι Κυρίου·
Blessed the coming One, the king, in the name of the Lord;
1515 3772 1391 1722 5310
εἰρήνη ἐν οὐρανῷ, καὶ δόξα ἐν ὑψίστοις.
peace in Heaven, and glory in highest places.
5100 5330 575 3793 2036 4314
39 Καί τινες τῶν Φαρισαίων ἀπὸ τοῦ ὄχλου εἶπον πρὸς
And some of the Pharisees from the crowd said to
846 1320 2008 3101 4675 611
40 αὐτόν, Διδάσκαλε, ἐπιτίμησον τοῖς μαθηταῖς σου. καὶ ἀπο-
Him, Teacher, rebuke the disciples of you. And
2036 846 3004 5213 3754 1437 3778 4623
κριθεὶς εἶπεν αὐτοῖς, Λέγω ὑμῖν ὅτι, ἐὰν οὗτοι σιωπήσωσιν,
answering He said to them, I say to you, — if these shall be silent,
3036 2896
οἱ λίθοι κεκράξονται.
the stones will cry out.
5613 1448 1492 4172 2799 1909 846
41 Καὶ ὡς ἤγγισεν, ἰδὼν τὴν πόλιν, ἔκλαυσεν ἐπ' αὐτῇ,
And as He drew near, seeing the city, He wept over it.

over it, 42 saying, If you had known, even you, even at least in this day of yours, the things for your peace! But now they were hidden from your eyes. 43 For the days will come on you, and your enemies will raise up a rampart to you, and will surround you, and will keep you in on every side; 44 and will tear you down, and your children in you, and will not leave a stone on a stone, because you did not know the time of your visitation.

45 And entering into the temple, He began to throw out those selling and buying in it, 46 saying to them, It has been written, "My house is a house of prayer," but you made it a den of robbers. 47 And He was teaching day by day in the temple. But the chief priests and the scribes and the chief men of the people sought to kill Him. 48 And *they* did not find what they might do; for all the people hung on Him, listening.

3004 3754 1487 1097 4771 1065 2250 4675 5026
42 λέγων ὅτι Εἰ ἔγνως καὶ σύ, καί γε ἐν τῇ ἡμέρᾳ σου ταύτῃ,
saying, If you knew, even you, even at least in day of you this,
4314 1515 1675 3568 2928 575 3788 4675 3754
43 τὰ πρὸς εἰρήνην σου· νῦν δὲ ἐκρύβη ἀπὸ ὀφθαλμῶν σου. ὅτι
the things for peace of you, now but were hid from the eyes of you. For
2250 2250 1909 4571 4016 2190 4675
ἥξουσιν ἡμέραι ἐπὶ σέ, καὶ περιβαλοῦσιν οἱ ἐχθροί σου
will come days on you, and will raise up the enemies of you
5482 4671 4033 4571 4912 4571 3840
χάρακά σοι, καὶ περικυκλώσουσί σε, καὶ συνέξουσί σε πάντο-
a rampart to you, and will surround you, and will keep in you on all
1474 4571 5043 4675 1722 4671 3756
44 θεν, καὶ ἐδαφιοῦσί σε καὶ τὰ τέκνα σου ἐν σοί, καὶ οὐκ
sides, and raze you, and the children of you in you, and not
863 1722 4671 3037 1909 3037 473 3739 3756 1097
ἀφήσουσιν ἐν σοὶ λίθον ἐπὶ λίθῳ· ἀνθ' ὧν οὐκ ἔγνως τὸν
will leave in you stone upon stone because not you knew the
2540 1984 4675
καιρὸν τῆς ἐπισκοπῆς σου.
time of the visitation of you.
1528 1519 2411 756 1544 4453
45 Καὶ εἰσελθὼν εἰς τὸ ἱερόν, ἤρξατο ἐκβάλλειν τοὺς πωλοῦν-
And entering into the Temple, He began to throw out the(ones) selling
1722 846 59 3004 846 1125
46 τας ἐν αὐτῷ καὶ ἀγοράζοντας, λέγων αὐτοῖς, Γέγραπται,
in it, and buying, saying to them, It has been written,
3624 3450 3624 4335 2076 5210 846 4160
Ὁ οἶκός μου οἶκος προσευχῆς ἐστίν· ὑμεῖς δὲ αὐτὸν ἐποιήσατε
The house of Me a house of prayer is; you but it made
4693 3027 2258 1321 2596 2250 1722
47 σπήλαιον λῃστῶν. καὶ ἦν διδάσκων τὸ καθ' ἡμέραν ἐν τῷ
a den of robbers. And He was teaching day by day in the
2411 749 1122 2212 846
ἱερῷ· οἱ δὲ ἀρχιερεῖς καὶ οἱ γραμματεῖς ἐζήτουν αὐτὸν
Temple. the But chief priests and the scribes sought Him
622 4413 2992 3756 2147 5101
48 ἀπολέσαι, καὶ οἱ πρῶτοι τοῦ λαοῦ· καὶ οὐχ εὕρισκον τὸ τί
to destroy, and the chief men of the people; and not did find — what
4160 2992 1063 537 1582 846 191
ποιήσωσιν, ὁ λαὸς γὰρ ἅπας ἐξεκρέματο αὐτοῦ ἀκούων.
they might do; the people for all hung upon Him, hearing.

CHAPTER 20

CHAPTER 20

1 And it happened on one of those days, *as* He was teaching the people and preaching the gospel in the temple, the chief priests and the scribes came up, along with the elders, 2 and spoke to Him, saying, Tell us by what authority you do these things, or who is it who gave to you this authority? 3 And answering He said to them, I will also ask you one thing, and you tell Me: 4 The baptism of John, was it from Heaven, or from men? 5 And they reasoned with themselves, saying, If we say, From Heaven, he will say, Why, then, did you not believe

1096 1722 3391 2250 1565 1321 846
1 Καὶ ἐγένετο ἐν μιᾷ τῶν ἡμερῶν ἐκείνων, διδάσκοντος αὐτοῦ
And it was, on one of — days those, teaching Him
2992 1722 2411 2097 2186
τὸν λαὸν ἐν τῷ ἱερῷ καὶ εὐαγγελιζομένου, ἐπέστησαν οἱ
the people in the Temple, and preaching the gospel; came upon the
749 1122 4862 4245 2036
2 ἀρχιερεῖς καὶ οἱ γραμματεῖς σὺν τοῖς πρεσβυτέροις, καὶ εἶπον
chief priests and the scribes with the elders, and spoke
4314 846 3004 2036 2254 1722 4169 1849 5023
πρὸς αὐτόν, λέγοντες, Εἰπὲ ἡμῖν, ἐν ποίᾳ ἐξουσίᾳ ταῦτα
to Him, saying, Tell us, by what authority these things
4160 2228 5101 2076 1325 4671 2849 5026 611
ποιεῖς, ἢ τίς ἐστιν ὁ δούς σοι τὴν ἐξουσίαν ταύτην; ἀπο-
you do, or who is the (one) giving you authority this?
2036 4314 846 2065 5209 2504 1520
3 κριθεὶς δὲ εἶπε πρὸς αὐτούς, Ἐρωτήσω ὑμᾶς κἀγὼ ἕνα
answering And He said to them, will ask you I also one
3056 2036 3427 908 2491 1537 3772
4 λόγον, καὶ εἴπατέ μοι· Τὸ βάπτισμα Ἰωάννου ἐξ οὐρανοῦ
word, and you tell Me: The baptism of John, from Heaven
2258 2228 1537 444 4817 4314 1438
5 ἦν, ἢ ἐξ ἀνθρώπων; οἱ δὲ συνελογίσαντο πρὸς ἑαυτούς,
was it, or from men? they And debated with themselves
3004 3756 1437 2036 1537 3772 2046 1302 3767 3756
λέγοντες ὅτι Ἐὰν εἴπωμεν, Ἐξ οὐρανοῦ, ἐρεῖ, Διατί οὖν οὐκ
saying, If we say, From Heaven, he will say, Why, then, not

him? [6]But if we say, From men, all the people will stone us, for *they* had been convinced that John was a prophet. [7]And they answered, they did not know from where. [8]And Jesus said to them, Neither do I tell you by what authority I do these things.

[9]And He began to speak this parable to the people: A certain man planted a vineyard, and let it out to vinedressers. And *he* left the country for long periods *of time*. [10]And in season he sent a slave to the vinedressers, that they might give him the fruit of the vineyard. But the vinedressers sent him away empty, beating *him*. [11]And he again sent another slave. But they also sent that one away empty, beating and insulting *him*. [12]And he again sent a third. But they also threw this one out, wounding *him*. [13]And the lord of the vineyard said, What shall I do? I will send my beloved son. Perhaps seeing this one, they will respect *him*. [14]And seeing him, the vinedressers reasoned with themselves, saying, This is the heir. Come let us kill him, so that the inheritance may become ours. [15]And throwing him out of the vineyard, they killed *him*. Therefore, what will the lord of the vineyard do to them? [16]He will come and will destroy these vinedressers, and will give the vineyard to others.

And hearing *this*, they said, Let it not be! [17]And looking at them He said, What, then, is this which has been written, *"The* stone that the builders rejected, this one came to be for *the* Head of *the* corner?

4100 846 1437 2036 1537 444 3956
6 ἐπιστεύσατε αὐτῷ ; ἐὰν δὲ εἴπωμεν, Ἐξ ἀνθρώπων, πᾶς ὁ
you believed him? if And we say From men, all the
2992 2642 2248 3982 0163 2076 2491
λαὸς καταλιθάσει ἡμᾶς· πεπεισμένος γάρ ἐστιν Ἰωάννην
people will stone us, having been convinced for John
4396 1511 611 3361 1492 4159
7 προφήτην εἶναι. καὶ ἀπεκρίθησαν μὴ εἰδέναι πόθεν. καὶ ὁ
a prophet was. And they answered not they knew from where. And
2424 2036 846 3761 1473 3004 5213 1722 4169 1849
8 Ἰησοῦς εἶπεν αὐτοῖς, Οὐδὲ ἐγὼ λέγω ὑμῖν ἐν ποίᾳ ἐξουσίᾳ
Jesus said to them, Neither do I tell you by what authority
5023 4160
ταῦτα ποιῶ.
these things I do.
756 4314 2992 3004 3850 5026
9 Ἤρξατο δὲ πρὸς τὸν λαὸν λέγειν τὴν παραβολὴν ταύτην·
He began And to the people to tell — parable this:
444 5100 5452 290 1554 846
Ἄνθρωπός τις ἐφύτευσεν ἀμπελῶνα, καὶ ἐξέδοτο αὐτὸν
A man certain planted a vineyard, and let out it
1092 589 5550 2425 1722 2540
10 γεωργοῖς, καὶ ἀπεδήμησε χρόνους ἱκανούς· καὶ ἐν καιρῷ
to vinedressers, and went away periods for considerable. And in time
649 4314 1092 1401 2443 575 2590
ἀπέστειλε πρὸς τοὺς γεωργοὺς δοῦλον, ἵνα ἀπὸ τοῦ καρποῦ
he sent to the vinedressers a slave, that from the fruit
290 1325 846 1092 1194 846
τοῦ ἀμπελῶνος δῶσιν αὐτῷ· οἱ δὲ γεωργοὶ δείραντες αὐτὸν
of the vineyard they will give him. the But vinedressers sent away him,
1821 2756 4369 3992 2087 1401
11 ἐξαπέστειλαν κενόν. καὶ προσέθετο πέμψαι ἕτερον δοῦλον·
beating (him), empty. And he added to send another slave,
2548 1194 818 1821 2756
οἱ δὲ κἀκεῖνον δείραντες καὶ ἀτιμάσαντες ἐξαπέστειλαν κενόν.
they but that one also, beating and insulting (him), sent away empty.
4369 3992 5154 5126 5135
12 καὶ προσέθετο πέμψαι τρίτον· οἱ δὲ καὶ τοῦτον τραυματί-
And he added to send a third. they But also this one, wounding,
1544 2036 2962 290 5101 4160
13 σαντες ἐξέβαλον. εἶπε δὲ ὁ κύριος τοῦ ἀμπελῶνος, Τί ποιήσω ;
(him) threw out. said And the lord of the vineyard, What shall I do?
3992 5207 3450 27 2481 5126 1492
πέμψω τὸν υἱόν μου τὸν ἀγαπητόν· ἴσως τοῦτον ἰδόντες
I will send the son of me, the beloved; perhaps this one seeing
1788 1492 846 1092 1260
14 ἐντραπήσονται. ἰδόντες δὲ αὐτὸν οἱ γεωργοὶ διελογίζοντο
they will respect. seeing And him, the vinedressers reasoned
4314 1438 3004 3778 2076 2818 1205
πρὸς ἑαυτούς, λέγοντες, Οὗτός ἐστιν ὁ κληρονόμος· δεῦτε,
with themselves, saying, This is the heir; come,
615 846 2443 2254 1096 2817
15 ἀποκτείνωμεν αὐτόν, ἵνα ἡμῶν γένηται ἡ κληρονομία. καὶ
let us kill him, that of us may become the inheritance. And
1544 846 1854 290 615 5101 3767
ἐκβαλόντες αὐτὸν ἔξω τοῦ ἀμπελῶνος, ἀπέκτειναν. τί οὖν
throwing out him out of the vineyard, they killed. What, then,
4160 846 2962 290 2064
16 ποιήσει αὐτοῖς ὁ κύριος τοῦ ἀμπελῶνος ; ἐλεύσεται καὶ
will do to them the lord of the vineyard? He will come and
622 1092 5128 1325 290
ἀπολέσει τοὺς γεωργοὺς τούτους, καὶ δώσει τὸν ἀμπελῶνα
will destroy vinedresses these, and will give the vineyard
243 191 2036 3361 1096 1689
ἄλλοις. ἀκούσαντες δὲ εἶπον, Μὴ γένοιτο. ὁ δὲ ἐμβλέψας
to others. hearing And, they said, Not let it be! He And looking at
846 2036 5101 3767 2076 1125 5124 3037 3739
17 αὐτοῖς εἶπε, Τί οὖν ἐστι τὸ γεγραμμένον τοῦτο, Λίθον ὃν
them said, What, then is having been written this: (The) stone that
593 3618 3778 1096 1519 2776
ἀπεδοκίμασαν οἱ οἰκοδομοῦντες, οὗτος ἐγενήθη εἰς κεφαλὴν
rejected those building, this one came to be for (the) head

[18]Everyone falling on that Stone will be broken in pieces; but on whomever it falls, it will grind him to powder.

[19]And the chief priests and the scribes sought to lay hands on Him in the same hour. And *they* feared the people, for they knew that He told this parable against them.

[20]And watching carefully, they sent spies, pretending themselves to be righteous, in order that they might seize upon a word of His, so as to deliver Him to the power and to the authority of the governor. [21]And they questioned Him, saying, Teacher, we know that you say and teach rightly, and do not receive a face, but you teach the way of God with truth. [22]Is it lawful to give tribute to Caesar, or not?[24]But perceiving their slyness, He said to them, Why do you tempt Me? [24]Show Me a denarius. Whose image and superscription does it have? And answering they said, Caesar's. [25]And He said to them, Then render the things of Caesar to Caesar, and the things of God to God. [26]And they were not able to lay hold of His speech before the people. And marveling at His answer, they were silent.

[27]And some of the Sadducees coming up, those speaking against a resurrection, *that it was* not to be, they questioned Him, [28]saying, Teacher, Moses wrote to us, If anyone's brother dies having a wife, and this one should die childless, that his brother should take the wife and raise up seed to his brother. [29]Then there were seven

1137 3956 4098 1909 1565 3037 4917 head
18 γωνίας ; πᾶς ὁ πεσὼν ἐπ' ἐκεῖνον τὸν λίθον συνθλασθή-
of (the) corner? Everyone falling on that – stone will be broken in
1909 3739 302 4098 3039 846
σεται ἐφ' ὃν δ' ἂν πέσῃ, λικμήσει αὐτόν.
pieces; on whomever but it falls, it will crush him.
2212 749 1122 1911
19 Καὶ ἐζήτησαν οἱ ἀρχιερεῖς καὶ οἱ γραμματεῖς ἐπιβαλεῖν
And sought the chief priests and the scribes to lay
1909 846 5495 1722 846 5610 5399
ἐπ' αὐτὸν τὰς χεῖρας ἐν αὐτῇ τῇ ὥρᾳ, καὶ ἐφοβήθησαν τὸν
on Him the hands in same the hour; and feared the
2992 1097 1063 3754 4314 846 3850 5026
λαόν· ἔγνωσαν γὰρ ὅτι πρὸς αὐτοὺς τὴν παραβολὴν ταύτην
people; they knew for that at them – parable this
2036 3906 649 1455 5271
20 εἶπε. καὶ παρατηρήσαντες ἀπέστειλαν ἐγκαθέτους ὑπο-
He told. And watching carefully they sent spies,
1438 1342 1511 2443 1949 846
κρινομένους ἑαυτοὺς δικαίους εἶναι, ἵνα ἐπιλάβωνται αὐτοῦ
pretending themselves righteous to be; that they might seize of Him
3056 1519 3860 846 746 1849
λόγου, εἰς τὸ παραδοῦναι αὐτὸν τῇ ἀρχῇ καὶ τῇ ἐξουσίᾳ
a word, in order to deliver Him to the power and to the authority
2232 1905 846 3004 1320
21 τοῦ ἡγεμόνος. καὶ ἐπηρώτησαν αὐτόν, λέγοντες, Διδάσκαλε,
of the governor And they questioned Him, saying, Teacher,
1492 3754 3723 3004 1321 3756 2983
οἴδαμεν ὅτι ὀρθῶς λέγεις καὶ διδάσκεις, καὶ οὐ λαμβάνεις
we know that rightly you speak, and teach, and not do receive
4383 235 1909 225 3598 2316 1321
πρόσωπον, ἀλλ' ἐπ' ἀληθείας τὴν ὁδὸν τοῦ Θεοῦ διδάσκεις.
a face, but upon truth the way – of God you teach.
1832 2254 2541 5411 1325 2228 3756 2657
22 ἔξεστιν ἡμῖν Καίσαρι φόρον δοῦναι, ἢ οὔ ; κατανοήσας δὲ
23 Is it lawful for us to Caesar tribute to give, or not? perceiving And
848 3834 2036 4314 846 5101 3165 3985
αὐτῶν τὴν πανουργίαν, εἶπε πρὸς αὐτούς, Τί με πειράζετε ;
of them the slyness, He said to them, Why Me do you tempt;
1925 3427 1220 5101 2192 1504 1923
24 ἐπιδείξατέ μοι δηνάριον· τίνος ἔχει εἰκόνα καὶ ἐπιγραφήν ;
show Me a denarius; of whom has it an image and superscription?
611 2036 2541 2036 846 591
25 ἀποκριθέντες δὲ εἶπον, Καίσαρος. ὁ δὲ εἶπεν αὐτοῖς, Ἀπόδοτε
answering And they said, Of Caesar. He And said to them, Render
5106 2541 2541 2316 2316
τοίνυν τὰ Καίσαρος Καίσαρι, καὶ τὰ τοῦ Θεοῦ τῷ Θεῷ.
then the things of Caesar to Caesar, and the things – of God – to God.
3756 2480 1949 848 4487 1726
26 καὶ οὐκ ἴσχυσαν ἐπιλαβέσθαι αὐτοῦ ῥήματος ἐναντίον τοῦ
And not they were able to lay hold of Him (the) speech before the
2992 2296 1909 612 848 4601
λαοῦ· καὶ θαυμάσαντες ἐπὶ τῇ ἀποκρίσει αὐτοῦ, ἐσίγησαν.
people and marveling at the answer of Him, they were silent
4334 5100 4523 483
27 Προσελθόντες δέ τινες τῶν Σαδδουκαίων, οἱ ἀντιλέγοντες
coming up And some of the Sadducees, those speaking against
386 3361 1511 1905 846 3004 1320
28 ἀνάστασιν μὴ εἶναι, ἐπηρώτησαν αὐτόν, λέγοντες, Διδά-
a resurrection not to be. They questioned Him, saying, Teacher,
3475 1125 2254 1437 5100 80 599
σκαλε, Μωσῆς ἔγραψεν ἡμῖν, ἐάν τινος ἀδελφὸς ἀποθάνῃ
Moses wrote to us, If of anyone a brother dies
2192 1135 3778 815 599 2443 2983
ἔχων γυναῖκα, καὶ οὗτος ἄτεκνος ἀποθάνῃ, ἵνα λάβῃ ὁ
having a wife, and this one childless should die, that should take the
80 848 1135 1817 4690
ἀδελφὸς αὐτοῦ τὴν γυναῖκα, καὶ ἐξαναστήσῃ σπέρμα τῷ
brother of him the wife, and raise up seed to the
80 848 2033 3767 80 2258 4413
29 ἀδελφῷ αὐτοῦ. ἑπτὰ οὖν ἀδελφοὶ ἦσαν· καὶ ὁ πρῶτος
brother of him. seven Then brothers there were, and the first

brothers. And having taken a wife, the first died childless. [30]And the second took the wife, and this one died childless. [31]And the third took her, and likewise also the seven died, and did not leave children. [32]And last of all the woman died. [33]Therefore, in the resurrection of which of them does she become wife? For the seven had her *as* wife. [34]And answering Jesus said to them, The sons of this world marry and are given in marriage. [35]But those counted worthy to obtain that world, and the resurrection from *the* dead, neither marry nor are given in marriage. [36]For they are not able to die *any* more; they are equal to angels, and are sons of God, being sons of the resurrection. [37]But that the dead are raised, even Moses pointed out at the Bush, when he calls *the* Lord the God of Abraham, and the God of Isaac, and the God of Jacob —[38]but He is not God of *the* dead, but of *the* living; for all live to Him. [39]And answering some of the scribes said, Teacher, you speak well. [40]And they did not dare to question Him any more—not a thing.

[41]And He said to them, How do they say the Christ is David's son? [42]Even David himself said in *the* Book of Psalms, "The Lord said to my Lord, Sit at My right *hand* [43]until I place Your enemies *as* a footstool of Your feet." [44]Then David calls Him Lord. And how is He his son?

[45]And *as* all the people were listening, He said to His disciples, [46]Beware of the scribes, those desiring to walk about in long robes,

2983 1135 599 815 2983 1208
30 λαβὼν γυναῖκα ἀπέθανεν ἄτεκνος· καὶ ἔλαβεν ὁ δεύτερος
having taken a wife died childless; and took the second
1135 3778 599 815 5154
τὴν γυναῖκα, καὶ οὗτος ἀπέθανεν ἄτεκνος. καὶ ὁ τρίτος
the wife, and this one died childless. And the third
2983 846 5615 2033 3756 2641
31 ἔλαβεν αὐτήν. ὡσαύτως δὲ καὶ οἱ ἑπτά· καὶ οὐ κατέλιπον
took her, likewise and also the seven even not did leave
5043 599 5305 3956 599 1135
32 τέκνα, καὶ ἀπέθανον. ὕστερον πάντων ἀπέθανε καὶ ἡ γυνή
children, and died. Lastly of all died also the woman.
1722 3767 386 5101 846 1096 1135 1063
33 ἐν τῇ οὖν ἀναστάσει, τίνος αὐτῶν γίνεται γυνή; οἱ γὰρ
in the Then resurrection, of which of them becomes she wife? the For
2033 2192 846 1135 611 2036 846
34 ἑπτὰ ἔσχον αὐτὴν γυναῖκα. καὶ ἀποκριθεὶς εἶπεν αὐτοῖς ὁ
seven had her (for) wife? And answering, said to them
2424 5207 165 5127 1060 1548
Ἰησοῦς, Οἱ υἱοὶ τοῦ αἰῶνος τούτου γαμοῦσι καὶ ἐκγαμί-
Jesus, The sons age of this marry and are given
2661 165 1565 5177
35 σκονται· οἱ δὲ καταξιωθέντες τοῦ αἰῶνος ἐκείνου τυχεῖν καὶ
marriage, those but counted worthy age of that to obtain, and
386 1537 3498 3777 1060 3777 1548
τῆς ἀναστάσεως τῆς ἐκ νεκρῶν οὔτε γαμοῦσιν οὔτε ἐκγαμί-
the resurrection the out of dead, neither marry nor are given
3777 1063 599 2089 1410 2465 1063
36 σκονται· οὔτε γὰρ ἀποθανεῖν ἔτι δύνανται· ἰσάγγελοι γάρ
in marriage; not even for to die (any more they are able, equal to angels for
1526 5207 1526 2316 386 5207 5607 3754
εἰσι, καὶ υἱοί εἰσι τοῦ Θεοῦ, τῆς ἀναστάσεως υἱοὶ ὄντες. ὅτι
they are; and sons are — of God, of the resurrection sons being. that
1453 3498 3475 3377 1909 942
37 δὲ ἐγείρονται οἱ νεκροί, καὶ Μωσῆς ἐμήνυσεν ἐπὶ τῆς βάτου,
But are raised the dead, even Moses pointed out at the Bush,
5613 3004 2962 2316 11 2316 2464
ὡς λέγει Κύριον τὸν Θεὸν Ἀβραὰμ καὶ τὸν Θεὸν Ἰσαὰκ καὶ
as he calls (the) Lord the God of Abraham and the God of Isaac and
2316 2384 2316 3756 2076 3498 235 2198
38 τὸν Θεὸν Ἰακώβ. Θεὸς δὲ οὐκ ἔστι νεκρῶν, ἀλλὰ ζώντων·
the God of Jacob. God but not He is of dead ones, but of living ones;
3956 1063 846 2198 611 5100 1122
39 πάντες γὰρ αὐτῷ ζῶσιν. ἀποκριθέντες δέ τινες τῶν γραμ-
all for to Him live. answering And some of the
2036 1320 2573 2036 3765 5111
40 ματέων εἶπον, Διδάσκαλε, καλῶς εἶπας. Οὐκέτι δὲ ἐτόλμων
scribes said, Teacher, Well you say. no more And they dared
1905 846 3752
ἐπερωτᾷν αὐτὸν οὐδέν.
to question Him, nothing.
2036 4314 846 4459 3004 5547 5207
41 Εἶπε δὲ πρὸς αὐτούς, Πῶς λέγουσι τὸν Χριστὸν υἱὸν
He said And to them, How do they say the Christ son
1138 1511 846 1138 3004 1722 976 5568
42 Δαβὶδ εἶναι; καὶ αὐτὸς Δαβὶδ λέγει ἐν βίβλῳ ψαλμῶν,
of David is? Even himself David says in (the) roll of Psalms:
2036 2962 2962 3450 2521 1537 1188 3450 2193 302
43 Εἶπεν ὁ Κύριος τῷ Κυρίῳ μου, Κάθου ἐκ δεξιῶν μου, ἕως ἂν
Said the Lord to the Lord of me, Sit at (the) right of Me until may
5087 2190 4675 5286 4228 4675 1138
44 θῶ τοὺς ἐχθρούς σου ὑποπόδιον τῶν ποδῶν σου. Δαβὶδ
I put the enemies of You a footstool of the foot of You. David
3767 2962 846 2564 4459 5207 848 2076
οὖν Κύριον αὐτὸν καλεῖ, καὶ πῶς υἱὸς αὐτοῦ ἐστιν;
then Lord Him calls. And how son of him is He?
191 3956 2992 2036 3101 848
45 Ἀκούοντος δὲ παντὸς τοῦ λαοῦ, εἶπε τοῖς μαθηταῖς αὐτοῦ,
hearing And all the people, He said to the disciples of Him,
4337 575 1122 2309 4043
46 Προσέχετε ἀπὸ τῶν γραμματέων τῶν θελόντων περιπατεῖν
Beware of the scribes, those desiring to walk about

and liking greetings in the markets, and chief seats in the synagogues, and chief couches in the suppers; [47]who devour the houses of the widows, and under pretense pray long. These will receive a more severe judgment.

CHAPTER 21

[1]And looking up He saw the rich ones putting their gifts into the treasury. [2]And He also saw a certain poor widow putting two lepta there. [3]And He said, Truly I say to you, This poor widow cast *in* more than all. [4]For all these out of their abundance cast into the gifts of God, but she out of her poverty cast *in* all the living which she had.

[5]And as some were speaking about the temple, that it had been adorned with beautiful stones and gifts, He said, [6]*As to* these things that you see, days will come in which a stone will not be left on a stone, which will not be thrown down.

[7]And they asked Him, saying, Teacher, then when will these things be? And what *will be* the sign when these things are about to occur? [8]And He said, Watch that you not be led astray. For many will come on My name, saying, I AM! Also, the time has come! Do not go after them. [9]And when you hear of wars and disturbances, do not be afraid. For these things must first occur; but the end *is* not at once. [10]Then He said to them, Nation will be lifted up against nation, and kingdom against kingdom.

1722 4749 5368 783 1722 58
ἐν στολαῖς, καὶ φιλούντων ἀσπασμοὺς ἐν ταῖς ἀγοραῖς, καὶ
in robes, and liking greetings in the markets, and
4410 1722 4864 4411 1722
πρωτοκαθεδρίας ἐν ταῖς συναγωγαῖς, καὶ πρωτοκλισίας ἐν
chief seats in the synagogues, and chief couches in
1173 3739 2719 3614 5503
47 τοῖς δείπνοις· οἳ κατεσθίουσι τὰς οἰκίας τῶν χηρῶν, καὶ
the suppers; those devouring the houses of the widows, and
4392 3117 4336 3778 2983 4054
προφάσει μακρὰ προσεύχονται. οὗτοι λήψονται περισσό-
under pretense long pray. These will receive a more
2917
τερον κρίμα.
severe judgment.

CHAPTER 21

308 1492 906 1435 848 1519
1 Ἀναβλέψας δὲ εἶδε τοὺς βάλλοντας τὰ δῶρα αὐτῶν εἰς
looking up And He saw those putting the gifts of them into
1049 4145 1492 5100 5503
2 τὸ γαζοφυλάκιον πλουσίους· εἶδε δὲ καί τινα χήραν
the treasury rich ones. He saw And also a certain widow
3998 906 1563 1417 3016 2036 230
3 πενιχρὰν βάλλουσαν ἐκεῖ δύο λεπτά, καὶ εἶπεν, Ἀληθῶς
poor putting there two lepta; and He said, Truly
3004 5213 3754 5503 4434 3778 4119 3956 906
λέγω ὑμῖν, ὅτι ἡ χήρα ἡ πτωχὴ αὕτη πλεῖον πάντων ἔβαλεν·
I say to you, widow poor This more (than) all cast.
537 1063 3778 1537 4052 846 906 1519
4 ἅπαντες γὰρ οὗτοι ἐκ τοῦ περισσεύοντος αὐτοῖς ἔβαλον εἰς
all For these out of the abundance to them cast into
1435 2316 3778 1537 5303 846
τὰ δῶρα τοῦ Θεοῦ, αὕτη δὲ ἐκ τοῦ ὑστερήματος αὐτῆς
the gifts to God, she but out of the want of her
537 979 3739 2192 906
ἅπαντα τὸν βίον ὃν εἶχεν ἔβαλε.
all the living which she had put.
5100 3004 4012 2411 3754 3037 2570
5 Καί τινων λεγόντων περὶ τοῦ ἱεροῦ, ὅτι λίθοις καλοῖς
And some speaking about the temple, that with stones
334 2885 2036 5023 3739 2334 beautiful
6 καὶ ἀναθήμασι κεκόσμηται, εἶπε, Ταῦτα ἃ θεωρεῖτε, ἐλεύ-
and gifts it has been decorated, He said, These things that you see, will
2064 2250 1722 3739 3756 863 3037 1909 3037 3739 3756
σονται ἡμέραι ἐν αἷς οὐκ ἀφεθήσεται λίθος ἐπὶ λίθῳ, ὃς οὐ
come days in which not will be left stone on stone which not
2647 1905 846 3004 1320
7 καταλυθήσεται. ἐπηρώτησαν δὲ αὐτόν, λέγοντες, Διδά-
will be thrown down. they questioned And Him, saying, Teacher,
4219 3767 5023 2071 5101 4592 3752 3195
σκαλε, πότε οὖν ταῦτα ἔσται : καὶ τί τὸ σημεῖον, ὅταν μέλλῃ
when, then, these things will be? And what the sign when are about
5023 1096 2036 991 3361 4105 4183
8 ταῦτα γίνεσθαι ; ὁ δὲ εἶπε, Βλέπετε μὴ πλανηθῆτε· πολλοὶ
these things to occur? He And said, Watch, lest you be led astray; many
1063 2064 1909 3686 3450 3004 3754 1473 1510
γὰρ ἐλεύσονται ἐπὶ τῷ ὀνόματί μου, λέγοντες ὅτι Ἐγώ εἰμι·
for will come on the name of Me, saying, — I AM;
2540 1448 3361 3767 4198 3694 846 3752
9 καί, Ὁ καιρὸς ἤγγικε. μὴ οὖν πορευθῆτε ὀπίσω αὐτῶν. ὅταν
and, The time has come. not Therefore go after them. when
191 4171 181 3361 4422
δὲ ἀκούσητε πολέμους καὶ ἀκαταστασίας, μὴ πτοηθῆτε·
And you hear of wars and disturbances, Do not be afraid.
1163 1063 5023 1096 4412 235 3756 2112 5056
δεῖ γὰρ ταῦτα γενέσθαι πρῶτον, ἀλλ' οὐκ εὐθέως τὸ τέλος.
must For these things occur first, but not at once the end.
5119 3004 846 1453 1484 1909 1484
10 Τότε ἔλεγεν αὐτοῖς, Ἐγερθήσεται ἔθνος ἐπὶ ἔθνος, καὶ
Then He said to them, will be raised Nation against nation, and

[11]Also there will be great earthquakes from place to place, and famines, and plagues. And also there will be terrors and great signs from Heaven. [12]But before all these things they will lay their hands on you, and will persecute *you,* delivering *you* into the synagogues and prisons, being led away before kings and governors on account of My name. [13]But it will return to you for a testimony. [14]Therefore, put into your hearts not to premeditate to make a defense. [15]For I will give you a mouth and wisdom, which those having been set against you will not be able to withstand or contradict. [16]But you will be betrayed also by parents, and brothers, and relatives, and friends. And they will put you to death. [17]And you will be hated by all because of My name. [18]And a hair of your head shall in no way perish. [19]By your patience you will gain your souls.

[20]And when you see Jerusalem being encircled by armies, then recognize that its destruction has come near. [21]Then let those in Judea flee into the mountains; and those in its midst, let them go out. And those in the open spaces, let them not go into her. [22]For these are days of vengeance *when* all things that have been written are to be fulfilled. [23]But woe to the pregnant women, and those suckling in those days; for great distress will be on the earth, and wrath on this people. [24]And they will fall by *the* mouth of *the* sword, and will be led captive to all the nations. And Jerusalem will be

932 1909 932 4578 5037 3173 2596 5117
11 βασιλεία ἐπὶ βασιλείαν· σεισμοί τε μεγάλοι κατὰ τόπους
kingdom against kingdom, earthquakes and great from place to place;
3042 3061 2071 5400 5037 4592 575
καὶ λιμοὶ καὶ λοιμοὶ ἔσονται, φόβητρά τε καὶ σημεῖα ἀπ'
and famines and plagues there will be; terrors both and signs from
3772 3173 2071 4253 5130 537 1911
12 οὐρανοῦ μεγάλα ἔσται. πρὸ δὲ τούτων ἁπάντων ἐπι-
Heaven great will be. before But these things all they
1909 5209 5495 848 1377 3860
βαλοῦσιν ἐφ' ὑμᾶς τὰς χεῖρας αὐτῶν, καὶ διώξουσι, παραδι-
will lay on you the hands of them, and will persecute, delivering
1519 4864 5438 71 1909 935
δόντες εἰς συναγωγὰς καὶ φυλακάς, ἀγομένους ἐπὶ βασιλεῖς
into the synagogues and prisons, being led away before kings
2232 1752 3686 3450 576
13 καὶ ἡγεμόνας, ἕνεκεν τοῦ ὀνόματός μου. ἀποβήσεται δὲ
and governors, on account of the name of Me. It will return But
5213 1519 3142 5087 3767 1519 2588 5216 3361
14 ὑμῖν εἰς μαρτύριον. θέσθε οὖν εἰς τὰς καρδίας ὑμῶν μὴ
to you for a testimony. put Therefore into the hearts of you not
4304 626 1473 1063 1325 5213 4750
15 προμελετᾶν ἀπολογηθῆναι· ἐγὼ γὰρ δώσω ὑμῖν στόμα καὶ
to premeditate to make a defense. I For will give you a mouth and
4678 3739 3756 1410 471 3761 436 3956
σοφίαν, ᾗ οὐ δυνήσονται ἀντειπεῖν οὐδὲ ἀντιστῆναι πάντες
wisdom, which not will be able to withstand nor contradict all
480 5213 3860 5259 1118
16 οἱ ἀντικείμενοι ὑμῖν. παραδοθήσεσθε δὲ καὶ ὑπὸ γονέων
those opposing you. you will be betrayed And also by parents
80 4773 5384 2289
καὶ ἀδελφῶν καὶ συγγενῶν καὶ φίλων, καὶ θανατώσουσιν
and brothers and relatives and friends, and they will execute
1537 5216 2071 3404 5259 3956 1223 3686
17 ἐξ ὑμῶν. καὶ ἔσεσθε μισούμενοι ὑπὸ πάντων διὰ τὸ ὄνομά
of you. And you will be hated by all because of the name
3450 2359 537 2776 5216 =3364= 622 1722
18 μου. καὶ θρὶξ ἐκ τῆς κεφαλῆς ὑμῶν οὐ μὴ ἀπόληται. ἐν τῇ
of Me. And a hair of the head of you in no way shall perish in the
5281 5216 2932 5590 5216
19 ὑπομονῇ ὑμῶν κτήσασθε τὰς ψυχὰς ὑμῶν.
patience of you, you will gain the souls of you.
3752 1492 2944 5259 4760
20 Ὅταν δὲ ἴδητε κυκλουμένην ὑπὸ στρατοπέδων τὴν
when And you see being encircled by armies
2419 5119 1097 3754 1448 2050 848
Ἱερουσαλήμ, τότε γνῶτε ὅτι ἤγγικεν ἡ ἐρήμωσις αὐτῆς
Jerusalem, then know that has come the ruin of it.
5119 1722 2449 5343 1519 3735 1722
21 τότε οἱ ἐν τῇ Ἰουδαίᾳ φευγέτωσαν εἰς τὰ ὄρη καὶ οἱ ἐν
Then those in Judea, let them flee into the mounts, and those in
3319 848 1633 1722 5561 3361 1525
μέσῳ αὐτῆς ἐκχωρείτωσαν· καὶ οἱ ἐν ταῖς χώραις μὴ εἰσερχέ-
midst of it, let them go out, and those in the open spaces not let them
1519 846 3754 2250 1557 3778 1526
22 σθωσαν εἰς αὐτήν. ὅτι ἡμέραι ἐκδικήσεως αὗταί εἰσι, τοῦ
enter into it. For days of vengenance these are.
4137 3956 1125 3759 1722 1064
23 πληρωθῆναι πάντα τὰ γεγραμμένα. οὐαὶ δὲ ταῖς ἐν γαστρὶ
to be fulfilled all the things having been written. woe But to the pregnant
2192 2337 1722 1565 2250
ἐχούσαις καὶ ταῖς θηλαζούσαις ἐν ἐκείναις ταῖς ἡμέραις·
women, and those giving suck in those days;
2071 2063 318 3173 1909 1092 3709 2992
ἔσται γὰρ ἀνάγκη μεγάλη ἐπὶ τῆς γῆς, καὶ ὀργὴ ἐν τῷ λαῷ
will be for distress great on the earth, and wrath on people
5129 4098 4750 3162 163
24 τούτῳ. καὶ πεσοῦνται στόματι μαχαίρας, καὶ αἰχμαλω-
this. And they will fall by (the) mouth of (the) sword, and will be led
1519 3956 1484 2419 2071
τισθήσονται εἰς πάντα τὰ ἔθνη· καὶ Ἱερουσαλὴμ ἔσται
captive to all the nations. And Jerusalem will be

[27]And then they will see the Son of man coming in a cloud with power and much glory. [28]But when these things begin to happen, stand up and lift up your heads, because your redemption draws near.

[29]And He spoke a parable to them: Watch the fig-tree and all the trees. [30]Now when they sprout leaves, seeing *it* you will know that now the summer is near. [31]So also when you see these things happening, you know that the kingdom of God is near. [32]Truly I say to you, In no way will this generation pass away until all *these* things occur. [33]The heaven and the earth will pass away, but My words in no way will pass away.

[34]But take heed to yourselves that your hearts not be loaded down with headaches, and drinking, and anxieties of life, and that trodden down by nations, until *the* times of *the* nations are fulfilled. [25]And there will be signs in sun and moon and stars. And on the earth *will be* anxiety of nations with bewilderment, roaring of sea and of surf, [26]men fainting at heart from fear, and expecting of the things which have come on the earth. For the powers of the heavens will be shaken. day come suddenly upon you [35]as a snare, for it will come in on all those sitting on *the* face of all the earth. [36]Then be watchful at every time, begging that you be counted worthy to escape all these things which are about to happen, and to stand before the Son of man.

[37]And *in* the days He was teaching in the temple. And *in* the nights going out, He

3961 5259 1484 891 4137 2540 1484
25 πατουμένη ὑπὸ ἐθνῶν, ἄχρι πληρωθῶσι καιροὶ ἐθνῶν. καὶ
trodden down by nations; until are fulfilled (the) times of nations. And
2071 4592 1722 2246 4582 798 1909
ἔσται σημεῖα ἐν ἡλίῳ καὶ σελήνῃ καὶ ἄστροις, καὶ ἐπὶ τῆς
will be signs in sun and moon and stars. And on the
1093 4928 1484 1722 640 2278 2281 4535
γῆς συνοχὴ ἐθνῶν ἐν ἀπορίᾳ, ἠχούσης θαλάσσης καὶ σάλου,
earth, anxiety of nations in perplexity of sound, of sea, and of surf,
674 444 575 5401 4329
26 ἀποψυχόντων ἀνθρώπων ἀπὸ φόβου καὶ προσδοκίας τῶν
fainting men from fear and expectation of the
1904 3625 1063 1411 3772
ἐπερχομένων τῇ οἰκουμένῃ· αἱ γὰρ δυνάμεις τῶν οὐρανῶν
things coming on the habitable earth; the for powers of the heavens
4531 5119 3700 5207 444
27 σαλευθήσονται. καὶ τότε ὄψονται τὸν υἱὸν τοῦ ἀνθρώπου
will be shaken. And then they will see the Son of man
2064 1722 3507 3326 1411 1391 4183 756
28 ἐρχόμενον ἐν νεφέλῃ μετὰ δυνάμεως καὶ δόξης πολλῆς. ἀρχο-
coming in a cloud with power and glory much. begin-
5130 1096 352 1869
μένων δὲ τούτων γίνεσθαι, ἀνακύψατε καὶ ἐπάρατε τὰς
ning And these things to happen, stand erect and lift up the
2776 5216 1360 1448 629 5216
κεφαλὰς ὑμῶν· διότι ἐγγίζει ἡ ἀπολύτρωσις ὑμῶν.
heads of you, because draws near the redemption of you.
2036 3850 846 1492 4808 3956
29 Καὶ εἶπε παραβολὴν αὐτοῖς, Ἴδετε τὴν συκῆν καὶ πάντα
And He told a parable to them: You see the fig-tree and all
1186 3752 4261 2235 991 575 1438
30 τὰ δένδρα· ὅταν προβάλωσιν ἤδη, βλέποντες ἀφ' ἑαυτῶν
the trees; when they sprout leaves now, seeing from yourselves
1097 3754 2235 1451 2330 2076 3779 5210
31 γινώσκετε ὅτι ἤδη ἐγγὺς τὸ θέρος ἐστίν. οὕτω καὶ ὑμεῖς,
you know that now near the summer is. So also you,
3752 1492 5023 1096 1097 3754 1451 2076
ὅταν ἴδητε ταῦτα γινόμενα, γινώσκετε ὅτι ἐγγύς ἐστιν ἡ
when you see these things occurring, know that near is the
932 2316 281 3004 5213 3754 =3364= 3928
32 βασιλεία τοῦ Θεοῦ. ἀμὴν λέγω ὑμῖν ὅτι οὐ μὴ παρέλθῃ ἡ
kingdom — of God. Truly I say to you that in no way will pass away
1074 3778 2193 302 3956 1096 3772 1093
33 γενεὰ αὕτη, ἕως ἂν πάντα γένηται. ὁ οὐρανὸς καὶ ἡ γῆ
generation this until shall all things occur. The heaven and the earth
3928 3056 3450 =3364= 3928
παρελεύσονται, οἱ δὲ λόγοι μου οὐ μὴ παρέλθωσι.
will pass away, the but words of Me in no way will pass away.
4337 1438 3779 925 5216
34 Προσέχετε δὲ ἑαυτοῖς, μήποτε βαρυνθῶσιν ὑμῶν αἱ
take heed And to yourselves, lest be loaded down of you the
2588 1722 2897 3178 3308 982
καρδίαι ἐν κραιπάλῃ καὶ μέθῃ καὶ μερίμναις βιωτικαῖς. καὶ
hearts in headaches and drinking and anxieties of life. And
160 1909 5209 2186 2250 1565 5613 3803 1063
35 αἰφνίδιος ἐφ' ὑμᾶς ἐπιστῇ ἡ ἡμέρα ἐκείνη· ὡς παγὶς γὰρ
come on you suddenly — day that; as a snare for
1904 1909 3956 2521 1909 4383
ἐπελεύσεται ἐπὶ πάντας τοὺς καθημένους ἐπὶ πρόσωπον
it will come in on all those sitting on (the) face
3956 1093 69 3767 1722 3956 2540 1189 2443
πάσης τῆς γῆς. ἀγρυπνεῖτε οὖν ἐν παντὶ καιρῷ δεόμενοι, ἵνα
of all the earth. you be watchful Then at every time, begging that
2661 1628 5023 3956 3195 1096
36 καταξιωθῆτε ἐκφυγεῖν ταῦτα πάντα τὰ μέλλοντα γίνεσθαι,
you be counted worthy to escape these all things being about to occur,
2476 1715 5207 444
καὶ σταθῆναι ἔμπροσθεν τοῦ υἱοῦ τοῦ ἀνθρώπου.
and to stand before the Son of man.
2258 2250 2411 1321 3571
37 Ἦν δὲ τὰς ἡμέρας ἐν τῷ ἱερῷ διδάσκων· τὰς δὲ νύκτας
He was And (in) the days in the Temple teaching, (in) the and nights

lodged in the Mount of Olives. 38 And all the people came early to Him in the temple, to hear Him.

CHAPTER 22

1 And the Feast of Unleavened *Bread*, being called Passover, drew near. 2 And the chief priests and the scribes sought how to destroy Him; for they feared the people.

3 And Satan entered into Judas, the *one* having been called Iscariot, being of the number of the Twelve. 4 And going, he talked with the chief priests and the commanders *as to* how he might betray Him. 5 And they exulted and they agreed to give him silver. 6 And he fully consented, and sought opportunity to betray Him to them, away from *the* crowd.

7 And the day of the Unleavened came, on which the passover must be killed. 8 And He sent Peter and John, saying, Going, prepare for us the passover, that we may eat. 9 And they said to Him, Where do You desire that we prepare? 10 And He said to them, Behold, you going into the city, you will meet a man carrying a pitcher of water. Follow him into the house where he goes in. 11 And you will say to the house-master, The Teacher says to you, Where is the guest-room where I may eat the passover with My disciples? 12 And he will show you a large upper room which *he* has spread. Prepare there. 13 And going they found as He had told them, and they prepared the passover.

14 And when the hour came, He reclined, and the twelve apostles with Him.

1831 835 1519 3735 2564 1636
38 ἐξερχόμενος ηὐλίζετο εἰς τὸ ὄρος τὸ καλούμενον ἐλαιῶν. καὶ
going out He lodged in the mountain being called of olives. And
3956 2992 3719 4314 846 2411 191 846
πᾶς ὁ λαὸς ὤρθριζε πρὸς αὐτὸν ἐν τῷ ἱερῷ ἀκούειν αὐτοῦ.
all the people came early to Him in the Temple to hear Him.

CHAPTER 22

1448 1859 106 3004 3957
1 Ἤγγιζε δὲ ἡ ἑορτὴ τῶν ἀζύμων, ἡ λεγομένη πάσχα.
drew near And the feast of the unleavened (bread), being called Passover.
2212 749 1122 4459 337
2 καὶ ἐζήτουν οἱ ἀρχιερεῖς καὶ οἱ γραμματεῖς τὸ πῶς ἀνέλωσιν
And sought the chief priests and the scribes – how to destroy
846 5399 1063 2992
αὐτόν· ἐφοβοῦντο γὰρ τὸν λαόν.
Him, they feared for the people.
1525 4567 1519 2455 1941
3 Εἰσῆλθε δὲ ὁ Σατανᾶς εἰς Ἰούδαν τον ἐπικαλούμενον
entered And Satan into Judas the (one) being called
2469 5607 1537 706 1427 565
4 Ἰσκαριώτην, ὄντα ἐκ τοῦ ἀριθμοῦ τῶν δώδεκα. καὶ ἀπελθὼν
Iscariot, being from the number of the twelve. And going
4814 749 4755 4459
συνελάλησε τοῖς ἀρχιερεῦσι καὶ τοις στρατηγοῖς τὸ πῶς
he talked with the chief priests and the captains (as to) how
846 3860 846 5463 4934 846
5 αὐτὸν παραδῷ αὐτοῖς. καὶ ἐχάρησαν, καὶ συνέθεντο αὐτῷ
he might betray Him. And they exulted, and they agreed him
694 1325 1843 2212 2120
6 ἀργύριον δοῦναι. καὶ ἐξωμολόγησε, καὶ ἐζήτει εὐκαιρίαν
silver to give. And he fully consented, and sought opportunity
3860 846 846 817 3793
τοῦ παραδοῦναι αὐτὸν αὐτοῖς ἄτερ ὄχλου.
to betray Him to them away from (the) crowd.
2064 2250 106 1722 3739 1163 2380 3957
7 Ἦλθε δὲ ἡ ἡμέρα τῶν ἀζύμων, ἐν ᾗ ἔδει θύεσθαι τὸ πασχα.
came And the day of the unleavened, on which must be the passover.
•2036 649 4074 2491 killed 4198
8 καὶ ἀπέστειλε Πέτρον καὶ Ἰωάννην, εἰπών, Πορευθέντες
And He sent Peter and John, saying, Going,
2090 2254 3957 2443 5315 2036 846
9 ἑτοιμάσατε ἡμῖν τὸ πάσχα, ἵνα φάγωμεν. οἱ δὲ εἶπον αὐτῷ,
prepare for us the passover, that we may eat. they And said to Him,
4226 2309 2090 2036 846 2400 1525
10 Ποῦ θέλεις ἑτοιμάσωμεν ; ὁ δὲ εἶπεν αὐτοῖς, Ἰδού, εἰσελθόντων
Where You desire we prepare? He And told them, Behold, going in
5216 1519 4172 4876 5213 444 2765
ὑμῶν εἰς τὴν πόλιν, συναντήσει ὑμῖν ἄνθρωπος κεράμιον
you into the city, will meet you a man a pitcher
5204 941 190 846 1519 3614 3757
ὕδατος βαστάζων· ἀκολουθήσατε αὐτῷ εἰς τὴν οἰκίαν οὗ
of water carrying. Follow him into the house where
1531 2046 3617 3614 3004
11 εἰσπορεύεται. καὶ ἐρεῖτε τῷ οἰκοδεσπότῃ τῆς οἰκίας, Λέγει
he goes in. And you will say to the house-master of the house, Says
4671 1320 4226 2076 2646 3699 3957
σοι ὁ διδάσκαλος, Ποῦ ἐστι τὸ κατάλυμα, ὅπου τὸ πάσχα
to you the Teacher, Where is the guest room where the passover
3326 3101 3450 5315 2548 5213 1166 508
12 μετὰ τῶν μαθητῶν μου φάγω ; κἀκεῖνος ὑμῖν δείξει ἀνώγεον
with the disciples of Me I may eat? And that one you will show an upper
3173 4766 1563 2090 565 214 room
13 μέγα ἐστρωμένον· ἐκεῖ ἑτοιμάσατε. ἀπελθόντες δὲ εὗρον
large having been spread; there prepare. going And they
2531 2046 846 2090 3957 found
καθὼς εἴρηκεν αὐτοῖς· καὶ ἡτοίμασαν τὸ πάσχα.
as He had told them, and they prepared the passover.
3753 1096 5610 377 1427 652
14 Καὶ ὅτε ἐγένετο ἡ ὥρα, ἀνέπεσε, καὶ οἱ δώδεκα ἀπόστολοι
And when came the hour, He reclined, and the twelve apostles

[15]And He said to them, With desire I desired to eat this passover with you before My suffering. [16]For I say to you that never in any way I will eat of it until it is fulfilled in the kingdom of God. [17]And taking a cup, giving thanks, He said, Take this and divide *it* among yourselves. [18]For I say to you that in no way will I drink from the produce of the vine until the kingdom of God has come. [19]And taking a loaf, giving thanks, He broke, and gave to them, saying, This is My body being given for you. Do this for My remembrance. [20]In the same way the cup also, after having supped, saying, This cup *is* the New Covenant in My blood, which is being poured out for you. [21]But, behold, the hand of My betrayer on the table with Me! [22] And, indeed, the Son of man goes according as was determined, but woe to that man by whom He is betrayed! [23]And they began to examine themselves who then it may be of them, the *one* being about to do this.

[24]And there was also a dispute among them, who of them seems to be greater. [25]And He said to them, The kings of the nations lord it over them, and the authorities over them are called benefactors.

[26]But you *be* not so, but the greater among you, let him be as the lesser; and the *one* governing as the *one* serving. [27]For who *is* greater, the *one* serving, or the *one* reclining. *Is it* not the *one* reclining? But I am in your midst as *One* serving. [28]But you are

4862 846 2036 4314 846 1939 1937 5124
15 σὺν αὐτῷ. καὶ εἶπε πρὸς αὐτούς, Ἐπιθυμίᾳ ἐπεθύμησα τοῦτο
with Him. And He said to them, With desire I desired this
3957 5315 3326 5216 4253 3165 3958 3004 1063
16 τὸ πάσχα φαγεῖν μεθ' ὑμῶν πρὸ τοῦ με παθεῖν· λέγω γὰρ
— passover to eat with you, before the Me to suffer. I say For
5213 3754 3765 =3364= 5315 1537 846 2193 3755 4137
ὑμῖν ὅτι οὐκέτι οὐ μὴ φάγω ἐξ αὐτοῦ, ἕως ὅτου πληρωθῇ ἐν
to you that never in any way I eat of it, until when it is fulfilled in
932 2316 1209 4221 2168
17 τῇ βασιλείᾳ τοῦ Θεοῦ. καὶ δεξάμενος ποτήριον, εὐχαριστή-
the kingdom of God. And taking a cup, having given thanks
2036 2983 5124 1260 1438 3004 1063
18 σας εἶπε, Λάβετε τοῦτο, καὶ διαμερίσατε ἑαυτοῖς· λέγω γὰρ
He said, Take this, and divide among you I say For
5213 3754=3364=4095 575 1081 288 2193
ὑμῖν ὅτι οὐ μὴ πίω ἀπὸ τοῦ γεννήματος τῆς ἀμπέλου, ἕως
to you that in no way I drink from the produce of the vine until
3755 932 2316 2064 2983 740 2168
19 ὅτου ἡ βασιλεία τοῦ Θεοῦ ἔλθῃ. καὶ λαβὼν ἄρτον, εὐχαριστή-
when the kingdom of God comes. And taking a loaf, having given
2806 1325 846 3004 5124 2076 4983
σας ἔκλασε, καὶ ἔδωκεν αὐτοῖς, λέγων, Τοῦτό ἐστι τὸ σῶμά
thanks, He broke, and gave to them, saying, This is the body
3450 5228 5216 1325 5124 4160 1519 1699
μου, τὸ ὑπὲρ ὑμῶν διδόμενον· τοῦτο ποιεῖτε εἰς τὴν ἐμὴν
of Me, — for you being given; this do for — My
364 5615 4221 3326 1172
20 ἀνάμνησιν. ὡσαύτως καὶ τὸ ποτήριον μετὰ τὸ δειπνῆσαι,
remembrance. In like manner And the cup after having supped,
3004 5124 4221 2537 1242 1722 129
λέγων, Τοῦτο τὸ ποτήριον ἡ καινὴ διαθήκη ἐν τῷ αἵματί
saying, This cup (is) the new covenant in the blood
3450 5228 5216 1632 4133 2400 5495
21 μου, τὸ ὑπὲρ ὑμῶν ἐκχυνόμενον πλὴν ἰδού, ἡ χεὶρ τοῦ
of Me, for you being poured out. But, behold, the hand of the
3860 3165 3326 1700 1909 5132 3303 5207
22 παραδιδόντος με μετ' ἐμοῦ ἐπὶ τῆς τραπέζης. καὶ ὁ μὲν υἱὸς
betrayer of Me with Me on the table. And, indeed the Son
444 4198 2596 3724 4133 3759
τοῦ ἀνθρώπου πορεύεται κατὰ τὸ ὡρισμένον· πλὴν οὐαὶ τῷ
— of man goes, according as was determined, but woe
444 1565 1223 3739 3860 846 756
23 ἀνθρώπῳ ἐκείνῳ δι' οὗ παραδίδοται. καὶ αὐτοὶ ἤρξαντο
man to that through whom He is betrayed! And they began
4802 4314 1438 5101 686 1498 1537 846 5124
συζητεῖν πρὸς ἑαυτοὺς τὸ τίς ἄρα εἴη ἐξ αὐτῶν ὁ τοῦτο
to examine with themselves who then it may be of them, he this
3195 4238
μέλλων πράσσειν.
being about to do.
1096 5379 1722 846 5101 846 1380
24 Ἐγένετο δὲ καὶ φιλονεικία ἐν αὐτοῖς τὸ τίς αὐτῶν δοκεῖ
there was And also a dispute among them, who of them seems
1511 3187 2036 846 935 1484
εἶναι μείζων. ὁ δὲ εἶπεν αὐτοῖς, Οἱ βασιλεῖς τῶν ἐθνῶν
to be greater. He And said to them, The kings of the nations
2961 846 1850 846 2110
25 κυριεύουσιν αὐτῶν, καὶ οἱ ἐξουσιάζοντες αὐτῶν εὐεργέται
lord it over them, and the authorities over them benefactors
2564 5210 3756 3779 235 3187 1722 5213
26 καλοῦνται. ὑμεῖς δὲ οὐχ οὕτως· ἀλλ' ὁ μείζων ἐν ὑμῖν
are called. you But not so, but the greater among you
1096 5613 3501 2233 5613 1247 5101
γενέσθω ὡς ὁ νεώτερος· καὶ ὁ ἡγούμενος ὡς ὁ διακονῶν. τίς
let him be as the lesser, and he governing as he serving. who
1063 3187 345 2228 1247 3780 345
27 γὰρ μείζων, ὁ ἀνακείμενος ἢ ὁ διακονῶν; οὐχὶ ὁ ἀνακεί-
For (is)greater, he reclining or he serving? (Is it) not he reclining?
1473 1510 1722 3319 5216 5613 1247 5210
28 μενος; ἐγὼ δέ εἰμι ἐν μέσῳ ὑμῶν ὡς ὁ διακονῶν. ὑμεῖς δέ
I But am in (the) midst of you as (one) serving. you But

those having continued with Me in My trials. 29And I appoint a kingdom to you, as My Father appointed to Me, 30that you may eat and drink at My table in My kingdom. And you will sit on thrones judging the twelve tribes of Israel.

31And the Lord said, Simon, Simon, behold! Satan asked for you, to sift *you* as wheat, 32but I prayed concerning you, that your faith might not fail. And when you have turned back, confirm your brothers. 33And he said to Him, Lord, I am ready to go both to prison and to death with You. 34And He said, Peter, I say to you, a cock will not crow today before you will deny knowing Me three times.

35And He said to them, When I sent you without a purse, or a wallet, or sandals, did you lack anything? And they said, Nothing. 36Then He said to them, But now the *one* having a purse, let him take *it*; likewise also a wallet. And the *one* not having, let him sell his garment and let him buy a sword. 37For I say to you that this that has been written must yet be fulfilled in Me, "And He was numbered with *the* lawless." For the things concerning Me also have an end. 38And they said, Lord, behold, here *are* two swords. And He said to them, It is enough.

39And going out, according to *His* custom, He went to the Mount of Olives; and His disciples also followed Him. 40And having come on the place, He said to them, Pray you *will* not

2075 1265 3326 1700 3986 3450
ἐστε οἱ διαμεμενηκότες μετ' ἐμοῦ ἐν τοῖς πειρασμοῖς μου·
are those having continued with Me in the temptation of Me;
2504 1303 5213 2531 1303 3450 3962 3450
29 κἀγὼ διατίθεμαι ὑμῖν, καθὼς διέθετό μοι ὁ πατήρ μου,
and I appoint to you, as appointed to Me the Father of Me
932 2443 2068 4095 1909 5132 3450
30 βασιλείαν, ἵνα ἐσθίητε καὶ πίνητε ἐπὶ τῆς τραπέζης μου
a kingdom, that you may eat and drink at the table of Me
1722 932 3450 2523 1909 2362 2919
ἐν τῇ βασιλείᾳ μου, καὶ καθίσησθε ἐπὶ θρόνων, κρίνοντες
in the kingdom of Me; and you will sit on thrones judging
1427 5443 2474 2036 2962 4613
31 τὰς δώδεκα φυλὰς τοῦ Ἰσραήλ. εἶπε δὲ ὁ Κύριος, Σίμων,
the twelve tribes of Israel. said And the Lord, Simon,
4613 2400 4567 1809 5209 4617 5613
Σίμων, ἰδού, ὁ Σατανᾶς ἐξῃτήσατο ὑμᾶς, τοῦ σινιάσαι ὡς
Simon, behold, — Satan asked for you — to sift (you) as
4621 1473 1189 4012 4675 2443 3361 1587 4102
32 τὸν σῖτον· ἐγὼ δὲ ἐδεήθην περὶ σοῦ, ἵνα μὴ ἐκλείπῃ ἡ πίστις
the wheat; I but entreated about you, that not might fail the faith
4675 4771 4218 1994 4741 80 4675
σου· καὶ σύ ποτε ἐπιστρέψας στήριξον τοὺς ἀδελφούς σου.
of you; and you when having turned confirm the brothers of you.
2036 846 2962 3326 4675 2092 1510 1519 5438
33 ὁ δὲ εἶπεν αὐτῷ, Κύριε, μετὰ σοῦ ἕτοιμός εἰμι καὶ εἰς φυλακὴν
he And said to him, Lord, with You prepared I am both to prison
1519 2288 4198 2036 3004 4675 4074 3756
34 καὶ εἰς θάνατον πορεύεσθαι. ὁ δὲ εἶπε, Λέγω σοι, Πέτρε, οὐ
and to death to go. He But said, I say to you, Peter, not
3361 5455 4594 220 4250 2228 5151 533 3361
μὴ φωνήσει σήμερον ἀλέκτωρ, πρὶν ἢ τρὶς ἀπαρνήσῃ μὴ
will sound today a cock before thrice you will deny —
1492 3165
εἰδέναι με.
knowing Me.
2036 846 3753 649 5209 817 905
35 Καὶ εἶπεν αὐτοῖς, Ὅτε ἀπέστειλα ὑμᾶς ἄτερ βαλαντίου καὶ
And He said to them, When I sent you without a purse and
4082 5266 3361 5100 5302 2036
πήρας καὶ ὑποδημάτων, μή τινος ὑστερήσατε; οἱ δὲ εἶπον,
a wallet and sandals, not anything you lacked? they And said,
3762 2036 3767 846 235 3568 2192 905
36 Οὐδενός. εἶπεν οὖν αὐτοῖς, Ἀλλὰ νῦν ὁ ἔχων βαλάντιον
Nothing. He said Then to them, But now he having a purse,
142 3668 4082 3361 2192 4453
ἀράτω, ὁμοίως καὶ πήραν· καὶ ὁ μὴ ἔχων, πωλησάτω τὸ
let him take; likewise also a wallet; and he not having, let him sell the
2440 848 59 3162 3004 1063 5213
37 ἱμάτιον αὐτοῦ, καὶ ἀγορασάτω μάχαιραν. λέγω γὰρ ὑμῖν
garment of him and let him buy a sword. I say For to you
3754 2089 5124 1125 1163 5055 1722 1698
ὅτι ἔτι τοῦτο τὸ γεγραμμένον δεῖ τελεσθῆναι ἐν ἐμοί, τὸ Καὶ
that yet this that has been written must be completed in Me: And
3326 459 3049 1063 4012 1700 5056 2192
μετὰ ἀνόμων ἐλογίσθη· καὶ γὰρ τὰ περὶ ἐμοῦ τέλος ἔχει. οἱ
with (the) lawless He was counted; also for that about Me an end has. they
2036 2962 2400 3162 5601 1417 2036 846
38 δὲ εἶπον, Κύριε, ἰδού, μάχαιραι ὧδε δύο. ὁ δὲ εἶπεν αὐτοῖς,
And said, Lord, behold, swords here (are) two. He And said to them,
2425 2076
Ἱκανόν ἐστι.
Enough it is.
1831 4198 2596 1485 1519 3735
39 Καὶ ἐξελθὼν ἐπορεύθη κατὰ τὸ ἔθος εἰς τὸ ὄρος τῶν
And going forth He went according to the custom to the mount of the
1636 190 846 3101 848 1096
ἐλαιῶν· ἠκολούθησαν δὲ αὐτῷ καὶ οἱ μαθηταὶ αὐτοῦ. γενό-
olives; followed and Him also the disciples of Him.
1909 5117 2036 846 4336 3361 1525
40 μενος δὲ ἐπὶ τοῦ τόπου, εἶπεν αὐτοῖς, Προσεύχεσθε μὴ εἰσελ-
coming And on the place, He said to them, Pray (you will) not enter

enter into temptation. [41]And He was withdrawn from them, about a stone's throw. And falling on *His* knees, He prayed, [42]saying, Father, if You will, take away this cup from Me; but let not My will be done, but Your *will*. [43]And an angel from Heaven appeared to Him, strengthening Him. [44]And being in an agony, He prayed more intently. And His sweat became as drops of blood falling down onto the earth. [45]And rising up from the prayer, coming to His disciples, He found them sleeping from grief. [46]And He said to them, Why do you sleep? Rising up, pray, that you do not enter into temptation. [47]And *as* He was yet speaking, behold, a crowd! And the *one* called Judas, one of the Twelve, came in front of them and drew near to Jesus to kiss Him. [48]And Jesus said to him, Judas, do you betray the Son of man with a kiss? [49]And those around Him seeing that about to occur, *they* said to Him, Lord, shall we strike with the sword?

[50]And a certain one of them struck the slave of the high priest, and cut off his right ear. [51]And answering Jesus said, Allow *it* until this. And touching his ear, He healed him.

[52]And Jesus said to those coming upon Him, chief priests, and commanders of the temple, and elders, Have you come out with swords and clubs as against a robber? [53]When I was with you day by day in the temple, you did not stretch out your hand on Me. But this is your hour, and the authority of the darkness.

1519 3986 846 645 575 846 5616
41 θεὶν εἰς πειρασμόν. καὶ αὐτὸς ἀπεσπάσθη ἀπ' αὐτῶν ὡσεὶ
into temptation. And He was withdrawn from them, about
3037 1000 5087 1119 4336 3004 3962
42 λίθου βολήν, καὶ θεὶς τὰ γόνατα προσηύχετο, λέγων, Πάτερ,
a stone's throw. And placing the knees, He prayed, saying, Father,
1487 1014 3911 4221 5124 575 1700 4133 3361
εἰ βούλει, παρένεγκε τὸ ποτήριον τοῦτο ἀπ' ἐμοῦ· πλὴν μὴ
If You will, take away — cup this from Me; but not
2307 3450 235 4674 1096 3700 846 32
43 τὸ θέλημά μου, ἀλλὰ τὸ σὸν γενέσθω. ὤφθη δὲ αὐτῷ ἄγγελος
the will of Me, but — of you let be. appeared And to Him an angel
575 3772 1765 846 1096 1722 74
44 ἀπ' οὐρανοῦ ἐνισχύων αὐτόν. καὶ γενόμενος ἐν ἀγωνίᾳ,
from Heaven strengthening Him. And becoming in an agony,
1617 4336 1096 2402 848 5616
ἐκτενέστερον προσηύχετο. ἐγένετο δὲ ὁ ἱδρὼς αὐτοῦ ὡσεὶ
more instantly He prayed. became And the sweat of Him as
2361 129 2597 1909 1093 450
45 θρόμβοι αἵματος καταβαίνοντες ἐπὶ τὴν γῆν. καὶ ἀναστὰς
drops of blood falling down onto the earth. And rising up
575 4335 2064 4314 3101 846
ἀπὸ τῆς προσευχῆς, ἐλθὼν πρὸς τοὺς μαθητὰς αὐτοῦ,
from the prayer, coming to the disciples of Him,
2147 846 2837 575 3077 2036 846
46 εὗρεν αὐτοὺς κοιμωμένους ἀπὸ τῆς λύπης, καὶ εἶπεν αὐτοῖς,
He found them sleeping from the grief, and said to them,
5101 2518 450 4336 2443 3361 1525
Τί καθεύδετε; ἀναστάντες προσεύχεσθε, ἵνα μὴ εἰσέλθητε
Why do you sleep? Rising up, pray, that not you enter
1519 3986
εἰς πειρασμόν.
into temptation.

2089 848 2980 2400 3793 3004
47 Ἔτι δὲ αὐτοῦ λαλοῦντος, ἰδού, ὄχλος, καὶ ὁ λεγόμενος
yet And Him speaking, behold, a crowd. And the (one) called
2455 1520 1427 4281 846 1448
Ἰούδας, εἷς τῶν δώδεκα, προήρχετο αὐτῶν. καὶ ἤγγισε τῷ
Judas, one of the twelve, came before them, and drew near to
2424 5368 846 2424 2036 846 2455
48 Ἰησοῦ φιλῆσαι αὐτόν. ὁ δὲ Ἰησοῦς εἶπεν αὐτῷ, Ἰούδα,
Jesus in order to kiss Him. But Jesus said to him, Judas,
5370 5207 444 3860 1497
49 φιλήματι τὸν υἱὸν τοῦ ἀνθρώπου παραδίδως; ἰδόντες δὲ οἱ
with a kiss the Son of man do you betray? seeing And those
4012 846 2071 2036 846 2962 1487 3960 1722
περὶ αὐτὸν τὸ ἐσόμενον εἶπον αὐτῷ, Κύριε, εἰ πατάξομεν ἐν
around him that about to occur said to Him, Lord, if we shall strike with
3162 3960 1520 5100 1535 846 1401
50 μαχαίρᾳ; καὶ ἐπάταξεν εἷς τις ἐξ αὐτῶν τὸν δοῦλον τοῦ
a sword? And struck a certain one of them of the slave of the
749 851 848 3775 1188 611
51 ἀρχιερέως, καὶ ἀφεῖλεν αὐτοῦ τὸ οὖς τὸ δεξιόν. ἀποκριθεὶς
high priest, and cut off of him the ear, the right. answering
2424 2036 1439 2193 5127 680
δὲ ὁ Ἰησοῦς εἶπεν, Ἐᾶτε ἕως τούτου. καὶ ἁψάμενος τοῦ
And Jesus said, Allow (it) until this. And touching the
5621 848 2390 846 2036 2424 4314
52 ὠτίου αὐτοῦ, ἰάσατο αὐτόν. εἶπε δὲ ὁ Ἰησοῦς πρὸς τοὺς
ear of him He cured him. said And Jesus to those
3854 1909 846 749 4755
παραγενομένους ἐπ' αὐτὸν ἀρχιερεῖς καὶ στρατηγοὺς τοῦ
coming upon Him, chief priests, and commanders of the
2411 4245 5613 1909 3027 1831 3326
ἱεροῦ καὶ πρεσβυτέρους, Ὡς ἐπὶ λῃστὴν ἐξεληλύθατε μετὰ
Temple, and elders: As against a robber did you come out with
3162 3586 2596 2250 5607 3450 3326 5216
53 μαχαιρῶν καὶ ξύλων; καθ' ἡμέραν ὄντος μου μεθ' ὑμῶν
swords and clubs? Day by day being Me with you
1722 2411 3756 1614 5495 1909 1691 235 3778
ἐν τῷ ἱερῷ, οὐκ ἐξετείνατε τὰς χεῖρας ἐπ' ἐμέ. ἀλλ' αὕτη
in the Temple, not you stretched the hand on Me. But this

[54]And laying hold of Him, they led Him away and led *Him* into the house of the high priest. And Peter followed at a distance. [55]And lighting a fire in *the* middle of the court, and they sitting down, Peter sat in their midst. [56]And a certain maidservant seeing him sitting near the light, and looking intently at him, *she* said, And this one was with him. [57]But he denied Him, saying, Woman, I do not know Him. [58]And after a while another seeing him said, You also are of them. But Peter said, Man, I am not. [59]And about an hour intervening, a certain other one boldly charged, saying, Truly this one also was with him, for he also is a Galilean. [60]And Peter said, Man, I do not know what you say. And immediately, while he yet spoke, the cock crowed.

[61]And turning, the Lord looked at Peter. And Peter remembered the word of the Lord, how He told him, Before a cock would crow, you will deny Me three times. [62]And going outside Peter wept bitterly.

[63]And the men who were holding Jesus mocked Him, beating *Him*. [64]And blindfolding Him, *they were* striking His face and questioning Him, saying, Prophesy, who is the *one* stinging you? [65]And many other things they said to Him, blaspheming.

[66]And when day came, the body of elders of the people, the chief priests and scribes, were gathered. And *they* led Him away into

5216 2076 5610 1849 4655
ὑμῶν ἐστιν ἡ ὥρα, καὶ ἡ ἐξουσία τοῦ σκότους.
your is — hour, and the authority of the darkness.

4815 846 71 1521 846
54 Συλλαβόντες δὲ αὐτὸν ἤγαγον, καὶ εἰσήγαγον αὐτὸν
having seized And Him, they led away, and brought Him

1519 3624 749 4074 190 3113
εἰς τὸν οἶκον τοῦ ἀρχιερέως. ὁ δὲ Πέτρος ἠκολούθει μακρόθεν.
into the house of the high priest. And Peter followed afar off.

681 4442 1722 3319 833 4776
55 ἁψάντων δὲ πῦρ ἐν μέσῳ τῆς αὐλῆς, καὶ συγκαθισάντων
lighting And a fire in (the) midst of the court, and sitting down

846 2521 4074 3319 846 1492 846
56 αὐτῶν, ἐκάθητο ὁ Πέτρος ἐν μέσῳ αὐτῶν. ἰδοῦσα δὲ αὐτὸν
they, sat Peter in (the) midst of them. seeing And him

3814 5100 2521 4314 5457 816 846
παιδίσκη τις καθήμενον πρὸς τὸ φῶς, καὶ ἀτενίσασα αὐτῷ,
maidservant a certain sitting near the light, and looking intently at him,

2036 3778 4862 846 2258 720 846 3004
57 εἶπε, Καὶ οὗτος σὺν αὐτῷ ἦν. ὁ δὲ ἠρνήσατο αὐτόν, λέγων,
said, And this one with him was. he But denied Him, saying,

1135 3756 1492 846 3326 1024 2087 1492 846
58 Γύναι, οὐκ οἶδα αὐτόν. καὶ μετὰ βραχὺ ἕτερος ἰδὼν αὐτὸν
Woman, not I know Him. And after a while another seeing him

5346 4771 1537 846 1488 4074 2036 444 3756
ἔφη, Καὶ σὺ ἐξ αὐτῶν εἶ. ὁ δὲ Πέτρος εἶπεν, Ἄνθρωπε, οὐκ
said, And you of them are. But Peter said, Man, not

1510 1339 5616 5610 3391 243 5100 1340
59 εἰμί. καὶ διαστάσης ὡσεὶ ὥρας μιᾶς, ἄλλος τις διϊσχυρίζετο,
I am. And intervening about hour one, other a certain boldly charged,

3004 1909 225 3778 3326 846 2258 1063
λέγων, Ἐπ' ἀληθείας καὶ οὗτος μετ' αὐτοῦ ἦν· καὶ γὰρ
saying, In truth also this one with him was, also for

1057 2076 2036 4074 444 3756 1492 3739
60 Γαλιλαῖός ἐστιν. εἶπε δὲ ὁ Πέτρος, Ἄνθρωπε, οὐκ οἶδα ὃ
a Galilean he is. said And Peter, Man, not I know what

3004 3916 2089 2980 846 5455
λέγεις. καὶ παραχρῆμα, ἔτι λαλοῦντος αὐτοῦ, ἐφώνησεν ὁ
you say. And immediately, yet speaking him, sounded the

220 4762 2962 1689 4074
61 ἀλέκτωρ. καὶ στραφεὶς ὁ Κύριος ἐνέβλεψε τῷ Πέτρῳ. καὶ
cock. And turning the Lord looked at — Peter. And

5279 4074 3056 2962 5613 2036 846
ὑπεμνήσθη ὁ Πέτρος τοῦ λόγου τοῦ Κυρίου, ὡς εἶπεν αὐτῷ
remembered Peter the word of the Lord, as He told him,

3754 4260 220 5455 533 3165 5151 1831
62 ὅτι Πρὶν ἀλέκτορα φωνῆσαι, ἀπαρνήσῃ με τρίς. καὶ ἐξελθὼν
Before a cock would sound, you will deny Me thrice. And going

1854 4074 2799 4090
ἔξω ὁ Πέτρος ἔκλαυσε πικρῶς.
outside Peter wept bitterly.

435 4912 2424 1702 846
63 Καὶ οἱ ἄνδρες οἱ συνέχοντες τὸν Ἰησοῦν ἐνέπαιζον αὐτῷ,
And the men having in charge Jesus mocked Him,

1194 4028 846 5180 848
64 δέροντες. καὶ περικαλύψαντες αὐτόν, ἔτυπτον αὐτοῦ τὸ
beating (Him). And blindfolding Him, striking of Him the

4383 1905 846 3004 4395
πρόσωπον, καὶ ἐπηρώτων αὐτόν, λέγοντες, Προφήτευσον·
face, and questioned Him, saying, Prophesy,

5101 2076 3817 4571 2087 4183 987
65 τίς ἐστιν ὁ παίσας σε; καὶ ἕτερα πολλὰ βλασφημοῦντες
who is the (one) stinging you? And other things many, blaspheming,

3004 1519 846
ἔλεγον εἰς αὐτόν.
they said to Him.

5610 1096 2250 4863 4244
66 Καὶ ὡς ἐγένετο ἡμέρα, συνήχθη τὸ πρεσβυτέριον τοῦ
And when came day, was assembled the body of elders of the

2992 749 5037 1122 321 846 1519
λαοῦ, ἀρχιερεῖς τε καὶ γραμματεῖς, καὶ ἀνήγαγον αὐτὸν εἰς
people, chief priests and scribes, and led away Him to

their sanhedrin, saying, [67]If you are the Christ, tell us. And He said to them, If I tell you, you will in no way believe. [68]And also if I ask, in no way will you answer Me, or let Me go. [69]From now on the Son of man will be sitting at the right *hand* of the power of God. [70]And they all said, Then are you the Son of God? And He said, You say *it*, because I AM! [71]And they said, Why do we yet have need of witness? For we ourselves heard *it* from his mouth.

4192 1438 3004 1487 4771 1488 5547 2036
67 τὸ συνέδριον ἑαυτῶν, λέγοντες, Εἰ σὺ εἶ ὁ Χριστός, εἰπὲ
the sanhedrin of themselves, saying, If you are the Christ, tell
2254 2036 846 1437 5213 2036 =3364= 4100
ἡμῖν. εἶπε δὲ αὐτοῖς, Ἐὰν ὑμῖν εἴπω, οὐ μὴ πιστεύσητε·
us. He said And to them, If you I tell, in no way will you believe.
1437 2065 =3364= 611 3427 630
68 ἐὰν δὲ καὶ ἐρωτήσω, οὐ μὴ ἀποκριθῆτέ μοι, ἢ ἀπολύσητε.
if And also I ask, in no way you will answer Me, or let Me go.
575 3568 2071 5207 444 2521 1537
69 ἀπὸ τοῦ νῦν ἔσται ὁ υἱὸς τοῦ ἀνθρώπου καθήμενος ἐκ
From now will be the Son of man sitting at
1188 1411 2316 2036 3956 4771 3767 1488
70 δεξιῶν τῆς δυνάμεως τοῦ Θεοῦ. εἶπον δὲ πάντες, Σὺ οὖν εἶ ὁ
the right of the power of God. they said And all, You, then, are the,
5207 2316 4314 846 5346 5210 3014 3754 1473
υἱὸς τοῦ Θεοῦ; ὁ δὲ πρὸς αὐτοὺς ἔφη, Ὑμεῖς λέγετε ὅτι ἐγώ
Son of God? He And to them said, You say (it), because I
1510 2036 5101 2089 5532 2192 3141 846 1063
71 εἰμι. οἱ δὲ εἶπον, Τί ἔτι χρείαν ἔχομεν μαρτυρίας; αὐτοὶ γὰρ
am. they And said, Why yet have we need of witness? ourselves For
191 575 4750 848
ἠκούσαμεν ἀπὸ τοῦ στόματος αὐτοῦ.
we heard from the mouth of Him.

CHAPTER 23

[1]And rising up, all the multitude of them led Him before Pilate. [2]And they began to accuse Him, saying, We found this one perverting the nation, and forbidding to give tribute to Caesar, saying himself to be a king, Christ. [3]And Pilate questioned Him, saying, Are you the king of the Jews? And answering him, He said, You say *it*. [4]And Pilate said to the chief priests and the crowd, I find nothing blameable in this man. [5]But they insisted, saying, He stirs up the people, teaching throughout all Judea, beginning from Galilee to here. [6]And hearing Galilee, Pilate asked if the man is a Galilean. [7]And knowing that He is from Herod's jurisdiction, he sent Him up to Herod, he also being in Jerusalem in these days. [8]And seeing Jesus, Herod greatly rejoiced; for he was wishing to see Him

450 537 4128 846 71 846 1909
1 Καὶ ἀναστὰν ἅπαν τὸ πλῆθος αὐτῶν, ἤγαγεν αὐτὸν ἐπὶ
And rising up all the multitude of them led him before
4091 756 2723 846 3004
2 τὸν Πιλάτον. ἤρξαντο δὲ κατηγορεῖν αὐτοῦ, λέγοντες,
– Pilate. they began And to accuse Him, saying,
5126 2147 1294 1484 2967 2541
Τοῦτον εὕρομεν διαστρέφοντα τὸ ἔθνος, καὶ κωλύοντα Καί-
This one we found perverting the nation, and forbidding to
5411 1325 3004 1438 5547 935 1511
σαρι φόρους διδόναι, λέγοντα ἑαυτὸν Χριστὸν βασιλέα εἶναι.
Caesar tribute to give, saying himself Christ a king to be.
4091 1905 846 3004 4771 1488 935
3 ὁ δὲ Πιλάτος ἐπηρώτησεν αὐτόν, λέγων, Σὺ εἶ ὁ βασιλεὺς
– And Pilate questioned Him, saying, you Are the king
2453 611 846 5346 4771 3004
4 τῶν Ἰουδαίων; ὁ δὲ ἀποκριθεὶς αὐτῷ ἔφη, Σὺ λέγεις. ὁ δὲ
of the Jews? He And answering him said, You say (it). And
4091 2036 4314 749 3793 3762
Πιλάτος εἶπε πρὸς τοὺς ἀρχιερεῖς καὶ τοὺς ὄχλους, Οὐδὲν
Pilate said to the chief priests and the crowds, Nothing
2147 158 444 5129 2001
5 εὑρίσκω αἴτιον ἐν τῷ ἀνθρώπῳ τούτῳ. οἱ δὲ ἐπίσχυον,
I find blameable in man this. they But insisted,
3004 3754 383 2992 1321 2596 3650
λέγοντες ὅτι Ἀνασείει τὸν λαόν, διδάσκων καθ' ὅλης τῆς
saying, He stirs up the people, teaching throughout all
2449 756 575 1056 2193 5602 4091
6 Ἰουδαίας, ἀρξάμενος ἀπὸ τῆς Γαλιλαίας ἕως ὧδε. Πιλάτος δὲ
Judea, beginning from Galilee to here. Pilate And
191 1056 1905 1487 444 1057
ἀκούσας Γαλιλαίαν ἐπηρώτησεν εἰ ὁ ἄνθρωπος Γαλιλαῖός
hearing Galilee, (he) asked if the man a Galilean
2076 1921 3754 1537 1849 2264 2076 375
7 ἐστι. καὶ ἐπιγνοὺς ὅτι ἐκ τῆς ἐξουσίας Ἡρώδου ἐστίν, ἀνέ-
is. And having known that from the jurisdiction of Herod He is, he
846 4314 2264 5607 846 2414
πεμψεν αὐτὸν πρὸς Ἡρώδην, ὄντα καὶ αὐτὸν ἐν Ἱεροσολύ-
sent up Him to Herod, being also him in Jerusalem
1722 5025 2250
μοις ἐν ταύταις ταῖς ἡμέραις.
in these – days.
2264 1492 2424 5463 3029 2258 1063
8 Ὁ δὲ Ἡρώδης ἰδὼν τὸν Ἰησοῦν ἐχάρη λίαν ἦν γὰρ
And Herod seeing Jesus rejoiced greatly; he was for

for a long *time*, because of hearing many things about Him. And he hoped to see some miracle brought about by Him. 9And he questioned Him in many words. But He answered him not a thing. 10And the chief priests and the scribes stood fiercely accusing Him. 11And having humiliated Him with his guardsmen, and mocking Him *by* putting luxurious clothing around *Him*, Herod sent Him back to Pilate. 12And on that same day both Pilate and Herod became friends with each other—for before they were at enmity *between* themselves.

13And having called together the chief priests and the rulers and the people, 14Pilate said to them, You brought this man to me as perverting the people. And, behold, examining him before you I found nothing blameable in this man *regarding that* which you charge against him. 15But neither did Herod; for I sent you up to him; and, behold, nothing worthy of death is done by him. 16Therefore, chastising him, I will release *him*. 17And he had to release to them one at *the* Feast. 18And they all together shouted, saying, Take this one, and release Barabbas to us—19*he* who was thrown into prison due to some revolt and murder occurring in the city.

20Then Pilate again called out, desiring to release Jesus. 21But they shouted, saying, Crucify! Crucify him! 22And a third *time* he said to them, For what evil did this

2309 1537 2425 1492 846 1223 191 4183 4012
θέλων ἐξ ἱκανοῦ ἰδεῖν αὐτόν, διὰ τὸ ἀκούειν πολλὰ περὶ
wishing of a long (time) to see Him, because of hearing many things abou
846 1679 5100 4592 1492 5259 846 1096
αὐτοῦ· καὶ ἤλπιζέ τι σημεῖον ἰδεῖν ὑπ' αὐτοῦ γινομενον.
Him. And he hoped some sign to see by Him brought about
1905 846 3056 2425 846 3762 611
9 ἐπηρώτα δὲ αὐτὸν ἐν λόγοις ἱκανοῖς· αὐτὸς δὲ οὐδὲν ἀπεκρί-
questioned And Him in words many. He But nothing
846 2476 749 1122
10 νατο αὐτῷ. εἱστήκεισαν δὲ οἱ ἀρχιερεῖς καὶ οἱ γραμματεῖς,
answered him. stood And the chief priests and the scribes
2159 2723 846 1848 846
εὐτόνως κατηγοροῦντες αὐτοῦ. ἐξουθενήσας δὲ αὐτὸν ὁ
vehemently accusing Him. having humiliated And Him,
2264 4862 4753 848 1702
11 Ἡρώδης σὺν τοῖς στρατεύμασιν αὐτοῦ, καὶ ἐμπαίξας,
Herod with the soldiery of him, and mocking
4016 846 2066 2986 375 846
περιβαλὼν αὐτὸν ἐσθῆτα λαμπράν, ἀνέπεμψεν αὐτὸν τῷ
putting around Him clothing luxurious, sent back Him
4091 1096 5384 3739 5037 4091 2264 1722
12 Πιλάτῳ. ἐγένοντο δὲ φίλοι ὅ τε Πιλάτος καὶ ὁ Ἡρώδης ἐν
to Pilate. became And friends both Pilate and Herod on
846 2250 3326 240 4391 1063 1722 2189
αὐτῇ τῇ ἡμέρᾳ μετ' ἀλλήλων· προϋπῆρχον γὰρ ἐν ἔχθρᾳ
same the day with each other; they before for in enmity
5607 4314 1438
ὄντες πρὸς ἑαυτούς.
being with themselves.
4091 4779 749 758
13 Πιλάτος δὲ συγκαλεσάμενος τοὺς ἀρχιερεῖς καὶ τοὺς ἄρχον
Pilate And calling together the chief priests and the leade
2992 2036 4314 846 4374 3427
14 τας καὶ τὸν λαόν, εἶπε πρὸς αὐτούς, Προσηνέγκατέ μοι τὸν
and the people, said to them, You brought to me
444 5126 5613 654 2992 2400
ἄνθρωπον τοῦτον, ὡς ἀποστρέφοντα τὸν λαόν· καὶ ἰδού,
man this, as perverting the people, and beho
1473 1799 5216 350 3762 2147 1722 444
ἐγὼ ἐνώπιον ὑμῶν ἀνακρίνας οὐδὲν εὗρον ἐν τῷ ἀνθρώπῳ
I before you examining nothing found in man
5129 158 3756 2723 2596 846 235 3761
15 τούτῳ αἴτιον ὧν κατηγορεῖτε κατ' αὐτοῦ· ἀλλ' οὐδ
this blameable of which you bring charge against him. But neithe
2265 375 1063 5209 4314 846 2400 3762
Ἡρώδης· ἀνέπεμψα γὰρ ὑμᾶς πρὸς αὐτόν, καὶ ἰδού, οὐδὲ
(did) Herod; I sent up for you to him, and, behold, nothi
514 2288 2076 4238 846 3811 376
16 ἄξιον θανάτου ἐστὶ πεπραγμένον αὐτῷ. παιδεύσας οὖ
worthy of death is done by him. Having chastised, th
846 630 318 2192 630 846 2596
17 αὐτὸν ἀπολύσω. ἀνάγκην δὲ εἶχεν ἀπολύειν αὐτοῖς κατ
him I will release. need And he had to release to them a
1859 1520 349 3826 3004 142 5126
18 ἑορτὴν ἕνα. ἀνέκραξαν δὲ παμπληθεί, λέγοντες, Αἶρε τοῦτον
(the) feast one. they shouted And, all enmass, saying, Take this one
630 2254 912 3748 2258 1223 4714 5100
ἀπόλυσον δὲ ἡμῖν τὸν Βαραββᾶν· ὅστις ἦν διὰ στάσιν τινὰ
release and to us Barabbas; who was due to revolt some
1096 4172 5408 906 1519 5438
19 γενομένην ἐν τῇ πόλει καὶ φόνον βεβλημένος εἰς φυλακήν
occurring in the city, and murder, thrown into prison.
3825 3767 4091 4377 2309 630
20 πάλιν οὖν ὁ Πιλάτος προσεφώνησε, θέλων ἀπολῦσαι τὸ
again Then Pilate called (to them), desiring to release
2424 2019 3004 4717 4717
21 Ἰησοῦν. οἱ δὲ ἐπεφώνουν, λέγοντες, Σταύρωσον, σταύρωσο
Jesus. they But shouted, saying, Crucify! Crucify
846 5154 2036 4314 846 5101 1063 2556 4160
22 αὐτόν. ὁ δὲ τρίτον εἶπε πρὸς αὐτούς, Τί γὰρ κακὸν ἐποίησε
him! he But a third said to them, what For evil did

one do? I found no cause of
death in him. Therefore,
chastising him, I will re-
ease *him*. [23]But with loud
voices they insisted, asking
or Him to be crucified. And
heir voices, and *that* of the
chief priests, prevailed.

[24]And Pilate adjudged their
equest to be done. [25]And
e released to them *the one*
hrown into prison due to
evolt and murder, whom
hey asked. But he de-
ivered Jesus to their will.

[26]And as they led Him
way, having laid hold on a
ertain Simon, a Cyrenian,
oming from a field, they
ut the cross on him, to
ear *it* behind Jesus.

[27]And a great multitude
f people were following
im, and of women who
so were bewailing and
menting Him. [28]And turn-
g to them, Jesus said,
aughters of Jerusalem, do
ot weep over Me, but
eep over yourselves and
ver your children. [29]For
ehold, days will come in
hich they will say, Blessed
e the barren, and the
ombs that did not bear,
d breasts that did not
ckle. [30]Then they will
gin to say to the
ountains, Fall on us! And
the hills, Cover us! [31]For
hey do these things in the
een tree, what may take
ace in the dry?

[32]And two others, two
iminals, were led with
m to be put to death.

[33]And when they came
the place being called
ull, they crucified Him
d the criminals there, one
the right, and one on *the*
t. [34]And Jesus said,

3778 3762 158 2288 2147 1722 846 3811 3767
οὗτος ; οὐδὲν αἴτιον θανάτου εὗρον ἐν αὐτῷ· παιδεύσας οὖν
this one? nothing cause of death I found in him; chastising, then,
846 630 1945 5456 3173 154
23 αὐτὸν ἀπολύσω. οἱ δὲ ἐπέκειντο φωναῖς μεγάλαις, αἰτού-
him I will release. they But insisted voices with great, asking
846 4717 2729 5456 846
μενοι αὐτὸν σταυρωθῆναι· καὶ κατίσχυον αἱ φωναὶ αὐτῶν
for Him to be crucified. And prevailed the voices of them
749 4091 1948 1096 155
24 καὶ τῶν ἀρχιερέων. ὁ δὲ Πιλάτος ἐπέκρινε γενέσθαι τὸ αἴτημα
and of the chief priests. And Pilate adjudged to be done the request
848 630 846 1223 4714 5408 906
25 αὐτῶν ἀπέλυσε δὲ αὐτοῖς τὸν διὰ στάσιν καὶ φόνον βεβλη-
of them. he released And to them (him) due to revolt and murder had been
1519 5438 3739 154 2424 3860
μένον εἰς τὴν φυλακήν, ὃν ἠτοῦντο· τὸν δὲ Ἰησοῦν παρέδωκε
thrown into the prison, whom they asked; but Jesus he delivered
2307 848
τῷ θελήματι αὐτῶν.
to the will of them.
5613 520 846 1949 4613 5100
26 Καὶ ὡς ἀπήγαγον αὐτόν, ἐπιλαβόμενοι Σίμωνός τινος
And as they led away Him, having laid hold on Simon a certain
2956 2064 575 68 2007 846
Κυρηναίου τοῦ ἐρχομένου ἀπ᾽ ἀγροῦ, ἐπέθηκαν αὐτῷ τὸν
a Cyrenian coming from a field, they put on him the
4716 5342 3693 2424
σταυρόν, φέρειν ὄπισθεν τοῦ Ἰησοῦ.
cross to bear (it) behind Jesus.
190 846 4183 4128 3992 1135
27 Ἠκολούθει δὲ αὐτῷ πολὺ πλῆθος τοῦ λαοῦ, καὶ γυναικῶν
were following And Him a much multitude of the people, and of women
2875 2354 846 4762 4314
28 αἳ καὶ ἐκόπτοντο καὶ ἐθρήνουν αὐτόν. στραφεὶς δὲ πρὸς
who also were bewailing and lamenting Him. turning And to
846 2424 2036 2364 2419 3361 2799
αὐτὰς ὁ Ἰησοῦς εἶπε, Θυγατέρες Ἱερουσαλήμ, μὴ κλαίετε
them Jesus said, Daughters of Jerusalem, not do weep
1909 1691 4133 1909 1438 2799 1909 5043 5216 3754
29 ἐπ᾽ ἐμέ, πλὴν ἐφ᾽ ἑαυτὰς κλαίετε καὶ ἐπὶ τὰ τέκνα ὑμῶν. ὅτι
over Me, but over yourselves weep, and over the children of you. For,
2400 2064 2250 1722 3739 2046 3107 4723
ἰδού, ἔρχονται ἡμέραι ἐν αἷς ἐροῦσι, Μακάριαι αἱ στεῖραι,
behold, will come days in which they will say, Blessed the barren,
2836 3739 3756 1080 3149 3756 2337
καὶ κοιλίαι αἳ οὐκ ἐγέννησαν, καὶ μαστοὶ οἳ οὐκ ἐθήλασαν.
and the wombs which not did bear, and breasts that not did give suck.
5119 756 3004 3735 4098 1909 2248
30 τότε ἄρξονται λέγειν τοῖς ὄρεσι, Πέσετε ἐφ᾽ ἡμᾶς· καὶ τοῖς
Then they will begin to say to the mountains, Fall on us! And to the
1015 2572 2248 3754 1487 1722 5200 3586 5023
31 βουνοῖς, Καλύψατε ἡμᾶς. ὅτι εἰ ἐν τῷ ὑγρῷ ξύλῳ ταῦτα
hills, Cover us, because if in the sappy tree these things
4160 1722 3584 5101 1096
ποιοῦσιν, ἐν τῷ ξηρῷ τί γένηται ;
they do, in the dry what may occur?
71 2087 1417 2557 4862 846 337
32 Ἤγοντο δὲ καὶ ἕτεροι δύο κακοῦργοι σὺν αὐτῷ ἀναι-
were led And also others, two criminals, with Him to be
ρεθῆναι.
executed.
3753 565 1909 5117 2563 2898
33 Καὶ ὅτε ἀπῆλθον ἐπὶ τὸν τόπον τὸν καλούμενον Κρανίον,
And when they came upon the place being called Skull,
1563 4717 846 2557 3739 3303 1537
ἐκεῖ ἐσταύρωσαν αὐτόν, καὶ τοὺς κακούργους, ὃν μὲν ἐκ
there they crucified Him, and the criminals, one on
1188 3739 1537 710 2424 3004 3962 863
34 δεξιῶν, ὃν δὲ ἐξ ἀριστερῶν. ὁ δὲ Ἰησοῦς ἔλεγε, Πάτερ, ἄφες
(the) right, and one on (the) left. – And Jesus said, Father, forgive

Father, forgive them, for they do not know what they are doing. And dividing His garments, they cast a lot. [35]And the people stood watching. And the rulers also *were* with them, scoffing, saying, He saved others; let him save himself, if this one is the Christ, the elect of God.

[36]And coming near the soldiers also mocked Him, and *were* offering vinegar [37]and saying, If you are the king of the Jews, save yourself. [38]And also a superscription was written over Him, in Greek and Latin and Hebrew letters: THIS IS THE KING OF THE JEWS

[39]And one of the hanged criminals blasphemed Him, saying, If you are the Christ, save yourself and us. [40]But answering, the other rebuked him, saying, Do you not fear God, for *you* are in the same judgment? [41]And we indeed justly, for we receive things worthy of what we did. But this One did nothing wrong. [42]And he said to Jesus, Lord, remember me when You come in Your kingdom. [43]And Jesus said to him, Truly I say to you, Today you will be with Me in Paradise.

[44]And it was about *the* sixth hour, and darkness came over all the land until *the* ninth hour. [45]And the sun was darkened; and the veil of the temple was torn in the middle. [46]And crying with a loud voice, Jesus said, Father, into Your hands I commit My spirit. And saying this, He breathed out the spirit.

[47]And seeing the thing happening, the centurion glorified God, saying, Truly, this Man was righteous.

846 3756 1063 1492 5101 4160 1266
αὐτοῖς· οὐ γὰρ οἴδασι τί ποιοῦσι. διαμεριζόμενοι δὲ τ
them, not for they know what they are doing. dividing And t
2440 848 906 2819 2476 2992 2334
35 ἱμάτια αὐτοῦ, ἔβαλον κλῆρον. καὶ εἱστήκει ὁ λαὸς θεωρῶν
garments of Him, they cast lots. And stood the people watching
1592 758 4862 846 3004
ἐξεμυκτήριζον δὲ καὶ οἱ ἄρχοντες σὺν αὐτοῖς, λέγοντες
scoffed And also the rulers with them, saying
243 4982 4982 1438 1487 3778 2076 5547
Ἄλλους ἔσωσε, σωσάτω ἑαυτόν, εἰ οὗτός ἐστιν ὁ Χριστός, ὁ
Others he saved, let him save himself, if this one is the Christ, the
2316 1588 1702 846 4757
36 τοῦ Θεοῦ ἐκλεκτός. ἐνέπαιζον δὲ αὐτῷ καὶ οἱ στρατιῶται
of God elect. mocked And Him also the soldiers,
4334 3690 4374 846 3004
37 προσερχόμενοι καὶ ὄξος προσφέροντες αὐτῷ, καὶ λέγοντες
having come near and vinegar offering to Him, and saying
•1488 1487 4775 • 935 2453 4982 4572 2258
38 Εἰ σὺ εἶ ὁ βασιλεὺς τῶν Ἰουδαίων, σῶσον σεαυτόν. ἦν δὲ κα
If you are the king of the Jews, save yourself. was And al
1923 1125 1909 846 1121 1673
ἐπιγραφὴ γεγραμμένη ἐπ' αὐτῷ γράμμασιν Ἑλληνικοῖς κα
an epigraph written over Him in letters Greek an
4513 1444 3778 2076 935
Ῥωμαϊκοῖς καὶ Ἑβραϊκοῖς, Οὗτός ἐστιν ὁ βασιλεὺς τῶν
Latin and Hebrew, THIS IS THE KING OF TH
2453
Ἰουδαίων.
JEWS.

1520 2910 2557 987 846
39 Εἷς δὲ τῶν κρεμασθέντων κακούργων ἐβλασφήμει αὐτό
one And of the hanged criminals blasphemed Him,
•1488 3004 1487 4775 • 5547 4982 4572 2248 611
λέγων, Εἰ σὺ εἶ ὁ Χριστός, σῶσον σεαυτὸν καὶ ἡμᾶς. ἀπο
saying, If you are the Christ, save yourself and us.
2087 2008 846 3004 3761 5399 4771
40 κριθεὶς δὲ ὁ ἕτερος ἐπετίμα αὐτῷ, λέγων, Οὐδὲ φοβῇ σὺ τὸ
answering But the other rebuked him, saying, Do not fear you
2316 3756 1722 846 2917 1488 2249 3303 1346 514
41 Θεόν, ὅτι ἐν τῷ αὐτῷ κρίματι εἶ; καὶ ἡμεῖς μὲν δικαίως, ἄξι
God, because in the same judgment are? And we indeed justly, thing
1063 3739 4238 618 3778 3762 824 worth
γὰρ ὧν ἐπράξαμεν ἀπολαμβάνομεν· οὗτος δὲ οὐδὲν ἄτοπο
for of what we did we receive. this One But nothing amis
4038 3004 2424 3415 3450 2962 375
42 ἔπραξε. καὶ ἔλεγε τῷ Ἰησοῦ, Μνήσθητί μου, Κύριε, ὅτα
did. And he said — to Jesus, Remember me, Lord, when
2064 932 4675 2036 846 2424 281
43 ἔλθῃς ἐν τῇ βασιλείᾳ σου. καὶ εἶπεν αὐτῷ ὁ Ἰησοῦς, Ἀμὴ
You come in the kingdom of You., And said to him Jesus, Truly
3004 4671 4594 3326 1700 2071 3857
λέγω σοι, σήμερον μετ' ἐμοῦ ἔσῃ ἐν τῷ παραδείσῳ.
I say to you, Today with Me you will be in Paradise.
2258 5616 5610 1622 4655 1096 1909 1650
44 Ἦν δὲ ὡσεὶ ὥρα ἕκτη, καὶ σκότος ἐγένετο ἐφ' ὅλην τὴ
it was And about hour sixth, and darkness came over all the
1093 2193 5610 1766 4654 2246 4977
45 γῆν ἕως ὥρας ἐννάτης. καὶ ἐσκοτίσθη ὁ ἥλιος, καὶ ἐσχίσθη τ
land, until hour ninth, and was darkened the sun, and was torn th
2665 3485 3319 5455 5456 3173
46 καταπέτασμα τοῦ ναοῦ μέσον. καὶ φωνήσας φωνῇ μεγάλῃ
veil of the Temple in two. And crying with a voice grea
2424 2036 3962 1519 5495 4675 3908 4151
Ἰησοῦς εἶπε, Πάτερ, εἰς χεῖράς σου παραθήσομαι τὸ πνεῦμ
Jesus said, Father, into the hands of You I commit the spi
3650 5023 2036 1606 1492 1543
47 μου· καὶ ταῦτα εἰπὼν ἐξέπνευσεν. Ἰδὼν δὲ ὁ ἑκατόνταρχ
of Me. And this saying, He breathed out seeing And, the centurio
•2316 1096 1392 the Spirit. 3004 3689 444
τὸ γενόμενον ἐδόξασε τὸν Θεός, λέγων, Ὄντως ὁ ἄνθρωπ
the thing happening glorified God, saying, Truly man

3778 1342 2258 3956 4836 3793
48 οὗτος δίκαιος ἦν. καὶ πάντες οἱ συμπαραγενόμενοι ὄχλοι
this righteous was. And all the having arrived together crowd
1909 2335 5026 2334 1096 5180
ἐπὶ τὴν θεωρίαν ταύτην, θεωροῦντες τὰ γενόμενα, τύπτοντες
at sight this, watching the things occurring, beating
1438 4738 5290 2476 3956
49 ἑαυτῶν τὰ στήθη ὑπέστρεφον. εἱστήκεισαν δὲ πάντες οἱ
of themselves the breasts, returned. stood And all those
1110 846 3113 1135 4870
γνωστοὶ αὐτοῦ μακρόθεν, καὶ γυναῖκες αἱ συνακολουθήσασαι
known to Him afar off, and women, those accompanying
846 575 1056 3708 5023
αὐτῷ ἀπὸ τῆς Γαλιλαίας, ὁρῶσαι ταῦτα.
Him from Galilee, seeing these things.
2400 435 3686 2501 1010 5225
50 Καὶ ἰδού, ἀνὴρ ὀνόματι Ἰωσήφ, βουλευτὴς ὑπάρχων
And behold, a man by name Joseph, a councillor being,
435 18 1342 3778 3756 2258 4783
ἀνὴρ ἀγαθὸς καὶ δίκαιος (οὗτος οὐκ ἦν συγκατατεθειμένος
a man good and righteous; this one not was agreeing with
1012 4234 848 575 707 4172
51 τῇ βουλῇ καὶ τῇ πράξει αὐτῶν), ἀπὸ Ἀριμαθαίας πόλεως
the counsel and the action of them; from Arimathea a city
2453 3739 4327 848 932
τῶν Ἰουδαίων, ὃς καὶ προσεδέχετο καὶ αὐτὸς τὴν βασιλείαν
of the Jews, who and was eagerly expecting also himself kingdom
2316 3778 4334 4091 154 4983
52 τοῦ Θεοῦ· οὗτος προσελθὼν τῷ Πιλάτῳ ᾐτήσατο τὸ σῶμα
of God; this one coming near to Pilate asked the body
2424 2507 846 1794 846 4616
53 τοῦ Ἰησοῦ. καὶ καθελὼν αὐτὸ ἐνετύλιξεν αὐτὸ σινδόνι, καὶ
of Jesus. And taking down it, he wrapped it in linen, and
5087 846 1722 3418 2991 3739 3756 2258 2764 3762
ἔθηκεν αὐτὸ ἐν μνήματι λαξευτῷ, οὗ οὐκ ἦν οὐδέπω οὐδεὶς
placed it in a tomb hewn, where not was no one not yet
2749 2250 2258 3904 4521 2020
54 κείμενος. καὶ ἡμέρα ἦν Παρασκευή, καὶ σάββατον ἐπέφωσκε.
laid. And day it was of preparation, and a sabbath was coming on.
2628 1135 3748 2258 4905
55 κατακολουθήσασαι δὲ καὶ γυναῖκες, αἵτινες ἦσαν συνεληλυ-
following And also women, who were accompanying
846 1537 1056 2300 3419 5613
θυῖαι αὐτῷ ἐκ τῆς Γαλιλαίας, ἐθεάσαντο τὸ μνημεῖον, καὶ ὡς
Him out of Galilee, watched the tomb, and how
5087 4983 848 5290 2090 759
56 ἐτέθη τὸ σῶμα αὐτοῦ. ὑποστρέψασαι δὲ ἡτοίμασαν ἀρώ-
was placed the body of Him. returning And prepared
3464
ματα καὶ μύρα.
spices and ointment.

CHAPTER 24

3303 4521 2270 2596 1785
1 Καὶ τὸ μὲν σάββατον ἡσύχασαν κατὰ τὴν ἐντολήν. τῇ δὲ
And (on) the indeed sabbath they rested according to the command. the But
3391 4521 3722 901 2064 1909 3418
μιᾷ τῶν σαββάτων, ὄρθρου βαθέος, ἦλθον ἐπὶ τὸ μνῆμα,
one of the week, while still very early, they came on the tomb,
5342 3739 2090 759 5100 4862 846 2147
2 φέρουσαι ἃ ἡτοίμασαν ἀρώματα, καί τινες σὺν αὐταῖς. εὗρον
carrying which they prepared spices, and some with them. they found
3037 617 575 3419
3 δὲ τὸν λίθον ἀποκεκυλισμένον ἀπὸ τοῦ μνημείου. καὶ
And the stone having been rolled away from the tomb. And
1525 3756 2147 4983 2962 2424
4 εἰσελθοῦσαι οὐχ εὗρον τὸ σῶμα τοῦ Κυρίου Ἰησοῦ. καὶ
going in not they found the body of the Lord Jesus. And
1096 1722 1280 846 4012 5127 2400
ἐγένετο ἐν τῷ διαπορεῖσθαι αὐτὰς περὶ τούτου, καὶ ἰδού,
It was in the perplexing (of) them about this; and behold,

48 And all the crowd arriving
together at this sight,
watching the things hap-
pening, beating their
breasts, *they* returned.
49 And all those known to
Him stood at a distance,
and *the* women, those who
accompanied Him from
Galilee, *were* seeing these
things.
50 And, behold, a man
named Joseph, being a
councillor, a good and
righteous man; 51 this one
was not assenting to their
counsel and deed—*he was*
from Arimathea, a city of the
Jews, and who himself was
eagerly expecting the kingdom of God— 52 coming
near to Pilate, this one
asked the body of Jesus.
53 And taking it down, he
wrapped it in linen, and
placed it in a quarried tomb,
where no one was ever yet
laid. 54 And it was Prep-
aration Day, and a sabbath
was coming on.
55 And also women *were*
following, who were ac-
companying Him out of
Galilee, *who* watched the
tomb, and how His body
was placed. 56 And returning, *they* prepared spices
and ointment.
And they remained quiet
on the sabbath, according
to the commandment.

CHAPTER 24

1 But *on* the indeed sabbath, while still very early,
they came on the tomb,
carrying spices which they
prepared; and some *were*
with them. 2 And they
found the stone having
been rolled away from the
tomb. 3 And going in, they
did not find the body of the
Lord Jesus. 4 And it hap-
pened, *as* they *were* perplexed about this, even

behold, two men in shining clothing stood by them.

5 And they becoming terrified, and bowing *their* faces to the earth, they said to them, Why do you seek the living with the dead? 6 He is not here, but was raised. Remember how He spoke to you, yet being in Galilee, 7 saying, The Son of man must be delivered into the hands of sinful men, and to be crucified, and the third day to rise again. 8 And they remembered His words.

9 And returning from the tomb, they reported all these things to the Eleven, and to all the rest. 10 And they were Mary Magdalene, and Joanna, and Mary *mother* of James, and the rest with them, who told these things to the apostles. 11 And their words seemed like foolishness to them, and they did not believe them. 12 But rising up, Peter ran to the tomb, and stooping down he saw the linen lying alone. And *he* went away wondering to himself *at what* had happened.

13 And, behold, two of them were going on the same day to a village being sixty furlongs distant from Jerusalem, which *was* named Emmaus. 14 And they talked to each other about all these things taking place. 15 And it happened, *as* they talked and reasoned, coming near Jesus Himself traveled with them. 16 But their eyes were held *so as* not to recognize Him. 17 And He said to them, What words *are* these which you exchange with each other *while*

1417 435 2186 846 1722 2067 797
δύο ἄνδρες ἐπέστησαν αὐταῖς ἐν ἐσθήσεσιν ἀστραπτούσαις·
two men stood by them in clothing shining.
1719 1096 846 2827 4383
5 ἐμφόβων δὲ γενομένων αὐτῶν, καὶ κλινουσῶν τὸ πρόσωπον
terrified And becoming them, and bending the faces
1519 1093 2036 4314 846 5101 2212 2198 332
εἰς τὴν γῆν, εἶπον πρὸς αὐτάς, Τί ζητεῖτε τὸν ζῶντα μετὰ
to the earth, they said to them, Why seek you the Living One with
3498 3756 2076 5602 235 1453 3415 561
6 τῶν νεκρῶν; οὐκ ἔστιν ὧδε, ἀλλ' ἠγέρθη· μνήσθητε ὡς
the dead ones? not He is here, but was raised. Remember how
1722 2980 5213 3208 5607 * 1056 3004 3754 1163 5207
7 ἐλάλησεν ὑμῖν, ἔτι ὢν ἐν τῇ Γαλιλαίᾳ, λέγων ὅτι δεῖ τὸν υἱὸν
He spoke to you, yet being in — Galilee, saying, that must the Son
444 3860 1519 5495 444 268
τοῦ ἀνθρώπου παραδοθῆναι εἰς χεῖρας ἀνθρώπων ἁμαρτω-
— of man be delivered into (the) hands men of sinfu
4717 5154 2250 450
λῶν, καὶ σταυρωθῆναι, καὶ τῇ τρίτῃ ἡμέρᾳ ἀναστῆναι.
and to be crucified, and the third day to rise aga
3415 4487 848 5290
8 καὶ ἐμνήσθησαν τῶν ῥημάτων αὐτοῦ, καὶ ὑποστρέψασαι
And they remembered the words of Him, and returning
575 3419 518 5023 3956 1733
9 ἀπὸ τοῦ μνημείου, ἀπήγγειλαν ταῦτα πάντα τοῖς ἕνδεκα
from the tomb reported these things all to the eleven,
3956 3062 2258 3094 3137
10 καὶ πᾶσι τοῖς λοιποῖς. ἦσαν δὲ ἡ Μαγδαληνὴ Μαρία καὶ
and to all the rest. they were And the Magdalene Mary, and
2489 3137 2385 3062 4862 846 373
Ἰωάννα καὶ Μαρία Ἰακώβου, καὶ αἱ λοιπαὶ σὺν αὐταῖς, αἳ
Joanna, and Mary of James, and the rest with them, who
3004 4314 652 5023 5316 1799
11 ἔλεγον πρὸς τοὺς ἀποστόλους ταῦτα. καὶ ἐφάνησαν ἐνώπιον
told to the apostles these things. And seemed before
846 5616 3026 4487 848 569 846
αὐτῶν ὡσεὶ λῆρος τὰ ῥήματα αὐτῶν, καὶ ἠπίστουν αὐταῖς
them as folly the words of them, and they disbelieved them
4074 450 5143 1909 3419 3879
12 ὁ δὲ Πέτρος ἀναστὰς ἔδραμεν ἐπὶ τὸ μνημεῖον, καὶ παρα-
And Peter having arisen ran to the tomb, and stooping
991 3608 2749 3441 565 4314
κύψας βλέπει τὰ ὀθόνια κείμενα μόνα· καὶ ἀπῆλθε πρὸς
down he sees the linen lying alone, and went away to
1438 2296 1096
ἑαυτὸν θαυμάζων τὸ γεγονός.
himself wondering (at what) had happened.
2400 1417 1537 846 2258 4198 1722 846
13 Καὶ ἰδού, δύο ἐξ αὐτῶν ἦσαν πορευόμενοι ἐν αὐτῇ τῇ
And behold, two of them were going on same the
2250 1519 2968 568 4712 1835 575
ἡμέρᾳ εἰς κώμην ἀπέχουσαν σταδίους ἑξήκοντα ἀπὸ
day to a village being distant furlongs sixty from
2419 3739 3686 1695 846 3656 4314
14 Ἰερουσαλήμ, ᾗ ὄνομα Ἐμμαούς. καὶ αὐτοὶ ὡμίλουν πρὸς
Jerusalem, to which name Emmaus; and they talked to
240 4012 3956 4819 5130
15 ἀλλήλους περὶ πάντων τῶν συμβεβηκότων τούτων. καὶ
each other about all having happened these things. And
1096 1722 3656 846 4802 846
ἐγένετο ἐν τῷ ὁμιλεῖν αὐτοὺς καὶ συζητεῖν, καὶ αὐτὸς ὁ
it was, in the talking (of) them and discussing, even Himself,
2424 1448 4848 846 3788 848
16 Ἰησοῦς ἐγγίσας συνεπορεύετο αὐτοῖς. οἱ δὲ ὀφθαλμοὶ αὐτῶν
Jesus, coming near traveled with them. the And eyes of them
2902 3361 1921 846 2036 4314 846
17 ἐκρατοῦντο τοῦ μὴ ἐπιγνῶναι αὐτόν. εἶπε δὲ πρὸς αὐτούς,
were held — not to recognize Him. He said And to them,
5101 3056 3778 3739 474 4314 240
Τίνες οἱ λόγοι οὗτοι οὓς ἀντιβάλλετε πρὸς ἀλλήλους
What — words these which you exchange with each other

walking, and are sad of
face? 18And answering, one
of them whose name *was*
Cleopas, said to Him, *Are*
you only a stranger in Jerusalem, and do not know the
things happening in it in
these days? 19And He said
to them, What things? And
they said to Him, The things
concerning Jesus the Nazarene, who was a man, a
prophet mighty in deed and
word before God and all the
people, 20how both the
chief priests and our rulers
delivered Him to *the*
judgment of death, and
crucified Him. 21But we
were hoping that He is the
One going to redeem Israel.
But then with all these
things, this third day comes
today since these things
happened. 22And also some
of our women astounded
us, having been early at the
tomb, 23and not finding His
body, *they* came saying to
have seen a vision of angels
also, who say Him to be
alive. 24And some of those
with us went to the tomb,
and found *it* so, even as the
women also said; but they
did not see Him. 25And He
said to them, O fools, and
slow of heart to believe on
all things which the
prophets spoke! 26Was it
not necessary for the Christ
to suffer these things, and
to enter into His glory?

27And beginning from
Moses, and from all the
prophets, He explained to
them all the Scriptures, the
things about Himself.
28And they drew near to
the village where they were
going, and He seemed to
be going further. 29And
they constrained Him, saying, Stay with us, for it is
toward evening, and the

4043 2075 4659 611 1519 3739
18 περιπατοῦντες, καί ἐστε σκυθρωποί ; ἀποκριθεὶς δὲ ὁ εἷς, ᾧ
(while) walking, and are downcast? answering And one, whose
3686 2810 2036 4314 846 4771 3441 3939 1722
ὄνομα Κλεόπας, εἶπε πρὸς αὐτόν, Σὺ μόνος παροικεῖς ἐν
name (was) Cleopas, said to Him, (Are) you only a stranger in
2419 3756 1097 1096 1722 846 1722
Ἱερουσαλήμ, καὶ οὐκ ἔγνως τὰ γενόμενα ἐν αὐτῇ ἐν ταῖς
Jerusalem, and not know the things occurring in it in —
2250 5025 2036 846 4169 2036 846
19 ἡμέραις ταύταις ; καὶ εἶπεν αὐτοῖς, Ποῖα ; οἱ δὲ εἶπον αὐτῷ
days these? And He said to them, What? they And said to Him,
4012 2424 3480 3739 1096 435 4396
Τὰ περὶ Ἰησοῦ τοῦ Ναζωραίου, ὃς ἐγένετο ἀνὴρ προφήτης
The things about Jesus the Nazarene, who was a man, a prophet
1415 1722 2014 3056 1726 2316 3956
δυνατὸς ἐν ἔργῳ καὶ λόγῳ ἐναντίον τοῦ Θεοῦ καὶ παντὸς
powerful in work and word before — God and all
2992 3704 5037 3860 846 749
20 τοῦ λαοῦ· ὅπως τε παρέδωκαν αὐτὸν οἱ ἀρχιερεῖς καὶ οἱ
the people, how both delivered Him the chief priests and the
758 2257 1519 2917 2288 4717 846
ἄρχοντες ἡμῶν εἰς κρίμα θανάτου, καὶ ἐσταύρωσαν αὐτόν.
rulers of us to (the) judgment of death, and crucified Him.
2249 1679 3754 846 2076 3195 3084
21 ἡμεῖς δὲ ἠλπίζομεν ὅτι αὐτός ἐστιν ὁ μέλλων λυτροῦσθαι τὸν
we But were hoping that He is the (One) going to redeem —
2474 235 1065 4862 3956 5125 5154 5026 2250
Ἰσραήλ. ἀλλά γε σὺν πᾶσι τούτοις τρίτην ταύτην ἡμέραν
Israel. But with all these things third this day
71 4594 575 3739 5023 1096 235 1135 5100
22 ἄγει σήμερον ἀφ' οὗ ταῦτα ἐγένετο. ἀλλὰ καὶ γυναῖκές τινες
comes today since these things occurred. But also women some
1537 2257 1839 2248 1096 3721 1909 3419
ἐξ ἡμῶν ἐξέστησαν ἡμᾶς, γενόμεναι ὄρθριαι ἐπὶ τὸ μνημεῖον·
of us astounded us, being early at the tomb,
3361 2147 4983 848 2064 3004 3701
23 καὶ μὴ εὑροῦσαι τὸ σῶμα αὐτοῦ, ἦλθον λέγουσαι καὶ ὀπτα-
and not finding the body of Him, came saying also a vision
32 3708 3004 846 2198 565
24 σίαν ἀγγέλων ἑωρακέναι, οἳ λέγουσιν αὐτὸν ζῆν. καὶ ἀπ-
of angels to have seen, who say Him to live. And
5100 4862 2254 1909 3419 2147 3779
ῆλθόν τινες τῶν σὺν ἡμῖν ἐπὶ τὸ μνημεῖον, καὶ εὗρον οὕτω
went some of those with us to the tomb, and found so
2531 1135 2036 846 3756 1492 846
25 καθὼς καὶ αἱ γυναῖκες εἶπον· αὐτὸν δὲ οὐκ εἶδον. καὶ αὐτὸς
as also the women said; Him but not they saw. And He
2036 4314 846 5599 453 1021 2588
εἶπε πρὸς αὐτούς, Ὦ ἀνόητοι καὶ βραδεῖς τῇ καρδίᾳ τοῦ
said to them, O fools and slow — in heart —
4100 1909 3956 3739 2980 4396 3780 5023
26 πιστεύειν ἐπὶ πᾶσιν οἷς ἐλάλησαν οἱ προφῆται· οὐχὶ ταῦτα
to believe on all things which spoke the prophets! Not these things
1163 3958 5547 1525 1519 1391 848
ἔδει παθεῖν τὸν Χριστόν, καὶ εἰσελθεῖν εἰς τὴν δόξαν αὐτοῦ ;
must suffer the Christ, and to enter into the glory of Him?
756 575 3475 575 3956 4396
27 καὶ ἀρξάμενος ἀπὸ Μωσέως καὶ ἀπὸ πάντων τῶν προφητῶν,
And beginning from Moses and from all the prophets,
1329 846 1722 3956 1124 4012 1438
διηρμήνευεν αὐτοῖς ἐν πάσαις ταῖς γραφαῖς τὰ περὶ ἑαυτοῦ.
He intepreted to them in all the Scriptures that about Himself.
1448 1519 2968 3757 4198 846
28 καὶ ἤγγισαν εἰς τὴν κώμην οὗ ἐπορεύοντο· καὶ αὐτὸς
And they drew near to the village where they were going, and He
4364 4208 4198 3849
29 προσεποιεῖτο πορρωτέρω πορεύεσθαι. καὶ παρεβιάσαντο
appeared further to be going. And they constrained
846 3004 3306 3326 2257 3754 4314 2073 2076
αὐτόν, λέγοντες, Μεῖνον μεθ' ἡμῶν, ὅτι πρὸς ἑσπέραν ἐστί,
Him, saying, Stay with us, because toward evening it is,

day has declined. And He went in to stay with them. [30]And it happened *as* He reclined with them, taking the loaf, He blessed; and breaking He gave to them. [31]And their their eyes were opened, and they knew Him. And He became invisible from them. [32]And they said to one another, Was not our heart burning in us as He spoke to us in the highway, and as He opened up to us the Scriptures? [33]And rising up in the same hour, they went back to Jerusalem, and *they* found the Eleven, and those with them, having been gathered, [34]saying, The Lord really was raised, and appeared to Simon. [35]And they related the things in the highway, and how He was known to them in the breaking of the loaf.

2827 2250 1525 3306 4862 846
30 καὶ κέκλικεν ἡ ἡμέρα. καὶ εἰσῆλθε τοῦ μεῖναι σὺν αὐτοῖς. καὶ
and has declined the day. And He went in to stay with them. And
1096 1722 2625 846 3326 846 2983
ἐγένετο ἐν τῷ κατακλιθῆναι αὐτὸν μετ' αὐτῶν, λαβὼν τὸν
it was, in the reclining (of) Him with them, taking the
740 2127 2806 1929 846 846
31 ἄρτον εὐλόγησε, καὶ κλάσας ἐπεδίδου αὐτοῖς. αὐτῶν δὲ
loaf He blessed, and breaking He gave to them. of them And
1272 3788 1921 846
διηνοίχθησαν οἱ ὀφθαλμοί, καὶ ἐπέγνωσαν αὐτόν· καὶ
were opened the eyes, and they remembered Him. And
846 855 1096 575 846 2036 4314 240
32 αὐτὸς ἄφαντος ἐγένετο ἀπ' αὐτῶν. καὶ εἶπον πρὸς ἀλλή-
He invisible became from them. And they said to each
3780 2588 2257 2545 2258 1722 2254 5613 2980
λους, Οὐχὶ ἡ καρδία ἡμῶν καιομένη ἦν ἐν ἡμῖν, ὡς ἐλάλει
other, Not the heart of us burning was in us as He spoke
2254 1722 3598 5613 1272 2254 1124
ἡμῖν ἐν τῇ ὁδῷ, καὶ ὡς διήνοιγεν ἡμῖν τὰς γραφάς; καὶ
to us in the way, and as He opened up to us the Scriptures? And
450 846 5610 5290 1519 2419
33 ἀναστάντες αὐτῇ τῇ ὥρᾳ ὑπέστρεψαν εἰς Ἱερουσαλήμ, καὶ
rising up same in the hour they returned to Jerusalem, and
2147 4867 1733 4862 846
εὗρον συνηθροισμένους τοὺς ἕνδεκα καὶ τοὺς σὺν αὐτοῖς,
found, having been gathered, the eleven and those with them,
3004 3754 1453 2962 3689 3700 4613
34 λέγοντας ὅτι Ἠγέρθη ὁ Κύριος ὄντως, καὶ ὤφθη Σίμωνι. καὶ
35 saying, was raised the Lord really, and appeared to Simon. And
846 1834 1722 3598 5613 1097 846
αὐτοὶ ἐξηγοῦντο τὰ ἐν τῇ ὁδῷ, καὶ ὡς ἐγνώσθη αὐτοῖς ἐν
they related the things in the way, and how He was known to them in
2800 740
τῇ κλάσει τοῦ ἄρτου.
the breaking of the loaf.

[36]And as they were telling these things, Jesus Himself stood in their midst, and said to them, Peace to you! [37]But being terrified and filled with fear, they thought they saw a spirit. [38]And He said to them, Why are you troubled? And why do reasonings come up in your hearts. [39]See My hands and My feet, that I am He? Feel Me and see, because a spirit does not have flesh and bones, as you see Me having. [40]And saying this, He showed them *His* hands and feet. [41]But yet they not believing from the joy, and marveling, He said to them, Have you any food here? [42]And they handed a broiled part of a fish to Him, and from a honeycomb. [43]And taking *these* before them, He ate.

5023 846 2980 846 2424 2476 1722
36 Ταῦτα δὲ αὐτῶν λαλούντων, αὐτὸς ὁ Ἰησοῦς ἔστη ἐν
these things And them saying, Himself, Jesus, stood in
3319 846 3004 846 1515 5213 4422
37 μέσῳ αὐτῶν, καὶ λέγει αὐτοῖς, Εἰρήνη ὑμῖν. πτοηθέντες δὲ
(the) midst of them, and says to them, Peace to you. terrified But
1719 1096 1380 4151 2334 2036
38 καὶ ἔμφοβοι γενόμενοι ἐδόκουν πνεῦμα θεωρεῖν. καὶ εἶπεν
and filled with fear being, they thought a spirit they beheld. And He said,
846 5101 5015 2075 1302 1261
αὐτοῖς, Τί τεταραγμένοι ἐστέ; καὶ διατί διαλογισμοὶ
to them, Why troubled are you? And why do reasonings
305 1722 2588 5216 1492 5495 3450
39 ἀναβαίνουσιν ἐν ταῖς καρδίαις ὑμῶν; ἴδετε τὰς χεῖράς μου
come up in the hearts of you? See the hands of Me
4228 3450 3754 846 1473 1510 5584 3165
καὶ τοὺς πόδας μου, ὅτι αὐτὸς ἐγώ εἰμι· ψηλαφήσατέ με καὶ
and the feet of Me, that He I am. Feel Me and
1492 3754 4151 4561 3747 3756 2192 2531 1691
ἴδετε, ὅτι πνεῦμα σάρκα καὶ ὀστέα οὐκ ἔχει, καθὼς ἐμὲ
see, because a spirit flesh and bones not has, as Me
2334 2192 5124 2036 1925 846
40 θεωρεῖτε ἔχοντα. καὶ τοῦτο εἰπὼν ἐπέδειξεν αὐτοῖς τὰς
you behold having. And this having said, He showed to them the
5495 4228 2089 569 846 575
41 χεῖρας καὶ τοὺς πόδας. ἔτι δὲ ἀπιστούντων αὐτῶν ἀπὸ τῆς
hands and the feet. yet And disbelieving them from the
5479 2296 2036 846 2192 5100 1034
χαρᾶς καὶ θαυμαζόντων, εἶπεν αὐτοῖς, Ἔχετέ τι βρώσιμον
joy and marveling, He said to them, Have you any food
1759 1929 846 2486 3702 3313 575
42 ἐνθάδε, οἱ δὲ ἐπέδωκαν αὐτῷ ἰχθύος ὀπτοῦ μέρος, καὶ ἀπὸ
here? they And handed to Him of a fish broiled part, and from
3193 2781 2983 1799 846 5315
43 μελισσίου κηρίου. καὶ λαβὼν ἐνώπιον αὐτῶν ἔφαγεν.
a honey-comb. And taking before them, He ate.

[44]And He said to them, These *are* the words which I spoke to you, yet being with you, that must be fulfilled, all the things having been written in the Law of Moses, and the Prophets, and the Psalms, concerning Me. [45]Then He opened up their mind to understand the Scriptures, [46]and said to them, So it has been written, and so it was necessary that the Christ should suffer, and to rise from *the* dead the third day; [47]and repentance and forgiveness of sins should be preached on His name to all the nations, beginning at Jerusalem. [48]And you are witnesses of these things. [49]And, behold, I send forth the promise of My Father on you. But you sit in the city of Jerusalem until you are clothed with power from on high.

[50]And He led them out as far as to Bethany. And lifting up His hands, He blessed them. [51]And it happened *as* He blessed them, He withdrew from them, and was carried into Heaven.

[52]And worshiping Him, they returned to Jerusalem with great joy. [53]And *they* were continually in the temple, praising and blessing God. Amen.

2036 846 3778 3056 3739 2980 4314 5209
44 Εἶπε δὲ αὐτοῖς, Οὗτοι οἱ λόγοι, οὓς ἐλάλησα πρὸς ὑμᾶς
He said And to them, These words which I spoke to you,
2089 • 4862 5213 3754 1163 4137 3956 1125
•5607 ἔτι ὢν σὺν ὑμῖν, ὅτι δεῖ πληρωθῆναι πάντα τὰ γεγραμμένα
yet being with you, that must be fulfilled all the things being written
1722 3551 3475 4396 5568 4012 1700
ἐν τῷ νόμῳ Μωσέως καὶ προφήταις καὶ ψαλμοῖς περὶ ἐμοῦ.
in the law of Moses and (the) prophets and Psalms, about Me.
5119 1272 848 3563 4920 1124
45 τότε διήνοιξεν αὐτῶν τὸν νοῦν, τοῦ συνιέναι τὰς γραφάς·
Then He opened up of them the mind — to understand the Scriptures;
2036 846 3754 3779 1125 3779 1163 3958
46 καὶ εἶπεν αὐτοῖς ὅτι Οὕτω γέγραπται, καὶ οὕτως ἔδει παθεῖν
and said to them, — Thus it is written, and thus must suffer
5547 450 1537 3498 5154 2250
τὸν Χριστόν, καὶ ἀναστῆναι ἐκ νεκρῶν τῇ τρίτῃ ἡμέρᾳ, καὶ
the Christ, and to rise from (the) dead the third day, and
2784 1909 3686 848 3341 849
47 κηρυχθῆναι ἐπὶ τῷ ὀνόματι αὐτοῦ μετάνοιαν καὶ ἄφεσιν
to be preached on the name of Him repentance and forgiveness
266 1519 3956 1484 756 575 2419
ἁμαρτιῶν εἰς πάντα τὰ ἔθνη, ἀρξάμενον ἀπὸ Ἱερουσαλήμ.
of sins to all the nations, beginning from Jerusalem.
5210 2076 3144 5130 2400 1473 649
48 ὑμεῖς δέ ἐστε μάρτυρες τούτων. καὶ ἰδού, ἐγὼ ἀποστέλλω
49 You And are witnesses of these things. And behold, I send forth
1860 3962 3450 1909 5209 5210 2523
τὴν ἐπαγγελίαν τοῦ πατρός μου ἐφ᾽ ὑμᾶς· ὑμεῖς δὲ καθίσατε
the promise of the Father of Me on you. you But sit
1722 4172 2419 2193 3739 1746 1411
ἐν τῇ πόλει Ἱερουσαλήμ, ἕως οὗ ἐνδύσησθε δύναμιν ἐξ
in the city of Jerusalem until you are clothed with power from
5311
ὕψους.
on high.

1806 846 1854 2193 1519 963 1869
50 Ἐξήγαγε δὲ αὐτοὺς ἔξω ἕως εἰς Βηθανίαν καὶ ἐπάρας τὰς
He led And them out until to Bethany, and lifting up the
5495 848 2127 846 1096 1722 2127
51 χεῖρας αὐτοῦ εὐλόγησεν αὐτούς. καὶ ἐγένετο ἐν τῷ εὐλογεῖν
hands of Him, He blessed them. And it was, in the blessing
846 846 1339 575 846 399 1519
αὐτὸν αὐτούς, διέστη ἀπ᾽ αὐτῶν, καὶ ἀνεφέρετο εἰς τὸ
(of) Him them, He withdrew from them, and was carried into
3772 846 4352 846 5290
52 οὐρανόν. καὶ αὐτοὶ προσκυνήσαντες αὐτόν, ὑπέστρεψαν
Heaven. And they having worshiped Him returned
1519 2419 3326 5472 3173 2258 1223 3956
53 εἰς Ἱερουσαλὴμ μετὰ χαρᾶς μεγάλης· καὶ ἦσαν διὰ παντὸς
to Jerusalem with joy great, and were continually
1722 2411 134 2127 2316 281
ἐν τῷ ἱερῷ, αἰνοῦντες καὶ εὐλογοῦντες τὸν Θεόν. Ἀμήν.
in the Temple, praising and blessing God. Amen.

THE

THE GOSPEL
ACCORDING TO
JOHN

A LITERAL TRANSLATION
OF THE BIBLE

CHAPTER 1

[1]In *the* beginning was the Word, and the Word was with God, and the Word was God. [2]He was in *the* beginning with God. [3]All things came into being through Him, and without Him not even one *thing* came into being that has come into being. [4]In Him was life, and the life was the light of men, [5]and the light shines in the darkness, and the darkness did not overtake it.

[6]There was a man sent from God, his name *was* John. [7]He came for a witness, that he might witness concerning the Light, that all might believe through Him. [8]He was not that Light, but that he might witness concerning the Light. [9]He was the true Light; He enlightens every man coming into the world. [10]He was in the world, and the world came into being through Him; yet the world did not know Him. [11]He came into *His* own, and *His* own did not receive Him. [12]But as many as received Him, to them He gave authority to become children of God, to the ones believing into His name; [13]who were born not of bloods, nor of *the* will of *the* flesh, nor of *the* will of man, but were born of God.

[14]And the Word became flesh, and tabernacled among us. And we beheld His glory, glory as of an only-begotten from *the* Father, full of grace and of truth. [15]John witnesses concerning Him, and has cried out, saying, This One

ΕΥΑΓΓΕΛΙΟΝ
THE GOSPEL
ΤΟ ΚΑΤΑ ΙΩΑΝΝΗΝ
ACCORDING TO JOHN

CHAPTER 1

1722 746 2258 3056 3056 2258 4314 2316
1 Ἐν ἀρχῇ ἦν ὁ λόγος, καὶ ὁ λόγος ἦν πρὸς τὸν Θεόν, καὶ
In (the) beginning was the Word, and the Word was with – God, and
2316/2258 3056 3778/2258/1722/746 4314 2316 3956
2 Θεὸς ἦν ὁ λόγος. οὗτος ἦν ἐν ἀρχῇ πρὸς τὸν Θεόν. πάντα
3 God was the Word. This One was in beginning with God. All things
1223 846 1096 5565 846 1096 3761/1520 1096
δι' αὐτοῦ ἐγένετο, καὶ χωρὶς αὐτοῦ ἐγένετο οὐδὲ ἓν ὃ γέγονεν.
through Him came into and without Him came into not even one that came into
1722 846 2222 being. 2222/2258 being (thing) 444 being.
*5457
4 ἐν αὐτῷ ζωὴ ἦν, καὶ ἡ ζωὴ ἦν τὸ φῶς *τῶν ἀνθρώπων, καὶ
5 In Him life was, and the life was the light of men, and
5457/1722 4653 5316 4653 846/3756/ 2638
τὸ φῶς ἐν τῇ σκοτίᾳ φαίνει, καὶ ἡ σκοτία αὐτὸ οὐ κατέλαβεν.
the light in the darkness shines, and the darkness it not did overtake
1096 444 649 3814 2316 3686 846
6 ἐγένετο ἄνθρωπος ἀπεσταλμένος παρὰ Θεοῦ, ὄνομα αὐτῷ
There was a man having been sent from God, name to him,
2491 3778 2064 1519 3141 2443 3140 4012
7 Ἰωάννης. οὗτος ἦλθεν εἰς μαρτυρίαν, ἵνα μαρτυρήσῃ περὶ
John; this one came for a witness, that he might witness about
5457 2443 3956 4100 1223 846 3756/2258 1565
8 τοῦ φωτός, ἵνα πάντες πιστεύσωσι δι' αὐτοῦ. οὐκ ἦν ἐκεῖνος
the light, that all might believe through Him. not He was that
5457 235/2443 3140 4012 5457 2258 5457
9 τὸ φῶς, ἀλλ' ἵνα μαρτυρήσῃ περὶ τοῦ φωτός. ἦν τὸ φῶς τὸ
light, but that he might witness about the light. He was the light
228 3739 5461 3956 444 2064 1519
ἀληθινόν, ὃ φωτίζει πάντα ἄνθρωπον ἐρχόμενον εἰς τὸν
true, which enlightens every man coming into the
2889 1722 2889 2258 2889 1223 846 1096
10 κόσμον. ἐν τῷ κόσμῳ ἦν, καὶ ὁ κόσμος δι' αὐτοῦ ἐγένετο, καὶ
world. In the world He was, and the world through Him became, and
2889 846 3756 1097 1519 2398/2064 2398 846
11 ὁ κόσμος αὐτὸν οὐκ ἔγνω. εἰς τὰ ἴδια ἦλθε, καὶ οἱ ἴδιοι αὐτὸν
the world Him did not know. Into (His) own He came, and (His) own Him
3756 3880 3745 2983 846 1325 846 1849
12 οὐ παρέλαβον. ὅσοι δὲ ἔλαβον αὐτόν, ἔδωκεν αὐτοῖς ἐξουσίαν
not did receive. as many as But received Him, He gave to them authority
5043 2316 1096 4100 1519 3686 848
τέκνα Θεοῦ γενέσθαι, τοῖς πιστεύουσιν εἰς τὸ ὄνομα αὐτοῦ·
children of God to become. to those believing into the name of Him,
3739/3756/1537/ 129 3761 1537 2307 4561 3761/1537/2307
13 οἳ οὐκ ἐξ αἱμάτων, οὐδὲ ἐκ θελήματος σαρκός, οὐδὲ ἐκ θελή-
who not of bloods, nor of (the) will of (the) flesh, nor of (the)
435 235/1537/2316 1080 3056 4561
14 ματος ἀνδρός, ἀλλ' ἐκ Θεοῦ ἐγεννήθησαν. καὶ ὁ λόγος σὰρξ
will of man, but of God were born. And the Word flesh
1096 4637 1722/2254 2300 1391
ἐγένετο, καὶ ἐσκήνωσεν ἐν ἡμῖν (καὶ ἐθεασάμεθα τὴν δόξαν
became, and tabernacled among us, and we beheld the glory
848 1391/5613 3439 3844 3962 4134 5485
αὐτοῦ, δόξαν ὡς μονογενοῦς παρὰ πατρός), πλήρης χάριτος
of Him, glory as of an only-begotten from (the) Father, full of grace
225 2491 3140 4012 846 2896
15 καὶ ἀληθείας. Ἰωάννης μαρτυρεῖ περὶ αὐτοῦ, καὶ κέκραγε
and of truth. John witnesses concerning Him, and has cried out
3004 3778 2258/3739/2036/ 3694 3450 2064 1715
λέγων, Οὗτος ἦν ὃν εἶπον, Ὁ ὀπίσω μου ἐρχόμενος ἔμπρο-
saying, This one was of whom I said, He after me coming before

was *He* of whom I said, He coming after me has been before me, for He was preceding me. [16]And out of His fullness we all received, and grace on top of grace. [17]For the Law came through Moses, *but* grace and truth came through Jesus Christ. [18]No one has seen God at any time; the only-begotten Son, who is in the bosom of the Father, He reveals *Him.*

[19]And this is the witness of John, when the Jews sent priests and Levites from Jerusalem that they might ask him, Who are you? [20]And he acknowledged and did not deny; yea, he acknowledged, I am not the Christ. [21]And they asked him, What, then? Are you Elijah? And he said, I am not. Are you the Prophet? And he answered, No. [22]They they said to him, Who are you, that we may give an answer to those who sent us? What do you say about yourself? [23]He said, *"I am* a voice crying in the wilderness: Make the way of the Lord straight," as Isaiah the prophet said. [24]And those who had been sent were of the Pharisees. [25]And they asked him and said to him, Why then do you baptize, if you are not the Christ, nor Elijah, nor the Prophet? [26]John answered them, saying, I baptize in water, but *One* stands in your midst whom you do not know; [27]He it is who comes after me, who has been before me, of whom I am not worthy that I should untie the latchet of His sandal. [28]These things took place in Bethabara beyond the Jordan, where John was baptizing.

[29]On the morrow, John sees Jesus coming toward

3450 1096 3754 4413 3450/2258 1537 4138
16 σθέν μου γέγονεν· ὅτι πρῶτός μου ἦν. καὶ ἐκ τοῦ πληρώματος
me has become, for preceding me He was. And out of the fullness
848 2249 3956 2983 5485 473 5485 3754
17 αὐτοῦ ἡμεῖς πάντες ἐλάβομεν, καὶ χάριν ἀντὶ χάριτος. ὅτι ὁ
of Him we all received, and grace on top of grace, because the
3551 1223 3475 1325 5485 225 1223 2424
νόμος διὰ Μωσέως ἐδόθη, ἡ χάρις καὶ ἡ ἀλήθεια διὰ Ἰησοῦ
Law through Moses was given, grace and truth through Jesus
5547 1096 2316 3762 3708 4415 3439
18 Χριστοῦ ἐγένετο. Θεὸν οὐδεὶς ἑώρακε πώποτε· ὁ μονογενὴς
Christ came into being. God No one has seen at any time; the only-begotten
5207 5607 /1519 2859 3962 1565 1834
υἱός, ὁ ὢν εἰς τὸν κόλπον τοῦ πατρός, ἐκεῖνος ἐξηγήσατο.
Son, who is in the bosom of the Father, that One explains (Him).
3778 2076 3141 2491 3753 649
19 Καὶ αὕτη ἐστὶν ἡ μαρτυρία τοῦ Ἰωάννου, ὅτε ἀπέστειλαν
And this is the witness — of John, when sent
2453 1537 2414 2409 3019 2443 2065
οἱ Ἰουδαῖοι ἐξ Ἱεροσολύμων ἱερεῖς καὶ Λευΐτας ἵνα ἐρωτή-
the Jews from Jerusalem priests and Levites, that they might
846 4771/5101/1488 3670 3756 720
20 σωσιν αὐτόν, Σὺ τίς εἶ; καὶ ὡμολόγησε, καὶ οὐκ ἠρνήσατο·
ask him, you Who are? And he acknowledged and not denied,
3670 3754/3756/1510/1473 5547 2065
21 καὶ ὡμολόγησεν ὅτι Οὐκ εἰμὶ ἐγὼ ὁ Χριστός. καὶ ἠρώτησαν
and he acknowledged, not am I the Christ. And they asked
846 5101/3767 2243/1488/4771 3004 3756 1510 4396
αὐτόν, Τί οὖν; Ἠλίας εἶ σύ; καὶ λέγει, Οὐκ εἰμί. Ὁ προφή-
him, What, then? Elijah you? And he says, not I am. The prophet
1488/4771 611 3756 2036 3767 846 5101/1488/2443
22 της εἶ σύ; καὶ ἀπεκρίθη, Οὔ. εἶπον οὖν αὐτῷ, Τίς εἶ; ἵνα
are you? And he answered, No. They said then to him, Who are you? that
612 1325 3992 2248 5101 3004 4012
ἀπόκρισιν δῶμεν τοῖς πέμψασιν ἡμᾶς. τί λέγεις περὶ
an answer we may give to those having sent us. What do you say about
4572 5346/1473/5456 994 1722 2048 2116
23 σεαυτοῦ; ἔφη, Ἐγὼ φωνὴ βοῶντος ἐν τῇ ἐρήμῳ, Εὐθύνατε
yourself? He said, I (am) a voice crying in the wilderness, Make straight
3598 2962 2531 2036 2268 4396
24 τὴν ὁδὸν Κυρίου. καθὼς εἶπεν Ἡσαΐας ὁ προφήτης. καὶ οἱ
the way of (the) Lord, as said Isaiah the prophet. And those
649 2258 1537 5330 2065
25 ἀπεσταλμένοι ἦσαν ἐκ τῶν Φαρισαίων. καὶ ἠρώτησαν
having been sent were of the Pharisees. And they asked
846 2036 846 5101/3767 907 1487/4771/3756/1487
αὐτόν, καὶ εἶπον αὐτῷ, Τί οὖν βαπτίζεις, εἰ σὺ οὐκ εἶ ὁ
him, and said to him, Why then do you baptize, if you not are the
5547 3777 2243 3777 4396 611 846
26 Χριστός, οὔτε Ἠλίας, οὔτε ὁ προφήτης; ἀπεκρίθη αὐτοῖς ὁ
Christ, nor Elijah, nor the prophet? Answered them —
2491 3004 1473 907 1722 5204 3319 5216
Ἰωάννης λέγων, Ἐγὼ βαπτίζω ἐν ὕδατι· μέσος δὲ ὑμῶν
John, saying, I baptize in water; amidst but you
2476 3739 5210 3756 1492 846 2076 3694 3450
27 ἕστηκεν ὃν ὑμεῖς οὐκ οἴδατε. αὐτός ἐστιν ὁ ὀπίσω μου
stands (One) whom you not do know. This One it is who after me
2064 3739 1715 3450 1096 3739/1473/3756/1510/514
ἐρχόμενος, ὃς ἔμπροσθέν μου γέγονεν· οὗ ἐγὼ οὐκ εἰμὶ ἄξιος
coming, who before me has become, of whom I not am worthy
2443 3089 846 2438 5266 5023 1722
28 ἵνα λύσω αὐτοῦ τὸν ἱμάντα τοῦ ὑποδήματος. ταῦτα ἐν
that I should loose of Him the latchet of the sandal. These things in
962 1096 4008 2446 3699/2258/2491
Βηθαβαρᾶ ἐγένετο πέραν τοῦ Ἰορδάνου, ὅπου ἦν Ἰωάννης
Bethabara occurred beyond the Jordan, where was John
907
βαπτίζων.
baptizing.

1887 991 2491 2424 2064
29 Τῇ ἐπαύριον βλέπει ὁ Ἰωάννης τὸν Ἰησοῦν ἐρχόμενον
On the morrow sees — John — Jesus coming

him, and said, Behold, the Lamb of God, who takes away the sin of the world! [30]This is He about whom I said, After me comes a Man who has been before me, for He was preceding me. [31]And I did not know Him; but that He be revealed to Israel, for this reason I came baptizing in water. [32]And John witnessed, saying, I have seen the Spirit coming down as a dove out of Heaven, and He abode on Him. [33]And I did not know Him, but He who sent me to baptize in water, that One said to me, On whomever you see the Spirit coming down and abiding on Him, this is He who baptizes in *the* Holy Spirit. [34]And I have seen, and have witnessed that this One is the Son of God.

[35]Again on the morrow, John and two from his disciples stood. [36]And looking at Jesus walking, he said, Behold, the Lamb of God! [37]And the two disciples heard him speaking, and followed Jesus. [38]But seeing them following, turning Jesus said to them, What do you seek? And they said to Him, Rabbi — which translated is called Teacher — where are You staying? [39]He said to them, Come and see. They went and saw where He stayed, and abode with him that day. And it was about *the* tenth hour.

[40]Andrew, the brother of Simon Peter was one of the two who heard this from John, and *had* followed Him. [41]This one first found his own brother Simon, and told him, We

4314 846 3004 2396 286 2316 142
πρὸς αὐτόν, καὶ λέγει, Ἴδε ὁ ἀμνὸς τοῦ Θεοῦ, ὁ αἴρων τὴν
toward him, and says, Behold, the Lamb – of God, taking the
266 2889 3778 2076 4012 3739/1473 2036
30 ἁμαρτίαν τοῦ κόσμου. οὗτός ἐστι περὶ οὗ ἐγὼ εἶπον,
sin of the world. This is He about whom I said,
3694 3450 2064 435 3739 1715 3450 1096 3754
Ὀπίσω μου ἔρχεται ἀνὴρ ὃς ἔμπροσθέν μου γέγονεν, ὅτι
After me comes a Man who before me has become, for
4413 3450/2258/2504/3756/ 1492 846 235 2443 5319
31 πρῶτός μου ἦν. κἀγὼ οὐκ ᾔδειν αὐτόν· ἀλλ' ἵνα φανερωθῇ
preceding me He was. And I not did know Him, but that He be revealed
2474 1223 5124 2064 1473/1722 5204 907
τῷ Ἰσραήλ, διὰ τοῦτο ἦλθον ἐγὼ ἐν τῷ ὕδατι βαπτίζων.
– to Israel, therefore came I in the water baptizing.
3140 2491 3004 3754 2300 4151
32 καὶ ἐμαρτύρησεν Ἰωάννης λέγων ὅτι Τεθέαμαι τὸ Πνεῦμα
And witnessed John saying, – I have beheld the Spirit
2597 5616 4058 1537 3772 3306 1909
καταβαῖνον ὡσεὶ περιστερὰν ἐξ οὐρανοῦ, καὶ ἔμεινεν ἐπ'
coming down as a dove out of Heaven, and He abode on
846 2504 3956 1492 846 235 3992 3165 907
33 αὐτόν. κἀγὼ οὐκ ᾔδειν αὐτόν· ἀλλ' ὁ πέμψας με βαπτίζειν
Him. And I did not know Him, but the (One) sending me to baptize
1722 5204 1565 3450 2036 1909/3739/302/1492 4151 2597
ἐν ὕδατι, ἐκεῖνός μοι εἶπεν, Ἐφ' ὃν ἂν ἴδῃς τὸ Πνεῦμα κατα-
in water, that One to me said, On whomever you see the Spirit coming
3306 1909 846 3778 2076 907
βαῖνον καὶ μένον ἐπ' αὐτόν, οὗτός ἐστιν ὁ βαπτίζων ἐν
down and abiding on Him, this is the (One) baptizing in
4151 40 2504 3708 3140 3754 3778
34 Πνεύματι Ἁγίῳ. κἀγὼ ἑώρακα, καὶ μεμαρτύρηκα ὅτι οὗτός
(the) Spirit Holy. And I have seen, and have witnessed that this One
2076 5207 2316
ἐστιν ὁ υἱὸς τοῦ Θεοῦ.
is the Son – of God.
1887 3825 2476 2491 1537
35 Τῇ ἐπαύριον πάλιν εἱστήκει ὁ Ἰωάννης, καὶ ἐκ τῶν
On the morrow again stood John, and out of the
3101 848 1417 1689 2424 4043
36 μαθητῶν αὐτοῦ δύο· καὶ ἐμβλέψας τῷ Ἰησοῦ περιπατοῦντι,
disciples of him two; and looking at Jesus walking,
3004 2396 286 2316 191 846 1417
37 λέγει, Ἴδε ὁ ἀμνὸς τοῦ Θεοῦ. καὶ ἤκουσαν αὐτοῦ οἱ δύο
he says, Behold, the Lamb of God! And heard him the two
3101 2980 190 2424 4762
38 μαθηταὶ λαλοῦντος, καὶ ἠκολούθησαν τῷ Ἰησοῦ. στραφεὶς
disciples speaking, and they followed Jesus. turning
2424 2300 846 190 3004
δὲ ὁ Ἰησοῦς καὶ θεασάμενος αὐτοὺς ἀκολουθοῦντας, λέγει
And Jesus and beholding them following, He says
846 5101 2212 2036 846 4461 3004
αὐτοῖς, Τί ζητεῖτε; οἱ δὲ εἶπον αὐτῷ, Ῥαββί (ὃ λέγεται
to them, What do you seek? they And said to Him Rabbi, which is called
2059 1320 4226 3306 3004 846 2064
39 ἑρμηνευόμενον, Διδάσκαλε), ποῦ μένεις; λέγει αὐτοῖς, Ἔρχε-
being translated, Teacher, where do you stay? He says to them, Come
1492 2064 1492 4226 3306 3844 846
σθε καὶ ἴδετε. ἦλθον καὶ εἶδον ποῦ μένει· καὶ παρ' αὐτῷ
and see. They went and saw where He stayed, and with Him
3306 2250 1565 5610 2258/5613 1182 2258
40 ἔμειναν τὴν ἡμέραν ἐκείνην· ὥρα δὲ ἦν ὡς δεκάτη. ἦν
abode. day that; (the) hour and was about (the) tenth. was
406 80 4613 4074 1520/1537 1417
Ἀνδρέας ὁ ἀδελφὸς Σίμωνος Πέτρου εἷς ἐκ τῶν δύο τῶν
Andrew the brother of Simon Peter, one of the two
191 3844 2491 190 846
ἀκουσάντων παρὰ Ἰωάννου καὶ ἀκολουθησάντων αὐτῷ.
hearing from John, and following Him.
2147 3778 4413 80 2398 4613
41 εὑρίσκει οὗτος πρῶτος τὸν ἀδελφὸν τὸν ἴδιον Σίμωνα, καὶ
finds This one first brother (his) own Simon, and

have found the Messiah, which being translated is the Christ. [42]And he led him to Jesus. And looking at him, Jesus said, You are Simon the son of Jonah; you shall be called Cephas — which translated is Peter.

[43]And on the morrow Jesus desired to go out into Galilee. And He found Philip, and said to him, Follow me! [44]And Philip was from Bethsaida, of the city of Andrew and Peter. [45]Philip found Nathanael, and said to him, We have found *the One* whom Moses wrote about in the Law and the Prophets, Jesus the son of Joseph, from Nazareth. [46]And Nathanael said to him, Can any good thing be out of Nazareth? Philip said to him, Come and see.

[47]Jesus saw Nathanael coming toward Him, and said concerning him, Behold, truly an Israelite in whom is no guile! [48]Nathanael said to Him, From where do You know me? Jesus answered and said to him, Before Philip called, you being under the fig-tree, I saw you.

[49]Nathanael answered and said to Him, Rabbi, You are the Son of God; You are the King of Israel. [50]Jesus answered and said to him, Because I said to you I saw you under the fig-tree, do you believe? You will see greater things than these. [51]And He said to him, Truly, truly, I say to you, From now on you will see Heaven opened, and the angels of God ascending and descending on the Son of man.

3004 846 2147 3323 3739/2076 3177
λέγει αὐτῷ, Εὑρήκαμεν τὸν Μεσσίαν (ὅ ἐστι μεθερμηνευό-
tells him, We have found the Messiah — which is, being translated
5547 71 846 4314 2424
42 μενον, ὁ Χριστός). καὶ ἤγαγεν αὐτὸν πρὸς τὸν Ἰησοῦν.
the Christ — and he led him to — Jesus
1689 846 2424 2036/4771/1488/4613 5207 2495
ἐμβλέψας δὲ αὐτῷ ὁ Ἰησοῦς εἶπε, Σὺ εἶ Σίμων ὁ υἱὸς Ἰωνᾶ·
looking at And him Jesus said, You are Simon the son of Jonah;
4771 2563 2786 3739 2059 4074
σὺ κληθήσῃ Κηφᾶς (ὃ ἑρμηνεύεται Πέτρος).
you shall be called Cephas—which translated is Peter.
1887 2309 2424 1831 1519 1056
43 Τῇ ἐπαύριον ἠθέλησεν ὁ Ἰησοῦς ἐξελθεῖν εἰς τὴν Γαλιλαίαν,
On the morrow decided Jesus to go out into Galilee.
2147 5376 3004 846 190 3427 2258
44 καὶ εὑρίσκει Φίλιππον, καὶ λέγει αὐτῷ, Ἀκολούθει μοι. ἦν δὲ
And he finds Philip, and says to him, Follow me. was And
5376 575 960 1537 4172 406
ὁ Φίλιππος ἀπὸ Βηθσαϊδά, ἐκ τῆς πόλεως Ἀνδρέου καὶ
— Philip from Bethsaida, of the city of Andrew and
4074 2147 5346 3482 3004 846
45 Πέτρου. εὑρίσκει Φίλιππος τὸν Ναθαναήλ, καὶ λέγει αὐτῷ,
Peter. finds Philip — Nathanael, and says to him,
3739 1125 3475/1722 3551 4396 2147
Ὃν ἔγραψε Μωσῆς ἐν τῷ νόμῳ καὶ οἱ προφῆται εὑρήκαμεν,
(He) whom wrote Moses in the Law and the Prophets, we have found
2424 5207 2501 575 3478 2036
46 Ἰησοῦν τὸν υἱὸν τοῦ Ἰωσὴφ τὸν ἀπὸ Ναζαρέθ. καὶ εἶπεν
Jesus the son — of Joseph — from Nazareth. And said
846 3482 1537 3478 1410 5100 18 1511
αὐτῷ Ναθαναήλ, Ἐκ Ναζαρὲθ δύναταί τι ἀγαθὸν εἶναι;
to him Nathanael, Out of Nazareth can anything good be?
3004 846 5376 2064 1492 1492 2424
47 λέγει αὐτῷ Φίλιππος, Ἔρχου καὶ ἴδε. εἶδεν ὁ Ἰησοῦς τὸν
Says to him Philip, Come and see. saw — Jesus —
3482 2064 4314 846 3004 4012 846
Ναθαναὴλ ἐρχόμενον πρὸς αὐτόν, καὶ λέγει περὶ αὐτοῦ, Ἴδε
Nathanael coming toward Him, and says about him, Behold,
230 2475 1722/3739 1388 3756 2076 3004 846
48 ἀληθῶς Ἰσραηλίτης, ἐν ᾧ δόλος οὐκ ἔστι. λέγει αὐτῷ
truly an Israelite, in whom guile not is. says to Him
3482 4159/3165 1097 611 2424
Ναθαναήλ, Πόθεν με γινώσκεις; ἀπεκρίθη ὁ Ἰησοῦς καὶ
Nathanael, From where me do You know? Answered Jesus and
2036 846 4253 4571 5376 5455 5607 5259
εἶπεν αὐτῷ, Πρὸ τοῦ σε Φίλιππον φωνῆσαι, ὄντα ὑπὸ τὴν
said to him, Before you Philip called, being under the
4808 1492/4571 611 3482 3004 846 4461
49 συκῆν, εἶδόν σε. ἀπεκρίθη Ναθαναὴλ καὶ λέγει αὐτῷ, Ῥαββί,
fig-tree, I saw you. answered Nathanael and says to Him, Rabbi,
4771/1488/5207 2316/4771/1488 935 2474 611
50 σὺ εἶ ὁ υἱὸς τοῦ Θεοῦ, σὺ εἶ ὁ βασιλεὺς τοῦ Ἰσραήλ. ἀπεκρίθη
You are the Son of God; You are the king of Israel. answered
2424 2036 846 3754 2036 4671 1492 4571 5270
Ἰησοῦς καὶ εἶπεν αὐτῷ, Ὅτι εἶπόν σοι, εἶδόν σε ὑποκάτω
Jesus and said to him, Because I told you I saw you underneath
4808 4100 3187 5130 3700 3004 846
51 τῆς συκῆς, πιστεύεις; μείζω τούτων ὄψει. καὶ λέγει αὐτῷ,
fig-tree, I saw you. answered Nathanael and says to Him, Rabbi,
281 281 3004 5213 575 737 3700 3772 455
Ἀμὴν ἀμὴν λέγω ὑμῖν, ἀπ' ἄρτι ὄψεσθε τὸν οὐρανὸν ἀνεῳ-
Truly, truly, I say to you, from now on you will see the heaven opened
32 2316 305 2597
γότα, καὶ τοὺς ἀγγέλους τοῦ Θεοῦ ἀναβαίνοντας καὶ κατα-
and the angels — of God ascending and
1909 5207 444
βαίνοντας ἐπὶ τὸν υἱὸν τοῦ ἀνθρώπου.
descending on the Son of man.

CHAPTER 2

[1]And on the third day a marriage took place in Cana of Galilee, and the mother of Jesus was there. [2]And Jesus and His disciples were also invited to the marriage. [3]And being short of wine, the mother of Jesus said to Him, They have no wine. [4]Jesus said to her, What is that to Me and to you, woman? My hour has not yet come. [5]His mother said to the servants, Whatever He says to you, do. [6]And there were six stone waterpots standing, according to the purification of the Jews, each containing two or three measures. [7]Jesus said to them, Fill the waterpots with water. And they filled them to *the* top. [8]And He said to them, Now draw out and carry to the master of the feast. And they carried *it.* [9]But when the master of the feast tasted the water that had become wine, and did not know from where it was—but the servants drawing the water knew—the master of the feast called the bridegroom, [10]and said to him, Every man first sets on the good wine; and when they have drunk freely, then the worse. You have kept the good wine until now. [11]This beginning of the miracles Jesus did in Cana of Galilee. And *it* revealed His glory, and His disciples believed in Him.

[12]After this He went down to Capernaum, He and His mother and His brothers and His disciples. And He remained there not many days. [13]And the Passover of the Jews was near. And Jesus went up to

CHAPTER 2

2250 5754 1062 1096 1722 2580
1 Καὶ τῇ ἡμέρᾳ τῇ τρίτῃ γάμος ἐγένετο ἐν Κανᾶ τῆς
And on the day third a wedding there was in Cana
1056 2258 3384 2424 1563 2564
2 Γαλιλαίας, καὶ ἦν ἡ μήτηρ τοῦ Ἰησοῦ ἐκεῖ· ἐκλήθη δὲ καὶ ὁ
of Galilee, and was the mother of Jesus there. was invited And also
2424 3101 848 1519 1062 5302
3 Ἰησοῦς καὶ οἱ μαθηταὶ αὐτοῦ εἰς τὸν γάμον. καὶ ὑστερή-
Jesus and the disciples of Him to the wedding. And being
3631 3004 3384 2424 4314 846 3631
σαντος οἴνου, λέγει ἡ μήτηρ τοῦ Ἰησοῦ πρὸς αὐτόν, Οἶνον
short of wine, says the mother of Jesus to Him, wine
3756 2192 3004 846 2424 5101/1698 4671 1135
4 οὐκ ἔχουσι. λέγει αὐτῇ ὁ Ἰησοῦς, Τί ἐμοὶ καὶ σοί, γύναι;
not They have. says to her Jesus, What to Me and to you, woman?
3768 2240 5610/3450 3004 3384 848 1249
5 οὔπω ἥκει ἡ ὥρα μου. λέγει ἡ μήτηρ αὐτοῦ τοῖς διακόνοις,
Not yet is come the hour of Me. Says the mother of Him to the servants,
=3748=302 3004 5213 4160 2258 1563 5201 3035
6 Ὅ τι ἂν λέγῃ ὑμῖν, ποιήσατε. ἦσαν δὲ ἐκεῖ ὑδρίαι λίθιναι
Whatever He says to you, do. were And there waterpots stone
1803 2749 2596 2512 2453 5562
ἓξ κείμεναι κατὰ τὸν καθαρισμὸν τῶν Ἰουδαίων, χωροῦσαι
six standing according to the purification of the Jews, containing
303 3355 1417/2228/5140/3004 846 2424 1072
7 ἀνὰ μετρητὰς δύο ἢ τρεῖς. λέγει αὐτοῖς ὁ Ἰησοῦς, Γεμίσατε
each measures two or three. says to them Jesus, Fill
5201 5204 1072 846 2193 507 3004
8 τὰς ὑδρίας ὕδατος. καὶ ἐγέμισαν αὐτὰς ἕως ἄνω. καὶ λέγει
the waterpots of water. And they filled them up to (the) top. And He says
846 501 3568 5342 755
αὐτοῖς, Ἀντλήσατε νῦν, καὶ φέρετε τῷ ἀρχιτρικλίνῳ. καὶ
to them, Draw out now, and carry to the master of the feast. And
5342 5613 1089 755 5204 3631
9 ἤνεγκαν. ὡς δὲ ἐγεύσατο ὁ ἀρχιτρίκλινος τὸ ὕδωρ οἶνον
they carried. as But tasted the master of the feast the water wine
1096 3756 1492 4159 2076 1249
γεγενημένον, καὶ οὐκ ᾔδει πόθεν ἐστίν (οἱ δὲ διάκονοι
having become, and not knew from where it is—the but servants
1492 501 5204 5455 3566
ᾔδεισαν οἱ ἠντληκότες τὸ ὕδωρ), φωνεῖ τὸν νυμφίον ὁ
knew, those having drawn the water calls the bridegroom the
755 3004 846 3956 444 4412
10 ἀρχιτρίκλινος, καὶ λέγει αὐτῷ, Πᾶς ἄνθρωπος πρῶτον τὸν
master of the feast, and says to him, Every man first the
2570 3631 5087 3752 3184 5119 1640
καλὸν οἶνον τίθησι, καὶ ὅταν μεθυσθῶσι, τότε τὸν ἐλάσσω·
good wine sets on, and when they have drunk, then the worse;
4771 5083 2570 3631 2193 737 5026 4160
11 σὺ τετήρηκας τὸν καλὸν οἶνον ἕως ἄρτι. ταύτην ἐποίησε
you have kept the good wine until now. This did
746 4592 2424 1722 2580 1056
τὴν ἀρχὴν τῶν σημείων ὁ Ἰησοῦς ἐν Κανᾶ τῆς Γαλιλαίας,
the beginning of the signs Jesus in Cana of Galilee.
5319 1391 848 4100 1519 846
καὶ ἐφανέρωσε τὴν δόξαν αὐτοῦ· καὶ ἐπίστευσαν εἰς αὐτὸν οἱ
And (it) revealed the glory of Him, and believed into Him the
3101 848
μαθηταὶ αὐτοῦ.
disciples of Him.

3325 5124 2597 1519 2584 846 3384
12 Μετὰ τοῦτο κατέβη εἰς Καπερναούμ, αὐτὸς καὶ ἡ μήτηρ
After this went down to Capernaum He, and the mother
848 80 848 3101 848 1563
αὐτοῦ, καὶ οἱ ἀδελφοὶ αὐτοῦ, καὶ οἱ μαθηταὶ αὐτοῦ· καὶ ἐκεῖ
of Him, and the brothers of Him, and the disciples of Him, and there
3306 3756 4183 2250
ἔμειναν οὐ πολλὰς ἡμέρας.
He abode not many days.

1451 2258 3957 2453 305 1519
13 Καὶ ἐγγὺς ἦν τὸ πάσχα τῶν Ἰουδαίων, καὶ ἀνέβη εἰς
And near was the Passover of the Jews. And went up to

Jerusalem. [14]And He found those selling oxen and sheep and doves in the Temple, and the moneychangers sitting. [15]And making a whip out of ropes, He threw all out of the temple, both the sheep, and the oxen, and the moneychangers, pouring out the money and overturning the tables. [16]And to the ones selling the doves, He said, Take these things from here! Do not make My Father's house a house of merchandise. [17]And His disciples remembered that it was written, "The zeal of Your house has consumed Me."

[18]Then answered the Jews and said to Him, What sign do you show to us, since you do these things? [19]Jesus said to them, Destroy this temple, and in three days I will raise it up. [20]Then the Jews said, This temple was forty-six years being built, and do you raise it up in three days? [21]But He spoke about the temple of His body. [22]Then when He was raised from *the* dead, His disciples recalled that He said this to them. And they believed the Scripture, and the word which Jesus spoke.

[23]And as He was in Jerusalem, at the Passover, at the Feast, many believed into His name, seeing the miracles which He did. [24]But Jesus Himself did not commit Himself to them, because He knew all; [25]and because He had no need that anyone should witness concerning man; for He knew what was in man.

2414 2424 2147/1722 2411 4453
14 Ἱεροσόλυμα ὁ Ἰησοῦς. καὶ εὗρεν ἐν τῷ ἱερῷ τοὺς πωλοῦντας
Jerusalem Jesus. And He found in the Temple those selling

1016 4263 4058 2773
βόας καὶ πρόβατα καὶ περιστεράς, καὶ τοὺς κερματιστὰς
oxen and sheep and doves, and the money merchants

2521 4160 5416 1537 4979 3956
15 καθημένους. καὶ ποιήσας φραγέλλιον ἐκ σχοινίων πάντας
sitting. And having made a whip out of ropes, all

1544 1537 2411 5037 4263 1016
ἐξέβαλεν ἐκ τοῦ ἱεροῦ, τά τε πρόβατα καὶ τοὺς βόας· καὶ τῶν
He threw out of the Temple, the both sheep and the oxen and the

2855 1632 2772 5132 390
κολλυβιστῶν ἐξέχεε τὸ κέρμα, καὶ τὰς τραπέζας ἀνέστρεψε·
moneychangers, pouring out the money, and the tables overturning.

4058 4453 2036 142 5023
16 καὶ τοῖς τὰς περιστερὰς πωλοῦσιν εἶπεν, Ἄρατε ταῦτα
And to those doves selling He said, Take these things

1782 3361 4160 3624 3962 3450 3624
ἐντεῦθεν· μὴ ποιεῖτε τὸν οἶκον τοῦ πατρός μου οἶκον
from here! Do not make the house of the Father of Me a house

1712 3415 3101 848 3754 1125
17 ἐμπορίου. ἐμνήσθησαν δὲ οἱ μαθηταὶ αὐτοῦ ὅτι γεγραμ-
of merchandise. remembered And the disciples of Him that having been

2076 2205 3624 4675 2719 3165 611
18 μένον ἐστίν, Ὁ ζῆλος τοῦ οἴκου σου κατέφαγέ με. ἀπεκρίθη-
written is: The zeal of the house of You has devoured Me. answered

3767 2453 2036 846 5101 4592 1166
σαν οὖν οἱ Ἰουδαῖοι καὶ εἶπον αὐτῷ, Τί σημεῖον δεικνύεις
Then the Jews and said to Him, What sign do you show

5213 3754 5024 4160 611 2424 2036 846
19 ἡμῖν, ὅτι ταῦτα ποιεῖς; ἀπεκρίθη ὁ Ἰησοῦς καὶ εἶπεν αὐτοῖς,
to us, since these things you do? answered Jesus and said to them,

3089 3485 5126 1722 5140 2250 1453 846
Λύσατε τὸν ναὸν τοῦτον, καὶ ἐν τρισὶν ἡμέραις ἐγερῶ αὐτόν.
Destroy Temple this, and in three days I will raise it.

2036 3767 2453 5062 1803 2094 3618
20 εἶπον οὖν οἱ Ἰουδαῖοι, Τεσσαράκοντα καὶ ἓξ ἔτεσιν ᾠκο-
said Then the Jews, Forty and six years is being

3485 3778 4771/1722/5140 2250 1453 846
δομήθη ὁ ναὸς οὗτος, καὶ σὺ ἐν τρισὶν ἡμέραις ἐγερεῖς αὐτόν;
built Temple this, and you in three days will raise it?

1565 3004 4012 3485 4983 848 3753
21 ἐκεῖνος δὲ ἔλεγε περὶ τοῦ ναοῦ τοῦ σώματος αὐτοῦ. ὅτε
22 that One But spoke about the temple of the body of Him. When

3767 1453 1537 3498 3415 3101 848 3754
οὖν ἠγέρθη ἐκ νεκρῶν, ἐμνήσθησαν οἱ μαθηταὶ αὐτοῦ ὅτι
then, He was raised from dead, recalled the disciples of Him that

5124 3004 846 4100 1124 3056
τοῦτο ἔλεγεν αὐτοῖς· καὶ ἐπίστευσαν τῇ γραφῇ, καὶ τῷ λόγῳ
this He said to them; and they believed the Scripture and the word

3739 2036 2424
ᾧ εἶπεν ὁ Ἰησοῦς.
which said Jesus.

5613 2258/1722 2414 1722 3957 1722 1859
23 Ὡς δὲ ἦν ἐν Ἱεροσολύμοις ἐν τῷ πάσχα, ἐν τῇ ἑορτῇ,
as And He was in Jerusalem, at the Passover, at the feast

4183 4100 1519 3686 848 2334 848
πολλοὶ ἐπίστευσαν εἰς τὸ ὄνομα αὐτοῦ, θεωροῦντες αὐτοῦ τὰ
many believed in the name of Him, beholding of Him the

4592 3739 4160 846 2424 3756 4100 1438
24 σημεῖα ἃ ἐποίει. αὐτὸς δὲ ὁ Ἰησοῦς οὐκ ἐπίστευεν ἑαυτὸν
signs which He did. Himself But, – Jesus not did commit Himself

846 1223 846 1097 3956 3754/3756/5532
25 αὐτοῖς, διὰ τὸ αὐτὸν γινώσκειν πάντας, καὶ ὅτι οὐ χρείαν
to them, because(of) Him knowing all, and because no need

2192 2443 5100 3140 4012 444 846 1063
εἶχεν ἵνα τις μαρτυρήσῃ περὶ τοῦ ἀνθρώπου· αὐτὸς γὰρ
He had that any should witness concerning – man; He for

1097 5101/2258/1722 444
ἐγίνωσκε τί ἦν ἐν τῷ ἀνθρώπῳ.
knew what was in man.

CHAPTER 3

[1]But there was a man from the Pharisees, Nicodemus his name, a ruler of the Jews. [2]This one came to Jesus by night, and said to Him, Rabbi, we know that You have come *as* a teacher from God. For no one is able to do these miracles which You do, except God be with Him. [3]Jesus answered and said to him, Truly, truly, I say to you, If one does not receive birth from above, he is not able to see the kingdom of God. [4]Nicodemus said to Him, How is a man able to be born, being old? He is not able to enter into his mother's womb a second *time* and be born? [5]Jesus answered, Truly, truly, I say to you, If one does not receive birth out of water and Spirit, he is not able to enter into the kingdom of God. [6]That receiving birth from the flesh is flesh; and that receiving birth from the Spirit is spirit. [7]Do not wonder because I told you, You must receive birth from above. [8]The Spirit breathes where He desires, and you hear His voice; but you do not know from where He comes, and where He goes —so is everyone who has received birth from the Spirit. [9]Nicodemus answered and said to Him, How can these things come about? [10]Jesus answered and said to him, You are the teacher of Israel, and you do not know these things? [11]Truly, truly, I say to you, That which we know, we speak; and that which we have seen, we testify. And you do not receive our testimony. [12]If I tell you earthly things, and you do not believe; how will you believe if I tell you heavenly things? [13]And no one has

CHAPTER 3

2258 444 1537 5330 3530 3686
1 Ἦν δὲ ἄνθρωπος ἐκ τῶν Φαρισαίων, Νικόδημος ὄνομα
was And a man out of the Pharisees, Nicodemus (the) name
848 758 2453 3778 2064 4314 2424
2 αὐτῷ, ἄρχων τῶν Ἰουδαίων· οὗτος ἦλθε πρὸς τὸν Ἰησοῦν
to him, a ruler of the Jews. This one came to Jesus
3571 2036 846 4461 1492 3754 575 2316 2064
νυκτός, καὶ εἶπεν αὐτῷ, Ῥαββί, οἴδαμεν ὅτι ἀπὸ Θεοῦ ἐλή-
by night, and said to Him, Rabbi, we know that from God You
1320 3762 1063 5023 4592 1410
λυθας διδάσκαλος· οὐδεὶς γὰρ ταῦτα τὰ σημεῖα δύναται
have come a teacher; no one for these signs is able
4160/3739/4771/4160 =3362= 2316 3326 846 611
3 ποιεῖν ἃ σὺ ποιεῖς, ἐὰν μὴ ᾖ ὁ Θεὸς μετ' αὐτοῦ. ἀπεκρίθη ὁ
to do which You do, except be God with Him. answered –
2424 2036 846 281 281 3004 4671 =3362= 5100
Ἰησοῦς καὶ εἶπεν αὐτῷ, Ἀμὴν ἀμὴν λέγω σοι, ἐὰν μή τις
Jesus and said to him, Truly, truly, I say to you, Except one
1080 509 3756 1410 1492 932 2316
γεννηθῇ ἄνωθεν, οὐ δύναται ἰδεῖν τὴν βασιλείαν τοῦ Θεοῦ.
receive birth from above, not he is able to see the kingdom of God.
3004 4314 846 3530 4459 1410 444
4 λέγει πρὸς αὐτὸν ὁ Νικόδημος, Πῶς δύναται ἄνθρωπος
says to Him Nicodemus, How is able a man
1080 1088 5607 3361 1410 1519 2836
γεννηθῆναι γέρων ὤν; μὴ δύναται εἰς τὴν κοιλίαν τῆς
to be born, old being? Not he is able into the womb of the
3384 848 1208 1525 1080 611
5 μητρὸς αὐτοῦ δεύτερον εἰσελθεῖν καὶ γεννηθῆναι; ἀπεκρίθη
mother of him a second (time) to enter and be born? answered
2424 281 281 3004 4671 =3362= 5100 1080 1537
ὁ Ἰησοῦς, Ἀμὴν ἀμὴν λέγω σοι, ἐὰν μή τις γεννηθῇ ἐξ
Jesus, Truly, truly, I say to you, Except one receive birth of
5204 4151 3756 1410 1525 1519 932
ὕδατος καὶ Πνεύματος, οὐ δύναται εἰσελθεῖν εἰς τὴν βασιλείαν
water and Spirit, not he is able to enter into the kingdom
2316 1080 1537 4561 4561 2076
6 τοῦ Θεοῦ. τὸ γεγεννημένον ἐκ τῆς σαρκὸς σάρξ ἐστι· καὶ τὸ
of God. That receiving birth from the flesh, flesh is; and that
1080 1537 4151 4151 2076 3361 2296
7 γεγεννημένον ἐκ τοῦ πνεύματος πνεῦμά ἐστι. μὴ θαυμάσῃς
receiving birth from the Spirit, spirit is. Do not wonder
3754 2036 4671 1163 5209 1080 509 4151 3699
8 ὅτι εἶπόν σοι, Δεῖ ὑμᾶς γεννηθῆναι ἄνωθεν. τὸ πνεῦμα ὅπου
because I told you, must You receive birth from above. The Spirit where
2309 4154 5456 848 191 235 3756 1492
θέλει πνεῖ, καὶ τὴν φωνὴν αὐτοῦ ἀκούεις, ἀλλ' οὐκ οἶδας
He desires breathes, and the voice of Him you hear, but not you know
4159 2064 4226 5217 3779 2076 3956 1080
πόθεν ἔρχεται καὶ ποῦ ὑπάγει· οὕτως ἐστὶ πᾶς ὁ γεγεννη-
from where He comes and where He goes; so is everyone having received
1537 4151 611 3530 2036
9 μένος ἐκ τοῦ πνεύματος. ἀπεκρίθη Νικόδημος καὶ εἶπεν αὐτῷ,
birth from the Spirit. answered Nicodemus and said to Him,
4459 1410 5023 1096 611 2424 2036
10 Πῶς δύναται ταῦτα γενέσθαι; ἀπεκρίθη ὁ Ἰησοῦς καὶ εἶπεν
How can these things come about? answered Jesus and said
846 4771 1488 1320 2474 5023 3756
αὐτῷ, Σὺ εἶ ὁ διδάσκαλος τοῦ Ἰσραήλ, καὶ ταῦτα οὐ
to him, You are the teacher of Israel, and these things not
3739 1097 281 281 3004 4671/3754/*/ 1492 2980
11 γινώσκεις; ἀμὴν ἀμὴν λέγω σοι ὅτι ὃ οἴδαμεν λαλοῦμεν, καὶ
you do know? Truly, truly, I say to you, what we know we speak, and
3739 3708 3140 3141 2257 3756
ὃ ἑωράκαμεν μαρτυροῦμεν· καὶ τὴν μαρτυρίαν ἡμῶν οὐ
what we have seen we witness, and the witness of us not
2983 1487 1919 2036 5213 3756 4100 4459
12 λαμβάνετε. εἰ τὰ ἐπίγεια εἶπον ὑμῖν καὶ οὐ πιστεύετε, πῶς,
you receive. If earthly things I told you and not you believe, how,
1437 2036 5213 2032 4100 3762 305
13 ἐὰν εἴπω ὑμῖν τὰ ἐπουράνια, πιστεύσετε; καὶ οὐδεὶς ἀναβέ-
if I tell you the heavenly things, will you believe? And no one has gone

gone up into Heaven, except He having come down out of Heaven, the Son of Man who is in Heaven. [14]And even as Moses lifted up the serpent in the wilderness, so must the Son of man be lifted up, [15]that everyone believing into Him should not perish, but have everlasting life.

[16]For God so loved the world that He gave His only-begotten Son, that everyone believing into Him should not perish, but have everlasting life. [17]For God did not send His Son into the world that He might judge the world, but that the world might be saved through Him. [18]The *one* believing into Him is not judged; but the *one* not believing has already been judged; for he has not believed into the name of the only-begotten Son of God. [19]And this is the judgment, that the Light has come into the world, and men loved the darkness more than the Light; for their works were evil. [20]For everyone practicing wickedness hates the Light, and does not come to the Light, that his works may not be exposed. [21]But the *one* doing the truth comes to the Light, that his works may be revealed, that they have been worked in God.

[22]After these things Jesus and His disciples came into the land of Judea. And *He* continued there with them, and baptized. [23]And John was also baptizing in Aenon, near Salim, for many waters were there. And they came and were being baptized. [24]For John had not yet been thrown into the prison.

1519 3772 =1508= 1537 3772 2597
βηκεν εἰς τὸν οὐρανόν, εἰ μὴ ὁ ἐκ τοῦ οὐρανοῦ καταβάς, ὁ
up into — Heaven except He out of — Heaven having come down the
5207 444 5607/1722 3772 2531 3475
14 υἱὸς τοῦ ἀνθρώπου ὁ ὢν ἐν τῷ οὐρανῷ. καὶ καθὼς Μωσῆς
Son — of man, who is in — Heaven. And as Moses
5312 3789 1722 2048 3779 5312 1163 5207
ὕψωσε τὸν ὄφιν ἐν τῇ ἐρήμῳ, οὕτως ὑψωθῆναι δεῖ τὸν υἱὸν
lifted up the serpent in the wilderness, so to be lifted up must the Son
444 2443/3956 4100 1519 846 3361 622
15 τοῦ ἀνθρώπου· ἵνα πᾶς ὁ πιστεύων εἰς αὐτὸν μὴ ἀπόληται,
— of man, that everyone believing in Him not may perish,
235/2192/2222 166
ἀλλ' ἔχῃ ζωὴν αἰώνιον.
but have life everlasting.
3779 1063 25 2316 2889 5620 5207
16 Οὕτω γὰρ ἠγάπησεν ὁ Θεὸς τὸν κόσμον, ὥστε τὸν υἱὸν
so For loved God the world, so as the Son
848 3439 1325 2443/3956 4100 1519 846
αὐτοῦ τὸν μονογενῆ ἔδωκεν, ἵνα πᾶς ὁ πιστεύων εἰς αὐτὸν
of Him, the only-begotten, He gave, that everyone believing into Him
3361 622 235 2192 2222 166 3756/1063 649
17 μὴ ἀπόληται, ἀλλ' ἔχῃ ζωὴν αἰώνιον. οὐ γὰρ ἀπέστειλεν ὁ
not may perish, but have life everlasting. not For sent
2316 5207 848 1519 2889 2443 2919 2889
Θεὸς τὸν υἱὸν αὐτοῦ εἰς τὸν κόσμον ἵνα κρίνῃ τὸν κόσμον,
God the Son of Him into the world that He judge the world,
235 2443 4982 2889 1223 846 4100 1519 846 3756
18 ἀλλ' ἵνα σωθῇ ὁ κόσμος δι' αὐτοῦ. ὁ πιστεύων εἰς αὐτὸν οὐ
but that may be saved the world via Him. The (one) believing into Him not
2919 3361 4100 2235 2919 3754/3361 4100
κρίνεται ὁ δὲ μὴ πιστεύων ἤδη κέκριται, ὅτι μὴ πεπί-
is judged; the (one) but not believing already has been judged, for not he has
1519 3686 3439 5207 2316 3778
19 στευκεν εἰς τὸ ὄνομα τοῦ μονογενοῦς υἱοῦ τοῦ Θεοῦ. αὕτη δέ
believed into the name of the only-begotten Son — of God. this And
2076 2920 3754 5457 2064 1519 2889
ἐστιν ἡ κρίσις, ὅτι τὸ φῶς ἐλήλυθεν εἰς τὸν κόσμον, καὶ
is the judgment, that the light has come into the world, and
25 444 3123 4655/2228 5457/2258
ἠγάπησαν οἱ ἄνθρωποι μᾶλλον τὸ σκότος ἢ τὸ φῶς· ἦν
loved — men more the darkness than the light; were
1063 4190 848 2041 3956/1063 5337 4238
20 γὰρ πονηρὰ αὐτῶν τὰ ἔργα. πᾶς γὰρ ὁ φαῦλα πράσσων
for evil of them the works. everyone For wickedness practicing
3404 5457 3756 2064 4314 5457 2443/3361 1651
μισεῖ τὸ φῶς, καὶ οὐκ ἔρχεται πρὸς τὸ φῶς, ἵνα μὴ ἐλεγχθῇ
hates the light, and not does come to the light, that not be reproved
2041 848 4160 225 2064 4314
21 τὰ ἔργα αὐτοῦ. ὁ δὲ ποιῶν τὴν ἀλήθειαν ἔρχεται πρὸς τὸ
the works of him. the (one) But doing the truth comes to the
5457 2443 5319 846 2041 3754/1722/2316 2076
φῶς, ἵνα φανερωθῇ αὐτοῦ τὰ ἔργα, ὅτι ἐν Θεῷ ἐστιν
light, that may be revealed of him the works, that in God they are
2038
εἰργασμένα.
having been worked.

3326 5023 2064 2424 3101 848 1519
22 Μετὰ ταῦτα ἦλθεν ὁ Ἰησοῦς καὶ οἱ μαθηταὶ αὐτοῦ εἰς
After these things came — Jesus and the disciples of Him into
2449 1093 1563 1304 3326 846 907
τὴν Ἰουδαίαν γῆν· καὶ ἐκεῖ διέτριβε μετ' αὐτῶν καὶ ἐβάπτι-
the Judean land, and there continued with them and baptized.
2258 2491 907 137 1451 4530
23 ζεν. ἦν δὲ καὶ Ἰωάννης βαπτίζων ἐν Αἰνὼν ἐγγὺς τοῦ Σαλείμ,
was And also John baptizing in Aenon near Salem,
3754 5204 4183/2258/1563 3854 907
ὅτι ὕδατα πολλὰ ἦν ἐκεῖ· καὶ παρεγίνοντο καὶ ἐβαπτίζοντο.
for waters many were there; and they came and were being baptized.
3768 1063 2258 906 1519 5438 2491
24 οὔπω γὰρ ἦν βεβλημένος εἰς τὴν φυλακὴν ὁ Ἰωάννης.
not yet For was having been cast into the prison John.

NOTE: Frequent words not numbered: δέ(1161); καί(2531)—and, but; ὁ, ἡ, τό (3588, the)— * above word, look in verse margin for No.

[25]Then a question from
John's disciples arose with
the Jews about purifying.
[26]And they came to John
and said to him, Teacher,
the one who was with you
beyond the Jordan, to
whom you have witnessed,
behold, this one baptizes,
and all are coming to Him.
[27]John answered and said,
A man is able to receive
nothing unless it has been
given to him from Heaven.
[28]You yourselves witness
to me, that I said, I am not
the Christ, but that having
been sent I am going
before that One. [29]The
one having the bride is *the*
bridegroom. But the friend
of the bridegroom, stand-
ing and hearing him, re-
joices with joy because of
the bridegroom's voice.
Then this my joy has been
fulfilled. [30]That One must
increase, but I *must*
decrease.

[31]The *One* coming from
above is above all. The *one*
being of the earth is earthy,
and speaks of the earth.
The *One* coming out of
Heaven is above all. [32]And
what He has seen and
heard, this He testifies;
and no one receives His
testimony. [33]The *one* receiving His testimony has
sealed that God is true;
[34]for *the One* whom God
sent speaks the words of
God; for God does not give
the Spirit by measure.
[35]The Father loves the Son,
and has given all things
into His hand. [36]The *one*
believing into the Son has
everlasting life; but the *one*
disobeying the Son will
not see life, but the wrath
of God remains on him.

CHAPTER 4

[1]Then when the Lord
knew that the Pharisees

1096 3767 2214 1537 3101 2491 3326
25 ἐγένετο οὖν ζήτησις ἐκ τῶν μαθητῶν Ἰωάννου μετὰ
was Therefore a questioning of the disciples of John with
2453 4012 2512 2064 4314 2491
26 Ἰουδαίων περὶ καθαρισμοῦ. καὶ ἦλθον πρὸς τὸν Ἰωάννην
Jews concerning purifying. And they came to — John
2036 846 4461/3739/2258/3326/4675/4008 2446
καὶ εἶπον αὐτῷ, Ῥαββί, ὃς ἦν μετὰ σοῦ πέραν τοῦ Ἰορδάνου,
and said to him, Rabbi, (He)who was with you beyond the Jordan,
3739/4771 3140 2396 3778 907 3956 2064
ᾧ σὺ μεμαρτύρηκας, ἴδε οὗτος βαπτίζει, καὶ πάντες ἔρχονται
to whom you have witnessed, behold, this one baptizes, and all are coming
4314 846 611 2491 2036 3756 1410
27 πρὸς αὐτόν. ἀπεκρίθη Ἰωάννης καὶ εἶπεν, Οὐ δύναται
to Him. answered John and said, not is able
444 2983 3762 3362=5600 1325 846 1537
ἄνθρωπος λαμβάνειν οὐδέν, ἐὰν μὴ ᾖ δεδομένον αὐτῷ ἐκ τοῦ
A man to receive nothing unless it is having been given to him from
3772 846 5210 3427 3140 3754 2036 3756 1510
28 οὐρανοῦ. αὐτοὶ ὑμεῖς μοι μαρτυρεῖτε ὅτι εἶπον, Οὐκ εἰμὶ
Heaven. (your)selves You to me witness that I said, not am
1473 5547 235 3754 649 1510 1715
ἐγὼ ὁ Χριστός, ἀλλ' ὅτι ἀπεσταλμένος εἰμὶ ἔμπροσθεν
I the Christ, but that having been sent I am preceding
1565 2192 3565 3566 2076 5384
29 ἐκείνου. ὁ ἔχων τὴν νύμφην νυμφίος ἐστίν· ὁ δὲ φίλος τοῦ
that One. He having the bride (the) bridegroom is, the but friend of the
3566 2476 191 846 5479 5463 1223
νυμφίου, ὁ ἑστηκὼς καὶ ἀκούων αὐτοῦ, χαρᾷ χαίρει διὰ τὴν
bridegroom, standing and hearing him, with joy rejoices for the
5456 3566 3778 3767 5479 1699 4137
φωνὴν τοῦ νυμφίου· αὕτη οὖν ἡ χαρὰ ἡ ἐμὴ πεπλήρωται.
voice of the bridegroom. this Then the joy of me has been fulfilled.
1565 1163 837 1691 1642
30 ἐκεῖνον δεῖ αὐξάνειν, ἐμὲ δὲ ἐλαττοῦσθαι.
That One must increase, me but to decrease.

509 2064 1883 3956 2076 5607 1537
31 Ὁ ἄνωθεν ἐρχόμενος ἐπάνω πάντων ἐστίν. ὁ ὢν ἐκ τῆς
The One from above coming above all is, the (one) being of the
1093/1537 1093/2076 1537 1093 2980 1537 3772
γῆς, ἐκ τῆς γῆς ἐστι, καὶ ἐκ τῆς γῆς λαλεῖ· ὁ ἐκ τοῦ οὐρανοῦ
earth of the earth is, and of the earth speaks. He from Heaven
2064 1883 3956 2076 3739 3708 191
32 ἐρχόμενος ἐπάνω πάντων ἐστί. καὶ ὃ ἑώρακε καὶ ἤκουσε,
coming above all is. And what He has seen and heard
5124 3140 3141 848 3762 2983
τοῦτο μαρτυρεῖ· καὶ τὴν μαρτυρίαν αὐτοῦ οὐδεὶς λαμβάνει.
this He witnesses, and the witness of Him no one receives.
2983 848 3141 4972 3754 2316 227
33 ὁ λαβὼν αὐτοῦ τὴν μαρτυρίαν ἐσφράγισεν ὅτι ὁ Θεὸς ἀληθής
He receiving of Him the witness has sealed that — God true.
2076 3739 1063 649 2316 4487 2316 2980
34 ἐστιν. ὃν γὰρ ἀπέστειλεν ὁ Θεός, τὰ ῥήματα τοῦ Θεοῦ λαλεῖ·
is. (He) whom For sent — God, the words — of God speaks;
3756/1063/1537/3358 1325 2316 4151 3962 25
35 οὐ γὰρ ἐκ μέτρου δίδωσιν ὁ Θεὸς τὸ Πνεῦμα. ὁ πατὴρ ἀγαπᾷ
not for by measure gives — God the Spirit. The Father loves
5207 3956 1325 5495 848 4100
36 τὸν υἱόν, καὶ πάντα δέδωκεν ἐν τῇ χειρὶ αὐτοῦ. ὁ πιστεύων
the Son, and all things has given into the hand of Him. The (one) believing
1519 5207/2192 2222 166 544 5207 3756
εἰς τὸν υἱὸν ἔχει ζωὴν αἰώνιον· ὁ δὲ ἀπειθῶν τῷ υἱῷ οὐκ
into the Son has life everlasting; the (one) but disobeying the Son not
3700 2222 235 3709 2316/3306/1909 846
ὄψεται ζωήν, ἀλλ' ἡ ὀργὴ τοῦ Θεοῦ μένει ἐπ' αὐτόν.
will see life, but the wrath — of God remains on him.

CHAPTER 4

5613 3767 1097 2962 3754 191 5330 3754
1 Ὡς οὖν ἔγνω ὁ Κύριος ὅτι ἤκουσαν οἱ Φαρισαῖοι ὅτι
As therefore knew the Lord that heard the Pharisees that

heard that Jesus made more disciples and baptized *more* than John—[2]though truly Jesus Himself did not baptize, but His disciples—[3]He left Judea and went away into Galilee again. [4]And it was needful for Him to pass through Samaria. [5]And He came to a Samaritan city called Sychar, near the piece of land Jacob gave to his son Joseph. [6]And Jacob's fountain was there. Then being wearied by the journey, Jesus sat thus on the fountain. *It* was about *the* sixth hour.

[7]A woman came out of Samaria to draw water. Jesus said to her, Give Me to drink. [8]For His disciples had gone away into the city that they might buy provisions. [9]Then the Samaritan woman said to Him, How do you, being a Jew, ask to drink from me, *I* being a Samaritan woman? For Jews do not associate with Samaritans. [10]Jesus answered and said to her, If you knew the gift of God, and who is the *One* saying to you, Give Me to drink, you would have asked Him, and He would give you living water. [11]The woman said to Him, Sir, you have no vessel, and the well is deep. From where then do you have living water? [12]Are you greater than our father Jacob who gave us the well, and he and his sons and his livestock drank out of it? [13]Jesus answered and said to her, Everyone drinking of this water will thirst again; [14]but whoever may drink of the water which I will give him will never ever thirst, but the water which I will give to him will become a

2424 4119 3101 4160 907 2228 2491
Ἰησοῦς πλείονας μαθητὰς ποιεῖ καὶ βαπτίζει ἢ Ἰωάννης
Jesus more disciples makes and baptizes than John,
2544 2424 848 3756 907 235 3101
2 (καίτοιγε Ἰησοῦς αὐτὸς οὐκ ἐβάπτιζεν, ἀλλ' οἱ μαθηταὶ
though Jesus Himself not baptized but the disciples
848 863 2449 565 3825 1519
3 αὐτοῦ), ἀφῆκε τὴν Ἰουδαίαν, καὶ ἀπῆλθε πάλιν εἰς τὴν
of Him; He left — Judea and went away again into —
1056 1163 846 1330 1223 4540 2064
4 Γαλιλαίαν. ἔδει δὲ αὐτὸν διέρχεσθαι διὰ τῆς Σαμαρείας. ἔρχε-
5 Galilee. it behoved And Him to pass through — Samaria. He
3767/1519/4172 4540 3004 4965 4139
ται οὖν εἰς πόλιν τῆς Σαμαρείας λεγομένην Συχάρ, πλησίον
comes then to a city of Samaria called Sychar, near
5564/3739/1325 2384 2501 5207 848 2258
6 τοῦ χωρίου ὃ ἔδωκεν Ἰακὼβ Ἰωσὴφ τῷ υἱῷ αὐτοῦ· ἦν δὲ
the piece of land that gave Jacob to Joseph the son of him. was And
1563 4077 2384 3767 2424 2872 1537
ἐκεῖ πηγὴ τοῦ Ἰακώβ. ὁ οὖν Ἰησοῦς κεκοπιακὼς ἐκ τῆς
there a fountain — of Jacob. Therefore, Jesus having wearied from the
3597 2516 3779 1909 4077 5610 2258 5616
ὁδοιπορίας ἐκαθέζετο οὕτως ἐπὶ τῇ πηγῇ. ὥρα ἦν ὡσεὶ
journey sat thus on the fountain; hour was about
1622 2064 1135/1537 4540 501 5204 3004
7 ἕκτη. ἔρχεται γυνὴ ἐκ τῆς Σαμαρείας ἀντλῆσαι ὕδωρ· λέγει
sixth. Comes a woman of — Samaria to draw water. says
846 2424 1325/3427 4095 1063 3101 848 565
8 αὐτῇ ὁ Ἰησοῦς, Δός μοι πιεῖν. οἱ γὰρ μαθηταὶ αὐτοῦ ἀπελη-
to her Jesus, Give Me to drink. the For disciples of Him had gone
1519 4172 2443 5160 59 3004 3767
9 λύθεισαν εἰς τὴν πόλιν, ἵνα τροφὰς ἀγοράσωσι. λέγει οὖν
away into the city, that foods they might buy. says Then
846 1135 4542 4459/4771 2453 5607/3844/1700
αὐτῷ ἡ γυνὴ ἡ Σαμαρεῖτις, Πῶς σὺ Ἰουδαῖος ὢν παρ' ἐμοῦ
to Him the woman Samaritan, How do you, a Jew being, from me
4095 154 5607 1135 4542 3756/1063 4798
πιεῖν αἰτεῖς, οὔσης γυναικὸς Σαμαρείτιδος; (οὐ γὰρ συγ-
to drink ask, (I) being woman a Samaritan? not for
2453 4541 611 2424 2036
10 χρῶνται Ἰουδαῖοι Σαμαρείταις.) ἀπεκρίθη Ἰησοῦς καὶ εἶπεν
associate Jews with Samaritans. answered Jesus and said
846 1487 1492 1431 2316 5101 2076 3004
αὐτῇ, Εἰ ᾔδεις τὴν δωρεὰν τοῦ Θεοῦ, καὶ τίς ἐστιν ὁ λέγων
to her, If you knew the gift — of God, and who is the (one) saying
4671 1325 3427 4095/4771/302 154 846 1325 302 4671
σοι, Δός μοι πιεῖν, σὺ ἂν ᾔτησας αὐτόν, καὶ ἔδωκεν ἄν σοι
to you, Give me to drink, you would have asked Him, and He would give you
5204/2198/ 3004 846 1135 2962 3777 502 2192
11 ὕδωρ ζῶν. λέγει αὐτῷ ἡ γυνή, Κύριε, οὔτε ἄντλημα ἔχεις, καὶ
water living. says to Him The woman, Lord, no vessel you have, and
5421 2076 901 4159 3767 2192 5204 2198/3361/4771
12 τὸ φρέαρ ἐστὶ βαθύ· πόθεν οὖν ἔχεις τὸ ὕδωρ τὸ ζῶν; μὴ σὺ
the well is deep; from where then have you water living? not You
3187 1488 3962 2257 2384/3739 1325 2254 5421
μείζων εἶ τοῦ πατρὸς ἡμῶν Ἰακώβ, ὃς ἔδωκεν ἡμῖν το φρέαρ,
greater are (than) the father of us, Jacob, who gave us the well,
848 1537/846 4095 5207 848 2353
καὶ αὐτὸς ἐξ αὐτοῦ ἔπιε, καὶ οἱ υἱοὶ αὐτοῦ, καὶ τὰ θρέμματα
and he out of it drank, and the sons of him, and the livestock
848 611 2424 2036 846 3956 4095 1537
13 αὐτοῦ; ἀπεκρίθη ὁ Ἰησοῦς καὶ εἶπεν αὐτῇ, Πᾶς ὁ πίνων ἐκ
of him? answered — Jesus and said to her, Everyone drinking of
5204 5127 1372 3825 3739 302 4095/1537
14 τοῦ ὕδατος τούτου, διψήσει πάλιν· ὃς δ' ἂν πίῃ ἐκ τοῦ
water this will thirst again; who but ever drinks of the
5204 3739/1473 1325 846 =3364= 1372 1519 165
ὕδατος οὗ ἐγὼ δώσω αὐτῷ, οὐ μὴ διψήσῃ εἰς τὸν αἰῶνα·
water which I will give him, in no way will thirst unto the age,
235 5204/3739/1325 846 1096 1722 846 4077
ἀλλὰ τὸ ὕδωρ ὃ δώσω αὐτῷ γενήσεται ἐν αὐτῷ πηγὴ
but the water which I will give him will become in him a fountain

fountain of water in him, springing up into everlasting life.

[15]The woman said to Him, Sir, give me this water, that I may not thirst, nor come here to draw. [16]Jesus said to her, Go, call your husband, and come here. [17]And the woman answered and said, I have no husband. Jesus said to her, Well did you say, I have no husband. [18]For you have had five husbands, and now *he* whom you have is not your husband. You have spoken this truly. [19]The woman said to Him, Sir, I perceive that you are a prophet. [20]Our fathers worshiped in this mountain, and you say that in Jerusalem is the place where it is necessary to worship. [21]Jesus said to her, Woman, believe Me that an hour is coming when you will worship the Father neither in this mountain nor in Jerusalem. [22]You worship what you do not know; we worship what we know, for salvation is of the Jews. [23]But an hour is coming, and now is, when the true worshipers will worship the Father in spirit and in truth. For the Father also seeks such *ones* that worship Him. [24]God *is* a spirit, and the ones worshiping Him must worship in spirit and truth. [25]The woman said to Him, I know that Messiah is coming, the *One* called Christ. When that One comes, He will announce to us all things. [26]Jesus said to her, I AM, the *One* speaking to you.

[27]And on this His disciples came and marveled that He was speaking with a woman. However, no one said, What do you seek? Or, Why do

5204 242 1519 2222 166 3004 4314 846
15 ὕδατος ἀλλομένου εἰς ζωὴν αἰώνιον. λέγει πρὸς αὐτὸν ἡ
of water springing to life everlasting. says to Him The
1135 2962 1325/3427 5124 5204 2443/3361/1372 3366
γυνή, Κύριε, δός μοι τοῦτο τὸ ὕδωρ, ἵνα μὴ διψῶ, μηδὲ
woman, Lord, give me this — water, that not I thirst, nor
2064 1757 501 3004 846 2424 5217
16 ἔρχωμαι ἐνθάδε ἀντλεῖν. λέγει αὐτῇ ὁ Ἰησοῦς, Ὕπαγε,
come here to draw. says to her Jesus, Go,
5455 435 4675 2064 1759 611 1135
17 φώνησον τὸν ἄνδρα σοῦ, καὶ ἐλθὲ ἐνθάδε. ἀπεκρίθη ἡ γυνὴ
call the husband of you, and come here. answered The woman
2036 3756 2192 435 3004 846 2424 2573 2036
καὶ εἶπεν, Οὐκ ἔχω ἄνδρα. λέγει αὐτῇ ὁ Ἰησοῦς, Καλῶς εἶπας
and said, not I have a husband. says to her Jesus, well You say,
3754 435 3756 2192 4002 1063 435 2192 3568 3739
18 ὅτι Ἄνδρα οὐκ ἔχω· πέντε γὰρ ἄνδρας ἔσχες, καὶ νῦν ὃν
A husband not I have; five for husbands you had, and now whom
2192/3756/2076/4675/435 5124 227 2046 3004 846
19 ἔχεις οὐκ ἔστι σου ἀνήρ· τοῦτο ἀληθὲς εἴρηκας. λέγει αὐτῷ
you have not is your husband; this truly you have said. says to Him
1135 2962 2334 3754 4396 1488/4771 3962 2257
20 ἡ γυνή, Κύριε, θεωρῶ ὅτι προφήτης εἶ σύ. οἱ πατέρες ἡμῶν
The woman, Lord, I perceive that a prophet are you. The fathers of us
1722 5129 3735 4352 5210 3004 3754/1722
ἐν τούτῳ τῷ ὄρει προσεκύνησαν· καὶ ὑμεῖς λέγετε ὅτι ἐν
in this mountain worshiped, and you say that in
2414 2076 5117 3699 1163 4352 3004
21 Ἱεροσολύμοις ἐστὶν ὁ τόπος ὅπου δεῖ προσκυνεῖν. λέγει
Jerusalem is the place where it is right to worship. says
846 2424 1135 4100 3427 3754 2064 5610
αὐτῇ ὁ Ἰησοῦς, Γύναι, πίστευσόν μοι, ὅτι ἔρχεται ὥρα,
to her Jesus, Woman, believe Me, that comes an hour
3753 3777/1722 3735 5129 3777/1722 2414 4352
ὅτε οὔτε ἐν τῷ ὄρει τούτῳ οὔτε ἐν Ἱεροσολύμοις προσκυνή-
when neither in mountain this, nor in Jerusalem, will you worship
3962 5210 4352 3739/3756 1492 5210
22 σετε τῷ πατρί. ὑμεῖς προσκυνεῖτε ὃ οὐκ οἴδατε· ἡμεῖς
the Father You worship what not you know, we
4352 3739 1492 3754 4991 1537 2453
προσκυνοῦμεν ὃ οἴδαμεν· ὅτι ἡ σωτηρία ἐκ τῶν Ἰουδαίων
worship what we know, since salvation of the Jews
2076 235 2064 5610 3568 2076 3753 228
23 ἐστίν. ἀλλ' ἔρχεται ὥρα καὶ νῦν ἐστιν, ὅτε οἱ ἀληθινοὶ
is. But is coming an hour, and now is, when the true
4353 4352 3962 1722 4151
προσκυνηταὶ προσκυνήσουσι τῷ πατρὶ ἐν πνεύματι καὶ
worshipers will worship the Father in spirit and
225 1063 3962 5108 2212 4352
ἀληθείᾳ· καὶ γὰρ ὁ πατὴρ τοιούτους ζητεῖ τοὺς προσ-
truth; also for the Father such seeks, those
846 4151 2316 4352
24 κυνοῦντας αὐτόν. Πνεῦμα ὁ Θεός· καὶ τοὺς προσκυνοῦντας
worshiping Him. A spirit God (is) and those worshiping
846 1722 4151 225 1163 4352 3004 846
25 αὐτόν, ἐν πνεύματι καὶ ἀληθείᾳ δεῖ προσκυνεῖν. λέγει αὐτῷ
Him in spirit and truth need to worship. says to Him
1135 1492 3754 3323 2064 3004 5547
ἡ γυνή, Οἶδα ὅτι Μεσσίας ἔρχεται (ὁ λεγόμενος Χριστός)·
The woman, I know that Messiah is coming, the (One) called Christ
3752 2064 1565 312 2215 3956 3004 846
26 ὅταν ἔλθῃ ἐκεῖνος, ἀναγγελεῖ ἡμῖν πάντα. λέγει αὐτῇ ὁ
when comes that One, He will announce to us all things. says to her
2424 1473/1510 2980 4671
Ἰησοῦς, Ἐγώ εἰμι, ὁ λαλῶν σοι.
Jesus, I AM, He speaking to you.
1909 5129 2064 3101 848 2296
27 Καὶ ἐπὶ τούτῳ ἦλθον οἱ μαθηταὶ αὐτοῦ, καὶ ἐθαύμασαν
And on this came the disciples of Him, and marveled
3754 3326 1135 2980 3762 3305 2036 5101 2212
ὅτι μετὰ γυναικὸς ἐλάλει· οὐδεὶς μέντοι εἶπε, Τί ζητεῖς;
that with a woman He was speaking; no one, though, said, What seek you?

You speak with her? [28]Then the woman left her waterpot and went away into the city, and said to the men, [29]Come, see a Man who told me all things, whatever I did. Is this One not the Christ? [30]Therefore, they went out of the city and came to Him.

[31]But in the meantime the disciples asked Him, saying, Rabbi, eat? [32]But He said to them, I have food to eat which you do not know. [33]Then the disciples said to one another, No one brought Him *food* to eat? [34]Jesus said to them, My food is that I should do the the will of *Him* who sent Me, and that I may finish His work. [35]You do not say, It is yet four months and the harvest comes. Behold, I say to you, Lift up your eyes and behold the fields, for they are already white to harvest. [36]And the *one* reaping receives reward, and gathers fruit to everlasting life, so that both the *one* sowing and the *one* reaping may rejoice together. [37]For in this the word is true, that another *is* the *one* sowing, and another the *one* reaping. [38]I sent you to reap what you have not labored over. Others have labored, and you have entered into their labor.

[39]And many of the Samaritans out of that city believed into Him, because of the word of the woman testifying, He told me all things, whatever I did. [40]Then as the Samaritans came to Him, they asked Him to remain with them. And He remained there two days. [41]And many more believed

2228/5102/2980/3326 846 863 3767 5201 848
28 ἤ, Τί λαλεῖς μετ' αὐτῆς; ἀφῆκεν οὖν τὴν ὑδρίαν αὐτῆς ἡ
or, Why speak You with her? left, then, the waterpot of her The
1135 565 1519 4172 3004 444
γυνή, καὶ ἀπῆλθεν εἰς τὴν πόλιν, καὶ λέγει τοῖς ἀνθρώποις,
woman, and went away into the city, and says to the men,
1205 1492 444 3739/2036/3427/3956 3745 4160 3385
29 Δεῦτε, ἴδετε ἄνθρωπον, ὃς εἶπέ μοι πάντα ὅσα ἐποίησα· μήτι
Come! See a man who told me all things whatever I did. Not
3778 2076 5547 1831 3767 1537 4172
30 οὗτός ἐστιν ὁ Χριστός; ἐξῆλθον οὖν ἐκ τῆς πόλεως, καὶ
this One is the Christ? They went out, then, from the city, and
2064 4314 846 1722 3342 2065 846
31 ἤρχοντο πρὸς αὐτόν. ἐν δὲ τῷ μεταξὺ ἠρώτων αὐτὸν οἱ
came to Him. in And the meantime asked Him the
3101 3004 4461 5315 2036 846 1473
32 μαθηταί, λέγοντες, Ῥαββί, φάγε. ὁ δὲ εἶπεν αὐτοῖς, Ἐγὼ
disciples, saying, Rabbi, eat. He but said to them, I
1035 2192 5315 3739/5210/3756 1492 3004 3767
33 βρῶσιν ἔχω φαγεῖν ἣν ὑμεῖς οὐκ οἴδατε. ἔλεγον οὖν οἱ
food have to eat which you not do know. said Then the
3101 4314 240 3387 5342 846 5315
μαθηταὶ πρὸς ἀλλήλους, Μήτις ἤνεγκεν αὐτῷ φαγεῖν;
disciples to one another, No one brought Him to eat?
3004 846 2424 1699 1033 2076/2443/4160 2307
34 λέγει αὐτοῖς ὁ Ἰησοῦς, Ἐμὸν βρῶμά ἐστιν, ἵνα ποιῶ τὸ θέλημα
says to them Jesus, My food is that I may do the will
3992 3165 5048 848 2041 3756 5210
35 τοῦ πέμψαντός με, καὶ τελειώσω αὐτοῦ τὸ ἔργον. οὐχ ὑμεῖς
of (Him) having sent Me, and I may finish of Him the work. Not you
3004 3754 2089 5072 2076 2326 2064
λέγετε ὅτι Ἔτι τετράμηνόν ἐστι, καὶ ὁ θερισμὸς ἔρχεται;
say, Yet four months it is, and the harvest comes.
2400 3004 5213 1869 3788 5216
ἰδού, λέγω ὑμῖν, Ἐπάρατε τοὺς ὀφθαλμοὺς ὑμῶν, καὶ
Behold, I say to you, Lift up the eyes of you, and
2300 5561 3754 3022 1520 4314 2326 2235
θεάσασθε τὰς χώρας, ὅτι λευκαί εἰσι πρὸς θερισμὸν ἤδη.
behold the fields, because white they are to harvest already.
2325 3408 2983 4863 2590 1519 2222
36 καὶ ὁ θερίζων μισθὸν λαμβάνει, καὶ συνάγει καρπὸν εἰς ζωὴν
And he reaping reward receives, and gathers fruit to life
166 2443 4687 3674 5463 2325
αἰώνιον· ἵνα καὶ ὁ σπείρων ὁμοῦ χαίρῃ καὶ ὁ θερίζων.
eternal, that also he sowing together may rejoice and he reaping.
1722/1063 5129 3056 2076 228 3754 243 2076
37 ἐν γὰρ τούτῳ ὁ λόγος ἐστὶν ἀληθινός, ὅτι ἄλλος ἐστὶν ὁ
In For this the word is true, that another is the (one)
4687 243 2325 1473 649 5209 2325
38 σπείρων, καὶ ἄλλος ὁ θερίζων. ἐγὼ ἀπέστειλα ὑμᾶς θερίζειν
sowing, and another the (one) reaping. I sent you to reap
3739/3756/5210 2872 243 2872 5210 1519
ὃ οὐχ ὑμεῖς κεκοπιάκατε· ἄλλοι κεκοπιάκασι, καὶ ὑμεῖς εἰς τὸν
what not you have labored over. Others have labored, and you into the
2873 848 1525
κόπον αὐτῶν εἰσεληλύθατε.
labor of them have entered.

1537 4172 1565 4183 4100 1519 846
39 Ἐκ δὲ τῆς πόλεως ἐκείνης πολλοὶ ἐπίστευσαν εἰς αὐτὸν
out of And the city that many believed in Him
4541 1223 3056 1135 3140
τῶν Σαμαρειτῶν διὰ τὸν λόγον τῆς γυναικὸς μαρτυρούσης
of the Samaritans because of the word of the woman testifying,
3754/2036/3427/3956 3745 4160 5613/3767 2064 4314 846
40 ὅτι Εἶπέ μοι πάντα ὅσα ἐποίησα. ὡς οὖν ἦλθον πρὸς αὐτὸν
He told me all things whatever I did. As then came to Him
4541 2065 846 3306 3844 846 3306
οἱ Σαμαρεῖται, ἠρώτων αὐτὸν μεῖναι παρ' αὐτοῖς· καὶ ἔμεινεν
the Samaritans, they asked Him to stay with them; and He stayed
1563/1417 2250 4183 4119 4100 1223
41 ἐκεῖ δύο ἡμέρας. καὶ πολλῷ πλείους ἐπίστευσαν διὰ τὸν
there two days. And more many believed through the

through His word. [42]And they said to the woman, We no longer believe because of your saying; for we *our*selves have heard, and we know that this One is truly the Savior of the world, the Christ.

[43]But after the two days, He went out from there, and went away into Galilee. [44]For Jesus Himself testified that a prophet has no honor in *his* own native-place. [45]Therefore, when He came into Galilee, the Galileans received Him, seeing all things which He did in Jerusalem at the Feast. For they also went to the Feast.

[46]Then Jesus came again to Cana of Galilee, where He made the water *into* wine. And there was a certain nobleman whose son was sick in Capernaum. [47]Hearing that Jesus was coming from Judea into Galilee, this one went out to Him, and asked Him that He would come and heal his son; for he was about to die. [48]Then Jesus said to him, Unless you see signs and wonders, you will not at all believe. [49]The nobleman said to Him, Sir, come down before my child dies. [50]Jesus said to him, Go! Your son lives. And the man believed the word which Jesus said to him, and went away. [51]But already, as he was going down, his slaves met him and reported, saying, Your child lives. [52]He then asked from them the hour in which he had gotten better. And they said to him, Yesterday, *at the* seventh hour, the fever left him. [53]Then the father knew that *it was* at that hour in which

3056 848 5037 1135 3004 3754 3765 1223 4674
42 λόγον αὐτοῦ, τῇ τε γυναικὶ ἔλεγον ὅτι Οὐκέτι διὰ τὴν σὴν
word of Him. to the And woman they said, No longer because of your
2981 4100 846 1063 191 1492 3754
λαλιὰν πιστεύομεν· αὐτοὶ γὰρ ἀκηκόαμεν, καὶ οἴδαμεν ὅτι
speaking we believe; (our)selves for we have heard, and we know that
3778 2076 230 4990 2889 5547
οὗτός ἐστιν ἀληθῶς ὁ Σωτὴρ τοῦ κόσμου, ὁ Χριστός.
this One is truly the Savior of the world, the Christ.
3326 1417 2250 1831 1564 565 1519
43 Μετὰ δὲ τὰς δύο ἡμέρας ἐξῆλθεν ἐκεῖθεν, καὶ ἀπῆλθεν εἰς
after And the two days, He went out from there, and went into
1056 848 1063 2424 3140 3754 4396
44 τὴν Γαλιλαίαν. αὐτὸς γὰρ ὁ Ἰησοῦς ἐμαρτύρησεν ὅτι προφή-
— Galilee. (Him)self For, - Jesus testified that a prophet
1722 2398 3968 5092 3756/2192/3753/3767/2064/1519
45 της ἐν τῇ ἰδίᾳ πατρίδι τιμὴν οὐκ ἔχει. ὅτε οὖν ἦλθεν εἰς τὴν
in the own native-place honor not has. When, then, He came into –
1056 1209 846 1057 3956 3708
Γαλιλαίαν, ἐδέξαντο αὐτὸν οἱ Γαλιλαῖοι, πάντα ἑωρακότες
Galilee, received Him the Galileans, all things having seen
3739/4160 1722 2414 1722 1859 846 1063 2064
ἃ ἐποίησεν ἐν Ἱεροσολύμοις ἐν τῇ ἑορτῇ· καὶ αὐτοὶ γὰρ ἦλθον
which He did in Jerusalem at the feast. also they For went
1519 1859
εἰς τὴν ἑορτήν.
to the feast.
2064 3767 2424 3825 1519 2580 1056
46 Ἦλθεν οὖν ὁ Ἰησοῦς πάλιν εἰς τὴν Κανᾶ τῆς Γαλιλαίας,
came then Jesus again to Cana of Galilee,
3699 4160 5204 3631 2258/5100 937 3739 5207
ὅπου ἐποίησε τὸ ὕδωρ οἶνον. καὶ ἦν τις βασιλικός, οὗ ὁ υἱὸς
where He made the water wine. And was one noble of whom the son
770 2584 3778 191 3754 2424 2240 1537
47 ἠσθένει ἐν Καπερναούμ. οὗτος ἀκούσας ὅτι Ἰησοῦς ἥκει ἐκ
was ill in Capernaum. This one hearing that Jesus comes from
2449 1519 1056 565 4314 846
τῆς Ἰουδαίας εἰς τὴν Γαλιλαίαν, ἀπῆλθε πρὸς αὐτόν, καὶ
— Judea into — Galilee, went out to Him, and
2065 846 2443 2597 2390 848 5207
ἠρώτα αὐτὸν ἵνα καταβῇ καὶ ἰάσηται αὐτοῦ τὸν υἱόν·
asked Him, that He would come and would cure of him the son;
3195 1063 599 2036 3767 2424 4314 846
48 ἤμελλε γὰρ ἀποθνήσκειν. εἶπεν οὖν ὁ Ἰησοῦς πρὸς αὐτόν,
he was For about to die. said Then — Jesus to him,
1437/3361 4592 5059 1492 =3364= 4100 3004
49 Ἐὰν μὴ σημεῖα καὶ τέρατα ἴδητε, οὐ μὴ πιστεύσητε. λέγει
Except signs and wonders you see, in no way you believe. says
4314 846 937 2962 2597 will 4250 599
πρὸς αὐτὸν ὁ βασιλικός, Κύριε, κατάβηθι πρὶν ἀποθανεῖν
to Him The noble Lord, come down before dies
3813 3427 3004 846 2424 4198 5207 4675
50 τὸ παιδίον μου. λέγει αὐτῷ ὁ Ἰησοῦς, Πορεύου· ὁ υἱός σου
the child of me. says to him Jesus, Go, the son of you
2198 4100 444 3056/3739/2036 846
ζῇ. καὶ ἐπίστευσεν ὁ ἄνθρωπος τῷ λόγῳ ᾧ εἶπεν αὐτῷ
lives. And believed the man the word which said to him
2424 4198 2235 846 2597
51 Ἰησοῦς, καὶ ἐπορεύετο. ἤδη δὲ αὐτοῦ καταβαίνοντος, οἱ
Jesus, and went away. already And (as) he (was) going down the
1401 848 528 846 518 3004
δοῦλοι αὐτοῦ ἀπήντησαν αὐτῷ, καὶ ἀπήγγειλαν λέγοντες
slaves of him met him, and reported, saying,
3754 3816 4675 2198 4441 3767/3844 848 5610/1722
52 ὅτι Ὁ παῖς σου ζῇ. ἐπύθετο οὖν παρ' αὐτῶν τὴν ὥραν ἐν
— The child of you lives. He asked then from them the hour in
37392866 2192 2036 846 3754/5504 5610 1442
ᾗ κομψότερον ἔσχε. καὶ εἶπον αὐτῷ ὅτι Χθὲς ὥραν ἑβδόμην
which better he had. And they said to him, Yesterday (at) hour seventh
863 846 4446 1097/3767 3962 3754/1722 1565
53 ἀφῆκεν αὐτὸν ὁ πυρετός. ἔγνω οὖν ὁ πατὴρ ὅτι ἐν ἐκείνῃ τῇ
left him the fever. Knew, then, the father that in that

Jesus said to him, Your son lives. And he himself, and his whole household, believed. 54Again, this second miracle Jesus did, coming from Judea into Galilee.

5610 1722/3739/2036 848 2424 3754 5207 4675 2198
ὥρᾳ, ἐν ᾗ εἶπεν αὐτῷ ὁ Ἰησοῦς ὅτι Ὁ υἱός σου ζῇ· καὶ
hour in which said to him — Jesus, — The son of you lives. And
4100 848 3614 848 3650 5124 3825
54 ἐπίστευσεν αὐτὸς καὶ ἡ οἰκία αὐτοῦ ὅλη. τοῦτο πάλιν
he believed, himself and the house of him whole. This again,
1208 4592 4160 2424 2064 1537 2449
δεύτερον σημεῖον ἐποίησεν ὁ Ἰησοῦς, ἐλθὼν ἐκ τῆς Ἰουδαίας
a second sign did — Jesus, having come from Judea
1519 1056
εἰς τὴν Γαλιλαίαν.
into — Galilee.

CHAPTER 5

1After these things there was a feast of the Jews, and Jesus went up to Jerusalem.

2And at Jerusalem is a pool at the Sheep Gate which *is* called in Hebrew, Bethesda, having five porches. 3In these was a great multitude of the infirm lying: blind ones, lame ones, withered ones; awaiting the stirring of the water. 4For an angel from time to time descended in the pool, and agitated the water. Then the *one* first entering after the agitation of the water became well, whatever disease he was held by.

5But a certain man was there, being in infirmity thirty-eight years. 6Seeing him lying, and knowing that he had already *spent* much time, Jesus said to him, Do you desire to become well? 7The infirm one answered Him, Lord, I do not have a man, that when the water is agitated he may throw me into the pool; but while I am coming, another goes down before me. 8Jesus said to him, Rise up, Take up your cot and walk! 9And instantly the man became well, and took up his cot and walked. And it was a sabbath that day. 10Therefore, the Jews said

CHAPTER 5

3326 5023 2258 1859 2453 305
1 Μετὰ ταῦτα ἦν ἑορτὴ τῶν Ἰουδαίων, καὶ ἀνέβη ὁ
After these things was a feast of the Jews, and went up —
2424 1519 2414
Ἰησοῦς εἰς Ἱεροσόλυμα.
Jesus to Jerusalem.
2076 1722 2414 1909 4262 2861
2 Ἔστι δὲ ἐν τοῖς Ἱεροσολύμοις ἐπὶ τῇ προβατικῇ κολυμ-
is And in — Jerusalem at the Sheep Gate a pool,
1951 1447 964 4002 4745
βήθρα, ἡ ἐπιλεγομένη Ἑβραϊστὶ Βηθεσδά, πέντε στοὰς
which (is) called in Hebrew Bethesda, five porches
2192 1722 5025 2621 4128 4183 770
3 ἔχουσα. ἐν ταύταις κατέκειτο πλῆθος πολὺ τῶν ἀσθενούν-
having. In these were lying a multitude great of the infirm,
5185 5560 3584 1551 5204
των, τυφλῶν, χωλῶν, ξηρῶν, ἐκδεχομένων τὴν τοῦ ὕδατος
blind ones, lame ones, withered ones, awaiting the of the water
2796 32 1063 2596 2540 2597
4 κίνησιν. ἄγγελος γὰρ κατὰ καιρὸν κατέβαινεν ἐν τῇ
stirring. an angel For at a time descended in the
2861 5015 5204 3767 4413 1684
κολυμβήθρᾳ, καὶ ἐτάρασσε τὸ ὕδωρ· ὁ οὖν πρῶτος ἐμβὰς
pool, and agitated the water. he Then first entering
3326 5016 5204 5199 1096 3739 1221
μετὰ τὴν ταραχὴν τοῦ ὕδατος, ὑγιὴς ἐγίνετο, ᾧ δήποτε
after the agitation of the water, whole became, to what ever
2722 3553 2258 5100 444 1563 5144
5 κατείχετο νοσήματι. ἦν δέ τις ἄνθρωπος ἐκεῖ τριάκοντα καὶ
he was held by disease. was But a certain man there thirty and
3638 2094 2192 1722 769 5126 1492 2424
6 ὀκτὼ ἔτη ἔχων ἐν τῇ ἀσθενείᾳ. τοῦτον ἰδὼν ὁ Ἰησοῦς
eight years being in infirmity. this one, seeing Jesus,
2621 1097 3754 4183 2235 5550 2192 3004
κατακείμενον, καὶ γνοὺς ὅτι πολὺν ἤδη χρόνον ἔχει, λέγει
lying (there) and knowing that much already time he has (spent), says
846 2309 5199 1096 61 846 770
7 αὐτῷ, Θέλεις ὑγιὴς γενέσθαι; ἀπεκρίθη αὐτῷ ὁ ἀσθενῶν,
to him, Desire you whole to become? answered Him The sick one,
2962 444 3756/2192/2443 3752 5015 5204
Κύριε, ἄνθρωπον οὐκ ἔχω ἵνα, ὅταν ταραχθῇ τὸ ὕδωρ,
Lord, a man not I have, that when is agitated the water
906 3165/1519 2861 1722/3739 2064 1473 243
βάλλῃ με εἰς τὴν κολυμβήθραν· ἐν ᾧ δὲ ἔρχομαι ἐγώ, ἄλλος
he cast me into the pool; while but am coming I, another
4253/1700 2597 3004 846 2424 1453 142
8 πρὸ ἐμοῦ καταβαίνει. λέγει αὐτῷ ὁ Ἰησοῦς, Ἔγειραι, ἆρον
before me goes down. says to him Jesus, Rise, Take up
2895 4675 4043 2112 1096 5199
9 τὸν κράββατόν σου, καὶ περιπάτει. καὶ εὐθέως ἐγένετο ὑγιὴς
the mattress of you, and walk! And instantly became whole
444 142 2895 848 4043
ὁ ἄνθρωπος, καὶ ἦρε τὸν κράββατον αὐτοῦ καὶ περιεπάτει.
the man, and took up the mattress of him and walked.
2258 4521 1722 1565 2250 3004 3767
10 Ἦν δὲ σάββατον ἐν ἐκείνῃ τῇ ἡμέρᾳ. ἔλεγον οὖν οἱ
it was And a sabbath on that — day. said Therefore the

to the *one* having been healed, It is a sabbath. It is not lawful for you to lift up the cot. [11]He answered them, The *One* making me well, that One said to me, Lift up your cot and walk. [12]Then they asked him, Who is the man who told you, Lift up your cot and walk? [13]But he did not know the *One* who cured him, for a crowd being in that place, Jesus had withdrawn.

[14]After these things Jesus found him in the temple, and said to him, Behold, you have become well; sin no more, that a worse thing not happen to you. [15]The man went away and told the Jews that Jesus is the *One* making him well. [16]And because of this, the Jews persecuted Jesus, and lusted to kill Him, because He did these things on a sabbath. [17]But Jesus answered them, My Father works until now, and I work. [18]Because of this, therefore, the Jews lusted the more to kill Him, for not only did He break the sabbath, but also called God His own Father, making Himself equal to God.

[19]Then Jesus answered and said to them, Truly, truly, I say to you, The Son is not able to do anything from Himself, except what He may see the Father doing; for whatever that One does, these things also the Son does the same way. [20]For the Father loves the Son, and shows to Him all things which He does. And He will show Him greater works than these in order that you may marvel. [21]For even as the Father raises the dead, and gives life, so also the Son gives life to whomever He wills. [22]For

2453 2323 4521 2076 3756 1832
Ἰουδαῖοι τῷ τεθεραπευμένῳ, Σάββατόν ἐστιν· οὐκ ἔξεστί
Jews to the (one) having been healed, A sabbath it is; not it is lawful

4671 142 2895 611 846 4160 3165
11 σοι ἆραι τὸν κράββατον. ἀπεκρίθη αὐτοῖς, Ὁ ποιήσας με
for you to lift the mattress. He answered them, The (One) making me

5199 1565 3427 2036 142 2895 4675
ὑγιῆ, ἐκεῖνός μοι εἶπεν, Ἆρον τὸν κράββατόν σου καὶ
whole, that One to me said, Lift up the mattress of you, and

4043 2065 3767 846 5101 2076 444
12 περιπάτει. ἠρώτησαν οὖν αὐτόν, Τίς ἐστιν ὁ ἄνθρωπος ὁ
walk. they asked Therefore him, Who is the man who

2036 4671 142 2895 4675 4043
13 εἰπών σοι, Ἆρον τὸν κράββατόν σου καὶ περιπάτει; ὁ δὲ
told you, Lift up the mattress of you and walk? he But

2390 3756 1492/5101 2076 1063 2424 1593 3793
ἰαθεὶς οὐκ ᾔδει τίς ἐστιν· ὁ γὰρ Ἰησοῦς ἐξένευσεν, ὄχλου
cured not did know who it is, For Jesus had withdrawn, a crowd

5607 1722 5117 3326 5023 2147 846 2424
14 ὄντος ἐν τῷ τόπῳ. μετὰ ταῦτα εὑρίσκει αὐτὸν ὁ Ἰησοῦς
being in the place. After these things finds him Jesus

1722 2411 2036 846 2396 5199 1096 3371
ἐν τῷ ἱερῷ, καὶ εἶπεν αὐτῷ, Ἴδε ὑγιὴς γέγονας· μηκέτι
in the Temple, and said to him, Behold, whole you have become; no more

264 2443 3361 5501/5100/4671 1096 565 444
15 ἁμάρτανε, ἵνα μὴ χεῖρόν τί σοι γένηται. ἀπῆλθεν ὁ ἄνθρω-
sin, lest a worse thing to you occur. went away The man

312 2453 3754 2424 2076 4160
πος, καὶ ἀνήγγειλε τοῖς Ἰουδαίοις ὅτι Ἰησοῦς ἐστιν ὁ ποιή-
and told the Jews that Jesus is He

846 5199 1223 5124 1377 2424
16 σας αὐτὸν ὑγιῆ. καὶ διὰ τοῦτο ἐδίωκον τὸν Ἰησοῦν οἱ
making him whole. And therefore persecuted — Jesus the

2453 2212 846 615 3754 5023 4160
Ἰουδαῖοι, καὶ ἐζήτουν αὐτὸν ἀποκτεῖναι, ὅτι ταῦτα ἐποίει
Jews, and sought Him to kill, because these things He did

1722 4521 2424 611 846 3962 3450
17 ἐν σαββάτῳ. ὁ δὲ Ἰησοῦς ἀπεκρίνατο αὐτοῖς, Ὁ πατήρ μου
on a sabbath. — But Jesus answered to them, The Father of Me

2193/737 2038 2504 2038 1223 5124 3767 3123
18 ἕως ἄρτι ἐργάζεται, κἀγὼ ἐργάζομαι. διὰ τοῦτο οὖν μᾶλλον
until now works, and I work. Because of this, then, the more

2212 846 2453 615 3754/3756/3440/3089
ἐζήτουν αὐτὸν οἱ Ἰουδαῖοι ἀποκτεῖναι, ὅτι οὐ μόνον ἔλυε τὸ
sought him the Jews to kill, because not only He broke the

4521 235 3962 2398 3004 2316 2470
σάββατον, ἀλλὰ καὶ πατέρα ἴδιον ἔλεγε τὸν Θεόν, ἴσον
sabbath, but also Father His own called — God, equal

1438 4160 2316
ἑαυτὸν ποιῶν τῷ Θεῷ.
Himself making — to God.

2919 3767 2424 2036 846 281 281
19 Ἀπεκρίνατο οὖν ὁ Ἰησοῦς καὶ εἶπεν αὐτοῖς, Ἀμὴν ἀμὴν
answered Therefore Jesus and said to them, Truly, truly

3004 5213 3756 1410 5207 4160 575 1438 3762 1437
λέγω ὑμῖν, οὐ δύναται ὁ υἱὸς ποιεῖν ἀφ' ἑαυτοῦ οὐδέν, ἐὰν
I say to you, not is able the Son to do from Himself nothing, un-

3361/510 1/991 3962 4160 3739/1063/302/ 1565 4160
μή τι βλέπῃ τὸν πατέρα ποιοῦντα· ἃ γὰρ ἂν ἐκεῖνος ποιῇ,
less what He may see the Father doing; what For ever that One does,

5023 5207 3668 4160 1063 3962 5268 5207
20 ταῦτα καὶ ὁ υἱὸς ὁμοίως ποιεῖ. ὁ γὰρ πατὴρ φιλεῖ τὸν υἱόν,
these things also the Son likewise does. the For Father loves the Son,

3956 1166 846/3739/846 4160 3187 5130
καὶ πάντα δείκνυσιν αὐτῷ ἃ αὐτὸς ποιεῖ καὶ μείζονα τούτων
and all things shows to Him which He does; and greater (than) these

1166 846 2041 2443 5210 2296 5618 1063 3962
21 δείξει αὐτῷ ἔργα, ἵνα ὑμεῖς θαυμάζητε. ὥσπερ γὰρ ὁ πατὴρ
He will show Him works, that you may marvel. even as For the Father

1453 3498 2227 3779 5207/3739/2309
ἐγείρει τοὺς νεκροὺς καὶ ζωοποιεῖ, οὕτω καὶ ὁ υἱὸς οὓς θέλει
raises up the dead and makes alive so also the Son whom He wills

the Father judges no one, but has given all judgment to the Son, [23]so that all may honor the Son, even as they honor the Father. The *one* not honoring the Son does not honor the Father who has sent Him. [24]Truly, truly, I say to you, The *one* who hears My word, and believes the *One* who has sent Me, has everlasting life, and does not come into judgment but has passed out of death into life. [25]Truly, truly, I say to you that an hour is coming, and now is, when the dead will hear the voice of the Son of God, and the ones hearing will live. [26]For even as the Father has life in Himself, so He gave also to the Son to have life in Himself. [27]And He also gave authority to Him to execute judgment, for He is *the* Son of man. [28]Do not marvel at this, for an hour is coming in which all those in the tombs will hear His voice. [29]And *they* will come out, the ones having done good into a resurrection of life; and the ones having practiced evil into a resurrection of judgment.

[30]Nothing I am able to do from Myself; just as I hear, I judge; and My judgment is just, for I do not seek My will, but the will of the *One* sending Me, *the* Father. [31]If I witness concerning Myself, My witness is not true; [32]it is Another that witnesses concerning Me, and I know that the witness which He witnesses concerning Me is true. [33]You have sent to John, and he has testified to the truth. [34]But I do not receive witness from man, but I say these things that you may be saved. [35]That one was the burning and shining lamp, and you were willing

2227 3761 1063 3962 2919 3762 235 2920
22 ζωοποιεῖ. οὐδὲ γὰρ ὁ πατὴρ κρίνει οὐδένα, ἀλλὰ τὴν κρίσιν
He makes alive. not for the Father judges no one, but judgment

3956 1325 5207 2443 3956 5091 5207 2531 5091
23 πᾶσαν δέδωκε τῷ υἱῷ· ἵνα πάντες τιμῶσι τὸν υἱόν, καθὼς τιμῶσι
all He has given to the Son, that all may honor the Son, even as they honor

3962 3361 5091 5207 3756 5091 3962
τὸν πατέρα ὁ μὴ τιμῶν τὸν υἱόν, οὐ τιμᾷ τὸν πατέρα τὸν πέμ-
the Father. He not honoring the Son not does honor the Father, the (One)

3992 846 281 281 3004 5213 3754 3056 3450
24 ψαντα αὐτόν. ἀμὴν ἀμὴν λέγω ὑμῖν ὅτι ὁ τὸν λόγον μου
having sent Him. Truly, truly, I say to you, The (one) the word of Me

191 4100 3992 3165 2192 2222 166
ἀκούων, καὶ πιστεύων τῷ πέμψαντί με, ἔχει ζωὴν αἰώνιον· καὶ
hearing, and believing the (One) having sent Me, has life everlasting and

1519 2920 3756 2064 235 3327 1537 2288 1519
εἰς κρίσιν οὐκ ἔρχεται, ἀλλὰ μεταβέβηκεν ἐκ τοῦ θανάτου εἰς τὴν
into judgment not comes, but has passed out of death into

2222 281 281 3004 5213 3754 2064 5610 3568 2076
25 ζωήν. ἀμὴν ἀμὴν λέγω ὑμῖν ὅτι ἔρχεται ὥρα καὶ νῦν ἐστιν,
life. Truly, truly, I say to you, comes An hour, and now is,

3753 5498 191 5456 5207 2316
ὅτε οἱ νεκροὶ ἀκούσονται τῆς φωνῆς τοῦ υἱοῦ τοῦ Θεοῦ,
when the dead will hear from the voice of the Son of God,

191 2198 5618 1063 3962 2192 2222
26 καὶ οἱ ἀκούσαντες ζήσονται. ὥσπερ γὰρ ὁ πατὴρ ἔχει ζωὴν
and those hearing will live. even as For the Father has life

1722/1438 3779 1325 5207 2222 2192/1722/1438
27 ἐν ἑαυτῷ, οὕτως ἔδωκε καὶ τῷ υἱῷ ζωὴν ἔχειν ἐν ἑαυτῷ· καὶ
in Himself. so He gave also to the Son life to have in Himself. And

1849 1325 846 2920 4160 3754 5207 444
ἐξουσίαν ἔδωκεν αὐτῷ καὶ κρίσιν ποιεῖν, ὅτι υἱὸς ἀνθρώπου
authority He gave to Him, also judgment to do, because Son of man

2739 2076/3361 2296 5124 3754/2064 5610/1722 3956 1722
28 ἐστί. μὴ θαυμάζετε τοῦτο· ὅτι ἔρχεται ὥρα, ἐν ᾗ πάντες οἱ ἐν
He is. not Marvel (at) this, for comes an hour in which all those in

3419 191 5456 848 1607
29 τοῖς μνημείοις ἀκούσονται τῆς φωνῆς αὐτοῦ, καὶ ἐκπορεύσ-
the tombs will hear the voice of Him, and will come out;

18 4160 1519 386 2222
ονται, οἱ τὰ ἀγαθὰ ποιήσαντες, εἰς ἀνάστασιν ζωῆς· οἱ δὲ
those the good having done, into a resurrection of life; those

5337 4238 1519 386 2920
τὰ φαῦλα πράξαντες, εἰς ἀνάστασιν κρίσεως.
and the evil having practiced into a resurrection of judgment.

3756 1410 1473 4160 575 1683 3762 2531 191
30 Οὐ δύναμαι ἐγὼ ποιεῖν ἀπ' ἐμαυτοῦ οὐδέν· καθὼς ἀκούω,
not am able I to do from Myself nothing; just as I hear,

2919 2920 1699 1342 2076 3754/3756/2212
κρίνω· καὶ ἡ κρίσις ἡ ἐμὴ δικαία ἐστίν· ὅτι οὐ ζητῶ τὸ
I judge; and judgment — My just is, because not I seek —

2307 1699 235 2307 3992 3165 3962
θέλημα τὸ ἐμόν, ἀλλὰ τὸ θέλημα τοῦ πέμψαντός με πατρός.
will — My, but the will of the (One) sending Me, (the) Father.

1437/1473 3140 4012 1683 3141 3450/3756/2076
31 ἐὰν ἐγὼ μαρτυρῶ περὶ ἐμαυτοῦ, ἡ μαρτυρία μου οὐκ ἔστιν
If I witness concerning Myself, the witness of Me not is

227 243 2076 3140 4012 1700 1492 3754
32 ἀληθής. ἄλλος ἐστὶν ὁ μαρτυρῶν περὶ ἐμοῦ, καὶ οἶδα ὅτι
true; another there is that witnesses concerning Me, and I know that

227 2076 3141 3739 3140 4012 1700 5210
33 ἀληθής ἐστιν ἡ μαρτυρία ἣν μαρτυρεῖ περὶ ἐμοῦ. ὑμεῖς
true is the witness which He witnesses concerning Me. You

649 4314 2491 3140 225
ἀπεστάλκατε πρὸς Ἰωάννην, καὶ μεμαρτύρηκε τῇ ἀληθείᾳ.
have sent to John, and he has witnessed to the truth;

1473 3756 3844 444 3141 2983 235
34 ἐγὼ δὲ οὐ παρὰ ἀνθρώπου τὴν μαρτυρίαν λαμβάνω, ἀλλὰ
I but not from man the witness receive, but

5023 3004/2443/5210 4982 1565 2258 3088 2545
35 ταῦτα λέγω ἵνα ὑμεῖς σωθῆτε. ἐκεῖνος ἦν ὁ λύχνος ὁ καιό-
these things I say that you may be saved. That one was the lamp

to exult in his light for an hour. [36]But I have the greater witness than John's, for the works which the Father has given Me, that I should finish them, the works which I do themselves witness concerning Me, that the Father has sent Me. [37]And the Father, He sending Me has Himself borne witness concerning Me. You have neither heard His voice at any time, nor have you seen His form. [38]And you do not have His word abiding in you, for He whom that One sent, you do not believe this One. [39]You search the Scriptures, for you think in them you have everlasting life. And they are the *ones* witnessing concerning Me. [40]And you are not willing to come to Me that you may have life. [41]I do not receive glory from men; [42]but I have known you, that you do not have the love of God in yourselves. [43]I have come in the name of My Father, and you do not receive Me. If another comes in *his* own name you will receive that one. [44]How are you able to believe, *you* receiving glory from one another, and the glory which *is* from the only God you do not seek? [45]Do not think that I will accuse you to the Father; there is *one* accusing you, Moses, in whom you have hoped. [46]For if you were believing Moses, you would then believe Me; for that one wrote concerning Me.

[47]But if you do not believe his writings, how will you believe My words?

5316 5210 2309 21 4314
μενος καὶ φαίνων, ὑμεῖς δὲ ἠθελήσατε ἀγαλλιασθῆναι πρὸς
burning and shining; you and were willing to exult for
5610/1722 5459 848 1473 2192 3141 3187
ὥραν ἐν τῷ φωτὶ αὐτοῦ. ἐγὼ δὲ ἔχω τὴν μαρτυρίαν μείζω
an hour in the light of him. I But have the witness greater
2491 1063 2041/3739 1325 3427 3962 2443
36 τοῦ Ἰωάννου· τὰ γὰρ ἔργα ἃ ἔδωκέ μοι ὁ πατὴρ ἵνα
than of John; the for works which has given Me the Father that
5048 846 848 2041/3739/1473/4160 3140 4012
τελειώσω αὐτά, αὐτὰ τὰ ἔργα ἃ ἐγὼ ποιῶ, μαρτυρεῖ περὶ
I may finish them, themselves the works that I do witness about
1700/3754 3962 3165 649 3992/3165/3962
37 ἐμοῦ ὅτι ὁ πατήρ με ἀπέσταλκε. καὶ ὁ πέμψας με πατήρ,
Me, that the Father Me has sent. And He having sent Me, (the) Father,
848 3140 4012 1700 3777 5456 848 191
αὐτὸς μεμαρτύρηκε περὶ ἐμοῦ. οὔτε φωνὴν αὐτοῦ ἀκηκόατε
He has witnessed concerning Me. Neither the voice of Him have you heard
4455 3777 1491 848 3708 3056 848
38 πώποτε, οὔτε εἶδος αὐτοῦ ἑωράκατε. καὶ τὸν λόγον αὐτοῦ
at any time, nor form His have you seen. And the word of Him
3756 2192 3306 1722/5213/3754/3739/ 649 1565 5129
οὐκ ἔχετε μένοντα ἐν ὑμῖν, ὅτι ὃν ἀπέστειλεν ἐκεῖνος, τούτῳ
not you have abiding in you, for whom sent that One, this One
5210/3756 4100 2045 1124 3754 5210 1380
39 ὑμεῖς οὐ πιστεύετε. ἐρευνᾶτε τὰς γραφάς, ὅτι ὑμεῖς δοκεῖτε
you do not believe. You search the Scriptures, because you think
1722 846 2222 166 2192 1565 1526 3140
ἐν αὐταῖς ζωὴν αἰώνιον ἔχειν, καὶ ἐκεῖναί εἰσιν αἱ μαρτυ-
in them life everlasting you have, and those are the (ones)
4012 1700 3756 2309 2064 4314/3165/2443/2222
40 ροῦσαι περὶ ἐμοῦ· καὶ οὐ θέλετε ἐλθεῖν πρός με, ἵνα ζωὴν
witnessing about Me. And not you desire to come to Me, that life
2192 1391 3844 444 3756 2983 235 1097
41 ἔχητε. δόξαν παρὰ ἀνθρώπων οὐ λαμβάνω· ἀλλ' ἔγνωκα
42 you may have. glory from men not I receive, but I have known
5209 3754 26 2316 3756 2192/1722/ 1438
ὑμᾶς, ὅτι τὴν ἀγάπην τοῦ Θεοῦ οὐκ ἔχετε ἐν ἑαυτοῖς
you, that the love — of God not you have in yourselves.
1473 2064 1722 3686 3962 3450
43 ἐγὼ ἐλήλυθα ἐν τῷ ὀνόματι τοῦ πατρός μου, καὶ οὐ
I have come in the name of the Father of Me, and not
2983 3165/1437 243 2064/1722 3686 2398 1565
λαμβάνετέ με· ἐὰν ἄλλος ἔλθῃ ἐν τῷ ὀνόματι τῷ ἰδίῳ, ἐκεῖνον
you receive Me; if another comes in — name the own, that one
2983 4459 1410 5210 4100 1391 3844 240
44 λήψεσθε. πῶς δύνασθε ὑμεῖς πιστεῦσαι, δόξαν παρὰ ἀλλή-
you will receive. How can you believe, glory from one
2983 1391 3844 3441 2316
λων λαμβάνοντες, καὶ τὴν δόξαν τὴν παρὰ τοῦ μόνου Θεοῦ
another receiving, and the glory — from the only God
3756 2212 3361 1380 3754/1473 2723 5216 4314
45 οὐ ζητεῖτε ; μὴ δοκεῖτε ὅτι ἐγὼ κατηγορήσω ὑμῶν πρὸς τὸν
not you seek? Do not think that I will accuse you to the
3962 2076 2723 5216 3475 1519/3739/5210
πατέρα· ἔστιν ὁ κατηγορῶν ὑμῶν, Μωσῆς, εἰς ὃν ὑμεῖς
Father; there is the (one) accusing you, Moses, in whom you
1679 1487/1063 4100 3475 4100 302 1698
46 ἠλπίκατε. εἰ γὰρ ἐπιστεύετε Μωσῇ, ἐπιστεύετε ἂν ἐμοί·
have hoped. if For you were believing Moses, you were believing then Me;
4012/1063/1700 1565 1125 1487 1565 1121
47 περὶ γὰρ ἐμοῦ ἐκεῖνος ἔγραψεν. εἰ δὲ τοῖς ἐκείνου γράμμασιν
about for Me that one wrote. if But the of that one writings
3756 4100 4459 1699 4487 4100
οὐ πιστεύετε, πῶς τοῖς ἐμοῖς ῥήμασι πιστεύσετε ;
not you believe, how — My words will you believe?

CHAPTER 6

[1]After these things Jesus went away over the Sea of

3326 5023 565 2424 4008 2281
1 Μετὰ ταῦτα ἀπῆλθεν ὁ Ἰησοῦς πέραν τῆς θαλάσσης τῆς
After these things went away Jesus across the sea —

Galilee, the Tiberian *Sea*. [2]And a great crowd followed Him, for they saw His miracles which He did on the sick ones. [3]And Jesus went up into the mountain, and sat there with His disciples. [4]And the Passover was near, the feast of the Jews.

[5]Then Jesus lifting up *His* eyes and seeing that a great crowd is coming to Him, He said to Philip, From where may we buy loaves that these may eat? [6]But He said this to test him, for He knew what He was about to do [7]Philip answered Him, Loaves for two hundred denarii are not enough for them, that each of them may receive a little. [8]One of His disciples said to Him, Andrew the brother of Simon Peter, [9]A little boy is here who has five barley loaves and two fish; but what are these for so many? [10]And Jesus said, Make the men to recline. And much grass was in the place. Then the men reclined, the number *was* about five thousand. [11]And Jesus took the loaves, and giving thanks distributed to the disciples, and the disciples to those reclining. And in the same way the fish, as much as they desired. [12]And when they were filled, He said to His disciples, Gather up the fragments left over, that not anything be lost. [13]Then they gathered and filled twelve handbaskets with fragments of the five barley loaves which were left over to those who had eaten.

[14]Then seeing what miracle Jesus did, the men said, This is truly the Prophet, the

1056 5085 190 846 3793 4183
2 Γαλιλαίας, τῆς Τιβεριάδος. καὶ ἠκολούθει αὐτῷ ὄχλος πολύς,
of Galilee, of Tiberias. And followed Him a crowd great
3754 3708 848 4592 3739 4160 1909 770
ὅτι ἑώρων αὐτοῦ τὰ σημεῖα ἃ ἐποίει ἐπὶ τῶν ἀσθενούντων.
for they saw of Him the signs which He did on the sick ones.
424 1519 3735 2424 1563 2521 3326
3 ἀνῆλθε δὲ εἰς τὸ ὄρος ὁ Ἰησοῦς, καὶ ἐκεῖ ἐκάθητο μετὰ τῶν
went up And to the mountain Jesus, and there sat with the
3101 848 2258 1451 3957 1859
4 μαθητῶν αὐτοῦ. ἦν δὲ ἐγγὺς τὸ πάσχα, ἡ ἑορτὴ τῶν
disciples of Him. was And near the Passover, the feast of the
2453 1869 3767 2424 3788
5 Ἰουδαίων. ἐπάρας οὖν ὁ Ἰησοῦς τοὺς ὀφθαλμούς, καὶ
Jews. lifting up Then Jesus the eyes, and
2300 3754 4183 3793 2064 4314 846 3004 4314
θεασάμενος ὅτι πολὺς ὄχλος ἔρχεται πρὸς αὐτόν, λέγει πρὸς
beholding that a great crowd is coming to Him, He says to
5376 4159 59 740 2443 5315
τὸν Φίλιππον, Πόθεν ἀγοράσομεν ἄρτους, ἵνα φάγωσιν
Philip, From where may we buy loaves that may eat
3778 5124 3004 3985 846 846 1063 1492/5101
6 οὗτοι; τοῦτο δὲ ἔλεγε πειράζων αὐτόν· αὐτὸς γὰρ ᾔδει τί
these? this And He said testing him; He for knew what
3195 4160 611 846 5376 1250
7 ἔμελλε ποιεῖν. ἀπεκρίθη αὐτῷ Φίλιππος, Διακοσίων
He was going to do. answered Him Philip, Of two hundred
1220 740 3756 714 846 2443 1538 846
δηναρίων ἄρτοι οὐκ ἀρκοῦσιν αὐτοῖς, ἵνα ἕκαστος αὐτῶν
denarii loaves not are enough for them, that each of them
1024/5100 2983 3004 846 1519/1537 3101 848
8 βραχύ τι λάβῃ. λέγει αὐτῷ εἷς ἐκ τῶν μαθητῶν αὐτοῦ,
a little may receive. says to Him one of the disciples of Him,
406 80 4613 4074 2076 3808 1520
9 Ἀνδρέας ὁ ἀδελφὸς Σίμωνος Πέτρου, Ἔστι παιδάριον ἓν
Andrew the brother of Simon Peter, There is little boy one
5602 2192 4002 740 2916 1417 3795 235
ὧδε, ὃ ἔχει πέντε ἄρτους κριθίνους καὶ δύο ὀψάρια· ἀλλὰ
here, who has five loaves (of) barley, and two fish; but
5023/5101/2076/1519 5118 2036 2424 4160
10 ταῦτα τί ἐστιν εἰς τοσούτους; εἶπε δὲ ὁ Ἰησοῦς, Ποιήσατε
these what are to so many? said And Jesus, Make
444 377 2258 5528 4183/1722 5117
τοὺς ἀνθρώπους ἀναπεσεῖν. ἦν δὲ χόρτος πολὺς ἐν τῷ τόπῳ.
the men to recline was And grass much in the place.
377 3767 435 706 5616 4000
ἀνέπεσον οὖν οἱ ἄνδρες τὸν ἀριθμὸν ὡσεὶ πεντακισχίλιοι.
Reclined, therefore, the men, the number about five thousand.
2983 740 2424 2168 1239
11 ἔλαβε δὲ τοὺς ἄρτους ὁ Ἰησοῦς, καὶ εὐχαριστήσας διέδωκε
took And the loaves Jesus, and having given thanks dealt out
3101 3101 345 3668 1537
τοῖς μαθηταῖς, οἱ δὲ μαθηταὶ τοῖς ἀνακειμένοις· ὁμοίως καὶ ἐκ
to the disciples, the and disciples to those reclining. likewise And of
3795 3765 2309 5613 1705 3004
12 τῶν ὀψαρίων ὅσον ἤθελον. ὡς δὲ ἐνεπλήσθησαν, λέγει τοῖς
the fish, as much as they desired. as And they were filled, He says to
3101 848 4863 4052 2801 the
μαθηταῖς αὐτοῦ, Συναγάγετε τὰ περισσεύσαντα κλάσματα,
disciples of Him, Gather together the left over fragments,
2443/3361/5100/ 622 4863 3756 1072 1427
13 ἵνα μή τι ἀπόληται. συνήγαγον οὖν, καὶ ἐγέμισαν δώδεκα
that not anything be lost. they gather Then, and filled twelve
2894 2801 1537 4002 740 2916 3739
κοφίνους κλασμάτων ἐκ τῶν πέντε ἄρτων τῶν κριθίνων, ἃ
baskets with fragments of the five loaves (of) barley which
4052 977 3767 444 1492 3739
14 ἐπερίσσευσε τοῖς βεβρωκόσιν. οἱ οὖν ἄνθρωποι ἰδόντες ὃ
were left over to those having eaten. the Therefore men seeing what
4160 4592 2424 3004 3754 3778 2076 230
ἐποίησε σημεῖον ὁ Ἰησοῦς, ἔλεγον ὅτι Οὗτός ἐστιν ἀληθῶς ὁ
did sign Jesus, said, This is truly the

one coming into the world. [15]Then knowing that they were about to come and seize Him, that they might make Him king, Jesus withdrew again to the mountain, alone *by* Himself.

[16]And when it became evening, His disciples went down on the sea. [17]And entering into the boat, they were going across the sea to Capernaum. And darkness already occurred, and Jesus had not come to them. [18]And the sea was aroused by a great wind blowing. [19]Then having rowed about twenty-five or thirty furlongs, they saw Jesus walking on the sea. And *He* having come near the boat, they were afraid. [20]But He said to them, I AM! Do not fear. [21]Then they desired to take Him into the boat. And instantly the boat came to be at the land to which they were going.

[22]On the morrow the crowd standing on the other side of the sea had seen that no other little boat was there, except one, that one into which His disciples entered, and that Jesus did not go with His disciples into the little boat, but that the disciples went away alone. [23]But other small boats came from Tiberias near the place where they ate the bread, the Lord having given thanks. [24]Therefore, when the crowd saw that Jesus was not there, nor His disciples, they themselves also entered into the boats and came to Capernaum seeking Jesus. [25]And finding Him across the sea, they said to Him, Rabbi, when did you come here? [26]Jesus answered

4396 2064 1519 2889 2424 3767 1097
15 προφήτης ὁ ἐρχόμενος εἰς τὸν κόσμον. Ἰησοῦς οὖν γνοὺς
prophet, the (one) coming into the world. Jesus Then knowing
3754 3195 2064 726 846 2443 4160
ὅτι μέλλουσιν ἔρχεσθαι καὶ ἁρπάζειν αὐτόν, ἵνα ποιήσωσιν
that they are about to come and seize Him, that they may make
846 935 402 3825 1519 3735 848 3441
αὐτὸν βασιλέα, ἀνεχώρησε πάλιν εἰς τὸ ὄρος αὐτὸς μόνος.
Him king, withdrew again into the mountain, Himself alone.
5613 3798 1096 2597 3101 848 1909
16 Ὡς δὲ ὀψία ἐγένετο, κατέβησαν οἱ μαθηταὶ αὐτοῦ ἐπὶ τὴν
when And evening it was, went down the disciples of Him on the
2281 1684 1519 4143 2064 4008
17 θάλασσαν, καὶ ἐμβάντες εἰς τὸ πλοῖον, ἤρχοντο πέραν τῆς
sea. And having entered into the boat, they were going across the
2281 2584 4653 2235 1096 3756
θαλάσσης εἰς Καπερναούμ. καὶ σκοτία ἤδη ἐγεγόνει, καὶ οὐκ
sea to Capernaum. And darkness already occurred, and not
2064 4314 846 2424 5037 2281 417 3173
18 ἐληλύθει πρὸς αὐτοὺς ὁ Ἰησοῦς. ἥ τε θάλασσα ἀνέμου μεγά-
had come to them — Jesus. And the sea by a wind great
4154 1326 1643 3767/5613 4712 1501
19 λου πνέοντος διηγείρετο. ἐληλακότες οὖν ὡς σταδίους εἰκοσι-
blowing was aroused. having rowed Then about furlongs twenty-
4002/2228/ 5144 2334 2424 4043 1909
πέντε ἢ τριάκοντα, θεωροῦσι τὸν Ἰησοῦν περιπατοῦντα ἐπὶ
five, or thirty, they behold — Jesus walking on
2281 1451 4143 1096 5399
τῆς θαλάσσης, καὶ ἐγγὺς τοῦ πλοίου γινόμενον· καὶ ἐφοβήθη-
the sea, and near the boat becoming; and they feared.
3004 846 1473 1510/3361 5399 2309 3767
20 σαν. ὁ δὲ λέγει αὐτοῖς, Ἐγώ εἰμι· μὴ φοβεῖσθε. ἤθελον οὖν
21 He But says to them, I AM! Do not fear. they desired Then
2983 846 1519 4143 2112 4143 1096
λαβεῖν αὐτὸν εἰς τὸ πλοῖον· καὶ εὐθέως τὸ πλοῖον ἐγένετο
to take Him into the boat; and instantly the boat became
1909 1093/1519/3739/ 5217
ἐπὶ τῆς γῆς εἰς ἣν ὑπῆγον.
at the land to which they were going.
1887 3793 2476 4008 2281
22 Τῇ ἐπαύριον ὁ ὄχλος ὁ ἑστηκὼς πέραν τῆς θαλάσσης,
On the morrow the crowd — standing across the sea
1492 3754 4142 243 3756/2258/1563=1508=1722 1565 1519
ἰδὼν ὅτι πλοιάριον ἄλλο οὐκ ἦν ἐκεῖ εἰ μὴ ἓν ἐκεῖνο εἰς ὃ
had seen that little boat another not was there, except one, that into which
1684 3101 848 3754/3756 4897
ἐνέβησαν οἱ μαθηταὶ αὐτοῦ, καὶ ὅτι οὐ συνεισῆλθε τοῖς
entered the disciples of Him; and that not went with the
3101 848 2424 1519 4142 235 3441
μαθηταῖς αὐτοῦ ὁ Ἰησοῦς εἰς τὸ πλοιάριον, ἀλλὰ μόνοι οἱ
disciples of Him — Jesus into the little boat but alone the
3101 848 565 243 2064 4142 1537
23 μαθηταὶ αὐτοῦ ἀπῆλθον, (ἄλλα δὲ ἦλθε πλοιάρια ἐκ
disciples of Him went away. other But came little boats from
5085 1451 5117 3699 5315 740
Τιβεριάδος ἐγγὺς τοῦ τόπου ὅπου ἔφαγον τὸν ἄρτον,
Tiberias near the place where they ate the loaves,
2168 2962 3753/3767 1492 3793 3754
24 εὐχαριστήσαντος τοῦ Κυρίου)· ὅτε οὖν εἶδεν ὁ ὄχλος ὅτι
having given thanks the Lord, when Therefore saw the crowd that
2424 3756 2076 1563 3761 3101 848 1684
Ἰησοῦς οὐκ ἔστιν ἐκεῖ οὐδὲ οἱ μαθηταὶ αὐτοῦ, ἐνέβησαν καὶ
Jesus not is there, nor the disciples of Him, they entered also
846 1519 4143 2064 1519 2584 2212
αὐτοὶ εἰς τὰ πλοῖα, καὶ ἦλθον εἰς Καπερναούμ, ζητοῦντες τὸν
themselves into the boats, and came to Capernaum seeking —
2424 2147 846 4008 2281 2036
25 Ἰησοῦν. καὶ εὑρόντες αὐτὸν πέραν τῆς θαλάσσης, εἶπον
Jesus. And having found Him across the sea, they said
846 4461 4219 5602 1096 611 846
26 αὐτῷ, Ῥαββί, πότε ὧδε γέγονας; ἀπεκρίθη αὐτοῖς ὁ
to Him, Rabbi, when here did you come? answered them —

them and said, Truly, truly, I say to you, you seek Me not because you saw miracles, but because you ate of the loaves and were satisfied. 27Do not labor *for* the food which perishes, but for the food which endures to everlasting life, which the Son of man will give to you; for God the Father sealed this One.

28Then they said to Him, What may we do that we may work the works of God? 29Jesus answered and said to them, This is the work of God, that you believe into *Him* whom that One sent. 30Then they said to Him, Then what miracle do you do, that we may see and may believe you? What do you work? 31Our fathers ate the manna in the wilderness, as it is written, "He gave them bread out of Heaven to eat." 32Then Jesus said to them, Truly, truly, I say to you, Moses has not given you the bread out of Heaven, but My Father gives you the true bread out of Heaven. 33For the bread of God is the *One* coming down out of Heaven and giving life to the world. 34Then they said to Him, Lord, always give us this bread.

35Jesus said to them, I am the Bread of life; the *one* coming to Me will not at all hunger, and the *one* believing into Me will never ever thirst. 36But I said to you that you also have seen Me and did not believe. 37All that the Father gives to Me will come to Me, and the *one* coming to Me I will in no way cast out. 38For I have come down out of Heaven, not that I should do My will, but the will of Him

2424 2036 281 281 3004 5213 2212/3165/3756/3754
Ἰησοῦς καὶ εἶπεν, Ἀμὴν ἀμὴν λέγω ὑμῖν, ζητεῖτέ με, οὐχ ὅτι
Jesus and said, Truly, truly, I say to you, You seek Me, not because
1492 4592 235 3754 5315 1537 740 5526
εἴδετε σημεῖα, ἀλλ' ὅτι ἐφάγετε ἐκ τῶν ἄρτων καὶ ἐχορτά-
you saw signs, but because you ate of the loaves and were
2038 3361 1035 622 235
27 σθητε. ἐργάζεσθε μὴ τὴν βρῶσιν τὴν ἀπολλυμένην, ἀλλὰ
satisfied. Work not (for) the food — perishing, but
1035 3306 1519 2222 166 3739 5207
τὴν βρῶσιν τὴν μένουσαν εἰς ζωὴν αἰώνιον, ἣν ὁ υἱὸς τοῦ
the food — enduring to life everlasting, which the Son —
444 5213 1325 5126 1063 3962 4972
ἀνθρώπου ὑμῖν δώσει· τοῦτον γὰρ ὁ πατὴρ ἐσφράγισεν,
of man to you will give; this One for the Father sealed,
2316 2036/3767/4314 846 5101 4160 2443 2038
28 ὁ Θεός. εἶπον οὖν πρὸς αὐτόν, Τί ποιῶμεν, ἵνα ἐργαζώμεθα
— God. they said Then to Him, What may we do that we may work
2041 2316 611 2424 2036 846
29 τὰ ἔργα τοῦ Θεοῦ; ἀπεκρίθη ὁ Ἰησοῦς καὶ εἶπεν αὐτοῖς,
the works — of God? answered — Jesus and said to them,
5124 2076 2041 2316 2443 4100 1519/3739
Τοῦτό ἐστι τὸ ἔργον τοῦ Θεοῦ, ἵνα πιστεύσητε εἰς ὃν
This is the work — of God, that you believe into whom
649 1565 2036 3767 846 5101/3767 4160 4771
30 ἀπέστειλεν ἐκεῖνος. εἶπον οὖν αὐτῷ, Τί οὖν ποιεῖς σὺ
sent that One. They said, then, to Him, What then do You
4592 2443 1492 4100 4671 5101 2038
31 σημεῖον, ἵνα ἴδωμεν καὶ πιστεύσωμέν σοι; τί ἐργάζῃ; οἱ
(as) a sign, that we may see and may believe You? What do You work? The
3962 2257 3131 5315 1722 2048 2531 2076
πατέρες ἡμῶν τὸ μάννα ἔφαγον ἐν τῇ ἐρήμῳ, καθώς ἐστι
fathers of us the manna ate in the wilderness, as it is
1125 740 1537 3772 1325 846 5315
γεγραμμένον, Ἄρτον ἐκ τοῦ οὐρανοῦ ἔδωκεν αὐτοῖς φαγεῖν.
having been written, Bread out of — Heaven He gave to them to eat.
2036 3767 846 2424 281 281 3004 5213 3756
32 εἶπεν οὖν αὐτοῖς ὁ Ἰησοῦς, Ἀμὴν ἀμὴν λέγω ὑμῖν, Οὐ
said therefore to them — Jesus, Truly, truly, I say to you, not
3475 1325 5213 740 1537 3772 235
Μωσῆς δέδωκεν ὑμῖν τὸν ἄρτον ἐκ τοῦ οὐρανοῦ· ἀλλ' ὁ
Moses has given you the bread out of — Heaven, but the
3962 3450 1325 5213 740 1537 3772
πατήρ μου δίδωσιν ὑμῖν τὸν ἄρτον ἐκ τοῦ οὐρανοῦ τὸν
Father of Me gives to you the bread out of — Heaven —
228 1063 740 2316 2076 2597 1537
33 ἀληθινόν. ὁ γὰρ ἄρτος τοῦ Θεοῦ ἐστιν ὁ καταβαίνων ἐκ τοῦ
true. the For bread — of God is the (One) coming down out of
3772 2222 1325 2889 2036 3767 4314 846
34 οὐρανοῦ καὶ ζωὴν διδοὺς τῷ κόσμῳ. εἶπον οὖν πρὸς αὐτόν,
Heaven and life giving to the world. They said, then, to Him,
2962 3842 1325/2254 740 5126 2036 846
35 Κύριε, πάντοτε δὸς ἡμῖν τὸν ἄρτον τοῦτον. εἶπε δὲ αὐτοῖς
Lord, always give us — bread this. said And to them
2424 1473 1510 740 2222 2064 4314/3165
ὁ Ἰησοῦς, Ἐγώ εἰμι ὁ ἄρτος τῆς ζωῆς· ὁ ἐρχόμενος πρός με
— Jesus, I am the bread — of life. the (one) coming to Me
3756/3361 3983 4100 1519/1691 =3364= 1372
οὐ μὴ πεινάσῃ· καὶ ὁ πιστεύων εἰς ἐμὲ οὐ μὴ διψήσῃ
not at all will hunger, and the (one) believing in Me in no way will thirst,
4455 235 2036 5213 3754 2708 3165 3756
36 πώποτε. ἀλλ' εἶπον ὑμῖν ὅτι καὶ ἑωράκατέ με, καὶ οὐ
ever! But I told you that both you have seen Me, and not
4100 3956/3739/ 1325 3427 3962 4314/1691/2240
37 πιστεύετε. πᾶν ὃ δίδωσί μοι ὁ πατὴρ πρὸς ἐμὲ ἥξει· καὶ τὸν
believe. All that gives to Me the Father to Me will come, and he
2064 4314/3165/3364/ 1544 1854 3754 2597 1537
38 ἐρχόμενον πρός με οὐ μὴ ἐκβάλω ἔξω. ὅτι καταβέβηκα ἐκ
coming to Me in no way I will cast out. For I have descended from
3772 3756 2443/4160 2309 1699 235
τοῦ οὐρανοῦ, οὐχ ἵνα ποιῶ τὸ θέλημα τὸ ἐμόν, ἀλλὰ τὸ
— Heaven not that I may do will — My, but the

who sent Me. [39]And this is the will of the Father who has sent Me, that *of* all that He has given Me, I shall not lose *any* of it, but shall raise it up in the last day. [40]And this is the will of the *One* who sent Me, that everyone seeing the Son and believing into Him should have everlasting life; and I will raise him up at the last day.

[41]Then the Jews murmured about Him, because He said, I am the Bread coming down out of Heaven. [42]And *they* said, Is this not Jesus the son of Joseph, of whom we know the father and the mother? How does this one now say, I have come down out of Heaven? [43]Then Jesus answered and said to them, Do not murmur with one another. [44]No one is able to come to Me unless the Father who sent Me draws him; and I will raise him up in the last day. [45]It has been written in the Prophets, "They shall all be taught of God." So then everyone who hears and learns from the Father comes to Me; [46]not that anyone has seen the Father, except the *One* being from God, He has seen the Father.

[47]Truly, truly, I say to you, the *one* believing into Me has everlasting life. [48]I am the Bread of life. [49]Your fathers ate the manna in the wilderness, and died. [50]This is the Bread coming down out of Heaven, that anyone may eat of it and not die. [51]I am the Living Bread that came down from Heaven. If anyone eats of this Bread, he will live forever. And indeed the bread which I will give is My flesh, which

2307 3992 3165 5124 2076 2307
39 θέλημα τοῦ πέμψαντός με. τοῦτο δέ ἐστι τὸ θέλημα τοῦ
will of the (One) sending Me. this And is the will of the
3992 3165 3962 2443 3956/3739 1325 3427/3361 622
πέμψαντός με πατρός, ἵνα πᾶν ὃ δέδωκέ μοι, μὴ ἀπολέσω
having sent Me Father, that all which He has given Me, not I shall lose
1537 846 235 450 846 1722 2078 2250 5124
40 ἐξ αὐτοῦ, ἀλλὰ ἀναστήσω αὐτὸ ἐν τῇ ἐσχάτῃ ἡμέρᾳ. τοῦτο
of it, but shall raise up it in the last day. this
2076 2307 3992 3165/2443/3956 2334
δέ ἐστι τὸ θέλημα τοῦ πέμψαντός με, ἵνα πᾶς ὁ θεωρῶν τὸν
And is the will of the (One) sending Me, that everyone seeing the
5207 4100 1519 846 2192 2222 166 450
υἱὸν καὶ πιστεύων εἰς αὐτόν, ἔχῃ ζωὴν αἰώνιον, καὶ ἀνα-
Son and believing in Him should have life everlasting; and will
846 1473 2072 2250
στήσω αὐτὸν ἐγὼ τῇ ἐσχάτῃ ἡμέρᾳ.
raise up him I at the last day.
1111 3767 2453 4012 846 3754 2036 1473
41 Ἐγόγγυζον οὖν οἱ Ἰουδαῖοι περὶ αὐτοῦ, ὅτι εἶπεν, Ἐγώ
murmured Then the Jews concerning Him, because He said, I
1510 740 2597 1537 3772 3004 3756
42 εἰμι ὁ ἄρτος ὁ καταβὰς ἐκ τοῦ οὐρανοῦ. καὶ ἔλεγον, Οὐχ
am the bread – coming down out of Heaven. And they said, not
3778 2076 2424 5207 2501 3739/ 2249 1492
οὗτός ἐστιν Ἰησοῦς ὁ υἱὸς Ἰωσήφ, οὗ ἡμεῖς οἴδαμεν τὸν
this is Jesus the son of Joseph, of whom we know the
3962 3384 4459/3767 3004 3778 3754/1537
πατέρα καὶ τὴν μητέρα; πῶς οὖν λέγει οὗτος ὅτι Ἐκ τοῦ
father and the mother? How now says this one – Out of –
3772 2597 611 3767 2424 2036 846
43 οὐρανοῦ καταβέβηκα; ἀπεκρίθη οὖν ὁ Ἰησοῦς καὶ εἶπεν αὐτοῖς,
Heaven I have come down? answered Then Jesus and said to them,
3361 1111 3326 240 3762 1410 2064 4314/3165
44 Μὴ γογγύζετε μετ' ἀλλήλων. οὐδεὶς δύναται ἐλθεῖν πρός με,
Do not murmur with one another. No one is able to come to Me
1437/3361 3962 3992 3165 1670 846 1473 450
ἐὰν μὴ ὁ πατὴρ ὁ πέμψας με ἑλκύσῃ αὐτόν, καὶ ἐγὼ ἀναστή-
unless the Father who sent Me draws him, and I will raise
846 2078 2250 2076 1125 1722 4396
45 σω αὐτὸν τῇ ἐσχάτῃ ἡμέρᾳ. ἔστι γεγραμμένον ἐν τοῖς προφή-
up him in the last day. It is having been written in the prophets,
2071 3956 1318 2316 3956 3767
ταις, Καὶ ἔσονται πάντες διδακτοὶ τοῦ Θεοῦ. πᾶς οὖν ὁ
And they shall be all taught – of God; everyone, then,
191 3844 3962 3129 2064 4314/3165/3756
46 ἀκούσας παρὰ τοῦ πατρὸς καὶ μαθών, ἔρχεται πρός με. οὐχ
hearing from the Father and learning, comes to Me. Not
3754 3962 5100 3708 = 1508= 5613 3844 2316
ὅτι τὸν πατέρα τις ἑώρακεν, εἰ μὴ ὁ ὢν παρὰ τοῦ Θεοῦ,
that the Father anyone has seen, except the (One) being from God,
3778 3708 3962 281 281 3004 5213 4100
47 οὗτος ἑώρακε τὸν πατέρα. ἀμὴν ἀμὴν λέγω ὑμῖν, ὁ πιστεύων
this One has seen the Father. Truly, truly, I say to you, he believing
1519/1691/2192/2222 166 1473 / 1510 740 2222
48 εἰς ἐμέ, ἔχει ζωὴν αἰώνιον. ἐγώ εἰμι ὁ ἄρτος τῆς ζωῆς. οἱ
49 in Me has life everlasting. I am the bread – of life. The
3962 5216 5315 3131 1722 2048 599
πατέρες ὑμῶν ἔφαγον τὸ μάννα ἐν τῇ ἐρήμῳ, καὶ ἀπέθανον.
fathers of you ate the manna in the wilderness, and died.
3778 2076 740 1537 3772 2597 2443/5100
50 οὗτός ἐστιν ὁ ἄρτος ὁ ἐκ τοῦ οὐρανοῦ καταβαίνων, ἵνα τις
This is the bread out of Heaven coming down, that anyone
1537 846 5315 3361 599 1473 1510 740 2198 1537
51 ἐξ αὐτοῦ φάγῃ καὶ μὴ ἀποθάνῃ. ἐγώ εἰμι ὁ ἄρτος ὁ ζῶν, ὁ ἐκ
of it may eat and not die. I am the bread living that from
3772 2597 1437/5100/5315/1537/ 5127 740
τοῦ οὐρανοῦ καταβάς· ἐάν τις φάγῃ ἐκ τούτου τοῦ ἄρτου,
– Heaven came down; if anyone eats of this – bread,
2198 1519 165 740 3739/1473 1325 4561
ζήσεται εἰς τὸν αἰῶνα. καὶ ὁ ἄρτος δὲ ὃν ἐγὼ δώσω, ἡ σάρξ
he will live to the age. indeed the bread And which I will give, the flesh

I will give for the life of the world.

[52]Then the Jews argued with one another, saying, How can this one give us *his* flesh to eat? [53]Then Jesus said to them, Truly, truly, I say to you, Except you eat the flesh of the Son of man, and drink His blood, you do not have life in yourselves. [54]The *one* partaking of My flesh and drinking of My blood has everlasting life, and I will raise him up at the last day. [55]For My flesh is truly food, and My blood is truly drink. [56]The *one* partaking of My flesh and drinking of My blood abides in Me, and I in him. [57]Even as the living Father sent Me, and I live through the Father, also the *one* partaking Me, even that one will live through Me. [58]This is the Bread which came down out of Heaven, not as your fathers ate the manna, and died; the *one* partaking of this Bread will live to the age. [59]He said these things teaching in a synagogue in Capernaum.

[60]Then hearing, many of His disciples said, This word is hard; who is able to hear it? [61]But knowing within Himself that His disciples were murmuring about this, Jesus said to them, Does this offend you? [62]Then *what* if you see the Son of man going up where He was at first? [63]It is the Spirit *that* makes alive. The flesh does not profit—nothing! The words which I speak to you are spirit and are life. [64]But there are some of you who are not believing. For Jesus

3450 2076/3739/1473 1325 5228 2889 2222
μου ἐστίν, ἣν ἐγὼ δώσω ὑπὲρ τῆς τοῦ κόσμου ζωῆς.
of Me is, which I will give for the of the world life.
3164 3767 4314 240 2453 3004 4459
52 Ἐμάχοντο οὖν πρὸς ἀλλήλους οἱ Ἰουδαῖοι λέγοντες, Πῶς
Argued therefore with one another the Jews, saying, How
1410 3778 2254 1325 4561 5315 2036 3767
53 δύναται οὗτος ἡμῖν δοῦναι τὴν σάρκα φαγεῖν; εἶπεν οὖν
can this one us give the flesh to eat? said Then
846 2424 281 281 3004 5213 1437 3361 5315
αὐτοῖς ὁ Ἰησοῦς, Ἀμὴν ἀμὴν λέγω ὑμῖν, ἐὰν μὴ φάγητε τὴν
to them — Jesus, Truly, truly, I say to you, Except you eat the
4561 5207 444 4095 848 129
σάρκα τοῦ υἱοῦ τοῦ ἀνθρώπου καὶ πίητε αὐτοῦ τὸ αἷμα,
flesh of the Son — of man and drink of Him the blood,
3756 2192 2222 1722 1438 5176 3450 4561
54 οὐκ ἔχετε ζωὴν ἐν ἑαυτοῖς. ὁ τρώγων μου τὴν σάρκα καὶ
not you do have life in yourselves. He partaking of Me the flesh and
4095 3450 129 2192 2222 166 1473 450
πίνων μου τὸ αἷμα, ἔχει ζωὴν αἰώνιον, καὶ ἐγὼ ἀναστήσω
drinking of Me the blood has life everlasting, and I will raise up
846 2078 2250 1063 4561 3450 230 2076
55 αὐτὸν τῇ ἐσχάτῃ ἡμέρᾳ. ἡ γὰρ σάρξ μου ἀληθῶς ἐστι
him at the last day the For flesh of Me truly is
1035 129 3450 230 2076 4213 5176 3450
56 βρῶσις, καὶ τὸ αἷμά μου ἀληθῶς ἐστι πόσις. ὁ τρώγων μου
food, and the blood of Me truly is drink. He partaking of Me
4561 4095 3450 129 1722/1698 3306 2504
τὴν σάρκα καὶ πίνων μου τὸ αἷμα, ἐν ἐμοὶ μένει, κἀγὼ ἐν
the flesh and drinking of Me the blood in Me abides, and I in
846 2531 649 3165 2198 3962 2504 2198/1223
57 αὐτῷ. καθὼς ἀπέστειλέ με ὁ ζῶν πατήρ, κἀγὼ ζῶ διὰ τὸν
him. Even as sent Me the living Father, and I live via the
3962 5176 3165 2548 2198 1223/1691 3778
58 πατέρα· καὶ ὁ τρώγων με, κἀκεῖνος ζήσεται δι' ἐμέ. οὗτός
Father, also he partaking Me, even that one will live via Me. This
2076 740 1537 3772 2597 3756 2531 5315
ἐστιν ὁ ἄρτος ὁ ἐκ τοῦ οὐρανοῦ καταβάς· οὐ καθὼς ἔφαγον
is the bread which out of Heaven came down, not as ate
3962 5216 3131 599 5176 5126
οἱ πατέρες ὑμῶν τὸ μάννα, καὶ ἀπέθανον· ὁ τρώγων τοῦτον
the fathers of you the manna, and died; he partaking this
740 2198 165 5023 2036 4864
59 τὸν ἄρτον, ζήσεται εἰς τὸν αἰῶνα. ταῦτα εἶπεν ἐν συναγωγῇ
— bread will live to the age. These things He said in a synagogue
1321 1722 2584
διδάσκων ἐν Καπερναούμ.
teaching in Capernaum.
4183 3767 191 1537 3101 848 2036
60 Πολλοὶ οὖν ἀκούσαντες ἐκ τῶν μαθητῶν αὐτοῦ εἶπον,
many Therefore hearing of the disciples of Him said,
4642 2076 3778 3056 5101 1410 848 191
Σκληρός ἐστιν οὗτος ὁ λόγος· τίς δύναται αὐτοῦ ἀκούειν;
Hard is this — word; who is able it to hear?
1402 2424 1722 1438 3754 1111 4012 5127
61 εἰδὼς δὲ ὁ Ἰησοῦς ἐν ἑαυτῷ ὅτι γογγύζουσι περὶ τούτου
knowing But Jesus in Himself that are murmuring about this
3101 848 2036 846 5124 5209 4624
οἱ μαθηταὶ αὐτοῦ, εἶπεν αὐτοῖς, Τοῦτο ὑμᾶς σκανδαλίζει;
the disciples of Him, He said to them, Does this you offend?
1437/3767 2334 5207 444 305 3699
62 ἐὰν οὖν θεωρῆτε τὸν υἱὸν τοῦ ἀνθρώπου ἀναβαίνοντα ὅπου
If then you behold the Son — of man going up where
2258 4386 4151 2076 2227 4561 3756
63 ἦν τὸ πρότερον; τὸ πνεῦμά ἐστι τὸ ζωοποιοῦν, ἡ σὰρξ οὐκ
He was at first? The Spirit it is (that) makes alive; the flesh not
5623 3762 4487 3739/1473 2980 5213 4151 2076
ὠφελεῖ οὐδέν· τὰ ῥήματα ἃ ἐγὼ λαλῶ ὑμῖν, πνεῦμά ἐστι
profits—nothing! The words which I speak to you spirit is
2222 2076 235 1526/1537/5216/5100 3756 4100
64 καὶ ζωή ἐστιν. ἀλλ' εἰσὶν ἐξ ὑμῶν τινες οἱ οὐ πιστεύουσιν.
and life are. But are of you some who not are believing.

knew from *the* beginning who the not believing ones were, and who was the *one* betraying Him. [65]And He said, For this reason I have told you that no one is able to come to Me except it is given to him from My Father.

[66]From this *time* many of His disciples went away into the things behind, and no longer walked with Him. [67]Therefore, Jesus said to the Twelve, Do you also wish to go? [68]Then Simon Peter answered Him, Lord, to whom shall we go? You have *the* words of everlasting life. [69]And we have believed and have known that You are the Christ, the Son of the living God. [70]Jesus answered them, Did I not choose you, the Twelve? Yet one *of* you is a devil! [71]But He spoke *of* Judas Iscariot, Simon's *son,* for this one was about to betray Him, being one of the Twelve.

CHAPTER 7

[1]And after these things Jesus was walking in Galilee; for He did not desire to walk in Judea, because the Jews were lusting to kill Him. [2]And the Jewish Feast of the Tabernacles was near. [3]Then His brothers said to Him, Move away from here and go to Judea, so that your disciples will also see your works which you do—[4]for no one does anything in secret, and himself seeks to be in public. If you do these things, reveal yourself to the world. [5]For His brothers did not believe into Him. [6]Then Jesus said

1492 1063/1537/ 746 2424 5101 1526 3361 4100
ᾔδει γὰρ ἐξ ἀρχῆς ὁ Ἰησοῦς, τίνες εἰσὶν οἱ μὴ πιστεύοντες,
knew For from beginning Jesus who are those not believing,
5101 2076 3860 846 3004 1223 5124
65 καὶ τίς ἐστιν ὁ παραδώσων αὐτόν. καὶ ἔλεγε, Διὰ τοῦτο
and who is the (one) betraying Him. And He said, Therefore
2046 5213 3754 3762 1410 2064 4314/3165/=3362=5600
εἴρηκα ὑμῖν, ὅτι οὐδεὶς δύναται ἐλθεῖν πρός με, ἐὰν μὴ ᾖ
I have told you, that no one is able to come to Me unless it be
1325 846 1537 3962 3450
δεδομένον αὐτῷ ἐκ τοῦ πατρός μου.
given to him from the Father of Me.
1537 5127 4183 565 3101 848
66 Ἐκ τούτου πολλοὶ ἀπῆλθον τῶν μαθητῶν αὐτοῦ εἰς
From this many went away of the disciples of Him into
3694 3765 3326 846 4043 2036 3767
67 τὰ ὀπίσω, καὶ οὐκέτι μετ' αὐτοῦ περιεπάτουν. εἶπεν οὖν ὁ
the things behind, and no longer with Him walked. said Therefore
2424 1427 3361 5210 2309 5217 611
68 Ἰησοῦς τοῖς δώδεκα, Μὴ καὶ ὑμεῖς θέλετε ὑπάγειν; ἀπεκρίθη
Jesus to the twelve, Not also you wish to go? answered
3767 846 4613 4074 2962 4314 5101 565
οὖν αὐτῷ Σίμων Πέτρος, Κύριε, πρὸς τίνα ἀπελευσόμεθα;
Then Him Simon Peter, Lord, to whom shall we go?
4487 2222 166 2192 2249 4100
69 ῥήματα ζωῆς αἰωνίου ἔχεις. καὶ ἡμεῖς πεπιστεύκαμεν καὶ
words of life eternal You have. And we have believed and
1097 3754/4771/1488/5547 5207 2316 2198
ἐγνώκαμεν ὅτι σὺ εἶ ὁ Χριστὸς ὁ υἱὸς τοῦ Θεοῦ τοῦ ζῶντος.
have known that You are the Christ, the Son — of God the living.
611 846 2424 3756/1473/ 5209 1427
70 ἀπεκρίθη αὐτοῖς ὁ Ἰησοῦς, Οὐκ ἐγὼ ὑμᾶς τοὺς δώδεκα
answered them — Jesus, Did not I you the twelve
1586 1537 5216 1519 1228 2076 3004
71 ἐξελεξάμην, καὶ ἐξ ὑμῶν εἷς διάβολός ἐστιν; ἔλεγε δὲ τὸν
choose? And of you one a devil is. He spoke And (of)
2455 4613 2469 3778 1063 3195 846
Ἰούδαν Σίμωνος Ἰσκαριώτην· οὗτος γὰρ ἤμελλεν αὐτὸν
Judas of Simon Iscariot; this one for was about Him
3860 1520/5607/1537 1427
παραδιδόναι, εἷς ὢν ἐκ τῶν δώδεκα.
to betray, one being of the twelve.

CHAPTER 7

4043 2424 3326 5023 1722 1056 3756
1 Καὶ περιεπάτει ὁ Ἰησοῦς μετὰ ταῦτα ἐν τῇ Γαλιλαίᾳ· οὐ
And was walking — Jesus after these things in — Galilee; not
1063 2309 1722 2449 4043 3754 2212 846
γὰρ ἤθελεν ἐν τῇ Ἰουδαίᾳ περιπατεῖν, ὅτι ἐζήτουν αὐτὸν
For He desired in — Judea to walk, because were seeking Him
2453 615 2258 1451 1859 2453
2 οἱ Ἰουδαῖοι ἀποκτεῖναι. ἦν δὲ ἐγγὺς ἡ ἑορτὴ τῶν Ἰουδαίων
the Jews to kill. was And near the feast of the Jews,
4634 2036 3767 4314 846 80 848
3 ἡ σκηνοπηγία. εἶπον οὖν πρὸς αὐτὸν οἱ ἀδελφοὶ αὐτοῦ,
The Tabernacles. said Therefore to Him the brothers of Him,
3327 1782 5217 2449 2443
Μετάβηθι ἐντεῦθεν, καὶ ὕπαγε εἰς τὴν Ἰουδαίαν, ἵνα καὶ οἱ
Depart from here, and go to — Judea, that also the
3101 4675 2334 2041 4675/3739/4160 3762 1063
4 μαθηταί σου θεωρήσωσι τὰ ἔργα σου ἃ ποιεῖς. οὐδεὶς γὰρ
disciples of you will behold the works of you which you do. no one For
1722 2927 5100 4160 2212 848 1722 3954 1511 1487
ἐν κρυπτῷ τι ποιεῖ, καὶ ζητεῖ αὐτὸς ἐν παρρησίᾳ εἶναι. εἰ
in secret anything does, and seeks himself in public to be. If
5023 4160 5319 4572 2889 3761 1063
5 ταῦτα ποιεῖς, φανέρωσον σεαυτὸν τῷ κόσμῳ. οὐδὲ γὰρ οἱ
these things you do, reveal yourself to the world. not even For the
80 848 4100 1519 846 3004 3767 846
6 ἀδελφοὶ αὐτοῦ ἐπίστευον εἰς αὐτόν. λέγει οὖν αὐτοῖς ὁ
brothers of Him believed in Him. says Then to them —

to them, My time is not yet here, but your time is always ready. [7]The world cannot hate you; but it hates Me because I witness about it, that its works are evil. [8]You go up to this feast. I am not yet going up to this feast, for My time has not yet been fulfilled. [9]And saying these things to them, He remained in Galilee.

[10]But when His brothers went up, then He also went up to the feast—not openly, but as in secret. [11]Then the Jews sought Him in the feast, and said, Where is He? [12]And there was much murmuring about Him in the crowds. Some said, He is a good one; but others said, No, but he deceives the crowd. [13]However, no one spoke publicly about Him, because of the fear of the Jews.

[14]But the feast being now half over, Jesus went up to the Temple and taught. [15]And the Jews marveled, saying, How does this one know letters, not being taught? [16]Jesus answered them and said, My teaching is not Mine, but of the *One* who sent Me. [17]If anyone desires to do His will, he will know concerning the teaching, whether it is of God, or I speak from Myself. [18]The *one* speaking from himself seeks *his* own glory. But the *one* seeking the glory of the *One* who sent Him, this One is true, and unrighteousness is not in Him. [19]Did not Moses give you the Law, and not one of you does the Law? Why do you seek to kill Me? [20]The

2424 2540 1699 3778 3918 2540
Ἰησοῦς, Ὁ καιρὸς ὁ ἐμὸς οὔπω πάρεστιν, ὁ δὲ καιρὸς ὁ
Jesus, The time — of Me not yet is present, but time --
5212 3842 2076 2092 3756 1410 2889
7 ὑμέτερος πάντοτέ ἐστιν ἕτοιμος. οὐ δύναται ὁ κόσμος
your always is ready. not is able The world
3404 5209/1691 3404/3754/1473/ 3140 4012 846 3754
μισεῖν ὑμᾶς· ἐμὲ δὲ μισεῖ, ὅτι ἐγὼ μαρτυρῶ περὶ αὐτοῦ, ὅτι
to hate you; Me but it hates, because I witness about it, that
2041 848 4190 2076 5210 305 1519 1859
8 τὰ ἔργα αὐτοῦ πονηρά ἐστιν. ὑμεῖς ἀνάβητε εἰς τὴν ἑορτὴν
the works of it evil are. You go up to feast
5026 1473 3768 305 1519 1859 5026 3754
ταύτην· ἐγὼ οὔπω ἀναβαίνω εἰς τὴν ἑορτὴν ταύτην, ὅτι ὁ
this; I not yet am going to — feast this, because
2540 1699 3768 4137 5023 2036 846
9 καιρὸς ὁ ἐμὸς οὔπω πεπλήρωται. ταῦτα δὲ εἰπὼν αὐτοῖς,
time My not yet has been fulfilled. these things And saying to them,
3306 1722 1056
ἔμεινεν ἐν τῇ Γαλιλαίᾳ.
He stayed in — Galilee.

5613 305 80 848 5119 846 305
10 Ὡς δὲ ἀνέβησαν οἱ ἀδελφοὶ αὐτοῦ, τότε καὶ αὐτὸς ἀνέβη
when But went up the brothers of Him, then also He went up
1519 1859 3756 5320 235 5613/1722 2927 3767
11 εἰς τὴν ἑορτήν, οὐ φανερῶς, ἀλλ' ὡς ἐν κρυπτῷ. οἱ οὖν
to the feast, not openly, but as in secret. the Then
2543 2212 846 1722 1859 3004 4226 2076
Ἰουδαῖοι ἐζήτουν αὐτὸν ἐν τῇ ἑορτῇ, καὶ ἔλεγον, Ποῦ ἐστιν
the Jews sought Him in the feast, and said, Where is
1565 1112 4183 4012 846/2258/1722 3793
12 ἐκεῖνος; καὶ γογγυσμὸς πολὺς περὶ αὐτοῦ ἦν ἐν τοῖς ὄχλοις·
that one? And murmuring much about Him was in the crowds;
3303 3004 3754 18 2076 243 3004 3756 235
οἱ μὲν ἔλεγον ὅτι Ἀγαθός ἐστιν· ἄλλοι δὲ ἔλεγον, Οὔ, ἀλλὰ
some said, — A good one He is; others but said, No, but
4105 3793 3762 3305 3954 2980/4012 846
13 πλανᾷ τὸν ὄχλον. οὐδεὶς μέντοι παρρησίᾳ ἐλάλει περὶ αὐτοῦ
he deceives the crowd. No one however publicly spoke about Him,
1223 5401 2453
διὰ τὸν φόβον τῶν Ἰουδαίων.
because of the fear of the Jews.

2235 1859 3322 305 2424 1519 2411
14 Ἤδη δὲ τῆς ἑορτῆς μεσούσης, ἀνέβη ὁ Ἰησοῦς εἰς τὸ ἱερόν,
now But the feast being in middle went up Jesus to the Temple
1321 2296 2453 3004 4459 3778
15 καὶ ἐδίδασκε. καὶ ἐθαύμαζον οἱ Ἰουδαῖοι λέγοντες, Πῶς οὗτος
and taught. And marveled the Jews, saying, How this one
1121 1492/3361 3129 611 846 2424
16 γράμματα οἶδε, μὴ μεμαθηκώς; ἀπεκρίθη αὐτοῖς ὁ Ἰησοῦς
letters knows, not being taught? answered them — Jesus
2036 1699 1322 3756 2076 1699/ 235 3992
καὶ εἶπεν, Ἡ ἐμὴ διδαχὴ οὐκ ἔστιν ἐμή, ἀλλὰ τοῦ πέμψαντός
and said, My teaching not is Mine, but of the (One) sending
3165/1437/5100/2309 2307 848 4160 1097 4012
17 με. ἐάν τις θέλῃ τὸ θέλημα αὐτοῦ ποιεῖν, γνώσεται περὶ τῆς
Me. If anyone desires the will of Him to do, he will know concerning the
1322 4220 1537 2316 2076 1473 575 1683
διδαχῆς, πότερον ἐκ τοῦ Θεοῦ ἐστιν, ἢ ἐγὼ ἀπ' ἐμαυτοῦ
teaching, whether of — God it is, or I from Myself
2980 575 1438 2980 1391 2398 2212
18 λαλῶ. ὁ ἀφ' ἑαυτοῦ λαλῶν, τὴν δόξαν τὴν ἰδίαν ζητεῖ· ὁ δὲ
speak. The (one) from himself speaking the glory — own seeks; he But
2212 1391 3992 846 3778 227 2076
ζητῶν τὴν δόξαν τοῦ πέμψαντος αὐτόν, οὗτος ἀληθής ἐστι,
seeking the glory of the (One) sending Him, this one true is,
93 1722 846 3756 2076 3756 3475 1325 5213
19 καὶ ἀδικία ἐν αὐτῷ οὐκ ἔστιν. οὐ Μωσῆς δέδωκεν ὑμῖν τὸν
and unrighteousness in him not is. Did not Moses give you the
3551 3762 1537 5216 4160 3551 5101/3165/2212
νόμον, καὶ οὐδεὶς ἐξ ὑμῶν ποιεῖ τὸν νόμον; τί με ζητεῖτε
law. and no one of you does the law. Why Me seek you

crowd answered and said, You have a demon. Who seeks to kill you? [21]Jesus answered and said to them, I did one work, and you all marvel. [22]Because of this Moses has given you circumcision; not that it is of Moses, but of the fathers, and on a sabbath you circumcise a man. [23]If a man receives circumcision on a sabbath, so that the Law of Moses is not broken, are you angry with Me because I made a man entirely sound on a sabbath? [24]Do not judge according to sight, but judge righteous judgment.

[25]Then some of the Jerusalemites said, Is this not the one they are seeking to kill? [26]And, behold, He speaks publicly, and they say nothing to him. Perhaps the rulers truly knew that this is indeed the Christ? [27]But we know this one, from where he is. But when the Christ comes, no one knows from where He is.

[28]Then teaching, Jesus cried out in the temple, even saying, You both know Me, and you know from where I am. And I have not come from Myself, but He sending Me is true, whom you do not know. [29]But I know Him, because I am from Him; and He sent Me. [30]Then they sought to seize Him; yet no one laid a hand on Him, because His hour had not yet come. [31]But many of the crowd believed into Him, and said, The Christ, when He comes, will He do more miracles than these which this One did?

[32]The Pharisees heard the crowd murmuring these things about Him, and the Pharisees and the chief priests sent officers that

615 611 3793 2036 1140 2192/5101
20 ἀποκτεῖναι ; ἀπεκρίθη ὁ ὄχλος καὶ εἶπε, Δαιμόνιον ἔχεις· τίς
to kill? answered the crowd and said, A demon you have; who
4571/2212 615 611 2424 2036 846
21 σε ζητεῖ ἀποκτεῖναι ; ἀπεκρίθη ὁ Ἰησοῦς καὶ εἶπεν αὐτοῖς,
you seeks to kill? answered — Jesus and said to them,
1520 2041 4160 3956 2296 1223 5124 3475
22 Ἓν ἔργον ἐποίησα, καὶ πάντες θαυμάζετε. διὰ τοῦτο Μωσῆς
One work I did, and all you marvel. Because of this Moses
1325 5213 4061 3756/3754/1537 3475 2076
δέδωκεν ὑμῖν τὴν περιτομήν (οὐχ ὅτι ἐκ τοῦ Μωσέως ἐστίν,
has given you circumcision; not that of Moses it is,
235 1537 3962 1722 4521 4059
ἀλλ' ἐκ τῶν πατέρων)· καὶ ἐν σαββάτῳ περιτέμνετε
but of the fathers; and on a sabbath you circumcise
444 1487 4061 2983 444 1722 4521
23 ἄνθρωπον. εἰ περιτομὴν λαμβάνει ἄνθρωπος ἐν σαββάτῳ,
a man. If circumcision receives a man on a sabbath,
2443/3363/3089 3551 3475 1698 5520 3754/3650 444
ἵνα μὴ λυθῇ ὁ νόμος Μωσέως, ἐμοὶ χολᾶτε ὅτι ὅλον ἄνθρω-
that not is broken the law of Moses, with Me are you angry that a whole man
5199 4160 1722 4521 3361 2919 2596 3799 235
24 πον ὑγιῆ ἐποίησα ἐν σαββάτῳ ; μὴ κρίνετε κατ' ὄψιν, ἀλλὰ
healthy I made on a sabbath? Do not judge by sight, but
1342 2920 2919
τὴν δικαίαν κρίσιν κρίνατε.
— righteous judgment judge.
3004 3767/5100/1537 2415 3756 3778 2076
25 Ἔλεγον οὖν τινες ἐκ τῶν Ἱεροσολυμιτῶν, Οὐχ οὗτός ἐστιν
said Therefore some of the Jerusalemites not this one Is it
3739 2212 615 2396 3954 2980 3762
26 ὃν ζητοῦσιν ἀποκτεῖναι ; καὶ ἴδε παρρησίᾳ λαλεῖ, καὶ οὐδὲν
whom they are seeking to kill? And behold, publicly He speaks, and nothing
846 3004 3379 230 1097 758 3754
αὐτῷ λέγουσι. μήποτε ἀληθῶς ἔγνωσαν οἱ ἄρχοντες ὅτι
to Him they say. Perhaps truly knew the rulers that
3778 2076 230 5547 235 5126 1492 4159
27 οὗτός ἐστιν ἀληθῶς ὁ Χριστός ; ἀλλὰ τοῦτον οἴδαμεν πόθεν
this is indeed the Christ? But this one we know from where
2076 5547 3752 2064 3762 1097 4159
ἐστίν· ὁ δε Χριστὸς ὅταν ἔρχηται, οὐδεὶς γινώσκει πόθεν
he is; the but Christ when comes, no one knows from where
2076 2896 3767/1722 2411 1321 2424 3004
28 ἐστίν. ἔκραξεν οὖν ἐν τῷ ἱερῷ διδάσκων ὁ Ἰησοῦς καὶ λέγων,
He is. cried out Then in the Temple teaching — Jesus, and saying,
2504 1492 1492 4159 1510 575 1683 3756
Κἀμὲ οἴδατε, καὶ οἴδατε πόθεν εἰμί· καὶ ἀπ' ἐμαυτοῦ οὐκ
And Me you know, and you know from where I am; and from Myself not
2064 235 2076 228 3992 3165/3739/5210/3756
ἐλήλυθα, ἀλλ' ἔστιν ἀληθινὸς ὁ πέμψας με, ὃν ὑμεῖς οὐκ
I have come, but He is true, the (One) sending Me, whom you not
1492 1473 1492 846 3754/3844 846 1510 2548 3165
29 οἴδατε. ἐγὼ δὲ οἶδα αὐτόν, ὅτι παρ' αὐτοῦ εἰμι, κἀκεῖνός με
do know. I But know Him, because from Him I am, and that One Me
649 2212 3767 846 4084 3762 1911
30 ἀπέστειλεν. ἐζήτουν οὖν αὐτὸν πιάσαι. καὶ οὐδεὶς ἐπέβαλεν
sent. they sought Then Him to seize; and no one laid
1909 846 5495 3754 3768 2064 5610 848
ἐπ' αὐτὸν τὴν χεῖρα, ὅτι οὔπω ἐληλύθει ἡ ὥρα αὐτοῦ.
on Him the hand, because not yet had come the hour of Him.
4183 1537 3793 4100 1519 846 3004
31 πολλοὶ δὲ ἐκ τοῦ ὄχλου ἐπίστευσαν εἰς αὐτόν, καὶ ἔλεγον
many But of the crowd believed in Him, and said,
3754 5547 3752 2064/3385 4119 4592 5130
ὅτι Ὁ Χριστὸς ὅταν ἔλθῃ, μήτι πλείονα σημεῖα τούτων
— The Christ when He comes, not greater signs than these
4160 3739 3778 4160 191 5330
32 ποιήσει ὧν οὗτος ἐποίησεν ; ἤκουσαν οἱ Φαρισαῖοι τοῦ
will He do which this One did? Heard the Pharisees the
3793 1111 4012 846 5023 649
ὄχλου γογγύζοντος περὶ αὐτοῦ ταῦτα· καὶ ἀπέστειλαν οἱ
crowd murmuring concerning Him these things and sent the

they might seize Him.
[33]Then Jesus said to them,
Yet a little while I am with
you, and I go to Him who
sent Me. [34]You will seek
Me, and will not find *Me*.
And where I am, you are not
able to come. [35]Then the
Jews said amongst them-
selves, Where is this one
about to go that we will not
find him? Is he about to go
to the Dispersion of the
Greeks? [36]What is this
word which he said, You
will seek Me and will not
find *Me*, and, Where I am,
you are not able to come?

[37]And in the last day of
the great feast, Jesus stood
and cried out, saying, If
anyone thirsts, let him
come to Me and drink.
[38]The *one* believing into
Me, as the Scripture said,
"Out of his belly will flow
rivers of living water." [39]But
He said this concerning the
Spirit, whom the ones
believing into Him were
about to receive; for *the*
Holy Spirit was not yet
given, because Jesus was
not yet glorified.

[40]Then hearing the word,
many of the crowd said,
This is truly the Prophet.
[41]Others said, This is the
Christ. But others said, *No!*
For does the Christ come
out of Galilee? [42]Has not
the Scripture said that the
Christ comes from the seed
of David, and from Bethlehem, the village where
David was? [43]Therefore, a
division occurred in the
crowd because of Him.
[44]And some of them desired
to seize Him, but no one
laid hands on Him.

5330 749 5257 2443 4084 846
Φαρισαῖοι καὶ οἱ ἀρχιερεῖς ὑπηρέτας ἵνα πιάσωσιν αὐτόν.
Pharisees and the chief priests officers, that they might seize Him.
2036 3767 846 2424 2089 3398 5550 3326 5216
33 εἶπεν οὖν αὐτοῖς ὁ Ἰησοῦς, Ἔτι μικρὸν χρόνον μεθ' ὑμῶν
said Therefore to them Jesus, Yet a little time with you
1510 5217 4314 3992 3165 2212 3165
34 εἰμι, καὶ ὑπάγω πρὸς τὸν πέμψαντά με. ζητήσετέ με, καὶ
I am, and I go to the (One) sending Me. You will seek Me, and
3756 2147 3699 1510/1473/ 5210/3756 1410 2064
οὐχ εὑρήσετε· καὶ ὅπου εἰμὶ ἐγώ, ὑμεῖς οὐ δύνασθε ἐλθεῖν.
not will find, and where am I, you not are able to come.
2036 3767 2453 4314 1438 4226 3778 3195
35 εἶπον οὖν οἱ Ἰουδαῖοι πρὸς ἑαυτούς, Ποῦ οὗτος μέλλει
said Then the Jews to themselves, Where this one is about
4198 3754 2249 3756 2147 846 3361 1519
πορεύεσθαι ὅτι ἡμεῖς οὐχ εὑρήσομεν αὐτόν; μὴ εἰς τὴν
to go that we not will find Him? not to the
1290 1672 3195 4198 1321
διασπορὰν τῶν Ἑλλήνων μέλλει πορεύεσθαι, καὶ διδάσκειν
Dispersion of the Greeks is he about to go, and to teach
1672 5101 2076 3778 3056 3739 2036 2212
36 τοὺς Ἕλληνας; τίς ἐστιν οὗτος ὁ λόγος ὃν εἶπε, Ζητήσετέ
the Greeks? What is this word which He said: You will seek
3165 3756 2147 3699 1510 1473 5210/3756 1410
με, καὶ οὐχ εὑρήσετε· καὶ ὅπου εἰμὶ ἐγώ, ὑμεῖς οὐ δύνασθε
Me, and not you will find, and where am I, you not are able
2064
ἐλθεῖν;
to come?
1722 2078 2250 3173 1859 2176
37 Ἐν δὲ τῇ ἐσχάτῃ ἡμέρᾳ τῇ μεγάλῃ τῆς ἑορτῆς εἱστήκει
in And the last day, the great, of the feast stood
2424 2896 3004 1437/5100/1372 2064 4314
ὁ Ἰησοῦς καὶ ἔκραξε, λέγων, Ἐάν τις διψᾷ, ἐρχέσθω πρός
— Jesus and cried out, saying, If anyone thirst, let him come to
3165 4095 4100 1519/1691 2531 2036 1124
38 με καὶ πινέτω. ὁ πιστεύων εἰς ἐμέ, καθὼς εἶπεν ἡ γραφή,
Me and drink. He believing into Me, as said the Writing,
4215 1537 2836 848 4412 5204 2198
ποταμοὶ ἐκ τῆς κοιλίας αὐτοῦ ῥεύσουσιν ὕδατος ζῶντος.
rivers out of the belly of him will flow water of living.
5124 2036 4012 4151 3756 3195 2983
39 τοῦτο δὲ εἶπε περὶ τοῦ Πνεύματος οὗ ἔμελλον λαμβάνειν οἱ
this But He said about the Spirit whom were about to receive those
4100 1519 846 3768 1063/2258 4151 40 3754
πιστεύοντες εἰς αὐτόν· οὔπω γὰρ ἦν Πνεῦμα Ἅγιον, ὅτι
believing in Him; not yet for was (the) Spirit Holy, because,
2424 3764 1392 4183 3767/1537 3793
40 ὁ Ἰησοῦς οὐδέπω ἐδοξάσθη. πολλοὶ οὖν ἐκ τοῦ ὄχλου
— Jesus not yet was glorified. Many therefore of the crowd
191 3056 3004 3778 2076 230 4396
ἀκούσαντες τὸν λόγον ἔλεγον, Οὗτός ἐστιν ἀληθῶς ὁ προφή-
hearing the word said, This is truly the prophet.
243 3004 3778 2076 5547 243 3004
41 της. ἄλλοι ἔλεγον, Οὗτός ἐστιν ὁ Χριστός. ἄλλοι δὲ ἔλεγον,
Others said, This is the Christ. others But said, (No!)
3361/1063/1537 1056 5547 2064 3780 1124
42 Μὴ γὰρ ἐκ τῆς Γαλιλαίας ὁ Χριστὸς ἔρχεται; οὐχὶ ἡ γραφὴ
not For out of — Galilee the Christ comes? Has not the Scripture
2036 3754/1537 4690 1138 575 965
εἶπεν ὅτι ἐκ τοῦ σπέρματος Δαβίδ, καὶ ἀπὸ Βηθλεέμ, τῆς
said that out of the seed of David, and from Bethlehem, the
2968 3699 /2258/1138 5547 2064 4978 3767/1722
43 κώμης ὅπου ἦν Δαβίδ, ὁ Χριστὸς ἔρχεται; σχίσμα οὖν ἐν
village where was David, the Christ comes? a division Then in
3793 1096 1223 846 5100 2309 1537 846
44 τῷ ὄχλῳ ἐγένετο δι' αὐτόν. τινὲς δὲ ἤθελον ἐξ αὐτῶν
the crowd occurred, because of Him. some And desired of them
4084 846 235 3762 1911 1909 846 5495
πιάσαι αὐτόν, ἀλλ' οὐδεὶς ἐπέβαλεν ἐπ' αὐτὸν τὰς χεῖρας.
to seize Him, but no one laid on Him the hands.

[45]Then the officers came to the chief priests and Pharisees. And they said to them, Why did you not bring him? [46]The officers answered, Never did a man so speak as does this man. [47]Then the Pharisees answered them, Have you not also been deceived? [48]Not any from the rulers or from the Pharisees believed into him? [49]But not knowing the Law this crowd is cursed. [50]Nicodemus said to them—the *one* coming *by* night to Him, being one of themselves—[51]Does our Law judge the man unless it hear from him first, and know what he does? [52]They answered and said to him, Are you also from Galilee? Search *the Scripture* and see that a prophet has not been raised out of Galilee.

[53]And they each one went to his house.

2064 3767 5257 4314 749 5330
45 Ἦλθον οὖν οἱ ὑπηρέται πρὸς τοὺς ἀρχιερεῖς καὶ Φαρι-
came Then the officers to the chief priests and
2036 846 1565 1302 3756 71 846
σαίους· καὶ εἶπον αὐτοῖς ἐκεῖνοι, Διατί οὐκ ἠγάγετε αὐτόν;
Pharisees, and said to them those, Why not did you bring him?
611 5257 3762 3779 2980
46 ἀπεκρίθησαν οἱ ὑπηρέται, Οὐδέποτε οὕτως ἐλάλησεν
answered The officers, Never so spoke
444 5613 3778 444 611 3767 846
47 ἄνθρωπος, ὡς οὗτος ὁ ἄνθρωπος. ἀπεκρίθησαν οὖν αὐτοῖς
a man as this man. answered Then them
5330 3361 5210 4105 =3387= 1537
48 οἱ Φαρισαῖοι, Μὴ καὶ ὑμεῖς πεπλάνησθε; μή τις ἐκ τῶν
the Pharisees, Not also you have been deceived? Not any from the
758 4100 1519 846 2228/1537 5330 235
49 ἀρχόντων ἐπίστευσεν εἰς αὐτόν, ἢ ἐκ τῶν Φαρισαίων; ἀλλ'
rulers have believed into him, or from the Pharisees? But
3793 3778 3361 1097 3551 1944 1526
ὁ ὄχλος οὗτος ὁ μὴ γινώσκων τὸν νόμον ἐπικατάρατοί εἰσι.
crowd this not knowing the Law cursed upon are
3004 3530 4314 846 2064 3571 4314 846
50 λέγει Νικόδημος πρὸς αὐτούς (ὁ ἐλθὼν νυκτὸς πρὸς αὐτόν,
says Nicodemus to them —he having come (by) night to Him.
1520/5607/1537/846 3361 3551 2257 2919 444
51 εἷς ὢν ἐξ αὐτῶν), Μὴ ὁ νόμος ἡμῶν κρίνει τὸν ἄνθρωπον,
one being of themselves—Not the Law of us does judge the man
=3362= 191 3844 846 4386 1097/5101/4160
ἐὰν μὴ ἀκούσῃ παρ' αὐτοῦ πρότερον καὶ γνῷ τί ποιεῖ;
unless it hear from him first and know what he does
611 2036 846 3361 4771/1537 1056 1488
52 ἀπεκρίθησαν καὶ εἶπον αὐτῷ, Μὴ καὶ σὺ ἐκ τῆς Γαλιλαίας εἶ;
They answered and said to him, Not also you of — Galilee are?
2045 1492 3754 4396 1537 1056 3756
ἐρεύνησον καὶ ἴδε ὅτι προφήτης ἐκ τῆς Γαλιλαίας οὐκ
Search (the) Scripture) and see that a prophet out of Galilee not
1453 4198 1538 1519 3614 898
53 ἐγήγερται. Καὶ ἐπορεύθη ἕκαστος εἰς τὸν οἶκον αὐτοῦ
has been raised. And they went each one to the house of him

CHAPTER 8

[1]But Jesus went to the Mount of Olives. [2]And at dawn He again arrived into the Temple, and all the people came to Him. And sitting down, He taught them. [3]And the scribes and the Pharisees brought to Him a woman having been taken in adultery. And standing her in *the* middle, [4]they said to Him, Teacher, this woman was taken in the very act, committing adultery. [5]And in the Law Moses commanded that such should be stoned. You, then, what do you say? [6]But they said this, tempting Him, that they may have *reason* to accuse Him. But bending down, Jesus wrote with the finger in the earth,

CHAPTER 8

2424 4198 1519
Ἰησοῦς δὲ ἐπορεύθη εἰς τὸ
Jesus And went to the
1
3735 1636 3722 3825 3854
ὄρος τῶν ἐλαιῶν. ὄρθρου δὲ πάλιν παρε-
2 mount of the olives. at dawn And again He
2411 3956 2992 2064 4314 846
γένετο εἰς τὸ ἱερόν, καὶ πᾶς ὁ λαὸς ἤρχετο πρὸς αὐτόν· καὶ
arrived in the Temple, and all the people came to Him, and
2523 1321 846 71 1122
3 καθίσας ἐδίδασκεν αὐτούς. ἄγουσι δὲ οἱ γραμματεῖς καὶ οἱ
sitting He taught them. lead And the scribes and the
5330 846 1135 1722 3430 2638
Φαρισαῖοι πρὸς αὐτὸν γυναῖκα ἐν μοιχείᾳ κατειλημμένην,
Pharisees to Him a woman in adultery having been taken,
2476 846 1722/3319 3004 846 1320
4 καὶ στήσαντες αὐτὴν ἐν μέσῳ, λέγουσιν αὐτῷ, Διδάσκαλε,
and standing her in (the) midst they say to Him, Teacher,
3778 1135 2638 1888 3431 1722
5 αὕτη ἡ γυνὴ κατειλήφθη ἐπαυτοφώρῳ μοιχευομένη. ἐν δὲ τῷ
this woman has been taken in the very act committing adultery. in And the
3551 3475 2254 1781 5108 3036
νόμῳ Μωσῆς ἡμῖν ἐνετείλατο τὰς τοιαύτας λιθοβολεῖσθαι·
Law Moses to us commanded such (women) to be stoned;
4771/3767/5101/3004 5124 3004 3985 846 2443
6 σὺ οὖν τί λέγεις; τοῦτο δὲ ἔλεγον πειράζοντες αὐτόν, ἵνα
you, then, what say you? this But they said tempting Him, that
2192 2723 846 2424 2736 2955
ἔχωσι κατηγορεῖν αὐτοῦ. ὁ δὲ Ἰησοῦς κάτω κύψας, τῷ
they may have to accuse Him. — But Jesus down stooping with th

not appearing *to hear.* [7]But as they continued questioning Him, bending back up, He said to them, The *one* among you without sin, let him cast the first stone at her. [8]And bending down again, He wrote in the earth. [9]But hearing, and being convicted by the conscience, they went out one by one, beginning from the older ones, until the last. And Jesus was left alone, and the woman standing in *the* middle. [10]And Jesus bending back up, and observing no one but the woman, He said to her, Woman, where are those, your accusers? Did not one give judgment against you? [11]And she said, No one, Lord. And Jesus said to her, Neither do I give judgment. Go, and sin no more.

[12]Then Jesus again spoke to them, saying, I am the Light of the world; he following Me will in no way walk in the darkness, but will have the light of life. [13]Then the Pharisees said to Him, You witnessed concerning yourself; your witness is not true. [14]Jesus answered and said to them, Even if I witness concerning Myself, My witness is true, for I know from where I came, and where I go. But you do not know from where I come, and where I go. [15]You judge according to the flesh. I judge no one. [16]But even if I judge, My judgment is true because I am not alone, but I and *the* Father who sent Me. [17]And in your Law it has been written that the witness of two men is true. [18]I am the *one* witnessing

1147 1125 1519 1093/3361 4364 5613
7 δακτύλῳ ἔγραφεν εἰς τὴν γῆν, μὴ προσποιούμενος. ὡς δὲ
finger wrote in the earth, not appearing (to hear). as And
1961 2065 846 352 2036 4314 846
ἐπέμενον ἐρωτῶντες αὐτόν, ἀνακύψας εἶπε πρὸς αὐτούς,
they continued questioning Him, bending back up, He said to them,
3361 5216 4413 3037 1909 846 906
Ὁ ἀναμάρτητος ὑμῶν, πρῶτος τὸν λίθον ἐπ' αὐτῇ βαλέτω.
The (one) sinless of you, first the stone on her let him cast.
3825 2736 2955 1125 1519 1093 191
8 καὶ πάλιν κάτω κύψας ἔγραφεν εἰς τὴν γῆν. οἱ δέ, ἀκούσαν-
9 And again down stooping He wrote in the earth. they But, having
5259 4893 1651 1831 =1527=
τες, καὶ ὑπὸ τῆς συνειδήσεως ἐλεγχόμενοι, ἐξήρχοντο εἷς καθ'
heard, and by the conscience being convicted, went out one by
1519 756 575 4245 2193 2078
εἷς, ἀρξάμενοι ἀπὸ τῶν πρεσβυτέρων ἕως τῶν ἐσχάτων· καὶ
one, beginning from the older ones, until the last. And
2641 3441 2424 1135 1722/3919 2476
κατελείφθη μόνος ὁ Ἰησοῦς, καὶ ἡ γυνὴ ἐν μέσῳ ἑστῶσα.
was left alone — Jesus, and the woman in (the) midst standing.
352 2424 3367 2300 4133
10 ἀνακύψας δὲ ὁ Ἰησοῦς, καὶ μηδένα θεασάμενος πλὴν τῆς
bending back up And Jesus, and no one observing but the
1135 2036 846 1135 4226/1526 1565 2725
γυναικός, εἶπεν αὐτῇ Ἡ γυνή, ποῦ εἰσιν ἐκεῖνοι οἱ κατήγοροί
woman, He said to her, Woman, where are those, the accusers
4675 3762/4571 2632 2036 3762 2962 2036
11 σου; οὐδείς σε κατέκρινεν; ἡ δὲ εἶπεν, Οὐδείς, Κύριε. εἶπε δὲ
of you? No one you judged? she And said, No one, Lord. said And
846 2424 3761 1473/4571 2632 4198 2371
αὐτῇ ὁ Ἰησοῦς, Οὐδὲ ἐγώ σε κατακρίνω· πορεύου καὶ μηκέτι
to her Jesus, Neither I you do judge; go, and no more
264
ἁμάρτανε.
sin.

3825 3767 2424 846 2980 3004 1473 1510
12 Πάλιν οὖν ὁ Ἰησοῦς αὐτοῖς ἐλάλησε λέγων, Ἐγώ εἰμι τὸ
Again, then, Jesus to them spoke, saying, I am the
5457 2889 190 1698 =3364= 4043 1722
φῶς τοῦ κόσμου· ὁ ἀκολουθῶν ἐμοὶ οὐ μὴ περιπατήσει ἐν τῇ
light of the world; the (one) following Me in no way will walk in the
4653 235 2192 5457 2222 2036 3767 846
13 σκοτίᾳ, ἀλλ' ἕξει τὸ φῶς τῆς ζωῆς. εἶπον οὖν αὐτῷ οἱ
darkness, but will have the light of life. said Then to Him the
5330 4771/4012 4572 3140 3141 4675 3756
Φαρισαῖοι, Σὺ περὶ σεαυτοῦ μαρτυρεῖς· ἡ μαρτυρία σου οὐκ
Pharisees, You about yourself witnessed. The witness of you not
2076 227 611 2424 2036 846 2579
14 ἔστιν ἀληθής. ἀπεκρίθη Ἰησοῦς καὶ εἶπεν αὐτοῖς, Κἂν
is true. answered Jesus and said to them, Even if
1473 3140 4012 1683 227 2076 3141 3450
ἐγὼ μαρτυρῶ περὶ ἐμαυτοῦ, ἀληθής ἐστιν ἡ μαρτυρία μου·
I witness about Myself, true is the witness of Me,
3754/1492 4159 2064 4226/5217 5210 3756 1492
ὅτι οἶδα πόθεν ἦλθον, καὶ ποῦ ὑπάγω· ὑμεῖς δὲ οὐκ οἴδατε
because I know from I came, and where I go; you but not do know
4159 2064 where 4226 5217 5210 2596 4561
15 πόθεν ἔρχομαι, καὶ ποῦ ὑπάγω. ὑμεῖς κατὰ τὴν σάρκα
from where I come, or where I go. You according to the flesh
2919 1473/3756 2919 3762 1437 2919 1473
16 κρίνετε· ἐγὼ οὐ κρίνω οὐδένα. καὶ ἐὰν κρίνω δὲ ἐγώ, ἡ
judge. I do not judge no one. even if judge But I,
2920 1699 227 2076 3754 3441/3756/1510/235/1473
κρίσις ἡ ἐμὴ ἀληθής ἐστιν· ὅτι μόνος οὐκ εἰμί, ἀλλ' ἐγὼ καὶ
judgment My true is, because alone not I am, but I and
3992 3165 3962 1722 3551 5212 1125
17 ὁ πέμψας με πατήρ. καὶ ἐν τῷ νόμῳ δὲ τῷ ὑμετέρῳ γέγρα-
He sending Me, (the) Father. Also in Law and your it has been
3754/1417 444 3141 227 2076 1473 1510
18 πται ὅτι δύο ἀνθρώπων ἡ μαρτυρία ἀληθής ἐστιν. ἐγώ εἰμι
written that of two men the witness true is. I am

concerning Myself, and He who sent Me, *the* Father, witnesses concerning Me. [19]Then they said to Him, Where is your father? Jesus answered, You neither know Me, nor My Father. If you had known Me, then you would have known My Father also.

[20]Jesus spoke these words in the treasury, teaching in the temple, and no one seized Him, for His hour had not yet come.

[21]Then Jesus said to them again, I go away, and you will seek Me. And you will die in your sin. Where I go, you are not able to come. [22]Then the Jews said, Will he kill himself, because he says, Where I go, you are not able to come? [23]And He said to them, You are from below; I am from above. You are from this world; I am not from this world. [24]Therefore, I said to you that you will die in your sins. For if you do not believe that I AM, you will die in your sins. [25]Then they said to Him, Who are you? And Jesus said to them, Altogether what I also say to you. [26]I have many things to say and to judge concerning you, but the *One* sending Me is true, and what I heard from Him, these things I say to the world. [27]They did not know that He spoke to them *of* the Father.

[28]Then Jesus said to them, When you lift up the Son of man, then you will know that I AM; and from Myself I do nothing; but *as* My Father taught Me, these things I speak. [29]And the *One* who sent Me is with Me. The Father

3140 4012 1683 3140 4012 1700 3992
ὁ μαρτυρῶν περὶ ἐμαυτοῦ, καὶ μαρτυρεῖ περὶ ἐμοῦ ὁ πέμψας
the (one) witnessing about Myself, and witnesses about Me He sending,
3165 3962 3004 3767 846 4226 2076 3962 4675
19 με πατήρ. ἔλεγον οὖν αὐτῷ, Ποῦ ἐστιν ὁ πατήρ σου
Me, (the) Father. they said Then to Him, Where is the father of you?
611 2424 3777/1691 1492 3777 3962 3450
ἀπεκρίθη ὁ Ἰησοῦς, Οὔτε ἐμὲ οἴδατε, οὔτε τὸν πατέρα μου·
answered Jesus, Neither Me you know, nor the Father of Me;
1487/1691/1492 3962 3450 1492 302 5023
20 εἰ ἐμὲ ᾔδειτε, καὶ τὸν πατέρα μου ᾔδειτε ἄν. ταῦτα τὰ
if Me you had known the Father of Me you had known then. These —
4487 2980 2424 1722 1049 1321
ῥήματα ἐλάλησεν ὁ Ἰησοῦς ἐν τῷ γαζοφυλακίῳ, διδάσκων
words spoke Jesus in the treasury, teaching
1722 2411 3762 4084 846 3754 3768 2064
ἐν τῷ ἱερῷ· καὶ οὐδεὶς ἐπίασεν αὐτόν, ὅτι οὔπω ἐληλύθει ἡ
in the Temple. And no one seized Him, because not yet had come the
5610 848
ὥρα αὐτοῦ.
hour of Him.
2036 3767 3825 846 2424 1473 5217
21 Εἶπεν οὖν πάλιν αὐτοῖς ὁ Ἰησοῦς, Ἐγὼ ὑπάγω, καὶ
said therefore again to them — Jesus, I go, and
2212 3165 1722 266 5216 599 3699
ζητήσετέ με, καὶ ἐν τῇ ἁμαρτίᾳ ὑμῶν ἀποθανεῖσθε· ὅπου
you will seek Me; and in the sin of you you will die. Where
1473 5217 5210 3756 1410 2064 3004 3767 2453
22 ἐγὼ ὑπάγω, ὑμεῖς οὐ δύνασθε ἐλθεῖν. ἔλεγον οὖν οἱ Ἰουδαῖοι,
I go, you not are able to come. said Then the Jews,
3385 615 1438 3754 3004 3699 1473 5217
Μήτι ἀποκτενεῖ ἑαυτόν, ὅτι λέγει, Ὅπου ἐγὼ ὑπάγω,
Not will he kill himself, because he says, Where I go,
5210/3756 1410 2064 2036 846 5210/1537 2736
23 ὑμεῖς οὐ δύνασθε ἐλθεῖν; καὶ εἶπεν αὐτοῖς, Ὑμεῖς ἐκ τῶν κάτω
you not are able to come? And He said to them, You from below
2075 1473/1537 507 1510 5210/1537 2889 5127 2075
ἐστέ, ἐγὼ ἐκ τῶν ἄνω εἰμί· ὑμεῖς ἐκ τοῦ κόσμου τούτου ἐστέ,
are; I from above am. You from world this are;
1473 3756/1510/1537 2889 5127 2036 3767/5213/3754
24 ἐγὼ οὐκ εἰμὶ ἐκ τοῦ κόσμου τούτου. εἶπον οὖν ὑμῖν ὅτι
I not am from — world this. I said therefore to you that
599 1722 266 5216 1437/1063/3361/ 4100
ἀποθανεῖσθε ἐν ταῖς ἁμαρτίαις ὑμῶν· ἐὰν γὰρ μὴ πιστεύσητε
you will die in the sins of you; if for not you believe
3754/1473/1510 599 1722 266 5216 3004
25 ὅτι ἐγώ εἰμι, ἀποθανεῖσθε ἐν ταῖς ἁμαρτίαις ὑμῶν. ἔλεγον
that I AM, you will die in the sins of you. They said
3767 846 4771/5101/1488 2036 846 2424 746
οὖν αὐτῷ, Σὺ τίς εἶ; καὶ εἶπεν αὐτοῖς ὁ Ἰησοῦς, Τὴν ἀρχὴν
then to Him, you Who are? And said to them — Jesus, Altogether
=3748= 2980 5213 4183 2192 4012 5216 2980
26 ὅ τι καὶ λαλῶ ὑμῖν. πολλὰ ἔχω περὶ ὑμῶν λαλεῖν καὶ
what even I say to you. Many things I have about you to say and
2919 235 3992/3165/ 227 2076 2504/3739/ 191 3844
κρίνειν· ἀλλ' ὁ πέμψας με ἀληθής ἐστι, κἀγὼ ἃ ἤκουσα παρ'
to judge, but the (One) sending Me true is, and I what I heard from
846 5023 3004 1519 2889 3756 1097 3754
27 αὐτοῦ, ταῦτα λέγω εἰς τὸν κόσμον. οὐκ ἔγνωσαν ὅτι τὸν
Him, these things I say to the world. not They knew that (of) the
3962 846 3004 2036 3767 846 2424 3752
28 πατέρα αὐτοῖς ἔλεγεν. εἶπεν οὖν αὐτοῖς ὁ Ἰησοῦς, Ὅταν
Father to them He spoke. said therefore to them Jesus, When
5312 5207 444 5119 1097 3754/1473
ὑψώσητε τὸν υἱὸν τοῦ ἀνθρώπου, τότε γνώσεσθε ὅτι ἐγώ
you lift up the Son — of man, then you will know that I
1510 575 1683 4160 3762 235 2531 1321 3165
εἰμι, καὶ ἀπ' ἐμαυτοῦ ποιῶ οὐδέν, ἀλλὰ καθὼς ἐδίδαξέ με ὁ
AM; and from Myself I do nothing, but as taught Me the
3962 3450 5023 2980 3992 3165/3326/1700/2076
29 πατήρ μου, ταῦτα λαλῶ. καὶ ὁ πέμψας με μετ' ἐμοῦ ἐστιν·
Father of Me. these things I say. And the (One) sending Me with Me is.

did not leave Me alone, for I always do the things pleasing to Him. [30]*As* He spoke these things, many believed into Him.

[31]Then Jesus said to the Jews who had believed in Him, If you continue in My word, you are truly My disciples. [32]And you will know the truth, and the truth will set you free. [33]They answered Him, We are Abraham's seed, and we have been enslaved to no one, never! How do you say, You will become free? [34]Jesus answered them, Truly, truly, I say to you, Everyone practicing sin is a slave of sin. [35]But the slave does not remain in the house forever; the son remains forever. [36]Then if the Son sets you free, you are free indeed. [37]I know that you are Abraham's seed, but you seek to kill Me because My word has no place in you. [38]I speak what I have seen with My Father. And therefore you do what you have seen with your father. [39]They answered and said to Him, Abraham is our father. Jesus said to them, If you were children of Abraham, you would do the works of Abraham. [40]But now you seek to kill Me, a man who has spoken the truth to you, which I heard alongside *of* God. Abraham did not do this. [41]You do the works of your father. Then they said to Him, We were not born of fornication; we have one father, God. [42]Then Jesus said to them, If God were your Father, you would love Me, for I went forth and have come

3756 863 3165 3441 3962 3754/1473 701 846 4160
οὐκ ἀφῆκέ με μόνον ὁ πατήρ. ὅτι ἐγὼ τὰ ἀρεστὰ αὐτῷ ποιῶ
Not left Me alone the Father, for I the things pleasing to Him do
3842 5023 846 2980 4183 4100
30 πάντοτε. ταῦτα αὐτοῦ λαλοῦντος πολλοὶ ἐπίστευσαν εἰς
always. These things He saying, many believed in
846
αὐτόν.
Him.

3004 3767 2424 4314 4100 846
31 Ἔλεγεν οὖν ὁ Ἰησοῦς πρὸς τοὺς πεπιστευκότας αὐτῷ
said Therefore Jesus to the having believed in Him
2453 1437 5210 3306 1722 3056 1699 230
Ἰουδαίους, Ἐὰν ὑμεῖς μείνητε ἐν τῷ λόγῳ τῷ ἐμῷ, ἀληθῶς
Jews, If you continue in the word – My, truly
3101 3450 2075 1097 225 225
32 μαθηταί μου ἐστέ· καὶ γνώσεσθε τὴν ἀλήθειαν, καὶ ἡ ἀλήθεια
disciples of Me you are; and you will know the truth, and the truth
1659 5209 611 846 4590 11
33 ἐλευθερώσει ὑμᾶς. ἀπεκρίθησαν αὐτῷ, Σπέρμα Ἀβραάμ
will set free you. They answered to Him, seed of Abraham
2010 3762 1398 4415 4459/4771/3004 3754
ἐσμεν, καὶ οὐδενὶ δεδουλεύκαμεν πώποτε· πῶς σὺ λέγεις ὅτι
We are, and to no one have we been enslaved; never! How do you say,
1658 1096 611 846 2424 281
34 Ἐλεύθεροι γενήσεσθε; ἀπεκρίθη αὐτοῖς ὁ Ἰησοῦς, Ἀμὴν
free You will become? answered them – Jesus, Truly,
281 3004 5213/3754/3956 4160 266 1401 2076
ἀμὴν λέγω ὑμῖν, ὅτι πᾶς ὁ ποιῶν τὴν ἁμαρτίαν δοῦλός ἐστι
truly, I say to you, that everyone doing – sin a slave is
266 1401 3756 3306/1722/3614 1519 165
35 τῆς ἁμαρτίας. ὁ δὲ δοῦλος οὐ μένει ἐν τῇ οἰκίᾳ εἰς τὸν αἰῶνα·
– of sin. the But slave not remains in the house to the age;
5207 3306 1519 165 1437/3767 5207 5209 1659
36 ὁ υἱὸς μένει εἰς τὸν αἰῶνα. ἐὰν οὖν ὁ υἱὸς ὑμᾶς ἐλευθερώσῃ,
the son remains to the age. If, then, the Son you sets free,
3689 1658 2071 1492 3754 4690 11 2075
37 ὄντως ἐλεύθεροι ἔσεσθε. οἶδα ὅτι σπέρμα Ἀβραάμ ἐστε·
really free you are. I know that the seed of Abraham you are
235 2212 3165 615 3754 3056 1699/3756 5562 1722
ἀλλὰ ζητεῖτέ με ἀποκτεῖναι, ὅτι ὁ λόγος ὁ ἐμὸς οὐ χωρεῖ ἐν
but you seek Me to kill, because word – My not has place in
5213 1473 3708 3844 3962 3450 2980 5210 3767
38 ὑμῖν. ἐγὼ ὃ ἑώρακα παρὰ τῷ πατρί μου, λαλῶ· καὶ ὑμεῖς οὖν
you. I what I have seen with the Father of Me, I speak; and you, then,
3739 3708 3844 3962 5216 4160 611
39 ὃ ἑωράκατε παρὰ τῷ πατρὶ ὑμῶν, ποιεῖτε. ἀπεκρίθησαν καὶ
what you have seen with the father of you, you do. They answered and
2036 846 3962 2257 11 2079 3004 846
εἶπον αὐτῷ, Ὁ πατὴρ ἡμῶν Ἀβραάμ ἐστι. λέγει αὐτοῖς ὁ
said to Him, The father of us Abraham is. says to them –
2424 1487 5043 11 2258 2041 11
Ἰησοῦς, Εἰ τέκνα τοῦ Ἀβραὰμ ἦτε, τὰ ἔργα τοῦ Ἀβραὰμ
Jesus, If children – of Abraham you were, the works – of Abraham
4160 302 3568 2212 3165 615 444 3739
40 ἐποιεῖτε ἄν. νῦν δὲ ζητεῖτέ με ἀποκτεῖναι, ἄνθρωπον ὃς τὴν
you would do. now And you seek Me to kill, a man who the
225 5213 2980 3739 191 3844 2316 5124
ἀλήθειαν ὑμῖν λελάληκα, ἣν ἤκουσα παρὰ τοῦ Θεοῦ· τοῦτο
truth to you has spoken, which I heard beside – God; this
11 3756 4160 5210 191 2041 3962
41 Ἀβραὰμ οὐκ ἐποίησεν. ὑμεῖς ποιεῖτε τὰ ἔργα τοῦ πατρὸς
Abraham not did do. You do the works of the father
5216 2036 3767 846 2249 1537 4202 3756 1080
ὑμῶν. εἶπον οὖν αὐτῷ, Ἡμεῖς ἐκ πορνείας οὐ γεγεννήμεθα·
of you. They said, then, to Him, We of fornication not were born;
1520 3962 2192 2316 2036 846 2424 1487
42 ἕνα πατέρα ἔχομεν, τὸν Θεόν. εἶπεν αὐτοῖς ὁ Ἰησοῦς, Εἰ ὁ
one father we have, – God. said to them – Jesus, If –
2316 3962 5216 2258 25 302/1691/1473/1063/1537 2316
Θεὸς πατὴρ ὑμῶν ἦν, ἠγαπᾶτε ἂν ἐμέ· ἐγὼ γὰρ ἐκ τοῦ Θεοῦ
God Father of you was, you would love Me; I for from – God

from God. For I have not
come from Myself, but that
One sent Me. 43 Why do
you not understand My
speech? *It is* because you
are not able to hear My
word. 44 You are of the
Devil *as* father, and the
lusts of your father you
desire to do. That one was
a murderer from *the* beginning, and he has not stood
in the truth because there
is no truth in him. When he
speaks *a* lie, he speaks
from *his* own, because he
is a liar, and the father of
it. 45 And because I speak
the truth, you do not be-
lieve Me. 46 Who of you
reproves Me concerning
sin? But if I speak truth,
why do you not believe
Me? 47 The *one* who is of
God hears the words of
God; for this reason you do
not hear, because you are
not of God. 48 Then the
Jews answered and said to
Him, Do we not say well
that you are a Samaritan,
and have a demon?
49 Jesus answered, I do not
have a demon, but I honor
My Father, and you
dishonor Me. 50 But I do
not seek My glory; there is
One who seeks and
judges. 51 Truly, truly, I say
to you, If anyone keeps My
word, he will never ever
see death.

52 Then the Jews said to
Him, Now we know that
you have a demon.
Abraham died, and the
prophets, and you say, If
anyone keeps My word, he
will never ever taste of
death. 53 Are you greater
than our father Abraham
who died? And the
prophets died! Whom do
you make yourself?
54 Jesus answered, If I
glorify Myself, My glory is
nothing; it is My Father

1831 2240 3761/1063 575 1683 2064 235
ἐξῆλθον καὶ ἥκω· οὐδὲ γὰρ ἀπ' ἐμαυτοῦ ἐλήλυθα, ἀλλ'
went forth, and have come; not for from Myself I have come, but
1565 3165 649 1302 2981 1699/3756/1097
43 ἐκεῖνός με ἀπέστειλε. διατί τὴν λαλιὰν τὴν ἐμὴν οὐ γινώ-
that One Me sent. Why — speech — My not you
3754/3756 1410 191 3056 1699 5210
44 σκετε; ὅτι οὐ δύνασθε ἀκούειν τὸν λόγον τὸν ἐμόν. ὑμεῖς
know? Because not you are able to hear word My. You
1537 3962 1228 2075 1939 3962
ἐκ πατρὸς τοῦ διαβόλου ἐστέ, καὶ τὰς ἐπιθυμίας τοῦ πατρὸς
from (your) father the Devil are; and the lusts of the father
5216 2309/4160 1565 443 2258/575 746
ὑμῶν θέλετε ποιεῖν. ἐκεῖνος ἀνθρωποκτόνος ἦν ἀπ' ἀρχῆς,
of you you desire to do. That one a murderer was from (the) first,
1722 225 3756 2476 3754/3756/2076 225 1722 846
καὶ ἐν τῇ ἀληθείᾳ οὐχ ἕστηκεν, ὅτι οὐκ ἔστιν ἀλήθεια ἐν αὐτῷ.
and in the truth not has stood, because not is truth in him.
3752 2980 5579 1537 2398 2980 3754 5583 2076
ὅταν λαλῇ τὸ ψεῦδος, ἐκ τῶν ἰδίων λαλεῖ· ὅτι ψεύστης ἐστὶ
When he speaks the lie, out of the own he speaks, for a liar he is,
3962 848 1473 3754 225 3004 3756/4100
45 καὶ ὁ πατὴρ αὐτοῦ. ἐγὼ δὲ ὅτι τὴν ἀλήθειαν λέγω, οὐ πι-
and the father of it. I But because the truth I say, not you
3427/5101/1537/5216/ 1651/3165/4012/ 266 1487 225
46 στεύετέ μοι. τίς ἐξ ὑμῶν ἐλέγχει με περὶ ἁμαρτίας; εἰ δὲ ἀλή-
believe Me. Who of you reproves Me concerning sin? if And
3004 1302 5210/3756 4100 3427 5607/1537 2316
47 θειαν λέγω, διατί ὑμεῖς οὐ πιστεύετέ μοι; ὁ ὢν ἐκ τοῦ Θεοῦ
truth I say, why you do not believe Me? He being of — God
4487 2316 191 1223 5124 5210 3756 191
τὰ ῥήματα τοῦ Θεοῦ ἀκούει· διὰ τοῦτο ὑμεῖς οὐκ ἀκούετε,
the words of God hears; therefore you do not hear,
3754/1537 2316 3756/2075 611 3767 2453
48 ὅτι ἐκ τοῦ Θεοῦ οὐκ ἐστέ. ἀπεκρίθησαν οὖν οἱ Ἰουδαῖοι καὶ
since from God not you are. answered, then, The Jews and
2036 846 3756 2573 3004 2249/3754 4541 1488/4771
εἶπον αὐτῷ, Οὐ καλῶς λέγομεν ἡμεῖς ὅτι Σαμαρείτης εἶ σύ,
said to Him, Not well say we that a Samaritan are you,
1140 2192 611 2424 1473 1140 3756
49 καὶ δαιμόνιον ἔχεις; ἀπεκρίθη Ἰησοῦς, Ἐγὼ δαιμόνιον οὐκ
and a demon you have? answered Jesus, I a demon not
2192 235 5091 3962 3450 5210 818 3165
ἔχω, ἀλλὰ τιμῶ τὸν πατέρα μου, καὶ ὑμεῖς ἀτιμάζετέ με.
have, but I honor the Father of Me, and you dishonor Me.
1473 3756/2212 1391 3450 2076 2212 2919
50 ἐγὼ δὲ οὐ ζητῶ τὴν δόξαν μου· ἔστιν ὁ ζητῶν καὶ κρίνων.
I But not do seek the glory of Me; is One seeking and judging
281 281 3004 5213/ 1537/5101 3056 1699 5083
51 ἀμὴν ἀμὴν λέγω ὑμῖν, ἐάν τις τὸν λόγον τὸν ἐμὸν τηρήσῃ,
Truly, truly, I say to you, if anyone — word — My keeps,
2288 3756/3361 2334 1519 165 2036 3767 846
52 θάνατον οὐ μὴ θεωρήσῃ εἰς τὸν αἰῶνα. εἶπον οὖν αὐτῷ
death in no way will he behold for ever. said, then, to Him
2453 3568 1097 3754 1140 2192 11
οἱ Ἰουδαῖοι, Νῦν ἐγνώκαμεν ὅτι δαιμόνιον ἔχεις. Ἀβραὰμ
The Jews, Now we have known that a demon you have. Abraham
599 4396 4771 3004 1437/5100 3056
ἀπέθανε καὶ οἱ προφῆται, καὶ σὺ λέγεις, Ἐάν τις τὸν λόγον
died, and the prophets, and you say, If anyone the word
3450 5083 =3364= 1089 2288 1519 165 3361/4771
53 μου τηρήσῃ, οὐ μὴ γεύσεται θανάτου εἰς τὸν αἰῶνα. μὴ σὺ
of Me keeps, in no way will he taste of death to the age. Not you
3187 1488 3962 2257 11 3748 599
μείζων εἶ τοῦ πατρὸς ἡμῶν Ἀβραάμ, ὅστις ἀπέθανε; καὶ
greater are than the father of us, Abraham, who died? Also
4376 599 5101 4572 4771 4160 611
54 οἱ προφῆται ἀπέθανον· τίνα σεαυτὸν σὺ ποιεῖς; ἀπεκρίθη
the prophets died. Whom Yourself you do make? answered
2424 1437/1473 1392 1683 1391 3450 3762 2076
Ἰησοῦς, Ἐὰν ἐγὼ δοξάζω ἐμαυτόν, ἡ δόξα μου οὐδέν ἐστιν·
Jesus, If I glorify Myself, the glory of Me nothing is;

who glorifies Me, whom you say is your God. [55]And you have not known Him; but I know Him, and if I say that I do not know Him, I shall be like you, a liar. But I know Him, and I keep His word. [56]Your father Abraham leaped for joy that he should see My day, and he saw, and rejoiced. [57]Then the Jews said to Him, You do not yet have fifty years, and have you seen Abraham? [58]Jesus said to them, Truly, truly, I say to you, Before Abraham came into being, I AM. [59]Then they took up stones that they might throw *them* on Him. But Jesus was hidden, and went forth out of the temple, going through *the* midst of them, and so passed by.

CHAPTER 9

[1]And passing by, He saw a man blind from birth. [2]And His disciples asked Him, saying, Teacher, who sinned, this one, or his parents, that he was born blind? [3]Jesus answered, Neither this one sinned nor his parents, but that the works of God might be revealed in him. [4]It is necessary for Me to work the works of Him who sent Me while it is day. Night comes when no one is able to work. [5]While I am in the world, I am *the* Light of the world. [6]Saying these things, He spat on the ground and made clay out of the spittle, and applied the clay on the blind one's eyes. [7]And He said to him, Go, wash in the pool of Siloam, which translated is Sent. Then he went, and washed, and came seeing.

2076 3962 3450 1392 3165/3739/5210/ 3004 3754/ 2316
ἔστιν ὁ πατήρ μου ὁ δοξάζων με, ὃν ὑμεῖς λέγετε ὅτι Θεὸς
it is the Father of Me glorifying Me, whom you say that God
5216 2076 3756 1097 846 1473 1492 846
55 ὑμῶν ἐστι, καὶ οὐκ ἐγνώκατε αὐτόν· ἐγὼ δὲ οἶδα αὐτόν,
of you is. And not you have known Him; I but know Him,
1437 2036 3754/3756 1492 846 2071 3664 5216
καὶ ἐὰν εἴπω ὅτι οὐκ οἶδα αὐτόν, ἔσομαι ὅμοιος ὑμῶν,
and if I say that not I know Him, I shall be like you,
5583 235 1492 846 3056 848 5083
ψεύστης· ἀλλ' οἶδα αὐτόν, καὶ τὸν λόγον αὐτοῦ τηρῶ.
a liar. But I know Him, and the word of Him I keep.
11 3962 5216 21 2443/1492 2250
56 Ἀβραὰμ ὁ πατὴρ ὑμῶν ἠγαλλιάσατο ἵνα ἴδῃ τὴν ἡμέραν
Abraham the father of you leaped for joy that he may see day
1699 1492 5463 2036 3767 2453 4314
57 τὴν ἐμήν, καὶ εἶδε καὶ ἐχάρη. εἶπον οὖν οἱ Ἰουδαῖοι πρὸς
— My, and he saw and rejoiced. said Then the Jews to
846 4004 2094 3768 2192 11 3708
αὐτόν, Πεντήκοντα ἔτη οὔπω ἔχεις, καὶ Ἀβραὰμ ἑώρακας;
Him, Fifty years not yet you have, and Abraham you have seen?
2036 846 2424 281 281 3004 5213 4950 11
58 εἶπεν αὐτοῖς ὁ Ἰησοῦς, Ἀμὴν ἀμὴν λέγω ὑμῖν, πρὶν Ἀβραὰμ
said to them — Jesus, Truly, truly I say to you, before Abraham
1096 1473/1510 142/3767 3037 2443 906 1909 846
59 γενέσθαι, ἐγώ εἰμι. ἦραν οὖν λίθους ἵνα βάλωσιν ἐπ' αὐτόν·
came into being, I AM. they took Then stones that they might cast on Him;
2424 2928 1831 1537 2411 1330 1223
Ἰησοῦς δὲ ἐκρύβη, καὶ ἐξῆλθεν ἐκ τοῦ ἱεροῦ, διελθὼν διὰ
Jesus but was hidden, and went forth out of the Temple, going through
3319 846 3855 3779
μέσου αὐτῶν· καὶ παρῆγεν οὕτως.
(the) midst of them, and passed by thus.

CHAPTER 9

3855 1492 444 5185 1537 1079
1 Καὶ παράγων εἶδεν ἄνθρωπον τυφλὸν ἐκ γενετῆς. καὶ
And passing by, He saw a man blind from birth. And
2065 846 3101 848 3004 4461 5101
2 ἠρώτησαν αὐτὸν οἱ μαθηταὶ αὐτοῦ λέγοντες, Ῥαββί, τίς
asked Him the disciples of Him, saying, Rabbi, who
264 3778 2228 1118 848 2443 5185 1080
ἥμαρτεν, οὗτος ἢ οἱ γονεῖς αὐτοῦ, ἵνα τυφλὸς γεννηθῇ;
sinned, this one, or the parents of him, that blind he was born?
611 2424 3777 3778 264 3777 1118
3 ἀπεκρίθη ὁ Ἰησοῦς, Οὔτε οὗτος ἥμαρτεν οὔτε οἱ γονεῖς
answered — Jesus, Neither this one sinned, nor the parents
848 235 2443 5319 2041 2316 1722 846
αὐτοῦ· ἀλλ' ἵνα φανερωθῇ τὰ ἔργα τοῦ Θεοῦ ἐν αὐτῷ.
of him, but that might be revealed the works — of God in Him.
1691/1163/2038 2041 3992 3165/2193 2250
4 ἐμὲ δεῖ ἐργάζεσθαι τὰ ἔργα τοῦ πέμψαντός με ἕως ἡμέρα
Me it behoves to work the works of the (One) sending Me while day
2076 2064 3571 3753 3762 1410 2038 3752 1722
5 ἐστίν· ἔρχεται νύξ, ὅτε οὐδεὶς δύναται ἐργάζεσθαι. ὅταν ἐν
it is. comes Night, when no one is able to work. When in
2889 5600/5457/1510 2889 5023 2036 4429
6 τῷ κόσμῳ ὦ, φῶς εἰμι τοῦ κόσμου. ταῦτα εἰπών, ἔπτυσε
the world I am, (the) light I am of the world. These things saying, He spat
5475 4160 4081 1537 4427 2025
χαμαί, καὶ ἐποίησε πηλὸν ἐκ τοῦ πτύσματος, καὶ ἐπέχρισε
on earth and made clay out of the spittle, and anointed
4081 1909 3788 5185 2036 846
7 τὸν πηλὸν ἐπὶ τοὺς ὀφθαλμοὺς τοῦ τυφλοῦ, καὶ εἶπεν αὐτῷ,
the clay on the eyes of the blind one, and said to him,
5217 3538 1519 2861 4611 3739 2059
Ὕπαγε νίψαι εἰς τὴν κολυμβήθραν τοῦ Σιλωάμ (ὃ ἑρμη-
Go, wash in the pool — of Siloam; which is
649 565 3767 3538 2064
νεύεται, ἀπεσταλμένος). ἀπῆλθεν οὖν καὶ ἐνίψατο, καὶ ἦλθε
translated, having been sent. He went then, and washed, and came

[8]Then the neighbors and those who formerly saw him, that he was blind, said, Is this one not the *one* who had sat and begged? [9]Some said, It is he; and others, He is like him. That one said, I am *he*. [10]Then they said to him, How were your eyes opened? [11]He answered and said, A man called Jesus made clay and applied *it to* my eyes, and told me, Go to the pool of Siloam, and wash. And going, and washing, I received sight. [12]Then they said to him, Where is that one? He said, I do not know.

[13]They brought him to the Pharisees, the *one* once blind. [14]And it was a sabbath when Jesus made the clay and opened his eyes. [15]Then also the Pharisees asked him again how he received sight. And he said to them, He put clay on my eyes, and I washed, and I see. [16]Then some of the Pharisees said, This man is not from God, because He does not keep the sabbath. Others said, How can a man, a sinner, do such miracles? And there was a division among them. [17]They said to the blind one again, What do you say about him, because he opened your eyes? And he said, He is a prophet. [18]Then the Jews did not believe concerning him, that he was blind and received sight, until they called the parents of the *one* who had received sight. [19]And they asked them, saying, Is this your son, whom you say that he was born blind?

991 3767 1069 2334 846 4386
8 βλέπων. οἱ οὖν γείτονες καὶ οἱ θεωροῦντες αὐτὸν τὸ πρό-
seeing. the Then neighbors and those beholding him formerly,
3754 5185 2258 3004 3756 3778 2076 2521
τερον ὅτι τυφλὸς ἦν, ἔλεγον, Οὐχ οὗτός ἐστιν ὁ καθή-
that blind he was, said, Not this one is the (one)
4319 243 3004 3754 3778 2076 243
9 μενος καὶ προσαιτῶν; ἄλλοι ἔλεγον ὅτι Οὗτός ἐστιν· ἄλλοι
sitting and begging? Others said, — This is he; others
3754 3664 846 2076 1565 3004 3754 1473/1510
δὲ ὅτι Ὅμοιος αὐτῷ ἐστιν. ἐκεῖνος ἔλεγεν ὅτι Ἐγώ εἰμι.
And, like him He is. That one said, I am.
3004 3767 846 4459 455 4675 3788
10 ἔλεγον οὖν αὐτῷ, Πῶς ἀνεῴχθησάν σου οἱ ὀφθαλμοί;
they said Then to him, How were opened of you the eyes?
611 1565 2036 444 3004 2424
11 ἀπεκρίθη ἐκεῖνος καὶ εἶπεν, Ἄνθρωπος λεγόμενος Ἰησοῦς
answered That one and said, (The) man being called Jesus
4081 4160 2025 3450 3788 2036
πηλὸν ἐποίησε, καὶ ἐπέχρισέ μου τοὺς ὀφθαλμούς, καὶ εἶπέ
clay made and anointed of me the eyes, and told
3427 5217 1519 2861 4611 3538
μοι, Ὕπαγε εἰς τὴν κολυμβήθραν τοῦ Σιλωάμ, καὶ νίψαι.
me, Go to the pool — of Siloam, and wash.
565 3538 308 2036 3767 846 4226
12 ἀπελθὼν δὲ καὶ νιψάμενος, ἀνέβλεψα. εἶπον οὖν αὐτῷ, Ποῦ
going And, and washing, I received sight. They said then to him, Where
2076 1565 3004 3756 1492
ἐστιν ἐκεῖνος; λέγει, Οὐκ οἶδα.
is that one? He says, Not I do know.
71 846 4314 5330 4218 5185
13 Ἄγουσιν αὐτὸν πρὸς τοὺς Φαρισαίους, τόν ποτε τυφλόν.
They lead him to the Pharisees, the (one) once blind.
2258 4521 3753 4081 4160 2424
14 ἦν δὲ σάββατον ὅτε τὸν πηλὸν ἐποίησεν ὁ Ἰησοῦς, καὶ
it was And a sabbath when the clay made Jesus, and
455 848 3788 3825 3767 2065 846
15 ἀνέῳξεν αὐτοῦ τοὺς ὀφθαλμούς. πάλιν οὖν ἠρώτων αὐτὸν
opened of him the eyes. Again, then, asked him
5330 4459 308 2036 846 4081
καὶ οἱ Φαρισαῖοι, πῶς ἀνέβλεψεν. ὁ δὲ εἶπεν αὐτοῖς, Πηλὸν
also the Pharisees how he received he And said to them, Clay
2007 1909 3788 sight. 3450 3538
ἐπέθηκεν ἐπὶ τοὺς ὀφθαλμούς μου, καὶ ἐνιψάμην, καὶ
He put on the eyes of me, and I washed, and
991 3004/ 3767/1537 5330 5100 3778 444
16 βλέπω. ἔλεγον οὖν ἐκ τῶν Φαρισαίων τινές, Οὗτος ὁ ἄνθρω-
I see. said Then of the Pharisees some, This man
3756 2076 3844 2316 3754 4521 3756 5083
πος οὐκ ἔστι παρὰ τοῦ Θεοῦ, ὅτι τὸ σάββατον οὐ τηρεῖ.
not is from — God, because the sabbath not He keeps.
243 3004 4459 1410 444 268 5108
ἄλλοι ἔλεγον, Πῶς δύναται ἄνθρωπος ἁμαρτωλὸς τοιαῦτα
Others said, How is able a man, a sinner, such
4592 4160 4978 2258/1722/846 3004 5185
17 σημεῖα ποιεῖν; καὶ σχίσμα ἦν ἐν αὐτοῖς. λέγουσι τῷ τυφλῷ
signs do? And a division was among them. They say to the blind one
3825 4771/5101/3004/4012 846 3754 455 4675 3788
πάλιν, Σὺ τί λέγεις περὶ αὐτοῦ, ὅτι ἤνοιξέ σου τοὺς ὀφθαλ-
again, you What say concerning him, because he opened of you the eyes?
2036 3754 4396 2076 3756 4100 3767
18 μούς; ὁ δὲ εἶπεν ὅτι Προφήτης ἐστίν. οὐκ ἐπίστευσαν οὖν οἱ
he And said, — A prophet He is. Not did believe, therefore, the
2453 4012 846 3754 5185 2258 308 2193
Ἰουδαῖοι περὶ αὐτοῦ, ὅτι τυφλὸς ἦν καὶ ἀνέβλεψεν, ἕως
Jews concerning Him, that blind he was and received sight, until
3755 5455 1118 846 308
19 ὅτου ἐφώνησαν τοὺς γονεῖς αὐτοῦ τοῦ ἀναβλέψαντος, καὶ
when they called the parents of him — having received sight; and
2065 846 3004 3778 2076 5207 5216 3739
ἠρώτησαν αὐτοὺς λέγοντες, Οὗτός ἐστιν ὁ υἱὸς ὑμῶν, ὃν
they asked them, saying, this Is the son of you, whom

Then how does he now see? [20]His parents answered them and said, We know that this is our son, and that he was born blind. [21]But how he now sees, we do not know; or who opened his eyes, we do not know. He is of age, ask him. He will speak about himself. [22]His parents said these things because they feared the Jews; for the Jews had already agreed that if anyone should confess Him *as* Christ, he would be expelled from the synagogue. [23]Because of this his parents said, He is of age, ask him.

[24]Then a second time they called the man who was blind, and *they* said to him, Give glory to God. We know that this man is a sinner. [25]Then he answered and said, Whether he is a sinner, I do not know. One *thing* I do know, that being blind, now I see. [26]And they said to him again, What did he do to you? How did he open your eyes? [27]He answered them, I told you already, and you did not hear. Why do you wish to hear again? Do you also desire to become disciples of Him? [28]Then they reviled him and said, You are a disciple of that one, but we are disciples of Moses. [29]We know that God has spoken by Moses, but this one, we do not know from where he is. [30]The man answered and said to them, For there is a marvel in this, that you do not know from where He is, and He opened my eyes. [31]But we know that God does not hear sinful ones, but if anyone is God-fearing, and does His will,

5210 3004 3754 5185 1080 4459 3767 737 991
ὑμεῖς λέγετε ὅτι τυφλὸς ἐγεννήθη; πῶς οὖν ἄρτι βλέπει;
you say that blind he was born? How, then, just now he sees?
611 846 1118 848 2036 1492 3754
20 ἀπεκρίθησαν αὐτοῖς οἱ γονεῖς αὐτοῦ καὶ εἶπον, Οἴδαμεν ὅτι
answered them The parents of him and said, We know that
3778 2076 5207 2257 3754 5185 1080 4459 3568
21 οὗτός ἐστιν ὁ υἱὸς ἡμῶν, καὶ ὅτι τυφλὸς ἐγεννήθη· πῶς δὲ νῦν
this is the son of us, and that blind he was born. how But now
991 3756 1492 2228/5101 455 848 3788
βλέπει, οὐκ οἴδαμεν· ἢ τίς ἤνοιξεν αὐτοῦ τοὺς ὀφθαλμούς,
he sees, not we know, or who opened of him the eyes
2249 3756 1492 846 2244 2192 846 2065
ἡμεῖς οὐκ οἴδαμεν· αὐτὸς ἡλικίαν ἔχει· αὐτὸν ἐρωτήσατε,
we not know. He age has, him ask.
846 4012 848 2980 5023 2036 1118 848 3754
22 αὐτὸς περὶ αὐτοῦ λαλήσει. ταῦτα εἶπον οἱ γονεῖς αὐτοῦ, ὅτι
He concerning himself will speak. These things said the parents of him, for
5399 2453 2235 1063 4934
ἐφοβοῦντο τοὺς Ἰουδαίους· ἤδη γὰρ συνετέθειντο οἱ
they feared the Jews; already for had agreed the
2453 2443/1437 846 3670 5547 656
Ἰουδαῖοι, ἵνα ἐάν τις αὐτὸν ὁμολογήσῃ Χριστόν, ἀποσυνά-
Jews that if anyone Him should confess (as) Christ, from
1096 1223 5124 1118 848 2036 synagogue
23 γωγος γένηται. διὰ τοῦτο οἱ γονεῖς αὐτοῦ εἶπον ὅτι
3754 expelled he would be. Because of this the parents of him said, —
2244 2192 846 2065 5455 3767/1537 1208
24 Ἡλικίαν ἔχει, αὐτὸν ἐρωτήσατε. ἐφώνησαν οὖν ἐκ δευτέρου
age He has, him ask. They called therefore a second time
444 3739/2258 5185 2036 846 1325 1391
τὸν ἄνθρωπον ὃς ἦν τυφλός, καὶ εἶπον αὐτῷ, Δὸς δόξαν τῷ
the man who was blind, and said to him, Give glory to
2316 5210 1492 3754 444 3778 268 2076
Θεῷ· ἡμεῖς οἴδαμεν ὅτι ὁ ἄνθρωπος οὗτος ἁμαρτωλός ἐστιν.
God; we know that man this a sinner is.
611 3767 1565 2036 1487 268 2076 3756
25 ἀπεκρίθη οὖν ἐκεῖνος καὶ εἶπεν, Εἰ ἁμαρτωλός ἐστιν, οὐκ
answered Then that one and said, If a sinner He is, not
1492 1722/1492/3754 5185 5607/737 991 2036 846
26 οἶδα· ἓν οἶδα, ὅτι τυφλὸς ὤν, ἄρτι βλέπω. εἶπον δὲ αὐτῷ
I know; one I know, that blind being, just now I see. they said And to him
3825 5101 4160 4671 4459 455 4675 3788
πάλιν, Τί ἐποίησέ σοι; πῶς ἤνοιξέ σου τοὺς ὀφθαλμούς;
again, What did he to you? How opened he of you the eyes?
611 846 2036 5213 2235 3756 191 5101 3825
27 ἀπεκρίθη αὐτοῖς, Εἶπον ὑμῖν ἤδη, καὶ οὐκ ἠκούσατε· τί πάλιν
He answered them, I told you already, and not you heard. Why again
2309 191 3361 5210 2309 848 3101 1096
θέλετε ἀκούειν; μὴ καὶ ὑμεῖς θέλετε αὐτοῦ μαθηταὶ γενέσθαι;
do you wish to hear? Not also you wish of Him disciples to become?
3058 3767 846 2036 4771/1488 3101 1565
28 ἐλοιδόρησαν οὖν αὐτόν, καὶ εἶπον, Σὺ εἶ μαθητὴς ἐκείνου·
they reviled Then him and said, You are a disciple of that one,
2249 3475 2070 3101 2249 1492 3754 3475
29 ἡμεῖς δὲ τοῦ Μωσέως ἐσμὲν μαθηταί. ἡμεῖς οἴδαμεν ὅτι Μωσῇ
we but — of Moses are disciples. We know that by Moses
2980 2316 5126 3756 1492 4159 2076
λελάληκεν ὁ Θεός· τοῦτον δὲ οὐκ οἴδαμεν πόθεν ἐστίν.
has spoken God, this one but not we know from where he is.
611 444 2036 846 1722 1063 5129
30 ἀπεκρίθη ὁ ἄνθρωπος καὶ εἶπεν αὐτοῖς, Ἐν γὰρ τούτῳ
answered The man and said to them, in For this
2298 2076 3754 5210 3756 1492 4192 2076
θαυμαστόν ἐστιν, ὅτι ὑμεῖς οὐκ οἴδατε πόθεν ἐστί, καὶ
a marvel is, that you do not know from where He is, and
455 3450 3788 1492 3754 268
31 ἀνέῳξέ μου τοὺς ὀφθαλμούς. οἴδαμεν δὲ ὅτι ἁμαρτωλῶν ὁ
He opened of me the eyes. we know And that sinful ones
2316 3756 191 235 1437/5100/ 2318 5600 2307
Θεὸς οὐκ ἀκούει· ἀλλ᾽ ἐάν τις θεοσεβὴς ᾖ, καὶ τὸ θέλημα
God not hears, but if anyone God-fearing is, and the will

He hears that one. 32 From the age it was not heard that anyone opened the eyes of one having been born blind. 33 If this One was not from God, He could not do anything. 34 They answered and said to him, You were born wholly in sins, and do you teach us? And they threw him outside.

35 Jesus heard that they threw him outside, and finding him, He said to him, Do you believe into the Son of God? 36 And he answered and said, Who is He, Lord, that I may believe into Him? 37 And Jesus said to him, Even you have seen Him, and He speaking with you is that One. 38 And he said, I believe, Lord! And he worshiped Him. 39 And Jesus said, I came into this world for judgment, that the ones who do not see may see; and they who see may become blind. 40 And those of the Pharisees who were with Him heard these things, and said to Him, Are we also blind? 41 Jesus said to them, If you were blind, you would have no sin. But now you say, We see; therefore, your sin remains.

848 4160 5127 191 1537 165 3756 191
32 αὐτοῦ ποιῇ, τούτου ἀκούει. ἐκ τοῦ αἰῶνος οὐκ ἠκούσθη
of Him does, this one He hears. From the age not it was heard
3754 455 5100 3788 5185 1080 =1508= 2258
33 ὅτι ἤνοιξέ τις ὀφθαλμοὺς τυφλοῦ γεγεννημένου. εἰ μὴ ἦν
that opened anyone eyes of one blind having been born. If not was
3778 3844 2316 3756 1410 4160 3762 611
34 οὗτος παρὰ Θεοῦ, οὐκ ἠδύνατο ποιεῖν οὐδέν. ἀπεκρίθησαν
this One from God, not He could do nothing. They answered
2036 846 1722 266 4771 1080 3650 4771
καὶ εἶπον αὐτῷ, Ἐν ἁμαρτίαις σὺ ἐγεννήθης ὅλος, καὶ σὺ
and said to him, In sins you were born wholly, and you
1321 2248 1544 846 1854
διδάσκεις ἡμᾶς; καὶ ἐξέβαλον αὐτὸν ἔξω.
teach us? And they threw him outside.
191 2424 3754 1544 846 1854 2147
35 Ἤκουσεν ὁ Ἰησοῦς ὅτι ἐξέβαλον αὐτὸν ἔξω· καὶ εὑρὼν
heard Jesus that they threw him outside, and finding
846 2036 846 4771 4100 1519 5207 2316 611
36 αὐτόν, εἶπεν αὐτῷ, Σὺ πιστεύεις εἰς τὸν υἱὸν τοῦ Θεοῦ; ἀπε-
him, He said to him, You do believe in the Son — of God?
1565 2036 5101 2076 2962 2443 4100 1519
κρίθη ἐκεῖνος καὶ εἶπε, Τίς ἐστι, Κύριε, ἵνα πιστεύσω εἰς
answered That one and said, Who is He, Lord, that I may believe in
846 2036 846 2424 3708 846
37 αὐτόν; εἶπε δὲ αὐτῷ ὁ Ἰησοῦς, Καὶ ἑώρακας αὐτόν, καὶ ὁ
Him? said And to him — Jesus, Even you have seen him, and He
2980 3326 4675 1565 2076 5346 4100 2962
38 λαλῶν μετὰ σοῦ ἐκεῖνός ἐστιν. ὁ δὲ ἔφη, Πιστεύω, Κύριε·
speaking with you that One is. he And said, I believe, Lord;
4352 846 2036 2424 1519 2919 1473
39 καὶ προσεκύνησεν αὐτῷ. καὶ εἶπεν ὁ Ἰησοῦς, Εἰς κρίμα ἐγὼ
and he worshiped Him. And said — Jesus, For judgment I
1519 2889 5126 2064 2443 3361 991 991
εἰς τὸν κόσμον τοῦτον ἦλθον, ἵνα οἱ μὴ βλέποντες βλέπω-
to — world this came, that the (ones) not seeing may see,
991 5185 1096 191 1537
40 σι, καὶ οἱ βλέποντες τυφλοὶ γένωνται. καὶ ἤκουσαν ἐκ τῶν
and those seeing blind may become. And heard of the
5330 5023 5607 3326 846 2036 846 3361
Φαρισαίων ταῦτα οἱ ὄντες μετ' αὐτοῦ, καὶ εἶπον αὐτῷ, Μὴ
Pharisees these things those being with Him, and said to Him, Not
2249 5185 2070 2036 846 2424 1487 5185
41 καὶ ἡμεῖς τυφλοί ἐσμεν; εἶπεν αὐτοῖς ὁ Ἰησοῦς, Εἰ τυφλοὶ
also we blind are? said to them Jesus, If blind
2258/3756/302 2192 266 3568 3004 3754 991
ἦτε, οὐκ ἂν εἴχετε ἁμαρτίαν· νῦν δὲ λέγετε ὅτι Βλέπομεν·
you were, not would you have sin; now but you say, We see;
3767 268 5216 3306
ἡ οὖν ἁμαρτία ὑμῶν μένει.
the then sin of you remains.

CHAPTER 10

1 Truly, truly, I say to you, the *one* not entering through the door into the sheepfold, but going up by another way, that one is a thief and a robber. 2 But the *one* entering through the door is the shepherd of the sheep. 3 The doorkeeper opens to him, and the sheep hear his voice, and he calls *his* own sheep by name, and leads them out. 4 And when he puts forth *his* own sheep, he

CHAPTER 10

281 281 3004 5213 3361 1525 1223 2374
1 Ἀμὴν ἀμὴν λέγω ὑμῖν, ὁ μὴ εἰσερχόμενος διὰ τῆς θύρας
Truly, truly I say to you, he not entering through the door
1519 833 4263 235 305 237
εἰς τὴν αὐλὴν τῶν προβάτων, ἀλλὰ ἀναβαίνων ἀλλαχόθεν,
into the fold of the sheep, but going up by another way,
1565 2812 2076 3027 1525 1223
2 ἐκεῖνος κλέπτης ἐστὶ καὶ λῃστής. ὁ δὲ εἰσερχόμενος διὰ τῆς
that one a thief is and a robber. he But entering through the
2374 4166 2076 4263 5129 2377
3 θύρας ποιμήν ἐστι τῶν προβάτων. τούτῳ ὁ θυρωρὸς
door shepherd is of the sheep, To this one the doorkeeper
455 4263 5456 848 191
ἀνοίγει, καὶ τὰ πρόβατα τῆς φωνῆς αὐτοῦ ἀκούει, καὶ τὰ
opens, and the sheep the voice of him hears, and the
2398 4263 2564 2590 3686 1806 846 3752
4 ἴδια πρόβατα καλεῖ κατ' ὄνομα, καὶ ἐξάγει αὐτά. καὶ ὅταν
own sheep he calls by name, and leads out them. And when

goes in front of them, and the sheep follow him because they know his voice. [5]But they never follow a stranger, but will flee from him, because they do not know the voice of the strangers. [6]Jesus spoke this allegory to them, but they did not know what it was which He spoke to them.

[7]Then Jesus again said to them, Truly, truly, I say to you that I am the door of the sheep. [8]All who came before Me are thieves and robbers; but the sheep did not hear them. [9]I am the door. If anyone enters through Me, he will be saved, and will go in, and will go out, and will find pasture. [10]The thief does not come except that he may steal, and kill, and destroy. I came that they may have life, and may have *it* abundantly. [11]I am the Good Shepherd! The Good Shepherd lays down His life for the sheep. [12]But the hireling, not even being a shepherd, who does not own the sheep, sees the wolf coming and forsakes the sheep, and flees. And the wolf seizes them, and scatters the sheep. [13]But the hireling flees because he is a hireling, and there is not a care to him concerning the sheep. [14]I am the Good Shepherd, and I know those that *are* Mine; and I am known by the *ones that are* Mine. [15]Even as the Father knows Me, I also know the Father; and I lay down My soul for the sheep. [16]And I have other sheep which are not of this fold. I must also lead those, and they will hear My voice; and there will be one flock,

2398 4263 1544 1715 846 4198
τὰ ἴδια πρόβατα ἐκβάλῃ, ἔμπροσθεν αὐτῶν πορεύεται· καὶ
the own sheep he passes, in front of them he passes, and
4263 846 190 3754 1492 5456 848
τὰ πρόβατα αὐτῷ ἀκολουθεῖ, ὅτι οἴδασι τὴν φωνὴν αὐτοῦ.
the sheep to him follow, because they know the voice of him.
245 =3364= 190 235 5343 575
5 ἀλλοτρίῳ δὲ οὐ μὴ ἀκολουθήσωσιν, ἀλλὰ φεύξονται ἀπ'
a stranger But in no way should they follow. but will flee from
846 3754/3756 1492 245 5456 5026
6 αὐτοῦ· ὅτι οὐκ οἴδασι τῶν ἀλλοτρίων τὴν φωνήν. ταύτην
him, because not they know of the strangers the voice. This
3942 2036 846 2424 1565 3756 1097
7 τὴν παροιμίαν εἶπεν αὐτοῖς ὁ Ἰησοῦς· ἐκεῖνοι δὲ οὐκ ἔγνωσαν
— allegory said to them — Jesus, those but not knew
5101/2258/3739/2980 846
τίνα ἦν ἃ ἐλάλει αὐτοῖς.
what it was which He spoke to them.
2036 3767 3825 846 2424 281 281 3004 5213
Εἶπεν οὖν πάλιν αὐτοῖς ὁ Ἰησοῦς, Ἀμὴν ἀμὴν λέγω ὑμῖν
said Therefore again to them — Jesus, Truly, truly, I say to you
3754 1473/1510 2374 4263 3956 3745/4253/1700
8 ὅτι Ἐγώ εἰμι ἡ θύρα τῶν προβάτων. πάντες ὅσοι πρὸ ἐμοῦ
that I am the door of the sheep. All who before Me
2064 2812 1526 3027 235 3756 191 846
ἦλθον κλέπται εἰσὶ καὶ λῃσταί· ἀλλ' οὐκ ἤκουσαν αὐτῶν τὰ
came thieves are and robbers; but did not hear them the
4263 1473 1510 2374 1223/1700/1437/5101/ 1525 4982
9 πρόβατα. ἐγώ εἰμι ἡ θύρα· δι' ἐμοῦ ἐάν τις εἰσέλθῃ, σωθή-
sheep. I am the door; through Me If anyone enter he will
1525 1831 3542 2147
σεται, καὶ εἰσελεύσεται καὶ ἐξελεύσεται, καὶ νομὴν εὑρήσει.
be saved, and will go in and will go out, and pasture will find.
2812 3756 2064 =1508=2443/2813 2380 622
10 ὁ κλέπτης οὐκ ἔρχεται εἰ μὴ ἵνα κλέψῃ καὶ θύσῃ καὶ ἀπολέσῃ·
The thief not comes except that he may steal and slay and destroy;
1473 2064 2443 2222 2192 4053 2192 1473/1510
11 ἐγὼ ἦλθον ἵνα ζωὴν ἔχωσι, καὶ περισσὸν ἔχωσιν. ἐγώ εἰμι
I came that life they may have, and abundantly may have. I am
4166 2570 4166 2570 5590 848
ὁ ποιμὴν ὁ καλός· ὁ ποιμὴν ὁ καλὸς τὴν ψυχὴν αὐτοῦ
the Shepherd — Good. The Shepherd — Good the soul of Him
5087 5228 4263 3411 3956/5607
12 τίθησιν ὑπὲρ τῶν προβάτων. ὁ μισθωτὸς δέ, καὶ οὐκ ὢν
lays down for the sheep. the hireling And, even not being
4166 3739/3756/1510 4263 2398 2334 3074
ποιμήν, οὗ οὐκ εἰσὶ τὰ πρόβατα ἴδια, θεωρεῖ τὸν λύκον
a shepherd, whose not are the sheep (his) own, beholds the wolf
2064 863 4263 5343 3074
ἐρχόμενον, καὶ ἀφίησι τὰ πρόβατα, καὶ φεύγει· καὶ ὁ λύκος
coming, and forsakes the sheep, and flees, and the wolf
726 846 4650 4263 3411
13 ἁρπάζει αὐτά, καὶ σκορπίζει τὰ πρόβατα. ὁ δὲ μισθωτὸς
seizes them and scatters the sheep. the Now hireling
5343 3754 3411 2076 3756 3199 846 4012
φεύγει, ὅτι μισθωτός ἐστι, καὶ οὐ μέλει αὐτῷ περὶ τῶν
flees because a hireling he is, and not is care to him about the
4263 1473/1510 4166 2570 1097 1699
14 προβάτων. ἐγώ εἰμι ὁ ποιμὴν ὁ καλός, καὶ γινώσκω τὰ ἐμά,
sheep. I am the Shepherd Good, and I know — Mine,
1097 5259 1699 2531 1097 3165 3962
15 καὶ γινώσκομαι ὑπὸ τῶν ἐμῶν. καθὼς γινώσκει με ὁ πατήρ,
and am known by — Mine. As knows Me the Father,
2504 1097 3962 5590 3450 5087 5228
κἀγὼ γινώσκω τὸν πατέρα· καὶ τὴν ψυχήν μου τίθημι ὑπὲρ
I also know the Father; and the soul of Me I lay down for
4263 243 4263 2192/3739/3756/2076/1537
16 τῶν προβάτων. καὶ ἄλλα πρόβατα ἔχω, ἃ οὐκ ἔστιν ἐκ τῆς
the sheep. And other sheep I have, which not are of
833 5023 2547 3165/1163 71 5456 3450
αὐλῆς ταύτης· κἀκεῖνά με δεῖ ἀγαγεῖν, καὶ τῆς φωνῆ μου
fold this; those also Me it is right to lead, and of the voice of Me

one Shepherd. [17]For this reason My Father loves Me, because I lay down My soul, that I may take it again. [18]No one takes it from Me, but I lay it down from Myself. I have authority to lay it down, and I have authority to take it again. I received this commandment from My Father.

[19]Then again a division occurred among the Jews, because of these words. [20]And many of them said, He has a demon and is insane. Why do you hear him? [21]Others said, These are not words of one having been possessed by a demon. A demon is not able to open *the* eyes of blind ones.

[22]And *the Feast* of Dedication took place in Jerusalem, and it was winter. [23]And Jesus was walking in the temple, in Solomon's Porch. [24]Then the Jews encircled Him, and said to Him, How long do you lift up our soul? If you are the Christ, tell us publicly. [25]Jesus answered them, I told you, and you did not believe. The works which I do in the name of My Father, these bear witness about Me. [26]But you do not believe, for you are not of My sheep, as I said to you. [27]My sheep hear My voice, and I know them, and they follow Me. [28]And I give eternal life to them, and they shall never perish to the age; and not anyone shall pluck them out of My hand. [29]My Father who has given *them* to Me is greater than all, and no one is able to pluck

191 1096 3391 4167 1520 4166 1223 5124
17 ἀκούσουσι· καὶ γενήσεται μία ποίμνη, εἷς ποιμήν. διὰ τοῦτο
they will hear, and will become one flock, one Shepherd. Therefore
3962 3165 25 3754/1473 5079 5590 3450/1473
ὁ πατήρ με ἀγαπᾷ, ὅτι ἐγὼ τίθημι τὴν ψυχήν μου, ἵνα
the Father Me loves, because I lay down the soul of Me. that
3825 2983 846 3762 142 846 575 1700 235/1473
18 πάλιν λάβω αὐτήν οὐδεὶς αἴρει αὐτὴν ἀπ' ἐμοῦ, ἀλλ' ἐγὼ
again I may take it. No one takes it from Me, but I
5087 846 575 1683 1849 2192 5087 846
τίθημι αὐτὴν ἀπ' ἐμαυτοῦ. ἐξουσίαν ἔχω θεῖναι αὐτήν, καὶ
lay down it from Myself. authority I have to lay down it, and
1849 2192 3825 2983 846 5026 1785
ἐξουσίαν ἔχω πάλιν λαβεῖν αὐτήν· ταύτην την ἐντολὴν
authority I have again to take it. This — commandment
2983 3844 3962 3450
ἔλαβον παρὰ τοῦ πατρός μου.
I received from the Father of Me.
4978 3767 3825 1096 1722 2453 1223
19 Σχίσμα οὖν πάλιν ἐγένετο ἐν τοῖς Ἰουδαίοις διὰ τοὺς
a division Therefore again occurred among the Jews, because of —
3056 5128 3004 4183 1537 846 1140 2192
20 λόγους τούτους. ἔλεγον δὲ πολλοὶ ἐξ αὐτῶν, Δαιμόνιον ἔχει
words these. said And many of them, A demon he has,
3105 5101 846 191 243 3004 5023
21 καὶ μαίνεται· τί αὐτοῦ ἀκούετε; ἄλλοι ἔλεγον, Ταῦτα τὰ
and is insane. Why him do you hear? Others said, These —
4487 3756 2076 1139 3361 1140 1410
ῥήματα οὐκ ἔστι δαιμονιζομένου· μὴ δαιμόνιον δύναται
words not are of one demon-possessed; not a demon is able
5185 3788 455
τυφλῶν ὀφθαλμοὺς ἀνοίγειν;
of blind ones eyes to open?
1096 1456 1722 2414
22 Ἐγένετο δὲ τὰ ἐγκαίνια· ἐν τοῖς Ἱεροσολύμοις, καὶ
occurred And the Dedication in Jerusalem; and
5494 2258 4043 2424 1722 2411 1722 4745
23 χειμὼν ἦν· καὶ περιεπάτει ὁ Ἰησοῦς ἐν τῷ ἱερῷ ἐν τῇ στοᾷ
winter it was. And walked — Jesus in the Temple in the porch
4672 2944 3767 846 2453
24 τοῦ Σολομῶντος. ἐκύκλωσαν οὖν αὐτὸν οἱ Ἰουδαῖοι, καὶ
— of Solomon. encircled Then Him the Jews, and
3004 846 2193 4219 5590 2257 142 1487/4771/1488
ἔλεγον αὐτῷ, Ἕως πότε τὴν ψυχὴν ἡμῶν αἴρεις; εἰ σὺ εἶ ὁ
said to Him, Until when the soul of us you lift up? If you are the
5547 2036 2254 3954 611 846 2424
25 Χριστός, εἰπὲ ἡμῖν παρρησίᾳ. ἀπεκρίθη αὐτοῖς ὁ Ἰησοῦς,
Christ, tell us publicly. answered them — Jesus,
2036 5213 3756 4100 2041/3739/1473/4160/1722
Εἶπον ὑμῖν, καὶ οὐ πιστεύετε· τὰ ἔργα ἃ ἐγὼ ποιῶ ἐν τῷ
I said to you, and not you believe; the works which I do in the
3686 3962 3450 5023 3140 4012 1700 235
26 ὀνόματι τοῦ πατρός μου, ταῦτα μαρτυρεῖ περὶ ἐμοῦ· ἀλλ'
name of the Father of Me, these witness concerning Me; but
5210/3756/ 4100 3756/1063/2075/1537 4263 1689
ὑμεῖς οὐ πιστεύετε· οὐ γάρ ἐστε ἐκ τῶν προβάτων τῶν ἐμῶν,
you not do believe not for you are of the sheep — of Me.
2531 2036 5213 4263 1699 5456 3450 191
27 καθὼς εἶπον ὑμῖν. τὰ πρόβατα τὰ ἐμὰ τῆς φωνῆς μου ἀκούει.
As I said to you, sheep — My of the voice of Me hear.
2504 1097 846 190 3427 2504 2222
28 κἀγὼ γινώσκω αὐτά, καὶ ἀκολουθοῦσί μοι· κἀγὼ ζωὴν
and I know them, and they follow Me; and I life
166 1325 846 =3364= 622 1519 165
αἰώνιον δίδωμι αὐτοῖς· καὶ οὐ μὴ ἀπόλωνται εἰς τὸν αἰῶνα,
eternal give to them; and in no way shall they perish for ever,
3756 726 5100 846 1537 5495 3450 3962 3450
29 καὶ οὐχ ἁρπάσει τις αὐτὰ ἐκ τῆς χειρός μου. ὁ πατήρ μου
and not shall pluck anyone them out of the hand of Me. The Father of Me
3739 1325 3427 3187 3956 2076 3762 1410
ὃς δέδωκέ μοι, μείζων πάντων ἐστί· καὶ οὐδεὶς δύναται
who has given to Me, greater than all is, and no one is able

out of My Father's hand. [30]I and the Father are one! [31]Then again the Jews took up stones, that they might stone Him. [32]Jesus answered them, I showed you many good works from My Father. For which work of them do you stone Me? [33]The Jews answered Him, saying, We do not stone you concerning a good work, but concerning blasphemy; and because you, being a man, make yourself God.

[34]Jesus answered them, Is it not written in your Law, "I said, you are gods"? [35]If He called those gods with whom the word of God was —and the Scripture cannot be broken—[36]do you say *of Him* whom the Father sanctified and sent into the world, You blaspheme, because I said, I am Son of God? [37]If I do not do the works of My Father, do not believe Me. [38]But if I do, even if you do not believe Me, believe the works, that you may perceive and may believe that the Father *is* in Me, and I in Him. [39]Then they again sought to seize Him. And He went forth out of their hand. [40]And He went away again across the Jordan to the place where John was at first baptizing, and remained there. [41]And many came to Him and said, John indeed did no miracle, but all things that John said concerning this One were true. [42]And many believed into Him there.

726 1537 5495 3962 3450 1473 3962
30 ἁρπάζειν ἐκ τῆς χειρὸς τοῦ πατρός μου. ἐγὼ καὶ ὁ πατὴρ
to pluck out of the hand of the Father of Me. I and the Father
1722 2070 941 3767 3825 3037 2453
31 ἕν ἐσμεν. ἐβάστασαν οὖν πάλιν λίθους οἱ Ἰουδαῖοι ἵνα
one are. took up Therefore again stones the Jews, that
3034 846 611 846 2424 4183 2570
32 λιθάσωσιν αὐτόν. ἀπεκρίθη αὐτοῖς ὁ Ἰησοῦς, Πολλὰ καλὰ
they might stone Him. answered them Jesus, Many good
2041 1166 5213/1537 3962 3450/1223 4169 846 2041
ἔργα ἔδειξα ὑμῖν ἐκ τοῦ πατρός μου· διὰ ποῖον αὐτῶν ἔργον
works I showed you from the Father of Me; for which of them work
3034 3165 611 846 2453 3004 4012
33 λιθάζετέ με; ἀπεκρίθησαν αὐτῷ οἱ Ἰουδαῖοι λέγοντες, Περὶ
do you stone Me? answered Him the Jews, saying, Con-
2570 2041 3756 3034 4571 235 4012 988 cerning
καλοῦ ἔργου οὐ λιθάζομέν σε, ἀλλὰ περὶ βλασφημίας, καὶ
a good work not we stone you, but concerning blasphemy, and
3754/3756 444 5607 4160 4572 2316 611 846
34 ὅτι σὺ ἄνθρωπος ὢν ποιεῖς σεαυτὸν Θεόν. ἀπεκρίθη αὐτοῖς
because you a man being make yourself God. answered them
2424 3756 2076 1125 1722 3551 5216 1473
ὁ Ἰησοῦς, Οὐκ ἔστι γεγραμμένον ἐν τῷ νόμῳ ὑμῶν, Ἐγὼ
— Jesus, not Is it having been written in the Law of you, I
2036 2316 2075/1487 1565 2036 2316 4314 3739 3056
35 εἶπα, θεοί ἐστε; εἰ ἐκείνους εἶπε θεούς, πρὸς οὓς ὁ λόγος τοῦ
said, gods you are. If those He called gods, with whom the word —
2316 1096 3756 1410 3089 1124 3739
36 Θεοῦ ἐγένετο (καὶ οὐ δύναται λυθῆναι ἡ γραφή), ὃν ὁ
of God was — and not can be broken the Scripture — whom the
3962 37 649 2889 5210 3004
πατὴρ ἡγίασε καὶ ἀπέστειλεν εἰς τὸν κόσμον, ὑμεῖς λέγετε
Father sanctified and sent into the world, you say,
3754 987 3754 2036 5207 2316 1510/1487/3756/4160
37 ὅτι Βλασφημεῖς, ὅτι εἶπον, Υἱὸς τοῦ Θεοῦ εἰμι; εἰ οὐ ποιῶ
— You blaspheme! Because I said, Son — of God I am? If not I do
2041 3962 3450 3361 4100 3427/1487 4160 2579
38 τὰ ἔργα τοῦ πατρός μου, μὴ πιστεύετέ μοι· εἰ δὲ ποιῶ, κἂν
the works of the Father of Me, not do believe Me. if But I do, even if
1698/3361 4100 2041 4100 2443 1097
ἐμοὶ μὴ πιστεύητε, τοῖς ἔργοις πιστεύσατε· ἵνα γνῶτε καὶ
Me not you believe, the works believe, that you may know and
4100 3754/1722/1698 3962 2504 1722 846 2212
39 πιστεύσητε ὅτι ἐν ἐμοὶ ὁ πατήρ, κἀγὼ ἐν αὐτῷ. ἐζήτουν
may believe that in Me the Father (is), and I in Him. they sought
3767 3825 846 4084 1831 1537 5495 848
οὖν πάλιν αὐτὸν πιάσαι· καὶ ἐξῆλθεν ἐκ τῆς χειρὸς αὐτῶν.
then again Him to seize. And He went out of the hand of them.
565 3825 4008 2446 1519 5117
40 Καὶ ἀπῆλθε πάλιν πέραν τοῦ Ἰορδάνου εἰς τὸν τόπον
And He went away again across the Jordan to the place
3699 2258 2491 4412 907 3306 1563
41 ὅπου ἦν Ἰωάννης τὸ πρῶτον βαπτίζων· καὶ ἔμεινεν ἐκεῖ. καὶ
where was John at first baptizing, and remained there. And
4183 2064 4314 846 3004 3754 2491 3303
πολλοὶ ἦλθον πρὸς αὐτόν, καὶ ἔλεγον ὅτι Ἰωάννης μὲν
many came to Him, and said, John indeed
4592 4160 3762 3956 3745 2036 2491 4012
σημεῖον ἐποίησεν οὐδέν· πάντα δὲ ὅσα εἶπεν Ἰωάννης περὶ
sign did none, all things but whatever said John concerning
5127 227 2258 4100 4183 1563 1519 846
42 τούτου, ἀληθῆ ἦν. καὶ ἐπίστευσαν πολλοὶ ἐκεῖ εἰς αὐτόν.
this One true were. And believed many there in Him.

CHAPTER 11

[1]And there was a certain sick one, Lazarus from Bethany, of the village of Mary and her sister Martha. [2]And it was Mary who

CHAPTER 11

2258 5100 770 2976 575 963 1537 2968
1 Ἦν δέ τις ἀσθενῶν Λάζαρος ἀπὸ Βηθανίας, ἐκ τῆς κώμης
was And a certain sick one, Lazarus from Bethany, of the village
3137 3136 79 848 2258 3137
2 Μαρίας καὶ Μάρθας τῆς ἀδελφῆς αὐτῆς. ἦν δὲ Μαρία ἡ
of Mary and Martha the sister of her. (it) was And Mary, she

anointed the Lord with ointment, and wiped His feet with her hair, whose brother Lazarus was sick. [3]Therefore, the sisters sent to Him, saying, Lord, behold, *the one* whom You love is sick. [4]And hearing, Jesus said, This is not sickness to death, but for the glory of God, that the Son of God be glorified by it. [5]And Jesus loved Martha, and her sister, and Lazarus. [6]Therefore, when He heard that he is sick, then, indeed, He remained in the place where He was two days. [7]Then after this he said to the disciples, Let us go to Judea again. [8]The disciples said to Him, Rabbi, just now the Jews were seeking to stone You, and do you go there again?

[9]Jesus answered, Are there not twelve hours in the day? If anyone walks in the day, he does not stumble because he sees the light of the world. [10]But if anyone walks in the night, he stumbles because the light is not in him. [11]He said these things. And after this He said to them, Our friend Lazarus has fallen asleep, but I am going that I may awaken him. [12]Then His disciples said, Lord, if he has fallen asleep, he will recover. [13]But Jesus had spoken about his death, but they thought that He spoke of the sleep of slumber. [14]Therefore, then Jesus said to them plainly, Lazarus has died. [15]And I rejoice because of you, in order that you may believe, that I was not there. But let us go to him. [16]Then Thomas, *he* having been called Twin, said to the fellow-disciples, Let us go, even we, that we may die with Him.

218 2962 3464 1591 4228 848
ἀλείψασα τὸν Κύριον μύρῳ, καὶ ἐκμάξασα τοὺς πόδας αὐτοῦ
rubbing the Lord with ointment, and wiping off the feet of Him
2359 848 3739 80 2976 770 649
3 ταῖς θριξὶν αὐτῆς, ἧς ὁ ἀδελφὸς Λάζαρος ἠσθένει. ἀπέστειλαν
with the hairs of her, of whom the brother Lazarus was sick. sent
3767 79 4314 846 3004 2962 2396/3739/5368
οὖν αἱ ἀδελφαὶ πρὸς αὐτὸν λέγουσαι, Κύριε, ἴδε ὃν φιλεῖς
Then the sisters to Him, saying, Lord, behold, whom You love
*2076 770 191 2424 2036 3778 769 3756 *
4 ἀσθενεῖ. ἀκούσας δὲ ὁ Ἰησοῦς εἶπεν, Αὕτη ἡ ἀσθένεια οὐκ ἔστι
is sick. hearing And,— Jesus said, This — sickness not is
4314 2288 235 5228 1391 2316 2443 1392
πρὸς θάνατον, ἀλλ' ὑπὲρ τῆς δόξης τοῦ Θεοῦ, ἵνα δοξασθῇ ὁ
to death, but for the glory — of God, that be glorified the
5207 2316 1223 846 25 2424 3136
5 υἱὸς τοῦ Θεοῦ δι' αὐτῆς. ἠγάπα δὲ ὁ Ἰησοῦς τὴν Μάρθαν καὶ
Son — of God by it. loved Now — Jesus — Martha and
79 848 2976 5613 3767 191 3754
6 τὴν ἀδελφὴν αὐτῆς καὶ τὸν Λάζαρον. ὡς οὖν ἤκουσεν ὅτι
the sister of her and — Lazarus. As, then, He heard that
3739 770 5119 3303 3306 1722/*/2258/5117/1417 2250 1899
7 ἀσθενεῖ, τότε μὲν ἔμεινεν ἐν ᾧ ἦν τόπῳ δύο ἡμέρας. ἔπειτα
he is sick, then, indeed, He abode in which was He place two days. Then
3326 5124 3004 3101 71 1519 2449
μετὰ τοῦτο λέγει τοῖς μαθηταῖς, Ἄγωμεν εἰς τὴν Ἰουδαίαν
after this He says to the disciples, Let us go to — Judea
3825 3004 846 3101 4461 3568 2212 4571
8 πάλιν. λέγουσιν αὐτῷ οἱ μαθηταί, Ῥαββί, νῦν ἐζήτουν σε
again. Say to Him the disciples, Rabbi, now were seeking You
3034 2453 3825 5217 1563 611
9 λιθάσαι οἱ Ἰουδαῖοι, καὶ πάλιν ὑπάγεις ἐκεῖ; ἀπεκρίθη ὁ
to stone the Jews, and again do You go there? answered —
2424 3778 1427 1526 5610 2250 1437/5100/4043
Ἰησοῦς, Οὐχὶ δώδεκά εἰσιν ὧραι τῆς ἡμέρας; ἐάν τις περι-
Jesus, Not twelve are there hours of the day? If anyone walks
1722 2250 3756 4350 3754 5457 2889
πατῇ ἐν τῇ ἡμέρᾳ, οὐ προσκόπτει, ὅτι τὸ φῶς τοῦ κόσμου
in the day, not he stumbles, because the light — world
5127 991 1437 5100 4043 1722 3571 4350
10 τούτου βλέπει. ἐὰν δέ τις περιπατῇ ἐν τῇ νυκτί, προσκόπτει,
this he sees. if But anyone walk in the night, he stumbles,
3754 5457/3756/2076/1722/846 5023 2036 3326 5124
11 ὅτι τὸ φῶς οὐκ ἔστιν ἐν αὐτῷ. ταῦτα εἶπε, καὶ μετὰ τοῦτο
because the light not is in him. These things He said, and after this
3004 846 2976 5384 2357 2837 235
λέγει αὐτοῖς, Λάζαρος ὁ φίλος ἡμῶν κεκοίμηται· ἀλλὰ
He says to them, Lazarus the friend of us has fallen asleep; but
4198 2443 1852 846 2036 3767 3101 848
12 πορεύομαι ἵνα ἐξυπνίσω αὐτόν. εἶπον οὖν οἱ μαθηταὶ αὐτοῦ,
I am going that I may awaken him. said Then the disciples of Him,
2962/1487/ 2837 4982 2046 2424 4012
13 Κύριε, εἰ κεκοίμηται, σωθήσεται. εἰρήκει δὲ ὁ Ἰησοῦς περὶ τοῦ
Lord, if he has slept, he will recover. had spoken And Jesus about the
2288 848 1565 1380/3754/4012 2838
θανάτου αὐτοῦ· ἐκεῖνοι δὲ ἔδοξαν ὅτι περὶ τῆς κοιμήσεως τοῦ
death of him, those but thought that about the sleep —
5258 3004 5119 3767 2036 846 2424 3954
14 ὕπνου λέγει. τότε οὖν εἶπεν αὐτοῖς ὁ Ἰησοῦς παρρησίᾳ,
of slumber He says. Then therefore told them — Jesus openly,
2976 599 5463 1223 5209 2443 4100 3754
15 Λάζαρος ἀπέθανε. καὶ χαίρω δι' ὑμᾶς, ἵνα πιστεύσητε, ὅτι
Lazarus has died. And I rejoice because of you, that you may believe, that
3756/2252/1563/235 71 4314 846 2036 3767 2381
16 οὐκ ἤμην ἐκεῖ· ἀλλ' ἄγωμεν πρὸς αὐτόν. εἶπεν οὖν Θωμᾶς, ὁ
not I was there. But let us go to him. said Then Thomas —
3004 1324 4827 71 2249 2443
λεγόμενος Δίδυμος, τοῖς συμμαθηταῖς, Ἄγωμεν καὶ ἡμεῖς, ἵνα
being called Twin, to the fellow-disciples, Let us go, even we, that
599 3326 846
ἀποθάνωμεν μετ' αὐτοῦ.
we may die with Him..

[17]Then coming, Jesus found him already being held in the tomb four days. [18]And Bethany was near Jerusalem, *about* fifteen furlongs off. [19]And many of the Jews had come to those around Martha and Mary, that they might console them concerning their brother. [20]Therefore, when Martha heard that Jesus is coming, she met Him; but Mary was sitting in the house. [21]Then Martha said to Jesus, Lord, if You had been here, my brother would not be dead.

[22]But even now I know that whatever You may ask God, God will give You. [23]Jesus said to her, Your brother will rise again. [24]Martha said to Him, I know that he will rise again in the resurrection in the last day. [25]Jesus said to her, I am the Resurrection and the Life; the *one* believing into Me, though he die, he shall live. [26]And everyone living and believing into Me shall die to the age. Do you believe this? [27]She said to Him, Yes, Lord, I have believed that You are the Christ, the Son of God who comes into the world.

[28]And saying these things, she went away and called her sister Mary secretly, saying, The Teacher is here and calls you. [29]That one, when she heard, rose up quickly and came to Him. [30]And Jesus had not yet come into the village, but was in the place where Martha met Him. [31]Then the Jews who were with her in the house, and consoling her, seeing that Mary quickly rose up and went out, *they* followed her, saying, She

2064 3767 2424 2147 846 5064 2250 2235
17 Ἐλθὼν οὖν ὁ Ἰησοῦς εὗρεν αὐτὸν τέσσαρας ἡμέρας ἤδη
coming Then — Jesus found him four days already
2192 1722 3419 2258 963 1451 2414
18 ἔχοντα ἐν τῷ μνημείῳ. ἦν δὲ ἡ Βηθανία ἐγγὺς τῶν Ἱεροσολύ-
being held in the tomb. was And Bethany near — Jerusalem,
5613 575 4712 1198 4183 1537
19 μων, ὡς ἀπὸ σταδίων δεκαπέντε· καὶ πολλοὶ ἐκ τῶν
as from stadia fifteen. And many of the
2453 2064 4314 4012 3136 3137
Ἰουδαίων ἐληλύθεισαν πρὸς τὰς περὶ Μάρθαν καὶ Μαρίαν,
Jews had come to those around Martha and Mary,
2443 3888 846 4012 80 848
20 ἵνα παραμυθήσωνται αὐτὰς περὶ τοῦ ἀδελφοῦ αὐτῶν. ἡ
that they might console them concerning the brother of them.
3767 3136 5613 191 3754 2424 2064 5221
οὖν Μάρθα, ὡς ἤκουσεν ὅτι ὁ Ἰησοῦς ἔρχεται, ὑπήντησεν
Therefore Martha, when she heard that Jesus is coming, met
846 3137 1722 3624 2516 2036 3767 3136
21 αὐτῷ· Μαρία δὲ ἐν τῷ οἴκῳ ἐκαθέζετο. εἶπεν οὖν ἡ Μάρθα
Him; Mary but in the house was sitting. said Then Martha
4314 2424 2962/1487/2258/5602 80 3450 3756 302
πρὸς τὸν Ἰησοῦν, Κύριε, εἰ ἦς ὧδε, ὁ ἀδελφός μου οὐκ ἂν
to — Jesus, Lord, if You were here, the brother of me not would
2348 235 3568 1492 3754/3745/302/ 154 2316
22 ἐτεθνήκει. ἀλλὰ καὶ νῦν οἶδα ὅτι ὅσα ἂν αἰτήσῃ τὸν Θεόν,
be dead. But also now I know that whatever you may ask — God,
1325 4671 2316 3004 846 2424 450
23 δώσει σοι ὁ Θεός. λέγει αὐτῇ ὁ Ἰησοῦς, Ἀναστήσεται ὁ
will give You God. says to her — Jesus, will rise again The
80 4675 3004 846 3136 1492 3754 450 1722
24 ἀδελφός σου. λέγει αὐτῷ Μάρθα, Οἶδα ὅτι ἀναστήσεται ἐν
brother of you. says to Him Martha, I know that he will rise again in
386 1722 2078 2250 2036 846 2424
25 τῇ ἀναστάσει ἐν τῇ ἐσχάτῃ ἡμέρᾳ. εἶπεν αὐτῇ ὁ Ἰησοῦς,
the resurrection in the last Day. said to her — Jesus,
1473/1510 386 2222 4100 1519/1691/2579
Ἐγώ εἰμι ἡ ἀνάστασις καὶ ἡ ζωή· ὁ πιστεύων εἰς ἐμέ, κἂν
I am the resurrection and the life; the (one) believing in Me, though
599 2198 3956 2198 4100 1519/1691/3756
26 ἀποθάνῃ, ζήσεται· καὶ πᾶς ὁ ζῶν καὶ πιστεύων εἰς ἐμέ, οὐ
he die, he shall live; and everyone living and believing in Me, in no
3361 599 1519 165 4100 5124 3004 846
27 μὴ ἀποθάνῃ εἰς τὸν αἰῶνα. πιστεύεις τοῦτο; λέγει αὐτῷ,
way shall die for ever. Do you believe this? She says to Him
3483 2962 1473 4100 3754/3756/1488/ 5547 5207
Ναί, Κύριε· ἐγὼ πεπίστευκα, ὅτι σὺ εἶ ὁ Χριστός, ὁ υἱὸς τοῦ
Yes, Lord, I have believed that You are the Christ, the Son —
2316 1519 2889 2064 5023 2036
28 Θεοῦ, ὁ εἰς τὸν κόσμον ἐρχόμενος. καὶ ταῦτα εἰποῦσα
of God, who into the world comes. And these things having said,
565 5455 3137 79 848 2977
ἀπῆλθε, καὶ ἐφώνησε Μαρίαν τὴν ἀδελφὴν αὐτῆς λάθρα,
she went away, and called Mary the sister of her secretly,
2036 1320 3918 5455 4571 1565 5613
29 εἰποῦσα, Ὁ διδάσκαλος πάρεστι καὶ φωνεῖ σε. ἐκείνη ὡς
saying, The Teacher is here and calls you. That one as
191 1453 5035 2064 4314 846 2768
30 ἤκουσεν, ἐγείρεται ταχὺ καὶ ἔρχεται πρὸς αὐτόν. (οὔπω
she heard rises up quickly and comes to Him. not yet
2064 2424 1519 2968 235/2258/1722 5117
δὲ ἐληλύθει ὁ Ἰησοῦς εἰς τὴν κώμην, ἀλλ' ἦν ἐν τῷ τόπῳ
And had come — Jesus into the village, but was in the place
3699 5221 846 3136 3767 2453 5607
31 ὅπου ὑπήντησεν αὐτῷ ἡ Μάρθα.) οἱ οὖν Ἰουδαῖοι οἱ ὄντες
where met Him Martha. the Then Jews, those being
3326 846/1722 3614 3888 846 1492
μετ' αὐτῆς ἐν τῇ οἰκίᾳ καὶ παραμυθούμενοι αὐτήν, ἰδόντες
with her in the house and consoling her, seeing
3137 3754 5030 450 1831 190
τὴν Μαρίαν ὅτι ταχέως ἀνέστη καὶ ἐξῆλθεν, ἠκολούθησαν
— Mary that quickly she rose up and went out, followed

is going to the tomb so that
she may weep there.
32 Then Mary, when she
came where Jesus was,
seeing Him, she fell at His
feet, saying to Him, Lord, if
You were here, my brother
would not have died.
33 Then when He saw her
weeping, and the Jews
who came down with her
weeping, Jesus groaned in
the spirit and troubled
Himself. 34 And *He* said,
Where have you put him?
They said to Him, Lord,
come and see. 35 Jesus
wept. 36 Then the Jews
said, See how He loved
him! 37 But some of them
said, Was this One, the *one*
opening the eyes of the
blind, not able to have
caused that this one should
not die? 38 Then groaning
again within Himself, Jesus
came to the tomb. And it
was a cave, and a stone was
lying on it. 39 Jesus said, Lift
the stone. Martha, the sister
of the one that had died,
said to Him, Lord, he
already smells, for it is *the*
fourth *day*. 40 Jesus said to
her, Did I not say to you that
if you would believe you will
see the glory of God?
41 Then they lifted the stone
where the dead one was
laid. And Jesus lifted *His*
eyes upward and said,
Father, I thank You that You
heard Me. 42 And I know
that You always hear Me;
but because of the crowd
standing around, I said *it*,
that they might believe that
You sent Me. 43 And saying
these things, He cried out
with a loud voice, Lazarus!
Here! Outside! 44 And the
one who had died came
out, the feet and the hands
having been bound with
sheets, and his face being
bound with a cloth. Jesus
said to them, Untie him,
and let *him* go

846 3004 3754 5217 1519 3419 2443 2799 1563
αὐτῇ, λέγοντες ὅτι ὑπάγει εἰς τὸ μνημεῖον, ἵνα κλαύσῃ ἐκεῖ.
her, saying that she goes to the tomb, that she may weep there.
3767 3137 5613 2064 3699 2258 2424 1492 846
32 ἡ οὖν Μαρία, ὡς ἦλθεν ὅπου ἦν ὁ Ἰησοῦς, ἰδοῦσα αὐτόν,
Then Mary, when she came where was — Jesus. seeing Him,
4098 1519 4228 848 3004 846 2962 1487/2258
ἔπεσεν εἰς τοὺς πόδας αὐτοῦ, λέγουσα αὐτῷ, Κύριε, εἰ ἦς
fell at the feet of Him, saying to Him, Lord, if You were
5602/3756/302 599 3450 80 2424 3756 5613 1492
33 ὧδε, οὐκ ἂν ἀπέθανέ μου ὁ ἀδελφός. Ἰησοῦς οὖν ὡς εἶδεν
here, not would have died of me the brother. Jesus Then, as He saw
846 2799 4905 846 2453
αὐτὴν κλαίουσαν, καὶ τοὺς συνελθόντας αὐτῇ Ἰουδαίους
her weeping, and the coming down with her Jews
2797 1690 4151 5015 1438
κλαίοντας, ἐνεβριμήσατο τῷ πνεύματι, καὶ ἐτάραξεν ἑαυτόν,
weeping, groaned in the spirit, and troubled Himself,
2036 4226 5087 846 3004 846 2962 2064
34 καὶ εἶπε, Ποῦ τεθείκατε αὐτόν; λέγουσιν αὐτῷ, Κύριε, ἔρχου
and said, Where have you put him? They say to Him, Lord, come
1492 1145 2424 3004 3767 2453 1492
35 καὶ ἴδε. ἐδάκρυσεν ὁ Ἰησοῦς. ἔλεγον οὖν οἱ Ἰουδαῖοι, Ἴδε
36 and see. shed tears — Jesus. said Therefore the Jews, See
4459 5368 846 5100 1537 846 2036 3756 1410
37 πῶς ἐφίλει αὐτόν. τινὲς δὲ ἐξ αὐτῶν εἶπον, Οὐκ ἠδύνατο
how He loved him. some And of them said, Not was able
3778 455 3788 5185 4160
οὗτος, ὁ ἀνοίξας τοὺς ὀφθαλμοὺς τοῦ τυφλοῦ, ποιῆσαι ἵνα
this One, He opening the eyes of the blind, to have caused that
3778 3361 599 2424 3767 3825 1690
38 καὶ οὗτος μὴ ἀποθάνῃ; Ἰησοῦς οὖν πάλιν ἐμβριμώμενος
also this one not should die. Jesus Then again groaning
1722 1438 2064 1519 3419 2258 4693 3037
ἐν ἑαυτῷ ἔρχεται εἰς τὸ μνημεῖον. ἦν δὲ σπήλαιον, καὶ λίθος
in Himself comes to the tomb. it was And a cave, and a stone
1945 1909 846 3004 2424 142 3037 3004
39 ἐπέκειτο ἐπ' αὐτῷ. λέγει ὁ Ἰησοῦς, Ἄρατε τὸν λίθον. λέγει
was lying on it. says — Jesus, Lift the stone. says
846 79 2348 3136 2962 2235 3605
αὐτῷ ἡ ἀδελφὴ τοῦ τεθνηκότος Μάρθα, Κύριε, ἤδη ὄζει·
to Him the sister of the (one) having died, Martha, Lord, already he smells,
5066 1063 2076 3004 846 2424 3756 2036 4671
40 τεταρταῖος γάρ ἐστι. λέγει αὐτῇ ὁ Ἰησοῦς, Οὐκ εἶπόν σοι,
(the) fourth (day) for it is. says to her — Jesus, Did not I say to you,
3754/1437 4100 3700 1391 2316 1423 3767
41 ὅτι ἐὰν πιστεύσῃς, ὄψει τὴν δόξαν τοῦ Θεοῦ; ἦραν οὖν τὸν
that if you believe you will see the glory — of God? they lifted Then the
3037 3757/2258 2348 2749 2424 142
λίθον, οὗ ἦν ὁ τεθνηκὼς κείμενος. ὁ δὲ Ἰησοῦς ἦρε τοὺς
stone, where was the dead one laid. And Jesus lifted the
3788 507 2036 3962 2168 4671 3754 191
ὀφθαλμοὺς ἄνω, καὶ εἶπε, Πάτερ, εὐχαριστῶ σοι ὅτι ἤκουσάς
eyes upward, and said, Father, I thank You that You heard
3450 1473 1492 3754 3842 3450 191 235 1223
42 μου. ἐγὼ δὲ ᾔδειν ὅτι πάντοτέ μου ἀκούεις· ἀλλὰ διὰ τὸν
Me. I And knew that always Me You hear. But because of the
3793 4026 2036 2443 4100 3754/3756/3165
ὄχλον τὸν περιεστῶτα εἶπον, ἵνα πιστεύσωσιν ὅτι σύ με
crowd — standing around I said, that they might believe that You Me
649 5023 2036 5456 3173 2905
43 ἀπέστειλας. καὶ ταῦτα εἰπών, φωνῇ μεγάλῃ ἐκραύγασε,
did send. And these things saying, with a voice great He cried out,
2976 1204 1854 1831 2348 1210
44 Λάζαρε, δεῦρο ἔξω. καὶ ἐξῆλθεν ὁ τεθνηκώς, δεδεμένος τοὺς
Lazarus, Here! Outside! And came out the (one) having died, being bound the
4228 5495 2750 3799 848 4676
πόδας καὶ τὰς χεῖρας κειρίαις, καὶ ἡ ὄψις αὐτοῦ σουδαρίῳ
feet and the hands with sheets, and the face of him with a cloth
4019 3004 846 2424 3089 846 863
περιεδέδετο. λέγει αὐτοῖς ὁ Ἰησοῦς, Λύσατε αὐτόν, καὶ ἄφετε
being bound. says to them — Jesus, Loosen him, and allow (him)

[45]Then many of the Jews, those coming to Mary, and having seen what Jesus did, believed into Him. [46]But some of them went away to the Pharisees, and told them what Jesus had done.

[47]Then the chief priests and the Pharisees assembled a sanhedrin, and said, What are we doing, for this man does many miracles? [48]If we let him alone this way, all will believe into him, and the Romans will come and will take away from us both the place and the nation. [49]But a certain one of them, Caiaphas, being high priest of that year, said to them, You know nothing, [50]nor consider that it is profitable for us that one man die for the people, and not all the nation to perish. [51]But he did not say this from himself, but being high priest that year he prophesied that Jesus was about to die on behalf of the nation, [52]and not only on behalf of the nation, but that He also might gather into one the children of God who had been scattered. [53]Then from that day they took counsel that they might kill Him.

[54]Therefore, Jesus no longer walked publicly among the Jews, but went away from there into the country near the desert, to a city being called Ephraim, and stayed there with His disciples.

[55]And the Passover of the Jews was near. And many went up to Jerusalem out of the country before the Passover, that they might

5217
ὑπάγειν.
to depart.

4183 3767/1537 2453 2064 4314 3137
45 Πολλοὶ οὖν ἐκ τῶν Ἰουδαίων, οἱ ἐλθόντες πρὸς τὴν Μαρίαν
Many therefore of the Jews, those coming to — Mary
2300 3739 4160 2424 4100 1519/846
καὶ θεασάμενοι ἃ ἐποίησεν ὁ Ἰησοῦς, ἐπίστευσαν εἰς αὐτόν.
and having beheld what did Jesus, believed in Him.

5100 1537 846 565 4314 5330 2036
46 τινὲς δὲ ἐξ αὐτῶν ἀπῆλθον πρὸς τοὺς Φαρισαίους, καὶ εἶπον
some But of them went away to the Pharisees and told
846 3739 4160 2424
αὐτοῖς ἃ ἐποίησεν ὁ Ἰησοῦς.
them what had done — Jesus.

4863 3767 749 5330 4892
47 Συνήγαγον οὖν οἱ ἀρχιερεῖς καὶ οἱ Φαρισαῖοι συνέδριον,
assembled Then the chief priests and the Pharisees a sanhedrin,
3004 5101 4160 3754 3778 444 4183
καὶ ἔλεγον, Τί ποιοῦμεν; ὅτι οὗτος ὁ ἄνθρωπος πολλὰ
and said, What are we doing, because this man many

4592 4160 1437 863 846 3779 3956 4100
48 σημεῖα ποιεῖ. ἐὰν ἀφῶμεν αὐτὸν οὕτω, πάντες πιστεύσουσιν
signs does? If we leave him thus, all will believe
1519 846 2064 4514 142 2257
εἰς αὐτόν· καὶ ἐλεύσονται οἱ Ῥωμαῖοι καὶ ἀροῦσιν ἡμῶν καὶ
in him, and will come the Romans and will take of us both

5117 1484/1519 5101/1537/846 2533 749
49 τὸν τόπον καὶ τὸ ἔθνος. εἷς δέ τις ἐξ αὐτῶν Καϊάφας, ἀρχιερεὺς
the place and the nation. one But man of them, Caiaphas, high priest
5607 1763 1565 2036 846 5210 3756 1492
ὢν τοῦ ἐνιαυτοῦ ἐκείνου, εἶπεν αὐτοῖς, Ὑμεῖς οὐκ οἴδατε
being of year that, said to them, You do not know

3762 3761 1260 3754 4851 2254/2443/1519/ 444
50 οὐδέν, οὐδὲ διαλογίζεσθε ὅτι συμφέρει ἡμῖν ἵνα εἷς ἄνθρωπος
nothing, nor consider that it is profitable for us that one man
599 5228 2992 3650 1484 622
ἀποθάνῃ ὑπὲρ τοῦ λαοῦ, καὶ μὴ ὅλον τὸ ἔθνος ἀπόληται.
die for the people, and not all the nation to perish.

5124 575 1438 3756 3004 235 749 5607 1763
51 τοῦτο δὲ ἀφ' ἑαυτοῦ οὐκ εἶπεν, ἀλλὰ ἀρχιερεὺς ὢν τοῦ ἐνιαυ-
this But from himself not he said, but high priest being — year
1565 4395 3754 3195 2424 599
τοῦ ἐκείνου, προεφήτευσεν ὅτι ἔμελλεν ὁ Ἰησοῦς ἀποθνή-
— that, he prophesied that was about — Jesus to die

5228 1484 3756 5228 1484 3440 235
52 σκειν ὑπὲρ τοῦ ἔθνους, καὶ οὐχ ὑπὲρ τοῦ ἔθνους μόνον, ἀλλ'
on behalf of the nation, and not on behalf of the nation only, but
2443 5043 2316 1287 4863
ἵνα καὶ τὰ τέκνα τοῦ Θεοῦ τὰ διεσκορπισμένα συναγάγῃ
that also the children — of God having been scattered He might gather

1519/1722/575 1565 3767 2250 4823 2443
53 εἰς ἕν. ἀπ' ἐκείνης οὖν τῆς ἡμέρας συνεβουλεύσαντο ἵνα
into one. from that Therefore — day, they took counsel that
615 846
ἀποκτείνωσιν αὐτόν.
they might kill Him.

2424 3767 3756 3954 4043 1722 2453
54 Ἰησοῦς οὖν οὐκέτι παρρησίᾳ περιεπάτει ἐν τοῖς Ἰουδαίοις,
Jesus Therefore no longer publicly walked among the Jews
235 565 1564 1519 5561 1451 2048
ἀλλὰ ἀπῆλθεν ἐκεῖθεν εἰς τὴν χώραν ἐγγὺς τῆς ἐρήμου, εἰς
but went away from there into the country near the desert, to
2187 3004 4172 2546 1304 3326 3101
Ἐφραῒμ λεγομένην πόλιν, κἀκεῖ διέτριβε μετὰ τῶν μαθητῶν
Ephraim being called a city, and there stayed with the disciples

848 2258 1451 3957 2453 305
55 αὐτοῦ. ἦν δὲ ἐγγὺς τὸ πάσχα τῶν Ἰουδαίων· καὶ ἀνέβησαν
of Him. was And near the Passover of the Jews, and went up
4183 1519 2414 1537 5561 4253 3957 2443
πολλοὶ εἰς Ἱεροσόλυμα ἐκ τῆς χώρας πρὸ τοῦ πάσχα, ἵνα
many to Jerusalem out of the country before the Passover, that

purify themselves. [56]Then they sought Jesus, and said with one another, standing in the temple, What does it seem to you? That He does not at all come to the Feast? [57]And all the chief priests and the Pharisees had given commands that if anyone knew where He is, he should inform so that they might seize Him.

CHAPTER 12

[1]Then six days before the Passover, Jesus came to Bethany, where Lazarus was, who had died, whom He raised from *the* dead. [2]Then they made Him a supper there, and Martha served. But Lazarus was one of those reclining with Him. [3]Then taking a pound of ointment of pure, costly spikenard, Mary anointed the feet of Jesus, and wiped off His feet with her hairs. And the house was filled with the odor of the ointment. [4]Then Simon's son, Judas Iscariot, one of His disciples, who was about to betray Him, said, [5]Why was this ointment not sold *for* three hundred denarii, and given to *the* poor? [6]But he said this, not that he was caring for the poor, but that he was a thief, and held the moneybag, and carried away the things being put *in*. [7]Then Jesus said, Allow her, for she has kept it for the day of My burial. [8]For you always have the poor with you, but you do not always have Me.

[9]Then a great crowd of the Jews learned that He was there. And they did not come because of Jesus alone, but that they also

48 1438 2212 3767 2424 3004 3326
56 ἁγνίσωσιν ἑαυτούς. ἐζήτουν οὖν τὸν Ἰησοῦν, καὶ ἔλεγον μετ'
they might purify themselves. they sought Then Jesus, and said with
240 1722 2411 2476 5101 1380 5213 3754/3756/3361
ἀλλήλων ἐν τῷ ἱερῷ ἑστηκότες, Τί δοκεῖ ὑμῖν; ὅτι οὐ μὴ
one another in the Temple standing, What seems it to you? That not at all
2064 1519 1859 1325 749
57 ἔλθῃ εἰς τὴν ἑορτήν; δεδώκεισαν δὲ καὶ οἱ ἀρχιερεῖς καὶ οἱ
He comes to the feast? had given And also the chief priests and the
5330 1785 2443/1437/5100/1097 2076 3377 3704
Φαρισαῖοι ἐντολήν, ἵνα ἐάν τις γνῷ ποῦ ἐστι, μηνύσῃ, ὅπως
Pharisees commands that if anyone knew where He is, he should inform so
4084 846
πιάσωσιν αὐτόν.
they might seize Him.

CHAPTER 12

3767 2424 42531803 2250 3957 2064
1 Ὁ οὖν Ἰησοῦς πρὸ ἓξ ἡμερῶν τοῦ πάσχα ἦλθεν εἰς
Therefore Jesus before six days the Passover came to
963 3699/2258 2976 2348 3739 1453 1537/3498
Βηθανίαν, ὅπου ἦν Λάζαρος ὁ τεθνηκώς, ὃν ἤγειρεν ἐκ νε-
Bethany, where was Lazarus, who had died, whom He raised out of
4160 3767 846 1173 1563 3136 1247
2 κρῶν. ἐποίησαν οὖν αὐτῷ δεῖπνον ἐκεῖ, καὶ ἡ Μάρθα διηκόνει·
(the) dead. they made Then for Him a supper there, and Martha served,
2976 1519/2258 4873 846 3767 3137
3 ὁ δὲ Λάζαρος εἷς ἦν τῶν συνανακειμένων αὐτῷ. ἡ οὖν Μαρία
but Lazarus one was of those reclining with Him. Then Mary
2983 3046 3464 3487 4101 4186
λαβοῦσα λίτραν μύρου νάρδου πιστικῆς πολυτίμου,
taking a pound of ointment of spikenard pure costly
218 4228 2424 1591 2359 848
ἤλειψε τοὺς πόδας τοῦ Ἰησοῦ, καὶ ἐξέμαξε ταῖς θριξὶν αὐτῆς
rubbed the feet — of Jesus, and wiped off with the hairs of her
4228 848 3614 4137 1537 3744
τοὺς πόδας αὐτοῦ· ἡ δὲ οἰκία ἐπληρώθη ἐκ τῆς ὀσμῆς τοῦ
the feet of Him. the And house was filled of the odor of the
3864 3004 3767/1519/1537 3101 848 2455 4613
4 μύρου. λέγει οὖν εἷς ἐκ τῶν μαθητῶν αὐτοῦ, Ἰούδας Σίμωνος
ointment. says Then one of the disciples of Him, Judas of Simon
2469 3195 846 3860 1302 5124
5 Ἰσκαριώτης, ὁ μέλλων αὐτὸν παραδιδόναι, Διατί τοῦτο τὸ
Iscariot, the (one) being about Him to betray, Why this —
3864 3756 4097 5145 1220 1325 4434
μύρον οὐκ ἐπράθη τριακοσίων δηναρίων, καὶ ἐδόθη πτω-
ointment not was sold (for) three hundred denarii, and given to (the)
2036 5124 3756/3754/4012 4434 3199 846
6 χοῖς; εἶπε δὲ τοῦτο, οὐχ ὅτι περὶ τῶν πτωχῶν ἔμελεν αὐτῷ,
poor? he said But this, not because about the poor was a care to him,
235 3754 2812 2258 1101 2192
ἀλλ' ὅτι κλέπτης ἦν, καὶ τὸ γλωσσόκομον εἶχε, καὶ τὰ
but that a thief he was, and the moneybag held and that
906 941 2036 3767 2424 863 846
7 βαλλόμενα ἐβάσταζεν. εἶπεν οὖν ὁ Ἰησοῦς, Ἄφες αὐτήν·
being put (in) carried away. said Therefore Jesus, Allow her;
1519 2250 1780 3450 5083 846
8 εἰς τὴν ἡμέραν τοῦ ἐνταφιασμοῦ μου τετήρηκεν αὐτό. τοὺς
for the day of the burial of Me she has kept it. the
4434 1063 3842 2192 3326 1438 1691 3756 3842
πτωχοὺς γὰρ πάντοτε ἔχετε μεθ' ἑαυτῶν, ἐμὲ δὲ οὐ πάντοτε
poor For always you have with yourselves, Me but not always
2192
ἔχετε.
you have.
1097 3767 3793 41831537 2453 3754/1563 2076
9 Ἔγνω οὖν ὄχλος πολὺς ἐκ τῶν Ἰουδαίων ὅτι ἐκεῖ ἐστι
knew Then crowd the much of the Jews that there He is,
2064 3756/1223 2424 3440 235 2443
καὶ ἦλθον οὐ διὰ τὸν Ἰησοῦν μόνον, ἀλλ' ἵνα καὶ τὸν
and they came not because of Jesus alone, but that also —

might see Lazarus whom He raised from *the* dead. [10]But the chief priests took counsel that they might put Lazarus to death also, [11]because through him many of the Jews went away and believed into Jesus.

[12]On the morrow, coming to the Feast, hearing that Jesus is coming to Jerusalem, a great crowd [13]took palm branches and went out to a meeting with Him, and were crying out, Hosanna! Blessed *is* He coming in *the* name of *the* Lord, the King of Israel! [14]And finding an ass colt, Jesus sat on it, even as it had been written, [15]"Do not fear, daughter of Zion. Behold, your king comes sitting on the foal of an ass." [16]But His disciples did not know these things at the first, but when Jesus was glorified, then they recalled that these things had been written on Him; and they did these things to Him. [17]Then the crowd which was with Him when He called Lazarus out of the tomb, and raised him from *the* dead, witnessed. [18]Because of this also the crowds met Him, because it heard *of* this miracle He had done. [19]Then the Pharisees said to themselves, Observe that you gain nothing. Behold, the world has gone after Him.

[20]And there were some Greeks among those coming up, that they might worship at the Feast. [21]Then these came to Philip, the *one* from Bethsaida of Galilee, and asked him, saying, Sir, we desire to see Jesus. [22]Philip came and told Andrew, and again Andrew and Philip told

2976 1492 3739 1453 1537 3698 1011
10 Λάζαρον ἴδωσιν, ὃν ἤγειρεν ἐκ νεκρῶν. ἐβουλεύσαντο δὲ οἱ
Lazarus they might see, whom He raised from dead. took counsel But the
749 2443 2976 615 3754 4183 1223
11 ἀρχιερεῖς ἵνα καὶ τὸν Λάζαρον ἀποκτείνωσιν· ὅτι πολλοὶ δι'
chief priests that also — Lazarus they might kill, because many through
846 5217 2453 4100 1519 2424
αὐτὸν ὑπῆγον τῶν Ἰουδαίων, καὶ ἐπίστευον εἰς τὸν Ἰησοῦν.
him departed of the Jews, and believed in — Jesus.
1887 3793 4183 2064 1519 1859 191
12 Τῇ ἐπαύριον ὄχλος πολὺς ὁ ἐλθὼν εἰς τὴν ἑορτήν, ἀκού-
On the morrow a crowd much coming to the feast,
3754 2064 2424 1519 2414 2983
13 σαντες ὅτι ἔρχεται ὁ Ἰησοῦς εἰς Ἱεροσόλυμα, ἔλαβον τὰ
hearing that is coming — Jesus to Jerusalem, took the
902 5404 1831 1519 5222 846
βαΐα τῶν φοινίκων, καὶ ἐξῆλθον εἰς ὑπάντησιν αὐτῷ, καὶ
branches of the palm-trees and went out to a meeting with Him, and
2896 5614 2127 2064 1722 3686
ἔκραζον, Ὡσαννά· εὐλογημένος ὁ ἐρχόμενος ἐν ὀνόματι
cried out, Hosanna! Blessed (is) He coming in (the) name
2962 935 2474 2147 2424 3678
14 Κυρίου, ὁ βασιλεὺς τοῦ Ἰσραήλ. εὑρὼν δὲ ὁ Ἰησοῦς ὀνάριον,
of (the) Lord, the king — of Israel. finding And Jesus an ass colt,
2323 1909 846 2531 2076 1125 3361 5399
15 ἐκάθισεν ἐπ' αὐτό, καθώς ἐστι γεγραμμένον, Μὴ φοβοῦ,
He sat upon it, even as it is having been written, Do not fear,
2364 4622 2400 935 4675 2064 2521 1909
θύγατερ Σιών· ἰδού, ὁ βασιλεύς σου ἔρχεται, καθήμενος ἐπὶ
daughter of Zion. Behold, the King of you comes, sitting on
4454 3688 5023 3756 1097 3101 848
16 πῶλον ὄνου. ταῦτα δὲ οὐκ ἔγνωσαν οἱ μαθηταὶ αὐτοῦ τὸ
the foal of an ass, these things But not did know the disciples of Him at the
4412 235 3753 1392 2424 5119 3415 3754
πρῶτον· ἀλλ' ὅτε ἐδοξάσθη ὁ Ἰησοῦς, τότε ἐμνήσθησαν ὅτι
first, but when was glorified Jesus, then they remembered that
5023 2258/1909/846 1125 5023 4160 846
ταῦτα ἦν ἐπ' αὐτῷ γεγραμμένα, καὶ ταῦτα ἐποίησαν αὐτῷ.
these things were on Him having been written, and these they did to Him.
3140 3767 3793 5607%3326 846 3753 2976
17 ἐμαρτύρει οὖν ὁ ὄχλος ὁ ὢν μετ' αὐτοῦ ὅτε τὸν Λάζαρον
witnessed Therefore the crowd which was with Him when — Lazarus
5455 1537 3419 1453 846 1537 3498 1223
18 ἐφώνησεν ἐκ τοῦ μνημείου, καὶ ἤγειρεν αὐτὸν ἐκ νεκρῶν. διὰ
He called out of the tomb, and raised him out of (the) dead There-
5124 5221 846 3793 3754 191 5124
τοῦτο καὶ ὑπήντησεν αὐτῷ ὁ ὄχλος, ὅτι ἤκουσε τοῦτο
fore also met with Him the crowd, because it heard this
846 4160 4592 3767 5330 2036 4314
19 αὐτὸν πεποιηκέναι τὸ σημεῖον. οἱ οὖν Φαρισαῖοι εἶπον πρὸς
(which) He had done sign. the Then Pharisees said to
1438 2334 3754/3756 5623 3762 2396 2889
ἑαυτούς, Θεωρεῖτε ὅτι οὐκ ὠφελεῖτε οὐδέν· ἴδε ὁ κόσμος
themselves, Observe, that not you profit nothing. Behold, the world
3694 846 565
ὀπίσω αὐτοῦ ἀπῆλθεν.
after Him has gone

2258 5100 1672 1537 305 2443 4352
20 Ἦσαν δέ τινες Ἕλληνες ἐκ τῶν ἀναβαινόντων ἵνα προσ-
were And some Greeks of those going up that they
1722 1859 3776 3767 4334 5376
21 κυνήσωσιν ἐν τῇ ἑορτῇ· οὗτοι οὖν προσῆλθον Φιλίππῳ
might worship at the feast. these Then came toward Philip
575 966 1056 2064 846
τῷ ἀπὸ Βηθσαϊδὰ τῆς Γαλιλαίας, καὶ ἠρώτων αὐτὸν
the (one) from Bethsaida — of Galilee, and asked him
3004 2962 2309 2424 1492 2064 5376
22 λέγοντες, Κύριε, θέλομεν τὸν Ἰησοῦν ἰδεῖν. ἔρχεται Φίλιππος
saying, Sir, we desire Jesus to see. Comes Philip
3004 406 3825 406 5376
καὶ λέγει τῷ Ἀνδρέᾳ· καὶ πάλιν Ἀνδρέας καὶ Φίλιππος
and tells — Andrew, and again Andrew and Philip

Jesus. [23]But Jesus answered them, saying, The hour has come that the Son of man should be glorified. [24]Truly, truly, I say to you, Unless the grain of wheat that falls into the earth dies, it remains alone. But if it dies, it bears much fruit. [25]The *one* who loves his soul loses it; and he who hates his soul in this world will keep it to everlasting life. [26]If anyone serves Me, let him follow Me; and where I am, there My servant will also be. And if anyone serves Me, the Father will honor him.

[27]And My soul is troubled, and what may I say? Father, save Me out of this hour? But on this account I came to this hour. [28]Father, glorify Your name. Then a voice came out of the heaven: I both glorified *it*, and again I will glorify *it*. [29]Then standing and hearing, the crowd said that thunder occurred. Others said, An angel has spoken to Him. [30]Jesus answered and said, This voice has not occurred because of Me, but because of you. [31]Now is *the* judgment of this world; now the ruler of this world shall be cast out. [32]And I, if I be lifted up from the earth, I will draw all to Myself.

[33]But He said this, signifying by what kind *of* death He was about to die. [34]The crowd answered Him, We heard out of the Law that the Christ remains forever. And how do you say that the Son of man must be lifted up? Who is this Son of man? [35]Then Jesus said to them, Yet a little while the Light is with you. Walk while you have the Light,

3004 2424 2424 611 846 3004
23 λέγουσι τῷ Ἰησοῦ. ὁ δὲ Ἰησοῦς ἀπεκρίνατο αὐτοῖς λέγων,
tell — Jesus. And Jesus answers them, saying,
2064 5610/2443 1392 5207 444 281
24 Ἐλήλυθεν ἡ ὥρα ἵνα δοξασθῇ ὁ υἱὸς τοῦ ἀνθρώπου. ἀμὴν
has come The hour that should be glorified the Son of man. Truly
281 3004 5213/1437/3361 2848 4621 4098 1519
ἀμὴν λέγω ὑμῖν, ἐὰν μὴ ὁ κόκκος τοῦ σίτου πεσὼν εἰς τὴν
truly, I say to you, Unless the grain of wheat falling into the
1093 599 846 3441 3306 1437 599 4183
γῆν ἀποθάνῃ, αὐτὸς μόνος μένει· ἐὰν δὲ ἀποθάνῃ, πολὺν
earth dies, it alone remains; if but it died much
2590 5342 5368 5590 848 622 846
25 καρπὸν φέρει. ὁ φιλῶν τὴν ψυχὴν αὐτοῦ ἀπολέσει αὐτήν·
fruit it bears. He loving the soul of him loses it;
3404 5590 846 1722 2889 5129 1519/2222
καὶ ὁ μισῶν τὴν ψυχὴν αὐτοῦ ἐν τῷ κόσμῳ τούτῳ εἰς ζωὴν
and he hating the soul of him in world this, to life
166 5442 846 1437/1698 1247 5100 1698 190
26 αἰώνιον φυλάξει αὐτήν. ἐὰν ἐμοὶ διακονῇ τις, ἐμοὶ ἀκολου-
eternal will keep it. If serves anyone, Me let him
3699 1510/1473/1563 1249 1699 2071
θείτω· καὶ ὅπου εἰμὶ ἐγώ, ἐκεῖ καὶ ὁ διάκονος ὁ ἐμὸς ἔσται·
follow; and where am I, there also servant My will be.
1437/5100/1698 1247 5091 846 3962 3568 5590
27 καὶ ἐάν τις ἐμοὶ διακονῇ, τιμήσει αὐτὸν ὁ πατήρ. νῦν ἡ ψυχή
And if anyone Me serves, will honor him the Father. Now the soul
3450 5015 5101 2036 3962 4982 3165/1537 5610
μου τετάρακται· καὶ τί εἴπω; πάτερ, σῶσόν με ἐκ τῆς ὥρας
of Me is agitated, and what may I say? Father, save Me out of hour
5126 235 1223 5124 2064 1519 5610 5026 3962
28 ταύτης. ἀλλὰ διὰ τοῦτο ἦλθον εἰς τὴν ὥραν ταύτην. πάτερ,
this. But on account of this I came to hour this. Father,
1392 4675 3686 2064 3767 5456 1537 3772
δόξασόν σου τὸ ὄνομα. ἦλθεν οὖν φωνὴ ἐκ τοῦ οὐρανοῦ,
glorify of You the name. came Then a voice out of Heaven:
1392 3825 1392 3767 3793 2476
29 Καὶ ἐδόξασα, καὶ πάλιν δοξάσω. ὁ οὖν ὄχλος ὁ ἑστὼς καὶ
Both I glorified and again I will glorify. the Then crowd standing and
191 3004 1027 1096 243 3004 32
ἀκούσας ἔλεγε βροντὴν γεγονέναι· ἄλλοι ἔλεγον, Ἄγγελος
hearing said thunder to have occurred. Others said, An angel
846 2980 611 2424 2036 3756/1223/1691
30 αὐτῷ λελάληκεν. ἀπεκρίθη ὁ Ἰησοῦς καὶ εἶπεν, Οὐ δι' ἐμὲ
to Him has spoken, answered — Jesus and said, Not via Me
3778 5456 1096 235 1223 5209/3568 2920 2076
31 αὕτη ἡ φωνὴ γέγονεν, ἀλλὰ δι' ὑμᾶς. νῦν κρίσις ἐστὶ τοῦ
this voice occurred, but because of you. Now judgment is —
2889 5127 3568 758 2889 5127 1544
κόσμου τούτου· νῦν ὁ ἄρχων τοῦ κόσμου τούτου ἐκβληθή-
of world this; now the ruler of world this shall be
1854 2504 1437 5312 1537 1093 3956 1670
32 σεται ἔξω. κἀγὼ ἐὰν ὑψωθῶ ἐκ τῆς γῆς, πάντας ἑλκύσω
thrown out. And I if I be lifted up from the earth. all I will draw
4314 1683 5124 3004 4591 4169 2288
33 πρὸς ἐμαυτόν. τοῦτο δὲ ἔλεγε, σημαίνων ποίῳ θανάτῳ
to Myself. this And He said, signifying by what kind (of) death
3195 599 611 846 3793 2249 191
34 ἤμελλεν ἀποθνήσκειν. ἀπεκρίθη αὐτῷ ὁ ὄχλος, Ἡμεῖς ἠκού-
He was about to die. answered Him The crowd, We heard
1537 3551 3754 5547 3306 1519 165 4459
σαμεν ἐκ τοῦ νόμου ὅτι ὁ Χριστὸς μένει εἰς τὸν αἰῶνα· καὶ πῶς
out of the law that the Christ abides to the age; and how
4771 3004 3754 1163 5312 5207 444 5101
σὺ λέγεις ὅτι Δεῖ ὑψωθῆναι τὸν υἱὸν τοῦ ἀνθρώπου; τίς
do you say that it behoves to be lifted up the Son — of man? Who
2076 3778 5207 444 2036 3767 846 2424
35 ἐστιν οὗτος ὁ υἱὸς τοῦ ἀνθρώπου; εἶπεν οὖν αὐτοῖς ὁ Ἰησοῦς,
Is this Son — of man? said Then to them Jesus,
2089 3398 5550 5457/3326/5216 2076 4043 2193
Ἔτι μικρὸν χρόνον τὸ φῶς μεθ' ὑμῶν ἐστι. περιπατεῖτε ἕως
Yet a little time the light with you is. Walk while

that darkness not overtake you. And the *one* walking in the darkness does not know where he is going. [36]While you have the Light, believe into the Light, that you may become sons of Light.

Jesus spoke these things, and going away was hidden from them.

[37]But *though* He had done so many miracles before them, they did not believe into Him, [38]so that the word of Isaiah the prophet might be fulfilled, which he said, "Lord, who has believed our report? And the arm of the Lord, to whom was it revealed?" [39]Because of this they could not believe, because Isaiah said again, [40]"He has blinded their eyes and has hardened their heart, that they might not see with the eyes, and understand with the heart, and be converted, and I should heal them." [41]Isaiah said these things when he saw His glory, and spoke about Him. [42]Still, however, even out of the rulers, many did believe into Him. But because of the Pharisees, they were not confessing, that they not be put out of the synagogue. [43]For they loved the glory of men more than the glory of God.

[44]But Jesus cried out and said, The *one* believing into Me does not believe into Me, but into the *One* sending Me. [45]And the *one* seeing Me sees the *One* who sent Me. [46]I have come *as* a Light to the world, that everyone who believes into Me may not remain in the darkness. [47]And if anyone hears My words, and does not believe, I do not judge him; for I did not come that I might judge the world, but that I might save the world. [48]The *one* who rejects Me and does not receive My

5457 2192 2443/3361 4653 5209 2638 4043
τὸ φῶς ἔχετε, ἵνα μὴ σκοτία ὑμᾶς καταλάβῃ· καὶ ὁ περιπα-
the light you have, lest darkness you overtake; and the (one) walk-
1722 4653 3756/1492/4226/ 5217 2193 5457 2192
36 τῶν ἐν τῇ σκοτίᾳ οὐκ οἶδε ποῦ ὑπάγει. ἕως τὸ φῶς ἔχετε,
ing in the darkness not knows where he is going. While the light you have,
4100 1519 5457/2443/5207 5457 1096
πιστεύετε εἰς τὸ φῶς, ἵνα υἱοὶ φωτὸς γένησθε.
believe in the light, that sons of light you may become.
5023 2980 2424 565 2928 575
Ταῦτα ἐλάλησεν ὁ Ἰησοῦς, καὶ ἀπελθὼν ἐκρύβη ἀπ'
These things spoke — Jesus, and going away was hidden from
846 5118 846 4592 4160 1715
37 αὐτῶν. τοσαῦτα δὲ αὐτοῦ σημεῖα πεποιηκότος ἔμπροσθεν
them. so many But He signs having done before
846 3756 4100 1519 846 2443 3056 2268
38 αὐτῶν, οὐκ ἐπίστευον εἰς αὐτόν· ἵνα ὁ λόγος Ἡσαΐου τοῦ
them, not they believed in Him that the word of Isaiah the
4396 4137 3739/2036 2962 5101 4100 189
προφήτου πληρωθῇ, ὃν εἶπε, Κύριε, τίς ἐπίστευσε τῇ ἀκοῇ
prophet might be fulfilled which he said, Lord, who has believed the report
2257 1023 2962 5101 601 1223 5124
39 ἡμῶν; καὶ ὁ βραχίων Κυρίου τίνι ἀπεκαλύφθη; διὰ τοῦτο
of us? And the arm of (the) Lord, to whom was it revealed? Therefore
3756 1410 4100 3754 3825 2036 2268 5186
40 οὐκ ἠδύναντο πιστεύειν, ὅτι πάλιν εἶπεν Ἡσαΐας, Τετύ-
not they could believe, because again said Isaiah, He has
848 3788 4456 848
φλωκεν αὐτῶν τοὺς ὀφθαλμούς, καὶ πεπώρωκεν αὐτῶν τὴν
blinded of them the eyes, and hardened of them the
2588 2443/3361 1492 3788 3539
41 καρδίαν· ἵνα μὴ ἴδωσι τοῖς ὀφθαλμοῖς, καὶ νοήσωσι τῇ
heart, that not they might see with the eyes, and understand with
2588 1994 2390 846 5023 2036 **the**
καρδίᾳ, καὶ ἐπιστραφῶσι, καὶ ἰάσωμαι αὐτούς. ταῦτα εἶπεν
heart, and be converted, and I should heal them. These things said
2268 3753/1492 1391 848 2980 4012 846
Ἡσαΐας, ὅτε εἶδε τὴν δόξαν αὐτοῦ, καὶ ἐλάλησε περὶ αὐτοῦ.
Isaiah when he saw the glory of Him, and spoke about Him.
3679 3305 1537 758 4183 4100
42 ὅμως μέντοι καὶ ἐκ τῶν ἀρχόντων πολλοὶ ἐπίστευσαν εἰς
Still, however, even of the rulers many believed in
846 235 1223 5330 3756 3670 2443/3361
αὐτόν· ἀλλὰ διὰ τοὺς Φαρισαίους οὐχ ὡμολόγουν, ἵνα μὴ
Him, but because of the Pharisees not were confessing lest
656 1096 25 1063 1391
43 ἀποσυνάγωγοι γένωνται. ἠγάπησαν γὰρ τὴν δόξαν τῶν
put out of the synagogue they be. they loved For the glory —
444 3123 2260 1391 2316
ἀνθρώπων μᾶλλον ἤπερ τὴν δόξαν τοῦ Θεοῦ.
of men more than the glory — of God.
2424 2896 2036 4100 1519/1691 3756
44 Ἰησοῦς δὲ ἔκραξε καὶ εἶπεν, Ὁ πιστεύων εἰς ἐμέ, οὐ
Jesus But cried out and said, The (one) believing in Me, not
4100 1519/1691/235/1519 3992 3165 2334
45 πιστεύει εἰς ἐμέ, ἀλλ' εἰς τὸν πέμψαντά με· καὶ ὁ θεωρῶν
believes in Me, but in the (One) sending Me; and he seeing
1691 2334 3992 3165 1473 5457 1519 2889
46 ἐμέ, θεωρεῖ τὸν πέμψαντά με. ἐγὼ φῶς εἰς τὸν κόσμον
Me sees the (One) sending Me. I a light to the world
2064 2443 3956 4100 1519/1691/1722 4653 3361 3306
ἐλήλυθα, ἵνα πᾶς ὁ πιστεύων εἰς ἐμέ, ἐν τῇ σκοτίᾳ μὴ μείνῃ.
have come, that everyone believing in Me in the darkness not may abide.
1437/5100/3450 191 4487 3361 4100
47 καὶ ἐάν τις μου ἀκούσῃ τῶν ῥημάτων καὶ μὴ πιστεύσῃ,
And if anyone of Me hears the words, and not believes,
1473/3756/2919 846 3756/1063 2064 2443 2919 2889
ἐγὼ οὐ κρίνω αὐτόν· οὐ γὰρ ἦλθον ἵνα κρίνω τὸν κόσμον,
I do not judge him; not for I came that I might judge the world,
235 2443 4982 2889 114 1691 3361 2983
48 ἀλλ' ἵνα σώσω τὸν κόσμον. ὁ ἀθετῶν ἐμὲ καὶ μὴ λαμβάνων
but that I might save the world. The (one) rejecting Me and not receiving

NOTE: Frequent words not numbered: δέ(1161); καί(2531)—and, but; ὁ, ἡ, τό (3588, the)— * above word, look in verse margin for No.

words has that judging him: the word which I spoke, that will judge him in the last Day. [49]For I did not speak from Myself, but He who sent Me, *the* Father, He has given Me command, what I should say, and what I should speak. [50]And I know that His command is everlasting life. Therefore, what things I speak, as the Father has said to Me, so I speak.

CHAPTER 13

[1]And before the feast of the Passover, Jesus knowing that His hour had come that He should move from this world to the Father, loving *His* own in the world, He loved them to *the* end. [2]And supper having occurred, the Devil having already put into the heart of Simon's *son* Judas Iscariot that he should betray Him, [3]Jesus knowing that His Father has given all things into *His* hands, and that He came out from God, and goes away to God, [4]He rose up from the supper, and laid aside *His* garments. And taking a towel, He girded Himself. [5]Then He put water into the basin and began to wash the feet of the disciples, and to wipe off with the towel with which He was girded. [6]He then came to Simon Peter. And that one said to Him, Lord, do You wash my feet? [7]Jesus answered and said to him, What I am doing, you do not yet know. But you will know after these things. [8]Peter said to Him, You may in no way wash my feet to the age. Jesus answered him, Unless I wash you, you have no part with Me. [9]Simon Peter said to Him, Lord, not my

4487 3450 2192 2919 846 3056 3739
τὰ ῥήματά μου, ἔχει τὸν κρίνοντα αὐτόν· ὁ λόγος ὃν
the words of Me has that judging him: the word which
2980 1565 2919 846 1722 2078 2250 3754/1473
49 ἐλάλησα, ἐκεῖνος κρινεῖ αὐτὸν ἐν τῇ ἐσχάτῃ ἡμέρᾳ. ὅτι ἐγὼ
I spoke, that will judge him in the last Day. Because I
1537 1683 3756 2980 235 3992 3165 3962 846 3427
ἐξ ἐμαυτοῦ οὐκ ἐλάλησα· ἀλλ' ὁ πέμψας με πατήρ, αὐτός μοι
from Myself not spoke, but He sending Me, (the) Father, He Me
1785 1325 5101 2036 5101 2980 1492 3754
50 ἐντολὴν ἔδωκε, τί εἴπω καὶ τί λαλήσω. καὶ οἶδα ὅτι ἡ
command has given, what I may say and what I may speak. And I know that the
1785 846 2222 166 2076/3739/3767/2980/1473 2531
ἐντολὴ αὐτοῦ ζωὴ αἰώνιός ἐστιν· ἃ οὖν λαλῶ ἐγώ, καθὼς
command of Him life eternal is. What things then speak I, as
2046 3427 3962 3779 2980
εἴρηκέ μοι ὁ πατήρ, οὕτω λαλῶ.
has said to Me the Father so I speak.

CHAPTER 13

4253 1859 3957 1492 2424 3754
1 Πρὸ δὲ τῆς ἑορτῆς τοῦ πάσχα, εἰδὼς ὁ Ἰησοῦς ὅτι
before And the feast of the Passover, knowing Jesus that
2064 848 5610 2443 3327 1537 2889 5127
ἐλήλυθεν αὐτοῦ ἡ ὥρα ἵνα μεταβῇ ἐκ τοῦ κόσμου τούτου
had come of Him the hour that He should move from world this,
4314 3962 25 2398 1722 2889
πρὸς τὸν πατέρα, ἀγαπήσας τοὺς ἰδίους τοὺς ἐν τῷ κόσμῳ,
to the Father, loving the own — in the world,
1519 5056 25 846 1173 1096
2 εἰς τέλος ἠγάπησεν αὐτούς. καὶ δείπνου γενομένου, τοῦ
to (the) end He loved them. And supper having occurred, the
1228 2235 906 2588 2455 4613
διαβόλου ἤδη βεβληκότος εἰς τὴν καρδίαν Ἰούδα Σίμωνος
Devil already having put into the heart of Judas of Simon
2469 2443 846 3860 1492 2424 3754 3956
3 Ἰσκαριώτου ἵνα αὐτὸν παραδῷ, εἰδὼς ὁ Ἰησοῦς ὅτι πάντα
Iscariot, that Him he should betray, knowing Jesus that all things
1325 846 3962 1519 5495 3754/575 2316
δέδωκεν αὐτῷ ὁ πατὴρ εἰς τὰς χεῖρας, καὶ ὅτι ἀπὸ Θεοῦ
has given Him the Father into the hands, and that from God
1831 4314 2316 5217 1453 1537 1173
4 ἐξῆλθε καὶ πρὸς τὸν Θεὸν ὑπάγει, ἐγείρεται ἐκ τοῦ δείπνου,
He came, and to — God departs, He rises from the supper
5087 2440 2983 3012 1241 1438
καὶ τίθησι τὰ ἱμάτια, καὶ λαβὼν λέντιον διέζωσεν ἑαυτόν.
and lays aside the garments, and taking a towel He girded Himself.
1534 906 5204 1519 3537 756 3538
5 εἶτα βάλλει ὕδωρ εἰς τὸν νιπτῆρα, καὶ ἤρξατο νίπτειν τοὺς
Then He put water into the basin, and began to wash the
4228 3101 1591 3012/3739/2258/1241
πόδας τῶν μαθητῶν, καὶ ἐκμάσσειν τῷ λεντίῳ ᾧ ἦν διεζω-
feet of the disciples, and to wipe off with the towel with which He
2064 3767 4314 4613 4074 3004 846
6 σμένος. ἔρχεται οὖν πρὸς Σίμωνα Πέτρον· καὶ λέγει αὐτῷ
was girded. He comes then to Simon Peter; and said to Him
1565 2962 4771/3450 3538 4228 611 2424
7 ἐκεῖνος, Κύριε, σύ μου νίπτεις τοὺς πόδας; ἀπεκρίθη Ἰησοῦς
that one, Lord, Do You of me wash the feet? answered Jesus
2036 846 3739/1473/4160 4771/3756/1492/737 1097
καὶ εἶπεν αὐτῷ, Ὃ ἐγὼ ποιῶ, σὺ οὐκ οἶδας ἄρτι, γνώσῃ
and said to him, What I am doing, you not know yet, you will know
3326 5023 3004 846 4074 =3364= 3538 4228
8 δὲ μετὰ ταῦτα. λέγει αὐτῷ Πέτρος, Οὐ μὴ νίψῃς τοὺς πόδας
but after these things, says to Him Peter, In no way may You wash the feet
3450/1519 165 611 846 2424 1437/3361/3538
μου εἰς τὸν αἰῶνα. ἀπεκρίθη αὐτῷ ὁ Ἰησοῦς, Ἐὰν μὴ νίψω
of me to the age. answered to him — Jesus, Unless I wash
4571/3756/1492 3313 3326 1700 3004 846 4613 4074
9 σε, οὐκ ἔχεις μέρος μετ' ἐμοῦ. λέγει αὐτῷ Σίμων Πέτρος,
you, not you have part with Me. says to Him Simon Peter,

feet only, but also the hands
and the head. [10]Jesus said
to him, The *one* having
been bathed has no need
other than to wash the feet,
but is wholly clean. And you
are clean, but not all. [11]For
He knew the *one* betraying
Him. For this reason He
said, You are not all clean.

[12]Then when He had
washed their feet, and had
taken His garments, re-
clining again, He said to
them, Do you know what I
have done to you? [13]You
call Me the Teacher, and,
The Lord. And you say well,
for I am. [14]If then I washed
your feet, the Lord and the
Teacher, you also ought to
wash the feet of one
another. [15]For I gave you
an example, that as I did to
you, you also should do.
[16]Truly, truly, I say to you, A
slave is not greater than his
lord, or a messenger greater
than the *one* sending him.
[17]If you know these things,
blessed are you if you do
them. [18]I do not speak
concerning all of you; I
know whom I chose out;
but that the Scripture might
be fulfilled, "The *one* eating
the bread with Me lifted up
his heel against Me."
[19]From this time I tell you,
before *it* happens, that
when it happens you may
believe that I AM. [20]Truly,
truly, I say to you, The *one*
who receives whomever I
may send receives Me; and
the *one* who receives Me
receives the *One* who sent
Me.

2962 3361 4228 3450 3440 235 5495
Κύριε, μὴ τοὺς πόδας μου μόνον, ἀλλὰ καὶ τὰς χεῖρας καὶ
Lord, not the feet of Me only but also the hands and
2776 3004 846 2424 3068 3756 5532
10 τὴν κεφαλήν. λέγει αὐτῷ ὁ Ἰησοῦς, Ὁ λελουμένος οὐ χρείαν
the head. says to him Jesus, He having bathed no need
2192 2228 4228 3538 235 2076 2513 3650
ἔχει ἢ τοὺς πόδας νίψασθαι, ἀλλ᾽ ἔστι καθαρὸς ὅλος· καὶ
has than the feet to wash, but is clean wholly; and
5210 2513 2076 235 3780 3956 1492 1063 3860
11 ὑμεῖς καθαροί ἐστε, ἀλλ᾽ οὐχὶ πάντες. ᾔδει γὰρ τὸν παραδι-
you clean are, but not all. He knew For the (one) betray-
846 1223 2036 3780 3956 2513 2075
δόντα αὐτόν· διὰ τοῦτο εἶπεν, Οὐχὶ πάντες καθαροί ἐστε.
ing Him; for this reason He said, Not all clean you are.
3753/3756/3538 4228 848 2983 2440
12 Ὅτε οὖν ἔνιψε τοὺς πόδας αὐτῶν, καὶ ἔλαβε τὰ ἱμάτια
When, therefore, He washed the feet of them, and took the garments
848 377 3825 2036 846 1097 5101 4160
αὐτοῦ, ἀναπεσὼν πάλιν, εἶπεν αὐτοῖς, Γινώσκετε τί πεποίη-
of Him. Reclining again, He said to them, Do you know what I have
5213 5210 5455 3165 1320 2962
13 κα ὑμῖν; ὑμεῖς φωνεῖτέ με, Ὁ διδάσκαλος, καὶ Ὁ κύριος· καὶ
done to you? You call Me, The Teacher, and, The Lord; and
2573 3004 1510/1063/1487/3767/1473/3538 5216 4228
14 καλῶς λέγετε, εἰμὶ γάρ. εἰ οὖν ἐγὼ ἔνιψα ὑμῶν τοὺς πόδας,
well you say; I am for. If, then, I washed of you the feet,
2962 1320 5210 3784 240
ὁ κύριος καὶ ὁ διδάσκαλος, καὶ ὑμεῖς ὀφείλετε ἀλλήλων
the Lord and the Teacher; also you ought of one another
3538 4228 5262 1063 1325 5213 2443 2531
15 νίπτειν τοὺς πόδας. ὑπόδειγμα γὰρ ἔδωκα ὑμῖν, ἵνα καθὼς
to wash the feet. an example For I gave you, that as
1473 4160 5213 5210 4160 281 281 3004 5213
16 ἐγὼ ἐποίησα ὑμῖν, καὶ ὑμεῖς ποιῆτε. ἀμὴν ἀμὴν λέγω ὑμῖν,
I did to you, also you should do. Truly, truly, I say to you,
3756/2076 1401 3187 2962 848 3761 652
Οὐκ ἔστι δοῦλος μείζων τοῦ κυρίου αὐτοῦ, οὐδὲ ἀπόστολος
not is A slave greater than the lord of him, nor a messenger
3187 3992 846 1487 5023 1492 3107
17 μείζων τοῦ πέμψαντος αὐτόν. εἰ ταῦτα οἴδατε, μακάριοί
greater than the (one) sending him. If these things you know, blessed
2075/1437 4160 846 3756/ 4012 3956 5216 3004 1473
18 ἐστε ἐὰν ποιῆτε αὐτά. οὐ περὶ πάντων ὑμῶν λέγω· ἐγὼ
are you if you do them. Not concerning all of you I speak; I
1492/3739 1586 235 2443 1124 4137 5176
οἶδα οὓς ἐξελεξάμην· ἀλλ᾽ ἵνα ἡ γραφὴ πληρωθῇ, Ὁ τρώγων
know whom I chose out, but that the Scripture be fulfilled: The (one) eating
3326/1700 740 1869 1909/1691 4418 848 575
19 μετ᾽ ἐμοῦ τὸν ἄρτον ἐπῆρεν ἐπ᾽ ἐμὲ τὴν πτέρναν αὐτοῦ. ἀπ᾽
with Me the bread lifted up against Me the heel of him. From
737 3004 5213 4253 1096 2443 3752 1096
ἄρτι λέγω ὑμῖν πρὸ τοῦ γενέσθαι, ἵνα, ὅταν γένηται,
now I tell you, before the happening, that when it happens
4100 3754/1473/1510/281 281 3004 5213 2983
20 πιστεύσητε ὅτι ἐγώ εἰμι. ἀμὴν ἀμὴν λέγω ὑμῖν, Ὁ λαμβάνων
you may believe that I AM. Truly, truly, I say to you, he receiving
1437/5100 3992 1691 2983 1691 2983 2983
ἐάν τινα πέμψω, ἐμὲ λαμβάνει· ὁ δὲ ἐμὲ λαμβάνων, λαμβάνει
whomever I may send, Me receives, he and Me receiving, receives
3992 3165
τὸν πέμψαντά με.
the (one) sending Me.

[21]Saying these things,
Jesus was troubled in spirit,
and testified and said,
Indeed I tell you truly that
one of you will betray Me.
[22]Then the disciples looked

5023 2036 2424 5015 4151
21 Ταῦτα εἰπὼν ὁ Ἰησοῦς ἐταράχθη τῷ πνεύματι, καὶ
These things saying — Jesus was agitated in the spirit, and
5216 3140 2036 281 281 3004 5213 3754/1520/1537/
ἐμαρτύρησε καὶ εἶπεν, Ἀμὴν ἀμὴν λέγω ὑμῖν ὅτι εἷς ἐξ ὑμῶν
witnessed and said, Truly, truly, I say to you that one of you
3860 3165 991 3767/1519 240 3101
22 παραδώσει με. ἔβλεπον οὖν εἰς ἀλλήλους οἱ μαθηταί,
will betray Me. looked Then at one another the disciples,

upon one another, doubting of whom He spoke. 23 But there was one of His disciples reclining at the bosom of Jesus, whom Jesus loved. 24 Then Simon Peter signaled to him to ask whom it might be of whom He spoke. 25 And leaning on the breast of Jesus, he said to Him, Lord, who is it? 26 Jesus answered, It is he to whom I, having dipped the morsel, shall give *it*. And dipping the morsel, He gave *it* to Judas Iscariot, *son* of Simon. 27 And after the morsel, then Satan entered into that one. Then Jesus said to him, What you do do quickly. 28 But no one of those reclining knew this, for what He spoke to him; 29 for some thought, since Judas held the moneybag, that Jesus was saying to him, Buy what things we have need *of* for the feast; or that he should give something to the poor. 30 Then, receiving the morsel, he immediately went out. And it was night.

31 Then when he had gone out, Jesus said, Now the Son of man was glorified, and God was glorified in Him. 32 If God was glorified in Him, God also will glorify Him in Himself, and immediately will glorify Him. 33 Little children, yet a little while I am with you. You will seek Me; and, as I said to the Jews, Where I go, you are not able to come; I also say to you now. 34 I give a new commandment to you, that you should love one another; according as I loved you, you should also love one another. 35 By this all shall know that you are My disciples, if you have love among one another.

639 4012 5101 3004 2258 345 1520
23 ἀπορούμενοι περὶ τίνος λέγει. ἦν δὲ ἀνακείμενος εἷς τῶν
being perplexed about whom He speaks. was And reclining one of the
3101 848 1722 2859 2424 3739 25
μαθητῶν αὐτοῦ ἐν τῷ κόλπῳ τοῦ Ἰησοῦ, ὃν ἠγάπα ὁ
disciples of Him on the bosom — of Jesus, whom loved —
2424 3506 3767 5129 4613 4074 4441 5101/302/1498
24 Ἰησοῦς· νεύει οὖν τούτῳ Σίμων Πέτρος πυθέσθαι τίς ἂν εἴη
Jesus; nods then to this one Simon Peter to ask who it might be
4012/3739/3004 1968 1565 1909 4738 2424
25 περὶ οὗ λέγει. ἐπιπεσὼν δὲ ἐκεῖνος ἐπὶ τὸ στῆθος τοῦ Ἰησοῦ,
about whom He speaks. leaning And that one on the breast — of Jesus,
3004 846 2962 5101 2076 611 2424
26 λέγει αὐτῷ, Κύριε, τίς ἐστιν; ἀποκρίνεται ὁ Ἰησοῦς,
he said to Him, Lord, who is it? answers — Jesus,
1565 2076/3739/1473 911 5596 1929 1686
Ἐκεῖνός ἐστιν ᾧ ἐγὼ βάψας τὸ ψωμίον ἐπιδώσω. καὶ ἐμβά-
That one it is to whom I having dipped the morsel shall give it. And dipping
5596 1325 2455 4613 2469
27 ψας τὸ ψωμίον, δίδωσιν Ἰούδᾳ Σίμωνος Ἰσκαριώτῃ. καὶ
the morsel, He gave to Judas of Simon Iscariot. And
3326 5596 5119 1525 1519 1565 4567 3004
μετὰ τὸ ψωμίον, τότε εἰσῆλθεν εἰς ἐκεῖνον ὁ Σατανᾶς. λέγει
after the morsel, then entered into that one Satan. says
3767 846 2424 4160 4160 5032 5124
28 οὖν αὐτῷ ὁ Ἰησοῦς, Ὃ ποιεῖς, ποίησον τάχιον. τοῦτο δὲ
Then to him Jesus, What you do, do quickly. this But
3762 1097 345 5101/2036/846 5100 1063
29 οὐδεὶς ἔγνω τῶν ἀνακειμένων πρὸς τί εἶπεν αὐτῷ. τινὲς γὰρ
no one knew of those reclining for what He spoke to him. some For
1380 1893 1101 2192 2455 3754 3004
ἐδόκουν, ἐπεὶ τὸ γλωσσόκομον εἶχεν ὁ Ἰούδας, ὅτι λέγει
thought, since the money-bag held — Judas, that tells
846 2424 59 3739 5532 2192 1519
αὐτῷ ὁ Ἰησοῦς, Ἀγόρασον ὧν χρείαν ἔχομεν εἰς τὴν
him Jesus, Buy of what things need we have for the
1859 2228 4434 2443/5100/1325/ 2983 3767 5596
30 ἑορτήν· ἢ τοῖς πτωχοῖς ἵνα τι δῷ. λαβὼν οὖν τὸ ψωμίον
feast; or, to the poor that a thing he give. Receiving, then, the morsel
1565 2112 1831 2258 3571
ἐκεῖνος, εὐθέως ἐξῆλθεν· ἦν δὲ νύξ.
that one, at once went out. it was And night.
3753/3767 1831 3004 2424 3568 1392 5207
31 Ὅτε οὖν ἐξῆλθε, λέγει ὁ Ἰησοῦς, Νῦν ἐδοξάσθη ὁ υἱὸς τοῦ
when Then he went, says Jesus, Now was glorified the Son —
444 2316 1392 1722 846/1487 2316 1392
32 ἀνθρώπου, καὶ ὁ Θεὸς ἐδοξάσθη ἐν αὐτῷ. εἰ ὁ Θεὸς ἐδοξάσθη
of man, and God was glorified in Him; if God was glorified
1722 846 2316 1392 846/1722 1438 2117
ἐν αὐτῷ, καὶ ὁ Θεὸς δοξάσει αὐτὸν ἐν ἑαυτῷ, καὶ εὐθὺς
in Him, both God will glorify Him in Himself, and at once
1392 846 5040 2089 3397 3327 5216 1510 2212
33 δοξάσει αὐτόν. τεκνία, ἔτι μικρὸν μεθ' ὑμῶν εἰμι. ζητήσετέ
will glorify Him. Children, yet a little with you I am. You will seek
3165 2531 2036 2453 3754 3699 5217 1473
με, καὶ καθὼς εἶπον τοῖς Ἰουδαίοις ὅτι Ὅπου ὑπάγω ἐγώ,
Me, and as I said to the Jews, Where go I,
5210 3756 1410 2064 5213 3004 737 1785
34 ὑμεῖς οὐ δύνασθε ἐλθεῖν, καὶ ὑμῖν λέγω ἄρτι. ἐντολὴν
you not are able to come, also to you I say now. A command
2537 1325 5213/2443 25 240 2531 25
καινὴν δίδωμι ὑμῖν, ἵνα ἀγαπᾶτε ἀλλήλους· καθὼς ἠγά-
A new I give you, that you love one another as I
5209/2443 5210 25 240 1722 5129 1097
35 πησα ὑμᾶς, ἵνα καὶ ὑμεῖς ἀγαπᾶτε ἀλλήλους. ἐν τούτῳ γνώ-
loved you that also you should love one another. By this will
3956/3756/1698 3101 2075/1437 26 2192
σονται πάντες ὅτι ἐμοὶ μαθηταί ἐστε, ἐὰν ἀγάπην ἔχητε ἐν
know all that to Me disciples you are, if love you have among
240
ἀλλήλοις.
one another.

[36]Simon Peter said to Him, Lord, where do You go? Jesus answered him, Where I go you are not able to follow Me now, but afterwards you shall follow Me. [37]Peter said to Him, Lord, why am I not able to follow You now? I will lay down my life for You! [38]Jesus answered him, Will you lay down your life for Me? Indeed, I tell you truly, in no way shall *the* cock crow until you shall deny Me three times.

3004 846 4613 4074 2962 4226 5217 611
36 Λέγει αὐτῷ Σίμων Πέτρος, Κύριε, ποῦ ὑπάγεις ; ἀπεκρίθη
says to Him Simon Peter, Lord, where do You go? answered
846 2424 3699 5217 3756 1410 3427/3568 190
αὐτῷ ὁ Ἰησοῦς, Ὅπου ὑπάγω, οὐ δύνασαί μοι νῦν ἀκο-
him Jesus, Where I go, not you are able Me now to
5305 190 3427 3004 846
37 λουθῆσαι, ὕστερον δὲ ἀκολουθήσεις μοι. λέγει αὐτῷ ὁ
follow; later but you will follow Me. says to Him
4074 2962 1302/3756 1410 4671 190 737
Πέτρος, Κύριε, διατί οὐ δύναμαί σοι ἀκολουθῆσαι ἄρτι ;
Peter, Lord, why not am I able You to follow now?
5590 3450 5228/4675/5087 611 846 2424
38 τὴν ψυχήν μου ὑπὲρ σοῦ θήσω. ἀπεκρίθη αὐτῷ ὁ Ἰησοῦς,
The soul of me for You I will lay down. answers him — Jesus,
5590 4675 5228 1700 5087 281 281 3004 4671/3756
Τὴν ψυχήν σου ὑπὲρ ἐμοῦ θήσεις ; ἀμὴν ἀμὴν λέγω σοι, οὐ
The soul of you for Me you will lay down? Truly, truly I say to you, in
3361 220 5455 2193/3739 533 3165 5151
μὴ ἀλέκτωρ φωνήσει ἕως οὗ ἀπαρνήσῃ με τρίς.
no way a cock will crow until you deny Me three times.

CHAPTER 14

[1]Do not let your heart be troubled; you believe in God, believe also in Me. [2]In My Father's house are many dwelling places. But if it were not so, I would have told you. I am going to prepare a place for you! [3]And if I go and prepare a place for you, I am coming again, and will receive you to Myself, that where I am you may be also. [4]And where I go you know, and the way you know.

[5]Thomas said to Him, Lord, we do not know where You go, and how can we know the way? [6]Jesus said to him, I am the Way, and the Truth, and the Life. No one comes to the Father except through Me. [7]If you had known Me, you would have known My Father also; and from now on you do know Him, and have seen Him. [8]And Philip said to Him, Lord, show us the Father, and it is enough for us. [9]Jesus said to him, Am I so long a time with you, and you have not known Me, Philip? The *one* seeing Me has seen the Father! And how do you say, Show us the Father? [10]Do you not believe that I *am* in the Father

CHAPTER 14

3361 5015 5216 2588 4100 1519 2316
1 Μὴ ταρασσέσθω ὑμῶν ἡ καρδία· πιστεύετε εἰς τὸν Θεόν,
Not let be agitated of you the heart; believe in God,
1519/1691 4100 1722 3614 3962 3450 3438
2 καὶ εἰς ἐμὲ πιστεύετε. ἐν τῇ οἰκίᾳ τοῦ πατρός μου μοναὶ
and in Me believe. In the house of the Father of Me dwellings
4183 1526 =1490= 2036 302 5213 4198 2090
πολλαί εἰσιν· εἰ δὲ μή, εἶπον ἂν ὑμῖν· πορεύομαι ἑτοιμάσαι
many are. Otherwise, I would have told you. I go to prepare
5117 5213 1437 4198 2090 5213 5117
3 τόπον ὑμῖν. καὶ ἐὰν πορευθῶ καὶ ἑτοιμάσω ὑμῖν τόπον,
a place for you, and if I go and prepare for you a place,
3825 2064 3880 5209 4314 1683 2443
πάλιν ἔρχομαι καὶ παραλήψομαι ὑμᾶς πρὸς ἐμαυτόν· ἵνα
again I am coming and will receive you to Myself, that
3699 1510/1473 5210/5600 3699 1473 5217 1492
4 ὅπου εἰμὶ ἐγώ, καὶ ὑμεῖς ἦτε. καὶ ὅπου ἐγὼ ὑπάγω οἴδατε,
where am I, also you may be. And where I go you know,
3598 1492 3004 846 2381 2962 3756 1492
5 καὶ τὴν ὁδὸν οἴδατε. λέγει αὐτῷ Θωμᾶς, Κύριε, οὐκ οἴδαμεν
and the way you know. says to Him Thomas, Lord, not we know
4226 5217 4459 1410 3598 1492 3004
6 ποῦ ὑπάγεις· καὶ πῶς δυνάμεθα τὴν ὁδὸν εἰδέναι ; λέγει
where You go, and how are we able the way to know? says
846 2424 1473 1510 3598 225 2222
αὐτῷ ὁ Ἰησοῦς, Ἐγώ εἰμι ἡ ὁδὸς καὶ ἡ ἀλήθεια καὶ ἡ ζωή·
to him — Jesus, I am the way and the truth and the life;
3762 2064 4314 3962 =1508=1223/1700/1487/ 1097
7 οὐδεὶς ἔρχεται πρὸς τὸν πατέρα, εἰ μὴ δι' ἐμοῦ. εἰ ἐγνώκειτέ
no one comes to the Father except through Me. If you had known
3165 3962 3450 1097 302 575 737 1097
με, καὶ τὸν πατέρα μου ἐγνώκειτε ἄν· καὶ ἀπ' ἄρτι γινώ-
Me, also the Father of Me you would have known, and from now you
846 3708 846 3004 846 5376
8 σκετε αὐτόν, καὶ ἑωράκατε αὐτόν. λέγει αὐτῷ Φίλιππος,
know Him, and have seen Him. says to Him Philip,
2962 1166 2254 3962 714 2254 3004 846
9 Κύριε, δεῖξον ἡμῖν τὸν πατέρα, καὶ ἀρκεῖ ἡμῖν. λέγει αὐτῷ
Lord, show us the Father, and it suffices us. **says** to him
2424 5118 5510 3326/5216/ 1510 3756 1097
ὁ Ἰησοῦς, Τοσοῦτον χρόνον μεθ' ὑμῶν εἰμι, καὶ οὐκ ἔγνωκάς
Jesus, so long a time with you am I, and not you know
3165 5376 3708 1691 3708 3962 4459/4771
με, Φίλιππε ; ὁ ἑωρακὼς ἐμέ, ἑώρακε τὸν πατέρα· καὶ πῶς σὺ
Me, Philip? The (one) seeing Me has seen the Father; and how do you
3004 1166 2254 3962 3756 4100 3754/1473/1722
10 λέγεις, Δεῖξον ἡμῖν τὸν πατέρα ; οὐ πιστεύεις ὅτι ἐγὼ ἐν τῷ
say, Show us the Father? Not do you believe that I in the

and the Father is in Me? The words which I speak to you I do not speak from Myself, but the Father who abides in Me, He does the works.

11Believe Me that I *am* in the Father, and the Father *is* in Me; but if not, believe Me because of the works themselves. 12Indeed, I tell you truly, He that believes in Me, the works which I do that one shall also do, and greater than these he will do, because I go to My Father. 13And whatever you may ask in My Name, this I will do, that the Father may be glorified in the Son. 14If you ask anything in My Name, I will do *it*. 15If you love Me, keep My commandments.

16And I will petition the Father, and He will give you another Comforter, that He may remain with you forever. 17the Spirit of Truth, whom the world cannot receive because it does not see Him nor know Him. But you know Him, for He abides with you, and shall be in you.

18I will not leave you orphans; I am coming to you. 19Yet a little *while* and the world no longer sees Me, but you see Me. Because I live, you also shall live. 20In that day you shall know that I *am* in My Father, and you *are* in Me, and I *am* in you. 21He that has My commandments and keeps them, it is that one who loves Me; and the *one* that loves Me shall be loved by My Father, and I shall love him and will reveal Myself to him.

22Judas, not the Iscariot, said to Him, Lord, what has happened that You are about to reveal Yourself to us and not at all to the world? 23Jesus answered and said to him, If anyone

3962 3962 1722/1698/2076 4487 3739/1473/2980
πατρί, καὶ ὁ πατὴρ ἐν ἐμοί ἐστι ; τὰ ῥήματα ἃ ἐγὼ λαλῶ
Father (am), and the Father in Me is? The words which I speak
5213 575 1683 3756 2980 3962 1722/1698 3306
ὑμῖν, ἀπ' ἐμαυτοῦ οὐ λαλῶ· ὁ δὲ πατὴρ ὁ ἐν ἐμοὶ μένων,
to you, from Myself not I speak, the but Father who in Me abides;
846 4160 2041 4100 3427/3754/1473/1722 3962
11 αὐτὸς ποιεῖ τὰ ἔργα. πιστεύετέ μοι ὅτι ἐγὼ ἐν τῷ πατρί,
He does the works. Believe Me, that I (am) in the Father,
3962 1722/1698 = 1490 = 1223 2041 848 4100
καὶ ὁ πατὴρ ἐν ἐμοί· εἰ δὲ μή, διὰ τὰ ἔργα αὐτὰ πιστεύετέ
and the Father in Me (is). if And not, for the works themselves believe
3427 281 281 3004 5213 4100 1519/1691 2041 1473
12 μοι. ἀμὴν ἀμὴν λέγω ὑμῖν, ὁ πιστεύων εἰς ἐμέ, τὰ ἔργα ἃ ἐγὼ
Me. Truly, truly, I say to you, the (one) believing in Me, the works that I
4160 2548 4160 3187 5130 4160 3754
ποιῶ κἀκεῖνος ποιήσει, καὶ μείζονα τούτων ποιήσει· ὅτι
do, also that one will do, and greater (than) these he will do, because
1473 4314 3962 3450 4198 5101/302 154
13 ἐγὼ πρὸς τὸν πατέρα μου πορεύομαι. καὶ ὅ τι ἂν αἰτήσητε
I to the Father of Me go. And whatever you may ask
1722 3686 3450 5124 4160 2443 1392 3962 1722
ἐν τῷ ὀνόματί μου, τοῦτο ποιήσω, ἵνα δοξασθῇ ὁ πατὴρ ἐν
in the name of Me, this I will do, that may be glorified the Father in
5207 1437/5100 154 1722 3686 3450 1473 4160
14 τῷ υἱῷ. ἐάν τι αἰτήσητε ἐν τῷ ὀνόματί μου, ἐγὼ ποιήσω.
the Son. If anything you ask in the name of Me, I will do
1437 25 3165 1785 1699 5083 1473
15 ἐὰν ἀγαπᾶτέ με, τὰς ἐντολὰς τὰς ἐμὰς τηρήσατε. καὶ ἐγὼ
16 If you love Me, commandments – My you will keep. And I
2065 3962 243 3875 1325 5213
ἐρωτήσω τὸν πατέρα, καὶ ἄλλον παράκλητον δώσει ὑμῖν,
will petition the Father, and another Paraclete He will give you.
2443/3306/3326/5216/1519 165 4151 225 3739
17 ἵνα μένῃ μεθ' ὑμῶν εἰς τὸν αἰῶνα, τὸ πνεῦμα τῆς ἀληθείας, ὃ
that He abide with you for ever, the Spirit – of Truth, whom
2889 3756 1410 2983 3754/3756/2334/846 3761 1097
ὁ κόσμος οὐ δύναται λαβεῖν, ὅτι οὐ θεωρεῖ αὐτό, οὐδὲ γινώ-
the world not is able to receive, because not it sees Him, nor knows.
846 5210 1097 846 3754/3844/5213/3306
σκει αὐτό· ὑμεῖς δὲ γινώσκετε αὐτό, ὅτι παρ' ὑμῖν μένει, καὶ
Him. you But know Him, because with you He abides, and
1722/5213 2071 3756 863 5209 3737 2064 4314
18 ἐν ὑμῖν ἔσται. οὐκ ἀφήσω ὑμᾶς ὀρφανούς· ἔρχομαι πρὸς
in you will be. Not I will leave you orphans; I am coming to
5209/2089 3397 2889 3165 2089 2334 5210 2334
19 ὑμᾶς. ἔτι μικρὸν καὶ ὁ κόσμος με οὐκέτι θεωρεῖ, ὑμεῖς δὲ θεω-
you. Yet a little and the world Me no longer beholds. you But behold
3165/3754/1473/2198 5210 2198 1722/1565 2250
20 ρεῖτέ με· ὅτι ἐγὼ ζῶ, καὶ ὑμεῖς ζήσεσθε. ἐν ἐκείνῃ τῇ ἡμέρᾳ
Me, because I live, also you will live. In that – day
1097 5210/3754/1473/1722 3962 3450 5210/1722/1698
γνώσεσθε ὑμεῖς ὅτι ἐγὼ ἐν τῷ πατρί μου, καὶ ὑμεῖς ἐν ἐμοί,
will know you that I (am) in the Father of Me, and you in Me,
2504 1722/5213 2192 1785 3450 5083 846
21 κἀγὼ ἐν ὑμῖν. ὁ ἔχων τὰς ἐντολάς μου καὶ τηρῶν αὐτάς,
and I in you. He having the commandments of Me and keeping them,
1565 2076 25 3165 25 3165 25
ἐκεῖνός ἐστιν ὁ ἀγαπῶν με· ὁ δὲ ἀγαπῶν με, ἀγαπηθήσεται
that one is the (one) loving Me; he And loving Me will be loved
5259 3962 3450 1473 25 846 1718
ὑπὸ τοῦ πατρός μου· καὶ ἐγὼ ἀγαπήσω αὐτόν, καὶ ἐμφανίσω
by the Father of Me, and I will love him, and will reveal
846 1683 3004 846 2455 3756 2469
22 αὐτῷ ἐμαυτόν. λέγει αὐτῷ Ἰούδας, οὐχ ὁ Ἰσκαριώτης,
to him Myself, says to Him Judas, not the Iscariot
2962 5101 1096 3754 5213 3195 1718 4572
Κύριε, τί γέγονεν ὅτι ἡμῖν μέλλεις ἐμφανίζειν σεαυτόν, καὶ
Lord, what has occurred that to us you are about to reveal Yourself, and
3780 2889 611 2424 2036 846 1437
23 οὐχὶ τῷ κόσμῳ ; ἀπεκρίθη ὁ Ἰησοῦς καὶ εἶπεν αὐτῷ, Ἐάν
not at all to the world? answered Jesus and said to him, If

loves Me, he will keep My word, and My Father will love him. And We will come to him and will make a dwelling-place with him. [24]The *one* who does not love Me does not keep My words — and the word which you hear is not Mine, but of the Father who sent Me!

[25]I have spoken these things to you, abiding with you; [26]but the Comforter, the Holy Spirit, whom the Father will send in My name, He shall teach you all things, and shall remind you *of* all things that I said to you. [27]I leave peace to you; My peace I give to you. I do not give to you as the world gives. Let not your heart be troubled, nor let it be timid. [28]You heard that I said to you, I am going away and I am coming *again* to you. If you loved Me, you would have rejoiced that I said, I am going to the Father; for My Father is greater than I. [29]And now I have told you before *it* occurs, that when it shall occur you may believe.

[30]I shall no longer speak many things with you, for the ruler of this world is coming, and he has nothing in Me. [31]But that the world may know that I love the Father, even as the Father commanded Me, so I do. Rise up, let us go from here.

5100 25 3165 3056 3450 5083 3962 3450
τις ἀγαπᾷ με, τὸν λόγον μου τηρήσει, καὶ ὁ πατήρ μου
anyone loves Me, the word of Me he will keep, and the Father of Me
25 846 4314 846 2064 3438
ἀγαπήσει αὐτόν, καὶ πρὸς αὐτὸν ἐλευσόμεθα, καὶ μονὴν
will love him, and to him We will come, and an abode
3844 846 4160 3361 25 3165 3056 3450
24 παρ' αὐτῷ ποιήσομεν. ὁ μὴ ἀγαπῶν με, τοὺς λόγους μου
with him we will make. the (one) not loving Me, the words of Me
3756 5083 3056 3739 191 3756 2076 1699 235
οὐ τηρεῖ· καὶ ὁ λόγος ὃν ἀκούετε οὐκ ἔστιν ἐμός, ἀλλὰ τοῦ
not keeps; and the word which you hear not is Mine, but of Him
3992 3165 3962
πέμψαντός με πατρός.
having sent Me (the) Father.

5023 2980 5213 3844/5213/3306 3875
25 Ταῦτα λελάληκα ὑμῖν παρ' ὑμῖν μένων. ὁ δὲ παράκλητος,
These things I have spoken to you with you abiding. the But Paraclete,
4151 40 3739 3992 3962/1722 3686 3450
26 τὸ Πνεῦμα τὸ Ἅγιον, ὃ πέμψει ὁ πατὴρ ἐν τῷ ὀνόματί μου,
the Spirit Holy which will send the Father in the name of Me
1565 5209 1321 3956 5279 5209 3956 3739
ἐκεῖνος ὑμᾶς διδάξει πάντα, καὶ ὑπομνήσει ὑμᾶς πάντα ἃ
that One you will teach all things, and remind you (of) all which
2036 5213 1515 863 5213 1515 1699 1325
27 εἶπον ὑμῖν. εἰρήνην ἀφίημι ὑμῖν, εἰρήνην τὴν ἐμὴν δίδωμι
I told you. Peace I leave to you; peace — My I give
5213/3756 2531 2889 1325 1473 1325 5213 3361
ὑμῖν· οὐ καθὼς ὁ κόσμος δίδωσιν, ἐγὼ δίδωμι ὑμῖν. μὴ
you; not as the world gives I give you. Not
5015 5216 2588 3366 1168 191 3754
28 ταρασσέσθω ὑμῶν ἡ καρδία, μηδὲ δειλιάτω. ἠκούσατε ὅτι
let be agitated of you the heart, nor let it be fearful. You heard that
1473 2036 5213 5217 2064 4314/5209/1487/ 25
ἐγὼ εἶπον ὑμῖν, Ὑπάγω καὶ ἔρχομαι πρὸς ὑμᾶς. εἰ ἠγαπᾶτέ
I told you: I go, and come to you. If you loved
3165 5463 302 3754 2036 4198 4314 3962
με, ἐχάρητε ἂν ὅτι εἶπον, Πορεύομαι πρὸς τὸν πατέρα·
Me, you would have rejoiced that I said, I am going to the Father,
3754 3962 3450 3187 3450/2076 3568 2046 5213 4250
29 ὅτι ὁ πατήρ μου μείζων μού ἐστι. καὶ νῦν εἴρηκα ὑμῖν πρὶν
for the Father of Me greater than Me is. And now I have told you before
1096 2443 3752 1096 4100 3756/2089 4183
30 γενέσθαι· ἵνα, ὅταν γένηται, πιστεύσητε. οὐκέτι πολλὰ
(it) happens, that when it happens you may believe. No longer many things
2980 3326 5216 2064 1063 2889 5127
λαλήσω μεθ' ὑμῶν· ἔρχεται γὰρ ὁ τοῦ κόσμου τούτου
I will speak with you, is coming for the of world this
758 1722/1698/3756/2192 3762 235 2443/1097 2889
31 ἄρχων, καὶ ἐν ἐμοὶ οὐκ ἔχει οὐδέν· ἀλλ' ἵνα γνῷ ὁ κόσμος
ruler, and in Me not He has nothing. But that may know the world
3754 25 3962 2531 1781 3427 3962
ὅτι ἀγαπῶ τὸν πατέρα, καὶ καθὼς ἐνετείλατό μοι ὁ πατήρ,
that I love the Father, and as commanded Me the Father,
3779 4160 1453 71 1782
οὕτω ποιῶ. ἐγείρεσθε, ἄγωμεν ἐντεῦθεν.
so I do. Rise, let us go from here.

CHAPTER 15

CHAPTER 15

[1]I am the True Vine, and My Father is the Vinedresser. [2]Every branch in Me not bearing fruit, He takes it away; and each one bearing fruit, He prunes so that it may bear more fruit. [3]You are already pruned because of the word which I

1473/1510 288 228 3962 3427
1 Ἐγώ εἰμι ἡ ἄμπελος ἡ ἀληθινή, καὶ ὁ πατήρ μου ὁ
I am the vine — true, and the Father of Me the
1092 2076 3956 2814/1722/1698/3361/5342 2590 142
2 γεωργός ἐστι. πᾶν κλῆμα ἐν ἐμοὶ μὴ φέρον καρπόν, αἴρει
Vinedresser is. Every branch in Me not bearing fruit, He takes
846 3956 2590 5342 2508 846 4119
αὐτό· καὶ πᾶν τὸ καρπὸν φέρον, καθαίρει αὐτό, ἵνα πλείονα
it. And each the fruit bearing, He prunes it so that more
2590 5342 2235 5210 2513 2073 1223 3004 3739
3 καρπὸν φέρῃ. ἤδη ὑμεῖς καθαροί ἐστε διὰ τὸν λόγον ὃν
fruit it may bear. Now you clean are because of the word which

have spoken to you. [4]Re-
main in Me, and I in you. As
the branch is not able to
bear fruit of itself, unless it
remain in the vine, so
neither *can* you unless you
remain in Me. [5]I am the
Vine; you *are* the branches.
He that remains in Me, and I
in him, this one bears much
fruit. For apart from Me you
are not able to do anything.
[6]Unless one remains in Me,
he is cast out as the branch,
and is dried up; and they
gather and throw them into
a fire, and they are burned.
[7]If you remain in Me, and
My words remain in you,
whatever you desire you
will ask, and it shall happen to you. [8]In this My
Father is glorified, that you
should bear much fruit; and
you will be My disciples.
[9]As the Father loved Me, I
also loved you; continue in
My love. [10]If you keep My
commandments, you will
continue in My love; as I
have kept My Father's
commandments and con-
tinue in His love. [11]I have
spoken these things to you
that My joy may abide in
you, and your joy may be
full. [12]This is My commandment, that you love one
another as I loved you.

[13]Greater love than this has
no one, that anyone should
lay down his soul for his
friends—[14]you are My
friends if you do whatever I
command you. [15]I no
longer call you slaves, for
the slave does not know
what his lord does. But I
called you friends, because
all things which I heard
from My Father I made
known to you. [16]You have
not chosen Me, but I chose
you out, and planted you,
that you should go and
should bear fruit, and your

2980 5213 3306 1722/1698 2504/1722/5213 2531
4 λελάληκα ὑμῖν. μείνατε ἐν ἐμοί,κἀγὼ ἐν ὑμῖν.καθὼς τὸ
I have spoken to you. Remain in Me, and I in you. As the
2814 3756 1410 2590 5342 575 1438 =3362= 3306
κλῆμα οὐ δύναται καρπὸν φέρειν ἀφ᾽ ἑαυτοῦ, ἐὰν μὴ μείνῃ
branch not is able fruit to bear from itself unless it remain
1722 288 3779 3761 5210/1437/3361/1722/1698/ 3306 1473
5 ἐν τῇ ἀμπέλῳ, οὕτως οὐδὲ ὑμεῖς, ἐὰν μὴ ἐν ἐμοὶ μείνητε. ἐγώ
in the vine, so neither you unless in Me you remain. I
1510 288 5210 2814 3306/1722/1698 2504 1722
εἰμι ἡ ἄμπελος, ὑμεῖς τὰ κλήματα. ὁ μένων ἐν ἐμοί, κἀγὼ ἐν
am the vine, you (are) the branches. He remaining in Me, and I in
846 3778 5322 2590 4183 3754 5565 1700/3756/ 1410
αὐτῷ, οὗτος φέρει καρπὸν πολύν· ὅτι χωρὶς ἐμοῦ οὐ δύνασθε
him, this one bears fruit much, because apart from Me not you can
4160 3762 =3362= 5100 3306/1722/1698 906 1854/5613
6 ποιεῖν οὐδέν. ἐὰν μή τις μείνῃ ἐν ἐμοί, ἐβλήθη ἔξω ὡς τὸ
do nothing. Unless anyone remains in Me, he is cast out as the
2814 3583 4863 846 1519 4442
κλῆμα, καὶ ἐξηράνθη, καὶ συνάγουσιν αὐτὰ καὶ εἰς πῦρ
branch, and is withered and they gather them and into a fire
906 2545 1437 3306 1722/1698 4487
7 βάλλουσι, καὶ καίεται. ἐὰν μείνητε ἐν ἐμοί, καὶ τὰ ῥήματά
they throw, and they are burned. If you remain in Me, and the words
3450/1722/5213/3306/3739/1437 2309 154 1096
μου ἐν ὑμῖν μείνῃ, ὃ ἐὰν θέλητε αἰτήσεσθε, καὶ γενήσεται
of Me in you remain, whatever you desire you will ask,and it shall happen
5213/1722/5129 1392 3962 3450/2443 2590 4183
8 ὑμῖν. ἐν τούτῳ ἐδοξάσθη ὁ πατήρ μου, ἵνα καρπὸν πολὺν
to you. In this is glorified the Father of Me, that fruit much
5342 2096 1698 3101 2531 25 3165
9 φέρητε· καὶ γενήσεσθε ἐμοὶ μαθηταί. καθὼς ἠγάπησέ με ὁ
you shall bear, and you will be to Me disciples. As loved Me the
3962 2504 25 5209 3306 1722 26 1699
πατήρ, κἀγὼ ἠγάπησα ὑμᾶς· μείνατε ἐν τῇ ἀγάπῃ τῇ ἐμῇ.
Father, I also loved you; remain in love — My.
1437 1785 3450 5083 3306 1722 26 3450
10 ἐὰν τὰς ἐντολάς μου τηρήσητε, μενεῖτε ἐν τῇ ἀγάπῃ μου·
If the commandments of Me you keep, you will remain in the love of Me,
2531 1473 1785 3962 3450 5083 3306
καθὼς ἐγὼ τὰς ἐντολὰς τοῦ πατρός μου τετήρηκα, καὶ μένω
as I the command of the Father of Me have kept, and remain
848 1722 26 5023 2980 5213/2443 5479
11 αὐτοῦ ἐν τῇ ἀγάπῃ. ταῦτα λελάληκα ὑμῖν, ἵνα ἡ χαρὰ ἡ
of Him in the love. These things I have spoken to you that joy
1699/1722/5213/3306 5479 5216 4137 3778 2076
12 ἐμὴ ἐν ὑμῖν μείνῃ, καὶ ἡ χαρὰ ὑμῶν πληρωθῇ. αὕτη ἐστὶν ἡ
of Me in you remain, and the joy of you may be filled. This is the
1785 1699 2443 25 240 2531 25
ἐντολὴ ἡ ἐμή, ἵνα ἀγαπᾶτε ἀλλήλους, καθὼς ἠγάπησα
commandment My, that you love one another even as I loved
5209 3187 5026 26 3762 2192/2443/5100 5590
13 ὑμᾶς. μείζονα ταύτης ἀγάπην οὐδεὶς ἔχει, ἵνα τις τὴν ψυχὴν
you. Greater than this love no one has, that anyone the soul
848/5087/5228 5384 848 5210 5384 3450 2075 1437
14 αὐτοῦ θῇ ὑπὲρ τῶν φίλων αὐτοῦ. ὑμεῖς φίλοι μου ἐστέ, ἐὰν
of him lay down for the friends of him. You friends of Me are, if
4160 3745/1473 1781 5213 3765 5209 3004 1401
15 ποιῆτε ὅσα ἐγὼ ἐντέλλομαι ὑμῖν. οὐκέτι ὑμᾶς λέγω δούλους,
you do whatever I command you. No longer you I call slaves,
3754 1401 3756/1492/5101/4160/ 848 2962 5209 2046
ὅτι ὁ δοῦλος οὐκ οἶδε τί ποιεῖ αὐτοῦ ὁ κύριος· ὑμᾶς δὲ εἴρηκα
for the slave not knows what does of him the lord; you but I called
5384 3754 3956 3739 191 3844 3962 3450 1107
φίλους, ὅτι πάντα ἃ ἤκουσα παρὰ τοῦ πατρός μου ἐγνώ-
friends because all things which I heard from the Father of Me I made
5213/3756/5210/3165/ 1585 235/1473 1586 5209
16 ρισα ὑμῖν. οὐχ ὑμεῖς με ἐξελέξασθε, ἀλλ᾽ ἐγὼ ἐξελεξάμην ὑμᾶς,
known to you.not You Me have chosen, but I chose out you,
5087 5209 2443 5210 5217 2590 5342
καὶ ἔθηκα ὑμᾶς, ἵνα ὑμεῖς ὑπάγητε καὶ καρπὸν φέρητε, καὶ ὁ
and planted you, that you should go and fruit should bear, and the

fruit remain; that whatever you should ask the Father in My name, He may give you.

[17]These things I command you, that you love one another. [18]If the world hates you, you know that it has hated Me before *it has hated* you. [19]If you were of the world, the world would love its own. But because you are not of the world, but I chose you out of the world, for this reason the world hates you. [20]Remember the word which I said to you, A slave is not greater than his lord. If they persecuted Me, they also will persecute you. If they kept My word, they also will keep yours. [21]But all these things they will do to you on account of My name, because they do not know the *One* who sent Me. [22]If I had not come and had not spoken to them, they had no sin. But now they do not have excuse as to their sin. [23]The *one* hating Me also hates My Father. [24]If I did not do the works among them which no other did, they had no sin. But now they both have seen and also have hated Me and My Father. [25]But that may be fulfilled the word that has been written in their Law, "They hated Me without a cause."

[26]And when the Comforter comes, whom I will send to you from the Father, the Spirit of truth who proceeds from the Father, that One will witness concerning Me. [27]And you also witness, because from *the* beginning you are with Me.

CHAPTER 16

[1]I have spoken these things to you so that you may not be offended. [2]They will put you out of *the*

2590 5216 3306 2443 = 3748= 154 3962 1722
καρπὸς ὑμῶν μένῃ· ἵνα ὅ τι ἂν αἰτήσητε τὸν πατέρα ἐν τῷ
fruit of you remain, that whatever you may ask the Father in the
3686 3450 1325 5213 5023 1781 5213
17 ὀνόματί μου, δῷ ὑμῖν. ταῦτα ἐντέλλομαι ὑμῖν, ἵνα
name of Me, He may give you. These things I command you, that
25 240 1487 2889 5209 3404 1097 3754
18 ἀγαπᾶτε ἀλλήλους. εἰ ὁ κόσμος ὑμᾶς μισεῖ, γινώσκετε ὅτι
you love one another. If the world you hates you know that
1691 4412 5216 3404 1487/1537 2889 2258 2889
19 ἐμὲ πρῶτον ὑμῶν μεμίσηκεν. εἰ ἐκ τοῦ κόσμου ἦτε, ὁ κόσμος
Me before you it has hated. If of the world you were, the world
302 2398 5368 3754 1537 2889 3756 2075 235 1473
ἂν τὸ ἴδιον ἐφίλει· ὅτι δὲ ἐκ τοῦ κόσμου οὐκ ἐστέ, ἀλλ' ἐγὼ
would the own have loved; that but of the world not you are, but I
1586 5209 1537 2889 1223 5124 3404 5209
ἐξελεξάμην ὑμᾶς ἐκ τοῦ κόσμου, διὰ τοῦτο μισεῖ ὑμᾶς ὁ
chose out you out of the world, therefore hates you the
2889 3421 3056 3739/1473/2036 5213 3756 2076
20 κόσμος. μνημονεύετε τοῦ λόγου οὗ ἐγὼ εἶπον ὑμῖν, Οὐκ ἔστι
world. Remember the word which I said to you: Not is
1401 3187 2962 840 1487/1691 1377 5209
δοῦλος μείζων τοῦ κυρίου αὐτοῦ. εἰ ἐμὲ ἐδίωξαν, καὶ ὑμᾶς
a slave greater than the lord of him. If Me they persecuted, also you
1377 1487 3056 3450 5083 5212
διώξουσιν· εἰ τὸν λόγον μου ἐτήρησαν, καὶ τὸν ὑμέτερον
they will persecute; if the word of Me they kept, also — yours
5083 235 5023 3956 4160 5213 1223
21 τηρήσουσιν. ἀλλὰ ταῦτα πάντα ποιήσουσιν ὑμῖν διὰ τὸ
they will keep. But these things all they will do to you because of
3686 3450 3754/3756 1492 3992 3165/1486/3361/2064
22 ὄνομά μου, ὅτι οὐκ οἴδασι τὸν πέμψαντά με. εἰ μὴ ἦλθον καὶ
name My, for not they know the (One) sending Me. Unless I came and
2980 846 166 3756 2192 3568 4392 3756
ἐλάλησα αὐτοῖς, ἁμαρτίαν οὐκ εἶχον· νῦν δὲ πρόφασιν οὐκ
spoke to them sin not they had; now but an excuse not
2192 4102 266 848 1691 3404
23 ἔχουσι περὶ τῆς ἁμαρτίας αὐτῶν. ὁ ἐμὲ μισῶν, καὶ τὸν
they have concerning the sin of them. The (one) Me hating also the
3962 3450 3404/1487 2041 3361/ 4160 1722 846 3739 3762
24 πατέρα μου μισεῖ. εἰ τὰ ἔργα μὴ ἐποίησα ἐν αὐτοῖς ἃ οὐδεὶς
Father **of Me hates.** If the works not I did among them which none
243 4160 266 3756 2192 3568 3708
ἄλλος πεποίηκεν, ἁμαρτίαν οὐκ εἶχον· νῦν δὲ καὶ ἑωράκασι
other did, sin not they had; now but both they have seen
3404 1691 3962 3450 235 2443 4137
25 καὶ μεμισήκασι καὶ ἐμὲ καὶ τὸν πατέρα μου. ἀλλ' ἵνα πλη-
and have hated both Me and the Father of Me. But that may be
3056 1125 1722 3551 848 3754 3404
ρωθῇ ὁ λόγος ὁ γεγραμμένος ἐν τῷ νόμῳ αὐτῶν ὅτι Ἐμίση-
fulfilled the word that has been written in the law of them, — They
3165 1432
σάν με δωρεάν.
hated Me freely.
3752 2064 3875 3739 1473 3992 5213 3844
26 Ὅταν δὲ ἔλθῃ ὁ παράκλητος, ὃν ἐγὼ πέμψω ὑμῖν παρὰ
when And comes the Paraclete, whom I will send to you from
3962 4151 225 3844 3962
τοῦ πατρός, τὸ πνεῦμα τῆς ἀληθείας, ὃ παρὰ τοῦ πατρὸς
the Father, the Spirit — of truth who from the Father
1607 1565 3140 4012 1700 5210
27 ἐκπορεύεται, ἐκεῖνος μαρτυρήσει περὶ ἐμοῦ· καὶ ὑμεῖς δὲ
proceeds, that One will witness concerning Me; also you and
3140 3754 575 746 3326/1700 2075
μαρτυρεῖτε, ὅτι ἀπ' ἀρχῆς μετ' ἐμοῦ ἐστε.
witness, because from (the) beginning with Me you are.

CHAPTER 16

5023 2960 5213 2443 3363 4624 656
1 Ταῦτα λελάληκα ὑμῖν, ἵνα μὴ σκανδαλισθῆτε. ἀπο-
2 These things I have spoken to you that not you may be offended. Out of

synagogue, but an hour is coming that everyone killing you will think to bear a service before God. [3]And they will do these things to you because they do not know the Father nor Me. [4]But I have spoken these things to you so that when the hour comes you may recall them, that I told you these things. But I did not say these things to you from *the* beginning because I was with you. [5]But now I am going to Him who sent Me. And not one of you asks Me, Where are you going? [6]But because I have said these things to you, grief has filled your heart. [7]But I tell you the truth, it is advantageous for you that I should go; for if I do not go away, the Comforter will not come to you. But if I go, I will send Him to you. [8]And when that One comes, *He* will convict the world concerning sin, and concerning righteousness, and concerning judgment. [9]Concerning sin, because they do not believe into Me; [10]and concerning righteousness because I am going to the Father, and you no longer see Me; [11]and concerning judgment because the ruler of this world has been judged. [12]Yet I have many things to tell you, but you are not able to bear now. [13]But when that One comes, the Spirit of truth, He will guide you into all truth; for He will not speak from Himself, but whatever He hears, He will speak; and He will announce the coming things to you. [14]That One will glorify Me, for He will receive from Mine and will announce to you. [15]All things which the Father has are Mine. For this reason I said that He receives from Mine, and will announce to you. [16]A little *while* and you do not see Me. And again a little *while,* and you will see

656 4160 5209 235 2064 5610 2443 3956
συναγώγους ποιήσουσιν ὑμᾶς· ἀλλ' ἔρχεται ὥρα, ἵνα πᾶς
(the) synagogue they will make you, but comes an hour that everyone
615 5209 1380 2999 4374 2316
3 ὁ ἀποκτείνας ὑμᾶς δόξῃ λατρείαν προσφέρειν τῷ Θεῷ. καὶ
killing you will think a service to bear before — God. And
5023 4160 5213 3754 3756 1097 3962 3761
ταῦτα ποιήσουσιν ὑμῖν, ὅτι οὐκ ἔγνωσαν τὸν πατέρα οὐδὲ
these things they will do to you because not they knew the Father nor
1691 235 5023 2980 5213 2443 3752 2064 5610
4 ἐμέ. ἀλλὰ ταῦτα λελάληκα ὑμῖν, ἵνα ὅταν ἔλθῃ ἡ ὥρα,
Me. But these things I have spoken to you that when comes the hour
3421 848 3754 1473 2036 5213 5023 5213 1537
μνημονεύητε αὐτῶν, ὅτι ἐγὼ εἶπον ὑμῖν. ταῦτα δὲ ὑμῖν ἐξ
you may recall them, that I told to you these things And to you from
746 3756 2036 3754 3326 5216 2252 3568 5217 4314
5 ἀρχῆς οὐκ εἶπον, ὅτι μεθ' ὑμῶν ἤμην. νῦν δὲ ὑπάγω πρὸς
(the) first not I said, because with you I was. now But I am going to
3992 3165 3762 1537/5216 2065 3165/4226 5217
τὸν πέμψαντά με, καὶ οὐδεὶς ἐξ ὑμῶν ἐρωτᾷ με, Ποῦ ὑπάγεις;
the (One) sending Me, and not one of you asks Me, Where are you going?
235 3754 5023 2980 5213 3077 4137 5216
6 ἀλλ' ὅτι ταῦτα λελάληκα ὑμῖν, ἡ λύπη πεπλήρωκεν ὑμῶν
But because these things I have said to you, grief has filled of you
2588 235 1473 225 3004 5213 4851
7 τὴν καρδίαν. ἀλλ' ἐγὼ τὴν ἀλήθειαν λέγω ὑμῖν· συμφέρει
the heart. But I the truth tell you, it is profitable
5213 2443/1473 565 1437/1063/3361/ 565 3875
ὑμῖν ἵνα ἐγὼ ἀπέλθω· ἐὰν γὰρ μὴ ἀπέλθω, ὁ παράκλητος
for you that I should go. if For not I go away, the Paraclete
3756 2064 4314 5209 1437 4198 3992 846
οὐκ ἐλεύσεται πρὸς ὑμᾶς· ἐὰν δὲ πορευθῶ, πέμψω αὐτὸν
not will come to you; if but I go, I will send Him
4314 5209 2064 1565 1651 2889 4012 266
8 πρὸς ὑμᾶς. καὶ ἐλθὼν ἐκεῖνος ἐλέγξει τὸν κόσμον περὶ ἁμαρ-
to you. And coming that One will convict the world concerning sin,
4012 1343 4012 2920 4012 266
9 τίας καὶ περὶ δικαιοσύνης καὶ περὶ κρίσεως· περὶ ἁμαρτίας
and concerning righteousness and concerning judgment; concerning sin
3363 3754/3756/4100 1519 1691 4012 1343 3754
10 μέν, ὅτι οὐ πιστεύουσιν εἰς ἐμέ· περὶ δικαιοσύνης δέ, ὅτι
because not they believe in Me· concerning righteousness and because
4314 3962 3450 5217 3756 2334 3165 4012
11 πρὸς τὸν πατέρα μου ὑπάγω, καὶ οὐκέτι θεωρεῖτέ με· περὶ
to the Father of Me I am going; and no longer you see Me; concerning
2920 3754 758 2889 5127 2919 2089
12 δὲ κρίσεως, ὅτι ὁ ἄρχων τοῦ κόσμου τούτου κέκριται. ἔτι
and judgment, because the ruler of world this has been judged. Yet
4183 2192 3004 5213 235 3756 1410 941 737
πολλὰ ἔχω λέγειν ὑμῖν, ἀλλ' οὐ δύνασθε βαστάζειν ἄρτι.
many things I have to tell you, but not you are able to bear now;
3752 2064 1565 4151 225 3594
13 ὅταν δὲ ἔλθῃ ἐκεῖνος, τὸ πνεῦμα τῆς ἀληθείας, ὁδηγήσει
when but comes that One, the Spirit — of truth, He will guide
5209 1519 3956 225 3756/1063 2980 575 1438
ὑμᾶς εἰς πᾶσαν τὴν ἀλήθειαν· οὐ γὰρ λαλήσει ἀφ' ἑαυτοῦ,
you into all the truth; not for will He speak from Himself,
235 3745/302 191 2980 2064 312
ἀλλ' ὅσα ἂν ἀκούσῃ λαλήσει, καὶ τὰ ἐρχόμενα ἀναγγελεῖ
but what ever He hears He will speak, and the coming things He will announce
5213 1565 1691 1392 3754/1537 1699 2983
14 ὑμῖν. ἐκεῖνος ἐμὲ δοξάσει, ὅτι ἐκ τοῦ ἐμοῦ λήψεται, καὶ
to you. That One Me will glorify because from Mine He will receive and
312 5213 3956 3745 2192 3962 1699/2076 1223
15 ἀναγγελεῖ ὑμῖν. πάντα ὅσα ἔχει ὁ πατὴρ ἐμά ἐστι· διὰ
will announce to you. All things which has the Father Mine are; for this
5124 2036 3754/1537 1699 2983 312 5213
τοῦτο εἶπον, ὅτι ἐκ τοῦ ἐμοῦ λήψεται, καὶ ἀναγγελεῖ ὑμῖν.
reason I said that from Mine He receives, and will announce to you.
3397 3756 2334 3165 3825 3397 3700 3165
16 μικρὸν καὶ οὐ θεωρεῖτέ με, καὶ πάλιν μικρὸν καὶ ὄψεσθέ με,
A little and not you behold Me, and again a little and you will see Me.

Me, because I go away to the Father.

17Then His disciples said to one another, What is this which He says to us, A little *while* and you do not see me; and again, A little and you will see Me? And, Because I go away to the Father? 18Then they said, What is this that He says, The little? We do not know what He says. 19Then Jesus knew that they desired to ask Him, and said to them, Do you seek *answers* with one another concerning this, because I said, A little *while*, and you do not see Me; and again a little and you will see Me? 20Truly, truly, I say to you that you will weep and will lament, but the world will rejoice. And you will be grieved, but your grief will become joy. 21The woman has grief when she bears, because her hour came, but when she brings forth the child, she no longer remembers the distress, because of the joy that a man was born into the world. 22And you, then, truly have grief now; but I will see you again, and your heart will rejoice; and no one takes your joy from you. 23And in that day you will ask Me nothing. Truly, truly, I say to you, Whatever you shall ask the Father in My name, He will give you. 24Until now you asked nothing in My name; ask, and you will receive, so that your joy may be full.

25I have spoken these things to you in allegories. An hour comes when I will no longer speak to you in allegories, but I will reveal the Father plainly to you. 26In that day you will ask in My name, and I do not tell you that I will petition the Father about you; 27for the

3754/1473 5217 4314 3962 2036 3767/1537
17 ὅτι ἐγὼ ὑπάγω πρὸς τὸν πατέρα. εἶπον οὖν ἐκ τῶν
because I go to the Father. said Therefore of the
3101 848 4314 240 5101/2076/5124 3004 5213
μαθητῶν αὐτοῦ πρὸς ἀλλήλους, Τί ἐστι τοῦτο ὃ λεγει ἡμῖν,
disciples of Him to one another, What is this which He tells us:
3397 3756 2334 3165 3825 3397 3700 3165
Μικρὸν καὶ οὐ θεωρεῖτέ με, καὶ πάλιν μικρὸν καὶ ὄψεσθέ με ;
A little and not you behold Me, and again a little and you will see Me?
3754/1473 5217 4314 3962 3004 3767 5124
18 καὶ ὅτι Ἐγὼ ὑπάγω πρὸς τὸν πατέρα ; ἔλεγον οὖν, Τοῦτο
Also, Because I go to the Father? they said Therefore, this
5101/2076 3004 3397 3756 1492 5101 2980 1097 3767
19 τί ἐστιν ὃ λέγει, τὸ μικρόν ; οὐκ οἴδαμεν τί λαλεῖ. ἔγνω οὖν
What is that He says, The little? do not We know what He says. knew Then
2424 3754 2309 846 2065 2036 846 4012
ὁ Ἰησοῦς ὅτι ἤθελον αὐτὸν ἐρωτᾷν, καὶ εἶπεν αὐτοῖς, Περὶ
Jesus that they desired Him to question, and said to them, Concerning
5127 2212 3326 240 3754 2036 3397 3756
τούτου ζητεῖτε μετ' ἀλλήλων, ὅτι εἶπον, Μικρὸν καὶ οὐ
this do you seek with one another, because I said, A little and not
2334 3165 3825 3397 3700 3165 281 281
20 θεωρεῖτέ με, καὶ πάλιν μικρὸν καὶ ὄψεσθέ με ; ἀμὴν ἀμὴν
you behold Me, and again a little and you will see Me? Truly, truly,
3004 5213/3754 2799 2354 5210 2889
λέγω ὑμῖν ὅτι κλαύσετε καὶ θρηνήσετε ὑμεῖς, ὁ δὲ κόσμος
I say to you that will weep and will lament you, the and world
5463 5210 3076 235 3077 5216 1519
χαρήσεται· ὑμεῖς δὲ λυπηθήσεσθε, ἀλλ' ἡ λύπη ὑμῶν εἰς
will rejoice you And will be grieved, but the grief of you into
5479 1096 1135 3752 5088 3077 2192/3754/2064
21 χαρὰν γενήσεται. ἡ γυνὴ ὅταν τίκτῃ λύπην ἔχει, ὅτι ἦλθεν
joy will become. The woman when she bears grief has, because came
5610 848 3752 1080 3813 3756/2089/3421
ἡ ὥρα αὐτῆς· ὅταν δὲ γεννήσῃ τὸ παιδίον, οὐκέτι μνημονεύει
the hour of her; when but she brings forth the child, no longer she remembers
2347 1223 5479 3754 1080 444
τῆς θλίψεως, διὰ τὴν χαρὰν ὅτι ἐγεννήθη ἄνθρωπος •εἰς
•1519 the distress, because of the joy that was born a man into
2889 5210/3767 3077 3303/3568/2192 3825
22 τὸν κόσμον. καὶ ὑμεῖς οὖν λύπην μὲν νῦν ἔχετε· πάλιν δὲ
the world. And you, therefore, grief indeed now have; again but
3700 5209 5463 5216 2588 5479
ὄψομαι ὑμᾶς, καὶ χαρήσεται ὑμῶν ἡ καρδία, καὶ τὴν χαρὰν
I will see you, and will rejoice of you the heart, and the joy
5216 3762 142 575 5216 1722 1565 2250 1691/3756
23 ὑμῶν οὐδεὶς αἴρει ἀφ' ὑμῶν. καὶ ἐν ἐκείνῃ τῇ ἡμέρᾳ ἐμὲ οὐκ
of you no one takes from you. And in that — day Me not
2065 3762 281 281 3004 5213 3754/3745/302/ 154
ἐρωτήσετε οὐδέν. ἀμὴν ἀμὴν λέγω ὑμῖν ὅτι ὅσα ἂν αἰτή-
you will question nothing. Truly, truly, I say to you that whatever you
3962 1722 3686 3450 1325 5213 2193 737
24 σητε τὸν πατέρα ἐν τῷ ὀνόματί μου, δώσει ὑμῖν. ἕως ἄρτι
may ask the Father in the name of Me, He will give you. Until now
3756 154 3762 1722 3686 3450 154 2983
οὐκ ᾐτήσατε οὐδὲν ἐν τῷ ὀνόματί μου· αἰτεῖτε, καὶ λήψεσθε,
not you asked nothing in the name of Me; ask, and you will receive
2443 5479 5216 5600/ 4137
ἵνα ἡ χαρὰ ὑμῶν ᾖ πεπληρωμένη.
that the joy of you may be filled.
5023 1722 3942 2980 5213 2064 5610 3753
25 Ταῦτα ἐν παροιμίαις λελάληκα ὑμῖν· ἔρχεται ὥρα ὅτε
These things in allegories I have spoken to you; comes an hour when
3756/2089 3942 2980 5213 235 3954 4012
οὐκέτι ἐν παροιμίαις λαλήσω ὑμῖν, ἀλλὰ παρρησίᾳ περὶ τοῦ
no longer in allegories I will speak to you, but plainly concerning the
3962 312 5213/1722/1565 2250 1722 3686 3450
26 πατρὸς ἀναγγελῶ ὑμῖν. ἐν ἐκείνῃ τῇ ἡμέρᾳ ἐν τῷ ὀνόματί μου
Father I will declare to you. In that day in the name of Me
154 3756 3004 5213 3754/1473 2065 3962
αἰτήσεσθε· καὶ οὐ λέγω ὑμῖν ὅτι ἐγὼ ἐρωτήσω τὸν πατέρα
you will ask, and not I tell you that I will petition the Father

NOTE: Frequent words not numbered: δέ(1161); καί(2531)—and, but; ὁ, ἡ, τό (3588, the)— • above word, look in verse margin for No.

Father Himself loves you,
because you have loved
Me, and have believed that I
came out from God. 28 I
came out from the Father,
and have come into the
world; I leave the world
again and go to the Father.
29 His disciples said to Him,
Behold, now You speak
plainly and You say no allegory. 30 Now we know that
You know all things and
have no need that anyone
question You. By this we
believe that You came out
from God. 31 Jesus an-
swered them, Do you be-
lieve now? 32 Behold, an
hour is coming, and now
has come, that you are
scattered, each one to *his*
own things, and you will
leave Me alone. Yet I am
not alone, because the
Father is with Me. 33 I have
spoken these things to you,
that you may have peace in
Me. You have distress in
the world; but be encour-
aged; I have overcome the
world.

4012/5216 8448 1063 3962 5368 5209 3754 5210 1691
27 περὶ ὑμῶν· αὐτὸς γὰρ ὁ πατὴρ φιλεῖ ὑμᾶς, ὅτι ὑμεῖς ἐμὲ
concerning you; Himself for the Father loves you, because you Me
5368 4100 3754/1473 3844 2316
πεφιλήκατε, καὶ πεπιστεύκατε ὅτι ἐγὼ παρὰ τοῦ Θεοῦ
have loved, and have believed that I from — God
1831 1831 3844 3962 2064 1519
28 ἐξῆλθον. ἐξῆλθον παρὰ τοῦ πατρός, καὶ ἐλήλυθα εἰς τὸν
came forth. I came forth from the Father, and have come into the
2889 3825 863 2889 4198 4314
κόσμον· πάλιν ἀφίημι τὸν κόσμον, καὶ πορεύομαι πρὸς τὸν
world; again I leave the world, and go to the
3962 3004 846 3101 848 2396 3568 3954
29 πατέρα. λέγουσιν αὐτῷ οἱ μαθηταὶ αὐτοῦ, Ἴδε, νῦν παρ-
Father. say to Him The disciples of Him, Behold, now
2980 3942 3762 3004 3568 1492
30 ρησίᾳ λαλεῖς, καὶ παροιμίαν οὐδεμίαν λέγεις. νῦν οἴδαμεν
plainly You speak, and allegory not one You say. Now we know
3754/1492 3956 3756 5532 2192 2443/5100/4571/2065 1722
ὅτι οἶδας πάντα, καὶ οὐ χρείαν ἔχεις ἵνα τίς σε ἐρωτᾷ· ἐν
that You know all things, and no need have that anyone You query; by
5129 4100 3754/575/2316 1831 611 846
31 τούτῳ πιστεύομεν ὅτι ἀπὸ Θεοῦ ἐξῆλθες. ἀπεκρίθη αὐτοῖς ὁ
this we believe that from God You came. answered them —
2424 737 4100 2400 2064 5610 3568 2064
32 Ἰησοῦς, Ἄρτι πιστεύετε; ἰδού, ἔρχεται ὥρα καὶ νῦν ἐλή-
Jesus, Now do you believe? Behold, comes an hour and now has
2443 4650 1538 1519 2398 1691 3441
λυθεν, ἵνα σκορπισθῆτε ἕκαστος εἰς τὰ ἴδια, καὶ ἐμὲ μόνον
come, that you are scattered, each one to the own things, and Me alone
863 3756/1510/3441/3754 3962 3326/1700/2076 5023
33 ἀφῆτε· καὶ οὐκ εἰμὶ μόνος, ὅτι ὁ πατὴρ μετ' ἐμοῦ ἐστι. ταῦτα
you leave; and not I am alone, because the Father with Me is. These things
2980 5213 2443/1722/1698 1515 2192 1722 2889
λελάληκα ὑμῖν, ἵνα ἐν ἐμοὶ εἰρήνην ἔχητε. ἐν τῷ κόσμῳ
I have spoken to you, that in Me peace you may have. In the world
2347 2192 235 2293 1473 3528 2889
θλίψιν ἕξετε· ἀλλὰ θαρσεῖτε, ἐγὼ νενίκηκα τὸν κόσμον.
distress you have, but be encouraged, I have overcome the world.

CHAPTER 17

1 Jesus spoke these
things, and lifted up His
eyes to Heaven, and said,
Father, the hour has come.
Glorify Your Son, that Your
Son may also glorify You.
2 As You gave to Him authority over all flesh, so that to
all which You gave to Him,
He may give to them ever-
lasting life. 3 And this is
everlasting life, that they
may know You, the only
true God, and Jesus Christ,
whom You have sent. 4 I
have glorified You on the
earth. I finished the work
that You gave Me to do.
5 And now Father, glorify Me
with Yourself, with the glory
which I had with You before
the existence of the world.
6 I revealed Your name to

CHAPTER 17

5023 2980 2424 1869 3788
1 Ταῦτα ἐλάλησεν ὁ Ἰησοῦς, καὶ ἐπῆρε τοὺς ὀφθαλμοὺς
These things spoke — Jesus, and lifting up the eyes
848 1519 3772 2036 3962 2064 5610
αὐτοῦ εἰς τὸν οὐρανόν, καὶ εἶπε, Πάτερ, ἐλήλυθεν ἡ ὥρα·
of Him to — Heaven, and said, Father, has come the hour
1392 4675 5207 2443 5207/4675/ 1392 4571 2531
2 δόξασόν σου τὸν υἱόν, ἵνα καὶ ὁ υἱός σου δοξάσῃ σε· καθὼς
glorify of You the Son, that also the Son of You may glorify You. As
1325 846 1849 3956 4561 2443 3956/3739/ 1325
ἔδωκας αὐτῷ ἐξουσίαν πάσης σαρκός, ἵνα πᾶν ὃ δέδωκας
You gave Him authority of all flesh, that all which You gave
846 1325 846 2222 166 3778 2076 166
3 αὐτῷ, δώσῃ αὐτοῖς ζωὴν αἰώνιον. αὕτη δέ ἐστιν ἡ αἰώνιος
to Him, He may give to them life everlasting. this And is everlasting
2222/2443 1097 4571 3441 228 2316 3739
ζωή, ἵνα γινώσκωσί σε τὸν μόνον ἀληθινὸν Θεόν, καὶ ὃν
life, that they may know You the only true God, and whom
649 2424 5547 1473/4571 1392 1909 1093
4 ἀπέστειλας Ἰησοῦν Χριστόν. ἐγώ σε ἐδόξασα ἐπὶ τῆς γῆς·
You sent, Jesus Christ. I You glorified on the earth,
2041 5048 3739 1325 3427/2443/ 4160 3568
5 τὸ ἔργον ἐτελείωσα ὃ δέδωκάς μοι ἵνα ποιήσω. καὶ νῦν
the work finishing which You gave to Me that I should do. And now
1392 3165/4771 3962 3844 4572 1391/3739/2192/4253
δόξασόν με σύ, πάτερ, παρὰ σεαυτῷ τῇ δόξῃ ᾗ εἶχον πρὸ
glorify Me You, Father, with Yourself with the glory that I had befo[re]
2889 1511 3844 4671 5319 4675 3686
6 τοῦ τὸν κόσμον εἶναι παρὰ σοί. ἐφανέρωσά σου τὸ ὄνομα
the of the world being with You. I revealed of You the name

the men whom You gave to
Me out of the world. They
were Yours, and You gave
them to Me; and they have
kept Your word. [7]Now they
have known that all things,
whatever You gave to Me,
are from You. [8]For the
words which You gave to
Me, I have given to them.
And they received, and truly
knew that I came out from
beside You; and they be-
lieved that You sent Me. [9]I
pray concerning them; I do
not pray concerning the
world, but for those whom
You gave to Me; for they are
Yours. [10]And all My things
are Yours, and Yours *are*
Mine; and I have been
glorified in them. [11]And I
no longer am in the world,
yet these are in the world;
and I come to You, Holy
Father; keep them in Your
name; those whom You
gave to Me, that *they* may
be one as We *are*.

[12]While I was with them
in the world, I kept them in
Your name; I guarded those
whom You gave to Me, and
not one of them was lost,
except the son of perdition,
that the Scripture might be
fulfilled. [13]And now I come
to You, and I speak these
things in the world that they
may have My joy fulfilled in
them. [14]I have given them
Your word, and the world
hated them because they
are not of the world, as I am
not of the world. [15]I do not
pray that You take them out
of the world, but that You
keep them from evil.

[16]They are not of the world,
even as I am not of the
world. [17]Sanctify them in
Your truth; Your word is
truth. [18]As You sent Me
into the world, I also sent
them into the world; [19]and I

444 3739 1325 3427/1537 2889 4674 2258
τοῖς ἀνθρώποις οὓς δέδωκάς μοι ἐκ τοῦ κόσμου· σοὶ ἦσαν,
to the men whom You gave to Me out of the world. To You they were,
1698 846 1325 3056 4675 5083
καὶ ἐμοὶ αὐτοὺς δέδωκας· καὶ τὸν λόγον σου τετηρήκασι.
and to Me them You gave; and the word of You they have kept.
3568 1097 3754 3956 3745 1325 3427 3844/4675 2076
7 νῦν ἔγνωκαν ὅτι πάντα ὅσα δέδωκάς μοι, παρὰ σοῦ ἐστιν·
Now they have known that all whatever You gave to Me from You is;
3754 4487 3739 1325 3427 1325 846 846
8 ὅτι τὰ ῥήματα ἃ δέδωκάς μοι, δέδωκα αὐτοῖς· καὶ αὐτοὶ
because the words which You gave to Me I have given to them, and they
2983 1097 230 3754 3844 4675 1831
ἔλαβον, καὶ ἔγνωσαν ἀληθῶς ὅτι παρὰ σοῦ ἐξῆλθον, καὶ
received, and knew truly that from beside You I came forth; and
4100 3754/3756/3165/ 649 1473 4012 846 2064
9 ἐπίστευσαν ὅτι σύ με ἀπέστειλας. ἐγὼ περὶ αὐτῶν ἐρωτῶ·
they believed that You Me sent. I concerning them petition;
3756/4012 2889 2065 235 4012 3739 1325 3427 3754
οὐ περὶ τοῦ κόσμου ἐρωτῶ, ἀλλὰ περὶ ὧν δέδωκάς μοι, ὅτι
not about the world I petition, but concerning whom You gave Me, for
4674/1526 1699 3956 4674 2076 4674/1699
10 σοί εἰσι· καὶ τὰ ἐμὰ πάντα σά ἐστι, καὶ τὰ σὰ ἐμά· καὶ
to You they are, and things My all Yours are, and Your things Mine; and
1392 1722 846 3756/2089/1510/1722 2889
11 δεδόξασμαι ἐν αὐτοῖς. καὶ οὐκέτι εἰμὶ ἐν τῷ κόσμῳ, καὶ
I have been glorified in them. And no longer am I in the world, and
3778 1722 2889 1526 1473 4314/4571 2064 3962
οὗτοι ἐν τῷ κόσμῳ εἰσί, καὶ ἐγὼ πρός σε ἔρχομαι. πάτερ
these in the world are, and I to You come. Father
40 5083 846 1722 3686 4675 3739 1325 3427
ἅγιε, τήρησον αὐτοὺς ἐν τῷ ὀνόματί σου, οὓς δέδωκάς μοι,
Holy, keep them in the name of You, whom You gave to Me
2443 5600/1520/2531/2249/3753/2252/3326 846 1722 2889
12 ἵνα ὦσιν ἕν, καθὼς ἡμεῖς. ὅτε ἤμην μετ᾽ αὐτῶν ἐν τῷ κόσμῳ,
that may be one, as we. When I was with them in the world,
1473 5083 846 1722 3686 4675/3739 1325 3427
ἐγὼ ἐτήρουν αὐτοὺς ἐν τῷ ὀνόματί σου· οὓς δέδωκάς μοι
I was keeping them in the name of You; whom You gave to Me
5442 3762 1537 846 622 =1508= 5207
ἐφύλαξα, καὶ οὐδεὶς ἐξ αὐτῶν ἀπώλετο, εἰ μὴ ὁ υἱὸς τῆς
I guarded, and not one of them perished, except the son —
684 2443 1124 4137 3568 4314/4571 2064
13 ἀπωλείας, ἵνα ἡ γραφὴ πληρωθῇ. νῦν δὲ πρός σε ἔρχομαι,
of perdition, that the Scripture might be fulfilled. now And to You I come,
5023 2980/1722 2889 2443 2192 5479
καὶ ταῦτα λαλῶ ἐν τῷ κόσμῳ, ἵνα ἔχωσι τὴν χαρὰν τὴν
and these things I speak in the world. that they have joy —
1699 4137 1722 848 1473 1325 846
14 ἐμὴν πεπληρωμένην ἐν αὐτοῖς. ἐγὼ δέδωκα αὐτοῖς τὸν
My having been fulfilled in them. I have given them the
3056 4675 2889 3404 846 3754/3756 1526 1537
λόγον σου, καὶ ὁ κόσμος ἐμίσησεν αὐτούς, ὅτι οὐκ εἰσὶν ἐκ
word of You, and the world hated them because not they are of
2889 1473/3756/1510/1537 2889 3756 2065
15 τοῦ κόσμου, καθὼς ἐγὼ οὐκ εἰμὶ ἐκ τοῦ κόσμου. οὐκ ἐρωτῶ
the world, even as I not am of the world. not I petition
2443 142 846 1537 2889 235 2443 5083 846
ἵνα ἄρῃς αὐτοὺς ἐκ τοῦ κόσμου, ἀλλ᾽ ἵνα τηρήσῃς αὐτοὺς
that You take them out of the world, but that You keep them
1537 4190 1537 2889 3756/1510 2531 1473/1537
16 ἐκ τοῦ πονηροῦ. ἐκ τοῦ κόσμου οὐκ εἰσί, καθὼς ἐγὼ ἐκ τοῦ
from evil. Of the world not they are, even as I of the
2889 3756/1510 37 846 1722 235 4675
17 κόσμου οὐκ εἰμί. ἁγίασον αὐτοὺς ἐν τῇ ἀληθείᾳ σου· ὁ
world not am. Sanctify them in the truth of You;
3056 4674 225 2076 2531 1691 649 1519
18 λόγος ὁ σὸς ἀλήθειά ἐστι. καθὼς ἐμὲ ἀπέστειλας εἰς τὸν
word Your truth is. Even as Me You sent into the
2889 2504 649 846 1519 2889 5228
19 κόσμον, κἀγὼ ἀπέστειλα αὐτοὺς εἰς τὸν κόσμον. καὶ ὑπὲρ
world, I also sent them into the world. And for

sanctify Myself for them, that they also may be sanctified in truth. [20]And I do not pray concerning these only, but also concerning those who will believe in Me through their word; [21]that all may be one, as You *are* in Me, Father, and I in You; that they also may be one in Us, that the world may believe that You sent Me. [22]And I have given them the glory which You have given Me, that they may be one, as We are one: [23]I in them, and You in Me, that they may be perfected in one, and that the world may know that You sent Me and loved them, even as You loved Me. [24]Father, I desire that *those* whom You have given Me, that where I am, they may also be with Me, that they may behold My glory which You gave Me, because You loved Me before *the* foundation of *the* world. [25]Righteous Father, indeed the world did not know You, but I knew You, and these have known that You sent Me. [26]And I made Your name known to them, and will make *it* known, that the love *with* which You loved Me may be in them, and I in them.

CHAPTER 18

[1]Having said these things, Jesus went out with His disciples across the winter-stream Kidron, where there was a garden into which He and His disciples entered. [2]And Judas, the *one* betraying Him, also knew the place, because Jesus many times assembled there with His disciples. [3]Therefore, receiving a cohort and under-officers from among the chief priests and the Pharisees, Judas came there with torches and lamps and weapons. [4]Then knowing

846 1473 37 1683 2443 846 5600 37
αὐτῶν ἐγὼ ἁγιάζω ἐμαυτόν, ἵνα καὶ αὐτοὶ ὦσιν ἡγιασμένοι
them I sanctify Myself, that also they may be sanctified
1722 225 3756/4012 5130 2065 3440 235 4012
20 ἐν ἀληθείᾳ. οὐ περὶ τούτων δὲ ἐρωτῶ μόνον, ἀλλὰ καὶ περὶ
in truth. not concerning these And I petition only, but also concerning
4100 1223 3056 848 1519/1691/2443 3956
21 τῶν πιστευσόντων διὰ τοῦ λόγου αὐτῶν εἰς ἐμέ· ἵνα πάντες
those who shall believe through the word of them into Me; that all
1520/5600/2531/4771/3962/1722/1698/2504/1722/4671/2443 846
ἓν ὦσι· καθὼς σύ, πάτερ, ἐν ἐμοί, κἀγὼ ἐν σοί, ἵνα καὶ αὐτοὶ
one may be, as You, Father, in Me, and I in You, that also they
1722/2254/1722/5600/2443/ 2889 4100 3754/4771/3165 649
ἐν ἡμῖν ἓν ὦσιν· ἵνα ὁ κόσμος πιστεύσῃ ὅτι σύ με ἀπέστειλας.
in Us one may be, that the world may believe that You Me sent.
1473 1391 3739 1325 3427 1325 846 2443
22 καὶ ἐγὼ τὴν δόξαν ἣν δέδωκάς μοι, δέδωκα αὐτοῖς, ἵνα
And I the glory which You have given Me have given to them, that
5600 1520 2531 2249 1520/2070/1473/1722/846 4771/1722/1698
23 ὦσιν ἕν, καθὼς ἡμεῖς ἕν ἐσμεν. ἐγὼ ἐν αὐτοῖς, καὶ σὺ ἐν ἐμοί,
they one, as We one are; I in them, and You in Me,
may be 5600/ 5048 1519/1722 2443 1097 2889 3754
2443 ἵνα ὦσι τετελειωμένοι εἰς ἕν, καὶ ἵνα γινώσκῃ ὁ κόσμος ὅτι
that they may be perfected into one, and that may know the world that
4771/3165/ 649 25 846 2531 1691 25
σύ με ἀπέστειλας, καὶ ἠγάπησας αὐτούς, καθὼς ἐμὲ ἠγάπη-
You Me sent and loved them even as Me You
3962 3739 1325 3427 2309 2443 3699/1510/1473
24 σας. πάτερ, οὓς δέδωκάς μοι, θέλω ἵνα ὅπου εἰμὶ ἐγώ,
loved. Father, whom You have given to Me, I desire that where am I,
2548 5600 3326/1700 2443 2334 1391 1699
κἀκεῖνοι ὦσι μετ' ἐμοῦ· ἵνα θεωρῶσι τὴν δόξαν τὴν ἐμήν,
those also may be with Me, that they may behold glory — My,
3799 1325 3427/3754 25 3165 4253 2602 2889
ἣν ἔδωκάς μοι, ὅτι ἠγάπησάς με πρὸ καταβολῆς κόσμου.
which You gave Me because You loved Me before foundation of (the) world.
3962 1342 2889 4571/3756/1097 1473 4571 1097
25 πάτερ δίκαιε, καὶ ὁ κόσμος σε οὐκ ἔγνω, ἐγὼ δέ σε ἔγνων,
Father Righteous, indeed the world You not knew, I but You knew,
3778 1097 3754/4771/3165/ 649 1107
26 καὶ οὗτοι ἔγνωσαν ὅτι σύ με ἀπέστειλας· καὶ ἐγνώρισα
and these knew that You Me sent; and I made known
846 3686 4675 1107 2443 26 3739
αὐτοῖς τὸ ὄνομά σου, καὶ γνωρίσω· ἵνα ἡ ἀγάπη, ἣν
to them the name of You, and will make known; that the love (with)
25 3165/1722/846/5600/2504/1722/846 which
ἠγάπησάς με, ἐν αὐτοῖς ᾖ, κἀγὼ ἐν αὐτοῖς.
You loved Me in them may be, and I in them.

CHAPTER 18

5023 2036 2424 1831 4862 3101 848
1 Ταῦτα εἰπὼν ὁ Ἰησοῦς ἐξῆλθε σὺν τοῖς μαθηταῖς αὐτοῦ
These things having said Jesus went forth with the disciples of Him
4008 5493 2748 3699/3739/2779 1519/3739
πέραν τοῦ χειμάρρου τῶν Κέδρων, ὅπου ἦν κῆπος, εἰς ὃν
across the torrent — of Kidron, where was a garden, into which
1525 846 3101 848 1492 2455
2 εἰσῆλθεν αὐτὸς καὶ οἱ μαθηταὶ αὐτοῦ. ᾔδει δὲ καὶ Ἰούδας, ὁ
entered He and the disciples of Him. knew And also Judas, he
3860 846 5117 3754 4178 4863
παραδιδοὺς αὐτόν, τὸν τόπον· ὅτι πολλάκις συνήχθη ὁ
betraying Him, the place, because many times assembled
2424 1563 3326 3101 848 2455 2983
3 Ἰησοῦς ἐκεῖ μετὰ τῶν μαθητῶν αὐτοῦ. ὁ οὖν Ἰούδας, λαβὼν
Jesus there with the disciples of Him. Therefore Judas, receiving
4686 1537 749 5330 5257
τὴν σπεῖραν, καὶ ἐκ τῶν ἀρχιερέων καὶ Φαρισαίων ὑπηρέτας,
the band, and from the chief priests and the Pharisees officers,
2064 1563/3326 5322 2985 3696 2424
4 ἔρχεται ἐκεῖ μετὰ φανῶν καὶ λαμπάδων καὶ ὅπλων. Ἰησοῦς
comes there with torches and lamps and weapons. Jesus

all the things come upon
Him, going forth Jesus
said to them, Whom do
you seek? [5]They answered
Him, Jesus the Nazarene.
Jesus said to them, I AM!
And Judas, the *one* betraying Him, also stood with
them. [6]Then when He
said to them, I AM, they
departed into the rear and
fell to the ground. [7]Then
again he asked, Whom do
you seek? And they said,
Jesus the Nazarene.
[8]Jesus answered, I told
you that I AM. Then if you
seek Me, allow these to
depart, — that the word
might be fulfilled which He
said, "*Of* those whom You
gave to Me, I lost not one
of them.

[10]Then having a sword,
Simon Peter drew it and
struck the slave of the high
priest, and cut off his right
ear. And the name of the
slave *was* Malchus. [11]Then
Jesus said to Peter, Put
your sword into the sheath;
the cup which the Father
has given Me, shall I not at
all drink it?

[12]Then the cohort, even
the commander and the
under-officers of the Jews
together seized Jesus and
bound Him. [13]And they
led Him away first to
Annas, for he was *the*
father-in-law of Caiaphas,
who was high priest that
year. [14]And Caiaphas was
the *one* who *had* given
counsel to the Jews that it
was advantageous *for* one
man to perish for the
people.

[15]And Simon Peter and
another disciple followed
Jesus, and that disciple
was known to the high
priest and entered together
with Jesus into the court of
the high priest. [16]But Peter
stood at the door outside.

3767 1492 3956 2064 1909 846 1831 2036
οὖν, εἰδὼς πάντα τὰ ἐρχόμενα ἐπ' αὐτόν, ἐξελθὼν εἶπεν
Then, knowing all the things coming on Him, going forth said
846 5101 2212 611 846 2424
5 αὐτοῖς, Τίνα ζητεῖτε; ἀπεκρίθησαν αὐτῷ, Ἰησοῦν τὸν
to them, Whom do you seek? They answered Him, Jesus the
3480 3004 846 2424 1473/1510 2476
Ναζωραῖον. λέγει αὐτοῖς ὁ Ἰησοῦς, Ἐγώ εἰμι. εἱστήκει δὲ
Nazarene. tells them Jesus, I AM. stood And
2455 3860 846 3326 846 5613/3767/2036
6 καὶ Ἰούδας ὁ παραδιδοὺς αὐτὸν μετ' αὐτῶν. ὡς οὖν εἶπεν
also Judas, the (one) betraying Him, with them. when Then He told
846 3754 1473 1510 565 1519 3694 4098
αὐτοῖς ὅτι Ἐγώ εἰμι, ἀπῆλθον εἰς τὰ ὀπίσω, καὶ ἔπεσον
them, — I AM, they went away into the rear, and fell
5476 3825 3767 846 1905 5101 2212
7 χαμαί. πάλιν οὖν αὐτοὺς ἐπηρώτησε, Τίνα ζητεῖτε; οἱ δὲ
to earth. Again, then, He inquired, Whom do you seek? they And
2036 2424 3480 611 2424 2036
8 εἶπον, Ἰησοῦν τὸν Ναζωραῖον. ἀπεκρίθη ὁ Ἰησοῦς, Εἶπον
said, Jesus the Nazarene. answered Jesus, I told
1487 5213/3754/1473/1510*/3767/1691 2212 863 5128 5217
ὑμῖν ὅτι ἐγώ εἰμι· εἰ οὖν ἐμὲ ζητεῖτε, ἄφετε τούτους ὑπάγειν·
you that I AM. If, then, Me you seek, allow these to go;
2443 4137 3056 3739 2036 3754/3739 1325 3427 3756
9 ἵνα πληρωθῇ ὁ λόγος ὃν εἶπεν ὅτι Οὓς δέδωκάς μοι, οὐκ
that might be fulfilled the word which said, — Whom You gave to Me, not
622 1537 846 3762 4613/3756 4074 2192 3162
10 ἀπώλεσα ἐξ αὐτῶν οὐδένα. Σίμων οὖν Πέτρος ἔχων μάχαιραν
I lost (any) of them, no one. Simon Then Peter having a sword,
1670 846 3817 749 1401
εἵλκυσεν αὐτήν, καὶ ἔπαισε τὸν τοῦ ἀρχιερέως δοῦλον, καὶ
drew it, and struck the of the high priest slave, and
609 848 5621 1188 2258 3686 1401
ἀπέκοψεν αὐτοῦ τὸ ὠτίον τὸ δεξιόν. ἦν δὲ ὄνομα τῷ δούλῳ
cut off of him the ear — right. was And a name to the slave,
3124 2036/3756 2424 4074 906 3162
11 Μάλχος. εἶπεν οὖν ὁ Ἰησοῦς τῷ Πέτρῳ, Βάλε τὴν μάχαιράν
Malchus. said Then — Jesus to Peter, Put the sword
4675/1519 2336 4221 3739 1325 3427 3962 =3364=
σου εἰς τὴν θήκην· τὸ ποτήριον ὃ δέδωκέ μοι ὁ πατήρ, οὐ μὴ
of you into the sheath; the cup which has given Me the Father, in no way
4095 846
πίω αὐτό;
shall I drink it?
3767 4686 5506 5257 2453
12 Ἡ οὖν σπεῖρα καὶ ὁ χιλίαρχος καὶ οἱ ὑπηρέται τῶν Ἰου-
the Then band and the chiliarch and the officers of the
4815 2424 1210 846 520
13 δαίων συνέλαβον τὸν Ἰησοῦν, καὶ ἔδησαν αὐτόν, καὶ ἀπή-
Jews together seized Jesus, and bound Him, and led
846 4314 452 4412 2258/1063 3995
γαγον αὐτὸν πρὸς Ἄνναν πρῶτον· ἦν γὰρ πενθερὸς τοῦ
away Him to Annas first, he was for father-in-law —
2533 3739/2258 749 1763 1565 2258 2533
14 Καϊάφα, ὃς ἦν ἀρχιερεὺς τοῦ ἐνιαυτοῦ ἐκείνου. ἦν δὲ Καϊάφας
of Caiaphas, who was high priest — of year that. was And Caiaphas
4823 2453 3754 4851 1520 444
ὁ συμβουλεύσας τοῖς Ἰουδαίοις, ὅτι συμφέρει ἕνα ἄνθρωπον
the (one) having advised the Jews that it is profitable for one man
622 5228 2992
ἀπολέσθαι ὑπὲρ τοῦ λαοῦ.
to perish for the people.
190 2424 4613 4074 243 3101
15 Ἠκολούθει δὲ τῷ Ἰησοῦ Σίμων Πέτρος, καὶ ἄλλος μαθητής.
followed And — Jesus Simon Peter and another disciple.
3101 1565 2258 1110 749 4897
ὁ δὲ μαθητὴς ἐκεῖνος ἦν γνωστὸς τῷ ἀρχιερεῖ, καὶ συνεισῆλθε
And disciple that was known to the high priest, and went in with
2424 1519 833 749 4074 2476
16 τῷ Ἰησοῦ εἰς τὴν αὐλὴν τοῦ ἀρχιερέως· ὁ δὲ Πέτρος εἱστήκει
Jesus into the court of the high priest; —but Peter stood

The other disciple who was known to the high priest therefore went out and spoke to the doorkeeper, and brought Peter in. 17 Then the maidservant, the doorkeeper, said to Peter, Are you not also of the disciples of this man? That one said, I am not. 18 Now the slaves and the under-officers were standing and warming, having made a fire of coals, for it was cold; and Peter was with them, standing and warming *himself*.

19 Then the high priest questioned Jesus about His disciples and about His teaching. 20 Jesus answered him, I publicly spoke to the world; I continually taught in the synagogue and in the temple where the Jews continually come together, and I spoke nothing in secret. 21 Why do you question Me? Question those hearing what I spoke to them: behold, these know what I said! 22 But *on* His having said these things, one of the under-officers standing by gave Jesus a blow with the palm, saying, Do you answer the high priest this way? 23 Jesus answered him, If I spoke evilly, bear witness concerning the evil; but if well, why do you strike Me? 24 Then Annas sent Him forth, having bound *Him*, to Caiaphas the high priest.

25 Now Simon Peter was standing and warming *himself*. They therefore said to him, Are you not also of His disciples? He denied and said, I am not. 26 One of the slaves of the high priest, being a relative *of him* of whom Peter cut off the ear, said, Did I not see you in the garden with Him? 27 Again then Peter denied, and

4314 2374/1854 1831 3767 3101 243 3739/2258
πρὸς τῇ θύρα ἔξω. ἐξῆλθεν οὖν ὁ μαθητὴς ὁ ἄλλος ὃς ἦν
at the door outside, went out Then the disciple other who was
1110 749 2036 2377 1521
γνωστὸς τῷ ἀρχιερεῖ, καὶ εἶπε τῇ θυρωρῷ, καὶ εἰσήγαγε τὸν
known to the high priest, and spoke to the portress, and brought in —
4074 3004 3767 3814 2377 4074 3361
17 Πέτρον. λέγει οὖν ἡ παιδίσκη ἡ θυρωρὸς τῷ Πέτρῳ, Μὴ καὶ
Peter. says Then the maidservant, the portress, to Peter, Not also
4771/1537 3101 1488 444 5127 3004 1565
σὺ ἐκ τῶν μαθητῶν εἶ τοῦ ἀνθρώπου τούτου; λέγει ἐκεῖνος,
you of the disciples are — of man this? says That one
3756/1510 2476 1401 5257 439
18 Οὐκ εἰμί. εἱστήκεισαν δὲ οἱ δοῦλοι καὶ οἱ ὑπηρέται ἀνθρακιὰν
Not I am. were standing And the slaves and the officers, a fire of coals
4160 3754 5592 2258 2328 2258 3326
πεποιηκότες, ὅτι ψῦχος ἦν, καὶ ἐθερμαίνοντο· ἦν δὲ μετ'
having made, because cold it was, and were warming; was and with
846 4074 2476 2328
αὐτῶν ὁ Πέτρος ἑστὼς καὶ θερμαινόμενος.
them — Peter standing and warming (himself)
3767 749 2065 2424 4012 3101
19 Ὁ οὖν ἀρχιερεὺς ἠρώτησε τὸν Ἰησοῦν περὶ τῶν μαθητῶν
the Then high priest questioned — Jesus concerning the disciples
848 4012 1322 848 611 846
20 αὐτοῦ, καὶ περὶ τῆς διδαχῆς αὐτοῦ. ἀπεκρίθη αὐτῷ ὁ
of Him, and concerning the teaching of Him. answered him —
2424 1473 3954 2980 2889 1473 3842
Ἰησοῦς, Ἐγὼ παρρησίᾳ ἐλάλησα τῷ κόσμῳ· ἐγὼ πάντοτε
Jesus, I publicly spoke to the world; I always
1321 1722 4864 1722 2411 3699 3842
ἐδίδαξα ἐν τῇ συναγωγῇ καὶ ἐν τῷ ἱερῷ, ὅπου πάντοτε οἱ
taught in the synagogue and in the Temple, where always the
2453 4905 1722 2927 2980 3762 5101/3165
21 Ἰουδαῖοι συνέρχονται, καὶ ἐν κρυπτῷ ἐλάλησα οὐδέν. τί με
Jews come together, and in secret I spoke nothing. Why Me
1905 1905 191 5101 2980 846
ἐπερωτᾷς; ἐπερώτησον τοὺς ἀκηκοότας, τί ἐλάλησα αὐτοῖς·
do you question? Question those having heard what I spoke to them.
2396 3778 1492 3739 2036 1473 5023 848 2036
22 ἴδε, οὗτοι οἴδασιν ἃ εἶπον ἐγώ. ταῦτα δὲ αὐτοῦ εἰπόντος,
Behold, these know what said I. these things And He saying,
1520 5257 3933 1325 4475 2424
εἷς τῶν ὑπηρετῶν παρεστηκὼς ἔδωκε ῥάπισμα τῷ Ἰησοῦ,
one of the officers standing by gave a blow — to Jesus,
2036 3779 611 749 611 846
23 εἰπών, Οὕτως ἀποκρίνῃ τῷ ἀρχιερεῖ; ἀπεκρίθη αὐτῷ ὁ
saying, Thus answer you the high priest? answered to him,
2424 1487 2560 2980 3140 4012 2556
Ἰησοῦς, Εἰ κακῶς ἐλάλησα, μαρτύρησον περὶ τοῦ κακοῦ·
Jesus, If evilly I spoke, bear witness concerning the evil;
1487 2573 5101/3165/1194 649 3767 846 452
24 εἰ δὲ καλῶς, τί με δέρεις; ἀπέστειλεν οὖν αὐτὸν ὁ Ἄννας
if but well, why Me do you beat? Sent therefore Him — Annas
1210 4314 2533 749
δεδεμένον πρὸς Καϊάφαν τὸν ἀρχιερέα.
being bound to Caiaphas the high priest.
2258 4613 4074 2476 2328 2036 3767
25 Ἦν δὲ Σίμων Πέτρος ἑστὼς καὶ θερμαινόμενος· εἶπον οὖν
was And Simon Peter standing and warming himself. they said Then
846 3361 4771/1537 3101 848 1488 720
αὐτῷ, Μὴ καὶ σὺ ἐκ τῶν μαθητῶν αὐτοῦ εἶ; ἠρνήσατο
to him, Not also you of the disciples of him are? denied
1565 2036 3756/1510 3004 1519/1537 1401
26 ἐκεῖνος, καὶ εἶπεν, Οὐκ εἰμί. λέγει εἷς ἐκ τῶν δούλων τοῦ
That one, and said, not I am. says One of the slaves of the
749 4773 5607 3739 609 4074 5621
ἀρχιερέως, συγγενὴς ὢν οὗ ἀπέκοψε Πέτρος τὸ ὠτίον,
high priest, a relative being of whom cut off Peter the ear,
3756/1473/4571/1492/1722 2779 3326 846 3825 3767
27 Οὐκ ἐγώ σε εἶδον ἐν τῷ κήπῳ μετ' αὐτοῦ; πάλιν οὖν
Not I you did see in the garden with Him? again Then

immediately a cock crowed.

[28]Then they led Jesus from Caiaphas into the praetorium, and it was early. And they did not enter into the praetorium, that they might not be defiled, but that they might eat the Passover. [29]Then Pilate went out to them and said, What accusation do you bring against this man? [30]They answered and said to him, If this one were not an evildoer, then we would not have delivered him to you. [31]Then Pilate said to them, You take him and judge him according to your *own* Law. Then the Jews said to him, It is not lawful for us to put anyone to death—[32]that the word of Jesus which He said might be fulfilled, signifying by what kind *of* death He was about to die.

[33]Then Pilate again went into the praetorium and called Jesus, and said to Him, Are you the king of the Jews? [34]Jesus answered him, Do you say this from yourself, or did others tell you about Me? [35]Pilate answered, Am I a Jew? Your nation, even the chief priests, delivered you up to me! What did you do? [36]Jesus answered, My kingdom is not of this world. If My kingdom were of this world, My servants would have fought, that I might not be delivered up to the Jews. But now My kingdom is not from here. [37]Then Pilate said to Him, Aare you really a king? Jesus answered, You say that I am a king. For this *purpose* I have been born, and for this

720 4074 2112 220 5455
ἠρνήσατο ὁ Πέτρος, καὶ εὐθέως ἀλέκτωρ ἐφώνησεν.
denied — Peter, and at once a cock sounded.
71 3767 2424 575 2533 1519 4232
28 Ἄγουσιν οὖν τὸν Ἰησοῦν ἀπὸ τοῦ Καϊάφα εἰς τὸ πραιτώ-
they lead Then — Jesus from — Caiaphas to the praetorium;
2258 4405 846 3756 1525 1519 4232
ριον· ἦν δὲ πρωΐα, καὶ αὐτοὶ οὐκ εἰσῆλθον εἰς τὸ πραιτώ-
it was and early; and they did not enter into the praetorium,
2443/3361 3392 235 2443 5315 3957 1831
29 ριον, ἵνα μὴ μιανθῶσιν, ἀλλ' ἵνα φάγωσι τὸ πάσχα. ἐξῆλθεν
lest they be defiled, but that they may eat the Passover. went out
3767 4091 4314 846 2036 5101 2724
οὖν ὁ Πιλάτος πρὸς αὐτούς, καὶ εἶπε, Τίνα κατηγορίαν
Therefore Pilate to them, and said, What accusation
5342 2996 444 5127 611 2036
30 φέρετε κατὰ τοῦ ἀνθρώπου τούτου; ἀπεκρίθησαν καὶ εἶπον
bring you against man this? They answered and said
846 1487/3361/2258/3778 2555 3756/302/4671 3860
αὐτῷ, Εἰ μὴ ἦν οὗτος κακοποιός, οὐκ ἂν σοι παρεδώκαμεν
to him, Unless was this one an evildoer, not then to you we had delivered
846 2036 3767 846 4091 2983 846 5210
31 αὐτόν. εἶπεν οὖν αὐτοῖς ὁ Πιλάτος, Λάβετε αὐτὸν ὑμεῖς, καὶ
him. said Then to them Pilate, take him You, and
2596 3551 5216 2919 846 2036 3767 846
κατὰ τὸν νόμον ὑμῶν κρίνατε αὐτόν. εἶπον οὖν αὐτῷ οἱ
according to the law of you judge him. said Then to him the
2453 2254/3756 1832 615 3762 2443 3056
32 Ἰουδαῖοι, Ἡμῖν οὐκ ἔξεστιν ἀποκτεῖναι οὐδένα· ἵνα ὁ λόγος
Jews, for us Not it is lawful to put to death no one; that the word
— 2424 4137 3739/2036 4591 4169 2288
τοῦ Ἰησοῦ πληρωθῇ, ὃν εἶπε, σημαίνων ποίῳ θανάτῳ
— of Jesus might be fulfilled, which He said, signifying by what kind (of) death
3195 599
ἤμελλεν ἀποθνήσκειν.
He was about to die.

1525 3767/1519 4232 3825 4091
33 Εἰσῆλθεν οὖν εἰς τὸ πραιτώριον πάλιν ὁ Πιλάτος, καὶ
entered Then into the praetorium again Pilate, and
5455 2424 2036 846 4771/1488 935
ἐφώνησε τὸν Ἰησοῦν, καὶ εἶπεν αὐτῷ, Σὺ εἶ ὁ βασιλεὺς τῶν
called Jesus, and said to Him, you Are the king of the
2453 611 846 2424 575 1438 4771 5124
34 Ἰουδαίων; ἀπεκρίθη αὐτῷ ὁ Ἰησοῦς, Ἀφ' ἑαυτοῦ σὺ τοῦτο
Jews? answered him Jesus, From yourself you this
3004/2228/243 4671 2036 4012/1700 611 4091
35 λέγεις, ἢ ἄλλοι σοι εἶπον περὶ ἐμοῦ; ἀπεκρίθη ὁ Πιλάτος,
say, or others you told about Me? answered Pilate,
3385 1473 2453 1510 1484 4674 749
Μήτι ἐγὼ Ἰουδαῖός εἰμι; τὸ ἔθνος τὸ σὸν καὶ οἱ ἀρχιερεῖς
Not I a Jew am? nation Your and the chief priests
3860 4571/1698/5101 4100 611 2424
36 παρέδωκάν σε ἐμοί· τί ἐποίησας; ἀπεκρίθη ὁ Ἰησοῦς, Ἡ
delivered up You to me; what did you do? answered — Jesus,
932 1699/3756/2076/1537 2889 5127 1487/1537
βασιλεία ἡ ἐμὴ οὐκ ἔστιν ἐκ τοῦ κόσμου τούτου· εἰ ἐκ τοῦ
kingdom My not is of world this; If of
2889 5127 2258 932 1699 5257 302 1699
κόσμου τούτου ἦν ἡ βασιλεία ἡ ἐμή, οἱ ὑπηρέται ἂν οἱ ἐμοὶ
world this was kingdom My, servants would My
75 2443/3361 3860 2453 3568
ἠγωνίζοντο, ἵνα μὴ παραδοθῶ τοῖς Ἰουδαίοις· νῦν δὲ ἡ
have fought, that not I should be delivered to the Jews. now But
932 1699/3756/2076 1782 2036/3767/846 4091
37 βασιλεία ἡ ἐμὴ οὐκ ἔστιν ἐντεῦθεν. εἶπεν οὖν αὐτῷ ὁ Πιλάτος,
kingdom My not is from here. said Then to Him Pilate,
3766 935 1488/4771 611 2424 4771 3004 3754
Οὐκοῦν βασιλεὺς εἶ σύ; ἀπεκρίθη ὁ Ἰησοῦς, Σὺ λέγεις ὅτι
Really not a king are you? answered — Jesus, You say that
935 1510/1473/1473/1519 5124 1080 1519 5124
βασιλεύς εἰμι ἐγώ. ἐγὼ εἰς τοῦτο γεγέννημαι, καὶ εἰς τοῦτο
a king am I I for this have been born, and for this

I have come into the world: that I might witness to the Truth. Everyone being of the Truth hears My voice. [38]Pilate said to Him, What is truth?

And saying this, he again went out to the Jews and said to them, I do not find even one crime in him! [39]But there is a common custom to you that I should release one *prisoner* to you at the Passover. Therefore, you decide: should I release the king of the Jews to you? [40]Then all cried out again, saying, Not this one, but Barabbas! But Barabbas was a robber.

CHAPTER 19

[1]Then Pilate then took Jesus and flogged *Him*. [2]And having plaited a wreath out of thorns, the soldiers put *it* on His head. And they threw a purple mantle around Him, [3]and said, Hail, king of the Jews! And they gave Him blows with the palm. [4]Then Pilate went outside again and said to them, Behold, I bring him out to you, that you may know that I do not find even one crime in him! [5]Then Jesus came outside, wearing the thorny wreath and the purple mantle. And he said to them, Behold, the Man! [6]Then when the chief priests and the under-officers saw Him, they cried out, saying, Crucify! Crucify! Pilate said to them, You take him and crucify *him*, for I do not find *one* crime in him! [7]Then the Jews answered him, We have a Law, and according to our Law he ought to die, because he made himself Son of God! [8]Then when Pilate

2064 1519 2889 2443 3140 225 3956
ἐλήλυθα εἰς τὸν κόσμον, ἵνα μαρτυρήσω τῇ ἀληθείᾳ. πᾶς ὁ
I have come into the world, that I might witness to the truth, everyone
5607/1537 225 191 3450 5456 3004 846
38 ὢν ἐκ τῆς ἀληθείας ἀκούει μου τῆς φωνῆς. λέγει αὐτῷ ὁ
being of the truth hears of Me the voice. says to Him
4091 5101 2076 225
Πιλάτος, Τί ἐστιν ἀλήθεια ;
Pilate, What is truth?
5124 2036 3825 1831 4314 2453
Καὶ τοῦτο εἰπών, πάλιν ἐξῆλθε πρὸς τοὺς Ἰουδαίους, καὶ
And this having said, again he went out to the Jews, and
3004 846 1473 3762 156 2147 1722 846 2076
39 λέγει αὐτοῖς, Ἐγὼ οὐδεμίαν αἰτίαν εὑρίσκω ἐν αὐτῷ. ἔστι
tells them, I not one crime find in him. is
4914 5213 2443/1520/5213 630 1722 3957
δὲ συνήθεια ὑμῖν, ἵνα ἕνα ὑμῖν ἀπολύσω ἐν τῷ πάσχα·
But a custom to you, that one to you I should release at the Passover;
1014 3767/5213 630 935 2453
βούλεσθε οὖν ὑμῖν ἀπολύσω τὸν βασιλέα τῶν Ἰουδαίων ;
decide you, then, to you I should release the king of the Jews?
2905 3767 3825 3956 3004 3361 5125 235
40 ἐκραύγασαν οὖν πάλιν πάντες, λέγοντες, Μὴ τοῦτον, ἀλλὰ
cried out Then again all, saying, Not this one, but
912 2258 912 3027
τὸν Βαραββᾶν· ἦν δὲ ὁ Βαραββᾶς λῃστής.
— Barabbas. was But Barabbas a robber.

CHAPTER 19

3767 2983 4091 2424 3146
1 Τότε οὖν ἔλαβεν ὁ Πιλάτος τὸν Ἰησοῦν, καὶ ἐμαστίγωσε.
Then, therefore, took Pilate — Jesus and scourged (Him).
4757 4120 4735 1537 173 2007
2 καὶ οἱ στρατιῶται πλέξαντες στέφανον ἐξ ἀκανθῶν ἐπέθηκαν
And the soldiers having plaited a wreath out of thorns put (it) on
848 2776 2440 4210 4016 846
αὐτοῦ τῇ κεφαλῇ, καὶ ἱμάτιον πορφυροῦν περιέβαλον αὐτόν,
of Him the head, and a garment purple threw around Him;
3004 5463 935 2453 1325
3 καὶ ἔλεγον, Χαῖρε, ὁ βασιλεὺς τῶν Ἰουδαίων· καὶ ἐδίδουν
and said, Hail, king of the Jews; and they gave
846 4475 1831 3767 3825 1854 4091
4 αὐτῷ ῥαπίσματα. ἐξῆλθεν οὖν πάλιν ἔξω ὁ Πιλάτος, καὶ
Him slaps. went out Then again outside Pilate and
3004 846 2396 71 5213 846 1854/2443 1097 3754/1722
λέγει αὐτοῖς, Ἴδε, ἄγω ὑμῖν αὐτὸν ἔξω, ἵνα γνῶτε ὅτι ἐν
said to them. Behold, I bring to you him out, that you may know that in
846 3762 156 2147 1831 3767 2424 1854
5 αὐτῷ οὐδεμίαν αἰτίαν εὑρίσκω. ἐξῆλθεν οὖν ὁ Ἰησοῦς ἔξω,
him not one crime I find. came out Then Jesus outside,
5409 174 4735 4210 2440
φορῶν τὸν ἀκάνθινον στέφανον καὶ τὸ πορφυροῦν ἱμάτιον.
bearing the thorny wreath and the purple garment.
3004 846 2396 444 3753/3768/1492 846
6 καὶ λέγει αὐτοῖς, Ἴδε, ὁ ἄνθρωπος. ὅτε οὖν εἶδον αὐτὸν οἱ
And he says to them, Behold, the man! when Then saw Him the
749 5257 2905 3004 4717
ἀρχιερεῖς καὶ οἱ ὑπηρέται, ἐκραύγασαν λέγοντες, Σταύρω-
chief priests and the officers, they cried out saying Crucify!
4717 3004 846 4091 2983 846
σον, σταύρωσον. λέγει αὐτοῖς ὁ Πιλάτος, Λάβετε αὐτὸν
Crucify! says to them Pilate, Take Him
5210 4717 1473/1063/3756/2147 1722 846 156
ὑμεῖς καὶ σταυρώσατε· ἐγὼ γὰρ οὐχ εὑρίσκω ἐν αὐτῷ αἰτίαν.
you, and crucify, I for not do find in him a crime.
611 846 2453 2249 3551 2192
7 ἀπεκρίθησαν αὐτῷ οἱ Ἰουδαῖοι, Ἡμεῖς νόμον ἔχομεν, καὶ
answered him The Jews, We a law have, and
2596 3551 2257 3784 599 3754 1438 5207
κατὰ τὸν νόμον ἡμῶν ὀφείλει ἀποθανεῖν, ὅτι ἑαυτὸν υἱὸν τοῦ
according to the law of us he ought to die, because himself Son —

heard this word, he was more afraid, 9and entered into the praetorium again, and said to Jesus, From where are you? But Jesus id not give him an answer. 10So Pilate said to Him, Do you not speak to me? Do you not know that I have authority to crucify you, and I have authority to release you? 11Jesus answered, You would not have authority against Me, not any, if it had not been given to you from above. Because of this he delivering Me to you has a greater sin. 12From this *time* Pilate sought to release Him. But the Jews cried oute, saying, If you release this one you are not a friend of Caesar. Everyone making himself a king speaks against Caesar.

13Then hearing this word, Pilate led Jesus out. And *he* sat down on the judgment seat, at a place called *The* Pavement, but in Hebrew, Gabbatha. 14And it was *the* preparation of the Passover, and about *the* sixth hour. And he said to the Jews, Behold, your king! 15But they cried out, Away, Away! Crucify him! Pilate said to them, Shall I crucify your king? The chief priests answered, We have no king except Caesar. 16Therefore, then, he delivered Him up to them, that He might be crucified.

And they took Jesus and led *Him* away.

17And He went out bearing His cross, to *the* place called Of a Skull; which is called in Hebrew, Golgotha; 18where they crucified Him, and two others with Him, on this side and on that side, and Jesus in the

2316 4160 3753/3767 191 4091 5126
8 Θεοῦ ἐποίησεν. ὅτε οὖν ἤκουσεν ὁ Πιλάτος τοῦτον τὸν
of God he has made. when Then heard Pilate this
3056 3123 5399 1525 1519 4232
9 λόγον, μᾶλλον ἐφοβήθη, καὶ εἰσῆλθεν εἰς τὸ πραιτώριον
word, more he was afraid, and entered into the praetorium m
3825 3004 2424 4159/1488/4771 2424 612
πάλιν, καὶ λέγει τῷ Ἰησοῦ, Πόθεν εἶ σύ; ὁ δὲ Ἰησοῦς ἀπό-
again and says — to Jesus, From where are You? But Jesus an
3756 1325 846 3004 3767 846 4091 1698
10 κρισιν οὐκ ἔδωκεν αὐτῷ. λέγει οὖν αὐτῷ ὁ Πιλάτος, Ἐμοὶ
answer did not give him. says Then to Him Pilate, To me
3756/2980 3756 1492 3754 1849 2192 4717 4571
οὐ λαλεῖς; οὐκ οἶδας ὅτι ἐξουσίαν ἔχω σταυρῶσαί σε, καὶ
not you speak? not you know that authority I have to crucify you, and
1849 2192 630 4571 611 2424 3756 2192
11 ἐξουσίαν ἔχω ἀπολῦσαί σε; ἀπεκρίθη ὁ Ἰησοῦς, Οὐκ εἶχες
authority I have to release you? answered Jesus, not You had
1849 3762 2596 1700/1487/3361/*/4571 1325 509
2258 ἐξουσίαν οὐδεμίαν κατ' ἐμοῦ, εἰ μὴ ἦν σοι δεδομένον ἄνωθεν·
authority, not any against Me, if not it was to you being given from above
1223 5124 3850 3165/4571 3187 266 21921537
12 διὰ τοῦτο ὁ παραδιδούς μέ σοι μείζονα ἁμαρτίαν ἔχει. ἐκ
therefore the (one) delivering Me to you a greater sin has. From
5127 2212 4091 630 846 2453
τούτου ἐζήτει ὁ Πιλάτος ἀπολῦσαι αὐτόν. οἱ δὲ Ἰουδαῖοι
this sought Pilate to release Him, the but Jews
2896 3004 1437 5126 630 3756/1488/5384
ἔκραζον λέγοντες, Ἐὰν τοῦτον ἀπολύσῃς, οὐκ εἶ φίλος τοῦ
cried out saying, If this one you release not you are friend —
2541 3956 935 848 4160 483
Καίσαρος· πᾶς ὁ βασιλέα αὑτὸν ποιῶν, ἀντιλέγει τῷ
of Caesar; everyone a king himself making speaks against
2541 3767 4091 191 5126 3056 71
13 Καίσαρι. ὁ οὖν Πιλάτος ἀκούσας τοῦτον τὸν λόγον ἤγαγεν
Caesar. Therefore Pilate hearing this word led
1854 2424 2523 1909 968 1519 5117
ἔξω τὸν Ἰησοῦν, καὶ ἐκάθισεν ἐπὶ τοῦ βήματος, εἰς τόπον
out — Jesus, and sat down on the judgment seat at a place
3004 3038 1447 1042 2258
14 λεγόμενον Λιθόστρωτον, Ἑβραϊστὶ δὲ Γαββαθᾶ· ἦν δὲ
called (The) Pavement, in Hebrew but, Gabbatha. it was And
3904 3957 5610 5616 1622 3004
Παρασκευὴ τοῦ πάσχα, ὥρα δὲ ὡσεὶ ἕκτη· καὶ λέγει τοῖς
preparation of the Passover, hour and about (the) sixth, and he says to the
2453 2396 935 5216 2905 142
15 Ἰουδαίοις, Ἴδε, ὁ βασιλεὺς ὑμῶν. οἱ δὲ ἐκραύγασαν, Ἆρον,
Jews, Behold, the king of you. they But cried out, Away,
142 4717 846 3004 846 4091
ἆρον, σταύρωσον αὐτόν. λέγει αὐτοῖς ὁ Πιλάτος, Τὸν
away, crucify him! says to them Pilate, The
935 5216 4717 611 749 3756
βασιλέα ὑμῶν σταυρώσω; ἀπεκρίθησαν οἱ ἀρχιερεῖς, Οὐκ
king of you shall I crucify? answered The chief priests, not
2192 935 =1508= 2541 5119 3767 3860 846
16 ἔχομεν βασιλέα εἰ μὴ Καίσαρα. τότε οὖν παρέδωκεν αὐτὸν
We have a king except Caesar. Then, therefore, he delivered up Him
846 2443 4717
αὐτοῖς, ἵνα σταυρωθῇ.
to them, that He might be crucified.
3880 2424 520 941
17 Παρέλαβον δὲ τὸν Ἰησοῦν καὶ ἀπήγαγον· καὶ βαστάζων
they took And Jesus and led away, and bearing
4716 848 1831 1519 3004 2898
τὸν σταυρὸν αὐτοῦ ἐξῆλθεν εἰς τὸν λεγόμενον Κρανίου
the cross of Him, He went out to that called Of a Skull,
5117 3739 3004 1447 1115 3699 846 4717
18 τόπον, ὃς λέγεται Ἑβραϊστὶ Γολγοθᾶ· ὅπου αὐτὸν ἐσταύ-
(the) place, which is called in Hebrew, Golgotha; where Him they
3326 846 243 1417 1782 1782
ρωσαν, καὶ μετ' αὐτοῦ ἄλλους δύο, ἐντεῦθεν καὶ ἐντεῦθεν,
crucified, and with him others two, on this side and on that side,

middle. [19]And Pilate also wrote a title and put *it* on the cross. And having been written, it was: JESUS THE NAZARENE—THE KING OF THE JEWS. [20]Therefore, many of the Jews read this title, because the place where Jesus was crucified was near the city. And it had been written in Hebrew, in Greek, in Latin. [21]Then the chief priests of the Jews said to Pilate, Do not write, The king of the Jews; but that that one said, I am king of the Jews. [22]Pilate answered, What I have written, I have written.

[23]Then when they crucified Jesus, the soldiers took His garments and made four parts, a part to each soldier; also the robe. And the robe was seamless, woven from the top throughout. [24]Then they said to one another, Let us not tear it, but let us cast lots about it, whose it will be—that the Scripture might be fulfilled which said, "They divided My garments among them, and they threw a lot *for* My garment." Therefore, the soldiers did these things.

[25]And His mother, and His mother's sister Mary, the *wife* of Clopas, and Mary Magdalene stood by the cross of Jesus. [26]Then seeing *His* mother, and the disciple whom He loved standing by, Jesus said to His mother, Woman, behold, your son! [27]Then He said to the disciple, Behold, your mother! And from that hour the disciple took her into *his* own *home*.

3319 2424 1125 5102 4091
19 μέσον δὲ τὸν Ἰησοῦν. ἔγραψε δὲ καὶ τίτλον ὁ Πιλάτος,
in center and Jesus. wrote And also a title Pilate,
5087/1909 4716 2258 1125 2424
καὶ ἔθηκεν ἐπὶ τοῦ σταυροῦ· ἦν δὲ γεγραμμένον, Ἰησοῦς ὁ
and put (it) on the cross; it was and having been written, JESUS THE
3480 935 2453 5126 3767
20 Ναζωραῖος ὁ βασιλεὺς τῶν Ἰουδαίων. τοῦτον οὖν τὸν
NAZARENE, THE KING OF THE JEWS. This, therefore —
5102 4183 314 2453 3754 1451 2258
τίτλον πολλοὶ ἀνέγνωσαν τῶν Ἰουδαίων, ὅτι ἐγγὺς ἦν
title many read of the Jews, because near was
4172 5117 3699 4717 2424 2258
τῆς πόλεως ὁ τόπος ὅπου ἐσταυρώθη ὁ Ἰησοῦς· καὶ ἦν
the city the place where was crucified Jesus; and it was
1125 1447 1676 4515 3004
21 γεγραμμένον Ἑβραϊστί, Ἑλληνιστί, Ῥωμαϊστί. ἔλεγον
having been written in Hebrew, in Greek, in Latin. said
3767 4091 749 2453 3361 1125
οὖν τῷ Πιλάτῳ οἱ ἀρχιερεῖς τῶν Ἰουδαίων, Μὴ γράφε,
Then to Pilate the chief priests of the Jews, Not do write,
935 2453 235 3754 1565 2036 935
Ὁ βασιλεὺς τῶν Ἰουδαίων· ἀλλ' ὅτι ἐκεῖνος εἶπε, Βασιλεύς
The king of the Jews; but that that one said, king
1510 2453 611 4091 3739 1125
22 εἰμι τῶν Ἰουδαίων. ἀπεκρίθη ὁ Πιλάτος, Ὃ γέγραφα,
I am of the Jews. answered Pilate, What I have written,
1125
γέγραφα.
I have written.
3767 4757 3753 4717 2424 2983
23 Οἱ οὖν στρατιῶται, ὅτε ἐσταύρωσαν τὸν Ἰησοῦν, ἔλαβον
the Then soldiers, when they crucified — Jesus, took
2440 848 4160 5064 3313 1538
τὰ ἱμάτια αὐτοῦ, καὶ ἐποίησαν τέσσαρα μέρη, ἑκάστῳ
the garments of Him, and made four parts, to each
4757 3313 5509 2258 5509 729
στρατιώτῃ μέρος, καὶ τὸν χιτῶνα· ἦν δὲ ὁ χιτὼν ἄρραφος,
soldier a part; also the tunic. was And the tunic seamless,
1537 509 5307 1223/3650 2036 3767 4314 240
24 ἐκ τῶν ἄνωθεν ὑφαντὸς δι' ὅλου. εἶπον οὖν πρὸς ἀλλήλους,
from the top woven throughout. They said, then, to one another,
3361 4977 846 235 2975 4012 846 5101
Μὴ σχίσωμεν αὐτόν, ἀλλὰ λάχωμεν περὶ αὐτοῦ, τίνος
Not let us tear it, but let us cast lots about it, whose
2071 2443 1124 4137 3004 1266
ἔσται· ἵνα ἡ γραφὴ πληρωθῇ ἡ λέγουσα, Διεμερίσαντο τὰ
it will be; that the Scripture be fulfilled which said, They divided the
2440 3450 1438 1909 2440 3450 906 2819
ἱμάτιά μου ἑαυτοῖς, καὶ ἐπὶ τὸν ἱματισμόν μου ἔβαλον κλῆρον.
the garments of Me to themselves and on the garment of Me cast a lot.
3303 3767 4757 5023 4160 2476
25 οἱ μὲν οὖν στρατιῶται ταῦτα ἐποίησαν. εἱστήκεισαν δὲ
the Therefore soldiers these things did. there stood But
3844 4716 2424 3384 848 79
παρὰ τῷ σταυρῷ τοῦ Ἰησοῦ ἡ μήτηρ αὐτοῦ, καὶ ἡ ἀδελφὴ
by the cross — of Jesus the mother of Him, and the sister
3384 848 3137 2832 3137
τῆς μητρὸς αὐτοῦ, Μαρία ἡ τοῦ Κλωπᾶ, καὶ Μαρία ἡ
of the mother of Him, Mary the (wife) of Clopas, and Mary the
3094 2424 3767/1492 3384 3101
26 Μαγδαληνή. Ἰησοῦς οὖν ἰδὼν τὴν μητέρα, καὶ τὸν μαθητὴν
Magdalene. Jesus Therefore seeing the mother, and the disciple
3936 3739 25 3004 3384 848 1135 2400
παρεστῶτα ὃν ἠγάπα, λέγει τῇ μητρὶ αὐτοῦ, Γύναι, ἰδοὺ ὁ
standing by, whom He loved, says to the mother of Him, Woman, behold the
5207/4675/1534/3004 3101 2400 3384 4675 575
27 υἱός σου. εἶτα λέγει τῷ μαθητῇ, Ἰδοὺ ἡ μήτηρ σου. καὶ ἀπ'
son of you. Then He says to the disciple. Behold, the mother of you. And from
1565 5610 2983 846 3101 1519 2398
ἐκείνης τῆς ὥρας ἔλαβεν αὐτὴν ὁ μαθητὴς εἰς τὰ ἴδια.
that — hour took her the disciple into the own (home).

[28]After this, knowing that all things have now been finished, that the Scripture be completed, Jesus said, I thirst. [29]Then a vessel full of vinegar was set, and having filled a sponge *with* vinegar, and putting hyssop around, they brought *it* to His mouth. [30]Then when Jesus took the vinegar, He said, It has been finished. And bowing *His* head, *He* delivered up the spirit.

[31]Then since it was Preparation, that the bodies not remain on the cross on the sabbath—for great was the day of that sabbath—the Jews asked Pilate that their legs might be broken, and they be taken away. [32]Then the soldiers came and broke the legs of the first, and of the other crucified with Him. [33]But on coming *to* Jesus, when they saw He already was dead, they did not break His legs. [34]But one of the soldiers pierced His side *with* a lance; and at once blood and water came out. [35]And the *one* seeing has borne witness, and his witness is true; and that one knows that he speaks truly, that you may believe. [36]For these things happened that the Scripture might be fulfilled, "Not a bone of Him shall be broken." [37]And again, a different Scripture says, "They shall look at *Him* whom they have pierced."

[38]And after these things, Joseph from Arimathea—being a disciple of Jesus, but concealed because of fear of the Jews—asked Pilate that he might take the body of Jesus. And Pilate

3326 5124 1492 2424 3754 3956 2235 5055
28 Μετὰ τοῦτο εἰδὼς ὁ Ἰησοῦς ὅτι πάντα ἤδη τετέλεσται,
After this, knowing Jesus that all things already have been done,
2443 5048 1124 3004 1372 4632 3767 2749 3690
29 ἵνα τελειωθῇ ἡ γραφή, λέγει, Διψῶ. σκεῦος οὖν ἔκειτο ὄξους
that be fulfilled the Scripture, says, I thirst. a vessel Then was set, of vinegar
3324 4130 4699 3690 5301
μεστόν· οἱ δέ, πλήσαντες σπόγγον ὄξους, καὶ ὑσσώπῳ
full; they and, filling a sponge (with) vinegar, and hyssop
4060 4374 846 4750 3753/3767/2983
30 περιθέντες, προσήνεγκαν αὐτοῦ τῷ στόματι. ὅτε οὖν ἔλαβε
putting around, they brought to of Him the mouth, when Then took
3690 2424 2036 5055 2827 2776
τὸ ὄξος ὁ Ἰησοῦς, εἶπε, Τετέλεσται· καὶ κλίνας τὴν κεφαλήν,
the vinegar Jesus, He said, It has been completed, and bowing the head
3860 4151
παρέδωκε τὸ πνεῦμα.
delivered up the spirit.
3767 2453 1893 3904 2258/2443/3361/3306/1909
31 Οἱ οὖν Ἰουδαῖοι, ἐπεὶ Παρασκευὴ ἦν, ἵνα μὴ μείνῃ ἐπὶ τοῦ
the Therefore Jews, since preparation it was, that not may remain on the
4716 4983 1722 4521 2258/1063 3173
σταυροῦ τὰ σώματα ἐν τῷ σαββάτῳ (ἦν γὰρ μεγάλη ἡ
cross the bodies on the sabbath, was for great the
2250 1565 4521 2065 4091 2443
ἡμέρα ἐκείνου τοῦ σαββάτου), ἠρώτησαν τὸν Πιλάτον ἵνα
day of that — sabbath; they asked Pilate that
2608 848 4628 142 2064 3767
32 κατεαγῶσιν αὐτῶν τὰ σκέλη, καὶ ἀρθῶσιν. ἦλθον οὖν οἱ
might be broken of them the legs, and they be taken. came Then the
4757 3303 4413 2608 4628
στρατιῶται, καὶ τοῦ μὲν πρώτου κατέαξαν τὰ σκέλη καὶ τοῦ
soldiers, and of the first broke the legs, and of the
243 4957 846 1909 2424 2064
33 ἄλλου τοῦ συσταυρωθέντος αὐτῷ· ἐπὶ δὲ τὸν Ἰησοῦν ἐλ-
other — crucified with Him; upon but — Jesus
5613 1492 846 2235 2348 3756 2608 848
θόντες, ὡς εἶδον αὐτὸν ἤδη τεθνηκότα, οὐ κατέαξαν αὐτοῦ
coming, when they saw He already was dead, not they broke of Him
4628 235 1520 4757 3057 848 4125
34 τὰ σκέλη· ἀλλ' εἷς τῶν στρατιωτῶν λόγχῃ αὐτοῦ τὴν πλευ-
the legs, but one of the soldiers a lance of him the side
3572 2117 1831 129 5204 3708
35 ρὰν ἔνυξε, καὶ εὐθὺς ἐξῆλθεν αἷμα καὶ ὕδωρ. καὶ ὁ ἑωρακὼς
pierced, and at once came out blood and water. And the (one) seeing
3140 228 848 2076 3141 2548
μεμαρτύρηκε, καὶ ἀληθινὴ αὐτοῦ ἐστιν ἡ μαρτυρία, κἀκεῖνος
has witnessed, and true of him is the witness, and that one
1492 3754 227 3004 2443 5210 4100 1096 1063
36 οἶδεν ὅτι ἀληθῆ λέγει, ἵνα ὑμεῖς πιστεύσητε. ἐγένετο γὰρ
knows that true he speaks, that you may believe. happened For
5023 2443 1124 4137 3747 3756 4937
ταῦτα ἵνα ἡ γραφὴ πληρωθῇ, Ὀστοῦν οὐ συντριβήσεται
these things that the Scripture be fulfilled: A bone not shall be splintered
848 3825 2087 1124 3004 3700 1519/3739
37 αὐτοῦ. καὶ πάλιν ἑτέρα γραφὴ λέγει, Ὄψονται εἰς ὃν
of Him. And again a different Scripture says, They shall look at whom
1574
ἐξεκέντησαν.
they have pierced.
3326 5023 2064 4091 2501 575
38 Μετὰ δὲ ταῦτα ἠρώτησε τὸν Πιλάτον ὁ Ἰωσὴφ ὁ ἀπὸ
after And these things asked Pilate Joseph from
707 5607 3101 2424 2928 1223
Ἀριμαθαίας, ὢν μαθητὴς τοῦ Ἰησοῦ, κεκρυμμένος δὲ διὰ
Arimathea, being a disciple — of Jesus, concealed but through
5401 2453 2443/142 4983 2424
τὸν φόβον τῶν Ἰουδαίων, ἵνα ἄρῃ τὸ σῶμα τοῦ Ἰησοῦ· καὶ
the fear of the Jews, that he take the body — of Jesus. And
2010 4091 2064/3767 142 4983 2424
ἐπέτρεψεν ὁ Πιλάτος. ἦλθεν οὖν καὶ ἦρε τὸ σῶμα τοῦ Ἰησοῦ.
allowed (it) Pilate. He came, then, and took the body — of Jesus.

gave permission. Then he came and took the body of Jesus. [39]And Nicodemus also came, the *one* coming at first to Jesus by night, bearing a mixture of myrrh and aloes, about a hundred Roman pounds. [40]Then they took the body of Jesus and bound it in linens, with the spices, as is usual with the Jews *in* burying. [41]And there was a garden in the place where He was crucified, and a new tomb in the garden, in which no one yet ever had been placed. [42]There, then, because of the Preparation of the Jews, because the tomb was near, they put Jesus.

CHAPTER 20

[1]But on the first of the sabbaths Mary Magdalene came early to the tomb, darkness yet being *on it.* And *she* saw the stone had been removed from the tomb. [2]Then she ran and came to Simon Peter, and to the other disciple whom Jesus loved, and said to them, They took away the Lord out of the tomb, and we do not know where they laid Him. [3]Then Peter and the other disciple went out and came to the tomb.

[4]And the two ran together, and the other disciple ran in front more quickly than Peter, and came first to the tomb. [5]And stooping down, he saw the linens lying; however, he did not go in. [6]Then Simon Peter came following him, and went into the tomb, and saw the linens lying. [7]And the gravecloth which was on His head *was* not lying with the linens, but was wrapped up in one place by itself. [8]Therefore, then the other disciple also entered, having come first to the tomb. And he saw and

2064 3530 2064 4314 2424 3571
39 ἦλθε δὲ καὶ Νικόδημος, ὁ ἐλθὼν πρὸς τὸν Ἰησοῦν νυκτὸς τὸ
came And also Nicodemus, the (one) coming to — Jesus (by) night at
4412 5342 3395 4666 250 5616 3046 1540
πρῶτον, φέρων μίγμα σμύρνης καὶ ἀλόης ὡσεὶ λίτρας ἑκατόν.
first, bearing a mixture of myrrh and aloes, about litrae a hundred.
2983 3767 4983 2424 1210 846 3608
40 ἔλαβον οὖν τὸ σῶμα τοῦ Ἰησοῦ, καὶ ἔδησαν αὐτὸ ὀθονίοις
they took Then the body — of Jesus, and bound it in linens
3326 759 2531 1485 2076 2453
μετὰ τῶν ἀρωμάτων, καθὼς ἔθος ἐστὶ τοῖς Ἰουδαίοις
with the spices, as custom is with the Jews
1779 2258 1722 5117 3699 4717 2779
41 ἐνταφιάζειν. ἦν δὲ ἐν τῷ τόπῳ ὅπου ἐσταυρώθη κῆπος, καὶ
to bury. was And in the place where He was crucified a garden and
1722 2779 3419 2537 1722/3739 3764 3762 5087 1563
42 ἐν τῷ κήπῳ μνημεῖον καινόν, ἐν ᾧ οὐδέπω οὐδεὶς ἐτέθη. ἐκεῖ
in the garden a tomb new, in which never yet no one was put. There,
3767/1223 3904 2453 3754 1451 2258
οὖν διὰ τὴν Παρασκευὴν τῶν Ἰουδαίων, ὅτι ἐγγὺς ἦν τὸ
then, because of the preparation of the Jews, because near was the
3419 5087 2424
μνημεῖον, ἔθηκαν τὸν Ἰησοῦν.
tomb, they put — Jesus.

CHAPTER 20

3391 4521 3137 3094 2064
1 Τῇ δὲ μιᾷ τῶν σαββάτων Μαρία ἡ Μαγδαληνὴ ἔρχεται
on the And first of the sabbaths, Mary the Magdalene comes
4404 4653 2089 5607/1519 3419 991
πρωΐ, σκοτίας ἔτι οὔσης, εἰς τὸ μνημεῖον, καὶ βλέπει τὸν
early, darkness yet being to the tomb, and sees the
3037 142 1537 3419 5143 3767 2064 4314
2 λίθον ἠρμένον ἐκ τοῦ μνημείου. τρέχει οὖν καὶ ἔρχεται πρὸς
stone being removed from the tomb. she runs Then and comes to
4613 4074 4314 243 3101 3739 5368
Σίμωνα Πέτρον καὶ πρὸς τὸν ἄλλον μαθητὴν ὃν ἐφίλει ὁ
Simon Peter, and to the other disciple whom loved
2424 3004 846 142 2962 1537 3419
Ἰησοῦς, καὶ λέγει αὐτοῖς, Ἦραν τὸν Κύριον ἐκ τοῦ μνημείου,
Jesus; and says to them, They took the Lord out of the tomb,
3756 1492 4228 5087 846 1831 3767 4074
3 καὶ οὐκ οἴδαμεν ποῦ ἔθηκαν αὐτόν. ἐξῆλθεν οὖν ὁ Πέτρος καὶ
and not we know where they put Him. went out Then Peter and
243 3101 2064 1519 3419 5143
4 ὁ ἄλλος μαθητής, καὶ ἤρχοντο εἰς τὸ μνημεῖον. ἔτρεχον δὲ οἱ
the other disciple, and came to the tomb. ran And the
1417 3674 243 3101 4390 5032
δύο ὁμοῦ· καὶ ὁ ἄλλος μαθητὴς προέδραμε τάχιον τοῦ
two together; and the other disciple ran in front. more quickly than
4074 2064 4413 1519 3419 3879
5 Πέτρου, καὶ ἦλθε πρῶτος εἰς τὸ μνημεῖον, καὶ παρακύψας
Peter, and came first to the tomb, and stooping
991 2749 3608 3756 3305 1525 2064 3767
6 βλέπει κείμενα τὰ ὀθόνια, οὐ μέντοι εἰσῆλθεν. ἔρχεται οὖν
sees lying the linens; not, however, he went in. Comes, therefore,
4613 4074 190 846 1525 1519 3419
Σίμων Πέτρος ἀκολουθῶν αὐτῷ, καὶ εἰσῆλθεν εἰς τὸ μνημεῖον,
Simon Peter following him, and entered into the tomb.
2334 3608 2749 4676 2258/1909
7 καὶ θεωρεῖ τὰ ὀθόνια κείμενα, καὶ τὸ σουδάριον ὃ ἦν ἐπὶ τῆς
And he beholds the linens lying, and the cloth which was on the
2776 848 3756/3326 3608 2749 235 5565
κεφαλῆς αὐτοῦ, οὐ μετὰ τῶν ὀθονίων κείμενον, ἀλλὰ χωρὶς
head of Him, not with the linens lying, but apart
1794 1519 1520 5117 5119 3767 1525 243
8 ἐντετυλιγμένον εἰς ἕνα τόπον. τότε οὖν εἰσῆλθε καὶ ὁ ἄλλος
being wrapped up into one place. Then, therefore entered also the other
3101 2064 4413 1519 3419 1492
μαθητὴς ὁ ἐλθὼν πρῶτος εἰς τὸ μνημεῖον, καὶ εἶδε, καὶ
disciple having come first to the tomb, and he saw, and

believed. [9]For they did not yet know the Scripture, that it was necessary for Him to rise from *the* dead. [10]Then the disciples went away again to themselves.

[11]But Mary stood outside at the tomb, weeping. Then as she wept, she stooped down into the tomb. [12]And *she* saw two angels in white, sitting one at the head, and one at the feet, where the body of Jesus had lain. [13]And they said to her, Woman, why do you weep? She said to them, Because they took away my Lord, and I do not know where they put Him. [14]And saying these things, she turned backward, and saw Jesus standing, and did not know that it was Jesus.

[15]Jesus said to her, Woman, why do you weep? Whom do you seek? Thinking that it was the gardener, she said to Him, Sir, if you carried Him away, tell me where you put Him, and I will take Him away. [16]Jesus said to her, Mary! Turning around, she said to Him, Rabboni!—that is to say, Teacher. [17]Jesus said to her, Do not touch Me, for I have not yet ascended to My Father, but go to My brothers and say to them, I am ascending to My Father and your Father, and My God, and your God. [18]Mary Magdalene came bringing word to the disciples that she had seen the Lord, and that He told her these things.

[19]Then it being evening on that day, the first of the sabbaths, and the doors having been locked where the disciples were assembled, because of fear

4100 3764 1063 1492 1124 3754 1163
9 ἐπίστευσεν· οὐδέπω γὰρ ᾔδεισαν τὴν γραφήν, ὅτι δεῖ
believed. not yet For they knew the Scripture, that it behoves
846 1537 3498 450 565 3767 3825 4314
10 αὐτὸν ἐκ νεκρῶν ἀναστῆναι. ἀπῆλθον οὖν πάλιν πρὸς
Him from (the) dead to rise. went away Then again to
1438 3101
ἑαυτοὺς οἱ μαθηταί.
themselves the disciples.
3137 2476 4314 3419 2799 1854 5613
11 Μαρία δὲ εἱστήκει πρὸς τὸ μνημεῖον κλαίουσα ἔξω· ὡς
Mary And stood at the tomb weeping outside. As
3767 2799 3879 1519 3419 2334 1417
12 οὖν ἔκλαιε, παρέκυψεν εἰς τὸ μνημεῖον, καὶ θεωρεῖ δύο
then she wept, she stooped into the tomb, and beholds two
32 1722 3022 2516 1520 4314 2776
ἀγγέλους ἐν λευκοῖς καθεζομένους, ἕνα πρὸς τῇ κεφαλῇ, καὶ
angels in white sitting, one at the head, and
1520/4314 4228 3699 2749 4983 2424
13 ἕνα πρὸς τοῖς ποσίν, ὅπου ἔκειτο τὸ σῶμα τοῦ Ἰησοῦ. καὶ
one at the feet, where had lain the body — of Jesus. And
3004 846 1565 1135 5101 2799 3004 846 3754
λέγουσιν αὐτῇ ἐκεῖνοι, Γύναι, τί κλαίεις; λέγει αὐτοῖς, Ὅτι
say to her those, Woman, why do you weep? She says to them, For
142 2962 3450 3756 1492 4226 5087 846
14 ἦραν τὸν Κύριόν μου, καὶ οὐκ οἶδα ποῦ ἔθηκαν αὐτόν. καὶ
they removed the Lord of me, and not I know where they put Him. And
5023 2036 4762 1519 3694 2334
ταῦτα εἰποῦσα ἐστράφη εἰς τὰ ὀπίσω, καὶ θεωρεῖ τὸν
these things saying, she turned into the rear, and beholds
2424 2476 3756/1492&3754 2424 2076 3004 846
15 Ἰησοῦν ἑστῶτα, καὶ οὐκ ᾔδει ὅτι ὁ Ἰησοῦς ἐστι. λέγει αὐτῇ
Jesus standing, and not knows that Jesus it is. says to her
2424 1135 5101 2799 5101 2212 1565 1380
ὁ Ἰησοῦς, Γύναι, τί κλαίεις; τίνα ζητεῖς; ἐκείνη, δοκοῦσα
Jesus, Woman, why do you weep? Whom seek you? That one, thinking
3754 2780 2076 3004 846 2962 1487/4771/ 941
ὅτι ὁ κηπουρός ἐστι, λέγει αὐτῷ, Κύριε, εἰ σὺ ἐβάστασας
that the gardener it is, says to Him, Sir, if you carried away
846 2036/3427/4226 846 5087 2504 846 142 3004
16 αὐτόν, εἰπέ μοι ποῦ αὐτὸν ἔθηκας, κἀγὼ αὐτὸν ἀρῶ. λέγει
Him, tell me where Him you put, and I Him will take. says
846 2424 3137 4762 1565 3004 846
αὐτῇ ὁ Ἰησοῦς, Μαρία. στραφεῖσα ἐκείνη λέγει αὐτῷ,
to her Jesus, Mary! turning That one says to Him
4462 3739/3004 1320 3004 846 2424 3361
17 Ῥαββουνί· ὃ λέγεται, Διδάσκαλε. λέγει αὐτῇ ὁ Ἰησοῦς, Μή
Rabboni, that is to say, Teacher. says to her Jesus, Do not
3450 680 3768 1063 305 4314 3962 3450
μου ἅπτου, οὔπω γὰρ ἀναβέβηκα πρὸς τὸν πατέρα μου·
Me touch, not yet for I have ascended to the Father of Me.
4198 4314 80 3450 2036 846
πορεύου δὲ πρὸς τοὺς ἀδελφούς μου, καὶ εἰπὲ αὐτοῖς,
go But to the brothers of Me, and say to them,
305 4314 3962 3450 3962 5216
Ἀναβαίνω πρὸς τὸν πατέρα μου καὶ πατέρα ὑμῶν, καὶ
I ascend to the Father of Me and the Father of you, and
2316 3450 2316 5216 2064 3137 3094
18 Θεόν μου καὶ Θεὸν ὑμῶν. ἔρχεται Μαρία ἡ Μαγδαληνὴ
the God of Me and the God of you. comes Mary the Magdalene
518 3101 3754 3708 2962
ἀπαγγέλλουσα τοῖς μαθηταῖς ὅτι ἑώρακε τὸν Κύριον, καὶ
bringing word to the disciples, that she has seen the Lord, and
5023 2036 846
ταῦτα εἶπεν αὐτῇ.
these things He told her.
5607/3756/3798 2250 1565 3391 4521
19 Οὔσης οὖν ὀψίας, τῇ ἡμέρᾳ ἐκείνῃ τῇ μιᾷ τῶν σαββάτων,
it being Then evening — day on that, the first of the sabbaths,
2374 2808 3699 2258 3101 4863
καὶ τῶν θυρῶν κεκλεισμένων ὅπου ἦσαν οἱ μαθηταὶ συνηγ-
and the doors having been locked where were the disciples gathered

of the Jews, Jesus came and stood in the midst, and said to them, Peace to you. [20]And saying this, He showed them His hands and side. Then seeing the Lord, the disciples rejoiced.

[21]Then Jesus said to them again, Peace to you. As the Father has sent Me, I also send you. [22]And saying this, He breathed on *them*, and said to them, Receive *the* Holy Spirit. [23]Of whomever you forgive the sins, they are forgiven to them. Or whomever you may retain, they are retained.

[24]But Thomas, one of the Twelve, the *one* called Twin, was not with them when Jesus came. [25]Then the other disciples said to him, We have seen the Lord. But he said to them, Unless I see the mark of the nails in His hands, and thrust my finger into the mark of the nails, and thrust my hand into His side, in no way will I believe.

[26]And after eight days His disciples were inside again, and Thomas was with them. The doors having been locked, Jesus came and stood in the midst, and said, Peace to you. [27]Then He said to Thomas, Bring your finger here and see My hands; and bring your hand and thrust into My side, and be not unbelieving, but believing. [28]And Thomas answered and said to Him, My Lord and my God! [29]Jesus said to him, Because you have seen Me, Thomas, you have believed. Blessed *are* the ones not seeing, and believing.

[30]Then truly Jesus did many other miracles in the

1223 5401 2453 2064 2424
μένοι, διὰ τὸν φόβον τῶν Ἰουδαίων, ἦλθεν ὁ Ἰησοῦς καὶ
together, because of the fear of the Jews, came Jesus and
2476 1519 3319 3004 846 1515 5213 5124
20 ἔστη εἰς τὸ μέσον, καὶ λέγει αὐτοῖς, Εἰρήνη ὑμῖν. καὶ τοῦτο
stood in the midst, and says to them, Peace to you. And this
2036 1166 846 5495 4125 848
εἰπὼν ἔδειξεν αὐτοῖς τὰς χεῖρας καὶ τὴν πλευρὰν αὐτοῦ.
saying He showed them the hands and the side of Him.
5463 3767 3101 1492 2962 2036 3767
21 ἐχάρησαν οὖν οἱ μαθηταὶ ἰδόντες τὸν Κύριον. εἶπεν οὖν
Rejoiced, therefore, the disciples seeing the Lord. said Then
846 2424 3825 1515 5213 2531 649 3165
αὐτοῖς ὁ Ἰησοῦς πάλιν, Εἰρήνη ὑμῖν· καθὼς ἀπέσταλκέ με ὁ
to them Jesus again, Peace to you. As has sent Me the
3962 2504 3992 5209 5124 2036 1720
22 πατήρ, κἀγὼ πέμπω ὑμᾶς. καὶ τοῦτο εἰπὼν ἐνεφύσησε καὶ
Father, I also send you. And this having said, He breathed on, and
3004 846 2983 4151 40 302 5100 863
23 λέγει αὐτοῖς, Λάβετε Πνεῦμα Ἅγιον. ἄν τινων ἀφῆτε τὰς
said to them, Receive (the) Spirit Holy. Ever of whom you forgive the
266 863 846 302 5100 2902 2902
ἁμαρτίας, ἀφίενται αὐτοῖς· ἄν τινων κρατῆτε, κεκράτηνται.
sins, they are forgiven to them; ever of whom you retain, they are retained.
2381 1520/1537 1427 3004 1324 3756/2258
24 Θωμᾶς δέ, εἷς ἐκ τῶν δώδεκα, ὁ λεγόμενος Δίδυμος, οὐκ ἦν
Thomas But, one of the twelve, the (one) called Twin, not was
3326 846 3753 2064 2424 3004/3767 846 243
25 μετ' αὐτῶν ὅτε ἦλθεν ὁ Ἰησοῦς. ἔλεγον οὖν αὐτῷ οἱ ἄλλοι
with them when came Jesus. said Then to him the other
3101 3708 2962 2036 846 =3362=
μαθηταί, Ἑωράκαμεν τὸν Κύριον. ὁ δὲ εἶπεν αὐτοῖς, Ἐὰν μὴ
disciples, We have seen the Lord. he But said to them, Unless
1492/1722 5495 848 5179 2247 906
ἴδω ἐν ταῖς χερσὶν αὐτοῦ τὸν τύπον τῶν ἥλων, καὶ βάλω
I see in the hands of Him the mark of the nails, and thrust
1147 3450 1519 5179 2247 906
τὸν δάκτυλόν μου εἰς τὸν τύπον τῶν ἥλων, καὶ βάλω τὴν
the finger of me into the mark of the nails, and thrust the
5495 3450 1519 4125 848 =3364= 4100
χεῖρά μου εἰς τὴν πλευρὰν αὐτοῦ, οὐ μὴ πιστεύσω.
hand of me into the side of Him, in no way will I believe.
3326 2250 3638 3825 2258 2080 3101 848
26 Καὶ μεθ' ἡμέρας ὀκτὼ πάλιν ἦσαν ἔσω οἱ μαθηταὶ αὐτοῦ,
And after days eight, again were inside the disciples of Him,
2381 3326 848 2064 2424 2374
καὶ Θωμᾶς μετ' αὐτῶν. ἔρχεται ὁ Ἰησοῦς, τῶν θυρῶν
and Thomas with them. comes — Jesus, the doors
2808 2476 1519 3319 2036 1515 5213
κεκλεισμένων, καὶ ἔστη εἰς τὸ μέσον καὶ εἶπεν, Εἰρήνη ὑμῖν.
having been locked, and stood in the midst, and said, Peace to you.
1534 3004 2381 5342 1147 4675 5602 1492
27 εἶτα λέγει τῷ Θωμᾷ, Φέρε τὸν δάκτυλόν σου ὧδε, καὶ ἴδε τὰς
Then He says to Thomas, Bring the finger of you here, and see the
5495 3450 5342 5495 4675 906 1519 4125
χεῖράς μου· καὶ φέρε τὴν χεῖρά σου, καὶ βάλε εἰς τὴν πλευ-
hands of Me, and bring the hand of you, and thrust into the side
3450 3361 1096 571 235 4103 611
28 ράν μου· καὶ μὴ γίνου ἄπιστος, ἀλλὰ πιστός. καὶ ἀπεκρίθη
of Me, and not become unbelieving, but believing. And answered
2381 2036 846 2962 3450 2316 3450 3004
29 ὁ Θωμᾶς, καὶ εἶπεν αὐτῷ, Ὁ Κύριός μου καὶ ὁ Θεός μου. λέγει
Thomas, and said to Him, The Lord of me and the God of me. says
846 2424 3754 3708 3165 2381 4100
αὐτῷ ὁ Ἰησοῦς, Ὅτι ἑώρακάς με, Θωμᾶ, πεπίστευκας·
to him Jesus, Because you have seen Me, Thomas, you have believed.
3107 3361 1492 4100
μακάριοι οἱ μὴ ἰδόντες, καὶ πιστεύσαντες.
Blessed those not seeing, and believing.
4183 3303 3767 243 4592 4160 2424 1799
30 Πολλὰ μὲν οὖν καὶ ἄλλα σημεῖα ἐποίησεν ὁ Ἰησοῦς ἐνώ-
Many, therefore, and other signs did Jesus in (the)

presence of His disciples which are not written in this book. [31]But these have been written that you may believe that Jesus is the Christ, the Son of God; and that believing you may have life in His name.

3101 848 3739/3756/2076 1125 1722
πιον τῶν μαθητῶν αὐτοῦ, ἃ οὐκ ἔστι γεγραμμένα ἐν τῷ
sight of the disciples of Him, which not is written in
975 5129 5023 1125 2443 4100 3754
31 βιβλίῳ τούτῳ. ταῦτα δὲ γέγραπται, ἵνα πιστεύσητε ὅτι ὁ
roll this. these things But have been written that you believe that
2424 2076 5547 5207 2316 2443 4100
Ἰησοῦς ἐστιν ὁ Χριστὸς ὁ υἱὸς τοῦ Θεοῦ, καὶ ἵνα πιστεύοντες
Jesus is the Christ the Son — of God, and that believing
2222 2192 1722 3686 848
ζωὴν ἔχητε ἐν τῷ ὀνόματι αὐτοῦ.
life you may have in the name of Him.

CHAPTER 21

[1]After these things Jesus revealed Himself again to the disciples at the Sea of Tiberias. And He revealed *Himself* this way: [2]Simon Peter, and Thomas, being called *The* Twin, and Nathanael from Cana of Galilee, and the *sons* of Zebedee, and two others of His disciples were together. [3]Simon Peter said to them, I am going out to fish. They said to him, We also are coming with you. They went and entered into the boat at once. And in that night they caught nothing. [4]And *it* now becoming early morning, Jesus stood on the shore. However, the disciples did not know that it was Jesus. [5]Then Jesus said to them, Children, Do you not have anything to eat? They answered Him, No. [6]And He said to them, Cast the net into the right side of the boat, and you will find. Then they cast, and they no longer had *the* strength to draw, from the multitude of the fish.

[7]Then the disciple whom Jesus loved said to Peter, It is the Lord. Then hearing that it is the Lord, Simon Peter girded on *his* coat—for he was naked—and threw himself into the sea. [8]And the other disciples came in the little boat; for they were not far from the land, only about

CHAPTER 21

3326 5023 5319 1438 3825 2424
1 Μετὰ ταῦτα ἐφανέρωσεν ἑαυτὸν πάλιν ὁ Ἰησοῦς τοῖς
After these things revealed Himself again Jesus to the
3101 1909 2281 5085 5319
μαθηταῖς ἐπὶ τῆς θαλάσσης τῆς Τιβεριάδος· ἐφανέρωσε δὲ
disciples on the sea — of Tiberias: He revealed and
3779 2258 3674 4613 4074 2381 3004
2 οὕτως. ἦσαν ὁμοῦ Σίμων Πέτρος, καὶ Θωμᾶς ὁ λεγόμενος
thus: Were together Simon Peter, and Thomas being called
1324 3482 575 2580 1056
Δίδυμος, καὶ Ναθαναὴλ ὁ ἀπὸ Κανᾶ τῆς Γαλιλαίας, καὶ οἱ
Twin, and Nathanael from Cana, of Galilee, and those
2199 243 1537 3101 848 1417
τοῦ Ζεβεδαίου, καὶ ἄλλοι ἐκ τῶν μαθητῶν αὐτοῦ δύο.
— of Zebedee, and others of the disciples of Him two.
3004 846 4613 4074 5217 232 3004
3 λέγει αὐτοῖς Σίμων Πέτρος, Ὑπάγω ἁλιεύειν. λέγουσιν
says to them Simon Peter, I am going out to fish. They say
846 2064 2249 4862/4571 1831 305
αὐτῷ, Ἐρχόμεθα καὶ ἡμεῖς σὺν σοί. ἐξῆλθον καὶ ἀνέβησαν
to him, are coming also We with you. They went and entered
1519 4143 2117 1722 1565 3571 4084 3762
εἰς τὸ πλοῖον εὐθύς, καὶ ἐν ἐκείνῃ τῇ νυκτὶ ἐπίασαν οὐδέν.
into the boat at once. And in that — night, they caught nothing.
4405 2235 1096 2476 2424 1519 123
4 πρωΐας δὲ ἤδη γενομένης ἔστη ὁ Ἰησοῦς εἰς τὸν αἰγιαλόν·
early morn But now (it) becoming, stood Jesus in the shore;
3756 3305 1492 3101 3754 2424 2076 3004 3767
5 οὐ μέντοι ᾔδεισαν οἱ μαθηταὶ ὅτι Ἰησοῦς ἐστι. λέγει οὖν
not, however, knew the disciples that Jesus it is. says Then
846 2424 3813 =3387= 4371 2192 611
αὐτοῖς ὁ Ἰησοῦς, Παιδία, μή τι προσφάγιον ἔχετε; ἀπεκρί-
to them Jesus, Children, not anything for eating have you? They
846 3756 2036 846 906 1519 1188
6 θησαν αὐτῷ, Οὔ. ὁ δὲ εἶπεν αὐτοῖς, Βάλετε εἰς τὰ δεξιὰ
answered Him, No. He And said to them, Cast to the right
3313 4143 1350 2147 906 3767
μέρη τοῦ πλοίου τὸ δίκτυον, καὶ εὑρήσετε. ἔβαλον οὖν, καὶ
parts of the boat the net, and you will find. They cast, then, and
3756/2089/846/1670 2480 575 4128 2486
οὐκέτι αὐτὸ ἑλκύσαι ἴσχυσαν ἀπὸ τοῦ πλήθους τῶν ἰχθύων.
no longer it to draw had they might from the multitude of the fish.
3004 3767 3101 1565 3739 25 2424 4074
7 λέγει οὖν ὁ μαθητὴς ἐκεῖνος ὃν ἠγάπα ὁ Ἰησοῦς τῷ Πέτρῳ,
says Then disciple that whom loved Jesus to Peter.
2962 2076 4613 3767 4074 191 3754 2962
Ὁ Κύριός ἐστι. Σίμων οὖν Πέτρος, ἀκούσας ὅτι ὁ Κύριός
The Lord it is. Simon Then Peter, hearing that the Lord
2076 1903 1241 2258 1063 1131
ἐστι, τὸν ἐπενδύτην διεζώσατο (ἦν γὰρ γυμνός), καὶ
it is, the coat (having) girded on—he was For naked — and
906 1438 1519 2281 243 3101
8 ἔβαλεν ἑαυτὸν εἰς τὴν θάλασσαν. οἱ δὲ ἄλλοι μαθηταὶ τῷ
threw himself into the sea. the And other disciples in the
4142 2064 3756/1063 2258 3112 575 1093 235
πλοιαρίῳ ἦλθον (οὐ γὰρ ἦσαν μακρὰν ἀπὸ τῆς γῆς, ἀλλ'
little boat came, not for they were far from the land, but

two hundred cubits, dragging the net of the fish. [9]Then when they went up on the land, they saw a coal fire lying, and a fish lying on *it*, and bread. [10]Jesus said to them, Bring from the little fish which you caught now. [11]Simon Peter went up and dragged the net onto the land, full of big fish, a hundred and fifty-three. And *though* being so many, the net was not torn. [12]Jesus said to them, Come, break fast. And no one of the disciples dared to ask Him, Who are You? knowing that it is the Lord. [13]Then Jesus came and took the bread, and gave to them; and in the same way the little fish. [14]This now *is* the three times *that* Jesus was revealed to His disciples, *He* being raised from *the* dead.

[15]Then when they broke fast, Jesus said to Simon Peter, Simon *son* of Jonah, do you love Me more than these? He said to Him, Yes, Lord; You know that I love You. He said to him, Feed My lambs! [16]Again He says to him, secondly, Simon *son* of Jonah, do you love Me? He says to Him, Yes, Lord; You know that I love You. He said to him, Shepherd My sheep! [17]Thirdly, He said to him, Simon *son* of Jonah, do you love Me? Peter was grieved that He said to him *a* third *time*, Do you love Me? And he said to him, Lord, You perceive all things; You know that I love You! Jesus said to him, Feed My sheep! [18]Truly, truly, I say to you, When you were younger, you girded yourself, and you walked where you desired. But when you grow old, you will stretch out your hands, and another will gird you, and will carry

5613 575 4083 1250 4951 1350
ὡς ἀπὸ πηχῶν διακοσίων), σύροντες τὸ δίκτυον τῶν
about from cubits two hundred, dragging the net of the
2486 5613/3767 576 1519 1093 991 439
9 ἰχθύων. ὡς οὖν ἀπέβησαν εἰς τὴν γῆν, βλέπουσιν ἀνθρακιὰν
fish. when Then they went up on the land, they saw a coal fire
2749 3795 1945 740 3004 846
10 κειμένην καὶ ὀψάριον ἐπικείμενον, καὶ ἄρτον. λέγει αὐτοῖς
lying, and a fish lying on, and bread. says to them
2424 5342 575 3795 3739 4084 3568
ὁ Ἰησοῦς, Ἐνέγκατε ἀπὸ τῶν ὀψαρίων ὧν ἐπιάσατε νῦν.
Jesus, Bring from the little fish which you caught now.
305 4613 4074 1670 1350 1909 1093
11 ἀνέβη Σίμων Πέτρος, καὶ εἵλκυσε τὸ δίκτυον ἐπὶ τῆς γῆς,
went up Simon Peter, and dragged the net onto the land,
3324 2486 3173 1540 4004/5140
μεστὸν ἰχθύων μεγάλων ἑκατὸν πεντηκοντατριῶν· καὶ
full of fish of great a hundred fifty-three. And
5118 5607 3756 4977 1350 3004 846
12 τοσούτων ὄντων, οὐκ ἐσχίσθη τὸ δίκτυον. λέγει αὐτοῖς ὁ
so many being not was torn the net. says to them
2424 1205 709 3762 5111 3101
Ἰησοῦς, Δεῦτε ἀριστήσατε. οὐδεὶς δὲ ἐτόλμα τῶν μαθητῶν
Jesus, Come, break fast. no one And dared of the disciples
1833 846 4771/5101/1488 1492 3754 2962 2076
ἐξετάσαι αὐτόν, Σὺ τίς εἶ; εἰδότες ὅτι ὁ Κύριός ἐστιν.
to question Him, You Who are, knowing that the Lord it is.
2064 3767 2424 2983 740 1325
13 ἔρχεται οὖν ὁ Ἰησοῦς, καὶ λαμβάνει τὸν ἄρτον, καὶ δίδωσιν
comes Then Jesus and takes the bread, and gives
846 3795 3668 5124 2235 5154 5319
14 αὐτοῖς, καὶ τὸ ὀψάριον ὁμοίως. τοῦτο ἤδη τρίτον ἐφανερώθη
to them, and the little fish likewise. This already thrice was revealed
2424 3101 848 1453 1537 3498
ὁ Ἰησοῦς τοῖς μαθηταῖς αὐτοῦ, ἐγερθεὶς ἐκ νεκρῶν.
Jesus to the disciples of Him, having been raised from (the) dead.
3753/3767 709 3004 4613 4074 2424
15 Ὅτε οὖν ἠρίστησαν, λέγει τῷ Σίμωνι Πέτρῳ ὁ Ἰησοῦς,
when Then they breakfasted, says to Simon Peter Jesus,
4613 2495 25 3165 4119 5130 3004 846 3483
Σίμων Ἰωνᾶ, ἀγαπᾷς με πλεῖόν τούτων; λέγει αὐτῷ, Ναί
Simon of Jonah, do you love Me more (than) these? He says to Him, Yes,
2962 4771 1492/3754/5368/4571/3004/846 1006 721 3450
Κύριε· σὺ οἶδας ὅτι φιλῶ σε λέγει αὐτῷ, Βόσκε τὰ ἀρνία μου.
Lord, You know that I love You. He says to him, Feed the lambs of Me.
3004 846 3825 1208 4513 2495 25 3165 3004
16 λέγει αὐτῷ πάλιν δεύτερον, Σίμων Ἰωνᾶ, ἀγαπᾷς με; λέγει
He says to him again secondly, Simon of Jonah, do you love Me? He says
846 3483 2962/4771/1492/3754/5368/4571/3004/846 4165
αὐτῷ, Ναὶ Κύριε· σὺ οἶδας ὅτι φιλῶ σε. λέγει αὐτῷ, Ποίμαινε
to Him, Yes, Lord, You know that I love You. He says to him, Shepherd
4263 3450 3004 846 5154 4613 2495 5368
17 τὰ πρόβατά μου. λέγει αὐτῷ τὸ τρίτον, Σίμων Ἰωνᾶ, φιλεῖς
the sheep of Me. He says to him thirdly, Simon of Jonah do you
3165 3076 4074 3754 2036 846 5154 5368 love*
*3165 με; ἐλυπήθη ὁ Πέτρος ὅτι εἶπεν αὐτῷ τὸ τρίτον, φιλεῖς με;
Me? was grieved Peter that He said to him thirdly, Do you love Me?
2036 846 2962 4771 3956 1492 4771 1097 3754
καὶ εἶπεν αὐτῷ, Κύριε, σὺ πάντα οἶδας· σὺ γινώσκεις ὅτι
And he said to Him, Lord, You all things perceive; You know that
5368/4571/3004/846 2424 1006 4263 3450 281
18 φιλῶ σε. λέγει αὐτῷ ὁ Ἰησοῦς, Βόσκε τὰ πρόβατά μου. ἀμὴν
I love You. says to him Jesus, Feed. the little sheep of Me. Truly,
281 3004 4671 3753/2258 3501 2224 4572
ἀμὴν λέγω σοι, ὅτε ἦς νεώτερος, ἐζώννυες σεαυτόν, καὶ
truly, I say to you, when you were younger you girded yourself, and
4043 3699 2309 3752 1095 1614
περιεπάτεις ὅπου ἤθελες· ὅταν δὲ γηράσῃς, ἐκτενεῖς τὰς
you walked where you desired, when but you grow old you will stretch the
5495 4675 243 4571 2224 5342 3699 3756 2309
χεῖράς σου, καὶ ἄλλος σε ζώσει, καὶ οἴσει ὅπου οὐ θέλεις.
hands of you, and another you will gird, and will carry where not you want

you where you do not desire. [19]But He said this signifying by what death he would glorify God. And having said this, He told him, Follow Me. [20]But turning, Peter saw the disciple whom Jesus loved following *them,* who also leaned on His breast at the Supper, and said, Lord, who is the *one* betraying You? [21]Seeing him, Peter said to Jesus, Lord, and what *of* this one? [22]Jesus said to him, If I desire him to remain until I come, what *is that* to you? You follow Me. [23]Therefore, the word went out to the brothers that that disciple does not die. Yet Jesus did not say to him that he does not die, but, If I desire him to remain until I come, what *is that* to you?

[24]This is the disciple witnessing about these other things, writing these things, and we know that his witness is true.

[25]And there are also many things, whatever Jesus did, which if they were written singly, I suppose the world itself *could* not contain the books having been written. Amen.

5124 2036 4591 4169 2288 1392 2316
19 τοῦτο δὲ εἶπε, σημαίνων ποίῳ θανάτῳ δοξάσει τὸν Θεόν.
this And He said, signifying by what death he will glorify God.
5124 2036 3004 846 190 3427 1994
20 καὶ τοῦτο εἰπὼν λέγει αὐτῷ, Ἀκολούθει μοι. ἐπιστραφεὶς δὲ
And this said, He tells him, Follow Me. turning And
4074 991 3101 3739 25 2424 190
ὁ Πέτρος βλέπει τὸν μαθητὴν ὃν ἠγάπα ὁ Ἰησοῦς ἀκολου-
Peter sees the disciple whom loved Jesus, following,
3739 377 1722 1173 1909 4738 848
θοῦντα, ὃς καὶ ἀνέπεσεν ἐν τῷ δείπνῳ ἐπὶ τὸ στῆθος αὐτοῦ
who also leaned at the supper on the breast of Him
2036 2962 5101 2076 3860 4571 5126 1492
21 καὶ εἶπε, Κύριε, τίς ἐστιν ὁ παραδιδούς σε; τοῦτον ἰδὼν ὁ
and said, Lord, who is the (one) betraying You? This one seeing
4074 3004 2424 2962 3778 5101 3004 846
22 Πέτρος λέγει τῷ Ἰησοῦ, Κύριε, οὗτος δὲ τί; λέγει αὐτῷ ὁ
Peter says to Jesus, Lord, this one and what? says to him
2424 1437 846 2309 3306 2193 2064 5101/4314/4571
Ἰησοῦς, Ἐὰν αὐτὸν θέλω μένειν ἕως ἔρχομαι, τί πρός σε;
Jesus, If him I desire to remain until I come, what to you?
4771 190 3427 1831 3767 3056 3778 1519 80
23 σὺ ἀκολούθει μοι. ἐξῆλθεν οὖν ὁ λόγος οὗτος εἰς τοὺς ἀδελ-
You follow Me. went out Therefore word this to the brothers,
3754 3101 1565 3756 599 3756 2036
φούς, ὅτι ὁ μαθητὴς ἐκεῖνος οὐκ ἀποθνήσκει· καὶ οὐκ εἶπεν
that disciple that not does die; and not said
846 2424 3754/3756 599 235 1437 846 2309
αὐτῷ ὁ Ἰησοῦς, ὅτι οὐκ ἀποθνήσκει· ἀλλ', Ἐὰν αὐτὸν θέλω
to him Jesus that not he does die; but, If him I desire
3306 2193 2064 5101 4314/4571
μένειν ἕως ἔρχομαι, τί πρός σε;
to remain until I come, what to you?
3778 2076 3101 3140 4012 5130
24 Οὗτός ἐστιν ὁ μαθητὴς ὁ μαρτυρῶν περὶ τούτων, καὶ
This is the disciple witnessing concerning other things
1125 5023 1492 3754 227 2076 3141
γράψας ταῦτα· καὶ οἴδαμεν ὅτι ἀληθής ἐστιν ἡ μαρτυρία
writing these things, and we know that true is the witness
848
αὐτοῦ.
of him.
2076 243 4183 3745 4160 2424 3748
25 Ἔστι δὲ καὶ ἄλλα πολλὰ ὅσα ἐποίησεν ὁ Ἰησοῦς, ἅτινα
are And also the things many, whatever did Jesus, which
1437 1125 2596/1520/3761/ 848 3633 2889 5562
ἐὰν γράφηται καθ' ἕν, οὐδὲ αὐτὸν οἶμαι τὸν κόσμον χωρῆσαι
if they were written singly, not itself I suppose the world to contain
1125 975 281
τὰ γραφόμενα βιβλία. Ἀμήν.
those being written rolls. Amen.

ACTS
OF THE
APOSTLES

A LITERAL TRANSLATION
OF THE BIBLE

CHAPTER 1

1Indeed, O Theophilus, I made the first report concerning all things which Jesus began both to do and to teach, 2until the day He was taken up, having given directions to the apostles whom He chose, through *the* Holy Spirit; 3to whom also He presented Himself living after His suffering, by many infallible proofs, being seen by them through forty days, and speaking the things concerning the kingdom of God. 4And having met with them, He charged them not to leave Jerusalem, but to await the promise of the Father, "which you heard of Me; 5for John indeed baptized in water, but you will be baptized in *the* Holy Spirit not many days after."

6Then, indeed, coming together they questioned Him, saying, Lord, do You restore the kingdom to Israel at this time? 7And He said to them, It is not yours to know times or seasons, which the Father placed in His own authority; 8but you will receive power, the Holy Spirit coming upon you, and you will be witnesses of Me both in Jerusalem, and in all Judea, and Samaria, and to *the* end of the earth. 9And saying these things, *as* they looked on, He was taken up; and a cloud received Him from their eyes.

10And as they were

ΠΡΑΞΕΙΣ
ACTS
ΤΩΝ ΑΠΟΣΤΟΛΩΝ
OF THE APOSTLES

CHAPTER 1

3303 4413 3056 4160 4012 3956 5599
1 Τὸν μὲν πρῶτον λόγον ἐποιησάμην περὶ πάντων, ὦ
The — first account I made concerning all things, O
2321 3739 756 2424 4160 1321
2 Θεόφιλε, ὧν ἤρξατο ὁ Ἰησοῦς ποιεῖν τε καὶ διδάσκειν, ἄχρι
Theophilus, which began — Jesus to do both and to teach, until
3739 2250 1781 652 1223 4151
ἧς ἡμέρας, ἐντειλάμενος τοῖς ἀποστόλοις διὰ Πνεύματος
which day, having given directions to the apostles through (the) Spirit
40 3739 1586 353 3739 3936 1438
3 Ἁγίου οὓς ἐξελέξατο, ἀνελήφθη· οἷς καὶ παρέστησεν ἑαυτὸν
Holy whom He chose, He was taken up; to whom also He showed Himself
2198 3326 3958 846 1722 4183 5039 1223
ζῶντα μετὰ τὸ παθεῖν αὐτὸν ἐν πολλοῖς τεκμηρίοις, δι'
living after the suffering (of) Him by many infallible proofs through
2250 5062 3700 846 3004
ἡμερῶν τεσσαράκοντα ὀπτανόμενος αὐτοῖς, καὶ λέγων τὰ
days forty being seen by them, and saying the things
4012 932 2316 4871 3326 846
4 περὶ τῆς βασιλείας τοῦ Θεοῦ. καὶ συναλιζόμενος μετ' αὐτῶν
about the kingdom — of God. And meeting with them
3853 846 575 2414 3361 5563
παρήγγειλεν αὐτοῖς ἀπὸ Ἱεροσολύμων μὴ χωρίζεσθαι,
He charged them from Jerusalem not to depart,
235 4037 1860 3962 3739 191
ἀλλὰ περιμένειν τὴν ἐπαγγελίαν τοῦ πατρός, ἣν ἠκούσατέ
but to await the promise of the Father, which you heard
3450 3754 2491 3303 907 5204 5210 907
5 μου· ὅτι Ἰωάννης μὲν ἐβάπτισεν ὕδατι, ὑμεῖς δὲ βαπτισθή-
of Me, because John indeed baptized in water, you but will be
1722 4151 40 3756 3326 4183 5025 2250
σεσθε ἐν Πνεύματι Ἁγίῳ οὐ μετὰ πολλὰς ταύτας ἡμέρας.
baptized in (the) Spirit Holy not after many these days.
3303/3767 4905 1905 846 3004 2962
6 Οἱ μὲν οὖν συνελθόντες ἐπηρώτων αὐτὸν λέγοντες, Κύριε,
those So then coming together questioned Him, saying, Lord,
1487/1722 5550 5129 600 932
εἰ ἐν τῷ χρόνῳ τούτῳ ἀποκαθιστάνεις τὴν βασιλείαν τῷ
if at — time this restore You the kingdom —
2474 2036 4314 846 3756 5216 2076 1097
7 Ἰσραήλ; εἶπε δὲ πρὸς αὐτούς, Οὐχ ὑμῶν ἐστι γνῶναι
to Israel? He said And to them, Not of you it is to know
5550 2228 2540 3739 3962 5087/1722 2398 1849
χρόνους ἢ καιροὺς οὓς ὁ πατὴρ ἔθετο ἐν τῇ ἰδίᾳ ἐξουσίᾳ.
times or seasons which the Father placed in the own authority.
235 2983 1411 1904 40 4151
8 ἀλλὰ λήψεσθε δύναμιν, ἐπελθόντος τοῦ Ἁγίου Πνεύματος
But you will receive power, coming the Holy Spirit
1909 5209 2071 3427 3144 1722/5037 2419 1722
ἐφ' ὑμᾶς· καὶ ἔσεσθέ μοι μάρτυρες ἔν τε Ἱερουσαλήμ, καὶ ἐν
upon you, and you will be of Me witnesses in both Jerusalem, and in
3956 2449 4540 2193 2078 1093
πάσῃ τῇ Ἰουδαίᾳ καὶ Σαμαρείᾳ, καὶ ἕως ἐσχάτου τῆς γῆς.
all — Judea, and Samaria, and unto (the) end of the earth.
5023 2036 991 846 1869 3507
9 καὶ ταῦτα εἰπών, βλεπόντων αὐτῶν ἐπήρθη, καὶ νεφέλη
And these things saying, looking them, He was taken up, and a cloud
5274 848 575 3788 848 5613 816
10 ὑπέλαβεν αὐτὸν ἀπὸ τῶν ὀφθαλμῶν αὐτῶν. καὶ ὡς ἀτενί-
received Him from the eyes of them. And as gazing

intently looking into the heaven, He having gone, even behold, two men in white clothing stood by them, [11]who also said, Men, Galileans, why do you stand looking up to the heaven? This Jesus, the *One* being taken from you into Heaven, will come in the way you saw Him going into Heaven.

[12]Then they returned to Jerusalem from *the* mount being called Of Olive Grove, which is near Jerusalem, a sabbath's *journey* away. [13]And when they went in, they went up to the upper room where they were waiting: both Peter and James, and John and Andrew, Philip and Thomas, Bartholomew and Matthew, James *the son* of Alpheus and Simon the Zealot, and Judas *the brother* of James. [14]These all were continuing steadfastly in prayer and in supplication with one mind, with *the* women, and *with* Mary the mother of Jesus, and with His brothers.

[15]And in these days, standing up in *the* middle of the disciples—and *the* number of names together *being* about a hundred and twenty — Peter said, [16]Men, brothers, it was necessary *for* this Scripture to be fulfilled which the Holy Spirit spoke before by David's mouth concerning Judas, the *one* having become guide to those seizing Jesus; [17]for he was numbered with us, and obtained a portion of this ministry. [18]Indeed, then, this one bought a field out of the reward of unrighteousness, and falling headlong, he burst in *the* middle, and poured out all

2258/1519 3772 4198 846 2400
ζοντες ἦσαν εἰς τὸν οὐρανόν, πορευομένου αὐτοῦ, καὶ ἰδοὺ
they were into the heaven, going Him, and behold,
435 1417 3936 846 1722 2066 3022
11 ἄνδρες δύο παρειστήκεισαν αὐτοῖς ἐν ἐσθῆτι λευκῇ, οἳ καὶ
men two stood by them in clothing white, who also
2036 435 1057 5101 2476 1689 1519
εἶπον, Ἄνδρες Γαλιλαῖοι, τί ἑστήκατε ἐμβλέποντες εἰς τὸν
said, Men, Galileans, why do you stand looking into the
3772 3779 2424 353 575 5216 1519
οὐρανόν ; οὗτος ὁ Ἰησοῦς, ὁ ἀναληφθεὶς ἀφ' ὑμῶν εἰς τὸν
heaven? This Jesus, the (One) being taken from you into the
3772 3779 2064 3739 5158 2300 846
οὐρανόν, οὕτως ἐλεύσεται ὃν τρόπον ἐθεάσασθε αὐτὸν
heaven, thus will come in the way you beheld Him
4198 1519 3772
πορευόμενον εἰς τὸν οὐρανόν.
going into the heaven.

5119 5290 1519 2419 575 3735 2564
12 Τότε ὑπέστρεψαν εἰς Ἱερουσαλὴμ ἀπὸ ὄρους τοῦ καλου-
Then they returned to Jerusalem from (the) mount being
1638 3739 2076 1451 2419 4521
μένου Ἐλαιῶνος, ὅ ἐστιν ἐγγὺς Ἱερουσαλήμ, σαββάτου
called Of olive grove, which is near Jerusalem, a sabbath's
2192 3598 3753 1525 305 1519 5253 3756
13 ἔχον ὁδόν. καὶ ὅτε εἰσῆλθον, ἀνέβησαν εἰς τὸ ὑπερῷον οὗ
having a way. And when they entered, they went up to the upper room where
2258 2650 5037 4074 2385 2491
ἦσαν καταμένοντες, ὅ τε Πέτρος καὶ Ἰάκωβος καὶ Ἰωάννης καὶ
they were waiting, both Peter and James and John and
406 5376 2381 918 3156
Ἀνδρέας, Φίλιππος καὶ Θωμᾶς, Βαρθολομαῖος καὶ Ματθαῖος,
Andrew, Philip and Thomas, Bartholomew and Matthew,
2385 256 4613 2208 2455 2385
Ἰάκωβος Ἀλφαίου καὶ Σίμων ὁ Ζηλωτής, καὶ Ἰούδας Ἰακώ-
James of Alpheus and Simon the Zealot, and Judas of
3778 3956 2258 4342 3661
14 βου. οὗτοι πάντες ἦσαν προσκαρτεροῦντες ὁμοθυμαδὸν τῇ
James. These all were continuing steadfastly with one mind —
4335 1162 4862 1135 3137 3384
προσευχῇ καὶ τῇ δεήσει, σὺν γυναιξὶ καὶ Μαρίᾳ τῇ μητρὶ τοῦ
in prayer and in supplication, with (the) women, and Mary the mother —
2424 4862 80 848
Ἰησοῦ, καὶ σὺν τοῖς ἀδελφοῖς αὐτοῦ.
of Jesus, and with the brothers of Him.

1722 2250 5025 450 4074 1722/3319
15 Καὶ ἐν ταῖς ἡμέραις ταύταις ἀναστὰς Πέτρος ἐν μέσῳ τῶν
And in — days these standing up Peter in (the) midst of the
3101 2036 2258/5037/3793 3686 1909 846 5613 1540
μαθητῶν εἶπεν (ἦν τε ὄχλος ὀνομάτων ἐπὶ τὸ αὐτὸ ὡς ἑκατὸν
disciples said; was and the crowd of names together about a hundred
1501 435 80 1163 4137 1124
16 εἴκοσιν), Ἄνδρες ἀδελφοί, ἔδει πληρωθῆναι τὴν γραφὴν
twenty; Men, brothers, it behoved to be fulfilled Scripture
5026 3739 4277 4151 40 1223 4750
ταύτην, ἣν προεῖπε τὸ Πνεῦμα τὸ Ἅγιον διὰ στόματος
this, which spoke the Spirit Holy through mouth
1138 4012 2455 1096 3595 4815
Δαβὶδ περὶ Ἰούδα, τοῦ γενομένου ὁδηγοῦ τοῖς συλλαβοῦσι
David's concerning Judas, the (one) being guide to the (ones) taking
2424 3754 2674 2258/4862/2254 2975
17 τὸν Ἰησοῦν. ὅτι κατηριθμημένος ἦν σὺν ἡμῖν, καὶ ἔλαχε τὸν
— Jesus; because being numbered he was with us, and obtained the
2819 1248 5026 3778 3303 3767 2932
18 κλῆρον τῆς διακονίας ταύτης. (οὗτος μὲν οὖν ἐκτήσατο
portion — of ministry this; this one therefore bought
5564 1537 3408 93 4248 1096
χωρίον ἐκ τοῦ μισθοῦ τῆς ἀδικίας, καὶ πρηνὴς γενόμενος
a field out of the reward of unrighteousness, and headlong becoming
2997 3319 1632 3956 4698 848
19 ἐλάκησε μέσος, καὶ ἐξεχύθη πάντα τὰ σπλάγχνα αὐτοῦ. καὶ
he burst in (the) middle, and poured out all the bowels of him. And

his bowels. 19And it became known to all those living in Jerusalem, so as that field to be called in their own dialect, Akeldama; that is, Field of Blood. 20For it has been written in *the* scroll of Psalms, "Let his estate become forsaken, and he not be living in it." And, "Let another take his office." 21Therefore, it is right that one of these men being with us all *the* time in which the Lord Jesus came in and went out among us, 22beginning from the baptism of John until the day when He was taken from us, one of these to become a witness of His resurrection with us. 23And they set out two: Joseph, he being called Barsabas, who was surnamed Justus; and Matthias. 24And having prayed, they said, You, Lord, knower of all hearts, show which one You chose from these two, 25to take the share of this ministry and apostleship, from which Judas fell, to go to *his* own place. 26And they gave their lots. And the lot fell on Matthias; and he was numbered with the eleven apostles.

1110 1096 3956 2730 2419 5620
γνωστὸν ἐγένετο πᾶσι τοις κατοικοῦσιν Ἱερουσαλήμ, ὥστε
known it became to all those inhabiting Jerusalem, so as

2564 5564 1565 2398 1258 848 184
κληθῆναι τὸ χωρίον ἐκεῖνο τῇ ἰδίᾳ διαλέκτῳ αὐτῶν Ἀκελ-
to be called — field that in the own dialect of them Akel-

5123 2076 5564 129 1125 1063/1722/976
20 δαμά, τοῦτ᾽ ἔστι, χωρίον αἵματος.) γέγραπται γὰρ ἐν βίβλῳ
dama, that is, Field of Blood. it has been written For in (the) roll

5568 1096 1886 848 2048 3361 2077
Ψαλμῶν, Γενηθήτω ἡ ἔπαυλις αὐτοῦ ἔρημος, καὶ μὴ ἔστω ὁ
of Psalms, Let become the estate of him forsaken, and not be he

2730 1722 846 1984 848 2983 2087
21 κατοικῶν ἐν αὐτῇ· καί, Τὴν ἐπισκοπὴν αὐτοῦ λάβοι ἕτερος.
dwelling in it; and, The office of him let take another.

1163/3767 4905 2254 435 1722 3956 5550 1722 *
δεῖ οὖν τῶν συνελθόντων ἡμῖν ἀνδρῶν ἐν παντὶ χρόνῳ ἐν ᾧ
*3739 must Then of the accompanying us men in all (the) time in which

1525 1831 1909/2248 2962 2424 756 575
εἰσῆλθε καὶ ἐξῆλθεν ἐφ᾽ ἡμᾶς ὁ Κύριος Ἰησοῦς, ἀρξάμενος ἀπὸ
went in and went out among us the Lord Jesus, beginning from

908 2491 2193 2250 3739 353 575
22 τοῦ βαπτίσματος Ἰωάννου, ἕως τῆς ἡμέρας ἧς ἀνελήφθη ἀφ᾽
the baptism of John until the day when He was taken from

2257 3144 386 848 1096 4862 2254
ἡμῶν, μάρτυρα τῆς ἀναστάσεως αὐτοῦ γενέσθαι σὺν ἡμῖν
us, a witness of the resurrection of Him to become with us

1520 5130 2476 1417 2501 2564
23 ἕνα τούτων. καὶ ἔστησαν δύο, Ἰωσὴφ τὸν καλούμενον
one of these. And they set two, Joseph the (one) being called

923 3739 1941 2459 3159 4336
24 Βαρσαβᾶν, ὃς ἐπεκλήθη Ἰοῦστος, καὶ Ματθίαν. καὶ προσ-
Barsabas, who was surnamed Justus, and Matthias. And

2036 4771 2962 2589 3956 322
ευξάμενοι εἶπον, Σὺ Κύριε καρδιογνῶστα πάντων, ἀνά-
praying they said, You, Lord, Heart-knower of all, show

1537 5130 1417/3739/1520/ 1586 2983 2819
25 δειξον ἐκ τούτων τῶν δύο ὃν ἕνα ἐξελέξω, λαβεῖν τὸν κλῆρον
out of these — two which one You chose to take the part

1248 5026 651 1537 3739/3845 2455
τῆς διακονίας ταύτης καὶ ἀποστολῆς, ἐξ ἧς παρέβη Ἰούδας,
of ministry this and apostleship, from which fell Judas,

4198 1519 5117 2398 1325 2819
26 πορευθῆναι εἰς τὸν τόπον τὸν ἴδιον. καὶ ἔδωκαν κλήρους
to go to the place — own. And they gave lots

848 4098 1819 1909 3159 4785
αὐτῶν, καὶ ἔπεσεν ὁ κλῆρος ἐπὶ Ματθίαν, καὶ συγκατεψη-
for them, and fell the lot on Matthias; and he was counted

3326 1733 652
φίσθη μετὰ τῶν ἕνδεκα ἀποστόλων.
with the eleven apostles.

CHAPTER 2

CHAPTER 2

1And in the fulfilling of the day of Pentecost, they were all with one mind in the same place. 2And suddenly a sound came out of the heaven, as being borne along by a violent wind! And it filled all the house where they were sitting. 3And tongues as of fire appeared to them *were* being distributed; and it sat on each one of them. 4And they were all filled of *the*

1722 4845 2250 4005
1 Καὶ ἐν τῷ συμπληροῦσθαι τὴν ἡμέραν τῆς Πεντηκοστῆς,
And in the fulfilling of the Day — of Pentecost,

2258 537 3661 1909 846 1096 869
2 ἦσαν ἅπαντες ὁμοθυμαδὸν ἐπὶ τὸ αὐτό. καὶ ἐγένετο ἄφνω
they were all with one mind in the same place. And was suddenly

1537 3772 2279 5618 5342 4157 972
ἐκ τοῦ οὐρανοῦ ἦχος ὥσπερ φερομένης πνοῆς βιαίας, καὶ
out of Heaven a sound as being borne of a wind violent, and

4137 3650 3624 3757/2258/ 2521 3700
3 ἐπλήρωσεν ὅλον τὸν οἶκον οὗ ἦσαν καθήμενοι. καὶ ὤφθησαν
it filled all the house where they were sitting. And appeared

846 1266 1100 5616 4442 2523 5037/1909
αὐτοῖς διαμεριζόμεναι γλῶσσαι ὡσεὶ πυρός, ἐκάθισέ τε ἐφ᾽
to them being distributed tongues as of fire, it sat and on

1520 1538 846 4130 537 4151
4 ἕνα ἕκαστον αὐτῶν. καὶ ἐπλήσθησαν ἅπαντες Πνεύματος
one each of them. And they were filled all of (the) Spirit

Holy Spirit, and began to speak in other languages, as the Spirit gave *ability* to them to speak.

[5]And Jews were living in Jerusalem, devout men from every nation of those under the heaven. [6]But this sound occurring, the multitude came together and were confounded, because they each heard them speaking in his own dialect.

[7]And all were amazed and marveled, saying to one another, Behold, are not all these, those speaking, Galileans? [8]And how do we hear each in our own dialect in which we were born, [9]Parthians, and Medes, and Elamites, and those living in Mesopotamia, both Judea and Cappadocia, Pontus and Asia, [10]both Phrygia and Pamphylia, Egypt, and the regions of Libya over against Cyrene, and the temporarily residing Romans, both Jews and proselytes, [11]Cretans and Arabians; we hear them speaking the great deeds of God in our own languages? [12]And all were amazed and puzzled, saying to one another, What would this wish to be? [13]But ridiculing, others said, They are full of sweet wine.

[14]But standing up with the Eleven, Peter lifted up his voice and spoke out to them, Men, Jews, and all those living in Jerusalem, let this be known to you, and listen to my words: [15]For these are not drunk, as you imagine, for it is *the* third hour of the day;, but

40 756 2980 2087 1100 2531
ʽΑγίου, καὶ ἤρξαντο λαλεῖν ἑτέραις γλώσσαις, καθὼς τὸ
Holy, and began to speak in other languages, as the
4151 1325 846 659
Πνεῦμα ἐδίδου αὐτοῖς ἀποφθέγγεσθαι.
Spirit gave to them to speak.
2258 1722 2419 2730 2453 435
5 Ἦσαν δὲ ἐν Ἱερουσαλὴμ κατοικοῦντες Ἰουδαῖοι, ἄνδρες
were And in Jerusalem living Jews, men
2126 575 3956 1484 5259 3772 1096
6 εὐλαβεῖς, ἀπὸ παντὸς ἔθνους τῶν ὑπὸ τὸν οὐρανόν. γενο-
devout from every nation of those under the heaven. happen-
5456 5026 4905 4128 4797
μένης δὲ τῆς φωνῆς ταύτης, συνῆλθε τὸ πλῆθος καὶ συνεχύθη.
ing And sound this, came together the multitude and were confounded
3754 191 1520 1538 2398 1258 2980
846 ὅτι ἤκουον εἷς ἕκαστος τῇ ἰδίᾳ διαλέκτῳ λαλούντων αὐτῶν.
because they heard each in the own dialect speaking them.
1839 3956 2296 3004 4314 240
7 ἐξίσταντο δὲ πάντες καὶ ἐθαύμαζον, λέγοντες πρὸς ἀλλή-
were amazed And all and marveled, saying to one
3756 2400 3956 3778 1526 2980 1057
λους, Οὐκ ἰδοὺ πάντες οὗτοί εἰσιν οἱ λαλοῦντες Γαλιλαῖοι ;
another, not, Behold, all these are those speaking Galileans?
4459 2249 191 1538 2398 1258 2257 1722
8 καὶ πῶς ἡμεῖς ἀκούομεν ἕκαστος τῇ ἰδίᾳ διαλέκτῳ ἡμῶν ἐν
And how we hear each in the own dialect of us in
1080 3934 3370 1639
9 ᾗ ἐγεννήθημεν ; Πάρθοι καὶ Μῆδοι καὶ Ἐλαμῖται, καὶ οἱ
which we were born, Parthians and Medes and Elamites, and those
2730 3318 2449 5037 2587
κατοικοῦντες τὴν Μεσοποταμίαν, Ἰουδαίαν τε καὶ Καπ-
inhabiting — Mesopotamia, Judea both and Cappa-
4195 773 5435 3828
10 παδοκίαν, Πόντον καὶ τὴν Ἀσίαν, Φρυγίαν τε καὶ Παμφυ-
docia, Pontus and — Asia, Phrygia both and Pam-
125 3313 3033 2596 2957
λίαν, Αἴγυπτον καὶ τὰ μέρη τῆς Λιβύης τῆς κατὰ Κυρήνην,
phylia, Egypt and the regions — of Libya — over against Cyrene,
2927 4514 2453 5037 4339
καὶ οἱ ἐπιδημοῦντες Ῥωμαῖοι, Ἰουδαῖοί τε καὶ προσήλυτοι,
and the temporarily residing Romans, Jews both and proselytes,
2912 690 191 2980 846
11 Κρῆτες καὶ Ἄραβες, ἀκούομεν λαλούντων αὐτῶν ταῖς
Cretans and Arabians, we hear speaking them in
2251 1100 3167 2316 1839
ἡμετέραις γλώσσαις τὰ μεγαλεῖα τοῦ Θεοῦ. ἐξίσταντο δὲ
our languages the great deeds — of God. were amazed And
3956 1280 243 4314 243 3004 5101 302
12 πάντες καὶ διηπόρουν, ἄλλος πρὸς ἄλλον λέγοντες, Τί ἂν
all and were puzzled, other to other saying, What would
2309 5124 1511 2087 5512 3004 3754 1098
13 θέλοι τοῦτο εἶναι ; ἕτεροι δὲ χλευάζοντες ἔλεγον ὅτι Γλεύκους
you wish this to be? others But mocking said, — Of sweet wine
3325 1526
μεμεστωμένοι εἰσί.
full they are.
2476 4074 4862 1733 1869 5456 848
14 Σταθεὶς δὲ Πέτρος σὺν τοῖς ἕνδεκα, ἐπῆρε τὴν φωνὴν αὐ-
standing But Peter with the eleven lifted up the voice of
669 846 435 2453 2730
τοῦ, καὶ ἀπεφθέγξατο αὐτοῖς, Ἄνδρες Ἰουδαῖοι, καὶ οἱ κατ-
him and spoke out to them, Men, Jews, and those
2419 537 5124 5213 1110
οικοῦντες Ἱερουσαλὴμ ἅπαντες, τοῦτο ὑμῖν γνωστὸν ἔστω,
inhabiting Jerusalem all, this to you known let be,
1801 4487 3450/3756/1063/5613/5210 5274
15 καὶ ἐνωτίσασθε τὰ ῥήματά μου. οὐ γάρ, ὡς ὑμεῖς ὑπολαμ-
and give ear to the words of me. not For, as you imagine,
3778 3184 2076 1063 5610 5154 2250
βάνετε, οὗτοι μεθύουσιν· ἔστι γὰρ ὥρα τρίτη τῆς ἡμέρας·
these are drunk, it is for hour third of the day;

this is that which has been
spoken by the prophet Joel,
[17]"And it shall be in the last
days, God says, I will pour
from My Spirit on all flesh,
and your sons and your
daughters shall prophesy;
and your young men shall
see visions; and your old
men shall dream dreams;
[18]and also I will pour out My
Spirit on My slaves and
slave-girls in those days,
and they shall prophesy.

[19]And I will give wonders
in the heaven above, and
miracles on the earth be-
low, blood and fire and
vapor of smoke. [20]The sun
will be turned into dark-
ness, and the moon into
blood, before the coming of
the great and notable day of
the Lord. [21]And it shall be
that everyone who shall call
on the name of *the* Lord will
be saved."

[22]Men, Israelites, hear
these words: Jesus the
Nazarene, a man from God,
having been approved
among you by powerful
deeds and wonders and
miracles, which God did
through Him in your midst,
as you yourselves also
know, [23]this One given to
you by the before-
determined counsel and
foreknowledge of God, *you*
having taken *Him* by lawless hands, having crucified
Him, you put *Him* to death.
[24]*But* God raised *Him* up,
loosing the throes of death,
because it was not possible
for Him to be held by it.
[25]For David said as to Him,
"I always foresaw the Lord
before Me, because He is at
My right *hand,* that I not be
moved. [26]For this reason
My heart rejoiced, and My
tongue was glad; and My
flesh also will dwell on
hope, [27]because You will

235 5124 2076 2045 1223 4396 2493
16 ἀλλὰ τοῦτό ἐστι τὸ εἰρημένον διὰ τοῦ προφήτου Ἰωήλ,
but this is the thing being spoken through the prophet Joel:
2071/1722 2078 2250 3004 2316 1632 575
17 Καὶ ἔσται ἐν ταῖς ἐσχάταις ἡμέραις, λέγει ὁ Θεός, ἐκχεῶ ἀπὸ
And it shall be in the last days, says – God, I will pour from
4151 3450 1909 3956 4561 4395
τοῦ πνεύματός μου ἐπὶ πᾶσαν σάρκα· καὶ προφητεύσουσιν
the Spirit of Me on all flesh, and will prophesy
5207 5216 2364 5216 3495 5216
οἱ υἱοὶ ὑμῶν καὶ αἱ θυγατέρες ὑμῶν. καὶ οἱ νεανίσκοι ὑμῶν
the sons of you, and the daughters of you, and the young men of you
3706 3700 4245 5216 1798 1797
ὁράσεις ὄψονται, καὶ οἱ πρεσβύτεροι ὑμῶν ἐνύπνια ἐνυπνια-
visions will see, and the old men of you dreams will
1065/1909 1401 3450 1909 1399
18 σθήσονται· καί γε ἐπὶ τοὺς δούλους μου καὶ ἐπὶ τὰς δούλας
dream, and – on the male slaves of Me, and on the female slaves
3450/1722 2250 1565 1632 575 4151 3450
μου ἐν ταῖς ἡμέραις ἐκείναις ἐκχεῶ ἀπὸ τοῦ πνεύματός μου, καὶ
of Me, in – days those I will pour from the Spirit of Me, and
4395 1325 5059 1722 3772 507
19 προφητεύσουσι. καὶ δώσω τέρατα ἐν τῷ οὐρανῷ ἄνω, καὶ
they will prophesy. And I will give wonders in the heaven above, and
4592 1909 1093 129 4442 822 2586
σημεῖα ἐπὶ τῆς γῆς κάτω, αἷμα καὶ πῦρ καὶ ἀτμίδα καπνοῦ
signs on the earth below, blood and fire and vapor of smoke.
2246 3344 1519 4655 4582 1519
20 ὁ ἥλιος μεταστραφήσεται εἰς σκότος, καὶ ἡ σελήνη εἰς
The sun will be turned into darkness and the moon into
129 4250/2228/2064 2250 2962 3173
αἷμα, πρὶν ἢ ἐλθεῖν τὴν ἡμέραν Κυρίου τὴν μεγάλην καὶ
blood, before comes the day of (the) Lord the great and
2016 2071 3956/3739/302/ 1941 3686 2962
21 ἐπιφανῆ· καὶ ἔσται, πᾶς ὃς ἂν ἐπικαλέσηται τὸ ὄνομα Κυρίου
notable. And it will be everyone whoever calls on the name of (the) Lord
4982 435 2475 191 3056
22 σωθήσεται. ἄνδρες Ἰσραηλῖται, ἀκούσατε τοὺς λόγους
will be saved. Men, Israelites, hear words
5128 2424 3480 435 575 2316
τούτους· Ἰησοῦν τὸν Ναζωραῖον, ἄνδρα ἀπὸ τοῦ Θεοῦ
these: Jesus the Nazarene, a man from God
584 1519/5209/ 1411 5059 4592
ἀποδεδειγμένον εἰς ὑμᾶς δυνάμεσι καὶ τέρασι καὶ σημείοις,
having been approved among you by powerful and wonders and signs,
•1722 3739 4160 1223 846 2316 deeds 5216 2531 846
•3319 οἷς ἐποίησε δι' αὐτοῦ ὁ Θεὸς ἐν μέσῳ ὑμῶν, καθὼς καὶ αὐτοὶ
which did through Him God amidst you, as also yourselves
1492 5126 3724 1012 4268 2316
23 οἴδατε, τοῦτον τῇ ὡρισμένῃ βουλῇ καὶ προγνώσει τοῦ Θεοῦ
you know, this One by the before-determined counsel and foreknowledge of God
1560 2983 5495 459 4362
•1223 ἔκδοτον λαβόντες, διὰ χειρῶν ἀνόμων προσπήξαντες
given up having taken by hands lawless, having crucified,
337 3739/ 2316 450 3089 5604 2288
24 ἀνείλετε· ὃν ὁ Θεὸς ἀνέστησε, λύσας τὰς ὠδῖνας τοῦ θανάτου,
you killed, whom God raised up, having loosed the throes – of death,
2530 3756/2258/ 1415 2902 846 5259 846 1138
25 καθότι οὐκ ἦν δυνατὸν κρατεῖσθαι αὐτὸν ὑπ' αὐτοῦ. Δαβὶδ
because not it was possible to be held Him by it. David
1063 3004 1519 846 4308 2962 1799 3450
γὰρ λέγει εἰς αὐτόν, Προωρώμην τὸν Κύριον ἐνώπιόν μου
For says (as) to Him, I foresaw the Lord before Me
1223 3956 3754/1537/ 1188 3450 2076 2443/3363 4531
26 διὰ παντός· ὅτι ἐκ δεξιῶν μου ἐστίν, ἵνα μὴ σαλευθῶ· διὰ
always, because on (the) right Me He is, that not I be moved. There-
5124 2165 2588 3450 21 1100
τοῦτο εὐφράνθη ἡ καρδία μου, καὶ ἠγαλλιάσατο ἡ γλῶσσά
fore was glad the heart of Me and exulted the tongue
3450 2089 4561 3450 2681 1909 1680 3754/3756
27 μου· ἔτι δὲ καὶ ἡ σάρξ μου κατασκηνώσει ἐπ' ἐλπίδι· ὅτι οὐκ
of Me; yet And also the flesh of Me will dwell on hope, because not

not leave My soul in Hades, nor will You give Your Holy One to see corruption.
[28]You revealed to Me paths of life; You will fill Me with joy with Your face."

[29]Men, brothers, it is permitted to say to you with plainness as to the patriarch David, that he both died and was buried, and his tomb is among us until this day. [30]Being a prophet, then, and knowing that God swore with an oath to him that of *the* fruit of his loin, as concerning flesh, to raise the Christ to sit on his throne; [31]foreseeing, he spoke about the resurrection of the Christ, that His soul was not left in Hades, nor did His flesh see corruption. [32]This Jesus God raised up, of which we all are witnesses. [33]Therefore, being exalted to the right of God, and receiving the promise of the Holy Spirit from the Father, He poured out this which you now see and hear. [34]For David did not ascend into Heaven, but he says, "The Lord said to my Lord, Sit at My right [35]until I place Your enemies as a footstool for Your feet." [36]Then assuredly, let all *the* house of Israel acknowledge that God made Him both Lord and Christ, this same Jesus whom you crucified.

[37]And hearing, they were stabbed in the heart, and said to Peter and the rest of the apostles, Men, brothers, What shall we do?
[38]And Peter said to them, Repent and be baptized, each of you on the name of Jesus Christ to forgiveness

1459 5590 3450 1519 86 3761 1325
ἐγκαταλείψεις τὴν ψυχήν μου εἰς ᾅδου, οὐδὲ δώσεις τὸν
You will leave the soul of Me in Hades, nor will You give the
3741 4675 1492 1312 1107 3427 3598 2222
28 ὅσιόν σου ἰδεῖν διαφθοράν. ἐγνώρισάς μοι ὁδοὺς ζωῆς·
Holy One of You to see corruption. You revealed to Me paths of life.
4137 3165 2167 3326 4383 4675 435
29 πληρώσεις με εὐφροσύνης μετὰ τοῦ προσώπου σου. ἄνδρες
You will fill Me with joy with the face of You. Men,
80 1832 2036 3326 3954 4314 5209 4012
ἀδελφοί, ἐξὸν εἰπεῖν μετὰ παρρησίας πρὸς ὑμᾶς περὶ τοῦ
brothers, it is permitted to say with plainness to you concerning the
3966 1138 3754 5053 2290
πατριάρχου Δαβίδ, ὅτι καὶ ἐτελεύτησε καὶ ἐτάφη, καὶ τὸ
patriarch David, that both he died and was buried, and the
3418 848 2076 1722/2254/891 2290 5026 4396
30 μνῆμα αὐτοῦ ἔστιν ἐν ἡμῖν ἄχρι τῆς ἡμέρας ταύτης. προφή-
tomb of him is among us until — day this. a prophet
3767 5225 1492 3754/3727 3660 846 2316
της οὖν ὑπάρχων, καὶ εἰδὼς ὅτι ὅρκῳ ὤμοσεν αὐτῷ ὁ Θεός,
Then being, and knowing that with an oath sworn to him God
1537 2590 3751 848 2596 4561 450
ἐκ καρποῦ τῆς ὀσφύος αὐτοῦ τὸ κατὰ σάρκα ἀναστήσειν
of (the) fruit of the loin of him as concerning flesh to raise up
5547 2523 1909 2362 848 4275
31 τὸν Χριστόν, καθίσαι ἐπὶ τοῦ θρόνου αὐτοῦ, προϊδὼν
the Christ, to sit on the throne of him, foreseeing
2980 4012 386 5547 3754/3756/ 2641
ἐλάλησε περὶ τῆς ἀναστάσεως τοῦ Χριστοῦ, ὅτι οὐ κατελείφθη
he spoke concerning the resurrection of the Christ, that not was left
5590 848 1519 86 3761 4561 848 1492 1312
ἡ ψυχὴ αὐτοῦ εἰς ᾅδου, οὐδὲ ἡ σὰρξ αὐτοῦ εἶδε διαφθοράν.
the soul of Him in Hades, nor the flesh of Him saw corruption.
5126 2424 450 2316 3756 3956 2249 2070
32 τοῦτον τὸν Ἰησοῦν ἀνέστησεν ὁ Θεός, οὗ πάντες ἡμεῖς ἐσμεν
This — Jesus raised up God, of which all we are
3144 1188 3767 2316 5312 5037 1860
33 μάρτυρες. τῇ δεξιᾷ οὖν τοῦ Θεοῦ ὑψωθείς, τήν τε ἐπαγγελίαν
witnesses; to the right, therefore, of God being exalted, the and promise
40 4151 2983 3844 3962 1632
τοῦ Ἁγίου Πνεύματος λαβὼν παρὰ τοῦ πατρός, ἐξέχεε
of the Holy Spirit receiving from the Father, He poured
5124/3739/3568/5210/ 991 191 3756/1063 1138 305
34 τοῦτο ὃ νῦν ὑμεῖς βλέπετε καὶ ἀκούετε. οὐ γὰρ Δαβὶδ ἀνέβη
this which now you see and hear. not For David ascended
1519 3772 3004 848 2036 2962 2962
εἰς τοὺς οὐρανούς, λέγει δὲ αὐτός, Εἶπεν ὁ Κύριος τῷ Κυρίῳ
to the heavens, says but he, said The Lord to the Lord
3450 2521 1537 1188 3450 2193/302/5087 2190 4675
35 μου, Κάθου ἐκ δεξιῶν μου, ἕως ἂν θῶ τοὺς ἐχθρούς σου
of me, Sit at (the) right of Me until I place the enemies of You
5286 4228 4675 806 3767 1097 3956
36 ὑποπόδιον τῶν ποδῶν σου. ἀσφαλῶς οὖν γινωσκέτω πᾶς
a footstool to the feet of You. Assuredly, therefore, let know all
3624 2474 3754 2962 5547 846 2316
οἶκος Ἰσραήλ, ὅτι καὶ Κύριον καὶ Χριστὸν αὐτὸν ὁ Θεὸς
the house of Israel that both Lord and Christ Him God
4160 5126 2424 3739 5210 4717
ἐποίησε, τοῦτον τὸν Ἰησοῦν ὃν ὑμεῖς ἐσταυρώσατε.
made this Jesus whom you crucified.
191 2660 2588 2036 5037 4314
37 Ἀκούσαντες δὲ κατενύγησαν τῇ καρδίᾳ, εἶπόν τε πρὸς
having heard And, They were stabbed in the heart, said and to
4074 3062 652 5101 4160
τὸν Πέτρον καὶ τοὺς λοιποὺς ἀποστόλους, Τί ποιήσομεν,
— Peter, and the remaining apostles, What may we do,
435 80 4074 5346 4314 846 3340
38 ἄνδρες ἀδελφοί; Πέτρος δὲ ἔφη πρὸς αὐτούς, Μετανοήσατε,
men, brothers? Peter And said to them, Repent
907 1538 5216 1909 3686 2424
καὶ βαπτισθήτω ἕκαστος ὑμῶν ἐπὶ τῷ ὀνόματι Ἰησοῦ
and be baptized each of you on the name of Jesus

of sins. And you will receive the gift of the Holy Spirit. 39 For the promise is to you and to your children, and to all those afar off, as many as *the* Lord our God shall call. 40 And with many other words he earnestly testified and exhorted, saying, Be saved from this perverse generation. 41 Then those who gladly welcomed his words were baptized. And about three thousand souls were added that day. 42 And they were continuing steadfastly in the teaching of the apostles, and in fellowship, and in the breaking of bread, and in prayers.

43 And fear came to every soul, and many wonders and miracles took place through the apostles. 44 And all the believers were together, and had all things common. 45 And they sold possessions and goods, and distributed them to all, according as anyone had need. 46 And continuing steadfastly with one mind day by day in the Temple, and breaking bread from house to house, they shared food in gladness and simplicity of heart, 47 praising God, and having favor with all the people. And the Lord added to the church those being saved from day to day.

5547 1519 859 266 2983 1431
Χριστοῦ εἰς ἄφεσιν ἁμαρτιῶν, καὶ λήψεσθε τὴν δωρεὰν
Christ to forgiveness of sins, and you will receive the gift
40 4151 5213 1063 2076 1860
39 τοῦ Ἁγίου Πνεύματος. ὑμῖν γάρ ἐστιν ἡ ἐπαγγελία, καὶ
of the Holy Spirit. to you For is the promise, and
5043 5216 3956 1519 3112 3745/302/4341
τοῖς τέκνοις ὑμῶν, καὶ πᾶσι τοῖς εἰς μακράν, ὅσους ἂν προσ-
to the children of you, even to all those at a distance, as many as may
2962 2316 2257 2087 5037 3056 4119
40 καλέσηται Κύριος ὁ Θεὸς ἡμῶν. ἑτέροις τε λόγοις πλείοσι
call (the) Lord, the God of us. with other And words many
1263 3870 3004 4982 575 1074
διεμαρτύρετο καὶ παρεκάλει λέγων, Σώθητε ἀπὸ τῆς γενεᾶς
he earnestly testified and exhorted, saying, Be saved from – generation
4646 5026 3303/3767 780 588
41 τῆς σκολιᾶς ταύτης. οἱ μὲν οὖν ἀσμένως ἀποδεξάμενοι τὸν
– perverse this. Those, then, gladly welcoming the
3056 848 907 4369 2250
λόγον αὐτοῦ ἐβαπτίσθησαν· καὶ προσετέθησαν τῇ ἡμέρᾳ
words of him were baptized, and there were added – day
1565 5590 5616 5153 2258 4342
42 ἐκείνῃ ψυχαὶ ὡσεὶ τρισχίλιαι. ἦσαν δὲ προσκαρτεροῦντες
that souls, about three thousand. they were And steadfastly continuing
1322 652 2842 2800
τῇ διδαχῇ τῶν ἀποστόλων καὶ τῇ κοινωνίᾳ, καὶ τῇ κλάσει
in the teaching of the apostles. and in the fellowship, and in the breaking
740 4335
τοῦ ἄρτου καὶ ταῖς προσευχαῖς.
of the bread, and in the prayers.

1096 3956 5590 5401 4183 5037 5059
43 Ἐγένετο δὲ πάσῃ ψυχῇ φόβος, πολλά τε τέρατα καὶ
came And to every soul fear; many and wonders and
4592 1223 652 1096 3956 4100
44 σημεῖα διὰ τῶν ἀποστόλων ἐγίνετο. πάντες δὲ οἱ πιστεύ-
signs through the apostles occurred. all And the believing
2258/1909 846 2192 537 2839
45 οντες ἦσαν ἐπὶ τὸ αὐτό, καὶ εἶχον ἅπαντα κοινά, καὶ τὰ
ones were together, and had all things common, and the
2933 5223 4097 1266 846
κτήματα καὶ τὰς ὑπάρξεις ἐπίπρασκον, καὶ διεμέριζον αὐτὰ
goods and the possessions they sold, and distributed them
3956 2530 302 5100/ 5532 2192 2596 2250 5037 4342
46 πᾶσι, καθότι ἄν τις χρείαν εἶχε. καθ' ἡμέραν τε προσκαρτε-
to all, according as anyone need had. from day to day And continuing
3661 1722 2411 2806 5037 2596 3624
ροῦντες ὁμοθυμαδὸν ἐν τῷ ἱερῷ, κλῶντές τε κατ' οἶκον
steadfastly with one mind in the Temple breaking and from house
740 3335 5160 1722 20 858 to house
ἄρτον, μετελάμβανον τροφῆς ἐν ἀγαλλιάσει καὶ ἀφελότητι
bread, they shared food in gladness and simplicity
2588 134 2316 2192 5485 4314 3650
47 καρδίας, αἰνοῦντες τὸν Θεόν, καὶ ἔχοντες χάριν πρὸς ὅλον
of heart, praising God, and having favor with all
2992 2962 4369 4982
τὸν λαόν. ὁ δὲ Κύριος προσετίθει τοὺς σωζομένους καθ'
the people. the And Lord added those being saved from
2250 1577
ἡμέραν τῇ ἐκκλησίᾳ.
day to day to the church.

CHAPTER 3

CHAPTER 3

1 And Peter and John were going up on the same *day* into the Temple at the hour of prayer, the ninth. 2 And a certain man, being lame from his mother's womb, was being carried,

1909 846 4074 2491 305 1519
1 Ἐπὶ τὸ αὐτὸ δὲ Πέτρος καὶ Ἰωάννης ἀνέβαινον εἰς τὸ
on the same And Peter and John were going into the
2411 1909 (day) 5610 4335 1766 5100
2 ἱερὸν ἐπὶ τὴν ὥραν τῆς προσευχῆς τὴν ἐννάτην. καί τις
Temple at the hour of prayer, the ninth, and a certain
435 5560/1537 2836 3384 848 5225 941
ἀνήρ χωλὸς ἐκ κοιλίας μητρὸς αὐτοῦ ὑπάρχων ἐβαστάζετο·
man lame from womb mother's his being. was being carried

whom day by day they put at the door of the Temple, being called Beautiful, to ask alms from those going into the Temple; [3]who seeing Peter and John about to go into the Temple, asked alms. [4]And with John, looking intently toward him, Peter said, Look to us! [5]And he paid heed to them, expecting to receive something from them. [6]But Peter said, There is no silver and gold to me, but what I have, this I give to you: In the name of Jesus Christ the Nazarean, rise up and walk! [7]And taking him by the right hand, he raised *him* up. And immediately his feet and ankle-bones were made firm. [8]And leaping up, he stood and walked, and went with them into the Temple, walking and leaping, and praising God. [9]And all the people saw him walking, and praising God. [10]And they recognized him, that it was the *one* who was sitting for alms at the Beautiful Gate of the Temple. And they were filled with amazement and ecstasy at the thing that happened to him.

[11]And the healed lame one *was* holding to Peter and John, *and* all the people ran together to them on the porch called Solomon's, greatly amazed. [12]And seeing *this*, Peter answered to the people, Men, Israelites, why do you marvel at this one? Or why do you stare at us, as *if* by our own power or godliness *we* have made him to walk? [13]The God of Abraham and Isaac and Jacob, the God of our fathers, glorified His

3739 5087 2596 2250 4314 2374 2411
ὃν ἐτίθουν καθ' ἡμέραν πρὸς τὴν θύραν τοῦ ἱεροῦ τὴν
whom they put from day to day at the door of the Temple —
3004 5611 154 1654 3844
λεγομένην Ὡραίαν, τοῦ αἰτεῖν ἐλεημοσύνην παρὰ τῶν
being called Beautiful, — to ask alms from those
1531 1519 2411 3738/1492 4074 2491
3 εἰσπορευομένων εἰς τὸ ἱερόν. ὃς ἰδὼν Πέτρον καὶ Ἰωάννην
going into the Temple, who seeing Peter and John
3195 1524 1519 2411 2065 1654 816
μέλλοντας εἰσιέναι εἰς τὸ ἱερόν, ἠρώτα ἐλεημοσύνην. ἀτενίσας
being about to go into the Temple, asked alms. gazing intently
4074/1519/846/4862 2491 2036 991 1519/2248
4 δὲ Πέτρος εἰς αὐτὸν σὺν τῷ Ἰωάννῃ, εἶπε, Βλέψον εἰς ἡμᾶς. ὁ
And Peter at him, with — John, he said, Look at us! he
1907 846 4328 5100/3844 846 2983 2036
5 δὲ ἐπεῖχεν αὐτοῖς, προσδοκῶν τι παρ' αὐτῶν λαβεῖν. εἶπε δὲ
And paid heed to them, expecting something from them to receive. said And
4074 694 5553 3756 5225 3427 2192
6 Πέτρος, Ἀργύριον καὶ χρυσίον οὐχ ὑπάρχει μοι· ὃ δὲ ἔχω,
Peter, Silver and gold not is to me, what but I have,
5124 4671 1325 1722 3686 2424 5547 3480
τοῦτό σοι δίδωμι. ἐν τῷ ὀνόματι Ἰησοῦ Χριστοῦ τοῦ Ναζω-
this to you I give, in the name of Jesus Christ the Naza-
1453 4043 4084 846 1188
7 ραίου, ἔγειραι καὶ περιπάτει. καὶ πιάσας αὐτὸν τῆς δεξιᾶς
rean, rise up and walk! And taking him by the right
5495 1453 3916 4732 848 939
χειρὸς ἤγειρε· παραχρῆμα δὲ ἐστερεώθησαν αὐτοῦ αἱ βάσεις
hand, he raised up, immediately and were strengthened of him the feet
4974 1814 2476 4043
8 καὶ τὰ σφυρά. καὶ ἐξαλλόμενος ἔστη καὶ περιεπάτει, καὶ
and the ankle-bones. And leaping up he stood, and walked, and
1525 4862 846 1519 2411 4043 242
εἰσῆλθε σὺν αὐτοῖς εἰς τὸ ἱερόν, περιπατῶν καὶ ἀλλόμενος
went in with them into the Temple, walking and leaping
134 2316 1492 846 3956 2992 4043
9 καὶ αἰνῶν τὸν Θεόν. καὶ εἶδεν αὐτὸν πᾶς ὁ λαὸς περιπα-
and praising — God. And saw him all the people walking
134 2316 1921 5037 846 3754
10 τοῦντα καὶ αἰνοῦντα τὸν Θεόν· ἐπεγίνωσκόν τε αὐτὸν ὅτι
and praising — God; they recognized and him, that
3778 2258 4314 1654 2521 1909 5611
οὗτος ἦν ὁ πρὸς τὴν ἐλεημοσύνην καθήμενος ἐπὶ τῇ Ὡραίᾳ
this was he for — alms sitting at the Beautiful
4439 2411 4130 2285 1611
πύλῃ τοῦ ἱεροῦ· καὶ ἐπλήσθησαν θάμβους καὶ ἐκστάσεως
Gate of the Temple. And they were filled of amazement and ecstasy
1909 4819 846
ἐπὶ τῷ συμβεβηκότι αὐτῷ.
at the thing having happened to him.

2902 2390 5560 4074
11 Κρατοῦντος δὲ τοῦ ἰαθέντος χωλοῦ τὸν Πέτρον καὶ
holding And the healed lame (one) Peter and
2491 4936 4314 846 3956 2992 1909 4745
Ἰωάννην, συνέδραμε πρὸς αὐτοὺς πᾶς ὁ λαὸς ἐπὶ τῇ στοᾷ
John, ran together to them all the people on the porch
2563 4672 1569 1492 4074 611
12 τῇ καλουμένῃ Σολομῶντος, ἔκθαμβοι. Ἰδὼν δὲ Πέτρος ἀπε-
— called Solomon's, greatly amazed. seeing And Peter
4314 2992 435 2475 5101 2296
κρίνατο πρὸς τὸν λαόν, Ἄνδρες Ἰσραηλῖται, τί θαυμάζετε
answered to the people, Men, Israelites, Why do you marvel
1909 5129 2228/2254/5101/ 816 5613/2398 1411 2228 2150
ἐπὶ τούτῳ, ἢ ἡμῖν τί ἀτενίζετε, ὡς ἰδίᾳ δυνάμει ἢ εὐσεβείᾳ
at this one, or at us why do you gaze, as by own power or piety
4160 4043 846 2316 11
13 πεποιηκόσι τοῦ περιπατεῖν αὐτόν; ὁ Θεὸς Ἀβραὰμ καὶ
having made — to walk him? The God of Abraham and
2464 2384 2316 3962 2257 1392
Ἰσαὰκ καὶ Ἰακώβ, ὁ Θεὸς τῶν πατέρων ἡμῶν, ἐδόξασε τὸν
of Isaac and of Jacob, the God of the fathers of us, glorified the

Child Jesus, whom you delivered up, and denied Him in the presence of Pilate, that one having decided to set *Him* free. [14]But you denied the holy and righteous *One*, and asked for a man, a murderer, to be granted to you. [15]And the Author of Life you killed, whom God raised up from *the* dead, of which we are witnesses. [16]And on the faith of His name, this one whom you see and know, *was* made firm *by* His name; and the faith which came through Him gave to him this complete soundness before you all. [17]And now, brothers, I know that you acted according to ignorance, as also *did* your rulers. [18]But what things God before announced through the mouth of all His prophets, *that* the Christ should suffer, He fulfilled in this manner. [19]Therefore, Repent, and convert, for the blotting out of your sins, so that times of refreshing may come from *the* face of the Lord, [20]and that He may send forth the *One* before proclaimed to you, Jesus Christ, [21]whom Heaven truly needs to receive until the times of restoration of all things, of which God spoke through *the* mouth of all His holy prophets from *the* age past. [22]For Moses indeed said to the fathers, "*The* Lord your God will raise up to you a Prophet from among your brothers, *One* like me; you shall hear Him according to all things, whatever He may speak to you. [23]And it shall be *that of* every soul, whoever should not hear that Prophet shall be utterly destroyed from among the people. [24]And also all the prophets, from Samuel and those following after, as many as spoke, also

3816 848 2424 3739 5210 3860 720
παῖδα αὐτοῦ Ἰησοῦν· ὃν ὑμεῖς παρεδώκατε, καὶ ἠρνήσασθε
servant of Him, Jesus, whom you delivered up, and denied
846 2596 4383 4091 2919 1565 630
αὐτὸν κατὰ πρόσωπον Πιλάτου, κρίναντος ἐκείνου ἀπο-
Him in the presence of Pilate, having decided that one to re-
5210 40 1342 720 154
14 λύειν. ὑμεῖς δὲ τὸν ἅγιον καὶ δίκαιον ἠρνήσασθε, καὶ ᾐτή-
lease (Him), you but the holy and righteous One denied, and
435 5406 5483 5213 747
15 σασθε ἄνδρα φονέα χαρισθῆναι ὑμῖν, τὸν δὲ ἀρχηγὸν τῆς
asked a man, a murderer, to be granted to you, the and Author —
2222 615 3739 2316 1453 1537 3498 3739/2249
ζωῆς ἀπεκτείνατε· ὃν ὁ Θεὸς ἤγειρεν ἐκ νεκρῶν, οὗ ἡμεῖς
of life you killed, whom God raised from (the) dead, of which we
3144 2070 1909 4102 3686 848
16 μάρτυρές ἐσμεν. καὶ ἐπὶ τῇ πίστει τοῦ ὀνόματος αὐτοῦ,
witnesses are. And on the faith of the name of Him,
5126 3739 2334 1492 4732 3686 848
τοῦτον ὃν θεωρεῖτε καὶ οἴδατε ἐστερέωσε τὸ ὄνομα αὐτοῦ·
this one whom you behold and know made strong the name of Him,
4102 1223 846 1325 846 3647
καὶ ἡ πίστις ἡ δι' αὐτοῦ ἔδωκεν αὐτῷ τὴν ὁλοκληρίαν
and the faith which through Him gave to him complete soundness
5026 561 3956 5216 3568 80 1492 3754
17 ταύτην ἀπέναντι πάντων ὑμῶν. καὶ νῦν, ἀδελφοί, οἶδα ὅτι
this before all of you. And now, brothers, I know that
2596 52 4238 5618 758 5216
18 κατὰ ἄγνοιαν ἐπράξατε, ὥσπερ καὶ οἱ ἄρχοντες ὑμῶν. ὁ δὲ
by way of ignorance you acted, as also the rulers of you, But
2316 3739 4293 1223 4750 3956 4396
Θεὸς ἃ προκατήγγειλε διὰ στόματος πάντων τῶν προ-
God that He before announced through (the) mouth of all the
848 3958 5547 4137 3779
φητῶν αὐτοῦ, παθεῖν τὸν Χριστόν, ἐπλήρωσεν οὕτω.
prophets of Him, to suffer the Christ, He fulfilled thus.
3340 3767 1994 1519 1813 5216
19 μετανοήσατε οὖν καὶ ἐπιστρέψατε, εἰς τὸ ἐξαλειφθῆναι ὑμῶν
Repent, therefore, and be converted, for the blotting out of you
266 3704 302 2064 2540 403 575 4383
τὰς ἁμαρτίας, ὅπως ἂν ἔλθωσι καιροὶ ἀναψύξεως ἀπὸ προσ-
the sins, so as may come times of refreshing from (the)
2962 649 4296
20 ώπου τοῦ Κυρίου, καὶ ἀποστείλῃ τὸν προκεκηρυγμένον
presence of the Lord, and He may send the (One) before proclaimed
5213 2424 5547 3739/1163 3772 3303 1209 891
21 ὑμῖν Ἰησοῦν Χριστόν· ὃν δεῖ οὐρανὸν μὲν δέξασθαι ἄχρι
to you, Jesus Christ, whom it is right Heaven to receive until
5550 605 3956 3739 2980 2316
χρόνων ἀποκαταστάσεως πάντων, ὧν ἐλάλησεν ὁ Θεὸς
(the) times of restitution of all things, which spoke God
1223 4750 3956 40 848 4396 575 165
διὰ στόματος πάντων ἁγίων αὐτοῦ προφητῶν ἀπ' αἰῶνος.
through (the) mouth of all holy of Him prophets from (the) age.
3475 3303 1063 4314 3962 2036 3754 4396
22 Μωσῆς μὲν γὰρ πρὸς τοὺς πατέρας εἶπεν ὅτι Προφήτην
Moses indeed For to the fathers said, — A prophet
5213 450 2962 2316 5216 1537 80 5216
ὑμῖν ἀναστήσει Κύριος ὁ Θεὸς ὑμῶν ἐκ τῶν ἀδελφῶν ὑμῶν
for you will raise up (the) Lord God of you from the brothers of you
5613/1691/846 191 2596 3956 3745/302 2980 4314
ὡς ἐμέ· αὐτοῦ ἀκούσεσθε κατὰ πάντα ὅσα ἂν λαλήσῃ πρὸς
like me; Him you shall hear according to all, whatever He may speak to
5209 2071 3956 5590 3748 302/3361 191 4396
23 ὑμᾶς. ἔσται δέ, πᾶσα ψυχή, ἥτις ἂν μὴ ἀκούσῃ τοῦ προφή-
you. It shall be And, every soul, whoever may not hear — prophet
1565 1842 1537 2992 3956
24 του ἐκείνου, ἐξολοθρευθήσεται ἐκ τοῦ λαοῦ. καὶ πάντες δὲ
that, will be utterly destroyed from the people. also all And
4396 4545 2517 3745 2980
οἱ προφῆται ἀπὸ Σαμουὴλ καὶ τῶν καθεξῆς, ὅσοι ἐλάλησαν,
the prophets from Samuel, and those in order, as many as spoke,

before announced these days.
25 You are sons of the prophets, and of the covenant which God appointed to our fathers, saying to Abraham, "Even in your Seed all the families of the earth shall be blessed."
26 Having raised up His child Jesus, God sent Him first to you, blessing you in turning away each one from your iniquities.

4293 2250 5025 5210 2075 5207
25 καὶ προκατήγγειλαν τὰς ἡμέρας ταύτας. ὑμεῖς ἐστε υἱοὶ τῶν
also before announced days these. You are sons of the
4396 1242 3739 1303 2316 4314
προφητῶν, καὶ τῆς διαθήκης ἧς διέθετο ὁ Θεὸς πρὸς τοὺς
prophets, and of the covenant which appointed God to the
3962 2257 3004 4314 11 4690 3675
πατέρας ἡμῶν, λέγων πρὸς Ἀβραάμ, Καὶ τῷ σπέρματί σου
fathers of us, saying to Abraham, And in the seed of you
1757 3956 3965 1093/5213 4412
26 ἐνευλογηθήσονται πᾶσαι αἱ πατριαὶ τῆς γῆς. ὑμῖν πρῶτον
shall be blessed all the families of the earth. To you first
2316 450 3816 848 2424 649
ὁ Θεός, ἀναστήσας τὸν παῖδα αὐτοῦ Ἰησοῦν, ἀπέστειλεν
God having raised up the Child of Him, Jesus, sent
846 2127 5209/1722 654 1538 575
αὐτὸν εὐλογοῦντα ὑμᾶς, ἐν τῷ ἀποστρέφειν ἕκαστον ἀπὸ
Him, blessing you in the turning away (of) each one from
4189 5216
τῶν πονηριῶν ὑμῶν.
the iniquities of you.

CHAPTER 4

1 And *as* they were speaking to the people, the priests, and the Temple commander, and the Sadducees stood near them,
2 being distressed because they taught the people and announced in Jesus the resurrection from *the* dead.
3 *And they* laid hands *on* them, and put *them* into custody until the morrow; for it was already evening.
4 But many of those hearing the word believed; and the number of the men became about five thousand.
5 And it happened on the morrow *that* the rulers and elders and scribes came together into Jerusalem;
6 also Annas the high priest, and Caiaphas, and John, and Alexander, and as many as were of the high-priestly family.
7 And standing them in the midst, *they* were inquiring, By what sort of power, or by what sort of name, did you do this?
8 Then filled of *the* Holy Spirit, Peter said to them, Rulers of the people, and elders of Israel:
9 if we are being examined today upon

2980 848 4314 2992 2186 846
1 Λαλούντων δὲ αὐτῶν πρὸς τὸν λαόν, ἐπέστησαν αὐτοῖς
speaking And they to the people, came upon them
2409 4755 2411 4523
οἱ ἱερεῖς καὶ ὁ στρατηγὸς τοῦ ἱεροῦ καὶ οἱ Σαδδουκαῖοι,
the priests and the commander of the Temple and the Sadducees,
1278 1223 1321 846 2992
2 διαπονούμενοι διὰ τὸ διδάσκειν αὐτοὺς τὸν λαόν, καὶ
being distressed because of the teaching (of) them the people, even
2605 1722 2424 386 1537 3498
καταγγέλλειν ἐν τῷ Ἰησοῦ τὴν ἀνάστασιν τὴν ἐκ νεκρῶν.
to announce by – Jesus the resurrection – from (the) dead.
1911 846 5495 5087 1519 5084 1519
3 καὶ ἐπέβαλον αὐτοῖς τὰς χεῖρας, καὶ ἔθεντο εἰς τήρησιν εἰς
And (they) laid on them the hands, and put into custody unto
839 2258/1063 2073 2235 4183 191
4 τὴν αὔριον· ἦν γὰρ ἑσπέρα ἤδη. πολλοὶ δὲ τῶν ἀκουσάντων
the morrow; it was for evening now. many And of those hearing
3056 4100 1096 706 435
τὸν λόγον ἐπίστευσαν· καὶ ἐγενήθη ὁ ἀριθμὸς τῶν ἀνδρῶν
the word believed. and became the number of the men
5616 5505 4002
ὡσεὶ χιλιάδες πέντε.
about thousands five.
1096 1909 839 4863 848
5 Ἐγένετο δὲ ἐπὶ τὴν αὔριον συναχθῆναι αὐτῶν τοὺς
it was And, on the morrow to be assembled of them the
758 4245 1122 1519 2419
ἄρχοντας καὶ πρεσβυτέρους καὶ γραμματεῖς εἰς Ἱερουσαλήμ,
rulers and elders and scribes to Jerusalem,
452 749 2533 2491
6 καὶ Ἄνναν τὸν ἀρχιερέα, καὶ Καϊάφαν, καὶ Ἰωάννην, καὶ
and Annas the high priest, and Caiaphas, and John, and
223 3745 2258/1537/1085 748
7 Ἀλέξανδρον, καὶ ὅσοι ἦσαν ἐκ γένους ἀρχιερατικοῦ. καὶ
Alexander, and as many as were of (the) family high priestly. And
2476 848 1722 3319 4441 1722 4169
στήσαντες αὐτοὺς ἐν τῷ μέσῳ ἐπυνθάνοντο, Ἐν ποίᾳ
having stood them in the midst inquired, By what
1411/2228/1722/4160 3686 4160 5124 5210 5119
8 δυνάμει ἢ ἐν ποίῳ ὀνόματι ἐποιήσατε τοῦτο ὑμεῖς; τότε
power or in what name did do this you? Then
4074 4130 4151 40 2036 4314 846
Πέτρος πλησθεὶς Πνεύματος Ἁγίου εἶπε πρὸς αὐτούς,
Peter filled of (the) Spirit Holy said to them,
758 2992 4345 2474 1487/2249
9 Ἄρχοντες τοῦ λαοῦ καὶ πρεσβύτεροι τοῦ Ἰσραήλ, εἰ ἡμεῖς
Rulers of the people and elders of Israel, if we

a good work *for* an infirm man, *regarding* by what this one has been healed, [10]let it be known to you all and to all the people of Israel that in the name of Jesus Christ the Nazarene, whom you crucified, whom God raised up from *the* dead — in this *name* this one stands near before you whole! [11]This *One* is the Stone counted worthless by you the builders, who has become *placed* into *the* Head of *the* corner; [12]and there is salvation in no other One, for neither is there any other name under Heaven having been given among men by which we must be saved.

[13]But seeing the boldness of Peter and John, and having perceived that they are untaught and uneducated men, they marveled. And they recognized them, that they were with Jesus. [14]But seeing the man standing with them, the *one* having been healed, they had nothing to say against *him*. [15]But commanding them to go outside the sanhedrin, they conferred with one another, [16]saying, What may we do to these men? For that a notable miracle has indeed occurred through them *is* plain to all those living in Jerusalem; and we are not able to deny *it*. [17]But that it may not spread abroad to the people, let us threaten them with a threat, *that* they no longer speak on this name to any men.

[18]And calling them, they ordered them not to speak at all, nor to teach on the name of Jesus. [19]But answering to them, Peter and John said, Whether it is right before God to listen to

4594 350 1909 2108 444 772
σήμερον ἀνακρινόμεθα ἐπὶ εὐεργεσίᾳ ἀνθρώπου ἀσθενοῦς,
today are being examined on a good work of a man infirm
1722/5101 3778 4982 1110 2077 3956 5213
10 ἐν τίνι οὗτος σέσωσται· γνωστὸν ἔστω πᾶσιν ὑμῖν καὶ
by what this one has been healed, known let it be to all of you and
3956 2992 2474 3754/1722 3686 2424 5547
παντὶ τῷ λαῷ Ἰσραήλ, ὅτι ἐν τῷ ὀνόματι Ἰησοῦ Χριστοῦ
to all the people of Israel, that in the name of Jesus Christ
3480 3739/5210/ 4717 3739 2316 1453
τοῦ Ναζωραίου, ὃν ὑμεῖς ἐσταυρώσατε, ὃν ὁ Θεὸς ἤγειρεν
the Nazarean, whom you crucified, whom God raised
1537 3498 1722 5129 3778 3936 1799 5216 5199
ἐκ νεκρῶν, ἐν τούτῳ οὗτος παρέστηκεν ἐνώπιον ὑμῶν ὑγιής.
from (the) dead, in this, this one stands before you whole.
3778 2076 3037 1848 5259 5216 3518
11 οὗτός ἐστιν ὁ λίθος ὁ ἐξουθενηθεὶς ὑφ' ὑμῶν τῶν οἰκοδο-
This is the Stone counted worthless by you the builders,
1096 1519 2776 1137 3756 2076 1722
μούντων, ὁ γενόμενος εἰς κεφαλὴν γωνίας. καὶ οὐκ ἔστιν ἐν
which has become to (be head of (the) corner. And not is in
3777 243 3762 4991 1063 3686 2076 2087 5259
12 ἄλλῳ οὐδενὶ ἡ σωτηρία οὔτε γὰρ ὄνομά ἐστιν ἕτερον ὑπὸ τὸν
other none the salvation, neither for name is another under -
3772 1325 1722 444 1722/3739/1163/ 4982 2248
οὐρανὸν τὸ δεδομένον ἐν ἀνθρώποις, ἐν ᾧ δεῖ σωθῆναι ἡμᾶς.
Heaven —having been given among men by which must be saved us.
2334 4074 3954 2491
13 Θεωροῦντες δὲ τὴν τοῦ Πέτρου παρρησίαν καὶ Ἰωάννου,
beholding And the — of Peter boldness and of John,
2638 3754 444 62 1526
καὶ καταλαβόμενοι ὅτι ἄνθρωποι ἀγράμματοί εἰσι καὶ
and having perceived that men unlettered they are, and
2399 2296 1921 5037 846 3754 4862
ἰδιῶται, ἐθαύμαζον, ἐπεγίνωσκόν τε αὐτοὺς ὅτι σὺν τῷ
private, they marveled, recognized and them that with —
2424 2258 444 991 4862 846 2476
14 Ἰησοῦ ἦσαν. τὸν δὲ ἄνθρωπον βλέποντες σὺν αὐτοῖς ἑστῶτα
Jesus they were. the And man seeing with them standing,
2323 3762 2192 471 2753
15 τὸν τεθεραπευμένον, οὐδὲν εἶχον ἀντειπεῖν. κελεύσαντες δὲ
the (one) having been healed, nothing they had to gainsay. commanding And
846 1854 4892 565 4820 4314 240
αὐτοὺς ἔξω τοῦ συνεδρίου ἀπελθεῖν, συνέβαλον πρὸς ἀλλή-
them outside the sanhedrin to go, they conferred with one
3004 5101 4160 444 5125 3754
16 λους, λέγοντες, Τί ποιήσομεν τοῖς ἀνθρώποις τούτοις; ὅτι
another, saying, What may we do to men these; that
3303/1063 1110 4592 1096 /1223/ 846 3956 2730
μὲν γὰρ γνωστὸν σημεῖον γέγονε δι' αὐτῶν, πᾶσι τοῖς κατοι-
indeed for a notable sign has occurred through them, to all those inhabit-
2419 5318 3756 1410 720
κοῦσιν Ἱερουσαλὴμ φανερόν, καὶ οὐ δυνάμεθα ἀρνήσασθαι.
ing Jerusalem (is) manifest, and not we are able to deny;
235 2443/3361/1909/ 4119 1268 1519 2992 547
17 ἀλλ' ἵνα μὴ ἐπὶ πλεῖον διανεμηθῇ εἰς τὸν λαόν, ἀπειλῇ
but that not more it be spread abroad to the people, let us with a threat
546 846 3371 2980 1909 3686 5127
ἀπειλησώμεθα αὐτοῖς μηκέτι λαλεῖν ἐπὶ τῷ ὀνόματι τούτῳ
threaten them no longer to speak on name this
3367 444 2564 846 3853
18 μηδενὶ ἀνθρώπων. καὶ καλέσαντες αὐτούς, παρήγγειλαν
to no one of men. And calling them, they ordered
846 2527 3361 5350 3366 1321 1909
αὐτοῖς τὸ καθόλου μὴ φθέγγεσθαι μηδὲ διδάσκειν ἐπὶ τῷ
them at all not to speak nor to teach on the
3686 2424 4074 2491 611
19 ὀνόματι τοῦ Ἰησοῦ. ὁ δὲ Πέτρος καὶ Ἰωάννης ἀποκριθέντες
name of Jesus. But Peter and John answering
4314 846 2036 1487 1342 2076 1799 2316 5216
πρὸς αὐτοὺς εἶπον, Εἰ δίκαιόν ἐστιν ἐνώπιον τοῦ Θεοῦ ὑμῶν
to them said, If right it is before God you

you rather than God, you judge. [20]For we are not able not to speak what we saw and heard. [21]But having threatened again, they let them go, finding nothing *as to* how they might punish them, on account of the people, because all glorified God on the thing happening. [22]For the man on whom this miracle of healing had occurred was more than forty years *of age*.

[23]And being let go, they came to their own and reported to them what the chief priests and elders said. [24]And hearing, *they* with one passion lifted voice to God and said, Master, You *are* the God who made the heaven and the earth and the sea, and all things in them, [25]who through *the* mouth of Your servant David said, "Why did the nations rage, and *the* peoples devised foolish things? [26]The kings of the earth stood up, and the rulers were assembled on the same *day* against the Lord, yea, against His Christ." [27]For truly both Herod and Pontius Pilate, with the nations and *the* peoples of Israel were gathered together against Your holy child Jesus, whom You anointed, [28]to do whatever Your hand and Your counsel before-determined to be done. [29]And now, Lord, look upon their threatenings, and give to Your slaves to speak Your word with all boldness, [30]in the extending of Your hand for healing and miracles and wonders to happen through the name of Your holy child Jesus. [31]And they having prayed, the place in which they were gathered was shaken, and they were all filled with

191 3123 2228 2316 2919 3756 1410 1063 2249
20 ἀκούειν μᾶλλον ἢ τοῦ Θεοῦ, κρίνατε. οὐ δυνάμεθα γὰρ ἡμεῖς,
to hear rather than God, you judge. not are able For we

1492 191 3361 2980 4324
21 ἃ εἴδομεν καὶ ἠκούσαμεν, μὴ λαλεῖν. οἱ δὲ προσαπειλησά-
what we saw and heard not to speak. they But having threatened

630 846 3367 2147 4459 2849
μενοι ἀπέλυσαν αὐτούς, μηδὲν εὑρίσκοντες τὸ πῶς κολάσων-
again released them, nothing finding how they might

846 1223 2992 3754 3956 1392 2316 1909
ται αὐτούς, διὰ τὸν λαόν, ὅτι πάντες ἐδόξαζον τὸν Θεὸν ἐπὶ
punish them, due to the people, because all glorified God on

1096 2094 1063/2258 4119 5062 444
22 τῷ γεγονότι. ἐτῶν γὰρ ἦν πλειόνων τεσσαράκοντα ὁ ἄν-
the thing occurring. of years For was more (than) forty the

1909/3739 1096 4592 5124 2392
θρωπος ἐφ' ὃν ἐγεγόνει τὸ σημεῖον τοῦτο τῆς ἰάσεως.
man on whom had happened sign this of healing.

630 2064 4314 2398 518
23 Ἀπολυθέντες δὲ ἦλθον πρὸς τοὺς ἰδίους, καὶ ἀπήγγειλαν
being released And they went to the own, and reported

3745 4314 846 749 4245 2036
ὅσα πρὸς αὐτοὺς οἱ ἀρχιερεῖς καὶ οἱ πρεσβύτεροι εἶπον. οἱ
what to them the chief priests and the elders said. they

191 3661 142 5456 4314 2316
24 δὲ ἀκούσαντες ὁμοθυμαδὸν ἦραν φωνὴν πρὸς τὸν Θεόν, καὶ
And having heard, with one passion lifted voice to God, and

2036 1203 4771 2316 4160 3772
εἶπον, Δέσποτα, σὺ ὁ Θεὸς ὁ ποιήσας τὸν οὐρανὸν καὶ τὴν
said, Master, You the God who made the heaven and the

1093 2281 3956 1722 846 1223 4753
γῆν καὶ τὴν θάλασσαν καὶ πάντα τὰ ἐν αὐτοῖς· ὁ διὰ στό-
earth and the sea and all things in them, who through (the)

1138 3816 4675 2036 2444 5433 1484
25 ματος Δαβὶδ τοῦ παιδός σου εἰπών, Ἱνατί ἐφρύαξαν ἔθνη,
mouth of David the child of You said, Why did rage the nations

2992 3191 2756 3936 935 1093
26 καὶ λαοὶ ἐμελέτησαν κενά; παρέστησαν οἱ βασιλεῖς τῆς γῆς,
and peoples meditate vain things? stood up The kings of the earth

758 4863 1909 846 2596 2962
καὶ οἱ ἄρχοντες συνήχθησαν ἐπὶ τὸ αὐτὸ κατὰ τοῦ Κυρίου,
and the rulers were assembled on the same against the Lord.

2596 5547 848 4863 1063 1909 225
27 καὶ κατὰ τοῦ Χριστοῦ αὐτοῦ· συνήχθησαν γὰρ ἐπ' ἀληθείας
and against the Christ of Him; were assembled for of a truth

1909 40 3816 4675 2424 3739 5548 2264 5037
ἐπὶ τὸν ἅγιον παῖδά σου Ἰησοῦν, ὃν ἔχρισας, Ἡρώδης τε
against the holy child of You, Jesus, whom You anointed, Herod both

4194 4091 4862 1484 2992 2474 4160
καὶ Πόντιος Πιλάτος, σὺν ἔθνεσι καὶ λαοῖς Ἰσραήλ, ποιῆσαι
and Pontius Pilate, with nations and peoples of Israel, to do

3745 5495 4675 1012 4675 4309 1096
28 ὅσα ἡ χείρ σου καὶ ἡ βουλή σου προώρισε γενέσθαι. καὶ
whatever the hand of You and the counsel of You predetermined to occur. And

3569 2962 1896 1909 547 848 1325
29 τὰ νῦν, Κύριε, ἔπιδε ἐπὶ τὰς ἀπειλὰς αὐτῶν, καὶ δὸς τοῖς
now, Lord, look upon the threatenings of them, and give to the

1401 4675 3326 3954 3956 2980 3056 4675
δούλοις σου μετὰ παρρησίας πάσης λαλεῖν τὸν λόγον σου,
slaves of You with boldness all to speak the word of You

1722 5495 4675 1614 4571/1519/2392 4592
30 ἐν τῷ τὴν χεῖρά σου ἐκτείνειν σε εἰς ἴασιν, καὶ σημεῖα καὶ
by the hand of You stretching You for healing, and signs and

5059 1096 1223 3686 40 3816 4675
τέρατα γίνεσθαι διὰ τοῦ ὀνόματος τοῦ ἁγίου παιδός σου
wonders to happen through the name of the holy child of You,

2424 1189 848 4531 5117/1722/3739/2258
31 Ἰησοῦ. καὶ δεηθέντων αὐτῶν ἐσαλεύθη ὁ τόπος ἐν ᾧ ἦσαν
Jesus. And having petitioned they, was shaken the place in which they were

4863 4130 537 4151 40
συνηγμένοι, καὶ ἐπλήσθησαν ἅπαντες Πνεύματος Ἁγίου,
assembled, and they were filled all with (the) Spirit Holy

the Holy Spirit, and spoke the word of God with boldness.

[32]And of the multitude of those who believed, the heart and the soul were one. And no one said any of his possessions to be his own, but all things were common to them. [33]And with great power the apostles gave testimony of the resurrection of the Lord Jesus. And great grace was upon them all. [34]For neither was anyone needy among them, for as many as were owners of lands or houses, selling *them*, they bore the value of the *things* being sold, [35]and laid them at the feet of the apostles. And it was distributed to each according as any had need.

[36]And Joses, the *one* surnamed Barnabas by the apostles, which is, being translated, Son of Consolation, a Levite, a Cypriot by race, [37]a field being his, selling *it*, he bore the proceeds and placed *them* at the feet of the apostles.

CHAPTER 5

[1]But a certain man named Ananias, with his wife Sapphira, sold a property, [2]and secretly kept back from the price, his wife also aware of *it;* and bringing a certain part, *he* placed *it* at the feet of the apostles. [3]But Peter said, Ananias, why did Satan fill your heart *for* you to lie to the Holy Spirit, and to secretly keep back from the price of the land? [4]Remaining, did it not remain yours? And being sold, was it *not* in your authority? Why *is it* that this action was put into

2980 3056 2316 3326 3954
καὶ ἐλάλουν τὸν λόγον τοῦ Θεοῦ μετὰ παρρησίας.
and spoke the word of God with boldness.
4128 4100 2258 2588
32 Τοῦ δὲ πλήθους τῶν πιστευσάντων ἦν ἡ καρδία καὶ ἡ
of the And multitude of those believing were the heart and the
5590 3391 3761 1520/5100 5224 846 3004
ψυχὴ μία· καὶ οὐδ' εἷς τι τῶν ὑπαρχόντων αὐτῷ ἔλεγεν
soul one, and not one anything of the possessions to him he said
2398 1511 235 2258 846 537 2839 3173
33 ἴδιον εἶναι, ἀλλ' ἦν αὐτοῖς ἅπαντα κοινά. καὶ μεγάλῃ
own to be, but were to them all things common. And with great
1411 591 3142 652 386
δυνάμει ἀπεδίδουν τὸ μαρτύριον οἱ ἀπόστολοι τῆς ἀναστά-
power gave the testimony the apostles of the resurrection
2962 2424 5485 5037 3173 2258 1909 3956
σεως τοῦ Κυρίου Ἰησοῦ, χάρις τε μεγάλη ἦν ἐπὶ πάντας
of the Lord Jesus, grace and great was upon all
846 3761 1063 1729 5100 5225 1722 846 3745 1063
34 αὐτούς. οὐδὲ γὰρ ἐνδεής τις ὑπῆρχεν ἐν αὐτοῖς· ὅσοι γὰρ
of them. neither For needy anyone was among them, as many as for
2935 5564 2228 3614 5225 4453 5342
κτήτορες χωρίων ἢ οἰκιῶν ὑπῆρχον, πωλοῦντες ἔφερον τὰς
owners of lands or houses were, having sold brought the
5092 4097 5087 3844 4228
35 τιμὰς τῶν πιπρασκομένων, καὶ ἐτίθουν παρὰ τοὺς πόδας
values of those being sold, and placed at the feet
652 1239 1538 2530 302/5100/5532
τῶν ἀποστόλων· διεδίδοτο δὲ ἑκάστῳ καθότι ἄν τις χρείαν
of the apostles; it was distributed and to each according to any need
2192
εἶχεν.
had.
2500 1941 921 5259 652
36 Ἰωσῆς δέ, ὁ ἐπικληθεὶς Βαρνάβας ὑπὸ τῶν ἀποστόλων
Joses And, he surnamed Barnabas by the apostles,
3739 2076 3177 5207 3874 3019
(ὅ ἐστι, μεθερμηνευόμενον, υἱὸς παρακλήσεως), Λευΐτης,
which is, being translated, Son of Consolation, a Levite,
2953 1085 5225 846 68 4453
37 Κύπριος τῷ γένει, ὑπάρχοντος αὐτῷ ἀγροῦ, πωλήσας
a Cypriot by race, being to him a field, having sold
5342 5536 5087 3844 4228 652
ἤνεγκε τὸ χρῆμα, καὶ ἔθηκε παρὰ τοὺς πόδας τῶν ἀποστόλων.
brought the proceeds and placed at the feet of the apostles.

CHAPTER 5

435 5100 367 3686 4862 4551 1135
1 Ἀνὴρ δέ τις Ἀνανίας ὀνόματι, σὺν Σαπφείρῃ τῇ γυναικὶ
man And a certain, Ananias by name, with Sapphira the wife
848 4453 2933 3557 575 5092
2 αὐτοῦ, ἐπώλησε κτῆμα, καὶ ἐνοσφίσατο ἀπὸ τῆς τιμῆς,
of him, sold a property, and secretly kept back from the price,
4894 1135 848 5342 3313 5100
συνειδυίας καὶ τῆς γυναικὸς αὐτοῦ, καὶ ἐνέγκας μέρος τι
aware of (it) also the wife of him, and bringing a part certain
3844 4228 652 5087 2036 4074
3 παρὰ τοὺς πόδας τῶν ἀποστόλων ἔθηκεν. εἶπε δὲ Πέτρος,
to the feet of the apostles placed (it). said But Peter,
367 1302 4137 4567 2588 4675
Ἀνανία, διατί ἐπλήρωσεν ὁ Σατανᾶς τὴν καρδίαν σου,
Ananias, why filled Satan the heart of you,
5574 4571 4151 40 3557 575
ψεύσασθαί σε τὸ Πνεῦμα τὸ Ἅγιον, καὶ νοσφίσασθαι ἀπὸ
to deceive you the Spirit Holy, and to secretly keep back from
5092 5564 3780 3306/4671/3306 4097 1722
4 τῆς τιμῆς τοῦ χωρίου; οὐχὶ μένον σοὶ ἔμενε, καὶ πραθὲν ἐν
the price of the land? not Remaining to you remain, and sold in
4674 1849 5225 5101/3754/5087/1722 2588 4675
τῇ σῇ ἐξουσίᾳ ὑπῆρχε; τί ὅτι ἔθου ἐν τῇ καρδίᾳ σου τὸ
your authority it was? What that was in the heart of you
(is it) put

your heart? You did not lie to men, but to God!
5And hearing these words, falling down, Ananias expired. And great fear came on all those hearing these things. 6And rising up the younger ones wrapped him; and carrying out, *they* buried *him*.

7And about three hours afterwards, his wife also entered, not knowing that happening. 8And Peter answered her, Tell me if you gave over the land *for* so much? And she said, Yes, *for* so much. 9And Peter said to her, Why *was it* that it was agreed with you to tempt the Spirit of *the* Lord? Behold, the feet of those burying your husband at the door! Yea, they will carry you out. 10And immediately she fell at his feet, and expired. And entering, the younger ones found her dead; and carrying *her* out, *they* buried her beside her husband. 11And great fear came on all the church, and on all those hearing these things.

12And many miracles and wonders among the people took place through the hands of the apostles. And they were all with one passion in Solomon's Porch. 13And of the rest, no one dared to be joined to them, but the people greatly magnified them.
14And more believing ones were added to *the* Lord, multitudes of both men and of women; 15so as to carry out the sick in the streets, and to place *them* on cots and mattresses, that *at the* coming *of* Peter, if even *his* shadow might overshadow some of them.

4229 5124 3756 5574 444 235 2316
πρᾶγμα τοῦτο ; οὐκ ἐψεύσω ἀνθρώποις, ἀλλὰ τῷ Θεῷ.
action this? not You lied to men, but to God.
191 367 3056 5128 4098 1634
5 ἀκούων δὲ Ἀνανίας τοὺς λόγους τούτους, πεσὼν ἐξέψυξε·
hearing And Ananias words these, falling expired.
1096 5401 3173/1909 3956 191 5023
καὶ ἐγένετο φόβος μέγας ἐπὶ πάντας τοὺς ἀκούοντας ταῦτα.
And came fear great on all those hearing these things
450 3501 4958 846 1627
6 ἀναστάντες δὲ οἱ νεώτεροι συνέστειλαν αὐτόν, καὶ ἐξενέγ-
rising up And the young men, they wrapped him, and carrying
2290
καντες ἔθαψαν.
out, buried (him).
1096 5613 5610 5140 1292 1135 848
7 Ἐγένετο δὲ ὡς ὡρῶν τριῶν διάστημα, καὶ ἡ γυνὴ αὐτοῦ
there was And about hours three afterwards and the wife of him
3361 1492 1096 1525 611 846 4074
8 μὴ εἰδυῖα τὸ γεγονὸς εἰσῆλθεν. ἀπεκρίθη δὲ αὐτῇ ὁ Πέτρος,
not knowing the happening, entered. answered And her — Peter,
2036/3427/1487/ 5118 5564 591 2036 3483
Εἰπέ μοι, εἰ τοσούτου τὸ χωρίον ἀπέδοσθε. ἡ δὲ εἶπε, Ναί,
Tell me, if of so much the land you gave over? she And said, Yes,
5118 4074 2036 4314 846 5101/3754/ 4856
9 τοσούτου. ὁ δὲ Πέτρος εἶπε πρὸς αὐτήν, Τί ὅτι συνεφωνήθη
of so much. And Peter said to her, What (was it) that it was agreed
2290 5213 3985 4151 2962 2400 4228
ὑμῖν πειράσαι τὸ Πνεῦμα Κυρίου ; ἰδού, οἱ πόδες τῶν θαψαν-
with you to tempt the Spirit of (the) Lord? Behold, the feet of those burying
435 4675 1909 2374 1627 4571 4098
10 των τὸν ἄνδρα σου ἐπὶ τῇ θύρᾳ, καὶ ἐξοίσουσί σε. ἔπεσε δὲ
the husband of you at the door and they will carry you. she fell And
3916 3844 4228 848 1634 1525
παραχρῆμα παρὰ τοὺς πόδας αὐτοῦ, καὶ ἐξέψυξεν· εἰσελ-
immediately at the feet of him, and expired. entering
3495 2147 846 3498 1627
θόντες δὲ οἱ νεανίσκοι εὗρον αὐτὴν νεκράν, καὶ ἐξενέγκαντες
And the young men found her dead, and carrying out
2290 4314 435 848 1096 5401 3173
11 ἔθαψαν πρὸς τὸν ἄνδρα αὐτῆς. καὶ ἐγένετο φόβος μέγας
buried her near the husband of her. And came fear great
1909 3650 1577 1909 3956 191
ἐφ' ὅλην τὴν ἐκκλησίαν, καὶ ἐπὶ πάντας τοὺς ἀκούοντας
on all the church, and on all those hearing
5023
ταῦτα.
these things.
1223 5495 652 1096 4592
12 Διὰ δὲ τῶν χειρῶν τῶν ἀποστόλων ἐγίνετο σημεῖα καὶ
through And the hands of the apostles happened signs and
5059 1722 2992 4183 2258 3661 537
τέρατα ἐν τῷ λαῷ πολλά· καὶ ἦσαν ὁμοθυμαδὸν ἅπαντες
wonders among the people many; and were with one passion all
1722 4745 4672 3062 3762 5111
13 ἐν τῇ στοᾷ Σολομῶντος. τῶν δὲ λοιπῶν οὐδεὶς ἐτόλμα
in the porch of Solomon. of the And rest, no one dared
2853 846 235 3170 846 2992 3123
κολλᾶσθαι αὐτοῖς, ἀλλ' ἐμεγάλυνεν αὐτοὺς ὁ λαός· μᾶλλον
to be joined to them, but magnified them the people; more
4369 4100 2962 4128 435 5037
14 δὲ προσετίθεντο πιστεύοντες τῷ Κυρίῳ, πλήθη ἀνδρῶν τε
and were added believing ones to (the) Lord, multitudes of men both
1135 5620 2596 4113 1627
15 καὶ γυναικῶν· ὥστε κατὰ τὰς πλατείας ἐκφέρειν τοὺς
and of women; so as in the streets to carry out the
772 5087 1909 2825 2895 2443 2064
ἀσθενεῖς, καὶ τιθέναι ἐπὶ κλινῶν καὶ κραββάτων, ἵνα ἐρχο-
sick, and to place on cots and mattresses, that coming
4074 2579 4639 1982 5100 846 4905
μένου Πέτρου κἂν ἡ σκιὰ ἐπισκιάσῃ τινὶ αὐτῶν. συνήρχετο
Peter, if even the shadow overshadow some of them. assembled

[16]And also the multitude came together *from* the cities around Jerusalem, bringing sick ones and those being tormented by unclean spirits; who were all healed.

[17]And rising up, the high priest and all those with him, which is *the* sect of the Sadducees, were filled with zeal, [18]and laid their hands on the apostles, and put them in public custody. [19]But an angel of *the* Lord opened the doors of the prison during the night, and leading them out, *he* said, [20]Go! And standing in the Temple, speak to the people all the words of this Life. [21]And hearing, they went into the Temple about dawn, and taught. But having come near, the high priest and those with him called together the sanhedrin and all the elderhood of the sons of Israel. And *they* sent to the jail to have them brought. [22]But having come near, the officers did not find them in the prison. And returning, they reported, [23]saying, Indeed we found the jail having been shut with all security, and the guards outside standing before the doors. But opening *it*, we found no one inside. [24]And when they heard these words, both the priest and the Temple commander and the chief priests were in doubt concerning them, what this might become.

[25]But having come, one reported to them, saying, Behold, the men whom you put in the prison are in the Temple, standing and teaching the people. [26]Then the commander going with the officers, *they* brought

4128 4038 4172 1519 2419
16 δὲ καὶ τὸ πλῆθος τῶν πέριξ πόλεων εἰς Ἱερουσαλήμ,
And also the multitude of the round about cities to Jerusalem,
5342 772 3791 5259 4151 169
φέροντες ἀσθενεῖς καὶ ὀχλουμένους ὑπὸ πνευμάτων ἀκαθάρ-
carrying sick (ones) and those being tormented by spirits unclean,
3748 2323 537
των, οἵτινες ἐθεραπεύοντο απαντες.
who were healed all.
450 749 3956 4862 846 5607
17 Ἀναστὰς δὲ ὁ ἀρχιερεὺς καὶ πάντες οἱ σὺν αὐτῷ (ἡ οὖσα
rising up And the high priest and all those with him, which is
139 4523 4130 2205 1911
αἵρεσις τῶν Σαδδουκαίων), ἐπλήσθησαν ζήλου, καὶ ἐπέ-
(the) sect of the Sadducees, were filled of jealousy and
5495 848 1909 652 5087
18 βαλον τὰς χεῖρας αὐτῶν ἐπὶ τοὺς ἀποστόλους, καὶ ἔθεντο
laid on the hands of them on the apostles, and put
846 1722 5084 1219 32 2962 1223 3571
19 αὐτοὺς ἐν τηρήσει δημοσίᾳ. ἄγγελος δὲ Κυρίου διὰ τῆς νυκτὸς
them in custody publicly. an angel But of (the) Lord by night
455 2374 5438 1806 5037 846 2036
ἤνοιξε τὰς θύρας τῆς φυλακῆς, ἐξαγαγών τε αὐτοὺς εἶπε,
opened the doors of the prison, leading out and them said,
4198 2476 2980 1722 2411 2992 3956
20 Πορεύεσθε, καὶ σταθέντες λαλεῖτε ἐν τῷ ἱερῷ τῷ λαῷ πάντα
Go, and standing speak in the Temple to the people all
4487 2222 5026 191 1525 5259
21 τὰ ῥήματα τῆς ζωῆς ταύτης. ἀκούσαντες δὲ εἰσῆλθον ὑπὸ
the words of life this. having heard And, they entered about
3722 1519 2411 1321 3854
τὸν ὄρθρον εἰς τὸ ἱερόν, καὶ ἐδίδασκον. παραγενόμενος δὲ ὁ
the dawn into the Temple, and taught. having come near And the
749 4862 846 4779 3892
ἀρχιερεὺς καὶ οἱ σὺν αὐτῷ, συνεκάλεσαν τὸ συνέδριον καὶ
high priest and those with him, he called together the sanhedrin and
3956 1087 5207 2474 649 1519
πᾶσαν τὴν γερουσίαν τῶν υἱῶν Ἰσραήλ, καὶ ἀπέστειλαν εἰς
all the elderhood of the sons of Israel. And they sent to
1201 71 846 5257 3854
22 τὸ δεσμωτήριον, ἀχθῆναι αὐτούς. οἱ δὲ ὑπηρέται παρα-
the jail to be brought them. the But officers having
3756 2147 846 1722 5438 390
γενόμενοι οὐχ εὗρον αὐτοὺς ἐν τῇ φυλακῇ· ἀναστρέψαντες
come near not did find them in the prison; having returned
518 3004 3754 3303 1201 2147
23 δὲ ἀπήγγειλαν, λέγοντες ὅτι Τὸ μὲν δεσμωτήριον εὕρομεν
and they reported, saying, the Indeed jail we found
2808 1722 3956 803 5441 1854
κεκλεισμένον ἐν πάσῃ ἀσφαλείᾳ, καὶ τοὺς φύλακας ἔξω
having been shut in all security and the guards outside
2476 4253 2374 455 2080 3762 2147
ἑστῶτας πρὸ τῶν θυρῶν· ἀνοίξαντες δέ, ἔσω οὐδένα εὕρο-
standing at the doors, having opened but, inside no one we
5613 191 3056 5128 3739/5037/2409
24 μεν. ὡς δὲ ἤκουσαν τοὺς λόγους τούτους ὅ τε ἱερεὺς καὶ ὁ
found. as And heard words these the both priest and the
4755 2411 749 1280 4012
στρατηγὸς τοῦ ἱεροῦ καὶ οἱ ἀρχιερεῖς, διηπόρουν περὶ
commander of the Temple and the chief priests, they were in doubt concerning
846 5101/302 1096 5124 3854 5100 518
25 αὐτῶν, τί ἂν γένοιτο τοῦτο. παραγενόμενος δέ τις ἀπηγ-
them, what might become this. having come And one reported
846 3004 3754 2400 435 3739 5087 1722
γειλεν αὐτοῖς λέγων ὅτι Ἰδού, οἱ ἄνδρες οὓς ἔθεσθε ἐν τῇ
to them, saying, Behold, the men whom you put in the
5438 1526 1722 2411 2476 1321 2992
φυλακῇ εἰσὶν ἐν τῷ ἱερῷ ἑστῶτες καὶ διδάσκοντες τὸν λαόν.
prison are in the Temple standing and teaching the people.
5119 565 4755 4862 5257 71
26 τότε ἀπελθὼν ὁ στρατηγὸς σὺν τοῖς ὑπηρέταις ἤγαγεν
Then going the commander with the officers brought

them, not with force, for they feared the people, that they might not be stoned. [27]And bringing them, they stood in the sanhedrin. And the high priest asked them, [28]saying, Did we not command you by a command *that* you not teach in this name? And, behold, you have filled Jerusalem with your teaching, and intend to bring on us the blood of this man. [29]But answering Peter and the apostles said, It is right to obey God rather than men. [30]The God of our fathers raised up Jesus, whom you laid hands on, hanging *Him* on a tree. [31]God *has* exalted this One *as* a Ruler and Savior to His right *hand*, to give to Israel repentance and forgiveness of sins. [32]And we are His witnesses of these things, and also the Holy Spirit, whom God gave to those obeying Him.

[33]But those hearing were cut, and *they* took counsel to do away with them. [34]But one standing up in the sanhedrin, a Pharisee named Gamaliel, a teacher of the Law honored by all the people, commanded the apostles to be put outside a little while. [35]And he said to them, Men, Israelites, take heed to yourselves what you intend to do on these men. [36]For before these days Theudas rose up, claiming himself to be somebody, to whom was joined a number of men, about four hundred; who was done away, and all, as many as obeyed him, were dispersed and came to nothing. [37]After this, Judas the Galilean rose up in the days

846 3756/3326 970 5399 1063 2992 2443/3361
αὐτους, οὐ μετὰ βίας, ἐφοβοῦντο γὰρ τὸν λαόν, ἵνα μὴ
them, not with force, they feared for the people, lest
3034 71 846 2476 1722 4892
27 λιθασθῶσιν. ἀγαγόντες δὲ αὐτοὺς ἔστησαν ἐν τῷ συνεδρίῳ.
they be stoned. bringing And them, they stood in the sanhedrin.
1905 846 749 3004 3756 3852
28 καὶ ἐπηρώτησεν αὐτοὺς ὁ ἀρχιερεύς, λέγων, Οὐ παραγ-
And questioned them the high priest, saying, Not by a
3853 5213/3361 1321 1909 3686
γελίᾳ παρηγγείλαμεν ὑμῖν μὴ διδάσκειν ἐπὶ τῷ ὀνόματι
charge did we charge to you not to teach on — name
5129 2400 4137 2419 1322
τούτῳ; καὶ ἰδοὺ πεπληρώκατε τὴν Ἱερουσαλὴμ τῆς δι-
this? And, behold, you have filled — Jerusalem of the
5216 1014 1863 1909 2248 129
δαχῆς ὑμῶν, καὶ βούλεσθε ἐπαγαγεῖν ἐφ' ἡμᾶς τὸ αἷμα τοῦ
teaching of you, and purpose to bring on us the blood —
444 5127 611 4074 652
29 ἀνθρώπου τούτου. ἀποκριθεὶς δὲ ὁ Πέτρος καὶ οἱ ἀπόστολοι
of man this. answering But — Peter and the apostles
2036 3980 1163/2316 3123 2228/ 444 2316
30 εἶπον, Πειθαρχεῖν δεῖ Θεῷ μᾶλλον ἢ ἀνθρώποις. ὁ Θεὸς τῶν
said, to obey It is right God rather than men. The God of the
3962 2257 1453 2424 3739/5210 1315
πατέρων ἡμῶν ἤγειρεν Ἰησοῦν, ὃν ὑμεῖς διεχειρίσασθε,
fathers of us raised Jesus, whom you laid hands upon,
2910 1909 3586 5126 2316 747 4990
31 κρεμάσαντες ἐπὶ ξύλου. τοῦτον ὁ Θεὸς ἀρχηγὸν καὶ σωτῆρα
hanging (Him) on a tree. This One God a Ruler and a Savior
5312 1188 848 1325 3341 2474
ὕψωσε τῇ δεξιᾷ αὐτοῦ, δοῦναι μετάνοιαν τῷ Ἰσραὴλ καὶ
exalted to the right (hand) of Him, to give repentance — to Israel and
859 266 2249 2070 848 3144
32 ἄφεσιν ἁμαρτιῶν. καὶ ἡμεῖς ἐσμεν αὐτοῦ μάρτυρες τῶν
forgiveness of sins. And we are of Him witnesses
4487 5130 4151 40 3739/ 1325
ῥημάτων τούτων, καὶ τὸ Πνεῦμα δὲ τὸ Ἅγιον, ὃ ἔδωκεν ὁ
of words these, also the Spirit and — Holy which gave
2316 3980 846
Θεὸς τοῖς πειθαρχοῦσιν αὐτῷ.
God to those obeying Him.

191 1282 1011 337
33 Οἱ δὲ ἀκούσαντες διεπρίοντο, καὶ ἐβουλεύοντο ἀνελεῖν
those And hearing were cut, and took counsel to take
3686 846 450 5100/1722 4892 5330 away
34 αὐτούς. ἀναστὰς δέ τις ἐν τῷ συνεδρίῳ Φαρισαῖος, ὀνό-
them. standing up But one in the sanhedrin, a Pharisee by
1059 3547 5093 3956 2992
ματι Γαμαλιήλ, νομοδιδάσκαλος, τίμιος παντὶ τῷ λαῷ,
name Gamaliel, a teacher of the Law, honored by all the people,
2753 1854 1024 5100 652 4160 2036 5037
35 ἐκέλευσεν ἔξω βραχύ τι τοὺς ἀποστόλους ποιῆσαι. εἶπέ τε
commanded outside a little while the apostles to put. he said And
4314 846 435 2475 4337 1438 1909
πρὸς αὐτούς, Ἄνδρες Ἰσραηλῖται, προσέχετε ἑαυτοῖς ἐπὶ
to them, Men, Israelites, take heed to yourselves on
444 5125 5101 3195 4238 4253 1063
36 τοῖς ἀνθρώποις τούτοις, τί μέλλετε πράσσειν. πρὸ γὰρ
— men these, what you intend to do. before For
5130 2250 450 2333 3004 1511 5100
τούτων τῶν ἡμερῶν ἀνέστη Θευδᾶς, λέγων εἶναί τινα
these — days stood up Theudas, saying to be someone
1438 3739 4347 706 435 5616 5071
ἑαυτόν, ᾧ προσεκολλήθη ἀριθμὸς ἀνδρῶν ὡσεὶ τετρακοσίων·
himself, to whom were joined a number of men, about four hundred,
3739 337 3956 3745 3982 846 1262
ὃς ἀνῃρέθη, καὶ πάντες ὅσοι ἐπείθοντο αὐτῷ διελύθησαν καὶ
who was taken away and all as many as obeyed him were dispersed and
1096 1519/3762 3326 5125 450 2455 1057
37 ἐγένοντο εἰς οὐδέν. μετὰ τοῦτον ἀνέστη Ἰούδας ὁ Γαλιλαῖος
came to nothing. After this stood up Judas the Galilean

of the Registration. And *he* drew considerable people after him. Yet that one perished, and all were scattered, as many as obeyed him. [38]And now I say to you, draw away from these men, and permit them; because if this counsel is of men, or this work, it will be destroyed. [39]But if it is from God, you will not be able to destroy it, lest you be found even fighters against God. [40]And they obeyed him. And having called the apostles, beating *them*, they charged *them* not to speak on the name of Jesus, and released them. [41]Then they indeed departed from *the* presence of the sanhedrin, rejoicing that they were deemed worthy to be dishonored on behalf of His name. [42]And every day they did not cease teaching and preachisng the gospel of Jesus the Christ in the Temple, and house to house.

1722 2250 582 868 2992 2425
ἐν ταῖς ἡμέραις τῆς ἀπογραφῆς. καὶ ἀπέστησε λαὸν ἱκανὸν
in the days of the registration, and drew away people much
3694 846 2548 622 3956 3745 3982
ὀπίσω αὐτοῦ· κἀκεῖνος ἀπώλετο, καὶ πάντες ὅσοι ἐπείθοντο
after him; and that one perished, and all as many as obeyed
846 1287 3569 3004 5213 868
38 αὐτῷ διεσκορπίσθησαν. καὶ τὰ νῦν λέγω ὑμῖν, ἀπόστητε
him were scattered. And now I say to you, draw away
575 444 5130 1439 848 3754/1437/•
5600 ἀπὸ τῶν ἀνθρώπων τούτων, καὶ ἐάσατε αὐτούς· ὅτι ἐὰν ᾖ
from men these, and allow them; because if be
1537 444 1012 3778/2228 2041 5124 2647
ἐξ ἀνθρώπων ἡ βουλὴ αὕτη ἢ τὸ ἔργον τοῦτο, καταλυθή-
of men counsel this, or work this, it will be
1487 1537/2316 2076 3756 1410 2647 846
39 σεται· εἰ δὲ ἐκ Θεοῦ ἐστιν, οὐ δύνασθε καταλῦσαι αὐτό,
destroyed. if But of God it is, not you will be able to destroy it,
3379 2314 2147 3982 846
40 μήποτε καὶ θεομάχοι εὑρεθῆτε. ἐπείσθησαν δὲ αὐτῷ· καὶ
lest even God-fighters you be found. they obeyed And him, and
4341 652 1194 3853
προσκαλεσάμενοι τοὺς ἀποστόλους, δείραντες παρήγγειλαν
having called the apostles, beating (them) they charged
3361 2980 1909 3686 2424 630 846
μὴ λαλεῖν ἐπὶ τῷ ὀνόματι τοῦ Ἰησοῦ, καὶ ἀπέλυσαν αὐτούς.
not to speak on the name — of Jesus, and released them.
3303/3767 4198 5463 575 4383 4892
41 οἱ μὲν οὖν ἐπορεύοντο χαίροντες ἀπὸ προσώπου τοῦ συνε-
They indeed then departed rejoicing from (the) presence of the san-
3754/5228 3686 848 2661 818
δρίου, ὅτι ὑπὲρ τοῦ ὀνόματος αὐτοῦ κατηξιώθησαν ἀτιμασθῆ-
hedrin, that for the name of Him they were deemed worthy to be
3956 5037 2250 1722 2411 2596 3624 3756 3973
42 ναι. πᾶσάν τε ἡμέραν, ἐν τῷ ἱερῷ καὶ κατ' οἶκον, οὐκ ἐπαύ-
dishonored every And day. in the Temple and house to house. not they
1321 2097 2424 5547
οντο διδάσκοντες καὶ εὐαγγελιζόμενοι Ἰησοῦν τὸν Χριστόν.
ceased teaching and preaching the gospel— Jesus the Christ.

CHAPTER 6

[1]But in those days, the disciples multiplying, a murmuring of the Hellenists toward the Hebrews occurred, because their widows were being overlooked in the daily serving. [2]And having called near the multitude of the disciples, the Twelve said, It is not pleasing to us to leave the word of God in order to serve tables! Then, brothers, be looking for men among you being witnessed to — seven full of *the* Holy Spirit and wisdom, whom we shall appoint over this duty. [4]But we shall continue steadfast to prayer and to the service of the word. [5]And the saying was pleasing before all the

1722 2250 5025 4129 3101
1 Ἐν δὲ ταῖς ἡμέραις ταύταις, πληθυνόντων τῶν μαθητῶν,
in And — days these, multiplying the disciples,
1096 1112 1675 4314 1445
ἐγένετο γογγυσμὸς τῶν Ἑλληνιστῶν πρὸς τοὺς Ἑβραίους,
there was a murmuring of the Hellenists against the Hebrews,
3754 3865 1722 1248 2522 5503
ὅτι παρεθεωροῦντο ἐν τῇ διακονίᾳ τῇ καθημερινῇ αἱ χῆραι
because were overlooked in the service near daily the widows
848 4341 1427 4128
2 αὐτῶν. προσκαλεσάμενοι δὲ οἱ δώδεκα τὸ πλῆθος τῶν
of them. having called near And the twelve the multitude of the
3101 2036 3756 701 2076 2248 2641
μαθητῶν, εἶπον, Οὐκ ἀρεστόν ἐστιν ἡμᾶς, καταλείψαντας
disciples, they said, not pleasing It is to us leaving
3056 2316 1247 5132 1980 3767
3 τὸν λόγον τοῦ Θεοῦ, διακονεῖν τραπέζαις. ἐπισκέψασθε οὖν,
the word — of God to serve tables. Look out, therefore,
80 435 1537 5216 3140 2033 4134
ἀδελφοί, ἄνδρας ἐξ ὑμῶν μαρτυρουμένους ἑπτά, πλήρεις
brothers, men from you being witnessed to, seven, full
4151 40 4678 3739 2525 1909
Πνεύματος Ἁγίου καὶ σοφίας, οὓς καταστήσομεν ἐπὶ τῆς
of (the) Spirit Holy, and of wisdom, whom we will appoint over —
5532 5026 2249 4335 1248
4 χρείας ταύτης. ἡμεῖς δὲ τῇ προσευχῇ καὶ τῇ διακονίᾳ τοῦ
duty this. we But to prayer and the service of the
3056 4342 700 3056 1799
5 λόγου προσκαρτερήσομεν. καὶ ἤρεσεν ὁ λόγος ἐνώπιον
word will continue steadfast. And was pleasing the word before

NOTE: Frequent words not numbered: δέ (1161); καί (2531)—and, but; ὁ, ἡ, τό (3588, the)— • above word, look in verse margin for No.

multitude. And they chose out Stephen a man full of faith and *the* Holy Spirit; and Philip, and Prochorus, and Nicanor, and Timon, and Parmenas, and Nicolas, a proselyte from Antioch—[6]*each of* whom they made stand before the apostles. And having prayed, they placed *their* hands on them. [7]And the word of God increased, and the number of the disciples in Jerusalem multiplyed exceedingly—even a great crowd of the priests were obeying the faith!

[8]And Stephen, full of faith and power, did wonders and great miracles among the people. [9]But some of those of the synagogue rose up, *those* called Libertines, also *some* Cyrenians and Alexandrians, and *some* of those from Cilicia and Asia *Minor*, disputing with Stephen. [10]And they had no strength to stand against the wisdom and the Spirit by which he spoke. [11]Then they induced men *to be* saying, We have heard him speaking blasphemous words against Moses and God! [12]And they stirred up the people and the elders and the scribes. And coming on, they together seized him, and led *him* into the sanhedrin. [13]And they stood up false witnesses, saying, This man does not cease speaking blasphemous words against this holy place and the Law; [14]for we have heard him saying that this Jesus the Nazarene will destroy this place, and will change the customs which Moses delivered over to us. [15]And looking intently at him, all those seating themselves in the sanhedrin

3956 4128 1586 4736 435 4134
παντὸς τοῦ πλήθους· καὶ ἐξελέξαντο Στέφανον, ἄνδρα πλήρη
all the multitude, and they chose Stephen, a man full
4102 4151 40 5376 4402
πίστεως καὶ Πνεύματος Ἁγίου, καὶ Φίλιππον, καὶ Πρόχο-
of faith and (the) Spirit Holy, and Philip, and Prochorus,
3527 5096 3937 3532
ρον, καὶ Νικάνορα, καὶ Τίμωνα, καὶ Παρμενᾶν, καὶ Νικόλαον
and Nicanor, and Timon, and Parmenas, and Nicolas
4339 491 3739 2476 1799 652
6 προσήλυτον Ἀντιοχέα, οὓς ἔστησαν ἐνώπιον τῶν ἀποστό-
a proselyte of Antioch; whom they set before the apostles;
4336 2007 846 5495
λων· καὶ προσευξάμενοι ἐπέθηκαν αὐτοῖς τὰς χεῖρας.
and having prayed they placed on them the hands.
3056 2316 837 4129 706
7 Καὶ ὁ λόγος τοῦ Θεοῦ ηὔξανε, καὶ ἐπληθύνετο ὁ ἀριθμὸς
And the word — of God increased, and was multiplied the number
3101 1722 2419 4970 4183 5037 3793
τῶν μαθητῶν ἐν Ἱερουσαλὴμ σφόδρα, πολύς τε ὄχλος τῶν
of the disciples in Jerusalem exceedingly; a much and crowd of the
2409 5219 4102
ἱερέων ὑπήκουον τῇ πίστει.
priests obeyed the faith.
4736 4134 4102 1411 4160 5059
8 Στέφανος δὲ πλήρης πίστεως καὶ δυνάμεως ἐποίει τέρατα
Stephen And full of faith and power did wonders
4592 3173 1722 2992 450 5100 1537
καὶ σημεῖα μεγάλα ἐν τῷ λαῷ. ἀνέστησαν δέ τινες τῶν ἐκ
and signs great among the people. rose up But some of those of
4864 3004 3032 2956
9 τῆς συναγωγῆς τῆς λεγομένης Λιβερτίνων, καὶ Κυρηναίων,
the synagogue — called of (the) Libertines, and of Cyrenians
221 575 2791 773 4802
καὶ Ἀλεξανδρέων, καὶ τῶν ἀπὸ Κιλικίας καὶ Ἀσίας, συζη-
and of Alexandrians, and of those from Cilicia and Asia,
4736 3756 2480 436 4678
10 τοῦντες τῷ Στεφάνῳ. καὶ οὐκ ἴσχυον ἀντιστῆναι τῇ σοφίᾳ
disputing with Stephen. And not were able to stand against the wisdom
4151 3739 2980 5119 5260 435 3004
11 καὶ τῷ πνεύματι ᾧ ἐλάλει. τότε ὑπέβαλον ἄνδρας λέγοντας
and the spirit with which he spoke. Then they suborned men, saying,
3754 191 846 2980 4487 989 1519
ὅτι Ἀκηκόαμεν αὐτοῦ λαλοῦντος ῥήματα βλάσφημα εἰς
— We have heard from him speaking words blasphemous against
3475 2316 4787 5037 2992
12 Μωσῆν καὶ τὸν Θεόν. συνεκίνησάν τε τὸν λαὸν καὶ τοὺς
Moses and — God. they stirred up And the people and the
4245 1122 2186 4884
πρεσβυτέρους καὶ τοὺς γραμματεῖς, καὶ ἐπιστάντες συν-
elders and the scribes, and coming on they
846 71 1519 4892 2476 5037
13 ήρπασαν αὐτόν, καὶ ἤγαγον εἰς τὸ συνέδριον, ἔστησάν τε
seized him, and led to the sanhedrin they stood And
3144 5571 3004 444 3778 3756 3973
μάρτυρας ψευδεῖς λέγοντας, Ὁ ἄνθρωπος οὗτος οὐ παύεται
witnesses false, saying, man This not ceases
4487 989 2980 2596 5117 40
ῥήματα βλάσφημα λαλῶν κατὰ τοῦ τόπου τοῦ ἁγίου
words blasphemous speaking against — place — holy
5127 3551 191 1063 846 3004 3754
14 τούτου καὶ τοῦ νόμου· ἀκηκόαμεν γὰρ αὐτοῦ λέγοντος ὅτι
this, and the Law; we have heard for from him, saying
2424 3480 3778 2647 5117 5126
Ἰησοῦς ὁ Ναζωραῖος οὗτος καταλύσει τὸν τόπον τοῦτον,
Jesus the Nazarene this One, will destroy — place this,
236 1485/3739/ 3860 2254 3475 816
15 καὶ ἀλλάξει τὰ ἔθη ἃ παρέδωκεν ἡμῖν Μωϋσῆς. καὶ ἀτενί-
and will change the customs which delivered to us Moses. And looking
1519 846 537 2516 1722 4892
σαντες εἰς αὐτὸν ἅπαντες οἱ καθεζόμενοι ἐν τῷ συνεδρίῳ,
intently at him, all those sitting in the sanhedrin

NOTE: Frequent words not numbered: δέ(1161); καί(2531)—and, but; ὁ, ἡ, τό (3588, the)— * above word, look in verse margin for No.

saw his face as if *it were the* face of an angel.

CHAPTER 7

[1]And the high priest said, *Tell me* if, then, you thus hold these things? [2]And he said, Men, brothers, and fathers, listen! The God of glory appeared to our father Abraham, being in Mesopotamia before he lived in Haran; [3]and said to him, Go out from your land and from your kindred, and come into a land which I will show to you. [4]Then going out from *the* land of the Chaldeans, he lived in Haran. And after his father died, *God* moved him from there into this land in which you now live. [5]And He did not give to him an inheritance in it, not even a foot-breadth. And *He* promised to give it to him for a possession, and to his seed after him, there being no child to him. [6]And God spoke thus, that his seed would be a sojourner in another land, and they would enslave *it* and oppress *it* four hundred years. [7]And God said, "I will judge the nation to which you will be in bondage." And, "After these things they will come out and will serve Me in this place." [8]And He gave to him a covenant of circumcision; and so he fathered Isaac, and circumcised him on the eighth day. And Isaac *fathered* Jacob, and Jacob the twelve patriarchs.

[9]And being jealous of Joseph, the patriarchs gave *him* over into Egupt. [10]And God was with him, and plucked him out from all his afflictions, and gave him

1492 4383 848 5616 4383 32
εἶδον τὸ πρόσωπον αὐτοῦ ὡσεὶ πρόσωπον ἀγγέλου.
saw the face of him as if a face of an angel.

CHAPTER 7

2036 749 1487/686 5023 3779 2192 5346
1 Εἶπε δὲ ὁ ἀρχιερεύς, Εἰ ἄρα ταῦτα οὕτως ἔχει ; ὁ δὲ ἔφη,
said And the high priest, If, then, these things thus hold? he And said,
435 80 3962 191 2316 1391
2 Ἄνδρες ἀδελφοὶ καὶ πατέρες, ἀκούσατε. ὁ Θεὸς τῆς δόξης
Men, brothers and fathers, hear: The God – of glory
3700 3962 2257 11 5607/1722 3318
ὤφθη τῷ πατρὶ ἡμῶν Ἀβραὰμ ὄντι ἐν τῇ Μεσοποταμίᾳ,
appeared to the father of us, Abraham, being in Mesopotamia
4250/2228/ 2730 846 1722 5488 2036 4314 846
3 πρὶν ἢ κατοικῆσαι αὐτὸν ἐν Χαρράν, καὶ εἶπε πρὸς αὐτόν,
before even dwelt him in Haran; and said to him,
1831/1537/ 1093/4675 1537 4772 4675 1204
Ἔξελθε ἐκ τῆς γῆς σου καὶ ἐκ τῆς συγγενείας σου, καὶ δεῦρο
Go out of the land of you and from the kindred of you, and come
3739 1519/1093//302/4671 1166 5119 1831 1537/1093 5466
4 εἰς γῆν ἣν ἄν σοι δείξω. τότε ἐξελθὼν ἐκ γῆς Χαλδαίων
into a land which to you I will show. Then going out of (the) land of Chaldea
2730 1722 5488 2547 3326 599
κατῴκησεν ἐν Χαρράν· κἀκεῖθεν, μετὰ τὸ ἀποθανεῖν τὸν
he dwelt in Haran. And from there, after the dying of the
3962 848 3351 846 1519 1093 5026 1519/3739
πατέρα αὐτοῦ, μετῴκισεν αὐτὸν εἰς τὴν γῆν ταύτην εἰς ἣν
father of him, (God) moved him into land this, in which
5210/3568 2730 3756 1325 846 2817 1722
5 ὑμεῖς νῦν κατοικεῖτε· καὶ οὐκ ἔδωκεν αὐτῷ κληρονομίαν ἐν
you now dwell. And not He gave to him an inheritance in
846 3761 968 4228 1861 846 1325 1519
αὐτῇ, οὐδὲ βῆμα ποδός· καὶ ἐπηγγείλατο αὐτῷ δοῦναι εἰς
it, nor space of a foot, and promised him to give for
2697 846 4690 848 3326 846 3756
κατάσχεσιν αὐτήν, καὶ τῷ σπέρματι αὐτοῦ μετ' αὐτόν, οὐκ
a possession it, and to the seed of him after him, not
5607 846 5043 2980 3779 2316 3754 2071
6 ὄντος αὐτῷ τέκνου. ἐλάλησε δὲ οὕτως ὁ Θεός, ὅτι ἔσται τὸ
being to him a child. spoke And thus – God, that will be the
4690 848 3941 1722 1093 245 1402
σπέρμα αὐτοῦ πάροικον ἐν γῇ ἀλλοτρίᾳ, καὶ δουλώσουσιν
seed of him a sojourner in a land another, and they will enslave
846 2559 2094 5071 1484 3739/1437
7 αὐτὸ καὶ κακώσουσιν, ἔτη τετρακόσια. καὶ τὸ ἔθνος, ᾧ ἐὰν
it, and will oppress years four hundred. And the nation to whom may
1398 2919 1473 2036 2316 3326 5023
δουλεύσωσι, κρινῶ ἐγώ, εἶπεν ὁ Θεός· καὶ μετὰ ταῦτα
they serve, will judge I; said God and, After these
1831 3000 3427/1722 5117 5129
8 ἐξελεύσονται, καὶ λατρεύσουσί μοι ἐν τῷ τόπῳ τούτῳ. καὶ
they will come out, and will do service to Me in – place this. And
1325 846 1242 4061 3779 1080
ἔδωκεν αὐτῷ διαθήκην περιτομῆς· καὶ οὕτως ἐγέννησε τὸν
He gave to him a covenant of circumcision; and thus he fathered –
2464 4059 846 2250 3590
Ἰσαάκ, καὶ περιέτεμεν αὐτὸν τῇ ἡμέρᾳ τῇ ὀγδόῃ· καὶ ὁ
Isaac, and circumcised him on the day – eighth. And
2464 2384 2384 1427 3966
Ἰσαὰκ τὸν Ἰακώβ, καὶ ὁ Ἰακὼβ τοὺς δώδεκα πατριάρχας.
Isaac (fathered) Jacob, and Jacob the twelve patriarchs.
3966 2206 2501 591 1519
9 καὶ οἱ πατριάρχαι ζηλώσαντες τὸν Ἰωσὴφ ἀπέδοντο εἰς
And the patriarchs being jealous – Joseph gave over into
125 2258 2316 3326 846 1807 846 1537
10 Αἴγυπτον· καὶ ἦν ὁ Θεὸς μετ' αὐτοῦ. καὶ ἐξείλετο αὐτὸν ἐκ
Egypt; and was – God with him, and plucked out him from
3950 2347 848 1325 846 5485
πασῶν τῶν θλίψεων αὐτοῦ, καὶ ἔδωκεν αὐτῷ χάριν καὶ
all the afflictions of him; and gave him favor and

favor and wisdom over against Pharaoh *the* king of Egypt. And he appointed him governor over Egypt and all his household. [11]But a famine came over all the land of Egypt and Canaan, and great affliction. And our fathers did not find food. [12]But hearing grain was in Egypt, Jacob sent our fathers out first. [13]And at the second *time*, Joseph was made known to his brothers, and Joseph's race became known to Pharaoh.

[14]And sending, Joseph called his father Jacob and all his kindred, seventy-five souls in *all*. [15]And Jacob went down into Egypt, and expired, he and our fathers. [16]And they were moved into Shechem, and were put in the tomb which Abraham bought *for* a price of silver from the sons of Hamor of Shechem. [17]But as the time of the promise drew near, which God swore to Abraham, the people increased and were multiplied in Egypt, [18]until another king rose up, who did not know Joseph.

[19]Dealing slyly with our race, this one oppressed our fathers, causing their infants to be exposed *so as* not to be kept alive.

[20]In which time Moses was born, and was beautiful to God; who was reared three months in his father's house. [21]And he being exposed, Pharaoh's daughter took him up and reared him for a son to her. [22]And Moses was instructed in all *the* wisdom of Egyptians; and was powerful in words and in works. [23]And when a period of forty years was fulfilled to him, it arose in

4878 1726 5328 935 125 2525
σοφίαν ἐναντίον Φαραὼ βασιλέως Αἰγύπτου, καὶ κατέστησεν
wisdom over against Pharaoh king of Egypt, and he appointed
846 2233/1909 125 3650 3624 848
αὐτὸν ἡγούμενον ἐπ' Αἴγυπτον καὶ ὅλον τὸν οἶκον αὐτοῦ.
him governor over Egypt and all the house of him.
2064 3042 1909 3650 1093 125 5477
11 ἦλθε δὲ λιμὸς ἐφ' ὅλην τὴν γῆν Αἰγύπτου καὶ Χαναάν, καὶ
came But a famine over all the land of Egypt and Canaan, and
2347 3173 3756 2147 5527 3962
θλῖψις μεγάλη· καὶ οὐχ εὕρισκον χορτάσματα οἱ πατέρες
affliction great; and not did find sustenance the fathers
2257 191 2384 5607 4621 1711/125 1821
12 ἡμῶν. ἀκούσας δὲ Ἰακὼβ ὄντα σῖτα ἐν Αἰγύπτῳ, ἐξαπέστειλε
of us. having heard But Jacob being grain in Egypt, he sent forth
3962 2257 4412 1722 1208 319
13 τοὺς πατέρας ἡμῶν πρῶτον. καὶ ἐν τῷ δευτέρῳ ἀνεγνωρίσθη
the fathers of us first. And in the second was made known
2501 80 848 5318 1096 5328
Ἰωσὴφ τοῖς ἀδελφοῖς αὐτοῦ, καὶ φανερὸν ἐγένετο τῷ Φαραὼ
Joseph to the brothers of him, and manifest became — to Pharaoh
1085 2501 649 2501 3333
14 τὸ γένος τοῦ Ἰωσήφ. ἀποστείλας δὲ Ἰωσὴφ μετεκαλέσατο
the race — of Joseph. sending And Joseph, called
3962 848 2384 3956 4772 848
τὸν πατέρα αὐτοῦ Ἰακώβ, καὶ πᾶσαν τὴν συγγένειαν αὐτοῦ,
the father of him, Jacob, and all the kindred of him,
1722 5590 1440 4002 2597 2384 1519 125
15 ἐν ψυχαῖς ἑβδομήκοντα πέντε. κατέβη δὲ Ἰακὼβ εἰς Αἴγυ-
in souls, seventy five. went down And Jacob into Egypt,
5053 846 3962 2257 3346
πτον, καὶ ἐτελεύτησεν αὐτὸς καὶ οἱ πατέρες ἡμῶν· καὶ μετετέ-
and expired he and the fathers of us, and they were
1519 4966 5087 1722 3418 3739/5608
16 θησαν εἰς Συχέμ, καὶ ἐτέθησαν ἐν τῷ μνήματι ὃ ὠνήσατο
moved into Shechem, and were placed in the tomb which bought
11 5092 894 3844 5207 1697 4966
Ἀβραὰμ τιμῆς ἀργυρίου παρὰ τῶν υἱῶν Ἐμὸρ τοῦ Συχέμ.
Abraham (for) a price of silver from the sons of Hamor of Shechem.
2531 1448 5550 1860 3739 3660 2316
17 καθὼς δὲ ἤγγιζεν ὁ χρόνος τῆς ἐπαγγελίας ἧς ὤμοσεν ὁ Θεὸς
as And drew near the time of the promise which swore God
11 837 2992 4129 1722 125
τῷ Ἀβραάμ, ηὔξησεν ὁ λαὸς καὶ ἐπληθύνθη ἐν Αἰγύπτῳ,
— to Abraham, grew the people, and were multiplied in Egypt,
891 3739 450 935 2087 3739/3756/1492 2501
18 ἄχρις οὗ ἀνέστη βασιλεὺς ἕτερος, ὃς οὐκ ᾔδει τὸν Ἰωσήφ.
until rose up king another, who not knew — Joseph.
3778 2686 1085 2257 2559 3962
19 οὗτος κατασοφισάμενος τὸ γένος ἡμῶν, ἐκάκωσε τοὺς πατέ-
This one dealing slyly with the race of us oppressed the fathers
2257 4160 1570 1025 848 1519 3361
ρας ἡμῶν, τοῦ ποιεῖν ἔκθετα τὰ βρέφη αὐτῶν, εἰς τὸ μὴ
of us, to make exposed the babes of them unto not
2225 1722/3739/2540 1080 3475 2258 791
20 ζωογονεῖσθαι. ἐν ᾧ καιρῷ ἐγεννήθη Μωσῆς, καὶ ἦν ἀστεῖος
being preserved alive. At which time was born Moses, and he was beautiful
2316 3739 397 3376 5140 1722 3624 3962
τῷ Θεῷ· ὃς ἀνετράφη μῆνας τρεῖς ἐν τῷ οἴκῳ τοῦ πατρὸς
— to God, who was reared months three in the house of the father
848 1620 846 337 846 2364
21 αὐτοῦ. ἐκτεθέντα δὲ αὐτόν, ἀνείλετο αὐτὸν ἡ θυγάτηρ
of him. being exposed And he, took up him, the daughter
5328 397 846 14381519/5207 3811
22 Φαραώ, καὶ ἀνεθρέψατο αὐτὸν ἑαυτῇ εἰς υἱόν. καὶ ἐπαιδεύθη
of Pharaoh, and reared him to herself for a son. And was instructed
3475 3956 4678 124 2258 1415 1722 3056
Μωσῆς πάσῃ σοφίᾳ Αἰγυπτίων· ἦν δὲ δυνατὸς ἐν λόγοις καὶ
Moses in all (the) wisdom of Egyptians, was and powerful in words and
1722/2041/5613 4137 846 5063 5550
23 ἐν ἔργοις. ὡς δὲ ἐπληροῦτο αὐτῷ τεσσαρακονταετὴς χρόνος,
in works. as But was fulfilled to him of forty years a time,

his heart to look upon his brothers, the sons of Israel. [24]And seeing one being wronged, he defended *him*, and he avenged the *one* getting the worse, striking the Egyptian. [25]And he thought his brothers *would* understand that God would give them deliverance by his hand. But they did not understand. [26]And on the following day he appeared to them *while* fighting. And *he* urged them to peace, saying, Men, you are brothers. Why do you wrong one another? [27]But the *one* wronging the neighbor thrust him away, saying, Who appointed you a ruler and a judge over us? [28]Do you not want to do away with me *in the* way you did away with the Egyptian yesterday? [29]And Moses fled at this word. And he became a sojourner in Midian land, where he fathered two sons.

[30]And forty years being fulfilled to him, *the* Angel of *the* Lord appeared to him in the desert of Mount Sinai, in a flame of fire *in* a bush. [31]And seeing, Moses marveled at the sight. And he coming up to look, a voice of *the* Lord came to him: [32]"I *am* the God of your fathers, the God of Abraham, and the God of Isaac, and the God of Jacob." But becoming trembly, Moses did not dare to look. [33]And the Lord said to him, "Untie the sandal from your feet, for the place where you stand is holy ground." [34]"I surely saw the affliction of My people in Egypt, and I have heard their groan; and I came down to pluck them out. And now, come, I will send you to Egypt."

[35]This Moses, whom they denied, saying, Who

305 1909 2588 848 1980 80
ἀνέβη ἐπὶ τὴν καρδίαν αὐτοῦ ἐπισκέψασθαι τοὺς ἀδελφοὺς
it arose on the heart of him to look upon the brothers
848 5207 2474 1492 5100 91 292
24 αὐτοῦ τοὺς υἱοὺς Ἰσραήλ. καὶ ἰδών τινα ἀδικούμενον, ἠμύ-
of him, the sons of Israel. And seeing one being wronged, he de-
4160 1557 2669 3950
νατο καὶ ἐποίησεν ἐκδίκησιν τῷ καταπονουμένῳ, πατάξας
fended, and he did vengeance for the (one) getting the worse, striking
124 3543 4920 80 848 3754
25 τὸν Αἰγύπτιον· ἐνόμιζε δὲ συνιέναι τοὺς ἀδελφοὺς αὐτοῦ ὅτι
the Egyptian. he thought And to understand the brothers of him that
2316/1223/5495 848 1325 846 4991 3756
ὁ Θεὸς διὰ χειρὸς αὐτοῦ δίδωσιν αὐτοῖς σωτηρίαν· οἱ δὲ οὐ
– God through hand of him would give to them deliverance; they but not
4920 1966 2250 3700 846 3164
26 συνῆκαν. τῇ δὲ ἐπιούσῃ ἡμέρᾳ ὤφθη αὐτοῖς μαχομένοις, καὶ
understood. the But following day he appeared to them fighting, and
4900 846 1519 1515 2036 435 80 2075
συνήλασεν αὐτοὺς εἰς εἰρήνην, εἰπών, Ἄνδρες, ἀδελφοί ἐστε
urged them to peace, saying, Men, brothers are
5210 2444 91 240 91 4139
27 ὑμεῖς· ἱνατί ἀδικεῖτε ἀλλήλους; ὁ δὲ ἀδικῶν τὸν πλησίον
you, why do you wrong one another? he But wronging the neighbor
683 846 2036 5101/4571 2525 758
ἀπώσατο αὐτόν, εἰπών, Τίς σε κατέστησεν ἄρχοντα καὶ
thrust away him, saying, Who you appointed a ruler and
1348 1909 2248/3361 337 3165/4771/2309/3739 5158 337
28 δικαστὴν ἐφ' ἡμᾶς; μὴ ἀνελεῖν με σὺ θέλεις, ὃν τρόπον ἀνεῖλες
a judge over us? Do not to take away me you desire, (in) what way you took away
5504 124 5343 3475 1722 3056 5129
29 χθὲς τὸν Αἰγύπτιον; ἔφυγε δὲ Μωσῆς ἐν τῷ λόγῳ τούτῳ,
yesterday the Egyptian? fled And Moses at – word this.
1096 3941 1722/1093 3099 3757 1080 5207 1417
καὶ ἐγένετο πάροικος ἐν γῇ Μαδιάμ, οὗ ἐγέννησεν υἱοὺς δύο.
And he became a sojourner in land Midian, where he fathered sons two.
4137 2094 5062 3700 846 1722
30 καὶ πληρωθέντων ἐτῶν τεσσαράκοντα, ὤφθη αὐτῷ ἐν τῇ
And being fulfilled years forty, appeared to him in the
2048 3735 4614 32 2962 1722 5395 4442
ἐρήμῳ τοῦ ὄρους Σινᾶ ἄγγελος Κυρίου ἐν φλογὶ πυρὸς
desert of the Mount Sinai, (the) angel of (the) Lord in a flame of fire
942 3475 1492 2296 3705 4334
31 βάτου. ὁ δὲ Μωσῆς ἰδὼν ἐθαύμασε τὸ ὅραμα· προσερχο-
of a bush. And Moses seeing marveled at the sight coming
846 2657 1096 5456 2962 4314
μένου δὲ αὐτοῦ κατανοῆσαι, ἐγένετο φωνὴ Κυρίου πρὸς
up And he to look, came a voice of (the) Lord to
846 1473 2316 3962 4675 2316 11
32 αὐτόν, Ἐγὼ ὁ Θεὸς τῶν πατέρων σου, ὁ Θεὸς Ἀβραὰμ καὶ
him. I (am) the God of the fathers of you, the God of Abraham, and
2316 2464 2316 2384 1790 1096
ὁ Θεὸς Ἰσαὰκ καὶ ὁ Θεὸς Ἰακώβ. ἔντρομος δὲ γενόμενος
the God of Isaac and the God of Jacob. trembling But becoming
3475 3756 5111 2657 2036 846 2962
33 Μωσῆς οὐκ ἐτόλμα κατανοῆσαι. εἶπε δὲ αὐτῷ ὁ Κύριος,
Moses not did dare to observe, said And to him the Lord,
3089 5266 4228 4675 1063 5117/1722/3739
Λῦσον τὸ ὑπόδημα τῶν ποδῶν σου· ὁ γὰρ τόπος ἐν ᾧ
Loosen the sandal of the feet of you, the for place on which
2476 1093 40 2076 1492 1492 2561 2992
34 ἕστηκας γῆ ἁγία ἐστίν. ἰδὼν εἶδον τὴν κάκωσιν τοῦ λαοῦ
you stand ground holy is. Seeing I saw the oppression of the people
3450 1722 125 4726 848 191
μου τοῦ ἐν Αἰγύπτῳ, καὶ τοῦ στεναγμοῦ αὐτῶν ἤκουσα·
of Me – in Egypt, and the groan of them I heard,
2597 1807 846 3568 1204 649 4571
καὶ κατέβην ἐξελέσθαι αὐτούς· καὶ νῦν δεῦρο, ἀποστελῶ σε
and I came down to rescue them; and now come, I will send you
1519 125 5126 3475 3739 720 2036
35 εἰς Αἴγυπτον. τοῦτον τὸν Μωϋσῆν ὃν ἠρνήσαντο εἰπόντες,
to Egypt. This – Moses whom they denied, saying,

appointed you a ruler and a judge, this one God has sent *as* ruler and redeemer by *the* hand of *the* Angel who appeared to him in the Bush. [36]This one led them out, working wonders and miracles in *the* land of Egypt, and in *the* Red Sea, and forty years in the wilderness. [37]This is the Moses who said to the sons of Israel, "*The* Lord your God will raise up a Prophet to you from your brothers, *One* like me. You shall hear Him." [38]This is the *one* who was in the congregation in the wilderness with the Angel who spoke to him in Mount Sinai, and *with* our fathers, who received living words to give to us; [39]to whom our fathers did not desire to be subject, but thrust *him* away, and turned their hearts back to Egypt,

[40]saying to Aaron, "Make for us gods which will go before us; for this Moses who led us out of *the* land of Egypt, we do not know what has happened to him." [41]And they made a calf in those days, and led up a sacrifice to the idol, and made merry in the works of their hands. [42]But God turned and gave them over to serve the host of the heaven; as it is written in *the* scroll of the Prophets: "Did you bring slain beasts and sacrifices to Me forty years in the wilderness, O house of Israel? [43]And you took up the the tent of Moloch, and the star of your god Remphan, the figures which you made in order to worship them. And I will remove you beyond Babylon." [44]The tabernacle of the testimony was among our fathers in

5101/4571 2525 758 1348 5126 2316
Τίς σε κατέστησεν ἄρχοντα καὶ δικαστήν ; τοῦτον ὁ Θεὸς
Who you appointed a ruler and a judge? This one – God
758 3086 649 1722 5495 32
ἄρχοντα καὶ λυτρωτὴν ἀπέστειλεν ἐν χειρὶ ἀγγέλου τοῦ
a ruler and a deliverer has sent by (the) hand of (the) Angel
3700 846 1722 942 3778 1806 846
36 ὀφθέντος αὐτῷ ἐν τῇ βάτῳ. οὗτος ἐξήγαγεν αὐτούς,
appearing to him in the Bush. This one led out them,
4160 5059 4592/1722/1093/ 125 1722 2063
ποιήσας τέρατα καὶ σημεῖα ἐν γῇ Αἰγύπτου καὶ ἐν Ἐρυθρᾷ
doing wonders and signs in (the) land of Egypt, and in (the) Red
2281 1722 2048 2094 5062 3778 2076
37 θαλάσσῃ, καὶ ἐν τῇ ἐρήμῳ ἔτη τεσσαράκοντα. οὗτός ἐστιν
Sea, and in the desert years forty. This is
3475 2036 5207 2474 4396 5213
ὁ Μωϋσῆς ὁ εἰπὼν τοῖς υἱοῖς Ἰσραήλ, Προφήτην ὑμῖν
the Moses – saying to the sons of Israel, A prophet for you
450 2962 2316 5216/1537 80 5216/5613/1691
ἀναστήσει Κύριος ὁ Θεὸς ὑμῶν ἐκ τῶν ἀδελφῶν ὑμῶν ὡς ἐμέ·
will raise up (the) Lord God of you from the brothers of you, like me.
846 191 3778 2076 1096 1722 1577
38 αὐτοῦ ἀκούσεσθε. οὗτός ἐστιν ὁ γενόμενος ἐν τῇ ἐκκλησίᾳ
Him you shall hear. This is the (one) having been in the assembly
1722 2048 3326 32 2980 846 1722
ἐν τῇ ἐρήμῳ μετὰ τοῦ ἀγγέλου τοῦ λαλοῦντος αὐτῷ ἐν τῷ
in the desert with the Angel speaking to him in the
3735/4614 3962 2257 3739/1209 3051 2198
ὄρει Σινᾶ καὶ τῶν πατέρων ἡμῶν· ὃς ἐδέξατο λόγια ζῶντα
Mount Sinai, and (with) the fathers of us, who received words living
1325 2254/3739/3756/ 2309 5255 1096 3962
39 δοῦναι ἡμῖν· ᾧ οὐκ ἠθέλησαν ὑπήκοοι γενέσθαι οἱ πατέρες
to give to us, to whom not desired subject to be the fathers
2257 235 683 4762 2588 848
ἡμῶν, ἀλλ' ἀπώσαντο, καὶ ἐστράφησαν ταῖς καρδίαις αὐτῶν
of us, but thrust away, and turned away the hearts of them
1519 125 2036 2 4160 2254 2316 3739
40 εἰς Αἴγυπτον, εἰπόντες τῷ Ἀαρών, Ποίησον ἡμῖν θεοὺς οἳ
to Egypt, saying to Aaron, Make for us gods which
4313 2257 1063 3475 3778 3739 1806
προπορεύσονται ἡμῶν· ὁ γὰρ Μωσῆς οὗτος, ὃς ἐξήγαγεν
will go before us; for Moses this, who led
2248/1537/1093 125 3756 1492 5101 1096 846
41 ἡμᾶς ἐκ γῆς Αἰγύπτου, οὐκ οἴδαμεν τί γέγονεν αὐτῷ. καὶ
us out of (the) land of Egypt, not we know what has occurred to him. And
3447 1722 2250 1565 321
ἐμοσχοποίησαν ἐν ταῖς ἡμέραις ἐκείναις, καὶ ἀνήγαγον
they made a calf in days those, and led up
2378 1497 2165 1722 2041
θυσίαν τῷ εἰδώλῳ, καὶ εὐφραίνοντο ἐν τοῖς ἔργοις τῶν
a sacrifice to the idol, and made merry in the works of the
5495 848 4762 2316 3860 846
42 χειρῶν αὐτῶν. ἔστρεψε δὲ ὁ Θεός, καὶ παρέδωκεν αὐτοὺς
hands of them. turned And God, and gave over them
3000 4756 3772 2531 1125 1722
λατρεύειν τῇ στρατιᾷ τοῦ οὐρανοῦ· καθὼς γέγραπται ἐν
to worship the host of heaven, as it has been written in
976 4396 3361 4968 2378 4374
βίβλῳ τῶν προφητῶν, Μὴ σφάγια καὶ θυσίας προσηνέγ-
(the) roll of the prophets, Not victims and sacrifices you brought
3427/2094 5062 1722 2048 3624 2474
κατέ μοι ἔτη τεσσαράκοντα ἐν τῇ ἐρήμῳ, οἶκος Ἰσραήλ ;
near to Me years forty in the desert, house of Israel;
353 4633 3434 798
43 καὶ ἀνελάβετε τὴν σκηνὴν τοῦ Μολόχ, καὶ τὸ ἄστρον τοῦ
and you took up the tent of Moloch, and the star of the
2316 5216 4481 5179 3739 4150 4352
θεοῦ ὑμῶν Ῥεμφάν, τοὺς τύπους οὓς ἐποιήσατε προσκυνεῖν
god of you, Remphan, the models which you made to worship
846 3351 5209 1900 897 4633
44 αὐτοῖς· καὶ μετοικιῶ ὑμᾶς ἐπέκεινα Βαβυλῶνος. ἡ σκηνὴ τοῦ
them, and I will remove you beyond Babylon. . The tent –

the wilderness, as He who spoke to Moses commanded to make it according to the pattern which he had seen; 45 which also *was* brought in, our fathers having inherited with Joshua, in the taking of possession of the nations; whom God expelled from the face of our fathers, until the days of David; 46 who found favor before God, and asked to find a tabernacle for the God of Jacob; 47 but Solomon built Him a house.

48 But the Most High does not dwell in temples made by hand; as the prophet says, 49 "Heaven *is* My throne, and the earth a footstool of My feet; what house will you build Me, says *the* Lord; or what the place of My rest? 50 Did not My hands make all these things?"

51 *O* stiffnecked and uncircumcised in heart and in the ears! You always fell against the Holy Spirit. As your fathers *did*, so you also *did*. 52 Which of the prophets did your fathers not persecute? And they killed those who before announced the coming of the Just One, of whom you now have become betrayers and murderers; 53 who received the Law by the disposition of angels, and did not keep *it*.

54 And hearing these things, they were cut to their hearts, and gnashed the teeth on him. 55 But being full of *the* Holy Spirit, looking intently into Heaven, he saw *the* glory of God, and Jesus standing at *the* right of God. 56 And *he* said, Behold, I see the heavens having been opened, and the Son of man standing at

3142 2258 3962 2257/1722 2048 2531
μαρτυρίου ἦν τοῖς πατράσιν ἡμῶν ἐν τῇ ἐρήμῳ, καθὼς
of witness was to the fathers of us in the desert, as
1299 2980 3475 4160 846 2596
διετάξατο ὁ λαλῶν τῷ Μωσῇ, ποιῆσαι αὐτὴν κατὰ τὸν
commanded the (One) speaking to Moses, to make it according to the
5179 3739 3708 3739 1521 1237 3962
45 τύπον ὃν ἑωράκει. ἣν καὶ εἰσήγαγον διαδεξάμενοι οἱ πατέρες
pattern which he had seen, which also was led, having inherited the fathers
2257 3326 2424/1722 2697 1484 3739 1856
ἡμῶν μετὰ Ἰησοῦ ἐν τῇ κατασχέσει τῶν ἐθνῶν, ὧν ἐξῶσεν ὁ
of us with Joshua in the taking of possession of the nations, whom put out
2316 575 4383 3962 2257 2193 2250
Θεὸς ἀπὸ προσώπου τῶν πατέρων ἡμῶν, ἕως τῶν ἡμερῶν
God from the face of the fathers of us, until the days
1138 3739/2147/5485 1799 2316 154 2147
46 Δαβίδ· ὃς εὗρε χάριν ἐνώπιον τοῦ Θεοῦ, καὶ ᾐτήσατο εὑρεῖν
of David, who found favor before — God, and asked to find
4638 2316 2384 4672 3618 846
47 σκήνωμα τῷ Θεῷ Ἰακώβ. Σολομῶν δὲ ᾠκοδόμησεν αὐτῷ
a tent for the God of Jacob. Solomon But built for Him
3624 235 3756 5310 1722 5499 3485 2730
48 οἶκον. ἀλλ' οὐχ ὁ ὕψιστος ἐν χειροποιήτοις ναοῖς κατοικεῖ,
a house. But not the Most High in made by hand temples dwells;
2531 4396 3004 3772 3427 2362 1093
49 καθὼς ὁ προφήτης λέγει, Ὁ οὐρανός μοι θρόνος, ἡ δὲ γῆ
as the prophet says, The Heaven to Me a throne, the and earth
5286 4228 3450 4169 3624 3618 3427
ὑποπόδιον τῶν ποδῶν μου· ποῖον οἶκον οἰκοδομήσετέ μοι ;
a footstool of the feet of Me; what sort of house will you build for Me,
3004 2962 2228/5101/5117 2863 3450 3780
50 λέγει Κύριος· ἢ τίς τόπος τῆς καταπαύσεώς μου ; οὐχὶ ἡ
says (the) Lord, or what place of the resting of Me? Did not the
5495 3450 4160 5023 3956
χείρ μου ἐποίησε ταῦτα πάντα ;
hand of Me make these things all?
4644 564 2588 3775
51 Σκληροτράχηλοι καὶ ἀπερίτμητοι τῇ καρδίᾳ καὶ τοῖς ὠσίν,
Stiffnecked and uncircumcised in the heart and in the ears,
5210/104 4151 40 496 5613 3962
ὑμεῖς ἀεὶ τῷ Πνεύματι τῷ Ἁγίῳ ἀντιπίπτετε· ὡς οἱ πατέρες
you always the Spirit — Holy fell against, as the fathers
5216 5210 5101 4396 3756 1377 3962
52 ὑμῶν, καὶ ὑμεῖς. τίνα τῶν προφητῶν οὐκ ἐδίωξαν οἱ πατέρες
of you, also you. Which of the prophets not persecuted the fathers
5216 615 4293 4012
ὑμῶν ; καὶ ἀπέκτειναν τοὺς προκαταγγείλαντας περὶ τῆς
of you? And they killed those before announcing concerning the
1660 1342 3739/3568/5210 4273 5406
ἐλεύσεως τοῦ δικαίου, οὗ νῦν ὑμεῖς προδόται καὶ φονεῖς
coming of the Just One, of whom now you betrayers and murderers
1096 3748 2983 3551/1519 1296 32
53 γεγένησθε· οἵτινες ἐλάβετε τὸν νόμον εἰς διαταγὰς ἀγγέλων,
have become, who received the Law by disposition of angels,
3756/5442
καὶ οὐκ ἐφυλάξατε.
and not kept (it).
191 5023 1282 2588 848
54 Ἀκούοντες δὲ ταῦτα, διεπρίοντο ταῖς καρδίαις αὐτῶν, καὶ
hearing And these things, they were cut to the hearts of them, and
1031 3599 1909 846 5225 4134
55 ἔβρυχον τοὺς ὀδόντας ἐπ' αὐτόν. ὑπάρχων δὲ πλήρης
gnashed the teeth at him. being But full
4151 40 816 1519 3772 1492 1391 2316
Πνεύματος Ἁγίου, ἀτενίσας εἰς τὸν οὐρανόν, εἶδε δόξαν Θεοῦ,
of (the) Spirit Holy looking intently into Heaven, he saw (the) glory of God,
2424 2476 1537 1188 2316 2036 2400
56 καὶ Ἰησοῦν ἑστῶτα ἐκ δεξιῶν τοῦ Θεοῦ, καὶ εἶπεν, Ἰδού,
and Jesus standing at (the) right — of God, and said, Behold,
2334 3772 455 5207 444
θεωρῶ τοὺς οὐρανοὺς ἀνεῳγμένους, καὶ τὸν υἱὸν τοῦ ἀνθρώ-
I see the heavens having been opened and the Son — of

the right of God! [57]And crying out with a loud voice, they held their ears, and rushed on him with one passion. [58]And throwing *him* outside the city, they stoned *him*. And the witnesses put off their garments at the feet of a young man called Saul. [59]And they stoned Stephen, invoking and saying, Lord Jesus, receive my spirit. [60]And placing the knees, he cried out with a loud voice, Lord, do not make this sin stand to them. And saying this, he fell asleep.

1537 1188 2476 2316 2896 5456 3173
57 που ἐκ δεξιῶν ἑστῶτα τοῦ Θεοῦ. κράξαντες δὲ φωνῇ μεγάλῃ,
man at (the) right standing of God. crying out And with a voice great,
4912 3775 848 3729 3661 1909
συνέσχον τὰ ὦτα αὐτῶν, καὶ ὥρμησαν ὁμοθυμαδὸν ἐπ᾽
they held the ears of them, and rushed with one passion on
846 1544 1854 4172 3036
58 αὐτόν· καὶ ἐκβαλόντες ἔξω τῆς πόλεως, ἐλιθοβόλουν· καὶ οἱ
him, and throwing outside the city, they stoned (him). And the
3144 659 2440 848 3844 4228
μάρτυρες ἀπέθεντο τὰ ἱμάτια αὐτῶν παρὰ τοὺς πόδας
witnesses put off the garments of them at the feet
3494 2563 4569 3036 4736
59 νεανίου καλουμένου Σαύλου. καὶ ἐλιθοβόλουν τὸν Στέφανον,
of a young man called Saul. And they stoned – Stephen
1941 3004 2962 2424 1209 4151
ἐπικαλούμενον καὶ λέγοντα, Κύριε Ἰησοῦ, δέξαι τὸ πνεῦμά
invoking (God) and saying, Lord Jesus, receive the spirit
3450 5087 1119 2896 5456 3173 2962 3361
60 μου. θεὶς δὲ τὰ γόνατα, ἔκραξε φωνῇ μεγάλῃ, Κύριε, μὴ
of me. placing And the knees, he cried with a voice great, Lord, Not
2476 846 266 5026 5124 2036
στήσῃς αὐτοῖς τὴν ἁμαρτίαν ταύτην. καὶ τοῦτο εἰπὼν
make stand to them sin this. And this having said,
2837
ἐκοιμήθη
he fell asleep.

CHAPTER 8

[1]And Saul was consenting to the doing away of him.

And in that day a great persecution took place on the church which *was* in Jerusalem; and all were scattered throughout the regions of Judea and Samaria, except the apostles. [2]And devout men together carried Stephen, and made a great lamentation over him. [3]But Saul ravaged the church, entering house by house, dragging both men and women, he delivered *them* to prison.

[4]Then, indeed, the ones who had been scattered passed through, preaching the gospel, the word. [5]And going down to a city of Samaria, Philip proclaimed Christ to them. [6]And with one passion the crowds heeded that being said by Philip, when they heard and saw the many miracles which he was doing. [7]For out of those having unclean spirits, many came out,

CHAPTER 8

4569 2258 4909 336 848
1 Σαῦλος δὲ ἦν συνευδοκῶν τῇ ἀναιρέσει αὐτοῦ.
Saul And was consenting to the doing away of him.
1096 1722 1565 2250 1375 3173
Ἐγένετο δὲ ἐν ἐκείνῃ τῇ ἡμέρᾳ διωγμὸς μέγας ἐπὶ τὴν
it was And in that – day a persecution great on the
1577 1722 2414 3956 5037 1289
ἐκκλησίαν τὴν ἐν Ἱεροσολύμοις· πάντες τε διεσπάρησαν
church – in Jerusalem, all and were scattered
2596 5561 2449 4540 4133
κατὰ τὰς χώρας τῆς Ἰουδαίας καὶ Σαμαρείας, πλὴν τῶν
through the countries – of Judea and Samaria, except the
652 4792 4736 435 2126
2 ἀποστόλων. συνεκόμισαν δὲ τὸν Στέφανον ἄνδρες εὐλαβεῖς,
apostles. together carried And – Stephen men devout,
4160 2870 3173 1909 846 4569
3 καὶ ἐποιήσαντο κοπετὸν μέγαν ἐπ᾽ αὐτῷ. Σαῦλος δὲ
and made a lamentation great over him. Saul And
3075 1577 2596 3624 1531
ἐλυμαίνετο τὴν ἐκκλησίαν, κατὰ τοὺς οἴκους εἰσπορευό-
ravaged the church, house by house, entering,
4951/5037/ 435 1135 3860 1519 5438
μενος, σύρων τε ἄνδρας καὶ γυναῖκας παρεδίδου εἰς φυλακήν.
dragging both men and women he delivered to prison.
3303/3767 1289 1330 2097
4 Οἱ μὲν οὖν διασπαρέντες διῆλθον, εὐαγγελιζόμενοι τὸν
Those, therefore, being scattered passed through preaching the gospel, the
3056 5376 2718 1519 4172 4540
5 λόγον. Φίλιππος δὲ κατελθὼν εἰς πόλιν τῆς Σαμαρείας,
word Philip And going down to a city of Samaria
2784 846 5547 4337 5037 3793
6 ἐκήρυσσεν αὐτοῖς τὸν Χριστόν. προσεῖχόν τε οἱ ὄχλοι τοῖς
proclaimed to them the Christ. heeded And the crowds that
3004 5259 5376 3661 1722 191
λεγομένοις ὑπὸ τοῦ Φιλίππου ὁμοθυμαδόν, ἐν τῷ ἀκούειν
being said by – Philip with one passion in the hearing
846 991 4592/3739/4160 4183 1063
7 αὐτοὺς καὶ βλέπειν τὰ σημεῖα ἃ ἐποίει. πολλῶν γὰρ τῶν
(of) them and seeing the signs which he was doing. many For of the
2192 4151 169 994 3173 5456
ἐχόντων πνεύματα ἀκάθαρτα, βοῶντα μεγάλῃ φωνῇ
(ones) having spirits unclean, crying with a great voice

crying with a loud voice. And *many* who had been paralyzed and lame were healed. [8]And great joy was in that city.

[9]But a certain man named Simon had long been conjuring in the city, and amazing the nation of Samaria, claiming himself to be some great one. [10]All were paying attention to *him,* from small to great, saying, This one is the great power of God. [11]And they were paying attention to him, because for a long time *he* had amazed them *with his* conjuring. [12]But when they believed Philip preaching the gospel, the things concerning the kingdom of God, and the name of Jesus Christ, they were baptized, both men and women. [13]And Simon himself also believed, and being baptized was continuing steadfastly with Philip. And seeing miracles and works of power happening, he was amazed.

[14]And the apostles in Jerusalem hearing that Samaria had received the word of God, they sent Peter and John to them, [15]who going down prayed concerning them, so that they might receive *the* Holy Spirit. [16]For He had not yet fallen on any of them, but they had only been baptized into the name of the Lord Jesus. [17]Then they laid hands on them, and they received *the* Holy Spirit.

[18]But Simon seeing that the Holy Spirit is given through the laying on of the hands of the apostles, he offered them money, [19]saying, Also give to me th authority, that on whomever I may lay on the hands, he may receive *the* Holy Spirit.

2192 4183 3886 5550 2323
ἐξήρχετο· πολλοὶ δὲ παραλελυμένοι καὶ χωλοὶ ἐθεραπεύθη-
came out; many and having been paralyzed and lame were healed.
1096 5479 3173 1722 4172 1565
8 σαν. καὶ ἐγένετο χαρὰ μεγάλη ἐν τῇ πόλει ἐκείνῃ.
And there was joy great in city that.
435 5100 3686 4613 4391 1722 4172
9 Ἀνὴρ δέ τις ὀνόματι Σίμων προϋπῆρχεν ἐν τῇ πόλει
a man And certain by name Simon had long been in the city
3096 1839 1484 4540 3004 1511
μαγεύων καὶ ἐξιστῶν τὸ ἔθνος τῆς Σαμαρείας, λέγων εἶναί
conjuring and amazing the nation — of Samaria, saying to be
5100 1438 3173 3739 4337 3956 575 3398 2193
10 τινα ἑαυτὸν μέγαν· ᾧ προσεῖχον πάντες ἀπὸ μικροῦ ἕως
someone himself great, to whom took heed all from small to
3173 3004 3778 2076 1411 2316
μεγάλου, λέγοντες, Οὗτός ἐστιν ἡ δύναμις τοῦ Θεοῦ ἡ
great. saying, This one is the power of God
3173 4337 846 1223 2425 5550
11 μεγάλη. προσεῖχον δὲ αὐτῷ, διὰ τὸ ἱκανῷ χρόνῳ ταῖς
great. they were heeding And him, because for a long time with the
3095 1839 846 3753 4100 5376
12 μαγείαις ἐξεστακέναι αὐτούς. ὅτε δὲ ἐπίστευσαν τῷ Φιλίππῳ
conjuring (he) had amazed them. when But they believed — Philip
2097 4012 932 2316
εὐαγγελιζομένῳ τὰ περὶ τῆς βασιλείας τοῦ Θεοῦ καὶ τοῦ
preaching the gospel, the things about the kingdom — of God, and the
3686 2424 5547 907 435 5037
ὀνόματος τοῦ Ἰησοῦ Χριστοῦ, ἐβαπτίζοντο ἄνδρες τε καὶ
name — of Jesus Christ, they were baptized, men both and
1135 4613 846 4100 907
13 γυναῖκες. ὁ δὲ Σίμων καὶ αὐτὸς ἐπίστευσε, καὶ βαπτισθεὶς
women. But Simon also himself believed, and being baptized
2258 4342 5376 2334 5037 1411
ἦν προσκαρτερῶν τῷ Φιλίππῳ· θεωρῶν τε δυνάμεις καὶ
was stedfastly continuing to Philip, beholding and works of power and
4592 1096 1839
σημεῖα γινόμενα, ἐξίστατο.
signs happening, he was amazed.
191 1722 2414 652 3754
14 Ἀκούσαντες δὲ οἱ ἐν Ἱεροσολύμοις ἀπόστολοι ὅτι
hearing And the in Jerusalem apostles that
1209 4540 3056 2316 649 4314
δέδεκται ἡ Σαμάρεια τὸν λόγον τοῦ Θεοῦ, ἀπέστειλαν πρὸς
has received Samaria the word of God, they sent to
846 4074 2491 3748 2597
15 αὐτοὺς τὸν Πέτρον καὶ Ἰωάννην· οἵτινες καταβάντες
them Peter and John, who going down
4336 4012 846 3704 2983 4151 40
προσηύξαντο περὶ αὐτῶν, ὅπως λάβωσι Πνεῦμα Ἅγιον·
prayed concerning them, so as they might receive (the) Spirit Holy
3768 1063/2258/1909/3762 846 1968 3440
16 οὔπω γὰρ ἦν ἐπ' οὐδενὶ αὐτῶν ἐπιπεπτωκός, μόνον δὲ
not yet for He was on no one of them having fallen, only but
907 5225 1519 3686 2962 2424
βεβαπτισμένοι ὑπῆρχον εἰς τὸ ὄνομα τοῦ Κυρίου Ἰησοῦ.
having been baptized they were in the name the Lord Jesus.
5119 2007 5495 1909 846 2983
17 τότε ἐπετίθουν τὰς χεῖρας ἐπ' αὐτούς, καὶ ἐλάμβανον
Then they laid on the hands on them, and they received
4151 40 2300 4613/3754/1223 1936
18 Πνεῦμα Ἅγιον. θεασάμενος δὲ ὁ Σίμων ὅτι διὰ τῆς ἐπιθέ-
(the) Spirit Holy beholding And Simon that through the laying
5495 652 1325 4151
σεως τῶν χειρῶν τῶν ἀποστόλων δίδοται τὸ Πνεῦμα τὸ
on of the hands of the apostles is given the Spirit
40 4374 846 5536 3004 1325 2504
19 Ἅγιον, προσήνεγκεν αὐτοῖς χρήματα, λέγων, Δότε κἀμοὶ
Holy, he offered them money, saying, Give also to
1849 5026 2443/3739/1437/2007 5495 2983 me
τὴν ἐξουσίαν ταύτην, ἵνα ᾧ ἐὰν ἐπιθῶ τὰς χεῖρας, λαμβάνῃ
authority this, that to may I lay on the hands, he may receive

[20]But Peter said to him, May your silver be with you into perdition, because you thought to get the gift of God through money. [21]There is neither part nor lot to you in this matter, for your heart is not upright in the sight of God. [22]Therefore, repent of this wickedness of yours, and petition God if perhaps the thought of your heart may be forgiven to you; [23]for I see you to be in *the* gall of bitterness and a bundle of unrighteousness. [24]And answering Simon said, You petition to the Lord for me, so that nothing of which you have spoken may come on me.

[25]Then having earnestly testified, and having spoken the word of the Lord, and having preached the gospel to many villages of the Samaritans, they returned to Jerusalem.

[26]But an angel of *the* Lord spoke to Philip, saying, Rise up and go along south on the highway going down from Jerusalem to Gaza; this is desert. [27]And rising up, he went. And, behold, an Ethiopian man, a eunuch, one in power *with* Candace the queen of *the* Ethiopians, who was over all her treasure, who had come to Jerusalem to worship. [28]And *he* was returning. And sitting on his chariot, he read the prophet Isaiah. [29]And the Spirit said to Philip, Come up and join yourself to this chariot. [30]And running near, Philip heard him reading the prophet Isaiah, and said, Then do you know what you

4151 40 4074 2036 4314 846 694 4675
20 Πνεῦμα Ἅγιον. Πέτρος δὲ εἶπε πρὸς αὐτόν, Τὸ ἀργύριόν σου
(the) Spirit Holy. Peter But said to him, The silver of you
4862/4671/1498/1519/ 684 3754 1431 2316 3543
σὺν σοὶ εἴη εἰς ἀπώλειαν, ὅτι τὴν δωρεὰν τοῦ Θεοῦ ἐνόμισας
with you be into perdition, because the gift of God you thought
1223 5536 2932 3756/2076/4671 3310/3761 2819 1722
21 διὰ χρημάτων κτᾶσθαι. οὐκ ἔστι σοι μερὶς οὐδὲ κλῆρος ἐν
through money to get. not There is to you part nor lot in
3056 5129 1063 2588 4675/3756/2076 2117 1799
τῷ λόγῳ τούτῳ. ἡ γὰρ καρδία σου οὐκ ἔστιν εὐθεῖα ἐνώπιον
– matter this. the For heart of you not is right before
2316 3340 3767 575 2549 4675 5025
22 τοῦ Θεοῦ. μετανόησον οὖν ἀπὸ τῆς κακίας σου ταύτης, καὶ
– God. Repent, therefore, from wickedness of you this, and
1189 2316 1487 686 863 4671 1963
δεήθητι τοῦ Θεοῦ, εἰ ἄρα ἀφεθήσεταί σοι ἡ ἐπίνοια τῆς
petition God if perhaps will be forgiven you the thought of the
2588 4675/1519/1063/5521 4088 4886 93
23 καρδίας σου. εἰς γὰρ χολὴν πικρίας καὶ σύνδεσμον ἀδικίας
heart of you. in For (the) gall of bitterness and a bundle of unrighteousness
3708/4571/5607 611 4613 2036 1189 5228
24 ὁρῶ σε ὄντα. ἀποκριθεὶς δὲ ὁ Σίμων εἶπε, Δεήθητε ὑμεῖς ὑπὲρ
I see you being. answering And Simon said, Petition you for
1700 4314 2962 3704 3367 1904 1909/1691/3739/2046
ἐμοῦ πρὸς τὸν Κύριον, ὅπως μηδὲν ἐπέλθῃ ἐπ' ἐμὲ ὧν εἰρη-
me to the Lord, so as not one may come on me of what you
κατε.
have spoken.

3303/3767 1263 2980 3056
25 Οἱ μὲν οὖν διαμαρτυράμενοι καὶ λαλήσαντες τὸν λόγον
They, therefore, having earnestly testified and having spoken the word
2962 5290 1519 2419 4183 5037 2968
τοῦ Κυρίου, ὑπέστρεψαν εἰς Ἱερουσαλήμ, πολλάς τε κώμας
of the Lord, returned to Jerusalem, many and villages
4541 2097
τῶν Σαμαρειτῶν εὐηγγελίσαντο.
of the Samaritans having preached the gospel.

32 2962 2980 4314 5376 3004
26 Ἄγγελος δὲ Κυρίου ἐλάλησε πρὸς Φίλιππον, λέγων,
an angel And of (the) Lord spoke to Philip, saying,
450 4198 2596 3314 1909 3598
Ἀνάστηθι καὶ πορεύου κατὰ μεσημβρίαν ἐπὶ τὴν ὁδὸν τὴν
Rise up and go along south, on the highway
2597 575 2419 1519 1048 3778 2076
καταβαίνουσαν ἀπὸ Ἱερουσαλὴμ εἰς Γάζαν· αὕτη ἐστὶν
going down from Jerusalem to Gaza; this is
2048 450 4198 2400 435 128 2135
27 ἔρημος. καὶ ἀναστὰς ἐπορεύθη· καὶ ἰδού, ἀνὴρ Αἰθίοψ εὐνοῦ-
desert. And rising up he went. And, behold, a man Ethiopian, a eunuch,
1413 2582 938 128 3739/2258/1909
χος δυνάστης Κανδάκης τῆς βασιλίσσης Αἰθιόπων, ὃς ἦν ἐπὶ
a power of Candace the queen of Ethiopians, who was over
3956 1047 848 3739 2064 4352 1519
πάσης τῆς γάζης αὐτῆς, ὃς ἐληλύθει προσκυνήσων εἰς
all the treasure of her, who had come to worship to
2419 2258/5037 5290 2521 1909
28 Ἱερουσαλήμ, ἦν τε ὑποστρέφων καὶ καθήμενος ἐπὶ τοῦ
Jerusalem, was and returning and sitting on the
716 848 314 4396 2268 2036
ἅρματος αὐτοῦ, ἀνεγίνωσκε τὸν προφήτην Ἡσαΐαν. εἶπε
chariot of him, he read the prophet Isaiah. said
4151 5376 4334 2853
29 δὲ τὸ Πνεῦμα τῷ Φιλίππῳ, Πρόσελθε καὶ κολλήθητι τῷ
And the Spirit – to Philip, Go near and join yourself to –
716 5129 4370 5376 191 846
30 ἅρματι τούτῳ. προσδραμὼν δὲ ὁ Φίλιππος ἤκουσεν αὐτοῦ
chariot this. running near And, Philip heard from him
314 4396 2268 2036 687
ἀναγινώσκοντος τὸν προφήτην Ἡσαΐαν, καὶ εἶπεν, Ἆρά
reading the prophet Isaiah, and said, Indeed.

are reading? [31]But he said, How should I be able, unless someone shall guide me? And he called Philip near, to come up and sit with him. [32]And *the* content of the Scripture which he was reading was this: "He was led as a sheep to slaughter, and as a lamb dumb before its shearer, so He does not open His mouth. [33]In His humiliation, His judgment was taken away; and who will recount His generation? For His life is taken away from the earth."

[34]And answering, the eunuch said to Philip, I beg you, about whom does the prophet say this? About himself, or about some other? [35]And opening his mouth, and beginning from this Scripture, Philip preached to him the gospel *of* Jesus. [36]And as they were going along the highway, they came on some water. And the eunuch said, Behold, water! What hinders me from being baptized? [37]And Philip said, If you believe out of all the heart, it is lawful. And answering, he said, I believe Jesus Christ to be the Son of God.

[38]And he commanded the chariot to stand still. And both went down into the water, both Philip and the eunuch; and he baptized him. [39]But when they came up out of the water, *the* Spirit of *the* Lord caught Philip away, and the eunuch did not see him any more; for he went his way rejoicing.

[40]And Philip was found at Azotus, and having passed through he preached the gospel *to* all the cities, until he came to Caesarea.

1065 1097 3739 314 2036 4459/1063/302/1410
31 γε γινώσκεις ἃ ἀναγινώσκεις ; ὁ δὲ εἶπε, Πῶς γὰρ ἂν δυναί-
do you know what you are reading? he And said, how For should I be
= 3362= 5100 3594 3165 3870 5037 5376
μην, ἐὰν μή τις ὁδηγήσῃ με ; παρεκάλεσέ τε τὸν Φίλιππον
able, unless someone shall guide me? he called near And – Philip
305 2523 4862 846 4042 1124 3739
32 ἀναβάντα καθίσαι σὺν αὐτῷ. ἡ δὲ περιοχὴ τῆς γραφῆς ἣν
coming up to sit with him. the And (the) content of the Scripture which
•1909 314 2258/3778 5613 4263 4967 71
ἀνεγίνωσκεν ἦν αὕτη, Ὡς πρόβατον ἐπὶ σφαγὴν ἤχθη, καὶ
he was reading was this: As a sheep to slaughter He was led, and
5613 286 1726 2751 846 880 3779 3756
ὡς ἀμνὸς ἐναντίον τοῦ κείροντος αὐτὸν ἄφωνος, οὕτως οὐκ
as a lamb before he shearing it (is) voiceless, so not
455 4750 848 1722 5014 848 2920
33 ἀνοίγει τὸ στόμα αὐτοῦ. ἐν τῇ ταπεινώσει αὐτοῦ ἡ κρίσις
He opens the mouth of Him. In the humiliation of Him, the judgment
848 142 1074 848 5101 1334 3754
αὐτοῦ ἤρθη, τὴν δὲ γενεὰν αὐτοῦ τίς διηγήσεται ; ὅτι
of Him was taken; the but generation of Him who will recount? Because
142 575 1093 2222 848 611 2135
34 αἴρεται ἀπὸ τῆς γῆς ἡ ζωὴ αὐτοῦ. ἀποκριθεὶς δὲ ὁ εὐνοῦχος
is taken from the earth the life of Him. answering And the eunuch
5376 2036 1189 4675 4012 5100 4396 3004
τῷ Φιλίππῳ εἶπε, Δέομαί σου, περὶ τίνος ὁ προφήτης λέγει
to Philip said, I ask you, about whom the prophet says
5124 4012 1438 2228 4012 2087 5101 455
35 τοῦτο ; περὶ ἑαυτοῦ, ἢ περὶ ἑτέρου τινός ; ἀνοίξας δὲ ὁ
this? (Is it) about himself, or about other someone? opening And
5376 4750 848 756 575 1124
Φίλιππος τὸ στόμα αὐτοῦ, καὶ ἀρξάμενος ἀπὸ τῆς γραφῆς
Philip the mouth of him, and beginning from Scripture
5026 2097 846 2424 5613 4198
36 ταύτης, εὐηγγελίσατο αὐτῷ τὸν Ἰησοῦν. ὡς δὲ ἐπορεύοντο
this, preached the gospel to him, Jesus. as And they were going
2596 3598 2064 1909/5100/5204 5346 2135
κατὰ τὴν ὁδόν, ἦλθον ἐπί τι ὕδωρ· καί φησιν ὁ εὐνοῦχος,
along the highway, they came on some water, and says the eunuch,
2400 5204/5101 2967 3165 907 2036 5376
37 Ἰδού, ὕδωρ· τί κωλύει με βαπτισθῆναι ; εἶπε δὲ ὁ Φίλιππος,
Behold, water! What prevents me to be baptized? said And Philip,
1487 4100 1537/3650 2588 1832 611 2036
Εἰ πιστεύεις ἐξ ὅλης τῆς καρδίας, ἔξεστιν. ἀποκριθεὶς δὲ εἶπε,
If you believe from all the heart, it is lawful. answering And he said,
4100 5207 2316 1511 2424 5547
38 Πιστεύω τὸν υἱὸν τοῦ Θεοῦ εἶναι τὸν Ἰησοῦν Χριστόν. καὶ
I believe the Son – of God to be – Jesus Christ. And
2753 2476 716 2597 297 1519
ἐκέλευσε στῆναι τὸ ἅρμα· καὶ κατέβησαν ἀμφότεροι εἰς τὸ
he ordered to stand the chariot, and went down both into the
5204 5037 5376 2135 907 846
ὕδωρ, ὅ τε Φίλιππος καὶ ὁ εὐνοῦχος· καὶ ἐβάπτισεν αὐτόν.
water, – both Philip and the eunuch, and he baptized him.
3753 305 1537 5204 4151 2962 726
39 ὅτε δὲ ἀνέβησαν ἐκ τοῦ ὕδατος, Πνεῦμα Κυρίου ἥρπασε τὸν
when And they came up out of the water (the) Spirit of (the) Lord caught away
5376 3756 1492 846 3765 2135 4198
Φίλιππον· καὶ οὐκ εἶδεν αὐτὸν οὐκέτι ὁ εὐνοῦχος, ἐπορεύετο
Philip, and not did see him any more the eunuch, he went
1063 3598 848 5463 5376 2147 1519 108
40 γὰρ τὴν ὁδὸν αὐτοῦ χαίρων. Φίλιππος δὲ εὑρέθη εἰς Ἄζωτον·
for the way of him rejoicing. Philip And was found at Azotus,
1330 2097 4172 3956 2193
καὶ διερχόμενος εὐηγγελίζετο τὰς πόλεις πάσας, ἕως τοῦ
and passing through he preached the gospel to the cities all, until the
2064 846/1519 2542
ἐλθεῖν αὐτὸν εἰς Καισάρειαν.
coming (of) him to Caesarea.

CHAPTER 9

[1]But still breathing threats and murder toward the disciples of the Lord, coming to the high priest, [2]Saul asked from him letters to Damascus, to the synagogues, so that if he found any being of the Way, both men and women, having bound them he might bring *them* to Jerusalem. [3]But in going, it happened *as* he drew near to Damascus; even suddenly a light from Heaven shone around him. [4]And falling on the earth, he heard a voice saying to him, Saul, Saul, why do you persecute Me? [5]And he said, Who are you, Sir? And the Lord said, I am Jesus whom you persecute. *It is* hard for you to kick against the prods. [6]Both trembling and being astonished, he said, Lord, what do You desire me to do? And the Lord *said* to him, Rise up and go into the city, and it will be told you what you must do. [7]But the men who were traveling with him had been standing speechless; hearing, indeed, the voice, but seeing no one.

[8]And Saul was lifted up from the ground, his eyes having been opened, *but* he saw no one. But leading him by the hand, they brought *him* to Damascus. [9]And he was three days not seeing, and did not eat or drink.

[10]And there was a certain disciple named Ananias in Damascus. And the Lord said to him in a vision, Ananias. And he said, Behold, I *am here*, Lord. [11]And the Lord *said* to him, Rising up, pass along on the street being called Straight, and seek a Tarsian named Saul in *the* house of Judas. For, behold, he is praying. [12]And

CHAPTER 9

4569 2089 1709 547 5408 1519
1 Ὁ δὲ Σαῦλος ἔτι ἐμπνέων ἀπειλῆς καὶ φόνου εἰς τοὺς
— But Saul still breathing in threats and murder toward the
3101 2962 4334 749 154
2 μαθητὰς τοῦ Κυρίου, προσελθὼν τῷ ἀρχιερεῖ, ᾐτήσατο
disciples of the Lord, having come to the high priest, asked
3844 846 1992 1519 1154 4314 4864
παρ' αὐτοῦ ἐπιστολὰς εἰς Δαμασκὸν πρὸς τὰς συναγωγάς,
from him letters to Damascus, to the synagogues,
3704/1437/5100/2147 3598 5607 435 5037 1135
ὅπως ἐάν τινας εὕρῃ τῆς ὁδοῦ ὄντας ἄνδρας τε καὶ γυναῖκας,
so that if any he found of the Way being, men both and women,
1210 71 1519 2419 1722 4198
3 δεδεμένους ἀγάγῃ εἰς Ἱερουσαλήμ. ἐν δὲ τῷ πορεύεσθαι,
binding (them) he may bring to Jerusalem. in And the going
1096 846 1448 1154 1810 4015
ἐγένετο αὐτὸν ἐγγίζειν τῇ Δαμασκῷ· καὶ ἐξαίφνης περι-
happened it he drew near — to Damascus, and suddenly shone
846 5457 575 3772 4098 1909
4 ήστραψεν αὐτὸν φῶς ἀπὸ τοῦ οὐρανοῦ· καὶ πεσὼν ἐπὶ τὴν
around him a light from — Heaven; and falling on the
1093 191 5456 3004 846 4549 4549 5101/3165
γῆν, ἤκουσε φωνὴν λέγουσαν αὐτῷ, Σαούλ, Σαούλ, τί με
earth, he heard a voice saying to him, Saul, Saul! Why Me
1377 2036 5101/1488/2962 2962 2036 1473 1510
5 διώκεις; εἶπε δέ, Τίς εἶ, Κύριε; ὁ δὲ Κύριος εἶπεν, Ἐγώ εἰμι
you persecute? he said And, Who are you, Sir? And the Lord said, I am
2424/3739/4771/ 1377 4642 4671 4314 2759 2979
Ἰησοῦς ὃν σὺ διώκεις· σκληρόν σοι πρὸς κέντρα λακτίζειν.
Jesus, whom you persecute; (It is) hard for you against prods to kick.
5141 5037 2284 2036 2962 5101/3165/2309 4160
6 τρέμων τε καὶ θαμβῶν εἶπε, Κύριε, τί με θέλεις ποιῆσαι; καὶ
trembling both And astonished, he said, Lord, what me desire You to do? And
2962 4314 846 450 1525 1519 4172
ὁ Κύριος πρὸς αὐτόν, Ἀνάστηθι καὶ εἴσελθε εἰς τὴν πόλιν,
the Lord (said) to him, Rise up and go into the city,
2980 4671/5101/4571/1163/4160 435 4922
7 καὶ λαληθήσεταί σοι τί σε δεῖ ποιεῖν. οἱ δὲ ἄνδρες οἱ συν-
and it shall be told you what you must do. the And men —
846 2476 1769 191 3303 5456
οδεύοντες αὐτῷ εἱστήκεισαν ἐννεοί, ἀκούοντες μὲν τῆς φω-
traveling with him had been standing speechless, hearing indeed the sound,
3367 2334 1453 4569 575
8 νῆς, μηδένα δὲ θεωροῦντες. ἠγέρθη δὲ ὁ Σαῦλος ἀπὸ τῆς
no one but beholding. was lifted And Saul from the
1093 455 3788 848 3762 991
γῆς· ἀνεῳγμένων δὲ τῶν ὀφθαλμῶν αὐτοῦ, οὐδένα ἔβλεπε,
earth, being opened but the eyes of him, no one he saw.
5496 846 1521 1519 1154 2258
χειραγωγοῦντες δὲ αὐτὸν εἰσήγαγον εἰς Δαμασκόν. καὶ ἦν
leading by the hand And him, they brought to Damascus. And he was
2250 5140/3361 991 3756 5315 3761 4095
9 ἡμέρας τρεῖς μὴ βλέπων, καὶ οὐκ ἔφαγεν οὐδὲ ἔπιεν.
days three not seeing, and did not eat nor drink.
2258 5100 3101 1722 1154 3686 367
10 Ἦν δέ τις μαθητὴς ἐν Δαμασκῷ ὀνόματι Ἀνανίας, καὶ
was And a certain disciple in Damascus by name Ananias, and
2036 4314 846 2962 1722 3705 367 2036
εἶπε πρὸς αὐτὸν ὁ Κύριος ἐν ὁράματι, Ἀνανία. ὁ δὲ εἶπεν,
said to him the Lord in a vision, Ananias! he And said.
2400 1473 2962 2962 4314 846 450
11 Ἰδοὺ ἐγώ, Κύριε. ὁ δὲ Κύριος πρὸς αὐτόν, Ἀναστὰς
Behold, I, Lord. the And Lord to him, Rising up
4198 1909 4505 2563 2117 2212
πορεύθητι ἐπὶ τὴν ῥύμην τὴν καλουμένην Εὐθεῖαν, καὶ ζήτη-
pass along on the street being called Straight, and seek
1722 3614 2455 4569 3686 5018 2400 1063
σον ἐν οἰκίᾳ Ἰούδα Σαῦλον ὀνόματι, Ταρσέα· ἰδοὺ γὰρ
in (the) house of Judas Saul by name a Tarsian; behold for

he has seen in a vision a man named Ananias coming and putting a hand on him, so that he may see again. [13]And Ananias answered, Lord, I have heard from many about this man, how many bad things he did to Your saints in Jerusalem.

[14]And here he has authority from the chief priests to bind all those calling on Your name. [15]And the Lord said to him, Go, for this one is a chosen vessel to Me, to bear My name before nations and kings and *the* sons of Israel; [16]for I will show him how much he must suffer for My name's sake.

[17]And Ananias went away and entered into the house. And putting hands on him, *he* said, Brother Saul, the Lord Jesus has sent me, the *One* who appeared to you in the highway *on* which you came, that you may see again, and be filled with *the* Holy Spirit. [18]And instantly scales as it were fell from his eyes, and he saw again. And rising up, *he* was baptized.

[19]And taking food, *he* was strengthened.

And Saul was with the disciples in Damascus some days. [20]And he at once proclaimed Christ in the synagogues, that this One is the Son of God. [21]And all those hearing were amazed, and said, Is this not the *one* destroying in Jerusalem those calling upon this Name, and he had come here for this, that binding them he may lead *them* before the chief priests? [22]But Saul was more filled with power, and confounded the Jews living in Damascus, proving that this

4336 1492 1722 3705 435 3686 367
12 προσεύχεται, καὶ εἶδεν ἐν ὁράματι ἄνδρα ὀνόματι Ἀνανίαν
he is praying, and has seen in a vision a man by name Ananias
1525 2007 846 5495 3704 308
εἰσελθόντα καὶ ἐπιθέντα αὐτῷ χεῖρα, ὅπως ἀναβλέψῃ.
coming in and putting on him a hand so as he may see again.
611 367 2962 191 575 4183 4012
13 ἀπεκρίθη δὲ ὁ Ἀνανίας, Κύριε, ἀκήκοα ἀπὸ πολλῶν περὶ
answered And – Ananias, Lord, I have heard from many about
435 5127 3745 2556 4160 40 4675 1722
τοῦ ἀνδρὸς τούτου, ὅσα κακὰ ἐποίησε τοῖς ἁγίοις σου ἐν
– man this, how many bad things he did to the saints of You in
2419 5602/2192 1849 3844 749
14 Ἱερουσαλήμ· καὶ ὧδε ἔχει ἐξουσίαν παρὰ τῶν ἀρχιερέων,
Jerusalem; and here he has authority from the chief priests
1210 3056 1941 3686 4675 2036
15 δῆσαι πάντας τοὺς ἐπικαλουμένους τὸ ὄνομά σου. εἶπε δὲ
to bind all the (ones) invoking the name of You. said But
4314 846 2962 4198 3754 4632 1589 3427 2076
πρὸς αὐτὸν ὁ Κύριος, Πορεύου, ὅτι σκεῦος ἐκλογῆς μοι ἐστὶν
to him the Lord, Go, because a vessel of election to Me is
3778 941 3686 3450 1799 1484
οὗτος, τοῦ βαστάσαι τὸ ὄνομά μου ἐνώπιον ἐθνῶν καὶ
this one, – to bear the name of Me before nations and
935 5207/5037 2474 1473/1063 5263 846 3745
16 βασιλέων, υἱῶν τε Ἰσραήλ· ἐγὼ γὰρ ὑποδείξω αὐτῷ ὅσα
kings, sons and of Israel; I for will show him how many
1163 846 5224 3686 3450 3958 565
17 δεῖ αὐτὸν ὑπὲρ τοῦ ὀνόματός μου παθεῖν. ἀπῆλθε δὲ
must he on behalf of the name of Me suffer. went away And
367 1525 1519 3614 2007 1909 846
Ἀνανίας καὶ εἰσῆλθεν εἰς τὴν οἰκίαν, καὶ ἐπιθεὶς ἐπ' αὐτὸν τὰς
Ananias and entered into the house, and putting on him the
5495 2036 4549 80 2962 649 3165 2424
χεῖρας εἶπε, Σαοὺλ ἀδελφέ, ὁ Κύριος ἀπέσταλκέ με, Ἰησοῦς
hands said, Saul Brother, the Lord has sent me, Jesus
3700 4671/1722 3598/3739/2064 3704 308 4130
ὁ ὀφθείς σοι ἐν τῇ ὁδῷ ᾗ ἤρχου, ὅπως ἀναβλέψῃς καὶ πλη-
He appearing to you in the way which you came, so as you may see and be
4151 40 2112 634 575
18 σθῇς Πνεύματος Ἁγίου. καὶ εὐθέως ἀπέπεσον ἀπὸ τῶν
filled of (the) Spirit Holy. And at once fell away from the
3788 848 5616 3013 308 5037 3916
ὀφθαλμῶν αὐτοῦ ὡσεὶ λεπίδες, ἀνέβλεψέ τε παραχρῆμα,
eyes of him as if scales, he saw again and, instantly
450 907 2983 5160 1765
19 καὶ ἀναστὰς ἐβαπτίσθη, καὶ λαβὼν τροφὴν ἐνίσχυσεν.
and rising up was baptized; and taking food was strengthened.
1096 4569 3326 1722 1154 3101
Ἐγένετο δὲ ὁ Σαῦλος μετὰ τῶν ἐν Δαμασκῷ μαθητῶν
was And – Saul with the in Damascus disciples
2250 5100 2112/1722 4864 2784
20 ἡμέρας τινάς. καὶ εὐθέως ἐν ταῖς συναγωγαῖς ἐκήρυσσε τὸν
days some, and at once in the synagogues he proclaimed the
5547 3754 3778 2076 5207 2316 1839
21 Χριστόν, ὅτι οὗτός ἐστιν ὁ υἱὸς τοῦ Θεοῦ. ἐξίσταντο δὲ
Christ, that this One is the Son – of God. were amazed And
3956 191 3004 3756 3778 2076 4199
πάντες οἱ ἀκούοντες καὶ ἔλεγον, Οὐχ οὗτός ἐστιν ὁ πορθήσας
all those hearing, and said, not this one Is the (one) destroying
1722 2419 1941 3686 5124
ἐν Ἱερουσαλὴμ τοὺς ἐπικαλουμένους τὸ ὄνομα τοῦτο, καὶ
in Jerusalem those invoking – name this, and
5602/1519/5124 2064 2443 1210 846 71 1909
ὧδε εἰς τοῦτο ἐληλύθει ἵνα δεδεμένους αὐτοὺς ἀγάγῃ ἐπὶ
here for this he had come, that binding them he may lead before
749 4569 3123 1743 4797
22 τοὺς ἀρχιερεῖς; Σαῦλος δὲ μᾶλλον ἐνεδυναμοῦτο, καὶ συνέ-
the chief priests? Saul And more was filled with power and con-
2453 2730 1722 1154
χυνε τοὺς Ἰουδαίους τοὺς κατοικοῦντας ἐν Δαμασκῷ,
founded the Jews living in Damascus,

One is the Christ.
[23]And when many days were fulfilled, the Jews plotted together to do away with him. [24]But their plot was known to Saul. And they carefully watched the gates both by day and by night, so that they might do away with him. [25]But taking him by night, the disciples let him down through the wall, lowering *him* in a basket.

[26]And Saul arriving in Jerusalem, he tried to be joined to the disciples; yet all feared him, not believing that he was a disciple. [27]But taking hold of him, Barnabas led him to the apostles. And *he* told them how he saw the Lord in the highway, and that He spoke to him; and how he spoke boldly in Damascus in the name of Jesus. [28]And he was with them, going in and going out in Jerusalem, and speaking boldly in the name of the Lord Jesus. [29]And he spoke and disputed with the Hellenists, but they seized him in order to do away with him. [30]But knowing *this*, the brothers brought him down to Caesarea, and sent him forth to Tarsus. [31]Then, indeed, the churches throughout all Judea, and Galilee, and Samaria, had peace, being built up and going on in the fear of the Lord. And *they* were increased in the comfort of the Holy Spirit.

[32]And it happened, passing through all, Peter also came down to the saints living in Lydda. [33]And he found that a certain man named Aeneas *was* there, *even* eight years lying on a

4822 3754 3778 2076 5547
συμβιβάζων ὅτι οὗτός ἐστιν ὁ Χριστός.
proving that this One is the Christ.
5613 4137 2250 2425 4823
23 Ὡς δὲ ἐπληροῦντο ἡμέραι ἱκαναί, συνεβουλεύσαντο οἱ
when And were fulfilled days many, plotted together the
2453 337 846 1097 4569 1917
24 Ἰουδαῖοι ἀνελεῖν αὐτόν· ἐγνώσθη δὲ τῷ Σαύλῳ ἡ ἐπιβουλὴ
Jews to kill him, was known but – to Saul the plot
848 3906 5037 4439 2250 5037 3571
αὐτῶν. παρετήρουν τε τὰς πύλας ἡμέρας τε καὶ νυκτός,
of them. they carefully watched And the gates by day both and by night,
3704 846 337 2983 846 3101 3571
25 ὅπως αὐτὸν ἀνέλωσι· λαβόντες δὲ αὐτὸν οἱ μαθηταὶ νυκτός,
so as him they may do away; taking but him the disciples by night
2524 1223 5038/ 5465 1722 4711
καθῆκαν διὰ τοῦ τείχους, χαλάσαντες ἐν σπυρίδι.
let down through the wall, lowering (him) in a basket.
3854 4569 1519 2419 3987
26 Παραγενόμενος δὲ ὁ Σαῦλος εἰς Ἱερουσαλήμ, ἐπειρᾶτο
arriving And Saul in Jerusalem, he tried
2853 3101 3956 5399 846 3361
κολλᾶσθαι τοῖς μαθηταῖς· καὶ πάντες ἐφοβοῦντο αὐτόν, μὴ
to be joined to the disciples; and all feared him, not
4100 3754 2076 3101 921 1949
27 πιστεύοντες ὅτι ἐστὶ μαθητής. Βαρνάβας δὲ ἐπιλαβόμενος
believing that he is a disciple. Barnabas But taking hold of
846 71 4314 652 1334 846
αὐτὸν ἤγαγε πρὸς τοὺς ἀποστόλους, καὶ διηγήσατο αὐτοῖς
him led to the apostles, and told them
4459/1722 3598 1492 2962 3754 2980 846
πῶς ἐν τῇ ὁδῷ εἶδε τὸν Κύριον, καὶ ὅτι ἐλάλησεν αὐτῷ,
how in the way he saw the Lord, and that He spoke to him,
4459/1722 1154 3955 1722 3686
καὶ πῶς ἐν Δαμασκῷ ἐπαρρησιάσατο ἐν τῷ ὀνόματι τοῦ
and how in Damascus he spoke boldly in the name –
2424 2258/3316 848 1531 1607
28 Ἰησοῦ. καὶ ἦν μετ' αὐτῶν εἰσπορευόμενος καὶ ἐκπορευό-
of Jesus. And he was with them going in and going
1722 2419 3955 1722 3686
μενος ἐν Ἱερουσαλήμ, καὶ παρρησιαζόμενος ἐν τῷ ὀνόματι
out in Jerusalem, and speaking boldly in the name
2962 2424 2980 5037 4802 4314
29 τοῦ Κυρίου Ἰησοῦ, ἐλάλει τε καὶ συνεζήτει πρὸς τοὺς
of the Lord Jesus. he spoke And and discussed with the
1675 2021 846 337 1921
30 Ἑλληνιστάς· οἱ δὲ ἐπεχείρουν αὐτὸν ἀνελεῖν. ἐπιγνόντες δὲ
Hellenists; they and took in hand him to do away. knowing But
80 2609 846 1519 2542 1821
οἱ ἀδελφοὶ κατήγαγον αὐτὸν εἰς Καισάρειαν, καὶ ἐξαπέ-
the brothers led down him to Caesarea, and sent
846 1519 5019 3303 3767 1577 2596
31 στειλαν αὐτὸν εἰς Ταρσόν. αἱ μὲν οὖν ἐκκλησίαι καθ'
forth him to Tarsus. the Therefore churches throughout
3650 2449 1056 4540 2192 1515
ὅλης τῆς Ἰουδαίας καὶ Γαλιλαίας καὶ Σαμαρείας εἶχον εἰρήνην
all Judea and Galilee and Samaria had peace,
3618 4198 5401 2962
οἰκοδομούμεναι, καὶ πορευόμεναι τῷ φόβῳ τοῦ Κυρίου καὶ
being built up, and going on in the fear of the Lord, and
3874 40 4151 4129
τῇ παρακλήσει τοῦ Ἁγίου Πνεύματος ἐπληθύνοντο.
in the comfort of the Holy Spirit were multiplied.
1096 4074 1330 1223 3956 2718
32 Ἐγένετο δὲ Πέτρον διερχόμενον διὰ πάντων κατελθεῖν καὶ
it was And, Peter passing through all came down also
4314 40 2730 3069 2147 1563
33 πρὸς τοὺς ἁγίους τοὺς κατοικοῦντας Λύδδαν. εὗρε δὲ ἐκεῖ
to the saints – inhabiting Lydda. he found And there
444 5100 132 3686 1537/2094/3638 2621
ἄνθρωπόν τινα Αἰνέαν ὀνόματι, ἐξ ἐτῶν ὀκτὼ κατακείμενον
a man certain, Aeneas by name, of years eight lying

a mattress, who was paralyzed. [34]And Peter said to him, Aeneas, Jesus the Christ heals you; rise up and spread for yourself! And he instantly rose up. [35]And all those living in Lydda and the Sharon *Plain* saw him, who *then* turned to the Lord.

[36]And in Joppa was a certain disciple named Tabitha, which translated is called Gazelle. She was full of good works and of alms which she did. [37]And it happened in those days, becoming ill, she died. And having washed her, they put *her* in an upper room. [38]And Lydda being near to Joppa, the disciples hearing that Peter is in it, they sent two men to him, begging *him* not to delay to come to them.

[39]And rising up, Peter went with them. *And he* having arrived, they led *him* up to the upper room, and all the widows stood by him, weeping and showing tunics and garments which Dorcas made, *while* being with them. [40]And putting all out, placing the knees, Peter prayed. And turning to the body, he said, Tabitha, Rise up! And she opened her eyes, and seeing Peter, she sat up. [41]And giving her a hand, he raised her up. And calling the saints and the widows, he presented her living. [42]And it became known throughout all Joppa, and many believed on the Lord. [43]And it was a considerable number of days *that* he remained in Joppa, with a certain Simon, a tanner.

1909 2895 3739/2258 3886 2036 846
34 ἐπὶ κραββάτῳ, ὃς ἦν παραλελυμένος. καὶ εἶπεν αὐτῷ ὁ
on a mattress, who was paralyzed. And said to him
4074 132 2390/4571 2424 5547 450
Πέτρος, Αἰνέα, ἰᾶταί σε Ἰησοῦς ὁ Χριστός· ἀνάστηθι καὶ
Peter, Aeneas, heals you Jesus the Christ; rise up and
4766 4572 2112 450 1492 846
στρῶσον σεαυτῷ. καὶ εὐθέως ἀνέστη. καὶ εἶδον αὐτὸν
spread for yourself. And instantly he rose up. And saw him
3956 2730 3069 4565 3748
35 πάντες οἱ κατοικοῦντες Λύδδαν καὶ τὸν Σάρωνα, οἵτινες
all those inhabiting Lydda and the Sharon (plain), who
1994 1909 2962
ἐπέστρεψαν ἐπὶ τὸν Κύριον.
turned to the Lord.
1722 2445 5100 2258/3102 3686 5000 3739 1329
36 Ἐν Ἰόππῃ δέ τις ἦν μαθήτρια ὀνόματι Ταβιθά, ἣ διερμη-
in Joppa And a certain was disciple, by name Tabitha, which being
3004 1393 3778/2258/4134 18 2041
νευομένη λέγεται Δορκάς· αὕτη ἦν πλήρης ἀγαθῶν ἔργων καὶ
translated is called Gazelle. She was full of good works and
1654 3739 4160 1096 1722 2250 1565
37 ἐλεημοσυνῶν ὧν ἐποίει. ἐγένετο δὲ ἐν ταῖς ἡμέραις ἐκείναις
of alms which she did. it was And, in — days those,
770 846 599 3068 846 5087
ἀσθενήσασαν αὐτὴν ἀποθανεῖν· λούσαντες δὲ αὐτὴν ἔθηκαν
having ailed, she died. having washed And, her they put
1722/5253 1451 5607 3069 2445 3101
38 ἐν ὑπερῴῳ. ἐγγὺς δὲ οὔσης Λύδδης τῇ Ἰόππῃ, οἱ μαθηταὶ
in an upper room. near And being Lydda to Joppa, the disciples
191 3754 4074 2076 1722 846 649 1417
ἀκούσαντες ὅτι Πέτρος ἐστὶν ἐν αὐτῇ, ἀπέστειλαν δύο
having heard that Peter is in it, they sent two
435 4314 846 3870 3361 3635 1330
ἄνδρας πρὸς αὐτόν, παρακαλοῦντες μὴ ὀκνῆσαι διελθεῖν
men to him, begging (him) not to delay to come
2193 846 450 4074 4905 846 3739 3854
39 ἕως αὐτῶν. ἀναστὰς δὲ Πέτρος συνῆλθεν αὐτοῖς· ὃν παρα-
to them. rising And Peter went with them; whom arriving
321 1519 5253 3936 846
γενόμενον ἀνήγαγον εἰς τὸ ὑπερῷον, καὶ παρέστησαν αὐτῷ
they led up to the upper room, and stood by him
3956 5503 2799 1925 5509
πᾶσαι αἱ χῆραι κλαίουσαι καὶ ἐπιδεικνύμεναι χιτῶνας καὶ
all the widows weeping and showing tunics and
2440 3745 4160 3326 846 5607 1393 1544
ἱμάτια ὅσα ἐποίει μετ᾽ αὐτῶν οὖσα ἡ Δορκάς. ἐκβαλὼν δὲ
garments such as made with them being — Dorcas. thrusting And
1854 3956 4074 5087 1119 4336
40 ἔξω πάντας ὁ Πέτρος θεὶς τὰ γόνατα προσηύξατο· καὶ
out all, Peter placing the knees prayed; and
1994 4314 4983 2036 5000 450
ἐπιστρέψας πρὸς τὸ σῶμα, εἶπε, Ταβιθά, ἀνάστηθι. ἡ δὲ
turning to the body, he said, Tabitha, Arise. she And
455 3788 848 1492 4074
ἤνοιξε τοὺς ὀφθαλμοὺς αὐτῆς· καὶ ἰδοῦσα τὸν Πέτρον,
opened the eyes of her and seeing — Peter,
339 1325 846 5495 450 846 5455
41 ἀνεκάθισε. δοὺς δὲ αὐτῇ χεῖρα, ἀνέστησεν αὐτήν· φωνήσας δὲ
she sat up. giving And her a hand, he raised up her; calling and
40 5503 3936 846 2198 1110
τοὺς ἁγίους καὶ τὰς χήρας, παρέστησεν αὐτὴν ζῶσαν. γνω-
the saints and the widows, he presented her living.
1096 2596 3650 2445 4183 4100
42 στὸν δὲ ἐγένετο καθ᾽ ὅλης τῆς Ἰόππης, καὶ πολλοὶ ἐπί-
known And it became through all — Joppa, and many
1909 2962 1096 2250 2425 3306
43 στευσαν ἐπὶ τὸν Κύριον. ἐγένετο δὲ ἡμέρας ἱκανὰς μεῖναι
believed on the Lord. it was And days sufficient remained
846 1722 2445 3844 5100 4613 1038
αὐτὸν ἐν Ἰόππῃ παρά τινι Σίμωνι βυρσεῖ.
he in Joppa with one Simon, a tanner.

CHAPTER 10

CHAPTER 10
1 But a certain man
named Cornelius was in
Caesarea, a centurion of a
cohort being called Italian;
2 *one* devout and fearing
God, with all his household,
both doing many alms to
the people, and praying
continually to God. 3 About
the ninth hour of the day, he
saw plainly in a vision an
angel coming to him, and
saying to him, Cornelius!
4 And he was staring at him,
and becoming terrified he
said, What is it, Sir? And he
said to him, Your prayers
and your alms went up for a
memorial before God. 5 And
now send men to Joppa,
and call for Simon who is
surnamed Peter. 6 This one
is lodged with one Simon, a
tanner, whose house is by
the sea. He will tell you
what you must do. 7 And
when the angel speaking to
Cornelius went away, calling two of his servants, and
a devout soldier of those
continually waiting on him,
8 and having explained all
things to them, he sent
them to Joppa.

9 And on the morrow,
these passing along on *the*
road, and drawing near to
the city, Peter went up on
the roof to pray, about *the*
sixth hour. 10 And he be-
came hungry, and wished
to taste *food*. But *as* they
were preparing, an ecstasy
fell on him. 11 And he saw
the heaven being opened,
and a certain vessel like a
great sheet coming down
on him, being bound by four
corners, and let down onto

435 5100/2258/1722/ 2542 3686 2883 1543
1 Ἀνὴρ δέ τις ἦν ἐν Καισαρείᾳ ὀνόματι Κορνήλιος, ἑκατοντ-
a man And certain was in Caesarea, by name Cornelius, a centurion
1537 4686 2564 2483 2152
2 άρχης ἐκ σπείρης τῆς καλουμένης Ἰταλικῆς, εὐσεβὴς καὶ
of a cohort — being called Italian; devout and
5399 2316/4862/3956 3624 848 4160 5037
φοβούμενος τὸν Θεὸν σὺν παντὶ τῷ οἴκῳ αὐτοῦ, ποιῶν τε
fearing — God with all the house of him, doing both
1654 4183 2992 1189 2316 1223
ἐλεημοσύνας πολλὰς τῷ λαῷ, καὶ δεόμενος τοῦ Θεοῦ διὰ
alms many to the people, and petitioning — God con-
3956 1492 1722 3705 5320 5616 5610 1766
3 παντός. εἶδεν ἐν ὁράματι φανερῶς, ὡσεὶ ὥραν ἐννάτην τῆς
tinually. He saw in a vision plainly, about hour ninth of the
2250 32 2316 1525 4314 846
ἡμέρας, ἄγγελον τοῦ Θεοῦ εἰσελθόντα πρὸς αὐτόν, καὶ
day, an angel — of God coming in to him, and
2036 846 2883 816 846 1719
4 εἰπόντα αὐτῷ, Κορνήλιε. ὁ δὲ ἀτενίσας αὐτῷ καὶ ἔμφοβος
saying to him, Cornelius! he And was gazing at him and terrified
1096 2036/5101/2076 2962 2036 846 4335
γενόμενος εἶπε, Τί ἐστι, Κύριε; εἶπε δὲ αὐτῷ, Αἱ προσευχαί
becoming he said, What is it, Sir? he said And to him, The prayers
4675 1654 4675 305 1519 3422
σου καὶ αἱ ἐλεημοσύναι σου ἀνέβησαν εἰς μνημόσυνον
of you and the alms of you went up for a memorial
1799 2316 3568 3992 1519 2445 435
5 ἐνώπιον τοῦ Θεοῦ. καὶ νῦν πέμψον εἰς Ἰόππην ἄνδρας, καὶ
before — God. And now send to Joppa men, and
3343 4613 3739 1941 4074 3778 3579
6 μετάπεμψαι Σίμωνα ὅς ἐπικαλεῖται Πέτρος· οὗτος ξενίζεται
call for Simon who is surnamed Peter; this one is lodged
3844 5100 4613 1038 * 2076 3614 3844 2281
3739 παρά τινι Σίμωνι βυρσεῖ, ᾧ ἐστιν οἰκία παρὰ θάλασσαν·
with one Simon, a tanner, to whom is a house by (the) sea
4571 3778 2980 4671/5101/*/1163/4160/5613 565 32
7 οὗτος λαλήσει σοι τί σε δεῖ ποιεῖν. ὡς δὲ ἀπῆλθεν ὁ ἄγγελος
this one will tell you what you must do. as And went away the angel
2980 2883 5455 1417 3610 848
ὁ λαλῶν τῷ Κορνηλίῳ, φωνήσας δύο τῶν οἰκετῶν αὐτοῦ,
— speaking — to Cornelius, having called two of the servants of him,
4757 2152 4342 846
καὶ στρατιώτην εὐσεβῆ τῶν προσκαρτερούντων αὐτῷ, καὶ
and a soldier devout of those continually waiting on him, and
1834 846 537 649 846 1519
8 ἐξηγησάμενος αὐτοῖς ἅπαντα, ἀπέστειλεν αὐτοὺς εἰς τὴν
having explained to them all things, he sent forth them to —
2445
Ἰόππην.
Joppa.

1887 3596 1565 4172
9 Τῇ δὲ ἐπαύριον, ὁδοιπορούντων ἐκείνων καὶ τῇ πόλει
on the And morrow, passing along (the) road these, and to the city
1448 305 4074 1909 1430 4336 4012
ἐγγιζόντων, ἀνέβη Πέτρος ἐπὶ τὸ δῶμα προσεύξασθαι, περὶ
drawing near, went up Peter on the roof to pray, about
5610 1622 1096 4361 2309 1089
10 ὥραν ἕκτην· ἐγένετο δὲ πρόσπεινος, καὶ ἤθελε γεύσασθαι·
hour sixth, he became And hungry, and desired to taste;
3903 1565 1968 1909 846 1611
παρασκευαζόντων δὲ ἐκείνων, ἐπέπεσεν ἐπ' αὐτὸν ἔκστασις,
preparing and they fell on him an ecstasy,
2334 3772 455 2597 1909
11 καὶ θεωρεῖ τὸν οὐρανὸν ἀνεῳγμένον, καὶ καταβαῖνον ἐπ'
And he beholds the heaven being opened, and coming down on
846 4632 5100/5613 3607 3173 5064 746
αὐτὸν σκεῦός τι ὡς ὀθόνην μεγάλην, τέσσαρσιν ἀρχαῖς
him a vessel certain like a sheet great, by four corners

the earth; [12]in which were all the four-footed animals of the earth, and the wild beasts, and the creeping things, and the birds of the heaven. [13]And a voice came to him, Rise up, Peter, slay and eat. [14]But Peter said, Not at all, Lord, because I never did eat anything common or unclean. [15]And again a voice *came* to him a second *time*, What things God made clean, you do not make common. [16]And this happened three *times*, and the vessel was taken up into the heaven again.

[17]And as Peter was doubting within himself what the vision which he saw might be, even behold, the men who had been sent from Cornelius stood on the porch asking out the house of Simon. [18]And calling out, they inquired if Simon being surnamed Peter is lodged here. [19]And *as* Peter pondered concerning the vision, the Spirit said to him, Behold, three men are seeking you. [20]But rising up, go down and go with them, not discriminating, because I have sent them. [21]And going down to the men, the ones sent from Cornelius to him, Peter said, Behold, I am *the one* you seek. What *is* the cause for which you are here? [22]And they said, Cornelius, a centurion, a just man and *one* fearing God, and being testified to by all the nation of the Jews, was divinely warned by a holy angel to call you to his house, and to hear words from you. [23]Then calling them in, he lodged *them*.

1210 2524 1909 1093/1722/3739/5225 3956
12 δεδεμένον, καὶ καθιέμενον ἐπὶ τῆς γῆς· ἐν ᾧ ὑπῆρχε πάντα
being bound, and let down onto the earth; in which were all
5074 1093 2342 2062
τὰ τετράποδα τῆς γῆς καὶ τὰ θηρία καὶ τὰ ἑρπετὰ καὶ τὰ
the quadrupeds of the earth, and the beasts, and the reptiles, and the
4071 3772 1096 5456 4314 846
13 πετεινὰ τοῦ οὐρανοῦ. καὶ ἐγένετο φωνὴ πρὸς αὐτόν,
birds of the heaven. And came a voice to him,
450 4074 2380 5315 4074 2036
14 Ἀναστάς, Πέτρε, θῦσον καὶ φάγε. ὁ δὲ Πέτρος εἶπε,
Rise up, Peter, slay and eat. – But Peter said,
3365 2962 3754 3762 5315 3956 2839/2228/ 169
Μηδαμῶς, Κύριε· ὅτι οὐδέποτε ἔφαγον πᾶν κοινὸν ἢ ἀκάθαρ-
Not at all, Lord, because never did I eat anything common or un-
5456 3825 1537 1208 4314 846 3739 2316
15 τον. καὶ φωνὴ πάλιν ἐκ δευτέρου πρὸς αὐτόν· ἃ ὁ Θεὸς
clean. And a voice again from a second (time) to him, what things God
2511 4771/3361/2840 5124 1096 1909 5151
16 ἐκαθάρισε, σὺ μὴ κοίνου. τοῦτο δὲ ἐγένετο ἐπὶ τρίς· καὶ
cleansed, you not make common. this And happened on three, and
3825 353 4632 1519 3772
πάλιν ἀνελήφθη τὸ σκεῦος εἰς τὸν οὐρανόν
again was taken up the vessel into the heaven.
5613 1722 1438 1280 4074 5101/302/1498 3705/3739
17 Ὡς δὲ ἐν ἑαυτῷ διηπόρει ὁ Πέτρος τί ἂν εἴη τὸ ὅραμα ὃ
as And in himself was doubting Peter, what might be the vision which
1492 2400 435 649 575 2883
εἶδε, καὶ ἰδού, οἱ ἄνδρες οἱ ἀπεσταλμένοι ἀπὸ τοῦ Κορνηλίου,
he saw, and behold, the men – having been sent from – Cornelius
1331 3614 4613 2186 1909
διερωτήσαντες τὴν οἰκίαν Σίμωνος, ἐπέστησαν ἐπὶ τὸν
having asked out the house of Simon stood at the
4440 5455 4441 1487 4613 1941
18 πυλῶνα, καὶ φωνήσαντες ἐπυνθάνοντο εἰ Σίμων, ὁ ἐπικαλού-
porch. And calling they inquired if Simon, – being
4074 1759 3579 4074 1760
19 μενος Πέτρος, ἐνθάδε ξενίζεται. τοῦ δὲ Πέτρου ἐνθυμουμένου
surnamed Peter, here is lodged. – And Peter pondering
4012 3705 2036 846 4151 2400 435
περὶ τοῦ ὁράματος, εἶπεν αὐτῷ τὸ Πνεῦμα, Ἰδού, ἄνδρες
about the vision, said to him the Spirit, Behold, men
5140 2212 4571 235 450 2597 4198 4862
20 τρεῖς ζητοῦσί σε. ἀλλὰ ἀναστὰς κατάβηθι, καὶ πορεύου σὺν
three are seeking you. But rising up, go down, and go with
846 3367 1252 1360 1473 649 846
αὐτοῖς, μηδὲν διακρινόμενος· διότι ἐγὼ ἀπέσταλκα αὐτούς.
them nothing discriminating, because I have sent them.
2597 4074 4314 435 649 575
21 καταβὰς δὲ Πέτρος πρὸς τοὺς ἄνδρας τοὺς ἀπεσταλμένους ἀπὸ
going down And Peter to the men, those sent from
2883 4314 846 2036 2400 1473 1510/3739/2212
τοῦ Κορνηλίου πρὸς αὐτόν, εἶπεν, Ἰδού, ἐγώ εἰμι ὃν ζητεῖτε·
– Cornelius to him, said, Behold, I am whom you seek;
5101 156/1223/3739/ 3918 2036 2883 1543
22 τίς ἡ αἰτία δι' ἣν πάρεστε; οἱ δὲ εἶπον, Κορνήλιος ἑκατοντάρ-
what (is) the cause for which you are here? they And said, Cornelius, a centurion
435 1342 5399 2316 3140
χης, ἀνὴρ δίκαιος καὶ φοβούμενος τὸν Θεόν, μαρτυρούμενός
a man just and fearing – God, being testified to
5037/5259/3650 1484 2453 5537 5259
τε ὑπὸ ὅλου τοῦ ἔθνους τῶν Ἰουδαίων, ἐχρηματίσθη ὑπὸ
and by all of the nation of the Jews, was warned by
32 40 3343 4571/1519 3624 848
ἀγγέλου ἁγίου μεταπέμψασθαί σε εἰς τὸν οἶκον αὐτοῦ, καὶ
an angel holy to call you to the house of him, and
191 4487 3844 4675 1528 3767 846
23 ἀκοῦσαι ῥήματα παρὰ σοῦ. εἰσκαλεσάμενος οὖν αὐτοὺς
to hear words from you. Calling in, therefore, them,
3579
ἐξένισε.
he lodged.

And on the morrow Peter went out with them. And some of the brothers from Joppa accompanied him. [24]And on the morrow they entered Caesarea. And Cornelius was awaiting them, having called together his relatives and *his* intimate friends. [25]And as Peter was coming in, meeting him, Cornelius fell at *his* feet *and* worshiped. [26]But Peter lifted him up, saying, Stand up! I myself am also a man.

[27]And talking with him, he went in and found many having come together. [28]And he said to them, You know how unlawful it is for a man, a Jew, to unite with or to come near to one of another race. Yet God showed to me not to call a man common or unclean. [29]Therefore, I also came without compalint, being summoned. Then for what reason did you send for me? [30]And Cornelius said, From *the* fourth day until this hour I have been fasting, and the ninth hour *I* was praying in my house. And, behold, a man stood before me in bright clothing. [31]And *he* said, Cornelius, your prayer was heard, and your alms were remembered before God.

[32]Therefore, send to Joppa and call for Simon who is surnamed Peter; this one is lodged in *the* house of Simon, a tanner, by *the* sea. Having come, *he* will speak to you. [33]Then at once I sent to you; and you did well *to* come. Now, then, we are all present before God to hear all the things having been commanded you by God.

1887 4074 1831 4862 846 5100
Τῇ δὲ ἐπαύριον ὁ Πέτρος ἐξῆλθε σὺν αὐτοῖς, καί τινες τῶν
on the And morrow, Peter went out with them, and some of the
80 575 2445 4905 846
24 ἀδελφῶν τῶν ἀπὸ τῆς Ἰόππης συνῆλθον αὐτῷ. καὶ τῇ
brothers – from – Joppa accompanied him. And on the
1887 1525 1519 2542 2883 2258
ἐπαύριον εἰσῆλθον εἰς τὴν Καισάρειαν. ὁ δὲ Κορνήλιος ἦν
morrow they entered into – Caesarea. And Cornelius was
4328 846 4779 4773 848
προσδοκῶν αὐτούς, συγκαλεσάμενος τοὺς συγγενεῖς αὐτοῦ
awaiting them, having called together the relatives of him
316 5384 5613 1096 1525
25 καὶ τοὺς ἀναγκαίους φίλους. ὡς δὲ ἐγένετο εἰσελθεῖν τὸν
and the intimate friends. when And was entering –
4074 4876 846 2883 4098 1909
Πέτρον, συναντήσας αὐτῷ ὁ Κορνήλιος, πεσὼν ἐπὶ τοὺς
Peter, meeting him – Cornelius, falling at the
4228 4352 4074 846 1453 3004
26 πόδας, προσεκύνησεν. ὁ δὲ Πέτρος αὐτὸν ἤγειρε λέγων,
feet worshiped. – But Peter him raised, saying,
450 2504 846 444 1510 4926 846
27 Ἀνάστηθι· κἀγὼ αὐτὸς ἄνθρωπός εἰμι. καὶ συνομιλῶν αὐτῷ
Stand up; also I (my)self a man am. And talking with him
1525 2147 4905 4183 5346/5037/4314
εἰσῆλθε, καὶ εὑρίσκει συνεληλυθότας πολλούς, ἔφη τε πρὸς
he entered, and finds having come together many, said and to
846 5210 1987 5613 111 2076 435 2453
28 αὐτούς, Ὑμεῖς ἐπίστασθε ὡς ἀθέμιτόν ἐστιν ἀνδρὶ Ἰουδαίῳ
them, You understand how unlawful it is for a man, a Jew,
2853 2228 4334 246 1698 2316
κολλᾶσθαι ἢ προσέρχεσθαι ἀλλοφύλῳ· καὶ ἐμοὶ ὁ Θεὸς
to unite with or to approach one of and to me God
1166 3367 2839/2228/169 another race 3000/ 444 1223
ἔδειξε μηδένα κοινὸν ἢ ἀκάθαρτον λέγειν ἄνθρωπον· διὸ καὶ
showed not one common or unclean to call a man. Because of this, also
•3767 369 2064 3343 4441 • 5101
29 ἀναντιρρήτως ἦλθον μεταπεμφθείς. πυνθάνομαι οὖν, τίνι
without complaint I came, being sent for. I ask, therefore, for what
3056 3343 3165 2883 5346 575 5067
30 λόγῳ μετεπέμψασθέ με. καὶ ὁ Κορνήλιος ἔφη, Ἀπὸ τετάρτης
reason you sent for me. And Cornelius said, From fourth
2250 3360 5026 5610 2252 3522
ἡμέρας μέχρι ταύτης τῆς ὥρας ἤμην νηστεύων, καὶ τὴν
day until this – hour, I have been fasting, and the
1766 5610 4336 1722 3624/3450 2400
ἐννάτην ὥραν προσευχόμενος ἐν τῷ οἴκῳ μου· καὶ ἰδού,
ninth hour was praying in the house of me, and behold
435 2476 1799 3450 1722 2066 2986 5346
31 ἀνὴρ ἔστη ἐνώπιόν μου ἐν ἐσθῆτι λαμπρᾷ, καί φησι,
a man stood before me in clothing bright, and says,
2883 1522 4675 4335 1654
Κορνήλιε, εἰσηκούσθη σου ἡ προσευχή, καὶ αἱ ἐλεημοσύναι
Cornelius, was listened (to) of you the prayer, and the alms
4675 3415 1799 2316 3992 3767/1519/ 2445
32 σου ἐμνήσθησαν ἐνώπιον τοῦ Θεοῦ. πέμψον οὖν εἰς Ἰόππην,
of you were remembered before – God. send Therefore to Joppa,
3333 4613 3739 1941 4074 3778 3579
καὶ μετακάλεσαι Σίμωνα ὃς ἐπικαλεῖται Πέτρος· οὗτος ξενί-
and call for Simon who is surnamed Peter; this one is
1722/3614 4613 1038 3844 2281 3739 3854
ζεται ἐν οἰκίᾳ Σίμωνος βυρσέως παρὰ θάλασσαν· ὃς παρα-
lodged in (the) house of Simon, a tanner, by (the) sea, who having
•5037 2980 4671 1824 3767 3992 4314/4571/4771/•
33 γενόμενος λαλήσει σοι. Ἐξαυτῆς οὖν ἔπεμψα πρός σε· σύ τε
come will speak to you. At once, then, I sent to you; you and
2573 4160 3854 3568/3767 3956 2249 1799
καλῶς ἐποίησας παραγενόμενος. νῦν οὖν πάντες ἡμεῖς ἐνώ-
well did having come. Now, then, all we
2316 3918 191 3956 4367
πιον τοῦ Θεοῦ πάρεσμεν ἀκοῦσαι πάντα τὰ προστεταγμένα
before – God are present to hear all the things being commanded

34And opening *his* mouth, Peter said, Truly I see that God is not an accepter of persons, 35but in every nation the *one* fearing Him and working righteousness is acceptable to Him. 36The word which He sent to the sons of Israel, preaching the gospel of peace through Jesus Christ, this One is lord of all—37you know the thing that happened throughout all Judea, beginning from Galilee after the baptism that John proclaimed—38*Jesus, the One* from Nazareth, how God anointed Him with *the* Holy Spirit and with power, who went through doing good, and healing all those having been oppressed by the Devil, because God was with Him. 39And we are witnesses of all things which He did, both in the country of the Jews, and in Jerusalem—they did away with *Him*, hanging *Him* on a tree—40God raised up this One the third day, and gave to Him to become visible; 41not to all the people, but to witnesses, the ones having been before hand-picked by God, to us who ate and drank with Him after His rising again from *the* dead. 42And He commanded us to proclaim to the people, and to witness solemnly that it is He who has been marked out by God *to be* Judge of *the* living and *the* dead. 43To this One all the prophets witness, *so that* through His name everyone believing into Him *will* receive forgiveness of sins.

44*As* Peter was yet speaking these words, the Holy Spirit fell on all those hearing the word. 45And

4671/5259 2316 455 4074 4750 2036
34 σοι ὑπὸ τοῦ Θεοῦ. ἀνοίξας δὲ Πέτρος τὸ στόμα εἶπεν,
you by — God. opening And Peter the mouth said,
1909 225 2638 3754/3756/2076/ 4381
Ἐπ᾽ ἀληθείας καταλαμβάνομαι ὅτι οὐκ ἔστι προσωπολή-
On truth, I perceive that not is a receiver of
2316 235/1722/3956 1484 5399 846
35 πτης ὁ Θεός· ἀλλ᾽ ἐν παντὶ ἔθνει ὁ φοβούμενος αὐτὸν καὶ
faces God, but in every nation he fearing Him and
2038 1343 1184 846 2076 3004 3739
36 ἐργαζόμενος δικαιοσύνην, δεκτὸς αὐτῷ ἐστι. τὸν λόγον ὃν
working righteousness acceptable to Him is. The word which
649 5207 2474 2097 1515 1223
ἀπέστειλε τοῖς υἱοῖς Ἰσραήλ, εὐαγγελιζόμενος εἰρήνην διὰ
He sent to the sons of Israel, preaching the gospel peace through
2424 5547 3778 2076 3956 2962 5210 1492
37 Ἰησοῦ Χριστοῦ (οὗτός ἐστι πάντων Κύριος)—ὑμεῖς οἴδατε,
Jesus Christ: this One is of all Lord. You know
1096 4487/2596/3650 2449 756 575
τὸ γενόμενον ῥῆμα καθ᾽ ὅλης τῆς Ἰουδαίας, ἀρξάμενον ἀπὸ
that happened the thing through all — of Judea, beginning from
1056 3326 908 3739 2784 2491
τῆς Γαλιλαίας, μετὰ τὸ βάπτισμα ὃ ἐκήρυξεν Ἰωάννης·
— Galilee after the baptism which proclaimed John;
2424 575 3478 5613 5548 846 2316 4151
38 Ἰησοῦν τὸν ἀπὸ Ναζαρέθ, ὡς ἔχρισεν αὐτὸν ὁ Θεὸς Πνεύ-
Jesus the (One) from Nazareth, how anointed Him God with (the)
40 1411 3739 1330 2109 2390
ματι Ἁγίῳ καὶ δυνάμει, ὃς διῆλθεν εὐεργετῶν καὶ ἰώμενος
Spirit Holy, and with power, who went about doing good and healing
3956 2616 5259 1228 3754
πάντας τοὺς καταδυναστευομένους ὑπὸ τοῦ διαβόλου, ὅτι
all those having been oppressed by the Devil, because
2316/2258/3326/ 846 2249 2070/ 3144 3956 3739
39 ὁ Θεὸς ἦν μετ᾽ αὐτοῦ. καὶ ἡμεῖς ἐσμεν μάρτυρες πάντων ὧν
God was with Him. And we are witnesses of all things which
4160 1722/5037 5561 2453 1722 2419
ἐποίησεν ἔν τε τῇ χώρᾳ τῶν Ἰουδαίων καὶ ἐν Ἱερουσαλήμ·
He did, in both the country of the Jews and in Jerusalem;
3739 337 2910 1909 3586 5126 2316 1453
40 ὃν ἀνεῖλον κρεμάσαντες ἐπὶ ξύλου. τοῦτον ὁ Θεὸς ἤγειρε τῇ
whom they did away (with) hanging on a tree. This One God raised the
5154 2250 1325 846 1717 1096 3756 3956
41 τρίτῃ ἡμέρᾳ, καὶ ἔδωκεν αὐτὸν ἐμφανῆ γενέσθαι, οὐ παντὶ
third day, and gave Him visible to become, not to all
2992 235 3144 4401 5259
τῷ λαῷ, ἀλλὰ μάρτυσι τοῖς προκεχειροτονημένοις ὑπὸ
the people, but to witnesses, those having been before hand-picked by
4844 2316 2254 3748 4906 846
τοῦ Θεοῦ, ἡμῖν, οἵτινες συνεφάγομεν καὶ συνεπίομεν αὐτῷ
— God, to us, who ate with and drank with Him
3326 450 846 1537 3498 3853
42 μετὰ τὸ ἀναστῆναι αὐτὸν ἐκ νεκρῶν. καὶ παρήγγειλεν
after the rising again (of) Him out of (the) dead. And He commanded
2254 2784 2992 1263 3754 846
ἡμῖν κηρύξαι τῷ λαῷ, καὶ διαμαρτύρασθαι ὅτι αὐτός
us to proclaim to the people, and to solemnly witness that He
2076 3724 5259 2316 2923 2198 3498
ἐστιν ὁ ὡρισμένος ὑπὸ τοῦ Θεοῦ κριτὴς ζώντων καὶ νεκρῶν.
it is who has been marked out by God (as) judge of living and of dead.
5129 3956 4396 3140 859 266
43 τούτῳ πάντες οἱ προφῆται μαρτυροῦσιν, ἄφεσιν ἁμαρτιῶν
To this One all the prophets witness, forgiveness of sins
2983 1223 3686 848 3956 4100
λαβεῖν διὰ τοῦ ὀνόματος αὐτοῦ πάντα τὸν πιστεύοντα
to receive through the name of Him everyone — believing
1519 846
εἰς αὐτόν.
in Him.
2089 2980 4074 4487 5023 1968
44 Ἔτι λαλοῦντος τοῦ Πέτρου τὰ ῥήματα ταῦτα, ἐπέπεσε τὸ
(As) yet speaking — Peter — words these, fell the

the faithful of *the* circumcision were amazed, as many as came with Peter, because the gift of the Holy Spirit was poured out on the nations also. [46]For they heard them speaking in languages, and magnifying God. Then Peter answered, [47]Can anyone forbid the water that these not be baptized, who the Holy Spirit received, even as we also? [48]And he commanded them to be baptized in the name of the Lord. Then they asked him to remain some days.

CHAPTER 11

[1]And the apostles and the brothers who were throughout Judea heard that the nations also received the word of God. [2]And when Peter went up to Jerusalem, those of the circumcision contended with him, [3]saying, You went in to uncircumcised men, and ate with them. [4]But beginning, Peter set out to them in order, saying, [5]I was being in *the* city of Joppa, praying. And in an ecstasy, I saw a vision: a certain vessel *was* coming down, like a huge sheet, being let down by four corners out of the heaven; and it came as far as me. [6]Looking intently on *this*, I observed. And I saw the four-footed animals of the earth, and the wild beasts, and the creeping things, and the birds of the heaven. [7]And I heard a voice saying to me, Peter, rise up, slay and eat. [8]But I said, Not at all, Lord, because never *has* anything common or unclean entered into my mouth. [9]But a voice answered me

4151 40 1909 3956 191 3056
Πνεῦμα τὸ Ἅγιον ἐπὶ πάντας τοὺς ἀκούοντας τὸν λόγον.
Spirit — Holy on all those hearing the word.
1839 1537 4061 4103 3745 4905
45 καὶ ἐξέστησαν οἱ ἐκ περιτομῆς πιστοί, ὅσοι συνῆλθον τῷ
And were amazed those of circumcision faithful, as many as came with —
4074/3754 1909 1484 1431 40 4151
Πέτρῳ, ὅτι καὶ ἐπὶ τὰ ἔθνη ἡ δωρεὰ τοῦ Ἁγίου Πνεύματος
Peter, because also on the nations the gift of the Holy Spirit
1632 191 1063 846 2980 1100
46 ἐκκέχυται. ἤκουον γὰρ αὐτῶν λαλούντων γλώσσαις, καὶ
was poured out. they heard For them speaking in languages, and
3170 2316 5119 611 4074 3385
μεγαλυνόντων τὸν Θεόν. τότε ἀπεκρίθη ὁ Πέτρος, Μήτι
magnifying — God. Then answered — Peter, Not
5204 2967 1410 5100 3361 907 5128
47 τὸ ὕδωρ κωλῦσαι δύναταί τις, τοῦ μὴ βαπτισθῆναι τούτους,
the water forbid can anyone, — not to be baptized these,
3748 4151 40 2983 2531 2249 4367
οἵτινες τὸ Πνεῦμα τὸ Ἅγιον ἔλαβον καθὼς καὶ ἡμεῖς; προσ-
who the Spirit — Holy received even as also we? he com-
5037 846 907 1722 3686 2962
48 έταξέ τε αὐτοὺς βαπτισθῆναι ἐν τῷ ὀνόματι τοῦ Κυρίου.
manded. And them to be baptized in the name of the Lord.
5119 2065 846 1961 2250 5100
τότε ἠρώτησαν αὐτὸν ἐπιμεῖναι ἡμέρας τινάς.
Then they asked him to remain days some.

CHAPTER 11

191 652 80 5607 2596
1 Ἤκουσαν δὲ οἱ ἀπόστολοι καὶ οἱ ἀδελφοὶ οἱ ὄντες κατὰ
heard And the apostles and the brothers — being throughout
2449 3754 1484 1209 3056 2316
τὴν Ἰουδαίαν ὅτι καὶ τὰ ἔθνη ἐδέξαντο τὸν λόγον τοῦ Θεοῦ.
— Judea that also the nations received the word — of God.
3753 305 4074 1519 2414 1252 4314 846
2 καὶ ὅτε ἀνέβη Πέτρος εἰς Ἱεροσόλυμα, διεκρίνοντο πρὸς αὐτὸν
And when went Peter to Jerusalem, disputed with him
1537 4061 3004 3754 4314 435 203
3 οἱ ἐκ περιτομῆς, λέγοντες ὅτι Πρὸς ἄνδρας ἀκροβυστίαν
those of circumcision, saying, — To men uncircumcision
2192 1525 4906 846 756
4 ἔχοντας εἰσῆλθες, καὶ συνέφαγες αὐτοῖς. ἀρξάμενος δὲ ὁ
having you went in, and you ate with them. beginning And,
4074 1620 846 2517 3004 1473 2252/1722/4172
5 Πέτρος ἐξετίθετο αὐτοῖς καθεξῆς λέγων, Ἐγὼ ἤμην ἐν πόλει
Peter explained to them in order, saying, I was being in (the) city
2445 4336 1492/1722/ 1611 3705 2597
Ἰόππῃ προσευχόμενος, καὶ εἶδον ἐν ἐκστάσει ὅραμα, κατα-
of Joppa praying, and I saw in an ecstasy a vision, coming
4632 5100/5613 3607 3173 5064 746
βαῖνον σκεῦός τι, ὡς ὀθόνην μεγάλην τέσσαρσιν ἀρχαῖς
down a vessel certain, as a sheet great by four corners
2524 1537 3772 2064 891 1700 1519/3739
6 καθιεμένην ἐκ τοῦ οὐρανοῦ, καὶ ἦλθεν ἄχρις ἐμοῦ· εἰς ἣν
being let down out of the heaven, and it came to me; into which
816 2657 1492 5074 1093
ἀτενίσας κατενόουν, καὶ εἶδον τὰ τετράποδα τῆς γῆς καὶ
gazing I perceived, and I saw the quadrupeds of the earth, and
2342 2062 4071 3772 191
7 τὰ θηρία καὶ τὰ ἑρπετὰ καὶ τὰ πετεινὰ τοῦ οὐρανοῦ. ἤκουσα
the beasts, and the reptiles, and the birds of the heaven. I heard
5456 3004 3427 450 4074 2380 5315
δὲ φωνῆς λεγούσης μοι, Ἀναστάς, Πέτρε, θῦσον καὶ φάγε.
And a voice saying to me, Rise up, Peter; slay and eat.
2036 3365 2962 3754 3956 2839 2228 169
8 εἶπον δέ, Μηδαμῶς, Κύριε· ὅτι πᾶν κοινὸν ἢ ἀκάθαρτον
I said And, Not at all, Lord, because anything common or unclean
3762 1525 1519 4750 3450 611 3427 5456
9 οὐδέποτε εἰσῆλθεν εἰς τὸ στόμα μου. ἀπεκρίθη δέ μοι φωνὴ
never entered into the mouth of me. answered And me a voice

the second *time* out of the heaven. What God has cleansed, you do not make common. [10]And this took place three *times;* and all things were pulled up into the heaven again.

[11]And, behold, at once three men stood at the house in which I was, having been sent from Caesarea to me. [12]And the Spirit said to me to go with them, not discriminating. And these six brothers also *were* with me,and we went into the man's house. [13]And he told us how he saw an angel in his house, standing and saying to him, Send men to Joppa, and send for Simon who is surnamed Peter, [14]who will speak words to you by which you and all your household will be saved. [15]And in my beginning to speak, the Holy Spirit fell on them, even as also on us in *the* beginning. [16]And I recalled the word of *the* Lord, how He said, John indeed baptized with water, but you shall be baptized in *the* Holy Spirit. [17]Then if God gave the same gift to them as also to us, believing on the Lord Jesus Christ,—and I, who was I *to be* able to prevent God? [18]And hearing these things, they kept silent, and glorified God, saying, Then God also has granted to the nations repentance unto life.

[19]Then, indeed, they who were scattered by the oppression taking place over Stephen passed through to Phoenicia and Cyprus and Antioch, speaking the word to no one except only to Jews. [20]But some men from them Cypriots and Cyrenians, who had come to Antioch,

1537 1208 1537 3772 3739 2316 2511 4771/3361
ἐκ δευτέρου ἐκ τοῦ οὐρανοῦ, Ἃ ὁ Θεὸς ἐκαθάρισε, σὺ μὴ
a second (time) out of — Heaven, What God has cleansed, you not
2840 5124 1096 1909 5151 3825 385
10 κοίνου. τοῦτο δὲ ἐγένετο ἐπὶ τρίς, καὶ πάλιν ἀνεσπάσθη
make common. this And happened on three, and again were pulled up
537 1519 3772 2400 1824 5140 435
11 ἅπαντα εἰς τὸν οὐρανόν. καὶ ἰδού, ἐξαυτῆς τρεῖς ἄνδρες
all things into — Heaven. And, behold, at once three men
2186 1909 3614 1722/3739/2252 549 575
ἐπέστησαν ἐπὶ τὴν οἰκίαν ἐν ᾗ ἤμην, ἀπεσταλμένοι ἀπὸ
stood at the house in which I was, having been sent from
2542 4314/3165/2036 3427 4151 4905 846
12 Καισαρείας πρός με. εἶπε δέ μοι τὸ Πνεῦμα συνελθεῖν αὐτοῖς,
Caesarea to me. said And to me the Spirit to go with them,
3367 1252 2064 4862 1698 1803 80
μηδὲν διακρινόμενον. ἦλθον δὲ σὺν ἐμοὶ καὶ οἱ ἓξ ἀδελφοὶ
nothing discriminating. came And with me also — six brothers
3778 1525 1519 3624 435 518
οὗτοι, καὶ εἰσήλθομεν εἰς τὸν οἶκον τοῦ ἀνδρός· ἀπήγγειλέ
these, and we entered into the house of the man. he reported
5037/2254/4459/1492 32 1722 3624 848 2476
13 τε ἡμῖν πῶς εἶδε τὸν ἄγγελον ἐν τῷ οἴκῳ αὐτοῦ σταθέντα,
And to us how he saw the angel in the house of him standing,
2036 846 649 1519 2445 435
καὶ εἰπόντα αὐτῷ, Ἀπόστειλον εἰς Ἰόππην ἄνδρας, καὶ
and saying to him, Send forth to Joppa men, and
3343 4613 1941 4074 3739 2980
14 μετάπεμψαι Σίμωνα, τὸν ἐπικαλούμενον Πέτρον, ὃς λαλήσει
send for Simon, the (one) surnamed Peter, who will speak
4487 4314/4571/1722/3739/ 4982 4771 3956 3624 4675
ῥήματα πρός σε, ἐν οἷς σωθήσῃ σὺ καὶ πᾶς ὁ οἶκός σου.
words to you, by which will be saved you and all the house of you.
1722 756 3165 2980 1968 4151 40
15 ἐν δὲ τῷ ἄρξασθαί με λαλεῖν, ἐπέπεσε τὸ Πνεῦμα τὸ Ἅγιον
in And beginning me to speak, fell the Spirit — Holy
1909 846 5618 1909 2248/1722/746 3415
16 ἐπ' αὐτούς, ὥσπερ καὶ ἐφ' ἡμᾶς ἐν ἀρχῇ. ἐμνήσθην δὲ τοῦ
on them, as also on us at first. I remembered And the
4487 2962 5613 3004 2491 3303 907 5204
ῥήματος Κυρίου, ὡς ἔλεγεν, Ἰωάννης μὲν ἐβάπτισεν ὕδατι,
word of (the) Lord, how He said, John indeed baptized with water,
5210 907 1722 4151 40 1487/3767 2470
17 ὑμεῖς δὲ βαπτισθήσεσθε ἐν Πνεύματι Ἁγίῳ. εἰ οὖν τὴν ἴσην
you but will be baptized in (the) Spirit Holy. If, then, the same
1431 1325 846 2316/5613 2254 4100 1909
δωρεὰν ἔδωκεν αὐτοῖς ὁ Θεὸς ὡς καὶ ἡμῖν, πιστεύσασιν ἐπὶ
gift gave them God, as also to us, having believed on
2962 2424 5547 1473 5101 2252 1415
τὸν Κύριον Ἰησοῦν Χριστόν, ἐγὼ δὲ τίς ἤμην δυνατὸς
the Lord Jesus Christ I, and who was able
2967 2316 191 5023 2270
18 κωλῦσαι τὸν Θεόν; ἀκούσαντες δὲ ταῦτα ἡσύχασαν, καὶ
to prevent God? hearing And these things, they kept silent, and
1392 2316 3004 686 1484 2316
ἐδόξαζον τὸν Θεόν, λέγοντες, Ἄραγε καὶ τοῖς ἔθνεσιν ὁ Θεὸς
glorified God, saying, Then also to the nations God
3341 1325 1519 2222
τὴν μετάνοιαν ἔδωκεν εἰς ζωήν.
— repentance has given unto life.
3303/3767 1289 575 2347 1096
19 Οἱ μὲν οὖν διασπαρέντες ἀπὸ τῆς θλίψεως τῆς γενομένης
they indeed Then who were scattered from the affliction — occurring
1909 4736 1330 2193 5403 2954
ἐπὶ Στεφάνῳ διῆλθον ἕως Φοινίκης καὶ Κύπρου καὶ
over Stephen passed through to Phoenicia and Cyprus and
490 3367 2980 3056 =1508= 3440
Ἀντιοχείας, μηδενὶ λαλοῦντες τὸν λόγον εἰ μὴ μόνον
Antioch, to no one speaking the word except only
2453 2258 5100/1537/846 435 2953 2956
20 Ἰουδαίοις. ἦσαν δέ τινες ἐξ αὐτῶν ἄνδρες Κύπριοι καὶ Κυρη-
to Jews. were But some of them men, Cypriots and Cyren-

spoke to the Hellenists, preaching the gospel of the Lord Jesus. [21]And *the* hand of *the* Lord was with them, and a great number believing, *they* turned to the Lord.

[22]And the word was heard in the ears of the church in Jerusalem concerning them. And they sent out Barnabas to go through as far as Antioch; [23]who having come, and seeing the grace of God, rejoiced. And *he* exhorted all with purpose of heart to abide near the Lord. [24]For he was a good man, and full of *the* Holy Spirit, and of faith. And a considerable crowd was added to the Lord. [25]And Barnabas went out to Tarsus to seek Saul. [26]And finding him, he brought him to Antioch. And it happened that *many* of them were gathered to them in the church a whole year. And they taught a considerable crowd. And the disciples were first called Christians *at* Antioch.

[27]And in these days prophets came down from Jerusalem to Antioch. [28]And one of them named Agabus rising up, *he* signified through the Spirit that a great famine was about to be over all the habitable earth—which also happened on Claudius Caesar's *time.* [29]And according as any was prospered, the disciples, each of them determined to send to those living in Judea to minister *to the;* brothers [30]which they also did, sending to the elders through *the* hand of Barnabas and Saul.

3748 1525 1519 490 2980 4314
ναῖοι, οἵτινες εἰσελθόντες εἰς Ἀντιόχειαν, ἐλάλουν πρὸς τοὺς
ians, who coming to Antioch spoke to the
1675 2097 2962 2424 2258
21 Ἑλληνιστάς, εὐαγγελιζόμενοι τὸν Κύριον Ἰησοῦν. καὶ ἦν
Hellenists, preaching the gospel of the Lord Jesus. And was
5495 2962 3326 846 4183 5037/706 4100 1994
χεὶρ Κυρίου μετ' αὐτῶν· πολύς τε ἀριθμὸς πιστεύσας ἐπέ-
hand (the) Lord's with them, a much and number, believing
1909 2962 191 3056/1519 3775
22 στρεψεν ἐπὶ τὸν Κύριον. ἠκούσθη δὲ ὁ λόγος εἰς τὰ ὦτα τῆς
turned upon the Lord. was heard And the word into the ears of the
1577 1722 2414 4012 846 1821
ἐκκλησίας τῆς ἐν Ἱεροσολύμοις περὶ αὐτῶν· καὶ ἐξαπέστειλαν
church — in Jerusalem about them; and they sent forth
921 1330 2193 490 3739 3854
23 Βαρνάβαν διελθεῖν ἕως Ἀντιοχείας· ὃς παραγενόμενος καὶ
Barnabas to go through to Antioch; who having come and
1492 5485 2316 5463 3870 3956
ἰδὼν τὴν χάριν τοῦ Θεοῦ ἐχάρη, καὶ παρεκάλει πάντας τῇ
seeing the grace of God rejoiced, and exhorted all —
4286 2588 4357 2962 3754/2258/435
24 προθέσει τῆς καρδίας προσμένειν τῷ Κυρίῳ· ὅτι ἦν ἀνὴρ
with purpose of heart to remain near the Lord; for he was a man
18 4134 4151 40 4102
ἀγαθὸς καὶ πλήρης Πνεύματος Ἁγίου καὶ πίστεως· καὶ
good, and full of (the) Spirit Holy and of faith. And
4369 3793 2425 2962 1831 1519 5019
25 προσετέθη ὄχλος ἱκανὸς τῷ Κυρίῳ. ἐξῆλθε δὲ εἰς Ταρσὸν ὁ
was added a crowd sufficient to the Lord. went And to Tarsus
921 327 4569 2147 846 71
26 Βαρνάβας ἀναζητῆσαι Σαῦλον, καὶ εὑρὼν αὐτὸν ἤγαγεν
Barnabas to seek Saul, and finding him he led
846 1519 490 1096 846 1763 3650
αὐτὸν εἰς Ἀντιόχειαν. ἐγένετο δὲ αὐτοὺς ἐνιαυτὸν ὅλον
him to Antioch. it was And, to them a year whole
4863 1722 1577 1321 3793 2425 5537
συναχθῆναι ἐν τῇ ἐκκλησίᾳ καὶ διδάξαι ὄχλον ἱκανόν, χρη-
were assembled in the church, and taught a crowd considerable,
5037 4412 1722 490 3101 5546
ματίσαι τε πρῶτον ἐν Ἀντιοχείᾳ τοὺς μαθητὰς Χριστιανούς.
were called and (at) first in Antioch the disciples Christians.
1722 5025 2250 2718 575 2414
27 Ἐν ταύταις δὲ ταῖς ἡμέραις κατῆλθον ἀπὸ Ἱεροσολύμων
in these And days came down from Jerusalem
4396 1519 490 450 1520/1537/846 3686
28 προφῆται εἰς Ἀντιόχειαν. ἀναστὰς δὲ εἷς ἐξ αὐτῶν ὀνόματι
prophets to Antioch. having risen And one of them by name
13 4591 1223 4151 3042 3173 3195
Ἄγαβος, ἐσήμανε διὰ τοῦ Πνεύματος λιμὸν μέγαν μέλλειν
Agabus signified through the Spirit a famine great to be about
1510 1909/3650 3625 3748 1096 1909
ἔσεσθαι ἐφ' ὅλην τὴν οἰκουμένην· ὅστις καὶ ἐγένετο ἐπὶ
to be over all the inhabited earth; which also happened on
2804 2541 3101 2531 2141 5100
29 Κλαυδίου Καίσαρος. τῶν δὲ μαθητῶν καθὼς ηὐπορεῖτό τις,
(the time) of Claudius Caesar. the And disciples, as was prospered any,
3724 1538 846 1519 1248 3992 2730
ὥρισαν ἕκαστος αὐτῶν εἰς διακονίαν πέμψαι τοῖς κατοι-
determined each of them for ministration to send to those
1722 2449 80 3739 4160 649
30 κοῦσιν ἐν τῇ Ἰουδαίᾳ ἀδελφοῖς· ὃ καὶ ἐποίησαν, ἀποστεί-
living in — Judea brothers; which also they did, sending
4314 4245 1223 5495 921
λαντες πρὸς τοὺς πρεσβυτέρους διὰ χειρὸς Βαρνάβα καὶ
to the elders through (the) hand of Barnabas and
4569
Σαύλου.
of Saul.

CHAPTER 12

CHAPTER 12

1And at that time Herod the king threw on the hands to oppress some of the church. 2And He did away with James the brother of John, with a sword. 3And seeing that it was pleasing to the Jews, he added also to seize Peter—and they were *the* days of unleavened *bread*—4also capturing *him*, he put *him* into prison, delivering *him* to four sets of four soldiers to guard him; intending to bring him up to the people after the Passover. 5Then Peter was indeed kept in the prison; but fervent prayer was made by the church to God on his behalf. 6But when Herod was about to bring him out, in that night Peter was sleeping between two soldiers, being bound with two chains, also guards were keeping the prison before the door. 7And, behold, an angel of *the* Lord stood by, and a light shone in the building. And striking Peter's side, he raised him up, saying, Rise up in haste! And the chains fell off from his hands. 8And the angel said to him, Gird yourself, and put on your sandals. And he did so. And he said to him, Throw around your garment, and follow me. 9And going out, he followed him, and did not know that this happening through the angel was real; but he thought he saw a vision. 10And going through a first and a second guard, they came on the iron gate carrying *one* into the city, which opened to them of itself. And going out, they went on one street; and instantly the

2596 1565 2540 1911 2254 935
1 Κατ' ἐκεῖνον δὲ τὸν καιρὸν ἐπέβαλεν Ἡρώδης ὁ βασιλεὺς
at that And – time threw on Herod the king
5495 2559 5100 575 1577 337
2 τὰς χεῖρας κακῶσαί τινας τῶν ἀπὸ τῆς ἐκκλησίας. ἀνεῖλε δὲ
the hands to oppress some of those from the church. he did away And
2385 80 2491 3162 1492/3754
3 Ἰάκωβον τὸν ἀδελφὸν Ἰωάννου μαχαίρᾳ. καὶ ἰδὼν ὅτι ἀρε-
James the brother of John with a sword. And seeing that
701 2076 2453 4369 4815 4074
στόν ἐστι τοῖς Ἰουδαίοις, προσέθετο συλλαβεῖν καὶ Πέτρον·
pleasing is to the Jews, he added to seize also Peter;
2258 2250 106 3739 4084 5087 1519/ 5438
4 ἦσαν δὲ ἡμέραι τῶν ἀζύμων· ὃν καὶ πιάσας ἔθετο εἰς φυλακήν,
were and days – of unleaven whom also capturing, he put in prison,
3860 5064 5069 4757 5442
παραδοὺς τέσσαρσι τετραδίοις στρατιωτῶν φυλάσσειν
delivering to four quaternions of soldiers to guard
846 1014 3326 3957 321 846
αὐτόν, βουλόμενος μετὰ τὸ πάσχα ἀναγαγεῖν αὐτὸν τῷ
him; intending after the Passover to lead up him to the
2992 3303/3767 4074 5083 1722 5438 4335
5 λαῷ. ὁ μὲν οὖν Πέτρος ἐτηρεῖτο ἐν τῇ φυλακῇ· προσευχὴ
people. indeed Then Peter was kept in the prison; prayer
2258/ 1618 1096 5259 1577 4314 2316
δὲ ἦν ἐκτενὴς γινομένη ὑπὸ τῆς ἐκκλησίας πρὸς τὸν Θεὸν
But was earnestly being made by the church to God
5228 846 3753 3195 846 4254 2264
6 ὑπὲρ αὐτοῦ. ὅτε δὲ ἔμελλεν αὐτὸν προάγειν ὁ Ἡρώδης, τῇ
about him. when And was about him to lead forth – Herod, –
3571 1565/2258 4074 2837 3342 1417 4757
νυκτὶ ἐκείνῃ ἦν ὁ Πέτρος κοιμώμενος μεταξὺ δύο στρατιω-
in night that was Peter sleeping between two soldiers,
1210 254 1417 5441 5037 4253 2374
τῶν, δεδεμένος ἁλύσεσι δυσί· φύλακές τε πρὸ τῆς θύρας
having been bound with chains two; guards and before the door
5083 5438 2400 32 2962 2186
7 ἐτήρουν τὴν φυλακήν. καὶ ἰδού, ἄγγελος Κυρίου ἐπέστη, καὶ
were keeping the prison. And behold, an angel of (the) Lord stood by, and
5457 2989 1722 3612 3960 4125
φῶς ἔλαμψεν ἐν τῷ οἰκήματι· πατάξας δὲ τὴν πλευρὰν τοῦ
a light shone in the building; striking and the side –
4074 1453 846 3004 450 1722/5034 1601
Πέτρου, ἤγειρεν αὐτὸν λέγων, Ἀνάστα ἐν τάχει. καὶ ἐξέπεσον
of Peter, he raised him, saying, Rise up in haste. And fell off
848 254 1537 5495 2036/5037 32 4314
8 αὐτοῦ αἱ ἁλύσεις ἐκ τῶν χειρῶν. εἶπέ τε ὁ ἄγγελος πρὸς
of him the chains from the hands. said And the angel to
846 4024 5265 4547 4675 4160
αὐτόν, Περίζωσαι καὶ ὑπόδησαι τὰ σανδάλιά σου. ἐποίησε
him, Gird yourself, and put on the sandals of you. he did
3779 3004 846 4016 2440 4675
δὲ οὕτω. καὶ λέγει αὐτῷ, Περιβαλοῦ τὸ ἱμάτιόν σου, καὶ
And so. And he says to him, Throw around the garment of you, and
190 3427 1831 190 846 3756/1492/3754
9 ἀκολούθει μοι. καὶ ἐξελθὼν ἠκολούθει αὐτῷ· καὶ οὐκ ᾔδει ὅτι
follow me. And going out he followed him, and not knew that
227 2076 1096 1223 32 1380 3705
ἀληθές ἐστι τὸ γινόμενον διὰ τοῦ ἀγγέλου, ἐδόκει δὲ ὅραμα
true was that happening through the angel; he thought but a vision
991 1330 4413 5438 1208 2064
10 βλέπειν. διελθόντες δὲ πρώτην φυλακὴν καὶ δευτέραν, ἦλθον
to see. going through And (the) first guard and (the) second, they came
1909 4439 4603 5342 1519 3825
ἐπὶ τὴν πύλην τὴν σιδηρᾶν, τὴν φέρουσαν εἰς τὴν πόλιν,
on the gate – iron – carrying (one) to the city,
3748 844 455 846 1831 4281
ἥτις αὐτομάτη ἠνοίχθη αὐτοῖς· καὶ ἐξελθόντες προῆλθον
which of itself was opened to them; and going out they went on

angel withdrew from him. [11]And having come, Peter said within himself, Now I know truly that *the* Lord sent out His angel and plucked me out of Herod's hand, and *out* of all the expectation of the people of the Jews. [12]And considering, he came to the house of Mary the mother of John, the *one* being surnamed Mark, where many were gathered together, and praying. [13]And Peter *was* knocking *at* the door of the porch, *and* a servant-girl named Rhoda came near to listen. [14]And recognizing Peter's voice, from joy she did not open the porch, but running in she reported Peter *was* standing before the porch. [15]But they said to her, You are raving. But she insisted, holding *it* to be so. And they said, It is his angel. [16]But Peter kept on knocking. And opening, they saw him, and were amazed. [17]And signaling to them with the hand to be silent, he told them how the Lord led him out of the prison. And he said, Report these things to James and the brothers. And going out, he went to another place.

[18]And day having come, there was not a little disturbance among the soldiers, *saying,* What, then, became of Peter? [19]And searching for him, and not finding *him,* examining the guards, Herod commanded *them* to be led away. And going down from Judea to Caesarea, *he* stayed.

[20]And Herod was in bitter hostility with *the* Tyrians and Sidonians. But with one passion they came to him. And persuading

4505 3391 2112 863 32 575 846
11 ῥύμην μίαν, καὶ εὐθέως ἀπέστη ὁ ἄγγελος ἀπ' αὐτοῦ. καὶ ὁ
street one; and instantly withdrew the angel from him. And
4074 1096 1722 1438 2036 3568 1492 230 3754
Πέτρος, γενόμενος ἐν ἑαυτῷ, εἶπε, Νῦν οἶδα ἀληθῶς ὅτι
Peter having come with in himself said, Now I know truly that
1821 2962 32 848 1807 3165/1537
ἐξαπέστειλε Κύριος τὸν ἄγγελον αὐτοῦ, καὶ ἐξείλετό με ἐκ
sent out (the) Lord the angel of Him, and plucked me out of
5495 2264 3956 4329 2992
χειρὸς Ἡρῴδου καὶ πάσης τῆς προσδοκίας τοῦ λαοῦ τῶν
hand Herod's, and of all the expectation of the people of the
2453 4894 5037 2064 1909 3614 3137
12 Ἰουδαίων. συνιδών τε ἦλθεν ἐπὶ τὴν οἰκίαν Μαρίας τῆς
Jews. considering And he came to the house of Mary the
3384 2491 1941 3138 3757 2258
μητρὸς Ἰωάννου τοῦ ἐπικαλουμένου Μάρκου, οὗ ἦσαν
mother of John, — surnamed Mark, where were
2425 4867 4336 2925
13 ἱκανοὶ συνηθροισμένοι καὶ προσευχόμενοι. κρούσαντος δὲ
many gathered together and praying. knocking And
4074 2374 4440 4334 3814
τοῦ Πέτρου τὴν θύραν τοῦ πυλῶνος, προσῆλθε παιδίσκη
— Peter (at) the door of the porch, came near a maidservant
5219 3686 4498 1921 5456
14 ὑπακοῦσαι, ὀνόματι Ῥόδη. καὶ ἐπιγνοῦσα τὴν φωνὴν τοῦ
to listen, by name Rhoda. And recognizing the voice —
4074 575 5479/3756 455 4440 1532
Πέτρου, ἀπὸ τῆς χαρᾶς οὐκ ἤνοιξε τὸν πυλῶνα, εἰσδραμοῦσα
of Peter, from — joy not she opened the porch, running
518 2476 4074 4253 4440
15 δὲ ἀπήγγειλεν ἑστάναι τὸν Πέτρον πρὸ τοῦ πυλῶνος. οἱ δὲ
but reported to stand — Peter before the porch. they But
4314 846 2036 3105 1340 3779 2192
πρὸς αὐτὴν εἶπον, Μαίνῃ. ἡ δὲ διϊσχυρίζετο οὕτως ἔχειν.
to her said, You are raving. she But insisted so (it) to hold.
3004 32 848 2076 4074 1961
16 οἱ δ' ἔλεγον, Ὁ ἄγγελος αὐτοῦ ἐστιν. ὁ δὲ Πέτρος ἐπέμενε
they And said, The angel of him it is. But Peter continued
2925 455 1492 846 1839 2678
κρούων· ἀνοίξαντες δὲ εἶδον αὐτόν, καὶ ἐξέστησαν. κατα-
knocking; having opened and they saw him, and were amazed.
846 5495 4601 1334 846 4459
17 σείσας δὲ αὐτοῖς τῇ χειρὶ σιγᾶν, διηγήσατο αὐτοῖς πῶς ὁ
signaling And to them with the hand to be silent, he told them how the
2962 846 1806 1537 5438 2036 518
Κύριος αὐτὸν ἐξήγαγεν ἐκ τῆς φυλακῆς. εἶπε δέ, Ἀπαγγεί-
Lord him led out from the prison. he said And, Report
2385 80 5023 1831 4198
λατε Ἰακώβῳ καὶ τοῖς ἀδελφοῖς ταῦτα. καὶ ἐξελθὼν ἐπορεύθη
to James and the brothers these things. And going out he went
1519 2087 5117 1096 2250 2258 5017 3756
18 εἰς ἕτερον τόπον. γενομένης δὲ ἡμέρας, ἦν τάραχος οὐκ
to another place. becoming And day, there was disturbance not
3641 1722 4757 686 4074 1096
ὀλίγος ἐν τοῖς στρατιώταις, τί ἄρα ὁ Πέτρος ἐγένετο.
a little among the soldiers: what then (of) Peter became?
2264 1934 846 3361 2147 350
19 Ἡρῴδης δὲ ἐπιζητήσας αὐτὸν καὶ μὴ εὑρών, ἀνακρίνας
Herod And searching for him, and not finding, examining
5441 2753 520 2718 575
τοὺς φύλακας, ἐκέλευσεν ἀπαχθῆναι. καὶ κατελθὼν ἀπὸ τῆς
the guards, commanded to be led away; and going down from —
2449 1519 2542 1304
Ἰουδαίας εἰς τὴν Καισάρειαν διέτριβεν.
Judea to — Caesarea stayed.
2258 2264 2371 5183 4506
20 Ἦν δὲ ὁ Ἡρῴδης θυμομαχῶν Τυρίοις καὶ Σιδωνίοις·
was And Herod in bitter hostility with Tyrians and Sidonians;
3661 3918 4314 846 3982 986
ὁμοθυμαδὸν δὲ παρῆσαν πρὸς αὐτόν, καὶ πείσαντες Βλάστον
with one mind and they came to him, and persuading Blastus,

Blastus, the *one* over the
king's bedroom, they
begged peace — because
their country was fed from
the royal *bounty.* [21]And on
a set day, having been
clothed in a regal garment,
and sitting on the tribunal,
Herod made a speech to
them. [22]And the mass *of*
people cried out, *The* voice
of a god, and not of a man!
[23]And instantly an angel of
the Lord struck him,
because he did not give the
glory to God. And having
been eaten by worms, his
soul went out.
[24]But the word of God
grew and increased.
[25]And Barnabas and Saul
returned from Jerusalem,
having fulfilled the service,
and taking with *them,* the
one surnamed Mark.

1909 2846 937 154 1515 1223
τὸν ἐπὶ τοῦ κοιτῶνος τοῦ βασιλέως, ᾐτοῦντο εἰρήνην, διὰ τὸ
the (one) over the bedroom of the king, they asked peace, because the
5142 848 5561 575 935 5002
21 τρέφεσθαι αὐτῶν τὴν χώραν ἀπὸ τῆς βασιλικῆς. τακτῇ δὲ
feeding of them the country from the royal (bounty). on a set And
2250 2264 1746 2066 937 2523
ἡμέρᾳ ὁ Ἡρώδης ἐνδυσάμενος ἐσθῆτα βασιλικήν, καὶ καθίσας
day, Herod being clothed in a garment regal, and sitting
1909 968 1215 4314 846 1218
22 ἐπὶ τοῦ βήματος, ἐδημηγόρει πρὸς αὐτούς· ὁ δὲ δῆμος
on the tribunal, made a speech to them. the And mass
2019 2316 5456 3756 444 3916
23 ἐπεφώνει, Θεοῦ φωνὴ καὶ οὐκ ἀνθρώπου. παραχρῆμα δὲ
cried out, of a god A voice, and not of a man! immediately And
3960 846 32 2962 473/3739/3756/1325
ἐπάταξεν αὐτὸν ἄγγελος Κυρίου, ἀνθ' ὧν οὐκ ἔδωκε τὴν
struck him an angel of (the) Lord, because not he gave the
1391 2316 1093 4662 1634
δόξαν τῷ Θεῷ· καὶ γενόμενος σκωληκόβρωτος, ἐξέψυξεν.
glory — to God. And becoming eaten by worms, his soul went out.
3056 2316 837 4129
24 Ὁ δὲ λόγος τοῦ Θεοῦ ηὔξανε καὶ ἐπληθύνετο.
the But word — of God grew and increased.
921 4569 5290 1537 2419
25 Βαρνάβας δὲ καὶ Σαῦλος ὑπέστρεψαν ἐξ Ἱερουσαλήμ,
Barnabas And and Saul returned out of Jerusalem
4137 1248 4838 2491
πληρώσαντες τὴν διακονίαν, συμπαραλαβόντες καὶ Ἰωάννην
having fulfilled the service, having taken with (them) and John,
1941 3138
τὸν ἐπικληθέντα Μάρκον.
— being surnamed Mark.

CHAPTER 13

[1]And in Antioch some
among the existing church
were prophets and teachers: both Barnabas and
Simeon, he being called
Niger; and Lucius the Cy-
renian; and Manaen *the*
foster-brother of Herod the
tetrarch; and Saul. [2]And
while they *were* doing
service to the Lord, and
fasting, the Holy Spirit said,
So, then, separate both
Barnabas and Saul to Me,
for the work to which I have
called them.
[3]Then, having fasted and
prayed, and placing hands
on them, they let *them* go.

[4]Then these indeed sent
out by the Holy Spirit went
down to Seleucia, and from
there sailed away to Cyprus.
[5]And having been in
Salamis, they announced

2258 5100/1722 490 2596 5607 1577
1 Ἦσαν δέ τινες ἐν Ἀντιοχείᾳ κατὰ τὴν οὖσαν ἐκκλησίαν
were And some in Antioch among the existing church
4396 1320 3739/5037 921 4826
προφῆται καὶ διδάσκαλοι, ὅ τε Βαρνάβας καὶ Συμεὼν ὁ
prophets and teachers. Both Barnabas and Simeon, he
2563 3526 3066 2956 3127 5037
καλούμενος Νίγερ, καὶ Λούκιος ὁ Κυρηναῖος, Μαναήν τε
being called Niger, and Luicius the Cyrenian, Manaen and
2264 5076 4939 4569 3008
2 Ἡρώδου τοῦ τετράρχου σύντροφος, καὶ Σαῦλος. λειτουρ-
of Herod the tetrarch foster-brother, and Saul. (while) doing service
846 2962 3522 2036
γούντων δὲ αὐτῶν τῷ Κυρίῳ καὶ νηστευόντων, εἶπε τὸ
And they to the Lord, and fasting, said the
4151 40 873 1211/3427 5037 921
Πνεῦμα τὸ Ἅγιον, Ἀφορίσατε δή μοι τόν τε Βαρνάβαν καὶ
Spirit — Holy, separate So then to me — both Barnabas and
4569 1519 2041/3739/ 4341 846 5119 3522
3 τὸν Σαῦλον εἰς τὸ ἔργον ὃ προσκέκλημαι αὐτούς. τότε νηστεύ-
— Saul for the work to which I have called them. Then having
4336 2007 5495 846
σαντες καὶ προσευξάμενοι καὶ ἐπιθέντες τὰς χεῖρας αὐτοῖς,
fasted and having prayed, and placing on the hands to them,
630
ἀπέλυσαν.
they let (them) go.
3778 3303/3756 1599 5259 4151
4 Οὗτοι μὲν οὖν, ἐκπεμφθέντες ὑπὸ τοῦ Πνεύματος τοῦ
These indeed therefore sent out by the Spirit —
40 2718 1519 4581 1564/5037 636
Ἁγίου, κατῆλθον εἰς τὴν Σελεύκειαν, ἐκεῖθέν τε ἀπέπλευσαν
Holy went down to — Seleucia, from there sailed away
1519 2954 1096 1722 4529 2605
5 εἰς τὴν Κύπρον. καὶ γενόμενοι ἐν Σαλαμῖνι, κατήγγελλον τὸν
to — Cyprus. And being in Salamis, they announced the

the word of God in the synagogues of the Jews. And they also had John *as* a helper. [6]And passing through the island as far as Paphos, they found a certain conjurer, a false prophet, a Jew whose name *was* Barjesus. [7]*He* was with the proconsul, Sergius Paulus, an intelligent man. This one having called Barnabas and Saul to *him, he* sought to hear the word of God. [8]But Elymas, the conjurer—for so his name was translated —withstood them, seeking to turn the proconsul away from the faith. [9]But Saul, who *is* also Paul, being filled with *the* Holy Spirit, and looking intently on him, [10]*he* said, O son of the Devil, full of all guile and of all cunning, enemy of all righteousness, will you not stop perverting the right ways of *the* Lord? [11]And now, behold, *the* hand of the Lord *is* on you, and you will be blind, not seeing the sun until a time. And instantly a mist and darkness fell on him; and going about he sought *some to* lead *him* by the hand. [12]Then seeing the thing happening, the proconsul believed, being astounded at the teaching of the Lord.

[13]And putting out from Paphos *with* those around *him*, Paul came to Perga of Pamphylia. And separating from them, John returned to Jerusalem. [14]But going through from Perga, they came to Antioch-Pisidia, and going into the synagogue on the day of the sabbaths, they sat down. [15]And after the reading of the Law, and of the Prophets, the synagogue rulers sent to them, saying,

3056 2316 1722 4864 2453 2192
λόγον τοῦ Θεοῦ ἐν ταῖς συναγωγαῖς τῶν Ἰουδαίων· εἶχον δὲ
word — of God in the synagogues of the Jews. they had And
2491 5257 1330 3520 891
6 καὶ Ἰωάννην ὑπηρέτην. διελθόντες δὲ τὴν νῆσον ἄχρι
also John (as) assistant. passing through And the island as far as
3974 2147 5100 3097 5578 2453 3739
Πάφου, εὗρόν τινα μάγον ψευδοπροφήτην Ἰουδαῖον, ᾧ
Paphos, they found a certain conjurer, a false prophet, a Jew, whose
3686 919 3739/2258/4862 446 4588 3972
7 ὄνομα Βαριησοῦς, ὃς ἦν σὺν τῷ ἀνθυπάτῳ Σεργίῳ Παύλῳ,
name (was) Barjesus, who was with the Proconsul, Sergius Paulus,
435 4908 3778 4341 921
ἀνδρὶ συνετῷ. οὗτος προσκαλεσάμενος Βαρνάβαν καὶ
a man intelligent. This one calling to (him) Barnabas and
4569 1934 191 3056 2316 436
Σαῦλον ἐπεζήτησεν ἀκοῦσαι τὸν λόγον τοῦ Θεοῦ. ἀνθίστατο
Saul sought to hear the word — of God. withstood
846 1681 3097 3779 1063 3177
8 δὲ αὐτοῖς Ἐλύμας, ὁ μάγος (οὕτω γὰρ μεθερμηνεύεται τὸ
But them Elymas, the conjurer so for was translated the
3686 848 2212 1294 446 575
ὄνομα αὐτοῦ), ζητῶν διαστρέψαι τὸν ἀνθύπατον ἀπὸ τῆς
name of him — seeking to turn away the Proconsul from the
4102 4569 3972 4130 4151
9 πίστεως. Σαῦλος δέ, ὁ καὶ Παῦλος, πλησθεὶς Πνεύματος
faith. Saul But, who also (is) Paul, being filled with (the) Spirit
40 816 1519 846 2036 5599 4134 3956
10 Ἁγίου, καὶ ἀτενίσας εἰς αὐτὸν εἶπεν, Ὦ πλήρης παντὸς
Holy, and looking intently on him said, O full of all
1388 3956/4468 5207 1228 2190 3956
δόλου καὶ πάσης ῥᾳδιουργίας, υἱὲ διαβόλου, ἐχθρὲ πάσης
deceit, and of all cunning, son of (the) Devil, enemy of all
1343 3756 3973 1294 3598 2962
δικαιοσύνης, οὐ παύσῃ διαστρέφων τὰς ὁδοὺς Κυρίου τὰς
righteousness, not will you cease turning away the ways of (the) Lord —
2117 3568/2400/5495 2962 1909/4571 2071 5185
11 εὐθείας; καὶ νῦν ἰδού, χεὶρ τοῦ Κυρίου ἐπὶ σέ, καὶ ἔσῃ τυφλός,
right? And now behold, hand the Lord's on you, and you will be blind,
3361 991 2246 891 2540 3916 1968
μὴ βλέπων τὸν ἥλιον ἄχρι καιροῦ. παραχρῆμα δὲ ἐπέπεσεν
not seeing the sun until a time. instantly And fell
1909 846 887 4655 4013 2212 5497
ἐπ' αὐτὸν ἀχλὺς καὶ σκότος, καὶ περιάγων ἐζήτει χειραγω-
on him a mist and darkness, and going about he sought leaders by
5119 1492 446 1096 4100
12 γούς. τότε ἰδὼν ὁ ἀνθύπατος τὸ γεγονὸς ἐπίστευσεν,
the hand. Then seeing the Proconsul the thing having occurred believed,
1805 1909 1322 2962
ἐκπλησσόμενος ἐπὶ τῇ διδαχῇ τοῦ Κυρίου.
being astounded at the teaching of the Lord.
321 575 3974 4012 3972 2064
13 Ἀναχθέντες δὲ ἀπὸ τῆς Πάφου οἱ περὶ τὸν Παῦλον ἦλθον
having put out And from — Paphos those around — Paul came
1519 4011 3828 2491 672 575
εἰς Πέργην τῆς Παμφυλίας. Ἰωάννης δὲ ἀποχωρήσας ἀπ'
to Perga — of Pamphylia. John And having separated from
846 5290 1519 2414 846 1330 575
14 αὐτῶν ὑπέστρεψεν εἰς Ἱεροσόλυμα. αὐτοὶ δὲ διελθόντες ἀπὸ
them returned to Jerusalem. they And going through from
4011 3854 1519 490 4099
τῆς Πέργης, παρεγένοντο εἰς Ἀντιόχειαν τῆς Πισιδίας, καὶ
— Perga arrived in Antioch the Pisidian. And
1525 1519 4864 2250 4521
εἰσελθόντες εἰς τὴν συναγωγὴν τῇ ἡμέρᾳ τῶν σαββάτων,
going into the synagogue on the day of the sabbaths
2523 3326 320 3551
15 ἐκάθισαν. μετὰ δὲ τὴν ἀνάγνωσιν τοῦ νόμου καὶ τῶν
sat down. after And the reading of the Law and of the
4396 649 752 4314 846
προφητῶν, ἀπέστειλαν οἱ ἀρχισυνάγωγοι πρὸς αὐτούς,
Prophets. sent forth the synagogue rulers to them,

Men, brothers, if there is a word of exhortation to the people, speak.

16 And rising up, and signaling with his hand, Paul said:

Men, Israelites, and the ones fearing God, listen. 17 The God of this people Israel chose out our fathers, and exalted the people in *their* stay in *the* land *of* Egypt. And with a high arm, He led them out of it. 18 And as forty years time *passed,* He endured them in the wilderness. 19 And *He* pulled down seven nations in Canaan land *and* gave their land to them as an inheritance.

20 And after these things, as four hundred and fifty years *passed,* He gave judges until Samuel the prophet. 21 And from there they asked *for* a king. And God gave Saul the son of Kish to them, a man of *the* tribe of Benjamin, *for* forty years. 22 And removing him, He raised up to them David for a king, to whom He also said, witnessing, "I found David the *son* of Jesse *to be* a man according to My *own* heart, who will do all My will." 23 Of the seed of this one, according to promise, God raised up to Israel a Savior, Jesus; 24 John going before to proclaim before the face of His entrance a baptism of repentance to all the people of Israel. 25 And as John fulfilled the course, he said, Whom do you suppose me to be? I am not *He*, but, behold, He comes after me, of whom I am not worthy to loosen the sandal of *His* feet. 26 Men, brothers, sons of *the* race of Abraham, and the ones among you fearing

3004 435 80 1487/2076 3056/1722/5213/ 3874
λέγοντες, Ἄνδρες ἀδελφοί, εἰ ἔστι λόγος ἐν ὑμῖν παρακλή-
saying, Men, brothers, if is a word among you of exhort-
4314 2992 3004 450 3972
16 σεως πρὸς τὸν λαόν, λέγετε. ἀναστὰς δὲ Παῦλος, καὶ
ation to the people, say (it). rising up And Paul, and
2678 5495 2036
κατασείσας τῇ χειρί, εἶπεν,
signaling with the hand, he said,
435 2475 5399 2316 191
Ἄνδρες Ἰσραηλῖται, καὶ οἱ φοβούμενοι τὸν Θεόν, ἀκού-
Men, Israelites, and those fearing God,
2316 2992 5127 2474 1586
17 σατε. ὁ Θεὸς τοῦ λαοῦ τούτου Ἰσραὴλ ἐξελέξατο τοὺς
hear: The God of people this Israel chose out the
3962 2257 2992 5312 1722 3940 1722 1093
πατέρας ἡμῶν, καὶ τὸν λαὸν ὕψωσεν ἐν τῇ παροικίᾳ ἐν γῇ
fathers of us, and the people exalted in the sojourn in land
125 3326 1023 5308 1806 846 1537
Αἰγύπτῳ, καὶ μετὰ βραχίονος ὑψηλοῦ ἐξήγαγεν αὐτοὺς ἐξ
(of) Egypt, and with an arm high He led out them out of
846 5613 5063 5550 5159
18 αὐτῆς. καὶ ὡς τεσσαρακονταετῆ χρόνον ἐτροποφόρησεν
it. And as (passed) forty years time, He endured
846 1722 2048 2507 1484 2033/1722/1093/ 5477
19 αὐτοὺς ἐν τῇ ἐρήμῳ. καὶ καθελὼν ἔθνη ἑπτὰ ἐν γῇ Χαναάν,
them in the desert And pulled down nations seven in land Canaan,
2624 846 1093 848 3326 5023
20 κατεκληροδότησεν αὐτοῖς τὴν γῆν αὐτῶν. καὶ μετὰ ταῦτα,
gave as an inheritance to them the land of them. And after these things,
5613 2094 5071 4004 1325 2923 2193
ὡς ἔτεσι τετρακοσίοις καὶ πεντήκοντα, ἔδωκε κριτὰς ἕως
as years four hundred and fifty, He gave judges, until
4545 4396 2547 154 935
21 Σαμουὴλ τοῦ προφήτου. κἀκεῖθεν ᾐτήσαντο βασιλέα, καὶ
Samuel the prophet. And from there they asked a king, and
1325 846 2316 4549 5207 2797 435 1537 5443
ἔδωκεν αὐτοῖς ὁ Θεὸς τὸν Σαοὺλ υἱὸν Κίς, ἄνδρα ἐκ φυλῆς
gave them God – Saul son of Kish, a man of tribe
958 2094 5062 3179 846 1453
22 Βενιαμίν, ἔτη τεσσαράκοντα. καὶ μεταστήσας αὐτόν, ἤγειρεν
of Benjamin, years forty. And removing him, He raised
846 1138 1519 935 3739 2036 3140 2147
αὐτοῖς τὸν Δαβὶδ εἰς βασιλέα, ᾧ καὶ εἶπε μαρτυρήσας, Εὗρον
to them – David for a king, to whom also He said, witnessing, I found
1138 2421 435 2596 2588 3450 3739
Δαβὶδ τὸν τοῦ Ἰεσσαί, ἄνδρα κατὰ τὴν καρδίαν μου, ὃς
David the (son) of Jesse a man according to the heart of Me, who
4160 3956 2307 3450 5127 2316 575
23 ποιήσει πάντα τὰ θελήματά μου. τούτου ὁ Θεὸς ἀπὸ τοῦ
will do all the desires of Me. Of this one God from the
4690 2596 1860 1453 2474 4990
σπέρματος κατ' ἐπαγγελίαν ἤγειρε τῷ Ἰσραὴλ σωτῆρα
seed according to promise raised – to Israel a Savior,
2424 4296 2491 4253 4383
24 Ἰησοῦν, προκηρύξαντος Ἰωάννου πρὸ προσώπου τῆς
Jesus. Previously proclaiming John, before (the) face of the
1529 848 908 3341 3956 2992 2474
εἰσόδου αὐτοῦ βάπτισμα μετανοίας παντὶ τῷ λαῷ Ἰσραήλ.
coming of Him a baptism of repentance to all the people of Israel.
5613 4137 2491 1408 3004 5101/3165
25 ὡς δὲ ἐπλήρου ὁ Ἰωάννης τὸν δρόμον, ἔλεγε, Τίνα με
as And fulfilled – John the course he said, Whom me
5282 1511 3756/1510/1473/235 2400 2064 3326 1691
ὑπονοεῖτε εἶναι; οὐκ εἰμὶ ἐγώ. ἀλλ' ἰδού, ἔρχεται μετ' ἐμέ,
do you suppose to be? not am I (He), but behold, He comes after me,
3739/3756/1510/514 5266 4228 3089 435
26 οὗ οὐκ εἰμὶ ἄξιος τὸ ὑπόδημα τῶν ποδῶν λῦσαι. ἄνδρες
of whom not I am worthy the sandal of (His) feet to loosen. Men,
80 5207 1085 11 1722/5213 5399
ἀδελφοί, υἱοὶ γένους Ἀβραάμ, καὶ οἱ ἐν ὑμῖν φοβούμενοι τὸν
brothers, sons of (the) race of Abraham, and those in you fearing –

God, to you the word of this salvation was sent. [27]For those dwelling in Jerusalem, and their rulers, not having known this One; and the voices of the prophets being read throughout every sabbath, judging *Him,* they fulfilled *the Scriptures.* [28]And finding not one cause of death, they asked Pilate to do away with Him. [29]And when they finished all the things having been written concerning Him, taking *Him* down from the tree, they laid *Him* in a tomb.

[30]But God raised Him from *the* dead; [31]who appeared for many days to those coming up with Him from Galilee to Jerusalem, who are witnesses of Him to the people. [32]And we preach the gospel *to* you, the promise made to the fathers, [33]that this God has fulfilled to us, their children, raising up Jesus; as also it has been written in the second Psalm, "You are My Son; today I have begotten You." [34]And that He raised Him from *the* dead, no more being about to return to corruption, so He has said, "I will give You the holy things of faithful David." [35]So He also said in another, "You will not give Your Holy One to see corruption." [36]For having served *his* own generation by the counsel of God, David truly fell asleep, and was added to his fathers, and saw corruption. [37]But *He* whom God raised up, this One did not see corruption. [38]Then let it be known to you, men, brothers, that through this One forgiveness of sin is announced to you. [39]And everyone believing in this One is justified from all

2316/5213 3056 4991 5026 649 1063
27 Θεόν, ὑμῖν ὁ λόγος τῆς σωτηρίας ταύτης ἀπεστάλη. οἱ γὰρ
God, to you the word of salvation this was sent forth. those For
2730 1722 2419 758 848 5126
κατοικοῦντες ἐν Ἱερουσαλὴμ καὶ οἱ ἄρχοντες αὐτῶν, τοῦτον
dwelling in Jerusalem and the rulers of them, this One
50 5456 4396 2596 3956
ἀγνοήσαντες, καὶ τὰς φωνὰς τῶν προφητῶν τὰς κατὰ πᾶν
not knowing, and the voices of the prophets throughout every
4521 314 2919 4137
28 σάββατον ἀναγινωσκομένας, κρίναντες ἐπλήρωσαν. καὶ
sabbath being read, having judged (Him), they fulfilled. And
3367 156 2298 2147 154 4091
μηδεμίαν αἰτίαν θανάτου εὑρόντες, ᾐτήσαντο Πιλάτον
not one cause of death having found, they asked Pilate
337 846 5613 5055 537 4012 846
29 ἀναιρεθῆναι αὐτόν. ὡς δὲ ἐτέλεσαν ἅπαντα τὰ περὶ αὐτοῦ
do away (with) Him. when And they finished all the things about Him
1125 2507 575 3586 5087 1519 3419
γεγραμμένα, καθελόντες ἀπὸ τοῦ ξύλου, ἔθηκαν εἰς μνημεῖον.
having been written, taking down from the tree, they laid in a tomb.
2316 1453 846 1537 3498 3739 3700 1909 2250
30 ὁ δὲ Θεὸς ἤγειρεν αὐτὸν ἐκ νεκρῶν· ὃς ὤφθη ἐπὶ ἡμέρας
31 But God raised Him from (the) dead; who appeared for days
4119 4872 846 575 1056 1519
πλείους τοῖς συναναβᾶσιν αὐτῷ ἀπὸ τῆς Γαλιλαίας εἰς
many to those coming up with Him from — Galilee to
2419 3748 1526 3144 848 4314 2992
32 Ἱερουσαλήμ, οἵτινές εἰσι μάρτυρες αὐτοῦ πρὸς τὸν λαόν. καὶ
Jerusalem, who are witnesses of Him to the people. And
2249 5209 2097 4314 3962 1860
ἡμεῖς ὑμᾶς εὐαγγελιζόμεθα τὴν πρὸς τοὺς πατέρας ἐπαγ-
we (to) you preach the gospel, the to the fathers promise
1096 3754 5026 2316 1603
γελίαν γενομένην, ὅτι ταύτην ὁ Θεὸς ἐκπεπλήρωκε τοῖς
having come, that this (promise) God has fulfilled to the
5043 848 2254 450 2424 5613 1722 5568
33 τέκνοις αὐτῶν ἡμῖν, ἀναστήσας Ἰησοῦν· ὡς καὶ ἐν τῷ ψαλμῷ
children of them to us, raising up Jesus, as also in the Psalm
1208 1125 5207 3450/1487/4771/1473 4594
τῷ δευτέρῳ γέγραπται, Υἱός μου εἶ σύ, ἐγὼ σήμερον
second, it has been written: Son of Me are You, I today
1080 4571/3754 450 846 1537 3498 3371
34 γεγέννηκά σε. ὅτι δὲ ἀνέστησεν αὐτὸν ἐκ νεκρῶν, μηκέτι
have begotten You. that And He raised up Him from (the) dead, no more
3195 5290 1519 1312 3779 2046 3754
μέλλοντα ὑποστρέφειν εἰς διαφθοράν, οὕτως εἴρηκεν ὅτι
being about to return to corruption, thus He has said, —
1325 5213 3741 1138 4103 1352 1722 2087 3004
35 Δώσω ὑμῖν τὰ ὅσια Δαβὶδ τὰ πιστά. διὸ καὶ ἐν ἑτέρῳ λέγει,
I will give You the holy things of David faithful. Thus also in another He says,
3756 1325 3741 4675 1492 1312 1138 3303 1063
36 Οὐ δώσεις τὸν ὅσιόν σου ἰδεῖν διαφθοράν. Δαβὶδ μὲν γὰρ
Not You will give the holy one of You to see corruption. David indeed For
2398 1074 5256 2316 1012 2837
ἰδίᾳ γενεᾷ ὑπηρετήσας τῇ τοῦ Θεοῦ βουλῇ ἐκοιμήθη, καὶ
own generation having served by the — of God counsel fell asleep, and
4369 4314 3962 848 1492 1312 3739
37 προσετέθη πρὸς τοὺς πατέρας αὐτοῦ, καὶ εἶδε διαφθοράν· ὃν
was added to the fathers of him, and saw corruption. whom
2316 1453 3756/1492 1312 1110 3756/2077
38 δὲ ὁ Θεὸς ἤγειρεν, οὐκ εἶδε διαφθοράν. γνωστὸν οὖν ἔστω
But God raised up, not He saw corruption. Known, therefore, let it be
5213 435 80 3754 1223 5127 5213 859 266
ὑμῖν, ἄνδρες ἀδελφοί, ὅτι διὰ τούτου ὑμῖν ἄφεσις ἁμαρτιῶν
to you, men, brothers, that through this One to you forgiveness of sins
2605 575 3956 3739/3756 1410 1722
39 καταγγέλλεται· καὶ ἀπὸ πάντων ὧν οὐκ ἠδυνήθητε ἐν τῷ
is announced, and from all things which not you could by the
3551 3475 1344 1722 5129 3956 4100
νόμῳ Μωσέως δικαιωθῆναι, ἐν τούτῳ πᾶς ὁ πιστεύων
law of Moses be justified, in this One everyone — believing

things which you could not be justified by the Law of Moses. [40]Then watch *that* the thing spoken in the Prophets may not come on you: [41]"Behold, you despisers, and marvel, and perish, because I work a work in your days, a work which you would in no way believe if anyone declares *it* to you."

[42]But the Jews having gone out of the synagogue, the Gentiles begged that these words be spoken to them on the next sabbath. [43]And the synagogue being broken up, many of the Jews and of the devout proselytes followed Paul and Barnabas; who speaking to them persuaded them to continue in the grace of God.

[44]And in the coming sabbath, almost all the city was gathered to hear the word of God. [45]And the Jews seeing the crowds, they were filled with jealousy, and contradicted the things being spoken by Paul, contradicting and blaspheming. [46]But speaking boldly, Paul and Barnabas said, It was necessary *for* the word of God to be spoken first to you; but since you indeed thrust it away, and judge yourselves not worthy of eternal life, behold, we turn to the Gentiles. [47]For so the Lord has commanded us, "I have set You for a Light of nations, that You be for salvation to *the* end of the earth."

[48]And hearing, the Gentiles rejoiced, and glorified the word of the Lord. And as many as had been appointed to eternal life believed.

[49]And the word of the Lord was carried through all the country. [50]But the Jews excited the devout and honorable women, and the

1344 991 3767 1904 1909/5209 2046 1722
40 δικαιοῦται. βλέπετε οὖν μὴ ἐπέλθῃ ἐφ' ὑμᾶς τὸ εἰρημένον ἐν
is justified. Look, then,(that) not come on you the thing spoken in
4396 1492 2707 2296
41 τοῖς προφήταις, Ἴδετε, οἱ καταφρονηταί, καὶ θαυμάσατε,
the prophets; See, the despisers, and marvel
853 3754 2041 1473 2038 1722 2250
καὶ ἀφανίσθητε· ὅτι ἔργον ἐγὼ ἐργάζομαι ἐν ταῖς ἡμέραις
and vanish, because a work I work in the days
5216 2041/3739/3364 4100 1437/5100 1555 5213
ὑμῶν, ἔργον ᾧ οὐ μὴ πιστεύσητε, ἐάν τις ἐκδιηγῆται ὑμῖν.
of you; a work which in no way you believe if anyone declare (it) to you.
1826 1537 4864 2453 3870
42 Ἐξιόντων δὲ ἐκ τῆς συναγωγῆς τῶν Ἰουδαίων, παρεκά-
going out And of the synagogue. the Jews begged
1484/1519 3342 4521 2980 846
λουν τὰ ἔθνη εἰς τὸ μεταξὺ σάββατον λαληθῆναι αὐτοῖς
the Gentiles on the next sabbath to be spoken to them
4487 5023 3089 4864 190
43 τὰ ῥήματα ταῦτα. λυθείσης δὲ τῆς συναγωγῆς, ἠκολούθησαν
words these. being broken And the synagogue, followed
4183 2453 4576 4339
πολλοὶ τῶν Ἰουδαίων καὶ τῶν σεβομένων προσηλύτων τῷ
many of the Jews and of the devout proselytes —
3972 921 3748 4354 846
Παύλῳ καὶ τῷ Βαρνάβᾳ· οἵτινες προσλαλοῦντες αὐτοῖς,
Paul and — Barnabas, who speaking to them
3982 846 1961 5485 2316
ἔπειθον αὐτοὺς ἐπιμένειν τῇ χάριτι τοῦ Θεοῦ.
persuaded them to continue in the grace of God.
2064 4521 4975 3956 4172 4863
44 Τῷ δὲ ἐρχομένῳ σαββάτῳ σχεδὸν πᾶσα ἡ πόλις συνήχθη
in the And coming sabbath almost all the city was gathered
191 3056 2316 1492 2453
45 ἀκοῦσαι τὸν λόγον τοῦ Θεοῦ. ἰδόντες δὲ οἱ Ἰουδαῖοι τοὺς
to hear the word — of God. seeing And the Jews the
3793 4130 2205 483 5259
ὄχλους ἐπλήσθησαν ζήλου, καὶ ἀντέλεγον τοῖς ὑπὸ τοῦ
crowds, they were filled of jealousy, and contradicted the things by
3972 3004 483 987
Παύλου λεγομένοις, ἀντιλέγοντες καὶ βλασφημοῦντες.
Paul, being spoken, contradicting and blaspheming.
3955 3972 921 2036 5213
46 παρρησιασάμενοι δὲ ὁ Παῦλος καὶ ὁ Βαρνάβας εἶπον, Ὑμῖν
speaking boldly But — Paul and — Barnabas said, To you
2258 316 4412 2980 3056 2316
ἦν ἀναγκαῖον πρῶτον λαληθῆναι τὸν λόγον τοῦ Θεοῦ.
it was necessary firstly to be spoken the word — of God.
1894 683 846 3756 514 2919 1438
ἐπειδὴ δὲ ἀπωθεῖσθε αὐτόν, καὶ οὐκ ἀξίους κρίνετε ἑαυτοὺς
since indeed But you put away it, and not worthy judge yourselves
166 2222 2400 4762 1519 1484 3779 1063
47 τῆς αἰωνίου ζωῆς, ἰδοὺ στρεφόμεθα εἰς τὰ ἔθνη. οὕτω γὰρ
of the eternal life, behold, we turn to the nations. so For
1781 2254 2962 5067 4571/1519/5457/1484
ἐντέταλται ἡμῖν ὁ Κύριος, Τέθεικά σε εἰς φῶς ἐθνῶν, τοῦ
has commanded us the Lord: I have set You for a light of nations —
1511/4571/1519/ 4991 2193 2078 1093 191
48 εἶναί σε εἰς σωτηρίαν ἕως ἐσχάτου τῆς γῆς. ἀκούοντα δὲ τὰ
to be You for salvation to (the) end of the earth. hearing And the
1484 5463 1392 3056 2962
ἔθνη ἔχαιρον, καὶ ἐδόξαζον τὸν λόγον τοῦ Κυρίου, καὶ
nations rejoiced, and glorified the word of the Lord. And
4100 3745 2258 5021 1519 2222 166 1308
49 ἐπίστευσαν ὅσοι ἦσαν τεταγμένοι εἰς ζωὴν αἰώνιον. διεφέ-
believed as many as were appointed to life eternal. was
3056 2962 1223/3650 5561
50 ρετο δὲ ὁ λόγος τοῦ Κυρίου δι' ὅλης τῆς χώρας. οἱ δὲ
carried And the word of the Lord through all the country. the But
2453 3951 4576 1135
Ἰουδαῖοι παρώτρυναν τὰς σεβομένας γυναῖκας καὶ τὰς
Jews urged on the devout women and —

chief ones of the city, and raised up a persecution against Paul and Barnabas, and threw them out from their borders. [51]But these shaking off the dust of their feet on them, they came into Iconium. [52]And the disciples were filled with joy and *the* Holy Spirit.

CHAPTER 14

[1]And it happened in Iconium, they went in together into the synagogue of the Jews, and spoke so as for a huge multitude of both Jews and Greeks to believe. [2]But the unbelieving Jews raised up and made malignant the souls of the Gentiles against the brothers. [3]Then, indeed, they stayed a considerable time, speaking boldly on the Lord, witnessing to the word of His grace, and *He* giving miracles and wonders to occur through their hands.

[4]And the multitude of the city was divided; and some were with the Jews, but others with the apostles. [5]And when a rush of the Gentiles occurred, and both the Jews and their rulers *came* to insult and to stone them; [6]perceiving *this*, they fled to the cities of Lycaonia, Lystra and Derbe, and the surrounding country. [7]And they were preaching the gospel there.

[8]And a certain man was sitting in Lystra, powerless in the feet, being lame from his mother's womb, who had never walked. [9]This one heard Paul speaking, who looking intently at him, and seeing that he had faith to be cured, [10]*he* said with a loud voice, Stand upright on your feet! And he leaped

2158 4413 4172 1892
εὐσχήμονας καὶ τοὺς πρώτους τῆς πόλεως, καὶ ἐπήγειραν
honorable, and the chief ones of the city; and raised up
1375 1909 3972 921 1544
διωγμὸν ἐπὶ τὸν Παῦλον καὶ τὸν Βαρνάβαν, καὶ ἐξέβαλον
persecution against – Paul and – Barnabas, and threw out
846 575 3725 848 1621
51 αὐτοὺς ἀπὸ τῶν ὁρίων αὐτῶν. οἱ δὲ ἐκτιναξάμενοι τὸν
them from the borders of them. they And shaking off the
2868 4228 848 1909 846 2064 1519 2430
κονιορτὸν τῶν ποδῶν αὐτῶν ἐπ' αὐτούς, ἦλθον εἰς Ἰκόνιον.
dust of the feet of them on them, they came into Iconium.
3101 4137 5479 4151 40
52 οἱ δὲ μαθηταὶ ἐπληροῦντο χαρᾶς καὶ Πνεύματος Ἁγίου.
the And disciples were filled from joy, and from (the) Spirit Holy.

CHAPTER 14

1096 1722 2430 2596 846 1525 846
1 Ἐγένετο δὲ ἐν Ἰκονίῳ, κατὰ τὸ αὐτὸ εἰσελθεῖν αὐτοὺς εἰς
it happened And in Iconium together entered them into
4864 2453 2980 3779 5620
τὴν συναγωγὴν τῶν Ἰουδαίων, καὶ λαλῆσαι οὕτως ὥστε
the synagogue of the Jews, and to speak so as
4100 2453 1672 4183 4128
πιστεῦσαι Ἰουδαίων τε καὶ Ἑλλήνων πολὺ πλῆθος. οἱ δὲ
to believe of Jews both and of Greeks, a much multitude. the But
544 2453 1892 2559 5590
2 ἀπειθοῦντες Ἰουδαῖοι ἐπήγειραν καὶ ἐκάκωσαν τὰς ψυχὰς
disobeying Jews raised up and embittered the souls
1484 2596 80 2425 3303 3767 5550
3 τῶν ἐθνῶν κατὰ τῶν ἀδελφῶν. ἱκανὸν μὲν οὖν χρόνον
of the Gentiles against the brothers. A considerable therefore time
1304 3955 1909 2962 3140
διέτριψαν παρρησιαζόμενοι ἐπὶ τῷ Κυρίῳ τῷ μαρτυροῦντι
they stayed speaking boldly on the Lord witnessing
3056 5485 848 1325 4592 5059
τῷ λόγῳ τῆς χάριτος αὐτοῦ, καὶ διδόντι σημεῖα καὶ τέρατα
to the word of the grace of Him, and giving signs and wonders
1096 1223 5495 848 4977 4128
4 γίνεσθαι διὰ τῶν χειρῶν αὐτῶν. ἐσχίσθη δὲ τὸ πλῆθος τῆς
to happen through the hands of them. was divided But the multitude of the
4172 3303 2258 4862 2453 4862
πόλεως· καὶ οἱ μὲν ἦσαν σὺν τοῖς Ἰουδαίοις, οἱ δὲ σὺν τοῖς
city, and some were with the Jews, others but with the
652 5613 1096 3730 1484 5037 2453
5 ἀποστόλοις. ὡς δὲ ἐγένετο ὁρμὴ τῶν ἐθνῶν τε καὶ Ἰουδαίων
apostles. when And occurred a rush of the Gentiles, even and Jews,
4862 758 848 5195 3036 846
σὺν τοῖς ἄρχουσιν αὐτῶν, ὑβρίσαι καὶ λιθοβολῆσαι αὐτούς,
with the rulers of them, to insult and to stone them;
4894 2703 1519 4172 3071 3082
6 συνιδόντες κατέφυγον εἰς τὰς πόλεις τῆς Λυκαονίας, Λύστραν
perceiving they fled to the cities – of Lycaonia, Lystra,
1191 4066 2546 2258 2097
7 καὶ Δέρβην, καὶ τὴν περίχωρον· κἀκεῖ ἦσαν εὐαγγελιζόμενοι.
and Derbe, and the surrounding country: and there they were evangelizing.
5100 435 1722 3082 102 4228 2521
8 Καί τις ἀνὴρ ἐν Λύστροις ἀδύνατος τοῖς ποσὶν ἐκάθητο,
And a certain man in Lystra powerless in the feet was sitting
1537 5560 3384 848 5225 3739 3762
χωλὸς ἐκ κοιλίας μητρὸς αὐτοῦ ὑπάρχων, ὃς οὐδέποτε
lame from (the) womb of (the) mother of him being, who never
4043 3778 191 3972 2980 3739
9 περιεπεπατήκει. οὗτος ἤκουε τοῦ Παύλου λαλοῦντος· ὃς
had walked. This one heard – Paul speaking, who
816 846 1492 3754 4102 2192 4982 2036
10 ἀτενίσας αὐτῷ, καὶ ἰδὼν ὅτι πίστιν ἔχει τοῦ σωθῆναι, εἶπε
looking at him and seeing that faith he has – to be cured, said
3173 5456 450 1909 4228 4675/ 3717
μεγάλῃ τῇ φωνῇ, Ἀνάστηθι ἐπὶ τοὺς πόδας σου ὀρθός. καὶ
with a great voice, Stand up on the feet of you erect. And

up and walked about [11]And seeing what Paul did, the crowd lifted up their voice in Lycaonian, saying, The gods have come down to us, becoming like men. [12]And they called Barnabas, Zeus; and Paul, Hermes, because he was the leader in speaking.

[13]And the priest of Zeus being before their city, carrying bulls and garlands to the gates, *he* wished to sacrifice along with the crowds. [14]But Paul and Barnabas, the apostles, hearing, tearing their garments, they sprang into the crowd, crying out, [15]and saying, Men, why do you do these things? We also are men of like feelings to you, preaching the gospel to you to turn *you* from these vanities to the living God, who made the heaven and the earth and the sea, and all things in them; [16]who in the generations which have passed allowed all the nations to go in their *own* ways, [17]though indeed He did not leave Himself without witness, doing good, giving rain and fruitful seasons to us from Heaven, filling our hearts with food and gladness. [18]And saying these things, they hardly stopped the crowds, *that they* not sacrifice to them.

[19]But Jews came there from Antioch and Iconium, and persuading the crowds, and stoning Paul, they dragged *him* outside the city, supposing him to have died. [20]But the disciples surrounding him, arising he entered into the city. And on the morrow he went away with Barnabas to Derbe. [21]And having

242 4043 3793 1492 4160
11 ἥλλετο καὶ περιεπάτει. οἱ δὲ ὄχλοι, ἰδόντες ὃ ἐποίησεν ὁ
he leaped and walked about. the And crowds seeing what did
3972 1869 5456 848 3072 3004
Παῦλος, ἐπῆραν τὴν φωνὴν αὐτῶν Λυκαονιστὶ λέγοντες, Οἱ
Paul lifted up the voice of them in Lycaonian, saying, The
2316 3666 444 2597 4314 2248 2564
12 θεοὶ ὁμοιωθέντες ἀνθρώποις κατέβησαν πρὸς ἡμᾶς. ἐκάλουν
gods having become like men have come down to us. they called
5037 3303 921 2203 3972 2060 1894
τε τὸν μὲν Βαρνάβαν, Δία· τὸν δὲ Παῦλον, Ἑρμῆν, ἐπειδὴ
And – Barnabas, Zeus; – and Paul, Hermes; since
846 2258 2233 3056 2409 2203
13 αὐτὸς ἦν ὁ ἡγούμενος τοῦ λόγου. ὁ δὲ ἱερεὺς τοῦ Διὸς τοῦ
he was the leader of the speaking. the But priest – of Zeus –
5607 4253 4172 846 5022 4725 1909
ὄντος πρὸ τῆς πόλεως αὐτῶν, ταύρους καὶ στέμματα ἐπὶ τοὺς
being before the city of them, bulls and garlands to the
4440 5342 4862 3793 2309 2380 191
14 πυλῶνας ἐνέγκας, σὺν τοῖς ὄχλοις ἤθελε θύειν. ἀκούσαντες δὲ
gates carrying, with the crowds wished to sacrifice. hearing And
652 921 3972 1284 2440
οἱ ἀπόστολοι Βαρνάβας καὶ Παῦλος, διαρρήξαντες τὰ ἱμάτια
the apostles Barnabas and Paul, having torn the garments
848 1530 1519 3793 2896 3004
αὐτῶν, εἰσεπήδησαν εἰς τὸν ὄχλον, κράζοντες καὶ λέγοντες,
of them, sprang into the crowd, crying out and saying,
435 5101 5023 4160 2249 3663 2070 5213
15 Ἄνδρες, τί ταῦτα ποιεῖτε; καὶ ἡμεῖς ὁμοιοπαθεῖς ἐσμεν ὑμῖν
Men, why these things do you? Also we of like feelings are to you
444 2097 5209 575 5130 3152
ἄνθρωποι, εὐαγγελιζόμενοι ὑμᾶς ἀπὸ τούτων τῶν ματαίων
men, preaching the gospel to you from these – vanities
1994 1909 2316 2198 3739 4160 3772
ἐπιστρέφειν ἐπὶ τὸν Θεὸν τὸν ζῶντα, ὃς ἐποίησε τὸν οὐρανὸν
to turn to the God living; who made the heaven
1093 2281 3956 1722 846 3739/1722
16 καὶ τὴν γῆν καὶ τὴν θάλασσαν καὶ πάντα τὰ ἐν αὐτοῖς· ὃς ἐν
and the earth and the sea, and all things in them; who in
3944 1074 1439 3956 1484 4198
ταῖς παρῳχημέναις γενεαῖς εἴασε πάντα τὰ ἔθνη πορεύεσθαι
the having passed by generations allowed all the nations to go
3598 848 = 2544 = 3756 267 1438 863
17 ταῖς ὁδοῖς αὐτῶν. καίτοιγε οὐκ ἀμάρτυρον ἑαυτὸν ἀφῆκεν
the ways of them. And yet not without witness Himself left,
15 3771 2254 5205 1305 2540
ἀγαθοποιῶν, οὐρανόθεν ἡμῖν ὑετοὺς διδοὺς καὶ καιροὺς
doing good, from Heaven to us, rain giving and seasons
2593 1705 5160 2167 2588
καρποφόρους, ἐμπιπλῶν τροφῆς καὶ εὐφροσύνης τὰς καρδίας
fruit-bearing filling of food and of gladness the hearts
2257 5023 3004 3433 2664 3793
18 ἡμῶν. καὶ ταῦτα λέγοντες, μόλις κατέπαυσαν τοὺς ὄχλους
of us. And these things saying, hardly they stopped the crowds
3361 2380 846
τοῦ μὴ θύειν αὐτοῖς.
– not to sacrifice to them.

1904 575 490 2430 2453
19 Ἐπῆλθον δὲ ἀπὸ Ἀντιοχείας καὶ Ἰκονίου Ἰουδαῖοι, καὶ
came over And from Antioch and Iconium Jews, and
3962 3793 3034 3972 4951
πείσαντες τοὺς ὄχλους, καὶ λιθάσαντες τὸν Παῦλον, ἔσυρον
persuading the crowds, and stoning – Paul, they dragged
1854 4172 3543 846 2348 2944
ἔξω τῆς πόλεως, νομίσαντες αὐτὸν τεθνάναι. κυκλωσάντων
outside the city, supposing him to have died. having surrounded
846 3101 450 1525 1519 4172
20 δὲ αὐτὸν τῶν μαθητῶν, ἀναστὰς εἰσῆλθεν εἰς τὴν πόλιν· καὶ
But him the disciples, rising up he entered into the city. And
1887 1831/4862 921 1519 1191 2097
21 τῇ ἐπαύριον ἐξῆλθε σὺν τῷ Βαρνάβᾳ εἰς Δέρβην. εὐαγγελι-
on the morrow he went with – Barnabas to Derbe. preaching

preached the gospel to that city, and having made many disciples, they returned to Lystra and Iconium and Antioch, [22]confirming the souls of the disciples, exhorting to continue in the faith, and that through many afflictions we must enter into the kingdom of God. [23]And having hand-picked elders for them in every church, having prayed with fastings, they committed them to the Lord into whom they had believed.

[24]And passing through Pisidia, they came to Pamphylia. [25]And speaking the word in Perga, they came down to Attalia, [26]and from there they sailed to Antioch, from where they had been committed to the grace of God for the work which they fulfilled.

[27]And having arrived, and gathering the church, they reported what things God did with them, and that He opened a door of faith to the nations. [28]And they remained there not a little time with the disciples.

5037 4172 1565 3100 2425
σάμενοί τε τὴν πόλιν ἐκείνην, καὶ μαθητεύσαντες ἱκανούς,
the gospel And — city to that, and having made disciples many,
5290 1519 3082 2430 490
ὑπέστρεψαν εἰς τὴν Λύστραν καὶ Ἰκόνιον καὶ Ἀντιόχειαν,
they returned to — Lystra and Iconium and Antioch,
1991 5590 3101 3870
22 ἐπιστηρίζοντες τὰς ψυχὰς τῶν μαθητῶν, παρακαλοῦντες
confirming the souls of the disciples, exhorting
1696 4102 3754/1223 4183 2347 1163 2248
ἐμμένειν τῇ πίστει, καὶ ὅτι διὰ πολλῶν θλίψεων δεῖ ἡμᾶς
to continue in the faith, and that through many afflictions must we
1525 1519 932 2316 5500
23 εἰσελθεῖν εἰς τὴν βασιλείαν τοῦ Θεοῦ. χειροτονήσαντες δὲ
enter into the kingdom — of God. having hand-picked And
846 4245 2596 1577 4336 3326
αὐτοῖς πρεσβυτέρους κατ' ἐκκλησίαν, προσευξάμενοι μετὰ
for them elders in (every) church praying with
3521 3908 846 2962 1519 302 4100
νηστειῶν, παρέθεντο αὐτοὺς τῷ Κυρίῳ εἰς ὃν πεπιστεύ-
fastings, they committed them to the Lord in whom they had
1330 4099 2064 1519 3828
24 κεισαν. καὶ διελθόντες τὴν Πισιδίαν ἦλθον εἰς Παμφυλίαν.
believed. And passing through — Pisidia, they came to Pamphylia
2980 1722 4011 3056 2597 1519 825
25 καὶ λαλήσαντες ἐν Πέργῃ τὸν λόγον, κατέβησαν εἰς Ἀττά-
And speaking in Perga the word, they came down to Attalia,
2547 636 1519 490 3606 2258
26 λειαν· κἀκεῖθεν ἀπέπλευσαν εἰς Ἀντιόχειαν, ὅθεν ἦσαν
and from there sailed away to Antioch, from where they had
3860 5485 2316 1519 2041 4137
παραδεδομένοι τῇ χάριτι τοῦ Θεοῦ εἰς τὸ ἔργον ὃ ἐπλή-
been committed to the grace of God for the work which they
3854 4863 1577
27 ρωσαν. παραγενόμενοι δὲ καὶ συναγαγόντες τὴν ἐκκλησίαν,
fulfilled having arrived And, and gathering the church,
312 3745 4160 2316 3326 846 3754 455
ἀνήγγειλαν ὅσα ἐποίησεν ὁ Θεὸς μετ' αὐτῶν, καὶ ὅτι ἤνοιξε
they reported what things did God with them, and that He opened
1484 2374 4102 1304 1563 5550 3756
28 τοῖς ἔθνεσι θύραν πίστεως. διέτριβον δὲ ἐκεῖ χρόνον οὐκ
to the Gentiles a door of faith. they continued And there a time not
3641/3862 3101
ὀλίγον σὺν τοῖς μαθηταῖς.
little with the disciples.

CHAPTER 15

[1]And going down from Judea, some taught the brothers, *saying,* If you are not circumcised *according* to the custom of Moses, you cannot be saved. [2]Then dissension and not a little disputation with them having taken place by Paul and Barnabas, they appointed Paul and Barnabas and some others of them to go up into Jerusalem to the apostles and elders concerning this question.

[3]Indeed, therefore, they, having been sent forward by the church, passed through Phoenicia and

CHAPTER 15

5100 2718 575 2449 1321
1 Καί τινες κατελθόντες ἀπὸ τῆς Ἰουδαίας, ἐδίδασκον τοὺς
And some going down from — Judea taught the
80 3754/1437/3361 4059 1485 3475 3756
ἀδελφοὺς ὅτι Ἐὰν μὴ περιτέμνησθε τῷ ἔθει Μωϋσέως, οὐ
brothers If not are circumcised by the custom of Moses, not
1410 4982 1096 3767 4714 4803
2 δύνασθε σωθῆναι. γενομένης οὖν στάσεως καὶ συζητήσεως
you can be saved. occurring Then discord and discussion
3756 3641 3972 921 4314 846 5021
οὐκ ὀλίγης τῷ Παύλῳ καὶ τῷ Βαρνάβᾳ πρὸς αὐτούς, ἔταξαν
not a little — by Paul and — Barnabas with them, they chose
305 3972 921 5100 243 1537
ἀναβαίνειν Παῦλον καὶ Βαρνάβαν καί τινας ἄλλους ἐξ
to go up Paul and Barnabas and some others of
846 4314 652 4245 1519 2419
αὐτῶν πρὸς τοὺς ἀποστόλους καὶ πρεσβυτέρους εἰς Ἱερου-
them to the apostles and elders to
4012 2213 5127 3303/3767 4311
3 σαλὴμ περὶ τοῦ ζητήματος τούτου. οἱ μὲν οὖν, προπεμ-
Jerusalem about — question this. they Therefore being set
5259 1577 1330 5403
φθέντες ὑπὸ τῆς ἐκκλησίας, διήρχοντο τὴν Φοινίκην καὶ
forward by the church, passed through — Phoenicia and

Samaria, telling about the conversion of the Gentiles and they caused great joy to all the brothers. [4]And having arrived in Jerusalem, they were welcomed by the church and the apostles and the elders. And they reported what things God did with them. [5]But some of those from the sect of the Pharisees, having believed, rose up, saying, It is necessary to circumcise them, and to command *them* to keep the Law of Moses.

[6]And the apostles and the elders were assembled to see about this matter. [7]And much disputation having occurred, rising up Peter said to them: Men, brothers, you recognize that from ancient days, God chose among us *that* through my mouth the nations *should* hear the word of the gospel, and to believe. [8]And the heart-knowing God testified to them, giving them the Holy Spirit, even as also to us. [9]And He made distinction in nothing between both us and them, having purified their hearts by faith.

[10]Now, then, why do you test God, *by* putting a yoke on the neck of the disciples which neither our fathers nor we had strength to bear? [11]But through the grace of *the* Lord Jesus Christ, we believe *in order* to be saved according to which manner they also *believed*.

[12]And all the multitude kept silent, and were hearing Barnabas and Paul recounting what things God did through them among the Gentiles, *even even* the signs and wonders.

[13]And after they were silent, James responded,

4540 1555 1995 1484
Σαμάρειαν, ἐκδιηγούμενοι τὴν ἐπιστροφὴν τῶν ἐθνῶν· καὶ
Samaria, telling about the conversion of the Gentiles and
4160 5479 3173 3956 80 3854
4 ἐποίουν χαρὰν μεγάλην πᾶσι τοῖς ἀδελφοῖς. παραγενό-
they caused joy great to all the brothers. having arrived
1519 2419 588 5259 1577
μενοι δὲ εἰς Ἱερουσαλήμ, ἀπεδέχθησαν ὑπὸ τῆς ἐκκλησίας
And to Jerusalem, they were welcomed by the church 5037
652 4245 312
καὶ τῶν ἀποστόλων καὶ τῶν πρεσβυτέρων, ἀνήγγειλάν τε
and the apostles and the elders, reported and
3745 2316 4160 3326 846 1817 5100
5 ὅσα ὁ Θεὸς ἐποίησε μετ' αὐτῶν. ἐξανέστησαν δέ τινες τῶν
what things God did with them. rise forth But some of those
575 139 5330 4100 3004
ἀπὸ τῆς αἱρέσεως τῶν Φαρισαίων πεπιστευκότες, λέγοντες
from the sect of the Pharisees having believed, saying,
3754/1163 4059 846 3853 5037 5083
ὅτι Δεῖ περιτέμνειν αὐτούς, παραγγέλλειν τε τηρεῖν τὸν
—It is right to circumcise them, to command and to keep the
3551 3475
νόμον Μωϋσέως.
law of Moses.
4863 652 4245 1492
6 Συνήχθησαν δὲ οἱ ἀπόστολοι καὶ οἱ πρεσβύτεροι ἰδεῖν
were assembled And the apostles and the elders to see
4012 3056 5127 4183 4803 1096
7 περὶ τοῦ λόγου τούτου. πολλῆς δὲ συζητήσεως γενομένης,
about — matter this. much And discussion having occurred,
450 4074 2036 4314 846
ἀναστὰς Πέτρος εἶπε πρὸς αὐτούς,
rising up Peter said to them,
435 80 5210 1987 3754/575/ 2250 744
Ἄνδρες ἀδελφοί, ὑμεῖς ἐπίστασθε ὅτι ἀφ' ἡμερῶν ἀρχαίων
Men, brothers, you understand that from days ancient
2316/1722/2254 1586 1223 4750 3450 191
ὁ Θεὸς ἐν ἡμῖν ἐξελέξατο, διὰ τοῦ στόματός μου ἀκοῦσαι
God among us chose through the mouth of me to hear
1484 3056 2098 4100
8 τὰ ἔθνη τὸν λόγον τοῦ εὐαγγελίου, καὶ πιστεῦσαι. καὶ ὁ
the nations the word of the gospel, and to believe. And the
2589 2316 3140 846 1325 846
καρδιογνώστης Θεὸς ἐμαρτύρησεν αὐτοῖς, δοὺς αὐτοῖς τὸ
heart-knowing God witnessed to them, giving them the
4151 40 2531 2254 3762 1252 3342
9 Πνεῦμα τὸ Ἅγιον, καθὼς καὶ ἡμῖν· καὶ οὐδὲν διέκρινε μεταξὺ
Spirit — Holy, as also to us, and nothing distinguished between
2257/5037 846 4102 2511 2588 848
ἡμῶν τε καὶ αὐτῶν, τῇ πίστει καθαρίσας τὰς καρδίας αὐτῶν.
us both and them, by faith having cleansed the hearts of them.
3568/3767/5101 3985 2316 2007 2218 1909
10 νῦν οὖν τί πειράζετε τὸν Θεόν, ἐπιθεῖναι ζυγὸν ἐπὶ τὸν
Now, then, why do you tempt — God, to put a yoke on the
5137 3101 3739/3777 3962 2257 3777/2249
τράχηλον τῶν μαθητῶν, ὃν οὔτε οἱ πατέρες ἡμῶν οὔτε ἡμεῖς
neck of the disciples, which neither the fathers of us nor we
2480 941 235/1223 5485 2962 2424
11 ἰσχύσαμεν βαστάσαι; ἀλλὰ διὰ τῆς χάριτος Κυρίου Ἰησοῦ
were able to bear? But through the grace of (the) Lord Jesus
5547 4100 4982 2596/3739/ 5158 2548
Χριστοῦ πιστεύομεν σωθῆναι, καθ' ὃν τρόπον κἀκεῖνοι.
Christ we believe to be saved by which means (as) even they.
4601 3956 4128 191 921
12 Ἐσίγησε δὲ πᾶν τὸ πλῆθος, καὶ ἤκουον Βαρνάβα καὶ
was silent And all the multitude, and heard Barnabas and
3972 1834 3745 4160 2316 4592
Παύλου ἐξηγουμένων ὅσα ἐποίησεν ὁ Θεὸς σημεῖα καὶ
Paul recounting what did — God signs and
5059 1722 1484/1223/846 3326 4601 846
13 τέρατα ἐν τοῖς ἔθνεσι δι' αὐτῶν. μετὰ δὲ τὸ σιγῆσαι αὐτούς,
wonders among the nations through them. after And the silence of them,

saying, Men, brothers, hear
me: [14]Simon recounted
how even as *at* first God
oversaw to take a people
out from *among the*
Gentiles for His name.
[15]And with this agree the
words of the prophets, as it
has been written, [16]"After
these things I will return
and I will build again the
tabernacle of David *which*
has fallen, and I will rebuild
the things which have been
demolished, and I will set it
up, [17]so as the rest of men
may seek the Lord, even all
the nations on whom My
name has been called, says
the Lord, who is doing
all these things." [18]All His
works are known to God
from eternity. [19]For this
reason I judge not to
trouble those from the
Gentiles turning to God;
[20]but to write to them to
hold back from the
pollutions of idols, and *from*
fornication, and that
strangled, and blood. [21]For
in every city from ancient
generations Moses has
those proclaiming him,
having been read in the
synagogues on every
sabbath.

611 2385 3004
ἀπεκρίθη Ἰάκωβος λέγων,
answered James, saying,
435 80 191 3450 4826 1834 2531
14 Ἄνδρες ἀδελφοί, ἀκούσατέ μου· Συμεὼν ἐξηγήσατο καθὼς
Men, brothers, hear me. Simeon recounted even as
4412 2316 1980 2983 1537 1484 2992 1909
πρῶτον ὁ Θεὸς ἐπεσκέψατο λαβεῖν ἐξ ἐθνῶν λαὸν ἐπὶ τῷ
first God oversaw to take out of nations a people for the
3686 848 5129 4856 3056 4396
15 ὀνόματι αὐτοῦ. καὶ τούτῳ συμφωνοῦσιν οἱ λόγοι τῶν προ-
name of Him. And to this agree together the words of the
2531 1125 3326 5023 390
16 φητῶν, καθὼς γέγραπται, Μετὰ ταῦτα ἀναστρέψω, καὶ
prophets, as it has been written, After these things I will return, and
456 4633 1138 4098
ἀνοικοδομήσω τὴν σκηνὴν Δαβὶδ τὴν πεπτωκυῖαν· καὶ τὰ
I will rebuild the tent of David — having fallen, and that
2679 848 456 461 846
κατεσκαμμένα αὐτῆς ἀνοικοδομήσω, καὶ ἀνορθώσω αὐτήν·
being demolished of it I will rebuild, and I will set up it,
3704/302 1567 2645 444
17 ὅπως ἂν ἐκζητήσωσιν οἱ κατάλοιποι τῶν ἀνθρώπων τὸν
so as — may seek the rest — of men the
2962 3956 1484/1909/3739/ 1941 3686 3450
Κύριον, καὶ πάντα τὰ ἔθνη, ἐφ' οὓς ἐπικέκληται τὸ ὄνομά μου
Lord, even all the nations on whom has been invoked the name of Me
1909 846 3004 2962 4160 5023 3956 1110
18 ἐπ' αὐτούς, λέγει Κύριος ὁ ποιῶν ταῦτα πάντα. γνωστὰ
upon them, says (the) Lord who is doing these things all. known
575 165 2076 2316 3956 2041 848 1352/1473
19 ἀπ' αἰῶνός ἐστι τῷ Θεῷ πάντα τὰ ἔργα αὐτοῦ. διὸ ἐγὼ
from eternity are to God All · the works of Him Because of this, I
2919 3361 3926 575 1484 1994
κρίνω μὴ παρενοχλεῖν τοῖς ἀπὸ τῶν ἐθνῶν ἐπιστρέφουσιν
judge not to trouble those from the nations turning
1909 2316 235 1989 846 567 575
20 ἐπὶ τὸν Θεόν· ἀλλὰ ἐπιστεῖλαι αὐτοῖς τοῦ ἀπέχεσθαι ἀπὸ
to God, but to write to them — to hold back from
234 1497 4202
τῶν ἀλισγημάτων τῶν εἰδώλων καὶ τῆς πορνείας καὶ τοῦ
pollutions of the idols, and — fornication, and the
4156 129 3475 1063/1537 1074 744
21 πνικτοῦ καὶ τοῦ αἵματος. Μωσῆς γὰρ ἐκ γενεῶν ἀρχαίων
strangled, and — blood. Moses For from generations ancient
2596 4172 2784 846 2192/1722 4864
κατὰ πόλιν τοὺς κηρύσσοντας αὐτὸν ἔχει, ἐν ταῖς συναγω-
in every city those proclaiming him he has, in the synagogues
2596 3956 4521 314
γαῖς κατὰ πᾶν σάββατον ἀναγινωσκόμενος.
on every sabbath having been read.

[22]Then it seemed *good* to
the apostles and the elders,
with all the church, to send
chosen men from them to
Antioch with Paul and
Barnabas: Judas having
been surnamed Barsabas,
and Silas, leading men
among the brothers,
[23]writing by their hand
these things: The apostles
and the elders and the
brothers, to those throughout Antioch, and Syria, and
Cilicia, brothers from *the*
Gentiles: Greeting.

5119 1380 652 4245 4862
22 Τότε ἔδοξε τοῖς ἀποστόλοις καὶ τοῖς πρεσβυτέροις σὺν
Then it seemed to the apostles and the elders, with
3650 1577 1586 435 1537 846 3992 1519
ὅλῃ τῇ ἐκκλησίᾳ, ἐκλεξαμένους ἄνδρας ἐξ αὐτῶν πέμψαι εἰς
all the church, chosen men of them to send to
490 4862 3972 921 2455
Ἀντιόχειαν σὺν τῷ Παύλῳ καὶ Βαρνάβᾳ, Ἰούδαν τὸν
Antioch with — Paul and Barnabas, Judas —
1941 923 4609 435 2233 1722
ἐπικαλούμενον Βαρσαβᾶν, καὶ Σίλαν, ἄνδρας ἡγουμένους ἐν
surnamed Barsabas, and Silas, men leading among
80 1125 1223 5495 848 3592
23 τοῖς ἀδελφοῖς, γράψαντες διὰ χειρὸς αὐτῶν τάδε, Οἱ ἀπό-
the brothers, writing through (the) hand of them these things: The
4245 80 2596
στολοι καὶ οἱ πρεσβύτεροι καὶ οἱ ἀδελφοὶ τοῖς κατὰ τὴν
apostles and the elders and the brothers to those throughout
490 4947 2791 80 1537 1484
Ἀντιόχειαν καὶ Συρίαν καὶ Κιλικίαν ἀδελφοῖς τοῖς ἐξ ἐθνῶν,
Antioch and Syria and Cilicia, brothers from (the) Gentiles.

[24]Since we heard that some of us having gone out have troubled you with words, unsettling your souls, saying, Be circumcised and keep the Law; to whom we gave no command; [25]it seemed *good* to us, having become of one mind, to send chosen men to you along with our beloved Barnabas and Paul, [26]men who have given up their souls on behalf of the name of our Lord, Jesus Christ. [27]Therefore, we have sent Judas and Silas, they by word also announcing the same things. [28]For it seemed *good* to the the Holy Spirit and to us to put not one greater burden on you than these necessary things: [29]To hold back from idol sacrifices, and blood, and that strangled, and *from* fornication; from which continually keeping yourselves, you will do well. Be prospered.

[30]Then they indeed being let go, they went to Antioch. And gathering the multitude, *they* delivered the letter. [31]And reading *it*, they rejoiced at the comfort. [32]And Judas and Silas, themselves also being prophets, exhorted the brothers through much speech, and confirmed *them*. [33]And continuing for a time, they were let go with peace from the brothers to the apostles.

[34]But it seemed *good* to Silas to remain. [35]And Paul and Barnabas stayed in Antioch, teaching and preaching the gospel, the word of the Lord, with many others also.

[36]And after some days Paul said to Barnabas,

5463 1894 191 3754 5100/1537/2257 1831 5015
24 χαίρειν· ἐπειδὴ ἠκούσαμεν ὅτι τινὲς ἐξ ἡμῶν ἐξελθόντες ἐτά-
Greeting. Since we heard that some of us having gone out
5209 3056 384 5590 5216
ραξαν ὑμᾶς λόγοις, ἀνασκευάζοντες τὰς ψυχὰς ὑμῶν,
troubled you with words, unsettling the souls of you,
3004 4059 5083 3551 3739/3756 1291
λέγοντες περιτέμνεσθαι καὶ τηρεῖν τὸν νόμον, οἷς οὐ διεστει-
saying, Be circumcised and keep the Law; to whom not we gave
1380 2254 1096 3661 1586
25 λάμεθα· ἔδοξεν ἡμῖν γενομένοις ὁμοθυμαδόν, ἐκλεξαμένους
command; it seemed to us becoming of one passion chosen
435 3992 4314 5209 4862 27 2257
ἄνδρας πέμψαι πρὸς ὑμᾶς, σὺν τοῖς ἀγαπητοῖς ἡμῶν
men to send to you, with the beloved of us
921 3972 444 3860 5590
26 Βαρνάβᾳ καὶ Παύλῳ, ἀνθρώποις παραδεδωκόσι τὰς ψυχὰς
Barnabas and Paul, men having given up the souls
848 5228 3686 2962 2257 2424 5547
αὐτῶν ὑπὲρ τοῦ ὀνόματος τοῦ Κυρίου ἡμῶν Ἰησοῦ Χρι-
of them on behalf of the name of the Lord of us, Jesus Christ.
649 3767 2455 4609 846 1223
27 στοῦ. ἀπεστάλκαμεν οὖν Ἰούδαν καὶ Σίλαν, καὶ αὐτοὺς διὰ
We have sent, therefore, Judas and Silas, and they through
3056 518 846 1380 1063 40
28 λόγου ἀπαγγέλλοντας τὰ αὐτά. ἔδοξε γὰρ τῷ Ἁγίῳ
word announcing, the same things. it seemed For to the Holy
4151 2254 3367 4119 2007 5213 922
Πνεύματι, καὶ ἡμῖν, μηδὲν πλέον ἐπιτίθεσθαι ὑμῖν βάρος,
Spirit and to us not one greater to put on you burden
4133 1876 5130 567 1494
29 πλὴν τῶν ἐπάναγκες τούτων, ἀπέχεσθαι εἰδωλοθύτων καὶ
than — necessary things these: to abstain from idol sacrifices, and
129 4156 4202 1537/3739 1301
αἵματος καὶ πνικτοῦ καὶ πορνείας· ἐξ ὧν διατηροῦντες
blood, and that strangled, and fornication; from which continually keeping
1438 2095 4238 4517
ἑαυτούς, εὖ πράξετε. ἔρρωσθε.
yourselves well you will do. Be prospered.
3303/3767 630 2064 1519 490 4863
30 Οἱ μὲν οὖν ἀπολυθέντες ἦλθον εἰς Ἀντιόχειαν· καὶ συν-
They, therefore, being let go, they went to Antioch; and having
4128 1929 1992 314
31 αγαγόντες τὸ πλῆθος, ἐπέδωκαν τὴν ἐπιστολήν. ἀναγνόντες
gathered the multitude, delivered the letter. having read
5463 1909 3874 2455 4609
32 δέ, ἐχάρησαν ἐπὶ τῇ παρακλήσει. Ἰούδας δὲ καὶ Σίλας, καὶ
And, they rejoiced at the comfort. Judas And and Silas, also
848 4396 5607 1223 3056 4183 3870
αὐτοὶ προφῆται ὄντες, διὰ λόγου πολλοῦ παρεκάλεσαν
themselves prophets being, through speech much exhorted
80 1991 4160 5550
33 τοὺς ἀδελφούς, καὶ ἐπεστήριξαν. ποιήσαντες δὲ χρόνον,
the brothers, and confirmed. having continued And a time,
630 3326 1515 575 80 4314
ἀπελύθησαν μετ' εἰρήνης ἀπὸ τῶν ἀδελφῶν πρὸς τοὺς
they were let go with peace from the brothers to the
652 1380 4609 1961 847 3972
34 ἀποστόλους. ἔδοξε δὲ τῷ Σίλᾳ ἐπιμεῖναι αὐτοῦ. Παῦλος δὲ
35 **apostles. it seemed (good) But to Silas to remain (there). Paul And**
921 1304 1722 490 1321
καὶ Βαρνάβας διέτριβον ἐν Ἀντιοχείᾳ, διδάσκοντες καὶ
and Barnabas stayed in Antioch, teaching and
2097 3326 2087 4183 3056
εὐαγγελιζόμενοι, μετὰ καὶ ἑτέρων πολλῶν, τὸν λόγον τοῦ
preaching the gospel, with also others many the word of the
2962
Κυρίου.
Lord.
3326 5100 2250 2036 3972 4314 921
36 **Μετὰ δέ τινας ἡμέρας εἶπε Παῦλος πρὸς Βαρνάβαν,**
after And some days said Paul to Barnabas,

Indeed, having turned back, let us look after our brothers throughout every city in which we announced the word of the Lord; how they are holding *it*. [37]But Barnabas purposed to take John with *them*, the *one* being called Mark. [38]But Paul thought *it* well not to take that one with *them, he* having withdrawn from them from Pamphylia, and not going with them to the work. [39]Then there was sharp feeling, so as to separate them from each other. And taking Mark, Barnabas sailed away to Cyprus. [40]But having chosen Silas, Paul went out, being commended to the grace of God by the brothers [41]And *he* went through Syria and Cilicia, making the churches strong.

CHAPTER 16

[1]And he arrived in Derbe and Lystra. And behold, a certain disciple named Timothy was there, *the* son of a certain believing Jewish woman—but *his* father *was* a Greek. [2]*This one* was being testified of by the brothers in Lystra and Iconium. [3]Paul desired this one to go forth with him, and taking *him he* circumcised him, because of the Jews being in those places—for they all knew his father, that he was a Greek. [4]And as they went through the cities, they delivered them *the need* to keep the decrees having been determined by the apostles and the elders in Jerusalem. [5]Then indeed the churches were being made stronger in the faith, and increased in number day by day.

[6]And passing through the Phrygian and the Galatian country—being

1994 1211 1980 80 2257
Ἐπιστρέψαντες δὴ ἐπισκεψώμεθα τοὺς ἀδελφοὺς ἡμῶν
Having turned back indeed let us look after the brothers of us
2596 3956 4172 1722/3739 2605 3056
κατὰ πᾶσαν πόλιν, ἐν αἷς κατηγγείλαμεν τὸν λόγον τοῦ
throughout every city in which we announced the word of the
2962 4459 2192 921 1011 4838
37 Κυρίου, πῶς ἔχουσι. Βαρνάβας δὲ ἐβουλεύσατο συμπαραλα-
Lord, how they are. : Barnabas And purposed to take with
holding.
2491 2563 3138 3972
38 βεῖν τὸν Ἰωάννην, τὸν καλούμενον Μάρκον. Παῦλος δὲ
(them) — John, — being called Mark. Paul But
515 868 575 846 575 3828 3361
ἠξίου, τὸν ἀποστάντα ἀπ' αὐτῶν ἀπὸ Παμφυλίας, καὶ μὴ
thought fit (he) having withdrawn from them from Pamphilia, and not
4905 846 1519 2041 3361 4838 5126
συνελθόντα αὐτοῖς εἰς τὸ ἔργον, μὴ συμπαραλαβεῖν τοῦτον.
going with them to the work, not to take with (them) that one.
1096 3767 3948 5620 673 846 575
39 ἐγένετο οὖν παροξυσμός, ὥστε ἀποχωρισθῆναι αὐτοὺς ἀπ'
there was Then sharp feeling, so as to separate them from
240 5037 921 3880 3138
ἀλλήλων, τόν τε Βαρνάβαν παραλαβόντα τὸν Μάρκον
each other; — and Barnabas taking — Mark
1602 1519 2954 3972 1951 4609 1831
40 ἐκπλεῦσαι εἰς Κύπρον· Παῦλος δὲ ἐπιλεξάμενος Σίλαν ἐξῆλθε,
to sail way to Cyprus. Paul But having chosen Silas went out,
3860 5485 2316 5259 80 1330
41 παραδοθεὶς τῇ χάριτι τοῦ Θεοῦ ὑπὸ τῶν ἀδελφῶν. διήρχετο
being commended to the grace of God by the brothers. went through
4947 2791 1991 1577
δὲ τὴν Συρίαν καὶ Κιλικίαν, ἐπιστηρίζων τὰς ἐκκλησίας.
And — Syria and Cilicia, making strong the churches.

CHAPTER 16

2658 1519 1191 3082 2400 3101
1 Κατήντησε δὲ εἰς Δέρβην καὶ Λύστραν· καὶ ἰδού, μαθητής
he came down And to Derbe and Lystra. And behold, a disciple
5100/2258/1563/ 3686 5095 5207 1135 5100 2453
τις ἦν ἐκεῖ, ὀνόματι Τιμόθεος, υἱὸς γυναικός τινος Ἰουδαίας
certain was there by name Timothy, son of a woman certain Jewish
4103 3962 1672 3739 3140 5259 1722
2 πιστῆς, πατρὸς δὲ Ἕλληνος· ὃς ἐμαρτυρεῖτο ὑπὸ τῶν ἐν
faithful, father but (was) a Greek; who was witnessed to by the in
3082 2430 80 5126 2309 3972
3 Λύστροις καὶ Ἰκονίῳ ἀδελφῶν. τοῦτον ἠθέλησεν ὁ Παῦλος
Lystra and Iconium brothers. This one desired — Paul
4862 848 1831 2983 4059 846 1223
σὺν αὐτῷ ἐξελθεῖν, καὶ λαβὼν περιέτεμεν αὐτόν, διὰ τοὺς
with him to go forth, and taking circumcised him because of the
2453 5607 1722 5117 1565 1492 1063
Ἰουδαίους τοὺς ὄντας ἐν τοῖς τόποις ἐκείνοις· ᾔδεισαν γὰρ
Jews — being in — places those; they knew for
537 3962 848 3754 1672 5225 5613
4 ἅπαντες τὸν πατέρα αὐτοῦ, ὅτι Ἕλλην ὑπῆρχεν. ὡς δὲ
all the father of him, that a Greek he was. as And
1279 4172 3860 846 5442
διεπορεύοντο τὰς πόλεις, παρεδίδουν αὐτοῖς φυλάσσειν τὰ
they went through the cities, they delivered to them to keep the
1378 2919 5259 652 4245
δόγματα τὰ κεκριμένα ὑπὸ τῶν ἀποστόλων καὶ τῶν πρεσ-
decrees — being decided by the apostles and the
1722/ 2419 3303/3767 1577 4732
5 βυτέρων τῶν ἐν Ἱερουσαλήμ. αἱ μὲν οὖν ἐκκλησίαι ἐστερεοῦν-
elders — in Jerusalem. the Therefore churches were made
4102 4052 706 2596 2250
το τῇ πίστει, καὶ ἐπερίσσευον τῷ ἀριθμῷ καθ' ἡμέραν.
strong in the faith, and increased — in number day by day.
1330 5435 1054 5561
6 Διελθόντες δὲ τὴν Φρυγίαν καὶ τὴν Γαλατικὴν χώραν,
having passed through And the Phrygia and the Galatian country,

forbidden by the Holy Spirit to speak the word in Asia—[7]coming against Mysia, they attempted to go along Bithynia; and the Spirit did not allow them. [8]And passing by Mysia, they came down into Troas. [9]And a vision appeared to Paul during the night: a certain man of Macedonia *was* standing, entreating him and saying, Passing over into Macedonia, help us! [10]And *as soon* as he saw the vision, we immediately sought to go forth into Macedonia, concluding that the Lord had called us to announce the gospel *to* them.

[11]Then having set sail from Troas, we ran a straight course into Samothrace, and on the morrow into Neapolis; [12]and from there into Philippi, which is the first city of *that* part of Macedonia, a colony. And we were in this city, staying some days. [13]And on the day of the sabbaths, we went outside the city beside a river, where it was customary *for* prayer to be *made*. And sitting down, we spoke to the women who came together *there*. [14]And a certain woman named Lydia, a seller of purple of *the* city of Thyatira, *one* reverencing God, listened, whose heart the Lord opened thoroughly to pay attention to the things being spoken by Paul. [15]And as she and her household were baptized, she entreated *Paul*, saying, If you have judged me to be believing in the Lord, entering into my house, remain *a while*. And she strongly urged us.

[16]And it happened, *as* we went into *a place of* prayer, a certain slavegirl having a Pythonic spirit met

2967 5259 40 4151 2980 3056
κωλυθέντες ὑπὸ τοῦ Ἁγίου Πνεύματος λαλῆσαι τὸν λόγον
being prevented by the Holy Spirit to speak the word
1722 773 2064 2596 3465 3985 2596
7 ἐν τῇ Ἀσίᾳ, ἐλθόντες κατὰ τὴν Μυσίαν ἐπείραζον κατὰ τὴν
in — Asia, coming against — Mysia, they attempted along
978 4198 3756 1439 846 4151
Βιθυνίαν πορεύεσθαι· καὶ οὐκ εἴασεν αὐτοὺς τὸ Πνεῦμα·
Bithynia to go, and not allowed them the Spirit.
3928 3465 2597 1519 5174
8 παρελθόντες δὲ τὴν Μυσίαν κατέβησαν εἰς Τρωάδα. καὶ
passing by And — Mysia they came down to Troas. And
3705 1223 3571 3700 3972 435/5100/2258/ 3110
9 ὅραμα διὰ τῆς νυκτὸς ὤφθη τῷ Παύλῳ· ἀνήρ τις ἦν Μακεδὼν
a vision during the night appeared — to Paul, a man certain was of Macedonia
2476 3870 846 3004 1224 1519 3109
ἑστώς, παρακαλῶν αὐτὸν καὶ λέγων, Διαβὰς εἰς Μακεδονίαν,
standing, begging him and saying, Passing over to Macedonia,
997 2254 5613 3705 1492 2112 2212
10 βοήθησον ἡμῖν. ὡς δὲ τὸ ὅραμα εἶδεν, εὐθέως ἐζητήσαμεν
help us. when And the vision he saw, at once we sought
1831 1519 3109 4822 3754 4341
ἐξελθεῖν εἰς τὴν Μακεδονίαν,συμβιβάζοντες ὅτι προσκέκλη-
to go forth to Macedonia concluding that has called
2248 2962 2097 846
ται ἡμᾶς ὁ Κύριος εὐαγγελίσασθαι αὐτούς.
us the Lord to preach the gospel to them.
321 3767 575 5174 2113 1519
11 Ἀναχθέντες οὖν ἀπὸ τῆς Τρῳάδος, εὐθυδρομήσαμεν εἰς
setting sail Then from — Troas, we ran a straight course to
4543 5037 1966 1519 3496 1564 5037/1519
12 Σαμοθρᾴκην, τῇ τε ἐπιούσῃ εἰς Νεάπολιν, ἐκεῖθέν τε εἰς
Samothrace, on the and next day to Neapolis, from there and to
5375 3748 2076 4413 3310 3109
Φιλίππους, ἥτις ἐστὶ πρώτη τῆς μερίδος τῆς Μακεδονίας
Philippi, which is (the) first of the part — of Macedonia
4172 2862 2258 1722 5026 4172 1304
πόλις, κολωνία· ἦμεν δὲ ἐν ταύτῃ τῇ πόλει διατρίβοντες
city, a colony. we were And in this — city staying
2250 5100 5037 2250 4521 1831 1854
13 ἡμέρας τινάς. τῇ τε ἡμέρᾳ τῶν σαββάτων ἐξήλθομεν ἔξω τῆς
days some. on the And day of the sabbaths, we went out outside the
4172 3844 4215 3757 3543 4335 1511
πόλεως παρὰ ποταμόν, οὗ ἐνομίζετο προσευχὴ εἶναι, καὶ
city by a river, where was customary prayer to be; and
2523 2980 4905 1135 5100
14 καθίσαντες ἐλαλοῦμεν ταῖς συνελθούσαις γυναιξί. καί τις
sitting down we spoke to the who came together women. And a certain
1135 3686 3070 4211 4172 2363
γυνὴ ὀνόματι Λυδία, πορφυρόπωλις πόλεως Θυατείρων,
woman, by name Lydia, a seller of purple, of (the) city of Thyatira,
4576 2316 191 3739 2962 1272 2588
σεβομένη τὸν Θεόν, ἤκουεν· ἧς ὁ Κύριος διήνοιξε τὴν καρδίαν,
revering — God, heard, of whom the Lord opened the heart
4337 2980 5259 3972 5613 907
15 προσέχειν τοῖς λαλουμένοις ὑπὸ τοῦ Παύλου. ὡς δὲ ἐβαπτί-
to attend to the things spoken by — Paul. when And she was
3624 848 3870 3004 1487 2919
σθη, καὶ ὁ οἶκος αὐτῆς, παρεκάλεσε λέγουσα, Εἰ κεκρίκατέ
baptized, and the house of her, she beseeched, saying, If you have judged
3165 4103 2962 1511 1525 1519 3624 3450
με πιστὴν τῷ Κυρίῳ εἶναι, εἰσελθόντες εἰς τὸν οἶκόν μου,
me believing in the Lord to be, entering into the house of me,
3306 3849 2248
μείνατε. καὶ παρεβιάσατο ἡμᾶς.
remain. And she urged us.
1096 4198 2257 1519 4335 3814
16 Ἐγένετο δὲ πορευομένων ἡμῶν εἰς προσευχήν, παιδίσκην
it was And, going us into (a place of) prayer, a girl
5100 2192 4151 4436 528 2254 3748
τινὰ ἔχουσαν πνεῦμα Πύθωνος ἀπαντῆσαι ἡμῖν, ἥτις
certain having a spirit of Python met us, who

us, whose divining brought much gain to her lords.

[17]Following after Paul and us, she cried out, saying, These men are slaves of the Most High God, who are announcing to us a way of salvation! [18]And she did this over many days. But becoming distressed, and turning to the *demonic* spirit, Paul said, In the name of Jesus Christ I command you to come out from her! And it came out in that *same* hour.

[19]And seeing that the hope of their gain went out, having seized Paul and Silas, her lords dragged *them* to the market before the rulers. [20]And bringing them near to the magistrates, *they* said, These men are very much troubling our city, being Jews, [21]and announce customs which it is not lawful for us to receive, nor to do, being Romans. [22]And the crowd rose up together against them. And tearing off their clothes, the magistrates commanded to flog *them*. [23]And laying on them many stripes, they threw *them* into prison, charging the jailer to keep them securely; [24]who, receiving such a charge, threw them into the inner prison, and locked their feet in the stocks.

[25]And having prayed, toward midnight Paul and Silas praised God in a hymn. And the prisoners listened to them. [26]And suddenly there was a great earthquake, so that the foundations of the jail were

2039 4183 3930 2962 848 3132
ἐργασίαν πολλὴν παρεῖχε τοῖς κυρίοις αὐτῆς, μαντευομένη.
gain much **brought** to the lords of her divining.
3778 2628 3972 2254 2896 3004
17 αὕτη κατακολουθήσασα τῷ Παύλῳ καὶ ἡμῖν, ἔκραζε λέγουσα
She following after — Paul and us, cried out saying,
3778 444 1401 2316 5310 1526
Οὗτοι οἱ ἄνθρωποι δοῦλοι τοῦ Θεοῦ τοῦ ὑψίστου εἰσίν,
These — men slaves of the God — most high are,
3748 2605 2254 3598 4991 5124
18 οἵτινες καταγγέλλουσιν ἡμῖν ὁδὸν σωτηρίας. τοῦτο δὲ
who announce to us a way of salvation. this And
4160/1909 4183 2250 1278 3972
ἐποίει ἐπὶ πολλὰς ἡμέρας. διαπονηθεὶς δὲ ὁ Παῦλος, καὶ
she did over many days. becoming distressed But Paul, and
1994 4151 2036 3853 4671 1722
ἐπιστρέψας, τῷ πνεύματι εἶπε, Παραγγέλλω σοι ἐν τῷ
turning to the spirit said, I command you in the
3686 2424 5547 1831 575 848 1831
ὀνόματι Ἰησοῦ Χριστοῦ, ἐξελθεῖν ἀπ᾿ αὐτῆς. καὶ ἐξῆλθεν
name of Jesus Christ to come out from her. And it came out
846 5610
αὐτῇ τῇ ὥρᾳ.
in that hour.
1492 2962 848 3754 1831 1680
19 Ἰδόντες δὲ οἱ κύριοι αὐτῆς ὅτι ἐξῆλθεν ἡ ἐλπὶς τῆς
seeing And the lords of her that went out the hope of the
2039 848 1949 3972 4609
ἐργασίας αὐτῶν, ἐπιλαβόμενοι τὸν Παῦλον καὶ τὸν Σίλαν,
gain of them, having seized — Paul and — Silas,
1670 1519 58 1909 758 4317
20 εἵλκυσαν εἰς τὴν ἀγορὰν ἐπὶ τοὺς ἄρχοντας, καὶ προσ-
dragged to the market before the rulers, and having
846 4755 2036 3778 444
αγαγόντες αὐτοὺς τοῖς στρατηγοῖς εἶπον, Οὗτοι οἱ ἄνθρω-
led near them to the magistrates, (they) said, These men
1613 2257 4172 2453 5225
21 ποι ἐκταράσσουσιν ἡμῶν τὴν πόλιν, Ἰουδαῖοι ὑπάρχοντες,
are exceedingly troubling of us the city, Jews being
2605 1485/3739/3756/ 1832 2254 3858
καὶ καταγγέλλουσιν ἔθη ἃ οὐκ ἔξεστιν ἡμῖν παραδέχεσθαι
and they announce customs which not it is lawful for us to receive,
3761 4160 4514 5607 4911 3793 2596
22 οὐδὲ ποιεῖν, Ῥωμαίοις οὖσι. καὶ συνεπέστη ὁ ὄχλος κατ᾿
nor to do, Romans being. And rose together the crowd against
846 4755 4048 846 2440
αὐτῶν, καὶ οἱ στρατηγοὶ περιρρήξαντες αὐτῶν τὰ ἱμάτια
them. And the governors, tearing off of them the clothes
2753 4463 4183 5037 2007 846 4127
23 ἐκέλευον ῥαβδίζειν. πολλάς τε ἐπιθέντες αὐτοῖς πληγὰς
commanded to flog; many and laying on them stripes
906 1519 5438 3853 1200
ἔβαλον εἰς φυλακήν, παραγγείλαντες τῷ δεσμοφύλακι
threw into prison, charging the jailer
806 5083 846 3739 3852 5108 2983
24 ἀσφαλῶς τηρεῖν αὐτούς· ὃς, παραγγελίαν τοιαύτην εἰληφώς,
securely to keep them; who a charge such having received,
906 846 1519 2082 5438 4228
ἔβαλεν αὐτοὺς εἰς τὴν ἐσωτέραν φυλακήν, καὶ τοὺς πόδας
threw them into the inner prison, and the feet
848 805 1519 3586 2596 3317
25 αὐτῶν ἠσφαλίσατο εἰς τὸ ξύλον. κατὰ δὲ τὸ μεσονύκτιον
of them secured in the stocks. about And — midnight,
3972 4609 4336 5214 2316 1874
Παῦλος καὶ Σίλας προσευχόμενοι ὕμνουν τὸν Θεόν, ἐπη-
Paul and Silas praying praised in a hymn — God,
846 1198 869 4578 1096
26 κροῶντο δὲ αὐτῶν οἱ δέσμιοι· ἄφνω δὲ σεισμὸς ἐγένετο
listened and to them the prisoners. suddenly And an earthquake was
3173 5620 4531 2310 1201
μέγας, ὥστε σαλευθῆναι τὰ θεμέλια τοῦ δεσμωτηρίου·
great, so as to be shaken the foundations of the jail.

shaken. And immediately all the doors were opened, and all of the bonds were loosened. [27]And having been awakened, and seeing that the doors of the prison had been opened, having drawn a sword, the jailer was about to do away with himself, supposing the prisoners to have escaped. [28]But Paul called out with a loud voice, saying, Do no harm *to* yourself! For we are all here. [29]And asking for lights, he rushed in. And becoming trembly, he fell before Paul and Silas. [30]And leading them outside, *he* said, Sirs, what must I do that I may be saved? [31]And they said, Believe on the Lord Jesus Christ, and you will be saved, you and your household. [32]And they spoke the word of the Lord to him, and to all those in his household. [33]And taking them in that hour of the night, he washed from *their* stripes. And he and those belonging to him were baptized all at once. [34]And bringing them up to the house, he set a table before *them*, and exulted with all his household, believing God.

[35]And day having come, the magistrates sent the floggers, saying, Let those men go. [36]And the jailer announced these words to Paul, The magistrates have sent that you be let go. Now, then, going out, proceed in peace. [37]But Paul said to them, Having beaten us publicly, being Romans *and* uncondemned men, they threw *us* into prison. And now do they throw us out secretly? No, indeed! But coming themselves, let them bring

455 5037 3916 2374 3956 3956
ἀνεῴχθησάν τε παραχρῆμα αἱ θύραι πᾶσαι, καὶ πάντων
were opened And immediately the doors all, and of all
1199 447 1853 1096 1200
27 τὰ δεσμὰ ἀνέθη. ἔξυπνος δὲ γενόμενος ὁ δεσμοφύλαξ, καὶ
the bonds were loosened. awake And becoming the jailer, and
1492 455 2374 5438 4685
ἰδὼν ἀνεῳγμένας τὰς θύρας τῆς φυλακῆς, σπασάμενος
seeing having been opened the doors of the prison, having drawn
3162 3195 1438 337 3543 1628
μάχαιραν, ἔμελλεν ἑαυτὸν ἀναιρεῖν, νομίζων ἐκπεφευγέναι
a sword, was about himself to do away, supposing to have escaped
1198 5455 5456 3173 3972 3004
28 τοὺς δεσμίους. ἐφώνησε δὲ φωνῇ μεγάλῃ ὁ Παῦλος λέγων,
the prisoners. called But with a voice great – Paul, saying,
3367 4238 4572 2556 537 1063 2070 1759
Μηδὲν πράξῃς σεαυτῷ κακόν· ἅπαντες γάρ ἐσμεν ἐνθάδε.
nothing Do (to) yourself harm, all for we are here.
154 5457 1530 1790 1096
29 αἰτήσας δὲ φῶτα εἰσεπήδησε, καὶ ἔντρομος γενόμενος
asking And lights, he rushed in, and trembling becoming
4363 3972 4609 4254 846
30 προσέπεσε τῷ Παύλῳ καὶ τῷ Σίλᾳ, καὶ προαγαγὼν αὐτοὺς
he fell before – Paul and – Silas, and having led them
1854/5346 2962 5101/3165/1163/4160/2443/ 4982 2036
31 ἔξω ἔφη, Κύριοι, τί με δεῖ ποιεῖν ἵνα σωθῶ; οἱ δὲ εἶπον,
outside said, Sirs, what me must do that I may be saved? they And said,
4100 1909 2962 2424 5547 4982
Πίστευσον ἐπὶ τὸν Κύριον Ἰησοῦν Χριστόν, καὶ σωθήσῃ
Believe on the Lord Jesus Christ, and you will be saved,
4771 3624 4675 2980 846 3056
32 σὺ καὶ ὁ οἶκός σου. καὶ ἐλάλησαν αὐτῷ τὸν λόγον τοῦ
you and the house of you. And they spoke to him the word of the
2962 3956 1722 3614 848 3880
33 Κυρίου, καὶ πᾶσι τοῖς ἐν τῇ οἰκίᾳ αὐτοῦ. καὶ παραλαβὼν
Lord, and all those in the house of him. And taking
846 1722 1565 5610 3571 3068 575 4127
αὐτοὺς ἐν ἐκείνῃ τῇ ὥρᾳ τῆς νυκτὸς ἔλουσεν ἀπὸ τῶν πλη-
them in that – hour of the night, he washed from the stripes,
1093 907 846 848 3956 3916
γῶν, καὶ ἐβαπτίσθη αὐτὸς καὶ οἱ αὐτοῦ πάντες παραχρῆμα.
and was baptized he and those of him all at once.
321 5037 846 1519 3624 848 3908 5132
34 ἀναγαγών τε αὐτοὺς εἰς τὸν οἶκον αὐτοῦ παρέθηκε τράπε-
bringing up and them to the house, he set before (them) a table,
21 3832 4100 2316
ζαν, καὶ ἠγαλλιάσατο πανοικὶ πεπιστευκὼς τῷ Θεῷ.
and exulted with all the house, having believed – God.
2250 1096 649 4755
35 Ἡμέρας δὲ γενομένης, ἀπέστειλαν οἱ στρατηγοὶ τοὺς
day And coming, sent the governors the
4465 3004 630 444 1565
ῥαβδούχους λέγοντες, Ἀπόλυσον τοὺς ἀνθρώπους ἐκείνους.
floggers, saying, Let go – men those.
518 1200 3056 5128 4314
36 ἀπήγγειλε δὲ ὁ δεσμοφύλαξ τοὺς λόγους τούτους πρὸς
announced And the jailer words these to
3972 3754 649 4755 2443 630
τὸν Παῦλον ὅτι Ἀπεστάλκασιν οἱ στρατηγοί, ἵνα ἀπο-
– Paul – have sent The governors, that you
3568/3767 1831 4198 1722 1515 3972
37 λυθῆτε· νῦν οὖν ἐξελθόντες πορεύεσθε ἐν εἰρήνῃ. ὁ δὲ Παῦλος
be let go. Now, then, going out proceed in peace. But Paul
5346 4314 846 1194 2248 1219 178
ἔφη πρὸς αὐτούς, Δείραντες ἡμᾶς δημοσίᾳ, ἀκατακρίτους,
said to them, Having beaten us publicly, uncondemned
444 4514 5225 906 1519 5438
ἀνθρώπους Ῥωμαίους ὑπάρχοντας, ἔβαλον εἰς φυλακήν, καὶ
men, Romans being, they threw into prison; and
3568 2977 2248 1544 3756/1063/ 235 2064 848
νῦν λάθρα ἡμᾶς ἐκβάλλουσιν; οὐ γάρ· ἀλλὰ ἐλθόντες αὐτοὶ
now secretly us they throw out? No indeed, but coming themselves

us out. [38]And the floggers
reported these words to the
magistrates. And hearing
that they were Romans,
they were afraid. [39]And
coming, *they* begged them.
And bringing *them* out,
they asked *them* to go out
of the city. [40]And going out
from the prison, *they* went
into the *house of* Lydia. And
seeing the brothers, they
exhorted them, and went
out.

CHAPTER 17

[1]And traveling through
Amphipolis and Apollonia,
they came to Thessalonica,
where a synagogue of the
Jews was. [2]And according
to Paul's custom, he went in
to them and reasoned with
them from the Scriptures on
three sabbaths, [3]opening
and setting forth that the
Christ must have suffered,
and to have risen from *the*
dead; and that this is the
Christ, Jesus, whom I
announce to you. [4]And
some of them were per-
suaded, and joined them-
selves to Paul and Silas,
both a great multitude of
the worshiping Greeks, and
not a few of the leading
women. [5]But becoming
jealous, and having taken
aside some wicked men of
the market-loafers, and
gathering a crowd, the disobeying Jews set the city
into turmoil. And coming on
the house of Jason, *they*
sought to bring them on to
the mob. [6]But not finding
them, they dragged Jason
and some brothers before
the city judges, crying,
Those turning the habitable
world upside down have
come here, too; [7]whom
Jason has received. And
these all act contrary to the
decrees of Caesar, saying

2248 1806 312 4755
38 ἡμᾶς ἐξαγαγέτωσαν. ἀνήγγειλαν δὲ τοῖς στρατηγοῖς οἱ
us let them bring out. reported And to the governors the
4465 4487 5023 5399 191
ῥαβδοῦχοι τὰ ῥήματα ταῦτα· καὶ ἐφοβήθησαν ἀκούσαντες
floggers — words these. And they were afraid, hearing
3754 4514 1526 2064 3870 846
39 ὅτι Ῥωμαῖοί εἰσι, καὶ ἐλθόντες παρεκάλεσαν αὐτούς, καὶ
that Romans they are; and coming begged them, and
1806 2065 1831 4172 1831 1537
40 ἐξαγαγόντες ἠρώτων ἐξελθεῖν τῆς πόλεως. ἐξελθόντες δὲ ἐκ
bringing out asked to go out of the city. going out And from
5438 1525 1519 3070 1492 80
τῆς φυλακῆς εἰσῆλθον εἰς τὴν Λυδίαν· καὶ ἰδόντες τοὺς ἀδελ-
the prison, entered into (the house of) Lydia, and seeing the brothers,
3870 846 1831
φούς, παρεκάλεσαν αὐτούς, καὶ ἐξῆλθον.
they exhorted them, and went forth.

CHAPTER 17

1353 295 624 2064
1 Διοδεύσαντες δὲ τὴν Ἀμφίπολιν καὶ Ἀπολλωνίαν, ἦλθον
traveling through And — Amphipolis and Apollonia, they came
1519 2332 3699/2258 4864 2453
εἰς Θεσσαλονίκην, ὅπου ἦν ἡ συναγωγὴ τῶν Ἰουδαίων·
to Thessalonica, where was a synagogue of the Jews.
2596 1486 3972 1525 4314 846 1909
2 κατὰ δὲ τὸ εἰωθὸς τῷ Παύλῳ εἰσῆλθε πρὸς αὐτούς, καὶ ἐπὶ
as And the custom with Paul, he entered to them, and on
4521 5140 1256 846 575 1124 1272
3 σάββατα τρία διελέγετο αὐτοῖς ἀπὸ τῶν γραφῶν, διανοίγων
sabbaths three reasoned with them from the Scriptures, opening
3908 3754 5547 1163 3958 450
καὶ παρατιθέμενος, ὅτι τὸν Χριστὸν ἔδει παθεῖν καὶ ἀναστῆ-
and setting forth that the Christ must have suffered and to have
1537 3498 3754 3778 2076 5547 2424 3739/1473
ναι ἐκ νεκρῶν, καὶ ὅτι οὗτός ἐστιν ὁ Χριστὸς Ἰησοῦς, ὃν ἐγὼ
risen from (the) dead, and that this is the Christ, Jesus, whom I
2605 5213 5100 1537 846 3982
4 καταγγέλλω ὑμῖν. καί τινες ἐξ αὐτῶν ἐπείσθησαν, καὶ
announce to you. And some of them were persuaded, and
4345 3972 4609 5037 4576
προσεκληρώθησαν τῷ Παύλῳ καὶ τῷ Σίλᾳ, τῶν τε σεβο-
joined themselves — to Paul and — Silas, of the both worship-
1672 4183 4128 1135 5037 4413
μένων Ἑλλήνων πολὺ πλῆθος, γυναικῶν τε τῶν πρώτων
ing Greeks a great multitude, of women and the chief,
3756 3641 2206 544 2453
5 οὐκ ὀλίγαι. ζηλώσαντες δὲ οἱ ἀπειθοῦντες Ἰουδαῖοι, καὶ
not a few. becoming jealous But the disobeying Jews, and
4355 60 5100 435 4190
προσλαβόμενοι τῶν ἀγοραίων τινὰς ἄνδρας πονηρούς, καὶ
taking aside of the market-loafers some men wicked and
3792 2350 4172 2186 5037
ὀχλοποιήσαντες, ἐθορύβουν τὴν πόλιν· ἐπιστάντες τε τῇ
gathering a crowd, set into turmoil the city, coming on and the
3614 2394 2212 846 71 1519 1218 3361
6 οἰκίᾳ Ἰάσονος, ἐζήτουν αὐτοὺς ἀγαγεῖν εἰς τὸν δῆμον. μὴ
house of Jason sought them to bring on to the mob; not
2147 846 4951 2394 5100 80
εὑρόντες δὲ αὐτούς, ἔσυρον τὸν Ἰάσονα καί τινας ἀδελφοὺς
finding but them, they dragged — Jason and some brothers
1909 4173 994 3754 3625
ἐπὶ τοὺς πολιτάρχας, βοῶντες ὅτι Οἱ τὴν οἰκουμένην
to the the city judges, crying, — Those the habitable world
387 3778 1759 3918 3739 5264
7 ἀναστατώσαντες, οὗτοι καὶ ἐνθάδε πάρεισιν, οὓς ὑποδέδε-
having turned upside down, these also here have come, whom has received
2394 3778 3956 561 1378
κται Ἰάσων· καὶ οὗτοι πάντες ἀπέναντι τῶν δογμάτων
Jason; and these all contrary to the decrees

there is another king, Jesus. [8]And hearing these things, they troubled the crowd and the city judges. [9]And taking security from Jason and the rest, they let them go.

[10]But the brothers at once sent both Paul and Silas to Berea during the night; who having arrived went into the synagogue of the Jews. [11]And these were more noble than those in Thessalonica; *for they* received the word with all readiness, daily examining the Scriptures if these things *are* so. [12]Then indeed many from among them believed, and not a few of the honorable Greek women and men. [13]But when the Jews from Thessalonica knew that the word of God was also announced in Berea by Paul, they came there also, shaking up the crowd. [14]And immediately, then, the brothers sent away Paul, to go as toward the sea. But both Silas and Timothy remained there. [15]But those conducting Paul brought him as far as Athens. And receiving a command to Silas and Timothy, that they come to him quickly, they departed.

[16]But awaiting them in Athens, Paul's spirit was pained within him, seeing the city full of images. [17]Then, indeed, he addressed the Jews in the synagogue, and those worshiping; also in the market every day, to those

2541 4138 935 3004 2087 1511 2424
Καίσαρος πράττουσι, βασιλέα λέγοντες ἕτερον εἶναι, Ἰησοῦν.
of Caesar act, king saying another to be, Jesus.
5015 3793 4173 191
8 ἐτάραξαν δὲ τὸν ὄχλον καὶ τοὺς πολιτάρχας ἀκούοντας
they troubled And the crowd and the city judges hearing
5023 2983 2425 3844 2394
9 ταῦτα. καὶ λαβόντες τὸ ἱκανὸν παρὰ τοῦ Ἰάσονος καὶ τῶν
these things. And taking the security from – Jason and the
3062 630 846
λοιπῶν, ἀπέλυσαν αὐτούς.
rest, they let go them.
80 2112 1223 3571 1599 5037
10 Οἱ δὲ ἀδελφοὶ εὐθέως διὰ τῆς νυκτὸς ἐξέπεμψαν τόν τε
the But brothers at once during the night sent – both
3962 4609 1519 960 3748 3854
Παῦλον καὶ τὸν Σίλαν εἰς Βέροιαν· οἵτινες παραγενόμενοι
Paul and – Silas to Berea, who having arrived
1519 4864 2453 549 3778 2258
11 εἰς τὴν συναγωγὴν τῶν Ἰουδαίων ἀπῄεσαν. οὗτοι δὲ ἦσαν
into the synagogue of the Jews went. these And were
2104 1722/2332 3748 1209
εὐγενέστεροι τῶν ἐν Θεσσαλονίκῃ, οἵτινες ἐδέξαντο τὸν
more noble (than) those in Thessalonica, who received the
3056 3326 3956 4288 2596/2250 350
λόγον μετὰ πάσης προθυμίας, τὸ καθ' ἡμέραν ἀνακρίνοντες
word with all readiness, daily examining
1124 1487/2192 5023 3779 4183 3303 3767/1537/846
12 τὰς γραφάς, εἰ ἔχοι ταῦτα οὕτως. πολλοὶ μὲν οὖν ἐξ αὐτῶν
the Scriptures, if have these things so. Many, therefore of them
4100 1674 1135 2158
ἐπίστευσαν, καὶ τῶν Ἑλληνίδων γυναικῶν τῶν εὐσχη-
believed and of the Greek women – honorable
435 3756 3641 5613 1097 575
13 μόνων καὶ ἀνδρῶν οὐκ ὀλίγοι. ὡς δὲ ἔγνωσαν οἱ ἀπὸ τῆς
and men not a few. when But knew the from –
2332 2453 3754 1722 960 2605
Θεσσαλονίκης Ἰουδαῖοι ὅτι καὶ ἐν τῇ Βεροίᾳ κατηγγέλη
Thessalonica Jews that also in – Berea was announced
5259 3972 3056 2316 2064 2546 4531
ὑπὸ τοῦ Παύλου ὁ λόγος τοῦ Θεοῦ, ἦλθον κἀκεῖ σαλεύοντες
by – Paul the word – of God, they came there also shaking
3793 2112 5119 3972 1821
14 τοὺς ὄχλους. εὐθέως δὲ τότε τὸν Παῦλον ἐξαπέστειλαν οἱ
the crowd. at once And, then, – Paul sent away the
80 4198 5613/1909 2281 5278
ἀδελφοὶ πορεύεσθαι ὡς ἐπὶ τὴν θάλασσαν· ὑπέμενον δὲ ὅ
brothers to go as to the sea. remained But –
5037 4609 5095 1563 2525 3972
15 τε Σίλας καὶ ὁ Τιμόθεος ἐκεῖ. οἱ δὲ καθιστῶντες τὸν Παῦλον,
both Silas and – Timothy there. those And conducting – Paul
71 846 2193 116 2983 1785 4314
ἤγαγον αὐτὸν ἕως Ἀθηνῶν· καὶ λαβόντες ἐντολὴν πρὸς
brought him as far as Athens; and having received a command to
4609 5095 2443 5613 5033 2064 4314 856
τὸν Σίλαν καὶ Τιμόθεον, ἵνα ὡς τάχιστα ἔλθωσι πρὸς αὐτόν,
– Silas and Timothy, that as quickly they come to him,
1826
ἐξῄεσαν.
they departed.
1722 116 1551 846 3972
16 Ἐν δὲ ταῖς Ἀθήναις ἐκδεχομένου αὐτοὺς τοῦ Παύλου,
in And – Athens awaiting them – Paul
3947 4151 848 1722 846 2334 2712
παρωξύνετο τὸ πνεῦμα αὐτοῦ ἐν αὐτῷ, θεωροῦντι κατεί-
was pained the spirit of him in him, beholding full of
5607 4172 1256 3303/3767/1722 4864
17 δωλον οὖσαν τὴν πόλιν. διελέγετο μὲν οὖν ἐν τῇ συναγωγῇ
images being the city. He addressed, therefore, in the synagogue
2453 4576 1722 58 2596
τοῖς Ἰουδαίοις καὶ τοῖς σεβομένοις, καὶ ἐν τῇ ἀγορᾷ κατὰ
the Jews and those worshiping; also in the market –

happening to be *there*. [18]And some of the Epicureans and of the Stoics, philosophers, fell in with him. And some said, What may this chatterer wish to say? And these *others*, He seems to be an announcer of foreign demons—because he announced Jesus and the resurrection to them. [19]And taking hold of him, they led *him* to the Areopagus, saying, Are we able to know what this new teaching being spoken by you *is*? [20]For you bring startling things to our ears. We are minded, then, to know what these things wish to be. [21]And all Athenians and the strangers living *there* have leisure for nothing else than to say and to hear newer *things*.

[22]And standing in *the* middle of the Areopagus, Paul said, Men, Athenians, I see how you in everything *are* fearful of gods; [23]for passing through and looking up at the objects of your worship, I also found an altar on which had been written, TO AN UNKNOWN GOD. Not knowing, then, whom you worship, I make Him known to you.

[24]The God who made the world and all things in it, this One being Lord of Heaven and of earth does not dwell in handmade temples, [25]nor is served by hands of men, *as* having need of anything. *For* He is giving life and breath and all things to all. [26]And He made every nation of men of one blood, to live on all the face of the earth, ordaining fore-appointed seasons and boundaries of their dwelling, [27]to seek the Lord, if perhaps they might feel after Him and might find Him, though indeed *He* not being far

3956 2250 4314 3909 5100
18 πᾶσαν ἡμέραν πρὸς τοὺς παρατυγχάνοντας. τινὲς δὲ τῶν
every day to those happening to be (there). some And of the
1946 4770 5386 4820 846
Ἐπικουρείων καὶ τῶν Στωϊκῶν φιλοσόφων συνέβαλλον αὐτῷ.
Epicureans and of the Stoics, philosophers, fell in with him.
5100 3004 5101/302/2309 4691 3778 3004
καί τινες ἔλεγον, Τί ἂν θέλοι ὁ σπερμολόγος οὗτος λέγειν;
And some said, What may desire — chatterer this to say?
3581 1140 1380 2604 1511 3754
οἱ δέ, Ξένων δαιμονίων δοκεῖ καταγγελεὺς εἶναι· ὅτι τὸν
these And, Of foreign demons he seems an announcer to be; because
2424 386 846 2097 1949
19 Ἰησοῦν καὶ τὴν ἀνάστασιν αὐτοῖς εὐηγγελίζετο. ἐπιλα-
Jesus and the resurrection to them he announced. taking
5037 846 1909 697 71 3004
βόμενοί τε αὐτοῦ, ἐπὶ τὸν Ἄρειον πάγον ἤγαγον λέγοντες,
hold And of him, to the Areopagus they led (him), saying,
1410 1097 5101 2537 3778 5259/4675/ 2980
Δυνάμεθα γνῶναι, τίς ἡ καινὴ αὕτη ἡ ὑπὸ σοῦ λαλουμένη
Are we able to know what — new this — by you being spoken
1322 3579 1063 5100 1533 1519 189 2257
20 διδαχή; ξενίζοντα γάρ τινα εἰσφέρεις εἰς τὰς ἀκοὰς ἡμῶν·
teaching (is)? startling things For some you bring to the ears of us;
1014 3767 1097 5101/302/2309/5023 1511 117
21 βουλόμεθα οὖν γνῶναι, τί ἂν θέλοι ταῦτα εἶναι. (Ἀθηναῖοι
we are minded, then, to know what wishes these things to be. Athenians
3956 1927 3581 1519 3762 2087 2119
δὲ πάντες καὶ οἱ ἐπιδημοῦντες ξένοι εἰς οὐδὲν ἕτερον εὐκαί-
And all and the living strangers for nothing different have
2228 3004 5100 191 2537
ρουν, ἢ λέγειν τι καὶ ἀκούειν καινότερον.)
leisure either to say something, and to hear newer (things).
2476 3972 1722 3319 697 5346
22 Σταθεὶς δὲ ὁ Παῦλος ἐν μέσῳ τοῦ Ἀρείου πάγου ἔφη,
standing And — Paul in (the) midst of the Areopagus said,
435 117 2596 3956 5613 1174 5209
Ἄνδρες Ἀθηναῖοι, κατὰ πάντα ὡς δεισιδαιμονεστέρους ὑμᾶς
Men, Athenians, in everything how very fearful of gods you
2334 1330 1063 333 4574
23 θεωρῶ. διερχόμενος γὰρ καὶ ἀναθεωρῶν τὰ σεβάσματα
I behold. passing through For and looking up at the objects of worship
•3739 5216 2147 1041/1722/ 1924 57 2316
ὑμῶν, εὗρον καὶ βωμὸν ἐν ᾧ ἐπεγέγραπτο, Ἀγνώστῳ Θεῷ.
of you, I found also an altar in which had been written, To an Unknown God.
3739/3767/ 50 2151 5126 1473 2605 5213
ὃν οὖν ἀγνοοῦντες εὐσεβεῖτε, τοῦτον ἐγὼ καταγγέλλω ὑμῖν.
Whom, then, not knowing you reverence, this One I announce to you.
2316 4160 2889 3956 1722 846 3778
24 ὁ Θεὸς ὁ ποιήσας τὸν κόσμον καὶ πάντα τὰ ἐν αὐτῷ, οὗτος,
The God, He having made the world and all things in it, this One
3772 1093 2962 5225 3756 1722 5499
οὐρανοῦ καὶ γῆς κύριος ὑπάρχων, οὐκ ἐν χειροποιήτοις
of Heaven and of earth Lord being, not in handmade
3485 2730 3761/5159 5495 444 2323
25 ναοῖς κατοικεῖ, οὐδὲ ὑπὸ χειρῶν ἀνθρώπων θεραπεύεται,
temples dwells, nor by hands of men is served
4326 5100 848 1325 3956 2222 4157
προσδεόμενός τινος, αὐτὸς διδοὺς πᾶσι ζωὴν καὶ πνοὴν καὶ
having need of anything. He is giving to all life and breath, and
3956 4160/5037/1537/1520/ 129 3956 1484 444
26 τὰ πάντα· ἐποίησέ τε ἐξ ἑνὸς αἵματος πᾶν ἔθνος ἀνθρώπων,
all things. He made And of one blood every nation of men,
2730 1909 3956 4383 1093 3724 4384
κατοικεῖν ἐπὶ πᾶν τὸ πρόσωπον τῆς γῆς, ὁρίσας προτεταγ-
to live on all the face of the earth, ordaining fore-appointed
•2212 2540 3734 2733 848
27 μένους καιροὺς καὶ τὰς ὁροθεσίας τῆς κατοικίας αὐτῶν· ζητεῖν
seasons and the boundaries of the dwelling of them, to seek
2962 1487 686/1065/ 5584 846 2147
τὸν Κύριον, εἰ ἄραγε ψηλαφήσειαν αὐτὸν καὶ εὕροιεν, καί-
the Lord, if perhaps they might feel after Him and might find,

from each one of us. [28]For in Him we live and move and are; as also some of the poets among you have said, For we are also His offspring. [29]Therefore, being offspring of God, we ought not to suppose that the Godhead is like gold or silver or stone, engraved by art and the imagination of man. [30]Truly, then, God overlooking the times of ignorance, now strictly charges all men everywhere to repent, [31]because He set a day in which He is going to judge the habitable world in righteousness, by a Man whom He appointed; having given proof to all *by* raising Him from *the* dead. [32]And hearing *of* a resurrection of *the* dead, some indeed ridiculed, and said, We will hear you again concerning this. [33]And so Paul went out from their midst. [34]But some men believed, joining themselves to him, among whom also *were* both Dionysius the Areopagite and a woman named Damaris, and others with them.

3756 3112 575 1520 1538 2257 5225 1722
τοιγε οὐ μακρὰν ἀπὸ ἑνὸς ἑκάστου ἡμῶν ὑπάρχοντα. ἐν
though not far from one each of us being. in
846 1063 2198 2795 2070 5613 5100
28 αὐτῷ γὰρ ζῶμεν καὶ κινούμεθα καὶ ἐσμεν· ὡς καὶ τινες τῶν
Him For we live and move and are, as indeed some of the
2596 5209 4163 2046 5120/1063 1085 2070 1085
29 καθ' ὑμᾶς ποιητῶν εἰρήκασι, Τοῦ γὰρ καὶ γένος ἐσμέν. γένος
among you poets have said: of Him For also offspring we are. offspring
3767 5225 2316 3756 3784 3543 5557 2228
οὖν ὑπάρχοντες τοῦ Θεοῦ, οὐκ ὀφείλομεν νομίζειν χρυσῷ ἢ
Then being — of God, not we ought to suppose to gold, or
696 3037 5480 5078 1761 444
ἀργύρῳ ἢ λίθῳ, χαράγματι τέχνης καὶ ἐνθυμήσεως ἀνθρώ-
to silver, or to stone, to an engraving of art and of imagination of man,
2304 1511 3664 3303/3767 5550 52
30 που, τὸ θεῖον εἶναι ὅμοιον. τοὺς μὲν οὖν χρόνους τῆς ἀγνοίας
the Godhead is like, the indeed Then times of ignorance
5237 2316 3569 3853 444 3956
ὑπεριδὼν ὁ Θεός, τὰ νῦν παραγγέλλει τοῖς ἀνθρώποις πᾶσι
overlooking, God now declares to men all
3837 3340 1360 2476 2250 1722 3739 3195
31 πανταχοῦ μετανοεῖν· διότι ἔστησεν ἡμέραν, ἐν ᾗ μέλλει
everywhere to repent, because He set a day in which He is
2919 3625 1722 1343 1722 435 3739 going
κρίνειν τὴν οἰκουμένην ἐν δικαιοσύνῃ, ἐν ἀνδρὶ ᾧ ὥρισε,
to judge the habitable world in righteousness, by a Man whom He appointed
4102 3930 3956 450 846 1537 3498
πίστιν παρασχὼν πᾶσιν, ἀναστήσας αὐτὸν ἐκ νεκρῶν.
proof having given to all having raised Him from (the) dead.
191 386 3498 3303 5512
32 'Ακούσαντες δὲ ἀνάστασιν νεκρῶν, οἱ μὲν ἐχλεύαζον· οἱ
hearing (of) And a resurrection of (the) dead, some indeed ridiculed;
2036 191 4675 3825 4012 5127 3779
33 δὲ εἶπον, 'Ακουσόμεθά σου πάλιν περὶ τούτου. καὶ οὕτως ὁ
but said, We will hear you again concerning this. And thus
3972 1831 1537 3319 846 5100 435 2853
34 Παῦλος ἐξῆλθεν ἐκ μέσου αὐτῶν. τινὲς δὲ ἄνδρες κολληθέντες
Paul went out from (the) midst of them. some But men adhering
846 4100 1722/3739 1354 698
αὐτῷ, ἐπίστευσαν· ἐν οἷς καὶ Διονύσιος ὁ 'Αρεοπαγίτης, καὶ
to him believed, among whom both Dionysius the Areopagite, and
1135 3686 1152 2087 4862 846
γυνὴ ὀνόματι Δάμαρις, καὶ ἕτεροι σὺν αὐτοῖς.
a woman by name Damaris, and others with them.

CHAPTER 18

[1]And after these things, departing from Athens, Paul came to Corinth. [2]And finding a certain Jew named Aquila, of Pontus by race, having recently come from Italy *with* his wife Priscilla—because Claudius had ordered all the Jews to leave Rome—he came to them. [3]And because *he* was of the same trade, he lived and worked with them; for they were tentmakers by trade. [4]And he reasoned in the synagogue on every sabbath

CHAPTER 18

3326 5023 5563 3972 1537 116 2064
1 Μετὰ δὲ ταῦτα χωρισθεὶς ὁ Παῦλος ἐκ τῶν 'Αθηνῶν ἦλθεν
after And these things departing Paul from Athens came
1519 2882 2147 5100 2453 3686 207
2 εἰς Κόρινθον. καὶ εὑρών τινα 'Ιουδαῖον ὀνόματι 'Ακύλαν,
to Corinth. And finding a certain Jew by name Aquila,
4193 1085 4373 2064 575 2482
Ποντικὸν τῷ γένει, προσφάτως ἐληλυθότα ἀπὸ τῆς 'Ιταλίας,
of Pontus by race, recently having come from Italy,
4252 1135 848 1223 1299 2804
καὶ Πρίσκιλλαν γυναῖκα αὐτοῦ, διὰ τὸ διατεταχέναι Κλαυ-
and Priscilla the wife of him, because had ordered Claudius
5563 3956 2453 1537 4516
διον χωρίζεσθαι πάντας τοὺς 'Ιουδαίους ἐκ τῆς 'Ρώμης,
to depart all the Jews from Rome,
4334 846 1223 3673 1511 3306 3844
3 προσῆλθεν αὐτοῖς· καὶ διὰ τὸ ὁμότεχνον εἶναι, ἔμενε παρ'
he came to them, and because the same trade being, he abode with
846 2038 2258/1063 4635 5078
αὐτοῖς καὶ εἰργάζετο· ἦσαν γὰρ σκηνοποιοὶ τὴν τέχνην.
them and worked; they were for tentmakers by trade.
1256 1722 4864 2596/3956 4521 3982 5037
4 διελέγετο δὲ ἐν τῇ συναγωγῇ κατὰ πᾶν σάββατον, ἔπειθέ τε
he reasoned And in the synagogue on every sabbath, persuading both

persuading both Jews and Greeks.

[5]And when both Silas and Timothy came down from Macedonia, Paul was pressed by the Spirit, earnestly testifying to the Jews *that* Jesus *is* the Christ. [6]But they having resisted, and blaspheming, having shaken *his* garments, he said to them, Your blood *be* on your head. I *am* pure *from it;* from now on I will go to the Gentiles. [7]And moving from there, he went into *the* house of one named Justus, *one* worshiping God, whose house was next door to the synagogue. [8]And Crispus, the synagogue ruler, believed the Lord along with all his household. And hearing, many of the Corinthians believed and were baptized. [9]And the Lord said to Paul through a vision in *the* night, Do not fear, but speak, and do not keep silence; [10]because I am with you, and no one shall set on you to oppress you; because there is much people to Me in this city. [11]And he remained a year and six months teaching the word of God among them.

[12]But Gallio *being* proconsul of Achaia, the Jews rushed against Paul with one passion, and led him to the tribunal, [13]saying, This one persuades men to worship God contrary to the Law. [14]But Paul being about to open *his* mouth, Gallio said to the Jews, If, indeed, then, it was some wrong or wicked criminality, O Jews, according to reason I would endure you.

2453 1672
Ἰουδαίους καὶ Ἕλληνας.
Jews and Greeks.
5613 2718 575 3109 5037 4609
5 Ὡς δὲ κατῆλθον ἀπὸ τῆς Μακεδονίας ὅ τε Σίλας καὶ ὁ
when And came down from Macedonia both Silas and
5095 4912 4151 3972 1263
Τιμόθεος, συνείχετο τῷ πνεύματι ὁ Παῦλος, διαμαρτυρό-
Timothy, was pressed by the Spirit Paul, earnestly testifying
2453 5547 2424 498
μενος τοῖς Ἰουδαίοις τὸν Χριστὸν Ἰησοῦν. ἀντιτασσο-
to the Jews (that) Christ Jesus (is). having re-
846 987 1621
6 μένων δὲ αὐτῶν καὶ βλασφημούντων, ἐκτιναξάμενος τὰ
sisted But they, and blaspheming, he having shaken the
2440 2036 4314 846 129 5216 1909 2776
ἱμάτια, εἶπε πρὸς αὐτούς, Τὸ αἷμα ὑμῶν ἐπὶ τὴν κεφαλὴν
garments said to them, The blood of you on the head
5216 2513 1473 575 3568/1519 1484 4198
ὑμῶν· καθαρὸς ἐγώ· ἀπὸ τοῦ νῦν εἰς τὰ ἔθνη πορεύσομαι.
of you (is); clean I from – now to the nations will go.
3327 1564 2064 1519 3614 5100 3686 2459
7 καὶ μεταβὰς ἐκεῖθεν ἦλθεν εἰς οἰκίαν τινὸς ὀνόματι Ἰούστου,
And moving from there he went into house of one by name Justus,
4576 2316 3739 3614/2258 4927
σεβομένου τὸν Θεόν, οὗ ἡ οἰκία ἦν συνομοροῦσα τῇ
(one) worshiping God, of whom the house was being next door to the
4864 2921 752 4100
8 συναγωγῇ. Κρίσπος δὲ ὁ ἀρχισυνάγωγος ἐπίστευσε τῷ
synagogue. Crispus And the synagogue ruler believed the
2962 4862/3650 3624 848 4183 2881
Κυρίῳ σὺν ὅλῳ τῷ οἴκῳ αὐτοῦ· καὶ πολλοὶ τῶν Κορινθίων
Lord with all the house of him, and many of the Corinthians
191 4100 907 2036 2962 1223
9 ἀκούοντες ἐπίστευον καὶ ἐβαπτίζοντο. εἶπε δὲ ὁ Κύριος δι'
hearing believed and were baptized. said And the Lord through
3705 1722 3571 3972 3361 5399 235 2980
ὁράματος ἐν νυκτὶ τῷ Παύλῳ, Μὴ φοβοῦ, ἀλλὰ λάλει καὶ
a vision in (the) night – to Paul, Do not fear, but speak and
3361 4623 1360/1473/1510/3326/4675 3762 2007
10 μὴ σιωπήσῃς· διότι ἐγώ εἰμι μετὰ σοῦ, καὶ οὐδεὶς ἐπιθή-
do not keep silence, because I am with you, and no one shall
4671 2559 4571/1360/2992 2076/3427/4183/1722
σεταί σοι τοῦ κακῶσαί σε· διότι λαός ἐστί μοι πολὺς ἐν τῇ
set on you – to oppress you; because people is to me much. in –
4172 5026 2523 5037 1763 3375 1803 1321
11 πόλει ταύτῃ. ἐκάθισέ τε ἐνιαυτὸν καὶ μῆνας ἕξ, διδάσκων
city this. he sat And a year and months six teaching
1722 846 3056 2316
ἐν αὐτοῖς τὸν λόγον τοῦ Θεοῦ.
among them the word – of God.
1058 445 882 2721
12 Γαλλίωνος δὲ ἀνθυπατεύοντος τῆς Ἀχαΐας, κατεπέστησαν
Gallio (being) And proconsul – of Achaia, rushed against
3661 2453 3972 71 846
ὁμοθυμαδὸν οἱ Ἰουδαῖοι τῷ Παύλῳ, καὶ ἤγαγον αὐτὸν
with one mind the Jews Paul, and led him
1909 968 3004 3754 3844 3551 3778 374
13 ἐπὶ τὸ βῆμα, λέγοντες ὅτι Παρὰ τὸν νόμον οὗτος ἀναπείθει
to the tribunal, saying, Contrary to the law, this one persuades
444 4576 2316 3195
14 τοὺς ἀνθρώπους σέβεσθαι τὸν Θεόν. μέλλοντος δὲ τοῦ
– men to worship – God. being about And –
3972 455 4750 2036 1058 4314
Παύλου ἀνοίγειν τὸ στόμα, εἶπεν ὁ Γαλλίων πρὸς τοὺς
Paul to open the mouth, said – Gallio to the
2453 1487/3303/3767/2258/ 92 5100/2228 4467
Ἰουδαίους, Εἰ μὲν οὖν ἦν ἀδίκημά τι ἢ ῥᾳδιούργημα
Jews, If indeed, then, it was wrong some or criminality
4190 5599 2453 2596 3056 302 430 5216
πονηρόν, ὦ Ἰουδαῖοι, κατὰ λόγον ἂν ἠνεσχόμην ὑμῶν·
wicked, O Jews, according to reason I would endure you;

15 But if it is a question about a word, and names, and the law according to you, you will see to *it* yourselves; for I do not wish to be a judge of these things. 16 And he drove them from the tribunal. 17 And all the Greeks having seized Sosthenes the ruler of the synagogue, they beat *him* before the tribunal. And not one of these things mattered to Gallio.

18 And having remained many days more, having taken leave of the brothers, Paul sailed to Syria—and Priscilla and Aquila *were* with him—having shaved *his* head in Cenchrea, for he had a vow. 19 And he came to Ephesus, and he left those there. But he going into the synagogue, he reasoned with the Jews. 20 And they asking *him* to remain over a longer time with them, he did not agree; 21 but took leave of them, saying, I must by all means keep the coming feast at Jerusalem; but I will come again to you, God willing. And he sailed from Ephesus. 22 And landing at Caesarea, having gone up and greeted the church, he went down to Antioch.

23 And spending some time, he went out, in order passing through the Galatian and Phrygian country, making all the disciples strong.

24 But a certain Jew named Apollos, an Alexandrian by birth, an eloquent man, came to Ephesus, being powerful in the Scriptures. 25 This one was taught by mouth in the way of the Lord; and *being* fervent in spirit, he spoke and taught accurately the

1487 2213 2076 4012 3056 3686 3551
15 εἰ δὲ ζήτημά ἐστι περὶ λόγου καὶ ὀνομάτων καὶ νόμου τοῦ
if but a question it is about a word and names and law the
2596 5209 3700 846 2923 1063/1473 5130 3756/1014
καθ᾽ ὑμᾶς, ὄψεσθε αὐτοί· κριτὴς γὰρ ἐγὼ τούτων οὐ βού-
according to you, you will (your) a judge for I of these things not
1511 see to (it) selves 846 575 968
16 λομαι εἶναι. καὶ ἀπήλασεν αὐτοὺς ἀπὸ τοῦ βήματος.
intend to be. And he drove them from the tribunal.
1949 3956 1672 4988 752[
17 ἐπιλαβόμενοι δὲ πάντες οἱ Ἕλληνες Σωσθένην τὸν ἀρχι-
seizing But all the Greeks Sosthenes the ruler
5180 1715 968 3762
συνάγωγον ἔτυπτον ἔμπροσθεν τοῦ βήματος. καὶ οὐδὲν
of the synagogue, they struck (him) before the tribunal; and not one
5130 1058 3199
τούτων τῷ Γαλλίωνι ἔμελεν.
of these things to Gallio mattered.
3972 2089 4357 2250 2425 80
18 Ὁ δὲ Παῦλος ἔτι προσμείνας ἡμέρας ἱκανάς, τοῖς ἀδελφοῖς
And Paul yet having remained days many, to the brothers
657 1602 1519 4947 4862 846
ἀποταξάμενος, ἐξέπλει εἰς τὴν Συρίαν, καὶ σὺν αὐτῷ
taking leave, he sailed to Syria, and with him
4252 207 2751 2776 1722 2747
Πρίσκιλλα καὶ Ἀκύλας, κειράμενος τὴν κεφαλὴν ἐν Κεγχρεαῖς·
Priscilla and Aquila, having shorn the head in Cenchrea;
2192 1063 2171 2658 1519 2181 2548 2641
19 εἶχε γὰρ εὐχήν. κατήντησε δὲ εἰς Ἔφεσον, κἀκείνους κατέ-
he had for a vow. he came down And to Ephesus, and those he
847 848 1525 1519 4864 1256
λιπεν αὐτοῦ· αὐτὸς δὲ εἰσελθὼν εἰς τὴν συναγωγὴν διε-
left there. he But entering into the synagogue reasoned
2453 2065 846 1909 4119
20 λέχθη τοῖς Ἰουδαίοις. ἐρωτώντων δὲ αὐτῶν ἐπὶ πλείονα
with the Jews. asking And they over a longer
5550 3306 3844 846 3756 1962 235 657
21 χρόνον μεῖναι παρ᾽ αὐτοῖς, οὐκ ἐπένευσεν· ἀλλ᾽ ἀπετάξατο
time to remain with them, not he did agree, but took leave
846 2036/1163/3165/ 3843 1859 2064 4160
αὐτοῖς εἰπών, Δεῖ με πάντως τὴν ἑορτὴν τὴν ἐρχομένην ποιῆ-
of them, saying, It behoves by all the feast coming to
1519 2414 me 3825 means 344 4314 5209 2316
σαι εἰς Ἱεροσόλυμα· πάλιν δὲ ἀνακάμψω πρὸς ὑμᾶς, τοῦ Θεοῦ
keep at Jerusalem, again but I will come to you, God
2309 321 575 2181 2718 1519
22 θέλοντος. καὶ ἀνήχθη ἀπὸ τῆς Ἐφέσου. καὶ κατελθὼν εἰς
willing. And he sailed from Ephesus. And landing at
2542 305 782 1577
Καισάρειαν, ἀναβὰς καὶ ἀσπασάμενος τὴν ἐκκλησίαν,
Caesarea, having gone up and having greeted the church,
2597 1519 490 4160 5550 5100 1831
23 κατέβη εἰς Ἀντιόχειαν. καὶ ποιήσας χρόνον τινὰ ἐξῆλθε,
he went down to Antioch. And having spent time some he went out,
1330 2517 1054 5561 5435
διερχόμενος καθεξῆς τὴν Γαλατικὴν χώραν καὶ Φρυγίαν,
passing through in order the Galatian country and Phrygia
1991 3956 3101
ἐπιστηρίζων πάντας τοὺς μαθητάς.
strengthening all the disciples.
2453 5100 625 3686 221
24 Ἰουδαῖος δέ τις Ἀπολλὼς ὀνόματι, Ἀλεξανδρεὺς τῷ
a Jew And certain, Apollos by name, an Alexandrian
1085 435 3052 2658 1519 2181 1415 5607/1722
γένει, ἀνὴρ λόγιος, κατήντησεν εἰς Ἔφεσον, δυνατὸς ὢν ἐν
by race, a man eloquent, came to Ephesus, powerful being in
1124 3778/2258 2727 3598 2962
25 ταῖς γραφαῖς. οὗτος ἦν κατηχημένος τὴν ὁδὸν τοῦ Κυρίου,
the Scriptures. This one was orally taught in the way of the Lord,
2204 4151 2980 1321 199 4012
καὶ ζέων τῷ πνεύματι ἐλάλει καὶ ἐδίδασκεν ἀκριβῶς τὰ περὶ
and fervent in spirit he spoke and taught accurately the about things

things about the Lord,
having understood only the
baptism of John. 26 And
this one began to speak
boldly in the synagogue.
And hearing him Priscilla
and Aquila took him and
more accurately expounded
the way of God to him.
27 And he having intended
to go through into Achaia,
having been encouraged
the brothers wrote to the
disciples to welcome him;
who, having arrived much
helped those who were be-
lieving through grace.
28 For he powerfully con-
futed the Jews publicly,
proving through the Scriptures Jesus to be the Christ.

2962 1987 3440 908 2491
τοῦ Κυρίου, ἐπιστάμενος μόνον τὸ βάπτισμα Ἰωάννου·
the Lord, having understood only the baptism of John.
3778/5037/756 3955 1722 4864 191
26 οὗτός τε ἤρξατο παρρησιάζεσθαι ἐν τῇ συναγωγῇ. ἀκού-
this one And began to speak boldly in the synagogue. hearing
846 207 4252 4355
σαντες δὲ αὐτοῦ Ἀκύλας καὶ Πρίσκιλλα, προσελάβοντο
And him, Aquila and Priscilla took
846 197 846 1620 2316 3598
αὐτόν, καὶ ἀκριβέστερον αὐτῷ ἐξέθεντο τὴν τοῦ Θεοῦ ὁδόν.
him and more accurately to him expounded the of God way.
1014 846 1330 1519 882 4389
27 βουλομένου δὲ αὐτοῦ διελθεῖν εἰς τὴν Ἀχαΐαν, προτρεψά-
intending And him to go through into Achaia, being encour-
80 1125 3101 588 846
μενοι οἱ ἀδελφοὶ ἔγραψαν τοῖς μαθηταῖς ἀποδέξασθαι αὐτόν·
aged, the brothers wrote to the disciples to welcome him;
3739 3854 4820 4183 4100 1223
ὃς παραγενόμενος συνεβάλετο πολὺ τοῖς πεπιστευκόσι διὰ
who having arrived helped much those believing through
5485 2159 1063 2453 1246
28 τῆς χάριτος· εὐτόνως γὰρ τοῖς Ἰουδαίοις διακατηλέγχετο
grace; vehemently for the Jews he confuted
1219 1925 1223 1124 1511 5547
δημοσίᾳ, ἐπιδεικνὺς διὰ τῶν γραφῶν εἶναι τὸν Χριστὸν
publicly, proving through the Scriptures to be the Christ
2424
Ἰησοῦν.
Jesus.

CHAPTER 19

1 And it happened, in the
time Apollos was in
Corinth, Paul *was* passing
through the higher parts to
come to Ephesus. And
finding some disciples, 2 he
said to them, Believing, did
you receive *the* Holy Spirit?
And they said to him, We
did not even hear whether
the Holy Spirit is. 3 And he
said to them, Then to what
were you baptized? And
they said, To the baptism of
John.
4 And Paul said, John
indeed baptized *with* a
baptism of repentance, saying to the people that they
should believe into the *One*
coming after him; that is,
into the Christ, Jesus. 5 And
hearing, they were baptized
into the name of the Lord
Jesus. 6 And Paul laying
hands on them, the Holy
Spirit came on them; and
they spoke in languages
and prophesied. 7 And all
the men were about twelve.

1096 1722 625 1511/1722 2882 3972
1 Ἐγένετο δέ, ἐν τῷ τὸν Ἀπολλὼ εἶναι ἐν Κορίνθῳ, Παῦλον
it happened And in the (time) Apollos was in Corinth, Paul
1330 510 3313 2064 1519 2181 2147
διελθόντα τὰ ἀνωτερικὰ μέρη ἐλθεῖν εἰς Ἔφεσον· καὶ εὑρών
passing through the higher parts came to Ephesus, and finding
5100 3101 2036 4314 846 1487 4151 40 2983
2 τινας μαθητὰς εἶπε πρὸς αὐτούς, Εἰ Πνεῦμα Ἅγιον ἐλάβετε
some disciples, said to them, If (the) Spirit Holy you received
4100 2036 4314/846 235 3761/1487/4151
πιστεύσαντες; οἱ δὲ εἶπον πρὸς αὐτόν, Ἀλλ' οὐδὲ εἰ Πνεῦμα
believing? they And said to him, But not even if (the) Spirit
40 2076 191 2036/5037/4314 846 1519/5101/3767
3 Ἅγιόν ἐστιν, ἠκούσαμεν. εἶπέ τε πρὸς αὐτούς, Εἰς τί οὖν
Holy is we did hear. he said And to them, To what, then
907 2036 1519 2491 908 2036
ἐβαπτίσθητε; οἱ δὲ εἶπον, Εἰς τὸ Ἰωάννου βάπτισμα; εἶπε
were you baptized? they And said, To the of John baptism. said
3972 2491 3303 907 908 3341
4 δὲ Παῦλος, Ἰωάννης μὲν ἐβάπτισε βάπτισμα μετανοίας, τῷ
And Paul, John indeed baptized a baptism of repentance to the
2992 3004 1519 2064 3326 846 2443 4100
λαῷ λέγων εἰς τὸν ἐρχόμενον μετ' αὐτὸν ἵνα πιστεύσωσι,
people, saying into the (One) coming after him that they should believe,
5123 2076 1519 5547 2424 191 907
5 τοῦτ' ἔστιν, εἰς τὸν Χριστὸν Ἰησοῦν. ἀκούσαντες δὲ ἐβαπτί-
this is, in the Christ, Jesus. hearing And they were
1519 3686 2962 2424 2007
6 σθησαν εἰς τὸ ὄνομα τοῦ Κυρίου Ἰησοῦ. καὶ ἐπιθέντος
baptized into the name of the Lord Jesus. And laying on
846 3972 5495 2064 4151 40
αὐτοῖς τοῦ Παύλου τὰς χεῖρας, ἦλθε τὸ Πνεῦμα τὸ Ἅγιον
them Paul the hands, came the Spirit Holy
1909 846 2980 5037 1100 4395 2258
7 ἐπ' αὐτούς, ἐλάλουν τε γλώσσαις καὶ προεφήτευον. ἦσαν
on them; the spoke and in languages and prophesied. were
3756 435 5616 1177
δὲ οἱ πάντες ἄνδρες ὡσεὶ δεκαδύο.
And the all men about twelve.

[8]And going into the synagogue, he spoke boldly over three months, having reasoned with *them*, and persuading concerning the things of the kingdom of God. [9]But when some were hardened, and did not obey, speaking evil of the Way before the multitude, departing from them He separated the disciples, conversing day by day in the school of a certain Tyrannus. [10]And this happened over two years, so as all those living in Asia heard the word of the Lord Jesus, both Jews and Greeks. [11]And God did works of power through the hands of Paul, not the common *works;* [12]*but* so as even handkerchiefs or aprons from his skin to be brought onto those sick, and the diseases to be released from them; and the evil spirits to go out from them.

[13]But certain from the strolling Jews, exorcists, undertook to name the name of the Lord Jesus over those having evil spirits, saying, We exorcise you *by* Jesus whom Paul preaches. [14]And there were seven sons of Sceva, a Jewish chief priest, doing this. [15]But answering the evil spirit said, I know Jesus, and I comprehend Paul, but who are you? [16]And the man in whom was the evil spirit leaped on them; and overcoming them, he was strong against them, so that they fled out of the house naked, and having been wounded. [17]And this became known to all, both Jews and Greeks, those living in Ephesus. And fear

1525 1519 4864 3955 1909
8 Εἰσελθὼν δὲ εἰς τὴν συναγωγὴν ἐπαρρησιάζετο, ἐπὶ
entering And into the synagogue, he spoke boldly over
3376 5140 1256 3982 4012 932
μῆνας τρεῖς διαλεγόμενος καὶ πείθων τὰ περὶ τῆς βασιλείας
months three conversing with and per- the things con- the kingdom
2316/5613 5100/4645 suading cerning 544 2551
9 τοῦ Θεοῦ. ὡς δέ τινες ἐσκληρύνοντο καὶ ἠπείθουν, κακολο-
of God. as But some were hardened and disobeyed, speaking
3598 1799 4128 868 575
γοῦντες τὴν ὁδὸν ἐνώπιον τοῦ πλήθους, ἀποστὰς ἀπ'
evil of the Way before the multitude, departing from
846 873 3101 2596 2250 1256
αὐτῶν ἀφώρισε τοὺς μαθητάς, καθ' ἡμέραν διαλεγόμενος
them, he separated the disciples, day by day conversing
1722 4981 5181 5100 5124 1096 1909/2094/1417
10 ἐν τῇ σχολῇ Τυράννου τινός. τοῦτο δὲ ἐγένετο ἐπὶ ἔτη δύο,
in the school of Tyrannus a certain. this And happened over years two.
5620 3956 2730 773 191
ὥστε πάντας τοὺς κατοικοῦντας τὴν Ἀσίαν ἀκοῦσαι τὸν
so as all those inhabiting Asia heard the
3056 2962 2424 2453 5037 1672
λόγον τοῦ Κυρίου Ἰησοῦ, Ἰουδαίους τε καὶ Ἕλληνας.
word of the Lord Jesus, Jews both and Greeks.
1411 5037/3756 5177 4160 2316/1223 5495
11 δυνάμεις τε οὐ τὰς τυχούσας ἐποίει ὁ Θεὸς διὰ τῶν χειρῶν
works of power And not the common did God through the hands
3972/5620 1909 770 2018 575
Παύλου, ὥστε καὶ ἐπὶ τοὺς ἀσθενοῦντας ἐπιφέρεσθαι ἀπὸ
of Paul, so as even onto those sick to be brought from
5559 848 4676 2228 4612 525
τοῦ χρωτὸς αὐτοῦ σουδάρια ἢ σιμικίνθια, καὶ ἀπαλλάσσε-
the skin of him handkerchiefs or aprons, and to be released
575 846 3554 5037 4151 4190
σθαι ἀπ' αὐτῶν τὰς νόσους, τά τε πνεύματα τὰ πονηρὰ
from them the diseases, the and spirits — evil
1831 575 846 2021 5100 575 4022
13 ἐξέρχεσθαι ἀπ' αὐτῶν. ἐπεχείρησαν δέ τινες ἀπὸ τῶν περιερ-
to go out from them. undertook But some from the strolling
2453 1845 3687 1909 2192
χομένων Ἰουδαίων ἐξορκιστῶν ὀνομάζειν ἐπὶ τοὺς ἔχοντας
Jews, exorcists, to name over those having
4151 4190 3686 2962 2424
τὰ πνεύματα τὰ πονηρὰ τὸ ὄνομα τοῦ Κυρίου Ἰησοῦ,
the spirits — evil the name of the Lord Jesus,
3004 3726 5209 2424/3739 3972 2784
λέγοντες, Ὁρκίζομεν ὑμᾶς τὸν Ἰησοῦν ὃν ὁ Παῦλος κηρύσ-
saying, we exorcise you (by) Jesus whom Paul proclaims.
2258 5100/5207 4630 2453 749 2033
14 σει. ἦσαν δέ τινες υἱοὶ Σκευᾶ Ἰουδαίου ἀρχιερέως ἑπτὰ οἱ
were And of one sons, of Sceva, a Jewish chief priest, seven
5124 4160 611 4151 4190
15 τοῦτο ποιοῦντες. ἀποκριθὲν δὲ τὸ πνεῦμα τὸ πονηρὸν
this doing. answering And the spirit — evil
2036 2424 1097 3972 1987
εἶπε, Τὸν Ἰησοῦν γινώσκω, καὶ τὸν Παῦλον ἐπίσταμαι·
said, — Jesus I know, and — Paul I comprehend,
5210 5101/2075 2177 1909 846 444
16 ὑμεῖς δὲ τίνες ἐστέ; καὶ ἐφαλλόμενος ἐπ' αὐτοὺς ὁ ἄνθρωπος
you but, who are? And leaping on them the man
1722/3739/2258 4151 4190 2634 846
ἐν ᾧ ἦν τὸ πνεῦμα τὸ πονηρόν, καὶ κατακυριεύσας αὐτῶν,
in whom was the spirit — evil, and overmastering them,
2480 2596 846 5620 1131 5135
ἴσχυσε κατ' αὐτῶν, ὥστε γυμνοὺς καὶ τετραυματισμένους
was strong against them, so as naked and having been wounded
1628 1537 3624 1565 5124 1096 1110
17 ἐκφυγεῖν ἐκ τοῦ οἴκου ἐκείνου. τοῦτο δὲ ἐγένετο γνωστὸν
to escape out of house that. this And became known
3956 2453 5037 1672 2730 2181
πᾶσιν Ἰουδαίοις τε καὶ Ἕλλησι τοῖς κατοικοῦσι τὴν Ἔφεσον,
to all, Jews both and Greeks, those inhabiting Ephesus;

fell on them all, and the name of the Lord Jesus was magnified. [18]And many of those who had believed came confessing, and declaring their deeds. [19]And many of the ones practicing the curious arts, bringing together the books, burned *them* before all. And they counted the prices of them, and found *it to be* five ten thousands of silver. [20]So with might, the word of the Lord increased and was strong.

[21]And when these things were fulfilled, passing through Macedonia and Achaia, Paul purposed in the Spirit to go to Jerusalem, saying, After I have come there, I must also see Rome. [22]And sending into Macedonia two who ministered to him, Timothy and Erastus, he stayed a time in Asia.

[23]And about that time there was no little disturbance about the Way. [24]For a certain silversmith named Demetrius *was* making silver shrines of Artemis, providing no little trade *for* the craftsmen. [25]And assembling the workmen about such things, he said, Men, you understand that from this trade is our wealth. [26]And you see and hear that not only Ephesus, but almost all of Asia this Paul persuading has perverted a huge crowd, saying that those being made by hands are not gods. [27]And not only is this dangerous to us, *lest our* part come to *be in* contempt, but also the temple of the great goddess Artemis will be counted nothing, and her

1968 5401 1909 3956 846 3170
καὶ ἔπεσε φόβος ἐπὶ πάντας αὐτούς, καὶ ἐμεγαλύνετο τὸ
and fell on fear on all them, and was magnified the
3686 2962 2424 4183 5037 4100
18 ὄνομα τοῦ Κυρίου Ἰησοῦ. πολλοί τε τῶν πεπιστευκότων
name of the Lord Jesus. many And of those having believed
2064 1843 312 4234
ἤρχοντο, ἐξομολογούμενοι, καὶ ἀναγγέλλοντες τὰς πράξεις
came confessing and telling the doings
848 2425 4021 4238 4851
19 αὐτῶν. ἱκανοὶ δὲ τῶν τὰ περίεργα πραξάντων συνενέγκαντες
of them. many And of those the curious arts practicing, bringing together
976 2618 1799 3956 4860
τὰς βίβλους κατέκαιον ἐνώπιον πάντων· καὶ συνεψήφισαν
the rolls, burned (them) before all, and they counted
5092 848 2147 694 3461 4002 3779
20 τὰς τιμὰς αὐτῶν, καὶ εὗρον ἀργυρίου μυριάδας πέντε. οὕτω
the prices of them, and found of silver ten thousands five. Thus
2596 2904 3056 2962 837 2480
κατὰ κράτος ὁ λόγος τοῦ Κυρίου ηὔξανε καὶ ἴσχυεν.
with might the word of the Lord increased and was strong.
5613 4137 5023 5087 3972 1722 4151
21 Ὡς δὲ ἐπληρώθη ταῦτα, ἔθετο ὁ Παῦλος ἐν τῷ πνεύματι,
when And were fulfilled these things, purposed Paul in the Spirit
1330 3109 882 4198 1519
διελθὼν τὴν Μακεδονίαν καὶ Ἀχαΐαν, πορεύεσθαι εἰς
passing through Macedonia and Achaia to go to
2419 2036 3754 3326 1096 3165/1563/1163/3165
Ἱερουσαλήμ, εἰπὼν ὅτι Μετὰ τὸ γενέσθαι με ἐκεῖ, δεῖ με καὶ
Jerusalem, saying, — After becoming me there, must me also
4516 1492 649 1519 3109 1417
22 Ῥώμην ἰδεῖν. ἀποστείλας δὲ εἰς τὴν Μακεδονίαν δύο τῶν
Rome see. sending And into — Macedonia two of those
1247 846 5095 2037 846 1907
διακονούντων αὐτῷ, Τιμόθεον καὶ Ἔραστον, αὐτὸς ἐπέσχε
ministering to him, Timothy and Erastus, he delayed
5550 1519 773
χρόνον εἰς τὴν Ἀσίαν.
a time in — Asia.
1096 2596 2540 1565 5017 3756 3641
23 Ἐγένετο δὲ κατὰ τὸν καιρὸν ἐκεῖνον τάραχος οὐκ ὀλίγος
there was And about — time that disturbance not a little
4012 3598 1216 1063 3686 695
24 περὶ τῆς ὁδοῦ. Δημήτριος γάρ τις ὀνόματι, ἀργυροκόπος,
about the Way. Demetrius For one by name, a silversmith,
4160 3485 693 735 3930 5079
ποιῶν ναοὺς ἀργυροῦς Ἀρτέμιδος, παρείχετο τοῖς τεχνίταις
making shrines silver of Artemis provided the craftsmen
2039 3756 3641 3739 4867 4012
25 ἐργασίαν οὐκ ὀλίγην· οὓς συναθροίσας, καὶ τοὺς περὶ τὰ
trade not a little; whom assembling also the about
5108 2040 2036 435 1987 3754/1537/5026
τοιαῦτα ἐργάτας, εἶπεν, Ἄνδρες, ἐπίστασθε ὅτι ἐκ ταύτης
such things workmen, he said, Men, you understand that from this
2039 2142 2257 2076 2334 191
26 τῆς ἐργασίας ἡ εὐπορία ἡμῶν ἐστι. καὶ θεωρεῖτε καὶ ἀκούετε
— trade the gain to us is. And you behold and hear
3754/3756/3440 2181 235 4975 3956 773
ὅτι οὐ μόνον Ἐφέσου, ἀλλὰ σχεδὸν πάσης τῆς Ἀσίας, ὁ
that not only Ephesus, but almost all — of Asia —
3972 3778 3982 3179 2425 3793 3005 3754
Παῦλος οὗτος πείσας μετέστησεν ἱκανὸν ὄχλον, λέγων ὅτι
Paul this persuading perverted a huge crowd, saying that
3756/1526/2316 1223 5495 1096 3756/ 3440 5124
27 οὐκ εἰσὶ θεοὶ οἱ διὰ χειρῶν γινόμενοι. οὐ μόνον δὲ τοῦτο
not are gods those through hands being made. not only And this,
2793 2254 3313 1519 557 2064 235
κινδυνεύει ἡμῖν τὸ μέρος εἰς ἀπελεγμὸν ἐλθεῖν, ἀλλὰ καὶ τὸ
is in danger to us the share into disrepute to come, but also the
3173 2299 735 2411 1519 3762 3049
τῆς μεγάλης θεᾶς Ἀρτέμιδος ἱερὸν εἰς οὐδὲν λογισθῆναι,
of the great goddess Artemis temple for nothing will be counted

majesty is also about to be destroyed, whom all Asia and the world worships.

[28]And hearing, and becoming full of anger, they cried out, saying, Great *is* Artemis of *the* Ephesians! [29]And all the city was filled with confusion. And they rushed with one passion into the theater, keeping a firm grip on Gaius and Aristarchus, Macedonians, traveling companions of Paul. [30]And Paul intending to go in to the mob, the disciples did not allow him. [31]And also some of the Asiarchs, being his friends, sending to him begged *him* not to give himself into the theater. [32]Then others indeed cried out a different thing, for the assembly was confused; and the majority did not know on what account they came together.

[33]But they dragged Alexander forward out of the crowd, the Jews pushing him in front. And waving *his* hand, Alexander desired to defend himself to the mob. [34]But knowing that he is a Jew, one voice was from all, as *they were* crying out over two hours, Great *is* Artemis of *the* Ephesians!

[35]And quieting the crowd,the town clerk said, Men, Ephesians, for what man is there who does not know the city of the Ephesians to be temple-keepers of the great goddess Artemis, and of That Fallen from the heaven? [36]Then these things being undeniable, it is necessary for you having been calmed to be *so*, and to do nothing rash. [37]For you brought these men, neither temple-robbers nor blaspheming your goddess. [38]If then, indeed, Demetrius and those craftsmen with him

3195 2507 3168 848/3739/3650
μέλλειν τε καὶ καθαιρεῖσθαι τὴν μεγαλειότητα αὐτῆς, ἣν ὅλη
is going and also to be diminished the greatness of her, whom all
773 3625 4576 191 1096
28 ἡ Ἀσία καὶ ἡ οἰκουμένη σέβεται. ἀκούσαντες δὲ καὶ γενό-
Asia and the habitable world worships. hearing And, and
4134 2372 2896 3004 3173 735
μενοι πλήρεις θυμοῦ, ἔκραζον λέγοντες, Μεγάλη ἡ Ἄρτεμις
becoming full of anger, they cried out saying, Great (is) Artemis
2180 4130 4172 3650 4799 3729 5037
29 Ἐφεσίων. καὶ ἐπλήσθη ἡ πόλις ὅλη συγχύσεως· ὥρμησάν τε
of (the) Ephesians! And was filled the city all of confusion, they rushed and
3661 1519 2302 4884 1050
ὁμοθυμαδὸν εἰς τὸ θέατρον, συναρπάσαντες Γάϊον καὶ
with one mind to the theatre, keeping a firm grip on Gaius and
708 3110 4898 3972
30 Ἀρίσταρχον Μακεδόνας, συνεκδήμους τοῦ Παύλου. τοῦ δὲ
Aristarchus, Macedonians, traveling companions of Paul. —And
3972 1014 1525 1519 1218 3756 1439 846
Παύλου βουλομένου εἰσελθεῖν εἰς τὸν δῆμον, οὐκ εἴων αὐτὸν
Paul intending to enter into the mob, not allowed him
3101 5100 775 5607 846 5384
31 οἱ μαθηταί. τινὲς δὲ καὶ τῶν Ἀσιαρχῶν, ὄντες αὐτῷ φίλοι,
the disciples. some And also of the Asiarchs, being of him friends,
3992 4314 846 3870 3361 1325 1438
πέμψαντες πρὸς αὐτόν, παρεκάλουν μὴ δοῦναι ἑαυτὸν εἰς
sending to him, begged not to give himself into
2302 243 3303 3767 243 5100 2896 2258/1063
32 τὸ θέατρον. ἄλλοι μὲν οὖν ἄλλο τι ἔκραζον· ἦν γὰρ ἡ
the theatre. Others indeed, then, other some cried out. was for the
1577 4797 4119 3756 1492 5101
ἐκκλησία συγκεχυμένη, καὶ οἱ πλείους οὐκ ᾔδεισαν τίνος
assembly confounded, and the majority not did know of what
1752 4905 1537 3793 4264 223
33 ἕνεκεν συνεληλύθεισαν. ἐκ δὲ τοῦ ὄχλου προεβίβασαν Ἀλέ-
on account they came together out of But the crowd, they dragged forward
4261 846 2453 223
ξανδρον, προβαλλόντων αὐτὸν τῶν Ἰουδαίων. ὁ δὲ Ἀλέξαν-
Alexander, thrusting forward him the Jews. And Alexander
2678 5495 2309 626 1218
δρος, κατασείσας τὴν χεῖρα, ἤθελεν ἀπολογεῖσθαι τῷ δήμῳ.
waving the hand desired to defend himself to the mob.
1921 3754 2453 2076 5456 1096 3391/1537
34 ἐπιγνόντων δὲ ὅτι Ἰουδαῖός ἐστι, φωνὴ ἐγένετο μια ἐκ
knowing But that a Jew he is, voice there was one from
3956 5613/1909/5610/1417 2896 3173 735
πάντων ὡς ἐπὶ ὥρας δύο κραζόντων, Μεγάλη ἡ Ἄρτεμις
all, as over hours two crying out, Great (is) Artemis
2180 2687 1122 3793 5346
35 Ἐφεσίων. καταστείλας δὲ ὁ γραμματεὺς τὸν ὄχλον φησίν,
of (the) Ephesians! quieting And the town clerk the crowd, he says,
435 2180 5101 1063 2076 444 3739/3756 1097
Ἄνδρες Ἐφέσιοι, τίς γάρ ἐστιν ἄνθρωπος ὃς οὐ γινώσκει
Men, Ephesians, what for is there man who not does know
2180 4172 3511 5607 3173 2299
τὴν Ἐφεσίων πόλιν νεωκόρον οὖσαν τῆς μεγάλης θεᾶς
the of (the) Ephesians city temple-keeper being of the great goddess
735 1356 368 3767 5607
36 Ἀρτέμιδος καὶ τοῦ Διοπετοῦς; ἀναντιρρήτων οὖν ὄντων
Artemis, and of that fallen from the sky? undeniable Then being
5130 1163 2076 5209 2687 5225
τούτων, δέον ἐστὶν ὑμᾶς κατεσταλμένους ὑπάρχειν, καὶ
these things, necessary it is you having been quietened to be (so), and
3367 4312 4238 71 1063 435
37 μηδὲν προπετὲς πράττειν. ἠγάγετε γὰρ τοὺς ἄνδρας
nothing rash to do. you brought For — men
5128 3777 2417 3777 987 2299
τούτους, οὔτε ἱεροσύλους οὔτε βλασφημοῦντας τὴν θεὰν
these, neither temple-robbers nor blaspheming the goddess
5216/1487/3303/3767/ 1216 4862 846 5079 4314
38 ὑμῶν. εἰ μὲν οὖν Δημήτριος καὶ οἱ σὺν αὐτῷ τεχνῖται πρός
of you. If indeed, then, Demetrius and those with him craftsmen against

have a matter against anyone, courts are being *held*, and there are proconsuls. Let them accuse one another. [39]But if you seek concerning other things, it will be settled in a lawful assembly. [40]For we are in danger to be accused of insurrection concerning today; there being no cause about which we will be able to give account of this crowding together. [41]And saying these things, he dismissed the assembly.

CHAPTER 20

[1]And after the ceasing of the tumult, having called the disciples, and having greeted *them*, Paul went away to go into Macedonia. [2]And passing through those parts, and exhorting them with much speech, he came into Greece. [3]And spending three months there, a plot by the Jews being *against* him, being about to sail into Syria, he was of a mind to return through Macedonia. [4]And Sopater, a Berean; and Aristarchus and Secundus of the Thessalonians; and Gaius of Derbe; and Timothy; and Tychicus and Trophimus of Asia accompanied him as far as Asia. [5]Going forward, these awaited us in Troas. [6]But we sailed along after the days of unleavened *bread* from Philippi, and came to them at Troas *in* five days, where we stayed seven days.

[7]And on the first of the sabaths, the disciples assembling to break bread, being about to depart on the morrow, Paul reasoned to them. And he continued his speech until midnight. [8]And many lamps

5100 3056 2192 60 71 446
τινα λόγον ἔχουσιν, ἀγοραῖοι ἄγονται, καὶ ἀνθύπατοί
anyone a matter have, courts are being (held), and proconsuls
1526 1458 140 1487/5100/4012 2087 1934
39 εἰσιν· ἐγκαλείτωσαν ἀλλήλοις. εἰ δέ τι περὶ ἑτέρων ἐπιζητεῖτε,
are; let them accuse one another. if But any about other things you seek,
1722 1772 1577 1956 1063 2793
40 ἐν τῇ ἐννόμῳ ἐκκλησίᾳ ἐπιλυθήσεται. καὶ γὰρ κινδυνεύομεν
in the lawful assembly it will be settled. also For we are in danger
1458 4714 4012 4594 3367 158
ἐγκαλεῖσθαι στάσεως περὶ τῆς σήμερον, μηδενὸς αἰτίου
to be accused of insurrection concerning today; nothing cause
5225 4012 3739 1410 591 3056
ὑπάρχοντος περὶ οὗ δυνησόμεθα ἀποδοῦναι λόγον τῆς
there being concerning which we shall be able to give account –
4963 5026 5023 2036 630 1577
41 συστροφῆς ταύτης. καὶ ταῦτα εἰπών, ἀπέλυσε τὴν ἐκκλησίαν.
crowding together of this. And these things saying, he dismissed the assembly.

CHAPTER 20

3326 3973 2351 4341
1 Μετὰ δὲ τὸ παύσασθαι τὸν θόρυβον, προσκαλεσάμενος
after And the ceasing of the tumult, having called
3972 3101 782 1831 4198
ὁ Παῦλος τοὺς μαθητάς, καὶ ἀσπασάμενος, ἐξῆλθε πορευθῆναι
Paul the disciples, and greeting, went away to go
1519 3109 1330 3313 1565 3870
2 εἰς τὴν Μακεδονίαν. διελθὼν δὲ τὰ μέρη ἐκεῖνα, καὶ παρα-
to Macedonia. passing through And parts those, and having
846 3056 4183 2064 1519 1671 4160
καλέσας αὐτοὺς λόγῳ πολλῷ, ἦλθεν εἰς τὴν Ἑλλάδα. ποιή-
exhorted them with speech much, he came into Greece. spending
5037 3376 5140 1096 846 1917 5259
3 σας τε μῆνας τρεῖς, γενομένης αὐτῷ ἐπιβουλῆς ὑπὸ τῶν
And months three, there being (against) him a plot by the
2453 3195 321 1519 4947 1096
Ἰουδαίων μέλλοντι ἀνάγεσθαι εἰς τὴν Συρίαν, ἐγένετο
Jews, being about to set sail to Syria, he was
1106 5290 1223 3109 4902
4 γνώμη τοῦ ὑποστρέφειν διὰ Μακεδονίας. συνείπετο δὲ
of a mind to return through Macedonia. accompanied And
846 891 773 4986 951 2331
αὐτῷ ἄχρι τῆς Ἀσίας Σώπατρος Βεροιαῖος· Θεσσαλονι-
him as far as Asia Sopater, a Berean, of Thessalonians
708 4580 1050 1190
κέων δέ, Ἀρίσταρχος καὶ Σεκοῦνδος, καὶ Γάϊος Δερβαῖος.
and, Aristarchus and Secundus; and Gaius of Derbe,
5095 774 5190 5161 3778
5 καὶ Τιμόθεος· Ἀσιανοὶ δέ, Τυχικὸς καὶ Τρόφιμος. οὗτοι
and Timothy, of Asia and, Tychicus and Trophimus. These
4281 3306 2248/1722 5174 2249 1602
6 προελθόντες ἔμενον ἡμᾶς ἐν Τρῳάδι. ἡμεῖς δὲ ἐξεπλεύσαμεν
going forward awaited us in Troas. we And sailed away
3326 2250 106 575 5375 2064
μετὰ τὰς ἡμέρας τῶν ἀζύμων ἀπὸ Φιλίππων, καὶ ἤλθομεν
after the days of unleavened from Philippi, and came
4314 846 1519 5174 891 2250 4002 3757
πρὸς αὐτοὺς εἰς τὴν Τρῳάδα ἄχρις ἡμερῶν πέντε, οὗ
to them in Troas until days five, where
1304 2250 2033
διετρίψαμεν ἡμέρας ἑπτά.
we remained days seven.
1722 3391 4521 4863 3101
7 Ἐν δὲ τῇ μιᾷ τῶν σαββάτων, συνηγμένων τῶν μαθητῶν
on And the one of the sabbaths, having been assembled the disciples
2806 740 3972 1256 846 3195
τοῦ κλάσαι ἄρτον, ὁ Παῦλος διελέγετο αὐτοῖς, μέλλων
– to break bread, Paul reasoned to them, being about to
1826 1887 3905/5037 3056 3360 3317
ἐξιέναι τῇ ἐπαύριον, παρέτεινέ τε τὸν λόγον μέχρι μεσονυ-
depart on the morrow; he continued and the discourse until midnight.

2258 2985 2425 1722 5253 3757 2258
8 κτίου. ἦσαν δὲ λαμπάδες ἱκαναὶ ἐν τῷ ὑπερῴῳ οὗ ἦσαν
there were And lamps many in the upper room where they were
4863 2521 5100 3494 3686 2161 1909
9 συνηγμένοι. καθήμενος δέ τις νεανίας ὀνόματι Εὔτυχος ἐπὶ
assembled. sitting And a certain young man by name Eutuchus on
2376 2702 2258 901 1256
τῆς θυρίδος, καταφερόμενος ὕπνῳ βαθεῖ, διαλεγομένου τοῦ
the window sill, being overborne by sleep deep, reasoning —
3972 1909 4119 2702 575 5258 4098 575
Παύλου ἐπὶ πλεῖον, κατενεχθεὶς ἀπὸ τοῦ ὕπνου ἔπεσεν ἀπὸ
Paul for a longer time, being overborne by the sleep, he fell from
5152 2736 142 3498 2597 3972
10 τοῦ τριστέγου κάτω, καὶ ἤρθη νεκρός. καταβὰς δὲ ὁ Παῦλος
the third floor down, and was taken up dead. going down But Paul
1968 846 4843 2036 3361 2350
ἐπέπεσεν αὐτῷ, καὶ συμπεριλαβὼν εἶπε, Μὴ θορυβεῖσθε
fell on him, and having embraced said, Do not be terrified;
1063 5590 848 1722 846 2076 305 2806
11 ἡ γὰρ ψυχὴ αὐτοῦ ἐν αὐτῷ ἐστιν. ἀναβὰς δὲ καὶ κλάσας
the for soul of him in him is. going up And, and breaking
740 1089 1909 2425 5037 3656 891 827
ἄρτον καὶ γευσάμενος, ἐφ' ἱκανόν τε ὁμιλήσας ἄχρις αὐγῆς,
bread, and tasting, over a long (time) and conversing until dawn,
3779 1831 71 3816 2198 3870
12 οὕτως ἐξῆλθεν. ἤγαγον δὲ τὸν παῖδα ζῶντα, καὶ παρεκλήθη-
thus he went out. they brought and the boy living. and were comforted
3756 3357
σαν οὐ μετρίως.
not moderately.

2259 4281 1909 4143 321 1519
13 Ἡμεῖς δέ, προελθόντες ἐπὶ τὸ πλοῖον, ἀνήχθημεν εἰς τὴν
we And, going before onto the ship, set sail for —
789 1564 3195 353 3972 3779
Ἄσσον, ἐκεῖθεν μέλλοντες ἀναλαμβάνειν τὸν Παῦλον· οὕτω
Assos, from there intending to take up — Paul; so
1063/2258 1299 3195 846 3978 5613 4820
14 γὰρ ἦν διατεταγμένος, μέλλων αὐτὸς πεζεύειν. ὡς δὲ συνέ-
For it was having been arranged, intending he to go afoot. When And he
2254/1519 789 353 846 2064 1519
βαλεν ἡμῖν εἰς τὴν Ἄσσον, ἀναλαβόντες αὐτὸν ἤλθομεν εἰς
met with us in — Assos, taking up him we came to
3412 2547 636 1966 2658
15 Μιτυλήνην. κἀκεῖθεν ἀποπλεύσαντες, τῇ ἐπιούσῃ κατηντή-
Mitylene; and from there sailing away on the next we
481 5508 2087 3846 1519 4544
σαμεν ἀντικρὺ Χίου· τῇ δὲ ἑτέρᾳ παρεβάλομεν εἰς Σάμον· καὶ
arrived off Chios, on the and other we crossed to Samos, and
3306 1722 5175 2192 2064 1519 3399
μείναντες ἐν Τρωγυλλίῳ, τῇ ἐχομένῃ ἤλθομεν εἰς Μίλητον.
having remained at Trogyllium, the next (day) we came to Miletus
2919 1063 3972 3896 2181 3704 3361
16 ἔκρινε γὰρ ὁ Παῦλος παραπλεῦσαι τὴν Ἔφεσον, ὅπως μὴ
had decided For Paul to sail past — Ephesus, so as not
1096 846 5551 1722 773 4692 1063 1487
γένηται αὐτῷ χρονοτριβῆσαι ἐν τῇ Ἀσίᾳ· ἔσπευδε γάρ, εἰ
be to him to spend time in — Asia; he hastened for, if
1415 2258 846 2250 4005 1096
δυνατὸν ἦν αὐτῷ, τὴν ἡμέραν τῆς Πεντηκοστῆς γενέσθαι
possible it was for him the day — of Pentecost to be
1519 2414 575 3399 3992 1519 2181
17 εἰς Ἱεροσόλυμα. Ἀπὸ δὲ τῆς Μιλήτου πέμψας εἰς Ἔφεσον
in Jerusalem. from And — Miletus sending to Ephesus
3333 4245 1577 5613 3854
18 μετεκαλέσατο τοὺς πρεσβυτέρους τῆς ἐκκλησίας. ὡς δὲ παρε-
he called for the elders of the church. when And they
4314 846 2036 846
γένοντο πρὸς αὐτόν, εἶπεν αὐτοῖς,
came to him, he said to them,
5210 1987 575 4413 2250 575/3739 1910 1519
Ὑμεῖς ἐπίστασθε, ἀπὸ πρώτης ἡμέρας ἀφ' ἧς ἐπέβην εἰς
You understand from (the) first day from which I set foot in

were in the upper room where they were gathered. [9]And a certain young man named Eutychus *was* sitting on the window sill, being overborne by deep sleep, Paul reasoning for a longer time, being overborne by the sleep, he fell from the third floor down, and was taken up dead. [10]But going down Paul fell on him, and embracing *him, he* said, Do not be terrified; for his soul is in him. [11]And going up, and breaking bread, and tasting, and conversing over a long *time,* until daybreak, he went out thus. [12]And they brought the boy alive, and were comforted not a little.

[13]But going before onto the ship, we set sail for Assos, being about to take Paul in there; for so it had been arranged, he being about to go on foot. [14]And when he met us in Assos, taking him up we came to Mitylene. [15]And sailing away from there, on the next *day* we arrived off Chios, and on the next we crossed to Samos. And remaining at Trogyllium, the next *day* we came to Miletus. [16]For Paul had decided to sail by Ephesus, so as it might not happen to him to spend time in Asia; for he hastened if it were possible for him to be in Jerusalem *on* the day of Pentecost.

[17]And sending to Ephesus from Miletus, he called for the elders of the church. [18]And when they came to him, he said to them:

You understand, from *the* first day *on* which I set foot

in Asia, how I was with you all the time, [19]serving the Lord with all humility, and many tears and trials happening to me by the plots of the Jews; [20]as I kept nothing back of what is profitable, *so as* not to tell you; and to teach you publicly, and from house to house, [21]earnestly testifying both to Jews and to Greeks repentance toward God and faith toward our Lord Jesus Christ. [22]And now, behold, I being bound by the Spirit go to Jerusalem, not knowing the things going to meet me in it, [23]but that the Holy Spirit testifies city by city saying that bonds and afflictions await me. [24]But I make no account, nor do I hold my soul precious to myself, so that I might finish my course with joy, and the ministry which I received from the Lord Jesus Christ, fully to testify the gospel of the grace of God. [25]And now, behold, I know that you all will see my face no more, among whom I went about proclaiming the kingdom of God. [26]Therefore, I testify to you on this day that I am pure from the blood of all. [27]For I did not keep back from declaring to you all the counsel of God.

[28]Therefore, take heed to yourselves and to all the flock, in which the Holy Spirit placed you *as* overseers, to shepherd the church of God, which He purchased through *His* own blood. [29]For I know this, that after my departure

773 4459/3326/5216 3956 5550 1096
τὴν Ἀσίαν, πῶς μεθ' ὑμῶν τὸν πάντα χρόνον ἐγενόμην,
– Asia, how with you the all time I was,

1398 2962 3326 3956 5012
19 δουλεύων τῷ Κυρίῳ μετὰ πάσης ταπεινοφροσύνης καὶ
serving the Lord with all humility and

4183 1144 3986 4819 3427/1722
πολλῶν δακρύων καὶ πειρασμῶν τῶν συμβάντων μοι ἐν
many tears and trials – happening to me by

1917 2453 5613 3762 5288
20 ταῖς ἐπιβουλαῖς τῶν Ἰουδαίων· ὡς οὐδὲν ὑπεστειλάμην τῶν
the plots of the Jews, as nothing I kept back of the

4851 3361 312 5213 1321 5209
συμφερόντων, τοῦ μὴ ἀναγγεῖλαι ὑμῖν καὶ διδάξαι ὑμᾶς
profitable (things), – not to tell you, and to teach you

1219 2596 3624 1263 2453 5037
21 δημοσίᾳ καὶ κατ' οἴκους, διαμαρτυρόμενος Ἰουδαίοις τε καὶ
publicly, and from house to house, earnestly testifying to Jews and also

1672 1519 2316 3341 4102 1519
Ἕλλησι τὴν εἰς τὸν Θεὸν μετάνοιαν, καὶ πίστιν τὴν εἰς τὸν
to Greeks – toward – God repentance, and faith – toward the

2962 2257 2424 5547 3568 2400/1473 1210
22 Κύριον ἡμῶν Ἰησοῦν Χριστόν. καὶ νῦν ἰδού, ἐγὼ δεδεμένος
Lord of us, Jesus Christ. And now behold, I being bound

4151 4198 1519 2419 1722/846 4876
τῷ πνεύματι πορεύομαι εἰς Ἱερουσαλήμ, τὰ ἐν αὐτῇ συναντή-
by the Spirit am going to Jerusalem, the things in it going

3427/3361/1492 4133 3754 4151 40 2596
23 σοντά μοι μὴ εἰδώς, πλὴν ὅτι τὸ Πνεῦμα τὸ Ἅγιον κατὰ
to meet me not knowing, but that the Spirit – Holy city

4172 1263 3004 3754 1199/3165 2347 3306
πόλιν διαμαρτύρεται λέγον ὅτι δεσμά με καὶ θλίψεις μένουσιν.
by city testifies saying that bonds me and afflictions await.

235 3762 3056 4160 3761 2192 5590 3450
24 ἀλλ' οὐδενὸς λόγον ποιοῦμαι, οὐδὲ ἔχω τὴν ψυχήν μου
But of nothing account I make, nor hold the soul of me

5093 1683 5613 5048 1408 3450 3326 5479
τιμίαν ἐμαυτῷ, ὡς τελειῶσαι τὸν δρόμον μου μετὰ χαρᾶς,
precious to myself, so as I may finish the course of me with joy,

1248 3739 2983 3844 2962 2424
καὶ τὴν διακονίαν ἣν ἔλαβον παρὰ τοῦ Κυρίου Ἰησοῦ,
and the ministry which I received from the Lord Jesus,

1263 2098 5485 2316
25 διαμαρτύρασθαι τὸ εὐαγγέλιον τῆς χάριτος τοῦ Θεοῦ. καὶ
to fully testify the gospel of the grace – of God. And

3568 2400 1473 1492..3754 3765 3700 4383 3450
νῦν ἰδού, ἐγὼ οἶδα ὅτι οὐκέτι ὄψεσθε τὸ πρόσωπόν μου
now behold, I know that no more will see the face of me

5210 3956 1722/3739/ 1330 2784 932
26 ὑμεῖς πάντες, ἐν οἷς διῆλθον κηρύσσων τὴν βασιλείαν τοῦ
you all, among whom I went about proclaiming the kingdom –

2316 1352 3143 5213/1722 4594 . 2250 3754 2513
Θεοῦ. διὸ μαρτύρομαι ὑμῖν ἐν τῇ σήμερον ἡμέρᾳ, ὅτι καθαρὸς
of God. Therefore I testify to you on – this day that clean

1473 575 129 3956 3756/1063 5288
27 ἐγὼ ἀπὸ τοῦ αἵματος πάντων. οὐ γὰρ ὑπεστειλάμην τοῦ
I am from the blood of all; not for I kept back –

3361 312 5213 3956 1012 2316 4337
μὴ ἀναγγεῖλαι ὑμῖν πᾶσαν τὴν βουλὴν τοῦ Θεοῦ. προσ-
not to declare to you all the counsel – of God. take

3767 1438 3956 4168 1722/3739/5209
28 έχετε οὖν ἑαυτοῖς καὶ παντὶ τῷ ποιμνίῳ, ἐν ᾧ ὑμᾶς τὸ
heed, therefore, to yourselves and to all the flock, in which you the

4151 40 5087 1985 4165 1577
Πνεῦμα τὸ Ἅγιον ἔθετο ἐπισκόπους, ποιμαίνειν τὴν ἐκκλη-
Spirit – Holy placed overseers, to shepherd the church

2316 3739 4046 1223 2398 129
σίαν τοῦ Θεοῦ, ἣν περιεποιήσατο διὰ τοῦ ἰδίου αἵματος.
– of God, which He purchased through the own blood.

1473/1063 1492 5124 3754 1525 3326 867
29 ἐγὼ γὰρ οἶδα τοῦτο, ὅτι εἰσελεύσονται μετὰ τὴν ἀφιξίν
I For know this, that will come in after the departure

grievous wolves will come in among you, not sparing the flock; 30and from among your own selves will rise up men speaking perverted things, in order to draw away the disciples after themselves.

31Because of this watch, remembering that I did not cease admonishing each one with tears night and day *for* three years. 32And now, brothers, I commend you to God and to the word of His grace, which is able to build up and to give you inheritance among all those having been sanctified. 33I have desired *the* silver, or gold, or clothing of no one. 34But you yourselves know that these hands ministered to my needs, and to those who were with me. 35I showed you all things, that working in this way we ought to help those being weak, and to remember the words of the Lord Jesus, that He said, It is more blessed to give than to receive.

36And saying these things, placing his knees, he prayed with them all. 37And there was much weeping of all, and falling on the neck of Paul, they ardently kissed him, 38most of all grieving for the word which he had said, that they no more were going to see his face. And they went with him to the ship.

3450 3074 926 1519 5209/3361 5339 4168
30 μου λύκοι βαρεῖς εἰς ὑμᾶς, μὴ φειδόμενοι τοῦ ποιμνίου· καὶ
of me wolves grievous into you, not sparing the flock, and
1537/5216/848 450 435 2980 1294
ἐξ ὑμῶν αὐτῶν ἀναστήσονται ἄνδρες λαλοῦντες διεστραμ-
out of you yourselves will rise up men speaking perverted
645 3101 3694 848 1352
31 μένα, τοῦ ἀποσπᾷν τοὺς μαθητὰς ὀπίσω αὐτῶν. διὸ
things, — to draw away the disciples after themselves. Therefore
1127 3421 3754 5148 3572 2250
γρηγορεῖτε, μνημονεύοντες ὅτι τριετίαν νύκτα καὶ ἡμέραν
watch, remembering that three years night and day
3767 3973 3326 1144 3560 1520 1538
32 οὐκ ἐπαυσάμην μετὰ δακρύων νουθετῶν ἕνα ἕκαστον. καὶ
not I ceased with tears admonishing one each. And
3568 3908 5209 80 2316 3056
τὰ νῦν παρατίθεμαι ὑμᾶς, ἀδελφοί, τῷ Θεῷ καὶ τῷ λόγῳ
— now I commend you, brothers, — to God and to the word
5485 848 1410 2026
τῆς χάριτος αὐτοῦ, τῷ δυναμένῳ ἐποικοδομῆσαι, καὶ
— of grace of Him, — being able to build up and
1325 5213 2817 1722 37 3956 694
33 δοῦναι ὑμῖν κληρονομίαν ἐν τοῖς ἡγιασμένοις πᾶσιν. ἀργυ-
to give you inheritance among those having been sanctified all. Silver
5553 2228 2441 3762 1937 846
34 ρίου ἢ χρυσίου ἢ ἱματισμοῦ οὐδενὸς ἐπεθύμησα. αὐτοὶ δὲ
or gold or clothing of no one I desired. yourselves But
1097 3754 5532 3450 5607 3326 1700
γινώσκετε ὅτι ταῖς χρείαις μου καὶ τοῖς οὖσι μετ' ἐμοῦ
know that to the needs of me and those being with me
5256 5495 3778 3956 5263 5213 3754
35 ὑπηρέτησαν αἱ χεῖρες αὗται. πάντα ὑπέδειξα ὑμῖν, ὅτι
ministered hands these. All things I showed to you, that
3779 2872 1135 482 770
οὕτω κοπιῶντας δεῖ ἀντιλαμβάνεσθαι τῶν ἀσθενούντων,
thus working it behoves to help those infirm (ones),
3421 5037 3056 2962 2424 3754 848
μνημονεύειν τε τῶν λόγων τοῦ Κυρίου Ἰησοῦ, ὅτι αὐτὸς
to remember and the word of the Lord Jesus, that He
2036 3107 2076 1325 3123/2228 2983
εἶπε, Μακάριόν ἐστι διδόναι μᾶλλον ἢ λαμβάνειν.
said, Blessed it is to give rather than to receive.
5023 2036 5087 1119 848 4862 3956
36 Καὶ ταῦτα εἰπών, θεὶς τὰ γόνατα αὐτοῦ, σὺν πᾶσιν
And these things having said, placing the knees of him, with all
846 4336 2425 1096 2805 3956
37 αὐτοῖς προσηύξατο. ἱκανὸς δὲ ἐγένετο κλαυθμὸς πάντων·
them he prayed. much And was weeping of all,
1968 1909 5137 3972 2705
καὶ ἐπιπεσόντες ἐπὶ τὸν τράχηλον τοῦ Παύλου κατεφίλουν
and falling on the neck of Paul they ardently kissed
846 3600 3122 1909 3056/3739 2046 3754
38 αὐτόν, ὀδυνώμενοι μάλιστα ἐπὶ τῷ λόγῳ ᾧ εἰρήκει, ὅτι
him, grieving most over the word which he said, that
3765 3195 4383 848 2334 4311
οὐκέτι μέλλουσι τὸ πρόσωπον αὐτοῦ θεωρεῖν. προέπεμπον
no more they are the face of him to behold. they escorted
848 1519 4143
δὲ αὐτὸν εἰς τὸ πλοῖον.
And him to the ship.

CHAPTER 21

1And when it was *time* to sail, we having been torn away from them, running direct we came to Coos; and on the next *day* to Rhodes, and from there to Patara. 2And finding a ship

CHAPTER 21

1096 321 2248 645 575
1 Ὡς δὲ ἐγένετο ἀναχθῆναι ἡμᾶς ἀποσπασθέντας ἀπ'
when And it was (time) to sail, we having been withdrawn from
846 2113 2064 1519 2972 1836
αὐτῶν, εὐθυδρομήσαντες ἤλθομεν εἰς τὴν Κῶν, τῇ δὲ ἑξῆς
them, having run direct, we came to — Coos; on the and next
1519 4499 2547 1519 3959 2147 4143
2 εἰς τὴν Ῥόδον, κἀκεῖθεν εἰς Πάταρα· καὶ εὑρόντες πλοῖον
to — Rhodes, and from there to Patara; and having found a ship

crossing over to Phoenice, going on board we set sail. [3]And sighting Cyprus, and leaving it on the left, we sailed to Syria, and came down to Tyre; for the ship was unloading the cargo there. [4]And finding disciples, we remained there seven days; who told Paul through the Spirit not to go up to Jerusalem. [5]But when it was *time for* us to complete the days, going out we traveled. *And they*, with all *the* women and children went with us as far as outside the city. And placing the knees on the shore, *we* prayed. [6]And giving parting greetings to one another, we went up into the ship; and those went back to their own.

[7]And completing the voyage from Tyre, we arrived at Ptolemais. And having greeted the brothers, we remained one day with them. [8]And on the morrow, those around *him* going out, Paul came to Caesarea. And going into the house of Philip the evangelist, *he* being of the Seven, we stayed with him.

[9]And there were four virgin daughters to this one, who prophesied. [10]And we remaining more days, a certain prophet from Judea named Agabus came down. [11]And coming to us, and taking Paul's girdle, and binding his hands and feet, he said, The Holy Spirit says these *things:* In Jerusalem the Jews will bind in this way the man whose girdle this is, and will deliver *him* up into *the* hands of *the* Gentiles. [12]And when we heard these things, both we and those of *the* place

1276 1519 5403 1910 321 398
διαπερῶν εἰς Φοινίκην, ἐπιβάντες ἀνήχθημεν. ἀναφάναντες
crossing over to Phoenice, entering we set sail. having sighted
2954 2641 846 2176 4126
3 δὲ τὴν Κύπρον, καὶ καταλιπόντες αὐτὴν εὐώνυμον, ἐπλέομεν
And – Cyprus, and leaving it on the left, we sailed
1519 4947 2609 1519 5184 1566 1063/2258
εἰς Συρίαν, καὶ κατήχθημεν εἰς Τύρον· ἐκεῖσε γὰρ ἦν τὸ
to Syria, and came down to Tyre; there for was the
4143 670 1117 429
4 πλοῖον ἀποφορτιζόμενον τὸν γόμον. καὶ ἀνευρόντες
ship unloading the cargo. And having found
3101 1961 847 2250 2033 3748 3972
μαθητάς, ἐπεμείναμεν αὐτοῦ ἡμέρας ἑπτά· οἵτινες τῷ Παύλῳ
disciples, we remained there days seven; who – Paul
3004 1223 4151 3361 305 1519 2419
ἔλεγον διὰ τοῦ Πνεύματος, μὴ ἀναβαίνειν εἰς Ἱερουσαλήμ.
told through the Spirit not to go up to Jerusalem.
3753 1096 2248 1822 2250 1831 4198
5 ὅτε δὲ ἐγένετο ἡμᾶς ἐξαρτίσαι τὰς ἡμέρας, ἐξελθόντες ἐπο-
when But it was (time) us to complete the days, having gone out we
4311 2248 3956 4862 1135
ρευόμεθα, προπεμπόντων ἡμᾶς πάντων σὺν γυναιξὶ καὶ
traveled, accompanying us all with women and
5043 2193 1854 4172 5087 1119 1909
τέκνοις ἕως ἔξω τῆς πόλεως· καὶ θέντες τὰ γόνατα ἐπὶ τὸν
children as far as outside the city; and placing the knees on the
123 4336 782 240 1910
6 αἰγιαλὸν προσηυξάμεθα. καὶ ἀσπασάμενοι ἀλλήλους, ἐπέ-
shore, praying. And giving parting greetings to each other, we
1519 4143 1565 5290 1519 2398
βημεν εἰς τὸ πλοῖον, ἐκεῖνοι δὲ ὑπέστρεψαν εἰς τὰ ἴδια.
went up into the ship, those and returned to the own.
2249 4144 1274 575 5184 2658
7 Ἡμεῖς δέ, τὸν πλοῦν διανύσαντες ἀπὸ Τύρου, κατηντή-
we And, the voyage completing from Tyre, arrived
1519 4424 782 80
σαμεν εἰς Πτολεμαΐδα, καὶ ἀσπασάμενοι τοὺς ἀδελφοὺς
at Ptolemais; and greeting the brothers,
3306 2250 3391 3844 846 1887 1831
8 ἐμείναμεν ἡμέραν μίαν παρ' αὐτοῖς. τῇ δὲ ἐπαύριον ἐξελθόντες
we remained day one with them. on the And morrow going out
4012 3972 2064 1519 2542 1525
οἱ περὶ τὸν Παῦλον ἤλθομεν εἰς Καισάρειαν· καὶ εἰσελθόντες
those around (him), Paul came to Caesarea, and having gone
1519 3624 5376 2099 5607 1537
εἰς τὸν οἶκον Φιλίππου τοῦ εὐαγγελιστοῦ, τοῦ ὄντος ἐκ τῶν
to the house of Philip the evangelist, – being of the
2033 3306 3844 846 5129 2258 2364
9 ἑπτά, ἐμείναμεν παρ' αὐτῷ. τούτῳ δὲ ἦσαν θυγατέρες
seven, we stayed with him. to this one And were daughters
3933 5064 4395 1961 2257
10 παρθένοι τέσσαρες προφητεύουσαι. ἐπιμενόντων δὲ ἡμῶν
virgin four prophesying. remaining And we
2250 4119 2718 5100 575 2449 4396
ἡμέρας πλείους, κατῆλθέ τις ἀπὸ τῆς Ἰουδαίας προφήτης
days more, came down a certain from Judea prophet,
3686 13 2064 4314/2248 142 2223
11 ὀνόματι Ἄγαβος. καὶ ἐλθὼν πρὸς ἡμᾶς, καὶ ἄρας τὴν ζώνην
by name Agabus, and coming to us, and taking the girdle
3972 1210/5037/848 5495 4228 2036
τοῦ Παύλου, δήσας τε αὐτοῦ τὰς χεῖρας καὶ τοὺς πόδας εἶπε,
of Paul, binding and of himself the hands and the feet, he said,
3592 3004 4151 40 435 3739 2076 2223
Τάδε λέγει τὸ Πνεῦμα τὸ Ἅγιον, Τὸν ἄνδρα οὗ ἐστιν ἡ ζώνη
These says the Spirit Holy, The man of whom is girdle
3778 3779 1210 1722 2419 2453
αὕτη, οὕτω δήσουσιν ἐν Ἱερουσαλὴμ οἱ Ἰουδαῖοι, καὶ
this, thus will bind in Jerusalem the Jews, and
3860 1519 5495 1484 5613 191 5023
12 παραδώσουσιν εἰς χεῖρας ἐθνῶν. ὡς δὲ ἠκούσαμεν ταῦτα,
will deliver into (the) hands of nations. when And we heard these things,

begged him not to go up to Jerusalem. [13]But Paul answered, What are you doing, weeping and breaking my heart? For I not only am ready to be bound, but also to die at Jerusalem for the name of the Lord Jesus. [14]And he not being persuaded, we were silent, saying, The will of the Lord be *done*.

[15]And after these days, having made ready, we went up to Jerusalem. [16]And also *some* of the disciples from Caesarea went with us, bringing Mnason, a certain Cypriot, an ancient disciple, with whom we might lodge.

[17]And we being in Jerusalem, the brothers joyfully received us. [18]And on the next *day*, Paul went in with us to James. And all the elders came. [19]And having greeted them, he related one by one what things God had worked among the nations through his ministry. [20]And hearing, they glorified the Lord, and said to him, You see, brother, how many myriads there are of Jews that have believed, and all are zealous ones of the Law. [21]And they were informed about you, that you teach falling away from Moses, telling all the Jews throughout the nations not to circumcise their children, nor to walk in the customs. [22]What then is it? At all events, a multitude must come together, for they will hear that you have come. [23]Therefore, do this, what we say to you: There are four men who have a vow

3870 2249/5037 1786 3361 305
παρεκαλοῦμεν ἡμεῖς τε καὶ οἱ ἐντόπιοι, τοῦ μὴ ἀναβαίνειν
begged we both and the residents – not to go up
846 1519 2419 611 3972 5101 4160
13 αὐτὸν εἰς Ἱερουσαλήμ. ἀπεκρίθη δὲ ὁ Παῦλος, Τί ποιεῖτε
him to Jerusalem. answered And Paul, What are you doing,
2799 4919 3450 2588 1473/1063 3756
κλαίοντες καὶ συνθρύπτοντές μου τὴν καρδίαν; ἐγὼ γὰρ οὐ
weeping and crushing of me the heart? I For not
3440 1210 235 599 1519 2419 2093
μόνον δεθῆναι, ἀλλὰ καὶ ἀποθανεῖν εἰς Ἱερουσαλὴμ ἑτοίμως
only to be bound, but also to die in Jerusalem readiness
2192/5228 3686 2962 2424 3361 3982
14 ἔχω ὑπὲρ τοῦ ὀνόματος τοῦ Κυρίου Ἰησοῦ. μὴ πειθομένου
I have for the name of the Lord Jesus. not being persuaded
846 2270 2036 2307 2962
δὲ αὐτοῦ, ἡσυχάσαμεν εἰπόντες, Τὸ θέλημα τοῦ Κυρίου
And him, we kept silence, having said, Of the will of the Lord
1096
γενέσθω.
let be (done).

3326 2250 5025 643 305
15 Μετὰ δὲ τὰς ἡμέρας ταύτας ἀποσκευασάμενοι ἀνεβαίνομεν
after And – days these having made ready, we went up
1519 2419 4905 3101 575 2542
16 εἰς Ἱερουσαλήμ. συνῆλθον δὲ καὶ τῶν μαθητῶν ἀπὸ Καισα-
to Jerusalem. went And also of the disciples from Caesarea
4862/2254 71 3844/3739 3579 3416 5100
ρείας σὺν ἡμῖν, ἄγοντες παρ' ᾧ ξενισθῶμεν, Μνάσωνί τινι
with us, bringing (one) with whom we may lodge, Mnason a certain
2953 744 3101
Κυπρίῳ, ἀρχαίῳ μαθητῇ.
Cypriot, an ancient disciple.

1096 2257/1519 2414 780 1209
17 Γενομένων δὲ ἡμῶν εἰς Ἱεροσόλυμα, ἀσμένως ἐδέξαντο
being And us in Jerusalem, joyfully received
2248 80 1966 1524 3972 4862/2254/4314
ἡμᾶς οἱ ἀδελφοί. τῇ δὲ ἐπιούσῃ εἰσῄει ὁ Παῦλος σὺν ἡμῖν πρὸς
us the brothers. on the And next went in Paul with us to
2385 3956 5037 3854 4245
18 Ἰάκωβον, πάντες τε παρεγένοντο οἱ πρεσβύτεροι. καὶ
James, all and came the elders. And
782 846 1834 2596/1520 1538 3739 4160
19 ἀσπασάμενος αὐτούς, ἐξηγεῖτο καθ' ἓν ἕκαστον ὧν ἐποίησεν
having greeted them, he related one by one of which did
2316/1722 1484 1223 1248 848 191
20 ὁ Θεὸς ἐν τοῖς ἔθνεσι διὰ τῆς διακονίας αὐτοῦ. οἱ δὲ ἀκού-
God among the nations through the ministry of him, they And
1392 2962 2036 5037/846 2334 80
σαντες ἐδόξαζον τὸν Κύριον· εἶπόν τε αὐτῷ, Θεωρεῖς, ἀδελφέ,
hearing glorified the Lord, said and to him, You see, brother
4214 3461 1526 2453 4100
πόσαι μυριάδες εἰσὶν Ἰουδαίων τῶν πεπιστευκότων· καὶ
how many myriads there are of Jews having believed, and
3956 2207 3551 5225 2727
21 πάντες ζηλωταὶ τοῦ νόμου ὑπάρχουσι· κατηχήθησαν δὲ
all zealous ones of the law are; they were informed and
4012 4675/3754 646 1321 575 3475
περὶ σοῦ, ὅτι ἀποστασίαν διδάσκεις ἀπὸ Μωσέως τοὺς
about you, that falling away you teach from Moses
2596 1484 3956 2453 3004 3361 4059
κατὰ τὰ ἔθνη πάντας Ἰουδαίους, λέγων μὴ περιτέμνειν
throughout the nations all Jews, telling not to circumcise
846 5043 3366 1485 4043 5101/3767/2076
22 αὐτοὺς τὰ τέκνα, μηδὲ τοῖς ἔθεσι περιπατεῖν. τί οὖν ἐστι;
them the children, nor in the customs to walk. What, then, is it?
3843 1135 4128 4905 191 1063/3754 2064
πάντως δεῖ πλῆθος συνελθεῖν· ἀκούσονται γὰρ ὅτι ἐλή-
At all events must a multitude come together, will hear for that you
524 3767 4160 3739/4671/3004 1526 2254 435
23 λυθας. τοῦτο οὖν ποίησον ὅ σοι λέγομεν· εἰσὶν ἡμῖν ἄνδρες
have come. This, then, do what you we tell. There are to us men

on themselves; [24]taking these, be purified with them, and be at expense on them, that they may shave the head. And all shall know that all what they have been told about you is nothing, but you yourself walk orderly, keeping the Law. [25]And as to the believing Gentiles, we joined in writing, judging them to observe no such thing, except to keep themselves from both idol sacrifice, and the blood, and a thing strangled, and *from* fornication. [26]Then taking the men on the next day, being purified with them, Paul went into the Temple, declaring the fulfillment of the days of the purification, until the offering should be offered for each one of them.

[27]But when the seven days were about to be completed, having seen him in the Temple, the Jews from Asia stirred up all the crowd, and laid hands on him, [28]crying out, Men, Israelites, help! This is the man who teaches all everywhere against the people and the Law and this place. And even more, *he* also brought Greeks into the Temple, and has defiled this holy place. [29]For they had before seen Trophimus the Ephesian in the city with him, whom they supposed that Paul brought into the Temple. [30]And the whole city was moved, and there was a running together of people. And having laid hold of Paul, they drew him outside of the Temple, and at once the doors were shut. [31]But *as* they *were* seeking to kill

5064 2171 2192 1909 1438 5128 3880
24 τέσσαρες εὐχὴν ἔχοντες ἐφ' ἑαυτῶν· τούτους παραλαβὼν
four having a vow upon themselves; these taking
48 4862 846 1159 1909 846 2443
ἁγνίσθητι σὺν αὐτοῖς, καὶ δαπάνησον ἐπ' αὐτοῖς, ἵνα
be purified with them, and be at expense on them, that
3587 2776 1097 3956 3754/3739 2727
ξυρήσωνται τὴν κεφαλήν, καὶ γνῶσι πάντες ὅτι ὧν κατη-
they may shave the head, and may know all that of which they
4012/4675/3762 2076 235 4748 848
χηνται περὶ σοῦ οὐδέν ἐστιν, ἀλλὰ στοιχεῖς καὶ αὐτὸς τὸν
have been told about you nothing is, but you walk also yourself the
3551 5442 4012 4100 1484 2249
25 νόμον φυλάσσων. περὶ δὲ τῶν πεπιστευκότων ἐθνῶν ἡμεῖς
Law keeping. concerning And the believing nations, we
1989 2919 3367 5108 5083 846 1487
ἐπεστείλαμεν, κρίναντες μηδὲν τοιοῦτον τηρεῖν αὐτούς, εἰ
joined in writing, judging no such thing to observe them, ex-
3361 5442 846 5037 1494 129
μὴ φυλάσσεσθαι αὐτοὺς τό τε εἰδωλόθυτον καὶ τὸ αἷμα καὶ
cept to keep from themselves the both idol sacrifice and the blood and
4156 4202 5119 3972 3880
26 πνικτὸν καὶ πορνείαν. τότε ὁ Παῦλος παραλαβὼν τοὺς
a thing strangled and fornication. Then Paul taking the
435 2192 2250 4862 846 48 1524 1519
ἄνδρας, τῇ ἐχομένῃ ἡμέρᾳ σὺν αὐτοῖς ἁγνισθεὶς εἰσῄει εἰς
men, on the next day with them having been purified went into
2411 1229 1604 2250
τὸ ἱερόν, διαγγέλλων τὴν ἐκπλήρωσιν τῶν ἡμερῶν τοῦ
the Temple, declaring the fulfillment of the days of the
49 2193/3739 4374 5228/1520 1538 846
ἁγνισμοῦ, ἕως οὗ προσηνέχθη ὑπὲρ ἑνὸς ἑκάστου αὐτῶν
purification, until should be offered for one each of them
4376
ἡ προσφορά.
the offering.

5613 3195 2033 2250 4931 575
27 Ὡς δὲ ἔμελλον αἱ ἑπτὰ ἡμέραι συντελεῖσθαι, οἱ ἀπὸ τῆς
as But about to be the seven days completed, the from
773 2453 2300 846 1722 2411 4797
Ἀσίας Ἰουδαῖοι, θεασάμενοι αὐτὸν ἐν τῷ ἱερῷ, συνέχεον
Asia Jews, having seen him in the Temple, stirred up
3956 3793 1911 5495 1909 846
πάντα τὸν ὄχλον, καὶ ἐπέβαλον τὰς χεῖρας ἐπ' αὐτόν,
all the crowd, and laid the hands on him,
2896 435 2475 997 3778 2076
28 κράζοντες, Ἄνδρες Ἰσραηλῖται, βοηθεῖτε. οὗτός ἐστιν ὁ
crying out, Men, Israelites, help! This is the
444 2596 2992 3551 5117
ἄνθρωπος ὁ κατὰ τοῦ λαοῦ καὶ τοῦ νόμου καὶ τοῦ τόπου
man who against the people and the Law and — place
5127 3956 3837 1321 2089/5037 1672
τούτου πάντας πανταχοῦ διδάσκων· ἔτι τε καὶ Ἕλληνας
this all everywhere teaching. further And also Greeks
1521 1519 2411 2840 40 5117
εἰσήγαγεν εἰς τὸ ἱερόν, καὶ κεκοίνωκε τὸν ἅγιον τόπον
brought in to the Temple, and has defiled — holy place
5126 2258 1063 4308 5161 2180 1722
29 τοῦτον. ἦσαν γὰρ προεωρακότες Τρόφιμον τὸν Ἐφέσιον ἐν
this, they were For previously seen Trophimus the Ephesian in
4172 4862 846 3739 3543 3754/1519 2411 1521
τῇ πόλει σὺν αὐτῷ, ὃν ἐνόμιζον ὅτι εἰς τὸ ἱερὸν εἰσήγαγεν
the city with him, whom they supposed that into the Temple brought in
3972 2795 5037 4172/3650 1096 4890
30 ὁ Παῦλος. ἐκινήθη τε ἡ πόλις ὅλη, καὶ ἐγένετο συνδρομὴ τοῦ
Paul, was moved And the city whole, and there was running together the
2992 1949 3972 1670 846 1854
λαοῦ· καὶ ἐπιλαβόμενοι τοῦ Παύλου εἷλκον αὐτὸν ἔξω τοῦ
people, and having seized — Paul, they drew him outside of the
2411 2112 2808 2374 2212 846
31 ἱεροῦ· καὶ εὐθέως ἐκλείσθησαν αἱ θύραι. ζητούντων δὲ αὐτὸν
Temple, and at once were shut the doors. they seeking And him

him, a report came up to the chiliarch of the cohort, that all Jerusalem is in a tumult. [32]*He* at once ran down to them, taking soldiers and centurions. And seeing the chiliarch and the soldiers, they stopped beating Paul. [33]Then going near, the chiliarch laid hold of him, and commanded *him* to be bound with two chains. And *he* asked who he might be, and what he is doing. [34]But others cried something else in the crowd, and not being able to know the certainty because of the uproar, he commanded him brought into the fortress.

[35]But when he came on the stairs, it happened he was borne by the soldiers because of the violence of the crowd. [36]For the multitude of the people followed, crying out, Take him away!

[37]But being about to be brought into the fortress, Paul said to the chiliarch, Is it lawful for me to say a thing to you? And he said, Do you know *to speak* in Greek? [38]Then are you not the Egyptian who before these days caused a riot, and led four thousand men of the assassins out into the desert? [39]But Paul said, I am indeed a man, a Jew of Tarsus, of Cilicia, a citizen *of* no mean city. And I beg you, allow me to speak to the people. [40]And he allowing him, standing on the stairs Paul signaled with *his* hand to the people. And much silence taking place, he spoke in the Hebrew dialect, saying,

615 305 5334 5506 4686 3754
ἀποκτεῖναι, ἀνέβη φάσις τῷ χιλιάρχῳ τῆς σπείρης, ὅτι
to kill, came up a report to the chiliarch of the cohort, that
3650 4797 2419 3739 1824 3880
32 ὅλη συγκέχυται Ἱερουσαλήμ· ὃς ἐξαυτῆς παραλαβὼν
all is in a tumult Jerusalem; who at once having taken
4757 1543 2701 1905 846
στρατιώτας καὶ ἑκατοντάρχους, κατέδραμεν ἐπ' αὐτούς·
soldiers and centurions ran down on them;
1492 5506 4757 3973
οἱ δέ, ἰδόντες τὸν χιλίαρχον καὶ τοὺς στρατιώτας, ἐπαύσαντο
they and seeing the chiliarch and the soldiers ceased
5180 3972 5119 1448 5506 1949
33 τύπτοντες τὸν Παῦλον. τότε ἐγγίσας ὁ χιλίαρχος ἐπελάβετο
beating — Paul. Then going near the chiliarch laid hold
846 2753 1210 254 1417 4441 5101
αὐτοῦ, καὶ ἐκέλευσε δεθῆναι ἁλύσεσι δυσί· καὶ ἐπυνθάνετο τίς
of him, and commanded to be bound with chains two, and asked who
302/1498 5101/2076 4160 243 243/5100 994/1722
34 ἂν εἴη, καὶ τί ἐστι πεποιηκώς. ἄλλοι δὲ ἄλλο τι ἐβόων ἐν τῷ
he may be, and what he is doing. others And else something cried in the
3793 3361 1410 1097 804 1223 2351
ὄχλῳ· μὴ δυνάμενος δὲ γνῶναι τὸ ἀσφαλὲς διὰ τὸν θόρυβον,
crowd, not being able and to know the certain thing for the uproar,
2753 71 846 1519 3925 3753 1096
35 ἐκέλευσεν ἄγεσθαι αὐτὸν εἰς τὴν παρεμβολήν. ὅτε δὲ ἐγένετο
he commanded to bring him into the fortress. when But he came
1909 304 4819 941 846 5259
ἐπὶ τοὺς ἀναβαθμούς, συνέβη βαστάζεσθαι αὐτὸν ὑπὸ τῶν
on the steps, it happened to be carried him by the
4757 1223 970 3793 191 1063
36 στρατιωτῶν διὰ τὴν βίαν τοῦ ὄχλου. ἠκολούθει γὰρ τὸ
soldiers because of the violence of the crowd. followed For the
4128 2992 2896 142 846
πλῆθος τοῦ λαοῦ κρᾶζον, Αἶρε αὐτόν.
multitude of the people crying out, Take away him.
3195 5037 1521 1519 3925 3972 3004
37 Μέλλων τε εἰσάγεσθαι εἰς τὴν παρεμβολὴν ὁ Παῦλος λέγει
being about And to be brought into the fortress, Paul said
5506 1487 1832 3427 2036/5100/4314/4571 5346
τῷ χιλιάρχῳ, Εἰ ἔξεστί μοι εἰπεῖν τι πρός σε; ὁ δὲ ἔφη,
to the chiliarch, If it is lawful for me to say a thing to you? he And said,
1676 1097 3756 686/4771/1487 124 4253
38 Ἑλληνιστὶ γινώσκεις; οὐκ ἄρα σὺ εἶ ὁ Αἰγύπτιος ὁ πρὸ
in Greek Do you know? Not, then, you are the Egyptian, he before
5130 2250 387 1806 1519
τούτων τῶν ἡμερῶν ἀναστατώσας καὶ ἐξαγαγὼν εἰς τὴν
these days caused a riot and leading out into the
2048 5070 435 4607 2036
39 ἔρημον τοὺς τετρακισχιλίους ἄνδρας τῶν σικαρίων; εἶπε δὲ ὁ
desert the four thousand men of the assassins? said And
3972 1473 444 3303 1510 2453 5018
Παῦλος, Ἐγὼ ἄνθρωπος μέν εἰμι Ἰουδαῖος, Ταρσεὺς τῆς
Paul, I a man indeed am, a Jew, a Tarsian
2791 3756 767 4172 4177 1189 4675 2010
Κιλικίας, οὐκ ἀσήμου πόλεως πολίτης· δέομαι δέ σου, ἐπί-
of Cilicia, not of a mean city a citizen. I beg And of you
3427 2980 4314 2992 2010 846
40 τρεψόν μοι λαλῆσαι πρὸς τὸν λαόν. ἐπιτρέψαντος δὲ αὐτοῦ,
allow me to speak to the people. he having allowed And him,
3972 2476 1909 304 2678 5495
ὁ Παῦλος ἑστὼς ἐπὶ τῶν ἀναβαθμῶν κατέσεισε τῇ χειρὶ τῷ
Paul, standing on the steps signaled with the hand to the
2992 4183 4602 1096 4377 1446
λαῷ· πολλῆς δὲ σιγῆς γενομένης, προσεφώνησε τῇ Ἑβραΐδι
people; much and silence occurring, he spoke in the Hebrew
1258 3004
διαλέκτῳ λέγων,
dialect, saying,

CHAPTER 22

1 Men, brothers, and fathers, hear my defense now to you.

2 And hearing that he spoke in the Hebrew dialect to them, they showed more quietness. And he said:

3 I am indeed a man, a Jew having been born in Tarsus of Cilicia, but having been brought up in this city at the feet of Gamaliel; having been trained according to the exactness of the ancestral law, being a zealous one of God, even as you all are today. 4 I persecuted this Way as far as death, binding and delivering up both men and women to prisons; 5 as also the high priest and all the elderhood witnesses to me. And having received letters from *them* to the brothers, I traveled into Damascus even to lead those to Jerusalem being bound there in order that they might be punished. 6 And it happened to me, traveling and drawing near to Damascus: suddenly, about midday, a great light out of the heaven shone around me. 7 And I fell to the ground, and I heard a voice saying to me, Saul, Saul, why do you persecute Me? 8 And I answered, Who are you, Sir? And He said to me, I am Jesus the Nazarene whom you persecute. 9 But those being with me indeed saw the light, and were alarmed, but did not hear His voice speaking to me.

10 And I said, What shall I do, Lord? And the Lord said to me, Rising up, go into Damascus, and there you will be told about all things

CHAPTER 22

435 80 3962 191 3450 4314
1 Ἄνδρες ἀδελφοὶ καὶ πατέρες, ἀκούσατέ μου τῆς πρὸς
Men, brothers and fathers, hear of me the to
5209 3568 627
ὑμᾶς νῦν ἀπολογίας.
you now defense.
191 3754 1446 1258 4377
2 Ἀκούσαντες δὲ ὅτι τῇ Ἑβραΐδι διαλέκτῳ προσεφώνει
hearing And that in the Hebrew dialect he spoke
846 3173 3930 2271 5346
αὐτοῖς, μᾶλλον παρέσχον ἡσυχίαν. καί φησιν,
to them, more they showed quietness. And he says,
1473/3303/1510/435/ 2453 1080 1722 5019
3 Ἐγὼ μέν εἰμι ἀνὴρ Ἰουδαῖος, γεγεννημένος ἐν Ταρσῷ τῆς
I indeed am a man, a Jew, having been born in Tarsus
2791 397 1722 4172 5026 3844
Κιλικίας, ἀνατεθραμμένος δὲ ἐν τῇ πόλει ταύτῃ παρὰ τοὺς
of Cilicia, having been brought up and in city this at the
4228 1059 3811 2596 195 3971
πόδας Γαμαλιήλ, πεπαιδευμένος κατὰ ἀκρίβειαν τοῦ πα-
feet of Gamaliel; having been trained according to exactness of the
3551 2207 5225 2316 2531 3956
τρῴου νόμου, ζηλωτὴς ὑπάρχων τοῦ Θεοῦ, καθὼς πάντες
ancestral Law, a zealous one being of God, even as all
5210/2075 4594 3739 5026 3598 1377 891 2288
4 ὑμεῖς ἐστε σήμερον· ὃς ταύτην τὴν ὁδὸν ἐδίωξα ἄχρι θανάτου,
you are today; who this Way persecuted as far as to death,
1195 3860 1519 5438 435 5037 1135
δεσμεύων καὶ παραδιδοὺς εἰς φυλακὰς ἄνδρας τε καὶ γυναῖκας.
binding and delivering to prisons men both and women.
5613 749 3140 3427 3956 4244
5 ὡς καὶ ὁ ἀρχιερεὺς μαρτυρεῖ μοι, καὶ πᾶν τὸ πρεσβυτέριον·
as Even the high priest witnesses to me, and all the elderhood;
3844/3739 1992 1209 4314 80 1519
παρ᾽ ὧν καὶ ἐπιστολὰς δεξάμενος πρὸς τοὺς ἀδελφούς, εἰς
from whom also letters having received to the brothers in
1159 4198 71 1566 5607 1210
Δαμασκὸν ἐπορευόμην, ἄξων καὶ τοὺς ἐκεῖσε ὄντας δεδεμένους
Damascus, I traveled leading also those there being bound
1519 2419 2443 5097 1096 3427 4198
6 εἰς Ἱερουσαλήμ, ἵνα τιμωρηθῶσιν. ἐγένετο δέ μοι πορευο-
to Jerusalem, that they might be punished. it was And to me traveling
1448 1154 4012 3314 1810
μένῳ καὶ ἐγγίζοντι τῇ Δαμασκῷ, περὶ μεσημβρίαν, ἐξαίφνης
and drawing near to Damascus, about midday suddenly
1537 3772 4015 5457 2425 4012/1691 4098
7 ἐκ τοῦ οὐρανοῦ περιαστράψαι φῶς ἱκανὸν περὶ ἐμέ. ἔπεσόν
out of the heaven shone light a great about me. I fell
5037/1519 1475 191 5456 3004 3427 4549
τε εἰς τὸ ἔδαφος, καὶ ἤκουσα φωνῆς λεγούσης μοι, Σαούλ,
And to the ground, and heard a voice saying to me, Saul,
4549 5101/3165 1377 1473 611 5101/1487/ 2962 2036
8 Σαούλ, τί με διώκεις; ἐγὼ δὲ ἀπεκρίθην, Τίς εἶ, Κύριε; εἶπέ
Saul, why Me you persecute? I And answered, Who are you, Sir? He said
5037/4314/3165/1473/1510 2424 3480 3739/4771/ 1377
τε πρός με, Ἐγώ εἰμι Ἰησοῦς ὁ Ναζωραῖος ὃν σὺ διώκεις.
And to me, I am Jesus the Nazarene, whom you persecute.
4862/1698/5607 3303/5951 2300 1719
9 οἱ δὲ σὺν ἐμοὶ ὄντες τὸ μὲν φῶς ἐθεάσαντο, καὶ ἔμφοβοι
those and with me being, the indeed light beheld, and alarmed
1096 5456 3756/ 191 2980 3427
ἐγένοντο· τὴν δὲ φωνὴν οὐκ ἤκουσαν τοῦ λαλοῦντός μοι.
were, the but voice not they heard of Him speaking to me.
2036 5101 4160 2962 2962 2036 4314/3165
10 εἶπον δέ, Τί ποιήσω, Κύριε; ὁ δὲ Κύριος εἶπε πρός με,
I said And, What may I do, Lord? the And Lord said to me,
450 4198 1519 1154 2546 4671 2980
Ἀναστὰς πορεύου εἰς Δαμασκόν· κἀκεῖ σοι λαληθήσεται
Rising up, go into Damascus, and there to you it will be told

which are appointed to you to do. 11 And as I did not see, from the glory of that light, being led by the hand by those being with me, I went into Damascus.

12 And a certain Ananias, a devout man according to the Law, testified *to* by all the Jews living *there*, 13 coming to me and standing by, *he* said to me, Brother Saul, look up. And in the same hour I looked up on him. 14 And he said, The God of our fathers appointed you to know His will, and to see the Just One, and to hear a voice out of His mouth; 15 for you shall be a witness for Him to all men, of what you have seen and heard. 16 And now what do you intend? Rising up, be baptized, and wash away your sins, calling on the name of the Lord. 17 And it happened to me, *I* returning to Jerusalem and praying in the Temple: I became in an ecstasy,

18 and I saw Him saying to me, Hurry and go out quickly from Jerusalem, because they will not receive your testimony concerning Me. 19 And I said, Lord, they understand that I was imprisoning and beating the ones believing on You throughout the synagogues. 20 And when the blood of Your witness Stephen was poured out, I myself also was standing by and consenting to his execution, and holding the garments of those killing him. 21 And He said to me, Go, for I will send you to the nations afar off.

22 And they heard him until this word, and lifted up

4012 3956 3739 5021 4671 4160 5613 3756 1689
11 περὶ πάντων ὧν τέτακταί σοι ποιῆσαι. ὡς δὲ οὐκ ἐνέβλεπον
about all things which is appointed to you to do. as And not I saw
575 1391 5457 1565 5496 5259
ἀπὸ τῆς δόξης τοῦ φωτὸς ἐκείνου, χειραγωγούμενος ὑπὸ
from the glory light of that, being led by the hand by
4895 3427 2064 1519 1154 367 5100
12 τῶν συνόντων μοι, ἦλθον εἰς Δαμασκόν. Ἀνανίας δέ τις,
the (ones) being with me, I went into Damascus. Ananias And a certain,
435 2152 2596 3551 3140 5259 3956
ἀνὴρ εὐσεβὴς κατὰ τὸν νόμον, μαρτυρούμενος ὑπὸ πάντων
a man devout according to the Law, testified (to) by all
2730 2453 2064 4314/3165 2186
13 τῶν κατοικούντων Ἰουδαίων, ἐλθὼν πρός με καὶ ἐπιστὰς
the living (there) Jews, coming to me and standing by
2036/3427/4549 80 308 2054 846 5610
εἰπέ μοι, Σαοὺλ ἀδελφέ, ἀνάβλεψον. κἀγὼ αὐτῇ τῇ ὥρᾳ
said to me, Saul, brother, look up. And I in that hour
308 1519/846 2036 2316 3962 2257
14 ἀνέβλεψα εἰς αὐτόν. ὁ δὲ εἶπεν, Ὁ Θεὸς τῶν πατέρων ἡμῶν
looked up at him. he And said, The God of the fathers of us
4400 4571 1097 2307 848 1492
προεχειρίσατό σε γνῶναι τὸ θέλημα αὐτοῦ, καὶ ἰδεῖν τὸν
before appointed you to know the will of Him, and to see the
1342 191 5456 1537 4750 848 3754/2071
15 δίκαιον, καὶ ἀκοῦσαι φωνὴν ἐκ τοῦ στόματος αὐτοῦ. ὅτι ἔσῃ
Just One, and to hear a voice out of the mouth of Him, for you will be
3144 846 4314 3956 444 3739 3708
μάρτυς αὐτῷ πρὸς πάντας ἀνθρώπους ὧν ἑώρακας καὶ
a witness to Him to all men of which you have seen and
191 3568/5101/3195 450 907 628
16 ἤκουσας. καὶ νῦν τί μέλλεις; ἀναστὰς βάπτισαι καὶ ἀπό-
heard. And now what intend you? Rising up, be baptized and wash
266 4675 1941 3686
λουσαι τὰς ἁμαρτίας σου, ἐπικαλεσάμενος τὸ ὄνομα τοῦ
away the sins of you, calling on the name of the
2962 1096 3427 5290 1519 2419
17 Κυρίου. ἐγένετο δέ μοι ὑποστρέψαντι εἰς Ἱερουσαλήμ, καὶ
Lord. it was And to me, having returned to Jerusalem, and
4336 3450/1722 2411/ 1096 3165/1722/ 1611
προσευχομένου μου ἐν τῷ ἱερῷ, γενέσθαι με ἐν ἐκστάσει, καὶ
praying me in the Temple, becoming me in an ecstasy, and
1492 846 3004 3427 4692 1831/1722/5034/1537
18 ἰδεῖν αὐτὸν λέγοντά μοι, Σπεῦσον καὶ ἔξελθε ἐν τάχει ἐξ
saw Him saying to me, Hurry and go out quickly from
2419 1360 3756 3888 4675 3141
Ἱερουσαλήμ· διότι οὐ παραδέξονταί σου τὴν μαρτυρίαν
Jerusalem, because not they will receive of you the testimony
4012 1700 2504 3036 2962 846 1987 3754 1473
19 περὶ ἐμοῦ. κἀγὼ εἶπον, Κύριε, αὐτοὶ ἐπίστανται ὅτι ἐγὼ
concerning Me. And I said, Lord, they understand that I
2252 5439 1194 2596 4864
ἤμην φυλακίζων καὶ δέρων κατὰ τὰς συναγωγὰς τοὺς
was imprisoning and beating throughout the synagogues those
4100 1909/4571 3753/ 1682 129 4736
20 πιστεύοντας ἐπὶ σέ· καὶ ὅτε ἐξεχεῖτο τὸ αἷμα Στεφάνου τοῦ
believing on You; and when was poured out the blood of Stephen the
3144 4675 848 2252 2186 4909
μάρτυρός σου, καὶ αὐτὸς ἤμην ἐφεστὼς καὶ συνευδοκῶν τῇ
witness of You, also myself I was standing by and consenting to the
336 848 5442 2440 337
ἀναιρέσει αὐτοῦ, καὶ φυλάσσων τὰ ἱμάτια τῶν ἀναιρούντων
execution of him, and keeping the garments of those killing
846 2036 4314 3165 4198 3754/1473/1519/1484/ 3112
21 αὐτόν. καὶ εἶπε πρός με, Πορεύου, ὅτι ἐγὼ εἰς ἔθνη μακρὰν
him And He said to me, Go, because I to the nations afar off
1821 4571
ἐξαποστελῶ σε.
will send you.
191 846 891 5127 3056 1869
22 Ἤκουον δὲ αὐτοῦ ἄχρι τούτου τοῦ λόγου, καὶ ἐπῆραν
they heard And him as far as to this — word, and lifted up

their voice, saying, Take such a one from the earth, for it is not fitting that he should live! 23And they shouting, and tearing the garments, and throwing dust into the air, 24the chiliarch ordered to bring him into the fortress, saying for him to be examined with scourges, that he may know for what crime they cried out so against him.

25But as they stretched him with the thongs, Paul said to the centurion standing by, Is it lawful for you to flog a man, even a Roman not found guilty? 26And hearing, coming near the centurion reported to the chiliarch, saying, Watch what you are about to do, for this man is a Roman. 27And coming up, the chiliarch said to him, Tell me, are you a Roman? And he said, Yes. 28And the chiliarch answered, I bought this citizenship with a great sum. And Paul said, But I even was born *free.* 29Then at once those being about to examine him stood away from him. And the chiliarch also feared, fully knowing that he was a Roman, and that he had bound him.

30And on the morrow, desiring to know the certainty *as to* why he was accused by the Jews, he freed him from the bonds. And *he* commanded the chief priests and all their sanhedrin to come. And bringing Paul down, *he* set *him* among them.

5456 848 3004 142 575 1093 5108
τὴν φωνὴν αὐτῶν λέγοντες, Αἶρε ἀπὸ τῆς γῆς τὸν τοιοῦτον·
the voice of them saying, Take from the earth – such a one;
3756/1063 2520 846 2198 2905 846
23 οὐ γὰρ καθῆκον αὐτὸν ζῆν. κραυγαζόντων δὲ αὐτῶν, καὶ
not for it is fitting he should live. shouting And them, and
4495 2440 2868 906 1519
ῥιπτούντων τὰ ἱμάτια, καὶ κονιορτὸν βαλλόντων εἰς τὸν
tearing the garments, and dust throwing into the
109 2753 846 5506 71 1519 3925
24 ἀέρα, ἐκέλευσεν αὐτὸν ὁ χιλίαρχος ἄγεσθαι εἰς τὴν παρεμβο-
air, commanded him the chiliarch to bring into the fortress,
2036 3148 426 846 2443 1921 3739
λήν. εἰπὼν μάστιξιν ἀνετάζεσθαι αὐτόν, ἵνα ἐπιγνῷ δι' ἣν
saying with scourges to be examined him, that he may know for what
156 3779 2019 846 5613 4385 846
25 αἰτίαν οὕτως ἐπεφώνουν αὐτῷ. ὡς δὲ προέτειναν αὐτὸν τοῖς
crime thus they cried against him. as But they stretched him with the
2438 2036 4314 2476 1543 3972 1487
ἱμᾶσιν, εἶπε πρὸς τὸν ἑστῶτα ἑκατόνταρχον ὁ Παῦλος, Εἰ
thongs, said to the standing by centurion – Paul, If
444 4514 178 1832 5213 3147
ἄνθρωπον Ῥωμαῖον καὶ ἀκατάκριτον ἔξεστιν ὑμῖν μαστίζειν;
a man, a Roman, and (one) not found guilty it is lawful for you to whip?
191 1543 4334 518
26 ἀκούσας δὲ ὁ ἑκατόνταρχος, προσελθὼν ἀπήγγειλε τῷ
hearing And the centurion coming near reported to the
5506 3004 3708/5101 3195 4160 1063 444
χιλιάρχῳ λέγων, Ὅρα τί μέλλεις ποιεῖν· ὁ γὰρ ἄνθρωπος
chiliarch, saying, See what you are about to do, for man
3778 4514 2076 4334 5506 2036 846
27 οὗτος Ῥωμαῖός ἐστι. προσελθὼν δὲ ὁ χιλίαρχος εἶπεν αὐτῷ,
this a Roman is. having come up And the chiliarch, he said to him,
3004/3427/1487/4771/ 4514/1487 5346 3483 611 5037
28 Λέγε μοι, εἰ σὺ Ῥωμαῖος εἶ; ὁ δὲ ἔφη, Ναί. ἀπεκρίθη τε ὁ
Tell me if you a Roman are, he And said, Yes. answered And the
5506 1473 4183 2774 4174 5026
χιλίαρχος, Ἐγὼ πολλοῦ κεφαλαίου τὴν πολιτείαν ταύτην
chiliarch, I of a much sum – citizenship this
2932 3972 5346 1473 1080
ἐκτησάμην. ὁ δὲ Παῦλος ἔφη, Ἐγὼ δὲ καὶ γεγέννημαι.
bought. And Paul said, I But even have been born.
2112 3767 868 575 846 3195 846 426
29 εὐθέως οὖν ἀπέστησαν ἀπ' αὐτοῦ οἱ μέλλοντες αὐτὸν ἀνε-
At once, then, stood away from him those being about him to
5506 5399 1921 3754 4514
τάζειν. καὶ ὁ χιλίαρχος δὲ ἐφοβήθη, ἐπιγνοὺς ὅτι Ῥωμαῖός
examine. also the chiliarch And feared, fully knowing that a Roman
2076 3754/2258/846 1210
ἐστι, καὶ ὅτι ἦν αὐτὸν δεδεκώς.
he is. and that he was him having bound.
1887 1014 1097 804 5101
30 Τῇ δὲ ἐπαύριον βουλόμενος γνῶναι τὸ ἀσφαλές, τὸ τί
on the And morrow, being minded to know the certain thing why
2723 3844 2453 3089 846 575
κατηγορεῖται παρὰ τῶν Ἰουδαίων, ἔλυσεν αὐτὸν ἀπὸ τῶν
he was accused by the Jews, he freed him from the
1199 2753 2064 749 3650
δεσμῶν, καὶ ἐκέλευσεν ἐλθεῖν τοὺς ἀρχιερεῖς καὶ ὅλον τὸ
bonds, and commanded to come the chief priests and all the
4892 848 2609 3972 2476 1519
συνέδριον αὐτῶν, καὶ καταγαγὼν τὸν Παῦλον ἔστησεν εἰς
sanhedrin of them; and having brought down Paul, (he) set (him)
846 among
αὐτούς.
them.

CHAPTER 23

1And looking on the sanhedrin, Paul said, Men,

816 3972 4892 2036 435 80
1 Ἀτενίσας δὲ ὁ Παῦλος τῷ συνεδρίῳ εἶπεν, Ἄνδρες ἀδελφοί,
having looked And Paul on the sanhedrin, he said, Men, brothers,

brothers, I in all good conscience have conducted myself toward God to this day. [2]But Ananias the high priest ordered those standing by him to strike his mouth. [3]Then Paul said to him, God is going to strike you, whitened wall! And do you sit judging me according to the Law, and contrary to the Law command me to be struck? [4]And those standing by said, Do you revile the high priest of God? [5]And Paul said, Brothers, I did not know that he is high priest; for it has been written, "You shall not speak evil of a ruler of your people." [6]But knowing that the one part consisted of Sadducees, and the other of Pharisees, Paul cried out in the sanhedrin, Men, brothers, I am a Pharisee, a son of Pharisees; I am being judged concerning hope and resurrection of *the* dead! [7]And *he* having spoken this, there was a discord between the Pharisees and the Sadducees; and the multitude was divided. [8]For the Sadducees indeed say there is no resurrection, nor angel, nor spirit. But Pharisees confess both. [9]And there was a great cry. And the scribes of the part of the Pharisees rising up, they were contending, saying, We find nothing evil in this man. And, If a spirit spoke to him, or an angel, let us not fight against God. [10]And discord having arisen, fearing lest Paul should be torn by them, the chiliarch commanded the soldiery to go down to snatch him out of their midst, and to bring *him* into the fortress.

[11]And coming to him in the following night the Lord said, Be cheered, Paul, for

1473 3956 4893 18 4176 2316 891
ἐγὼ πάσῃ συνειδήσει ἀγαθῇ πεπολίτευμαι τῷ Θεῷ ἄχρι
I in all conscience good have lived — to God until

5026 2250 749 367 2004
2 ταύτης τῆς ἡμέρας. ὁ δὲ ἀρχιερεὺς Ἀνανίας ἐπέταξε τοῖς
this — day. the But high priest, Ananias, ordered those

3936 846 5180 848 4750 5119 3972
3 παρεστῶσιν αὐτῷ τύπτειν αὐτοῦ τὸ στόμα. τότε ὁ Παῦλος
standing by him to strike of him the mouth. Then Paul

4314 846 2036 5180 4571 3195 2316 5109 2867
πρὸς αὐτὸν εἶπε, Τύπτειν σε μέλλει ὁ Θεός, τοῖχε κεκονιαμένε·
to him said, to strike you is about God, wall whitened!

4771 2521 2919 3165 2596 3551 3891
καὶ σὺ κάθῃ κρίνων με κατὰ τὸν νόμον, καὶ παρανομῶν
And you sit judging me according to the Law, and contrary to law

2753/3165 5180 3936 2036 749
4 κελεύεις με τύπτεσθαι; οἱ δὲ παρεστῶτες εἶπον, Τὸν ἀρχιερέα
command me to be struck? those And standing by said, The high priest

2316 3058 5346/5037 3972 3756 1496 80
5 τοῦ Θεοῦ λοιδορεῖς; ἔφη τε ὁ Παῦλος, Οὐκ ᾔδειν, ἀδελφοί,
— of God do you revile? said And Paul, Not I knew, brothers,

3754/2076 749 1125 1063 758 2992 4675
ὅτι ἐστὶν ἀρχιερεύς· γέγραπται γάρ, Ἄρχοντα τοῦ λαοῦ σου
that he is high priest; it has been written for, A ruler of the people of you

3756/2046 2560 1097 3972 3754 1722 3313 2076
6 οὐκ ἐρεῖς κακῶς. γνοὺς δὲ ὁ Παῦλος ὅτι τὸ ἓν μέρος ἐστὶ
not speak of evilly. knowing And Paul that the one part is

4523 2087 5330 2896 1722
Σαδδουκαίων, τὸ δὲ ἕτερον Φαρισαίων, ἔκραξεν ἐν τῷ
of Sadducees, the and other of Pharisees, cried out in the

4892 435 80 1473 5330 1510/5207 5330
συνεδρίῳ, Ἄνδρες ἀδελφοί, ἐγὼ Φαρισαῖός εἰμι, υἱὸς Φαρι-
sanhedrin, Men, brothers, I a Pharisee am, a son of Phari-

4012 1680 386 3498 1473 2919
σαίου· περὶ ἐλπίδος καὶ ἀναστάσεως νεκρῶν ἐγὼ κρίνομαι.
sees; concerning hope and resurrection of (the) dead I am being judged.

5124 846 2980 1096 4714 5330
7 τοῦτο δὲ αὐτοῦ λαλήσαντος, ἐγένετο στάσις τῶν Φαρισαίων
this And him having spoken, there was a discord of the Pharisees

4523 4977 4128 4523
8 καὶ τῶν Σαδδουκαίων, καὶ ἐσχίσθη τὸ πλῆθος. Σαδδουκαῖοι
and the Sadducees, and was divided the multitude. Sadducees

3303/1063/3004 3361/1511 386 3366 32 3383
μὲν γὰρ λέγουσι μὴ εἶναι ἀνάστασιν, μηδὲ ἄγγελον, μήτε
indeed For say not to be a resurrection, neither angel nor

4151 5330 3670 287 1096
9 πνεῦμα· Φαρισαῖοι δὲ ὁμολογοῦσι τὰ ἀμφότερα. ἐγένετο δὲ
spirit. Pharisees But confess — both. there was And

2906 3173 450 1122 3313
κραυγὴ μεγάλη· καὶ ἀναστάντες οἱ γραμματεῖς τοῦ μέρους
a cry great, and having risen up the scribes of the part

5330 1264 3004 3762 2556 2147
τῶν Φαρισαίων διεμάχοντο λέγοντες, Οὐδὲν κακὸν εὑρί-
the Pharisees, they were contending, saying, Nothing evil we

1722 444 5129 1487 4151 2980 846
σκομεν ἐν τῷ ἀνθρώπῳ τούτῳ· εἰ δὲ πνεῦμα ἐλάλησεν αὐτῷ
find in — man this; if and a spirit spoke to him

2228 32 3361 2313 4183 1096 4714
10 ἢ ἄγγελος, μὴ θεομαχῶμεν. πολλῆς δὲ γενομένης στάσεως,
or an angel, not let us fight against God. much And having arisen discord

2125 5506 3361 1288 3972/5259 846
εὐλαβηθεὶς ὁ χιλίαρχος μὴ διασπασθῇ ὁ Παῦλος ὑπ' αὐτῶν,
fearing the chiliarch lest should be torn Paul by them,

2753 4253 2597 726 846 1537 3319
ἐκέλευσε τὸ στράτευμα καταβὰν ἁρπάσαι αὐτὸν ἐκ μέσου
commanded the soldiery going down to seize him out of (the) midst

848 71 5037/1519 3925
αὐτῶν, ἄγειν τε εἰς τὴν παρεμβολήν.
of them, to bring and into the fortress.

1966 3571 2186 846 2962 2036 2293
11 Τῇ δὲ ἐπιούσῃ νυκτὶ ἐπιστὰς αὐτῷ ὁ Κύριος εἶπε, Θάρσει
in the And following night coming on to him the Lord said, Be cheered,

as you fully testified the things concerning Me in Jerusalem, so you must also testify at Rome.

[12]And day having come about, some of the Jews making a conspiracy cursed themselves, saying neither to eat nor to drink until they should kill Paul. [13]And those making this plot were more than forty; [14]who coming near to the chief priests and to the elders said, With a curse we have cursed ourselves to taste of nothing until we may kill Paul. [15]Now, then, you with the sanhedrin inform the chiliarch, so that tomorrow he may bring him down to you, as intending more accurately to find out about him. And before his drawing near, we are ready to kill him.

[16]But the son of Paul's sister hearing of the ambush, having come near and entering into the fortress, reported to Paul. [17]And calling near one of the centurions, Paul said, Bring this young man to the chiliarch, for he has something to report to him. [18]Then indeed taking him, he brought *him* to the chiliarch, and said, Paul the prisoner having called me near asked me to bring this young man to you, having a thing to tell you. [19]And laying hold of his hand, and drawing aside privately, the chiliarch asked, What is *it* that you have to report to me? [20]And he said, The Jews agreed to ask you that tomorrow you bring down

3972 5613 1063 1263 4012/1700/1519 2419
Παῦλε· ὡς γὰρ διεμαρτύρω τὰ περὶ ἐμοῦ εἰς Ἱερουσαλήμ,
Paul; as for you fully testified the things about Me in Jerusalem,
3779/4571/1163 1519 4516 3140
οὕτω σε δεῖ καὶ εἰς Ῥώμην μαρτυρῆσαι.
so you must also in Rome testify.
1096 2250 4160 5100 2453
12 Γενομένης δὲ ἡμέρας, ποιήσαντές τινες τῶν Ἰουδαίων
becoming And day, making some of the Jews
4963 332 1438 3004 3383 5315
συστροφήν, ἀνεθεμάτισαν ἑαυτούς, λέγοντες μήτε φαγεῖν
a conspiracy, cursed themselves, saying neither to eat
3383 4095/2193/3756/ 615 3972 2258 4119
13 μήτε πιεῖν ἕως οὗ ἀποκτείνωσι τὸν Παῦλον. ἦσαν δὲ πλείους
nor to drink until they should kill — Paul. were And more (than)
5062 5026 4945 4160
τεσσαράκοντα οἱ ταύτην τὴν συνωμοσίαν πεποιηκότες·
forty those this * — plot making;
3748 4334 749 4245
14 οἵτινες προσελθόντες τοῖς ἀρχιερεῦσι καὶ τοῖς πρεσβυτέροις
who having come near to the chief priests and to the elders
2036 331 332 1438 3367 1089
εἶπον, Ἀναθέματι ἀνεθεματίσαμεν ἑαυτούς, μηδενὸς γεύσα-
said, With a curse we cursed ourselves of nothing to taste
2193/3739 615 3972 3568/3767/5210 1718
15 σθαι ἕως οὗ ἀποκτείνωμεν τὸν Παῦλον. νῦν οὖν ὑμεῖς ἐμφανί-
until we may kill — Paul. Now, then, you inform
5506 4862 4892 3704 839 846
σατε τῷ χιλιάρχῳ σὺν τῷ συνεδρίῳ, ὅπως αὔριον αὐτὸν
the chiliarch with the sanhedrin, so as tomorrow him
2609 4314 5209/5613 3195 1231 197
καταγάγῃ πρὸς ὑμᾶς, ὡς μέλλοντας διαγινώσκειν ἀκριβέ-
he bring down to you as intending to ascertain more
4012 846 2249 4253 1448 846
στερον τὰ περὶ αὐτοῦ· ἡμεῖς δέ, πρὸ τοῦ ἐγγίσαι αὐτόν,
accurately that about him; we and before the drawing near of him
2092 2070 332 846 191 5207
16 ἕτοιμοί ἐσμεν τοῦ ἀνελεῖν αὐτόν. ἀκούσας δὲ ὁ υἱὸς τῆς
ready are — to kill him. hearing And the son of the
79 3972 1749 3854 1525
ἀδελφῆς Παύλου τὴν ἐνέδραν, παραγενόμενος καὶ εἰσελθὼν
sister of Paul of the ambush, having come near and entering
1519 3925 518 3972 4341
εἰς τὴν παρεμβολήν, ἀπήγγειλε τῷ Παύλῳ. προσκαλεσά-
into the fortress reported — to Paul. calling to (him)
3972 1520 1543 5346 3494
17 μενος δὲ ὁ Παῦλος ἕνα τῶν ἑκατοντάρχων ἔφη, Τὸν νεανίαν
And Paul one of the centurions said, — youth
5126 520 4314 5506 2192/1063/5100/ 518
τοῦτον ἀπάγαγε πρὸς τὸν χιλίαρχον· ἔχει γάρ τι ἀπαγγεῖ-
This bring up to the chiliarch, he has for something to
846 3303/3767 3880 846 71 4314
18 λαι αὐτῷ. ὁ μὲν οὖν παραλαβὼν αὐτὸν ἤγαγε πρὸς τὸν
report to him. he Then taking him brought to the
5506 5346 1198 3972 4341
χιλίαρχον, καί φησιν, Ὁ δέσμιος Παῦλος προσκαλεσάμενός
chiliarch, and says, The prisoner Paul calling near
3165 2065 5126 3494 71 4314/4571 2192 5100
με ἠρώτησε τοῦτον τὸν νεανίαν ἀγαγεῖν πρός σε, ἔχοντά τι
me asked this — youth to bring to you, having a thing
2980 4671 1949 5495 848 5506
19 λαλῆσαί σοι. ἐπιλαβόμενος δὲ τῆς χειρὸς αὐτοῦ ὁ χιλίαρχος,
to tell you. laying hold And of the hand of him the chiliarch
402 2596 2398 4441 5101/ 2076/3739/2192
καὶ ἀναχωρήσας κατ' ἰδίαν ἐπυνθάνετο, Τί ἐστιν ὃ ἔχεις
and having withdrawn privately asked, What is (it) which you have
518 3427 2036 3754 2453 4934
20 ἀπαγγεῖλαί μοι; εἶπε δὲ ὅτι Οἱ Ἰουδαῖοι συνέθεντο τοῦ
to report to me? he said And, — The Jews agreed —
2065 4571/3704 839 1519 4892 2609
ἐρωτῆσαί σε, ὅπως αὔριον εἰς τὸ συνέδριον καταγάγῃς τὸν
to ask you so as tomorrow to the sanhedrin you bring down —

NOTE: Frequent words not numbered: δέ (1161); καί (2531)—and, but; ὁ, ἡ, τό (3588, the)— * above word, look in verse margin for No.

Paul into the sanhedrin, as being about to inquire more accurately concerning him. [21]Therefore, you *must* not be not persuaded by them, for more than forty men of them lie in wait for him, who put themselves under a curse neither to eat nor to drink until they kill him. And now they are ready, awaiting the promise from you. [22]Then the chiliarch sent away the young man, charging *him*, Tell no one that you reported these things to me.

[23]And having called near a certain two of the centurions, he said, Get two hundred soldiers ready, so that they may go to Caesarea, and seventy horsemen, and two hundred spearmen, from the third hour of the night; [24]and animals to stand by, so that setting Paul on, they may bring *him* to Felix the governor. [25]*For he was* writing a letter, having this form:

[26]Claudius Lysias to the most excellent governor, Felix, greeting: [27]This man being seized by the Jews, and being about to be killed by them, coming on with the soldiers I rescued him, learning that he was a Roman. [28]And being minded to know the charge for which they were accusing him, I brought him down to their sanhedrin; [29]I found *him* to be accused concerning questions of their law, and having no charge worthy of death or of bonds. [30]And it being revealed to me that a plot against the man was about to be *executed* by the Jews, I at once sent to you, also commanding the accusers to say the things against him before you. Farewell.

3972 5613 3195 5101 197 4441 4012
Παῦλον, ὡς μέλλοντές τι ἀκριβέστερον πυνθάνεσθαι περὶ
Paul, as intending something more accurately to inquire concerning
846 4771/3767/3361 3982 846 1748 1063 846
21 αὐτοῦ. σὺ οὖν μὴ πεισθῇς αὐτοῖς· ἐνεδρεύουσι γὰρ αὐτὸν
him. You, then, not be persuaded by them; lie in wait for for him
1537/846 435 4119 5062 3748 332
ἐξ αὐτῶν ἄνδρες πλείους τεσσαράκοντα, οἵτινες ἀνεθεμάτισαν
of them men more (than) forty, who cursed
1438 3383 5315 3383 4095 2195/3756 337 846
ἑαυτοὺς μήτε φαγεῖν μήτε πιεῖν ἕως οὗ ἀνέλωσιν αὐτόν· καὶ
themselves neither to eat nor drink until they kill him, and
3568 2092 1526 4327 575/4675 1860
νῦν ἕτοιμοί εἰσι προσδεχόμενοι τὴν ἀπὸ σοῦ ἐπαγγελίαν. ὁ
now ready they are, awaiting the from you promise. the
3303/3767 5506 630 3494 3853 3367
22 μὲν οὖν χιλίαρχος ἀπέλυσε τὸν νεανίαν, παραγγείλας μηδενὶ
Then chiliarch dismissed the youth, charging (him) no one
1583 3754 5023 1718 4314/3165 4341
23 ἐκλαλῆσαι ὅτι ταῦτα ἐνεφάνισας πρός με. καὶ προσκαλεσά-
to tell that these things you reported to me. And calling near
1417 5100 1543 2036 2090
μενος δύο τινὰς τῶν ἑκατοντάρχων εἶπεν, Ἑτοιμάσατε
two a certain of the centurions he said, Prepare
4757 1250 3704 4198 2193 2542
στρατιώτας διακοσίους ὅπως πορευθῶσιν ἕως Καισαρείας,
soldiers two hundred, so as they may go to Caesarea,
2460 1440 1187 1250 575
καὶ ἱππεῖς ἑβδομήκοντα, καὶ δεξιολάβους διακοσίους, ἀπὸ
and horsemen seventy, and spearmen two hundred, from
5154 5610 3571 2934/5037/3936 2443 1913
24 τρίτης ὥρας τῆς νυκτός· κτήνη τε παραστῆσαι, ἵνα ἐπιβιβά-
third hour of the night; beasts and to stand by, that having
3972 1295 4314 5344 2232
σαντες τὸν Παῦλον διασώσωσι πρὸς Φήλικα τὸν ἡγεμόνα·
set on — Paul they may bring to Felix the governor;
1125 1982 4023 5179 5126
25 γράψας ἐπιστολὴν περιέχουσαν τὸν τύπον τοῦτον·
writing a letter having — form this:
2804 3079 2903 2232 5344 5463
26 Κλαύδιος Λυσίας τῷ κρατίστῳ ἡγεμόνι Φήλικι χαίρειν.
Claudius Lysias to the most excellent governor, Felix, greeting.
435 5226 4815 5259 2453
27 τὸν ἄνδρα τοῦτον συλληφθέντα ὑπὸ τῶν Ἰουδαίων, καὶ
— man This having been seized by the Jews, and
3195 337 5259 846 2186 4862 4753
μέλλοντα ἀναιρεῖσθαι ὑπ' αὐτῶν, ἐπιστὰς σὺν τῷ στρατεύ-
being about to be killed by them, coming on with the soldiery
1807 846 3129 3754 4514 2076 1014
28 ματι ἐξειλόμην αὐτόν, μαθὼν ὅτι Ῥωμαῖός ἐστι. βουλόμενος
I rescued him, having learned that a Roman he is. being minded
1097 156 1223/2258/ 1458 846 2609
δὲ γνῶναι τὴν αἰτίαν δι' ἣν ἐνεκάλουν αὐτῷ, κατήγαγον
And to know the charge for which they were accusing him, I brought down
846 1519 4892 848 3739/2147 1458 4012
29 αὐτὸν εἰς τὸ συνέδριον αὐτῶν· ὃν εὗρον ἐγκαλούμενον περὶ
him to the sanhedrin of them; whom I found being accused concerning
2213 3551 848 3367 514 2288
ζητημάτων τοῦ νόμου αὐτῶν, μηδὲν δὲ ἄξιον θανάτου ἢ
questions of the law of them, nothing and worthy of death, or
1193 1462 2192 3377 3427 1917 1519
30 δεσμῶν ἔγκλημα ἔχοντα. μηνυθείσης δέ μοι ἐπιβουλῆς εἰς τὸν
of bonds charge having. being revealed And to me a plot against the
435 3195 1510 5259 2453 1824 3992
ἄνδρα μέλλειν ἔσεσθαι ὑπὸ τῶν Ἰουδαίων, ἐξαυτῆς ἔπεμψα
man being about to be by the Jews, at once I sent
4314/4571 3853 2725 3004 4314
πρός σε, παραγγείλας καὶ τοῖς κατηγόροις λέγειν τὰ πρὸς
to you commanding also the accusers to say the things to
846 1909/4675 4517
αὐτὸν ἐπὶ σοῦ. ἔρρωσο.
him before you. Farewell.

[31]Then indeed taking up Paul, according to the thing appointed to them, the soldiers brought *him* through the night to Antipatris. [32]And on the morrow, allowing the horsemen to go with him, they returned to the fortress. [33]Entering into Caesarea, and giving the letter to the governor, *they* also presented Paul to him. [34]And reading *it*, the governor asked from what province he is. And having learned that *he was* from Cilicia, [35]he said, I will hear you fully when your accusers arrive. And *he* commanded him to be kept in the praetorium of Herod.

3303/3767 4757 2596 1299 846
31 Οἱ μὲν οὖν στρατιῶται, κατὰ τὸ διατεταγμένον αὐτοῖς,
the Therefore soldiers, according to the thing appointed to them,
353 3972 71 1223 3571 1519
ἀναλαβόντες τὸν Παῦλον, ἤγαγον διὰ τῆς νυκτὸς εἰς τὴν
taking up — Paul, brought through the night to —
494 1837 1439 2460 4198
32 Ἀντιπατρίδα. τῇ δὲ ἐπαύριον ἐάσαντες τοὺς ἱππεῖς πορεύ-
Antipatris; on the and morrow, allowing the horsemen to go
4862 846 5290 1519 3925 3748
33 εσθαι σὺν αὐτῷ, ὑπέστρεψαν εἰς τὴν παρεμβολήν· οἵτινες
with him, they returned to the fortress; who
1525 2542 325 1992
εἰσελθόντες εἰς τὴν Καισάρειαν, καὶ ἀναδόντες τὴν ἐπιστολὴν
having entered into — Caesarea, and giving over the letter
2232 3936 3972 846 314
34 τῷ ἡγεμόνι, παρέστησαν καὶ τὸν Παῦλον αὐτῷ. ἀναγνοὺς
to the governor, presented also — Paul to him. having read
2232 1905 1537/4169 1885 2076
δὲ ὁ ἡγεμών, καὶ ἐπερωτήσας ἐκ ποίας ἐπαρχίας ἐστί, καὶ
And the governor, and asking of what province he is, and
4441 3754/575 2791 1251 4675/5346 3752
35 πυθόμενος ὅτι ἀπὸ Κιλικίας, Διακούσομαί σου, ἔφη, ὅταν καὶ
learning that from Cilicia, I will hear you. he said, when also
2725 4675 3854 2753 5037/846 1722
οἱ κατήγοροί σου παραγένωνται· ἐκέλευσέ τε αὐτὸν ἐν τῷ
the accusers of you arrive; commanding and him in the
4232 2264 5442
πραιτωρίῳ τοῦ Ἡρώδου φυλάσσεσθαι.
praetorium of Herod to be kept.

CHAPTER 24

[1]And after five days Ananias the high priest came down with the elders, and a certain orator, Tertullus, who made a statement to the governor against Paul. [2]And Tertullus being called, he began to accuse, saying, [3]Obtaining much peace through you, and excellent accomplishments having come to this nation due to your forethought, in everything and everywhere we accept with all thankfulness, most excellent Felix. [4]But that I not hinder you more, I beseech you to hear us briefly in your fairness.

[5]For finding this man pestilent, and moving insurrection among all the Jews throughout the world, and a ringleader of the Nazarene sect; [6]who also attempted to profane the Temple; whom we also seized and wished to judge

3326 4002 2250 2597 749 367 3326
1 Μετὰ δὲ πέντε ἡμέρας κατέβη ὁ ἀρχιερεὺς Ἀνανίας μετὰ
after And five days came down the high priest, Ananias, with
4245 4489 5061 5100 3748
τῶν πρεσβυτέρων καὶ ῥήτορος Τερτύλλου τινός, οἵτινες
the elders and an orator, Tertullus one, who
1718 2232 2596 3972 2564
2 ἐνεφάνισαν τῷ ἡγεμόνι κατὰ τοῦ Παύλου. κληθέντος δὲ
informed the governor against Paul. being called And
846 756 2723 5061 3004
αὐτοῦ, ἤρξατο κατηγορεῖν ὁ Τέρτυλλος λέγων,
him, began to accuse Tertullus, saying,
4183 1515 5177 1223/4675 2735
3 Πολλῆς εἰρήνης τυγχάνοντες διὰ σοῦ, καὶ κατορθωμάτων
Much peace obtaining through you, and excellent measures
1096 1484 5129 1223 4674 4307 3859 5037
γινομένων τῷ ἔθνει τούτῳ διὰ τῆς σῆς προνοίας, πάντῃ τε
coming to nation this through your forethought, in everything
3837 588 2903 5344 3326 3956
καὶ πανταχοῦ ἀποδεχόμεθα, κράτιστε Φῆλιξ, μετὰ πάσης
and everywhere we welcome, most excellent Felix, with all
2169 2443 3361/1909/4119/4571 1465 3870
4 εὐχαριστίας. ἵνα δὲ μὴ ἐπὶ πλεῖόν σε ἐγκόπτω, παρακαλῶ
thankfulness. that But not more you I hinder, I beseech
191 4571/2257 4935 4674 1932 2147 1063
5 ἀκοῦσαί σε ἡμῶν συντόμως τῇ σῇ ἐπιεικείᾳ. εὑρόντες γὰρ
to hear you us briefly in your forbearance. finding For
435 5126 3061 2795 4714 3956
τὸν ἄνδρα τοῦτον λοιμόν, καὶ κινοῦντα στάσιν πᾶσι τοῖς
man this pestilent and moving insurrection among all the
2453 2596 3625 4414 5037
Ἰουδαίοις τοῖς κατὰ τὴν οἰκουμένην, πρωτοστάτην τε τῆς
Jews throughout the habitable world, a ringleader and of the
3840 139 3739 2411 3985 953
6 τῶν Ναζωραίων αἱρέσεως· ὃς καὶ τὸ ἱερὸν ἐπείρασε βεβηλῶ-
— Nazarene sect, who also the temple attempted to profane,
3739 2902 2596 2251 3551 2309
σαι· ὃν καὶ ἐκρατήσαμεν καὶ κατὰ τὸν ἡμέτερον νόμον ἠθελή-
whom also we seized, and according to our law wished

according to our law; [7]but Lysias the chiliarch coming up with much force took him away out of our hands, commanding his accusers to come to you; [8]from whom you will be able yourself to know, having examined as to all these things of which we accuse him. [9]And the Jews also joined in, alleging these things to be so.

[10]But the governor signaling to him to speak, Paul answered:

Understanding you as being *a* judge to this nation many years, I cheerfully defend myself *as to* the things concerning myself. [11]You *are* able to know that not more than twelve days are to me since I went worshiping in Jerusalem; [12]and neither did they find me reasoning with anyone in the Temple, or making a gathering of a crowd; neither in the synagogues, nor throughout the city; [13]nor are they able to prove that concerning which they now accuse me. [14]But I confess this to you, that according to the Way, which they say *is* a sect, so I worship the ancestral God, believing all things according to that having been written *in* the Law and the Prophets, [15]having hope toward God, which these themselves admit, *of* a resurrection being about to be of *the* dead, both of just and unjust ones. [16]And in this I exercise myself to have always a blameless conscience toward God and men. [17]And after many years I arrived doing alms and offerings to my nation, [18]among which they found me purified in the Temple,

2919 3928 3079 5506 3326 4183
7 σαμεν κρίνειν. παρελθὼν δὲ Λυσίας ὁ χιλίαρχος μετὰ πολλῆς
to judge. coming up But Lysias the chiliarch with much
970/1537 5495 2257 520 2753 2725
βίας ἐκ τῶν χειρῶν ἡμῶν ἀπήγαγε, κελεύσας τοὺς κατηγό-
force out of the hands of us took commanding the accusers
848 2069 1909/4571/3844/3756/ 1410 848 350
8 ρους αὐτοῦ ἔρχεσθαι ἐπὶ σέ· παρ' οὗ δυνήσῃ, αὐτὸς ἀνα-
of him to come to you; from whom you can yourself, having
4012 3956 5130 1921 3739/2249 2723
κρίνας, περὶ πάντων τούτων ἐπιγνῶναι ὧν ἡμεῖς κατηγο-
examined about all these things, know fully of which we accuse
846 4934 2453 5335
9 ροῦμεν αὐτοῦ. συνέθεντο δὲ καὶ οἱ Ἰουδαῖοι, φάσκοντες
him. joined in And also the Jews, alleging
5023 3779 2192
ταῦτα οὕτως ἔχειν.
these things so to be.
611 3972 3506 846 2232
10 Ἀπεκρίθη δὲ ὁ Παῦλος, νεύσαντος αὐτῷ τοῦ ἡγεμόνος
answered And Paul, having signaled to him the governor
3004
λέγειν,
to speak,
1537 4183 2094/5651/4571/ 2923 1484 5129 1987
Ἐκ πολλῶν ἐτῶν ὄντα σε κριτὴν τῷ ἔθνει τούτῳ ἐπιστά-
Of many years being you a judge nation to this under-
2115 4012 1683 626 1410
μενος, εὐθυμότερον τὰ περὶ ἐμαυτοῦ ἀπολογοῦμαι, δυνα-
standing, cheerfully (as to) the things about myself I defend myself. being
4675 1097 3754 4119/1526/3427/ 2250 1177
11 μένου σου γνῶναι ὅτι οὐ πλείους εἰσί μοι ἡμέραι ἢ δεκαδύο,
able you to know that not more are to me days twelve
575/3739/ 305 4352 1722 2419 3777/1722
12 ἀφ' ἧς ἀνέβην προσκυνήσων ἐν Ἱερουσαλήμ· καὶ οὔτε ἐν τῷ
from which I went worshiping in Jerusalem and neither int the
2411 2147/3165/4314 5100 1256 1999
ἱερῷ εὗρόν με πρός τινα διαλεγόμενον ἢ ἐπισύστασιν
Temple they found me with anyone reasoning, or a gathering
4160 3793 3777/1722 4864 3777 2596
ποιοῦντα ὄχλου, οὔτε ἐν ταῖς συναγωγαῖς, οὔτε κατὰ τὴν
making of a crowd, neither in the synagogues, nor throughout the
•3739 4172 3777 3936 1410 4012/•/3568/ 2723
13 πόλιν. οὔτε παραστῆσαι δύνανται περὶ ὧν νῦν κατηγοροῦσί
city, nor to prove they are able about which now they accuse
3450 3670 5124 4671/3754/2596 2598/3739/ 3004
14 μου. ὁμολογῶ δὲ τοῦτό σοι, ὅτι κατὰ τὴν ὁδὸν ἣν λέγουσιν
me. I confess But this to you, that according to the Way which they say
139 3779 3000 3971 2316 4100 3956
αἵρεσιν, οὕτω λατρεύω τῷ πατρῴῳ Θεῷ, πιστεύων πᾶσι
a sect (is), thus I worship the ancestral God, believing all
2596 3551 4396 1125
τοῖς κατὰ τὸν νόμον καὶ τοῖς προφήταις γεγραμμένοις·
the things as to the Law and the Prophets having been written
1680 2192/1519 2316/3739 846 3778 4327
15 ἐλπίδα ἔχων εἰς τὸν Θεόν, ἣν καὶ αὐτοὶ οὗτοι προσδέχονται,
hope having toward God, which also themselves these admit,
386 3195 1510 3498 1342 5037 94
ἀνάστασιν μέλλειν ἔσεσθαι νεκρῶν, δικαίων τε καὶ ἀδίκων.
a resurrection being about to be of (the) dead, of just both and unjust.
1722/5129 848 778 677 4893 2192 4314
16 ἐν τούτῳ δὲ αὐτὸς ἀσκῶ, ἀπρόσκοπον συνείδησιν ἔχειν πρὸς
by this And myself I exercise a blameless conscience to have toward
2316 444 1223 3956 1223 2094
17 τὸν Θεὸν καὶ τοὺς ἀνθρώπους διὰ παντός. δι' ἐτῶν δὲ
– God and men always after years And
4119 3854 1654 4160 1519 1484
πλειόνων παρεγενόμην ἐλεημοσύνας ποιήσων εἰς τὸ ἔθνος
many I arrived alms doing to the nation
3450 4376 1722 2147/3165/ 48 1722 2411
18 μου καὶ προσφοράς· ἐν οἷς εὗρόν με ἡγνισμένον ἐν τῷ ἱερῷ,
of me and offerings, among which they found me purified in the temple.

from Asia, [19]who ought to be present before you and to accuse, if they have anything against me. [20]Or these themselves say if they found anything unjust in me, I standing before the sanhedrin, [21]than concerning this one voice which I cried out standing among them, that concerning a resurrection of *the* dead I am being judged today before you.

[22]And hearing these things, Felix put them off, knowing more accurately about the Way, saying, When Lysias the chiliarch comes down, I will examine the things as to you. [23]And having ordered the centurion to keep Paul, and to have ease, and not to forbid anyone of his own to minister or to come to him.

[24]And after some days, Felix having arrived with his wife Drusilla, who was a Jewess, he sent for Paul. And *he* heard him concerning the faith in Christ. [25]And he having reasoned concerning righteousness and self-control, and the Judgment that is about to be, becoming afraid Felix answered, For the present, go; but taking time later, I will call for you; [26]and with it all also hoping that silver would be given to him by Paul, that he might free him. Because of this *he* also more frequently sent for him *and* conversed with him. [27]But two years being completed, Felix welcomed a successor, Porcius Festus. And wishing to show a favor to the Jews, Felix left Paul bound.

3756/3326/ 3793 3762 3326 2351 5100 575 723
οὐ μετὰ ὄχλου οὐδὲ μετὰ θορύβου, τινὲς ἀπὸ τῆς Ἀσίας
not with a crowd, nor with tumult; some from Asia
2453 3739/ 1163/1909/4675 3918 2723 1487/5101
19 Ἰουδαῖοι· οὓς ἔδει ἐπὶ σοῦ παρεῖναι καὶ κατηγορεῖν εἴ τι
Jews, whom it is right before you to be present and to accuse if a thing
2192 4314/3165 846 3778 2036 =1536= 2147/1722/1698
20 ἔχοιεν πρός με. ἢ αὐτοὶ οὗτοι εἰπάτωσαν, εἴ τι εὗρον ἐν ἐμοὶ
they have against me. Or them these let say if anything they found in
92 2476 3450/1909 4892 4012/3391 5026 me
21 ἀδίκημα, στάντος μου ἐπὶ τοῦ συνεδρίου, ἢ περὶ μιᾶς ταύτης
unjust, standing me before the sanhedrin, than about one this
5456 3739 2896 2476 1722 846 3754 4012 386
φωνῆς, ἧς ἔκραξα ἑστὼς ἐν αὐτοῖς, ὅτι Περὶ ἀναστάσεως
voice which I cried out standing among them, that concerning a resurrection
3498 1473 2919 4594 5259 5216
νεκρῶν ἐγὼ κρίνομαι σήμερον ὑφ' ὑμῶν.
of (the) dead I am being judged today before you.
191 5023 5344 306 846 187
22 Ἀκούσας δὲ ταῦτα ὁ Φῆλιξ ἀνεβάλετο αὐτούς, ἀκριβέ-
having heard And these things Felix put off them, more
1492 4012 3598 2036 3752 3079 5506
στερον εἰδὼς τὰ περὶ τῆς ὁδοῦ, εἰπών, Ὅταν Λυσίας ὁ χιλί-
accurately knowing about the Way, saying, When Lysias the chili-
2597 1231 2596 5209 1299 5037
23 αρχος καταβῇ, διαγνώσομαι τὰ καθ' ὑμᾶς· διαταξάμενός τε
arch comes down I will examine the things as to you; having ordered and
1543 5083 3972 2192/5037/ 425
τῷ ἑκατοντάρχῃ τηρεῖσθαι τὸν Παῦλον, ἔχειν τε ἄνεσιν, καὶ
the centurion to keep — Paul, to have and ease, and
3367 2967 2398 848 5256 4334
μηδένα κωλύειν τῶν ἰδίων αὐτοῦ ὑπηρετεῖν ἢ προσέρχεσθαι
no one to forbid of the own him to minister or to come
846
αὐτῷ.
to him.
3326 2250 5100 3854 5344 4862
24 Μετὰ δὲ ἡμέρας τινάς, παραγενόμενος ὁ Φῆλιξ σὺν
after And days some, having arrived Felix with
1409 1135 848 5607 2453 3343
Δρουσίλλῃ τῇ γυναικὶ αὐτοῦ οὔσῃ Ἰουδαίᾳ, μετεπέμψατο
Drusilla the wife of him, being a Jewess, he sent for
3972 191 846 4012 1519 5547 4102
τὸν Παῦλον, καὶ ἤκουσεν αὐτοῦ περὶ τῆς εἰς Χριστὸν πί-
Paul, and heard him concerning the in Christ
1256 846 4012 1343 1466
25 στεως. διαλεγομένου δὲ αὐτοῦ περὶ δικαιοσύνης καὶ ἐγκρατείας
faith. reasoning And him concerning righteousness and self-control
2917 3195 1510 1719 1096
καὶ τοῦ κρίματος τοῦ μέλλοντος ἔσεσθαι, ἔμφοβος γενόμενος
and the judgment — being about to be, afraid becoming
5344 611 3568/2192 4198 2540 3335
ὁ Φῆλιξ ἀπεκρίθη, Τὸ νῦν ἔχον πορεύου· καιρὸν δὲ μεταλα-
Felix answered, For the present go, time but taking
3333 4571/260 1679 3754 5536
26 βὼν μετακαλέσομαί σε· ἅμα δὲ καὶ ἐλπίζων ὅτι χρήματα
later I will send for you; withal but also hoping that silver
1325 846 5259 3972 3704 3089 846 1417
δοθήσεται αὐτῷ ὑπὸ τοῦ Παύλου, ὅπως λύσῃ αὐτόν· διὸ
will be given him by — Paul; that he might free him. So
4437 846 3343 3656 846
καὶ πυκνότερον αὐτὸν μεταπεμπόμενος ὡμίλει αὐτῷ.
also more frequently him sending for, he conversed with him.
1333 4137 2983 1240 3344 4201
27 διετίας δὲ πληρωθείσης, ἔλαβε διάδοχον ὁ Φῆλιξ Πόρκιον
two years And being completed, received a successor Felix, Porcius
5347 2309 5485 2698 2453 5344
Φῆστον· θέλων τε χάριτας καταθέσθαι τοῖς Ἰουδαίοις ὁ Φῆλιξ
Festus; wishing and a favor to show to the Jews, Felix
2641 3972 1210
κατέλιπε τὸν Παῦλον δεδεμένον.
left Paul bound.

CHAPTER 25

CHAPTER 25

[1]Then entering the province, after three days Festus went up to Jerusalem from Caesarea. [2]And the high priest and the chief of the Jews made a statement before him against Paul, and they begged him, [3]asking a favor against him, so as he might send for him to Jerusalem, making a plot to kill him on the way. [4]Then indeed Festus answered that Paul should be kept at Caesarea, he himself even being about to go shortly. [5]Then he said, those having power among you may go down with *me*. If there is a thing amiss in this man, let them accuse him.

[6]And remaining among them more than ten days, going down to Caesarea, on the next day sitting on the tribunal, he ordered Paul to be brought. [7]And he having arrived, the Jews coming down from Jerusalem stood around, also bringing many weighty charges against Paul, which they were not able to prove. [8]Defending himself, *Paul* said, Neither against the Law of the Jews, nor against the Temple, nor against Caesar have I sinned *in* anything. [9]But desiring to show a favor to the Jews, answering Paul, Festus said, Do you desire to go up to Jerusalem to be judged before me there about these things? [10]But Paul said, I am standing before the tribunal of Caesar where I ought to be judged. I did nothing to the Jews, as also you very well know. [11]For if I indeed do wrong and have done anything worthy of death, I

5347 3767 1910 1885 3326/5140 2250 305
1 Φῆστος οὖν ἐπιβὰς τῇ ἐπαρχίᾳ, μετὰ τρεῖς ἡμέρας ἀνέβη
Festus, therefore, entering the province after three days went up
1519 2414 575 2542 1718 846
2 εἰς Ἱεροσόλυμα ἀπὸ Καισαρείας. ἐνεφάνισαν δὲ αὐτῷ ὁ
to Jerusalem from Caesarea. made a statement And to him the
749 4413 2453 2596 3972
ἀρχιερεὺς καὶ οἱ πρῶτοι τῶν Ἰουδαίων κατὰ τοῦ Παύλου,
chief priest and the chief of the Jews against – Paul.
3870 846 154 5485 2596 846 3704
3 καὶ παρεκάλουν αὐτόν, αἰτούμενοι χάριν κατ' αὐτοῦ, ὅπως
And they besought him, asking a favor against him, so as
3343 846 1519 2419 1747 4160
μεταπέμψηται αὐτὸν εἰς Ἱερουσαλήμ, ἐνέδραν ποιοῦντες
he might send for him to Jerusalem, a plot making
337 846 2596 3598 3303/3767 5347 611
4 ἀνελεῖν αὐτὸν κατὰ τὴν ὁδόν. ὁ μὲν οὖν Φῆστος ἀπεκρίθη,
to kill him by the way. Therefore Festus answered
5083 3972 1722 2542 1438 3195
τηρεῖσθαι τὸν Παῦλον ἐν Καισαρείᾳ, ἑαυτὸν δὲ μέλλειν ἐν
to be kept – Paul in Caesarea, himself and being about to
5034 1607 3767 1415 1722/5213/5346 4782
5 τάχει ἐκπορεύεσθαι. οἱ οὖν δυνατοὶ ἐν ὑμῖν, φησί, συγκατα-
quickly go forth. the Then able ones among you, he says, going down
=1536= 2076 824 1722 435 5129 2723
βάντες, εἴ τι ἐστὶν ἄτοπον ἐν τῷ ἀνδρὶ τούτῳ, κατηγορεί-
with (me), if a thing is amiss in – man this, let them
846
τωσαν αὐτοῦ.
accuse him.

1304 1722 846 2250 4119 1176 2597
6 Διατρίψας δὲ ἐν αὐτοῖς ἡμέρας πλείους ἢ δέκα, καταβὰς
having stayed And among them days more than ten, going down
1519 2542 1887 2523 1909 968 2753
εἰς Καισάρειαν, τῇ ἐπαύριον καθίσας ἐπὶ τοῦ βήματος ἐκέ-
to Caesarea, on the morrow sitting on the tribunal he
3972 71 3854 846
7 λευσε τὸν Παῦλον ἀχθῆναι. παραγενομένου δὲ αὐτοῦ,
ordered Paul to be brought. having arrived And him,
4026 575 2414 2597 2453
περιέστησαν οἱ ἀπὸ Ἱεροσολύμων καταβεβηκότες Ἰουδαῖοι,
stood around the from Jerusalem having come down Jews,
4183 926 157 5342 2596 3972
πολλὰ καὶ βαρέα αἰτιάματα φέροντες κατὰ τοῦ Παύλου, ἃ
many and weighty charges bringing against Paul, which
3756 2480 584 626 846 3754/3777/1519
8 οὐκ ἴσχυον ἀποδεῖξαι, ἀπολογουμένου αὐτοῦ ὅτι Οὔτε εἰς
not they had strength to prove. Defending himself, he said, Neither against
3551 2453 3777/1519 2411 3777/1519 2541
τὸν νόμον τῶν Ἰουδαίων, οὔτε εἰς τὸ ἱερόν, οὔτε εἰς Καίσαρά
the law of the Jews, nor against the temple, nor against Caesar
5101/264 5347 2453 2309 5485
9 τι ἥμαρτον. ὁ Φῆστος δὲ τοῖς Ἰουδαίοις θέλων χάριν
anything I sinned. Festus But the Jews wishing a favor
2698 611 3972 2036 2309 1519 2414
καταθέσθαι, ἀποκριθεὶς τῷ Παύλῳ εἶπε, Θέλεις εἰς Ἱεροσό-
to show, answering – Paul said, Desire you to Jerusalem
305 1563/4012 5130 2919 1909 1700 2036
10 λυμα ἀναβάς, ἐκεῖ περὶ τούτων κρίνεσθαι ἐπ' ἐμοῦ; εἶπε δὲ
to go up, there about these things to be judged before me? said And
3972 1909 968 2541 2476 1510/3757/3165/1163
ὁ Παῦλος, Ἐπὶ τοῦ βήματος Καίσαρος ἑστώς εἰμι, οὗ με δεῖ
Paul, Before the tribunal of Caesar standing I am; where me must
2919 2453 3762 91 5613 4771 2573
κρίνεσθαι· Ἰουδαίους οὐδὲν ἠδίκησα, ὡς καὶ σὺ κάλλιον
be judged. Jews nothing I have wronged, as indeed you very well
1921 1487/3303/1063/91 514 2288 4238
11 ἐπιγινώσκεις. εἰ μὲν γὰρ ἀδικῶ καὶ ἄξιον θανάτου πέπραχά
know, if indeed For I do wrong and worthy of death I have done

do not refuse to die. But if there is nothing of which they accuse me, no one can give me up to them. I appeal to Caesar. [12]Then conferring with the sanhedrin, Festus answered, You have appealed to Caesar; you shall go before Caesar.

[13]And some days having passed, Agrippa the king and Bernice arrived at Caesarea, greeting Festus. [14]And when they stayed there more days, Festus set out to the king the things as to Paul, saying, A certain man has been left a prisoner by Felix, [15]about whom, on my being in Jerusalem, the chief priests and the elders of the Jews made a statement, asking judgment against him; [16]to whom I answered, It is not a custom with Romans to give up any man to destruction before the *one* being accused may have the accusers face to face, and may receive place of defense concerning the charge. [17]Then they coming together here, making no delay, sitting on the tribunal on the next *day,* I commanded the man to be brought; [18]about whom, standing up, the accusers brought no charge of which I suspected, [19]but they had certain questions about *their* own demon-worship, and about a certain Jesus dying, whom Paul claimed to live.

[20]And being puzzled as to this inquiry, I said, Did he desire to go to Jerusalem, and to be judged there concerning these things? [21]But Paul having appealed for himself to be kept to the

5100/3756/ 3868 599 1487 3762 2076 5613 3778
τι, οὐ παραιτοῦμαι τὸ ἀποθανεῖν· εἰ δὲ οὐδέν ἐστιν ὧν οὗτοι
a thing, not I refuse — to die; if but not one is of which these
2723 3450 3762/3165/ 1410 846 5483
κατηγοροῦσί μου, οὐδείς με δύναται αὐτοῖς χαρίσασθαι.
accuse me, no one me is able to them to grant.
2541 1941 5119 5347 4814 3326
12 Καίσαρα ἐπικαλοῦμαι. τότε ὁ Φῆστος συλλαλήσας μετὰ τοῦ
Caesar I appeal to. Then Festus having conferred with the
4824 611 2541 1941 1909 2541
συμβουλίου ἀπεκρίθη, Καίσαρα ἐπικέκλησαι ; ἐπὶ Καίσαρα
sanhedrin answered, Caesar you have appealed to, before Caesar
4198
πορεύσῃ.
you shall go.

2250 1230 5100 67 935
13 Ἡμερῶν δὲ διαγενομένων τινῶν, Ἀγρίππας ὁ βασιλεὺς
days And passing some, Agrippa the king
959 2658 1519 2542 782
καὶ Βερνίκη κατήντησαν εἰς Καισάρειαν, ἀσπασόμενοι τὸν
and Bernice arrived at Caesarea, greeting
5347 5613 4119 2250 1304 1563 5347
14 Φῆστον. ὡς δὲ πλείους ἡμέρας διέτριβον ἐκεῖ, ὁ Φῆστος τῷ
Festus. as And more days they stayed there, Festus to the
935 394 2596 3972 3004 435/5100/2076
βασιλεῖ ἀνέθετο τὰ κατὰ τὸν Παῦλον, λέγων, Ἀνήρ τίς ἐστι
king set out the things as to — Paul, saying, a man certain is
2641 5259 5344 1198 4012/3756 1096
15 καταλελειμμένος ὑπὸ Φήλικος δέσμιος, περὶ οὗ, γενομένου
having been left by Felix a prisoner, about whom, being
3450/1519 2414 1718 749 4245
μου εἰς Ἱεροσόλυμα, ἐνεφάνισαν οἱ ἀρχιερεῖς καὶ οἱ πρεσ-
me in Jerusalem, made a statement the chief priests and the
2453 154 2596 846 1349 4314
16 βύτεροι τῶν Ἰουδαίων, αἰτούμενοι κατ' αὐτοῦ δίκην. πρὸς
elders of the Jews, asking against him sentence; to
3739 611 3754/3756/2076/1485 4514 5483 5100
οὓς ἀπεκρίθην, ὅτι οὐκ ἔστιν ἔθος Ῥωμαίοις χαρίζεσθαί τινα
whom I answered that not it is a custom with Romans to grant any
444 1519 684 4250 2723 2596
ἄνθρωπον εἰς ἀπώλειαν, πρὶν ἢ ὁ κατηγορούμενος κατὰ
man to destruction before the (one) being accused face
4383 2192 2725 5117/5037/627
πρόσωπον ἔχοι τοὺς κατηγόρους, τόπον τε ἀπολογίας
to face should have the accusers, place and of defense
2983 4012 1462 4905 3767 846 1759
17 λάβοι περὶ τοῦ ἐγκλήματος. συνελθόντων οὖν αὐτῶν ἐνθάδε,
receive concerning the charge. Coming together, then, they to here,
311 3367 4160 1836 2523 1909
ἀναβολὴν μηδεμίαν ποιησάμενος, τῇ ἑξῆς καθίσας ἐπὶ τοῦ
delay no making, on the next sitting on the
968 2753 71 435 4012/3756/ 2476
18 βήματος, ἐκέλευσα ἀχθῆναι τὸν ἄνδρα· περὶ οὗ σταθέντες οἱ
tribunal, I commanded to be brought the man; about whom standing the
2725 3762 156 2018 3739 5283 1473
κατήγοροι οὐδεμίαν αἰτίαν ἐπέφερον ὧν ὑπενόουν ἐγώ,
accusers no charge brought of which suspected I,
2213 5100 4012 2398 1175 2192 4314
19 ζητήματα δέ τινα περὶ τῆς ἰδίας δεισιδαιμονίας εἶχον πρὸς
questions but certain about the own demon-worship they had with
846 4012/5100/2424 2348 3739 5335 3972
αὐτόν, καὶ περί τινος Ἰησοῦ τεθνηκότος, ὃν ἔφασκεν ὁ Παῦλος
him, and about a certain Jesus having died, whom claimed Paul
2198 639 1473/1519 4012 5127 2214
20 ζῆν. ἀπορούμενος δὲ ἐγὼ εἰς τὴν περὶ τούτου ζήτησιν,
to live. being puzzled And I as to the concerning this inquiry,
3004 1487 1014 4198 1519 2419 2546 2919
ἔλεγον, εἰ βούλοιτο πορεύεσθαι εἰς Ἱερουσαλήμ, κἀκεῖ κρίνε-
said if he desired to go to Jereusalem and there to be
4012 5130 3972 1941 5083
21 σθαι περὶ τούτων. τοῦ δὲ Παύλου ἐπικαλεσαμένου τηρηθῆναι
judged about these things. But Paul having appealed to be kept

examination of Augustus, I
commanded him to be held
until I might send him to
Caesar. 22And Agrippa said
to Festus, I also was myself
minded to hear the man.
And he said, Tomorrow you
shall hear him.

23Then on the next day,
Agrippa and Bernice
coming with much pomp
and entering into the auditorium, with both the chiliarchs and the chief men,
being of the city; also Festus
commanding, Paul was led
out.

24And Festus said, King
Agrippa, and all those men
present with us, you see this
one about whom all the
multitude of the Jews
pleaded with me both here
and in Jerusalem, crying out
that he ought to live no
longer. 25But I having perceived nothing he had done
worthy of death, also this
one himself having ap-
pealed to Augustus, I de-
cided to send him; 26about
whom I have nothing cer-
tain to write to *my* lord. For
this reason I brought him
before you, and most of all
before you, king Agrippa, so
as the examination taking
place, I may have some-
what to write to *my* lord.
27For it seems unreasonable
to me to send a prisoner, and
not also to signify the
charges against him.

846 1519 4575 1233 2753 5083
αὐτὸν εἰς τὴν τοῦ Σεβαστοῦ διάγνωσιν, ἐκέλευσα τηρεῖσθαι
him to the of Augustus examination, I commanded to be kept
846 2193/3756/ 3992 846 4314 2541 67
22 αὐτόν, ἕως οὗ πέμψω αὐτὸν πρὸς Καίσαρα. Ἀγρίππας δὲ
him until I may send him to Caesar. Agrippa And
4314 5347 5346 1014 848 444
πρὸς τὸν Φῆστον ἔφη, Ἐβουλόμην καὶ αὐτὸς τοῦ ἀνθρώπου
to Festus said, I was minded also myself the man
191 839 5346 191 846
ἀκοῦσαι. ὁ δέ, Αὔριον, φησίν, ἀκούσῃ αὐτοῦ.
to hear. he And, Tomorrow, said, you will hear him.

3767 1887 2064 67 959
23 Τῇ οὖν ἐπαύριον, ἐλθόντος τοῦ Ἀγρίππα καὶ τῆς Βερνίκης
on the Then morrow coming — Agrippa and — Bernice
3326 4183 5325 1525 1519 201
μετὰ πολλῆς φαντασίας, καὶ εἰσελθόντων εἰς τὸ ἀκροατήριον,
with much pomp, and entering into the auditorium,
4862/5037 5506 435 2596 1851 5607
σύν τε τοῖς χιλιάρχοις καὶ ἀνδράσι τοῖς κατ' ἐξοχὴν οὖσι τῆς
with both the chiliarchs and men the chief being of the
4172 2753 5347 71 3972
24 πόλεως, καὶ κελεύσαντος τοῦ Φήστου, ἤχθη ὁ Παῦλος. καί
city, and having commanded Festus, was brought Paul. And
5346 5347 67 935 3956 4840
φησιν ὁ Φῆστος, Ἀγρίππα βασιλεῦ, καὶ πάντες οἱ συμπαρόν-
says Festus, Agrippa King, and all those present with
2254 435 2334 5126 4012/3739/3956 4128
τες ἡμῖν ἄνδρες, θεωρεῖτε τοῦτον περὶ οὗ πᾶν τὸ πλῆθος τῶν
us, men, you behold this one about whom all the multitude of
*5037 2453 1793 3427/1722/•/ 2414 1759 the
Ἰουδαίων ἐνέτυχόν μοι ἔν τε Ἱεροσολύμοις καὶ ἐνθάδε, ἐπι-
Jews petitioned me in both Jerusalem and here,
1916 3361/1163/2198/ 846 3371 1473 2638
25 βοῶντες μὴ δεῖν ζῆν αὐτὸν μηκέτι. ἐγὼ δὲ καταλαβόμενος
crying not ought to live him no longer. I And having perceived
3367 514 2288 846 4238 848 5127
μηδὲν ἄξιον θανάτου αὐτὸν πεπραχέναι, καὶ αὐτοῦ δὲ τοῦτον
nothing worthy of death he had done, also himself but this one
1941 4575 2919 3992 846 4012
26 ἐπικαλεσαμένου τὸν Σεβαστόν, ἔκρινα πέμπειν αὐτόν. περὶ
having appealed to Augustus, I decided to send him. About
3756 804 5101 1125 2962 3756/2192/1352 4254
οὗ ἀσφαλές τι γράψαι τῷ κυρίῳ οὐκ ἔχω. διὸ προήγαγον
whom certain anything to write to the lord not I have. So I brought forth
846 1909/5216 3122 1909/4675 935 67
αὐτὸν ἐφ' ὑμῶν, καὶ μάλιστα ἐπὶ σοῦ, βασιλεῦ Ἀγρίππα,
him before you, and most before you, king Agrippa,
3704 351 1096 2192/5100/1125 249
27 ὅπως τῆς ἀνακρίσεως γενομένης σχῶ τι γράψαι. ἄλογον
• so as the examination being, I may have what to write, unreasonable
1063/3427/1380 3992 1198 3361 2596 846
γάρ μοι δοκεῖ, πέμποντα δέσμιον, μὴ καὶ τὰς κατ' αὐτοῦ
For to me it seems sending a prisoner, not also the against him
156 4591
αἰτίας σημᾶναι.
charges to signify.

CHAPTER 26

CHAPTER 26
1And Agrippa said to Paul,
It is allowed for you yourself
to speak. Then Paul made a
defense, stretching out the
hand:

2Concerning all of which I
am accused by Jews, king

67 4314 3972 5346 2010 4671
1 Ἀγρίππας δὲ πρὸς τὸν Παῦλον ἔφη, Ἐπιτρέπεταί σοι
Agrippa And to Paul said, It is allowed for you
5228 4572 3004 5119 3972 626 1614
ὑπὲρ σεαυτοῦ λέγειν. τότε ὁ Παῦλος ἀπελογεῖτο, ἐκτείνας
for yourself to speak. Then Paul made a defense, stretching
5495
τὴν χεῖρα,
the hand,
4012 3956 3739 1458 5259 2453 935
2 Περὶ πάντων ὧν ἐγκαλοῦμαι ὑπὸ Ἰουδαίων, βασιλεῦ
Concerning all things of which I am accused by Jews, king

Agrippa, I count myself
happy being about to make
defense before you today,
[3]you being most of all
expert, knowing of all the
customs and questions also
among the Jews. Because
of this, I beg you patiently to
hear me. [4]Truly, then, all the
Jews know my way of life
from youth, which from *the*
beginning had been in my
nation in Jerusalem; [5]who
before knew me from the
first, if they will testify, that
according to the most exact
sect of our religion, I lived a
Pharisee. [6]And now for *the*
hope of the promise having
been made by God to the
fathers, I stand being
judged; [7]to which our
twelve tribes hope to arrive,
worshiping in earnestness
night and day; concerning
which hope I am accused by
the Jews, king Agrippa.

[8]Why is it judged unbe-
lievable by you if God
raises *the* dead? [9]I indeed
then thought to myself
that I ought to do many
things contrary to the
name of Jesus the Naza-
rene. [10]Which I also did in
Jerusalem; I also shut up
many of the saints in
prisons, receiving authority
from the chief priests; and
they being put to death, I
cast a vote. [11]And often
punishing them through all
the synagogues, I com-
pelled *them* to blaspheme.
And *being* exceedingly
furious against them, I even
persecuted as far as the
outer cities.

[12]In which also traveling
to Damascus with authority
and decision-power from
the chief priests, [13]at midday along the highway, *O*
king, I and those with me
saw a light from heaven
shining around me, above

67 2233 1683 3107 3195 626
Ἀγρίππα, ἥγημαι ἐμαυτὸν μακάριον μέλλων ἀπολογεῖσθαι
Agrippa, I count myself happy being about to make defense
1909/4675 4594 3122 1109 5607/4571/1492 3956
3 ἐπὶ σοῦ σήμερον· μάλιστα γνώστην ὄντα σὲ εἰδὼς πάντων
before you today, most of all an expert being you knowing of all
2596 2453 1485/5037 2213 1352 1189/4675
τῶν κατὰ Ἰουδαίους ἐθῶν τε καὶ ζητημάτων· διὸ δέομαί σου,
the among Jews customs both and questions; therefore I beg you,
3116 191 3450 3303/3767 981 3450 1537
4 μακροθύμως ἀκοῦσαί μου. τὴν μὲν οὖν βίωσίν μου τὴν ἐκ
patiently to hear me. the Indeed then way of life of me from
3503 575 746 1096 1722 1484/3450/1722
νεότητος, τὴν ἀπ' ἀρχῆς γενομένην ἐν τῷ ἔθνει μου ἐν
youth — from the beginning having been in the nation of me in
2414 2467 3956 2453 4267
5 Ἱεροσολύμοις, ἴσασι πάντες οἱ Ἰουδαῖοι, προγινώσκοντές
Jerusalem, know all the Jews, before knowing
3165/509 1437 2309 3140 3754 2596 196
με ἄνωθεν, ἐὰν θέλωσι μαρτυρεῖν, ὅτι κατὰ τὴν ἀκριβεστά-
me from the first, if they will to testify, that according to the most exact
139 2251 2356 2198 5330
6 την αἵρεσιν τῆς ἡμετέρας θρησκείας ἔζησα Φαρισαῖος. καὶ
sect — of our religion I lived a Pharisee. And
3568/1909/1680 4314 3962 1860 1096
νῦν ἐπ' ἐλπίδι τῆς πρὸς τοὺς πατέρας ἐπαγγελίας γενομένης
now on hope of the to the fathers promise having been
5259 2316 2476 2919 1519/3739 1429
7 ὑπὸ τοῦ Θεοῦ ἕστηκα κρινόμενος, εἰς ἣν τὸ δωδεκάφυλον
by — God, I stand being judged, to which the twelve tribes
2257/1722/1616 3571 2250 3000 1679 2658
ἡμῶν ἐν ἐκτενείᾳ νύκτα καὶ ἡμέραν λατρεῦον ἐλπίζει καταν-
of us in earnestness night and day worshiping hopes to
4012/3739/1680 1458 935 67 5259
τῆσαι· περὶ ἧς ἐλπίδος ἐγκαλοῦμαι, βασιλεῦ Ἀγρίππα, ὑπὸ
arrive; concerning which hope I am accused, king Agrippa, by
2453 5101 571 2919 3844/5213/1487 2316
8 τῶν Ἰουδαίων. τί ἄπιστον κρίνεται παρ' ὑμῖν, εἰ ὁ Θεὸς
the Jews. Why unbelievable is it judged by you if God
3498 1453 1473/3303/3767/1380 1683 4314 3686
9 νεκροὺς ἐγείρει; ἐγὼ μὲν οὖν ἔδοξα ἐμαυτῷ πρὸς τὸ ὄνομα
(the) dead raises? I indeed then thought to myself to the name
2424 3480 1163 4183 1727 4238
10 Ἰησοῦ τοῦ Ναζωραίου δεῖν πολλὰ ἐναντία πρᾶξαι· ὃ καὶ
of Jesus the Nazarene ought many things contrary to do; which also
4160 1722 2414 4183 90 1473
ἐποίησα ἐν Ἱεροσολύμοις, καὶ πολλοὺς τῶν ἁγίων ἐγὼ
I did in Jerusalem, and many of the saints I
5438 2628 3844 749 1849
φυλακαῖς κατέκλεισα, τὴν παρὰ τῶν ἀρχιερέων ἐξουσίαν
in prisons shut up, the from the chief priests authority
2983 337 5037/846 2702 5586 2596
11 λαβών, ἀναιρουμένων τε αὐτῶν κατήνεγκα ψῆφον. καὶ κατὰ
receiving, being killed and them, I cast a vote. And through
3956 4864 4173 5097 846 315
πάσας τὰς συναγωγὰς πολλάκις τιμωρῶν αὐτούς, ἠνάγ-
all the synagogues often punishing them, I
987 4057 5037 1693 846
καζον βλασφημεῖν· περισσῶς τε ἐμμαινόμενος αὐτοῖς,
compelled to blaspheme, exceedingly and furious against them,
1377 2193 1519 1854 4172/1722/3739 4198
12 ἐδίωκον ἕως καὶ εἰς τὰς ἔξω πόλεις. ἐν οἷς καὶ πορευόμενος
I persecuted until even to the outside cities. In which also traveling
1519 1154 3326 1849 2011 3844
εἰς τὴν Δαμασκὸν μετ' ἐξουσίας καὶ ἐπιτροπῆς τῆς παρὰ τῶν
to — Damascus with authority and decision-power from the
749 2250 3319 2596 3598 1492 935
13 ἀρχιερέων, ἡμέρας μέσης, κατὰ τὴν ὁδὸν εἶδον, βασιλεῦ,
chief priests, at day mid- along the way I saw, king,
3771 5228 2987 2246 4034
οὐρανόθεν ὑπὲρ τὴν λαμπρότητα τοῦ ἡλίου, περιλάμψαν
from Heaven above the brightness of the sun shining around

the brightness of the sun. [14]And all of us falling to the ground, I heard a voice speaking to me, and saying in the Hebrew dialect, Saul, Saul why do you persecute Me? *It is* hard for you to kick against the prods. [15]And I said, Who are you, Sir? And He said, I am Jesus whom you persecute; [16]but rise up and stand on your feet, for *it is* for this reason I appeared to you, to appoint you a servant and a witness both of what you saw, and in what I shall appear to you, [17]having delivered you from the people and the nations, to whom I now send you, [18]to open their eyes, and to turn *them* from darkness to light, and *from* the authority of Satan to God; in order that they *may* receive forgiveness of sins, and an inheritance among those being sanctified by faith in Me. [19]Upon this, king Agrippa, I was not disobedient to the heavenly vision; [20]but to those first in Damascus, and Jerusalem, and to all the country of Judea, and to the nations, I announced *the command* to repent and to turn to God, doing works worthy of repentance.

[21]Because of these things, having seized *me* in the Temple, the Jews tried to kill *me*. [22]Then obtaining help from God, I stand until this day, witnessing both to small and to great, saying nothing else than what the prophets and Moses also said was going to happen: [23]*that* Christ *was* to suffer, *that* by a resurrection of *the* dead He was first going to proclaim light to the people and to the nations.

3165/5457 4862/1698 4198 3956 2667
14 με φῶς καὶ τοὺς σὺν ἐμοὶ πορευομένους. πάντων δὲ κατα-
me a light, also those with me traveling. all And having
2257/1519 1093 191 5456 2980 4314
πεσόντων ἡμῶν εἰς τὴν γῆν, ἤκουσα φωνὴν λαλοῦσαν πρός
fallen down us to the earth, I heard a voice speaking to
3165 3004 1446 1258 4549 4549/5101
με καὶ λέγουσαν τῇ Ἑβραΐδι διαλέκτῳ, Σαούλ, Σαούλ, τί
me, and saying in the Hebrew dialect, Saul, Saul, why
3165 1377 4642 4671 4314 2759 2979 1473
15 με διώκεις; σκληρόν σοι πρὸς κέντρα λακτίζειν. ἐγὼ δὲ
Me persecute you? (It is) hard for you to kick against the prods. I And
2036 5100/1487/2962 2036 1473/1510 2424/3739/4771
εἶπον, Τίς εἶ, Κύριε; ὁ δὲ εἶπεν, Ἐγώ εἰμι Ἰησοῦς ὃν σὺ
said, Who are you, Sir? He And said, I am Jesus whom you
1377 235 450 2476/1909 4228/ 4675/1519
16 διώκεις. ἀλλὰ ἀνάστηθι, καὶ στῆθι ἐπὶ τοὺς πόδας σου· εἰς
persecute. But rise up, and stand on the feet of you, for
5124 1063 3700 4671 4400 4571 5257
τοῦτο γὰρ ὤφθην σοι, προχειρίσασθαί σε ὑπηρέτην καὶ
this For I appeared to you, to appoint you a servant and
3739 3144 3739/5037/1492/*/5037 3700 4671 1807 4571
17 μάρτυρα ὧν τε εἶδες ὧν τε ὀφθήσομαί σοι, ἐξαιρούμενός σε
a witness of what both you saw of what and I will appear to you, delivering you
1537 2992 1484 1519/3739/3568/4571/ 649
ἐκ τοῦ λαοῦ καὶ τῶν ἐθνῶν, εἰς οὓς νῦν σε ἀποστέλλω,
from the people and the nations, to whom now you I send,
455 3788 846 1994 575 4655
18 ἀνοῖξαι ὀφθαλμοὺς αὐτῶν, καὶ ἐπιστρέψαι ἀπὸ σκότους
to open the eyes of them, and to turn from darkness
1519/5457 1849 4567 1909 2316
εἰς φῶς καὶ τῆς ἐξουσίας τοῦ Σατανᾶ ἐπὶ τὸν Θεόν, τοῦ
to light, and the authority of Satan to God,
2983 846 859 266 2819 1722 37
λαβεῖν αὐτοὺς ἄφεσιν ἁμαρτιῶν, καὶ κλῆρον ἐν τοῖς ἡγια-
to receive them forgiveness of sins, and a lot among those being
4102 1519/1691/3606 935 67 3756
19 σμένοις πίστει τῇ εἰς ἐμέ. ὅθεν, βασιλεῦ Ἀγρίππα, οὐκ
sanctified by faith in Me. Upon this, king Agrippa, not
1096 545 3770 3701 235 1722
20 ἐγενόμην ἀπειθὴς τῇ οὐρανίῳ ὀπτασίᾳ· ἀλλὰ τοῖς ἐν
I was disobedient to the heavenly vision, but to those in
1154 4412 2414 1519 3956 5037
Δαμασκῷ πρῶτον καὶ Ἱεροσολύμοις, εἰς πᾶσάν τε τὴν
Damascus firstly, and (in) Jerusalem, to all and the
5561 2449 1484 518 3340
χώραν τῆς Ἰουδαίας, καὶ τοῖς ἔθνεσιν, ἀπήγγελλον μετανοεῖν,
country of Judea, and to the nations, I announced to repent
1994 1909 2316 514 3341 2041
καὶ ἐπιστρέφειν ἐπὶ τὸν Θεόν, ἄξια τῆς μετανοίας ἔργα
and to turn to God, worthy of the repentance works
4238 1752 5130/3165 2453 4815 1722
21 πράσσοντας. ἕνεκα τούτων με οἱ Ἰουδαῖοι συλλαβόμενοι ἐν
doing. Because of these things me the Jews having seized in
2411 3987 1315 1947 3767 5177
22 τῷ ἱερῷ ἐπειρῶντο διαχειρίσασθαι. ἐπικουρίας οὖν τυχὼν
the Temple tried to kill (me). Help, then, obtaining
3844 2316 891 2250 5026 2476
τῆς παρὰ τοῦ Θεοῦ, ἄχρι τῆς ἡμέρας ταύτης ἕστηκα
— from God until day this, I stand
3140 3398/5037 3173 3762 1623 3004/3739
μαρτυρούμενος μικρῷ τε καὶ μεγάλῳ, οὐδὲν ἐκτὸς λέγων ὧν
witnessing to small and also to great, nothing else than saying what
5037 4396 2980 3195 1096 3475 1487
23 τε οἱ προφῆται ἐλάλησαν μελλόντων γίνεσθαι καὶ Μωσῆς, εἰ
both the prophets said being about to happen and Moses, if
3805 5547 1487 4413 1537 386 3498 5457
παθητὸς ὁ Χριστός, εἰ πρῶτος ἐξ ἀναστάσεως νεκρῶν φῶς
to suffer the Christ, if first by a resurrection of (the) dead a light
3195 2605 2992 1484
μέλλει καταγγέλλειν τῷ λαῷ καὶ τοῖς ἔθνεσι.
He is going to announce to the people and to the nations.

[24]And he defending himself *with* these things, Festus said with a loud voice, Paul, You rave! Your many letters turned *you* into madness. [25]But he said, Not to madness, most excellent Festus, but I speak words of truth and sanity. [26]For the king understands about these things, to whom I speak, even being bold of speech. For I am persuaded not any of these things are hidden *from* him, nothing. For *the* doing of this is not in a corner. [27]Do you believe the prophets, king Agrippa? I know that you believe. [28]And Agrippa said to Paul, Do you persuade me to become a Christian in *but* a little?

[29]And Paul said, I would pray to God, both in a little and in much, not only you, but also these hearing me today to become as I also am, except for these bonds.

[30]And saying these things, the king and the governor and Bernice rose up, and those who sat with them. [31]And withdrawing, they spoke to one another saying, This man does nothing worthy of death or of bonds. [32]And Agrippa said to Festus, This man was able to have been let go, if he had not appealed to Caesar.

5023 848 626 5347 3173
24 Ταῦτα δὲ αὐτοῦ ἀπολογουμένου, ὁ Φῆστος μεγάλῃ τῇ
these things And him defending himself, Festus great with the
5456 5346 3105 3972 4183 1121 1519 3130
φωνῇ ἔφη, Μαίνῃ Παῦλε· τὰ πολλά σε γράμματα εἰς μανίαν
voice says, You rave, Paul; the many of you letters to madness
4062 3105 5346 2903 5347 235
25 περιτρέπει. ὁ δέ. Οὐ μαίνομαι, φησί, κράτιστε Φῆστε, ἀλλ'
turn (you). But, Not to madness, he says, most excellent Festus, but
225 4997 4487 659 1987
ἀληθείας καὶ σωφροσύνης ῥήματα ἀποφθέγγομαι. ἐπίσταται
of truth and sanity words I speak. understands
1063/4012 5130 935 4314/3739 3955
26 γὰρ περὶ τούτων ὁ βασιλεύς, πρὸς ὃν καὶ παρρησιαζόμενος
For about these things the king, to whom even being bold of speech
2980 2990 1063 846 5100 5130 3756 3982 3762
λαλῶ· λανθάνειν γὰρ αὐτόν τι τούτων οὐ πείθομαι οὐδέν·
I speak, to be hidden for (from) him any of these not, I am persuaded nothing.
3756/1063/2076/1722/ 1137 4238 5124 4100
27 οὐ γάρ ἐστιν ἐν γωνίᾳ πεπραγμένον τοῦτο. πιστεύεις,
not For is in a corner (the) doing of this. Do you believe,
935 67 4396 1492/3756/ 4100
28 βασιλεῦ Ἀγρίππα, τοῖς προφήταις; οἶδα ὅτι πιστεύεις. ὁ δὲ
king Agrippa, the prophets? I know that you believe. And
67 4314 3972 5346/1722/ 3641 3165 3982
Ἀγρίππας πρὸς τὸν Παῦλον ἔφη, Ἐν ὀλίγῳ με πείθεις
Agrippa to Paul said, In a little me you persuade
5546 1086 3972 2036 2172 302
Χριστιανὸν γενέσθαι. ὁ δὲ Παῦλος εἶπεν, Εὐξαίμην ἂν τῷ
a Christian to become? And Paul said, I would pray
2316 1722 3641 1722 4183 3756/3440 4571 235
29 Θεῷ, καὶ ἐν ὀλίγῳ καὶ ἐν πολλῷ οὐ μόνον σε, ἀλλὰ καὶ
God, both in a little and in much, not only you, but also
3956 191 3450 4594 1096 5108
πάντας τοὺς ἀκούοντάς μου σήμερον, γενέσθαι τοιούτους
all those hearing me today, to become such
3697 2504 1510 3924 1199 5130
ὁποῖος κἀγώ εἰμι, παρεκτὸς τῶν δεσμῶν τούτων.
as also I am, except — bonds these.
5023 2036 846 450 935
30 Καὶ ταῦτα εἰπόντος αὐτοῦ, ἀνέστη ὁ βασιλεὺς καὶ ὁ
And these things having said he, rose up the king and the
2232/ 3739/ 5037 959 4775 846
ἡγεμών, ἥ τε Βερνίκη, καὶ οἱ συγκαθήμενοι αὐτοῖς· καὶ
governor, and Bernice, and those sitting with them; and
402 2980 4314 240 3004 3754
31 ἀναχωρήσαντες ἐλάλουν πρὸς ἀλλήλους, λέγοντες ὅτι
having left spoke to one another, saying, —
3762 2288 514/2228/ 1199 4238 444 3778
Οὐδὲν θανάτου ἄξιον ἢ δεσμῶν πράσσει ὁ ἄνθρωπος οὗτος.
Nothing of death worthy or bonds does man this.
67 5347 5346 630 1410
32 Ἀγρίππας δὲ τῷ Φήστῳ ἔφη, Ἀπολελύσθαι ἐδύνατο ὁ
Agrippa And to Festus said, to have been released was able
444 3778/1487/3361/ 1941 2541
ἄνθρωπος οὗτος, εἰ μὴ ἐπεκέκλητο Καίσαρα.
man this, if not he had appealed to Caesar.

CHAPTER 27

[1]And when it was decided for us to sail to Italy, they delivered up both Paul and certain other prisoners to a centurion named Julius, of a cohort of Augustus. [2]And boarding a ship of Adramyttium which was about to sail alongside Asian places, we set sail;

5613 2919 636 2248/1519 2482 3860
1 Ὡς δὲ ἐκρίθη τοῦ ἀποπλεῖν ἡμᾶς εἰς τὴν Ἰταλίαν, παρεδί-
when And it was decided to sail us to — Italy, they de-
5037 3972 5100 2087 1202 1543
δουν τόν τε Παῦλον καί τινας ἑτέρους δεσμώτας ἑκατοντ-
livered — both Paul and some other prisoners to a cen-
3686 2457 4686 4575 1910
2 άρχῃ, ὀνόματι Ἰουλίῳ, σπείρης Σεβαστῆς. ἐπιβάντες δὲ
turion, by name Julius, of a cohort Augustan. embarking And
4143 98 3195 4126 2596 773
πλοίῳ Ἀδραμυττηνῷ, μέλλοντες πλεῖν τοὺς κατὰ τὴν Ἀσίαν
a ship of Adramyttium, being about to sail to the alongside Asia

Aristarchus a Macedonian of Thessalonica being with us. [3]And on the next *day* we landed at Sidon. And treating Paul kindly, Julius allowed *him* to go to *his* friends to receive care. [4]And setting sail from there, we sailed close to Cyprus, because of the winds being contrary.

[5]And sailing over the sea against Cilicia and Pamphylia, we came to Myra of Lycia. [6]And the centurion finding there an Alexandrian ship sailing to Italy, he put us into it. [7]And in many days, sailing slowly and with difficulty, hardly coming against Cnidus, the wind not allowing us, we sailed close to Crete against Salmone. [8]And coasting along it with difficulty, we came to a certain place named Fair Havens, near to which was a city, Lasea.

[9]And much time having passed, and the voyage already being dangerous, because the Fast already had gone by, Paul warned them, [10]saying, Men, I see that the voyage is about to be with injury, and not only much loss of the cargo and of the ship, but also of our souls.

[11]But the centurion was rather persuaded by the helmsman and the shipmaster, than by the things spoken by Paul. [12]And the port not being fit for wintering, the most gave counsel to set sail from there, if somehow they may be able to pass the winter, arriving at Phoenice, a port of Crete

5117 321 5607 4862/2254 708 3110
τόπους, ἀνήχθημεν, ὄντος σὺν ἡμῖν Ἀριστάρχου Μακεδόνος
places, we set sail, being with us Aristarchus, a Macedonian
2331 5037/2087 2509 1519 4605 5364
3 Θεσσαλονικέως. τῇ τε ἑτέρᾳ κατήχθημεν εἰς Σιδῶνα· φιλαν-
of Thessalonica. on the And next we were landed at Sidon, kindly
5037 2457 3972 5530 2010 4314
θρώπως τε ὁ Ἰούλιος τῷ Παύλῳ χρησάμενος ἐπέτρεψε πρὸς
And Julius Paul treating allowed to
5384 4198 1958 5177 2547 321
4 τοὺς φίλους πορευθέντα ἐπιμελείας τυχεῖν. κἀκεῖθεν ἀναχθέν-
the friends going care to receive. And from there putting
5284 2954 1223 417 1511
τες ὑπεπλεύσαμεν τὴν Κύπρον, διὰ τὸ τοὺς ἀνέμους εἶναι
to sea, we sailed close to Cyprus, because of the winds being
1727 5037 3989 2596 2791 3828
5 ἐναντίους. τό τε πέλαγος τὸ κατὰ τὴν Κιλικίαν καὶ Παμφυ-
contrary the And sea – against – Cilicia and Pam-
1277 2718 1519 3460 3073 2546
6 λίαν διαπλεύσαντες, κατήλθομεν εἰς Μύρα τῆς Λυκίας. κἀκεῖ
phylia sailing over we came down to Myra – of Lycia. And there
2147 1543 4143 222 4126 1519
εὑρὼν ὁ ἑκατόνταρχος πλοῖον Ἀλεξανδρῖνον πλέον εἰς τὴν
having found the centurion ship an Alexandrian sailing to –
2482 1688 2248/1519/846/1722/ 2425 2250
7 Ἰταλίαν, ἐνεβίβασεν ἡμᾶς εἰς αὐτό. ἐν ἱκαναῖς δὲ ἡμέραις
Italy, he placed us in it. in many And days
1020 3433 1096 2596 2834 3361
βραδυπλοοῦντες, καὶ μόλις γενόμενοι κατὰ τὴν Κνίδον, μὴ
sailing slowly, and hardly coming against Cnidus, not
4330 2248 4171 5284 2914
προσεῶντος ἡμᾶς τοῦ ἀνέμου, ὑπεπλεύσαμεν τὴν Κρήτην
allowing us the wind, we sailed close to Crete
2596 4534 3433/5037 3881 846 2064
8 κατὰ Σαλμώνην· μόλις τε παραλεγόμενοι αὐτὴν ἤλθομεν
against Salmone, hardly and having sailed along it we came
1519 5117 5100 2563 2570 3040 3739 1451 2258
εἰς τόπον τινὰ καλούμενον Καλοὺς Λιμένας, ᾧ ἐγγὺς ἦν
to a place certain being called Fair Haven, to which near was
4172 2996
πόλις Λασαία.
a city, Lasea.
2425 5550 1230 5607 2235 2000
9 Ἱκανοῦ δὲ χρόνου διαγενομένου, καὶ ὄντος ἤδη ἐπισφα-
much And time having passed, and being now dangerous
4144 1223 3521 2235 3928
λοῦς τοῦ πλοός, διὰ τὸ καὶ τὴν νηστείαν ἤδη παρεληλυ-
the voyage, because also the Fast now to have gone
3867 3972 3004 846 435 2334 3754
10 θέναι, παρῄνει ὁ Παῦλος λέγων αὐτοῖς, Ἄνδρες, θεωρῶ ὅτι
by, advised Paul saying to them, Men, I see that
3326 5196 4183 2209 3756 3440 5414
μετὰ ὕβρεως καὶ πολλῆς ζημίας, οὐ μόνον τοῦ φόρτου καὶ
with injury and much loss, not only of the cargo and
4143 235 5590 2257 3195 1510
τοῦ πλοίου ἀλλὰ καὶ τῶν ψυχῶν ἡμῶν, μέλλειν ἔσεσθαι τὸν
of the ship, but also the souls of us, to be about to be the
4144 1543 2942 3490
11 πλοῦν. ὁ δὲ ἑκατόνταρχος τῷ κυβερνήτῃ καὶ τῷ ναυκλήρῳ
voyage. the But centurion by the steersman and the shipmaster
3982 3123 2228 5259 3972 3004
ἐπείθετο μᾶλλον ἢ τοῖς ὑπὸ τοῦ Παύλου λεγομένοις.
was persuaded rather than the things by Paul said.
428 3040 5225 4314 3915
12 ἀνευθέτου δὲ τοῦ λιμένος ὑπάρχοντος πρὸς παραχειμασίαν,
not fit And the port being for wintering,
4119 5087 1012 321 2547 1513 1410
οἱ πλείους ἔθεντο βουλὴν ἀναχθῆναι κἀκεῖθεν, εἴπως δύ-
the most gave counsel to set sail from there, if somehow they
2658 1519 5405 3914 3040
ναιντο καταντήσαντες εἰς Φοίνικα παραχειμάσαι, λιμένα τῆς
may be able having arrived at Phoenice to pass the winter, a port

looking toward *the* southwest and toward *the* northwest. [13]And a south wind
blowing gently, thinking to
have gained the purpose,
raising *anchor* they sailed
along close by Crete.
[14]And not much after, a
stormy wind being called
Euroclydon beat down *on* it.
[15]And the ship being seized,
and not being able to beat
against the wind, giving way
we were borne along. [16]But
running under an islet being
called Clauda, we were
hardly able to get mastery of
the boat; [17]which taking,
they used helps, undergirding the ship. And fearing lest
they fall into Syrtis, lowering
the tackle, so they were
borne along.
[18]But we having been
exceedingly storm-tossed,
they made a casting on the
next *day*. [19]And on the third
day they threw out the ship's
tackle with their hands.
[20]And neither sun nor stars
appearing over many days,
and no small tempest pressing hard, now all hope of our
being saved was taken
away. [21]And there being
much fasting, then standing
up in their midst, Paul said,
Truly, O men, being obed-
ient to me *you* ought not to
have set sail from Crete, and
to have come by this injury
and loss. [22]And now I
exhort you to be cheered, for
there will be no casting
away of soul from among
you, only of the ship. [23]For
tonight stood by me an
angel of God, whose I am,
and whom I serve, [24]say-
ing, Do not fear, Paul, You
must stand before Caesar.
And, behold, God has
granted to you all those
sailing with you. [25]There-
fore, be cheered, men, for I
believe God, that it will be
so, according to the way it

2914 991 2596 3047 2596 5566 5285
13 Κρήτης βλέποντα κατὰ λίβα καὶ κατὰ χῶρον. ὑποπνεύ-
of Crete looking toward southwest and toward northwest. blowing
3558 1380 4286 2902
σαντος δὲ νότου, δόξαντες τῆς προθέσεως κεκρατηκέναι,
gently And a south wind, thinking the purpose to have gained,
142 788 3881 2914 3326/3756/4183
14 ἄραντες ἆσσον παρελέγοντο τὴν Κρήτην. μετ' οὐ πολὺ δὲ
raising (anchor) close they sailed by — Crete. after not much And
906 2596 846 417 5189 2564 2148
ἔβαλε κατ' αὐτῆς ἄνεμος τυφωνικός, ὁ καλούμενος Εὐροκλύ-
beat down it wind a stormy, being called Euroclydon,
4884 4143 3361 1410
15 δων· συναρπασθέντος δὲ τοῦ πλοίου, καὶ μὴ δυναμένου
being seized and the ship, and not being able
503 417 1929 5342 3519 5100
16 ἀντοφθαλμεῖν τῷ ἀνέμῳ, ἐπιδόντες ἐφερόμεθα. νησίον δέ τι
to beat against the wind, giving way we were borne. islet But an
5295 2563 2802 3433 2480 4031
ὑποδραμόντες καλούμενον Κλαύδην μόλις ἰσχύσαμεν περι-
running under, being called Clauda, hardly we were able
1096 4627 3739 142 996 5530
17 κρατεῖς γενέσθαι τῆς σκάφης· ἣν ἄραντες, βοηθείαις ἐχρῶντο,
mastery to get of the boat, which taking helps they used,
5269 4143 5399 5037/3361/1519 4950
ὑποζωννύντες τὸ πλοῖον· φοβούμενοί τε μὴ εἰς τὴν σύρτιν
undergirding the ship; fearing and not into Syrtis
1601 5465 4632 3779 5342 4971
18 ἐκπέσωσι, χαλάσαντες τὸ σκεῦος, οὕτως ἐφέροντο. σφοδρῶς
they fall, lowering the tackle, thus they were borne. exceedingly
5492 2257 1836 1546 4160
19 δὲ χειμαζομένων ἡμῶν, τῇ ἑξῆς ἐκβολὴν ἐποιοῦντο· καὶ τῇ
But being tempest-tossed we, on the next a casting out they made, and on the
5154 849 4631 4143 4496 3383
τρίτῃ αὐτόχειρες τὴν σκευὴν τοῦ πλοίου ἐρρίψαμεν. μήτε
third with their hands the tackle of the ship they threw. neither
2246 3383 798 2014 1909 4119 2250
20 δὲ ἡλίου μήτε ἄστρων ἐπιφαινόντων ἐπὶ πλείονας ἡμέρας,
And sun nor stars appearing over many days,
5494 5037/3756 3641 1945 3063 4014 3956
χειμῶνός τε οὐκ ὀλίγου ἐπικειμένου, λοιπὸν περιηρεῖτο πᾶσα
tempest and no small pressing hard, now was taken away all
1680 4982 2248 4183 776 5225
21 ἐλπὶς τοῦ σῴζεσθαι ἡμᾶς. πολλῆς δὲ ἀσιτίας ὑπαρχούσης,
hope — to be saved us. much And fasting being,
5119 2476 3972 1722/3319 848 2036 1163/3303/5599
τότε σταθεὶς ὁ Παῦλος ἐν μέσῳ αὐτῶν εἶπεν, Ἔδει μέν, ὦ
then standing Paul in (the) midst of them said, (You) ought, O
435 3980 3427/3361 321 575 2914
ἄνδρες, πειθαρχήσαντάς μοι μὴ ἀνάγεσθαι ἀπὸ τῆς Κρήτης,
men, having been obedient to me not to have set sail from — Crete,
2770 5037 5196 5026 2209 3569
22 κερδῆσαί τε τὴν ὕβριν ταύτην καὶ τὴν ζημίαν. καὶ τὰ νῦν
to come by and — injury this and — loss. And — now
3867 5209 2114 580 1063 5590 3762 2071
παραινῶ ὑμᾶς εὐθυμεῖν· ἀποβολὴ γὰρ ψυχῆς οὐδεμία ἔσται
I advise you to be cheered, casting away for of soul no will be
1537/5216/4133 4143 3936 1063/3427 3571 5026
23 ἐξ ὑμῶν, πλὴν τοῦ πλοίου. παρέστη γάρ μοι τῇ νυκτὶ ταύτῃ
of you, but of the ship. stood by For me — night this
32 2316 3739/1510/3739 3000 3004 3361
24 ἄγγελος τοῦ Θεοῦ, οὗ εἰμι, ᾧ καὶ λατρεύω, λέγων, Μὴ
an angel — of God, whose I am, whom also I serve, saying, Do not
5399 3972 2541 4571/1163 3936 2400 5483
φοβοῦ, Παῦλε· Καίσαρί σε δεῖ παραστῆναι· καὶ ἰδού, κεχάρι-
fear, Paul, Caesar you must stand before, and behold, has given
4671 2316 3956 4126 3326/4675/1352/ 2114
25 σταί σοι ὁ Θεὸς πάντας τοὺς πλέοντας μετὰ σοῦ. διὸ εὐθυμεῖτε
you God all those sailing with you. So be cheered,
435 4100 1063 2316 3754 3779 2071 2596/3739
ἄνδρες· πιστεύω γὰρ τῷ Θεῷ ὅτι οὕτως ἔσται καθ' ὃν
men, I believe for — God. that so it will be in the way

was spoken to me. [26]But we must fall on a certain island.

[27]And when *the* fourteenth night came, we being carried about in the Adriatic *Sea*, toward the middle of the night the sailors supposed *us to* come near some country. [28]And sounding, they found twenty fathoms; and moving a little and sounding again, they found fifteen fathoms. [29]And fearing lest they should fall on rock places, and casting four anchors out of *the* stern, they wished day to come. [30]But the sailors seeking to flee out of the ship, and lowering the boat into the sea, pretending to be about to cast out anchors from *the* prow, [31]Paul said to the centurion, and to the soldiers, Unless these remain in the ship, you cannot be saved. [32]Then the soldiers cut away the ropes of the boat, and let it fall.

[33]And until day was about to come, Paul begged all to partake of food, saying, Today *is the* fourteenth day you continued waiting without food, not having taken anything. [34]Therefore, I beg you to take of food, for this is to your deliverance; for not a hair of your head shall perish. [35]And saying these things, and taking bread, he gave thanks to God before all; and breaking, he began to eat.

[36]And all having become cheered, they took food. [37]And we were in the ship altogether two hundred seventy-six souls. [38]And being filled *with* food, they lightened the ship, throwing the wheat out into the sea.

5158 2980 3427/1519 3520 5100/1163/2248 1601
26 τρόπον λελάληταί μοι. εἰς νῆσον δέ τινα δεῖ ἡμᾶς ἐκπεσεῖν.
of which it was spoken to me. Onto island But an must we fall off.
5613 5065 3571 1096 1308
27 Ὡς δὲ τεσσαρεσκαιδεκάτη νὺξ ἐγένετο, διαφερομένων
when And (the) fourteenth night came, being carried about
2257/1722 99 2596 3319 3571 5282
ἡμῶν ἐν τῷ Ἀδρίᾳ, κατὰ μέσον τῆς νυκτὸς ὑπενόουν οἱ
us in the Adriatic, toward the middle of the night supposed the
3492 4317 5100 848 5561 1001 2147
28 ναῦται προσάγειν τινὰ αὐτοῖς χώραν· καὶ βολίσαντες εὗρον
sailors to approach some to them country. And sounding they found
3711 1501 1024 1339 3825 1001
ὀργυιὰς εἴκοσι· βραχὺ δὲ διαστήσαντες, καὶ πάλιν βολί-
fathoms twenty, a little and having moved also again sounding,
2147 3712 1178 5399 5037/3381 1519
29 σαντες, εὗρον ὀργυιὰς δεκαπέντε· φοβούμενοί τε μήπως εἰς
they found fathoms fifteen; fearing and lest on
5138 5117 1601 1537 4403 4496 45
τραχεῖς τόπους ἐκπέσωμεν, ἐκ πρύμνης ῥίψαντες ἀγκύρας
rough places they may fall off, out of (the) stern throwing anchors
5064 2172 2250 1096 3492 2212
30 τέσσαρας, ηὔχοντο ἡμέραν γενέσθαι. τῶν δὲ ναυτῶν ζητούν-
four, they wished day to come. the And sailors seeking
5343/1537 4143 5465 4627 1519
των φυγεῖν ἐκ τοῦ πλοίου, καὶ χαλασάντων τὴν σκάφην εἰς
to flee out of the ship, and lowering the boat into
2281 4392 5613/1537 4408 3195 45
τὴν θάλασσαν, προφάσει ὡς ἐκ πρώρας μελλόντων ἀγκύρας
the sea, pretending as out of (the) prow being about anchors
1614 2036 3972 1543 4757
31 ἐκτείνειν, εἶπεν ὁ Παῦλος τῷ ἑκατοντάρχῃ καὶ τοῖς στρατιώ-
to cast out, said Paul to the centurion and to the soldiers
=3362= 3778 3306 1722 4143 5210 4982 3756
ταις, Ἐὰν μὴ οὗτοι μείνωσιν ἐν τῷ πλοίῳ, ὑμεῖς σωθῆναι οὐ
If not these remain in the ship, you to be saved not
1410 5119 4757 609 4979
32 δύνασθε. τότε οἱ στρατιῶται ἀπέκοψαν τὰ σχοινία τῆς
are able. Then the soldiers cut away the ropes of the
4627 1439 846 1601 891 3739 3195 2250
33 σκάφης, καὶ εἴασαν αὐτὴν ἐκπεσεῖν. ἄχρι δὲ οὗ ἔμελλεν ἡμέρα
boat, and let it fall off. until And was about day
1096 3870 3972 537 3335 5160
γίνεσθαι, παρεκάλει ὁ Παῦλος ἅπαντας μεταλαβεῖν τροφῆς,
to come, begged Paul all to partake of food,
3004 5065 4594 2250 4328
λέγων, Τεσσαρεσκαιδεκάτην σήμερον ἡμέραν προσδοκῶντες
saying, (The) fourteenth today (is) day waiting
777 1300 3367 4355 1352 3870
34 ἄσιτοι διατελεῖτε, μηδὲν προσλαβόμενοι. διὸ παρακαλῶ
without food you continued, nothing having taken. Therefore I beg
5209 4355 5160 5124 1063 4314 5212
ὑμᾶς προσλαβεῖν τροφῆς· τοῦτο γὰρ πρὸς τῆς ὑμετέρας
you to take of food; this for to – your
4991 5225 3762 1063 5216 2359/1537 3776
σωτηρίας ὑπάρχει· οὐδενὸς γὰρ ὑμῶν θρὶξ ἐκ τῆς κεφαλῆς
salvation is; of no one for of you a hair from the head
4098 2036 5023 2983 740 2168
35 πεσεῖται. εἰπὼν δὲ ταῦτα, καὶ λαβὼν ἄρτον, εὐχαρίστησε
shall perish. saying And these things, and taking bread, he gave thanks
2316 1799 3956 2906 756 2068 2115
36 τῷ Θεῷ ἐνώπιον πάντων· καὶ κλάσας ἤρξατο ἐσθίειν. εὔθυμοι
– to God before all, and breaking began to eat. cheered
1096 3956 848 4355 5160 2258
δὲ γενόμενοι πάντες καὶ αὐτοὶ προσελάβοντο τροφῆς. ἦμεν
And having become all, also they took food. we were
1722 4143 3956 5590 1250 1440 1803
δὲ ἐν τῷ πλοίῳ αἱ πᾶσαι ψυχαί, διακόσιαι ἑβδομηκονταέξ.
And in the ship the all souls, two hundred seventy-six.
2880 5160 2893 4143 1544
38 κορεσθέντες δὲ τροφῆς ἐκούφιζον τὸ πλοῖον, ἐκβαλλόμενοι
having been filled And of food, they lightened the ship, throwing out

39 And when day came, they did not recognize the land, but they noted a certain bay having a shore, into which they purposed, if they were able, to drive the ship. 40 And casting off the anchors, they left *them* in the sea, at the same time loosening the bands of the rudders, and raising the foresail to the breeze, they held to the shore. 41 And coming on a place between two seas, they drove the vessel. And indeed the prow having stuck firmly, *it* remained. But the stern was broken by the violence of the waves. 42 And the mind of the soldiers was that they should kill the prisoners, lest any swimming out should escape. 43 But being minded to save Paul, the centurion kept them back *from their* purpose, and commanded those able to swim, first casting *themselves* overboard, to go out on the land. 44 And the rest *went*, some indeed on boards, and others on some of the things from the ship. And so it happened that all *were* saved on the land.

4621/1519 2281 3753 2250 1096 1093
39 τὸν σῖτον εἰς τὴν θάλασσαν. ὅτε δε ἡμέρα ἐγένετο, τὴν γῆν
the wheat into the sea. when And day came, the land
3756 1921 2859 5100 2657 2192 123
οὐκ ἐπεγίνωσκον· κόλπον δέ τινα κατενόουν ἔχοντα αἰγια-
not did recognize, a bay but certain they noted having a shore,
1519/3739/ 1011 1487 1410 1856 4143
40 λόν, εἰς ὃν ἐβουλεύσαντο, εἰ δύναιντο, ἐξῶσαι τὸ πλοῖον. καὶ
into which they purposed, if they could, to drive the ship. And
45 4014 1439/1519 2281 260 447
τὰς ἀγκύρας περιελόντες εἴων εἰς τὴν θάλασσαν, ἅμα ἀνέντες
the anchors having cast off they left in the sea, at the same time freeing
2202 4079 1869 736
τὰς ζευκτηρίας τῶν πηδαλίων· καὶ ἐπάραντες τὸν ἀρτέμονα
the bands of the rudders, and raising the foresail
4154 2722 1519 123 4045 1519
41 τῇ πνεούσῃ κατεῖχον εἰς τὸν αἰγιαλόν. περιπεσόντες δὲ εἰς
to the breeze, they held to the shore. coming upon And —
5117 1337 2027 3491 3303 4408
τόπον διθάλασσον ἐπώκειλαν τὴν ναῦν· καὶ ἡ μὲν πρῷρα
a place between two seas, they drove the vessel, and the prow
2043 3306 761 4403 3089 5259
ἐρείσασα ἔμεινεν ἀσάλευτος, ἡ δὲ πρύμνα ἐλύετο ὑπὸ τῆς
having stuck remained immovable, the but stern was loosed by the
970 2949 4757 1012 1096
42 βίας τῶν κυμάτων. τῶν δὲ στρατιωτῶν βουλὴ ἐγένετο ἵνα
violence of the waves. of the And soldiers (the) mind was that
1202 615 3361/5100 1579 1309
τοὺς δεσμώτας ἀποκτείνωσι, μήτις ἐκκολυμβήσας διαφύγοι.
the prisoners they should kill, lest any swimming out should escape.
1543 1014 1295 3972
43 ὁ δὲ ἑκατόνταρχος, βουλόμενος διασῶσαι τὸν Παῦλον,
the But centurion being minded to save — Paul,
2967 846 1013 2753 5037 1410
ἐκώλυσεν αὐτοὺς τοῦ βουλήματος, ἐκέλευσέ τε τοὺς δυνα-
prevented them the purpose, commanded and those being
2860 641 4413 1909 1093
μένους κολυμβᾷν ἀπορρίψαντας πρώτους ἐπὶ τὴν γῆν
able to swim, throwing overboard first, onto the land
1826 3062 3739/3303/1909 4548 3739 1909
44 ἐξιέναι· καὶ τοὺς λοιπούς, οὓς μὲν ἐπὶ σανίσιν, οὓς δὲ ἐπί
to go out. And the rest, some indeed on planks, others and on
5100 575 4143 3779 1096 3956
τινων τῶν ἀπὸ τοῦ πλοίου. καὶ οὕτως ἐγένετο πάντας
some of the things from the ship. And so it was, all
1295 1909 1093
διασωθῆναι ἐπὶ τὴν γῆν.
to be saved on the land.

CHAPTER 28

1 And being saved, then they knew that the island is called Melita. 2 And the foreigners *were* showing not the common kindness to us, for having kindled a fire because of the rain coming on, and because of the cold, they welcomed us all. 3 And Paul gathering a bunch of sticks, and putting *them* on the fire, a snake coming out from the heat fastened on his hand. 4 And when the foreigners saw the beast hanging from his

CHAPTER 28

1295 5119 1921 3754 3194 3520
1 Καὶ διασωθέντες, τότε ἐπέγνωσαν ὅτι Μελίτη ἡ νῆσος
And having been saved, then they knew that Melita the island
2564 915 3930 3756 5177
2 καλεῖται. οἱ δὲ βάρβαροι παρεῖχον οὐ τὴν τυχοῦσαν
is called. the And foreigners showed not the common
5363 2254 381 1063 4443 4355
φιλανθρωπίαν ἡμῖν· ἀνάψαντες γὰρ πυράν, προσελάβοντο
kindness us; having kindled for a fire, they welcomed
3956 2248/1223 5205 2186 1223 5592
πάντας ἡμᾶς, διὰ τὸν ὑετὸν τὸν ἐφεστῶτα, καὶ διὰ τὸ ψῦχος.
all us, because of the rain — coming on, and due to the cold.
4962 3972 5434 4128
3 συστρέψαντος δὲ τοῦ Παύλου φρυγάνων πλῆθος, καὶ
having gathered And — Paul of sticks a bunch, and
2007 1909 4443 2191 1537 2329 1831
ἐπιθέντος ἐπὶ τὴν πυράν, ἔχιδνα ἐκ τῆς θέρμης ἐξελθοῦσα
putting on the fire, a snake from the heat coming out
2510 5495 848 5613 1492 915 2910
4 καθῆψε τῆς χειρὸς αὐτοῦ. ὡς δὲ εἶδον οἱ βάρβαροι κρεμά-
fastened on the hand of him. when And saw the foreigners hanging

hand, they said to one another, By all means this man is a murderer, whom being saved out of the sea, Justice did not permit to live. [5]Then he indeed shaking the beast off into the fire, *he* suffered no harm. [6]But they expected him to be about to become inflamed, or suddenly to fall down dead. But over much *time*, they expecting and seeing nothing amiss happening to him, changing their minds, they said him to be a god.

2342 1537 5495 848 3004 4314 240
μενον τὸ θηρίον ἐκ τῆς χειρὸς αὐτοῦ, ἔλεγον πρὸς ἀλλήλους,
the beast from the hand of him, they said to one another,
3972 5406 2076 444 3778/3739 1295
Πάντως φονεύς ἐστιν ὁ ἄνθρωπος οὗτος, ὃν διασωθέντα ἐκ
By all means a murderer is man this, whom being saved out of
2281 1349/2198/3756/1439 3303/3767 660
5 τῆς θαλάσσης ἡ Δίκη ζῆν οὐκ εἴασεν. ὁ μὲν οὖν, ἀποτινάξας
the sea — justice to live not allowed. He then, shaking off
2342/1519 4442 3958 3762 2556 4328
6 τὸ θηρίον εἰς τὸ πῦρ, ἔπαθεν οὐδὲν κακόν. οἱ δὲ προσεδόκων
the beast into the fire, suffered no harm. they But expected
846 3195 4092 2228 2667 869 3498 1909
αὐτὸν μέλλειν πίμπρασθαι ἢ καταπίπτειν ἄφνω νεκρόν· ἐπὶ
him to be about to swell, or to fall down suddenly dead. over
4183 846 4328 2334 3367
πολὺ δὲ αὐτῶν προσδοκώντων, καὶ θεωρούντων μηδὲν
much But they expecting, and beholding nothing
824 1519 846 1096 3328 3004 2316
ἄτοπον εἰς αὐτὸν γινόμενον, μεταβαλλόμενοι ἔλεγον θεὸν
amiss to him happening, changing their minds they said a god
846 1511
αὐτὸν εἶναι.
him to be.

[7]And in the *parts* about that place were lands to the chief of the island, Publius by name. Welcoming us, *he* housed us three days in a friendly way. [8]And it happened the father of Publius was lying down, suffering from fevers and dysentery; to whom Paul, entering and praying, laying on his hands, cured him. [9]Then, this taking place, the rest who *were* having infirmities in the island also came up, and *they* were healed. [10]*They* also honored us with many honors. And on *our* setting sail, they laid on *us* the things for *our* need.

1722 4012 5117 1565 5225 5564
7 Ἐν δὲ τοῖς περὶ τὸν τόπον ἐκεῖνον ὑπῆρχε χωρία τῷ
in And the (parts) about place that, were lands to the
4413 3520 3686 4196 3739 324 2248
πρώτῳ τῆς νήσου, ὀνόματι Ποπλίῳ, ὃς ἀναδεξάμενος ἡμᾶς
chief of the island, by name Publius, who welcoming us
5140 2250 5390 3579 1096 3962
8 τρεῖς ἡμέρας φιλοφρόνως ἐξένισεν. ἐγένετο δὲ τὸν πατέρα τοῦ
three days in a friendly way lodged (us). it was And, the father —
4196 4446 1420 4912 2621
Ποπλίου πυρετοῖς καὶ δυσεντερίᾳ συνεχόμενον κατακεῖσθαι·
of Publius fevers and dysentery suffering from was lying down
4314/3739 3972 1525 4336 2007
πρὸς ὃν ὁ Παῦλος εἰσελθών, καὶ προσευξάμενος, ἐπιθεὶς τὰς
to whom Paul having entered and praying, laying on the
5495 846 2390 846 5127 3767 1096
9 χεῖρας αὐτῷ, ἰάσατο αὐτόν. τούτου οὖν γενομένου, καὶ οἱ
hands him, cured him. this Then happening, also the
3062 2192 769 1722 3520 4334
λοιποὶ οἱ ἔχοντες ἀσθενείας ἐν τῇ νήσῳ προσήρχοντο καὶ
rest of those having infirmities in the island came up and
2323 3739 4183 5091 · 5092 2248
10 ἐθεραπεύοντο· οἳ καὶ πολλαῖς τιμαῖς ἐτίμησαν ἡμᾶς, καὶ
were healed; who also with many honors honored us, and
321 2007 4314 5532
ἀναγομένοις ἐπέθεντο τὰ πρὸς τὴν χρείαν.
on our sailing laid on the things for the needs (of us).

[11]And after three months we sailed in a ship which had wintered in the island, an Alexandrian with an ensign, *The* Twin Brothers. [12]And landing at Syracuse, we remained three days. [13]Going around from there, we arrived at Rhegium. And after one day, a south wind having come on, on the second we came to Puteoli; [14]where finding brothers, we were begged by them to remain seven days. And so we went toward Rome.

3326 3376 321 1722 4143 3914
11 Μετὰ δὲ τρεῖς μῆνας ἀνήχθημεν ἐν πλοίῳ παρακεχει-
after And three months we sailed in a ship having
1722 3520 222 3902 1359
μακότι ἐν τῇ νήσῳ, Ἀλεξανδρίνῳ, παρασήμῳ Διοσκούροις.
wintered in the island, an Alexandrian, with an ensign, Twin Brothers.
2609 1519 4946 1961 2250 5140
12 καὶ καταχθέντες εἰς Συρακούσας ἐπεμείναμεν ἡμέρας τρεῖς·
And having been landed at Syracuse, we remained days three,
3606 4022 2658 1519 4484 3326 3391
13 ὅθεν περιελθόντες κατηντήσαμεν εἰς Ῥήγιον, καὶ μετὰ μίαν
from where tacking we arrived at Rhegium. And after one
2250 1920 3558 1206 2064 1519 4223
ἡμέραν ἐπιγενομένου νότου, δευτεραῖοι ἤλθομεν εἰς Ποτιό-
day, coming on a south wind, on the second we came to Puteoli,
3757 2147 80 3870 1909 846
14 λους· οὗ εὑρόντες ἀδελφούς, παρεκλήθημεν ἐπ' αὐτοῖς
where having found brothers, we were besought by them
1961 2250 2033 3779 1519 4516 2064
ἐπιμεῖναι ἡμέρας ἑπτά· καὶ οὕτως εἰς τὴν Ῥώμην ἤλθομεν.
to remain days seven; and thus to Rome we went.

[15]And the brothers from there hearing about us, *they* came out to meet us, as far as *the* market-place of Appius, and Three Taverns; whom Paul seeing, thanking God, he took courage.

[16]And when we went into Rome, the centurion delivered the prisoners to the camp commander. But Paul was allowed to remain by himself, with the soldier guarding him.

[17]And after three days, it happened that Paul called together those being chief of the Jews. And they coming together, he said to them, Men, brothers, I did nothing contrary to the people, or to the ancestral customs. I was delivered a prisoner from Jerusalem into the hands of the Romans; [18]who examining me were of a mind to let me go, because no cause of death was in me. [19]But the Jews speaking against *it*, I was compelled to appeal to Caesar, not as having anything to accuse my nation. [20]On account of this, then, I called for you, to see and to speak to *you*. For I have this chain around *me* for the sake of the hope of Israel.

[21]And they said to him, We neither received letters concerning you from the Jews, nor having arrived has any one of the brothers reported or spoken anything evil concerning you. [22]But we think *it* fitting to hear from you *as to* what you think, for truly as concerning this sect, it is known to us that it is spoken against everywhere.

[23]And having appointed him a day, more came to him in the lodging, to whom he

2547 80 191 4012 2257 1831 1519
15 κἀκεῖθεν οἱ ἀδελφοὶ ἀκούσαντες τὰ περὶ ἡμῶν, ἐξῆλθον εἰς
And from there the brothers having heard about us came out to
529 2254 891 675 5410 5140 4999
ἀπάντησιν ἡμῖν ἄχρις Ἀππίου Φόρου καὶ Τριῶν Ταβερνῶν·
meet us as far as Appius Forum and Three Taverns,
3739/1492 3972 2168 2316 2983 2294
οὓς ἰδὼν ὁ Παῦλος, εὐχαριστήσας τῷ Θεῷ, ἔλαβε θάρσος.
whom seeing Paul, thanking God, he took courage.
3753 2064 1519 4516 1543 3860
16 Ὅτε δὲ ἤλθομεν εἰς Ῥώμην, ὁ ἑκατόνταρχος παρέδωκε
when And we went into Rome, the centurion delivered
1198 4759 3972 2010
τοὺς δεσμίους τῷ στρατοπεδάρχῃ· τῷ δὲ Παύλῳ ἐπετράπη
the prisoners to the camp commander; but Paul was allowed
3306 2596 1438 4862 5442 846 4757
μένειν καθ' ἑαυτόν, σὺν τῷ φυλάσσοντι αὐτὸν στρατιώτῃ.
to remain by himself, with the guarding him soldier.
1096 3326 2250 5140 4779 3972
17 Ἐγένετο δὲ μετὰ ἡμέρας τρεῖς συγκαλέσασθαι τὸν Παῦλον
it was And, after days three called together — Paul
5607 2453 4413 4905 848
τοὺς ὄντας τῶν Ἰουδαίων πρώτους· συνελθόντων δὲ αὐτῶν,
those being of the Jews chief. coming together And them,
3004 4314 846 435 80 1473 3762 1727
ἔλεγε πρὸς αὐτούς, Ἄνδρες ἀδελφοί, ἐγὼ οὐδὲν ἐναντίον
he said to them, Men, brothers, I nothing contrary
4160 2992/2228 1485 3971 1198 1537
ποιήσας τῷ λαῷ ἢ τοῖς ἔθεσι τοῖς πατρῴοις, δέσμιος ἐξ
did to the people or to the customs ancestral, a prisoner from
2414 3860 1519 5495 4514
Ἱεροσολύμων παρεδόθην εἰς τὰς χεῖρας τῶν Ῥωμαίων·
Jerusalem I was delivered to the hands of the Romans,
3748 350 3165 1014 630 1223 3367
18 οἵτινες ἀνακρίναντές με ἐβούλοντο ἀπολῦσαι, διὰ τὸ μηδε-
who having examined me were minded to let me go, because no
156 2288 5225 1722/1698 483
19 μίαν αἰτίαν θανάτου ὑπάρχειν ἐν ἐμοί. ἀντιλεγόντων δὲ τῶν
cause of death to be in me. speaking against But the
2453 315 1941 2541 3756/5613
Ἰουδαίων, ἠναγκάσθην ἐπικαλέσασθαι Καίσαρα, οὐχ ὡς
Jews, I was compelled to appeal to Caesar; not as
1484 3450/2192/5100/ 2723 1223 5026 3767
20 τοῦ ἔθνους μου ἔχων τι κατηγορῆσαι. διὰ ταύτην οὖν τὴν
the nation of me having anything to accuse. Because of this, then,
156 3870 5209 1492 4354 1752 1063
αἰτίαν παρεκάλεσα ὑμᾶς ἰδεῖν καὶ προσλαλῆσαι· ἕνεκεν γὰρ
cause I called fo you to see and to speak to; for the sake of for
1680 2474 254 5026 4029
τῆς ἐλπίδος τοῦ Ἰσραὴλ τὴν ἅλυσιν ταύτην περίκειμαι.
the hope — of Israel, — chain this I have around (me).
4314 846 2036 2249 3777 1121 4012/4675
21 οἱ δὲ πρὸς αὐτὸν εἶπον, Ἡμεῖς οὔτε γράμματα περὶ σοῦ
they And to him said, We neither letters about you
1209 575 2449 3777 3854 5100
ἐδεξάμεθα ἀπὸ τῆς Ἰουδαίας, οὔτε παραγενόμενός τις τῶν
received from the Jews, nor arriving anyone of the
80 518 2229 2980 5100 4012/4675 4190
ἀδελφῶν ἀπήγγειλεν ἢ ἐλάλησέ τι περὶ σοῦ πονηρόν.
brothers told or spoke anything about you evil.
515 3844/4675 191 3739 5426 4012/3303/1063
22 ἀξιοῦμεν δὲ παρὰ σοῦ ἀκοῦσαι ἃ φρονεῖς περὶ μὲν γὰρ τῆς
we think fit But from you to hear what you think about indeed for
139 5026 1110 2076 2254/3754 3837 483
αἱρέσεως ταύτης γνωστόν ἐστιν ἡμῖν ὅτι πανταχοῦ ἀντιλέ-
sect this known is us, that everywhere it is
γεται.
spoken against.
5021 846 2250 2240 4314 846 1519
23 Ταξάμενοι δὲ αὐτῷ ἡμέραν, ἧκον πρὸς αὐτὸν εἰς τὴν
appointing And him a day, came to him in the

expounded, earnestly testifying the kingdom of God, and persuaded them the things concerning Jesus, both from the law of Moses and the Prophets, from morning until evening. [24]And some indeed were persuaded by that being said; others disbelieved. [25]And disagreeing with one another, they were let go, Paul saying one word: Well did the Holy Spirit speak through the prophet Isaiah to our fathers, [26]saying, "Go to this people and say, You will surely hear, and not at all understand; and you will surely see, and not at all perceive; [27]for the heart of this people was fattened, and they have heard with the ears heavily; and they closed their eyes lest at any time they see with *their* eyes and hear with *their* ears, and understand with *their* heart, and be converted, and I should heal them." [28]Therefore, let it be known to you that the salvation of God was sent to the nations; and they will hear. [29]And he saying these things, the Jews went away, having much discussion among themselves.

[30]And Paul remained two whole years in *his* own rented place, and *he* welcomed all those coming in to him, [31]proclaiming the kingdom of God, and teaching the things concerning the Lord Jesus Christ, with all freedom, *and* without hindrance.

3578 4119 3739 1620 1263 932
ξενίαν πλείονες· οἷς ἐξετίθετο διαμαρτυρόμενος τὴν βασι-
lodging more, to whom he set forth earnestly testifying the king
2316 3982 5037 846 4012 2424 575
λείαν τοῦ Θεοῦ, πείθων τε αὐτοὺς τὰ περὶ τοῦ Ἰησοῦ, ἀπό
dom — of God, persuading and them the things concerning · Jesus. from
5037 3551 3475 4396 575 4404 2193
τε τοῦ νόμου Μωσέως καὶ τῶν προφητῶν, ἀπὸ πρωῒ ἕως
and the law of Moses and the Prophets, from morning until
2073 3303/ 3982 3004 569
24 ἑσπέρας. καὶ οἱ μὲν ἐπείθοντο τοῖς λεγομένοις, οἱ δὲ ἠπίστουν.
evening. And some were persuaded by that being said, others disbelieved.
800 5607 4314 240 630 2036
25 ἀσύμφωνοι δὲ ὄντες πρὸς ἀλλήλους ἀπελύοντο, εἰπόντος
being disagreed And being with one another, they were let go, having said
3972 4487/1520/3754/2573 4151 40
τοῦ Παύλου ῥῆμα ἕν, ὅτι Καλῶς τὸ Πνεῦμα τὸ Ἅγιον
— Paul word one, — Well the Spirit — Holy
2980 1223 2268 4396 4314 3962
ἐλάλησε διὰ Ἡσαΐου τοῦ προφήτου πρὸς τοὺς πατέρας
spoke through Isaiah the prophet to the fathers
2257 3004 4198 4314 2992 5126 2036
26 ἡμῶν, λέγον, Πορεύθητι πρὸς τὸν λαὸν τοῦτον καὶ εἰπέ,
of us, saying, Go to — people this and say:
189 191 =3364= 4920 991 991
Ἀκοῇ ἀκούσετε, καὶ οὐ μὴ συνῆτε· καὶ βλέποντες βλέψετε,
in hearing you will hear, and not at all understand, and seeing you will see
=3364= 1492 3975 1063 2588 2992 5127
27 καὶ οὐ μὴ ἴδητε· ἐπαχύνθη γὰρ ἡ καρδία τοῦ λαοῦ τούτου,
and not at all perceive, was fattened for the heart people of this,
3775 917 191 3788 848
καὶ τοῖς ὠσὶ βαρέως ἤκουσαν, καὶ τοὺς ὀφθαλμοὺς αὐτῶν
and with the ears heavily they heard, and the eyes of them
2576 3379 1492 3788 3775
ἐκάμμυσαν· μήποτε ἴδωσι τοῖς ὀφθαλμοῖς, καὶ τοῖς ὠσὶν
they closed, lest at any time they see with the eyes, and with the ears
191 2588 4920 1994
ἀκούσωσι, καὶ τῇ καρδίᾳ συνῶσι, καὶ ἐπιστρέψωσι, καὶ
hear, and with the heart understand, and be converted, and
2390 846 1110 3767 2077/5213/3754 1484
28 ἰάσωμαι αὐτούς. γνωστὸν οὖν ἔστω ὑμῖν, ὅτι τοῖς ἔθνεσι
I should heal them. Known, therefore, be it to you, that to the nations
649 4992 2316 846 191
ἀπεστάλη τὸ σωτήριον τοῦ Θεοῦ, αὐτοὶ καὶ ἀκούσονται.
was sent the salvation of God, they and will hear.
5023 846 2036 565 2453 4183
29 καὶ ταῦτα αὐτοῦ εἰπόντος, ἀπῆλθον οἱ Ἰουδαῖοι, πολλὴν
And these things he having said, went away the Jews much
2192 1722 1438 4803
ἔχοντες ἐν ἑαυτοῖς συζήτησιν.
having among themselves discussion.
3306 3972 1333 3650/1722/2398 3410
30 Ἔμεινε δὲ ὁ Παῦλος διετίαν ὅλην ἐν ἰδίῳ μισθώματι, καὶ
remained And Paul two years a whole in (his) own rented place, and
588 3956 1531 4314 846
ἀπεδέχετο πάντας τοὺς εἰσπορευομένους πρὸς αὐτόν,
welcomed all those coming in to him,
2784 932 2316 1321 4012
31 κηρύσσων τὴν βασιλείαν τοῦ Θεοῦ, καὶ διδάσκων τὰ περὶ
proclaiming the kingdom — of God, and teaching the things about
2962 2424 5547 3326 3956 3954
τοῦ Κυρίου Ἰησοῦ Χριστοῦ, μετὰ πάσης παρρησίας,
the Lord Jesus Christ, with all freedom,
209
ἀκωλύτως.
without hindrance.

ΠΑΥΛΟΥ ΤΟΥ ΑΠΟΣΤΟΛΟΥ
PAUL THE APOSTLE

Η ΠΡΟΣ
TO (THE)

ΡΩΜΑΙΟΥΣ ΕΠΙΣΤΟΛΗ
ROMANS EPISTLE

THE
EPISTLE TO
THE ROMANS

A LITERAL TRANSLATION
OF THE BIBLE

CHAPTER 1

1 Paul, a slave of Jesus
Christ, a called apostle,
separated to the gospel of
God, 2 which He promised
before through His
prophets in holy Scriptures,
3 concerning His Son who
came of the seed of David
according to flesh, 4 who
was marked out Son of God
in power, according to *the*
Spirit of holiness, by resurrection of *the* dead, Jesus
Christ our Lord; 5 by whom
we received grace and
apostleship to obedience of
faith among all the nations,
for His name's sake,
6 among whom are you also,
called-out ones of Jesus
Christ; 7 to all those who
are in Rome, beloved of
God, called-out saints,
grace and peace to you
from God our Father and
the Lord Jesus Christ.

8 First, I thank my God
through Jesus Christ for you
all, that your faith is spoken
of in all the world. 9 For God
is my witness, whom I serve
in my spirit in the gospel of
His Son, how without
ceasing I make mention of
you 10 always at my prayers,
beseeching if by any means
now at length I shall be
blessed by the will of God
to come to you. 11 For I long
to see you, that I may impart
some spiritual gift to you,
for the establishing of you;
12 and this is, to be
comforted together among
you, through the faith in one

CHAPTER 1

3972 1401 2424 5547 2822 652
1 Παῦλος, δοῦλος Ἰησοῦ Χριστοῦ, κλητὸς ἀπόστολος,
Paul, a slave of Jesus Christ, called (to be) an apostle,
873 1519 2098 2316/3739/ 4279 1223
2 ἀφωρισμένος εἰς εὐαγγέλιον Θεοῦ, ὃ προεπηγγείλατο διὰ
being separated to (the) gospel of God, which He promised before through
4396 848 1722 1124 40 4012 5207
3 τῶν προφητῶν αὐτοῦ ἐν γραφαῖς ἁγίαις, περὶ τοῦ υἱοῦ
the prophets of Him in Scriptures holy, concerning the Son
848 1096 1537 4690 1138 2596 4561
αὐτοῦ, τοῦ γενομένου ἐκ σπέρματος Δαβὶδ κατὰ σάρκα,
of Him, come of the seed of David according to flesh,
3724 5207 2316/1722 1411 2596 4151 42
4 τοῦ ὁρισθέντος υἱοῦ Θεοῦ ἐν δυνάμει, κατὰ πνεῦμα ἁγιω-
– marked out Son of God in power according to (the) Spirit of
1537 386 3498 2424 5547 2962
σύνης, ἐξ ἀναστάσεως νεκρῶν, Ἰησοῦ Χριστοῦ τοῦ Κυρίου
holiness, by resurrection of (the) dead, Jesus Christ the Lord
2257 1223/3739 2983 5485 651 1519 5218
5 ἡμῶν, δι' οὗ ἐλάβομεν χάριν καὶ ἀποστολὴν εἰς ὑπακοὴν
of us, through whom we received grace and apostleship to obedience
4102 1722/3956 1484 5228 3686 848 1722
6 πίστεως ἐν πᾶσι τοῖς ἔθνεσιν, ὑπὲρ τοῦ ὀνόματος αὐτοῦ, ἐν
of faith among all the nations, for the sake of the name of Him, among
3739/2075 5210 2822 2424 5547 3956 5607
7 οἷς ἐστε καὶ ὑμεῖς, κλητοὶ Ἰησοῦ Χριστοῦ· πᾶσι τοῖς οὖσιν
whom are also you called out ones of Jesus Christ. To all those being
1722/4516 27 2316 2822 40 5485/5213
ἐν Ῥώμῃ ἀγαπητοῖς Θεοῦ, κλητοῖς ἁγίοις· χάρις ὑμῖν καὶ
in Rome beloved of God, called out saints, grace to you and
1515 575 2316 3962 2257 2962 2424 5597
εἰρήνη ἀπὸ Θεοῦ πατρὸς ἡμῶν καὶ Κυρίου Ἰησοῦ Χριστοῦ.
peace from God (the) Father of us, and (the) Lord Jesus Christ
4412 3303 2168 2316/3450/1223/2424 5547
8 Πρῶτον μὲν εὐχαριστῶ τῷ Θεῷ μου διὰ Ἰησοῦ Χριστοῦ
Firstly, truly I thank the God of me through Jesus Christ
5228 3956 5216 3754 4102 5216 2605 1722
ὑπὲρ πάντων ὑμῶν, ὅτι ἡ πίστις ὑμῶν καταγγέλλεται ἐν
for all of you, that the faith of you is spoken of in
3650 2889 3144 1063/3450/2076 2316/3739/ 3000
9 ὅλῳ τῷ κόσμῳ. μάρτυς γάρ μού ἐστιν ὁ Θεός, ᾧ λατρεύω
all the world, the witness For of me is God, whom I serve
1722 4151 3450/1722 2098 5207/848 5613
ἐν τῷ πνεύματί μου ἐν τῷ εὐαγγελίῳ τοῦ υἱοῦ αὐτοῦ, ὡς
in the spirit of me in the gospel of the Son of Him, how
89 3417 5216 4160 3842 1909
10 ἀδιαλείπτως μνείαν ὑμῶν ποιοῦμαι, πάντοτε ἐπὶ τῶν
without ceasing mention of you I make always on the
4335 3450 1189 1513 2235 4218 2137 1722
προσευχῶν μου δεόμενος, εἴπως ἤδη ποτὲ εὐοδωθήσομαι ἐν
prayers of me beseeching, if at all now at length I shall be blessed by
2307 2316 2064 4314/5209 1971 1063 1492
11 τῷ θελήματι τοῦ Θεοῦ ἐλθεῖν πρὸς ὑμᾶς. ἐπιποθῶ γὰρ ἰδεῖν
the will of God to come to you. I long For to see
5209 2443/5100/ 3330 5496 5213 4152 1519
ὑμᾶς, ἵνα τι μεταδῶ χάρισμα ὑμῖν πνευματικόν, εἰς τὸ
you, that some I may impart gift to you spiritual, for the

another, both yours and mine.

[13]But I do not wish you to be ignorant, brothers, that often I purposed to come to you, and was kept back until the present; that I might have some fruit among you also, even as among the other nations. [14]I am a debtor both to Greeks and to foreigners, both to wise, and to foolish, [15]so as far as in me *lies*, I am eager to preach the gospel to you in Rome also. [16]For I am not ashamed of the gospel of Christ, for it is *the* power of God to salvation to everyone believing, both to Jew first, and to Greek; [17]for in it the righteousness of God is revealed from faith to faith; even as it has been written, "But the just shall live by faith."

[18]For God's wrath is revealed from Heaven on all ungodliness and unrighteousness of men, holding the truth in unrighteousness, [19]because the thing known of God is clearly known within them, for God revealed *it* to them—[20]for the unseen things of Him from *the* creation of the world are clearly seen, being understood by the things made, both His eternal power and Godhead, for them to be without excuse. [21]Because knowing God, they did not glorify Him as God, nor were thankful; but became vain in their reasonings, and their undiscerning heart was darkened. [22]Professing to be wise, they became foolish, [23]and changed the glory of the incorruptible God into a likeness of an image of corruptible man, and of birds, and four-footed animals, and creeping

4741 5209 5124 2076 4837 1722/5213
12 **στηριχθῆναι ὑμᾶς. τοῦτο δέ ἐστι, συμπαρακληθῆναι ἐν ὑμῖν**
establishing of you. this And is to be comforted together among you
1223 1722 240 4102 5216/5037 1700/3756/2309
13 διὰ τῆς ἐν ἀλλήλοις πίστεως ὑμῶν τε καὶ ἐμοῦ. οὐ θέλω δὲ
through the in one another faith of you both and of me. not I wish But
5209 50 80 3754 4178 4388 2064 4314
ὑμᾶς ἀγνοεῖν, ἀδελφοί, ὅτι πολλάκις προεθέμην ἐλθεῖν πρὸς
you to be ignorant, brothers, that often I purposed to come to
5209 2967 891 1204 2443 2590 5100/2192
ὑμᾶς (καὶ ἐκωλύθην ἄχρι τοῦ δεῦρο), ἵνα καρπόν τινα σχῶ
you, and was hindered until the present, that fruit some I have
1722/5213/2531 1722 3062 1484 1672 5037
14 καὶ ἐν ὑμῖν, καθὼς καὶ ἐν τοῖς λοιποῖς ἔθνεσιν. Ἕλλησί τε καὶ
also among you, even as also in the remaining nations. To Greeks Both and
915 4680/5037 453 3781 1510 3779
βαρβάροις, σοφοῖς τε καὶ ἀνοήτοις ὀφειλέτης εἰμί· οὕτω τὸ
to foreigners, to wise both and foolish, a debtror I am; so as
2596/1691/ 4289 5213 1722/ 4516 2097
κατ᾽ ἐμὲ πρόθυμον καὶ ὑμῖν τοῖς ἐν Ῥώμῃ εὐαγγελίσασθαι.
far as in me (lies) I am eager also to you in Rome to preach the gospel.
3756/1063/ 1870 2098 5547 1411
οὐ γὰρ ἐπαισχύνομαι τὸ εὐαγγέλιον τοῦ Χριστοῦ· δύναμις
not For I am ashamed of the gospel of Christ, power
1063/2316/2076/1519/ 4991 3956 4100 2453
γὰρ Θεοῦ ἐστιν εἰς σωτηρίαν παντὶ τῷ πιστεύοντι, Ἰουδαίῳ
for of God it is to salvation to everyone believing; to Jew
5037 4412 1672 1343 1063 2316/1722/846
17 τε πρῶτον καὶ Ἕλληνι. δικαιοσύνη γὰρ Θεοῦ ἐν αὐτῷ
both firstly, and to Greek. a righteousness For of God in it
601 1537/ 4102 1519 4102 2531 1125
ἀποκαλύπτεται ἐκ πίστεως εἰς πίστιν. καθὼς γέγραπται,
is revealed from faith to faith, even as it has been written,
1342/1537/ 4102 2198
Ὁ δὲ δίκαιος ἐκ πίστεως ζήσεται.
the But just by faith shall live.
601 1063 3709 2316 575 3772 1909 3956
18 Ἀποκαλύπτεται γὰρ ὀργὴ Θεοῦ ἀπ᾽ οὐρανοῦ ἐπὶ πᾶσαν
is revealed For (the) wrath of God from Heaven on all
763 93 444 225 1722/93
ἀσέβειαν καὶ ἀδικίαν ἀνθρώπων τῶν τὴν ἀλήθειαν ἐν ἀδικίᾳ
ungodliness and unrighteousness of men the truth in unrighteousness
2722 1360 1110 2316 5318 2076/1722
19 κατεχόντων· διότι τὸ γνωστὸν τοῦ Θεοῦ φανερόν ἐστιν ἐν
holding; because the thing known of God clearly known is in
846 1063 2316 846 5319 1063/ 517 846
20 αὐτοῖς· ὁ γὰρ Θεὸς αὐτοῖς ἐφανέρωσε. τὰ γὰρ ἀόρατα αὐτοῦ
them, for God to them revealed (it). the For unseen things of Him
575 2937 2889 4161 3539 2529
ἀπὸ κτίσεως κόσμου τοῖς ποιήμασι νοούμενα καθορᾶται.
from creation of of (the) world by the things made being realized is being understood
3739/5037/126 848 1411 2305 1519 1511
ἥ τε ἀΐδιος αὐτοῦ δύναμις καὶ θειότης, εἰς τὸ εἶναι αὐτοὺς
the both eternal of Him power and Godhead; for to be them
379 1360 1097 2316 3756/5613/2316
21 ἀναπολογήτους· διότι γνόντες τὸν Θεόν, οὐχ ὡς Θεὸν
without excuse. Because having known God, not as God
1392 2228 2168 235 3154 1722
ἐδόξασαν ἢ εὐχαρίστησαν, ἀλλ᾽ ἐματαιώθησαν ἐν τοῖς
they glorified, nor were thankful; but became vain in the
1261 848 4654 801 848
διαλογισμοῖς αὐτῶν, καὶ ἐσκοτίσθη ἡ ἀσύνετος αὐτῶν
reasonings of them, and was darkened the undiscerning of them
2588 5335 1511 4680 3471 236
22 καρδία. φάσκοντες εἶναι σοφοὶ ἐμωράνθησαν, καὶ ἤλλαξαν
heart. Professing to be wise, they became foolish, and changed
1391 862 2316/1722/ 3667 1504 5349
23 τὴν δόξαν τοῦ ἀφθάρτου Θεοῦ ἐν ὁμοιώματι εἰκόνος φθαρτοῦ
the glory of the incorruptible God into a likeness of an image of corruptible
444 4071 5074 2062
ἀνθρώπου καὶ πετεινῶν καὶ τετραπόδων καὶ ἑρπετῶν.
man, and birds, and four-footed animals, and reptiles.

things. [24]Because of this, God gave them up to uncleanness in the lusts of their hearts, their bodies to be dishonored among themselves; [25]who changed the truth of God into the lie, and worshiped and served the created thing more than the Creator, who is blessed forever. Amen.

[26]Because of this, God gave them up to dishonorable passions, for even their females changed the natural use to that contrary to nature. [27]And likewise, the males also forsaking the natural use of the female burned in their lust toward one another, males with males working out shamefulness, and receiv-ing back in themselves the reward which was fitting for their error.

[28]And even as they did not think fit to have God in *their* knowledge, God gave them up to a reprobate mind, to do the things not right, [29]having been filled with all unrighteousness, fornication, iniquity, covetousness, malice; *being* full of envy, murder, quarrels, deceit, evil habits; *becoming* whisperers, [30]slanderers, God-haters, insolent, proud, braggarts, devisers of evil things, disobedient to parents, [31]without discernment, perfidious, without natural affection, unforgiving, unmerciful—[32]who knowing the righteous order of God, that those practicing such things are worthy of death, not only do them, but also applaud those practicing *them*.

1352 3860 846 2316/1722 1939
24 Διὸ καὶ παρέδωκεν αὐτοὺς ὁ Θεὸς ἐν ταῖς ἐπιθυμίαις τῶν
Therefore also gave up them God in the lusts of the
2588 848 1519 167 818 4983
καρδιῶν αὐτῶν εἰς ἀκαθαρσίαν τοῦ ἀτιμάζεσθαι τὰ σώματα
hearts of them to uncleanness, — to be dishonored the bodies
848 1722 1438 3748 3337 225
25 αὐτῶν ἐν ἑαυτοῖς· οἵτινες μετήλλαξαν τὴν ἀλήθειαν τοῦ
of them among themselves; who changed the truth —
2316/1722 5579 4573 3000
Θεοῦ ἐν τῷ ψεύδει, καὶ ἐσεβάσθησαν καὶ ἐλάτρευσαν τῇ
of God into the lie, and worshiped and served the
2937 3844 2936 3739 2076 2128 1519
κτίσει παρὰ τὸν κτίσαντα, ὅς ἐστιν εὐλογητὸς εἰς τοὺς
creature rather than the Creator, who is blessed to the
165 281
αἰῶνας. ἀμήν.
ages. Amen.

1223 5124 3860 846 2316/1519/3806 819
26 Διὰ τοῦτο παρέδωκεν αὐτοὺς ὁ Θεὸς εἰς πάθη ἀτιμίας·
Because of this gave up them God to passions of dishonor;
5037/1063/ 2338 848 3337 5446 5540
αἵ τε γὰρ θήλειαι αὐτῶν μετήλλαξαν τὴν φυσικὴν χρῆσιν
the even for females of them changed the natural use
1519 3844 5449 3668 5037 730 863
27 εἰς τὴν παρὰ φύσιν· ὁμοίως τε καὶ οἱ ἄρσενες, ἀφέντες τὴν
to the (use) against nature; likewise and also the males having forsaken the
5446 5540 2338 1572 1722 3715 848
φυσικὴν χρῆσιν τῆς θηλείας, ἐξεκαύθησαν ἐν τῇ ὀρέξει αὐτῶν
natural use of the female, burned in the lust of them
1519 240 730 1722 730 808 2716
εἰς ἀλλήλους, ἄρσενες ἐν ἄρσεσι τὴν ἀσχημοσύνην κατερ-
toward one another, males among males the shamefulness working
489 3739/1163 4106 848
γαζόμενοι, καὶ τὴν ἀντιμισθίαν ἣν ἔδει τῆς πλάνης αὐτῶν
out, and the reward which behoved the straying of them,
1722 1438 618
ἐν ἑαυτοῖς ἀπολαμβάνοντες.
in themselves receiving back.

2531/3756/ 1381 2316 1492/1722/ 1922
28 Καὶ καθὼς οὐκ ἐδοκίμασαν τὸν Θεὸν ἔχειν ἐν ἐπιγνώσει,
And even as not they thought fit — God to have in knowledge,
3860 846 2316/1519 96 3563 4160 3361
παρέδωκεν αὐτοὺς ὁ Θεὸς εἰς ἀδόκιμον νοῦν, ποιεῖν τὰ μὴ
gave up them God to a reprobate mind, to do the things not
2520 4137 3956 93 4202 4189
29 καθήκοντα, πεπληρωμένους πάσῃ ἀδικίᾳ, πορνείᾳ, πονηρίᾳ,
right, having been filled with all unrighteousness, fornication, iniquity,
4124 2549 3324 5355 5408 2054 1388
πλεονεξίᾳ, κακίᾳ· μεστοὺς φθόνου, φόνου, ἔριδος, δόλου,
covetousness, malice, full of envy, murder, quarrels, deceit,
2550 5588 2637 2319 5197
30 κακοηθείας· ψιθυριστάς, καταλάλους, θεοστυγεῖς, ὑβριστάς,
evil habits, whisperers, slanderers, God-haters, insolent,
5244 213 2182 2556 1118 545
ὑπερηφάνους, ἀλαζόνας, ἐφευρετὰς κακῶν, γονεῦσιν ἀπει-
proud, braggarts, devisers of evil things, to parents diso-
801 802 794 786 415
31 θεῖς, ἀσυνέτους, ἀσυνθέτους, ἀστόργους, ἀσπόνδους, ἀνελεή-
bedient, undiscerning, perfidious, without affection, implacable, unmerci-
3748 1345 2316 1921 3754
32 μονας· οἵτινες τὸ δικαίωμα τοῦ Θεοῦ ἐπιγνόντες, ὅτι οἱ τὰ
ful; who the righteous order of God having known, that those
5108 4238 514 2288 1526/3756/3440 846
τοιαῦτα πράσσοντες ἄξιοι θανάτου εἰσίν, οὐ μόνον αὐτὰ
such things practicing worthy of death are, not only them
4160 235 4909 4238
ποιοῦσιν, ἀλλὰ καὶ συνευδοκοῦσι τοῖς πράσσουσι.
do, but also consent to those practicing (them).

CHAPTER 2

[1]Therefore, O man, you are without excuse, everyone who judges, for in that in which you judge the other, you condemn yourself; for you who judge practice the same things. [2]But we know that the judgment of God is according to truth on those that practice such things. [3]And, O man, the *one* judging those practicing such things, and doing them, do you think that you will escape the judgment of God? [4]Or do you despise the riches of His kindness, and the forbearance and the long-suffering, not knowing that the kindness of God leads you to repentance? [5]But according to your hardness and *your* impenitent heart, do you treasure up to yourself wrath in a day of wrath, and revelation of a righteous judgment of God, [6]who will give to each according to his works: [7]everlasting life truly to those who with patience *in* good work *are* seeking glory and honor and incorruptibility; [8]but to those even disobeying the truth out of self-interest, and obeying unrighteousness, *will be* anger and wrath, [9]trouble and pain on every soul of man that works out evil, both of Jew first, and of Greek. [10]But glory and honor and peace *will be* to everyone that works out good, both to *the* Jew first, and to *the* Greek. [11]For there is no respect of persons with God. [12]For as many as sinned without Law will also perish without Law. And as many as sinned within Law will be judged through Law. [13]For not the hearers of the law are just with God, but the doers of the law shall be justified. [14]For when

CHAPTER 2

1352 379 1488/5599/ 444 3956 2919 1722/*/1063
1 Διὸ ἀναπολόγητος εἶ, ὦ ἄνθρωπε πᾶς ὁ κρίνων· ἐν ᾧ γὰρ
*3739 Therefore without excuse are you, O man, everyone judging;in what for
2919 2087 4572 2632 1063 846 4238
κρίνεις τὸν ἕτερον, σεαυτὸν κατακρίνεις, τὰ γὰρ αὐτὰ πράσ-
you judge the other, yourself you condemn; the for same things you
2919 1492 3754 2917 2316 2076 2596
2 σεις ὁ κρίνων. οἴδαμεν δὲ ὅτι τὸ κρίμα τοῦ Θεοῦ ἐστι κατὰ
practice those judging. we know But that the judgment of God is according to
225 1909 5108 4238 3049 5124
3 ἀλήθειαν ἐπὶ τοὺς τὰ τοιαῦτα πράσσοντας. λογίζῃ δὲ τοῦτο,
truth on those that such things practice. do you think And this,
5599 444 2919 5108 4238 4160
ὦ ἄνθρωπε ὁ κρίνων τοὺς τὰ τοιαῦτα πράσσοντας καὶ ποιῶν
O man, he judging those such things practicing and doing
846 3754/4771/ 1628 2917 2316 4149
4 αὐτά, ὅτι σὺ ἐκφεύξῃ τὸ κρίμα τοῦ Θεοῦ; ἢ τοῦ πλούτου
them, that you will escape the judgment — of God? Or the riches
5544 848 463 3115
τῆς χρηστότητος αὐτοῦ καὶ τῆς ἀνοχῆς καὶ τῆς μακροθυμίας
of the kindness of Him, and the forbearance and the longsuffering
2706 50 3754 5543 2316/1519/ 3341
καταφρονεῖς, ἀγνοῶν ὅτι τὸ χρηστὸν τοῦ Θεοῦ εἰς μετάνοιάν
do you despise, not knowing that the kindness – of God to repentance
4571/ 71 2596 4543 4675 279
5 σε ἄγει; κατὰ δὲ τὴν σκληρότητά σου καὶ ἀμετανόητον
you leads? according to But the hardness of you and the impenitent
2588 2343 4572 3709/1722/ 2250 3709
καρδίαν θησαυρίζεις σεαυτῷ ὀργὴν ἐν ἡμέρᾳ ὀργῆς καὶ
heart, do you treasure for yourself wrath in a day of wrath, and
602 1341 2316/3739/ 591 1538
6 ἀποκαλύψεως δικαιοκρισίας τοῦ Θεοῦ, ὃς ἀποδώσει ἑκάστῳ
revelation of a righteous judgment of God, who will give to each one
2596 2041 846 3303/2596 5281 2041 18
7 κατὰ τὰ ἔργα αὐτοῦ· τοῖς μὲν καθ' ὑπομονὴν ἔργου ἀγαθοῦ
according the works of him to those truly by patience work good,
1391 to 5092 861 2212 2222 166
δόξαν καὶ τιμὴν καὶ ἀφθαρσίαν ζητοῦσι, ζωὴν αἰώνιον· τοῖς
glory and honor and incorruptibility seeking, life everlasting. to those
1537 2052 544 3303 225 3982
8 δὲ ἐξ ἐριθείας, καὶ ἀπειθοῦσι μὲν τῇ ἀληθείᾳ, πειθομένοις δὲ
But out of self-interest even disobeying indeed the truth, obeying but
93 2372 3709 2347 4730 1909
9 τῇ ἀδικίᾳ, θυμὸς καὶ ὀργή, θλῖψις καὶ στενοχωρία, ἐπὶ
unrighteousness, anger and wrath, trouble and pain on
3956 5590 444 2716 2556
πᾶσαν ψυχὴν ἀνθρώπου τοῦ κατεργαζομένου τὸ κακόν,
every soul of man working out the evil,
2453 5037 4412 1672 1391 5092
10 Ἰουδαίου τε πρῶτον καὶ Ἕλληνος· δόξα δὲ καὶ τιμὴ καὶ
of Jew both firstly, and of Greek glory But and honor and
1515 3956 2038 18 2453 5037 4412
εἰρήνη παντὶ τῷ ἐργαζομένῳ τὸ ἀγαθόν, Ἰουδαίῳ τε πρῶτον
peace to everyone working out the good, to Jew both firstly,
1672 3756/1063/2076 4382 3844 2316
11 καὶ Ἕλληνι· οὐ γάρ ἐστι προσωποληψία παρὰ τῷ Θεῷ.
and to Greek. not For is respect of persons with God.
3745/1063 460 264 460 622
12 ὅσοι γὰρ ἀνόμως ἥμαρτον, ἀνόμως καὶ ἀπολοῦνται· καὶ
as many as For without law sinned, without law also will perish; and
3745/1722/3551 264 1223 3551 2919 3756/1063
13 ὅσοι ἐν νόμῳ ἥμαρτον, διὰ νόμου κριθήσονται· οὐ γὰρ οἱ
as many as in law sinned, through law will be judged; not for the
202 3551 1342 3844 2316 235 4163
ἀκροαταὶ τοῦ νόμου δίκαιοι παρὰ τῷ Θεῷ, ἀλλ' οἱ ποιηταὶ
hearers of the law are just with God, but the doers
3551 1344 3752/1063/1484 3361 3551
14 τοῦ νόμου δικαιωθήσονται. ὅταν γὰρ ἔθνη τὰ μὴ νόμον
of the law shall be justified. when For nations not law

nations not having Law do by nature the things of the Law, they not having Law are a law to themselves; 15who show the work of the law written in their hearts, their conscience witnessing with *them*; and the thoughts between one another accusing or excusing, 16in a day when God judges the hidden things of men, according to my gospel, through Jesus Christ.

17Behold, you are called a Jew, and rest in the Law, and boast in God, 18and know the will, and approve the things excelling, being instructed out of the Law; 19and persuading yourself to be a guide of blind ones, a light to those in darkness, 20an instructor of foolish ones, a teacher of infants, having the form of knowledge and of the truth in the Law—21then the *one* teaching another, do you not teach yourself? The *one* proclaiming not to steal, do you steal? 22He saying not to commit adultery, do you commit adultery? The *one* detesting the idols, do you rob temples? 23*You* who boast in Law, do you dishonor God through transgression of the Law? 24For the name of God is blasphemed among the nations through you, even as it has been written: 25"For truly circumcision profits if you practice *the* Law, but if you are a transgressor of Law, your circumcision becomes uncircumcision. 26If, then, the uncircumcision keeps the demands of the Law, *will* not his uncircumcision be counted for circumcision? 27And will *not* the uncircumcision by nature *by* keeping the Law judge you, the *one who* through letter and circumcision *becomes*

2192 5449 3551 4160 3778 3551 3361 2192
ἔχοντα φύσει τὰ τοῦ νόμου ποιῇ, οὗτοι, νόμον μὴ ἔχοντες,
having by nature the things of the law do, these law not having
1438 1526 3551 3748 1731 2041 3551
15 ἑαυτοῖς εἰσι νόμος· οἵτινες ἐνδείκνυνται τὸ ἔργον τοῦ νόμου
to themselves are a law; who show the work of the law
1123 1722 2588 848 4828 848
γραπτὸν ἐν ταῖς καρδίαις αὐτῶν, συμμαρτυρούσης αὐτῶν
written in the hearts of them, witnessing with of them
4893 3342 240 3953
τῆς συνειδήσεως, καὶ μεταξὺ ἀλλήλων τῶν λογισμῶν
the conscience, and between one another the thoughts
2723 2228 626 1722/2250/3753/2919
16 κατηγορούντων ἢ καὶ ἀπολογουμένων, ἐν ἡμέρᾳ ὅτε κρινεῖ
accusing or even excusing, in a day when judges
2316 2927 444 2596 2098 3450
ὁ Θεὸς τὰ κρυπτὰ τῶν ἀνθρώπων, κατὰ τὸ εὐαγγέλιόν μου
God the hidden things of men according to the gospel of me
1223 2424 5547
διὰ Ἰησοῦ Χριστοῦ.
through Jesus Christ.
2396/4771/ 2453 2028 1879
17 Ἴδε σὺ Ἰουδαῖος ἐπονομάζῃ, καὶ ἐπαναπαύῃ τῷ νόμῳ.
Behold, you a Jew are named, and rest in the law,
2744 1722 2316 1097 2307 1381
18 καὶ καυχᾶσαι ἐν Θεῷ, καὶ γινώσκεις τὸ θέλημα, καὶ δοκι-
and boast in God, and know the will, and approve
1308 2727 1537 3551 3982
19 μάζεις τὰ διαφέροντα, κατηχούμενος ἐκ τοῦ νόμου, πέποιθάς
the things excelling, being instructed out of the law, having persuaded
5037 4572 3595 1511 5185 5457 1722 4655 3810
τε σεαυτὸν ὁδηγὸν εἶναι τυφλῶν, φῶς τῶν ἐν σκότει, παι-
and yourself a guide to be of blind ones, a light to those in darkness, an
878 1320 3516 2192 3446
20 δευτὴν ἀφρόνων, διδάσκαλον νηπίων, ἔχοντα τὴν μόρφωσιν
instructor of foolish ones, a teacher of infants, having the from
1108 225 1722 3551 3767 1321
21 τῆς γνώσεως καὶ τῆς ἀληθείας ἐν τῷ νόμῳ· ὁ οὖν διδάσκων
of knowledge and of the truth in the law; he, then, teaching
2087 4572 3756 1321 2784 3361 2813
ἕτερον, σεαυτὸν οὐ διδάσκεις; ὁ κηρύσσων μὴ κλέπτειν,
another, yourself not do you teach? He proclaiming not to steal,
2813 3004 3361 3431 3431 948
22 κλέπτεις; ὁ λέγων μὴ μοιχεύειν, μοιχεύεις; ὁ βδελυσσόμενος
do you steal? He saying not to commit do you commit He detesting
1497 2416 adultery adultery? 2774 1223
23 τὰ εἴδωλα, ἱεροσυλεῖς; ὃς ἐν νόμῳ καυχᾶσαι διὰ τῆς
the idols, do you rob temples? Who in law boast through
3847 3551 2316 818 1063 3686
24 παραβάσεως τοῦ νόμου τὸν Θεὸν ἀτιμάζεις; τὸ γὰρ ὄνομα
transgression of law God do you dishonor? the For name
2316/1223/5209 987 1722 1484 2531
τοῦ Θεοῦ δι' ὑμᾶς βλασφημεῖται ἐν τοῖς ἔθνεσι, καθὼς
of God through you is blasphemed among the nations; even as
1125 4061 3303/1063 5623 1437 3551 4238
25 γέγραπται. περιτομὴ μὲν γὰρ ὠφελεῖ, ἐὰν νόμον πράσσῃς·
it has been written, circumcision truly For profits, if law you practice;
1437 3848 3551 5600 4061 4675 203
ἐὰν δὲ παραβάτης νόμου ᾖς, ἡ περιτομή σου ἀκροβυστία
if if but a transgressor of law you are, the circumcision of you uncircumcision
1096 1437/3767 203 1345 3551
26 γέγονεν. ἐὰν οὖν ἡ ἀκροβυστία τὰ δικαιώματα τοῦ νόμου
becomes. If, then, the uncircumcision the ordinances of the law
5442 3780 203 848 1519 4061 3049
φυλάσσῃ, οὐχὶ ἡ ἀκροβυστία αὐτοῦ εἰς περιτομὴν λογισθή-
keeps, (will) not the uncircumcision of him for circumcision be counted?
2919 1537 5449 203 3551
27 σεται; καὶ κρινεῖ ἡ ἐκ φύσεως ἀκροβυστία, τὸν νόμον
And will judge the by nature uncircumcision the law
5055 4571 1223 1121 4061 3848
τελοῦσα, σὲ τὸν διὰ γράμματος καὶ περιτομῆς παραβάτην
keeping you the through letter and circumcision transgressor

transgressor of Law? [28]For he is not a Jew that *is one* outwardly, nor *is* circumcision that outwardly in flesh; [29]but he *is* a Jew that *is one* inwardly; and circumcision *is* of heart, in spirit, not in letter; of whom the praise *is* not from men, but from God.

CHAPTER 3

[1]What then *is* the superiority of the Jew? Or what the profit of circumcision? [2]Much by every way. For first, indeed, that they were entrusted with the oracles of God. [3]For what if some did not believe? Will their unbelief not nullify the faith of God? [4]Let it not be! But let God be true, and every man a liar; even as it has been written, "That You should be justified in Your words, and will overcome in Your being judged."

[5]But if our unrighteousness commends the righteousness of God, what shall we say? *Is* God unrighteous *in* laying on wrath? I speak according to man. [6]Let it not be! Otherwise, how will God judge the world? [7]for if in my lie the truth of God abounded to His glory, why am I yet also judged as a sinner? [8]And not, as we are wrongly accused, and as some report us to say, Let us do bad things so that good things may come, *the* judgment of whom is just.

[9]What, then? Do we excel? Not at all! For we before charged both. Jews and Greeks all to be under sin; [10]according as it has been written, "There is none righteous, no, not one! [11]There is none that understands, there is not one that seeks after God. [12]All turned away; *they*

3551/3756/1063 1722 5318 2453 2076 3761 1722
28 νόμου ; οὐ γὰρ ὁ ἐν τῷ φανερῷ Ἰουδαῖός ἐστιν, οὐδὲ ἡ ἐν τῷ
of law? not For the in the open Jew is, nor (is) in the
5318 1722/4561 4061 235 1722 2927 2453
29 φανερῷ ἐν σαρκὶ περιτομή· ἀλλ' ὁ ἐν τῷ κρυπτῷ Ἰουδαῖος,
open in flesh circumcision, but the in private Jew (is)
4061 2588 1722 4151 3756 1121 3739
καὶ περιτομὴ καρδίας ἐν πνεύματι, οὐ γράμματι· οὗ ὁ
and circumcision (is) of heart, in spirit, not in letter; of whom the
1868 3756/1537 444 235/1537 2316
ἔπαινος οὐκ ἐξ ἀνθρώπων, ἀλλ' ἐκ τοῦ Θεοῦ.
praise (is) not from men, but from God.

CHAPTER 3

5101/3767 4053 2453 2228/5101 5622
1 Τί οὖν τὸ περισσὸν τοῦ Ἰουδαίου, ἢ τίς ἡ ὠφέλεια τῆς
What, then, the superiority of the Jew, or what the profit
4061 4183 2596 3956 5158 4412 3303/1063/3754
2 περιτομῆς ; πολὺ κατὰ πάντα τρόπον· πρῶτον μὲν γὰρ ὅτι
of circumcision? Much by every way. firstly, indeed, For, that
4100 3051 2316/5101/1063/1487/ 569
3 ἐπιστεύθησαν τὰ λόγια τοῦ Θεοῦ. τί γὰρ εἰ ἠπίστησάν
they were entrusted with the oracles of God. what For? If disbelieved
5100/3361 570 848 4102 2316 2673
τινες· μὴ ἡ ἀπιστία αὐτῶν τὴν πίστιν τοῦ Θεοῦ καταργή-
some, Not the unbelief of them the faith of God destroy?
3361 1096 1096 2316 227 3956 444
4 σει ; μὴ γένοιτο· γινέσθω δὲ ὁ Θεὸς ἀληθής, πᾶς δὲ ἄνθρωπος
Not let it be! let be But God true, every and man
5583 2531 1125 3704 302 1344 1722
ψεύστης, καθὼς γέγραπται, Ὅπως ἂν δικαιωθῇς ἐν τοῖς
a liar, even as it has been written, So as you may be justified in the
3056 4675 3528 1722 2919 4571/1487 93
5 λόγοις σου, καὶ νικήσῃς ἐν τῷ κρίνεσθαί σε. εἰ δὲ ἡ ἀδικία
sayings of you, and will overcome in the being judged you. if But the unrighteousness
2257 2316 1343 4921 5101 2046 3361 94
ἡμῶν Θεοῦ δικαιοσύνην συνίστησι, τί ἐροῦμεν ; μὴ ἄδικος
of us of God a righteousness commends, what shall we say? unrighteous
2316 2018 3709 2596 444 3004 3361
6 ὁ Θεὸς ὁ ἐπιφέρων τὴν ὀργήν (κατὰ ἄνθρωπον λέγω) ; μὴ
(Is) God inflicting wrath? —according to man I say — not
1096 1893 4459 2919 2316 2889 1487/1063
7 γένοιτο· ἐπεὶ πῶς κρινεῖ ὁ Θεὸς τὸν κόσμον ; εἰ γὰρ ἡ
let it be! Otherwise how will judge God the world? if For the
225 2316/1722 1699 5582 4052 1519
ἀλήθεια τοῦ Θεοῦ ἐν τῷ ἐμῷ ψεύσματι ἐπερίσσευσεν εἰς τὴν
truth of God by my lie abounded to the
1391 848 5101/2089/2504/5613/ 268 2919 3361
8 δόξαν αὐτοῦ, τί ἔτι κἀγὼ ὡς ἁμαρτωλὸς κρίνομαι ; καὶ μὴ
glory of Him, why yet I also as a sinner am judged? And not
2531 987 2531 5346 5100/2248 3004
(καθὼς βλασφημούμεθα, καὶ καθώς φασί τινες ἡμᾶς λέγειν
—as we are wrongly accused, and as report some us to say—
3754 4160 2556 2443/2064 18 3739 2917
ὅτι), Ποιήσωμεν τὰ κακὰ ἵνα ἔλθῃ τὰ ἀγαθά ; ὧν τὸ κρίμα
Let us do bad things that may come good things. Of whom judgment
1738 2076
ἔνδικόν ἐστι.
just is.
5101 3767 4284 3756 3843 4256 1063
9 Τί οὖν ; προεχόμεθα ; οὐ πάντως· προῃτιασάμεθα γὰρ
What, then? Do we excel? Not at all! we before charged For
2453 5037 1672 3956 5259 266 1511 2531
10 Ἰουδαίους τε καὶ Ἕλληνας πάντας ὑφ' ἁμαρτίαν εἶναι, καθὼς
Jews both and Greeks all under sin to be, even as
1125 3754/3756/2076/ 1342 3761/1519/3756/2076 4920
11 γέγραπται ὅτι Οὐκ ἔστι δίκαιος οὐδὲ εἷς· οὐκ ἔστιν ὁ συνιῶν,
has been written, Not a righteous, not one; not is (one) understanding;
3756/2076 1567 2316 3956 1578 260 889
12 οὐκ ἔστιν ὁ ἐκζητῶν τὸν Θεόν· πάντες ἐξέκλιναν, ἅμα ἠχρειώ-
not is (one) seeking — God; all turned away, together became

became worthless together; not *one* is doing kindness, not so much as one! 13Their throat *is* an opened grave; they used deceit with their tongues; *the* poison of asps *is* under their lips; 14whose mouth is full of cursing and bitterness. 15Their feet *are* swift to shed blood; 16ruin and misery *are* in their way; 17and they do not know a way of peace; 18there is no fear of God before their eyes."

19Now we know that whatever the Law says, it speaks to those within the Law, so that every mouth may be stopped, and all the world be under judgment to God. 20Because by works of law no flesh will be justified before Him—for through law *is* full knowledge of sin.

21But now a righteousness of God has been revealed apart from Law, being witnessed by the Law and the Prophets, 22even the righteousness of God through *the* faith of Jesus Christ toward all and upon all those believing; for there is no difference, 23for all sinned and come short of the glory of God, 24being justified as a free gift by His grace through the redemption in Christ Jesus; 25whom God set forth *as* a propitiation through faith in His blood, for a showing forth of His righteousness through the passing by of the sins that had taken place before, in the forbearance of God; 26for *the* showing forth of His righteousness in the present time, for His being just and justifying him that *is* of *the* faith of Jesus. 27Then where *is* the boasting? It was excluded. Through what law? Of works? No, but through a law of faith. 28Then we conclude a man

3756/2076 4160 5544 3756/2076 2193 1520
θησαν· οὐκ ἔστι ποιῶν χρηστότητα, οὐκ ἔστιν ἕως ἑνός·
worthless, not is (one) doing kindness, not is so much as one.
5028 455 2995 848 1100 848
13 τάφος ἀνεῳγμένος ὁ λάρυγξ αὐτῶν, ταῖς γλώσσαις αὐτῶν
A grave opened (is) the throat of them, with the tongues of them
1387 2447 785 5259 5491 848 3739 4750
14 ἐδολιοῦσαν· ἰὸς ἀσπίδων ὑπὸ τὰ χείλη αὐτῶν· ὧν τὸ στόμα
they used deceit, poison of asps under the lips of them; of whom the mouth
685 4088 1073 3691 4228 848 1632 129
15 ἀρᾶς καὶ πικρίας γέμει· ὀξεῖς οἱ πόδες αὐτῶν ἐκχέαι αἷμα·
of cursing and bitterness is full; swift the feet of them to shed blood:
4938 5004 1722 3598 848 3598
16 σύντριμμα καὶ ταλαιπωρία ἐν ταῖς ὁδοῖς αὐτῶν, καὶ ὁδὸν
ruin and misery in the way of them: and a way
1515 3756 1097 3756/2076 5401 2316 561
17 εἰρήνης οὐκ ἔγνωσαν· οὐκ ἔστι φόβος Θεοῦ ἀπέναντι τῶν
18 **of peace not they knew. Not is fear of God before the**
3788 848
ὀφθαλμῶν αὐτῶν.
eyes of them.
1492 3754/3745 3551 3004 1722 3551 2980
19 Οἴδαμεν δὲ ὅτι ὅσα ὁ νόμος λέγει, τοῖς ἐν τῷ νόμῳ λαλεῖ,
we know But that what the law says, to those in the law it speaks,
2443/3956 4750 5420 5267 1096 3956 2889
ἵνα πᾶν στόμα φραγῇ, καὶ ὑπόδικος γένηται πᾶς ὁ κόσμος
that every mouth be stopped, and under judgment may become all the world
2316 1320/1537/2041/3551 3756 1344 3956 4561
20 τῷ Θεῷ· διότι ἐξ ἔργων νόμου οὐ δικαιωθήσεται πᾶσα σάρξ
to God; because by works of law not will be justified all flesh
1799 846 1223/1063 3551 1922 266 3570
21 ἐνώπιον αὐτοῦ· διὰ γὰρ νόμου ἐπίγνωσις ἁμαρτίας. νυνὶ δὲ
before Him; through for law (is) full knowledge of sin. now But
5565 3551 1343 2316 5319 3140
22 χωρὶς νόμου δικαιοσύνη Θεοῦ πεφανέρωται, μαρτυρουμένη
without law a righteousness of God has been revealed, being witnessed
5259 3551 4396 1343 2316/1223
ὑπὸ τοῦ νόμου καὶ τῶν προφητῶν· δικαιοσύνη δὲ Θεοῦ διὰ
by the Law and the Prophets, a righteousness and of God via
4102 2424 5547 1519 3956 1909 3956
πίστεως Ἰησοῦ Χριστοῦ εἰς πάντας καὶ ἐπὶ πάντας τοὺς
faith of Jesus Christ to all and upon all those
4100 3756/1063/2076 1293 3956 1063 264
23 πιστεύοντας· οὐ γάρ ἐστι διαστολή· πάντες γὰρ ἥμαρτον
believing; not for there is a difference; all for sinned
5302 1391 2316 1344 1432
24 καὶ ὑστεροῦνται τῆς δόξης τοῦ Θεοῦ, δικαιούμενοι δωρεὰν
and come short of the glory — of God, being justified freely
848 5485 1223 629 1722 5547
τῇ αὐτοῦ χάριτι διὰ τῆς ἀπολυτρώσεως τῆς ἐν Χριστῷ
by the of Him grace through the redemption — in Christ
2424 3739 4388 2316 2435 1223 4102
25 Ἰησοῦ· ὃν προέθετο ὁ Θεὸς ἱλαστήριον, διὰ τῆς πίστεως,
Jesus; whom set forth God a propitiation through — faith,
1722 848 129 1519 1732 1343 848 1223
ἐν τῷ αὐτοῦ αἵματι, εἰς ἔνδειξιν τῆς δικαιοσύνης αὐτοῦ, διὰ
by the of Him blood, for a display of the righteousness of Him, through
3929 4266 265 1722 463
τὴν πάρεσιν τῶν προγεγονότων ἁμαρτημάτων, ἐν τῇ ἀνοχῇ
the passing by of the that before had occurred sins, in the forbearance
2316 4314 1732 1343 848 1722 3568
26 τοῦ Θεοῦ· πρὸς ἔνδειξιν τῆς δικαιοσύνης αὐτοῦ ἐν τῷ νῦν
— of God for the display of the righteousness of Him in the present
2540 1519 1511 848 1342 1344 1537
καιρῷ, εἰς τὸ εἶναι αὐτὸν δίκαιον καὶ δικαιοῦντα τὸν ἐκ
time, for the being (of) Him just and justifying the (one) of
4102 2424 4226/3767 2746 1576 1223 4169
27 πίστεως Ἰησοῦ. ποῦ οὖν ἡ καύχησις; ἐξεκλείσθη. διὰ ποίου
faith of Jesus. Where, then, the boasting? It was excluded. Through what
3551 2041 3780 235 1223 3551 4102 3049
28 νόμου; τῶν ἔργων; οὐχί, ἀλλὰ διὰ νόμου πίστεως. λογιζό-
law? Of works? No, but through a law of faith. we con-

to be justified without works of Law. [29]Or *is He* the God of Jews only, and not also of *the* nations? [30]Yes, also of nations, since *it is* one God who will justify circumcision by faith, and uncircumcision through faith. [31]Then do we make Law of no effect through faith? Let is not be! But we establish Law.

CHAPTER 4

[1]What then shall we say our father Abraham to have found according to flesh? [2]For if Abraham was justified by works, he has a boast — but not with God. [3]For what does the Scripture say? "And Abraham believed God, and it was counted to him for righteousness." [4]Now *to one* working, the reward is not counted according to grace, but according to debt. [5]But to the *one* not working, but believing on Him justifying the ungodly, his faith is counted for righteousness. [6]Even as also David says of the blessedness of the man to whom God counts righteousness apart from works: [7]"Blessed *are those* whose lawlessnesses are forgiven, and whose sins are covered; [8]blessed *the* man to whom *the* Lord will in no way charge sin."

[9]*Is* this blessedness then on the circumcision, or also on the uncircumcision? For we say the faith was counted to Abraham for righteousness. [10]How then was it counted? Being in circumcusion, or in uncircumcision? Not in circumcision, but in uncircumcision! [11]And he received a sign of circumcision *as* a seal of the righteousness of faith *while* in uncircumcision, for him to be a father of all the believing ones through uncircumcision, for

3767 4102 1344 444 5565 2041 3551
μεθα οὖν πίστει δικαιοῦσθαι ἄνθρωπον, χωρὶς ἔργων νόμου.
clude Then by faith to be justified a man without works of law.
2228 2453 2316 3440 3780 1484 3483
29 ἢ Ἰουδαίων ὁ Θεὸς μόνον ; οὐχὶ δὲ καὶ ἐθνῶν ; ναὶ καὶ
Or of Jews (is He) the God only, not and also of nations? Yes, also
1484 1897/1519 2316 3739 1344 4061 1537/4102
30 ἐθνῶν· ἐπείπερ εἷς ὁ Θεός, ὃς δικαιώσει περιτομὴν ἐκ πί-
of nations, since (it is) one God who will justify circumcision by
203 1223 4102 3551 3767/2673
31 στεως, καὶ ἀκροβυστίαν διὰ τῆς πίστεως. νόμον οὖν καταρ-
faith, and uncircumcision through the faith. law Then do we
1223 4102 3361 1096 235 3551 2476
γοῦμεν διὰ τῆς πίστεως ; μὴ γένοιτο· ἀλλὰ νόμον ἱστῶμεν.
destroy though the faith? Not let it be! But law we establish.

CHAPTER 4

5101/3767/ 2046 11 3962 2257 2147 2596
1 Τί οὖν ἐροῦμεν Ἀβραὰμ τὸν πατέρα ἡμῶν εὑρηκέναι κατὰ
What then shall we say Abraham the father of us to have found according
4561 1487/1063 11 1537 2041 1344 2192 2745
2 σάρκα ; εἰ γὰρ Ἀβραὰμ ἐξ ἔργων ἐδικαιώθη, ἔχει καύχημα,
to flesh? if For Abraham by works was justified, he has a boast;
235/3756/4314 2316/5101/1063 1124 3004 4100
3 ἀλλ' οὐ πρὸς τὸν Θεόν. τί γὰρ ἡ γραφὴ λέγει ; Ἐπίστευσε
but not with — God. what For the Scripture says? believed
11 2316 3049 846 1519 1343
δὲ Ἀβραὰμ τῷ Θεῷ, καὶ ἐλογίσθη αὐτῷ εἰς δικαιοσύνην. τῷ
And Abraham God, and it was counted to him for righteousness. to the
2038 3408 3756 3049 2596 5485 235
4 δὲ ἐργαζομένῳ ὁ μισθὸς οὐ λογίζεται κατὰ χάριν, ἀλλὰ
Now (one) working the reward not is counted according to grace, but
2596 3783 3361 2038 4100 1909
5 κατὰ τὸ ὀφείλημα. τῷ δὲ μὴ ἐργαζομένῳ, πιστεύοντι δὲ ἐπὶ
according to debt. to the But not working (one), believing but on
1344 765 3049 4102 848 1519
τὸν δικαιοῦντα τὸν ἀσεβῆ, λογίζεται ἡ πίστις αὐτοῦ εἰς
the (One) justifying the ungodly, is counted the faith of him for
1343 2509 1138 3004 3107
6 δικαιοσύνην. καθάπερ καὶ Δαβὶδ λέγει τὸν μακαρισμὸν τοῦ
righteousness, even as also David says of the blessedness of the
444 3739 2316 3049 1343 5565 2041
ἀνθρώπου, ᾧ ὁ Θεὸς λογίζεται δικαιοσύνην χωρὶς ἔργων,
man to whom God counts righteousness without works,
3107 3739 863 458 3739 1943
7 Μακάριοι ὧν ἀφέθησαν αἱ ἀνομίαι, καὶ ὧν ἐπεκαλύφθησαν
Blessed of whom are forgiven the lawlessnesses, and of whom are covered
266 3107 435 3739/=3364= 3049 2962
8 αἱ ἁμαρτίαι. μακάριος ἀνὴρ ᾧ οὐ μὴ λογίσηται Κύριος
the sins; Blessed (the) man to whom in no way will charge (the) Lord
266 3107 3767 3778/1909 4061 2228
9 ἁμαρτίαν. ὁ μακαρισμὸς οὖν οὗτος ἐπὶ τὴν περιτομήν, ἢ καὶ
sin. (Is) blessedness then this on the circumcision, or also
1909 203 3004 1063/3754 3049
ἐπὶ τὴν ἀκροβυστίαν ; λέγομεν γὰρ ὅτι Ἐλογίσθη τῷ
on the uncircumcision? we say For, — was counted
11 4102 1519 1343 4459/3767 3049 1722
10 Ἀβραὰμ ἡ πίστις εἰς δικαιοσύνην. πῶς οὖν ἐλογίσθη ; ἐν
to Abraham The faith for righteousness. How, then, was it counted? In
4061 5607 1722 203 3756/1722 4061 235 1722
περιτομῇ ὄντι, ἢ ἐν ἀκροβυστίᾳ ; οὐκ ἐν περιτομῇ, ἀλλ' ἐν
circumcision being, or in uncircumcision? Not in circumcision, but in
203 4592 2983 4061 4973
11 ἀκροβυστίᾳ· καὶ σημεῖον ἔλαβε περιτομῆς, σφραγῖδα τῆς
uncircumcision; and a sign he received of circumcision, a seal of the
1343 4102 1722 203 1519
δικαιοσύνης τῆς πίστεως τῆς ἐν τῇ ἀκροβυστίᾳ εἰς τὸ
righteousness of the faith (while) in — uncircumcision, for the
1511 846 3962 3956 4100 1223 203
εἶναι αὐτὸν πατέρα πάντων τῶν πιστευόντων δι' ἀκροβυ-
being (of) him a father of all the believing ones through uncir-

righteousness to be counted to them also; [12]and a father of circumcision to those not of circumcision only, but also to thsoe walking by the steps of the faith of our father Abraham during uncircumcision.

[13]For the promise *was* not through law to Abraham, or to his seed, *for* him to be the heir of the world, but through a righteousness of faith. [14]For if the heirs *are* of Law, faith has been made of no effect, and the promise has been nullified. [15]For the Law works out wrath; for where no law is, neither *is* transgression. [16]On account of this, *it is* of faith, that *it be* according to grace, for the promise to be made sure to all the seed—not to that of the Law only, but also to that of *the* faith of Abraham, who is father of us all—[17]according as it has been written, "I have appointed you a father of many nations;"—before God, whom he believed, the *One* making the dead live, and calling the things that are not as *as if* they were. [18]*He* against hope believed in hope, for him to become father of many nations, according to what was said, "So shall your seed be."

[19]And being about a hundred years *old*, not weakening in faith, he did not consider his body already to have died, nor yet the death of Sarah's womb, [20]and did not stagger by unbelief at the promise of God, but was empowered by faith, giving glory to God, [21]and being fully persuaded that what He has promised, He is also able to do. [22]Therefore, it was also counted to him for righteousness. [23]But it was not written for him only, that it was counted to him, [24]but also

1519 3049 846 1343
στίας, εἰς τὸ λογισθῆναι καὶ αὐτοῖς τὴν δικαιοσύνην· καὶ
cumcision, for to be counted also to them – righteousness, and
3962 4061 3756/1537 4061 3440 235
12 πατέρα περιτομῆς τοῖς οὐκ ἐκ περιτομῆς μόνον, ἀλλὰ καὶ
a father of circumcision to those not of circumcision only, but also
4748 2487 1722 203 4102
τοῖς στοιχοῦσι τοῖς ἴχνεσι τῆς ἐν τῇ ἀκροβυστίᾳ πίστεως
to those walking in the steps of the in uncircumcision faith
3962 2257 11 3756/1063/1223/3551 1860
13 τοῦ πατρὸς ἡμῶν Ἀβραάμ. οὐ γὰρ διὰ νόμου ἡ ἐπαγγελία
of the father of us, Abraham. not For through law the promise
11 2228 4690 848 2818 846
τῷ Ἀβραὰμ η τῷ σπέρματι αὐτοῦ, τὸ κληρονόμον αὐτὸν
to Abraham, or to the seed of him, the heir him
1511 2889 235 1223 1343 4102 1487/1063
14 εἶναι τοῦ κόσμου, ἀλλὰ διὰ δικαιοσύνης πίστεως. εἰ γὰρ οἱ
to be of the world, but through a righteousness of faith, if For the
1537/3551 2818 2758 4102 2673
ἐκ νόμου κληρονόμοι, κεκένωται ἡ πίστις, καὶ κατήργηται ἡ
of law (are) heirs, has been voided faith, and has been the
1860 1063 3551 3709 2716 destroyed 3756
15 ἐπαγγελία· ὁ γὰρ νόμος ὀργὴν κατεργάζεται· οὗ γὰρ οὐκ
3757 promise. the For law wrath works out, where for not
*1063 2076/3551/3761 3847 1223 5124 1537 4102 2443 2596
16 ἔστι νόμος, οὐδὲ παράβασις. διὰ τοῦτο ἐκ πίστεως, ἵνα κατὰ
is law, neither (is) transgression. Therefore (it is) of faith, that according
5485 1519 1511 949 1860 3956 to
χάριν, εἰς τὸ εἶναι βεβαίαν τὴν ἐπαγγελίαν παντὶ τῷ
grace, for the being made sure the promise to all the
4690 3756 1537 3551 3440 235 1537
σπέρματι, οὐ τῷ ἐκ τοῦ νόμου μόνον, ἀλλὰ καὶ τῷ ἐκ
seed, not to the (seed) of the law only, but also to (that) of
4102 11 3739 2076 3962 3956 2257 2531
πίστεως Ἀβραάμ, ὅς ἐστι πατὴρ πάντων ἡμῶν (καθὼς
(the) faith of Abraham who is father of all us even as
1125 3754 3962 4183 1484 5087/4571 2713
17 γέγραπται ὅτι Πατέρα πολλῶν ἐθνῶν τέθεικά σε) κατέναντι
it has been written, A father of many nations I have appointed you – before
3739 4100 2316 2227 3498
οὗ ἐπίστευσε Θεοῦ, τοῦ ζωοποιοῦντος τοὺς νεκροὺς, καὶ
whom he believed God, the (one) making live the dead, and
2564 3361 5607/5613/5607/3739/3844 1680 1909 1680
18 καλοῦντος τὰ μὴ ὄντα ὡς ὄντα. ὃς παρ' ἐλπίδα ἐπ' ἐλπίδι
calling the things not being as being; who beyond hope on hope
4100 1519 1096 846 3962 4183 1484
ἐπίστευσεν, εἰς τὸ γενέσθαι αὐτὸν πατέρα πολλῶν ἐθνῶν,
believed, for the becoming (of) him a father of many nations,
2596 2046 3779 2071 4690 4675 3361
19 κατὰ τὸ εἰρημένον, Οὕτως ἔσται τὸ σπέρμα σου. καὶ μὴ
according to what was said, So shall be the seed of you. And not
770 4102 3756 2657 1438 4983 2235
ἀσθενήσας τῇ πίστει, οὐ κατενόησε τὸ ἑαυτοῦ σῶμα ἤδη
weakening – in faith, not he considered the of himself body already
3499 1541 4225 5225 3500
νενεκρωμένον (ἑκατονταέτης που ὑπάρχων), καὶ τὴν νέ-
to have died, a hundred years about being, and the
3388 4564 1519 1860 2316
20 κρωσιν τῆς μήτρας Σάρρας· εἰς δὲ τὴν ἐπαγγελίαν τοῦ Θεοῦ
death of the womb of Sarah; at but the promise of God
3756 1252 570 235 1743 4102 1325
οὐ διεκρίθη τῇ ἀπιστίᾳ, ἀλλ' ἐνεδυναμώθη τῇ πίστει, δοὺς
not hesitated – by unbelief, but was empowered – by faith, giving
1391 2316 4135 3754 1861
21 δόξαν τῷ Θεῷ, καὶ πληροφορηθεὶς ὅτι ὃ ἐπήγγελται,
glory – to God, and being fully persuaded that what He has promised
1415 2076 4160 1352 3049 846 1519 1343
22 δυνατός ἐστι καὶ ποιῆσαι. διὸ καὶ ἐλογίσθη αὐτῷ εἰς δικαιο-
able He is also to do. Therefore also it was counted to him for right-
3756/1125 1223 846 3440 3754 3049 846
23 σύνην. οὐκ ἐγράφη δὲ δι' αὐτὸν μόνον, ὅτι ἐλογίσθη αὐτῷ·
eousness. not it was written But for him only that it was counted to him,

also on account of us, to whom it is about to be counted, to the ones believing on Him who has raised our Lord Jesus from *the* dead, [25]who was delivered for our offenses, and was raised for our justification.

235 1223/2248 3739 3195 3049 4100
24 ἀλλὰ καὶ δι' ἡμᾶς, οἷς μέλλει λογίζεσθαι, τοῖς πιστεύουσιν
but also for us, to whom it is going to be counted, to those believing
1909 1453 2424 2962 2257 1537 3498 3739
25 ἐπὶ τὸν ἐγείραντα Ἰησοῦν τὸν Κύριον ἡμῶν ἐκ νεκρῶν, ὃς
on the (One) having raised Jesus the Lord of us out of (the) dead, who
3860 1223 3900 2257 1453 1223
παρεδόθη διὰ τὰ παραπτώματα ἡμῶν, καὶ ἠγέρθη διὰ τὴν
was delivered for the offenses of us, and was raised for the
1347 2257
δικαίωσιν ἡμῶν.
justification of us.

CHAPTER 5

CHAPTER 5

[1]Then being justified by faith, we have peace with God through our Lord Jesus Christ; [2]through whom also we have had access by faith into this grace in which we stand, and *we* glory on the hope of the glory of God. [3]And not only so, but we also glory in afflictions, knowing that affliction works out patience, [4]and patience *works out* proven character; and proven character, hope. [5]And the hope does not put *us* to shame, because the love of God has been poured out in our hearts through *the* Holy Spirit given to us; [6]for we yet being without strength, in due time Christ died on behalf of ungodly ones. [7]For one will with difficulty die for a just one—for perhaps one even dares to die for the sake of the good one—[8]but God commends His love to us in that we yet being sinners, Christ died for us. [9]Much more, then, being justified now by His blood, we will be saved through Him from wrath.

1344 3767/1537 4102 1515 2192 4314
1 Δικαιωθέντες οὖν ἐκ πίστεως, εἰρήνην ἔχομεν πρὸς τὸν
having been justified Then by faith, peace we have with
2316/1223 2962 2257 2424 5547 1223/3739
2 Θεὸν διὰ τοῦ Κυρίου ἡμῶν Ἰησοῦ Χριστοῦ. δι' οὗ καὶ τὴν
God through the Lord of us, Jesus Christ, through whom also the
4318 2192 4102 1519 5485 5026 1722
προσαγωγὴν ἐσχήκαμεν τῇ πίστει εἰς τὴν χάριν ταύτην ἐν
access we have had by faith into grace this in
3739/2476 2744 1909 1680 1391 2316
ᾗ ἑστήκαμεν, καὶ καυχώμεθα ἐπ' ἐλπίδι τῆς δόξης τοῦ Θεοῦ.
which we stand, and boast on the hope of the glory — of God.
3756/3440 235 2744 1722 2347 1492
3 οὐ μόνον δέ, ἀλλὰ καὶ καυχώμεθα ἐν ταῖς θλίψεσιν, εἰδότες
not only And (so), but also we boast in — troubles, knowing
3754 2347 5281 2716 5281 1382
4 ὅτι ἡ θλῖψις ὑπομονὴν κατεργάζεται, ἡ δὲ ὑπομονὴ δοκιμήν,
that trouble patience works out, and patience proof,
1382 1680 1680/3756 2617 3754 26
5 ἡ δὲ δοκιμὴ ἐλπίδα· ἡ δὲ ἐλπὶς οὐ καταισχύνει, ὅτι ἡ ἀγάπη
and proof hope, and hope not does put to shame, for the love
2316 1632 1722 2588 2257/1223 4151
τοῦ Θεοῦ ἐκκέχυται ἐν ταῖς καρδίαις ἡμῶν διὰ Πνεύματος
of God has been poured out in the hearts of us through (the) Spirit
40 1325 2254 2089/1063 5547 5607 2257
6 Ἁγίου τοῦ δοθέντος ἡμῖν. ἔτι γὰρ Χριστός, ὄντων ἡμῶν
Holy — given to us. yet For Christ — being us
772 2596 2540 5228 765 599 3433/1063/5228
7 ἀσθενῶν, κατὰ καιρὸν ὑπὲρ ἀσεβῶν ἀπέθανε. μόλις γὰρ ὑπὲρ
weak — according to time for ungodly ones died. hardly For for
1342 5100 599 5228/1063 18 5029 5100
δικαίου τις ἀποθανεῖται· ὑπὲρ γὰρ τοῦ ἀγαθοῦ τάχα τις·
a just one anyone will die; on behalf of for the good one perhaps one
5111 599 4921 1438 26 1519
8 καὶ τολμᾷ ἀποθανεῖν. συνίστησι δὲ τὴν ἑαυτοῦ ἀγάπην εἰς
even dares to die; commends but the of Himself love to
2248 2316/3754/2089/ 268 5607 2257 5547 5228
ἡμᾶς ὁ Θεός, ὅτι ἔτι ἁμαρτωλῶν ὄντων ἡμῶν Χριστὸς ὑπὲρ
us God, that yet sinners being us, Christ for
2257 599 4183 3767 3123 1344 3568/1722
9 ἡμῶν ἀπέθανε. πολλῷ οὖν μᾶλλον, δικαιωθέντες νῦν ἐν τῷ
us died. much Then more having been justified now by the
129 848 4982 1223 846 575 3709 1487
αἵματι αὐτοῦ, σωθησόμεθα δι' αὐτοῦ ἀπὸ τῆς ὀργῆς. εἰ
blood of Him, we shall be saved through Him from the wrath. if

[10]For if being enemies, we were reconciled to God through the death of His Son, much more being reconciled we shall be saved by His life. [11]And not only *so*, but also glorying in God through our Lord Jesus Christ, through whom we

1063 2190 5607 2644 2316/1223 2288
10 γὰρ ἐχθροὶ ὄντες κατηλλάγημεν τῷ Θεῷ διὰ τοῦ θανάτου
For enemies being we were reconciled — to God through the death
5207 848 4183 3123 2644 4982
τοῦ υἱοῦ αὐτοῦ, πολλῷ μᾶλλον καταλλαγέντες σωθησό-
of the Son of Him, by much more having been reconciled we shall be
1722 2222 848 3756 3440 235 1744 1722
11 μεθα ἐν τῇ ζωῇ αὐτοῦ· οὐ μόνον δέ, ἀλλὰ καὶ καυχώμενοι ἐν
saved by the life of Him; not only (so) And, but also boasting in
2316/1223 2962 2257 2424 5547 1223/3756/3568
τῷ Θεῷ διὰ τοῦ Κυρίου ἡμῶν Ἰησοῦ Χριστοῦ, δι' οὗ νῦν τὴν
— God through the Lord of us, Jesus Christ, through whom now the

now received the reconciliation. [12]Because of this, even as sin entered the world through one man, and death through sin, so also death passed to all men, inasmuch as all sinned; [13]for sin was in *the* world until Law, but sin is not charged *where* there is no law; [14]but death reigned from Adam until Moses, even over those who had not sinned in the likeness of Adam's transgression, who is a type of the coming *One*. [15]But the free gift *shall* not *be* also like the offense. for if by the offense of the one the many died, much more the grace of God, and the gift in grace, which *is* of the one Man, Jesus Christ, did abound to the many. [16]And the gift *shall* not *be* as by one having sinned; for indeed the judgment *was* of one to condemnation; but the free gift *is* of many offenses to justification. [17]For if by the offense of the one death reigned by the one, much more those who are receiving the abundance of grace and the gift of righteousness shall rule in life by the One, Jesus Christ. [18]So, then, as through one offense *it was* toward all men to condemnation, so also by one accomplished righteousness toward all men to justification of life. [19]For as through the one man's disobedience the many were constituted sinners, so also by the obedience of the One the many shall be constituted righteous. [20]But Law came

2643 2983
καταλλαγὴν ἐλάβομεν.
reconciliation we received.
1223 5124 5618/1223/1520 444 266 1519
12 Διὰ τοῦτο, ὥσπερ δι' ἑνὸς ἀνθρώπου ἡ ἁμαρτία εἰς τὸν
Therefore as through one man sin into the
2889 1525 1223 266 2288 3779
κόσμον εἰσῆλθε, καὶ διὰ τῆς ἁμαρτίας ὁ θάνατος, καὶ οὕτως
world entered, and through sin death, also so
1519 3956 444 2288 1330 1909/3739/ 3956
13 εἰς πάντας ἀνθρώπους ὁ θάνατος διῆλθεν, ἐφ' ᾧ πάντες
to all men death passed, inasmuch as all
264 891 1063 3551 266 2258/1722/ 2889 266
ἥμαρτον· ἄχρι γὰρ νόμου ἁμαρτία ἦν ἐν κόσμῳ· ἁμαρτία
sinned —until for law sin was in (the) world, sin
3756 1677 3361 5607 3551 235 936
14 δὲ οὐκ ἐλλογεῖται, μὴ ὄντος νόμου. ἀλλ' ἐβασίλευσεν ὁ
but not is charged there not being law; but reigned
2288 575 76 3360 3475 1909 3361 264
θάνατος ἀπὸ Ἀδὰμ μέχρι Μωσέως καὶ ἐπὶ τοὺς μὴ ἁμαρτή-
death from Adam until Moses even over those not sinning
1909 3667 3847 76 3739/2076
σαντας ἐπὶ τῷ ὁμοιώματι τῆς παραβάσεως Ἀδάμ, ὅς ἐστι
on the likeness of the transgression of Adam, who is
5179 3195 235 3756/5613 3900 3779
15 τύπος τοῦ μέλλοντος. ἀλλ' οὐχ ὡς τὸ παράπτωμα, οὕτω
a type of the (One) coming. But not as the offense, so
5486 1487/1063 1520 3900
καὶ τὸ χάρισμα. εἰ γὰρ τῷ τοῦ ἑνὸς παραπτώματι οἱ
also the free gift; if for by the of the one offense the
4183 599 4183 3123 5485 2316
πολλοὶ ἀπέθανον, πολλῷ μᾶλλον ἡ χάρις τοῦ Θεοῦ καὶ ἡ
many died, much more the grace — of God and the
1431 1722 5485 1520 444 2424 5547 1519
δωρεὰ ἐν χάριτι τῇ τοῦ ἑνὸς ἀνθρώπου Ἰησοῦ Χριστοῦ εἰς
gift in grace — of the one Man, Jesus Christ, to
4183 4052 3756/5613/1223/1520/ 264
16 τοὺς πολλοὺς ἐπερίσσευσε. καὶ οὐχ ὡς δι' ἑνὸς ἁμαρτή-
the many abounded. And not as through one sinning
1434 3303/1063 2917/1537/1520/1519/ 2631
σαντος, τὸ δώρημα· τὸ μὲν γὰρ κρίμα ἐξ ἑνὸς εἰς κατάκριμα,
(be) the gift; the indeed for judgment of one to condemnation,
5486 1537 4183 3900 1519 1345
17 τὸ δὲ χάρισμα ἐκ πολλῶν παραπτωμάτων εἰς δικαίωμα. εἰ
the But free gift (is) of many offenses to justification. if
1063 1520 3900 2288 936 1223
γὰρ τῷ τοῦ ἑνὸς παραπτώματι ὁ θάνατος ἐβασίλευσε διὰ
For by the of the one offense death reigned through
1520 4183 3123 4050 5485
τοῦ ἑνός, πολλῷ μᾶλλον οἱ τὴν περισσείαν τῆς χάριτος καὶ
the one, much more those the abundance of the grace and
1431 1343 2983 1722/2222 936
τῆς δωρεᾶς τῆς δικαιοσύνης λαμβάνοντες ἐν ζωῇ βασιλεύ-
of the gift of righteousness receiving in life will
1223 1520 2424 5547 686/3767/5613/1223/1520
18 σουσι διὰ τοῦ ἑνὸς Ἰησοῦ Χριστοῦ. ἄρα οὖν ὡς δι' ἑνὸς
reign through the One, Jesus Christ. So then, as through one
3900 1519 3956 444 1519 2631 3779
παραπτώματος εἰς πάντας ἀνθρώπους εἰς κατάκριμα, οὕτω
offense to all men to condemnation, so
1223/1520 1345 1519/3956 444 1519 1347
καὶ δι' ἑνὸς δικαιώματος εἰς πάντας ἀνθρώπους εἰς δικαίωσιν
also through one righteous act to all men to justification
2222 5618 1063/1223 3876 1520 444
19 ζωῆς. ὥσπερ γὰρ διὰ τῆς παρακοῆς τοῦ ἑνὸς ἀνθρώπου
of life. as For through the disobedience of the one man
268 2525 4183 3779 1223
ἁμαρτωλοὶ κατεστάθησαν οἱ πολλοί, οὕτω καὶ διὰ τῆς
sinners were constituted the many, so also through the
5218 1520 1342 2525 4183
ὑπακοῆς τοῦ ἑνὸς δίκαιοι κατασταθήσονται οἱ πολλοί.
obedience of the One righteous will be constituted the many.

in beside, that the offense might abound. But where sin abounded, grace much more abounded, [21]that as sin ruled in death, so also grace might rule through righteousness to everlasting life, through Jesus Christ our Lord.

CHAPTER 6

[1]What then shall we say? Shall we continue in sin that grace may abound? [2]Let it not be! We who died to sin, how shall we still live in it? [3]Or are you ignorant that all who were baptized into Christ Jesus were baptized into His death? [4]Then we were buried with Him through baptism into death, that as Christ was raised up from *the* dead by the glory of the Father, so also we should walk in newness of life. [5]For if we have been joined together in the likeness of His death, so also shall we be in the resurrection; [6]knowing this, that our old man was crucified with *Him*, that the body of sin might be annulled, so that we no longer serve sin. [7]For the *one* that died has been justified from sin. [8]But if we died with Christ, we believe that also we shall live with Him, [9]knowing that Christ being raised from *the* dead dies no more; death no longer lords it over Him. [10]For in that He died, He died to sin once for all; but in that He lives, He lives to God. [11]So also you count yourselves to be truly dead to sin, but alive to God, in Christ Jesus our Lord.

3551 3922 2443 4121 3900 3757
20 νόμος δὲ παρεισῆλθεν, ἵνα πλεονάσῃ τὸ παράπτωμα· οὗ
Law But came in beside, that might abound the offense; where
4121 266 5248 5485 2443
δὲ ἐπλεόνασεν ἡ ἁμαρτία, ὑπερεπερίσσευσεν ἡ χάρις· ἵνα
but abounded the sin, more abounded grace, that
5618 936 266 1722 2288 3779
21 ὥσπερ ἐβασίλευσεν ἡ ἁμαρτία ἐν τῷ θανάτῳ, οὕτω καὶ ἡ
as reigned sin in death, so also
5485 936 1223 1343 1519 2222 166 1223
χάρις βασιλεύσῃ διὰ δικαιοσύνης εἰς ζωὴν αἰώνιον, διὰ
grace might reign through righteousness to life everlasting through
2424 5547 2962 2257
Ἰησοῦ Χριστοῦ τοῦ Κυρίου ἡμῶν.
Jesus Christ the Lord of us.

CHAPTER 6

5101/3767 2046 1961 266 2443 5485
1 Τί οὖν ἐροῦμεν; ἐπιμενοῦμεν τῇ ἁμαρτίᾳ, ἵνα ἡ χάρις
What, then, shall we say? Shall we continue in sin, that grace
4121 3361 1096 3748 599 266
2 πλεονάσῃ; μὴ γένοιτο. οἵτινες ἀπεθάνομεν τῇ ἁμαρτίᾳ,
may abound? Not let it be! who We died to sin,
4459/2089 2198/1722/846/2228/ 50 3754/3745 907
3 πῶς ἔτι ζήσομεν ἐν αὐτῇ; ἢ ἀγνοεῖτε ὅτι ὅσοι ἐβαπτίσθημεν
how still shall we live in it? Or are you ignorant that all who were baptized
1519 5547 2424 1519 2288 848 907
εἰς Χριστὸν Ἰησοῦν, εἰς τὸν θάνατον αὐτοῦ ἐβαπτίσθημεν;
into Christ Jesus, into the death of Him were baptized?
4916 3767 846 1223 908 1519
4 συνετάφημεν οὖν αὐτῷ διὰ τοῦ βαπτίσματος εἰς τὸν
we were buried with Then Him through — baptism into
2288 2443 5618 1453 5547 1537 3498 1223
θάνατον· ἵνα ὥσπερ ἠγέρθη Χριστὸς ἐκ νεκρῶν διὰ τῆς
death, that as was raised Christ from (the) dead through the
1391 3962 3779 2249/1722/ 2538 2222 4043
δόξης τοῦ πατρός, οὕτω καὶ ἡμεῖς ἐν καινότητι ζωῆς περι-
glory of the Father, so also we in newness of life might
1487/1063 4854 1096 3667
5 πατήσωμεν. εἰ γὰρ σύμφυτοι γεγόναμεν τῷ ὁμοιώματι τοῦ
walk. if For united with we have become in the likeness of the
2288 848 235 386 2071 5124
θανάτου αὐτοῦ, ἀλλὰ καὶ τῆς ἀναστάσεως ἐσόμεθα· τοῦτο
death of Him, but also of the resurrection we shall be. this
1097 3754 3820 2257 444 4957
6 γινώσκοντες, ὅτι ὁ παλαιὸς ἡμῶν ἄνθρωπος συνεσταυρώθη,
Knowing, that the old of us man was crucified with,
2443 2673 4983 266 3371 1398
ἵνα καταργηθῇ τὸ σῶμα τῆς ἁμαρτίας, τοῦ μηκέτι δουλεύειν
that might be annulled the body of sin, no longer to serve
2248 266 1063 599 1344 575
7 ἡμᾶς τῇ ἁμαρτίᾳ· ὁ γὰρ ἀποθανὼν δεδικαίωται ἀπὸ τῆς
us sin; the (one) for having died has been justified from
266 1487 599 4862 5547 4100 3754
8 ἁμαρτίας. εἰ δὲ ἀπεθάνομεν σὺν Χριστῷ, πιστεύομεν ὅτι καὶ
sin. if But we died with Christ, we believe that also
4800 846 1492 3754 5547 1453 1537 3498
9 συζήσομεν αὐτῷ· εἰδότες ὅτι Χριστὸς ἐγερθεὶς ἐκ νεκρῶν
we shall live with Him, knowing that Christ having been raised from dead
3765 599 2288 846 3765 2961 1063
10 οὐκέτι ἀποθνήσκει· θάνατος αὐτοῦ οὐκέτι κυριεύει. ὃ γὰρ
no more dies; death Him no more lords it over. that For
599 266 599 2178 3739 2198/2198 2316
ἀπέθανε, τῇ ἁμαρτίᾳ ἀπέθανεν ἐφάπαξ· ὃ δὲ ζῇ, ζῇ τῷ Θεῷ.
He died, to sin He died once for all in that but he lives, he lives to God.
3779 5210 3049 1438 3498 3303 1511
11 οὕτω καὶ ὑμεῖς λογίζεσθε ἑαυτοὺς νεκροὺς μὲν εἶναι τῇ
So also you count yourselves dead indeed to be —
266 2198 2316/1722/ 5547 2424 2962
ἁμαρτίᾳ, ζῶντας δὲ τῷ Θεῷ ἐν Χριστῷ Ἰησοῦ τῷ Κυρίῳ
to sin, living but to God in Christ Jesus the Lord

[12]Therefore, do not let sin rule in your mortal body, to obey it in its lusts. [13]Do not yield your members *as* instruments of unrighteousness to sin; but yield yourselves to God as living from *the* dead, and your members instruments of righteousness to God. [14]For your sin shall not lord it over you, for you are not under law, but under grace.

[15]What then? Shall we sin because we are not under law, but under grace? Let it not be! [16]Do you not know that to whom you yield yourselves slaves for obedience, you are slaves to whom you obey, whether of sin to death, or obedience to righteousness? [17]But thanks to God that you were slaves of sin, but you obeyed from *the* heart the form of teaching to which you were delivered. [18]And having been set free from sin, you were enslaved to righteousness. [19]I speak as a man on account of the weakness of your flesh. For as you yielded your members *as* slaves to uncleanness and to lawless act unto lawless act, so now yield your members *as* slaves to righteousness unto sanctification. [20]For when you were slaves of sin, you were free as to righteousness. [21]Therefore, what fruit did you have then in the *things* over which you now are ashamed? For the end of those things *is* death. [22]But now being set free from sin, and being enslaved to God, you have your fruit unto sanctification, and the end everlasting life. [23]For the wages of sin *is* death; but the free gift of God *is* everlasting

2257
ἡμῶν.
of us.
3361/3767 936 266 1722 2349 5216 4983
12 Μὴ οὖν βασιλευέτω ἡ ἁμαρτία ἐν τῷ θνητῷ ὑμῶν σώματι,
Do not, therefore, let reign sin in the mortal of you body,
1519 5219 846/1722 1939 848 3366 3936
13 εἰς τὸ ὑπακούειν αὐτῇ ἐν ταῖς ἐπιθυμίαις αὐτοῦ· μηδὲ παρι-
to obey it in the lusts of it, neither
3196 5216 3696 93 266 235
στάνετε τὰ μέλη ὑμῶν ὅπλα ἀδικίας τῇ ἁμαρτίᾳ· ἀλλὰ
yield the members of you weapons of unrighteousness to sin, but
3936 1438 2316/5613/1537/3498 2198
παραστήσατε ἑαυτοὺς τῷ Θεῷ ὡς ἐκ νεκρῶν ζῶντας, καὶ τὰ
yield yourselves to God as from (the) dead living, and the
3196 5216 3696 1343 2316 266 1063 5216/3756
14 μέλη ὑμῶν ὅπλα δικαιοσύνης τῷ Θεῷ. ἁμαρτία γὰρ ὑμῶν οὐ
members of you weapons of righteousness to God; sin for of you not
2961 3756/1063/2075/5259/3551 235/5259 5485
κυριεύσει· οὐ γάρ ἐστε ὑπὸ νόμον, ἀλλ᾽ ὑπὸ χάριν.
shall lord it over, not for you are under law, but under grace.
5101/3767 264 3754/3756/2070/5259/3551 235 5259
15 Τί οὖν; ἁμαρτήσομεν, ὅτι οὐκ ἐσμὲν ὑπὸ νόμον, ἀλλ᾽ ὑπὸ
What then? Shall we sin because not we are under law, but under
5485 3361 1096 3756 1492 3754/3739 3936 1438
16 χάριν; μὴ γένοιτο. οὐκ οἴδατε ὅτι ᾧ παριστάνετε ἑαυτοὺς
grace? Not let it be! not Know you that to whom you yield yourselves
1401 1519 5218 1401 2075/3739 5219 2273 266
δούλους εἰς ὑπακοήν, δοῦλοί ἐστε ᾧ ὑπακούετε, ἤτοι ἁμαρ-
slaves for obedience, slaves you are whom you obey, whether of
1519 2288 2228 5218 1519 1343 5485
17 τίας εἰς θάνατον, ἢ ὑπακοῆς εἰς δικαιοσύνην; χάρις δὲ τῷ
sin unto death, or obedience unto righteousness? thanks But
2316/3754/2258/ 1401 266 5219 1537 2588
Θεῷ, ὅτι ἦτε δοῦλοι τῆς ἁμαρτίας, ὑπηκούσατε δὲ ἐκ καρδίας
to God that you were slaves of sin, you obeyed and from the heart
1519/3739 3860 5179 1322 1659 575
18 εἰς ὃν παρεδόθητε τύπον διδαχῆς· ἐλευθερωθέντες δὲ ἀπὸ
to which you were delivered a form of teaching; having been freed And from
266 1402 1343 442 3004
19 τῆς ἁμαρτίας, ἐδουλώθητε τῇ δικαιοσύνῃ. ἀνθρώπινον λέγω
sin, you were enslaved to righteousness. As a man I speak
1223 769 4561 5216 5618 1063 3936
διὰ τὴν ἀσθένειαν τῆς σαρκὸς ὑμῶν· ὥσπερ γὰρ παρεστή-
because of the weakness of the flesh of you. as For you yielded
3196 5216 1400 167 458 1519
σατε τὰ μέλη ὑμῶν δοῦλα τῇ ἀκαθαρσίᾳ καὶ τῇ ἀνομίᾳ εἰς
the members of you slaves — to uncleanness and to iniquity unto
458 3779 3568 3936 3196 5216 1400
τὴν ἀνομίαν, οὕτω νῦν παραστήσατε τὰ μέλη ὑμῶν δοῦλα
iniquity, so now yield the members of you slaves
1343 1519 38 3753/1063 1401 2258
20 τῇ δικαιοσύνῃ εἰς ἁγιασμόν. ὅτε γὰρ δοῦλοι ἦτε τῆς
to righteousness unto sanctification. when For slaves you were
266 1658 2258 1343 5101/3767 2590
21 ἁμαρτίας, ἐλεύθεροι ἦτε τῇ δικαιοσύνῃ. τίνα οὖν καρπὸν
of sin, free you were to righteousness. what Therefore fruit
3739 2192 5119/1909//3568 1870 1063 5056 1565
εἴχετε τότε ἐφ᾽ οἷς νῦν ἐπαισχύνεσθε; τὸ γὰρ τέλος ἐκείνων
had you then? Over which now you are ashamed? the for end of those
2288 3570 1659 575 266 1402
22 θάνατος. νυνὶ δὲ ἐλευθερωθέντες ἀπὸ τῆς ἁμαρτίας, δουλω-
(is) death. now But having been freed from sin, having been
2316 2192 2590 5216/1519 38
θέντες δὲ τῷ Θεῷ, ἔχετε τὸν καρπὸν ὑμῶν εἰς ἁγιασμόν, τὸ
enslaved and to God, you have the fruit of you to sanctification, the
5056 2222 166 1063 3800 266
23 δὲ τέλος ζωὴν αἰώνιον. τὰ γὰρ ὀψώνια τῆς ἁμαρτίας
and end life everlasting. the For wages of sin
2288 5486 2316 2222 166 1722 5547
θάνατος, τὸ δὲ χάρισμα τοῦ Θεοῦ ζωὴ αἰώνιος ἐν Χριστῷ
(is) death, the and gift of God life everlasting in Christ

life in Christ Jesus our Lord.

CHAPTER 7

[1]Or, brothers, are you ignorant—for I speak to those knowing law—that the law rules over the man for as long a time as he may live? [2]For the married woman was bound by law to the living husband; but if the husband dies, she is set free from the law of the husband. [3]So, then, *if* the husband *is* living, she will be called an adulteress if she becomes another man's. But if the husband dies, she is free from the law, *so as for* her not to be an adulteress *by* becoming another man's *wife*. [4]So that, my brothers, you also were made dead to the law through the body of Christ, *for* you to become Another's, to *One* raised from *the* dead, so that we may bear fruit to God. [5]For when we were in the flesh, the passions of sin worked in our members through the law for the bearing of fruit unto death. [6]But now we have been set free from the law, having died *to that* in which we were held, so that we serve in newness of spirit, and not *in* oldness of letter.

[7]What, then, shall we say? *Is* the law sin? Let it not be! But I did not know sin except through law; for also I did not know lust except the law said, You shall not lust. [8]But sin taking occasion through the commandment worked every lust in me; for apart from law, sin was dead. [9]And I was alive apart from law once, but the commandment came, and sin

2424 2962 2257
Ἰησοῦ τῷ Κυρίῳ ἡμῶν.
Jesus the Lord of us.

CHAPTER 7

2228/50 80 1097 1063 3551 2980
1 Ἢ ἀγνοεῖτε, ἀδελφοί (γινώσκουσι γὰρ νόμον λαλῶ),
Or are you ignorant, brothers — to those knowing for law I speak —
3754 3551 3961 444 1909 3745 5550 2198
ὅτι ὁ νόμος κυριεύει τοῦ ἀνθρώπου ἐφ' ὅσον χρόνον ζῇ; ἢ
that the law lords it over the man over such time (as) He lives. the
1063 5220 1135 2198 435 1210 3551 1437
2 γὰρ ὕπανδρος γυνὴ τῷ ζῶντι ἀνδρὶ δέδεται νόμῳ· ἐὰν δὲ
For married woman to the living husband was bound by law; if but
599 435 2673 575 3551 435
ἀποθάνῃ ὁ ἀνήρ, κατήργηται ἀπὸ τοῦ νόμου τοῦ ἀνδρός.
dies the husband, she is freed from the law of the husband.
686 3767 2198 435 3428 5537 1437
3 ἄρα οὖν ζῶντος τοῦ ἀνδρὸς μοιχαλὶς χρηματίσει, ἐὰν
Therefore living the husband, an adulteress she will be called, if
1096 435 2087 1437 599 435 1658
γένηται ἀνδρὶ ἑτέρῳ· ἐὰν δὲ ἀποθάνῃ ὁ ἀνήρ, ἐλευθέρα
she becomes man to another. if But dies the husband, free
2076 575 3551 3361/1511/846 3428 1096
ἐστὶν ἀπὸ τοῦ νόμου, τοῦ μὴ εἶναι αὐτὴν μοιχαλίδα, γενομέ-
she is from the law, not being her an adulteress becoming
435 2087 5620 80 3450 5210 2289
4 νην ἀνδρὶ ἑτέρῳ. ὥστε, ἀδελφοί μου, καὶ ὑμεῖς ἐθανατώθητε
(wife) man to another. So, brothers of me, also you were made dead
3551/1223 4983 5547 1519 1096
τῷ νόμῳ διὰ τοῦ σώματος τοῦ Χριστοῦ, εἰς τὸ γενέσθαι
to the law through the body — of Christ, to become
5209 2087 1537 3498 1453 2443 2592
ὑμᾶς ἑτέρῳ, τῷ ἐκ νεκρῶν ἐγερθέντι, ἵνα καρποφορήσωμεν
you to Another, to (One) from dead raised, that we may bear fruit
2316 3753/1063/2258 1722 4561 3804
5 τῷ Θεῷ. ὅτε γὰρ ἦμεν ἐν τῇ σαρκί, τὰ παθήματα τῶν
to God. when For we were in the flesh, the passions
266 1223 3551 1754 1722 3196
ἁμαρτιῶν τὰ διὰ τοῦ νόμου ἐνηργεῖτο ἐν τοῖς μέλεσιν
of sin through the law working in the members
2257/1519 2592 2288 3570 2673
6 ἡμῶν εἰς τὸ καρποφορῆσαι τῷ θανάτῳ. νυνὶ δὲ κατηργήθη-
of us for the bearing of fruit to death. now But we having been
575 3551 599 1722/3739/ 2722 5620
μεν ἀπὸ τοῦ νόμου, ἀποθανόντος ἐν ᾧ κατειχόμεθα, ὥστε
freed from the law, dying (to that) in which we were held, so as
1398 2248/1722/ 2538 4151 3756/ 3821
δουλεύειν ἡμᾶς ἐν καινότητι πνεύματος, καὶ οὐ παλαιότητι
to serve us in newness of spirit and not (in) oldness
1121
γράμματος.
of letter.

5101/3767 2046 3551 266 3361 1096 235
7 Τί οὖν ἐροῦμεν; ὁ νόμος ἁμαρτία; μὴ γένοιτο· ἀλλὰ τὴν
What then shall we say? (is) the law sin? Not let it be! But
266 3756/ 1097 =1508= 1223 3551 5037/1063/ 1939
ἁμαρτίαν οὐκ ἔγνων, εἰ μὴ διὰ νόμου· τήν τε γὰρ ἐπιθυμίαν
sin not I knew, except through law also For lust
3756/1492 =1508= 3551 3004 3756 1937 874
8 οὐκ ᾔδειν, εἰ μὴ ὁ νόμος ἔλεγεν, Οὐκ ἐπιθυμήσεις· ἀφορμὴν
not I knew, except the law said, not You shall lust. occasion
2983 266 1223 1785 2716 1722
δὲ λαβοῦσα ἡ ἁμαρτία διὰ τῆς ἐντολῆς κατειργάσατο ἐν
But taking sin through the commandment worked in
1698 3956 1939 5565 1063 3551 266 3498
ἐμοὶ πᾶσαν ἐπιθυμίαν· χωρὶς γὰρ νόμου ἁμαρτία νεκρά.
me every lust; without for law sin (is) dead.
1473 2198 5565 3551 4218 2064 1785
9 ἐγὼ δὲ ἔζων χωρὶς νόμου ποτέ· ἐλθούσης δὲ τῆς ἐντολῆς,
I And was living without law then, coming but the commandmen

came alive, and I died.
[10]And the commandment
which *was* to life, this was
found *to be* death to me;
[11]for sin taking occasion
through the command-
ment deceived me, and
through it killed *me.*

[12]So indeed the law *is*
holy, and the command-
ment holy and just and
good. [13]Then that which *is*
good, has it become death
to me? Let it not be! But sin,
that it might appear *to be*
sin, having worked out
death to me through the
good, in order that sin
might become excessive-
ly sinful through the commandment. [14]For we know
that the law is spiritual, and
I am fleshly, having been
sold under sin. [15]For what
I work out, I do not know.
For what I do not desire,
this I do. But what I hate,
this I do. [16]But if I do what I
do not desire, I agree with
the law, that *it is* good.

[17]But now I no longer work
it out, but the sin dwelling
in me. [18]For I know that
in me, that is in my flesh,
dwells no good. For to desire is present to me, but to
work out the good I do not
find. [19]For what good I
desire, I do not. But the evil
I do not desire, this I do.
[20]But if I do what I do not
desire, *it is* no longer I
working it out, but the sin
dwelling in me. [21]I find
then the law, *when* I desire
to do the right, that evil is
present with me. [22]For I
delight in the law of God
according to the inward
man; [23]but I see another
law in my members war-
ring against the law of my
mind, and taking me cap-
tive by the law of sin being
in my members. [24]O
wretched man *that* I *am*!

266 326 1473 599 2147 3427
10 ἡ ἁμαρτία ἀνέζησεν, ἐγὼ δὲ ἀπέθανον· καὶ εὑρέθη μοι ἡ
sin revived, I and died, and was found to me the
1785 1519 2222 3778 1519 2288 1063 266
11 ἐντολὴ ἡ εἰς ζωήν, αὕτη εἰς θάνατον· ἡ γὰρ ἁμαρτία
command-ment for life, this to death (was). For sin
2983 1223 1785 3165 1223
ἀφορμὴν λαβοῦσα διὰ τῆς ἐντολῆς ἐξηπάτησέ με, καὶ δι'
occasion taking through the command deceived me, and through
846 615 5620 3303 3551 40 1785
12 αὐτῆς ἀπέκτεινεν. ὥστε ὁ μὲν νόμος ἅγιος, καὶ ἡ ἐντολὴ
it killed (me). So the indeed law (is) holy, and the command-ment
40 1342 18 3767 18 1698 1096
13 ἁγία καὶ δικαία καὶ ἀγαθή. τὸ οὖν ἀγαθὸν ἐμοὶ γέγονε
holy and just and good. the Then good to me (has it) become
2288 3361 1096 235 266 2443 5316 266
θάνατος; μὴ γένοιτο. ἀλλὰ ἡ ἁμαρτία, ἵνα φανῇ ἁμαρτία,
death? Not let it be! But sin, that it appear sin.
1223 18 3427 2716 2288 2443 1096
διὰ τοῦ ἀγαθοῦ μοι κατεργαζομένη θάνατον,—ἵνα γένηται
through the good to me having worked out death, that may become
2596 5236 268 266 1223 1785
καθ' ὑπερβολὴν ἁμαρτωλὸς ἡ ἁμαρτία διὰ τῆς ἐντολῆς.
excessively sinful sin through the commandment.
1492 1063/3754 3551 4152 2076/1473 4559
14 οἴδαμεν γὰρ ὅτι ὁ νόμος πνευματικός ἐστιν· ἐγὼ δὲ σαρκικός
we know For that the law spiritual is; I but fleshly
1510 4097 5259 266 1063 2716
15 εἰμι, πεπραμένος ὑπὸ τὴν ἁμαρτίαν. ὃ γὰρ κατεργάζομαι,
am, having been sold under sin. what For I work,
3756 1097 3756/1063 2309 5124 4238 235/3739/3404
οὐ γινώσκω· οὐ γὰρ ὃ θέλω, τοῦτο πράσσω· ἀλλ' ὃ μισῶ,
not I know; not for what I desire, this I practice; but what I hate,
5124 4160/1487 3739/3756/2309 5124 4160 4852
16 τοῦτο ποιῶ. εἰ δὲ ὃ οὐ θέλω, τοῦτο ποιῶ, σύμφημι τῷ
this I do. if But what not I desire, this I do, I agree with the
3551 3754 2570 3570 3765 1473 2716 846
17 νόμῳ ὅτι καλός. νυνὶ δὲ οὐκέτι ἐγὼ κατεργάζομαι αὐτό,
law that (it is) good. now But no longer I work out it,
235 3611 1722/1698/ 266 1492/1063/3754/3756/3611/1722
18 ἀλλ' ἡ οἰκοῦσα ἐν ἐμοὶ ἁμαρτία. οἶδα γὰρ ὅτι οὐκ οἰκεῖ ἐν
but the indwelling in me sin. I know For that not dwells in
1698 5123 2076/1722 4561 3450 18 1063 2309
ἐμοί, τοῦτ' ἔστιν ἐν τῇ σαρκί μου, ἀγαθόν· τὸ γὰρ θέλειν
me this is in the flesh of me the good; for to desire
3873 3427 2716 2570 3756 2147
παράκειταί μοι, τὸ δὲ κατεργάζεσθαι τὸ καλὸν οὐχ εὑρίσκω.
Is present to me, but to work out the good not I find.
3756/1063 2309 4160 18 235/3739/3756/2309/2556 5124
19 οὐ γὰρ ὃ θέλω, ποιῶ ἀγαθόν· ἀλλ' ὃ οὐ θέλω κακόν, τοῦτο
not For what I desire I do good, but what not I desire, evil this
4238 1487/3739/3756/2309/1473/5124 4160 3765 1473 2716
20 πράσσω. εἰ δὲ ὃ οὐ θέλω ἐγώ, τοῦτο ποιῶ, οὐκέτι ἐγὼ κατερ-
I practice. if But what not desire I, this I do, no longer I work
846 235 3611 1722/1698/ 266 2147 686
21 γάζομαι αὐτό, ἀλλ' ἡ οἰκοῦσα ἐν ἐμοὶ ἁμαρτία. εὑρίσκω ἄρα
out it, but the dwelling in me sin. I find, then,
3551 2309 1698 4160 2570 3754/1698 2556
τὸν νόμον τῷ θέλοντι ἐμοὶ ποιεῖν τὸ καλόν, ὅτι ἐμοὶ τὸ κακὸν
the law, the (one) desiring me to do the good, that to me the evil
3873 4913 1063 3551 2316 2596
22 παράκειται. συνήδομαι γὰρ τῷ νόμῳ τοῦ Θεοῦ κατὰ τὸν
is present. I delight For in the law of God according to the
2080 444 991 2087 3551/1722 3196 3450
23 ἔσω ἄνθρωπον· βλέπω δὲ ἕτερον νόμον ἐν τοῖς μέλεσί μου
inner man. I see But another law in the members of me
497 3551 3563/3450 163
ἀντιστρατευόμενον τῷ νόμῳ τοῦ νοός μου, καὶ αἰχμαλωτί-
having warred against the law of the mind of me, and taking captive
3165 3551 266 5607/1722 3196 3450
ζοντά με τῷ νόμῳ τῆς ἁμαρτίας τῷ ὄντι ἐν τοῖς μέλεσί μου.
me by the law of sin, the (one) being in the members of me.

Who will deliver me from the body of this death? [25]I thank God through Jesus Christ our Lord! So then I myself with the mind truly serve *the* law of God, and *with* the flesh *the* law of sin.

CHAPTER 8

[1]*There is* therefore now no condemnation to those in Christ Jesus, who do not walk according to flesh, but according to Spirit. [2]For the law of the Spirit of life in Christ Jesus set me free from the law of sin and of death. [3]For the law *being* powerless, in that it was weak through the flesh, God sending His own Son in *the* likeness of sinful flesh, and concerning sin, condemned sin in the flesh. [4]So that the righteous demand of the law might be fulfilled in us, those not walking according to flesh, but according to Spirit. [5]For the ones that are according to flesh mind the things of the flesh. And the ones according to Spirit *mind* the things of the Spirit. [6]For the mind of the flesh *is* death; but the mind of the Spirit *is* life and peace; [7]because of this the mind of the flesh *is* enmity towards God; for it is not subject to the law of God, for neither can *it be*. [8]And those being in the flesh are not able to please God. [9]But you are not in flesh, but in Spirit, since *the* Spirit of God dwells in you. But if anyone has not *the* Spirit of Christ, this one is not His. [10]But if Christ *is* in you, the body indeed is dead because of sin, but the Spirit *is* life because of righteousness. [11]But if the Spirit of the *One* having raised Jesus from *the* dead

5005 1473 444 5101/3165/ 4506/1537 4983
24 ταλαίπωρος ἐγὼ ἄνθρωπος· τίς με ῥύσεται ἐκ τοῦ σώματος
Wretched I man! Who me will deliver from the body
2288 5127 2168 2316/1223/2424 5547
25 τοῦ θανάτου τούτου; εὐχαριστῶ τῷ Θεῷ διὰ Ἰησοῦ Χρι-
death of this? I thank God through Jesus Christ
2962 2257 686/3767/848/1473 3303/3583/1398
στοῦ τοῦ Κυρίου ἡμῶν. ἄρα οὖν αὐτὸς ἐγὼ τῷ μὲν νοῒ δουλεύω
the Lord of us. So then myself, I truly with the serve
3551/2316 4561 3551 266 mind
νόμῳ Θεοῦ, τῇ δὲ σαρκὶ νόμῳ ἁμαρτίας.
(the) law of God, the and flesh (the) law of sin.

CHAPTER 8

3762 686 3568 2631 1722 5547 2424 3361 2596
1 Οὐδὲν ἄρα νῦν κατάκριμα τοῖς ἐν Χριστῷ Ἰησοῦ, μὴ κατὰ
no Therefore now condemnation to those in Christ Jesus, not accor-
4561 4043 235 2596 151 1063 3551 ding to
2 σάρκα περιπατοῦσιν, ἀλλὰ κατὰ πνεῦμα. ὁ γὰρ νόμος τοῦ
flesh walking, but according to Spirit. the For law of the
4151 2222/1722/ 5547 2424 1659 3165 575
πνεύματος τῆς ζωῆς ἐν Χριστῷ Ἰησοῦ ἠλευθέρωσέ με ἀπὸ
Spirit of life in Christ Jesus set free me from
3551 266 2288 1063 102
3 τοῦ νόμου τῆς ἁμαρτίας καὶ τοῦ θανάτου. τὸ γὰρ ἀδύνατον
the law of sin and of death. the For powerless
3551/1722/3739/770 1223 4561 2316 1438
τοῦ νόμου, ἐν ᾧ ἠσθένει διὰ τῆς σαρκός, ὁ Θεὸς τὸν ἑαυτοῦ
law, in which it was weak via the flesh, God the of Himself
5207 3992 1722 3667 4561 266 4012 266
υἱὸν πέμψας ἐν ὁμοιώματι σαρκὸς ἁμαρτίας καὶ περὶ ἁμαρ-
Son sending in likeness of flesh of sin, and concerning sin
2632 266 1722 4561 2443 1345
4 τίας κατέκρινε τὴν ἁμαρτίαν ἐν τῇ σαρκί· ἵνα τὸ δικαίωμα
condemned sin in the flesh, that righteous demand
3551 4137 1722/2254 3361 2596 4561 4043
τοῦ νόμου πληρωθῇ ἐν ἡμῖν, τοῖς μὴ κατὰ σάρκα περιπατοῦ-
of the law may be fulfilled in us, those not by flesh walking,
235 2596 4151 1063 2596 4561 5607
5 σιν, ἀλλὰ κατὰ πνεῦμα. οἱ γὰρ κατὰ σάρκα ὄντες τὰ τῆς
but according to Spirit. those For according to flesh being the things
4561 5426 2596 4151 4151
σαρκὸς φρονοῦσιν· οἱ δὲ κατὰ πνεῦμα τὰ τοῦ πνεύματος. τὸ
of flesh mind; those but by Spirit the things of the Spirit. the
1063 5427 4561 2288 5427 4151
6 γὰρ φρόνημα τῆς σαρκὸς θάνατος· τὸ δὲ φρόνημα τοῦ πνεύ-
For mind of the flesh (is) death; the but mind of the Spirit
2222 1515 1360 5427 4561 2189
7 ματος ζωὴ καὶ εἰρήνη· διότι τὸ φρόνημα τῆς σαρκὸς ἔχθρα
(is) life and peace. Therefore the mind of the flesh (is) enmity
1519/2316 1063 3551 2316 3756 5293 3761
εἰς Θεόν, τῷ γὰρ νόμῳ τοῦ Θεοῦ οὐχ ὑποτάσσεται, οὐδὲ
against God, to the for law of God not it is subject, neither
1063 1410 1722 4561 5607 2316 700 3756 1410
8 γὰρ δύναται· οἱ δὲ ἐν σαρκὶ ὄντες Θεῷ ἀρέσαι οὐ δύνανται.
for can (be); those and in flesh being God to please not are able
5210 3756/2075/1722/4561 235/1722/ 4151 1512 4151
9 ὑμεῖς δὲ οὐκ ἐστὲ ἐν σαρκί, ἀλλ' ἐν πνεύματι, εἴπερ Πνεῦμα
you But not are in flesh, but in Spirit, since (the) Spirit
2316/3611/1722/5213/1487/5100 4150 5547 3756/2192 3778
Θεοῦ οἰκεῖ ἐν ὑμῖν. εἰ δέ τις Πνεῦμα Χριστοῦ οὐκ ἔχει, οὗτος
of God dwells in you. if But anyone (the) Spirit of Christ not has, this one
3756/2076 848 1487 5547 1722/5213 3303 4983 3498
10 οὐκ ἔστιν αὐτοῦ. εἰ δὲ Χριστὸς ἐν ὑμῖν, τὸ μὲν σῶμα νεκρὸν
not is of Him. if But Christ (is) in you, the indeed body (is) dead
1223 266 4151 2222/1223 1343 1487
11 δι' ἁμαρτίαν, τὸ δὲ πνεῦμα ζωὴ διὰ δικαιοσύνην. εἰ δὲ τὸ
because of sin, the but Spirit (is) life because of righteousness. if But the
4151 1453 2424 1537 3498 3611/1722/5213
Πνεῦμα τοῦ ἐγείραντος Ἰησοῦν ἐκ νεκρῶν οἰκεῖ ἐν ὑμῖν, ὁ
Spirit of the (One) raising Jesus from (the) dead dwells in you, the (One)

dwells in you, the *One* having raised the Christ from *the* dead will also make your mortal bodies live through the indwelling of His Spirit in you.

[12]So, then, brothers, we are debtors, not to the flesh, to live according to flesh; [13]for if you live according to flesh, you are going to die. But if by *the* Spirit you put to death the practices of the body, you will live. [14]For as many as are led by *the* Spirit of God, these are sons of God. [15]For you did not receive a spirit of slavery again to fear, but you received a Spirit of adoption by which we cry, Abba! Father! [16]The Spirit Himself witnesses with our spirit that we are children of God. [17]And if children, also heirs; truly heirs of God, and joint-heirs of Christ; if indeed we suffer together, that we may also be glorified together.

[18]For I calculate that the sufferings of the present time *are* not worthy *to compare* to the coming glory to be revealed in us. [19]For the earnest expectation of the creation is eagerly expecting the revelation of the sons of God. [20]For the creation was not willingly subjected to vanity, but through Him subjecting *it*, on hope; [21]that also the creation will be freed from the slavery of corruption to the freedom of the glory of the children of God. [22]For we know that all the creation groans together and travails together until now. [23]And not only *so*, but we ourselves having the firstfruit of the Spirit, also we ourselves groan within ourselves, eagerly expecting adoption, the redemption of our body;

1453 5547 1537 3498 2227 2349
ἐγείρας τὸν Χριστὸν ἐκ νεκρῶν ζωοποιήσει καὶ τὰ θνητὰ
having raised the Christ from (the) dead will make live also the mortal
4983 5216 1223 1774 848 4151 1722
σώματα ὑμῶν, διὰ τοῦ ἐνοικοῦντος αὐτοῦ Πνεύματος ἐν
bodies of you, through the indwelling of Him Spirit in
5213
ὑμῖν.
you.

686/3767 80 3781 2070/3756 4561 2596
12 Ἄρα οὖν, ἀδελφοί, ὀφειλέται ἐσμέν, οὐ τῇ σαρκί, τοῦ κατὰ
So then, brothers, debtors we are, not to the flesh — according to
4561 2198/1487/1063/2596/ 4561 2198 3195 599
13 σάρκα ζῆν· εἰ γὰρ κατὰ σάρκα ζῆτε, μέλλετε ἀποθνήσκειν·
flesh to live. if For according to flesh you live, you are going to die;
1487 4151 4234 4983 2289 2198
εἰ δὲ πνεύματι τὰς πράξεις τοῦ σώματος θανατοῦτε, ζήσεσθε.
if but by (the) Spirit the practices of the body you put to death, you will live.
3745/1063 4151 2316 71 3778 1526 5207 2316
14 ὅσοι γὰρ Πνεύματι Θεοῦ ἄγονται, οὗτοί εἰσιν υἱοὶ Θεοῦ.
as many as For by Spirit of God are led, these are sons of God.
3756/1063 2983 4151 1397 3825 1519 5401 235
15 οὐ γὰρ ἐλάβετε πνεῦμα δουλείας πάλιν εἰς φόβον, ἀλλ'
not For you received a spirit of slavery again to fear, but
2983 4151 5206 1722/3739/ 2896 5 3962
ἐλάβετε πνεῦμα υἱοθεσίας, ἐν ᾧ κράζομεν, Ἀββᾶ, ὁ πατήρ.
you received a Spirit of adoption, by which we cry. Abba, Father!
846 4151 4828 4151 2257 3754 2070
16 αὐτὸ τὸ Πνεῦμα συμμαρτυρεῖ τῷ πνεύματι ἡμῶν, ὅτι ἐσμὲν
itself The Spirit bears witness with the spirit of us, that we are
5043 2316 1487 5043 2818 2818 3303
17 τέκνα Θεοῦ· εἰ δὲ τέκνα, καὶ κληρονόμοι· κληρονόμοι μὲν
children of God. if And children, also heirs; heirs truly
2316 4789 5547 1512 4841 2443
Θεοῦ, συγκληρονόμοι δὲ Χριστοῦ· εἴπερ συμπάσχομεν, ἵνα
of God, joint-heirs and of Christ; if indeed we suffer together, that
4888
καὶ συνδοξασθῶμεν.
also we may be glorified together.

3049 1063/3754/3756/514 3804 3568 2540
18 Λογίζομαι γὰρ ὅτι οὐκ ἄξια τὰ παθήματα τοῦ νῦν καιροῦ
I calculate For that not worthy the sufferings of the present time
4314 3195 1391 601 1519/2248 1063
19 πρὸς τὴν μέλλουσαν δόξαν ἀποκαλυφθῆναι εἰς ἡμᾶς. ἡ γὰρ
to the coming glory to be revealed in us. the For
603 2937 602 5207
ἀποκαραδοκία τῆς κτίσεως τὴν ἀποκάλυψιν τῶν υἱῶν τοῦ
earnest expectation of the creation the revelation of the sons
2316 553 1063 3153 2937 5293
20 Θεοῦ ἀπεκδέχεται. τῇ γὰρ ματαιότητι ἡ κτίσις ὑπετάγη,
of God is eagerly expecting. For to vanity the creation was subjected,
3756 1635 235 1223 5293 1909 1680 3754
21 οὐχ ἑκοῦσα, ἀλλὰ διὰ τὸν ὑποτάξαντα, ἐπ' ἐλπίδι· ὅτι καὶ
not willingly, but through Him subjecting, on hope, that also
848 2937 1659 575 1397
αὐτὴ ἡ κτίσις ἐλευθερωθήσεται ἀπὸ τῆς δουλείας τῆς
itself the creation will be freed from the slavery —
5356 1519 1657 1391 5043 2316
φθορᾶς εἰς τὴν ἐλευθερίαν τῆς δόξης τῶν τέκνων τοῦ Θεοῦ.
of corruption to the freedom of the glory of the children — of God.
1492 1063/3754/3956 2937 4959 4944
22 οἴδαμεν γὰρ ὅτι πᾶσα ἡ κτίσις συστενάζει καὶ συνωδίνει
we know For that all the creation groans together and travails
891 3568/3756/3440 235 848 536
23 ἄχρι τοῦ νῦν. οὐ μόνον δέ, ἀλλὰ καὶ αὐτοὶ τὴν ἀπαρχὴν
until now. not only And (so) but also ourselves the firstfruit
4151 2192 2249 848 1722 1438 4727
τοῦ Πνεύματος ἔχοντες, καὶ ἡμεῖς αὐτοὶ ἐν ἑαυτοῖς στενά-
of the Spirit having, also we ourselves in ourselves having
5206 553 629
ζομεν, υἱοθεσίαν ἀπεκδεχόμενοι, τὴν ἀπολύτρωσιν τοῦ
groaned, adoption eagerly expecting, the redemption of the

[24]for we were being saved by hope; but hope being seen is not hope; for what anyone sees, why does he also hope? [25]But if we hope for what we do not see, through patience we eagerly expect.

[26]And likewise the Spirit also joins in to help our weakness. For we do not know what we should pray *for* as we ought, but the Spirit Himself pleads our case for us with groanings that cannot be uttered. [27]But the *One* searching the hearts knows what *is the* mind of the Spirit, because He intercedes for the saints according to God. [28]But we know that all things work together for good to those who love God, to those who are called according to purpose; [29]because whom He foreknew, He also predestinated *to be* conformed to the image of His Son, for Him to be *the* firstborn among many brothers. [30]But whom He predestinated, these He also called; and whom He called, these He also justified; but whom He justified, these He also glorified.

[31]What then shall we say to these things? If God *be* for us, who against us? [32]Truly *He* who did not spare His own Son, but gave Him up for us all, how will He not freely give us all things with Him? [33]Who will bring any charge against God's elect? God *is* the *One* justifying! [34]Who *is he* condemning. Christ *is* the *One* who has died, but rather also *is* raised, who also is at *the* right *hand* of God; who also intercedes for us. [35]Who shall separate us from the love of Christ? *Shall* tribulation, or distress, or persecution, or famine, or nakedness, or

4983 2257 1063 1680 4982 1680 991
24 σώματος ἡμῶν. τῇ γὰρ ἐλπίδι ἐσώθημεν· ἐλπὶς δὲ βλεπομένη
body of us. For by hope we were being hope but being seen
3756/2076/1680 1063 991 5101 saved,1679 1487 3739/3756
25 οὐκ ἔστιν ἐλπίς· ὃ γὰρ βλέπει τις, τί καὶ ἐλπίζει ; εἰ δὲ ὃ οὐ
not is hope; what for sees anyone, why also he hopes? if But what not
991 1679 1223 5281 553
βλέπομεν ἐλπίζομεν, δι' ὑπομονῆς ἀπεκδεχόμεθα.
we see we hope (for). through patience we eagerly expect.
5615 4151 4878
26 Ὡσαύτως δὲ καὶ τὸ Πνεῦμα συναντιλαμβάνεται ταῖς
likewise And also the Spirit joins in to help the
769 2257 1063/5101 4336 2526/1163/3756
ἀσθενείαις ἡμῶν· τὸ γὰρ τί προσευξώμεθα καθὸ δεῖ, οὐκ
weaknesses of us, for what we may pray (for) as we ought, not
1492 235 848 4151 5241 5228 2257
οἴδαμεν, ἀλλ' αὐτὸ τὸ πνεῦμα ὑπερεντυγχάνει ὑπὲρ ἡμῶν
we know, but itself the Spirit pleads our case for us
4726 215 2045 2588 1492/5101
27 στεναγμοῖς ἀλαλήτοις· ὁ δὲ ἐρευνῶν τὰς καρδίας οἶδε τί τὸ
with groanings unutterable. He But searching the hearts knows what (is)
5427 4151 3754/2596/ 2316 1793 5228
φρόνημα τοῦ Πνεύματος, ὅτι κατὰ Θεὸν ἐντυγχάνει ὑπὲρ
(the) mind of the Spirit, because according to God He intercedes for
40 1492 3754 25 2316 3956
28 ἁγίων. οἴδαμεν δὲ ὅτι τοῖς ἀγαπῶσι τὸν Θεὸν πάντα
saints. we know And that to the (ones) loving God, all things
4903/1519 18 2596 4286 2822 5607 3754
29 συνεργεῖ εἰς ἀγαθόν, τοῖς κατὰ πρόθεσιν κλητοῖς οὖσιν. ὅτι
work together for good, to those according to purpose called being. Because
3739 4267 4309 4832 1504 5207
οὓς προέγνω, καὶ προώρισε συμμόρφους τῆς εἰκόνος τοῦ υἱοῦ
whom He foreknew also He predestinated conformed to the image of the Son
848 1519 1511 846 4416 1722 4183 80
αὐτοῦ, εἰς τὸ εἶναι αὐτὸν πρωτότοκον ἐν πολλοῖς ἀδελφοῖς·
of Him, for to be Him firstborn among many brothers;
3739 4309 5128 2563 3739 2564 5128
30 οὓς δὲ προώρισε, τούτους καὶ ἐκάλεσε· καὶ οὓς ἐκάλεσε, τού-
whom but He predestinated,these also He called, and whom He called,
1344 3739 1344 5128 1392
τους καὶ ἐδικαίωσεν· οὓς δὲ ἐδικαίωσε, τούτους καὶ ἐδόξασε.
these also He justified; whom but He justified, these also He glorified.
5101/3767/2046 4314 5023 1487 2316 5228 2257 5101
31 Τί οὖν ἐροῦμεν πρὸς ταῦτα ; εἰ ὁ Θεὸς ὑπὲρ ἡμῶν, τίς
What then shall we say to these things? If God (be) for us, who
2596 2257 3739/1065 2398 5207/3756 5339 235 5228
32 καθ' ἡμῶν ; ὅς γε τοῦ ἰδίου υἱοῦ οὐκ ἐφείσατο, ἀλλ' ὑπὲρ
against us? (He) who truly the own Son not spared, but for
2257 3956 3860 846 4459 3780 4862 846
ἡμῶν πάντων παρέδωκεν αὐτόν, πῶς οὐχὶ καὶ σὺν αὐτῷ
us all gave up Him, how not also with Him
3956 2254 5483 5101 1458 2596 1588
33 τὰ πάντα ἡμῖν χαρίσεται ; τίς ἐγκαλέσει κατὰ ἐκλεκτῶν
all things to us will He freely give? Who will bring charge against the elect
2316 2316 1344 5101 2632 5547 599
34 Θεοῦ ; Θεὸς ὁ δικαιῶν· τίς ὁ κατακρίνων ; Χριστὸς ὁ ἀπο-
of God? God (is) He justifying. Who condemning? Christ (is) He having
3123 1453 3739 2076/1722/1188 2316
θανών, μᾶλλον δὲ καὶ ἐγερθείς, ὃς καὶ ἔστιν ἐν δεξιᾷ τοῦ Θεοῦ,
died, rather but also raised, who also is at (the) right (hand) of God,
3739 1793 5228 2257 5101 2248 5563 575
35 ὃς καὶ ἐντυγχάνει ὑπὲρ ἡμῶν. τίς ἡμᾶς χωρίσει ἀπὸ τῆς
who also intercedes for us. Who us shall separate from the
26 5547 2347 2228 4730 2228 1375 2228
ἀγάπης τοῦ Χριστοῦ ; θλῖψις, ἢ στενοχωρία, ἢ διωγμός, ἢ
love of Christ? (Shall tribulation, or distress, or persecuting, or
3042/2228/ 1132 2228 2794 2228 3162 2531 1125
36 λιμός, ἢ γυμνότης, ἢ κίνδυνος, ἢ μάχαιρα ; καθὼς γέγραπται
famine, or nakedness, or danger, or sword? Even as it has been written,
3754 1752 4675 2289 3650 2250 3049
ὅτι Ἕνεκά σου θανατούμεθα ὅλην τὴν ἡμέραν· ἐλογίσθημεν
For the sake of You we are killed all the day; we are counted

danger, or sword? [36]Even
as it has been written, "For
Your sake we are killed all
the day *long;* we are
counted as sheep of
slaughter." [37]But in all
these things we more than
conquer through the *One*
loving us. [38]For I am
persuaded that neither
death, nor life, nor angels,
nor rulers, nor powers, nor
things present, nor things
to come, [39]nor height, nor
depth, nor any other
creature will be able to
separate us from the love
of God in Christ Jesus, our
Lord.

CHAPTER 9

[1]I tell *the* truth in Christ, I
do not lie, my conscience
bearing witness with me in
the Holy Spirit, [2]that my
grief is great, and *a* never-
ceasing pain *is* in my heart,
[3]for I myself was wishing
to be a curse from Christ on
behalf of my brothers, my
kinsmen according to flesh;
[4]who are Israelites; whose
are the adoption and the
glory, and the covenants,
and the Law-giving, and the
service, and the promises;
[5]whose *are* the fathers; and
of whom *is* the Christ
according to flesh, He
being God over all, blessed
forever. Amen.

[6]Not, however, that the
word of God has failed. For
not all those of Israel *are*
Israel; [7]nor because they
are Abraham's seed *are* all
children, but "In Isaac a
Seed will be called to you."
[8]That is: Not the children of
the flesh *are* children of
God, but the children of the
promise *are* counted for a
seed. [9]For the word of
promise *is* this, "According
to this time I will come, and
a son will be to Sarah."
[10]And not only *so,* but also
Rebekah conceiving from
one, our father Isaac; [11]for
the children not yet being
born, nor having done any

5613 4263 4967 235/1722/5125 3956 5245 1223
37 ὡς πρόβατα σφαγῆς. ἀλλ' ἐν τούτοις πᾶσιν ὑπερνικῶμεν διὰ
as sheep of slaughter. But in these things all we overconquer through
25 2248 3982 1063/3754/3777 2288
38 τοῦ ἀγαπήσαντος ἡμᾶς. πέπεισμαι γὰρ ὅτι οὔτε θάνατος
the (One) loving us. I have been persuaded For that not death
3777 2222 3777 32 3777 746 3777 1411 3777
οὔτε ζωὴ οὔτε ἄγγελοι οὔτε ἀρχαὶ οὔτε δυνάμεις οὔτε
nor life nor angels nor rulers nor powers nor
1764 3777 3195 3777 5313 3777 899 3777/5100
39 ἐνεστῶτα οὔτε μέλλοντα οὔτε ὕψωμα οὔτε βάθος οὔτε τις
things present nor things coming nor height nor depth nor any
2937 2087 1410 2248 5583 575 26
κτίσις ἑτέρα δυνήσεται ἡμᾶς χωρίσαι ἀπὸ τῆς ἀγάπης τοῦ
creature other will be able us to separate from the love
2316 1722 5547 2424 2962 2257
Θεοῦ τῆς ἐν Χριστῷ Ἰησοῦ τῷ Κυρίῳ ἡμῶν.
of God in Christ Jesus the Lord of us.

CHAPTER 9

225 3004/1722/5547/3756/ 5574 4828
1 Ἀλήθειαν λέγω ἐν Χριστῷ, οὐ ψεύδομαι, συμμαρτυρούσης
(the) truth I tell in Christ, not I lie, bearing witness with
3427 4893 3450/1722/ 4151 40 3754 3077 3427
2 μοι τῆς συνειδήσεώς μου ἐν Πνεύματι Ἁγίῳ. ὅτι λύπη μοι
me the conscience of me in (the) Spirit Holy, that grief to me
2076 3173 88 3601 2588 3450 2172
3 ἐστὶ μεγάλη, καὶ ἀδιάλειπτος ὀδύνη τῇ καρδίᾳ μου. ηὐχόμην
is great and never ceasing pain in the heart of me. was wishing
1063 848 1473 331 1511 575 5547 5228
γὰρ αὐτὸς ἐγὼ ἀνάθεμα εἶναι ἀπὸ τοῦ Χριστοῦ ὑπὲρ τῶν
For myself I a curse to be from Christ on behalf of the
80 3450 4773 3450/2596/ 4561 3748 1526
4 ἀδελφῶν μου, τῶν συγγενῶν μου κατὰ σάρκα· οἵτινές εἰσιν
brothers of me, the kinsmen of me according to flesh; who are
2475 3739 5206 1391 1242
Ἰσραηλῖται, ὧν ἡ υἱοθεσία καὶ ἡ δόξα καὶ αἱ διαθῆκαι καὶ ἡ
Israelites, of whom the adoption and the glory, and the covenants and the
3548 2999 1860 3739 3962
5 νομοθεσία καὶ ἡ λατρεία καὶ αἱ ἐπαγγελίαι, ὧν οἱ πατέρες,
law-giving, and the service and the promises; of whom the fathers,
1537/3739 5547 2596 4561 3739/1909/3956 2316
καὶ ἐξ ὧν ὁ Χριστὸς τὸ κατὰ σάρκα, ὁ ὢν ἐπὶ πάντων, Θεὸς
and from whom the Christ according to flesh, He being over all, God
2128 1519 165 281 3756/3634 3754 1601
6 εὐλογητὸς εἰς τοὺς αἰῶνας. ἀμήν. οὐχ οἷον δὲ ὅτι ἐκπέπτωκεν
blessed to the ages. Amen. Not, however, that has failed
3056 2316 3756/1063 3956 1537 2474 3778
ὁ λόγος τοῦ Θεοῦ. οὐ γὰρ πάντες οἱ ἐξ Ἰσραήλ, οὗτοι
the word — of God. not For all those of Israel, these
2474 3761/3754/1526/ 4690 11 3956 5043 235
7 Ἰσραήλ· οὐδ' ὅτι εἰσὶ σπέρμα Ἀβραάμ, πάντες τέκνα· ἀλλ'
(are) Israel; nor because they are seed of Abraham (are they) all children, but
1722 2464 2564 4671 4690 5123 2076 3756
8 Ἐν Ἰσαὰκ κληθήσεταί σοι σπέρμα. τοῦτ' ἔστιν, οὐ τὰ
In Isaac will be called to you a Seed This is, not the
5043 4561 5023 5043 2316 235 5043
τέκνα τῆς σαρκός, ταῦτα τέκνα τοῦ Θεοῦ· ἀλλὰ τὰ τέκνα τῆς
children of the flesh these children — of God, but the children of the
1860 3049 1519 4690 1860 1063 3056
9 ἐπαγγελίας λογίζεται εἰς σπέρμα. ἐπαγγελίας γὰρ ὁ λόγος
promise (is) counted for a seed. of promise For the word
3778 2596 2540 5126 2064 2071
οὗτος, Κατὰ τὸν καιρὸν τοῦτον ἐλεύσομαι, καὶ ἔσται τῇ
this (is): According to time this I will come, and will be —
4564 5207/3756/3440 235 4479 1537/1520 2845
10 Σάρρᾳ υἱός. οὐ μόνον δέ, ἀλλὰ καὶ Ῥεβέκκα ἐξ ἑνὸς κοίτην
to Sarah a son. not only (so) And, but also Rebekah from one con-
2192 2464 3962 2257 3380/1063 1080
11 ἔχουσα, Ἰσαὰκ τοῦ πατρὸς ἡμῶν—μήπω γὰρ γεννηθέντων,
ceiving, Isaac the father of us; not yet for being born,

good or evil, that the purpose of God according to election might stand, not of works, but of the *One* calling, [12]it was said to her, "The greater shall serve the lesser;" [13]even as it has been written, "I loved Jacob, and I hated Esau."

[14]What then shall we say? *Is there* not unrighteousness with God? Let it not be! [15]For He said to Moses, "I will have mercy on whomever I have mercy, and I will pity whomever I pity." [16]So, then, *it is* not of the *one* willing, nor of the *one* running, but of the *One* showing mercy—of God. [17]For the Scripture says to Pharaoh, "For this very thing I raised you up, so that I might show forth My power in you, and so that My name might be publicized in all the earth." [18]So, then, to whom He desires, He has mercy, And whom He desires, He hardens. [19]You will then say to me, Why does He yet find fault? For who has resisted His counsel? [20]Yes, rather, O man, who are you answering against God? Shall the thing formed say to the *One* forming *it*, Why did You make me like this? [21]Or does not the potter have authority *over* the clay, out of the same lump to make one vessel to honor, and one to dishonor? [22]But if God, desiring to show forth wrath, and to make His power known, endured in much long-suffering vessels of wrath having been fitted out for destruction; [23]and that He make known the riches of His glory on vessels of mercy which He before prepared for glory—[24]whom He also called, not only us, of Jews, but also out of nations. [25]As also He says in Hosea, "I will call those not My people, My people! And those not beloved, Beloved! [26]And it shall be, in the place where it was said

3366 4238 5100 18 2228 2556/2443 2596 1589
μηδὲ πραξάντων τι ἀγαθὸν ἢ κακόν, ἵνα ἡ κατ' ἐκλογὴν τοῦ
nor practicing anything good or evil, that the according to election
2316 4286 3306/3756/1537/2041/ 235/1537 2564
Θεοῦ πρόθεσις μένῃ, οὐκ ἐξ ἔργων, ἀλλ' ἐκ τοῦ καλοῦντος,
of God purpose might stand, not of works, but of the (One) calling,
4483 846 3754 3187 1398 1640 2531
12 ἐρρήθη αὐτῇ ὅτι Ὁ μείζων δουλεύσει τῷ ἐλάσσονι. καθὼς
13 it was said to her — The greater shall serve the lesser; even as
1125 2384 25 2269 3404
γέγραπται, Τὸν Ἰακὼβ ἠγάπησα, τὸν δὲ Ἠσαῦ ἐμίσησα.
it has been written: Jacob I loved, — and Esau I hated.
5101/3767/2046 3361 93 3844 2316 3361 1096
14 Τί οὖν ἐροῦμεν; μὴ ἀδικία παρὰ τῷ Θεῷ; μὴ γένοιτο.
What then shall we say Not unrighteousness with God Not let it be!
1063 3475 3004 1653 3739/302 1653 3627
15 τῷ γὰρ Μωσῇ λέγει, Ἐλεήσω ὃν ἂν ἐλεῶ, καὶ οἰκτειρήσω
— For to Moses He says: I will have mercy on, whomever I have mercy and I will pity
3739/302 3627 686/3767, 3756 2309 3761 5143
16 ὃν ἂν οἰκτείρω. ἄρα οὖν οὐ τοῦ θέλοντος, οὐδὲ τοῦ τρέ-
whomever I pity. So therefore not of the (one) willing, nor of the (one)
235 1653 2316 3004/1063 1124
17 χοντος, ἀλλὰ τοῦ ἐλεοῦντος Θεοῦ. λέγει γὰρ ἡ γραφὴ τῷ
running, but of the (One) showing mercy, God, says For the Scripture —
5328 3754/1519/846 5124 1825 4571 3704 1731
Φαραὼ ὅτι Εἰς αὐτὸ τοῦτο ἐξήγειρά σε, ὅπως ἐνδείξωμαι
to Pharaoh, — For this very thing I raised up you, so as I may show forth
1722/4671 1411 3450 3704 1229 3686 3450
ἐν σοὶ τὴν δύναμίν μου, καὶ ὅπως διαγγελῇ τὸ ὄνομά μου
in you the power of Me, and so as might be publicized in the name of Me
1722/3956 1093 686/3767/302/2309/1653/3739 2309 4645
18 ἐν πάσῃ τῇ γῇ. ἄρα οὖν ὃν θέλει ἐλεεῖ· ὃν δὲ θέλει σκληρύνει.
in all the earth. So, then, to He He has whom and He hardens.
*5101 2046/3767/3427/5101/2089 whom wills mercy 1063 He wills 1013 848
*3201 Ἐρεῖς οὖν μοι, Τί ἔτι μέμφεται; τῷ γὰρ βουλήματι αὐτοῦ
19 You will say then to me, Why yet finds He fault? the For counsel of Him
5101 436 3304 5599 444 4771/5101/1488 470
1063 τίς ἀνθέστηκε; μενοῦνγε, ὦ ἄνθρωπε, σὺ τίς εἶ ὁ ἀνταπο-
20 who resisted? Yes, rather, O man, you who are the (one)
2316/3361/2046 4110 4111 5101/3165
κρινόμενος τῷ Θεῷ; μὴ ἐρεῖ τὸ πλάσμα τῷ πλάσαντι, Τί με
answering against God; not will say, that formed to the Former: Why me
4160 3779 2228/3756/2192/ 1849 2763 4081
21 ἐποίησας οὕτως; ἢ οὐκ ἔχει ἐξουσίαν ὁ κεραμεὺς τοῦ πηλοῦ,
made You this way? Or not has authority the potter of the clay,
1537 846 5445 4160 3739/3303/1519/5092/ 4632/3739
ἐκ τοῦ αὐτοῦ φυράματος ποιῆσαι ὃ μὲν εἰς τιμὴν σκεῦος, ὃ
out of the same lump to make one to honor vessel
1519 819 1487 2309 2316 1731 3709
22 δὲ εἰς ἀτιμίαν; εἰ δὲ θέλων ὁ Θεὸς ἐνδείξασθαι τὴν ὀργήν,
and one to dishonor? if But desiring God to show forth wrath
1107 1415 848 5342 1722 4183 3115
καὶ γνωρίσαι τὸ δυνατὸν αὐτοῦ, ἤνεγκεν ἐν πολλῇ μα-
and to make known the power of Him, endured in much long-
4632 3709 2675 1519 684 2443
κροθυμίᾳ σκεύη ὀργῆς κατηρτισμένα εἰς ἀπώλειαν· καὶ ἵνα
suffering vessels of wrath having been fitted for destruction; and that
1107 4149 1391 848 1909 4632 1656
23 γνωρίσῃ τὸν πλοῦτον τῆς δόξης αὐτοῦ ἐπὶ σκεύη ἐλέους,
He make known the riches of the glory of Him on vessels of mercy,
3739 4282 1519 1391 3739 2564 2248/3739/3440
24 ἃ προητοίμασεν εἰς δόξαν, οὓς καὶ ἐκάλεσεν ἡμᾶς οὐ μόνον
which He before prepared for glory, whom also He called, us not only,
1537/2453 235 1537 1484/5613 1722 5617 3004
25 ἐξ Ἰουδαίων, ἀλλὰ καὶ ἐξ ἐθνῶν; ὡς καὶ ἐν τῷ Ὡσηὲ λέγει,
of Jews, but also of nations. As also in Hosea He says:
2564 3756/2992/3450/2992/3450 3756 25
Καλέσω τὸν οὐ λαόν μου λαόν μου· καὶ τὴν οὐκ ἠγαπη-
I will call the not people of Me a people of Me, and the not beloved
25 2071/1722 5117/3757/4483 846
26 μένην ἠγαπημένην. καὶ ἔσται, ἐν τῷ τόπῳ οὗ ἐρρήθη αὐτοῖς,
ones, Beloved; and it shall be, in the place where it was said to them,

to them, You are not
My people—there they
will be called, Sons of the
living God." 27But Isaiah
cries on behalf of Israel,
"If the number of the sons
of Israel be as the sand of
the sea, the remnant will
be saved. 28For *He is*
bringing *the* matter to an
end, and cutting short in
righteousness, because
the Lord will do a thing
having been cut short on
the earth." 29And as
Isaiah has said before,
"Except *the* Lord of hosts
left a seed to us, we would
have become as Sodom,
and we would have be-
come as Gomorrah."
30What then shall we
say? That *the* nations not
following after righteousness have taken on righ-
teousness, but a righteousness of faith; 31but Israel
following after a law of
righteousness did not arrive
at a law of righteousness?
32Why? Because *it was* not
of faith, but as of works of
Law. For they stumbled at
the Stone-of-stumbling,
33as it has been written,
"Behold, I place in Zion a
Stone-of-stumbling, and a
Rock-of-offense; and everyone believing on Him will
not be put to shame."

CHAPTER 10

1Brothers, truly my heart's
pleasure and request to
God on behalf of Israel is for
it to be saved. 2For I testify
to them that they have zeal
to God, but not according to
knowledge. 3For being ig-
norant of the righteousness
of God, and seeking to
establish their own
righteousness, they did not
submit to the righteousness
of God. 4For Christ *is* the
end of law for righteous-
ness to every one that believes. 5For Moses writes
of the righteousness

3756 2992 3450 5210 1563 2564 5207 2316 2198
Οὐ λαός μου ὑμεῖς, ἐκεῖ κληθήσονται υἱοὶ Θεοῦ ζῶντος.
not a people of Me you, there they will be called sons God of a living.
2268 2896 5228 2474 1437/5600 706
27 Ἡσαΐας δὲ κράζει ὑπὲρ τοῦ Ἰσραήλ, Ἐὰν ᾖ ὁ ἀριθμὸς τῶν
Isaiah But cries on behalf of — Israel, If be the number of the
5207 2474 5613 285 2281 2640
υἱῶν Ἰσραὴλ ὡς ἡ ἄμμος τῆς θαλάσσης, τὸ κατάλειμμα
sons of Israel as the sand of the sea, the remnant
4982 3056 1063 4931 4932 1722 1343
28 σωθήσεται· λόγον γὰρ συντελῶν καὶ συντέμνων ἐν δικαιο-
will be saved; the matter for bringing to an end and cutting short in righteous-
3754 3056 4932 4160 2962 1909
σύνῃ· ὅτι λόγον συντετμημένον ποιήσει Κύριος ἐπὶ τῆς
ness, because a matter having been cut short will do (the) Lord on the
1093 2531 4280 2268/=1508= 2962 4519
29 γῆς. καὶ καθὼς προείρηκεν Ἡσαΐας, Εἰ μὴ Κύριος Σαβαὼθ
earth. And as has said before, Isaiah: Except (the) Lord of hosts
1459 2254 4690 5613 4670 302 1096 5613
ἐγκατέλιπεν ἡμῖν σπέρμα, ὡς Σόδομα ἂν ἐγενήθημεν, καὶ ὡς
left to us a seed, as Sodom we would have become, and as
1116 302 3666
Γόμορρα ἂν ὡμοιώθημεν.
Gomorrah we would have become.
5101/3767 2046 3754/1484 3361 1377 1343
30 Τί οὖν ἐροῦμεν; ὅτι ἔθνη, τὰ μὴ διώκοντα δικαιοσύνην,
What then shall we say? That nations not following after righteousness
2638 1343 1343 1537 4102 2474
κατέλαβε δικαιοσύνην, δικαιοσύνην δὲ τὴν ἐκ πίστεως· Ἰσ-
have taken on righteousness, a righteousness but of faith;
1377 3551 1343 1519 3551 1343
31 ραὴλ δέ, διώκων νόμον δικαιοσύνης, εἰς νόμον δικαιοσύνης
Israel but following after a law of righteousness at a law of righteousness
3756 5348 1302 3754/3756/1537/ 4102 235/5613/1537/ 2041
32 οὐκ ἔφθασε. διατί; ὅτι οὐκ ἐκ πίστεως, ἀλλ' ὡς ἐξ ἔργων
not did arrive. Why? Because not of faith, but as of works
3551 4350 1063 3037 4348 2531
33 νόμου. προσέκοψαν γὰρ τῷ λίθῳ τοῦ προσκόμματος, καθὼς
of law. they stumbled For at the Stone- of-stumbling, even as
1125 2400/5087/1722/ 4622 3037 4348
γέγραπται, Ἰδοὺ τίθημι ἐν Σιὼν λίθον προσκόμματος καὶ
it was written: Behold, I place in Zion a Stone- of-stumbling and
4073 4625 3956 4100 1909 846 3756 2617
πέτραν σκανδάλου· καὶ πᾶς ὁ πιστεύων ἐπ' αὐτῷ οὐ καται-
a Rock-of-offense, and everyone believing on Him not will be
σχυνθήσεται.
put to shame.

CHAPTER 10

80 3303 2107 1699 2588 1162
1 Ἀδελφοί, ἡ μὲν εὐδοκία τῆς ἐμῆς καρδίας καὶ ἡ δέησις ἡ
Brothers, the indeed pleasure of My heart and the request
4314 2316 5228 2474 2076 1519 4991 3140
2 πρὸς τὸν Θεὸν ὑπὲρ τοῦ Ἰσραήλ ἐστιν εἰς σωτηρίαν. μαρ-
to God on behalf of Israel is for to be saved. I
1063 846 3754 2205 2316 2192 235 3756 2596
τυρῶ γὰρ αὐτοῖς ὅτι ζῆλον Θεοῦ ἔχουσιν, ἀλλ' οὐ κατ'
testify For to them that zeal to God they have, but not according to
1922 50 1063 2316 1343
3 ἐπίγνωσιν. ἀγνοοῦντες γὰρ τὴν τοῦ Θεοῦ δικαιοσύνην, καὶ
knowledge. being ignorant For the — of God righteousness, and
2398 1343 2212 2476 1343
τὴν ἰδίαν δικαιοσύνην ζητοῦντες στῆσαι, τῇ δικαιοσύνῃ τοῦ
the own righteousness seeking to establish, to the righteousness —
2316/3756 5293 5056 1063 3551 5547 1519 1343
4 Θεοῦ οὐχ ὑπετάγησαν. τέλος γὰρ νόμου Χριστὸς εἰς δικαιο-
of God not they submitted. the end For of law Christ (is) for righteous-
3956 4100 3475 1063 1125 1343
5 σύνην παντὶ τῷ πιστεύοντι. Μωσῆς γὰρ γράφει τὴν δι-
ness to everyone believing. Moses For writes: The

which is of the law: "The man doing these things shall live by them." [6]But the righteousness of faith says this: "Do not say in your heart, Who will go up into Heaven?"—that is, to bring down Christ; or, [7]"Who will go down into the abyss?"—that is, to bring Christ up from *the* dead. [8]But what does it say? "The word is near you, in your mouth and in your heart"—that is, the word of faith which we proclaim. [9]Because if you confess *the* Lord Jesus with your mouth, and believe in your heart that God raised Him from *the* dead, you will be saved. [10]For with *the* heart *one* believes unto righteousness, and with *the* mouth *one* confesses unto salvation. [11]For the Scripture says, "Everyone believing on Him will not be put to shame." [12]For there is no difference both of Jew and of Greek, for the same Lord of all is rich toward all the ones calling on Him. [13]For everyone, whoever may call on the name of *the* Lord, will be saved. [14]How then may they call on *One* in whom they have not believed? And how may they believe *One* of whom they have not heard? And how may they hear without preaching? [15]And how may they preach if they are not sent? Even as it has been written, "How beautiful the feet of those preaching the gospel of peace, of those preaching the gospel of good things."

[16]But not all obeyed the gospel, for Isaiah says, "Lord, who has believed our report?" [17]Then faith *is* of hearing, and hearing through the word of God. [18]But I say, Did they not hear? Yes, rather, into all the earth their voice went

1343 1537 3551 3754 4160 846 444
καιοσύνην τὴν ἐκ τοῦ νόμου, ὅτι ὁ ποιήσας αὐτὰ ἄνθρωπος
righteousness of law. the doing of these things man
2198 1722 846 1537 4102 1343 3779 3004
6 ζήσεται ἐν αὐτοῖς. ἡ δὲ ἐκ πίστεως δικαιοσύνη οὕτω λέγει,
shall live by them. the But of faith righteousness thus says:
3361/2036/1722 2588 4675/5101 305 1519 3772
Μὴ εἴπῃς ἐν τῇ καρδίᾳ σου, Τίς ἀναβήσεται εἰς τὸν οὐρανόν;
not Say in the heart of you, Who will go up into Heaven?
= 5123 = 5547 2609 2228/5101 2597 1519
7 (τοῦτ' ἔστι Χριστὸν καταγαγεῖν·) ἤ, Τίς καταβήσεται εἰς
—this is, Christ to bring down— or, Who will go down into
12 = 5123 = 5547 1537 3498 321
τὴν ἄβυσσον; (τοῦτ' ἔστι Χριστὸν ἐκ νεκρῶν ἀναγαγεῖν.)
the abyss —this is, Christ from (the) dead to bring up—
235/5101/3004 1451 4675 4487 2076/1722 4750
8 ἀλλὰ τί λέγει; Ἐγγύς σου τὸ ῥῆμά ἐστιν, ἐν τῷ στόματί
but what says it? near you the word is, in the mouth
4675 1722 2588 4675 =5123 = 4487 4102
σου καὶ ἐν τῇ καρδίᾳ σου· τοῦτ' ἔστι τὸ ῥῆμα τῆς πίστεως
of you and in the heart of you; this is the word of faith
2784 3754/1437 3670 1722 4750 4675
9 ὃ κηρύσσομεν· ὅτι ἐὰν ὁμολογήσῃς ἐν τῷ στόματί σου
which we proclaim. Because if you confess with the mouth of you
2962 2424 4100 1722 2588 4675/3754/2316
Κύριον Ἰησοῦν, καὶ πιστεύσῃς ἐν τῇ καρδίᾳ σου ὅτι ὁ Θεὸς
(the) Lord Jesus, and believe in the heart of you that God
846 1453 1537 3498 4982 2588 1063 4100
10 αὐτὸν ἤγειρεν ἐκ νεκρῶν, σωθήσῃ· καρδίᾳ γὰρ πιστεύεται
Him raised from (the) dead, you will be saved. with heart For (one) believes
1519 1343 4750 3670 1519 4991 3004
11 εἰς δικαιοσύνην, στόματι δὲ ὁμολογεῖται εἰς σωτηρίαν. λέγει
to righteousness, with mouth and (one) confesses to salvation. says
1063 1124 3956 4100 1909 846/3756 2617
γὰρ ἡ γραφή, Πᾶς ὁ πιστεύων ἐπ' αὐτῷ οὐ καταισχυνθή-
For the Scripture: Everyone believing on Him not will be put to
3756/1063/2076 1293 2453 1672
12 σεται. οὐ γάρ ἐστι διαστολὴ Ἰουδαίου τε καὶ Ἕλληνος· ὁ
shame. not For is difference of Jew both and of Greek, the
1063 846 2962 3956 4147 1519 3956 1941
γὰρ αὐτὸς Κύριος πάντων, πλουτῶν εἰς πάντας τοὺς ἐπι-
for same Lord of all is rich to all those
846 3956/1063/3739/302 1941 3686
13 καλουμένους αὐτόν. πᾶς γὰρ ὃς ἂν ἐπικαλέσηται τὸ ὄνομα
calling on Him. everyone For whoever calls on the name
2962 4982 4459/3767 1941 1519/3739/3756/4100
14 Κυρίου σωθήσεται. πῶς οὖν ἐπικαλέσονται εἰς ὃν οὐκ ἐπί-
of (the) Lord will be saved. How then may they call on (One) in whom not
4459 4100 3739/3756 191 4459
στευσαν; πῶς δὲ πιστεύσουσιν οὗ οὐκ ἤκουσαν; πῶς δὲ
they believed? how And may they believe of whom not they heard? how And
191 5565 2784 4459 2784 1437/3361
15 ἀκούσουσι χωρὶς κηρύσσοντος; πῶς δὲ κηρύξουσιν ἐὰν μὴ
may they hear without preaching? how And may they preach if not
649 2531 1125 3739 5611 4228
ἀποσταλῶσι; καθὼς γέγραπται, Ὡς ὡραῖοι οἱ πόδες τῶν
they are sent? Even as it has been written: How beautiful the feet of those
2097 1515 2097 18
εὐαγγελιζομένων εἰρήνην, τῶν εὐαγγελιζομένων τὰ ἀγαθά.
preaching the gospel of peace, of those preaching the gospel of good things.
235/3756 3956 5219 2098 2268 1063
16 Ἀλλ' οὐ πάντες ὑπήκουσαν τῷ εὐαγγελίῳ. Ἡσαΐας γὰρ
But not all obeyed the gospel. Isaiah For
3004 2962 5101 4100 189 2257 686 4102 1537
17 λέγει, Κύριε, τίς ἐπίστευσε τῇ ἀκοῇ ἡμῶν; ἄρα ἡ πίστις ἐξ
says, Lord, who has believed the report of us? Then faith (is) of
189 189 1223 4487 2316 235 3004 3361/3756
18 ἀκοῆς, ἡ δὲ ἀκοὴ διὰ ῥήματος Θεοῦ. ἀλλὰ λέγω, Μὴ οὐκ
hearing, the and hearing through a word of God. But I say, Did not
191 3304 1519 3956 1093 1831 5353
ἤκουσαν; μενοῦνγε εἰς πᾶσαν τὴν γῆν ἐξῆλθεν ὁ φθόγγος
they hear? Yes, rather, to all the earth went out, the utterance

out, and to the ends of the world their words. [19]But I say, Did not Israel know? First, Moses says, "I will provoke you to jealousy by a not-nation; by an unwise nation I will anger you." [20]But Isaiah *is* very bold and says, "I was found by those not seeking Me; I came to be revealed to those not inquiring after Me." [21]But to Israel He says, "All the day I stretched out My hands to a disobeying and contradicting people."

CHAPTER 11

[1]I say, then, Did not God thrust away His people? Let it not be! For I also am an Israelite, out of Abraham's seed, of *the* tribe of Benjamin. [2]God did not thrust away His people whom He foreknew. Or do you not know what the Scripture said in Elijah, how he pleads with God against Israel, saying, [3]"Lord, they killed Your prophets, and they dug down Your altars; and only I am left; and they seek my soul." [4]But what does the Divine answer say to him, "I reserved to Myself seven thousand men who did not bow a knee to Baal." [5]So then, also in the present time a remnant according to election of grace has come into being. [6]But if by grace, no longer *is* it of works; else grace no longer becomes grace. But if of works, it is no longer grace; else work is no longer work. [7]What then? What Israel seeks, this he did not obtain, but the election obtained *it*, and the rest were hardened; [8]even as it has been written, "God gave to them a spirit of slumber, eyes not seeing and ears not

848 1519 4009 3625 4487 848
αὐτῶν, καὶ εἰς τὰ πέρατα τῆς οἰκουμένης τὰ ῥήματα αὐτῶν.
of them, and to the ends of the habitable world the words of them.
235 3004 = 3378= 1097 2474 4413 3475 3004
ἀλλὰ λέγω, Μὴ οὐκ ἔγνω Ἰσραήλ; πρῶτος Μωσῆς λέγει,
But I say, Did not know Israel? First, Moses says,
1473 3863 5209 1909/3767/1484/1909/1484 801
19 Ἐγὼ παραζηλώσω ὑμᾶς ἐπ' οὐκ ἔθνει, ἐπὶ ἔθνει ἀσυνέτῳ
I will provoke to jealousy you by not a nation, by a nation unwise
3949 5209 2268 662 3004 2147
20 παροργιῶ ὑμᾶς. Ἠσαΐας δὲ ἀποτολμᾷ καὶ λέγει, Εὑρέθην
I will anger you. Isaiah But (is) very bold and says, I was found
1691/3361 2212 1717 1096 1691/3361/ 1905
τοῖς ἐμὲ μὴ ζητοῦσιν, ἐμφανὴς ἐγενόμην τοῖς ἐμὲ μὴ ἐπερω-
by those Me not seeking; revealed I became to those Me not inquiring
4314 2474 3004 3650 2250 1600
21 τῶσι. πρὸς δὲ τὸν Ἰσραὴλ λέγει, Ὅλην τὴν ἡμέραν ἐξεπέ-
after. to But Israel He says, All the day I stretched
5495 3650/4314/2992 544 483
τασα τὰς χεῖράς μου πρὸς λαὸν ἀπειθοῦντα καὶ ἀντιλέγοντα.
out the hands of Me to a people disobeying and contradicting.

CHAPTER 11

3004 3767 3361 683 2316 2992 848 3361
1 Λέγω οὖν, Μὴ ἀπώσατο ὁ Θεὸς τὸν λαὸν αὐτοῦ; μὴ
I say, then, Did not put away God the people of Him? Not
1096 1063/1473 2475 5110/1537 4690
γένοιτο. καὶ γὰρ ἐγὼ Ἰσραηλίτης εἰμί, ἐκ σπέρματος
let it be! even For I an Israelite am, out of (the) seed
11 5443 958 3756 683 2316 2992
2 Ἀβραάμ, φυλῆς Βενϊαμίν. οὐκ ἀπώσατο ὁ Θεὸς τὸν λαὸν
of Abraham, of tribe of Benjamin, not did thrust away God the people
848 3739 4267 3756 1492/1722/2243/5101/3004 1124
αὐτοῦ ὃν προέγνω. ἢ οὐκ οἴδατε ἐν Ἠλίᾳ τί λέγει ἡ γραφή;
of Him whom He fore- Or not you know in Eli- what says the Scripture,
5613 1793 knew 2316/2596 jah 2474 3004 2962
3 ὡς ἐντυγχάνει τῷ Θεῷ κατὰ τοῦ Ἰσραήλ, λέγων, Κύριε,
how he pleads with God against — Israel, saying: Lord,
4396 4675 615 2379 4675
τοὺς προφήτας σου ἀπέκτειναν, καὶ τὰ θυσιαστήριά σου
the prophets of You they killed, and the altars of You
2679 2504 5275 3441 2212
κατέσκαψαν· κἀγὼ ὑπελείφθην μόνος, καὶ ζητοῦσι τὴν
they dug down, and I am left alone, and they seek the
5590 3450 235/5101/3004/846 5538 2641
4 ψυχήν μου. ἀλλὰ τί λέγει αὐτῷ ὁ χρηματισμός; Κατέλιπον
soul of me. But what says to him the divine answer? I reserved
1683 2035 435 3748 3756 2578 1119
ἐμαυτῷ ἑπτακισχιλίους ἄνδρας, οἵτινες οὐκ ἔκαμψαν γόνυ
to Myself seven thousand men who not bowed (the) knee
896 3779 3767 1722 3568 2540 3005 2596
5 τῇ Βάαλ. οὕτως οὖν καὶ ἐν τῷ νῦν καιρῷ λεῖμμα κατ'
to Baal. So, then, also in the present time a remnant according
1589 5485 1096 1487 5485 3765 1537/2041 to
6 ἐκλογὴν χάριτος γέγονεν. εἰ δὲ χάριτι, οὐκέτι ἐξ ἔργων·
election of grace has become. if And by grace, no longer of works;
1893 5485 3765 1096 5485/1487 1537/2041 3765 2076
ἐπεὶ ἡ χάρις οὐκέτι γίνεται χάρις. εἰ δὲ ἐξ ἔργων, οὐκέτι ἐστὶ
else grace no longer becomes grace. if But of works, no longer is it
5485 1893 2041 3765 2076 2041/5101/3767/3739/ 1934
7 χάρις· ἐπεὶ τὸ ἔργον οὐκέτι ἐστὶν ἔργον. τί οὖν; ὃ ἐπιζητεῖ
grace, else work no longer is work. What then? What seeks for
2474 5127 3756 2013 1589 2013
Ἰσραήλ, τούτου οὐκ ἐπέτυχεν, ἡ δὲ ἐκλογὴ ἐπέτυχεν, οἱ δὲ
Israel, this not he obtained; the but election obtained (it), the and
3062 4456 2531 1125 1325 846
8 λοιποὶ ἐπωρώθησαν· καθὼς γέγραπται, Ἔδωκεν αὐτοῖς ὁ
rest were hardened; as it has been written: gave to them
2316 4151 2659 3788 3361 991
Θεὸς πνεῦμα κατανύξεως, ὀφθαλμοὺς τοῦ μὴ βλέπειν, καὶ
God a spirit of slumber, eyes not seeing, and

hearing" until this day. [9]And David said, "Let their table become for a snare and a trap, and for a stumbling-block, and a recompense to them; [10]let their eyes be darkened, not to see, and their back always bowing."

[11]I say, then, Did not they stumble that they fall? Let it not be! But by their slipping away *came* salvation to the nations, to provoke them to jealousy. [12]But if their slipping away *is the* riches of *the* world, and their default *the* riches of *the* nations, how much more their fullness? [13]For I speak to you, the nations, since I am an apostle of *the* nations—I glorify my ministry, [14]if somehow I may provoke to jealousy my flesh, and may save some of them. [15]For if their casting away *is the* reconciliation of *the* world, what the reception, except life from *the* dead? [16]Now if the firstfruit *is* holy, also the lump. And if the root *is* holy, also the branches. [17]But if some of the branches were broken off, and you being a wild olive tree were grafted in among them, and became a sharer of the root and the fatness of the olive-tree, [18]do not boast against the branches. But if you do boast, *it is* not you *that* bears the root, but the root bears you. [19]You will then say, The branches were broken off that I might be grafted in. [20]Well! For unbelief they were broken off. And you stand by faith. Do not *be* high-minded, but fear. [21]For if God did not spare the natural branches, lest it may be He will not spare you either. [22]Behold, then, *the* kindness and severity of God: On those having fallen, severity. But

3775 3361 191 2193 4594 2250 1138
9 ὦτα τοῦ μὴ ἀκούειν, ἕως τῆς σήμερον ἡμέρας. καὶ Δαβὶδ
ears not hearing; until the present day. And David
3004 1096 5132 848 1519 3803 1519 2339
λέγει, Γενηθήτω ἡ τράπεζα αὐτῶν εἰς παγίδα, καὶ εἰς θήραν,
says: Let become the table of them for a snare, and for a trap,
1519 4625 1519 468 846 4654
10 καὶ εἰς σκάνδαλον, καὶ εἰς ἀνταπόδομα αὐτοῖς· σκοτισθή-
and for a stumbling-block, and for a recompense to them; let be darkened
3788 848 3361 991 3577
τωσαν οἱ ὀφθαλμοὶ αὐτῶν τοῦ μὴ βλέπειν καὶ τὸν νῶτον
the eyes of them not to see, and the back
848 1223 3956 4781 3004/3767/3361/ 4417 2443
11 αὐτῶν διὰ παντὸς σύγκαμψον. λέγω οὖν, μὴ ἔπταισαν ἵνα
of them always bowing. I say, then, Did not they stumble that
4098 3361 1096 235 848 3900
πέσωσι; μὴ γένοιτο· ἀλλὰ τῷ αὐτῶν παραπτώματι ἡ
they fall? Not let it be! But by the of them slipping away (came)
4991 1484 1519 3863 846 1487
σωτηρία τοῖς ἔθνεσιν, εἰς τὸ παραζηλῶσαι αὐτούς. εἰ δὲ τὸ
salvation to the nations, to provoke to jealousy them. if But the
3900 848 4149 2889 2275 848
12 παράπτωμα αὐτῶν πλοῦτος κόσμου, καὶ τὸ ἥττημα αὐτῶν
slipping away of them (is the) riches of (the) world, and the default of them
4149 1484 4214 3123 4138 848
πλοῦτος ἐθνῶν, πόσῳ μᾶλλον τὸ πλήρωμα αὐτῶν;
(the) riches of (the) nations, how much more the fullness of them!
5213/1063 3004 1484 1909/3745/3303/1510/1473/1484
13 Ὑμῖν γὰρ λέγω τοῖς ἔθνεσιν. ἐφ' ὅσον μέν εἰμι ἐγὼ ἐθνῶν
to you For I speak, the nations, since indeed am I of nations
652 1248 3450 1392 =1513= 3863
14 ἀπόστολος, τὴν διακονίαν μου δοξάζω· εἴ πως παραζηλώσω
an apostle, the ministry of me I glorify, if somehow I may provoke to jealousy
3450 4561 4982 5100/1537 846 1487/1063
15 μου τὴν σάρκα, καὶ σώσω τινὰς ἐξ αὐτῶν. εἰ γὰρ ἡ ἀπο-
of me the flesh and may save some of them. if For the casting
580 846 2643 2889 5101 4356 =1508=
βολὴ αὐτῶν καταλλαγὴ κόσμου, τίς ἡ πρόσληψις, εἰ μὴ
away of them (the) reconciliation of world, what the reception, except
2222/1537/ 3498/1487 536 40 5445
16 ζωὴ ἐκ νεκρῶν; εἰ δὲ ἡ ἀπαρχὴ ἁγία, καὶ τὸ φύραμα· καὶ εἰ
life from (the) dead? if Now the firstfruit (is) holy, also the lump; and if
4491/40 2798 1487 5100 2798 1575
17 ἡ ῥίζα ἁγία, καὶ οἱ κλάδοι. εἰ δέ τινες τῶν κλάδων ἐξεκλάσθη-
the root (is) holy also the branches. if But some of the branches were broken
4771 65 5607 1461 1722 846
σαν, σὺ δὲ ἀγριέλαιος ὢν ἐνεκεντρίσθης ἐν αὐτοῖς, καὶ
off, you and, a wild olive being were grafted in among them, and
4791 4491 4096 1636 1096
συγκοινωνὸς τῆς ῥίζης καὶ τῆς πιότητος τῆς ἐλαίας ἐγένου,
a partaker of the root and of the fatness of the olive-tree became,
3361 2620 2798 1487 2620 3756/4771
18 μὴ κατακαυχῶ τῶν κλάδων· εἰ δὲ κατακαυχᾶσαι, οὐ σὺ τὴν
do not boast against the branches; if but you boast, not you the
4491 941 235 4491/4571/2046/3767 1575
19 ῥίζαν βαστάζεις, ἀλλ' ἡ ῥίζα σέ. ἐρεῖς οὖν, Ἐξεκλάσθησαν οἱ
root bears, but the root you. You will say then, were broken off the
2798 2443 1473 1461 2573 570 1575
20 κλάδοι, ἵνα ἐγὼ ἐγκεντρισθῶ. καλῶς· τῇ ἀπιστίᾳ ἐξεκλά-
Branches that I might be grafted in. Well, for unbelief they were
4771 4102 2476 3361 5309 235
σθησαν, σὺ δὲ τῇ πίστει ἕστηκας. μὴ ὑψηλοφρόνει, ἀλλὰ
broken off, you and by faith stand. not high-minded (Be), but
5399 1487/1063 2316 2596 5449 2798 3756 5339
21 φοβοῦ· εἰ γὰρ ὁ Θεὸς τῶν κατὰ φύσιν κλάδων οὐκ ἐφείσατο,
fear; if for God the according to nature branches not did spare,
3381 3761 4675 5339 1492/3767 5544 663
22 μήπως οὐδὲ σου φείσηται. ἴδε οὖν χρηστότητα καὶ ἀποτο-
lest neither you He will spare. behold, then, (the) kindness and severity
2316 1909/3303 4098 663 1909 4571
μίαν Θεοῦ· ἐπὶ μὲν τοὺς πεσόντας, ἀποτομίαν· ἐπὶ δέ σε,
of God on indeed those having fallen severity; on but you,

on you, kindness—if you continue in the kindness. Otherwise, you will also be cut off. [23]And those also, if they do not continue in unbelief, will be grafted in. For God is able to graft them in again. [24]For if you were cut out of the natural wild olive tree, and were against nature grafted into a good olive tree, how much more these *being* according to nature will be grafted into *their* own olive tree?

[25]For I do not want you to be ignorant of this mystery, brothers—so that you may not be wise within yourselves—that hardness *in* part has happened to Israel, until the fullness of the nations comes in; [26]and so all Israel will be saved, even as it has been written, "The Deliverer will come out of Zion, and He will turn away ungodliness from Jacob. [27]And this *is* My covenant with them, when I take away their sins." [28]Indeed, as regards the gospel, enemies for you; but as regards the election, beloved for the sake of the fathers. [29]For the free gifts and the calling of God *are* without repentance. [30]For as you also then disobeyed God, but now have obtained mercy by the disobedience of these; [31]so also these now *have* disobeyed, so that they also may obtain mercy by your mercy. [32]For God shut up all in disobedience, that He may show mercy to all.

[33]O *the* depth of *the* riches and of *the* wisdom and *the* knowledge of God! How unsearchable *are* His judgments, and His ways past finding out! [34]For who has known the mind of *the* Lord? Or who became His

5544 1437 1961 5544 1893 4771
χρηστότητα, ἐὰν ἐπιμείνῃς τῇ χρηστότητι· ἐπεὶ καὶ σὺ
kindness. if you continue in the kindness, otherwise also you
1581 1565 =3362= 1961 570
23 ἐκκοπήσῃ. καὶ ἐκεῖνοι δέ, ἐὰν μὴ ἐπιμείνωσι τῇ ἀπιστίᾳ,
will be cut off also those And, if not they continue in unbelief,
1461 1415 1063 2076 2316 3825 1461
ἐγκεντρισθήσονται· δυνατὸς γάρ ἐστιν ὁ Θεὸς πάλιν ἐγκεν-
will be grafted in; able for is God again to graft
1537 846/1487/1063/3756/*/ 2596 5449 1581 65
24 τρίσαι αὐτούς. εἰ γὰρ σὺ ἐκ τῆς κατὰ φύσιν ἐξεκόπης ἀγρι-
in them. if For you out of the natural were cut out wild
3844 5449 1461 1519 2565 4214
ἐλαίου, καὶ παρὰ φύσιν ἐνεκεντρίσθης εἰς καλλιέλαιον, πόσῳ
olive, and against nature were grafted in into a good olive, how much
3123 3778 2596 5449 1461 2398
μᾶλλον οὗτοι, οἱ κατὰ φύσιν, ἐγκεντρισθήσονται τῇ ἰδίᾳ
more these, those according to nature, will be grafted in the own
1636
ἐλαίᾳ;
olive-tree?

3756/1063/2309/5209/ 50 80 3466 5124
25 Οὐ γὰρ θέλω ὑμᾶς ἀγνοεῖν, ἀδελφοί, τὸ μυστήριον τοῦτο,
not For I wish you to be ignorant, brothers, (of) mystery this,
2443/3361/5600/3844 1438 5429 3754 4457 575 3313
ἵνα μὴ ἦτε παρ' ἑαυτοῖς φρόνιμοι, ὅτι πώρωσις ἀπὸ μέρους
that not you be in yourselves wise, that hardness from (in) part
2474 1096 891/3739 4138 1484 1525
τῷ Ἰσραὴλ γέγονεν, ἄχρις οὗ τὸ πλήρωμα τῶν ἐθνῶν εἰσ-
to Israel has happened, until the fullness of the nations comes
3779/3956 2474 4982 2531 1125
26 έλθῃ· καὶ οὕτω πᾶς Ἰσραὴλ σωθήσεται· καθὼς γέγραπται,
in, and so all Israel will be saved, even as it has been written:
2240/1537/4622 4506 654 763 575
Ἥξει ἐκ Σιὼν ὁ ῥυόμενος, καὶ ἀποστρέψει ἀσεβείας ἀπὸ
Will come out of Zion the Deliverer, and He will turn away ungodliness from
2384 3778 846 3844 1700 1242 3752 851
27 Ἰακώβ· καὶ αὕτη αὐτοῖς ἡ παρ' ἐμοῦ διαθήκη, ὅταν ἀφέλω-
Jacob. And this (is) with them the from Me covenant, when I take away
266 848 2596/3303 2098 2190 1223
28 μαι τὰς ἁμαρτίας αὐτῶν. κατὰ μὲν τὸ εὐαγγέλιον, ἐχθροὶ δι'
the sins of them as regards Indeed the gospel, enemies for
5209 2596 1589 27 1223 3962
ὑμᾶς· κατὰ δὲ τὴν ἐκλογήν, ἀγαπητοὶ διὰ τοὺς πατέρας.
you; as regards but the election, beloved for the sake of the fathers.
278 1063 5486 2921 2316
29 ἀμεταμέλητα γὰρ τὰ χαρίσματα καὶ ἡ κλῆσις τοῦ Θεοῦ.
without repentance For the free gifts and the calling — of God.
5618 1063 5210 4218 544 2316 3568
30 ὥσπερ γὰρ καὶ ὑμεῖς ποτὲ ἠπειθήσατε τῷ Θεῷ, νῦν δὲ
as For also you then disobeyed God, now but
1653 5130 543 3779 3778 3568 544
31 ἠλεήθητε τῇ τούτων ἀπειθείᾳ· οὕτω καὶ οὗτοι νῦν ἠπείθη-
you obtained mercy by the of these disobedience, so also these now disobeyed
5212 1653 2443 846 1656 4788
32 σαν, τῷ ὑμετέρῳ ἐλέει ἵνα καὶ αὐτοὶ ἐλεηθῶσι. συνέκλεισε
by your mercy that also they may obtain mercy. shut up
1063 2316 3956 1519 543 2443 3956
γὰρ ὁ Θεὸς τοὺς πάντας εἰς ἀπείθειαν, ἵνα τοὺς πάντας
For God — all in disobedience that — to all
1653
ἐλεήσῃ.
He may show mercy.

899 4149 4678 1108 2316 5613
33 Ὦ βάθος πλούτου καὶ σοφίας καὶ γνώσεως Θεοῦ. ὡς
O (the) depth of (the) riches and of (the) wisdom and (the) knowledge of God: how
419 2917 848 421 3598
ἀνεξερεύνητα τὰ κρίματα αὐτοῦ, καὶ ἀνεξιχνίαστοι αἱ ὁδοὶ
unsearchable the judgments of Him, and past finding out the ways
848 5101/1063/1097/3563 2962 5101 4825 848
34 αὐτοῦ. τίς γὰρ ἔγνω νοῦν Κυρίου; ἢ τίς σύμβουλος αὐτοῦ
of Him! who For has known the mind of (the) Lord? or who His counselor

counselor? [35]Or who first gave to Him, and it will be repaid to him? [36]Because of Him, and through Him, and to Him *are* all things. To Him be the glory forever! Amen.

CHAPTER 12

[1]Therefore, brothers, I call on you through the mercies of God to present your bodies a living sacrifice, holy, pleasing to God, *which is* your reasonable service. [2]And be not conformed to this age, but be transformed by the renewing of your mind, in order to prove by you what *is* the good and pleasing and perfect will of God. [3]For I say through the grace which is given to me, to everyone being among you, not to have high thoughts beyond what is right to think. But set your mind to be right-minded, even as God divided a measure of faith to each.

[4]For even as we have many members in one body, but all members do not have the same function; [5]so we the many are one body in Christ, and each one members of one another. [6]But having different gifts according to the grace given to us, whether prophecy, according to the proportion of faith; [7]or ministry, in the ministry; or the *one* teaching, in the teaching; [8]or the *one* exhorting, in the encouragement; the *one* sharing, in simplicity; the *one* taking the lead, in diligence; the *one* showing mercy, in cheerfulness.

[9]*Let* love *be* without dissimulation, shrinking from evil, cleaving to good; [10]In brotherly love to one another loving fervently, having gone before one another in

1096 5101 4272 846 467
35 ἐγένετο ; ἢ τίς προέδωκεν αὐτῷ, καὶ ἀνταποδοθήσεται
became? or who first gave to Him, and it will be repaid
848 3754/1537/846 1223 846 1519 846 3956
36 αὐτῷ ; ὅτι ἐξ αὐτοῦ καὶ δι' αὐτοῦ καὶ εἰς αὐτὸν τὰ πάντα·
to him? Because of Him, and through Him, and to Him (are) all things;
846 1391/1519 164 281
αὐτῷ ἡ δόξα εἰς τοὺς αἰῶνας. ἀμήν.
to Him be the glory to the ages! Amen.

CHAPTER 12

3870 3767/5209 80 1223 3628
1 Παρακαλῶ οὖν ὑμᾶς, ἀδελφοί, διὰ τῶν οἰκτιρμῶν τοῦ
I beseech Therefore you, brothers, through the compassions
2316 3936 4983 5216 2378 2198 40
Θεοῦ, παραστῆσαι τὰ σώματα ὑμῶν θυσίαν ζῶσαν, ἁγίαν,
of God, to present the body of you sacrifice a living, holy,
2101 2316 3050 2999 5216 3361
2 εὐάρεστον τῷ Θεῷ, τὴν λογικὴν λατρείαν ὑμῶν. καὶ μὴ
well-pleasing to God, the reasonable service of you. And not
4964 165 5129 235 3339
συσχηματίζεσθε τῷ αἰῶνι τούτῳ, ἀλλὰ μεταμορφοῦσθε τῇ
be conformed to age this, but be transformed by the
342 3563 5216 1519 1381 5209 5101
ἀνακαινώσει τοῦ νοὸς ὑμῶν, εἰς τὸ δοκιμάζειν ὑμᾶς τί τὸ
renewing of the mind of you, to prove you what the
2307 2316 18 2101 5046
θέλημα τοῦ Θεοῦ τὸ ἀγαθὸν καὶ εὐάρεστον καὶ τέλειον.
will of God, the good and well-pleasing and perfect.
3004/1063/1223 5485 1325 3427 3956
3 Λέγω γάρ, διὰ τῆς χάριτος τῆς δοθείσης μοι, παντὶ τῷ
I say For, through the grace — given to me to everyone
5607/1722/5213/3361/ 5252 3844/3739/1163/ 5426 235
ὄντι ἐν ὑμῖν, μὴ ὑπερφρονεῖν παρ' ὃ δεῖ φρονεῖν, ἀλλὰ
being among you, not to have high thoughts beyond what is right to think, but
5426 1519 4993 1538/5613 2316 3307 3358
φρονεῖν εἰς τὸ σωφρονεῖν, ἑκάστῳ ὡς ὁ Θεὸς ἐμέρισε μέτρον
to think to be sober-minded, to each as God divided a measure
4102 2509 1063/1722/1520/ 4983 3196 4183 2192
4 πίστεως. καθάπερ γὰρ ἐν ἑνὶ σώματι μέλη πολλὰ ἔχομεν, τὰ
of faith. as For in one body members many we have, the
3196 3956 3756 846 2192 4234 3779 4183
5 δὲ μέλη πάντα οὐ τὴν αὐτὴν ἔχει πρᾶξιν· οὕτως οἱ πολλοὶ
but members all not the same have function, so the many
1722 4983 2070 1722 5547 2596/1519/ 240 3196
ἓν σῶμά ἐσμεν ἐν Χριστῷ, ὁ δὲ καθ' εἷς ἀλλήλων μέλη.
one body we are in Christ, and each one of one another members
2192 5486 2596 5485 1325 2254
6 ἔχοντες δὲ χαρίσματα κατὰ τὴν χάριν τὴν δοθεῖσαν ἡμῖν
having And gifts according to the grace given to us
1313 1535 4394 2596 356 4102
διάφορα, εἴτε προφητείαν, κατὰ τὴν ἀναλογίαν τῆς πίστεως·
differing, whether prophecy, according to the proportion of faith:
1535 1248 1722 1248 1535 1321 1722
7 εἴτε διακονίαν, ἐν τῇ διακονίᾳ· εἴτε ὁ διδάσκων, ἐν τῇ
or ministry, in the ministry; or the (one) teaching, in the
1319 1535 3870 1722 3874 3330
8 διδασκαλίᾳ· εἴτε ὁ παρακαλῶν, ἐν τῇ παρακλήσει· ὁ μεταδι-
teaching; or the (one) exhorting, in the exhortation; the (one) sharing,
1722 572 4291 1722 4710 1653 1722
δούς, ἐν ἁπλότητι· ὁ προϊστάμενος, ἐν σπουδῇ· ὁ ἐλεῶν ἐν
in simplicity; the (one) taking the lead in diligence, he showing mercy, in
2432 26 505 655
9 ἱλαρότητι. ἡ ἀγάπη ἀνυπόκριτος. ἀποστυγοῦντες τὸ
cheerfulness. (let) Love (be) without dissimulation; shrinking from
4190 2853 18 5360 1519 240
10 πονηρόν, κολλώμενοι τῷ ἀγαθῷ. τῇ φιλαδελφίᾳ εἰς ἀλλή-
evil, cleaving to the good; in brotherly love to one
5387 5092 240 4285
λους φιλόστοργοι· τῇ τιμῇ ἀλλήλους προηγούμενοι· τῇ
another loving fervently, in honor one another having gone before

honor. [11]As to diligence not slothful; warm in spirit, serving the Lord; [12]in hope, rejoicing; in affliction, enduring; in prayer, steadfastly continuing, [13]imparting to the needs of the saints; pursuing hospitality.

[14]Bless those who persecute you; bless, and do not curse. [15]Rejoice with rejoicing ones, and weep with weeping ones; [16]minding the same thing toward one another, not minding high things, but yielding to the lowly. Do not become wise within yourselves. [17]Repay no one evil for evil; providing right things before all men. [18]If possible, as far as *is* in you, seeking peace with all men; [19]not avenging yourselves, beloved, but giving place to wrath — for it has been written, "Vengeance *is* Mine, I will repay, says the Lord." [20]Then if your enemy hungers, feed him; if he thirsts, give drink to him; for doing this you will heap coals of fire on his head. [21]Do not be overcome by evil, but overcome the evil with good.

4710 3361 3636 4151 2204 2962 1398
11 σπουδῇ μὴ ὀκνηροί· τῷ πνεύματι ζέοντες· τῷ Κυρίῳ δου-
in diligence, not slothful; in spirit burning, the Lord
1680 5463 2347 5278
12 λεύοντες· τῇ ἐλπίδι χαίροντες· τῇ θλίψει ὑπομένοντες· τῇ
serving; in hope, rejoicing; in trouble, enduring;
4335 4342 5532 40
13 προσευχῇ προσκαρτεροῦντες· ταῖς χρείαις τῶν ἁγίων
in prayer, steadfastly continuing, to the needs of the saints
2841 5381 1377 2127
14 κοινωνοῦντες· τὴν φιλοξενιαν διώκοντες. εὐλογεῖτε τοὺς
imparting, hospitality pursuing. Bless those
1377 5209 2127 3361 2672 5463 3326
15 διώκοντας ὑμᾶς· εὐλογεῖτε, καὶ μὴ καταρᾶσθε. χαίρειν μετὰ
persecuting you; bless, and do not curse. Rejoice with
5463 2799 3326 2799 846 1519 240
16 χαιρόντων, καὶ κλαίειν μετὰ κλαιόντων. τὸ αὐτὸ εἰς ἀλλή-
rejoicing ones; and weep with weeping ones. The same toward one
5426 3361 5308 5426 235
λους φρονοῦντες. μὴ τὰ ὑψηλὰ φρονοῦντες, ἀλλὰ τοῖς
another minding; not the things high minding, but to the
5011 4879 3361 1096 5429 3844 1438
ταπεινοῖς συναπαγόμενοι. μὴ γίνεσθε φρόνιμοι παρ' ἑαυτοῖς.
humble yield, do not become wise with yourselves.
3367 2556 473 2556 591 4306 2570
17 μηδενὶ κακὸν ἀντὶ κακοῦ ἀποδιδόντες. προνοούμενοι καλὰ
To no one evil for evil returning; providing for right things
1799 3956 444 1487 1415 1537/5216 3326
18 ἐνώπιον πάντων ἀνθρώπων. εἰ δυνατόν, τὸ ἐξ ὑμῶν, μετὰ
before all men; if possible, as far as in you, with
3956 444 1514 3361 1438 1556
19 πάντων ἀνθρώπων εἰρηνεύοντες. μὴ ἑαυτοὺς ἐκδικοῦντες,
all men seeking peace; not yourselves avenging,
27 235 1325 5117 3709 1125 1063
ἀγαπητοί, ἀλλὰ δότε τόπον τῇ ὀργῇ· γέγραπται γάρ,
beloved, but give place to wrath, it has been written for,
1695 1557 1473 467 3004 2962 1437/3767/ 3983
20 'Εμοὶ ἐκδίκησις, ἐγὼ ἀνταποδώσω, λέγει Κύριος. ἐὰν οὖν πεινᾷ
To Me (is) vengeance, I will repay, says (the) Lord. if Then hungers
2190 4675 5595 846 1437/1372 4222 846 5124
ὁ ἐχθρός σου, ψώμιζε αὐτόν· ἐὰν διψᾷ, πότιζε αὐτόν· τοῦτο
the enemy of you, feed him; if he thirsts, give drink to him; this
1063/ 4160 440 4442 4987 1909 2776 848
γὰρ ποιῶν, ἄνθρακας πυρὸς σωρεύσεις ἐπὶ τὴν κεφαλὴν αὐτοῦ.
for doing, coals of fire you will heap on the head of him
3361/3528/5259 2556 235 3528/1722 18 2556
21 μὴ νικῶ ὑπὸ τοῦ κακοῦ. ἀλλὰ νίκα ἐν τῷ ἀγαθῷ τὸ κακόν.
Not be conquered by evil, but conquer with good the evil.

CHAPTER 13

CHAPTER 13

[1]Let every soul be subject to higher authorities, for there is no authority except from God; but the authorities that exist have been ordained by God. [2]So that the *one* resisting authority has opposed the ordinance of God; and the ones opposing will receive judgment to themselves. [3]For the rulers are not a terror to good works, but to the bad. And do you desire not to be afraid of the authority? Do the good, and you will have

3956 5590 1849 5242 5293 3756
1 Πᾶσα ψυχὴ ἐξουσίαις ὑπερεχούσαις ὑποτασσέσθω· οὐ
Every soul authorities to higher let be subject to. no
1063/2076 1849 =1508= 575 2316 5607 1849 5259
γάρ ἐστιν ἐξουσία εἰ μὴ ἀπὸ Θεοῦ, αἱ δὲ οὖσαι ἐξουσίαι ὑπὸ
For there is authority except from God, the but existing authorities by
2316 5021 1526 5620 498
2 τοῦ Θεοῦ τεταγμέναι εἰσίν. ὥστε ὁ ἀντιτασσόμενος τῇ
— God having been ordained are. So the (one) resisting the
1849 2316 1296 436 436
ἐξουσίᾳ, τῇ τοῦ Θεοῦ διαταγῇ ἀνθέστηκεν· οἱ δὲ ἀνθεστη-
authority the of God ordinance has opposed; those and having
1438 2917 2983 1063 758 3756/1526
3 κότες ἑαυτοῖς κρίμα λήψονται. οἱ γὰρ ἄρχοντες οὐκ εἰσὶ
opposed, to themselves judgment will receive. the For rulers not are
5401 18 2041 235 2556 2309 3361
φόβος τῶν ἀγαθῶν ἔργων, ἀλλὰ τῶν κακῶν. θέλεις δὲ μὴ
a terror to good works, but to the bad. wish you And not
5399 1849 18 4160 2192/ 1868
φοβεῖσθαι τὴν ἐξουσίαν; τὸ ἀγαθὸν ποίει, καὶ ἕξεις ἔπαινον
to fear the authority? the good Do, and you will have praise

praise from it; [4]for it is a servant of God to you for good. But if you practice evil, be afraid; for he does not bear the sword in vain; for he is a servant of God, an avenger for wrath to the *one* practicing evil. [5]Because of this, *it is* necessary to be subject, not only on account of wrath, but also on account of conscience. [6]For on this account you also pay taxes; for they are ministers of God, always giving attention to this very thing. [7]Then give to all *their* dues: to the *one due* tax, the tax; to the *one due* tribute, the tribute; to the *one due* fear, the fear; to the *one due* honor, the honor. [8]Owe no one anything, except to love one another. For the *one* loving the other has fulfilled the law. [9]For, "Do not commit adultery; do not murder; do not steal; do not bear false witness; do not lust," and if *there is* any other commandment, it is summed up in this word: "You shall love your neighbor as yourself." [10]Love does not work evil to the neighbor. Then love *is* the fulfillment of law.

[11]Also this, knowing the time, that *it is* now the hour for you to be aroused from sleep, for now our salvation is nearer than when we believed. [12]The night is far gone, and the day has drawn near; therefore, let us cast off the works of darkness, and let us put on the weapons of the light. [13]Let us walk becomingly, as in *the* day; not in carousings and drinking; not in cohabitation and lustful acts; not in fighting and envy. [14]But put on the Lord Jesus Christ and do not take thought beforehand for the lusts of the flesh.

1537/846 2316 1063 1249 2076/4671/1519 18 1437
4 ἐξ αὐτῆς· Θεοῦ γὰρ διάκονός ἐστί σοι εἰς τὸ ἀγαθόν. ἐὰν δὲ
from it; of God For a servant he is to you for the good. if But
2556 4160 5399 3756/1063/1500 3162 5409
τὸ κακὸν ποιῇς, φοβοῦ· οὐ γὰρ εἰκῇ τὴν μάχαιραν φορεῖ·
the evil you do, fear; not for in vain the sword he bears;
2316/1063 1249 2076 1558 1519 3709 2556
Θεοῦ γὰρ διάκονός ἐστιν, ἔκδικος εἰς ὀργὴν τῷ τὸ κακὸν
of God for a servant he is, an avenger for wrath to the (one) evil
4238 1352 318 5293 3756 3440 1223
5 πράσσοντι. διὸ ἀνάγκη ὑποτάσσεσθαι, οὐ μόνον διὰ τὴν
practicing. Therefore it is necessary to be subject, not only because of
3709 235 1223 4893 1223 5124 1063
ὀργήν, ἀλλὰ καὶ διὰ τὴν συνείδησιν. διὰ τοῦτο γὰρ καὶ
wrath, but also, because of conscience. on account of this For also
5411 5055 3011 1063 2316 1526/1519/846 5124
6 φόρους τελεῖτε· λειτουργοὶ γὰρ Θεοῦ εἰσιν, εἰς αὐτὸ τοῦτο
taxes you pay; ministers for of God they are, for this very thing
4342 591 3767 3956 3782
7 προσκαρτεροῦντες. ἀπόδοτε οὖν πᾶσι τὰς ὀφειλάς· τῷ τὸν
always giving attention. give Then to all the dues: to the (one) the
5411 5411 5056 5056 5401
φόρον τὸν φόρον· τῷ τὸ τέλος τὸ τέλος· τῷ τὸν φόβον τὸν
tax (due) the tax; to the (one) the tribute, the tribute; fear (due), the
5401 5092 5092
φόβον· τῷ τὴν τιμὴν τὴν τιμήν.
fear; honor (due) the honor.
3367 3367 3784 1508 25 240 1063
8 Μηδενὶ μηδὲν ὀφείλετε, εἰ μὴ τὸ ἀγαπᾷν ἀλλήλους· ὁ γὰρ
To no one nothing owe, except to love one another; he for
25 2087 3551 4137 1063/3756 3431
9 ἀγαπῶν τὸν ἕτερον, νόμον πεπλήρωκε. τὸ γάρ, Οὐ μοιχεύ-
loving the other, the law has fulfilled. – For: Do not commit
3756 5407 3756 2813 3756 5576 3756
σεις, οὐ φονεύσεις, οὐ κλέψεις, οὐ ψευδομαρτυρήσεις, οὐκ
adultery; not do murder; not do steal; Do not bear false witness; not
1937 1487/5101/2087 1785 1722 5129 3056
ἐπιθυμήσεις, καὶ εἴ τις ἑτέρα ἐντολή, ἐν τούτῳ τῷ λόγῳ
lust; and if any other commandment, in this word
346 1722 25 4139 4675/5613
ἀνακεφαλαιοῦται, ἐν τῷ, Ἀγαπήσεις τὸν πλησίον σου ὡς
it is summed up: You shall love the neighbor of you as
1438 26 4139 2556 3756 2038
10 ἑαυτόν. ἡ ἀγάπη τῷ πλησίον κακὸν οὐκ ἐργάζεται·
yourself Love to the neighbor evil does not work;
4138 3767 3551 26
πλήρωμα οὖν νόμου ἡ ἀγάπη.
fulfillment then of law (is) love.
5124 1492 2540 3754/5610/2248/2235/1537/5258
11 Καὶ τοῦτο, εἰδότες τὸν καιρόν, ὅτι ὥρα ἡμᾶς ἤδη ἐξ ὕπνου
And this, knowing the time, that an hour (is for you) now out of sleep
1453 3568/1093/ 1452 2257 4991 3753 4100
ἐγερθῆναι· νῦν γὰρ ἐγγύτερον ἡμῶν ἡ σωτηρία ἢ ὅτε ἐπι-
to be raised: now for nearer of us the salvation than when we
3571 4298 2250 1448 659
12 στεύσαμεν. ἡ νὺξ προέκοψεν, ἡ δὲ ἡμέρα ἤγγικεν· ἀποθώμεθα
believed. The night (is) far gone, the and day has drawn near. Let us cast off
3767 2041 4655 1746 3696
οὖν τὰ ἔργα τοῦ σκότους, καὶ ἐνδυσώμεθα τὰ ὅπλα τοῦ
then the works of the darkness, and let us put on the weapons of the
5457/5613/1722/2250 2156 4043 3361 2970
13 φωτός. ὡς ἐν ἡμέρᾳ, εὐσχημόνως περιπατήσωμεν, μὴ κώμοις
light. As in (the) day, becomingly let us walk, not in carousing
3178 3361 2845 766 3361 2054 2205 235
14 καὶ μέθαις, μὴ κοίταις καὶ ἀσελγείαις, μὴ ἔριδι καὶ ζήλῳ. ἀλλ
and drinking, not in cohabi-tation and lustful acts, not in fighting and envy. But
1746 2424 5547 4561
ἐνδύσασθε τὸν Κύριον Ἰησοῦν Χριστόν, καὶ τῆς σαρκὸς
put on the Lord Jesus Christ, and of the flesh
4307 3361 4160 1519 1939
πρόνοιαν μὴ ποιεῖσθε, εἰς ἐπιθυμίας.
forethought do not make for (its) lusts.

CHAPTER 14

[1]And receive the *one* who is weak in the faith, not to judgments of *your* thoughts. [2]One indeed believes to eat all things; but being weak, *another* one eats vegetables. [3]The *one* eating do not despise the *one* not eating. And the *one* not eating, do not judge the *one* eating—for God received him. [4]Who are you judging another's servant? To his own master he stands or falls. But he will stand, for God is able to make him stand. [5]One indeed judges a day above *another* day; and *another* one judges every day *alike*. Let each one be fully assured in his own mind. [6]The *one* minding the day, *he* minds *it* to *the* Lord. And the *one* not minding the day, he does not mind *it* to *the* Lord. The *one* eating, he eats to *the* Lord; for he gives thanks to God. And the *one* not eating, he does not eat to *the* Lord, and gives thanks to God. [7]For no one of us lives to himself; and no one dies to himself. [8]For both if we live, we live to *the* Lord; and if we die, we die to *the* Lord. Then both if we live, and if we die, we are the Lord's. [9]For this Christ both died and rose and lived again, that He might be Lord over both *the* dead and the living.

[10]But why do you judge your brother? Or why do you also despise your brother? For all shall stand before the judgment seat of Christ. [11]For it has been written, "I live, says *the* Lord, that every knee will bow to Me, and every tongue confess to God." [12]So then each one of us will give account concerning himself to God.

CHAPTER 14

770 4102 4355 3361/1519
1 Τὸν δὲ ἀσθενοῦντα τῇ πίστει προσλαμβάνεσθε, μὴ εἰς
the (one) And being weak in the faith receive, not to
1253 1261 3739/3303/ 4100 5315 3956
2 διακρίσεις διαλογισμῶν. ὃς μὲν πιστεύει φαγεῖν πάντα, ὁ
judgments of thoughts. One indeed believes to eat all things, one
770 3001 2068 2068 3361 2068 3361
3 δὲ ἀσθενῶν λάχανα ἐσθίει. ὁ ἐσθίων τὸν μὴ ἐσθίοντα μὴ
but being weak vegetables eats. The (one) eating the (one) not eating do not
1848 3361 2068 2068 3361 2919
ἐξουθενείτω, καὶ ὁ μὴ ἐσθίων τὸν ἐσθίοντα μὴ κρινέτω· ὁ
despise; and the (one) not eating the (one) eating do not judge. —
2316 1063 846 4355 4771/5101/1487/ 2919 245
4 Θεὸς γὰρ αὐτὸν προσελάβετο. σὺ τίς εἶ ὁ κρίνων ἀλλότριον
God For him received. You who are judging of another
3610 2398 2962 2476/2228/ 4098 2476
οἰκέτην; τῷ ἰδίῳ κυρίῳ στήκει ἢ πίπτει. σταθήσεται δέ·
a servant, to the own lord he stands or falls; he will stand but
1415 1063 2076 2316 4739 846 3739/3303 2919
5 δυνατὸς γάρ ἐστιν ὁ Θεὸς στῆσαι αὐτόν. ὃς μὲν κρίνει
able for is God to stand him. One indeed judges
2250 3844 2250 3739 2919 3956 2250 1538
ἡμέραν παρ' ἡμέραν, ὃς δὲ κρίνει πᾶσαν ἡμέραν. ἕκαστος
a day above a day; one and judges every day (alike). Each
1722 2398 3563 4135 5426 2250
6 ἐν τῷ ἰδίῳ νοῒ πληροφορείσθω. ὁ φρονῶν τὴν ἡμέραν,
in the own mind let him be fully assured. He minding the day,
2962 5426 3361 5426 2250 2962 3756
Κυρίῳ φρονεῖ· καὶ ὁ μὴ φρονῶν τὴν ἡμέραν, Κυρίῳ οὐ
to (the) Lord he minds; and he not minding the day, to (the) Lord not
5426 2068 2962 2068 2168 1063 2316
φρονεῖ. ὁ ἐσθίων Κυρίῳ ἐσθίει, εὐχαριστεῖ γὰρ τῷ Θεῷ· καὶ
he minds. He eating, to (the) Lord he eats; he gives thanks for to God; and
3361 2068 2962 3756 2068 2168 2316
ὁ μὴ ἐσθίων Κυρίῳ οὐκ ἐσθίει, καὶ εὐχαριστεῖ τῷ Θεῷ.
he not eating, to (the) Lord not he eats; and gives thanks to God.
3762 1063 5216 1438/2198 3762 1438 599
7 οὐδεὶς γὰρ ἡμῶν ἑαυτῷ ζῇ, καὶ οὐδεὶς ἑαυτῷ ἀποθνήσκει.
no one For of us to himself lives, and no one to himself dies.
1437/5037/1063/ 2198 2962 2198 1437/5037/ 599
8 ἐάν τε γὰρ ζῶμεν, τῷ Κυρίῳ ζῶμεν· ἐάν τε ἀποθνήσκωμεν,
if both For we live, to (the) Lord we live; if and we die,
2962 599 1437/6037/3767/2198/1437/5037/ 599
τῷ Κυρίῳ ἀποθνήσκομεν· ἐάν τε οὖν ζῶμεν, ἐάν τε ἀποθνή-
to (the) Lord we die. if And therefore we live, if and we
2962 2068 1519 5124 1063 5547
9 σκωμεν, τοῦ Κυρίου ἐσμέν. εἰς τοῦτο γὰρ Χριστὸς καὶ
die, of the Lord we are. for this For Christ also
599 450 326 2443 3498
ἀπέθανε καὶ ἀνέστη καὶ ἀνέζησεν, ἵνα καὶ νεκρῶν καὶ
died and rose and lived again, that both of dead and
2198 2961 4771 5101 2919 80 4675 2228
10 ζώντων κυριεύσῃ. σὺ δὲ τί κρίνεις τὸν ἀδελφόν σου; ἢ καὶ
of living He might be Lord. you And why judge the brother of you? Or also
4771/5101/ 1848 80 4675 3956 1063 3936
σὺ τί ἐξουθενεῖς τὸν ἀδελφόν σου; πάντες γὰρ παραστη-
you why despise the brother of you? all For shall stand
968 5547 1125 1063/2198/1473
11 σόμεθα τῷ βήματι τοῦ Χριστοῦ. γέγραπται γάρ, Ζῶ ἐγώ,
before the judgment seat of Christ. it has been written For, live I,
3004 2962/3754/1698 2578 3956 1119 3956 1100
λέγει Κύριος· ὅτι ἐμοὶ κάμψει πᾶν γόνυ, καὶ πᾶσα γλῶσσα
says (the) Lord, that to Me will bow every knee, and every tongue
1843 2316 686 3767 1538 2257 4012
12 ἐξομολογήσεται τῷ Θεῷ. ἄρα οὖν ἕκαστος ἡμῶν περὶ
will confess to God. So then, each one of us concerning
1438 3056 1325 2316
ἑαυτοῦ λόγον δώσει τῷ Θεῷ.
himself account will give to God.

[13]Then let us no longer judge one another, but rather judge this, not to put a stumbling-block or an offense toward a brother. [14]I know and am persuaded in *the* Lord Jesus that nothing by itself *is* common; except to the *one* counting anything to be common, *it is* common. [15]But if your brother is grieved because of *your* food, you no longer walk according to love. Do not by your food destroy that one for whom Christ died. [16]Then do not let your good be spoken evil of. [17]For the kingdom of God is not eating and drinking, but righteousness and peace and joy in *the* Holy Spirit. [18]For the *one* serving Christ in these things *is* well-pleasing to God, and approved by men.

[19]So then let us pursue the things of peace, and the things for building up one another. [20]Do not undo the work of God because of food. Truly, all things *are* clean, but *it is* bad to the man who eats through a stumbling-block. [21]*It is* good not to eat flesh, nor to drink wine, nor *anything* by which your brother stumbles, or is offended, or is weak.

[22]Do you have faith? Have *it* to yourself before God. Blessed *is* the *one* not condemning himself in what he approves. [23]But the *one* doubting, if he eats, *he* has been condemned, because it is not of faith—and whatever *is* not of faith is sin.

CHAPTER 15

[1]But we who *are* strong ought to bear the weaknesses of those not strong, and not to please ourselves. [2]For let everyone of us please his neighbor for good, to building up.

3371 3767 240 2919 235 5124 2919
13 Μηκέτι οὖν ἀλλήλους κρίνωμεν· ἀλλὰ τοῦτο κρίνατε
No longer, then, one another let us judge; but this judge
3123 3361 5087 4348 80 4625
μᾶλλον, τὸ μὴ τιθέναι πρόσκομμα τῷ ἀδελφῷ ἢ σκάνδαλον.
rather, not to put a stumbling-block to the brother or an offense
1492 3982 1722 2962 2424 3754/3762 2839 1223
14 οἶδα καὶ πέπεισμαι ἐν Κυρίῳ Ἰησοῦ, ὅτι οὐδὲν κοινὸν δι'
I know and am persuaded in (the) Lord Jesus, that nothing (is) common by
1438 =1508= 3049 5100 2839 1511 1565 2839
ἑαυτοῦ· εἰ μὴ τῷ λογιζομένῳ τι κοινὸν εἶναι, ἐκείνῳ κοινόν.
itself, except to the (one) counting anything common to be, to that comm
1487 1223 1033 80 4675 3076 3765 2596 26
15 εἰ δὲ διὰ βρῶμα ὁ ἀδελφός σου λυπεῖται, οὐκέτι κατὰ ἀγάπην
if And for (your) food the brother of you is grieved, no longer according to lo
4043 3361 1033 4675 1565 622 5228 373
περιπατεῖς. μὴ τῷ βρώματί σου ἐκεῖνον ἀπόλλυε, ὑπὲρ οὗ
do you walk. Not by the food of you that one destroy, for whom
5547 599 3361 987 3767/5216/ 18
16 Χριστὸς ἀπέθανε. μὴ βλασφημείσθω οὖν ὑμῶν τὸ ἀγαθόν·
Christ died, let not be evil spoken of Then of you the good.
3756/1063/2076 932 2316 1035 4213 235
17 οὐ γάρ ἐστιν ἡ βασιλεία τοῦ Θεοῦ βρῶσις καὶ πόσις, ἀλλὰ
not For is the kingdom Of God eating and drinking, but
1343 1515 5479/1722 4151 40 1063
18 δικαιοσύνη καὶ εἰρήνη καὶ χαρὰ ἐν Πνεύματι Ἁγίῳ. ὁ γὰρ
righteousness and peace and joy in (the) Spirit Holy. the For
1722 5125 1398 5547 2101 2316
ἐν τούτοις δουλεύων τῷ Χριστῷ εὐάρεστος τῷ Θεῷ, καὶ
in these serving Christ (is) well-pleasing to God, and
1384 444 686/3767 1515 1377
19 δόκιμος τοῖς ἀνθρώποις. ἄρα οὖν τὰ τῆς εἰρήνης διώκωμεν,
approved by men. So then the things of peace let us pursue
3619 1519 240 3361/1752 1033
20 καὶ τὰ τῆς οἰκοδομῆς τῆς εἰς ἀλλήλους. μὴ ἕνεκεν βρώματος
and the things for building up for one another. Do not because of food
2647 2041 2316 3956 3303/ 2513 235 2556
κατάλυε τὸ ἔργον τοῦ Θεοῦ. πάντα μὲν καθαρά, ἀλλὰ κακὸν
undo the work of God. All things truly (are) clean, but bad
444 1223 4348 2068 2570 3361
21 τῷ ἀνθρώπῳ τῷ διὰ προσκόμματος ἐσθίοντι. καλὸν τὸ μὴ
to the man through a stumbling-block eating. (It is) good not
5315 2907 3366 4095 3631 3366/1722/3739 80 4675
φαγεῖν κρέα, μηδὲ πιεῖν οἶνον, μηδὲ ἐν ᾧ ὁ ἀδελφός σου
to eat flesh, nor to drink wine, nor (any) by which the brother of y
4350 2228 4624 2228 770 4771 4102 2192
22 προσκόπτει ἢ σκανδαλίζεται ἢ ἀσθενεῖ. σὺ πίστιν ἔχεις
stumbles, or be offended, or be weak. Do you faith have?
2596 4572 2192 1799 2316 3107 3361 2919
κατὰ σαυτὸν ἔχε ἐνώπιον τοῦ Θεοῦ. μακάριος ὁ μὴ κρίνων
By yourself have (it) before God. Blessed the (one) not judging
1438 1722/3739/ 1381 1252 1437 5315 2632
23 ἑαυτὸν ἐν ᾧ δοκιμάζει. ὁ δὲ διακρινόμενος, ἐὰν φάγῃ, κατα-
himself in what he approves; he but doubting, if he eats, has been
3754/3756/1537/ 4102 3956 3739/3756/1537/4102
κέκριται, ὅτι οὐκ ἐκ πίστεως· πᾶν δὲ ὃ οὐκ ἐκ πίστεως
condemned, because not of faith; all and not of faith
266 2076
ἁμαρτία ἐστίν.
sin is.

CHAPTER 15

3784 2249 1415 771 102
1 Ὀφείλομεν δὲ ἡμεῖς οἱ δυνατοὶ τὰ ἀσθενήματα τῶν ἀδυνά-
ought And we the strong the weaknesses of the not
941 3361 1438 700 1538 1063
2 των βαστάζειν, καὶ μὴ ἑαυτοῖς ἀρέσκειν. ἕκαστος γὰρ
strong to bear, and not (our)selves to please. each one For
2257 4139 700 1519 18 4314 3619
ἡμῶν τῷ πλησίον ἀρεσκέτω εἰς τὸ ἀγαθὸν πρὸς οἰκοδομήν
of us the neighbor let him please for good, to building up

[3]For also Christ did not please Himself, but even as it has been written, "The curses of those cursing You fell on Me." [4]For whatever things were written before were written for our instruction, that through patience and encouragement of the Scriptures we might have hope. [5]And may the God of patience and encouragement give to you to mind the same among one another according to Christ Jesus, [6]that with one accord *and* with one mouth you may glorify *the* God and Father of our Lord Jesus Christ. [7]Therefore, receive one another as Christ also received us, to *the* glory of God. [8]And I say, Jesus Christ has become a minister of circumcision for *the* truth of God, to confirm the promises of the fathers, [9]and for the nations to glorify God for mercy, even as it has been written, "Because of this I will confess to You in the nations, and I will give praise to Your name." [10]And again He says, "Rejoice, nations, with His people." [11]And again, "Praise the Lord, all the nations, and praise Him all the peoples." [12]And again Isaiah says, "The Root of Jesse shall be, and He rising up to rule the nations; on Him nations will hope." [13]And may the God of hope fill you with all joy and peace in believing, for you to abound in hope, in power of *the* Holy Spirit.

[14]But, my brothers, I myself also am persuaded concerning you, that you yourselves are also full of goodness, being filled with all knowledge, being able to warn one another. [15]But I wrote to you more boldly,

1063 5547 3756 1438 700 235 2531
3 καὶ γὰρ ὁ Χριστὸς οὐχ ἑαυτῷ ἤρεσεν, ἀλλά, καθὼς
even For Christ not Himself pleased, but even as
1125 3680 3679 4571 1968
γέγραπται, Οἱ ὀνειδισμοὶ τῶν ὀνειδιζόντων σε ἐπέπεσον
it has been written: The reproaches of those reproaching You fell
1909/1691/3745/1063 4270 1519 2251 1319
4 ἐπ' ἐμέ. ὅσα γὰρ προεγράφη, εἰς τὴν ἡμετέραν διδασκαλίαν
on Me. what- For were written for our teaching
•1223 4270 ever 2443/•/ before. 5281 3874
προεγράφη, ἵνα διὰ τῆς ὑπομονῆς καὶ τῆς παρακλήσεως
were written before, that through patience and encouragement
1124 1680 2192 2316 5281
5 τῶν γραφῶν τὴν ἐλπίδα ἔχωμεν. ὁ δὲ Θεὸς τῆς ὑπομονῆς
of the Scriptures hope we might have. the And God of patience
3874 1325/5213 846 5426 1722 240
καὶ τῆς παρακλήσεως δῴη ὑμῖν τὸ αὐτὸ φρονεῖν ἐν ἀλλήλοις
and of encouragement give to you the same, to mind among one another
2596 5547 2424 2443 3661 1722/1520 4750
6 κατὰ Χριστὸν Ἰησοῦν· ἵνα ὁμοθυμαδὸν ἐν ἑνὶ στόματι
according to Christ Jesus, that with one accord, with one mouth
1392 2316 3962 2962 2257 2424
δοξάζητε τὸν Θεὸν καὶ πατέρα τοῦ Κυρίου ἡμῶν Ἰησοῦ
you may glorify the God and Father of the Lord of us Jesus,
5547 1352 4355 240 2531 5547
7 Χριστοῦ. διὸ προσλαμβάνεσθε ἀλλήλους, καθὼς καὶ ὁ Χρι-
Christ. Therefore receive one another, even as also Christ
4355 2248/1519/1391 2316 3004 2424
8 στὸς προσελάβετο ἡμᾶς, εἰς δόξαν Θεοῦ. λέγω δέ, Ἰησοῦν
received us, to (the) glory of God. I say And, Jesus
5547 1249 1096 4061 5228 225
Χριστὸν διάκονον γεγενῆσθαι περιτομῆς ὑπὲρ ἀληθείας
Christ a minister has become of circumcision for (the) truth
2316/1519 950 1860 3962
Θεοῦ, εἰς τὸ βεβαιῶσαι τὰς ἐπαγγελίας τῶν πατέρων· τὰ
of God, to confirm the promises of the fathers, the
1484 5228 1656 1392 2316 2531 1125
9 δὲ ἔθνη ὑπὲρ ἐλέους δοξάσαι τὸν Θεόν, καθὼς γέγραπται,
and nations for mercy to glorify God, even as it has been written,
1223/5124 1843 4671/1722/1484 3686 4675
Διὰ τοῦτο ἐξομολογήσομαί σοι ἐν ἔθνεσι, καὶ τῷ ὀνόματί σου
Therefore I will confess to You among nations, and to Your name
5567 3825 3004 2165 1484 3326 2992
10 ψαλῶ. καὶ πάλιν λέγει, Εὐφράνθητε, ἔθνη, μετὰ τοῦ λαοῦ
I will praise. And again he says, Rejoice, nations, with the people
848 3825 134 2962 3956 1484
11 αὐτοῦ. καὶ πάλιν, Αἰνεῖτε τὸν Κύριον πάντα τὰ ἔθνη, καὶ
of Him. And again, Praise the Lord all the nations, and
1867 846 3956 2992 3825 2268 3004
12 ἐπαινέσατε αὐτὸν πάντες οἱ λαοί. καὶ πάλιν Ἠσαΐας λέγει,
praise Him all the peoples And again, Isaiah says,
2071 4491 2421 450 757 1484
Ἔσται ἡ ῥίζα τοῦ Ἰεσσαί, καὶ ὁ ἀνιστάμενος ἄρχειν ἐθνῶν·
Shall be the Root of Jesse, and the (One) rising up to rule the nations;
1909/846 1484 1679 2316 1680 4137
13 ἐπ' αὐτῷ ἔθνη ἐλπιοῦσιν. ὁ δὲ Θεὸς τῆς ἐλπίδος πληρῶσαι
on Him nations will hope. the And God of hope fill
5209 3956 5479 1515/1722 4100 1519 4052
ὑμᾶς πάσης χαρᾶς καὶ εἰρήνης ἐν τῷ πιστεύειν, εἰς τὸ περισ-
you of all joy and peace in believing, for to
5209/1722 1680 1722 1411 4151 40
σεύειν ὑμᾶς ἐν τῇ ἐλπίδι, ἐν δυνάμει Πνεύματος Ἁγίου.
abound you in hope, in power of (the) Spirit Holy.
3982 80 3450 848 1473/4012/5216/3754
14 Πέπεισμαι δέ, ἀδελφοί μου, καὶ αὐτὸς ἐγὼ περὶ ὑμῶν, ὅτι
I am persuaded But, brothers of me, even myself, I, concerning you, that
848 3324/2075 19 4137 3956
καὶ αὐτοὶ μεστοί ἐστε ἀγαθωσύνης, πεπληρωμένοι πάσης
also yourselves full you are of goodness, having been filled of all
1108 1410 240 3560 5112
15 γνώσεως, δυνάμενοι καὶ ἀλλήλους νουθετεῖν. τολμηρότερον
knowledge, being able also one another to warn. more boldly

brothers, as reminding you in part, because of the grace given to me by God, [16]for me to be a minister of Jesus Christ to the nations, sacredly ministering the gospel of God, that the offering of the nations might be acceptable *and* sanctified by *the* Holy Spirit. [17]Therefore, I have boasting in Christ Jesus *as to* the things pertaining to God. [18]For I will not dare to speak of anything which Christ did not work out through me for *the* obedience of the nations in word and work, [19]in power of miracles and wonders, in power of *the* Spirit of God, so as *for* me to have fulfilled the gospel of Christ from Jerusalem and in a circle as far as Illyricum. [20]And so eagerly striving to preach the gospel where Christ was named, so that I should not build on another's foundation; [21]but even as it has been written, "They shall see, to whom nothing was announced concerning Him; and the ones that have not heard, they shall understand."

[22]Therefore, I also was much hindered from coming to you, [23]but now having no more place in these regions, and having a longing to come to you for many years, [24]whenever I may go into Spain, I will come to you; for I hope *in* traveling through to see you, and to be set forward there by you, if first I may be filled of you in part. [25]But now I am going to Jerusalem, doing service to the saints. [26]For Macedonia and Achaia thought it good to make certain gifts to the poor of the saints in

1125 5213 80 575 3313/5613/ 1878
δὲ ἔγραψα ὑμῖν, ἀδελφοί, ἀπὸ μέρους, ὡς ἐπαναμιμνήσκων
And I wrote to you, brothers, in part as reminding
5209/1223 5485 1325 3427 5259 2316 1519
16 ὑμᾶς, διὰ τὴν χάριν τὴν δοθεῖσάν μοι ὑπὸ τοῦ Θεοῦ, εἰς τὸ
you, because of the grace given to me by God, for
1511/3165/ 3011 2424 5547 1519 1484 2418
εἶναί με λειτουργὸν Ἰησοῦ Χριστοῦ εἰς τὰ ἔθνη, ἱερουρ-
to be me a minister of Jesus Christ to the nations, sacredly
2098 2316 2443 1096 4376
γοῦντα τὸ εὐαγγέλιον τοῦ Θεοῦ, ἵνα γένηται ἡ προσφορὰ
ministering the gospel of God, that may be the offering
1484 2144 37 1722 4151 40 2192
17 τῶν ἐθνῶν εὐπρόσδεκτος, ἡγιασμένη ἐν Πνεύματι Ἁγίῳ. ἔχω
of the nations acceptable, sanctified by (the) Spirit Holy. I have
3767 2746 1722 5547 2424 4314 2316 3756/1063
18 οὖν καύχησιν ἐν Χριστῷ Ἰησοῦ τὰ πρὸς Θεόν. οὐ γὰρ
therefore boasting in Christ Jesus the things with God. not for
5111 2980/5100/3739/3756/ 2716 5547 1223/1700
τολμήσω λαλεῖν τι ὧν οὐ κατειργάσατο Χριστὸς δι' ἐμοῦ,
I will dare to speak anything which not did work out Christ through me,
1519 5218 1484 of 3056 2041 1722 1411 4592
19 εἰς ὑπακοὴν ἐθνῶν λόγῳ καὶ ἔργῳ, ἐν δυνάμει σημείων καὶ
for obedience of (the) nations in word and work, in power of signs and
5059 2722 1411 4151 2316 5620/3165/575 2419
τεράτων, ἐν δυνάμει Πνεύματος Θεοῦ· ὥστε με ἀπὸ Ἱερου-
wonders, in power of (the) Spirit of God, so as me from Jerus-
2945 3360 2437 4137
σαλὴμ καὶ κύκλῳ μέχρι τοῦ Ἰλλυρικοῦ πεπληρωκέναι τὸ
alem and around to — Illyricum to have fulfilled the
2098 5547 3779 5389 2097
20 εὐαγγέλιον τοῦ Χριστοῦ· οὕτω δὲ φιλοτιμούμενον εὐαγγελί-
gospel of Christ. so And eagerly striving to preach the
3756/3699 3687 5547 2443/3361/1909 245
ζεσθαι, οὐχ ὅπου ὠνομάσθη Χριστός, ἵνα μὴ ἐπ' ἀλλότριον
gospel, not where was named Christ, that not on another's
2310 3618 235 2531 1125 3739 3756
21 θεμέλιον οἰκοδομῶ· ἀλλά, καθὼς γέγραπται, Οἷς οὐκ
foundation I should build, but, even as it has been written: To whom no
312 4012 846 3700 3739/3756 191
ἀνηγγέλη περὶ αὐτοῦ, ὄψονται· καὶ οἳ οὐκ ἀκηκόασι,
it was announced about Him, they shall see; and those not having heard,
4820
συνήσουσι.
they shall understand.

1352 1465 4183 2064 4314 5209
22 Διὸ καὶ ἐνεκοπτόμην τὰ πολλὰ τοῦ ἐλθεῖν πρὸς ὑμᾶς·
Therefore also I was hindered much to come to you;
3570 3371 5117 2192/1722 2824 5125 1974
23 νυνὶ δὲ μηκέτι τόπον ἔχων ἐν τοῖς κλίμασι τούτοις, ἐπιποθίαν
now but no longer place having in — regions these, a desire
2192 2064 4314 5209 575 4183 2094/5613/1437
24 δὲ ἔχων τοῦ ἐλθεῖν πρὸς ὑμᾶς ἀπὸ πολλῶν ἐτῶν, ὡς ἐὰν
and having to come to you from many years, whenever
4198 1519 4681 2064 4314/5209 1679
πορεύωμαι εἰς τὴν Σπανίαν, ἐλεύσομαι πρὸς ὑμᾶς· ἐλπίζω
I may go into Spain, I will come to you; I hope
1063 1279 2300 5209 5259 5216 4311
γὰρ διαπορευόμενος θεάσασθαι ὑμᾶς, καὶ ὑφ' ὑμῶν προ-
for traveling through to behold you, and by you to be
1563/1437 5216 4412 575 3313 1705
πεμφθῆναι ἐκεῖ, ἐὰν ὑμῶν πρῶτον ἀπὸ μέρους ἐμπλησθῶ.
set forward there. if of you firstly in part I may be filled.
3570 4198 1519 2419 1247 40
25 νυνὶ δὲ πορεύομαι εἰς Ἱερουσαλήμ, διακονῶν τοῖς ἁγίοις.
now And I am going to Jerusalem ministering to the saints.
2106 1063 3109 882 2842 5100
26 εὐδόκησαν γὰρ Μακεδονία καὶ Ἀχαΐα κοινωνίαν τινὰ
thought it good For Macedonia and Achaia gifts certain
4160 1519 4434 40 1722 2419
ποιήσασθαι εἰς τοὺς πτωχοὺς τῶν ἁγίων τῶν ἐν Ἱερου-
to make to the poor of the saints — in Jeru-

Jerusalem. [27]For they thought it good, also being debtors of them; for if the nations shared in their spiritual things, they ought also to minister to them in the fleshly things. [28]Then completing and having sealed this fruit to them, I will go through you into Spain. [29]And I know that I will come to you in the fullness of *the* blessing of the gospel of Christ *when* I come.

2106 1063 3781 848 1526 1487/1063
27 σαλήμ. εὐδόκησαν γάρ, καὶ ὀφειλέται αὐτῶν εἰσιν. εἰ γὰρ
salem. they thought it good For, and debtors of them are. if For
4152 848 2841 1484 3784
τοῖς πνευματικοῖς αὐτῶν ἐκοινώνησαν τὰ ἔθνη, ὀφείλουσι
in the spiritual things of them shared the nations, they ought
1722 4559 3008 846 5124 3767
28 καὶ ἐν τοῖς σαρκικοῖς λειτουργῆσαι αὐτοῖς. τοῦτο οὖν
also in the fleshly things to minister to them. this Then
2005 4972 846 2590 5126
ἐπιτελέσας, καὶ σφραγισάμενος αὐτοῖς τὸν καρπὸν τοῦτον,
having finished, and having sealed to them fruit this,
565 1223/5216/1519 4681 1492 3754 2064
29 ἀπελεύσομαι δι' ὑμῶν εἰς τὴν Σπανίαν. οἶδα δὲ ὅτι ἐρχό-
I will go away through you to Spain. I know And that coming
4314/5209/1722/ 4138 2129 2098
μενος πρὸς ὑμᾶς ἐν πληρώματι εὐλογίας τοῦ εὐαγγελίου τοῦ
to you in the fullness of (the) blessing of the gospel
5547 2064
Χριστοῦ ἐλεύσομαι.
of Christ I will come.

[30]But, brothers, I exhort you by our Lord Jesus Christ, and by the love of the Spirit, to strive together with me in *your* prayers to God on my behalf, [31]that I be delivered from those disobeying in Judea, and that my ministry to Jerusalem may be acceptable to the saints; [32]that *I may* come to you in joy through *the* will of God, and that I may be refreshed with you. [33]And the God of peace *be* with all of you. Amen.

3870 5209 80 1223 2962 2257 2424
30 Παρακαλῶ δὲ ὑμᾶς, ἀδελφοί, διὰ τοῦ Κυρίου ἡμῶν Ἰησοῦ
I exhort And you, brothers, by the Lord of us, Jesus
5547 1223 26 4151 4865
Χριστοῦ, καὶ διὰ τῆς ἀγάπης τοῦ Πνεύματος, συναγωνί-
Christ, and by the love of the Spirit, to strive
3427/1722 4335 5228 1700/4314 2316
σασθαί μοι ἐν ταῖς προσευχαῖς ὑπὲρ ἐμοῦ πρὸς τὸν Θεόν·
together with me in the prayers on behalf of me to — God,
2443 4506 575 544 1722 2449 2443
31 ἵνα ῥυσθῶ ἀπὸ τῶν ἀπειθούντων ἐν τῇ Ἰουδαίᾳ, καὶ ἵνα ἡ
that I be delivered from those disobeying in — Judea, and that the
1248 3450 1519 2419 2144 1096
διακονία μου ἡ εἰς Ἱερουσαλὴμ εὐπρόσδεκτος γένηται τοῖς
ministry of me which (is) to Jerusalem acceptable may be to the
40 2443/1722/5479/2064 4314/5209/1223/ 2307 2316
32 ἁγίοις· ἵνα ἐν χαρᾷ ἔλθω πρὸς ὑμᾶς διὰ θελήματος Θεοῦ, καὶ
saints, that in joy coming to you through (the) will of God, and
4875 5216 2316 1515 3326 3956
33 συναναπαύσωμαι ὑμῖν. ὁ δὲ Θεὸς τῆς εἰρήνης μετὰ πάντων
I may be refreshed with you. the And God of peace with all
5216 281
ὑμῶν. ἀμήν.
of you. Amen.

CHAPTER 16

[1]But I commend to you our sister Phoebe, being a servant of the church in Cenchrea; [2]that you may receive her in *the* Lord, *as is* worthy of the saints, and may assist her in whatever she may need of you. For she also became a helper of many, and of myself.

4921 5213 5402 79 2259 5607
1 Συνίστημι δὲ ὑμῖν Φοίβην τὴν ἀδελφὴν ἡμῶν, οὖσαν
I commend And to you Phoebe the sister of us, being
1249 1577 1722 2747 2443 846 4327
διάκονον τῆς ἐκκλησίας τῆς ἐν Κεγχρεαῖς· ἵνα αὐτὴν προσδέ-
a servant of the church in Cenchrea, that her you may
3739 1722 2962 516 40 3936 846/1722//
2 ξησθε ἐν Κυρίῳ ἀξίως τῶν ἁγίων, καὶ παραστῆτε αὐτῇ ἐν ᾧ
receive in (the) Lord worthily of the saints, and may assist her in what-
302/5216 5535 4229 1063/3778 4368 4183
ἂν ὑμῶν χρῄζῃ πράγματι· καὶ γὰρ αὕτη προστάτις πολλῶν
ever of you she may matter. also For she a helper of many
1096 have need 848 1700
ἐγενήθη, καὶ αὐτοῦ ἐμοῦ.
became, and of myself.

[3]Greet Priscilla and Aquila, my fellow-workers in Christ Jesus, [4]who laid down their neck for my soul; to whom I not only give thanks, but also all the

782 4252 207 4904 3450
3 Ἀσπάσασθε Πρίσκιλλαν καὶ Ἀκύλαν τοὺς συνεργούς μου
Greet Priscilla and Aquilla the fellow-workers of me
1722 5547 2424 3748 5228 5590 3450 1438
4 ἐν Χριστῷ Ἰησοῦ, οἵτινες ὑπὲρ τῆς ψυχῆς μου τὸν ἑαυτῶν
In Christ Jesus, who for the soul of me the of themselves
5137 5294 3756/1473/3441 2168 235
τράχηλον ὑπέθηκαν, οἷς οὐκ ἐγὼ μόνος εὐχαριστῶ, ἀλλὰ
neck they laid down; to whom not I only give thanks, but

churches of the nations. [5]And greet the church at their house, and my beloved Epenetus, who is a firstfruit of Achaia for Christ. [6]Greet Mary, who did much labor for us. [7]Greet Andronicus and Junias, my kinsmen and fellow-prisoners, noted among the apostles, who also were in Christ before me. [8]Greet Amplias my beloved in the Lord.

3956 1577 1484 2596 3624 848
5 καὶ πᾶσαι αἱ ἐκκλησίαι τῶν ἐθνῶν· καὶ τὴν κατ' οἶκον αὐτῶν
also all the churches of the nations; and the in house of them
1577 782 1866 27 3450/3739
ἐκκλησίαν. ἀσπάσασθε Ἐπαίνετον τὸν ἀγαπητόν μου, ὅς
church. Greet Epenetus the beloved of me, who
2076 536 882 1519 5547 782 3137
ἐστιν ἀπαρχὴ τῆς Ἀχαΐας εἰς Χριστόν. ἀσπάσασθε Μαριάμ,
is firstfruit of Achaia for Christ. Greet Mariam,
3748 4183 2872 1519/5209 782 408
6 ἥτις πολλὰ ἐκοπίασεν εἰς ἡμᾶς. ἀσπάσασθε Ἀνδρόνικον καὶ
who many things labored for you. Greet Andronicus and
2458 4773 3450 4869 3450
7 Ἰουνίαν τοὺς συγγενεῖς μου καὶ συναιχμαλώτους μου,
Junias the kinsmen of me and fellow-prisoners of me,
3748 1526 1978 1722 652 3739 4253/1700
οἵτινές εἰσιν ἐπίσημοι ἐν τοῖς ἀποστόλοις, οἳ καὶ πρὸ ἐμοῦ
who are notable among the apostles, who and before me
1096 1722 5547 782 291 27
8 γεγόνασιν ἐν Χριστῷ. ἀσπάσασθε Ἀμπλίαν τὸν ἀγαπητόν
have been in Christ. Greet Amplias the beloved

[9]Greet Urbanus, our helper in Christ, and my beloved Stachys. [10]Greet Apelles, the approved in Christ; Greet those of Aristobulus.

3450/1722/2962 782 3773 4904 2257/1722
9 μου ἐν Κυρίῳ. ἀσπάσασθε Οὐρβανὸν τὸν συνεργὸν ἡμῶν ἐν
of me in (the) Lord. Greet Urbanus the fellow-worker of us in
5547 4720 27 3450 782 559
10 Χριστῷ, καὶ Στάχυν τὸν ἀγαπητόν μου. ἀσπάσασθε Ἀπελ-
Christ, and Stachys the beloved of me. Greet Apelles
1384 1722 5547 782 1537 711
λῆν τὸν δόκιμον ἐν Χριστῷ. ἀσπάσασθε τοὺς ἐκ τῶν Ἀριστο-
the approved in Christ. Greet those of Aristo-

[11]Greet Herodion, my kinsman. Greet those of Narcissus, those being in *the* Lord. [12]Greet Tryphena and Tryphosa, those laboring in *the* Lord. Greet Persis the beloved, who *has* labored *in* many things in *the* Lord. [13]Greet Rufus, the chosen in *the* Lord, and his mother and mine. [14]Greet Asyncritus, Phlegon, Hermas, Patrobas, Hermes, and the brothers with them. [15]Greet Philologus and Julias, Nereus and his sister, and Olympas, and all the saints with them. [16]Greet one another with a holy kiss. The churches of Christ greet you.

782 2267 4773 3450 782
11 βούλου. ἀσπάσασθε Ἡροδίωνα τὸν συγγενῆ μου. ἀσπά-
bulus. Greet Herodian the kinsman of me. Greet
1537 3488 5607 1722 2962 782
12 σασθε τοὺς ἐκ τῶν Ναρκίσσου, τοὺς ὄντας ἐν Κυρίῳ. ἀσπά-
those of Narcissus, those being in (the) Lord. Greet
5170 5173 2872 1722 2962
σασθε Τρύφαιναν καὶ Τρυφῶσαν τὰς κοπιώσας ἐν Κυρίῳ.
Tryphena and Tryphosa, those laboring in (the) Lord.
782 4069 27 3748 4183 2872
ἀσπάσασθε Περσίδα τὴν ἀγαπητήν, ἥτις πολλὰ ἐκοπίασεν
Greet Persis the beloved, who many things labored
1722/2962 782 4504 1588 1722 2962
13 ἐν Κυρίῳ. ἀσπάσασθε Ῥοῦφον τὸν ἐκλεκτὸν ἐν Κυρίῳ, καὶ τὴν
in (the) Lord. Greet Rufus the chosen in (the) Lord, and the
3384 848 1700 782 799 5393
μητέρα αὐτοῦ καὶ ἐμοῦ. ἀσπάσασθε Ἀσύγκριτον, Φλέγοντα,
mother of him and of me. Greet Asyncritus, Phlegon,
2057 3969 2060 4862 846 80
14 Ἑρμᾶν, Πατρόβαν, Ἑρμῆν, καὶ τοὺς σὺν αὐτοῖς ἀδελφούς.
Hermas, Patrobas, Hermes, and the with them brothers.
782 5378 2456 3517 79
15 ἀσπάσασθε Φιλόλογον καὶ Ἰουλίαν, Νηρέα καὶ τὴν ἀδελφὴν
Greet Philologus and Julias, Nereus and the sister
848 3652 4862 846 3956 40
αὐτοῦ, καὶ Ὀλυμπᾶν, καὶ τοὺς σὺν αὐτοῖς πάντας ἁγίους.
of him, and Olympas, and the with him all saints.
782 240 1722 5370 40 782 5209
16 ἀσπάσασθε ἀλλήλους ἐν φιλήματι ἁγίῳ. ἀσπάζονται ὑμᾶς
Greet one another with a kiss holy. Greet you
1577 5547
αἱ ἐκκλησίαι τοῦ Χριστοῦ.
the churches of Christ.

[17]And I exhort you, brothers, to watch those making divisions and causes of stumbling contrary to the teaching which you learned; and turn away from them. [18]For such

3870 5209 80 4648 1370
17 Παρακαλῶ δὲ ὑμᾶς, ἀδελφοί, σκοπεῖν τοὺς τὰς διχοστα-
I exhort And you, brothers, to watch those the divisions
4625 3844 1322 3739/5210 3129
σίας καὶ τὰ σκάνδαλα, παρὰ τὴν διδαχὴν ἣν ὑμεῖς ἐμάθετε,
and the offenses, against the teaching which you learned,
4160 1578 575 846 1063 5108
18 ποιοῦντας· καὶ ἐκκλίνατε ἀπ' αὐτῶν. οἱ γὰρ τοιοῦτοι τῷ
making. and turn away from them. For such ones the

ones do not serve our Lord Jesus Christ, but their own belly; and by smooth speaking and flattering *they* deceive the hearts of those without guile. [19]For your obedience reached to all; therefore, I rejoice over you. But I desire you to be truly wise *as* to good, but simple toward evil. [20]And the God of peace will bruise Satan under your feet shortly.

The grace of our Lord Jesus Christ be with you. Amen.

[21]My fellow-worker Timothy, and Lucius, and Jason, and Sosipater my kinsman, greet you. [22]I, Tertius, the *one* writing the epistle, greet you in *the* Lord. [23]Gaius, the host of all the church and me, greets you. Erastus, the steward of the city, and Quartus the brother, greet you. [24]The grace of our Lord Jesus Christ be with you all. Amen.

[25]Now to Him *who is* able to establish you according to my gospel, and the preaching of Jesus Christ, according to the revelation of *the* mystery having been kept unvoiced during eternal times, [26]but now has been made plain, and by prophetic Scriptures, according to the command of the eternal God, made known for obedience of faith to all the nations; [27]the only wise God through Jesus Christ, to whom *be* the glory forever. Amen.

2962 2257 2424 5547 3756 1398 235
Κυρίῳ ἡμῶν Ἰησοῦ Χριστῷ οὐ δουλεύουσιν, ἀλλὰ τῇ
Lord of us, Jesus Christ, not do serve; but the
1438 2836 1223 5542 2129
ἑαυτῶν κοιλίᾳ· καὶ διὰ τῆς χρηστολογίας καὶ εὐλογίας
of themselves belly; and through smooth speech and flattering
1818 2588 172 1063 5216 5218
19 ἐξαπατῶσι τὰς καρδίας τῶν ἀκάκων. ἡ γὰρ ὑμῶν ὑπακοὴ
deceive the hearts of the guileless. the For of you obedience
1519 3956 864 5463 3767 1909/5213/ 2309 5209
εἰς πάντας ἀφίκετο. χαίρω οὖν τὸ ἐφ᾽ ὑμῖν· θέλω δὲ ὑμᾶς
to all reached. I rejoice Therefore over you; I desire and you
4680 3303 1511/1519 18 185 1519 2556
σοφοὺς μὲν εἶναι εἰς τὸ ἀγαθόν, ἀκεραίους δὲ εἰς τὸ κακόν.
wise truly to be to the good; simple but toward the evil.
2316 1515 4937 4567 5259
20 ὁ δὲ Θεὸς τῆς εἰρήνης συντρίψει τὸν Σατανᾶν ὑπὸ τοὺς
the And God of peace will crush Satan under the
4228 5216/1722/5034
πόδας ὑμῶν ἐν τάχει.
feet of you shortly.
5485 2962 5216 2424 5547 3326 5216
Ἡ χάρις τοῦ Κυρίου ἡμῶν Ἰησοῦ Χριστοῦ μεθ᾽ ὑμῶν.
The grace of the Lord of us, Jesus Christ, (be) with you.
281
ἀμήν.
Amen.
782 5209 5095 4904 3450 3066
21 Ἀσπάζονται ὑμᾶς Τιμόθεος ὁ συνεργός μου, καὶ Λούκιος
greets you Timothy the fellow-worker of me, and Lucius
2394 4989 4773 3450 782
καὶ Ἰάσων καὶ Σωσίπατρος οἱ συγγενεῖς μου. ἀσπάζομαι
and Jason, and Sosipater the kinsman of me. greet
5209 1473 5060 1125 1992 1722 2962
22 ὑμᾶς ἐγὼ Τέρτιος, ὁ γράψας τὴν ἐπιστολήν, ἐν Κυρίῳ.
you I, Tertius, the (one) writing the epistle, in (the) Lord.
782 5209 1050 3581/3450 1577 3650
23 ἀσπάζεται ὑμᾶς Γάϊος ὁ ξένος μου καὶ τῆς ἐκκλησίας ὅλης.
greets you Gaius the host of me, and the church of all.
782 5209 2037 3623 4172
ἀσπάζεται ὑμᾶς Ἔραστος ὁ οἰκονόμος τῆς πόλεως, καὶ
greets you Erastus the treasurer of the city, and
2890 80
Κουαρτος ὁ ἀδελφός.
Quartus the brother.
5485 2962 2257 2424 5547 3326 3956
24 Ἡ χάρις τοῦ Κυρίου ἡμῶν Ἰησοῦ Χριστοῦ μετὰ πάντων
The grace of the Lord of us, Jesus Christ, with all
5216 281 1410 5209 4741 2596
25 ὑμῶν. ἀμήν. Τῷ δὲ δυναμένῳ ὑμᾶς στηρίξαι κατὰ τὸ
you. Amen. to the (One) And able you to establish according to
2098 3450 2782 2424 5547 2596
εὐαγγέλιόν μου καὶ τὸ κήρυγμα Ἰησοῦ Χριστοῦ, κατὰ
the gospel of me, and the proclamation of Jesus Christ, according
602 3466 5550 166 4601
ἀποκάλυψιν μυστηριου χρονοις αἰωνίοις σεσιγημένου,
to the revelation of (the) mystery in times eternal having been kept silent,
5319 3558/1223/5037/ 1124 4397 2596
26 φανερωθέντος δὲ νῦν, διά τε γραφῶν προφητικῶν, κατ᾽
revealed but now, through and writings prophetic, according
2003 166 2316 1519 5218 4102 1519
ἐπιταγὴν τοῦ αἰωνίου Θεοῦ, εἰς ὑπακοὴν πίστεως εἰς
to the command of the eternal God for obedience of faith to
3956 1484 1107 3441 4680 2316 1223
27 παντα τὰ ἔθνη γνωρισθέντος, μόνῳ σοφῷ Θεῷ, διὰ
all the nations made known, only wise to God through
2424 5547 1391/1519 165 281
Ἰησοῦ Χριστοῦ, ἡ δόξα εἰς τούς· αἰῶνας. ἀμήν.
Jesus Christ, to whom (be) glory to the ages. Amen.

ΠΑΥΛΟΥ ΤΟΥ ΑΠΟΣΤΟΛΟΥ
PAUL THE APOSTLE

Η ΠΡΟΣ
THE TO

ΚΟΡΙΝΘΙΟΥΣ
(THE) CORINTHIANS

ΕΠΙΣΤΟΛΗ ΠΡΩΤΗ
EPISTLE FIRST

THE FIRST EPISTLE TO THE CORINTHIANS

A LITERAL TRANSLATION OF THE BIBLE

CHAPTER 1

1 Paul, a called apostle of Jesus Christ, by *the* will of God, and Sosthenes the brother, 2 to the church of God existing in Corinth, those having been sanctified in Christ Jesus, called-out saints, with all those calling on the name of our Lord Jesus Christ in every place, both theirs and ours: 3 Grace to you, and peace, from God our Father and (the) Lord Jesus Christ.

4 I give thanks to my God always concerning you *for* the grace of God given to you in Christ Jesus, 5 that in everything you were enriched in Him, in all discourse and all knowledge, 6 even as the testimony of Christ was confirmed in you, 7 so that you *are* not lacking in any gift, awaiting the revelation of our Lord, Jesus Christ, 8 who also will confirm you until *the* end, blameless in the day of our Lord Jesus Christ.

9 God *is* faithful, through whom you were called into *the* fellowship of His Son, Jesus Christ, our Lord.

10 Now I exhort you, brothers, through the name

CHAPTER 1

3962 2822 652 2424 5547 1223 2307
1 Παῦλος κλητὸς ἀπόστολος Ἰησοῦ Χριστοῦ διὰ θελήματος
Paul a called apostle of Jesus Christ through (the) will
2316 4988 80 1577 2316
2 Θεοῦ, καὶ Σωσθένης ὁ ἀδελφός, τῇ ἐκκλησίᾳ τοῦ Θεοῦ τῇ
of God, and Sosthenes the brother, to the church of God
5607/1722 2882 37 1722 5547 2424 2822
οὔσῃ ἐν Κορίνθῳ, ἡγιασμένοις ἐν Χριστῷ Ἰησοῦ, κλητοῖς
existing in Corinth, those having been sanctified in Christ Jesus called out
40 4862 3956 1941 3686 2962
ἁγίοις, σὺν πᾶσι τοῖς ἐπικαλουμένοις τὸ ὄνομα τοῦ Κυρίου
saints, with all those calling on the name of the Lord
2257 2424 5547 1722 3956 5117 848 5037 2257
ἡμῶν Ἰησοῦ Χριστοῦ ἐν παντὶ τόπῳ, αὐτῶν τε καὶ ἡμῶν·
of us Jesus Christ, in every place, of them both and of us;
5485 5213 1515 475 2316 3962 2257 2962
3 χάρις ὑμῖν καὶ εἰρήνη ἀπὸ Θεοῦ πατρὸς ἡμῶν καὶ Κυρίου
grace to you, and peace, from God (the) Father of us and (the) Lord
2424 5547
Ἰησοῦ Χριστοῦ.
Jesus Christ.

2168 2316 3450 3956 4012 5216 1909
4 Εὐχαριστῶ τῷ Θεῷ μου πάντοτε περὶ ὑμῶν, ἐπὶ τῇ
I gave thanks to the God of me always concerning you, on the
5485 2316 1325 5213/1722/ 5547 2424 3754/1722
5 χάριτι τοῦ Θεοῦ τῇ δοθείσῃ ὑμῖν ἐν Χριστῷ Ἰησοῦ· ὅτι ἐν
grace of God given to you in Christ Jesus, that in
3956 4148 1722 846 1722 3956 3056 3956
παντὶ ἐπλουτίσθητε ἐν αὐτῷ, ἐν παντὶ λόγῳ καὶ πάσῃ
everything you were enriched in Him, in all discourse and all
1108 2531 3142 5547 950 1722
6 γνώσει, καθὼς τὸ μαρτύριον τοῦ Χριστοῦ ἐβεβαιώθη ἐν
knowledge, even as the testimony of Christ was confirmed in
5213 5620/5209/3361 5302 1722 3367 5486 553
7 ὑμῖν· ὥστε ὑμᾶς μὴ ὑστερεῖσθαι ἐν μηδενὶ χαρίσματι, ἀπεκ-
you, so as you not to be lacking in no gift, having
602 2962 2257 2424
δεχομένους τὴν ἀποκάλυψιν τοῦ Κυρίου ἡμῶν Ἰησοῦ
been awaiting the revelation of the Lord of us, Jesus
5547 3739 950 5209/2193 5056 410 1722
8 Χριστοῦ, ὃς καὶ βεβαιώσει ὑμᾶς ἕως τέλους, ἀνεγκλήτους ἐν
Christ, who also will confirm you until (the) end, blameless in
2250 2962 2257 2424 5547 4103 2316
9 τῇ ἡμέρᾳ τοῦ Κυρίου ἡμῶν Ἰησοῦ Χριστοῦ. πιστὸς ὁ Θεός,
the day of the Lord of us, Jesus Christ. Faithful (is) God
1223/3739/ 2564 1519 2842 5207 848 2424 5547
δι' οὗ ἐκλήθητε εἰς κοινωνίαν τοῦ υἱοῦ αὐτοῦ Ἰησοῦ Χριστοῦ
through whom you were called into fellowship of the Son of Him, Jesus Christ
2962 2257
τοῦ Κυρίου ἡμῶν.
the Lord of us.

3870 5209 80 1223 3686
10 Παρακαλῶ δὲ ὑμᾶς, ἀδελφοί, διὰ τοῦ ὀνόματος τοῦ
I exhort Now you, brothers, through the name of the

of our Lord Jesus Christ that you all say the same thing, and there not be divisions among you; but you be united in the same mind and in the same judgment. [11]For, my brothers, concerning you it was shown to me by those of Chloe that there are strifes among you. [12]But I say this, that each of you says, Truly I am of Paul, and I of Apollos, and I of Cephas, and I of Christ. [13]Has Christ been divided? Was Paul crucified for you? Or were you baptized into the name of Paul? [14]I give thanks to God that I did not baptize one of you, except Crispus and Gaius, [15]that not anyone should say that you were baptized in my name. [16]And I also baptized the household of Stephanas. For the rest, I do not know if I baptized any other. [17]For Christ did not send me to baptize, but to preach the gospel; not in wisdom of words, that the cross of Christ not be nullified.

[18]For the word of the cross is truly foolishness to those being lost; but to us being saved, *it* is *the* power of God. [19]For it has been written, "I will destroy the wisdom of the wise, and I will set aside the understanding of those perceiving." [20]Where *is the* wise? Where *the* scribe? Where *the* lawyer of this world? Did God not make the wisdom of this world foolish? [21]For since in the wisdom of God the world did not know God through wisdom, God was pleased through the foolishness of preaching to save the ones believing. [22]And since Jews ask for a sign, and Greeks seek wisdom, [23]but we preach Christ having been crucified—truly an offense to Jews,

2962 2257 2424 5547 2443 846 3004 3956
Κυρίου ἡμῶν Ἰησοῦ Χριστοῦ, ἵνα τὸ αὐτὸ λέγητε πάντες,
Lord of us, Jesus Christ, that the same thing you say all,
3361 1722/5213/ 4978 5600 2675 1722 846
καὶ μὴ ᾖ ἐν ὑμῖν σχίσματα, ἦτε δὲ κατηρτισμένοι ἐν τῷ αὐτῷ
and not be among you divisions, you be but united in the same
3563 1722 846 1106 1213 1063/3427/4012/5216
11 νοῒ καὶ ἐν τῇ αὐτῇ γνώμῃ. ἐδηλώθη γάρ μοι περὶ ὑμῶν,
mind and in the same judgment. it was shown For to me about you
80 3427 5259 5514 3754/2054/1722/5213/1526/3004
12 ἀδελφοί μου, ὑπὸ τῶν Χλόης, ὅτι ἔριδες ἐν ὑμῖν εἰσι. λέγω
brothers of me, by those of Chloe, that strifes among you are. I say
5124 3754 1538 5216 3004 1473/3303/1510/ 3972
δὲ τοῦτο, ὅτι ἕκαστος ὑμῶν λέγει, Ἐγὼ μὲν εἰμι Παύλου,
And this, that each of you says, I indeed am of Paul,
1473 625 1473 2786 1473 5547 3307
13 Ἐγὼ δὲ Ἀπολλώ, Ἐγὼ δὲ Κηφᾶ, Ἐγὼ δὲ Χριστοῦ. μεμέ-
I and of Apollos, I and of Cephas, I and of Christ. Has
5547 3361 3972 4717 5228/5216/2228/1519
ρισται ὁ Χριστός; μὴ Παῦλος ἐσταυρώθη ὑπὲρ ὑμῶν, ἢ εἰς
been divided Christ? Not Paul was crucified for you? Or in
3686 3972 907 2168 2316/3754
14 τὸ ὄνομα Παύλου ἐβαπτίσθητε; εὐχαριστῶ τῷ Θεῷ ὅτι
the name of Paul were you baptized? I give thanks to God that
3762 5216 907 =1508= 2921 1050/2443/3361/5100
15 οὐδένα ὑμῶν ἐβάπτισα, εἰ μὴ Κρίσπον καὶ Γάϊον· ἵνα μή τις
not one of you I baptized, except Crispus and Gaius; lest anyone
2036/3754/1519 1699 3686 907 907 4734
16 εἴπῃ ὅτι εἰς τὸ ἐμὸν ὄνομα ἐβάπτισα. ἐβάπτισα δὲ καὶ τὸν Στε-
should say that in my name you were baptized. I baptized But also the of
3624 3063 3756/1492=1536= 243 907 3756/1063
17 φανᾶ οἶκον· λοιπὸν οὐκ οἶδα εἴ τινα ἄλλον ἐβάπτισα. οὐ γὰρ
Stephanas house. For the rest not I know if any other I baptized. not For
649 3165 5547 907 235 2097 3756
ἀπέστειλέ με Χριστὸς βαπτίζειν, ἀλλ' εὐαγγελίζεσθαι οὐκ
sent me Christ to baptize, but to preach the gospel, not
1722/4678 3056 2443/3361/ 2758 4716 5547
ἐν σοφίᾳ λόγου, ἵνα μὴ κενωθῇ ὁ σταυρὸς τοῦ Χριστοῦ.
in wisdom of words, lest be nullified the cross of Christ.
3056 1063 4716 3303 622
18 Ὁ λόγος γὰρ ὁ τοῦ σταυροῦ τοῖς μὲν ἀπολλυμένοις
the word For of the cross to those truly perishing
3472 2076 4982 2254 1411 2316 2076
μωρία ἐστί, τοῖς δὲ σωζομένοις ἡμῖν δύναμις Θεοῦ ἐστι.
foolishness is; and being saved to us (the) power of God is.
1125 1063 622 4678 4680
19 γέγραπται γάρ, Ἀπολῶ τὴν σοφίαν τῶν σοφῶν, καὶ τὴν
it has been written For, I will destroy the wisdom of the wise, and the
4907 4908 114 4226 4680 4226 1122
20 σύνεσιν τῶν συνετῶν ἀθετήσω. ποῦ σοφός; ποῦ γραμ-
understanding of the perceiving I will set aside. Where (the) wise? Where (the)
4226 4804 165 5127 3780 3471
ματεύς; ποῦ συζητητὴς τοῦ αἰῶνος τούτου; οὐχὶ ἐμώ-
scribe? Where (the) disputer age of this? Did not make
2316 4678 2889 5127 1894 1063
21 ρανεν ὁ Θεὸς τὴν σοφίαν τοῦ κόσμου τούτου; ἐπειδὴ γὰρ
foolish God the wisdom of world this? since For,
1722 4678 2316/3756/1097 2889 1223 4678
ἐν τῇ σοφίᾳ τοῦ Θεοῦ οὐκ ἔγνω ὁ κόσμος διὰ τῆς σοφίας τὸν
in the wisdom of God, not knew the world through the wisdom
2316 2106 2316/1223 3472 2782
Θεόν, εὐδόκησεν ὁ Θεὸς διὰ τῆς μωρίας τοῦ κηρύγματος
God, was pleased God through the foolishness of preaching
4982 4100 1894 2453 4592
22 σῶσαι τοὺς πιστεύοντας. ἐπειδὴ καὶ Ἰουδαῖοι σημεῖον
to save those believing. since And Jews ask
154 1672 4678 2212 2249 2784
23 αἰτοῦσι, καὶ Ἕλληνες σοφίαν ζητοῦσιν· ἡμεῖς δὲ κηρύσσομεν
a sign and Greeks wisdom seek, we but preach
5547 4717 2453 3303 4625 1672
Χριστὸν ἐσταυρωμένον, Ἰουδαίοις μὲν σκάνδαλον, Ἕλλησι
Christ having been crucified; to Jews indeed an offense; to Greeks,

and foolishness to Greeks
—[24]but to the called-out
ones, both to Jews and to
Greeks, Christ *is* the power
of God and *the* wisdom of
God; [25]because the foolish thing of God is wiser
than men; and the weak
thing of God is stronger
than men.
[26]For you see your
calling, brothers, that *there
are* not many wise according to flesh, nor many
powerful, not many well-
born. [27]But God chose the
foolish things of the world
that the wise might be put
to shame, and God chose
the weak things of the
world so that He might put
to shame the strong things.
[28]And God chose the low-
born of the world, and the
things having been de-
spised, and the things that
are not, so that He might
bring to nothing the things
that are; [29]so that no flesh
might glory in His presence.
[30]But of Him, you are in
Christ Jesus, who was
made to us wisdom from
God, both righteousness
and sanctification and
redemption, [31]so that
even as it has been written,
"He that glories, let him
glory in *the* Lord."

CHAPTER 2

[1]And when I came to
you, brothers, I did not
come with excellency of
word or wisdom, declaring
to you the testimony of
God. [2]For I decided not to
know anything among you
except Jesus Christ, and
Him having been crucified.
[3]And I was with you in
weakness, and in fear, and
in much trembling. [4]And
my word and my preaching
was not in moving words of
human wisdom, but in
proof of *the* Spirit and of
power, [5]that your faith
might not be in *the* wisdom
of men, but in *the* power of
God.

3472 846 2822 2453 5037 1672
24 δε μωρίαν· αὐτοῖς δὲ τοῖς κλητοῖς, Ἰουδαίοις τε καὶ Ἕλλησι,
and foolishness; to them but the called ones, to Jews both and to Greeks,
5547 2316 1411 2316 4678 3754 3474
25 Χριστὸν Θεοῦ δύναμιν καὶ Θεοῦ σοφίαν. ὅτι τὸ μωρὸν τοῦ
Christ of God (the) power and of God (the) wisdom. For the foolish thing
2316 4680 444 2076 772
Θεοῦ σοφώτερον τῶν ἀνθρώπων ἐστί, καὶ τὸ ἀσθενὲς του
of God wiser (than) men is; and the weak thing
2316 2478 444 2076
Θεοῦ ἰσχυρότερον τῶν ἀνθρώπων ἐστί.
of God stronger (than) men is.
991 1063 2821 5216 80 3754/3756/4183
26 Βλέπετε γὰρ τὴν κλῆσιν ὑμῶν, ἀδελφοί, ὅτι οὐ πολλοὶ
you see For the calling of you, brothers, that not many
4680 2596 4561/3756/4183 1415 3756 4183 2104
σοφοὶ κατὰ σάρκα, οὐ πολλοὶ δυνατοί, οὐ πολλοὶ εὐγενεῖς·
wise ones as to flesh, not many powerful, not many well-born;
235 3474 2889 1586 2316 2443
27 ἀλλὰ τὰ μωρὰ τοῦ κόσμου ἐξελέξατο ὁ Θεός, ἵνα τοὺς
but the foolish things of the world chose God, that the
4680 2617 772 2889 1586
28 σοφοὺς καταισχύνῃ· καὶ τὰ ἀσθενῆ τοῦ κόσμου ἐξελέξατο ὁ
wise might be shamed; and the weak things of the world chose
2316 2443 2617 2478 36 2889
Θεός, ἵνα καταισχύνῃ τὰ ἰσχυρά· καὶ τὰ ἀγενῆ του κοσμου
God, that He might shame the strong things; and the base things of the world
1848 1586 2316 3361/5607/2443
καὶ τὰ ἐξουθενημένα ἐξελέξατο ὁ Θεός, καὶ τα μὴ ὄντα, ἵνα
and the things despised chose God, and the things not being, that
5607 2673 3704 3361 2744 3956 4561
29 τὰ ὄντα καταργήσῃ· ὅπως μὴ καυχήσηται πᾶσα σὰρξ
the things being He nullify; so as not might boast all flesh
1799 846 1537 846 5210 2075/1722/ 5547 2424
30 ἐνώπιον αὐτοῦ. ἐξ αὐτοῦ δὲ ὑμεῖς ἐστε ἐν Χριστῷ Ἰησοῦ,
before Him. of Him And you are in Christ Jesus,
3739/ 1096 2254 4678 575 2316 1343 5037
ὃς ἐγενήθη ἡμῖν σοφία ἀπὸ Θεοῦ, δικαιοσύνη τε καὶ
who became to us wisdom from God, righteousness both and
38 629 2443 2531 1125
31 ἁγιασμός, καὶ ἀπολύτρωσις· ἵνα, καθὼς γέγραπται, Ὁ
sanctification and redemption, that even as has been written: Those
2605 1722 2962 2744
καυχώμενος, ἐν Κυρίῳ καυχάσθω.
boasting, in (the) Lord let him boast.

CHAPTER 2

2504 2064 4314 5209 80 2064/3756/2596 5247
1 Κἀγὼ ἐλθὼν πρὸς ὑμᾶς, ἀδελφοί, ἦλθον οὐ καθ' ὑπεροχὴν
And I coming to you, brothers, came not according to excellence
3056 4678 2605 5213 3142 2316
λόγου ἢ σοφίας καταγγέλλων ὑμῖν τὸ μαρτύριον τοῦ Θεοῦ.
of word or wisdom, announcing to you the testimony of God.
3756/1063 2919 1492/5100/*/5213/*1508= 2424 5547
2 οὐ γὰρ ἔκρινα τοῦ εἰδέναι τι ἐν ὑμῖν, εἰ μὴ Ἰησοῦν Χριστόν,
1722 not For I decided to know anything among you, except Jesus Christ,
5126 4717 1473/1722/ 769 1722 5401
3 καὶ τοῦτον ἐσταυρωμένον. καὶ ἐγὼ ἐν ἀσθενείᾳ καὶ ἐν φόβῳ
and this (One) having been crucified. And I in weakness and in fear
1722 5156 4183 1096 4314 5209 3056 3450
4 καὶ ἐν τρόμῳ πολλῷ ἐγενόμην πρὸς ὑμᾶς. καὶ ὁ λόγος μου
and in trembling much was with you. And the word of me
2782 3450 3756/1722/ 3981 442 4678
καὶ τὸ κήρυγμά μου οὐκ ἐν πειθοῖς ἀνθρωπίνης σοφίας
and the preaching of me not in persuasive of human wisdom
3056 235/1722 585 4151 1411 2443
5 λόγοις, ἀλλ' ἐν ἀποδείξει πνεύματος καὶ δυνάμεως· ἵνα ἡ
words but in proof of (the) Spirit and of power; that the
5600 4102 5216/3361/*/1722/4678 444 235/1722 1411 2316
πίστις ὑμῶν μὴ ᾖ ἐν σοφίᾳ ἀνθρώπων, ἀλλ' ἐν δυνάμει Θεοῦ.
faith of you not be in wisdom of men, but in power of God.

δέ(1161); καί(2531)—and, but; ὁ, ἡ, τό (3588, the)— * above word, look in verse margin for No.

[6]But we speak wisdom among the perfect; but not the wisdom of this age, nor of the rulers of this age, those being brought to nothing. [7]But we speak *the* wisdom of God in a mystery, having been hidden, which God predetermined before the ages for our glory; [8]which not one of the rulers of this age has known. For if they had known, they would not have crucified the Lord of glory. [9]according as it has been written, "Eye has not seen, and ear has not heard," nor has it risen up into the heart of man, "the things which God has prepared for those that love Him." [10]But God revealed *them* to us by His Spirit, for (the) Spirit searches all things, even the deep things of God. [11]For who among men knows the things of a man, except the spirit of a man within him? So also no one has known the things of God except the Spirit of God. [12]But we have not received the spirit of the world, but the Spirit from God; that we may know the things freely given to us by God; [13]which things we also speak, not in words taught in human wisdom, but in *words* taught of (the) Holy Spirit, comparing spiritual things with spiritual *things*. [14]But a natural man does not receive the things of *the* Spirit of God, for they are foolishness to him, and he is not able to know *them*, because they are spiritually discerned. [15]But the spiritual one discerns all things, but he is discerned by no one. [16]For who knew *the* mind of *the* Lord? Who will teach Him? But we have *the* mind of Christ.

4678 2980 1722 5046 4678 3756
6 Σοφίαν δὲ λαλοῦμεν ἐν τοῖς τελείοις· σοφίαν δὲ οὐ τοῦ
wisdom But we speak among the perfect; the wisdom but not—
165 5127 3761 758 165 5127
αἰῶνος τούτου, οὐδὲ τῶν ἀρχόντων τοῦ αἰῶνος τούτου,
age of this, neither of the rulers — age of this,
2673 235 2980 4678 2316/1722/3466
7 τῶν καταργουμένων· ἀλλὰ λαλοῦμεν σοφίαν Θεοῦ ἐν μυστη-
those being brought to nothing; but we speak a wisdom of God in mystery,
613 3739 4309 2316 4253
ρίῳ, τὴν ἀποκεκρυμμένην, ἣν προώρισεν ὁ Θεὸς πρὸ τῶν
— having been hidden, which predetermined God before the
165 1519 1391 2257/3739/3762 758 165
8 αἰώνων εἰς δόξαν ἡμῶν· ἣν οὐδεὶς τῶν ἀρχόντων τοῦ αἰῶνος
ages for glory of us; which not one of the rulers — age
5127 1097 1487/1063 1097 3756/302 2962
τούτου ἔγνωκεν· εἰ γὰρ ἔγνωσαν, οὐκ ἂν τὸν Κύριον τῆς
of this has known; if for they knew, not the Lord —
1391 4717 235 2531 1125 3739/3788
9 δόξης ἐσταύρωσαν· ἀλλὰ καθὼς γέγραπται, Ἃ ὀφθαλμὸς
of glory they had crucified. But even as it has been written: Things that eye
3756/1492 3775/3756 191 1909 2588 444 3756
οὐκ εἶδε, καὶ οὖς οὐκ ἤκουσε, καὶ ἐπὶ καρδίαν ἀνθρώπου οὐκ
did not see, and ear not did hear, and on the heart of man not
305 3739 2090 2316 25 846 2254
10 ἀνέβη, ἃ ἡτοίμασεν ὁ Θεὸς τοῖς ἀγαπῶσιν αὐτόν. ἡμῖν δὲ ὁ
came up, how prepared God those loving Him. to us But
2316 601 1223 4151 848 1063 4151
Θεὸς ἀπεκάλυψε διὰ τοῦ πνεύματος αὐτοῦ· τὸ γὰρ πνεῦμα
God revealed through the Spirit of Him, the for Spirit
3956 2045 899 2316/5101/1063/1492 444
11 πάντα ἐρευνᾷ, καὶ τὰ βάθη τοῦ Θεοῦ. τίς γὰρ οἶδεν ἀνθρώ-
all things searches, even the deep things of God. who For knows of men
444 =1508= 4151 444 1722
πων τὰ τοῦ ἀνθρώπου, εἰ μὴ τὸ πνεῦμα τοῦ ἀνθρώπου τὸ ἐν
the things of a man, except the spirit of a man in
846 3779 2316 3762 1492 =1508= 4151
αὐτῷ ; οὕτω καὶ τὰ τοῦ Θεοῦ οὐδεὶς οἶδεν, εἰ μὴ τὸ Πνεῦμα
him? So also the things of God no one has known except the Spirit
2316 2249 3756 4151 2889 2983 235
12 τοῦ Θεοῦ. ἡμεῖς δὲ οὐ τὸ πνεῦμα τοῦ κόσμου ἐλάβομεν, ἀλλὰ
of God. we And not the spirit of the world received, but
4151 1537 2316 2443/1492 5259 2316
τὸ πνεῦμα τὸ ἐκ τοῦ Θεοῦ, ἵνα εἰδῶμεν τὰ ὑπὸ τοῦ Θεοῦ
the Spirit from God, that we may know the things by God
5483 2254 2980 3756/1722 1318 442
13 χαρισθέντα ἡμῖν. ἃ καὶ λαλοῦμεν, οὐκ ἐν διδακτοῖς ἀνθρω-
freely given to us; which things also we speak, not in taught of
4678 3056 235/1722 1318 4151 40
πίνης σοφίας λόγοις, ἀλλ' ἐν διδακτοῖς Πνεύματος Ἁγίου,
human wisdom words, but in (words) taught of (the) Spirit Holy,
4152 4152 4793 5591 444
14 πνευματικοῖς πνευματικὰ συγκρίνοντες. ψυχικὸς δὲ ἄνθρω-
with spiritual things spiritual things comparing. a natural But man
3756 1209 4151 2316 3472 1062
πος οὐ δέχεται τὰ τοῦ Πνεύματος τοῦ Θεοῦ· μωρία γὰρ
not receives the things of (the) Spirit of God; foolishness for
846 2076 3756 1410 1097 3754 4153 350
αὐτῷ ἐστι, καὶ οὐ δύναται γνῶναι, ὅτι πνευματικῶς ἀνακρί-
to him they are and not he is able to know, because spiritually they are dis-
4152 350 3303 3956 846 5259
15 νεται. ὁ δὲ πνευματικὸς ἀνακρίνει μὲν πάντα, αὐτὸς δὲ ὑπ'
cerned. the But spiritual one discerns indeed all things, he but by
3762 350 5102/1063/ 1097/3563/ 2962/3739 4822
16 οὐδενὸς ἀνακρίνεται. τίς γὰρ ἔγνω νοῦν Κυρίου, ὃς συμβιβά-
no one is discerned. who For knew (the) mind of Lord, who will teach
846 2249 3563 5547 2192
σει αὐτόν ; ἡμεῖς δὲ νοῦν Χριστοῦ ἔχομεν.
Him? we But (the) mind of Christ have.

CHAPTER 3

[1]And, brothers, I was not able to speak to you as to spiritual ones, but as to fleshly ones, as to babes in Christ. [2]I gave you milk to drink, and not food, for you were not then able; but neither now are you yet able. [3]For you are yet fleshly. For where among you *is* jealousy, and strife, and divisions, are you not fleshly and walk according to man? [4]For when one may say, Truly I am of Paul; and another, I of Apollos; are you not fleshly? [5]What then is Paul? And what Apollos, but ministers through whom you believed, and toe ach as the Lord gave? [6]I planted; Apollos watered, but God made to grow. [7]So as neither he planting is anything, nor he watering, but God making to grow. [8]So he planting and he watering are one, and each one will receive *his* own reward according to *his* own labor. [9]For we are fellow-workers of God, a field of God; *and* you are a building of God.

[10]According to God's grace given to me, as a wise master-builder, I laid a foundation; but another builds on *it*. But let each one observe how he builds. [11]For no one is able to lay *any* other foundation beside the *One* having been laid, who is Jesus Christ. [12]And if anyone builds on this foundation gold, silver, precious stones, wood, grass, straw, [13]the work of each will be revealed; for the Day will make *it* known, because it is revealed in fire; and the fire will prove the work of each, what sort it is. [14]If the work of anyone which he built remains,

CHAPTER 3

1473 80 3756 1410 2980 5213/5613/4152
1 Καὶ ἐγώ, ἀδελφοί, οὐκ ἠδυνήθην λαλῆσαι ὑμῖν ὡς πνευ-
And I, brothers, not was able to speak to you as spiritual
235/5613/ 4559 5613 3516 1722 5547 1051
2 ματικοῖς, ἀλλ' ὡς σαρκικοῖς, ὡς νηπίοις ἐν Χριστῷ. γάλα
ones but as to fleshly, as to infants in Christ. milk
5209 4222 3756 1033 3768 1063 1410 235
ὑμᾶς ἐπότισα, καὶ οὐ βρῶμα· οὔπω γὰρ ἠδύνασθε. ἀλλ'
you I gave to drink, and not food, not then for you were able, but
3777/2089/3568 1410 2089/1063 4559 2075 3699 1063/1722
3 οὔτε ἔτι νῦν δύνασθε· ἔτι γὰρ σαρκικοί ἐστε· ὅπου γὰρ ἐν
neither yet now are you able; yet for fleshly you are. where For among
5213 2205 2054 1370 3780 4559 2075
ὑμῖν ζῆλος καὶ ἔρις καὶ διχοστασίαι, οὐχὶ σαρκικοί ἐστε,
you (is) jealousy and strife and division, not fleshly are you
2596 444 4043 3752 1063 3004/5100/1473
4 καὶ κατὰ ἄνθρωπον περιπατεῖτε; ὅταν γὰρ λέγῃ τις, Ἐγὼ
and according to man walk? when For may say one, I
3303/1510 3972 2087 1473 625 3780 4559
μέν εἰμι Παύλου, ἕτερος δέ, Ἐγὼ Ἀπολλώ, οὐχὶ σαρκικοί
truly am of Paul, another and, I of Apollos, not fleshly
2075/5101/3767/2076 3972 5100 625 235/2228/ 1249
5 ἐστε; τίς οὖν ἐστι Παῦλος, τίς δὲ Ἀπολλώς ἀλλ' ἢ διάκονοι
are you? What then is Paul; what and Apollos? But ministers
1223/3739/ 4100 1538 5613 2962 1325 1473
6 δι' ὧν ἐπιστεύσατε, καὶ ἑκάστῳ ὡς ὁ Κύριος ἔδωκεν; ἐγὼ
through whom you believed, and to each as the Lord gave. I
5452 625 4222 235 2316 837 5620
7 ἐφύτευσα, Ἀπολλὼς ἐπότισεν, ἀλλ' ὁ Θεὸς ηὔξανεν. ὥστε
planted, Apollos watered, but God made to grow. So as
3777 5452 2076/5100/3777 4222 235 837
οὔτε ὁ φυτεύων ἐστί τι, οὔτε ὁ ποτίζων, ἀλλ' ὁ αὐξάνων.
neither he planting is anything, nor he watering, but He making grow
2316 5452 4222 1520 1526 1538
8 Θεός. ὁ φυτεύων δὲ καὶ ὁ ποτίζων ἕν εἰσιν· ἕκαστος δὲ τὸν
God. he planting So and he watering one are, each one and the
2398 3408 2983 2596 2398 2873 2316/1063/2070
9 ἴδιον μισθὸν λήψεται κατὰ τὸν ἴδιον κόπον. Θεοῦ γάρ ἐσμεν
own reward will receive according to the own labor. of God For we are
4904 2316 1091 2316 3619 2075
συνεργοί· Θεοῦ γεώργιον, Θεοῦ οἰκοδομή ἐστε.
fellow-workers; Of God, a field; of God, a building you are.
2596 5485 2316 1325 3427/5613 4680
10 Κατὰ τὴν χάριν τοῦ Θεοῦ τὴν δοθεῖσάν μοι, ὡς σοφὸς
According to the grace of God given to me, as a wise
753 2310 5087 243 2026 1538
ἀρχιτέκτων θεμέλιον τέθεικα, ἄλλος δὲ ἐποικοδομεῖ. ἕκαστος
master builder a foundation I laid, another but builds on (it). each one
991 4459 2026 2310 1063 243 3762
11 δὲ βλεπέτω πῶς ἐποικοδομεῖ. θεμέλιον γὰρ ἄλλον οὐδεὶς
But let him look how he builds on(it). foundation For other no one
1410 5087 3844 2749 3739 2076 2424
δύναται θεῖναι παρὰ τὸν κείμενον, ὅς ἐστιν Ἰησοῦς ὁ
is able to lay beside the (One) being laid, who is Jesus the
5547 1487 5100 2026 1909 2310 5126
12 Χριστός. εἰ δέ τις ἐποικοδομεῖ ἐπὶ τὸν θεμέλιον τοῦτον
Christ. if And anyone builds on foundation this
5557 696 3037 5093 3586 5528 2562
χρυσόν, ἄργυρον, λίθους τιμίους, ξύλα, χόρτον, καλάμην,
gold, silver, stones precious, woods, hay, stubble,
1538 2041 5318 1096 1063 2250 1213
13 ἑκάστου τὸ ἔργον φανερὸν γενήσεται· ἡ γὰρ ἡμέρα δηλώσει,
of each one the work manifest will be; the for day will declare,
3754/1722/4442/ 601 1538 2041 3697
ὅτι ἐν πυρὶ ἀποκαλύπτεται· καὶ ἑκάστου τὸ ἔργον ὁποῖόν
for by fire it is revealed, and of each one the work of what sort
2076 4442 1381 =1536= 2041 3306/3739/ 2026
14 ἐστι τὸ πῦρ δοκιμάσει. εἴ τινος τὸ ἔργον μένει ὃ ἐπῳκοδό-
it is, the fire it will prove. If of someone the work remains, which he built

he will receive a reward. [15]If the work of anyone shall be consumed, he shall suffer loss; but he will be saved, but so as through fire.

[16]Do you not know that you are a temple of God, and the Spirit of God dwells in you? [17]If anyone corrupts the temple of God, God will bring that one to corruption; for the temple of God is holy, which you are.

[18]Let no one deceive himself, if anyone thinks to be wise among you in this age, let him become foolish, that he may become wise. [19]For the wisdom of this world is foolishness with God; for it has been written, "He has taken the wise in their own craftiness." [20]And again, "*The* Lord knows the reasonings of the wise, that they are worthless." [21]So let no one glory in men; for all things are yours, [22]whether Paul, or Apollos, or Cephas, or *the* world, or life, or death, or things present, or things to come —all are yours, [23]and you are Christ's, and Christ *is* God's.

3408 2983 =1536= 2041 2618
15 μησε, μισθὸν λήψεται. εἴ τινος τὸ ἔργον κατακαήσεται,
on, a reward he will receive. If anyone the work will be consumed,
2210 848 4982 3779 5613/1223/4442
ζημιωθήσεται· αὐτὸς δὲ σωθήσεται, οὕτω δὲ ὡς διὰ πυρός.
he will suffer loss, he but will be saved, so but as through fire.
3756 1492/3756/3485/2316/2075 4151 2316
16 Οὐκ οἴδατε ὅτι ναὸς Θεοῦ ἐστε, καὶ τὸ Πνεῦμα τοῦ Θεοῦ
Do not you know that a temple of God you are, and the Spirit of God
3611/1722/5213/1487 5101 3485 2316 5351 5351
17 οἰκεῖ ἐν ὑμῖν; εἴ τις τὸν ναὸν τοῦ Θεοῦ φθείρει, φθερεῖ
dwells in you? If anyone the temple of God corrupts, will corrupt
5126 2316 1063/3485 2316 40 2076 3748
τοῦτον ὁ Θεός· ὁ γὰρ ναὸς τοῦ Θεοῦ ἅγιός ἐστιν, οἵτινές
this one God. the For temple of God holy is, who
2075 5210
ἐστε ὑμεῖς.
are you.

3367 1438 1818 =1536= 1380 4680 1511/1722
18 Μηδεὶς ἑαυτὸν ἐξαπατάτω· εἴ τις δοκεῖ σοφὸς εἶναι ἐν
No one himself let deceive; if anyone thinks wise to be among
5213/1722 165 5129 3474 1096 2443 1096 4680
ὑμῖν ἐν τῷ αἰῶνι τούτῳ, μωρὸς γενέσθω, ἵνα γένηται σοφός.
you in age this, foolish let him become, that he become wise.
1063 4078 2889 5127 3472 3844 2316 2076
19 ἡ γὰρ σοφία τοῦ κόσμου τούτου μωρία παρὰ τῷ Θεῷ ἐστι.
the For wisdom world of this foolishness with God is.
1125 1063 1405 4680/1722 3834
γέγραπται γάρ, Ὁ δρασσόμενος τοὺς σοφοὺς ἐν τῇ πανουρ-
it has been written For: He (is) taking the wise in the craftiness
848 3825 2962 1097 1261
20 γίᾳ αὐτῶν. καὶ πάλιν, Κύριος γινώσκει τοὺς διαλογισμοὺς
of them. And again: (The) Lord knows the reasonings
4680 3754/1526 3152 5620 3367 2744 1722
21 τῶν σοφῶν, ὅτι εἰσὶ μάταιοι. ὥστε μηδεὶς καυχάσθω ἐν
of the wise, that they are vain. So as no one let boast in
444 3956 1063 5216 2076 1535 3972 1535
22 ἀνθρώποις· πάντα γὰρ ὑμῶν ἐστιν, εἴτε Παῦλος, εἴτε
men; all things for of you is, whether Paul, or
625 1535 2786 1535 2889 1535/2222/1535 2288
Ἀπολλώς, εἴτε Κηφᾶς, εἴτε κόσμος, εἴτε ζωή, εἴτε θάνατος
Apollos, or Cephas, or (the) world, or life, or death,
1535 1764 1535 3195 3956 5216 2076 5210
23 εἴτε ἐνεστῶτα, εἴτε μέλλοντα· πάντα ὑμῶν ἐστιν, ὑμεῖς δὲ
or things present, or things coming, all things of you are, you and
5547 5547 2316
Χριστοῦ, Χριστὸς δὲ Θεοῦ.
of Christ, Christ and of God.

CHAPTER 4

[1]So let a man think of us as ministers of Christ and stewards of *the* mysteries of God. [2]And the rest, it is sought among stewards that one be found faithful. [3]But to me it is a small thing that I am judged by you, or by a man's day. But neither do I judge myself. [4]For I know nothing against myself, but I have not been justified by this; but He judging me is *the* Lord. [5]So then do not judge anything before time, until the Lord comes, who will both

CHAPTER 4

3779 2248 3049 444 5613 5257 5547
1 Οὕτως ἡμᾶς λογιζέσθω ἄνθρωπος, ὡς ὑπηρέτας Χριστοῦ
So us let count a man as ministers of Christ,
3623 3466 2316 3063 2212 1722
2 καὶ οἰκονόμους μυστηρίων Θεοῦ. ὃ δὲ λοιπόν, ζητεῖται ἐν
and stewards of (the) mysteries of God. the And rest, it is sought among
3623 2443 4103 5100 2147 1698 1519 1646
3 τοῖς οἰκονόμοις, ἵνα πιστός τις εὑρεθῇ. ἐμοὶ δὲ εἰς ἐλάχιστόν
— stewards, that faithful anyone be found. to me And for a little thing
2076 2443/5259/5216 350 5259 442 2250
ἐστιν ἵνα ὑφ' ὑμῶν ἀνακριθῶ, ἢ ὑπὸ ἀνθρωπίνης ἡμέρας·
it is that by you I am judged, or by a man's day;
235 3761 1683 350 3762 1063 1683 4894
4 ἀλλ' οὐδὲ ἐμαυτὸν ἀνακρίνω. οὐδὲν γὰρ ἐμαυτῷ σύνοιδα,
but not myself I judge; nothing for against myself I know,
235/3767/1722/ 5129 1344 350 3165 2962
ἀλλ' οὐκ ἐν τούτῳ δεδικαίωμαι· ὁ δὲ ἀνακρίνων με Κύριός
but not by this have I been justified; He but judging me Lord
2076 5620/3361/4253/2540/5100/2919/2193/302/2064 2962
5 ἐστιν. ὥστε μὴ πρὸ καιροῦ τι κρίνετε, ἕως ἂν ἔλθῃ ὁ Κύριος,
is. So as not before time anything judge, until comes the Lord,

shed light on the hidden things of darkness, and will reveal the counsels of the hearts. And then the praise will be to each one from God.

[6]And, brothers, I transferred these things to myself and Apollos because of you, that in us you may learn not to think above what has been written, that you not *be* puffed up one over the other. [7]For who makes you to differ? And what do you have that you did not receive? And if you received *it*, why do you boast as *if you* did not receive? [8]You are already satisfied; you already became rich; you reigned without us—and oh that you really did reign, so that we also might reign with you! [9]For I think that God set us out last, the apostles, as appointed to death, because we became a spectacle to the world, even to angels and to men. [10]We *are* fools because of Christ, but you *are* wise in Christ. We *are* weak, but you *are* strong. You *are* honored, but we not honored. [11]Until the present hour we also hunger and thirst, and are naked, and are buffeted, and wander homeless, [12]and labor, working with our own hands. Being cursed, we bless; persecuted, we bear; [13]defamed, we entreat—we have become as filth of the world, dirt wiped off by all until now. [14]I do not write these things shaming you, but warning you as my beloved children. [15]For if you have myriads of teachers in Christ, yet not many fathers; for I fathered you in Christ Jesus through the gospel.

[16]Then I urge you, be imitators of me.

3739 5461 2927 4655 1519
ὅς καὶ φωτίσει τὰ κρυπτὰ τοῦ σκότους, καὶ φανερώσει τὰς
who both will shed light on the hidden things of darkness, and will reveal the
1012 2588 5119 1868 1096 1538
βουλὰς τῶν καρδιῶν· καὶ τότε ὁ ἔπαινος γενήσεται ἑκάστῳ
counsels of the hearts; and then the praise will be to each one
575 2316
ἀπὸ τοῦ Θεοῦ.
from God.
5023 80 3345 1519 1683
6 Ταῦτα δέ, ἀδελφοί, μετεσχημάτισα εἰς ἐμαυτὸν καὶ
these things And, brothers, I transferred to myself and
625 1223/5209/2443/1722/5213/ 3129 3361/5228/3739/1125
Ἀπολλὼ δι' ὑμᾶς, ἵνα ἐν ἡμῖν μάθητε τὸ μὴ ὑπὲρ ὃ γέγρα-
Apollos because of you, that in us you may learn not above what has been
5426 2443/3361/1519/5228 1520 5448 2596
πται φρονεῖν, ἵνα μὴ εἷς ὑπὲρ τοῦ ἑνὸς φυσιοῦσθε κατὰ τοῦ
written to think, that not one over one you are puffed up against the
2087/5101/1063/4571/ 1252 5101 2192/3739/3756 2983 1487
7 ἑτέρου. τίς γάρ σε διακρίνει; τί δὲ ἔχεις ὃ οὐκ ἔλαβες; εἰ δὲ
other. who For you makes differ? what And have you not you received? if
2983 5101 2744 5613/3361/2983 2235 2880
8 καὶ ἔλαβες, τί καυχᾶσαι ὡς μὴ λαβών; ἤδη κεκορεσμένοι
And you received, why boast you as not receiving? Already being sated
2075 2235 4147 5565 2257 936
ἐστέ, ἤδη ἐπλουτήσατε, χωρὶς ἡμῶν ἐβασιλεύσατε· καὶ
you are; already you became rich; without us you reigned, and
3785 1065 936 2443 2249 5213 4821
ὄφελόν γε ἐβασιλεύσατε, ἵνα καὶ ἡμεῖς ὑμῖν συμβασιλεύσω-
oh that really you did reign, that also we you might reign with.
1380 1063/3754 2316/5209 652 2078
9 μεν. δοκῶ γὰρ ὅτι ὁ Θεὸς ἡμᾶς τοὺς ἀποστόλους ἐσχάτους
I think For that God us, the apostles, last
584 5613 1935 3754 2302 1096
ἀπέδειξεν ὡς ἐπιθανατίους· ὅτι θέατρον ἐγενήθημεν τῷ
set out, as appointed to death, because a spectacle we became to the
2889 32 444 2249 3474 1223
10 κόσμῳ, καὶ ἀγγέλοις, καὶ ἀνθρώποις. ἡμεῖς μωροὶ διὰ
world, and to angels and to men. We (are) fools because of
5547 5210 5429 1722 5547 2249 772 5210
Χριστόν, ὑμεῖς δὲ φρόνιμοι ἐν Χριστῷ· ἡμεῖς ἀσθενεῖς, ὑμεῖς
Christ, you but prudent in Christ; we (are) weak, you
2478 5210 1741 2249 820 891 737
11 δὲ ἰσχυροί ὑμεῖς ἔνδοξοι, ἡμεῖς δὲ ἄτιμοι. ἄχρι τῆς ἄρτι
but strong; you (are) honored, we but unhonored. Until the present
5610 3983 1372 1130
ὥρας καὶ πεινῶμεν, καὶ διψῶμεν, καὶ γυμνητεύομεν, καὶ
hour both we hunger, and thirst, and are naked, and
2852 790 2872 2038
12 κολαφιζόμεθα, καὶ ἀστατοῦμεν, καὶ κοπιῶμεν ἐργαζόμενοι
are buffeted, and wander homeless, and labor, working
2398 5495 3058 2127 1377
ταις ἰδίαις χερσί· λοιδορούμενοι εὐλογοῦμεν· διωκόμενοι
with the own hands. Cursed, we bless; persecuted
430 987 3870 5613 4027
13 ἀνεχόμεθα· βλασφημούμενοι παρακαλοῦμεν· ὡς περικαθάρ-
we bear; having been defamed, we entreat; as filth
2889 1096 3956 4067 2193 737
ματα τοῦ κόσμου ἐγενήθημεν, πάντων περίψημα ἕως ἄρτι.
of the world, we are become; of all dirt wiped off until now.
3756 1788 5209 1125 5023 235 5613 5043 3450
14 Οὐκ ἐντρέπων ὑμᾶς γράφω ταῦτα, ἀλλ' ὡς τέκνα μου
not shaming you I write these things, but as children of me
27 3560 1437/1063/3463 3807 2192 1722
15 ἀγαπητὰ νουθετῶ. ἐὰν γὰρ μυρίους παιδαγωγοὺς ἔχητε ἐν
beloved warning. if For myriads teachers you have in
5547 235/3756 4183 3962 1722/1063 5547 2424
Χριστῷ, ἀλλ' οὐ πολλοὺς πατέρας· ἐν γὰρ Χριστῷ Ἰησοῦ
Christ, yet not many fathers; in for Christ Jesus
1223 2098 1473/5209 1080 3870 3767
16 διὰ τοῦ εὐαγγελίου ἐγὼ ὑμᾶς ἐγέννησα. παρακαλῶ οὖν
through the gospel I you fathered. I urge then,

[17]Because of this I sent
Timothy to you, who is my
beloved child, and faithful
in *the* Lord, who will remind
you *of* my ways in Christ,
even as I teach everywhere
in every church. [18]As to my
not coming to you now,
some were puffed up. [19]But
if the Lord wills, I will come
to you shortly. And I will not
know the word of those
who have been puffed up,
but the power. [20]For the
kingdom of God *is* not in
word, but in power. [21]What
do you desire? *Shall* I come
to you with a rod, or in love
and a spirit of meekness?

5209 3402 3450 1096 1223 5124 3992 5213 5095
17 ὑμᾶς, μιμηταί μου γίνεσθε. διὰ τοῦτο ἔπεμψα ὑμῖν Τιμόθεον,
you, imitators of me become. Because of this I sent to you Timothy,
3739/2076 5043/3450 27 4103 1722 2962 3739/5209
ὅς ἐστι τέκνον μου ἀγαπητὸν καὶ πιστὸν ἐν Κυρίῳ, ὅς ὑμᾶς
who is a child of me, beloved and faithful in (the) Lord, who you
363 3598 3450 1722 5547 2531 3837
ἀναμνήσει τὰς ὁδούς μου τὰς ἐν Χριστῷ, καθὼς πανταχοῦ
will remind (of) the ways of me in Christ, as everywhere
1722/3956 1577 1321 5613/3361/ 2064 3450/ 4314
18 ἐν πάσῃ ἐκκλησίᾳ διδάσκω. ὡς μὴ ἐρχομένου δέ μου πρός
in every church I teach. When not coming now me to
5209 5448 5100 2064 5030 4314 5209
19 ὑμᾶς ἐφυσιώθησάν τινες. ἐλεύσομαι δὲ ταχέως πρὸς ὑμᾶς,
you were puffed up some. I will come But shortly to you,
1437 2962 2309 1097 3756 3056
ἐάν ὁ Κύριος θελήσῃ, καὶ γνώσομαι οὐ τὸν λόγον τῶν
if the Lord wills, and I will know not the word of those
5448 235 1411 3756/1063/1722/3056
20 πεφυσιωμένων, ἀλλὰ τὴν δύναμιν. οὐ γὰρ ἐν λόγῳ ἡ
having been puffed up, but the power. not For in word the
932 2316 235/1722 1411 5101 2309 1722 4464
21 βασιλεία τοῦ Θεοῦ, ἀλλ᾽ ἐν δυνάμει. τί θέλετε; ἐν ῥάβδῳ
kingdom of God, but in power. What desire you? With a rod
2064 4314/5209 1722 26 4151 5037 4236
ἔλθω πρὸς ὑμᾶς, ἢ ἐν ἀγάπῃ πνεύματί τε πρᾳότητος;
I come to you, or in love, a spirit and of meekness?

CHAPTER 5

[1]Everywhere *it* is heard
that fornication *is* among
you, and such fornication
which *is* not named among
the heathen, so as one to
have *his* father's wife. [2]And
you are puffed up, and have
not rather mourned, that he
that did this deed might be
taken from your midst. [3]For
as being absent in body, but
being present in spirit,
indeed I have already
judged the *one* who has
worked out this thing, as *if I*
were present: [4]In the name
of our Lord Jesus Christ—
you being gathered to-
gether with my spirit, with
the power of our Lord Jesus
Christ—[5]to deliver such a
one to Satan for destruction
of the flesh, that the spirit
may be saved in the day of
the Lord Jesus. [6]Your
boast *is* not good. Do you
not know that a little leaven
leavens all the lump?
[7]Therefore, purge out the
old leaven so that you may
be a new lump, even as you
are unleavened. For also
Christ our Passover was

CHAPTER 5

3654 191 1722/5213 4202 5108 4202
1 Ὅλως ἀκούεται ἐν ὑμῖν πορνεία, καὶ τοιαύτη πορνεία,
Everywhere (it) is heard among you fornication, and such fornication
3748/3761/1722 1484 3687 5620 1135 5100
ἥτις οὐδὲ ἐν τοῖς ἔθνεσιν ὀνομάζεται, ὥστε γυναῖκά τινα
which (is) not among the nations named, so as (the) wife one
3962 2192 5210 5448 2075 3780
2 τοῦ πατρὸς ἔχειν. καὶ ὑμεῖς πεφυσιωμένοι ἐστέ, καὶ οὐχὶ
of the father to have. And you having been puffed up are, and not
3123 3996 2443 1808 1537 3319 5216 2041
μᾶλλον ἐπενθήσατε, ἵνα ἐξαρθῇ ἐκ μέσου ὑμῶν ὁ τὸ ἔργον
rather mourned, that might be taken from your midst he deed
5124 4160 1473/3303/1063/5613/548 4983 3918
3 τοῦτο ποιήσας. ἐγὼ μὲν γὰρ ὡς ἀπὼν τῷ σώματι παρὼν
this did, I indeed For as being absent in the body, but present
4151 2235 2919 5613 3779 5124
δὲ τῷ πνεύματι, ἤδη κέκρικα ὡς παρών, τὸν οὕτω τοῦτο
in the spirit, already have judged as being present he thus this thing
2716 1722 3686 2962 2257 2424
4 κατεργασάμενον, ἐν τῷ ὀνόματι τοῦ Κυρίου ἡμῶν Ἰησοῦ
having worked out. In the name of the Lord of us, Jesus
5547 4863 5216 1699 4151 4862
Χριστοῦ, συναχθέντων ὑμῶν καὶ τοῦ ἐμοῦ πνεύματος, σὺν
Christ, being gathered together you and the of me spirit, with
1411 2962 2257 2424 5547 3860
5 τῇ δυνάμει τοῦ Κυρίου ἡμῶν Ἰησοῦ Χριστοῦ, παραδοῦναι
the power of the Lord of us, Jesus Christ, to deliver
5108 4567 1519 3639 4561 2443
τὸν τοιοῦτον τῷ Σατανᾷ εἰς ὄλεθρον τῆς σαρκός, ἵνα τὸ
such a one to Satan for destruction of the flesh, that the
4151 4982/1722 2250 2962 2424 3756 2570
6 πνεῦμα σωθῇ ἐν τῇ ἡμέρᾳ τοῦ Κυρίου Ἰησοῦ. οὐ καλὸν τὸ
spirit may be saved in the day of the Lord Jesus. Not good (is) the
2745 5216 3756 1492/3754 3398 2219/3650 5445
καύχημα ὑμῶν. οὐκ οἴδατε ὅτι μικρὰ ζύμη ὅλον τὸ φύραμα
boast of you. Do not you know that a little leaven all the lump
2220 1571 3767 3820 2219 2443/5600/3501
7 ζυμοῖ; ἐκκαθάρατε οὖν τὴν παλαιὰν ζύμην, ἵνα ἦτε νέον
leavens? purge out Then the old leaven, that you be a new
5445 2531 2075 106 1063 3957 2257 5228
φύραμα, καθώς ἐστε ἄζυμοι. καὶ γὰρ τὸ πάσχα ἡμῶν ὑπὲρ
lump, as you are unleavened. also For the Passover of us for

NOTE: Frequent words not numbered: δέ(1161); καί(2531)—and, but; ὁ, ἡ, τό (3588, the)— * above word, look in verse margin for No.

sacrificed for us. 8So let us
keep *the* feast, not with old
leaven, nor with leaven of
malice and of evil, but with
unleavened *bread* of sincerity and truth.
9I wrote to you in the
letter not to associate
intimately with fornicators;
10and not altogether with
the fornicators of this world,
or with the covetous, or
with plunderers, or with
idolaters, since then you
must go out of the world.
11But now I wrote to you
not to associate intimately;
if anyone *is* called a brother
and is either a fornicator, or
a covetous one, or an
idolater, or a reviler, or a
drunkard, or a plunderer,
with such a one not to eat.
12For what *is it* to me also
to judge the ones outside?
Do you not judge those
inside? 13But God will
judge the ones outside.
And you shall put out the
evil one from you.

CHAPTER 6

1Does anyone of you
having a matter against
another dare to be judged
before the unjust, and not
before the saints? 2Do you
not know that the saints
will judge the world? And if
the world is judged by you,
are you unworthy of small
judgments? 3Or do you not
know that we shall judge
angels, not to speak of this
life? 4If, then, you truly
have judgments of this life,
those being least esteemed
in the church, you sit these.
5For I speak shame to you.
So, is there not a wise one
among you, not even one
who will be able to give
judgment on his brother in
your midst? 6But brother is
judged with brother, and
this before unbelievers!
7Indeed, then, there is
already a failure with you all,
that you have lawsuits with
yourselves. Why not in-
stead be wronged? Why not

2257 2380 5547 5620 1858 3361/1722/2219 3820
8 ἡμῶν ἐθύθη Χριστός· ὥστε ἑορτάζωμεν, μὴ ἐν ζύμῃ παλαιᾷ,
us was sacrificed, Christ, so as let us keep feast, not with leaven old,
3366/1722/2219 2549 4189 235 1722 106 1505
μηδὲ ἐν ζύμῃ κακίας καὶ πονηρίας, ἀλλ' ἐν ἀζύμοις εἰλι-
not with leaven of malice and of evil: but with unleavened of
225
κρινείας καὶ ἀληθείας.
sincerity and truth.
1125 5213/1722 1992 3361 4874
9 Ἔγραψα ὑμῖν ἐν τῇ ἐπιστολῇ μὴ συναναμίγνυσθαι
I wrote to you in the epistle not to associate intimately
4205 3756 3843 4205 2889 5127
10 πόρνοις· καὶ οὐ πάντως τοῖς πόρνοις τοῦ κόσμου τούτου,
with fornicators, and not altogether with the fornicators world of this,
4123 2228 727 2228 1496 1893
ἢ τοῖς πλεονέκταις, ἢ ἅρπαξιν, ἢ εἰδωλολάτραις· ἐπεὶ
or with the covetous, or with plunderers, or with idolaters, since
3784 686/1537 2889 1831 3570 1125 5213
11 ὀφείλετε ἄρα ἐκ τοῦ κόσμου ἐξελθεῖν. νυνὶ δὲ ἔγραψα ὑμῖν
you ought then out of the world to go out. now But I wrote to you
3361 4874 1437 5100 80 3687 2228
μὴ συναναμίγνυσθαι, ἐάν τις ἀδελφὸς ὀνομαζόμενος ᾖ
not to associate intimately if anyone a brother is called (is) either
4205 2228 4123 2228 1496 2228 3060 2228
πόρνος, ἢ πλεονέκτης, ἢ εἰδωλολάτρης, ἢ λοίδορος, ἢ
a fornicator, or a covetous, or an idolater, or a reviler, or
3183 2228 727 5101 3366 4906 5101/1063/3427
12 μέθυσος, ἢ ἅρπαξ· τῷ τοιούτῳ μηδὲ συνεσθίειν. τί γάρ μοι
drunkard, or a plunderer, with such a one not to eat. what For to me
1854 2919 3780 2080 5210 2919
13 καὶ τοὺς ἔξω κρίνειν; οὐχὶ τοὺς ἔσω ὑμεῖς κρίνετε; τοὺς δὲ
also those outside to judge? Do not those inside you judge? those But
1854 2316 2919 1808 4190 1537/5216 848
ἔξω ὁ Θεὸς κρίνει. καὶ ἐξαρεῖτε τὸν πονηρὸν ἐξ ὑμῶν αὐτῶν
outside God will judge. And you shall put out the evil one from yourselves.

CHAPTER 6

5111/5100/5216/4229 2192 4314 2087 2919
1 Τολμᾷ τις ὑμῶν, πρᾶγμα ἔχων πρὸς τὸν ἕτερον, κρίνεσθαι
Dares anyone of you a matter having against another to be judged
1909 94 3780/1909 40 3756 1492 3753
2 ἐπὶ τῶν ἀδίκων, καὶ οὐχὶ ἐπὶ τῶν ἁγίων; οὐκ οἴδατε ὅτι οἱ
before the unjust, and not before the saints? Do not you know that the
40 2889 2918 1487/1722/5213/2919 2889
ἅγιοι τὸν κόσμον κρινοῦσι; καὶ εἰ ἐν ὑμῖν κρίνεται ὁ κόσμος,
saints the world will judge? And if by you is judged the world,
370 2075 2922 1646 3756 1492 3754/32
3 ἀνάξιοί ἐστε κριτηρίων ἐλαχίστων; οὐκ οἴδατε ὅτι ἀγγέ-
unworthy are you judgments of small? Do not you know that angels
2919 = 3386= 982 982 3303/3777/ 2922
4 λους κρινοῦμεν; μήτι γε βιωτικά; βιωτικὰ μὲν οὖν κριτήρια
we will judge, not to speak of this life? Of this life truly then judgments
1437/2192 1848 1722 1577 5128
ἐὰν ἔχητε, τοὺς ἐξουθενημένους ἐν τῇ ἐκκλησίᾳ, τούτους
if you have, those being least esteemed in the church, these
2523 4314 1791 5213 3004 3779 3756 2076 1722
5 καθίζετε. πρὸς ἐντροπὴν ὑμῖν λέγω. οὕτως οὐκ ἔστιν ἐν
sit you. For shame to you I say. Thus, not is among
5213 4680 3761/1519/3739/ 1410 1252 303 3319
ὑμῖν σοφὸς οὐδὲ εἷς, ὃς δυνήσεται διακρῖναι ἀνὰ μέσον τοῦ
you a wise one, not one who will be able to discern in your midst the
80 848 235 80 3326 80 2919
6 ἀδελφοῦ αὐτοῦ, ἀλλὰ ἀδελφὸς μετὰ ἀδελφοῦ κρίνεται, καὶ
brother of him? But brother with brother is judged, and
5124 1909 571 2235/3303/3767/3654/ 2275/1722/5213/2076
7 τοῦτο ἐπὶ ἀπίστων; ἤδη μὲν οὖν ὅλως ἥττημα ἐν ὑμῖν ἐστιν,
this before unbelievers. Already indeed, then all a failure with you is,
3754 2917 2192 3326 1438 1302 3780 3123 91
ὅτι κρίματα ἔχετε μεθ' ἑαυτῶν. διατί οὐχὶ μᾶλλον ἀδικεῖσθε;
that lawsuits you have with yourselves. Why not instead be wronged?

instead be defrauded? [8]But you do wrong, and defraud; and these things to brothers! [9]Or do you not know that unjust ones will not inherit *the* kingdom of God? Do not be led astray, neither fornicators, nor idolaters, nor adulterers, nor abusers, nor homosexuals, [10]nor thieves, nor covetous ones, nor drunkards, nor revilers, nor plunderers shall inherit *the* kingdom of God. [11]And some were these things, but you were washed; but you were sanctified; but you were justified in the name of the Lord Jesus, and in the Spirit of our God.

[12]All things are lawful to me, but not all things contribute. All things are lawful to me, but I will not be ruled by any. [13]Foods for the belly, and the belly for foods; but God will destroy both this and these. But the body *is* not for fornication, but for the Lord, and the Lord for the body. [14]And God also raised up the Lord, and will raise us up through His power. [15]Do you not know that your bodies are members of Christ? Then taking the members of Christ, shall I make *them* members of a harlot? Let it not be! [16]Or do you not know that he being joined to a harlot is one body? For He says, "The two *shall be* into one flesh." [17]But he being joined to the Lord is one spirit. [18]Flee fornication. Every sin which a man may do is outside the body, but he doing fornication sins against *his* own body. [19]Or do you not know that your body is a temple of *the* Holy Spirit in you, which you have from God; and you are not of

1302 3780 3123 650 235 5210 91
8 διατί οὐχὶ μᾶλλον ἀποστερεῖσθε ; ἀλλὰ ὑμεῖς ἀδικεῖτε καὶ
Why not instead be despoiled? But you do wrong and
650 5023 80 2228/3756 1492 3754 94
9 ἀποστερεῖτε, καὶ ταῦτα ἀδελφούς. ἢ οὐκ οἴδατε ὅτι ἄδικοι
despoil, and these things (to) brothers. Or not you know that unjust ones
932 2316/3756 2816 3361 4105 3777
βασιλείαν Θεοῦ οὐ κληρονομήσουσι ; μὴ πλανᾶσθε· οὔτε
(the) kingdom of God not will inherit? Be not led astray; not
4205 3777 1496 3777 3432 3777 3120 3777
πόρνοι, οὔτε εἰδωλολάτραι, οὔτε μοιχοί, οὔτε μαλακοί, οὔτε
fornicators, nor idolaters, nor adulterers, nor abusers, nor
733 3777 2812 3777 4123 3777 3183
10 ἀρσενοκοῖται, οὔτε κλέπται, οὔτε πλεονέκται, οὔτε μέθυσοι,
homosexuals, nor thieves, nor covetous ones, nor drunkards,
3756 3060 3756 727 932 2316 3756 2816
οὐ λοίδοροι, οὐχ ἅρπαγες, βασιλείαν Θεοῦ οὐ κληρονομή-
not revilers, not plunderers (the) kingdom of God not shall
5023 5100 2258 235 628 235
11 σουσι. καὶ ταῦτά τινες ἦτε· ἀλλὰ ἀπελούσασθε, ἀλλὰ
inherit. And these things some were. But you were washed; but
37 235 1344 1722 3686 2962
ἡγιάσθητε, ἀλλ' ἐδικαιώθητε ἐν τῷ ὀνόματι τοῦ Κυρίου
you were sanctified; but you were justified in the name of the Lord
2424 1722 4151 2316 2257
Ἰησοῦ, καὶ ἐν τῷ Πνεύματι τοῦ Θεοῦ ἡμῶν.
Jesus and in the Spirit God of us.
3956 3427 1832 235 3756 3956 4851 3956 3427
12 Πάντα μοι ἔξεστιν, ἀλλ' οὐ πάντα συμφέρει· πάντα μοι
All things to me are lawful, but not all things contribute. All things to me
1832 235 3756/1473 1850 5259 5100
ἔξεστιν, ἀλλ' οὐκ ἐγὼ ἐξουσιασθήσομαι ὑπό τινος. τὰ
are lawful, but not I will be ruled by any
1033 2836 2836 1033 2316
13 βρώματα τῇ κοιλίᾳ, καὶ ἡ κοιλία τοῖς βρώμασιν· ὁ δὲ Θεὸς
Foods for the belly, and the belly – for foods; but God
5026 5023 2673 4983 3756
καὶ ταύτην καὶ ταῦτα καταργήσει. τὸ δὲ σῶμα οὐ τῇ
both this and these will destroy. the But body not (is)
4202 235 2962 2962 4983
14 πορνείᾳ, ἀλλὰ τῷ Κυρίῳ, καὶ ὁ Κύριος τῷ σώματι· ὁ δὲ
for fornication, but for the Lord, and the Lord for the body. And
2316 2962 1453 2248 1825 1223
Θεὸς καὶ τὸν Κύριον ἤγειρε, καὶ ἡμᾶς ἐξεγερεῖ διὰ τῆς
God also the Lord raised, and us will raise up through the
1411 848 3756 1492 3754 4983 5216 3196
15 δυνάμεως αὐτοῦ. οὐκ οἴδατε ὅτι τὰ σώματα ὑμῶν μέλη
power of Him. Do not you know that the bodies of you members
5547 2076 142 3767 3196 5547 4160
Χριστοῦ ἐστιν ; ἄρας οὖν τὰ μέλη τοῦ Χριστοῦ ποιήσω
of Christ are? having taken Then the members of Christ, Shall I make
4204 3196 3361 1096 /2228/3756/1492/3754 2853
16 πόρνης μέλη ; μὴ γένοιτο. ἢ οὐκ οἴδατε ὅτι ὁ κολλώμενος τῇ
of a harlot members? Not let it be! Or not you know that he being joined
4204/1722/4983/2076 2071 1063 5346 1417/1519/4562
πόρνῃ ἓν σῶμά ἐστιν ; Ἔσονται γάρ, φησίν, οἱ δύο εἰς σάρκα
to a harlot one body is? will be For, He says, the two into flesh
3391 2853 2962 1520/ 4151 2076 5343
17 μίαν. ὁ δὲ κολλώμενος τῷ Κυρίῳ ἓν πνεῦμά ἐστι. φεύγετε τὴν
18 one. he But being joined to the Lord one spirit is. Flee –
4202 3956 265 3739/1437/ 4160 444 1623
πορνείαν. πᾶν ἁμάρτημα ὃ ἐὰν ποιήσῃ ἄνθρωπος ἐκτὸς τοῦ
fornication. Every sin which if may do a man outside the
4983 2076 4203 1519 2398 4983 264
σώματός ἐστιν· ὁ δὲ πορνεύων εἰς τὸ ἴδιον σῶμα ἁμαρτάνει.
body is, he but doing fornication against the own body sins.
2228/3756 1492 3754 4983 5216 3485 1722 5213 40
19 ἢ οὐκ οἴδατε ὅτι τὸ σῶμα ὑμῶν ναὸς τοῦ ἐν ὑμῖν Ἁγίου
Or not you know that the body of you a temple of the in you Holy
4151 2076 3756/2192 575 2316 3756/2075 1438
Πνεύματός ἐστιν, οὗ ἔχετε ἀπὸ Θεοῦ ; καὶ οὐκ ἐστὲ ἑαυτῶν,
Spirit is, which you have from God; and not are you of yourselves?

NOTE: Frequent words not numbered: δέ(1161); καί(2531)–and, but; ὁ, ἡ, τό (3588, the)— * above word, look in verse margin for No.

yourselves? [20]For you were bought with a price; then glorify God in your body, and in your spirit, which are of God.

CHAPTER 7

[1]But concerning what you wrote to me, *it is* good for a man not to touch a woman; [2]but because of fornication, let each have his *own* wife, and let each have *her* own husband. [3]Let the husband give due kindness to the wife; and likewise the wife also to the husband. [4]The wife does not have authority of *her* own body, but the husband. And likewise also the husband does not have authority *over his* own body, but the wife. [5]Do not deprive one another, unless by agreement for a time, that you may be free for fasting and for prayer. And come together again on the same *place,* that Satan may not tempt you through your incontinence. [6]But I say this by permission, not by command. [7]But I desire all men also to be as myself. But each has his own gift from God, one this way, and one that way.

[8]But I say to the unmarried men, and to the widows, it is good for them if they also remain as I. [9]But if they do not have self-control, let them marry; for it is better to marry than to be inflamed. [10]But I enjoin the ones being married—not I, but the Lord—a woman not to be separated from *her* husband; [11]but if she indeed is separated, remain unmarried; or be reconciled to the husband. And a husband *is* not to leave *his* wife. [12]But to the rest I say, not the Lord, if any brother has an unbelieving wife, and she consents to

59 1063 5092 1392 1211 2316/1722 4983
20 ἠγοράσθητε γὰρ τιμῆς· δοξάσατε δὴ τὸν Θεὸν ἐν τῷ σώματι
you were bought For of a price; glorify then God in the body
5216 1722 4151 5216 3748/2076 2316
ὑμῶν, καὶ ἐν τῷ πνεύματι ὑμῶν, ἅτινά ἐστι τοῦ Θεοῦ.
of you, and in the spirit of you, which are of God.

CHAPTER 7

4012 3739 1125 3427 2570 444 1135 3361
1 Περὶ δὲ ὧν ἐγράψατέ μοι, καλὸν ἀνθρώπῳ γυναικὸς μὴ
concerning But what you wrote to me, (it is) good for a man a woman not
680 1223 4202 1538 1438 1135
2 ἅπτεσθαι. διὰ δὲ τὰς πορνείας ἕκαστος τὴν ἑαυτοῦ γυναῖκα
to touch; because of but the fornications each one the of himself wife
2192 1538 2398 435 2192 1135 435
3 ἐχέτω, καὶ ἑκάστη τὸν ἴδιον ἄνδρα ἐχέτω. τῇ γυναικὶ ὁ ἀνὴρ
have; and each one the own husband have. To the wife the husband
3784 2133 591 3668 1135
τὴν ὀφειλομένην εὔνοιαν ἀποδιδότω· ὁμοίως δὲ καὶ ἡ γυνὴ
due kindness let pay; likewise and also the wife
435 1135 2398 4983 3756 1850 235
4 τῷ ἀνδρί. ἡ γυνὴ τοῦ ἰδίου σώματος οὐκ ἐξουσιάζει, ἀλλ'
to the husband. The wife of the own body not has authority, but
435 3668 435 2398 4983 3756 1850
ὁ ἀνήρ· ὁμοίως δὲ καὶ ὁ ἀνὴρ τοῦ ἰδίου σώματος οὐκ ἐξου-
the husband; likewise and also the husband the own body not has
235 1135 3361 650 240 =1509= 302
5 σιάζει, ἀλλ' ἡ γυνή. μὴ ἀποστερεῖτε ἀλλήλους, εἰ μή τι ἂν
authority, but the wife. Do not deprive one another, unless
1537 4859 4314 2540 2443 4980 3521
ἐκ συμφώνου πρὸς καιρόν, ἵνα σχολάζητε τῇ νηστείᾳ καὶ
by agreement for a time, that you may be free for fasting and
4335 3825 1909 846 4905 2443/3361
τῇ προσευχῇ, καὶ πάλιν ἐπὶ τὸ αὐτὸ συνέρχησθε, ἵνα μὴ
for prayer; and again on the same come together, that not
3985 5209 4567 1223 (place) 192 5216 5124
6 πειράζῃ ὑμᾶς ὁ Σατανᾶς διὰ τὴν ἀκρασίαν ὑμῶν. τοῦτο δὲ
may tempt you Satan through the incontinence of you. this And
3004 2596 4774 3756 2596 2003 2309 1063
7 λέγω κατὰ συγγνώμην, οὐ κατ' ἐπιταγήν. θέλω γὰρ
I say by permission, not by command. I desire For
3956 444 1511/5613 1683 235 1538 2398
πάντας ἀνθρώπους εἶναι ὡς καὶ ἐμαυτόν· ἀλλ' ἕκαστος ἴδιον
all men to be as also myself; but each one (the) ow
•1537 5486 2192/•/2316/3739/3303/3779/3739 3779
χάρισμα ἔχει ἐκ Θεοῦ, ὃς μὲν οὕτως, ὃς δὲ οὕτως.
gift has from God, one thus, one and thus.
3004 22 5503 2570 846
8 Λέγω δὲ τοῖς ἀγάμοις καὶ ταῖς χήραις, καλὸν αὐτοῖς
I say And to the bachelors and to the widows, good for them
2076 1437 3306 5613 2504 1487 3756 1467
9 ἐστιν ἐὰν μείνωσιν ὡς κἀγώ. εἰ δὲ οὐκ ἐγκρατεύονται,
it is if they remain as I also. if But not have self-control,
1060 2909 1063 2076 1060 2228 4448
γαμησάτωσαν· κρεῖσσον γάρ ἐστι γαμῆσαι ἢ πυροῦσθαι.
let them marry; better for it is to marry than to be inflamed.
1060 3853 3756/1473 235 2962
10 τοῖς δὲ γεγαμηκόσι παραγγέλλω, οὐκ ἐγώ, ἀλλ' ὁ Κύριος,
to those But having married I enjoin, not I, but the Lord,
1135 575 435 3361 5563 1437 5563
11 γυναῖκα ἀπὸ ἀνδρὸς μὴ χωρισθῆναι (ἐὰν δὲ καὶ χωρισθῇ,
a woman from (her) husband not to be separated if but indeed she is
3306 22 2228 435 2644 separated,
•435 μενέτω ἄγαμος, ἢ τῷ ἀνδρὶ καταλλαγήτω)· καὶ ἄνδρα
remain unmarried, or to the husband be reconciled – and a husband
1135 3361 863 3062 1473 3004 3756
12 γυναῖκα μὴ ἀφιέναι. τοῖς δὲ λοιποῖς ἐγὼ λέγω, οὐχ ὁ
(his) wife not to leave. to the And rest I say, not the
2962 =1536= 80 1135 2192 571 846
Κύριος· εἴ τις ἀδελφὸς γυναῖκα ἔχει ἄπιστον, καὶ αὐτὴ
Lord: If any brother a wife has unbelieving, and she

live with him, let him not leave her. [13]And a woman who has an unbelieving husband, and he consents to live with her, let her not leave him. [14]For the unbelieving husband has been sanctified by the wife; and the unbelieving wife has been sanctified by the husband; else, then, your children are unclean; but now they are holy. [15]But if the unbelieving one separates, let *them* be separated; the brother or the sister is not in bondage in such matters; but God has called us in peace. [16]For what do you know, wife, whether you will save the husband; or what do you know, husband, whether you will save the wife? [17]Only as God has divided to each, each as the Lord has called, so let him walk. So I command in the churches.

[18]Was anyone called having been circumcised? Do not be uncircumcised. *Was* anyone called in uncircumcision? Do not be circumcised. [19]Circumcision is nothing, and uncircumcision is nothing; but the keeping of God's commands. [20]Each one in the calling in which he was called, in this remain. [21]Were you called *as* a slave? It does not matter to you. But if you are able to be free, rather use *it*. [22]For the *one* called a slave in *the* Lord is a freed man of *the* Lord. And likewise, the *one* called a free man is a slave of Christ. [23]You were redeemed with a price; do not become slaves of men. [24]Each in whatever *state* called, brothers, in this remain with God.

[25]But about virgins, I have no command of *the* Lord. But I give judgment, as having received mercy by *the* Lord to be faithful.

[26]Then I think this to be good, because of the present necessity: that *it is*

4909 3611 3326 846 3361 863 846 1135
13 συνευδοκεῖ οἰκεῖν μετ' αὐτοῦ, μὴ ἀφιέτω αὐτήν. καὶ γυνὴ
consents to live with him, not let him leave her. And a woman
3748/2192 435 571 846 4909 3611 3326
ἥτις ἔχει ἄνδρα ἄπιστον, καὶ αὐτὸς συνευδοκεῖ οἰκεῖν μετ'
who has a husband unbelieving, and he consents to live with
846 3361 863 846 37 1063 435 571
14 αὐτῆς, μὴ ἀφιέτω αὐτόν. ἡγίασται γὰρ ὁ ἀνὴρ ὁ ἄπιστος
her, not let her leave him. has been sanctified For the husband unbelieving
1722 1135 37 1135 571 1722 435
ἐν τῇ γυναικί, καὶ ἡγίασται ἡ γυνὴ ἡ ἄπιστος ἐν τῷ ἀνδρί·
by the wife; and has been sanctified the wife unbelieving by the husband;
1893 686 5043 5216 169 2076/3568 40 2076
ἐπεὶ ἄρα τὰ τέκνα ὑμῶν ἀκάθαρτά ἐστι, νῦν δὲ ἅγιά ἐστιν.
else then the children of you unclean is; now but holy they are.
1487 571 5563 5563 3756 1402
15 εἰ δὲ ὁ ἄπιστος χωρίζεται, χωριζέσθω. οὐ δεδούλωται ὁ
if But the unbelieving separates, let be separated, not is in bondage the
80 2228 79 1722 5108 1722 1515 2564
ἀδελφὸς ἢ ἡ ἀδελφὴ ἐν τοῖς τοιούτοις· ἐν δὲ εἰρήνῃ κέκληκεν
brother or the sister in such matters; in but peace has called
2248 2316/5101/1063/ 1492 1135 1487 435 4983/2228/5101
16 ἡμᾶς ὁ Θεός. τί γὰρ οἶδας, γύναι, εἰ τὸν ἄνδρα σώσεις ; ἢ τί
us God. what For know you, wife, if the husband you will save; or what
1492 435 1487 1135 4982 =1508=/ 1538/5613/ 3307
17 οἶδας, ἄνερ, εἰ τὴν γυναῖκα σώσεις ; εἰ μὴ ἑκάστῳ ὡς ἐμέρισεν
know you, husband, if the wife you will save? Only to each as has divided
2316 1538 5613 2564 2962 3779 4043
ὁ Θεός, ἕκαστον ὡς κέκληκεν ὁ Κύριος, οὕτω περιπατείτω.
God, each as has called the Lord, so let him walk.
3779 1722 1577 3956 1299 4059
18 καὶ οὕτως ἐν ταῖς ἐκκλησίαις πάσαις διατάσσομαι. περι-
And so in the churches all I command. Having
5100 2564 3361 1986 1722 203 5100
τετμημένος τις ἐκλήθη ; μὴ ἐπισπάσθω. ἐν ἀκροβυστίᾳ τις
been circumcised any was called not be uncircumcised; in uncircumcision any
2564 3361 4059 4061 3762 2076
ἐκλήθη ; μὴ περιτεμνέσθω. ἡ περιτομὴ οὐδέν ἐστι, καὶ ἡ
was called, not be circumcised. Circumcision nothing is, and
203 3762 2076 235 5084 1785 2316
19 ἀκροβυστία οὐδέν ἐστιν, ἀλλὰ τήρησις ἐντολῶν Θεοῦ.
uncircumcision nothing is, but the keeping of the commands of God.
1538 1722 2821/3739/ 2564 1722/ 5026 3306 1401
20 ἕκαστος ἐν τῇ κλήσει ᾗ ἐκλήθη, ἐν ταύτῃ μενέτω. δοῦλος
Each one in the calling in which he was called, in this remain. a slave
2563 3361 4671 3199 235 1487 1410 1658
21 ἐκλήθης ; μή σοι μελέτω· ἀλλ' εἰ καὶ δύνασαι ἐλεύθερος
Were you called? Not to you it matters. But if also you are able free,
1096 3123 5530 1063/1722/2962 2564 1401
22 γενέσθαι, μᾶλλον χρῆσαι. ὁ γὰρ ἐν Κυρίῳ κληθεὶς δοῦλος,
to become, rather use (it). the (one) For in (the) Lord called a slave
558 2962 2076 3668 1658 2563
ἀπελεύθερος Κυρίου ἐστίν· ὁμοίως καὶ ὁ ἐλεύθερος κληθείς,
a freed man of (the) Lord is. likewise And the (one) a free man called,
1401 2076 5547 5092 59 3361 1096 1401
23 δοῦλός ἐστι Χριστοῦ. τιμῆς ἠγοράσθητε· μὴ γίνεσθε δοῦλοι
a slave is of Christ. Of a price you were bought; not become slaves
444 1538 1722/3739/ 2564 80 1722 5129 3306
24 ἀνθρώπων. ἕκαστος ἐν ᾧ ἐκλήθη, ἀδελφοί, ἐν τούτῳ μενέτω
of men. Each one in what-ever (state) called, brothers, in this remain
3844 2316
παρὰ τῷ Θεῷ.
with God.
4012 3933 2063 2962· 3756/2192 1106
25 Περὶ δὲ τῶν παρθένων ἐπιταγὴν Κυρίου οὐκ ἔχω· γνώμην
about And the virgins a command of (the) lord not I have. judgment
1325/5613/ 1653 5259 2962 4103 1511 3543 3767
26 δὲ δίδωμι ὡς ἠλεημένος ὑπὸ Κυρίου πιστὸς εἶναι. νομίζω οὖν
but I give as having had mercy by (the) Lord faithful to be. I think, then,
5124 2570 5225 1223 1764 318 3754
τοῦτο καλὸν ὑπάρχειν διὰ τὴν ἐνεστῶσαν ἀνάγκην, ὅτι
this good to be because of the present necessity; that (is)

good for a man to be thus. [27]Have you been bound to a wife? Do not seek to be released. Have you been released from a wife? Do not seek a wife. [28]But if you also marry, you do not sin. And if the virgin marries, she does not sin. But such will have trouble in the flesh. But I am sparingyou. [29]But, brothers, I say this, that the time has been cut short. For the rest is that even the *ones* having wives should be as not having; [30]and the *ones* weeping as not weeping; and the *ones* rejoicing as not rejoicing; and the *ones* buying as not possessing; [31]and the *ones* using this world as not abusing *it*; for the mode of this world is passing away.

[32]But I desire you to be without care. The one unmarried cares for the things of *the* Lord; [33]but the *one* married cares for the things of the world, how to please the wife. [34]The wife and the virgin *are* different. The unmarried one cares for the things of *the* Lord, that she be holy in both body and spirit. But the married one cares for the things of the world, how to please the husband. [35]And I say this for your advantage, not that I put a snare *before* you; but for the fitting thing, and waiting on the Lord without distraction.

[36]But if anyone thinks *it* behaving indecently toward his virginity—if he *is* beyond *his* prime, and so *it* ought to be—let him do what he desires; he does not sin; let them marry. [37]But *he* who stands firm in heart, not having necessity, but has authority as to *his* own will, and has judged this in his heart, to keep his virginity; he does well. [38]So that he that gives in marriage does well; and he that does not give in marriage does better.

2570 444 3779 1511 1210 1135 3361 2212
27 καλὸν ἀνθρώπῳ τὸ οὕτως εἶναι. δέδεσαι γυναικί; μὴ ζήτει
good for a men — so to be. Have you been bound to a woman? Not seek
3089 3089 575 1135 3361/2212 1135 1437
28 λύσιν. λέλυσαι ἀπὸ γυναικός; μὴ ζήτει γυναῖκα. ἐὰν δὲ καὶ
to be loosed. Have you been loosed from a woman? Not seek a woman. if But indeed
1060 3756 264 1437 1060 3933 3756 264
γήμῃς, οὐχ ἥμαρτες· καὶ ἐὰν γήμῃ ἡ παρθενος, οὐχ ἥμαρτε.
you marry, not you sin. And if marries the virgin, not she sinned.
2347 4561 2192 5108 1473 5216 5339
θλῖψιν δὲ τῇ σαρκὶ ἕξουσιν οἱ τοιοῦτοι· ἐγὼ δὲ ὑμῶν φείδομαι.
trouble But in the flesh will have such. I But you am sparing
5124 5346 80 3754 2540 4958
29 τοῦτο δέ φημι, ἀδελφοί, ὅτι ὁ καιρὸς συνεσταλμένος· τὸ
this But I say, brothers, that the time has been shortened; for
3063 2076/2443 2192 1135 5613/3361/2192 5600
λοιπόν ἐστιν ἵνα καὶ οἱ ἔχοντες γυναῖκας ὡς μὴ ἔχοντες ὦσιν
the rest is, that even those having wives, as not having be:
2799 5613/3361/ 2799 5463 5613/3361
30 καὶ οἱ κλαίοντες, ὡς μὴ κλαίοντες· καὶ οἱ χαίροντες, ὡς μὴ
and those weeping, as not weeping; and those rejoicing, as not
5463 59 5613/3361/ 2722
31 χαίροντες· καὶ οἱ ἀγοράζοντες, ὡς μὴ κατέχοντες· καὶ οἱ
rejoicing; and those buying, as not possessing; and those
5530 2889 5129 5613/3361/ 2710 3855
χρώμενοι τῷ κόσμῳ τούτῳ, ὡς μὴ καταχρώμενοι· παράγει
using world this, as not abusing (it); is passing away
1063 4976 2889 5127 2309 5209 275
32 γὰρ τὸ σχῆμα τοῦ κόσμου τούτου. θέλω δὲ ὑμᾶς ἀμερίμνους
for the mode world of this. I desire But you without care
1511 22 3308 2962 4459 700
33 εἶναι. ὁ ἄγαμος μεριμνᾷ τὰ τοῦ Κυρίου, πῶς ἀρέσει τῷ
to be. The unmarried one cares for the things of (the) Lord, how to please the
2962 1060 3309 2889 4459 700
Κυρίῳ· ὁ δὲ γαμήσας μεριμνᾷ τὰ τοῦ κόσμου, πῶς ἀρέσει
Lord; he but having married cares for the things of the world, how to please
1135 3307 1135 3933 22
34 τῇ γυναικί. μεμέρισται ἡ γυνὴ καὶ ἡ παρθένος. ἡ ἄγαμος
the wife. Different (are) the wife and the virgin. The unmarried
3309 2962 2443 40 4983 4151
μεριμνᾷ τὰ τοῦ Κυρίου, ἵνα ᾖ ἁγία καὶ σώματι καὶ πνεύματι·
cares for the things of (the) Lord, that she be holy both in body and in spirit;
1060 3309 2889 4459 700
ἡ δὲ γαμήσασα μεριμνᾷ τὰ τοῦ κόσμου, πῶς ἀρέσει τῷ
the but married cares for the things of (the) world, how to please the
435 5124 4314 5216 846 4851 3004 3756
35 ἀνδρί. τοῦτο δὲ πρὸς τὸ ὑμῶν αὐτῶν συμφέρον λέγω· οὐχ
husband. this And for the of yourselves advantage I say, not
2443 1029 5213 1911 235 4314 2158
ἵνα βρόχον ὑμῖν ἐπιβάλω, ἀλλὰ πρὸς τὸ εὔσχημον καὶ
that a snare (before) you I put; but for the thing fitting and
2145 2962 563 1487 5100 807
36 εὐπρόσεδρον τῷ Κυρίῳ ἀπερισπάστως. εἰ δέ τις ἀσχημονεῖν
waiting on the Lord without distraction. if But any to behave indecently 3779
1909 3933 848 3543 1437/5600/ 5230
ἐπὶ τὴν παρθένον αὐτοῦ νομίζει, ἐὰν ᾖ ὑπέρακμος, καὶ οὕτως
toward the virginity of him thinks — if he is beyond (his) prime, and so
3784 1096 3739/2309 4160 3756 264 1060
ὀφείλει γίνεσθαι, ὃ θέλει ποιείτω· οὐχ ἁμαρτάνει· γαμείτω-
(it) ought to be, what he desires let him do; not he sins; let them
3739 2476 1476/1722 2588/3361/ 2192 318
37 σαν. ὃς δὲ ἕστηκεν ἑδραῖος ἐν τῇ καρδίᾳ, μὴ ἔχων ἀνάγκην,
marry. (he) but stands firm in the heart, not having necessity,
1849 who 2192/4012 2398 2307 5124
ἐξουσίαν δὲ ἔχει περὶ τοῦ ἰδίου θελήματος, καὶ τοῦτο
authority but has concerning the own will, and this
2919 1722 2588 848 5083 1438
κέκρικεν ἐν τῇ καρδίᾳ αὐτοῦ, τοῦ τηρεῖν τὴν ἑαυτοῦ
has judged in the heart of him, to keep the of himself
3933 2573 4160 5620 1547 2573 4160
38 παρθένον, καλῶς ποιεῖ. ὥστε καὶ ὁ ἐκγαμίζων καλῶς ποιεῖ·
virginity, well he does. So as both he giving in marriage well does,

[39]A wife is bound by law for as long a time as her husband lives; but if her husband sleeps, she is free to be married to whomever she desires, only in *the* Lord. [40]But she is happier if she remains so, according to my judgment. And I think I also have *the* Spirit of God.

CHAPTER 8

[1]But concerning the sacrifices to idols, we know that we have all knowledge. Knowledge puffs up, but love builds up. [2]But if anyone thinks to know anything, he still has known nothing as he ought to know. [3]But if anyone loves God, this one has been known by Him. [4]Then concerning the eating of things sacrificed to idols, we know that an idol *is* nothing in *the* world, and that *there is* no other God except one. [5]For even if *some* are called gods, either in Heaven or on the earth; even as there are many gods, and many lords; [6]but to us *is* one God, the Father, of whom *are* all things, and we for Him; and one Lord, Jesus Christ, through whom *are* all things, and we by Him. [7]But the knowledge *is* not in all; but some being aware of the idol eat as an idolatrous sacrifice until now; and their conscience being weak is defiled. [8]But food will not commend us to God. For neither if we eat do we excel, nor if we do not eat are we behind. [9]But be careful lest this authority of yours become a cause of stumbling to the weak ones. [10]For if anyone sees you, the (one) having knowledge, sitting in an idol-temple, will not the weak one's conscience be

3361 1547 2908 4160 1135 1210 3551/1909
39 ὁ δὲ μὴ ἐκγαμίζων κρεῖσσον ποιεῖ. γυνὴ δέδεται νόμῳ ἐφ'
he and not giving in marriage better does. A wife has been bound by law for
4735 5550 2198 435 848 1437 2837 435 848
ὅσον χρόνον ζῇ ὁ ἀνὴρ αὐτῆς· ἐὰν δὲ κοιμηθῇ ὁ ἀνὴρ αὐτῆς,
as long a time as lives her husband; if but sleeps the husband of her,
1658 2076 3739/2309 1060 3440/1722 2962 3107
ἐλευθέρα ἐστὶν ᾧ θέλει γαμηθῆναι, μόνον ἐν Κυρίῳ. μακα-
free she is to whom she desires to be married, only in (the) Lord.
2076 1437 3779 3306 2596 1699 1106
40 ριωτέρα δέ ἐστιν ἐὰν οὕτω μείνῃ, κατὰ τὴν ἐμὴν γνώμην·
happier But she is if so she remains, according to my judgment;
1380 2504 4151 2316 2192
δοκῶ δὲ κἀγὼ Πνεῦμα Θεοῦ ἔχειν.
I think and I also (the) Spirit of God have.

CHAPTER 8

4012 1494 1492 3754 3956 1108
1 Περὶ δὲ τῶν εἰδωλοθύτων. οἴδαμεν ὅτι πάντες γνῶσιν
concerning And the idolatrous sacrifices, we know that all knowledge
2192 1108 5448 26 3618 1487 5100
2 ἔχομεν. ἡ γνῶσις φυσιοῖ, ἡ δὲ ἀγάπη οἰκοδομεῖ. εἰ δέ τις
we have. Knowledge puffs up, but love builds up. if But any
1380 1492 5100 3764 3762 1097 2531 1163 1097
δοκεῖ εἰδέναι τι, οὐδέπω οὐδὲν ἔγνωκε καθὼς δεῖ γνῶναι·
thinks to know anything, nothing yet he has known as ought he to know.
1487 5100 25 2316 3778 1097 5259 846
3 εἰ δέ τις ἀγαπᾷ τὸν Θεόν, οὗτος ἔγνωσται ὑπ' αὐτοῦ.
if But anyone loves God, this one has been known by Him.
4012 1035 3767 1494 1492 3754 3762
4 περὶ τῆς βρώσεως οὖν τῶν εἰδωλοθύτων, οἴδαμεν ὅτι οὐδὲν
about the eating Then of the idolatrous sacrifices, we know that (is) not
1497 1722 2889 3754 3762 2316 2087 =1508= 1520
εἴδωλον ἐν κόσμῳ, καὶ ὅτι οὐδεὶς Θεὸς ἕτερος εἰ μὴ εἷς.
an idol in (the) world, and that (there is) no God other except one.
1063 1512 1526 3004 2316/1535/1722/ 3772 1535/1909
5 καὶ γὰρ εἴπερ εἰσὶ λεγόμενοι θεοί, εἴτε ἐν οὐρανῷ, εἴτε ἐπὶ
even For if there are (that) called gods, either in Heaven, or upon
1093 5618 1526/2316 4183 2962 4183 235
6 τῆς γῆς· ὥσπερ εἰσὶ θεοὶ πολλοί, καὶ κύριοι πολλοί· ἀλλ'
the earth; even as there are gods many, and lords many, but
5213/1519/2316 3962/1537/3739 3956 2249/1519/ 846
ἡμῖν εἷς Θεὸς ὁ πατήρ, ἐξ οὗ τὰ πάντα, καὶ ἡμεῖς εἰς αὐτόν·
to us one God the Father, of whom things all, and we for Him,
1520 2962 2424 5547 1223/3739 3956 2249
καὶ εἷς Κύριος Ἰησοῦς Χριστός, δι' οὗ τὰ πάντα, καὶ ἡμεῖς
and one Lord Jesus Christ, through whom things all, and we
1223 846 235 3756/1722/3956 1108 5100 4893
7 δι' αὐτοῦ. ἀλλ' οὐκ ἐν πᾶσιν ἡ γνῶσις· τινὲς δὲ τῇ συνειδήσει
by Him. But not in all (is) the knowledge; some and conscious
1497 2193 737 5613 1494 2068
τοῦ εἰδώλου ἕως ἄρτι ὡς εἰδωλόθυτον ἐσθίουσι, καὶ ἡ
of the idol until now as an idolatrous sacrifice eat, and the
4893 848 772 5607 3435 1033 2248
8 συνείδησις αὐτῶν ἀσθενὴς οὖσα μολύνεται. βρῶμα δὲ ἡμᾶς
conscience of them weak being is defiled. food But us
3756 3936 2316 3777 1063 1437 5315 4052
οὐ παρίστησι τῷ Θεῷ· οὔτε γὰρ ἐὰν φάγωμεν περισσεύο-
not will commend to God, neither for if we eat do we excel,
3777/1437/3361/ 5315 5302 992 3381
9 μεν, οὔτε ἐὰν μὴ φάγωμεν ὑστερούμεθα. βλέπετε δὲ μήπως
nor if not we eat are we behind. watch But lest
1849 5216 3778 4348 1096 770
ἡ ἐξουσία ὑμῶν αὕτη πρόσκομμα γένηται τοῖς ἀσθενοῦσιν.
the authority of yours this a stumbling-block becomes to the weak ones.
1437/1063/5100/*/4571 2192 1108 1722 1493 2621
10 ἐάν γάρ τις ἴδῃ σε τὸν ἔχοντα γνῶσιν ἐν εἰδωλείῳ κατακεί-
if For anyone sees you, the having knowledge in an idol temple
3780 4893 (one) 846 772 5607 3618
μενον, οὐχὶ ἡ συνείδησις αὐτοῦ ἀσθενοῦς ὄντος οἰκοδομηθή-
sitting, not the conscience of him, weak being, be built up

lifted up so as to eat things sacrificed to idols? [11]And on your knowledge the weak brother will fall, *he* for whom Christ died. [12]And sinning in this way against *your* brothers, and wounding their conscience, being weak, you sin against Christ. [13]Therefore, if food offends my brother, I will not at all eat flesh forever, so that I do not offend my brother.

CHAPTER 9

[1]Am I not an apostle? Am I not free? (Have) I not seen our Lord Jesus Christ? Are you not my work in *the* Lord? [2]If I am not an apostle to others, yet I am indeed to you; for you are the seal of my apostleship in *the* Lord. [3]My defense to those examining me is this: [4]Have we not authority to eat and to drink? [5]Have we not authority to lead about a sister, a wife, as the rest of the apostles also, and Cephas, and the Lord's brothers *do*? [6]Or *is it* only Barnabas and I *who* have no authority to quit work? [7]Who serves as a soldier at *his* own wages at any time? Who plants a vineyard, and does not eat of its fruit? Or who shepherds a flock, and does not eat of the milk of the flock? [8]Do I speak these things according to man, or does not the Law say these things? [9]For it has been written in the Law of Moses, "You shall not muzzle an ox treading grain." Is it *that* it matters to God *as to* oxen? [10]Or does He say *it* altogether because of us? It is written because of us, so that the *one* plowing ought to plow *in* hope; and the *one* threshing *in* hope to partake of his hope.

1519 1494 2068 622 770
11 σεται εἰς τὸ τὰ εἰδωλόθυτα ἐσθίειν ; καὶ ἀπολεῖται ὁ ἀσθε-
— — the idolatrous sacrifices to eat? And is destroyed the weak
80 1909 4674 1108 1223/3739 5547 599
νῶν ἀδελφὸς ἐπὶ τῇ σῇ γνώσει, δι' ὃν Χριστὸς ἀπέθανεν ;
brother by the of you knowledge, for whom Christ died.
3779 264 1519 80 5180
12 οὕτω δὲ ἁμαρτάνοντες εἰς τοὺς ἀδελφούς, καὶ τύπτοντες
so And sinning against the brothers, and wounding
848 4893 770 1519 5547 264
αὐτῶν τὴν συνείδησιν ἀσθενοῦσαν, εἰς Χριστὸν ἁμαρτάνετε.
of them the conscience being weak, against Christ you sin.
1355/1487/ 1033 4624 80 3450 =3364= 5315
13 διόπερ εἰ βρῶμα σκανδαλίζει τὸν ἀδελφόν μου, οὐ μὴ φάγω
Therefore, if food offends the brother of me, in no way I eat
2907/1519 165 2443/3361 80 3450 4624
κρέα εἰς τὸν αἰῶνα, ἵνα μὴ τὸν ἀδελφόν μου σκανδαλίσω.
flesh to the age, that not the brother of me I offend.

CHAPTER 9

3756/1510 652 3756/1510 1658 3780 2424
1 Οὐκ εἰμὶ ἀπόστολος ; οὐκ εἰμὶ ἐλεύθερος ; οὐχὶ Ἰησοῦν
not Am I an apostle? not Am I free? (Have) not Jesus
5547 2962 2257 3708 3756 2041 3450 5210
Χριστὸν τὸν Κύριον ἡμῶν ἑώρακα ; οὐ τὸ ἔργον μου ὑμεῖς
Christ the Lord of us I have seen? not the work of me you
1722 2075/*/2962/1487/243 3756/1510 652 135/1065/5213
2 ἐστε ἐν Κυρίῳ ; εἰ ἄλλοις οὐκ εἰμὶ ἀπόστολος, ἀλλά γε ὑμῖν
Are in (the) Lord? If to others not I am an apostle, yet indeed to you
1510 1063 4973 1699 651 5210 2075/1722/2962
εἰμι· ἡ γὰρ σφραγὶς τῆς ἐμῆς ἀποστολῆς ὑμεῖς ἐστε ἐν Κυρίῳ.
I am; the for seal of my apostleship you are in (the) Lord.
1699 627 1691 350 3778 2076 =3378=
3 ἡ ἐμὴ ἀπολογία τοῖς ἐμὲ ἀνακρίνουσιν αὕτη ἐστί. μὴ οὐκ
My defense to those me examining this is. not
2192 1849 5315 4095 =3378= 2192 1849
4 ἔχομεν ἐξουσίαν φαγεῖν καὶ πιεῖν ; μὴ οὐκ ἔχομεν ἐξουσίαν
5 Have we authority to eat and to drink? not Have we authority
79 1135 4013 5613 3062 652
ἀδελφὴν γυναῖκα περιάγειν, ὡς καὶ οἱ λοιποὶ ἀπόστολοι,
a sister, a wife, to lead about, as also the rest of (the) apostles,
80 2962 2786 2228/3441/1473
6 καὶ οἱ ἀδελφοὶ τοῦ Κυρίου, καὶ Κηφᾶς ; ἢ μόνος ἐγὼ καὶ
and the brothers of the Lord, and Cephas? Or only I and
921 3756 2192 1849 3361 2038 5101
7 Βαρνάβας οὐκ ἔχομεν ἐξουσίαν τοῦ μὴ ἐργάζεσθαι ; τίς
Barnabas not we have authority not to work? Who
4754 2398 3800 4218 5101 5452 290
στρατεύεται ἰδίοις ὀψωνίοις ποτέ ; τίς φυτεύει ἀμπελῶνα,
soldiers at (his) own wages at any time? Who plants a vineyard
1537 2590 848 3756 2068 /2228/5101/ 4165 4167
καὶ ἐκ τοῦ καρποῦ αὐτοῦ οὐκ ἐσθίει ; ἢ τίς ποιμαίνει ποίμνην,
and from the fruit of it not eats? Or who shepherds a flock,
1537 1051 4167 3756 2068 3361/2596 444
8 καὶ ἐκ τοῦ γάλακτος τῆς ποίμνης οὐκ ἐσθίει ; μὴ κατὰ ἄνθρω-
and of the milk of the flock not eats? Not according to
5023 2980 2228/3780 3551 5023 3004 1722/1063
9 πον ταῦτα λαλῶ ; ἢ οὐχὶ καὶ ὁ νόμος ταῦτα λέγει ; ἐν γὰρ
man these things I speak, or not also the law these things says? in For
3475 3551 1135 3756 5392 1016 248
10 τῷ Μωσέως νόμῳ γέγραπται, Οὐ φιμώσεις βοῦν ἀλοῶντα.
the of Moses law it has been written: not You shall muzzle an ox threshing
3362 1016 3199 2316/2228/1223/5209 3843 3004 1223
μὴ τῶν βοῶν μέλει τῷ Θεῷ ; ἢ δι' ἡμᾶς πάντως λέγει ; δι'
Not of oxen matters it to God, or because of us altogether He says? For
5209 1063 1125 3754/1909 1680 3784 722
ἡμᾶς γὰρ ἐγράφη, ὅτι ἐπ' ἐλπίδι ὀφείλει ὁ ἀροτριῶν
us, for it was written; because on hope ought the (one) plowing
722 248 1680 848 3348 1909 1680
ἀροτριᾷν, καὶ ὁ ἀλοῶν τῆς ἐλπίδος αὐτοῦ μετέχειν ἐπ' ἐλπίδι.
to plow; and he threshing of his hope to partake on hope.

[11]If we have sowed spiritual things to you, *is it* a great thing if we shall reap of your fleshly things? [12]If others have a share of the authority *over* you, *should* not rather we? But we did not use this authority, but we endured all things, so that we might not give a hindrance to the gospel of Christ. [13]Do you not know that those who have labored eat of the holy things of the Temple? Those attending *on* the altar partake with the altar. [14]So also the Lord ordained those preaching the gospel to live from the gospel.

[15]But I have not used one of these. And I do not write these things that it be so with me. For *it is* good to me rather to die than that anyone nullify my glorying. [16]For if I preach the gospel, there is no glory to me; for necessity is laid on me, and it is woe to me if I do not preach the gospel. [17]For if I do this willingly, I have a reward; but if unwillingly, I am entrusted with a stewardship. [18]What then is my reward? That preaching the gospel I may make the gospel of Christ without charge, so as not to use fully my authority in the gospel. [19]For being free of all, I enslaved myself to all, that I might gain the more. [20]And I became as a Jew to the Jews, that I might gain Jews; to those under Law as under Law, that I might gain those under Law; [21]to those without Law as without Law—not being without law of God, but under *the* law of Christ—that I might gain *those* without Law. [22]I became to the weak as weak, that I might gain the weak. To all I have become all things, that in any and

1487/2249/5213 4152 4687 3173/1487/2249/5216
11 εἰ ἡμεῖς ὑμῖν τὰ πνευματικὰ ἐσπείραμεν, μέγα εἰ ἡμεῖς ὑμῶν
If we to you spiritual things sowed, (is it) a great thing if we of you
4559 2325 1487/243 1849 5216 3348
12 τὰ σαρκικὰ θερίσομεν; εἰ ἄλλοι τῆς ἐξουσίας ὑμῶν μετέ-
fleshly things shall reap? If others of the authority of you have a
3756 3123 2249 235 3756 5330 1849
χουσιν, οὐ μᾶλλον ἡμεῖς; ἀλλ' οὐκ ἐχρησάμεθα τῇ ἐξουσίᾳ
share, not rather we? But not we used authority
5026 235 3956 4722 2443/3361 1464 5100 1325
ταύτῃ· ἀλλὰ πάντα στέγομεν, ἵνα μὴ ἐγκοπήν τινα δῶμεν
this, but all things we endured, that not an obstacle anyone we give
2098 5447 3756 1492 3754 2413
13 τῷ εὐαγγελίῳ τοῦ Χριστοῦ. οὐκ οἴδατε ὅτι οἱ τὰ ἱερὰ
to the gospel of Christ Do not you know that those holy things
2038 1537 2411 2068 2379
ἐργαζόμενοι ἐκ τοῦ ἱεροῦ ἐσθίουσιν, οἱ τῷ θυσιαστηρίῳ
laboring (about) of the temple eat, those the altar
4332 2379 4829 3779
14 προσεδρεύοντες τῷ θυσιαστηρίῳ συμμερίζονται; οὕτω καὶ
attending (on), the altar partake with. So also
2962 1299 2098 2605 1537
ὁ Κύριος διέταξε τοῖς τὸ εὐαγγέλιον καταγγέλλουσιν ἐκ τοῦ
the Lord ordained those of the gospel announcing, of the
2098 2198 1473 3762 5530 5130 3756
15 εὐαγγελίου ζῆν. ἐγὼ δὲ οὐδενὶ ἐχρησάμην τούτων· οὐκ
gospel to live. I But not one have used of these. not
1125 5023 2443/3779 1096 1722/1698 2570 1063/3427
ἔγραψα δὲ ταῦτα ἵνα οὕτω γένηται ἐν ἐμοί· καλὸν γάρ μοι
I write And these things that so it should be with me; good For to me
3123 599 2228 2745 3450/2443/5100 2758 1437
μᾶλλον ἀποθανεῖν ἢ τὸ καύχημά μου ἵνα τις κενώσῃ. ἐὰν
rather to die, than the glorying of me that anyone void. if
1063 2097 3756/2076/3427 2745 318 1063
16 γὰρ εὐαγγελίζωμαι, οὐκ ἔστι μοι καύχημα· ἀνάγκη γάρ
For I preach the gospel, not there is to me glory; necessity for
3427 1945 3759 3427 2076 1437/3361 2097 1487
μοι ἐπίκειται· οὐαὶ δέ μοι ἐστίν, ἐὰν μὴ εὐαγγελίζωμαι. εἰ
me is laid on; woe and to me is, if not I preach the gospel. if
1063/1635 5124 4238 3408 2192/1487 210 3622
17 γὰρ ἑκὼν τοῦτο πράσσω, μισθὸν ἔχω· εἰ δὲ ἄκων, οἰκονομίαν
For willingly this I do, a reward I have; if but unwillingly, a stewardship
4100 5101/3767/3427/2076 3408 2443 2097
18 πεπίστευμαι. τίς οὖν μοί ἐστιν ὁ μισθός; ἵνα εὐαγγελιζό-
I am entrusted with. What then of me is the reward? That preaching the
77 5087 2098 5547 1519 3361
μενος ἀδάπανον θήσω τὸ εὐαγγέλιον τοῦ Χριστοῦ, εἰς τὸ μὴ
gospel without charge I place the gospel of Christ, so as not
2710 1849 3450/1722 2098 1658
19 καταχρήσασθαι τῇ ἐξουσίᾳ μου ἐν τῷ εὐαγγελίῳ. ἐλεύ-
to use to the full the authority of me in the gospel. free
1063/5607/1537/ 3956 3956 1683 1402 2443
θερος γὰρ ὢν ἐκ πάντων, πᾶσιν ἐμαυτὸν ἐδούλωσα, ἵνα
For being of all, to all myself I enslaved, that
4119 2770 1096 2453 5613
20 τοὺς πλείονας κερδήσω. καὶ ἐγενόμην τοῖς Ἰουδαίοις ὡς
the more I might gain. And I became to the Jews as
2453 2443 2453 2770 5259 3551/5613/5259
Ἰουδαῖος, ἵνα Ἰουδαίους κερδήσω· τοῖς ὑπὸ νόμον ὡς ὑπὸ
a Jew, that Jews I might gain; to those under law as under
3551 2443 5259 3551 2770 459 5613 459
21 νόμον, ἵνα τοὺς ὑπὸ νόμον κερδήσω· τοῖς ἀνόμοις ὡς ἄνομος,
law, that those under law I might gain; to those without law as without law
3361/5608 459 2316 235 1772 5547 2443 2770 459
μὴ ὢν ἄνομος Θεῷ ἀλλ' ἔννομος Χριστῷ, ἵνα κερδήσω ἀνό-
not being without law of God, but under law of Christ, that I might gain with-
1096 772 5613 772 2443 772
22 μους. ἐγενόμην τοῖς ἀσθενέσιν ὡς ἀσθενής, ἵνα τοὺς ἀσθενεῖς
out law. I became to the weak as weak, that the weak
2770 3956 1096 3956 2443 3843 5100
κερδήσω. τοῖς πᾶσι γέγονα τὰ πάντα, ἵνα πάντως τινὰς
I might gain. To all I have become all things, that in any case some

every way I might save
some. [23]And I do this for
the gospel, that I might
become a fellow-partaker
of it.
[24]Do you not know that
those running in a stadium
indeed all run, but one
receives the prize? So run
that you may obtain. [25]But
everyone striving *in* all
things controls himself.
Then those truly that they
may receive a corruptible
crown, but we an
incorruptible. [26]So I run
accordingly, not as uncertainly; so I fight, as not
beating air; [27]but I buffet
my body and lead *it* captive,
that proclaiming to others I
myself might not be
rejected.

4982 5124 4160 1223 2098 2443 4792
23 σώσω. τοῦτο δὲ ποιῶ διὰ τὸ εὐαγγέλιον, ἵνα συγκοινωνὸς
I might save. this And I do for the gospel, that a fellow-partaker
846 1096 3756 1492 3754 1722 4712 5143 3956
24 αὐτοῦ γένωμαι. οὐκ οἴδατε ὅτι οἱ ἐν σταδίῳ τρέχοντες πάν-
of it I might become. Not know you that those in a stadium running all
3303 5143 1520 2983 1017 3779
τες μὲν τρέχουσιν, εἷς δὲ λαμβάνει τὸ βραβεῖον; οὕτω
indeed run, one but receives the prize? So
5143 2443 2638 3956 75 3956
25 τρέχετε, ἵνα καταλάβητε. πᾶς δὲ ὁ ἀγωνιζόμενος πάντα
run that you may obtain. everyone And striving (in) all things
1467 1565 3303/3767/2443/ 5349 4735 2983
ἐγκρατεύεται· ἐκεῖνοι μὲν οὖν ἵνα φθαρτὸν στέφανον λάβω-
controls himself; those truly, then, that a corruptible crown they may
2249 862 1473 5106 3779 5143/5613/3756
26 σιν, ἡμεῖς δὲ ἄφθαρτον. ἐγὼ τοίνυν οὕτω τρέχω, ὡς οὐκ
receive, we but an incorruptible. I accordingly so run, as not
84 3779 4438 5613/3756/109 1194 235 5299
27 ἀδήλως· οὕτω πυκτεύω, ὡς οὐκ ἀέρα δέρων· ἀλλ' ὑπωπιάζω
uncertainly; so I fight, as not air beating; but I buffet
3430 4983 1396 3381 243 2784
μου τὸ σῶμα καὶ δουλαγωγῶ, μήπως, ἄλλοις κηρύξας,
of me the body and lead (it) captive, lest to others proclaiming,
848 96 1096
αὐτὸς ἀδόκιμος γένωμαι.
myself rejected I may become.

CHAPTER 10

[1]And I do not want you
to be ignorant, brothers,
that our fathers were all
under the cloud; and all
passed through the Sea.
[2]And all were baptized to
Moses in the cloud, and in
the Sea; [3]and all ate the
same spiritual food. [4]And
all drank the same spiritual
drink; for they drank of the
spiritual rock following—
and that Rock was Christ.
[5]Yet God was not pleased
with most of them; for they
were scattered in the
desert. [6]But these things
were examples for us, so
that we may not be lusters
after evil, even as those
indeed lusted. [7]Neither be
idolaters, even as some of
them, as it has been
written, "The people sat
down to eat and drink, and
stood up to play." [8]Nor
should we commit fornica-
tion, as some of them
fornicated, and twenty-
three thousand fell in one
day. [9]Neither overtempt
Christ, as some of them

CHAPTER 10

3756/2309 5209 50 80 3754 3962 2257
1 Οὐ θέλω δὲ ὑμᾶς ἀγνοεῖν, ἀδελφοί, ὅτι οἱ πατέρες ἡμῶν
not I desire And you to be ignorant, brothers, that the fathers of us
3956 5259 3507 2258 3956 1223 2281
πάντες ὑπὸ τὴν νεφέλην ἦσαν, καὶ πάντες διὰ τῆς θαλάσσης
all under the cloud were, and all through the sea
1330 3956/1519 3475 907 1722 3507
2 διῆλθον, καὶ πάντες εἰς τὸν Μωσῆν ἐβαπτίσαντο ἐν τῇ νεφέλῃ
passed and all to Moses were baptized in the cloud
1722 2281 3956 846 1033 4152
3 καὶ ἐν τῇ θαλάσσῃ, καὶ πάντες τὸ αὐτὸ βρῶμα πνευματικὸν
and in the sea, and all the same food spiritual
5315 3956 846 4188 4152 4095
4 ἔφαγον, καὶ πάντες τὸ αὐτὸ πόμα πνευματικὸν ἔπιον·
ate, and all the same drink spiritual drank;
4095 1063/1537/ 4152 190 4073
ἔπινον γὰρ ἐκ πνευματικῆς ἀκολουθούσης πέτρας· ἡ δὲ
they drank for of a spiritual following rock, the and
4073/2258 5547 235/3756/1722 4119 846
5 πέτρα ἦν ὁ Χριστός. ἀλλ' οὐκ ἐν τοῖς πλείοσιν αὐτῶν
Rock was Christ. But not in the most of them
2106 2316 2693 1063/1722 2048 5023
εὐδόκησεν ὁ Θεός· κατεστρώθησαν γὰρ ἐν τῇ ἐρήμῳ. ταῦτα
was well-pleased God; they were scattered for in the desert. these things
5179 2257 1096 1519 3361/1511/2248 1938
6 δὲ τύποι ἡμῶν ἐγενήθησαν, εἰς τὸ μὴ εἶναι ἡμᾶς ἐπιθυμητὰς
And examples of us were, for not to be us lusters after
2556 2531 2548 1937 3366 1496
7 κακῶν, καθὼς κἀκεῖνοι ἐπεθύμησαν. μηδὲ εἰδωλολάτραι
evil, even as those indeed lusted. Neither idolaters
1096 2531 51 00 846 5613 1125 2523 2992
γίνεσθε, καθώς τινες αὐτῶν· ὡς γέγραπται, Ἐκάθισεν ὁ λαὸς
be, even as some of them, as it has been written: Sat the people
5315 4095 450 3815 3366 4203
8 φαγεῖν καὶ πιεῖν, καὶ ἀνέστησαν παίζειν. μηδὲ πορνεύωμεν,
to eat and drink, and stood up to play. Neither do fornication.
2531 5100 846 4203 4098 1722/3391/2250
καθώς τινες αὐτῶν ἐπόρνευσαν, καὶ ἔπεσον ἐν μιᾷ ἡμέρᾳ
even as some of them fornicated, and fell in one day
1501 - 5140 5505 3366 1598 5547 2531
9 εἰκοσιτρεῖς χιλιάδες. μηδὲ ἐκπειράζωμεν τὸν Χριστόν, καθὼς
twenty-three thousands. Neither overtempt the Christ. even as

tempted, and perished by serpents. [10]Neither should you murmur, as also some of them murmured, and perished by the destroyer. [11]And all these things happened to those *as* examples, and *it* was written for our warning, on whom the ends of the ages have come. [12]So that he that thinks to stand, let him watch that he not fall. [13]No temptation has taken you except *what is* human; but God is faithful, who will not allow you to be tempted above what you are able. But with the tempation, *He* will also make the way out, so that you may be able to bear *it*.

[14]On account of this, my beloved, flee from idolatry. [15]I speak as to prudent ones; you judge what I say. [16]The cup of blessing that we bless, is *it* not a partaking of the blood of Christ? The bread which we break, is it not a partaking of the body of Christ? [17]Because we, the many, are one bread, one body, for we all partake of the one Bread. [18]Look at Israel according to flesh. Are not those eating the sacrifices partakers of the altar? [19]What then do I say, that an idol is anything, or that an idolatrous sacrifice is anything? [20]But the things the nations sacrifice, *they* sacrifice to demons, and not to God. But I do not want you to become sharers of demons; [21]you are not able to drink *the* cup of the Lord and a cup of demons; you cannot partake of the table of *the* Lord and a table of demons. [22]Or do we provoke the Lord to jealousy? Are we stronger than He?

[23]All things are lawful to me, but not all things

5100 846 3985 5259 3789 622
καὶ τινες αὐτῶν ἐπείρασαν, καὶ ὑπὸ τῶν ὄφεων ἀπώλοντο.
also some of them tempted, and by serpents were destroyed.
3366 1111 2531 5100 846 1111
10 μηδὲ γογγύζετε, καθὼς καί τινες αὐτῶν ἐγόγγυσαν, καὶ
Neither murmur even as also some of them murmured, and
622 5259 3644 5023 3956 5179
11 ἀπώλοντο ὑπὸ τοῦ ὀλοθρευτοῦ. ταῦτα δὲ πάντα τύποι
were destroyed by the destroyer. these things And all (as) examples
4819 1565 1125 4314 3559 2257 1519
συνέβαινον ἐκείνοις· ἐγράφη δὲ πρὸς νουθεσίαν ἡμῶν, εἰς
happened to those, was written and for warning of us,, to
5056 165 2568 5620 1380
12 οὓς τὰ τέλη τῶν αἰώνων κατήντησεν. ὥστε ὁ δοκῶν
whom the ends of the ages has arrived. So as the (one) thinking
2476 991 3361/4098 3986 5209/3756 2983 1487
13 ἑστάναι, βλεπέτω μὴ πέσῃ. πειρασμὸς ὑμᾶς οὐκ εἴληφεν εἰ
to stand, let watch lest he falls. Temptation you not has taken ex-
3361 442 4103 2316/3739/3756/1439/5209 3985
μὴ ἀνθρώπινος· πιστὸς δὲ ὁ Θεός, ὃς οὐκ ἐάσει ὑμᾶς πει-
cept (what is) human; faithful but (is) God, who not will allow you to be
5228/3739/ 1410 235 4160 4862 3986
ρασθῆναι ὑπὲρ ὃ δύνασθε, ἀλλὰ ποιήσει σὺν τῷ πειρασμῷ
tempted beyond what you are able; but will make with the temptation
1545 1410 5209 5297
καὶ τὴν ἔκβασιν, τοῦ δύνασθαι ὑμᾶς ὑπενεγκεῖν.
also the way out, to be able you to bear (it).
1355 27 3450 5343 575 1495
14 Διόπερ, ἀγαπητοί μου, φεύγετε ἀπὸ τῆς εἰδωλολατρείας.
Therefore, beloved of me, flee from idolatry.
5613 5429 3004 2919 5210/3739/5346 4221
15 ὡς φρονίμοις λέγω, κρίνατε ὑμεῖς ὅ φημι. τὸ ποτήριον τῆς
As to prudent ones I say, judge you what I say. The cup
2129/3739/ 2127 3780 2842 129
16 εὐλογίας ὃ εὐλογοῦμεν, οὐχὶ κοινωνία τοῦ αἵματος τοῦ
of blessing which we bless, not a partaking of the blood
5547 2076 740 3739 2806 3780 2842
Χριστοῦ ἐστί; τὸν ἄρτον ὃν κλῶμεν, οὐχὶ κοινωνία τοῦ
of Christ is? The bread which we break, not a partaking of the
4983 5547 2076 3754/1519/740 1722 4983
17 σώματος τοῦ Χριστοῦ ἐστίν; ὅτι εἷς ἄρτος, ἓν σῶμα, οἱ
body of Christ is it? Because one bread, one body the
4183 2070 1063 3956 1537 1520 740 3348
πολλοί ἐσμεν· οἱ γὰρ πάντες ἐκ τοῦ ἑνὸς ἄρτου μετέχομεν.
many we are; for all of the one bread we partake.
991 2474 2596 4561 3780 2068
18 βλέπετε τὸν Ἰσραὴλ κατὰ σάρκα· οὐχὶ οἱ ἐσθίοντες τὰς
See Israel acording to flesh; not those eating the
2378 2844 2379 1526/5101/3767/5346 3754
19 θυσίας κοινωνοὶ τοῦ θυσιαστηρίου εἰσί; τί οὖν φημι; ὅτι
sacrifices sharers of the altar are? What then do I say, that
1497 5100/2076/2228/3754/ 1494 5100/2076 235 3754/3739
20 εἴδωλόν τί ἐστιν; ἢ ὅτι εἰδωλόθυτόν τί ἐστιν; ἀλλ' ὅτι ἃ
an idol anything is? Or that an idol sacrifice anything is? But that what
2380 1484 1140 2380 3756/2316/3756/2309 5209
θύει τὰ ἔθνη, δαιμονίοις θύει, καὶ οὐ Θεῷ· οὐ θέλω δὲ ὑμᾶς
sacrifice the nations, to demons sacrifice, and not to God. not I want But you
2844 1140 1096 3756 1410 4221
21 κοινωνοὺς τῶν δαιμονίων γίνεσθαι. οὐ δύνασθε ποτήριον
sharers of demons to become. not You are able a cup
2962 4095 4221 1140 3756 1410 5132
Κυρίου πίνειν καὶ ποτήριον δαιμονίων· οὐ δύνασθε τραπέζης
of (the) Lord to drink and a cup of demons; not you are able of a table
2962 3348 5232 1140 2228 3863
22 Κυρίου μετέχειν καὶ τραπέζης δαιμονίων. ἢ παραζηλοῦμεν
of (the) Lord to partake and a table of demons. Or do we make jealous
2962 3361 2478 846 2070
τὸν Κύριον; μὴ ἰσχυρότεροι αὐτοῦ ἐσμέν;
the Lord? Not stronger (than) He we are?
3956 3427 1832 235 3756 3956 4851 3956 3427
23 Πάντα μοι ἔξεστιν, ἀλλ' οὐ πάντα συμφέρει. πάντα μοι
All things to me are lawful, but not all things contribute. All things to me

contribute. All things are lawful to me, but not all things build up. 24 Let no one seek his own things, but each one that of the other. 25 Eat everything being sold in a meat market, examining nothing because of conscience, 26 for "the earth *is* the Lord's, and the fullness of it." 27 And if any of the unbelievers invites you, and you desire to go, eat everything set before you, examining nothing because of conscience. 28 But if anyone tells you, This is slain in sacrifice to idols; do not eat, because of that one pointing *it* out, and the conscience; for "the earth *is* the Lord's, and the fullness of it." 29 But I say conscience, not that of himself, but that of the other. For why is my freedom judged by the conscience of another? 30 But if I partake by grace, why am I evil spoken of for the sake of what I give thanks? 31 Then whether you eat or drink, or whatever you do, do all things to the glory of God. 32 Be without offense both to Jews and Greeks, and to the church of God. 33 Even as I also please all *in* all things, not seeking my own advantage, but that of the many, that they may be saved.

CHAPTER 11

1 Be imitators of me, as I also of Christ.

2 But, brothers, I praise you that in all things you have remembered me; and even as I delivered to you, you hold fast the traditions. 3 But I want you to know that Christ is the Head of every man, and the man *is the* head of a woman, and God *is the* head of Christ. 4 Every man praying or prophesying, having *anything* down over *his* head shames his Head. 5 And

1832 235/3756 3956 3618 3367 1438 2212
24 ἔξεστιν, ἀλλ' οὐ πάντα οἰκοδομεῖ. μηδεὶς τὸ ἑαυτοῦ ζητείτω,
are lawful, but not all things build up. No one the thing of himself seeks,
235 2087 1538 3956 1722 3111 4453
25 ἀλλὰ τὸ τοῦ ἑτέρου ἕκαστος. πᾶν τὸ ἐν μακέλλῳ πωλού-
but that of the other each one. Everything in a meat market being
2068 3367 350 1223 4893
26 μενον ἐσθίετε, μηδὲν ἀνακρίνοντες διὰ τὴν συνείδησιν· τοῦ
sold eat, nothing examining because of conscience: of the
1063 2962 1093 4138 848 1487 5100/2564/5209
27 γὰρ Κυρίου ἡ γῆ καὶ τὸ πλήρωμα αὐτῆς. εἰ δέ τις καλεῖ ὑμᾶς
for Lord the earth and the fullness of it. if And anyone invites you
571 2309 4198 3956 3908
τῶν ἀπίστων, καὶ θέλετε πορεύεσθαι, πᾶν τὸ παρατιθέ-
of the unbelievers, and you desire to go, everything set before
5213 2068 3367 350 1223 4893
μενον ὑμῖν ἐσθίετε, μηδὲν ἀνακρίνοντες διὰ τὴν συνείδησιν.
you eat, nothing examining because of conscience.
1437 5100/5213/2036 5124 1494 2076/3361/2068/1223
28 ἐὰν δέ τις ὑμῖν εἴπῃ, Τοῦτο εἰδωλόθυτόν ἐστι, μὴ ἐσθίετε, δι'
if But anyone you tells, This slain in sacrifice is, do not eat, because
1565 3377 4983 1063 2962
ἐκεῖνον τὸν μηνύσαντα καὶ τὴν συνείδησιν· τοῦ γὰρ Κυρίου
that one pointing out, and conscience; the for (is the) Lord's
1093 4138 848 4893 3004 3780
29 ἡ γῆ καὶ τὸ πλήρωμα αὐτῆς. συνείδησιν δὲ λέγω, οὐχὶ τὴν
the earth and the fullness of it. conscience But I say, not the (one)
1438 235 2087 2444 1063 1657 3450
ἑαυτοῦ, ἀλλὰ τὴν τοῦ ἑτέρου· ἱνατί γὰρ ἡ ἐλευθερία μου
of himself, but the (one) of the other. why For the freedom of me
2919 5259 243 4893 1487 1473 5485 3348 5101
30 κρίνεται ὑπὸ ἄλλης συνειδήσεως; εἰ δὲ ἐγὼ χάριτι μετέχω, τί
is judged by another's conscience? if And I by grace partake, why
987 5228/3739/1473 2168 1535/3767 2068
31 βλασφημοῦμαι ὑπὲρ οὗ ἐγὼ εὐχαριστῶ; εἴτε οὖν ἐσθίετε,
am I evil spoken of because of what I give thanks (for)? Whether then you eat
1535 4095 1535/5100/4160 3956 1519/1391 2316 4160
εἴτε πίνετε, εἴτε τι ποιεῖτε, πάντα εἰς δόξαν Θεοῦ ποιεῖτε.
or drink, or what you do, all things to the glory of God do.
677 1096 2453 1672
32 ἀπρόσκοποι γίνεσθε καὶ Ἰουδαίοις καὶ Ἕλλησι καὶ τῇ
without offense Be both to Jews and to Greeks and to the
1577 2316 2531 2504 3956 3956 700 3361
33 ἐκκλησίᾳ τοῦ Θεοῦ· καθὼς κἀγὼ πάντα πᾶσιν ἀρέσκω, μὴ
church of God, as I also (in) all things all please, not
2212 1683 4851 235 4183 2443
ζητῶν τὸ ἐμαυτοῦ συμφέρον, ἀλλὰ τὸ τῶν πολλῶν, ἵνα
seeking the of myself advantage, but of the many, that
4982
σωθῶσι.
they may be saved.

CHAPTER 11

3402 3450 1096 2531 2504 5547
1 μιμηταί μου γίνεσθε, καθὼς κἀγὼ Χριστοῦ.
imitators of me Be, as also I of Christ.
1867 5209 80 3754 3956 3450 3415
2 Ἐπαινῶ δὲ ὑμᾶς, ἀδελφοί, ὅτι πάντα μου μέμνησθε, καὶ
I praise But you, brothers, because all things of me you recalled, and
2531 3860 5213 3862 2722 2309
3 καθὼς παρέδωκα ὑμῖν τὰς παραδόσεις κατέχετε. θέλω δὲ
as I delivered to you, the traditions you hold fast. I wish But
5209 1492 3754 3956 435 2776 5547 2076
ὑμᾶς εἰδέναι, ὅτι παντὸς ἀνδρὸς ἡ κεφαλὴ ὁ Χριστός ἐστι·
you to know, that of every man the head Christ is;
2776 1135 435 2776 5547 2316/3956
4 κεφαλὴ δὲ γυναικός, ὁ ἀνήρ· κεφαλὴ δὲ Χριστοῦ, ὁ Θεός. πᾶς
head and of a woman, the man; (the) head and of Christ, God. Every
435 4336 2228 4395 2596 2776 2192
ἀνὴρ προσευχόμενος ἢ προφητεύων, κατὰ κεφαλῆς ἔχων,
man praying or prophesying down over (his) head having,

every woman praying or prophesying with the head uncovered shames her head; for it is the same *as* being shaved. [6]For if a woman is not covered, let her also be shorn. But if *it is* shameful for a woman to be shorn, or to be shaved, let her be covered. [7]For truly a man ought not to have the head covered, being *the* image and glory of God. But woman is *the* glory of man—[8]for man is not of the woman, but woman of man; [9]for also man was not created through the woman, but woman through the man; [10]because of this, the woman ought to have authority on the head, because of the angels—[11]however, man *is* not apart from woman, nor woman apart from man, in *the* Lord. [12]For as the woman *is* out of the man, so also the man through the woman; but all things from God. [13]You judge among yourselves: is it fitting *for* a woman to pray to God uncovered? [14]Or does not nature herself teach you that if a man indeed adorns the hair, it is a dishonor to him[15]But if a woman should adorn the hair, it is a glory to her; because the long hair has been given to her instead of a veil. [16]But if anyone thinks to be contentious, we do not have such a custom, nor the churches of God.

[17]But enjoining this, I do not praise *you*, because you come together not for the better, but for the worse. [18]Indeed, first, I hear divisions to be among you *when* you have come together in the church. And I believe some part. [19]For there must also be heresies among you, so that the

2617 2776 848 3956 1135 4336
5 καταισχύνει τὴν κεφαλὴν αὐτοῦ. πᾶσα δὲ γυνὴ προσευχο-
shames the Head of him. every But woman praying
2228 4395 177 2776 2617
μένη ἢ προφητεύουσα ἀκατακαλύπτῳ τῇ κεφαλῇ, καται-
or prophesying uncovered with the head, shames
2776 1438/1520/1063/2076 846 3587
σχύνει τὴν κεφαλὴν ἑαυτῆς· ἓν γάρ ἐστι καὶ τὸ αὐτὸ τῇ ἐξυρη-
the head of herself, one for it is and the same with being
1487/1063/3756/ 2619 1135 2751 1487
6 μένῃ. εἰ γὰρ οὐ κατακαλύπτεται γυνή, καὶ κειράσθω· εἰ δὲ
shaved. If For not is covered a woman, also let her be shorn. if But
149 1135 2751 2228 3587 2619
αἰσχρὸν γυναικὶ τὸ κείρασθαι ἢ ξυρᾶσθαι, κατακαλυ-
shameful for a woman to be shorn or to be shaved, let her be
435 3303 1063 3756 3784 2619
7 πτέσθω. ἀνὴρ μὲν γὰρ οὐκ ὀφείλει κατακαλύπτεσθαι τὴν
covered. a man indeed For not ought to be covered the
2776 1504 1391 2316 5225 1135 1391
κεφαλήν, εἰκὼν καὶ δόξα Θεοῦ ὑπάρχων· γυνὴ δὲ δόξα
head, (the) image and glory of God being. the woman But glory
435 2076 3756/1063/2076 435 1537 1135 235 1135
8 ἀνδρός ἐστιν. οὐ γάρ ἐστιν ἀνὴρ ἐκ γυναικός, ἀλλὰ γυνὴ
of a man is. not For is man of woman, but woman
1537/435 1063/3756 2936 435 1223 1135 235
9 ἐξ ἀνδρός· καὶ γὰρ οὐκ ἐκτίσθη ἀνὴρ διὰ τὴν γυναῖκα, ἀλλὰ
of man; also for not was created man because of the woman, but
1135 1223 435 1223 5124 3784 1135 1849
10 γυνὴ διὰ τὸν ἄνδρα· διὰ τοῦτο ὀφείλει ἡ γυνὴ ἐξουσίαν
woman because of the man. Therefore ought the woman authority
2192/1909 2776 1223 32 4133 3777 435
11 ἔχειν ἐπὶ τῆς κεφαλῆς διὰ τοὺς ἀγγέλους. πλὴν οὔτε ἀνὴρ
to have on the head because of the angels. But neither man
5565 1135 3777 1135 5565 435 1722 2962 5618
12 χωρὶς γυναικός, οὔτε γυνὴ χωρὶς ἀνδρός, ἐν Κυρίῳ. ὥσπερ
without woman, nor woman without man, in (the) Lord. as
1063 1135/1537 435 3779 435 1223
γὰρ ἡ γυνὴ ἐκ τοῦ ἀνδρός, οὕτω καὶ ὁ ἀνὴρ διὰ τῆς
For the woman of the man, so also the man through the
1135 3956/1537 2316/1722/5213 846 2919
13 γυναικός, τὰ δὲ πάντα ἐκ τοῦ Θεοῦ. ἐν ὑμῖν αὐτοῖς κρίνατε·
woman, but all things of God. Among you yourselves judge:
4241 2076 1135 177 2316 4336
πρέπον ἐστὶ γυναῖκα ἀκατακάλυπτον τῷ Θεῷ προσεύχε-
fitting Is it (for) a woman uncovered to God to pray?
2228/3761 846 5449 1321 5209 3754/435/3303/1437
14 σθαι; ἢ οὐδὲ αὐτὴ ἡ φύσις διδάσκει ὑμᾶς, ὅτι ἀνὴρ μὲν ἐὰν
Does not herself nature teach you that a man indeed if
2863 819 846 2076 1135 1437 2863 1391 846
15 κομᾷ, ἀτιμία αὐτῷ ἐστί; γυνὴ δὲ ἐὰν κομᾷ. δόξα αὐτῇ
adorns the hair, a dishonor to him it is; a woman but if should adorn the hair, a glory to her
2076 3754 2864 473 4018 1325 846/1487/5100
16 ἐστιν. ὅτι ἡ κόμη ἀντὶ περιβολαίου δέδοται αὐτῇ. εἰ δέ τις
it is? Because the beautified hair instead of a veil has been given to her. if But any
1380 5380 1511/2249 5108 4914 3756 2192
δοκεῖ φιλόνεικος εἶναι, ἡμεῖς τοιαύτην συνήθειαν οὐκ ἔχομεν,
thinks contentious to be, we such a custom do not have,
3761 1577 2316
οὐδὲ αἱ ἐκκλησίαι τοῦ Θεοῦ.
neither the churches of God.
5124 3853 3756 1867 3754/3756/1519
17 Τοῦτο δὲ παραγγέλλων οὐκ ἐπαινῶ, ὅτι οὐκ εἰς τὸ
this But enjoining, not I praise (you), because not for the
2909 235 1519 2276 4905 4412 3303/1063
18 ρεῖττον ἀλλ᾽ εἰς τὸ ἧττον συνέρχεσθε. πρῶτον μὲν γὰρ
better, but for the worse you come together. firstly indeed For
4905 5216/1722 1577 191 4978 1722
συνερχομένων ὑμῶν ἐν τῇ ἐκκλησίᾳ, ἀκούω σχίσματα ἐν
coming together you, in the church, I hear divisions among
5213 5225 3313/5100 4100 1163/1063 139 1722
19 ὑμῖν ὑπάρχειν, καὶ μέρος τι πιστεύω. δεῖ γὰρ καὶ αἱρέσεις ἐν
you to be, and part some I believe. must For also heresies among

approved ones may become manifest among you. [20]Then you having come together into one place, it is not to eat *the* Lord's supper. [21]For each one takes his own supper first in the eating; and one is hungry, and another drunken. [22]For do you not have houses to eat and to drink? Or do you despise the church of God, and shame those who have not? What do I say to you? Shall I praise you in this? I do not praise.

[23]For I received from the Lord what also I delivered to you, that the Lord Jesus in the night in which He was betrayed took bread; [24]and giving thanks He broke and said, Take, eat; this is My body which *is* broken on behalf of you; this do for remembrance of Me. [25]In the same way the cup also, after supping, saying, This cup is the New Covenant in My blood; as often as you drink, do this for remembrance of Me. [26]For *as* often as you may eat this bread, and drink this cup, you solemnly proclaim the death of the Lord, until He shall come. [27]So that whoever should eat this bread, or drink the cup of the Lord, unworthily, *that one* will be guilty of the body and of the blood of the Lord. [28]But let a man examine himself, and so let him eat of the bread, and let him drink of the cup; [29]for the (one) eating and drinking unworthily eats and drinks judgment to himself, not discerning the body of the Lord. [30]For this reason many among you *are* weak and feeble, and many sleep. [31]For if we discerned ourselves, we would not be

5213/1511/2443 1384 5318 1096 1722/5213 4905
20 ὑμῖν εἶναι, ἵνα οἱ δόκιμοι φανεροὶ γένωνται ἐν ὑμῖν. συνερχο-
you be, that the approved ones revealed may become among you. Coming
3767 5216 1909 846 3756/2076 2960 1173
μένων οὖν ὑμῶν ἐπὶ τὸ αὐτό, οὐκ ἔστι Κυριακὸν δεῖπνον
together, then, you together, not it is of the Lord a supper
5315 1538 1063 2398 1173 4301 1722
21 φαγεῖν. ἕκαστος γὰρ τὸ ἴδιον δεῖπνον προλαμβάνει ἐν τῷ
to eat. each one For the own supper takes before
5315 3739/3303 3983 3739 3184 3361/1063 3614 3756
22 φαγεῖν, καὶ ὃς μὲν πεινᾷ, ὃς δὲ μεθύει. μὴ γὰρ οἰκίας οὐκ
to eat; and one hungers, another drunken. not For houses not
2192 1519 2068 4095 2228 1577 2316 2706
ἔχετε εἰς τὸ ἐσθίειν καὶ πίνειν ; ἢ τῆς ἐκκλησίας τοῦ Θεοῦ κατα-
you have to eat and to drink? Or the church of God do you
2617 3361 2192 5101/5213/2036
φρονεῖτε, καὶ καταισχύνετε τοὺς μὴ ἔχοντας ; τί ὑμῖν εἴπω ;
despise, and shame those not having? What to you do I say?
1867 5209/1722/5129/3756 1867 1473/1063 3880
23 ἐπαινέσω ὑμᾶς ἐν τούτῳ ; οὐκ ἐπαινῶ. ἐγὼ γὰρ παρέλαβον
Shall I praise you in this? not I praise. I For I received
575 2962 3860 5213/3754 2962
ἀπὸ τοῦ Κυρίου, ὃ καὶ παρέδωκα ὑμῖν, ὅτι ὁ Κύριος
from the Lord what also I delivered to you, that the Lord
2424 1722 3571 3739 3860 2983 740
24 Ἰησοῦς ἐν τῇ νυκτὶ ᾗ παρεδίδοτο ἔλαβεν ἄρτον, καὶ
Jesus in the night in which He was betrayed took bread, and
2168 2806 2036 2983 5315 5124 3450
εὐχαριστήσας ἔκλασε, καὶ εἶπε, Λάβετε, φάγετε, τοῦτό μού
giving thanks broke and said, Take, eat, this of Me
2076 4983 5228 5216 2806 5124 4160 1519
ἐστι τὸ σῶμα τὸ ὑπὲρ ὑμῶν κλώμενον· τοῦτο ποιεῖτε εἰς
is the body on behalf of you broken; this do for
1699 364 5615 4221 3326
25 τὴν ἐμὴν ἀνάμνησιν. ὡσαύτως καὶ τὸ ποτήριον, μετὰ τὸ
My remembrance. In the same way And the cup, after the
1172 3004 5124 4221 2537 1242
δειπνῆσαι, λέγων, Τοῦτο το ποτήριον ἡ καινὴ διαθήκη
supping, saying This cup the new covenant
2076/1722 1699 129 5124 4160 3740 302 4095
ἐστὶν ἐν τῷ ἐμῷ αἵματι· τοῦτο ποιεῖτε, ὁσάκις ἂν πίνητε,
is in My blood; this do, as often as may you drink,
1519 1699 364 3740 1063 302 2068 740
26 εἰς τὴν ἐμὴν ἀνάμνησιν. ὁσάκις γὰρ ἂν ἐσθίητε τὸν ἄρτον
for My remembrance. as often For (as) may you eat bread
5126 4221 5124 4095 2288
τοῦτον, καὶ τὸ ποτήριον τοῦτο πίνητε, τὸν θάνατον τοῦ
this, and cup this drink, the death of the
2962 2605 891/3739/302/2064 5620/3739/302/ 2068
27 Κυρίου καταγγέλλετε ἄχρις οὗ ἂν ἔλθῃ. ὥστε ὃς ἂν ἐσθίῃ
Lord you declare, until He may come. So as whoever may eat
740 5126 2228/4095 4221 2962 371
τὸν ἄρτον τοῦτον ἢ πίνῃ τὸ ποτήριον τοῦ Κυρίου ἀναξίως,
the bread this, or drinks the cup of the Lord unworthily
1777 2071 4983 129 2962 1381
28 ἔνοχος ἔσται τοῦ σώματος καὶ αἵματος τοῦ Κυρίου. δοκι-
guilty will be of the body and of the blood of the Lord. let
444 1438 3779 /1537 740
μαζέτω δὲ ἄνθρωπος ἑαυτόν, καὶ οὕτως ἐκ τοῦ ἄρτου
prove. But a man himself, and so of the bread
2068 1537 4221 4095 1063/ 2068 4095
29 ἐσθιέτω, καὶ ἐκ τοῦ ποτηρίου πινέτω. ὁ γὰρ ἐσθίων καὶ πίνων
let him eat, and of the cup let him drink. he For eating and drinking
371 2917 1438 2068 4095 3361 1252
ἀναξίως, κριμα ἑαυτῷ ἐσθίει καὶ πίνει, μὴ διακρίνων τὸ
unworthily judgment to himself eats and drinks, not discerning the
4983 2962 1223 5124 1722/5213 4183 772
30 σῶμα τοῦ Κυρίου. διὰ τοῦτο ἐν ὑμῖν πολλοὶ ἀσθενεῖς καὶ
body of the Lord. Because of this among you (are) many weak and
732 2837 2425/1487/1063/1438 1252
31 ἄρρωστοι, καὶ κοιμῶνται ἱκανοί. εἰ γὰρ ἑαυτοὺς διεκρίνομεν,
feeble, and sleep many. if For ourselves we discerned,

judged. [32]But being judged, we are disciplined by *the* Lord, that we not be condemned with the world. [33]So that, my brothers, coming together to eat, wait for one another. [34]But if anyone hungers, let him eat at home, that you may not come together for judgment. And the other things, whenever I come, I will set in order.

CHAPTER 12

[1]But as to spiritual things, brothers, I do not wish you to be ignorant. [2]You know that being led away, you Gentiles were led to dumb idols. [3]Therefore I make known to you that no one speaking by *the* Spirit of God says, Jesus *is* a curse. And no one is able to say Jesus *is* Lord, except by *the* Holy Spirit.

[4]But there are differences of gifts, but the same Spirit;

[5]and there are differences of ministries, yet the same Lord. [6]And there are differences of workings, but the same God is working all things in all. [7]But to each one is given the showing forth of the Spirit to *our* profit. [8]For through the Spirit is given to one a word of wisdom; and to another, a word of knowledge, according to the same Spirit; [9]and to another, faith by the same Spirit; and to another, gifts of healing by the same Spirit; [10]and to another workings of powers; and to another, prophecy; and to another, discernings of spirits; and to another, interpretations of languages. [11]But the one and the same Spirit works all these things, distributing separately to each as He wills.

[12]Even as the body is one, and has many

3756/302 2919 2919 5259 2962 3811
32 οὐκ ἂν ἐκρινόμεθα. κρινόμενοι δέ, ὑπὸ Κυρίου παιδευόμεθα,
not we would be judged. being judged But by (the) Lord, we are chastened,
2443/3363/4862 2889 2632 5620 80 3450
33 ἵνα μὴ σὺν τῷ κόσμῳ κατακριθῶμεν. ὥστε, ἀδελφοί μου,
lest with the world we are condemned. So as, brothers of me,
4905 1519 5315 240 1551 1487 5100
34 συνερχόμενοι εἰς τὸ φαγεῖν, ἀλλήλους ἐκδέχεσθε. εἰ δέ τις
coming together to eat, one another await. if And anyone
3983/1722/3624 2068 2443/3361/1519/2917 4905
πεινᾷ, ἐν οἴκῳ ἐσθιέτω· ἵνα μὴ εἰς κρίμα συνέρχησθε. τὰ δὲ
hungers, at home let him eat, lest to judgment you come together. the And
3062 5613/302/2064 1299
λοιπά, ὡς ἂν ἔλθω, διατάξομαι.
rest, whenever I come, I will set in order.

CHAPTER 12

4017 4152 80 3756/2309/5209 50
1 Περὶ δὲ τῶν πνευματικῶν, ἀδελφοί, οὐ θέλω ὑμᾶς ἀγνοεῖν.
about And the spiritual matters, brothers, not I wish you to be ignorant.
1492 3754/1484/2258/ 4314 1497 880 5613 302
2 οἴδατε ὅτι ἔθνη ἦτε πρὸς τὰ εἴδωλα τὰ ἄφωνα, ὡς ἂν
You know that nations you were to the idols dumb,
71 520 1352 1107 5213/3754 3762/1722/4151
3 ἤγεσθε, ἀπαγόμενοι. διὸ γνωρίζω ὑμῖν, ὅτι οὐδεὶς ἐν Πνεύ-
you were led, being led away. Therefore I make known to you that no one by
2316 2980 3004 331 2424 3762 1410
ματι Θεοῦ λαλῶν λέγει ἀνάθεμα Ἰησοῦν· καὶ οὐδεὶς δύναται
(the) Spirit of God speaking says, A curse (is) Jesus; and no one is able
2036 2962 2424 =1508=1722 4151 40
εἰπεῖν Κύριον Ἰησοῦν, εἰ μὴ ἐν Πνεύματι Ἁγίῳ.
to say, Lord Jesus, except by (the) Spirit Holy.
1243 5486 1526 846 4151
4 Διαιρέσεις δὲ χαρισμάτων εἰσί, τὸ δὲ αὐτὸ Πνεῦμα. καὶ
differences But of gifts there are, the but same Spirit. And
1243 1248 1526 846 2962 1243
5 διαιρέσεις διακονιων εἰσί, καὶ ὁ αὐτὸς Κύριος. καὶ διαιρέσεις
6 differences of ministries there are, yet the same Lord. And differences
1755 1526 846 2076 2316 1754
ἐνεργημάτων εἰσίν, ὁ δὲ αὐτός ἐστι Θεός, ὁ ἐνεργῶν τὰ
of workings there are, the and same is God working
3956/1722 3956 1538 1325 5321
7 πάντα ἐν πᾶσιν. ἑκάστῳ δὲ δίδοται ἡ φανέρωσις τοῦ
all things in all. to each one But is given the showing forth of the
4151 4314 4851 3739/3303/1063/1223 4151
Πνεύματος πρὸς τὸ συμφέρον. ᾧ μὲν γὰρ διὰ τοῦ Πνεύματος
Spirit to the advantage. to one For through the Spirit
1325 3056 4678 243 3056 1108 2596 846
8 δίδοται λόγος σοφίας, ἄλλῳ δὲ λόγος γνώσεως, κατὰ τὸ αὐτὸ
is given a word of wisdom; to another and a word of knowledge per the same
4151 2087 4102/1722 846 4151 243
9 Πνεῦμα· ἑτέρῳ δὲ πίστις, ἐν τῷ αὐτῷ Πνεύματι· ἄλλῳ δὲ
Spirit; to another and faith, by the same Spirit; to another and
5486 2386 1722 846 4151 243 1755
10 χαρίσματα ἰαμάτων, ἐν τῷ αὐτῷ Πνεύματι· ἄλλῳ δὲ ἐνεργή-
gifts of healing, by the same Spirit, to another and workings
1411 243 4394 243 1253
ματα δυνάμεων, ἄλλῳ δὲ προφητεία, ἄλλῳ δὲ διακρίσεις
of powers; to another and prophecy; to another and discerning
4151 2087 1085 1100 243 2058
πνευμάτων, ἑτέρῳ δὲ γένη γλωσσῶν, ἄλλῳ δὲ ἑρμηνεία
of spirits; to another and kinds of languages; to another and interpretation
1100 3956 5023 1754 1520 846 4151
11 γλωσσῶν· πάντα δὲ ταῦτα ἐνεργεῖ τὸ ἓν καὶ τὸ αὐτὸ Πνεῦμα,
of languages; all and these things works the one and the same Spirit,
1244 2398 1538 2531 1014
διαιροῦν ἰδίᾳ ἑκάστῳ καθὼς βούλεται.
distributing separately to each as He purposes.
2509 1063 4983 1722/2076 3196 2192 4183
12 Καθάπερ γὰρ τὸ σῶμα ἕν ἐστι, καὶ μέλη ἔχει πολλά,
as For the body one is, and members has many,

members, but all the members of the one body, being many, *make up* one body; so also *is* Christ. [13]For also we all were baptized by one Spirit into one body, whether Jews or Greeks, whether slaves or free, even all were given to drink into one Spirit. [14]For also the body is not one member, but many. [15]If the foot says, Because I am not a hand, I am not of the body; on account of this, is it not of the body? [16]And if the ear says, Because I am not an eye, I am not of the body; on account of this, is it not of the body? [17]If all the body *were* an eye, where *would be* the hearing? If all hearing, where the smelling? [18]But now God set the members, each one of them, in the body, even as He desired. [19]But if all were one member, where *would* the body *be*? [20]But now, indeed, many *are* the members, but one body. [21]And the eye is not able to say to the hand, I have no need of you; or again the head to the feet, I have no need of you. [22]But much rather the members of the body seeming to be weaker are necessary. [23]And those of the body we think to be less honorable, to these we put more abundant honor around *them*. And our unpresentable *members* have more abundant propriety. [24]But our presentable *members* have no need. But God tempered the body together, giving more abundant honor to the *member* having need, [25]that there not be division in the body, but that the members might have the same care for one another. [26]And if one member suffers, all the members suffer with *it*. If one member is glorified, all the members rejoice with *it*.

3956 3196 4983 1520 4183 5607 1520
πάντα δὲ τὰ μέλη τοῦ σώματος τοῦ ἑνός, πολλὰ ὄντα, ἕν
all but the members of the body one, many being, one
2076 4983 3779 5547 1063/1722/1520 4151
13 ἐστι σῶμα· οὕτω καὶ ὁ Χριστός. καὶ γὰρ ἐν ἑνὶ Πνεύματι
is body; so also the Christ. also For by one Spirit
2249 3956 1519/1520/4983 907 1535 2453 1535
ἡμεῖς πάντες εἰς ἓν σῶμα ἐβαπτίσθημεν, εἴτε Ἰουδαῖοι εἴτε
we all into one body were baptized, whether Jews or
1672 1535 1401 1535 1658 3956 1519/1520/4151
Ἕλληνες, εἴτε δοῦλοι εἴτε ἐλεύθεροι· καὶ πάντες εἰς ἓν Πνεῦμα
Greeks, whether slaves or free, and all into one Spirit
4222 1063 4983 3756/ 2076/1722/3196 235
14 ἐποτίσθημεν. καὶ γὰρ τὸ σῶμα οὐκ ἔστιν ἓν μέλος, ἀλλὰ
we were given to drink. also For the body not is one member, but
4183 1437 2036 4228/3754/3756/1510/5495/3756/1510/1537
15 πολλά. ἐὰν εἴπῃ ὁ πούς, Ὅτι οὐκ εἰμὶ χείρ, οὐκ εἰμὶ ἐκ τοῦ
many. If says the foot: Because not I am a hand, not I am of the
4983 3756 3844 5124 3756 2076/1537 4983
16 σώματος· οὐ παρὰ τοῦτο οὐκ ἔστιν ἐκ τοῦ σώματος; καὶ
body; on account of this not is it of the body? And
1437/2036 3775 3754/3756/1510 3788 3756/1510/1537
ἐὰν εἴπῃ τὸ οὖς, Ὅτι οὐκ εἰμὶ ὀφθαλμός, οὐκ εἰμὶ ἐκ τοῦ
if says the ear: Because not I am an eye, not I am of the
4983 3756 3844 5124 3756 2076 1537 4983 1487
17 σώματος· οὐ παρὰ τοῦτο οὐκ ἔστιν ἐκ τοῦ σώματος; εἰ
body; on account of this, not is it of the body; If
3650 4983 3788 4226 189 1487/3650/189 4226
ὅλον τὸ σῶμα ὀφθαλμός, ποῦ ἡ ἀκοή; εἰ ὅλον ἀκοή, ποῦ
all the body (was) an eye, where the hearing? If all hearing, where
3750 3570 2316 5087 3196/1722/ 1538 846
18 ἡ ὄσφρησις; νυνὶ δὲ ὁ Θεὸς ἔθετο τὰ μέλη ἓν ἕκαστον αὐτῶν
the smelling. now But God set the members, one each of them
1722 4983 2531 2309 1487 2258 3956 1722 3196
19 ἐν τῷ σώματι, καθὼς ἠθέλησεν. εἰ δὲ ἦν τὰ πάντα ἓν μέλος,
in the body, as He desired. if And was all one member,
4226 4983 3568 4183 3303/3196/1520 4983 3756
20 ποῦ τὸ σῶμα; νῦν δὲ πολλὰ μὲν μέλη, ἓν δὲ σῶμα. οὐ
where the body? now But many indeed members, one but body. not
1410 3788 2036 5495 5532 5675/3756/2192
21 δύναται δὲ ὀφθαλμὸς εἰπεῖν τῇ χειρί, Χρείαν σου οὐκ ἔχω·
can And the eye say to the hand need of you not I have;
2228/3825 2776 4228 5532 5216/3756/2192 235
22 ἢ πάλιν ἡ κεφαλὴ τοῖς ποσί, Χρείαν ὑμῶν οὐκ ἔχω. ἀλλὰ
or again the head to the feet, need of you not I have. But
4183 3123 1380 3196 4983 772
πολλῷ μᾶλλον τὰ δοκοῦντα μέλη τοῦ σώματος ἀσθενέ-
by much more the seeming members of the body weaker
5225 314 2076 3739/ 1380 820
23 στερα ὑπάρχειν, ἀναγκαῖά ἐστι· καὶ ἃ δοκοῦμεν ἀτιμότερα
to be, necessary is; and those which we think less honorable
1511 4983 5125 5092 4055 4060
εἶναι τοῦ σώματος, τούτοις τιμὴν περισσοτέραν περιτίθεμεν·
to be of the body, to these honor more abundant we put around;
809 2257 2157 4055 2192
καὶ τὰ ἀσχήμονα ἡμῶν εὐσχημοσύνην περισσοτέραν ἔχει·
and the unpresentable of us propriety more abundant has;
2158 2257 3756 5532 2192 235 2316 4786
24 τὰ δὲ εὐσχήμονα ἡμῶν οὐ χρείαν ἔχει· ἀλλ' ὁ Θεὸς συνε-
the but presentable (members) of us not need has. But God tempered
4983 5302 4055 1325 5092
κέρασε τὸ σῶμα, τῷ ὑστεροῦντι περισσοτέραν δοὺς τιμήν,
together the body, to the (member) lacking, more abundant giving honor,
2443/3361/*/ 4978/1722 4983 235 846 5228 240
25 ἵνα μὴ ᾖ σχίσμα ἐν τῷ σώματι, ἀλλὰ τὸ αὐτὸ ὑπὲρ ἀλλήλων
*5600 lest be division in the body; but the same on behalf of one another
3309 3196 1535 3958 1520 3196 4841
26 μεριμνῶσι τὰ μέλη. καὶ εἴτε πάσχει ἓν μέλος, συμπάσχει
should care the members. And whether suffers one member, suffers with (it)
3956 3196 1535 1392 1520 3196 4796 3956
πάντα τὰ μέλη· εἴτε δοξάζεται ἓν μέλος, συγχαίρει πάντα
all the members; or is glorified one member, rejoices with (it) all

[27]And you are a body of Christ, and members in part. [28]And God placed some in the church: firstly apostles; secondly, prophets; thirdly, teachers; then works of power; then gifts of healing, helps, governings, kinds of languages. [29]*Are* all apostles? All prophets? All teachers? All workers of power? [30]Do all have gifts of healing? Do all speak languages? Do all interpret? [31]But zealously strive after the better gifts. And yet I show you a way according to excellence:

3196 5210 2075 4983 5547 3196/1537/3313
27 τὰ μέλη. ὑμεῖς δέ ἐστε σῶμα Χριστοῦ, καὶ μέλη ἐκ μέρους.
the members. you And are a body of Christ. and members in part.
3739/3303/5087 2316/1722 1577 4412 652
28 καὶ οὓς μὲν ἔθετο ὁ Θεὸς ἐν τῇ ἐκκλησίᾳ πρῶτον ἀποστόλους,
And some placed God in the church firstly apostles;
1208 4396 5154 1320 1899 1411
δεύτερον προφήτας, τρίτον διδασκάλους, ἔπειτα δυνάμεις,
secondly prophets; thirdly, teachers; then works of power;
1534 5486 2386 484 2941 1085
εἶτα χαρίσματα ἰαμάτων, ἀντιλήψεις, κυβερνήσεις, γένη
then gifts of healing; helps; governings; kinds
1100 3361 3956 652 3361 3956 4396
29 γλωσσῶν. μὴ πάντες ἀπόστολοι; μὴ πάντες προφῆται;
of languages. Not all (are) apostles? Not all (are) prophets?
3361 3956 1320 3361 3956 1411 3361 3956
30 μὴ πάντες διδάσκαλοι; μὴ πάντες δυνάμεις; μὴ πάντες
Not all (are) teachers? Not all workers of power? Not all
5486 2192 2386 3361 3956 1100 2980
χαρίσματα ἔχουσιν ἰαμάτων; μὴ πάντες γλώσσαις λαλοῦσι;
gifts have of healings? Not all languages speak?
3361 3956 1329 2206 5486
31 μὴ πάντες διερμηνεύουσι; ζηλοῦτε δὲ τὰ χαρίσματα τὰ
Not all interpret? zealously strive after But the gifts
2909 2089/2596 5236 3598/5213 1166
κρείττονα. καὶ ἔτι καθ' ὑπερβολὴν ὁδὸν ὑμῖν δείκνυμι.
better. And yet according to excellence a way to you I show.

CHAPTER 13

[1]If I speak with the tongues of men and of angels, but I do not have love, I have become *as* sounding brass or a clanging cymbal. [2]And if I have prophecies, and know all mysteries and all knowledge, and if I have all faith so as to move mountains, but do not have love, I am nothing. [3]And if I give out all my goods, and if I deliver my body that I be burned, but I do not have love, I am not profited anything. [4]Love has patience, is kind; love is not envious; love is not vain, is not puffed up; [5]does not behave indecently; does not pursue its own things; is not easily provoked; thinks no evil; [6]does not rejoice over wrong, but rejoices with the truth; [7]quietly covers all things; believes all things; hopes all things; endures all things; [8]love never fails. But if *there are* prophecies, they will be abolished; if tongues, they shall cease; if knowledge, it will be

1437 1100 444 2980
1 Ἐὰν ταῖς γλώσσαις τῶν ἀνθρώπων λαλῶ καὶ τῶν
If in the languages of men I speak, even
32 26 3361 2192 1096 5475 2278/2228
ἀγγέλων, ἀγάπην δὲ μὴ ἔχω, γέγονα χαλκὸς ἠχῶν ἢ
of angels, love and not I have, I have become brass sounding, or
2950 214 1437/2192 4394 1492
2 κύμβαλον ἀλαλάζον. καὶ ἐὰν ἔχω προφητείαν, καὶ εἰδῶ τὰ
a cymbal tinkling. And if I have prophecies, and know
3466 3956 3956 1108 1437/1473/3956
μυστήρια πάντα καὶ πᾶσαν τὴν γνῶσιν, καὶ ἐὰν ἔχω πᾶσαν
mysteries all, and all knowledge, and if I have all
4102 5620/3735 3179 26 3361/2192 3762
τὴν πίστιν, ὥστε ὄρη μεθιστάνειν, ἀγάπην δὲ μὴ ἔχω, οὐδέν
faith, so as mountains to move, love but not have, nothing
1510 1437 5595 3956 5224 3450 1437
3 εἰμι. καὶ ἐὰν ψωμίσω πάντα τὰ ὑπάρχοντά μου, καὶ ἐὰν
I am. And if I give out all the goods of me, and if
3860 4983 3450/2443/ 2545 26 3361/2192
παραδῶ τὸ σῶμά μου ἵνα καυθήσωμαι, ἀγάπην δὲ μὴ ἔχω,
I deliver the body of me that I be burned, love but not I have,
3762 5623 26 3114 5541
4 οὐδὲν ὠφελοῦμαι. ἡ ἀγάπη μακροθυμεῖ, χρηστεύεται· ἡ
nothing I am profited. Love suffers long, is kind;
26 3756/2206 26 3756 4068 3756 5448
ἀγάπη οὐ ζηλοῖ· ἡ ἀγάπη οὐ περπερεύεται, οὐ φυσιοῦται,
love not is envious; love not vaunts itself, not is puffed up,
3756 807 3756 2212 1438 3756 3947 3756
5 οὐκ ἀσχημονεῖ, οὐ ζητεῖ τὰ ἑαυτῆς, οὐ παροξύνεται, οὐ
not behaves indecently, not seeks things of itself, not is provoked, not
3049 2556 3756/5463/1909 93 4796
6 λογίζεται τὸ κακόν, οὐ χαίρει ἐπὶ τῇ ἀδικίᾳ, συγχαίρει δὲ τῇ
thinks evil, not rejoices over the wrong, rejoices with but the
225 3956 4722 3956 4100 3956 1679
7 ἀληθείᾳ, πάντα στέγει, πάντα πιστεύει, πάντα ἐλπίζει,
truth; all things covers quietly, all things believes, all things hopes,
3956 5278 26 3762 1601 1535 4394
8 πάντα ὑπομένει. ἡ ἀγάπη οὐδέποτε ἐκπίπτει· εἴτε δὲ προφη-
all things endures. Love never fails; whether but prophesies,
2673 1535 1100 3973 1535
τεῖαι, καταργηθήσονται· εἴτε γλῶσσαι, παύσονται· εἴτε
they will be abolished; if languages, they shall cease; if

abolished. [9]For we know in part, and we prophesy in part; [10]but when the perfect thing comes, then that *which* is in part will be caused to cease.

[11]When I was an infant, I spoke as an infant, I thought as an infant, I reasoned as an infant. But when I became a man, I did away with the things of the infant. [12]For now we see through a mirror in dimness, but then face to face. Now I know in part, but then I will fully know even as I also was fully known. [13]And now faith, hope, and love, these three things remain; but the greatest of these *is* love.

CHAPTER 14

[1]Pursue love, and seek eagerly the spiritual things, but rather that you may prophesy. [2]For the *one* speaking in a tongue does not speak to men, but to God; for no one hears, but in spirit he speaks mysteries. [3]But the *one* prophesying to men speaks *for* building up, and encouragement, and comfort. [4]The *one* speaking in a tongue builds himself up; but the *one* prophesying builds up a church. [5]And I wish all of you to speak in languages, but rather that you may prophesy—for greater is the *one* prophesying than the *one* speaking in tongues, unless he interpret that the church may receive building up. [6]But now, brothers, if I come to you speaking in tongues, what will I profit you, except I speak to you either in revelation, or in knowledge, or in prophecy, or in teaching? [7]Yet lifeless things giving a sound, whether pipe or harp, if they do not give a distinction in the sound, how will it be known what *is* being piped or harped? [8]For also if a

1108 2673 1537/3313/1063 1097 1537
9 γνῶσις, καταργηθήσεται. ἐκ μέρους γὰρ γινώσκομεν, καὶ ἐκ
knowledge, it shall be abolished. in part For we know, and in
3313 4395 3752 2064 5046 5119 1537
10 μέρους προφητεύομεν· ὅταν δὲ ἔλθῃ τὸ τέλειον, τότε τὸ ἐκ
part we prophesy; when but comes the perfect thing, then that in
3313 2673 3753 2252 3516 5613 3516
11 μέρους καταργηθήσεται. ὅτε ἤμην νήπιος, ὡς νήπιος
part will be abolished. When I was an infant, as an infant
2980 5613 3516 5426 5613 3516 3049 3753
ἐλάλουν, ὡς νήπιος ἐφρόνουν, ὡς νήπιος ἐλογιζόμην· ὅτε δὲ
I spoke, as an infant I thought, as an infant I reasoned; when but
1096 435 2673 3516 991 1063
12 γέγονα ἀνήρ, κατήργηκα τὰ τοῦ νηπίου. βλέπομεν γὰρ
I became a man, I did away with the things of the infant. we see For
737 1223 2072 1722 135 5119 4383 4314
ἄρτι δι' ἐσόπτρου ἐν αἰνίγματι, τότε δὲ πρόσωπον πρὸς
yet through a mirror in obscureness, then but face to
4383 737 1097 1537 3313 5119 1921
πρόσωπον· ἄρτι γινώσκω ἐκ μέρους, τότε δὲ ἐπιγνώσομαι
face; yet I know in part, then but I will fully know
2531 1921 3570 3306 4102 1680 26
13 καθὼς καὶ ἐπεγνώσθην. νυνὶ δὲ μένει πίστις, ἐλπίς, ἀγάπη,
even as also I was fully known. now But remains faith, hope, love,
5140 5023 3187 5130 26
τὰ τρία ταῦτα· μείζων δὲ τούτων ἡ ἀγάπη.
three things these (the) greater and of these (is) love.

CHAPTER 14

1377 26 2206 4152 3123
1 Διώκετε τὴν ἀγάπην· ζηλοῦτε δὲ τὰ πνευματικά, μᾶλλον
Pursue love, seek eagerly and the spiritual things; rather
2443 4395 1063 2980 1100 3756 444
2 δὲ ἵνα προφητεύητε. ὁ γὰρ λαλῶν γλώσσῃ οὐκ ἀνθρώποις
and that you may prophesy he for speaking in a tongue not to men
2980 235 2316 3762 1063 191 4151 2980
3 λαλεῖ, ἀλλὰ τῷ Θεῷ· οὐδεὶς γὰρ ἀκούει, πνεύματι δὲ λαλεῖ
speaks, but to God; no one for hears, in spirit but he speaks
3466 4395 444 2980 3619
μυστήρια. ὁ δὲ προφητεύων ἀνθρώποις λαλεῖ οἰκοδομὴν καὶ
mysteries. the (one) but prophesying to men speaks (for) building up and
3874 3889 2980 1100 1438 3618
4 παράκλησιν καὶ παραμυθίαν ὁ λαλῶν γλώσσῃ ἑαυτὸν οἰκο-
encouragement and comfort. The (one) speaking in a tongue himself builds
4395 1577 3618 2309 3956
5 δομεῖ, ὁ δὲ προφητεύων ἐκκλησίαν οἰκοδομεῖ. θέλω δὲ πάντας
up, the (one) but prophesying a church builds up. I desire And all
5209 2980 1100 3123 2443 4395 3187
ὑμᾶς λαλεῖν γλώσσαις, μᾶλλον δὲ ἵνα προφητεύητε· μείζων
you to speak in languages, rather but that you may prophesy; greater
1063 4395 2228 2980 1100 1623=1508= 1329
γὰρ ὁ προφητεύων ἢ ὁ λαλῶν γλώσσαις, ἐκτὸς εἰ μὴ διερμη-
for the (one) prophesying than he speaking in tongues, unless he interpret
2443 1577 3619 2983 3570 80 1437
6 νεύῃ, ἵνα ἡ ἐκκλησία οἰκοδομὴν λάβῃ. νυνὶ δέ, ἀδελφοί, ἐὰν
that the church building up may receive. now But, brothers, if
2064 4314 5209 1100 2980 5101/5209 5623 =3362=
ἔλθω πρὸς ὑμᾶς γλώσσαις λαλῶν, τί ὑμᾶς ὠφελήσω, ἐὰν μὴ
I come to you in languages speaking, what you will I profit, except
5213 2980 2228/1722/ 602 2228/1722/ 1108/2228/1722/ 4394
ὑμῖν λαλήσω ἢ ἐν ἀποκαλύψει, ἢ ἐν γνώσει, ἢ ἐν προφητείᾳ,
to you I speak either in revelation, or in knowledge, or in prophecy,
2228/1722/ 1322 3676 895 5456 1325 1535 836
7 ἢ ἐν διδαχῇ; ὅμως τὰ ἄψυχα φωνὴν διδόντα, εἴτε αὐλός,
or in teaching? Yet lifeless things a sound giving, whether pipe
1535 2788 1437 1293 5353 3361 1325 4459
εἴτε κιθάρα, ἐὰν διαστολὴν τοῖς φθόγγοις μὴ δῷ, πῶς
or harp, if a distinction in the sound not they give, how
1097 832 2228 2789 1063
8 γνωσθήσεται τὸ αὐλούμενον ἢ τὸ κιθαριζόμενον; καὶ γὰρ
will it be known the thing being piped or the thing being harped? indeed For

trumpet gives an uncertain
sound, who will get himself
ready for war?
[9]So also you, if you do not
give a clear word through
the language, how will it be
known what *is* being said?
For you will be speaking
into air. [10]So it may be
many kinds of sounds are in
the world, and not one is
without *distinct* sound. [11]If,
then, I do not know the
power of the sound, I will be
a foreigner to the *one*
speaking, and the *one*
speaking a foreigner *to* me.
[12]So also you, since you are
zealots of spiritual things,
seek to build up the church
that you may abound. [13]So
then, the *one* speaking in a
language, let him pray that
he may interpret. [14]For if I
pray in a tongue, my spirit
prays, but my mind is un-
fruitful. [15]What then is it? I
will pray with the spirit, and
I will also pray with the
mind; I will sing with the
spirit, and I will also sing
with the mind. [16]Else, if you
bless in the spirit, the *one*
occupying the place of the
unlearned, how will he say
the amen at your giving of
thanks, since he does not
know what you say? [17]For
you truly give give thanks
well, but the other is not
built up. [18]I thank my God
that I speak more
languages than all of you.
[19]But in a church I desire to
speak five words with my
mind, that I may also in-
struct others, than myriads
of words in a foreign
language.
[20]Brothers, do not be
children in your minds, but
in malice be like infants,
and in *your* minds be
mature. [21]It has been written in the Law, "By other
tongues and by other lips I
will speak to this people,
and even so they will not
hear Me, says *the* Lord."

1437 82 5456 4536 1325/5101 3903 1519
ἐὰν ἄδηλον φωνὴν σάλπιγξ δῷ, τίς παρασκευάσεται εἰς
if an uncertain sound a trumpet gives, who will get himself ready for
4171 3779 5210/1223 1100 1437/3361/ 2154
9 πόλεμον ; οὕτω καὶ ὑμεῖς διὰ τῆς γλώσσης ἐὰν μὴ εὔσημον
war? So also you through the language if not a clear
3056 1325 4459 1097 2980 2071 1063
λόγον δῶτε, πῶς γνωσθήσεται τὸ λαλούμενον ; ἔσεσθε γὰρ
word give, how will it be known the thing being said? you For
1519/109 2980 5118 1487 5177/1085 5456 2076
10 εἰς ἀέρα λαλοῦντες. τοσαῦτα, εἰ τύχοι, γένη φωνῶν ἐστὶν
into air will be speaking. So many it may be kinds of sounds are
1722/2889 3762 880 1437/3767/3361/1492 1411
11 ἐν κόσμῳ καὶ οὐδὲν ἄφωνον. ἐὰν οὖν μὴ εἰδῶ τὴν δύναμιν
in (the) world, and not one is voiceless. If, then, not I know the power
5456 2071 2980 915 2980 1722
τῆς φωνῆς, ἔσομαι τῷ λαλοῦντι βάρβαρος, καὶ ὁ λαλῶν ἐν
of the sound, I will be to the (one) speaking a foreigner, and he speaking in
1698 915 3779 5210 1893 2207 2075 4151
12 ἐμοὶ βάρβαρος. οὕτω καὶ ὑμεῖς, ἐπεὶ ζηλωταί ἐστε πνευ-
me a foreigner. So also you, since zealots you are of
4314 3619 1577 2212 2443 4052
μάτων, πρὸς τὴν οἰκοδομὴν τῆς ἐκκλησίας ζητεῖτε ἵνα περισ-
spiritual things, to the building up of the church seek, that you may
1355 2980 1100 4336 2443 1329
13 σεύητε. διόπερ ὁ λαλῶν γλώσσῃ προσευχέσθω ἵνα διερμη-
abound. Therefore, he speaking in a language let him pray that he may
1437 1063 4336 1100 4151 3450
14 νεύῃ. ἐὰν γὰρ προσεύχωμαι γλώσσῃ, τὸ πνεῦμά μου
interpret. If For I pray in a tongue, the spirit of me
4336 3563 3450 175 2076/5101/3767/2076
15 προσεύχεται, ὁ δὲ νοῦς μου ἄκαρπός ἐστι. τί οὖν ἐστί ;
prays, the but mind of me unfruitful is. What then is it?
4336 4151 4336 3563 5567
προσεύξομαι τῷ πνεύματι, προσεύξομαι δὲ καὶ τῷ νοΐ· ψαλῶ
I will pray with the spirit, I will pray and also with the mind; I sing
4151 5567 3563/1893/1437 2127
16 τῷ πνεύματι, ψαλῶ δὲ καὶ τῷ νοΐ. ἐπεὶ ἐὰν εὐλογήσῃς τῷ
with the spirit, I sing and also with the mind. Else if you bless in the
4151 378 5117 2399 4459 2046
πνεύματι, ὁ ἀναπληρῶν τὸν τόπον τοῦ ἰδιώτου πῶς ἐρεῖ
spirit, the (one) occupying the place of the unlearned, how will he say
281/1909 4674 2169 1894 5101 3004 3756/1492
τὸ ἀμὴν ἐπὶ τῇ σῇ εὐχαριστίᾳ, ἐπειδὴ τί λέγεις οὐκ οἶδε ;
the amen at your giving thanks? Since what you say not he knows;
4771/3303/1063 2573 2168 235 2087 3756/3618
17 σὺ μὲν γὰρ καλῶς εὐχαριστεῖς, ἀλλ' ὁ ἕτερος οὐκ οἰκοδο-
you indeed for well give thanks, but the other not is built up
2168 2316 3450 3956 5216 3123
18 μεῖται. εὐχαριστῶ τῷ Θεῷ μου, πάντων ὑμῶν μᾶλλον
I thank the God of me, all of you more than
1100 2980 235/1722 1577 2309 4002 3056 1223
19 γλώσσαις λαλῶν· ἀλλ' ἐν ἐκκλησίᾳ θέλω πέντε λόγους διὰ
in languages I speak, but in a church I desire five words with
3563/3450/ 2980 2443 243 2727 2228 3463
τοῦ νοός μου λαλῆσαι, ἵνα καὶ ἄλλους κατηχήσω, ἢ μυρίους
the mind of me to speak, that also others I may instruct, than myriads
3056 1722 1100
λόγους ἐν γλώσσῃ.
of words in a foreign language.
80 3361 3813 1096 5424 235 2549
20 Ἀδελφοί, μὴ παιδία γίνεσθε ταῖς φρεσίν· ἀλλὰ τῇ κακίᾳ
Brothers, not children be in the minds., but in malice
3515 5424 5046 1096 1722 3551
21 νηπιάζετε, ταῖς δὲ φρεσὶ τέλειοι γίνεσθε. ἐν τῷ νόμῳ
be like infants in the and minds mature be. In the law
1125 3754/1722 2084 1722 5491 2087
γέγραπται ὅτι Ἐν ἑτερογλώσσοις καὶ ἐν χείλεσιν ἑτέροις
it has been written: In other tongues and in lips other
2980 2992 5129 3761 3779 1522 3450
λαλήσω τῷ λαῷ τούτῳ, καὶ οὐδ' οὕτως εἰσακούσονταί μου,
I will speak to people this, and not so will they hear Me,

22 So that tongues are not a
sign to those believing, but
to those not believing. But
prophecy is not to those not
believing, but to those
believing. 23 Therefore, if
the whole church comes
together, and all speak in
languages, and unin-
structed ones or unbelievers come in, will they not
say that you rave? 24 But if
all prophesy, and some unbeliever or one not in-
structed comes in, he is
convicted by all, he is
judged by all. 25 And so the
secrets of his heart become
revealed; and so, falling on
his face, he will worship
God, declaring that God is
truly among you.

26 Then, brothers, what is
it? When you come to-
gether, each one of you has
a psalm; he has a teaching;
he has a language; he has a
revelation; he has an interpretation. Let all things be
for building up. 27 If one
speaks in a language, *let it
be* by two or three *at* the
most; and in turn, also let
one interpret. 28 And if there
is no interpreter, let him be
silent in church; and let him
speak to himself and to
God. 29 And *if there are* two
or three prophets, let them
speak, and let the others
discern. 30 But if a *revelation* is revealed to another
sitting by, let the first be
silent. 31 For you can all
prophesy one by one, that
all may learn, and all may be
encouraged. 32 And the
spirits of prophets *are*
subject to prophets. 33 For
God is not *God* of con-
fusion, but of peace, as in all
the churches of the saints.
34 Let your women be
silent in the churches, for it
is not allowed to them to
speak, but to be in sub-
jection, as also the Law

3004 2962 5620 1100 1519 4592 1526 3756
22 λέγει Κύριος. ὥστε αἱ γλῶσσαι εἰς σημεῖόν εἰσιν, οὐ τοῖς
says (the) Lord. So as tongues for a sign are, not to those
4100 235 571 4394 3756
πιστεύουσιν, ἀλλὰ τοῖς ἀπίστοις· ἡ δὲ προφητεία, οὐ τοῖς
believing, but to those not believing; and prophecy (is) not to th
571 235 4100 1437 3767 4905
23 ἀπίστοις, ἀλλὰ τοῖς πιστεύουσιν. ἐὰν οὖν συνέλθῃ ἡ
unbelievers, but to those believing. If therefore, comes the
1577 3650/1909 846 3956 1100 2980
ἐκκλησία ὅλη ἐπὶ τὸ αὐτό, καὶ πάντες γλώσσαις λαλῶσιν,
church whole together, and all in languages speak,
1525 2399 2228/571 3756/2046 3754 3105
εἰσέλθωσι δὲ ἰδιῶται ἢ ἄπιστοι, οὐκ ἐροῦσιν ὅτι μαίνεσθε;
come in and uninstructed or unbelievers, not will they say that you rave?
1437 3956 4395 1525 5100 571 2228
24 ἐὰν δὲ πάντες προφητεύωσιν, εἰσέλθῃ δέ τις ἄπιστος ἢ
if But all prophesy, comes in and some unbeliever or
2399 1651 5259 3956 350 5259 3956
ἰδιώτης, ἐλέγχεται ὑπὸ πάντων, ἀνακρίνεται ὑπὸ πάντων,
uninstructed, he is convicted by all, he is judged by all;
3779 2927 2588 848 5318 1096
25 καὶ οὕτω τὰ κρυπτὰ τῆς καρδίας αὐτοῦ φανερὰ γίνεται· καὶ
and so the secrets of the heart of him revealed become, and
3779 4098 1909 4383 4352 2316 518
οὕτω πεσὼν ἐπὶ πρόσωπον προσκυνήσει τῷ Θεῷ ἀπαγ-
so falling on (his) face, he will worship God, declaring
3754 2316 3779/1722/5213/2076
γέλλων ὅτι ὁ Θεὸς ὄντως ἐν ὑμῖν ἐστι.
that God truly among you is.
5101/3767/2076 80 3752 4905 1538 5216
26 Τί οὖν ἐστίν, ἀδελφοί; ὅταν συνέρχησθε, ἕκαστος ὑμῶν
What then is it, brothers? When you come together, each one of yo
5568 2192 1322 2192 1100 2192 602 2192
ψαλμὸν ἔχει, διδαχὴν ἔχει, γλῶσσαν ἔχει, ἀποκάλυψιν ἔχει,
a psalm has, a teaching he has, a language he has, a revelation he ha
2058 2192 3956 4314 3619 1096 1535
27 ἑρμηνείαν ἔχει. πάντα πρὸς οἰκοδομὴν γενέσθω. εἴτε
an interpretation he has. all things for building up let be. If
1100 5100 2980 2596 1417/2228 4118 5140 303
γλώσσῃ τις λαλεῖ, κατὰ δύο ἢ τὸ πλεῖστον τρεῖς, καὶ ἀνὰ
in a language one speaks, by two or the most three, and in
3313 1520 1329 1437 3361/5600/ 1328 4601
28 μέρος, καὶ εἷς διερμηνευέτω· ἐὰν δὲ μὴ ᾖ διερμηνευτής, σιγάτω
turn, and one let interpret; if but not (is) an interpreter, be silen
1722 1577 1438 2980 2316 4396
29 ἐν ἐκκλησίᾳ· ἑαυτῷ δὲ λαλείτω καὶ τῷ Θεῷ. προφῆται δὲ
in church, to himself and let him speak, and to God. prophets An
1417/2228/5140/ 2980 243 1252 1437
30 δύο ἢ τρεῖς λαλείτωσαν, καὶ οἱ ἄλλοι διακρινέτωσαν. ἐὰν δὲ
two or three let them speak, and the others let discern; if an
243 601 2521 4413 4601 1410
31 ἄλλῳ ἀποκαλυφθῇ καθημένῳ, ὁ πρῶτος σιγάτω. δύνασθε
to another is revealed sitting the first let be silent. you can
1063/2596/1520 3956 4395 2443 3956 3129
γὰρ καθ᾽ ἕνα πάντες προφητεύειν, ἵνα πάντες μανθάνωσι,
For one by one all prophesy, that all may learn
3956 3870 4151 4396 4396
32 καὶ πάντες παρακαλῶνται· καὶ πνεύματα προφητῶν προφή-
and all may be encouraged. And the spirits of prophets to prophet
5293 3756/1063/2076 181 2316 235
33 ταις ὑποτάσσεται. οὐ γάρ ἐστιν ἀκαταστασίας ὁ Θεός, ἀλλ᾽
(are) subject. not For is of confusion God, but
1515 5613/1722/ 3956 1577 40
εἰρήνης, ὡς ἐν πάσαις ταῖς ἐκκλησίαις τῶν ἁγίων.
of peace, as in all the churches of the saints.
1135 5216/1722 1577 4601 3756/1063
34 Αἱ γυναῖκες ὑμῶν ἐν ταῖς ἐκκλησίαις σιγάτωσαν· οὐ γὰρ
Let the women of you in the churches be silent, not for
2010 846 2980 235 5293 2531
ἐπιτέτραπται αὐταῖς λαλεῖν, ἀλλ᾽ ὑποτάσσεσθαι, καθὼς καὶ
it is allowed to them to speak but let them be subject, as also

says. [35]But if they desire to learn anything, let them question their husbands at home; for it is a shame for a woman to speak in a church. [36]Or did the word of God go out from you? Or did it reach only to you?

[37]If anyone thinks to be a prophet, or a spiritual one, let him recognize what I write to you, that they are a command of the Lord.
[38]But if any be ignorant, let him be ignorant.

[39]So then, brothers, seek eagerly to prophesy, and do not forbid to speak in languages. [40]And let all things be done decently and in order.

CHAPTER 15

[1]But, brothers, I reveal to you the gospel which I preached to you, which you also received, in which you also stand, [2]by which you also are being saved, if you hold fast the word which I preached to you; unless you believed in vain. [3]For I delivered to you in the first place what I also received, that Christ died for our sins, according to the Scriptures; [4]and that He was buried; and that *He* has been raised the third day, according to the Scriptures; [5]and that He was seen by Peter, then to the Twelve. [6]Then He was seen by over five hundred brothers at once, of whom the most remain until now; but some also fell asleep. [7]Then He was seen by James; then by all the apostles; [8]and last of all, even as if to *one* born out of time, He was also seen by me. [9]For I am the least of the apostles, who am not sufficient to be called an apostle, because I persecuted the church of God. [10]But by the grace of God I

3551 3004 1487 5100 3129 2309 1722 3624 2398
35 ὁ νόμος λέγει. εἰ δέ τι μαθεῖν θέλουσιν, ἐν οἴκῳ τοὺς ἰδίους
the law says. if But anything to learn they desire, at home the own
435 1905 149 1063 2076 1135 1722
ἄνδρας ἐπερωτάτωσαν· αἰσχρὸν γάρ ἐστι γυναιξὶν ἐν
husbands let them question; a shame for it is for women in
1577 2980/2228/575/5216 3056 2316 1831 2228
36 ἐκκλησίᾳ λαλεῖν. ἢ ἀφ' ὑμῶν ὁ λόγος τοῦ Θεοῦ ἐξῆλθεν ; ἢ
a church to speak. Or from you the word of God went out, or
1519/5209/ 3441 2658
εἰς ὑμᾶς μόνους κατήντησεν·
to you only did it reach?
*1536= 1380 4396 1511/2228/ 4152 1921
37 Εἴ τις δοκεῖ προφήτης εἶναι ἢ πνευματικός, ἐπιγινωσκέτω
If anyone thinks a prophet to be, or a spiritual one, let him recognize
3739 1125/5213/3754 2962 1526 1785 1487 5100 50
38 ἃ γράφω ὑμῖν, ὅτι τοῦ Κυρίου εἰσὶν ἐντολαί. εἰ δέ τις ἀγνοεῖ,
what I write to you, that of the Lord they are a command. if But any be ignorant,
50
ἀγνοείτω.
let him be ignorant.
5620 80 2206 4395 2980
39 Ὥστε, ἀδελφοί, ζηλοῦτε τὸ προφητεύειν, καὶ τὸ λαλεῖν
So as, brothers, seek eagerly to prophesy, and to speak
1100 3361 2967 3956 2156 2596 5010
40 γλώσσαις μὴ κωλύετε. πάντα εὐσχημόνως καὶ κατὰ τάξιν
in languages not do forbid; all things decently and according to order
1096
γινέσθω.
let be done.

CHAPTER 15

1107 5213 80 2098 3739 2097
1 Γνωρίζω δὲ ὑμῖν, ἀδελφοί, τὸ εὐαγγέλιον ὃ εὐηγγελισάμην
I make known And to you, brothers, the gospel which I preached
5213 3880 1722/3739 2476 1223/3739 4982
2 ὑμῖν, ὃ καὶ παρελάβετε, ἐν ᾧ καὶ ἑστήκατε, δι' οὗ καὶ σώζεσθε·
to you, which also you received, in which also you stand, by which also you are saved.
1500 5101 3056 2097 5213/1487/ 2722 1623 =1508=
τίνι λόγῳ εὐηγγελισάμην ὑμῖν, εἰ κατέχετε, ἐκτὸς εἰ μὴ εἰκῆ
to what word I announced to you; if you hold fast unless in vain
4100 3860 1063 5213/1722 4413/3739 3880
3 ἐπιστεύσατε. παρέδωκα γὰρ ὑμῖν ἐν πρώτοις, ὃ καὶ παρέ-
you believed. I delivered For to you among the first what also I
3754 5547 599 5228 266 2257
λαβον, ὅτι Χριστὸς ἀπέθανεν ὑπὲρ τῶν ἁμαρτιῶν ἡμῶν
received, that Christ died for the sins of us
2596 1124 3754 2290 3754 1453 5154
4 κατὰ τὰς γραφάς· καὶ ὅτι ἐτάφη· καὶ ὅτι ἐγήγερται τῇ τρίτῃ
according to the Scriptures, and that He was buried, and has been raised the third
2250 2596 1124 3754/3700 2786 1427
5 ἡμέρᾳ κατὰ τὰς γραφάς· καὶ ὅτι ὤφθη Κηφᾷ, εἶτα τοῖς δώδεκα·
day according to the Scriptures, and that He was seen by Cephas, then by the twelve;
3739 1899 3700 1883 4001 80 2178 1537
6 ἔπειτα ὤφθη ἐπάνω πεντακοσίοις ἀδελφοῖς ἐφάπαξ, ἐξ ὧν οἱ
afterward He was seen over by five hundreds brothers at one time, of whom the
4119 3306 2193/737 5100 2837 1899
7 πλείους μένουσιν ἕως ἄρτι τινὲς δὲ καὶ ἐκοιμήθησαν· ἔπειτα
most remain until now, some but also fell asleep. Afterward
3700 2385 1534 652 3956 2078
8 ὤφθη Ἰακώβῳ, εἶτα τοῖς ἀποστόλοις πᾶσιν· ἔσχατον δὲ
He was seen by James, then by the apostles all; lastly and
3956 5619 1626 3700 2504/1473 1063
9 πάντων, ὡσπερεὶ τῷ ἐκτρώματι, ὤφθη κἀμοί. ἐγὼ γάρ
of all, even as if to the untimely birth, He was seen by me also. I For
1510 1646 652 3739/3756/1510/2425 2564
10 εἰμι ὁ ἐλάχιστος τῶν ἀποστόλων, ὃς οὐκ εἰμὶ ἱκανὸς καλεῖσθαι
am the least of the apostles, who not am sufficient to be called
652 1360 1377 1577 2316 5485
ἀπόστολος, διότι ἐδίωξα τὴν ἐκκλησίαν τοῦ Θεοῦ. χάριτι δὲ
an apostle, because I persecuted the church of God. by grace But

am what I am, and His grace which *was* toward me was not without fruit, but I labored more abundantly than all of them—yet not I, but the grace of God with me. [11]Therefore, whether they or I, so we preach, and so you believed.

[12]But if Christ is proclaimed, that He was raised from *the* dead, how do some among you say that there is not a resurrection of *the* dead? [13]But if there is not a resurrection of *the* dead, neither has Christ been raised. [14]But if Christ has not been raised, then our proclamation is worthless, and your faith is also worthless. [15]And also we are found *to be* false witnesses of God, because we witnessed as to God that He raised Christ, whom He did not raise, then, if *the* dead are not raised.

[16]For if *the* dead are not raised, neither has Christ been raised. [17]But if Christ has not been raised, your faith *is* foolish; you are still in your sins. [18]And then those that fell asleep in Christ were lost. [19]If we have hoped in Christ only in this life, we are of all men most miserable.

[20]But now Christ has been raised from *the* dead; He became the firstfruit of those having fallen asleep. [21]For since death *is* through man, also through a Man *is* a resurrection of *the* dead—[22]for as all die in Adam, so also all will be made alive in Christ, [23]but each in *his* own order: Christ, the firstfruit; afterward those of Christ at His coming. [24]Then *is* the end—when He delivers the kingdom to God, even the Father; when

2316 / 1510/1510 5485 848 1519/1691/3756/2756/ 1096
Θεοῦ εἰμὶ ὅ εἰμι, καὶ ἡ χάρις αὐτοῦ ἡ εἰς ἐμὲ οὐ κενὴ ἐγενήθη,
of God I am what I am, and His grace to me not empty was,
235 4054 846 3956 2872 3756 / 1473
ἀλλὰ περισσότερον αὐτῶν πάντων ἐκοπίασα· οὐκ ἐγὼ δέ,
but more abundantly (than) them all I labored, not I yet,
235 5485 2316 4862/1698/1535/3767/1473/1535/ 1565
11 ἀλλ' ἡ χάρις τοῦ Θεοῦ ἡ σὺν ἐμοί. εἴτε οὖν ἐγώ, εἴτε ἐκεῖνοι
but the grace of God with me. Whether, then, I or those,
3779 2784 3779 4100
οὕτω κηρύσσομεν, καὶ οὕτως ἐπιστεύσατε.
so we proclaim, and so you believed.
1487 5547 2784 3754/1537/3498 1453 4459
12 Εἰ δὲ Χριστὸς κηρύσσεται ὅτι ἐκ νεκρῶν ἐγήγερται, πῶς
if But Christ is proclaimed that from (the) dead He was raised, how
3004 5100/1722/5213/3754/ 386 3498 3756 2076 1487
13 λέγουσί τινες ἐν ὑμῖν ὅτι ἀνάστασις νεκρῶν οὐκ ἔστιν; εἰ δὲ
say some among you that a resurrection of dead not is? if But
386 3498 3756 2076 3761 5547 1453
ἀνάστασις νεκρῶν οὐκ ἔστιν, οὐδὲ Χριστὸς ἐγήγερται·
a resurrection of dead not is, neither Christ has been raised;
1487 5547 3756 1453 2756 686 2782
14 εἰ δὲ Χριστὸς οὐκ ἐγήγερται, κενὸν ἄρα τὸ κήρυγμα
if and Christ not has been raised, worthless then the proclamation
2257 2756 4102 5216 2147 5575
15 ἡμῶν, κενὴ δὲ καὶ ἡ πίστις ὑμῶν. εὑρισκόμεθα δὲ καὶ ψευδο-
of us, worthless and also the faith of you. we are found And also false
2316 3754 3140 2596 2316 3754
μάρτυρες τοῦ Θεοῦ, ὅτι ἐμαρτυρήσαμεν κατὰ τοῦ Θεοῦ ὅτι
witnesses of God, because we witnessed as to God that
1453 5547 3739/3756 1453 1512 686 3498 3756
16 ἤγειρε τὸν Χριστόν, ὃν οὐκ ἤγειρεν, εἴπερ ἄρα νεκροὶ οὐκ
He raised Christ, whom not He raised if then dead ones not
1453 1487/1063 3498 3756 1453 3761 5547
ἐγείρονται. εἰ γὰρ νεκροὶ οὐκ ἐγείρονται, οὐδὲ Χριστὸς
are raised. if For dead ones not are raised, neither Christ
1453 1487 5547 3756 1453 3152 4102
17 ἐγήγερται· εἰ δὲ Χριστὸς οὐκ ἐγήγερται, ματαία ἡ πίστις
has been raised; if but Christ not has been raised, foolish the faith
5216/2089/2075/1722 266 5216 686 2837
18 ὑμῶν· ἔτι ἐστὲ ἐν ταῖς ἁμαρτίαις ὑμῶν. ἄρα καὶ οἱ κοιμη-
of you; still you are in the sins of you. Then also those having
1722 5547 622 1487/1722 2222 5026 1679
19 θέντες ἐν Χριστῷ ἀπώλοντο. εἰ ἐν τῇ ζωῇ ταύτῃ ἠλπικότες
slept in Christ were lost. If in life this having hoped
2070/1722 5547 3440 1652 3956 444
ἐσμὲν ἐν Χριστῷ μόνον, ἐλεεινότεροι πάντων ἀνθρώπων
we are in Christ only, more miserable of all men
2070
ἐσμέν.
we are.
3570 5547 1453 1537 3498 536
20 Νυνὶ δὲ Χριστὸς ἐγήγερται ἐκ νεκρῶν, ἀπαρχὴ τῶν
now But Christ has been raised from (the) dead, firstfruit of those
2837 1096 1894/1063/1223/ 444 2288
21 κεκοιμημένων ἐγένετο. ἐπειδὴ γὰρ δι' ἀνθρώπου ὁ θάνατος,
having fallen asleep He became. since For through man (is) death,
1223 444 386 3498 5618 1063/1722
22 καὶ δι' ἀνθρώπου ἀνάστασις νεκρῶν. ὥσπερ γὰρ ἐν τῷ
and through a Man a resurrection of (the) dead. as For in
76 3956 599 3779 1722 5547
Ἀδὰμ πάντες ἀποθνήσκουσιν, οὕτω καὶ ἐν τῷ Χριστῷ
Adam all die, so also in Christ
3956 2227 1538 1722 2398 5001
23 πάντες ζωοποιηθήσονται. ἕκαστος δὲ ἐν τῷ ἰδίῳ τάγματι·
all will be made alive. each But in the own order:
536 5547 1899 5547 1722 3952 848
ἀπαρχὴ Χριστός, ἔπειτα οἱ Χριστοῦ ἐν τῇ παρουσίᾳ αὐτοῦ.
the firstfruit Christ, afterward those of Christ in the coming of Him.
1534 5056 3752 3860 932 2316
24 εἶτα τὸ τέλος, ὅταν παραδῷ τὴν βασιλείαν τῷ Θεῷ καὶ
Then the end — when He delivers the kingdom to God, even

He makes to cease all rule and all authority and power —[25]for it is right for Him to reign until He puts all the enemies under His feet; [26]*the* last enemy made to cease is death. [27]For He subjected all things under His feet; but when He says that all things have been subjected, *it is* plain that *it* excepts Him who has subjected all things to Him. [28]But when all things are subjected to Him, then the Son Himself also will be subjected to the *One* who has subjected all things to Him, that God may be all things in all.

[29]Otherwise, what will they do, those being baptized on behalf of the dead? If *the* dead are not at all raised, why indeed are they baptized on behalf of the dead? [30]Why are we also in danger every hour? [31]Day by day I die, by your glorying, which I have in Christ Jesus our Lord. [32]If according to man I fought with beasts in Ephesus, what the profit to me if *the* dead are not raised?—"Let us eat and drink, for tomorrow we die." [33]Do not be led astray; bad companionships ruin good habits. [34]Be aroused ighteously, and do not sin; for some have ignorance of God. I speak shame to you.

[35]But someone will say, How are the dead raised? And with what body do they come?
[36]Foolish one! What you sow is not made alive unless it dies. [37]And what you sow, you do not sow the body that *is* going to be, but a bare grain—it may be of wheat, or of some of the rest—[38]and God gives it a body according as He willed, and to each of the

3962 3752 2673 3956 746 3956 1849
πατρί, ὅταν καταργήσῃ πᾶσαν ἀρχὴν καὶ πᾶσαν ἐξουσίαν
the Father; when He abolishes all rule and all authority
1411 1163/1063 846 935 891 3756/302/5087
25 καὶ δύναμιν. δεῖ γὰρ αὐτὸν βασιλεύειν, ἄχρις οὗ ἂν θῇ
and power — it is right For Him to reign until He puts
3956 2190 5259 4228 848 2078
26 πάντας τοὺς ἐχθροὺς ὑπὸ τοὺς πόδας αὐτοῦ. ἔσχατος
all the enemies under the feet of Him—(the) last
2190 2673 2288 3956 1063 5293 5259
27 ἐχθρὸς καταργεῖται ὁ θάνατος. Πάντα γὰρ ὑπέταξεν ὑπὸ
enemy is abolished, death— all things for He subjected under
4228 848 3752 2036 3754 3956 5293
τοὺς πόδας αὐτοῦ. ὅταν δὲ εἴπῃ ὅτι Πάντα ὑποτέτακται,
the feet of Him. when But He says that all things have been subjected.
1212/3754 1623 5293 846 3956 3752
28 δῆλον ὅτι ἐκτὸς τοῦ ὑποτάξαντος αὐτῷ τὰ πάντα. ὅταν δὲ
(it is) plain that excepted the (One) having subjected to Him all things. when But
5293 846 3956 5119 848 5207 5293
ὑποταγῇ αὐτῷ τὰ πάντα, τότε καὶ αὐτὸς ὁ υἱὸς ὑποταγή-
is subjected to Him all things, then also Himself, the Son, will be sub-
5293 846 3956 2443 2316
σεται τῷ ὑποτάξαντι αὐτῷ τὰ πάντα, ἵνα ᾖ ὁ Θεὸς τὰ
jected to the (One) having subjected to Him all things, that may be God
3956/1722/3956
πάντα ἐν πᾶσιν.
all things in all.
1893/5101/ 4160 907 5228 3498
29 Ἐπεὶ τί ποιήσουσιν οἱ βαπτιζόμενοι ὑπὲρ τῶν νεκρῶν;
Otherwise what will they do, those being baptized on behalf of the dead?
1487/3654/3498/3756 1453 5101 907 5228
εἰ ὅλως νεκροὶ οὐκ ἐγείρονται, τί καὶ βαπτίζονται ὑπὲρ τῶν
If not at all dead ones not are raised, why indeed are they baptized for the
3498 5101 2249 2793 3956 5610 2596 2250
30 νεκρῶν; τί καὶ ἡμεῖς κινδυνεύομεν πᾶσαν ὥραν; καθ' ἡμέραν
31 dead; why also we are in danger every hour? Day by day
599 3513 5212 2746 3739/2192/1722/ 5547
ἀποθνήσκω, νὴ τὴν ὑμετέραν καύχησιν, ἣν ἔχω ἐν Χριστῷ
I die, by your boasting, which I have in Christ
2424 2962 2257/1487/2596 444 2341
32 Ἰησοῦ τῷ Κυρίῳ ἡμῶν. εἰ κατὰ ἄνθρωπον ἐθηριομάχησα
Jesus the Lord of us. If according to man I fought with beasts
1722 2181 5101/3427 3786 1487 3498 3756 1453
ἐν Ἐφέσῳ τί μοι τὸ ὄφελος, εἰ νεκροὶ οὐκ ἐγείρονται;
in Ephesus, what to me the profit? If dead ones not are raised,
5315 4095 839 1063 599 3361 4105
33 φάγωμεν καὶ πίωμεν, αὔριον γὰρ ἀποθνήσκομεν. μὴ πλανᾶ-
let us eat and drink, tomorrow for we die. not Be led
5351 2239 5543 3657 2556 1594 1345
34 σθε· Φθείρουσιν ἤθη χρήσθ' ὁμιλίαι κακαί. ἐκνήψατε δικαίως,
astray, will corrupt habits good companionships bad. Be aroused righteously,
3361 264 56 1063 2316 5100 2192 4314
καὶ μὴ ἁμαρτάνετε· ἀγνωσίαν γὰρ Θεοῦ τινὲς ἔχουσι· πρὸς
and not sin; ignorance for of God some have; for
1791 5213 3004
ἐντροπὴν ὑμῖν λέγω.
shame to you I speak.
235 2046/5100/4459/ 1453 3498 4169 4983
35 Ἀλλ' ἐρεῖ τις, Πῶς ἐγείρονται οἱ νεκροί; ποίῳ δὲ σώματι
But will say someone, How are raised the dead? with what And body
2064 878 4771/3739/ 4687 3756 2227 =3362=
36 ἔρχονται; ἄφρον, σὺ ὃ σπείρεις, οὐ ζωοποιεῖται, ἐὰν μὴ
do they come? Foolish one, you what sow, not is made alive unless
599 3739 4687 3756 4983 1096 4687
37 ἀποθάνῃ· καὶ ὃ σπείρεις, οὐ τὸ σῶμα τὸ γενησόμενον σπεί-
it dies; and what you sow, not the body going to become you
235 1131 2848 1487 5177 4621/2228/5100
ρεις, ἀλλὰ γυμνὸν κόκκον, εἰ τύχοι, σίτου ἤ τινος τῶν
sow, but a naked grain it may be of wheat or some of the
3062 2316 846 1325 4983 2531 2309
38 λοιπῶν· ὁ δὲ Θεὸς αὐτῷ δίδωσι σῶμα καθὼς ἠθέλησε, καὶ
rest; but God to it gives a body as He desired, and

seeds its own body. [39]Not every flesh *is* the same flesh, but one flesh of men, and another flesh of beasts, and another of fish, and another of birds. [40]And *there are* heavenly bodies, and earthly bodies. But the glory of the heavenly *is* truly different, and that of the earthly different; [41]one glory of *the* sun, and another glory of *the* moon, and another glory of *the* stars; for a star differs from star in glory. [42]So also the resurrection of the dead. It is sown in corruption; it is raised in incorruption. [43]It is sown in dishonor, it is raised in glory. It is sown in weakness, it is raised in power. [44]It is sown a natural body, it is raised a spiritual body; there is a natural body, and there is a spiritual body. [45]So also it has been written, "The first man, Adam, became a living soul," the last Adam *became* a life-giving Spirit.

[46]But not the spiritual first, but the natural; afterward the spiritual. [47]The first man *was* out of earth, earthy. The second Man *was* the Lord out of Heaven. [48]Such the earthy man, such also the earthy ones. And such the heavenly Man, such also the heavenly ones. [49]And as we bore the image of the earthy man, we shall also bear the image of the heavenly Man.

[50]And I say this, brothers, that flesh and blood is not able to inherit *the* kingdom of God, nor does corruption inherit incorruption. [51]Behold, I speak a mystery to you: indeed we shall not all sleep, but we shall all be changed, [52]in a moment, in a glance of an eye, at the last trumpet; for a trumpet

1538 4690 2398 4983 3756 3956 4561
39 ἑκάστῳ τῶν σπερμάτων τὸ ἴδιον σῶμα. οὐ πᾶσα σὰρξ ἡ
to each of the seeds the own body. (is) not All flesh the
846 4561 235 243 3303 4561 444 243 4561
αὐτὴ σάρξ· ἀλλὰ ἄλλη μὲν σὰρξ ἀνθρώπων, ἄλλη δὲ σὰρξ
same flesh, but other indeed flesh of men, other and flesh
2934 243 2486 243 4421 4983
40 κτηνῶν, ἄλλη δὲ ἰχθύων, ἄλλη δὲ πτηνῶν. καὶ σώματα
of animals, other and of fish other and of birds. And (are) bodies
2032 4983 1919 235 2087/3303 2032
ἐπουράνια, καὶ σώματα ἐπίγεια· ἀλλ᾽ ἑτέρα μὲν ἡ τῶν ἐπου-
heavenly, and bodies earthly, but other (is) truly the of the
1391 2087 1919 243 1391 2246
41 ρανίων δόξα, ἑτέρα δὲ ἡ τῶν ἐπιγείων. ἄλλη δόξα ἡλίου, καὶ
heavenly glory, other and that of the earthly; other glory of the sun, and
243 1391 4582 243 1391 792 792 1063
ἄλλη δόξα σελήνης, καὶ ἄλλη δόξα ἀστέρων· ἀστὴρ γὰρ
other glory of the moon, and others glory of (the) stars; star for
792 1308 1722/1391 3779 386
42 ἀστέρος διαφέρει ἐν δόξῃ. οὕτω καὶ ἡ ἀνάστασις τῶν
from star differs in glory. So also the resurrection of the
3498 4687 1722 5356 1453 1722 861 4687
νεκρῶν. σπείρεται ἐν φθορᾷ, ἐγείρεται ἐν ἀφθαρσίᾳ· σπεί-
dead. It is sown in corruption; it is raised in incorruption; it is
1722 819 1453 1722/1391 4687 1722 769
43 ρεται ἐν ἀτιμίᾳ, ἐγείρεται ἐν δόξῃ· σπείρεται ἐν ἀσθενείᾳ,
sown in dishonor; it is raised in glory; it is sown in weakness;
1453 1722 1411 4687 4983 5591 1453
44 ἐγείρεται ἐν δυνάμει· σπείρεται σῶμα ψυχικόν, ἐγείρεται
it is raised in power; it is sown a body natural; it is raised
4983 4152 2076 4983 5591 2076 4983
σῶμα πνευματικόν. ἔστι σῶμα ψυχικόν, καὶ ἔστι σῶμα
body spiritual. There is a body natural, and there is a body
4152 3779 1125 1096 4413
45 πνευματικόν. οὕτω καὶ γέγραπται, Ἐγένετο ὁ πρῶτος
spiritual. So also it has been written: became The first
444 76 1519 5590 2198 2078 76 1519
ἄνθρωπος Ἀδὰμ εἰς ψυχὴν ζῶσαν. ὁ ἔσχατος Ἀδὰμ εἰς
man Adam soul a living; the last Adam
4151 2227 235 3756 4412 4152 235
46 πνεῦμα ζωοποιοῦν. ἀλλ᾽ οὐ πρῶτον τὸ πνευματικόν, ἀλλὰ
Spirit a life-giving. But not firstly the spiritual (body), but
5591 1899 4152 4413 444 1537
47 τὸ ψυχικόν, ἔπειτα τὸ πνευματικόν. ὁ πρῶτος ἄνθρωπος ἐκ
the natural; afterward the spiritual. The first man (was) out of
1093 5517 1208 444 2962 1537 3772
γῆς, χοϊκός· ὁ δεύτερος ἄνθρωπος, ὁ Κύριος ἐξ οὐρανοῦ.
earth, earthy; the second Man the Lord out of Heaven.
3634 5517 5108 5517 3634 2032
48 οἷος ὁ χοϊκός, τοιοῦτοι καὶ οἱ χοϊκοί· καὶ οἷος ὁ ἐπουράνιος,
Such the earthy, such also the earthy ones; and such the heavenly Man,
5108 man 2032 2531 5409 1504
49 τοιοῦτοι καὶ οἱ ἐπουράνιοι· καὶ καθὼς ἐφορέσαμεν τὴν εἰκόνα
such also the heavenly ones. And as we bore the image
5517 5409 1504 2032
τοῦ χοϊκοῦ, φορέσομεν καὶ τὴν εἰκόνα τοῦ ἐπουρανίου.
of the earthy man, we shall bear also the image of the heavenly Man.
5124 5346 80 3754 4561 129 932
50 Τοῦτο δέ φημι, ἀδελφοί, ὅτι σὰρξ καὶ αἷμα βασιλείαν
this And I say, brothers, that flesh and blood (the) kingdom
2316 2816 3756 1410 3761 5356 861
Θεοῦ κληρονομῆσαι οὐ δύνανται, οὐδὲ ἡ φθορὰ τὴν ἀφθαρ-
of God inherit not is able to, nor corruption incorrup-
2816 2400 3466 5213 3004 3956 3303/3756
51 σίαν κληρονομεῖ. ἰδού, μυστήριον ὑμῖν λέγω· Πάντες μὲν οὐ
tion inherit. Behold, a mystery to you I tell: all indeed not
2837 3956 236 1722 823 1722 4493
52 κοιμηθησόμεθα, πάντες δὲ ἀλλαγησόμεθα, ἐν ἀτόμῳ, ἐν ῥιπῇ
we shall fall asleep, all but we shall be changed, in a moment, in a glance
3788 1722 2078 4536 4537 1063
ὀφθαλμοῦ, ἐν τῇ ἐσχάτῃ σάλπιγγι· σαλπίσει γάρ, καὶ οἱ
of an eye, at the last trumpet; will trumpet for, and the

will sound, and the dead will be raised incorruptible, and we shall all be changed. [53]For this corruptible must put on incorruption, and this mortal must put on immortality. [54]But when this corruptible shall put on incorruption, and this mortal shall put on immortality, then will take place the word that has been written, "Death was swallowed up in victory. [55]O death, where *is your* sting? Hades, where *is your* victory?" [56]Now the sting of death *is* sin, and the power of sin *is* the law; [57]but thanks *be* to God, He giving us the victory through our Lord Jesus Christ! [58]So that, my beloved brothers, *you* be firm, unmoveable, abounding in the work of the Lord always, knowing that your labor is not without fruit in *the* Lord.

3498 1453 862 2249 236
νεκροὶ ἐγερθήσονται ἄφθαρτοι, καὶ ἡμεῖς ἀλλαγησόμεθα.
dead will be raised incorruptible and we shall be changed.
1163/1063 5349 5124 1746 861
53 δεῖ γὰρ τὸ φθαρτὸν τοῦτο ἐνδύσασθαι ἀφθαρσίαν, καὶ τὸ
must For corruptible this put on incorruption, and
2349 5124 1746 110 3752 5349
54 θνητὸν τοῦτο ἐνδύσασθαι ἀθανασίαν. ὅταν δὲ τὸ φθαρτὸν
mortal this put on immortality. when And corruptible
5124 1746 861 2349 5124 1746
τοῦτο ἐνδύσηται ἀφθαρσίαν καὶ τὸ θνητὸν τοῦτο ἐνδύσηται
this shall put on incorruption, and mortal this put on
110 5119 1096 3056 1125 2666
ἀθανασίαν, τότε γενήσεται ὁ λόγος ὁ γεγραμμένος, Κατε-
immortality, then will occur the word having been written: was
2288 1519/3534 4226/4675 2288 2759 4226
55 πόθη ὁ θάνατος εἰς νῖκος. Ποῦ σου, θάνατε, τὸ κέντρον ; ποῦ
swallowed Death in victory. Where of you, death the sting; where
4675/86 3534 2759 2288 266
56 σου, ᾅδη, τὸ νῖκος ; τὸ δὲ κέντρον τοῦ θανάτου ἡ ἁμαρτία· ἡ
of you Hades the victory? the And sting of death (is) sin,
1411 266 3551 2316 5485
57 δὲ δύναμις τῆς ἁμαρτίας ὁ νόμος· τῷ δὲ Θεῷ χάρις τῷ
and the power of sin (is) the law; but to God thanks, He
1325 2254 3534 1223 2962 2257 2424 5547
διδόντι ἡμῖν τὸ νῖκος διὰ τοῦ Κυρίου ἡμῶν Ἰησοῦ Χριστοῦ.
giving to us the victory through the Lord of us, Jesus Christ.
5620 80 3450 27 1476 1096 277
58 ὥστε, ἀδελφοί μου ἀγαπητοί, ἑδραῖοι γίνεσθε, ἀμετακίνητοι,
So as, brothers of me, beloved, firm be, unmoveable,
4052 1722 2041 2962 3842 1492 3754
περισσεύοντες ἐν τῷ ἔργῳ τοῦ Κυρίου πάντοτε, εἰδότες ὅτι
abounding in the work of the Lord always, knowing that
2873 5216 3756/2076/2756/1722/2962
ὁ κόπος ὑμῶν οὐκ ἔστι κενὸς ἐν Κυρίῳ.
the labor of you not is fruitless in (the) Lord.

CHAPTER 16

CHAPTER 16

[1]And about the collection for the saints, as I charged the churches of Galatia, so also you do. [2]On the first of a week, let each of you put by himself, storing up whatever he is prospered, that there not be then collections when I come. [3]And when I arrive, whomever you approve, through these epistles, I will send to carry your grace to Jerusalem. [4]And if it is suitable for me to go also, they shall go with me. [5]But I will come to you when I go through Macedonia. For I am going through Macedonia. [6]And possibly I will stay with you, or even spend the winter, that you may set me forward wherever I may go. [7]For I do not desire to see

4012 3048 1519 40 5618 1299
1 Περὶ δὲ τῆς λογίας τῆς εἰς τοὺς ἁγίους, ὥσπερ διέταξα ταῖς
about And the collection for the saints, as I charged the
1577 1053 3779 5210 4160 2596
2 ἐκκλησίας τῆς Γαλατίας, οὕτω καὶ ὑμεῖς ποιήσατε. κατὰ
churches of Galatia, so also you do. Every
3391 4521 1538 5216 3844 1438 5087 2343
μίαν σαββάτων ἕκαστος ὑμῶν παρ' ἑαυτῷ τιθέτω, θησαυ-
one of a week each of you by himself let him put, storing
3748/302 2137 2443/3361 3752 2064 5119 3048
ῥίζων ὅ τι ἂν εὐοδῶται, ἵνα μή, ὅταν ἔλθω, τότε λογίαι
up whatever he is prospered, that not when I come then collections
1096 3752 3854 3739/1437/ 1381 1223
3 γίνωνται. ὅταν δὲ παραγένωμαι, οὓς ἐὰν δοκιμάσητε δι'
there be. when But I arrive, whomever you approve, through
1992 5128 3992 667 5485 5216/1519
ἐπιστολῶν, τούτους πέμψω ἀπενεγκεῖν τὴν χάριν ὑμῶν εἰς
epistles these I will send to carry the grace of you to
2419 1437 5600/514 2504 4198 4862/1698
4 Ἱερουσαλήμ· ἐὰν δὲ ᾖ ἄξιον τοῦ κἀμὲ πορεύεσθαι, σὺν ἐμοὶ
Jerusalem. if But it is suitable me also to go, with me
4198 2064 4314 5209 3752 3109
5 πορεύσονται. ἐλεύσομαι δὲ πρὸς ὑμᾶς, ὅταν Μακεδονίαν
they shall go. I will come And to you when Macadonia
1330 3109 1063 1330 4314 5209 5177
6 διέλθω· Μακεδονίαν γὰρ διέρχομαι· πρὸς ὑμᾶς δὲ τυχὸν
I go through. Macedonia For I am going through, with you and possibly
3887 2228 3914 2443/5210/3165/ 4311 3757
παραμενῶ, ἢ καὶ παραχειμάσω, ἵνα ὑμεῖς με προπέμψητε οὗ
I will stay, or even spend the winter, that you me may set forward
1437 4198 3756/2309/1063/5209 737/1722 3938 1492
7 ἐὰν πορεύωμαι. οὐ θέλω γὰρ ὑμᾶς ἄρτι ἐν παρόδῳ ἰδεῖν·
wherever I may go. not I desire For you yet in passage to see;

you now in passage, but I am hoping to remain some time with you, if the Lord permits. 8But I will remain in Ephesus until Pentecost. 9For a door opened to me, great and effective; and many *are* opposing.

10But if Timothy comes, see that he is with you without fear; for he works the work of the Lord, even as I. 11Then do not let any despise him, but set him forward in peace, that he may come to me; for I am waiting for him with the brothers. 12And concerning the brother Apollos, I much urged him that he come to you with the brothers; but it was not altogether *his* will that he come now. But he will come when he has opportunity.

13Watch! Stand fast in the faith! Be men! Be strong! 14Let all your things be in love.

15But, brothers, I exhort you. You know the house of Stephanas, that it is the firstfruit of Achaia, and they appointed themselves to ministry to the saints. 16*See* that you also may submit to such ones, and to everyone working and laboring with *me*. 17And I rejoice at the coming of Stephanas, and of Fortunatus and Achaicus, because these supplied your lack. 18For they refreshed my spirit and yours. Then recognize such ones.

19The churches of Asia greet you. Aquila and Priscilla much greet you in *the* Lord, with the church in their house. 20The brothers all greet you. Greet one another with a holy kiss.

21The greeting with my hand, Paul. 22If anyone does not love the Lord

1679 5550 5100 1961 4314 5209/1437 2962
ἐλπίζω δὲ χρόνον τινὰ ἐπιμεῖναι πρὸς ὑμᾶς, ἐὰν ὁ Κύριος
I am hoping and time some to remain with you, if the Lord
2010 1961 1722 2181 2193 4005 2374
8 ἐπιτρέπῃ. ἐπιμενῶ δὲ ἐν Ἐφέσῳ ἕως τῆς Πεντηκοστῆς· θύρα
permits. I will remain But in Ephesus until Pentecost, a door
1063/3427 455 3173 1756 480 4183
9 γάρ μοι ἀνέῳγε μεγάλη καὶ ἐνεργής, καὶ ἀντικείμενοι πολλοί.
for to me opened great and effective, and (are) opposing many.
1437 2064 5095 991 2443 870 1096 4314
10 Ἐὰν δὲ ἔλθῃ Τιμόθεος, βλέπετε ἵνα ἀφόβως γένηται πρὸς
if But comes Timothy, see that without fear he is with
5209 1063 2041 2962 2036 5613 1473 3361/5100
11 ὑμᾶς· τὸ γὰρ ἔργον Κυρίου ἐργάζεται ὡς καὶ ἐγώ. μή τις
you, the for work of (the) Lord he works, as also I. Let not any
3767 846 1848 4311 846/1722/ 1515 2443
οὖν αὐτὸν ἐξουθενήσῃ· προπέμψατε δὲ αὐτὸν ἐν εἰρήνῃ, ἵνα
then him despise, set forward but him in peace, that
2064 4314 3165 1551 1063 846 3326 80 4012
12 ἔλθῃ πρός με· ἐκδέχομαι γὰρ αὐτὸν μετὰ τῶν ἀδελφῶν. περὶ
he come to me; I am awaiting for him with the brothers. about
625 80 4183 3870 846 2443
δὲ Ἀπολλὼ τοῦ ἀδελφοῦ, πολλὰ παρεκάλεσα αὐτὸν ἵνα
And Apollos the brother, much I besought him that
2064 4314 5209 3326 80 3843 3756/2258
ἔλθῃ πρὸς ὑμᾶς μετὰ τῶν ἀδελφῶν· καὶ πάντως οὐκ ἦν
he come to you with the brothers, and altogether not it was
2307 2443 3568 /2064 2064 3752 2119
θέλημα ἵνα νῦν ἔλθῃ, ἐλεύσεται δὲ ὅταν εὐκαιρήσῃ
(his) will that now he come; he will come but when he has opportunity.
1127 4739 1722 4102 407 2901
13 Γρηγορεῖτε, στήκετε ἐν τῇ πίστει, ἀνδρίζεσθε, κραταιοῦ-
Watch! Stand in the faith! Be men! Be strong!
3956 5216/1722/ 26 1096
14 σθε. πάντα ὑμῶν ἐν ἀγάπῃ γινέσθω.
All things of you in love let it be.
3870 5209 80 1492 3614 4734
15 Παρακαλῶ δὲ ὑμᾶς, ἀδελφοί (οἴδατε τὴν οἰκίαν Στεφανᾶ,
I beseech And you, brothers, you know the house of Stephanas,
3754 2076 536 882 1519 1248 40
ὅτι ἐστὶν ἀπαρχὴ τῆς Ἀχαΐας, καὶ εἰς διακονίαν τοῖς ἁγίοις
that it is firstfruit of Achaia, and to ministry to the saints
5021 1438 2443 5210 5293 5108
16 ἔταξαν ἑαυτούς), ἵνα καὶ ὑμεῖς ὑποτάσσησθε τοῖς τοιούτοις,
they appointed themselves, that also you may submit to such ones,
3956 4903 2872 5463 1909
17 καὶ παντὶ τῷ συνεργοῦντι καὶ κοπιῶντι. χαίρω δὲ ἐπὶ τῇ
and to everyone working with (me) and laboring. I rejoice And at the
3952 4734 5415 883 3754
παρουσίᾳ Στεφανᾶ καὶ Φουρτουνάτου καὶ Ἀχαϊκοῦ ὅτι τὸ
presence of Stephanas, and of Fortunatus, and of Achaicus, that
5216 5303 3778 378 373 1063 1699
18 ὑμῶν ὑστέρημα οὗτοι ἀνεπλήρωσαν. ἀνέπαυσαν γὰρ τὸ ἐμὸν
your lack these supplied; they refreshed for my
4151 5216 1921 3767 5108
πνεῦμα καὶ τὸ ὑμῶν· ἐπιγινώσκετε οὖν τοὺς τοιούτους.
spirit and of you. Recognize, therefore, such ones.
782 5209 1577 773 782
19 Ἀσπάζονται ὑμᾶς αἱ ἐκκλησίαι τῆς Ἀσίας· ἀσπάζονται
Greet you the churches of Asia Greets
5209/1722/2962 4183 207 4252 4862 2596
ὑμᾶς ἐν Κυρίῳ πολλὰ Ἀκύλας καὶ Πρίσκιλλα, σὺν τῇ κατ'
you in (the) Lord much Aquila and Priscilla, with the in
3624 848 1577 782 5209 80 3956
20 οἶκον αὐτῶν ἐκκλησίᾳ. ἀσπάζονται ὑμᾶς οἱ ἀδελφοὶ πάντες.
(the) house of them church. Greet you the brothers all.
782 240 1722 5370 40
ἀσπάσασθε ἀλλήλους ἐν φιλήματι ἁγίῳ.
Greet one another with kiss a holy.
783 1699 5495 3972 =1536=3756/5388
21 Ὁ ἀσπασμὸς τῇ ἐμῇ χειρὶ Παύλου. εἴ τις οὐ φιλεῖ τὸν
22 The greeting with my hand, Paul. If anyone not love the

Jesus Christ, let him be a curse. The Lord comes!

[23]The grace of the Lord Jesus Christ *be* with you. [24]My love *be* with all of you in Christ Jesus. Amen.

2962 2424 5547 2277 331 =3134= 5485
23 Κύριον Ἰησοῦν Χριστόν, ἤτω ἀνάθεμα. Μαρὰν ἀθά. ἡ χάρις
Lord Jesus Christ, let him be a curse. The Lord comes. The grace
2962 2424 5547 3326 5216 24 3450 3326
24 τοῦ Κυρίου Ἰησοῦ Χριστοῦ μεθ' ὑμῶν. ἡ ἀγάπη μου μετὰ
of the Lord Jesus Christ (be) with you. The love of me (be) with
3956 5216/1722 5547 2424 281
πάντων ὑμῶν ἐν Χριστῷ Ἰησοῦ. ἀμήν.
all of you in Christ Jesus. Amen.

ΠΑΥΛΟΥ ΤΟΥ ΑΠΟΣΤΟΛΟΥ
PAUL THE APOSTLE

Η ΠΡΟΣ
THE TO

ΚΟΡΙΝΘΙΟΥΣ
(THE) CORINTHIANS

ΕΠΙΣΤΟΛΗ ΔΕΥΤΕΡΑ
EPISTLE SECOND
CORINTHIANS

THE SECOND EPISTLE TO THE CORINTHIANS
A LITERAL TRANSLATION OF THE BIBLE

CHAPTER 1

[1]Paul, an apostle of Jesus Christ, through the will of God, and Timothy the brother, to the church of God being in Corinth, with all the saints being in all Achaia, [2]Grace to you and peace from God our Father and *the* Lord Jesus Christ.

[3]Blessed *be* the God and Father of our Lord Jesus Christ, the Father of compassions and God of all comfort, [4]the *One* comforting us on all our affliction, through the comfort by which we ourselves are comforted by God. [5]Because the sufferings of Christ abound in us, so also our comfort abounds through Christ. [6]But if we are afflicted, *it is* for your comfort and salvation, being worked out in *the* endurance of the same sufferings which we also suffer. If we are comforted, *it is* for your comfort and salvation; [7]and our hope for you *is* certain, knowing that even as you are sharers of the sufferings, so also of the comfort.

CHAPTER 1

3972 652 2424 5547 1223 2307 2316
1 Παῦλος ἀπόστολος Ἰησοῦ Χριστοῦ διὰ θελήματος Θεοῦ,
Paul an apostle of Jesus Christ through (the) will of God,
5095 80 1577 2316 5607/1722
καὶ Τιμόθεος ὁ ἀδελφός, τῇ ἐκκλησίᾳ τοῦ Θεοῦ τῇ οὔσῃ ἐν
and Timothy the brother to the church of God being in
2882 4862 40 3956 5607/1722/3650 882
Κορίνθῳ, σὺν τοῖς ἁγίοις πᾶσι τοῖς οὖσιν ἐν ὅλῃ τῇ Ἀχαΐᾳ·
Corinth, with the saints all being in all Achaia:
5485 5213 1515 575 2316 3962 2257 2962
2 χάρις ὑμῖν καὶ εἰρήνη ἀπὸ Θεοῦ πατρὸς ἡμῶν καὶ Κυρίου
Grace to you and peace from God (the) Father of us and (the) Lord
2424 5547
Ἰησοῦ Χριστοῦ.
Jesus Christ.
2128 2316 3962 2962 2257 2424
3 Εὐλογητὸς ὁ Θεὸς καὶ πατὴρ τοῦ Κυρίου ἡμῶν Ἰησοῦ
Blessed (be) the God and Father of the Lord of us, Jesus
5547 3962 3628 2316 3956 3874
Χριστοῦ ὁ πατὴρ τῶν οἰκτιρμῶν καὶ Θεὸς πάσης παρα-
Christ, the Father of compassions and the God of all com-
3870 2248/1909 3956 2347 2257
4 κλήσεως, ὁ παρακαλῶν ἡμᾶς ἐπὶ πάσῃ τῇ θλίψει ἡμῶν,
fort, the (One) comforting us on all the trouble of us,
1519 1410 2248 3870 1722 3956 2347 1223
εἰς τὸ δύνασθαι ἡμᾶς παρακαλεῖν τοὺς ἐν πάσῃ θλίψει, διὰ
for to be able us to comfort those in every trouble, through
3874 3739 3870 848 5259 2316
τῆς παρακλήσεως ἧς παρακαλούμεθα αὐτοὶ ὑπὸ τοῦ Θεοῦ.
the comfort of which we are comforted ourselves by God.
3754 2531 4052 3804 5547 1519 2248
5 ὅτι καθὼς περισσεύει τὰ παθήματα τοῦ Χριστοῦ εἰς ἡμᾶς,
Because as abounds the sufferings of Christ in us,
3779 1223 5547 4052 3874 2257 1535
6 οὕτω διὰ Χριστοῦ περισσεύει καὶ ἡ παράκλησις ἡμῶν. εἴτε
so through Christ abounds also the comfort of us. whether
2346 5228 5216 3874 4992
δὲ θλιβόμεθα, ὑπὲρ τῆς ὑμῶν παρακλήσεως καὶ σωτηρίας,
And we are troubled for the of you comfort and salvation
1754 1722 5281 848 3804 3739
τῆς ἐνεργουμένης ἐν ὑπομονῇ τῶν αὐτῶν παθημάτων ὧν
being worked out in (the) endurance of the same sufferings which
2249 3958 1535 3870 5228 5216
καὶ ἡμεῖς πάσχομεν· εἴτε παρακαλούμεθα, ὑπὲρ τῆς ὑμῶν
also we suffer, whether we are comforted (it is) for your
3874 4991 1680 2257 949 5228
7 παρακλήσεως καὶ σωτηρίας· καὶ ἡ ἐλπὶς ἡμῶν βεβαία ὑπὲρ
comfort and salvation; and the hope of us (is) certain for
5216 1492 3754 5618 3844 2075 3804
ὑμῶν· εἰδότες ὅτι ὥσπερ κοινωνοί ἐστε τῶν παθημάτων,
you, knowing that as sharers you are of the sufferings,

[8]For, brothers, we do not want you to be ignorant as to our affliction having happened to us in Asia, that we were excessively pressed down beyond *our* power, so as for us even to despair of living. [9]But we ourselves have the sentence of death in ourselves, that we should not trust on ourselves, but on God, the *One* rising the dead; [10]who delivered us from so great a death, and does deliver; in whom we have hope that He will still deliver *us*, [11]you also laboring together for us in prayer, that the gracious gift by many persons be *the cause of* thanksgiving through many for us.

[12]For our glorying is this, the testimony of our conscience, that we had our conduct in the world in simplicity and sincerity of God, not in fleshly wisdom, but in the grace of God, and more abundantly toward you. [13]For we do not write other things to you than what you read, or even recognize; and I hope that you will recognize even to *the* end, [14]even as you also *in* part recognized us, that we are your glorying, even as also you *are* ours in the day of the Lord Jesus.

[15]And in this confidence, I purposed to come to you before now, that you might have a second benefit, [16]and to go through you into Macedonia, and again from Macedonia to come to you; and to be set forward by you to Judea. [17]Then purposing this, did I indeed use lightness? Or what I purposed, did I purpose according to flesh, that may be with me yes, yes, and no,

3779 3874 3756/1063/ 2309 5209 50
8 οὕτω καὶ τῆς παρακλήσεως. οὐ γὰρ θέλομεν ὑμᾶς ἀγνοεῖν,
so also of the comfort. not For we desire you to be ignorant
80 5228 2347 2257 1096 2254/1722
ἀδελφοί, ὑπὲρ τῆς θλίψεως ἡμῶν τῆς γενομένης ἡμῖν ἐν τῇ
brothers, as to the trouble of us having happened to us in
773 3754/2596 5236 916 5228 1411 5620
Ἀσίᾳ, ὅτι καθ' ὑπερβολὴν ἐβαρήθημεν ὑπὲρ δύναμιν, ὥστε
Asia that – excessively – we were burdened beyond power, so as
1820 2248 2198 235 848 1722 1438
9 ἐξαπορηθῆναι ἡμᾶς καὶ τοῦ ζῆν. ἀλλὰ αὐτοὶ ἐν ἑαυτοῖς τὸ
to despair us, even to live. But (our)selves in ourselves the
610 2288 4506 2443/3361 3982 5600
ἀπόκριμα τοῦ θανάτου ἐσχήκαμεν, ἵνα μὴ πεποιθότες ὦμεν
sentence of death we have, that not should trust we
1909 1438 235/1909 2316 1453 3498 3739
10 ἐφ' ἑαυτοῖς, ἀλλ' ἐπὶ τῷ Θεῷ τῷ ἐγείροντι τοὺς νεκρούς· ὃς
on ourselves, but on God, the (One) raising the dead; who
1537 5082 2288 4506 2248 4506 1519/3739
ἐκ τηλικούτου θανάτου ἐρρύσατο ἡμᾶς καὶ ῥύεται, εἰς ὃν
out of so great a death delivered us and does deliver, in whom
1679 3754 2089 4506 4943 5216
11 ἠλπίκαμεν ὅτι καὶ ἔτι ῥύσεται· συνυπουργούντων καὶ ὑμῶν
we have hope that even yet He will deliver, laboring together also you
5228 2257 1162 2443/1537 4183 4383 1519
ὑπὲρ ἡμῶν τῇ δεήσει, ἵνα ἐκ πολλῶν προσώπων τὸ εἰς
for us in prayer, that by many persons the for
2248 5486 1223 4183 2168 5228 2257
ἡμᾶς χάρισμα διὰ πολλῶν εὐχαριστηθῇ ὑπὲρ ἡμῶν.
us gift through many thanks may be given for us.

1063 2746 2257 3778 2076 3142
12 Ἡ γὰρ καύχησις ἡμῶν αὕτη ἐστί, τὸ μαρτύριον τῆς
the For boasting of us this is, the testimony of the
4893 2257/3754/1722 572 1505 2316
συνειδήσεως ἡμῶν, ὅτι ἐν ἁπλότητι καὶ εἰλικρινείᾳ Θεοῦ,
conscience of us, that in simplicity and sincerity of God,
3756/1722/4678 4559 235 1722 5485 2316 390
οὐκ ἐν σοφίᾳ σαρκικῇ, ἀλλ' ἐν χάριτι Θεοῦ, ἀνεστράφημεν
not in wisdom fleshly, but in the grace of God we behaved
1722 2889 4056 4314/5209/3756/1063 243
13 ἐν τῷ κόσμῳ, περισσοτέρως δὲ πρὸς ὑμᾶς. οὐ γὰρ ἄλλα
in the world, more abundantly and toward you. not For other things
3739 1125 5213 235/2228// 314 2228 1921
γράφομεν ὑμῖν, ἀλλ' ἢ ἃ ἀναγινώσκετε ἢ καὶ ἐπιγινώσκετε,
we write to you, other than what you read, or even perceive,
1679 3754 2193 5056 1921 2531 1921
14 ἐλπίζω δὲ ὅτι καὶ ἕως τέλους ἐπιγνώσεσθε· καθὼς καὶ ἐπέ-
I hope and that also until the end you will perceive, as also you
2248 575 3313 3754 2745 5216 2070 2509
γνωτε ἡμᾶς ἀπὸ μέρους, ὅτι καύχημα ὑμῶν ἐσμέν, καθάπερ
perceived us from (in) part, because boasting of you we are, even as
5210 2257/1722 2250 2962 2424
καὶ ὑμεῖς ἡμῶν, ἐν τῇ ἡμέρᾳ τοῦ Κυρίου Ἰησοῦ.
also you of us, in the day of the Lord Jesus.

5026 4006 1014 4314 5209 2064
15 Καὶ ταύτῃ τῇ πεποιθήσει ἐβουλόμην πρὸς ὑμᾶς ἐλθεῖν
And in this confidence I purposed to you to come
4386 2443 1208 5485/2192 1223 5216 1330 1519
16 πρότερον, ἵνα δευτέραν χάριν ἔχητε· καὶ δι' ὑμῶν διελθεῖν εἰς
previously, that a second benefit you have, and through you to go through to
3109 3825 575 3109 2064 4314 5209
Μακεδονίαν, καὶ πάλιν ἀπὸ Μακεδονίας ἐλθεῖν πρὸς ὑμᾶς,
Macedonia, and again from Macedonia to come to you,
5259 5216 4311 1519 2449 5124 3767
17 καὶ ὑφ' ὑμῶν προπεμφθῆναι εἰς τὴν Ἰουδαίαν. τοῦτο οὖν
and by you to be set forward to Judea. This, then,
,3739 1011 =3385=686 1644 5530 2228/*/1011
βουλευόμενος, μή τι ἄρα τῇ ἐλαφρίᾳ ἐχρησάμην; ἢ ἃ βου-
purposing, not indeed lightness I used? Or what I
2596 4561 1011 2443/5600/3844/1698 3483/3483
λεύομαι, κατὰ σάρκα βουλεύομαι, ἵνα ᾖ παρ' ἐμοὶ τὸ ναὶ ναὶ
purposed, according to flesh do I purpose, that may be with me the Yes, Yes,

no? [18]But God *is* faithful; that our word to you did not become Yes and No. [19]For Jesus Christ the Son of God, the *One* proclaimed among you by us, through me and Silvanus and Timothy, was not Yes and No, but has been Yes in Him. [20]For as many promises as *are* of God, in Him *they are* Yes, and in Him *are* Amen, for glory to God through us. [21]But He confirming us and anointing us with you in Christ *is* God. [22]And He having sealed us, and giving the earnest of the Spirit in our hearts.

[23]And I call God *as* witness to my soul that to spare you I came no more to Corinth. [24]Not that we rule over your faith, but we are fellow-workers of your joy. For by faith you stand.

3756/3756 4103 2316/3754 3056 2257 4314
18 καὶ τὸ οὒ οὔ ; πιστὸς δὲ ὁ Θεός, ὅτι ὁ λόγος ἡμῶν ὁ πρὸς
and the No, No? faithful But (is) God, that the word of us to
5209/3756 1096 3483 3756 1063 2316 5207 2424
19 ὑμᾶς οὐκ ἐγένετο ναὶ καὶ οὔ. ὁ γὰρ τοῦ Θεοῦ υἱὸς Ἰησοῦς
you not became Yes, and No. For the of God Son, Jesus
5547 1722/5213/1223/2257 2784 1223/1700 4610
Χριστὸς ὁ ἐν ὑμῖν δι' ἡμῶν κηρυχθείς, δι' ἐμοῦ καὶ Σιλουανοῦ
Christ, the (One) among you by us proclaimed, through me and Silvanus
5095 3756 1096 3483 3756 235 3483/1722/846
καὶ Τιμοθέου, οὐκ ἐγένετο ναὶ καὶ οὔ, ἀλλὰ ναὶ ἐν αὐτῷ
and Timothy, not became Yes, and No, but Yes in Him
1096 3745 1063 1860 2316/1722/846 3483 1722
20 γέγονεν. ὅσαι γὰρ ἐπαγγελίαι Θεοῦ, ἐν αὐτῷ τὸ ναί, καὶ ἐν
has been, as many as For (are) promises of God, in Him the Yes, and in
846 281 2316 4314 1391/1223/2257 950
21 αὐτῷ τὸ ἀμήν, τῷ Θεῷ πρὸς δόξαν δι' ἡμῶν. ὁ δὲ βεβαιῶν
Him the Amen, to God unto glory through us. He But confirming
2248 4862 5213/1519 5547 5548 2248 2316
22 ἡμᾶς σὺν ὑμῖν εἰς Χριστόν, καὶ χρίσας ἡμᾶς, Θεός· ὁ καὶ
us with you in Christ, and anointing us (is) God, He and
4972 2248 1325 728 4151
σφραγισάμενος ἡμᾶς, καὶ δοὺς τὸν ἀρραβῶνα τοῦ Πνεύ-
having sealed us and having given the earnest of the Spirit
1722 2588 2257
ματος ἐν ταῖς καρδίαις ἡμῶν.
in the hearts of us.
1473 3144 2316 1941 1909 1699
23 Ἐγὼ δὲ μάρτυρα τὸν Θεὸν ἐπικαλοῦμαι ἐπὶ τὴν ἐμὴν
I And (as) witness God call on my
5590 3754 5339 5216 3765 2064 1519 2882 3756
24 ψυχήν, ὅτι φειδόμενος ὑμῶν οὐκέτι ἦλθον εἰς Κόρινθον. οὐχ
soul, that sparing you no more I came to Corinth. Not
3754 2961 5216 4102 235 4904 2070
ὅτι κυριεύομεν ὑμῶν τῆς πίστεως, ἀλλὰ συνεργοί ἐσμεν τῆς
that we rule over of you the faith, but fellow-workers we are of the
5479 5216 1063 4102 2476
χαρᾶς ὑμῶν· τῇ γὰρ πίστει ἑστήκατε.
joy of you; for by faith you stand.

CHAPTER 2

[1]But I decided this within myself, not to come to you again in grief. [2]For if I grieved you, who yet will be making me glad, if not the *one* being grieved by me? [3]And I wrote this same thing to you, lest coming I might have grief from *those* of whom I ought to rejoice; trusting in you all that my joy is *the joy of* all of you. [4]For out of much affliction and agony of heart I wrote to you, through many tears, not that you be grieved, but that you know the love which I have more abundantly toward you.

[5]But if anyone has grieved, he has not grieved me, but in part, that I not

2919 1683 5124 3361 3825 2064/1722/3077
1 ἔκρινα δὲ ἐμαυτῷ τοῦτο, τὸ μὴ πάλιν ἐλθεῖν ἐν λύπῃ
I decided And in myself this, not again to come in grief
4314/5209/1487 1063/1473 3077 5209 5101/2076
2 πρὸς ὑμᾶς. εἰ γὰρ ἐγὼ λυπῶ ὑμᾶς, καὶ τίς ἐστιν ὁ
to you. if For I grieve you, even who is it
2165 3165=1508= 3076 1537 1700 1125
3 εὐφραίνων με, εἰ μὴ ὁ λυπούμενος ἐξ ἐμοῦ ; καὶ ἔγραψα
making glad me, if not the (one) being grieved by me? And I wrote
5213 5124 846 2443/3361/2064 3077 2192/575/3739/1163
ὑμῖν τοῦτο αὐτό, ἵνα μὴ ἐλθὼν λύπην ἔχω ἀφ' ὧν ἔδει
to you this same thing, that not coming grief I should have from whom it behoved
3165/5463 3982 1909 3956 5209 3754 1699
5479 με χαίρειν, πεποιθὼς ἐπὶ πάντας ὑμᾶς, ὅτι ἡ ἐμὴ χαρὰ
4 me to rejoice, trusting in all of you, that my joy
3956 5216 2076/1537/1063/4183 2347 4928
πάντων ὑμῶν ἐστίν. ἐκ γὰρ πολλῆς θλίψεως καὶ συνοχῆς
all of you is, out of For much trouble and anxiety
2588 1125 5213 1223 4183 1144 3756/2443
καρδίας ἔγραψα ὑμῖν διὰ πολλῶν δακρύων, οὐχ ἵνα
of heart I wrote to you through many tears, not that
3076 235 26 2443 1097 3739/2192 4056
λυπηθῆτε, ἀλλὰ τὴν ἀγάπην ἵνα γνῶτε ἣν ἔχω περισ-
you be grieved, but the love that you know which I have more
1519 5209
σοτέρως εἰς ὑμᾶς.
abundantly to you.
1487 5100 3076 3756/1691/ 3076 235 575 3313
5 Εἰ δέ τις λελύπηκεν, οὐκ ἐμὲ λελύπηκεν, ἀλλ' ἀπὸ μέρους·
if But anyone has grieved, not me he has grieved, but from part,

overbear all of you. [6]This censure by the majority *is* enough for such a one. [7]So that on the contrary, you should rather forgive and comfort such a one, that *he* not be swallowed up *by* the overflowing grief. [8]So I beseech you to confirm *your* love to him. [9]For to this end I also wrote, that I might know the proof of you, if you are obedient in all things. [10]But to whom you forgive anything, I also. For also if I have forgiven anything, of whom I have forgiven *it, it is* for you, in Christ's person; [11]so that we should not be overreached by Satan, for we are not ignorant of his devices.

[12]And coming to Troas for the gospel of Christ, and a door having been opened to me in *the* Lord, [13]I had no ease in my spirit at my not finding my brother Titus; but saying farewell to them, I went out to Macedonia. [14]But thanks *be* to God, He always leading us in triumph in Christ, and *the One* revealing through us the odor of the knowledge of Him in every place. [15]For we are a sweet smell to God because of Christ in those being saved, and in those being lost— [16]to the one, an odor of death unto death; and to the other an odor of life unto life. And who is sufficient for these things? [17]For we are not as the many, hawking the word of God; but as of sincerity, but as of God. We speak in Christ, in the sight of God.

2443/3361/ 1912 3956 5209 2425 5108 2009
6 ἵνα μὴ ἐπιβαρῶ πάντας ὑμᾶς. ἱκανὸν τῷ τοιούτῳ ἡ ἐπιτιμία
that not I overbear all of you. Enough for such a one censure
3778 5259 4119 5620 5121 3123 5209
7 αὕτη ἡ ὑπὸ τῶν πλειόνων· ὥστε τοὐναντίον μᾶλλον ὑμᾶς
this by the majority. so as on the contrary rather you
5483 3870 3361 4459 4055
χαρίσασθαι καὶ παρακαλέσαι, μή πως τῇ περισσοτέρᾳ
to forgive and to comfort. lest (by) the more abundant
3077 2666 5108 1352 3870 5209 2964
8 λύπῃ καταποθῇ ὁ τοιοῦτος. διὸ παρακαλῶ ὑμᾶς κυρῶσαι
grief be swallowed such a one. Therefore I beseech you to confirm
1519 846 26 1519 5124 1063 1125 2443 1097
9 εἰς αὐτὸν ἀγάπην. εἰς τοῦτο γὰρ καὶ ἔγραψα, ἵνα γνῶ τὴν
to him (your) love. to this For also I wrote, that I might know
1382 5216/1487/1519/3956 5255 2075/3739 5100/ 5483
10 δοκιμὴν ὑμῶν, εἰ εἰς πάντα ὑπήκοοί ἐστε. ᾧ δέ τι χαρίζεσθε,
proof of you, if in all things obedient you are. to But any- you forgive
1473 1063/1473=1536= 5483 3739 5483
whom thing
καὶ ἐγώ· καὶ γὰρ ἐγὼ εἴ τι κεχάρισμαι, ᾧ κεχάρισμαι, δι
also I; indeed for I if anything I have of I have forgiven, for
5209/1722 4383 5547 2443 forgiven whom 4122 5259
11 ὑμᾶς ἐν προσώπῳ Χριστοῦ, ἵνα μὴ πλεονεκτηθῶμεν ὑπὸ
you (it is) in (the) person of Christ, that not we be overreached by
4567 3756/1063 848 3540 50
τοῦ Σατανᾶ· οὐ γὰρ αὐτοῦ τὰ νοήματα ἀγνοοῦμεν.
Satan, not for of him the devices we are ignorant.
2064 1519 5174 1519 2098 5547
12 Ἐλθὼν δὲ εἰς τὴν Τρῳάδα εἰς τὸ εὐαγγέλιον τοῦ Χριστοῦ
having come And to Troas in the gospel of Christ,
2374/3427 455 1722 2962 3756 2192 425
13 καὶ θύρας μοι ἀνεῳγμένης ἐν Κυρίῳ, οὐκ ἔσχηκα ἄνεσιν τῷ
and a door to me having been opened in (the) Lord, not I had rest to the
4151 3450 3361 2147/3165/5103 80 3450 235
πνεύματί μου, τῷ μὴ εὑρεῖν με Τίτον τὸν ἀδελφόν μου· ἀλλὰ
spirit of me, in the not finding me Titus the brother of me, but
657 846 1831 1519 3109 2316
14 ἀποταξάμενος αὐτοῖς ἐξῆλθον εἰς Μακεδονίαν. τῷ δὲ Θεῷ
saying farewell to them, I went out to Macedonia. But to God
5485 3842 2358 2248/1722 5547
χάρις τῷ πάντοτε θριαμβεύοντι ἡμᾶς ἐν τῷ Χριστῷ, καὶ τὴν
thanks, He always leading in triumph us in Christ, and the
3744 1108 848 5319 1223/2257/1722 3956
ὀσμὴν τῆς γνώσεως αὐτοῦ φανεροῦντι δι' ἡμῶν ἐν παντὶ
odor of the knowledge of Him revealing through us in every
5117 3754 5547 2175 2070 2316/1722 4982
15 τόπῳ. ὅτι Χριστοῦ εὐωδία ἐσμὲν τῷ Θεῷ ἐν τοῖς σωζομένοις
place; because of Christ a sweet smell we are to God in those being saved
1722 622 3739/3303/3744 2288 1519 2288
16 καὶ ἐν τοῖς ἀπολλυμένοις· οἷς μὲν ὀσμὴ θανάτου εἰς θάνατον,
and in those being lost; to the one, an odor of death unto death;
3739 3744 2222 1519 2222 4314 5023 5102 2425 3756
17 οἷς δὲ ὀσμὴ ζωῆς εἰς ζωήν. καὶ πρὸς ταῦτα τίς ἱκανός; οὐ
the other and an odor of life unto life. And for these things who is enough? not
1063 2070/5613 4183 2585 3056 2316
γάρ ἐσμεν ὡς οἱ πολλοί, καπηλεύοντες τὸν λόγον τοῦ Θεοῦ·
For we are as the many, hawking the word of God,
235/5613/1537/ 1505 235/5613/1537/2316/ 2714
ἀλλ' ὡς ἐξ εἰλικρινείας, ἀλλ' ὡς ἐκ Θεοῦ, κατενώπιον τοῦ
but as of sincerity, but as of God, in the sight of
2316/1722 5547 2980
Θεοῦ, ἐν Χριστῷ λαλοῦμεν.
God, in Christ, we speak.

CHAPTER 3

[1]Do we begin again to commend ourselves? Or do we, as some, need commendatory letters to you, or commendatory *ones* from

CHAPTER 3

756 3825 1438 4921 3361 5535
1 Ἀρχόμεθα πάλιν ἑαυτοὺς συνιστάνειν; ἢ μὴ χρῄζομεν,
Do we begin again ourselves to commend? or not need we
5613/5100 4956 1992 4314 5209/2228/1537/5216
ὥς τινες, συστατικῶν ἐπιστολῶν πρὸς ὑμᾶς, ἢ ἐξ ὑμῶν
as some commendatory epistles to you or from you

you? [2]You are our letter, having been inscribed in our hearts, being known and being read by all men, [3]*it* having been made plain that you are Christ's letter, served by us; not having been inscribed by ink, but by *the* Spirit of *the* living God; not in tablets of stone, but in fleshly tablets *of the* heart.

[4]And we have such confidence through Christ toward God; [5]not that we are sufficient of ourselves to reason out anything as out of ourselves, but our sufficiency *is* of God, [6]who also made us able ministers of a new covenant; not of letter, but of Spirit. For the letter kills, but the Spirit makes alive. [7]But if the ministry of death having been engraved in letters in stone was with glory, so as the sons of Israel could not gaze into the face of Moses because of the glory of his face; which was to cease, [8]how much rather the ministry of the Spirit will be in glory! [9]For if the ministry of condemnation *was* glory, much rather the ministry of righteousness abounds in glory. [10]For even that which has been made glorious has not been made glorious in this respect, because of the surpassing glory. [11]For if the thing done away *was* through glory, much rather the thing remaining in glory.

[12]Therefore, having such hope, we use much boldness. [13]And not as Moses *who* put a veil over his face, for the sons of Israel not to gaze at the end of the *thing* being done away, [14]but their thoughts were

4956 1992 2257 5210 2075 1449
2 συστατικῶν; ἡ ἐπιστολὴ ἡμῶν ὑμεῖς ἐστέ, ἐγγεγραμμένη
commendatory (ones)? The epistle of us you are, having been inscribed
1722 2588 2257 1097 314
ἐν ταῖς καρδίαις ἡμῶν, γινωσκομένη καὶ ἀναγινωσκομένη
in the hearts of us, being known and being read
5259 3956 444 5319 3754/2075 1992
3 ὑπὸ πάντων ἀνθρώπων· φανερούμενοι ὅτι ἐστὲ ἐπιστολὴ
by all men, being manifested that you are an epistle
5547 1247 5259 2257 1449 3756 3188
Χριστοῦ διακονηθεῖσα ὑφ' ἡμῶν, ἐγγεγραμμένη οὐ μέλανι,
of Christ ministered by us, having been inscribed not by ink,
235 4151 2316 2198 3756/1722 4109 3035 235 1722
ἀλλὰ Πνεύματι Θεοῦ ζῶντος, οὐκ ἐν πλαξὶ λιθίναις, ἀλλ' ἐν
but by (the) Spirit of God a living, not in tables of stone, but in
4109 2588 4560 4006 5108 2192
4 πλαξὶ καρδίας σαρκίναις. πεποίθησιν δὲ τοιαύτην ἔχομεν
tablets (of the) heart fleshly. confidence And such we have
1223 5547 4314 2316 3756/3754/2425 2070 575
5 διὰ τοῦ Χριστοῦ πρὸς τὸν Θεόν· οὐχ ὅτι ἱκανοί ἐσμεν ἀφ'
through Christ toward God. Not that sufficient we are of
•1537 1438 3049 5100/5613/•/ 1438 235 2425 2257
ἑαυτῶν λογίσασθαί τι ὡς ἐξ ἑαυτῶν, ἀλλ' ἡ ἱκανότης ἡμῶν
ourselves to reason out any as out ourselves, but the sufficiency of us
thing of
1537 2316 2426 2248 1249 2537
6 ἐκ τοῦ Θεοῦ· ὃς καὶ ἱκάνωσεν ἡμᾶς διακόνους καινῆς
(is) of God, who also made sufficient us (as) ministers of a new
1242 3756 1121 235 4151 1063 1121
διαθήκης, οὐ γράμματος, ἀλλὰ πνεύματος· τὸ γὰρ γράμμα
covenant, not of letter, but of spirit; the for letter
615 4151 2226 1487 1248
7 ἀποκτείνει, τὸ δὲ πνεῦμα ζωοποιεῖ. εἰ δὲ ἡ διακονία τοῦ
kills, the but Spirit makes alive. if And the ministry
2288 1722 1121 1795 1722 3037 1096 1722
θανάτου ἐν γράμμασιν, ἐντετυπωμένη ἐν λίθοις, ἐγενήθη ἐν
of death in letters having been engraved in stone was in
1391 5620/3361 1410 816 5207 2474 1519
δόξῃ, ὥστε μὴ δύνασθαι ἀτενίσαι τοὺς υἱοὺς Ἰσραὴλ εἰς τὸ
glory, so as not to be able to gaze the sons of Israel into the
4383 3475 1223 1391 4383 848
πρόσωπον Μωσέως διὰ τὴν δόξαν τοῦ προσώπου αὐτοῦ,
face of Moses because of the glory of the face of him,
2673 4459/3780 3123 1248 4151
8 τὴν καταργουμένην· πῶς οὐχὶ μᾶλλον ἡ διακονία τοῦ πνεύ-
being done away, how not rather the ministry of the Spirit
2071/1722/1391/1487/1063 1248 2633
9 ματος ἔσται ἐν δόξῃ; εἰ γὰρ ἡ διακονία τῆς κατακρίσεως
will be in glory? if For the ministry of condemnation
1391 4183 3123 4052 1248 1343
δόξα, πολλῷ μᾶλλον περισσεύει ἡ διακονία τῆς δικαιοσύνης
(was) glory, much rather abounds the ministry of righteousness
1722/1391 1063/3761 1392 1392 1722 5129
10 ἐν δόξῃ. καὶ γὰρ οὐδὲ δεδόξασται τὸ δεδοξασμένον ἐν τούτῳ
in glory. indeed For not has been glorified the thing glorified in this
3313 1752 5235 1391/1487/1063 2673
11 τῷ μέρει, ἕνεκεν τῆς ὑπερβαλλούσης δόξης. εἰ γὰρ τὸ κατ-
respect, because of of the excelling glory. if For the thing
1223/1391 4183 3123 3306/1722/1391
αργούμενον, διὰ δόξης, πολλῷ μᾶλλον τὸ μένον, ἐν δόξῃ.
being done away (was) via glory, much rather the thing remaining in glory.
2192 3767 5108 1680 4183 3954 5530
12 Ἔχοντες οὖν τοιαύτην ἐλπίδα, πολλῇ παρρησίᾳ χρώ-
having Therefore such hope, much boldness we
3756 2509 3475 5087 2571 1909 4383
13 μεθα· καὶ οὐ καθάπερ Μωσῆς ἐτίθει κάλυμμα ἐπὶ τὸ πρόσω-
use, and not as Moses put a veil over the face
1438 4314 3361 816 5207 2474 1519
πον ἑαυτοῦ, πρὸς τὸ μὴ ἀτενίσαι τοὺς υἱοὺς Ἰσραὴλ εἰς τὸ
of himself, for not to gaze the sons of Israel at the
5056 2673 235 4456 3540
14 τέλος τοῦ καταργουμένου· ἀλλ' ἐπωρώθη τὰ νοήματα
end of the (thing) being done away. But were hardened the thoughts

hardened. For until the present the same veil remains on the reading of the Old Covenant, not being unveiled that it is being done away in Christ. 15But until today, when Moses is being read, a veil lies on their heart. 16But whenever it turns to *the* Lord the veil is taken away. 17And the Lord is the Spirit, and where the Spirit of *the* Lord *is*, there *is* freedom. 18But we all with *our* face having been unveiled, having beheld the glory of *the* Lord in a mirror, are being changed *into* the same image from glory to glory, as from *the* Lord Spirit.

CHAPTER 4

1Therefore, having this ministry, even as we obtained mercy, we do not faint. 2But we have renounced the hidden things of shame, not walking in craftiness, nor adulterating the word of God, but *by* the revelation of the truth commending ourselves to every conscience of men before God. 3But also if our gospel is being hidden, it has been hidden in those being lost; 4in whom the god of this age has blinded the thoughts of the unbelieving, so that the brightness of the gospel of the glory of Christ, who is the image of God, should not dawn on them. 5For we do not proclaim ourselves, but Christ Jesus *as* Lord, and ourselves your slaves for the sake of Jesus. 6Because *it is* God who said,

848 891 1063 4594 846 2571 1909
αὐτῶν· ἄχρι γὰρ τῆς σήμερον τὸ αὐτὸ κάλυμμα ἐπὶ τῇ
of them. until For the present the same veil on the
320 3820 1242 3306/3361/ 343
ἀναγνώσει τῆς παλαιᾶς διαθήκης μένει μὴ ἀνακαλυπτόμενον,
reading of the Old Covenant remains, not being unveiled
=3748=1722 5547 2673 235 2193 4594 2259
15 ὅ τι ἐν Χριστῷ καταργεῖται. ἀλλ' ἕως σήμερον, ἡνίκα
that in Christ it is being done away. But until today, when
314 3475 2571 1909 2588 848
ἀναγινώσκεται Μωσῆς, κάλυμμα ἐπὶ τὴν καρδίαν αὐτῶν
is being read Moses, a veil on the heart of them
2749 2259 302 1994 4314 2962 4014
16 κεῖται. ἡνίκα δ' ἂν ἐπιστρέψῃ πρὸς Κύριον, περιαιρεῖται τὸ
lies; whenever But may it turn to (the) Lord, is taken away the
2571 2962 4151 2076 3756 4151
17 κάλυμμα. ὁ δὲ Κύριος τὸ Πνεῦμά ἐστιν· οὗ δὲ τὸ Πνεῦμα
veil. the And Lord the Spirit is, where and the Spirit
2962 1563 1657 2249 3956 343
18 Κυρίου, ἐκεῖ ἐλευθερία. ἡμεῖς δὲ πάντες, ἀνακεκαλυμμένῳ
of (the) Lord (is), there freedom (is). we But all, having been unveiled
4383 1391 2962 2734 846
προσώπῳ τὴν δόξαν Κυρίου κατοπτριζόμενοι, τὴν αὐτὴν
with face the glory of (the) Lord beholding in a mirror, the same
1504 3339 575 1391 1519 1391 2509 575
εἰκόνα μεταμορφούμεθα ἀπὸ δόξης εἰς δόξαν, καθάπερ ἀπὸ
image are being changed (into), from glory to glory, even as from
2962 4151
Κυρίου Πνεύματος.
(the) Lord Spirit.

CHAPTER 4

1223 5124 2192 1248 5026 2531 1653
1 Διὰ τοῦτο ἔχοντες τὴν διακονίαν ταύτην, καθὼς ἠλεήθη-
Because of this, having ministry this, even as we obtained
3756 1573 235 550 2927
2 μεν, οὐκ ἐκκακοῦμεν· ἀλλ' ἀπειπάμεθα τὰ κρυπτὰ τῆς
mercy, not we faint; but we have renounced the hidden things
152 3361 4043 1722 3834 3366 1389
αἰσχύνης, μὴ περιπατοῦντες ἐν πανουργίᾳ μηδὲ δολοῦντες
of shame, not walking in craftiness, nor adulterating
3056 2316 235 5321 225
τὸν λόγον τοῦ Θεοῦ, ἀλλὰ τῇ φανερώσει τῆς ἀληθείας
the word of God, but the revelation of the truth
4921 1438 4314 3956 4893 444
συνιστῶντες ἑαυτοὺς πρὸς πᾶσαν συνείδησιν ἀνθρώπων
commending ourselves to every conscience of men
1799 2316/1487 2076 2572 2098
3 ἐνώπιον τοῦ Θεοῦ. εἰ δὲ καὶ ἔστι κεκαλυμμένον τὸ εὐαγγέλιον
before God. if But indeed is being hidden the gospel
2257/1722 622 2076 2572 1722/3739 2316
4 ἡμῶν, ἐν τοῖς ἀπολλυμένοις ἐστὶ κεκαλυμμένον· ἐν οἷς ὁ Θεὸς
of us, in those being lost it is hidden, in whom the god
165 5127 5186 3540 571
τοῦ αἰῶνος τούτου ἐτύφλωσε τὰ νοήματα τῶν ἀπίστων,
age of this has blinded the thoughts of the unbelieving.
1519 3361 826 846 5462 2098
εἰς τὸ μὴ αὐγάσαι αὐτοῖς τὸν φωτισμὸν τοῦ εὐαγγελίου
to not dawn on them the brightness of the gospel
1391 5547 3739/2076 1504 2316/3756/1063
5 τῆς δόξης τοῦ Χριστοῦ, ὅς ἐστιν εἰκὼν τοῦ Θεοῦ. οὐ γὰρ
of the glory of Christ, who is (the) image of God. not For
1438 2784 235 5547 2424 2962
ἑαυτοὺς κηρύσσομεν, ἀλλὰ Χριστὸν Ἰησοῦν Κύριον·
ourselves we proclaim, but Christ Jesus (as) Lord,
1438 1401 5216 1223 2424 3754 2316 2036/1537
6 ἑαυτοὺς δὲ δούλους ὑμῶν διὰ Ἰησοῦν. ὅτι ὁ Θεὸς ὁ εἰπὼν ἐκ
ourselves and slaves of you for the sake of Jesus. Because God saying: Out of
4655 5457 2989 3739 2989 1722 2588 2257
σκότους φῶς λάμψαι, ὃς ἔλαμψεν ἐν ταῖς καρδίαις ἡμῶν,
darkness light shall shine, Who shone in the hearts of us

hearts to *give the* brightness of the knowledge of the glory of God in *the* face of Jesus Christ.

[7]But we have this treasure in earthen vessels, so that the excellence of the power may be of God, and not from us; [8]in every *way* being troubled, but not being hemmed in; being perplexed, but not utterly at a loss; [9]being persecuted, but not having been forsaken; being thrown down, but not having been destroyed; [10]always bearing about the dying of the Lord Jesus in the body, that also the life of Jesus may be revealed in our body. [11]For we who live are always being delivered up to death on account of Jesus, that also the life of Jesus may be revealed in our mortal flesh; [12]so that death indeed works in us, and life in you. [13]But having the same spirit of faith, according to what has been written, "I believed, therefore I spoke," we also believe, therefore we also speak; [14]knowing that He who raised up the Lord Jesus will also raise us up through Jesus, and will present *us* with you. [15]For all things *are* for your sake, that the superabounding grace may be made to abound through the thanksgiving of the greater number, to the glory of God.

[16]Therefore, we do not faint, but if indeed our outward man is being decayed, yet the inward *man* is being renewed day by day. [17]For the lightness of our present affliction works out for us an eternal weight of glory surpassing *moment* by surpassing *moment*; [18]we not considering the things seen, but the things not being seen; for the things seen

4314 5462 1108 1391 2316 1722
πρὸς φωτισμὸν τῆς γνώσεως τῆς δόξης τοῦ Θεοῦ ἐν
to (give the) brightness of the knowledge of the glory of God in
4383 2424 5547
προσώπῳ Ἰησοῦ Χριστοῦ.
(the) face of Jesus Christ.
2192 2344 5126/1722/ 3749 4632
7 Ἔχομεν δὲ τὸν θησαυρὸν τοῦτον ἐν ὀστρακίνοις σκεύεσιν,
we have And treasure this in earthen vessels.
2443 5236 1411 2316 3361/1537/2257
ἵνα ἡ ὑπερβολὴ τῆς δυνάμεως ᾖ τοῦ Θεοῦ, καὶ μὴ ἐξ ἡμῶν·
that the excellence of the power may be of God, and not of us;
1722/3956 2346 235 3756 4729 639
8 ἐν παντὶ θλιβόμενοι, ἀλλ' οὐ στενοχωρούμενοι· ἀπορού-
in every (way) being troubled, but not being hemmed in; being per-
235 3756 1820 1377 235 3756 1459
9 μενοι, ἀλλ' οὐκ ἐξαπορούμενοι· διωκόμενοι, ἀλλ' οὐκ ἐγκατα-
plexed, but not utterly at a loss; being persecuted, but not having been
2598 235 3756 622 3842
10 λειπόμενοι· καταβαλλόμενοι, ἀλλ' οὐκ ἀπολλύμενοι· πάν-
forsaken; being thrown down, but not having been destroyed; always
3500 2962 2424/1722 4983 4064
τοτε τὴν νέκρωσιν τοῦ Κυρίου Ἰησοῦ ἐν τῷ σώματι περιφέ-
the dying of the Lord Jesus in the body bearing
2443 2222 2424 1722 4983 2257
ροντες, ἵνα καὶ ἡ ζωὴ τοῦ Ἰησοῦ ἐν τῷ σώματι ἡμῶν
about, that also the life of Jesus in the body of us
5319 104/1063 2249 2198 1519 2288 3860
11 φανερωθῇ. ἀεὶ γὰρ ἡμεῖς οἱ ζῶντες εἰς θάνατον παραδιδό-
may be revealed. always For we the (ones) living to death are being deliv-
1223 2424 2443 2222 2424 5319 1722
μεθα διὰ Ἰησοῦν, ἵνα καὶ ἡ ζωὴ τοῦ Ἰησοῦ φανερωθῇ ἐν τῇ
ered on account of Jesus, that also the life of Jesus may be revealed in the
2349 4561 2257 5620 3303 2288 1722/2254 1754
12 θνητῇ σαρκὶ ἡμῶν. ὥστε ὁ μὲν θάνατος ἐν ἡμῖν ἐνεργεῖται,
mortal flesh of us. So as indeed death in us works
2222/1722/5213 2192 846 4151 4102
13 ἡ δὲ ζωὴ ἐν ὑμῖν. ἔχοντες δὲ τὸ αὐτὸ πνεῦμα τῆς πίστεως,
and life in you. having But the same spirit of faith,
2596 1125 4100 1223 2980 2249
κατὰ τὸ γεγραμμένον, Ἐπίστευσα, διὸ ἐλάλησα, καὶ ἡμεῖς
according to that having been written: I believed, so I spoke; both we
4100 1352 2980 1492 3754 1453
14 πιστεύομεν, διὸ καὶ λαλοῦμεν· εἰδότες ὅτι ὁ ἐγείρας τὸν
believe, therefore and we speak, knowing that He having raised the
2962 2424 2248/1223 2424 1453 3936
Κύριον Ἰησοῦν καὶ ἡμᾶς διὰ Ἰησοῦ ἐγερεῖ, καὶ παραστήσει
Lord Jesus also us with Jesus will raise, and will present (us)
3767/5213 1063 3956/1223/5209/2443 5485 4121
15 σὺν ὑμῖν. τὰ γὰρ πάντα δι' ὑμᾶς, ἵνα ἡ χάρις πλεονάσασα
with you. For all things for you sake, that grace may superabound
1223 4119 2169 4052 1519
διὰ τῶν πλειόνων τὴν εὐχαριστίαν περισσεύσῃ εἰς τὴν
through the greater number the thanksgiving may make abound to the
1391 2316
δόξαν τοῦ Θεοῦ.
glory of God.
1352/3756 1573 235 =1499= 1854 2257 444
16 Διὸ οὐκ ἐκκακοῦμεν· ἀλλ' εἰ καὶ ὁ ἔξω ἡμῶν ἄνθρωπος
Therefore not we faint, but if indeed, outward of us man
1311 235 2081 341 the 2250 2250
διαφθείρεται, ἀλλ' ὁ ἔσωθεν ἀνακαινοῦται ἡμέρᾳ καὶ ἡμέρᾳ.
is being decayed, yet the inward (man) is being renewed day by day
1063 3910 1645 2347 2257 2596 5228
17 τὸ γὰρ παραυτίκα ἐλαφρὸν τῆς θλίψεως ἡμῶν καθ' ὑπερ-
the For present lightness of the affliction of us surpassing
1519 5236 166 922 1391 2716
βολὴν εἰς ὑπερβολὴν αἰώνιον βάρος δόξης κατεργάζεται
(moment) by surpassing (moment) an eternal weight of glory work out
2254 3361 4648 2257 991 235 3361
18 ἡμῖν, μὴ σκοπούντων ἡμῶν τὰ βλεπόμενα, ἀλλὰ τὰ μὴ
for us, not considering us the things being seen, but the things not

are not lasting, but the things not seen *are* everlasting.

CHAPTER 5

[1]For we know that if our earthly house of *this* tabernacle is taken down, we have a building from God, a house not made with hands, eternal in Heaven. [2]For indeed in this we groan, greatly desiring to be clothed with our dwelling place out of Heaven; [3]if indeed *in* being clothed, we shall not be found naked. [4]For indeed being in the tabernacle, we groan, having been weighted down, inasmuch as we do not wish to be unclothed, but to be clothed, so that the mortal may be swallowed up by the life. [5]And He having worked in us for this same thing *is* God, who also *is* giving us the earnest of the Spirit. [6]Then always being fully assured, and knowing that being at home in the body we are away from home from the Lord—[7]for we walk by faith, not by sight— [8]we are fully assured, then, and are pleased rather to go away from home out of the body, and to come home to the Lord. [9]Because of this, we also are striving to be well-pleasing to Him, whether being at home, or being away from home. [10]For we all must appear before the judgment-seat of Christ, so that each one may receive the things *done* through the body, according to what he did, whether good or bad.

[11]Then knowing the fear of the Lord, we persuade men, and we have been manifest to God, and I also hope to have been manifest in your consciences. [12]For we do not again commend ourselves to you, but are

991 1063 991 4340 3361 991
βλεπόμενα· τὰ γὰρ βλεπόμενα πρόσκαιρα· τὰ δὲ μὴ βλεπό-
being seen. the things For being seen (are) temporary, the things but not
166
μενα αἰώνια.
being seen (are) everlasting.

CHAPTER 5

1492 1063/3754/1437 1919 2257 3614 4636
1 Οἴδαμεν γὰρ ὅτι ἐὰν ἡ ἐπίγειος ἡμῶν οἰκία τοῦ σκήνους
we know For that if the earthly of us house of the tabernacle
2647 3619 1537 2316 2192 3614 886
καταλυθῇ, οἰκοδομὴν ἐκ Θεοῦ ἔχομεν, οἰκίαν ἀχειροποίητον.
is destroyed, a building of God we have, a house not made by hands.
166 1722 3772 1063/1722/5129 4727
2 αἰώνιον ἐν τοῖς οὐρανοῖς. καὶ γὰρ ἐν τούτῳ στενάζομεν, τὸ
eternal in the heavens. indeed For in this we groan, the
3613 2257 1537 3772 1902 1971
οἰκητήριον ἡμῶν τὸ ἐξ οὐρανοῦ ἐπενδύσασθαι ἐπιποθοῦντες·
dwelling place of us out of Heaven to put on greatly desiring,
1489 1746 3756 1131 2147 1063
3 εἴ γε καὶ ἐνδυσάμενοι οὐ γυμνοὶ εὑρεθησόμεθα. καὶ γὰρ οἱ
4 if indeed being clothed, not naked we shall be found. indeed For
5600 5607/1722 4636 4727 916 1909//3756 2309
ὄντες ἐν τῷ σκήνει στενάζομεν βαρούμενοι· ἐφ' ᾧ οὐ θέλομεν
being in the tabernacle, we groan, being burdened, inasmuch as not we wish
1562 235 1902 2443 2666 2349
ἐκδύσασθαι, ἀλλ' ἐπενδύσασθαι, ἵνα καταποθῇ τὸ θνητὸν
to be unclothed, but to be clothed, that may be swallowed the mortal
5259 2222 2716 2248/1519/846 5124
5 ὑπὸ τῆς ζωῆς. ὁ δὲ κατεργασάμενος ἡμᾶς εἰς αὐτὸ τοῦτο
by the life. He And having worked in us for this same thing
2316 1325 2254 728 4151
Θεός, ὁ καὶ δοὺς ἡμῖν τὸν ἀρραβῶνα τοῦ Πνεύματος.
(is) God, he also giving us the earnest of the Spirit.
2292 3767 3842 1492 3754 1736 1722
6 θαρροῦντες οὖν πάντοτε, καὶ εἰδότες ὅτι ἐνδημοῦντες ἐν τῷ
being assured Then always, and knowing that being at home in the
4983 1553 575 2962 1223 4102 1063
7 σώματι ἐκδημοῦμεν ἀπὸ τοῦ Κυρίου (διὰ πίστεως γὰρ
body we are away from home from the Lord — through faith for
4043 3756/1223 1491 2292 2106
8 περιπατοῦμεν, οὐ διὰ εἴδους), θαρροῦμεν δέ, καὶ εὐδοκοῦμεν
we walk, not through sight —we are assured, then, and think it good
3123 1553 1537 4983 1736 4314
μᾶλλον ἐκδημῆσαι ἐκ τοῦ σώματος, καὶ ἐνδημῆσαι πρὸς τὸν
rather to go away from home out of the body, and to come home to the
2962 1352 5389 1535 1736 1535 1553
9 Κύριον. διὸ καὶ φιλοτιμούμεθα, εἴτε ἐνδημοῦντες, εἴτε ἐκδη-
Lord. Therefore also we are striving, whether being at home, or being away
2101 846 1511 1063 3956 2248
10 μοῦντες, εὐάρεστοι αὐτῷ εἶναι. τοὺς γὰρ πάντας ἡμᾶς
from home, well-pleasing to Him to be. For all us
5319 1163 1715 968 5547 2443
φανερωθῆναι δεῖ ἔμπροσθεν τοῦ βήματος τοῦ Χριστοῦ, ἵνα
to be revealed it behoves before the judgment-seat of Christ, that
2865 1538 1223 4983 4314/3739 4238
κομίσηται ἕκαστος τὰ διὰ τοῦ σώματος, πρὸς ἃ ἔπραξεν,
may receive each one the things through the body, according to what he did
1535 18 1535 2556
εἴτε ἀγαθόν, εἴτε κακόν.
whether good or bad.
1492 3767 5401 2962 444 3982
11 Εἰδότες οὖν τὸν φόβον τοῦ Κυρίου ἀνθρώπους πείθομεν,
Knowing, then, the fear of the Lord, men we persuade,
2316 5319 1679 1722 4893
Θεῷ δὲ πεφανερώμεθα· ἐλπίζω δὲ καὶ ἐν ταῖς συνειδήσεσιν
to God and we have been manifest; I hope and also in the consciences
5216 5319 3756/1063 3825 1438 4921
12 ὑμῶν πεφανερῶσθαι. οὐ γὰρ πάλιν ἑαυτοὺς συνιστάνομεν
of you to have been manifest. not For again ourselves we commend

giving you occasion of glorying on our behalf, that you may have *it* toward those boasting in appearance, and not in heart. [13]For if we are insane, *it is* to God; or *if* we are in our senses, *it is* for you. [14]For the love of Christ constrains us, having judged this, that if One died for all, then the all died; [15]and He died for all, that the living ones may live no more to themselves, but to the *One* having died for them, and having been raised. [16]So as we now know no one according to flesh, but even if we have known Christ according to flesh, yet now we no longer know. [17]So that if anyone *is* in Christ, *that one* is a new creation; the old things have passed away; behold, all things have become new! [18]And all things *are* of God, who reconciled us to Himself through Jesus Christ, and giving to us the ministry of reconciliation; [19]whereas God was in Christ reconciling *the* world to Himself, not charging their trespasses to them, and putting the word of reconciliation in us.

[20]Therefore, on behalf of Christ, we are ambassadors, as God *is* exhorting through us, we beseech on behalf of Christ, Be reconciled to God. [21]For He made Him who knew no sin *to be* sin for us, that we might become *the* righteousness of God in Him.

CHAPTER 6

[1]But working together, we also call on you not to receive the grace of God in vain. [2]For He says, "In an acceptable time I heard you, and in a day of salvation I helped you;" Behold, now *is* the acceptable

5213 235 874 1325 5213 2745 5228 2257
ὑμῖν, ἀλλὰ ἀφορμὴν διδόντες ὑμῖν καυχήματος ὑπὲρ ἡμῶν,
to you, but an occasion giving to you of boasting on behalf of us,

2443 2192 4314 1722 4383 2744 3756
ἵνα ἔχητε πρὸς τοὺς ἐν προσώπῳ καυχωμένους, καὶ οὐ
that you may have (it) toward those in appearance boasting, and not

2588 1535/1063 1839 2316/1535 4993 5213
13 καρδίᾳ. εἴτε γὰρ ἐξέστημεν, Θεῷ· εἴτε σωφρονοῦμεν, ὑμῖν.
in heart. whether For we are insane, (it is) to God; or we are in our senses, for you.

1063 26 5547 4912 2248 2919 5124
14 ἡ γὰρ ἀγάπη τοῦ Χριστοῦ συνέχει ἡμᾶς, κρίναντας τοῦτο,
the For love of Christ constrains us, having judged this

3754/1487/1519/5228/ 3956 599 686 3956 599
ὅτι εἰ εἷς ὑπὲρ πάντων ἀπέθανεν, ἄρα οἱ πάντες ἀπέθανον·
that if One for all died, then the all died;

5228 3956 599 2443 2198 3371 1438
15 καὶ ὑπὲρ πάντων ἀπέθανεν, ἵνα οἱ ζῶντες μηκέτι ἑαυτοῖς
and for all He died, that those living no more to themselves

2198 235 5228 846 599 1453 5620
16 ζῶσιν, ἀλλὰ τῷ ὑπὲρ αὐτῶν ἀποθανόντι καὶ ἐγερθέντι. ὥστε
may live, but to the (One) for them having died, and having been raised So as

2249 575 3568 3762 1492 2596 4561/1487
ἡμεῖς ἀπὸ τοῦ νῦν οὐδένα οἴδαμεν κατὰ σάρκα· εἰ δὲ καὶ
we from now no one know according to flesh; if but even

1097 2596 4561 5547 235 3568 3765 1097
ἐγνώκαμεν κατὰ σάρκα Χριστόν, ἀλλὰ νῦν οὐκέτι γινώ-
we have known according to flesh Christ, but now no more we know

5620/1487/5101/1722/5547 2537 2937 744
17 σκομεν. ὥστε εἴ τις ἐν Χριστῷ, καινὴ κτίσις· τὰ ἀρχαῖα
(Him). So as if anyone (is) in Christ, (he is) a new creation; the old things

3928 2400 1096 2537 3956 3956 1537
18 παρῆλθεν, ἰδοὺ γέγονε καινὰ τὰ πάντα. τὰ δὲ πάντα ἐκ τοῦ
passed away behold, have become new all things. the things and all (are) out of

2316 2644 2248 1438 1223 2424 5547
Θεοῦ, τοῦ καταλλάξαντος ἡμᾶς ἑαυτῷ διὰ Ἰησοῦ Χριστοῦ,
God, the (One) having reconciled us to Himself through Jesus Christ,

1325 2254 1248 2643 5613/3754/2316
19 καὶ δόντος ἡμῖν τὴν διακονίαν τῆς καταλλαγῆς· ὡς ὅτι Θεὸς
and having given to us the ministry of reconciliation, as that God

2258/1722/5547 2889 2644 1438 3361 3049
ἦν ἐν Χριστῷ κόσμον καταλλάσσων ἑαυτῷ, μὴ λογιζό-
was in Christ (the) world reconciling to Himself, not charging

846 3900 848 5087/1722/2254
μενος αὐτοῖς τὰ παραπτώματα αὐτῶν, καὶ θέμενος ἐν ἡμῖν
to them the trespasses of them, and putting in us

3056 2643
τὸν λόγον τῆς καταλλαγῆς.
the word of reconciliation.

5228 5547 3767 4243 5613 2316 3870
20 Ὑπὲρ Χριστοῦ οὖν πρεσβεύομεν, ὡς τοῦ Θεοῦ παρακαλ-
On behalf of Christ, therefore, we are ambassadors as God exhorting

1223 2257 1189 5228 5547 2644
οῦντος δι' ἡμῶν· δεόμεθα ὑπὲρ Χριστοῦ, καταλλάγητε τῷ
through us; we beseech on behalf of Christ, be reconciled

2316 1063/3361 1097 266 5228 2257 266
21 Θεῷ. τὸν γὰρ μὴ γνόντα ἁμαρτίαν, ὑπὲρ ἡμῶν ἁμαρτίαν
to God. the (One) For not knowing sin on behalf of us sin

4160 2443/2249 1096 1343 2316/1722 846
ἐποίησεν, ἵνα ἡμεῖς γινώμεθα δικαιοσύνη Θεοῦ ἐν αὐτῷ.
He made, so that we might become (the) righteousness of God in Him.

CHAPTER 6

4903 3870 3361/1519/2756 5485
1 συνεργοῦντες δὲ καὶ παρακαλοῦμεν μὴ εἰς κενὸν τὴν χάριν
working together And also we exhort not to in vain the grace

2316 1209 5209 3004 1063 2540 1184 1873
2 τοῦ Θεοῦ δέξασθαι ὑμᾶς (λέγει γάρ, Καιρῷ δεκτῷ ἐπήκουσά
of God to receive you — He says For, In a time acceptable I heard

4675 1722 2250 4991 997 4671 2400 3568 2540
σου, καὶ ἐν ἡμέρᾳ σωτηρίας ἐβοήθησά σοι· ἰδού, νῦν καιρὸς
you, and in a day of salvation I helped you — behold, now a time

time! Behold now *is* the day of salvation! [3]*Let us* not give a cause of stumbling in anything, that the ministry may not be blamed, [4]but in everything commending ourselves as God's servants, in much patience, in afflictions, in emergencies, in difficulties, [5]in stripes, in imprisonments, in riots, in labors, in watchings, in fastings, [6]in pureness, in knowledge, in long-suffering, in kindness, in the Holy Spirit, in unfeigned love, [7]in *the* word of truth, in *the* power of God, through the weapons of righteousness on the right *hand* and on the left, [8]through glory and dishonor; through evil report and good report — as deceivers, and yet true; [9]as unknown, and yet well-known; as dying, and yet, look, we live!; as flogged, and yet not put to death; [10]as sorrowful, but yet always rejoicing; as poor, but yet enriching many; as having nothing, yet possessing all things.

[11]Our mouth is opened to you, Corinthians, our heart has been made larger. [12]You are not restrained in us, but you are restrained in your *own* bowels. [13]But for the same reward — I speak as to children — you also be made larger.

[14]Do not be unequally yoked *with* unbelievers. For what partnership does righteousness *have* with lawlessness? And what fellowship does light *have* with darkness? [15]And what agreement does Christ *have* with Belial? Or what part does a believer *have* with an unbeliever? [16]And what agreement does a temple of God *have* with idols? For you are a temple of *the* living God, even as

2144 2400 3568 2250 4991 3367 1722
3 εὐπρόσδεκτος, ἰδού, νῦν ἡμέρα σωτηρίας) μηδεμίαν ἐν
acceptable; behold, now a day of salvation – no in
3367 1325 4349 2443/3361/ 3469 1248 235
4 μηδενὶ διδόντες προσκοπήν, ἵνα μὴ μωμηθῇ ἡ διακονία· ἀλλ'
nothing giving cause of stumbling, that not be blamed the ministry, but
1722/3956 4921 1438/5613/2316 1249 1722 5281
ἐν παντὶ συνιστῶντες ἑαυτοὺς ὡς Θεοῦ διάκονοι, ἐν ὑπομονῇ
in everything commending ourselves as of God ministers, in patience
4183 1722 2347 1722 318 1722 4730 1722 4127
5 πολλῇ, ἐν θλίψεσιν, ἐν ἀνάγκαις, ἐν στενοχωρίαις, ἐν πλη-
much, in troubles, in emergencies, in difficulties, in stripes,
1722 5438 1722 181 1722 2873 1722 70
γαῖς, ἐν φυλακαῖς, ἐν ἀκαταστασίαις, ἐν κόποις, ἐν ἀγρυ-
in imprisonments, in riots, in labors, in watchings,
1722 3521 1722 54 1722 1108 1722 3115
6 πνίαις, ἐν νηστείαις, ἐν. ἁγνότητι, ἐν γνώσει, ἐν μα-
in fastings, in pureness, in knowledge, in
1722 5544 1722 4151 40 1722 26
κροθυμίᾳ, ἐν χρηστότητι, ἐν Πνεύματι Ἁγίῳ, ἐν ἀγάπῃ
long-suffering, in kindness, in spirit a holy, in love
505 1722 3056 225 1722 1411 2316/1223
7 ἀνυποκρίτῳ, ἐν λόγῳ ἀληθείας, ἐν δυνάμει Θεοῦ, διὰ τῶν
unfeigned, in a word of truth, in (the) power of God, through the
3696 1343 1188 710 1223
8 ὅπλων τῆς δικαιοσύνης τῶν δεξιῶν καὶ ἀριστερῶν, διὰ
weapons of righteousness on the right and of left; through
1391 819 1223 1426 2162 5613 4108
δόξης καὶ ἀτιμίας, διὰ δυσφημίας καὶ εὐφημίας· ὡς πλάνοι,
glory and dishonor; through evil report and good report, as deceivers
227 5613 50 1921 5613
9 καὶ ἀληθεῖς· ὡς ἀγνοούμενοι, καὶ ἐπιγινωσκόμενοι· ὡς
and (yet) true; as unknown, and (yet) well-known; as
599 2400 2198 5613 3811 3361
ἀποθνήσκοντες, καὶ ἰδού, ζῶμεν· ὡς παιδευόμενοι, καὶ μὴ
dying, and behold, we live; as flogged, and not
2289 5613 3076 104 5463 5613 4434
10 θανατούμενοι· ὡς λυπούμενοι, ἀεὶ δὲ χαίροντες· ὡς πτωχοί,
put to death; as grieved, always and rejoicing; as poor,
4183 4148 5613 3367 2192 3956
πολλοὺς δὲ πλουτίζοντες· ὡς μηδὲν ἔχοντες, καὶ πάντα
many but enriching; as nothing having, and all things
2722
κατέχοντες.
possessing.
4750 2257 455 4314 5209 2881 1588
11 Τὸ στόμα ἡμῶν ἀνέῳγε πρὸς ὑμᾶς, Κορίνθιοι, ἡ καρδία
The mouth of us is opened to you, Corinthians, the heart
2257 4115 3756 4729 1722/2254 4729
12 ἡμῶν πεπλάτυνται. οὐ στενοχωρεῖσθε ἐν ἡμῖν, στενοχω-
of us has been made larger. not You are restrained in us, you are
1722 4698 5216 846 489
13 ρεῖσθε δὲ ἐν τοῖς σπλάγχνοις ὑμῶν. τὴν δὲ αὐτὴν ἀντιμισθίαν
restrained but in the bowels of you. for the But same reward
5613 5043 3004 4115 5210
(ὡς τέκνοις λέγω), πλατύνθητε καὶ ὑμεῖς.
–as to children I speak – be enlarged also you.
3361 1096 2086 571 5101/1063 3352
14 Μὴ γίνεσθε ἑτεροζυγοῦντες ἀπίστοις· τίς γὰρ μετοχὴ
Do not become unequally yoked (with) unbelievers, what for partnership
1343 458 5101 2842 5457 4314 4655
δικαιοσύνῃ καὶ ἀνομίᾳ ; τίς δὲ κοινωνία φωτὶ πρὸς σκότος ;
(have) righteousness and lawlessness? what And fellowship light with darkness?
5101 4857 5547 4314 955 5101/3310 4103
15 τίς δὲ συμφώνησις Χριστῷ πρὸς Βελίαλ ; ἢ τίς μερὶς πιστῷ
what And agreement (has) Christ with Belial? Or what part a believer
3326 571 5101 4783 3485 2316 3326 1497
16 μετὰ ἀπίστου : τίς δὲ συγκατάθεσις ναῷ Θεοῦ μετὰ εἰδώλων ;
with an unbeliever? what And union a temple of God with idols?
5210 1063 3485 2316 2075 2198 2531 2036 2316 3754
ὑμεῖς γὰρ ναὸς Θεοῦ ἐστε ζῶντος, καθὼς εἶπεν ὁ Θεὸς ὅτι
you For a temple of God are of a living, even as said God;

God said, "I will dwell in them, and walk among *them*; and I will be their God, and they shall be My people." [17]Because of this, come out from among them, and be separated, says *the* Lord, and do not touch *the* unclean thing; and I will receive you. [18]And I will be a Father to you, and you will be sons and daughters to Me, says *the* Lord Almighty.

CHAPTER 7

[1]Then having these promises, beloved, let us cleanse ourselves from all defilements of flesh and of spirit, perfecting holiness in *the* fear of God. [2]Make room for us. We wronged no one; we plundered no one; we overreached no one. [3]I do not speak to condemnation, for I have said before that you are in our hearts, for *us* to die together, and to live together. [4]My boldness toward you *is* great. My boasting on your behalf *is* much. I have been filled with comfort; I overflow with joy on all our trouble.

[5]For, indeed, we coming into Macedonia, our flesh had no rest, but being troubled in every way, *with* fightings *on the* outside, and fears *on the* inside. [6]But He who comforts the lowly comforted us by the presence of Titus. [7]And not only by his coming, but also by the comfort with which he was comforted over you, telling us your longing, your mourning, your zeal for me; so as for me to rejoice more. [8]For even if I grieved you in the letter, I do not regret; if

1774 1722 846 1704 2071 848
Ἐνοικήσω ἐν αὐτοῖς, καὶ ἐμπεριπατήσω· καὶ ἔσομαι αὐτῶν
I will dwell among them, and I will walk among (them), and I will be of them
2316 846 2071 3427 2992 1352 1831 1537 3319
17 Θεός, καὶ αὐτοὶ ἔσονταί μοι λαός. διὸ Ἐξέλθετε ἐκ μέσου
God, and they shall be of Me a people. Therefore come out from amidst
846 873 3004 2962 169 3361
αὐτῶν καὶ ἀφορίσθητε, λέγει Κύριος, καὶ ἀκαθάρτου μὴ
them, and be separated, says (the) Lord, and an unclean thing not
680 2504 1523 5209 2071 5213/1519/3962
18 ἅπτεσθε· κἀγὼ εἰσδέξομαι ὑμᾶς, καὶ ἔσομαι ὑμῖν εἰς πατέρα,
touch, and I will receive you, and I will be to you for a Father
5210 2071 3427/1519/5207 2364 3004 2962
καὶ ὑμεῖς ἔσεσθέ μοι εἰς υἱοὺς καὶ θυγατέρας, λέγει Κύριος
and you will be to Me for sons and daughters, says (the) Lord
3841
παντοκράτωρ.
Almighty.

CHAPTER 7

5025 3767 2192 2860 27
1 ταύτας οὖν ἔχοντες τὰς ἐπαγγελίας, ἀγαπη-
these Then having promises, beloved,
2511 1438 575 3956 3436 4561
τοί, καθαρίσωμεν ἑαυτοὺς ἀπὸ παντὸς μολυσμοῦ σαρκὸς
let us cleanse ourselves from all defilements of flesh
4151 2005 42 1722/5401 2316
καὶ πνεύματος, ἐπιτελοῦντες ἁγιωσύνην ἐν φόβῳ Θεοῦ.
and of spirit, perfecting holiness in (the) fear of God.
5562 2248 3762 91 3762 5351
2 Χωρήσατε ἡμᾶς· οὐδένα ἠδικήσαμεν, οὐδένα ἐφθείραμεν,
Make room for us; no one we wronged, no one we corrupted,
3762 4122 3756/4314 2633 3004 4280
3 οὐδένα ἐπλεονεκτήσαμεν. οὐ πρὸς κατάκρισιν λέγω· προεί-
no one we overreached. Not for condemnation I speak, I have
1063/3754/1722 2588 2257 2075/1519 4880
ρηκα γάρ, ὅτι ἐν ταῖς καρδίαις ἡμῶν ἐστὲ εἰς τὸ συναποθα-
before for that in the hearts of us you are, for to die with (you)
said 4800 4183 3427 3954 4314 5209 4183 3427
4 νεῖν καὶ συζῆν. πολλή μοι παρρησία πρὸς ὑμᾶς, πολλή μοι
and to live with (you) Great (is) my boldness toward you. Much to me
2746 5216 4137 3874 5248
καύχησις ὑπὲρ ὑμῶν· πεπλήρωμαι τῇ παρακλήσει, ὑπερ-
boasting on behalf of you. I have been filled with comfort, I
5479/1909/3956 2347 2257
περισσεύομαι τῇ χαρᾷ ἐπὶ πάσῃ τῇ θλίψει ἡμῶν.
overflow with joy on all the trouble of us.
1063 2064 2257/1519 3109 3762 2192
5 Καὶ γὰρ ἐλθόντων ἡμῶν εἰς Μακεδονίαν οὐδεμίαν ἔσχηκεν
indeed For coming us into Macedonia no has had
425 4561 2257 235/1722/3956/ 2346 1855 3163
ἄνεσιν ἡ σὰρξ ἡμῶν, ἀλλ' ἐν παντὶ θλιβόμενοι· ἔξωθεν μάχαι,
rest the flesh of us, but in every way being troubled; without fightings,
2081 5401 235 3870 5011 3870
6 ἔσωθεν φόβοι. ἀλλ' ὁ παρακαλῶν τοὺς ταπεινοὺς παρε-
within fears. But the (One) comforting the lowly
2248 2316/1722 3952 5103 3756/ 3440 1722
7 κάλεσεν ἡμᾶς, ὁ Θεός, ἐν τῇ παρουσίᾳ Τίτου· οὐ μόνον δὲ ἐν
comforted us, God, by the presence of Titus; not only and by
3952 235 1722 3874 3739 3870
τῇ παρουσίᾳ αὐτοῦ, ἀλλὰ καὶ ἐν τῇ παρακλήσει ᾗ παρεκλήθη
the presence of him, but also by the comfort with which he was comforted
1909/5213 312 2254 2257 1972 5216
ἐφ' ὑμῖν, ἀναγγέλλων ἡμῖν τὴν ὑμῶν ἐπιπόθησιν, τὸν ὑμῶν
over you, telling us your longing, your
3602 5216 2205 5228 1700 5620/3165 3123
ὀδυρμόν, τὸν ὑμῶν ζῆλον ὑπὲρ ἐμοῦ, ὥστε με μᾶλλον
mourning, your zeal for me, so as for me more
5463 3754/1487 3076 5209/1722 1992 3756/3338
8 χαρῆναι. ὅτι εἰ καὶ ἐλύπησα ὑμᾶς ἐν τῇ ἐπιστολῇ, οὐ μετα-
to rejoice. Because if even I grieved you by the epistle, not I

indeed I did regret; for I see that that letter grieved you for an hour. [9]Now I rejoice, not that you were grieved, but that you were grieved to repentance. For you were grieved according to God, that you might suffer loss in nothing by us. [10]For the grief according to God works repentance to salvation, not to be regretted. But the grief of the world works out death. [11]For behold this same thing, you being grieved according to God, how much it worked out earnestness in you; but *also* defense; but *also* indignation; but *also* fear; but *also* desire; but *also* zeal; but *also* vengeance! In everything you commended yourselves to be clear in the matter. [12]Then even if I wrote to you, *it was* not for the sake of him who did wrong, nor for the sake of him having suffered wrong, but for the sake of revealing our earnestness on your behalf, for you before God. [13]For this reason we have been comforted in your comfort, and we rejoice the rather more abundantly over the joy of Titus, because his spirit has been refreshed by all of you.

[14]Because if I have boasted anything to him about you, I was not ashamed. But as we spoke all things in truth to you, so also our boasting as to Titus became truth. [15]And his tender feelings are abundant toward you, remembering the obedience of all of you, as you received him with fear and trembling. [16]Therefore, I rejoice, that in everything I am fully assured in you.

CHAPTER 8

[1]But we make known to you the grace of God,

1487 3338 991 1063/3754 1992
μέλομαι, εἰ καὶ μετεμελόμην· βλέπω γὰρ ὅτι ἡ ἐπιστολὴ
regret; if indeed I regretted, I see for that epistle
1565 =1499= 4314 5610 3076 5209 3568 5463 3756
9 ἐκείνη, εἰ καὶ πρὸς ὥραν, ἐλύπησεν ὑμᾶς. νῦν χαίρω, οὐχ
that if indeed for an hour it grieved you, now I rejoice, not
3754 3076 235 3754 3076 1519 3341 3076
ὅτι ἐλυπήθητε, ἀλλ' ὅτι ἐλυπήθητε εἰς μετάνοιαν· ἐλυπήθητε
that you were grieved, but that you were grieved to repentance; you grieved
1063 2596 2316 2443/1722/3367 2210 1537 2257 1063
10 γὰρ κατὰ Θεόν, ἵνα ἐν μηδενὶ ζημιωθῆτε ἐξ ἡμῶν. ἡ γὰρ
for according to God, that in nothing you might suffer loss by us. the For
2596 2316 3077 3341 1519 4991 278
κατὰ Θεὸν λύπη μετάνοιαν εἰς σωτηρίαν ἀμεταμέλητον
according to God grief repentance to salvation unregrettable
2716 3889 3077 2288 2716
κατεργάζεται· ἡ δὲ τοῦ κόσμου λύπη θάνατον κατεργά-
works: the but of the world grief death works
2400/1063 846 5124 2596 2316 3076 5209
11 ζεται. ἰδοὺ γάρ, αὐτὸ τοῦτο, τὸ κατὰ Θεὸν λυπηθῆναι ὑμᾶς,
out. behold For this same thing, according to God to be grieved you
4214 2716 5213 4710 235 627
πόσην κατειργάσατο ὑμῖν σπουδήν, ἀλλὰ ἀπολογίαν,
how much it worked out in you earnestness, but defense,
235 24 235 5401 235 1972 235
ἀλλὰ ἀγανάκτησιν, ἀλλὰ φόβον, ἀλλὰ ἐπιπόθησιν, ἀλλὰ
but indignation, but fear, but eager desire, but
2205 235 1557 1722/3956 4921 1438 53
ζῆλον, ἀλλ' ἐκδίκησιν. ἐν παντὶ συνεστήσατε ἑαυτοὺς ἁγνοὺς
zeal, but vengeance! In everything you commended yourselves clear
1511/1722 4229 686 =1499= 1125 5213 3756 1752
12 εἶναι ἐν τῷ πράγματι. ἄρα εἰ καὶ ἔγραψα ὑμῖν, οὐχ εἵνεκεν
to be in the affair. Then if even I wrote to you (it was) not for
91 3761 1752 91 235 1752
τοῦ ἀδικήσαντος, οὐδὲ εἵνεκεν τοῦ ἀδικηθέντος, ἀλλ' εἵνεκεν
the (one) doing wrong, nor for the (one) being wronged, but for
5319 4710 2257 5228 5216 4314
τοῦ φανερωθῆναι τὴν σπουδὴν ἡμῶν τὴν ὑπὲρ ὑμῶν πρὸς
to be revealed the earnestness of us on behalf of you toward
5209 1799 2316 1223 5124 3870 1909
13 ὑμᾶς ἐνώπιον τοῦ Θεοῦ. διὰ τοῦτο παρακεκλήμεθα ἐπὶ τῇ
you before God. For this reason we have been comforted over the
3874 5216 4056 3123 5463 1909
παρακλήσει ὑμῶν· περισσοτέρως δὲ μᾶλλον ἐχάρημεν ἐπὶ τῇ
comfort of you, abundantly and more we rejoice over the
5479 5103 3754 373 4151 848 575 3956
χαρᾷ Τίτου, ὅτι ἀναπέπαυται τὸ πνεῦμα αὐτοῦ ἀπὸ πάντων
joy of Titus, because has been rested the spirit of him from all
5216 3754=1536= 846/5228/5216 2744 3756 2617
14 ὑμῶν. ὅτι εἴ τι αὐτῷ ὑπὲρ ὑμῶν κεκαύχημαι, οὐ κατησχύν-
you, because if anything to him for you I have boasted, not I was ashamed
235/5613/3956/1722/225 2980 5213 3779
θην· ἀλλ' ὡς πάντα ἐν ἀληθείᾳ ἐλαλήσαμεν ὑμῖν, οὕτω καὶ ἡ
but as all things in truth we spoke to you, so also the
2746 2257 1909 5103 225 1096 4698
15 καύχησις ἡμῶν, ἡ ἐπὶ Τίτου, ἀλήθεια ἐγενήθη. καὶ τὰ σπλάγ-
boasting of us as to Titus truth became, and the bowels
848 4056 1519 5209 2076 363
χνα αὐτοῦ περισσοτέρως εἰς ὑμᾶς ἐστίν, ἀναμιμνησκομένου
of him abundantly toward you are, remembering
3956 5216 5218 5613/3326 5401 5156
τὴν πάντων ὑμῶν ὑπακοήν, ὡς μετὰ φόβου καὶ τρόμου
the of all of you obedience, as with fear and trembling
1209 846 5463 3767/3754/1722/3956/2292/1722/5213
16 ἐδέξασθε αὐτόν. χαίρω οὖν ὅτι ἐν παντὶ θαρρῶ ἐν ὑμῖν.
you received him. I rejoice Then that in everything I am assured in you.

CHAPTER 8

1107 5213 80 5485 2316
1 Γνωρίζομεν δὲ ὑμῖν, ἀδελφοί, τὴν χάριν τοῦ Θεοῦ τὴν
we make known But to you, brothers, the grace of God

brothers, which has been given among the churches of Macedonia, [2]that in much testing of trouble, the overflowing of their joy, and the depth of their poverty, abounded to the riches of their generosity. [3]For I testify *that* according to *their* ability, and beyond *their* ability, *they* willingly *gave*, [4]with much entreating, begging us *that they might* receive of us the grace and the fellowship of the ministry to the saints. [5]And not as we hoped, but *they* first gave themselves to the Lord, and to us, through *the* will of God, [6]for us to call on Titus, that even as he began before, so also he might complete this grace to you also. [7]But even as you abound in everything—in faith, and in word, and in knowledge, and in all earnestness, and in your love in us—that you also should abound in this grace. [8]I do not speak according to command, but through the earnestness of others, and testing the trueness of your love.

[9]For you know the grace of our Lord Jesus Christ, that being rich, He became poor for your sake, so that you might become rich by the poverty of that One. [10]And I give judgment in this, for this is profitable for you, who began before not only to do, but also to be willing from last year. [11]But now also finish the doing *of it*, so that even as *there was* the eagerness *in* the willing, so also the finishing, *giving* out of what *giving* out of what *you* have. [12]For if the eagerness is present, it is acceptable according to *what* one has, not according to *what* one does not have. [13]For *it is* not that others *have* ease, but you trouble; [14]but by equality in the present time: your abundance for their need, so that their abundance

1325 1722 1577 3109 3754/1722/4183
2 δεδομένην ἐν ταῖς ἐκκλησίαις τῆς Μακεδονίας· ὅτι ἐν πολλῇ
being given among the churches of Macedonia, that in much
1382 2347 4050 5479 848 2596
δοκιμῇ θλίψεως ἡ περισσεία τῆς χαρᾶς αὐτῶν καὶ ἡ κατὰ
testing of trouble the overflowing of the joy of them, and the
899 4432 848 4052 1519 4149
βάθους πτωχεία αὐτῶν ἐπερίσσευσεν εἰς τὸν πλοῦτον τῆς
depth poverty of them abounded to the riches of the
572 848 3754 2596 1411 3140 5228
3 ἁπλότητος αὐτῶν. ὅτι κατὰ δύναμιν, μαρτυρῶ, καὶ ὑπὲρ
liberality of them. Because according to ability, I witness, and beyond
1411 830 3326 4183 3874 1189
4 δύναμιν αὐθαίρετοι, μετὰ πολλῆς παρακλήσεως δεόμενοι
(their) ability voluntarily with much beseeching begging
2257 5485 2842 1248 1519
ἡμῶν, τὴν χάριν καὶ τὴν κοινωνίαν τῆς διακονίας τῆς εἰς
us the grace and the fellowship of the ministry to
40 1209 2248 3756 2531 1679 235
5 τοὺς ἁγίους δέξασθαι ἡμᾶς· καὶ οὐ καθὼς ἠλπίσαμεν, ἀλλ᾽
the saints to receive of us, and not as we hoped, but
1438 1325 4412 2962 2254/1223/ 2307
ἑαυτοὺς ἔδωκαν πρῶτον τῷ Κυρίῳ, καὶ ἡμῖν διὰ θελήματος
themselves gave firstly to the Lord, and to us, through the will
2316/1519 3870 2248 5103 2443 2531 4278
6 Θεοῦ. εἰς τὸ παρακαλέσαι ἡμᾶς Τίτον, ἵνα καθὼς προενήρ-
of God. For to call us on Titus, that as he began
3779 2005 1519/5209 5485 5026
ξατο, οὕτω καὶ ἐπιτελέσῃ εἰς ὑμᾶς καὶ τὴν χάριν ταύτην.
before, so also he should complete to you also grace this.
235 5618/1722 3956 4052 4102 3056
7 ἀλλ᾽ ὥσπερ ἐν παντὶ περισσεύετε, πίστει, καὶ λόγῳ, καὶ
But as in everything you abound, in faith, and in word, and
1108 3956 4710 1537/5216/1722/2254/ 26
γνώσει, καὶ πάσῃ σπουδῇ, καὶ τῇ ἐξ ὑμῶν ἐν ἡμῖν ἀγάπῃ,
in knowledge and all earnestness, and the of you in us love—
2443 1722/5026 5485 4052 3756/2596 2003
8 ἵνα καὶ ἐν ταύτῃ τῇ χάριτι περισσεύητε. οὐ κατ᾽ ἐπιταγὴν
that also in this grace you may abound. Not by command
3004 235 1223 2087 4710 5212
λέγω, ἀλλὰ διὰ τῆς ἑτέρων σπουδῆς καὶ τὸ τῆς ὑμετέρας
I say, but through the of others earnestness also the of your
26 1103 1381 1097 1063 5485
9 ἀγάπης γνήσιον δοκιμάζων. γινώσκετε γὰρ τὴν χάριν τοῦ
love trueness testing; you know for the grace of the
2962 2257 2424 5547 3754/1223/5209/ 4433
Κυρίου ἡμῶν Ἰησοῦ Χριστοῦ, ὅτι δι᾽ ὑμᾶς ἐπτώχευσε,
Lord of us, Jesus Christ that on account of you He became poor
4145 5607/2443/5210 1565 4432 4147
10 πλούσιος ὤν, ἵνα ὑμεῖς τῇ ἐκείνου πτωχείᾳ πλουτήσητε. καὶ
rich being, that you by the of that One poverty might become rich. And
1106 1722 5129 1325 5124 1063/5213 4851 3748
γνώμην ἐν τούτῳ δίδωμι· τοῦτο γὰρ ὑμῖν συμφέρει, οἵτινες
a judgment in this I give, this for to you is profitable, who
3756/3440 4160 235 2309 4278 575
οὐ μόνον τὸ ποιῆσαι ἀλλὰ καὶ τὸ θέλειν προενήρξασθε ἀπὸ
not only the to do but also the to will you before began from
4070 3570 4160 2005 3704 2509
11 πέρυσι. νυνὶ δὲ καὶ τὸ ποιῆσαι ἐπιτελέσατε, ὅπως, καθάπερ
last year. now But also the doing (of it) finish, so as, as
4288 2309 3779 2005 1537 2192
ἡ προθυμία τοῦ θέλειν, οὕτω καὶ τὸ ἐπιτελέσαι ἐκ τοῦ ἔχειν
the eagerness of the willing, so also the finishing out of (what) you have
1487/1063 4288 4295 2526/1437/2192/5100/, 2144
12 εἰ γὰρ ἡ προθυμία πρόκειται, καθὸ ἐὰν ἔχῃ τις, εὐπρόσδε-
if For the eagerness is present, according to what one has, it is acceptable,
3756/2526/3756/2192/3756/1063/2443/, 243 425 5213
13 κτος, οὐ καθὸ οὐκ ἔχει. οὐ γὰρ ἵνα ἄλλοις ἄνεσις, ὑμῖν δὲ
not according (what) one to not has. not For that to others ease, you but
2347 235 1537 2471 1722 3568 2540 5216 4051
14 θλίψις· ἀλλ᾽ ἐξ ἰσότητος, ἐν τῷ νῦν καιρῷ τὸ ὑμῶν περίσ-
trouble but by equality, in the present time the of you abun-

may also be for your need, so that there may be equality — [15]as it has been written: "He *taking* much, he had nothing over and he *taking* little, he did not have less."

[16]But thanks *be* to God, who gives the same earnestness for you in the heart of Titus. [17]For truly he received the entreating; but being more earnest, he went out to you of his own accord. [18]But we sent with him the brother whose praise *is* in the gospel all through the churches; [19]and not only *so*, but also he having been chosen by the churches *as* a traveling companion to us with this gift being ministered by us to the glory of the Lord Himself, and your eagerness; [20]avoiding this, lest anyone should blame us in this bounty being ministered by us; [21]providing right things not only before *the* Lord, but also before men. [22]And we sent with them our brother whom we often proved in many things to be earnest, and now much more earnest by the great assurance which *I have* toward you. [23]If *any asks* as to Titus, *he is* my partner, and a fellow-worker for you; or *about* our brothers, *they are* messengers of the churches, *the* glory of Christ. [24]Then show them a proof of your love and of our boastings toward you, even in the sight of the churches.

1519 1565 5303 2443 1565 4051
σευμα εἰς τὸ ἐκείνων ὑστέρημα, ἵνα καὶ τὸ ἐκείνων περίσσευμα
dance for the of those lack, that also the of those abundance
1096 1519 5216 5303 3704 1096 2471
γένηται εἰς τὸ ὑμῶν ὑστέρημα· ὅπως γένηται ἰσότης,
may be for the of you lack, so as may be equality,
2531 1125 4183 3756 4121
15 καθὼς γέγραπται, Ὁ τὸ πολύ, οὐκ ἐπλεόνασε· καὶ ὁ τὸ
even as it has been written: He (taking) much, not he had over, and he (taking)
3641 3756 1641
ὀλίγον, οὐκ ἠλαττόνησε.
little, not had less.
5485 2316 1325 846 4710 5228
16 Χάρις δὲ τῷ Θεῷ τῷ διδόντι τὴν αὐτὴν σπουδὴν ὑπὲρ
thanks But to God giving the same earnestness for
5216/1722 2588 5103 3754 3303 3874 1209
17 ὑμῶν ἐν τῇ καρδίᾳ Τίτου. ὅτι τὴν μὲν παράκλησιν ἐδέξατο,
you in the heart of Titus, because the indeed beseeching he received,
4707 5225 830 1831 4314 5209
σπουδαιότερος δὲ ὑπάρχων, αὐθαίρετος ἐξῆλθε πρὸς ὑμᾶς.
more earnest and being, of his own accord he went out to you.
4842 3326 846 80 3756 1868 1722
18 συνεπέμψαμεν δὲ μετ' αὐτοῦ τὸν ἀδελφόν, οὗ ὁ ἔπαινος ἐν τῷ
we sent And with him the brother, of whom the praise is in the
2098 1223 3956 1577 3756 3440 235
19 εὐαγγελίῳ διὰ πασῶν τῶν ἐκκλησιῶν· οὐ μόνον δέ, ἀλλὰ
gospel throughout all the churches, not only and, but
5500 5259 1577 4898 2257
καὶ χειροτονηθεὶς ὑπὸ τῶν ἐκκλησιῶν συνέκδημος ἡμῶν
also having been chosen by the churches a traveling companion to us
4862 5485 5026 1247 5259 2257 4314
σὺν τῇ χάριτι ταύτῃ τῇ διακονουμένῃ ὑφ' ἡμῶν πρὸς τὴν
with gift this being ministered by us to the
848 2962 1391 4288 5216 4724
20 αὐτοῦ τοῦ Κυρίου δόξαν, καὶ προθυμίαν ὑμῶν· στελλόμενοι
Himself of the Lord glory, and (the) eagerness of you; avoiding
5124 3361/5100/2248 3469 1722 100 5026
τοῦτο, μή τις ἡμᾶς μωμήσηται ἐν τῇ ἁδρότητι ταύτῃ τῇ
this, lest anyone us should blame in bounty this
1247 5259 2257 4306 2570/3756 3440
21 διακονουμένῃ ὑφ' ἡμῶν· προνοούμενοι καλὰ οὐ μόνον
being ministered by us; providing right things not only
1799 2962 235 1799 444 4842
22 ἐνώπιον Κυρίου ἀλλὰ καὶ ἐνώπιον ἀνθρώπων. συνεπέμψα-
before (the) Lord, but also before men. we sent with
846 80 2257 3739 1381 1722 4183
μεν δὲ αὐτοῖς τὸν ἀδελφὸν ἡμῶν, ὃν ἐδοκιμάσαμεν ἐν πολλοῖς
And them the brother of us, whom we proved in many things
4178 4705 5607 3570 4183 4707
πολλάκις σπουδαῖον ὄντα, νυνὶ δὲ πολὺ σπουδαιότερον,
many times earnest being, now and much more earnest,
4006 4183 1519/5209/1535/5228 5103 2844
23 πεποιθήσει πολλῇ τῇ εἰς ὑμᾶς. εἴτε ὑπὲρ Τίτου, κοινωνὸς
in assurance much toward you. Whether as to Titus, partner
1699 1519 5209 4904 1535 80 2257 652
ἐμὸς καὶ εἰς ὑμᾶς συνεργός· εἴτε ἀδελφοὶ ἡμῶν, ἀπόστολοι
my and for you fellow-worker, or brothers of us, apostles
1577 1391 5547 3767 1732 26
24 ἐκκλησιῶν, δόξα Χριστοῦ. τὴν οὖν ἔνδειξιν τῆς ἀγάπης
of churches, (the) glory of Christ. the Therefore proof of the love
5216 2257 2746 5228 5216/1519/846 1731
ὑμῶν, καὶ ἡμῶν καυχήσεως ὑπὲρ ὑμῶν, εἰς αὐτοὺς ἐνδείξασθε
of you and of us the boasting as to you to them showing forth
1519 4383 1577
καὶ εἰς πρόσωπον τῶν ἐκκλησιῶν.
and in the presence of the churches.

CHAPTER 9

[1]For indeed concerning the ministry to the saints, it is unnecessary for me to

4012/3303/1063 1248 1519 40 4053
1 Περὶ μὲν γὰρ τῆς διακονίας τῆς εἰς τοὺς ἁγίους περισσόν
concerning indeed For the ministry to the saints, superfluous

write to you. [2]For I know your eagerness, *of* which I boast to Macedonia on your behalf, that Achaia has made ready from last year; and your zeal arouses the greater number. [3]But I sent the brothers that our boasting which *is* on your behalf should not be in vain in this respect, that as I said, you were ready; [4]lest if Macedonians come with me, and find you not ready, that we—we do not say you—should be ashamed in this assurance of boasting. [5]Therefore, I thought *it* necessary to exhort the brothers, that they go forward to you, and arrange beforehand your promised blessing; this to be ready, thus as a blessing, and not as greediness.

[6]And this: the *one* sowing sparingly will also reap sparingly; and the *one* sowing on *hope of* blessing will also reap on blessing. [7]Each one as he purposes in his heart, not of grief or of necessity, for God loves a cheerful giver. [8]And God is able to make all grace to abound toward you, that in everything, always having all self-sufficiency, you may abound to every good work; [9]even as it has been written, "He scattered; he gave to the poor; his righteousness abides forever."

[10]Now He that supplies seed to the sower, and bread for eating, may He supply and multiply your seed, and increase the fruits of your righteousness, [11]in everyting *you* being enriched to all generosity, which works out thanksgiving to God through us.

3427/2076 1125 5213 1492/1063 4288 5216 3739
2 μοί ἐστι τὸ γράφειν ὑμῖν· οἶδα γὰρ τὴν προθυμίαν ὑμῶν, ἣν
to me it is to write you; I know for the eagerness of you,which
5228 5216 2744 3110 3754 882 3903
ὑπὲρ ὑμῶν καυχῶμαι Μακεδόσιν, ὅτι Ἀχαΐα παρεσκεύασται
as to you I boast to Macedonia, that Achaia has made ready
575 4070 1537/5216 2205 2042 4119
ἀπὸ πέρυσι· καὶ ὁ ἐξ ὑμῶν ζῆλος ἠρέθισε τοὺς πλείονας.
from last year, and the of you zeal arouses the greater number.
3992 80 2443/3361 1745 2257 5228
3 ἔπεμψα δὲ τοὺς ἀδελφούς, ἵνα μὴ τὸ καύχημα ἡμῶν τὸ ὑπὲρ
I sent And the brothers, lest the boast of us as to
5216 2758 1722 3313 5129 2443 2531 3004 3903
ὑμῶν κενωθῇ ἐν τῷ μέρει τούτῳ· ἵνα, καθὼς ἔλεγον, παρε-
you should be in vain in respect this, that, as I said, having
5600/3361/4459/1437/2064 4862/1698 3110
4 σκευασμένοι ἦτε· μή πως, ἐὰν ἔλθωσι σὺν ἐμοὶ Μακεδόνες καὶ
been ready you were, lest if come with me Macedonians and
2147 5209 532 2617 2249 2443
εὕρωσιν ὑμᾶς ἀπαρασκευάστους, καταισχυνθῶμεν ἡμεῖς (ἵνα
find you not ready should be ashamed we that
3361 3004 5210 1722 5287 5026 2746
μὴ λέγωμεν ὑμεῖς) ἐν τῇ ὑποστάσει ταύτῃ τῆς καυχήσεως.
not we say you – in assurance this of boasting.
316 3767 2233 3870 80 2443
5 ἀναγκαῖον οὖν ἡγησάμην παρακαλέσαι τοὺς ἀδελφούς, ἵνα
necessary Therefore I thought (it) to exhort the brothers, that
4281 1519 5209 4294 4293
προέλθωσιν εἰς ὑμᾶς, καὶ προκαταρτίσωσι τὴν προκατηγ-
they go forward to you, and arrange beforehand the having been
2129 5216 5026 2092 1511 3779/5613
γελμένην εὐλογίαν ὑμῶν, ταύτην ἑτοίμην εἶναι, οὕτως ὡς
promised blessing of you, this ready to be, thus as
2129 3361 5618 4124
εὐλογίαν, καὶ μὴ ὥσπερ πλεονεξίαν.
a blessing, and not as greediness.
5124 4687 5340 5340 2325
6 Τοῦτο δέ, ὁ σπείρων φειδομένως, φειδομένως καὶ θερίσει·
this And: he sowing sparingly, sparingly also will reap;
4687 1909 2129 1909 2129 2325
καὶ ὁ σπείρων ἐπ' εὐλογίαις, ἐπ' εὐλογίαις καὶ θερίσει.
and he sowing on (hope of) blessing on blessing also will reap.
1537 1538 2531 4255 2588 3361/1537/3077/2228/*/
7 ἕκαστος καθὼς προαιρεῖται τῇ καρδίᾳ· μὴ ἐκ λύπης ἢ ἐξ
Each one as he purposes in the heart, not of grief or of
318 2431 1063 1395 25 2316 1415
8 ἀνάγκης· ἱλαρὸν γὰρ δότην ἀγαπᾷ ὁ Θεός. δυνατὸς δὲ ὁ
necessity; a cheerful for giver loves God. is able And
2316 3956 5485 4052 1519 5209 2443/1722 3956
Θεὸς πᾶσαν χάριν περισσεῦσαι εἰς ὑμᾶς, ἵνα ἐν παντὶ
God all grace to make abound toward you, that in everything
3842 3956 841 2192 4052 1519 3956
πάντοτε πᾶσαν αὐτάρκειαν ἔχοντες περισσεύητε εἰς πᾶν
always all self-sufficiency having you may abound to every
2041 18 2531 1125 4650 1325
9 ἔργον ἀγαθόν· καθὼς γέγραπται, Ἐσκόρπισεν, ἔδωκε τοῖς
work good; even as it has been written: He scattered; he gave to the
3993 1343 848 3306/1519 165
10 πένησιν· ἡ δικαιοσύνη αὐτοῦ μένει εἰς τὸν αἰῶνα. ὁ δὲ
poor; the righteousness of him remains to the age. He Now
2023 4690 4687 740 1519 1035
ἐπιχορηγῶν σπέρμα τῷ σπείροντι, καὶ ἄρτον εἰς βρῶσιν
that supplies seed to the sower, and bread for eating,
5524 4129 4703 5216 837
χορηγήσαι, καὶ πληθύναι τὸν σπόρον ὑμῶν, καὶ αὐξήσαι
may He supply and multiply the seed of you, and increase
1081 1343 5216 1711 3956 4148
11 τὰ γεννήματα τῆς δικαιοσύνης ὑμῶν· ἐν παντὶ πλουτιζό-
the fruits of the righteousness of you in everything being en-
1519 3956 572 3748 2716 1223 2257
μενοι εἰς πᾶσαν ἁπλότητα, ἥτις κατεργάζεται δι' ἡμῶν
riched to all liberality, which works out through us

12 Because the ministry of
this service is not only
making up the things
lacking of the saints, but
also multiplying through
many thanksgivings to God,
13 through the proof of this
service, *they* glorifying God
by your freely expressed
submission to the gospel of
Christ, and *the* generosity
of the fellowship toward
them and toward all; 14 and
in their prayer for you, a
longing after you, because
of the overflowing grace of
God on you. 15 But thanks
be to God for His
unspeakable free gift.

CHAPTER 10

1 And I myself, Paul, call
on you through the meek-
ness and gentleness of
Christ—I, who indeed to
look upon am lowly among
you, but being absent am
bold toward you; 2 but I ask,
not being present, that I
may be bold with the
confidence which I think to
be daring against some,
those having thought *of* us
as walking according to
flesh; 3 for walking about in
flesh, we do not war ac-
cording to flesh; 4 for the
weapons of our warfare *are*
not fleshly, but powerful to
God in order to pull down
strongholds; 5 pulling down
imaginations and every
high thing lifting up *itself*
against the knowledge of
God, and bringing into
captivity every thought into
the obedience of Christ;
6 and having readiness to
avenge all disobedience,
whenever your obedience
is fulfilled. 7 Do you look at
things according to appearance? If anyone has per-
suaded himself to be of
Christ, let him think this

2169 2316/3754 1248 3009 5026
12 εὐχαριστίαν τῷ Θεῷ. ὅτι ἡ διακονία τῆς λειτουργίας ταύτης
thanksgiving to God. Because the ministry service of this
3756 3440 2076 4322 5303
οὐ μόνον ἐστὶ προσαναπληροῦσα τὰ ὑστερήματα τῶν
not only is making up the things lacking of the
40 235 4052 1223 4183 2169
ἁγίων, ἀλλὰ καὶ περισσεύουσα διὰ πολλῶν εὐχαριστιῶν
saints, but also abounding through many thanksgivings
2316 1223 1382 1248 5026 1392
13 τῷ Θεῷ· διὰ τῆς δοκιμῆς τῆς διακονίας ταύτης δοξάζοντες
to God, through the proof ministry of this glorifying
2316 1909 5292 3671 5216/1519
τὸν Θεὸν ἐπὶ τῇ ὑποταγῇ τῆς ὁμολογίας ὑμῶν εἰς τὸ
God on the submission by the confession of you to the
2098 5547 572 2842 1519
εὐαγγέλιον τοῦ Χριστοῦ, καὶ ἁπλότητι τῆς κοινωνίας εἰς
gospel of Christ, and (the) liberality of the fellowship toward
846 1519 3956 848 1162 5228 5216
14 αὐτοὺς καὶ εἰς πάντας· καὶ αὐτῶν δεήσει ὑπὲρ ὑμῶν
them and toward all; and them with petition for you
1971 5209/1223 5235 5485
ἐπιποθούντων ὑμᾶς διὰ τὴν ὑπερβάλλουσαν χάριν τοῦ
longing after you on account of the surpassing grace
2316/1909/5213 5485 2316/1909 411 848
15 Θεοῦ ἐφ' ὑμῖν. χάρις δὲ τῷ Θεῷ ἐπὶ τῇ ἀνεκδιηγήτῳ αὐτοῦ
of God upon you. thanks But to God for the unspeakable of Him
1431
δωρεᾷ.
gift.

CHAPTER 10

848 1473 3972 3870 5209/1223 4236
1 Αὐτὸς δὲ ἐγὼ Παῦλος παρακαλῶ ὑμᾶς διὰ τῆς πρᾳότητος
myself And I, Paul, exhort you through the meekness
1932 5547 3739/2596 4383 3303 5011
καὶ ἐπιεικείας τοῦ Χριστοῦ, ὃς κατὰ πρόσωπον μὲν ταπεινὸς
and forbearance of Christ, who according to face indeed humble
1722/5213/ 548 2292 1519/5209 1189 3361 3918
2 ἐν ὑμῖν, ἀπὼν δὲ θαρρῶ εἰς ὑμᾶς· δέομαι δέ, τὸ μὴ παρὼν
among you being, but am bold toward you; I ask but, not being present,
2292 absent,4006 3739 3049 5111 1909 5100
θαρρῆσαι τῇ πεποιθήσει ᾗ λογίζομαι τολμῆσαι ἐπί τινας
to be bold in the confidence which I think to be daring toward some,
3049 2248/5613 2596 4561 4043
τοὺς λογιζομένους ἡμᾶς ὡς κατὰ σάρκα περιπατοῦντας.
those thinking us as according to flesh walking.
1722/4561/1063 4043 3756 2596 4561 4754
3 ἐν σαρκὶ γὰρ περιπατοῦντες, οὐ κατὰ σάρκα στρατευόμεθα
in flesh For walking, not according to flesh we war;
1063 3696 4752 2257 3756 4559 235
4 (τὰ γὰρ ὅπλα τῆς στρατείας ἡμῶν οὐ σαρκικά, ἀλλὰ
the for weapons of the warfare of us (are) not fleshly, but
1415 2316 4314 2506 3794 3053
5 δυνατὰ τῷ Θεῷ πρὸς καθαίρεσιν ὀχυρωμάτων), λογισμοὺς
powerful to God in order to demolish strongholds, imaginations
2507 3956 5313 1869 2596 1108
καθαιροῦντες καὶ πᾶν ὕψωμα ἐπαιρόμενον κατὰ τῆς γνώσεως
demolishing, and every high thing lifting up (itself) against the knowledge
2316 163 3956 3540/1519 5218
τοῦ Θεοῦ, καὶ αἰχμαλωτίζοντες πᾶν νόημα εἰς τὴν ὑπακοὴν
of God, and bringing into captivity every thought into the obedience
5547 1722 2092 2192 1556 3956
6 τοῦ Χριστοῦ, καὶ ἐν ἑτοίμῳ ἔχοντες ἐκδικῆσαι πᾶσαν
of Christ, and readiness having to avenge all
3876 3752 4137 5216 5218 2596
7 παρακοήν, ὅταν πληρωθῇ ὑμῶν ἡ ὑπακοή. τὰ κατὰ
disobedience, whenever is fulfilled of you the obedience. the things as to
4383 991 =1536= 3982 1438 5547 1511
πρόσωπον βλέπετε; εἴ τις πέποιθεν ἑαυτῷ Χριστοῦ εἶναι,
face you look (at)? If anyone has persuaded himself of Christ to be,

again as to himself, that as he *is* of Christ, so also we *are* of Christ. [8]For even if I also somewhat more fully should boast about our authority—which the Lord gave us for building up, and not for pulling you down—I will not be put to shame; [9]so that I may not seem to frighten you by letters—[10]because, he says, truly the letters *are* weighty and strong, but the bodily presence *is* weak, and *his* speech being despised —[11]let such a one think this, that such as we are in word through letters, being absent, such *we are* also being present in deed. [12]For we dare not rank or compare ourselves with some of those commending themselves—but they measuring themselves among themselves, and comparing themselves to themselves, *are* not perceptive. [13]But we will not boast beyond measure, but according to measure of the rule which the God of measure distributed to us, to reach even to you. [14]For we do not overstretch ourselves as *if* not reaching to you; for we also came to you in the gospel of Christ; [15]not boasting beyond measure in the labors of others, but having hope that the growing faith among you will be made larger according to our rule, to overflowing, [16]in order to preach the gospel to that beyond you, not to boast in another's rule in things ready. [17]But the *one* glorying, let him glory in *the* Lord. [18]For not the *one* commending himself is the one approved, but *the one* whom the Lord commends.

5124 3049 3825 575 1438 3754 2531 846
τοῦτο λογιζέσθω πάλιν ἀφ' ἑαυτοῦ, ὅτι καθὼς αὐτὸς
this let him think again as to himself, that as he (is)
5547 3779 2249 5547 1437/5037/1063 4055
8 Χριστοῦ, οὕτω καὶ ἡμεῖς Χριστοῦ. ἐάν τε γὰρ καὶ περισσό-
of Christ, so also we of Christ. if even For also more abun-
5100 2744 4012 1849 2257 3739 1325
τερόν τι καυχήσωμαι περὶ τῆς ἐξουσίας ἡμῶν (ἧς ἔδωκεν ὁ
dantly some- I should more about the authority of us—which gave the
what fully boast
1519 2962 2254 3619 3756/1519 2506 5216
Κύριος ἡμῖν εἰς οἰκοδομήν, καὶ οὐκ εἰς καθαίρεσιν ὑμῶν),
Lord to us for building up, and not for pulling down of you;
3756 153 2443/3361/1380/5613/302/ 1629 5209 1223
9 οὐκ αἰσχυνθήσομαι· ἵνα μὴ δόξω ὡς ἂν ἐκφοβεῖν ὑμᾶς διὰ
not I will be put to shame, that not I seem as though to scare you through
1992 3754 3303 1992 5346 926
10 τῶν ἐπιστολῶν. ὅτι Αἱ μὲν ἐπιστολαί, φησί, βαρεῖαι καὶ
the epistles. Because the truly epistles, he says, (are) weighty and
2478 3952 4983 772 3056
ἰσχυραί ἡ δὲ παρουσία τοῦ σώματος ἀσθενής, καὶ ὁ λόγος
strong, the but presence of the body (is) weak, and the speech
1848 5124 3049 5108 3754/3634 2070
11 ἐξουθενημένος. τοῦτο λογιζέσθω ὁ τοιοῦτος, ὅτι οἷοί ἐσμεν
being despised. this Let think such a one, that such as we are
3056/1223 1992 548 5108 3918
τῷ λόγῳ δι' ἐπιστολῶν ἀπόντες, τοιοῦτοι καὶ παρόντες
in word through epistles being absent, such also being present
2041 3756/1063 5111 1469 2228 4793 1438
12 τῷ ἔργῳ. οὐ γὰρ τολμῶμεν ἐγκρῖναι ἢ συγκρῖναι ἑαυτούς
in work. not For we dare to rank with or compare ourselves
5100 1438 4921 235 846/1722 1438
τισι τῶν ἑαυτοὺς συνιστανόντων· ἀλλὰ αὐτοὶ ἐν ἑαυτοῖς
with some of those themselves commending—but they among themselves
1438 3354 4793 1438 1438 3756
ἑαυτοὺς μετροῦντες, καὶ συγκρίνοντες ἑαυτοὺς ἑαυτοῖς, οὐ
themselves measuring, and comparing themselves to themselves, not
4920 2249 3780/1519 280 2744 235
13 συνιοῦσιν. ἡμεῖς δὲ οὐχὶ εἰς τὰ ἄμετρα καυχησόμεθα, ἀλλὰ
(are) perceptive. we But not beyond measure will boast, but
2596 3358 2583 3739 3307 2254 2316 3358
κατὰ τὸ μέτρον τοῦ κανόνος οὗ ἐμέρισεν ἡμῖν ὁ Θεός, μέτρου
according to measure of the rule which divided to us the God of measure,
2185 891 5216/3756/1062/5613/3361/ 2185 1519 5209
14 ἐφικέσθαι ἄχρι καὶ ὑμῶν. οὐ γὰρ ὡς μὴ ἐφικνούμενοι εἰς ὑμᾶς
to reach as far as even you. not For as not reaching to you
5239 1438 891 1063 5216 5348 1722
ὑπερεκτείνομεν ἑαυτούς· ἄχρι γὰρ καὶ ὑμῶν ἐφθάσαμεν ἐν τῷ
do we overstretch ourselves until for even to you we came in the
2098 5547 3756/1519 280 2744 1722
15 εὐαγγελίῳ τοῦ Χριστοῦ· οὐκ εἰς τὰ ἄμετρα καυχώμενοι, ἐν
gospel of Christ, not beyond measure boasting in
245 2873 1680 2192 837
ἀλλοτρίοις κόποις, ἐλπίδα δὲ ἔχοντες, αὐξανομένης τῆς
of others the labors, hope but having growing the
4102 5216/1722/5213/ 3170 2596 2583 2257
πίστεως ὑμῶν, ἐν ὑμῖν μεγαλυνθῆναι κατὰ τὸν κανόνα ἡμῶν
faith of you among you to be magnified according to the rule of us
1519 4050 1519 5238 5216 2097 3756
16 εἰς περισσείαν, εἰς τὰ ὑπερέκεινα ὑμῶν εὐαγγελίσασθαι, οὐκ
to overflowing, in order to (in) that beyond you to preach the gospel, not
1722 245 2583 1519 2092 2744 2744
17 ἐν ἀλλοτρίῳ κανόνι εἰς τὰ ἕτοιμα καυχήσασθαι. ὁ δὲ καυχώ-
in of another (the rule) in things ready to boast. he But boasting,
1722 2962 2744 3756/1063 1438 4921
18 μενος, ἐν Κυρίῳ καυχάσθω. οὐ γὰρ ὁ ἑαυτὸν συνιστῶν,
in (the) Lord let him boast. not For the (one) himself commending,
1565 2076 1384 235/3739 2962 4921
ἐκεῖνός ἐστι δόκιμος, ἀλλ' ὃν ὁ Κύριος συνίστησιν.
that one is approved, but whom the Lord commends.

CHAPTER 11

[1]I would that you were bearing with me a little in foolishness; but, indeed, bear with me. [2]For I am jealous *over* you with a jealousy of God. For I have promised you to one Man, to present *you* a pure virgin to Christ. [3]But I fear lest by any means, as the serpent deceived Eve in his craftiness, so your thoughts should be corrupted from the purity which *is due* to Christ. [4]For if, indeed, the *one* coming proclaims another Jesus, whom we have not proclaimed, or *if* you receive another spirit which you have not received, or another gospel which you never accepted, you might well endure *these*. [5]For I judge *myself* to have come behind the highest apostles *in* nothing. [6]But even if *I am* unskilled in speech, yet not in knowledge. But in every way *I* have been clearly revealed to you in all things. [7]Or did I commit sin, humbling myself that you might be exalted, because I preached the gospel of God to you without charge? [8]I stripped other churches, receiving wages for the serving of you. [9]And being present with you, and lacking, I was not a burden to anyone. The brothers coming from Macedonia completely made up for my lack. And in every way I kept myself without burden *to you*; and I will keep *myself*.

[10]The truth of Christ is in me, that this boasting shall not be silenced in me in the regions of Achaia. [11]Why? Because I do not love you? God knows. [12]But what I do, I also will do, that I may cut off the opportunity of those desiring an opportunity, so that in that which they boast, they be found

CHAPTER 11

3785 430 3450 3398 877 235
1 Ὄφελον ἀνείχεσθέ μου μικρὸν τῇ ἀφροσύνῃ· ἀλλὰ καὶ
I would that you endured me a little of foolishness, but, indeed,
430 3450 2206/1063/5209 2316 2205 718 1063
2 ἀνέχεσθέ μου. ζηλῶ γὰρ ὑμᾶς Θεοῦ ζήλῳ· ἡρμοσάμην γὰρ
bear with me. I am jealous For (over) you of God with a jealousy, I joined for
5209/1520/435 3933 53 3936 5547
ὑμᾶς ἑνὶ ἀνδρὶ παρθένον ἁγνὴν παραστῆσαι τῷ Χριστῷ.
you to one husband a virgin pure to present to Christ.
5399 3361/4459/5613/3789/2096 1816 1722 3834
3 φοβοῦμαι δὲ μή πως ὡς ὁ ὄφις Εὔαν ἐξηπάτησεν ἐν τῇ πανουρ-
I fear And lest somehow as the serpent Eve deceived in the craftiness
848 3779 5351 3540 5216 575 572
γίᾳ αὐτοῦ, οὕτω φθαρῇ τὰ νοήματα ὑμῶν ἀπὸ τῆς ἁπλό-
of him so should be spoiled the thoughts of you from the simplic-
1519 5547 1487/3303/1063 2064 243
4 τητος τῆς εἰς τὸν Χριστόν. εἰ μὲν γὰρ ὁ ἐρχόμενος ἄλλον
ity (due) to Christ. if indeed For the *one* coming another
2424 2784 3739/3756 2784 2228 4151 2087 2983
Ἰησοῦν κηρύσσει ὃν οὐκ ἐκηρύξαμεν, ἢ πνεῦμα ἕτερον λαμ-
Jesus proclaims whom not we have proclaimed, or spirit another you
3739/3756/2983/2228/ 2098 2087/3739/3756 1209
βάνετε ὃ οὐκ ἐλάβετε, ἢ εὐαγγέλιον ἕτερον ὃ οὐκ ἐδέξασθε,
receive which not you received, or gospel another which not you accepted,
2573 430 3049 1063 3367 5302
5 καλῶς ἠνείχεσθε. λογίζομαι γὰρ μηδὲν ὑστερηκέναι τῶν
(these) well you endure. I judge For nothing to have come behind the
5228/3029 652 1487 2399 3056 235 3756
6 ὑπὲρ λίαν ἀποστόλων. εἰ δὲ καὶ ἰδιώτης τῷ λόγῳ, ἀλλ' οὐ
highest apostles. if But indeed unskilled in speech, yet not
1108 235/1722/3956 5319 1722 3956/1519/5209/2228
7 τῇ γνώσει· ἀλλ' ἐν παντὶ φανερωθέντες ἐν πᾶσιν εἰς ὑμᾶς. ἢ
in knowledge, but in every way having been revealed in all things to you. Or
266 4160 1683 5013 2443/5210 5312
ἁμαρτίαν ἐποίησα ἐμαυτὸν ταπεινῶν ἵνα ὑμεῖς ὑψωθῆτε,
sin did I commit myself humbling that you might be exalted,
3754 1432 2316 2098 2097 5213
ὅτι δωρεὰν τὸ τοῦ Θεοῦ εὐαγγέλιον εὐηγγελισάμην ὑμῖν;
because freely the of God gospel I preached to you?
243 1577 4813 2983 3800 4314 5216
8 ἄλλας ἐκκλησίας ἐσύλησα, λαβὼν ὀψώνιον πρὸς τὴν ὑμῶν
Other churches I stripped, having received wages for the of you
1248 3918 4314/5209 5302 3756 2655
9 διακονίαν· καὶ παρὼν πρὸς ὑμᾶς καὶ ὑστερηθείς, οὐ κατενάρ-
ministry, and being present with you and lacking, not I was a
3762 1063 5303 3450 4322
κησα οὐδενός· τὸ γὰρ ὑστέρημά μου προσανεπλήρωσαν
burden of no one; the for lack of me made up completely
80 2064 575 3109 1722 3956 4
οἱ ἀδελφοί, ἐλθόντες ἀπὸ Μακεδονίας· καὶ ἐν παντὶ ἀβαρῆ
the brothers coming from Macedonia; and in every way without burden
5213 1683 5083 5083 2076 225 5547
10 ὑμῖν ἐμαυτὸν ἐτήρησα καὶ τηρήσω. ἔστιν ἀλήθεια Χριστοῦ
to you, myself I kept and I will keep. is (The) truth of Christ
1722/1698/3754 2746 3778/3756 5420 1519/1691/1722
ἐν ἐμοί, ὅτι ἡ καύχησις αὕτη οὐ φραγήσεται εἰς ἐμὲ ἐν τοῖς
in me, that boasting this not shall be silenced in me in the
2824 882 1302 3754/3756 25 5209 2316
11 κλίμασι τῆς Ἀχαΐας. διατί; ὅτι οὐκ ἀγαπῶ ὑμᾶς; ὁ Θεὸς
regions of Achaia. Why? Because not I love you? God
1492/3739 4160 4160 2443 1581 874
12 οἶδεν. ὃ δὲ ποιῶ, καὶ ποιήσω, ἵνα ἐκκόψω τὴν ἀφορμὴν τῶν
knows. what But I do, also I will do, that I may cut off the opportunity of those
2309 874 2443/1722/3739/ 2744 2147 2531
θελόντων ἀφορμήν, ἵνα ἐν ᾧ καυχῶνται, εὑρεθῶσι καθὼς
desiring an opportunity, that in that which they boast, they be found as
2249 1063 5108 5570 2040 1386
13 καὶ ἡμεῖς. οἱ γὰρ τοιοῦτοι ψευδαπόστολοι, ἐργάται δόλιοι,
also we (are). For such (are) false apostles, workers deceitful.

also as we. 13For such ones
are false apostles, deceitful
workers transforming themselves into apostles of
Christ. 14Did not Satan
marvelously transform himself into an angel of light?
15*It is* not a great thing,
then, if also his ministers
transform themselves as
ministers of righteousness;
whose end will be accord-
ing to their works.
16Again I say, let not
anyone think me to be
foolish. But if not, even if as
foolish, receive me, that I
also may boast a little.
17What I speak, I speak not
according to *the* Lord, but
as in foolishness, in this
boldness of boasting.
18Since many boast according to the flesh, I also will
boast. 19For you gladly
endure fools, being wise.
20For you endure if anyone
enslaves you, if anyone
devours, if anyone receives,
if anyone exalts *self*, if
anyone beats you in the
face. 21I speak according to
dishonor, as *if* we have
been weak. But in what-
ever anyone dares—I say *it*
in foolishness—I also dare.
22Are they Hebrews? I also.
Are they Israelites? I also.
Are they Abraham's seed? I
also. 23Are they ministers
of Christ?—I speak as
beside myself—I *being*
beyond *them*: in labors,
more abundantly; in stripes,
beyond measure; in prisons,
much more; in deaths,
many times. 24Five times I
received forty *stripes* minus
one from the Jews. 25I was
flogged three times; I was
stoned once; I was ship-
wrecked three times; I have
spent a night and a day in
the deep. 26*I have been* in
travels often, in dangers of
rivers; in dangers of
robbers; in dangers from
my race; in dangers from
the nations; in dangers in
the city; in dangers in *the*
desert; in dangers on *the*
sea; in dangers among false

3345 1519 652 5547 3756
14 μετασχηματιζόμενοι εἰς ἀποστόλους Χριστοῦ. καὶ οὐ
transforming themselves into apostles of Christ. And not
2298 848 1063 4567 3345 1519
θαυμαστόν· αὐτὸς γὰρ ὁ Σατανᾶς μετασχηματίζεται εἰς
marvelously himself For Satan transform himself into
32 5457 3756 3173 3767 =1499= 1249 848
15 ἄγγελον φωτός. οὐ μέγα οὖν εἰ καὶ οἱ διάκονοι αὐτοῦ
an angel of light? (It is) not a great then, if also the ministers of him
3345 5613/1249 thing, 1343 3739 5056
μετασχηματίζονται ὡς διάκονοι δικαιοσύνης, ὧν τὸ τέλος
transform themselves as ministers of righteousness; of whom the end
2071/2596 2041 848
ἔσται κατὰ τὰ ἔργα αὐτῶν.
will be according to the works of them.
•3165 3825 3004/3361/5100/*/1380 878 1511=1490=1490= 2579
16 Πάλιν λέγω, μή τίς με δόξῃ ἄφρονα εἶναι· εἰ δὲ μή γε, κἂν
Again I say, not anyone me think foolish to be; if but not, even if
5613/878 1209 3165/2443 3398 5100 2504 2744 3739
17 ὡς ἄφρονα δέξασθέ με, ἵνα μικρόν τι κἀγὼ καυχήσωμαι. ὃ
as foolish receive me, that a little I also may boast. What
2980/3756/ 2980/2596 2962 235/5613/1722/ 877 1722 5026
λαλῶ, οὐ λαλῶ κατὰ Κύριον, ἀλλ' ὡς ἐν ἀφροσύνῃ, ἐν ταύτῃ
I speak, not I speak according to (the) Lord, but as in foolishness, in this
5287 2746 1893 4183 2744 2596
18 τῇ ὑποστάσει τῆς καυχήσεως. ἐπεὶ πολλοὶ καυχῶνται κατὰ
boldness of boasting. Since many boast according to
4561 2504 2744 2234 1063 430
19 τὴν σάρκα, κἀγὼ καυχήσομαι. ἡδέως γὰρ ἀνέχεσθε τῶν
the flesh, I also will boast. gladly For you endure
878 5429 5607 430 1063 =1536= 5209 2615
20 ἀφρόνων, φρόνιμοι ὄντες. ἀνέχεσθε γάρ, εἴ τις ὑμᾶς κατα-
fools, wise being. you endure For, if anyone you
=1536= 2719 =1536= 2983 =1536= 1869 =
δουλοῖ, εἴ τις κατεσθίει, εἴ τις λαμβάνει, εἴ τις ἐπαίρεται, εἴ
enslaves, if anyone devours, if anyone receives (you), if anyone lifts (him- if
•5613 1536=5209/1519 4383 1184 2596 819 3004 self) 3754
21 τις ὑμᾶς εἰς πρόσωπον δέρει. κατὰ ἀτιμίαν λέγω, ὡς ὅτι
anyone you in the face beats. According to dishonor I say, as that
•302 2249 770 1722/3739/1161/*/5100 5111 1722 877
ἡμεῖς ἠσθενήσαμεν· ἐν ᾧ δ' ἄν τις τολμᾷ (ἐν ἀφροσύνῃ
we have been weak; in what but ever anyone dares—in foolishness
3004 5111 2504 1445 1526/ 2504 2475
22 λέγω), τολμῶ κἀγώ. Ἑβραῖοί εἰσι; κἀγώ· Ἰσραηλῖταί
I say (it) — dare I also. Hebrews Are they? I also! Israelites
1526 2504 4690 11 1526 2504 1249 5547
23 εἰσι; κἀγώ· σπέρμα Ἀβραάμ εἰσι; κἀγώ· διάκονοι Χριστοῦ
are they? I also! Seed of Abraham are they? I also! Ministers of Christ
1526 3912 2980 5228/1473/1722/ 2873 4056
εἰσι; (παραφρονῶν λαλῶ) ὑπὲρ ἐγώ· ἐν κόποις περισσοτέ-
are they? As beside myself I speak—beyond I in labors more abun-
•1722 1722 4127 5234 (them) 5438 4056
ρως, ἐν πληγαῖς ὑπερβαλλόντως, ἐν φυλακαῖς περισσοτέρως,
dently, in stripes surpassing measure, in prisons more abundantly,
1722 2288 4178 5259 2453 3999 5062
24 ἐν θανάτοις πολλάκις. ὑπὸ Ἰουδαίων πεντάκις τεσσαρά-
in deaths many times. By Jews five times forty
3844/3391 2983 5151 4463 530 3034
25 κοντα παρὰ μίαν ἔλαβον. τρὶς ἐρραβδίσθην, ἅπαξ ἐλιθάσθην,
(stripes) less one I received; thrice I was flogged; once I was stoned;
5151 3489 3574 1722 1037 4160
τρὶς ἐναυάγησα, νυχθήμερον ἐν τῷ βυθῷ πεποίηκα·
thrice I was shipwrecked; a night and a day in the deep I have done;
3597 4178 2794 4215 2794 3027
26 ὁδοιπορίαις πολλάκις, κινδύνοις ποταμῶν, κινδύνοις λῃ-
in travels many times; in dangers of rivers, in dangers of
2794 1537 1085 2794 1537 1484 2794 1722
στῶν, κινδύνοις ἐκ γένους, κινδύνοις ἐξ ἐθνῶν, κινδύνοις ἐν
robbers, in dangers from (my) race, in dangers from nations; in dangers in
4172 2794 1722 2047 2794 1722 2281 2794
πόλει, κινδύνοις ἐν ἐρημίᾳ, κινδύνοις ἐν θαλάσσῃ, κινδύνοις
a city; in dangers in a desert; in dangers in sea; in dangers

brothers; [27]in hardship and toil; often in watchings; in hunger and thirst; often in fastings, in cold and nakedness. [28]Besides the things outside conspiring against me day by day, the care of all the churches. [29]Who is weak, and I am not weak?

Who is offended, and I do not burn? [30]If it is right to boast, I will boast the things of my weakness. [31]The God and Father of our Lord Jesus Christ knows, He who is blessed forever, that I am not lying. [32]In Damascus, the governor of Aretas the king guarded the city of *the* Damascenes, desiring to seize me. [33]And I was let down through a window through the wall in a basket, and escaped their hands.

1722 5569 1722 2873 3449 1722 70
27 ἐν ψευδαδέλφοις· ἐν κόπῳ καὶ μόχθῳ, ἐν ἀγρυπνίαις
among false brothers; in labor and hardship; in watchings
4178 1722 3042 1372/1722/3521 4178 1722 5592
πολλάκις, ἐν λιμῷ καὶ δίψει, ἐν νηστείαις πολλάκις, ἐν ψύχει
many times; in hunger and thirst; in fastings many times; in cold
1132 5565 3924 1999 3450
28 καὶ γυμνότητι. χωρὶς τῶν παρεκτός, ἡ ἐπισύστασίς μου
and nakedness; apart from the things outside, the conspiring against me
2596 2250 3308 3956 1577 5101
29 ἡ καθ᾽ ἡμέραν, ἡ μέριμνα πασῶν τῶν ἐκκλησιῶν. τίς
day by day; the care of all the churches. Who
770 3756 770 5101 4624 3756 1473
ἀσθενεῖ, καὶ οὐκ ἀσθενῶ; τίς σκανδαλίζεται, καὶ οὐκ ἐγὼ
is weak, and not I am weak? Who is offended, and not I
4448 1487 2744 1163 769 3450 2744
30 πυροῦμαι; εἰ καυχᾶσθαι δεῖ, τὰ τῆς ἀσθενείας μου καυχήσο-
burn? If to boast it is right, the things of my weakness I will
2316 3962 2962 2257 2424 5547
31 μαι. ὁ Θεὸς καὶ πατὴρ τοῦ Κυρίου ἡμῶν Ἰησοῦ Χριστοῦ
boast. The God and Father of the Lord of us, Jesus Christ,
1492 5607 2128 1519 165 3754/3756 5574 1722
32 οἶδεν, ὁ ὢν εὐλογητὸς εἰς τοὺς αἰῶνας, ὅτι οὐ ψεύδομαι. ἐν
knows, He being blessed to the ages, that not I am lying. In
1154 1481 702 935 5432
Δαμασκῷ ὁ ἐθνάρχης Ἀρέτα τοῦ βασιλέως ἐφρούρει τὴν
Damascus the governor of Aretas the king guarded the
1153 4172 4084 3165 2309 1223 2376 1722
33 Δαμασκηνῶν πόλιν, πιάσαι με θέλων· καὶ διὰ θυρίδος ἐν
of (the) Damascenes city, to seize me desiring, and through a window in
4553 5465 1223 5038 1628
σαργάνῃ ἐχαλάσθην διὰ τοῦ τείχους, καὶ ἐξέφυγον τὰς
a basket I was lowered through the wall and escaped the
5495 848
χεῖρας αὐτοῦ.
hands of them.

CHAPTER 12

CHAPTER 12

[1]Indeed, to boast *is* not profitable to me; for I will come to visions and revelations of *the* Lord. [2]I know a man in Christ fourteen years ago—whether in the body, I do not know; or out of the body, I do not know; God knows—such a one *was* caught up to *the* third Heaven. [3]And I know such a man—whether in *the* body, or outside the body, I do not know; God knows— [4]that he was caught up into Paradise and heard unspeakable words, which it is not allowed to a man to speak. [5]On behalf of such a one I will boast; but I will not boast on my behalf, except in my weaknesses. [6]For if I desire to boast, I will not be foolish; for I speak the truth. But I spare, that not any may reckon me *to be* beyond

2744 1211/3756 4851 3427 2064 1063 1519 3701
1 Καυχᾶσθαι δὴ οὐ συμφέρει μοι· ἐλεύσομαι γὰρ εἰς ὀπτα-
To boast indeed not (is) profitable to me, I will come for to visions
602 2962 1492 444 1722 5547
2 σίας καὶ ἀποκαλύψεις Κυρίου. οἶδα ἄνθρωπον ἐν Χριστῷ
and revelations of (the) Lord. I know a man in Christ
4253 2094 1180 1535/1722/ 4983 3756 1492/1535/1623
πρὸ ἐτῶν δεκατεσσάρων (εἴτε ἐν σώματι, οὐκ οἶδα· εἴτε ἐκτὸς
before years fourteen —whether in (the) body, not I know; or outside
4983 3756 1492 2316 1492 726 5108
τοῦ σώματος, οὐκ οἶδα· ὁ Θεὸς οἶδεν), ἁρπαγέντα τὸν τοιοῦ-
the body, not I know; God knows — caught up such
2193 5154 3772 1492 5108 444
3 τον ἕως τρίτου οὐρανοῦ. καὶ οἶδα τὸν τοιοῦτον ἄνθρωπον
a one to third Heaven. And I know such a man
1535/1722 4983 1535 1623 4983 3756 1492 2316
4 (εἴτε ἐν σώματι, εἴτε ἐκτὸς τοῦ σώματος, οὐκ οἶδα· ὁ Θεὸς
—whether in (the) body, or outside the body, not I know; God
1492 3754 726 1519 3857 191 731
5 οἶδεν), ὅτι ἡρπάγη εἰς τὸν παράδεισον, καὶ ἤκουσεν ἄρρητα
knows— that he was caught into Paradise and heard unspeakable
4487 3739/3756/1832/444 2980 5228 5108
ῥήματα, ἃ οὐκ ἐξὸν ἀνθρώπῳ λαλῆσαι. ὑπὲρ τοῦ τοιούτου
words, which not it is allowed a man to speak. On behalf of such a one
2744 5228 1683 3756 2744 1508 1722
καυχήσομαι· ὑπὲρ δὲ ἐμαυτοῦ οὐ καυχήσομαι, εἰ μὴ ἐν ταῖς
I will boast; on behalf of but myself not I will boast, except in the
769 3450/1437/1063 2309 2744 3756 2071
6 ἀσθενείαις μου· ἐὰν γὰρ θελήσω καυχήσασθαι, οὐκ ἔσομαι
weaknesses of me, if For I should desire to boast, not I shall be
1691 878 225 1063/2046 5339 3361/5100/1519/*/ 3049
ἄφρων· ἀλήθειαν γὰρ ἐρῶ· φείδομαι δέ, μή τις εἰς ἐμὲ λογίση-
foolish, truth for I will speak; I spare but, lest anyone to me reckons

what he sees me, or hears of me; [7]and by the surpassing revelations, that I not be made haughty, a thorn in the flesh was given to me, a messenger of Satan, that he might buffet me, that I not be made haughty. [8]As to this I entreated the Lord three times, that it depart from me. [9]And he said to me, My grace is sufficient for you; for My power is perfected in weakness. Therefore, I will rather gladly boast in my weaknesses, that the power of Christ may overshadow me. [10]Because of this, I am pleased in weaknesses, in insults, in dire needs, in persecutions, in distresses, for the sake of Christ. For when I may be weak, then I am powerful.

[11]Boasting, I have become foolish. You compelled me. For I ought to be commended by you, for I lacked nothing of the highest apostles, even though I am nothing. [12]Truly the signs of the apostle were worked out among you in all patience, in miracles, and in wonders, and by works of power. [13]For what is it in which you were less than the rest of the churches, except that I myself did not burden you? Forgive me this wrong.

[14]Behold, I am ready to come to you a third *time*. And I will not burden you, for I do not seek your things, but you. For the children ought not to lay up treasure for the parents, but the parents for the children. [15]But I will most gladly spend and be spent for your souls, even if loving you more and more, I am loved *the* less. [16]But let it be *so*, I did not burden you; but being crafty, I caught you

1537 5228 991 3165/2228/ 191/5100//1700 5236
7 ται ὑπὲρ ὅ βλέπει με, ἢ ἀκούει τι ἐξ ἐμοῦ. καὶ τῇ ὑπερβολῇ
beyond what he sees me, or hears of me. and by surpassing
602 2443/3361 5229 1325 3427 4647
τῶν ἀποκαλύψεων ἵνα μὴ ὑπεραίρωμαι, ἐδόθη μοι σκόλοψ
revelations, that not I be made haughty, was given to me a thorn
4561 32 4566 2443/3165 2852 2443/3363/ 5229
τῇ σαρκί, ἄγγελος Σατᾶν ἵνα με κολαφίζῃ, ἵνα μὴ ὑπεραί-
in the flesh, a messenger of Satan, that me he might buffet, lest I be made
5228 5127 5151 2962 3870 2443 868
8 ρωμαι. ὑπὲρ τούτου τρὶς τὸν Κύριον παρεκάλεσα, ἵνα ἀποστῇ
haughty. As to this thrice the Lord I besought, that it depart
575 1700 2046 3427 714 4671 5485 3450 1063
9 ἀπ' ἐμοῦ. καὶ εἴρηκέ μοι, Ἀρκεῖ σοι ἡ χάρις μου· ἡ γὰρ
from me. And He said to me, Enough for you (is) the grace of Me; the for
1411 3450/1722 769 5048 2236 3756 3123
δύναμίς μου ἐν ἀσθενείᾳ τελειοῦται. ἥδιστα οὖν μᾶλλον
power of Me in weakness is perfected. gladly Therefore rather
2744 1722 769 3450/2443 1981 1909/1691
καυχήσομαι ἐν ταῖς ἀσθενείαις μου, ἵνα ἐπισκηνώσῃ ἐπ' ἐμὲ
I will boast in the weaknesses of me, that may overshadow me
1411 5547 1352 2106 1722 769 1722 5196
10 ἡ δύναμις τοῦ Χριστοῦ. διὸ εὐδοκῶ ἐν ἀσθενείαις, ἐν ὕβρεσιν,
the power of Christ. Therefore I am pleased in weaknesses, in insults,
1722 318 1722 1375 1722 4730 5228 5547
ἐν ἀνάγκαις, ἐν διωγμοῖς, ἐν στενοχωρίαις, ὑπὲρ Χριστοῦ·
in dire needs, in persecutions, in distresses, for the sake of Christ.
3752/1063 770 5119 1415 1510
ὅταν γὰρ ἀσθενῶ, τότε δυνατός εἰμι.
when For I may be weak, then powerful I am.
1096 878 2744 5210/3165/ 315 1473
11 Γέγονα ἄφρων καυχώμενος· ὑμεῖς με ἠναγκάσατε· ἐγὼ
I have become foolish boasting you me compelled. I
1063 3784 5259 5216 4921 3762 1063 5302
γὰρ ὤφειλον ὑφ' ὑμῶν συνίστασθαι· οὐδὲν γὰρ ὑστέρησα
For ought by you to be commended. nothing For I lacked
5228 3029 652 =1499=3762 1510 3303 4592
12 τῶν ὑπὲρ λίαν ἀποστόλων, εἰ καὶ οὐδέν εἰμι. τὰ μὲν σημεῖα
of the highest apostles, if even nothing I am. the Indeed signs
652 2716 1722/5213/1722/3956 5281 1722
τοῦ ἀποστόλου κατειργάσθη ἐν ὑμῖν ἐν πάσῃ ὑπομονῇ, ἐν
of the apostle were worked out among you in all patience, by
4592 5059 1411 5101/1065/2076 2274
13 σημείοις καὶ τέρασι καὶ δυνάμεσι. τί γάρ ἐστιν ὃ ἡττήθητε
signs and wonders, and by works of power. what For is it which you were
5228 3062 1577 =1508=3754/ 848 1473/3756 less
ὑπὲρ τὰς λοιπὰς ἐκκλησίας, εἰ μὴ ὅτι αὐτὸς ἐγὼ οὐ κατε-
than the rest of the churches, except that myself I not
2655 5216 5483 3427 93 5026
νάρκησα ὑμῶν; χαρίσασθέ μοι τὴν ἀδικίαν ταύτην.
burdened you? Forgive me wrong this.
2400 5154 2093 2192 2064 4314 5209 3756
14 Ἰδού, τρίτον ἑτοίμως ἔχω ἐλθεῖν πρὸς ὑμᾶς, καὶ οὐ
Behold, a third (time) I am ready to come to you, and not
2655 5216 3756/1063/2212 5216 235 5209 3756
καταναρκήσω ὑμῶν· οὐ γὰρ ζητῶ τὰ ὑμῶν, ἀλλ' ὑμᾶς· οὐ
I will burden you; not for I seek the things of you, but you. not
1063 3784 5043 1118 2343 235
γὰρ ὀφείλει τὰ τέκνα τοῖς γονεῦσι θησαυρίζειν, ἀλλ' οἱ
For ought the children for the parents to lay up treasure, but the
1118 5043 1473 2236 1159 1550
15 γονεῖς τοῖς τέκνοις. ἐγὼ δὲ ἥδιστα δαπανήσω καὶ ἐκδα-
parents for the children. I But most gladly will spend and be
5228 5590 5216 =1499= 4056
πανηθήσομαι ὑπὲρ τῶν ψυχῶν ὑμῶν, εἰ καὶ περισσοτέρως
spent out on behalf of the souls of you; if even more abundantly
5209 25 2276 25 2077 1473 3756 2599
16 ὑμᾶς ἀγαπῶν, ἧττον ἀγαπῶμαι. ἔστω δέ, ἐγὼ οὐ κατε-
you I love, (the) less I am loved. let it be But, I not
5209 235 5225 3835 1388 5209
βάρησα ὑμᾶς· ἀλλ' ὑπάρχων πανοῦργος, δόλῳ ὑμᾶς
burdened you: but being crafty, with guile you

with bait. [17]By any whom I
have sent to you, did I
overreach you by him?
[18]I begged Titus, and sent
the brother with *him*. Did
Titus overreach you? Did we
not walk in the same spirit?
Did *we* not *walk* in the
same steps?

[19]Again, do you think we
are defending to you? We
speak before God in Christ,
but in all things for your
building up, beloved. [20]For
I fear lest somehow coming
I not find you as I wish, and I
be found by you such as you
do not wish; lest somehow
there be strifes, envyings,
angers, rivalries, evil
speakings, whisperings,
proud thoughts, disturb-
ances; [21]that *in* my coming
again my God may not
humble me with you, and I
shall mourn many of those
previously sinning, and not
repenting over the uncleanness, and fornication, and
lustfulness which they have
practiced.

2983 3361/5100/3739 649 4314 5209/1223 846
17 ἔλαβον. μή τινα ὧν ἀπέσταλκα πρὸς ὑμᾶς, δι᾽ αὐτοῦ
I took. Not anyone whom I have sent to you, through him
4122 5209 3870 5103 4862
18 ἐπλεονέκτησα ὑμᾶς; παρεκάλεσα Τίτον, καὶ συναπέστειλα
did I overreach you? I besought Titus, and sent with (him)
80 =3387= 4122 5209 5103 3756 846
τὸν ἀδελφόν· μή τι ἐπλεονέκτησεν ὑμᾶς Τίτος; οὐ τῷ αὐτῷ
the brother, not overreached you Titus? Did not in the same
4151 4043 3756 846 2487
Πνεύματι περιεπατήσαμεν; οὐ τοῖς αὐτοῖς ἴχνεσι;
spirit we walk? Did not in the same steps (we walk)?
3825 1380 3754 5213 626 2714
19 Πάλιν δοκεῖτε ὅτι ὑμῖν ἀπολογούμεθα; κατενώπιον τοῦ
Again, do you think that to you we are defending? Before
2316/1722/ 5547 2980 3956 27 5228
Θεοῦ ἐν Χριστῷ λαλοῦμεν· τὰ δὲ πάντα, ἀγαπητοί, ὑπὲρ
God in Christ we speak; things but in all, beloved, on behalf of
5216 3619 5399 1063 3361/4459 2064 3756
20 τῆς ὑμῶν οἰκοδομῆς. φοβοῦμαι γάρ, μή πως ἐλθὼν οὐχ
the of you building up. I fear For lest some-how coming not
3634 2309 2147 5209 2504 2147 5213 3634 3756/2309/3361
οἵους θέλω εὕρω ὑμᾶς, κἀγὼ εὑρεθῶ ὑμῖν οἷον οὐ θέλετε· μή
such as I wish I find you, and I am found by you such as not you wish, lest
4459 2054 2205 2372 2052 2636 5587
πως ἔρεις, ζῆλοι, θυμοί, ἐριθεῖαι, καταλαλιαί, ψιθυρισμοί,
some-how (be) strifes, envyings, angers, rivalries, evil speakings, whisperings
5450 181 3361 3825 2064 3165 5013
21 φυσιώσεις, ἀκαταστασίαι· μὴ πάλιν ἐλθόντα με ταπεινώσῃ
proud thoughts, disturbances; lest again coming me may humble
2316/3450/4314 5209 3996 4183 4258
ὁ Θεός μου πρὸς ὑμᾶς, καὶ πενθήσω πολλοὺς τῶν προη-
the God of me with you, and I shall mourn many of those having
3361 3340 1909 167
μαρτηκότων, καὶ μὴ μετανοησάντων ἐπὶ τῇ ἀκαθαρσίᾳ καὶ
previously sinned, and not repenting over the uncleanness and
4202 766 3739 4238
πορνείᾳ καὶ ἀσελγείᾳ ᾗ ἔπραξαν.
fornication and lustfulness which they have practiced.

CHAPTER 13

CHAPTER 13

[1]I am coming to you this
third *time*. In *the* mouth of
two or three witnesses
every matter shall be
established. [2]I said
before, and I say before-
hand, as being present the
second *time*, and being
absent now. I write to those
previously sinning, and all
the rest, that if I come again
I will not spare. [3]Since you
seek a proof of Christ
speaking in me; who is
not weak toward you, but is
powerful in you—[4]for even
if He was crucified out of
weakness, yet He lives by
the power of God toward
you—[5]examine yourselves,
whether you are in the faith;
prove yourselves. Or do you
not yourselves know that

5154 5124 2064 4314 5209 1909 4750 1417
1 Τρίτον τοῦτο ἔρχομαι πρὸς ὑμᾶς. ἐπὶ στόματος δύο
(The) third (time) this (is) I am coming to you. At (the) mouth of two
3144 5140 2476 3956 4487 4280
2 μαρτύρων καὶ τριῶν σταθήσεται πᾶν ῥῆμα. προείρηκα καὶ
witnesses and of three shall be established every matter. I said before, and
4302 5613 3918 1208 548 3568 1125
προλέγω, ὡς παρὼν τὸ δεύτερον, καὶ ἀπὼν νῦν γράφω
I say beforehand, as being present the second, and being absent now, I write
4258 3062 3956 3756/1437/2064
τοῖς προημαρτηκόσι καὶ τοῖς λοιποῖς πᾶσιν, ὅτι ἐὰν ἔλθω
to those having previously sinned, and the rest all, that if I come
1519 3825 3756 5339 1893 1382 2212 1722/1698
3 εἰς τὸ πάλιν, οὐ φείσομαι· ἐπεὶ δοκιμὴν ζητεῖτε τοῦ ἐν ἐμοὶ
— — again, not I will spare, since a proof you seek in me
2980 5547 3739/1519/5209/3756 770 235 1414
λαλοῦντος Χριστοῦ, ὃς εἰς ὑμᾶς οὐκ ἀσθενεῖ, ἀλλὰ δυνατεῖ
speaking of Christ, who toward you not is weak, but is powerful
1722/5213 1063/1487/ 4717 1537 769 235/2198/1537
4 ἐν ὑμῖν· καὶ γὰρ εἰ ἐσταυρώθη ἐξ ἀσθενείας, ἀλλὰ ζῇ ἐκ
in you. even For if He was crucified out of weakness, but He lives by
1411 2316 1063 2249 770 1722/846 235
δυνάμεως Θεοῦ. καὶ γὰρ καὶ ἡμεῖς ἀσθενοῦμεν ἐν αὐτῷ, ἀλλὰ
(the) power of God. indeed For even we are weak in Him, but
2198 4862 846/1537 1411 2316/1519/5209 1438
5 ζησόμεθα σὺν αὐτῷ ἐκ δυνάμεως Θεοῦ εἰς ὑμᾶς. ἑαυτοὺς
we shall live with Him by (the) power of God toward you. Yourselves
3985 1487/2075/1722 4102 1438 1381 2228/3756
πειράζετε εἰ ἐστὲ ἐν τῇ πίστει, ἑαυτοὺς δοκιμάζετε. ἢ οὐκ
examine, if you are in the faith, yourselves test; or do not

Jesus Christ is in you, unless you are reprobates?
[6]And I hope you will know that we are not reprobates.
[7]But I pray to God *for* you not to do evil, none. *And* not that we may appear approved, but that you may do the good; but we *being deemed* to be reprobates.
[8]For we have no power against the truth, but for the truth. [9]For we rejoice when we are weak, and you are powerful. But we pray for this also, your perfection.
[10]Because of this, I write these things while absent, that being present I may not deal sharply *with you* according to the authority which the Lord gave me for building up, and not for pulling down.

[11]For the rest, brothers, rejoice! Perfect yourselves; encourage yourselves; mind the same thing; be at peace; and the God of love and of peace will be with you.

[12]Greet one another with a holy kiss.

[13]All the saints greet you.

[14]The grace of the Lord Jesus Christ, and the love of God, and the fellowship of the Holy Spirit *be* with you all. Amen.

1921 1438 3754 2424 5547 1722/5213/2076
ἐπιγινώσκετε ἑαυτούς, ὅτι Ἰησοῦς Χριστὸς ἐν ὑμῖν ἐστίν;
you perceive yourselves that Jesus Christ in you is.
=1508= 96 2075 1679 3754 1097 3754/2249/3756
6 εἰ μή τι ἀδόκιμοί ἐστε. ἐλπίζω δὲ ὅτι γνώσεσθε ὅτι ἡμεῖς οὐκ
unless reprobates you are. I hope And that you will know that we not
2070 96 2172 4314 2316/3361 4160 5209
7 ἐσμὲν ἀδόκιμοι. εὔχομαι δὲ πρὸς τὸν Θεόν, μὴ ποιῆσαι ὑμᾶς
are reprobates. I pray And to God not to do you
2556 3367 3756/2443/2249 1384 5316 235/2443/2249
κακὸν μηδέν, οὐχ ἵνα ἡμεῖς δόκιμοι φανῶμεν, ἀλλ' ἵνα ὑμεῖς
evil, none; not that we approved may appear, but that you
2570 4160 2249 5613 96 5600 3756/1063/ 1410
8 τὸ καλὸν ποιῆτε, ἡμεῖς δὲ ὡς ἀδόκιμοι ὦμεν. οὐ γὰρ δυνά-
the good may do; we and (deemed) reprobates to be. not For we can
5100/2596 225 235 5228 225 5463
9 μεθά τι κατὰ τῆς ἀληθείας, ἀλλ' ὑπὲρ τῆς ἀληθείας. χαίρομεν
power any against the the truth, but for the truth. we rejoice
1063/ 3752 2249 770 5210 1415 5600 5124
γὰρ ὅταν ἡμεῖς ἀσθενῶμεν, ὑμεῖς δὲ δυνατοὶ ἦτε· τοῦτο δὲ
For when we are weak, you and powerful are; this also
2172 5216 2676 1223 5124 5023 548
10 καὶ εὐχόμεθα, τὴν ὑμῶν κατάρτισιν. διὰ τοῦτο ταῦτα ἀπὼν
and we pray, the of you perfection. Therefore these things being absent
1125 2443 3918 3361 664 5530 2596
γράφω, ἵνα παρὼν μὴ ἀποτόμως χρήσωμαι, κατὰ τὴν
I write, that being present not sharply I may deal according to the
1849 3739 1325/3427 2962 1519 3619 3756/1519
ἐξουσίαν ἣν ἔδωκέ μοι ὁ Κύριος εἰς οἰκοδομήν, καὶ οὐκ εἰς
authority which gave me the Lord for building up and not for
2506
καθαίρεσιν.
pulling down.
3063 80 5463 2675 3870
11 Λοιπόν, ἀδελφοί, χαίρετε· καταρτίζεσθε, παρακαλεῖσθε,
For the rest, brothers, rejoice; perfect yourselves, encourage yourselves
846 5426 1514 2316 26
τὸ αὐτὸ φρονεῖτε, εἰρηνεύετε· καὶ ὁ Θεὸς τῆς ἀγάπης καὶ
the same thing mind, be at peace, and the God of love and
1515 2071/3326/ 5216 782 240 1722 40
12 εἰρήνης ἔσται μεθ' ὑμῶν. ἀσπάσασθε ἀλλήλους ἐν ἁγίῳ
of peace will be with you. Greet one another with a holy
5370
φιλήματι.
kiss.
782 5209 40 3956
13 Ἀσπάζονται ὑμᾶς οἱ ἅγιοι πάντες.
Greet you the saints all.
5485 2962 2424 5547 26
14 Ἡ χάρις τοῦ Κυρίου Ἰησοῦ Χριστοῦ, καὶ ἡ ἀγάπη τοῦ
The grace of the Lord Jesus Christ, and the love
2316 2842 40 4151 3326 3956
Θεοῦ, καὶ ἡ κοινωνία τοῦ Ἁγίου Πνεύματος μετὰ πάντων
of God, and the fellowship of the Holy Spirit (be) with all
5216 281
ὑμῶν. ἀμήν.
you. Amen.

ΠΑΥΛΟΥ
PAUL
Η ΠΡΟΣ
THE TO
ΓΑΛΑΤΑΣ ΕΠΙΣΤΟΛΗ
(THE) GALATIANS EPISTLE

THE EPISTLE TO *THE* GALATIANS

A LITERAL TRANSLATION OF THE BIBLE

CHAPTER 1

1 Paul, an apostle, not
from men, nor through man,
but through Jesus Christ
and God *the* Father; the *One*
raising Him from *the* dead;
2 and all the brothers with
me, to the churches of
Galatia. 3 Grace to you, and
peace, from God *the* Father
and our Lord Jesus Christ,
4 who gave Himself for our
sins, so that He might
deliver us out of the present
evil age, according to the
will of our God and Father,
5 to whom *be* the glory
forever and ever. Amen.

6 I wonder that you are so
quickly being transferred
from Him having called you
by *the* grace of Christ to
another gospel, 7 which is
not another; only some
there are troubling you and
desiring to pervert the
gospel of Christ. 8 But even
if we, or an angel out of
Heaven, should preach a
gospel to you beside what
we preached to you, let him
be accursed. 9 As we have
said before, and now I say
again, If anyone preaches a
gospel to you beside what
you received, let him be
accursed.
10 For do I now persuade
men, or God? Or do I seek to
please men? For if I yet
pleased men, I would not
have been a slave of Christ.

CHAPTER 1

3972 652 3756 575 444 3761 1223
1 Παῦλος ἀπόστολος (οὐκ ἀπ' ἀνθρώπων, οὐδὲ δι'
Paul an apostle not from men, nor through
444 235 1223 2424 5547 2316 3962
ἀνθρώπου, ἀλλὰ διὰ Ἰησοῦ Χριστοῦ, καὶ Θεοῦ πατρὸς
man, but through Jesus Christ, and God (the) Father
1453 846/1537 3498 4862/1698 3956
2 τοῦ ἐγείραντος αὐτὸν ἐκ νεκρῶν), καὶ οἱ σὺν ἐμοὶ πάντες
He having raised Him from (the) dead; and those with me all
80 1577 1053 5485/5213 1515
3 ἀδελφοί, ταῖς ἐκκλησίαις τῆς Γαλατίας· χάρις ὑμῖν καὶ εἰρήνη
brothers, to the churches of Galatia, Grace to you and peace
575 2316 3962 2962 2257 2424 5547
4 ἀπὸ Θεοῦ πατρός, καὶ Κυρίου ἡμῶν Ἰησοῦ Χριστοῦ, τοῦ
from God (the) Father, and (the) Lord of us, Jesus Christ, the (One)
1325 1438 5228 266 2257 3704 1807
δόντος ἑαυτὸν ὑπὲρ τῶν ἁμαρτιῶν ἡμῶν, ὅπως ἐξέληται
having given Himself for the sins of us, so as He might deliver
5209/1537 1764 165 4190 2596 2307
ἡμᾶς ἐκ τοῦ ἐνεστῶτος αἰῶνος πονηροῦ, κατὰ τὸ θέλημα
us out of the present age of evil, according to the will
2316 3962 2257/3739 1391/1519 165
5 τοῦ Θεοῦ καὶ πατρὸς ἡμῶν· ᾧ ἡ δόξα εἰς τοὺς αἰῶνας τῶν
of the God and Father of us, whose (is) the glory to the ages of the
165 281
αἰώνων. ἀμήν.
ages. Amen.
2296 3754 3779 5030 3346 575 2564
6 Θαυμάζω ὅτι οὕτω ταχέως μετατίθεσθε ἀπὸ τοῦ καλέ-
I wonder that so quickly are being transferred from the (One) hav-
5209/1722/5485 5547 1519 2087 2098 3739
7 σαντος ὑμᾶς ἐν χάριτι Χριστοῦ εἰς ἕτερον εὐαγγέλιον· ὅ
ing called you by (the) grace of Christ to another gospel, which
3756/2076 243 =1508= 5100 1526 5015 5209
οὐκ ἔστιν ἄλλο, εἰ μή τινές εἰσιν οἱ ταράσσοντες ὑμᾶς καὶ
not is another, only some there are troubling you and
2309 3344 2098 5547 235
8 θέλοντες μεταστρέψαι τὸ εὐαγγέλιον τοῦ Χριστοῦ. ἀλλὰ
desiring to pervert the gospel of Christ. But
1437/2249/2228/ 32 1537 3772 2097 5213/3844
καὶ ἐὰν ἡμεῖς ἢ ἄγγελος ἐξ οὐρανοῦ εὐαγγελίζηται ὑμῖν παρ'
even if we or an angel out of Heaven preach a gospel to you beside
3739 2097 5213 331 2077 5613 4280
9 ὃ εὐηγγελισάμεθα ὑμῖν, ἀνάθεμα ἔστω. ὡς προειρήκαμεν,
what we preached to you, accursed let him be. As we have said before,
*3739 737 3825 3004 =1536= 5209 2097 3844 *
καὶ ἄρτι πάλιν λέγω, εἴ τις ὑμᾶς εὐαγγελίζεται παρ' ὅ
and now again I say, if anyone you preaches a gospel beside what
3880 331 2077 737 1063 444 3982
10 παρελάβετε, ἀνάθεμα ἔστω. ἄρτι γὰρ ἀνθρώπους πείθω
you received, accursed let him be. now For men do I persuade,
2228 2316/2228/2212 444 700 1487/1063/2089/ 444
ἢ τὸν Θεόν ; ἢ ζητῶ ἀνθρώποις ἀρέσκειν ; εἰ γὰρ ἔτι ἀνθρώ-
or God? Or do I seek men to please? if For yet men
700 5547 1401 3756/302/2252
ποις ἤρεσκον, Χριστοῦ δοῦλος οὐκ ἂν ἤμην.
I pleased, of Christ a slave not would I be

NOTE: Frequent words not numbered: δέ(1161); καί(2531)—and, but; ὁ, ἡ, τό (3588, the)— * above word, look in verse margin for No.

[11]And, brothers, I make known to you the gospel preached by me, that it is not according to man. [12]For I did not receive it from man, nor was I taught *it*, but by a revelation of Jesus Christ. [13]For you heard my way of life when *I was* in Judaism, that with surpassing *zeal* I persecuted the church of God, and ravaged it. [14]And *I* progressed in Judaism beyond many contemporaries in my race, being much more a zealot of the traditions of my ancestors.

[15]But when God was pleased, He having separated me from my mother's womb, and having called through His grace, [16]to reveal His Son in me, that I might preach Him among the nations; immediately I did not confer with flesh and blood, [17]nor did I go up to Jerusalem to the apostles before me; but I went away into Arabia, and returned again to Damascus.

[18]Then after three years I went up to Jerusalem to learn from Peter, and remained with him fifteen days. [19]But I saw *no* other of the apostles, except James the brother of the Lord. [20]And what I write to you, behold, before God I do not lie. [21]Then I went into the regions of Syria and of Cilicia; [22]but I was not known by face to the churches of Judea in Christ. [23]But only they were hearing that the *one* who then *was* persecuting us now preaches the gospel, the faith which he ravaged then. [24]And they glorified God in me.

1107 5213 80 2098 2097
11 Γνωρίζω δὲ ὑμῖν, ἀδελφοί, τὸ εὐαγγέλιον τὸ εὐαγγελισθὲ
I make known And to you, brothers, the gospel preached
5259/1700/3754/3756/2076/2596 444 3761/1063/1473/3844
12 ὑπ' ἐμοῦ, ὅτι οὐκ ἔστι κατὰ ἄνθρωπον. οὐδὲ γὰρ ἐγὼ παρὰ
by me, that not it is according to man. not For I from
444 3880 846 3777 1321 235 1223
ἀνθρώπου παρέλαβον αὐτό, οὔτε ἐδιδάχθην, ἀλλὰ δι'
man received it, nor was I taught (by man), but by
602 2424 5547 191 1063 1699
13 ἀποκαλύψεως Ἰησοῦ Χριστοῦ. ἠκούσατε γὰρ τὴν ἐμὴν
a revelation of Jesus Christ. you heard For my
391 4218/1722 2454 3754/2596 5236
ἀναστροφήν ποτε ἐν τῷ Ἰουδαϊσμῷ, ὅτι καθ' ὑπερβολὴν
way of life when in the Judaism, that with surpassing (zeal)
1377 1577 2316 4199 846
14 ἐδίωκον τὴν ἐκκλησίαν τοῦ Θεοῦ, καὶ ἐπόρθουν αὐτήν· καὶ
I persecuted the church of God, and ravaged it, and
4298 1722 2454 5228 4183 4915
προέκοπτον ἐν τῷ Ἰουδαϊσμῷ ὑπὲρ πολλοὺς συνηλικιώτας
progressed in Judaism beyond many contemporarie
1722 1085/3450 4056 2207 5225
ἐν τῷ γένει μου, περισσοτέρως ζηλωτὴς ὑπάρχων τῶν
in the race of me, much more a zealot being of the
3987 3450 3862 3753 2106 2316
15 πατρικῶν μου παραδόσεων. ὅτε δὲ εὐδόκησεν ὁ Θεός, ὁ
ancestral of me traditions. when But was pleased God, He
873 3165/1537 2836 3384 3450 2564 1223
ἀφορίσας με ἐκ κοιλίας μητρός μου καὶ καλέσας διὰ τῆς
separating me from belly mother's my, and calling through the
5485 848 601 5207 848 1722/1698/2443
16 χάριτος αὐτοῦ, ἀποκαλύψαι τὸν υἱὸν αὐτοῦ ἐν ἐμοί, ἵνα
grace of Him to reveal the Son of Him in me, that
2097 846/1722 1484 2112 3756 4323
εὐαγγελίζωμαι αὐτὸν ἐν τοῖς ἔθνεσιν, εὐθέως οὐ προσανε-
I might preach Him among the nations, immediately not I conferred
4561 129 3761 424 1519 2414 4314
17 θέμην σαρκὶ καὶ αἵματι· οὐδὲ ἀνῆλθον εἰς Ἱεροσόλυμα πρὸς
with flesh and blood, neither did I go up to Jerusalem to
4253/1700 652 235 565 1519 688
τοὺς πρὸ ἐμοῦ ἀποστόλους, ἀλλ' ἀπῆλθον εἰς Ἀραβίαν, καὶ
the before me apostles, but I went away into Arabia, and
3825 5290 1519 1154
πάλιν ὑπέστρεψα εἰς Δαμασκόν.
again returned to Damascus.
1899 3326/2094/5140 424 1519 2414 2477
18 Ἔπειτα μετὰ ἔτη τρία ἀνῆλθον εἰς Ἱεροσόλυμα ἱστορῆσαι
Then after years three I went up to Jerusalem to learn from
4074 1961 4314 846 2250 1178 2087
19 Πέτρον, καὶ ἐπέμεινα πρὸς αὐτὸν ἡμέρας δεκαπέντε. ἕτερον
Peter, and remained with him days fifteen, other
652 3756 1492 =1508= 2385 80
δὲ τῶν ἀποστόλων οὐκ εἶδον, εἰ μὴ Ἰάκωβον τὸν ἀδελφὸν
but of the apostles not I saw, except James the brother
2962 3739 1125 5213 2400 1799 2316/3754
20 τοῦ Κυρίου. ἃ δὲ γράφω ὑμῖν, ἰδοὺ ἐνώπιον τοῦ Θεοῦ, ὅτι
of the Lord. what And I write to you, behold before God, that
3756 5574 1899 2064/1519 2824 4947
21 οὐ ψεύδομαι. ἔπειτα ἦλθον εἰς τὰ κλίματα τῆς Συρίας καὶ τῆς
not I lie. Then I went into the regions of Syria and
2791 2257 50 4383 1577
22 Κιλικίας. ἤμην δὲ ἀγνοούμενος τῷ προσώπῳ ταῖς ἐκκλησίαις
of Cilicia. I was And unknown by face to the churches
2449 1722 5547 3440 191 2258 3754
23 τῆς Ἰουδαίας ταῖς ἐν Χριστῷ· μόνον δὲ ἀκούοντες ἦσαν ὅτι
of Judea in Christ. only But hearing they were that
1377 2248/4218 3568 2097 4102 3739/4218
Ὁ διώκων ἡμᾶς ποτέ, νῦν εὐαγγελίζεται τὴν πίστιν ἥν ποτε
the (one) persecuting us then now preaches the gospel, the faith which then
4199 1392 1722/1698 2316
24 ἐπόρθει. καὶ ἐδόξαζον ἐν ἐμοὶ τὸν Θεόν.
he ravaged; and they glorified in me God.

CHAPTER 2

[1]Then through fourteen years I again went up to Jerusalem with Barnabas, also taking Titus with *me*. [2]And I went up according to revelation. And I put before them the gospel which I proclaim in the nations, but privately to the ones seeming *to be pillars*, lest I run, or I ran, into vanity. [3]But not even Titus, the *one* with me, a Greek, was compelled to be circumcised. [4]But because of those false brothers stealing in, who stole in to spy on our freedom which we have in Christ Jesus, they desiring to enslave us; [5]to whom not even for an hour we yielded in subjection, that the truth of the gospel might continue with you; [6]but from those seeming to be something—of what kind they were then does not matter to me; God does not accept the face of man —for those seeming *important* conferred nothing to me; [7]but on the contrary, seeing that I have been entrusted *with* the gospel of the uncircumcision, even as Peter to the circumcision —[8]for He working in Peter to an apostleship of the circumcision also worked in me to the nations—[9]and knowing the grace given to me, James and Cephas and John, those seeming to be pillars, gave right *hands* of fellowship to Barnabas and to me, that we *go* to the nations, but they to the circumcision; [10]only that we might remember the poor, which same thing I was eager to do.

[11]But when Peter came to Antioch, I opposed *him* to his face, because he was to be blamed. [12]For before

CHAPTER 2

1899 1223 1180 2094 3825 305 1519 2414
1 Ἔπειτα διὰ δεκατεσσάρων ἐτῶν πάλιν ἀνέβην εἰς Ἱεροσό-
Then through fourteen years again I went up to Jerusa-
3326 921 4838 5103 305
2 λυμα μετὰ Βαρνάβα, συμπαραλαβὼν καὶ Τίτον. ἀνέβην δὲ
lem with Barnabas, taking with (me) also Titus. I went up And
2596 602 394 846 2098
κατὰ ἀποκάλυψιν, καὶ ἀνεθέμην αὐτοῖς τὸ εὐαγγέλιον ὃ
according to a revelation, and I put before them the gospel which
2784 1722 1484 2596 2398 1380 =3381=1519
κηρύσσω ἐν τοῖς ἔθνεσι, κατ' ἰδίαν δὲ τοῖς δοκοῦσι, μή πως εἰς
I proclaim in the nations, privately but to those seeming, lest into
2756 5143/2228/ 5143 235 3761 5103 4862/1698 1672
3 κενὸν τρέχω ἢ ἔδραμον. ἀλλ' οὐδὲ Τίτος ὁ σὺν ἐμοί, Ἕλλην
vanity I run or I ran. But not even Titus, he with me, a Greek
5607 314 4059 1223 3920
4 ὤν, ἠναγκάσθη περιτμηθῆναι· διὰ δὲ τοὺς παρεισάκτους
being, was compelled to be circumcised; on ac- but those stealing
5569 3748 3922 count of 2684
ψευδαδέλφους, οἵτινες παρεισῆλθον κατασκοπῆσαι τὴν
false brothers, who stole in to spy on the
1657 2257 3739 2192 1722 5547 2424 2443 2248
ἐλευθερίαν ἡμῶν ἣν ἔχομεν ἐν Χριστῷ Ἰησοῦ, ἵνα ἡμᾶς
freedom of us which we have in Christ Jesus, that us
2615 3739/3761/4314/5610 1502 5292
5 καταδουλώσωνται· οἷς οὐδὲ πρὸς ὥραν εἴξαμεν τῇ ὑποταγῇ,
they desire to enslave; to whom not for an hour yielded we in subjection
2443 225 2098 1265 4314/5209 575
6 ἵνα ἡ ἀλήθεια τοῦ εὐαγγελίου διαμείνῃ πρὸς ὑμᾶς. ἀπὸ δὲ
that the truth of the gospel might continue with you. from But
1380 1511/5100 3697 4218 2258 3762 3427
τῶν δοκούντων εἶναί τι (ὁποῖοί ποτε ἦσαν οὐδέν μοι
those seeming to be something – of what kind then they were not to me
1308 4383 2316 444 3756 2983 1698
διαφέρει· πρόσωπον Θεὸς ἀνθρώπου οὐ λαμβάνει)—ἐμοὶ
matters; the face God of man does not accept – to me
1063 1380 3762 4323 235 5121
7 γὰρ οἱ δοκοῦντες οὐδὲν προσανέθεντο· ἀλλὰ τοὐναντίον,
for those seeming nothing conferred but on the contrary
1492 3754 4100 2098 203
ἰδόντες ὅτι πεπίστευμαι τὸ εὐαγγέλιον τῆς ἀκροβυστίας,
knowing that I have been entrusted (with) the gospel of the uncircumcision,
2531 4074 4061 1063 1754 4074 1519
8 καθὼς Πέτρος τῆς περιτομῆς (ὁ γὰρ ἐνεργήσας Πέτρῳ εἰς
even as Peter to the circumcision – the (One) for working in Peter to
651 4061 1754 1698/1519 1484
ἀποστολὴν τῆς περιτομῆς, ἐνήργησε καὶ ἐμοὶ εἰς τὰ ἔθνη),
an apostleship of the circumcision, worked also in me to the nations–
1097 5485 1325 3427 2385
9 καὶ γνόντες τὴν χάριν τὴν δοθεῖσάν μοι, Ἰάκωβος καὶ
and knowing the grace given to me, James and
2786 2491 1380 4769 1511 1188
Κηφᾶς καὶ Ἰωάννης, οἱ δοκοῦντες στύλοι εἶναι, δεξιὰς
Cephas and John, those seeming pillars to be, right (hands)
1325 1698 921 2842 2443 2249/1519 1484
ἔδωκαν ἐμοὶ καὶ Βαρνάβᾳ κοινωνίας, ἵνα ἡμεῖς εἰς τὰ ἔθνη,
gave to me and to Barnabas of fellowship, that we to the nations,
846 1519 4061 3440 4434 2443 3421
10 αὐτοὶ δὲ εἰς τὴν περιτομήν· μόνον τῶν πτωχῶν ἵνα μνημο-
they but to the circumcision; only the poor that we might
4704 846 5124 4160
νεύωμεν, ὃ καὶ ἐσπούδασα αὐτὸ τοῦτο ποιῆσαι.
remember, which indeed I was eager this same thing to do.
3753 2064 4074 1519 490 2596 4383
11 Ὅτε δὲ ἦλθε Πέτρος εἰς Ἀντιόχειαν, κατὰ πρόσωπον
when But came Peter to Antioch, against face
846 436 3754 2607 2258 4253 1063 2064
12 αὐτῷ ἀντέστην, ὅτι κατεγνωσμένος ἦν. πρὸ τοῦ γὰρ ἐλθεῖν
to him I opposed, because to be condemned he was. before the for coming

some came from James, he
ate with the Gentiles. But
when they came, he drew
back and separated him-
self, being afraid of those of
the circumcision. [13]And
also the rest of the Jews
dissembled with him, so as
even Barnabas was led
away with their dissem-
bling. [14]But when I saw
that they did not walk
uprightly with the truth of
the gospel, I said to Peter
before all, If you being a
Jew live *as* a Gentile, and
not *as the* Jews, why do
you compel the Gentiles to
Judaize? [15]We Jews by
nature, and not sinners of
the Gentiles—[16]knowing
that a man is not justified by
works of law, but through
faith *in* Jesus Christ—we
also believed in Christ
Jesus, that we may be justified by faith *in* Christ, and
not by works of law, be-
cause all flesh will not be
justified by works of law.
[17]But if seeking to be justified in Christ, we ourselves
also were found *to be*
sinners, *is* Christ then a
minister of sin? Let it not be!
[18]For if I build again these
things which I destroyed, I
confirm myself *as* a transgressor. [19]For through law I
died to law, that I might live
to God. [20]I have been
crucified with Christ; and I
live, *yet* no longer I, but
Christ lives in me. And that
life I now live in the flesh, I
live by faith toward the Son
of God, the *One* loving me
and giving Himself over on
my behalf. [21]I do not set
aside the grace of God; for if
righteousness is through
law, then Christ died
without cause.

5100 575 2385 3326 1484 4906 3753
τινὰς ἀπὸ Ἰακώβου, μετὰ τῶν ἐθνῶν συνήσθιεν· ὅτε δὲ
of some from James, with the nations he ate; when but
2064 5288 873 1438 5399 1537
ἦλθον, ὑπέστελλε καὶ ἀφώριζεν ἑαυτόν, φοβούμενος τοὺς ἐκ
they came, he drew back and separated himself, being afraid of those of
4061 4942 846 3062 2453
13 περιτομῆς. καὶ συνυπεκρίθησαν αὐτῷ καὶ οἱ λοιποὶ Ἰουδαῖοι,
the circumcision. And dissembled with him also the rest of the Jews,
5620 921 4879 848 5272 235
14 ὥστε καὶ Βαρνάβας συναπήχθη αὐτῶν τῇ ὑποκρίσει. ἀλλ'
so as even Barnabas was led away with of them the dissembling. But
3753 1492 3754/3756 3716 4314 225
ὅτε εἶδον ὅτι οὐκ ὀρθοποδοῦσι πρὸς τὴν ἀλήθειαν τοῦ
when I saw that not they walked uprightly with the truth of the
2098 2036 4074 1715 3956 1487/4771
εὐαγγελίου, εἶπον τῷ Πέτρῳ ἔμπροσθεν πάντων, Εἰ σύ,
gospel, I said to Peter, in front of all, If you
2453 5225 1483 2198 3756 2452 5101
Ἰουδαῖος ὑπάρχων, ἐθνικῶς ζῇς καὶ οὐκ Ἰουδαϊκῶς, τί τὰ
a Jew being, a Gentile live, and not (as the) Jews why the
1484 314 2450 2249 5449 2453 3756
15 ἔθνη ἀναγκάζεις Ἰουδαΐζειν; ἡμεῖς φύσει Ἰουδαῖοι, καὶ οὐκ
Gentiles you compel to judaize? We by nature Jews, and not
1537 1484 268 1492 3754/3756 1344 444
16 ἐξ ἐθνῶν ἁμαρτωλοί, εἰδότες ὅτι οὐ δικαιοῦται ἄνθρωπος
of (the) Gentiles sinners, knowing that not is justified a man
1537 2041 3551 1437/3361/1223/ 4102 2424 5547
ἐξ ἔργων νόμου, ἐὰν μὴ διὰ πίστεως Ἰησοῦ Χριστοῦ, καὶ
by works of law, except through faith (in) Jesus Christ, even
2249/1519 5547 2424 4100 2443 1344 1537
ἡμεῖς εἰς Χριστὸν Ἰησοῦν ἐπιστεύσαμεν, ἵνα δικαιωθῶμεν ἐκ
we in Christ Jesus believed that we may be justified by
4102 5547 3756 1537/2041/3551 1360/3756/ 1344
πίστεως Χριστοῦ, καὶ οὐκ ἐξ ἔργων νόμου· διότι οὐ δικαιωθή-
faith (in) Christ, and not of works of law, because not will be justi-
1537/2041 3551 3956 4561/1487 2212 1344
17 σεται ἐξ ἔργων νόμου πᾶσα σάρξ. εἰ δέ, ζητοῦντες δικαιωθῆ-
fied by works of law all flesh. if But seeking to be justified
1722 5547 2147 848 268 687
ναι ἐν Χριστῷ, εὑρέθημεν καὶ αὐτοὶ ἁμαρτωλοί, ἄρα
in Christ we were found also ourselves sinners, then
5547 266 1249 3361/ 1096 1487/1063/3739/ 2647
18 Χριστὸς ἁμαρτίας διάκονος; μὴ γένοιτο. εἰ γὰρ ἃ κατέλυσα,
(is) Christ of sin a minister? Not let it be! if For what I destroyed,
5023 3825 3618 3848 1683 4921 1473
19 ταῦτα πάλιν οἰκοδομῶ, παραβάτην ἐμαυτὸν συνίστημι. ἐγὼ
these things again I build, a transgressor myself I establish. I
1063/1223/ 3551 3551 599 2443 2316 2198 5547
20 γὰρ διὰ νόμου νόμῳ ἀπέθανον, ἵνα Θεῷ ζήσω. Χριστῷ
For through law to law died, that to God I might live. With Christ
4957 2198 3765 1473/2198 1722/1698 5547
συνεσταύρωμαι· ζῶ δέ, οὐκέτι ἐγώ, ζῇ δὲ ἐν ἐμοὶ Χριστός·
I have been crucified; I live and, no longer I, lives but in me Christ;
3739 3568/2198/1722/4561/1722/4102/2198 5207 2316
ὃ δὲ νῦν ζῶ ἐν σαρκί, ἐν πίστει ζῶ τῇ τοῦ υἱοῦ τοῦ Θεοῦ, τοῦ
the (life) but now I live in flesh, by faith I live to the Son of God, He
25 3165 3860 1438 5228 1700 3756
21 ἀγαπήσαντός με καὶ παραδόντος ἑαυτὸν ὑπὲρ ἐμοῦ. οὐκ
loving me and giving over Himself on behalf of me. not
114 5485 2316/1487/1063/1223/3551 1343
ἀθετῶ τὴν χάριν τοῦ Θεοῦ· εἰ γὰρ διὰ νόμου δικαιοσύνη,
I set aside the grace of God; if for through law righteousness,
686 5547 1432 599
ἄρα Χριστὸς δωρεὰν ἀπέθανεν.
then Christ without cause died.

CHAPTER 3

[1]O foolish Galatians, who
bewitched you not to obey
the truth, to whom before

CHAPTER 3

453 1052 5101/5209 940 225 3361
1 Ὦ ἀνόητοι Γαλάται, τίς ὑμᾶς ἐβάσκανε τῇ ἀληθείᾳ μὴ
O foolish Galatians, who you bewitched the truth not

your eyes Jesus Christ was written among you crucified? [2]This only I desire to learn from you: Did you receive the Spirit by works of law, or by hearing of faith? [3]Are you so foolish? Having begun in *the* Spirit, do you now perfect *yourself* in *the* flesh? [4]Did you suffer so much vainly? If indeed *it* also *was* vainly? [5]Then He supplying the Spirit to you, and working works of power in you, *is it* by works of law, or by hearing of faith? [6]Even as Abraham believed God, and it was counted to him for righteousness. [7]Know, then, that those of faith, these are sons of Abraham. [8]And the Scripture foreseeing that God would justify the nations by faith, preached the gospel before to Abraham: "All the nations will be blessed in you." [9]So that those of faith are blessed with the faithful Abraham.

[10]For as many as are out of works of law, *these* are under a curse. For it has been written, "Cursed *is* everyone who does not continue in all the things having been written in the book of the Law, to do them." [11]And that no one is justified by law before God *is* clear, because, "The just shall live by faith."

[12]But the Law is not of faith, but, "The man doing these things shall live in them." [13]Christ redeemed us from the curse of the law, having become a curse for us; for it has been written, "Cursed *is* everyone having been hung on a tree;" [14]that the blessing of Abraham might be to the nations in Christ Jesus, that we might receive the promise of the Spirit through faith.

[15]Brothers, I speak according to man, a covenant having been ratified, even

3982 3739/2596 3788 2424 5547 4270
πείθεσθαι, οἷς κατ' ὀφθαλμοὺς Ἰησοῦς Χριστὸς προεγράφη
to obey, to whom before the eyes Jesus Christ was written afore
1722/5213/ 4717 5124 3440 2309 3129 575 5216
2 ἐν ὑμῖν ἐσταυρωμένος; τοῦτο μόνον θέλω μαθεῖν ἀφ' ὑμῶν,
among you crucified? This only I desire to learn from you,
1537/2041 3551 4151 2983 2228/1537 189 4102
ἐξ ἔργων νόμου τὸ Πνεῦμα ἐλάβετε, ἢ ἐξ ἀκοῆς πίστεως;
by works of law the Spirit did you receive, or by hearing of faith?
3779 453 2075 1728 4151 3568 4561
3 οὕτως ἀνόητοί ἐστε; ἐναρξάμενοι Πνεύματι, νῦν σαρκὶ
so foolish Are you? Having begun in (the) Spirit, now in (the) flesh
2005 5118 3958 1500/1489= 1500 3767
4 ἐπιτελεῖσθε; τοσαῦτα ἐπάθετε εἰκῇ; εἴ γε καὶ εἰκῇ. ὁ οὖν
5 do you finish? So much suffered you vainly? If indeed even vainly? He then
2023 5213 4151 1754 1411 1722/5213
ἐπιχορηγῶν ὑμῖν τὸ Πνεῦμα καὶ ἐνεργῶν δυνάμεις ἐν ὑμῖν,
supplying to you the Spirit and working works of power in you,
1537/2041 3551 1537 189 4102 2531 11
6 ἐξ ἔργων νόμου, ἢ ἐξ ἀκοῆς πίστεως; καθὼς Ἀβραὰμ ἐπί-
by works of law, or by hearing of faith? As Abraham
4100 2316 3049 846 1519 1343 1097
7 στευσε τῷ Θεῷ, καὶ ἐλογίσθη αὐτῷ εἰς δικαιοσύνην. γινώ-
believed God, and it was counted to him for righteousness. Know
686/3754 1537 4102 3778 1526 5207 11
σκετε ἄρα ὅτι οἱ ἐκ πίστεως, οὗτοί εἰσιν υἱοὶ Ἀβραάμ.
then that those of faith, these are sons of Abraham.
4275 1124 3754/1537/ 4102 1344 1484
8 προϊδοῦσα δὲ ἡ γραφὴ ὅτι ἐκ πίστεως δικαιοῖ τὰ ἔθνη ὁ
foreseeing And the Scripture that by faith would justify the nations
2316 4283 11 3754 2127
Θεός, προευηγγελίσατο τῷ Ἀβραὰμ ὅτι Εὐλογηθήσονται
God, preached the gospel before to Abraham that will be blessed
1722/4671/3956 1484 5620 1537 4102 2127
9 ἐν σοὶ πάντα τὰ ἔθνη. ὥστε οἱ ἐκ πίστεως εὐλογοῦνται σὺν
in you all the nations. So as those of faith are blessed with
4103 11 3745/1063/1537/2041 3551 1526 5259
τῷ πιστῷ Ἀβραάμ. ὅσοι γὰρ ἐξ ἔργων νόμου εἰσίν, ὑπὸ
the faithful Abraham. as many as For out of works of law are under
2671 1526 1125 1063 1944 3956/3739/3756
10 κατάραν εἰσί· γέγραπται γάρ, Ἐπικατάρατος πᾶς ὃς οὐκ
a curse are; it has been written for: Cursed (is) everyone who not
1696 1722/3956 1125 1722 975 3551
ἐμμένει ἐν πᾶσι τοῖς γεγραμμένοις ἐν τῷ βιβλίῳ τοῦ νόμου,
continues in all the things having been written in the roll of the law
4160 846 3754 1722/3551 3762 1344 3844
11 τοῦ ποιῆσαι αὐτά. ὅτι δὲ ἐν νόμῳ οὐδεὶς δικαιοῦται παρὰ
to do them. that And by law no one is justified before
2316 1212 3754 1342 1537 4102 2198
12 τῷ Θεῷ, δῆλον· ὅτι Ὁ δίκαιος ἐκ πίστεως ζήσεται· ὁ δὲ
God (is) clear, because the just one by faith will live; the and
3551/3756/2076/1537/4102 235 4160 846 444
νόμος οὐκ ἔστιν ἐκ πίστεως, ἀλλ' Ὁ ποιήσας αὐτὰ ἄνθρωπος
law not is of faith, but: The doing these things man
2198 1722 846 5547 2248 1805 1537 2671
13 ζήσεται ἐν αὐτοῖς. Χριστὸς ἡμᾶς ἐξηγόρασεν ἐκ τῆς κατάρας
shall live in them. Christ us redeemed out of the curse
3551 1096 5228 2257 2671 1125 1063
τοῦ νόμου, γενόμενος ὑπὲρ ἡμῶν κατάρα· γέγραπται γάρ,
of the law, having become for us a curse; it has been written for:
1944 3956 2910 1909 3586 2443/1519 1484
14 Ἐπικατάρατος πᾶς ὁ κρεμάμενος ἐπὶ ξύλου· ἵνα εἰς τὰ ἔθνη
Cursed (is) everyone who has been hung on a tree; that to the nations
2129 11 1096 1722 5547 2424 2443
ἡ εὐλογία τοῦ Ἀβραὰμ γένηται ἐν Χριστῷ Ἰησοῦ, ἵνα τὴν
the blessing of Abraham might be in Christ Jesus, that the
1860 4151 2983 1223 4102
ἐπαγγελίαν τοῦ Πνεύματος λάβωμεν διὰ τῆς πίστεως.
promise of the Spirit we might receive through faith.
80 2596 444 3004 3676 444 2964
15 Ἀδελφοί, κατὰ ἄνθρωπον λέγω· ὅμως ἀνθρώπου κεκυρω-
Brothers, according to man I say, even of man having been

among mankind, no one sets aside or adds to *it*.
[16]But the promises were spoken to Abraham and to his Seed—it does not say, And to seeds, as of many; but as of one, "And to your Seed," which is Christ.
[17]And I say this, A covenant having been ratified before to Christ by God, *the* Law coming into being four hundred and thirty years after does not annul the promise, so as to abolish *it*. [18]For if the inheritance *is* of law, *it is* no more of promise; but God has given *it* to Abraham through promise. [19]Why, then, the Law? It was added because of transgressions, until the Seed should come, to whom it had been promised, being ordained through angels in a mediator's hand. [20]But the Mediator is not of one, but God is one.
[21]Then *is* the Law against the promises of God? Let it not be! For if a law had been given which had been able to make alive, indeed righteousness would have been out of law. [22]But the Scripture locked up all under sin, that the promise by faith of Jesus Christ might be given to the ones believing. [23]But before the coming of faith, we were guarded under law, having been locked up to the faith being about to be revealed.
[24]So that the Law has become a trainer of us *until* Christ, that we might be justified by faith. [25]But faith coming, we are no longer under a trainer; [26]for you are all sons of God through faith in Christ Jesus. [27]For as many as were baptized into Christ, you put on Christ. [28]There cannot be Jew nor Greek; there is no slave nor freeman; there is no male and female; for you

1242 3762 114 2228 1928
16 μένην διαθήκην οὐδεὶς ἀθετεῖ ἢ ἐπιδιατάσσεται. τῷ δὲ
ratified a covenant, no one sets aside or addes to (it). And
11 4483 1860 4690 848
Ἀβραὰμ ἐρρήθησαν αἱ ἐπαγγελίαι, καὶ τῷ σπέρματι αὐτοῦ.
to Abraham were said the promises, and to the Seed of him.
3756/3004 4690 5613/1909/4183 235 5613/1909
οὐ λέγει, Καὶ τοῖς σπέρμασιν, ὡς ἐπὶ πολλῶν, ἀλλ' ὡς ἐφ'
Not it says, And to the seeds, as upon many, but as of
1520 4690 4675/3739/2076 5547 5124 3004
17 ἑνός, Καὶ τῷ σπέρματί σου, ὅς ἐστι Χριστός. τοῦτο δὲ λέγω,
One: And to the Seed of you, who is Christ. this And I say,
1242 4300 5259 2316/1519 5547 3326
διαθήκην προκεκυρωμένην ὑπὸ τοῦ Θεοῦ εἰς Χριστὸν ὁ μετὰ
A covenant having been ratified before by God to Christ, the after
2094 5071 5144 1096 3551/3756/ 208/1519
ἔτη τετρακόσια καὶ τριάκοντα γεγονὼς νόμος οὐκ ἀκυροῖ, εἰς
years four hundred and thirty coming into being Law not annuls, so
2673 1860 1487/1063/1637/3551 2817
18 τὸ καταργῆσαι τὴν ἐπαγγελίαν. εἰ γὰρ ἐκ νόμου ἡ κληρονο-
as to abolish the promise. if For of law the inheritance
3765/1537/ 1860 11 1223 1860
μία, οὐκέτι ἐξ ἐπαγγελίας· τῷ δὲ Ἀβραὰμ δι' ἐπαγγελίας
(is), no more (is it) of promise; but to Abraham through promise
5483 2316/5101/3767 3551 3847 5484
19 κεχάρισται ὁ Θεός. τί οὖν ὁ νόμος; τῶν παραβάσεων χάριν
has given (it) God. Why, then, the law? the transgressions because of
4369 891/3756/2064 4690 3739 1861 1299
προσετέθη, ἄχρις οὗ ἔλθῃ τὸ σπέρμα ᾧ ἐπήγγελται, διατα-
it was added, until should come the Seed to whom it had been being promised,
1223 32 1722 5495 3316 3316 1520/3756
20 γεὶς δι' ἀγγέλων ἐν χειρὶ μεσίτου. ὁ δὲ μεσίτης ἑνὸς οὐκ
ordained through angels in hand a mediator's. the But mediator of one not
2076 2316/1519/2076 3767 3551 2596 1860
21 ἔστιν, ὁ δὲ Θεὸς εἷς ἐστιν. ὁ οὖν νόμος κατὰ τῶν ἐπαγγελιῶν
is, but God one is. the Then law against the promises
2316 3361 1096 1487/1063 1325 3551 1410
τοῦ Θεοῦ; μὴ γένοιτο. εἰ γὰρ ἐδόθη νόμος ὁ δυνάμενος
God (is)? Not let it be! if For had been given a law which was able
2227 3689 302/1537/3551/2258 1343 235
22 ζωοποιῆσαι, ὄντως ἂν ἐκ νόμου ἦν ἡ δικαιοσύνη. ἀλλὰ
to make alive, indeed would out of law been the righteousness. But
4788 1124 3956 5259 266 2443
συνέκλεισεν ἡ γραφὴ τὰ πάντα ὑπὸ ἁμαρτίαν, ἵνα ἡ
locked up the Scripture all under sin, that the
1860 1537 4102 2424 5547 1325 4100
ἐπαγγελία ἐκ πίστεως Ἰησοῦ Χριστοῦ δοθῇ τοῖς πιστεύουσι.
promise by faith of Jesus Christ might be given to those believing.
4253 2064 4102 5259 3551 5432
23 Πρὸ τοῦ δὲ ἐλθεῖν τὴν πίστιν, ὑπὸ νόμον ἐφρουρούμεθα,
before the But coming of faith, under law we were guarded,
4788 1519 3195 4102 601
συγκεκλεισμένοι εἰς τὴν μέλλουσαν πίστιν ἀποκαλυφθῆναι.
having been locked up to the being about faith to be revealed.
5620 3551 3807 2257 1096 1519 5547 2443
24 ὥστε ὁ νόμος παιδαγωγὸς ἡμῶν γέγονεν εἰς Χριστόν, ἵνα
So as the law a trainer of us has become (until) Christ, that
1537 4102 1344 2064 4102 3765
25 ἐκ πίστεως δικαιωθῶμεν. ἐλθούσης δὲ τῆς πίστεως, οὐκέτι
by faith we might be justified. having come But faith, no more
5259 3807 2070 3956 1063/5207 2316 2075/1223
26 ὑπὸ παιδαγωγόν ἐσμεν. πάντες γὰρ υἱοὶ Θεοῦ ἐστε διὰ τῆς
under a trainer we are. all For sons of God you are through
4102 1722 5547 2424 3745 1063/1519 5547 907
27 πίστεως ἐν Χριστῷ Ἰησοῦ. ὅσοι γὰρ εἰς Χριστὸν ἐβαπτί-
faith in Christ Jesus. as many as For into Christ were
5547 1746 3756/1762 2453 3761 1672
28 σθητε, Χριστὸν ἐνεδύσασθε. οὐκ ἔνι Ἰουδαῖος οὐδὲ Ἕλλην,
baptized, Christ you put on. not There is Jew nor Greek,
3756/1762/1401 3761 1658 3756/1762/730 2338 3956
οὐκ ἔνι δοῦλος οὐδὲ ἐλεύθερος, οὐκ ἔνι ἄρσεν καὶ θῆλυ· πάντες
not is slave nor freeman; not is male and female; all

are all one in Christ Jesus. 29And if you *are* of Christ, then you are a seed of Abraham, even heirs according to promise.

1063/5210/1519/2075/•/ 5547 2424 1487 5210 5547 686
1722 γὰρ ὑμεῖς εἷς ἐστὲ ἐν Χριστῷ Ἰησοῦ. εἰ δὲ ὑμεῖς Χριστοῦ, ἄρα
for you one are in Christ Jesus. if And you (are) of Christ, then
11 4690 2075 2596 1860 2818
29 τοῦ Ἀβραὰμ σπέρμα ἐστέ, καὶ κατ' ἐπαγγελίαν κληρονό-
of Abraham a seed you are, even according to promise heirs.
μοι.

CHAPTER 4

1But I say, Over so long a time the heir is an infant; he being lord of all does not differ *from* a slave, 2but is under guardians and housemasters until the *term* set before by the father. 3So we also, when we were infants, we were under the elements of the world, being enslaved. 4But when the fullness of the time came, God sent forth His Son, having come out of a woman, having come under law, 5that He might redeem the ones under law, that we might receive the adoption of sons. 6And because you are sons, God sent forth the Spirit of His Son into your hearts, crying, Abba! Father! 7So that you no more are a slave, but a son; and if a son, also an heir of God through Christ.

3004 1909/3745 5550 2818 3516 2076
1 Λέγω δέ, ἐφ' ὅσον χρόνον ὁ κληρονόμος νήπιός ἐστιν,
I say But, over so long a time the heir an infant is,
3762 1308 1401 2962 3956 5607 235 5259
2 οὐδὲν διαφέρει δούλου, κύριος πάντων ὤν· ἀλλὰ ὑπὸ
nothing he differs (from) a slave, lord of all being, but under
2012 2076 3623 891 4287
ἐπιτρόπους ἐστὶ καὶ οἰκονόμους, ἄχρι τῆς προθεσμίας τοῦ
guardians is, and housemasters, until the (term) set before by the
3962 3779 2249 3753/2258 3516 5259 4747
3 πατρός. οὕτω καὶ ἡμεῖς, ὅτε ἦμεν νήπιοι, ὑπὸ τὰ στοιχεῖα
father. So also we, when we were infants, under the elements
2889 2258 1402 3753 2064 4138
4 τοῦ κόσμου ἦμεν δεδουλωμένοι· ὅτε δὲ ἦλθε τὸ πλήρωμα
of the world we were, being enslaved; when but came the fullness
5550 1821 2316 5207 848 1096
τοῦ χρόνου, ἐξαπέστειλεν ὁ Θεὸς τὸν υἱὸν αὐτοῦ, γενό-
of the time sent forth God the Son of Him, becoming
1537 1135 1096 5259 3551 2443 5259
5 μενον ἐκ γυναικός, γενόμενον ὑπὸ νόμον, ἵνα τοὺς ὑπὸ
of a woman, becoming under law, that those under
3551 1805 2443 5206 618 3754
6 νόμον ἐξαγοράσῃ, ἵνα τὴν υἱοθεσίαν ἀπολάβωμεν. ὅτι δέ
law He might redeem, that the adoption of sons we may receive. because And
2075/ 5207 1821 2316 4151 5207 848
ἐστε υἱοί, ἐξαπέστειλεν ὁ Θεὸς τὸ Πνεῦμα τοῦ υἱοῦ αὐτοῦ
you are sons, sent forth God the Spirit of the Son of Him
1519 2588 5216 2896 5 3962 5620 3765
7 εἰς τὰς καρδίας ὑμῶν, κρᾶζον, Ἀββᾶ, ὁ πατήρ. ὥστε οὐκέτι
into the hearts of you, crying, Abba, Father! So as no more
1487/1401 235 5207/1487 5207 2818 2316 1223
εἶ δοῦλος, ἀλλ' υἱός· εἰ δὲ υἱός, καὶ κληρονόμος Θεοῦ διὰ
are you a slave, but a son; if and a son, also an heir of God by
5547
Χριστοῦ.
Christ.

8But then, indeed, not knowing God, you served as slaves *to* the ones not by nature being gods. 9But now, knowing God, but rather being known by God, how do you turn again to the weak and poor elements, *to* which you again desire to slave anew? 10You observe days, and months, and seasons, and years. 11I fear *for* you, lest somehow I have labored among you in vain.

12Brothers, I beg of you, be as I *am*, because I *am* as you. You wronged me *in* nothing. 13But you know that because of weakness of the flesh, I preached the

235 5119/3303/3756/ 1492 2316 1398 3361
8 Ἀλλὰ τότε μέν, οὐκ εἰδότες Θεόν, ἐδουλεύσατε τοῖς μὴ
But then indeed not knowing God, you served as slaves those not
5449 5607 2316/3568 1097 2316 3123 1097
9 φύσει οὖσι θεοῖς· νῦν δέ, γνόντες Θεόν, μᾶλλον δὲ γνωσθέντες
by nature being gods; now but knowing God, rather but being known
5259 2316 4459 1994 3825 1909 772
ὑπὸ Θεοῦ, πῶς ἐπιστρέφετε πάλιν ἐπὶ τὰ ἀσθενῆ καὶ
by God, how do you turn again upon the weak and
4434 4747 3739 3825 509 1398 2309 2250
10 πτωχὰ στοιχεῖα, οἷς πάλιν ἄνωθεν δουλεύειν θέλετε; ἡμέρας
poor elements, which again anew to slave for you desire? days
3906 3376 2540 1763 5399
11 παρατηρεῖσθε, καὶ μῆνας, καὶ καιρούς, καὶ ἐνιαυτούς. φοβοῦ-
You observe, and months, and seasons, and years. I fear
5209/3361/4459/1500/ 2872 1519 5209
μαι ὑμᾶς, μή πως εἰκῇ κεκοπίακα εἰς ὑμᾶς.
(for) you, lest some in vain I have labored among you.
•5613 1096 •how 1473/3754/1504/5613/5210 80 1189 5216
12 Γίνεσθε ὡς ἐγώ, ὅτι κἀγὼ ὡς ὑμεῖς, ἀδελφοί, δέομαι ὑμῶν.
Be as I because I also as you, brothers, I beg of you.
3762/3165/ 91 1492 3754/1223 769 4561
13 οὐδέν με ἠδικήσατε· οἴδατε δὲ ὅτι δι' ἀσθένειαν τῆς σαρκὸς
Nothing me you wronged; you know and that because weakness of the flesh

gospel to you before; [14]and you did not despise my temptation in my flesh, nor spurn *it*, but you received me as an angel of God, as Christ Jesus. [15]What then was your blessedness? For I testify to you that if you were able, plucking out your eyes, *you* would have given *them* to me. [16]So then did I become your enemy speaking truth to you? [17]They are zealous for you, *but* not well; but they *only* desire to shut you out, that you be zealous *to* them. [18]But *it is* good to be zealous always in a good thing, and not only in my being present with you. [19]My children, *for* whom I again travail until Christ should be formed in you, [20]even now I desired to be present with you, and to change my voice; for I am in doubt *as to* you.

[21]Tell me, those desiring to be under Law, do you not hear the Law? [22]For it has been written: Abraham had two sons, one out of the slave-woman, and one out of the free woman. [23]But, indeed, he of the slave-woman has been born according to flesh; and he out of the free woman through the promise; [24]which things are being allegorized; for these are two covenants, one, indeed, from Mount Sinai bringing forth to slavery—which is Hagar, [25]for Hagar is Mount Sinai in Arabia, and corresponds to the present Jerusalem, and she slaves with her children—[26]but the Jerusalem *from* above is free, who is the mother of us all; [27]for it has been written, "Be glad, barren *one* not bearing; break forth and shout, the *one* not travailing, for more *are* the children of the desolate rather than she having the husband."

2097 5213 4386 of 3906 3450
14 εὐηγγελισάμην ὑμῖν τὸ πρότερον. καὶ τὸν πειρασμόν μου
I preached the gospel to you before, and the temptation of me
1722 4561 3450/3756 1848 3761 1609
τὸν ἐν τῇ σαρκί μου οὐκ ἐξουθενήσατε οὐδὲ ἐξεπτύσατε,
in the flesh of me not you despised, not disdained,
235/5613 32 2316 1209 3165/5613 5547 2424
ἀλλ' ὡς ἄγγελον Θεοῦ ἐδέξασθέ με, ὡς Χριστὸν Ἰησοῦν.
but as an angel of God you received me, as Christ Jesus.
5101/3767/2258 3107 5217 3140 1063 5213/3754/1487
15 τίς οὖν ἦν ὁ μακαρισμὸς ὑμῶν; μαρτυρῶ γὰρ ὑμῖν ὅτι, εἰ
What then was the blessedness of you? I witness for to you that, if
1415 3788 5216 1846 302 1325 3427
δυνατόν, τοὺς ὀφθαλμοὺς ὑμῶν ἐξορύξαντες ἂν ἐδώκατέ μοι.
you could, the eyes of you plucking out would have given me.
5620 2190 5216 1096 226 5213 2206 5209
16 ὥστε ἐχθρὸς ὑμῶν γέγονα ἀληθεύων ὑμῖν; ζηλοῦσιν ὑμᾶς
17 **So then an enemy of you became I speaking truth to you? They are zealous for you,**
3756/2573 235 1576 5209 2309 2443 846 2206
οὐ καλῶς, ἀλλὰ ἐκκλεῖσαι ὑμᾶς θέλουσιν, ἵνα αὐτοὺς ζηλοῦτε.
not well, but to shut out you they desire, that(to) them you be zealous:
2570 2206 1722/2570 3842 3361 3440/1722
18 καλὸν δὲ τὸ ζηλοῦσθαι ἐν καλῷ πάντοτε, καὶ μὴ μόνον ἐν
(it is) good but to be zealous in a good thing always, and not only in
3918 3165/4314 5209 5040 3450 3739 3825 5605
19 τῷ παρεῖναί με πρὸς ὑμᾶς. τεκνία μου, οὓς πάλιν ὠδίνω,
being present me with you. Children of me, (for) whom again I travail,
891 3756 3445 5547 1722/5213 2309 3918 4314
20 ἄχρις οὗ μορφωθῇ Χριστὸς ἐν ὑμῖν, ἤθελον δὲ παρεῖναι πρὸς
until should be formed Christ in you, I desired and to be present with
5209 737 236 5456 3450/3754 639 1722
ὑμᾶς ἄρτι, καὶ ἀλλάξαι τὴν φωνήν μου. ὅτι ἀποροῦμαι ἐν
you now, and to change the voice of me because I am in doubt in
5213
ὑμῖν.
you.
3004 3427 5259 3551 2309 1511 3551 3756
21 Λέγετέ μοι, οἱ ὑπὸ νόμον θέλοντες εἶναι, τὸν νόμον οὐκ
Tell me, those under law desiring to be, the law do not
191 1125 1063/3754 11 1417 5207 2192 1520
22 ἀκούετε; γέγραπται γάρ, ὅτι Ἀβραὰμ δύο υἱοὺς ἔσχεν· ἕνα
you hear? it has been written For: — Abraham two sons had, one
1537 3814 1520/1537 1658 235 3303/1537
23 ἐκ τῆς παιδίσκης, καὶ ἕνα ἐκ τῆς ἐλευθέρας. ἀλλ' ὁ μὲν ἐκ τῆς
of the slave-woman, and one of the free woman. But he indeed of the
3814 2596 4561 1080 1537 1658 1223
παιδίσκης κατὰ σάρκα γεγέννηται, ὁ δὲ ἐκ τῆς ἐλευθέρας διὰ
slave-woman according to flesh has been born; he and of the free woman via
1860 3748 2076 238 3778 1063
24 τῆς ἐπαγγελίας. ἅτινά ἐστιν ἀλληγορούμενα· αὗται γάρ
the promise. Which things is being allegorized; these for
1526 1417 1242 3391/3303/575/3735 4614/1519 1397
εἰσιν αἱ δύο διαθῆκαι· μία μὲν ἀπὸ ὄρους Σινᾶ, εἰς δουλείαν
are two covenants: one indeed from Mount Sinai, to slavery
1080 3748 2076 28 1063 28 4614/3735/2076/1722
25 γεννῶσα, ἥτις ἐστὶν Ἄγαρ. τὸ γὰρ Ἄγαρ Σινᾶ ὄρος ἐστὶν ἐν
bringing forth, which is Hagar. the For Hagar Sinai Mount is in
688 4960 3568 2419 1398
τῇ Ἀραβίᾳ, συστοιχεῖ δὲ τῇ νῦν Ἱερουσαλήμ, δουλεύει δὲ
Arabia, corresponds and to the now Jerusalem, she slaves and
3326 5043 848 507 2419 1658 2076
26 μετὰ τῶν τέκνων αὐτῆς. ἡ δὲ ἄνω Ἱερουσαλὴμ ἐλευθέρα ἐστίν,
with the children of her. the But above Jerusalem free is,
3748/2076 3384 3956 2257 1125 1063 2165
27 ἥτις ἐστὶ μήτηρ πάντων ἡμῶν. γέγραπται γάρ, Εὐφράνθητι
who is mother of all of us; it has been written for: Be glad
4723 3756 5088 4486 994 3756 5605
στεῖρα ἡ οὐ τίκτουσα· ῥῆξον καὶ βόησον ἡ οὐκ ὠδίνουσα·
barren (one) not bearing, break forth and shout, the (one) not travailing;
3754 4183 5043 2048 3123/2228 2192
ὅτι πολλὰ τὰ τέκνα τῆς ἐρήμου μᾶλλον ἢ τῆς ἐχούσης τὸν
because more the children of the desolate rather than she having the

NOTE: Frequent words not numbered: [illegible] 531)—and, but; ὁ, ἡ, τό (3588, the)— * above word, look in verse margin for No.

435 2249 80 2596 2464 1860 5043
28 ἄνδρα. ἡμεῖς δέ, ἀδελφοί, κατα Ἰσαάκ, ἐπαγγελίας τέκνα
husband. we But, brothers, according to Isaac, of promise children
2070 235 5618 5119 2596 4561 1080 1377
29 ἐσμέν. ἀλλ' ὥσπερ τότε ὁ κατὰ σάρκα γεννηθεὶς ἐδίωκε τὸν
we are. But even as then he according to flesh born persecuted the (one)
2596 4151 3779 3568 235/5101/3004 1124 1544
30 κατὰ Πνεῦμα, οὕτω καὶ νῦν. ἀλλὰ τί λέγει ἡ γραφή ; Ἔκβαλε
according to Spirit, so also now. But what says the Scripture? Cast out
3814 5207 848 3364/1063/3361/ 2816
τὴν παιδίσκην καὶ τὸν υἱὸν αὐτῆς, οὐ γὰρ μὴ κληρονομήσῃ
the slave-woman and the son of her, in any For not shall inherit
5207 3814 3326 5207 1658 686 80
31 ὁ υἱὸς τῆς παιδίσκης μετὰ τοῦ υἱοῦ τῆς ἐλευθέρας. ἄρα, ἀδελ-
the son of the slave-woman with the Son of the free woman. Then, brothers,
3756 2070 3814 5043 235 1658
φοί, οὐκ ἐσμὲν παιδίσκης τέκνα, ἀλλὰ τῆς ἐλευθέρας.
not we are of a slave-woman children, but of the free woman.

CHAPTER 5

1657 3767 5547 2248 1659 4739
1 τῇ ἐλευθερίᾳ οὖν ᾗ Χριστὸς ἡμᾶς ἠλευθέρωσε, στήκετε, καὶ
in the freedom, then, with which Christ us made free, stand firm, and
3361/3825/ 2218 1758
*1397 μὴ πάλιν ζυγῷ δουλείας ἐνέχεσθε.
not again with a yoke of slavery be held.
2396/1473 3972 3004 5213/3754/1437/ 4059 5547
2 Ἴδε, ἐγὼ Παῦλος λέγω ὑμῖν, ὅτι ἐὰν περιτέμνησθε, Χριστὸς
Behold, I, Paul, tell you, that if you are circumcised, Christ
5209 3762 5623 3143 3825 3956 444
3 ὑμᾶς οὐδὲν ὠφελήσει. μαρτύρομαι δὲ πάλιν παντὶ ἀνθρώπῳ
you nothing will profit. I testify And again to every man
4059 3754 3781 2076 3650 3551 4160
περιτεμνομένῳ, ὅτι ὀφειλέτης ἐστὶν ὅλον τὸν νόμον ποιῆσαι.
being circumcised, that a debtor he is all the law to do.
2673 575 5547 3748 1722/3551 1344
4 κατηργήθητε ἀπὸ τοῦ Χριστοῦ, οἵτινες ἐν νόμῳ δικαιοῦσθε·
You were passed away from Christ, whoever by law are justified,
5485 1601 2249 1063 4151 1537 4102
5 τῆς χάριτος ἐξεπέσατε. ἡμεῖς γὰρ Πνεύματι ἐκ πίστεως
grace you fell from. we For by (the) Spirit from faith
1680 1343 553 1722/1063 5547 2424
6 ἐλπίδα δικαιοσύνης ἀπεκδεχόμεθα. ἐν γὰρ Χριστῷ Ἰησοῦ
(the) hope of righteousness eagerly wait. in For Christ Jesus
3777 4061 5100 2480 3777 203 235 4102 1223
οὔτε περιτομή τι ἰσχύει, οὔτε ἀκροβυστία, ἀλλὰ πίστις δι'
neither circumcision any strength has nor uncircumcision, but faith through
26 1754 5143 2573 5101/5209 348
7 ἀγάπης ἐνεργουμένη. ἐτρέχετε καλῶς· τίς ὑμᾶς ἀνέκοψε τῇ
love working. You were running well, who you held back the
225 3361 3982 3988 3756/1537 2564
8 ἀληθείᾳ μὴ πείθεσθαι ; ἡ πεισμονὴ οὐκ ἐκ τοῦ καλοῦντος
truth not you obey? the persuasion (is) not from Him calling
5209 3398 2219 3650 5445 2220 1473 3982 1519
9 ὑμᾶς. μικρὰ ζύμη ὅλον τὸ φύραμα ζυμοῖ. ἐγὼ πέποιθα εἰς
10 you. A little leaven all the lump leavens. I trust as to
5209/1722/2962/3754 3762 235 5426 5015
ὑμᾶς ἐν Κυρίῳ, ὅτι οὐδὲν ἄλλο φρονήσετε· ὁ δὲ ταράσσων
you in (the) Lord, that nothing other you will think; the (one) but troubling
5209 941 291 3748 302/5600/1473 80 1487
11 ὑμᾶς βαστάσει τὸ κρίμα, ὅστις ἂν ᾖ. ἐγὼ δέ, ἀδελφοί, εἰ
you shall bear the judgment, whoever he may be. I But, brothers, if
4061 2089 2784 5101/2089/ 1377 686 2673
περιτομὴν ἔτι κηρύσσω, τί ἔτι διώκομαι ; ἄρα κατήργηται
circumcision still proclaim, why yet am I persecuted? Then has passed away
4625 4716 3785 609
12 τὸ σκάνδαλον τοῦ σταυροῦ. ὄφελον καὶ ἀποκόψονται οἱ
the offense of the cross. Would that also will cut themselves off those
387 5209
ἀναστατοῦντες ὑμᾶς.
causing to doubt you.

[28]But, brothers, we are children of promise according to Isaac. [29]But then even as he born according to flesh persecuted the *one* according to Spirit, so also now. [30]But what says the Scripture? "Cast out the slave-woman and her son, for in no way shall the son of the slave-woman inherit with the son of the free *woman*." [31]Then, brothers, we are not children of a slave-woman, but of the free *woman*.

CHAPTER 5

[1]Then stand firm in the freedom with which Christ made us free, and do not again be held with a yoke of slavery.

[2]Behold, I, Paul, say to you that if you are circumcised, Christ will profit you nothing. [3]And I testify again to every man being circumcised, that he is a debtor to do all the Law; [4]you who are justified by law are deprived of all effect from Christ—you fell from grace. [5]For we through *the* Spirit eagerly wait for *the* hope of righteousness out of faith. [6]For in Christ Jesus neither circumcision nor uncircumcision has any strength, but faith working through love. [7]You were running well; who held you back *that* you do not obey the truth? [8]The persuasion *is* not from Him calling you. [9]A little leaven leavens all the lump. [10]I trust as to you in *the* Lord that you will think nothing else, but that the *one* troubling you shall bear the judgment, whoever he may be. [11]But I, brothers, if I proclaim circumcision, why am I still persecuted? Then the offense of the Cross has passed away. [12]I would that the ones causing you to doubt will cut themselves off.

[13]For, brothers, you were called to freedom. Only do not *use* the freedom for gain to the flesh. But serve one another as slaves by love. [14]For the whole law is fulfilled in one word, in *this*: "You shall love your neighbor as yourself." [15]But if you bite and devour one another, watch, that you not be consumed by one another.

[16]But I say, Walk in *the* Spirit, and you will not fulfill *the* lust of *the* flesh. [17]For the flesh lusts against the Spirit, and the Spirit against the flesh; and these are contrary to one another; lest whatever you may will, these things you do. [18]But if you are led by *the* Spirit, you are not under law. [19]Now the works of the flesh are clearly revealed, which are: adultery, fornication, uncleanness, lustfulness, [20]idolatry, sorcery, hatreds, fightings, jealousies, angers, rivalries, divisions, heresies, [21]envyings, murders, drunkennesses, wild parties, and things like these; *of* which I tell you beforehand, as I also said before, that the ones practicing such things will not inherit *the* kingdom of God.

[22]But the fruit of the Spirit is: love, joy, peace, long-suffering, kindness, goodness, faith, [23]meekness, self-control—against such things there is not a law. [24]But the ones belonging to Christ crucified the flesh with *its* passions and lusts.

[25]If we live in *the* Spirit, let us also walk in *the* Spirit. [26]Let us not become glory-seeking ones, provoking one another, envying one another.

5210/1063/1909 1657 2563 80 3440/3361
13 Ὑμεῖς γὰρ ἐπ' ἐλευθερίᾳ ἐκλήθητε, ἀδελφοί· μόνον μὴ τὴν
you For for freedom were called, brothers, only not the
1657 1519 874 4561 235 1223 26
ἐλευθερίαν εἰς ἀφορμὴν τῇ σαρκί, ἀλλὰ διὰ τῆς ἀγάπης
freedom for gain to the flesh, but through love
1722 1398 240 1063/3956/3551//1520/3056 4137
14 δουλεύετε ἀλλήλοις. ὁ γὰρ πᾶς νόμος ἐν ἑνὶ λόγῳ πληροῦται,
serve as slaves to one the For whole law in one word is fulfilled
1722 25 another. 4139 4675/5613 1438 1487
15 ἐν τῷ, Ἀγαπήσεις τὸν πλησίον σου ὡς ἑαυτόν. εἰ δὲ
in the (word): You shall love the neighbor of you as yourself. if But
240 1143 2719 991 3361/5259 240
ἀλλήλους δάκνετε καὶ κατεσθίετε, βλέπετε μὴ ὑπὸ ἀλλήλων
one another you bite and devour, see lest by one another
355
ἀναλωθῆτε.
you are consumed.

3004 4151 4043 1939 4561 3756
16 Λέγω·δέ, Πνεύματι περιπατεῖτε, καὶ ἐπιθυμίαν σαρκὸς οὐ
I say And, in (the) Spirit walk, and (the) lust of (the) flesh not
3361 5055 1063/4561 1937 2596 4151
17 μὴ τελέσητε. ἡ γὰρ σὰρξ ἐπιθυμεῖ κατὰ τοῦ Πνεύματος, τὸ
at all you will fulfill. the For flesh lusts against the Spirit the
4151 2596 4561 5023 480 240
δὲ Πνεῦμα κατὰ τῆς σαρκός· ταῦτα δὲ ἀντίκειται ἀλλήλοις,
and (the) Spirit against the flesh, these and (are) contrary to one another
2443/3361/*/302 2309 5023 4160 1487 4151 71
18 ἵνα μὴ ἃ ἂν θέλητε, ταῦτα ποιῆτε. εἰ δὲ Πνεύματι ἄγεσθε,
3363 that not what ever you may will, these things you do. if But by (the) Spirit you are led
3756/2075/5259/3551 /5318 2076 2041 4561
19 οὐκ ἐστὲ ὑπὸ νόμον. φανερὰ δέ ἐστι τὰ ἔργα τῆς σαρκός,
not you are under law. clearly revealed Now are the works of the flesh,
3748 2076 3430 4202 167 766 1495
20 ἅτινά ἐστι μοιχεία, πορνεία, ἀκαθαρσία, ἀσέλγεια, εἰδω-
which are: adultery, fornication, uncleanness, lustfulness, idol-
5331 2189 2054 2205 2372 2052
λολατρεία, φαρμακεία, ἔχθραι, ἔρεις, ζῆλοι, θυμοί, ἐριθεῖαι,
service, sorcery, enmities, fightings, jealousies, angers, rivalries,
1370 139 5355 5408 3178 2970
21 διχοστασίαι, αἱρέσεις, φθόνοι, φόνοι, μέθαι, κῶμοι, καὶ τὰ
divisions, heresies, envyings, murders, drunkennesses, revellings, and
3664 5125 3739 4302 5213 2531 4277 3754
ὅμοια τούτοις· ἃ προλέγω ὑμῖν, καθὼς καὶ προεῖπον, ὅτι
like things to these, which I tell before you, as also I said previously, that
5108 4238 932 2316/3756 2816
οἱ τὰ τοιαῦτα πράσσοντες βασιλείαν Θεοῦ οὐ κληρονομή-
those the(se) things practicing (the) kingdom of God not will inherit.
2590 4151 2076 26 5479
22 σουσιν. ὁ δὲ καρπὸς τοῦ Πνεύματός ἐστιν ἀγάπη, χαρά,
the But fruit of the Spirit is: love, joy,
1515 3115 5544 19 4102 4236
23 εἰρήνη, μακροθυμία, χρηστότης, ἀγαθωσύνη, πίστις, πρᾳό-
peace, long-suffering, kindness, goodness, faith, meek-
1466 2596 5108 3756/2076/3551
24 της, ἐγκράτεια· κατὰ τῶν τοιούτων οὐκ ἔστι νόμος. οἱ δὲ τοῦ
ness, self-control; against such things not is a law. those And
5547 4561 4717 4862 3804
Χριστοῦ, τὴν σάρκα ἐσταύρωσαν σὺν τοῖς παθήμασι καὶ
of Christ the flesh crucified with the passions and
1939
ταῖς ἐπιθυμίαις.
the lusts.
1487 2198 4151 4151 4748 3361 1096
25 Εἰ ζῶμεν Πνεύματι, Πνεύματι καὶ στοιχῶμεν. μὴ γινώ-
26 If we live in (the) Spirit, in (the) Spirit also let us walk. not Let us be-
2755 240 4292 240 5354
μεθα κενόδοξοι, ἀλλήλους προκαλούμενοι, ἀλλήλοις φθονοῦντες
come vainglorious, one another provoking, one another envying.

CHAPTER 6

1 Brothers, if a man is taken in some fault, you, the spiritual ones, restore such a one in the spirit of meekness, considering yourself, that you not also be tempted. 2 Bear one another's burden's, and so you will fulfill the law of Christ. 3 For if anyone thinks to be something, he deceives himself, being nothing. 4 But let each one prove his work, and then he alone will have *a* boast in himself, and not as to another. 5 For each one will bear *his* own load.

6 But let the *one* being taught in the word share with the *one* teaching, in all good things. 7 Do not be deceived, God is not mocked. For whatever a man may sow, that he also will reap. 8 For the *one* sowing to his flesh will reap corruption of the flesh. But the *one* sowing to the Spirit will reap everlasting life from the Spirit. 9 But we should not lose heart in doing good, for in due time we shall reap, if *we* do not faint. 10 So, then, as we have time, let us work good toward all, and especially toward the household of the faith.

11 See in what large letters I write to you with my hand. 12 As many as desire to look well in *the* flesh, these compel you to be circumcised; only that they may not be persecuted for the cross of Christ. 13 For they themselves having been circumcised do not even keep *the* Law; but they desire you to be circumcised so that they may boast in your flesh. 14 But may it never be for me to boast, except in the cross of

80 1437 4301 444 1722/5100 3900
1 Ἀδελφοί, ἐὰν καὶ προληφθῇ ἄνθρωπος ἔν τινι παραπτώ-
Brothers, if indeed is overtaken a man in some fault,
5210 4152 2675 5101 1722
ματι, ὑμεῖς οἱ πνευματικοὶ καταρτίζετε τὸν τοιοῦτον ἐν
you the spiritual ones restore such a one in
4151 4236 4648 4572 3361 4771/3985
πνεύματι πρᾳότητος, σκοπῶν σεαυτὸν μὴ καὶ σὺ πειρασθῇς.
the spirit of meekness, considering yourself, lest also you be tempted
240 922 941 3779 378
2 ἀλλήλων τὰ βάρη βαστάζετε, καὶ οὕτως ἀναπληρώσατε τὸν
Of one another the burdens bear, and so you will fulfill the
3551 5547 1487/1063/1380/5100/1511/5100/3367/5607
3 νόμον τοῦ Χριστοῦ. εἰ γὰρ δοκεῖ τις εἶναί τι, μηδὲν ὤν,
law of Christ. if For thinks anyone to be something, nothing being,
1438 5422 2041 1438 1381 1538
4 ἑαυτὸν φρεναπατᾷ. τὸ δὲ ἔργον ἑαυτοῦ δοκιμαζέτω ἕκαστος,
himself he deceives. the But work of himself let prove each one,
1519 1438 3440 2745 2192 3756/1519
καὶ τότε εἰς ἑαυτὸν μόνον τὸ καύχημα ἕξει, καὶ οὐκ εἰς τὸν
and then in himself alone the boast he will have, and not in the
2087 1538 1063 2398 5413 941
5 ἕτερον. ἕκαστος γὰρ τὸ ἴδιον φορτίον βαστάσει.
other one. each one For the own load will bear.

2841 2727 3056 2727
6 Κοινωνείτω δὲ ὁ κατηχούμενος τὸν λόγον τῷ κατηχοῦντι
let him share And, he being taught in the word, with the (one) teaching
1722/3956 18 3361 4105 2316/3756/3456 3739/1063
7 ἐν πᾶσιν ἀγαθοῖς. μὴ πλανᾶσθε, Θεὸς οὐ μυκτηρίζεται· ὃ γὰρ
in all good things. not Be led astray, God not is mocked; what For
1437 4687 444 5124 2325 3754 4687 1519
8 ἐὰν σπείρῃ ἄνθρωπος, τοῦτο καὶ θερίσει. ὅτι ὁ σπείρων εἰς
ever may sow a man, this also he will reap.; because he sowing to
4561 1438 1537 4561 2325 5356 4687
τὴν σάρκα ἑαυτοῦ, ἐκ τῆς σαρκὸς θερίσει φθοράν· ὁ δὲ σπεί-
the flesh of himself, of the flesh will reap corruption; he but
1519 4151 1537 4151 2325 2222 166
ρων εἰς τὸ Πνεῦμα, ἐκ τοῦ Πνεύματος θερίσει ζωὴν αἰώνιον.
sowing to the Spirit, of the Spirit will reap life everlasting
2570 4160 3361 1573 2540/1063/2398 2325
9 τὸ δὲ καλὸν ποιοῦντες μὴ ἐκκακῶμεν· καιρῷ γὰρ ἰδίῳ θερίσο-
the And good doing, not let us weaken. in time For in its own we shall
3361 1590 686/3767/5613/2540 2192 2038
10 μεν, μὴ ἐκλυόμενοι. ἄρα οὖν ὡς καιρὸν ἔχομεν, ἐργαζώμεθα
reap, not (we are) fainting. So then as time we have, let us work
18 4314 3956 3122 4314 3609
τὸ ἀγαθὸν πρὸς πάντας, μάλιστα δὲ πρὸς τοὺς οἰκείους τῆς
the good to all, most of all and to the household of the
4102
πίστεως.
faith.

1492 4080 5213 1121 1125 1699 5495 3745
11 Ἴδετε πηλίκοις ὑμῖν γράμμασιν ἔγραψα τῇ ἐμῇ χειρί. ὅσοι
12 See in how large to you letters I write with my hand. As many as
2309 2146 1722 4561 3778 314
θέλουσιν εὐπροσωπῆσαι ἐν σαρκί, οὗτοι ἀναγκάζουσιν
desire to look well in (the) flesh, these compel
5209 4059 3440/2443/3361 4716 5547
ὑμᾶς περιτέμνεσθαι, μόνον ἵνα μὴ τῷ σταυρῷ τοῦ Χριστοῦ
you to be circumcised, only that not for the cross of Christ
1377 3761/1063 4059 846 3551 5442
13 διώκωνται. οὐδὲ γὰρ οἱ περιτεμνόμενοι αὐτοὶ νόμον φυλάσ-
they are persecuted; not even For those having been circumcised themselves law keep.
235 2309 5209 4059 2443/1722 5212
σουσιν· ἀλλὰ θέλουσιν ὑμᾶς περιτέμνεσθαι, ἵνα ἐν τῇ ὑμετέρᾳ
but they desire you to be circumcised that in your
4561 2744 1698 3361 1096 2744 =1508=1722
14 σαρκὶ καυχήσωνται. ἐμοὶ δὲ μὴ γένοιτο καυχᾶσθαι εἰ μὴ ἐν
flesh they may boast. to me But not it may be to boast, except in

our Lord Jesus Christ, through whom the world has been crucified to me, and I to the world. [15]For in Christ Jesus neither circumcision *has* any strength, nor uncircumcision; but a new creation. [16]And as many as shall walk by this rule, peace and mercy *be* on them, and on the Israel of God.

[17]For the rest, let no one give troubles to me, for I bear in my body the brands of the Lord Jesus.

[18]The grace of our Lord Jesus Christ *be* with your spirit, brothers. Amen.

4716 2962 2257 2424 5547 1223/3739/1698
τῷ σταυρῷ τοῦ Κυρίου ἡμῶν Ἰησοῦ Χριστοῦ· δι' οὗ ἐμοὶ
the cross of (the) Lord of us, Jesus Christ through whom to me
2889 4717 2504 2889 1722/1063 5547 2424
15 κόσμος ἐσταύρωται, κἀγὼ τῷ κόσμῳ. ἐν γὰρ Χριστῷ Ἰησοῦ
(the) world has been crucified, and I to the world. in For Christ Jesus
3777 4061 5100 2480 3777 203 235 2537
οὔτε περιτομή τι ἰσχύει, οὔτε ἀκροβυστία, ἀλλὰ καινὴ
neither circumcision any strength has, not uncircumcision, but a new
2937 3745 2583 5129 4748 1515 1909
16 κτίσις. καὶ ὅσοι τῷ κανόνι τούτῳ στοιχήσουσιν, εἰρήνη ἐπ'
creation. And as many as by rule this shall walk, peace on
846 1656 1909 2474 2316
αὐτούς, καὶ ἔλεος, καὶ ἐπὶ τὸν Ἰσραὴλ τοῦ Θεοῦ.
them, and mercy, and on the Israel of God.
3064 2873 3427 3367 3930 1473 1063
17 Τοῦ λοιποῦ, κόπους μοι μηδεὶς παρεχέτω· ἐγὼ γὰρ τὰ
For the rest, troubles to me no one let cause; I for the
4742 2962 2424/1722 4983 3450 941
στίγματα τοῦ Κυρίου Ἰησοῦ ἐν τῷ σώματί μου βαστάζω.
brands of the Lord Jesus in the body of me bear.
5485 2962 5216 2424 5547 3326
18 Ἡ χάρις τοῦ Κυρίου ἡμῶν Ἰησοῦ Χριστοῦ μετὰ τοῦ
The grace of the Lord of us, Jesus Christ,(be)with the
4151 5216 80 281
πνεύματος ὑμῶν, ἀδελφοί. ἀμήν.
spirit of you, brothers. Amen.

ΠΑΥΛΟΥ ΤΟΥ ΑΠΟΣΤΟΛΟΥ
PAUL THE APOSTLE

Η ΠΡΟΣ
TO THE

ΕΦΕΣΙΟΥΣ ΕΠΙΣΤΟΛΗ
EPHESIANS EPISTLE

THE EPISTLE
TO THE
EPHESIANS

A LITERAL TRANSLATION
OF THE BIBLE

CHAPTER 1

[1]Paul, *an* apostle of Jesus Christ through *the* will of God, to the saints being in Ephesus, and faithful in Christ Jesus: [2]Grace to you and peace from God our Father and the Lord Jesus Christ.

[3]Blessed *is* the God and Father of our Lord Jesus Christ, who blessed us with every spiritual blessing in the heavenlies with Christ; [4]according as He chose us in Him before *the* foundation of *the* world, for us to be holy and without blemish before Him in love; [5]predestinating us to adoption through Jesus Christ to Himself, according to the good pleasure of His will, [6]to *the* praise of *the* glory of His grace, in which He favored us in the Beloved, [7]in whom we have redemption through His blood, the forgiveness of sins, according to the riches of His grace; [8]which He caused to abound toward us in all wisdom and understanding, [9]making known to us the mystery of His will, according to His good pleasure which He purposed in Himself, [10]for the administration of the fullness of time; to head up all things in Christ, both the things in Heaven, and the things on earth, in Him,

CHAPTER 1

3972 652 2424 5547 1223 2307 2316
1 Παῦλος, ἀπόστολος Ἰησοῦ Χριστοῦ διὰ θελήματος Θεοῦ,
Paul, an apostle of Jesus Christ through (the) will of God,
40 5607/1722 2181 4103 1722 5547
τοῖς ἁγίοις τοῖς οὖσιν ἐν Ἐφέσῳ καὶ πιστοῖς ἐν Χριστῷ
to the saints being in Ephesus and faithful in Christ
2424 5485 5213 1515 575 2316 3962 2257
2 Ἰησοῦ· χάρις ὑμῖν καὶ εἰρήνη ἀπὸ Θεοῦ πατρὸς ἡμῶν καὶ
Jesus: Grace to you and peace from God the Father of us, and
2962 2424 5547
Κυρίου Ἰησοῦ Χριστοῦ.
(the) Lord Jesus Christ.
2128 2316 3962 2962 2257 2424
3 Εὐλογητὸς ὁ Θεὸς καὶ πατὴρ τοῦ Κυρίου ἡμῶν Ἰησοῦ
Blessed (is) the God and Father of the Lord of us, Jesus
5547 2127 2248/1722/3956 2129 4152
Χριστοῦ, ὁ εὐλογήσας ἡμᾶς ἐν πάσῃ εὐλογίᾳ πνευματικῇ
Christ, who blessed us with every blessing spiritual
1722 2032 1722 5547 2531 1586 2248/1722
4 ἐν τοῖς ἐπουρανίοις ἐν Χριστῷ· καθὼς ἐξελέξατο ἡμᾶς ἐν
in the heavenlies in Christ; according as He chose us in
846 4253 2602 2889 1511 2248 40
αὐτῷ πρὸ καταβολῆς κόσμου, εἶναι ἡμᾶς ἁγίους καὶ
Him before (the) foundation of (the) world, to be us holy and
299 2714 846/1722/ 26, 4309 2248/1519
5 ἀμώμους κατενώπιον αὐτοῦ ἐν ἀγάπῃ, προορίσας ἡμᾶς εἰς
unblemished before Him, in love predestinating us to
5206 1223 2424 5547 1519 848 2596 2107
υἱοθεσίαν διὰ Ἰησοῦ Χριστοῦ εἰς αὐτόν, κατὰ τὴν εὐδοκίαν
adoption through Jesus Christ to Himself, according to the good pleasure
2307 848 1519 1868 1391 5485 848
6 τοῦ θελήματος αὐτοῦ, εἰς ἔπαινον δόξης τῆς χάριτος αὐτοῦ,
of the will of Him, to (the) praise of (the) glory of the grace of Him,
1722/3739/ 5487 2248/1722 25 1722/3739/ 2192
7 ἐν ᾗ ἐχαρίτωσεν ἡμᾶς ἐν τῷ ἠγαπημένῳ· ἐν ᾧ ἔχομεν τὴν
with which He favored us in the (One) having been loved; in whom we have the
629 1223 129 848 859
ἀπολύτρωσιν διὰ τοῦ αἵματος αὐτοῦ, τὴν ἄφεσιν τῶν
redemption through the blood of Him, the forgiveness
3900 2596 4149 5485 848
παραπτωμάτων, κατὰ τὸν πλοῦτον τῆς χάριτος αὐτοῦ,
of trespasses, according to the riches of the grace of Him,
3739 4052 1519 2248/1722 3956 4678 5428
8 ἧς ἐπερίσσευσεν εἰς ἡμᾶς ἐν πάσῃ σοφίᾳ καὶ φρονήσει,
which he caused to abound to us in all wisdom and intelligence,
1107 2254 3466 2307 848 2596
9 γνωρίσας ἡμῖν τὸ μυστήριον τοῦ θελήματος αὐτοῦ, κατὰ
making known to us the mystery of the will of Him, according to
2107 848 3739 4388 1722/848/1519 3622
10 τὴν εὐδοκίαν αὐτοῦ, ἣν προέθετο ἐν αὐτῷ εἰς οἰκονομίαν τοῦ
the good pleasure of Him, which He purposed in Himself for a stewardship of the
4138 2540 346 3956
πληρώματος τῶν καιρῶν, ἀνακεφαλαιώσασθαι τὰ πάντα
fullness of the times, to head up all things
1722 5547 5037/1722 3772 1909 1093
ἐν τῷ Χριστῷ, τά τε ἐν τοῖς οὐρανοῖς καὶ τὰ ἐπὶ τῆς γῆς·
in Christ, the things both in the heavens and the things on the earth

11 in whom we also have been chosen to an inheritance, being predestinated according to *the* purpose of the *One* working all things according to the counsel of His *own* will, 12 for us to be to *the* praise of His glory, the ones first trusting in Christ; 13 in whom also you, hearing the word of truth, the gospel of your salvation, in whom also believing, you were sealed with the Holy Spirit of promise, 14 who is an earnest of our inheritance, to *the* redemption of the purchased possession, to *the* praise of His glory.

15 Because of this, hearing of your faith in the Lord Jesus, and love toward all the saints, I also 16 do not cease giving thanks on your behalf, making mention of you in my prayers, 17 that the God of our Lord Jesus Christ, the Father of glory, may give to you a spirit of wisdom and revelation in *the* knowledge of Him, 18 the eyes of your mind having been enlightened for you to know what is the hope of His calling, and what the riches of the glory of His inheritance in the saints, 19 and what is the surpassing greatness of His power toward us, the ones believing according to the working of His mighty strength 20 which He worked in Christ *in* raising Him from *the* dead—yea, *He* seated *Him* at His right *hand* in the heavenlies, 21 far above all principality, and authority, and power, and lordship, and every name being named, not only in this age, but also in

1722 846 1722/3739 2820 4309 2596
11 ἐν αὐτῷ, ἐν ᾧ καὶ ἐκληρώθημεν, προορισθέντες κατὰ
in Him, in whom also we have been chosen to an inheritance being predestinated according to
1012 4286 3956 1754 2596
πρόθεσιν τοῦ τὰ πάντα ἐνεργοῦντος κατὰ τὴν βουλὴν τοῦ
(the) purpose of the (One) all things working according to the counsel of the
2307 848 1519 1511 2248/1519 1868 1391
12 θελήματος αὐτοῦ, εἰς τὸ εἶναι ἡμᾶς εἰς ἔπαινον τῆς δόξης
will of Him, for to be us to (the) praise of the glory
848 4276 1722 5547 1722/3739 5210
13 αὐτοῦ, τοὺς προηλπικότας ἐν τῷ Χριστῷ· ἐν ᾧ καὶ ὑμεῖς,
of Him, those having previously trusted in Christ; in whom also you,
191 3056 225 2098
ἀκούσαντες τὸν λόγον τῆς ἀληθείας, τὸ εὐαγγέλιον τῆς
hearing the word of truth, the gospel of the
4991 5216 1722/3739 4100 4972
σωτηρίας ὑμῶν,—ἐν ᾧ καὶ πιστεύσαντες ἐσφραγίσθητε τῷ
salvation of you, in whom also believing you were sealed with the
4151 1860 40 3739/2076 728
14 Πνεύματι τῆς ἐπαγγελίας τῷ Ἁγίῳ, ὅς ἐστιν ἀρραβὼν τῆς
Spirit of promise the Holy, who is an earnest of the
2817 2257 1519 629 4047 1519
κληρονομίας ἡμῶν, εἰς ἀπολύτρωσιν τῆς περιποιήσεως, εἰς
inheritance of us, until (the) redemption of the possession, to
1868 1391 848
ἔπαινον τῆς δόξης αὐτοῦ.
(the) praise of the glory of Him.
1223 5124 2504 191 2596/5209 4102/1722
15 Διὰ τοῦτο κἀγώ, ἀκούσας τὴν καθ' ὑμᾶς πίστιν ἐν τῷ
Therefore I also, hearing the among you faith in the
2962 2424 26 1519 3956 40
Κυρίῳ Ἰησοῦ καὶ τὴν ἀγάπην τὴν εἰς πάντας τοὺς ἁγίους,
Lord Jesus and the love to all the saints.
3756 3973 2188 5228 5216 3417 5216 4160
16 οὐ παύομαι εὐχαριστῶν ὑπὲρ ὑμῶν, μνείαν ὑμῶν ποιού-
not do cease giving thanks on behalf of you, mention of you making
1909 4335 3450/2443 2316 2962 2257
17 μενος ἐπὶ τῶν προσευχῶν μου· ἵνα ὁ Θεὸς τοῦ Κυρίου ἡμῶν
on the prayers of me, that the God of the Lord of us,
2424 5547 3962 1391 1325 5213 4151
Ἰησοῦ Χριστοῦ, ὁ πατὴρ τῆς δόξης, δῴη ὑμῖν πνεῦμα
Jesus Christ, the Father of glory, may give to you a spirit
4678 602 1722 1922 848 5461
18 σοφίας καὶ ἀποκαλύψεως, ἐν ἐπιγνώσει αὐτοῦ· πεφωτι-
of wisdom and revelation in (the) knowledge of Him, having been
3788 1271 2257/1519 1492
σμένους τοὺς ὀφθαλμοὺς τῆς διανοίας ὑμῶν, εἰς τὸ εἰδέναι
enlightened the eyes of the mind of you, for to know
5209/5101/2076 1680 2821 848 5101 4149
ὑμᾶς τίς ἐστιν ἡ ἐλπὶς τῆς κλήσεως αὐτοῦ, καὶ τίς ὁ πλοῦτος
you what is the hope of the calling of Him, and what the riches
1391 1817 848 1722 40 5101
19 τῆς δόξης τῆς κληρονομίας αὐτοῦ ἐν τοῖς ἁγίοις, καὶ τί τὸ
of the glory of the inheritance of Him in the saints; and what the
5235 3174 1411 848 1519 2248
ὑπερβάλλον μέγεθος τῆς δυνάμεως αὐτοῦ εἰς ἡμᾶς τοὺς
surpassing greatness of the power of Him toward us, those
4100 2596 1753 2904 2479
πιστεύοντας, κατὰ τὴν ἐνέργειαν τοῦ κράτους τῆς ἰσχύος
believing according to the working of the might of the strength
848 3739 1754 1722 5547 1453 846 1537 3498
20 αὐτοῦ ἣν ἐνήργησεν ἐν τῷ Χριστῷ, ἐγείρας αὐτὸν ἐκ νεκρῶν,
of Him, which He worked in Christ raising Him from (the) dead;
2523 1722 1188 848 1722 2032 5231
21 καὶ ἐκάθισεν ἐν δεξιᾷ αὐτοῦ ἐν τοῖς ἐπουρανίοις, ὑπεράνω
and He seated (Him) at the right of Him in the heavenlies far above
3956 746 1849 1411 2963
πάσης ἀρχῆς καὶ ἐξουσίας καὶ δυνάμεως καὶ κυριότητος,
all rule and authority and power and lordship,
3956 3686 3687 3756 3440 1722 165
καὶ παντὸς ὀνόματος ὀνομαζομένου οὐ μόνον ἐν τῷ αἰῶνι
and every name being named not only in age

the coming *age;* [22]and He
put all things under His feet,
and gave Him *to be* Head
over all things to the
church, [23]which is His
body, the fullness of Him
filling all things in all—

5129 235 1722 3195 3956 5293 5259
22 τούτῳ, ἀλλὰ καὶ ἐν τῷ μέλλοντι· καὶ πάντα ὑπέταξεν ὑπὸ
this, but also in the coming (age), and all things subjected under
4228 848 846 1325 2776 5228 3956
τοὺς πόδας αὐτοῦ, καὶ αὐτὸν ἔδωκε κεφαλὴν ὑπὲρ πάντα τῇ
the feet of Him, and Him gave (to be) Head over all things to the
1577 3748 2076 4983 848 4138 3956
23 ἐκκλησίᾳ, ἥτις ἐστὶ τὸ σῶμα αὐτοῦ, τὸ πλήρωμα τοῦ πάντα
church, which is the body of Him, the fullness of the (One) all things
1722/3956 4137
ἐν πᾶσι πληρουμένου.
with all things filling.

CHAPTER 2

CHAPTER 2

[1]and *He worked in* you
who were once dead in
trespasses and sins, [2]in
which you then walked
according to the course of
this world, according to the
ruler of the authority of the
air, the spirit now working
in the sons of dis-
obedience; [3]among whom
we also all conducted
ourselves in times past in
the lusts of our flesh, doing
the things willed of the
flesh and of the under-
standings, and were by
nature the children of
wrath, even as the rest.

[4]But God, being rich in
mercy, because of His
great love *with* which He
loved us, [5]even we being
dead in sins, *He* made us
alive together with Christ
— by grace you are being
saved —[6]and raised *us* up
together and seated *us* together in the heavenlies
in Christ Jesus, [7]that He
might show in the coming
ages the exceeding great
riches of His grace in
kindness toward us in
Christ Jesus. [8]For by
grace you are being saved,
through faith, and this not
of yourselves; *it is* the gift
of God; [9]not of works, that
not anyone should boast;
[10]for we are *His* workman-
ship, created in Christ
Jesus unto good works,
which God before pre-
pared that we should walk
in them.

5209 5607 3498 3900
1 Καὶ ὑμᾶς ὄντας νεκροὺς τοῖς παραπτώμασι καὶ ταῖς
And you being dead in the trespasses and in the
266 1722/3739/4218 3900 2596 165
2 ἁμαρτίαις, ἐν αἷς ποτὲ περιεπατήσατε κατὰ τὸν αἰῶνα τοῦ
sins, in which then you walked according to the age
2889 5127 2596 758 1849 109
κόσμου τούτου, κατὰ τὸν ἄρχοντα τῆς ἐξουσίας τοῦ ἀέρος,
world of this, according to the ruler of the authority of the air,
4151 3568 1754 1722 5207 543
τοῦ πνεύματος τοῦ νῦν ἐνεργοῦντος ἐν τοῖς υἱοῖς τῆς ἀπει-
the spirit now working in the sons of dis-
1722/3739 2249 3956 390 4218/1722
3 θείας· ἐν οἷς καὶ ἡμεῖς πάντες ἀνεστράφημέν ποτε ἐν ταῖς
obedience, among whom also we all conducted ourselves then in the
1939 4561 2257 4160 2307
ἐπιθυμίαις τῆς σαρκὸς ἡμῶν, ποιοῦντες τὰ θελήματα τῆς
lusts of the flesh of us, doing the things willed of the
4561 1271 2258 5043 5449 3709 5613
σαρκὸς καὶ τῶν διανοιῶν, καὶ ἦμεν τέκνα φύσει ὀργῆς, ὡς
flesh and of the understandings, and were children by nature of wrath, as
3062 2316 4145 5607/1722/1656/1223
4 καὶ οἱ λοιποί· ὁ δὲ Θεός, πλούσιος ὢν ἐν ἐλέει, διὰ τὴν
also the rest but God rich being in mercy, because of the
4183 26 848 3739 25 2248 5607 2248
5 πολλὴν ἀγάπην αὐτοῦ ἣν ἠγάπησεν ἡμᾶς, καὶ ὄντας ἡμᾶς
much love of Him (with) which He loved us, even being us
3498 3900 4806 5547
νεκροὺς τοῖς παραπτώμασι συνεζωοποίησε τῷ Χριστῷ
dead in trespasses (He) made us alive with Christ;
5485 2075 4982 4891 4776
6 (χάριτί ἐστε σεσωσμένοι), καὶ συνήγειρε, καὶ συνεκάθισεν
by grace you are being saved; and raised (us) with, and seated (us) with
1722 2032 1722 5547 2424 2443 1731 1722
7 ἐν τοῖς ἐπουρανίοις ἐν Χριστῷ Ἰησοῦ· ἵνα ἐνδείξηται ἐν τοῖς
in the heavenlies in Christ Jesus, that He might show in the
165 1904 5235 4149
αἰῶσι τοῖς ἐπερχομένοις τὸ ὑπερβάλλοντα πλοῦτον τῆς
ages coming on the surpassing riches of the
5485 848 1722 5544 1909/2248/1722 5547 2424
χάριτος αὐτοῦ ἐν χρηστότητι ἐφ' ἡμᾶς ἐν Χριστῷ Ἰησοῦ·
grace of Him in kindness toward us in Christ Jesus.
1063 [illegible] 2075 4982 1223 4102 5124
8 τῇ γὰρ [illegible] ἐστε σεσωσμένοι διὰ τῆς πίστεως, καὶ τοῦτο
For by grace you are being saved, through faith, and this
3756/1[illegible] 2316 1435 3756/1537/2041 2443/3361/5100
9 οὐκ ἐξ ὑμῶν· Θεοῦ τὸ δῶρον· οὐκ ἐξ ἔργων, ἵνα μή τις
not of you, of God (is) the gift; not of works, lest anyone
2744 848 1063 2070 4161 2936 1722 5547
10 καυχήσηται αὐτοῦ γάρ ἐσμεν ποίημα, κτισθέντες ἐν Χριστῷ
should boast. of Him For we are (His) doing, created in Christ
2424 1909 2041 18 3739 4282 2316 2443
Ἰησοῦ ἐπὶ ἔργοις ἀγαθοῖς, οἷς προητοίμασεν ὁ Θεός, ἵνα
Jesus unto works good, which before prepared God that
1722/846 4043
ἐν αὐτοῖς περιπατήσωμεν.
in them we should walk

[11]Therefore, remember that you, the nations, *were* then in *the* flesh, those having been called Uncircumcision by those having been called Circumcision in *the* flesh made by hand, [12]that at that time you were without Christ, alienated from the commonwealth of Israel and strangers of the covenants of promise, having no hope, and without God in the world. [13]But now in Christ Jesus you who then were afar off came to be near by the blood of Christ. [14]For He is our peace, He making *us* both one, and breaking down the middle wall of partition, [15]annulling in His flesh the enmity, the Law of the commandments in decrees, that He might in Himself create the two into one new man, making peace; [16]and might reconcile both in one body to God through the cross, slaying the enmity in Himself. [17]And coming, *He* preached peace to you, the ones afar off, and to the ones near. [18]For through Him we both have access by one Spirit to the Father. [19]So, then, you are no longer strangers and tenants, but *you are* fellow-citizens of the saints and *of the* household of God, [20]being built up on the foundation of the apostles and prophets, Jesus Christ Himself being *the* cornerstone; [21]in whom all the building fitted together grows into a holy temple in *the* Lord; [22]in whom you also are being built together into a dwelling-place of God in *the* Spirit.

1352 3421 3754 5210 4218 1484/1722/4561
11 Διὸ μνημονεύετε, ὅτι ὑμεῖς ποτὲ τὰ ἔθνη ἐν σαρκί, οἱ
Therefore remember that you then the nations in (the) flesh, those
3004 203 5259 3004 4061 1722
λεγόμενοι ἀκροβυστία ὑπὸ τῆς λεγομένης περιτομῆς ἐν
being called uncircumcision by those being called circumcision in
4561 5499 3754/2258/1722 2540 1565 5565
12 σαρκὶ χειροποιήτου, ὅτι ἦτε ἐν τῷ καιρῷ ἐκείνῳ χωρὶς
(the) flesh made by hand, that you were at time that without
5547 526 4174 2474
Χριστοῦ, ἀπηλλοτριωμένοι τῆς πολιτείας τοῦ Ἰσραήλ, καὶ
Christ, having been alienated from the commonwealth of Israel, and
3581 1242 1860 1680/3361/ 2192
ξένοι τῶν διαθηκῶν τῆς ἐπαγγελίας, ἐλπίδα μὴ ἔχοντες,
strangers of the covenants of promise hope not having.
112 1722 2889 3570 1722 5547 2424 5210
13 καὶ ἄθεοι ἐν τῷ κόσμῳ. νυνὶ δὲ ἐν Χριστῷ Ἰησοῦ ὑμεῖς οἱ
and godless in the world. now But in Christ Jesus you, those
4218 5607 3112 1451 1096 1722 129
ποτὲ ὄντες μακρὰν ἐγγὺς ἐγενήθητε ἐν τῷ αἵματι τοῦ
then being afar off, near became by the blood
5547 846 1063 2076 1515 2257 4160
14 Χριστοῦ. αὐτὸς γάρ ἐστιν ἡ εἰρήνη ἡμῶν, ὁ ποιήσας τὰ
of Christ. He For is the peace of us, the (One) making
297 1722 3320 5418 3089
15 ἀμφότερα ἕν, καὶ τὸ μεσότοιχον τοῦ φραγμοῦ λύσας, τὴν
both one, and the middle wall of partition having broken, the
2189 1722 4561 848 3551 1785 1722
ἔχθραν ἐν τῇ σαρκὶ αὐτοῦ, τὸν νόμον τῶν ἐντολῶν ἐν
enmity in the flesh of Him, the law of the commandments in
1378 2673 2443 1417 2936/1722/1438/1519/1520
δόγμασι, καταργήσας· ἵνα τοὺς δύο κτίσῃ ἐν ἑαυτῷ εἰς ἕνα
decrees, having abolished, that the two He create in Himself into one
2537 444 4160 1515 604
16 καινὸν ἄνθρωπον, ποιῶν εἰρήνην, καὶ ἀποκαταλλάξῃ τοὺς
new man, making peace, and might reconcile
297 1722/1520 4983 2316 1223 4716
ἀμφοτέρους ἐν ἑνὶ σώματι τῷ Θεῷ διὰ τοῦ σταυροῦ,
both in one body to God through the cross
615 2189 1722/846 2064 2097
17 ἀποκτείνας τὴν ἔχθραν ἐν αὐτῷ· καὶ ἐλθὼν εὐηγγελίσατο
slaying the enmity in Himself, and coming preached
1515 5213 3112 1451 3754/1223 846
18 εἰρήνην ὑμῖν τοῖς μακρὰν καὶ τοῖς ἐγγύς· ὅτι δι᾽ αὐτοῦ
peace to you, those afar off, and to the (ones) near, for through Him
2192 4318 297 1722/1520 4151 4314
ἔχομεν τὴν προσαγωγὴν οἱ ἀμφότεροι ἐν ἑνὶ Πνεύματι πρὸς
we have access both by one Spirit unto
3962 686/3767 3765 2075 3581 3941 235
19 τὸν πατέρα. ἄρα οὖν οὐκέτι ἐστὲ ξένοι καὶ πάροικοι, ἀλλὰ
the Father. Then therefore no more are you strangers and sojourners, but
4847 40 3609 2316 2026
20 συμπολῖται τῶν ἁγίων καὶ οἰκεῖοι τοῦ Θεοῦ, ἐποικοδομη-
fellow-citizens of the saints and (of the) household of God, having been
1909 2310 652 4396 5607
θέντες ἐπὶ τῷ θεμελίῳ τῶν ἀποστόλων καὶ προφητῶν, ὄντος
built on the foundation of the apostles and prophets, being
204 848 2424 5547 1722/3739/3956 3619
21 ἀκρογωνιαίου αὐτοῦ Ἰησοῦ Χριστοῦ, ἐν ᾧ πᾶσα ἡ οἰκοδομὴ
(the) cornerstone (Him)self Jesus Christ, in whom all the building
4883 837 1519/3485/ 40/1722 2962/1722/3739
22 συναρμολογουμένη αὔξει εἰς ναὸν ἅγιον ἐν Κυρίῳ, ἐν ᾧ καὶ
fitted together grows into a temple holy in (the) Lord, in whom also
5210 4925 1519 2732 2316 1722
ὑμεῖς συνοικοδομεῖσθε εἰς κατοικητήριον τοῦ Θεοῦ ἐν
you are being built together into a dwelling-place of God in
4151
Πνεύματι.
(the) Spirit.

CHAPTER 3

[1]For this reason I, Paul, the prisoner of Christ Jesus on behalf of you, the nations, [2]if, indeed, you heard of the stewardship of the grace of God given to me for you, [3]that by revelation He made known to me the mystery, as I wrote before in brief, [4]by the reading of which you are able to realize my understanding in the mystery of Christ; [5]which was not made known to the sons of men in other generations, as it now has been revealed to His holy apostles and prophets in *the* Spirit, [6]*for* the nations to be joint-heirs, and of the same body, and sharers of His promise in Christ, through the gospel; [7]of which I was made a minister, according to the gift of the grace of God given to me, according to the working of His power.

[8]This grace was given to me, less than the least of all the saints, to preach the gospel of the unsearchable riches of Christ among the nations, [9]and to bring all to light, what *is* the fellowship of the mystery having been hidden from eternity in God, the *One* creating all things through Jesus Christ, [10]so that now to the rulers and to the authorities in the heavenlies might be made known through the church the manifold wisdom of God, [11]according to the eternal purpose which He accomplished in Christ Jesus our Lord, [12]in whom we have boldness and access in confidence through His faith. [13]Because of this I beg *you* not to faint at my

CHAPTER 3

5127 5484/1473 3972 1198 5547 2424
1 Τούτου χάριν ἐγὼ Παῦλος ὁ δέσμιος τοῦ Χριστοῦ Ἰησοῦ
of this By reason I, Paul, the prisoner of Christ Jesus
5228 5216 1484 1489 191 3622
2 ὑπὲρ ὑμῶν τῶν ἐθνῶν,—εἴγε ἠκούσατε τὴν οἰκονομίαν τῆς
on behalf of you the nations—if indeed you heard of the stewardship of the
5485 2316 1325 3427/1519/5209/3754/2596
3 χάριτος τοῦ Θεοῦ τῆς δοθείσης μοι εἰς ὑμᾶς, ὅτι κατὰ
grace of God given to me for you, that by way of
602 1107 3427 3466 2531 4270
ἀποκάλυψιν ἐγνώρισέ μοι τὸ μυστήριον, καθὼς προέγραψα
revelation was made known to me the mystery, as I wrote before
1722 3641 4314/3739/ 1410 314 3539
4 ἐν ὀλίγῳ, πρὸς ὃ δύνασθε ἀναγινώσκοντες νοῆσαι τὴν
in brief, as to which you are able reading to realize the
4907 3450/1722 3466 5547/3739/1722 2087
5 σύνεσίν μου ἐν τῷ μυστηρίῳ τοῦ Χριστοῦ· ὃ ἐν ἑτέραις
understanding of me in the mystery of Christ, which in other
1074 3756 1107 5207 444 5613 3568
γενεαῖς οὐκ ἐγνωρίσθη τοῖς υἱοῖς τῶν ἀνθρώπων, ὡς νῦν
generations not was made known to the sons of men as now
601 40 652 848 4396
ἀπεκαλύφθη τοῖς ἁγίοις ἀποστόλοις αὐτοῦ καὶ προφήταις
it was revealed to the holy apostles of Him and prophets
1722 4151 1511 1484 4789 4954
6 ἐν Πνεύματι· εἶναι τὰ ἔθνη συγκληρονόμα καὶ σύσσωμα καὶ
in (the) Spirit to be the nations joint-heirs and a joint-body and
4830 1860 848 1722 5547 1223
συμμέτοχα τῆς ἐπαγγελίας αὐτοῦ ἐν τῷ Χριστῷ, διὰ τοῦ
joint-sharers of the promise of Him in Christ, through the
2098 3739 1096 1249 2596 1431
7 εὐαγγελίου, οὗ ἐγενόμην διάκονος κατὰ τὴν δωρεὰν τῆς
gospel, of which I became a minister according to the gift of the
5485 2316 1325 3427 2596 1753
χάριτος τοῦ Θεοῦ, τὴν δοθεῖσάν μοι κατὰ τὴν ἐνέργειαν τῆς
grace of God, given to me according to the working of the
1411 848 1698 1647 3956
8 δυνάμεως αὐτοῦ. ἐμοὶ τῷ ἐλαχιστοτέρῳ πάντων τῶν
power of Him. To me, the least of all the
40 1325 5485 3778/1722 1484 2097
ἁγίων ἐδόθη ἡ χάρις αὕτη, ἐν τοῖς ἔθνεσιν εὐαγγελίσασθαι
saints, was given grace this, in the nations to preach the gospel,
421 4149 5547 5461
9 τὸν ἀνεξιχνίαστον πλοῦτον τοῦ Χριστοῦ, καὶ φωτίσαι
the unsearchable riches of Christ, and to bring to light
3956 5101 2842 3466 613
πάντας τίς ἡ κοινωνία τοῦ μυστηρίου τοῦ ἀποκεκρυμμένου
all, what (is) the fellowship of the mystery having been hidden
575 165 1722 2316 3956 2936 1223
ἀπὸ τῶν αἰώνων ἐν τῷ Θεῷ τῷ τὰ πάντα κτίσαντι διὰ
from the ages in God, the (One) all things having created through
2424 5547 2443 1107 3568 746
10 Ἰησοῦ Χριστοῦ, ἵνα γνωρισθῇ νῦν ταῖς ἀρχαῖς καὶ ταῖς
Jesus Christ, that might be made known now to the rulers and to the
1849 1722 2032 1223 1577 4182
ἐξουσίαις ἐν τοῖς ἐπουρανίοις διὰ τῆς ἐκκλησίας ἡ πολυποί-
authorities in the heavenlies through the church the manifold
4678 2316/2596 4286 165 3739/4160
11 κιλος σοφία τοῦ Θεοῦ, κατὰ πρόθεσιν τῶν αἰώνων ἣν ἐποίη-
wisdom of God, according to the purpose of the ages which He
1722 5547 2424 2962 2257/1722/3739/2192
12 σεν ἐν Χριστῷ Ἰησοῦ τῷ Κυρίῳ ἡμῶν· ἐν ᾧ ἔχομεν τὴν
made in Christ Jesus the Lord of us, in whom we have
3954 4318 1722 4006 1223
παρρησίαν καὶ τὴν προσαγωγὴν ἐν πεποιθήσει διὰ τῆς
boldness and access in confidence through the
4102 848 1223 154 3361 1573 1722 2347 3450
13 πίστεως αὐτοῦ. διὸ αἰτοῦμαι μὴ ἐκκακεῖν ἐν ταῖς θλίψεσί μου
faith of Him. Therefore I ask (you) not to faint among the troubles of me

troubles on your behalf, which is your glory.

[14]For this reason I bow my knees to the Father of our Lord Jesus Christ, [15]of whom every family in Heaven and on earth is named, [16]that He may give you according to the riches of His glory by *His* power to become mighty in the inward man through His Spirit, [17]that through faith Christ may dwell in your hearts, having been rooted and founded in love, [18]that you may be given strength to grasp, with all the saints, what *is* the breadth and length and depth and height, [19]and to know the love of Christ which surpasses knowledge, that you may be filled with all the fullness of God. [20]Now to Him being able to do exceedingly above all that we ask or think, according to the power working in us, [21]to Him *be* the glory in the church in Christ Jesus, to all the generations of the age forever. Amen.

5228 5216 3748/2076/1391/5216
ὑπὲρ ὑμῶν, ἥτις ἐστὶ δόξα ὑμῶν.
on your behalf, which is glory of you.
5127 5484 2578 1119 3450 4314 3962
14 Τούτου χάριν κάμπτω τὰ γόνατά μου πρὸς τὸν πατέρα
of this By reason I bow the knees of me to the Father
2962 2257 2424 5547 1537/3739/3956 3965/1722/3772
15 τοῦ Κυρίου ἡμῶν Ἰησοῦ Χριστοῦ, ἐξ οὗ πᾶσα πατριὰ ἐν οὐ-
of the Lord of us, Jesus Christ, of whom every family in
1909/1093 3687 2443/1325/5213/2596 4149
16 ρανοῖς καὶ ἐπὶ γῆς ὀνομάζεται, ἵνα δῴη ὑμῖν, κατὰ τὸν πλοῦ-
Heaven and on earth is named, that He may give you per the riches
1391 848 1411 2901 1223 4151
τον τῆς δόξης αὐτοῦ, δυνάμει κραταιωθῆναι διὰ τοῦ Πνεύ-
of the glory of Him by power to become mighty through the
848 1519 2080 444 2730 5547
17 ματος αὐτοῦ εἰς τὸν ἔσω ἄνθρωπον, κατοικῆσαι τὸν Χριστὸν
Spirit of Him in the inward man, to dwell Christ
1223 4102 1722 2588 5216 1722 26 4492
διὰ τῆς πίστεως ἐν ταῖς καρδίαις ὑμῶν· ἐν ἀγάπῃ ἐρριζω-
through faith in the hearts of you, in love having been
2311 2443 1840 2638 4862
18 μένοι καὶ τεθεμελιωμένοι ἵνα ἐξισχύσητε καταλαβέσθαι σὺν
rooted and having been founded, that you be strengthened to grasp with
3956 40/5101 4114 3372 899 5311
πᾶσι τοῖς ἁγίοις, τί τὸ πλάτος καὶ μῆκος καὶ βάθος καὶ ὕψος,
all the saints, what (is) the breadth and length and depth and height,
1097 5037 5235 1108 26
19 γνῶναί τε τὴν ὑπερβάλλουσαν τῆς γνώσεως ἀγάπην τοῦ
to know and the surpassing knowledge love
5547 2443 4137 1519/3956 4138 2316
Χριστοῦ, ἵνα πληρωθῆτε εἰς πᾶν τὸ πλήρωμα τοῦ Θεοῦ.
of Christ, that you may be filled to all the fullness of God.
1410 5228 3956 4160 5228/1537 4053
20 Τῷ δὲ δυναμένῳ ὑπὲρ πάντα ποιῆσαι ὑπὲρ ἐκ περισσοῦ
to Him Now being able beyond all things to do exceedingly above
3739 154 2228 3539 2596 1411 1754
ὧν αἰτούμεθα ἢ νοοῦμεν, κατὰ τὴν δύναμιν τὴν ἐνεργου-
what we ask or think, according to the power working
1722/2254/846 1391/1722 1577 1722 5547 2424
21 μένην ἐν ἡμῖν, αὐτῷ ἡ δόξα ἐν τῇ ἐκκλησίᾳ ἐν Χριστῷ Ἰησοῦ
in us, to Him (be) the glory in the church in Christ Jesus
1519 3956 1074 165 165 281
εἰς πάσας τὰς γενεὰς τοῦ αἰῶνος τῶν αἰώνων. ἀμήν.
to all the generations of the age of the ages. Amen.

CHAPTER 4

[1]Therefore, I, the prisoner in *the* Lord, exhort you to walk worthily of the calling in which you were called, [2]with all humility and meekness, with longsuffering, bearing with one another in love; [3]being eager to keep the unity of the Spirit in the bond of peace. [4]*There is* one body and one Spirit, even as you also were called in one hope of your calling; [5]one Lord, one faith, one baptism, [6]one God and Father of all, He above all and in you all.

CHAPTER 4

3870 3767 2248 1473 1198 1722 2962 516
1 Παρακαλῶ οὖν ὑμᾶς ἐγώ, ὁ δέσμιος ἐν Κυρίῳ, ἀξίως
exhort therefore you I, the prisoner in (the) Lord, worthily
4043 2821 3739 2564 3326 3956 5012
2 περιπατῆσαι τῆς κλήσεως ἧς ἐκλήθητε, μετὰ πάσης ταπει-
to walk of the calling of which you were called, with all
4236 3326 3115 430
νοφροσύνης καὶ πρᾳότητος, μετὰ μακροθυμίας, ἀνεχό-
humility, and meekness, with longsuffering, bearing
240 1722 26 4704 5083 1775
3 μενοι ἀλλήλων ἐν ἀγάπῃ, σπουδάζοντες τηρεῖν τὴν ἑνότητα
with one another, in love, being eager to keep the unity
4151 1722 4886 1515 1722 4983
4 τοῦ Πνεύματος ἐν τῷ συνδέσμῳ τῆς εἰρήνης. ἓν σῶμα καὶ
of the Spirit in the bond of peace. One body and
1520 4151 2531 2564 1722/3391/1680 2821
ἓν Πνεῦμα, καθὼς καὶ ἐκλήθητε ἐν μιᾷ ἐλπίδι τῆς κλήσεως
one Spirit (is, as also you were called in one hope of the calling
5216 1519 2962 3391 4102 1722 908 1520 2316
5 ὑμῶν· εἷς Κύριος, μία πίστις, ἓν βάπτισμα, εἷς Θεὸς καὶ
6 **of you, one Lord, one faith, one baptism, one God and**
3962 3956 1909 3956 1223 3956 1722
πατὴρ πάντων, ὁ ἐπὶ πάντων, καὶ διὰ πάντων, καὶ ἐν
Father of all, the (One) above all, and through all, and in

7But to each one of us was
given grace according to
the measure of the gift of
Christ. 8Therefore, He says,
"Having gone up on high,
He led captivity captive,
and gave gifts to men."—
9but that He went up, what
is it except that He also first
came down into the lower
parts of the earth? 10He that
came down is the same
who also went up above all
the heavens, that He might
fill all things. 11And He
gave some *to be* apostles;
some, prophets; some,
evangelists; some, pastors,
and teachers; 12with a
view to the perfecting of the
saints, for the work of the
ministry, for the building up
of the body of Christ; 13until
we all may come to the
unity of the faith and of the
knowledge of the Son of
God, to a full-grown man, to
the measure of *the* stature
of the fullness of Christ,
14so that we may no longer
be infants, having been
blown and carried to and fro
by every wind of doctrine, in
the underhandedness of
men, in craftiness with a
view to the trickery of error;
15but speaking the truth in
love, we may grow up into
Him in all things, who is the
head, the Christ; 16from
whom all the body having
been fitted and compacted
together through every
assisting bond, according
to *the* working of one
measure *in* each part,
producing the growth of
the body to the building up
of itself in love.

17Therefore, I say this,
and testify in *the* Lord, that
you no longer walk even as
also the rest *of the* nations
walk, in *the* vanity of their

3956 5213 1520 1538 2257 1325 5485 2596
7 πᾶσιν ὑμῖν. ἑνὶ δὲ ἑκάστῳ ἡμῶν ἐδόθη ἡ χάρις κατὰ τὸ
all you. to one But each of us was given grace according to the
3358 1431 5547 1352 3004 305 1519
8 μέτρον τῆς δωρεᾶς τοῦ Χριστοῦ. διὸ λέγει, Ἀναβὰς εἰς
measure of the gift of Christ. Therefore He says, Having gone up on
5311 162 161 1325 1390
ὕψος ᾐχμαλώτευσεν αἰχμαλωσίαν, καὶ ἔδωκε δόματα τοῖς
high, He led captive captivity, and gave gifts
444 305 5101/2076/=1508=3754 2597
9 ἀνθρώποις. (τὸ δέ, Ἀνέβη, τί ἐστιν εἰ μὴ ὅτι καὶ κατέβη
to men —the Now: He went up; what is it except that also He came down
4412 1519 2737 3313 1093 2597 846
10 πρῶτον εἰς τὰ κατώτερα μέρη τῆς γῆς; ὁ καταβάς, αὐτός
first into the lower parts of the earth? The (one) coming down himself
2076 305 5231 3956 3772
ἐστι καὶ ὁ ἀναβὰς ὑπεράνω πάντων τῶν οὐρανῶν, ἵνα
is also the (one) going up far above all the heavens, that
4137 3956 846 1325 3303 652
11 πληρώσῃ τὰ πάντα.) καὶ αὐτὸς ἔδωκε τοὺς μὲν ἀποστό-
He might fill the things all. And he gave some apostles,
4396 2099
λους, τοὺς δὲ προφήτας, τοὺς δὲ εὐαγγελιστάς, τοὺς δὲ
some prophets, some evangelists, some
4166 1320 4314 2677
12 ποιμένας καὶ διδασκάλους, πρὸς τὸν καταρτισμὸν τῶν
pastors, and teachers, for the perfecting of the
40/1519/2041 1248 1519 3619 4983
ἁγίων, εἰς ἔργον διακονίας, εἰς οἰκοδομὴν τοῦ σώματος τοῦ
saints, for (the) work of ministry, to building of the body
5547 3360 2658 3956 1519 1775
13 Χριστοῦ· μέχρι καταντήσωμεν οἱ πάντες εἰς τὴν ἑνότητα
of Christ, until we may come all to the unity
4102 1922 5207 2316 1519
τῆς πίστεως καὶ τῆς ἐπιγνώσεως τοῦ υἱοῦ τοῦ Θεοῦ, εἰς
of the faith and of the knowledge of the Son of God to
435 5046 1519 3358 2244 4138
ἄνδρα τέλειον, εἰς μέτρον ἡλικίας τοῦ πληρώματος τοῦ
a man full-grown, to (the) measure of (the) stature of the fullness
5547 2443 3371 5600 3516 2831
14 Χριστοῦ· ἵνα μηκέτι ὦμεν νήπιοι, κλυδωνιζόμενοι καὶ
of Christ, that no longer we may be infants, being blown and
4064 3956 417 1319 1722 2940
περιφερόμενοι παντὶ ἀνέμῳ τῆς διδασκαλίας, ἐν τῇ κυβείᾳ
being carried about by every wind of doctrine, in the sleight
444 1722 3834 4314 3180
τῶν ἀνθρώπων, ἐν πανουργίᾳ, πρὸς τὴν μεθοδείαν τῆς
of men, in craftiness to the trickery
4106 226 1722 26 837 1519 846
15 πλάνης· ἀληθεύοντες δὲ ἐν ἀγάπῃ αὐξήσωμεν εἰς αὐτὸν τὰ
of error; speaking truth but in love we may grow into Him (in) the things
3956 3739/2076 2776 5547 1537/3739/3956 4983
16 πάντα, ὅς ἐστιν ἡ κεφαλή, ὁ Χριστός, ἐξ οὗ πᾶν τὸ σῶμα
all, who is the Head, Christ, of whom all the body
4883 4822 1223 3956 860
συναρμολογούμενον καὶ συμβιβαζόμενον διὰ πάσης ἁφῆς
being fitted together and being brought together through every bond
2024 2596 1753 1722 3358 1520 1538
τῆς ἐπιχορηγίας, κατ' ἐνέργειαν ἐν μέτρῳ ἑνὸς ἑκάστου
of assistance, according to (the) working in measure of one each
3313 838 4983 4160 1519 3619
μέρους, τὴν αὔξησιν τοῦ σώματος ποιεῖται εἰς οἰκοδομὴν
part, the growth of the body producing, to the building up
1438 1722 26
ἑαυτοῦ ἐν ἀγάπῃ.
of itself in love.
5124 3767 3004 3143 1722 2962 3371 5209
17 Τοῦτο οὖν λέγω καὶ μαρτύρομαι ἐν Κυρίῳ, μηκέτι ὑμᾶς
this Therefore I say, and testify in (the) Lord, no longer you
4043 2531 3062 1484 4043 1722 3153
περιπατεῖν, καθὼς καὶ τὰ λοιπὰ ἔθνη περιπατεῖ ἐν ματαιό-
walk even as also the rest nations walk, in vanity
(of the)

mind, 18having been darkened in the understanding, being alienated *from* the life of God through the ignorance which is in them because of the hardness of their heart, 19who having cast off all feeling gave themselves up to lust, for *the* working of all uncleanness with greediness. 20But you have not so learned Christ, 21if indeed you heard Him, and were taught in Him, as *the* truth is in Jesus; 22for you have put off the old man, as regards the former behavior, having been corrupted according to the deceitful lusts; 23and to be renewed in the spirit of your mind; 24and to have put on the new man *which* according to God *was* created in righteousness and true holiness.

25Therefore, putting off the false, speak truth each with his neighbor, because we are members of one another. 26Be angry, but do not sin; do not let the sun go down on your wrath, 27nor give place to the Devil. 28The *one* stealing, let him steal no more, but rather let him labor, working what is good with the hands, that he may have *something* to give to the *one* that has need. 29Let not every filthy word go out of your mouth, but if any*thing*, for good to building up in respect of need, that it may give grace to the ones hearing. 30And do not grieve the Holy Spirit of God, by whom you were sealed to *the* day of redemption. 31Let all bitterness, and anger, and wrath, and tumult, and evil speaking be put away from you, along with all evil things. 32And be kind to one another,

3563 848 4654 1271 5607
18 τητι τοῦ νοὸς αὐτῶν, ἐσκοτισμένοι τῇ διανοίᾳ, ὄντες
of the mind of them, having been darkened in the intellect, being
526 2222 2316 1223 52
ἀπηλλοτριωμένοι τῆς ζωῆς τοῦ Θεοῦ διὰ τὴν ἄγνοιαν τὴν
alienated (from) the life of God through the ignorance
5607/1722/ 846 1223 4457 2588 848
οὖσαν ἐν αὐτοῖς, διὰ τὴν πώρωσιν τῆς καρδίας αὐτῶν·
being in them, on account of the hardness of the heart of them,
3748 524 1438 3860 766 1519
19 οἵτινες ἀπηλγηκότες ἑαυτοὺς παρέδωκαν τῇ ἀσελγείᾳ, εἰς
who having cast off all feeling themselves gave up to lust, to
2039 167 3956 1722 4124 5210 3756
20 ἐργασίαν ἀκαθαρσίας πάσης ἐν πλεονεξίᾳ. ὑμεῖς δὲ οὐχ
(the) working of uncleanness all with greediness. you But not
3779 3129 5547 1489 846 191 1722
21 οὕτως ἐμάθετε τὸν Χριστόν, εἴγε αὐτὸν ἠκούσατε καὶ ἐν
so learned Christ, if indeed Him you heard and by
846 1321 2531 2076 225 1722 2424
αὐτῷ ἐδιδάχθητε, καθώς ἐστιν ἀλήθεια ἐν τῷ Ἰησοῦ·
Him were taught, even as is (the) truth in Jesus,
659 5209 2596 4387 391
22 ἀποθέσθαι ὑμᾶς, κατὰ τὴν προτέραν ἀναστροφήν, τὸν
to put off you, as regards the former behavior of the
3820 444 5351 2596 1939
παλαιὸν ἄνθρωπον, τὸν φθειρόμενον κατὰ τὰς ἐπιθυμίας
old man, being corrupted according to the lusts
539 365 4151 3563 5216
23 τῆς ἀπάτης· ἀνανεοῦσθαι δὲ τῷ πνεύματι τοῦ νοὸς ὑμῶν,
of deceit, to be renewed and in the spirit of the mind of you,
1746 2537 444 2596 2316 2936
24 καὶ ἐνδύσασθαι τὸν καινὸν ἄνθρωπον, τὸν κατὰ Θεὸν κτι-
and to put on the new man according to God
1722 1343 3742 225
σθέντα ἐν δικαιοσύνῃ καὶ ὁσιότητι τῆς ἀληθείας.
created in righteousness and holiness of truth.
1352 659 5579 2980 225 1538 3326
25 Διὸ ἀποθέμενοι τὸ ψεῦδος λαλεῖτε ἀλήθειαν ἕκαστος μετὰ
Therefore putting off the false, speak truth each with
4139 848 3754/2070 240 3196 3710
26 τοῦ πλησίον αὐτοῦ· ὅτι ἐσμὲν ἀλλήλων μέλη. ὀργίζεσθε καὶ
the neighbor of him, because we are one another's members. Be angry and
3361 264 2246/3361 1931 1909 3950
μὴ ἁμαρτάνετε· ὁ ἥλιος μὴ ἐπιδυέτω ἐπὶ τῷ παροργισμῷ
do not sin, the sun not let set on the provocation
5216 3383 1325 5117 1228 2813 3371
27 ὑμῶν· μήτε δίδοτε τόπον τῷ διαβόλῳ. ὁ κλέπτων μηκέτι
28 of you; nor give place to the Devil. The (one) stealing, no more
2813 3123 2872 2036 18
κλεπτέτω· μᾶλλον δὲ κοπιάτω, ἐργαζόμενος τὸ ἀγαθὸν ταῖς
let him steal, rather but let him labor, working the good with the
5495 2443/2192 3330 5532 2192 3956 3056
29 χερσίν, ἵνα ἔχῃ μεταδιδόναι τῷ χρείαν ἔχοντι. πᾶς λόγος
hands, that he may have to give to the (one) need having. Every word
4550 1537 4750 5216/3361 1607 235=1536=
σαπρὸς ἐκ τοῦ στόματος ὑμῶν μὴ ἐκπορευέσθω, ἀλλ᾽ εἴ τις
corrupt out of the mouth of you not let go, but if any
18 4314 3619 5532 2443/1326/5485 191
ἀγαθὸς πρὸς οἰκοδομὴν τῆς χρείας, ἵνα δῷ χάριν τοῖς ἀκου-
(is) good to building up the need, that it may give grace to those
3361 3076 4151 40 2316 1722/3739
30 ουσι. καὶ μὴ λυπεῖτε τὸ Πνεῦμα τὸ Ἅγιον τοῦ Θεοῦ, ἐν ᾧ
hearing. And not do grieve the Spirit Holy of God, by whom
4972 1519 2250 629 3956 4088
31 ἐσφραγίσθητε εἰς ἡμέραν ἀπολυτρώσεως. πᾶσα πικρία καὶ
you were sealed for a day of redemption. All bitterness and
2372 3709 2906 988 142 575 5216
θυμὸς καὶ ὀργὴ καὶ κραυγὴ καὶ βλασφημία ἀρθήτω ἀφ᾽ ὑμῶν,
anger and wrath and tumult and evil speaking put away from you,
4862 3956 2549 1096 1519 240 5543 2155
32 σὺν πάσῃ κακίᾳ· γίνεσθε δὲ εἰς ἀλλήλους χρηστοί, εὔσπλαγ-
with all evil things. be And to one another kind, tender-

tenderhearted, having forgiven one another, even as also God forgave you in Christ.

CHAPTER 5

[1]Then be imitators of God, as beloved children, [2]and walk in love, even as Christ also loved us, and gave Himself for us, an offering and a sacrifice to God for an odor of a sweet smell.

[3]But let not be named among you fornication, and all uncleanness, or greediness, as is fitting for saints; [4]also filthiness, and foolish talking, or joking—the things not becoming—but rather thanksgiving. [5]For be knowing this, that every fornicator, or unclean one, or covetous *one*, who is an idolater, has no inheritance in the kingdom of Christ and of God. [6]Let no one deceive you with empty words, for through these the wrath of God comes on the sons of disobedience. [7]Then do not be partners with them; [8]for you then were darkness, but now light in *the* Lord—walk as children of light. [9]For the fruit of the Spirit *is* in all goodness and righteousness and truth, [10]proving what is well-pleasing to the Lord. [11]And have no fellowship with the unfruitful works of darkness, but rather even reprove *them*. [12]For it is shameful even to speak of the things being done by them in secret. [13]But all things being exposed by the light are clearly revealed, for everything having been revealed *is* light. [14]Therefore, He says, "Arise, sleeping one, and stand up out of the dead ones, and Christ will shine on you."

5483 1438 2531 2316/1722/5547 5483
χνοι, χαριζόμενοι ἑαυτοῖς, καθὼς καὶ ὁ Θεὸς ἐν Χριστῷ ἐχαρί-
hearted, forgiving yourselves, as also God in Christ
5213
σατο ὑμῖν.
forgave you.

CHAPTER 5

1096 3767 3402 2316 5613 5043 27
1 Γίνεσθε οὖν μιμηταὶ τοῦ Θεοῦ, ὡς τέκνα ἀγαπητά καὶ
be Then imitators of God, as children beloved, and
4043 1722 26 2531 5547 25 2248
2 περιπατεῖτε ἐν ἀγάπῃ, καθὼς καὶ ὁ Χριστὸς ἠγάπησεν ἡμᾶς,
walk in love, even as also Christ loved us
3860 1438 5228 2257 4376 2378
καὶ παρέδωκεν ἑαυτὸν ὑπὲρ ἡμῶν προσφορὰν καὶ θυσίαν
and gave up Himself for us an offering and a sacrifice
2316/1519/3744 2175 4202 3956 167
3 τῷ Θεῷ εἰς ὀσμὴν εὐωδίας. πορνεία δὲ καὶ πᾶσα ἀκαθαρσία
to God for an odor of sweet smell. fornication But and all uncleanness
4124 3366 3687 1722/5213 2531 4241 40
ἢ πλεονεξία μηδὲ ὀνομαζέσθω ἐν ὑμῖν, καθὼς πρέπει ἁγίοις·
or greediness not let it be named among you, as is fitting for saints,
151 3473 2228 2160 3756 433
4 καὶ αἰσχρότης, καὶ μωρολογία ἢ εὐτραπελία, τὰ οὐκ ἀνη-
and filthiness, and foolish talking or joking, the things not be-
235 3123 2169 5124 1063 2075 1097
5 κοντα· ἀλλὰ μᾶλλον εὐχαριστία. τοῦτο γὰρ ἔστε γινώ-
coming, but rather thanksgiving. this For be
3754/3956 4205/2228/ 169 2228 4123 3739/2076
σκοντες, ὅτι πᾶς πόρνος, ἢ ἀκάθαρτος, ἢ πλεονέκτης, ὅς ἐστιν
knowing, that every fornicator; or unclean one; or greedy, who is
1496 3756/2192 2818 1722 932
εἰδωλολάτρης, οὐκ ἔχει κληρονομίαν ἐν τῇ βασιλείᾳ τοῦ
an idolater; not has inheritance in the kingdom
5547 2316 3367 5209 538 2756 3056
6 Χριστοῦ καὶ Θεοῦ. μηδεὶς ὑμᾶς ἀπατάτω κενοῖς λόγοις·
of Christ and of God. Let no one you deceive with empty words;
1223 5023 1063 2064 3709 2316/1909 5207
διὰ ταῦτα γὰρ ἔρχεται ἡ ὀργὴ τοῦ Θεοῦ ἐπὶ τοὺς υἱοὺς
through these for comes the wrath of God on the sons
543 3361/3767 1096 4830 846 2258/1063
7 τῆς ἀπειθείας. μὴ οὖν γίνεσθε συμμέτοχοι αὐτῶν· ἦτε γὰρ
8 **of disobedience. not Then be partners with them; you were for**
4218 4655 3568 5457/1722/2962/5613/5043/ 5457 4043
ποτε σκότος, νῦν δὲ φῶς ἐν Κυρίῳ· ὡς τέκνα φωτὸς περι-
then darkness, now and light in (the) Lord, as children of light walk,
1063 2590 4151 1722 3956 19
9 πατεῖτε (ὁ γὰρ καρπὸς τοῦ Πνεύματος ἐν πάσῃ ἀγαθωσύνῃ
—the for fruit of the Spirit (is) in all goodness
1343 225 1381 5101 2076 2101
10 καὶ δικαιοσύνῃ καὶ ἀληθείᾳ), δοκιμάζοντες τί ἐστιν εὐάρε-
and righteousness and truth — proving what is well-
2962 3361 4790 2041
11 στον τῷ Κυρίῳ· καὶ μὴ συγκοινωνεῖτε τοῖς ἔργοις τοῖς
pleasing to the Lord; and do not have fellowship with the works
175 4655 3123 1651 1063
12 ἀκάρποις τοῦ σκότους, μᾶλλον δὲ καὶ ἐλέγχετε· τὰ γὰρ
unfruitful of darkness, rather but even reprove; the for
2931 1096 5259 846 149 2076 3004
13 κρυφῆ γινόμενα ὑπ' αὐτῶν αἰσχρόν ἐστι καὶ λέγειν. τὰ δὲ
hidden things being done by them shameful it is even to speak; but
3956 1651 5259 5457 5319 3956 1063
πάντα ἐλεγχόμενα ὑπὸ τοῦ φωτὸς φανεροῦται· πᾶν γὰρ
all things being reproved by the light is revealed; everything for
5319 5457/2076/1223/3004 1453 2518
14 τὸ φανερούμενον φῶς ἐστί. διὸ λέγει, Ἔγειραι ὁ καθεύδων
being revealed light is. Therefore He says: Arise sleeping one
450 1537 3498 2017 4671 5547
καὶ ἀνάστα ἐκ τῶν νεκρῶν, καὶ ἐπιφαύσει σοι ὁ Χριστός.
and stand up from the dead ones. and will shine on you Christ.

[15]Then watch how carefully you walk, not as unwise, but as wise ones, [16]redeeming the time, because the days are evil. [17]For this reason, do not be foolish, but understanding what the will of the Lord *is*. [18]And do not be drunk with wine, in which is debauchery, but be filled by *the* Spirit, [19]speaking to yourselves in psalms and hymns and spiritual songs, singing and praising in your heart to the Lord, [20]giving thanks at all times for all things in the name of our Lord Jesus Christ, even to God *the* Father, [21]having been subject to one another in *the* fear of God.

[22]Wives, subject yourselves to *your* own husbands, as to the Lord; [23]because a husband is head of the wife, as also Christ *is* Head of the church, and He is Savior of the body. [24]But even as the church is subject to Christ, so also the wives to their own husbands in everything.

[25]Husbands, love your wives, even as Christ also loved the church and gave Himself up on its behalf, [26]that He might sanctify it, cleansing *it* by the washing of the water in *the* word, [27]that He might present it to Himself *as* the glorious church, not having spot or wrinkle, or any such things; but that it be holy and without blemish. [28]So, husbands ought to love their wives as their *own* bodies—he loving his wife loves himself—[29]for then no one hated his *own* flesh, but nourishes and cherishes it, even as also the

991 3767/4459 199 4043 3361/5613 781
15 Βλέπετε οὖν πῶς ἀκριβῶς περιπατεῖτε, μὴ ὡς ἄσοφοι,
See, therefore, how carefully you walk, not as unwise,
235/5613/4680 1805 2540 3754 2250
16 ἀλλ' ὡς σοφοί, ἐξαγοραζόμενοι τὸν καιρόν, ὅτι αἱ ἡμέραι
but as wise ones, redeeming the time, because the days
4190 1526/1223 5124/3361/ 1096 878 235 4920
17 πονηραί εἰσι. διὰ τοῦτο μὴ γίνεσθε ἄφρονες, ἀλλὰ συνιέντες
evil are. Because of this, do not be foolish, but understanding
5101 2307 2962 3361 3182 3631/1722/3739
18 τί τὸ θέλημα τοῦ Κυρίου. καὶ μὴ μεθύσκεσθε οἴνῳ, ἐν ᾧ
what the will of the Lord (is). And do not be drunk with wine, in which
2076 810 235 4137 1722 4151 2980
19 ἐστὶν ἀσωτία, ἀλλὰ πληροῦσθε ἐν Πνεύματι, λαλοῦντες
is debauchery, but be filled by (the) Spirit, speaking
1438 5568 5215 5603 4152 103
ἑαυτοῖς ψαλμοῖς καὶ ὕμνοις καὶ ᾠδαῖς πνευματικαῖς, ᾄδοντες
to yourselves in psalms and hymns and songs spiritual, singing
5567 1722 2588 5216 2962 2168
20 καὶ ψάλλοντες ἐν τῇ καρδίᾳ ὑμῶν τῷ Κυρίῳ, εὐχαριστοῦντες
and psalming in the heart of you to the Lord, giving thanks
3842 5228 3956 1722 3686 2962 2257 2424
πάντοτε ὑπὲρ πάντων ἐν ὀνόματι τοῦ Κυρίου ἡμῶν Ἰησοῦ
always for all things in the name of the Lord of us, Jesus
5547 2316 3962 5293 240 1722
21 Χριστοῦ τῷ Θεῷ καὶ πατρί, ὑποτασσόμενοι ἀλλήλοις ἐν
Christ, to God, even (the) Father, being subject to one another in
5401 2316
φόβῳ Θεοῦ.
(the) fear of God.

1135 2398 435 5293 5613
22 Αἱ γυναῖκες, τοῖς ἰδίοις ἀνδράσιν ὑποτάσσεσθε, ὡς τῷ
The wives to the own husbands subject yourselves, as to the
2962 3754 435 2076 2776 1135 5613
23 Κυρίῳ. ὅτι ὁ ἀνήρ ἐστι κεφαλὴ τῆς γυναικός, ὡς καὶ ὁ
Lord, because a man is head of the woman, as also the
5547 2776 1577 846 2076 4990
Χριστὸς κεφαλὴ τῆς ἐκκλησίας, καὶ αὐτός ἐστι σωτὴρ τοῦ
Christ (is) Head of the church, and He is Savior of the
4983 235 5618 1577 5293 5547
24 σώματος. ἀλλ' ὥσπερ ἡ ἐκκλησία ὑποτάσσεται τῷ Χριστῷ,
body. But as the church is subject to Christ,
3779 1135 2398 435 1722 3956
25 οὕτω καὶ αἱ γυναῖκες τοῖς ἰδίοις ἀνδράσιν ἐν παντί. οἱ
so also the wives to the own husbands in everything. The
435 25 1135 1438 2531 5547
ἄνδρες, ἀγαπᾶτε τὰς γυναῖκας ἑαυτῶν, καθὼς καὶ ὁ Χριστὸς
husbands, love the wives (of) yourselves, even as also Christ
25 1577 1438 3860 5228 846
ἠγάπησε τὴν ἐκκλησίαν, καὶ ἑαυτὸν παρέδωκεν ὑπὲρ αὐτῆς·
loved the church, and Himself gave up on behalf of it,
2443 846 37 2511 3067 5204 1722
26 ἵνα αὐτὴν ἁγιάσῃ, καθαρίσας τῷ λουτρῷ τοῦ ὕδατος ἐν
that it He might sanctify, cleansing by the washing of the water by
4487 2443 3936 846 1438 1741 1577
27 ῥήματι, ἵνα παραστήσῃ αὐτὴν ἑαυτῷ ἔνδοξον τὴν ἐκκλη-
(the) word, that might present it to Himself glorious the church,
3361/2192 4695 2228/4512/2228/5100 5101 235
σίαν, μὴ ἔχουσαν σπῖλον ἢ ῥυτίδα ἤ τι τῶν τοιούτων, ἀλλ'
not having spot or wrinkle or any of the such things, but
2443/5600/40 299 3779 3784 435 25
28 ἵνα ᾖ ἁγία καὶ ἄμωμος. οὕτως ὀφείλουσιν οἱ ἄνδρες ἀγαπᾶν
that it be holy and unblemished. So ought the husbands to love
1438 1135 5613 1438 4983 25
τὰς ἑαυτῶν γυναῖκας ὡς τὰ ἑαυτῶν σώματα. ὁ ἀγαπῶν τὴν
the of themselves wives as the of themselves bodies. The (one) loving the
1438 1135 1438 25 3762 1063/4218 1438
29 ἑαυτοῦ γυναῖκα ἑαυτὸν ἀγαπᾷ· οὐδεὶς γάρ ποτε τὴν ἑαυτοῦ
of himself wife himself loves; no one for then the of himself
4561 3404 235 1625 2282 846 2531
σάρκα ἐμίσησεν, ἀλλ' ἐκτρέφει καὶ θάλπει αὐτήν, καθὼς καὶ
flesh hated, but nourishes and cherishes it, even as also

Lord the church. [30]For we are members of His body, of His flesh, and of His bones. [31]"For this a man shall leave his father and mother, and shall be joined to his wife; and the two shall be one flesh." [32]The mystery is great, but I speak as to Christ and as to the church. [33]However, you also, everyone, let each love his wife as himself, and the wife, that she fears the husband.

2962 1577 3754/3196/2070 4983 848
30 ὁ Κύριος τὴν ἐκκλησίαν· ὅτι μέλη ἐσμὲν τοῦ σώματος αὐτοῦ,
the Lord the church, because members we are of the body of Him,
1537 4561 848 1537 3747 848 473 5127
31 ἐκ τῆς σαρκὸς αὐτοῦ καὶ ἐκ τῶν ὀστέων αὐτοῦ. Ἀντὶ τού-
of the flesh of Him and of the bones of Him. For this
2641 444 3962 848
του καταλείψει ἄνθρωπος τὸν πατέρα αὐτοῦ καὶ τὴν
shall leave a man the father of him and the
3384 4347 4314 1135 848
μητέρα, καὶ προσκολληθήσεται πρὸς τὴν γυναῖκα αὐτοῦ,
mother and shall cleave to the wife of him,
2071 1417/1519/4561/3391 3466 5124 3173
32 καὶ ἔσονται οἱ δύο εἰς σάρκα μίαν. τὸ μυστήριον τοῦτο μέγα
and shall be the two for flesh one. mystery This great
2076 1473 3004/1519 5547 1519 1577 4133
ἐστίν· ἐγὼ δὲ λέγω εἰς Χριστόν, καὶ εἰς τὴν ἐκκλησίαν. πλὴν
is, I but say as to Christ and as to the church. But
5210 2596/1520 1538 1438 1135 3779
33 καὶ ὑμεῖς οἱ καθ' ἕνα, ἕκαστος τὴν ἑαυτοῦ γυναῖκα οὕτως
also you one by one, each the of himself wife, so
25 5613 1438 1135/2443/5399 435
ἀγαπάτω ὡς ἑαυτόν· ἡ δὲ γυνὴ ἵνα φοβῆται τὸν ἄνδρα.
let him love as himself, the and wife that she fears the husband.

CHAPTER 6

[1]Children, obey your parents in *the* Lord, for this is right. [2]Honor your father and mother, which is *the* first commandment with a promise, [3]that it may be well with you, and you may be long-lived on the earth. [4]And fathers, do not provoke your children, but bring them up in *the* discipline and admonition of *the* Lord.

5043 5219 1118 5216/1722/2962 5124
1 Τὰ τέκνα, ὑπακούετε τοῖς γονεῦσιν ὑμῶν ἐν Κυρίῳ· τοῦτο
The children: obey the parents of you in (the) Lord, this
1063 2076 1342 5091 3962 4675 3384
2 γάρ ἐστι δίκαιον. Τίμα τὸν πατέρα σου καὶ τὴν μητέρα
for is right. Honor the father of you and the mother
3748 2076 1785 4413 1722 1860 2443/2095/4671
3 (ἥτις ἐστὶν ἐντολὴ πρώτη ἐν ἐπαγγελίᾳ), ἵνα εὖ σοι
—which is commandment (the) first with a promise — that well with you
1096 2071 3118 1909 1093 3962
4 γένηται, καὶ ἔσῃ μακροχρόνιος ἐπὶ τῆς γῆς. καὶ οἱ πατέρες,
it may be, and you may be long-lived on the earth. And the fathers:
3361 3949 5043 5216 235 1625 846 1722
μὴ παροργίζετε τὰ τέκνα ὑμῶν, ἀλλ' ἐκτρέφετε αὐτὰ ἐν
do not provoke the children of you, but nurture them in
3809 3559 2962
παιδείᾳ καὶ νουθεσίᾳ Κυρίου.
(the) discipline and admonition of (the) Lord.

[5]Slaves, obey *your* lords according to flesh, with fear and trembling, in singleness of your heart, as to Christ; [6]not with eye-service as men-pleasers, but as slaves of Christ doing the will of God from *the* soul, [7]serving as slaves with good will to the Lord, and not *as to* men; [8]each one knowing that whatever good thing he does, this he shall receive from the Lord, whether a slave, or a freeman. [9]And lords, do the same things toward them, forbearing threatening, knowing that the Lord of you and of them is in Heaven, and there is no respect of persons with Him.

1401 5219 2962/2596 4561 3326 5401
5 Οἱ δοῦλοι, ὑπακούετε τοῖς κυρίοις κατὰ σάρκα μετὰ φόβου
The slaves: obey the lords according to flesh with fear
5156 1722 572 2588 5216/5613 5547
καὶ τρόμου, ἐν ἁπλότητι τῆς καρδίας ὑμῶν, ὡς τῷ Χριστῷ·
and trembling, in singleness of the heart of you, as to Christ
3361/2596/3787 5613 441 235/5613/1401
6 μὴ κατ' ὀφθαλμοδουλείαν ὡς ἀνθρωπάρεσκοι, ἀλλ' ὡς δοῦλοι
not by way of eye-service as men-pleasers, but as slaves
5547 4160 2307 2316/1537/5590 3326
7 τοῦ Χριστοῦ, ποιοῦντες τὸ θέλημα τοῦ Θεοῦ ἐκ ψυχῆς, μετ'
of Christ doing the will of God from (the) soul, with
2133 1398 5613 2962 3756 444
εὐνοίας δουλεύοντες ὡς τῷ Κυρίῳ καὶ οὐκ ἀνθρώποις·
goodwill serving as slaves as to the Lord and not (as to) men,
1492 3754/•/1437 5100/1538 4160 18 5124 2865
8 εἰδότες ὅτι ὃ ἐάν τι ἕκαστος ποιήσῃ ἀγαθόν, τοῦτο κομιεῖται
knowing that whatever each one he does good thing, this he will get
3844 2962 1535 1401 1535 1658 2962
9 παρὰ τοῦ Κυρίου, εἴτε δοῦλος, εἴτε ἐλεύθερος. καὶ οἱ κύριοι,
from the Lord, whether a slave, or a freeman. And the lords:
846 4160 4314 846 447 547 1492
τὰ αὐτὰ ποιεῖτε πρὸς αὐτούς, ἀνιέντες τὴν ἀπειλήν· εἰδότες
the same things do toward them, forbearing the threatening, knowing
3754 5216 846 2962 2076/1722/3772 4382
ὅτι καὶ ὑμῶν αὐτῶν ὁ Κύριός ἐστιν ἐν οὐρανοῖς, καὶ προσω-
that also of you of them the Lord is in Heaven, and respect

[10]For the rest, my
brothers, be made power-
ful in *the* Lord, and in the
might of His strength. [11]Put
on all the armor of God, for
you to be able to stand
against the wiles of the
Devil; [12]because we are not
wrestling against flesh and
blood, but against the
rulers, against the authorities, against the rulers of
this world, of the darkness
of this age, against the
spiritual *powers* of evil in
the heavenlies. [13]Because
of this, take up all of the
armor of God, that you may
be able to resist in the evil
day, and having worked out
all things, to stand. [14]Then
stand firm, having girded
your loins about with truth,
and having put on the
breastplate of righteous-
ness, [15]and having shod
the feet with *the* preparation of the gospel of peace;
[16]above all, taking up the
shield of faith, with which
you will be able to quench
all the darts of the evil one,
the things having been
made fiery. [17]Also, take the
helmet of salvation, and the
sword of the Spirit, which is
the word of God; [18]through
all prayer and petition,
praying at every time in *the*
Spirit, and watching to this
same thing with all perseverance and petition con-
cerning all the saints.

[19]*Pray* also for me, that to
me may be given speech in
the opening of my mouth
with boldness to make
known the mystery of the
gospel, [20]for which I am an
ambassador in a chain, that
in it I may speak boldly as it
is right for me to speak.

3756/2076/3844/ 846
πολυψία οὐκ ἔστι παρ' αὐτῷ.
of persons not is with Him.
3063 80 3450 1743 1722 2962 1722
10 Τὸ λοιπόν, ἀδελφοί μου, ἐνδυναμοῦσθε ἐν Κυρίῳ, καὶ ἐν
For the rest, brothers of me, be empowered in (the) Lord, and in
2904 2479 848 1746 3833
11 τῷ κράτει τῆς ἰσχύος αὐτοῦ. ἐνδύσασθε τὴν πανοπλίαν τοῦ
the might of the strength of Him. Put on the whole armor
2316 4314 1410 5209 2476 4314 3180
Θεοῦ, πρὸς τὸ δύνασθαι ὑμᾶς στῆναι πρὸς τὰς μεθοδείας τοῦ
of God, for to be able you to stand against the wiles of the
1228 3754/3756/2076/ 2254 3823 4314 129 4561
12 διαβόλου. ὅτι οὐκ ἔστιν ἡμῖν ἡ πάλη πρὸς αἷμα καὶ σάρκα,
Devil. Because not is to us wrestling against blood and flesh,
235 4314 746 4314 1849 4314
ἀλλὰ πρὸς τὰς ἀρχάς, πρὸς τὰς ἐξουσίας, πρὸς τοὺς κο-
but against the rulers, against the authorities, against the
2888 4655 165 5127 4314
σμοκράτορας τοῦ σκότους τοῦ αἰῶνος τούτου, πρὸς τὰ
world's rulers of the darkness age of this, against the
4152 4189 1722 2032 1223 5124
13 πνευματικὰ τῆς πονηρίας ἐν τοῖς ἐπουρανίοις. διὰ τοῦτο
spiritual (powers) of evil in the heavenlies. Because of this
353 3833 2316/2443 1410 436
ἀναλάβετε τὴν πανοπλίαν τοῦ Θεοῦ, ἵνα δυνηθῆτε ἀντιστῆ-
take up the whole armor of God, that you be able to resist
1722 2250 4190 537 2716
ναι ἐν τῇ ἡμέρᾳ τῇ πονηρᾷ καὶ ἅπαντα κατεργασάμενοι
in the day evil, and all things having worked out
2476 2476 3767 4024 3751 5216 1722
14 στῆναι. στῆτε οὖν περιζωσάμενοι τὴν ὀσφὺν ὑμῶν ἐν
to stand. Stand, therefore, having girded about the loins of you with
225 1746 2382 1343
15 ἀληθείᾳ, καὶ ἐνδυσάμενοι τὸν θώρακα τῆς δικαιοσύνης, καὶ
truth, and putting on the breastplate of the righteousness, and
5265 4228 1722 2091 2098
ὑποδησάμενοι τοὺς πόδας ἐν ἑτοιμασίᾳ τοῦ εὐαγγελίου τῆς
having shod the feet with (the) preparation of the gospel
1515 1909 3956 353 2375 4102
16 εἰρήνης· ἐπὶ πᾶσιν ἀναλαβόντες τὸν θυρεὸν τῆς πίστεως,
of peace; above all, having taken up the shield of faith,
1722/3739/ 1410 3956 956 4190 4448
ἐν ᾧ δυνήσεσθε πάντα τὰ βέλη τοῦ πονηροῦ τὰ πεπυρωμένα
by which you will be able all the darts of the evil one having been made fiery
4570 4030 4992 1209
17 σβέσαι. καὶ τὴν περικεφαλαίαν τοῦ σωτηρίου δέξασθε, καὶ
to quench. And the helmet of salvation take, and
3162 4151 =3063= 4487 2316/1223/ 3956
18 τὴν μάχαιραν τοῦ Πνεύματος, ὅ ἐστι ῥῆμα Θεοῦ· διὰ πάσης
the sword of the Spirit, which is (the) word of God via all
4335 1162 4336 1722 3956 2540/1722
προσευχῆς καὶ δεήσεως προσευχόμενοι ἐν παντὶ καιρῷ ἐν
prayer and petition, praying at every time in
4151 1519 846 5124 69 1722 3956
Πνεύματι, καὶ εἰς αὐτὸ τοῦτο ἀγρυπνοῦντες ἐν πάσῃ
(the) Spirit, and to same thing this watching in all
4343 1162 4012 3956 40
19 προσκαρτερήσει καὶ δεήσει περὶ πάντων τῶν ἁγίων, καὶ
perseverance and petition concerning all the saints, and
5228 1700 2443/3427/ 1325 3056/1722 457 4750
ὑπὲρ ἐμοῦ, ἵνα μοι δοθείη λόγος ἐν ἀνοίξει τοῦ στόματός
for me, that to me may be given speech in opening of the mouth
3450/1722/ 3954 1107 3466 2098
μου ἐν παρρησίᾳ, γνωρίσαι τὸ μυστήριον τοῦ εὐαγγελίου,
of me in boldness, to make known the mystery of the gospel,
5228/3756 4243 1722 254 2443/1722/846 3955
20 ὑπὲρ οὗ πρεσβεύω ἐν ἁλύσει, ἵνα ἐν αὐτῷ παρρησιάσωμαι,
for which I am an ambassador in a chain, that in it I may speak boldly
5613/1163/3165/2980
ὡς δεῖ με λαλῆσαι.
as it behoves me to speak.

[21]But that you also may
know the things about me,
what I am doing, Tychicus,
the beloved brother and
faithful minister in *the* Lord
will make known all things
to you, [22]whom I sent to
you for this same thing, that
you might know the things
about us, and *he* may
comfort your hearts.

[23]Peace to the brothers,
and love with faith from
God *the* Father and *the* Lord
Jesus Christ. [24]Grace *be*
with all those that love our
Lord Jesus Christ in
incorruptibility.

2443 1492 5210 2596/1691/5101/ 4238 3956
21 Ἵνα δὲ εἰδῆτε καὶ ὑμεῖς τὰ κατ' ἐμέ, τί πράσσω, πάντα
that Now may know also you the things about me, what I am doing, all things
5213 1107 5190 27 80 4103
ὑμῖν γνωρίσει Τυχικὸς ὁ ἀγαπητὸς ἀδελφὸς καὶ πιστὸς
to you will make known Tychicus the beloved brother and faithful
1249 1722 2962 3739 3992 4314/ 5209/1519/846 5124
22 διάκονος ἐν Κυρίῳ· ὃν ἔπεμψα πρὸς ὑμᾶς εἰς αὐτὸ τοῦτο,
minister in (the) Lord whom I sent to you for this same thing,
2443 1097 4012 2257 3870 2588
ἵνα · γνῶτε τὰ περὶ ἡμῶν, καὶ παρακαλέσῃ τὰς καρδίας
that you may know the things about us, and may comfort the hearts
5216
ὑμῶν.
of you.
1515 80 26 3326 4102 575 2316
23 Εἰρήνη τοῖς ἀδελφοῖς καὶ ἀγάπη μετὰ πίστεως ἀπὸ Θεοῦ
Peace to the brothers and love with faith from God
3962 2962 2424 5547 5485 3326 3956
24 πατρὸς καὶ Κυρίου Ἰησοῦ Χριστοῦ. ἡ χάρις μετὰ πάντων
(the) Father and (the) Lord Jesus Christ. Grace (be) with all
25 2962 2257 2424 5547 1722
τῶν ἀγαπώντων τὸν Κύριον ἡμῶν Ἰησοῦν Χριστὸν ἐν
those loving the Lord of us, Jesus Christ in
861
ἀφθαρσίᾳ.
incorruptibility.

ΠΑΥΛΟΥ ΤΟΥ ΑΠΟΣΤΟΛΟΥ
PAUL THE APOSTLE
Η ΠΡΟΣ
TO (THE)
ΦΙΛΙΠΠΗΣΙΟΥΣ ΕΠΙΣΤΟΛΗ
PHILIPPIANS EPISTLE

THE EPISTLE
TO THE
PHILIPPIANS
A LITERAL TRANSLATION
OF THE BIBLE

CHAPTER 1

[1]Paul, and Timothy, slaves of Jesus Christ, to all the saints in Christ Jesus who are in Philippi, with the overseers and ministers: [2]Grace to you and peace from God our Father and *the* Lord Jesus Christ.

[3]I thank my God on all the remembrance of you, [4]always in my every prayer on your behalf making *my* prayer with joy [5]over your fellowship in the gospel, from *the* first day until now, [6]being persuaded of this very thing, that the *One* having begun a good work in you will finish *it* until *the* day of Jesus Christ; [7]as it is righteous for me to think this of you all, because you have me in *your* heart; both in my bonds and in the defense and confirmation of the gospel, you are all sharers of the grace with me. [8]For God is my witness how I long after you all in *the* bowels of Jesus Christ.

[9]And this I pray, that your love may yet abound more and more in full knowledge and all perception, [10]for you *to* distinguish the things that differ, that you may be sincere and without blame for *the* day of Christ, [11]being filled *with the* fruits of righteousness through

CHAPTER 1

3972 5095 1401 2424 5547 3956
1 Παῦλος καὶ Τιμόθεος, δοῦλοι Ἰησοῦ Χριστοῦ, πᾶσι τοῖς
Paul and Timothy, slaves of Jesus Christ, to all the
40 1722 5547 2424 5607/1722 5375 4862 1985
ἁγίοις ἐν Χριστῷ Ἰησοῦ τοῖς οὖσιν ἐν Φιλίπποις, σὺν ἐπι-
saints in Christ Jesus being in Philippi with
1249 5485 5213 1515 575 2316
2 σκόποις καὶ διακόνοις· χάρις ὑμῖν καὶ εἰρήνη ἀπὸ Θεοῦ
overseers and ministers: Grace to you and peace from God
3962 2257 2962 2424 5547
πατρὸς ἡμῶν καὶ Κυρίου Ἰησοῦ Χριστοῦ.
(the) Father of us and (the) Lord Jesus Christ.
2168 2316/3450/1909/3956 3417 5216 3956
3 Εὐχαριστῶ τῷ Θεῷ μου ἐπὶ πάσῃ τῇ μνείᾳ ὑμῶν, πάντοτε
4 I thank the God of me at all the remembrance of you, always
1722/3956 1162 3450 5228 3956 5216 3326 5479
ἐν πάσῃ δεήσει μου ὑπὲρ πάντων ὑμῶν μετὰ χαρᾶς τὴν
in every petition of me on behalf of all you with joy the
1162 4160 1909 2842 5216/1519 2098
5 δέησιν ποιούμενος, ἐπὶ τῇ κοινωνίᾳ ὑμῶν εἰς τὸ εὐαγγέλιον,
petition making, over the fellowship of you in the gospel
575 4413 2250 891 3568 3982 846 5124
6 ἀπὸ πρώτης ἡμέρας ἄχρι τοῦ νῦν· πεποιθὼς αὐτὸ τοῦτο,
from (the) first day until now, being persuaded very this thing,
3754 1728 1722/5213 2041 18 2005 891
ὅτι ὁ ἐναρξάμενος ἐν ὑμῖν ἔργον ἀγαθὸν ἐπιτελέσει ἄχρις
that He having begun in you a work good will finish (it) until
2250 2424 5547 2531 2076 1342 1698 5124
7 ἡμέρας Ἰησοῦ Χριστοῦ· καθώς ἐστι δίκαιον ἐμοὶ τοῦτο
(the) day of Jesus Christ. as it is righteous for me this
5426 5228 3956 5216 1223 2192/3165/1722 2588
φρονεῖν ὑπὲρ πάντων ὑμῶν, διὰ τὸ ἔχειν με ἐν τῇ καρδίᾳ
to think of all you, because of having me in the heart
5209/1722/5037 1199 3450 627 951
ὑμᾶς, ἔν τε τοῖς δεσμοῖς μου καὶ τῇ ἀπολογίᾳ καὶ βεβαιώσει
you, in both the bonds of me and in the defense and confirmation
2098 4791 3450 5485 3956
τοῦ εὐαγγελίου, συγκοινωνούς μου τῆς χάριτος πάντας
of the gospel, sharers with me of the grace all
5209 5607 3144 1063 3450 2076 2316 5613 1971
8 ὑμᾶς ὄντας. μάρτυς γάρ μού ἐστιν ὁ Θεός, ὡς ἐπιποθῶ
you being. witness For of me is God, how I long after
3956 5209/1722 4698 2424 5547 5124
9 πάντας ὑμᾶς ἐν σπλάγχνοις Ἰησοῦ Χριστοῦ. καὶ τοῦτο
all you in (the) bowels of Jesus Christ. And this
4336 2443 26 5216 2089 3123 3123
προσεύχομαι, ἵνα ἡ ἀγάπη ὑμῶν ἔτι μᾶλλον καὶ μᾶλλον
I pray, that the love of you yet more and more
4052 1722 1922 3956 144 1519 1381
10 περισσεύῃ ἐν ἐπιγνώσει καὶ πάσῃ αἰσθήσει, εἰς τὸ δοκιμάζειν
may abound in full knowledge and all perception, for the approving
5209 1308 2443/5600 1506 677 1519
ὑμᾶς τὰ διαφέροντα, ἵνα ἦτε εἰλικρινεῖς καὶ ἀπρόσκοποι εἰς
of you the things differing, that you be sincere and without blame for
2250 5547 4137 2590 1343
11 ἡμέραν Χριστοῦ, πεπληρωμένοι καρπῶν δικαιοσύνης τῶν
(the) day of Christ, having been filled (with) fruits of righteousness

Jesus Christ, to *the* glory
and praise of God. 12But I
want you to know, brothers,
that the things concerning
me have more fully come to
the advancement of the
gospel, 13so that in all the
praetorium, and to all the
rest, my bonds have
become clearly revealed *to*
be in Christ; 14and the most
of the brothers in *the* Lord,
being confident in my
bonds, more exceedingly
dare to speak the word
fearlessly. 15Some, indeed,
even proclaim Christ be-
cause of envy and strife; but
some also because of good
will. 16These, indeed, announce Christ out of party
spirit, not sincerely, thinking to add affliction to my
bonds. 17But these *others*
out of love, knowing that I
am set for defense of the
gospel.

18For what? Yet in every
way, whether in pretense or
in truth, Christ is an-
nounced; and I rejoice in
this; I will also yet rejoice.
19For I know that this will
result in salvation to me
through your petition, and
the supply of the Spirit of
Jesus Christ, 20according
to my earnest expectation
and hope, that in nothing I
shall be ashamed, but as
always in all boldness even
now Christ will be magni-
fied in my body, whether
through life or through
death.
21For to me to live *is*
Christ, and to die is gain.
22But if I live in *the* flesh, this
is to me fruit of *my* labor;
and what I shall choose, I
do not know. 23For I am
pressed together by the
two: having a desire to
depart and be with Christ,
which is far better—24but to
remain in the flesh *is* more
necessary on account of
you. 25And being persuaded

1223 2424 5547 1519 1391 1868 2316
διὰ Ἰησοῦ Χριστοῦ, εἰς δόξαν καὶ ἔπαινον Θεοῦ.
through Jesus Christ, to (the) glory and praise of God.
1097 5209 1014 80 3754 2596
12 Γινώσκειν δὲ ὑμᾶς βούλομαι, ἀδελφοί, ὅτι τὰ κατ' ἐμὲ
to know And you I want, brothers, that the things about me
3123 1519 4297 2098 2064 5620
13 μᾶλλον εἰς προκοπὴν τοῦ εὐαγγελίου ἐλήλυθεν· ὥστε τοὺς
rather to (the) advance of the gospel has come, so as the
1199 3450 5318 1722/ 5547 1096 1722/3650 4232
δεσμούς μου φανερούς ἐν Χριστῷ γενέσθαι ἐν ὅλῳ τῷ πραι-
bonds of me clearly revealed in Christ become in all the prae-
3062 3956 4119 80
14 τωρίῳ καὶ τοῖς λοιποῖς πᾶσι, καὶ τοὺς πλείονας τῶν ἀδελφῶν
torium, and to the rest all, and the most of the brothers
1722 2962 3982 1199 3450 4056
ἐν Κυρίῳ, πεποιθότας τοῖς δεσμοῖς μου, περισσοτέρως
in (the) Lord being confident in the bonds of me, more exceedingly
5111 870 3056 2980 5100/3303 1223 5355
15 τολμᾷν ἀφόβως τὸν λόγον λαλεῖν. τινὲς μὲν καὶ διὰ φθόνον
to dare fearlessly the word to speak. Some indeed even through envy
2054 5100 1223 2509 5547 2784
καὶ ἔριν, τινὲς δὲ καὶ δι' εὐδοκίαν τὸν Χριστὸν κηρύσσουσιν·
and strife, some but also through good will Christ proclaim;
3303/1537/ 2052 5547 2605 3756 55
16 οἱ μὲν ἐξ ἐριθείας τὸν Χριστὸν καταγγέλλουσιν, οὐχ ἁγνῶς,
These indeed of rivalry Christ announce, not sincerely,
3363 2347 2018 1199 3450 1537 26
17 οἰόμενοι θλίψιν ἐπιφέρειν τοῖς δεσμοῖς μου· οἱ δὲ ἐξ ἀγάπης,
thinking trouble to add to the bonds of me. these But out of love,
1492 3754 1519 627 2098 2249 5100 1063
18 εἰδότες ὅτι εἰς ἀπολογίαν τοῦ εὐαγγελίου κεῖμαι. τί γάρ;
knowing that for defense of the gospel I am set. what For?
4133 3956 5158 1535 4392 1535 225 5547
πλὴν παντὶ τρόπῳ, εἴτε προφάσει εἴτε ἀληθείᾳ, Χριστὸς
Yet in every way, whether in pretense or in truth, Christ
2605 1722 5129 5463 235 5463
καταγγέλλεται· καὶ ἐν τούτῳ χαίρω, ἀλλὰ καὶ χαρήσομαι.
is announced, and in this I rejoice; yet also I will rejoice.
2092/1063/3754/5124/3427 576 1519 4991 1223
19 οἶδα γὰρ ὅτι τοῦτό μοι ἀποβήσεται εἰς σωτηρίαν διὰ τῆς
I know For that this to me will result in salvation through the
5216 1162 2024 4151 2424
ὑμῶν δεήσεως, καὶ ἐπιχορηγίας τοῦ Πνεύματος Ἰησοῦ
of you petition, and supply of the Spirit of Jesus
5547 2596 603 1680 3450 3754/1722
20 Χριστοῦ, κατὰ τὴν ἀποκαραδοκίαν καὶ ἐλπίδα μου, ὅτι ἐν
Christ, according to the earnest expectation and hope of me, that in
3762 153 235/1722/3956 3054 5613 3842
οὐδενὶ αἰσχυνθήσομαι, ἀλλ' ἐν πάσῃ παρρησίᾳ, ὡς πάν-
nothing I shall be ashamed, but in all boldness, as always,
3568 3170 5547 1722 4983 3450
τοτε, καὶ νῦν μεγαλυνθήσεται Χριστὸς ἐν τῷ σώματί μου,
and now will be magnified Christ in the body of me,
1535/1223/2222/1535/1223/ 2288 1698/1063 2198 5547
21 εἴτε διὰ ζωῆς εἴτε διὰ θανάτου. ἐμοὶ γὰρ τὸ ζῆν, Χριστός·
whether via life or via death. to me For to live (is) Christ,
599 2771 1487 2198/1722/4561 5124/3427
22 καὶ τὸ ἀποθανεῖν, κέρδος. εἰ δὲ τὸ ζῆν ἐν σαρκί, τοῦτό μοι
and to die is gain. if But to live in (the) flesh, this to me
2590 2041 5101 138 3756 1107 4912
23 καρπὸς ἔργου· καὶ τί αἱρήσομαι οὐ γνωρίζω. συνέχομαι
(is) fruit of (my) work, and what I shall choose not I perceive. I am constrained
1063/1537 1417 1939 2192/1519 360 4862
γὰρ ἐκ τῶν δύο, τὴν ἐπιθυμίαν ἔχων εἰς τὸ ἀναλῦσαι καὶ σὺν
For by the two, the desire having to depart and with
5547 1511 4183 3123 2909 1961 1722
24 Χριστῷ εἶναι, πολλῷ μᾶλλον κρεῖσσον· τὸ δὲ ἐπιμένειν ἐν
Christ be, much rather better; but to remain in
4561 316 1223 5209 5124 3982
25 τῇ σαρκὶ ἀναγκαιότερον δι' ὑμᾶς. καὶ τοῦτο πεποιθὼς
the flesh (is) more necessary on account of you. And this being assured

of this, I know that I will remain and will continue with you all for your advancement and joy of faith; [26]so that your glorying may abound in Christ Jesus in me, through my presence with you again. [27]Only behave yourself worthily of the gospel of Christ, so that whether coming and seeing you, or being absent, I hear the things concerning you, that you stand fast in one spirit and one soul, striving together in the faith of the gospel, [28]and not being terrified in anything by those who oppose, which to them truly is a proof of destruction, but to you of salvation, and this from God; [29]because it was granted to you on behalf of Christ not only to believe in Him, but also to suffer on His behalf, [30]having the same struggle which you saw in me, and now hear *to be* in me.

CHAPTER 2

[1]Then if *there is* any comfort in Christ, if any consolation of love, if any fellowship of *the* Spirit, if any tendernesses and compassions, [2]fulfill my joy, that you think the same, having the same love, one in soul, minding the one thing, [3]*doing* nothing according to party spirit or self-glory, but in humility esteeming one another to surpass themselves; [4]each not looking at their own things, but each also *at the* things of others. [5]For let this mind be in you which also *was* in Christ Jesus, [6]who subsisting in the form of God thought *it* not robbery to be equal with God, [7]but emptied Himself, taking *the* form of a slave, having become in *the*

1492/3754/3306 4893 3956 5213/1519 5216
οἶδα ὅτι μενῶ, καὶ συμπαραμενῶ πᾶσιν ὑμῖν εἰς τὴν ὑμῶν
I know that I will remain, and will continue with all you for the of you
4297 5479 4102 2443 2745 5216
26 προκοπὴν καὶ χαρὰν τῆς πίστεως, ἵνα τὸ καύχημα ὑμῶν
advancement and joy of the faith, that the boast of you
4052 1722 5547 2424/1722/1698/1223 1699 3952
περισσεύῃ ἐν Χριστῷ Ἰησοῦ ἐν ἐμοί, διὰ τῆς ἐμῆς παρου-
may abound in Christ Jesus in me, through my presence
3825 4314 5209 3440 516 2098
27 σίας πάλιν πρὸς ὑμᾶς. μόνον ἀξίως τοῦ εὐαγγελίου τοῦ
again with you. Only worthily of the gospel
5547 4176 2443/1535 2064 1492 5209 1535
Χριστοῦ πολιτεύεσθε, ἵνα εἴτε ἐλθὼν καὶ ἰδὼν ὑμᾶς, εἴτε
of Christ conduct yourself, that whether coming and seeing you, or
548 191 4012 5216 3754 4739 1722/1520/ 4151
ἀπών, ἀκούσω τὰ περὶ ὑμῶν, ὅτι στήκετε ἐν ἑνὶ πνεύματι,
being absent, I hear the things about you, that you stand in one spirit,
3391 5590 4866 4102 2098 3361
28 μιᾷ ψυχῇ συναθλοῦντες τῇ πίστει τοῦ εὐαγγελίου, καὶ μὴ
with one soul striving together in the faith of the gospel, and not
4426 1722 3367 5259 480 3748 846
πτυρόμενοι ἐν μηδενὶ ὑπὸ τῶν ἀντικειμένων· ἥτις αὐτοῖς
being terrified in nothing by those opposing, which to them
3303/2076 1732 684 5213 4991 5124
μέν ἐστιν ἔνδειξις ἀπωλείας, ὑμῖν δὲ σωτηρίας, καὶ τοῦτο
indeed is a proof of destruction, to you but of salvation, and this
575 2316/3754/5213 5483 5228 5547 3756 3440
29 ἀπὸ Θεοῦ· ὅτι ὑμῖν ἐχαρίσθη τὸ ὑπὲρ Χριστοῦ, οὐ μόνον τὸ
from God, because to you it was granted for Christ, not only
1519 846 4100 235 5228 846 3958
30 εἰς αὐτὸν πιστεύειν, ἀλλὰ καὶ τὸ ὑπὲρ αὐτοῦ πάσχειν· τὸν
in Him to believe, but also on behalf of Him to suffer, the
846 73 2192 3634 1492/1722/1698 3568 191 1722
αὐτὸν ἀγῶνα ἔχοντες οἷον εἴδετε ἐν ἐμοί, καὶ νῦν ἀκούετε ἐν
same struggle having which you saw in me, and now hear in
1698
ἐμοί.
me.

CHAPTER 2

1487/5101/3767/ 3874 1722 5547 =1536= 3890
1 Εἴ τις οὖν παράκλησις ἐν Χριστῷ, εἴ τι παραμύθιον
If (is) any Then comfort in Christ, if any consolation
26 =1536= 2842 4151 =1536= 4698
ἀγάπης, εἴ τις κοινωνία Πνεύματος, εἴ τινα σπλάγχνα καὶ
of love, if any fellowship of (the) Spirit, if any compassions and
3628 4137 3450 5479 2443 846 5426
2 οἰκτιρμοί, πληρώσατέ μου τὴν χαράν, ἵνα τὸ αὐτὸ φρονῆτε,
pities, fulfill of me the joy, that the same you think,
846 26 2192 4861 1722 5426
τὴν αὐτὴν ἀγάπην ἔχοντες, σύμψυχοι, τὸ ἓν φρονοῦντες·
the same love having, one in soul, the one thing minding,
3367 2596 2052/2228/ 2754 235 5012
3 μηδὲν κατὰ ἐρίθειαν ἢ κενοδοξίαν, ἀλλὰ τῇ ταπεινοφροσύνῃ
nothing according to rivalry or self-glory, but in humility
240 2233 5242 1438 3361 1438
4 ἀλλήλους ἡγούμενοι ὑπερέχοντας ἑαυτῶν· μὴ τὰ ἑαυτῶν
one another esteeming surpassing themselves; not their own things
1538 4648 235 2087 1538 5124 1063
5 ἕκαστος σκοπεῖτε, ἀλλὰ καὶ τὰ ἑτέρων ἕκαστος. τοῦτο γὰρ
each looking at, but also other's things each. this For
5426 1722/5213/3739/1722 5547 2424/3739/1722/3444 2316
6 φρονείσθω ἐν ὑμῖν ὃ καὶ ἐν Χριστῷ Ἰησοῦ· ὃς ἐν μορφῇ Θεοῦ
think among you, which also (was) in Christ Jesus, who in (the) form of God
5225 3756 725 2233 1511/2470/2316/ 235
7 ὑπάρχων, οὐχ ἁρπαγμὸν ἡγήσατο τὸ εἶναι ἴσα Θεῷ, ἀλλ'
subsisting, not robbery thought (it) to be equal with God, but
1438 2758 3444 1401 2983/1722/ 3667 444
ἑαυτὸν ἐκένωσε, μορφὴν δούλου λαβών, ἐν ὁμοιώματι ἀνθρώ-
Himself emptied, (the) form of a slave taking, in likeness of men

likeness of men, 8 and being found in fashion as a man, He humbled Himself, having become obedient until death, even *the* death of a cross. 9 Therefore, also God highly exalted Him and gave Him a name above every name, 10 that at the name of Jesus every knee should bow, of *those* of Heaven, and *those* of earth, and *those* under *the* earth; 11 and every tongue should confess that Jesus Christ *is* Lord, to *the* glory of God *the* Father.

12 So, then, my beloved, even as you always obeyed, not as in my presence only, but now much rather in my absence, work out your salvation with fear and trembling, 13 for it is God who is working in you both to will and to work for the sake of *His* good pleasure.

14 Do all things without murmurings and disputings, 15 that you may be blameless and harmless, children of God, without fault in the midst of a crooked generation, even having been perverted—among whom you shine as luminaries in *the* world, 16 holding up a word of life, for a boast to me in *the* day of Christ, that I ran not in vain, nor labored in vain. 17 But if indeed I am poured out on the sacrifice and service of your faith, I rejoice; and I rejoice with you all. 18 And you also rejoice *in* the same, and rejoice with me.

19 But I hope in the Lord Jesus to send Timothy to you soon, that I may also be of good cheer, knowing the things about you. 20 For I have no one likeminded, who genuinely will care for the things about you. 21 For all seek their own things, not the things of Christ Jesus. 22 But you know the

1096 4976 2147/5613/ 444 5013
8 πων γενόμενος· καὶ σχήματι εὑρεθεὶς ὡς ἄνθρωπος, ἐταπείνω-
becoming; and in fashion being found as a man, He humbled
1438 1096 5255 3360 2288 2288
σεν ἑαυτόν, γενόμενος ὑπήκοος μέχρι θανάτου, θανάτου δὲ
Himself, becoming obedient until death, (the) death even
4716 1352 2316 846 5251 5483
9 σταυροῦ. διὸ καὶ ὁ Θεὸς αὐτὸν ὑπερύψωσε, καὶ ἐχαρίσατο
of a cross. Therefore also God Him highly exalted, and gave
846 3686 5228/3956 3686 2443/1722 3686 2424
10 αὐτῷ ὄνομα τὸ ὑπὲρ πᾶν ὄνομα· ἵνα ἐν τῷ ὀνόματι Ἰησοῦ
to Him a name above every name, that in the name of Jesus
3956/1063 2578 2032 1919 2709
πᾶν γόνυ κάμψῃ ἐπουρανίων καὶ ἐπιγείων καὶ καταχθονίων,
every knee should bow, of heavenly and of earthly and those under earth,
3956 1100 1843 3754 2962 2424
11 καὶ πᾶσα γλῶσσα ἐξομολογήσηται ὅτι Κύριος Ἰησοῦς
and every tongue should confess that Lord Jesus
5547 1519 1391 2316 3962
Χριστός, εἰς δόξαν Θεοῦ πατρός.
Christ (is), to (the) glory of God (the) Father.
5620 27 3450 2531/3842 5219 3361/5613
12 Ὥστε, ἀγαπητοί μου, καθὼς πάντοτε ὑπηκούσατε, μὴ ὡς
So as, beloved of me, as always you obeyed, not as
1722 3952 3450 3440 235 3568 4183 3123 1722
ἐν τῇ παρουσίᾳ μου μόνον, ἀλλὰ νῦν πολλῷ μᾶλλον ἐν τῇ
in the presence of me only, but now by more rather in the
666 3450 3326 5401 5156 1438 4991
ἀπουσίᾳ μου, μετὰ φόβου καὶ τρόμου τὴν ἑαυτῶν σωτηρίαν
absence of me, with fear and trembling the of yourselves salvation
2716 2316 1063 2076 1754 1722/5213
13 κατεργάζεσθε· ὁ Θεὸς γάρ ἐστιν ὁ ἐνεργῶν ἐν ὑμῖν καὶ τὸ
work out; God for is the (One) working in you both
2309 1754 5228 2107 3956 4160
14 θέλειν καὶ τὸ ἐνεργεῖν ὑπὲρ τῆς εὐδοκίας. πάντα ποιεῖτε
to will and to work on behalf of (His) good pleasure. All things do
5565 1112 1261 2443 1096 273
15 χωρὶς γογγυσμῶν καὶ διαλογισμῶν, ἵνα γένησθε ἄμεμπτοι
without murmurings and disputings, that you may be blameless
185 5043 2316 298 1722/3319 1074 4646
καὶ ἀκέραιοι, τέκνα Θεοῦ ἀμώμητα ἐν μέσῳ γενεᾶς σκολιᾶς
and harmless, children of God faultless amidst a generation crooked
1294 1722/3739 5316 5613 5458 1722 2889
καὶ διεστραμμένης, ἐν οἷς φαίνεσθε ὡς φωστῆρες ἐν κόσμῳ,
and having been perverted, among whom you shine as luminaries in (the) world
3056 2222 1907 1519 2745 1698/1513/2250 5547
16 λόγον ζωῆς ἐπέχοντες, εἰς καύχημα ἐμοὶ εἰς ἡμέραν Χριστοῦ,
a word of life holding up, for a boast to me in (the) day of Christ,
3754/3756/1513/2756 5143 3761/1519/2756/2872 235/1487
17 ὅτι οὐκ εἰς κενὸν ἔδραμον, οὐδὲ εἰς κενὸν ἐκοπίασα. ἀλλ' εἰ
that not in vain I ran, nor in vain labored. But if
4689 1909 2378 3009 4102
καὶ σπένδομαι ἐπὶ τῇ θυσίᾳ καὶ λειτουργίᾳ τῆς πίστεως
indeed I am poured out on the sacrifice and service of the faith
5216 5453 4796 3956/5213 1223/846 5210
18 ὑμῶν, χαίρω καὶ συγχαίρω πᾶσιν ὑμῖν· τὸ δ' αὐτὸ καὶ ὑμεῖς
of you, I rejoice, and I rejoice with all you; the and same also you
5463 4796 3427
χαίρετε καὶ συγχαίρετέ μοι.
rejoice, and rejoice with me.
1679 1722 2962 2424 5095 5030 3992
19 Ἐλπίζω δὲ ἐν Κυρίῳ Ἰησοῦ, Τιμόθεον ταχέως πέμψαι
I hope But in (the) Lord Jesus Timothy shortly to send
5213/2443/2504 2174 1097 4012/5216 3762 1063/2192
20 ὑμῖν, ἵνα κἀγὼ εὐψυχῶ, γνοὺς τὰ περὶ ὑμῶν. οὐδένα γὰρ ἔχω
to you, that I also may be of good cheer knowing the things about you. no one For I have
2473 3748 1104 4012 5216 3309 3956
21 ἰσόψυχον, ὅστις γνησίως τὰ περὶ ὑμῶν μεριμνήσει. οἱ πάντες
likeminded, who genuinely the things about you will care for all
1063 1438 2212 3756 5547 2424
22 γὰρ τὰ ἑαυτῶν ζητοῦσιν, οὐ τὰ τοῦ Χριστοῦ Ἰησοῦ. τὴν δὲ
For the things of themselves seek, not the things of Christ Jesus. the But

proof of him, that as a child to a father, he served with me for the gospel. [23]Therefore, I hope to send this one at once, whenever I shall see the things about me. [24]But I trust in *the* Lord that I myself also will come soon. [25]But I thought it needful to send to you Epaphroditus, my brother and fellow-worker, and my fellow-soldier, and your messenger and minister of my need; [26]since he was longing for you all, and has been troubled because you heard that he was sick. [27]For indeed he was sick, coming near to death; but God had mercy on him, and not only on him, but also me, lest I should have grief on grief. [28]Therefore, I sent him more eagerly, that seeing him again you may rejoice, and I may be less grieved. [29]Then receive him in *the* Lord with all joy, and hold such in honor; [30]that through the work of Christ he drew near to death, exposing *his* soul, that he may fill up your lack of service toward me.

that he may fill up your lack of service toward me.

1382 846 1097 3754/5613 3962 5043 4862/1698
δοκιμὴν αὐτοῦ γινώσκετε, ὅτι ὡς πατρὶ τέκνον, σὺν ἐμοὶ
proof of him you know, that as to a father a child, with me
1398 1519 2098 5126 3303/3767/ 1679 3992
23 ἐδούλευσεν εἰς τὸ εὐαγγέλιον. τοῦτον μὲν οὖν ἐλπίζω πέμψαι,
he served for the gospel. This one, therefore, I hope to send,
5613/302/872 4012/1691 1824 3982 1722/2962 3754
24 ὡς ἂν ἀπίδω τὰ περὶ ἐμέ, ἐξαυτῆς· πέποιθα δὲ ἐν Κυρίῳ, ὅτι
whenever I shall see the things about me at once; I trust but in (the) Lord that
848 5030/ 2064 316 2233
25 καὶ αὐτὸς ταχέως ἐλεύσομαι. ἀναγκαῖον δὲ ἡγησάμην
also myself shortly I will come. necessary But I thought (it)
1891 80 4904 4961
Ἐπαφρόδιτον τὸν ἀδελφὸν καὶ συνεργὸν καὶ συστρατιώτην
Epaphroditus the brother and fellow-worker and fellow-soldier
3450 5216 652 3011 5532 3450
μου, ὑμῶν δὲ ἀπόστολον, καὶ λειτουργὸν τῆς χρείας μου,
of me, of you and, apostle and minister of the need of me,
3992 4314 5209 1894 1971 2258 3956 5209
26 πέμψαι πρὸς ὑμᾶς· ἐπειδὴ ἐπιποθῶν ἦν πάντας ὑμᾶς, καὶ
to send to you since longing after he was all you, and
85 1360 191 3754 770 1063 770
27 ἀδημονῶν, διότι ἠκούσατε ὅτι ἠσθένησε· καὶ γὰρ ἠσθένησε
being troubled, because you heard that he was sick, indeed For he was sick,
3997 2288 235 2316 846 1653 3756 846
παραπλήσιον θανάτῳ· ἀλλ' ὁ Θεὸς αὐτὸν ἠλέησεν, οὐκ αὐτὸν
coming near to death, but God him had mercy on, not on him
3440 235 1691/2443/3361/3077/1909/3077/2192 4708
28 δὲ μόνον, ἀλλὰ καὶ ἐμέ, ἵνα μὴ λύπην ἐπὶ λύπῃ σχῶ. σπου-
and only, but also me, lest grief on grief I should have. More
3767 3992 846 2443 1492 846 3825
δαιοτέρως οὖν ἔπεμψα αὐτόν, ἵνα, ἰδόντες αὐτὸν πάλιν,
eagerly, therefore, I sent him, that seeing him again
5463 2504 253 5600 4327 3767 846 1722
29 χαρῆτε, κἀγὼ ἀλυπότερος ὦ. προσδέχεσθε οὖν αὐτὸν ἐν
you may rejoice, and I less grieved may be. receive Therefore him in
2962 3326 3956 5479 5108 1784 2192
Κυρίῳ μετὰ πάσης χαρᾶς, καὶ τοὺς τοιούτους ἐντίμους ἔχετε·
(the) Lord with all joy, and such ones honored hold,
3754/1223 2041 5547 3360 2288 1448
30 ὅτι διὰ τὸ ἔργον τοῦ Χριστοῦ μέχρι θανάτου ἤγγισε,
that through the work of Christ as far as death he drew near,
3851 5590 2443 378 5216
παραβουλευσάμενος τῇ ψυχῇ, ἵνα ἀναπληρώσῃ τὸ ὑμῶν
exposing the soul, that he might fill up the of you
5303 4314/3165/ 3009
ὑστέρημα τῆς πρός με λειτουργίας.
lack toward me of service.

CHAPTER 3

[1]For the rest, my brothers, rejoice in *the* Lord. To write the same things to you truly *is* not tiresome to me, but safe for you. [2]Look out *for* the dogs; look out *for* the evil workers; look out *for* the concision *party*. [3]For we are the circumcision, the ones who worship by the Spirit of God, and who glory in Christ Jesus, and who do not trust in flesh. [4]Though I also might have trust in flesh—if any other thinks to trust in flesh, I more—[5]in circumcision, *the* eighth

CHAPTER 3

3063 80 3450 5463 1722 2962 846
1 Τὸ λοιπόν, ἀδελφοί μου, χαίρετε ἐν Κυρίῳ. τὰ αὐτὰ
For the rest, brothers of me, rejoice in (the) Lord. The same things
1125 5213/1698/3303/3756/ 3636 5213 804 991
2 γράφειν ὑμῖν, ἐμοὶ μὲν οὐκ ὀκνηρόν, ὑμῖν δὲ ἀσφαλές. βλέπετε
to write to you for me indeed not is tiresome, for you but safe. Look (to)
2965 991 2556 2040 991
τοὺς κύνας, βλέπετε τοὺς κακοὺς ἐργάτας, βλέπετε τὴν
the dogs, Look (to) the evil workers, look (to) the
2699 2249/1063/2070 4061 4151 2316
3 κατατομήν· ἡμεῖς γάρ ἐσμεν ἡ περιτομή, οἱ πνεύματι Θεῷ
concision. we For are the circumcision, those by Spirit of God
3000 2744 1722 5547 2424 3756/1722
λατρεύοντες, καὶ καυχώμενοι ἐν Χριστῷ Ἰησοῦ, καὶ οὐκ ἐν
worshiping, and boasting in Christ Jesus, and not in
4561 3982 2539 1473 2192 4006 1722 4561
4 σαρκὶ πεποιθότες· καίπερ ἐγὼ ἔχων πεποίθησιν καὶ ἐν σαρκί·
(the) flesh trusting; even though I having trust also in (the) flesh
=1536= 1380 243 3982 1722 4561 1473 3123 4061
5 εἴ τις δοκεῖ ἄλλος πεποιθέναι ἐν σαρκί, ἐγὼ μᾶλλον· περιτομῇ
—if any thinks other to trust in (the) flesh, I more: in circumcision

day; of *the* race of Israel, *the* tribe of Benjamin; a Hebrew of the Hebrews, according to Law, a Pharisee; [6]according to zeal, persecuting the church; according to righteousness in Law, being blameless. [7]But what things were gain to me, these I have counted loss because of Christ. [8]But, nay, rather I also count all things to be loss because of the excellency of the knowledge of Christ Jesus, my Lord, for whose sake I have suffered the loss of all things, and count *them* to be trash, that I might gain Christ, [9]and be found in Him; not having my own righteousness of Law, but through *the* faith of Christ *having* the righteousness of God *based* on faith, [10]to know Him and the power of His resurrection, and the fellowship of His sufferings, having been conformed to His death; [11]if somehow I may attain to the resurrection from the dead. [12]Not that I already received, or already have been perfected, but I press on, if I also may lay hold, inasmuch as I also was laid hold of by Christ Jesus. [13]Brothers, I do not count myself to have laid hold, but one *thing I do*, forgetting the things behind, and

stretching forward to those things before, [14]I press on after the mark, for the prize of the high calling of God in Christ Jesus. [15]Then as many as *are* perfect, let us be of this mind; and if you think anything differently, God will also reveal this to you.

[16]Yet *as* to where we have reached, *let us* walk by the same rule, *being* of the same mind. [17]Be fellow-imitators of me, brothers, and consider those walking this way, even as you have us *for* a pattern. [18]For many walk *as* the enemies of the cross of Christ—of whom I

3637 1537 1085 2474 5443 958 1445 1537
ὀκταήμερος, ἐκ γένους Ἰσραήλ, φυλῆς Βενιαμίν, Ἑβραῖος ἐξ
(the) eighth day; of (the) race of Israel; (the) tribe of Benjamin; a Hebrew of
1445 2596 3551 5330 2596 2205 1377
6 Ἑβραίων, κατὰ νόμον Φαρισαῖος, κατα ζῆλον διώκων τὴν
Hebrews; according to law, a Pharisee; according to zeal, persecuting the
1577 2596 1343 1722 3551 1096 273
ἐκκλησίαν, κατὰ δικαιοσύνην τὴν ἐν νόμῳ γενόμενος ἄμεμ-
church; according to righteousness in (the) law, being blame-
235 3748/2258/3427/2771 5023 2233 1223 5547
7 πτος. ἀλλ' ἅτινα ἦν μοι κέρδη, ταῦτα ἥγημαι διὰ τὸν Χριστὸν
less. But what things were to me gain, these I have counted because of Christ
2209 235 3304 2233 3956 2209 1511 1223
8 ζημίαν. ἀλλὰ μενοῦνγε καὶ ἡγοῦμαι πάντα ζημίαν εἶναι διὰ
loss. But nay, rather also I count all things loss to be because of
5242 1108 5547 2424 2962 3450
τὸ ὑπερέχον τῆς γνώσεως Χριστοῦ Ἰησοῦ τοῦ Κυρίου μου·
the excellency of the knowledge of Christ Jesus the Lord of me,
1223/3739 3956 2210 2233 4657 1511 2443
δι' ὃν τὰ πάντα ἐζημιώθην, καὶ ἡγοῦμαι σκύβαλα εἶναι, ἵνα
for whose sake all things I suffered loss, and count refuse to be, that
5547 2770 2147/1722/846/3361/2192 1699 1343
9 Χριστὸν κερδήσω, καὶ εὑρεθῶ ἐν αὐτῷ, μὴ ἔχων ἐμὴν δικαιο-
Christ I might gain, and be found in Him, not having my right-
1537/3551 235 1223 4102 5547 1537
σύνην τὴν ἐκ νόμου, ἀλλὰ τὴν διὰ πίστεως Χριστοῦ, τὴν ἐκ
eousness of law, But the through faith of Christ, the of
2316 1343 1909 4102 1097 846
10 Θεοῦ δικαιοσύνην ἐπὶ τῇ πίστει· τοῦ γνῶναι αὐτόν, καὶ
God righteousness (based) on faith, to know Him and
1411 386 848 2842
τὴν δύναμιν τῆς ἀναστάσεως αὐτοῦ, καὶ τὴν κοινωνίαν τῶν
the power of the resurrection of Him, and the fellowship of the
3804 848 4833 2288 848 1487
11 παθημάτων αὐτοῦ, συμμορφούμενος τῷ θανάτῳ αὐτοῦ, εἴ
sufferings of Him, being conformed to the death of Him; if
4459 2658 1519 1815 3498 3756/3754
12 πως καταντήσω εἰς τὴν ἐξανάστασιν τῶν νεκρῶν. οὐχ ὅτι
somehow I may attain to the resurrection out of the dead. Not that
2235 2983 2228/2235 5048 1377 =1499= 2638
ἤδη ἔλαβον, ἢ ἤδη τετελείωμαι· διώκω δέ, εἰ καὶ καταλάβω
already I received, or already been perfected. I follow but, if also I may lay hold,
1909/3739 2638 5259 5547 2424 80
13 ἐφ' ᾧ καὶ κατελήφθην ὑπὸ τοῦ Χριστοῦ Ἰησοῦ. ἀδελφοί,
inasmuch as also I was laid hold of by Christ Jesus. Brothers,
1473 1683 3756 3049 2638 1520 3303 3694
ἐγὼ ἐμαυτὸν οὐ λογίζομαι κατειληφέναι· ἓν δέ, τὰ μὲν ὀπίσω
I myself not reckon to have laid hold, one but, the things behind
1950 1715 1901 2596
14 ἐπιλανθανόμενος, τοῖς δὲ ἔμπροσθεν ἐπεκτεινόμενος, κατὰ
forgetting the things and before stretching forward to, after
4649 1377 1909 1017 507 2821 2316
σκοπὸν διώκω ἐπὶ τὸ βραβεῖον τῆς ἄνω κλήσεως τοῦ Θεοῦ
a mark I pursue, for the prize of the high calling of God
1722 5547 2424 3745/3767/5046 5124 5426 =1536
15 ἐν Χριστῷ Ἰησοῦ. ὅσοι οὖν τέλειοι, τοῦτο φρονῶμεν· καὶ εἴ
in Christ Jesus. as many as Then (are) perfect, this let us think; and if
= 2088 5426 5124 2316 5213 601 4133
16 τι ἑτέρως φρονεῖτε, καὶ τοῦτο ὁ Θεὸς ὑμῖν ἀποκαλύψει· πλὴν
anything other you think, even this God to you will reveal. Yet
1519/3739/ 5348 846 4748 2583 846 5426
εἰς ὃ ἐφθάσαμεν, τῷ αὐτῷ στοιχεῖν κανόνι, τὸ αὐτὸ φρονεῖν.
to what we arrived, by the same to walk rule, of the same mind.
4831 3450 1096 80 4648 3779
17 Συμμιμηταί μου γίνεσθε, ἀδελφοί, καὶ σκοπεῖτε τοὺς οὕτω
fellow-imitators of me Be, brothers, and mark those thus
4043 2531 2192 5179 2248 4183 1063 4043
18 περιπατοῦντας, καθὼς ἔχετε τύπον ἡμᾶς. πολλοὶ γὰρ περι-
walking, as you have an example us. many For
3739 4183 3004 5213/3568 2799 3004
πατοῦσιν, οὓς πολλάκις ἔλεγον ὑμῖν, νῦν δὲ καὶ κλαίων λέγω,
walk —of whom often I told you, now and also weeping I say —

often told you, and now even weeping I say *it*— [19]whose end *is* destruction, whose god *is* the belly, and *who* glory in their shame, those who mind earthly things.

[20]For our citizenship is in Heaven, from where we also wait for a Savior, *the* Lord Jesus Christ, [21]who will transform our body of humiliation, for it to be conformed to His body of glory, according to the working of His power, even to put all things under Himself.

CHAPTER 4

[1]So that, my brothers, ones loved and longed for, my joy and crown, so stand firm in *the* Lord, beloved ones.

[2]I entreat Euodia, and I entreat Syntyche, to mind the same thing in *the* Lord. [3]And I also ask you, true yokefellow, help those who struggled along with me and with Clement, and the rest, fellow-workers with me, whose names *are* in *the* Scroll of Life.

[4]Rejoice in *the* Lord always. Again I say, Rejoice! [5]Let your reasonableness be known to all men. The Lord *is* near. [6]Do not be anxious about anything, but in everything by prayer and by petition, with thanksgivings, let your requests be made known to God; [7]and the peace of God which surpasses all understanding will keep your hearts and your minds in Christ Jesus. [8]For the rest, brothers, whatever is true, whatever honorable, whatever *is* right, whatever pure, whatever lovely, whatever of good report; if *of* any virtue, and if *of* any

2190 4716 5547 3739 5056 684
19 τοὺς ἐχθροὺς τοῦ σταυροῦ τοῦ Χριστοῦ· ὧν τὸ τέλος ἀπώ-
(as) the enemies of the cross of Christ, of whom the end (is) destruc-
3739 2316 2836 1391/1722 152 848
λεια, ὧν ὁ θεὸς ἡ κοιλία, καὶ ἡ δόξα ἐν τῇ αἰσχύνῃ αὐτῶν, οἱ
tion, of whom the god the belly (is) and the glory in the shame of them, those
1919 5426 2257/1063 4175 1722 3772
20 τὰ ἐπίγεια φρονοῦντες. ἡμῶν γὰρ τὸ πολίτευμα ἐν οὐρανοῖς
the earthly things thinking. of us For the citizenship in Heaven
5225 1537/3739 4990 553 2962 2424
ὑπάρχει, ἐξ οὗ καὶ Σωτῆρα ἀπεκδεχόμεθα, Κύριον Ἰησοῦν
is, from where also a Savior we wait for, (the) Lord Jesus
5547 3739 3345 4983 5014
21 Χριστόν· ὃς μετασχηματίσει τὸ σῶμα τῆς ταπεινώσεως
Christ, who will change the body of the humiliation
2257/1519 1096 846 4832 4983 1391
ἡμῶν, εἰς τὸ γενέσθαι αὐτὸ σύμμορφον τῷ σώματι τῆς δόξης
of us for to be it conformed to the body of the glory
848 2596 1753 1410 846 5293
αὐτοῦ, κατὰ τὴν ἐνέργειαν τοῦ δύνασθαι αὐτὸν καὶ ὑποτάξαι
of Him, according to the working of the ability (of) Him, even to subject
1438 3956
ἑαυτῷ τὰ πάντα.
to Himself all things.

CHAPTER 4

5620 80 3450 27 1973 5479
1 Ὥστε, ἀδελφοί μου ἀγαπητοὶ καὶ ἐπιπόθητοι, χαρὰ καὶ
So as, brothers of me, beloved and longed for, joy and
4735 3450 3779 4739 1722 2962 27
στέφανός μου, οὕτω στήκετε ἐν Κυρίῳ, ἀγαπητοί.
crown of me, so stand in (the) Lord, beloved.
2136 3870 4941 3870 846
2 Εὐοδίαν παρακαλῶ, καὶ Συντύχην παρακαλῶ, τὸ αὐτὸ
Euodia I beseech, and Syntyche I beseech, the same thing
5426 1722 2962 2065 4571 4805 1103 4815
3 φρονεῖν ἐν Κυρίῳ. καὶ ἐρωτῶ καί σε, σύζυγε γνήσιε, συλλαμ-
to think in (the) Lord. And I ask also you, yoke-fellow true, help
846 3748/1722 2098 4866 3427
βάνου αὐταῖς, αἵτινες ἐν τῷ εὐαγγελίῳ συνήθλησάν μοι,
them, who in the gospel struggled with me,
3326 2815 3062 4904 3450/3739
μετὰ καὶ Κλήμεντος, καὶ τῶν λοιπῶν συνεργῶν μου, ὧν τὰ
with and Clement, and the rest, fellow-workers with me of whom the
3686 1722 976 2222
ὀνόματα ἐν βίβλῳ ζωῆς.
names (are) in (the) Scroll of Life.
5463 1722 2962 3842 3825 2046 5463 1933
4 Χαίρετε ἐν Κυρίῳ πάντοτε· πάλιν ἐρῶ, χαίρετε. τὸ ἐπιεικὲς
5 Rejoice in (the) Lord always; again I will say, Rejoice. The mildness
5216 1097 3956 444 2962 1451 3367
6 ὑμῶν γνωσθήτω πᾶσιν ἀνθρώποις. ὁ Κύριος ἐγγύς. μηδὲν
of you let it be known to all men. The Lord (is) near. Nothing
3309 235 1722 3956 4335 1162 3326
μεριμνᾶτε, ἀλλ' ἐν παντὶ τῇ προσευχῇ καὶ τῇ δεήσει μετὰ
be anxious about, but in everything by prayer and by petition with
2169 155 5216 1107 4314 2316
εὐχαριστίας τὰ αἰτήματα ὑμῶν γνωριζέσθω πρὸς τὸν Θεόν.
thanksgivings, the requests of you let be made known to God.
1515 2316 5242 3956 3563 5432
7 καὶ ἡ εἰρήνη τοῦ Θεοῦ, ἡ ὑπερέχουσα πάντα νοῦν, φρουρήσει
And the peace of God which surpasses all understanding will keep
2588 5216 3540 5216/1722 5547 2424
τὰς καρδίας ὑμῶν καὶ τὰ νοήματα ὑμῶν ἐν Χριστῷ Ἰησοῦ.
the hearts of you and the minds of you in Christ Jesus.
3063 80 3745 2076 227 3745 4586 3745
8 Τὸ λοιπόν, ἀδελφοί, ὅσα ἐστὶν ἀληθῆ, ὅσα σεμνά, ὅσα
For the rest, brothers whatever is true, whatever honorable, whatever
1342 3745 53 3745 4375 3745 2163 =1536= 703
δίκαια, ὅσα ἁγνά, ὅσα προσφιλῆ, ὅσα εὔφημα, εἴ τις ἀρετὴ
just, whatever pure, whatever lovable, whatever of good report, if any virtue

praise, think on these things. [9]And what things you learned and received and heard and saw in me, practice these things; and the God of peace will be with you.

[10]But I rejoiced in *the* Lord greatly that now at last you revived *your* thinking of me—although you indeed did think, but lacked opportunity. [11]Not that I speak as to great need; for I have learned to be content in whatever state I am. [12]But I know to be humbled, and I know to abound; in everything, and in all things, I am taught both to be filled, and to hunger; both to abound, and to lack. [13]I can do all things through Christ, the *One* giving me power. [14]Yet you did well in sharing my troubles. [15]And you know, too, Philippians, that in *the* beginning of the gospel, when I went out from Macedonia, not one church shared with me in *the* matter of giving and receiving, except you only. [16]Because truly in Thessalonica you sent to my need, both once and twice. [17]Not that I seek a gift, but I seek the fruit multiplying to your account. [18]But I have all things, and more than enough; I have been filled, receiving from Epaphroditus the things from you, an odor of sweet smell, an acceptable sacrifice, well-pleasing to God.

[19]And my God will fill your every need according to His riches in glory, in Christ Jesus. [20]Now may glory be to our God and Father forever and ever. Amen.

[21]Greet every saint in Christ Jesus. The brothers with me greet you. [22]All the saints greet you, most

=1536= 1868 5023 3049 3739 3129 3880
9 καὶ εἴ τις ἔπαινος, ταῦτα λογίζεσθε. ἃ καὶ ἐμάθετε καὶ παρε-
and if any praise, these things consider. What things you learned and re-
191 1492/1722/1698 5023 4238
λάβετε καὶ ἠκούσατε καὶ εἴδετε ἐν ἐμοί, ταῦτα πράσσετε· καὶ
ceived, and heard and saw, in me, these things practice; and
2316 1515 2071 3326 5216
ὁ Θεὸς τῆς εἰρήνης ἔσται μεθ' ὑμῶν.
the God of peace will be with you.
5463 1722 2962 3171 3754/2235/4218 330
10 Ἐχάρην δὲ ἐν Κυρίῳ μεγάλως, ὅτι ἤδη ποτὲ ἀνεθάλετε τὸ
I rejoiced And in (the) Lord greatly, that now at last you revived
5228 1700 5426 1909/3739 5426 170 3756
11 ὑπὲρ ἐμοῦ φρονεῖν· ἐφ' ᾧ καὶ ἐφρονεῖτε, ἠκαιρεῖσθε δέ. οὐχ
of me thinking, as to which indeed you thought, lacked opportunity. but Not
•1722 3754/2596 5304 3004 1473 1063 3129 1510
ὅτι καθ' ὑστέρησιν λέγω· ἐγὼ γὰρ ἔμαθον, ἐν οἷς εἰμι
3739 that as to lack, say I for learned in what (state) I am
842 1511 1492 5013 1492 4052
12 αὐτάρκης εἶναι. οἶδα καὶ ταπεινοῦσθαι, οἶδα καὶ περισ-
self-sufficient to be. I know both to be humbled, I know and to
1722 3956 1722 3956 3453 5526
σεύειν· ἐν παντὶ καὶ ἐν πᾶσι μεμύημαι καὶ χορτάζεσθαι καὶ
abound; in everything and in all things I am taught both to be filled and
3983 4052 5302 3956 2480 1722
13 πεινᾶν, καὶ περισσεύειν καὶ ὑστερεῖσθαι. πάντα ἰσχύω ἐν
to hunger, both to abound and to lack. All things I can do in
1743 3165 5547 4133 2573 4160
14 τῷ ἐνδυναμοῦντί με Χριστῷ. πλὴν καλῶς ἐποιήσατε
the (One) empowering me, Christ. Yet well you did
4790 3450 2347 1492 5210
15 συγκοινωνήσαντές μου τῇ θλίψει. οἴδατε δὲ καὶ ὑμεῖς,
sharing in of me the troubles. know And also you,
5374 3754/1722/746 2098 3753 1831
Φιλιππήσιοι, ὅτι ἐν ἀρχῇ τοῦ εὐαγγελίου, ὅτε ἐξῆλθον
Philippians, that in (the) beginning of the gospel, when I went out
575 3109 3762 3427 1577 2841 1519
ἀπὸ Μακεδονίας, οὐδεμία μοι ἐκκλησία ἐκοινώνησεν εἰς
from Macedonia, not one me church shared with in
3056 1394 3028 =1508= 5210 3440 3754 1722
16 λόγον δόσεως καὶ λήψεως, εἰ μὴ ὑμεῖς μόνοι· ὅτι καὶ ἐν
(the) matter of giving and receiving, except you only, because even in
2332 530 1364/1519 5532 3427 3992
Θεσσαλονίκῃ καὶ ἅπαξ καὶ δὶς εἰς τὴν χρείαν μοι ἐπέμψατε.
Thessalonica both once and twice to the need of me you sent.
3756/3754 1934 1390 235 1934 2590
17 οὐχ ὅτι ἐπιζητῶ τὸ δόμα, ἀλλ' ἐπιζητῶ τὸν καρπὸν τὸν
Not that I seek the gift, but I seek the fruit
4121 1519 3056 5216 588 3956 4052
18 πλεονάζοντα εἰς λόγον ὑμῶν. ἀπέχω δὲ πάντα καὶ περισ-
multiplying to (the) account of you. I have But all things and abound;
4137 1209 3844 1891 3844
σεύω· πεπλήρωμαι, δεξάμενος παρὰ Ἐπαφροδίτου τὰ παρ'
I have been filled, receiving from Epaphroditus the things from
5216 3744 2175 2378 1184 2101 2316
ὑμῶν, ὀσμὴν εὐωδίας, θυσίαν δεκτήν, εὐάρεστον τῷ Θεῷ.
you, an odor of sweet smell, a sacrifice acceptable, well-pleasing to God.
2316 3450 4137 3956 5532 5216 2596
19 ὁ δὲ Θεός μου πληρώσει πᾶσαν χρείαν ὑμῶν κατὰ τὸν
the And God of me will fill every need of you according to the
4149 848 1722 1391/1722 5547 2424 2316
20 πλοῦτον αὐτοῦ ἐν δόξῃ, ἐν Χριστῷ Ἰησοῦ. τῷ δὲ Θεῷ καὶ
riches of Him in glory, in Christ Jesus. to the Now God and
3962 2257 1391/1519 165 165 281
πατρὶ ἡμῶν ἡ δόξα εἰς τοὺς αἰῶνας τῶν αἰώνων. ἀμήν.
Father of us (be) the glory to the ages of the ages. Amen.
782 3956 40 1722 5547 2424 782
21 Ἀσπάσασθε πάντα ἅγιον ἐν Χριστῷ Ἰησοῦ. ἀσπά-
Greet every saint in Christ Jesus. Greet
5209 4862 1698 80 782 5209 3956
22 ζονται ὑμᾶς οἱ σὺν ἐμοὶ ἀδελφοί. ἀσπάζονται ὑμᾶς πάντες
you the with me brothers. Greet you all

of all those of Caesar's
house.
23 The grace of our Lord
Jesus Christ be with all of
you. Amen.

40 3122 1537 2541 3614
οἱ ἅγιοι, μάλιστα δὲ οἱ ἐκ τῆς Καίσαρος οἰκίας.
the saints, most of all but those of the of Caesar house.
5485 2962 2257 2424 5547 3326 3956
23 Ἡ χάρις τοῦ Κυρίου ἡμῶν Ἰησοῦ Χριστοῦ μετὰ πάντων
The grace of the Lord of us, Jesus Christ (be) with all
5216 281
ὑμῶν. ἀμήν.
of you. Amen.

ΠΑΥΛΟΥ ΤΟΥ ΑΠΟΣΤΟΛΟΥ
PAUL THE APOSTLE

Η ΠΡΟΣ
THE TO

ΚΟΛΟΣΣΑΕΙΣ ΕΠΙΣΤΟΛΗ
(THE) COLOSSIANS EPISTLE

THE EPISTLE
TO THE
COLOSSIANS

A LITERAL TRANSLATION
OF THE BIBLE

CHAPTER 1

[1]Paul, *an* apostle of Jesus Christ through the will of God, and Timothy the brother, [2]to the saints and faithful brothers in Christ in Colosse: Grace and peace to you from God our Father and *the* Lord Jesus Christ.

[3]We give thanks to God and *the* Father of our Lord Jesus Christ, praying continually about you, [4]hearing of your faith in Christ Jesus, and the love which *you have* toward all the saints, [5]through the hope being laid up for you in Heaven; which you heard before in the word of the truth of the gospel, [6]coming to you, as also in all the world, and it is bearing fruit, even also among you, from the day in which you heard and knew the grace of God in truth; [7]even as you also learned from Epaphras our beloved fellow-slave, who is a faithful minister of Christ for you, [8]he also showing to us your love in *the* Spirit.

[9]For this cause also, from the day in which we heard, we do not cease praying for you and asking that you may be filled *with* the knowledge of His will in all wisdom and spiritual

CHAPTER 1

3972 652 2424 5547 1223 2307 2316
1 Παῦλος ἀπόστολος Ἰησοῦ Χριστοῦ διὰ θελήματος Θεοῦ,
Paul an apostle of Jesus Christ through (the) will of God,
5095 80 1722 2857 40 4103
2 καὶ Τιμόθεος ὁ ἀδελφός, τοῖς ἐν Κολοσσαῖς ἁγίοις καὶ πιστοῖς
and Timothy the brother, to the in Colosse saints and faithful
80 1722 5547 5485 5213 1515 575 2316 3962
ἀδελφοῖς ἐν Χριστῷ· χάρις ὑμῖν καὶ εἰρήνη ἀπὸ Θεοῦ πατρὸς
brothers in Christ: Grace to you and peace from God (the) Father
2257 2962 2424 5547
ἡμῶν καὶ Κυρίου Ἰησοῦ Χριστοῦ.
of us and (the) Lord Jesus Christ.
2168 2316 3962 2962 2257
3 Εὐχαριστοῦμεν τῷ Θεῷ καὶ πατρὶ τοῦ Κυρίου ἡμῶν
We give thanks to God and Father of the Lord of us,
2424 5547 3842 4012 5216 4336 191
4 Ἰησοῦ Χριστοῦ, πάντοτε περὶ ὑμῶν προσευχόμενοι, ἀκού-
Jesus Christ, always concerning you praying, having
4102 5216/1722/5547 2424 26
σαντες τὴν πίστιν ὑμῶν ἐν Χριστῷ Ἰησοῦ, καὶ τὴν ἀγάπην
heard the faith of you in Christ Jesus, and the love
1519 3956 40 1223 1680 606
5 τὴν εἰς πάντας τοὺς ἁγίους, διὰ τὴν ἐλπίδα τὴν ἀποκειμένην
of all the saints, through the hope being laid up
5213/1722 3772 3739 4257 1722 3056
ὑμῖν ἐν τοῖς οὐρανοῖς, ἣν προηκούσατε ἐν τῷ λόγῳ τῆς
for you in the heavens, which you heard before in the word of the
225 2098 3918 1519 5209 2531
6 ἀληθείας τοῦ εὐαγγελίου, τοῦ παρόντος εἰς ὑμᾶς, καθὼς καὶ
truth of the gospel, coming to you, as also
1722/3956 2889 2076 2592 2531
ἐν παντὶ τῷ κόσμῳ, καὶ ἔστι καρποφορούμενον, καθὼς καὶ
in all the world, and it is bearing fruit, even also
1722/5213/575/3739/2250 191 3129 5485
ἐν ὑμῖν, ἀφ' ἧς ἡμέρας ἠκούσατε καὶ ἐπέγνωτε τὴν χάριν τοῦ
among you, from which day you heard and fully knew the grace
2316/1722 225 2531 3129 575 1889
7 Θεοῦ ἐν ἀληθείᾳ· καθὼς καὶ ἐμάθετε ἀπὸ Ἐπαφρᾶ τοῦ
of God in truth, as also you learned from Epaphras the
27 4889 2257 3739/2076 4103 5228 5216
ἀγαπητοῦ συνδούλου ἡμῶν, ὅς ἐστι πιστὸς ὑπὲρ ὑμῶν
beloved fellow-slave of us, who is a faithful for you
1249 5547 1213 2254 5216 26
8 διάκονος τοῦ Χριστοῦ, ὁ καὶ δηλώσας ἡμῖν τὴν ὑμῶν ἀγάπην
minister of Christ, he also showing us the of you love
1722 4151
ἐν Πνεύματι.
in (the) Spirit.
1223 5124 5210 575/3739/2250 191 3756 3973
9 Διὰ τοῦτο καὶ ἡμεῖς, ἀφ' ἧς ἡμέρας ἠκούσαμεν, οὐ παυό-
Because of this also we, from which day we heard, do not cease
5228 5216 4336 154 2443 4137
μεθα ὑπὲρ ὑμῶν προσευχόμενοι, καὶ αἰτούμενοι ἵνα πλη-
on behalf of you praying and asking that you
1922 2307 848/1722/3956 4678
ρωθῆτε τὴν ἐπίγνωσιν τοῦ θελήματος αὐτοῦ ἐν πάσῃ σοφίᾳ
may be filled (with) the knowledge of the will of Him in all wisdom

understanding, 10*for* you to walk worthily of the Lord to all pleasing, bearing fruit in every good work, and growing into the full knowledge of God; 11being empowered with all power according to the might of His glory, to all patience and long-suffering with joy; 12giving thanks to the Father, who has made us fit for a share of the inheritance of the saints in light, 13who delivered us out of the power of darkness, and translated *us* into the kingdom of the Son of His love; 14in whom we have redemption through His blood, the forgiveness of sins; 15who is *the* image of the invisible God, *the* Firstborn of all creation—16for all things were created in Him, the things in the heavens, and the things on the earth; the visible and the invisible; whether thrones, or lordships, or rulers, or authorities, all things have been created through Him and for Him.

17And He is before all things, and all things consist in Him. 18And He is the Head of the body, the church; who is *the* Beginning, *the* Firstborn from *the* dead, that He be pre-eminent in all things; 19because all the fullness was pleased to dwell in Him, 20and through Him making peace by the blood of His cross, to reconcile all things to Himself through Him, whether the things on the earth, or the things in the heavens. 21And you then were once alienated and enemies in *your* mind by evil works. But now He reconciled 22in the body of His flesh, through death, to

4907 4152 4043 5209 516 2962
10 καὶ συνέσει πνευματικῇ, περιπατῆσαι ὑμᾶς ἀξίως τοῦ Κυρίου
and understanding spiritual, to walk you worthily of the Lord
1519/3956 699 1722/3956/2041 18 2592
εἰς πᾶσαν ἀρέσκειαν, ἐν παντὶ ἔργῳ ἀγαθῷ καρποφοροῦντες
to all pleasing, in every work good bearing fruit
837 1519 1922 2316/1722/3956/ 1411
11 καὶ αὐξανόμενοι εἰς τὴν ἐπίγνωσιν τοῦ Θεοῦ· ἐν πάσῃ δυνάμει
and growing into the full knowledge of God, with all power
1412 2596 2904 1391 848 1519 3956
δυναμούμενοι, κατὰ τὸ κράτος τῆς δόξης αὐτοῦ, εἰς πᾶσαν
being empowered, according to the might of the glory of Him, to all
5281 3115 3326 5479 2168
12 ὑπομονὴν καὶ μακροθυμίαν μετὰ χαρᾶς· εὐχαριστοῦντες τῷ
patience and long-suffering, with joy, giving thanks to the
3962 2427 2248/1519 3310 2819
πατρὶ τῷ ἱκανώσαντι ἡμᾶς εἰς τὴν μερίδα τοῦ κλήρου τῶν
Father having made fit us for the share of the lot of the
40 1722 5457/3739/ 4506 2248/1537 1849
13 ἁγίων ἐν τῷ φωτί, ὃς ἐρρύσατο ἡμᾶς ἐκ τῆς ἐξουσίας τοῦ
saints in light, who delivered us out of the authority
4655 3179 1519 932 5207
σκότους, καὶ μετέστησεν εἰς τὴν βασιλείαν τοῦ υἱοῦ τῆς
of darkness, and translated (us) into the kingdom of the Son of the
26 848 1722/3739/ 2192 629 1223
14 ἀγάπης αὐτοῦ, ἐν ᾧ ἔχομεν τὴν ἀπολύτρωσιν διὰ τοῦ
love of Him, in whom we have redemption through the
129 848 859 266 3739/2076 1504
15 αἵματος αὐτοῦ, τὴν ἄφεσιν τῶν ἁμαρτιῶν· ὅς ἐστιν εἰκὼν
blood of Him, the forgiveness of sins; who is (the) image
2316 517 4416 3956 2937 3754
16 τοῦ Θεοῦ τοῦ ἀοράτου, πρωτότοκος πάσης κτίσεως· ὅτι
of God the invisible, (the) firstborn of all creation, because
1722/846 2936 3956 1722 3772 1909
ἐν αὐτῷ ἐκτίσθη τὰ πάντα, τὰ ἐν τοῖς οὐρανοῖς καὶ τὰ ἐπὶ
in Him were created all things, the things in the heavens, and the things on
1093 3707 517 1535 2362 1535 2963
τῆς γῆς, τὰ ὁρατὰ καὶ τὰ ἀόρατα, εἴτε θρόνοι, εἴτε κυριό-
the earth, the visible and the invisible, whether thrones, or lordships
1535 746 1535 1849 3956 1223 846 1519
τητες, εἴτε ἀρχαί, εἴτε ἐξουσίαι· τὰ πάντα δι' αὐτοῦ καὶ εἰς
or rulers, or authorities; all things through Him and for
846 2936 846 2076/4253 3956 3956
17 αὐτὸν ἔκτισται· καὶ αὐτός ἐστι πρὸ πάντων, καὶ τὰ πάντα
Him have been created, and He is before all things, and all things
1722/846 4921 846 2076 2776 4983
18 ἐν αὐτῷ συνέστηκε. καὶ αὐτός ἐστιν ἡ κεφαλὴ τοῦ σώματος,
in Him consisted; and He is the Head of the body,
1577 3739/2076 746 4416 1537 3498
τῆς ἐκκλησίας· ὅς ἐστιν ἀρχή, πρωτότοκος ἐκ τῶν νεκρῶν,
the church, who is (the) beginning, firstborn from the dead,
2443 1096 1722 3956 846 4409 3754/1722/846 2106
19 ἵνα γένηται ἐν πᾶσιν αὐτὸς πρωτεύων· ὅτι ἐν αὐτῷ εὐδόκησε
that may be in all things He pre-eminent, because in Him was pleased
3956 4138 2730 1223 846 604
20 πᾶν τὸ πλήρωμα κατοικῆσαι, καὶ δι' αὐτοῦ ἀποκαταλλάξαι
all the fullness to dwell, and through Him to reconcile
3956 1519 848 1517 1223 129
τὰ πάντα εἰς αὐτόν, εἰρηνοποιήσας διὰ τοῦ αἵματος τοῦ
all things to Himself, making peace through the blood of the
4716 848 1223 848 1535 1909 1093 1535 1722
σταυροῦ αὐτοῦ, δι' αὐτοῦ, εἴτε τὰ ἐπὶ τῆς γῆς, εἴτε τὰ ἐν
cross of Him, through Him, whether the things on the earth, or the things
3772 5209 4218 5607 526
21 τοῖς οὐρανοῖς. Καὶ ὑμᾶς ποτὲ ὄντας ἀπηλλοτριωμένους καὶ
the heavens. And you, then being alienated and
2190 1271 1722 2041 4190 3570
ἐχθροὺς τῇ διανοίᾳ ἐν τοῖς ἔργοις τοῖς πονηροῖς, νυνὶ δὲ
enemies in the mind by (your) works evil. now But
604 1722 4983 4561 848 1223
22 ἀποκατήλλαξεν ἐν τῷ σώματι τῆς σαρκὸς αὐτοῦ διὰ τοῦ
He reconciled in the body of the flesh of Him through the

present you holy and without blame, and without charge before Him, [23]if you continue in the faith grounded and settled, and not being moved away from the hope of the gospel which you heard proclaimed in all the creation under Heaven, of which I, Paul, became a minister.

2288 3936 5209 40 299
θανάτου, παραστῆσαι ὑμᾶς ἁγίους καὶ ἀμώμους καὶ
death (of Him), to present you holy and blameless and
410 2714 846 1489 1961 4102
23 ἀνεγκλήτους κατενώπιον αὐτοῦ· εἴγε ἐπιμένετε τῇ πίστει
without charge before Him, if indeed you continue in the faith
2311 1476 3361 3334 575
τεθεμελιωμένοι καὶ ἑδραῖοι, καὶ μὴ μετακινούμενοι ἀπὸ τῆς
having been founded and steadfast, and not being moved away from the
1680 2098 3739 191 2784 1722
ἐλπίδος τοῦ εὐαγγελίου οὗ ἠκούσατε, τοῦ κηρυχθέντος ἐν
hope of the gospel which you heard proclaimed in
3956 2937 5259 3772 3739 1096 1473
πάσῃ τῇ κτίσει τῇ ὑπὸ τὸν οὐρανόν, οὗ ἐγενόμην ἐγὼ
all the creation under Heaven, of which became I,
3972 1249
Παῦλος διάκονος.
Paul, a minister.

[24]Now *I* rejoice in my sufferings on your behalf, and I fill up in my flesh the things lacking of the afflictions of Christ, on behalf of His body, which is the church; [25]of which I became a minister, according to the administration of God given to me for you to fulfill the word of God, [26]the mystery having been hidden from the ages, and from the generations, but now was revealed to His saints; [27]to whom God desired to make known what *are* the riches of the glory of this mystery among the nations, which is Christ in you, the hope of glory; [28]whom we announce, warning every man and teaching every man in all wisdom, that we may present every man full-grown in Christ Jesus. [29]For which also I labor, working according to the working of Him who works in me in power.

3739 3568 5463/1722 3804 3450 5228 5216
24 Ὃς νῦν χαίρω ἐν τοῖς παθήμασί μου ὑπὲρ ὑμῶν, καὶ
Who now rejoice in the sufferings of me on behalf of you, and
466 5303 2347 5547
ἀνταναπληρῶ τὰ ὑστερήματα τῶν θλίψεων τοῦ Χριστοῦ
fill up the things lacking of the afflictions of Christ
1722 4561 3450 5228 4983 848 3603/2076
ἐν τῇ σαρκί μου ὑπὲρ τοῦ σώματος αὐτοῦ, ὅ ἐστιν ἡ
in the flesh of me on behalf of the body of Him, which is the
1577 3739 1096 1473 1249 2596 3622
25 ἐκκλησία· ἧς ἐγενόμην ἐγὼ διάκονος, κατὰ τὴν οἰκονομίαν
church, of which became I a minister as regards the stewardship
2316 1325 3427/1519/5209 4137 3056
τοῦ Θεοῦ τὴν δοθεῖσάν μοι εἰς ὑμᾶς, πληρῶσαι τὸν λόγον
of God given to me for you, to fulfill the word
2316 3466 613 575
26 τοῦ Θεοῦ, τὸ μυστήριον τὸ ἀποκεκρυμμένον ἀπὸ τῶν
of God, the mystery having been hidden from the
165 575 1074 3570 5319 40
αἰώνων καὶ ἀπὸ τῶν γενεῶν· νυνὶ δὲ ἐφανερώθη τοῖς ἁγίοις
ages and from the generations, now but was revealed to the saints
848 3739 2309 2316 1107 5101 4149
27 αὐτοῦ, οἷς ἠθέλησεν ὁ Θεὸς γνωρίσαι τίς ὁ πλοῦτος τῆς
of Him, to whom desired God to make known what (are) the riches of the
1391 3466 5127 1722 1484/3739/2076 5547
δόξης τοῦ μυστηρίου τούτου ἐν τοῖς ἔθνεσιν, ὅς ἐστι Χριστὸς
glory mystery of this among the nations, who is Christ
1722/5213 1680 1391 3739/2249 2605 3560
28 ἐν ὑμῖν, ἡ ἐλπὶς τῆς δόξης· ὃν ἡμεῖς καταγγέλλομεν, νου-
in you, the hope of the glory, whom we announce,
3956 444 1321 3956 444
θετοῦντες πάντα ἄνθρωπον, καὶ διδάσκοντες πάντα ἄνθρω-
warning every man, and teaching every man
1722/3956 4678 2443 3936 3956 444
πον ἐν πάσῃ σοφίᾳ, ἵνα παραστήσωμεν πάντα ἄνθρωπον
in all wisdom that we may present every man
5046 1722 5547 2424 1519/3739 2872 75
29 τέλειον ἐν Χριστῷ Ἰησοῦ· εἰς ὃ καὶ κοπιῶ, ἀγωνιζόμενος
full-grown in Christ Jesus, for which also I labor, struggling
2596 1753 848 1754 1722/1698/1722
κατὰ τὴν ἐνέργειαν αὐτοῦ, τὴν ἐνεργουμένην ἐν ἐμοὶ ἐν
according to the working of Him, the (One) working in me in
1411
δυνάμει.
power.

CHAPTER 2

[1]For I want you to know how great a struggle I have concerning you, and those in Laodicea, and as many as have not seen my face in

2309/1063/5209 1492 2245 73 2192/4012/5216
1 Θέλω γὰρ ὑμᾶς εἰδέναι ἡλίκον ἀγῶνα ἔχω περὶ ὑμῶν καὶ
I want For you to know how great a struggle I have as to , you and
1722 2993 3745 3756 3708 4383 3450
τῶν ἐν Λαοδικείᾳ, καὶ ὅσοι οὐχ ἑωράκασι τὸ πρόσωπόν μου
those in Laodicea, and as many as not have seen the face of me

the flesh; [2]that their hearts may be comforted, being joined together in love, and to all riches of the full assurance of the understanding, to *the* full knowledge of the mystery of God, even of *the* Father and of Christ, [3]in whom are hidden all the treasures of wisdom and of knowledge. [4]And I say this, that no one may beguile you with persuasive words. [5]For though I am indeed absent in the flesh, yet I am with you in spirit, rejoicing and seeing your order, and the firmness of your faith in Christ. [6]Therefore, as you received Christ Jesus the Lord, walk in Him, [7]having been rooted and built up in Him, and having been confirmed in the faith, even as you were taught, abounding in it with thanksgiving.

[8]Watch, that there not be one robbing you through philosophy and empty deceit, according to the tradition of men, according to the elements of the world, and not according to Christ. [9]For in Him dwells all the fullness of the Godhead bodily; [10]and having been filled, you are in Him, who is the Head of all rule and authority, [11]in whom also you were circumcised with a circumcision not made by hand, in the putting off of the body of the sins of the flesh, by the circumcision of Christ; [12]being buried with Him in baptism, in whom also you were raised through the faith of the working of God, raising Him from the dead. [13]And you, being dead in the offenses and the uncircumcision of your flesh, He made alive together with Him, having forgiven you all the offenses; [14]blotting

1722/4561/2443/ 3870 2588 848 4822
2 ἐν σαρκί, ἵνα παρακληθῶσιν αἱ καρδίαι αὐτῶν, συμβιβασθέν-
in (the) flesh, that may be comforted the hearts of them, being joined to-
1722 26 1519 3956 4149 4136
των ἐν ἀγάπῃ, καὶ εἰς πάντα πλοῦτον τῆς πληροφορίας τῆς
gether in love, and for all riches of the full assurance of the
4907 1519 1922 3466 2316 3962
συνέσεως, εἰς ἐπίγνωσιν τοῦ μυστηρίου τοῦ Θεοῦ καὶ πατρὸς
understanding, for full knowledge of the mystery of God, and of Father,
5547 1722/3739/1526/3956 2344 4678
3 καὶ τοῦ Χριστοῦ, ἐν ᾧ εἰσὶ πάντες οἱ θησαυροὶ τῆς σοφίας
and of Christ, in whom are all the treasures of wisdom
5100 1108 614 5124 3004/2443/3361/*/5209
4 καὶ τῆς γνώσεως ἀπόκρυφοι. τοῦτο δὲ λέγω, ἵνα μή τις ὑμᾶς
and knowledge hidden. this And I say, that not anyone you
3884 1722 4086 1487/1063 4561 548
5 παραλογίζηται ἐν πιθανολογίᾳ. εἰ γὰρ καὶ τῇ σαρκὶ ἄπειμι,
beguile by persuasive words. if For indeed in the flesh I am
235 4151 4862 5213/1510 5463 991 absent
ἀλλὰ τῷ πνεύματι σὺν ὑμῖν εἰμί, χαίρων καὶ βλέπων ὑμων
yet in the spirit with you I am, rejoicing and seeing of you.
5010 4733 1519 5547 4102 5216
τὴν τάξιν, καὶ τὸ στερέωμα τῆς εἰς Χριστὸν πίστεως ὑμῶν.
the order, and the firmness of the in Christ faith of you.
3739/3767 3880 5547 2424 2962 1722
6 Ὡς οὖν παρελάβετε τὸν Χριστὸν Ἰησοῦν τὸν Κύριον, ἐν
As, therefore, you received Christ Jesus the Lord, in
846 4043 4492 2026 1722
7 αὐτῷ περιπατεῖτε, ἐρριζωμένοι καὶ ἐποικοδομούμενοι ἐν
Him walk, having been rooted and having been built up in
846 950 1722 4102 2531 1321
αὐτῷ, καὶ βεβαιούμενοι ἐν τῇ πίστει, καθὼς ἐδιδάχθητε,
Him, and being confirmed in the faith, as you were taught,
4052 1722/846/1722/ 2169
περισσεύοντες ἐν αὐτῇ ἐν εὐχαριστίᾳ.
abounding in it in thanksgiving.
991 3361/5100/5209/2071 4812 1223 5385
8 Βλέπετε μή τις ὑμᾶς ἔσται ὁ συλαγωγῶν διὰ τῆς φιλοσο-
Watch, lest anyone you shall be robbing through philoso-
2756 539 2596 3862 444
φίας καὶ κενῆς ἀπάτης, κατὰ τὴν παράδοσιν τῶν ἀνθρώπων,
phy and vain deceit, according to the tradition of men,
2596 4747 2889 3756 2596 5547 3754/1722
9 κατὰ τὰ στοιχεῖα τοῦ κόσμου, καὶ οὐ κατὰ Χριστόν· ὅτι ἐν
according to the elements of the world, and not according to Christ; for in
846 2730 3956 4138 2320 4985
αὐτῷ κατοικεῖ πᾶν τὸ πλήρωμα τῆς θεότητος σωματικῶς,
Him dwells all the fullness of the Godhead bodily,
2075/1722/846 4137 3739/2076 2776 3956
10 καὶ ἐστε ἐν αὐτῷ πεπληρωμένοι, ὅς ἐστιν ἡ κεφαλὴ πασης
and you are in Him having been filled, who is the Head of all
746 1849 1722/3739 4059 4061 886
11 ἀρχῆς καὶ ἐξουσίας· ἐν ᾧ καὶ περιετμήθητε περιτομῇ ἀχει-
rule and authority, in whom also you were circumcised with a circumcision not
1722 555 4983 266
ροποιήτῳ, ἐν τῇ ἀπεκδύσει του σώματος τῶν αμαρτιῶν
made by hand, by the putting off of the body of the sins
4561 1722 4061 5547 4916 846
12 τῆς σαρκός, ἐν τῇ περιτομῇ τοῦ Χριστοῦ, συνταφέντες αὐτῷ
of the flesh, by the circumcision of Christ, co-buried with Him
1722 908 1722/3739 4891 1223 4102
ἐν τῷ βαπτίσματι, ἐν ᾧ καὶ συνηγέρθητε διὰ τῆς πίστεως τῆς
in the baptism, in whom also you were raised through the faith of the
1753 2316 1453 846 1537 3498
ἐνεργείας τοῦ Θεοῦ, τοῦ ἐγείραντος αὐτὸν ἐκ τῶν νεκρῶν.
working of God, raising Him from the dead;
5209 3498 5607/1722 3900 203
13 καὶ ὑμᾶς, νεκροὺς ὄντας εν τοῖς παραπτώμασι καὶ τῇ ἀκρο-
and you dead being in the offenses and the uncir-
4561 5216 4806 4862/846 5483
βυστίᾳ τῆς σαρκὸς ὑμῶν, συνεζωοποίησε σὺν αὐτῷ, χαρισά-
cumcision of the flesh of you, He made alive with Him, having for-

out the handwriting in the
ordinances against us,
which were contrary to us,
even *He* has taken it out of
the midst, nailing it to the
cross; 15 having stripped
the rulers and the authorities, He made a show of
them in public, triumphing
over them in it.

16 Then do not let anyone
judge you in eating or in
drinking, or in respect of a
feast, or the new moon, or
of sabbaths, 17 which are a
shadow of coming things;
but the body *is* of Christ.
18 Let no one judge you
unworthy, willing in
humility and worship of the
angels, pushing into things
which he has not seen,
being puffed up by the mind
of his flesh without a cause,
19 and not holding fast the
Head, from whom all the
body having been supplied
with the joints and bands,
and having been joined
together, will grow with
the growth *which comes*
from God.

20 If, then, you died with
Christ from the elements
of the world, why are you
under *its* decrees, as living
in *the* world? 21 Do not
handle; do not taste; do not
touch—22 which things are
all to rot away in the using,
according to the injunc-
tions and teachings of men.
23 Which things indeed have
a reputation of wisdom in
will-worship and humility,
and unsparing *abuse* of *the*
body, not in any honor for
satisfaction of the flesh.

5213 3956 3900 1813 2596 2257
14 μενος ὑμῖν πάντα τὰ παραπτώματα, ἐξαλείψας τὸ καθ' ἡμῶν
given you all the offenses; blotting out the against us
5498 1378 3739/2258/ 5227 2254 846
χειρόγραφον τοῖς δόγμασιν, ὃ ἦν ὑπεναντίον ἡμῖν· καὶ αὐτὸ
handwriting in ordinances which were contrary to us, and it
142/1537 3319 4338 846 4716 554
15 ἦρκεν ἐκ τοῦ μέσου, προσηλώσας αὐτὸ τῷ σταυρῷ· ἀπεκδυ-
has taken out of the midst, nailing it to the cross; having
746 1849 1165 1722 3954
σάμενος τὰς ἀρχὰς καὶ τὰς ἐξουσίας, ἐδειγμάτισεν ἐν παρ-
stripped the rulers and the authorities, He displayed (them) in
2358 846 1722 846
ρησίᾳ, θριαμβεύσας αὐτοὺς ἐν αὐτῷ.
public, triumphing (over) them in it.
•2228 3361/3767/5100/5209/ 2919/1722/1035/2228/1722/4213/•/1722/3313
16 Μὴ οὖν τις ὑμᾶς κρινέτω ἐν βρώσει ἢ ἐν πόσει, ἢ ἐν μέρει
Not, therefore, anyone you let judge in eating or in drinking, or in respect
1859 2228 3561 2228 4521 3739/2076/4639 3195
17 ἑορτῆς ἢ νουμηνίας ἢ σαββάτων· ἅ ἐστι σκιὰ τῶν μελλόν-
of a feast, or of a new moon, or of sabbaths, which is a shadow of things
4983 5547 3367 5209 2603
18 των, τὸ δὲ σῶμα τοῦ Χριστοῦ. μηδεὶς ὑμᾶς καταβραβευέτω
coming, the but body (is) of Christ. No one you let give judgment
2309 1722 5012 2356 32 3739
θέλων ἐν ταπεινοφροσύνῃ καὶ θρησκείᾳ τῶν ἀγγέλων, ἃ
wishing in humility and worship of the angels, things which
3361 3708 1687 1500 5448 5259 3563
μὴ ἑώρακεν ἐμβατεύων, εἰκῇ φυσιούμενος ὑπὸ τοῦ νοὸς
not he has seen pushing into, without a cause puffed up by the mind
4561 848 3756 2902 2776 1537/3739/3956
19 τῆς σαρκὸς αὐτοῦ, καὶ οὐ κρατῶν τὴν κεφαλήν, ἐξ οὗ πᾶν
of the flesh of him, and not holding the Head, from whom all
2983 1223 860 4886 2023
τὸ σῶμα, διὰ τῶν ἀφῶν καὶ συνδέσμων ἐπιχορηγούμενον
the body, through the joints and bands having been supplied
4822 837 838 2316
καὶ συμβιβαζόμενον, αὔξει τὴν αὔξησιν τοῦ Θεοῦ.
and having been joined together will grow with the growth of God.
1487 3767 599 4862 5547 575 4747
20 Εἰ οὖν ἀπεθάνετε σὺν τῷ Χριστῷ ἀπὸ τῶν στοιχείων
If, then, you died with Christ from the elements
2889 5101/5613 2198 1722 2889 1379 3361
21 τοῦ κόσμου, τί, ὡς ζῶντες ἐν κόσμῳ, δογματίζεσθε, Μὴ
of the world, why as living in (the) world, are you under decrees: Not
680 3366 1089 3366 2345 3739/2076 3956 1519 5356
22 ἅψῃ, μηδὲ γεύσῃ, μηδὲ θίγῃς (ἅ ἐστι πάντα εἰς φθορὰν τῇ
touch, nor taste, nor handle which things are all for corruption in the
671 2596 1778 1319
ἀποχρήσει), κατὰ τὰ ἐντάλματα καὶ διδασκαλίας τῶν
using — according to the injunctions and teachings
444 3748 2076 3056 3303/2192 4678 1722/1479
23 ἀνθρώπων; ἅτινά ἐστι λόγον μὲν ἔχοντα σοφίας ἐν ἐθε-
of men? Which things is a repute indeed having of wisdom in self-
5012 857 4483 3756
λοθρησκείᾳ καὶ ταπεινοφροσύνῃ καὶ ἀφειδίᾳ σώματος, οὐκ
imposed worship and humility and unsparing (abuse) of (the) body, not
1722/5092/5100/4314 4140 4561
ἐν τιμῇ τινὶ πρὸς πλησμονὴν τῆς σαρκός.
in honor any for satisfaction of the flesh.

CHAPTER 3

1 If, then, you were raised
with Christ, seek the things
above, where Christ is
sitting at *the* right of God;
2 mind the things above, not
the things on the earth,
3 for you died, and your life
has been hidden with

CHAPTER 3

1487/3767 4891 5547 507 2212 3757
1 Εἰ οὖν συνηγέρθητε τῷ Χριστῷ, τὰ ἄνω ζητεῖτε, οὗ ὁ
If, then, you were raised with Christ, the things above seek, where
5547 2076/1722/1188 2316 2521 507 5426
2 Χριστός ἐστιν ἐν δεξιᾷ τοῦ Θεοῦ καθήμενος. τὰ ἄνω φρονεῖτε,
Christ is at (the) right of God sitting; the things above mind,
3361 1909 1093 599 1063 2222 5216 2928
3 μὴ τὰ ἐπὶ τῆς γῆς. ἀπεθάνετε γάρ, καὶ ἡ ζωὴ ὑμῶν κέκρυ-
not the things on the earth, you died For, and the life of you has been

Christ in God. [4]Whenever Christ our life is revealed, then also you will be revealed in glory with Him.

[5]Then put to death your members which *are* on the earth: fornication, uncleanness, passion, evil lust, and covetousness, which is idolatry; [6]on account of which things the wrath of God is coming on the sons of disobedience; [7]among whom you also walked at one time, when you were living in these. [8]But now, you also put off all *these* things: wrath, anger, malice, evil speaking, shameful words out of your mouth.

[9]Do not lie to one another, having put off the old man with his practices. [10]And having put on the new, having been renewed in full knowledge according to *the* image of the *One* creating him; [11]where there is no Greek and Jew, circumcision and uncircumcision, foreigner, Scythian, slave *or* freeman — but Christ *is* is all things and in all.

[12]Then put on as the elect of God, holy and beloved, tender feelings of compassions, kindness, humility, meekness, long-suffering, [13]bearing with one another, and forgiving each other, if any has a complaint against anyone; even as Christ forgave you, so also *should* you. [14]And above all these, *add* love, which is *the* bond of perfectness. [15]And let the peace of God rule in your hearts, to which you also were called in one body, and be thankful.

[16]Let the word of Christ live in you richly, in all

4862 5547/1722 2316 3552 5547 5319
4 πται σὺν τῷ Χριστῷ ἐν τῷ Θεῷ. ὅταν ὁ Χριστὸς φανερωθῇ,
hidden with Christ in God. Whenever Christ is revealed,
2222 2257 5119 5210 4862 846 5319 1722
ἡ ζωὴ ἡμῶν, τότε καὶ ὑμεῖς σὺν αὐτῷ φανερωθήσεσθε ἐν
the life of us, then also you with Him will be revealed in
1391
δόξῃ.
glory.
3499 3767 3196 5216 1909 1093 4202
5 Νεκρώσατε οὖν τὰ μέλη ὑμῶν τὰ ἐπὶ τῆς γῆς, πορνείαν,
put to death Therefore the members of you on the earth, fornication,
167 3806 1939 2556 4124
ἀκαθαρσίαν, πάθος, ἐπιθυμίαν κακήν, καὶ τὴν πλεονεξίαν,
uncleanness, passion, lust, evil, and covetousness,
3748 2076 1495 1223/3739/ 2064 3709 2316
6 ἥτις ἐστὶν εἰδωλολατρεία, δι' ἃ ἔρχεται ἡ ὀργὴ τοῦ Θεοῦ
which is idolatry; for which things is coming the wrath of God
1909 5207 543 1722/3739 5210 4043
7 ἐπὶ τοὺς υἱοὺς τῆς ἀπειθείας· ἐν οἷς καὶ ὑμεῖς περιεπατήσατέ
on the sons of disobedience, among whom also you walked
4218 3753 2198 1722 846 3570 659 5210
8 ποτε, ὅτε ἐζῆτε ἐν αὐτοῖς. νυνὶ δὲ ἀπόθεσθε καὶ ὑμεῖς τὰ
then, when you were living in these. now But, put off also you
3956 3709 2372 2549 988 148
πάντα, ὀργήν, θυμόν, κακίαν, βλασφημίαν, αἰσχρολογίαν
all things: wrath, anger, malice, evil speaking, shameful words
1537 4750 5216/3361 5574 1519 240 554
ἐκ τοῦ στόματος ὑμῶν· μὴ ψεύδεσθε εἰς ἀλλήλους, ἀπεκδυσά-
out of the mouth of you. Do not lie to one another, having put
3820 444 4862 4234 848
9 μενοι τὸν παλαιὸν ἄνθρωπον σὺν ταῖς πράξεσιν αὐτοῦ,
off the old man with the practices of him,
1746 3501 341 1519 1922
10 καὶ ἐνδυσάμενοι τὸν νέον, τὸν ἀνακαινούμενον εἰς ἐπίγνωσιν
and having put on the new (man) being renewed in full knowledge
2596 1504 2936 848 3699/3756/1762/ 1672
11 κατ' εἰκόνα τοῦ κτίσαντος αὐτόν· ὅπου οὐκ ἔνι Ἕλλην καὶ
according to (the) image of Him creating him, where not there is Greek and
2453 4061 203 915 4658
Ἰουδαῖος, περιτομὴ καὶ ἀκροβυστία, βάρβαρος, Σκύθης,
Jew, circumcision and uncircumcision, foreigner, Scythian,
1401 1658 235 3956 1722 3956 5547
δοῦλος, ἐλεύθερος· ἀλλὰ τὰ πάντα καὶ ἐν πᾶσι Χριστός.
slave, freeman, but all things and in all Christ (is).
1746 3767 5613 1588 2316 40
12 Ἐνδύσασθε οὖν, ὡς ἐκλεκτοὶ τοῦ Θεοῦ, ἅγιοι καὶ
put on Therefore, as elect ones of God, holy and
25 4698 3628 5544 5012
ἠγαπημένοι, σπλάγχνα οἰκτιρμῶν, χρηστότητα, ταπεινο-
having been loved, bowels of compassions, kindness, humility,
4236 3115 430 240
13 φροσύνην, πρᾳότητα, μακροθυμίαν· ἀνεχόμενοι ἀλλήλων,
meekness, long-suffering, forbearing one another,
5483 1438 1437/5100/4314/5100/2192/ 3437 2531
καὶ χαριζόμενοι ἑαυτοῖς, ἐάν τις πρός τινα ἔχῃ μομφήν· καθὼς
and forgiving yourselves, if anyone against any has a complaint; as
5547 5483 5213 3779 5210 1909 3956
14 καὶ ὁ Χριστὸς ἐχαρίσατο ὑμῖν, οὕτω καὶ ὑμεῖς· ἐπὶ πᾶσι δὲ
indeed Christ forgave you, so also you; above all and
5125 26 3748 2076 4886 5047
τούτοις τὴν ἀγάπην, ἥτις ἐστὶ σύνδεσμος τῆς τελειότητος.
these things love, which is (the) bond of perfectness
1515 2316 1018 1722 2588 5216
15 καὶ ἡ εἰρήνη τοῦ Θεοῦ βραβευέτω ἐν ταῖς καρδίαις ὑμῶν,
And the peace of God let rule in the hearts of you,
1519/2258 2564 1722/1520/ 4983 2170 1096
16 εἰς ἣν καὶ ἐκλήθητε ἐν ἑνὶ σώματι· καὶ εὐχάριστοι γίνεσθε. ὁ
to which truly you were called in one body, and thankful be. The
3056 5547 1774 1722 5213 4146 1722 3956
λόγος τοῦ Χριστοῦ ἐνοικείτω ἐν ὑμῖν πλουσίως ἐν πάσῃ
word of Christ let dwell in you richly, in all

wisdom teaching and exhorting yourselves in psalms and hymns and spiritual songs, singing with grace in your hearts to the Lord. [17]And everything, whatever you do in word or in work, *do* all things in the name of *the* Lord Jesus, giving thanks to God and *the* Father through Him.

[18]Wives, be subject to *your* own husbands, as is becoming in *the* Lord. [19]Husbands, love the wives, and do not be bitter against them. [20]Children, obey the parents in all things; for this is well-pleasing to the Lord. [21]Fathers, do not provoke your children, that they may not be disheartened. [22]Slaves, obey the lords according to flesh in all respects, not with eye-service as men-pleasers, but in singleness of heart, fearing God. [23]And whatever you may do, work from the soul, as to the Lord, and not to men, [24]knowing that from *the* Lord you shall receive the reward of the inheritance. For you serve *the* Lord Christ. [25]But the *one* doing wrong will receive what he did wrong, and there is no respect of persons.

CHAPTER 4

[1]Lords, give that which *is* just and that which *is* equal to the slaves, knowing that you also have a Lord in Heaven.

[2]Steadfastly continue in prayer, watching in it with thanksgiving, [3]praying together about us also, that God may open to us a door of the word, to speak the mystery of Christ, on

4678 1321 3560 1438 5568
σοφίᾳ· διδάσκοντες καὶ νουθετοῦντες ἑαυτούς, ψαλμοῖς, καὶ
wisdom teaching and exhorting yourselves, in psalms and
5215 5603 4152 1722 5485 103 1722
17 ὕμνοις, καὶ ᾠδαῖς πνευματικαῖς, ἐν χάριτι ᾄδοντες ἐν τῇ
hymns and songs spiritual, with grace singing in the
2588 5216 2962 3956=3748=302/4160 1722 3056/2228
καρδίᾳ ὑμῶν τῷ Κυρίῳ. καὶ πᾶν ὅ τι ἂν ποιῆτε, ἐν λόγῳ ἢ
hearts of you to the Lord. And everything, what-ever you do in word or
1722/2041 3956 1722 3686 2962 2424 2168
ἐν ἔργῳ, πάντα ἐν ὀνόματι Κυρίου Ἰησοῦ, εὐχαριστοῦντες
in work, all things (do) in the name of (the) Lord Jesus, giving thanks
2316 3962/1223/846
τῷ Θεῷ καὶ πατρὶ δι' αὐτοῦ.
to God and (the) Father through Him.
1135 5293 2398 435 5613 433
18 Αἱ γυναῖκες, ὑποτάσσεσθε τοῖς ἰδίοις ἀνδράσιν, ὡς ἀνῆκεν
The wives: be subject to the own husbands, as is befitting
1722 2962 435 25 1135 3361 4087
19 ἐν Κυρίῳ. οἱ ἄνδρες, ἀγαπᾶτε τὰς γυναῖκας, καὶ μὴ πικραί-
in (the) Lord. The husbands: love the wives, and not be
4314 846 5043 5219 1118 2596
20 νεσθε πρὸς αὐτάς. τὰ τέκνα, ὑπακούετε τοῖς γονεῦσι κατὰ
bitter toward them. The children: obey the parents all in
3956 5124 1063 2076 2101 2962 3962
21 πάντα· τοῦτο γάρ ἐστιν εὐάρεστον τῷ Κυρίῳ. οἱ πατέρες,
all, this for is well-pleasing to the Lord. The fathers:
3361 2042 5043 5216 2443/3361 120 1401
22 μὴ ἐρεθίζετε τὰ τέκνα ὑμῶν, ἵνα μὴ ἀθυμῶσιν. οἱ δοῦλοι,
do not provoke the children of you, that not they be disheartened. The slaves:
5219 2596 3956 2596 4561 2962 3361/1722
ὑπακούετε κατὰ πάντα τοῖς κατὰ σάρκα κυρίοις, μὴ ἐν
obey all in all those according to flesh lords, not with
3787 5613 441 235 1722 572
ὀφθαλμοδουλείαις ὡς ἀνθρωπάρεσκοι, ἀλλ' ἐν ἁπλότητι
eye-services as men-pleasers, but in singleness
2588 5399 2316 3956/3748=1437 4160 1537
23 καρδίας, φοβούμενοι τὸν Θεόν· καὶ πᾶν ὅ τι ἐὰν ποιῆτε, ἐκ
of heart, fearing God. And everything whatever you do, from
5590 2036 5613 2962 3756 444 1492
24 ψυχῆς ἐργάζεσθε, ὡς τῷ Κυρίῳ καὶ οὐκ ἀνθρώποις· εἰδότες
the soul work as to the Lord and not to men, knowing
3754/575 2962 618 469 2817
ὅτι ἀπὸ Κυρίου ἀπολήψεσθε τὴν ἀνταπόδοσιν τῆς κληρονο-
that from (the) Lord you will receive the reward of the inheritance.
1063 2962 5547 1398 91
25 μίας· τῷ γὰρ Κυρίῳ Χριστῷ δουλεύετε. ὁ δὲ ἀδικῶν
the For Lord Christ you serve; the (one) and doing wrong
2865 3739 91 3756/2076 4382
κομιεῖται ὃ ἠδίκησε· καὶ οὐκ ἔστι προσωποληψία.
will receive what he did wrong, and not is (any) respect of persons.

CHAPTER 4

2962 1342
1 οἱ κύριοι, τὸ δίκαιον καὶ τὴν
The lords: the just thing and the
2471 1401 3930 1492 3754 5210 2192
ἰσότητα τοῖς δούλοις παρέχεσθε, εἰδότες ὅτι καὶ ὑμεῖς ἔχετε
equality to the slaves supply, knowing that also you have
2962/1722/ 3772
Κύριον ἐν οὐρανοῖς.
a Lord in Heaven.
4335 4342 1127 1722 846/1722
2 Τῇ προσευχῇ προσκαρτερεῖτε, γρηγοροῦντες ἐν αὐτῇ ἐν
In the prayer steadfastly continue, watching in it with
2169 4336 260 4012 2257/2443 2316
3 εὐχαριστίᾳ· προσευχόμενοι ἅμα καὶ περὶ ἡμῶν, ἵνα ὁ Θεὸς
thanksgiving, praying together also about us, that God
455 2254 2374 3056 2980 3466
ἀνοίξῃ ἡμῖν θύραν τοῦ λόγου, λαλῆσαι τὸ μυστήριον τοῦ
may open to us a door of the word, to speak the mystery

account of which I also have bound, [4]that I may make it clear, as I ought to speak. [5]Walk in wisdom toward the ones outside, redeeming the time. [6]Let your word be always with grace, being seasoned with salt, to know how you ought to answer each one.

[7]Tychicus the beloved brother and faithful minister, and fellow-slave in *the* Lord, will make known to you all the things about me, [8]whom I sent to you for this very thing, that he know the things about you, and that he might comfort your hearts; [9]with Onesimus the faithful and beloved brother, who is of you. They will make known to you all the things here.

[10]Aristarchus, my fellow-prisoner, greets you; also Mark the cousin of Barnabas, about whom you received orders —if he comes to you, receive him —[11]and Jesus, the *one* being called Justus, those being of the circumcision, these only fellow-workers for the kingdom of God, who became a comfort to me.

[12]Epaphras greets you, he of you, a slave of Christ, always striving for you in prayers, that you may stand full-grown and being complete in every will of God. [13]For I bear witness to him, that he has much zeal on your behalf, and those in Laodicea, and those in Hierapolis. [14]Luke the beloved physician greets you, also Demas. [15]Greet the brothers in Laodicea, and Nymphas, and the church in his house.

[16]And when this letter is read before you, cause that it be read also in the Laodicean church; and

5547 1223/3739 1210 2443 5319 846/5613/1163/3165
4 Χριστοῦ, δι' ὃ καὶ δέδεμαι ἵνα φανερώσω αὐτό, ὡς δεῖ με
•4043 of Christ, for which also I have been bound, that I may reveal it as ought me
2980 1722 4678 4314 1854 2540
5 λαλῆσαι. ἐν σοφίᾳ περιπατεῖτε πρὸς τοὺς ἔξω, τὸν καιρὸν
to speak; In wisdom walk toward those outside, the time
1805 3056 5216 3842 1722 5485 217
6 ἐξαγοραζόμενοι. ὁ λόγος ὑμῶν πάντοτε ἐν χάριτι, ἅλατι
redeeming. The speech of you (let be) always with grace, with salt
741 1492 4459/1163/5209/1520/ 1538 611
ἠρτυμένος, εἰδέναι πῶς δεῖ ὑμᾶς ἑνὶ ἑκάστῳ ἀποκρίνεσθαι.
being seasoned, to know how it behoves you one each to answer.
2596/1691/ 3956 1107 5213 5190 27
7 Τὰ κατ' ἐμὲ πάντα γνωρίσει ὑμῖν Τυχικός, ὁ ἀγαπητὸς
The things about me all will make known to you Tychicus the beloved
80 4103 1249 4889/1722 2962 3739
8 ἀδελφὸς καὶ πιστὸς διάκονος καὶ σύνδουλος ἐν Κυρίῳ, ὃν
brother and faithful minister, and fellow-slave in (the) Lord, whom
3992 4314/5209/1519/846 5124 2443/1097 4012 5216
ἔπεμψα πρὸς ὑμᾶς εἰς αὐτὸ τοῦτο, ἵνα γνῷ τὰ περὶ ὑμῶν καὶ
I sent to you for this same thing, that he know things the about you, and
3682 3870 2588 5216 4862 4103
9 παρακαλέσῃ τὰς καρδίας ὑμῶν· σὺν Ὀνησίμῳ τῷ πιστῷ
he might comfort the hearts of you, with Onesimus the faithful
27 80 3739 2076 1537 5216 3956 5213
καὶ ἀγαπητῷ ἀδελφῷ, ὅς ἐστιν ἐξ ὑμῶν. πάντα ὑμῖν
and beloved brother, who is of you; all to you
1107 5602
γνωριοῦσι τὰ ὧδε.
they will make known the things here.
782 5209 708 4869 3450
10 Ἀσπάζεται ὑμᾶς Ἀρίσταρχος ὁ συναιχμάλωτός μου,
Greets you Aristarchus the fellow-captive of me,
3138 431 921 4012/3739/ 2983 1785
καὶ Μάρκος ὁ ἀνεψιὸς Βαρνάβα (περὶ οὗ ἐλάβετε ἐντολάς·
and Mark the cousin of Barnabas about whom you received orders;
1437/2064 4315 5209 1209 846 2424 3004
11 ἐὰν ἔλθῃ πρὸς ὑμᾶς, δέξασθε αὐτόν), καὶ Ἰησοῦς ὁ λεγό-
if he comes to you, receive him — and Jesus, the (one)
2459 5607/1537/ 4061 3778 3441 4904
μενος Ἰοῦστος, οἱ ὄντες ἐκ περιτομῆς· οὗτοι μόνοι συνεργοὶ
named Justus, those being of the circumcision, these only fellow-workers
1519 932 2316 3748 1096 3427
εἰς τὴν βασιλείαν τοῦ Θεοῦ, οἵτινες ἐγενήθησάν μοι
for the kingdom of God. who became to me
3931 782 5209 1889 1537 5216 1401
12 παρηγορία. ἀσπάζεται ὑμᾶς Ἐπαφρᾶς ὁ ἐξ ὑμῶν, δοῦλος
a comfort. Greets you Epaphras the (one) of you, a slave
5547 3842 75 5228 5216/1722 4335
Χριστοῦ, πάντοτε ἀγωνιζόμενος ὑπὲρ ὑμῶν ἐν ταῖς προσ-
of Christ, always struggling on behalf of you in the
2443 2476 5046 4137 1722 3956
ευχαῖς, ἵνα στῆτε τέλειοι καὶ πεπληρωμένοι ἐν παντὶ
prayers, that you may stand full-grown and being complete in all
2307 2316/ 3140 1063 846 3754 2192 2205
13 θελήματι τοῦ Θεοῦ. μαρτυρῶ γὰρ αὐτῷ ὅτι ἔχει ζῆλον
(the) will of God. I bear witness For to him that he has zeal
4183 5228 5216 1722 2993 1722 2404
πολὺν ὑπὲρ ὑμῶν καὶ τῶν ἐν Λαοδικείᾳ καὶ τῶν ἐν Ἱεραπό-
much on behalf of you, and those in Laodicea, and those in Hierapolis.
782 5209 3065 2395 27
14 λει. ἀσπάζεται ὑμᾶς Λουκᾶς ὁ ἰατρὸς ὁ ἀγαπητός, καὶ
Greets you Luke the physician beloved, and
1214 782 1722 2993 80 3564
15 Δημᾶς. ἀσπάσασθε τοὺς ἐν Λαοδικείᾳ ἀδελφούς, καὶ Νυμφᾶν,
Demas. Greet the in Laodicea brothers, and Nymphas
2596 3624 848 1577 3752 314
16 καὶ τὴν κατ' οἶκον αὐτοῦ ἐκκλησίαν. καὶ ὅταν ἀναγνωσθῇ
and the at (the) house of him church. And whenever is read
3844 5213 1992 4160 2443 1722 2993
παρ' ὑμῖν ἡ ἐπιστολή, ποιήσατε ἵνα καὶ ἐν τῇ Λαοδικέων
before you the epistle, cause that also in the Laodicean

the *one* of Laodicea, that you also read. [17]And say to Archippus, Look to the ministry which you received in *the* Lord, that you may fulfill it.

[18]The greeting of Paul by my own hand. Remember my bonds. Grace *be* with you. Amen.

1577 314 1537 2993 2443 5210
ἐκκλησίᾳ ἀναγνωσθῇ, καὶ τὴν ἐκ Λαοδικείας ἵνα καὶ ὑμεῖς
church it is read, and the (one) of Laodicea, that also you
314 2036 751 991 1248 3739
17 ἀναγνῶτε. καὶ εἴπατε Ἀρχίππῳ, Βλέπε τὴν διακονίαν ἣν
read. And tell Archippus: Look (to) the ministry which
3880 1722 2962 2443 846 4137
παρέλαβες ἐν Κυρίῳ, ἵνα αὐτὴν πληροῖς.
you received in (the) Lord, that it you may fulfill.
783 1699 5495 3972 3421 3450
18 Ὁ ἀσπασμὸς τῇ ἐμῇ χειρὶ Παύλου. μνημονεύετέ μου τῶν
The greeting by my hand, of Paul. Remember of me the
1199 5485/3326 5216 281
δεσμῶν. ἡ χάρις μεθ' ὑμῶν. ἀμήν.
bonds. Grace (be) with you. Amen.

ΠΑΥΛΟΥ ΤΟΥ ΑΠΟΣΤΟΛΟΥ
PAUL THE APOSTLE
Η ΠΡΟΣ
TO THE
ΘΕΣΣΑΛΟΝΙΚΕΙΣ
THESSALONIANS
ΕΠΙΣΤΟΛΗ ΠΡΩΤΗ
EPISTLE FIRST

THE FIRST EPISTLE
TO THE
THESSALONIANS
A LITERAL TRANSLATION
OF THE BIBLE

CHAPTER 1

[1]Paul and Silvanus and Timothy to the church of Thessalonians in God *the* Father and *the* Lord Jesus Christ: Grace and peace to you from God our Father and *the* Lord Jesus Christ.

[2]We give thanks to God always concerning you all, making mention of you at our prayers, [3]remembering without ceasing your work of faith and labor of love, and the patience of hope of our Lord Jesus Christ, before our God and Father; [4]knowing, brothers, beloved by God, your election.

[5]For our gospel did not come to you in word only, but also in power, and in *the* Holy Spirit, and in much assurance, even as you know what we were among you for your sake. [6]And you became imitators of us and of the Lord, welcoming the word in much affliction with joy of *the* Holy Spirit, [7]so that you became examples to all those believing in Macedonia and Achaia. [8]For the word of the Lord sounded out from you, not only in Macedonia and

CHAPTER 1

3972 4610 5095 1577 2331
1 Παῦλος καὶ Σιλουανὸς καὶ Τιμόθεος, τῇ ἐκκλησίᾳ Θεσ-
Paul and Silvanus and Timothy to the church of
1722/2316/3962 2962 2424 5547 5485
σαλονικέων ἐν Θεῷ πατρί, καὶ Κυρίῳ Ἰησοῦ Χριστῷ· χάρις
Thessalonians in God (the) Father, and (the) Lord Jesus Christ: Grace
5213 1515 575 2316 3962 2257 2962 2424
ὑμῖν καὶ εἰρήνη ἀπὸ Θεοῦ πατρὸς ἡμῶν καὶ Κυρίου Ἰησοῦ
to you and peace from God (the) Father of us and (the) Lord Jesus
5547
Χριστοῦ.
Christ.
2168 2316 3842 4012 3956 5216
2 Εὐχαριστοῦμεν τῷ Θεῷ πάντοτε περὶ πάντων ὑμῶν,
We give thanks to God always concerning all you,
3417 5216 4160 1909 4335 2257 89
3 μνείαν ὑμῶν ποιούμενοι ἐπὶ τῶν προσευχῶν ἡμῶν, ἀδια-
mention of you making on the prayers of us, un-
3421 5216 2041 4102
λείπτως μνημονεύοντες ὑμῶν τοῦ ἔργου τῆς πίστεως, καὶ
ceasingly remembering of you the work of faith, and
2873 36 5281 1680
τοῦ κόπου τῆς ἀγάπης, καὶ τῆς ὑπομονῆς τῆς ἐλπίδος τοῦ
the labor of love, and the patience of hope of the
2962 2257 2424 5547 1715 2316
Κυρίου ἡμῶν Ἰησοῦ Χριστοῦ, ἔμπροσθεν τοῦ Θεοῦ καὶ
Lord of us, Jesus Christ, before the God and
3962 2257 1492 80 25 5259 2316
4 πατρὸς ἡμῶν· εἰδότες, ἀδελφοὶ ἠγαπημένοι, ὑπὸ Θεοῦ τὴν
Father of us, knowing, brothers, having been loved by God the
1589 5216 3754 2098 2257 3756 1096 1519/5209
5 ἐκλογὴν ὑμῶν· ὅτι τὸ εὐαγγέλιον ἡμῶν οὐκ ἐγενήθη εἰς ὑμᾶς
election of you; because the gospel of us not came to you
1722/3056 3440 235 1722 1411 1722 4151 40
ἐν λόγῳ μόνον, ἀλλὰ καὶ ἐν δυνάμει, καὶ ἐν Πνεύματι Ἁγίῳ,
in word only, but also in power, and in (the) Spirit Holy,
1722 4136 4183 2531 1492/3634 1096 1722
καὶ ἐν πληροφορίᾳ πολλῇ, καθὼς οἴδατε οἷοι ἐγενήθημεν ἐν
and in assurance much, as you know what sort we were among
5213/1223/5209 5210 3402 2257 1096
6 ὑμῖν δι' ὑμᾶς. καὶ ὑμεῖς μιμηταὶ ἡμῶν ἐγενήθητε καὶ τοῦ
you because of you. And you imitators of us became and of the
2962 1209 3056/1722 2347 4183 3326 5479
Κυρίου, δεξάμενοι τὸν λόγον ἐν θλίψει πολλῇ μετὰ χαρᾶς
Lord, welcoming the word in affliction much with joy
4151 40 5620 1096 5209 5179 3956
7 Πνεύματος Ἁγίου, ὥστε γενέσθαι ὑμᾶς τύπους πᾶσι τοῖς
of (the) Spirit Holy, so as to become you patterns to all those
4100 1722 3109 882 575, 5209 1063
8 πιστεύουσιν ἐν τῇ Μακεδονίᾳ καὶ τῇ Ἀχαΐᾳ. ἀφ' ὑμῶν γὰρ
believing in Macedonia and Achaia. from you For
1837 3056 2962 3756 3440 1722 3109
ἐξήχηται ὁ λόγος τοῦ Κυρίου οὐ μόνον ἐν τῇ Μακεδονίᾳ
sounded the word of the Lord not only in Macedonia

Achaia, but also in every place your faith toward God has gone out, so that there is no need for us to have to say anything. 9 For they themselves announce concerning us, what kind of entrance we have to you, and how you had turned to God from the idols, to serve *the* true and living God, 10 and eagerly to await His Son from Heaven, whom He raised from *the* dead, Jesus, the *One* delivering us from the wrath to come.

CHAPTER 2

1 For brothers, you yourselves know our entrance to you, that it has not been without fruit. 2 But also suffering before and being insulted in Philippi, as you know, we were bold in our God to speak the gospel of God to you in much agony. 3 For our exhortation *was* not of error, nor of uncleanness, nor in guile; 4 but even as we have been approved by God to be entrusted *with* the gospel, so we speak; not as pleasing men, but God, who tests our hearts. 5 For neither were we then *found* with words of flattery, even as you know, nor with pretense of covetousness—God is witness—6 nor seeking glory from men; neither from you, nor from others, having been able to be *so* with heaviness as apostles of Christ. 7 But we were gentle in your midst, even as a nurse should warmly cherish her children.

8 Longing over you in this way, we were pleased to impart to you not only the gospel of God, but also our own souls, because you

882 235 1722/3956 5117 4102 5216 4314
καὶ Ἀχαΐᾳ, ἀλλὰ καὶ ἐν παντὶ τόπῳ ἡ πίστις υμῶν ἡ πρὸς
and Achaia, but also in every place the faith of you toward
2316 1831 5620/3361 5532 2248 2192 2980/5100
τὸν Θεὸν ἐξελήλυθεν, ὥστε μὴ χρείαν ἡμᾶς ἔχειν λαλεῖν τι.
*2192 God has gone out, so as not need for us to have to speak anything;
846 1063 4012 2257 518 3697 1529
9 αὐτοὶ γὰρ περὶ ἡμῶν ἀπαγγέλλουσιν ὁποίαν εἴσοδον ἔσχο-
themselves for about us announce what kind of entrance we
4314 5209 4459 1994 4314 2316 575
μεν πρὸς ὑμᾶς, καὶ πῶς ἐπεστρέψατε πρὸς τὸν Θεὸν ἀπὸ τῶν
have to you, and how you had turned to God from the
1497 1398 2316 2198 228 362
10 εἰδώλων, δουλεύειν Θεῷ ζῶντι καὶ ἀληθινῷ καὶ ἀναμένειν
idols, to serve God living and true, and to await
5207 848 1537 3772 3739 1453 1537 3498
τὸν υἱὸν αὐτοῦ ἐκ τῶν οὐρανῶν, ὃν ἤγειρεν ἐκ νεκρῶν,
the Son of Him from the heavens, whom He raised from (the) dead,
2424 4506 2248 575 3709 2064
Ἰησοῦν, τὸν ῥυόμενον ἡμᾶς ἀπὸ τῆς ὀργῆς τῆς ἐρχομένης.
Jesus, He delivering us from the wrath coming.

CHAPTER 2

846 1063 1492 80 1529 2257 4314
1 Αὐτοὶ γὰρ οἴδατε, ἀδελφοί, τὴν εἴσοδον ἡμῶν τὴν πρὸς
yourselves For, you know, brothers the entrance of us to
5209 3754/3756/2756 1096 235 4310
2 ὑμᾶς, ὅτι οὐ κενὴ γέγονεν· ἀλλὰ καὶ προπαθόντες καὶ
you, that not in vain it has been, but also having suffered before and
5195 2531 1492 1722 5375 3955
ὑβρισθέντες, καθὼς οἴδατε, ἐν Φιλίπποις, ἐπαρρησιασάμεθα
having been insulted, as you know, in Philippi we were bold
1722 2316 5216 2980 4314 5209 2098
ἐν τῷ Θεῷ ἡμῶν λαλῆσαι πρὸς ὑμᾶς τὸ εὐαγγέλιον τοῦ
in the God of us to speak to you the gospel
2316/1722/4183 73 1063 3874 2257 3756/1537
3 Θεοῦ ἐν πολλῷ ἀγῶνι. ἡ γὰρ παράκλησις ἡμῶν οὐκ ἐκ
of God, in much struggle. the For exhortation of us not of
4106 3761/1537 167 3777/1722/ 1388 235 2531
πλάνης, οὐδὲ ἐξ ἀκαθαρσίας, οὔτε ἐν δόλῳ· ἀλλὰ καθὼς
error, nor of uncleanness, nor in guile, but as
1381 5259 2316 4100 2098
4 δεδοκιμάσμεθα ὑπὸ τοῦ Θεοῦ πιστευθῆναι τὸ εὐαγγέλιον,
we have been approved by God to be entrusted (with) the gospel,
3779 2980 3756/5613/ 444 700 235 2316
οὕτω λαλοῦμεν, οὐχ ὡς ἀνθρώποις ἀρέσκοντες, ἀλλὰ τῷ Θεῷ
so we speak, not as men pleasing, but God
1381 2588 2257 3777/1063/4218/1722/3056
5 τῷ δοκιμάζοντι τὰς καρδίας ἡμῶν. οὔτε γάρ ποτε ἐν λόγῳ
the (one) testing the hearts of us. neither For then in word
2850 1096 2531 1492 3777/1722/ 4392
κολακείας ἐγενήθημεν, καθὼς οἴδατε, οὔτε ἐν προφάσει
of flattery were we, as you know, not with pretext
4124 2316 3144 3777 2212 1537 444
6 πλεονεξίας· Θεὸς μάρτυς· οὔτε ζητοῦντες ἐξ ἀνθρώπων
of covetousness—God (is) witness— nor seeking from men
1391 3777 575 5216 3777 575 243 1410 1722 922
δόξαν, οὔτε ἀφ' ὑμῶν οὔτε ἀπ' ἄλλων, δυνάμενοι ἐν βάρει
glory, neither from you, nor from others, being able with heaviness
1511 5613 5547 652 235 1096 2261/1722
7 εἶναι, ὡς Χριστοῦ ἀπόστολοι, ἀλλ' ἐγενήθημεν ἤπιοι ἐν
to be, as of Christ apostles; but we were gentle in
3319 5216/5613/302/ 5162 2282 1438 5043 3779
8 μέσῳ ὑμῶν, ὡς ἂν τροφὸς θάλπῃ τὰ ἑαυτῆς τέκνα· οὕτως,
(the) midst of you, as if a nurse should cherish the of herself children, so
2442 5216 2206 3330 5213/3756/3440
ἱμειρόμενοι ὑμῶν, εὐδοκοῦμεν μεταδοῦναι ὑμῖν οὐ μόνον τὸ
longing for you, we were well-pleased to impart to you not only the
2098 2316 235 1438 5590 1360
εὐαγγέλιον τοῦ Θεοῦ, ἀλλὰ καὶ τὰς ἑαυτῶν ψυχάς, διότι
gospel of God, but also the of ourselves souls, because

have become beloved to us. 9For, brothers, you remember our labor and toil, night and day, working in order not to put a burden on any one of you, we proclaimed to you the gospel of God. 10You and God *are* witnesses how holily and righteously and blamelessly we were to you, those believing; 11even as you know how *I was to* each one of you, as a father *to* his children, exhorting and consoling you, 12testifying for you to walk worthily of God, He calling you to His kingdom and glory.

13And because of this we give thanks to God without ceasing, that having received *the* word of hearing from us, you welcomed *it as* of God, not *as* a word of men, but as it is, truly *the* word of God, which also works in you, the *ones* believing. 14For, brothers, you became imitators of the churches of God being in Judea in Christ Jesus, because you also suffered these things by *your* own fellow-countrymen, as they also by the Jews, 15who both killed the Lord Jesus and *their* own prophets, also driving us out, and not pleasing God, and *being* contrary to all men; 16hindering us from speaking to the nations in order that they be saved, to fill up their sins always. But the wrath has come on them to *the* uttermost.

17But, brothers, we being taken away from you for an hour's time, in presence, not in heart, we were much more eager with much desire to see your face.

27 2254 1096 3421 1063 80
9 ἀγαπητοὶ ἡμῖν γεγένησθε. μνημονεύετε γάρ, ἀδελφοί, τὸν
beloved to us you have become. you remember For, brothers, the
2873 2257 3449 3571 1063 2250 2036
κόπον ἡμῶν καὶ τὸν μόχθον· νυκτὸς γὰρ καὶ ἡμέρας ἐργαζό-
labor of us and the toil, night for and day working
4314 3361 1912 5100 5216 2784 1519
μενοι, πρὸς τὸ μὴ ἐπιβαρῆσαί τινα ὑμῶν, ἐκηρύξαμεν εἰς
in order to not put a burden on anyone of you, we proclaimed to
5209 2098 2316 5210 3144 2316
10 ὑμᾶς τὸ εὐαγγέλιον τοῦ Θεοῦ. ὑμεῖς μάρτυρες καὶ ὁ Θεός,
you the gospel of God. You (are) witnesses, and God,
5613/3743 1346 274 5213 4100
ὡς ὁσίως καὶ δικαίως καὶ ἀμέμπτως ὑμῖν τοῖς πιστεύουσιν
how holily and righteously and blamelessly to you, those believing,
1096 2509 1492/5613/1520/ 1538 5216/5613/ 3962
11 ἐγενήθημεν· καθάπερ οἴδατε ὡς ἕνα ἕκαστον ὑμῶν, ὡς πατὴρ
we were, even as you know how one each of you, as a father
5043 1438 3870 5209 3888
τέκνα ἑαυτοῦ, παρακαλοῦντες ὑμᾶς καὶ παραμυθούμενοι καὶ
children of himself, exhorting you and consoling, and
3140 1519 4043 5209 516 2316
12 μαρτυρούμενοι, εἰς τὸ περιπατῆσαι ὑμᾶς ἀξίως τοῦ Θεοῦ
testifying for to have walked you worthily of God,
2564 5209/1519 1438 932 1391
τοῦ καλοῦντος ὑμᾶς εἰς τὴν ἑαυτοῦ βασιλείαν καὶ δόξαν.
the (One) calling you to the of Himself kingdom and glory.
1223/5124 2249 2168 2316 89
13 Διὰ τοῦτο καὶ ἡμεῖς εὐχαριστοῦμεν τῷ Θεῷ ἀδιαλείπτως,
therefore And we give thanks to God without ceasing,
3754 3880 3056 189 3844 2257 2316
ὅτι παραλαβόντες λόγον ἀκοῆς παρ' ἡμῶν τοῦ Θεοῦ,
that having received (the) word of hearing from us, of God,
1209/3756/3056 444 235 2531 2076 230
ἐδέξασθε οὐ λόγον ἀνθρώπων, ἀλλὰ καθώς ἐστιν ἀληθῶς,
you welcomed, not (as) a word of men, but as it is truly,
3056 2316/3739 1754 1722 5213 4100
λόγον Θεοῦ, ὃς καὶ ἐνεργεῖται ἐν ὑμῖν τοῖς πιστεύουσιν.
a word of God, which also works in you, those believing.
5210 1063 3402 1096 80 1577
14 ὑμεῖς γὰρ μιμηταὶ ἐγενήθητε, ἀδελφοί, τῶν ἐκκλησιῶν τοῦ
you For imitators became, brothers, of the churches
2316 5607 1722 2449/1722 5547 2424 3754 5024
Θεοῦ τῶν οὐσῶν ἐν τῇ Ἰουδαίᾳ ἐν Χριστῷ Ἰησοῦ· ὅτι ταυτὰ
of God being in Judea in Christ Jesus, because these things
3958 5210/5209 2398 4853 2531
ἐπάθετε καὶ ὑμεῖς ὑπὸ τῶν ἰδίων συμφυλετῶν, καθὼς καὶ
suffered also you by the own fellow-countrymen, as also
846 5259 2453 2962 615
15 αὐτοὶ ὑπὸ τῶν Ἰουδαίων, τῶν καὶ τὸν Κύριον ἀποκτεινάν-
they by the Jews, those both the Lord killing,
2424 2398 4396 2248 1559
των Ἰησοῦν καὶ τοὺς ἰδίους προφήτας, καὶ ἡμᾶς ἐκδιωξ-
Jesus, and the own prophets, and us driving
2316/3361 700 3956 444
των, καὶ Θεῷ μὴ ἀρεσκόντων, καὶ πᾶσιν ἀνθρώποις
and God not pleasing, and to all men
1727 2967 2248 1484 2980 2443 4982
16 ἐναντίων, κωλυόντων ἡμᾶς τοῖς ἔθνεσι λαλῆσαι ἵνα σωθῶσιν,
contrary, hindering us to the nations to speak, that they be saved,
1519 378 848 266 3842 5348
εἰς τὸ ἀναπληρῶσαι αὐτῶν τὰς ἁμαρτίας πάντοτε· ἔφθασε
to fill up of them the sins always. has come
1909 846 3709/1519/5056
δὲ ἐπ' αὐτοὺς ἡ ὀργὴ εἰς τέλος.
But on them the wrath to (the) end.
2249 80 642 575 5216 4314 2540
17 Ἡμεῖς δέ, ἀδελφοί, ἀπορφανισθέντες ἀφ' ὑμῶν πρὸς καιρὸν
we But, brothers being taken away from you for time
5610 4383 3756 2588 4056 4704
ὥρας, προσώπῳ οὐ καρδίᾳ, περισσοτέρως ἐσπουδάσαμεν
of an hour, in face, not in heart, more abundantly were eager

[18]Therefore, we desired to come to you, truly I, Paul, both once and twice, but Satan hindered us. [19]For what *is* our hope or joy, or crown of glorying? *Are* you not even *to be* before our Lord Jesus Christ at His coming? [20]For you are our glory and our joy.

CHAPTER 3

[1]So no longer enduring, we were pleased to be left in Athens alone, [2]and sent Timothy, our brother and minister of God, and our fellow-worker in the gospel of Christ, in order to establish you and to encourage you concerning your faith, [3]that no one be drawn aside by these afflictions. For you yourselves know that we are appointed to this. [4]For even when we were with you, we said to you before that we are about to be afflicted; as it also hapened, even you know. [5]Because of this, no longer enduring, I also sent to know your faith, that the tempting *one* not somehow tempt you, and our labor should become to no avail. [6]But now Timothy coming to us from you, and announcing good news to us *of* your love and faith, and that you have good remembrance of us always, longing to see us, even as also we *long to see* you, [7]because of this we were comforted as to you, brothers, on *knowing* all our affliction and distress through your faith, [8]for we now live, if you should stand fast in *the* Lord. [9]For what thanks are we able to

4383 5216 1492/1722/4183 1939 1352 2309
18 τὸ πρόσωπον ὑμῶν ἰδεῖν ἐν πολλῇ ἐπιθυμίᾳ· διὸ ἠθελήσαμεν
the face of you to see with much desire. Therefore we desired
2064 4314 5209 1473/3303 3972 530 1354 1465
ἐλθεῖν πρὸς ὑμᾶς, ἐγὼ μὲν Παῦλος καὶ ἅπαξ καὶ δίς, καὶ ἐνέ-
to come to you, I indeed Paul, both once and twice, and
2248 4567 5101/1063/2257 1680/2228/5479/2228/
19 κοψεν ἡμᾶς ὁ Σατανᾶς. τίς γὰρ ἡμῶν ἐλπὶς ἢ χαρὰ ἢ στέ-
hindered us Satan. what For of us hope or joy or
4735 2746 2228/3780 5210 1715 2962
φανος καυχήσεως ; ἢ οὐχὶ καὶ ὑμεῖς, ἔμπροσθεν τοῦ Κυρίου
crown of boasting? Not even you before the Lord
2257 2424 5547 1722 848 3952 5210 1063
20 ἡμῶν Ἰησοῦ Χριστοῦ ἐν τῇ αὐτοῦ παρουσίᾳ ; ὑμεῖς γάρ
of us, Jesus Christ at the of Him coming? you For
2075 1391 2257 5479
ἐστε ἡ δόξα ἡμῶν καὶ ἡ χαρά.
are the glory of us and the joy.

CHAPTER 3

1352 3371 4722 2106 2641 1722
1 Διὸ μηκέτι στέγοντες, εὐδοκήσαμεν καταλειφθῆναι ἐν
So no longer enduring, we were pleased to be left in
116 3441 3992 5095 80 2257
2 Ἀθήναις μόνοι, καὶ ἐπέμψαμεν Τιμόθεον τὸν ἀδελφὸν ἡμῶν
Athens alone, and sent Timothy the brother of us
1249 2316 4904 2257/1722 2098
καὶ διάκονον τοῦ Θεοῦ καὶ συνεργὸν ἡμῶν ἐν τῷ εὐαγγελίῳ
and minister of God, and fellow-worker of us in the gospel
5547 1519 4741 5209 3870 5209 4012
τοῦ Χριστοῦ, εἰς τὸ στηρίξαι ὑμᾶς καὶ παρακαλέσαι ὑμᾶς περὶ
of Christ, to establish you and to encourage you about
4102 5216 3367 4525 1722 2347
3 τῆς πίστεως ὑμῶν, τῷ μηδένα σαίνεσθαι ἐν ταῖς θλίψεσι
the faith of you no one to be drawn aside by afflictions
5025 846 1063 1492 3754/1519 5124 2749 1063
4 ταύταις· αὐτοὶ γὰρ οἴδατε ὅτι εἰς τοῦτο κείμεθα. καὶ γὰρ
these. yourselves For you know that to this we are appointed. even For
3753 4314 5209 2258 4302 5213/3754 3195 2345
ὅτε πρὸς ὑμᾶς ἦμεν, προελέγομεν ὑμῖν ὅτι μέλλομεν θλί-
when with you we were, we said before to you that we are about to be
2531 1096 1492 1223 5124 2504
5 βεσθαι, καθὼς καὶ ἐγένετο καὶ οἴδατε. διὰ τοῦτο κἀγώ,
afflicted, as also it happened, and you know. Therefore I also
3371 4722 3992 1519 1097 4102 5216 3361
μηκέτι στέγων, ἔπεμψα εἰς τὸ γνῶναι τὴν πίστιν ὑμῶν, μή
no longer enduring sent to know the faith of you, lest
4459 3985 5209 3985 1519 2756 1096
πως ἐπείρασεν ὑμᾶς ὁ πειράζων, καὶ εἰς κενὸν γένηται ὁ
somehow tempted you the tempting (one), and in vain became the
2873 2257 737 2064 5095 4314 2248 575
6 κόπος ἡμῶν. ἄρτι δὲ ἐλθόντος Τιμοθέου πρὸς ἡμᾶς ἀφ'
labor of us. now But coming Timothy to us from
5216 2097 2254 4102 26
ὑμῶν, καὶ εὐαγγελισαμένου ἡμῖν τὴν πίστιν καὶ τὴν ἀγάπην
you, and announcing good news to us (of) the faith and the love
5216 3754 2192 3417 2257 18 3842 1971
ὑμῶν, καὶ ὅτι ἔχετε μνείαν ἡμῶν ἀγαθὴν πάντοτε, ἐπιπο-
of you, and that you have remembrance of us good always, longing
2248 1492 2509 2249 5209 1223 5124
7 θοῦντες ἡμᾶς ἰδεῖν, καθάπερ καὶ ἡμεῖς ὑμᾶς· διὰ τοῦτο
us to see, even as also we you, for this reason
3870 80 1909/5213/1909/3956 2341
παρεκλήθημεν, ἀδελφοί, ἐφ' ὑμῖν ἐπὶ πάσῃ τῇ θλίψει καὶ
we were comforted, brothers, over you on all the aflcition and
318 2257/1223 5216 4102 3754/3568/ 2198 1437
8 ἀνάγκῃ ἡμῶν διὰ τῆς ὑμῶν πίστεως· ὅτι νῦν ζῶμεν, ἐὰν
distress of us through the of you faith, because now we live if
5210 4739 1722 2962 5100 1063/ 2169 1410
9 ὑμεῖς στήκητε ἐν Κυρίῳ. τίνα γὰρ εὐχαριστίαν δυνάμεθα τῷ
you stand in (the) Lord. what For thanks are we able

return to God as to you, as to all the joy *with* which we rejoice because of you before our God, [10]night and day praying exceedingly to see your face, and to complete the things lacking in your faith?

[11]But may our God and Father Himself, and our Lord Jesus Christ, direct our way to you. [12]And may the Lord make you to increase and to abound in love toward one another and toward all, even as we also toward you, [13]in order to establish your hearts blameless in holiness before our God and Father at the coming of our Lord Jesus Christ with all His saints.

2316 467 4012 5216 1909 3956 5479/3739/5463
Θεῷ ἀνταποδοῦναι περὶ ὑμῶν, ἐπὶ πάσῃ τῇ χαρᾷ ᾗ χαί-
to God to return concerning you, over all the joy (with) which
1223/5209 1715 2316 2257 3571 2250
10 ρομεν δι' ὑμᾶς ἔμπροσθεν τοῦ Θεοῦ ἡμῶν, νυκτὸς καὶ ἡμέρας
we rejoice by you before the God of us, night and day
5228/1537/ 4053 1189 1519 1492 5216 4383
ὑπὲρ ἐκ περισσοῦ δεόμενοι εἰς τὸ ἰδεῖν ὑμῶν τὸ πρόσωπον,
superabundantly petitioning for to see of you the face,
2675 5303 4102 5216
καὶ καταρτίσαι τὰ ὑστερήματα τῆς πίστεως ὑμῶν;
and to complete the things lacking in the faith of you?
846 2316 3962 2257 2962 2257
11 Αὐτὸς δὲ ὁ Θεὸς καὶ πατὴρ ἡμῶν, καὶ ὁ Κύριος ἡμῶν
Himself And the God and Father of us, and the Lord of us,
2424 5547 2720 3598 2257 4314 5209 5209
12 Ἰησοῦς Χριστός, κατευθύναι τὴν ὁδὸν ἡμῶν πρὸς ὑμᾶς· ὑμᾶς
Jesus Christ, may He direct the way of us to you, you
2962 4121 4052 26 1519 240
δὲ ὁ Κύριος πλεονάσαι καὶ περισσεύσαι τῇ ἀγάπῃ εἰς ἀλλή-
and the Lord make to abound and to exceed in love toward one
1519 3956 2509 2249/1519/5209/1519
λους καὶ εἰς πάντας, καθάπερ καὶ ἡμεῖς εἰς ὑμᾶς, εἰς τὸ
another and toward all, even as also we toward you, to
4741 5216 2588 273 1722 42
13 στηρίξαι ὑμῶν τὰς καρδίας ἀμέμπτους ἐν ἁγιωσύνῃ,
establish of you the hearts blameless in holiness,
1715 2316 3962 2257/1722 3952
ἔμπροσθεν τοῦ Θεοῦ καὶ πατρὸς ἡμῶν, ἐν τῇ παρουσίᾳ τοῦ
before the God and Father of us, in the presence of the
2962 2257 2424 5547 3326 3956 40
Κυρίου ἡμῶν Ἰησοῦ Χριστοῦ μετὰ πάντων τῶν ἁγίων
Lord of us, Jesus Christ, with all the saints
848
αὐτοῦ.
of Him.

CHAPTER 4

[1]For the rest, then, brothers, we beg you and we exhort in *the* Lord Jesus, even as you received from us how you ought to walk and to please God, that you abound more. [2]For you know what injunctions we gave you through the Lord Jesus. [3]For this is God's will, your sanctification, *for* you to abstain from fornication, [4]each one of you to know to possess his vessel in sanctification and honor, [5]not in passion of lust, even as also the nations not knowing God *do*; [6]not to go beyond and to overreach in the matter of his brother; because *the* avenger concerning all these *is* the Lord, even as we told you before, and solemnly testified.

CHAPTER 4

3063 3767 80 2065 5209 3870
1 Τὸ λοιπὸν οὖν, ἀδελφοί, ἐρωτῶμεν ὑμᾶς καὶ παρακαλοῦ-
For the rest, then, brothers, we beseech you and we exhort
1722 2962 2424 2531 3880 3844 2257 4459
μεν ἐν Κυρίῳ Ἰησοῦ καθὼς παρελάβετε παρ' ἡμῶν τὸ πῶς
in (the) Lord Jesus, even as you received from us how
1163/5209 4043 700 2316 2443 4052
δεῖ ὑμᾶς περιπατεῖν καὶ ἀρέσκειν Θεῷ, ἵνα περισσεύητε
it behoves you to walk and to please God, that you abound
3123 1491 1063/5100 3852 1325 5213/1223
2 μᾶλλον. οἴδατε γὰρ τίνας παραγγελίας ἐδώκαμεν ὑμῖν διὰ
more. you know For what injunctions we gave you through
2962 2424 5124 1063 2076 2307 2316
3 τοῦ Κυρίου Ἰησοῦ. τοῦτο γάρ ἐστι θέλημα τοῦ Θεοῦ, ὁ
the Lord Jesus. this For is (the) will of God, the
38 5216 567 5209 575 4202 1492
4 ἁγιασμὸς ὑμῶν, ἀπέχεσθαι ὑμᾶς ἀπὸ τῆς πορνείας· εἰδέναι
sanctification of you, to abstain you from fornication, to know
1538 5216 1438 4632 2932 1722 38 5092
ἕκαστον ὑμῶν τὸ ἑαυτοῦ σκεῦος κτᾶσθαι ἐν ἁγιασμῷ καὶ τιμῇ,
each one of you the of himself vessel to possess in purity and honor,
3361/1722/3806 1939 2509 1484 3361/ 1492
5 μὴ ἐν πάθει ἐπιθυμίας, καθάπερ καὶ τὰ ἔθνη τὰ μὴ εἰδότα τὸν
not in passion of lust, even as also the nations not knowing
2316 3361 5233 4122 1722 4229
6 Θεόν· τὸ μὴ ὑπερβαίνειν καὶ πλεονεκτεῖν ἐν τῷ πράγματι
God, not to go beyond and to overreach in the matter
80 848 1360 1558 2962 4012 3956
τὸν ἀδελφὸν αὐτοῦ· διότι ἔκδικος ὁ Κύριος περὶ πάντων
the brother of him, because (the) avenger the Lord (is) concerning all
5130 2531 4277 5213 1263
τούτων, καθὼς καὶ προείπαμεν ὑμῖν καὶ διεμαρτυράμεθα.
these, as indeed we before told you and solemnly witnessed.

[7]For God did not call us to uncleanness, but in sanctification. [8]Therefore, the *one* that despises does not despise man, but God, even He giving His Holy Spirit to us.

[9]Now as to brotherly love, you have no need *for me* to write to you, for you yourselves are taught by God to love one another. [10]For you also do it toward the brothers in all Macedonia. But, brothers, we exhort you to abound more. [11]And try earnestly to be quiet, and to do *your* own things, and to work with your own hands, as we enjoined you, [12]that you may walk becomingly toward those outside, and that you may have need of nothing.

[13]But I do not want you to be ignorant, brothers, concerning those who sleep, that you not grieve, as the rest also, not having hope. [14]For if we believe that Jesus died and rose again, even so God will also bring with Him all those who have fallen asleep through Jesus. [15]For we say this to you in *the* word of *the* Lord, that we the living who remain to the coming of the Lord not at all will go before those who have fallen asleep; [16]because the Lord Himself shall come down from Heaven with a commanding shout of an archangel's voice, and with God's trumpet. And the dead in Christ will rise again first, [17]then we who remain alive will be caught up together with them in *the* clouds to a meeting with the Lord in *the* air. And so we will always be with *the* Lord. [18]So, then, comfort each other with these words.

3756/1063 2564 2248 2316 1909 167 235 1722
7 οὐ γὰρ ἐκάλεσεν ἡμᾶς ὁ Θεὸς ἐπὶ ἀκαθαρσίᾳ, ἀλλ' ἐν
not For called us God to uncleanness, but in
38 5105 114 3756 444 114 235
8 ἁγιασμῷ. τοιγαροῦν ὁ ἀθετῶν οὐκ ἄνθρωπον ἀθετεῖ, ἀλλὰ
purity. Therefore those despising not man despises, but
2316 1325 4151 848 40 1519 2248
τὸν Θεὸν τὸν καὶ δόντα τὸ Πνεῦμα αὐτοῦ τὸ Ἅγιον εἰς ἡμᾶς.
God, the (One) also giving the Spirit of him the Holy to you.
4012 5360 3756 5532 2192 1125 5213
9 Περὶ δὲ τῆς φιλαδελφίας οὐ χρείαν ἔχετε γράφειν ὑμῖν·
concerning And brotherly love, no need you have to write to you,
846 1063 5210 2312 2075/1519 25 240
αὐτοὶ γὰρ ὑμεῖς θεοδίδακτοί ἐστε εἰς τὸ ἀγαπᾷν ἀλλήλους·
yourselves for you taught by God are to love one another;
1063 4160 846/1519 3956 80 1722/3650
10 καὶ γὰρ ποιεῖτε αὐτὸ εἰς πάντας τοὺς ἀδελφοὺς τοὺς ἐν ὅλῃ
indeed for you do it toward all the brothers in all
3109 3870 5209 80 4052
τῇ Μακεδονίᾳ. παρακαλοῦμεν δὲ ὑμᾶς, ἀδελφοί, περισσεύειν
Macedonia. we exhort But you, brothers, to abound
3123 5389 2270 4238 2398
11 μᾶλλον, καὶ φιλοτιμεῖσθαι ἡσυχάζειν, καὶ πράσσειν τὰ ἴδια,
more, and to try earnestly to be quiet, and to practice the own,
2036 2398 5495 5216 2531 5213 3853
καὶ ἐργάζεσθαι ταῖς ἰδίαις χερσὶν ὑμῶν, καθὼς ὑμῖν παρηγ-
and to work with the own hands of you, as you we
2443 4043 2156 4314 1854
12 γείλαμεν· ἵνα περιπατῆτε εὐσχημόνως πρὸς τοὺς ἔξω, καὶ
enjoined, that you may walk becomingly toward those outside, and
3367 5532 2192
μηδενὸς χρείαν ἔχητε.
of nothing need you may have.
3756/2309 5209 50 80 4012 2837
13 Οὐ θέλω δὲ ὑμᾶς ἀγνοεῖν, ἀδελφοί, περὶ τῶν κεκοιμη-
not I do desire And you to be ignorant, brothers, about those sleeping,
2443/3361 3076 2531 3062 3361 2192
μένων, ἵνα μὴ λυπῆσθε, καθὼς καὶ οἱ λοιποὶ οἱ μὴ ἔχοντες
lest you grieve as also the rest not having
1680/1487/1063/ 4100 3754 2424 599 450
14 ἐλπίδα. εἰ γὰρ πιστεύομεν ὅτι Ἰησοῦς ἀπέθανε καὶ ἀνέστη,
hope. if For we believe that Jesus died and rose again,
3779 2316 2837 1223 2424 71 4862
οὕτω καὶ ὁ Θεὸς τοὺς κοιμηθέντας διὰ τοῦ Ἰησοῦ ἄξει σὺν
so also God those having slept through Jesus will bring with
846 5124 1063 5213 3004 1722 3056 2962 3754 2249
15 αὐτῷ. τοῦτο γὰρ ὑμῖν λέγομεν ἐν λόγῳ Κυρίου, ὅτι ἡμεῖς οἱ
Him. this For to you we say by a word of (the) Lord, that we the
2198 4035 1519 3952 2962 3756
ζῶντες οἱ περιλειπόμενοι εἰς τὴν παρουσίαν τοῦ Κυρίου, οὐ
living remaining to the coming of the Lord, not
3361 5348 2837 3754 848 2962/1722/2752
μὴ φθάσωμεν τοὺς κοιμηθέντας. ὅτι αὐτὸς ὁ Κύριος ἐν κελεύ-
at all may go before those having slept; because Himself the Lord with a word
1722/5456 743 1722 4536 2316 2597
16 σματι, ἐν φωνῇ ἀρχαγγέλου, καὶ ἐν σάλπιγγι Θεοῦ καταβή-
of command by a voice of an archangel, and with a trumpet of God, will
575 2772 3498/1722 5547 450
σεται ἀπ' οὐρανοῦ, καὶ οἱ νεκροὶ ἐν Χριστῷ ἀναστήσονται
descend from Heaven, and the dead in Christ will rise again
4412 1899 2249 2198 4035 260 4862
17 πρῶτον· ἔπειτα ἡμεῖς οἱ ζῶντες, οἱ περιλειπόμενοι, ἅμα σὺν
firstly, then we the living remaining together with
846 726 1722 3507 1519 529 2962
αὐτοῖς ἁρπαγησόμεθα ἐν νεφέλαις εἰς ἀπάντησιν τοῦ Κυρίου
them will be caught up in clouds to a meeting of the Lord
1519/109 3779 3842 4862 2962 2071 5620 3870
18 εἰς ἀέρα· καὶ οὕτω πάντοτε σὺν Κυρίῳ ἐσόμεθα. ὥστε παρα-
in (the) air, and so always with (the) Lord we will be. So then
240 1722 3056 5125
καλεῖτε ἀλλήλους ἐν τοῖς λόγοις τούτοις.
comfort one another with words these.

CHAPTER 5

[1]But as to the times and
the seasons, brothers, you
have no need for you to be
written *to*, [2]for you yourselves know accurately the
day of *the* Lord comes as a
thief in the night. [3]For
when they say, Peace and
safety! Then suddenly de-
struction comes upon
them, like travail to the
pregnant woman, and they
shall not at all escape. [4]But
you, brothers, are not in
darkness, that the Day
should overtake you as a
thief. [5]You are all sons of
light and sons of day; we
are not of night, nor of
darkness. [6]So, then, we
should not sleep as the rest
also *do*, but we should
watch and be calm. [7]For
the *ones* who sleep sleep
by night, and the *ones*
having been drunk are
drunk by night; [8]but we
being of day should be
calm, having put on *the*
breastplate of faith and
love, and *the* hope of salvation *as* a helmet; [9]be-
cause God has not ap-
pointed us to wrath, but for
obtaining salvation through
our Lord Jesus Christ, [10]He
dying on our behalf, so that
whether we watch or we
sleep, we may live together
with Him. [11]Therefore,
comfort one another, and
build up one another, as
you indeed do.

[12]But, brothers, we beg
you to know those laboring
among you, and taking the
lead of you in *the* Lord, and
warning you; [13]even es-
teem them most exceed-
ingly in love because of
their work. Be at peace
among yourselves.
[14]And we exhort you,
brothers, to warn the unruly
ones, comfort those *that*

CHAPTER 5

4012 5550 2540 80 3756 5532
1 Περὶ δὲ τῶν χρόνων καὶ τῶν καιρῶν, ἀδελφοί, οὐ χρείαν
concerning And the times and the seasons, brothers, not need
2192/5213 1125 846 1063 199 1492 3754 2250
2 ἔχετε ὑμῖν γράφεσθαι. αὐτοὶ γὰρ ἀκριβῶς οἴδατε ὅτι ἡ ἡμέρα
have you to be written, yourselves for accurately you know that (the) day
2962 5613 2812 1722 3571 3779 2064 3752 1063
3 Κυρίου ὡς κλέπτης ἐν νυκτὶ οὕτως ἔρχεται· ὅταν γὰρ
of (the) Lord as a thief at night so it comes. when For
3004 1515 803 5119 160 846
λέγωσιν, Εἰρήνη καὶ ἀσφάλεια, τότε αἰφνίδιος αὐτοῖς
they say, Peace and safety! Then sudden them
2186 3639 5618 5604 1722 1064 2192
ἐφίσταται ὄλεθρος, ὥσπερ ἡ ὠδὶν τῇ ἐν γαστρὶ ἐχούσῃ, καὶ
comes on destruction, as the travail to the pregnant woman, and
=3364= 1628 5210 80 3756/2075/1722/ 4655 2443
4 οὐ μὴ ἐκφύγωσιν. ὑμεῖς δέ, ἀδελφοί, οὐκ ἐστὲ ἐν σκότει, ἵνα
not at all may they escape. you But, brothers, not are in darkness, that
2250 5209/5613 2812 2638 3956 5210/5207 5457
5 ἡ ἡμέρα ὑμᾶς ὡς κλέπτης καταλάβῃ· πάντες ὑμεῖς υἱοὶ φωτός
the day you as a thief should overtake; all you sons of light
2075 5207 2250 3756 2070 3571 3761 4655 686/3767
6 ἐστε καὶ υἱοὶ ἡμέρας· οὐκ ἐσμὲν νυκτὸς οὐδὲ σκότους· ἄρα οὖν
are, and sons of day. not We are of night, nor of darkness; therefore
3361 2518 5613 3062 235 1127
μὴ καθεύδωμεν ὡς καὶ οἱ λοιποί, ἀλλὰ γρηγορῶμεν καὶ
not let us sleep as also the rest, but let us watch and
3525 1063 2518 2571 2518
7 νήφωμεν. οἱ γὰρ καθεύδοντες νυκτὸς καθεύδουσι· καὶ οἱ
be sober. those For sleeping, by night sleep, and those
3184 3571 3182 2249 2250 5607 3525
8 μεθυσκόμενοι νυκτὸς μεθύουσιν. ἡμεῖς δέ, ἡμέρας ὄντες, νήφω-
being drunk by night are drunk; we but, of day being, let us be
1746 2382 4102 26 4030
μεν, ἐνδυσάμενοι θώρακα πίστεως καὶ ἀγάπης, καὶ περικεφα-
sober, putting on a breastplate of faith and of love, and a helmet
1680 4991 3754/3756 5087 2248 2316/1519
9 λαίαν, ἐλπίδα σωτηρίας. ὅτι οὐκ ἔθετο ἡμᾶς ὁ Θεὸς εἰς
of hope of salvation; because not appointed us God to
3709 235/1519 4047 4991 1223 2962 2257
ὀργήν, ἀλλ' εἰς περιποίησιν σωτηρίας διὰ τοῦ Κυρίου ἡμῶν
wrath, but for obtainment of salvation through the Lord of us,
2424 5547 599 5228 2257 2443 1535
10 Ἰησοῦ Χριστοῦ, τοῦ ἀποθανόντος ὑπὲρ ἡμῶν, ἵνα, εἴτε
Jesus Christ, the (One) having died on behalf of us, that whether
1127 1535 2518 260/ 4862/ 846 2198 1352
11 γρηγορῶμεν εἴτε καθεύδωμεν, ἅμα σὺν αὐτῷ ζήσωμεν. διὸ
we watch or we sleep, together with Him we may live. So
3870 240 3618 1519 1520 2531
παρακαλεῖτε ἀλλήλους, καὶ οἰκοδομεῖτε εἷς τὸν ἕνα, καθὼς
comfort one another, and build up one the other, as
4160
καὶ ποιεῖτε.
indeed you do.

2065 5209 80 1492 2872 1722
12 Ἐρωτῶμεν δὲ ὑμᾶς, ἀδελφοί, εἰδέναι τοὺς κοπιῶντας ἐν
we ask And you, brothers, to know those laboring among
5213 4291 5216/1722/2962 3560
ὑμῖν, καὶ προϊσταμένους ὑμῶν ἐν Κυρίῳ, καὶ νουθετοῦντας
you, and taking the lead of you in (the) Lord, and warning
5209 2233 846 5228/1537/ 4053 1722 26 1223
13 ὑμᾶς, καὶ ἡγεῖσθαι αὐτοὺς ὑπὲρ ἐκ περισσοῦ ἐν ἀγάπῃ διὰ
you, and esteem them most exceedingly in love because of
2041 848 1514 1722 1438 3870
14 τὸ ἔργον αὐτῶν. εἰρηνεύετε ἐν ἑαυτοῖς. παρακαλοῦμεν δὲ
the work of them. Be at peace among yourselves. we exhort And
5209 80 3560 813 3888
ὑμᾶς, ἀδελφοί, νουθετεῖτε τοὺς ἀτάκτους, παραμυθεῖσθε τοὺς
you, brothers, warn the insubordinate, comfort the

are faint-hearted, sustain the weak, be patient towards all. [15]See *that* no one returns evil for evil to anyone, but always pursue the good, both towards one another and towards all.

[16]Rejoice always. [17]Pray without ceasing. [18]In everything give thanks, for this *is the* will of God in Christ Jesus toward you. [19]Do not quench the Spirit. [20]Do not despise prophecies. [21]Test all things, hold fast to the good. [22]Keep back from every form of evil.

[23]And may the God of peace Himself fully sanctify you, and may your whole spirit and soul and body be kept blameless at the coming of our Lord Jesus Christ. [24]*He* who calls you *is* faithful, who also will perform *it*.

[25]Brothers, pray concerning us.

[26]Greet all the brothers with a holy kiss. [27]I charge you by the Lord that this letter be read to all the holy brothers.

[28]The grace of our Lord Jesus Christ *be* with you. Amen.

3642 472 772 3114 4314
ὀλιγοψύχους, ἀντέχεσθε τῶν ἀσθενῶν, μακροθυμεῖτε πρὸς
faint-hearted, care for those being weak, be long-suffering toward
3956 3708/3361/5100/2556/ 473 2556 5100 591 235
15 πάντας. ὁρᾶτε μή τις κακὸν ἀντὶ κακοῦ τινὶ ἀποδῷ· ἀλλὰ
all. See (that) not anyone evil for evil to anyone returns, but
3842 18 1377 1519 240 1519 3956
πάντοτε τὸ ἀγαθὸν διώκετε καὶ εἰς ἀλλήλους καὶ εἰς πάντας.
always the good follow even toward one another and toward all.
3842 5463 89 4336 1722 3956
16 πάντοτε χαίρετε· ἀδιαλείπτως προσεύχεσθε· ἐν παντὶ
17 **always Rejoice. without ceasing Pray. In everything**
2168 5124 1063 2307 2316/1722/5547 2424 1519
18 εὐχαριστεῖτε· τοῦτο γὰρ θέλημα Θεοῦ ἐν Χριστῷ Ἰησοῦ εἰς
give thanks, this for (is) (the) will of God in Christ Jesus to
5209 4151 3361 4570 4394 3361 1848
19 ὑμᾶς. τὸ Πνεῦμα μὴ σβέννυτε· προφητείας μὴ ἐξουθενεῖτε·
20 **you. The Spirit not do quench. Prophecies not despise.**
3956 1381 2570 2722 575 3956 1491
21 πάντα δοκιμάζετε· τὸ καλὸν κατέχετε· ἀπὸ παντὸς εἴδους
22 **All things test, the good hold fast. From every form**
4190 567
πονηροῦ ἀπέχεσθε.
of evil keep back.
848 2316 1515 37 5209 3651
23 Αὐτὸς δὲ ὁ Θεὸς τῆς εἰρήνης ἁγιάσαι ὑμᾶς ὁλοτελεῖς· καὶ
Himself And the God of peace, may He sanctify you fully, and
3648 5216 4151 5590 4983
ὁλόκληρον ὑμῶν τὸ πνεῦμα καὶ ἡ ψυχὴ καὶ τὸ σῶμα
whole of you the spirit, and the soul, and the body,
274 1722 3952 2962 2257 2424 5547
ἀμέμπτως ἐν τῇ παρουσίᾳ τοῦ Κυρίου ἡμῶν Ἰησοῦ Χριστοῦ
blamelessly at the coming of the Lord of us, Jesus Christ
5083 4103 2564 5209/3739 4160
24 τηρηθείη. πιστὸς ὁ καλῶν ὑμᾶς, ὃς καὶ ποιήσει.
may be kept. Faithful (is) He calling you, who also will do (it).
80 4336 4012 2257
25 Ἀδελφοί, προσεύχεσθε περὶ ἡμῶν.
Brothers, pray concerning us.
782 80 3956 1722 5370 40
26 Ἀσπάσασθε τοὺς ἀδελφοὺς πάντας ἐν φιλήματι ἁγίῳ.
Greet the brothers all with kiss a holy.
3726 5209 2962 314 1992
27 ὁρκίζω ὑμᾶς τὸν Κύριον, ἀναγνωσθῆναι τὴν ἐπιστολὴν
I charge you by the Lord to be read the epistle
3956 40 80
πᾶσι τοῖς ἁγίοις ἀδελφοῖς.
to all the holy brothers.
5485 2962 2257 2424 5547 3326 5216
28 Ἡ χάρις τοῦ Κυρίου ἡμῶν Ἰησοῦ Χριστοῦ μεθ' ὑμῶν.
The grace of the Lord of us, Jesus Christ, (be) with you.
281
ἀμήν.
Amen.

ΠΑΥΛΟΥ ΤΟΥ ΑΠΟΣΤΟΛΟΥ
PAUL THE APOSTLE
Η ΠΡΟΣ
THE TO
ΘΕΣΣΑΛΟΝΙΚΕΙΣ
(THE) THESSALONIANS
ΕΠΙΣΤΟΛΗ ΔΕΥΤΕΡΑ
EPISTLE SECOND

THE SECOND EPISTLE TO THE THESSALONIANS

A LITERAL TRANSLATION OF THE BIBLE

CHAPTER 1

[1]Paul and Silvanus and Timothy to the church of Thessalonians in God our Father and *the* Lord Jesus Christ: [2]Grace to you and peace from God our Father and *the* Lord Jesus Christ.

[3]Brothers, we are bound to give thanks to God always concerning you, even as it is right, because your faith grows exceedingly, and the love of each one of you all multiplies toward one another; [4]so as for us to boast ourselves in you in the churches of God for your patience and faith in all your persecutions, and the afflictions which you endure, [5]a clear token of the just judgment of God, for you to be counted worthy of the kingdom of God, for which you indeed suffer; [6]since *it is* a just thing with God to repay affliction to the ones afflicting you; [7]and to you, those being afflicted, rest with us at the revelation of the Lord Jesus from Heaven with angels of His power, [8]in flaming fire giving full vengeance to those not knowing God, and to those not obeying the gospel of our Lord Jesus Christ,

CHAPTER 1

3972 4610 5095 1577 2331
1 Παῦλος καὶ Σιλουανὸς καὶ Τιμόθεος τῇ ἐκκλησίᾳ Θεσσα-
Paul and Silvanus and Timothy to the church of Thess-
1722/2316/3962 2257 2962 2424 5547
λονικέων ἐν Θεῷ πατρὶ ἡμῶν καὶ Κυρίῳ Ἰησοῦ Χριστῷ·
alonians in God (the) Father of us and (the) Lord Jesus Christ :
5485 5213 1515 575 2316 3962 2257 2962
2 χάρις ὑμῖν καὶ εἰρήνη ἀπὸ Θεοῦ πατρὸς ἡμῶν καὶ Κυρίου
Grace to you and peace from God (the) Father of us and (the) Lord
2424 5547
Ἰησοῦ Χριστοῦ.
Jesus Christ.
2168 3784 2316 3482 4012 2257
3 Εὐχαριστεῖν ὀφείλομεν τῷ Θεῷ πάντοτε περὶ ὑμῶν,
to give thanks We ought to God always concerning you,
80 514 2076 3754 5232 4102 2257
ἀδελφοί, καθὼς ἄξιόν ἐστιν, ὅτι ὑπεραυξάνει ἡ πίστις ὑμῶν,
brothers, even as right it is; because grows exceedingly the faith of you,
4121 26 1520 1538 3956 5216/1722/240
καὶ πλεονάζει ἡ ἀγάπη ἑνὸς ἑκάστου πάντων ὑμῶν εἰς ἀλλή-
and multiplies the love one of each all of you to one
5620 2248 846 1722/5213 2744 1722 1577
4 λους· ὥστε ἡμᾶς αὐτοὺς ἐν ὑμῖν καυχᾶσθαι ἐν ταῖς ἐκκλησίαις
another, so as us ourselves in you to boast among the churches
2316 5228 5281 5216 4102 1722 3956
τοῦ Θεοῦ ὑπὲρ τῆς ὑπομονῆς ὑμῶν καὶ πίστεως ἐν πᾶσι
of God for the patience of you and faith in all
1375 5216 2347 3739 430 1730
5 τοῖς διωγμοῖς ὑμῶν καὶ ταῖς θλίψεσιν αἷς ἀνέχεσθε· ἔνδειγμα
the persecutions of you and the afflictions which you endure, a clear token
1342 2920 2316 1519 2661 5209
τῆς δικαίας κρίσεως τοῦ Θεοῦ, εἰς τὸ καταξιωθῆναι ὑμᾶς τῆς
of the just judgment of God for to be counted worthy you of the
932 2316 5228/3739 3958 1512 1342 3844
6 βασιλείας τοῦ Θεοῦ, ὑπὲρ ἧς καὶ πάσχετε· εἴπερ δίκαιον παρὰ
kingdom of God, for which indeed you suffer, since a just thing with
2316 467 2346 5209 2347 5213
Θεῷ ἀνταποδοῦναι τοῖς θλίβουσιν ὑμᾶς θλῖψιν, καὶ ὑμῖν τοῖς
God to repay to those afflicting you affliction, and to you those
2346 425 3326 2257/1722 602 2962
7 θλιβομένοις ἄνεσιν μεθ' ἡμῶν, ἐν τῇ ἀποκαλύψει τοῦ Κυρίου
being afflicted rest with us, at the revelation of the Lord
2424 575 3772 3326 32 1411 848 1722/4442
8 Ἰησοῦ ἀπ' οὐρανοῦ μετ' ἀγγέλων δυνάμεως αὐτοῦ, ἐν πυρὶ
Jesus from Heaven with angels of power of Him, in fire
5395 1325 1557 3361 1492 2316
φλογός, διδόντος ἐκδίκησιν τοῖς μὴ εἰδόσι Θεόν, καὶ τοῖς
of flame, giving full vengeance to those not knowing God, and to those
3361 5219 2098 2962 2257 2424
μὴ ὑπακούουσι τῷ εὐαγγελίῳ τοῦ Κυρίου ἡμῶν Ἰησοῦ
not obeying the gospel of the Lord of us Jesus

9 who will pay the penalty: eternal destruction from *the* face of the Lord, and from the glory of His strength, 10 when He comes to be glorified in His saints, and to be admired in all those who believe in that Day, because our testimony to you was believed. 11 For which we also always pray concerning you, that our God may count you worthy of the calling, and may fulfill every good pleasure of goodness, and work of faith in power, 12 so that the name of our Lord Jesus Christ may be glorified in you, and you in Him, according to the grace of our God and of *the* Lord Jesus Christ.

5547 3748/1349 5099 3639 166 575 4383
9 Χριστοῦ· οἵτινες δίκην τίσουσιν, ὄλεθρον αἰώνιον ἀπὸ προσ-
Christ, who (the) penalty will pay, destruction eternal from (the)
2962 575 1391 2479 848
ώπου τοῦ Κυρίου καὶ ἀπὸ τῆς δόξης τῆς ἰσχύος αὐτοῦ,
face of the Lord and from the glory of the strength of Him,
3752 2064 1740 1722 40 848 2296
10 ὅταν ἔλθῃ ἐνδοξασθῆναι ἐν τοῖς ἁγίοις αὐτοῦ, καὶ θαυμασθῆ-
when He comes to be glorified in the saints of Him, and to be admired
1722/3956 4100 3754 4100 3142
ναι ἐν πᾶσι τοῖς πιστεύουσιν (ὅτι ἐπιστεύθη τὸ μαρτύριον
in all those believing, because was believed the testimony
2257/1909/5209/1722 2250 1565 1519/3739 4336
11 ἡμῶν ἐφ' ὑμᾶς) ἐν τῇ ἡμέρᾳ ἐκείνῃ. εἰς ὃ καὶ προσευχόμεθ
of us to you in day that. For which indeed we pray
4012/2257 2443/5209 515 2821 2316
πάντοτε περὶ ὑμῶν, ἵνα ὑμᾶς ἀξιώσῃ τῆς κλήσεως ὁ Θεὸς
always concerning you, that you may count worthy of the calling the God
2257 4137 3956 2107 19 2041
ἡμῶν, καὶ πληρώσῃ πᾶσαν εὐδοκίαν ἀγαθωσύνης καὶ ἔργον
of us, and may fulfill every good pleasure of goodness and work
4102 1722 1411 3704 1740 3686 2962
12 πίστεως ἐν δυνάμει· ὅπως ἐνδοξασθῇ τὸ ὄνομα τοῦ Κυρίου
of faith in power, so as may be glorified the name of the Lord
2257 2424 5547 1722/5213 5210/1722/846 2596
ἡμῶν Ἰησοῦ Χριστοῦ ἐν ὑμῖν, καὶ ὑμεῖς ἐν αὐτῷ, κατὰ τὴν
of us. Jesus Christ in you, and you in Him, according to the
5485 2316/2257 2962 2424 5547
χάριν τοῦ Θεοῦ ἡμῶν καὶ Κυρίου Ἰησοῦ Χριστοῦ.
grace of the God of us and (the) Lord Jesus Christ.

CHAPTER 2

1 And, brothers, we beg you, by the coming of our Lord Jesus Christ, and of our gathering together to Him, 2 for you not to be quickly shaken *in* the mind, nor to be troubled; neither through a spirit, nor through speech, nor through letter, as through us, as if the Day of Christ has come. 3 Do not let anyone deceive you in any way, because *that Day will not come* unless first comes the falling away, and the man of sin is revealed, the son of perdition, 4 the *one* opposing and exalting himself over everything being called God, or object of worship, so as *for* him to sit in the temple of God as God, showing himself that he is a god. 5 Do you not remember that I told you these things, *I* yet being with you? 6 And now you know the thing holding back, for him to be revealed in his time. 7 For the mystery

2065 5209 80 5228 3952
1 Ἐρωτῶμεν δὲ ὑμᾶς, ἀδελφοί, ὑπὲρ τῆς παρουσίας τοῦ
we ask And you, brothers, by the presence of the
2962 2257 2424 5547 2257 1997 1909
Κυρίου ἡμῶν Ἰησοῦ Χριστοῦ, καὶ ἡμῶν ἐπισυναγωγῆς ἐπ'
Lord of us, Jesus Christ, and of us gathering together to
846 1519 3361 5030 4531 5209 575 3563
2 αὐτόν, εἰς τὸ μὴ ταχέως σαλευθῆναι ὑμᾶς ἀπὸ τοῦ νοός,
Him, for not quickly to be shaken you from the mind,
3383 2360 3383/1223 4151 3383/1223 3056 3383
μήτε θροεῖσθαι, μήτε διὰ πνεύματος, μήτε διὰ λόγου, μήτε
nor to be troubled, neither through a spirit, nor through speech, nor
1223 1992 5613/1223/2257/5613/3754 1764 2250
δι' ἐπιστολῆς ὡς δι' ἡμῶν, ὡς ὅτι ἐνέστηκεν ἡ ἡμέρα τοῦ
through epistle, as through us, as that is come the day of the
5547 3361/5101/5209 1818 2596 3367 5158 3754
3 Χριστοῦ· μή τις ὑμᾶς ἐξαπατήσῃ κατὰ μηδένα τρόπον· ὅτι
Christ. Let not anyone you deceive, by no way, because
1437/3361/2064 646 4412 601 444
ἐὰν μὴ ἔλθῃ ἡ ἀποστασία πρῶτον, καὶ ἀποκαλυφθῇ ὁ ἄνθρω-
unless comes the falling away first, and is revealed the man
266 5207 684 480
4 πος τῆς ἁμαρτίας, ὁ υἱὸς τῆς ἀπωλείας, ὁ ἀντικείμενος καὶ
of sin, the son of perdition, he opposing and
5229 1909/3956 3004 2316 4574 5620
ὑπεραιρόμενος ἐπὶ πᾶν τὸ λεγόμενον Θεὸν ἢ σέβασμα, ὥστε
exalting himself over everything being called God, or object of worship, so as
846 1519 3485 2316/5613/2316 2523 584
αὐτὸν εἰς τὸν ναὸν τοῦ Θεοῦ ὡς Θεὸν καθίσαι, ἀποδεικνύντα
him in the temple of God as God to sit, showing
1438 3754/2076/2316/3756 3421 3754/2089/5607/4314/5209
5 ἑαυτὸν ὅτι ἐστὶ Θεός. οὐ μνημονεύετε ὅτι ἔτι ὢν πρὸς ὑμᾶς
himself that he is a God. Do not you remember that yet being with you,
5023 3004 5213 3568 2722 1492 1519 601
6 ταῦτα ἔλεγον ὑμῖν; καὶ νῦν τὸ κατέχον οἴδατε, εἰς τὸ ἀπο-
these things I told you? And now the thing restraining you know, for to be
846/1722 1438 2540 1063 3466
7 καλυφθῆναι αὐτὸν ἐν τῷ ἑαυτοῦ καιρῷ. τὸ γὰρ μυστήριον
revealed him in the of him time. the For mystery

of lawlessness already is working, only he holding back now, until it comes out of *the* midst; [8]and then the Lawless One will be revealed, whom the Lord will consume by the spirit of His mouth; and *He* will bring to nothing by the brightness of His coming; [9]*His* coming is according to the working of Satan in all power and miracles and lying wonders, [10]and in all deceit of unrighteousness in those being lost, because they did not receive the love of the truth in order for them to be saved. [11]And because of this, God will send to them a working of error, for them to believe the lie, [12]that all may be judged, those not believing the truth, but who have delighted in unrighteousness.

[13]But we ought to thank God always concerning you, brothers, beloved by *the* Lord, because God chose you from the beginning to salvation in sanctification of *the* Spirit and belief of *the* truth, [14]to which He called you through our gospel, to obtain *the* glory of our Lord Jesus Christ. [15]So, then, brothers, stand firm and strongly hold the teachings you were taught, whether by word or by our letter. [16]But may our Lord Himself, Jesus Christ, and our God and Father, He who loves and gives us everlasting encouragement and good hope by grace, [17]encourage your hearts, and may He establish you in every good word and work.

CHAPTER 3

[1]For the rest, brothers, pray concerning us, that the

2235 1754 458 3440 2722 737 2193/1537
ἤδη ἐνεργεῖται τῆς ἀνομίας· μόνον ὁ κατέχων ἄρτι, ἕως ἐκ
already works of lawlessness, only he restraining now, until out of
3319 1096 5119 601 459 3739
8 μέσου γένηται. καὶ τότε ἀποκαλυφθήσεται ὁ ἄνομος, ὃν ὁ
(the) midst it comes. And then will be revealed the lawless one, whom the
2962 355 4151 4750 848
Κύριος ἀναλώσει τῷ πνεύματι τοῦ στόματος αὐτοῦ, καὶ
Lord will consume by the spirit of the mouth of Him, and
2673 2015 3952 848 3739 2076
9 καταργήσει τῇ ἐπιφανείᾳ τῆς παρουσίας αὐτοῦ· οὗ ἐστιν
bring to nothing by the brightness of the coming of Him; of whom is
3952 2596 1753 4567 1722/3956 1411
ἡ παρουσία κατ' ἐνέργειαν τοῦ Σατανᾶ ἐν πάσῃ δυνάμει καὶ
the coming according to the working of Satan in all power and
4592 5059 5579 1722 3956 539 93
10 σημείοις καὶ τέρασι ψεύδους, καὶ ἐν πάσῃ ἀπάτῃ τῆς ἀδικίας
signs and wonders of a lie, and with all deceit of unrighteousness
1722 622 473/3739 26 225
ἐν τοῖς ἀπολλυμένοις, ἀνθ' ὧν τὴν ἀγάπην τῆς ἀληθείας
in those being lost; because the love of the truth
3756 1209 1519 4982 846 1223 5124 3992
11 οὐκ ἐδέξαντο εἰς τὸ σωθῆναι αὐτούς. καὶ διὰ τοῦτο πέμψει
not they received for to be saved them. And because of this will send
846 2316 1753 4106 1519 4100 846
αὐτοῖς ὁ Θεὸς ἐνέργειαν πλάνης, εἰς τὸ πιστεῦσαι αὐτοὺς
to them God a working of error for to believe them
5579 2443 2919 3956 3361 4100
12 τῷ ψεύδει· ἵνα κριθῶσι πάντες οἱ μὴ πιστεύσαντες τῇ
the lie, that may be judged all those not believing the
225 235 2106 1722 93
ἀληθείᾳ, ἀλλ' εὐδοκήσαντες ἐν τῇ ἀδικίᾳ.
truth, but having had pleasure in unrighteousness.
2249 3784 2168 2316 3842 4012
13 Ἡμεῖς δὲ ὀφείλομεν εὐχαριστεῖν τῷ Θεῷ πάντοτε περὶ
we But ought to thank God always concerning
5216 80 25 5259 2962 3754 138 5209
ὑμῶν, ἀδελφοὶ ἠγαπημένοι ὑπὸ Κυρίου, ὅτι εἵλετο ὑμᾶς
you, brothers, having been loved by (the) Lord, because chose you
2316/575 746 1519 4991 1722 38 4151
ὁ Θεὸς ἀπ' ἀρχῆς εἰς σωτηρίαν ἐν ἁγιασμῷ Πνεύματος καὶ
God from (the) beginning to salvation in sanctification of (the) Spirit and
4102 225 1519/3739/ 2564 5209/1223 2098
14 πίστει ἀληθείας· εἰς ὃ ἐκάλεσεν ὑμᾶς διὰ τοῦ εὐαγγελίου
belief of (the) truth, to which He called you through the gospel
2257 1519 4047 1391 2962 2257 2424
ἡμῶν, εἰς περιποίησιν δόξης τοῦ Κυρίου ἡμῶν Ἰησοῦ
of us, to obtainment of (the) glory of the Lord of us, Jesus
5547 686/3767 80 4739 2902 3862
15 Χριστοῦ. ἄρα οὖν, ἀδελφοί, στήκετε, καὶ κρατεῖτε τὰς παρα-
Christ. So then, brothers, stand, and hold the tra-
3739 1321 1535/1223/3056 1535/1223/ 1992 2257
δόσεις ἃς ἐδιδάχθητε, εἴτε διὰ λόγου εἴτε δι' ἐπιστολῆς ἡμῶν.
ditions which you were taught either by word or by an epistle of us.
846 2962 2257 2424 5547 2316
16 Αὐτὸς δὲ ὁ Κύριος ἡμῶν Ἰησοῦς Χριστός, καὶ ὁ Θεὸς καὶ
Himself And the Lord of us, Jesus Christ, and the God and
3962 2257 25 2248 1325 3874 166
πατὴρ ἡμῶν ὁ ἀγαπήσας ἡμᾶς καὶ δοὺς παράκλησιν αἰωνίαν
Father of us, the (One) loving us and giving comfort eternal
1680 18 1722 5485 3870 5216
17 καὶ ἐλπίδα ἀγαθὴν ἐν χάριτι, παρακαλέσαι ὑμῶν τὰς
and a hope good by grace, may He comfort of you the
2588 4741 5209/1722/3956/3056 2041 18
καρδίας καὶ στηρίξαι ὑμᾶς ἐν παντὶ λόγῳ καὶ ἔργῳ ἀγαθῷ.
hearts and establish you in every word and work good.

CHAPTER 3

3063 4336 80 4012/2257/2443 3056
1 Τὸ λοιπόν, προσεύχεσθε, ἀδελφοί, περὶ ἡμῶν, ἵνα ὁ λόγος
For the rest, pray, brothers, about us, that the word

word of the Lord may run and be glorified, even as also with you, [2]and that we may be delivered from perverse and evil men—for faith *is* not in all. [3]But the Lord is faithful, who will establish and will guard you from the evil one. [4]But we are persuaded in *the* Lord as to you, that whatever things we enjoin you, you both do and will do. [5]And the Lord direct your hearts into the love of God and into the patience of Christ.

[6]And we enjoin you, brothers, in the name of our Lord Jesus Christ, to draw yourselves back from every brother walking *in an* unruly *way*, and not according to the teaching which you received from us. [7]for you yourselves know how it is right to act like us, because we were not disorderly among you; [8]nor did we eat bread from anyone *as* a gift; but by labor and toil working night and day in order not to burden anyone of you. [9]Not that we do not have authority, but that we give ourselves an example to you, for *you* to act like us. [10]For even when we were with you, we enjoined this to you: If anyone does not desire to work, let him not eat. [11]For we hear some *are* walking in a disorderly way among you, not working at all, but being busybodies. [12]And we enjoin such and exhort through our Lord Jesus Christ that working with quietness they may eat their own bread. [13]And you, brothers, do not lose heart *in* welldoing. [14]But if anyone does not obey our word through the letter, mark that

2962 5143 1392 2531 4314 5209
2 τοῦ Κυρίου τρέχῃ καὶ δοξάζηται, καθὼς καὶ πρὸς ὑμᾶς, καὶ
of the Lord may run and be glorified, as indeed with you, and
2443 4506 575 824 4190 444
ἵνα ῥυσθῶμεν ἀπὸ τῶν ἀτόπων καὶ πονηρῶν ἀνθρώπων·
that we be delivered from perverse and evil men;
3756/1063/3956 4102 4103 2076 2962 3739
3 οὐ γὰρ πάντων ἡ πίστις. πιστὸς δέ ἐστιν ὁ Κύριος, ὃς
(is not for of all the faith. faithful But is the Lord, who
4741 5209 5442 575 4190 3982
4 στηρίξει ὑμᾶς καὶ φυλάξει ἀπὸ τοῦ πονηροῦ. πεποίθαμεν
will establish you and will guard from the evil one. we are persuaded
1722 2962 1909 5209 3754/3739 3853 5213
δὲ ἐν Κυρίῳ ἐφ' ὑμᾶς, ὅτι ἃ παραγγέλλομεν ὑμῖν καὶ
And in (the) Lord as to you, that what things we enjoin you both
4160 4160 3739 2962 2720 5216
5 ποιεῖτε καὶ ποιήσετε. ὁ δὲ Κύριος κατευθύναι ὑμῶν τὰς
you do and will do. the And Lord direct of you the
2588 1519 26 2316 1519 5281
καρδίας εἰς τὴν ἀγάπην τοῦ Θεοῦ, καὶ εἰς τὴν ὑπομονὴν τοῦ
hearts into the love of God, and into the patience
5547
Χριστοῦ.
of Christ.

3853 5213 80 1722 3686 2962
6 Παραγγέλλομεν δὲ ὑμῖν, ἀδελφοί, ἐν ὀνόματι τοῦ Κυρίου
we enjoin And you, brothers, in the name of the Lord
2257 2424 5547 4724 5209 575 3956 80
ἡμῶν Ἰησοῦ Χριστοῦ, στέλλεσθαι ὑμᾶς ἀπὸ παντὸς ἀδελφοῦ
of us, Jesus Christ, to draw back you from every brother
814 4043 3361 2596 3862 3739
ἀτάκτως περιπατοῦντος, καὶ μὴ κατὰ τὴν παράδοσιν ἣν
insubordinately walking, and not according to the tradition which
3880 3844 2257 846 1063 1492 4459/1163 3401
7 παρέλαβε παρ' ἡμῶν. αὐτοὶ γὰρ οἴδατε πῶς δεῖ μιμεῖσθαι
you received from us. yourselves For, you know how it is right to imitate
2248 3754 3756 812 1722 5213 3761 1432 740
8 ἡμᾶς· ὅτι οὐκ ἠτακτήσαμεν ἐν ὑμῖν, οὐδὲ δωρεὰν ἄρτον
us, because not we were disorderly among you, nor (as) a gift bread
5315 3844 5100 235/1722/2873 3449 3571
ἐφάγομεν παρά τινος, ἀλλ' ἐν κόπῳ καὶ μόχθῳ, νύκτα καὶ
ate from anyone, but by labor and toil night and
2250 2036 4314 3361 1912 5100 2257
ἡμέραν ἐργαζόμενοι, πρὸς τὸ μὴ ἐπιβαρῆσαί τινα ὑμῶν·
day working for not to burden anyone of you;
3756/3754/3756/ 2192 1849 235/2443/ 1438 5179 1325
9 οὐχ ὅτι οὐκ ἔχομεν ἐξουσίαν, ἀλλ' ἵνα ἑαυτοὺς τύπον δῶμεν
not that not we have authority, but that ourselves an example we give
5213/1519 3401 2248 1063/3753/2258/4314/5209 5124
10 ὑμῖν εἰς τὸ μιμεῖσθαι ἡμᾶς. καὶ γὰρ ὅτε ἦμεν πρὸς ὑμᾶς, τοῦτο
to you for to imitate us. even For when we were with you, this
3853 5213/3754=1536=/3756/2309 2036 3366
παρηγγέλλομεν ὑμῖν ὅτι Εἴ τις οὐ θέλει ἐργάζεσθαι, μηδὲ
we enjoined you, – If anyone not desires to work, not
2068 191 1063 5100 4043 1722/5213
11 ἐσθιέτω. ἀκούομεν γάρ τινας περιπατοῦντας ἐν ὑμῖν
let him eat. we hear (of) For some walking among you
814 3367 2036 235 4020
12 ἀτάκτως, μηδὲν ἐργαζομένους, ἀλλὰ περιεργαζομένους. τοῖς
disorderly, nothing working, but working all about,
5108 3853 3870 1223
δὲ τοιούτοις παραγγέλλομεν, καὶ παρακαλοῦμεν διὰ τοῦ
and such we enjoin and exhort through the
2962 2257 2424 5547 2443 3326 2271 2036
Κυρίου ἡμῶν Ἰησοῦ Χριστοῦ, ἵνα μετὰ ἡσυχίας ἐργαζόμενοι
Lord of us, Jesus Christ, that with quietness working
1438 740)68 5210 80 3361 1573
13 τὸν ἑαυτῶν ἄρτον ἐσθίωσιν. ὑμεῖς δέ, ἀδελφοί, μὴ ἐκκακήσητε
the of themselves bread they may eat. you And, brothers, do not lose heart
2569 1487 5100/3756/ 5219 3056 2257/1223
14 καλοποιοῦντες. εἰ δέ τις οὐχ ὑπακούει τῷ λόγῳ ἡμῶν διὰ τῆς
(in) welldoing. if And any not obeys the word of us via the

one, and do not associate with him, that he be shamed; [15]but do not count *him* an enemy, but warn *him* as a brother.

[16]And may the Lord of peace Himself continually give peace to you in every way. The Lord *be* with all of you.

[17]The greeting of Paul by my hand is *the* sign in every letter; so I write. [18]The grace of our Lord Jesus Christ *be* with you all. Amen.

1992 5126 4593 3361 4874 846
ἐπιστολῆς, τοῦτον σημειοῦσθε, καὶ μὴ συναναμίγνυσθε αὐτῷ,
epistle, this one mark, and do not associate with him,
2443 1788 3361/5613/2190 2233 235 3560 5613
15 ἵνα ἐντραπῇ· καὶ μὴ ὡς ἐχθρὸν ἡγεῖσθε, ἀλλὰ νουθετεῖτε ὡς
that he be shamed; and not as an enemy esteem (him), but warn as
80
ἀδελφόν.
a brother.
846 2962 1515 1325/5213 1515 1223
16 Αὐτὸς δὲ ὁ Κύριος τῆς εἰρήνης δῴη ὑμῖν τὴν εἰρήνην διὰ
Himself And, the Lord of peace give to you the peace con-
3956 /1722/3956 5158 2962 3326 3956 5216
παντὸς ἐν παντὶ τρόπῳ. ὁ Κύριος μετὰ πάντων ὑμῶν.
tinually in every way. The Lord (be) with all you.
783 1699/5495 3972 2076 4592 1722/3956
17 Ὁ ἀσπασμὸς τῇ ἐμῇ χειρὶ Παύλου, ὅ ἐστι σημεῖον ἐν πάσῃ
The greeting by my hand, of Paul, which is a sign in every
1992 3779 1125 5485 2962 2257 2424
18 ἐπιστολῇ· οὕτω γράφω. ἡ χάρις τοῦ Κυρίου ἡμῶν Ἰησοῦ
epistle; thus I write. The grace of the Lord of us, Jesus
5547 3326 3956 2257 281
Χριστοῦ μετὰ πάντων ὑμῶν. ἀμήν.
Christ (be) with all you. Amen.

ΠΑΥΛΟΥ ΤΟΥ ΑΠΟΣΤΟΛΟΥ

PAUL THE APOSTLE

Η ΠΡΟΣ

THE TO

ΤΙΜΟΘΕΟΝ

TIMOTHY

ΕΠΙΣΤΟΛΗ ΠΡΩΤΗ

EPISTLE FIRST

THE FIRST EPISTLE
TO
TIMOTHY

A LITERAL TRANSLATION
OF THE BIBLE

CHAPTER 1

[1]Paul, an apostle of Jesus Christ according to a command of God our Savior, even *the* Lord Jesus Christ, our Hope, [2]to Timothy, a true child in *the* faith: Grace, mercy, peace from God our Father and our Lord Jesus Christ.

[3]Even as I begged you to remain *in* Ephesus —*I* going to Macedonia—that you might charge some not to teach other doctrines, [4]nor to give heed to fables and to endless genealogies—which provide doubts rather than a stewardship of God in faith—[5]but the end of the commandment is love out of a pure heart and a good conscience, and faith not pretended; [6]from which having missed the mark some turned aside to empty talking, [7]wishing to be teachers of Law, neither understanding what they say, nor about that which they strongly affirm. [8]And we know that the Law *is* good, if anyone uses it lawfully; [9]knowing this, that law is not laid down for a righteous one but for lawless and unruly ones, for ungodly and sinful ones, for unholy and profane ones, for slayers of fathers and slayers of mothers, for murderers, [10]for fornicators,

CHAPTER 1

3972 652 2424 5547 2596 2003 2316
1 Παῦλος ἀπόστολος Ἰησοῦ Χριστοῦ κατ' ἐπιταγὴν Θεοῦ
Paul an apostle of Jesus Christ according to a command of God
4990 2257 2962 2424 5547 1680
σωτῆρος ἡμῶν, καὶ Κυρίου Ἰησοῦ Χριστοῦ τῆς ἐλπίδος
the Savior of us, even (the) Lord Jesus Christ the hope
2257 5095 1103 5043 1722 4102 5485 1656 1515
2 ἡμῶν, Τιμοθέῳ γνησίῳ τέκνῳ ἐν πίστει· χάρις, ἔλεος, εἰρήνη
of us, to Timothy, a true child in (the) faith; Grace, mercy, peace
575 2316 3962 2257 2424 5547 2962
ἀπὸ Θεοῦ πατρὸς ἡμῶν καὶ Ἰησοῦ Χριστοῦ τοῦ Κυρίου
from God (the) Father of us, and Jesus Christ the Lord
2257
ἡμῶν.
of us.

2531 3870 4571 4357 1722 2181 4198
3 Καθὼς παρεκάλεσά σε προσμεῖναι ἐν Ἐφέσῳ, πορευό-
As I besought you to remain in Ephesus, (I) going
1519 3109 2443 3853 5100/3361/2085
μενος εἰς Μακεδονίαν, ἵνα παραγγείλῃς τισὶ μὴ ἑτεροδιδα-
into Macedonia, that you might enjoin certain ones not to teach
3366 4337 3454 1076 562
4 σκαλεῖν, μηδὲ προσέχειν μύθοις καὶ γενεαλογίαις ἀπεράντοις,
other doctrines, nor to attend to tales and to genealogies endless,
3748 2214 3930 3123 2228/3622 2316
αἵτινες ζητήσεις παρέχουσι μᾶλλον ἢ οἰκοδομίαν Θεοῦ τὴν
which doubts provide rather than a stewardship of God
1722/4102 5056 3852 2076 26 1537
5 ἐν πίστει—.τὸ δὲ τέλος τῆς παραγγελίας ἐστὶν ἀγάπη ἐκ
in faith. the But end of the commandment is love out of
2513 2588 4893 18 4102
καθαρᾶς καρδίας καὶ συνειδήσεως ἀγαθῆς καὶ πίστεως
a clean heart and a conscience good and faith
505 5613 5100 795 1624 1519
6 ἀνυποκρίτου· ὧν τινὲς ἀστοχήσαντες ἐξετράπησαν εἰς
unpretended, which some missing the mark turned aside to
3150 2309 1511 3547 3361 3539
7 ματαιολογίαν, θέλοντες εἶναι νομοδιδάσκαλοι, μὴ νοοῦντες
empty talking, wishing to be teachers of law, not understanding
3383/3739/3004 3383 4012 5100 1226 1492
8 μήτε ἃ λέγουσι, μήτε περὶ τίνων διαβεβαιοῦνται. οἴδαμεν
either what they say, or about what things they strongly affirm. we know
3754/2570 3551 1437/5100/846 3545 5530 1492
9 δὲ ὅτι καλὸς ὁ νόμος, ἐάν τις αὐτῷ νομίμως χρῆται, εἰδὼς
And that (is) good the law, if anyone it lawfully uses, knowing
5124 3754 1342 3551/3756/2749 459 506
τοῦτο, ὅτι δικαίῳ νόμος οὐ κεῖται, ἀνόμοις δὲ καὶ ἀνυπο-
this, that for a just one law not is laid down, for lawless but and for in-
765 268 462 952
τάκτοις, ἀσεβέσι καὶ ἁμαρτωλοῖς, ἀνοσίοις καὶ βεβήλοις,
subordinate, for ungodly and sinful ones, for unholy and profane ones,
3964 3389 409 4205 733
10 πατραλῴαις καὶ μητραλῴαις, ἀνδροφόνοις, πόρνοις, ἀρσενο-
for father-slayers and mother-slayers, for men-slayers, for fornicators, for

for homosexuals, for slave-traders, for liars, for perjurers, and if any other thing opposes sound teaching, 11according to the gospel of the glory of the blessed God *with* which I was entrusted.

12And I have thanks to Him empowering me, our Lord Jesus Christ, because He counted me faithful, putting *me* into the ministry, 13the *one* who before was a blasphemer, and a persecutor, and insolent; but I obtained mercy, because being ignorant I did *it* in unbelief. 14But the grace of our Lord abounded exceedingly with faith and love in Christ Jesus. 15Faithful *is* the word, and worthy of all acceptance, that Christ Jesus came into the world to save sinners, of whom I am chief. 16But for this reason I obtained mercy, that in me first Jesus Christ might show forth all long-suffering, for an example to those being about to believe on Him to everlasting life. 17Now to the King eternal, incorruptible, invisible, *the* only wise God, *be* honor and glory forever and ever. Amen.

18This charge I commit to you, *my* child Timothy, according to the prophecies going before as to you, that you might war the good warfare by them, 19having faith and a good conscience, which some having thrust away made shipwreck concerning the faith; 20of whom are Hymeneus and Alexander, whom I delivered to Satan, that they may be taught not to blaspheme.

405 5583 1965 = 1536 =
κοίταις, ἀνδραποδισταῖς, ψεύσταις, ἐπιόρκοις, καὶ εἴ τι
homosexuals, for slave-traders, for liars, for perjurers, and if any

2087 5198 1319 480 2596
11 ἕτερον τῇ ὑγιαινούσῃ διδασκαλίᾳ ἀντίκειται, κατὰ τὸ
other thing the sound teaching opposes, according to the

2098 1391 3107 2316/3739/ 4100
εὐαγγέλιον τῆς δόξης τοῦ μακαρίου Θεοῦ, ὃ ἐπιστεύθην
gospel of the glory of the blessed God, which was entrusted (with)

1473
ἐγώ.
I

5485 2192 1743 3165 5547 2424
12 Καὶ χάριν ἔχω τῷ ἐνδυναμώσαντί με Χριστῷ Ἰησοῦ τῷ
And thanks I have to the (One) empowering me, Christ Jesus the

2962 2257 3754 4103/3165/ 2233 5087 1519 1248
Κυρίῳ ἡμῶν, ὅτι πιστόν με ἡγήσατο, θέμενος εἰς διακονίαν,
Lord of us, because faithful me He counted, putting (me) into ministry

4386 5607 989 1376 5197
13 τὸν πρότερον ὄντα βλάσφημον καὶ διώκτην καὶ ὑβριστήν·
the (one) before being a blasphemer and a peresecutor and insolent;

235 1653 3754 50 4160 1722 570 5250
14 ἀλλ' ἠλεήθην, ὅτι ἀγνοῶν ἐποίησα ἐν ἀπιστίᾳ· ὑπερ-
but I obtained mercy, because being ignorant I did (it) in unbelief, super-

5485 2962 2257 3326 4102
επλεόνασε δὲ ἡ χάρις τοῦ Κυρίου ἡμῶν μετὰ πίστεως καὶ
abounded the grace of the Lord, of us with faith and

26 1722 5547 2424 4103 3056 3956
15 ἀγάπης τῆς ἐν Χριστῷ Ἰησοῦ. πιστὸς ὁ λόγος καὶ πάσης
love in Christ Jesus. Faithful (is) the word and of all

594 514 3754 5547 2424 2064/1519 2889
ἀποδοχῆς ἄξιος, ὅτι Χριστὸς Ἰησοῦς ἦλθεν εἰς τὸν κόσμον
acceptance worthy, that Christ Jesus came into the world

268 4982 3739 4413 1510/1473/235/1223 5124
16 ἁμαρτωλοὺς σῶσαι, ὧν πρῶτός εἰμι ἐγώ· ἀλλὰ διὰ τοῦτο
sinners to save, of whom chief am I; but because of this

1653 2443/1722/1698/ 4413 1731 2424 5547
ἠλεήθην, ἵνα ἐν ἐμοὶ πρώτῳ ἐνδείξηται Ἰησοῦς Χριστὸς τὴν
I obtained mercy. that in me first might show forth Jesus Christ

3115 4314 5296 3195
πᾶσαν μακροθυμίαν, πρὸς ὑποτύπωσιν τῶν μελλόντων
all long-suffering, for a pattern to those being about

4100 1909 846/1519/2222 166 935
17 πιστεύειν ἐπ' αὐτῷ εἰς ζωὴν αἰώνιον. τῷ δὲ βασιλεῖ τῶν
to believe on Him for life everlasting. to the Now King of the

165 862 517 3441 4680 2316 5092 1391
αἰώνων, ἀφθάρτῳ, ἀοράτῳ, μόνῳ σοφῷ Θεῷ, τιμὴ καὶ δόξα
ages, incorruptible, invisible, (the) only wise God, (be) honor and glory

1519 165 165 281
εἰς τοὺς αἰῶνας τῶν αἰώνων. ἀμήν.
to the ages of the ages. Amen.

5026 3852 3908 4671 5043
18 Ταύτην τὴν παραγγελίαν παρατίθεμαί σοι, τέκνον
This charge I commit to you, child,

5095 2596 4254 1909/4571 4394 2443
Τιμόθεε, κατα τὰς προαγούσας ἐπὶ σε προφητείας, ἵνα
Timothy, according to the going before as to you prophecies that

4754 1722 846 2570 4752 2192 4102
19 στρατεύῃ ἐν αὐταῖς τὴν καλὴν στρατείαν, ἔχων πίστιν καὶ
you might war by them the good warfare, having faith and

18 4893 3739/5100 683 4012 4102
ἀγαθὴν συνείδησιν, ἥν τινες ἀπωσάμενοι περὶ τὴν πίστιν
a good conscience, which some having thrust away concerning the faith

3489 3739 2076 5211 223 3739
20 ἐναυάγησαν· ὧν ἐστιν Ὑμέναιος καὶ Ἀλέξανδρος, οὓς
made shipwreck; of whom is Hymeneus and Alexander, whom

3860 4567 2443 3811 3361 987
παρέδωκα τῷ Σατανᾷ, ἵνα παιδευθῶσι μὴ βλασφημεῖν.
I delivered to Satan, that they may be taught not to blaspheme.

CHAPTER 2

[1]First of all, then, I exhort *that* petitions, prayers, intercessions, *and* thanksgivings be made on behalf of all men; [2]for kings and all the ones being in high position, that we may lead a tranquil and quiet existence in all godliness and reverence. [3]For this *is* good and acceptable before God our deliverer, [4]who desires all men to be delivered, and to come to a full knowledge of truth. [5]For God *is* one, also *there is* one Mediator of God and of men, *the* Man Christ Jesus, [6]the *One* having given Himself a ransom on behalf of all, the testimony *to be given* in its own times; [7]to which I was appointed a herald and apostle—I speak the truth in Christ, I do not lie—a teacher of *the* nations, in faith and truth.

[8]Therefore, I desire the men to pray in every place, lifting up holy hands without wrath and doubting. [9]Likewise also the women to adorn themselves in decent clothing, with modesty and sensibleness, not with plaiting, or gold, or pearls, or expensive garments, [10]but what becomes women professing fear of God, through good works.

[11]Let a woman learn in silence, in all subjection. [12]But I do not allow a woman to teach, nor to exercise authority *over* a man, but to be in silence. [13]For Adam was formed first, then Eve. [14]And Adam was not deceived, but the woman being deceived has come to be in transgression; [15]but she will be delivered through the bearing of children, if they remain in

CHAPTER 2

3870 3767 4412 3956 4160 1162 4335
1 Παρακαλῶ οὖν πρῶτον πάντων ποιεῖσθαι δεήσεις, προσ-
I exhort Therefore firstly of all to be made petitions, prayers,
1783 2169 5228 3956 444
ευχάς, ἐντεύξεις, εὐχαριστίας, ὑπὲρ πάντων ἀνθρώπων·
intercessions, thanksgivings on behalf of all men;
5228 935 3956 1722 5247 5607 2443
2 ὑπὲρ βασιλέων καὶ πάντων τῶν ἐν ὑπεροχῇ ὄντων, ἵνα
for kings and all those in high position being, that
2263 2272 979 1236 1722 3956 2150
ἤρεμον καὶ ἡσύχιον βίον διάγωμεν ἐν πάσῃ εὐσεβείᾳ καὶ
a tranquil and quiet existence we may lead in all godliness and
4587 5124 1063 2570 587 1799
3 σεμνότητι. τοῦτο γὰρ καλὸν καὶ ἀπόδεκτον ἐνώπιον τοῦ
reverence. this (is) For good and acceptable before the
4990 2257 2316/3739/3956 444 2309 4982
4 σωτῆρος ἡμῶν Θεοῦ, ὃς πάντας ἀνθρώπους θέλει σωθῆναι
deliverer of us, God, who all men desires to be delivered
1519 1922 225 2064 1520/1063 2316 1519
5 καὶ εἰς ἐπίγνωσιν ἀληθείας ἐλθεῖν. εἷς γὰρ Θεός, εἷς καὶ
and to a full knowledge of truth to come. one For God (is), one also
3316 2316 444 444 5547 2424
μεσίτης Θεοῦ καὶ ἀνθρώπων, ἄνθρωπος Χριστὸς Ἰησοῦς,
Mediator of God and of men, (the) man Christ Jesus,
1325 1438 487 5228 3956 3142
6 ὁ δοὺς ἑαυτὸν ἀντίλυτρον ὑπὲρ πάντων, τὸ μαρτύριον
He having given Himself a ransom on behalf of all, the testimony
2540 2398 1519 5087 1473 2783 652 225
7 καιροῖς ἰδίοις, εἰς ὃ ἐτέθην ἐγὼ κήρυξ καὶ ἀπόστολος (ἀλή-
in its own times; to which was appointed I a herald and apostle — truth
3004/1722/ 5547 3756 5574 1320 1484/1722
θειαν λέγω ἐν Χριστῷ, οὐ ψεύδομαι), διδάσκαλος ἐθνῶν ἐν
I say in Christ, do not I lie — a teacher of nations in
4102 225
πίστει καὶ ἀληθείᾳ.
faith and truth.

1014 3767 4336 435 1722 3956 5117
8 Βούλομαι οὖν προσεύχεσθαι τοὺς ἄνδρας ἐν παντὶ τόπῳ,
I desire Therefore to pray the men in every place,
1869 3741 5495 5565 3709 1261
ἐπαίροντας ὁσίους χεῖρας, χωρὶς ὀργῆς καὶ διαλογισμοῦ.
lifting up holy hands, without wrath and doubting.
5615 1135 1722/ 2689 2887 3326 127
9 ὡσαύτως καὶ τὰς γυναῖκας ἐν καταστολῇ κοσμίῳ, μετὰ αἰδοῦς
Likewise also the women in clothing decent, with modesty
1722 4997 2885 1438 3361// 4117 2228/ 5557
καὶ σωφροσύνης, κοσμεῖν ἑαυτάς, μὴ ἐν πλέγμασιν, ἢ χρυσῷ,
and sensibleness to adorn themselves, not with plaiting, or gold,
2228/3135 2228 2441 4185 235 3739/4241
10 ἢ μαργαρίταις, ἢ ἱματισμῷ πολυτελεῖ, ἀλλ' (ὃ πρέπει
or pearls, or garments expensive, but what becomes
1135 1861 2317 1223 2041 18
γυναιξὶν ἐπαγγελλομέναις θεοσέβειαν) δι' ἔργων ἀγαθῶν.
women professing fear of God, by means of works good.
1135 1722/ 2271 3129 1722 3956 5292 1135
11 γυνὴ ἐν ἡσυχίᾳ μανθανέτω ἐν πάσῃ ὑποταγῇ. γυναικὶ δὲ
A woman in silence let learn in all subjection. a woman But
1321 3756 2010 3761 831 435 235 1511
12 διδάσκειν οὐκ ἐπιτρέπω, οὐδὲ αὐθεντεῖν ἀνδρός, ἀλλ' εἶναι
to teach not I allow, nor to exercise authority of a man, but to be
1722 2271 76 1063 4413 4111 1534 2096
13 ἐν ἡσυχίᾳ. Ἀδὰμ γὰρ πρῶτος ἐπλάσθη, εἶτα Εὕα· καὶ
in silence. Adam For first was formed, then Eve. And
76 3756 538 1135 538 1722 3847
14 Ἀδὰμ οὐκ ἠπατήθη, ἡ δὲ γυνὴ ἀπατηθεῖσα ἐν παραβάσει
Adam not was deceived, the but woman being deceived in transgression
1096 4982 1223 5042 1437 3306 1711
15 γέγονε· σωθήσεται δὲ διὰ τῆς τεκνογονίας, ἐὰν μείνωσιν ἐν
has become; she will be saved but through the childbearing, if they remain in

faith and love and holiness,
with sensibleness.

CHAPTER 3

[1]Faithful *is* the word: If
anyone reaches out to overseership, he desires a good
work. [2]Then the overseer
must be blameless, hus-
band of one wife, temper-
ate, sensible, modest, hospitable, apt at teaching;
[3]not a drinker, not a contentious one, not greedy of
ill gain—but gentle, not
quarrelsome, not loving
money; [4]ruling his own
house well, having children
in subjection with all reverence—[5]but if anyone
does not know to rule *his*
own house, how will he
care for a church of God?—
[6]not a novice, lest being
puffed up he may fall into
the judgment of the Devil.
[7]But he must also have a
good witness from those
outside, that he not fall into
reproach, and *into* a snare
of the Devil.

[8]Likewise, deacons *to*
be reverent, not double-
tongued, not addicted to
much wine, not greedy of ill
gain, [9]having the mystery
of the faith with a pure
conscience. [10]And also let
these be tested first, then
let them serve, being
blameless.[11]Likewise, *their*
wives *to be* reverent, not
slanderers, temperate, faithful in all things. [12]Let
deacons be husbands of
one wife, ruling *their* own
households and children
well. [13]For those having
served well gain a good
grade for themselves, and
much boldness in faith,
those in Christ Jesus.
[14]I write these things to
you, hoping to come to you
shortly. [15]But if I delay, that
you may know how to be-
have in the house of God,

4102 26 38 3326 4997
πίστει καὶ ἀγάπη καὶ ἁγιασμῷ μετὰ σωφροσυνης.
faith and love and holiness with sensibleness.

CHAPTER 3

4103 3056 =1536= 1984 3713 2570 2041
1 Πιστὸς ὁ λόγος· Εἴ τις ἐπισκοπῆς ὀρέγεται, καλοῦ ἔργου
Faithful (is) the word: If anyone overseership aspires to, a good work
1937 1163/3767 1985 423 1511 3391
2 ἐπιθυμεῖ. δεῖ οὖν τὸν ἐπίσκοπον ἀνεπίληπτον εἶναι, μιᾶς
he desires. It behoves, then, the overseer without reproach to be, of one
1135 435 3524 4998 2887 5382
γυναικὸς ἄνδρα, νηφάλιον, σώφρονα, κόσμιον, φιλόξενον,
wife husband, temperate, sensible, modest, hospitable,
1317 3361 3943 3361 4131 3361 146
3 διδακτικόν· μὴ πάροινον, μὴ πλήκτην, μὴ αἰσχροκερδῆ,
apt at teaching, not a drinker, not a striker, not greedy of ill gain,
235 1933 269 866 2398 3624 2573
4 ἀλλ' ἐπιεικῆ, ἄμαχον, ἀφιλάργυρον· τοῦ ἰδίου οἴκου καλῶς
but gentle, not quarrelsome, not avaricious, the own house well
4291 5043 2192 1722 5292 3326 3956
προϊστάμενον, τέκνα ἔχοντα ἐν ὑποταγῇ μετὰ πάσης
ruling, children having in subjection with all
4587 1487 5100 2398 3624 4291 3756 1492
5 σεμνότητος (εἰ δέ τις τοῦ ἰδίου οἴκου προστῆναι οὐκ οἶδε,
reverence — if but anyone the own house to rule not knows,
4459 1577 2316 1959 3361 3504 2443/3361
6 πῶς ἐκκλησίας Θεοῦ ἐπιμελήσεται ;)· μὴ νεόφυτον, ἵνα μὴ
how a church of God will he care for? — not a novice, lest
5187 1519 2917 1706 1228 1163 846
7 τυφωθεὶς εἰς κρίμα ἐμπέσῃ τοῦ διαβόλου. δεῖ δὲ αὐτὸν καὶ
being puffed up into judgment he fall of the Devil. it behoves And him also
3141 2570 2192 575 1855 2443/3361/1519/ 3680
μαρτυρίαν καλὴν ἔχειν ἀπὸ τῶν ἔξωθεν, ἵνα μὴ εἰς ὀνειδισμὸν
a witness good to have from those outside, lest into reproach
1706 3803 1228 1249 5615
8 ἐμπέσῃ καὶ παγίδα τοῦ διαβόλου. διακόνους ὡσαύτως
he fall, and (into) a snare of the Devil. deacons Likewise
4586 3361 1351 3361 3631 4183 4337 3361
σεμνούς, μὴ διλόγους, μὴ οἴνῳ πολλῷ προσέχοντας, μὴ
reverent (to be), not double-tongued, not wine to much addicted, not
146 2192 3466 4102 1722 2513
9 αἰσχροκερδεῖς, ἔχοντας τὸ μυστήριον τῆς πίστεως ἐν καθαρᾷ
greedy of ill gain, having the mystery of the faith with a clean
4893 3778 1381 4412 1534
10 συνειδήσει. καὶ οὗτοι δὲ δοκιμαζέσθωσαν πρῶτον, εἶτα
conscience. also these And let be tested first, then
1247 410 5607 1135 5615
11 διακονείτωσαν, ἀνέγκλητοι ὄντες. γυναῖκας ὡσαύτως
let them minister, without reproach being. wives Likewise
4586/3361/ 1228 3524 4103 1722/3956 1249
12 σεμνάς, μὴ διαβόλους, νηφαλίους, πιστὰς ἐν πᾶσι. διάκονοι
reverent (to be), not slanderers, temperate, faithful in all things. deacons
2077 3391 1135 435 5043 2573 4291
ἔστωσαν μιᾶς γυναικὸς ἄνδρες, τέκνων καλῶς προϊστάμενοι
Let be of one wife husbands children well ruling
2398 3624 1063 2573 1247 898
13 καὶ τῶν ἰδίων οἴκων. οἱ γὰρ καλῶς διακονήσαντες βαθμὸν
and the own households. those For well having ministered a grade
1438 2570 4046 4183 3954 1722
ἑαυτοῖς καλὸν περιποιοῦνται, καὶ πολλὴν παρρησίαν ἐν
for themselves good gain, and much boldness in
4102 1722 5547 2424
πίστει τῇ ἐν Χριστῷ Ἰησοῦ.
faith, those in Christ Jesus.
5023 4671 1125 1679 2064 4314/4571/ 5032 1437
14 Ταῦτά σοι γράφω, ἐλπίζων ἐλθεῖν πρός σε τάχιον· ἐὰν δὲ
These things to you I write, hoping to come to you shortly; if but
1019 2443 1492 4459/1163/1722/3624/2316 390
15 βραδύνω, ἵνα εἰδῇς πῶς δεῖ ἐν οἴκῳ Θεοῦ ἀναστρέφεσθαι,
I delay, that you may know how must in (the) house of God to behave

which is *the* church of the living God, *the* pillar and foundation of the truth. [16]And confessedly, great is the mystery of godliness: God was manifested in flesh, was justified in Spirit, was seen by angels, was proclaimed among nations, was believed on in *the* world, was taken up in glory.

CHAPTER 4

[1]But the Spirit expressly says that in the latter times some will depart from the faith, cleaving to deceiving spirits and teachings of demons, [2]in hypocrisy of liars, being seared in *their* own conscience, [3]forbidding to marry, *saying* to abstain from foods, which God created for partaking with thanksgiving by the believers, and *those* knowing the truth. [4]Because every creature of God *is* good and nothing to be thrust away, but having been received with thanksgiving; [5]for through God's word and prayerfully coming together, it is sanctified. [6]Having suggested these things to the brothers, you will be a good minister of Jesus Christ, having been nourished by the words of faith, and by the good teaching which you have followed. [7]But refuse the profane and old-womanish tales. And exercise yourself to godliness. [8]For bodily exercise is profitable for a little, but godliness is profitable to all things, having promise of the present life, and of that coming. [9]Faithful *is* the word, and worthy of all acceptance; [10]for to this we also labor and *are* reproached, because we hope on *the* living God,

3748 2076 1577 2316 2198 4769 1477
ἥτις ἐστὶν ἐκκλησία Θεοῦ ζῶντος, στύλος καὶ ἑδραίωμα τῆς
which is (the) church of God (the) living, pillar and foundation of the
225 3672 3173 2076 2150
16 ἀληθείας. καὶ ὁμολογουμένως μέγα ἐστὶ τὸ τῆς εὐσεβείας
truth. And confessedly, great is the of godliness
3466 2316 5319 1722 4561 1344 1722 4151
μυστήριον· Θεὸς ἐφανερώθη ἐν σαρκί, ἐδικαιώθη ἐν πνεύματι,
mystery, God was manifested in flesh, was justified in spirit,
3700 32 2784 1722 1484 4100/1722/ 2889
ὤφθη ἀγγέλοις, ἐκηρύχθη ἐν ἔθνεσιν, ἐπιστεύθη ἐν κόσμῳ,
was seen by angels, was proclaimed among nations, was believed in (the) world,
353 1722 1391
ἀνελήφθη ἐν δόξῃ.
was taken up in glory.

CHAPTER 4

4151 4490 3004 3754/1722/ 5306 2540 868
1 Τὸ δὲ Πνεῦμα ῥητῶς λέγει, ὅτι ἐν ὑστέροις καιροῖς ἀποστή-
the But Spirit in words says that in latter times will
5100 4102 4337 4151 4108
σονταί τινες τῆς πίστεως, προσέχοντες πνεύμασι πλάνοις
depart from some the faith, adhering to spirits deceiving
1319 1140 1722 5272 5573
2 καὶ διδασκαλίαις δαιμονίων, ἐν ὑποκρίσει ψευδολόγων,
and teachings of demons, in hypocrisy of liars,
2743 2398 4893 2967 1060
3 κεκαυτηριασμένων τὴν ἰδίαν συνείδησιν, κωλυόντων γαμεῖν,
having been seared on the own conscience, forbidding to marry,
567 1033 3739 2316 2936 1519 3336 3326
ἀπέχεσθαι βρωμάτων, ἃ ὁ Θεὸς ἔκτισεν εἰς μετάληψιν μετὰ
(saying) to abstain from foods which God created for partaking with
2169 4103 1921 225 3754
4 εὐχαριστίας τοῖς πιστοῖς καὶ ἐπεγνωκόσι τὴν ἀλήθειαν. ὅτι
thanksgiving by the believers and (those) knowing the truth. Because
3956 2938 2316 2570 3762 579 3326 2169
πᾶν κτίσμα Θεοῦ καλόν, καὶ οὐδὲν ἀπόβλητον, μετὰ εὐχαρι-
every creature of God (is) good, and nothing to be put away, with thanks-
2983 37 1063/1223/3056 2316
5 στίας λαμβανόμενον· ἁγιάζεται γὰρ διὰ λόγου Θεοῦ καὶ
giving having been received; it is sanctified for through a word of God and
1783
ἐντεύξεως.
prayerful intercourse.
5023 5294 80 2570 2071 1249
6 Ταῦτα ὑποτιθέμενος τοῖς ἀδελφοῖς καλὸς ἔσῃ διάκονος
These things having suggested to the brothers, good you will be minister
2424 5547 1789 3056 4102
Ἰησοῦ Χριστοῦ, ἐντρεφόμενος τοῖς λόγοις τῆς πίστεως, καὶ
of Jesus Christ, being nourished by the words of the faith, and
2570 1319 3739 3877 952
7 τῆς καλῆς διδασκαλίας ᾗ παρηκολούθηκας. τοὺς δὲ βεβήλους
by the good teaching which you have followed. the But profane
1126 3454 3868 1128 4572 4314
καὶ γραώδεις μύθους παραιτοῦ. γύμναζε δὲ σεαυτὸν πρὸς
and old-womanish tales refuse. exercise And yourself to
2150 1063 4984 1129 4314 3641 2076
8 εὐσέβειαν· ἡ γὰρ σωματικὴ γυμνασία πρὸς ὀλίγον ἐστὶν
godliness. For bodily exercise for a little is
5624 2150 4314 3956 5624 2076 1860
ὠφέλιμος· ἡ δὲ εὐσέβεια πρὸς πάντα ὠφέλιμός ἐστιν, ἐπαγ-
profitable, but godliness to all things profitable is,
2192 2222 3568 3195 4103
9 γελίαν ἔχουσα ζωῆς τῆς νῦν καὶ τῆς μελλούσης. πιστὸς ὁ
promise having life of the now and of the coming. Faithful (is) the
3056 3956 594 514 1519/5124/1063 2872
10 λόγος καὶ πάσης ἀποδοχῆς ἄξιος. εἰς τοῦτο γὰρ καὶ κοπιῶ-
word and of all acceptance worthy. to this For also we labor
3679 3754 1679 1909 2316 2198 3739/2076
μεν καὶ ὀνειδιζόμεθα, ὅτι ἠλπίκαμεν ἐπὶ Θεῷ ζῶντι, ὅς ἐστι
and (are) reproached because we have set hope on God (the) living, who is

who is deliverer of all men, especially of believers. [11]Enjoin and teach these things.

[12]Let no one despise your youth, but become an example of the believers in word, in conduct, in love, in spirit, in faith, in purity. [13]Until I come, attend to reading, to exhortation, to teaching. [14]Do not be neglectful of the gift in you, which was given to you through prophecy, with laying on of the hands of the elderhood. [15]Meditate on these things; be in these things in order that your progress may be plain to all. [16]Hold on to yourself and to the teaching; continue in them; for doing this, you will both deliver yourself and those hearing you.

CHAPTER 5

[1]Do not sharply rebuke an elder, but exhort as a father, *and* younger ones as brothers; [2]elder women as mothers; younger women as sisters in all purity. [3]Honor widows, the *ones* really being widows; [4]but if any widow has children or grandchildren, let them learn first to be godly to their own house, and to make a return payment to *their* forebears; for this is good and pleasing before God. [5]But she being really a widow, even having been left alone, has set *her* hope on God, and continues in petitions and prayers night and day. [6]But she who lives in self-pleasure has died *while* living. [7]And enjoin these things that they may be blameless. [8]But if anyone does not provide for *his* own, and especially *his* family, he has denied the faith, and is worse than an unbeliever. [9]Let a widow be enrolled having become not less than sixty years, wife of one man, [10]being witnessed by good works; if

4990 3956 444 3122 4103 3853
11 σωτὴρ παντων ἀνθρώπων, μάλιστα πιστῶν. παράγγελλε
deliverer of all men, especially of believers. Enjoin
5023 1321 3367 4675 3503 2706
12 ταῦτα καὶ δίδασκε. μηδείς σου τῆς νεότητος καταφρονείτω,
these things and teach. no one of you the youth Let despise,
235 5179 1096 4103 1722 3056/1722/ 391 1722
ἀλλὰ τύπος γίνου τῶν πιστῶν ἐν λόγῳ, ἐν ἀναστροφῇ, ἐν
but an example become of the believers in word, in conduct, in
26 1722 4151 1722 4102 1722/47 2193 2064
13 ἀγάπῃ, ἐν πνεύματι, ἐν πίστει, ἐν ἁγνείᾳ. ἕως ἔρχομαι,
love, in spirit, in faith, in purity. Until I come,
4337 320 3874 1319 3361
14 πρόσεχε τῇ ἀναγνώσει, τῇ παρακλήσει, τῇ διδασκαλίᾳ. μὴ
attend to the reading, to the exhortation, to the teaching. Do not
272 1722/4671 5486 3739 1325 4675/1223 4394
ἀμέλει τοῦ ἐν σοὶ χαρίσματος, ὃ ἐδόθη σοι διὰ προφητείας
be neglectful of the in you gift, which was given you via prophecy
3326 1936 5495 4244 5023 3191
15 μετὰ ἐπιθέσεως τῶν χειρῶν τοῦ πρεσβυτερίου. ταῦτα μελέτα,
with laying on of the hands of the elderhood. these things Give care to
1722/5125 2468/2443/4675 4297 5318/5600/1722/3956 1907
16 ἐν τούτοις ἴσθι, ἵνα σου ἡ προκοπὴ φανερὰ ᾖ ἐν πᾶσιν. ἔπεχε
in these things be, that of you the progress plain may be to all. Hold on
4572 1319 1961 846 5124/1063 4160
σεαυτῷ καὶ τῇ διδασκαλίᾳ. ἐπίμενε αὐτοῖς· τοῦτο γὰρ ποιῶν
to yourself and to the teaching; continue in them; this for doing
4572 4982 191 4675
καὶ σεαυτὸν σώσεις καὶ τοὺς ἀκούοντάς σου.
both yourself you will deliver, and those hearing you.

CHAPTER 5

4245 3361 1969 235 3870 5613 3962
1 Πρεσβυτέρῳ μὴ ἐπιπλήξῃς, ἀλλὰ παρακάλει ὡς πατέρα·
an older man Do not rebuke, but exhort as a father;
3501 5613 80 4245 5613 3384 3501
2 νεωτέρους, ὡς ἀδελφούς· πρεσβυτέρας, ὡς μητέρας· νεωτέρας,
younger ones as brothers; older women as mothers; younger women
5613 80 1722/3956 47 5503 5091 3689 5503
3 ὡς ἀδελφάς, ἐν πάσῃ ἁγνείᾳ. χήρας τίμα τὰς ὄντως χήρας.
as sisters, in all purity. widows Honor, those being really widows.
1487/5100/5503 5043 1549 2192 3129 4412
4 εἰ δέ τις χήρα τέκνα ἢ ἔκγονα ἔχει, μανθανέτωσαν πρῶτον
if But any widow children or grandchildren has, let them learn firstly
2398 3624 2151 287 591 4269
τὸν ἴδιον οἶκον εὐσεβεῖν, καὶ ἀμοιβὰς ἀποδιδόναι τοῖς προγό-
the (one) own house to be godly to, and repayments return to the fore-
5124/1063/2076/2570 587 1799 2316
νοις· τοῦτο γάρ ἐστι καλὸν καὶ ἀπόδεκτον ἐνώπιον τοῦ Θεοῦ.
bears; this for is good and acceptable before God.
3689 5503 3443 1679 1909 2316
5 ἡ δὲ ὄντως χήρα καὶ μεμονωμένη ἤλπικεν ἐπὶ τὸν Θεόν,
the But being really widow even having been left has set hope on God,
4357 1162 4335 3571
καὶ προσμένει ταῖς δεήσεσι καὶ ταῖς προσευχαῖς νυκτὸς καὶ
and continues in the petitions and the prayers night and
2250 4684 2198 2348 5023 3853
6 ἡμέρας. ἡ δὲ σπαταλῶσα, ζῶσα τέθνηκε. καὶ ταῦτα παράγ-
7 day. the But (one) living in self-pleasure (while) living has died. And these things enjoin
2443/423 5600/1487 5100 2398
8 γελλε, ἵνα ἀνεπίληπτοι ὦσιν. εἰ δέ τις τῶν ἰδίων καὶ
that without reproach they may be. if But anyone the own, and
3122 3609 3756 4306 4102 720
μάλιστα τῶν οἰκείων οὐ προνοεῖ, τὴν πίστιν ἤρνηται, καὶ
especially the family, not provides for, the faith he has denied, and
2076 571 5501 5503 2639 3361 1640 2094
9 ἔστιν ἀπίστου χείρων. χήρα καταλεγέσθω μὴ ἔλαττον ἐτῶν
is an unbeliever worse than. A widow let be enrolled not less (than) years
1835 1096 1520 435 1135/1722/2041 2570
10 ἑξήκοντα, γεγονυῖα ἑνὸς ἀνδρὸς γυνή, ἐν ἔργοις καλοῖς
sixty having become, of one man wife, by works good

she brought up children; if she hosted strangers; if she washed the feet of the saints; if she relieved afflicted ones; if she followed after every good work.

[11]But refuse younger widows; for whenever they grow lustful against Christ, they desire to marry, [12]having guilt because they set aside the first faith; [13]and with it all, they also learn *to be* idle, going around the houses, and not only idle but also gossips and busy-bodies, speaking the things not proper. [14]Therefore, I desire *the* young women to marry, to bear children, to rule the house, giving no occasion to the adversary on account of reproach. [15]For some already have turned aside behind Satan. [16]If any believing man or believing woman has widows, let them relieve *them*; and do not burden the church, that it may relieve those being really widows.

[17]Let the elders who take the lead well be counted worthy of double honor, especially those laboring in word and teaching. [18]For the Scripture says, "You shall not muzzle an ox treading out *grain*"—and, "The laborer *is* worthy of his pay."

[19]Do not receive an accusation against an elder unless on *the testimony of* two or three witnesses. [20]The ones sinning before all, rebuke; that the rest also may have fear. [21]I solemnly witness before God and *the* Lord Jesus Christ, and the elect angels, that you should guard these things without prejudice, doing nothing by way of partiality.

[22]Lay hands quickly on no one, nor share in *the* sins of others. Keep yourself pure. [23]No longer drink water, but

3140 1487 5044 1487 3580 1487 40
μαρτυρουμένη, εἰ ἐτεκνοτρόφησεν, εἰ ἐξενοδόχησεν, εἰ ἁγίων
being witnessed, if she brought up children, if she hosted strangers, if of saints
4228 3538 1487 2346 1884 1487 3956 2041
πόδας ἔνιψεν, εἰ θλιβομένοις ἐπήρκεσεν, εἰ παντὶ ἔργῳ
feet she washed, if afflicted ones she relieved, if every work
18 1872 3501 5503 3868 3752
11 ἀγαθῷ ἐπηκολούθησε. νεωτέρας δὲ χήρας παραιτοῦ· ὅταν
good she followed after. younger But widows refuse; whenever
1063 2691 5547 1060 2309
γὰρ καταστρηνιάσωσι τοῦ Χριστοῦ, γαμεῖν θέλουσιν,
for they grow lustful against Christ, to marry they desire,
2192 2917 3754 4413 4102 114 260
12 ἔχουσαι κρίμα, ὅτι τὴν πρώτην πίστιν ἠθέτησαν. ἅμα δὲ
having (a) judgment, because the first faith they set aside; withal and
692 3129 4022 3614 3756 3440
13 καὶ ἀργαὶ μανθάνουσι, περιερχόμεναι τὰς οἰκίας, οὐ μόνον
also idle they learn (to be), going around the houses, not only
692 235 5397 4021 2980
δὲ ἀργαί, ἀλλὰ καὶ φλύαροι καὶ περίεργοι, λαλοῦσαι τὰ
and idle, but also gossips and busybodies, speaking the things
3361 1163 1014 3767 3501 1060 5041
14 μὴ δέοντα. βούλομαι οὖν νεωτέρας γαμεῖν, τεκνογονεῖν,
not proper. I will, therefore, younger women to marry, to bear children,
3616 3367 874 1325 480
οἰκοδεσποτεῖν, μηδεμίαν ἀφορμὴν διδόναι τῷ ἀντικειμένῳ
to rule the house, no occasion to give to the (one) opposing
3059 5484/ 2235/ 1063/ 5100 1624 3694
15 λοιδορίας χάριν. ἤδη γάρ τινες ἐξετράπησαν ὀπίσω τοῦ
reproach on account of. already For some turned aside behind
4567 = 1536= 4103/2228/4103/2192/5503 1884 846
16 Σατανᾶ. εἴ τις πιστὸς ἢ πιστὴ ἔχει χήρας, ἐπαρκείτω αὐταῖς,
Satan. If any believing man or believing woman has widows, relieve them,
3361 916 1577 2443 3689 5503 1884
καὶ μὴ βαρείσθω ἡ ἐκκλησία, ἵνα ταῖς ὄντως χήραις ἐπαρ-
and not burden the church, that those being really widows it may
κέσῃ.
relieve.

2573 4291 4245 1362 5092 515
17 Οἱ καλῶς προεστῶτες πρεσβύτεροι διπλῆς τιμῆς ἀξιού-
The well ruling elders of double honor count
3122 2872/1722/3056 1319
σθωσαν, μάλιστα οἱ κοπιῶντες ἐν λόγῳ καὶ διδασκαλίᾳ.
worthy, expecially those laboring in word and teaching.
3004/1063 1124 1016 248 3756 5392 514
18 λέγει γὰρ ἡ γραφή, Βοῦν ἀλοῶντα οὐ φιμώσεις. καί, Ἄξιος
says For the Scripture: An ox threshing not you shall muzzle. and, Worthy
2040 3408 848 2596 4245 2724
19 ὁ ἐργάτης τοῦ μισθοῦ αὐτοῦ. κατὰ πρεσβυτέρου κατη-
the workman of the pay of him. Against an elder
3361 3858 1623 =1508=1909/1417 5140 3144
γορίαν μὴ παραδέχου, ἐκτὸς εἰ μὴ ἐπὶ δύο ἢ τριῶν μαρτύ-
accusation not receive, unless on two or three wit-
264 1799 3956 1651 2443
20 ρων. τοὺς ἁμαρτάνοντας ἐνώπιον πάντων ἔλεγχε, ἵνα καὶ
nesses. Those sinning before all, reprove; that also
3062 5401 2192 1263 1799 2316
21 οἱ λοιποὶ φόβον ἔχωσι. διαμαρτύρομαι ἐνώπιον τοῦ Θεοῦ
the rest fear may have. I solemnly witness before God
2962 2424 5547 1588 32 2443
καὶ Κυρίου Ἰησοῦ Χριστοῦ καὶ τῶν ἐκλεκτῶν ἀγγέλων, ἵνα
and (the) Lord Jesus Christ, and the elect angels, that
5023 5442 5565 4299 3367 4160 2596
ταῦτα φυλάξῃς χωρὶς προκρίματος, μηδὲν ποιῶν κατὰ
these things you guard without prejudice, nothing doing by way of
4346 5495 5030 3367 2007 3366 2841
22 πρόσκλισιν. χεῖρας ταχέως μηδενὶ ἐπιτίθει, μηδὲ κοινώνει
partiality. hands quickly no one Lay on, nor share in
266 245 4572 53 5083 3371 5202
23 ἁμαρτίαις ἀλλοτρίαις· σεαυτὸν ἁγνὸν τήρει. μηκέτι ὑδροπό-
sins of others; yourself pure keep. No longer drink

use a little wine on account of your stomach and your frequent infirmities. 24The sins of some men are plain before, going before to judgment; but indeed some follow after. 25Likewise, also the good works are plain beforehand, and those otherwise cannot be hidden.

CHAPTER 6

1Let as many as *are* slaves under a yoke count their masters worthy of all honor, that the name and teaching of God may not be blasphemed. 2And those having believing masters, let them not despise *them* because they are brothers, but rather let them serve as slaves because they are believing and beloved ones, those receiving of the good service in return. Teach and exhort these things.

3If anyone teaches differently, and does not consent to sound words, those of our Lord Jesus Christ, and the teaching according to godliness, 4he has been puffed up, understanding nothing, but *is* sick concerning doubts and arguments, out of which comes envy, strife, evil-speakings, evil suspicions, 5meddling, of men whose mind has been corrupted and deprived of the truth, supposing gain to be godliness. Withdraw from such *persons*. 6But godliness with contentment is great gain. 7For we have brought nothing into the world, *and it is* plain that neither can we carry anything out. 8But having food and clothing, we will be satisfied with these. 9But those having purposed to be rich fall into many foolish and hurtful

235 3631 3641 5530/1223 4751 4675
τει, ἀλλ' οἴνῳ ὀλίγῳ χρῶ, διὰ τὸν στόμαχόν σου καὶ τὰς
water, but wine a little use, because of the stomach of you and the
4437 4675 769 5100 444 266
24 πυκνάς σου ἀσθενείας. τινῶν ἀνθρώπων αἱ ἁμαρτίαι
frequent of you weaknesses. of some men The sins
4271 1526 4254 1519 2920 5100 1872
πρόδηλοί εἰσι, προάγουσαι εἰς κρίσιν· τισὶ δὲ καὶ ἐπακο-
plain before are, going before to judgment; some but indeed they
5615 2570 2041 4271 2076
25 λουθοῦσιν. ὡσαύτως καὶ τὰ καλὰ ἔργα πρόδηλά ἐστι· καὶ
follow on; likewise also the good works plain before are, and
247 2192 2928 3756 1410
τὰ ἄλλως ἔχοντα κρυβῆναι οὐ δύναται.
those otherwise (being) be hidden not can.

CHAPTER 6

3745/1526/5259/2218 1401 2398 1203 3956
1 Ὅσοι εἰσὶν ὑπὸ ζυγὸν δοῦλοι, τοὺς ἰδίους δεσπότας πάσης
As many as are under a yoke, slaves, the own masters of all
5092 514 2233 2443/3361 3686 2316
τιμῆς ἀξίους ἡγείσθωσαν, ἵνα μὴ τὸ ὄνομα τοῦ Θεοῦ καὶ ἡ
honor worthy esteem, that not the name of God and the
1319 987 4103 2192 1203
2 διδασκαλία βλασφημῆται. οἱ δὲ πιστοὺς ἔχοντες δεσπότας
teaching be blasphemed, those And believing having masters,
3361 2706 3754 80 1526 235 3123 1398
μὴ καταφρονείτωσαν, ὅτι ἀδελφοί εἰσιν· ἀλλὰ μᾶλλον δου-
not let them despise because brothers they are, but rather let them
3754 4103 1526 27 2108
λευέτωσαν, ὅτι πιστοί εἰσι καὶ ἀγαπητοὶ οἱ τῆς εὐεργεσίας
serve as slaves, because believing are and beloved those of the good service
482 5023 1321 3870
ἀντιλαμβανόμενοι. ταῦτα δίδασκε καὶ παρακάλει.
receiving in return. these things Teach and exhort.
=1536= 2085 3361 4334 5198
3 Εἴ τις ἑτεροδιδασκαλεῖ, καὶ μὴ προσέρχεται ὑγιαίνουσι
If anyone teaches differently, and not consents to sound
3056 2962 2257 2424 5547 2596
λόγοις, τοῖς τοῦ Κυρίου ἡμῶν Ἰησοῦ Χριστοῦ, καὶ τῇ κατ'
words, those of the Lord of us, Jesus Christ, and to the according to
2150 1319 5187 3367 1987 *
•235 4 εὐσέβειαν διδασκαλίᾳ, τετύφωται, μηδὲν ἐπιστάμενος, ἀλλὰ
godliness teaching, he has been puffed up, nothing understanding, but
3552 4012 2214 3055 1537/3739 1096 5355
νοσῶν περὶ ζητήσεις καὶ λογομαχίας, ἐξ ὧν γίνεται φθόνος,
is sick concerning doubts and arguments, out of which comes envy,
2054 988 5283 4190 3859 1311
5 ἔρις, βλασφημίαι, ὑπόνοιαι πονηραί, παραδιατριβαὶ διε-
strife, evil-speakings, suspicions evil, wearing disputes, having
444 3563 650
φθαρμένων ἀνθρώπων τὸν νοῦν, καὶ ἀπεστερημένων τῆς
been corrupted of men the mind, and deprived of the
225 3543 4200 1511 2150 868
ἀληθείας, νομιζόντων πορισμὸν εἶναι τὴν εὐσέβειαν. ἀφί-
truth, supposing gain to be godliness; with-
575 5108 2076 4200 3173 2150
6 στασο ἀπὸ τῶν τοιούτων. ἔστι δὲ πορισμὸς μέγας ἡ εὐσέβεια
draw from such. is But gain great godliness
3326 841 3762 1063 1533 1519 2889
7 μετὰ αὐταρκείας· οὐδὲν γὰρ εἰσηνέγκαμεν εἰς τὸν κόσμον,
with contentment; nothing for we have brought into the world,
1212/3754/3761 1627 5100 1410 2192 1305
8 δῆλον ὅτι οὐδὲ ἐξενεγκεῖν τι δυνάμεθα· ἔχοντες δὲ διατροφὰς
(it is) plain that neither carry out anything can we; having but foods
4629 5125 714 1014
9 καὶ σκεπάσματα τούτοις ἀρκεσθησόμεθα. οἱ δὲ βουλόμενοι
and clothings, with these things we will be satisfied. those but resolving
4147 1706 1519 3986 3803 1939
πλουτεῖν ἐμπίπτουσιν εἰς πειρασμὸν καὶ παγίδα καὶ ἐπιθυ-
to be rich fall into temptation and a snare, and lusts

δέ(1161); καί(2531)—and, but; ὁ, ἡ, τό (3588, the)— • above word, look in verse margin for No.

4183 453 983 3748 1036
μίας πολλὰς ἀνοήτους καὶ βλαβεράς, αἵτινες βυθίζουσι τοὺς
many foolish, and hurtful, which cause to sink
444 1519 3639 684 4491/1063 3956
10 ἀνθρώπους εἰς ὄλεθρον καὶ ἀπώλειαν. ῥίζα γὰρ πάντων τῶν
men into ruin and destruction. a root For of all
2556 2076 5365 3739/5100 3713 635
κακῶν ἐστὶν ἡ φιλαργυρία· ἧς τινὲς ὀρεγόμενοι ἀπεπλανήθη-
evils is the love of money, of which some lusting after were seduced
575 4102 1438 4044 3601
σαν ἀπὸ τῆς πίστεως, καὶ ἑαυτοὺς περιέπειραν ὀδύναις
from the faith, and themselves pierced around pains
4183
πολλαῖς.
by many.
4771 3739/ 444 2316 5023 5343 1377 1343
11 Σὺ δέ, ὦ ἄνθρωπε τοῦ Θεοῦ, ταῦτα φεῦγε· δίωκε δὲ δικαιο-
you But, O man of God, these things flee, pursue and righ-
2150 4102 26 5281 4236
σύνην, εὐσέβειαν, πίστιν, ἀγάπην, ὑπομονήν, πρᾳότητα.
teousness, godliness, faith, love, patience, meekness.
75 2570 73 4102 1949
12 ἀγωνίζου τὸν καλὸν ἀγῶνα τῆς πίστεως, ἐπιλαβοῦ τῆς
Fight the good fight of faith. Lay hold on
166 2222/1519/3739 2564 3670 2570
αἰωνίου ζωῆς, εἰς ἣν καὶ ἐκλήθης, καὶ ὡμολόγησας τὴν καλὴν
everlasting life, to which also you were called, and confessed the good
3671 1799 4183 3144 3853 4671
13 ὁμολογίαν ἐνώπιον πολλῶν μαρτύρων. παραγγέλλω σοι
confession before many witnesses. I enjoin you
1799 2316 2227 3956 5547
ἐνώπιον τοῦ Θεοῦ τοῦ ζωοποιοῦντος τὰ πάντα, καὶ Χριστοῦ
before God, the (One) making alive all things, and Christ
2424 3140 1909 4194 4091 2570
Ἰησοῦ τοῦ μαρτυρήσαντος ἐπὶ Ποντίου Πιλάτου τὴν καλὴν
Jesus, the (One) having witnessed on Pontius Pilate the good
3671 5083 4571 1785 784 423
14 ὁμολογίαν, τηρῆσαί σε τὴν ἐντολὴν ἄσπιλον, ἀνεπίληπτον,
confession, to keep you the commandment unspotted, irreproachable,
3360 2015 2962 2257 2424 5547 3739
15 μέχρι τῆς ἐπιφανείας τοῦ Κυρίου ἡμῶν Ἰησοῦ Χριστοῦ, ἣν
until the appearing of the Lord of us, Jesus Christ, which
2540 2398 1166 3107 3441 1413 935
καιροῖς ἰδίοις δείξει ὁ μακάριος καὶ μόνος δυνάστης, ὁ Βασι-
in its own time will reveal the blessed and only Potentate, the King
936 2962 2961
16 λεὺς τῶν βασιλευόντων, καὶ Κύριος τῶν κυριευόντων, ὁ
of kings, and Lord of lords, the
3441 2192 110 5457 3611 676 3739 1492 3762
μόνος ἔχων ἀθανασίαν, φῶς οἰκῶν ἀπρόσιτον, ὃν εἶδεν οὐδεὶς
only (One) having immortality, light living in unapproachable, whom saw no one
444 3761 1492 1410 3739 5092 2904 166
ἀνθρώπων, οὐδὲ ἰδεῖν δύναται· ᾧ τιμὴ καὶ κράτος αἰώνιον.
of men, nor see can; to whom honor and might everlasting.
281
ἀμήν.
Amen.
4145 1722 3568 165 3853 3361 5309
17 Τοῖς πλουσίοις ἐν τῷ νῦν αἰῶνι παράγγελλε, μὴ ὑψη-
The rich in the present age enjoin not to be
3366 1679 1909 4149 83 235/1722
λοφρονεῖν, μηδὲ ἠλπικέναι ἐπὶ πλούτου ἀδηλότητι, ἀλλ' ἐν
highminded, nor to set hope on of riches (the) uncertainty, but on
2316 2198 3930 2254 4146 3956
τῷ Θεῷ τῷ ζῶντι, τῷ παρέχοντι ἡμῖν πλουσίως πάντα
God the living, the (One) offering to us richly all things
1519 619 14 4147 1722 2041 2570
18 εἰς ἀπόλαυσιν· ἀγαθοεργεῖν, πλουτεῖν ἐν ἔργοις καλοῖς,
for enjoyment, to work good, to be rich in works good,
2130 1511 2843 597 1438
19 εὐμεταδότους εἶναι, κοινωνικούς, ἀποθησαυρίζοντας ἑαυτοῖς
ready to impart to be, generous, treasuring away for themselves

lusts which plunge men into death and destruction. [10]For the love of money is a root of all kinds of evils, *by means* of which some having lusted after *it* were seduced from the faith, and *they* themselves pierced through by many pains.

[11]But you, O man of God, flee these things, and pursue righteousness, godliness, faith, love, patience, *and* meekness. [12]Fight the good fight of faith. Lay hold on eternal life, to which you were also called, and confessed the good confession before many witnesses. [13]I charge you before God, He making all things alive, and Christ Jesus, He witnessing the good confession *to* Pontius Pilate, [14]that you keep the commandment spotless, blameless, until the appearing of our Lord Jesus Christ; [15]who in His own time will reveal the blessed and only Potentate, the King of kings and Lord of lords; [16]the only *One* having immortality, living in light that cannot be approached; whom no one of men saw, nor can see; to whom be honor and everlasting might. Amen.

[17]Charge the rich in the present age not to be highminded, nor to set hope on *the* uncertainty of riches, but in the living God, He offering to us richly all things for enjoyment; [18]to do good, to be rich in good works, to be ready to share, generous, [19]treasuring up for themselves a good

temptation and a snare, and foundation for the coming *age*, that they may lay hold on everlasting life.

[20]O Timothy, guard the deposit, having turned away from the profane, empty babblings and opposing theories of the falsely named knowledge, [21]which some having asserted have missed the mark concerning the faith.

Grace *be* with you. Amen.

2310 2570/1519 3195 2443 1949 166
θεμέλιον καλὸν εἰς τὸ μέλλον, ἵνα ἐπιλάβωνται τῆς αἰωνίου
foundation a good for the coming (age), that they lay hold on everlasting
2222
ζωῆς.
life.
5095 3872 5442 1624
20 Ὦ Τιμόθεε, τὴν παρακαταθήκην φύλαξον, ἐκτρεπόμενος
O Timothy, the deposit guard, having turned from
952 2757 477 5581
τὰς βεβήλους κενοφωνίας καὶ ἀντιθέσεις τῆς ψευδωνύμου
the profane, empty babblings and opposing theories of the falsely named
1108 3739 5100 1861 4012 4102
21 γνώσεως· ἥν τινες ἐπαγγελλόμενοι περὶ τὴν πίστιν
knowledge, which some asserting concerning the faith
795
ἠστόχησαν.
have missed the mark.
5485 3326/4675 281
Ἡ χάρις μετὰ σοῦ. ἀμήν.
Grace (be) with you. Amen.

ΠΑΥΛΟΥ ΤΟΥ ΑΠΟΣΤΟΛΟΥ
PAUL THE APOSTLE

Η ΠΡΟΣ
THE TO

ΤΙΜΟΘΕΟΝ
TIMOTHY

ΕΠΙΣΤΟΛΗ ΔΕΥΤΕΡΑ
EPISTLE SECOND

THE SECOND EPISTLE TO TIMOTHY
A LITERAL TRANSLATION OF THE BIBLE

CHAPTER 1

[1]Paul *an* apostle of Jesus Christ by *the* will of God, according to the promise of life which *is* in Christ Jesus, [2]to *my* beloved child Timothy: Grace, mercy, peace from God *the* Father and Christ Jesus our Lord.

[3]I have thanks to God, whom I worship from *my* forebears in a pure conscience, how unceasingly I have remembrance concerning you in my petitions night and day, [4]longing to see you, being reminded of your tears, that I may be filled with joy; [5]taking recollection of the unpretended faith in you, which first dwelt in your grandmother Lois, and *in* your mother Eunice; and I am assured that *it is* also in you. [6]For which cause I remind you to fan the flame of the gift of God, which is in you through the laying on of my hands. [7]For God did not give a spirit of fearfulness to us, but of power, and of love, and of self-control.

[8]Then do not be ashamed of the testimony of our Lord, nor *of* me, His prisoner. But suffer hardship with the gospel, according to *the* power of God, [9]He having saved us and having called us with a holy calling, not according to our works, but

CHAPTER 1

3972 652 2424 5547 1223 2307 2316
1 Παῦλος, ἀπόστολος Ἰησοῦ Χριστοῦ διὰ θελήματος Θεοῦ,
Paul an apostle of Jesus Christ through (the) will of God
2596 1860 2222 1722 5547 2424 3095
2 κατ' ἐπαγγελίαν ζωῆς τῆς ἐν Χριστῷ Ἰησοῦ, Τιμοθέῳ
by way of a promise of life in Christ Jesus, to Timothy
27 5043 5485 1656 1515 575 2316 3962
ἀγαπητῷ τέκνῳ· χάρις, ἔλεος, εἰρήνη ἀπὸ Θεοῦ πατρὸς καὶ
beloved child: Grace, hope, peace from God (the) Father and
5547 2424 2962 2257
Χριστοῦ Ἰησοῦ τοῦ Κυρίου ἡμῶν.
Christ Jesus the Lord of us.
5485/2192 2316/3739/3000 575 4269 1722 2513
3 Χάριν ἔχω τῷ Θεῷ, ᾧ λατρεύω ἀπὸ προγόνων ἐν καθαρᾷ
Thanks I have to God, whom I worship from (my) forebears in a clean
4893 5613 88 2192 4012/4675/3417/1722
συνειδήσει, ὡς ἀδιάλειπτον ἔχω τὴν περὶ σοῦ μνείαν ἐν ταῖς
conscience, as without ceasing I have the concerning you remembrance in the
1162 3450/3571 2250 1971 4571/1492 3415
4 δεήσεσί μου νυκτὸς καὶ ἡμέρας, ἐπιποθῶν σε ἰδεῖν, μεμνημένος
petitions of me night and day, longing you to see, being reminded
4675 1144 2443 5479 4137 5280 2983
5 σου τῶν δακρύων, ἵνα χαρᾶς πληρωθῶ, ὑπόμνησιν λαμ-
of you the tears, that with joy I may be filled, recollection taking
1722/4671 505 4102 3748 1774
βάνων τῆς ἐν σοὶ ἀνυποκρίτου πίστεως, ἥτις ἐνῴκησε
of the in you unpretended faith, which indwelt
4412 1722 3125 4675 3090 3384 4675 2131
πρῶτον ἐν τῇ μάμμῃ σου Λωΐδι καὶ τῇ μητρί σου Εὐνίκῃ,
firstly in your grandmother Lois, and (in) the mother of you Eunice,
3982 3754 1722/4671/1223/3739/156 363 4571
6 πέπεισμαι δὲ ὅτι καὶ ἐν σοί. δι' ἣν αἰτίαν ἀναμιμνήσκω σε
I am assured and that also in you (is). For which cause I remind you
329 5486 2316/3739/2076/1722/4771/1223
ἀναζωπυρεῖν τὸ χάρισμα τοῦ Θεοῦ, ὅ ἐστιν ἐν σοὶ διὰ τῆς
to fan the flame of the gift of God, which is in you through the
1936 5495 3450/3756/1063 1325 2254 2316
7 ἐπιθέσεως τῶν χειρῶν μου. οὐ γὰρ ἔδωκεν ἡμῖν ὁ Θεὸς
laying on of the hands of me. not For gave to us God
4151 1167 235 1411 26 4995
πνεῦμα δειλίας, ἀλλὰ δυνάμεως καὶ ἀγάπης καὶ σωφρονι-
a spirit of cowardice, but of power and of love and of self-
3361/3767 1870 3142 2962 2257
8 σμοῦ. μὴ οὖν ἐπαισχυνθῇς τὸ μαρτύριον τοῦ Κυρίου ἡμῶν,
control. not Therefore be ashamed of the testimony of the Lord of us,
3366/1691 1198 848 235 4777
μηδὲ ἐμὲ τὸν δέσμιον αὐτοῦ· ἀλλὰ συγκακοπάθησον τῷ
nor (of) me, the prisoner of Him, but suffer hardship with the
2098 2596 1411 2316 4982 2248
9 εὐαγγελίῳ κατὰ δύναμιν Θεοῦ, τοῦ σώσαντος ἡμᾶς καὶ
gospel according to (the) power of God, the (One) having saved us and
2564 2821 40/3756/2596 2041 2257 235 2596
καλέσαντος κλήσει ἁγίᾳ, οὐ κατὰ τὰ ἔργα ἡμῶν, ἀλλὰ κατ'
having called calling with a holy, not according to the works of us, but by

according to *His* own purpose and grace given to us in Christ Jesus before eternal times, [10]but now revealed through the appearance of our Savior, Jesus Christ, making death of no effect *and* bringing life and incorruption to light through the gospel; [11]for which I was appointed a herald and apostle, and a teacher of nations. [12]For which cause I also suffer these things; but I am not ashamed, for I know whom I have believed, and I am persuaded that He is able to guard my deposit until that Day. [13]Hold a pattern of sound words which you heard from me, in faith and love in Christ Jesus. [14]Guard the good deposit *given* through *the* Holy Spirit indwelling in us.

2398 4286 5485 1325 2254/1722/5547 2424
ἰδίαν πρόθεσιν καὶ χάριν τὴν δοθεῖσαν ἡμῖν ἐν Χριστῷ Ἰησοῦ
(His) own purpose and grace given to us in Christ Jesus
4253 5550 166 5319 3568/1223 2015
10 πρὸ χρόνων αἰωνίων, φανερωθεῖσαν δὲ νῦν διὰ τῆς ἐπι-
before times eternal; revealed but now through the
4990 2257 2424 5547 2673
φανείας τοῦ σωτῆρος ἡμῶν Ἰησοῦ Χριστοῦ, καταργήσαντος
appearance of the Savior of us, Jesus Christ, making of no effect
3303 2288 5461 2222 861 1223
μὲν τὸν θάνατον, φωτίσαντος δὲ ζωὴν καὶ ἀφθαρσίαν διὰ τοῦ
death, bringing to light and life and incorruption through the
2098 1519/3739/5087/1473 2783 652
11 εὐαγγελίου, εἰς ὃ ἐτέθην ἐγὼ κῆρυξ καὶ ἀπόστολος καὶ
gospel, for which was appointed I a herald and apostle and
1320 1484/1223/3739/156 5023 3958 235, 3756
12 διδάσκαλος ἐθνῶν· δι' ἣν αἰτίαν καὶ ταῦτα πάσχω, ἀλλ' οὐκ
a teacher of nations; for which cause also these things I suffer, but not
1870 1492/1063/3739/ 4100 3982 3754
ἐπαισχύνομαι· οἶδα γὰρ ᾧ πεπίστευκα, καὶ πέπεισμαι ὅτι
I am ashamed, I know for whom I have believed, and I am persuaded that
1415 2076 3866 3450 5442 1519 1565
δυνατός ἐστι τὴν παραθήκην μου φυλάξαι εἰς ἐκείνην τὴν
able He is the deposit of me to guard unto that
2250 5296 2192/ 5198 3056/3739/3844/1700
13 ἡμέραν. ὑποτύπωσιν ἔχε ὑγιαινόντων λόγων ὧν παρ' ἐμοῦ
Day. a pattern Have of sound words which from me
191 1722 4102 26 1722 5547 2424
14 ἤκουσας, ἐν πίστει καὶ ἀγάπῃ τῇ ἐν Χριστῷ Ἰησοῦ. τὴν
you heard, in faith and love in Christ Jesus. The
2570 3872 5442 1223 4151 40
καλὴν παρακαταθήκην φύλαξον διὰ Πνεύματος Ἁγίου τοῦ
good deposit guard through (the) Spirit Holy
1774 1722 2254
ἐνοικοῦντος ἐν ἡμῖν.
indwelling in us.

[15]You know this, that all those in Asia turned away from me, of whom are Phygellus and Hermogenes. [16]May the Lord give mercy to the house of Onesiphorus, because he often refreshed me, and he was not ashamed *of* my chain; [17]but having come to Rome, he more diligently sought and found me. [18]May the Lord give to him to find mercy from *the* Lord in that Day. And what things he served in Ephesus, you know very well.

1492 5124 3754 654 3165 3956 1722 773
15 Οἶδας τοῦτο, ὅτι ἀπεστράφησάν με πάντες οἱ ἐν τῇ Ἀσίᾳ,
You know this, that turned away from me all those in Asia,
3739/2076 5436 2061 1325 1656 2962
16 ὧν ἐστι Φύγελλος καὶ Ἑρμογένης. δῴη ἔλεος ὁ Κύριος τῷ
of whom is Phygellus and Hermogenes. May give mercy the Lord to the
3683 3624 3754 4178 3165/404 254
Ὀνησιφόρου οἴκῳ· ὅτι πολλάκις με ἀνέψυξε, καὶ τὴν ἅλυσίν
of Onesiphorus house because often me he refreshed, and the chain
3450/3756 1870 235 1096 1722 4516 4706
17 μου οὐκ ἐπῃσχύνθη, ἀλλὰ γενόμενος ἐν Ῥώμῃ, σπουδαιό-
of me not he was ashamed (of); but having come to Rome more diligently
2212 3165 2147 1325 846 2962 2147 1656
18 τερον ἐζήτησέ με καὶ εὗρε (δῴη αὐτῷ ὁ Κύριος εὑρεῖν ἔλεος
he sought me and found —may give to him the Lord to find mercy
3844 2962/1722 1565 2250 3745/1722 2181
παρὰ Κυρίου ἐν ἐκείνῃ τῇ ἡμέρᾳ)· καὶ ὅσα ἐν Ἐφέσῳ
from (the) Lord in that Day — and what things in Ephesus
1247 957 4771 1097
διηκόνησε, βέλτιον σὺ γινώσκεις.
he served, very well you know.

CHAPTER 2

[1]Therefore, my child, you be empowered by grace in Christ Jesus. [2]And what things you heard from me through many witnesses, commit these things to faithful men, such as will be competent also to teach others. [3]Therefore, you suffer hardship as a good

CHAPTER 2

4771/3767 5043 /3450 1743 1722 5485 1722 5547
1 Σὺ οὖν, τέκνον μου, ἐνδυναμοῦ ἐν τῇ χάριτι τῇ ἐν Χριστῷ
You, therefore, child of me, be empowered by grace in Christ
2424 3739/ 191 3844 1700/1223 4183 3144
2 Ἰησοῦ. καὶ ἃ ἤκουσας παρ' ἐμοῦ διὰ πολλῶν μαρτύρων,
Jesus. And what things you heard from me through many witnesses,
5023 3908 4103 444 3748 2425 2071
ταῦτα παράθου πιστοῖς ἀνθρώποις, οἵτινες ἱκανοὶ ἔσονται
these things commit to faithful men, who competent will be
2087 1321 4771/3767/ 2553 5613/2570 4757
3 καὶ ἑτέρους διδάξαι. σὺ οὖν κακοπάθησον ὡς καλὸς στρατιώ-
also others to teach. You, then, suffer hardship as a good soldier

soldier of Jesus Christ. [4]No one serving as a soldier tangles with the affairs of this life, so that he might please the *one* enlisting *him*.

[5]And also if anyone competes, he is not crowned unless he competes lawfully. [6]*It is* right *that* the laboring farmer partake first of the fruits. [7]Consider what I say, for the Lord will give you understanding in all things. [8]Remember Jesus Christ having been raised from *the* dead, of *the* seed of David, according to my gospel, [9]in which I suffer ill as an evildoer, unto bonds; but the word of God has not been bound. [10]Because of this, I endure all things on account of the elect, that they also may obtain salvation in Christ Jesus, with everlasting glory. [11]Faithful *is* the word: for if we died with *Him*, we also shall live with *Him*. [12]If we endure, we also shall reign with *Him*. If we deny *Him*, that One will deny us. [13]If we are unfaithful, that One remains faithful—He is not able to deny Himself.

[14]Remind *them of* these things, solemnly testifying before the Lord not to dispute about words for nothing useful, to *the* throwing down *of* those hearing. [15]Earnestly *study* to show yourself approved to God, a workman unashamed, rightly dividing the Word of Truth. [16]But shun profane, empty babblings, for they will go on to more ungodliness, [17]and their word will have growth like gangrene—of whom is Hymeneus and Philetus; [18]who missed the mark concerning the truth, saying the resurrection already has come, and overturn the faith of some. [19]However, the foundation of God stands firm, having this

2424 5547 3762 4754 1707
4 της Ἰησοῦ Χριστοῦ. οὐδεὶς στρατευόμενος ἐμπλέκεται ταῖς
of Jesus Christ. No one serving as a soldier tangles with the
979 4230 2443 4758 700
τοῦ βίου πραγματείαις, ἵνα τῷ στρατολογήσαντι ἀρέσῃ.
of life affairs, that the (One) having enlisted (him) he please.
1437 118 5100/3756/ 4737 =3362= 3545 118
5 ἐὰν δὲ καὶ ἀθλῇ τις, ου στεφανοῦται ἐὰν μὴ νομίμως ἀθλήσῃ.
if And also competes any, not he is crowned unless lawfully he competes.
2872 1092 1163 4413 2590 3335
6 τὸν κοπιῶντα γεωργὸν δεῖ πρῶτον τῶν καρπῶν μετα-
The laboring farmer it behoves firstly of the fruits to
3539/3739/3004/1325/1063/4671 2962 4907 1722
7 λαμβάνειν. νόει ἃ λέγω· δῴη γάρ σοι ὁ Κύριος σύνεσιν ἐν
partake. Consider what I say, will give for you the Lord understanding in
3956 3421 2424 5547 1453 1537 3498
8 πᾶσι. μνημόνευε Ἰησοῦν Χριστὸν ἐγηγερμένον ἐκ νεκρῶν,
all. Remember Jesus Christ having been raised from (the) dead,
1537 4690 1138 2596 2098 3450/1722/3739/2553
9 ἐκ σπέρματος Δαβίδ, κατὰ τὸ εὐαγγέλιόν μου· ἐν ᾧ κακο-
of (the) seed of David, according to the gospel of me; in which I
3360 1199 5613 2557 235 3056 2316
παθῶ μέχρι δεσμῶν, ὡς κακοῦργος· ἀλλ' ὁ λόγος τοῦ Θεοῦ
suffer ill unto bonds as an evildoer; but the word of God
3756 1210 1223/5124 3956 5278 1223 1588
10 οὐ δέδεται. διὰ τοῦτο πάντα ὑπομένω διὰ τοὺς ἐκλεκτούς,
not has been bound. Therefore all things I endure on account of the elect
2443 846 4991 5177 1722 5547 2424 3326
ἵνα καὶ αὐτοὶ σωτηρίας τύχωσι τῆς ἐν Χριστῷ Ἰησοῦ, μετὰ
that also they salvation may obtain in Christ Jesus, with
1391 166 4103 3056 1487/1063/ 4880
11 δόξης αἰωνίου. πιστὸς ὁ λόγος· Εἰ γὰρ συναπεθάνομεν, καὶ
glory everlasting. Faithful (is) the word; if for we died with (Him), also
4800 1487 5278 4821 1487 569
12 συζήσομεν· εἰ ὑπομένομεν, καὶ συμβασιλεύσομεν· εἰ ἀρνού-
we shall live if we endure, also we shall reign with (Him); if we deny
2548 720 2248/1487 569 1565 4103
13 μεθα, κἀκεῖνος ἀρνήσεται ἡμᾶς· εἰ ἀπιστοῦμεν, ἐκεῖνος πιστὸς
(Him), that One will deny us; if we are unfaithful, that One faithful
3305 720 1438 3756 1410
μένει· ἀρνήσασθαι ἑαυτὸν οὐ δύναται.
remains; to deny Himself not He is able.
5023 5279 1263 1799
14 Ταῦτα ὑπομίμνησκε, διαμαρτυρόμενος ἐνώπιον τοῦ
These things remind (them), solemnly testifying before the
2962/3361/ 3054 1519/3762 5539 1909 2692
Κυρίου μὴ λογομαχεῖν εἰς οὐδὲν χρήσιμον, ἐπὶ καταστροφῇ
Lord not to dispute about words for nothing useful, to throwing down
191 4704 4572 1384 3936
15 τῶν ἀκουόντων. σπούδασον σεαυτὸν δόκιμον παραστῆσαι
those hearing. Earnestly (study) yourself approved to show
2316 2040 422 3718 3056
τῷ Θεῷ, ἐργάτην ἀνεπαίσχυντον, ὀρθοτομοῦντα τὸν λόγον
to God a workman unashamed, rightly dividing the word
225 952 2757 4026 1909
16 τῆς ἀληθείας. τὰς δὲ βεβήλους κενοφωνίας περιΐστασο· ἐπὶ
of truth. the But profane, empty babblings shun; to
4119 1063 4298 763 3056 848 5613
17 πλεῖον γὰρ προκόψουσιν ἀσεβείας, καὶ ὁ λόγος αὐτῶν ὡς
more for they will advance ungodliness, and the word of them as
1044 3542 2192/3739/2076 5211 5372 3748
18 γάγγραινα νομὴν ἕξει· ὧν ἐστιν Ὑμέναιος καὶ Φιλητός· οἵτινες
gangrene feeding will have; of whom is Hymeneus and Philetus, who
4012 225 795 3004 386
περὶ τὴν ἀλήθειαν ἠστόχησαν, λέγοντες τὴν ἀνάστασιν
concerning the truth missed the mark, saying the resurrection
2235 1096 396 5100 4102 3305
19 ἤδη γεγονέναι, καὶ ἀνατρέπουσι τήν τινων πίστιν. ὁ μέντοι
already to have come, and overturn the of some faith. the However
4731 2310 2316 2476 2192 4973
στερεὸς θεμέλιος τοῦ Θεοῦ ἕστηκεν, ἔχων τὴν σφραγῖδα
firm foundation of God stands, having seal

seal, "*The* Lord knew those being His;" also, "Let everyone naming the name of Christ depart from unrighteousness."
[20]But in a great house not only are there vessels of gold and silver, but also of wood and of earth; and some to honor, and some to dishonor. [21]Then if anyone purifies himself from these, he will be a vessel to honor, having been sanctified and made useful to the Master, having been prepared to every good work. [22]But flee youthful lusts, and pursue righteousness, faith, love, peace, with the *ones* calling on the Lord out of a pure heart. [23]But refuse the foolish and uninstructed questionings, knowing that they generate quarrels. [24]But a slave of *the* Lord ought not to quarrel, but to be gentle towards all, apt to teach, forbearing, [25]in meekness teaching those who have opposed, *if* perhaps God may give them repentance for a full knowledge of *the* truth, [26]and they may awake out of the snare of the Devil, having been taken captive by him, so as to do the will of that one.

5026 1097 2962 5607 848 868
ταύτην, Ἔγνω Κύριος τοὺς ὄντας αὐτοῦ, καί, Ἀποστήτω
this, knew (the) Lord those being His, and, Let depart
575 93 3956 3687 3686 5547 1722 3173
20 ἀπὸ ἀδικίας πᾶς ὁ ὀνομάζων τὸ ὄνομα Χριστοῦ. ἐν μεγάλῃ
from iniquity everyone naming the name of Christ. in a great
3614/3756/2076/3440 4632 5552 693 235
δὲ οἰκίᾳ οὐκ ἔστι μόνον σκεύη χρυσᾶ καὶ ἀργυρᾶ, ἀλλὰ καὶ
Now house, not is there only vessels golden and silver, but also
3585 3749 3739/3303/1519/5092/3739 1519 819
ξύλινα καὶ ὀστράκινα, καὶ ἃ μὲν εἰς τιμήν, ἃ δὲ εἰς ἀτιμίαν.
wooden and earthen; and some to honor, and some to dishonor
1437/3767/5100/ 1571 1438 575 5130 2071 4632 1519
21 ἐὰν οὖν τις ἐκκαθάρῃ ἑαυτὸν ἀπὸ τούτων, ἔσται σκεῦος εἰς
If, therefore, any cleanses himself from these, he will be a vessel to
5092 37 2173 1203 1519 3956
τιμήν, ἡγιασμένον, καὶ εὔχρηστον τῷ δεσπότῃ, εἰς πᾶν
honor, having been sanctified, and useful to the master, to every
2041 18 2090 3512 1939
22 ἔργον ἀγαθὸν ἡτοιμασμένον. τὰς δὲ νεωτερικὰς ἐπιθυμίας
work good having been prepared. the And youthful lusts
5343 1377 1343 4102 26 1515 3326
φεῦγε· δίωκε δὲ δικαιοσύνην, πίστιν, ἀγάπην, εἰρήνην, μετὰ
flee, pursue but righteousness, faith, love, peace, with
1941 2962 1537 2513 2588
23 τῶν ἐπικαλουμένων τὸν Κύριον ἐκ καθαρᾶς καρδίας. τὰς δὲ
those calling on the Lord out of a clean heart. But
3474 521 2414 3868 1492 3754
μωρὰς καὶ ἀπαιδεύτους ζητήσεις παραιτοῦ, εἰδὼς ὅτι
foolish and uninstructed questionings refuse, knowing that
1080 3163 1401 2962 3756/1163 3164 235
24 γεννῶσι μάχας. δοῦλον δὲ Κυρίου οὐ δεῖ μάχεσθαι, ἀλλ'
they generate quarrels; a slave and of (the) Lord not it behoves to quarrel, but
2261 1511 4314 3956 1317 420 1722 4236
25 ἤπιον εἶναι πρὸς πάντας, διδακτικόν, ἀνεξίκακον, ἐν πρᾳό-
gentle to be toward all, apt to teach, forbearing, in meek-
3811 475 3379 1325 856
τητι παιδεύοντα τοὺς ἀντιδιατιθεμένους· μήποτε δῷ αὐτοῖς
ness teaching those opposing, (if) perhaps may give them
2316 3341 1519 1922 225 366
26 ὁ Θεὸς μετάνοιαν εἰς ἐπίγνωσιν ἀληθείας, καὶ ἀνανήψωσιν
God repentance for a full knowledge of truth, and they regain senses
1537 1228 3803 2221 5259 846 1519
ἐκ τῆς τοῦ διαβόλου παγίδος, ἐζωγρημένοι ὑπ' αὐτοῦ εἰς τὸ
out of the devil snare, having been captured by him to (do) the
1565 2307
ἐκείνου θέλημα.
of that one will.

CHAPTER 3

[1]But know this, that in *the* last days grievous times will be at hand. [2]For men will be lovers of themselves, lovers of money, braggarts, arrogant, blasphemers, disobedient to parents, unthankful, unholy, [3]without natural feeling, unyielding, slanderers, without self-control, savage, haters of good, [4]betrayers, reckless, puffed up, lovers of pleasure rather than lovers of God, [5]having a form of godliness, but denying the power of it—even turn away from

5124 1097 3754/1722/ 2078 2250 1764
1 Τοῦτο δὲ γίνωσκε, ὅτι ἐν ἐσχάταις ἡμέραις ἐνστήσονται
this And know, that in (the) last days will be at hand
2540 5467 2071 1063 444 5367 5366
2 καιροὶ χαλεποί. ἔσονται γὰρ οἱ ἄνθρωποι φίλαυτοι, φιλ-
times grievous. will be For men self-lovers, money-
213 5244 989 1118 545
άργυροι, ἀλαζόνες, ὑπερήφανοι, βλάσφημοι, γονεῦσιν ἀπει-
lovers, braggarts, arrogant, blasphemers, to parents diso-
884 462 794 786 1228
3 θεῖς, ἀχάριστοι, ἀνόσιοι, ἄστοργοι, ἄσπονδοι. διάβολοι,
bedient, unthankful, unholy, without natural feeling, implacable, slanderers,
193 434 865 4273 4312 5187
4 ἀκρατεῖς, ἀνήμεροι, ἀφιλάγαθοι, προδόται, προπετεῖς, τετυ-
without self-control savage, haters of good, betrayers, reckless, puffed
5369 3123 2228 5377 2192 3446
5 φωμένοι, φιλήδονοι μᾶλλον ἢ φιλόθεοι, ἔχοντες μόρφωσιν
up, pleasure-lovers rather than God-lovers, having a form
2150 1411 848 720 5128
εὐσεβείας, τὴν δὲ δύναμιν αὐτῆς ἠρνημένοι· καὶ τούτους
of godliness, the but power of it having denied—even these

these. [6]For of these are those creeping into houses and leading silly women captive, *the ones* having been heaped with sins, being led away by various lusts, [7]always learning, but never being able to come to a full knowledge of *the* truth. [8]But in the way Jannes and Jambres withstood Moses, so also these withstand the truth, men having been corrupted *in* mind, found worthless as to the faith. [9]But they will not go further, for their foolishness will be plain to all, as also that of those became.

[10]But you have closely followed my teaching, the conduct, the purpose, the faith, the long-suffering, the love, the patient endurance, [11]the persecutions, the sufferings, such as happened to me in Antioch, in Iconium, in Lystra; what persecutions I bore. And the Lord delivered me out of all. [12]And, indeed, all desiring to live godly in Christ Jesus will be persecuted.

[13]But evil men and pretenders will go forward to worse, leading astray, and being led astray. [14]But you keep on in what you learned and were assured of, knowing from whom you learned, [15]and that from a babe you know the Holy Scriptures, those being able to make you wise to salvation through belief in Christ Jesus. [16]Every Scripture *is* God-breathed and profitable for teaching, for reproof, for correction, for instruction in righteousness; [17]so that the man of God may be perfect, fully furnished for every good work.

665 1537 5130 1063/1526 1744 1519 3614
6 ἀποτρέπου. ἐκ τούτων γάρ εἰσιν οἱ ἐνδύνοντες εἰς τὰς οἰκίας,
turn away from. of these For are those creeping into houses,

162 1133 4987 266
καὶ αἰχμαλωτεύοντες τὰ γυναικάρια σεσωρευμένα ἁμαρ-
and leading captive silly women having been heaped with

71 1939 4164 3842 3129
7 τίαις, ἀγόμενα ἐπιθυμίαις ποικίλαις, πάντοτε μανθάνοντα,
sins, being led lusts by various, always learning

3368 1519 1922 225 2064 1410 3739
8 καὶ μηδέποτε εἰς ἐπίγνωσιν ἀληθείας ἐλθεῖν δυνάμενα. ὃν
and never to a full knowledge of truth to come being able. by

5158 2389 2387 436 3475 3779
τρόπον δὲ Ἰαννῆς καὶ Ἰαμβρῆς ἀντέστησαν Μωϋσεῖ, οὕτω
what way And Jannes and Jambres opposed Moses, so

3778 436 225 444 2704
καὶ οὗτοι ἀνθίστανται τῇ ἀληθείᾳ, ἄνθρωποι κατεφθαρ-
also these oppose the truth, men having been

3563 96 4012 4102 235 3756/ 4298
9 μένοι τὸν νοῦν, ἀδόκιμοι περὶ τὴν πίστιν. ἀλλ᾽ οὐ προκό-
corrupted the mind, reprobate concerning the faith. But not they will

1909 4119 1063 454 848 1552 2071 3956
ψουσιν ἐπὶ πλεῖον· ἡ γὰρ ἄνοια αὐτῶν ἔκδηλος ἔσται πᾶσιν,
advance to more; the for folly of them plain will be to all,

5613 1565 1096 4771 3877 3450
10 ὡς καὶ ἡ ἐκείνων ἐγένετο. σὺ δὲ παρηκολούθηκάς μου τῇ
as also the (folly) of those became. you But have closely followed of me the

1319 72 4286 4102 3115
διδασκαλίᾳ, τῇ ἀγωγῇ, τῇ προθέσει, τῇ πίστει. τῇ μα-
teaching, the conduct, the purpose, the faith, the long-

26 5281 1375 3804
11 κροθυμίᾳ, τῇ ἀγάπῃ, τῇ ὑπομονῇ, τοῖς διωγμοῖς, τοῖς παθή-
suffering, the love, the patience, the persecutions, the sufferings

3634/3427/ 1096/1722 490 1722 2430 3082
μασιν, οἷά μοι ἐγένετο ἐν Ἀντιοχείᾳ, ἐν Ἰκονίῳ, ἐν Λύστροις,
which to me happened in Antioch, in Iconium, in Lystra;

3634 1375 5297 1537 3956 3165 4506
οἵους διωγμοὺς ὑπήνεγκα· καὶ ἐκ πάντων με ἐρρύσατο ὁ
what persecutions I bore; yet out of all me delivered the

2962 3956 2309 2153 2198/1722/5547
12 Κύριος. καὶ πάντες δὲ οἱ θέλοντες εὐσεβῶς ζῆν ἐν Χριστῷ
Lord. indeed all And those desiring godly to live in Christ

2424 1377 4190 444 1114
13 Ἰησοῦ διωχθήσονται. πονηροὶ δὲ ἄνθρωποι καὶ γόητες
Jesus will be persecuted. evil But men and pretenders

4298 1909 5501 4105 4105
προκόψουσιν ἐπὶ τὸ χεῖρον, πλανῶντες καὶ πλανώμενοι.
will go forward to worse, deceiving and being deceived.

4771 3306/1722/3739/3129 4104 1492 3844 5101
14 σὺ δὲ μένε ἐν οἷς ἔμαθες καὶ ἐπιστώθης, εἰδὼς παρὰ τίνος
you But continue in what you learned and were assured of, knowing from whom

3129 3754 575 1025 2413 1121 1492
15 ἔμαθες, καὶ ὅτι ἀπὸ βρέφους τὰ ἱερὰ γράμματα οἶδας, τὰ
you learned, and that from a babe the holy scriptures you know, those

1410 4571 4679 1519 4991 1223 4102 1722
δυνάμενά σε σοφίσαι εἰς σωτηρίαν διὰ πίστεως τῆς ἐν
being able you to make wise to salvation through belief in

5547 2424 3956 1124 2315 5624
16 Χριστῷ Ἰησοῦ. πᾶσα γραφὴ θεόπνευστος καὶ ὠφέλιμος
Christ Jesus. Every Scripture (is) God-breathed and profitable

4314 3809 4314 1650 4314 1882 4314
πρὸς διδασκαλίαν, πρὸς ἔλεγχον, πρὸς ἐπανόρθωσιν, πρὸς
for teaching, for reproof, for correction, for

3809 1722 1343 2443 739 5600 2316
17 παιδείαν τὴν ἐν δικαιοσύνῃ· ἵνα ἄρτιος ᾖ ὁ τοῦ Θεοῦ
instruction in righteousness, that fitted may be the of God

444 4314/3956 2041 18 1822
ἄνθρωπος, πρὸς πᾶν ἔργον ἀγαθὸν ἐξηρτισμένος.
man, for every work good having been furnished.

CHAPTER 4

CHAPTER 4

[1]Then I solemnly witness before God and the Lord Jesus Christ, He being about to judge living and dead according to His appearance and His kingdom: [2]preach the word; be urgent in season, out of season; convict, warn, encourage with all long-suffering and teaching. [3]For a time will be when they will not endure sound doctrine, but according to their own lusts, they will heap up to themselves teachers tickling the ear; [4]and *they* will turn away the ear from the truth, and will be turned aside to myths. [5]But you be clear-minded in all; suffer hardship, do *the* work of an evangelist; fully carry out your ministry. [6]For I am already being poured out, and the time of my release is here. [7]I have fought the good fight. I have finished the course. I have kept the faith. [8]For the rest, the crown of righteousness is laid up for me, which the Lord, the righteous Judge, will give to me in that Day—and not only to me, but also to all the ones loving His appearance.

1263 3767/1473 1799 2316
1 Διαμαρτύρομαι οὖν ἐγὼ ἐνώπιον τοῦ Θεοῦ, καὶ τοῦ
solemnly witness Then I before God, and the
2962 2424 5547 3195 2919 2198
Κυρίου Ἰησοῦ Χριστοῦ, τοῦ μέλλοντος κρίνειν ζῶντας καὶ
Lord Jesus Christ, the (One) being about to judge living ones and
3498 2596 2015 848 932
νεκροὺς κατὰ τὴν ἐπιφάνειαν αὐτοῦ καὶ τὴν βασιλείαν
dead, according to the appearance of Him and the kingdom
848 2784 3056 2186 2122 171
2 αὐτοῦ, κήρυξον τὸν λόγον, ἐπίστηθι εὐκαίρως, ἀκαίρως,
of Him, proclaim the word, be urgent in season, out of season,
1651 2008 3870 1722 3956 3115
ἔλεγξον, ἐπιτίμησον, παρακάλεσον, ἐν πάσῃ μακροθυμίᾳ
reprove, warn, encourage with all long-suffering
1322 2071 1063 2540 3753 5198 1319
3 καὶ διδαχῇ. ἔσται γὰρ καιρὸς ὅτε τῆς ὑγιαινούσης διδα-
and teaching. there will For a time when the sound
3756 430 235 2596 1939 2398
σκαλίας οὐκ ἀνέξονται, ἀλλὰ κατὰ τὰς ἐπιθυμίας τὰς ἰδίας
doctrine not they will bear, but according to the lusts the own
1438 2002 1320 2833 189
ἑαυτοῖς ἐπισωρεύσουσι διδασκάλους, κνηθόμενοι τὴν ἀκοήν·
to themselves they will heap up teachers tickling the ear:
575/3303 225 189 654 1909
4 καὶ ἀπὸ μὲν τῆς ἀληθείας τὴν ἀκοὴν ἀποστρέψουσιν, ἐπὶ
and from indeed the truth the ear will turn away, to
3454 1624 4771 3525/1722/3956 2553
5 δὲ τοὺς μύθους ἐκτραπήσονται. σὺ δὲ νῆφε ἐν πᾶσι, κακοπά-
and myths will be turned. you But be sober in all, suffer
2041 4160 2099 1248 4675
θησον, ἔργον ποίησον εὐαγγελιστοῦ, τὴν διακονίαν σου
evil, (the) work do of an evangelist, the ministry of you
4135 1473/1063/2235 4689 2540
6 πληροφόρησον. ἐγὼ γὰρ ἤδη σπένδομαι, καὶ ὁ καιρὸς τῆς
fulfill. I For already am being poured out, and the time of the
1699 359 2186 73 2570 75
7 ἐμῆς ἀναλύσεως ἐφέστηκε. τὸν ἀγῶνα τὸν καλὸν ἠγώνισμαι,
of me departure has arrived. The fight good I have fought,
1408 5055 4102 5083 3063 606
8 τὸν δρόμον τετέλεκα, τὴν πίστιν τετήρηκα· λοιπόν, ἀπό-
the course I have finished, the faith I have kept; for the rest, is laid
3427 1343 4735 3739 591 3427
κειταί μοι ὁ τῆς δικαιοσύνης στέφανος, ὃν ἀποδώσει μοι ὁ
up for me the of righteousness crown, which will give to me the
2962/1722/1565 2250 1342 2923 3756/3440
Κύριος ἐν ἐκείνῃ τῇ ἡμέρᾳ, ὁ δίκαιος κριτής· οὐ μόνον δὲ
Lord in that Day, the righteous Judge; not only and
1698 235 3956 25 2015 848
ἐμοί, ἀλλὰ καὶ πᾶσι τοῖς ἠγαπηκόσι τὴν ἐπιφάνειαν αὐτοῦ.
to me; but also all those having loved the appearance of Him.

[9]Make haste to come to me shortly; [10]for Demas deserted me, loving the present age; and *he* went to Thessalonica. Crescens *went* to Galatia, Titus to Dalmatia. [11]Only Luke is with me. Taking Mark, bring *him* with you, for he is useful to me for ministry. [12]But I sent Tychicus to Ephesus. [13]When you come, bring the cloak which I left in Troas

4704 2064 4314/3165/5030 1214 1063/3165/1459
Σπούδασον ἐλθεῖν πρός με ταχέως· Δημᾶς γάρ με ἐγκατέ-
Make haste to come to me shortly. Demas For me deserted
25 3568 165 4198 1519 2316
9 λιπεν, ἀγαπήσας τὸν νῦν αἰῶνα, καὶ ἐπορεύθη εἰς Θεσ-
10 loving the present age, and went to Thessa-
2913 1519 1053 5103 1519 1149
σαλονίκην· Κρήσκης εἰς Γαλατίαν, Τίτος εἰς Δαλματίαν.
lonica, Crescens to Galatia; Titus to Dalmatia.
3065 2076 3441 3326 1700 3138 353 71 3326
11 Λουκᾶς ἐστι μόνος μετ' ἐμοῦ. Μάρκον ἀναλαβὼν ἄγε μετὰ
Luke is only with me. Mark having taken, bring with
4572 2076 1063/3427 2173 1519 1248 5190
12 σεαυτοῦ· ἔστι γάρ μοι εὔχρηστος εἰς διακονίαν. Τυχικὸν δὲ
yourself, he is for to me useful for ministry. Tychicus But
649 1519 2181 5341 3739 620 1722 5174
13 ἀπέστειλα εἰς Ἔφεσον. τὸν φελόνην ὃν ἀπέλιπον ἐν Τρωάδι
I sent to Ephesus. The cloak which I left in Troas

with Carpus, and the books, especially the parchments. [14]Alexander the coppersmith showed many evil things to me. The Lord will give to him according to his works. [15]You also guard against *him*, for he greatly resisted our words.

[16]In my first defense, no one was beside me, but all deserted me. May it not be reckoned to them. [17]But the Lord stood with me and gave me power, that through me the preaching might be fulfilled, and all the nations might hear. And I was delivered out of *the* mouth of the lion. [18]And the Lord will deliver me from every wicked work, and will save *me* for His heavenly kingdom; to whom *be* the glory forever and ever. Amen.

[19]Greet Prisca and Aquila, and the house of Onesiphorus. [20]Erastus remained in Corinth, but I left Trophimus sick in Miletus.

[21]Try to come before winter. Eubulus greets you, and Pudens, and Linus, and Claudia, and all the brothers.

[22]The Lord Jesus Christ *be* with your spirit. Grace *be* with you. Amen.

3844 2591 2064 5342 975 3122
παρὰ Κάρπῳ, ἐρχόμενος φέρε, καὶ τὰ βιβλία, μάλιστα τὰς
with Carpus, coming bring, and the scrolls, especially the
3200 223 5471 4183 3427/2556 1731
14 μεμβράνας. Ἀλέξανδρος ὁ χαλκεὺς πολλά μοι κακὰ ἐνεδεί-
parchments. Alexander the coppersmith much to me evils showed;
591 846 2962 2596 2041 848 3739
15 ξατο· ἀποδῴη αὐτῷ ὁ Κύριος κατὰ τὰ ἔργα αὐτοῦ· ὃν καὶ
will give to him the Lord according to the works of him; whom also
4771 5442 3029 1063 436 2251 3056
σὺ φυλάσσου, λίαν γὰρ ἀνθέστηκε τοῖς ἡμετέροις λόγοις.
you guard (against), greatly for he opposed our words.
1722 4413 3450 627 3762 3317 4836 235
16 ἐν τῇ πρώτῃ μου ἀπολογίᾳ οὐδείς μοι συμπαρεγένετο, ἀλλὰ
At the first of me defense no one me was beside, but
3956 3165 1459 3361 846 3049 2962
17 πάντες με ἐγκατέλιπον· μὴ αὐτοῖς λογισθείη. ὁ δὲ Κύριός
all me deserted. May it not to them be reckoned. the But Lord
3427 3936 1743 3165/2443/1223/1700 2782
μοι παρέστη, καὶ ἐνεδυνάμωσέ με, ἵνα δι᾽ ἐμοῦ τὸ κήρυγμα
me stood with, and empowered me, that through me the preaching
4135 191 3956 1484 4506 1537
πληροφορηθῇ, καὶ ἀκούσῃ πάντα τὰ ἔθνη· καὶ ἐρρύσθην ἐκ
might be fulfilled, and might hear all the nations. And I was delivered out of
4750 3023 4506 3165 2962 575 3956 2041
18 στόματος λέοντος. καὶ ῥύσεταί με ὁ Κύριος ἀπὸ παντὸς ἔργου
(the) mouth of (the) lion. And will deliver me The Lord from every work
4190 4982 1519 932 848 2032
πονηροῦ. καὶ σώσει εἰς τὴν βασιλείαν αὐτοῦ τὴν ἐπουράνιον·
wicked, and will save for the kingdom of Him heavenly;
3739 1391/1519 165 165 281
ᾧ ἡ δόξα εἰς τοὺς αἰῶνας τῶν αἰώνων. ἀμήν.
to whom (be) the glory to the ages of the ages. Amen.
782 4251 207 3683
19 Ἀσπασαι Πρίσκαν καὶ Ἀκύλαν, καὶ τὸν Ὀνησιφόρου
Greet Priscilla and Aquila, and the of Onesiphorus
3624 2037 3306 1722 2882 5161 620
20 οἶκον. Ἔραστος ἔμεινεν ἐν Κορίνθῳ· Τρόφιμον δὲ ἀπέλιπον
house. Erastus remained in Corinth, Trophimus But I left
1722 3399 770 4704 4253 5494 2064
21 ἐν Μιλήτῳ ἀσθενοῦντα. σπούδασον πρὸ χειμῶνος ἐλθεῖν.
in Miletus sick. Make haste before winter to come.
782 4571 2103 4227 3044 2803
ἀσπάζεταί σε Εὔβουλος, καὶ Πούδης, καὶ Λῖνος, καὶ Κλαυδία,
Greets you Eubulus and Pudens and Linus and Claudia,
80 3956
καὶ οἱ ἀδελφοὶ πάντες.
and the brothers all.
2962 2424 5547 3326 4151 4675
22 Ὁ Κύριος Ἰησοῦς Χριστὸς μετὰ τοῦ πνεύματός σου. ἡ
The Lord Jesus Christ (be) with the spirit of you.
5485 3326 5216 281
χάρις μεθ᾽ ὑμῶν. ἀμήν.
Grace (be) with you. Amen.

THE EPISTLE
TO
TITUS
A LITERAL TRANSLATION
OF THE BIBLE

CHAPTER 1

1 Paul, a slave of God and an apostle of Jesus Christ according to *the* faith of *the* elect of God and full knowledge of *the* truth according to godliness, 2 on hope of eternal life which the God that does not lie promised before *the* eternal times, 3 but revealed in its own times in a proclamation of His word, with which I was entrusted by *the* command of our Savior God: 4 to Titus, a true child according to *our* common faith. Grace, mercy, peace from God *the* Father and *the* Lord Jesus Christ our Savior.

5 For this cause I left you in Crete, that you might set in order the things lacking, and appoint elders in every city, as I ordered you:

6 If anyone is blameless, husband of one wife, having believing children, not in accusation of loose behavior, or unruly. 7 For the overseer must be blameless, as a steward of God, not self-pleasing, not full of passion, not given to wine, not a quarreler, not greedy of ill gain; 8 but hospitable, a lover of good, discreet, just, holy, temperate, 9 clinging to the faithful word according to the teaching, that he may be able both to encourage with sound teaching, and to convict the *ones* speaking against.

ΠΑΥΛΟΥ
PAUL
Η ΠΡΟΣ
THE TO
ΤΙΤΟΝ ΕΠΙΣΤΟΛΗ
TITUS EPISTLE

CHAPTER 1

3972 1401 2316 652 2424 5547 2596
1 Παῦλος, δοῦλος Θεοῦ, ἀπόστολος δὲ Ἰησοῦ Χριστοῦ, κατὰ
Paul, a slave of God, an apostle and of Jesus Christ, according to
4102 1588 2316 1922 225 2596
πίστιν ἐκλεκτῶν Θεοῦ καὶ ἐπίγνωσιν ἀληθείας τῆς κατ'
(the) faith of (the) elect of God and full knowledge of (the) truth according to
2150 1909 1680 2222 166 3739 1861
2 εὐσέβειαν, ἐπ' ἐλπίδι ζωῆς αἰωνίου, ἣν ἐπηγγείλατο ὁ
godliness, on hope life of eternal which promised the
893 2316 4253 5550 166 5319 2540
3 ἀψευδὴς Θεὸς πρὸ χρόνων αἰωνίων, ἐφανέρωσε δὲ καιροῖς
not lying God before times eternal, revealed but times
2398 3056 848/1722 2782 3739 4100 1473 2596
ἰδίοις τὸν λόγον αὐτοῦ ἐν κηρύγματι ὃ ἐπιστεύθην ἐγὼ κατ'
in its own the word of Him in a proclamation which was entrusted I by
2003 4990 2257 2316 5103 1103 5043
4 ἐπιταγὴν τοῦ σωτῆρος ἡμῶν Θεοῦ, Τίτῳ γνησίῳ τέκνῳ
(the) command of the Savior of us, God, to Titus a true child
2596 3839 4102 5485 1656 1515 575 2316 3962
κατὰ κοινὴν πίστιν· χάρις, ἔλεος, εἰρήνη ἀπὸ Θεοῦ πατρός,
according to a common faith: Grace, mercy, peace from God (the) Father
2962 2424 5547 4990 2257
καὶ Κυρίου Ἰησοῦ Χριστοῦ τοῦ σωτῆρος ἡμῶν.
and (the) Lord Jesus Christ, the Savior of us.
5127 5484 2641 4571/1722/2914 2443 3007
5 Τούτου χάριν κατέλιπόν σε ἐν Κρήτῃ, ἵνα τὰ λείποντα
For this cause I left you in Crete, that the things lacking
1930 2525 2596 4172 4245
ἐπιδιορθώσῃ, καὶ καταστήσῃς κατὰ πόλιν πρεσβυτέρους,
you set in order, and appoint in every city elders,
5613/1473/4671 1299 =1536= 2076 410 3391
6 ὡς ἐγώ σοι διεταξάμην· εἴ τίς ἐστιν ἀνέγκλητος, μιᾶς
as I you ordered; if anyone is blameless, of one
1135 435 5043 2192 4103/3361/1722/ 2724 810
γυναικὸς ἀνήρ, τέκνα ἔχων πιστά, μὴ ἐν κατηγορίᾳ ἀσωτίας
wife husband, children having believing, not in accusation of looseness
506 1163/1063 1985 410 1511
7 ἢ ἀνυπότακτα. δεῖ γὰρ τὸν ἐπίσκοπον ἀνέγκλητον εἶναι,
or unruly. it behoves For the overseer blameless to be,
5613/2316/ 3623 3361 829 3361 3711 3361 3943
ὡς Θεοῦ οἰκονόμον· μὴ αὐθάδη, μὴ ὀργίλον, μὴ πάροινον,
as of God a steward, not self-pleasing, not passionate, not given to wine,
3361 4131 3361 146 235 5382 5358
8 μὴ πλήκτην, μὴ αἰσχροκερδῆ, ἀλλὰ φιλόξενον, φιλάγαθον,
not a quarreler, not greedy of ill gain, but hospitable, a lover of good,
4998 1342 3741 1468 472 2596
9 σώφρονα, δίκαιον, ὅσιον, ἐγκρατῆ, ἀντεχόμενον τοῦ κατὰ
discreet, just, holy, temperate, clinging to the according to
1322 4103 3056 2443 1415/5600 3870
τὴν διδαχὴν πιστοῦ λόγου, ἵνα δυνατὸς ᾖ καὶ παρακαλεῖν
the teaching faithful word, that able he may be both to exhort
1722 1319 5198 483
ἐν τῇ διδασκαλίᾳ τῇ ὑγιαινούσῃ, καὶ τοὺς ἀντιλέγοντας
by the teaching sound, and those contradicting
1651
ἐλέγχειν.
to convict

[10]For there are indeed many unruly men, empty talkers and mind-deluders, especially those of *the* circumcision, [11]whose mouth *you* must stop, who overturn whole houses, teaching things which *they* ought not for the sake of ill gain. [12]One of them, a prophet of their own, said: Cretans *are* always liars, evil beasts, lazy gluttons. [13]This testimony is true; for which cause convict them severely, that they may be sound in the faith, [14]not listening to Jewish myths and commandments of men, having turned away from the truth. [15]Truly, all things *are* pure to the pure; but to the ones having been defiled and unbelieving, nothing is pure, but even their mind and conscience has been defiled. [16]They profess to know God, but by *their* works they deny *Him*, being abominable and disobedient, and reprobate to every good work.

CHAPTER 2

[1]But you speak things which become sound doctrine: [2]aged men to be temperate, sensible, discreet, sound in faith, in love, in patience; [3]aged women likewise in reverent behavior, not slanderers, not having been enslaved by much wine, teachers of good, [4]that they might train the young women to be lovers of husbands, lovers of children, [5]discreet, chaste, keepers at home, good, subject to their own husbands, so that the word of God may not be spoken against; [6]the younger men in the same way exhort to be discreet; [7]having shown yourself a pattern of good works about all things, in teaching, in purity, sensibleness, incorruption, [8]*in* sound speech,

1526 1063 4183 506 3151
10 Εἰσὶ γὰρ πολλοὶ καὶ ἀνυπότακτοι, ματαιολόγοι καὶ
there are For many indeed unruly men, empty talkers, and
5423 3122 1537 4061 3739/1163/ 1993
11 φρεναπάται, μάλιστα οἱ ἐκ περιτομῆς, οὓς δεῖ ἐπιστομίζειν·
mind-deluders, especially those of circum- cision of (you) must stop the mouth
3748 3650 3624 396 whom 1321 3739/3361/1163
οἵτινες ὅλους οἴκους ἀνατρέπουσι, διδάσκοντες ἃ μὴ δεῖ,
who whole houses overturn, teaching things not right,
150 2771 5484 2036/5100/1537/848 2398 848
12 αἰσχροῦ κέρδους χάριν. εἶπέ τις ἐξ αὐτῶν, ἴδιος αὐτῶν
ill gain for the sake of. said One of them, an own of them
4396 2912/104/5583 2556 2342 1064 692
προφήτης, Κρῆτες ἀεὶ ψεῦσται, κακὰ θηρία, γαστέρες ἀργαί.
prophet, Cretans (are) always liars, evil beasts, gluttons idle.
3141 3778 2076 227 1223/3739/ 156 1651 846
13 ἡ μαρτυρία αὕτη ἐστὶν ἀληθής. δι' ἣν αἰτίαν ἔλεγχε αὐτοὺς
witness This is true; for which cause convict them
664 2443 5198 1722 4102 3361 4337
14 ἀποτόμως, ἵνα ὑγιαίνωσιν ἐν τῇ πίστει, μὴ προσέχοντες
severely, that they may be sound in the faith, not listening
2451 3454 1785 444 654
Ἰουδαϊκοῖς μύθοις καὶ ἐντολαῖς ἀνθρώπων ἀποστρεφομένων
to Jewish myths and commandments of men having perverted
225 3956 3303 2513 2513
15 τὴν ἀλήθειαν· πάντα μὲν καθαρὰ τοῖς καθαροῖς· τοῖς δὲ
the truth. All things indeed (are) clean to the clean, to those but
3392 571 3762 2513 235 3392
μεμιασμένοις καὶ ἀπίστοις οὐδὲν καθαρόν· ἀλλὰ μεμίανται
having been defiled and unbelieving nothing (is) clean, but has been defiled
848 3563 4893 2316 3670
16 αὐτῶν καὶ ὁ νοῦς καὶ ἡ συνείδησις. Θεὸν ὁμολογοῦσιν
of them even the mind and the conscience. God They profess
1492 2041 720 947 5620
εἰδέναι, τοῖς δὲ ἔργοις ἀρνοῦνται, βδελυκτοὶ ὄντες καὶ
to know, by the but works they deny (Him), abominable being and
545 4314/3956 2041 18 96
ἀπειθεῖς καὶ πρὸς πᾶν ἔργον ἀγαθὸν ἀδόκιμοι.
disobedient and to every work good reprobate.

CHAPTER 2

4771 2980/3739/4241 5198 1319 4246
1 Σὺ δὲ λάλει ἃ πρέπει τῇ ὑγιαινούσῃ διδασκαλίᾳ· πρεσ-
you But speak things which becomes the sound teaching. Aged
3524 1511 4586 4998 5198
2 βύτας νηφαλίους εἶναι, σεμνούς, σώφρονας, ὑγιαίνοντας τῇ
men temperate to be, sensible, discreet, sound in the
4102 26 5281 4247 5615 1722
3 πίστει, τῇ ἀγάπῃ, τῇ ὑπομονῇ· πρεσβύτιδας ὡσαύτως ἐν
faith; in love, in patience; aged women likewise in
2688 2412 3361 1223 3361 3631 4183
καταστήματι ἱεροπρεπεῖς, μὴ διαβόλους, μὴ οἴνῳ πολλῷ
behavior reverent, not slanderers, not wine by much
1402 2567 2443 4994 3501
4 δεδουλωμένας, καλοδιδασκάλους, ἵνα σωφρονίζωσι τὰς νέας
having been enslaved, teachers of good, that they may train the young women
5362 1511 5388 4998 53 3626
5 φιλάνδρους εἶναι, φιλοτέκνους, σώφρονας, ἁγνάς, οἰκουρούς,
lovers of husbands to be, child-lovers, discreet, chaste, homeworkers,
18 5293 2398 435 2443/3361 3056
ἀγαθάς, ὑποτασσομένας τοῖς ἰδίοις ἀνδράσιν, ἵνα μὴ ὁ λόγος
good, being subject to the own husbands, that not the word
2316 987 3501 5615 3870
6 τοῦ Θεοῦ βλασφημῆται· τοὺς νεωτέρους ὡσαύτως παρακάλει
of God be blasphemed. The younger men likewise exhort
4993 4012 3956 4572 3930 5179 2570
7 σωφρονεῖν· περὶ πάντα σεαυτὸν παρεχόμενος τύπον καλῶν
to be discreet; about all things yourself showing a pattern of good
2041 1722 1319 90 4587 861
ἔργων, ἐν τῇ διδασκαλίᾳ ἀδιαφθορίαν, σεμνότητα, ἀφθ-
works, in the teaching, in purity, sensibleness, incor-

not to be condemned; that he who is opposed may be ashamed, having nothing bad to say about you.

[9]Let slaves be subject to *their* own masters, well-pleasing in all things, not speaking against *them*, [10]not stealing, but showing all good faith, that they may adorn the teaching of our Savior God in all things. [11]For the grace of God which brings salvation appeared to all men, [12]instructing us that having denied ungodliness and worldly lusts, we should live discreetly and righteously and godly in the present age, [13]looking for the blessed hope and appearance of the glory of our great God and Savior Jesus Christ, [14]who gave Himself on our behalf, that He might redeem us from all iniquity, and purify a special people for Himself, zealous of good works.

[15]Speak these things, and exhort, and convict with all authority. Let no one despise you.

CHAPTER 3

[1]Remind them to be subject to rulers and authorities, to be obedient, to be ready in every good work; [2]to speak evil of no one, not quarrelsome, *but* forbearing, having displayed all meekness to all men. [3]For we also once *were* senseless, disobedient, led astray, slaving for various lusts and pleasures, living in malice and envy, hateful, hating one another. [4]But when the kindness and love of God our Savior toward

3056 5199 176 2443 1537 1727
8 αρσίαν, λόγον ὑγιῆ, ἀκατάγνωστον, ἵνα ὁ ἐξ ἐναντίας
ruption, speech sound, irreprehensible, that he of opposition
1788 3367 2192 4012 5216 3004 5337 1401 2398
9 ἐντραπῆ, μηδὲν ἔχων περὶ ὑμῶν λέγειν φαῦλον. δούλους ἰδίοις
be ashamed, nothing having about us to say bad. Slaves to own
1203 5293 1722 3956 2101 1511 3361
δεσπόταις ὑποτάσσεσθαι, ἐν πᾶσιν εὐαρέστους εἶναι, μὴ
masters to be subject in all things well-pleasing to be, not
483 3361 3557 235 4102 3956 1731
10 ἀντιλέγοντας, μὴ νοσφιζομένους, ἀλλὰ πίστιν πᾶσαν ἐνδει-
contradicting, not stealing, but faith all
18 2443 1319 4990 2257
κνυμένους ἀγαθήν, ἵνα τὴν διδασκαλίαν τοῦ σωτῆρος ἡμῶν
showing good, that the teaching of the Savior of us,
2316/2885 1722 3956 2014 1063 5485 2316
11 Θεοῦ κοσμῶσιν ἐν πᾶσιν. ἐπεφάνη γὰρ ἡ χάρις τοῦ Θεοῦ ἡ
God, they may adorn in all things. appeared For the grace of God
4992 3956 444 3811 2248/2443 720
12 σωτήριος πᾶσιν ἀνθρώποις, παιδεύουσα ἡμᾶς ἵνα, ἀρνησά-
saving to all men, instructing us that having
763 2886 1939 4996
μενοι τὴν ἀσέβειαν καὶ τὰς κοσμικὰς ἐπιθυμίας, σωφρόνως καὶ
denied ungodliness and worldly lusts, discreetly and
1346 2153 2198 1722 3568 165 4327
13 δικαίως καὶ εὐσεβῶς ζήσωμεν ἐν τῷ νῦν αἰῶνι, προσδεχό-
righteously and godly we might live in the present age, expecting
3107 1680 2015 1391
μενοι τὴν μακαρίαν ἐλπίδα καὶ ἐπιφάνειαν τῆς δόξης τοῦ
the blessed hope and appearance of the glory of the
3173 2316 4990 2257 2424 5547 3739 1325
14 μεγάλου Θεοῦ καὶ σωτῆρος ἡμῶν Ἰησοῦ Χριστοῦ, ὃς ἔδωκεν
great God and Savior of us, Jesus Christ, who gave
1438 5228 2257 2443 3084 2248 575 3956
ἑαυτὸν ὑπὲρ ἡμῶν, ἵνα λυτρώσηται ἡμᾶς ἀπὸ πάσης
Himself on behalf of us, that He might redeem us from all
458 2511 1438 2992 4041 2207
ἀνομίας, καὶ καθαρίσῃ ἑαυτῷ λαὸν περιούσιον, ζηλωτὴν
iniquity and cleanse for Himself a people special, zealous
2570 2041
καλῶν ἔργων.
of good works.
5023 2980 3870 1651 3326 3956
15 Ταῦτα λάλει, καὶ παρακάλει, καὶ ἔλεγχε μετὰ πάσης
These things speak, and exhort, and convict with all
2003 3367 4675 4065
ἐπιταγῆς. μηδείς σου περιφρονείτω.
authority. no one you Let despise.

CHAPTER 3

5279 846 746 1849 5293
1 Ὑπομίμνησκε αὐτοὺς ἀρχαῖς καὶ ἐξουσίαις ὑποτάσσεσθαι,
Remind them to rulers and authorities to be subject,
3980 4314/3956 2041 18 2092 1511 3367
2 πειθαρχεῖν, πρὸς πᾶν ἔργον ἀγαθὸν ἑτοίμους εἶναι, μηδένα
to be obedient, in every work good ready to be no one
987 269 1511 1933 3956 1731
βλασφημεῖν, ἀμάχους εἶναι, ἐπιεικεῖς, πᾶσαν ἐνδεικνυμένους
to speak evil of, uncontentious to be, forbearing, all showing forth
4236 4314 3956 444 2258 1063 4218
3 πρᾳότητα πρὸς πάντας ἀνθρώπους. ἦμεν γάρ ποτε καὶ
meekness to all men. were For then also
2249 453 545 4105 1398 1939
ἡμεῖς ἀνόητοι, ἀπειθεῖς, πλανώμενοι, δουλεύοντες ἐπιθυμίαις
we senseless, disobedient, led astray, slaving for lusts
2237 4164 1722 2549 5355 1236
καὶ ἡδοναῖς ποικίλαις, ἐν κακίᾳ καὶ φθόνῳ διάγοντες,
and pleasures various, in evil and envy living;
4767 3404 240 3753 5544
4 στυγητοί, μισοῦντες ἀλλήλους. ὅτε δὲ ἡ χρηστότης καὶ ἡ
hateful, hating one another. when But the kindness and

man appeared, [5]not by works in righteousness which we had done, but according to His mercy He saved us, through *the* washing of regeneration and renewal of *the* Holy Spirit, [6]which He poured out on us richly through Jesus Christ, our Savior; [7]that being justified by His grace, we should become heirs according to *the* hope of eternal life. [8]Faithful is the word, and concerning these things I desire you strongly to affirm that the *ones* believing God should take thought to maintain good works. These things are good and profitable to men.

[9]But keep back from foolish questionings, and genealogies, and arguments, and quarrels of law, for they are unprofitable and vain. [10]After the first and second warning, avoid a man of heresy, [11]knowing that such a one has been perverted, and sins, being self-condemned.

[12]When I shall send Artemas to you, or Tychicus, hasten to come to me at Nicopolis. For I have decided to winter there. [13]Diligently set forward Zenas the lawyer, and Apollos, that nothing be lacking to them. [14]And let ours also learn to maintain good works for necessary uses, that they may not be without fruit.

[15]All those with me greet you. Greet those who love us in *the* faith.

Grace *be* with you all. Amen.

5363 2014 4990 2257 2316 3756/1537
5 φιλανθρωπία ἐπεφάνη τοῦ σωτῆρος ἡμῶν Θεοῦ, οὐκ ἐξ
love toward man appeared of the Savior of us God, not by
2041 1722 1343 3739 4160 2249 235 2596
ἔργων τῶν ἐν δικαιοσύνῃ ὧν ἐποιήσαμεν ἡμεῖς, ἀλλὰ κατὰ
works in righteousness which had done we, but according to
848 1656 4982 2248/1223 3067 3824
τὸν αὐτοῦ ἔλεον ἔσωσεν ἡμᾶς, διὰ λουτροῦ παλιγγενεσίας
the of Him mercy He saved us, through (the) washing of regeneration
342 4151 40 3739 1632/1909 2248
6 καὶ ἀνακαινώσεως Πνεύματος Ἁγίου, οὗ ἐξέχεεν ἐφ' ἡμᾶς
and renewal of (the) Spirit Holy, which He poured out on us
4146 1223 2424 5547 4990 2257 2443
7 πλουσίως, διὰ Ἰησοῦ Χριστοῦ τοῦ σωτῆρος ἡμῶν, ἵνα
richly through Jesus Christ the Savior of us, that
1344 1565 5485 2818 1096 2596
δικαιωθέντες τῇ ἐκείνου χάριτι, κληρονόμοι γενώμεθα κατ'
being justified by the of that One grace, heirs we might become according to
1680 2222 166 4103 3056 4012 5130
8 ἐλπίδα ζωῆς αἰωνίου. πιστὸς ὁ λόγος, καὶ περὶ τούτων
(the) hope of life eternal. Faithful (is) the word, and as to these things
1014 4571 1226 2443 5431 2570 2041
βούλομαί σε διαβεβαιοῦσθαι, ἵνα φροντίζωσι καλῶν ἔργων
I desire you to strongly affirm that may take thought of good works
4291 4100 2316 5023 2076
προΐστασθαι οἱ πεπιστευκότες τῷ Θεῷ. ταῦτά ἐστι τὰ
to maintain those having believed God. These things are
2570 5624 444 3474 2214
9 καλὰ καὶ ὠφέλιμα τοῖς ἀνθρώποις· μωρὰς δὲ ζητήσεις καὶ
good and profitable to men. foolish But questionings and
1076 2054 3163 3544 4026 1526
γενεαλογίας καὶ ἔρεις καὶ μάχας νομικὰς περιΐστασο· εἰσὶ
genealogies, and arguments, and quarrels of law keep back from; they are
*3391 1063 512 3152 141 444 3326
10 γὰρ ἀνωφελεῖς καὶ μάταιοι. αἱρετικὸν ἄνθρωπον μετὰ μίαν
for unprofitable and vain. A heretic man after one
1208 3559 3868 1492/3754 1612
11 καὶ δευτέραν νουθεσίαν παραιτοῦ, εἰδὼς ὅτι ἐξέστραπται ὁ
and a second warning avoid, knowing that has been perverted
5108 264 5607 843
τοιοῦτος, καὶ ἁμαρτάνει, ὢν αὐτοκατάκριτος.
such a one and sins, being self-condemned.

3752 3992 734 4314/4571 5190 4704
12 Ὅταν πέμψω Ἀρτεμᾶν πρός σε ἢ Τυχικόν, σπούδασον
When I shall send Artemas to you, or Tychicus, hasten
2064 4314/3165/1519/ 3533 1563/1063 2919 3914
ἐλθεῖν πρός με εἰς Νικόπολιν· ἐκεῖ γὰρ κέκρικα παραχειμάσαι.
to come to me at Nicopolis; there for I have decided to winter.
2211 3544 625 4709 4311
13 Ζηνᾶν τὸν νομικὸν καὶ Ἀπολλὼ σπουδαίως πρόπεμψον,
Zenas the lawyer and Apollos urgently set forward,
2443 3367 846 3007 3129 2251
14 ἵνα μηδὲν αὐτοῖς λείπῃ. μανθανέτωσαν δὲ καὶ οἱ ἡμέτεροι
that nothing to them be lacking. let learn And also our (own)
2570 2041 4291 1519 316 5532 2443/3361
καλῶν ἔργων προΐστασθαι εἰς τὰς ἀναγκαίας χρείας, ἵνα μὴ
of good works to maintain for necessary uses, that not
5600 175
ὦσιν ἄκαρποι.
they be without fruit.

782 4571 3326 1700 3956 782
15 Ἀσπάζονταί σε οἱ μετ' ἐμοῦ πάντες. ἄσπασαι τοὺς
Greet you those with me all. Greet those
5368 2248/1722/4102
φιλοῦντας ἡμᾶς ἐν πίστει.
loving us in faith.
5485 3326 3956 5216 281
Ἡ χάρις μετὰ πάντων ὑμῶν. ἀμήν.
Grace (be) with all you. Amen.

ΠΑΥΛΟΥ
PAUL
Η ΠΡΟΣ
THE TO
ΦΙΛΗΜΟΝΑ ΕΠΙΣΤΟΛΗ
PHILEMON EPISTLE

THE EPISTLE
TO
PHILEMON
A LITERAL TRANSLATION
OF THE BIBLE

[1]Paul, *a* prisoner of Christ Jesus, and Timothy the brother, to Philemon the beloved and our fellow-worker, [2]and to Apphia the beloved, and to Archippus our fellow-soldier, and to the church in your house: [3]Grace to you and peace from God our Father and *the* Lord Jesus Christ.

[4]I thank my God always making mention of you in my prayers, [5]hearing of your love and faith which you have toward the Lord Jesus, and toward all the saints, [6]so that the fellowship of your faith may operate in a full knowledge of every good thing in you for Jesus Christ. [7]For we have much joy and encouragement over your love, in that the hearts of the saints have been refreshed through you, brother.

[8]Therefore, having much boldness in Christ to enjoin you *to do* what *is* becoming—[9]rather because of love I entreat, being such a one as Paul *the* aged, and now also a prisoner of Jesus Christ; [10]I entreat you concerning my child Onesimus, whom I fathered in my bonds, [11]the *one* once worthless to you, but now useful to you and to me;

3972 1198 5547 2424 5095 80
1 Παῦλος δέσμιος Χριστοῦ Ἰησοῦ, καὶ Τιμόθεος ὁ ἀδελφός,
Paul, a prisoner of Christ Jesus, and Timothy the brother,
5371 27 4904 2257 682
2 Φιλήμονι τῷ ἀγαπητῷ καὶ συνεργῷ ἡμῶν, καὶ Ἀπφίᾳ τῇ
to Philemon the beloved and fellow-worker to us, and to Apphia the
27 751 4961 2257
ἀγαπητῇ, καὶ Ἀρχίππῳ τῷ συστρατιώτῃ ἡμῶν, καὶ τῇ
beloved, and to Archippus the fellow-soldier of us, and to the
2596 3624/4675 1577 5485 5213 1515 575 2316
3 κατ᾽ οἶκόν σου ἐκκλησίᾳ· χάρις ὑμῖν καὶ εἰρήνη ἀπὸ Θεοῦ
at house of you church: Grace to you and peace from God
3962 2257 2962 2424 5547
πατρὸς ἡμῶν καὶ Κυρίου Ἰησοῦ Χριστοῦ.
(the) Father of us and (the) Lord Jesus Christ.
2168 2316/3450 3842 3417 4675 4160
4 Εὐχαριστῶ τῷ Θεῷ μου, πάντοτε μνείαν σου ποιούμενος
I thank the God of me, always mention of you making
1909 4335 3450 191 4675 26
5 ἐπὶ τῶν προσευχῶν μου, ἀκούων σου τὴν ἀγάπην, καὶ τὴν
at the prayers of me, hearing of you the love and the
4102/3739/2192/4314 2962 2424 1519 3956
πίστιν ἣν ἔχεις πρὸς τὸν Κύριον Ἰησοῦν καὶ εἰς πάντας τοὺς
faith which you have to the Lord Jesus, and to all the
40 3704 2842 4102 4675 1756 1096
6 ἁγίους, ὅπως ἡ κοινωνία τῆς πίστεώς σου ἐνεργὴς γένηται
saints, so as the fellowship of the faith of you operative may be
1722 1922 3956 18 1722/5213/1519/ 5547 2424
ἐν ἐπιγνώσει παντὸς ἀγαθοῦ τοῦ ἐν ὑμῖν εἰς Χριστὸν Ἰησοῦν.
in a full knowledge of every good thing in you for Christ Jesus.
5485 1063 2192 4183 3874 1909 26
7 χαρὰν γὰρ ἔχομεν πολλὴν καὶ παράκλησιν ἐπὶ τῇ ἀγάπῃ
joy For we have much, and encouragement over the love
4675/3754 4698 40 373 1223/4675
σου, ὅτι τὰ σπλάγχνα τῶν ἁγίων ἀναπέπαυται διὰ σοῦ,
of you, that the bowels of the saints have been refreshed through you,
80
ἀδελφέ.
brother.
1352 4183 1722 5547 3954 2192 2004 4671
8 Διὸ πολλὴν ἐν Χριστῷ παρρησίαν ἔχων ἐπιτάσσειν σοι
Therefore, much in Christ boldness having to enjoin you
433 1223 26 3123 3870 5108
9 τὸ ἀνῆκον, διὰ τὴν ἀγάπην μᾶλλον παρακαλῶ, τοιοῦτος
the thing fitting, because of love rather I beseech; such a one
5607/5613 3972 4246 3570 1198 2424
ὢν ὡς Παῦλος πρεσβύτης, νυνὶ δὲ καὶ δέσμιος Ἰησοῦ
being as Paul (the) aged one, now and also a prisoner of Jesus
5547 3870 4571/4012 1699 5043 3739 1080 1722
10 Χριστοῦ. παρακαλῶ σε περὶ τοῦ ἐμοῦ τέκνου, ὃν ἐγέννησα ἐν
Christ. I beseech you concerning the of me child, whom I fathered in
1199 3450 3682 4218/4671 990 3570
11 τοῖς δεσμοῖς μου, Ὀνήσιμον, τόν ποτέ σοι ἄχρηστον, νυνὶ δὲ
the bonds of me, Onesimus, the (one) then to you useless, now but

whom I sent back. [12]Even
receive him, that is, my
heart; [13]whom I resolved to
hold with myself, that for
you he might minister to me
in the bonds of the gospel.

[14]But I was willing to do
nothing without your con-
sent, that your good might
not be by way of necessity,
but by way of willingness.
[15]For perhaps for this he
was separated for an hour,
that you might receive him
eternally; [16]no longer as a
slave, but beyond a slave, a
beloved brother, especially
to me, and how much more
to you, both in *the* flesh and
in the Lord.
[17]Then if you have me as
a partner, receive him as
me. [18]And if he wronged
you *in* anything, or owes,
put this to my account. [19]I,
Paul, wrote with my hand; I
will repay; that I not say to
you that you even owe
yourself to me also. [20]Yes,
brother, *that* I may have
your help in *the* Lord,
refresh my heart in *the* Lord.
[21]Trusting to your obedience, I wrote to you, knowing that you will do even
beyond what I say. [22]But at
once prepare lodging for
me; for I hope that through
your prayers I shall be given
to you.

[23]Epaphras, my fellow-
prisoner in Christ Jesus,
greets you, [24]*also* my
fellow-workers Mark, Aristarchus, Demas, *and* Luke.

[25]The grace of our Lord
Jesus Christ *be* with your
spirit. Amen.

4671 1698 2173 3739 375 4771 846 5123 2076
12 σοὶ καὶ ἐμοὶ εὔχρηστον, ὃν ἀνέπεμψα· σὺ δὲ αὐτόν, τοῦτ᾽ ἔστι
to you and to me useful, whom I sent back to you, even him, this is,
1699 4698 4355 3739/1473 1014 4314
13 τὰ ἐμὰ σπλάγχνα, προσλαβοῦ· ὃν ἐγὼ ἐβουλόμην πρὸς
the of me bowels, receive (him), whom I resolved with
1683 2722 2443/5228/4675 1247 3427/1722 1199
ἐμαυτὸν κατέχειν, ἵνα ὑπὲρ σοῦ διακονῇ μοι ἐν τοῖς δεσμοῖς
myself to hold, that for you he minister to me in the bonds
2098 5565 4674 1106 3762 2309
14 τοῦ εὐαγγελίου· χωρὶς δὲ τῆς σῆς γνώμης οὐδὲν ἠθέλησα
of the gospel. without But your consent nothing I was willing
4160 2443/3361/5613/2596/ 318 18 4675/5600/235
ποιῆσαι, ἵνα μὴ ὡς κατὰ ἀνάγκην τὸ ἀγαθόν σου ᾖ, ἀλλὰ
to do, that not as by way of necessity the good of you be, but
2596 1595 5029 1063/1223/5124 5563 4314 5610
15 κατὰ ἑκούσιον. τάχα γὰρ διὰ τοῦτο ἐχωρίσθη πρὸς ὥραν,
by way of willingness. perhaps For for this he was separated for an hour,
2443 166 846 568 3765 5613 1401 235 5228
16 ἵνα αἰώνιον αὐτὸν ἀπέχῃς· οὐκέτι ὡς δοῦλον, ἀλλ᾽ ὑπὲρ
that eternally him you might receive no longer as a slave, but beyond
1402 80 27 3122 1698 4214 3123
δοῦλον, ἀδελφὸν ἀγαπητόν, μάλιστα ἐμοί, πόσῳ δὲ μᾶλλον
a slave, a brother beloved, especially to me, how much and more
4671 1722 4561 1722 2962 1487/3767/1691/2192 2844
17 σοὶ καὶ ἐν σαρκὶ καὶ ἐν Κυρίῳ. εἰ οὖν ἐμὲ ἔχεις κοινωνόν,
to you both in flesh and in (the) Lord. if Then me you have a partner,
4355 846 5613/1691/1487/5100/ 91 4571 3784 5124
18 προσλαβοῦ αὐτὸν ὡς ἐμέ. εἰ δέ τι ἠδίκησέ σε ἢ ὀφείλει, τοῦτο
receive him as me. if And anything he wronged you, or owes, this
1698 1677 1473 3972 1125 1699 5495 1473/ 661
19 ἐμοὶ ἐλλόγει· ἐγὼ Παῦλος ἔγραψα τῇ ἐμῇ χειρί, ἐγὼ ἀπο-
to me reckon: I Paul wrote with my hand, I will
2443/3361/3004/4671/3754 4572 3427 4359 3483
20 τίσω· ἵνα μὴ λέγω σοι ὅτι καὶ σεαυτόν μοι προσοφείλεις. ναί,
repay, that not I say to you that indeed yourself to me you owe also. Yes,
80 1473 4675 3685 1722 2962 373 3450
ἀδελφέ, ἐγώ σου ὀναίμην ἐν Κυρίῳ· ἀνάπαυσόν μου τὰ
brother, I of you may have help in (the) Lord, refresh of me the
4698 1722 2962 3982 5218 4675 1125
21 σπλάγχνα ἐν Κυρίῳ. πεποιθὼς τῇ ὑπακοῇ σου ἔγραψά
bowels in (the) Lord. Having trusted to the obedience of you, I wrote
4671 1492/3754 5228/3739/3004/ 4160 260 2090
22 σοι, εἰδὼς ὅτι καὶ ὑπὲρ ὃ λέγω ποιήσεις. ἅμα δὲ καὶ ἑτοίμαζέ
to you, knowing that even beyond what I say you will do. at once And also prepare
3427 3578 1679 1063 3754/1223 4335 5216
μοι ξενίαν· ἐλπίζω γὰρ ὅτι διὰ τῶν προσευχῶν ὑμῶν
for me lodging, I hope for that through the prayers of you
5483 5213
χαρισθήσομαι ὑμῖν.
I shall be given to you.
782 4571 1889 4869 3450 1722
23 Ἀσπάζονταί σε Ἐπαφρᾶς ὁ συναιχμάλωτός μου ἐν
Greet you Epaphras the fellow-captive of me in
5547 2424 3138 708 1214 3065
24 Χριστῷ Ἰησοῦ, Μάρκος, Ἀρίσταρχος, Δημᾶς, Λουκᾶς, οἱ
Christ Jesus, Mark, Aristarchus, Demas, Luke, the
4904 3450
συνεργοί μου.
fellowworkers of me.
5485 2962 2257 2424 5547 3326
25 Ἡ χάρις τοῦ Κυρίου ἡμῶν Ἰησοῦ Χριστοῦ μετὰ τοῦ
The grace of the Lord of us, Jesus Christ, with the
4151 5216 281
πνεύματος ὑμῶν. ἀμήν.
spirit of you (be). Amen.

ΠΑΥΛΟΥ ΤΟΥ ΑΠΟΣΤΟΛΟΥ
PAUL THE APOSTLE

Η ΠΡΟΣ
THE TO

ΕΒΡΑΙΟΥΣ ΕΠΙΣΤΟΛΗ
(THE) HEBREWS EPISTLE

THE EPISTLE
TO THE
HEBREWS
A LITERAL TRANSLATION
OF THE BIBLE

CHAPTER 1

[1]In many parts and in many ways of old, God spoke to the fathers in the prophets; [2]in these last days *He* spoke to us in *the* Son, whom He appointed heir of all; through whom He indeed made the ages; [3]who being *the* shining splendor of *His* glory, and the express image of His essence, and upholding all things by the word of His power, having made purification of our sins through Himself, *He* sat down on *the* right of the Majesty on high, [4]having become so much better than the angels, He has inherited a name more excellent than they. [5]For to which of the angels did He ever say, "You are My Son; today I have begotten You"? And again, "I will be a Father to Him, and He shall be a Son to Me." [6]And again, when He brought the Firstborn into the world, He said, "And let all *the* angels of God worship Him."

[7]And as to the angels, He said, "Who makes His angels spirits, and His ministers a flame of fire;" [8]but as to the Son, "Your throne, *O* God, *is* forever and ever, A sceptre of righteousness *is* the sceptre of Your kingdom; [9]You have loved righteousness and hated lawlessness; because of this God, Your God, has anointed You *with* the oil of

CHAPTER 1

4181 4187 3819 2316 2980
1 Πολυμερῶς καὶ πολυτρόπως πάλαι ὁ Θεὸς λαλήσας τοῖς
In many parts and in many ways of old God spoke to the
3962 1722 4396 1909 2078 2250
2 πατράσιν ἐν τοῖς προφήταις, ἐπ' ἐσχάτων τῶν ἡμερῶν τού-
fathers by the prophets, in (the) last days of
2980 2254/1722/5207/• 5087 2818 3956 1223
των ἐλάλησεν ἡμῖν ἐν υἱῷ, ὃν ἔθηκε κληρονόμον πάντων, δι'
these spoke to us in (the) Son, whom He appointed heir of all, through
3739 165 4160 3739/5607/ 541 1391
3 οὗ καὶ τοὺς αἰῶνας ἐποίησεν, ὃς ὢν ἀπαύγασμα τῆς δόξης
whom indeed the ages He made; who being (the) radiance of the glory
5481 5287 848 5342/5037 3956
καὶ χαρακτὴρ τῆς ὑποστάσεως αὐτοῦ, φέρων τε τὰ πάντα
and the express image of the essence of Him, upholding and all things
4487 1411 848 1223 1438 2512
τῷ ῥήματι τῆς δυνάμεως αὐτοῦ, δι' ἑαυτοῦ καθαρισμὸν
by the word of the power of Him, through Himself cleansing
4160 266 2257 2523 1722 1188
ποιησάμενος τῶν ἁμαρτιῶν ἡμῶν, ἐκάθισεν ἐν δεξιᾷ τῆς
having made of the sins of us, sat down on (the) right the
3172 1722 5308 5118 2909 1096
4 μεγαλωσύνης ἐν ὑψηλοῖς, τοσούτῳ κρείττων γενόμενος τῶν
Majesty on high; by so much better becoming (than) the
32 3745 1313 3844 846 2816
ἀγγέλων, ὅσῳ διαφορώτερον παρ' αὐτοὺς κεκληρονόμηκεν
angels, as a more excellent than them He has inherited
•1488 3686 5101/1063/2036/4218 32 3745/3450/•/4771/1473
5 ὄνομα. τίνι γὰρ εἶπέ ποτε τῶν ἀγγέλων, Υἱός μου εἶ σύ, ἐγὼ
name. to which For said He ever of the angels, Son of Me are you, I
4594 1080 4571 3825 1473 2071 846 1519
σήμερον γεγέννηκά σε; καὶ πάλιν, Ἐγὼ ἔσομαι αὐτῷ εἰς
today have begotten You? And again, I will be to Him for
3962 846 2071/3427/1519/5207/3752 3825 1521
6 πατέρα, καὶ αὐτὸς ἔσται μοι εἰς υἱόν; ὅταν δὲ πάλιν εἰσα-
a Father, and He shall be to me for a Son? when And again He
4416 1519 3625 3004 4352
γάγῃ τὸν πρωτότοκον εἰς τὴν οἰκουμένην λέγει, Καὶ προσ-
brings the Firstborn into the habitable world He says, And let
846 3956 32 2316 4314/3303
7 κυνησάτωσαν αὐτῷ πάντες ἄγγελοι Θεοῦ. καὶ πρὸς μὲν τοὺς
worship Him all angels of God. And as to the
32 3004 4160 32 848 4151
ἀγγέλους λέγει, Ὁ ποιῶν τοὺς ἀγγέλους αὐτοῦ πνεύματα,
angels, He says, Who (is) making the angels of Him spirits,
3011 848 4442 5395 4314 5207
8 καὶ τοὺς λειτουργοὺς αὐτοῦ πυρὸς φλόγα· πρὸς δὲ τὸν υἱόν,
and the ministers of Him of fire a flame as to but the Son,
2262 4675 2316/1519 165 165 4464
Ὁ θρόνος σου, ὁ Θεός, εἰς τὸν αἰῶνα τοῦ αἰῶνος· ῥάβδος
The throne of You, God, (is) to the ages of the ages, (the) rod
2118 4464 932 4675 25 1343
9 εὐθύτητος ἡ ῥάβδος τῆς βασιλείας σου. ἠγάπησας δικαιο-
of uprightness (is the) rod of the kingdom of You. You loved righteous-
3404 458 1223 5124 5548/4571 2316
σύνην, καὶ ἐμίσησας ἀνομίαν· διὰ τοῦτο ἔχρισέ σε ὁ Θεός, ὁ
ness, and hated lawlessness; therefore anointed You God, the

gladness above Your companions." [10]And, "You, Lord, at *the* beginning founded the earth, and the heavens are works of Your hands. [11]They will vanish away, but You will continue; and *they* will all become old, like a garment, [12]and You shall fold them up like a covering, and *they* shall be changed. But You are the same, and Your years shall not fail." [13]But to which of the angels did He ever say, "Sit at My right *hand* until I place Your enemies *as* a footstool of Your feet"? [14]Are they not all ministering spirits for service, being sent out because of the *ones* being about to inherit salvation?

2316/4675 1637 20 3844 3353 4675
10 Θεός σου, ἔλαιον ἀγαλλιάσεως παρὰ τοὺς μετόχους σου. καί,
God of You, (with) oil of gladness above the partners of You. And:
4771/2596/746 2962 1093 2311 2041
Σὺ κατ' ἀρχάς, Κύριε, τὴν γῆν ἐθεμελίωσας, καὶ ἔργα τῶν
You at (the) beginning Lord, the earth founded, and works of the
5495 4675/1526 3772 846 622 4771 1265
11 χειρῶν σου εἰσιν οἱ οὐρανοί· αὐτοὶ ἀπολοῦνται, σὺ δὲ δια-
hands of You are the heavens; they will perish, You but will
3956 5613 2440 3822 5616
12 μένεις· καὶ πάντες ὡς ἱμάτιον παλαιωθήσονται, καὶ ὡσεὶ
remain and all as a garment shall become old, and as
4018 1667 846 236 4771 846
περιβόλαιον ἑλίξεις αὐτοὺς καὶ ἀλλαγήσονται· σὺ δὲ ὁ αὐτὸς
a covering You shall roll them, and shall be changed. You but the same
1488 2094 4675 3756 1587 4314 5101
13 εἶ, καὶ τὰ ἔτη σου οὐκ ἐκλείψουσι. πρὸς τίνα δὲ τῶν
are, and the years of You not shall fail. to which But of the
32 2046 4218 2521/1537/1188/3450/2193/3739/5087
ἀγγέλων εἴρηκέ ποτε. Κάθου ἐκ δεξιῶν μου, ἕως ἂν θῶ τοὺς
angels has He said at any time, Sit on (the) right of Me, until I may put the
2190 4675/5286 4228 4675 3780 3956 1526
14 ἐχθρούς σου ὑποπόδιον τῶν ποδῶν σου; οὐχὶ πάντες εἰσὶ
enemies of You a footstool of the feet of You not all Are they
3010 4151 1519 1248 649 1223
λειτουργικὰ πνεύματα, εἰς διακονίαν ἀποστελλόμενα διὰ
ministering spirits for service being sent out because of
3195 2816 4991
τοὺς μέλλοντας κληρονομεῖν σωτηρίαν;
those being about to inherit salvation?

CHAPTER 2

[1]For this reason we ought to give the more earnest heed to the things heard, that we should not slip away at any time. [2]For if the word spoken by angels was confirmed, and every transgression and disobedience received a just repayment; [3]how shall we escape *if we* neglect so great a salvation? Which having received a beginning to be spoken through the Lord, was confirmed to us by the ones hearing; [4]God bearing witness with *them* by both miracles and wonders, and by various works of power, even by distribution *of the* Holy Spirit, according to His will.

[5]For He did not put the coming world under angels, about which we speak, [6]but one fully testified somehere, saying, "What is man, that You are mindful of him; or the son of man, that You look upon him? [7]You made him a little less than *the*

CHAPTER 2

1223 5124 1163 4056 2248 4337 191
1 Διὰ τοῦτο δεῖ περισσοτέρως ἡμᾶς προσέχειν τοῖς ἀκου-
For this reason ought more abundantly us to give heed to the things
3361 4218 3901 1487/1063 1223 32
2 σθεῖσι, μή ποτε παραρρυῶμεν. εἰ γὰρ ὁ δι' ἀγγέλων
heard, lest at any time we should slip away. if For the through angels
2980 3056 1096 949 3956 3847
λαληθεὶς λόγος ἐγένετο βέβαιος. καὶ πᾶσα παράβασις καὶ
spoken word was confirmed, and every transgression and
3876 2983 1738 3405 4459 2249 1628
3 παρακοὴ ἔλαβεν ἔνδικον μισθαποδοσίαν, πῶς ἡμεῖς ἐκφευ-
disobedience received a just recompense, how we shall escape
5082 272 4991 3748 746
ξόμεθα τηλικαύτης ἀμελήσαντες σωτηρίας; ἥτις, ἀρχὴν
so great neglecting a salvation? Which a beginning
2983 2980 1223 2962 5259 191
λαβοῦσα λαλεῖσθαι διὰ τοῦ Κυρίου, ὑπὸ τῶν ἀκουσάντων
receiving to be spoken through the Lord, by those hearing
1519/2248 950 4901 2316 4592
4 εἰς ἡμᾶς ἐβεβαιώθη, συνεπιμαρτυροῦντος τοῦ Θεοῦ σημείοις
to us was confirmed, bearing witness with God by signs
5037 5059 4164 1411 4151 40
τε καὶ τέρασι. καὶ ποικίλαις δυνάμεσι, καὶ Πνεύματος Ἁγίου
both and wonders, and by various works of power, and (the) Spirit Holy
3311 2596 848 2308
μερισμοῖς, κατὰ τὴν αὐτοῦ θέλησιν.
by distribution, according to the of Him will.
3756/1063 32 5293 3625 3195
5 Οὐ γὰρ ἀγγέλοις ὑπέταξε τὴν οἰκουμένην τὴν μέλλουσαν,
not For to angels subjected He the habitable world coming.
4012/3739 2980 1263 4225/5100 3004
6 περὶ ἧς λαλοῦμεν. διεμαρτύρατο δέ πού τις λέγων, Τί
about which we speak. solemnly witnessed But somewhere one, saying, What
2076 444 3754 3403 846 2228/5207 444
ἐστιν ἄνθρωπος, ὅτι μιμνήσκῃ αὐτοῦ; ἢ υἱὸς ἀνθρώπου,
is man that You remember him? Or the son of man
3754 1980 846 1642 846 1024/5100/3844
7 ὅτι ἐπισκέπτῃ αὐτόν; ἠλάττωσας αὐτὸν βραχύ τι παρ'
that You observed him? You made less him a little than

angels; You crowned him with glory and honor, and You set him over the works of Your hands; [8]You put all things under his feet." For in putting all things under him, He left nothing not subjected to him. But now we do not yet see all things being subjected to him; [9]but we do see Jesus crowned with glory and honor, who on account of the suffering of death *was* made a little less than the angels, so that by *the* grace of God He might taste of death for every *son*. [10]For it was fitting for Him, because of whom *are* all things, and through whom *are* all things, bringing many sons to glory, to perfect *Him as* the Author of their salvation through sufferings. [11]For both He sanctifying and the *one* being sanctified *are* all of one; for which cause He is not ashamed to call them brothers, [12]saying, "I will announce Your name to My brothers; I will sing to You in *the* midst of *the* church." [13]And again, "I will be trusting on Him." And again, "Behold, I and the children whom God gave to Me."

[14]Since, then, the children have partaken of flesh and blood, in like manner He Himself also shared the same things, that through death He might cause to cease the *one* having the power of death, that is, the Devil; [15]and might set these free, as many as by fear of death were subject to slavery through all the *time* to live. [16]For indeed He does not take hold of angels, but He takes hold of *the* seed of Abraham. [17]Therefore, He ought by all means to become like *His* brothers, that He might become a merciful and faithful high priest *in* the things respecting God, in

32 1391 5092 4737 846 2525
ἀγγέλους· δόξῃ καὶ τιμῇ ἐστεφάνωσας αὐτόν, καὶ κατέ-
the angels with glory and with honor You crowned him; and,
846 1909 2041 5495 4675 3956 5293
8 στησας αὐτὸν ἐπὶ τὰ ἔργα τῶν χειρῶν σου· πάντα ὑπέταξας
You set him over the works of the hands of You; all things You subjected
5270 4228 848 1722/1063 5293 846
ὑποκάτω τῶν ποδῶν αὐτοῦ. ἐν γὰρ τῷ ὑποτάξαι αὐτῷ
under the feet of him. in order For to subject to him
3956 3762 863 846 506 3568 3768
τὰ πάντα, οὐδὲν ἀφῆκεν αὐτῷ ἀνυπότακτον. νῦν δὲ οὔπω
all things, nothing He left to him not subjected. now But not yet
3708 846 3956 5293 1024 5100
9 ὁρῶμεν αὐτῷ τὰ πάντα ὑποτεταγμένα. τὸν δὲ βραχύ τι
do we see to him all things having been subjected. the (One) But a little
3844 32 1642 991 2424 1223
παρ' ἀγγέλους ἠλαττωμένον βλέπομεν Ἰησοῦν, διὰ τὸ
than the angels having been made less we see, Jesus, because of the
3804 2288 1391 5092 4737 3704
πάθημα τοῦ θανάτου δόξῃ καὶ τιμῇ ἐστεφανωμένον, ὅπως
suffering of death with glory and with honor having been crowned so as
5485 2316 5228 3956 1089 2288 4241 1063
10 χάριτι Θεοῦ ὑπὲρ παντὸς γεύσηται θανάτου. ἔπρεπε γὰρ
by grace God's for every (son) He might taste of death. it was fitting For
846 1223/3739 3956 1223/3739 3956 4183 5207
αὐτῷ, δι' ὃν τὰ πάντα, καὶ δι' οὗ τὰ πάντα, πολλοὺς υἱοὺς
for Him, because of whom (are) all things, and through whom (are) all things, many sons
1519/1391 71 747 4991 848
εἰς δόξαν ἀγαγόντα, τὸν ἀρχηγὸν τῆς σωτηρίας αὐτῶν
to glory bringing, the Author of the salvation of them
1223 3804 5048 5037/1063/ 37 37
11 διὰ παθημάτων τελειῶσαι. ὅ τε γὰρ ἁγιάζων καὶ οἱ ἁγιαζό-
through sufferings to perfect. He both For sanctifying and the (one) being
1537/1520 3956 1223/3739/ 156 3756 1870
μενοι, ἐξ ἑνὸς πάντες· δι' ἣν αἰτίαν οὐκ ἐπαισχύνεται
sanctified of one all (are); for which cause not He is ashamed
80 846 2564 3004 518 3686 4675
12 ἀδελφοὺς αὐτοὺς καλεῖν, λέγων, Ἀπαγγελῶ τὸ ὄνομά σου
brothers them to call, saying, I will announce the name of You
80 3450/1722/3319 1577 5214/4571 3825
13 τοῖς ἀδελφοῖς μου, ἐν μέσῳ ἐκκλησίας ὑμνήσω σε. καὶ πάλιν,
to the brothers of Me; in (the) midst of (the) church I will hymn You. And again,
1473 2071 3982 1909 846 3825 2400/1473
Ἐγὼ ἔσομαι πεποιθὼς ἐπ' αὐτῷ. καὶ πάλιν, Ἰδοὺ ἐγὼ καὶ
I will be trusting on Him. And again, Behold, I and
3813 3739/3427 1325 2316/1893/3767 3813 2841
14 τὰ παιδία ἅ μοι ἔδωκεν ὁ Θεός. ἐπεὶ οὖν τὰ παιδία κεκοινώ-
the children whom to Me gave God. Since, then, the children have partaken
4561 129 846 3898 3348
νηκε σαρκὸς καὶ αἵματος, καὶ αὐτὸς παραπλησίως μετέσχε
of flesh and blood, also Himself, in like manner He shared
846 2443/1223 2288 2673 2904
τῶν αὐτῶν, ἵνα διὰ τοῦ θανάτου καταργήσῃ τὸν τὸ κράτος
the same things, that through the death He might annul the (one) the power
2192 2288 5123 2076 1228 525
15 ἔχοντα τοῦ θανάτου, τοῦτ' ἔστι τὸν διάβολον, καὶ ἀπαλ-
having of death, this is the Devil, and might set
5128 3745 5401 2288 1223 3956 2198
λάξῃ τούτους, ὅσοι φόβῳ θανάτου διὰ παντὸς τοῦ ζῆν
free these, as many as by fear of death through all the (time) to live
1777 2258 1397 3756/1063 1222 32 1949
16 ἔνοχοι ἦσαν δουλείας. οὐ γὰρ δήπου ἀγγέλων ἐπιλαμβά-
subject were to slavery. not For indeed of angels He takes hold,
235 4690 11 1949 3606 3784
17 νεται, ἀλλὰ σπέρματος Ἀβραὰμ ἐπιλαμβάνεται. ὅθεν ὤφειλε
but of (the) seed of Abraham He takes hold. Therefore He ought
2596 3956 80 3666 2443 1655 1096
κατὰ πάντα τοῖς ἀδελφοῖς ὁμοιωθῆναι, ἵνα ἐλεήμων γένηται
by all means to the brothers to become like, that a merciful He might be
4103 749 4314 2316/1519 2433
καὶ πιστὸς ἀρχιερεὺς τὰ πρὸς τὸν Θεόν. εἰς τὸ ἱλάσκεσθαι
and faithful High Priest (in) the things as to God, in order to make propitiation for

order to make propitiation for the sins of *His* people. [18]For in what He has suffered, being tried, He is able to help those having been tried.

CHAPTER 3

[1]For which reason, holy brothers called *to be* partakers of a heavenly *calling,* consider the Apostle and High Priest of our confession, Christ Jesus, [2]being faithful to Him who appointed Him, as also Moses in all his house. [3]For He was counted worthy of more glory than Moses, by so much as the *one* having built the house has more honor than the house. [4]For every house is built by someone; but He who built all things *is* God. [5]And Moses truly *was* faithful in all his house as a ministering servant, for a testimony of the things having been spoken; [6]but Christ as Son over His house, whose house we are, if truly we hold fast the boldness and rejoicing of the hope firm to the end.

[7]For this reason even as the Holy Spirit says, "Today, if you will hear His voice, [8]do not harden your hearts, as in the provocation, in the day of temptation in the wilderness, [9]there where your fathers tempted Me, testing Me, and saw My works forty years. [10]Because of this, I was angry with that generation, and said, They always go astray in heart; and they did not know My ways; [11]so I swore in My wrath, They shall not enter into My rest."

[12]Watch, brothers, lest perhaps shall be in any one of you a heart of evil unbelief in falling away from *the* living God. [13]But exhort

266 2992/1722/3739/1063/ 3958 848 3985
18 τὰς ἁμαρτίας τοῦ λαοῦ. ἐν ᾧ γὰρ πέπονθεν αὐτὸς πειρα-
the sins of the people. in what For has suffered He, having been
1410 3985 997
σθείς, δύναται τοῖς πειραζομένοις βοηθῆσαι.
tempted, He is able those being tempted to help.

CHAPTER 3

3606 80 40 2821 2032 3353
1 Ὅθεν, ἀδελφοὶ ἅγιοι, κλήσεως ἐπουρανίου μέτοχοι,
Therefore, brothers holy, called (to be) of a heavenly sharers,
2657 652 748 3671
κατανοήσατε τὸν ἀπόστολον καὶ ἀρχιερέα τῆς ὁμολογίας
consider the Apostle and High Priest of the confession
2257 5547 2424 4103 5607 4160 846
2 ἡμῶν Χριστὸν Ἰησοῦν, πιστὸν ὄντα τῷ ποιήσαντι αὐτόν,
of us, Christ Jesus, faithful being to the (One) making Him (these)
5613 3475/1722/3650 3624 848 4119 1063 1391
3 ὡς καὶ Μωσῆς ἐν ὅλῳ τῷ οἴκῳ αὐτοῦ. πλείονος γὰρ δόξης
as also Moses in all the house of him. of more For glory
3778 3844 3475 515 2596 3745 4119 5092 2192
οὗτος παρὰ Μωσῆν ἠξίωται, καθ' ὅσον πλείονα τιμὴν ἔχει
this (One) than Moses has been by so much as more honor has (than)
3624 2680 counted worthy, 3956/1063/3624 2680
4 τοῦ οἴκου ὁ κατασκευάσας αὐτόν. πᾶς γὰρ οἶκος κατασκευά-
the house the (one) building it. every For house is prepared
5259 5100 3956 2680 2316
5 ζεται ὑπό τινος· ὁ δὲ τὰ πάντα κατασκευάσας, Θεός. καὶ
by someone, He but all things having prepared (is) God. And
3475 3303 4103/1722/3650 3624 848 5613 2324 1519
Μωσῆς μὲν πιστὸς ἐν ὅλῳ τῷ οἴκῳ αὐτοῦ ὡς θεράπων, εἰς
Moses indeed (was) faithful in all the house of him as a servant, for
3142 2980 5547 5613/5207/1909
6 μαρτύριον τῶν λαληθησομένων· Χριστὸς δὲ ὡς υἱὸς ἐπὶ τὸν
a testimony of the things having been spoken; Christ but as a Son over the
3624 848 3739/3624 2070 2249/1437-4007 3954
οἶκον αὐτοῦ· οὗ οἶκός ἐσμεν ἡμεῖς, ἐάνπερ τὴν παρρησίαν καὶ
house of Him, of whom a house are we, if truly the confidence and
2745 1680 3360 5056 949 2722
τὸ καύχημα τῆς ἐλπίδος μέχρι τέλους βεβαίαν κατάσχωμεν.
the boast of the hope until (the) end firm we hold fast.
1352 2531 3004 4151 40 4594 1437
7 διό, καθὼς λέγει τὸ Πνεῦμα τὸ Ἅγιον, Σήμερον ἐὰν τῆς
Therefore, as says the Spirit — Holy, Today, if the
5456 848 191 3361 4645 2588 5216
8 φωνῆς αὐτοῦ ἀκούσητε, μὴ σκληρύνητε τὰς καρδίας ὑμῶν,
voice of Him you hear, do not harden the hearts of you,
5613/1722 3894 2596 2250 3986
ὡς ἐν τῷ παραπικρασμῷ, κατὰ τὴν ἡμέραν τοῦ πειρασμοῦ
as in the provocation in the day of the temptation
1722 2048 3757 3985 3165 3962 5216 1381
9 ἐν τῇ ἐρήμῳ, οὗ ἐπείρασάν με οἱ πατέρες ὑμῶν, ἐδοκίμασάν
in the wilderness, when tempted Me the fathers of you, testing
3165 1492 2041 3450 5062 2094 1352 4360
10 με, καὶ εἶδον τὰ ἔργα μου τεσσαράκοντα ἔτη. διὸ προσ-
Me, and saw the works of Me forty years. Therefore I was
1074 1565 2036 104 4105 2588
ώχθισα τῇ γενεᾷ ἐκείνῃ, καὶ εἶπον, Ἀεὶ πλανῶνται τῇ καρδίᾳ·
angry with generation that, and I said, Always they err in the heart,
846 3756 1097 3598 3450/5613/3660/1722 3709
11 αὐτοὶ δὲ οὐκ ἔγνωσαν τὰς ὁδούς μου· ὡς ὤμοσα ἐν τῇ ὀργῇ
they and not did know the ways of Me; as I swore in the wrath
3450/1487 1525 1519 2663 3450 991
12 μου, Εἰ εἰσελεύσονται εἰς τὴν κατάπαυσίν μου. βλέπετε,
of Me, If they shall enter into the rest of Me. Watch,
80 3361/4218/2071/1722/5100/5216/ 2588 4190 570
ἀδελφοί, μή ποτε ἔσται ἔν τινι ὑμῶν καρδία πονηρὰ ἀπιστίας
brothers, lest perhaps shall be in anyone of you a heart evil of unbelief
1722 868 575 2316 2198 235 3870
13 ἐν τῷ ἀποστῆναι ἀπὸ Θεοῦ ζῶντος· ἀλλὰ παρακαλεῖτε
in departing from God a living; but exhort

yourselves each day, as long as it is being called today, that not any of you be hardened by *the* deceit of sin. [14]For we have become sharers of Christ, if truly we hold the beginning of the assurance firm to *the* end; [15]*as* in the saying, "Today, if you hear His voice, do not harden your hearts, as in the provocation." [16]For hearing, some provoked *Him*, but not all those coming out of Egypt through Moses. [17]But with whom was He angry forty years? *Was it* not with the ones sinning, whose corpses fell in the wilderness? [18]And to whom did He swear *they would* not enter into His rest, except to those not obeying? [19]And we see that they were not able to enter in because of unbelief.

1438 2596 1538 2250 891 4594 2564
ἑαυτοὺς καθ' ἑκάστην ἡμέραν, ἄχρις οὗ τὸ σήμερον καλεῖται,
yourselves each day, while today it is being called,
2443/3361/ 4645 5100/1537/5216/ 539 266 3353
14 ἵνα μὴ σκληρυνθῇ τις ἐξ ὑμῶν ἀπάτῃ τῆς ἁμαρτίας· μέτοχοι
that not be hardened anyone of you by(the) deceit of sin. sharers
1063 1096 5547 1437-4007 746 5287
γὰρ γεγόναμεν τοῦ Χριστοῦ, ἐάνπερ τὴν ἀρχὴν τῆς ὑπο-
For we have become of Christ, if truly the beginning of the
3360 5056 949 2722 1722 3004
15 στάσεως μέχρι τέλους βεβαίαν κατάσχωμεν· ἐν τῷ λέγεσθαι,
assurance until (the) end firm we hold fast. In the saying
4594 1437 5456 848 191 3361/ 4645
Σήμερον ἐὰν τῆς φωνῆς αὐτοῦ ἀκούσητε, μὴ σκληρύνητε τὰς
Today, if the voice of Him you hear, do not harden the
2588 5216/5613/1722 3894 5100 1063 191
16 καρδίας ὑμῶν, ὡς ἐν τῷ παραπικρασμῷ. τινὲς γὰρ ἀκού-
hearts of you, as in the provocation. some For
3893 235 3756 3956 1831 1537
σαντες παρεπίκραναν, ἀλλ' οὐ πάντες οἱ ἐξελθόντες ἐξ
hearing provoked, but not all those coming out of
125 1223 3475 5101 4360 5062
17 Αἰγύπτου διὰ Μωσέως. τίσι δὲ προσώχθισε τεσσαράκοντα
Egypt through Moses. with whom But was He angry forty
2094 3780 264 3739 2966 4098 1722
ἔτη; οὐχὶ τοῖς ἁμαρτήσασιν, ὧν τὰ κῶλα ἔπεσεν ἐν τῇ
years? Not with those sinning, of whom the corpses fell in the
2048 5101 3660/3361 1525 1519 2663
18 ἐρήμῳ; τίσι δὲ ὤμοσε μὴ εἰσελεύσεσθαι εἰς τὴν κατάπαυσιν
wilderness? to whom And swore He not to enter into the rest
848 =1508= 544 991 3754/3756/ 1410
19 αὐτοῦ, εἰ μὴ τοῖς ἀπειθήσασι; καὶ βλέπομεν ὅτι οὐκ ἠδυνή-
of Him, except to those not obeying? And we see that not they were
1525 1223 570
θησαν εἰσελθεῖν δι' ἀπιστίαν.
able to enter in because of unbelief.

CHAPTER 4

[1]Therefore, let us fear lest perhaps a promise being left to enter into His rest, any of you might seem to come short. [2]For, indeed, we have had the gospel preached *to us*, even as they also; but the word did not profit those hearing *it*, not having been mixed with faith in the ones who heard.

[3]For we, the ones believing, enter into the rest, even as He said, "As I swore in My wrath, they shall not enter into My rest," though the works had come into being from *the* foundation of the world. [4]For He has spoken somewhere about the seventh *day* this way, "And God rested from all His works in the seventh *day*." [5]And in this *place* again, "They shall not enter into

5399 3767/3361 5218 2641 1860
1 Φοβηθῶμεν οὖν μή ποτε καταλειπομένης ἐπαγγελίας
let us fear Therefore, lest perhaps being left a promise
1525 1519 2663 848 1380/5100/1537/5216
εἰσελθεῖν εἰς τὴν κατάπαυσιν αὐτοῦ, δοκῇ τις ἐξ ὑμῶν
to enter into the rest of Him, seems anyone of you
5302 1063 2070 2097 2509
2 ὑστερηκέναι. καὶ γὰρ ἐσμεν εὐηγγελισμένοι, καθάπερ
to come short. indeed For we are having had the gospel preached, even as
2548 235 3756/5623 3056 189 1565 3361
κἀκεῖνοι· ἀλλ' οὐκ ὠφέλησεν ὁ λόγος τῆς ἀκοῆς ἐκείνους, μὴ
those also; but did not profit the word of hearing those, not
4786 4102 191 1525 1063
3 συγκεκραμένος τῇ πίστει τοῖς ἀκούσασιν. εἰσερχόμεθα γὰρ
having been mixed with faith in those hearing. we enter For
1519 2663 4100 2531 2046 5613
εἰς τὴν κατάπαυσιν οἱ πιστεύσαντες, καθὼς εἴρηκεν, Ὡς
into the rest, those believing, even as He said, As
3660 1722 3709 3450 1487 1525 1519 2663
ὤμοσα ἐν τῇ ὀργῇ μου, Εἰ εἰσελεύσονται εἰς τὴν κατά-
I swore in the wrath of Me, If they shall enter into the rest
3450 2543 2041 575 2602 2889
παυσίν μου· καίτοι τῶν ἔργων ἀπὸ καταβολῆς κόσμου
of Me; though the works from (the) foundation of world
1096 2046 1063/4225/4012 1442 3779
4 γενηθέντων. εἴρηκε γάρ που περὶ τῆς ἑβδόμης οὕτω, Καὶ
coming into being. He has said For somewhere about the seventh (day) thus: And
2664 2316/1722 2250 1442 575 3956
κατέπαυσεν ὁ Θεὸς ἐν τῇ ἡμέρᾳ τῇ ἑβδόμῃ ἀπὸ πάντων
rested God in the day seventh from all
2041 848 1722 5129 3825/1487 1525
5 τῶν ἔργων αὐτοῦ· καὶ ἐν τούτῳ πάλιν, Εἰ εἰσελεύσονται εἰς
the works of Him; and in this (place) again, If they shall enter into

My rest." 6 Therefore, since it remains *for* some to enter into it, and those who formerly had the gospel preached did not enter in on account of disobedience, 7 He again marks out a certain day, saying in David, "Today"—after so long a time, according as He has said—"Today, if you hear His voice, do not harden your hearts." 8 For if Joshua gave them rest, then He would not have afterwards spoken about another day. 9 So, then, there remains a rest to the people of God. 10 For He entering into His rest, *He* Himself also rested from His works, as God *had done* from His own.

11 Therefore, let us labor to enter into that rest, that not anyone fall in the same example of disobedience. 12 For the word of God *is* living, and powerfully working, and sharper than every two-edged sword, even piercing as far as *the* dividing apart of both soul and spirit, of both joints and marrow, and able to judge of the thoughts and intentions of the heart; 13 and there is no creature unrevealed before Him; but all things *are* naked and laid open to His eyes, with whom *is* our account.

14 Therefore, having a great High Priest *who* has passed through the heavens, Jesus the Son of God, let us hold fast the confession. 15 For we do not have a high priest not being able to sympathize with our infirmities, but *One* having been tried in all respects according to *our* likeness, apart from sin. 16 Therefore, let us draw near with confidence to the throne of grace, that we may receive mercy, and we may find grace for help in time of need.

2663 3450 1893/3767 620 5100 1525
6 τὴν κατάπαυσίν μου. ἐπεὶ οὖν ἀπολείπεται τινὰς εἰσελθεῖν
the rest of Me. Since therefore it remains (for) some to enter
1519 846 4386 2097 3756 1525 1223
εἰς αὐτήν, καὶ οἱ πρότερον εὐαγγελισθέντες οὐκ εἰσῆλθον δι'
into it, and those before having had the gospel preached not entered for
543 3825 5100 3724 2250 4594 1722 1138
7 ἀπείθειαν, πάλιν τινὰ ὁρίζει ἡμέραν, Σήμερον, ἐν Δαβὶδ
disobedience, again a certain marks out day: Today; in David
3004 3326 5118 5550 2531 2046 4594 1437
λέγων, μετὰ τοσοῦτον χρόνον, καθὼς εἴρηται, Σήμερον ἐὰν
saying after such a time, as He has said, Today, if
5456 848 191 3361 4645 2588
τῆς φωνῆς αὐτοῦ ἀκούσητε, μὴ σκληρύνητε τὰς καρδίας
the voice of Him you hear, do not harden the hearts
5216/1487/1063/846 2424 2664 3756/302/4012/243
8 ὑμῶν. εἰ γὰρ αὐτοὺς Ἰησοῦς κατέπαυσεν, οὐκ ἂν περὶ ἄλλης
of you. if For them (Joshua) rested, not concerning another
2980 /3326 5023 2250 686 620 4520
9 ἐλάλει μετὰ ταῦτα ἡμέρας. ἄρα ἀπολείπεται σαββατισμὸς
he would after these things day. Then remains a sabbath rest
*2992 have spoken 2316 1063 1525/1519 2663 848
10 τῷ λαῷ τοῦ Θεοῦ. ὁ γὰρ εἰσελθὼν εἰς τὴν κατάπαυσιν αὐτοῦ
to the people of God. He For having entered into the rest of Him,
846 2664 575 2041 848 5618 575
καὶ αὐτὸς κατέπαυσεν ἀπὸ τῶν ἔργων αὐτοῦ, ὥσπερ ἀπὸ
also Himself rested from the works of Him, as from
2398 2316 4704 3767 1525 1519 1565
11 τῶν ἰδίων ὁ Θεός. σπουδάσωμεν οὖν εἰσελθεῖν εἰς ἐκείνην τὴν
the own (did) God. Let us be eager, therefore, to enter into that
2663 2443/3361/1722 846/5100/ 5262 4098
κατάπαυσιν, ἵνα μὴ ἐν τῷ αὐτῷ τις ὑποδείγματι πέσῃ τῆς
rest, that not in the same anyone example falls
543 2198/1063 3056 2316 1756
12 ἀπειθείας. ζῶν γὰρ ὁ λόγος τοῦ Θεοῦ, καὶ ἐνεργής, καὶ
of disobedience. (is) living For the word of God, and working, and
*5228 5114 3956 3162 1366 1338
τομώτερος ὑπὲρ πᾶσαν μάχαιραν δίστομον, καὶ διϊκνού-
sharper than every sword two-mouthed, and piercing
841 3311 5590/5037 4151 719 5037
μενος ἄχρι μερισμοῦ ψυχῆς τε καὶ πνεύματος, ἁρμῶν τε καὶ
as far as (the) division of soul both and spirit, of joints both and
3452 2924 1761 1771 2588
13 μυελῶν, καὶ κριτικὸς ἐνθυμήσεων καὶ ἐννοιῶν καρδίας. καὶ
of marrows, and able to judge of thoughts and intentions of a heart; and
3756/2076/ 2937 852 1799 846 3956 1131
οὐκ ἔστι κτίσις ἀφανὴς ἐνώπιον αὐτοῦ· πάντα δὲ γυμνὰ καὶ
not is (a) creature not revealed before Him, all things but (are) naked and
5136 3788 848 4314/3739/2254 3056
τετραχηλισμένα τοῖς ὀφθαλμοῖς αὐτοῦ πρὸς ὃν ἡμῖν ὁ λόγος.
laid open to the eyes of Him with whom (is) our account.
2192 3767 749 3173 1330 3772
14 Ἔχοντες οὖν ἀρχιερέα μέγαν, διεληλυθότα τοὺς οὐρανούς,
Having therefore a high priest great, having passed through the heavens,
2424 5207 2316 2902 3671 3756/1063
15 Ἰησοῦν τὸν υἱὸν τοῦ Θεοῦ, κρατῶμεν τῆς ὁμολογίας. οὐ γὰρ
Jesus, the Son of God, let us hold fast the confession. not For
2192 749 3361 1410 4834 769
ἔχομεν ἀρχιερέα μὴ δυνάμενον συμπαθῆσαι ταῖς ἀσθενείαις
we have a high priest not being able to sympathize with the infirmities
2257 3985 2596 3956 2596 3665 5565
ἡμῶν, πεπειρασμένον δὲ κατὰ πάντα καθ' ὁμοιότητα, χωρὶς
of us, having been tempted but (One) in all respects according to (our) likeness apart from
266 4334 3767/ 3326 3954 2362
16 ἁμαρτίας. προσερχώμεθα οὖν μετὰ παρρησίας τῷ θρόνῳ τῆς
sin. let us draw near Therefore with confidence to the throne —
5485 2443 2983 1656 5485 2147 1519 2121
χάριτος, ἵνα λάβωμεν ἔλεον, καὶ χάριν εὕρωμεν εἰς εὔκαιρον
of grace, that we may receive mercy, and grace we may find for timely
996
βοήθειαν.
help.

CHAPTER 5

[1]For every high priest being taken from men is appointed on behalf of men *in* the things respecting God, that he may offer both gifts and sacrifices for sins; [2]being able to feel in due measure for those not knowing and having been led astray, since he also is circled about *with* weakness. [3]And because of this he ought to offer for sins as concerning the people and concerning himself. [4]And no one takes the honor to himself, but he being called by God, even as Aaron also. [5]So also Christ did not glorify Himself to become a high priest, but He speaking to Him, "You are My Son; today I have begotten You." [6]As He also says in another, "You *are* a priest forever according to the order of Melchizedek, [7]who in the days of His flesh offering both petitions and entreaties to Him being able to save Him from death, with strong crying and tears, and being heard from *His* godly fear; —[8]though being a Son, He learned obedience from what He suffered—[9]and being perfected, He became *the* Author of eternal salvation to all those obeying Him, [10]having been called out by God *as* a High Priest according to the order of Melchizedek.

[11]Concerning whom we *have* much to say, and hard to interpret, since you have become dull in hearing. [12]For indeed because of the time *you are* due to be teachers, you need to have someone to teach you again the rudiments of the beginning of the oracles of God, and you have become *in* need of milk, and not of solid food; [13]for

CHAPTER 5

3956/1063 749 1537 444 2983 5228
1 Πᾶς γαρ ἀρχιερεύς, ἐξ ἀνθρώπων λαμβανόμενος, ὑπὲρ
every For high priest out of men having been taken on behalf of
444 2525 4314 2316/2443 4374
ἀνθρώπων καθίσταται τὰ πρὸς τὸν Θεόν, ἵνα προσφέρῃ
men is appointed (in) the things as to God. that he may offer
1435/5037 2378 5228 266 3356 1410
2 δῶρά τε καὶ θυσίας ὑπὲρ ἁμαρτιῶν· μετριοπαθεῖν δυνάμενος
gifts both and sacrifices on behalf of sins, to feel in due measure being able
50 4105 1893 848 4029
τοῖς ἀγνοοῦσι καὶ πλανωμένοις, ἐπεὶ καὶ αὐτὸς περίκειται
for those not knowing and being led astray, since also he is encompassed
769 1223 5026 3784 2531 4012 2992 3779
3 ἀσθένειαν· καὶ διὰ ταύτην ὀφείλει, καθὼς περὶ τοῦ λαοῦ, οὕτω
(with) weakness and for this he ought, as concerning the people, so
4012 1438 4374 5228 266 3756 1438
4 καὶ περὶ ἑαυτοῦ, προσφέρειν ὑπὲρ ἁμαρτιῶν. καὶ οὐχ ἑαυτῷ
also concerning himself to offer on behalf of sins. And not to himself
5100/2983 5092 235 2564 5259 2316
τις λαμβάνει τὴν τιμήν, ἀλλὰ ὁ καλούμενος ὑπὸ τοῦ Θεοῦ,
anyone takes the honor, but the (one) being called by God,
2504 2 3779 5547 3756 1438
5 καθάπερ καὶ ὁ Ἀαρών. οὕτω καὶ ὁ Χριστὸς οὐχ ἑαυτὸν
even as indeed Aaron. So also Christ not Himself
1392 1096 749 235 2980 4314 846
ἐδόξασε γενηθῆναι ἀρχιερέα, ἀλλ' ὁ λαλήσας πρὸς αὐτόν,
glorified to become a high priest, but the (One) speaking to Him:
1488 5207/3450//4771/1473/ 4594 1080 4571 2531 1722/2087
6 Υἱός μου εἶ σύ, ἐγὼ σήμερον γεγέννηκά σε. καθὼς καὶ ἐν ἑτέρῳ
Son of Me are You, I today have begotten You; as also in another
3004/4771/2409/1519 165 2596 5010 3198
λέγει, Σὺ ἱερεὺς εἰς τὸν αἰῶνα κατὰ τὴν τάξιν Μελχισεδέκ.
He says, You (are) a priest to the age according to the order of Melchizedek;
3739/1722 2250 4561 848 1162/5037 2428
7 ὃς ἐν ταῖς ἡμέραις τῆς σαρκὸς αὐτοῦ, δεήσεις τε καὶ ἱκετηρίας
who in the days of the flesh of Him petitions both and entreaties
4314 1410 4982 846 1537 2288 3326 2906
πρὸς τὸν δυνάμενον σώζειν αὐτὸν ἐκ θανάτου μετὰ κραυγῆς
to the (One) being able to save Him out of death, with crying
2478 1144 4374 1522 575
ἰσχυρᾶς καὶ δακρύων προσενέγκας, καὶ εἰσακουσθεὶς ἀπὸ τῆς
strong and tears, offering and being heard from the
2124 2539 5607/5207 3129 575/3739/3958 5218
8 εὐλαβείας, καίπερ ὢν υἱός, ἔμαθεν ἀφ' ὧν ἔπαθε τὴν ὑπακοήν,
godly fear, though being a Son, He learned from (that) which He suffered obedience,
5048 1096 5219 846 3956 159
9 καὶ τελειωθεὶς ἐγένετο τοῖς ὑπακούουσιν αὐτῷ πᾶσιν αἴτιος
and having perfected He became those obeying Him to all (the) cause
4991 166 4316 5259 2316 749
10 σωτηρίας αἰωνίου· προσαγορευθεὶς ὑπὸ τοῦ Θεοῦ ἀρχιερεὺς
of salvation eternal having been called out by God a High Priest
2596 5010 3198
κατὰ τὴν τάξιν Μελχισεδέκ.
according to the order of Melchizedek.

4012/3739/4183/2254 3056 1421 3004
11 Περὶ οὗ πολὺς ἡμῖν ὁ λόγος καὶ δυσερμήνευτος λέγειν,
Concerning whom much to us the word, and hard to interpret to say,
1893 3576 1096 189 1063 3784 1511
12 ἐπεὶ νωθροὶ γεγόνατε ταῖς ἀκοαῖς. καὶ γὰρ ὀφείλοντες εἶναι
since dull you have become in the hearing For being due to be
1320 1223 5550 3825 5532 2192 1321
διδάσκαλοι διὰ τὸν χρόνον, πάλιν χρείαν ἔχετε τοῦ διδά-
teachers because of the time, again need you have to
5209 5101 4747 746 3051 2316
σκειν ὑμᾶς, τίνα τὰ στοιχεῖα τῆς ἀρχῆς τῶν λογίων τοῦ Θεοῦ·
teach you someone the rudiments of the beginning of the oracles of God,
1096 5532 2192 1051 3756 4731
καὶ γεγόνατε χρείαν ἔχοντες γάλακτος, καὶ οὐ στερεᾶς
and you become (in) need having of milk, and not of solid

everyone partaking of milk *is* not skilled *in the* word of righteousness, for he is an infant. [14]But solid food is for those full-grown, having exercised the faculties through habit, for distinguishing both good and bad.

CHAPTER 6

[1]Therefore, leaving the discourse of the beginning of Christ, let us be borne on to full growth, not laying down again a foundation of repentance from dead works, and of faith toward God, [2]of *the* baptisms, of teaching, of laying on of hands, and of resurrection of dead ones, and of eternal judgment. [3]And this we will do, if indeed God permits. [4]For those being once enlightened, and having tasted of the heavenly gift, and becoming partakers of *the* Holy Spirit, [5]and having tasted *the* good word of God, and *the* works of power of a coming age, [6]and falling away, *it is* impossible *for them* again to renew to repentance, *for they* again *will be* crucifying to themselves the Son of God, and putting *Him* to open shame. [7]For the earth drinking in the rain often coming upon it, and producing plants fit for those for whom it is also worked, receives blessing from God; [8]but bearing thorns and thistles, *it is* deemed unfit and near a curse, of which the end *is* for burning.

[9]But, loved ones, even if we indeed speak so, we have been persuaded better things concerning you, even holding fast salvation. [10]For God is not unjust, to forget your work and the labor of love which you

5160 3956/1063 3348 1051 552 3056 1343
13 τροφῆς. πᾶς γὰρ ὁ μετέχων γάλακτος ἄπειρος λόγου δι-
food. everyone For partaking of milk (is) not skilled of(the) word
3516 1063 2076 5046 2076 4731
14 καιοσύνης· νήπιος γάρ ἐστι. τελείων δέ ἐστιν ἡ στερεὰ
of righteousness, an infant for he is; of full-grown but is solid
5160 1223 1838 145 1128
τροφή, τῶν διὰ τὴν ἕξιν τὰ αἰσθητήρια γεγυμνασμένα
food, of those through habit the faculties exercised
2192 4314 1253 2570/5037 2556
ἐχόντων πρὸς διάκρισιν καλοῦ τε καὶ κακοῦ.
having, for distinguishing good both and bad.

CHAPTER 6

1352 863 746 5547 3056 1909
1 Διό, ἀφέντες τὸν τῆς ἀρχῆς τοῦ Χριστοῦ λόγον, ἐπὶ τὴν
Therefore, leaving the of the beginning of Christ discourse, on to
5047 5342 3361 3825 2310 2598
τελειότητα φερώμεθα, μὴ πάλιν θεμέλιον καταβαλλόμενοι
full growth let us be borne, not again a foundation laying down
3341 575 3498 2041 4102 1909 2316 909
2 μετανοίας ἀπὸ νεκρῶν ἔργων, καὶ πίστεως ἐπὶ Θεόν, βαπτι-
of repentance from dead works, and of faith upon God, of baptisms,
1322 1936 5037 5495 386 5037 3498
σμῶν διδαχῆς, ἐπιθέσεώς τε χειρῶν, ἀναστάσεώς τε νεκρῶν,
of teaching, of laying on and of hands, of resurrection and of dead ones
2917 166 5124 4160 1437 4007
3 καὶ κρίματος αἰωνίου. καὶ τοῦτο ποιήσομεν, ἐάνπερ ἐπι-
and judgment of eternal. And this we will do if indeed
2010 2316 102 1063 530 5461
4 τρέπῃ ὁ Θεός. ἀδύνατον γὰρ τοὺς ἅπαξ φωτισθέντας,
permits God. (it is) impossible For (for) those once being enlightened,
1089 5037 1431 2032 3353
γευσαμένους τε τῆς δωρεᾶς τῆς ἐπουρανίου, καὶ μετόχους
having tasted and of the gift heavenly, and sharers
1096 4151 40 2570 1089 2316
5 γενηθέντας Πνεύματος Ἁγίου, καὶ καλὸν γευσαμένους Θεοῦ
becoming Spirit of (the) Holy, and (the) good tasting of God
4487 1411 5037 3195 165 3895
6 ῥῆμα, δυνάμεις τε μέλλοντος αἰῶνος, καὶ παραπεσόντας,
word, works of power and of a coming age. and falling away
3825 340 1519 3341 388 1438
πάλιν ἀνακαινίζειν εἰς μετάνοιαν, ἀνασταυροῦντας ἑαυτοῖς
again to renew to repentance, crucifying again for themselves
5207 2316 3856 1093/1063
7 τὸν υἱὸν τοῦ Θεοῦ καὶ παραδειγματίζοντας. γῆ γὰρ ἡ
the Son of God. and putting (Him) to open shame. earth For
4095 1909 846 4178 2065 5205
πιοῦσα τὸν ἐπ' αὐτῆς πολλάκις ἐρχόμενον ὑετόν, καὶ
drinking the upon it often coming rain, and
5088 1008 2111 1565 1223/3739 1090
τίκτουσα βοτάνην εὔθετον ἐκείνοις δι' οὓς καὶ γεωργεῖται,
producing plants fit for those for whom indeed it is worked
3335 2129 575 2316 1627 173
8 μεταλαμβάνει εὐλογίας ἀπὸ τοῦ Θεοῦ· ἐκφέρουσα δὲ ἀκάνθας
receives blessing from God; bringing forth but thorns
5146 96 2671 1451/3739 5056/1519
καὶ τριβόλους, ἀδόκιμος καὶ κατάρας ἐγγύς, ἧς τὸ τέλος εἰς
and thistles (it is) disapproved and a curse near, of which the end (is) for
2740
καῦσιν.
burning.
3982 4012 5216 27 2909
9 Πεπείσμεθα δὲ περὶ ὑμῶν, ἀγαπητοί, τὰ κρείττονα καὶ
we have been persuaded But about you, loved ones, the things better, even
2192 4991 =1499= 3779 2980 3756/1063 94
10 ἐχόμενα σωτηρίας, εἰ καὶ οὕτω λαλοῦμεν· οὐ γὰρ ἄδικος ὁ
holding fast salvation, if indeed so we speak. not For unjust
2316 1950 2041 5216 2873
Θεὸς ἐπιλαθέσθαι τοῦ ἔργου ὑμῶν, καὶ τοῦ κόπου τῆς
God (is) to be forgetful of the work of you, and of the labor

showed to His name, ministering to the saints, and *now are* ministering. 11 But we desire each of you to show the same eagerness, to the full assurance of the hope to *the* end; 12 that you not become dull, but imitators of those who through faith and long-suffering *are* inheriting the promises.

13 For God having made promise to Abraham, since He had no greater to swear by, *He* swore by Himself, 14 saying, "Surely blessing I will bless you, and multiplying I will multiply you." 15 And so, being long-suffering, he obtained the promise. 16 For men indeed swear by the greater, and an oath to make things sure *is* to them the end of all gainsaying. 17 In which way, desiring to more fully declare to the heirs of the promise the unchangeableness of His counsel, God interposed by an oath, 18 that through two unchangeable things, in which *it was* not possible *for* God to lie, we might have a strong consolation, those having fled to lay hold on the hope set before *us*, 19 which we have as an anchor of the soul, both certain and sure, and entering into the inner *side* of the veil; 20 where Jesus entered *as* forerunner for us, having become a High Priest forever, according to the order of Melchizedek.

26 3739 1731 1519 3686 848 1247
ἀγάπης ἧς ἐνδείξασθε εἰς τὸ ὄνομα αὐτοῦ, διακονήσαντες
of love which you showed to the name of Him, having ministered
40 1247 1937 1538 5216
11 τοῖς ἁγίοις καὶ διακονοῦντες. ἐπιθυμοῦμεν δὲ ἕκαστον ὑμῶν
to the saints, and (now) ministering. we desire But each one of you
846 1731 4710 4314 4136
τὴν αὐτὴν ἐνδείκνυσθαι σπουδὴν πρὸς τὴν πληροφορίαν τῆς
the same to show eagerness to the full assurance of the
1680 891 5056 2443/3361 3576 1096 3402
12 ἐλπίδος ἄχρι τέλους· ἵνα μὴ νωθροὶ γένησθε, μιμηταὶ δὲ
hope unto (the) end, lest dull you become; imitators but
1223 4102 3115 2816
τῶν διὰ πίστεως καὶ μακροθυμίας κληρονομούντων τὰς
of those through faith and long-suffering inheriting the
1860
ἐπαγγελίας.
promises.
1063 11 1861 2316 1893 2596
13 Τῷ γὰρ Ἀβραὰμ ἐπαγγειλάμενος ὁ Θεός, ἐπεὶ κατ'
For to Abraham having made promise God, since by
3762 2192 3187 3660 3660 2596 1438 3004
14 οὐδενὸς εἶχε μείζονος ὀμόσαι, ὤμοσε καθ' ἑαυτοῦ, λέγων,
no one he had greater to swear, swore by Himself, saying,
=2229= 2127 2127 4571 4129 4129 4571
Ἦ μὴν εὐλογῶν εὐλογήσω σε, καὶ πληθύνων πληθυνῶ σε.
If surely blessing I will bless you, and multiplying I will multiply you.
3779 3114 2013 1860 444
15 καὶ οὕτω μακροθυμήσας ἐπέτυχε τῆς ἐπαγγελίας. ἄνθρωποι
16 And so being long-suffering, he obtained the promise. men
3303/1063/2596 3187 3660 3956 846
μὲν γὰρ κατὰ τοῦ μείζονος ὀμνύουσι, καὶ πάσης αὐτοῖς
indeed For by the greater swear, and of all (is) to them
485 4009/1519 951 3527 1722/3739/ 4054
17 ἀντιλογίας πέρας εἰς βεβαίωσιν ὁ ὅρκος. ἐν ᾧ περισσότερον
contradiction an end for confirmation the oath. In which more abundantly
1014 2316 1925 2818 1860
βουλόμενος ὁ Θεὸς ἐπιδεῖξαι τοῖς κληρονόμοις τῆς ἐπαγ-
resolving God to show to the heirs of the promise
276 1012 848 3315 3727
γελίας τὸ ἀμετάθετον τῆς βουλῆς αὐτοῦ, ἐμεσίτευσεν ὅρκῳ
the unchangeableness of the counsel of Him, He interposed by an oath,
2443/1223/1417 4229 276 1722/3739 102
18 ἵνα διὰ δύο πραγμάτων ἀμεταθέτων, ἐν οἷς ἀδύνατον
that through two things unchangeable, in which (it was) impossible
5574 2316 2478 3874 2192 2703
ψεύσασθαι Θεόν, ἰσχυρὰν παράκλησιν ἔχωμεν οἱ κατα-
to lie God, a strong consolation we might have, those
2902 4295 1680/3739/5613/ 45
19 φυγόντες κρατῆσαι τῆς προκειμένης ἐλπίδος· ἣν ὡς ἄγκυραν
having fled to lay hold of the set before (us) hope; which as an anchor
2192 5590 804/ 5037 949 1525
ἔχομεν τῆς ψυχῆς ἀσφαλῆ τε καὶ βεβαίαν, καὶ εἰσερχομένην
we have of the soul, secure both and firm, and entering
1519 2082 2665 3699 4274 5228
20 εἰς τὸ ἐσώτερον τοῦ καταπετάσματος· ὅπου πρόδρομος ὑπὲρ
into the inner (side) of the veil, where a forerunner for
2257 1525 2424 2596 5010 3198 749
ἡμῶν εἰσῆλθεν Ἰησοῦς, κατὰ τὴν τάξιν Μελχισεδὲκ ἀρχιερεὺς
us entered, Jesus, according to the order of Melchizedek a high priest
1096 1519 165
γενόμενος εἰς τὸν αἰῶνα.
becoming to the age.

CHAPTER 7

CHAPTER 7

1 For this Melchizedek, king of Salem, priest of the most high God, the *one* meeting Abraham returning from the slaughter of the

3778/1063 3198 935 4532 2409 2316
1 Οὗτος γὰρ ὁ Μελχισεδέκ, βασιλεὺς Σαλήμ, ιερεὺς τοῦ Θεοῦ
this For Melchizedek, king of Salem, priest of God
5310 4876 11 5290 575
τοῦ ὑψίστου, ὁ συναντήσας Ἀβραὰμ ὑποστρέφοντι ἀπὸ τῆς
the most high, the (one) meeting Abraham returning from the

kings, and blessing him;
[2]to whom also Abraham
divided a tenth from all—
first being interpreted, king
of righteousness; and then
also king of Salem, which
is, king of peace, [3]without
father, without mother,
without genealogy, nor
beginning of days, nor
having end of life, but
having been made like the
Son of God, *he* remains a
priest in perpetuity.

[4]Now behold how great
this *one was*, to whom even
the patriarch Abraham gave
a tenth of the spoils; [5]and
indeed those of the sons of
Levi receiving the priesthood have a command to
tithe the people according
to Law—that is, from their
brothers, though coming
forth out of Abraham's loins
—[6]but he not counting *his*
genealogy from them has
tithed Abraham, and has
blessed the *one* having the
promises. [7]But without contradiction, the lesser is
blessed by the better. [8]And
here dying men indeed re-
ceive tithes, but there
it having been witnessed
that he lives; [9]and as a
word to say, through
Abraham Levi also, the *one*
receiving tithes, has been
tithed. [10]For he was yet in
his father's loins when Melchizedek met him.

[11]Truly, then, if perfection
was through the Levitical
priestly office — for the
people has been given Law
under it—why yet need *for*
another priest to arise according to the order of
Melchizedek, and not to be
called according to the
order of Aaron? [12]For the
priestly office having been
changed, of necessity a
change of law also occurs.
[13]For the *One* of whom
these things are said has
partaken of another tribe,
from which no one has
given devotion at the altar.

2871 935 2127 846 3739 1181
2 κοπῆς τῶν βασιλέων καὶ εὐλογήσας αὐτόν, ᾧ καὶ δεκάτην
slaughter of the kings and blessing him, to whom indeed a tenth
575 3956 3307 11 4412 3303 2059
ἀπὸ πάντων ἐμέρισεν Ἀβραάμ (πρῶτον μὲν ἑρμηνευόμενος
from all divided Abraham firstly being interpreted,
935 1343 1899 935 4532 2076
βασιλεὺς δικαιοσύνης, ἔπειτα δὲ καὶ βασιλεὺς Σαλήμ, ὅ ἐστι
king of righteousness, then and also king of Salem, which is,
935 1515 540 282 35 3383
3 βασιλεὺς εἰρήνης· ἀπάτωρ, ἀμήτωρ, ἀγενεαλόγητος, μήτε
king of peace, without father, without mother, without pedigree, nor
746 2250 3383 2222 5056 2192 871
ἀρχὴν ἡμερῶν μήτε ζωῆς τέλος ἔχων, ἀφωμοιωμένος δὲ τῷ
beginning of days, nor of life end having, having been made like but the
5207 2316 3306 2409/1519 1336
υἱῷ τοῦ Θεοῦ), μένει ἱερεὺς εἰς τὸ διηνεκές.
Son of God – remains a priest in perpetuity.
2334 4080 3778/3739 1181 11 1325
4 Θεωρεῖτε δὲ πηλίκος οὗτος, ᾧ καὶ δεκάτην Ἀβραὰμ ἔδωκεν
behold Now how great this to even a tenth Abraham gave
1537 205 **(one was) whom**
3966 3303/1537 5207
5 ἐκ τῶν ἀκροθινίων ὁ πατριάρχης. καὶ οἱ μὲν ἐκ τῶν υἱῶν
of the spoils the patriarch. And those of the sons
3017 2405 2983 1785 2192 586
Λευὶ τὴν ἱερατείαν λαμβάνοντες ἐντολὴν ἔχουσιν ἀποδεκα-
of Levi the priesthood receiving a commandment have to tithe
2992/2596 3551 5123 2076 80
τοῦν τὸν λαὸν κατὰ τὸν νόμον, τοῦτ᾽ ἔστι τοὺς ἀδελφοὺς
the people according to the law, this is the brothers
848 2539 1831 1537 3751 11
6 αὐτῶν, καίπερ ἐξεληλυθότας ἐκ τῆς ὀσφύος Ἀβραάμ· ὁ δὲ
of them, though having come forth out of the loins of Abraham; he but
3361 1075 1537 846 1183 11
μὴ γενεαλογούμενος ἐξ αὐτῶν δεδεκάτωκε τὸν Ἀβραάμ, καὶ
not counting (his) pedigree from them has tithed Abraham, and
2192 1860 2127 5565 3956 485
7 τὸν ἔχοντα τὰς ἐπαγγελίας εὐλόγηκε. χωρὶς δὲ πάσης ἀντι-
the (one) having the promises (he) has blessed. without And all con-
1640 5259 2909 2127 5602
8 λογίας, τὸ ἔλαττον ὑπὸ τοῦ κρείττονος εὐλογεῖται. καὶ ὧδε
tradiction, the lesser by the better is blessed. And here
3303 1181 599 444 2983 1563
μὲν δεκάτας ἀποθνήσκοντες ἄνθρωποι λαμβάνουσιν· ἐκεῖ δέ,
indeed tithes dying men receive, there but
3140 3754/2198 5613/2031 2036 1223 11
9 μαρτυρούμενος ὅτι ζῇ. καί, ὡς ἔπος εἰπεῖν, διὰ Ἀβραὰμ καὶ
being witnessed that he lives. And as a word to say, through Abraham also
3017 1181 2983 1183 2089/1063/1722 3751
10 Λευὶ ὁ δεκάτας λαμβάνων δεδεκάτωται· ἔτι γὰρ ἐν τῇ ὀσφύϊ
Levi, the (one) tithes receiving, has been tithed. yet For in the loins
3962 2258/3753/4876 846 3198
τοῦ πατρὸς ἦν, ὅτε συνήντησεν αὐτῷ ὁ Μελχισεδέκ.
of the father he was when met him Melchizedek.
1487/3303/3767 5050 1223 3020 2420 2258
11 Εἰ μὲν οὖν τελείωσις διὰ τῆς Λευϊτικῆς ἱερωσύνης ἦν (ὁ
If therefore perfection through the Levitical priestly office was, the
2992 1063/1909/846 3549 5101/2089/5532/2596
λαὸς γὰρ ἐπ᾽ αὐτῇ νενομοθέτητο), τίς ἔτι χρεία, κατὰ τὴν
people for under it has been given law, why yet need according to the
5010 3198 2087 450 2409 3756 2596
τάξιν Μελχισεδὲκ ἕτερον ἀνίστασθαι ἱερέα, καὶ οὐ κατὰ τὴν
order of Melchizedek another to arise priest, and not according to the
5010 2 3004 3346 1063 2420
12 τάξιν Ἀαρὼν λέγεσθαι; μετατιθεμένης γὰρ τῆς ἱερωσύνης,
order of Aaron to be said? being changed For the priestly office,
1537 318 3551 3331 1096 1909/3739/1063/3004
13 ἐξ ἀνάγκης καὶ νόμου μετάθεσις γίνεται. ἐφ᾽ ὃν γὰρ λέγεται
of necessity also of law a change occurs. of whom For are said
5023 5443 2087 3348 575/3739 3762 4337
ταῦτα, φυλῆς ἑτέρας μετέσχηκεν, ἀφ᾽ ἧς οὐδεὶς προσέσχηκε
these things, tribe of another has partaken, from which no one has given devotion

14 For it is clear that our Lord
has risen out of Judah, as to
which tribe Moses spoke
nothing concerning priesthood. 15 And it is still more
abundantly clear *that* if another priest arises according to the likeness of Melchizedek, 16 who has not become *so* according to a law
of a fleshly command, but
according to *the* power of an
indissoluble life— 17 for it is
testified, "You *are* a priest
forever according to the
order of Melchizedek." 18 For
a voiding of *the* preceding
command comes about be-
cause of its weak*ness* and
unprofitableness. 19 For the
Law perfected nothing, but a
bringing in of a better hope,
through which we draw near
to God. 20 And by how much
it was not apart from *the*
swearing of an oath—for
they have become priests
without *the* swearing of an
oath, 21 but He with *the*
swearing through Him who
says to Him, "*The* Lord
swore, and will not repent,
You *are* a priest forever
according to the order of
Melchizedek"— 22 by so
much Jesus has become
Surety of a better covenant.
23 And they truly are many
priests, being hindered from
continuing because of
death; 24 but He has the
priesthood not to be passed
on, because of His con
tinuing forever. 25 From this
also He is able to save to
perfection those who
come to God through Him,
ever living to intercede for
them.

26 For such a High Priest
was fitting for us: holy,
harmless, undefiled, and
separated from sinners,
and having become higher
than the heavens; 27 who
has no need, as do the high
priests, to offer sacrifices
day by day, first for *his* own

2379 4271 1063/3754/1537/2455 393
14 τῷ θυσιαστηρίῳ. πρόδηλον γὰρ ὅτι ἐξ Ἰούδα ἀνατέταλκεν
at the altar. it is clear For that out of Judah has risen
2962 2257 1519/3739/5443 3762 4012 2420 3475
ὁ Κύριος ἡμῶν, εἰς ἣν φυλὴν οὐδὲν περὶ ἱερωσύνης Μωσῆς
the Lord of us, as to which tribe nothing concerning priesthood Moses
2980 4054 2089 2612 2076/1487/2596
15 ἐλάλησε. καὶ περισσότερον ἔτι κατάδηλόν ἐστιν, εἰ κατὰ τὴν
spoke. And more abundantly still quite clear is it, if according to the
3756 3665 3198 450 2409 2087 3739 2596
16 ὁμοιότητα Μελχισεδὲκ ἀνίσταται ἱερεὺς ἕτερος, ὃς οὐ κατὰ
likeness of Melchizedek arises priest another, who not according to
3551 1785 4559 1096 235 2596 1411 2222
νόμον ἐντολῆς σαρκικῆς γέγονεν, ἀλλὰ κατὰ δύναμιν ζωῆς
(the) law of a command fleshly has become, but according to (the) power life
179 3140 1063/3754/4771 2409 1519 165 2596
17 ἀκαταλύτου· μαρτυρεῖ γὰρ ὅτι Σὺ ἱερεὺς εἰς τὸν αἰῶνα κατὰ
of an indissoluble. it is testified for: — You (are) a priest to the age according to
5010 3198 115 3303/1063/1096 4254
18 τὴν τάξιν Μελχισεδέκ. ἀθέτησις μὲν γὰρ γίνεται προαγούσης
the order of Melchizedek. an annulment For comes about of (the) preceding
1785 1223 848 772 512 3762 1063
19 ἐντολῆς, διὰ τὸ αὐτῆς ἀσθενὲς καὶ ἀνωφελές· οὐδὲν γὰρ
command, because of the of it weak(ness) and unprofitable(ness), nothing for
5048 3551 1898 2909 1680 1223
ἐτελείωσεν ὁ νόμος, ἐπεισαγωγὴ δὲ κρείττονος ἐλπίδος, δι'
perfected the law, a bringing in but of a better hope, through
3739/1448 2316 2596/3745/3756/5565 3728
20 ἧς ἐγγίζομεν τῷ Θεῷ. καὶ καθ' ὅσον οὐ χωρὶς ὁρκωμοσίας
which we draw near to God. And by how much (it was) not without oath-taking
3303/1063/5565 3728 1526 2409 1096
21 (οἱ μὲν γὰρ χωρὶς ὁρκωμοσίας εἰσὶν ἱερεῖς γεγονότες, ὁ δὲ
—those tr. for without oath-taking are priests becoming He but
3326 3728 1223 3004 4314 846 3660
μετὰ ὁρκωμοσίας, διὰ τοῦ λέγοντος πρὸς αὐτόν, Ὤμοσε
with oath-taking through Him saying to Him, Swore
2962 3756 3338 4771 2409 1519 165 2596
Κύριος καὶ οὐ μεταμεληθήσεται, Σὺ ἱερεὺς εἰς τὸν αἰῶνα κατὰ
(the) Lord, and not will change (His) mind, You a priest to the age; by
5010 3198 2596 5117 2909 1242
22 τὴν τάξιν Μελχισεδέκ)· κατὰ τοσοῦτον κρείττονος διαθήκης
the order of Melchizedek— by so much of a better covenant
1096 1450 2424 3303 4119 1526 1096
23 γέγονεν ἔγγυος Ἰησοῦς. καὶ οἱ μὲν πλείονές εἰσι γεγονότες
has become surety Jesus. And those indeed many are, having become
2409 1223 2288 2967 3887 1223
24 ἱερεῖς, διὰ τὸ θανάτῳ κωλύεσθαι παραμένειν· ὁ δέ, διὰ τὸ
priests because of by death being prevented to continue; He but, because of
3306 846/1519 165 531 2192 2420
μένειν αὐτὸν εἰς τὸν αἰῶνα, ἀπαράβατον ἔχει τὴν ἱερωσύνην.
remaining Him to the age, not to be passed on has the priestly office
3606 4982/1519 3638 1410 4334
25 ὅθεν καὶ σώζειν εἰς τὸ παντελὲς δύναται τοὺς προσερχο-
from this also to save to perfection He is able those drawing near
1223 846 2316 3842 2198/1519 1793
μένους δι' αὐτοῦ τῷ Θεῷ, πάντοτε ζῶν εἰς τὸ ἐντυγχάνειν
through Him to God, ever living to intercede
5228 846
ὑπὲρ αὐτῶν.
on behalf of them.

5108 1063 2254 4241 749 3741 172
26 Τοιοῦτος γὰρ ἡμῖν ἔπρεπεν ἀρχιερεύς, ὅσιος, ἄκακος,
such For to us was fitting a High Priest, holy, harmless,
283 5563 575 268 5308
ἀμίαντος, κεχωρισμένος ἀπὸ τῶν ἁμαρτωλῶν, καὶ ὑψηλό-
undefiled, having been separated from sinners, and higher
3772 2096 3739/3756/2192/2596 2250
27 τερος τῶν οὐρανῶν γενόμενος· ὃς οὐκ ἔχει καθ' ἡμέραν
than the heavens becoming; who not has day by day
318 5618 749 4386 5228 2398
ἀνάγκην, ὥσπερ οἱ ἀρχιερεῖς, πρότερον ὑπὲρ τῶν ἰδίων
need, as do the high priests, firstly for the own

sins, then *for* those of the people. For He did this once for all, offering up Himself. [28]For the Law makes men high priests who have infirmity, but the word of the swearing of an oath, after the Law, *appoints the* Son forever, having been perfected.

CHAPTER 8

[1]Now a summary of the things being said *is*: We have such a High Priest, who sat down on *the* right of the throne of the Majesty in Heaven, [2]Minister of the holies, and of the true tabernacle which the Lord pitched, and not man.

[3]For every high priest is set in place to offer both gifts and sacrifices; from which *it is* necessary *for* this One also to have something which He may offer. [4]For if indeed He were on earth, He would not even be a priest, there being those priests offering gifts according to the Law, [5]who serve *the* pattern and shadow of heavenly things, even as Moses was divinely warned, being about to make the tabernacle: For He says, "See that you make all things according to the pattern shown to you in the mount." [6]But now He has gotten a more excellent ministry, also by so much as He is a Mediator of a better covenant, which has been enacted on better promises. [7]For if that first was faultless, place would not have been sought for a second. [8]For finding fault, He said to them, "Behold, days are coming, says *the* Lord, and I will make an end on the house of Israel, and on the house of Judah; a new covenant *shall be*, [9]not according to the covenant which I made with their fathers in *the* day of My taking hold of their hand to

266 2378 399 1899 2992 5124
ἁμαρτιῶν θυσίας ἀναφέρειν, ἔπειτα τῶν τοῦ λαοῦ· τοῦτο
sins sacrifices to offer up; then (for) those of the people; this
1063 4160 2178 1438 399 3551 1063
28 γὰρ ἐποίησεν ἐφάπαξ, ἑαυτὸν ἀνενέγκας. ὁ νόμος γὰρ
for He did once for all, Himself offering up. the law For
444 2525 749 2192 769
ἀνθρώπους καθίστησιν ἀρχιερεῖς, ἔχοντας ἀσθένειαν· ὁ
men appoints high priests having infirmity; the
3056 3728 3326 3551 5207/1519
λόγος δὲ τῆς ὁρκωμοσίας τῆς μετὰ τὸν νόμον, υἱὸν εἰς τὸν
word but of the oath-taking after the law (appoints) a Son to the
165 5048
αἰῶνα τετελειωμένον.
age, having been perfected.

CHAPTER 8

2774 1909 3004 5108 2192
1 Κεφάλαιον δὲ ἐπὶ τοῖς λεγομένοις· τοιοῦτον ἔχομεν
a summary Now over the things being said, such we have
749 3739 2523 1722/1188 2362 3172
ἀρχιερέα, ὃς ἐκάθισεν ἐν δεξιᾷ τοῦ θρόνου τῆς μεγαλωσύνης
a High Priest, who sat at (the) right of the throne of the Majesty
1722 3772 39 3011 4633
2 ἐν τοῖς οὐρανοῖς, τῶν ἁγίων λειτουργός, καὶ τῆς σκηνῆς τῆς
in Heaven, of the holy things a minister, and of the tabernacle
228 3739 4078 2962 3756 444 3956/1063
3 ἀληθινῆς, ἣν ἔπηξεν ὁ Κύριος, καὶ οὐκ ἄνθρωπος. πᾶς γὰρ
true, which raised up the Lord, and not man. every For
749 1519 4374 1435/5037 2378 2525
ἀρχιερεὺς εἰς τὸ προσφέρειν δῶρά τε καὶ θυσίας καθίσταται·
high priest to offer gifts both and sacrifices is appointed;
3606 316 2192/5100 5126/3739/4374 1487/3303/1063
4 ὅθεν ἀναγκαῖον ἔχειν τι καὶ τοῦτον ὃ προσενέγκῃ. εἰ μὲν γὰρ
from which (it is) needful to have some thing also this One which He may offer. if truly For
2258/1909/1093/3761/302/2258/2409 5607 2409
ἦν ἐπὶ γῆς, οὐδ' ἂν ἦν ἱερεύς, ὄντων τῶν ἱερέων τῶν
He were on earth, He would not be a priest, being those priests
4374 2596 3551 1435 3748 5262
5 προσφερόντων κατὰ τὸν νόμον τὰ δῶρα, οἵτινες ὑποδείγματι
offering according to the law the gifts; who an example
4639 3000 2032 2531 5537
καὶ σκιᾷ λατρεύουσι τῶν ἐπουρανίων, καθὼς κεχρημάτισται
and a shadow serve of the heavenly things, as has been warned
3475 3195 2005 4633 3708 1063 5346
Μωσῆς μέλλων ἐπιτελεῖν τὴν σκηνήν, Ὅρα, γάρ φησι,
Moses being about to make the tabernacle: see For,He says,
4160 3956 2596 5179 1166 4671/1722 3735
ποιήσῃς πάντα κατὰ τὸν τύπον τὸν δειχθέντα σοι ἐν τῷ ὄρει
you make all things according to the pattern shown to you in the mount.
3570 1313 5177 3009 3745 2909
6 νυνὶ δὲ διαφορωτέρας τέτευχε λειτουργίας, ὅσῳ καὶ κρείτ-
now And a more excellent He has gotten ministry, by so much also of a
2076 1242 3316 3748/1909/ 2909 1860
τονός ἐστι διαθήκης μεσίτης, ἥτις ἐπὶ κρείττοσιν ἐπαγγελίαις
better He is covenant Mediator, which on better promises
3549 1487/1063 4413 1565 2258 273 3756/302
7 νενομοθέτηται. εἰ γὰρ ἡ πρώτη ἐκείνη ἦν ἄμεμπτος, οὐκ ἂν
has been enacted. if For first that was faultless, not would
1208 2212 5117 3201 1063/846 3004 2400
8 δευτέρας ἐζητεῖτο τόπος. μεμφόμενος γὰρ αὐτοῖς λέγει, Ἰδού,
of a second have been sought place. finding fault For them He says, Behold,
2250 2064 3004 2962 4931 1909 3624
ἡμέραι ἔρχονται, λέγει Κύριος, καὶ συντελέσω ἐπὶ τὸν οἶκον
days are coming, says (the) Lord, and I will make an end upon the house
2474 1909 3624 2455 1242 2537 3756/2596
9 Ἰσραὴλ καὶ ἐπὶ τὸν οἶκον Ἰούδα διαθήκην καινήν· οὐ κατὰ
of Israel, and upon the house of Judah, covenant a new, not according to
1242 3739 4160 3962 848 1722/2250
τὴν διαθήκην ἣν ἐποίησα τοῖς πατράσιν αὐτῶν ἐν ἡμέρᾳ
the covenant which I made with the fathers of them, in (the) day

lead them out of *the* land of Egypt; because they did not continue in My covenant, and I did not regard them, says *the* Lord. [10]Because this *is* the covenant which I will covenant with the house of Israel after those days, says *the* Lord, giving My laws into their mind, and I will write them on their hearts, and I will be their God, and they shall be My people. [11]And they shall no more teach each one his neighbor, and each one his brother, saying, Know the Lord; because all shall know Me, from the least of them to their great ones. [12]For I will be merciful to their unrighteousnesses, and I will not at all remember their sins and their lawless deeds."

[13]In the saying, "New," He has made the first old. And the thing having been made old and growing aged *is* near disappearing.

1949 3450 5495 838 1806 846 1537
ἐπιλαβομένου μου τῆς χειρὸς αὐτῶν ἐξαγαγεῖν αὐτοὺς ἐκ
taking hold Me the hand of them to lead forth them out of
1093 125 3754 846 3756 1696 1722 1242 3450
γῆς Αἰγύπτου· ὅτι αὐτοὶ οὐκ ἐνέμειναν ἐν τῇ διαθήκῃ μου,
(the) land of Egypt, because they not continued in the covenant of Me,
2505 272 846 3004 2962 3754/3778 1242 3739
10 κἀγὼ ἠμέλησα αὐτῶν, λέγει Κύριος. ὅτι αὕτη ἡ διαθήκη ἣν
and I not regarded them, says (the) Lord. Because this the covenant which
1303 3624 2474 3326 2250 1565 3004
διαθήσομαι τῷ οἴκῳ Ἰσραὴλ μετὰ τὰς ἡμέρας ἐκείνας, λέγει
I will covenant with the house of Israel after days those, says
2962 1325 3551 3450/1519 1271 848 1909
Κύριος, διδοὺς νόμους μου εἰς τὴν διάνοιαν αὐτῶν, καὶ ἐπὶ
(the) Lord, giving laws of Me into the mind of them, and on
2588 848 1924 846 2071 846/1519 2316
καρδίας αὐτῶν ἐπιγράψω αὐτούς· καὶ ἔσομαι αὐτοῖς εἰς Θεόν,
hearts of them I will write them, and I will be to them for God,
846 2071 3427/1519/2992 =3364= 1321 1538
11 καὶ αὐτοὶ ἔσονταί μοι εἰς λαόν. καὶ οὐ μὴ διδάξωσιν ἕκαστος
and they will be to Me for a people; and not at all may they teach each one
4139 848 1538 80 848 3004
τὸν πλησίον αὐτοῦ, καὶ ἕκαστος τὸν ἀδελφὸν αὐτοῦ, λέγων,
the neighbor of him, and each one the brother of him, saying,
1097 2962 3754 3956 1492 3165 575 3398
Γνῶθι τὸν Κύριον· ὅτι πάντες εἰδήσουσί με, ἀπὸ μικροῦ
Know the Lord; because all will know Me, from little
846 2193 3173 846 3754 2436 2071 93
12 αὐτῶν ἕως μεγάλου αὐτῶν. ὅτι ἵλεως ἔσομαι ταῖς ἀδικίαις
of them to (the) great of them. Because merciful I will be to the unrighteousnesses
848 266 848
αὐτῶν, καὶ τῶν ἁμαρτιῶν αὐτῶν καὶ τῶν ἀνομιῶν αὐτῶν
of them, and the sins of them, and the lawlessnesses of them.
=3364= 3415 2089/1722 3004 2537 3822
13 οὐ μὴ μνησθῶ ἔτι. ἐν τῷ λέγειν, Καινήν, πεπαλαίωκε τὴν
not at all I may remember still. In the saying, New, He has made old the
4413 3822 1095 1451 854
πρώτην. τὸ δὲ παλαιούμενον καὶ γηράσκον, ἐγγὺς ἀφανι-
first; the thing and being made old and growing aged (is) near dis-

σμοῦ.
appearing.

CHAPTER 9

[1]Truly, then, the first *tabernacle* also had ordinances of service, and the worldly holy place. [2]For the first tabernacle was prepared, in which *was* both the lampstand and the table, and the setting out of the loaves, which is called holy; [3]but behind the second veil *is* a tabernacle, that called Holy of Holies, [4]having a golden altar of incense, and the ark of the covenant covered around on all sides with gold, in which *was* the golden pot having the manna, and Aaron's rod that budded, and the tablets of the covenant; [5]and above it *the* cherubim of glory overshadowing the mercy-seat —about which now is not

2192/3303/3767 4413 1345 2999 5037
1 Εἶχε μὲν οὖν καὶ ἡ πρώτη δικαιώματα λατρείας, τό τε
had So then also the first (tabernacle) ordinances of service, the and
•1063 39 3886 4633 2680 4413/1722/3739
2 ἅγιον κοσμικόν. σκηνὴ γὰρ κατεσκευάσθη ἡ πρώτη, ἐν ᾗ ἥ
holy place worldly. a tabernacle For was prepared, the first, in which the
5037/3087 5132 4286 740 3748
τε λυχνία καὶ ἡ τράπεζα καὶ ἡ πρόθεσις τῶν ἄρτων, ἥτις
both lampstand and the table, and the setting out of the loaves, which
3004 39 3326 1208 2665 4633
3 λέγεται ἅγια. μετὰ δὲ τὸ δεύτερον καταπέτασμα σκηνὴ ἡ
is called Holy; after and the second veil a tabernacle, that
3004 39 39 5552 2192 2369
4 λεγομένη ἅγια ἁγίων, χρυσοῦν ἔχουσα θυμιατήριον, καὶ
called Holy of Holies, golden having an altar, and
2787 1242 4028 3840
τὴν κιβωτὸν τῆς διαθήκης περικεκαλυμμένην πάντοθεν
the ark of the covenant having been covered around on all sides
5552 1722/3739/4713 5553 2192 3131 4464
χρυσίῳ, ἐν ᾗ στάμνος χρυσῆ ἔχουσα τὸ μάννα, καὶ ἡ ῥάβδος
with gold, in which a pot golden having the manna, and the rod
2 985 4109 1242 5231
5 Ἀαρὼν ἡ βλαστήσασα, καὶ αἱ πλάκες τῆς διαθήκης· ὑπερ-
of Aaron budded, and the tablets of the covenant, above
846 5502 1391 2683 2435
άνω δὲ αὐτῆς Χερουβὶμ δόξης κατασκιάζοντα τὸ ἱλαστή-
and it cherubim of glory overshadowing the mercy-

time to speak piece by piece. [6]And these having been prepared thus, the priests go into the first tabernacle through all, completing the services. [7]But into the second the high priest *goes* alone once *in* the year, not without blood, which he offers for himself and the ignorances of the people; [8]the Holy Spirit signifying *by* this *that* the way of the Holies has not yet been made manifest, the first tabernacle still having standing; [9]which *has* a parable for the present time, according to which both gifts and sacrifices are offered, *but* as regards conscience, not being able to perfect the *one* serving, [10]but only on foods and drinks, and various washings, and fleshly ordinances, until *the* time of setting things right has been imposed.

[11]But Christ having appeared *as* a High Priest of the coming good things, through the greater and more perfect tabernacle not made with hands, that is, not of this creation, [12]nor through *the* blood of goats and of calves, but through *His* own blood, *He* entered once for all into the Holies, having procured everlasting redemption. [13]For if the blood of bulls and goats, and ashes of a heifer sprinkling those having been defiled, sanctifies to the purity of the flesh, [14]by how much more the blood of Christ, who through *the* eternal Spirit offered Himself without spot to God, will purify your conscience from dead works for *the* serving of *the* living God! [15]And because of this He is Mediator of a new covenant, so that, death having occurred for redemption of transgressions under the

4012/3739/3756/2076/3568/3004/2596/ 3313 5130 3779
6 ριον· περὶ ὧν οὐκ ἔστι νῦν λέγειν κατὰ μέρος. τούτων δὲ οὕτω
seat, about which not is now to speak piece by piece. these And thus
2680 1519/3303 4413 4633 1223 3956
κατεσκευασμένων, εἰς μὲν τὴν πρώτην σκηνὴν διὰ παντὸς
having been prepared, into the first tabernacle through all
1524 2409 2999 2005 1519
7 εἰσίασιν οἱ ἱερεῖς, τὰς λατρείας ἐπιτελοῦντες· εἰς δὲ τὴν
go the priests the services completing, into but the
1208 530 1763 3441 749 3756/5565
δευτέραν ἅπαξ τοῦ ἐνιαυτοῦ μόνος ὁ ἀρχιερεύς, οὐ χωρὶς
second once (in) the year (goes) alone the high priest, not without
129/3739/4374 5228 1438 2992 51
αἵματος, ὃ προσφέρει ὑπὲρ ἑαυτοῦ καὶ τῶν τοῦ λαοῦ ἀγνοη-
blood,, which he offers for himself and the of the people ignorances;
5124 1213 4151 40 3380
8 μάτων· τοῦτο δηλοῦντος τοῦ Πνεύματος τοῦ Ἁγίου, μήπω
this showing the Spirit Holy, not yet
5319 39 3598/2089 4413 4633
πεφανερῶσθαι τὴν τῶν ἁγίων ὁδόν, ἔτι τῆς πρώτης σκηνῆς
having been revealed the of the Holies way, yet the first tabernacle
2192 4714 3748 3850 1519 2540 1764
9 ἐχούσης στάσιν· ἥτις παραβολὴ εἰς τὸν καιρὸν τὸν ἐνεστη-
having standing, which (was) a parable for the time present,
2596/3739/1435/5037 2378 4374 3361 1410
κότα, καθ' ὃν δῶρά τε καὶ θυσίαι προσφέρονται, μὴ δυνά-
according to which gifts both and sacrifices are being offered, not being
2596 4893 5048 3000 3440
10 μεναι κατὰ συνείδησιν τελειῶσαι τὸν λατρεύοντα, μόνον
able as to conscience to perfect the (one) serving, only
1909 1033 4188 1313 909
ἐπὶ βρώμασι καὶ πόμασι καὶ διαφόροις βαπτισμοῖς καὶ
on foods and drinks and various washings, even
1345 4561 3360 2540 1357 1945
δικαιώμασι σαρκός, μέχρι καιροῦ διορθώσεως ἐπικείμενα.
ordinances of flesh until a time of setting things right being imposed.
5547 3854 749 3195
11 Χριστὸς δὲ παραγενόμενος ἀρχιερεὺς τῶν μελλόντων
Christ But having appeared (as) a High Priest of the coming
18 1223 3187 5046 4633 3756
ἀγαθῶν, διὰ τῆς μείζονος καὶ τελειοτέρας σκηνῆς, οὐ
good things, through the greater and more perfect tabernacle not
5499 5123 2076/3756/5026 2937 3761/1223
12 χειροποιήτου, τοῦτ' ἔστιν, οὐ ταύτης τῆς κτίσεως, οὐδὲ δι'
made with hands, this is not of this creation; nor through
129 5131 3448 1223 2398 129
αἵματος τράγων καὶ μόσχων, διὰ δὲ τοῦ ἰδίου αἵματος
blood of goats and of calves, through but the own blood
1525 2178 1519 39 166 3085 2147
εἰσῆλθεν ἐφάπαξ εἰς τὰ ἅγια, αἰωνίαν λύτρωσιν εὑράμενος.
entered once for all into the Holies, eternal redemption having found.
1487/1063 129 5022 5131 4700 1151
13 εἰ γὰρ τὸ αἷμα ταύρων καὶ τράγων, καὶ σποδὸς δαμάλεως
if For the blood of bulls and goats, and ashes of a heifer
4472 2840 37 4314
ῥαντίζουσα τοὺς κεκοινωμένους, ἁγιάζει πρὸς τὴν τῆς
sprinkling those having been polluted sanctifies to the of the
4561 2514 4214 3123 129 5547
14 σαρκὸς καθαρότητα, πόσῳ μᾶλλον τὸ αἷμα τοῦ Χριστοῦ,
flesh cleanness, by how much more the blood of Christ,
3739/1223/ 4151 166 1438 4374 299
ὃς διὰ Πνεύματος αἰωνίου ἑαυτὸν προσήνεγκεν ἄμωμον τῷ
who through (the) Spirit Eternal Himself offered without spot
2316 2511 4893 5216 575 3498 2041 1519
Θεῷ, καθαριεῖ τὴν συνείδησιν ὑμῶν ἀπὸ νεκρῶν ἔργων, εἰς
to God, will cleanse the conscience of you from dead works, for
3000 2316 2198 1223 5124 1242 2537
15 τὸ λατρεύειν Θεῷ ζῶντι; καὶ διὰ τοῦτο διαθήκης καινῆς
serving God of (the) living. And because of this covenant of a new
3316 2076 3704 2288 1096 1519 629
μεσίτης ἐστίν, ὅπως, θανάτου γενομένου εἰς ἀπολύτρωσιν
Mediator He is, so as death having occurred for redemption

first covenant, those having been called out might
receive the promise of the
everlasting inheritance.
[16]For where a covenant
is, *the* death of him covenanting must be offered.
[17]For a covenant is affirmed
over *those* dead, since it
never has force when he
covenanting *is* living.
[18]From which: Neither the
first was dedicated without
blood. [19]For every com-
mand being spoken by
Moses to all the people,
according to Law *he* took
the blood of the calves and
goats, with water and scarlet wool and hyssop, *and*
he sprinkled both the scroll
and all the people, [20]say-
ing, This *is* the blood of the
covenant which God en-
joined to you. [21]And he
likewise sprinkled both the
tabernacle and all the
service vessels with the
blood. [22]And almost all
things are cleansed by
blood according to the
Law; and apart from shed-
ding of blood no remission
occurs. [23]Then *it was*
needful for the figures of
the things in the heavens to
be cleansed *with* these; but
the heavenly things them-
selves by better sacrifices
than these. [24]For Christ did
not enter into *the* Holies
made by hand, types of the
true things, but into
Heaven itself, now to
appear in the presence of
God on our behalf—[25]not
that He often should offer
Himself, even as the high
priest enters into the
Holies year by year with
blood of others; [26]since He
must often have suffered
from *the* foundation of the
world. But now once, at the
completion of the ages, He
has been manifested for
putting away of sin through
the sacrifice of Himself.
[27]And as it is reserved to
men once to die, and after

1909 4413 1242 3847 1860
τῶν ἐπὶ τῇ πρώτῃ διαθήκῃ παραβάσεων, τὴν ἐπαγγελίαν
of the under the first covenant transgressions, the promise
2983 2564 166 2817 3699 1063
16 λάβωσιν οἱ κεκλημένοι τῆς αἰωνίου κληρονομίας. ὅπου γὰρ
may receive those being called of the eternal inheritance. where (is) For
1242 2288 318 5342 1303 1242
17 διαθήκη, θάνατον ἀνάγκη φέρεσθαι τοῦ διαθεμένου. διαθήκη
a covenant (the) death (is) needful to be offered of him covenanting a covenant
2198 1063/1909/3498 949/1893/3361/4218 2480/3753/
γὰρ ἐπὶ νεκροῖς βεβαία, ἐπεὶ μή ποτε ἰσχύει ὅτε ζῇ ὁ διαθέ-
for over (those) dead (is) firm, since not ever has it strength when living he cove-
1303 3606 3761 4413 5565 129 1457
18 μενος. ὅθεν οὐδ' ἡ πρώτη χωρὶς αἵματος ἐγκεκαίνισται.
nanting. From which neither the first without blood was dedicated.
2980 1063 3956 1785 2596 3551 5259 3475
λαληθείσης γὰρ πάσης ἐντολῆς κατὰ νόμον ὑπὸ Μωϋσέως
being spoken For every command according to law by Moses
3956 2992 2983 129 3448 5131
19 παντὶ τῷ λαῷ, λαβὼν τὸ αἷμα τῶν μόσχων καὶ τράγων,
to all the people, taking the blood of the calves and of goats,
3326 5204 2053 2847 5301 846/5037
μετὰ ὕδατος καὶ ἐρίου κοκκίνου καὶ ὑσσώπου, αὐτό τε τὸ
with water and wool scarlet and hyssop, it(self) both the
975 3956 2992 4472 3004 5124
20 βιβλίον καὶ πάντα τὸν λαὸν ἐρράντισε, λέγων, Τοῦτο τὸ
scroll and all the people he sprinkled, saying, This (is) the
129 1242 3739 1781 4314 5209 2316
21 αἷμα τῆς διαθήκης ἧς ἐνετείλατο πρὸς ὑμᾶς ὁ Θεός. καὶ τὴν
blood of the covenant which enjoined to you God. both the
4633 3956 4632 3009 129
σκηνὴν δὲ καὶ πάντα τὰ σκεύη τῆς λειτουργίας τῷ αἵματι
tabernacle And and all the vessels of the service with the blood
3688 4472 4975/1722/129 3956 2511
22 ὁμοίως ἐρράντισε. καὶ σχεδὸν ἐν αἵματι πάντα καθαρίζεται
likewise he sprinkled. And almost by blood all things are cleansed
2596 3551 5565 130 3756 1096 859
κατὰ τὸν νόμον, καὶ χωρὶς αἱματεκχυσίας οὐ γίνεται ἄφεσις.
according to the law, and without bloodshedding no there comes remission.
318 3767 3303 5262 1722 3772
23 Ἀνάγκη οὖν τὰ μὲν ὑποδείγματα τῶν ἐν τοῖς οὐρανοῖς,
(It was) needful then, the things truly examples of the in the heavens
*5125 2511 848 2032 2909
τούτοις καθαρίζεσθαι, αὐτὰ δὲ τὰ ἐπουράνια κρείττοσι
these to be cleansed; them(selves) But the heavenly things by better
2378 3844 5025 3756/1063/1519/5499 39 1525
24 θυσίαις παρὰ ταύτας. οὐ γὰρ εἰς χειροποίητα ἅγια εἰσῆλθεν
sacrifices than these. not For into made by hands Holies entered
5547 499 228 235/1519 846
ὁ Χριστός, ἀντίτυπα τῶν ἀληθινῶν, ἀλλ' εἰς αὐτὸν τὸν
Christ, figures of the true things, but into it(self)
3772 3568 1718 4383 2316 5228
οὐρανόν, νῦν ἐμφανισθῆναι τῷ προσώπῳ τοῦ Θεοῦ ὑπὲρ
Heaven, now to appear in the presence of God for
2257 3761 2443 4178 4374 1438 5618
25 ἡμῶν· οὐδ' ἵνα πολλάκις προσφέρῃ ἑαυτόν, ὥσπερ ὁ
us; not that often He should offer Himself, even as the
749 1525 1519 39 2596 1763 1722 129
ἀρχιερεὺς εἰσέρχεται εἰς τὰ ἅγια κατ' ἐνιαυτὸν ἐν αἵματι
high priest enters into the Holies year by year with blood
245 1893/1163/846 4178 3958 575 2602
26 ἀλλοτρίῳ· ἐπεὶ ἔδει αὐτὸν πολλάκις παθεῖν ἀπὸ καταβολῆς
of others—since must He often have suffered from foundation
2889 3568 530 1909 4930 165 1519 115
κόσμου· νῦν δὲ ἅπαξ ἐπὶ συντελείᾳ τῶν αἰώνων εἰς ἀθέτησιν
of (the) world—now but once at the completion of the ages for putting away
266 1223 2378 848 5319 2596 3745
27 ἁμαρτίας διὰ τῆς θυσίας αὐτοῦ πεφανέρωται. καὶ καθ' ὅσον
of sin through the sacrifice of Him He has been revealed. And as
606 444 530 599 3326 5124
ἀπόκειται τοῖς ἀνθρώποις ἅπαξ ἀποθανεῖν, μετὰ δὲ τοῦτο
it is reserved to men once to die, after and this

this Judgment; [28]so being once offered to bear *the* sins of many, Christ shall appear a second *time* without sin to those expecting Him for salvation.

CHAPTER 10

[1]For the Law had a shadow of the coming good things, not the image it*self* of *those* things. *Appearing* year by year with the same sacrifices, which they offer continually, *they* never are able to perfect the ones drawing near. [2]Otherwise, would they not have ceased to be offered because those serving did not still have conscience of sins, having once been cleansed? [3]But in these *there is* a remembrance of sins year by year —[4]for *it is* not possible *for the* blood of bulls and goats to take away sins. [5]For this reason, coming into the world, He says, "Sacrifice and offering You did not desire, but You prepared a body for Me. [6]You did not delight in burnt offerings and *sacrifices* as to sins. [7]Then I said, Lo, I come—in *the* heading of the Book, it was written concerning Me —to do Your will, *O* God."

[8]Above, saying, "You did not desire nor were pleased *with* offering and burnt offerings and *sacrifices* about sins," which are offered according to the Law, [9]then He said, "Lo, I come to do Your will, *O* God." He takes away the first in order that He may set up the second; [10]by which will we are sanctified through the offering of the body of Jesus Christ once for all. [11]And indeed every priest stands day by day ministering, and often offering the same sacrifices, which can never take

2920 3779 5547 530 4374 1519 4183
κρίσις· οὕτως ὁ Χριστός, ἅπαξ προσενεχθεὶς εἰς τὸ πολλῶν
judgment, so Christ, once having been offered of many
399 266 1537 1208 5565 266 3700
28 ἀνενεγκεῖν ἁμαρτίας, ἐκ δευτέρου χωρὶς ἁμαρτίας ὀφθήσεται
to bear sins, a second (time) without sin will appear
846 553 1519 4991
τοῖς αὐτὸν ἀπεκδεχομένοις, εἰς σωτηρίαν.
to those Him expecting for salvation.

CHAPTER 10

4639 1063 2192 3551 3195 18 3756
1 Σκιὰν γὰρ ἔχων ὁ νόμος τῶν μελλόντων ἀγαθῶν, οὐκ
a shadow For having the law of the coming good things, not
846 1504 4229 2596 1763
αὐτὴν τὴν εἰκόνα τῶν πραγμάτων, κατ' ἐνιαυτὸν ταῖς
it(self) the image of those things, year by year with the
846 2378 3739 4374 1519 1336 3762
αὐταῖς θυσίαις ἃς προσφέρουσιν εἰς τὸ διηνεκές, οὐδέποτε
same sacrifices which they offer continually never
1410 4334 5048 1893 3756/302
2 δύναται τοὺς προσερχομένους τελειῶσαι. ἐπεὶ οὐκ ἂν
are able those drawing near to perfect. ; since not would
3973 4374 1223 3367 2192/2089/4893
ἐπαύσαντο προσφερόμεναι, διὰ τὸ μηδεμίαν ἔχειν ἔτι συνείδη-
they have ceased being offered because of not having still conscience
266 3000 530 2508 235
3 σιν ἁμαρτιῶν τοὺς λατρεύοντας, ἅπαξ κεκαθαρμένους ; ἀλλ'
of sins those serving, once having been cleansed; but
1722/846 364 266 2596 1763 102 1063
4 ἐν αὐταῖς ἀνάμνησις ἁμαρτιῶν κατ' ἐνιαυτόν· ἀδύνατον γὰρ
in them a remembrance of sins year by year; it is impossible for
129 5022 5131 851 266 1352 1525
5 αἷμα ταύρων καὶ τράγων ἀφαιρεῖν ἁμαρτίας. διὸ εἰσερχό-
blood of bulls and of goats to take away sins. Therefore entering
1519 2889 3004 2378 4376 3756
μενος εἰς τὸν κόσμον λέγει, Θυσίαν καὶ προσφορὰν οὐκ
into the world, He says, Sacrifice and offering not
2309 4983 2675 3427 3646 4012
6 ἠθέλησας, σῶμα δὲ κατηρτίσω μοι· ὁλοκαυτώματα καὶ περὶ
You desired, a body but You prepared for Me; burnt offerings and (sacrifices) as to
*1722 266 3756 2106 5119 2036 2400 2240 2777
7 ἁμαρτίας οὐκ εὐδόκησας· τότε εἶπον, Ἰδού, ἥκω (ἐν κεφαλίδι
sins not You were pleased. Then I said, Behold, I come—in a heading
275 1125 4012 1700 4160 2316
βιβλίου γέγραπται περὶ ἐμοῦ) τοῦ ποιῆσαι, ὁ Θεός, τὸ
of (the) Book it was written about Me — to do God the
2307 4675 511 3004 3754 2378 4374
8 θέλημά σου. ἀνώτερον λέγων ὅτι Θυσίαν καὶ προσφορὰν
will of You. Above saying that sacrifice and offering
3646 4012 266 3756 2309 3761
καὶ ὁλοκαυτώματα καὶ περὶ ἁμαρτίας οὐκ ἠθέλησας, οὐδὲ
and burnt offerings and (sacrifices) as to sins not You desired, not
2106 3748 2596 3551 4376 5119
9 εὐδόκησας (αἵτινες κατὰ τὸν νόμον προσφέρονται), τότε
were pleased - which according to the law are offered — then
2046 2400 2240 4160 2316 2307 4675
εἴρηκεν. Ἰδού, ἥκω τοῦ ποιῆσαι, ὁ Θεός, τὸ θέλημά σου.
He said, Behold, I come to do God the will of You.
337 4413 2443 1208 2476 1722/3739/2307
10 ἀναιρεῖ τὸ πρῶτον, ἵνα τὸ δεύτερον στήσῃ. ἐν ᾧ θελήματι
He takes away the first, that the second He may set up, by which will
37 2070 1223 4376 4983
ἡγιασμένοι ἐσμὲν διὰ τῆς προσφορᾶς τοῦ σώματος τοῦ
sanctified we are through the offering of the body
2424 5547 2178 3956/3303 2409 2476 2596
11 Ἰησοῦ Χριστοῦ ἐφάπαξ. καὶ πᾶς μὲν ἱερεὺς ἕστηκε καθ'
of Jesus Christ once for all. And every indeed priest stands day
2250 3008 846 4178 4374
ἡμέραν λειτουργῶν, καὶ τὰς αὐτὰς πολλάκις προσφέρων
by day ministering, and the same often offering

away sins. [12]But He, offering but one sacrifice for sins, sat down in perpetuity at *the* right *hand* of God, [13]from then on expecting until His enemies are placed *as* a footstool of His feet. [14]For by one offering He has perfected in perpetuity the ones being sanctified.

[15]And the Holy Spirit witnesses to us also. For after having said before, [16]"This *is* the covenant which I will covenant to them after those days, says *the* Lord: Giving My laws on their hearts, and I will write them on their minds; [17]and I will not at all still remember their sins and their lawless deeds." [18]But where forgiveness of these *is*, there *is* no longer offering concerning sins.

[19]Then, brothers, having confidence for the entering of the Holies by the blood of Jesus, [20]which He consecrated for us, a new and living way through the veil; that is, His flesh; [21]and *having* a great priest over the house of God, [22]let us draw near with a true heart in full assurance of faith, *our* hearts having been sprinkled from an evil conscience, and *our* body having been washed in pure water; [23]let us hold fast the confession of the hope without yielding, for He who has promised *is* faithful. [24]And let us consider one another, to incitement of love and of good works, [25]not forsaking the assembling together of ourselves, as *is the* custom of some, but exhorting; and by so much more as you see the Day drawing near.

2378 3748 3762 1410 4014 266 846
12 θυσίας, αἵτινες οὐδέποτε δύνανται περιελεῖν ἁμαρτίας· αὐτὸς
sacrifices, which never can take away sins; He
3391 5228 266 4374 2378 1519 1336
δὲ μίαν ὑπὲρ ἁμαρτιῶν προσενέγκας θυσίαν εἰς τὸ διηνεκές,
but one on behalf of sins having offered sacrifice, in perpetuity,
2523 1722 1188 2316 3063 1551 2193
13 ἐκάθισεν ἐν δεξιᾷ τοῦ Θεοῦ, τὸ λοιπὸν ἐκδεχόμενος ἕως
sat down at (the) right of God, from then on expecting until
5087 2190 848 5286 4228 848 3391
14 τεθῶσιν οἱ ἐχθροὶ αὐτοῦ ὑποπόδιον τῶν ποδῶν αὐτοῦ. μιᾷ
are put the enemies of Him (as) a footstool of the feet of Him. by one
1063 4376 5048 1519 1336 37
γὰρ προσφορᾷ τετελείωκεν εἰς τὸ διηνεκὲς τοὺς ἁγιαζο-
For offering He has perfected in perpetuity those being sanct-
3140 2254 4151 40 3316 1063
15 μένους. μαρτυρεῖ δὲ ἡμῖν καὶ τὸ Πνεῦμα τὸ Ἅγιον· μετὰ γὰρ
ified. witnesses And to us also the Spirit Holy; after for
4280 3778 1242 3739 1303 4314
16 τὸ προειρηκέναι, Αὕτη ἡ διαθήκη ἣν διαθήσομαι πρὸς
having said before, This (is) the covenant which I will covenant to
846 3326 2250 1565 3004 2962 1325 3551
αὐτοὺς μετὰ τὰς ἡμέρας ἐκείνας, λέγει Κύριος, διδοὺς νόμους
them after days those, says (the) Lord: Giving laws
3450 1909 2588 848 1909 1271 848
μου ἐπὶ καρδίας αὐτῶν, καὶ ἐπὶ τῶν διανοιῶν αὐτῶν
of Me on hearts of them, also on the minds of them
1924 846 266 848
17 ἐπιγράψω αὐτούς· καὶ τῶν ἁμαρτιῶν αὐτῶν καὶ τῶν
I will write them, and the sins of them and the
458 848 =3364= 3415 2089/3699 859 5130
18 ἀνομιῶν αὐτῶν οὐ μὴ μνησθῶ ἔτι. ὅπου δὲ ἄφεσις τούτων,
lawlessnesses of them not at all I will remember still. where Now forgiveness of these (is),
3765 4376 4012 266
οὐκέτι προσφορὰ περὶ ἁμαρτίας.
no longer (is) offering concerning sins.
2192 3767 80 3954 1519 1529
19 Ἔχοντες οὖν, ἀδελφοί, παρρησίαν εἰς τὴν εἴσοδον τῶν
Having, therefore, brothers, confidence for the entering of the
39 1722 129 2424 3739 1457 2254 3598
20 ἁγίων ἐν τῷ αἵματι Ἰησοῦ, ἣν ἐνεκαίνισεν ἡμῖν ὁδὸν
Holies by the blood of Jesus, which He consecrated for us, a way
4372 2198 1223 2665 5123
πρόσφατον καὶ ζῶσαν, διὰ τοῦ καταπετάσματος, τοῦτ'
new and living through the veil, this
2076 4561 848 2409 3173/1909 3624
21 ἔστι, τῆς σαρκὸς αὐτοῦ, καὶ ἱερέα μέγαν ἐπὶ τὸν οἶκον τοῦ
is, the flesh of Him; and (having) a priest great over the house
2316 4334 3326 228 2588 1722 4136
22 Θεοῦ, προσερχώμεθα μετὰ ἀληθινῆς καρδίας ἐν πληρο-
of God, let us draw near with a true heart in full
4102 4472 2588 575 4893
φορίᾳ πίστεως, ἐρραντισμένοι τὰς καρδίας ἀπὸ συνειδήσεως
assurance of faith, having been sprinkled the hearts from a conscience
4190 3068 4983 5204 2513 2722
23 πονηρᾶς, καὶ λελουμένοι τὸ σῶμα ὕδατι καθαρῷ· κατέχω-
evil, and having been washed the body water in clean; let us hold
3671 1680 186 4103 1063
μεν τὴν ὁμολογίαν τῆς ἐλπίδος ἀκλινῆ, πιστὸς γὰρ ὁ
fast the confession of the hope unyieldingly, faithful for (is) He
1861 2657 240 1519 3948
24 ἐπαγγειλάμενος· καὶ κατανοῶμεν ἀλλήλους εἰς παροξυσμὸν
having promised; and let us consider one another to incitement
26 2570/2041 3361 1459 1997
25 ἀγάπης καὶ καλῶν ἔργων, μὴ ἐγκαταλείποντες τὴν ἐπισυν-
of love and of good works, not forsaking the assembling
1438 2531 1485 5100 235 3870
αγωγὴν ἑαυτῶν, καθὼς ἔθος τισίν, ἀλλὰ παρακαλοῦντες,
of ourselves as (the) custom of some (is), but exhorting,
5118 3123 3745 991 1448 2250
καὶ τοσούτῳ μᾶλλον, ὅσῳ βλέπετε ἐγγίζουσαν τὴν ἡμέραν.
and by so much more as you see drawing near the Day.

NOTE: Frequent words not numbered: δέ(1161); καί(2531)—and, but; ὁ, ἡ, τό (3588, the)— * above word, look in verse margin for No.

[26]For *if* we *are* willfully sinning after receiving the full knowledge of the truth, there remains no more sacrifice concerning sins, [27]but a certain fearful expectation of judgment and zealous fire being about to consume the adversaries. [28]*If* anyone did not regard *the* Law of Moses, *that one* dies without pities on *the word of* two or three witnesses. [29]How much worse punishment do you think he will be thought worthy *to receive* having trampled on the Son of God, and having counted the blood of the covenant in which he was sanctified common, and having insulted the Spirit of grace? [30]For we know Him who has said, "Vengeance *belongs* to Me; I will repay, says *the* Lord." And again, "*The* Lord will judge His people." [31]*It is* a fearful thing to fall into *the* hands of *the* living God.

[32]But call to mind the former days in which being enlightened you endured much conflict of sufferings; [33]partly being exposed both to reproaches and to afflictions; and partly having become partners of those so conducting themselves. [34]For also you suffered together in my bonds; and you accepted the seizure of your possessions with joy, knowing yourselves to have a better and abiding possession in Heaven. [35]Then do not throw away your confidence, which has great reward. [36]For you have need of patience, that having done the will of God you may obtain the promise. [37]For, "yet a very little *and* the *One* coming will come, and will not delay." [38]But the just shall live by faith; and if he draws back, My soul is not pleased in him.

1596 1063 264 2257 3326 2983
26 Ἑκουσίως γὰρ ἁμαρτανόντων ἡμῶν μετὰ τὸ λαβεῖν τὴν
willfully For sinning us after receiving the

1922 225 3765 4012 266 620
ἐπίγνωσιν τῆς ἀληθείας, οὐκέτι περὶ ἁμαρτιῶν ἀπολείπεται
full knowledge of the truth, no more concerning sins remains

2378 5398 5100 1561 2920 4442 2205
27 θυσία, φοβερὰ δέ τις ἐκδοχὴ κρίσεως, καὶ πυρὸς ζῆλος
a sacrifice, fearful but some expectation of judgment, and of fire zeal

2068 3195 5227 114 5100 3551
28 ἐσθίειν μέλλοντος τοὺς ὑπεναντίους. ἀθετήσας τις νόμον
to consume being about the adversaries. disregarding Anyone law

3475 5565 3628 1909 1417/2228/5140 3144
Μωσέως χωρὶς οἰκτιρμῶν ἐπὶ δυσὶν ἢ τρισὶ μάρτυσιν
of Moses without pities on (the word of) two or three witnesses

599 4214 1380 5501 515 5098
29 ἀποθνήσκει· πόσῳ, δοκεῖτε, χείρονος ἀξιωθήσεται τιμωρίας
dies; by how much think you of worse will be thought worthy (to receive) punishment

5207 2316 2662 129 1242
ὁ τὸν υἱὸν τοῦ Θεοῦ καταπατήσας, καὶ τὸ αἷμα τῆς διαθή-
he the Son of God having trampled, and the blood of the cove-

2839 2233 1722/3739 37 4151
κης κοινὸν ἡγησάμενος ἐν ᾧ ἡγιάσθη, καὶ τὸ Πνεῦμα τῆς
nant common having deemed by which he was sanctified, and the Spirit

5485 1796 1492 1063 2036 1698 1557
30 χάριτος ἐνυβρίσας; οἴδαμεν γὰρ τὸν εἰπόντα, Ἐμοὶ ἐκδίκη-
of grace having insulted; we know for the (One) having said, To Me (is) ven-

1473 467 3004 2962 3825 2962
σις, ἐγὼ ἀνταποδώσω, λέγει Κύριος· καὶ πάλιν, Κύριος
geance, I will repay, says (the) Lord; and again, (The) Lord

2919 2992 848 5398 1706 1519 5495 2316
31 κρινεῖ τὸν λαὸν αὐτοῦ. φοβερὸν τὸ ἐμπεσεῖν εἰς χεῖρας Θεοῦ
will judge the people of Him. A fearful thing (it is) to fall into (the) hands God

2198
ζῶντος.
of (the) living.

363 4386 2250 1722 5461
32 Ἀναμιμνήσκεσθε δὲ τὰς πρότερον ἡμέρας, ἐν αἷς φωτι-
call to mind But the former days in which having

4183 119 5278 3804 5124 3303
33 σθέντες πολλὴν ἄθλησιν ὑπεμείνατε παθημάτων· τοῦτο μέν,
been enlightened much struggle you endured of sufferings; this *partly*

3680 5037 2347 2301 5124 2844
ὀνειδισμοῖς τε καὶ θλίψεσι θεατριζόμενοι· τοῦτο δέ, κοινωνοὶ
to reproaches both and to afflictions being exposed; this and, sharers

3779 390 1096 1063
34 τῶν οὕτως ἀναστρεφομένων γενηθέντες. καὶ γὰρ τοῖς
of those so living becoming. indeed For in the

1199 3450 4834 724 5224
δεσμοῖς μου συνεπαθήσατε, καὶ τὴν ἁρπαγὴν τῶν ὑπαρχόν-
bonds of me you suffered together, and the seizure of the possessions

5216 3326 5479 4327 1097 2192/1722
των ὑμῶν μετὰ χαρᾶς προσεδέξασθε, γινώσκοντες ἔχειν ἐν
of you with joy you accepted, knowing to have in

1438 2909 5223 1722 3772 3306 3361
35 ἑαυτοῖς κρείττονα ὕπαρξιν ἐν οὐρανοῖς καὶ μένουσαν. μὴ
yourselves a better possession in Heaven and abiding. do not

577 3767 3954 5216 3748/2192/ 3405
ἀποβάλητε οὖν τὴν παρρησίαν ὑμῶν, ἥτις ἔχει μισθαποδο-
cast away Therefore the confidence of you, which has reward

3173 5281 1063 2192 5532 2443 2307
36 σίαν μεγάλην. ὑπομονῆς γὰρ ἔχετε χρείαν, ἵνα τὸ θέλημα
great. of patience For you have need, that the will

2316 4160 2865 1860 2089/1063
37 τοῦ Θεοῦ ποιήσαντες κομίσησθε τὴν ἐπαγγελίαν. ἔτι γὰρ
of God having done, you may obtain the promise. yet For

3398 3745 2064 2240 3756/ 5549
38 μικρὸν ὅσον ὅσον, Ὁ ἐρχόμενος ἥξει, καὶ οὐ χρονιεῖ. ὁ δὲ
little a very, the coming (One) will come, and not delay; the but

1342 1537 4102 2198 1437 5288 3756
δίκαιος ἐκ πίστεως ζήσεται· καὶ ἐὰν ὑποστείληται, οὐκ
just by faith will live. and if he draws back, not

[39]But we are not of *those* drawing back to destruction, but of faith, to *the* preservation of *the* soul.

CHAPTER 11

[1]Now faith is *the* substance of things hoped for, *the* evidence of things not being seen. [2]For by this the elders obtained witness. [3]By faith we understand the worlds to have been framed by *the* word of God, so that the things seen *should* not come into being out of things that appear.

[4]By faith Abel offered a greater sacrifice to God than Cain, by which he obtained witness to be righteous, God testifying over his gifts; and through it, having died, he yet speaks. [5]By faith Enoch was translated *so as* not to see death, and was not found, because God translated him. For before his translation, he had obtained witness to have been pleasing to God. [6]But without faith it is impossible to please *God*. For it is right *that* the *one* drawing near to God should believe that He is, and *that* He becomes a rewarder to the ones seeking Him out. [7]Being warned by God about the things not yet having been seen, moved with fear, by faith Noah prepared an ark for *the* salvation of his house; through which he condemned the world, and became heir of the righteousness according to faith.

[8]Having been called out by faith, Abraham obeyed to go forth to a place which he was going to receive for an inheritance, and went out not understanding where he went. [9]By faith he resided as a foreigner in a land of promise, living in tents with Isaac and Jacob, the co-heirs of the same

2106 5590 3450/1722/846 2249 3756 2070 5289
39 εὐδοκεῖ ἡ ψυχή μου ἐν αὐτῷ. ἡμεῖς δὲ οὐκ ἐσμὲν ὑποστολῆς
is pleased the soul of Me in him. we But not are of (those) drawing
1519 684 235 4102 1519 4047 5590
εἰς ἀπώλειαν, ἀλλὰ πίστεως εἰς περιποίησιν ψυχῆς.
to destruction, but of faith to preservation of (the) soul.

CHAPTER 11

2076 4102 1679 5287 4229
1 Ἔστι δὲ πίστις ἐλπιζομένων ὑπόστασις, πραγμάτων
is Now faith of things being hoped, (the) substance of things
1650/3756/ 991 1722 5026 1063 3140
2 ἔλεγχος οὐ βλεπομένων. ἐν ταύτῃ γὰρ ἐμαρτυρήθησαν οἱ
(the) evidence not being seen. by this For obtained witness the
4245 4102 3539 2675 165
3 πρεσβύτεροι. πίστει νοοῦμεν κατηρτίσθαι τοὺς αἰῶνας
elders. By faith we understand to have been framed the worlds
4487 2316/1519 3361/1537/ 5316 991 1096
ῥήματι Θεοῦ, εἰς τὸ μὴ ἐκ φαινομένων τὰ βλεπόμενα γεγονέ-
by a word of God, so as not out of things appearing the seen to have come into
*2535 4102 4119 2378 6 3844 things 4374
4 ναι. πίστει πλείονα θυσίαν Ἄβελ παρὰ Κάϊν προσήνεγκε τῷ
being. By faith a greater sacrifice Abel than Cain offered
2316/1223/3739/ 3140 1511 1342 3140 1909
Θεῷ, δι᾽ ἧς ἐμαρτυρήθη εἶναι δίκαιος, μαρτυροῦντος ἐπὶ τοῖς
to God by which he obtained to be righteous, testifying over the
1435 848 witness 2316 1223 846 599 2089/2980
δώροις αὐτοῦ τοῦ Θεοῦ· καὶ δι᾽ αὐτῆς ἀποθανὼν ἔτι λαλεῖ.
gifts of him God, and through it having died yet he speaks.
4102 1802 3346 3361 1492 2288 3756
5 πίστει Ἐνὼχ μετετέθη τοῦ μὴ ἰδεῖν θάνατον, καὶ οὐχ
By faith Enoch was translated not to see death, and not
2146 1360 3346 846 2316/4253/1063 3346
εὑρίσκετο, διότι μετέθηκεν αὐτὸν ὁ Θεός· πρὸ γὰρ τῆς μεταθέ-
was found, because translated him God. before For the trans-
848 3140 2100 2316 5565
6 σεως αὐτοῦ μεμαρτύρηται εὐηρεστηκέναι τῷ Θεῷ· χωρὶς δὲ
lating of him he obtained witness to have been pleasing to God; without but
4102 102 2100 4100 1063 1163
πίστεως ἀδύνατον εὐαρεστῆσαι· πιστεῦσαι γὰρ δεῖ τὸν
faith it is impossible to please (God); to believe for it is right the (one)
4334 2316/3754/2076 1567 846
προσερχόμενον τῷ Θεῷ, ὅτι ἔστι, καὶ τοῖς ἐκζητοῦσιν αὐτὸν
approaching God that He is, and to those seeking out Him
3405 1096 4102 5537 3575 4012
7 μισθαποδότης γίνεται. πίστει χρηματισθεὶς Νῶε περὶ τῶν
a rewarder He becomes. By faith being warned by God Noah about the
3369 991 2125 2680 2787 things
μηδέπω βλεπομένων, εὐλαβηθεὶς κατεσκεύασε κιβωτὸν εἰς
not yet being seen, moved with fear prepared an ark for
4991 3624 848 1223/3739/ 2632 2889
σωτηρίαν τοῦ οἴκου αὐτοῦ· δι᾽ ἧς κατέκρινε τὸν κόσμον, καὶ
(the) salvation of the house of him, by which he condemned the world, and
2596 4102 1343 1096 2818 4102
8 τῆς κατὰ πίστιν δικαιοσύνης ἐγένετο κληρονόμος. πίστει
of the according to faith righteousness became heir. By faith
2564 11 5219 1831 1519 5117 3739
καλούμενος Ἀβραὰμ ὑπήκουσεν ἐξελθεῖν εἰς τὸν τόπον ὃν
having been called, Abraham obeyed to go forth to a place which
3195 2983 1519 2817 1831 3361 1987
ἤμελλε λαμβάνειν εἰς κληρονομίαν, καὶ ἐξῆλθε μὴ ἐπιστά-
he was about to receive for an inheritance, and went forth not under-
4226 2064 4102 3939 1519 1093 1860
9 μενος ποῦ ἔρχεται. πίστει παρῴκησεν εἰς τὴν γῆν τῆς ἐπαγ-
standing where he went. By faith he sojourned in a land of
5613 245 1722 4633 2730 3326 2464
γελίας, ὡς ἀλλοτρίαν, ἐν σκηναῖς κατοικήσας μετὰ Ἰσαὰκ
promise, as a foreigner, in tents dwelling with Isaac
2384 4789 1860 846
καὶ Ἰακώβ, τῶν συγκληρονόμων τῆς ἐπαγγελίας τῆς αὐτῆς·
and Jacob, the co-heirs of the promise same;

promise. [10]For he looked for a city having the foundations of which the builder and maker *is* God. [11]Also by faith Sarah herself received power for conceiving seed even beyond *the* time of age, *and* gave birth; since she deemed the *One* having promised *to be* faithful. [12]Because of this came into being from one—and that *from* one having died —*seed* even as the stars of the heaven in multitude, and countless as sand by the seaside.

[13]These all died by way of faith, not having received the promises, but seeing them from afar, and being persuaded, and having embraced and confessed that they are aliens and sojourners on the earth. [14]For those saying such things make clear that they seek a fatherland. [15]And truly if they remembered that from which they came out, they had time to return. [16]But now they stretch forth to a better, that is, a heavenly *land*. Therefore, God is not ashamed *of* them, to be called their God; for He prepared a city for them.

[17]By faith, being tested, Abraham offered up Isaac; and he receiving the promises was offering up the only-begotten, [18]as to whom it was said, "In Isaac your Seed shall be called;" [19]reckoning that God *was* able to raise even from *the* dead; from where indeed he obtained him in a parable. [20]Concerning coming things, by faith Isaac blessed Jacob and Esau. [21]By faith dying Jacob blessed each of the sons of Joseph, and worshiped on the top of his staff.

1551 1063 2310 2192 4172 3739 5079
10 ἐξεδέχετο γὰρ τὴν τοὺς θεμελίους ἔχουσαν πόλιν, ἧς τεχνίτης
looked forward for to the the foundations having city, of which builder
1217 2316 4102 848 4564 1411 1519
11 καὶ δημιουργος ὁ Θεός. πίστει καὶ αὐτὴ Σάρρα δύναμιν εἰς
and maker (was) God. By faith also her(self) Sarah power for
2602 4690 2983 3844 2540 2244
καταβολὴν σπέρματος ἔλαβε, καὶ παρὰ καιρὸν ἡλικίας
conception of seed received even beyond time of age,
5088 1893 4103 2233 1861 1352
12 ἔτεκεν, ἐπεὶ πιστὸν ἡγήσατο τὸν ἐπαγγειλάμενον. διὸ καὶ
gave birth, since faithful she deemed the (One) having promised. Therefore
575 1520 1080 5023 3499 2531
ἀφ' ἑνὸς ἐγεννήθησαν, καὶ ταῦτα νενεκρωμένου, καθὼς τὰ
from one came into being —and that (of) one having died — even as the
798 3772 4128 5616 285 3844
ἄστρα τοῦ οὐρανοῦ τῷ πλήθει, καὶ ὡσεὶ ἄμμος ἡ παρὰ τὸ
stars of the heaven in multitude, and as sand by the
5491 2281 382
χεῖλος τῆς θαλάσσης ἡ ἀναρίθμητος.
lip of the sea countless.
2596 4102 599 3778 3956 3361 2983
13 Κατὰ πίστιν ἀπέθανον οὗτοι πάντες, μὴ λαβόντες τὰς
By way of faith died these all, not having received the
1860 235 4207 846 1492 3982
ἐπαγγελίας, ἀλλὰ πόρρωθεν αὐτὰς ἰδόντες, καὶ πεισθέντες,
promises, but from afar them seeing, and being persuaded
782 3670 3754 3581 3927
καὶ ἀσπασάμενοι, καὶ ὁμολογήσαντες ὅτι ξένοι καὶ παρ-
and having embraced, and having confessed that aliens and so-
1526/1909 1093 1063 5108 3004 1718
14 επίδημοί εἰσιν ἐπὶ τῆς γῆς. οἱ γὰρ τοιαῦτα λέγοντες ἐμφανί-
journers they are on the earth. those For such things saying make
3754 3968 1934 1487/3303 1565 3421
15 ζουσιν ὅτι πατρίδα ἐπιζητοῦσι. καὶ εἰ μὲν ἐκείνης ἐμνη-
clear that a fatherland they seek. And if indeed that they
575/3739/ 1831 2192/302/ 2540 344 2570
16 μόνευον ἀφ' ἧς ἐξῆλθον, εἶχον ἂν καιρὸν ἀνακάμψαι. νυνὶ δὲ
remembered from which they came out, they had time to return. now But
2909 3713 5123 2076 2032 1352/3756
κρείττονος ὀρέγονται, τοῦτ' ἔστιν, ἐπουρανίου· διὸ οὐκ
a better stretch forth to, the is, a heavenly. Therefore, not
1870 846 2316 2316 1941 848
ἐπαισχύνεται αὐτοὺς ὁ Θεός, Θεὸς ἐπικαλεῖσθαι αὐτῶν
is ashamed (of) them God, God to be called of them;
2090 1063 846 4172
ἡτοίμασε γὰρ αὐτοῖς πόλιν.
He prepared for them a city.
4102 4374 11 2464 3985
17 Πίστει προσενήνοχεν Ἀβραὰμ τὸν Ἰσαὰκ πειραζόμενος,
By faith offered up Abraham Isaac, being tested
3439 4374 1860 324
καὶ τὸν μονογενῆ προσέφερεν ὁ τὰς ἐπαγγελίας ἀναδεξά-
and the only-begotten was offering up the (one) the promises having
4314/3739/ 2980 3754/1722 2464 4671
18 μενος, πρὸς ὃν ἐλαλήθη ὅτι Ἐν Ἰσαὰκ κληθήσεταί σοι
accepted, as to whom it was spoken: In Isaac shall be called of you
4690 3049 3754 1537 3498 1453 1415
19 σπέρμα· λογισάμενος ὅτι καὶ ἐκ νεκρῶν ἐγείρειν δυνατὸς ὁ
the seed, reckoning that even from (the) dead to raise (was) able
2316 3606 846 1722 3850 2865 4102 4012
20 Θεός· ὅθεν αὐτὸν καὶ ἐν παραβολῇ ἐκομίσατο. πίστει περὶ
God, from where him indeed in a parable he obtained. By faith concerning
3195 2127 2464 2384 2269
μελλόντων εὐλόγησεν Ἰσαὰκ τὸν Ἰακὼβ καὶ τὸν Ἠσαῦ.
coming things blessed Isaac Jacob and Esau.
4102 2384 599 1538 5207 2501
21 πίστει Ἰακὼβ ἀποθνήσκων ἕκαστον τῶν υἱῶν Ἰωσὴφ
By faith Jacob dying each of the sons of Joseph
2127 4352 1909 206 4464 848
εὐλόγησε, καὶ προσεκύνησεν ἐπὶ τὸ ἄκρον τῆς ῥάβδου αὐτοῦ.
blessed, and worshiped on the top of the staff of him.

22By faith dying Joseph made mention concerning the Exodus of the sons of Israel, and gave orders concerning his bones. 23Moses being born, *he* was by faith hidden by his parents *for* three months, because they saw the child *was* beautiful; and they did not fear the king's decree. 24By faith Moses having become great refused to be called *the* son of Pharaoh's daughter, 25having chosen instead to suffer affliction with the people of God, than for a time to have enjoyment of sin; 26having counted the reproach of Christ greater riches than the treasures of Egypt— for he was looking to the reward.

27By faith he left Egypt, not fearing the anger of the king; for he kept on as seeing the Invisible *One*. 28By faith he made the Passover, and the sprinkling of blood, that the destroyer of the firstborn might not touch them. 29By faith they passed through the Red Sea, as through dry *land; by* which trial the Egyptians were swallowed. 30By faith the walls of Jericho fell down, having been circled during seven days. 31By faith Rahab the harlot did not perish with those disobeying, having received the spies with peace.

32And what more may I say? For the times will fail me telling about Gideon, Barak, and also Samson and Jephthah, and also David and Samuel, and the prophets, 33who through faith overcame kingdoms, worked out righteousness, obtained promises, stopped the mouths of lions, 34quenched *the* power of fire, escaped *the* mouths of *the* sword, acquired power from weakness, became

4102 2501 5053 4012 1841 5207 2474
22 πίστει Ἰωσὴφ τελευτῶν περὶ τῆς ἐξόδου τῶν υἱῶν Ἰσραὴλ
By faith Joseph dying concerning the exodus of the sons of Israel
3421 4012 3747 848 1781
ἐμνημόνευσε, καὶ περὶ τῶν ὀστέων αὐτοῦ ἐνετείλατο.
remembered, and concerning the bones of him gave orders.
4102 3475 1080 2928 5150 5259 3962
23 πίστει Μωσῆς γεννηθεὶς ἐκρύβη τρίμηνον ὑπὸ τῶν πατέρων
By faith Moses having been born was hidden three months by the parents
848 1360 1492 791 3813 3756 5399
αὐτοῦ, διότι εἶδον ἀστεῖον τὸ παιδίον· καὶ οὐκ ἐφοβήθησαν
of him, because they saw (was) fair the child, and not they feared
1297 935 4102 3475 3173 1096
24 τὸ διάταγμα τοῦ βασιλέως. πίστει Μωσῆς μέγας γενόμενος
the decree of the king. By faith Moses great having become
720 3004 5207 2364 5328 3123 138
25 ἠρνήσατο λέγεσθαι υἱὸς θυγατρὸς Φαραω, μᾶλλον ἑλόμενος
refused to be called son of (the) daughter of Pharaoh, rather choosing
4778 2992 2316/2228/ 4340 2192
συγκακουχεῖσθαι τῷ λαῷ τοῦ Θεοῦ ἢ πρόσκαιρον ἔχειν
to suffer affliction with the people of God, than for a time to have
266 619 3187 4149 2233
26 ἁμαρτίας ἀπόλαυσιν· μείζονα πλοῦτον ἡγησάμενος τῶν
of sin enjoyment, greater riches deeming (than) the
1722 125 2344 3680 5547 578
ἐν Αἰγύπτῳ θησαυρῶν τὸν ὀνειδισμὸν τοῦ Χριστοῦ· ἀπέ-
of Egypt treasures the reproach of Christ; he was
1063/ 1519 3405 4102 2641
27 βλεπε γὰρ εἰς τὴν μισθαποδοσίαν. πίστει κατέλιπεν
looking for to the reward. By faith he left
125 3361 5399 2372 935 1063
Αἴγυπτον, μὴ φοβηθεὶς τὸν θυμὸν τοῦ βασιλέως· τὸν γὰρ
Egypt, not fearing the anger of the king; the for
517 5613/3708 2594 4102 4160 3957
28 ἀόρατον ὡς ὁρῶν ἐκαρτέρησε. πίστει πεποίηκε τὸ πάσχα
Invisible (One) as seeing he kept on. By faith he made the Passover
4378 129 2443/3361 3645
καὶ τὴν πρόσχυσιν τοῦ αἵματος, ἵνα μὴ ὁ ὀλοθρεύων τὰ
and the sprinkling of blood, that not He destroying the
4416 2345 846 4102 1224 2063
29 πρωτότοκα θίγῃ αὐτῶν. πίστει διέβησαν τὴν ἐρυθρὰν
firstborns should touch them. By faith they went through the Red
2281 5613/1223/3584/3739 3984 2983 124
θάλασσαν ὡς διὰ ξηρᾶς· ἧς πεῖραν λαβόντες οἱ Αἰγύπτιοι
Sea as through dry, which trial taking the Egyptians
2666 4102 5038 2410 4098 2944
30 κατεπόθησαν. πίστει τὰ τείχη Ἰεριχὼ ἔπεσε, κυκλωθέντα
were swallowed. By faith the walls of Jericho fell, having been circle
1909/2033 2250 4102 4460 4204/3756 4881
31 ἐπὶ ἑπτὰ ἡμέρας. πίστει Ῥαὰβ ἡ πόρνη οὐ συναπώλετο
during seven days. By faith Rahab the harlot did not perish
544 1209 2685 3326 1515
τοῖς ἀπειθήσασι, δεξαμένη τοὺς κατασκόπους μετ' εἰρήνης.
with those disobeying, receiving the spies with peace.
5101/2089/3004 1952 1063/3165/ 1334 5550 4012
32 καὶ τί ἔτι λέγω; ἐπιλείψει γάρ με διηγούμενον ὁ χρόνος περὶ
And what still may I say? will fail For me telling the times concernir
1066 918 5037 4546 2422 1138/5037
Γεδεών, Βαράκ τε καὶ Σαμψὼν καὶ Ἰεφθάε, Δαβίδ τε καὶ
Gideon, Barak, both and Samson and Jephthah, David both and
4545 4396 1223 4102 2610
33 Σαμουὴλ καὶ τῶν προφητῶν· οἳ διὰ πίστεως κατηγωνίσαντο
Samuel, and the prophets, who through faith overcame
932 2038 1343 2013 1860
βασιλείας, εἰργάσαντο δικαιοσύνην, ἐπέτυχον ἐπαγγελιῶν,
kingdoms, worked out righteousness, obtained promises,
5420 4750 3023 1743 1411 4442 5343
34 ἔφραξαν στόματα λεόντων, ἔσβεσαν δύναμιν πυρός, ἔφυγον
stopped mouths of lions, quenched (the) power of fire, escaped
4750 3162 1743 575 769 1096
στόματα μαχαίρας, ἐνεδυναμώθησαν ἀπὸ ἀσθενείας, ἐγενή-
mouths of (the) sword, acquired power from weakness, became

strong in war, made armies
of foreigners to yield.
35 Women received their
dead by resurrection; but
others were beaten to
death, not accepting deliverance, that they might
obtain a better resurrec-
tion. 36 And others re-
ceived trial of mockings and
of floggings; yea, more, of
bonds and of prison: 37 they
were stoned; they were
tried; they were sawn in
two; they died by murder of
sword; they went about in
sheepskins *and* in goat-
skins, being in need, being
afflicted, being ill-treated;
38 of whom the world was
not worthy, wandering in
deserts, and mountains,
and caves, and the holes of
the earth. 39 And having
obtained witness through
the faith, these all did not
obtain the promise, 40 God
having foreseen something
better concerning us, that
they should not be per-
fected apart from us.

2478 1722 4171 3925 2827 245
υησαν ἰσχυροὶ εν πολέμῳ, παρεμβολὰς ἔκλιναν ἀλλοτρίων.
strong in war, armies made to yield of foreigners,
2983 1135 1537 386 3498 848 243
35 ἔλαβον γυναῖκες ἐξ ἀναστάσεως τοὺς νεκροὺς αὐτῶν· ἄλλοι
received women by resurrection the dead of them; others
5178 3756 4327 629
δὲ ἐτυμπανίσθησαν, οὐ προσδεξάμενοι τὴν ἀπολύτρωσιν,
but were beaten to death, not accepting deliverance,
2443 2909 386 5177 2087 1701
36 ἵνα κρείττονος ἀναστάσεως τύχωσιν· ἕτεροι δὲ ἐμπαιγμῶν
that a better resurrection they might obtain; others and of mockings
3148 3984 2983 2089 1199 5438
καὶ μαστίγων πεῖραν ἔλαβον, ἔτι δὲ δεσμῶν καὶ φυλακῆς·
and of floggings trial received, more and, bonds and of prison;
3034 3984 4249 1722/5408 3162
37 ἐλιθάσθησαν, ἐπρίσθησαν, ἐπειράσθησαν, ἐν φόνῳ μαχαίρας
they were stoned, they were tried, they were sawn apart, by murder of sword
599 4022 1722 3374 1722 122 1192
ἀπέθανον· περιῆλθον ἐν μηλωταῖς, ἐν αἰγείοις δέρμασιν,
they died, they went about in sheepskins, in goatskins,
5302 2346 2558 3739/3756/2258/514
38 ὑστερούμενοι, θλιβόμενοι, κακουχούμενοι (ὧν οὐκ ἦν ἄξιος
being in need, being afflicted, being ill-treated, of whom not was worthy
2889 1722 2047 4105 3735 4693
ὁ κόσμος), ἐν ἐρημίαις πλανώμενοι καὶ ὄρεσι καὶ σπηλαίοις
the world, over deserts wandering and mountains and caves
3692 1093 3778 3956 3140
39 καὶ ταῖς ὀπαῖς τῆς γῆς. καὶ οὗτοι πάντες, μαρτυρηθέντες
and the holes of the earth. And these all having obtained witness
1223 4102 3756 2865 1860
40 διὰ τῆς πίστεως, οὐκ ἐκομίσαντο τὴν ἐπαγγελίαν, τοῦ
through the faith did not obtain the promise,
2316/4012 2257 2909 5100 4265 2443/3361/5565
Θεοῦ περὶ ἡμῶν κρεῖττόν τι προβλεψαμένου, ἵνα μὴ χωρὶς
God concerning us better something having foreseen, that not without
2257 5048
ἡμῶν τελειωθῶσι.
us they should be perfected.

CHAPTER 12

1 So therefore we, having
so great a cloud of wit-
nesses encircling us, having laid aside every weight
and the easily-surrounding
sin, let us through patience
run the race set before us,
2 looking to the Author and
Finisher of *our* faith, Jesus,
who because of the joy set
before Him endured *the*
cross, despising the shame,
and sat down at *the* right of
the throne of God. 3 For
consider Him who had
endured such gainsaying of
sinners against Himself,
that you do not grow weary,
fainting in your souls. 4 You
did not yet resist unto
blood, wrestling against

CHAPTER 12

5105 2249 5118 2192 4029 2254
1 Τοιγαροῦν καὶ ἡμεῖς, τοσοῦτον ἔχοντες περικείμενον ἡμῖν
So therefore also we, such having encircling us
3509 3144 3591 659 3956 2139
νέφος μαρτύρων, ὄγκον ἀποθέμενοι πάντα καὶ τὴν εὐπερί-
a cloud of witnesses, weight laying aside every and the easily sur-
266 1223 5281 5143 4295
στατον ἁμαρτίαν, δι' ὑπομονῆς τρέχωμεν τὸν προκείμενον
rounding sin, through patience let us run the set before
2254 73 872 1519 4102 747
2 ἡμῖν ἀγῶνα, ἀφορῶντες εἰς τὸν τῆς πίστεως ἀρχηγὸν καὶ
us race, looking to the of the faith Author and
5051 2424 3739/473 4295 846 5479
τελειωτὴν Ἰησοῦν, ὅς, ἀντὶ τῆς προκειμένης αὐτῷ χαρᾶς,
Finisher, Jesus, who against the set before Him joy
5278 4716 152 2706 1722/1188/5037
ὑπέμεινε σταυρόν, αἰσχύνης καταφρονήσας, ἐν δεξιᾷ τε τοῦ
endured (the) cross, (the) shame despising, at (the) right and of the
2362 2316 2523 357 1063 5108
3 θρόνου τοῦ Θεοῦ ἐκάθισεν. ἀναλογίσασθε γὰρ τὸν τοιαυτην
throne of God sat down. consider For the (One) such
5278 5259 268 1519 848 485
ὑπομεμενηκότα ὑπὸ τῶν ἁμαρτωλῶν εἰς αὐτὸν ἀντιλογίαν,
having endured by of sinners against Himself contradiction,
2443/3361/2577 5590 5216 1590 3768 3360
4 ἵνα μὴ κάμητε ταῖς ψυχαῖς ὑμῶν ἐκλυόμενοι. οὔπω μέχρις
lest you grow weary in the souls of you fainting Not yet unto
129 478 4314 266 464
αἵματος ἀντικατέστητε πρὸς τὴν ἁμαρτίαν ἀνταγωνιζόμε-
blood you resisted against sin wrestling,

sin. [5]And you have forgotten the exhortation which *He* speaks with you, as with sons, "My sons, do not despise the chastening of *the* Lord, nor faint *while* being corrected by Him. [6]For whom *the* Lord loves, He disciplines, and whips every son whom He receives." [7]If you endure discipline, God is dealing with you as with sons; for who is *the* son whom a father does not discipline? [8]But if you are without discipline, of which all have become sharers, then you are bastards, and not sons. [9]Moreover, we have had fathers of our flesh *as* correctors, and we respected *them*. Shall we not much more be subject to the Father of spirits, and we shall live? [10]For they truly disciplined *us* for a few days according to the thing seeming good to them; but He for *our* profit, in order *for us* to partake of His holiness. [11]And all discipline for the present indeed does not seem to be joyous, but grievous; but afterward it gives back peaceable fruit of righteousness to the ones having been exercised by it.

[12]Therefore, straighten up the hands hanging alongside, and the enfeebled knees; [13]and make straight tracks for your feet, that the lame not be turned aside, but rather healed.

[14]Eagerly pursue peace and holiness with all, without which no one will see the Lord, [15]watching diligently that not any lack from the grace of God, that no root of bitterness growing up may disturb *you*, and through this many be defiled; [16]that not any fornicator, or profane one—as Esau, who for one feeding gave up his birthright; [17]for you know also that afterwards desiring to inherit the

1585 3874 3748 5213/5613/5207
5 νοι· καὶ ἐκλέλησθε τῆς παρακλήσεως, ἥτις ὑμῖν ὡς υἱοῖς
and you have forgotten the exhortation, which with you as with sons
1256 5207/3450/3361 3643 3809 2962 3366
διαλέγεται, Υἱέ μου, μὴ ὀλιγώρει παιδείας Κυρίου, μηδὲ
(He) speaks: Son of Me, do not despise (the) chastening of (the) Lord, nor
1590 5259 846 1651 3739/1063 25 2962
6 ἐκλύου ὑπ' αὐτοῦ ἐλεγχόμενος· ὃν γὰρ ἀγαπᾷ Κύριος
faint by Him being corrected, whom for loves (the) Lord
3811 3146 3956 5207/3739 3858 1487
7 παιδεύει· μαστιγοῖ δὲ πάντα υἱὸν ὃν παραδέχεται. εἰ
He disciplines, whips and every son whom He receives. If
3809 5278 5613/5207/5213 4374 2316/5101
παιδείαν ὑπομένετε, ὡς υἱοῖς ὑμῖν προσφέρεται ὁ Θεός· τίς
discipline you endure, as with sons with you is dealing God, who
1063 2076 5207/3739/3756/ 3811 3962 1487 5565 2075
8 γάρ ἐστιν υἱὸς ὃν οὐ παιδεύει πατήρ; εἰ δὲ χωρίς ἐστε
for is son, whom not disciplines a father? if But without you are
3809 3739 3353 1096 3956 686 3541/2075
παιδείας, ἧς μέτοχοι γεγόνασι πάντες, ἄρα νόθοι ἐστὲ καὶ
discipline, of which sharers have become all, then bastards you are and
3756/ 5207 1534 3303 4561 2257 3962 2192
9 οὐχ υἱοί. εἶτα τοὺς μὲν τῆς σαρκὸς ἡμῶν πατέρας εἴχομεν
not sons. Moreover the of the flesh of us fathers we had
3810 1788 3756 4183 3123 5293
παιδευτάς, καὶ ἐνετρεπόμεθα· οὐ πολλῷ μᾶλλον ὑποταγησό-
(as) correctors, and we respected (them); not much more shall we be subject
3962 4151 2198 3303/1063
10 μεθα τῷ πατρὶ τῶν πνευμάτων, καὶ ζήσομεν; οἱ μὲν γὰρ
to the Father of spirits, and we shall live? they truly For
4314 3641 2250 2596 1380 846 3811
πρὸς ὀλίγας ἡμέρας κατὰ τὸ δοκοῦν αὐτοῖς ἐπαίδευον· ὁ δὲ
for a few days according to the seeming thing good to them disciplined (us). He But
1909 4851 1519 3335 41 848
ἐπὶ τὸ συμφέρον, εἰς τὸ μεταλαβεῖν τῆς ἁγιότητος αὐτοῦ.
for the profit, to partake of the holiness of Him.
3956 3809 4314/3303 3918 3756 1380 5479 1511
11 πᾶσα δὲ παιδεία πρὸς μὲν τὸ παρὸν οὐ δοκεῖ χαρᾶς εἶναι,
all And discipline for indeed the present does not seem of joy to be,
235 3077 5305 2590 1516 1223 846
ἀλλὰ λύπης· ὕστερον δὲ καρπὸν εἰρηνικὸν τοῖς δι' αὐτῆς
but of grief; later but fruit peaceable to those through it
1128 591 1343 1352 3935
12 γεγυμνασμένοις ἀποδίδωσι δικαιοσύνης. διὸ τὰς παρειμένας
having been exercised it gives back of righteousness. Therefore the alongside
5495 3886 1119 461
13 χεῖρας καὶ τὰ παραλελυμένα γόνατα ἀνορθώσατε· καὶ
hands and the enfeebled knees straighten up, and
5163 3717 4160 4228 5216 2443/3361 5560
τροχιὰς ὀρθὰς ποιήσατε τοῖς ποσὶν ὑμῶν, ἵνα μὴ τὸ χωλὸν
tracks straight make for the feet of you, that not the lame
1624 2390 3123
ἐκτραπῇ, ἰαθῇ δὲ μᾶλλον.
be turned aside, be healed but rather.
1515 1377 3326 3956 38 3739
14 Εἰρήνην διώκετε μετὰ πάντων, καὶ τὸν ἁγιασμόν, οὗ
peace Follow with all and holiness, which
5565 3762 3700 2962 1983 3361/5100
15 χωρὶς οὐδεὶς ὄψεται τὸν Κύριον· ἐπισκοποῦντες μή τις
without no one will see the Lord. watching diligently lest any
5302 575 5485 2316/3361/5100/4491 4088
ὑστερῶν ἀπὸ τῆς χάριτος τοῦ Θεοῦ· μή τις ῥίζα πικρίας
lack from the grace of God, lest any root of bitterness
507 5453 1776 1223 5026 3392 4183 3361
16 ἄνω φύουσα ἐνοχλῇ, καὶ διὰ ταύτης μιανθῶσι πολλοί· μή
up growing disturb, and through this be defiled many; lest
5100 4205 2228 952 5613 2269/3739/473 1035 3391
τις πόρνος, ἢ βέβηλος, ὡς Ἠσαῦ, ὃς ἀντὶ βρώσεως μιᾶς
any fornicator, or profane one, as Esau, who for feeding one
591 4415 848 2467/1063/3754 3347
17 ἀπέδοτο τὰ πρωτοτόκια αὐτοῦ. ἴστε γὰρ ὅτι καὶ μετέπειτα,
gave up the birthright of him. you know For that indeed afterwards

blessing, he was rejected, for he found no place of repentance, although seeking it with tears.

[18]For you have not drawn near to *the* mountain being touched, and having been lit with fire, and to gloom, and darkness, and tempest, [19]and to a sound of trumpet, and to a voice of words, which those hearing begged not a word be added to them; [20]for they could not bear that *which* was enjoined: "Even if a beast touches the mountain, it will be stoned, or shot through with a dart." [21]And so fearful was the thing appearing, Moses said, "I am terrified and trembling." [22]But you have drawn near Mount Zion, even the city of *the* living God, to a heavenly Jerusalem, and to myriads of angels, [23]and to an assembly, a church of the firstborn ones having been enrolled in Heaven; and to God *the* judge of all; and to spirits of just ones who have been perfected; [24]and to Jesus *the* Mediator of a new covenant, and to blood of sprinkling speaking better things than *that* of Abel. [25]Watch *that* you do not refuse the *One* speaking; for if these did not escape who refused Him who divinely warned *them* on earth, much rather we, those turning away from Heaven; [26]whose voice shook the earth then, but now He has promised, saying, "Yet once I will shake not only the earth, but the heaven." [27]Now the *words* "Yet once" make clear the removal of the *things* being shaken, as having been made, so that the things not shaken may remain. [28]For this reason, receiving an unshakable kingdom, let us have grace, by which we may serve God pleasingly, with reverence and awe; [29]for also, "Our God *is* a

2309 2816 2129 593 3341
θέλων κληρονομῆσαι τὴν εὐλογίαν, ἀπεδοκιμάσθη· μετανοίας
desiring to inherit the blessing, he was rejected, of repentance
1063 5117/3756/2147 2539 3326 1144 1567 846
γὰρ τόπον οὐχ εὗρε, καίπερ μετὰ δακρύων ἐκζητήσας αὐτήν.
for place not he found, though with tears seeking it.
3756/1063 4334 5584 3735 2545
18 Οὐ γὰρ προσεληλύθατε ψηλαφωμένῳ ὄρει, καὶ κεκαυ-
not For you have drawn near being touched (the) mountain, and
4442 1105 4655 2366 4536 having
19 μένῳ πυρί, καὶ γνόφῳ, καὶ σκότῳ, καὶ θυέλλῃ, καὶ σάλπιγ-
been lit with fire, and to gloom and darkness and tempest, and of trumpet
2279 5456 4487 3739 191 3868
γος ἤχῳ, καὶ φωνῇ ῥημάτων, ἧς οἱ ἀκούσαντες παρῃτή-
to a sound, and to a voice of words, which those hearing begged
3361 4369 846 3056 3756 5342 1063
20 σαντο μὴ προστεθῆναι αὐτοῖς λόγον· οὐκ ἔφερον γὰρ τὸ
not to be added to them a word; not they bore for that
1291 2579 2342 2345 3735 3036
διαστελλόμενον, Κἂν θηρίον θίγῃ τοῦ ὄρους, λιθοβοληθή-
being enjoined: If even a beast touches the mountain, it will be stoned;
1002 2700 3779 5398 2258
21 σεται ἢ βολίδι κατατοξευθήσεται· καί, οὕτω φοβερὸν ἦν τὸ
or with a dart shot through; and, so fearful was the thing
5324 3475 2036 1630 1510 1790
φανταζόμενον, Μωσῆς εἶπεν, Ἔκφοβός εἰμι καὶ ἔντρομος.
appearing, Moses said, terrified I am, and trembling.
235 4334 4622 3735 4172 2316 2198
22 ἀλλὰ προσεληλύθατε Σιὼν ὄρει, καὶ πόλει Θεοῦ ζῶντος,
But you have drawn near Zion Mount, and a city God of (the) living.
2419 2032 3461 32 3831
23 Ἱερουσαλὴμ ἐπουρανίῳ, καὶ μυριάσιν ἀγγέλων, πανηγύρει
Jerusalem to a heavenly, and to myriads of angels, to an assembly
1577 4416 1722 3772 583
καὶ ἐκκλησίᾳ πρωτοτόκων ἐν οὐρανοῖς ἀπογεγραμμένων,
and, a church of firstborn ones in Heaven having been enrolled,
2923 2316 3956 4151 1342 5048
καὶ κριτῇ Θεῷ πάντων, καὶ πνεύμασι δικαίων τετελειω-
and (the) judge God of all, and to spirits of just ones having been
1242 3501 3316 2424 129 4473
24 μένων, καὶ διαθήκης νέας μεσίτῃ Ἰησοῦ, καὶ αἵματι ῥαντι-
perfected, and covenant of a new Mediator to Jesus, and to blood of
2909 2980 3844 6 991 3361
25 σμοῦ κρεῖττονα λαλοῦντι παρὰ τὸ Ἄβελ. βλέπετε μὴ
sprinkling better things speaking than (that) of Abel. Watch (that) not
3868 2980 1487/1063/1565/3756/5343
παραιτήσησθε τὸν λαλοῦντα. εἰ γὰρ ἐκεῖνοι οὐκ ἔφυγον, τὸν
you refuse the (One) speaking; if for these did not escape
1909 1093 3868 5537 4183 3123
ἐπὶ τῆς γῆς παραιτησάμενοι χρηματίζοντα, πολλῷ μᾶλλον
on the earth having refused (the One) divinely warning, much rather
2249 575/3772 854 3739 5456
26 ἡμεῖς οἱ τὸν ἀπ' οὐρανῶν ἀποστρεφόμενοι· οὗ ἡ φωνὴ τὴν
we, those from Heaven turning away; of whom the voice the
1093 4531 5119 3568 1861 3004 2089 530
γῆν ἐσάλευσε τότε, νῦν δὲ ἐπήγγελται, λέγων, Ἔτι ἅπαξ
earth shook then, now but He has promised, saying, Yet once
1473 4579/3756/3440 1093 235 3772
27 ἐγὼ σείω οὐ μόνον τὴν γῆν, ἀλλὰ καὶ τὸν οὐρανόν. τὸ δέ,
I shake not only the earth, but also the Heaven. the Now
2089 530 1213 4531 3331 (words) 5613
Ἔτι ἅπαξ, δηλοῖ τῶν σαλευομένων τὴν μετάθεσιν, ὡς
Yet once, makes clear of the (things) being shaken the removal, as
4160 2443 3306 3361 4531 1352 932
28 πεποιημένων, ἵνα μείνῃ τὰ μὴ σαλευόμενα. διὸ βασιλείαν
having been made, that may remain the things not shaken. Therefore kingdom
761 3880 2192 5485 1223/3739 3000
ἀσάλευτον παραλαμβάνοντες, ἔχωμεν χάριν, δι' ἧς λα-
an unshakeable receiving, let us have grace, through which we
2102 2316/3326 127 2128
29 τρεύωμεν εὐαρέστως τῷ Θεῷ μετὰ αἰδοῦς καὶ εὐλαβείας· καὶ
may serve well-pleasingly God with reverence and fear; truly

NOTE: Frequent words not numbered: δέ(1161); καί(2531)—and, but; ὁ, ἡ, τό (3588, the)— * above word, look in verse margin for No.

consuming fire."

CHAPTER 13

[1]Let brotherly love continue. [2]Do not forget hospitality, for by this some unknowingly took in angels as guests. [3]Be mindful of the prisoners, as having been bound with *them*; of those ill-treated, as also being in the body yourselves. [4]Marriage *is* honorable in all, and the bed undefiled; but God will judge fornicators and adulterers. [5]*Set your* way of life without money-loving, being satisfied with present things; for He has said, "I will never leave you, nor will I ever forsake you." [6]So that we may boldly say, *The* Lord *is* my helper, and I will not be afraid; what shall man do to me?

[7]Remember your leaders who spoke the word of God to you, considering the issue of *their* conduct, imitate *their* faith: [8]Jesus Christ, the same yesterday and today and forever. [9]Do not be carried away by various and strange teaching; for *it is* good *that* the heart be confirmed by grace, not by foods, in which those walking *in them* were not profited. [10]We have an altar of which those serving the tabernacle have no authority to eat. [11]For of the animals *whose* blood is brought by the high priest into the Holies concerning sins, of these the bodies are burned outside the camp. [12]Therefore, that He might sanctify the people by His own blood, Jesus also suffered outside the gate. [13]So now let us go forth to Him outside the camp, bearing His reproach. [14]For we do not have here a continuing

1063 2316 2257 4442 2654
γὰρ ὁ Θεὸς ἡμῶν πῦρ καταναλίσκον.
for the God of us fire a consuming (is).

CHAPTER 13

5360 3306 5381 3361 1950
1 Ἡ φιλαδελφία μενέτω. τῆς φιλοξενίας μὴ ἐπιλανθάνεσθε·
brotherly love Let remain. of hospitality Be not forgetful,
1223 5026 1063 2990 5100 3579 32 3403
2 διὰ ταύτης γὰρ ἔλαθόν τινες ξενίσαντες ἀγγέλους. μιμνή-
3 through this for unknowingly some entertained angels. Be
1198 5613 4887 2558
σκεσθε τῶν δεσμίων, ὡς συνδεδεμένοι· τῶν κακουχουμένων,
mindful of the prisoners, as being bound with (them), of those ill-treated,
5613 848 5607/1722/4983 5093 1062/1722/3956
4 ὡς καὶ αὐτοὶ ὄντες ἐν σώματι. τίμιος ὁ γάμος ἐν πᾶσι, καὶ ἡ
as also yourselves, being in the body, honorable marriage (is) in all, and the
2845 283 4205 3432 2919 2316 866
5 κοίτη ἀμίαντος· πόρνους δὲ καὶ μοιχοὺς κρινεῖ ὁ Θεός. ἀφιλ-
bed undefiled; fornicators but and adulterers will judge God. (Let be)
5158 714 3918 846 1063
άργυρος ὁ τρόπος, ἀρκούμενοι τοῖς παροῦσιν· αὐτὸς γὰρ
without money-loving the way of life, being satisfied with the things present; He for
3756 2046 3361/4571/447/3761/3364/4771 1459 5624
6 εἴρηκεν, Οὐ μή σε ἀνῶ, οὐδ' οὐ μή σε ἐγκαταλίπω. ὥστε
has said, Not at all you will I leave, nor in any way you will I forsake. So that
2292 2248/3004 2962 1698 998 3756 5399
θαρροῦντας ἡμᾶς λέγειν, Κύριος ἐμοὶ βοηθός, καὶ οὐ φοβηθή-
may confidently we say, (The) Lord to me (is) a helper, and not I will be
5101 4160 3427 444
σομαι τί ποιήσει μοι ἄνθρωπος.
afraid; what shall do to me man?
3421 2233 5216 3748 2980 5213
7 Μνημονεύετε τῶν ἡγουμένων ὑμῶν, οἵτινες ἐλάλησαν ὑμῖν
Remember the leaders of you, who spoke to you
3056 2316 3739 333 1545
τὸν λόγον τοῦ Θεοῦ· ὧν ἀναθεωροῦντες τὴν ἔκβασιν τῆς
the word of God, of whom considering the issue of the
391 3401 4102 2424 5547 5504
8 ἀναστροφῆς, μιμεῖσθε τὴν πίστιν. Ἰησοῦς Χριστὸς χθὲς καὶ
conduct, imitate (their) faith; Jesus Christ yesterday and
4594 846 1519 165 1322 4164
9 σήμερον ὁ αὐτός, καὶ εἰς τοὺς αἰῶνας. διδαχαῖς ποικίλαις καὶ
today (is) the same, even to the ages. teaching By various and
3581/3361 4064 2570 1063 5485 950
ξέναις μὴ περιφέρεσθε· καλὸν γὰρ χάριτι βεβαιοῦσθαι τὴν
strange not do be carried away; good (it is) for by grace to be confirmed the
2588 3756 1033 1722/3739/3756/ 5623 4043
καρδίαν, οὐ βρώμασιν, ἐν οἷς οὐκ ὠφελήθησαν οἱ περιπατή-
heart, not by foods, by which not were profited those walking
2192 2379 1537/3739/5315/3756 2192
10 σαντες. ἔχομεν θυσιαστήριον, ἐξ οὗ φαγεῖν οὐκ ἔχουσιν
We have an altar of which to eat not have
1849 4633 3000 3739/1063/ 1533 2226
11 ἐξουσίαν οἱ τῇ σκηνῇ λατρεύοντες. ὧν γὰρ εἰσφέρεται ζώων
authority those the tabernacle serving. of what For is brought animals
129 4012 266 1519 39/1223 749 5130
τὸ αἷμα περὶ ἁμαρτίας εἰς τὰ ἅγια διὰ τοῦ ἀρχιερέως, τούτων
the blood concerning sins into the Holies via the high priest, of these
4983 2618 1854 3925 1352
12 τὰ σώματα κατακαίεται ἔξω τῆς παρεμβολῆς. διὸ καὶ
the bodies are burned outside the camp. Therefore, indeed
2424 2443 37 1223 2398 129 2992 1854
Ἰησοῦς, ἵνα ἁγιάσῃ διὰ τοῦ ἰδίου αἵματος τὸν λαόν, ἔξω τῆς
Jesus, that He might sanctify through the own blood the people, outside the
4439 3958 5106/1831 4314 846 1854 3925
13 πύλης ἔπαθε. τοίνυν ἐξερχώμεθα πρὸς αὐτὸν ἔξω τῆς παρ-
gate suffered. So let us go forth to Him outside the
3680 848 5342 3756/1063 2192 5602
14 εμβολῆς, τὸν ὀνειδισμὸν αὐτοῦ φέροντες. οὐ γὰρ ἔχομεν ὧδε
camp. the reproach of Him bearing. not For we have here

city, but we seek the *city*
coming. [15]Then through
Him let us offer up a sacrifice of praise to God always,
that is, *the* fruit of the lips,
confessing to His name.
[16]But do not be forgetful of
doing good and sharing, for
God is well-pleased with
such sacrifices.

[17]Obey those taking the
lead of you, and submit, for
they watch for your souls,
giving account, that they
may do this with joy, and
not *with* groaning; for this
would be no profit to you.

[18]Pray for us, for we are
persuaded that we have a
good conscience, in all
things wishing to behave
well. [19]But I much more
urge *you* to do this, that I
may sooner be restored to
you.

[20]Now the God of Peace,
He leading up out of *the*
dead, the great Shepherd of
the sheep, in *the* blood of
the everlasting covenant,
our Lord Jesus, [21]perfect
you in every good work, to
do His will, doing in you
that *which is* pleasing in His
sight, through Jesus Christ,
to whom *be* the glory
forever and ever. Amen.

[22]And, brothers, I exhort
you, endure the word of
exhortation, for I indeed
wrote to you by *a* few
words. [23]You know the
brother, Timothy, with
whom if I come sooner,
having been freed, I will see
you.

[24]Greet all those leading
you, also all the saints.

3306 4172 235 3195 1934 1223
15 μένουσαν πόλιν, ἀλλὰ τὴν μέλλουσαν ἐπιζητοῦμεν. δι᾽
a continuing city, but the (one) coming we seek. Through
846 3767 399 2378 133 1223/3956 2316
αὐτοῦ οὖν ἀναφέρωμεν θυσίαν αἰνέσεως διὰ παντὸς τῷ Θεῷ,
Him, therefore, let us offer up a sacrifice of praise always to God,
5123 2076 2590 5491 3670 3686
τοῦτ᾽ ἔστι, καρπὸν χειλέων ὁμολογούντων τῷ ὀνόματι
this is, (the) fruit of the lips, confessing to the name
848 2140 2842 3361 1950
16 αὐτοῦ. τῆς δὲ εὐποιΐας καὶ κοινωνίας μὴ ἐπιλανθάνεσθε·
of Him. of the But doing good and sharing, do not be forgetful;
5108 1063 2378 2100 2316 3982
17 τοιαύταις γὰρ θυσίαις εὐαρεστεῖται ὁ Θεός. πείθεσθε τοῖς
with such for sacrifices is well-pleased God. Obey those
2233 5216 5226 846 1063 69
ἡγουμένοις ὑμῶν, καὶ ὑπείκετε· αὐτοὶ γὰρ ἀγρυπνοῦσιν
leading of you, and submit to (them), they for watch
5228 5590 5216 5613 3056 591 2443 3326
ὑπὲρ τῶν ψυχῶν ὑμῶν, ὡς λόγον ἀποδώσοντες· ἵνα μετὰ
for the souls of you, an account giving, that with
5479 5124 4160 3361 4727 255 1063
χαρᾶς τοῦτο ποιῶσι, καὶ μὴ στενάζοντες· ἀλυσιτελὲς γὰρ
joy this they may do, and not (with) groaning.; profitless for
5213 5124
ὑμῖν τοῦτο.
to you this (would be).
4336 4012 2257 3982 1063 3754 2570
18 Προσεύχεσθε περὶ ἡμῶν· πεποίθαμεν γὰρ ὅτι καλὴν
Pray concerning us, we are persuaded for that a good
4893 2192/1722/3956/ 2573 2309 390
συνείδησιν ἔχομεν, ἐν πᾶσι καλῶς θέλοντες ἀναστρέφεσθαι.
conscience we have, in all well desiring to conduct (ourselves)
4056 3870 5124 4160 2443 5032
19 περισσοτέρως δὲ παρακαλῶ τοῦτο ποιῆσαι, ἵνα τάχιον
more abundantly But I exhort (you) this to do, that sooner
600 5213
ἀποκατασταθῶ ὑμῖν.
I may be restored to you.
2316 1515 321 1537 3498
20 Ὁ δὲ Θεὸς τῆς εἰρήνης, ὁ ἀναγαγὼν ἐκ νεκρῶν τὸν
the Now God of peace, He having led up out of (the) dead, the
4166 4263 3173/1722/ 129 1242
ποιμένα τῶν προβάτων τὸν μέγαν ἐν αἵματι διαθήκης
Shepherd of the sheep great, in (the) blood of a covenant
166 2962 2257 2424 2675 5209/1722
21 αἰωνίου, τὸν Κύριον ἡμῶν Ἰησοῦν, καταρτίσαι ὑμᾶς ἐν
eternal, the Lord of us, Jesus, perfect you in
3956 2041 18 1519 4160 2307 848 4160
παντὶ ἔργῳ ἀγαθῷ εἰς τὸ ποιῆσαι τὸ θέλημα αὐτοῦ, ποιῶν
every work good, in order to do the will of Him, doing
1722/5213 2101 1799 846 1223 2424 5547
ἐν ὑμῖν τὸ εὐάρεστον ἐνώπιον αὐτοῦ, διὰ Ἰησοῦ Χριστοῦ·
in you the thing pleasing before Him, through Jesus Christ,
3739 1391/1519 165 165 281
ᾧ ἡ δόξα εἰς τοὺς αἰῶνας τῶν αἰώνων. ἀμήν.
to whom (be) the glory to the ages of the ages. Amen.
3870 5209 80 430 3056
22 Παρακαλῶ δὲ ὑμᾶς, ἀδελφοί, ἀνέχεσθε τοῦ λόγου τῆς
I exhort And you, brothers, endure the word
3874 1063/1223/ 1024 1989 5213 1097
23 παρακλήσεως· καὶ γὰρ διὰ βραχέων ἐπέστειλα ὑμῖν. γινώ-
of exhortation; indeed for through few (words) I wrote to you. Know
80 5095 630 3326/3739/1437/5032
σκετε τὸν ἀδελφὸν Τιμόθεον ἀπολελυμένον, μεθ᾽ οὗ, ἐὰν τάχιον
the brother, Timothy, having been freed, with whom, if sooner
2064 3700 5209
ἔρχηται, ὄψομαι ὑμᾶς.
I come, I will see you.
782 3956 2233 5216 3956
24 Ἀσπάσασθε πάντας τοὺς ἡγουμένους ὑμῶν, καὶ πάντας
Greet all those leading of you, and all

greet you. Those from
Italy greet you.
25 Grace *be* with you all.
Amen.

40		782	5209	575	2482
τοὺς	ἁγίους.	ἀσπάζονται	ὑμᾶς οἱ	ἀπὸ τῆς	Ἰταλίας.
the	saints.	greet	you Those	from	Italy.

25 Ἡ χάρις μετὰ πάντων ὑμῶν. ἀμήν.
Grace (be) with all of you. Amen.

THE GENERAL EPISTLE
OF
JAMES
A LITERAL TRANSLATION
OF THE BIBLE

CHAPTER 1

[1]James, a slave of God and of *the* Lord Jesus Christ, to the twelve tribes in the Dispersion, greeting:

[2]My brothers, count *it* all joy when you fall into various temptations, [3]knowing that the proving of your faith works patience. [4]But let patience have *its* perfect work, that you may be perfect and complete, lacking nothing.

[5]But if any of you lacks wisdom, let him ask from God, *who* gives to all freely and with no reproach, and it will be given to him. [6]But let him ask in faith, doubting nothing. For the *one* who doubts *is* like a wave of *the* sea, being driven by wind and being tossed; [7]for do not let that man suppose that he will receive anything from the Lord—[8]*he is* a double-souled man, not dependable in all his ways.

[9]But let *the* lowly brother rejoice in his lifting up; [10]and the rich one *rejoice* in his humiliation, because he will pass away like *the* flower of *the* grass. [11]For the sun rose with the hot wind and dried up the grass, and its flower fell out, and the beauty of its appearance perished—so also the rich one will fade away in his ways.

ΙΑΚΩΒΟΥ
OF JAMES
ΕΠΙΣΤΟΛΗ ΚΑΘΟΛΙΚΗ
EPISTLE GENERAL

CHAPTER 1

2385 2316 2962 2424 5547 1401
1 Ἰάκωβος, Θεοῦ καὶ Κυρίου Ἰησοῦ Χριστοῦ δοῦλος, ταῖς
James, of God and of (the) Lord Jesus Christ a slave, to the
1427 5443 1722 1290 5463
δώδεκα φυλαῖς ταῖς ἐν τῇ διασπορᾷ, χαίρειν.
twelve tribes in the dispersion, greeting.
3956 5479 2233 80 3450 3752 3986
2 Πᾶσαν χαρὰν ἡγήσασθε, ἀδελφοί μου, ὅταν πειρασμοῖς
all joy Count (it), brothers of me, when temptations
4045 4164 1097 3754 1383 5216
3 περιπέσητε ποικίλοις, γινώσκοντες ὅτι τὸ δοκίμιον ὑμῶν τῆς
you fall into various, knowing that the proving of you the
4102 2716 5281 5281 2041
4 πίστεως κατεργάζεται ὑπομονήν· ἡ δὲ ὑπομονὴ ἔργον
faith works patience. And patience work
5046 2192/2443/5600/5046 3648 1722/3367 3007
τέλειον ἐχέτω, ἵνα ἦτε τέλειοι καὶ ὁλόκληροι, ἐν μηδενὶ λειπό-
perfect let it have, that you may be perfect and entire, in nothing having
μενοι.
lacked.
1487 5100/5216 3007 4678 154 3844 1325
5 Εἰ δέ τις ὑμῶν λείπεται σοφίας, αἰτείτω παρὰ τοῦ διδόντος
if But any of you lacks wisdom, let him ask from giving
2316 3956 574 3361/3679 1325 846
Θεοῦ πᾶσιν ἁπλῶς, καὶ μὴ ὀνειδίζοντος, καὶ δοθήσεται αὐτῷ.
God to all freely, and not reproaching, and it will be given to him.
154 1722 4102 3367 1252 1063 1252
6 αἰτείτω δὲ ἐν πίστει, μηδὲν διακρινόμενος· ὁ γὰρ διακρινό-
let him ask But in faith, nothing doubting, the (one) for doubting
1503 2830 2281 416 4494
μενος ἔοικε κλύδωνι θαλάσσης ἀνεμιζομένῳ καὶ ῥιπιζομένῳ.
(is) like a wave of (the) sea, being driven by wind and tossed.
3361/1063 3633 444 1565 3754 2983 5100/3844
7 μὴ γὰρ οἰέσθω ὁ ἄνθρωπος ἐκεῖνος ὅτι λήψεταί τι παρὰ τοῦ
not For let suppose man that that he will receive any-thing from the
2962 435 1374 182 3956 3598
8 Κυρίου. ἀνὴρ δίψυχος ἀκατάστατος ἐν πάσαις ταῖς ὁδοῖς
Lord, a man two-souled undependable in all the ways
848
αὐτοῦ.
of him.
2744 80 5011 1722 5311 848
9 Καυχάσθω δὲ ὁ ἀδελφὸς ὁ ταπεινὸς ἐν τῷ ὕψει αὐτοῦ· ὁ
10 let boast But the brother humble in the height of him; the
4145 1722 5014 848 3754/5623/438 5528
δὲ πλούσιος ἐν τῇ ταπεινώσει αὐτοῦ· ὅτι ὡς ἄνθος χόρτου
and the rich one in the humiliation of him, because as a flower of grass
3928 393 1063 2246 4862 2742
11 παρελεύσεται. ἀνέτειλε γὰρ ὁ ἥλιος σὺν τῷ καύσωνι, καὶ
he will pass away. rose For the sun with the hot wind and
3583 5528 438 848 1601 2143
ἐξήρανε τὸν χόρτον, καὶ τὸ ἄνθος αὐτοῦ ἐξέπεσε, καὶ ἡ εὐπρέ-
dried the grass, and the flower of it fell out, and the beauty
4383 848 622 3779 4145
πεια τοῦ προσώπου αὐτοῦ ἀπώλετο· οὕτω καὶ ὁ πλούσιος
of the appearance of it perished; so also the rich one
1722 4197 848 3133
ἐν ταῖς πορείαις αὐτοῦ μαρανθήσεται.
in the goings of him will fade away.

[12]Blessed *is the* man who endures temptation, because having been approved he will receive the crown of life which the Lord promised to the ones loving Him.
[13]Let no one being tempted say, I am tempted from God. For God is not tempted by evils, and He tempts no one. [14]But each one is tempted by *his* lusts, having been drawn out and having been seduced *by them*. [15]Then being conceived lust brings forth sin. And sin being fully formed brings forth death. [16]Do not go astray, my beloved brothers, [17]every *act of* giving good and every perfect gift is from above, coming down from the Father of lights, with whom is no change or shadow of turning. [18]Having purposed, He brought us forth by *the* word of truth, for us to be a certain firstfruit of His creatures.

[19]So that, my beloved brothers, let every man be swift to hear, slow to speak, slow to wrath. [20]For *the* wrath of man does not work out *the* righteousness of God. [21]On account of this, having put aside all filthiness and overflowing of evil, in meekness receive the implanted word being able to save your souls.

[22]But become doers of *the* word, and not hearers only, deceiving yourselves. [23]Because if anyone *is* a hearer of *the* word, and not a doer, this one is like a man studying his natural face in a mirror; [24]for he studied himself, and has gone away, and immediately *he* forgot of what kind he was. [25]But the *one* looking into the perfect law of liberty, and continuing in *it*, this

3107 435 3739 5278 3986 3754 1384 1096
12 Μακάριος ἀνὴρ ὃς ὑπομένει πειρασμόν· ὅτι δόκιμος γενό-
Blessed (the) man who endures temptation, because approved having
2983 4735 2222 3739 1861
μενος λήψεται τὸν στέφανον τῆς ζωῆς, ὃν ἐπηγγείλατο ὁ
become he will receive the crown of life, which promised the
2962 25 846 3367 3985 3004
13 Κύριος τοῖς ἀγαπῶσιν αὐτόν. μηδεὶς πειραζόμενος λεγέτω
Lord to those loving Him. no one being tempted Let say,
3754 575 2316/3985 1063 2316/551 2076
ὅτι Ἀπὸ τοῦ Θεοῦ πειράζομαι· ὁ γὰρ Θεὸς ἀπείραστός ἐστι
From God I am tempted. For God not tempted is
2556 3985 848 3762 1538 3985
14 κακῶν, πειράζει δὲ αὐτὸς οὐδένα· ἕκαστος δὲ πειράζεται,
by evils, tempts and He no one. each one But is tempted
5259 2398 1939 1828 1185 1534
15 ὑπὸ τῆς ἰδίας ἐπιθυμίας ἐξελκόμενος καὶ δελεαζόμενος. εἶτα
by the own lusts being drawn out and being seduced; then
1939 4815 5088 266 266
ἡ ἐπιθυμία συλλαβοῦσα τίκτει ἁμαρτίαν· ἡ δὲ ἁμαρτία
lust having conceived produces sin; and sin
658 616 2288 3361 4105 80
16 ἀποτελεσθεῖσα ἀποκύει θάνατον. μὴ πλανᾶσθε, ἀδελφοί
being fully formed brings forth death. Do not go astray, brothers
3450 27 3956 1394 18 3956 1434 5046
17 μου ἀγαπητοί. πᾶσα δόσις ἀγαθὴ καὶ πᾶν δώρημα τέλειον
of me beloved. Every giving good and every gift perfect
509 2076 2597 575 3962 5457 3844
ἄνωθέν ἐστι, καταβαῖνον ἀπὸ τοῦ πατρὸς τῶν φώτων, παρ'
from above is, coming down from the Father of lights, with
3739/3756/1762/ 3883 2228 5157 644 1014
18 ᾧ οὐκ ἔνι παραλλαγή, ἢ τροπῆς ἀποσκίασμα. βουληθεὶς
whom not there is variation or of turning shadow. Having purposed
616 2248 5056 225 1519 1511/2248 536
ἀπεκύησεν ἡμᾶς λόγῳ ἀληθείας, εἰς τὸ εἶναι ἡμᾶς ἀπαρχήν
He brought forth us by a word of truth, for to be us firstfruit
5100 848 2938
τινα τῶν αὐτοῦ κτισμάτων.
a certain of the of Him creatures.
5620 80 3450 27 2077 3956 444 5036
19 Ὥστε, ἀδελφοί μου ἀγαπητοί, ἔστω πᾶς ἄνθρωπος ταχὺς
So that, brothers of me beloved, let be every man swift
1519 191 1021 1519 2980 1021 1519 3709
εἰς τὸ ἀκοῦσαι, βραδὺς εἰς τὸ λαλῆσαι, βραδὺς εἰς ὀργήν·
to hear, slow to speak, slow to wrath;
3709/ 1063 435 1343 2316/3756/ 2716 1352
20 ὀργὴ γὰρ ἀνδρὸς δικαιοσύνην Θεοῦ οὐ κατεργάζεται. διὸ
(the) wrath for of man (the) righteousness of God not works. Therefore,
659 3956 4507 4050 2549/1722/4140
21 ἀποθέμενοι πᾶσαν ῥυπαρίαν καὶ περισσείαν κακίας, ἐν πραΰ-
putting away all filthiness and overflowing of evil, in meek-
1209 1721 3056 1410 4982
τητι δέξασθε τὸν ἔμφυτον λόγον, τὸν δυνάμενον σῶσαι τὰς
ness receive the implanted word being able to save the
5590 5216 1096 4163 3056 3361 3440
22 ψυχὰς ὑμῶν. γίνεσθε δὲ ποιηταὶ λόγου, καὶ μὴ μόνον
souls of you. become And doers of the word, and not only
202 3884 1438 3754/1536= 202
23 ἀκροαταί, παραλογιζόμενοι ἑαυτούς. ὅτι εἴ τις ἀκροατὴς
hearers, deceiving yourselves. Because if anyone a hearer
3056/2076 3756 4161 3778 1503 435 2657
λόγου ἐστὶ καὶ οὐ ποιητής, οὗτος ἔοικεν ἀνδρὶ κατανοοῦντι
of (the) word is, and not a doer, this one is like a man perceiving
4383 1078 848 1722 2072 2657
24 τὸ πρόσωπον τῆς γενέσεως αὐτοῦ ἐν ἐσόπτρῳ· κατενόησε
the face of the birth of him in a mirror; he perceived
1063 1438 565 2112 1950 3697 2258
γὰρ ἑαυτὸν καὶ ἀπελήλυθε, καὶ εὐθέως ἐπελάθετο ὁποῖος ἦν.
for himself and has gone away, and immediately forgot what sort he was
3979 1519 3551 5046 1657
25 ὁ δὲ παρακύψας εἰς νόμον τέλειον τὸν τῆς ἐλευθερίας καὶ
he But having looked into law perfect the of freedom, and

one not having become a forgetful hearer, but a doer of *the* work, this one will be blessed in his doing. 26 If anyone thinks to be religious among you, *yet* not bridling his tongue, but deceiving his heart, this one's religion *is* vain.

27 Pure and undefiled religion before God and *the* Father *is* this: to visit orphans and widows in their afflictions, *and* to keep oneself unspotted from the world.

3887 3778 3756 202 1953 1096
παραμείνας, οὗτος οὐκ ἀκροατὴς ἐπιλησμονῆς γενόμενος
continuing, this one not a hearer of forgetfulness becoming,
235 4161 2041 3778 3107 1722 4161 848
ἀλλὰ ποιητὴς ἔργου, οὗτος μακάριος ἐν τῇ ποιήσει αὐτοῦ
but a doer of (the) work, this one blessed in the doing of him
2071 1536 1380 2357 1511/1722/5213/3361/ 5468
26 ἔσται. εἴ τις δοκεῖ θρῆσκος εἶναι ἐν ὑμῖν, μὴ χαλιναγωγῶν
will be. If anyone thinks religious to be among you, not bridling
1100 848 235 538 2588 848 5127
γλῶσσαν αὐτοῦ, ἀλλ' ἀπατῶν καρδίαν αὐτοῦ, τούτου
the tongue of him, but deceiving (the) heart of himself, this one's
3152 2356 2356 2513 283 3844
27 μάταιος ἡ θρησκεία. θρησκεία καθαρὰ καὶ ἀμίαντος παρὰ
vain the religion (is). religion Clean and undefiled before
2316 3962 3778 2076 1980 3737
τῷ Θεῷ καὶ πατρὶ αὕτη ἐστίν, ἐπισκέπτεσθαι ὀρφανοὺς καὶ
the God and Father this is to visit orphans and
5503/1722 2347 848 784 1438 5083 575
χήρας ἐν τῇ θλίψει αὐτῶν, ἄσπιλον ἑαυτὸν τηρεῖν ἀπὸ τοῦ
widows in the affliction of them, unspotted himself to keep from the
2889
κόσμου.
world.

CHAPTER 2

1 My brothers, do not with partiality to persons have the faith of our Lord Jesus Christ, the *Lord* of glory. 2 For if a gold-fingered man in splendid clothing comes into your synagogue, and a poor one in shabby clothing also comes in; 3 and you look on the *one* wearing the splendid clothing, and say to him, You sit here comfortably; and to the poor one you say, You stand there, or, Sit here under my footstool; 4 did you not also make a difference among yourselves and became judges *with* evil thoughts? 5 Hear, my beloved brothers, did not God choose the poor of this world *to be* rich in faith, and heirs of the kingdom which He promised to the *ones* loving Him? 6 But you dishonored the poor one. Do not the rich ones oppress you, and they drag you to judgment seats? 7 Do they not blaspheme the good Name called on you? 8 If you truly fulfill *the* royal law

CHAPTER 2

80 3450/3361/1722/ 4382 2192 4102
1 Ἀδελφοί μου, μὴ ἐν προσωποληψίαις ἔχετε τὴν πίστιν
Brothers of me, not in respects of persons have the faith
2962 2257 2424 5547 1391 1437/1063/1525
2 τοῦ Κυρίου ἡμῶν Ἰησοῦ Χριστοῦ τῆς δόξης. ἐὰν γὰρ εἰσ-
the Lord of us, Jesus Christ, of the (Lord) of glory. If For
1519 4864 5216 435 5554 1722
έλθῃ εἰς τὴν συναγωγὴν ὑμῶν ἀνὴρ χρυσοδακτύλιος ἐν
comes into the synagogue of you a man gold-fingered, in
2066 2986 1525 4434 1722 4508 2066
ἐσθῆτι λαμπρᾷ, εἰσέλθῃ δὲ καὶ πτωχὸς ἐν ῥυπαρᾷ ἐσθῆτι,
clothing fancy, comes in and also a poor one in shabby clothing,
1914 1909 5409 2066 2986
3 καὶ ἐπιβλέψητε ἐπὶ τὸν φοροῦντα τὴν ἐσθῆτα τὴν λαμπράν,
and you look on the (one) wearing the clothing fancy,
2036 846 4771 2521 5602 2578 4434
καὶ εἴπητε αὐτῷ, Σὺ κάθου ὧδε καλῶς, καὶ τῷ πτωχῷ
and say to him, You sit here well, and to the poor one
2036 4771/2476/1563/2228/2521/5602/5259 5286 3450
εἴπητε, Σὺ στῆθι ἐκεῖ, ἢ κάθου ὧδε ὑπὸ τὸ ὑποπόδιόν μου·
you say, You stand there, or sit here under the footstool of me,
3756 1252 1722 1438 1096 2923 1261
4 καὶ οὐ διεκρίθητε ἐν ἑαυτοῖς, καὶ ἐγένεσθε κριταὶ διαλογισμῶν
even did make a among yourselves, and became judges thoughts
4190 not difference 191 80 3450 27 3756 2316
5 πονηρῶν; ἀκούσατε, ἀδελφοί μου ἀγαπητοί. οὐχ ὁ Θεὸς
of evil? Hear, brothers of me beloved, Did not God
1586 4434 2889 5127 4145
ἐξελέξατο τοὺς πτωχοὺς τοῦ κόσμου τούτου, πλουσίους
choose the poor world of this rich
1722/4102 2918 932 3739 1861
ἐν πίστει, καὶ κληρονόμους τῆς βασιλείας ἧς ἐπηγγείλατο
in faith, and heirs of the kingdom which He promised
25 846 5210 818 4434 3756
6 τοῖς ἀγαπῶσιν αὐτόν; ὑμεῖς δὲ ἠτιμάσατε τὸν πτωχόν. οὐχ
to those loving Him. you But dishonored the poor one. Do not
4145 2616 5216 846 1670
οἱ πλούσιοι καταδυναστεύουσιν ὑμῶν, καὶ αὐτοὶ ἕλκουσιν
the rich ones oppress you, and they drag
5209/1519/ 2922 3756 846 907 2570 3686
7 ὑμᾶς εἰς κριτήρια; οὐκ αὐτοὶ βλασφημοῦσι τὸ καλὸν ὄνομα
you to judgment seats? Do not they blaspheme the good name
1941 1909 5209/1487/ 3305 3551 5055 937
8 τὸ ἐπικληθὲν ἐφ' ὑμᾶς; εἰ μέντοι νόμον τελεῖτε βασιλικόν,
called upon you? If indeed law you fulfill a royal

according to the Scripture, "You shall love your neighbor as yourself," you do well. [9]But if you have partiality to persons, you work sin, having been found guilty as transgressors by the law. [10]For whoever shall keep all the law, but stumbles in one, he has become guilty of all. [11]For He who said, "You shall not commit adultery," also said, "You shall not murder." But if you do not commit adultery, but commit murder, you have become a transgressor of *the* law. [12]So speak and so do as being about to be judged by *the* law of liberty. [13]For Judgment *will be* without mercy to the one not doing mercy. And mercy rejoices over judgment.

[14]My brothers, what *is* the gain if anyone says *he* has faith, but he does not have works? Is faith able to save him? [15]But if a brother or a sister is naked and may be lacking in daily food, [16]and any one of you say to them, Go in peace; be warmed and filled—but does not give them the things the body needs—what gain *is it*? [17]So also faith, if it does not have works, is dead by itself. [18]But someone will say, You have faith, and I have works. Show me your faith apart from your works, and I will show you my faith by from my works. [19]You believe that God is one. You do well; even the demons believe and shudder. [20]But are you willing to know, O vain man, that faith apart from works is dead? [21]Was not our father Abraham justified by works, offering up his son Isaac on the altar? [22]You see that faith worked with his works, and by the works the faith was

2596 1124 25 4139 4675/5613/4572
κατὰ τὴν γραφήν, Ἀγαπήσεις τὸν πλησίον σου ὡς σεαυ-
according to the Scripture: You shall love the neighbor of you as your-
2573 4160 1487 4380 266 2036
9 τόν, καλῶς ποιεῖτε· εἰ δὲ προσωποληπτεῖτε, ἁμαρτίαν ἐργά-
self, well you do; if but you respect persons, sin you work,
1651 5259 3551/5613 3848 3748 1063
10 ζεσθε, ἐλεγχόμενοι ὑπὸ τοῦ νόμου ὡς παραβάται. ὅστις γὰρ
being reproved by the law as transgressors, (he) who For
3650 3551 5083 4417 1722/1520/1096 3956
ὅλον τὸν νόμον τηρήσει, πταίσει δὲ ἐν ἑνί, γέγονε πάντων
all the law keeps, stumbles but in one, he has become of all
1777 1063 2036 3361 3431 2056 3361 5407
11 ἔνοχος. ὁ γὰρ εἰπών, Μὴ μοιχεύσῃς, εἶπε καί, Μὴ φονεύσῃς·
guilty He For saying, Do not do adultery, said also, Do not murder
1487/3756/3431 5407 1096 3848 3551
εἰ δὲ οὐ μοιχεύσεις, φονεύσεις δέ, γέγονας παραβάτης νόμου.
if but not you do adultery, murder but, you have become a transgressor of law.
3779 2980 3779 4160 5613/1223/3551 1657
12 οὕτω λαλεῖτε καὶ οὕτω ποιεῖτε, ὡς διὰ νόμου ἐλευθερίας
So speak and so do, as through a law of freedom
3195 2919 1063 2920 448 3361 4160
13 μέλλοντες κρίνεσθαι. ἡ γὰρ κρίσις ἀνίλεως τῷ μὴ ποιήσαντι
being about to be judged. the For Judgment will be unmerciful to the *one* not doing
1656 2620 1656 2920
ἔλεος· καὶ κατακαυχᾶται ἔλεος κρίσεως.
mercy; and exults over mercy judgment.
5101 3786 80 3450/1437/4102 3004/5100/2192/2041
14 Τί τὸ ὄφελος, ἀδελφοί μου, ἐὰν πίστιν λέγῃ τις ἔχειν, ἔργα
What (is) the profit, brothers of me, if faith says anyone to have, works
3361/2192/3361 1410 4102 4982 846 1437
15 δὲ μὴ ἔχῃ; μὴ δύναται ἡ πίστις σῶσαι αὐτόν; ἐὰν δὲ
but not he has? Is able the faith to save him? if But
80 2228 79 1131 5226 3007 5600
ἀδελφὸς ἢ ἀδελφὴ γυμνοὶ ὑπάρχωσι καὶ λειπόμενοι ὦσι
a brother or a sister naked are, and lacking may be
2184 5160 2036 5100 846 1537/5216 5217
16 τῆς ἐφημέρου τροφῆς, εἴπῃ δέ τις αὐτοῖς ἐξ ὑμῶν, Ὑπάγετε
of daily food, says and anyone to them of you, Go
1722/1515 2328 5526 3361 1325 846
ἐν εἰρήνῃ, θερμαίνεσθε καὶ χορτάζεσθε, μὴ δῶτε δὲ αὐτοῖς
in peace, be warmed and filled, not you give but them
2006 4983 5101 3786 3779 4102
17 τὰ ἐπιτήδεια τοῦ σώματος, τί τὸ ὄφελος; οὕτω καὶ ἡ πίστις,
the necessities of the body, what (is) the profit? So indeed faith,
1437/3361/2041/2192/3498 2076/3596 1438 235 2046 5100/4771
18 ἐὰν μὴ ἔργα ἔχῃ, νεκρά ἐστι καθ' ἑαυτήν. ἀλλ' ἐρεῖ τις, Σὺ
if not works it has, dead is by itself. But will say one, You
4102 2192 2504 2041 2192 1166 3427 4102 4675
πίστιν ἔχεις, κἀγὼ ἔργα ἔχω· δεῖξόν μοι τὴν πίστιν σου
faith have, and I works have: show me the faith of you
5565 2041 4675 2504 1166/4671/1537 2041 3450
χωρὶς τῶν ἔργων σου, κἀγὼ δείξω σοι ἐκ τῶν ἔργων μου
without the works of you, and I will show you by the works of me
4102 3450/4771/4100 3754 2316 1520/2076 2573
19 τὴν πίστιν μου. σὺ πιστεύεις ὅτι ὁ Θεὸς εἷς ἐστί· καλῶς
the faith of me. You believe that God one is? well
4160 1140 4100 5425 2309
20 ποιεῖς· καὶ τὰ δαιμόνια πιστεύουσι, καὶ φρίσσουσι. θέλεις
You do; also the demons believe and tremble. are you willing
1097 5599 444 2756/3754 4102 5565 2041
δὲ γνῶναι, ὦ ἄνθρωπε κενέ, ὅτι ἡ πίστις χωρὶς τῶν ἔργων
But to know, O man vain, that faith without works
3498 2076 11 3962 2257/3756/1537/2041/1344
21 νεκρά ἐστιν; Ἀβραὰμ ὁ πατὴρ ἡμῶν οὐκ ἐξ ἔργων ἐδικαιώθη,
dead is? Abraham the father of us not by works Was justified,
399 2464 5207 848 1909 2379
ἀνενέγκας Ἰσαὰκ τὸν υἱὸν αὐτοῦ ἐπὶ τὸ θυσιαστήριον;
offering up Isaac the son of him on the altar?
991/3754 4102 4903 2041 848 1537
22 βλέπεις ὅτι ἡ πίστις συνήργει τοῖς ἔργοις αὐτοῦ, καὶ ἐκ τῶν
You see that faith worked with the works of him, and by the

made complete. [23]And
the Scripture was fulfilled,
saying, "And Abraham believed
God, and it was
counted for righteousness
to him;" and he was called,
"Friend of God." [24]You see,
then, that a man is justified
by works, and not by faith
only. [25]But in the same
way Rahab the harlot was
also justified by works,
having received the messengers,
and sending *them*
out by another way. [26]For
as the body is dead apart
from *the* spirit, so also faith
is dead apart from works.

CHAPTER 3

[1]My brothers, do not be
many teachers, knowing
that we will receive greater
judgment. [2]For we all
stumble *in* many *ways*. If
any one does not stumble
in word, this *one is* a mature
man, able also to bridle the
whole body. [3]Behold, we
put bits in the mouths of the
horses, for them to obey us;
and we turn about their
whole body. [4]Behold, the
ships also, being so great,
and being driven by violent
winds, *they are* directed by
a very small rudder, where
the impulse of the *one*
steering purposes. [5]So
also the tongue is a little
member, and boasts great
things. Behold, how little a
fire kindles how large a
forest! [6]And the tongue *is* a
fire, the world of iniquity. So
the tongue is set among our
members, spotting all the
body, and inflaming the
course of nature, and
having been inflamed by
Hell. [7]For every species of
beasts, both indeed of
birds, of creeping things,
and of sea-animals, is
tamed, and has been tamed

2041 4102 5048 4137 1124
23 ἔργων ἡ πίστις ἐτελειώθη; καὶ ἐπληρώθη ἡ γραφὴ ἡ
works the faith was perfected, and was fulfilled the Scripture,
3004 4100 11 2316 3049
λέγουσα, Ἐπίστευσε δὲ Ἀβραὰμ τῷ Θεῷ, καὶ ἐλογίσθη
saying, believed And Abraham God, and it was counted
846 1519 1343 5384 2316 2564 3708 5106
24 αὐτῷ εἰς δικαιοσύνην, καὶ φίλος Θεοῦ ἐκλήθη. ὁρᾶτε τοίνυν
to him for righteousness, and friend of God he was called. You see then
3754/1537/2041 1344 444 3756/1537/4102 3440
ὅτι ἐξ ἔργων δικαιοῦται ἄνθρωπος, καὶ οὐκ ἐκ πίστεως μόνον.
that by works is justified a man, and not by faith only.
3668 4460 4204/3756/1537/2041/ 1344 5264
25 ὁμοίως δὲ καὶ Ῥαὰβ ἡ πόρνη οὐκ ἐξ ἔργων ἐδικαιώθη, ὑποδε-
likewise And also Rahab the harlot not by works was justified, enter-
32 2087 3598 1544 5618
ξαμένη τοὺς ἀγγέλους, καὶ ἑτέρᾳ ὁδῷ ἐκβαλοῦσα; ὥσπερ
taining the messengers, and by another way sending out? as
1063 4983 5565 4151 3498 2076 3779
26 γὰρ τὸ σῶμα χωρὶς πνεύματος νεκρόν ἐστιν, οὕτω καὶ ἡ
For the body without spirit dead is, so also
4102 5565 2041 3498 2076
πίστις χωρὶς τῶν ἔργων νεκρά ἐστι.
faith without works dead is.

CHAPTER 3

3361/4183 1320 1096 80 3450 1492 3756
1 Μὴ πολλοὶ διδάσκαλοι γίνεσθε, ἀδελφοί μου, εἰδότες ὅτι
not many teachers Become, brothers of me, knowing that
3187 2917 2983 4183 1063 4417 537 =1536
2 μεῖζον κρίμα ληψόμεθα. πολλὰ γὰρ πταίομεν ἅπαντες. εἴ
greater judgment we will receive. (in) many For (ways) we stumble all. If
=1722/3056/3756/4417 3778 5046 435 1415 5468
τις ἐν λόγῳ οὐ πταίει, οὗτος τέλειος ἀνήρ, δυνατὸς χαλιν-
anyone in word not stumbles, this (is) a mature man, able to
3650 4983 2400 2462 5469
3 αγωγῆσαι καὶ ὅλον τὸ σῶμα. ἰδού, τῶν ἵππων τοὺς χαλι-
bridle also the whole body. Behold, of the horses the bits
1519 4750 906 4314 3982 846
νοὺς εἰς τὰ στόματα βάλλομεν πρὸς τὸ πείθεσθαι αὐτοὺς
in the mouths we put, for to obey them
2254 3650 4983 848 3329 2400
4 ἡμῖν, καὶ ὅλον τὸ σῶμα αὐτῶν μετάγομεν. ἰδού, καὶ τὰ
us, and whole the body of them we turn about. Behold, also the
4143 5082 5607 5259 4642 417 1643
πλοῖα, τηλικαῦτα ὄντα, καὶ ὑπὸ σκληρῶν ἀνέμων ἐλαυνό-
ships so great being, and by hard winds being
3329 5250 1646 4079 3699/302 3730
μενα, μετάγεται ὑπὸ ἐλαχίστου πηδαλίου, ὅπου ἂν ἡ ὁρμὴ
driven, is directed by a very little rudder, where the impulse
2116 1014 3779 1100 3398 3196
5 τοῦ εὐθύνοντος βούληται. οὕτω καὶ ἡ γλῶσσα μικρὸν μέλος
of the (one) steering purposes. So also the tongue a little member
2076 3166 2400 3641 4442 2245 5208
ἐστί, καὶ μεγαλαυχεῖ. ἰδού, ὀλίγον πῦρ ἡλίκην ὕλην
is, and great things boast. Behold, how little a fire how great wood
381 1100 4442 2889 93 3779
6 ἀνάπτει. καὶ ἡ γλῶσσα πῦρ, ὁ κόσμος τῆς ἀδικίας· οὕτως
kindles; and the tongue (is) a fire, the world of iniquity; so
1100 2525 1722 3196 2257 4696
ἡ γλῶσσα καθίσταται ἐν τοῖς μέλεσιν ἡμῶν, ἡ σπιλοῦσα
the tongue is set among the members of us, spotting
3650 4983 5394 5164 1078
ὅλον τὸ σῶμα, καὶ φλογίζουσα τὸν τροχὸν τῆς γενέσεως,
all the body, and inflaming the course of nature,
5394 5259 1067 3956 1063 5449 2342
7 καὶ φλογιζομένη ὑπὸ τῆς γεέννης. πᾶσα γὰρ φύσις θηρίων
and being inflamed by Gehenna. every For nature of beasts
5037 4071 2062 5037 1724 1150
τε καὶ πετεινῶν, ἑρπετῶν τε καὶ ἐναλίων, δαμάζεται καὶ
both and of birds of reptiles both and of sea animals, is tamed and

by the human species; [8]but no one of men is able to tame the tongue—it is an evil that cannot be restrained, full of death-dealing poison. [9]By this we bless God and *the* Father; and by this we curse men having come into being according to *the* image of God. [10]Out of the same mouth comes forth blessing and cursing. My brothers, it is not fitting *for* these things to be so. [11]*Does* the fountain out of the same hole send forth the sweet and the bitter? [12]My brothers, is a fig-tree able to produce olives, or a vine figs? So neither *can* a fountain produce *both* salt and sweet water.

[13]Who *is* wise and knowing among you? Let him show his works by *his* good behavior, in meekness of wisdom. [14]But if you have bitter jealousy and contention in your heart, do not boast and lie against the truth. [15]This is not the wisdom coming down from above, but *is* earthly, beastly, devilish. [16]For where jealousy and contention *are*, there *is* confusion and every foul deed. [17]But the wisdom from above is firstly truly pure, then peaceable, forbearing, yielding, full of mercy and of good fruits, not partial and not pretended. [18]And *the* fruit of righteousness is sown in peace for the *ones* making peace.

CHAPTER 4

[1]From where do wars and fightings among you *come*? *Is it* not from this, from your lusts warring in your members? [2]You desire and do not have. You murder, and are jealous, and are not able

1150 5449 442 1100
8 δεδάμασται τῇ φύσει τῇ ἀνθρωπίνῃ· τὴν δὲ γλῶσσαν
has been tamed by the nature human; the but tongue
3762 1410 444 1150 183 2556
οὐδεὶς δύναται ἀνθρώπων δαμάσαι· ἀκατασχετον κακόν,
no one is able of men to tame; (it is) an unrestrainable evil,
3324 2447 2287 1722/846 2127 2316
9 μεστὴ ἰοῦ θανατηφόρου. ἐν αὐτῇ εὐλογοῦμεν τὸν Θεὸν καὶ
full of poison death-dealing. By this we bless God and
3962 1722/846 2672 444 2596
πατέρα, καὶ ἐν αὐτῇ καταρώμεθα τοὺς ἀνθρώπους τοὺς καθ'
(the) Father, and by this we curse men according to
3669 2316 1096 1537 846 4750 1831
10 ὁμοίωσιν Θεοῦ γεγονότας· ἐκ τοῦ αυτοῦ στόματος ἐξέρχεται
(the) image of God having come being, into out of the same mouth comes forth
2129 2671 3756/5534/ 80 3450 5023 3779
εὐλογία καὶ κατάρα. οὐ χρή, ἀδελφοί μου, ταῦτα οὕτω
blessing and cursing. not it is fitting, brothers of me, these things so
1096 3385 4077/1537 846 3692 1032 1099
11 γίνεσθαι. μήτι ἡ πηγὴ ἐκ τῆς αὐτῆς ὀπῆς βρύει τὸ γλυκὺ
to be. (Does) the fountain out of the same hole send forth the sweet
4089 3361 1410 80 3450 4808 1636
12 καὶ τὸ πικρόν; μὴ δύναται, ἀδελφοί μου, συκῆ ἐλαίας
and the bitter? Not is able, brothers of me, a fig-tree olives
4160/2228/ 288 4810 3779 3762 4077 252
ποιῆσαι, ἢ ἄμπελος σῦκα; οὕτως οὐδεμία πηγὴ ἁλυκὸν καὶ
to produce, or a vine figs? So neither a fountain salt and
1099 4160 5204
γλυκὺ ποιῆσαι ὕδωρ.
sweet to produce water.
5101 4680 1990 1722/5213 1166 1537 2570
13 Τίς σοφὸς καὶ ἐπιστήμων ἐν ὑμῖν; δειξάτω ἐκ τῆς καλῆς
Who (is) wise and knowing **among you? Let him show by the good**
391 1041 848 1722 4240 4678 1487 2205
14 ἀναστροφῆς τὰ ἔργα αὐτοῦ ἐν πραΰτητι σοφίας. εἰ δὲ ζῆλον
behavior the works of him in meekness of wisdom. if But jealousy
4089 2192 2052 1722 2588 5216/3361/ 2620
πικρὸν ἔχετε καὶ ἐρίθειαν ἐν τῇ καρδίᾳ ὑμῶν, μὴ κατα-
bitter you have, and contention in the heart of you, do not exult
5574 2596 225 3756/2076 3778
15 καυχᾶσθε καὶ ψεύδεσθε κατὰ τῆς ἀληθείας. οὐκ ἔστιν αὕτη ἡ
over and lie against the truth. not is This the
4678 509 2718 235 1919 5591 1141
σοφία ἄνωθεν κατερχομένη, ἀλλ' ἐπίγειος, ψυχική, δαι-
wisdom from above coming down, but (is) earthly, beastly,
3699/1063 2205 2052 1563 181
16 μονιώδης. ὅπου γὰρ ζῆλος καὶ ἐρίθεια, ἐκεῖ ἀκαταστασία καὶ
devilish. where For jealousy and contention, there is confusion and
3956/5337 4229 509 4678 4412 3303 53
17 πᾶν φαῦλον πρᾶγμα. ἡ δὲ ἄνωθεν σοφία πρῶτον μὲν ἁγνή
every foul deed. the But from above wisdom firstly truly pure
2076 1899 1516 1933 2138 3324 1656
ἐστιν, ἔπειτα εἰρηνική, ἐπιεικής, εὐπειθής, μεστὴ ἐλέους καὶ
is, then peacable, forbearing, yielding full of mercy and
2590 18 87 505 2590
18 καρπῶν ἀγαθῶν, ἀδιάκριτος καὶ ἀνυπόκριτος. καρπὸς δὲ τῆς
fruits of good, not partial and not pretended. (the) fruit And
1343 1722 1515 4687 4160 1515
δικαιοσύνης ἐν εἰρήνῃ σπείρεται τοῖς ποιοῦσιν εἰρήνην.
of righteousness in peace is sown for those making peace.

CHAPTER 4

4159 4171 3163/1722/5213/3756/ 1782 1537
1 Πόθεν πόλεμοι καὶ μάχαι ἐν ὑμῖν; οὐκ ἐντεῦθεν, ἐκ τῶν
From where wars and fights among you? Not from this, from the
2237 5216 4754 1722 3196 5216
ἡδονῶν ὑμῶν τῶν στρατευομένων ἐν τοῖς μέλεσιν ὑμῶν;
lusts of you warring in the members of you?
1937 3756/2192 5407 2206 3756 1410
2 ἐπιθυμεῖτε, καὶ οὐκ ἔχετε· φονεύετε καὶ ζηλοῦτε, καὶ οὐ δύνα-
You desire, and not have; you murder and are jealous, and not are

to obtain. You fight and you war, and you do not have, because you do not ask *God*. [3]You ask, and do not receive, because you ask wrongly, in order that you may spend on your lusts. [4]Adulterers and adulteresses! Do you not know that the friendship of the world is enmity *with* God? Whoever, then, purposes to be a friend of the world is shown to be an enemy of God.

[5]Or do you think that vainly the Scripture says, "The spirit which has dwelt in us yearns with envy"? [6]But He gives greater grace. Because of this it says, "God sets *Himself* against proud ones; but He gives grace to humble ones." [7]Then be subject to God. Resist the Devil, and he will flee from you. [8]Draw near to God, and He will draw near to you. Cleanse your hands, sinners! And purify *your* hearts, double-minded ones! [9]Be distressed, and mourn, and weep. Let your laughter be turned to mourning, and *your* joy into shame. [10]Be humbled before the Lord, and He will exalt you.

[11]Do not speak against one another, brothers. He that speaks against a brother, and *is* judging a brother, *he* speaks against law, and judges law. But if you judge law, you are not a doer of law, but a judge. [12]One is the Lawgiver, who is able to save and to destroy. Who are you who judges another?

[13]Come now, those saying, Today or tomorrow we will go into this city, and we will spend one year there, and we will trade and will make a profit; [14]who do not know of the morrow. For what *is* your life? For it is a mist, which for a little *while*

2013 3164 4170 3756/2192 1223 3361
σθε ἐπιτυχεῖν· μάχεσθε καὶ πολεμεῖτε, οὐκ ἔχετε δέ, διὰ τὸ μὴ
able to obtain; you fight and you war, do not you have and, because not
154 5209 154 3756 2983 1360 2560
3 αἰτεῖσθαι ὑμᾶς· αἰτεῖτε, καὶ οὐ λαμβάνετε, διότι κακῶς
ask you; you ask, and not you receive, because wrongly
154 2443/1722 2237 5216 1159 3432
4 αἰτεῖσθε, ἵνα ἐν ταῖς ἡδοναῖς ὑμῶν δαπανήσητε. μοιχοὶ καὶ
you ask, that on the lusts of you you may spend. Adulterers and
3428 3756 1492/3754 5373 2889 2189
μοιχαλίδες, οὐκ οἴδατε ὅτι ἡ φιλία τοῦ κόσμου ἔχθρα τοῦ
adulteresses, do not you know that the friendship of the world enmity
2316 2076/3739/302/3767 1014 5384 1511 2889
Θεοῦ ἐστίν; ὃς ἂν οὖν βουληθῇ φίλος εἶναι τοῦ κόσμου,
of God is? Whoever, then, purposes a friend to be of the world,
2190 2316 2525 2228 1380 3754 2761 1124
5 ἐχθρὸς τοῦ Θεοῦ καθίσταται. ἢ δοκεῖτε ὅτι κενῶς ἡ γραφὴ
an enemy of God is shown to be. Or do you think that vainly the Scripture
3004 4314 5355 1971 4151 3739 2730 1722/2254
λέγει, Πρὸς φθόνον ἐπιποθεῖ τὸ πνεῦμα ὃ κατῴκησεν ἐν ἡμῖν
says: to envy yearns 'The spirit which has dwelt in us?
3187 1325 5485 1352 3004 2316 5244
6 μείζονα δὲ δίδωσι χάριν· διὸ λέγει, Ὁ Θεὸς ὑπερηφάνοις
greater But He gives grace, therefore it says: God proud ones
498 5011 1325 5485 5293 3767
7 ἀντιτάσσεται, ταπεινοῖς δὲ δίδωσι χάριν. ὑποτάγητε οὖν
sets (Himself) against, to humble ones but He gives grace. Be subject, therefore
2316 436 1228 5343 575 5216
τῷ Θεῷ· ἀντίστητε τῷ διαβόλῳ, καὶ φεύξεται ἀφ' ὑμῶν.
to God; oppose the devil, and he will flee from you.
1448 2316 1448 5213 2511 5495
8 ἐγγίσατε τῷ Θεῷ, καὶ ἐγγιεῖ ὑμῖν· καθαρίσατε χεῖρας,
Draw near to God, and He will draw near to you. Cleanse (the) hands,
268 48 2588 1374 5003
9 ἁμαρτωλοί, καὶ ἁγνίσατε καρδίας, δίψυχοι. ταλαιπωρή-
sinners, and purify (your) hearts, two-souled ones. Be distressed
3996 2799 1071 5216/1519 3997
σατε καὶ πενθήσατε καὶ κλαύσατε· ὁ γέλως ὑμῶν εἰς πένθος
and mourn and weep, the laughter of you to mourning
3344 5479/1519/ 2726 5013
10 μεταστραφήτω, καὶ ἡ χαρὰ εἰς κατήφειαν. ταπεινώθητε
let it be turned, and the joy to shame. Be humbled
1799 2962 5312 5209
ἐνώπιον τοῦ Κυρίου, καὶ ὑψώσει ὑμᾶς.
before the Lord, and He will exalt you.
3361 2635 240 80 2635
11 Μὴ καταλαλεῖτε ἀλλήλων, ἀδελφοί. ὁ καταλαλῶν
Do not speak against one another, brothers. He speaking against
80 2919 80 848 2635 3551
ἀδελφοῦ, καὶ κρίνων τὸν ἀδελφὸν αὐτοῦ, καταλαλεῖ νόμου,
a brother, and judging the brother of him, speaks against law,
2919 3551 1487 3551 2919 3756/1488/ 4163 3551
καὶ κρίνει νόμον· εἰ δὲ νόμον κρίνεις, οὐκ εἶ ποιητὴς νόμου,
and judges law; if and law you judge, not you are a doer of law,
235 2923 1520/2076 3550 1410 4982
12 ἀλλὰ κριτής. εἷς ἐστιν ὁ νομοθέτης, ὁ δυνάμενος σῶσαι καὶ
but a judge. One is the Lawgiver, who is able to save and
3739 622 4771/5101/1488/*/ 2919 2087
ἀπολέσαι· σὺ τίς εἶ ὃς κρίνεις τὸν ἕτερον;
to destroy; you who are who judges the other?
33 3568 3004 4594 839 4198 1519
13 Ἄγε νῦν οἱ λέγοντες, Σήμερον ἢ αὔριον πορευσόμεθα εἰς
Come now those saying, Today or tomorrow we will go into
3592 4172 4160 1563 1763 1520
τήνδε τὴν πόλιν, καὶ ποιήσομεν ἐκεῖ ἐνιαυτὸν ἕνα, καὶ
this city, and we will spend there year one, and
1710 2770 3748 3756 1987
14 ἐμπορευσόμεθα, καὶ κερδήσομεν· οἵτινες οὐκ ἐπίστασθε τὸ
we will trade and will make a profit; who not know of the
839 4169/1063 2222 5216 822 1063 2076 4314
τῆς αὔριον. ποία γὰρ ἡ ζωὴ ὑμῶν; ἀτμὶς γάρ ἐστιν ἡ πρὸς
morrow; what for the life of you? a mist For it is, which for

appears, and then disappears. [15]Instead of you saying, If the Lord wills, even we will live, and we will do this or that; [16]but now you boast in your presumptions. All such boastings is evil. [17]Therefore, to *anyone* knowing to do good, and not doing *it*, it is sin to him.

3641 5316 1899 853 473 3004
15 ὀλίγον φαινομένη, ἔπειτα δὲ ἀφανιζομένη. ἀντὶ τοῦ λέγειν
a little (while) appears, then and disappears. Instead of saying

5209 1437 2962 2309 2198 4160
ὑμᾶς, Ἐὰν ὁ Κύριος θελήσῃ, καὶ ζήσομεν, καὶ ποιήσομεν
you, If the Lord wills, even we will live, and we will do

5124 1565 3568 2744 1722 212 5216
16 τοῦτο ἢ ἐκεῖνο. νῦν δὲ καυχᾶσθε ἐν ταῖς ἀλαζονείαις ὑμῶν·
this or that. now But you boast in the vauntings of you;

3956 2746 5108 4190 2076 1492 3756 2570
17 πᾶσα καύχησις τοιαύτη πονηρά ἐστιν. εἰδότι οὖν καλὸν
all boastings such evil is. to (one) knowing Then good

4160 3361 4160 266 846 2076
ποιεῖν καὶ μὴ ποιοῦντι, ἁμαρτία αὐτῷ ἐστίν.
to do, and not doing (it), sin to him it is.

CHAPTER 5

[1]Come now, rich ones, weep, howling over your hardships coming on. [2]Your riches have rotted, and your garments have become moth-eaten. [3]Your gold and silver have rusted over, and their poison will be a testimony to you, and will eat your flesh as fire. You heaped treasure in *the* last days. [4]Behold, the wages of the workmen who have reaped your fields cry out, being kept back by you. And the cries of the ones who have reaped have entered into the ears of *the* Lord of Hosts. [5]You lived luxuriously on the earth, and lived in self-gratification; you nourished your hearts as in a day of slaughter; [6]you condemned; you murdered the righteous—he does not resist you.

[7]Therefore, brothers, be long-suffering until the coming of the Lord. Behold, the farmer waits for the precious fruit of the earth, being long-suffering over it until it may receive *the* early and the latter rain. [8]You also be long-suffering. Set your hearts firmly, because the coming of the Lord has drawn near. [9]Do not murmur against one another, brothers, that you not be condemned. Behold, *the* Judge stands before the door.

CHAPTER 5

33 3568 4145 2799 3649 1909
1 Ἄγε νῦν οἱ πλούσιοι, κλαύσατε ὀλολύζοντες ἐπὶ ταῖς
Come now rich ones, weep, crying aloud over the

5004 5216 1904 4149 5216
2 ταλαιπωρίαις ὑμῶν ταῖς ἐπερχομέναις. ὁ πλοῦτος ὑμῶν
hardships of you coming upon. The riches of you

4595 2440 5216 4598 1096 5557
3 σέσηπε, καὶ τὰ ἱμάτια ὑμῶν σητόβρωτα γέγονεν· ὁ χρυσὸς
have rotted, and the garments of you moth-eaten have become; the gold

5216 696 2728 2447 848 1519/3142
ὑμῶν καὶ ὁ ἄργυρος κατίωται, καὶ ὁ ἰὸς αὐτῶν εἰς μαρτύ-
of you and the silver have rusted over, and the poison of them for a test-

5213/2071 5315 4561 5216/5613/4442
ριον ὑμῖν ἔσται, καὶ φάγεται τὰς σάρκας ὑμῶν ὡς πῦρ.
imony to you will be, and will eat the flesh of you as fire.

2343 1722 2078 2250 2400 3408
4 ἐθησαυρίσατε ἐν ἐσχάταις ἡμέραις. ἰδού, ὁ μισθὸς τῶν
You heaped treasure in (the) last days. Behold, the wages of the

2040 270 5561 5216 650
ἐργατῶν τῶν ἀμησάντων τὰς χώρας ὑμῶν, ὁ ἀπεστερη-
workmen having reaped the fields of you being kept

575/5216 2896 995 2325 1519
μένος ἀφ' ὑμῶν, κράζει· καὶ αἱ βοαὶ τῶν θερισάντων εἰς τὰ
back from you cries out, and the cries of those having reaped into the

3775 2962 4519 1525 5171 1909
5 ὦτα Κυρίου Σαβαὼθ εἰσεληλύθασιν. ἐτρυφήσατε ἐπὶ τῆς
ears of (the) Lord of Hosts have entered. You lived luxuriously on the

1093 4684 5142 2588 5216/5613/1722
γῆς καὶ ἐσπαταλήσατε· ἐθρέψατε τὰς καρδίας ὑμῶν ὡς ἐν
earth, and lived riotously, you nourished the hearts of you as in

2250 4967 2613 5407 1342 3756
6 ἡμέρᾳ σφαγῆς. κατεδικάσατε, ἐφονεύσατε τὸν δίκαιον· οὐκ
a day of slaughter. You condemned, you murdered the righteous; not

498 5213
ἀντιτάσσεται ὑμῖν.
he resists you.

3114 3767 80 2193 3952
7 Μακροθυμήσατε οὖν, ἀδελφοί, ἕως τῆς παρουσίας τοῦ
Be longsuffering, then, brothers, until the coming of the

2962 2400 1092 1551 5093 2590
Κυρίου. ἰδού, ὁ γεωργὸς ἐκδέχεται τὸν τίμιον καρπὸν τῆς
Lord. Behold, the farmer awaits the precious fruit of the

1093 3114 1909 846 2193/302 2983 5205 4406
γῆς, μακροθυμῶν ἐπ' αὐτῷ, ἕως ἂν λάβῃ ὑετὸν πρώϊμον
earth, being longsuffering over it until it may receive rain (the) early

3797 3114 5210 4741 2588
8 καὶ ὄψιμον. μακροθυμήσατε καὶ ὑμεῖς, στηρίξατε τὰς καρδίας
and latter. Be long-suffering also you, establish the hearts

5216 3754 3952 2962 1448 3361 4727 2596
9 ὑμῶν, ὅτι ἡ παρουσία τοῦ Κυρίου ἤγγικε. μὴ στενάζετε κατ'
of you, because the coming of the Lord has drawn near. not Murmur against

240 80 2443/3363/ 2632 2400 2923/4253
ἀλλήλων, ἀδελφοί, ἵνα μὴ κατακριθῆτε· ἰδού, ὁ κριτὴς πρὸ
one another, brothers, that not you be judged; behold, the Judge before

[10]My brothers, *as* an example of suffering ill, and of long-suffering, take the prophets who spoke in the name of *the* Lord. [11]Behold, we call those blessed who endure. You have heard *of* the patience of Job, and you saw the end of *the* Lord, that the Lord is full of tender mercy and pity.

[12]But before all things, my brothers, do not swear, neither by the heaven, nor by the earth, nor any other oath. But let your yes be yes, and the no, no, that you may not fall under judgment. [13]Does anyone suffer ill among you? Let him pray. Is anyone cheerful? Let him praise. [14]Is any among you sick? Let him call the elders of the church, and let them pray over him, anointing him with oil in the name of the Lord. [15]And the prayer of faith will cure those being sick, and the Lord will raise him up. And if he may have committed sin, it will be forgiven him.

[16]Confess faults to one another, and pray for one another, that you may be healed. *The* prayer of a righteous one *has* great strength, having been made effective. [17]Elijah was a man of like feeling to us, and he prayed in prayer *for it* not to rain; and it did not rain on the earth three years and six months. [18]And he prayed again, and the heaven gave rain, and the earth caused its fruit to sprout.

[19]If anyone among you goes astray from the truth, brothers, and anyone turns him back, [20]know that the *one* turning a sinner from

2374 2476 5262 2983 2552
10 τῶν θυρῶν ἕστηκεν. ὑπόδειγμα λάβετε τῆς κακοπαθείας,
the door stands. an example Take of suffering ill,
80 3450 3115 4396
ἀδελφοί μου, καὶ τῆς μακροθυμίας, τοὺς προφήτας οἳ
brothers of me, and of longsuffering: the prophets who
2980 3686 2962 2400 3106
11 ἐλάλησαν τῷ ὀνόματι Κυρίου. ἰδού, μακαρίζομεν τοὺς
spoke in the name of (the) Lord. Behold, we count blessed those
5278 5281 2492 191 5056
ὑπομένοντας· τὴν ὑπομονὴν Ἰὼβ ἠκούσατε, καὶ τὸ τέλος
enduring. the patience of Job You heard (of), and the end
2962 1492 3754 4184 2076 2962
Κυρίου εἴδετε, ὅτι πολύσπλαγχνός ἐστιν ὁ Κύριος καὶ
of (the) Lord you saw, that very compassionate is the Lord and
3629
οἰκτίρμων.
pitying.
4253 3956 80 3450 3361 3660 3383
12 Πρὸ πάντων δέ, ἀδελφοί μου, μὴ ὀμνύετε, μήτε τὸν
before all things But, brothers of me, do not swear, neither by the
3772 3383 1093 3383 243 5100 3727 2277
οὐρανόν, μήτε τὴν γῆν, μήτε ἄλλον τινὰ ὅρκον· ἤτω δὲ
heaven, not by the earth, nor other any oath; let be but
5216 3483/3483 3756/3739/2443/3361/5259/2920 4098
ὑμῶν τὸ ναί, ναί, καὶ τὸ οὔ, οὔ· ἵνα μὴ ὑπὸ κρίσιν πέσητε.
of you the yes, yes, and the no, no, that not under judgment you fall.
2553 5100/1722/5213 4336 2114 5100
13 Κακοπαθεῖ τις ἐν ὑμῖν; προσευχέσθω. εὐθυμεῖ τις;
Suffers ill any among you? Let him pray. Is cheerful any?
5567 770 5100/1722/5213 4341 4245
14 ψαλλέτω. ἀσθενεῖ τις ἐν ὑμῖν; προσκαλεσάσθω τοὺς πρεσ-
Let him sing. Is infirm any among you? Let him summon the elders
1577 4336 1909 846
βυτέρους τῆς ἐκκλησίας, καὶ προσευξάσθωσαν ἐπ' αὐτόν,
of the church, and let them pray over him,
218 846 1637/1722 3686 2962
15 ἀλείψαντες αὐτὸν ἐλαίῳ ἐν τῷ ὀνόματι τοῦ Κυρίου· καὶ ἡ
having anointed him with oil in the name of the Lord. And the
2171 4102 4982 2577 1453 846
εὐχὴ τῆς πίστεως σώσει τὸν κάμνοντα, καὶ ἐγερεῖ αὐτὸν ὁ
prayer of faith will cure those being sick, and will raise him the
2962 2579 266 5600 4160 863 846
Κύριος· κἂν ἁμαρτίας ᾖ πεποιηκώς, ἀφεθήσεται αὐτῷ.
Lord; and if sin he may be having done it will be forgiven him.
1843 240 3900 2172
16 ἐξομολογεῖσθε ἀλλήλοις τὰ παραπτώματα, καὶ εὔχεσθε
Confess to one another the offenses, and pray
5228 240 3704 2390 4183 2480 1162 1342
ὑπὲρ ἀλλήλων, ὅπως ἰαθῆτε. πολὺ ἰσχύει δέησις δικαίου
for one another, so as you may be healed. much (is) strong a petition of one
1754 2243 444 2258 3663 2254 righteous
17 ἐνεργουμένη. Ἠλίας ἄνθρωπος ἦν ὁμοιοπαθὴς ἡμῖν, καὶ
being made effective. Elijah a man was of like feeling to us, and
4335 4336 3361 1026 3756 1026 1909
προσευχῇ προσηύξατο τοῦ μὴ βρέξαι· καὶ οὐκ ἔβρεξεν ἐπὶ
in prayer he prayed not to rain, and not it rained on
1093 1763 5140 3376/1803 3825 4336
18 τῆς γῆς ἐνιαυτοὺς τρεῖς καὶ μῆνας ἕξ. καὶ πάλιν προσηύξατο,
the earth years three and months six. And again he prayed,
3772 5205 1325 1093/ 985 2590
καὶ ὁ οὐρανὸς ὑετὸν ἔδωκε, καὶ ἡ γῆ ἐβλάστησε τὸν καρπὸν
and the heaven rain gave, and the earth produced the fruit
848
αὐτῆς.
of it.
80 1437/5100/1722/5213/ 4105 575 225
19 Ἀδελφοί, ἐάν τις ἐν ὑμῖν πλανηθῇ ἀπὸ τῆς ἀληθείας, καὶ
Brothers, if anyone among you errs from the truth, and
1994 5100 846 1097 3754 1994 268
20 ἐπιστρέψῃ τις αὐτόν, γινωσκέτω ὅτι ὁ ἐπιστρέψας ἁμαρ-
turns anyone him, know that the (one) turning a

the error of his way will save *the* soul from death, and will hide a multitude of sins.

1537 4106 3598 848 4982 5590/1537/2288
τωλὸν ἐκ πλάνης ὁδοῦ αὐτοῦ σώσει ψυχὴν ἐκ θανάτου, καὶ
sinner from (the) error of way of him will save (the) soul from death, and
2572 4128 266
καλύψει πλῆθος ἁμαρτιῶν.
will hide a multitude of sins.

ΠΕΤΡΟΥ
OF PETER
ΕΠΙΣΤΟΛΗ ΚΑΘΟΛΙΚΗ ΠΡΩΤΗ
EPISTLE GENERAL FIRST

THE FIRST GENERAL
EPISTLE OF
PETER
A LITERAL TRANSLATION
OF THE BIBLE

CHAPTER 1

[1]Peter, an apostle of
Jesus Christ, to *the* elect
sojourners of *the* dis-
persion of Pontus, of Galatia, of Cappadocia, of Asia,
and of Bithynia, [2]accord-
ing to the foreknowledge of
God the Father, in sanctification of *the* Spirit to
obedience and sprinkling
of *the* blood of Jesus
Christ: Grace and peace be
multiplied to you.
[3]Blessed *be* the God and
Father of our Lord Jesus
Christ, He according to His
great mercy having regen-
erated us to a living hope
through *the* resurrection of
Jesus Christ from *the* dead,
[4]to an inheritance incorruptible and undefiled, and
unfading, having been kept
in Heaven for you [5]by *the*
power of God, having been
guarded through faith to a
salvation ready to be re-
vealed in *the* last time; [6]in
which you exult; yet a little
while, if need be, grieving
in manifold trials, [7]so that
the proving of your faith,
much more precious than
perishing gold, but having
been proved through fire,
may be found to praise and
honor and glory at *the* revelation of Jesus Christ;
[8]whom you love, not
having seen *Him;* in whom
you exult with unspeakable
joy, and have glorified;
believing in *Him,* yet not
seeing, [9]obtaining the end
of your faith, the salvation
of *your* souls.

[10]About which salvation
the prophets sought out

CHAPTER 1

4074 652 2424 5547 1588 3927
1 Πέτρος, ἀπόστολος Ἰησοῦ Χριστοῦ, ἐκλεκτοῖς παρεπιδή-
Peter, an apostle of Jesus Christ, to (the) elect sojourners
1290 4195 1053 2587 773
μοις διασπορᾶς Πόντου, Γαλατίας, Καππαδοκίας, Ἀσίας,
of (the) dispersion of Pontus, of Galatia, of Cappadocia, of Asia,
978 2596 4268 2316 3962 1722 38
2 καὶ Βιθυνίας, κατὰ πρόγνωσιν Θεοῦ πατρός, ἐν ἁγιασμῷ
and of Bithynia, according to foreknowledge God's, the Father, in sanctification
4151 1519 5218 4473 129 2424
Πνεύματος, εἰς ὑπακοὴν καὶ ῥαντισμὸν αἵματος Ἰησοῦ
of (the) Spirit, to obedience and sprinkling of (the) blood of Jesus
5547 5485 5213 1515 4129
Χριστοῦ· χάρις ὑμῖν καὶ εἰρήνη πληθυνθείη.
Christ: Grace to you, and peace, be multiplied.
2128 2316 3962 2962 2257 2424
3 Εὐλογητὸς ὁ Θεὸς καὶ πατὴρ τοῦ Κυρίου ἡμῶν Ἰησοῦ
Blessed (be) the God and Father of the Lord of us, Jesus
5547 2596 4183 848 1656 313 2248
Χριστοῦ, ὁ κατὰ τὸ πολὺ αὐτοῦ ἔλεος ἀναγεννήσας ἡμᾶς
Christ, the (One) according to much of Him mercy, having regenerated us
1519/1680 2198/1223 386 2424 5547 3498
εἰς ἐλπίδα ζῶσαν δι' ἀναστάσεως Ἰησοῦ Χριστοῦ ἐκ νεκρῶν,
to a hope living through (the) resurrection of Jesus Christ from (the) dead,
1519 2817 862 283 263
4 εἰς κληρονομίαν ἄφθαρτον καὶ ἀμίαντον καὶ ἀμάραντον,
to an inheritance incorruptible and undefiled and unfading,
5083 1722 3772 1519/5209 1722 1411 2316
5 τετηρημένην ἐν οὐρανοῖς εἰς ὑμᾶς, τοὺς ἐν δυνάμει Θεοῦ
having been kept in Heaven for you by (the) power of God,
5432 1223 4102/1519 4991 2092 601
φρουρουμένους διὰ πίστεως εἰς σωτηρίαν ἑτοίμην ἀποκαλυ-
being guarded through faith to a salvation ready to be reveal-
1722 2540 2078 1722/3739 21 3641 737
6 φθῆναι ἐν καιρῷ ἐσχάτῳ. ἐν ᾧ ἀγαλλιᾶσθε, ὀλίγον ἄρτι,
ed in time (the) last. In which you exult, a little yet
1487/1163/2076 3076 1722 4164 3986 2443
7 εἰ δέον ἐστί, λυπηθέντες ἐν ποικίλοις πειρασμοῖς, ἵνα τὸ
if needful it is grieving by manifold trials, that the
1383 5216 4102 4183 5093 5553
δοκίμιον ὑμῶν τῆς πίστεως πολὺ τιμιώτερον χρυσίου τοῦ
proving of you of the faith, much more precious than gold
622 1223 4442 1381 2147 1519
ἀπολλυμένου, διὰ πυρὸς δὲ δοκιμαζομένου, εὑρεθῇ εἰς
of perishing, through fire yet being proved, may be found to
1868 5092 1391 1722/602 2424 5547
ἔπαινον καὶ τιμὴν καὶ δόξαν ἐν ἀποκαλύψει Ἰησοῦ Χριστοῦ·
praise and honor and glory at (the) revelation of Jesus Christ;
3739/3756 1492 25 1519/3739/737/3361/ 3708 4100
8 ὃν οὐκ ἰδόντες ἀγαπᾶτε, εἰς ὃν ἄρτι μὴ ὁρῶντες, πιστεύοντες
whom not having seen, you love, in whom yet not seeing, believing,
21 5479 412 1392 2865
9 δέ, ἀγαλλιᾶσθε χαρᾷ ἀνεκλαλήτῳ καὶ δεδοξασμένῃ, κομιζό-
but; you exult with joy unspeakable and glorified, obtaining
5056 4102 5216 4992 5590
μενοι τὸ τέλος τῆς πίστεως ὑμῶν, σωτηρίαν ψυχῶν.
the end of the faith of you, (the) salvation of (your) souls.
4012/3739/ 4991 1567 1830 4396
10 περὶ ἧς σωτηρίας ἐξεζήτησαν καὶ ἐξηρεύνησαν προφῆται οἱ
About which salvation sought out and searched out prophets the

and searched out, prophesying concerning the grace for you, 11searching for what, or what sort of time the Spirit of Christ made clear within them; testifying beforehand of the sufferings *belonging* to Christ, and the glories after these. 12To whom it was revealed that not to themselves, but to us they ministered the same things, which now were announced to you by those having preached the gospel to you in *the* Holy Spirit sent from Heaven—into which things angels long to look into.

13Therefore, girding up the loins of your mind, being sober, perfectly hope on the grace being brought to you at *the* revelation of Jesus Christ, 14as obedient children, not in ignorance fashioning yourselves to your former lusts, 15but according to the Holy One who has called you, you also become holy in all conduct; 16because it has been written, "Be holy, because I am holy." 17And if you call on *Him as* Father, He judging without respect to persons, according to the work of each one, pass the time of your sojourning in fear, 18knowing that not with corruptible things, silver or gold, you were redeemed from your worthless way of life handed down from *your* fathers, 19but with precious blood of Christ, as of an unblemished and unspotted lamb, 20indeed having been foreknown before *the* foundation of *the* world, but revealed in *the* last times because of you, 21the ones believing in God through Him, He raising Him from *the* dead, and giving glory to Him so that your faith and hope may be in God. 22Purifying your souls in the obedience of the truth

4012 1519/5209/ 5485 4395 2045 1519
11 περὶ τῆς εἰς ὑμᾶς χάριτος προφητεύσαντες· ἐρευνῶντες εἰς
concerning the for you grace prophesying, searching for
5101/2228/4169/2540 1213 1722 846 4151 5547
τίνα ἢ ποῖον καιρὸν ἐδήλου τὸ ἐν αὐτοῖς Πνεῦμα Χριστοῦ,
what or what sort of time made clear the in them Spirit of Christ,
4303 1519 5547 3804 3326
προμαρτυρόμενον τὰ εἰς Χριστὸν παθήματα, καὶ τὰς μετὰ
testifying beforehand of (belonging) the to Christ sufferings, and the after
5023 1391/3739 601 3754/3756/ 1438 2254
12 ταῦτα δόξας. οἷς ἀπεκαλύφθη ὅτι οὐχ ἑαυτοῖς, ἡμῖν δὲ
these glories. To whom it was revealed that not to themselves, to us but
1247 846/3739/3568/ 312 5213/1223 2097
διηκόνουν αὐτά, ἃ νῦν ἀνηγγέλη ὑμῖν διὰ τῶν εὐαγγελισα-
they ministered the same, which now were announced to you through those having preached
5209/1722 4151 40 649 575 3772
μένων ὑμᾶς ἐν Πνεύματι Ἁγίῳ ἀποσταλέντι ἀπ' οὐρανοῦ,
the gospel to you in (the) Spirit Holy sent from Heaven,
1519/3739 1937 32 3879
εἰς ἃ ἐπιθυμοῦσιν ἄγγελοι παρακύψαι.
into which things long angels to look into.
1352 328 3751 1271 5216
13 Διὸ ἀναζωσάμενοι τὰς ὀσφύας τῆς διανοίας ὑμῶν,
Therefore, girding up the loins of the mind of you,
3525 5049 1679 1909 5342 5213 5485
νήφοντες, τελείως ἐλπίσατε ἐπὶ τὴν φερομένην ὑμῖν χάριν
being sober, perfectly hope on the being brought to you grace
1722 602 2424 5547 5613 5043 5218 3361
14 ἐν ἀποκαλύψει Ἰησοῦ Χριστοῦ· ὡς τέκνα ὑπακοῆς, μὴ
at (the) revelation of Jesus Christ. As children of obedience, not
4964 4386 1722 52 5216 1939
συσχηματιζόμενοι ταῖς πρότερον ἐν τῇ ἀγνοίᾳ ὑμῶν ἐπιθυ-
fashioning yourselves to the formerly in the ignorance of you lusts,
235 2596 2564 5209 40 846/40
15 μίαις, ἀλλὰ κατὰ τὸν καλέσαντα ὑμᾶς ἅγιον καὶ αὐτοὶ ἅγιοι
but according to the calling you Holy One, also yourselves holy
1722/3956 391 1096 1360 1125 40
16 ἐν πάσῃ ἀναστροφῇ γενήθητε· διότι γέγραπται, Ἅγιοι
in all conduct become. Because it has been written: holy
1096 3754/1473/40 1510 1487/3962 1941
17 γένεσθε, ὅτι ἐγὼ ἅγιός εἰμι. καὶ εἰ πατέρα ἐπικαλεῖσθε τὸν
Be, because I holy am. And if (as) Father you call on (Him) the (One)
678 2919 2596 1538 2041/1722
ἀπροσωπολήπτως κρίνοντα κατὰ τὸ ἑκάστου ἔργον, ἐν
without respect to persons judging according to the of each one work, in
5401 3940 5216 5550 390 1492
18 φόβῳ τὸν τῆς παροικίας ὑμῶν χρόνον ἀναστράφητε· εἰδότες
fear the of the sojourning of you time pass, knowing
3754/3756/ 5349 694 2228/5563 3084 1537
ὅτι οὐ φθαρτοῖς, ἀργυρίῳ ἢ χρυσίῳ, ἐλυτρώθητε ἐκ τῆς
that not with corruptible things, silver or gold, you were redeemed from the
3152 5216 391 3970 235 5093
19 ματαίας ὑμῶν ἀναστροφῆς πατροπαραδότου, ἀλλὰ τιμίῳ
worthless of you living handed down from fathers, but with precious
129 5613 286 299 784 5547 4267
20 αἵματι ὡς ἀμνοῦ ἀμώμου καὶ ἀσπίλου Χριστοῦ, προεγνω-
blood, as of a lamb unblemished and unspotted, of Christ, having been
3303/4253 2602 2889 5319 1909
σμένου μὲν πρὸ καταβολῆς κόσμου, φανερωθέντος δὲ ἐπ'
foreknown before (the) foundation of (the) world, revealed but in
2078 5550/1223/5209 1223 846 4100
21 ἐσχάτων τῶν χρόνων δι' ὑμᾶς, τοὺς δι' αὐτοῦ πιστεύοντας
(the) last of the times because of you, those through Him believing
1519/2316 1453 846 1537/3498 1391 846
εἰς Θεόν, τὸν ἐγείραντα αὐτὸν ἐκ νεκρῶν, καὶ δόξαν αὐτῷ
in God, the (One) raising Him from (the) dead, and glory to Him
1325 5620 4102 5216 1680 1511/1519/2316
22 δόντα, ὥστε τὴν πίστιν ὑμῶν καὶ ἐλπίδα εἶναι εἰς Θεόν. τὰς
having given, so as the faith of you and hope to be in God. The
5590 5216 48 1722 5218 225 1223 4151
ψυχὰς ὑμῶν ἡγνικότες ἐν τῇ ὑπακοῇ τῆς ἀληθείας διὰ Πνεύ-
souls of you having purified in the obedience of the truth, through (the)

through *the* Spirit to unpretended brotherly love, love one another fervently out of a pure heart, [23]having been born again, not by corruptible seed, but incorruptible, through the living word of God, and remaining forever. [24]Because all flesh *is* as grass, and all *the* glory of men as *the* flower of grass—the grass was dried, and its flower fell out —[25]but *the* word of *the* Lord remains forever. And this is the word preached as gospel to you.

1519 5360 505 1537 2513 2588
ματος εἰς φιλαδελφίαν ἀνυπόκριτον, ἐκ καθαρᾶς καρδίας
Spirit to brotherly love unpretended, from (the) pure heart
240 25 1619 313 3756/1537
23 ἀλλήλους ἀγαπήσατε ἐκτενῶς· ἀναγεγεννημένοι οὐκ ἐκ
one another love fervently, having been regenerated not by
4701 5349 235 862 1223 3056 2198 2316
σπορᾶς φθαρτῆς, ἀλλὰ ἀφθάρτου διὰ λόγου ζῶντος Θεοῦ
seed corruptible, but incorruptible through word (the) living of God
3306 1519 165 1360/3956 4561/5613 5528
24 καὶ μένοντος εἰς τὸν αἰῶνα. διότι πᾶσα σὰρξ ὡς χόρτος,
and remaining to the age. Because all flesh (is) as grass,
3956 1391 444 5613/438 5528 3583
καὶ πᾶσα δόξα ἀνθρώπου ὡς ἄνθος χόρτου. ἐξηράνθη ὁ
and all (the) glory of man as (the) flower of grass; was dried the
5528 438 848 1601 4487 2962
25 χόρτος, καὶ τὸ ἄνθος αὐτοῦ ἐξέπεσε· τὸ δὲ ῥῆμα Κυρίου
grass, and the flower of it fell out, the but word of (the) Lord
3306 1519 165 5124 2076 4487 2097
μένει εἰς τὸν αἰῶνα. τοῦτο δέ ἐστι τὸ ῥῆμα τὸ εὐαγγελισθὲν
remains to the age. this And is the word preached as gospel
1519/5209
εἰς ὑμᾶς.
to you.

CHAPTER 2

[1]Then laying aside all malice, and all guile, and hypocrisies, and envies, and all evil words, [2]as newborn babes desire the pure soul-nourishing milk, that you may grow by it; [3]if indeed you tasted that the Lord *is* good. [4]Having drawn near to *Him*, a living Stone, indeed having been rejected by men, but chosen by God, precious; [5]you also as living stones are being built a spiritual house, a holy priesthood, to offer spiritual sacrifices acceptable to God through Jesus Christ. [6]Because of this, it is also contained in the Scripture: "Behold, I lay in Zion an elect, precious Stone, a Corner-foundation; and the *one* believing in Him shall never in any way be ashamed."

[7]Then to you who believe *belongs* the honor. But to disobeying ones, *He is the* Stone which those building rejected—this One became *the* Head-of-the-corner, [8]and a Stone-of-stumbling, and a Rock-of-offense to those disobeying, stumbling at the word, to which they were also appointed. [9]But you are an

CHAPTER 2

659 3767 3956 2549 3956 1388
1 Ἀποθέμενοι οὖν πᾶσαν κακίαν καὶ πάντα δόλον καὶ
laying aside Then all malice and all guile, and
5272 5355 3956 2636 5613 738
2 ὑποκρίσεις καὶ φθόνους καὶ πάσας καταλαλιάς, ὡς ἀρτιγέν-
hypocrisies, and envies, and all evil words, as newborn
1025 3050 97 1051 1971 2443/1722
νητα βρέφη, τὸ λογικὸν ἄδολον γάλα ἐπιποθήσατε, ἵνα ἐν
babes, the spiritual pure milk desire, that by
846 837 1512 1089 3754 5543 2962 4314
3 αὐτῷ αὐξηθῆτε, εἴπερ ἐγεύσασθε ὅτι χρηστὸς ὁ Κύριος· πρὸς
4 it you may grow, if indeed you tasted that good the Lord (is), to
3739 4334 3037 2198 5259 444 3303 593
ὃν προσερχόμενοι, λίθον ζῶντα, ὑπὸ ἀνθρώπων μὲν ἀποδε-
whom drawing near, a stone living, by men indeed having
3844/ 2316 1588 1784 848
5 δοκιμασμένον, παρὰ δὲ Θεῷ ἐκλεκτόν, ἔντιμον, καὶ αὐτοὶ
been rejected by but God elect, precious, also yourselves
5613/3037 2198 3618 3624 4152 2406
ὡς λίθοι ζῶντες οἰκοδομεῖσθε οἶκος πνευματικός, ἱεράτευμα
as stones living are being built a house spiritual, a priesthood
40 399 4152 2378 2144
ἅγιον, ἀνενέγκαι πνευματικὰς θυσίας εὐπροσδέκτους τῷ
holy, to offer spiritual sacrifices acceptable
2316/1223 2424 5547 1352 4023 1722 1124
6 Θεῷ διὰ Ἰησοῦ Χριστοῦ. διὸ καὶ περιέχει ἐν τῇ γραφῇ,
to God through Jesus Christ. Because indeed it is contained in the Scripture
2400 5087/1722/4622/3037 204 1588 1784
Ἰδού, τίθημι ἐν Σιὼν λίθον ἀκρογωνιαῖον, ἐκλεκτόν, ἔντιμον·
Behold, I lay in Zion a stone corner foundation elect, precious,
4100 1909/846 =3364= 2617 5213 3767
7 καὶ ὁ πιστεύων ἐπ' αὐτῷ οὐ μὴ καταισχυνθῇ. ὑμῖν οὖν ἡ
and the (one) believing on Him not at all shall be shamed. To you, then, the
5092 4100 544 3037/3739/ 593
τιμὴ τοῖς πιστεύουσιν· ἀπειθοῦσι δέ, Λίθον ὃν ἀπεδοκί-
honor, those believing. to disobeying ones, But a stone which rejected
3618 3778 1096 1519 2776 1137
μασαν οἱ οἰκοδομοῦντες, οὗτος ἐγενήθη εἰς κεφαλὴν γωνίας,
those building. This (One) came to be for Head of (the) corner,
3037 4348 4073 4625 3739 4350
8 καί, Λίθος προσκόμματος καὶ πέτρα σκανδάλου· οἳ προσ-
and, a Stone-of-stumbling, and a Rock- of-offense to those
3056 544 1519/3739 5087 5210
9 κόπτουσι τῷ λόγῳ ἀπειθοῦντες· εἰς ὃ καὶ ἐτέθησαν. ὑμεῖς
stumbling at the word disobeying, to which indeed they were appointed. you

elect race, a royal priesthood, a holy nation, a people for possession, so that you may openly speak of the virtues of the *One* who has called you out of darkness into His marvelous light; [10]*you* who then were not a people, but now *are* the people of God; the one not pitied *then* but now pitied.

[11]Beloved, I exhort *you* as sojourners and aliens to abstain from fleshly lusts which war against the soul; [12]having your behavior good among the nations, in that which they speak against you as evildoers, by observing *your* good works, they may glorify God in a day of visitation.

[13]Then be in obedience to every ordinance of men because of the Lord; whether to a king, as being supreme; [14]or to governors, as through Him having indeed been sent for vengeance *on* evildoers—but praise *on* welldoers—[15]because so is the will of God, doing good to silence the ignorance of foolish men; [16]as free, and not having freedom as a cover of evil, but as slaves of God; [17]honor all, love the brotherhood, fear God, honor the king.

[18]Servants, be obedient to *your* masters in all fear, not only to those good and forbearing, but also to the perverse *ones*. [19]For this *is* a grace, if because of conscience *toward* God anyone bears grief, suffering unjustly. [20]For what glory *is it* if you patiently endure *while* sinning and

1085 1588 934 2406 1484 40 2992
δὲ γένος ἐκλεκτόν, βασίλειον ἱεράτευμα, ἔθνος ἅγιον, λαὸς
But a race elect, a royal priesthood, a nation holy, a people
1519 4047 3704 703 1804 1537
εἰς περιποίησιν, ὅπως τὰς ἀρετὰς ἐξαγγείλητε τοῦ ἐκ
for possession, so as the virtues you may speak out of He from
4655 5209 2564 1519 2298 848 5457
σκότους ὑμᾶς καλέσαντος εἰς τὸ θαυμαστὸν αὐτοῦ φῶς·
darkness you calling into the marvelous of Him light;
4218/3756/2992/3568 2992 2316 3756 1653 3568
10 οἱ ποτὲ οὐ λαός, νῦν δὲ λαὸς Θεοῦ· οἱ οὐκ ἠλεημένοι, νῦν δὲ
who then not a people, now but people God's, those not pitied, now but
1653
ἐλεηθέντες.
pitied.
27 3870 5613 3941 3927
11 Ἀγαπητοί, παρακαλῶ ὡς παροίκους καὶ παρεπιδή-
Beloved, I exhort (you) as sojourners and aliens
567 4559 1939 3748 4754
μους, ἀπέχεσθαι τῶν σαρκικῶν ἐπιθυμιῶν, αἵτινες στρατεύον-
to abstain from fleshly lusts, which war
2596 5590 391 5216/1722 1484
12 ται κατὰ τῆς ψυχῆς· τὴν ἀναστροφὴν ὑμῶν ἐν τοῖς ἔθνεσιν
against the soul, the behavior of you among the nations
2192 2570 2443/1722/3739/ 2635 5216/5613/ 2555
ἔχοντες καλήν, ἵνα, ἐν ᾧ καταλαλοῦσιν ὑμῶν ὡς κακοποιῶν
having good, that in which they speak against you as evildoers,
1537 2570 2041 2029 1392 2316
ἐκ τῶν καλῶν ἔργων, ἐποπτεύσαντες, δοξάσωσι τὸν Θεὸν
by the good works having witnessed, they may glorify God
1722/2250 1984
ἐν ἡμέρᾳ ἐπισκοπῆς.
in a day of visitation.
5293 3767 3956 442 2937/1223 2962
13 Ὑποτάγητε οὖν πάσῃ ἀνθρωπίνῃ κτίσει διὰ τὸν Κύριον·
Be obedient, then, to every of men ordinance because of the Lord;
1535 935 5613 5242 1535 2232 5613/1223/846
14 εἴτε βασιλεῖ, ὡς ὑπερέχοντι· εἴτε ἡγεμόσιν, ὡς δι' αὐτοῦ
whether to a king as being supreme, or to governors, as through Him
3992 1519 1557 3303 2555 1868
πεμπομένοις εἰς ἐκδίκησιν μὲν κακοποιῶν, ἔπαινον δὲ
having been sent for vengeance indeed (on) evildoers, praise but
17 3754/3779/2076 2307 2316 15
15 ἀγαθοποιῶν. ὅτι οὕτως ἐστὶ τὸ θέλημα τοῦ Θεοῦ, ἀγαθο-
of welldoers; because so is the will of God, doing
5392 878 444 56
ποιοῦντας φιμοῦν τὴν τῶν ἀφρόνων ἀνθρώπων ἀγνωσίαν·
good to silence the of foolish men ignorance;
5613 1658 3361/5613/ 1942 2192 2549
16 ὡς ἐλεύθεροι, καὶ μὴ ὡς ἐπικάλυμμα ἔχοντες τῆς κακίας τὴν
as free, and not as a cover having of evil
1657 235/5613 1401 2316 3956 5091
17 ἐλευθερίαν, ἀλλ' ὡς δοῦλοι Θεοῦ. πάντας τιμήσατε. τὴν
freedom but as slaves of God. all Honor, the
81 25 2316 5399 935
ἀδελφότητα ἀγαπᾶτε. τὸν Θεὸν φοβεῖσθε. τὸν βασιλέα
brotherhood love, God fear, the king
5091
τιμᾶτε.
honor.
3610 5293 1722/3956 5401 1203
18 Οἱ οἰκέται, ὑποτασσόμενοι ἐν παντὶ φόβῳ τοῖς δεσπόταις,
Servants, be obedient in all fear to the masters (of you),
3756 3440 18 1933 235 4646
οὐ μόνον τοῖς ἀγαθοῖς καὶ ἐπιεικέσιν, ἀλλὰ καὶ τοῖς σκολιοῖς.
not only to the good and forbearing but also to the perverse.
5124 1063 5485/1487/1223 4893 2316 5297 5100
19 τοῦτο γὰρ χάρις, εἰ διὰ συνείδησιν Θεοῦ ὑποφέρει τις
this For (is) a grace, if because of conscience of God bears anyone
3077 3958 95 4169 1063 2811/1487 264
20 λύπας, πάσχων ἀδίκως. ποῖον γὰρ κλέος, εἰ ἁμαρτάνοντες
grief, suffering unjustly. what For glory (is it) if sinning

being buffeted? But if you *are* suffering *while* doing good, and patiently endure, this *is* a grace from God. [21]For you were called to this, for even Christ suffered on our behalf, leaving behind an example for us, that you should follow His steps; [22]who did not sin, nor was guile found in His mouth; [23]who, having been reviled, did not revile in return; suffering, He did not threaten, but gave *Himself* up to Him who *was* judging righteously; [24]who Himself bore in His body our sins onto the tree; that dying to sins, we might live to righteousness; of whom, by His wound, you were healed. [25]For you were straying sheep, but now you *are* turned to the Shepherd and Overseer of your souls.

2852 5278 235/1487 15
καὶ κολαφιζόμενοι ὑπομενεῖτε ; ἀλλ' εἰ ἀγαθοποιοῦντες καὶ
and being buffeted you patiently endure? But if doing good and
3958 5278 5124 5485 3844 2316/1519/5124
21 πάσχοντες ὑπομενεῖτε, τοῦτο χάρις παρὰ Θεῷ. εἰς τοῦτο
suffering you patiently endure, this (is) a grace from God. to this
1063 2564 3756 5547 3958 5228 2257 2254
γὰρ ἐκλήθητε, ὅτι καὶ Χριστὸς ἔπαθεν ὑπὲρ ἡμων, ἡμῖν
For you were called even Christ suffered on behalf of us, for us
5277 5251 2443 1872
ὑπολιμπάνων ὑπογραμμόν, ἵνα ἐπακολουθήσητε τοῖς
leaving behind an example that you should follow the
2487 848 3739 296 3756 4160 3761 2147 1388
22 ἴχνεσιν αὐτοῦ· ὃς ἁμαρτίαν οὐκ ἐποίησεν, οὐδὲ εὑρέθη δόλος
steps of Him; who sin did not do, nor was found guile
1722 4750 848 3739 3058 3756 486
23 ἐν τῷ στόματι αὐτοῦ· ὃς λοιδορούμενος οὐκ ἀντελοιδόρει,
in the mouth of Him; who being reviled did not revile in return;
3958 3756/546 3860 2919 1346 3739
24 πάσχων οὐκ ἠπείλει, παρεδίδου δὲ τῷ κρίνοντι δικαίως· ὃς
suffering, not He threatened, gave (Himself) but to Him judging righteously,
•1722 266 2257 848 399 4983 848
τὰς ἁμαρτίας ἡμῶν αὐτὸς ἀνήνεγκεν ἐν τῷ σώματι αὐτοῦ
the sins of us who Himself carried up in the body of Him
1909 3586 2443 266 581 1343
ἐπὶ τὸ ξύλον, ἵνα, ταῖς ἁμαρτίαις ἀπογενόμενοι, τῇ δικαιο-
onto the tree, that to sins dying, to righteous-
2198 3739 3468 848 2390 2258/1063/5613
25 σύνῃ ζήσωμεν· οὗ τῷ μώλωπι αὐτοῦ ἰάθητε. ἦτε γὰρ ὡς
ness we might live; of whom by the wound of Him you were healed. you were For as
4263 4105 235 1994 3568/1909 4166
πρόβατα πλανώμενα· ἀλλ' ἐπεστράφητε νῦν ἐπὶ τὸν ποι-
sheep wandering, but you turned now to the
1985 5590 5216
μένα καὶ ἐπίσκοπον τῶν ψυχῶν ὑμῶν.
Shepherd and Overseer of the souls of you.

CHAPTER 3

CHAPTER 3

[1]Likewise, wives, submitting yourselves to *your* own husbands, that even if any disobey the word, through the behavior of the wives, they will without a word be won, [2]observing your pure behavior in fear. [3]Of whom let it not be the outward *act* of braiding of hairs, and of putting gold around, or of clothing, *the* adorning of garments, [4]but the hidden man of the heart, in the incorruptible *adornment* of the meek and quiet spirit, which is of great value before God. [5]For so once indeed the holy women *who were* hoping on God adorned themselves, submitting themselves to their own husbands, [6]as Sarah obeyed Abraham, calling him lord; whose children you became, doing good,

3668 1135 5293 2398 435
1 Ὁμοίως, αἱ γυναῖκες, ὑποτασσόμεναι τοῖς ἰδίοις ἀν-
Likewise, wives, submitting yourselves to the own
2443 =1536= 544 3056 1223
δράσιν, ἵνα, καὶ εἴ τινες ἀπειθοῦσι τῷ λόγῳ, διὰ τῆς τῶν
husbands, that even if any disobey the word, through the of the
1135 391 427 3056 2770 2029
2 γυναικῶν ἀναστροφῆς ἄνευ λόγου κερδηθήσωνται, ἐπο-
wives behavior, without a word they will be won, having
1722/5401 53 391 5216/3739/2077
3 πτεύσαντες τὴν ἐν φόβῳ ἁγνὴν ἀναστροφὴν ὑμῶν. ὧν ἔστω
witnessed the in fear pure behavior of you. Of whom let it be
3756 1855 1708 2359 4025 5553
οὐχ ὁ ἔξωθεν ἐμπλοκῆς τριχῶν, καὶ περιθέσεως χρυσίων,
not the outward of braiding of hairs, and of putting around gold (jewelry)
1745 2440 2889 235 2927 2588
4 ἢ ἐνδύσεως ἱματίων κόσμος· ἀλλ' ὁ κρυπτὸς τῆς καρδίας
or of clothing of garments adorning; but the hidden of the heart
444 1722 862 4239 2272 4151
ἄνθρωπος, ἐν τῷ ἀφθάρτῳ τοῦ πραέος καὶ ἡσυχίου πνεύ-
man in the incorruptible of the meek and quiet spirit
3739/2076 1799 2316 4185 3779/1063/4218
5 ματος, ὅ ἐστιν ἐνώπιον τοῦ Θεοῦ πολυτελές. οὕτω γάρ ποτε
which is before God of great value. so For then
40 1135 1679 1909 2316 2885
καὶ αἱ ἅγιαι γυναῖκες αἱ ἐλπίζουσαι ἐπὶ τὸν Θεὸν ἐκόσμουν
also the holy women hoping on God adorned
1438 5293 2398 435 5613 4564
6 ἑαυτάς, ὑποτασσόμεναι τοῖς ἰδίοις ἀνδράσιν· ὡς Σάρρα
themselves, submitting themselves to the own husbands, as Sarah
5219 11 2962 846 2564 3739 1096
ὑπήκουσε τῷ Ἀβραάμ, κύριον αὐτὸν καλοῦσα, ἧς ἐγενήθητε
obeyed Abraham, lord him calling, of whom you became

and fearing no terror. [7]Likewise, husbands, dwelling together according to knowledge, as with a weaker vessel, the female, bestowing honor, as truly *being* co-heirs of *the* grace of life, not cutting off your prayers.

[8]And, finally, *be* all of one mind, sympathetic, loving *the* brothers, tenderhearted, friendly, [9]not giving back evil for evil, or reviling against reviling; but, on the contrary, *give* blessing; knowing that you were called to this in order that you might inherit blessing. [10]For the *one* desiring to love life, and to see good days, let him restrain his tongue from evil, even his lips not to speak guile. [11]Let him turn aside from evil, and let him do good. Let him seek peace, and pursue it; [12]because the eyes of *the* Lord *are* on the righteous, and His ears *open* to their prayer. But *the* face of *the* Lord *is* against *any* doing bad things.

[13]And who *is* the *one* harming you, if you become imitators of the good? [14]But if you truly suffer because of righteousness, *you are* blessed. And do not fear their fear, nor be troubled. [15]But sanctify the Lord God in your hearts, and always *be* ready to give an answer to everyone asking you a reason concerning the hope in you, with meekness and fear, [16]having a good conscience, that while they speak against you as evildoers, they may be shamed, those falsely accusing your good behavior in Christ. [17]For *it is* better, if the will of God wills *it*, to suffer *for* doing good than

5043 15 3361 5399 3367 4423
τέκνα, ἀγαθοποιοῦσαι καὶ μὴ φοβούμεναι μηδεμίαν πτόησιν.
children, doing good and fearing no terror.
435 3668 4924 2596 1108 5613 772
7 Οἱ ἄνδρες ὁμοίως, συνοικοῦντες κατὰ γνῶσιν, ὡς ἀσθενε-
Husbands likewise, dwelling together accord- knowledge, as with a
4632 1134 632 ing to 5092 5613
στέρῳ σκεύει τῷ γυναικείῳ ἀπονέμοντες τιμήν, ὡς καὶ
weaker vessel the female, bestowing honor, as truly
4789 5485 2222/1519 3361 1581
συγκληρονόμοι χάριτος ζωῆς, εἰς τὸ μὴ ἐκκόπτεσθαι τὰς
co-heirs of (the) grace of life, unto not cutting off the
4335 5216
προσευχὰς ὑμῶν.
prayers of you.
5056 3956 3675 4835 5361
8 Τὸ δὲ τέλος, πάντες ὁμόφρονες, συμπαθεῖς, φιλάδελφοι,
And finally, all of one mind, sympathetic, loving (the) brothers,
2155 5391/3361/ 591 2556 473 2556
9 εὔσπλαγχνοι, φιλόφρονες· μὴ ἀποδιδόντες κακὸν ἀντὶ κακοῦ,
tenderhearted, friendly, not giving back evil against evil,
2228 3059 473 3059 5121 2127
ἢ λοιδορίαν ἀντὶ λοιδορίας· τοὐναντίον δὲ εὐλογοῦντες,
or reviling against reviling, on the contrary but, blessing,
1492 3754/1519/5124 2564 2443 2129 2816
εἰδότες ὅτι εἰς τοῦτο ἐκλήθητε, ἵνα εὐλογίαν κληρονομήσητε.
knowing that to this you were called that blessing you might inherit.
1063 2309 2222 25 1492 2250 18
10 Ὁ γὰρ θέλων ζωὴν ἀγαπᾷν, καὶ ἰδεῖν ἡμέρας ἀγαθάς,
the (one) For desiring life to love, and to see days good,
3973 1100 848 575 2556 5491 848
παυσάτω τὴν γλῶσσαν αὐτοῦ ἀπὸ κακοῦ, καὶ χείλη αὐτοῦ
let him hold back the tongue of him from evil, even (the) lips of him
3361 2980 1388 1578 575 2556 4160
11 τοῦ μὴ λαλῆσαι δόλον· ἐκκλινάτω ἀπὸ κακοῦ, καὶ ποιησάτω
not to speak guile; let him turn away from evil, and let him do
18 2212 1515 1377 846 3754
12 ἀγαθόν· ζητησάτω εἰρήνην, καὶ διωξάτω αὐτήν. ὅτι οἱ
good; let him seek peace and pursue it; because the
3788 2962 1909 1342 3775 848 1519 1162
ὀφθαλμοὶ Κυρίου ἐπὶ δικαίους, καὶ ὦτα αὐτοῦ εἰς δέησιν
eyes of (the) Lord (are) on the righteous, and His ears (open) to petition
848 4383 2962 1909 4160 2556
αὐτῶν· πρόσωπον δὲ Κυρίου ἐπὶ ποιοῦντας κακά.
of them; (the) face but of (the) Lord against (any) doing evil things.
5101 2559 5209/1437 18 3402 1096
13 Καὶ τίς ὁ κακώσων ὑμᾶς, ἐὰν τοῦ ἀγαθοῦ μιμηταὶ γένησθε;
And who (is) he harming you, if of the good imitators you become?
235/1487 3958 1223 1343 3107
14 ἀλλʼ εἰ καὶ πάσχοιτε διὰ δικαιοσύνην, μακάριοι· τὸν δὲ
But if truly you suffer because of righteousness, blessed (are you). the But
5401 848 /3361/ 5399 3366 5015 2962
15 φόβον αὐτῶν μὴ φοβηθῆτε, μηδὲ ταραχθῆτε· Κύριον δὲ τὸν
fear of them do not fear, nor be troubled, Lord but the
2316 37 1722 2588 5216 2092 104 4314
Θεὸν ἁγιάσατε ἐν ταῖς καρδίαις ὑμῶν· ἕτοιμοι δὲ ἀεὶ πρὸς
God sanctify in the hearts of you ready and always to
627 3956 154 5209/3056 4012 1722/5213
ἀπολογίαν παντὶ τῷ αἰτοῦντι ὑμᾶς λόγον περὶ τῆς ἐν ὑμῖν
give an answer to everyone asking you a word concerning the in you
1680 3326 4240 5401 4893 2192
16 ἐλπίδος, μετὰ πραΰτητος καὶ φόβου· συνείδησιν ἔχοντες
hope; with meekness and fear, conscience having
18 2443/1722/3739/ 2635 5216 5613 2555
ἀγαθήν, ἵνα, ἐν ᾧ καταλαλῶσιν ὑμῶν ὡς κακοποιῶν,
a good, that while they speak against you as evildoers,
2617 1908 5216 18 1722
καταισχυνθῶσιν οἱ ἐπηρεάζοντες ὑμῶν τὴν ἀγαθὴν ἐν
they may be shamed, those abusing of you the good in
5547 391 2909 1063 15 1487
17 Χριστῷ ἀναστροφήν. κρεῖττον γὰρ ἀγαθοποιοῦντας, εἰ
Christ behavior. (it is) better For doing good if

for doing evil. [18]Because even Christ once suffered concerning sins, the just for the unjust, that He might bring us to God; indeed being put to death in *the* flesh, but made alive in the Spirit; [19]in which also, going in to the spirits in prison, He then proclaimed [20]to disobeying ones, when once the long-suffering of God waited in *the* days of Noah, an ark having been prepared in which a few, that is, eight souls, were saved through water. [21]Which figure now also saves us, baptism—not a putting away of *the* filth of *the* flesh, but *the* answer of a good conscience toward God through *the* resurrection of Jesus Christ; [22]who going into Heaven is at *the* right of God, *the* angels, and authorities, and powers being subjected to Him.

2309 2307 2316 3958 2228 2554 3754
18 θέλει τὸ θέλημα τοῦ Θεοῦ, πάσχειν, ἢ κακοποιοῦντας. ὅτι
wills the will of God, to suffer, than (for) doing evil. Because
5547 530 4012 266 3958 1342 5228
καὶ Χριστὸς ἅπαξ περὶ ἁμαρτιῶν ἔπαθε, δίκαιος ὑπὲρ
even Christ once concerning sins suffered, the just for
94 2443 2248 4317 2316 2289 3303
ἀδίκων, ἵνα ἡμᾶς προσαγάγῃ τῷ Θεῷ, θανατωθεὶς μὲν
the unjust, that us He might bring to God, being put to death truly
4561 2227 4151 1722/3739 1722 5438
19 σαρκί, ζωοποιηθεὶς δὲ τῷ πνεύματι, ἐν ᾧ καὶ τοῖς ἐν φυλακῇ
in (the) flesh, made alive but in the Spirit; in which also to the in prison
4151 4198 2784 544 4218 3753 530
20 πνεύμασι πορευθεὶς ἐκήρυξεν, ἀπειθήσασί ποτε, ὅτε ἅπαξ
spirits going He proclaimed to disobeying ones then, when once
1544 2316 3115 1722 2250 3575 2680
ἐξεδέχετο ἡ τοῦ Θεοῦ μακροθυμία ἐν ἡμέραις Νῶε, κατα-
waited the of God longsuffering in (the) days of Noah, having
2787 1519/3739/3641 5123 2076 3638
σκευαζομένης κιβωτοῦ, εἰς ἣν ὀλίγαι, τοῦτ' ἔστιν ὀκτὼ
been prepared an ark, in which a few, this is, eight
5590 1295 1223 5204/3739 2248 499 3568
21 ψυχαί, διεσώθησαν δι' ὕδατος· ᾧ καὶ ἡμᾶς ἀντίτυπον νῦν
souls, were saved through water. Which also us figure now
4982 908 3756 4561 595 4509 235 4893
σώζει βάπτισμα, οὐ σαρκὸς ἀπόθεσις ῥύπου, ἀλλὰ συνειδή-
saves, baptism, not of (the) flesh a putting away of (the) filth, but of a conscience
18 1906 1519/2316 1223 386 2424
σεως ἀγαθῆς ἐπερώτημα εἰς Θεόν, δι' ἀναστάσεως Ἰησοῦ
good an answer toward God, through (the) resurrection of Jesus
5547/3739/2076/1722/1188 2316 4198 1519 3772
22 Χριστοῦ, ὅς ἐστιν ἐν δεξιᾷ τοῦ Θεοῦ, πορευθεὶς εἰς οὐρανόν,
Christ, who is at (the) right of God, having gone into Heaven,
5293 846 32 1849 1411
ὑποταγέντων αὐτῷ ἀγγέλων καὶ ἐξουσιῶν καὶ δυνάμεων.
being subjected to Him angels and authorities and powers.

CHAPTER 4

[1]Therefore, Christ having suffered for us in *the* flesh, you also arm yourselves *with* the same mind, because the *one* suffering in flesh has ceased from sin, [2]for *him* no longer to live in *the* lusts of men, but in *the* will of God the remaining time in *the* flesh. [3]For *the* time of life having passed *is* sufficient for us to have worked out the will of the nations, having gone *on* in wantonness, lusts, drunkennesses, parties, carousings, and unlawful idolatries; [4]in which they are surprised, you not running with *them* into the same overflow of unsavedness, blaspheming; [5]who will give account to Him having readiness to judge *the* living and dead. [6]For to this *end* also the gospel was preached to *the* dead, that they might be judged according to men in *the*

CHAPTER 4

5547 3767 3958 5228 2257 4561 5210
1 Χριστοῦ οὖν παθόντος ὑπὲρ ἡμῶν σαρκί, καὶ ὑμεῖς τὴν
Christ Therefore having suffered for us in (the) flesh, also you the
846 1771 3695 3754 3958 1722 4561 3973
αὐτὴν ἔννοιαν ὁπλίσασθε· ὅτι ὁ παθὼν ἐν σαρκί, πέπαυται
same mind arm yourselves, because he suffering in (the) flesh has ceased
266 1519 3371 444 1939 235 2307
2 ἁμαρτίας· εἰς τὸ μηκέτι ἀνθρώπων ἐπιθυμίαις, ἀλλὰ θελή-
from sin; for the no longer of men in (the) lusts, but in (the) will
2316 1954 1722 4561 980 5550 713
3 ματι Θεοῦ τὸν ἐπίλοιπον ἐν σαρκὶ βιῶσαι χρόνον. ἀρκετὸς
of God the remaining in (the) flesh to live time. sufficient
1063 2254 3928 5550 979 2307
γὰρ ἡμῖν ὁ παρεληλυθὼς χρόνος τοῦ βίου τὸ θέλημα τῶν
For to us the having passed away time of life of the will of the
1484 2716 4198 1722 766 1939
ἐθνῶν κατεργάσασθαι, πεπορευμένους ἐν ἀσελγείαις, ἐπιθυ-
nations having worked out, having gone (on) in wantonness, lusts,
3632 2970 4224 111 1495
μίαις, οἰνοφλυγίαις, κώμοις, πότοις, καὶ ἀθεμίτοις εἰδωλο-
drunkennesses, parties, carousings, and unlawful idol-
1722/3739/ 3579 3361 4936 5216/1519
4 λατρείαις· ἐν ᾧ ξενίζονται, μὴ συντρεχόντων ὑμῶν εἰς τὴν
atries. While they are surprised not running with you into the
846 810 401 987 3739 591
5 αὐτὴν τῆς ἀσωτίας ἀνάχυσιν, βλασφημοῦντες· οἳ ἀποδώ-
same of dissoluteness overflow, blaspheming; who will give
3056 2093 2192 2919 2198 3498
σουσι λόγον τῷ ἑτοίμως ἔχοντι κρῖναι ζῶντας καὶ νεκρούς.
account to the (One) ready having to judge living and dead.
1519/5124/1063 3498/ 2097 2443 2919 3303 2596
6 εἰς τοῦτο γὰρ καὶ νεκροῖς εὐηγγελίσθη, ἵνα κριθῶσι μὲν κατὰ
for this For indeed to dead ones was preached the gospel that they might be judged in-deed according to

flesh, but might live according to God in *the* Spirit.

[7]But the end of all things has drawn near. Be of sound mind, then, and be sensible to prayers; [8]and above all things having fervent love to yourselves, because love will cover a multitude of sins. [9]Be hospitable to one another without murmurings, [10]each one as he received a gift, ministering it to yourselves as good stewards of *the* manifold grace of God. [11]If anyone speaks, *let it be* as *the* words of God; if anyone ministers, as by strength which God supplies, that in all things God may be glorified through Jesus Christ; to whom is the glory and the might forever and ever. Amen.

[12]Beloved, do not be astonished *at* the fiery trial happening among you for your testing, as *if* a surprise *were* occurring to you; [13]but according as you share the sufferings of Christ, rejoice; so that you may rejoice exultingly at the revelation of His glory.

[14]If you are reviled in *the* name of Christ, *you are* blessed, because the Spirit of God and of glory rests on you. Truly, according to them, He is blasphemed; but according to you, He is glorified. [15]For do not let any of you suffer as a murderer, or a thief, or an evildoer, or as a meddler in the affairs of others. [16]But if *he suffers* as a Christian, do not let him be ashamed, but to glorify God in this respect. [17]Because the time *has come* to begin the judgment from the house of God; and if firstly from us, what *will be* the end of the ones disobeying the gospel of God? [18]And if the righteous is scarcely saved,

444 4561 2198 2596 2316 4151
ἀνθρώπους σαρκί, ζῶσι δὲ κατα Θεὸν πνευματι.
men in (the) flesh; might live but according to God in (the) Spirit.
3956 5056 1448 4993 3767
7 Πάντων δὲ τὸ τέλος ἤγγικε· σωφρονήσατε οὖν καὶ
of all things But the end has drawn near. Be disciplined, then, and
3525 1519 4335 4253 3956 1519 1438
8 νήψατε εἰς τὰς προσευχάς· πρὸ πάντων δὲ τὴν εἰς ἑαυτοὺς
be sensible to prayers; before all things and to yourselves
26 1618 2192 3754 26 2572 4128
ἀγάπην ἐκτενῆ ἔχοντες, ὅτι ἡ ἀγάπη καλύψει πλῆθος
love fervent having, because love will cover a multitude
266 5382 1519 240 427 1112
9 ἁμαρτιῶν· φιλόξενοι εἰς ἀλλήλους ἄνευ γογγυσμῶν·
of sins. Be hospitable to one another without murmurings;
1538 2531 2983 5486 1519 1438 846 1247
10 ἕκαστος καθὼς ἔλαβε χάρισμα, εἰς ἑαυτοὺς αὐτὸ διακονοῦν-
each one as he received a gift, to yourselves it ministering
5613 2570 3623 4164 5485 2316/1536= 2980
11 τες, ὡς καλοὶ οἰκονόμοι ποικίλης χάριτος Θεοῦ· εἴ τις λαλεῖ,
as good stewards of (the) manifold grace of God; If any speaks,
5613/3051 2316 =1536= 1247 5613/1537/2479/3739/ 5524
ὡς λόγια Θεοῦ· εἴ τις διακονεῖ, ὡς ἐξ ἰσχύος ἧς χορηγεῖ ὁ
as (the) words of God; if any ministers, as by strength which supplies
2316/2443/1722/3956 1392 2316 1223/2424 5547
Θεός· ἵνα ἐν πᾶσι δοξάζηται ὁ Θεὸς διὰ Ἰησοῦ Χριστοῦ,
God, that in all things may be glorified God through Jesus Christ,
3739/2076 1391 2904 1519 165 165
ᾧ ἐστιν ἡ δόξα καὶ τὸ κράτος εἰς τοὺς αἰῶνας τῶν αἰώνων.
to whom is the glory and the might to the ages of the ages.
281
ἀμήν.
Amen
27 3361 3579 1722/5213 4451 4314 3986
12 Ἀγαπητοί, μὴ ξενίζεσθε τῇ ἐν ὑμῖν πυρώσει πρὸς πειρα-
Beloved, do not be astonished (at) among you fiery trial, for trial
5213 1096 5613/3581 5213/ 4819 235 2526
13 σμὸν ὑμῖν γινομένῃ, ὡς ξένου ὑμῖν συμβαίνοντος· ἀλλὰ καθὸ
of you happening, as a surprise to you occurring, but as
2841 5547 3804 5463 2443 1722
κοινωνεῖτε τοῖς τοῦ Χριστοῦ παθήμασι, χαίρετε, ἵνα καὶ ἐν
you share the of Christ sufferings, rejoice, that also at
602 1391 848 5463 21 1487
14 τῇ ἀποκαλύψει τῆς δόξης αὐτοῦ χαρῆτε ἀγαλλιώμενοι. εἰ
the revelation of the glory of Him you may rejoice exultingly If
3679 1722/3686 5547 3107 3754 1391
ὀνειδίζεσθε ἐν ὀνόματι Χριστοῦ, μακάριοι· ὅτι τὸ τῆς δόξης
you are reviled in (the) name of Christ, blessed (are you), for the of glory
2316 4151 1909/5209 373 2596 3303
καὶ τὸ τοῦ Θεοῦ Πνεῦμα ἐφ' ὑμᾶς ἀναπαύεται· κατὰ μὲν
and the of God Spirit on you rests; according to truly
846 987 2596 5209 1392 3361/1063/5100
15 αὐτοὺς βλασφημεῖται, κατὰ δὲ ὑμᾶς δοξάζεται. μὴ γάρ τις
them, He is blasphemed; according to but you, He is glorified. not For any
5216 3958 5613 5406/2228/ 2812 2228 2555 2228/5613
ὑμῶν πασχέτω ὡς φονεύς, ἢ κλέπτης, ἢ κακοποιός, ἢ ὡς
of you let suffer as a murderer, or a thief, or an evildoer, or as
244 1487 5613 5546 3361 153
16 ἀλλοτριοεπίσκοπος· εἰ δὲ ὡς Χριστιανός, μὴ αἰσχυνέσθω,
a meddler; if but as a Christian, not let him be ashamed,
1392 2316/1722 3313 5129/3754 2540
17 δοξαζέτω δὲ τὸν Θεὸν ἐν τῷ μέρει τούτῳ. ὅτι ὁ καιρὸς τοῦ
to glorify but God in respect this. Because the time
756 2917 575 3624 2316/1487 4412
ἄρξασθαι τὸ κρίμα ἀπὸ τοῦ οἴκου τοῦ Θεοῦ· εἰ δὲ πρῶτον
to begin the judgment from the house of God; if and firstly
575 2257 5101 5056 544 2316
ἀφ' ἡμῶν, τί τὸ τέλος τῶν ἀπειθούντων τῷ τοῦ Θεοῦ
from us, what (will be) the end of those disobeying the of God
2098 1342 3433 4982 765
18 εὐαγγελίῳ; καὶ εἰ ὁ δίκαιος μόλις σώζεται, ὁ ἀσεβὴς καὶ
gospel? And if the righteous one scarcely is saved, the ungodly and

where will the ungodly and
sinner appear? [19]So as indeed the ones suffering according to God's will, as to a
faithful Creator, let them
commit their souls in welldoing.

CHAPTER 5

[1]I, a fellow-elder, exhort
the elders among you, *I*
being also witness of the
sufferings of Christ, and
being sharer of the glory
about to be revealed:
[2]Shepherd the flock of God
among you, exercising oversight, not by compulsion,
but willingly; nor eagerly for
base gain, but readily; [3]nor
as exercising lordship over
the ones allotted *to you*, but
becoming examples of the
flock. [4]And *at* the appearing of the Chief Shepherd,
you will receive the never-
fading crown of glory.
[5]Likewise, younger ones
be subject to older ones;
and all being subject to one
another. Put on humility,
because God sets *Himself*
against proud ones, but He
gives grace to humble
ones. [6]Then be humbled
under the mighty hand of
God, that He may exalt you
in time; [7]casting all your
anxiety onto Him, because
it matters to Him con-
cerning you. [8]Be sensible,
watch, because your adversary *the* Devil walks about
as a roaring lion seeking
someone he may devour;
[9]whom firmly resist in the
faith, knowing the same
sufferings *that are* in the
world are being completed
in your brotherhood. [10]Now
the God of all grace, the
One calling you to His
eternal glory in Christ
Jesus, *you* having suffered
a little, *He* Himself will

268 4226 5316 5620 3958 2596
19 ἁμαρτωλὸς ποῦ φανεῖται ; ὥστε καὶ οἱ πάσχοντες κατὰ τὸ
sinner where will appear? So as indeed those suffering according to
2307 2316/5613 4103 2939 3908
θέλημα τοῦ Θεοῦ, ὡς πιστῷ κτίστῃ παρατιθέσθωσαν τὰς
will God's, as to a faithful Creator, let them commit the
5590 1438/1722/ 16
ψυχὰς ἑαυτῶν ἐν ἀγαθοποιΐᾳ.
souls of themselves in welldoing.

CHAPTER 5

4245 1722/5213 3870 4850
1 Πρεσβυτέρους τοὺς ἐν ὑμῖν παρακαλῶ ὁ συμπρεσβύτερος
elders The among you I exhort, he a fellow-elder (being),
3144 5547 3804 3195
καὶ μάρτυς τῶν τοῦ Χριστοῦ παθημάτων, ὁ καὶ τῆς μελλού-
and witness of the of Christ sufferings, the also of the being
601 1391 2844 4165 1722/5213
2 σης ἀποκαλύπτεσθαι δόξης κοινωνός· ποιμάνατε τὸ ἐν ὑμῖν
about to be revealed glory sharer; shepherd the among you
4168 2316 1983 3361 317 235
ποίμνιον τοῦ Θεοῦ, ἐπισκοποῦντες μὴ ἀναγκαστῶς, ἀλλ'
flock of God, exercising oversight not by compulsion, but
1596 3366 147 235 4290 3366/5613
3 ἑκουσίως· μηδὲ αἰσχροκερδῶς, ἀλλὰ προθύμως· μηδ' ὡς
willingly, nor eagerly for base gain, but readily; nor as
2634 2819 235 5179 1096
κατακυριεύοντες τῶν κλήρων, ἀλλὰ τύποι γινόμενοι τοῦ
as exercising lordship over the allotments, but examples becoming of the
4168 5319 750 2865
4 ποιμνίου. καὶ φανερωθέντος τοῦ ἀρχιποίμενος, κομιεῖσθε τὸν
flock; and (at) the appearing of the chief Shepherd, you will receive the
162 1391 4735 3668 3501 5293
5 ἀμαράντινον τῆς δόξης στέφανον. ὁμοίως, νεώτεροι, ὑποτά-
unfading of glory crown. Likewise, younger ones be sub-
4245 3956 240 5293
γητε πρεσβυτέροις· πάντες δὲ ἀλλήλοις ὑποτασσόμενοι, τὴν
ject to older ones; all and to one another being subject,
5012 1463 3754 2316 5244
ταπεινοφροσύνην ἐγκομβώσασθε· ὅτι ὁ Θεὸς ὑπερηφάνοις
humility put on, because God proud ones
498 5011 1325 5485 5013
6 ἀντιτάσσεται, ταπεινοῖς δὲ δίδωσι χάριν. ταπεινώθητε
sets (Himself) against, to humble ones but He gives grace. Be humbled,
3767/5259 2900 5495 2316/2443/5209 5312 1722
οὖν ὑπὸ τὴν κραταιὰν χεῖρα τοῦ Θεοῦ, ἵνα ὑμᾶς ὑψώσῃ ἐν
then, under the mighty hand of God, that you He may exalt in
2540 3956 3308 5216 1977 1909 846
7 καιρῷ, πᾶσαν τὴν μέριμναν ὑμῶν ἐπιρρίψαντες ἐπ' αὐτόν,
time; all the anxiety of you casting onto Him,
3754 846 3199 4012/5216 3525 1127 3754
8 ὅτι αὐτῷ μέλει περὶ ὑμῶν. νήψατε, γρηγορήσατε, ὅτι ὁ
because to Him it concerning you. Be sensible, watch, because the
476 matters 1228 5613 3023 5612 4043
•5216 ἀντίδικος ὑμῶν διάβολος, ὡς λέων ὠρυόμενος, περιπατεῖ
adversary of you, (the) devil, as a lion roaring walks about
2212 5101 2666 3739 436 4731 4102
9 ζητῶν τίνα καταπίῃ· ᾧ ἀντίστητε στερεοὶ τῇ πίστει,
seeking someone he may devour; whom resist firm in the faith,
1492 846 3804 1722 2889 5216 81
εἰδότες τὰ αὐτὰ τῶν παθημάτων τῇ ἐν κόσμῳ ὑμῶν ἀδελ-
knowing the same sufferings in the in (the) world of you brother-
2005 2316 3956 5485 2564
10 φότητι ἐπιτελεῖσθαι. ὁ δὲ Θεὸς πάσης χάριτος, ὁ καλέσας
hood are being completed. the Now God of all grace, the (One) calling
2248/1519 166 848 1391/1722/5547 2424 3641
ἡμᾶς εἰς τὴν αἰώνιον αὐτοῦ δόξαν ἐν Χριστῷ Ἰησοῦ, ὀλίγον
us to the eternal of Him glory in Christ Jesus, a little
3958 848 2675 5209 4741 4599
παθόντας αὐτὸς καταρτίσαι ὑμᾶς, στηρίξαι, σθενώσαι,
having suffered Himself perfect you, confirm, strengthen.

perfect, confirm, strengthen, establish you. [11]To Him *be* the glory and the might forever and ever. Amen.

[12]I wrote to you by a few *words* by way of Silvanus the faithful brother, as I reckon, exhorting and witnessing this to be *the* true grace of God, in which you stand. [13]The fellow-elected in Babylon greet you; also Mark my son. [14]Greet one another with a kiss of love.

Peace to you, all those in Christ Jesus. Amen.

2311 846 1391 2904/1519 165
11 θεμελιώσαι. αὐτῷ ἡ δόξα καὶ τὸ κράτος εἰς τοὺς αἰῶνας τῶν
establish (you). To Him the glory and the might to the ages of the
165 281
αἰώνων. ἀμήν.
ages. Amen.
1223 4610 5213 4103 80 5613 3049
12 Διὰ Σιλουανοῦ ὑμῖν τοῦ πιστοῦ ἀδελφοῦ, ὡς λογίζομαι,
Through Silvanus to you the faithful brother, as I reckon,
1223 3641 1125 3870 1957 5026
δι' ὀλίγων ἔγραψα, παρακαλῶν καὶ ἐπιμαρτυρῶν ταύτην
via a few (words) I wrote, exhorting and witnessing this
1511 227 5485 2316/1519/3739/ 2476 782
13 εἶναι ἀληθῆ χάριν τοῦ Θεοῦ εἰς ἣν ἑστήκατε. ἀσπάζεται
to be (the) true grace of God, in which you stand. Greets
5209 1722 897 4899 3138 5207/3450
ὑμᾶς ἡ ἐν Βαβυλῶνι συνεκλεκτή, καὶ Μάρκος ὁ υἱός μου.
you the in Babylon fellow-elected, and Mark the son of me.
782 240 1722 5370 26
14 ἀσπάσασθε ἀλλήλους ἐν φιλήματι ἀγάπης.
Greet one another with a kiss of love.
1515 5213 /3956 1722 5547 2424 281
Εἰρήνη ὑμῖν πᾶσι τοῖς ἐν Χριστῷ Ἰησοῦ. ἀμήν.
Peace to you, all those in Christ Jesus. Amen.

THE SECOND GENERAL EPISTLE OF PETER

A LITERAL TRANSLATION OF THE BIBLE

ΠΕΤΡΟΥ
OF PETER

ΕΠΙΣΤΟΛΗ ΚΑΘΟΛΙΚΗ ΔΕΥΤΕΡΑ
EPISTLE GENERAL SECOND

CHAPTER 1

[1]Simon Peter, a slave and apostle of Jesus Christ, to those equally precious with us, having obtained faith in *the* righteousness of our God and our Savior, Jesus Christ: [2]Grace to you, and peace be multiplied by a full knowledge of God, and of Jesus our Lord.

[3]As His divine power has given to us all things pertaining to life and godliness through the full knowledge of the *One* calling us through glory and virtue, [4]by which means He has given to us the very great and precious promises, so that through these you might be partakers of *the* divine nature, escaping from the corruption in *the* world by lust. [5]But also in this very thing, bringing in all diligence, filling out your faith *with* virtue; and virtue *with* knowledge; [6]and knowledge *with* self-control; and self-control *with* patience; and patience *with* godliness; [7]and godliness *with* brotherly love; and brotherly love *with* love. [8]For these things being in you, and abounding, makes *you* not barren, not unfruitful in the full knowledge of our Lord Jesus Christ. [9]For the *one* in whom these things *are* not present is blind, being short-sighted, taking on forgetfulness of the cleansing of his sins in time past. [10]On account of this, brothers, rather be diligent to make sure of your calling

4824 4074 1401 652 2424 5547
1 Σίμων Πέτρος, δοῦλος καὶ ἀπόστολος Ἰησοῦ Χριστοῦ,
Simon Peter, a slave and apostle of Jesus Christ,
2472 2254 2975 4102 1722/1343 2316
τοῖς ἰσότιμον ἡμῖν λαχοῦσι πίστιν ἐν δικαιοσύνῃ τοῦ Θεοῦ
to those equally precious with us having obtained faith in (the) righteousness of the God
2257 4990 2257 2424 5547 5485 5213
2 ἡμῶν καὶ σωτῆρος ἡμῶν Ἰησοῦ Χριστοῦ· χάρις ὑμῖν καὶ
of us and Savior of us, Jesus Christ: Grace to you and
1515 4129 1722 1922 2316 2424
εἰρήνη πληθυνθείη ἐν ἐπιγνώσει τοῦ Θεοῦ, καὶ Ἰησοῦ τοῦ
peace be multiplied by a full knowledge of God, and of Jesus the
2962 2257/5613 3956 2254 2304 1411 848
3 Κυρίου ἡμῶν· ὡς πάντα ἡμῖν τῆς θείας δυνάμεως αὐτοῦ τὰ
Lord of us. As all things to us the divine power of Him
4314 2222 2150 1433 1223 1922
πρὸς ζωὴν καὶ εὐσέβειαν δεδωρημένης, διὰ τῆς ἐπιγνώσεως
as to life and godliness having been given, through the full knowledge
2564 2248/1223/1391 703 1223/3739 3176
4 τοῦ καλέσαντος ἡμᾶς διὰ δόξης καὶ ἀρετῆς· δι' ὧν τὰ μέγιστα
of the (One) calling us via glory and virtue, through which the very great
2254 5093 1862 1433 2443/1223/5130
ἡμῖν καὶ τίμια ἐπαγγέλματα δεδώρηται, ἵνα διὰ τούτων
to us and precious promises He has given, that through these
1096 2304 2844 5449 668 1722/2889
γένησθε θείας κοινωνοὶ φύσεως, ἀποφυγόντες τῆς ἐν κόσμῳ
you might be of a divine partakers nature, escaping from the in (the) world
1722/1939 5356 846 5124 4710 3956
5 ἐν ἐπιθυμίᾳ φθορᾶς. καὶ αὐτὸ τοῦτο δέ, σπουδὴν πᾶσαν
by lust corruption. also in this very thing But, diligence all
3923 2023 1722 4102 5216
παρεισενέγκαντες, ἐπιχορηγήσατε ἐν τῇ πίστει ὑμῶν τὴν
bringing in, fill out in the faith of you
703 1722 703 1108 1722 1108
6 ἀρετήν, ἐν δὲ τῇ ἀρετῇ τὴν γνῶσιν, ἐν δὲ τῇ γνώσει τὴν
virtue; with and virtue, knowledge; with and knowledge,
1466 1722 1466 5281 1722
ἐγκράτειαν, ἐν δὲ τῇ ἐγκρατείᾳ τὴν ὑπομονήν, ἐν δὲ τῇ
self-control; with and self-control, patience; with and
5281 2150 1722 2150 5360
7 ὑπομονῇ τὴν εὐσέβειαν, ἐν δὲ τῇ εὐσεβείᾳ τὴν φιλαδελφίαν,
patience, godliness, with and godliness, brotherly love;
1722 5360 26 5023/1063/5213 5225
8 ἐν δὲ τῇ φιλαδελφίᾳ τὴν ἀγάπην. ταῦτα γὰρ ὑμῖν ὑπάρ-
with and brotherly love, love. these things For in you being
4121 3756 692 3761 175 5225
χοντα καὶ πλεονάζοντα, οὐκ ἀργοὺς οὐδὲ ἀκάρπους καθί-
and abounding, not barren not unfruitful
1519 2962 2257 2424 5547 1922
στησιν εἰς τὴν τοῦ Κυρίου ἡμῶν Ἰησοῦ Χριστοῦ ἐπίγνωσιν.
makes (you) in the of the Lord of us Jesus Christ full knowledge.
3739 1063/3361 3918 5023 5185 2076 3467 3024
9 ᾧ γὰρ μὴ πάρεστι ταῦτα, τυφλός ἐστι, μυωπάζων, λήθην
(he) in whom For not is present these things, blind is, being short-sighted, forgetfulness
•1352 2983 2512 3819 848 266
10 λαβὼν τοῦ καθαρισμοῦ τῶν πάλαι αὐτοῦ ἁμαρτιῶν. διὸ
taking of the cleansing of the in time past of him sins. Therefore
3123 80 4704 949 5216 2821
μᾶλλον, ἀδελφοί, σπουδάσατε βεβαίαν ὑμῶν τὴν κλῆσιν
rather, brothers, be diligent sure of you the calling

and election; for doing these things, you will not ever fall. [11]For so will be richly furnished to you the entrance into the everlasting kingdom of our Lord and Savior, Jesus Christ.

[12]For this reason I will not neglect to cause you to remember always concerning these things, though *you* know and have been confirmed in the present truth. [13]But I deem *it* right, so long as I am in this tabernacle, to stir you up by a reminder, [14]knowing that the putting off of my tabernacle is soon, as indeed our Lord Jesus Christ made clear to me. [15]And I will also be diligent to cause you always to have memory of these things after my departure. [16]For not following fables which had been cleverly devised, but becoming eyewitnesses of the majesty of Jesus Christ, that *One* made known to you the power and coming of our Lord. [17]For receiving honor and glory from God *the* Father—such a voice being borne to Him from the magnificent glory, "This is My Son, the Beloved, in whom I was well-pleased," [18]even we heard this voice being borne out of Heaven, being with Him in the holy mountain—[19]and we have the more established prophetic word, in which you do well to take heed, as to a lamp shining in a murky place, until day dawns and the Daystar rises in your hearts; [20]knowing this first, that every prophecy of Scripture did not come into being of *its* own interpretation; [21]for prophecy was not at any time borne by *the*

1589 4160 5023 1063 4160 =3364= 4417
καὶ ἐκλογὴν ποιεῖσθαι· ταῦτα γὰρ ποιοῦντες οὐ μὴ πταίσητέ
and election to make; these things for doing not at all you will fall
4218 3779/1063 4146 2023 5213 1529
11 ποτε· οὕτω γὰρ πλουσίως ἐπιχορηγηθήσεται ὑμῖν ἡ εἴσοδος
ever. so For richly will be furnished to you the entrance
1519 166 932 2962 2257 4990
εἰς τὴν αἰώνιον βασιλείαν τοῦ Κυρίου ἡμῶν καὶ σωτῆρος
into the eternal kingdom of the Lord of us and Savior,
2424 5547
Ἰησοῦ Χριστοῦ.
Jesus Christ.

1352/3756 272 5209/104 5279 4012 5130
12 Διὸ οὐκ ἀμελήσω ὑμᾶς ἀεὶ ὑπομιμνήσκειν περὶ τούτων,
Therefore not I will neglect you always to cause to remember about these,
2539 1492 4741 1722 3918 225
καίπερ εἰδότας, καὶ ἐστηριγμένους ἐν τῇ παρούσῃ ἀληθείᾳ.
though knowing and having been confirmed in the present truth.
1342 2233 1909 3745/1510/1722/5129 4638
13 δίκαιον δὲ ἡγοῦμαι, ἐφ' ὅσον εἰμὶ ἐν τούτῳ τῷ σκηνώματι,
right And I deem (it), so long as I am in this tabernacle,
1326 5209/1722 5280 1492 3754 5031 2076
14 διεγείρειν ὑμᾶς ἐν ὑπομνήσει· εἰδὼς ὅτι ταχινή ἐστιν ἡ
to arouse you by a reminder, knowing that soon is the
595 4638 3450 2531 2962 2257
ἀπόθεσις τοῦ σκηνώματός μου, καθὼς καὶ ὁ Κύριος ἡμῶν
putting off of the tabernacle of me, as indeed the Lord of us,
2424 5547 1213 3427 4704 1539
15 Ἰησοῦς Χριστὸς ἐδήλωσέ μοι. σπουδάσω δὲ καὶ ἑκάστοτε
Jesus Christ, made clear to me. I will be diligent And also always
2192 5209 3326 1699 1841 5130 3420
ἔχειν ὑμᾶς μετὰ τὴν ἐμὴν ἔξοδον τὴν τούτων μνήμην
to have you after my departure the of these things memory
4160 3756/1063 4679 3454 1811
16 ποιεῖσθαι. οὐ γὰρ σεσοφισμένοις μύθοις ἐξακολουθήσαντες
to cause. not For having been cleverly devised fables following,
1107 5213 2962 2257 2424 5547
ἐγνωρίσαμεν ὑμῖν την τοῦ Κυρίου ἡμῶν Ἰησοῦ Χριστοῦ
we made known to you the of the Lord of us, Jesus Christ,
1411 3952 235 2030 1096
δύναμιν καὶ παρουσίαν, ἀλλ' ἐπόπται γενηθέντες τῆς
power and coming, but eyewitnesses having become of the
1565 3168 2983 1063 3844 2316 3962
17 ἐκείνου μεγαλειότητος. λαβὼν γὰρ παρὰ Θεοῦ πατρὸς
of that (One) majesty. receiving For from God (the) Father
5092 1391 5456 5342 846 5107 5259
τιμὴν καὶ δόξαν, φωνῆς ἐνεχθείσης αὐτῷ τοιᾶσδε ὑπὸ τῆς
honor and glory, a voice being borne to Him such from the
3169 1391 3778 2076 5207/3450 27
μεγαλοπρεποῦς δόξης, Οὗτός ἐστιν ὁ υἱός μου ὁ ἀγαπητός,
magnificent glory: This is the Son of Me, the Beloved,
1519/3739/1473/ 2106 5026 5456 2249 191
18 εἰς ὃν ἐγὼ εὐδόκησα· καὶ ταύτην τὴν φωνὴν ἡμεῖς ἠκού-
in whom I was well-pleased. And this voice we heard
1537/ 3772 5342 4862 846 5607 1722 3735
σαμεν ἐξ οὐρανοῦ ἐνεχθεῖσαν, σὺν αὐτῷ ὄντες ἐν τῷ ὄρει τῷ
out of Heaven being borne, with Him being in the mountain
40 2192 949 4397 3056 3739
19 ἁγίῳ. καὶ ἔχομεν βεβαιότερον τὸν προφητικὸν λόγον, ᾧ
holy. And we have more firm the prophetic word, in which
2573 4160 4337 5613 3088 5316 1722/850
καλῶς ποιεῖτε προσέχοντες, ὡς λύχνῳ φαίνοντι ἐν αὐχμηρῷ
well you do taking heed, as to a lamp shining in murky
5117 2193/3739/2250 1306 5459 393 1722
τόπῳ, ἕως οὗ ἡμέρα διαυγάσῃ, καὶ φωσφόρος ἀνατείλῃ ἐν
place, until day dawns, and the Daystar rises in
2588 5216 5124 4412 1097 3754 3956
20 ταῖς καρδίαις ὑμῶν· τοῦτο πρῶτον γινώσκοντες, ὅτι πᾶσα
the hearts of you; this firstly knowing, that every
4394 1124 2398 1955 3756 1096 3756/1063
21 προφητεία γραφῆς ἰδίας ἐπιλύσεως οὐ γίνεται. οὐ γὰρ
prophecy of Scripture of (its) own unloosing did not come into being. not For

will of man, but having been borne along by *the* Holy Spirit, holy men of God spoke.

CHAPTER 2

1 But false prophets were also among the people, as also false teachers will be among you, who will secretly bring in destructive heresies, and denying the Master who has bought them, bringing swift destruction on themselves. 2 And many will follow their destructive ways, by whom the way of truth will be evil spoken of. 3 And by covetousness, with well-turned words, they will use you for gain—for whom judgment of old does not linger, and their destruction does not slumber. 4 For if God did not spare sinning angels, but delivered *them* to chains of darkness, thrust down into Tartarus, having been kept to judgment; 5 and did not spare *the* ancient world, but preserved Noah *the* eighth, a herald of righteousness, bringing a flood on a world of ungodly ones; 6 and covering the cities *of* Sodom and Gomorrah with ashes, *He* condemned *them* with an overthrow, setting an example to men intending to live ungodly. 7 And He delivered righteous Lot, who had been oppressed by the behavior of the lawless in lustfulness. 8 For that righteous one living among them day after day, in seeing and in hearing, *his* righteous soul *was* tormented with *their* lawless deeds.

9 *But the* Lord knows to deliver the godly out of temptation, and to keep the unjust for a day of judgment, being punished, 10 and most of all those going after flesh in *the* lust of defilement,

2307 444 5342 4218 4394 235 5259
θελήματι ἀνθρώπου ἠνέχθη ποτὲ προφητεία, ἀλλ' ὑπὸ
by (the)will of man was borne at any time prophecy, but by
4151 40 5342 2980 40 2316 444
Πνεύματος Ἁγίου φερόμενοι ἐλάλησαν ἅγιοι Θεοῦ ἄνθρωποι.
(the) Spirit Holy being borne along spoke (the) holy of God men.

CHAPTER 2

1096 5578 1722 2992/5613 1722
1 Ἐγένοντο δὲ καὶ ψευδοπροφῆται ἐν τῷ λαῷ, ὡς καὶ ἐν
there were But also false prophets among the people, as also among
5213 2071 5572 3748 3919
ὑμῖν ἔσονται ψευδοδιδάσκαλοι, οἵτινες παρεισάξουσιν
you will be false teachers, who will secretly bring in
139 684 59 846 1203
αἱρέσεις ἀπωλείας, καὶ τὸν ἀγοράσαντα αὐτοὺς δεσπότην
heresies of destruction, and the having bought them Master
720 1863 1438 5031 684
2 ἀρνούμενοι, ἐπάγοντες ἑαυτοῖς ταχινὴν ἀπώλειαν. καὶ
denying, bringing on themselves swift destruction. And
4183 1811 848 684 1223 3739
πολλοὶ ἐξακολουθήσουσιν αὐτῶν ταῖς ἀπωλείαις, δι' οὓς
many will follow of them the destructive ways, by whom
3598 225 987 1722 4124
3 ἡ ὁδὸς τῆς ἀληθείας βλασφημηθήσεται. καὶ ἐν πλεονεξίᾳ
the way of the truth will be evil spoken of. And by covetousness
4112 3056 5209 1710 3739 2917 1597
πλαστοῖς λόγοις ὑμᾶς ἐμπορεύσονται· οἷς τὸ κρίμα ἔκπαλαι
with well-turned words you they will use for gain for whom the judgment of old
3756 691 684 848 3756 3573/1487/1063,
4 οὐκ ἀργεῖ, καὶ ἡ ἀπώλεια αὐτῶν οὐ νυστάζει. εἰ γὰρ ὁ
not lingers, and the destruction of them not slumbers. if For
2316 32 264 3756 5339 235 4577
Θεὸς ἀγγέλων ἁμαρτησάντων οὐκ ἐφείσατο, ἀλλὰ σειραῖς
God angels sinning did not spare, but to chains
2217 5020 3860 1519 2920 5083
5 ζόφου ταρταρώσας παρέδωκεν εἰς κρίσιν τετηρημένους· καὶ
of darkness thrust down into Tartarus delivered (them) to judgment having been kept; and
744 2889 3756 5339 235 3590 3575 1343
ἀρχαίου κόσμου οὐκ ἐφείσατο, ἀλλ' ὄγδοον Νῶε δικαιοσύνης
(the) ancient world not spared, but (the) eighth, Noah, of righteousness
2783 5442 2627 2889 765 1863
6 κήρυκα ἐφύλαξε, κατακλυσμὸν κόσμῳ ἀσεβῶν ἐπάξας· καὶ
a herald preserved, a flood a world of ungodly ones bringing and
4172 4670 1116 5077 2692
πόλεις Σοδόμων καὶ Γομόρρας τεφρώσας καταστροφῇ
the cities, Sodom and Gomorrah, covering with ashes by an overthrow
2632 5262 3195 754 5087
7 κατέκρινεν, ὑπόδειγμα μελλόντων ἀσεβεῖν τεθεικώς· καὶ
condemned, an example of men intending to live ungodly setting; and
1342 3091 2669 5259 133 1722
δίκαιον Λώτ, καταπονούμενον ὑπὸ τῆς τῶν ἀθέσμων ἐν
righteous Lot, having been oppressed by the of the lawless in
766 391 4506 990 1063 189
8 ἀσελγείᾳ ἀναστροφῆς, ἐρρύσατο (βλέμματι γὰρ καὶ ἀκοῇ ὁ
lustfulness conduct delivered — in seeing for and hearing, the
1342 1460 1722 846 2250 1537 2250 5590
δίκαιος, ἐγκατοικῶν ἐν αὐτοῖς, ἡμέραν ἐξ ἡμέρας ψυχὴν
righteous one dwelling among them day after day (his) soul
1342 459 2041 928 1492 2962 2152
9 δικαίαν ἀνόμοις ἔργοις ἐβασάνιζεν)· οἶδε Κύριος εὐσεβεῖς
righteous with (the) lawless works tormented — knows (the) Lord the godly
1537/ 3986 4506 94 1519/2250 2920 2849
ἐκ πειρασμῶν ῥύεσθαι, ἀδίκους δὲ εἰς ἡμέραν κρίσεως κολαζο-
out of temptation to deliver, the unjust but for a day of judgment being
5083 3122 3694 4561 1722 1939
10 μένους τηρεῖν· μάλιστα δὲ τοὺς ὀπίσω σαρκὸς ἐν ἐπιθυμίᾳ
punished to keep; most of all and the after flesh in lust
3394 4198 2963 2706
μιασμοῦ πορευομένους, καὶ κυριότητος καταφρονοῦντας.
of defilement (ones) going, and dominion despising,

and despising rulership, darers, self-satisfied; they do not tremble *at* glories, speaking evil; 11 where angels being greater in strength and power do not bring against them a reproaching charge before *the* Lord. 12 But these as unreasoning natural beasts, having been born for capture and corruption, speaking evil in that *of* which they are ignorant, they shall utterly perish in their corruption, 13 being about to receive *the* wages of unrighteousness, having deemed indulgence in the day *to be* pleasure; reveling *in* spots and blemishes, feasting along with you in their deceits; 14 having eyes full of an adulteress, and never ceasing from sin; alluring unsettled souls; having a heart busied *with* covetousness; cursed children; 15 forsaking a straight path, they went astray, following the way of Balaam the *son* of Beor, who loved *the* wages of unrighteousness, 16 but had reproof of *his* own transgression—the dumb ass speaking in a man's voice held back the madness of the prophet. 17 These are springs without water, clouds being driven by tempest, for whom the blackness of darkness is kept forever. 18 For speaking great swelling *words* of vanity, by *the* lusts of the flesh, by unbridled lusts, they allure those who *were* escaping the ones living in error, 19 promising them freedom, *though* themselves being slaves of corruption; for by whom anyone has been overcome, even to this one he has been enslaved. 20 For if by a full knowledge of the Lord and Savior, Jesus Christ, *they* have escaped the defilements of the world, and again being entangled *they* have been

5113 829 1391 3756 5141 987
τολμηταί, αὐθάδεις, δόξας οὐ τρέμουσι βλασφημοῦντες·
darers, self-satisfied, glories not they tremble (at), speaking evil,
3699 32 2479 1411 3187 5607/3756/5342
11 ὅπου ἄγγελοι, ἰσχύϊ καὶ δυνάμει μείζονες ὄντες, οὐ φέρουσι
where angels in strength and in power greater being do not bring
2596 846 3844 2962 989 2920 3778 5613
12 κατ' αὐτῶν παρὰ Κυρίῳ βλάσφημον κρίσιν. οὗτοι δέ, ὡς
against them before (the) Lord a reproaching charge. these But, as
249 2226 5446 1080 1519 259 5356 1722
ἄλογα ζῶα φυσικὰ γεγενημένα εἰς ἅλωσιν καὶ φθοράν, ἐν
unreasoning beasts natural having been born for capture and corruption, in
3739 50 987 1722 5356 848 2704
οἷς ἀγνοοῦσι βλασφημοῦντες, ἐν τῇ φθορᾷ αὐτῶν καταφθαρή-
which they are ignorant (of) speaking evil; in the corruption of them, they shall utterly
2865 3408 93 2237 2233
13 σονται, κομιούμενοι μισθὸν ἀδικίας, ἡδονὴν ἡγούμενοι τὴν
perish; being about to receive wages of wrong, (as) pleasure deeming
1722 2250 5172 4695 3470 1792 1722
ἐν ἡμέρᾳ τρυφήν, σπῖλοι καὶ μῶμοι, ἐντρυφῶντες ἐν ταῖς
in (the) day indulgence, spots and blemishes revelling (in); in the
539 848 4910 5213 3788 2192
14 ἀπάταις αὐτῶν συνευωχούμενοι ὑμῖν, ὀφθαλμοὺς ἔχοντες
deceits of them feasting along with you; eyes having
3324 3428 180 266 1185
μεστοὺς μοιχαλίδος καὶ ἀκαταπαύστους ἁμαρτίας, δελεά-
full of an adulteress, and not ceasing from sin, alluring
5590 793 2588 1128 4124
ζοντες ψυχὰς ἀστηρίκτους, καρδίαν γεγυμνασμένην πλεονε-
souls unsettled; a heart having been busied covet-
2192 2671 5043 2641 2117 3598
15 ξίαις ἔχοντες, κατάρας τέκνα· καταλιπόντες τὴν εὐθεῖαν ὁδὸν
ousness having; of curse children; forsaking a straight way,
4105 1811 3598 903
ἐπλανήθησαν, ἐξακολουθήσαντες τῇ ὁδῷ τοῦ Βαλαὰμ τοῦ
they erred, following the way of Balaam the (son)
1007 3739 3408 93 25 1649 2192 2398
16 Βοσόρ, ὃς μισθὸν ἀδικίας ἠγάπησεν, ἔλεγξιν δὲ ἔσχεν ἰδίας
of Beor, who (the) wages of wrong loved, reproof and had of own
3892 5268 880 1722/444 5456 5350
παρανομίας· ὑποζύγιον ἄφωνον, ἐν ἀνθρώπου φωνῇ φθεγξά-
transgression; ass a dumb with of a man voice speaking
2967 4396 3913 3778/1526
17 μενον, ἐκώλυσε τὴν τοῦ προφήτου παραφρονίαν. οὗτοί εἰσι
restrained the of the prophet madness. These are
4077 504 3507 5259 2978 1643 3739
πηγαὶ ἄνυδροι, νεφέλαι ὑπὸ λαίλαπος ἐλαυνόμεναι, οἷς ὁ
springs without water, clouds by tempest being driven, for whom th
2217 4655 1519 165 5083 5246 1063
18 ζόφος τοῦ σκότους εἰς αἰῶνα τετήρηται. ὑπέρογκα γὰρ
blackness of darkness to ages is kept. overswollen (words) For
3153 5350 1185 1722 1939 4561
ματαιότητος φθεγγόμενοι, δελεάζουσιν ἐν ἐπιθυμίαις σαρκός,
of vanity speaking, they allure by (the) lusts of (the) flesh,
1722 766 3689 668 1722 4106
ἐν ἀσελγείαις, τοὺς ὄντως ἀποφυγόντας τοὺς ἐν πλάνῃ
in unbridled lusts, those indeed escaping the (ones) in error
390 1657 846 1861 846
19 ἀναστρεφομένους, ἐλευθερίαν αὐτοῖς ἐπαγγελλόμενοι, αὐτοὶ
living, freedom to them promising, themselves
1401 5225 5356/3739/1063/5100/ 2274 5129
δοῦλοι ὑπάρχοντες τῆς φθορᾶς· ᾧ γάρ τις ἥττηται, τούτῳ
slaves being of corruption; by for any- has been de- to this one
1402 1487/1063/668 whom one 3393 feated,
20 καὶ δεδούλωται. εἰ γὰρ ἀποφυγόντες τὰ μιάσματα τοῦ
also he has been enslaved. if For having escaped the defilements of the
2889 1722 1922 2962 4990 2424 5547
κόσμου ἐν ἐπιγνώσει τοῦ Κυρίου καὶ σωτῆρος Ἰησοῦ Χρι-
world by a full knowledge of the Lord and Savior Jesus Christ,
5125 3825 1707 2274 1096 846
21 στοῦ, τούτοις δὲ πάλιν ἐμπλακέντες ἡττῶνται, γέγονεν αὐτοῖς
by these and again being entangled have been defeated have become to them

overcome by these, *then their* last things *are* worse *than* the first. [21]For it was better for them not to have fully known the way of righteousness, than fully knowing to turn from the holy commandment delivered to them. [22]But the *word* of the true proverb has happened to them: *The* dog turning to *his* own vomit; also *The* washed sow to wallowing *in* mud.

CHAPTER 3

[1]Beloved, I now write this second epistle to you, in which by reminder I stir up your sincere mind to remember [2]the words having been spoken before by the holy prophets, and the command of the Lord and and Savior—by us, the apostles; [3]first, knowing this, that during *the* last days scoffers will come, walking according to their own lusts, [4]and saying, Where is the promise of His coming? For since the fathers fell asleep, all things continue this way from *the* beginning of creation. [5]For this is hidden from them *by their* willing *it so,* that heavens were of old, and earth by water, and through water, being held together by the word of God, [6]through which the world which then *was,* being flooded by water, perished. [7]But the heavens and the earth now, having been stored up by the same word, are being kept for fire to a day of judgment and destruction of ungodly men.

[8]But let not this one thing be hidden *from* you, beloved, that one day with *the* Lord *is* as a thousand years, and a thousand years as one day. [9]The Lord is not slow *as to* the promise, as some deem slowness, but

2078 5501 4413 2909 1063/2258/846
τὰ ἔσχατα χείρονα τῶν πρώτων. κρεῖττον γὰρ ἦν αὐτοῖς
the last things worse (than) the first. better For it was for them
3361 1921 3598 1343 2228 1921
μὴ ἐπεγνωκέναι τὴν ὁδὸν τῆς δικαιοσύνης, ἢ ἐπιγνοῦσιν
not to have fully known the way of righteousness, than fully knowing
1994 1537 3860 846 40 1785
ἐπιστρέψαι ἐκ τῆς παραδοθείσης αὐτοῖς ἁγίας ἐντολῆς.
to turn from the – delivered to them holy commandment.
4819 846 227 3942 2965
22 συμβέβηκε δὲ αὐτοῖς τὸ τῆς ἀληθοῦς παροιμίας, Κύων
has happened But to them the (word) of the true proverb: (the) dog
1994 1909 2398 1829 5300 3068 1519
ἐπιστρέψας ἐπὶ τὸ ἴδιον ἐξέραμα, καί ὗς λουσαμένη εἰς
turning to the own vomit; and, (The) sow washed, to
2946 1004
κύλισμα βορβόρου.
wallowing of mud.

CHAPTER 3

5026 2235 27 1208 5213 1125 1992
1 Ταύτην ἤδη, ἀγαπητοί, δευτέραν ὑμῖν γράφω ἐπιστολήν,
This now, beloved, second to you I write epistle,
1722/3739 / 1326 5216/1722 5280 1506 1271
ἐν αἷς διεγείρω ὑμῶν ἐν ὑπομνήσει τὴν εἰλικρινῆ διάνοιαν,
in which I arouse you by reminder the sincere mind,
3415 4280 4487 5259 40
2 μνησθῆναι τῶν προειρημένων ῥημάτων ὑπὸ τῶν ἁγίων
to remember the having been before spoken words by the holy
4396 652 2257 1785
προφητῶν, καὶ τῆς τῶν ἀποστόλων ἡμῶν ἐντολῆς τοῦ
prophets, and the of the apostles by us command of the
2962 4990 5124 4412 1097 3754
3 Κυρίου καὶ σωτῆρος· τοῦτο πρῶτον γινώσκοντες, ὅτι
Lord and Savior; this firstly knowing, that
2064 1909 2078 2250 1703 2596
ἐλεύσονται ἐπ' ἐσχάτου τῶν ἡμερῶν ἐμπαῖκται, κατὰ τὰς
will come during (the) last of the days scoffers, according to the
2398 848 1939 4198 3004 4226
4 ἰδίας αὐτῶν ἐπιθυμίας πορευόμενοι, καὶ λέγοντες, Ποῦ
own of them lusts walking, and saying, Where
2076 1860 3952 848 575/3739/1063
ἐστιν ἡ ἐπαγγελία τῆς παρουσίας αὐτοῦ; ἀφ' ἧς γὰρ οἱ
is the promise of the coming of Him? from which for the
3962 2837 3956 3779 1265 575 746
πατέρες ἐκοιμήθησαν, πάντα οὕτω διαμένει ἀπ' ἀρχῆς
fathers fell asleep, all things so remain from (the) be-
3772 2937 2990 1063 846 5124 2309 3754/ ginning
5 κτίσεως. λανθάνει γὰρ αὐτοὺς τοῦτο θέλοντας, ὅτι οὐρανοὶ
of creation. is hidden (from) For them this (by their) willing, that heavens
2258 1597 1093/1537/ 5204 1223 5204 4921
ἦσαν ἔκπαλαι, καὶ γῆ ἐξ ὕδατος καὶ δι' ὕδατος συνεστῶσα,
were of old, and earth by water, and through water having been held
2316 3056 1223/3739 5119 2889 5204/2626 together
6 τῷ τοῦ Θεοῦ λόγῳ, δι' ὧν ὁ τότε κόσμος ὕδατι κατακλυ-
by the of God word, by which the then world by water being
622 3568 3772 1093 846 3056
7 σθεὶς ἀπώλετο· οἱ δὲ νῦν οὐρανοὶ καὶ ἡ γῆ τῷ αὐτῷ λόγῳ
flooded perished. the But now heavens and the earth by the same word
2343 1526 4442 5083 1519 2250 2920
τεθησαυρισμένοι εἰσί, πυρὶ τηρούμενοι εἰς ἡμέραν κρίσεως
having been stored up are for fire being kept unto a day of judgment
684 765 444
καὶ ἀπωλείας τῶν ἀσεβῶν ἀνθρώπων.
and destruction of ungodly men.
1722 5124 3361/ 2990 5209 27 3754 3391
8 Ἓν δὲ τοῦτο μὴ λανθανέτω ὑμᾶς, ἀγαπητοί, ὅτι μία
one But this thing not let be hidden from you, beloved, that one
2250 3844 2962/5613/5507/2094 5507/2094/5613/2250
ἡμέρα παρὰ Κυρίῳ ὡς χίλια ἔτη, καὶ χίλια ἔτη ὡς ἡμέρα
day with (the) Lord (is) as a thousand and a thousand as day
years years
3391/3756 1019 2962 1860 5100 1022
9 μία. οὐ βραδύνει ὁ Κύριος τῆς ἐπαγγελίας, ὥς τινες βραδυ-
one. not is slow The Lord of the promise, as some slowness

is long-suffering toward us, not having purposed any *of us* to perish, but all *of us* to come to repentance. [10]But the day of *the* Lord will come as a thief in *the* night, in which the heavens will pass away with rushing sound, and having burned *the* elements will be dissolved, and earth and the works in it will be burned up. [11]Then all these being *about* to be dissolved, what sort ought you to be in holy behavior and godliness, [12]looking for and hastening the coming of the Day of God, through which *the* heavens being set afire will be dissolved, and *the* elements will melt? [13]But according to His promise, we look for new heavens and a new earth, in which righteousness dwells.

[14]Because of this, beloved, looking for these things, be diligent, spotless, and without blemish, to be found in peace by Him. [15]And think of the long-suffering of our Lord *as* salvation, as also our beloved brother Paul wrote to you, according to the wisdom given to him; [16]as also in all *his* epistles, speaking in them concerning these things, in which are some things hard to understand, which the unlearned and unsettled pervert, as also *they do* the rest of the Scriptures, to *their* own destruction. [17]Then beloved, you knowing beforehand, watch lest being led away by the error of the lawless you fall from *your* own steadfastness.

[18]But grow in grace and knowledge of our Lord and Savior, Jesus Christ. To Him *be* the glory, both now and to *the* day of eternity. Amen.

2233 235 3114 1519/2248/3361 1014
τῆτα ἡγοῦνται· ἀλλὰ μακροθυμεῖ εἰς ἡμᾶς, μὴ βουλόμενός
deem, but is long-suffering toward us, not having purposed
5100 622 235 3956 1519 3341 5562
τινας ἀπολέσθαι, ἀλλὰ πάντας εἰς μετάνοιαν χωρῆσαι.
any to perish, but all to repentance to come.
•3739 2240 2250 2962/5613/2812/1722/3571/1722/•/ 3772
10 ἥξει δὲ ἡ ἡμέρα Κυρίου ὡς κλέπτης ἐν νυκτί, ἐν ᾗ οἱ οὐρανοὶ
will come But the day of (the) as a thief in (the) night, in which the heavens
4500 3928 Lord 4747 2741 3089
ῥοιζηδὸν παρελεύσονται, στοιχεῖα δὲ καυσούμενα λυθή-
with rushing sound will pass away, (the) elements and burning will be
1093 1722 846 2041 2618 5130
11 σονται, καὶ γῆ καὶ τὰ ἐν αὐτῇ ἔργα κατακαήσεται. τούτων
dissolved, and earth and the in it works will be burned up. these things
3767 3956 3089 4217 1163 5225 5209 172
οὖν πάντων λυομένων, ποταποὺς δεῖ ὑπάρχειν ὑμᾶς ἐν
Then all being dissolved, what sort ought to be you in
40 391 2150 4328
12 ἁγίαις ἀναστροφαῖς καὶ εὐσεβείαις, προσδοκῶντας καὶ
holy behavior and godliness, looking for and
4692 3952 2316 2250 1223/3739
σπεύδοντας τὴν παρουσίαν τῆς τοῦ Θεοῦ ἡμέρας, δι' ἣν
rushing the coming of the of God day, for which
3772 4448 3089 4747 2741
οὐρανοὶ πυρούμενοι λυθήσονται, καὶ στοιχεῖα καυσούμενα
•5080 (the) having been set afire will be dissolved, and (the) elements burning
•heavens 2537 3772 1093 2537 2596
13 τήκεται; καινοὺς δὲ οὐρανοὺς καὶ γῆν καινὴν κατὰ τὸ
will melt. new But heavens and an earth new according to the
1862 848 4328 1722/3739/ 1343 2730
ἐπάγγελμα αὐτοῦ προσδοκῶμεν, ἐν οἷς δικαιοσύνη κατοικεῖ.
promise of Him we look for, in which righteousness dwells.
1352 27 5023 4328 4704
14 Διό, ἀγαπητοί, ταῦτα προσδοκῶντες, σπουδάσατε
Therefore, beloved, these things looking for, be diligent,
784 298 846 2147 1722/1515
15 ἄσπιλοι καὶ ἀμώμητοι αὐτῷ εὑρεθῆναι ἐν εἰρήνῃ. καὶ τὴν
spotless and without blemish, by Him to be found in peace, and the
2962 2257 3115 4991 2233 2531
τοῦ Κυρίου ἡμῶν μακροθυμίαν σωτηρίαν ἡγεῖσθε, καθὼς
of the Lord of us longsuffering salvation deem, as
27 2257 80 3972 2596 846
καὶ ὁ ἀγαπητὸς ἡμῶν ἀδελφὸς Παῦλος κατὰ τὴν αὐτῷ
also the beloved of us brother, Paul, according to the to him
1325 4678 1125 5213/5613 1722 3956
16 δοθεῖσαν σοφίαν ἔγραψεν ὑμῖν· ὡς καὶ ἐν πάσαις ταῖς
given wisdom, wrote to you, as also in all (his)
1992 2980/1722/846 4012/ 5130 1722/3739/2076/1425
ἐπιστολαῖς, λαλῶν ἐν αὐταῖς περὶ τούτων· ἐν οἷς ἐστι δυσνόη-
epistles, speaking in them concerning these, in which are hard to understand
5100/3739/ 261 793 4761 5613
τά τινα, ἃ οἱ ἀμαθεῖς καὶ ἀστήρικτοι στρεβλοῦσιν, ὡς καὶ τὰς
some things, which the unlearned and unsettled pervert, as also the
3062 1124 4314 2398 848 684 5210 3767
17 λοιπὰς γραφάς, πρὸς τὴν ἰδίαν αὐτῶν ἀπώλειαν. ὑμεῖς οὖν,
remaining Scriptures, to the own of them destruction. You, then,
27 4267 5442 2443/3361
ἀγαπητοί, προγινώσκοντες φυλάσσεσθε, ἵνα μή, τῇ τῶν
beloved, knowing beforehand, watch that not by the of the
113 4106 4879 1601 2398 4740
ἀθέσμων πλάνῃ συναπαχθέντες, ἐκπέσητε τοῦ ἰδίου στηριγ-
lawless error being led away you fall from the own steadfast-
837 1722 5485 1108 2962 2257
18 μοῦ. αὐξάνετε δὲ ἐν χάριτι καὶ γνώσει τοῦ Κυρίου ἡμῶν καὶ
ness; grow but in grace and knowledge of the Lord of us and
4990 2424 5547 846 1391 3568 1519
σωτῆρος Ἰησοῦ Χριστοῦ. αὐτῷ ἡ δόξα καὶ νῦν καὶ εἰς
Savior, Jesus Christ. To Him (be) the glory both now and to
2250 165 281
ἡμέραν αἰῶνος. ἀμήν.
a day of eternity. Amen.

THE FIRST GENERAL
EPISTLE OF
JOHN

A LITERAL TRANSLATION
OF THE BIBLE

CHAPTER 1

[1]*We announce to you* what was from *the* beginning, what we have heard, what we have seen with our eyes, what we beheld, and *what* our hands touched, as regards the Word of Life. [2]And the Life was revealed, and we have seen, and we bear witness, and we announce to you the everlasting Life which was with the Father, and was revealed to us. [3]We announce to you what we have seen, and *what* we have heard, that you also may have fellowship with us. And truly our fellowship *is* with the Father and with His Son, Jesus Christ. [4]And we write these things to you, that your joy may be full.

[5]And this is the message which we have heard from Him, and we announce to you: God is light, and no darkness is in Him—none. [6]If we say that we have fellowship with Him, and we walk in darkness, we lie and are not practicing the truth. [7]But if we walk in the light, as He is in the light, we have fellowship with one another, and the blood of His Son Jesus Christ cleanses us from all sin. [8]If we say that we have no sin, we deceive ourselves, and the truth is not in us. [9]If we confess our sins, He is faithful and righteous that

ΙΩΑΝΝΟΥ
OF JOHN
ΕΠΙΣΤΟΛΗ ΚΑΘΟΛΙΚΗ ΠΡΩΤΗ
EPISTLE GENERAL FIRST

CHAPTER 1

3739/2258/575 746/3739 191 3739 3708 3788
1 Ὃ ἦν ἀπ' ἀρχῆς, ὃ ἀκηκόαμεν, ὃ ἑωράκαμεν τοῖς ὀφθαλ-
What was from (the) what we have heard, what we have seen with
2257 beginning 2300 5495 2257 5584 the
μοῖς ἡμῶν, ὃ ἐθεασάμεθα, καὶ αἱ χεῖρες ἡμῶν ἐψηλάφησαν
eyes of us, what we beheld, and the hands of us touched,
4012 3056 2222 2222 5319
2 περὶ τοῦ λόγου τῆς ζωῆς (καὶ ἡ ζωὴ ἐφανερώθη, καὶ
concerning the Word of life —and the Life was revealed, and
3708 3140 518 5213
ἑωράκαμεν, καὶ μαρτυροῦμεν, καὶ ἀπαγγέλλομεν ὑμῖν τὴν
we have seen, and we bear witness, and we announce to you the
2222 166 3748/2258/4314 3962 5319
ζωὴν τὴν αἰώνιον, ἥτις ἦν πρὸς τὸν πατέρα, καὶ ἐφανερώθη
Life everlasting, which was with the Father, and was revealed
2254 3739 3708 191 518 5213
3 ἡμῖν)· ὃ ἑωράκαμεν καὶ ἀκηκόαμεν, ἀπαγγέλλομεν ὑμῖν,
to us— what we have seen, and we have heard, we announce to you,
2443 5210 2842 2192 3326 2257 2842
ἵνα καὶ ὑμεῖς κοινωνίαν ἔχητε μεθ' ἡμῶν· καὶ ἡ κοινωνία δὲ
that also you fellowship may have with us, truly fellowship And
2251 3326 3962 3326 5207 848 2424
ἡ ἡμετέρα μετὰ τοῦ πατρὸς καὶ μετὰ τοῦ υἱοῦ αὐτοῦ Ἰησοῦ
our (is) with the Father and with the Son of Him, Jesus
5547 5023 1125 5213/2443 5479 5216
4 Χριστοῦ· καὶ ταῦτα γράφομεν ὑμῖν, ἵνα ἡ χαρὰ ὑμῶν ᾖ
Christ. And these things write to you, that the joy of you be
4137
πεπληρωμένη.
fulfilled.

3778 2076 1860 3739 191 575 846
5 Καὶ αὕτη ἐστὶν ἡ ἀγγελία ἣν ἀκηκόαμεν ἀπ' αὐτοῦ καὶ
And this is the message which we have heard from Him, and
312 5213/3754 2316/5457/2076 4653/1722/846
ἀναγγέλλομεν ὑμῖν, ὅτι ὁ Θεὸς φῶς ἐστί, καὶ σκοτία ἐν αὐτῷ
we announce to you, that God light is, and darkness in Him
3756 2076 3762 1437 2036 3754 2842 2192 3316
6 οὐκ ἔστιν οὐδεμία. ἐὰν εἴπωμεν ὅτι κοινωνίαν ἔχομεν μετ'
not is, none. If we say that fellowship we have with
846 1722 4655 4043 5574 3756
αὐτοῦ, καὶ ἐν τῷ σκότει περιπατῶμεν, ψευδόμεθα, καὶ οὐ
Him, and in the darkness we walk, we lie, and not
4160 225 1437 1722 5457 4043
7 ποιοῦμεν τὴν ἀλήθειαν· ἐὰν δὲ ἐν τῷ φωτὶ περιπατῶμεν,
are doing the truth. if But in the light we walk,
5607/846 2076/1722 5457 2842 2192 3326 240
ὡς αὐτός ἐστιν ἐν τῷ φωτί, κοινωνίαν ἔχομεν μετ' ἀλλήλων,
as He is in the light, fellowship we have with one another,
129 2424 5547 5207 846 2511 2248
καὶ τὸ αἷμα Ἰησοῦ Χριστοῦ τοῦ υἱοῦ αὐτοῦ καθαρίζει ἡμᾶς
and the blood of Jesus Christ the Son of Him cleanses us
575 3956 266 1437/ 2036 3754 266 3756 2192
8 ἀπὸ πάσης ἁμαρτίας. ἐὰν εἴπωμεν ὅτι ἁμαρτίαν οὐκ ἔχομεν,
from all sin. If we say that sin not we have,
1438 4105 225 3756 2076/1722/2254/1437
9 ἑαυτοὺς πλανῶμεν, καὶ ἡ ἀλήθεια οὐκ ἔστιν ἐν ἡμῖν. ἐὰν
ourselves we deceive, and the truth not is in us. If
3670 266 2257 4103 2076 1342
ὁμολογῶμεν τὰς ἁμαρτίας ἡμῶν, πιστός ἐστι καὶ δίκαιος
we confess the sins of us, faithful He is and righteous,

He may forgive us the sins, and may cleanse us from all unrighteousness. [10]If we say that we have not sinned, we make Him a liar, and His word is not in us.

CHAPTER 2

[1]My little children, I write these things to you so that you do not sin. And if anyone sins, we have an advocate with the Father, Jesus Christ *the* righteous. [2]And He is *the* propitiation relating to our sins, and not relating to ours only, but also relating to all the world. [3]And by this we know that we have known Him, if we keep His commands. [4]The *one* saying, I have known Him, and not keeping His commands is a liar, and the truth is not in that one. [5]But whoever keeps His word, truly in this one the love of God has been perfected. By this we know that we are in Him. [6]The *one* saying to rest in Him ought so to walk himself as that *One* walked.

[7]Brothers, I do not write a new commandment to you, but an old commandment which you had from *the* beginning. The old commandment is the word which you heard from *the* beginning. [8]Again I write a new commandment to you which is true in Him and in you, because the darkness is passing away, and the true Light already shines. [9]The *one* saying to be in the light, yet hating his brother, is in the darkness until now. [10]The *one* loving his brother rests in the light, and no offense is in him. [11]But the *one* hating his brother is in the darkness, and walks in the darkness, and does not

2443/863/ 2254 266 2511 2248 575 3956
ἵνα ἀφῇ ἡμῖν τὰς ἁμαρτίας, καὶ καθαρίσῃ ἡμᾶς ἀπὸ πάσης
that He may forgive us the sins, and may cleanse us from all
93 1437/ 2036 3754/3756/ 264 5583 4160
10 ἀδικίας. ἐὰν εἴπωμεν ὅτι οὐχ ἡμαρτήκαμεν, ψεύστην ποιοῦ-
unrighteousness. If we say that not we have sinned, a liar we
846 3056 848/ 3756 2076/1722/2254
μεν αὐτόν, καὶ ὁ λόγος αὐτοῦ οὐκ ἔστιν ἐν ἡμῖν.
make Him, and the word of Him not is in us.

CHAPTER 2

5040/3450 5024 1125 5213/2443/3363/ 264 1437
1 Τεκνία μου, ταῦτα γράφω ὑμῖν, ἵνα μὴ ἁμάρτητε. καὶ ἐάν
Little children of me, these I write to you, that not you sin. And if
5100 264 3875 2192 4314 3962 2424
τις ἁμάρτῃ, παράκλητον ἔχομεν πρὸς τὸν πατέρα, Ἰησοῦν
anyone sins, an advocate we have with the Father, Jesus
5547 1342 846 2434 2076/4012 266
2 Χριστὸν δίκαιον· καὶ αὐτὸς ἱλασμός ἐστι περὶ τῶν ἁμαρτιῶν
Christ (the) righteous; and He a propitiation is concerning the sins
2257/3756/4012 2251 3440 235 4012 3650
ἡμῶν· οὐ περὶ τῶν ἡμετέρων δὲ μόνον, ἀλλὰ καὶ περὶ ὅλου
of us; not concerning ours and only, but also concerning all
2889 1722 5129 1097 3754 1097 846
3 τοῦ κόσμου. καὶ ἐν τούτῳ γινώσκομεν ὅτι ἐγνώκαμεν αὐτόν,
the world. And by this we know that we have known Him,
1437 1785 848 5083 3004 1097 846
4 ἐὰν τὰς ἐντολὰς αὐτοῦ τηρῶμεν. ὁ λέγων, Ἔγνωκα αὐτόν,
if the commands of Him we keep. The (one) saying, I have known Him,
1785 848 3361 5083 5583 2076 1722 5129
καὶ τὰς ἐντολὰς αὐτοῦ μὴ τηρῶν, ψεύστης ἐστί, καὶ ἐν τούτῳ
and the commands of Him not keeping a liar is, and in this one
1223 225 3756/2076/3739/302/5083 848 3056 230
5 ἡ ἀλήθεια οὐκ ἔστιν· ὃς δ᾽ ἂν τηρῇ αὐτοῦ τὸν λόγον, ἀληθῶς
the truth not is. whoever But keeps of Him the word, truly
1722 5129 26 2316 5048 1722 5129 1097
ἐν τούτῳ ἡ ἀγάπη τοῦ Θεοῦ τετελείωται. ἐν τούτῳ γινώ-
in this one the love of God has been perfected. By this we know
3754/1722/846 2070 3004/1722/ 846 3306 3784
6 σκομεν ὅτι ἐν αὐτῷ ἐσμέν· ὁ λέγων ἐν αὐτῷ μένειν ὀφείλει,
that in Him we are. The (one) saying in Him to remain ought
2531 1565 4043 848 3779 4043
καθὼς ἐκεῖνος περιεπάτησε, καὶ αὐτὸς οὕτω περιπατεῖν.
as that (One) walked, also himself so to walk.
80 3756 1785 2537 1125 5213 235 1785
7 Ἀδελφοί, οὐκ ἐντολὴν καινὴν γράφω ὑμῖν, ἀλλ᾽ ἐντολὴν
Brothers, not a commandment new I write to you, but a commandment
3820 3739 2192 575 746 1785 3820 2076
παλαιάν, ἣν εἴχετε ἀπ᾽ ἀρχῆς· ἡ ἐντολὴ ἡ παλαιά ἐστιν ὁ
old, which you had from (the) beginning the commandment old is the
3056/3739/ 191 575 746 3825 1785 2537 1125
8 λόγος ὃν ἠκούσατε ἀπ᾽ ἀρχῆς. πάλιν ἐντολὴν καινὴν γράφω
word which you have heard from (the) beginning. Again commandment new I write
5213/3739/2076/ 227/1722/846 1722/5213/3754 4653 3855
ὑμῖν, ὅ ἐστιν ἀληθὲς ἐν αὐτῷ καὶ ἐν ὑμῖν· ὅτι ἡ σκοτία παρ-
to you, what is true in Him and in you, because the darkness is
5457 228 2235 5316 3004/1722 5457
9 άγεται, καὶ τὸ φῶς τὸ ἀληθινὸν ἤδη φαίνει. ὁ λέγων ἐν τῷ φωτὶ
passing away, and the light true already shines. He saying in the light
1511 80 848 3404/1722 4653 2076 2193
εἶναι καὶ τὸν ἀδελφὸν αὐτοῦ μισῶν, ἐν τῇ σκοτίᾳ ἐστὶν ἕως
to be and the brother of him hating in the darkness is until
737 25 80 848/1722 5457 3306
10 ἄρτι. ὁ ἀγαπῶν τὸν ἀδελφὸν αὐτοῦ ἐν τῷ φωτὶ μένει, καὶ
now. He loving the brother of him, in the light rests, and
4625 1722 846/3756 2076 3404 80
11 σκάνδαλον ἐν αὐτῷ οὐκ ἔστιν. ὁ δὲ μισῶν τὸν ἀδελφὸν
offense in him not is. the (one) But hating the brother
848/1722 4653 2076 1722 4653 4043 3756
αὐτοῦ ἐν τῇ σκοτίᾳ ἐστί, καὶ ἐν τῇ σκοτίᾳ περιπατεῖ, καὶ οὐκ
of him, in the darkness is, and in the darkness walks, and not

know where he is going, because the darkness blinded his eyes.

[12]Little children, I write to you because you have been forgiven *your* sins through His name. [13]Fathers, I write to you because you have known Him from *the* beginning. I write to you, young men, because you overcome the evil one. I write to you, young ones, because you have known the Father. [14]Fathers, I wrote to you because you have known Him from *the* beginning. I wrote to you, young men, because you are strong, and the word of God abides in you, and you have overcome the evil one.

[15]Do not love the world nor the things in the world. If anyone loves the world, the love of the Father is not in him, [16]because all that which *is* in the world: the lust of the flesh, and the lust of the eyes, and the pride of life, is not of the Father, but is of the world. [17]And the world is passing away, and its lust. But the *one* doing the will of God abides forever.

[18]Young ones, it is a last hour, and as you heard that the antichrist is coming, even now many antichrists have risen up; from which you know that it is a last hour. [19]They went out from us, but they were not of us. For if they were of us, they would have remained with us; but *they left* so that it might be revealed that they all are not of us. [20]And you have an anointing from the Holy One, and you know all things. [21]I did not write to you because you do not know the truth, but because you know it, and because every lie is not of the truth. [22]Who is the liar, except the *one* denying, *saying* that Jesus is not the Christ? This

1492/4226 5217 3754 4653 5186 3788
οἶδε ποῦ ὑπάγει, ὅτι ἡ σκοτία ἐτύφλωσε τοὺς ὀφθαλμοὺς
knows where he is going; for the darkness blinded • the eyes
848
αὐτοῦ.
of him.
1125/5213 5040 3754 863 5213 266 1223
12 Γράφω ὑμῖν, τεκνία, ὅτι ἀφέωνται ὑμῖν αἱ ἁμαρτίαι διὰ
I write to you, little children, for have been forgiven you the sins because of
3686 848 1125/5213 3962 3754 1097
13 τὸ ὄνομα αὐτοῦ. γράφω ὑμῖν, πατέρες, ὅτι ἐγνώκατε τὸν
the name of Him. I write to you, fathers, because you have known the (One)
575 746 1125 5213 3495 3754 3528 4190
ἀπ᾽ ἀρχῆς. γράφω ὑμῖν, νεανίσκοι, ὅτι νενικήκατε τὸν πονη-
from beginning. I write to you, young men, because you have overcome. the evil
*3962 1125 5213 3813 3754 1097 1125
14 ρόν. γράφω ὑμῖν, παιδία, ὅτι ἐγνώκατε τὸν πατέρα. ἔγραψα
one. I wrote to you, young ones, for you have known the Father. I wrote
5213 3962 3754 1097 575 746 1125 5213
ὑμῖν, πατέρες, ὅτι ἐγνώκατε τὸν ἀπ᾽ ἀρχῆς. ἔγραψα ὑμῖν,
to you, fathers, because you have known * the (One) from beginning. I wrote to you
*2075 3495 3754 2478 3056 2316/1722/5213
νεανίσκοι, ὅτι ἰσχυροί ἐστε, καὶ ὁ λόγος τοῦ Θεοῦ ἐν ὑμῖν
young men, that strong you are, and the word of God in you
3306 3528 4190 3361 25 2889
15 μένει, καὶ νενικήκατε τὸν πονηρόν. μὴ ἀγαπᾶτε τὸν κόσμον,
remains, and you have overcome the evil one. Do not love the world,
3366 1722 2889 1437/5100/ 25 2889 3756 2076
μηδὲ τὰ ἐν τῷ κόσμῳ. ἐάν τις ἀγαπᾷ τὸν κόσμον, οὐκ ἔστιν
nor the things in the world. If anyone loves the world, not is
26 3962/1722/ 846 3754/3956 1722 2889
16 ἡ ἀγάπη τοῦ πατρὸς ἐν αὐτῷ. ὅτι πᾶν τὸ ἐν τῷ κόσμῳ, ἡ
the love of the Father in him; because all that in the world. the
1939 4561 1939 which (is) 3788
ἐπιθυμία τῆς σαρκός, καὶ ἡ ἐπιθυμία τῶν ὀφθαλμῶν, καὶ ἡ
lust of the flesh, and the lust of the eyes, and the
212 979 3756 2076/1537 3962 235/1537
ἀλαζονεία τοῦ βίου, οὐκ ἔστιν ἐκ τοῦ πατρός, ἀλλ᾽ ἐκ τοῦ
pride of life, not is of the Father, but of the
2889 2076 2889 3855 1939 848
17 κόσμου ἐστί. καὶ ὁ κόσμος παράγεται, καὶ ἡ ἐπιθυμία αὐτοῦ·
world is. And the world is passing away, and the lust of it;
4160 2307 2316 3306/1519 165
ὁ δὲ ποιῶν τὸ θέλημα τοῦ Θεοῦ μένει εἰς τὸν αἰῶνα.
he but doing the will of God remains to the age.
3813 2078 5610 2076 2531 191 3754
18 Παιδία, ἐσχάτη ὥρα ἐστί· καὶ καθὼς ἠκούσατε ὅτι ὁ
Young ones, a last hour it is, and as you heard that the
500 2064 3568 500 4183 1096
ἀντίχριστος ἔρχεται, καὶ νῦν ἀντίχριστοι πολλοὶ γεγόνασιν·
antichrist is coming, even now antichrists many have come to be;
3606 1097 3754 2078 5610 2076/1537/2257 1831
19 ὅθεν γινώσκομεν ὅτι ἐσχάτη ὥρα ἐστίν. ἐξ ἡμῶν ἐξῆλθον,
from which you know that a last hour it is. From us they went out
235 3756 2258/1537/2257/1487/1063/2258/1537/2257 3306
ἀλλ᾽ οὐκ ἦσαν ἐξ ἡμῶν· εἰ γὰρ ἦσαν ἐξ ἡμῶν, μεμενήκεισαν
but not they were of us; if for they were of us, they have remained
302/3326/2257 235 2443 5319 3754/3756/1526/3956
ἂν μεθ᾽ ἡμῶν· ἀλλ᾽ ἵνα φανερωθῶσιν ὅτι οὐκ εἰσὶ πάντες
would with us; but that it might be revealed that not they are all
1537/2257 5210 5545 2192 575 40 1492
20 ἐξ ἡμῶν. καὶ ὑμεῖς χρίσμα ἔχετε ἀπὸ τοῦ ἁγίου, καὶ οἴδατε
of us And you an anointing have from the Holy One, and you know
3956 3756 1125 5213/3754/3756 1492 225 235
21 πάντα. οὐκ ἔγραψα ὑμῖν, ὅτι οὐκ οἴδατε τὴν ἀλήθειαν, ἀλλ᾽
all. Not I wrote to you because not you know the truth, but
3754 1492 846 3754/3956/5579/1537 225 3756
ὅτι οἴδατε αὐτήν, καὶ ὅτι πᾶν ψεῦδος ἐκ τῆς ἀληθείας οὐκ
because you know it, and because every lie of the truth not
2076/5101/2076 5583 =1508= 720 3754 2424 3756
22 ἐστι. τίς ἐστιν ὁ ψεύστης, εἰ μὴ ὁ ἀρνούμενος ὅτι Ἰησοῦς οὐκ
is. Who is the liar, except the (one) denying that Jesus not

is the antichrist, the *one* denying the Father and the Son. [23]Everyone denying the Son does not have the Father. The *one* confessing the Son also has the Father. [24]Then what you heard from *the* beginning, let it abide in you. If what you heard from *the* beginning abides in you, you will abide both in the Son and in the Father. [25]And this is the promise which He promised us: everlasting life.

[26]I wrote these things to you concerning the ones leading you astray. [27]And the anointing which you received from Him abides in you, and you have no need that anyone teach you. But as His anointing teaches you concerning all things, and is true, and is not a lie, and as He taught you, abide in Him. [28]And now, little children, abide in Him, that when He is revealed we may have confidence, and not be shamed from Him in His coming. [29]If you know that He is righteous, know that everyone doing righteousness has been born of Him.

CHAPTER 3

[1]See what manner of love the Father has given us, that we may be called children of God. For this reason the world does not know us, because it did not know Him. [2]Beloved, now we are the children of God, and it was not yet revealed what we shall be. But we know that if He is revealed, we shall be like Him, because we shall see Him as He is. [3]And everyone having this hope on Him purifies himself, even as that *One* is pure. [4]Everyone practicing sin also

2076 5547 3778 2076 500 720
ἐστιν ὁ Χριστός; οὗτός ἐστιν ὁ ἀντίχριστος, ὁ ἀρνούμενος
is the Christ? This is the antichrist, the (one) denying
3962 5207 3956 720 5207 3761
23 τὸν πατέρα καὶ τὸν υἱόν. πᾶς ὁ ἀρνούμενος τὸν υἱὸν οὐδὲ
the Father and the Son. Everyone denying the Son neither
3962 2192 3671 5207 3962 2192
τὸν πατέρα ἔχει· ὁ ὁμολογῶν τὸν υἱὸν καὶ τὸν πατέρα ἔχει.
the Father has; the (one) confessing the Son also the Father has.
5210 3767/3739/ 191 575 746 1722/5213/ 3306 1437/1722
24 ὑμεῖς οὖν ὃ ἠκούσατε ἀπ' ἀρχῆς, ἐν ὑμῖν μενέτω. ἐὰν ἐν
you then What you heard from (the) beginning, in you let it remain. If in
5213 3306/3739/575/ 746 191 5210/1722 5207
ὑμῖν μείνῃ ὃ ἀπ' ἀρχῆς ἠκούσατε, καὶ ὑμεῖς ἐν τῷ υἱῷ καὶ
you remains what from beginning you heard, both you in the Son and
1722 3962 3306 3778/2076 1860 3739 846
25 ἐν τῷ πατρὶ μενεῖτε. καὶ αὕτη ἐστὶν ἡ ἐπαγγελία ἣν αὐτὸς
in the Father will remain. And this is the promise which He
1861 5213 2222 166 5023 1125
26 ἐπηγγείλατο ἡμῖν, τὴν ζωὴν τὴν αἰώνιον. ταῦτα ἔγραψα
promised us the life everlasting. These things I wrote
5213 4012 4105 5209 5210 5545/3739
27 ὑμῖν περὶ τῶν πλανώντων ὑμᾶς. καὶ ὑμεῖς, τὸ χρίσμα ὃ
to you concerning those leading astray you. And you the anointing which
2983 575 846/1722/5213/3306 3756 5532 2192/2443/5100
ἐλάβετε ἀπ' αὐτοῦ ἐν ὑμῖν μένει, καὶ οὐ χρείαν ἔχετε ἵνα τις
received from Him in you remains, and no need you have that anyone
1321 5209 235/5613 846 5545 1321 5209 4012
διδάσκῃ ὑμᾶς· ἀλλ' ὡς τὸ αὐτὸ χρίσμα διδάσκει ὑμᾶς περὶ
teach you; but as the of Him anointing teaches you concerning
3956 227 2076 3756 2076 5579 2531
πάντων, καὶ ἀληθές ἐστι, καὶ οὐκ ἔστι ψεῦδος, καὶ καθὼς
all things, and true is, and not is a lie, and as
1321 5209 3306/1722 846 3568 5040 3306 1722
28 ἐδίδαξεν ὑμᾶς, μενεῖτε ἐν αὐτῷ. καὶ νῦν, τεκνία, μένετε ἐν
He taught you, remain in Him. And now, little children, remain in
846 2443 3752 5319 2192 3954 3361
αὐτῷ· ἵνα ὅταν φανερωθῇ, ἔχωμεν παρρησίαν, καὶ μὴ
in Him, that when He is revealed we may have confidence, and not
153 575 846/1722 3952 848 1437 1492
29 αἰσχυνθῶμεν ἀπ' αὐτοῦ ἐν τῇ παρουσίᾳ αὐτοῦ. ἐὰν εἰδῆτε
be shamed from Him in the coming of Him. If you know
3754 1342 2076 1097 3754 3956 4160 1343
ὅτι δίκαιός ἐστι, γινώσκετε ὅτι πᾶς ὁ ποιῶν τὴν δικαιοσύνην
that righteous He is, know that everyone doing the righteousness,
1537/846 1080
ἐξ αὐτοῦ γεγέννηται.
of Him has been born.

CHAPTER 3

1492 4217 26 1325 2254 3962 2443 5043
1 Ἴδετε ποταπὴν ἀγάπην δέδωκεν ἡμῖν ὁ πατήρ, ἵνα τέκνα
See what manner of love has given us the Father, that children
2316 2564 1223 5124 2889 3656/ 1097 2248 3754
Θεοῦ κληθῶμεν. διὰ τοῦτο ὁ κόσμος οὐ γινώσκει ἡμᾶς, ὅτι
of God we may be called. Therefore the world not knows us, because
3756/1097 846 27 5043 2316 2070 3768
2 οὐκ ἔγνω αὐτόν. ἀγαπητοί, νῦν τέκνα Θεοῦ ἐσμέν, καὶ οὔπω
not it knew Him. Beloved, now children of God we are, and not yet
5319 5101 2071 1492 3754/1437 5319 3664
ἐφανερώθη τί ἐσόμεθα· οἴδαμεν δὲ ὅτι ἐὰν φανερωθῇ, ὅμοιοι
was it revealed what we shall be, we know but that if He is revealad, like
846 2071 3754 3700 846 2531 2076 3956
3 αὐτῷ ἐσόμεθα, ὅτι ὀψόμεθα αὐτὸν καθώς ἐστι. καὶ πᾶς ὁ
Him we shall be, because we shall see Him as He is. And everyone
2192 1680 5026 1909 846 48 1438 2531
ἔχων τὴν ἐλπίδα ταύτην ἐπ' αὐτῷ ἁγνίζει ἑαυτόν, καθὼς
having hope this on him purifies himself, as
1565 53 2076 3956 4160 266
4 ἐκεῖνος ἁγνός ἐστι. πᾶς ὁ ποιῶν τὴν ἁμαρτίαν, καὶ τὴν
that (One) pure is. Everyone doing sin, also

practices lawlessness, and sin is lawlessness. [5]And you know that He was revealed that He might bear our sins; and sin is not in Him.

[6]Everyone remaining in Him does not sin. Everyone sinning has not seen Him, nor known Him. [7]Little children, let no one lead you astray; the *one* practicing righteousness is righteous, even as that One is righteous. [8]The *one* practicing sin is of the Devil, because the Devil sins from *the* beginning. For this the Son of God was revealed, that He undo the works of the Devil. [9]Everyone who has been begotten of God does not sin, because His seed abides in him, and he is not able to sin, because he has been born of God. [10]By this the children of God and the children of the Devil are revealed: Everyone not practicing righteousness is not of God; also the *one* not loving his brother. [11]Because this is the message which you heard from *the* beginning, that we should love one another, [12]not as Cain was of the evil one, and killed his brother. And for what did he kill him? Because his works were evil, but the things of his brother *were* righteous.

[13]Do not marvel, my brothers, if the world hates you. [14]We know that we have passed from death to life because we love the brothers. The *one* not loving the brother remains in death. [15]Everyone hating the brother is a murderer, and you know that every murderer does not have everlasting life abiding in him.

[16]By this we have known the love of God, because

458 4160 266 2076 458 1492
5 ἀνομίαν ποιεῖ· καὶ ἡ ἁμαρτία ἐστὶν ἡ ἀνομία. καὶ οἴδατε ὅτι
lawlessness does; and sin is lawlessness. And you know that
1565 5319 2443 266 2257 142 266
ἐκεῖνος ἐφανερώθη, ἵνα τὰς ἁμαρτίας ἡμῶν ἄρῃ· καὶ ἁμαρτία
that (One) was revealed that the sins of us He might bear, and sin
1722/846/3756/2076/3956 1722/846 3306 3756 264 3956
6 ἐν αὐτῷ οὐκ ἔστι. πᾶς ὁ ἐν αὐτῷ μένων οὐχ ἁμαρτάνει· πᾶς
in Him not is. Everyone in Him remaining not sins; everyone
264 3756 3708 846 3761 1097 846
ὁ ἁμαρτάνων οὐχ ἑώρακεν αὐτόν, οὐδὲ ἔγνωκεν αὐτόν.
sinning not has seen Him, nor known Him.
5038 3367 4105 5209 4160 1343
7 τεκνία, μηδεὶς πλανάτω ὑμᾶς· ὁ ποιῶν τὴν δικαιοσύνην
Little children, no one let lead astray you; he doing righteousness
1342 2076 2531 1565 1342 2076 4160
8 δίκαιός ἐστι, καθὼς ἐκεῖνος δίκαιός ἐστιν· ὁ ποιῶν τὴν
righteous is, even as that One righteous is. The (one) doing
266 1537 1228 2076 3754/575 746 1228
ἁμαρτίαν ἐκ τοῦ διαβόλου ἐστίν, ὅτι ἀπ' ἀρχῆς ὁ διάβολος
sin of the Devil is, because from (the) beginning the Devil
264 1519 5124 5319 5207 2316/2443/3089
ἁμαρτάνει. εἰς τοῦτο ἐφανερώθη ὁ υἱὸς τοῦ Θεοῦ, ἵνα λύσῃ
sins. For this was revealed the Son of God, that He undo
2041 1228 3956 1080 1537 2316
9 τὰ ἔργα τοῦ διαβόλου. πᾶς ὁ γεγεννημένος ἐκ τοῦ Θεοῦ
the works of the Devil. Everyone having been begotten of God
266 3756/4160/3754 4690 848/1722/846 3306 3756
ἁμαρτίαν οὐ ποιεῖ, ὅτι σπέρμα αὐτοῦ ἐν αὐτῷ μένει· καὶ οὐ
sin not does, because seed of Him in him remains; and not
1410 264 3754/1537 2316 1080 1722 5129
10 δύναται ἁμαρτάνειν, ὅτι ἐκ τοῦ Θεοῦ γεγέννηται. ἐν τούτῳ
he is able to sin, because of God he has been born. By this
5318 2076 5043 2316 5043 1228
φανερά ἐστι τὰ τέκνα τοῦ Θεοῦ καὶ τὰ τέκνα τοῦ διαβόλου·
revealed are the children of God and the children of the Devil:
3956 3361 4160 1343 3756/2076/1537 2316 3361
πᾶς ὁ μὴ ποιῶν δικαιοσύνην οὐκ ἔστιν ἐκ τοῦ Θεοῦ, καὶ ὁ μὴ
Everyone not doing righteousness not is of God; also he not
25 80 848 3754 3778 2076 31 3739
11 ἀγαπῶν τὸν ἀδελφὸν αὐτοῦ. ὅτι αὕτη ἐστὶν ἡ ἀγγελία ἣν
loving the brother of him. Because this is the message which
191 575 746 2443 25 240 3756 2531
12 ἠκούσατε ἀπ' ἀρχῆς, ἵνα ἀγαπῶμεν ἀλλήλους· οὐ καθὼς
you heard from (the) beginning, that we should love one another; not as
2535/1737 4190 2258 4969 80 848
Κάϊν ἐκ τοῦ πονηροῦ ἦν, καὶ ἔσφαξε τὸν ἀδελφὸν αὐτοῦ. καὶ
Cain of the evil one was, and killed the brother of him; and
5484 5101 4969 846 3754 2041 848 4190 2258
χάριν τίνος ἔσφαξεν αὐτόν; ὅτι τὰ ἔργα αὐτοῦ πονηρὰ ἦν,
for the sake of what did he kill him? because the works of him evil were;
80 848 1342
τὰ δὲ τοῦ ἀδελφοῦ αὐτοῦ δίκαια.
the things but of the brother of him (were) righteous.
3361/ 2296 80 3450/1487/3404/5209 2889 2249
13 Μὴ θαυμάζετε, ἀδελφοί μου, εἰ μισεῖ ὑμᾶς ὁ κόσμος· ἡμεῖς
14 Do not marvel, brothers of me, if hates you the world. We
1492 3754 3327 1537 2288 1519 2222 3754
οἴδαμεν ὅτι μεταβεβήκαμεν ἐκ τοῦ θανάτου εἰς τὴν ζωήν, ὅτι
know that we have passed from death to life, because
25 80 3361 25 80
ἀγαπῶμεν τοὺς ἀδελφούς. ὁ μὴ ἀγαπῶν τὸν ἀδελφόν,
we love the brothers. The (one) not loving the brother
3306/1722 2288 3956 3404 80 848 443
15 μένει ἐν τῷ θανάτῳ. πᾶς ὁ μισῶν τὸν ἀδελφὸν αὐτοῦ ἀνθρω-
remains in death. Everyone hating the brother of him a murderer
2076 1492/3754/3956/ 443 3756 2192
ποκτόνος ἐστί· καὶ οἴδατε ὅτι πᾶς ἀνθρωποκτόνος οὐκ ἔχει
is, and you know that every murderer not has
2222 166 1722 846 3306 1722 5129 1097
16 ζωὴν αἰώνιον ἐν αὐτῷ μένουσαν. ἐν τούτῳ ἐγνώκαμεν τὴν
life everlasting in him remaining. By this we have known the

that *One* laid down His soul for us; and on behalf of the brothers we ought to lay down *our* souls. [17]Whoever has the means of life of the world, and sees his brother having need, and shuts up his bowels from him, how does the love of God abide in him?

[18]My little children, let us not love in word, or in tongue, but in deed and in truth. [19]And in this we shall know that we are of the truth, and shall persuade our hearts before Him, [20]that if our heart accuses us, *we know* that God is greater than our heart and knows all things. [21]Beloved, if our heart does not accuse us, we have confidence with God. [22]And whatever we ask, we receive from Him, because we keep His commandments, and we do the things pleasing before Him. [23]And this is His commandment, that we should believe the name of His Son, Jesus Christ, and love one another, even as He gave command to us. [24]And the *one* keeping His commandments abides in Him, and He in him. And by this we know that He abides in us, by the Spirit, which He gave to us.

26 2316 3754 1565 5228 2257 5590 848
ἀγάπην τοῦ Θεοῦ, ὅτι ἐκεῖνος ὑπὲρ ἡμῶν τὴν ψυχὴν αὐτοῦ
love of God, because that (One) for us the soul of Him
5087 2249 3784 5228 80 5590
ἔθηκε· καὶ ἡμεῖς ὀφείλομεν ὑπὲρ τῶν ἀδελφῶν τὰς ψυχὰς
laid down; and we ought on behalf of the brothers the souls
5087 3739/1223/302/2192 979 2889 2334
17 τιθέναι. ὃς δ' ἂν ἔχῃ τὸν βίον τοῦ κόσμου, καὶ θεωρῇ τὸν
to lay down. Whoever has the means of life of the world, and beholds the
80 848 5532 2192 2808 4698
ἀδελφὸν αὐτοῦ χρείαν ἔχοντα, καὶ κλείσῃ τὰ σπλάγχνα
brother of him need having, and shuts up the bowels
848 575 856 4459 26 2316 3306/1722/846
αὐτοῦ ἀπ' αὐτοῦ, πῶς ἡ ἀγάπη τοῦ Θεοῦ μένει ἐν αὐτῷ;
of him from him, how the love of God remains in him?
5038 3450/3361/ 25 3056 3366 1100 235 2041
18 τεκνία μου, μὴ ἀγαπῶμεν λόγῳ μηδὲ γλώσσῃ ἀλλ' ἔργῳ
Little children of me, not let us love in word, nor in tongue, but in work
225 1722 5129 1097 3754/1537 225
19 καὶ ἀληθείᾳ. καὶ ἐν τούτῳ γινώσκομεν ὅτι ἐκ τῆς ἀληθείας
and truth. And in this we shall know that of the truth
2070 1715 846 3982 2588 2257
ἐσμέν, καὶ ἔμπροσθεν αὐτοῦ πείσομεν τὰς καρδίας ἡμῶν,
we are, and before Him shall persuade the heart of us,
3754/1437 2607 2257 2588 3754 3187 2076
20 ὅτι ἐὰν καταγινώσκῃ ἡμῶν ἡ καρδία, ὅτι μείζων ἐστὶν ὁ
that if accuses of us the heart, that greater is
2316 2588 2257 1097 3956 27
21 Θεὸς τῆς καρδίας ἡμῶν, καὶ γινώσκει πάντα. ἀγαπητοί,
God (than) the heart of us and knows all things. Beloved,
1437 2588 2257/3361 2607 2257 3954
ἐὰν ἡ καρδία ἡμῶν μὴ καταγινώσκῃ ἡμῶν, παρρησίαν
if the heart of us not accuses us, confidence
2192 4314 2316 3739/1437 154 2983 3844
22 ἔχομεν πρὸς τὸν Θεόν, καὶ ὃ ἐὰν αἰτῶμεν, λαμβάνομεν παρ'
we have with God, and whatever we ask we receive from
846 3754 1785 848 5083 701
αὐτοῦ, ὅτι τὰς ἐντολὰς αὐτοῦ τηροῦμεν, καὶ τὰ ἀρεστὰ
Him, because the commandments of Him we keep, and the things pleasing
1799 846 4160 3778 2076 1785 848
23 ἐνώπιον αὐτοῦ ποιοῦμεν. καὶ αὕτη ἐστὶν ἡ ἐντολὴ αὐτοῦ,
before Him we do. And this is the commandment of Him,
2443 4100 3686 5207 848 2424 5547
ἵνα πιστεύσωμεν τῷ ὀνόματι τοῦ υἱοῦ αὐτοῦ Ἰησοῦ Χρι-
that we should believe the name of the Son of Him, Jesus Christ,
25 240 2531 1325 1785 2254
στοῦ, καὶ ἀγαπῶμεν ἀλλήλους, καθὼς ἔδωκεν ἐντολὴν ἡμῖν.
and love one another, even as He gave command to us.
5083 1785 848 1722 846 3306 846 1722
24 καὶ ὁ τηρῶν τὰς ἐντολὰς αὐτοῦ ἐν αὐτῷ μένει, καὶ αὐτὸς ἐν
And he keeping the commandments of Him in Him remains, and He in
1722 846 1722 5129 1097 3754 3306 /*/ 2254/1537
αὐτῷ. καὶ ἐν τούτῳ γινώσκομεν ὅτι μένει ἐν ἡμῖν, ἐκ τοῦ
him. And by this we know that He remains in us, by the
4151 3739/2254/ 1325
Πνεύματος οὗ ἡμῖν ἔδωκεν.
Spirit which to us He gave.

CHAPTER 4

[1]Beloved, do not believe every spirit, but test the spirits, whether they are from God; for many false prophets have gone forth into the world. [2]By this know the Spirit of God: every spirit which confesses that Jesus Christ

CHAPTER 4

27 3361 3956 4151 4100 235 1381
1 Ἀγαπητοί, μὴ παντὶ πνεύματι πιστεύετε, ἀλλὰ δοκι-
Beloved, not every spirit believe, but test
4151 1487/1537 2316 2076 3754 4183
μάζετε τὰ πνεύματα, εἰ ἐκ τοῦ Θεοῦ ἐστίν· ὅτι πολλοὶ
the spirits, if of God they are, because many
5578 1831 1519 2889 1722 5129
2 ψευδοπροφῆται ἐξεληλύθασιν εἰς τὸν κόσμον. ἐν τούτῳ
false prophets have gone forth into the world. By this
1097 4151 2316 3956 4151 3670
γινώσκετε τὸ Πνεῦμα τοῦ Θεοῦ· πᾶν πνεῦμα ὃ ὁμολογεῖ
know the Spirit of God: every spirit which confesses

has come in *the* flesh is from God. [3]And every spirit which does not confess that Jesus Christ has come in *the* flesh is not from God; and this is the antichrist which you heard is coming, and now is already in the world. [4]Little children, you are of God and have overcome them, because He in you is greater than he in the world. [5]They are of the world; therefore they speak of the world, and the world hears them. [6]We are of God; the *one* knowing God hears us. Whoever is not of God does not hear us. From this we know the spirit of truth and the spirit of error.

2424 5547 1722/4561 2064 1537 2316 2076
Ἰησοῦν Χριστὸν ἐν σαρκὶ ἐληλυθότα ἐκ τοῦ Θεοῦ ἐστί·
Jesus Christ in (the) flesh having come, of God is.
3956 4151 3739/3361/ 3670 2424 5547 1722
3 καὶ πᾶν πνεῦμα ὃ μὴ ὁμολογεῖ τὸν Ἰησοῦν Χριστὸν ἐν
And every spirit which not confesses Jesus Christ in
4561 2064 1537 2316 3756 2076 5124 2076
σαρκὶ ἐληλυθότα, ἐκ τοῦ Θεοῦ οὐκ ἔστι· καὶ τοῦτό ἐστι τὸ
(the) flesh having come, of God not is; and this is the
500 3739 191 3754 2064 3568/1722
τοῦ ἀντιχρίστου, ὃ ἀκηκόατε ὅτι ἔρχεται, καὶ νῦν ἐν τῷ
antichrist which you heard that it is coming, and now in the
2889 2076 2235 5210/1537 2316 2076 5040
4 κόσμῳ ἐστὶν ἤδη. ὑμεῖς ἐκ τοῦ Θεοῦ ἐστέ, τεκνία, καὶ
world is already. You of God are, little children, and
3528 846 3754 3187 2076 1722 5213/2228 1722
νενικήκατε αὐτούς· ὅτι μείζων ἐστὶν ὁ ἐν ὑμῖν ἢ ὁ ἐν τῷ
have overcome them, because greater is the (One) in you than the in the
2889 846/1537 2889 1526 1223 5124/1537 (one) 2889
5 κόσμῳ. αὐτοὶ ἐκ τοῦ κόσμου εἰσί· διὰ τοῦτο ἐκ τοῦ κόσμου
world. They of the world are; therefore of the world
2980 2889 846 191 2249/1537 2316
6 λαλοῦσι, καὶ ὁ κόσμος αὐτῶν ἀκούει. ἡμεῖς ἐκ τοῦ Θεοῦ
they speak, and the world them hears. We of God
2070 1097 2316 191 2257/3739/3756/2076/1537
ἐσμέν· ὁ γινώσκων τὸν Θεόν, ἀκούει ἡμῶν· ὃς οὐκ ἔστιν ἐκ
are; the (one) knowing God hears us; (he) who not is of
2316 3756 191 2257 1537 5127 1097
τοῦ Θεοῦ, οὐκ ἀκούει ἡμῶν. ἐκ τούτου γινώσκομεν τὸ
God not hears us. From this we know the
4151 225 4151 4106
πνεῦμα τῆς ἀληθείας καὶ τὸ πνεῦμα τῆς πλάνης.
spirit of truth, and the spirit of error.

[7]Beloved, let us love one another, because love is of God, and everyone who loves has been born of God, and knows God. [8]The *one* who does not love has not known God, because God is love. [9]By this the love of God was revealed in us, because His Son, the Only-begotten, God has sent into the world that we might live through Him. [10]In this is love, not that we loved God, but that He loved us, and sent His Son *to be* a propitiation relating to our sins.

27 25 240 3754 26 1537
7 Ἀγαπητοί, ἀγαπῶμεν ἀλλήλους· ὅτι ἡ ἀγάπη ἐκ τοῦ
Beloved, let us love one another, because love of
2316/2076 3956 25 1537 2316 1080
Θεοῦ ἐστί, καὶ πᾶς ὁ ἀγαπῶν ἐκ τοῦ Θεοῦ γεγέννηται, καὶ
God is, and everyone loving, of God has been born, and
1097 2316 3361 25 3756 1097 2316/3754
8 γινώσκει τὸν Θεόν. ὁ μὴ ἀγαπῶν οὐκ ἔγνω τὸν Θεόν· ὅτι
knows God. The (one) not loving not knew God, because
2316 26 2076 1722 5129 5319 26
9 ὁ Θεὸς ἀγάπη ἐστίν. ἐν τούτῳ ἐφανερώθη ἡ ἀγάπη τοῦ
God love is. By this was revealed the love
2316/1722/2254/3754 5207 848 3439 849
Θεοῦ ἐν ἡμῖν, ὅτι τὸν υἱὸν αὐτοῦ τὸν μονογενῆ ἀπέσταλκεν
of God in us, because the Son of Him the only-begotten has sent
2316/1519 2889 2443 2198 1223 846 1722 5129
10 ὁ Θεὸς εἰς τὸν κόσμον, ἵνα ζήσωμεν δι᾽ αὐτοῦ. ἐν τούτῳ
God into the world, that we might live through Him. In this
2076 26 3756/3756/2249 25 2316 235
ἐστὶν ἡ ἀγάπη, οὐχ ὅτι ἡμεῖς ἠγαπήσαμεν τὸν Θεόν, ἀλλ᾽
is love, not that we loved God, but
3754 846 25 2248 649 5207 848
ὅτι αὐτὸς ἠγάπησεν ἡμᾶς, καὶ ἀπέστειλε τὸν υἱὸν αὐτοῦ
that He loved us, and sent the Son of Him
2434 4012 266 2257 27 1487/3779

[11]Beloved, if God so loved us, we also ought to love one another. [12]No one has seen God at any time. If we love one another, God abides in us, and His love having been perfected is in us. [13]By this we know that we abide in Him, and He in us, because of His Spirit He

11 ἱλασμὸν περὶ τῶν ἁμαρτιῶν ἡμῶν. ἀγαπητοί, εἰ οὕτως ὁ
a propitiation concerning the sins of us. Beloved, if so
2316 25 2248 2249 3784 240 25
Θεὸς ἠγάπησεν ἡμᾶς, καὶ ἡμεῖς ὀφείλομεν ἀλλήλους ἀγαπᾷν.
God loved us, also we ought one another to love.
2316 3762 4455 2300 1437 25 240
12 Θεὸν οὐδεὶς πώποτε τεθέαται· ἐὰν ἀγαπῶμεν ἀλλήλους,
God No one ever has beheld; if we love one another,
2316/1722/2254/3306 26 848 5048
ὁ Θεὸς ἐν ἡμῖν μένει, καὶ ἡ ἀγάπη αὐτοῦ τετελειωμένη
God in us remains, and the love of Him having been per-fected
2076/1722/2254/1722/5129 1097 3754/1722/846 3306
13 ἐστὶν ἐν ἡμῖν. ἐν τούτῳ γινώσκομεν ὅτι ἐν αὐτῷ μένομεν καὶ
is in us. By this we know that in Him we remain, and

has given to us. 14 And we have beheld and bear witness that the Father has sent the Son *as* Savior of the world. 15 Whoever confesses that Jesus is the Son of God, God abides in him, and he in God. 16 And we have known and have believed the love which God has in us. God is love, and the *one* abiding in love abides in God, and God in him. 17 By this love has been perfected with us, that we have confidence in the day of judgment, that as He is, we are also in this world.

18 There is no fear in love, but perfect love casts out fear, because fear has punishment; and the *one* fearing has not been perfected in love. 19 We love Him because He first loved us. 20 If anyone says, I love God, and hates his brother, he is a liar. For the *one* not loving his brother whom he has seen, how is he able to love God whom he has not seen? 21 And we have this commandment from Him, that the *one* who loves God also loves his brother.

846/1722/2254/3754/1537 4151 848 1325 2254
αὐτὸς ἐν ἡμῖν, ὅτι ἐκ τοῦ Πνεύματος αὐτοῦ δέδωκεν ἡμῖν.
He in us, because of the Spirit of Him He has given us.

2249 2300 3140 3754 3962 649
14 καὶ ἡμεῖς τεθεάμεθα καὶ μαρτυροῦμεν ὅτι ὁ πατὴρ ἀπέσταλκε
And we we have beheld and bear witness that the Father has sent

5207 4990 2889 3739/302/ 3670 3754 2424
15 τὸν υἱὸν σωτῆρα τοῦ κόσμου. ὃς ἂν ὁμολογήσῃ ὅτι Ἰησοῦς
the Son (as) Savior of the world. Whoever confesses that Jesus

2076 5207 2316 2316/1722/846/3306 846 1722
ἐστὶν ὁ υἱὸς τοῦ Θεοῦ, ὁ Θεὸς ἐν αὐτῷ μένει, καὶ αὐτὸς ἐν
is the Son of God, God in him remains, and he in

2306 2249 1097 4100 26
16 τῷ Θεῷ. καὶ ἡμεῖς ἐγνώκαμεν καὶ πεπιστεύκαμεν τὴν ἀγάπην
God. And we have known and have believed the love

3739/2192 2316/1722/2254 2316 26 2076 3306/1722
ἣν ἔχει ὁ Θεὸς ἐν ἡμῖν. ὁ Θεὸς ἀγάπη ἐστί, καὶ ὁ μένων ἐν τῇ
which has God in us. God love is, and he remaining in

26 1722 2316 3306 2316/1722/846/1722/5129/5048
17 ἀγάπῃ, ἐν τῷ Θεῷ μένει, καὶ ὁ Θεὸς ἐν αὐτῷ. ἐν τούτῳ τετε-
love, in God remains, and God in him. By this has

26 3326/2257/1443 3954 2192/1722
λείωται ἡ ἀγάπη μεθ' ἡμῶν, ἵνα παρρησίαν ἔχωμεν ἐν τῇ
been perfected love with us, that confidence we have in the

2250 2920 3754/2531 1565 2076 2249 2070/1722
ἡμέρᾳ τῆς κρίσεως, ὅτι καθὼς ἐκεῖνός ἐστι, καὶ ἡμεῖς ἐσμὲν ἐν
day of judgment, that as that (One) is, also we are in

2889 5129 5401 3756 2076/1722 26 235
18 τῷ κόσμῳ τούτῳ. φόβος οὐκ ἔστιν ἐν τῇ ἀγάπῃ, ἀλλ' ἡ
world this. Fear not is in love, but

5046 26 1854 906 5401 3754 5401 2851
τελεία ἀγάπη ἔξω βάλλει τὸν φόβον, ὅτι ὁ φόβος κόλασιν
perfect love out casts fear, because fear punishment

2192 5399 3756 5048 1722 26 2249
19 ἔχει ὁ δὲ φοβούμενος οὐ τετελείωται ἐν τῇ ἀγάπῃ. ἡμεῖς
has, the (one) and having feared not has been perfected in love. We

25 846 3754 846 4413 25 2248 1437
20 ἀγαπῶμεν αὐτόν, ὅτι αὐτὸς πρῶτος ἠγάπησεν ἡμᾶς. ἐάν
love Him, because He first loved us. If

5100/2036/3754 25 2316 80 848 3404
τις εἴπῃ ὅτι Ἀγαπῶ τὸν Θεόν, καὶ τὸν ἀδελφὸν αὐτοῦ μισῇ,
anyone says, I love God, and the brother of him hates,

5583 2076 1063/3361 25 80 848 3739
ψεύστης ἐστίν· ὁ γὰρ μὴ ἀγαπῶν τὸν ἀδελφὸν αὐτοῦ ὃν
a liar he is; the (one) for not loving the brother of him whom

3708 2316/3739/3756/3708 4459 1410 25
21 ἑώρακε, τὸν Θεὸν ὃν οὐχ ἑώρακε πῶς δύναται ἀγαπᾶν ; καὶ
he has seen, God whom not he has seen, how is he able to love? And

5026 1785 2192 575 846 2443 25
ταύτην τὴν ἐντολὴν ἔχομεν ἀπ' αὐτοῦ, ἵνα ὁ ἀγαπῶν τὸν
this commandment we have from Him, that the (one) loving

2316/25 80 848
Θεόν, ἀγαπᾷ καὶ τὸν ἀδελφὸν αὐτοῦ.
God, loves also the brother of him.

CHAPTER 5

1 Everyone who believes that Jesus is the Christ has been born of God. And everyone who loves Him who begets also loves the *one* who has been born of Him. 2 By this we know that we love the children of God: when we love God and keep His commandments. 3 For this is the love

CHAPTER 5

3956 4100 3754 2424 2076 5547 1537 2316
1 Πᾶς ὁ πιστεύων ὅτι Ἰησοῦς ἐστὶν ὁ Χριστός, ἐκ τοῦ Θεοῦ
Everyone believing that Jesus is the Christ, of God

1080 3956 25 1080 25
γεγέννηται· καὶ πᾶς ὁ ἀγαπῶν τὸν γεννήσαντα ἀγαπᾷ καὶ
has been born; and everyone loving the (One) begetting, loves also

1080 1537 846 1722 5129 1097 3754
2 τὸν γεγεννημένον ἐξ αὐτοῦ. ἐν τούτῳ γινώσκομεν ὅτι
the (one) having been born of Him. By this we know that

25 5043 2316 3752 2316 25
ἀγαπῶμεν τὰ τέκνα τοῦ Θεοῦ, ὅταν τὸν Θεὸν ἀγαπῶμεν,
we love the children of God, whenever God we love,

1785 848 5083 3778 1063 2076 26
3 καὶ τὰς ἐντολὰς αὐτοῦ τηρῶμεν. αὕτη γάρ ἐστιν ἡ ἀγάπη
and the commandments of Him we keep. this For is the love

of God, that we keep His commandments; and His commandments are not heavy. [4]Because everything having been born of God overcomes the world, and this is the victory overcoming the world, our faith. [5]Who is the *one* overcoming the world except the *one* who believes that Jesus is the Son of God? [6]This is the *One* coming through water and blood, Jesus Christ; not by the water only, but by the water and the blood. And the Spirit is the *One* witnessing, because the Spirit is the truth. [7]*For there are three bearing witness in Heaven: the Father, the Word, and the Holy Spirit; and these three are one.*

[8]And there are three who bear witness on the earth: The Spirit, and the water, and the blood; and the three are to the one. [9]If we receive the witness of men, the witness of God is greater; because this is the witness of God which He has witnessed about His Son: [10]The *one* believing in the Son of God has the witness in himself. The *one* not believing God has made Him a liar, because he has not believed in the witness which God has witnessed concerning His Son. [11]And this is the witness: that God gave us everlasting life, and this life is in His Son. [12]The *one* having the Son has life. The *one* not having the Son of God does not have life.

[13]I wrote these things to you, the ones believing in the name of the Son of God, that you may know that you have everlasting life, and that you may believe in the name of the Son of God. [14]And this is the

2316/2443 1785 848 5083 1785
τοῦ Θεοῦ, ἵνα τὰς ἐντολὰς αὐτοῦ τηρῶμεν· καὶ αἱ ἐντολαὶ
of God, that the commandments of Him we keep; and the commands
848 926 3756/1526 3754/3956 1080 1537
4 αὐτοῦ βαρεῖαι οὐκ εἰσίν. ὅτι πᾶν τὸ γεγεννημένον ἐκ τοῦ
of Him heavy not are, because everything having been born of
2316/3528 2889 3778 2076 3529 3528
Θεοῦ νικᾷ τὸν κόσμον· καὶ αὕτη ἐστὶν ἡ νίκη ἡ νικήσασα τὸν
God overcomes the world, and this is the victory overcoming the
2889 4102 2257/5101/2076 3528 2889 =1508=
5 κόσμον, ἡ πίστις ἡμῶν. τίς ἐστιν ὁ νικῶν τὸν κόσμον, εἰ μὴ ὁ
world, the faith of us. Who is the (one) over-coming the world, except the (one)
4100 3754 2424 2076 5207 2316 3778 2076
6 πιστεύων ὅτι Ἰησοῦς ἐστὶν ὁ υἱὸς τοῦ Θεοῦ; οὗτός ἐστιν ὁ
believing that Jesus is the Son of God? This is the (One)
2064/1223/5204 129 2424 5547 3756/1722
ἐλθὼν δι' ὕδατος καὶ αἵματος, Ἰησοῦς ὁ Χριστός· οὐκ ἐν τῷ
coming through water and blood, Jesus Christ; not by the
5204 3440 235/1722 5204 129 4151
ὕδατι μόνον, ἀλλ' ἐν τῷ ὕδατι καὶ τῷ αἵματι. καὶ τὸ Πνεῦμά
water only, but by the water and the blood. And the Spirit
2076 3140 3754 4151 2076 225 3754 5140
7 ἐστι τὸ μαρτυροῦν, ὅτι τὸ Πνεῦμά ἐστιν ἡ ἀλήθεια. ὅτι τρεῖς
is the (One) witnessing, for the Spirit is the truth. (Because three
1526 3140 1722 3772 3962 3056
εἰσὶν οἱ μαρτυροῦντες ἐν τῷ οὐρανῷ, ὁ πατήρ, ὁ λόγος, καὶ
there are bearing witness in Heaven, the Father, the Word, and
40 4151 3778 5140/1520/1526 5140 1526
8 τὸ Ἅγιον Πνεῦμα· καὶ οὗτοι οἱ τρεῖς ἕν εἰσι. καὶ τρεῖς εἰσὶν
the Holy Spirit, and these three One is.) And three there are
3140 1722 1093 4151 5204
οἱ μαρτυροῦντες ἐν τῇ γῇ, τὸ Πνεῦμα, καὶ τὸ ὕδωρ, καὶ τὸ
who bear witness on the earth, the Spirit, and the water, and the
129 5140/1519 1722/1526/1487 3140
9 αἷμα· καὶ οἱ τρεῖς εἰς τὸ ἕν εἰσιν. εἰ τὴν μαρτυρίαν τῶν
blood; and the three to the one are. If the witness
444 2983 3141 2316 3187 2076
ἀνθρώπων λαμβάνομεν, ἡ μαρτυρία τοῦ Θεοῦ μείζων ἐστίν·
of men we receive, the witness of God greater is,
3754/3778 2076 3141 2316 3739 3140 4012
ὅτι αὕτη ἐστὶν ἡ μαρτυρία τοῦ Θεοῦ, ἣν μεμαρτύρηκε περὶ
because this is the witness of God, which He has witnessed about
5207 848 4100 1519 5207 2316 2192
10 τοῦ υἱοῦ αὐτοῦ. ὁ πιστεύων εἰς τὸν υἱὸν τοῦ Θεοῦ ἔχει τὴν
the Son of Him. The (one) believing in the Son of God has the
3141 1722 1438 3361 4100 2316 5583 4160
μαρτυρίαν ἐν ἑαυτῷ· ὁ μὴ πιστεύων τῷ Θεῷ ψεύστην πεποί-
witness in himself. The (one) not believing God a liar has
846 3754/3756 4100 1519 3141 3739
ηκεν αὐτόν, ὅτι οὐ πεπίστευκεν εἰς τὴν μαρτυρίαν, ἣν
made Him, because not he has believed in the witness which
3140 2316/4012 5207 848 3778 2076
11 μεμαρτύρηκεν ὁ Θεὸς περὶ τοῦ υἱοῦ αὐτοῦ. καὶ αὕτη ἐστὶν
has witnessed God concerning the Son of Him. And this is
3141 3754 2222 166 1325 2254 2316 3778
ἡ μαρτυρία, ὅτι ζωὴν αἰώνιον ἔδωκεν ἡμῖν ὁ Θεός, καὶ αὕτη
the witness, that life everlasting gave us God, and this
2222/1722 5207 848 2076 2192 5207/2192 2198
12 ἡ ζωὴ ἐν τῷ υἱῷ αὐτοῦ ἐστίν. ὁ ἔχων τὸν υἱὸν ἔχει τὴν ζωήν
life in the Son of Him is. The (one) having the Son has life.
3361/2192 5207 2316 2222/3756/2192
ὁ μὴ ἔχων τὸν υἱόν τοῦ Θεοῦ τὴν ζωὴν οὐκ ἔχει.
he not having the Son of God. life not has.
5023 1125 5213 4100 1519 3686
13 Ταῦτα ἔγραψα ὑμῖν τοῖς πιστεύουσιν εἰς τὸ ὄνομα τοῦ
These things I wrote to you, those believing in the name of the
5207 2316/2443 1492/3754/2222 2192 166 2443
υἱοῦ τοῦ Θεοῦ, ἵνα εἰδῆτε ὅτι ζωὴν ἔχετε αἰώνιον, καὶ ἵνα
Son of God, that you may know that life you have eternal, and that
4100 1519 3686 5207 2316 3778 2076
14 πιστεύητε εἰς τὸ ὄνομα τοῦ υἱοῦ τοῦ Θεοῦ. καὶ αὕτη ἐστὶν
you may believe in the name of the Son of God. And this is

confidence we have toward Him, that if we ask anything according to His will, He hears us. 15 And if we know that He hears us, whatever we ask, we know that we have the requests which we have asked from Him.

16 If anyone sees his brother sinning a sin not unto death, he shall ask, and He shall give life to him, to the ones not sinning unto death. There is a sin unto death. I do not say that he should ask about that. 17 All unrighteousness is sin, and there is a sin not unto death.

18 We know that everyone having been born of God does not sin, but the *one* born of God guards himself, and the evil one does not touch him. 19 We know that we are of God, and the whole world lies in evil. 20 And we know that the Son of God has come, and has given to us an understanding that we might know the true *One*, and we are in the true *One*, in His Son Jesus Christ. This is the true God, and the life everlasting.

21 Little children, guard yourselves from idols.

Amen.

3954 3739 2192 4314 846 3754/1437/5100/154
ἡ παρρησία ἣν ἔχομεν πρὸς αὐτόν, ὅτι ἐάν τι αἰτώμεθα
the confidence which we have toward Him, that if anything we ask
2596 2307 848 191 2257 1437 1492 3754
15 κατὰ τὸ θέλημα αὐτοῦ, ἀκούει ἡμῶν· καὶ ἐὰν οἴδαμεν ὅτι
according to the will of Him, He hears us. And if we know that
191 2257/3739/302 154 1492 3754 2192
ἀκούει ἡμῶν, ὃ ἂν αἰτώμεθα, οἴδαμεν ὅτι ἔχομεν τὰ
He hears us, whatever we ask, we know that we have the
155 154 3844 846 1437/5100/1492 80
16 αἰτήματα ἃ ἠτήκαμεν παρ' αὐτοῦ. ἐάν τις ἴδῃ τὸν ἀδελφὸν
requests which we have asked from Him. If anyone sees the brother
848 264 266 3361 4314 2288 154
αὐτοῦ ἁμαρτάνοντα ἁμαρτίαν μὴ πρὸς θάνατον, αἰτήσει,
of him sinning a sin not unto death, he shall ask,
1325 846 2222 264 3361 4314 2288
καὶ δώσει αὐτῷ ζωὴν τοῖς ἁμαρτάνουσι μὴ πρὸς θάνατον.
and He will give to him life to those sinning not unto death.
2076 266 4314 2288 3756/4012 1565 3004 2443
ἔστιν ἁμαρτία πρὸς θάνατον· οὐ περὶ ἐκείνης λέγω ἵνα
There is a sin unto death; not concerning that I say that
2065 3956 93 266 2076 2076 266 3756
17 ἐρωτήσῃ. πᾶσα ἀδικία ἁμαρτία ἐστί· καὶ ἔστιν ἁμαρτία οὐ
he should ask. All unrighteousness sin is, and there is a sin not
4314 2288
πρὸς θάνατον.
unto death.
1492 3754/3956 1080 1537 2316/3756 264
18 Οἴδαμεν ὅτι πᾶς ὁ γεγεννημένος ἐκ τοῦ Θεοῦ οὐχ ἁμαρ-
We know that everyone having been born of God not sins,
235 1080 1537 2316 5083 1438
τάνει· ἀλλ' ὁ γεννηθεὶς ἐκ τοῦ Θεοῦ τηρεῖ ἑαυτόν, καὶ ὁ
but the (one) born of God keeps himself, and the
4190 3756 680 846 1492 3754/1537 2316
19 πονηρὸς οὐχ ἅπτεται αὐτοῦ. οἴδαμεν ὅτι ἐκ τοῦ Θεοῦ
evil one does not touch him. We know that of God
2070 2889 3650/1722 4190 2749 1492
20 ἐσμέν, καὶ ὁ κόσμος ὅλος ἐν τῷ πονηρῷ κεῖται. οἴδαμεν δὲ
we are, and the world whole in evil lies. we know And
3754 5207 2316 2240 1325 2254 1271 2443
ὅτι ὁ υἱὸς τοῦ Θεοῦ ἥκει, καὶ δέδωκεν ἡμῖν διάνοιαν ἵνα
that the Son of God is come, and has given to us an understanding that
1097 228 2070/1722 228 1722
γινώσκωμεν τὸν ἀληθινόν· καί ἐσμεν ἐν τῷ ἀληθινῷ, ἐν τῷ
we might know the true (One), and we are in the true (One), in the
5207 848 2424 5547 3778 2076 228 2316
υἱῷ αὐτοῦ Ἰησοῦ Χριστῷ. οὗτός ἐστιν ὁ ἀληθινὸς Θεός,
Son of Him, Jesus Christ. This is the true God,
2222 166 5038 5442 1438 575
21 καὶ ἡ ζωὴ αἰώνιος. Τεκνία, φυλάξατε ἑαυτοὺς ἀπὸ τῶν
and the life everlasting. Little children, guard yourselves from
1497 281
εἰδώλων. ἀμήν.
idols. Amen.

ΙΩΑΝΝΟΥ
JOHN
ΕΠΙΣΤΟΛΗ ΔΕΥΤΕΡΑ
EPISTLE SECOND

THE SECOND EPISTLE
OF
JOHN

A LITERAL TRANSLATION
OF THE BIBLE

1 The elder to *the* elect lady and her children, whom I love in truth; and not I only, but also all those who have known the truth, 2 because of the truth remaining among us, and will be with us forever. 3 Grace, mercy, peace will be with you from God *the* Father and from *the* Lord Jesus Christ, the Son of the Father, in truth and love.

4 I rejoiced greatly because I found your children walking in truth, as we received command from the Father. 5 And I now request you, lady, not writing as a new commandment, but *one* which we had from *the* beginning, that we should love one another. 6 And this is love, that we should walk according to His commandments. This is the commandment, even as you heard from *the* beginning, that you should walk in it. 7 Because many deceivers went out into the world, those not confessing Jesus Christ to have come in *the* flesh—this is the deceiver and the antichrist.

8 Watch yourselves, that we may not lose the things we worked out, but that we may receive a full reward. 9 Everyone transgressing and not abiding in the teaching of

4245 1588 2959 5043 848
1 Ὁ πρεσβύτερος ἐκλεκτῇ κυρίᾳ καὶ τοῖς τέκνοις αὐτῆς,
The elder to (the) elect lady and the children of her,
3739/1473 25 1722 225 3756/1473 3440 235
οὓς ἐγὼ ἀγαπῶ ἐν ἀληθείᾳ, καὶ οὐκ ἐγὼ μόνος, ἀλλὰ καὶ
whom I love in truth,- and not I only, but also
3956 1097 225 1223 225
2 πάντες οἱ ἐγνωκότες τὴν ἀλήθειαν, διὰ τὴν ἀλήθειαν τὴν
all those who have known the truth, because of the truth
3306 1722/2254 3326 2257 2071/1519 165 2071
3 μένουσαν ἐν ἡμῖν, καὶ μεθ' ἡμῶν ἔσται εἰς τὸν αἰῶνα· ἔσται
remaining among us, and with us will be unto the age. will be
3326/5216 5485 1656 1515 3844 2316 3962 3844
μεθ' ὑμῶν χάρις, ἔλεος, εἰρήνη παρὰ Θεοῦ πατρός, καὶ παρὰ
with you Grace, mercy, peace, from God (the) Father, and from
2962 2424 5547 5207 3962/1722 225
Κυρίου Ἰησοῦ Χριστοῦ τοῦ υἱοῦ τοῦ πατρός, ἐν ἀληθείᾳ καὶ
(the) Lord Jesus Christ the Son of the Father, in truth and
26
ἀγάπῃ.
love.
5463 3029/3754 2147/1537 5043 4675 4043
4 Ἐχάρην λίαν ὅτι εὕρηκα ἐκ τῶν τέκνων σου περιπατοῦν-
I rejoiced greatly because I found of the children of you walking
1722 225 2531 1785 2983 3844 3962
τας ἐν ἀληθείᾳ, καθὼς ἐντολὴν ἐλάβομεν παρὰ τοῦ πατρός.
in truth, as commandment we received from the Father.
3568 2065/4571/2959/3756/5613/ 1785 1125 4671 2537
5 καὶ νῦν ἐρωτῶ σε, κυρία, οὐχ ὡς ἐντολὴν γράφων σοι καινήν,
And now I request you, lady, not as a command writing to you new,
235/3739 2192 575 746 2443 25 240
6 ἀλλὰ ἣν εἴχομεν ἀπ' ἀρχῆς, ἵνα ἀγαπῶμεν ἀλλήλους. καὶ
but which we had from (the) beginning, that we should love one another. And
3778 2076 26 2443 4043 2596 1785
7 αὕτη ἐστὶν ἡ ἀγάπη, ἵνα περιπατῶμεν κατὰ τὰς ἐντολὰς
this is love, that we should walk according to the commands
848 3778 2076 1785 2531 191 575 746
αὐτοῦ. αὕτη ἐστὶν ἡ ἐντολή, καθὼς ἠκούσατε ἀπ' ἀρχῆς,
of Him. This is the command, even as you heard from beginning
2443/1722/846 4043 3754 4183 4108 1525 1519
ἵνα ἐν αὐτῇ περιπατῆτε. ὅτι πολλοὶ πλάνοι εἰσῆλθον εἰς τὸν
that in it you should walk. Because many deceivers went out into the
2889 3361 3670 2424 5547 2064 1722
κόσμον, οἱ μὴ ὁμολογοῦντες Ἰησοῦν Χριστὸν ἐρχόμενον ἐν
world, those not confessing Jesus Christ coming in
4561 3778 2076 4108 500 991
8 σαρκί. οὗτός ἐστιν ὁ πλάνος καὶ ὁ ἀντίχριστος. βλέπετε
(the) flesh. This is the deceiver and the antichrist. Watch
1438 2443/3361 622 3739 2038 235 3408
ἑαυτούς, ἵνα μὴ ἀπολέσωμεν ἃ εἰργασάμεθα, ἀλλὰ μισθὸν
yourselves, lest we may lose the things we worked out, but a reward
4134 618 3956 3845 3361 3306/1722
9 πλήρη ἀπολάβωμεν. πᾶς ὁ παραβαίνων καὶ μὴ μένων ἐν
full we may receive. Everyone transgressing and not abiding in
1322 5547 2316/3756/2192 3306 1722
τῇ διδαχῇ τοῦ Χριστοῦ, Θεὸν οὐκ ἔχει· ὁ μένων ἐν τῇ
the teaching of Christ, God not has The (one) abiding in the

Christ does not have God. The *one* abiding in the teaching of Christ, this one has the Father and the Son. [10]If anyone comes to you and does not bear this teaching, do not receive him into *the* house, and do not speak a greeting to him. [11]For the *one* speaking a greeting shares in his evil works.

[12]Having many things to write to you, I do not intend *to speak* by means of paper and ink, but I am hoping to come to you, and to speak mouth to mouth, that our joy may be full.

[13]The children of your elect sister greet you.

Amen.

1322 5547 3778 3962 5207
διδαχῇ τοῦ Χριστοῦ, οὗτος καὶ τὸν πατέρα καὶ τὸν υἱὸν
teaching of Christ, this one even the Father and the Son
2192=1536= 2064 4314 5209 5026 1322 3756
10 ἔχει. εἴ τις ἔρχεται πρὸς ὑμᾶς, καὶ ταύτην τὴν διδαχὴν οὐ
has. If anyone comes to you, and this teaching not
5342/3361/2983 846/1519 3614 5463 846/3361
φέρει, μὴ λαμβάνετε αὐτὸν εἰς οἰκίαν, καὶ χαίρειν αὐτῷ μὴ
bears, not do receive him into (the) house, and a greeting to him not
3004 1063 3004 846 5463 2841 2041
11 λέγετε· ὁ γὰρ λέγων αὐτῷ χαίρειν κοινωνεῖ τοῖς ἔργοις
do speak. he For speaking to him a greeting shares in the works
848 4190
αὐτοῦ τοῖς πονηροῖς.
of him evil.
4183 2192 5213 1125 3756 1014 1223 5489
12 Πολλὰ ἔχων ὑμῖν γράφειν οὐκ ἠβουλήθην διὰ χάρτου
Many things having to you to write not I intend by means of paper
3188 235 1679 2064 4314/5209 4750 4314
καὶ μέλανος· ἀλλὰ ἐλπίζω ἐλθεῖν πρὸς ὑμᾶς, καὶ στόμα πρὸς
and ink, but I am hoping to come to you, and mouth to
4750 2980 2443 5479 2257/5600/ 4137 782
13 στόμα λαλῆσαι, ἵνα ἡ χαρὰ ἡμῶν ᾖ πεπληρωμένη. ἀσπά-
mouth to speak, that the joy of us may be fulfilled. greet
4571 5043 79 4675 1588 281
ζεταί σε τὰ τέκνα τῆς ἀδελφῆς σου τῆς ἐκλεκτῆς. ἀμήν.
you The children of the sister of you elect. Amen.

ΙΩΑΝΝΟΥ
OF JOHN
ΕΠΙΣΤΟΛΗ ΤΡΙΤΗ
EPISTLE THIRD

THE THIRD EPISTLE
OF
JOHN
A LITERAL TRANSLATION
OF THE BIBLE

[1]The elder to Gaius the beloved, whom I love in truth.

[2]Beloved, in regard to all things, I pray *for* you to do well, and to be in health, as your soul does well. [3]For I rejoiced greatly *at the* coming of *the* brothers, also bearing witness of you in the truth, as you walk in truth. [4]I have no greater joy than these things, that I hear my children are walking in truth.

[5]Beloved, you do faithfully whatever you work for the brothers and for the strangers, [6]who in love bore witness of you before *the* church, whom you will do well to send forward worthily of God. [7]For on behalf of His name they went out, taking nothing from the Gentiles. [8]Therefore, we ought to entertain such *men*, that we may become co-workers in the truth.

[9]I wrote to the church, but he loving to be first of them, Diotrephes, does not receive us. [10]Because of this, if I come, I will recall his works which he does, ranting against us with evil words. And not being satisfied *with* these, neither does he receive the brothers; and those intending *it* he prevents, and

4245 1050 27 3739/1473 25 1722
1 Ὁ πρεσβύτερος Γαΐῳ τῷ ἀγαπητῷ, ὃν ἐγὼ ἀγαπῶ ἐν
The elder to Gaius the beloved, whom I love in
225
ἀληθείᾳ.
truth.
27 4012 3956 2172 4571 2137
2 Ἀγαπητέ, περὶ πάντων εὔχομαί σε εὐοδοῦσθαι καὶ
Beloved, concerning all things I pray you to do well, and
5198 2531 2137 4675 5590 5463 1063 3029
3 ὑγιαίνειν, καθὼς εὐοδοῦταί σου ἡ ψυχή. ἐχάρην γὰρ λίαν,
to be in health, as does well of you the soul. I rejoiced For greatly,
2064 80 3140 4675 225
ἐρχομένων ἀδελφῶν καὶ μαρτυρούντων σου τῇ ἀληθείᾳ,
coming (the) brothers and bearing witness of you in the truth
2531 3771/1722/ 225 4043 3186 5130 3756
4 καθὼς σὺ ἐν ἀληθείᾳ περιπατεῖς. μειζοτέραν τούτων οὐκ
as you in truth walk. greater (than) these things not
2192 5479 2443 191 1699 5043/1722 225 4043
ἔχω χαράν, ἵνα ἀκούω τὰ ἐμὰ τέκνα ἐν ἀληθείᾳ περι-
I have joy, that I hear my children in (the) truth are
πατοῦντα.
walking.

27 4103 4160/3739/1437/2038/1519 80
5 Ἀγαπητέ, πιστὸν ποιεῖς ὃ ἐὰν ἐργάσῃ εἰς τοὺς ἀδελφοὺς
Beloved, faithfully you do whatever you work for the brothers
1519 3581/3739 3140 4675 26 1799
6 καὶ εἰς τοὺς ξένους, οἳ ἐμαρτύρησάν σου τῇ ἀγάπῃ ἐνώπιον
and for the strangers, who bore witness of you in love in sight of
1577 3739 2573 4160 4311 516 2316
ἐκκλησίας· οὓς καλῶς ποιήσεις προπέμψας ἀξίως τοῦ Θεοῦ.
(the) church, whom well you will do sending forward worthily of God.
5228 1063 3686 846 1831 3367 2983
7 ὑπὲρ γὰρ τοῦ ὀνόματος αὐτοῦ ἐξῆλθον μηδὲν λαμβάνοντες
on behalf of For the name of Him they went out, nothing taking
575 1484 2249 3767 3784 618
8 ἀπὸ τῶν ἐθνῶν. ἡμεῖς οὖν ὀφείλομεν ἀπολαμβάνειν τοὺς
from the Gentiles. We therefore ought to entertain
5108 2443 4904 1096 225
τοιούτους, ἵνα συνεργοὶ γινώμεθα τῇ ἀληθείᾳ.
such (men) that co-workers we may become in the truth.
1125 1577 235 5383 848
9 Ἔγραψα τῇ ἐκκλησίᾳ· ἀλλ' ὁ φιλοπρωτεύων αὐτῶν
I wrote to the church, but the (one) loving to be first of them,
1361 3756 1926 2248 1223 5124 1437 2064
10 Διοτρεφὴς οὐκ ἐπιδέχεται ἡμᾶς. διὰ τοῦτο, ἐὰν ἔλθω,
Diotrephes, not does receive us. Therefore, If I come,
5279 846 2041/3739/4160/3056 4190 5396
ὑπομνήσω αὐτοῦ τὰ ἔργα ἃ ποιεῖ, λόγοις πονηροῖς φλυαρῶν
I will recall of him the works which he does, with words evil prating against
2248 3361 714 1909 5125 3777 848 1926
ἡμᾶς· καὶ μὴ ἀρκούμενος ἐπὶ τούτοις, οὔτε αὐτὸς ἐπιδέχεται
us, and not being satisfied on these, neither he receives
80 1014 2967 1537
τοὺς ἀδελφούς, καὶ τοὺς βουλομένους κωλύει, καὶ ἐκ τῆς
the brothers, and those intending (to do so), he prevents, and from the

thrusts them out from the church.

[11]Beloved, do not imitate the bad, but the good. The *one* doing good is of God; but the *one* doing bad has not seen God.

[12]Witness has been borne to Demetrius by all, and by the truth itself. And we also bear witness, and you know that our witness is true.

[13]I had many things to write, but I do not desire to write by means of pen and ink. [14]But I am hoping to see you at once, and we will speak mouth to mouth.

Peace to you. The friends greet you. Greet the friends by name.

1577 1544 27 3361 3401 2556 235
11 ἐκκλησίας ἐκβάλλει. ἀγαπητέ, μὴ μιμοῦ τὸ κακόν, ἀλλὰ τὸ
church thrusts out. Beloved, not do imitate the bad, but the
18 15 1537 2316 2076 2554
ἀγαθόν. ὁ ἀγαθοποιῶν ἐκ τοῦ Θεοῦ ἐστίν· ὁ δὲ κακοποιῶν
good. The (one) doing good of God is; the (one) but doing ill
3756 3708 2316 1216 3140 5259
12 οὐχ ἑώρακε τὸν Θεόν. Δημητρίῳ μεμαρτύρηται ὑπὸ
not has seen God. To Demetrius witness has been borne by
3956 5259 846 225 2249 3140
πάντων, καὶ ὑπ' αὐτῆς τῆς ἀληθείας· καὶ ἡμεῖς δὲ μαρτυροῦ-
all, and by its (own) the truth; also we and bear witness
1492/3754 self 3141 2257 227 2076
μεν, καὶ οἴδατε ὅτι ἡ μαρτυρία ἡμῶν ἀληθής ἐστι.
and you know that the witness of us true is.
4183 2192 1125 235 3756 2309 1223 3188
13 Πολλὰ εἶχον γράφειν, ἀλλ' οὐ θέλω διὰ μέλανος καὶ
Many things I had to write, but not I desire via ink and
2563 4671 1125 1679 2112 1492 4571 4750
14 καλάμου σοι γράψαι· ἐλπίζω δὲ εὐθέως ἰδεῖν σε, καὶ στόμα
pen to you to write; I am hoping but at once to see you, and mouth
4314 4750 2980 1515 4671 782 4571
15 πρὸς στόμα λαλήσομεν. εἰρήνη σοι. ἀσπάζονταί σε οἱ
to mouth we will speak. Peace to you. Greet you The
5384 782 5384 2596 3686
φίλοι. ἀσπάζου τοὺς φίλους κατ' ὄνομα.
friends. Greet the friends by name.

THE GENERAL EPISTLE
OF
JUDE
A LITERAL TRANSLATION
OF THE BIBLE

[1]Jude, a slave of Jesus Christ, and brother of James, to the *ones* called in God *the* Father, having been set apart, and having been kept to Jesus Christ: [2]Mercy and peace, and love be multiplied to you.

[3]Having made all diligence to write to you about the common salvation, beloved, I had need to write to you *to* exhort you to contend earnestly for the faith once delivered to the saints. [4]For certain men crept in secretly, those having been of old marked out to this condemnation, ungodly ones perverting the grace of God for unbridled lust, and denying the only Master, God, even our Lord Jesus Christ.

[5]But I intend to remind you, you once knowing these things, that the Lord having saved a people out of *the* land of Egypt, in the second place destroyed the ones not believing. [6]And those angels not having kept their first place, but having deserted *their* dwelling-place, He has kept in everlasting chains under darkness for *the* judgment of a great Day; [7]as Sodom and Gomorrah, and the cities around them, in like manner to these, committing fornication, and going away after other flesh, laid down an example beforetimes, undergoing vengeance of everlasting fire. [8]Likewise, indeed, also those dreaming ones even defile flesh, and despise rulership, and

ΙΟΥΔΑ
JUDE
ΕΠΙΣΤΟΛΗ ΚΑΘΟΛΙΚΗ
EPISTLE GENERAL

2455 2424 5547 1401 80 2385
1 Ἰούδας Ἰησοῦ Χριστοῦ δοῦλος, ἀδελφὸς δὲ Ἰακώβου,
Jude, of Jesus Christ a slave, brother and of James,
1722/2316 3962 37 2424 5547 5083
τοῖς ἐν Θεῷ πατρὶ ἡγιασμένοις, καὶ Ἰησοῦ Χριστῷ τετηρη-
to those in God (the) Father having been set apart, and by Jesus Christ having been
2822 1656/5213 1515 26 4129
2 μένοις, κλητοῖς· ἔλεος ὑμιν καὶ εἰρήνη καὶ ἀγάπη πληθυνθείη.
kept, called: Mercy to you and peace and love be multiplied.
27 3956 4710 4160 1125 5213/4012
3 Ἀγαπητοί, πᾶσαν σπουδὴν ποιούμενος γράφειν ὑμῖν περὶ
Beloved, all diligence making to write to you, about
2839 4991 318 2192 1125 5213 3870
τῆς κοινῆς σωτηρίας, ἀνάγκην ἔσχον γράψαι ὑμῖν, παρα-
the common salvation, necessity I had to write to you, ex-
1864 530 3860 40
καλῶν ἐπαγωνίζεσθαι τῇ ἅπαξ παραδοθείσῃ τοῖς ἁγίοις
horting to earnestly contend for the once delivered to the saints
4102 3921 1063/5100 444 3819 4270
4 πίστει. παρεισέδυσαν γάρ τινες ἄνθρωποι, οἱ πάλαι προγε-
faith, crept in For certain men, those of old having been
1519/5124 2917 765 2316 2257
γραμμένοι εἰς τοῦτο τὸ κρίμα, ἀσεβεῖς, τὴν τοῦ Θεοῦ ἡμῶν
previously into this judgment, ungodly the of the God of us
•5485 written 3346 1519 766 ones. 3441 1203
χάριν μετατιθέντες εἰς ἀσέλγειαν, καὶ τὸν μόνον δεσπότην
grace, perverting for unbridled lust, and the only Master
2316 2962 2257 2424 5547 720
Θεόν, καὶ Κύριον ἡμῶν Ἰησοῦν Χριστὸν ἀρνούμενοι.
God, and Lord of us, Jesus Christ denying.
5279 5209 1014 1492 5209 530 5124
5 Ὑπομνῆσαι δὲ ὑμᾶς βούλομαι, εἰδότας ὑμᾶς ἅπαξ τοῦτο,
to remind But you I intend, knowing you once these things,
3754 2962 2992/1537/1093/ 125 4982 1208
ὅτι ὁ Κύριος, λαὸν ἐκ γῆς Αἰγύπτου σώσας, τὸ δεύτερον
that the Lord people out of land of Egypt having saved, in the second place
3361 4100 622 32/5037 3361
6 τοὺς μὴ πιστεύσαντας ἀπώλεσεν. ἀγγέλους τε τοὺς μὴ
those not believing He destroyed; angels and those not
5083 1438 746 235 620
τηρήσαντας τὴν ἑαυτῶν ἀρχήν, ἀλλὰ ἀπολιπόντας τὸ
having kept the of themselves first place, but having deserted the
2398 3613 1519 2920 3173 2250 1199 126
ἴδιον οἰκητήριον, εἰς κρίσιν μεγάλης ἡμέρας δεσμοῖς ἀϊδίοις
own dwelling-place, for (the) Judgment of a great Day in chains eternal
5259 2217 5083 5613 4670 1116 4012
7 ὑπὸ ζόφον τετήρηκεν. ὡς Σόδομα καὶ Γόμορρα, καὶ αἱ περὶ
under blackness He has kept; as Sodom and Gomorrah and the around
846 4172 3664 5125 5158 1608
αὐτὰς πόλεις, τὸν ὅμοιον τούτοις τρόπον ἐκπορνεύσασαι,
them cities, in the similar to these manner committing fornication
565 3694 4561 2087 4295 1164
καὶ ἀπελθοῦσαι ὀπίσω σαρκὸς ἑτέρας, πρόκεινται δεῖγμα,
and going away after flesh other, laid beforetimes an example
4442 166 1349 5254 3668 3305 3778
8 πυρὸς αἰωνίου δίκην ὑπέχουσαι. ὁμοίως μέντοι καὶ οὗτοι
of fire everlasting vengeance undergoing. Likewise indeed also these
1797 4561 3303 3392 2963 114
ἐνυπνιαζόμενοι σάρκα μὲν μιαίνουσι, κυριότητα δὲ ἀθετοῦσι,
dreaming (ones) flesh even defile, lordship and despise,

speak evil of glories. 9But Michael the archangel, when contending with the Devil, he argued about the body of Moses—he dared not bring a judgment of blasphemy, but said, Let *the* Lord rebuke you! 10But what things they do not know, they speak evil of these. And what things they understand naturally, like the animals without reason, they are corrupted by these.

11Woe to them, because they went the way of Cain, and gave themselves up to the error of Balaam *for* reward, and perished in the speaking against of Korah! 12These are sunken rocks in your love feasts, feasting together with you; feeding themselves without fear, waterless clouds being carried about by winds; fruitless autumn trees, having died twice, having been plucked up by the roots; 13wild waves of *the* sea foaming up their shames; wandering stars for whom blackness of darkness has been kept forever.

14And *the* seventh from Adam, Enoch also prophesied to these men, saying, Behold, *the* Lord came with myriads of His saints, 15to do judgment against all, and to rebuke all the ungodly of them concerning all their ungodly works which they ungodly did, and concerning all the hard things ungodly sinners spoke against Him. 16These are murmurers, complainers, leading lives according to their lusts, and their mouth speaks proud things, admiring faces for the sake of gain. 17But you, beloved, remember the words spoken before by the apostles of our Lord Jesus Christ,

1391 987 3413 743 3753
9 δόξας δὲ βλασφημοῦσιν. ὁ δὲ Μιχαὴλ ὁ ἀρχάγγελος, ὅτε τῷ
glories and speak evil of. But Michael the archangel, when with the
1228 1252 1256 4012 3475 4983
διαβόλῳ διακρινόμενος διελέγετο περὶ τοῦ Μωσέως σώ-
Devil contending, he argued about the of Moses
3756 5111 2920 2018 988 235
ματος, οὐκ ἐτόλμησε κρίσιν ἐπενεγκεῖν βλασφημίας, ἀλλ'
body, not he dared a judgment to bring of blasphemy, but
2036 2008 4671 2962 3778 3745/3303/3756/1492
10 εἶπεν, Ἐπιτιμήσαι σοι Κύριος. οὗτοι δὲ ὅσα μὲν οὐκ οἴδασι
said, Let rebuke you (the) Lord. these But what things not they know,
987 3745 5447 5613 249 2226 1987
βλασφημοῦσιν· ὅσα δὲ φυσικῶς, ὡς τὰ ἄλογα ζῷα, ἐπί-
they speak evil of; what things and naturally – as the without reason animals – they
3754 1722/5125 5351 3759 846 3598
11 στανται, ἐν τούτοις φθείρονται. οὐαὶ αὐτοῖς· ὅτι τῇ ὁδῷ τοῦ
understand, by these they are corrupted. Woe to them, because in the way
2535 4198 4106 903 3408
Κάϊν ἐπορεύθησαν, καὶ τῇ πλάνῃ τοῦ Βαλαὰμ μισθοῦ
of Cain they went, and to the error of Balaam (for) reward
1632 485 2079 622 3778
12 ἐξεχύθησαν, καὶ τῇ ἀντιλογίᾳ τοῦ Κορὲ ἀπώλοντο. οὗτοί
gave themselves, and in the gainsaying of Korah perished! These
1526/1722 26 5216 4694 4910 5213
εἰσιν ἐν ταῖς ἀγάπαις ὑμῶν σπιλάδες, συνευωχούμενοι ὑμῖν,
are in the love feasts of you rocky reefs feasting together with you,
870 1438 4165 3507 504 5259
ἀφόβως ἑαυτοὺς ποιμαίνοντες· νεφέλαι ἄνυδροι, ὑπὸ
without fear themselves feeding, clouds waterless by
417 4064 1186 5352 175 1364
ἀνέμων περιφερόμεναι· δένδρα φθινοπωρινά, ἄκαρπα, δὶς
winds having been carried about trees autumn without fruit, twice
599 1610 2949 66 2281 1890
13 ἀποθανόντα, ἐκριζωθέντα· κύματα ἄγρια θαλάσσης, ἐπ-
dying having been uprooted, waves wild of (the) sea
1438 152 792 4107 3739
αφρίζοντα τὰς ἑαυτῶν αἰσχύνας· ἀστέρες πλανῆται, οἷς ὁ
foaming up the of themselves shames, stars wandering, for whom
2217 4655 1519 165 5083 4395
14 ζόφος τοῦ σκότους εἰς τὸν αἰῶνα τετήρηται. προεφήτευσε
blackness of darkness to the age has been kept. prophesied
5125 1442 575 76 1802 3004 2400
δὲ καὶ τούτοις ἕβδομος ἀπὸ Ἀδὰμ Ἐνώχ, λέγων, Ἰδού,
And also to these (the) seventh from Adam, Enoch, saying, Behold,
2064 2962/1722/ 3461 40 848 4160 2920 2596
15 ἦλθε Κύριος ἐν μυριάσιν ἁγίαις αὐτοῦ, ποιῆσαι κρίσιν κατὰ
came (the) Lord with myriads saints of Him, to do judgment against
3956 1827 3956 765 846 4012
πάντων, καὶ ἐξελέγξαι πάντας τοὺς ἀσεβεῖς αὐτῶν περὶ
all, and to rebuke all the ungodly of them concerning
3956 2041 763 848/3739/ 764 4012
πάντων τῶν ἔργων ἀσεβείας αὐτῶν ὧν ἠσέβησαν, καὶ περὶ
all the works ungodly of them which they ungodly did, and about
3956 4642 3739 2980 2596 846 268
πάντων τῶν σκληρῶν ὧν ἐλάλησαν κατ' αὐτοῦ ἁμαρτωλοὶ
all the hard things which spoke against Him sinners
765 3778 1526 1113 3202 2596
16 ἀσεβεῖς. οὗτοί εἰσι γογγυσταί, μεμψίμοιροι, κατὰ τὰς
ungodly. These are murmurers, complainers, according to the
1939 848 4198 4750 848 2980
ἐπιθυμίας αὐτῶν πορευόμενοι, καὶ τὸ στόμα αὐτῶν λαλεῖ
lusts of them following and the mouth of them speaks
5246 2296 4383 5622 5484
ὑπέρογκα, θαυμάζοντες πρόσωπα ὠφελείας χάριν.
proud things, admiring faces gain for the sake of
5210 27 3415 4487
17 Ὑμεῖς δέ, ἀγαπητοί, μνήσθητε τῶν ῥημάτων τῶν
you But, beloved, remember the words
4280 5259 652 2962 2257
προειρημένων ὑπὸ τῶν ἀποστόλων τοῦ Κυρίου ἡμῶν
spoken before by the apostles of the Lord of us,

[18]because they told you that at *the* last time there will be mockers according to their lusts, leading ungodly lives. [19]These are the *ones* setting themselves apart, animal-like ones, not having *the* Spirit.

[20]But you, beloved, building yourselves up by your most holy faith, praying in *the* Holy Spirit, [21]keep yourselves in *the* love of God, eagerly awaiting the mercy of our Lord Jesus Christ to everlasting life. [22]And pity some, making distinction. [23]But save others with fear, snatching *them* out of the fire, hating even the garment having been stained from the flesh.

[24]Now to Him being able to keep you without stumbling, and to set *you* before His glory without blemish, with unspeakable joy; [25]to *the* only wise God, our Savior, *be* glory and majesty and might and authority, even now and forever. Amen.

2424 5547 3754 3004 5213 3754/1722/ 2078 5550
18 Ἰησοῦ Χριστοῦ· ὅτι ἔλεγον ὑμῖν, ὅτι ἐν ἐσχάτῳ χρόνῳ
Jesus Christ, because they told you that at (the) last time
2071 1703 2596 1438 1939 4198
ἔσονται ἐμπαῖκται, κατὰ τὰς ἑαυτῶν ἐπιθυμίας πορευό-
will be mockers according to the of themselves lusts following
763 3778 1526 592 1438
19 μενοι τῶν ἀσεβειῶν. οὗτοί εἰσιν οἱ ἀποδιορίζοντες ἑαυτούς,
the ungodly. These are they dividing apart themselves,
5591 4151 3361 2192 5210 27 40
20 ψυχικοί, Πνεῦμα μὴ ἔχοντες. ὑμεῖς δέ, ἀγαπητοί, τῇ ἁγιω-
animal-like, (the) Spirit not having. you But, beloved, by the most
2257 4102 2026 1438 1722 4151
τάτῃ ὑμῶν πίστει ἐποικοδομοῦντες ἑαυτούς, ἐν Πνεύματι
holy of you faith building up yourselves, in (the) Spirit
40 4336 1438 1722 26 2316 5083
21 Ἁγίῳ προσευχόμενοι, ἑαυτοὺς ἐν ἀγάπῃ Θεοῦ τηρήσατε,
Holy praying, yourselves in (the) love of God keep,
4327 1656 2962 2257 2424 5547
προσδεχόμενοι τὸ ἔλεος τοῦ Κυρίου ἡμῶν Ἰησοῦ Χριστοῦ
eagerly awaiting the mercy of the Lord of us, Jesus Christ
1519 2222 166 3739/3303/1653 1252 3739
22 εἰς ζωὴν αἰώνιον. καὶ οὓς μὲν ἐλεεῖτε διακρινόμενοι· οὓς δὲ
23 to life everlasting. And some truly pity, making distinction, others but
1722/5401 4982 1537 4442 726 3404
ἐν φόβῳ σῴζετε, ἐκ τοῦ πυρὸς ἁρπάζοντες, μισοῦντες καὶ
with fear save, out of the fire snatching (them), hating even
575 4561 4696 5509
τὸν ἀπὸ τῆς σαρκὸς ἐσπιλωμένον χιτῶνα.
the from the flesh stained garment.
1410 5442 5209 679 2476
24 Τῷ δὲ δυναμένῳ φυλάξαι ὑμᾶς ἀπταίστους, καὶ στῆσαι
to Him Now being able to keep you without stumbling, and to set
2714 1391 848 299 1722 20
κατενώπιον τῆς δόξης αὐτοῦ ἀμώμους ἐν ἀγαλλιάσει,
(you) before the glory of Him without blemish with exultation,
3441 4680 2316 4990 2257 1391 3172
25 μόνῳ σοφῷ Θεῷ σωτῆρι ἡμῶν, δόξα καὶ μεγαλωσύνη,
to (the) only wise God Savior of us, (be) glory and greatness,
2904 1849 3568 1519 3956 165
κράτος καὶ ἐξουσία, καὶ νῦν καὶ εἰς πάντας τοὺς αἰῶνας.
might and majesty, even now and to all the ages.
281
ἀμήν.
Amen.

ΑΠΟΚΑΛΥΨΙΣ
REVELATION

ΤΟΥ ΑΓΙΟΥ
THE HOLY

ΙΩΑΝΝΟΥ ΤΟΥ ΘΕΟΛΟΓΟΥ
OF JOHN THE DIVINE

THE HOLY REVELATION
OF
JOHN THE DIVINE
A LITERAL TRANSLATION
OF THE BIBLE

CHAPTER 1

[1]A revelation of Jesus Christ, which God gave to Him to show to His slaves things which must occur quickly. And He signified *by* sending through His angel to His slave, John, [2]who testified of the word of God and the witness of Jesus Christ, even as many things as he saw. [3]Blessed *is* the *one* reading, and those hearing, the words of this prophecy, and keeping the things having been written; for the time *is* near.

[4]John to the seven churches in Asia:

Grace to you, and peace, from the *One* who is, and who was, and who *is* coming, and from the seven spirits which are before His throne; [5]even from Jesus Christ the faithful witness, the Firstborn from the dead, and the Ruler of the kings of the earth. To Him loving us and having washed us from our sins by His blood, [6]and made us kings and priests to God, even His Father. To Him *is* the glory and the might forever and ever. Amen.

[7]Behold, He comes with the clouds, and every eye will see Him, and the ones who pierced Him, and all the tribes of the earth will wail on account of Him. Yes, Amen.

CHAPTER 1

602 2424 5547 3739 1325 846 2316
1 Ἀποκάλυψις Ἰησοῦ Χριστοῦ, ἣν ἔδωκεν αὐτῷ ὁ Θεὸς
A revelation of Jesus Christ, which gave to Him God,
1166 1401 848/3739/1163 1096 1722/5034 4591
δεῖξαι τοῖς δούλοις αὐτοῦ, ἃ δεῖ γενέσθαι ἐν τάχει, καὶ ἐσή-
to show to the slaves of Him things which must occur with speed; and He
649 1223 32 848 1401 848
μανεν ἀποστείλας διὰ τοῦ ἀγγέλου αὐτοῦ τῷ δούλῳ αὐτοῦ
signified sending through the angel of Him to the slave of Him,
2491 3739 3140 3056 2316 3141
2 Ἰωάννῃ, ὃς ἐμαρτύρησε τὸν λόγον τοῦ Θεοῦ καὶ τὴν μαρτυ-
John, who testified of the word of God and the witness
2424 5547 3745/5037/1492/ 3107 314
3 ρίαν Ἰησοῦ Χριστοῦ, ὅσα τε εἶδε. μακάριος ὁ ἀναγινώσκων,
of Jesus Christ, as many as even he saw. Blessed the (one) reading
191 3056 4394 5083
καὶ οἱ ἀκούοντες τοὺς λόγους τῆς προφητείας καὶ τηροῦντες
and those hearing the words of the prophecy, and keeping
1722/846 1125 1063 2540 1451
τὰ ἐν αὐτῇ γεγραμμένα· ὁ γὰρ καιρὸς ἐγγύς.
the things in it having been written, the for time (is) near.
2491 2033 1577 1722 773 5485 5213
4 Ἰωάννης ταῖς ἑπτὰ ἐκκλησίαις ταῖς ἐν τῇ Ἀσίᾳ· χάρις ὑμῖν
John to the seven churches in Asia: Grace to you,
1515 575 5607 2258 2064 575
5 καὶ εἰρήνη ἀπὸ τοῦ ὁ ὢν καὶ ὁ ἦν καὶ ὁ ἐρχόμενος· καὶ ἀπὸ
and peace from the (One) being, who was and who is coming; and from
2033/4151 2076 1799 2362 848
τῶν ἑπτὰ πνευμάτων ἃ ἐστιν ἐνώπιον τοῦ θρόνου αὐτοῦ·
the seven spirits which are before the throne of Him,
575 2424 5547 3144 4103 4416
καὶ ἀπὸ Ἰησοῦ Χριστοῦ, ὁ μάρτυς ὁ πιστός, ὁ πρωτότοκος
and from Jesus Christ the witness faithful, the firstborn
1537 3498 758 935 1093
ἐκ τῶν νεκρῶν, καὶ ὁ ἄρχων τῶν βασιλέων τῆς γῆς. τῷ
out of the dead, and the Ruler of the kings of the earth. To the (One)
25 2248 3068 2248 575 266
ἀγαπήσαντι ἡμᾶς, καὶ λούσαντι ἡμᾶς ἀπὸ τῶν ἁμαρτιῶν
loving us, and having washed us from the sins
2257/1722 129 848 4160 2248 935
6 ἡμῶν ἐν τῷ αἵματι αὐτοῦ· καὶ ἐποίησεν ἡμᾶς βασιλεῖς καὶ
of us by the blood of Him, and made us kings and
2409 2316 3962 848 846 1391 2904
ἱερεῖς τῷ Θεῷ καὶ πατρὶ αὐτοῦ· αὐτῷ ἡ δόξα καὶ τὸ κράτος
priests to the God and Father of Him, to Him (is) the glory and the might
1519 165 165 281 2400 2064 3326
7 εἰς τοὺς αἰῶνας τῶν αἰώνων. ἀμήν. Ἰδού, ἔρχεται μετὰ τῶν
to the ages of the ages. Amen. Behold, He comes with the
3507 3700 846 3956 3788 3748 846
νεφελῶν, καὶ ὄψεται αὐτὸν πᾶς ὀφθαλμός, καὶ οἵτινες αὐτὸν
clouds, and will see Him every eye and those who Him
1574 2875 1909 846 3956 5443
ἐξεκέντησαν· καὶ κόψονται ἐπ' αὐτὸν πᾶσαι αἱ φυλαὶ τῆς
pierced, and will wail due to Him all the tribes of the
1093 281
γῆς. ναί, ἀμήν.
earth. Yes, Amen.

[8]I am the Alpha and the Omega, *the* Beginning and *the* Ending, says the Lord, the *One* who is, and who was, and who *is* coming—the Almighty.

[9]I, even your brother John, and co-sharer in the affliction, and in the kingdom and patience of Jesus Christ, came to be in the island being called Patmos because of the word of God, and because of the witness of Jesus Christ. [10]I came to be in *the* Spirit on the Lord's day, and I heard behind me a great voice, as of a trumpet, [11]saying, I am the Alpha and the Omega, the First and the Last; also, What you see, write in a scroll, and send to the seven churches of Asia: to Ephesus, and to Smyrna, and to Pergamos, and to Thyatira, and to Sardis, and to Philadelphia, and to Laodicea. [12]And I turned to see the voice which spoke with me. [13]And turning, I saw seven golden lampstands, and in *the* midst of the seven lampstands *One* like *the* Son of man, having been clothed to *the* feet, and having been girded with a golden girdle at the breasts. [14]And the hairs of His head *were* white as white wool, as snow, and His eyes as a flame of fire;

[15]and His feet like burnished metal having been fired in a furnace; and His voice as a sound of many waters; [16]and having in His right hand seven stars; and a sharp, two-edged sword proceeding out of His mouth; and His face shining as the sun in its power. [17]And when I saw Him, I fell at His feet, as dead. And He

1473/1510 1 5598 746 2078 3004 2962
8 Ἐγώ εἰμι τὸ Α καὶ τὸ Ω, ἀρχὴ καὶ τέλος, λέγει ὁ Κύριος,
I am the Alpha and the, Beginning and Ending, says the Lord,
*2064 5607 2258 •Omega, 3841
ὁ ὢν καὶ ὁ ἦν καὶ ὁ ἐρχόμενος, ὁ παντοκράτωρ.
the being, and who was, and (is) coming, the Almighty.
1473 2491 80 5216 4791 1722
9 Ἐγὼ Ἰωάννης, ὁ καὶ ἀδελφὸς ὑμῶν καὶ συγκοινωνὸς ἐν
I, John, the even brother of you, and co-sharer in
2347 1722 932 5281 2424 5547
τῇ θλίψει καὶ ἐν τῇ βασιλείᾳ καὶ ὑπομονῇ Ἰησοῦ Χριστοῦ,
the affliction and in the kingdom and patience of Jesus Christ,
1096 1722 3520 2564 3963 1223 3056
ἐγενόμην ἐν τῇ νήσῳ τῇ καλουμένῃ Πάτμῳ, διὰ τὸν λόγον
came to be in the island being called Patmos, for the word
2116 1223 3141 2424 5547 1096
10 τοῦ Θεοῦ καὶ διὰ τὴν μαρτυρίαν Ἰησοῦ Χριστοῦ. ἐγενόμην
of God and because of the witness of Jesus Christ. I came to be
1722 4151 1722 2960 2250 191 3694 3450
ἐν Πνεύματι ἐν τῇ Κυριακῇ ἡμέρᾳ· καὶ ἤκουσα ὀπίσω μου
in (the) Spirit on the (of) the Lord day, and I heard behind me
5456 3173 5613 4536 3004 1473/1510 1
11 φωνὴν μεγάλην ὡς σάλπιγγος, λεγούσης. Ἐγώ εἰμι τὸ Α καὶ
a voice great, as of a trumpet, saying, I am the Alpha and
5598 4413 2078 3739 991 1125 1519
τὸ Ω, ὁ πρῶτος καὶ ὁ ἔσχατος· καί, Ὃ βλέπεις γράψον εἰς
the Omega, the First and the Last; and, What you see write in
975 3992 2033 1577 1722 773 1519
βιβλίον, καὶ πέμψον ταῖς ἑπτὰ ἐκκλησίαις ταῖς ἐν Ἀσίᾳ, εἰς
a roll, and send to the seven churches in Asia, to
2181 1519 4667 1519 4010 1519 2363
Ἔφεσον, καὶ εἰς Σμύρναν, καὶ εἰς Πέργαμον, καὶ εἰς Θυάτειρα,
Ephesus, and to Smyrna, and to Pergamos, and to Thyatira,
1519 4554 1519 5359 1519 2993
καὶ εἰς Σάρδεις, καὶ εἰς Φιλαδέλφειαν, καὶ εἰς Λαοδίκειαν.
and to Sardis, and to Philadelphia, and to Laodicea.
1994 991 5456 3748 2980 3326/1700
12 καὶ ἐπέστρεψα βλέπειν τὴν φωνὴν ἥτις ἐλάλησε μετ' ἐμοῦ.
And I turned to see the voice which spoke with me.
1994 1492 2033 3087 5552 1722 3319
13 καὶ ἐπιστρέψας εἶδον ἑπτὰ λυχνίας χρυσᾶς, καὶ ἐν μέσῳ
And having turned I saw seven lampstands of gold, and in (the) midst
2033 3087 3664 5207 444 1746
τῶν ἑπτὰ λυχνιῶν ὅμοιον υἱῷ ἀνθρώπου, ἐνδεδυμένον
of the seven lampstands (One) like (the) Son of man, having been clothed
4158 4024 4314 3149 2223
ποδήρη, καὶ περιεζωσμένον πρὸς τοῖς μαστοῖς ζώνην
to (the) feet, and having been girded with at the breasts a girdle
5552 2776 848 2359 3022 5616 2053
14 χρυσῆν. ἡ δὲ κεφαλὴ αὐτοῦ καὶ αἱ τρίχες λευκαὶ ὡσεὶ ἔριον
of gold. the And head of Him, and the hairs white as wool
3022 5613/5510 3788 848 5613 5395 4442
λευκόν, ὡς χιών· καὶ οἱ ὀφθαλμοὶ αὐτοῦ ὡς φλὸξ πυρός·
white, as snow, and the eyes of Him as a flame of fire,
4228 848 3664 5474 5613/1722 2575
15 καὶ οἱ πόδες αὐτοῦ ὅμοιοι χαλκολιβάνῳ, ὡς ἐν καμίνῳ
and the feet of Him like burnished metal as in a furnace
4448 5456 848 5613 5456 5204 4183
πεπυρωμένοι· καὶ ἡ φωνὴ αὐτοῦ ὡς φωνὴ ὑδάτων πολλῶν.
having been fired, and the voice of Him as a sound of waters many,
2192/1722 1188 848 5495 792 2033 1537
16 καὶ ἔχων ἐν τῇ δεξιᾷ αὐτοῦ χειρὶ ἀστέρας ἑπτά· καὶ ἐκ τοῦ
and having in the right of Him hand stars seven, and out of the
4750 848 4501 1366 3691 1607
στόματος αὐτοῦ ῥομφαία δίστομος ὀξεῖα ἐκπορευομένη· καὶ
mouth of Him a sword two-mouthed sharp proceeding, and
3799 848 5613 2246 5316/1722 1411 848 3753
17 ἡ ὄψις αὐτοῦ, ὡς ὁ ἥλιος φαίνει ἐν τῇ δυνάμει αὐτοῦ. καὶ ὅτε
the face of Him as the sun shines in the power of it. And when
1492 846 4098 4314 4228 848 5613 3498
εἶδον αὐτόν, ἔπεσα πρὸς τοὺς πόδας αὐτοῦ ὡς νεκρός· καὶ
I saw Him, I fell at the feet of Him as dead; and

put His right hand on me, saying to me, Do not fear. I am the First and the Last, [18]and the Living One; and I became dead; and, behold, I am living forever and ever. Amen. And I have the keys to Hades, and of death. [19]Write what things you saw, and what things are, and what things are about to occur after these things.

[20]The mystery of the seven stars which you saw on My right, and the seven golden lampstands. The seven stars are the angels of the seven churches, and the seven lampstands you saw are seven churches.

CHAPTER 2

[1]To the angel of the Ephesian church, write:

[2]These things says the *One* holding the seven stars in His right *hand*, He walking in *the* midst of the seven golden lampstands: I know your works, and your labor, and your patience, and that you cannot bear evil ones; and *you* tried those pretending to be apostles, and are not, and found them *to be* liars. [3]And *I know* you bore up and on account of My name you have labored and have not wearied. [4]But I have against you that you left your first love. [5]Then remember from where you have fallen, and repent, and do the first works. And if not, I am coming to you quickly, and will remove your lampstand from its place, unless you repent.

[6]But you have this, that you hate the works of the Nicolaitans, which I also hate. [7]The *one* having an ear, hear what the Spirit says to

2007 1188 848 5495/1909/1691 3004 3427/3361
ἐπέθηκε τὴν δεξιὰν αὐτοῦ χεῖρα ἐπ' ἐμέ, λέγων μοι, Μὴ
He placed the right of Him hand on me, saying to me, Not
5399 1473/1510 4413 2078 2198
18 φοβοῦ· ἐγώ εἰμι ὁ πρῶτος καὶ ὁ ἔσχατος, καὶ ὁ ζῶν, καὶ
fear; I am the First and the Last, and the living One, and
1096 3498 2400 2198/1510/1519 165
ἐγενόμην νεκρός, καὶ ἰδού, ζῶν εἰμὶ εἰς τοὺς αἰῶνας τῶν
I became dead, and, behold, living I am to the ages of the
165 281 2192 2807 86 2288
αἰώνων, ἀμήν· καὶ ἔχω τὰς κλεῖς τοῦ ᾅδου καὶ τοῦ θανάτου
ages, Amen. And I have the keys of Hades and of death.
1125 3739/1492 3739/1526 3739/3195 1096 3326 5023
19 γράψον ἃ εἶδες, καὶ ἅ εἰσι. καὶ ἃ μέλλει γίνεσθαι μετὰ ταῦτα·
Write what things you saw, and what things are, and what things are about to occur after these things.
3466 2033 792 3739 1492/1909 1188
20 τὸ μυστήριον τῶν ἑπτὰ ἀστέρων ὧν εἶδες ἐπὶ τῆς δεξιᾶς
The mystery of the seven stars which you saw on the right
3450 2033 3087 5552 2033 792
μου, καὶ τὰς ἑπτὰ λυχνίας τὰς χρυσᾶς. οἱ ἑπτὰ ἀστέρες
of me, and the seven lampstands of gold the seven stars
32 2033 1577 1526 2033 3087 3739
ἄγγελοι τῶν ἑπτὰ ἐκκλησιῶν εἰσί· καὶ αἱ ἑπτὰ λυχνίαι ἃς
angels of the seven churches are, and the seven lampstands
1492 2033 1577 1526
εἶδες ἑπτὰ ἐκκλησίαι εἰσί.
you saw seven churches are.

CHAPTER 2

32 2179 1577 1125
1 Τῷ ἀγγέλῳ τῆς Ἐφεσίνης ἐκκλησίας γράψον,
To the angel of the Ephesian church write:
3592 3004 2902 2033 792 1722 1188
Τάδε λέγει ὁ κρατῶν τοὺς ἑπτὰ ἀστέρας ἐν τῇ δεξιᾷ
These things says the (One) holding the seven stars in the right
848 4043 1722 3319 2033 3087
αὐτοῦ, ὁ περιπατῶν ἐν μέσῳ τῶν ἑπτὰ λυχνιῶν τῶν
of Him, the (One) walking in (the) midst of the seven lampstands
5552 1492 2041 3675 2873 4675
2 χρυσῶν· Οἶδα τὰ ἔργα σου, καὶ τὸν κόπον σου, καὶ τὴν
of gold: I know the works of you, and the labor of you, and the
5281 4675 3754/3756/1410 941 2556
ὑπομονήν σου, καὶ ὅτι οὐ δύνῃ βαστάσαι κακούς, καὶ
patience of you, and that you cannot bear evil ones; and
3985 5335 1511 642 3756/1526
ἐπειράσω τοὺς φάσκοντας εἶναι ἀποστόλους καὶ οὐκ εἰσί,
(you) tried those pretending to be apostles, and not are,
2147 846 5571 941 5281 2192
3 καὶ εὗρες αὐτοὺς ψευδεῖς, καὶ ἐβάστασας καὶ ὑπομονὴν ἔχεις,
and found them liars; and you bore up and patience have,
1223 3686 3450 2872 3756 2577 235 2192
4 καὶ διὰ τὸ ὄνομά μου κεκοπίακας καὶ οὐ κέκμηκας. ἀλλ' ἔχω
even due to the name of Me you have labored and not have wearied. But I have
2596 4675/3754 26 4675 4413 863 3421
5 κατὰ σοῦ, ὅτι τὴν ἀγάπην σου τὴν πρώτην ἀφῆκας. μνημό-
against you that the love of you the first you left. Remember
3767 4159 1601 3340 4413
νευε οὖν πόθεν ἐκπέπτωκας, καὶ μετανόησον, καὶ τὰ πρῶτα
therefore whence you have fallen, and repent, and the first
2041 4160 1487 3361 2064 4671/5034 2795
ἔργα ποίησον· εἰ δὲ μή, ἔρχομαί σοι ταχύ, καὶ κινήσω τὴν
works do; if and not, I am coming to you quickly, and will move the
3087 4675/1537 5117 848 =3362= 3340 235
6 λυχνίαν σου ἐκ τοῦ τόπου αὐτῆς, ἐὰν μὴ μετανοήσῃς. ἀλλὰ
lampstand of you from the place of it, unless you repent. But
5124 2192 3754 3404 2041 3531 3739/2504
τοῦτο ἔχεις, ὅτι μισεῖς τὰ ἔργα τῶν Νικολαϊτῶν, ἃ κἀγὼ
this you have, that you hate the works of the Nicolaitans, which I also
3404 2192 3739 191 5101 4151 3004 1577
7 μισῶ. ὁ ἔχων οὖς ἀκουσάτω τί τὸ Πνεῦμα λέγει ταῖς ἐκκλη-
hate. The (one) having an ear, hear what the Spirit says to the churches.

the churches. To the *one* overcoming, I will give to him to eat of the Tree of Life which is in *the* midst of the Paradise of God.

[8]And to the angel of the church of Smyrna, write:

[9]These things says the First and the Last, who became dead, and lived: I know your works, and the affliction, and the poverty; but you are rich. And *I know* the evil speaking of those saying themselves to be Jews, and they are not, but *are* a synagogue of Satan. [10]Do not at all fear what you are about to suffer. Behold, the Devil is about to throw you into prison, so that you may be tried; and you will have affliction ten days. Be faithful until death, and I will give you the crown of life. [11]The *one* who has an ear, hear what the Spirit says to the churches. The *one* overcoming will not at all be hurt by the second death.

[12]And to the angel of the church in Pergamos, write:

These things says the *One* having the sharp, two-edged sword: [13]I know your works, and where you dwell, where the throne of Satan *is*. And you hold My name, and did not deny My faith even in the days in which Antipas *was* My faithful witness; who was killed alongside you, where Satan dwells. [14]But I have a few things against you, that you have there those holding the teachings of Balaam, who taught Balak to throw a stumbling-block before the sons of Israel, to eat idol-sacrifices, and to commit fornication. [15]So you also have those holding the teaching of the Nicolaitans, which thing I hate. [16]Repent! But if not, I

3528 1325 846 5315/1537 3586 2222
σίαις. τῷ νικῶντι δώσω αὐτῷ φαγεῖν ἐκ τοῦ ξύλου τῆς ζωῆς,
To the (one) over-coming I will give to him to eat of the tree of life,
3739/2076/1722 3857 2316
•3319 ὅ ἐστιν ἐν μέσῳ τοῦ παραδείσου τοῦ Θεοῦ.
which is in (the) midst of the Paradise of God.

32 1577 4668 1125
8 Καὶ τῷ ἀγγέλῳ τῆς ἐκκλησίας Σμυρναίων γράψον,
And to the angel of the church of Smyrna write:
3592/3004 4413 2078 3739/1096 3498
Τάδε λέγει ὁ πρῶτος καὶ ὁ ἔσχατος, ὃς ἐγένετο νεκρὸς καὶ
These things says the First and the Last, who became dead and
2198 1492/4675 2041 2347 4432
9 ἔζησεν· Οἶδά σου τὰ ἔργα καὶ τὴν θλίψιν καὶ τὴν πτωχείαν
lived: I know of you the works and the affliction and the poverty,
4145 1488 988 3004 2453
(πλούσιος δὲ εἶ), καὶ τὴν βλασφημίαν τῶν λεγόντων Ἰου-
rich but you are, and the evil speaking of those saying Jews
1511 1438 3756/1526 235 4864
δαίους εἶναι ἑαυτούς, καὶ οὐκ εἰσίν, ἀλλὰ συναγωγὴ τοῦ
to be themselves, and not they are, but a synagogue of
4567 3367 5399/3739/3195 3958 2400 3195 906
10 Σατανᾶ. μηδὲν φοβοῦ ἃ μέλλεις πάσχειν· ἰδού, μέλλει βαλεῖν
Satan. Not at all do fear what you are about to suffer. Behold, is about to cast
1537/5216 1228 1519 5438 2443 3985 2192
ἐξ ὑμῶν ὁ διάβολος εἰς φυλακήν, ἵνα πειρασθῆτε· καὶ ἕξετε
of you the Devil into prison, that you may be tried, and you will have
2347 2250 1176 1096 4103 891 2288 1325
θλίψιν ἡμερῶν δέκα. γίνου πιστὸς ἄχρι θανάτου, καὶ δώσω
affliction days ten. Be faithful until death, and I will give
4671 4735 2222 2192/3739 191 5101
11 σοι τὸν στέφανον τῆς ζωῆς. ὁ ἔχων οὖς ἀκουσάτω τί τὸ
you the crown of life. The (one) having an ear, hear what the
4151 3004 1577 3528/3756/3361/ 91 1537
Πνεῦμα λέγει ταῖς ἐκκλησίαις. ὁ νικῶν οὐ μὴ ἀδικηθῇ ἐκ τοῦ
Spirit says to the churches. The (one) over-coming not at all will be hurt by the
2288 1208
θανάτου τοῦ δευτέρου.
death second.

32 1722 4010 1577 1125
12 Καὶ τῷ ἀγγέλῳ τῆς ἐν Περγάμῳ ἐκκλησίας γράψον,
And to the angel of the in Pergamos church write:
3592 3004 2192 4501 1366
Τάδε λέγει ὁ ἔχων τὴν ῥομφαίαν τὴν δίστομον τὴν
These things says He having the sword two-mouthed
3691 1492 2041/4675 4226 2730 3699 2362
13 ὀξεῖαν· Οἶδα τὰ ἔργα σου καὶ ποῦ κατοικεῖς, ὅπου ὁ θρόνος
sharp: I know the works of you and where you dwell, where the throne
4567 2902 3686/3450 3756 720
τοῦ Σατανᾶ· καὶ κρατεῖς τὸ ὄνομά μου, καὶ οὐκ ἠρνήσω τὴν
(is) of Satan: and you hold the name of Me, and not did deny the
4102 3450 1722 2250/1722/3739/ 493 3144 3450
πίστιν μου καὶ ἐν ταῖς ἡμέραις ἐν αἷς Ἀντίπας ὁ μάρτυς μου,
faith of Me even in the days in which (was) Antipas the witness of Me
•5213 4103 3739 615 3844 3699/ 2730 4567
ὁ πιστός, ὃς ἀπεκτάνθη παρ' ὑμῖν, ὅπου κατοικεῖ ὁ Σατανᾶς.
faithful, who was killed alongside you, where dwells Satan.
235 1473 2596/4675 3641 3754/2192/1563 2902
14 ἀλλ' ἔχω κατὰ σοῦ ὀλίγα, ὅτι ἔχεις ἐκεῖ κρατοῦντας τὴν
But I have against you a few things, for you have there those holding the
1322 903 3739 1321 906 906 4625
διδαχὴν Βαλαάμ, ὃς ἐδίδασκε τὸν Βαλὰκ βαλεῖν σκάνδαλον
teachings of Balaam, who taught Balak to throw a stumbling-block
1799 5207 2474 5315 1494 4203
ἐνώπιον τῶν υἱῶν Ἰσραήλ, φαγεῖν εἰδωλόθυτα καὶ πορνεῦ-
before the sons of Israel, to eat idol sacrifices and to commit
3779 2192 4771 2902 1322
15 σαι. οὕτως ἔχεις καὶ σὺ κρατοῦντας τὴν διδαχὴν τῶν
fornication So have also you those holding the teaching of the
3531 3739/3404 3340 =1490= 2064 4671
16 Νικολαϊτῶν· ὃ μισῶ. μετανόησον· εἰ δὲ μή, ἔρχομαί σοι
Nicolaitans which thing I hate. Repent! if But not, I will come to you

will come to you quickly, and I will make war with them by the sword of My mouth. [17]The *one* who has an ear, hear what the Spirit says to the churches. To the *one* overcoming, I will give him to eat from the hidden manna. And I will give to him a white stone, and on the stone a new name having been written, which no one knows except the *one* receiving *it*.

[18]And to the angel of the church in Thyatira, write:

These things says the Son of God, the *One* having His eyes as a flame of fire, and His feet like burnished metal: [19]I know your works, and the love, and the ministry, and the faith, and your patience, and your works; and the last more than the first. [20]But I have a few things against you, that you allow the woman Jezebel to teach, she saying herself *to be* a prophetess, and to cause My slaves to go astray, and to commit fornication, and to eat idol-sacrifices. [21]And I gave time to her that she might repent of her fornication. And she did not repent. [22]Behold, I am throwing her into a bed, and those committing adultery with her into great affliction, unless they repent of their works. [23]And I will kill her children with death; and all the churches will know that I am the *One* searching the inner parts and hearts. And I will give to each of you according to your works. [24]But I say to you and to the rest in Thyatira, as many as do not have this teaching, and who did not know the deep things of Satan, as they say; I am not casting another burden on you; [25]but what you have, hold

5035 4170 3326 846 1722 4501 4750
ταχύ, καὶ πολεμήσω μετ᾽ αὐτῶν ἐν τῇ ῥομφαίᾳ τοῦ στό-
quickly, and I will make war with them by the sword of the mouth

3450 2192/3775 191 5101 4151 3004
17 ματός μου. ὁ ἔχων οὖς ἀκουσάτω τί τὸ Πνεῦμα λέγει ταῖς
of Me. The (one) having an ear, hear what the Spirit says to the

1577 3528 1325 846 5315 575 3131
ἐκκλησίαις. τῷ νικῶντι δώσω αὐτῷ φαγεῖν ἀπὸ τοῦ μάννα
churches. To the (one) overcoming, I will give him to eat from the manna

2928 1325 846 5386 3022 1909
τοῦ κεκρυμμένου, καὶ δώσω αὐτῷ ψῆφον λευκήν, καὶ ἐπὶ
hidden. And I will give to him a stone white, and on

5586 3686 2537 1125 3739/3762 1097/=1508=
τὴν ψῆφον ὄνομα καινὸν γεγραμμένον, ὃ οὐδεὶς ἔγνω εἰ μὴ
the stone a name new being written, which no one knows except

2983
ὁ λαμβάνων.
the (one) receiving (it).

32 1722 2363 1577 1125
18 Καὶ τῷ ἀγγέλῳ τῆς ἐν Θυατείροις ἐκκλησίας γράψον,
And to the angel of the in Thyatira church write:

3592/3004 5207 2316 2192 3788 848
Τάδε λέγει ὁ υἱὸς τοῦ Θεοῦ, ὁ ἔχων τοὺς ὀφθαλμοὺς αὐτοῦ
These things says the Son of God, He having the eyes of Him

5613 5395/4442 4228 848 3664 5474
ὡς φλόγα πυρός, καὶ οἱ πόδες αὐτοῦ ὅμοιοι χαλκολιβάνῳ·
as a flame of fire, and the feet of Him like burnished metal

1492/4675 2041 26 1248
19 Οἶδά σου τὰ ἔργα, καὶ τὴν ἀγάπην καὶ τὴν διακονίαν, καὶ
I know of you the works, and the love and the ministry, and

4102 5281 4675 2041/4675
τὴν πίστιν καὶ τὴν ὑπομονήν σου, καὶ τὰ ἔργα σου, καὶ τὰ
the faith and the patience of you, and the works of you, and the

2078 4119 4413 235 2192 2596 4675 3641
20 ἔσχατα πλείονα τῶν πρώτων. ἀλλ᾽ ἔχω κατὰ σοῦ ὀλίγα
last more than the first. But I have against you a few things,

3754/1439 1135 2403 3004 1438/4398
ὅτι ἐᾷς τὴν γυναῖκα Ἰεζαβήλ, τὴν λέγουσαν ἑαυτὴν προφῆ-
that you allow the woman Jezebel, the (one) saying herself a prophet-

1321 4105 1699 1401 4203
τιν, διδάσκειν καὶ πλανᾶσθαι ἐμοὺς δούλους πορνεῦσαι καὶ
tess, to teach and to cause to err My slaves to commit fornication and

1494 5315 1325 846 5550/2443 3340
21 εἰδωλόθυτα φαγεῖν. καὶ ἔδωκα αὐτῇ χρόνον ἵνα μετανοήσῃ
idol sacrifices to eat. And I gave to her time that she might repent

1537 4202 848 3756 3340 2400/1473 906
22 ἐκ τῆς πορνείας αὐτῆς, καὶ οὐ μετενόησεν. ἰδού, ἐγὼ βάλλω
of the fornication of her, and not she repented. Behold, I am casting

846 1519 2825 3431 3326 846/1519 2347
αὐτὴν εἰς κλίνην, καὶ τοὺς μοιχεύοντας μετ᾽ αὐτῆς εἰς θλῖψιν
her into a bed, and those committing adultery with her into affliction

3173 1437/3361/ 3340 1537 2041 848
23 μεγάλην, ἐὰν μὴ μετανοήσωσιν ἐκ τῶν ἔργων αὐτῶν. καὶ τὰ
great, unless they may repent of the works of them. And the

5043 848 615 1722 2288 1097 3956
τέκνα αὐτῆς ἀποκτενῶ ἐν θανάτῳ· καὶ γνώσονται πᾶσαι
children of her I will kill with death; and will know all

1577 3754/1473/1510 2045 3510 2588
αἱ ἐκκλησίαι ὅτι ἐγώ εἰμι ὁ ἐρευνῶν νεφροὺς καὶ καρδίας·
the churches that I am the (One) searching kidneys and hearts,

1325 5213 1538 2596 2041 5216 5213
24 καὶ δώσω ὑμῖν ἑκάστῳ κατὰ τὰ ἔργα ὑμῶν. ὑμῖν δὲ
and I will give to you each according to the works of you. to you But

3004 3062 1722 2363 3745 3756 2192
λέγω καὶ λοιποῖς τοῖς ἐν Θυατείροις, ὅσοι οὐκ ἔχουσι τὴν
I say and to the rest in Thyatira, as many as not have

1322 5026 3748 3756 1097 899
διδαχὴν ταύτην, καὶ οἵτινες οὐκ ἔγνωσαν τα βάθη τοῦ
teaching this, and who not did know the deep things

4567 5613 3004 3756 906/1909/ 5209 235 922 4133
25 Σατανᾶ, ὡς λέγουσιν, Οὐ βαλῶ ἐφ᾽ ὑμᾶς ἄλλο βάρος. πλὴν
of Satan, as they say, not I am casting on you another load, but

until I shall come. [26]And the *one* overcoming, and the *one* keeping My works until *the* end, I will give to him authority over the nations, [27]and he will shepherd them with an iron staff—they are broken to pieces like clay vessels — as I also have received from My Father. [28]And I will give to him the morning star. [29]The *one* who has an ear, hear what the Spirit says to the churches.

CHAPTER 3

[1]And to the angel of the church in Sardis, write:

These things says the *One* having the seven spirits of God, and the seven stars: I know your works, that you have the name that you live, and are dead. [2]Be watching, and establish the things left, which are about to die. For I have not found your works being fulfilled before God. [3]Then remember how you received and heard, and keep, and repent. If, then, you do not watch, I will come upon you like a thief, and you will not at all know what hour I come upon you. [4]You also have a few names in Sardis which did not defile their robes, and they shall walk with Me in white because they are worthy.

[5]The *one* overcoming, this *one* shall be clothed in white garments, and I will not at all blot his name out of the Book of Life; and I will acknowledge his name before My Father, and before His angels. [6]The *one* who has an ear, hear what the Spirit says to the churches.

[7]And to the angel of the church in Philadelphia, write:

These things says the Holy One, the True One, the *One* having the key of

2192 2902 891/3739/302/2240 3528
26 ὃ ἔχετε κρατήσατε, ἄχρις οὗ ἂν ἥξω. καὶ ὁ νικῶν καὶ ὁ
what you have hold until I shall come. And the over-coming (one) and the (one)
5083 891 5056 2041 3450 1325 846 1849 1909
τηρῶν ἄχρι τέλους τὰ ἔργα μου, δώσω αὐτῷ ἐξουσίαν ἐπὶ
keeping until (the) end the works of Me, I will give him authority over
1484 4165 846 1722 4464 4603 5613
27 τῶν ἐθνῶν· καὶ ποιμανεῖ αὐτοὺς ἐν ῥάβδῳ σιδηρᾷ· ὡς τὰ
the nations, and he will shepherd them with a staff iron, as
4632 2764 4937 5613/2504 2983 3844
σκεύη τὰ κεραμικά, συντρίβεται· ὡς κἀγὼ εἴληφα παρὰ τοῦ
vessels clay, they are broken, as I also have received from the
3962 3450 1325 846 792 4407
28 πατρός μου· καὶ δώσω αὐτῷ τὸν ἀστέρα τὸν πρωϊνόν.
Father of Me, and I will give him the star morning.
2192/3775 191 5101 4151 3004 1577
29 ὁ ἔχων οὖς ἀκουσάτω τί τὸ Πνεῦμα λέγει ταῖς ἐκκλησίαις.
he having an ear, hear what the Spirit says to the churches.

CHAPTER 3

32 1722 4554 1577 1125
1 Καὶ τῷ ἀγγέλῳ τῆς ἐν Σάρδεσιν ἐκκλησίας γράψον,
And to the angel of the in Sardis church write:
3592/3004 2192 2033 4151 2316
Τάδε λέγει ὁ ἔχων τὰ ἑπτὰ πνεύματα τοῦ Θεοῦ καὶ τοὺς
These things says He having the seven spirits of God, and the
2033 792 1492 4675 2041/3754 3686 2192/3754
ἑπτὰ ἀστέρας· Οἶδά σου τὰ ἔργα, ὅτι τὸ ὄνομα ἔχεις ὅτι
seven stars: I know of you the works, that the name you have that
2198 3498/1488/1096 1125 4741 3062
2 ζῇς, καὶ νεκρὸς εἶ. γίνου γρηγορῶν, καὶ στήριξον τὰ λοιπὰ
you live, and dead are. Be watching, and establish the things left
3739/3195 599 3756/1063 2147 4675 2041 4137
ἃ μέλλει ἀποθανεῖν· οὐ γὰρ εὕρηκά σου τὰ ἔργα πεπληρω-
which are about to die; not for I have found of you the works being ful-
1799 2316 3421 3767/4459 2983
3 μένα ἐνώπιον τοῦ Θεοῦ. μνημόνευε οὖν πῶς εἴληφας καὶ
filled before God Remember, then, how you received and
191 5083 3340 1437/3767/3361 1127
ἤκουσας, καὶ τήρει, καὶ μετανόησον. ἐὰν οὖν μὴ γρηγορή-
heard, and keep, and repent. If, then, not you watch,
2240/1909/4571/5613/ 2812 =3364= 1097 4169 5610
4 σῃς, ἥξω ἐπί σε ὡς κλέπτης, καὶ οὐ μὴ γνῷς ποίαν ὥραν
I will come on you as a thief, and not at all you know what hour
2240/1909/4571/2192/ 3641 3686 1722 4554 3739/3756
ἥξω ἐπί σε. ἔχεις ὀλίγα ὀνόματα καὶ ἐν Σάρδεσιν, ἃ οὐκ
I come on you. You have a few names also in Sardis which not
3435 2440 848 4043 3326/1700/1722
ἐμόλυναν τὰ ἱμάτια αὐτῶν· καὶ περιπατήσουσι μετ' ἐμοῦ ἐν
defile the robes of them, and they shall walk with Me in
3022 3754/514 1526 3528 3778 4016 1722
5 λευκοῖς, ὅτι ἄξιοί εἰσιν. ὁ νικῶν, οὗτος περιβαλεῖται ἐν
white, because worthy they are. he overcoming, he shall be clothed in
2440 3022 =3364= 1813 3686 848 1537
ἱματίοις λευκοῖς· καὶ οὐ μὴ ἐξαλείψω τὸ ὄνομα αὐτοῦ ἐκ τῆς
garments white, and not at all will I blot the name of him out of the
976 2222 1843 3686 848
βίβλου τῆς ζωῆς, καὶ ἐξομολογήσομαι τὸ ὄνομα αὐτοῦ
Scroll of Life, and I will acknowledge the name of him
1799 3962 3450 1799 32 848
ἐνώπιον τοῦ πατρός μου, καὶ ἐνώπιον τῶν ἀγγέλων αὐτοῦ.
before the Father of Me, and before the angels of Him.
2192/3775 191 5101 4151 3004 1577
6 ὁ ἔχων οὖς ἀκουσάτω τί τὸ Πνεῦμα λέγει ταῖς ἐκκλησίαις.
The (one) having an ear, hear what the Spirit says to the churches.
32 1722 5359 1577 1125
7 Καὶ τῷ ἀγγέλῳ τῆς ἐν Φιλαδελφείᾳ ἐκκλησίας γράψον,
And to the angel of the in Philadelphia, church write:
3592/3004 40 228 2192 2807
Τάδε λέγει ὁ ἅγιος, ὁ ἀληθινός, ὁ ἔχων τὴν κλεῖδα τοῦ
These things says the Holy One, the True One, He having the key

David, the *One* opening, and no one shuts, and shuts and no one opens; [8]I know your works. Behold, I have given a door being opened before you, and no one is able to shut it, for you have a little power and have kept My word, and have not denied My name. [9]Behold, I give out of the synagogue of Satan those saying themselves to be Jews, and they are not, but they lie. Behold, I will make them come and bow down before your feet, and they shall know that I loved you. [10]Because you kept the word of My patience, I also will keep you out of the hour of trial which is going to come on all the habitable world in order to try those dwelling on the earth. [11]Behold, I am coming quickly. Hold what you have that no one take your crown. [12]The *one* overcoming, I will make him a pillar in the temple of My God, and he shall not go out any more. And I will write the name of My God on him, and the name of the city of My God, the new Jerusalem which comes down out of Heaven from My God, and My new name.

[13]The *one* who has an ear, hear what the Spirit says to the churches.

[14]And to the angel of the church of Laodicea, write:

These things says the Amen, the faithful and true Witness, the Head of the creation of God: [15]I know your works, that you are neither cold nor hot. I would that you were cold, or hot. [16]So, because you are lukewarm, and neither cold nor hot, I am about to

1138 455 3762 2808 2808 3762
Δαβίδ, ὁ ἀνοίγων καὶ οὐδεὶς κλείει, καὶ κλείει καὶ οὐδεὶς
of David, the (One) opening and no one shuts, and shuts, and no one
455 1492/4675 2041 2400 1325 1799 4675/2374
8 ἀνοίγει· Οἶδά σου τὰ ἔργα (ἰδού, δέδωκα ἐνώπιόν σου θύραν
opens: I know of you the works. Behold, I have given before you a door
455 3762 1410 2808 846 3754 3398
ἀνεῳγμένην, καὶ οὐδεὶς δύναται κλεῖσαι αὐτήν), ὅτι μικρὰν
being opened, and no one is able to shut it, because a little
2192 1411 5083 3450 3056 3756 720
ἔχεις δύναμιν, καὶ ἐτήρησάς μου τὸν λόγον, καὶ οὐκ ἠρνήσω
you have power, and have kept of Me the word, and not denied
3686 3450 2400 1325/1537 4864 4567
9 τὸ ὄνομά μου. ἰδού, δίδωμι ἐκ τῆς συναγωγῆς τοῦ Σατανᾶ,
the name of Me. Behold, I give out of the synagogue of Satan,
3004 1438 2453 1511 3756/1526 235
τῶν λεγόντων ἑαυτοὺς Ἰουδαίους εἶναι, καὶ οὐκ εἰσίν, ἀλλὰ
those saying themselves Jews to be, and not they are, but
5574 2400 4160 846 2443 2240 4352
ψεύδονται· ἰδού, ποιήσω αὐτοὺς ἵνα ἥξωσι καὶ προσκυνή-
they lie; behold, I will make them that they shall come and shall
1799 4228 4675 1097 3754 1473
σωσιν ἐνώπιον τῶν ποδῶν σου, καὶ γνῶσιν ὅτι ἐγὼ
bow before the feet of you, and they shall know that I
25 4571/3754 5083 3056 5281 3450
10 ἠγάπησά σε. ὅτι ἐτήρησας τὸν λόγον τῆς ὑπομονῆς μου,
loved you. Because you kept the word of the patience of Me,
2504/4571/ 5083/1537 5610 3986 3195
κἀγώ σε τηρήσω ἐκ τῆς ὥρας τοῦ πειρασμοῦ, τῆς μελλούσης
I also you will keep out of the hour of trial being about
2064 1909 3625 3650 3985 2730
ἔρχεσθαι ἐπὶ τῆς οἰκουμένης ὅλης, πειράσαι τοὺς κατοι-
to come upon the habitable world all, to try those dwelling
1909 1093/2400 2064 5035 2902/3739/2192/2443
11 κοῦντας ἐπὶ τῆς γῆς. ἰδού, ἔρχομαι ταχύ· κράτει ὃ ἔχεις, ἵνα
on the earth. Behold, I am coming quickly; hold what you have that
3367 2983 4735 4675 3528 4160 846
12 μηδεὶς λάβῃ τὸν στέφανόν σου. ὁ νικῶν, ποιήσω αὐτὸν
no one take the crown of you. The over- (One) coming I will make him
4769 1722 3485 2316/3450 •/=3364= 1831 2089
στύλον ἐν τῷ ναῷ τοῦ Θεοῦ μου, καὶ ἔξω οὐ μὴ ἐξέλθῃ ἔτι,
a pillar in the temple of the God of Me, and out not at all he will go yet,
1125 1909 846 3686 2316/3450 3686
καὶ γράψω ἐπ' αὐτὸν τὸ ὄνομα τοῦ Θεοῦ μου, καὶ τὸ ὄνομα
and I will write on him the name of the God of Me, and the name
4172 2316/3450 2537 2419 2597
τῆς πόλεως τοῦ Θεοῦ μου, τῆς καινῆς Ἱερουσαλήμ, ἡ κατα-
of the city of the God of Me, the new Jerusalem which comes
1537 3772 575 2316/3450 3686/3450
βαίνει ἐκ τοῦ οὐρανοῦ ἀπὸ τοῦ Θεοῦ μου, καὶ τὸ ὄνομά μου
down out of Heaven from the God of Me, and the name of Me
2537 2192/3775 191 5101 4151 3004
13 τὸ καινόν. ὁ ἔχων οὖς ἀκουσάτω τί τὸ Πνεῦμα λέγει ταῖς
new. The (one) having an ear, hear what the Spirit says to the
1577
ἐκκλησίαις.
churches.

32 1577 2993 1125
14 Καὶ τῷ ἀγγέλῳ τῆς ἐκκλησίας Λαοδικέων γράψον,
And to the angel of the church in Laodicea write:
3592/3004 281 3144 4103 228
Τάδε λέγει ὁ Ἀμήν, ὁ μάρτυς ὁ πιστὸς καὶ ἀληθινός, ἡ
These things says the Amen, the Witness faithful and true, the
746 2937 2316 1492/4675 2041 3754 3777
15 ἀρχὴ τῆς κτίσεως τοῦ Θεοῦ· Οἶδά σου τὰ ἔργα, ὅτι οὔτε
Head of the creation of God: I know of you the works, that neither
5593/1488/3777 2200 3785 5593 1498/2228/2200 3779
16 ψυχρὸς εἶ οὔτε ζεστός· ὄφελον ψυχρὸς εἴης ἢ ζεστός. οὕτως
cold are you, nor hot; I would that cold you were, or hot. So
3754/ 5513/1488 3777 5593 3777 2200 3195/4571/1692
ὅτι χλιαρὸς εἶ, καὶ οὔτε ψυχρὸς οὔτε ζεστός, μέλλω σε ἐμέσαι
because luke- warm you are, and neither cold nor hot, I am about you to vomit

vomit you out of My mouth. [17]Because you say, I am rich, and I am made rich, and I have need of nothing, and do not know that you are wretched and miserable and poor and blind and naked. [18]I advise you to buy from Me gold having been fired by fire, that you may be rich; and white garments, that you may be clothed, and your shame and nakedness may not be revealed. And anoint your eyes with eye-salve, that you may see. [19]I, as many as I love, I rebuke and I chasten. Be zealous, then, and repent. [20]Behold, I stand at the door and knock: If anyone hears My voice and opens the door, I will go in to him, and I will dine with him, and he with Me. [21]The *one* overcoming, I will give to him to sit with Me in My throne, as I also overcame and sat with My Father in His throne. [22]The *one* who has an ear, hear what the Spirit says to the churches.

CHAPTER 4

[1]After these things I saw. And behold, a door being opened in Heaven! And I heard the first voice as a trumpet speaking with me, saying, Come up here, and I will show you what needs to happen after these things.

[2]And at once I became in spirit. And, behold, a throne was set in Heaven, and *One* sitting on the throne. [3]And the *One* sitting was in appearance like a jasper stone, and a sardius; and a rainbow *was* around the throne, in appearance like an emerald. [4]And around the throne /

1537 4750 3450 3754 3004 3754 4145 1510
17 ἐκ τοῦ στοματός μου. ὅτι λέγεις ὅτι Πλούσιός εἰμι, καὶ
out of the mouth of Me. Because you say, — rich I am, and
4147 3762 5532/2192 3756/1492/3754/4771
πεπλούτηκα, καὶ οὐδενὸς χρείαν ἔχω, καὶ οὐκ οἶδας ὅτι σὺ
I am made rich, and of nothing need I have, and not know that you
1488 5005 1652 4434 5185
εἶ ὁ ταλαίπωρος καὶ ἐλεεινὸς καὶ πτωχὸς καὶ τυφλὸς καὶ
are the wretched (one) and miserable and poor and blind and
1131 4823 4671 59 3844 1700 5553
18 γυμνός· συμβουλεύω σοι ἀγοράσαι παρ' ἐμοῦ χρυσίον
naked I advise you to buy from Me gold
4448 1537/4442/2443 4147 2440 3022
πεπυρωμένον ἐκ πυρός, ἵνα πλουτήσῃς, καὶ ἱμάτια λευκά,
having been fired by fire, that you may be rich; and garments white,
2443 4016 3361/ 5319 152 1132
ἵνα περιβάλῃ, καὶ μὴ φανερωθῇ ἡ αἰσχύνη τῆς γυμνότητός
that you be clothed, and not may be revealed the shame and the nakedness
4675 2854 1472 3788 4675 2443
σου· καὶ κολλούριον ἔγχρισον τοὺς ὀφθαλμούς σου, ἵνα
of you, and with eyesalve anoint the eyes of you, that
991 1473 3745/1437/5368 1651 3811 2206
19 βλέπῃς. ἐγὼ ὅσους ἐὰν φιλῶ, ἐλέγχω καὶ παιδεύω· ζήλωσον
you may see. I as many if I love, I rebuke, and I chasten; be zealous,
3767 3340 2400 2476/1909 2374 2925
20 οὖν καὶ μετανόησον. Ἰδού, ἕστηκα ἐπὶ τὴν θύραν καὶ κρούω·
then, and repent. Behold, I stand at the door and knock;
1437/5100 191 5456 3450 455 2374
ἐάν τις ἀκούσῃ τῆς φωνῆς μου, καὶ ἀνοίξῃ τὴν θύραν,
If anyone hear the voice of Me, and opens the door,
1525 4314 846 1172 3326 846
εἰσελεύσομαι πρὸς αὐτόν, καὶ δειπνήσω μετ' αὐτοῦ, καὶ
I will enter to him, and I will dine with him, and
846 3326 1700 3528 1325 846 2523 3326 1700
21 αὐτὸς μετ' ἐμοῦ. ὁ νικῶν, δώσω αὐτῷ καθίσαι μετ' ἐμοῦ
he with Me. The (one) overcoming I will give to him to sit with Me
1722 2362 3450/5613/2504 3528 2523 3326
ἐν τῷ θρόνῳ μου, ὡς κἀγὼ ἐνίκησα. καὶ ἐκάθισα μετὰ τοῦ
in the throne of Me, as I also overcame and sat with the
3962 3450/1722 2362 848 2192/3775 191 5101
22 πατρός μου ἐν τῷ θρόνῳ αὐτοῦ. ὁ ἔχων οὖς ἀκουσάτω τί
Father of Me in the throne of Him. The (one) having an ear, hear what
4151 3004 1577
τὸ Πνεῦμα λέγει ταῖς ἐκκλησίαις.
the Spirit says to the churches.

CHAPTER 4

3326 5023 1492 2400 2374 455 1722
1 Μετὰ ταῦτα εἶδον, καὶ ἰδού, θύρα ἠνεῳγμένη ἐν τῷ
After these things I saw, and behold, a door having been opened in
3772 5456 4413/3739 191 5613 4536
οὐρανῷ, καὶ ἡ φωνὴ ἡ πρώτη ἣν ἤκουσα ὡς σάλπιγγος
Heaven, and the voice first which I heard as a trumpet
2980 3326/1700 3004 305 5602 1166 4671
λαλούσης μετ' ἐμοῦ, λέγουσα, Ἀνάβα ὧδε, καὶ δείξω σοι
speaking with me, saying, Come up here, and I will show you
3739/1163 1096 3326 5023 2112 1096/1722/ 4151
2 ἃ δεῖ γενέσθαι μετὰ ταῦτα. καὶ εὐθέως ἐγενόμην ἐν πνεύματι·
what needs to occur after these things. And at once I became in spirit,
2400 2362 2749/1722 3772 1909 2362
καὶ ἰδού, θρόνος ἔκειτο ἐν τῷ οὐρανῷ, καὶ ἐπὶ τοῦ θρόνου
and behold, a throne was set in Heaven, and on the throne
2521 2521 2258 3664 3706 3037 2393
3 καθήμενος· καὶ ὁ καθήμενος ἦν ὅμοιος ὁράσει λίθῳ ἰάσπιδι
(One) sitting, and He sitting was like in appearance a stone jasper;
4555 2463 2943 2362 3664 3706
καὶ σαρδίνῳ· καὶ ἶρις κυκλόθεν τοῦ θρόνου ὁμοία ὁράσει
and a sardius, and a rainbow (was) around the throne like in appearance
4664 2943 2362 2362 1501
4 σμαραγδίνῳ. καὶ κυκλόθεν τοῦ θρόνου θρόνοι εἴκοσι καὶ
to an emerald And around the throne (I saw) thrones twenty and

saw twenty-four thrones, and on the thrones I saw twenty-four elders sitting, having been clothed in white garments. And they had golden crowns on their heads. [5]And out of the throne come forth lightnings and thunders and voices. And seven lamps of fire *are* burning before the throne, which are the seven Spirits of God; [6]and a glassy sea before the throne, like crystal. And in *the* midst of the throne and around the throne *were* four living creatures, full of eyes before and behind.

[7]And the first living creature *was* like a lion; and the second living creature like a calf; and the third living creature having a face like a man; and the fourth living creature like an eagle flying. [8]And the four living creatures each one had six wings around, and within being full of eyes. And they had no rest day and night, saying, Holy, holy, holy, Lord God Almighty, the *One who* was, and is, and *is* coming!

[9]And when the living creatures shall give glory and honor and thanks to the *One* sitting on the throne, to the *One* living forever and ever, [10]the twenty-four elders fall down before Him sitting on the throne; and they will worship the *One* living forever and ever, and will throw their crowns before the throne, saying, [11]Lord, You are worthy to receive the glory and the honor and the power, because You created all things, and through Your will they exist.

5064 1909 2362 1492 1501 5064
τέσσαρες· καὶ ἐπὶ τοὺς θρόνους εἶδον τοὺς εἴκοσι καὶ τέσσαρας
four, and on the thrones I saw twenty and four
4245 2521 4016 1722 2440
πρεσβυτέρους καθημένους, περιβεβλημένους ἐν ἱματίοις
elders sitting, having been clothed in garments
3022 2192 1909 2776 848 4735
λευκοῖς, καὶ ἔσχον ἐπὶ τὰς κεφαλὰς αὐτῶν στεφάνους
white, and they had on the heads of them crowns
5552 1537 2362 1607 796
5 χρυσοῦς. καὶ ἐκ τοῦ θρόνου ἐκπορεύονται ἀστραπαὶ καὶ
of gold. And out of the throne come forth lightnings and
1027 5456 2033 2985 4442 2545
βρονταὶ καὶ φωναί. καὶ ἑπτὰ λαμπάδες πυρὸς καιόμεναι
thunders and voices. And seven lamps of fire (are) burning
1799 2362 3739/1526 2033 4151 2316
ἐνώπιον τοῦ θρόνου, αἵ εἰσι τὰ ἑπτὰ πνεύματα τοῦ Θεοῦ·
before the throne, which are the seven Spirits of God;
1799 2362 2281 5193 3664 2930
6 καὶ ἐνώπιον τοῦ θρόνου θάλασσα ὑαλίνη, ὁμοία κρυστάλλῳ.
and before the throne sea a glassy like to crystal;
1722/3319 2362 2945 2362 5064 2226
καὶ ἐν μέσῳ τοῦ θρόνου καὶ κύκλῳ τοῦ θρόνου τέσσαρα ζῷα
and in (the) midst of the throne and around the throne four living creatures
1073 3788 1715 3693 2226
7 γέμοντα ὀφθαλμῶν ἔμπροσθεν καὶ ὄπισθεν. καὶ τὸ ζῷον
full of eyes before and behind and the living creature
4413 3664 3023 1208 2226 3664
τὸ πρῶτον ὅμοιον λέοντι, καὶ τὸ δεύτερον ζῷον ὅμοιον
first (was) like a lion, and the second living creature like
3448 5154 2226/2192 4383 5613 444
μόσχῳ, καὶ τὸ τρίτον ζῷον ἔχον τὸ πρόσωπον ὡς ἄνθρωπος,
a calf, and the third living creature having the face as of a man,
5067 2226 3664 105 4072 5064
8 καὶ τὸ τέταρτον ζῷον ὅμοιον ἀετῷ πετωμένῳ. καὶ τέσσαρα
and the fourth living creature like an eagle flying. And (the) four
2226/1520/2596/1438 2192/303 4420 1803 2943
ζῷα, ἓν καθ' ἑαυτὸ εἶχον ἀνὰ πτέρυγας ἓξ κυκλόθεν, καὶ
living creatures one by one having each wings six around and
2081 1073 3788 372 3756 2192
ἔσωθεν γέμοντα ὀφθαλμῶν, καὶ ἀνάπαυσιν οὐκ ἔχουσιν
within being full of eyes; and respite not they have
2250 3571 3004 40 40 40 2962
ἡμέρας καὶ νυκτός, λέγοντα, Ἅγιος, ἅγιος, ἅγιος Κύριος ὁ
day and night, saying, Holy, holy, holy, Lord
2316 3841 2258 5607 2064
9 Θεὸς ὁ παντοκράτωρ, ὁ ἦν καὶ ὁ ὢν καὶ ὁ ἐρχόμενος. καὶ
God, the Almighty, the (One who) was and is and (is) coming. And
3752 1325 2226 1391 5092 2169
ὅταν δώσουσι τὰ ζῷα δόξαν καὶ τιμὴν καὶ εὐχαριστίαν τῷ
when shall give the living creatures glory and honor and thanks to the (One)
2521 1909 2362 2198 1519 165
καθημένῳ ἐπὶ τοῦ θρόνου, τῷ ζῶντι εἰς τοὺς αἰῶνας τῶν
sitting on the throne, to the (One) living to the ages of the
164 4098 1501 5064 4245
10 αἰώνων, πεσοῦνται οἱ εἴκοσι καὶ τέσσαρες πρεσβύτεροι
ages, will fall down the twenty and four elders
1799 2521 1909 2362 4352
ἐνώπιον τοῦ καθημένου ἐπὶ τοῦ θρόνου, καὶ προσκυνοῦσι τῷ
before the (One) sitting on the throne, and they will worship the (One)
2198 1519 165 165 906
ζῶντι εἰς τοὺς αἰῶνας τῶν αἰώνων, καὶ βάλλουσι τοὺς
living to the ages of the ages, and will cast the
4735 848 1799 2362 3004 514/1488
11 στεφάνους αὐτῶν ἐνώπιον τοῦ θρόνου, λέγοντες, Ἄξιος εἶ,
crowns of them before the throne, saying, worthy are You
2962 2983 1391 5092 1411 3754/4771
Κύριε, λαβεῖν τὴν δόξαν καὶ τὴν τιμὴν καὶ τὴν δύναμιν· ὅτι σὺ
Lord, to receive the glory and the honor and the power, because You
2936 3956 1223 2307 4675/1526 2936
ἔκτισας τὰ πάντα, καὶ διὰ τὸ θέλημά σου εἰσὶ καὶ ἐκτίσθησαν.
created all things, and because of the will of You they exist and were created.

CHAPTER 5

1And I saw on the right of the *One* sitting on the throne a scroll having been written within and on the back, having been sealed with seven seals. 2And I saw a strong angel proclaiming with a great voice: Who is worthy to open the scroll, and to loosen its seals? 3And no one in Heaven was able to open the scroll nor to see it, neither on the earth, nor underneath the earth. 4And I wept very much, because no one worthy was found to open and to read the scroll, nor to see it. 5And one of the elders said to me, Do not weep. Behold, the Lion being of the tribe of Judah, the Root of David, overcame *so as* to open the scroll, and to loose its seven seals.

6And I saw, and behold, in *the* midst of the throne, and of the four living creatures, and in *the* midst of the elders, *was* a Lamb standing, as having been slain, having seven horns and seven eyes, which are the seven Spirits of God, having been sent out into all the earth. 7And He came and took the scroll out of the right *hand* of Him sitting on the throne. 8And when He took the scroll, the four living creatures and the twenty-four elders fell down before the Lamb, each one having harps, and golden bowls full of incenses, which are the prayers of the saints. 9And they sing a new song, saying, Worthy are You to receive the scroll, and to open its seals, because You were slain, and by Your blood purchased us to God out of every tribe and tongue and people and nation, 10and

CHAPTER 5

1492/1909 1188 2521 1909 2362
1 Καὶ εἶδον ἐπὶ τὴν δεξιὰν τοῦ καθημένου ἐπὶ τοῦ θρόνου
And I saw on the right of the (One) sitting on the throne
975 1125 2081 3693 2696
βιβλίον γεγραμμένον ἔσωθεν καὶ ὄπισθεν, κατεσφραγισμένον
a scroll having been written within and on the back, having been sealed
4973 2033 1492 32 2478 2784
2 σφραγῖσιν ἑπτά. καὶ εἶδον ἄγγελον ἰσχυρὸν κηρύσσοντα
with seals seven,. And I saw an angel strong proclaiming
5101 2076 514 455 975 3089
φωνῇ μεγάλῃ, Τίς ἐστιν ἄξιος ἀνοῖξαι τὸ βιβλίον, καὶ λῦσαι
with a voice great, Who is worthy to open the scroll, and to loosen
4973 848 3762 1410 1722 3772
3 τὰς σφραγῖδας αὐτοῦ; καὶ οὐδεὶς ἠδύνατο ἐν τῷ οὐρανῷ,
the seals of it? And no one was able in Heaven,
3761/1909 1093 3761 5270 1093 455 975
οὐδὲ ἐπὶ τῆς γῆς, οὐδὲ ὑποκάτω τῆς γῆς, ἀνοῖξαι τὸ βιβλίον,
nor on the earth, nor underneath the earth, to open the scroll
3761 991 846 1473 2799 4183 3754 3762/514
4 οὐδὲ βλέπειν αὐτό. καὶ ἐγὼ ἔκλαιον πολλά, ὅτι οὐδεὶς ἄξιος
nor to see it. And I wept much, because no one worthy
2147 455 314 975 3777 991 846
εὑρέθη ἀνοῖξαι καὶ ἀναγνῶναι τὸ βιβλίον, οὔτε βλέπειν αὐτό.
was found to open and to read the scroll, nor to see it.
1519/1537 4245 3004/3427/3361 2799 2400
5 καὶ εἷς ἐκ τῶν πρεσβυτέρων λέγει μοι, Μὴ κλαῖε· ἰδού,
And one of the elders says to me, Not do weep; behold,
3528 3023 5607/1537 5443 2455 4491 1138
ἐνίκησεν ὁ λέων ὁ ὢν ἐκ τῆς φυλῆς Ἰούδα, ἡ ῥίζα Δαβίδ,
overcame the Lion being of the tribe of Judah, the Root of David,
455 975 3089 2033 4973 848
ἀνοῖξαι τὸ βιβλίον καὶ λῦσαι τὰς ἑπτὰ σφραγῖδας αὐτοῦ.
to open the scroll and to loose the seven seals of it.
1492 2400/1722/3319 2362 5064
6 καὶ εἶδον, καὶ ἰδού, ἐν μέσῳ τοῦ θρόνου καὶ τῶν τεσσάρων
And I saw and behold, in (the) midst of the throne and of the four
2226 1722 3319 4245 721 2476 5613
ζώων, καὶ ἐν μέσῳ τῶν πρεσβυτέρων, ἀρνίον ἑστηκὸς ὡς
living creatures, and amidst the elders, a Lamb standing as
4969 2192 2768 2033 3788 2033 3739/1526
ἐσφαγμένον, ἔχον κέρατα ἑπτὰ καὶ ὀφθαλμοὺς ἑπτά, οἵ εἰσι
having been slain, having horns seven and eyes seven, which are
2033 2316 4151 649 1519 3956
τὰ ἑπτὰ τοῦ Θεοῦ πνεύματα τὰ ἀπεσταλμένα εἰς πᾶσαν τὴν
the seven of God Spirits, having been sent out into all the
1093 2064 2983 975 1537 1188
7 γῆν. καὶ ἦλθε, καὶ εἴληφε τὸ βιβλίον ἐκ τῆς δεξιᾶς τοῦ
earth. And He came, and took the scroll out of the right of the
2521 1909 2362 3753 2983 975
8 καθημένου ἐπὶ τοῦ θρόνου. καὶ ὅτε ἔλαβε τὸ βιβλίον, τὰ
(One) sitting on the throne. And when He took the scroll, the
5064 2226 1501-- 5064 4245 4098
τέσσαρα ζῷα καὶ οἱ εἰκοσιτέσσαρες πρεσβύτεροι ἔπεσον
four living creatures and the twenty-four elders fell down
1799 721 2192 1538 2788 5357
ἐνώπιον τοῦ ἀρνίου, ἔχοντες ἕκαστος κιθάρας, καὶ φιάλας
before the Lamb, having each one harps, and bowls
5552 1073 2368 3739/1526 4335
χρυσᾶς γεμούσας θυμιαμάτων, αἵ εἰσιν αἱ προσευχαὶ τῶν
of gold full of incenses, which are the prayers of the
40 103 5603 2537 3004 514/1488/2983
9 ἁγίων. καὶ ᾄδουσιν ᾠδὴν καινήν, λέγοντες, Ἄξιος εἶ λαβεῖν
saints. And they sing a song new, saying, Worthy are You to re-
975 455 4973 848 3754 4969 ceive
τὸ βιβλίον, καὶ ἀνοῖξαι τὰς σφραγῖδας αὐτοῦ· ὅτι ἐσφάγης,
the scroll, and to open the seals of it, because You were slain,
59 2316/2248/1722 129 4675/1537/3956 5443
καὶ ἠγόρασας τῷ Θεῷ ἡμᾶς ἐν τῷ αἵματί σου ἐκ πάσης φυλῆς
and purchased the God of us by the blood of You out of every tribe

made us kings and priests to our God, and we shall reign over the earth. 11And I saw, and I heard a sound of many angels around the throne, and the living creatures, and the elders, and their number was myriads of myriads, and thousands of thousands, 12saying with a great voice, Worthy is the Lamb having been slain to receive the power and riches and wisdom and strength and honor and glory and blessing. 13And every creature which is in Heaven, and in the earth, and underneath the earth, and the things that are on the sea, and the things in all of them, I heard saying: To Him sitting on the throne, and to the Lamb *be* the blessing and the honor and the glory and the might forever and ever.

14And the four living creatures said, Amen. And the twenty-four elders fell down and worshiped *the* Living One forever and ever.

CHAPTER 6

1And I saw when the Lamb opened one of the seals. And I heard one of the four living creatures, like a sound of thunder, saying, Come and see. 2And I saw, and behold, a white horse! And the *one* sitting on it had a bow. And a crown was given to him, and he went out overcoming, and that he might overcome.

3And when He opened the second seal, I heard the second living creature saying, Come and see. 4And another horse went out, red. And it was given to the

1100 2992 1484 4160 2248 2316
10 καὶ γλώσσης καὶ λαοῦ καὶ ἔθνους, καὶ ἐποίησας ἡμᾶς τῷ Θεῷ
and tongue and people and nation, and made us to the God
2257 935 2409 936 1909 1093
11 ἡμῶν βασιλεῖς καὶ ἱερεῖς, καὶ βασιλεύσομεν ἐπὶ τῆς γῆς. καὶ
of us kings and priests, and we shall reign over the earth. And
1492 191 5456 32 4183 2943
εἶδον, καὶ ἤκουσα φωνὴν ἀγγέλων πολλῶν κυκλόθεν τοῦ
I saw, and I heard a sound of angels many around the
2362 2226 4245 2258
θρόνου καὶ τῶν ζώων καὶ τῶν πρεσβυτέρων· καὶ ἦν ὁ
throne, and the living creatures and of the elders, and was the
706 846 3463 3463 5505 5505
ἀριθμὸς αὐτῶν μυριάδες μυριάδων, καὶ χιλιάδες χιλιάδων,
number of them myriads of myriads, and thousands of thousands,
3004 5456 3173 514 2076 721 4969
12 λέγοντες φωνῇ μεγάλῃ, Ἄξιόν ἐστι τὸ ἀρνίον τὸ ἐσφαγ-
saying with a voice great, Worthy is the Lamb having been
2983 1411 4149 4678
μένον λαβεῖν τὴν δύναμιν καὶ πλοῦτον καὶ σοφίαν καὶ
slain to receive the power and riches and wisdom and
2479 5092 1391 2129 3956 2938 3739
ἰσχὺν καὶ τιμὴν καὶ δόξαν καὶ εὐλογίαν. καὶ πᾶν κτίσμα ὅ
13 strength and honor and glory and blessing. And every creature which
2076/1722 3772 1722 1093 5270 1093
ἐστιν ἐν τῷ οὐρανῷ, καὶ ἐν τῇ γῇ, καὶ ὑποκάτω τῆς γῆς, καὶ
is in Heaven, and in the earth, and underneath the earth, and
1909 2281 3739/2076 1722 846 3956 191
ἐπὶ τῆς θαλάσσης ἅ ἐστι, καὶ τὰ ἐν αὐτοῖς πάντα, ἤκουσα
on the sea the things that are, and the things in them all, I heard
3004 2521 1909 2362 721
λέγοντας, Τῷ καθημένῳ ἐπὶ τοῦ θρόνου καὶ τῷ ἀρνίῳ ἡ
saying, To the (one) sitting on the throne and to the Lamb the
2129 5092 1391 2904 1519 165
εὐλογία καὶ ἡ τιμὴ καὶ ἡ δόξα καὶ τὸ κράτος εἰς τοὺς αἰῶνας
blessing and the honor and the glory and the might to the ages
165 5064 2226 3004 281
14 τῶν αἰώνων. καὶ τὰ τέσσαρα ζῶα ἔλεγον, Ἀμήν. καὶ οἱ
of the ages. And the four living creatures said, Amen; and the
1501 -- 5064 4245 4098 4352
εἰκοσιτέσσαρες πρεσβύτεροι ἔπεσαν καὶ προσεκύνησαν
twenty-four elders fell down and worshiped
1519 165 165
ζῶντι εἰς τοὺς αἰῶνας τῶν αἰώνων.
(the) Living One to the ages of the ages.

CHAPTER 6

1492/3753/ 455 721 3391/1537 4973
1 Καὶ εἶδον ὅτε ἤνοιξε τὸ ἀρνίον μίαν ἐκ τῶν σφραγίδων,
And I saw when opened the Lamb one of the seals
191 1520/1537 5064 2226 3004 5613 5456
καὶ ἤκουσα ἑνὸς ἐκ τῶν τεσσάρων ζώων λέγοντος, ὡς φωνῆς
and I heard one of the four living creatures saying, as of a sound
1027 2064 991 1492 2400 2462
2 βροντῆς, Ἔρχου καὶ βλέπε. καὶ εἶδον, καὶ ἰδού, ἵππος
of thunder, Come and see; and I saw. And behold, a horse
3022 2521 1909 846 2192 5115 1325
λευκός, καὶ ὁ καθήμενος ἐπ' αὐτῷ ἔχων τόξον· καὶ ἐδόθη
white, and the (one) sitting on it having a bow, and was given
846 4735 1831 3528 2443 3528
αὐτῷ στέφανος, καὶ ἐξῆλθε νικῶν, καὶ ἵνα νικήσῃ.
to him a crown, and he went out overcoming, and that he might overcome
3753 455 1208 4973 191
3 Καὶ ὅτε ἤνοιξε τὴν δευτέραν σφραγῖδα, ἤκουσα τοῦ
And when He opened the second seal, I heard the
1208 2226 3004 2064 991 1831
4 δευτέρου ζώου λέγοντος, Ἔρχου καὶ βλέπε. καὶ ἐξῆλθεν
second living creature saying, Come and see. And went out
243 2462 4450 2521 1909 846 1325
ἄλλος ἵππος πυρρός· καὶ τῷ καθημένῳ ἐπ' αὐτῷ ἐδόθη
another horse, red; and to the (one) sitting on it was given

one sitting on *it* to take peace from the earth, and that they should slay one another. And a great sword was given to him.

[5]And when He opened the third seal, I heard the third living creature saying, Come and see. And I saw, and behold, a black horse, and the *one* sitting on it having a balance in his hand. [6]And I heard a voice in *the* midst of the four living creatures saying, A choenix of wheat *for* a denarius, and three choenixes of barley *for* a denarius; and do not harm the oil and the wine.

[7]And when He opened the fourth seal, I heard a voice of the fourth living creature saying, Come and see. [8]And I saw, and behold, a pale green horse, and the name of the *one* sitting on it *was* Death; and Hades followed after him. And authority was given to them to kill over the fourth of the earth with sword, and with famine, and with death, and by the wild beasts of the earth.

[9]And when He opened the fifth seal, I saw under the altar the souls of those having been slain for the word of God, and for the witness which they had. [10]And they cried with a great voice, saying, Until when, holy and true Master, do You not judge and take vengeance *for* our blood, from those dwelling on the earth? [11]And there was given to each one a white robe. And it was said to them that they should rest yet a little time, until might be fulfilled also *the number* of their fellow-slaves and their brothers, those being about to be killed, even as they.

846 2983 1515 575 1093 2443 240
αὐτῷ λαβεῖν τὴν εἰρήνην ἀπὸ τῆς γῆς, καὶ ἵνα ἀλλήλους
to him to take peace from the earth, and that one another
4969 1325 846 3162 3173
σφάξωσι· καὶ ἐδόθη αὐτῷ μάχαιρα μεγάλη.
they shall slay; and was given to him a sword great.
3753 455 5154 4973 191 5154
5 Καὶ ὅτε ἤνοιξε τὴν τρίτην σφραγῖδα, ἤκουσα τοῦ τρίτου
And when He opened the third seal, I heard the third
2226 3004 2064 991 1492 2400 2462
ζώου λέγοντος, Ἔρχου καὶ βλέπε. καὶ εἶδον, καὶ ἰδού, ἵππος
living creature saying, Come and see And I saw, and behold, a horse
3189 2521 1909 846 2192 2218 1722 5495
μέλας, καὶ ὁ καθήμενος ἐπ' αὐτῷ ἔχων ζυγὸν ἐν τῇ χειρὶ
black, and the (one) sitting on it having a balance in the hand
848 191 5456 1722/3319 5064 2226
6 αὐτοῦ. καὶ ἤκουσα φωνὴν ἐν μέσῳ τῶν τεσσάρων ζώων
of him. And I heard a voice in (the) midst of the four living creatures
3004 5518 4621 1220 5140 5518 2915
λέγουσαν, Χοῖνιξ σίτου δηναρίου, καὶ τρεῖς χοίνικες κριθῆς
saying, A choenix of wheat (for) a denarius, and three choenixes of barley
1220 1637 3631/3361 91
δηναρίου· καὶ τὸ ἔλαιον καὶ τὸν οἶνον μὴ ἀδικήσῃς.
(for) a denarius; and the oil and the wine not harm.
3753 455 4973 5067 191
7 Καὶ ὅτε ἤνοιξε τὴν σφραγῖδα τὴν τετάρτην, ἤκουσα
And when He opened the seal fourth, I heard
5456 5067 2226 3004 2064 991
8 φωνὴν τοῦ τετάρτου ζώου λέγουσαν, Ἔρχου καὶ βλέπε. καὶ
(the) voice of the fourth living creature saying, Come and see. And
1492 2400 2462 5515 2521 1883
εἶδον, καὶ ἰδού, ἵππος χλωρός, καὶ ὁ καθήμενος ἐπάνω
I saw. And behold, a horse pale green, and the (one) sitting upon
846 3686 846 2288 86 190 3326
αὐτοῦ, ὄνομα αὐτῷ ὁ θάνατος, καὶ ὁ ᾅδης ἀκολουθεῖ μετ'
it, name to him death, and Hades followed with
846 1325 846 1849 615 1909 5067
αὐτοῦ. καὶ ἐδόθη αὐτοῖς ἐξουσία ἀποκτεῖναι ἐπὶ τὸ τέταρτον
him, and was given to them authority to kill over the fourth
1093/1722/4501 1722/3042 1722 2288 5259
τῆς γῆς ἐν ῥομφαίᾳ καὶ ἐν λιμῷ καὶ ἐν θανάτῳ, καὶ ὑπὸ τῶν
of the earth with sword and with famine and with death, and by the
2342 1093
θηρίων τῆς γῆς.
wild beasts of the earth.
3753 455 3991 4973 1492 5270
9 Καὶ ὅτε ἤνοιξε τὴν πέμπτην σφραγῖδα, εἶδον ὑποκάτω
And when He opened the fifth seal I saw underneath
2379 5590 4969 1223 3056
τοῦ θυσιαστηρίου τὰς ψυχὰς τῶν ἐσφαγμένων διὰ τὸν λόγον
the altar the souls of those having been slain for the word
2316 1223 3141 3739/2192 2896 5456
10 τοῦ Θεοῦ, καὶ διὰ τὴν μαρτυρίαν ἣν εἶχον, καὶ ἔκραζον φωνῇ
of God, and for the witness which they had. And they cried with a voice
3173 3004 2193/4219 1203 40 228
μεγάλῃ, λέγοντες, Ἕως πότε, ὁ δεσπότης, ὁ ἅγιος καὶ ὁ ἀλη-
great saying, Until when, Master holy and true,
3756/2919 1556 129 2257 575 2730
θινός, οὐ κρίνεις καὶ ἐκδικεῖς τὸ αἷμα ἡμῶν ἀπὸ τῶν κατοι-
not do You judge and avenge the blood of us from those dwelling
1909 1093 1325 1538 4749 3022
11 κούντων ἐπὶ τῆς γῆς; καὶ ἐδόθησαν ἑκάστοις στολαὶ λευκαί,
on the earth? And was given to each one a robe white,
4483 846 2443 373 2089 5550 3398 2193
καὶ ἐρρέθη αὐτοῖς ἵνα ἀναπαύσωνται ἔτι χρόνον μικρόν, ἕως
and it was said to them that they should rest yet a time little, until
3739 4137 4889 848 80
οὗ πληρώσονται καὶ οἱ σύνδουλοι αὐτῶν καὶ οἱ ἀδελφοὶ
should be fulfilled also the fellow-slaves of them and the brothers
848 3195 615 5613 848
αὐτῶν, οἱ μέλλοντες ἀποκτείνεσθαι ὡς καὶ αὐτοί.
of them, those being about to be killed as also they.

12 And I saw when He opened the sixth seal. And behold, a great earthquake occurred. And the sun became black as sackcloth made of hair; and the moon became as blood; 13 and the stars of the heaven fell to the earth, as a fig-tree being shaken by a great wind casts its unripe figs. 14 And *the* heaven departed like a scroll being rolled up. And every mountain and island were moved out of their places. 15 And the kings of the earth, and the great ones, and the rich ones, and the commanders, and the powerful ones, and every slave, and every freeman hid themselves in the caves and in the rocks of the mountains. 16 And they said to the mountains and to the rocks, Fall on us, and hide us from *the* face of the *One* sitting on the throne, and from the wrath of the Lamb, 17 because the great day of His wrath has come; and who is able to stand?

1492/3753 455 4973 1622 2400
12 Καὶ εἶδον ὅτε ἤνοιξε τὴν σφραγῖδα τὴν ἕκτην, καὶ ἰδού,
And I saw when He opened the seal sixth, and behold,
4578 3173 1096 2246 1096 3189/5613/4526
σεισμὸς μέγας ἐγένετο, καὶ ὁ ἥλιος ἐγένετο μέλας ὡς σάκκος
an earthquake great occurred, and the sun became black as sackcloth
5155 4582 1096/5613/129 792
13 τρίχινος, καὶ ἡ σελήνη ἐγένετο ὡς αἷμα, καὶ οἱ ἀστέρες τοῦ
made of hair, and the moon became as blood, and the stars of th
3772 4098 1519 1093/5613/4808 906 3653
οὐρανοῦ ἔπεσαν εἰς τὴν γῆν, ὡς συκῆ βάλλει τοὺς ὀλύνθους
heaven fell to the earth, as a fig-tree casts the unripe figs
848 5259 3173 417 4579 3772 673
14 αὐτῆς, ὑπὸ μεγάλου ἀνέμου σειομένη. καὶ οὐρανὸς ἀπεχω-
of it, by a great wind being shaken. And (the) heaven departe
5613 975 1507 3956 3735 3520 153
ρίσθη ὡς βιβλίον εἱλισσόμενον, καὶ πᾶν ὄρος καὶ νῆσος ἐκ
as a scroll being rolled up, and every mountain and island o
5117 848 2795 935 1093
15 τῶν τόπων αὐτῶν ἐκινήθησαν. καὶ οἱ βασιλεῖς τῆς γῆς, καὶ
of the places of them were moved. And the kings of the earth, and
3175 4145 5506
οἱ μεγιστᾶνες, καὶ οἱ πλούσιοι, καὶ οἱ χιλίαρχοι, καὶ οἱ
the great ones, and the rich, and the chiliarchs, and the
1415 3956 1401 3956 1658 2928 1438
δυνατοί, καὶ πᾶς δοῦλος καὶ πᾶς ἐλεύθερος, ἔκρυψαν ἑαυτοὺς
powerful, and every slave, and every freeman, hid themselves
1519 4693 1519 4073 3735 3004
16 εἰς τὰ σπήλαια καὶ εἰς τὰς πέτρας τῶν ὀρέων, καὶ λέγουσι
in the caves and in the rocks of the mountains; and they say
3735 4073 4098/1909/2248 2928
τοῖς ὄρεσι καὶ ταῖς πέτραις, Πέσετε ἐφ' ἡμᾶς, καὶ κρύψατε
to the mountains and to the rocks, Fall on us and hide
2248 575 4383 2521 1909 2362
ἡμᾶς ἀπὸ προσώπου τοῦ καθημένου ἐπὶ τοῦ θρόνου, καὶ
us from (the) face of the (One) sitting on the throne, and
575 3709 721 3754 2064 2250 3173
17 ἀπὸ τῆς ὀργῆς τοῦ ἀρνίου· ὅτι ἦλθεν ἡ ἡμέρα ἡ μεγάλη
from the wrath of the Lamb, because came the day great
3709 848 5101 1410 2476
τῆς ὀργῆς αὐτοῦ, καὶ τίς δύναται σταθῆναι;
of the wrath of Him, and who is able to stand?

CHAPTER 7

1 And after these things I saw four angels standing on the four corners of the earth, holding the four winds of the earth, that wind should not blow on the earth, nor on the sea, nor on every tree. 2 And I saw another angel coming up from *the* rising of the sun, having a seal of *the* living God. And he cried with a great voice to the four angels to whom it was given to them to harm the earth and the sea, saying, 3 Do not harm the earth, nor the sea, nor the trees, until we seal the slaves of our

CHAPTER 7

3326 5023 1492 5064 32 2476 1909
1 Καὶ μετὰ ταῦτα εἶδον τέσσαρας ἀγγέλους ἑστῶτας ἐπὶ τὰς
And after these things I saw four angels standing on the
5064 1137 1093 2902 5064
τέσσαρας γωνίας τῆς γῆς, κρατοῦντας τοὺς τέσσαρας
four corners of the earth, holding the four
417 1093/2443/3361/4154/417 1909 1093 3383 1909
ἀνέμους τῆς γῆς, ἵνα μὴ πνέῃ ἄνεμος ἐπὶ τῆς γῆς, μήτε ἐπὶ
winds of the earth, that not should blow wind on the earth, nor on
2281 3383 1909/3956 1186 1492 243
2 τῆς θαλάσσης, μήτε ἐπὶ πᾶν δένδρον. καὶ εἶδον ἄλλον
the sea, nor on every tree. And I saw another
32 305 575 395 2246 2192 4973
ἄγγελον ἀναβαίνοντα ἀπὸ ἀνατολῆς ἡλίου, ἔχοντα σφρα-
angel coming up from (the) rising of (the) sun, having a sea
2316 2198 2896 5456 3173 5064
γῖδα Θεοῦ ζῶντος· καὶ ἔκραξε φωνῇ μεγάλῃ τοῖς τέσσαρσι
of God (the) living, and he cried with a voice great to the four
32 3739 1325 846 91 1093
ἀγγέλοις, οἷς ἐδόθη αὐτοῖς ἀδικῆσαι τὴν γῆν καὶ τὴν
angels to whom it was given to them to harm the earth and th
2281 3004 3361 91 1093 3383 2281
3 θάλασσαν, λέγων, Μὴ ἀδικήσητε τὴν γῆν, μήτε τὴν θάλασ-
sea, saying, Not do harm the earth, nor the sea
3383 1186 891 3739 4972 1401
σαν, μήτε τὰ δένδρα, ἄχρις οὗ σφραγίσωμεν τοὺς δούλους
nor the trees, until we may seal the slaves

God on their foreheads.
4And I heard the number of
those having been sealed:
one hundred forty-four
thousands, having been
sealed out of every tribe of
the sons of Israel:

5Out of *the* tribe of Judah,
twelve thousand having
been sealed. Out of *the*
tribe of Reuben, twelve
thousand having been
sealed. Out of *the* tribe of
Gad, twelve thousand
having been sealed.
6Out of *the* tribe of Asher,
twelve thousand having
been sealed. Out of *the*
tribe of Naphtali, twelve
thousand having been
sealed. Out of *the* tribe of
Manasseh, twelve thous-
and having been sealed.
7Out of *the* tribe of Simeon, twelve thousand hav-
ing been sealed. Out of *the*
tribe of Levi, twelve thousand having been sealed.
Out of *the* tribe of Issachar,
twelve thousand having
been sealed.
8Out of *the* tribe of
Zebulun, twelve thousand
having been sealed. Out of
the tribe of Joseph, twelve
thousand having been
sealed. Out of *the* tribe of
Benjamin, twelve thousand
having been sealed.
9After these things I saw,
and behold, a great crowd
which no one was able to
number them, out of every
nation, even tribes and
peoples and tongues standing in front of the throne,
and before the Lamb, hav-
ing been clothed *with*
white robes, and palms in
their hands. 10And they cry
with a great voice, saying,
Salvation to our God sitting
on the throne, and to the
Lamb.

11And all the angels
and of the elders and of the
four living creatures stood
around the throne. And *they*
fell before the throne on

2316 2257 1909 3359 848 191
4 τοῦ Θεοῦ ἡμῶν ἐπὶ τῶν μετώπων αὐτῶν. καὶ ἤκουσα τὸν
of the God of us on the foreheads of them. And I heard the
*1540 706 4972 * 5505 4972
-5062 ἀριθμὸν τῶν ἐσφραγισμένων, ρμδ' χιλιάδες, ἐσφραγισμένοι
-5064 **number of those having been sealed, 144 thousands, having been sealed**
(=144) 1537/3956/5443 5207 2474
ἐκ πάσης φυλῆς υἱῶν Ἰσραήλ.
out of every tribe of (the) sons of Israel:

1537 5443 2455 1427 5505 4972
5 Ἐκ φυλῆς Ἰούδα, ιβ' χιλιάδες ἐσφραγισμένοι·
Of (the) tribe of Judah, twelve thousands having been sealed.
1537 5443 4502 1427 5505 4972
Ἐκ φυλῆς Ῥουβήν, ιβ' χιλιάδες ἐσφραγισμένοι·
Of (the) tribe of Reuben, twelve thousands having been sealed.
1537 5443 1045 1427 5505 4972
Ἐκ φυλῆς Γάδ, ιβ' χιλιάδες ἐσφραγισμένοι·
Of (the) tribe of Gad, twelve thousands having been sealed.
1537 5443 768 1427 5505 4972
6 Ἐκ φυλῆς Ἀσήρ, ιβ' χιλιάδες ἐσφραγισμένοι·
Of (the) tribe of Asher, twelve thousands having been sealed.
1537 5443 3508 1427 5505 4972
Ἐκ φυλῆς Νεφθαλείμ, ιβ' χιλιάδες ἐσφραγισμένοι·
Of (the) tribe of Naphtali, twelve thousands having been sealed.
1537 5443 3128 1427 5505 4972
Ἐκ φυλῆς Μανασσῆ, ιβ' χιλιάδες ἐσφραγισμένοι·
Of (the) tribe of Manasseh, twelve thousands having been sealed.
1537 5443 4826 1427 5505 4972
7 Ἐκ φυλῆς Συμεών, ιβ' χιλιάδες ἐσφραγισμένοι·
Of (the) tribe of Simeon, twelve thousands having been sealed.
1537 5443 3017 1427 5505 4972
Ἐκ φυλῆς Λευΐ, ιβ' χιλιάδες ἐσφραγισμένοι·
Of (the) tribe of Levi, twelve thousands having been sealed.
1537 5443 2466 1427 5505 4972
Ἐκ φυλῆς Ἰσαχάρ, ιβ' χιλιάδες ἐσφραγισμένοι·
Of (the) tribe of Issachar, twelve thousands having been sealed.
1537 5443 2194 1427 5505 4972
8 Ἐκ φυλῆς Ζαβουλῶν, ιβ' χιλιάδες ἐσφραγισμένοι·
Of (the) tribe of Zebulun, twelve thousands having been sealed.
1537 5443 2501 1427 5505 4972
Ἐκ φυλῆς Ἰωσήφ, ιβ' χιλιάδες ἐσφραγισμένοι·
Of (the) tribe of Joseph, twelve thousands having been sealed.
1537 5443 958 1427 5505 4972
Ἐκ φυλῆς Βενιαμίν, ιβ' χιλιάδες ἐσφραγισμένοι.
Of (the) tribe of Benjamin, twelve thousands having been sealed.
3326 5023 1492 2400 3793 4183/3739/705
9 Μετὰ ταῦτα εἶδον, καὶ ἰδού, ὄχλος πολύς, ὃν ἀριθμῆσαι
After these things I saw, and behold, a crowd much, which to number
846 3762 1410 1537 3956 1484 5443
αὐτὸν οὐδεὶς ἠδύνατο, ἐκ παντὸς ἔθνους καὶ φυλῶν καὶ
them no one was able, out of every nation, even tribes and
2992 1100 2476 1799 2362
λαῶν καὶ γλωσσῶν, ἑστῶτες ἐνώπιον τοῦ θρόνου καὶ
peoples and tongues, standing before the throne and
1799 721 4016 4749 3022
ἐνώπιον τοῦ ἀρνίου, περιβεβλημένοι στολὰς λευκάς, καὶ
before the Lamb, having been clothed (with) robes white, and
5404 1722 5495 848 2896 5456 3173
10 φοίνικες ἐν ταῖς χερσὶν αὐτῶν· καὶ κράζοντες φωνῇ μεγάλῃ,
palms in the hands of them. And they cry with a voice great,
3004 4991 2316 2257 2521 1909
λέγοντες, Ἡ σωτηρία τῷ Θεῷ ἡμῶν τῷ καθημένῳ ἐπὶ τοῦ
saying, Salvation to the God of us sitting on the
2362 721 3956 32 2476
11 θρόνου, καὶ τῷ ἀρνίῳ. καὶ πάντες οἱ ἄγγελοι ἑστήκεσαν
throne, and to the Lamb. And all the angels stood
2945 2362 4245 5064
κύκλῳ τοῦ θρόνου καὶ τῶν πρεσβυτέρων καὶ τῶν τεσ-
around the throne, and of the elders, and of the four
2226 4098 1799 2362 1909 4383
σάρων ζώων, καὶ ἔπεσον ἐνώπιον τοῦ θρόνου ἐπὶ πρόσ-
living creatures, and they fell before the throne on (the)

their faces, and worshiped God, [12]saying, Amen, Blessing and glory and wisdom and thanksgiving and honor and power and strength to our God forever and ever. Amen.

848 4352 2316 3004 281
12 ωπον αὐτῶν, καὶ προσεκύνησαν τῷ Θεῷ, λέγοντες, Ἀμήν·
face of them, and worshiped God, saying, Amen,
2129 1391 4678 2169
ἡ εὐλογία καὶ ἡ δόξα καὶ ἡ σοφία καὶ ἡ εὐχαριστία καὶ ἡ
blessing and glory and wisdom and thanksgiving and
5092 1411 2479 2316 2257/1519 165
τιμὴ καὶ ἡ δύναμις καὶ ἡ ἰσχὺς τῷ Θεῷ ἡμῶν εἰς τοὺς αἰῶνας
honor and power and strength to the God of us to the ages
165 281
τῶν αἰώνων. ἀμήν.
of the ages. Amen.

[13]And one of the elders answered, saying to me, These, the ones having been clothed *in* the white robes, who are they, and from where did they come? [14]And I said to him, Sir, you know. And he said to me, These are those coming out of the great tribulation; and *they* washed their robes and whitened them in the blood of the Lamb. [15]Because of this they are before the throne of God, and serve Him day and night in His temple. And He sitting on the throne will spread *His skirt* over them. [16]And they will not hunger still, nor will they thirst still, nor at all shall fall on them the sun, nor any *kind of* heat. [17]Because the Lamb in the midst of the throne will shepherd them, and will lead them on the living fountains of waters; and God will wipe off every tear from their eyes.

611 1519 /1537 4245 3004 3427 3778
13 Καὶ ἀπεκρίθη εἷς ἐκ τῶν πρεσβυτέρων, λέγων μοι, Οὗτοι
And answered one of the elders, saying to me, These,
4016 4749 3022 5101/1526 4159
οἱ περιβεβλημένοι τὰς στολὰς τὰς λευκάς, τίνες εἰσί, καὶ πόθεν
those having been clothed (in) robes the white, who are they, and from where
2064 2046 848 2962/4771/1492 2036/3427 3778
14 ἦλθον; καὶ εἴρηκα αὐτῷ, Κύριε, σὺ οἶδας. καὶ εἶπέ μοι, Οὗτοί
came they? And I said to him, Sir, you know. And he told me, These
1526 2064 1537 2347 3173 4150
εἰσιν οἱ ἐρχόμενοι ἐκ τῆς θλίψεως τῆς μεγάλης, καὶ ἔπλυναν
are those coming out of the affliction great, and they washed
4749 848 3021 846 1722 129
τὰς στολὰς αὐτῶν, καὶ ἐλεύκαναν αὐτὰς ἐν τῷ αἵματι τοῦ
the robes of them, and whitened them in the blood of the
721 1223 5124 1526 1799 2362 2316
15 ἀρνίου. διὰ τοῦτό εἰσιν ἐνώπιον τοῦ θρόνου τοῦ Θεοῦ,
Lamb. Therefore are they before the throne of God,
3000 846 2250 3571/1722 3485 848
καὶ λατρεύουσιν αὐτῷ ἡμέρας καὶ νυκτὸς ἐν τῷ ναῷ αὐτοῦ·
and serve Him day and night in the temple of Him,
2521 1909 2362 4637 1909 846 3756
16 καὶ ὁ καθήμενος ἐπὶ τοῦ θρόνου σκηνώσει ἐπ' αὐτούς. οὐ
and the(One) sitting on the throne tabernacled over them. not
3983 2089 3761 1372 2089 3761/3361/4098 1909
πεινάσουσιν ἔτι, οὐδὲ διψήσουσιν ἔτι, οὐδὲ μὴ πέσῃ ἐπ'
they will hunger longer, nor will they thirst longer, nor not shall fall on
846 2246 3761 3956 2738 3754 721 303
17 αὐτοὺς ὁ ἥλιος, οὐδὲ πᾶν καῦμα· ὅτι τὸ ἀρνίον τὸ ἀνὰ
them the sun, nor every (kind of) heat, because the Lamb in the
2362 4165 846 3594 846 1909
μέσον τοῦ θρόνου ποιμανεῖ αὐτούς, καὶ ὁδηγήσει αὐτοὺς ἐπὶ
midst of the throne will shepherd them, and will lead them upon
2198 4077 5204 1813 2316/3956 1144
ζώσας πηγὰς ὑδάτων, καὶ ἐξαλείψει ὁ Θεὸς πᾶν δάκρυον
living fountains of waters, and will wipe off God every tear
575 3788 848
ἀπὸ τῶν ὀφθαλμῶν αὐτῶν.
from the eyes of them.

CHAPTER 8

CHAPTER 8

[1]And when He opened the seventh seal, a silence occurred in Heaven, about a half-hour. [2]And I saw the seven angels who stood before God, and seven trumpets were given to them.

3753 455 4973 1442 1096 4602
1 Καὶ ὅτε ἤνοιξε τὴν σφραγῖδα τὴν ἑβδόμην, ἐγένετο σιγὴ
And when He opened the seal seventh, occurred a silence
1722 3772 5613 2256 1492 2033 32 3739
2 ἐν τῷ οὐρανῷ ὡς ἡμιώριον. καὶ εἶδον τοὺς ἑπτὰ ἀγγέλους οἳ
in Heaven about a half-hour. And I saw the seven angels who
1799 2316 2476 1325 846 2033
ἐνώπιον τοῦ Θεοῦ ἑστήκασι, καὶ ἐδόθησαν αὐτοῖς ἑπτὰ
before God stood, and were given to them seven
4536
σάλπιγγες.
trumpets.

[3]And another angel came and stood at the altar, having a golden censer. And much incense was

243 32 2064 2476 1909 2379
3 Καὶ ἄλλος ἄγγελος ἦλθε, καὶ ἐστάθη ἐπὶ τὸ θυσιαστήριον,
And another angel came and stood at the altar
2192 3031 5552 1325 846 2368 4183
ἔχων λιβανωτὸν χρυσοῦν· καὶ ἐδόθη αὐτῷ θυμιάματα πολλά,
having a censer of gold, and was given to him incense much,

given to him, that he give *them* with the prayers of all the saints at the golden altar before the throne. [4]And the smoke of the incenses went up with the prayers of the saints out of *the* hand of the angel before God. [5]And the angel has taken the censer and filled it from the fire of the altar, and *he* cast *it* into the earth. And sounds and thunders and lightnings and earthquakes occurred. [6]And the seven angels having the seven trumpets prepared themselves, that they might trumpet. [7]And the first angel trumpeted. And hail and fire mixed with blood occurred. And it was cast onto the earth; and the third *part* of the trees was burned; and all green grass was burned.

[8]And the second angel trumpeted. And as a great mountain burning with fire, it was thrown into the sea. And the third *part* of the sea became blood; [9]and the third *part* of the creatures having souls died in the sea; and the third *part* of the ships was destroyed.

[10]And the third angel trumpeted. And a great burning star, like a lamp, fell out of the heaven. And it fell onto the third *part* of the rivers, and onto the fountains of waters. [11]And the name of the star is said *to be* Wormwood. And the third *part* of the waters became *changed* into wormwood. And many men died from the waters, because they were bitter.

[12]And the fourth angel trumpeted. And the third *part* of the sun, and the

2443/1325 4335 40 3956 1909 2379
ἵνα δώσῃ ταῖς προσευχαῖς τῶν ἁγίων πάντων ἐπὶ τὸ θυσια-
that he give with the prayers of the saints all at the altar
5552 1799 2362 305
4 στήριον τὸ χρυσοῦν τὸ ἐνώπιον τοῦ θρόνου. καὶ ἀνέβη ὁ
of gold before the throne. And went up the
2586 2368 4335 40 1537
καπνὸς τῶν θυμιαμάτων ταῖς προσευχαῖς τῶν ἁγίων ἐκ
smoke of the incenses with the prayers of the saints out of
5495 32 1799 2316 2983
5 χειρὸς τοῦ ἀγγέλου ἐνώπιον τοῦ Θεοῦ. καὶ εἴληφεν ὁ
(the) hand of the angel before God. And has taken the
32 3031 1072 846/1537 4442
ἄγγελος τὸ λιβανωτόν, καὶ ἐγέμισεν αὐτὸ ἐκ τοῦ πυρὸς τοῦ
angel the censer, and filled it from the fire of the
2379 906 1519 1093 1096 5456
θυσιαστηρίου, καὶ ἔβαλεν εἰς τὴν γῆν· καὶ ἐγένοντο φωναὶ καὶ
altar, and cast it into the earth, and occurred sounds and
1027 796 4578
βρονταὶ καὶ ἀστραπαὶ καὶ σεισμός.
thunders and lightnings and an earthquake.
2033 32 2192 2033 4536
6 Καὶ οἱ ἑπτὰ ἄγγελοι οἱ ἔχοντες τὰς ἑπτὰ σάλπιγγας
And the seven angels having the seven trumpets
2090 1438 2443 4537
ἡτοίμασαν ἑαυτοὺς ἵνα σαλπίσωσι.
prepared themselves that they might trumpet.
4413 32 4537 1096 5464
7 Καὶ ὁ πρῶτος ἄγγελος ἐσάλπισε, καὶ ἐγένετο χάλαζα καὶ
And the first angel trumpeted, and occurred hail and
4442 3396 129 906 1519 1093 5154
πῦρ μεμιγμένα αἵματι, καὶ ἐβλήθη εἰς τὴν γῆν· καὶ τὸ τρίτον
fire being mixed with blood, and it was cast to the earth, and the third (part)
1186 2618 3956 5528 5515 2618
τῶν δένδρων κατεκάη, καὶ πᾶς χόρτος χλωρὸς κατεκάη.
of the trees was burned down; and all grass green was burned down
1208 32 4537 5613 3735 3173 4442
8 Καὶ ὁ δεύτερος ἄγγελος ἐσάλπισε, καὶ ὡς ὄρος μέγα πυρὶ
And the second angel trumpeted, and as a mountain great with fire
2545 906 1519 2281 1096 5154
καιόμενον ἐβλήθη εἰς τὴν θάλασσαν· καὶ ἐγένετο τὸ τρίτον
burning it was cast into the sea; and became the third (part)
2281 129 599 5154 2938
9 τῆς θαλάσσης αἷμα· καὶ ἀπέθανε τὸ τρίτον τῶν κτισμάτων
of the sea blood, and died the third (part) of the creatures
1722 2281 2192 5590 5154
τῶν ἐν τῇ θαλάσσῃ, τὰ ἔχοντα ψυχάς, καὶ τὸ τρίτον τῶν
in the sea those having souls; and the third (part) of the
4143 1311
πλοίων διεφθάρη.
ships was destroyed.
5154 32 4537 4098/1537 3772
10 Καὶ ὁ τρίτος ἄγγελος ἐσάλπισε, καὶ ἔπεσεν ἐκ τοῦ οὐρανοῦ
And the third angel trumpeted, and fell out of the heaven
792 3173 2545 5613 2985 4098 1909 5154
ἀστὴρ μέγας καιόμενος ὡς λαμπάς, καὶ ἔπεσεν ἐπὶ τὸ τρίτον
a star great burning as a lamp, and it fell onto the third (part)
4215 1909 4077 5204 3686
11 τῶν ποταμῶν, καὶ ἐπὶ τὰς πηγὰς ὑδάτων. καὶ τὸ ὄνομα τοῦ
of the rivers, and onto the fountains of waters. And the name of the
792 3004 894 1096 5154 5204
ἀστέρος λέγεται Ἄψινθος· καὶ γίνεται τὸ τρίτον τῶν ὑδάτων
star is said (to be) Wormwood. And became the third (part) of the waters
1519 894 4183 444 599 1537 5204
εἰς ἄψινθον, καὶ πολλοὶ ἀνθρώπων ἀπέθανον ἐκ τῶν ὑδάτων,
into wormwood, and many of men died from the waters,
3754 4087
ὅτι ἐπικράνθησαν.
because they were bitter.
5067 32 4537 4141 5154
12 Καὶ ὁ τέταρτος ἄγγελος ἐσάλπισε, καὶ ἐπλήγη τὸ τρίτον
And the fourth angel trumpeted, and was struck the third (part)

third *part* of the moon, and the third *part* of the stars, was struck, that the third *part* of them might be darkened, and the third *part* of the day might not appear, and in the same way the night.

[13]And I saw, and I heard one angel flying in mid-heaven, saying with a great voice, Woe! Woe! Woe to those dwelling on the earth, from the rest of *the* voices of the trumpet of the three angels being about to trumpet.

CHAPTER 9

[1]And the fifth angel trumpeted. And I saw a star out of the heaven falling onto the earth. And the key to the pit of the abyss was given to it. [2]And he opened the pit of the abyss. And smoke went up out of the pit, like smoke of a great furnace. And the sun was darkened, and the air, by the smoke of the pit. [3]And out of the smoke locusts came forth to the earth. And authority was given to them, as the scorpions of the earth have authority. [4]And it was said to them that they should not harm the grass of the earth, nor every green thing, nor every tree, except only the men who do not have the seal of God on their foreheads. [5]And it was given to them that they should not kill them, but that they be tormented five months. And their torment *is* as *the* torment of a scorpion when it stings a man. [6]And in those days men will seek death, and they will not find it. And they will long to die, yet death will flee from them.

2246 5154 4582 5154
τοῦ ἡλίου καὶ τὸ τρίτον τῆς σελήνης καὶ τὸ τρίτον τῶν
of the sun and the third (part) of the moon and the third (part) of the
792 2443 4654 5154 848 2250 3361
ἀστέρων, ἵνα σκοτισθῇ το τρίτον αὐτῶν, καὶ ἡ ἡμέρα μὴ
stars, that might be darkened the third of them, and the day not
5316 5154 848 3571 3668
φαίνῃ τὸ τρίτον αὐτῆς, καὶ ἡ νὺξ ὁμοίως.
might appear the third of it, and the night likewise.
1492 191 1520 32 4072 1722 3221
13 Καὶ εἶδον, καὶ ἤκουσα ἑνὸς ἀγγέλου πετωμένου ἐν μεσου-
And I saw, and I heard one angel flying in mid-
3004 5456 3173 3759 3759 3759
ρανήματι, λέγοντος φωνῇ μεγάλῃ, Οὐαί, οὐαί, οὐαί τοῖς
heaven, saying, with a voice great, Woe! Woe! Woe to those
2730 1909 1093/1537 3062 5456 4536
κατοικοῦσιν ἐπὶ τῆς γῆς, ἐκ τῶν λοιπῶν φωνῶν τῆς σάλ-
dwelling on the earth, from the rest of (the) voices of the
5140 32 3195 4537
πιγγος τῶν τριῶν ἀγγέλων τῶν μελλόντων σαλπίζειν.
trumpet of the three angels being about to trumpet.

CHAPTER 9

3991 32 4537 1492 792 1537
1 Καὶ ὁ πέμπτος ἄγγελος ἐσάλπισε, καὶ εἶδον ἀστέρα ἐκ τοῦ
And the fifth angel trumpeted, and I saw a star out of
3772 4098 1519 1093 1325 846 2807
οὐρανοῦ πεπτωκότα εἰς τὴν γῆν, καὶ ἐδόθη αὐτῷ ἡ κλεὶς
heaven having fallen onto the earth. And was given to it the key
5421 12 455 5421 12
2 τοῦ φρέατος τῆς ἀβύσσου. καὶ ἤνοιξε τὸ φρέαρ τῆς ἀβύσσου,
to the pit of the abyss. and he opened the pit of the abyss;
305 2586 1537 5421 5613 2586 2575
και ἀνέβη καπνὸς ἐκ τοῦ φρέατος ὡς καπνὸς καμίνου
and went up a smoke out of the pit as smoke of a furnace
3173 4654 2246 109/1537 2586
μεγάλης, καὶ ἐσκοτίσθη ὁ ἥλιος καὶ ὁ ἀὴρ ἐκ τοῦ καπνοῦ
great. And was darkened the sun and the air from the smoke
5421 1537 2586 1831 200 1519 1093
3 τοῦ φρέατος. καὶ ἐκ τοῦ καπνοῦ ἐξῆλθον ἀκρίδες εἰς τὴν γῆν,
of the pit. And out of the smoke came forth locusts to the earth,
1325 846 1849 5613 2192 1849 4651
καὶ ἐδόθη αὐταῖς ἐξουσία, ὡς ἔχουσιν ἐξουσίαν οἱ σκορπίοι
and was given to them authority, as have authority the scorpions
1093 4483 846 2443/3361 91 5528
4 τῆς γῆς. καὶ ἐρρέθη αὐταῖς ἵνα μὴ ἀδικήσωσι τὸν χόρτον
of the earth. And it was said to them that not they should harm the grass
1093 3761 3956 5515 3761 3956 1186 =1508=
τῆς γῆς, οὐδὲ πᾶν χλωρόν, οὐδὲ πᾶν δένδρον, εἰ μὴ τοὺς
of the earth, nor every green thing, nor every tree, except the
444 3441 3748 3756 2192 4973
ἀνθρώπους μόνους οἵτινες οὐκ ἔχουσι τὴν σφραγῖδα τοῦ
men only who not have the seal
2316/1909 3359 848 1325 846 2443/3361
5 Θεοῦ ἐπὶ τῶν μετώπων αὐτῶν. καὶ ἐδόθη αὐταῖς ἵνα μὴ
of God on the foreheads of them. And it was given to them that not
615 846 235 2443 928 3376 4002
ἀποκτείνωσιν αὐτούς, ἀλλ' ἵνα βασανισθῶσι μῆνας πέντε·
they should kill them, but that they be tormented months five;
929 848 5613 929 4651 3752
καὶ ὁ βασανισμὸς αὐτῶν ὡς βασανισμὸς σκορπίου, ὅταν
and the torment of them (is) as (the) torment of a scorpion when
3817 444 1722 2250 1565 2212
6 παίσῃ ἄνθρωπον. καὶ ἐν ταῖς ἡμέραις ἐκείναις ζητήσουσιν
it stings a man. And in days those will seek
444 2288 3756 2147 846
οἱ ἄνθρωποι τὸν θάνατον, καὶ οὐχ εὑρήσουσιν αὐτόν·
men death, and not they will find it,
1937 599 5343 2288 575
καὶ ἐπιθυμήσουσιν ἀποθανεῖν, καὶ φεύξεται ὁ θάνατος ἀπ'
and they will long to die, and will flee death from

[7]And the likenesses of the locusts *were* like horses having been prepared for war; and on their heads as crowns, like gold; and their faces like the faces of men. [8]And they had hairs like *the* hairs of women; and their teeth were like *those* of lions. [9]And they had breastplates like iron breastplates; and the sound of their wings *was* like *the* sound of chariots with many horses running to war. [10]And they have tails like scorpions, and their stings were in their tails; and their authority *is* to harm men five months.

[11]And they have a king over them, the angel of the abyss. In Hebrew his name *was* Abaddon, and in Greek he has *the* name Apollyon.
[12]The first woe has departed; behold, after these things yet comes two woes.

[13]And the sixth angel trumpeted. And I heard one voice out of the four horns of the golden altar before God, [14]saying to the sixth angel who had the trumpet, Release the four angels, those having been bound at the great river Euphrates. [15]And the four angels were released, those having been prepared for the hour and day and month and year, that they should kill the third *part* of men.

[16]And the number of the armies of the cavalry *was* two myriads of myriads; and I heard their number. [17]And so I saw in the vision the horses, and those sitting on them, having fire-colored breastplates, even dusky red and brimstone-

846 3667 200 3664 2462 2090
7 αὐτῶν. καὶ τὰ ὁμοιώματα τῶν ἀκρίδων ὅμοια ἵπποις ἡτοι-
them. And the likenesses of the locusts like horses having
1519 4171 1909 2776 848 5613
μασμένοις εἰς πόλεμον, καὶ ἐπὶ τὰς κεφαλὰς αὐτῶν ὡς
been prepared for war, and on the heads of them as
4735 3664 5557 4383 848 5613
στέφανοι ὅμοιοι χρυσῷ, καὶ τὰ πρόσωπα αὐτῶν ὡς
crowns like gold; and the faces of them as
4383 444 2192 5359/5613/2359 1135
8 πρόσωπα ἀνθρώπων. καὶ εἶχον τρίχας ὡς τρίχας γυναικῶν,
the faces of men; and they had hairs as hairs of women;
3599 848 5613 3023 2258 2192 2382
9 καὶ οἱ ὀδόντες αὐτῶν ὡς λεόντων ἦσαν. καὶ εἶχον θώρακας
and the teeth of them as of lions were; and they had breastplates
5613 2382 4603 5456 4420 848
ὡς θώρακας σιδηροῦς, καὶ ἡ φωνὴ τῶν πτερύγων αὐτῶν
as breastplates iron; and the sound of the wings of them
5613/5456 716 2462 4183 5143 1519 4171
ὡς φωνὴ ἁρμάτων ἵππων πολλῶν τρεχόντων εἰς πόλεμον.
as sound chariots of horses many running to war.
2192 3769 3664 4551 2759 2258/1722
10 καὶ ἔχουσιν οὐρὰς ὁμοίας σκορπίοις, καὶ κέντρα ἦν ἐν ταῖς
And they have tails like scorpions, and stings were in the
3769 848 1849 848 91 444
οὐραῖς αὐτῶν· καὶ ἡ ἐξουσία αὐτῶν ἀδικῆσαι τοὺς ἀνθρώ-
tails of them and the authority of them (is) to harm men
3376 4002 2192 1909 848 935
11 πους μῆνας πέντε. καὶ ἔχουσιν ἐπ' αὐτῶν βασιλέα τὸν
months five. And they have over them a king, the
32 12 3686 846 1447 3
ἄγγελον τῆς ἀβύσσου· ὄνομα αὐτῷ Ἑβραϊστὶ Ἀβαδδών,
angel of the abyss, name to him in Hebrew, Abaddon,
1722 1673 3686 2192 623 3759 3391
12 καὶ ἐν τῇ Ἑλληνικῇ ὄνομα ἔχει Ἀπολλύων. ἡ οὐαὶ ἡ μία
and in the Greek (the) name he has (is) Apollyon. The woe one
565 2400 2064 2089/1417/3759/3326/ 5023
ἀπῆλθεν· ἰδού, ἔρχονται ἔτι δύο οὐαὶ μετὰ ταῦτα.
has departed; behold, comes yet two woes after these things.
1622 32 4537 191 5456 3391/1537
13 Καὶ ὁ ἕκτος ἄγγελος ἐσάλπισε, καὶ ἤκουσα φωνὴν μίαν ἐκ
And the sixth angel trumpeted. And I heard a voice one out of
5064 2768 2379 5552
τῶν τεσσάρων κεράτων τοῦ θυσιαστηρίου τοῦ χρυσοῦ
the four horns of the altar of gold
1799 2316 3004 1622 32 3739/2192
14 τοῦ ἐνώπιον τοῦ Θεοῦ, λέγουσαν τῷ ἕκτῳ ἀγγέλῳ ὃς εἶχε
before God, saying to the sixth angel who had
4536 3089 5064 32 1210
τὴν σάλπιγγα, Λῦσον τοὺς τέσσαρας ἀγγέλους τοὺς δεδε-
the trumpet, Loose the four angels, those having
1909 4215 3173 2166 3089
15 μένους ἐπὶ τῷ ποταμῷ τῷ μεγάλῳ Εὐφράτῃ. καὶ ἐλύθησαν
been bound at the river great Euphrates. And were loosed
5064 32 2090 1519 5610
οἱ τέσσαρες ἄγγελοι οἱ ἡτοιμασμένοι εἰς τὴν ὥραν καὶ
the four angels, those having been prepared for the hour and
2250 3376 1763 2443 615 5154
ἡμέραν καὶ μῆνα καὶ ἐνιαυτόν, ἵνα ἀποκτείνωσι τὸ τρίτον
day and month and year, that they should kill the third (part)
444 706 4753 2461
16 τῶν ἀνθρώπων. καὶ ὁ ἀριθμὸς στρατευμάτων τοῦ ἱππικοῦ
of men. And the number of the armies of the cavalry
1417 3461 3461 191 706 848
17 δύο μυριάδες μυριάδων· καὶ ἤκουσα τὸν ἀριθμὸν αὐτῶν. καὶ
two myriads of myriads; and I heard the number of them. And
3779 1492 2462 1722 3706 2521
οὕτως εἶδον τοὺς ἵππους ἐν τῇ ὁράσει, καὶ τοὺς καθημένους
thus I saw the horses in the vision, and those sitting
1909 846 2192 2382 4447 5191
ἐπ' αὐτῶν, ἔχοντας θώρακας πυρίνους καὶ ὑακινθίνους
on them, having breastplates fire-colored and dusky red

like; and the heads of the horses as heads of lions; and out of their mouths comes fire and smoke and brimstone. [18]By these three were killed the third *part* of men, by the fire, and by the smoke, and by the brimstone coming out of their mouths. [19]For their authority is in their mouth, and in their tails; for their tails *are* like snakes, having heads, and they do harm with them.

[20]And the rest of men, those not killed by these plagues, did not repent of the works of their hands, that they will not worship demons, and golden idols, and silver, and bronze, and stone, and wooden *idols*, which neither are able to see, nor to hear, nor to walk. [21]And they did not repent of their murders, nor of their sorceries, nor of their fornications, nor of their thefts.

2306 2776 2462 5613 2776 3023
καὶ θειώδεις· καὶ αἱ κεφαλαὶ τῶν ἵππων ὡς κεφαλαὶ λεόντων,
and brimstone-like; and the heads of the horses as heads of lions;
1537 4750 848 1607 4442 2586
καὶ ἐκ τῶν στομάτων αὐτῶν ἐκπορεύεται πῦρ καὶ καπνὸς
and out of the mouths of them proceeds fire and smoke
2303 5259 5140 5130 615 5154
18 καὶ θεῖον. ὑπὸ τῶν τριῶν τούτων ἀπεκτάνθησαν τὸ τρίτον
and brimstone. By three these were killed the third (part)
444 1537 4442 1537 2586 1537
τῶν ἀνθρώπων, ἐκ τοῦ πυρὸς καὶ ἐκ τοῦ καπνοῦ καὶ ἐκ τοῦ
of men, from the fire and from smoke and from the
2303 1607 1537 4750 848 1063
19 θείου τοῦ ἐκπορευομένου ἐκ τῶν στομάτων αὐτῶν. ἡ γὰρ
brimstone coming out from the mouths of them. the For
1849 848 1722 4750 848 1526 1722 3769
ἐξουσία αὐτῶν ἐν τῷ στόματι αὐτῶν ἐστί, καὶ ἐν ταῖς οὐραῖς
authority of them in the mouth of them is, and in the tails
848 1063 3769 848 3664 3789 2192 2776
αὐτῶν· αἱ γὰρ οὐραὶ αὐτῶν ὅμοιαι ὄφεσιν, ἔχουσαι κεφαλάς,
of them;the for tails of them (are) like snakes, having heads
1722 846 91 3062 444 3739/3756
20 καὶ ἐν αὐταῖς ἀδικοῦσι. καὶ οἱ λοιποὶ τῶν ἀνθρώπων, οἳ οὐκ
and with them they do harm. And the rest of men, who not
615 1722 4127 5025 3756 3340 1537
ἀπεκτάνθησαν ἐν ταῖς πληγαῖς ταύταις, οὐ μετενόησαν ἐκ
were killed by plagues these, not repented of
2041 5495 848 2443/3361/ 4352
τῶν ἔργων τῶν χειρῶν αὐτῶν, ἵνα μὴ προσκυνήσωσι τὰ
the works of the hands of them, that not they will worship
1140 1497 5552 693
δαιμόνια, καὶ εἴδωλα τὰ χρυσᾶ καὶ τὰ ἀργυρᾶ καὶ τὰ
demons and idols gold and silver and
5470 3035 3585 3739/3777 991 1410
χαλκᾶ καὶ τὰ λίθινα καὶ τὰ ξύλινα, ἃ οὔτε βλέπειν δύναται,
bronze and stone and wood, which neither to see are able.
3777 191 3777 4043 3756 3340 1537
21 οὔτε ἀκούειν, οὔτε περιπατεῖν· καὶ οὐ μετενόησαν ἐκ τῶν
nor to hear, nor to walk; and not they repented of the
5408 848 3777/1537 5331 848 3777/1537
φόνων αὐτῶν, οὔτε ἐκ τῶν φαρμακειῶν αὐτῶν, οὔτε ἐκ τῆς
murders of them, nor of the sorceries of them, nor of the
4202 848 3777/1537 2809 848
πορνείας αὐτῶν, οὔτε ἐκ τῶν κλεμμάτων αὐτῶν.
fornications of them nor of the thefts of them.

CHAPTER 10

CHAPTER 10

[1]And I saw another strong angel coming down out of Heaven, having been clothed *with* a cloud, and a rainbow on the head; and his face as the sun, and his feet as pillars of fire. [2]And he had in his hand a little scroll having been opened. And he placed his right foot on the sea, and the left on the land, [3]and cried with a great voice, as a lion roars. And when he cried, the seven thunders spoke their sounds. [4]And when the seven thunders spoke their

1492 243 32 2478 2597 1537
1 Καὶ εἶδον ἄλλον ἄγγελον ἰσχυρὸν καταβαίνοντα ἐκ τοῦ
And I saw another angel strong coming down out of
3772 4016 3507 2463/1909 2776
οὐρανοῦ, περιβεβλημένον νεφέλην, καὶ ἶρις ἐπὶ τῆς κεφαλῆς,
Heaven, having been clothed (with) a cloud, and a rainbow on the head
4383 848 5613 2246 4228 848 5613
καὶ τὸ πρόσωπον αὐτοῦ ὡς ὁ ἥλιος, καὶ οἱ πόδες αὐτοῦ ὡς
and the face of him as the sun, and the feet of him as
4769 4442 2192/1722 5495 848 974
2 στῦλοι πυρός· καὶ εἶχεν ἐν τῇ χειρὶ αὐτοῦ βιβλαρίδιον
pillars of fire, and he had in the hand of him a little scroll
455 5087 4228 848 1188 1909
ἀνεῳγμένον· καὶ ἔθηκε τὸν πόδα αὐτοῦ τὸν δεξιὸν ἐπὶ τὴν
having been opened And he placed the foot of him the right on the
2281 2176 1909 1093 2896 5456
3 θάλασσαν, τὸν δὲ εὐώνυμον ἐπὶ τὴν γῆν, καὶ ἔκραξε φωνῇ
sea, the and left on the land, and cried with a voice
3173 5618 3023 3455 3753 2896 2980
μεγάλῃ ὥσπερ λέων μυκᾶται· καὶ ὅτε ἔκραξεν, ἐλάλησαν αἱ
great as a lion roars. And when he cried, spoke the
2033 1027 1438 5456 3753 2980 2033
4 ἑπτὰ βρονταὶ τὰς ἑαυτῶν φωνάς. καὶ ὅτε ἐλάλησαν αἱ ἑπτὰ
seven thunders the of themselves voices. And when spoke the seven

sounds, I was about to write. And I heard a voice out of Heaven saying to me, Seal what things the seven thunders spoke, and do not write these things. [5]And the angel whom I saw standing on the sea and on the land lifted his hand to Heaven, [6]and swore by Him living forever and ever, who created the heaven and the things in it, and the earth and the things in it, and the sea and the things in it, that time shall no longer be; [7]but in the days of the voice of the seventh angel, whenever he is about to trumpet, was even ended the mystery of God, as He preached to His slaves, the prophets.

[8]And the voice which I heard out of Heaven *was* again speaking to me, and saying, Go, take the little scroll having been opened in the hand of the angel standing on the sea and on the land. [9]And I went away toward the angel, saying to him, Give the little scroll to me. And he said to me, Take and eat it up, and it will make your belly bitter, but it will be sweet as honey in your mouth. [10]And I took the little scroll out of the angel's hand, and ate it up. And it was sweet like honey in my mouth; and when I ate it, my belly was made bitter. [11]And he said to me, You must again prophesy before peoples and nations and tongues and many kings.

1027 5456 1438 3195 1125 191
βρονταὶ τὰς φωνὰς ἑαυτῶν, ἔμελλον γράφειν· καὶ ἤκουσα
thunders the voices of themselves, I was about to write; and I heard
5456 1537 3772 3004 3427 4972 3739/2980
φωνὴν ἐκ τοῦ οὐρανοῦ, λέγουσάν μοι, Σφράγισον ἃ ἐλά-
a voice out of Heaven, saying to me, Seal what things
2033 1027 3361 5023 1125
5 λησαν αἱ ἑπτὰ βρονταί, καὶ μὴ ταῦτα γράψῃς. καὶ ὁ
spoke the seven thunders, and not these things write. And the
32 3739 1492 2476 1909 2281 1909 1093
ἄγγελος ὃν εἶδον ἑστῶτα ἐπὶ τῆς θαλάσσης καὶ ἐπὶ τῆς γῆς
angel whom I saw standing on the sea and on the land
142 5495 848/1519 3772 3660 1722
6 ἦρε τὴν χεῖρα αὐτοῦ εἰς τὸν οὐρανόν, καὶ ὤμοσεν ἐν τῷ
lifted the hand of him to Heaven, and swore by Him
2198/1519 165 165 3739 2936 3772
ζῶντι εἰς τοὺς αἰῶνας τῶν αἰώνων, ὃς ἔκτισε τὸν οὐρανὸν
living to the ages of the ages, who created the heaven
1722/846 1093 1722/846 2281
καὶ τὰ ἐν αὐτῷ, καὶ τὴν γῆν καὶ τὰ ἐν αὐτῇ, καὶ τὴν θάλασ-
and the things in it, and the earth and the things in it, and the sea
1722/846 3754 5550/3756 2071/2089 235 1722
7 σαν καὶ τὰ ἐν αὐτῇ, ὅτι χρόνος οὐκ ἔσται ἔτι· ἀλλ᾽ ἐν ταῖς
and the things in it, that time not shall be longer, but in the
2250 5456 1442 32 3752 3195
ἡμέραις τῆς φωνῆς τοῦ ἑβδόμου ἀγγέλου, ὅταν μέλλῃ
days of the voice of the seventh angel, whenever he is about
4537 5055 3456 2316 5613 1097
σαλπίζειν, καὶ τελεσθῇ τὸ μυστήριον τοῦ Θεοῦ, ὡς εὐηγ-
to trumpet, even may be ended the mystery of God, as He
1438 1401 4396 5456 3739
8 γέλισε τοῖς ἑαυτοῦ δούλοις τοῖς προφήταις. καὶ ἡ φωνὴ ἣν
preached to the of Himself slaves the prophets. And the voice which
191 1537 3772 3825 2980 3326 1700
ἤκουσα ἐκ τοῦ οὐρανοῦ, πάλιν λαλοῦσα μετ᾽ ἐμοῦ, καὶ
I heard out of Heaven, again speaking with me, and
3004 5217 2983 974 455 1722
λέγουσα, Ὕπαγε, λάβε τὸ βιβλαρίδιον τὸ ἠνεῳγμένον ἐν
saying, Go, take the little scroll having been opened in
5495 32 2476 1909 2281 1909
τῇ χειρὶ ἀγγέλου τοῦ ἑστῶτος ἐπὶ τῆς θαλάσσης καὶ ἐπὶ
the hand of the angel standing on the sea and on
1093 565 4314 32 3004 846 1325
9 τῆς γῆς. καὶ ἀπῆλθον πρὸς τὸν ἄγγελον, λέγων αὐτῷ, Δός
the land. And I went away toward the angel, saying to him, Give
3427 974 3004/3427 2983 2719 846
μοι τὸ βιβλαρίδιον. καὶ λέγει μοι, Λάβε καὶ κατάφαγε αὐτό·
to me the little scroll. And he said to me, Take and eat up it.
4087 4675 2836 235 1722 4750 4675 2071
καὶ πικρανεῖ σου τὴν κοιλίαν, ἀλλ᾽ ἐν τῷ στόματί σου ἔσται
and it will embitter of you the belly, but in the mouth of you it will be
1099/5613/3192 2983 974 1537 5495
10 γλυκὺ ὡς μέλι. καὶ ἔλαβον τὸ βιβλαρίδιον ἐκ τῆς χειρὸς τοῦ
sweet as honey. And I took the little scroll out of the hand of the
32 2719 846 2258/1722 4750 3450
ἀγγέλου, καὶ κατέφαγον αὐτό, καὶ ἦν ἐν τῷ στόματί μου
angel and devoured it. and it was in the mouth of me
5613/2192 1099 3753 5315 846 4087 2836
ὡς μέλι, γλυκύ· καὶ ὅτε ἔφαγον αὐτό, ἐπικράνθη ἡ κοιλία
as honey, sweet; and when I ate it, was made bitter the belly
3450 3004/3427/1163/4571/3825 4395 1909 2992
11 μου. καὶ λέγει μοι, Δεῖ σε πάλιν προφητεῦσαι ἐπὶ λαοῖς καὶ
of me. And he says to me, must You again prophesy before peoples and
1484 1100 935 4183
ἔθνεσι καὶ γλώσσαις καὶ βασιλεῦσι πολλοῖς.
nations and tongues and kings many.

CHAPTER 11

[1]And a reed like a staff was given to me, and the angel stood, saying, Rise

CHAPTER 11

1325/3427 2563 3664 4464 32
1 Καὶ ἐδόθη μοι κάλαμος ὅμοιος ῥάβδῳ, καὶ ὁ ἄγγελος
And was given to me a reed like a staff, and the angel

and measure the temple of God and the altar, and those worshiping in it. [2]And cast aside the outside court of the temple, and do not measure it. For it was given to the nations, and they will trample the holy city forty-two months. [3]And I will give to My two witnesses, and they will prophesy a thousand, two hundred and sixty days, dressed *in* sackcloth. [4]These are the two olive trees, and the two lampstands, standing before the God of the earth. [5]And if anyone desires to harm them, fire comes out of their mouth and devours their enemies. And if anyone desires to harm them, so it is right for him to be killed.

[6]These have the authority to shut up the heaven, that no rain may rain in the days of their prophecy. And they have authority over the waters, to turn them into blood, and to strike the earth *with* every plague, as often as they desire. [7]And when they complete their witness, the beast coming up out of the abyss will make war with them, and will overcome them, and will kill them. [8]And their bodies *will be* on the street of the great city, which spiritually is called Sodom, and Egypt—where our Lord was crucified. [9]And *some* from the peoples and tribes and tongues and nations will see their dead bodies three days and a half; and they do not allow their dead bodies to be put in tombs. [10]And those living on the earth will rejoice over them, and will

2476 3004 1453 3354 3485 2316
εἱστήκει, λέγων, Ἔγειραι, καὶ μέτρησον τὸν ναὸν τοῦ Θεοῦ,
stood, saying, Rise and measure the temple of God,
2379 4352 1722/846
2 καὶ τὸ θυσιαστήριον, καὶ τοὺς προσκυνοῦντας ἐν αὐτῷ. καὶ
and the altar, and those worshiping in it. And
833 2081 3485 1544 1854 3361 846
τὴν αὐλὴν τὴν ἔξωθεν τοῦ ναοῦ ἔκβαλε ἔξω, καὶ μὴ αὐτὴν
the court outside of the temple cast outside, and not it
3354 3754 1325 1484 4172 40
μετρήσῃς, ὅτι ἐδόθη τοῖς ἔθνεσι· καὶ τὴν πόλιν τὴν ἁγίαν
do measure, for it was given to the nations, and the city holy
3961 3376 5062 1417 1325 1417
3 πατήσουσι μῆνας τεσσαράκοντα δύο. καὶ δώσω τοῖς δυσὶ
they will trample months forty-two. And I will give to the two
3144 3450 4395 2250 5507 1250
μάρτυσί μου, καὶ προφητεύσουσιν ἡμέρας χιλίας διακοσίας
witnesses of Me, and they will prophesy days a thousand, two hundred
1835 4016 4526 3778 1526 1417 1636
4 ἑξήκοντα περιβεβλημένοι σάκκους. οὗτοί εἰσιν αἱ δύο ἐλαῖαι,
sixty, having been clothed (in) sackcloth. These are the two olive-trees,
1417 3087 1799 2316 1093 2476
καὶ αἱ δύο λυχνίαι αἱ ἐνώπιον τοῦ Θεοῦ τῆς γῆς ἑστῶσαι.
and the two lampstands before the God of the earth standing.
=1536= 846 2309 91 4442 1607 1537
5 καὶ εἴ τις αὐτοὺς θέλῃ ἀδικῆσαι, πῦρ ἐκπορεύεται ἐκ τοῦ
And if anyone them desires to harm, fire proceeds out of the
4750 848 2719 2190 848 1487
στόματος αὐτῶν, καὶ κατεσθίει τοὺς ἐχθροὺς αὐτῶν· καὶ εἴ
mouth of them and devours the enemies of them; and if
5100 846 2309 91 3779/1163 846 615
τις αὐτοὺς θέλῃ ἀδικῆσαι, οὕτω δεῖ αὐτὸν ἀποκτανθῆναι.
anyone them desires to harm, thus it behoves him to be killed.
3778 2192 1849 2808 3772 2443/3361/1026
6 οὗτοι ἔχουσιν ἐξουσίαν κλεῖσαι τὸν οὐρανόν, ἵνα μὴ βρέχῃ
These have authority to shut the heaven, that not may rain
5205/1722/2250 848 4394 1849 2192
ὑετὸς ἐν ἡμέραις αὐτῶν τῆς προφητείας· καὶ ἐξουσίαν ἔχου-
rain in days of them of the prophecy, and authority they
1909 5204 4762 846 1519/129 3960
σιν ἐπὶ τῶν ὑδάτων, στρέφειν αὐτὰ εἰς αἷμα, καὶ πατάξαι
have over the waters, to turn them into blood, and to strike
1093 3956 4127 3740 1437 2309 3752
7 τὴν γῆν πάσῃ πληγῇ, ὁσάκις ἐὰν θελήσωσι. καὶ ὅταν
the earth (with) every plague, as often as if they desire. And whenever
5055 3141 848 2342 305 1537
τελέσωσι τὴν μαρτυρίαν αὐτῶν, τὸ θηρίον τὸ ἀναβαῖνον ἐκ
they finish the witness of them, the beast coming up out of
12 4160 4171 3326 846 3528
τῆς ἀβύσσου ποιήσει πόλεμον μετ' αὐτῶν, καὶ νικήσει
the abyss will make war with them, and will overcome
846 615 846 4430 848 1909
8 αὐτούς, καὶ ἀποκτενεῖ αὐτούς. καὶ τὰ πτώματα αὐτῶν ἐπὶ
them, and will kill them. And the bodies of them on
4113 4172 3173 3748 2564 4153
τῆς πλατείας πόλεως τῆς μεγάλης, ἥτις καλεῖται πνευ-
the street of city the great, which is called spirit-
4670 125 3699 2962 2257
ματικῶς Σόδομα καὶ Αἴγυπτος, ὅπου καὶ ὁ Κύριος ἡμῶν
ually Sodom, and, Egypt, where indeed the Lord of us
4717 991 1537 2992 5443
9 ἐσταυρώθη. καὶ βλέψουσιν ἐκ τῶν λαῶν καὶ φυλῶν καὶ
was crucified. And will see (some) from the peoples and tribes and
1100 1484 4430 848 2250 5140
γλωσσῶν καὶ ἐθνῶν τὰ πτώματα αὐτῶν ἡμέρας τρεῖς καὶ
tongues and nations the bodies of them days three and
2255 4430 848 3756 863 5087 1519
ἥμισυ, καὶ τὰ πτώματα αὐτῶν οὐκ ἀφήσουσι τεθῆναι εἰς
a half; and the bodies of them not they allow to be placed in
3418 2730 1909 1093 5463 1909
10 μνήματα. καὶ οἱ κατοικοῦντες ἐπὶ τῆς γῆς χαροῦσιν ἐπ'
tombs. And those dwelling on the earth will rejoice over

make merry. And they will send one another gifts, because these two prophets tormented those living on the earth.

[11]And after three days and a half, a spirit of life from God entered into them, and they stood on their feet. And great fear fell on the ones beholding them.

[12]And they heard a great voice out of Heaven saying to them, Come up here. And they went up into the heaven in the cloud. And their enemies saw them. [13]And in that hour a great earthquake occurred, and the tenth *part* of the city fell. And there were killed in the earthquake seven thousand names of men. And the rest became terrified, and gave glory to the God of Heaven.

[14]The second woe departed. And, behold, the third woe is coming quickly.

[15]And the seventh angel trumpeted. And there were great voices in Heaven, saying, The kingdoms of the world became our Lord's, even of His Christ; and He shall reign forever *and* ever. [16]And the twenty-four elders sitting before God on their thrones fell on their faces and worshiped God, [17]saying, We thank You, Lord God Almighty, the *One* who is, and who was, and who *is* coming, because You took Your great power and reigned. [18]And the nations were full of wrath; and Your wrath came, and the time

846 2165 1435 3992 240
αὐτοῖς, καὶ εὐφρανθήσονται, καὶ δῶρα πέμψουσιν ἀλλήλοις,
them and will make merry. And gifts they will send one another
3754/3778 1417 4396 928 2730
ὅτι οὗτοι οἱ δύο προφῆται ἐβασάνισαν τοὺς κατοικοῦντας
because these two prophets tormented those dwelling
1909 1093 3326 5140 2250 2255 4151
11 ἐπὶ τῆς γῆς. καὶ μετὰ τὰς τρεῖς ἡμέρας καὶ ἥμισυ, πνεῦμα
on the earth. And after the three days and a half, a spirit
2222/1537 2316 1525 1909 846 2476 1909
ζωῆς ἐκ τοῦ Θεοῦ εἰσῆλθεν ἐπ' αὐτούς καὶ ἔστησαν ἐπὶ
of life out of God entered into them, and they stood on
4228 848 5401 3173 4098 1909 2334
τοὺς πόδας αὐτῶν, καὶ φόβος μέγας ἔπεσεν ἐπὶ τοὺς θεωροῦν-
the feet of them, and fear great fell on those beholding
846 191 5456 3173 1537 3772
12 τας αὐτούς. καὶ ἤκουσαν φωνὴν μεγάλην ἐκ τοῦ οὐρανοῦ,
them. And they heard a voice great out of Heaven,
3004 846 305 5602 305 1519
λέγουσαν αὐτοῖς, Ἀνάβητε ὧδε. καὶ ἀνέβησαν εἰς τὸν
saying to them, Come up here. And they went up into
3772 1722 3507 2334 846 2190
οὐρανὸν ἐν τῇ νεφέλῃ, καὶ ἐθεώρησαν αὐτοὺς οἱ ἐχθροὶ
Heaven in the cloud; and beheld them the enemies
848 1722/1565 5610 1096 4578 3173
13 αὐτῶν. καὶ ἐν ἐκείνῃ τῇ ὥρᾳ ἐγένετο σεισμὸς μέγας, καὶ τὸ
of them. And in that hour occurred an earthquake great, and the
1182 4172 4098 615 1722 4578
δέκατον τῆς πόλεως ἔπεσε, καὶ ἀπεκτάνθησαν ἐν τῷ σεισμῷ
tenth (part) of the city fell, and were killed in the earthquake
3686 444 5505 2033 3062 1719
ὀνόματα ἀνθρώπων, χιλιάδες ἑπτά· καὶ οἱ λοιποὶ ἔμφοβοι
names of men, thousands seven, and the rest terrified
1096 1325 1391 2316 3772
ἐγένοντο, καὶ ἔδωκαν δόξαν τῷ Θεῷ τοῦ οὐρανοῦ.
became, and gave glory to the God of Heaven.
3759 1208 32 2400 3759 5154
14 Ἡ οὐαὶ ἡ δευτέρα ἀπῆλθεν· καὶ ἰδού, ἡ οὐαὶ ἡ τρίτη
The woe second passed away; and behold, the woe third
2064 5035
ἔρχεται ταχύ.
is coming quickly.
1442 32 4537 1096 5456
15 Καὶ ὁ ἕβδομος ἄγγελος ἐσάλπισε, καὶ ἐγένοντο φωναὶ
And the seventh angel trumpeted. And there were voices
3173 1722 3772 3004 1096 932
μεγάλαι ἐν τῷ οὐρανῷ, λέγουσαι, Ἐγένοντο αἱ βασιλεῖαι
great in Heaven, saying, became The kingdoms
2889 2962 2257 5547 848
τοῦ κόσμου, τοῦ Κυρίου ἡμῶν, καὶ τοῦ Χριστοῦ αὐτοῦ,
of the world of the Lord of us, and of the Christ of Him,
936 1519 165 165 1501
16 καὶ βασιλεύσει εἰς τοὺς αἰῶνας τῶν αἰώνων. καὶ οἱ εἴκοσι καὶ
and He shall reign to the ages of the ages. And the twenty and
5064 4245 1799 2316 2521 1909
τέσσαρες πρεσβύτεροι οἱ ἐνώπιον τοῦ Θεοῦ καθήμενοι ἐπὶ
four elders before God sitting on
2362 848 4098 1909 4383 848
τοὺς θρόνους αὐτῶν, ἔπεσαν ἐπὶ τὰ πρόσωπα αὐτῶν, καὶ
the thrones of them, fell on the faces of them, and
4352 2316 3004 2168 4671 2962
17 προσεκύνησαν τῷ Θεῷ, λέγοντες, Εὐχαριστοῦμέν σοι, Κύριε
worshiped God, saying, We thank You, Lord
2316 3841 5607 2258 2064
ὁ Θεὸς ὁ παντοκράτωρ, ὁ ὢν καὶ ὁ ἦν καὶ ὁ ἐρχόμενος,
God Almighty, the (One) being, and who was, and who (is) coming,
3754 2983 1411 4675 3173 936
ὅτι εἴληφας τὴν δύναμίν σου τὴν μεγάλην, καὶ ἐβασίλευσας.
because You took the power of You great, and reigned.
1484 3710 2064 3709 4675
18 καὶ τὰ ἔθνη ὠργίσθησαν, καὶ ἦλθεν ἡ ὀργή σου, καὶ ὁ
And the nations were wrathful, and came the wrath of You, and the

of the judging of the dead, and to give the reward to Your slaves the prophets, and to the saints, and to the ones fearing Your name— to the small and to the great—and to destroy those destroying the earth.

[19]And the temple of God in Heaven was opened, and the ark of His covenant was seen in His temple, and lightnings, and voices, and thunders, and earthquake, and a great hail occurred.

CHAPTER 12

[1]And a great sign was seen in Heaven, a woman having been clothed *with* the sun, and the moon *was* underneath her feet; and on her head a crown of twelve stars; [2]and having *a babe* in womb. She cries, being in labor, and having been distressed to bear.

[3]And another sign was seen in Heaven. And, behold, a great red dragon having seven heads and ten horns! And on his heads *were* seven diadems, [4]and his tail drew the third *part* of the stars of the heaven. And *he* throws them to the earth. And the dragon stood before the woman being about to bear, so that when she bears he might devour her child. [5]And she bore a son, a male, who is going to shepherd all the nations with an iron staff. And her child was caught away to God, and to His throne. [6]And the woman fled into the wilderness, where she had a place, *it* having been prepared from God, that there they might nourish her a thousand two

2540 3498 2919 1325 3408
καιρὸς τῶν νεκρῶν κριθῆναι, καὶ δοῦναι τὸν μισθὸν τοῖς
time of the dead to be judged and to give the reward to the
1401 4675 4396 40 5399
δούλοις σου τοῖς προφήταις καὶ τοῖς ἁγίοις καὶ τοῖς φοβου-
slaves of You, to the prophets and to the saints, and to those fearing
3686 4675 3398 3173
μένοις τὸ ὄνομά σου, τοῖς μικροῖς καὶ τοῖς μεγάλοις, καὶ
the name of You, to the small and to the great, and
1311 1311 1093
διαφθεῖραι τοὺς διαφθείροντας τὴν γῆν.
to destroy those destroying the earth.
455 3485 2316/1722 3772 3700
19 Καὶ ἠνοίγη ὁ ναὸς τοῦ Θεοῦ ἐν τῷ οὐρανῷ, καὶ ὤφθη ἡ
And was opened the temple of God in Heaven, and was seen the
2787 1242 848/1722 3485 848 1096
κιβωτὸς τῆς διαθήκης αὐτοῦ ἐν τῷ ναῷ αὐτοῦ· καὶ ἐγένοντο
ark of the covenant of Him in the temple of Him, and occurred
796 5456 1027 4578 5464
ἀστραπαὶ καὶ φωναὶ καὶ βρονταὶ καὶ σεισμὸς καὶ χάλαζα
lightnings and voices and thunders and an earthquake and a hail
3173
μεγάλη.
great.

CHAPTER 12

4592 3173 3700/1722 3772 1135 4016
1 Καὶ σημεῖον μέγα ὤφθη ἐν τῷ οὐρανῷ, γυνὴ περιβεβλη-
And a sign great was seen in Heaven a woman having been
2246 4582 5270 4228 848
μένη τὸν ἥλιον, καὶ ἡ σελήνη ὑποκάτω τῶν ποδῶν αὐτῆς,
clothed (with) the sun, and the moon underneath the feet of her,
1909 2776 848 4735 792 1427
2 καὶ ἐπὶ τῆς κεφαλῆς αὐτῆς στέφανος ἀστέρων δώδεκα· καὶ
and on the head of her a crown of stars twelve and
1722/1064 2192 2896 5605 928
ἐν γαστρὶ ἔχουσα, κράζει ὠδίνουσα, καὶ βασανιζομένη
in womb having; she cries, being in travail, and having been distressed
5088 3700 243 4592 1722 3772 2400
3 τεκεῖν. καὶ ὤφθη ἄλλο σημεῖον ἐν τῷ οὐρανῷ, καὶ ἰδού,
to bear. And was seen another sign in Heaven, and behold,
1404 3173 4450 2192 2776 2033 2768 1176
δράκων μέγας πυρρός, ἔχων κεφαλὰς ἑπτὰ καὶ κέρατα δέκα,
a dragon great red, having heads seven and horns ten,
1909 2776 848 1238 2033 3769
4 καὶ ἐπὶ τὰς κεφαλὰς αὐτοῦ διαδήματα ἑπτά. καὶ ἡ οὐρὰ
and on the heads of him diadems seven, and the tail
848 4951 5154 792 3772
αὐτοῦ σύρει τὸ τρίτον τῶν ἀστέρων τοῦ οὐρανοῦ, καὶ
of him draws the third (part) of the stars of heaven, and
906 846 1519 1093 1404 2476 1799
ἔβαλεν αὐτοὺς εἰς τὴν γῆν· καὶ ὁ δράκων ἕστηκεν ἐνώπιον
throws them to the earth. And the dragon stood before
1135 3195 5088 2443/3752 5088 5043
τῆς γυναικὸς τῆς μελλούσης τεκεῖν, ἵνα, ὅταν τέκῃ, τὸ τέκνον
the woman being about to bear, that, when she bears, the child
848 2719 5088 5207 730 3739 3195 4165
5 αὐτῆς καταφάγῃ. καὶ ἔτεκεν υἱὸν ἄρρενα, ὃς μέλλει ποι-
of her he may devour. And she bore a son, a male, who is about to
3956 1484/1722/4464 4603 726
μαίνειν πάντα τὰ ἔθνη ἐν ῥάβδῳ σιδηρᾷ· καὶ ἡρπάσθη τὸ
shepherd all the nations with a staff iron. And was seized the
5043 848 4314 2316 2362 848
6 τέκνον αὐτῆς πρὸς τὸν Θεὸν καὶ τὸν θρόνον αὐτοῦ. καὶ ἡ
child of her to God and the throne of Him. And the
1135 5343 1519 2048 3699 2192 5117 2090
γυνὴ ἔφυγεν εἰς τὴν ἔρημον, ὅπου ἔχει τόπον ἡτοιμασμένον
woman fled into the wilderness, where she has a place having been prepared
575 2316 2443/1563 5142 846 2250/5507
ἀπὸ τοῦ Θεοῦ, ἵνα ἐκεῖ τρέφωσιν αὐτὴν ἡμέρας χιλίας
from God, that there they might nourish her days a thousand

hundred *and* sixty days.

[7]And war occurred in Heaven, Michael and his angels making war against the dragon. And the dragon and his angels made war, [8]but they did not have strength, nor was place yet found *for* them in Heaven. [9]And the great dragon was cast out—the old serpent being called Devil, and, Satan, he deceiving the whole habitable world—was cast out onto the earth, and his angels were cast with him.

[10]And I heard a great voice saying in Heaven, Now has come the salvation and power and the kingdom of our God, and the authority of His Christ, because the accuser of our brothers is thrown down, the *one* accusing them before our God day and night. [11]And they overcame him because of the blood of the Lamb, and because of the word of their testimony. And they did not love their soul *even* until death. [12]Because of this, be glad, the heavens and those tabernacling in them. Woe *to* the ones dwelling on the earth, and in the sea, because the Devil came down to you having great anger, knowing that he has a little time!

[13]And when the dragon saw that he was cast out onto the earth, he pursued the woman who bore the male. [14]And two wings of the great eagle were given to the woman, that she might fly into the wilderness, to her place, where she is nourished there a time, and times, and half a time, away from *the* serpent's face. [15]And the

1250 1835
διακοσίας ἑξήκοντα.
two hundred (and) sixty.
1096 4171 1722 3772 3413
7 Καὶ ἐγένετο πόλεμος ἐν τῷ οὐρανῷ· ὁ Μιχαὴλ καὶ οἱ
And occurred war in Heaven, Michael and the
32 848 4170 2596 1404
ἄγγελοι αὐτοῦ ἐπολέμησαν κατὰ τοῦ δράκοντος· καὶ ὁ
angels of him made war against the dragon. And the
1404 4170 32 848 3756 2480
8 δράκων ἐπολέμησε, καὶ οἱ ἄγγελοι αὐτοῦ, καὶ οὐκ ἴσχυσαν,
dragon warred, and the angels of him, and not they had strength.
906 3777 5117 2147 848 2089/1722 3772
9 οὔτε τόπος εὑρέθη αὐτῶν ἔτι ἐν τῷ οὐρανῷ. καὶ ἐβλήθη
not even place was found of them still in Heaven. And was cast
1404 3173 3789 744 2564 1228
ὁ δράκων ὁ μέγας, ὁ ὄφις ὁ ἀρχαῖος, ὁ καλούμενος διάβολος
the dragon great, the serpent old, being called Devil
4567 4105 3625 3650 906
καὶ ὁ Σατανᾶς, ὁ πλανῶν τὴν οἰκουμένην ὅλην· ἐβλήθη
and Satan the (one) deceiving the habitable world whole; was cast
1519 1093 32 848 3326 846 906
εἰς τὴν γῆν, καὶ οἱ ἄγγελοι αὐτοῦ μετ' αὐτοῦ ἐβλήθησαν.
onto the earth, and the angels of him with him were cast.
191 5456 3173 3004 1722 3772 737
10 καὶ ἤκουσα φωνὴν μεγάλην λέγουσαν ἐν τῷ οὐρανῷ, Ἄρτι
And I heard a voice great saying in Heaven, Now
1096 4991 1411 932 2316
ἐγένετο ἡ σωτηρία καὶ ἡ δύναμις καὶ ἡ βασιλεία τοῦ Θεοῦ
has come into being the salvation and the power and the kingdom of the God
*2257 1849 5547 848 3754 2598
ἡμῶν, καὶ ἡ ἐξουσία τοῦ Χριστοῦ αὐτοῦ· ὅτι κατεβλήθη
of us, and the authority of the Christ of Him, because is thrown down
2725 80 2257 2723 846
ὁ κατήγορος τῶν ἀδελφῶν ἡμῶν, ὁ κατηγορῶν αὐτῶν
the accuser of the brothers of us, the (one) accusing them
1799 2316 2257 2250 3571 846
11 ἐνώπιον τοῦ Θεοῦ ἡμῶν ἡμέρας καὶ νυκτός. καὶ αὐτοὶ
before the God of us day and night. And they
3528 846 1223 129 721 1223 3056
ἐνίκησαν αὐτὸν διὰ τὸ αἷμα τοῦ ἀρνίου, καὶ διὰ τὸν λόγον
overcame him because of the blood of the Lamb, and because of the word
3141 848 3756 25 5590 848
τῆς μαρτυρίας αὐτῶν, καὶ οὐκ ἠγάπησαν τὴν ψυχὴν αὐτῶν
of the witness of them; and no they loved the soul of them
891 2288 1223 5124 2165 3772 1722
12 ἄχρι θανάτου. διὰ τοῦτο εὐφραίνεσθε, οἱ οὐρανοὶ καὶ οἱ ἐν
until death. Therefore, be glad, the heavens and those in
846 4637 3759 2730 1093
αὐτοῖς σκηνοῦντες· οὐαὶ τοῖς κατοικοῦσι τὴν γῆν καὶ τὴν
them tabernacling Woe (to) those inhabiting the earth and the
2281 3754 2597 1228 4314 5209 2192 2372
θάλασσαν, ὅτι κατέβη ὁ διάβολος πρὸς ὑμᾶς ἔχων θυμὸν
sea, because came down the Devil to you having anger
3173 1492 3754 3641 2540 2192
μέγαν, εἰδὼς ὅτι ὀλίγον καιρὸν ἔχει.
great, knowing that a little time he has.
3753/1492 1404 3754 906 1519 1093 1377
13 Καὶ ὅτε εἶδεν ὁ δράκων ὅτι ἐβλήθη εἰς τὴν γῆν, ἐδίωξε τὴν
And when saw the dragon that he was cast onto the earth, he pursued the
1135 3748 5088 730 1325 1135
14 γυναῖκα ἥτις ἔτεκε τὸν ἄρρενα. καὶ ἐδόθησαν τῇ γυναικὶ
woman who bore the male. And were given to the woman
1417 4420 105 3173 2443 4072 1519
δύο πτέρυγες τοῦ ἀετοῦ τοῦ μεγάλου, ἵνα πέτηται εἰς τὴν
two wings of the eagle great, that she may fly into the
2048 1519 5117 848 3699 5142 1563 2540
ἔρημον εἰς τὸν τόπον αὐτῆς, ὅπου τρέφεται ἐκεῖ καιρόν, καὶ
wilderness, to the place of her, where she is nourished there a time, and
2540 2255 2540 575 4383 3789
15 καιρούς, καὶ ἥμισυ καιροῦ, ἀπὸ προσώπου τοῦ ὄφεως. καὶ
times, and half a time, from (the) face of the serpent. And

serpent threw water out of his mouth like a river after the woman, that he might cause her *to be* carried off *by the* river. [16]And the earth helped the woman, and the earth opened its mouth and swallowed the river which the dragon threw out of his mouth. [17]And the dragon was enraged over the woman, and went away to make war with the rest of her seed, those keeping the commandments of God, and having the testimony of Jesus Christ.

906 3789 3694 1135 1537 4750 848
ἔβαλεν ὁ ὄφις ὀπίσω τῆς γυναικὸς ἐκ τοῦ στόματος αὐτοῦ
cast the serpent after the woman out of the mouth of him

5204 5613 4215 2443 5026 4216 4160
ὕδωρ ὡς ποταμόν, ἵνα ταύτην ποταμοφόρητον ποιήσῃ.
water as a river, that she carried off (a) river he might make.

997 1093 1135 455 1093 4750
16 καὶ ἐβοήθησεν ἡ γῆ τῇ γυναικί, καὶ ἤνοιξεν ἡ γῆ τὸ στόμα
And helped the earth the woman, and opened the earth the mouth

848 2666 4215 3739 906 1404/1537
αὐτῆς, καὶ κατέπιε τὸν ποταμὸν ὃν ἔβαλεν ὁ δράκων ἐκ τοῦ
of it and swallowed the river which cast the dragon out of the

4750 848 3710 1404 1909 1135
17 στόματος αὐτοῦ. καὶ ὠργίσθη ὁ δράκων ἐπὶ τῇ γυναικί, καὶ
mouth of him. And was enraged the dragon over the woman, and

565 4160 4171 3326 3062 4690
ἀπῆλθε ποιῆσαι πόλεμον μετὰ τῶν λοιπῶν τοῦ σπέρματος
went away to make war with the rest of the seed

848 5083 1785 2316 2192
αὐτῆς, τῶν τηρούντων τὰς ἐντολὰς τοῦ Θεοῦ καὶ ἐχόντων
of her, those keeping the commandments of God, and having

3141 2424 5547
τὴν μαρτυρίαν τοῦ Ἰησοῦ Χριστοῦ
the witness of Jesus Christ.

CHAPTER 13

[1]And I stood on the sand of the sea.

And I saw a beast coming up out of the sea, having seven heads and ten horns, and on his horns ten diadems, and on its heads names of blasphemy. [2]And the beast which I saw was like a leopard, and its feet as of a bear, and its mouth as a lion's mouth. And the dragon gave its power to it, and its throne, and great authority. [3]And I saw one of its heads, as having been slain to death, and its deadly wound was healed. And all the earth marveled after the beast.

[4]And they worshiped the dragon who gave authority to the beast; and they worshiped the beast, saying, Who *is* like the beast; who is able to make war with it?

[5]And a mouth speaking great things and blasphemies was given to it. And authority to act forty-two months was given to it.

2476 1909 285 2281
1 καὶ ἐστάθην ἐπὶ τὴν ἄμμον τῆς θαλάσσης.
And I stood on the sand of the sea.

1492/1537 2281 2342 305 2192 2776
Καὶ εἶδον ἐκ τῆς θαλάσσης θηρίον ἀναβαῖνον, ἔχον κεφαλὰς
And I saw out of the sea a beast coming up, having heads

2033 2768 1176 1909 2768 848 1176
ἑπτὰ καὶ κέρατα δέκα, καὶ ἐπὶ τῶν κεράτων αὐτοῦ δέκα
seven and horns ten, and on the horns of it ten

1238 1909 2776 848 3686 988
διαδήματα, καὶ ἐπὶ τὰς κεφαλὰς αὐτοῦ ὄνομα βλασφημίας.
diadems, and on the heads of it names of blasphemy.

2342 1492 2258 3664 3917 4228
2 καὶ τὸ θηρίον, ὃ εἶδον, ἦν ὅμοιον παρδάλει, καὶ οἱ πόδες
And the beast which I saw was like a leopard, and the feet

848 5613 715 4750 848 5613 4750 3023
αὐτοῦ ὡς ἄρκτου, καὶ τὸ στόμα αὐτοῦ ὡς στόμα λέοντος·
of it as of a bear, and the mouth of it as (the) mouth of a lic

1325 846 1404 1411 848
καὶ ἔδωκεν αὐτῷ ὁ δράκων τὴν δύναμιν αὐτοῦ, καὶ τὸν
And gave to it the dragon the power of it and the

2362 848 1849 3173 1492 3391
3 θρόνον αὐτοῦ, καὶ ἐξουσίαν μεγάλην. καὶ εἶδον μίαν τῶν
throne of it and authority great. And I saw one of the

2776 848 5613 4969 1519 2288 4127
κεφαλῶν αὐτοῦ ὡς ἐσφαγμένην εἰς θάνατον· καὶ ἡ πληγὴ τοῦ
heads of it as having been slain to death, and the wound of the

2288 848 2323 2296 3650 1093 3694
θανάτου αὐτοῦ ἐθεραπεύθη· καὶ ἐθαύμασεν ὅλη ἡ γῆ ὀπίσω
death of it was healed. And marveled all the earth after

2342 4352 1404 3739 1325
4 τοῦ θηρίου· καὶ προσεκύνησαν τὸν δράκοντα ὃς ἔδωκεν
the beast; and they worshiped the dragon who gave

1849 2342 4352 2342 3004
ἐξουσίαν τῷ θηρίῳ, καὶ προσεκύνησαν τὸ θηρίον, λέγοντες,
authority to the beast, and they worshiped the beast, saying,

5101 3664 2342 5101 1410 4170 3326 846
Τίς ὅμοιος τῷ θηρίῳ; τίς δύναται πολεμῆσαι μετ' αὐτοῦ;
Who (is) like the beast, who is able to make war with it?

1325 846 4750 2980 3173 988
5 καὶ ἐδόθη αὐτῷ στόμα λαλοῦν μεγάλα καὶ βλασφημίας· καὶ
And was given to it a mouth speaking great things and blasphemies; and

1325 846 1849 4160 3376 5062 1417
6 ἐδόθη αὐτῷ ἐξουσία ποιῆσαι μῆνας τεσσαράκοντα δύο. καὶ
was given to it authority to act months forty- two. And

[6]And it opened its mouth in blasphemy toward God, to blaspheme His name and His tabernacle, and those tabernacling in Heaven.

[7]And it was given to it to war with the saints, and to overcome them. And authority was given to it over every tribe and tongue and nation. [8]And all those dwelling in the earth will worship it, *those* of whom the names now were written in the Scroll of Life of the Lamb having been slain from *the* foundation of *the* 4 world. [9]If anyone has an ear, let him hear. [10]If anyone gathers captivity, into captivity he goes. If anyone will kill by a sword, by a sword he must be killed. Here is the patience and the faith of the saints.

[11]And I saw another beast coming up out of the earth. And it had two horns like a lamb, but spoke like a dragon. [12]And it executes all the authority of the first beast before it. And it causes that the earth and those dwelling in it should worship the first beast, of which was healed its deadly wound. [13]And it does great signs, that even fire it causes to come down out of the heaven onto the earth before men. [14]And it deceives those dwelling on the earth, because of the signs which were given to it to do before the beast, saying to those dwelling on the earth to make an image to the beast who has the wound of the sword, and lived. [15]And was given to it to give a spirit to the image of the beast, so that the image of the beast might

455 4750 848 1519 988 4314 2316
ἤνοιξε τὸ στόμα αὐτοῦ εἰς βλασφημίαν πρὸς τὸν Θεόν,
it opened the mouth of it in blasphemy toward God,
987 3686 848 4633 848
βλασφημῆσαι τὸ ὄνομα αὐτοῦ, καὶ τὴν σκηνὴν αὐτοῦ, καὶ
to blaspheme the name of Him, and the tabernacle of Him, and
1722 3772 4637 1325 846 4171
7 τοὺς ἐν τῷ οὐρανῷ σκηνοῦντας. καὶ ἐδόθη αὐτῷ πόλεμον
those in Heaven tabernacling. And was given to it war
4160 3326 40 3528 846 1325
ποιῆσαι μετὰ τῶν ἁγίων, καὶ νικῆσαι αὐτούς· καὶ ἐδόθη
to make with the saints, and to overcome them. And was given
846 1849 1909 3956 5443 1100 1484
αὐτῷ ἐξουσία ἐπὶ πᾶσαν φυλὴν καὶ γλῶσσαν καὶ ἔθνος.
to it authority over every tribe and tongue and nation
4352 846 3956 2730 1909
8 καὶ προσκυνήσουσιν αὐτῷ πάντες οἱ κατοικοῦντες ἐπὶ τῆς
And will worship it all those dwelling on the
1093/3739/3756/ 1125 3686 1722 976 2222
γῆς, ὧν οὐ γέγραπται τὰ ὀνόματα ἐν τῇ βίβλῳ τῆς ζωῆς
earth, of whom not was written the names in the Scroll of Life
721 4969 575 2602 2889/=1536=2192
9 τοῦ ἀρνίου ἐσφαγμένου ἀπὸ καταβολῆς κόσμου. εἴ τις ἔχει
of the Lamb having been slain from (the) foundation world's. If any-has one
3779 191 =1536= 161 4863 1519 161
10 οὖς, ἀκουσάτω. εἴ τις αἰχμαλωσίαν συνάγει, εἰς αἰχμαλω-
an ear, let him hear. If anyone captivity gathers into captivity
5217 =1536=1722 3162 615 1163 846 1722
σίαν ὑπάγει· εἴ τις ἐν μαχαίρᾳ ἀποκτενεῖ, δεῖ αὐτὸν ἐν
he goes. If anyone by a sword will kill, must he by
3162 615 5602/2076 5281 4102
μαχαίρᾳ ἀποκτανθῆναι. ὧδέ ἐστιν ἡ ὑπομονὴ καὶ ἡ πίστις
a sword be killed. Here is the patience and the faith
40
τῶν ἁγίων.
of the saints.
1492 243 2342 305 1537 1093 2192
11 Καὶ εἶδον ἄλλο θηρίον ἀναβαῖνον ἐκ τῆς γῆς, καὶ εἶχε
And I saw another beast coming up out of the earth, and it had
2768 1417 3664 721 2980 5613 1404
12 κέρατα δύο ὅμοια ἀρνίῳ, καὶ ἐλάλει ὡς δράκων. καὶ τὴν
horns two like a lamb, and spoke as a dragon. And the
1849 4413 2342 3956 4160 1799 846
ἐξουσίαν τοῦ πρώτου θηρίου πᾶσαν ποιεῖ ἐνώπιον αὐτοῦ.
authority of the first beast all it does before it.
4160 1093 2730 1722 846 2443
καὶ ποιεῖ τὴν γῆν καὶ τοὺς κατοικοῦντας ἐν αὐτῇ ἵνα
And it makes the earth and those dwelling in it that
4352 2342 4413 3739 2323
προσκυνήσωσι τὸ θηρίον τὸ πρῶτον, οὗ ἐθεραπεύθη ἡ
they should worship the beast the first, of which was healed the
4127 2288 848 4160 4592 3173 2443
πληγὴ τοῦ θανάτου αὐτοῦ. καὶ ποιεῖ σημεῖα μεγάλα, ἵνα
wound of death of it. And it does signs great, that
4442 4160 2597 1537 3772 1519 1093
13 καὶ πῦρ ποιῇ καταβαίνειν ἐκ τοῦ οὐρανοῦ εἰς τὴν γῆν
even fire it makes to come down out of the heaven onto the earth
1799 444 4105 2730
14 ἐνώπιον τῶν ἀνθρώπων. καὶ πλανᾷ τοὺς κατοικοῦντας
before men. And it deceives those dwelling
1909 1093/1223 4592 3739 1325 846 4160 1799
ἐπὶ τῆς γῆς διὰ τὰ σημεῖα ἃ ἐδόθη αὐτῷ ποιῆσαι ἐνώπιον
on the earth, because of the signs which were given it to do before
2342 3004 2730 1909 1093 4160
τοῦ θηρίου, λέγων τοῖς κατοικοῦσιν ἐπὶ τῆς γῆς ποιῆσαι
the beast, saying to those dwelling on the earth to make
1504 2342/3739/2192 4127 3162 2198
εἰκόνα τῷ θηρίῳ ὃ ἔχει τὴν πληγὴν τῆς μαχαίρας καὶ ἔζησε.
an image to the beast who has the wound of the sword, and lived.
1325 846 1325 4151 1504 2342 2443
15 καὶ ἐδόθη αὐτῷ δοῦναι πνεῦμα τῇ εἰκόνι τοῦ θηρίου, ἵνα καὶ
And was given to it to give a spirit to the image of the beast, that even

even speak, and might cause as many as would not worship the image of the beast to be killed. [16]And the small and the great, and the rich and the poor, and the freemen and the slaves, it causes that they give to them all a mark on their right hand, or on their foreheads, [17]even that not any could buy or sell, except the *one* having the mark, or the name of the beast, or the number of its name. [18]Here is wisdom: Let the *one* having reason count the number of the beast, for it is *the* number of a man—and its number *is* six hundred *and* sixty-six.

2980 1504 2342 4160 3745 302/3361
λαλήσῃ ἡ εἰκὼν τοῦ θηρίου, καὶ ποιήσῃ, ὅσοι ἂν μὴ
might speak the image of the beast, and might make as many as not

4352 1504 2342 2443 615
προσκυνήσωσι τὴν εἰκόνα τοῦ θηρίου, ἵνα ἀποκτανθῶσι.
would worship the image of the beast, that (they) be killed.

4160 3956 3398 3173
16 καὶ ποιεῖ πάντας, τοὺς μικροὺς καὶ τοὺς μεγάλους, καὶ τοὺς
And it makes all, the small and the great, and the

4145 4434 1658
πλουσίους καὶ τοὺς πτωχούς, καὶ τοὺς ἐλευθέρους καὶ τοὺς
rich and the poor, and the freemen and the

1401 2443 1325 846 5480 1909 5495 848
δούλους, ἵνα δώσῃ αὐτοῖς χάραγμα ἐπὶ τῆς χειρὸς αὐτῶν
slaves, that it may give to them a mark on the hand of them

1188 1909 3359 848 2443/3361/5100
17 τῆς δεξιᾶς, ἢ ἐπὶ τῶν μετώπων αὐτῶν. καὶ ἵνα μή τις
right, or on the foreheads of them, even that not any

1410 59 2228 4453 =1508= 2192 5480
δύνηται ἀγοράσαι ἢ πωλῆσαι, εἰ μὴ ὁ ἔχων τὸ χάραγμα ἢ
could buy or sell, except he having the mark, or

3686 2342/2228 706 3686 848 5602
18 τὸ ὄνομα τοῦ θηρίου ἢ τὸν ἀριθμὸν τοῦ ὀνόματος αὐτοῦ. ὧδε
the name of the beast, or the number of the name of it. Here

4678 2076 2192 3563 5585 706
ἡ σοφία ἐστίν. ὁ ἔχων τὸν νοῦν ψηφισάτω τὸν ἀριθμὸν τοῦ
wisdom is. The (one) having reason let him count the number of the

*1812- 2342 706 1063 444 2076 706 848 *
1835- θηρίου· ἀριθμὸς γὰρ ἀνθρώπου ἐστί, καὶ ὁ ἀριθμὸς αὐτοῦ χξς΄.
1803 **beast; (the) number for of a man it is. And the number of it (is) 666.**
(=666)

CHAPTER 14

[1]And I saw, and behold, *the* Lamb standing on Mount Zion! And with Him *were* a hundred *and* forty-four thousands, *with* the name of His Father having been written on their foreheads. [2]And I heard a sound out of the heaven, as a sound of many waters, and as a sound of great thunder. Also I heard a sound of harpers harping on their harps. [3]And they sing as a new song before the throne, and before the four living creatures and the elders. And no one was able to learn the song except the hundred *and* forty-four thousands, those having been redeemed from the earth. [4]These are the ones who were not defiled with women, for they are virgins. These are the ones following the Lamb wherever He may go. These were redeemed from among men as first-fruit to God and to the Lamb.

1492 2400 721 2476 1909 3735 4622
1 Καὶ εἶδον, καὶ ἰδού, ἀρνίον ἑστηκὸς ἐπὶ τὸ ὄρος Σιών, καὶ
And I saw, and behold, (the) Lamb standing on the mount Zion, and

3326 846 1540 5062 5064 5505 2192
μετ᾽ αὐτοῦ ἑκατὸν τεσσαρακοντατέσσαρες χιλιάδες, ἔχουσαι
with Him a hundred (and) forty-four thousands, having

3686 3962 848 1125 1909 3359
τὸ ὄνομα τοῦ πατρὸς αὐτοῦ γεγραμμένον ἐπὶ τῶν μετώπων
the name of the Father of Him having been written on the foreheads

848 191 5456/1537 3772 5613 5456 5204
2 αὐτῶν. καὶ ἤκουσα φωνὴν ἐκ τοῦ οὐρανοῦ, ὡς φωνὴν ὑδάτων
of them. And I heard a sound out of Heaven, as a sound of waters

4183 5613/5456 1027 3173 5456 191
πολλῶν, καὶ ὡς φωνὴν βροντῆς μεγάλης· καὶ φωνὴν ἤκουσα
many, and as a sound of thunder great; and a sound I heard

2790 2789 1722 2788 848
3 κιθαρῳδῶν κιθαριζόντων ἐν ταῖς κιθάραις αὐτῶν. καὶ
of harpers harping on the harps of them. And

103 5613/5603 2537 1799 2362 1799
ᾄδουσιν ὡς ᾠδὴν καινὴν ἐνώπιον τοῦ θρόνου, καὶ ἐνώπιον
they sing as a song new before the throne, and before

5064 2226 4245 3762 1410
τῶν τεσσάρων ζώων καὶ τῶν πρεσβυτέρων· καὶ οὐδεὶς ἠδύ-
the four living creatures and the elders; and no one was

3129 5603 =1508= 1540 5062 5064
νατο μαθεῖν τὴν ᾠδήν, εἰ μὴ αἱ ἑκατὸν τεσσαρακοντατέσ-
able to learn the song, except the hundred (and) forty-four

5505 59 575 1093 3778 1526
4 σαρες χιλιάδες, οἱ ἠγορασμένοι ἀπὸ τῆς γῆς. οὗτοί εἰσιν οἳ
thousands, those being redeemed from the earth. These are who

3326 1135 3756 3435 3933 1063 1526 3778
μετὰ γυναικῶν οὐκ ἐμολύνθησαν· παρθένοι γάρ εἰσιν. οὗτοί
with women not were defiled, virgins for they are. These

1526 190 721 3699 302/5217 3778
εἰσιν οἱ ἀκολουθοῦντες τῷ ἀρνίῳ ὅπου ἂν ὑπάγῃ. οὗτοι
are those following the Lamb wherever He may go. These

59 575 444 536 2316
ἠγοράσθησαν ἀπὸ τῶν ἀνθρώπων, ἀπαρχὴ τῷ Θεῷ καὶ τῷ
were redeemed from men firstfruit to God and to the

[5]And no guile was found in their mouth, for they are without blemish before the throne of God.

[6]And I saw another angel flying in mid-heaven, having an everlasting gospel to proclaim to those dwelling on the earth, even *to* every nation and tribe and tongue and people, [7]saying in a great voice, Fear God, and give glory to Him, because the hour of His judgment has come; also, Worship Him who has made the heaven, and the earth, and and the sea, and the fountains of waters.

[8]And another angel followed, saying, The great city, Babylon, has fallen, has fallen; because of the wine of the anger of her fornication, *she* made all nations to drink.

[9]And a third angel followed them, saying in a great voice, If anyone worships the beast and its image, and receives a mark on his forehead, or in his hand, [10]he also shall drink of the wine of the anger of God having been mixed undiluted in the cup of His wrath. And *he* will be tormented by fire and brimstone before the holy angels and before the Lamb. [11]And the smoke of their torment goes up forever *and* ever. And those worshiping the beast and its image have no rest night and day, even if anyone receives the mark of its name. [12]Here *is* the patience of the saints; here *are* the ones keeping the commands of God, and the faith of Jesus. [13]And I

721 1722 4750 848 3756 2147 1388 299
5 ἀρνίῳ. καὶ ἐν τῷ στόματι αὐτῶν οὐχ εὑρέθη δόλος· ἄμωμοι
Lamb. And in the mouth of them not was found guile; unmarked
1063/1526 1799 2362 2316
γάρ εἰσιν ἐνώπιον τοῦ θρόνου τοῦ Θεοῦ.
for they are before the throne of God.
1492 243 32 4072 1722 3321
6 Καὶ εἶδον ἄλλον ἄγγελον πετώμενον ἐν μεσουρανήματι,
And I saw another angel flying in mid-heaven,
2192 2098 166 2097 2730
ἔχοντα εὐαγγέλιον αἰώνιον, εὐαγγελίσαι τοὺς κατοικοῦντας
having a gospel everlasting to preach to those dwelling
1909 1093 3956 1484 5443 1100 2992
ἐπὶ τῆς γῆς, καὶ πᾶν ἔθνος καὶ φυλὴν καὶ γλῶσσαν καὶ λαόν,
on the earth, even every nation and tribe and tongue and people,
3004 1722/5456 3173 5399 2316 1325 846
7 λέγοντα ἐν φωνῇ μεγάλῃ, Φοβήθητε τὸν Θεόν, καὶ δότε αὐτῷ
saying in a voice great, Fear God, and give to Him
1391 3754/2064 5610 2920 848 4352
δόξαν, ὅτι ἦλθεν ἡ ὥρα τῆς κρίσεως αὐτοῦ, καὶ προσκυνή-
glory, because came the hour of the judgment of Him; and, Worship
4160 3772 1093 2281
σατε τῷ ποιήσαντι τὸν οὐρανὸν καὶ τὴν γῆν καὶ τὴν θάλασ-
Him having made the heaven and the earth and the sea
4077 5204
σαν καὶ πηγὰς ὑδάτων.
and fountains of waters.
243 32 190 3004 4098 4098
8 Καὶ ἄλλος ἄγγελος ἠκολούθησε, λέγων, Ἔπεσεν ἔπεσε
And another angel followed, saying, Fell, fell
897 4172 3173 3754/1537 3631 2372
Βαβυλὼν ἡ πόλις ἡ μεγάλη, ὅτι ἐκ τοῦ οἴνου τοῦ θυμοῦ τῆς
Babylon the city great, because of the wine of the anger of the
4202 848 4222 3956 1484
πορνείας αὐτῆς πεπότικε πάντα ἔθνη.
fornication of her she made to drink all nations.
5154 32 190 846 3004/1722/5456
9 Καὶ τρίτος ἄγγελος ἠκολούθησεν αὐτοῖς, λέγων ἐν φωνῇ
And a third angel followed them, saying in a voice
3173 =1536= 2342 4352 1504 848
μεγάλῃ, Εἴ τις τὸ θηρίον προσκυνεῖ καὶ τὴν εἰκόνα αὐτοῦ,
great, If anyone the beast worships and the image of it,
2983 5480 1909 3359 848 2228/1909
καὶ λαμβάνει χάραγμα ἐπὶ τοῦ μετώπου αὐτοῦ, ἢ ἐπὶ τὴν
and receives a mark on the forehead of him, or on the
5495 848 846 4095 1537 3631 2372
10 χεῖρα αὐτοῦ, καὶ αὐτὸς πίεται ἐκ τοῦ οἴνου τοῦ θυμοῦ τοῦ
hand of him, even he shall drink of the wine of the anger of the
2316 2767 194 1722 4221 3709
Θεοῦ, τοῦ κεκερασμένου ἀκράτου ἐν τῷ ποτηρίῳ τῆς ὀργῆς
God, having been mixed undiluted in the cup of the wrath
848 928 1722/4442 2303 1799
αὐτοῦ, καὶ βασανισθήσεται ἐν πυρὶ καὶ θείῳ ἐνώπιον τῶν
of Him, and will be tormented by fire and brimstone before the
40 32 1799 721 2586
11 ἁγίων ἀγγέλων, καὶ ἐνώπιον τοῦ ἀρνίου· καὶ ὁ καπνὸς τοῦ
holy angels, and before the Lamb. And the smoke of the
929 848 305 1519 165 165 3756
βασανισμοῦ αὐτῶν ἀναβαίνει εἰς αἰῶνας αἰώνων· καὶ οὐκ
torment of them goes up to ages of ages; and not
2192 372 2250 3571 4352
ἔχουσιν ἀνάπαυσιν ἡμέρας καὶ νυκτὸς οἱ προσκυνοῦντες τὸ
have rest day and night those worshiping the
2342 1504 848 =1536= 2983 5480
θηρίον καὶ τὴν εἰκόνα αὐτοῦ, καὶ εἴ τις λαμβάνει τὸ χάραγμα
beast and the image of it; even if anyone receives the mark
3686 848 5602 5281 40 2076 5602
12 τοῦ ὀνόματος αὐτοῦ. ὧδε ὑπομονὴ τῶν ἁγίων ἐστίν· ὧδε
of the name of it. Here (the) patience of the saints is. Here
5083 1785 2316 4102 2424
οἱ τηροῦντες τὰς ἐντολὰς τοῦ Θεοῦ καὶ τὴν πίστιν Ἰησοῦ.
those keeping the commandments of God and the faith of Jesus.

heard a voice out of Heaven saying to me, Write: Blessed *are* the dead, the ones dying in *the* Lord from now. Yes, says the Spirit, they shall rest from their labors, and their works follow with them.

14 And I saw; and behold, a white cloud; and on the cloud *One* sitting, like *the* Son of man, having on His head a golden crown, and in His hand a sharp sickle. 15 And another angel went forth out of the temple, crying in a great voice to the *One* sitting on the cloud, Send Your sickle and reap, because Your hour to reap came, because the harvest of the earth was dried. 16 And the *One* sitting on the cloud thrust His sickle onto the earth, and the earth was reaped.

17 And another angel went forth out of the temple in Heaven, he also having a sharp sickle.

18 And another angel went forth out of the altar having authority over the fire. And he spoke with a great cry to the *one* having the sharp sickle, saying, Send your sharp sickle and gather the clusters of the vine of the earth, because its grapes are ripened. 19 And the angel thrust his sickle into the earth and gathered the vine of the earth, and threw into the winepress of the great anger of God. 20 And the winepress was trodden outside the city, and blood went out of the winepress as far as the bridles of the horses, from a thousand, six hundred stadia.

191 5456 1537 3772 3004 3427 1125
13 Καὶ ἤκουσα φωνῆς ἐκ τοῦ οὐρανοῦ λεγούσης μοι, Γράψον,
And I heard a voice out of Heaven saying to me, Write:
3107 3498 1722 2962 599 575 737
Μακάριοι οἱ νεκροὶ οἱ ἐν Κυρίῳ ἀποθνήσκοντες ἀπ' ἄρτι·
Blessed (are) the dead, those in (the) Lord dying from now.
3483 3004 4151 2443 373 1537 2873
ναί, λέγει τὸ Πνεῦμα, ἵνα ἀναπαύσωνται ἐκ τῶν κόπων
Yes, says the Spirit, that they shall rest from the labors
848 2041 848 190 3326 846
αὐτῶν· τὰ δὲ ἔργα αὐτῶν ἀκολουθεῖ μετ' αὐτῶν.
of them; the and works of them follow with them.

1492 2400 3507 3022 1909 3507
14 Καὶ εἶδον, καὶ ἰδού, νεφέλη λευκή, καὶ ἐπὶ τὴν νεφέλην
And I saw, and behold, a cloud white, and on the cloud
2521 3664 5207 444 2192 1909 2776
καθήμενος ὅμοιος υἱῷ ἀνθρώπου, ἔχων ἐπὶ τῆς κεφαλῆς
(One) sitting like (the) Son of man, having on the head
848 4735 5552 1722 5495 848 1407
αὐτοῦ στέφανον χρυσοῦν, καὶ ἐν τῇ χειρὶ αὐτοῦ δρέπανον
of Him a crown of gold and in the hand of Him a sickle
3691 243 32 1831 1537 3485 2896 1722
15 ὀξύ. καὶ ἄλλος ἄγγελος ἐξῆλθεν ἐκ τοῦ ναοῦ, κράζων ἐν
sharp. And another angel went forth out of the temple, crying in
3173 5456 2521 1909 3507 3992
μεγάλῃ φωνῇ τῷ καθημένῳ ἐπὶ τῆς νεφέλης, Πέμψον τὸ
a great voice to the (One) sitting on the cloud, Send the
1407 4675 2325 3754/2064/4671 5610 2325
δρέπανόν σου καὶ θέρισον· ὅτι ἦλθέ σοι ἡ ὥρα τοῦ θερίσαι,
sickle of You and reap because came You the hour to reap,
3754 3583 2326 1093 906 2521
16 ὅτι ἐξηράνθη ὁ θερισμὸς τῆς γῆς. καὶ ἔβαλεν ὁ καθήμενος
because was dried the harvest of the earth. And thrust the (One) sitting
1909 3507 1407 848 1909 1093
ἐπὶ τὴν νεφέλην τὸ δρέπανον αὐτοῦ ἐπὶ τὴν γῆν. καὶ
on the cloud the sickle of Him on the earth, and
2325 1093
ἐθερίσθη ἡ γῆ.
was reaped the earth.

243 32 1821 1537 3485 1722
17 Καὶ ἄλλος ἄγγελος ἐξῆλθεν ἐκ τοῦ ναοῦ τοῦ ἐν τῷ
And another angel went forth out of the temple in
3772 2192 846 1407 3691 243 32
18 οὐρανῷ, ἔχων καὶ αὐτὸς δρέπανον ὀξύ. καὶ ἄλλος ἄγγελος
Heaven, having also he a sickle sharp. And another angel
1831 1537 2379 2192 1849 1909 4442
ἐξῆλθεν ἐκ τοῦ θυσιαστηρίου, ἔχων ἐξουσίαν ἐπὶ τοῦ πυρός,
went forth out of the altar, having authority over the fire,
5455 2906 3173 2192 1407 3691
καὶ ἐφώνησε κραυγῇ μεγάλῃ τῷ ἔχοντι τὸ δρέπανον τὸ ὀξύ,
and he spoke with a cry great to the (one) having the sickle sharp,
3004 4151 4675 1407 3691 5166
λέγων, Πέμψον σου τὸ δρέπανον τὸ ὀξὺ καὶ τρύγησον τοὺς
saying, Send of you the sickle sharp and gather the
1009 288 1093/3754 187 4718
βότρυας τῆς ἀμπέλου τῆς γῆς, ὅτι ἤκμασαν αἱ σταφυλαὶ
clusters of the vine of the earth, because are ripened the grapes
848 906 32 1407 848 1519 1093
19 αὐτῆς. καὶ ἔβαλεν ὁ ἄγγελος τὸ δρέπανον αὐτοῦ εἰς τὴν γῆν,
of it. And thrust the angel the sickle of him into the earth.
5166 288 1093 906 1519 3025
καὶ ἐτρύγησε τὴν ἄμπελον τῆς γῆς, καὶ ἔβαλεν εἰς τὴν ληνὸν
and gathered the vine of the earth, and threw into the winepress
2372 2316 3173 3961 3025
20 τοῦ θυμοῦ τοῦ Θεοῦ τὴν μεγάλην. καὶ ἐπατήθη ἡ ληνὸς
of the anger of God great. And was trodden the winepress
1854 4172 1831 129 1537 3025 891
ἔξω τῆς πόλεως, καὶ ἐξῆλθεν αἷμα ἐκ τῆς ληνοῦ ἄχρι τῶν
outside the city, and came forth blood out of the winepress until the
5469 2462 575 4712 5507 1812
χαλινῶν τῶν ἵππων, ἀπὸ σταδίων χιλίων ἑξακοσίων.
bridles of the horses, and stadia a thousand six hundred.

NOTE: Frequent words not numbered: δέ(1161); καί(2531)—and, but; ὁ, ἡ, τό (3588, the)— • above word, look in ... se margin for No

CHAPTER 15

[1]And I saw another sign in Heaven, great and marvelous: seven angels having the last seven plagues, because the anger of God was completed in them.

[2]And I saw, as a glassy sea having been mixed with fire. And the ones overcoming the beast, and its image, and its mark, of the number of its name, *were* standing on the glassy sea, having harps of God. [3]And they sing the song of Moses the slave of God, and the song of the Lamb, saying, Great and marvelous *are* Your works, Lord God Almighty, righteous and true *are* Your ways, King of the saints. [4]Who will not fear You, Lord, and glorify Your name? For *You* only *are* holy. For all the nations will come and will worship before You, because Your righteousnesses were made known.

[5]And after these things I saw; and behold, the temple of the tabernacle of the testimony in Heaven was opened! [6]And the seven angels having the seven plagues came forth out of the temple, having been clothed *in* clean and bright linen, and golden bands having been girded around the breasts. [7]And one of the four living creatures gave to the seven angels seven golden bowls filled with the anger of the living God, forever *and* ever. [8]And the temple was filled with *the* smoke of the glory of God, and with His power. And no one was able to enter into the temple until

CHAPTER 15

1492 243 4592 1722 3772 3173 2298
1 Καὶ εἶδον ἄλλο σημεῖον ἐν τῷ οὐρανῷ μέγα καὶ θαυμα-
And I saw another sign in Heaven, great and marvelous
32 2033 2192 4127 2033 2078
στόν, ἀγγέλους ἑπτὰ ἔχοντας πληγὰς ἑπτὰ τὰς ἐσχάτας,
angels seven having plagues seven the last.
3754/1722/846 5055 2372 2316
ὅτι ἐν αὐταῖς ἐτελέσθη ὁ θυμὸς τοῦ Θεοῦ.
because in them was completed the anger of God.
1492 5613 2281 5193 3396 4442
2 Καὶ εἶδον ὡς θάλασσαν ὑαλίνην μεμιγμένην πυρί, καὶ
And I saw as a sea glassy having been mixed with fire, and
3528 1537 2342 1537 1504 848
τοὺς νικῶντας ἐκ τοῦ θηρίου καὶ ἐκ τῆς εἰκόνος αὐτοῦ καὶ
those overcoming of the beast and of the image of it, and
1537 5480 848 1537 706 3686
ἐκ τοῦ χαράγματος αὐτοῦ, ἐκ τοῦ ἀριθμοῦ τοῦ ὀνόματος
of the mark of it, of the number of the name
848 2476 1909 2281 5193 2192
αὐτοῦ, ἑστῶτας ἐπὶ τὴν θάλασσαν τὴν ὑαλίνην, ἔχοντας
of it, standing on the sea glassy, having
2788 2316 103 5603 3475 1401
3 κιθάρας τοῦ Θεοῦ. καὶ ᾄδουσι τὴν ᾠδὴν Μωσέως τοῦ δούλου
harps of God. And they sing the song of Moses the slave
2316 5603 721 3004 3173
τοῦ Θεοῦ, καὶ τὴν ᾠδὴν τοῦ ἀρνίου, λέγοντες, Μεγάλα
of God, and the song of the Lamb, saying, Great
2293 2041 4675 2962 2316 3841
καὶ θαυμαστὰ τὰ ἔργα σου, Κύριε ὁ Θεὸς ὁ παντοκράτωρ·
and marvelous the works of You, Lord God Almighty,
1342 228 3598 4675 935 40 5101
4 δίκαιαι καὶ ἀληθιναὶ αἱ ὁδοί σου, ὁ βασιλεὺς τῶν ἁγίων. τίς
righteous and true the ways of You, the King of the saints. Who
=3364= 5399 4571 2962 1392 3686 4675 3754
οὐ μὴ φοβηθῇ σε, Κύριε, καὶ δοξάσῃ τὸ ὄνομά σου; ὅτι
in no way fear You, Lord, and glorify the name of You? For
3440 3741 3754 3956 1484 2240 4352
μόνος ὅσιος· ὅτι πάντα τὰ ἔθνη ἥξουσι καὶ προσκυνή-
(You) only (are) holy, for all the nations will come and will worship
1799 4675/3754 1345 4675 5319
σουσιν ἐνώπιόν σου, ὅτι τὰ δικαιώματά σου ἐφανερώθησαν.
before You, because the righteousnesses of You were revealed.
3326 5023 1492 2400 455 3485 4633
5 Καὶ μετὰ ταῦτα εἶδον, καὶ ἰδού, ἠνοίγη ὁ ναὸς τῆς σκηνῆς
And after these things I saw, and behold, was opened the temple of the tent
3142 1722 3772 1831 2033 32
6 τοῦ μαρτυρίου ἐν τῷ οὐρανῷ· καὶ ἐξῆλθον οἱ ἑπτὰ ἄγγελοι
of the testimony in Heaven; and came forth the seven angels
2192 2033 4127/1537 3485 1746 3043
ἔχοντες τὰς ἑπτὰ πληγὰς ἐκ τοῦ ναοῦ, ἐνδεδυμένοι λίνον
having the seven plagues out of the temple. Being clothed (with) linen
2513 2986 4024 4012 4738
καθαρὸν καὶ λαμπρόν, καὶ περιεζωσμένοι περὶ τὰ στήθη
clean and bright, and having been girded around the breasts
2223 5552 1520/1537 5064 2226 1325
7 ζώνας χρυσᾶς. καὶ ἓν ἐκ τῶν τεσσάρων ζώων ἔδωκε τοῖς
(with) girdles of gold And one of the four living creatures gave to the
2033 32 2033 5357 5552 1073 2372
ἑπτὰ ἀγγέλοις ἑπτὰ φιάλας χρυσᾶς γεμούσας τοῦ θυμοῦ
seven angels seven bowls of gold filled of the anger
2316 2198 1519 165 165
8 τοῦ Θεοῦ τοῦ ζῶντος εἰς τοὺς αἰῶνας τῶν αἰώνων. καὶ
of God the living, to the ages of the ages. And
1072 3485 2586 1537 1391 2316 1537
ἐγεμίσθη ὁ ναὸς καπνοῦ ἐκ τῆς δόξης τοῦ Θεοῦ, καὶ ἐκ τῆς
was filled the temple of smoke of the glory of God, and of the
1411 848 3762 1410 1525 1519 3485
δυνάμεως αὐτοῦ· καὶ οὐδεὶς ἠδύνατο εἰσελθεῖν εἰς τὸν ναόν,
power of Him. And no one could enter into the temple,

the seven plagues of the seven angels should be completed.

891 5055 2033 4127 2033 32
ἄχρι τελεσθῶσιν αἱ ἑπτὰ πληγαὶ τῶν ἑπτὰ ἀγγέλων.
until should be finished the seven plagues of the seven angels.

CHAPTER 16

[1]And I heard a great voice out of the temple saying to the seven angels: Go and pour out the bowls of the anger of God onto the earth.

[2]And the first went away and poured out his bowl onto the earth. And it became a bad and evil sore onto the men, the *ones* having the mark of the beast, and the ones worshiping its image.

[3]And the second angel poured out his bowl onto the sea. And it became blood, as of a dead one, and every soul of life died in the sea.

[4]And the third angel poured out his bowl onto the rivers, and onto the fountains of the waters; and it became blood. [5]And I heard the angel of the waters saying, You are righteous, Lord, the *One* who is, and who was, and who will be, because You judged these things, [6]since they poured out *the* blood of the saints and of *the* prophets; and You gave blood to them to drink, for they were deserving.

[7]And I heard another out of the altar saying, Yes, Lord God Almighty, Your judgments *are* true and righteous.

[8]And the fourth angel poured out his bowl onto the sun. And it was given to him to burn men with fire. [9]And men were burned *with* great heat. And they blasphemed the name

CHAPTER 16

191 5456 3173 1537 3485 3004
1 Καὶ ἤκουσα φωνῆς μεγάλης ἐκ τοῦ ναοῦ, λεγούσης τοῖς
And I heard a voice great out of the temple, saying to the
2033 32 5217 1632 5357 2372
ἑπτὰ ἀγγέλοις, Ὑπάγετε, καὶ ἐκχέατε τὰς φιαλας τοῦ θυμοῦ
seven angels, Go, and pour out the bowls of the anger
2316/1519 1093
τοῦ Θεοῦ εἰς τὴν γῆν.
of God onto the earth.

565 4413 1632 5357 848 1909
2 Καὶ ἀπῆλθεν ὁ πρῶτος, καὶ ἐξέχεε τὴν φιάλην αὐτοῦ ἐπὶ
And went away the first, and poured out the bowl of him onto
1093 1096 1668 2556 4190 1519
τὴν γῆν· καὶ ἐγένετο ἕλκος κακὸν καὶ πονηρὸν εἰς τοὺς
the earth; and it became a sore bad and evil into the
444 2192 5480 2342
ἀνθρώπους τοὺς ἔχοντας τὸ χάραγμα τοῦ θηρίου, καὶ τοὺς
men having the mark of the beast, and those
1504 848 4352
τῇ εἰκόνι αὐτοῦ προσκυνοῦντας.
the image of it worshiping.

1208 32 1632 5357 848 1519
3 Καὶ ὁ δεύτερος ἄγγελος ἐξέχεε τὴν φιάλην αὐτοῦ εἰς τὴν
And the second angel poured out the bowl of him onto the
2281 1096 129/5613 3498 3956 5590
θάλασσαν· καὶ ἐγένετο αἷμα ὡς νεκροῦ, καὶ πᾶσα ψυχὴ
sea; and it became blood, as of a dead one, and every soul
2198 599 1722 2281
ζῶσα ἀπέθανεν ἐν τῇ θαλάσσῃ.
living died in the sea.

5154 32 1632 5357 848 1519
4 Καὶ ὁ τρίτος ἄγγελος ἐξέχεε τὴν φιάλην αὐτοῦ εἰς τοὺς
And the third angel poured out the bowl of him onto the
4215 1519 4077 5204 1096 129
ποταμοὺς καὶ εἰς τὰς πηγὰς τῶν ὑδάτων· καὶ ἐγένετο αἷμα.
rivers and onto the fountains of the waters; and it became blood.
191 32 5204 3004 1342
5 καὶ ἤκουσα τοῦ ἀγγέλου τῶν ὑδάτων λέγοντος, Δίκαιος,
And I heard the angel of the waters saying, Righteous
2962/1488 5607 2258 3741 3754 5023 2919
Κύριε, εἶ, ὁ ὢν καὶ ὁ ἦν καὶ ὁ ἐσόμενος, ὅτι ταῦτα ἔκρινας·
Lord You are: He being, who was and who will be, because these You judged;
3754 129 40 4396 1632 129 846
6 ὅτι αἷμα ἁγίων καὶ προφητῶν ἐξέχεαν, καὶ αἷμα αὐτοῖς
since (the) blood of saints and of prophets they poured out and blood to them
1325 4095 514 1063/1526 191 243 1537
7 ἔδωκας πιεῖν· ἄξιοι γάρ εἰσι. καὶ ἤκουσα ἄλλου ἐκ τοῦ
You gave to drink; deserving for they are. And I heard another out of the
2379 3004 3483 2962 2316 3841
θυσιαστηρίου λέγοντος, Ναί, Κύριε ὁ Θεὸς ὁ παντοκράτωρ,
altar saying, Yes, Lord God Almighty,
228 1342 2920 4675
ἀληθιναὶ καὶ δίκαιαι αἱ κρίσεις σου.
true and righteous the judgments of You.

5067 32 1632 5357 848 1909
8 Καὶ ὁ τέταρτος ἄγγελος ἐξέχεε τὴν φιάλην αὐτοῦ ἐπὶ τὸν
And the fourth angel poured out the bowl of him onto the
2246 1325 846 2739 444 1722/4442
ἥλιον· καὶ ἐδόθη αὐτῷ καυματίσαι τοὺς ἀνθρώπους ἐν πυρί.
sun, and it was given to it to burn the men with fire.
2739 444 2738 3173 987
9 καὶ ἐκαυματίσθησαν οἱ ἄνθρωποι καῦμα μέγα, καὶ ἐβλασφή-
And were burned men (with) heat great, and they blas-

of God, the *One* having authority over these plagues — and they did not repent to give Him glory.

[10]And the fifth angel poured out his bowl onto the throne of the beast. And its kingdom became darkened; and they gnawed their tongues from the pain. [11]And they blasphemed the God of Heaven, from their pains and from their sores. And they did not repent of their works.

[12]And the sixth angel poured out his bowl onto the great river Euphrates, and its water was dried up so that might be prepared the way of the kings from *the* rising of *the* sun. [13]And I saw three unclean spirits like frogs out of the mouth of the dragon, and out of the mouth of the beast, and out of the mouth of the false prophet. [14]For they are spirits of demons doing signs, which go forth to the kings of the earth, even of the whole habitable world to assemble them to the war of that day, the great *day* of God Almighty.

[15]Behold, I am coming as a thief. Blessed *is* the *one* watching and keeping his garments, that he does not walk naked, and they may see his shame. [16]And He assembled them in the place having been called in Hebrew, Armageddon.

[17]And the seventh angel poured out his bowl into the air, and a great voice came from the throne from the temple of Heaven, saying,

3686 2316 2192 1849 1909
μησαν τὸ ὄνομα τοῦ Θεοῦ τοῦ ἔχοντος ἐξουσίαν ἐπὶ τὰς
phemed the name of God, the (One) having authority over
4127 5025 3756 3340 1325 846 1391
πληγὰς ταύτας, καὶ οὐ μετενόησαν δοῦναι αὐτῷ δόξαν.
plagues these; and not they repented to give Him glory.
3991 32 1632 5357 848 1909
10 Καὶ ὁ πέμπτος ἄγγελος ἐξέχεε τὴν φιάλην αὐτοῦ ἐπὶ τὸν
And the fifth angel poured out the bowl of him onto the
2362 2342 1096 932 848 4656
θρόνον τοῦ θηρίου· καὶ ἐγένετο ἡ βασιλεία αὐτοῦ ἐσκοτω-
throne of the beast; and became the kingdom of it darkened,
3145 1100 848 1537 4192
μένη· καὶ ἐμασσῶντο τὰς γλώσσας αὐτῶν ἐκ τοῦ πόνου,
and they gnawed the tongues of them from the pain;
987 2316 3772 1537 4192
11 καὶ ἐβλασφήμησαν τὸν Θεὸν τοῦ οὐρανοῦ ἐκ τῶν πόνων
and they blasphemed the God of Heaven from the pains
848 1537 1668 848 3756 3340 1537
αὐτῶν καὶ ἐκ τῶν ἑλκῶν αὐτῶν, καὶ οὐ μετενόησαν ἐκ τῶν
of them and from the sores of them; and not they repented of the
2041 848
ἔργων αὐτῶν.
works of them.

1622 32 1632 5357 848 1909
12 Καὶ ὁ ἕκτος ἄγγελος ἐξέχεε τὴν φιάλην αὐτοῦ ἐπὶ τὸν
And the sixth angel poured out the bowl of him onto the
4215 3173 2166 3583 5204
ποταμὸν τὸν μέγαν τὸν Εὐφράτην· καὶ ἐξηράνθη τὸ ὕδωρ
river great Euphrates, and was dried up the water
848 2443 2090 3598 935 575
αὐτοῦ, ἵνα ἑτοιμασθῇ ἡ ὁδὸς τῶν βασιλέων τῶν ἀπὸ
of it, that might be prepared the way of the kings from
395 2246 1492/1537 4750 1404
13 ἀνατολῶν ἡλίου. καὶ εἶδον ἐκ τοῦ στόματος τοῦ δράκοντος,
(the) rising of (the) sun. And I saw out of the mouth of the dragon,
1537 4750 2342 1537 4750
καὶ ἐκ τοῦ στόματος τοῦ θηρίου, καὶ ἐκ τοῦ στόματος τοῦ
and out of the mouth of the beast, and out of the mouth of the
5578 4151 5140 169 3664 944
ψευδοπροφήτου, πνεύματα τρία ἀκάθαρτα ὅμοια βατρά-
false prophet, spirits three unclean like frogs;
1526/1063 4151 1142 4160 4592 3739
14 χοις· εἰσὶ γὰρ πνεύματα δαιμόνων ποιοῦντα σημεῖα, ἃ
they are for spirits of demons doing signs, which
1607 1909 935 1093 3625
ἐκπορεύεται ἐπὶ τοὺς βασιλεῖς τῆς γῆς καὶ τῆς οἰκουμένης
go forth to the kings of the earth, even of the habitable world
3650 4863 846 1519 4171 2250 1565
ὅλης, συναγαγεῖν αὐτοὺς εἰς τὸν πόλεμον τῆς ἡμέρας ἐκείνης
whole, to assemble them to the war of day that
3173 2316 3841 2400
15 τῆς μεγάλης τοῦ Θεοῦ τοῦ παντοκράτορος. (Ἰδού,
the great (day) of God Almighty. Behold,
2064 5613 2812 3107 1127 5083
ἔρχομαι ὡς κλέπτης. μακάριος ὁ γρηγορῶν καὶ τηρῶν τὰ
I am coming as a thief, blessed the (one) watching and keeping the
2440 848 2443/3361 1131 4043 991
ἱμάτια αὐτοῦ, ἵνα μὴ γυμνὸς περιπατῇ, καὶ βλέπωσι τὴν
garments of him, that not naked he may walk, and they may see the
808 848 4863 846 1519 5117
16 ἀσχημοσύνην αὐτοῦ.) καὶ συνήγαγεν αὐτοὺς εἰς τὸν τόπον
shame of him. And He assembled them in the place
2564 1447 717
τὸν καλούμενον Ἑβραϊστὶ Ἀρμαγεδδών.
having been called in Hebrew, Armageddon.

1442 32 1632 5357 848 1519
17 Καὶ ὁ ἕβδομος ἄγγελος ἐξέχεε τὴν φιάλην αὐτοῦ εἰς τὸν
And the seventh angel poured out the bowl of him into the
109 1831 5456 3173 575 3485 3772
ἀέρα· καὶ ἐξῆλθε φωνὴ μεγάλη ἀπὸ τοῦ ναοῦ τοῦ οὐρανοῦ,
air, and came a voice great from the temple of Heaven,

it has happened! 18And voices and thunders and lightnings occurred. And a great earthquake occurred, such as did not occur since man came into being on the earth, such a huge earthquake, so great! 19And the great city came to be into three parts, and the cities of the nations fell. And Babylon the great was remembered before God, to give to her the cup of the wine of the anger of His wrath. 20And every island fled away, and mountains were not found. 21And a great hail, as the size of a talent, came down out of the heaven upon men. And men blasphemed God from the plague of the hail, because its plague is exceedingly great.

575 2362 3004 1096 1096 5456
18 ἀπὸ τοῦ θρόνου, λέγουσα, Γέγονε. καὶ ἐγένοντο φωναὶ καὶ
from the throne, saying, It has happened. And occurred voices and
1027 796 4578 1096 3173 3634/3756
βρονταὶ καὶ ἀστραπαί, καὶ σεισμὸς ἐγένετο μέγας, οἷος οὐκ
thunders and lightnings, and an earthquake occurred great such as not
1096 575 3739 444 1096 1909 1093 5082
ἐγένετο ἀφ' οὗ οἱ ἄνθρωποι ἐγένοντο ἐπὶ τῆς γῆς, τηλι-
occurred from when men came into being on the earth, such a
4578 3779 3173 1096 4172 3173
19 κοῦτος σεισμός, οὕτω μέγας. καὶ ἐγένετο ἡ πόλις ἡ μεγάλη
huge earthquake, so great. And came to be the city great
1519/5140/3313 4172 1484 4098 897
εἰς τρία μέρη, καὶ αἱ πόλεις τῶν ἐθνῶν ἔπεσον· καὶ Βαβυλὼν
into three parts, and the cities of the nations fell. And Babylon
3173 3415 1799 2316 1325 846 4221
ἡ μεγάλη ἐμνήσθη ἐνώπιον τοῦ Θεοῦ, δοῦναι αὐτῇ τὸ ποτή-
the great was remembered before God, to give to her the cup
3631 2372 3709 848 3956 3520
20 ριον τοῦ οἴνου τοῦ θυμοῦ τῆς ὀργῆς αὐτοῦ. καὶ πᾶσα νῆσος
of the wine of the anger of the wrath of Him. And every island
5343 3735/3756 2147 5464 3173 5613 5006
21 ἔφυγε, καὶ ὄρη οὐχ εὑρέθησαν. καὶ χάλαζα μεγάλη, ὡς ταλαν-
fled, and mountains not were found. And a hail great, as talent-
2597 1537 3772 1909 444
τιαία, καταβαίνει ἐκ τοῦ οὐρανοῦ ἐπὶ τοὺς ἀνθρώπους· καὶ
sized, comes down out of the heaven on men, and
987 444 2316 1537 4127
ἐβλασφήμησαν οἱ ἄνθρωποι τὸν Θεὸν ἐκ τῆς πληγῆς
blasphemed men God from the plague
5464 3754 3173 2076 4127 848 4970
τῆς χαλάζης· ὅτι μεγάλη ἐστὶν ἡ πληγὴ αὐτῆς σφόδρα.
of the hail, because great is the plague of it exceedingly.

CHAPTER 17

CHAPTER 17

1And one of the seven angels having the seven bowls came and spoke with me, saying to me, Come, I will show you the judgment of the great harlot sitting on the many waters, 2with whom the kings of the earth committed fornication, and the ones inhabiting the earth became drunk from the wine of her fornication. 3And he carried me away into a desert, by *the* Spirit. And I saw a woman sitting on a scarlet beast, filled *with* names of blasphemy, having seven heads and ten horns. 4And the woman was clothed *in* purple and scarlet, and being gilded with gold and precious stone and pearls, having a golden cup in her hand, filled *with* abominations and unclean things of her fornication. 5And on her

2064/1520/1537 2033 32 2192
1 Καὶ ἦλθεν εἷς ἐκ τῶν ἑπτὰ ἀγγέλων τῶν ἐχόντων τὰς
And came one of the seven angels having the
2033 5357 2980 3326/1700 3004 3427 1204 1166
ἑπτὰ φιάλας, καὶ ἐλάλησε μετ' ἐμοῦ, λέγων μοι, Δεῦρο, δείξω
seven bowls, and spoke with me, saying to me, Come, I will show
4671 2917 4204 3173 2521 1909
σοι τὸ κρίμα τῆς πόρνης τῆς μεγάλης, τῆς καθημένης ἐπὶ τῶν
you the judgment of the harlot great sitting on the
5204 4183 3326/3739/ 4203 935
2 ὑδάτων τῶν πολλῶν· μεθ' ἧς ἐπόρνευσαν οἱ βασιλεῖς τῆς
waters many, with whom committed fornication the kings of the
1093 3184 1537 3631 4202 848
γῆς, καὶ ἐμεθύσθησαν ἐκ τοῦ οἴνου τῆς πορνείας αὐτῆς οἱ
earth, and became drunk from the wine of the fornication of her, those
2730 1093 667 3165/1519 2048 1722
3 κατοικοῦντες τὴν γῆν. καὶ ἀπήνεγκέ με εἰς ἔρημον ἐν
inhabiting the earth. And he carried away me into a desert by
4151 1492 1135 2521 1909 2342 2847
Πνεύματι· καὶ εἶδον γυναῖκα καθημένην ἐπὶ θηρίον κόκκινον,
(the) Spirit. And I saw a woman sitting on beast a scarlet,
1073 3686 988 2192 2776 2033 2768
γέμον ὀνομάτων βλασφημίας, ἔχον κεφαλὰς ἑπτὰ καὶ κέρατα
full of names of blasphemy, having heads seven and horns
1176 1135 4016 4209 2847
4 δέκα. καὶ ἡ γυνὴ ἦν περιβεβλημένη πορφύρᾳ καὶ κοκκίνῳ,
ten. And the woman was clothed (in) purple and scarlet,
5558 5557 3037 5093 3135
καὶ κεχρυσωμένη χρυσῷ καὶ λίθῳ τιμίῳ καὶ μαργαρίταις,
and being gilded with gold and stone precious and pearls,
2192 5552 4221 1722 5495 848 1073 946
ἔχουσα χρυσοῦν ποτήριον ἐν τῇ χειρὶ αὐτῆς, γέμον βδε-
having a golden cup in the hand of her, full of
168 4202 848 1909
5 λυγμάτων καὶ ἀκαθάρτητος πορνείας αὐτῆς, καὶ ἐπὶ τὸ
abominations and uncleanness of (the) fornication of her. And on the

forehead *was* a name having been written: MYSTERY, BABYLON THE GREAT, THE MOTHER OF THE HARLOTS AND OF THE ABOMINATIONS OF THE EARTH.

[6]And I saw the woman being drunk from the blood of the saints, and from the blood of the witnesses of Jesus. And I marveled, seeing her *with* a great marveling. [7]And the angel said to me, Why did you marvel? I will tell you the mystery of the woman, and of the beast supporting her, the *one* having the seven heads and the ten horns. [8]The beast which you saw was, and is not, and is about to come up out of the abyss, and goes to perdition. And those dwelling on the earth will marvel, *the ones* whose names have not been written on the Scroll of Life from *the* foundation of *the* world, seeing the beast, that it was a thing, and is not, yet now is. [9]Here is the mind having wisdom: the seven heads are seven mountains, where the woman sits on them. [10]And *the* kings are seven. The five fell, and the one is, and the other has not yet come. And when he does come, he must remain a little. [11]And the beast which was, and is not, even he is *the* eighth, and is of the seven, and goes to perdition. [12]And the ten horns you saw are ten kings who have not yet received a kingdom, but will receive authority as kings one hour with the beast. [13]These have one mind, and their power and authority they shall give up to the beast.

[14]These will make war with the Lamb, and the Lamb will overcome them, because He is Lord of lords and King of kings, and the ones with

3359 848 3686 1125 3466 897
μέτωπον αὐτῆς ὄνομα γεγραμμένον, Μυστήριον, Βαβυλὼν
forehead of her a name having been written: MYSTERY, BABYLON
3173 3384 4204 946
ἡ μεγάλη, ἡ μήτηρ τῶν πορνῶν καὶ τῶν βδελυγμάτων τῆς
THE GREAT, The Mother of the Harlots and of the Abominations of the
1093 1492 1135 3184 1537 129
6 γῆς. καὶ εἶδον τὴν γυναῖκα μεθύουσαν ἐκ τοῦ αἵματος τῶν
Earth. And I saw the woman being drunk from the blood of the
40 1537 129 3144 2424
ἁγίων, καὶ ἐκ τοῦ αἵματος τῶν μαρτύρων Ἰησοῦ. καὶ
saints, and from the blood of the witnesses of Jesus. And
2296 1492 846 2294 3173 3427
7 ἐθαύμασα, ἰδὼν αὐτήν, θαῦμα μέγα. καὶ εἶπέ μοι ὁ
I marveled seeing her (with) a marvel great. And said to me the
32 1302 2296 1473/4671/2046 3466
ἄγγελος, Διατί ἐθαύμασας; ἐγώ σοι ἐρῶ τὸ μυστήριον τῆς
angel, Why did you wonder? I you will tell the mystery of the
1135 2342 941 846
γυναικός, καὶ τοῦ θηρίου τοῦ βαστάζοντος αὐτήν, τοῦ
woman, and of the beast supporting her, the (one)
2192 2033 2776 1176 2768 2342/3739
8 ἔχοντος τὰς ἑπτὰ κεφαλὰς καὶ τὰ δέκα κέρατα. τὸ θηρίον, ὃ
having the seven heads and the ten horns. The beast which
1492/2258 3756/2076 3195 305 1537 12
εἶδες, ἦν, καὶ οὐκ ἔστι, καὶ μέλλει ἀναβαίνειν ἐκ τῆς ἀβύσσου,
you saw was, and not is, and is about to come up out of the abyss,
1519/684 5217 2296 2730
καὶ εἰς ἀπώλειαν ὑπάγειν. καὶ θαυμάσονται οἱ κατοικοῦντες
and to perdition goes; and will marvel those dwelling
1909 1093/3739/3756/ 1125 3686 1909 975
ἐπὶ τῆς γῆς, ὧν οὐ γέγραπται τὰ ὀνόματα ἐπὶ τὸ βιβλίον
on the earth, of whom not has been written the names on the Scroll
2222 575 2602 2889 991 2342 =3748=
τῆς ζωῆς ἀπὸ καταβολῆς κόσμου, βλέποντες τὸ θηρίον ὅ, τι
of Life from (the) foundation of (the) world, seeing the beast, that a thing
2258 3756/2076 2539 2076 5602 3563 2192 4678
9 ἦν, καὶ οὐκ ἔστι, καίπερ ἔστιν. ὧδε ὁ νοῦς ὁ ἔχων σοφίαν. αἱ
it was, and not is, although it is. Here (is) the mind having wisdom. The
2033 2776 3735 1526 2033 3609 1135 2521 1909
ἑπτὰ κεφαλαὶ ὄρη εἰσὶν ἑπτά, ὅπου ἡ γυνὴ κάθηται ἐπ'
seven heads mountains are seven, where the woman sits on
846 935 2033 1526 4002 4098 1520
10 αὐτῶν. καὶ βασιλεῖς ἑπτά εἰσιν· οἱ πέντε ἔπεσαν, καὶ ὁ εἷς
them; and kings seven are: the five fell, and the one
2076 243 3768 2064 3752 2064 3641 846 1163
ἔστιν, ὁ ἄλλος οὔπω ἦλθε· καί, ὅταν ἔλθῃ, ὀλίγον αὐτὸν δεῖ
is, the other not yet came, and when he comes, a little he must
3306 2342/3739/2258 3756/2076 846 3590
11 μεῖναι. καὶ τὸ θηρίον ὃ ἦν, καὶ οὐκ ἔστι, καὶ αὐτὸς ὄγδοός
remain. And the beast which was, and not is, even he eighth
2076 1537 2033/2076 1519 684 5217
12 ἐστι, καὶ ἐκ τῶν ἑπτά ἐστι, καὶ εἰς ἀπώλειαν ὑπάγει. καὶ τὰ
is, and of the seven it is, and to perdition goes. And the
1176 2768 3739/1492/1176 935 1526 3748 932
δέκα κέρατα, ἃ εἶδες, δέκα βασιλεῖς εἰσίν, οἵτινες βασιλείαν
ten horns which you saw, ten kings are, who a kingdom
3768 2983 235 1849 5613 935 3391 5610 2983
οὔπω ἔλαβον, ἀλλ' ἐξουσίαν ὡς βασιλεῖς μίαν ὥραν λαμβά-
not yet received, but authority as kings one hour receive
3326 2342 3778 3391 1106 2192
13 νουσι μετὰ τοῦ θηρίου. οὗτοι μίαν γνώμην ἔχουσι, καὶ τὴν
with the beast. These one mind have, and the
1411 1849 1438 2342 1239
δύναμιν καὶ τὴν ἐξουσίαν ἑαυτῶν τῷ θηρίῳ διαδιδώσουσιν.
power and the authority of themselves to the beast they shall give up.
3778 3326 721 4170 721 3528
14 οὗτοι μετὰ τοῦ ἀρνίου πολεμήσουσι, καὶ τὸ ἀρνίον νικήσει
These with the Lamb will make war, and the Lamb will overcome
846 3754 2962 2962 2076 935 935
αὐτούς, ὅτι Κύριος κυρίων ἐστὶ καὶ Βασιλεὺς βασιλέων, καὶ
them, because Lord of lords He is and King of kings, and

Him *are the* called and elect and faithful ones.

[15]And he says to me, The waters which you saw, where the harlot sits, are peoples and crowds and nations and tongues. [16]And the ten horns which you saw on the beast, these will hate the harlot, and will make her desolated and naked. And *they* will eat her flesh, and will burn her down with fire. [17]For God gave into their hearts to do His mind, and to act in one mind, and to give their kingdom to the beast, until the words of God shall be fulfilled. [18]And the woman whom you saw is the great city, having a kingdom over the kings of the earth.

CHAPTER 18

[1]And after these things I saw another angel coming down out of Heaven having great authority, and the earth was lighted up from his glory. [2]And he cried in a strong, great voice, saying, Babylon the great has fallen! *It* has fallen, and it has become a dwelling-place of demons, and a prison of every unclean spirit, and a prison of every unclean bird, even having been hated; [3]because of the wine of the anger of her fornication *which* all the nations have drunk, even the kings of the earth have committed fornication with her; and the merchants of the earth became rich from the power of her luxury.

[4]And I heard another voice out of Heaven saying, My people, come out of her, that you may not share

3326 846 2822 1588 4103 3004/3427
15 οἱ μετ' αὐτοῦ, κλητοὶ καὶ ἐκλεκτοὶ καὶ πιστοί. καὶ λέγει μοι,
those with Him (the) called and elect and faithful ones. And he says to me,
5204/3739/1492/3757 4204 2521 2992 3793/2076
Τὰ ὕδατα, ἃ εἶδες, οὗ ἡ πόρνη κάθηται, λαοὶ καὶ ὄχλοι εἰσί,
The waters which you saw, where the harlot sits, peoples and crowds are,
1484 1100 1176 2768 3739/1492/1909
16 καὶ ἔθνη καὶ γλῶσσαι. καὶ τὰ δέκα κέρατα, ἃ εἶδες, ἐπὶ τὸ
even nations and tongues. And the ten horns which you saw on the
2342 3778 3404 4204 2049
θηρίον, οὗτοι μισήσουσι τὴν πόρνην, καὶ ἠρημωμένην
beast, these will hate the harlot, and desolated
4160 846 1131 4561 848
ποιήσουσιν αὐτὴν καὶ γυμνήν, καὶ τὰς σάρκας αὐτῆς
will make her and naked, and the flesh of her
4315 846 2618 1722/4442 1063 2316
17 φάγονται, καὶ αὐτὴν κατακαύσουσιν ἐν πυρί. ὁ γὰρ Θεὸς
they will eat, and her will burn down with fire. For God
1325 1519 2588 848 4160 1106 848
ἔδωκεν εἰς τὰς καρδίας αὐτῶν ποιῆσαι τὴν γνώμην αὐτοῦ,
gave into the hearts of them to do the mind of Him,
4160 3391 1106 1325 932 848
καὶ ποιῆσαι μίαν γνώμην, καὶ δοῦναι τὴν βασιλείαν αὐτῶν
and to do one mind, and to give the kingdom of them
2342 891 5055 4487 2316 1135
18 τῷ θηρίῳ, ἄχρι τελεσθῇ τὰ ῥήματα τοῦ Θεοῦ. καὶ ἡ γυνή,
to the beast, until shall be completed the words of God. And the woman
3739/1492 2076 4172 3173 2192 932 1909
ἣν εἶδες, ἐστὶν ἡ πόλις ἡ μεγάλη, ἡ ἔχουσα βασιλείαν ἐπὶ
whom you saw is the city great, having a kingdom over
935 1093
τῶν βασιλέων τῆς γῆς.
the kings of the earth.

CHAPTER 18

3326 5023 1492 243 32 2597 1537
1 Καὶ μετὰ ταῦτα εἶδον ἄλλον ἄγγελον καταβαίνοντα ἐκ
And after these things I saw another angel coming down out of
3772 2192 1849 3173 1093 5461
τοῦ οὐρανοῦ, ἔχοντα ἐξουσίαν μεγάλην· καὶ ἡ γῆ ἐφωτίσθη
Heaven, having authority great, and the earth was lighted up
1537 1391 848 2896 1722 2479 5456 3173
2 ἐκ τῆς δόξης αὐτοῦ. καὶ ἔκραξεν ἐν ἰσχύϊ, φωνῇ μεγάλῃ,
from the glory of him. And he cried in a strong, with a a voice great,
3004 4098 4098 897 3173 1096
λέγων, Ἔπεσεν ἔπεσε Βαβυλὼν ἡ μεγάλη, καὶ ἐγένετο
saying, Fell, fell Babylon the great, and has become
2732 1142 5438 3956 4151
κατοικητήριον δαιμόνων, καὶ φυλακὴ παντὸς πνεύματος
a dwelling-place of demons, and a prison of every spirit
169 5438 3956 3732 169
ἀκαθάρτου, καὶ φυλακὴ παντὸς ὀρνέου ἀκαθάρτου καὶ
unclean, and a prison of every bird unclean and
3404 3754/1537 3631 2372 4202 848
3 μεμισημένου. ὅτι ἐκ τοῦ οἴνου τοῦ θυμοῦ τῆς πορνείας αὐτῆς
being hated, because of the wine of the anger of the fornication of her
4095 3956 1484 935 1093/3326/846
πέπωκε πάντα τὰ ἔθνη, καὶ οἱ βασιλεῖς τῆς γῆς μετ' αὐτῆς
have drunk all the nations, and the kings of the earth with her
4203 1713 1093/1537 1411
ἐπόρνευσαν, καὶ οἱ ἔμποροι τῆς γῆς ἐκ τῆς δυνάμεως τοῦ
committed fornication, and the merchants of the earth from the power of the
4764 846 4147
στρήνους αὐτῆς ἐπλούτησαν.
luxury of her became rich.
191 243 5456 1537 3772 3004
Καὶ ἤκουσα ἄλλην φωνὴν ἐκ τοῦ οὐρανοῦ, λέγουσαν,
And I heard another voice out of Heaven, saying,
1831 1537 846 2992 3450/2443/3361/ 4790
4 Ἐξέλθετε ἐξ αὐτῆς ὁ λαός μου, ἵνα μὴ συγκοινωνήσητε ταῖς
Come out of her, people of Me, that not you share in the

in her sins, and that you may not receive of her plagues; [5]because her sins joined together, *even* up to Heaven, and God remembered her unjust deeds. [6]Give back to her as also she gave back to you, and double to her double, according to her works. In the cup which she mixed, mix to her double. [7]By what things she glorified herself, and luxuriated, by so much give back to her torment and mourning. Because she says in her heart, I sit *as* a queen, and I am not a widow; and I do not see mourning at all. [8]Because of this, in one day her plagues shall come: death, and mourning, and famine; and she will be consumed with fire, for *the* Lord God judging her *is* strong. [9]And the kings of the earth will weep for her, and will wail over her, those having fornicated and having luxuriated with her, when they see the smoke of her burning; [10]standing from afar because of the fear of her torment, saying, Woe! Woe to the great city, Babylon, the strong city! For in one hour your judgment came.

[11]And the merchants of the earth weep and mourn over her, because no one buys their cargo any more, [12]cargo of gold, and silver, and of precious stone, and of pearls, and of fine linen, and of purple, and of silk, and of scarlet, and all thyine wood, and every ivory vessel, and every vessel of very precious wood, and of bronze, and of iron, and of marble, [13]and cinnamon, and incenses, and ointment, and frankincense, and wine, and oil, and fine meal, and wheat, and

266 848 2443/3361/2983/1537 4127 848
ἁμαρτίαις αὐτῆς, καὶ ἵνα μὴ λάβητε ἐκ τῶν πληγῶν αὐτῆς·
sins of her, and that not you receive of the plagues of her;
3754 190 848 266 891 3772
5 ὅτι ἐκολλήθησαν αὐτῆς αἱ ἁμαρτίαι ἄχρι τοῦ οὐρανοῦ, καὶ
because joined together of her the sins up to Heaven, and
3421 2316 92 848 591 846
6 ἐμνημόνευσεν ὁ Θεὸς τὰ ἀδικήματα αὐτῆς. ἀπόδοτε αὐτῇ
remembered God the unjust deeds of her. Return to her
5613 846 591 5213 1363 846 1362
ὡς καὶ αὐτὴ ἀπέδωκεν ὑμῖν, καὶ διπλώσατε αὐτῇ διπλᾶ
as also she returned to you, and double to her double
2596 2041 848 1722 4221 3739 2767 2767
κατὰ τὰ ἔργα αὐτῆς· ἐν τῷ ποτηρίῳ ᾧ ἐκέρασε κεράσατε
according to the works of her; in the cup in which she mixed, mix
846 1362 3745 1392 1438 4763
7 αὐτῇ διπλοῦν. ὅσα ἐδόξασεν ἑαυτὴν καὶ ἐστρηνίασε,
to her double By what things she glorified herself and luxuriated,
5118 1325 846 929 3997 3754/1722
τοσοῦτον δότε αὐτῇ βασανισμὸν καὶ πένθος· ὅτι ἐν τῇ
by so much give to her torment and mourning. Because in the
2588 848 3004 2521 938 5503/3756/1510
καρδίᾳ αὐτῆς λέγει, Κάθημαι βασίλισσα, καὶ χήρα οὐκ εἰμί,
heart of her she says, I sit a queen, and a widow not I am,
3997 =3364= 1492 1223 5124/1722/3391/2250/ 2240
8 καὶ πένθος οὐ μὴ ἴδω. διὰ τοῦτο ἐν μιᾷ ἡμέρᾳ ἥξουσιν αἱ
and mourning not at all I see. Therefore in one day shall come the
4127 848 2288 3997 3042 1722/4442
πληγαὶ αὐτῆς, θάνατος καὶ πένθος καὶ λιμός, καὶ ἐν πυρὶ
plagues of her, death and mourning and famine, and with fire
2618 3754 2478 2962 2316 2919 846
κατακαυθήσεται, ὅτι ἰσχυρὸς Κύριος ὁ Θεὸς ὁ κρίνων αὐτήν.
she will be consumed, because strong (is the) Lord God judging her.
2799 846 2875 1909 846 935
9 καὶ κλαύσονται αὐτήν, καὶ κόψονται ἐπ' αὐτῇ οἱ βασιλεῖς τῆς
And will weep for her, and will wail over her the kings of the
1093 3326 846 4203 4763 3752
γῆς οἱ μετ' αὐτῆς πορνεύσαντες καὶ στρηνιάσαντες, ὅταν
earth, those with her having fornicated and having luxuriated, when
991 2586 4451 848 575 3113
10 βλέπωσι τὸν καπνὸν τῆς πυρώσεως αὐτῆς, ἀπὸ μακρόθεν
they see the smoke of the burning of her, from afar
2476 1223 5401 929 848 3004
ἑστηκότες διὰ τὸν φόβον τοῦ βασανισμοῦ αὐτῆς, λέγοντες,
standing because of the fear of the torment of her, saying,
3759 3759 4172 3173 897 4172 2478
Οὐαί, οὐαί, ἡ πόλις ἡ μεγάλη Βαβυλών, ἡ πόλις ἡ ἰσχυρά,
Woe! Woe, to the city great, Babylon, the city strong,
3754/1722/3391/5610/2064 2920 4675 1713 1093
11 ὅτι ἐν μιᾷ ὥρᾳ ἦλθεν ἡ κρίσις σου. καὶ οἱ ἔμποροι τῆς γῆς
for in one hour came the judgment of you. And the merchants of the earth
2799 3996 1909 846 3754 1117 848
κλαίουσι καὶ πενθοῦσιν ἐπ' αὐτῇ, ὅτι τὸν γόμον αὐτῶν
weep and mourn over her, because the cargo of them
3762 59 3765 1117 5557 696
12 οὐδεὶς ἀγοράζει οὐκέτι· γόμον χρυσοῦ, καὶ ἀργύρου, καὶ
no one buys no more, cargo of gold, and of silver, and
3037 5093 3135 1040 4209
λίθου τιμίου, καὶ μαργαρίτου, καὶ βύσσου, καὶ πορφύρας,
of stone precious, and of pearls, and of fine linen, and of purple,
4596 2847 3956 3586 2367 3956
καὶ σηρικοῦ, καὶ κοκκίνου· καὶ πᾶν ξύλον θύϊνον, καὶ πᾶν
and of silk, and of scarlet, and all wood sandarac, and every
4632 1661 3956 4632/1537 3586 5093
σκεῦος ἐλεφάντινον, καὶ πᾶν σκεῦος ἐκ ξύλου τιμιωτάτου,
vessel ivory, and every vessel of wood very precious,
5475 4604 3139 2792
13 καὶ χαλκοῦ, καὶ σιδήρου, καὶ μαρμάρου· καὶ κινάμωμον, καὶ
and of bronze, and of iron, and of marble, and cinnamon, and
2368 3464 3030 3631 1637
θυμιάματα, καὶ μύρον, καὶ λίβανον, καὶ οἶνον, καὶ ἔλαιον,
incenses, and ointment, and frankincense, and wine, and oil,

beasts, and sheep, and horses, and chariots, and of bodies and souls of men. [14]And the ripe fruits of the lust of your soul went away from you, and all the fat things, and the bright things went away from you, and you will find them no more, not at all. [15]The merchants of these things, the ones being enriched from her, will stand from afar because of the fear of her torment, weeping and mourning; [16]and saying, Woe! Woe *to* the great city having been clothed in linen and purple and scarlet, and having been gilded with gold and precious stone, and pearls!

[17]For in one hour such great wealth was desolated. And every ship-pilot and all company on the ships, and sailors, and as many as work the sea, stood from afar, [18]and cried out, seeing the smoke of her burning, saying, What *is* like the great city? [19]And they threw dust on their heads, and cried out, weeping and mourning, saying, Woe! Woe *to* the great city, by which all those having ships in the sea were rich, from her costliness, because in one hour she was ruined. [20]Rejoice over her, Heaven, and the holy apostles, and the prophets, because God judged your judgment on her.

[21]And one strong angel lifted a stone like a great millstone, and threw *it* into the sea, saying, This way, on an impulse, Babylon the great city will be thrown down, and *it* will never more still be found. [22]And the sound of harpers, and of musicians, and flutists, and of trumpeters will never

4585 4621 2934 4263 2462
καὶ σεμίδαλιν, καὶ σῖτον, καὶ κτήνη, καὶ πρόβατα· καὶ ἵππων,
and fine meal, and wheat, and beasts, and sheep, and horses,
4480 4983 5590 444
14 καὶ ῥεδῶν, καὶ σωμάτων· καὶ ψυχὰς ἀνθρώπων. καὶ ἡ
and chariots, and of bodies, and souls of men. And the
3703 1939 5590 4675 565 575 4675
ὀπώρα τῆς ἐπιθυμίας τῆς ψυχῆς σου ἀπῆλθεν ἀπὸ σοῦ, καὶ
ripe fruits of the lust of the soul of you went away from you, and
3956 3045 2986 565 575 4675
πάντα τὰ λιπαρὰ καὶ τὰ λαμπρὰ ἀπῆλθεν ἀπὸ σοῦ, καὶ
all the fat things, and the bright things went away from you, and
3765 =3364= 2147 846 1713 5130 4147
15 οὐκέτι οὐ μὴ εὑρήσῃς αὐτά. οἱ ἔμποροι τούτων, οἱ πλουτή-
no more, not at all you will find them. The merchants of these, those being
575 846 575 3113 2476 1223 5401
σαντες ἀπ' αὐτῆς, ἀπὸ μακρόθεν στήσονται διὰ τὸν φόβον
enriched from her, from afar will stand because of the fear
929 848 2799 3996
16 τοῦ βασανισμοῦ αὐτῆς, κλαίοντες καὶ πενθοῦντες, καὶ
of the torment of her, weeping and mourning and
3004 3759 3759 4172 3173 4016
λέγοντες, Οὐαί, οὐαί, ἡ πόλις ἡ μεγάλη, ἡ περιβεβλημένη
saying, Woe, woe, the city great, having been clothed in
1039 4210 2847 5558 1722
βύσσινον καὶ πορφυροῦν καὶ κόκκινον, καὶ κεχρυσωμένη ἐν
linen and purple and scarlet, and having been gilded with
5557 3037 5093 3135 3754/3391/5610/2049
17 χρυσῷ καὶ λίθῳ τιμίῳ καὶ μαργαρίταις· ὅτι μιᾷ ὥρᾳ ἠρη-
gold and stone precious, and pearls; because in one hour was
5118 4149 3956 2942 3956/1909
μώθη ὁ τοσοῦτος πλοῦτος. καὶ πᾶς κυβερνήτης, καὶ πᾶς ἐπὶ
desolated such great wealth. And every helmsman and all on
4143 3658 3492 3745 2281
τῶν πλοίων ὁ ὅμιλος, καὶ ναῦται, καὶ ὅσοι τὴν θάλασσαν
the ships the company, and sailors, and as many as the sea
2038 575 3113 2476 2896 3708
18 ἐργάζονται, ἀπὸ μακρόθεν ἔστησαν, καὶ ἔκραζον, ὁρῶντες
work, from afar stood, and cried out seeing
2586 4451 848 3004 5101 3664
τὸν καπνὸν τῆς πυρώσεως αὐτῆς, λέγοντες, Τίς ὁμοία τῇ
the smoke of the burning of her, saying, What (is) like the
4172 3173 906 5522/1909 2776 848
19 πόλει τῇ μεγάλῃ; καὶ ἔβαλον χοῦν ἐπὶ τὰς κεφαλὰς αὐτῶν,
city great? And they threw dust on the heads of them,
2896 2799 3996 3004 3759 3759
καὶ ἔκραζον κλαίοντες καὶ πενθοῦντες, λέγοντες, Οὐαί, οὐαί,
and cried out weeping and mourning, saying, Woe! Woe,
4172 3173 1722/3739/4147 3956 2192 4143
ἡ πόλις ἡ μεγάλη, ἐν ᾗ ἐπλούτησαν πάντες οἱ ἔχοντες πλοῖα
(to) the city great, by which were rich all those having ships
1722 2281 1537 5094 848 3754/3391/5610/2049
ἐν τῇ θαλάσσῃ ἐκ τῆς τιμιότητος αὐτῆς, ὅτι μιᾷ ὥρᾳ ἠρη-
in the sea, from the costliness of her, because in one hour was
2165 1909/846 3772 40 652
20 μώθη. εὐφραίνου ἐπ' αὐτήν, οὐρανέ, καὶ οἱ ἅγιοι ἀπόστολοι,
she ruined. Be glad over her, Heaven and the holy apostles
4396 3754 2919 2316 2917 5216/1537 846
καὶ οἱ προφῆται, ὅτι ἔκρινεν ὁ Θεὸς τὸ κρίμα ὑμῶν ἐξ αὐτῆς.
and the prophets, because judged God the judgment of you upon her.
142 1520 32 2478 3067 5613 3458 3173
21 Καὶ ἦρεν εἷς ἄγγελος ἰσχυρὸς λίθον ὡς μύλον μέγαν, καὶ
And lifted one angel strong a stone as a millstone great, and
906 1519 2281 3004 3779 3731 906
ἔβαλεν εἰς τὴν θάλασσαν, λέγων, Οὕτως ὁρμήματι βληθή-
threw (it) into the sea, saying, Thus on an impulse will be
897 3173 4172 =3364= 2147 2089
22 σεται Βαβυλὼν ἡ μεγάλη πόλις, καὶ οὐ μὴ εὑρεθῇ ἔτι. καὶ
thrown Babylon the great city, and not at all will be found yet. And
5456 2790 3451 834 4538
φωνὴ κιθαρῳδῶν καὶ μουσικῶν καὶ αὐλητῶν καὶ σαλπιστῶν
sound of harpers, and of musicians, and flutists, and of trumpeters,

be heard in you longer, and
every craftsman of every
craft will never be found in
you still; and *the* sound of a
mill will never be heard in
you still. [23]And the light of
a lamp *will* never more
shine in you. And *the* voice
of the bridegroom and bride
will never more be heard in
you. For your merchants
were the great ones of the
earth, for by your sorcery all
the nations were led astray.
[24]And in her was found *the*
blood of prophets, and of
saints, and of all the ones
having been slain on the
earth.

CHAPTER 19

[1]And after these things, I
heard a great voice of a
numerous crowd in Heaven,
saying, Hallelujah! The salvation and the glory and the
honor and the power of *the*
Lord our God! [2]For true and
righteous *are* His judg-
ments, because He judged
the great harlot who defiled
the earth with her fornication. And He avenged the
blood of His slaves out of
her hand. [3]And secondly
they said, Hallelujah! Also
her smoke goes up forever
and ever. [4]And the twenty-
four elders, and the four
living creatures fell down
and worshiped God sitting
on the throne, saying,
Amen! Hallelujah! [5]And a
voice came out from the
throne, saying, Praise our
God, all His slaves, and the
ones fearing Him, the small
and the great.

=3364= 191 1722/4671/2089 3956 5079 3956 5078
οὐ μὴ ἀκουσθῇ ἐν σοὶ ἔτι. καὶ πᾶς τεχνίτης πάσης τέχνης
not at all will be heard in you longer, and every craftsman of every craft
=3364= 2147 1722/4671/2089 5456 3458 =3364= 191 1722
οὐ μὴ εὑρεθῇ ἐν σοὶ ἔτι, καὶ φωνὴ μύλου οὐ μὴ ἀκουσθῇ ἐν
not at all will be found in you longer; and sound of a mill not at all be heard in
4671/2089 5456 3566 =3364= 5316/1722/4671/2089 5456
23 σοὶ ἔτι, καὶ φῶς λύχνου οὐ μὴ φανῇ ἐν σοὶ ἔτι, καὶ φωνὴ
you longer; and light of a lamp not at all (will) shine in you still; and voice
3566 3565 =3364= 191 1722/4675/2089/3754 1713
νυμφίου καὶ νύμφης οὐ μὴ ἀκουσθῇ ἐν σοὶ ἔτι· ὅτι οἱ ἔμποροί
of groom and bride not at all will be heard in you still. For the merchants
4675 2258 3175 1093/3754/1722 5331 4675
σου ἦσαν οἱ μεγιστᾶνες τῆς γῆς· ὅτι ἐν τῇ φαρμακείᾳ σου
of you were the great ones of the earth, for by the sorcery of you
4105 3956 1484 1722 846 129 4396
24 ἐπλανήθησαν πάντα τὰ ἔθνη. καὶ ἐν αὐτῇ αἷμα προφητῶν
were misled all the nations, and in her (the) blood of prophets
40 2147 3956 4969 1909 1093
καὶ ἁγίων εὑρέθη, καὶ πάντων τῶν ἐσφαγμένων ἐπὶ τῆς γῆς.
and saints was found, and of all those having been slain on the earth.

CHAPTER 19

3326 5023 191 5456 3793 4183 3173
1 Καὶ μετὰ ταῦτα ἤκουσα φωνὴν ὄχλου πολλοῦ μεγάλην
And after these things I heard a voice of a crowd much great
1722 3772 3004 239 4991
2 ἐν τῷ οὐρανῷ, λέγοντος, Ἀλληλούϊα· ἡ σωτηρία καὶ ἡ
in Heaven, saying, Hallelujah! The salvation and the
1391 5092 1411 2962 2316 2257 3754
δόξα καὶ ἡ τιμὴ καὶ ἡ δύναμις Κυρίῳ τῷ Θεῷ ἡμῶν· ὅτι
glory and the honor and the power of (the) Lord God of us, because
228 1342 2920 848 3754 2919 4204
ἀληθιναὶ καὶ δίκαιαι αἱ κρίσεις αὐτοῦ· ὅτι ἔκρινε τὴν πόρνην
true and righteous the judgments of Him, for He judged the harlot
3173 3748 5351 1093/1722 4202 848
τὴν μεγάλην, ἥτις ἔφθειρε τὴν γῆν ἐν τῇ πορνείᾳ αὐτῆς,
great, who defiled the earth with the fornication of her,
1556 129 1401 848 1537 5495 848
καὶ ἐξεδίκησε τὸ αἷμα τῶν δούλων αὐτοῦ ἐκ τῆς χειρὸς αὐτῆς.
and He avenged the blood of the slaves of Him out of the hand of her.
1208 2046 239 2586 848
3 καὶ δεύτερον εἴρηκαν, Ἀλληλούϊα· καὶ ὁ καπνὸς αὐτῆς
And secondly, they said, Hallelujah! And the smoke of her
305 1519 165 165 4098
4 ἀναβαίνει εἰς τοὺς αἰῶνας τῶν αἰώνων. καὶ ἔπεσαν οἱ
goes up to the ages of the ages. And fell down the
4245 1501 5064 5064 2226
πρεσβύτεροι οἱ εἴκοσι καὶ τέσσαρες, καὶ τὰ τέσσαρα ζῷα,
elders twenty and four, and the four living creatures,
4352 2316 2521 1909 2362
καὶ προσεκύνησαν τῷ Θεῷ τῷ καθημένῳ ἐπὶ τοῦ θρόνου,
and worshiped God sitting on the throne
3004 281 239 5456 1537 2362
5 λέγοντες, Ἀμήν· Ἀλληλούϊα. καὶ φωνὴ ἐκ τοῦ θρόνου
saying, Amen! Hallelujah! And a voice from the throne
1831 3004 134 2316 2257 3956 1401
ἐξῆλθε, λέγουσα, Αἰνεῖτε τὸν Θεὸν ἡμῶν πάντες οἱ δοῦλοι
came out, saying, Praise the God of us, all the slaves
848 5399 846 3398 3173
αὐτοῦ, καὶ οἱ φοβούμενοι αὐτόν, καὶ οἱ μικροὶ καὶ οἱ μεγάλοι.
of Him, and those fearing Him, even the small and the great.

[6]And I heard as a sound
of a numerous crowd, and
as a sound of many waters,
and as a sound of strong
thunders, saying, Hallelujah! Because *the* Lord God

191 5613 5456 3793 4183 5613 5456 5204
6 καὶ ἤκουσα ὡς φωνὴν ὄχλου πολλοῦ, καὶ ὡς φωνὴν ὑδάτων
And I heard as a sound of a crowd much, and as a sound of waters
4183 5613 5456 1027 2478 3004
πολλῶν, καὶ ὡς φωνὴν βροντῶν ἰσχυρῶν, λέγοντας,
many, and as a sound thunders of strong, saying,
239 3754 936 2962 2316 3841
Ἀλληλούϊα· ὅτι ἐβασίλευσε Κύριος ὁ Θεὸς ὁ παντοκράτωρ.
Hallelujah, because reigned (the) Lord God Almighty.

Almighty reigned. [7]Let us rejoice and let us exult, and we will give glory to Him, because the marriage of the Lamb came, and His wife prepared herself. [8]And it was given to her that she be clothed *in* fine linen, pure and bright; for the fine linen is the righteousnesses of the saints.

[9]And he says to me, Write: Blessed *are* the ones having been called to the supper of the marriage of the Lamb. And he says to me, These words of God are true. [10]And I fell before his feet to worship him, but he said to me, Behold! Stop! I am your fellow-slave, and of your brothers, having the testimony of Jesus. Worship God. For the testimony of Jesus is the spirit of prophecy.

[11]And I saw Heaven being opened. And, behold! A white horse, and He sitting on it having been called Faithful and True. And He judges and wars in righteousness. [12]And His eyes *were* as a flame of fire, and on His head many diadems, having a name that had been written, which no one knows except Himself; [13]and having been clothed *in* a garment which had been dipped in blood. And His name is called The Word of God.

[14]And the armies in Heaven followed Him on white horses, being dressed *in* fine linen, white and pure. [15]And out of His mouth goes forth a sharp sword, that with it He might smite the nations. And He will shepherd them with an iron rod. And He treads the winepress of the wine of the anger and of the wrath of God Almighty. [16]And He has on His

5463 21 1325 1391 846
7 χαίρωμεν καὶ ἀγαλλιώμεθα, καὶ δῶμεν τὴν δόξαν αὐτῷ·
Let us rejoice and let us exult, and we will give the glory to Him,
3754 2064 1062 721 1135 848 2090
ὅτι ἦλθεν ὁ γάμος τοῦ ἀρνίου, καὶ ἡ γυνὴ αὐτοῦ ἡτοίμασεν
because came the marriage of the Lamb, and the wife of Him prepared
1438 1325 846/2443 4016 1039 2513
8 ἑαυτήν. καὶ ἐδόθη αὐτῇ ἵνα περιβάληται βύσσινον καθαρὸν
herself, and it was given to her that she be clothed (with) fine linen clean
2986 1063 1039 1345 2076
καὶ λαμπρόν· τὸ γὰρ βύσσινον τὰ δικαιώματά ἐστι τῶν
and bright; the for fine linen the righteousnesses is of the
40 3004/3427 1125 3107 1519 1173
9 ἁγίων. καὶ λέγει μοι, Γράψον, Μακάριοι οἱ εἰς τὸ δεῖπνον
saints. And he says to me, Write: Blessed those to the supper
1062 721 2564 3004 3427 3778
τοῦ γάμου τοῦ ἀρνίου κεκλημένοι. καὶ λέγει μοι, Οὗτοι οἱ
of the marriage of the Lamb having been called. And he says to me, These
3056 228 1526 2316 4098 1715
10 λόγοι ἀληθινοί εἰσι τοῦ Θεοῦ. καὶ ἔπεσον ἔμπροσθεν τῶν
words true are of God, And I fell before the
4228 848 4352 846 3004 3427 3708 3361
ποδῶν αὐτοῦ προσκυνῆσαι αὐτῷ· καὶ λέγει μοι, Ὅρα μή·
feet of him to worship him; and he says to me, See, do not.
4889 4675/1510 80 4675 2192
σύνδουλός σου εἰμι καὶ τῶν ἀδελφῶν σου τῶν ἐχόντων τὴν
A fellow-slave of you I am, and of the brothers of you, having the
3141 2424 2316 4352 1063
μαρτυρίαν τοῦ Ἰησοῦ· τῷ Θεῷ προσκύνησον· ἡ γὰρ
witness of Jesus; To God, give worship. the For
3141 2424 2076 4151 4394
μαρτυρία τοῦ Ἰησοῦ ἐστὶ τὸ πνεῦμα τῆς προφητείας.
witness of Jesus is the spirit of prophecy.
1492 3772 455 2400 2462
11 Καὶ εἶδον τὸν οὐρανὸν ἀνεῳγμένον, καὶ ἰδού, ἵππος
And I saw Heaven having been opened, and behold, a horse
3022 2521 1909 846 2564 4103
λευκός, καὶ ὁ καθήμενος ἐπ' αὐτόν, καλούμενος πιστὸς καὶ
white, and the (One) sitting on it being called faithful and
228 1722 1343 2919 4170 3788
12 ἀληθινός, καὶ ἐν δικαιοσύνῃ κρίνει καὶ πολεμεῖ. οἱ δὲ ὀφθαλμοὶ
true. And in righteousness He judges and wars. the And eyes
848 5613/5395/4442 1909 2776 848 1238
αὐτοῦ ὡς φλὸξ πυρός, καὶ ἐπὶ τὴν κεφαλὴν αὐτοῦ διαδήματα
of Him as a flame of fire, and on the head of Him diadems
4183 2192 3686 1125 3739/3761 1492 =3364= 848
πολλά· ἔχων ὄνομα γεγραμμένον ὃ οὐδεὶς οἶδεν εἰ μὴ αὐτός,
many, having a name having been written which no one knows except Him;
4016 2440 911 129 2564
13 καὶ περιβεβλημένος ἱμάτιον βεβαμμένον αἵματι· καὶ καλεῖται
and being clothed (in) a garment having been dipped in blood, and is called
3686 848 3056 2316 4753
14 τὸ ὄνομα αὐτοῦ, Ὁ λόγος τοῦ Θεοῦ. καὶ τὰ στρατεύματα
the name of Him, The Word of God. And the armies
1722 3772 190 846 1909 2462 3022 1746
ἐν τῷ οὐρανῷ ἠκολούθει αὐτῷ ἐφ' ἵπποις λευκοῖς, ἐνδεδυ-
in Heaven followed Him on horses white, having been
1039 3022 2513 1537 4750
15 μένοι βύσσινον λευκὸν καὶ καθαρόν. καὶ ἐκ τοῦ στόματος
dressed (in) fine linen, white and clean. And out of the mouth
848 1607 4501 3691/2443/1722/846 3960
αὐτοῦ ἐκπορεύεται ῥομφαία ὀξεῖα, ἵνα ἐν αὐτῇ πατάσσῃ τὰ
of Him goes forth a sword sharp, that with it He may smite the
1484 846 4165 846 1722 4464 4603 846
ἔθνη· καὶ αὐτὸς ποιμανεῖ αὐτοὺς ἐν ῥάβδῳ σιδηρᾷ· καὶ αὐτὸς
nations; and He will shepherd them with a rod iron. And He
3961 3025 3631 2372 3709
πατεῖ τὴν ληνὸν τοῦ οἴνου τοῦ θυμοῦ καὶ τῆς ὀργῆς τοῦ
treads the press of the wine of the anger and of the wrath
2316 3841 2192/1909 2440 1909
16 Θεοῦ τοῦ παντοκράτορος. καὶ ἔχει ἐπὶ τὸ ἱμάτιον καὶ ἐπὶ τὸν
of God Almighty. And He has on the garment and on the

garment and on His thigh a name having been written: KING OF KINGS AND LORD OF LORDS.

[17]And I saw one angel standing in the sun. And he cried with a great voice, saying to all the birds flying in mid-heaven, Come and gather together to the supper of the great God, [18]that you may eat *the* flesh of kings, and *the* flesh of commanders, and *the* flesh of strong ones, and *the* flesh of horses, and of the *ones* sitting on them, and *the* flesh of all, both freemen and slaves, even of *the* small and great.

[19]And I saw the beast and the kings of the earth, and their armies being assembled to make war with the *One* sitting on the horse, and with His army. [20]And the beast was seized, and with this *one* the false prophet doing signs before it, by which he led astray those having received the mark of the beast, and those worshiping its image. The two were thrown alive into the Lake of Fire burning with brimstone. [21]And the rest were killed with the sword of the *One* sitting on the horse, *it* having gone out of His mouth. And all the birds were filled from their flesh.

CHAPTER 20

[1]And I saw an angel coming down out of Heaven, having the key of the abyss, and a great chain on his hand. [2]And he laid hold of the dragon, the old

3382 848 3686 1125 935 935
μηρὸν αὐτοῦ ὄνομα γεγραμμένον, Βασιλεὺς βασιλέων καὶ
thigh of Him a name having been written: KING OF KINGS, AND
2962 2962
Κύριος κυρίων.
LORD OF LORDS.
1492 1520 32 2476 1722 2246 2896
17 Καὶ εἶδον ἕνα ἄγγελον ἑστῶτα ἐν τῷ ἡλίῳ· καὶ ἔκραξε
And I saw one angel standing in the sun and he cried
5456 3173 3004 3956 3732 4072 1722
φωνῇ μεγάλῃ, λέγων πᾶσι τοῖς ὀρνέοις τοῖς πετωμένοις ἐν
with a voice great, saying to all the birds flying in
3321 1205 4863 1519 1173
μεσουρανήματι, Δεῦτε καὶ συνάγεσθε εἰς τὸ δεῖπνον τοῦ
mid-heaven, Come and gather together to the supper of the
3173 2316 2443 5315 4561 935 4561
18 μεγάλου Θεοῦ, ἵνα φάγητε σάρκας βασιλέων, καὶ σάρκας
great God, that you may eat (the) flesh of kings, and (the) flesh
5506 4561 2478 4561 2462
χιλιάρχων, καὶ σάρκας ἰσχυρῶν, καὶ σάρκας ἵππων καὶ τῶν
of chiliarchs, and (the) flesh of strong ones, and (the) flesh of horses, and of those
2521 1909 846 4561 3956 1658 5037
καθημένων ἐπ' αὐτῶν, καὶ σάρκας πάντων, ἐλευθέρων τε καὶ
sitting on them, and (the) flesh of all, freemen both and
1401 3398 3173
δούλων, καὶ μικρῶν καὶ μεγάλων.
slaves, even of (the) small and great.
1492 2342 935 1093
19 Καὶ εἶδον τὸ θηρίον, καὶ τοὺς βασιλεῖς τῆς γῆς, καὶ τὰ
And I saw the beast, and the kings of the earth, and the
4753 848 4863 4160 4171 3326
στρατεύματα αὐτῶν συνηγμένα ποιῆσαι πόλεμον μετὰ τοῦ
armies of them being assembled to make war with the (One)
2521 1909 2462 3326 4753 848
καθημένου ἐπὶ τοῦ ἵππου, καὶ μετὰ τοῦ στρατεύματος αὐτοῦ.
sitting on the horse, and with the army of Him.
4084 2342 3326 5127 5578
20 καὶ ἐπιάσθη τὸ θηρίον, καὶ μετὰ τούτου ὁ ψευδοπροφήτης
And was seized the beast, and with this (one) the false prophet
4160 4592 1799 846 1722/3739 4105
ὁ ποιήσας τὰ σημεῖα ἐνώπιον αὐτοῦ, ἐν οἷς ἐπλάνησε τοὺς
doing the signs before it, by which he misled those
2983 5480 2342 4352
λαβόντας τὸ χάραγμα τοῦ θηρίου, καὶ τοὺς προσκυνοῦντας
having received the mark of the beast, and those worshiping
1504 848 2198 906 1417/1519 3041
τῇ εἰκόνι αὐτοῦ ζῶντες ἐβλήθησαν οἱ δύο εἰς τὴν λίμνην τοῦ
the image. of it. living were thrown the two into the Lake
4442 2545 1722 2303 3062 615
21 πυρὸς τὴν καιομένην ἐν τῷ θείῳ· καὶ οἱ λοιποὶ ἀπεκτάνθησαν
of Fire burning with brimstone. And the rest were killed
1722 4501 2521 1909 2462 1607
ἐν τῇ ῥομφαίᾳ τοῦ καθημένου ἐπὶ τοῦ ἵππου, τῇ ἐκπορευο-
with the sword of the (One) sitting on the horse, having gone
1537 4750 848 3956 3732 5526
μένῃ ἐκ τοῦ στόματος αὐτοῦ· καὶ πάντα τὰ ὄρνεα ἐχορτάσθη-
forth out of the mouth of Him, and all the birds were filled
1537 4561 848
σαν ἐκ τῶν σαρκῶν αὐτῶν.
from the flesh of them.

CHAPTER 20

1492 32 2597 1537 3772
1 Καὶ εἶδον ἄγγελον καταβαίνοντα ἐκ τοῦ οὐρανοῦ,
And I saw an angel coming down out of Heaven,
2192 2807 12 254 3173 1909
ἔχοντα τὴν κλεῖδα τῆς ἀβύσσου, καὶ ἅλυσιν μεγάλην ἐπὶ
having the key of the abyss, and a chain great on
5495 848 2902 1404 3789
2 τὴν χεῖρα αὐτοῦ. καὶ ἐκράτησε τὸν δράκοντα, τὸν ὄφιν τὸν
the hand of him. And he laid hold of the dragon, the serpent

serpent who is *the* Devil, and Satan, and bound him a thousand years, [3]and threw him into the abyss, and shut him up, and sealed over him, that he should not still lead astray the nations, until the thousand years are fulfilled. And after these things, he must be set loose a little time.

[4]And I saw thrones, and they sat on them. And judgment was given to them, and the souls of the *ones* having been beheaded because of the witness of Jesus, and because of the word of God, and who had not worshiped the beast nor its image, and had not received the mark on their forehead and on their hand. And they lived and reigned with Christ a thousand years. [5]But the rest of the dead did not live again until the thousand years were ended. This *is* the first resurrection. [6]Blessed and holy *is* the *one* having part in the first resurrection. The second death has no authority over these, but they will be priests of God and of Christ, and will reign with Him a thousand years.

[7]And whenever the thousand years are ended, Satan will be set loose out of his prison, [8]and he will go to mislead the nations in the four corners of the earth—Gog and Magog—to assemble them in war, whose number *is* as the sand of the sea. [9]And they went up over the breadth of the land and encircled the camp of the saints, and the beloved city. And fire from God came down out of

744 3739/2076 1228 4567 1210 846
ἀρχαῖον, ὅς ἐστι διάβολος καὶ Σατανᾶς, καὶ ἔδησεν αὐτὸν
old, who is Devil and Satan, and bound him
5507 2094 906 846 1519 12 2808
3 χίλια ἔτη, καὶ ἔβαλεν αὐτὸν εἰς τὴν ἄβυσσον, καὶ ἔκλεισεν
a thousand years and threw him into the abyss, and shut up
846 4972 1883 846 2443/3361 4105
αὐτόν, καὶ ἐσφράγισεν ἐπάνω αὐτοῦ, ἵνα μὴ πλανήσῃ τὰ
him, and sealed over him, that not he should mis-lead the
1484/2089/891 5055 5507 2094 3326/5023 1163
ἔθνη ἔτι, ἄχρι τελεσθῇ τὰ χίλια ἔτη· καὶ μετὰ ταῦτα δεῖ
nations still, until are ended the thousand years; and after these things must
846 3089 3398 5550
αὐτὸν λυθῆναι μικρὸν χρόνον.
he be loosed a little time.
1492 2362 2523 1909 846 2917
4 Καὶ εἶδον θρόνους, καὶ ἐκάθισαν ἐπ' αὐτούς, καὶ κρίμα
And I saw thrones, and they sat on them, and judgment
1325 846 5590 3990 1223
ἐδόθη αὐτοῖς· καὶ τὰς ψυχὰς τῶν πεπελεκισμένων διὰ τὴν
was given to them, and the souls of those having been beheaded due to the
3141 2424 1223 3056 2316 3748
μαρτυρίαν Ἰησοῦ, καὶ διὰ τὸν λόγον τοῦ Θεοῦ, καὶ οἵτινες
witness of Jesus, and because of the word of God, and who
3756 4352 2342 3777 1504 848
οὐ προσεκύνησαν τῷ θηρίῳ, οὔτε τὴν εἰκόνα αὐτοῦ, καὶ
not had worshiped the beast nor the image of it, and
3756 2983 5480 1909 3359 848 1909
οὐκ ἔλαβον τὸ χάραγμα ἐπὶ τὸ μέτωπον αὐτῶν, καὶ ἐπὶ
not received the mark on the forehead of them, and on
5495 848 2198 936 3326
τὴν χεῖρα αὐτῶν· καὶ ἔζησαν, καὶ ἐβασίλευσαν μετὰ
the hand of them; and they lived and reigned with
5547 5507 2094 3062 3498 3756 326
5 Χριστοῦ χίλια ἔτη. οἱ δὲ λοιποὶ τῶν νεκρῶν οὐκ ἀνέζησαν
Christ a thousand years. the But rest of the dead not did live again
2193 5065 5507 2094 3778 396 4413
ἕως τελεσθῇ τὰ χίλια ἔτη. αὕτη ἡ ἀνάστασις ἡ πρώτη.
until, were ended the thousand years. This (is) the resurrection first.
3107 40 2192 3313/1722 386 4413
6 μακάριος καὶ ἅγιος ὁ ἔχων μέρος ἐν τῇ ἀναστάσει τῇ πρώτῃ·
Blessed and holy the (one) having part in the resurrection first;
1909 5130 2288 1208 3756/2192 1849 235
ἐπὶ τούτων ὁ θάνατος ὁ δεύτερος οὐκ ἔχει ἐξουσίαν, ἀλλ'
over these the death second not has authority, but
2071 2409 2316 5547 936
ἔσονται ἱερεῖς τοῦ Θεοῦ καὶ τοῦ Χριστοῦ, καὶ βασιλεύσουσι
they will be priests of God and of Christ, and will reign
3326 846 5507 2094
μετ' αὐτοῦ χίλια ἔτη.
with Him a thousand years.
3752 5055 5507/2094 3089 4567 1537
7 Καὶ ὅταν τελεσθῇ τὰ χίλια ἔτη, λυθήσεται ὁ Σατανᾶς ἐκ
And whenever are ended the thousand years will be loosed Satan out of
5438 848 1831 4105 1484
8 τῆς φυλακῆς αὐτοῦ, καὶ ἐξελεύσεται πλανῆσαι τὰ ἔθνη τὰ
the prison of him, and he will go out to mislead the nations
1722 5064 1137 1093 1136 3098
ἐν ταῖς τέσσαρσι γωνίαις τῆς γῆς, τὸν Γὼγ καὶ τὸν Μαγώγ,
in the four corners of the earth, Gog and Magog,
4863 846 1519 4171 3739 706 5613 285
συναγαγεῖν αὐτοὺς εἰς πόλεμον· ὧν ὁ ἀριθμὸς ὡς ἡ ἄμμος
to assemble them in war, of whom the number (is) as the sand
2281 305 1909 4114 1093
9 τῆς θαλάσσης. καὶ ἀνέβησαν ἐπὶ τὸ πλάτος τῆς γῆς, καὶ
of the sea. And they went up over the breadth of the land and
2944 3925 40 4172
ἐκύκλωσαν τὴν παρεμβολὴν τῶν ἁγίων καὶ τὴν πόλιν τὴν
encircled the camp of the saints, and the city
25 2597 4442 575 2316/1537 3772
ἠγαπημένην· καὶ κατέβη πῦρ ἀπὸ τοῦ Θεοῦ ἐκ τοῦ οὐρανοῦ,
beloved, and came down fire from God out of Heaven

Heaven and burned them down. [10]And the Devil leading them astray was thrown into the Lake of Fire and Brimstone, where the beast and the false prophet *were*. And they were tormented day and night forever *and* ever.

[11]And I saw a great white throne, and the *One* sitting on it, from whose face the earth and the heaven fled; and a place was not found for them. [12]And I saw the dead, *the* small and the great, standing before God. And scrolls were opened. And another Scroll was opened, which is the *Scroll* of Life. And the dead were judged out of the things written in the scrolls, according to their works. [13]And the sea gave up the dead in it. And death and Hades gave up the dead in them. And they were each judged according to their works. [14]And death and Hades were thrown into the Lake of Fire. This is the second death. [15]And if anyone was not found having been written in the Scroll of Life, he was thrown into the Lake of Fire.

CHAPTER 21

[1]And I saw a new heaven and a new earth, for the first heaven and the first earth passed away, and the sea no longer is. [2]And I, John, saw the holy city, New Jerusalem, coming down out of Heaven from God, having been prepared as a bride, having been adorned for her Husband. [3]And I heard a great voice out of Heaven, saying, Behold, the tabernacle of God with men! And He will tabernacle with them, and they

2719 846 1228 4105 846
10 καὶ κατέφαγεν αὐτούς. καὶ ὁ διάβολος ὁ πλανῶν αὐτοὺς
and burned down them. And the Devil misleading them
906 1519 3041 4442 2303 3699 2342
ἐβλήθη εἰς τὴν λίμνην τοῦ πυρὸς καὶ θείου, ὅπου τὸ θηρίον
was thrown into the Lake of Fire and brimstone, where the beast
5578 928 2250
καὶ ὁ ψευδοπροφήτης· καὶ βασανισθήσονται ἡμέρας καὶ
and the false prophet (were); and they will be tormented day and
3571/1519 165 165
νυκτὸς εἰς τοὺς αἰῶνας τῶν αἰώνων.
night to the ages of the ages.
1492 2362 3022 3173 2521 1909 846
11 Καὶ εἶδον θρόνον λευκὸν μέγαν, καὶ τὸν καθήμενον ἐπ' αὐτοῦ
And I saw a throne white great, and the (One) sitting on it,
3739/575 4383 5343 1093 3772 5117
οὗ ἀπὸ προσώπου ἔφυγεν ἡ γῆ καὶ ὁ οὐρανός, καὶ τόπος
of whom from (the) face fled the earth and the heaven; and a place
3756 2147 846 1492 3498 3398
12 οὐχ εὑρέθη αὐτοῖς. καὶ εἶδον τοὺς νεκρούς, μικροὺς καὶ
not was found for them. And I saw the dead, (the)small and
3173 2476 1799 2316 975 455
μεγάλους, ἑστῶτας ἐνώπιον τοῦ Θεοῦ, καὶ βιβλία ἠνεῴχθη-
great, standing before God, and scrolls were opened.
975 243 455 3739/2076 2222 2919
σαν· καὶ βιβλίον ἄλλο ἠνεῴχθη, ὅ ἐστι τῆς ζωῆς· καὶ ἐκρί-
And Scroll another was opened, which is the (Scroll) of Life. And were
3498 1537 1125 1722 975 2596
θησαν οἱ νεκροὶ ἐκ τῶν γεγραμμένων ἐν τοῖς βιβλίοις, κατὰ
judged the dead out of those having been written in the scrolls, according to
2041 848 1325 2281 1722/846 3498
13 τὰ ἔργα αὐτῶν. καὶ ἔδωκεν ἡ θάλασσα τοὺς ἐν αὐτῇ νεκρούς,
the works of them. And gave the sea the in it dead,
2288 86 1325 1722 846 3498
καὶ ὁ θάνατος καὶ ὁ ᾅδης ἔδωκαν τοὺς ἐν αὐτοῖς νεκρούς· καὶ
and death and Hades gave the in them dead; and
2919 1538 2596 2041 848 2288
14 ἐκρίθησαν ἕκαστος κατὰ τὰ ἔργα αὐτῶν. καὶ ὁ θάνατος καὶ
they were judged each one according to their works. And death and
86 906 1519 3042 4442 3778 2076
ὁ ᾅδης ἐβλήθησαν εἰς τὴν λίμνην τοῦ πυρός· οὗτός ἐστιν ὁ
Hades were thrown into the Lake of Fire. This is the
1208 2288 =1536=3756/2147/1722 976 2222
15 δεύτερος θάνατος. καὶ εἴ τις οὐχ εὑρέθη ἐν τῇ βίβλῳ τῆς ζωῆς
second death. And if anyone not was found in the Scroll of Life
1125 906 1519 3041 4442
γεγραμμένος, ἐβλήθη εἰς τὴν λίμνην τοῦ πυρός.
having been written, he was thrown into the Lake of Fire.

CHAPTER 21

1492 3772 2537 1093 2537 1063 4413
1 Καὶ εἶδον οὐρανὸν καινὸν καὶ γῆν καινήν· ὁ γὰρ πρῶτος
And I saw a heaven new and an earth new; the for first
3772 4413 1093 3928 2281 3756 2076
οὐρανὸς καὶ ἡ πρώτη γῆ παρῆλθε, καὶ ἡ θάλασσα οὐκ ἔστιν
heaven and the first earth went away, and the sea not is
2089 1473 2491 1492 4172 40 2419
2 ἔτι. καὶ ἐγὼ Ἰωάννης εἶδον τὴν πόλιν τὴν ἁγίαν, Ἱερουσαλὴμ
still. And I John, saw the city holy, Jerusalem
2537 2597 575 2316/1537 3772 2090
καινήν, καταβαίνουσαν ἀπὸ τοῦ Θεοῦ ἐκ τοῦ οὐρανοῦ, ἡτοι-
New, coming down from God out of Heaven, having
5613 3565 2885 435 848
3 μασμένην ὡς νύμφην κεκοσμημένην τῷ ἀνδρὶ αὐτῆς. καὶ
been prepared as a bride having been adorned for the Husband of her. And
191 5456 3173 1537 3772 3004 2400
ἤκουσα φωνῆς μεγάλης ἐκ τοῦ οὐρανοῦ, λεγούσης, Ἰδού, ἡ
I heard a voice great out of Heaven, saying, Behold, the
4633 2316 3326 444 4637 3326
σκηνὴ τοῦ Θεοῦ μετὰ τῶν ἀνθρώπων, καὶ σκηνώσει μετ'
tabernacle of God with men! And He will tabernacle with

will be His people, and God Himself will be with them as their God. 4And God will wipe away every tear from their eyes. And death shall be no longer, nor mourning, nor outcry, nor pain will be any longer; for the first things passed away. 5And the *One* sitting on the throne said, Behold, I make all things new. And He says to me, Write, because these words are faithful and true.

6And He said to me, It is done! I am the Alpha and the Omega, the Beginning and the Ending. To the *one* thirsting, I will freely give of the fountain of the water of life. 7The *one* overcoming will inherit all things, and I will be God to him, and he will be the son to Me. 8But for the cowardly and unbelieving, and those having become foul, and murderers, and fornicators, and sorcerers, and idolaters, and all the lying ones, their part *will be* in the Lake burning with fire and brimstone, which is *the* second death.

9And one of the seven angels came to me, he having the seven bowls being filled *with* the seven last plagues, and spoke with me, saying, Come, I will show you the bride, the wife of the Lamb. 10And he carried me in spirit onto a great and high mountain, and showed me the great city, holy Jerusalem, coming down out of Heaven from God, 11having the glory of God. And its light *was* like a very precious stone, as a jasper stone, being clear as crystal, 12and having a great and high wall, having twelve gates, and twelve angels at the gates, and

846 846 2992 848 2071 848 2316 2071
αὐτῶν, καὶ αὐτοὶ λαοὶ αὐτοῦ ἔσονται, καὶ αὐτὸς ὁ Θεὸς ἔσται
them, and they peoples of Him will be, and Himself God will b
3326 846 2316 848 1813 2316 3956 1144
4 μετ' αὐτῶν, Θεὸς αὐτῶν· καὶ ἐξαλείψει ὁ Θεὸς πᾶν δάκρυον
with them (the) God of them. And will wipe away God every tear
575 3788 848 2288 3756 2071/2089/3777
ἀπὸ τῶν ὀφθαλμῶν αὐτῶν, καὶ ὁ θάνατος οὐκ ἔσται ἔτι· οὔτε
from the eyes of them; and death not will be longer, nor
3997 3777 2906 3777 4192 3756 2071 2089/3754 4413
πένθος, οὔτε κραυγή, οὔτε πόνος οὐκ ἔσται ἔτι· ὅτι τὰ πρῶτα
mourning, nor outcry, nor pain not will be longer, for the things first
565 2036 2521 1909 2362 2400
5 ἀπῆλθον. καὶ εἶπεν ὁ καθήμενος ἐπὶ τοῦ θρόνου, Ἰδού,
went away. And said the (One) sitting on the throne, Behold
2537 3956 4160 3004/3427 1125 3754 3778 3056
καινὰ πάντα ποιῶ. καὶ λέγει μοι, Γράψον· ὅτι οὗτοι οἱ λόγοι
new all things I make. And He says to me, Write, because these words
228 4103 1526 2036/3427 1096 1473/1510
6 ἀληθινοὶ καὶ πιστοί εἰσι. καὶ εἶπέ μοι, Γέγονε. ἐγώ εἰμι τὸ
true and faithful are; and He said to me, It is done. I am the
1 5598 746 5056 1473 1372 1325 153
Α καὶ τὸ Ω, ἡ ἀρχὴ καὶ τὸ τέλος. ἐγὼ τῷ διψῶντι δώσω ἐκ
Alpha and the Omega, the Head and the End. I to (the one) thirsting will give
4077 5204 2222 1432 3528 2816
7 τῆς πηγῆς τοῦ ὕδατος τῆς ζωῆς δωρεάν. ὁ νικῶν κληρονομή-
the fountain of the water of life freely. The (one) overcoming will in
3956 2071 846 2316 846 2071/3427 5207
σει πάντα, καὶ ἔσομαι αὐτῷ Θεός, καὶ αὐτὸς ἔσται μοι ὁ υἱός
herit all things, and I will be to him God, and he will be to Me the son
1169 571 949 5406
8 δειλοῖς δὲ καὶ ἀπίστοις καὶ ἐβδελυγμένοις καὶ φονεῦσι καὶ
to fearful But and unbelieving and abominable and murderers and
4205 5332 1496 3956
πόρνοις καὶ φαρμακεῦσι καὶ εἰδωλολάτραις, καὶ πᾶσι τοῖς
fornicators and sorcerers and idolaters and all the
5571 3313 848 1722 3041 2545 4442
ψευδέσι, τὸ μέρος αὐτῶν ἐν τῇ λίμνῃ τῇ καιομένῃ πυρὶ κα
lying ones, the part of them in the Lake burning with fire and
2303/3603/2076/1208 2288
θείῳ, ὅ ἐστι δεύτερος θάνατος.
brimstone, which is (the) second death.
2064/4314/3165/1519 2033 32 2192
9 Καὶ ἦλθε πρός με εἷς τῶν ἑπτὰ ἀγγέλων τῶν ἐχόντων τὰς
And came to me one of the seven angels he having the
2033 5357 1073 2033 4127 2078
ἑπτὰ φιάλας τὰς γεμούσας τῶν ἑπτὰ πληγῶν τῶν ἐσχάτων
seven bowls being filled of the seven plagues last,
2980 3326/1700 3004 1204 1166 4671 3565
καὶ ἐλάλησε μετ' ἐμοῦ, λέγων, Δεῦρο, δείξω σοι τὴν νύμφην
and spoke with me, saying, Come, I will show you the bride,
721 1135 667 3165/1722 4151 1909
10 τοῦ ἀρνίου τὴν γυναῖκα. καὶ ἀπήνεγκέ με ἐν Πνεύματι ἐπ'
of the Lamb the wife. And he carried me in Spirit onto
3735 3173 5308 1166/3427 4172 3173
ὄρος μέγα καὶ ὑψηλόν, καὶ ἔδειξέ μοι τὴν πόλιν τὴν μεγάλην,
a mount great and high, and showed me the city great,
40 2419 2597 1537 3772
τὴν ἁγίαν Ἱερουσαλήμ, καταβαίνουσαν ἐκ τοῦ οὐρανοῦ
Holy Jerusalem coming down out of Heaven
575 2316 2192 1391 2316 5458
11 ἀπὸ τοῦ Θεοῦ, ἔχουσαν τὴν δόξαν τοῦ Θεοῦ· καὶ ὁ φωστὴρ
from God having the glory of God. And the lighting
848 3664 3037 5093 5613/3037/2393 2929
αὐτῆς ὅμοιος λίθῳ τιμιωτάτῳ, ὡς λίθῳ ἰάσπιδι κρυσταλλί-
of it (was) like a stone very precious, as stone a jasper being clear as
2192/5037 5038 3173 5308 2192 4440
12 ζοντι· ἔχουσάν τε τεῖχος μέγα καὶ ὑψηλόν, ἔχουσαν πυλῶνας
crystal, having and wall a great and high, having gates
1437 1909 4440 32 3686
δώδεκα, καὶ ἐπὶ τοῖς πυλῶσιν ἀγγέλους δώδεκα, καὶ ὀνόματα
twelve, and at the gates angels twelve, and names

twelve tribes of the sons of Israel. [13]From *the* east, three gates; from *the* north, three gates; from *the* south, three gates; and from *the* west, three gates.

[14]And the wall of the city had twelve foundations, and in them *the* names of the twelve apostles of the Lamb. [15]And he speaking with me had a golden reed, that he may measure the city, and its gates, and its wall. [16]And the city lies four-cornered, even its length as much as the width also. And he measured the city with the reed at twelve thousand stadia; its length and width and height are equal. [17]And he measured its wall, a hundred *and* forty-four cubits, a measure of a man, which is of an angel. [18]And the structure of its wall *was* jasper; and the city *was* pure gold, like pure glass.

[19]And the foundation of the wall of the city having been adorned with every precious stone: The first foundation, jasper; the second, sapphire; the third, chalcedony; the fourth, emerald; [20]the fifth, sardonyx; the sixth, sardius; the seventh, chrysolite; the eighth, beryl; the ninth, topaz; the tenth, chrysoprasus; the eleventh, hyacinth; the twelfth, amethyst. [21]And the twelve gates *were* twelve pearls; respectively each one of the gates was of one pearl. And the street of the city *was* pure gold, as transparent glass. [22]And I saw no temple in it, for *the* Lord

1924 3739/2076 1427 5443 5207 2474
ἐπιγεγραμμένα, ἅ ἐστι τῶν δώδεκα φυλῶν τῶν υἱῶν Ἰσραήλ.
having been inscribed, which are of the twelve tribes of the sons of Israel.
575 395 4440 5140 575 1005 4440 5140
13 ἀπ' ἀνατολῆς, πυλῶνες τρεῖς· ἀπὸ βορρᾶ, πυλῶνες τρεῖς·
From (the) east, gates three; from (the) north, gates three;
575 3558 4440 5140 575 1424 4440 5140
ἀπὸ νότου, πυλῶνες τρεῖς· καὶ ἀπὸ δυσμῶν, πυλῶνες τρεῖς.
from (the) south gates three; and from (the) west gates three.
5038 4172 2192 2310 1427 1722
14 καὶ τὸ τεῖχος τῆς πόλεως ἔχον θεμελίους δώδεκα, καὶ ἐν
And the wall of the city having foundations twelve, and in
846 3686 1427 652 721
15 αὐτοῖς ὀνόματα τῶν δώδεκα ἀποστόλων τοῦ ἀρνίου. καὶ
them names of the twelve apostles of the Lamb. And
2980 3326 1700 2192 2563 5552 2443 3354
ὁ λαλῶν μετ' ἐμοῦ εἶχε κάλαμον χρυσοῦν, ἵνα μετρήσῃ τὴν
he speaking with me had a reed of gold, that he may measure the
4172 4440 848 5038 848
16 πόλιν, καὶ τοὺς πυλῶνας αὐτῆς, καὶ τὸ τεῖχος αὐτῆς. καὶ
city, and the gates of it, and the wall of it. And
4172 5068 2749 3372 848 5118
ἡ πόλις τετράγωνος κεῖται, καὶ τὸ μῆκος αὐτῆς τοσοῦτόν
the city four-cornered lies, and the length of it so much
2076 3745 4114 3354 4172
ἐστιν ὅσον καὶ τὸ πλάτος. καὶ ἐμέτρησε τὴν πόλιν τῷ
is as much as also the width. And he measured the city with the
2563 1909 4712 1427 5505 3372
καλάμῳ ἐπὶ σταδίων δώδεκα χιλιάδων· τὸ μῆκος καὶ τὸ
reed at stadia twelve thousands; the length and the
4114 5311 848 2470/2076 3354 5038
17 πλάτος καὶ τὸ ὕψος αὐτῆς ἴσα ἐστί. καὶ ἐμέτρησε τὸ τεῖχος
width and the height of it equal are. And he measured the wall
848 1540 5062 5064 4083 3358
αὐτῆς ἑκατὸν τεσσαρακοντατεσσάρων πηχῶν, μέτρον
of it, a hundred (and) forty-four cubits, a measure
444 3739/2076 32 2258 1739 5038
18 ἀνθρώπου, ὅ ἐστιν ἀγγέλου. καὶ ἦν ἡ ἐνδόμησις τοῦ τείχους
of a man, which is of an angel. And was the structure of the wall
848 2393 4172 5553 2513 3664 5194
αὐτῆς, ἴασπις· καὶ ἡ πόλις χρυσίον καθαρόν, ὁμοία ὑάλῳ
of it jasper; and the city (was) gold clean, like glass
2513 2310 5038 4172 3956 3037
19 καθαρῷ. καὶ οἱ θεμέλιοι τοῦ τείχους τῆς πόλεως παντὶ λίθῳ
clean. And the foundations of the wall of the city with every stone
5093 2885 2310 4413 2393 1208
τιμίῳ κεκοσμημένοι. ὁ θεμέλιος ὁ πρῶτος, ἴασπις· ὁ δεύτερος,
precious was adorned; the foundation first, jasper; the second,
4552 5154 5472 5067 4665
20 σάπφειρος· ὁ τρίτος, χαλκηδών· ὁ τέταρτος, σμάραγδος· ὁ
sapphire; the third, chalcedony; the fourth, emerald; the
3991 4557 1622 4556 1442 5555
πέμπτος, σαρδόνυξ· ὁ ἕκτος, σάρδιος· ὁ ἕβδομος, χρυσόλιθος·
fifth, sardonyx; the sixth, sardius; the seventh, chrysolite;
3590 969 1766 5116 1182
ὁ ὄγδοος, βήρυλλος· ὁ ἔννατος, τοπάζιον· ὁ δέκατος,
the eighth, beryl; the ninth, topaz; the tenth,
5556 1734 5192 1428 271
χρυσόπρασος· ὁ ἑνδέκατος, ὑάκινθος· ὁ δωδέκατος, ἀμέ-
chrysoprasus; the eleventh, hyacinth; the twelfth, ame-
1427 4440 1427 3135 303
21 θυστος. καὶ οἱ δώδεκα πυλῶνες, δώδεκα μαργαρῖται· ἀνὰ
thyst. And the twelve gates (were) twelve pearls; respectively
1520 1538 4440 2258/1537/1520/ 3135
εἷς ἕκαστος τῶν πυλώνων ἦν ἐξ ἑνὸς μαργαρίτου· καὶ ἡ
one each of the gates was of one pearl. And the
4113 4172 5553 2513 5613/5194 1307
πλατεῖα τῆς πόλεως χρυσίον καθαρόν, ὡς ὕαλος διαφανής.
street of the city (was) of gold clean, as glass transparent.
3485/3756/1492/1722/846 1063 2962 2316 3841
22 καὶ ναὸν οὐκ εἶδον ἐν αὐτῇ· ὁ γὰρ Κύριος ὁ Θεὸς ὁ παντο-
And a temple not I saw in it, the for Lord God Al-

God Almighty is its temple, even the Lamb.

[23]And the city had no need of the sun, nor of the moon, that they might shine in it, for the glory of God illuminated it, even its lamp *is* the Lamb. [24]And the nations of the ones saved will walk in its light; and the kings of the earth bring their glory and honor into it. [25]And its gates may not at all be shut by day, for no night will be there. [26]And they will bring the glory and the honor of the nations into it. [27]And all profaning may not at all enter into it, or *any* making an abomination or a lie; but only the ones having been written in the Scroll of Life of the Lamb.

3485 848 2076 721 4172 3756
23 κράτωρ ναὸς αὐτῆς ἐστί, καὶ τὸ ἀρνίον. καὶ ἡ πόλις οὐ
mighty temple of it is, and the Lamb. And the city not
5532 2192 2246 3761 4582 2443 5316 1722
χρείαν ἔχει τοῦ ἡλίου, οὐδὲ τῆς σελήνης, ἵνα φαίνωσιν ἐν
need has of the sun, nor of the moon, that they might shine in
846 1063/1391 2316 5461 846 3088
αὐτῇ· ἡ γὰρ δόξα τοῦ Θεοῦ ἐφώτισεν αὐτήν, καὶ ὁ λύχνος
it, the for glory of God enlightened it, and the lamp
848 721 1484 4982 1722 5457
24 αὐτῆς τὸ ἀρνίον. καὶ τὰ ἔθνη τῶν σωζομένων ἐν τῷ φωτὶ
of it (is) the Lamb. And the nations of those saved in the light
848 4043 935 1093 5342
αὐτῆς περιπατήσουσι· καὶ οἱ βασιλεῖς τῆς γῆς φέρουσι τὴν
of it will walk; and the kings of the earth bring the
1391 5092 848 1519 846 4440
25 δόξαν καὶ τὴν τιμὴν αὐτῶν εἰς αὐτήν. καὶ οἱ πυλῶνες
glory and the honor of them into it. And the gates
848 =3364= 2808 2250 3571/1063/3756/2071/1563
26 αὐτῆς οὐ μὴ κλεισθῶσιν ἡμέρας (νὺξ γὰρ οὐκ ἔσται ἐκεῖ) καὶ
of it not at all may be shut by day—night for not will be there — and
5342 1391 5092 1484 1519 846
27 οἴσουσι τὴν δόξαν καὶ τὴν τιμὴν τῶν ἐθνῶν εἰς αὐτήν· καὶ
they will bring the glory and the honor of the nations into it. And
=3364= 1525/1519/846 3956 2840 4160 946
οὐ μὴ εἰσέλθῃ εἰς αὐτὴν πᾶν κοινοῦν, καὶ ποιοῦν βδέλυγμα
not at all may enter into it all profaning and (any) making an abomination
5579 =1508= 1125 1722 975 2222
καὶ ψεῦδος· εἰ μὴ οἱ γεγραμμένοι ἐν τῷ βιβλίῳ τῆς ζωῆς τοῦ
and a lie, except those having been written in the Scroll of Life of the
721
ἀρνίου.
Lamb.

CHAPTER 22

[1]And he showed me a pure river of water of life, bright as crystal, coming forth out of the throne of God and of the Lamb. [2]In *the* midst of its street and of the river, from here and from there, *was* a tree of life producing twelve fruits: according to one month each yielding its fruit. And the leaves of the tree *were* for healing of the nations. [3]And every curse will no longer be. And the throne of God and the Lamb will be in it; and His slaves will serve Him. [4]And they will see His face; and His name *will be* on their foreheads. [5]And night will not be there; and they have no need of a lamp or a light of *the* sun, because *the* Lord God will shed light on them. And

1186/3427 2513 4215 5204 2222 2986
1 καὶ ἔδειξέ μοι καθαρὸν ποταμὸν ὕδατος ζωῆς, λαμ-
And he showed me a clean river of water of life,
5613 2930 1607 1537 2362 2316
πρὸν ὡς κρύσταλλον, ἐκπορευόμενον ἐκ τοῦ θρόνου τοῦ Θεοῦ
bright as crystal, coming forth out of the throne of God
721 1722 3319 4113 848
2 καὶ τοῦ ἀρνίου. ἐν μέσῳ τῆς πλατείας αὐτῆς, καὶ τοῦ
and of the Lamb. In (the) midst of the street of it, and of the
4215 1782 1782 3586 2222 4160 2590
ποταμοῦ ἐντεῦθεν καὶ ἐντεῦθεν, ξύλον ζωῆς, ποιοῦν καρποὺς
river, from here and from there, a tree of life, producing fruits
1427 2596 3376/1520 1538 591 2590
δώδεκα, κατὰ μῆνα ἕνα ἕκαστον ἀποδιδοῦν τὸν καρπὸν
twelve, according to month one each yielding the fruit
848 5444 3586/1519 2322 1484
αὐτοῦ· καὶ τὰ φύλλα τοῦ ξύλου εἰς θεραπείαν τῶν ἐθνῶν.
of it. And the leaves of the tree (will be) for healing of the nations.
3956 2652 3756/2071/2089 2362 2316
3 καὶ πᾶν κατανάθεμα οὐκ ἔσται ἔτι· καὶ ὁ θρόνος τοῦ Θεοῦ καὶ
And every curse not will be longer. And the throne of God and
721/1722/846 2071 1401 848 3000
τοῦ ἀρνίου ἐν αὐτῇ ἔσται· καὶ οἱ δοῦλοι αὐτοῦ λατρεύσουσιν
of the Lamb in it will be, and the slaves of Him will do service
846 3700 4383 848 3686
4 αὐτῷ, καὶ ὄψονται τὸ πρόσωπον αὐτοῦ· καὶ τὸ ὄνομα
to Him, and they will see the face of Him, and the name
848 1909 3359 848 3571/3756/2071/1563
5 αὐτοῦ ἐπὶ τῶν μετώπων αὐτῶν. καὶ νὺξ οὐκ ἔσται ἐκεῖ, καὶ
of Him (will be) on the foreheads of them. And night not will be there, and
5532 3756 2192 3088 5457 2246 3754 2962
χρείαν οὐκ ἔχουσι λύχνου καὶ φωτὸς ἡλίου, ὅτι Κύριος ὁ
need not they have of a lamp and a light of sun, because (the) Lord
2316 5461 846 936 1519 165
Θεὸς φωτίζει αὐτούς· καὶ βασιλεύσουσιν εἰς τοὺς αἰῶνας τῶν
God will enlighten them, and they will reign to the ages of the

they shall reign forever *and* ever.

[6]And he said to me, These words *are* faithful and true. And *the* Lord God of the holy prophets sent His angel to show His slaves what must happen quickly. [7]Behold, I am coming quickly. Blessed *is* the *one* keeping the words of the prophecy of this Scroll.

[8]And I, John, *was* the *one* seeing and hearing these things. And when I heard and saw, I fell down to worship before the feet of the angel showing me these things. [9]And he said to me, Behold! Stop! For I am your fellow-slave, and of your brothers the prophets, and of the *ones* keeping the words of this Scroll. Do worship to God.

[10]And he said to me, Do not seal the words of the prophecy of this Scroll, because the time is near. [11]The *one* acting unjustly, let him still act unjustly; and the filthy, let *him* still be filthy; and the righteous, let *him* still *do* righteousness; and the holy, let *him* still be holy.

[12]And, behold, I am coming quickly, and My reward *is* with Me, to give to each as his work is. [13]I am the Alpha and the Omega, the Beginning and the Ending, the First and the Last. [14]Blessed *are* the *ones* doing His commands that their authority will be over the Tree of Life,, and they may enter into the city by the gates. [15]But outside *are* the dogs and the sorcerers, and the fornicators, and the murderers, and the idolaters, and everyone loving a lie, and making *it*. [16]I, Jesus, sent My angel to testify these things to

165
αἰώνων.
ages.
2036/3427 3778 3056 4103 228
6 Καὶ εἰπέ μοι, Οὗτοι οἱ λόγοι πιστοὶ καὶ ἀληθινοί· καὶ
And he said to me, These words (are) faithful and true, and
2962 2316 40 4396 649 32
Κύριος ὁ Θεὸς τῶν ἁγίων προφητῶν ἀπέστειλε τὸν ἄγγελον
(the) Lord God of the holy prophets sent the angel
848 1166 1401 848/3739/1163 1096 1722 5034
αὐτοῦ δεῖξαι τοῖς δούλοις αὐτοῦ ἃ δεῖ γενέσθαι ἐν τάχει.
of Him to show the slaves of Him what must happen with speed.
2400 2064 5035 3107 5083 3056
7 Ἰδού, ἔρχομαι ταχύ. μακάριος ὁ τηρῶν τοὺς λόγους τῆς
Behold, I am coming quickly. Blessed the (one) keeping the words of the
4394 975 5127
προφητείας τοῦ βιβλίου τούτου.
prophecy of Scroll this.
1473 2491 991 5023 191 3753
8 Καὶ ἐγὼ Ἰωάννης ὁ βλέπων ταῦτα καὶ ἀκούων. καὶ ὅτε
And I, John, the (one) seeing these things and hearing; and when
191 991 4098 4352 1715
ἤκουσα καὶ ἔβλεψα, ἔπεσα προσκυνῆσαι ἔμπροσθεν τῶν
I heard and saw, I fell down to worship before the
4228 32 1166 3427 5023 3004
9 ποδῶν τοῦ ἀγγέλου τοῦ δεικνύοντός μοι ταῦτα. καὶ λέγει
feet of the angel showing me these things. And he says
3427 3708/3361 4889 4675/1063/1510 80 4675
μοι, Ὅρα μή· σύνδουλός σου γάρ εἰμι, καὶ τῶν ἀδελφῶν σου
to me, See, no! a fellow-slave of you For I am, and of the brothers of you,
4396 5083 3056
τῶν προφητῶν, καὶ τῶν τηρούντων τοὺς λόγους τοῦ
the prophets, and of those keeping the words
975 5127 2316 4352
βιβλίου τούτου· τῷ Θεῷ προσκύνησον.
Scroll of this. To God, do worship.
3004/3427/3361/ 4972 3056 4394
10 Καὶ λέγει μοι, Μὴ σφραγίσῃς τοὺς λόγους τῆς προφητείας
And he says to me, Not do seal the words of the prophecy
975 5127 3754 2540 1451 2076 91
11 τοῦ βιβλίου τούτου· ὅτι ὁ καιρὸς ἐγγύς ἐστιν. ὁ ἀδικῶν
Scroll of this, because the time near is. He acting unjustly
91 2089 4510 4510 2089 1342
ἀδικησάτω ἔτι· καὶ ὁ ῥυπῶν ῥυπωσάτω ἔτι· καὶ ὁ δίκαιος
let him act unjustly still; and the filthy, let be filthy still; and the righteous,
1344 2089 40 37 2089 2400
12 δικαιωθήτω ἔτι· καὶ ὁ ἅγιος ἁγιασθήτω ἔτι. καὶ ἰδού,
righteousness (do) still; and the holy, let him be holy still. And behold,
2064 5035 3408 3427/3326/1700 591 1538
ἔρχομαι ταχύ, καὶ ὁ μισθός μου μετ᾽ ἐμοῦ, ἀποδοῦναι ἑκάστῳ
I am coming quickly, and My reward (is) with Me, to render to each
5613 2041 848 2071 1473/1510 1 5598 746
13 ὡς τὸ ἔργον αὐτοῦ ἔσται. ἐγώ εἰμι τὸ Α καὶ τὸ Ω, ἀρχὴ
as the work of him is. I am the Alpha and the Omega the Head
5056 4413 2078 3107 4160
14 καὶ τέλος, ὁ πρῶτος καὶ ὁ ἔσχατος. μακάριοι οἱ ποιοῦντες
and Ending, the First and the Last. Blessed (are) those doing
1785 848 2443 2071 1849 848 1909 3586
τὰς ἐντολὰς αὐτοῦ, ἵνα ἔσται ἡ ἐξουσία αὐτῶν ἐπὶ τὸ ξύλον
the commands of Him, that will be the authority of them over the tree
2222 4440 1525 1519 4172
τῆς ζωῆς, καὶ τοῖς πυλῶσιν εἰσέλθωσιν εἰς τὴν πόλιν.
of life, and by the gates they may enter into the city
1854 2965 5333 4205 5406
15 ἔξω δὲ οἱ κύνες καὶ οἱ φαρμακοὶ καὶ οἱ πόρνοι καὶ οἱ φονεῖς
(are) outside But the dogs and the sorcerers, and the fornicators and the murderers
1496 3956 5368 4160 5579
καὶ οἱ εἰδωλολάτραι, καὶ πᾶς ὁ φιλῶν καὶ ποιῶν ψεῦδος.
and the idolaters, and everyone loving and making a lie.
1473 2491 3992 32 3450 3140
16 Ἐγὼ Ἰησοῦς ἔπεμψα τὸν ἄγγελόν μου μαρτυρῆσαι
I, Jesus, sent the angel of Me to witness

you over the churches. I am the Root and Offspring of David, the bright and morning Star.

[17]And the Spirit and the bride say, Come! And the *one* hearing, let him say, Come! And the *one* thirsting, let *him* come; and the *one* desiring, let him take of the water of life freely.

[18]For I testify together with everyone hearing the words of the prophecy of this Book: If anyone adds to these things, God will add upon him the plagues having been written in this Book. [19]And if anyone takes away from the words of *the* Book of this prophecy, God will take away his part from *the* Book of Life, and out of the holy city, and of the things having been written in this Book.

[20]The *One* testifying these things says, Yes, I am coming quickly. Amen. Yes, come, Lord Jesus!

[21]The grace of our Lord Jesus Christ *be* with all of you. Amen.

5213 5023 /1909 1577 1473/1510 4491 108
ὑμῖν ταῦτα ἐπὶ ταῖς ἐκκλησίαις. ἐγώ εἰμι ἡ ῥίζα καὶ τὸ γένο
to you these things over the churches. I am the Root and the Offsprir
1138 792 2986 3720
τοῦ Δαβίδ, ὁ ἀστὴρ ὁ λαμπρὸς καὶ ὀρθρινός.
of David, the Star bright and morning.
4151 3555 3004 2064 191
17 Καὶ τὸ Πνεῦμα καὶ ἡ νύμφη λέγουσιν, Ἐλθέ. καὶ ὁ ἀκούω
And the Spirit and the bride say, Come! And he hearing,
2036 2064 1372 2064 2309 2983
εἰπάτω, Ἐλθέ. καὶ ὁ διψῶν ἐλθέτω· καὶ ὁ θέλων λαμβανέτ
let him say, Come! And he thirsting let come; and he willing, let him take
5204 2222 1432
τὸ ὕδωρ ζωῆς δωρεάν.
of the water of life freely.
4828 1063 3956 191 3056
18 Συμμαρτυροῦμαι γὰρ παντὶ ἀκούοντι τοὺς λόγους τῆ
I testify together For everyone hearing the words of the
4394 975 5127 1437/5100 2007 431
προφητείας τοῦ βιβλίου τούτου, Ἐάν τις ἐπιτιθῇ πρ
prophecy of Scroll this, If anyone add to
5023 2007 2316/1909 846 4127 1125
ταῦτα, ἐπιθήσει ὁ Θεὸς ἐπ' αὐτὸν τὰς πληγὰς τὰς γεγρα
these things, will add God upon him the plagues having beer
1722 975 5129 1437/5100/851 575 3056
μένας ἐν βιβλίῳ τούτῳ· καὶ ἐάν τις ἀφαιρῇ ἀπὸ τῶν λόγω
19
written in Scroll this; and if anyone take away from the words
975 4394 5026 851 2316 3313
βίβλου τῆς προφητείας ταύτης, ἀφαιρήσει ὁ Θεὸς τὸ μέρο
of (the) Scroll of prophecy this, will take away God the part
848 575 975 2222 1537 4172 40
αὐτοῦ ἀπὸ βίβλου τῆς ζωῆς, καὶ ἐκ τῆς πόλεως τῆς ἁγίας
of him from (the) Scroll of Life, and out of the city holy,
1125 1722 975 5129
καὶ τῶν γεγραμμένων ἐν βιβλίῳ τούτῳ.
and of the things having been written in Scroll this.
3004 3140 5023 3483 2064 5035 281 348
20 Λέγει ὁ μαρτυρῶν ταῦτα, Ναί, ἔρχομαι ταχύ. ἀμήν. Να
says The (One) testifying these things, Yes, I am coming quickly. Amen. Ye
2064 2962 2424 5485 2962 2257 2424
21 ἔρχου, Κύριε Ἰησοῦ. Ἡ χάρις τοῦ Κυρίου ἡμῶν Ἰησοῦ
come, Lord Jesus. The grace of the Lord of us, Jesus
5547 3326 3956 5216 281
Χριστοῦ μετὰ πάντων ὑμῶν. αμήν.
Christ, (be) with all of you. Amen.